HUMAN RIGHTS
AND THE
UNITED STATES

HUMAN RIGHTS AND THE UNITED STATES

Third Edition
Volume 1

H. Victor Condé
Charles F. Gelsinger

GREY HOUSE PUBLISHING

PUBLISHER: Leslie Mackenzie
EDITORIAL DIRECTOR: Laura Mars
PRODUCTION MANAGER: Kristen Hayes
MARKETING DIRECTOR: Jessica Moody

AUTHORS: H. Victor Condé, Charles F. Gelsinger

CONTRIBUTING AUTHORS: Karly H. Bennett — A Human Right to Healthcare
Trezlen D. Drake — Bibliography
Tina M. Ramirez — Chronology; Freedom of Thought,
Conscience, Religion or Belief
PEER REVIEW EDITORS: Trezlen Drake, Tina M. Ramirez

Grey House Publishing, Inc.
4919 Route 22
Amenia, NY 12501
518.789.8700 • Fax: 845.373.6390
www.greyhouse.com • e-mail: books@greyhouse.com

Publisher's Cataloging-In-Publication Data
(Prepared by The Donohue Group, Inc.)

Names: Condé, H. Victor, 1947- | Gelsinger, Charles F.
Title: Human rights and the United States / H. Victor Condé, Charles F. Gelsinger.
Other Titles: Human rights in the United States
Description: Third edition. | Amenia, NY : Grey House Publishing, [2017] | Previously published as: Human rights in the United States. | Includes bibliographical references and index.
Identifiers: ISBN 978-1-68217-346-6 (hardcover)
Subjects: LCSH: Human rights—United States—Dictionaries. | Human rights—United States—Encyclopedias. | Human rights—United States—History—Sources. | LCGFT: Reference works.
Classification: LCC KF4747.5 .C37 2017 | DDC 342.73/085/03—dc23

DEDICATION

This book is dedicated to all those who educate and train in, for, and about human rights and to all human rights defenders in the United States. Americans require a clear knowledge, and full and free exercise of our human rights. Striving for human rights demands constant oversight that all peoples worldwide fully exercise and completely enjoy theirs on an equal basis.

We dedicate our efforts to the American public's gradual acknowledgement of human rights issues in the U.S. and the important applicability of International Human Rights Law and related areas of law in analyzing and resolving those issues. We do this as we seek ways to better understand human rights as normative thinking, essential to reformulating a realistic and just American dream.

We also dedicate this book to the on-going struggles of Central American communities in the U.S. and in Central America.

In Memoriam
SIR NIGEL RODLEY

ACKNOWLEDGMENTS

Special acknowledgment goes to our dear colleagues, Tina M. Ramirez, Trezlen Drake and Karly H. Bennett, for their valuable help and human rights expertise without which this book would not have happened.

We would also especially like to thank our patient and supportive spouses and our children—who are the reason we write this work— for their competent and heartfelt help and encouragement in making this book possible.

Also, we expressly thank Nancy Flowers for her help and encouragement with the subject of education and human rights.

H. Victor specifically acknowledges: Sir Nigel Rodley, Jean Condé, Simone Condé, Fran Fagen, William B. Bennett, Melanie Popovich, Prof. David Kaye, Prof. Dinah Shelton. Prof. Stephen Kennedy, Ginger Pisano, Robert Savage, John Felcyn, Ric Nicol, Pierre and Karin, Christian and Kristine, Pascal and Martha, Jean Noel and Eveline, Leif and Kiera, Catherine and Esther.

Charles specifically acknowledges: all the teachers of human rights I encountered in France, including H. Victor Condé and Karen Parker; to my courageous wife, Carolina, and to our amazing son, Diego, whose beautiful existence was born in equal parts out of his parents' love for each other and for justice and respect for human rights.

In recognition of the Institut International des Droits de l'Homme/International Institute of Human Rights in Strasbourg, France, whose founder, Nobel Peace Prize laureate René Cassin, never knew the effect he would have on us who, long ago, studied international human rights in depth, thereby receiving the Diplôme of the Institute, for acquired knowledge of human rights, humanitarian law and international criminal law. We also gratefully honor the memory of Professors Jean-Francois Flauss, and Alexandre Kiss, its late Secretaries-General, and acknowledge the past leadership of Jean Bernard Marie, and present leadership of Sebastian Touzé and Jean-Paul Costa.

In recognition of the U.N. Office of the High Commissioner for Human Rights for its critically important work.

In recognition of the 1980s Sanctuary Movement and to all those Central Americans who struggle still for respect for their citizen, immigrant, refugee, and humanitarian law rights, whose struggle for human rights for themselves challenge us to study and learn the human rights of all. Mil gracias.

TABLE OF CONTENTS

Publisher's Note

Grey House Publishing is excited to offer this third edition of *Human Rights and the United States*. Previously titled *An Encyclopedia of Human Rights in the United States*, the new title reflects the major reorganization and new content in this new, two-volume edition. Here's what's new:

■ **New Chapters**

This new edition is organized into 23 thoughtful chapters, designed to offer readers focused content on specific areas of human rights, including Education, the United Nations, Climate Change, Immigrants, Criminal Justice, Children, Torture, and so much more. Plus, Chapter Two presents a detailed chronology of human rights that spans hundreds of years, ending with relevant events of 2017.

■ **Chapter Arrangement**

Each chapter follows a helpful format, starting with a leader page that summarizes, in clear language, what the chapter is about, and why it's important. These explanations are only a paragraph or two, giving the reader a quick, clear sense of what's to follow.

Following the leader page are a handful of carefully chosen **Quotes & Key Text Excerpts**, designed to give a sense of public and private sentiment about the chapter's focus. These are fully cited and sourced, making it easy to research the complete quote or text and put it in further context.

What You Should Know is the next part of each chapter. This is where the authors explain the background, current situation, and future options as they relate to the human rights issue at hand and the United States, as well as the world at large. Here is where you will learn what your human rights are, how they are being protected, how they may have been violated, and what steps you can take. You will learn what steps can be and have been taken to "punish" violators, and how our national, and the international, legal systems fits into the picture. This also includes how various U.S. administrations—from President Washington to President Trump—view human rights issues as we know them today, and how various interpretations come into play.

Following the What You Should Know narrative, is the **Primary Source Documents** section. Here you will find reprints of actual documents that create the Human Rights Law, International Law, Humanitarian Law, etc. designed to protect our human rights. These include treaties, protocols, letters, mission statements, country reports, review processes, court cases, and more. Each document includes a concise introduction by the authors to ground the reader in time, place and purpose. Due to the length of these documents, many are thoughtfully excerpted and all have full source information for further research.

■ **Appendices**

Following the 23 chapters, readers will find 3 appendices designed to support the material in these two volumes:

Appendix A – U.S. Law & Legislation, Resolution & the Restatement of Law – includes and explains 28 legal sources in U.S. domestic law that relate to International Human Rights Law and its place in the U.S. legal system.

Appendix B – Case Law Decisions from U.S. Courts & International Courts – presents several significant decisions where International Human Rights Law and Humanitarian Law are involved in relation to the U.S.

Appendix C – Reports of Selected U.S. & International NGOs – offers reports from Amnesty International, Human Rights Watch, and others, that rate the actions of the U.S. and others regarding human rights issues.

■ **Bibliography**

A comprehensive bibliography includes hundreds of resources used to compile the extensive material in this work. To help readers find the exact resources they are looking for, including full text documents of the many reprinted excerpts, its entries are categorized into 27 topics, such as U.S. Related, Law, Treaties, etc.

■ **Finding Guides**

Two guides designed to help the reader quickly find exactly what he or she needs:

Primary Source Documents Index makes easy work of searching through all 237 primary documents to find just the one you are looking for.

General Index lists all significant people, places, laws, organizations, and events in this work.

Grey House Publishing sincerely thanks authors Victor Condé and Charles Gelsinger, who diligently took apart the content of the previous edition, rearranged it, and put it back together so that this third edition is the most valuable, informative, and accessible work on the subject, for both students and the general population. Also, their detailed Introduction and User's Guide that follows this Publisher's Note offers more information on how to get the most out of the incredible amount of content in this work.

Foreword

Integer vitae scelerisque purus non eget Mauris iaculis neque arcu nec venenatis gravida sagittis, Fusce, pharetra, sive per Syrtis iter aestuosas sive facturus per inhospitalem Caucasum vel quae loca fabulosus lambit Hydaspes.*

—Quintus Horatius Flaccus, Horace's Ode 1.22

Two thousand years ago the famous Roman lyric poet, Horace, penned the above verse. Its universal message speaks to our time in this age of terrorism, threats to human security, and our weaponized response. He states that those who are morally upright, law-abiding and who do no moral or criminal wrong need not fear misfortune. He infers that something metaphysical happens to a person who does justice and avoids evil, and that they are protected by an invisible force. Horace was satirizing the Roman society that wielded power primarily with that time's latest and most terrifying weapons—poisoned arrows—weaponized drones of his day.

Horace's words raise the issue of whether weapons and military intelligence are what keeps us safe, or whether being just, righteous and respectful of human rights is a more powerful source of security. The world today continues to combat evil, terrorism, and extremism with massive, expensive military operations and intelligence hardware systems, which often puts justice and human rights on the back burner.

Based on years as international human rights activists and educators, and close observation of how different states, including our own, treat human beings, it is our opinion that the nation with a rule-of-law system which more fully respects human rights, regardless of domestic or external threats, is more just, safe, and secure than a nation without such a system. History is replete with nations fallen or defeated in battle, though militarily superior to their enemy. As idealistic as it sounds, might does not make right. It does not always achieve victory, much less justice. Too often, might is wielded by a side which is not doing right. Horace has the more universally correct view. History has proven him right: Soft power has longer staying power than hard power. Education is stronger than bullets. More and better weapons do not make a society safer and more secure, but a better system of law and justice and respect for human dignity does.

The premise of this work is that the more this great nation respects and complies with International Human Rights Law and related areas such as Humanitarian Law, Refugee Law, and International Criminal Law, the stronger, safer and more respected it will be. It is our deep desire that the U.S. continue to improve respect for and compliance with obligations within international human rights and related areas of International Law. To accomplish this, government officials, and the population at large, need to understand human rights and the international legal obligations the U.S. voluntarily assumes in the area of international human rights and related areas of law. This work provides the information necessary to inform individuals about our human rights law, our listed human rights, and our country's legal obligations to respect those rights domestically and abroad.

Throughout years of working and teaching with other American and international experts in the field of international human rights, we have found that the general American public is largely unaware of International Human Rights Law, and actions of the U.S. government regarding human rights on behalf of the American people within international institutions such as the U.N. The same is true for International Humanitarian Law and International Criminal Law. This work includes material on international human rights as they relate to the U.S., and as they are understood within International Human Rights Law, the fastest developing area of International Law, and content on International Humanitarian Law, International Criminal Law, and International Refugee Law as it impacts the U.S.

Every country, including the U.S., commits human rights violations. Increased respect for human rights world wide can, in our opinion, be accomplished not by focusing international actions against states, such as North Korea, Iran or Cuba, but by increasing American education, awareness, and respect for human rights by and for the American people. The U.S. is not just any nation when it comes to human rights. It is the nation most able to set the tone and example of respect for human rights for other countries, especially as we struggle against terrorism. No country has done more than the U.S. to establish the global system of international human rights laws and institutions concerning human rights and related areas of International Law. Yet, it has not always lived up to the standards placed on other countries regarding those international, especially human rights, legal norms. The U.S. has the opportunity to create momentum for positive change internationally by improving its human rights' record at home.

The reason this matters to the U.S. is that, when states do not respect human rights and humanitarian law norms, they give ammunition and motivation to their enemies, which creates the very terrorism they are fighting to overcome. Moral and legal righteousness brings with them a strength of spirit that cannot be conquered by human weapons.

Human rights and humanitarian law violators are not simplistically evil, heartless, or godless fanatics. They are often the "good people" in a society, people of otherwise good character, high government office, importance, deep faith and unquestioned patriotism. They do what they think is right for their government, their region, their state, their country, and the world, and what they feel is absolutely necessary, even to the point of taking life. However, when countries believe that their cause is just, often god-ordained, and their opponent is evil, godless and deserving of evil, they commit atrocious acts they believe are necessary to protect their values, beliefs, and the very existence of their society. Without knowledge of the human rights tools to set the permissible limits of our government's power, the American people can not assure that their government does not commit human rights and humanitarian law violations in our name.

This work is designed as a tool to help Americans learn about U.S. laws, policies, procedures, opinions and records within the international human rights and related law arena. Chapters include concise descriptions of various areas of human rights, relevant quotations and key text excerpts, a short narrative, and human rights and related documents that offer instruction and explanation. This material offers students of human rights and related areas of law the opportunity to take positive active in influencing leadership to improve the human rights record of the U.S. assuring that it sets the gold standard when it comes to promoting and protecting human rights domestically.

The events of 9/11 has had tremendous impact on the U.S. psyche, its laws, and its policies in the so-called war on terrorism. As a result, this third edition includes significant material related to human rights, counter-terrorism measures, the protection of human security, and the question of the balance between human rights and national security.

Additionally, in the current political climate, we see the Rule of Law being threatened, not by a foreign enemy, but by the U.S. government. It's important that the U.S. stays the course of protecting the human dignity of all persons in the country, not just our citizens. Every human being within our borders holds human rights recognized historically by the U.S. as articulated by the international community as basic minimum standards of state conduct vis à vis individual human beings for the protection of their inalienable inherent human dignity.

The contents of this work is designed for both students and educators at all academic levels, complete with straightforward answers to straightforward questions, and more complicated answers and questions alike. This third edition is a tool with resources for further study. Human rights are part of every subject.

The authors thank the following dedicated human rights scholars for their critical contributions to this third edition: Karly H. Bennett, A Human Right to Healthcare; Trezlen Drake, Bibliography; and Tina M. Ramirez, Chronology and Freedom of Thought, Conscience, Religion or Belief. They are responsible for the information and ideas set forth in these sections.

Finally, it is our hope that the issues raised in this work encourage human rights NGOs in the U.S. to come together to create a National Human Rights Institution, consistent with the Paris Principles, as a place to educate our people about human rights. Because the government refuses to do so, and is actually planning to take the terms "advancing democracy and human rights" out of our foreign affairs discourse, we must take this initiative ourselves in the civil society sector.

We have a dream...

–H. Victor Condé and Charles F. Gelsinger

The person who leads a wholesome and law-abiding life, and is free from wickedness, O Fuscus, has no need of Moorish bow, or javelins, or a quiver full of poison arrows, whether he is journeying through the glowing hot sands of the Syrtes or he is passing through the inhospitable Caucasus, or through those places celebrated in story and washed by the Hydaspes.

Translation by H. Victor Condé, BA cum laude in Classical Latin and Greek

Introduction and User's Guide

"Nothing could be more irrational than to give the people power and withhold from them information without which power is abused."

—James Madison

The Subject

This third edition of *Human Rights and the United States* is the second post 9/11 edition. It contains a broad range of information about international human rights in the United States, from the Declaration of Independence to the present. It covers select areas and subjects of human rights chosen to introduce the reader to International Human Rights Law as it relates to U.S. National Law, and how it is interpreted and applied by the U.S. both within and outside the country. Especially relevant at this particular time in American history, this work discusses what Americans need to know to ensure that their government recognizes, respects, and implements human rights norms.

This work is primarily about the field of International Law known as Human Rights Law, which covers the treatment of individuals by the state (the government), individuals who are under the jurisdiction of that state, both citizens and non-citizens. Chapter 1 lists our 40 human rights. Subsequent chapters discuss how these human rights are affected by various issues—education, climate, discrimination, rights of women and children, war, etc.—and how these human rights are recognized by, and inform the actions of, the U.S.

Because of the current state of conflict around the globe, this work also includes the Law of Armed Conflict, usually referred to as the Law of War. In today's world, we see human rights issues relate to the Law of Armed Conflict, part of which is known as International Humanitarian Law. To further define this area, this work includes new legal norms from the field of the Law of Armed Conflict, particularly from Humanitarian Law, such as the use of biological and chemical weapons and indiscriminate bombings, both of which are key issues in the ongoing conflicts around the globe. Also included is material from International Criminal Law, such as the Statute of the International Criminal Court, or the Rome Statute. These issues involve legal norms found in Public International Law, or the Law of Nations. There has been a gradual convergence of these legal systems and their case-law/jurisprudence.

We see incidents today where the same act/acts violate both Human Rights Law and Humanitarian Law; this work provides the broadest legal picture of an issue involving actions of the U.S. either at home or abroad, enabling the reader to judge all international issues and events by the same international standards and terminology which, for the most part, apply to most countries of the world. All countries are judged by the standards set by the international community as the minimum standards for the protection of human dignity of all human beings. These standards are, for the most part, part of U.S. law, and accepted as being reflective of American values.

Human Rights and the United States is directed at average Americans who want to know more about human rights in general, and International Human Rights Law in particular. Two related areas of law also covered are the Law of Armed Conflict and International Criminal Law. These two volumes include the tools to help familiarize the reader with human rights and related areas of law, allowing understanding of the international norms and rights as they are found in U.S. legal and political policy and practice. Although it would be extremely difficult to fully cover all areas of the fast-growing human rights and related areas of International Law this work provides a strong foundation.

The lack of significant human rights curriculum in the U.S. educational system has resulted in a failure to fully support human rights and related area causes. Indeed, the term "human rights" is often misunderstood by many Americans. This work offers basic concepts, definitions, and theory of international human rights, Humanitarian Law and International Criminal Law as they are presently understood in the national and international context.

Your human rights are listed in Chapter 1. Studying and understanding human rights concepts, theories, and events, is made more meaningful by knowing not only your internationally recognized human rights, but states' limitations and obligations regarding these rights, and consequences for violations. Knowledge gives you the power to stand up for your own, or another's, human rights.

Human Rights and the United States is meant as a broad introduction to human rights and related laws, and discusses certain subjects, instruments, and institutions in the human rights arena and related areas of law as they impact the U.S. and its domestic law, policy and practice of the U.S. It is about legal standards of compliance. It looks at the U.S and human rights in a number of different areas to familiarize readers with U.S. action and international law, and is designed to encourage further study.

The third edition of *Human Rights and the United States* is thoughtfully organized:

Front Matter
- Detailed Table of Contents
- Foreword by the Authors
- Introduction and User's Guide
- Abbreviations of terms and names of human rights and related areas documents

Chapter Arrangement
- Each chapter opens with a **Leader Page** that quickly anchors the reader to a particular subject. It includes *This Chapter is About...* and *This is Important Because...* sections, as well as a list of Primary Source Documents.
- The Leader Page is followed by **Selected Quotes & Key Text Excerpts**—2 to 12 items, fully sourced, chosen for a sense of the meaning, message, and historical connection of the subject with the U.S. historical experience of human rights.
- Selected Quotes & Key Text Excerpts is followed by **What You Should Know**. This narrative of 2 to 20 pages gives a clear, easy-to-understand introduction of the topic with technical, theoretical, conceptual, historical and institutional background information to lead into the Primary Source Document section.
- **Primary Source Documents**, the major component of each chapter, are from the U.S., U.N., and other sources. They provide an introduction to real language, procedures and legal standards of human rights and related areas of International Law. Each chapter includes 4 to 24 documents, some reprinted in their entirety, others carefully excerpted. Chosen for their instructive value, they provide an authoritative and accurate source of information that grounds the reader with an understanding of the legal dimensions of human rights and related legal norms. An important part of understanding these primary documents is the terminology, much of it legal, of human rights. All documents include an informative introduction, and are fully sourced.

Content

This Introduction provides conceptual background material on human rights and related areas from an academic, theoretical perspective, and lays a conceptual, philosophical and legal foundation for the issues and norms that are detailed in the following 23 chapters, summarized below.

Chapter 1—Human Rights Law: Background, Concepts & Tools

Introduces the reader to 1. International Human Rights Law, 2. International Humanitarian Law (applicable during armed conflicts), and 3. International Criminal Law (dealing with crimes against humankind). These areas of law are mainly based on treaties—written legal instruments—which are international contracts among countries that create legal obligations and standards of government conduct. This chapter defines and explains human rights from the legal perspective.

This chapter includes theoretical and conceptual tools, and legal and historical charts and information about human rights law that discuss the nature of human rights; where human rights come from; various human rights; how human rights are established in international law; how human rights are "enforced"; human rights law and U.S. law; and the historical evolution of international legal norms in U.S. law. It also introduces the related areas of International Humanitarian Law and International Criminal Law and their legal relationship to International Human Rights Law.

Certainly one of the most important pieces of information of this chapter, indeed of the entire book, is the List of Your Human Rights. Human rights are composed of four main human rights instruments known as the "International Bill of Rights." All the rights set forth in those instruments and listed here use the first person, instead of the language used by the Universal Declaration of Human Rights. For example, "Everyone has the right to freedom of movement" has been changed to "I/We have the right to freedom of movement" to help remember and internalize the rights. The full text of these human rights instruments is included in this chapter's Primary Source Documents.

Next, this chapter provides a background on International Human Rights Law with the legal concepts, terms, and principles that describe sources, interpretation, and application of human rights laws. It focuses on the process by which an international law treaty, like any human rights treaty, is made, using a flow chart of the usual steps, sometimes called "standard setting." Next are charts showing how an International Treaty Norm is transformed into U.S. law, and the spectrum of different laws that are applicable to the U.S. This spectrum of Different Sets of Laws Applicable in the U.S. shows both national and international laws.

In order to understand the meaning of a treaty and how to apply it to an issue, this chapter also includes rules and resources on interpreting, understanding and applying a human rights treaty to a given situation, discusses permissible government limitations/restrictions on the exercise of human rights in certain situations, and describes the procedural processes for filing and deciding written complaints alleging that a state has violated human rights.

Finally, Chapter 1 discusses the relationship between International Human Rights Law, International Humanitarian Law, and International Criminal Law and their growing convergence as bodies of law.

Chapter 2—Chronology of Human Rights Movements & Events

Sets forth a complete and up-to-date Chronology of Human Rights in relation to the U.S. These are the events and actions where U.S. law, policy and practice most closely touched international human rights and related areas of law, both within the U.S. and with the U.S. internationally. It starts with the Magna Carta in 1215, and ends with events of 2017. It includes Presidential Proclamations on Human Rights Day from both Democratic and Republican Presidents, and events from the beginning of the Trump administration, which is having an enormous impact on human rights in the U.S. both domestically and in terms of foreign policy. The Presidential proclamations demonstrate that the U.S. human rights experience is not just a liberal or Democrat value, but has been supported historically by all American presidents and Americans, both Democrat and Republican.

Chapter 3—U.S. State Department, Secretary of State, & Human Rights

Presents the role of the U.S. Department of State and Secretary of State in relation to government policies and understanding of human rights and related legal norms, created by the international community, including the U.S. The State Department, through its Secretary, speaks for the U.S. to the international community about: how the U.S. is doing in respecting human rights; how the State Department (and the U.S.) receives information from the international community; and how various human rights institutions see U.S. performance. The U.S. State Department executes foreign policy and law, and speaks the President's position on given international matters. It attends and participates at international inter-governmental organizations, like the U.N.

Chapter 4—U.N. Charter Based Bodies: Focus on the Human Rights Council and the Universal Periodic Review

As the first of a three-chapter unit of the U.S. in the U.N., Chapter 4 focuses on the procedure known as the Universal Periodic Review (UPR). Chapter 5 deals with the Human Rights Council and its special mechanisms or special procedures. Chapter 6 deals with U.N. treaty-based bodies.

The U.S. interfaces with the U.N., its various bodies, and other States on human rights issues. The U.S. helped found the U.N. in 1945 at an international event held in the U.S., and has continuously acted as a key player in promoting and propelling human rights into the international community in hopes of avoiding another world war or holocaust. The U.N. is where the U.S. most importantly, extensively, and legally is involved in international laws, procedures and organs which articulate, create, and implement international human rights and relate legal standards, particularly in the U.N. Human Rights Council. This is where: the U.S interacts with, reports to, and appears before the members of the international community about its human rights record; the international community interacts with and reports back to the U.S. about how the international organs and procedures see U.S. law and practice; the U.S. learns how it could improve its human rights practice.

This chapter focuses on the UPR and includes Primary Source Documents related to U.S. participation in the UPR process, which marks the first time that the U.S. general human rights record (and that of every other country), is examined by the international community, represented by the Human Rights Council, under all the legal standards which apply to it. It involves self-reporting, and response and recommendations by the Council and other States.

Chapter 5—U.N. Human Rights Council Special Procedures & Complaint Procedure

Covers the many special procedures, also called special mechanisms, in addition to the UPR, established by the U.N. Human Rights Council (HRC) to study human rights issues, such as racism and xenophobia. These procedures are established by adopting a resolution mandating someone to do something, such as prepare a study of access to water, for example, or research the independence of a judiciary. Most of the procedures involve the appointment of persons called Special Rapporteurs who are given a mandate by the HRC and report back periodically, or when their work is done. There are also persons who are designated as independent experts on a subject and advise the HRC on the subject. Country-specific mandates, and a complaint procedure for continuing patterns of gross and reliably attested violations in a particular State are also covered in Chapter 5.

Chapter 6—U.S., U.N. & Human Rights Law: Treaties and Treaty Bodies

Covers the U.N bodies that are established by human rights treaties. These are called treaty-based bodies or treaty-supervising bodies. The U.S. has ratified some U.N. human rights treaties, which it is obliged to comply with. The State compliance with the treaty is supervised by the treaty body. An example is the HRC, which was established in the International Covenant on Civil and Political Rights (ICCPR). These treaty obligations include submitting periodic reports to the treaty body. This chapter records various interaction between the U.S. and aspects of treaty bodies, such as the issuing of general comments on the interpretation and application of the norms of the treaty.

Chapter 7—The Organization of American States: The U.S. and the Inter-American Human Rights System

Concerns the U.S. in relation to a regional human rights system involving the Western Hemisphere nations—the Organization of American States (OAS). The OAS has a human rights system that includes both a Human Rights Commission and a Human Rights Court. The Commission is called the Inter-American Commission on Human Rights, and the Court is called the Inter-American Court of Human Rights. This system is based on a declaration—American Declaration on the Rights and Duties of Man (ADRDM)—and a treaty—American Convention on Human Rights (ACHR). The Commission sits in Washington, D.C., hears complaints of U.S. human rights violations, and makes decisions on further action. This chapter describes some of the case complaints received by the OAS human rights bodies and the U.S. response.

Chapter 8—The Organization for Security & Cooperation in Europe (OSCE)

Is about the Organization on Security and Cooperation in Europe (OSCE), a 57-member political organization of mostly European State members, of which the U.S. is a member. The OSCE deals with a wide range of security-related concerns, including arms control, confidence- and security-building measures, human rights, national minorities, democratization, policing strategies, counter-terrorism and economic and environmental activities. It incorporated human rights norms into its post-World War II political processes and is now very much engaged in a variety of human rights activities. The organization runs principally under the Helsinki Final Act of 1972, which is not a treaty, but which contains non-legally binding "commitments," and other follow up documents. The OSCE also does international election monitoring and reporting. The Primary Source Documents in this chapter come directly from the OSCE, and relate directly to the U.S. participation in this organization.

Chapter 9—Equality, Non-discrimination & Racism

Covers the principle and human right of equality before the law and the principle and human right against discrimination in general. Of recent importance to the U.S., it covers racial inequality and discrimination, especially in the context of racially motivated law enforcement police abuse of force. It also applies to other characteristics of unlawful discrimination, such as ethnic, national, gender, linguistic, and religious discrimination. Non-discrimination and equality are basic principles of Human Rights Law and apply to all human rights. This chapter focuses on the Convention on the Elimination of All Forms of Racial Discrimination (CEAFRD).

Chapter 10—Rights of Indigenous Peoples

Discusses indigenous rights as human rights. It focuses largely around the U.N. Declaration on the Rights of Indigenous People and the indigenous peoples related activities within the U.N. Special human rights apply to such groups as Native Americans, Eskimos, and Native Hawaiians, who are known in human rights law as Indigenous Peoples.

Chapter 11—Rights of the Child

Is about children's rights—the human rights that children hold because of their unique condition and status. There was a time when children were treated as property, abused and exploited, and were helpless and deemed right-less with no effective remedies for protection. The focal base of children's rights is the International Convention on the Rights of the Child and two of its protocols. The Children's Convention, as it is known, is the most ratified treaty in the world. This area of human rights seeks to protect the vulnerable group known as children, and to protect their human rights in accordance with their evolving capacities as they age through childhood. Most of this chapter focuses on U.S. participation in U.N. activities and treaties to protect children's human rights. It covers the activities and procedures of the Committee on the Rights of the Child (CRC), the treaty body that supervises implementation of that treaty.

Chapter 12—Women's and Girls' Rights

Covers women's human rights, the human rights that specifically address both the protection of women, and those human rights, such as the right to vote, that impact the equality and human dignity of women. The focal point of women's rights is the U.N. Convention on the Elimination of Discrimination against Women (CEDAW). CEDAW also seeks to cover the rights of the "girl child" as a unique gender subject, different from children's rights. This chapter discusses the activities and procedures of the CEDAW.

Chapter 13—Immigration, Migrant Workers, Refugees and Asylum

Deals with the human rights of persons who are not citizens of the U.S., either those in the U.S, or those trying to enter the U.S. (legally or illegally) as immigrants, migrant workers, and asylum seekers. This involves not only International Human Rights Law, but International Humanitarian Law (in the case of, for example, Syrian refugees) and International Refugee Law as well. The work of the U.N, and the OAS will be discussed and further, how International Human Rights law sees human beings as human beings and not as citizens of any particular State.

Chapter 14—Freedom of Thought, Conscience, Religion or Belief

Covers the international human right to have and manifest any religion or belief, or no belief, and the freedom of conscience. After an historical overview, this chapter focuses on the legal norms of the Universal Declaration of Human Rights, and the International Covenant on Civil and Political Rights and other non-binding declaration and international organizational procedures, such as general comments and periodic states reports, that are used in the supervision of implementation of those norms. It primarily covers activity within the context of the U.N., particularly on the Special Rapporteur on Freedom of Religion or Belief. It sets forth U.S. laws meant to implement those norms and tie them to U.S foreign policy, with the goal of U.S. action aimed at protection for freedom of religion or belief in the world.

Chapter 15—Freedom of Expression & Opinion, Including Freedom of the Press

Covers a specific civil human right: freedom of speech and expression in all its forms, including political, literary, artistic and commercial speech. This right includes freedom of the press and all media, and the right to seek and receive information from any source. It is focused around the international legal norms on freedom of expression, etc., found in the Universal Declaration of Human Rights, and the International Covenant on Civil and Political Rights, and the international organizational procedures to supervise implementation of those norms.

Chapter 16—Law Enforcement and Criminal Justice: Arrest, Detention, Punishment and the Death Penalty

Discusses law enforcement, criminal justice and procedure, conditions of detention, treatment of persons in detention, and the death penalty. This chapter covers human rights norms which apply from the moment of arrest to execution of sentence, and includes many Primary Source Documents that set forth non-legally binding ("soft law") guidelines, basic principles, standard minimum rules, and codes of conduct on all aspects of the deprivation of human liberty, especially in the jail and prison context.

Chapter 17—Torture, Cruel, Inhuman or Degrading Treatment or Punishment

Covers the human right to be free from torture, cruel, inhuman or degrading treatment or punishment, under the Universal Declaration of Human Rights, and the International Covenant on Civil and Political Rights. It focuses on the U.N. International Convention against Torture and Other Cruel, Inhuman or Degrading Treatment or Punishment and the procedures of the U.N. Committee against Torture, and the place of torture prevention in the U.S. legal system. It includes coverage of mostly U.N. bodies, particularly the Human Rights Committee, the Human Rights Council, and the Committee against Torture, tasked with monitoring and supervising the activities of states, including the U.S. relating to this human right.

Chapter 18—Human Right to Healthcare

Establishes that access to healthcare is an internationally recognized human right, not a privilege, and sets forth the legal sources that support that position. It calls for politicians and Americans in political discourse to call healthcare a human right, and not just "a right." It challenges Americans to transform the national dialogue and debate concerning healthcare from one about the economics of medical service as a market commodity, to one about a human-rights-based approach and the need for the American government to provide healthcare for everyone.

Chapter 19—Climate Change

Discusses the slow and recent convergence of the fields of Environmental Law and International Human Rights Law, due to the proven impact of global warming upon the lives of human beings around the world. Because we are seeing concrete and quantifiable damage to human beings caused by climate change, natural or man-made, this is a major topic of increasing concern. This chapter shows the link between human rights and climate change, the specific human rights involved, and what the U.S. and the international community are doing to address climate change and the damage it's causing, including the recent Paris Agreement of 2015, which the Trump Administration abandoned in mid 2017.

Chapter 20—Human Right to Education and to a Human Rights Education (HRE)

Deals with education in two different forms: the international human right to an education, at least an elementary education, and the human right to a human rights education (HRE), a goal of this work. This chapter sets forth international norms on the right to an education, so that humans can grow, develop, and intelligently participate in the governance of society. Also discussed are efforts to bring human rights education into the formal and informal education systems of all countries, to create a human rights-educated populace. This chapter explains that there is a human right of every individual to receive an education in human rights, and shows the programs at the international level to bring human rights education into different sectors of society.

Chapter 21—International Criminal Law

Introduces the reader to the area of International Law involved in the criminalization and punishment of certain acts that are considered to be an offense against all of humankind, such as slavery or genocide. Certain human rights violations can be punished as international crimes. This chapter shows what International Criminal Laws could potentially impact the U.S., and what international criminal norms can be applied to atrocities happening in other countries, such as the Syrian chemical weapons used against civilians, use of human hostage shields by ISIS in Mosul, or genocide against Yazidis in Iraq. This area of International Law is increasingly considered and applied in contemporary international crises along with Human Rights Law and Humanitarian Law.

Chapter 22—International Humanitarian Law

Introduces, like Chapter 21, an area of International Law related to International Human Rights Law. International Humanitarian Law (IHL) is the International Law which applies during armed conflicts to limit the impact of armed violence on victims of that violence, such as on wounded or captured soldiers, interned civilians, or inhabitants of militarily occupied territories. IHL protects civilians and combatants. This area of law is conceptually different from International Human Rights Law, but its goal is parallel, existing to minimize physical and mental harm to a person and to maintain the inherent dignity of human beings in the context of any form of armed conflict. This chapter deals with international treaties, such as the well-known Geneva Conventions, and highlights the role and work of the International Committee of the Red Cross, whose primary mission continues to be assuring that States fully implement, comply with, and enforce all the norms of International Humanitarian Law. Violations of this body of law, known as grave breaches, are international crimes, and are covered in Chapter 21.

Chapter 23—Human Rights and National Security/Counter Terrorism Measures

Discusses national security, counter-terrorism measures (surveillance, capture, detention, interrogation), and access to justice for the accused, in light of certain International Laws. This chapter is specifically about how to protect U.S. national security while countering terrorism, and what international legal limits can be placed on specific measures taken by the U.S. in that fight—for example, a drone strike assassination of a suspected terrorist. This is about how the U.S. struggles for human security and national security in relation to international human rights and related law standards, and about how the U.S. is looked to as a leader of the international community. Allowing that there are many differing political and legal viewpoints concerning the U.S. and the war on terrorism, both in the U.S. and between the U.S. and the international community, the Primary Source Documents in this chapter set forth the international standards for the U.S. regarding its international legal obligations.

Primary Source Documents

Major elements of this reference text are the Primary Source Document sections, found at the end of every chapter. Together, there are 237 documents, representative of the many human rights and related area law documents that relate to the U.S. These documents are intended to show the reader how a particular subject, event, or topic of human rights is handled within various subject area, i.e. rights of children, or freedom of expression. The documents reprinted here comprise several types—historical, international, U.N., Humanitarian Law, criminal, etc.—and demonstrate the various types of documents that one encounters in this field of law and politics, particularly International Law and politics. These documents do not comprise all the documents that have been written on human rights and related law areas, but do offer a solid, wide-ranging representation. Most of the documents are from international organizations of which the U.S. is a member and key player. Some are legal instruments (i.e. treaties), some are political, and some are executive-administrative (i.e. country reports).

The Primary Source Documents are listed on the Leader Page of each Chapter. All documents include a brief introduction that addresses its context and significance. The document itself (excerpted or complete), is followed by online source availability.

For example:

Document title: 2. INTERNATIONAL COVENANT ON CIVIL AND POLITICAL RIGHTS

Document introduction: *It was always intended that the rights set forth in the UDHR would be transformed into binding legal instruments called treaties to make the obligations to protect human rights legally binding on all states who chose to become bound by them, as a "state-party....*

The actual text of the document is usually preceded by the bracketed word: [Text]

Many of the documents are excerpted; ellipses (...) indicate missing text.

The end of the document is usually marked by the bracketed word: [End text]

The text of the document is followed by an internet source address where that document can be found in full, often with related materials, i.e.: *Source: http://www.ohchr.org/EN/ProfessionalInterest/Pages/CCPR.aspx*

The Primary Source Documents are not presented to advance a particular political agenda or ideology, but to provide a representative sample of information from the field of International Human Rights and related areas of law as they relate to the U.S. This material is the official world of human rights, and constitutes today's political and institutional human rights discourse as it relates to the U.S. and vice versa.

Neither are the Primary Source Documents presented here the final word about a subject. This information was valid and up-to-date at press time. Situations are constantly changing, and updates to the material presented—whether it be state reports, government policy, or court opinion—can be found by researching the bibliography and the internet sources given throughout this work.

Cross References and See Alsos

Primary Source Documents are cross-referenced throughout this book by the chapter and document number, for example: see Chapter 1, Document 1. This particular cross reference refers the reader back to the Universal Declaration of Human Rights.

Appendices

Following the 23 chapters are three appendices. They are designed to supplement and amplify understanding of the Primary Source Documents in the chapters, in terms of U.S. national laws and case law. They also present several reports by American-based human rights organizations, our civil society watchdogs, in relation to the United States. The appendices contain material that applies to many different subjects, and are meant to reinforce the legal and political reality that human rights are a part of the historical, political and legal fabric of the U.S. Human rights are a part of who we are as a nation, and why we even exist as a country.

Appendix A—Selected summaries and excerpts of U.S. legislation, both enacted and proposed, aimed at the promotion and protection of human rights here and abroad, and human rights-related congressional resolutions. This material sets forth general human rights laws and country-specific laws that are seen as the will of the American people, which, so far as it is constitutional, must be carried out by the executive branch and enforced by the judicial branch of the government. Also included are several congressional resolutions regarding human rights, showing how Congress expresses its understanding of a human rights issue or country's human rights record. In some cases, only the reference citation and name of the legislation is included. Note that legislation is subject to change by amendment, or by repeal. The current status and content of a law can be found in the appropriate U.S. legal texts, on websites of congressional representatives listed in the Bibliography, or after certain Primary Source Documents.

Appendix B—Excerpts of selected case decisions involving the U.S., human rights and related law. Appendix B includes not only cases decided solely within the U.S. Constitution and Bill of Rights framework, but also case decisions that have a specific connection to the international law of human rights and related areas. These decisions from U.S. courts, the U.S. Supreme Court, and federal courts provide examples of how human rights have been interpreted and applied in U.S. jurisprudence by U.S. courts, offering insight into the struggle of the courts to deal with the area of human rights law, a field not commonly studied in law school. Also included are decisions arising from international judicial and quasi-judicial bodies in which either the U.S. is a party to the case, or whose case involves action by the U.S. in an area affecting human rights. The reference citation given for each case includes the full case decision for further study.

Appendix C—Selected reports of U.S.-based, non-governmental human rights organizations, such as Amnesty International USA and Human Rights Watch, two key international human rights organizations. These are also called "civil society organizations," or CSOs. These reports are written by human rights scholars and activists about how governments are complying with their international legal obligations. There are many other human rights organizations in the U.S, each with its own focus and strengths, and each with a varying degree of objectiveness and credibility.

Bibliography

This Bibliography not only makes it easy to find complete text of documents that are excerpted in the document sections of this work, but also offers valuable guidance for further research from a variety of sources, including more complete works on the history of human rights. Special resources and links for educators are included.

Index

A detailed subject index offers the reader a quick and easy way to access the enormous amount and variety of material in these two volumes, including individual names, laws, and organizations.

In conclusion, the Introductory Narrative, Quotes, and Key Text Excerpts of each chapter, together with the Primary Source Documents, Appendices, Bibliography, detailed Index, and carefully chosen resources for further research combine to give the reader an unparallelled, informative overview of human rights and related areas of law, specific examples, and practical tools for understanding this complex field.

৵৹৶

"Democracy can be an effective form of government only to the degree that the public (that rule it in theory) are well-informed about national and international events and can think independently and critically about those events."

—President James Madison

ABBREVIATIONS

ACHR	American Convention on Human Rights
ADHR	American Declaration of the Rights and Duties of Man
ATCA	Alien Tort Claims Act
CAT	Convention against Torture, Cruel, Inhuman, or Degrading Treatment or Punishment
CEDAW	Convention on the Elimination of All Forms of Discrimination Against Women
CERD	Convention on the Elimination of All Forms of Racial Discrimination
ECOSOC	United Nations Economic and Social Council
EIF	Entry into Force
EA	Executive Agreement
EO	Executive Order
FSIA	Foreign Sovereign Immunities Act
GA (UNGA)	General Assembly (of the United Nations)
GAOR	General Assembly Official Records
GC	Geneva Conventions of 1949
HFA	Helsinki Final Act
HRCee	Human Rights Committee (U.N.)
HRC	Human Rights Council (U.N.)
I-AComHR	Inter-American Commission on Human Rights
I-ACourtHR	Inter-American Court of Human Rights
ICC	International Criminal Court
ICCPR	International Covenant on Civil and Political Rights
ICESCR	International Covenant on Economic, Social and Cultural Rights
ICRC	International Committee of the Red Cross
ICJ	International Court of Justice
ICTR	International Criminal Tribunal for Rwanda
ICTY	International Criminal Tribunal for the Former Yugoslavia
IDP	Internally Displaced Person
IFI	International Financial Institution
IGO	Inter-Governmental Organization
ILO	International Labour Organization
IRFA	International Religious Freedom Act of 1998
NGO	Non-Governmental Organization
POW	Prisoner of War
R2P	Responsibility to Protect
RDUs/RUDs	Reservations, Declarations, and Understandings
SuR	State Under Review
TVPA	Torture Victim Protection Act
UDHR	Universal Declaration of Human Rights
U.N.	United Nations
UNCH	United Nations Charter
UNESCO	United Nations Educational, Scientific, and Cultural Organization
UNHCHR	United Nations High Commissioner for Human Rights
UNHCR	United Nations High Commissioner for Refugees
UPR	Universal Periodic Review

Human Rights Law: Background, Theory, Concepts & Tools

Chapter 1

This Chapter is About understanding what human rights are and where they come from. It's about the theory, concepts, terminology and other legal tools for understanding International Human Rights Law and the relation of Human Rights Law to International Humanitarian Law and International Criminal Law. It is also an introduction to human rights legal instruments.

This is Important Because without an understanding of what human rights are and how to understand and use them, they risk being reduced to a mere abstract concept with no concrete social utility. They could remain academic and aspirational at best. A knowledge of human rights law, its concepts and terminology along with a history of human rights gives the reader an understanding of a whole field of international law which is absolutely necessary for assuring that governments respect human dignity. No one can stand up for rights he or she does not know exist. Without an understanding of the relationship between and application of International Human Rights Law, International Humanitarian Law and International Criminal Law, one has an incomplete legal picture of human rights.

Quotes & Key Text Excerpts

Whatever career you may choose for yourself — doctor, lawyer, teacher — let me propose an avocation to be pursued along with it. Become a dedicated fighter for civil rights. Make it a central part of your life. It will make you a better doctor, a better lawyer, a better teacher. It will enrich your spirit as nothing else possibly can. It will give you that rare sense of nobility that can only spring from love and selflessly helping your fellow man. Make a career of humanity. Commit yourself to the noble struggle for human rights. You will make a greater person of yourself, a greater nation of your country and a finer world to live in.

—*Martin Luther King, Jr.*

༺ঌ༺ঌ༺ঌ༺ঌ

The protection of fundamental human rights was a foundation stone in the establishment of the United States over 200 years ago. Since then, a central goal of U.S. foreign policy has been the promotion of respect for human rights, as embodied in the *Universal Declaration of Human Rights*. The United States understands that the existence of human rights helps secure the peace, deter aggression, promote the rule of law, combat crime and corruption, strengthen democracies, and prevent humanitarian crises.

Because the promotion of human rights is an important national interest, the United States seeks to:

- Hold governments accountable to their obligations under universal human rights norms and international human rights instruments;
- Promote greater respect for human rights, including freedom from torture, freedom of expression, press freedom, women's rights, children's rights, and the protection of minorities;
- Promote the rule of law, seek accountability, and change cultures of impunity;
- Assist efforts to reform and strengthen the institutional capacity of the Office of the U.N. High Commissioner for Human Rights and the U.N. [Human Rights Council]; and
- Coordinate human rights activities with important allies, including the EU, and regional organizations.

Source: U.S. Department of State, Diplomacy in Action, Website, 2016: http://www.state.gov/j/drl/hr/

༺ঌ༺ঌ༺ঌ༺ঌ

The desire to live freely under a government that would respect and protect human rights was the fundamental motivation of our country's Founders — human rights have not only been part of the United States since the beginning, they were the reason our nation was created. From its adoption in 1789, the U.S. Constitution has been the central legal instrument of government and the supreme law of the land....

The Constitution's first ten amendments, adopted in 1791 and known as the Bill of Rights, along with the Thirteenth, Fourteenth, and Fifteenth Amendments, adopted in the wake of the Civil War, protect many rights that, in the twentieth century, became recognized and protected under international human rights law.

Source: U.S. Government National Report to the U.N. Human Rights Council for the Universal Periodic Review, First Cycle, 2010, para. 9.

ళ్ళ~ళ్ళ~ళ్ళ~ళ్ళ

Liberty cannot be preserved without a general knowledge among the people.

—*John Adams, Second U.S. President*

What You Should Know

Your Human Rights

A critical goal of this work is to make the reader aware of his or her human rights. Below is the list of our human rights, set forth in what is known as the *International Bill of Rights*. The *International Bill of Rights* consists of the following four international human rights instruments:

1. Universal Declaration of Human Rights (UDHR)

2. International Covenant on Civil and Political Rights (ICCPR)

3. International Covenant on Economic, Social and Cultural Rights (ICESCR)

4. First Optional Protocol to the ICCPR

The list of all human rights we hold as human beings:

I/We have the right to the exercise of all the following rights without discrimination based on race, religion, color, sex, language, political or other opinion, national/social origin, property, birth/other status.

I/We have the right to life.

I/We have the right to liberty and security of person.

I/We have the right to be free from slavery and forced labor.

I/We have the right to be free from torture, cruel, inhuman, or degrading treatment or punishment.

I/We have the right to recognition as a legal person before the law.

I/We have the right to equal protection (equality) of the law.

I/We have the right to access to effective domestic legal remedies for human rights violations.

I/We have the right to be free from arbitrary arrest or detention.

I/We have the right to a fair public hearing/trial before a competent, independent, impartial judiciary.

I/We have the right to be presumed innocent against criminal charges and to all procedural due process rights.

I/We have the right to be free from retroactive (*ex post facto*) criminal laws, and from double jeopardy.

I/We have the right, if detained, to be treated with humanity (humanely) and with respect for my/our human dignity.

I/We have the right to be free from interference with privacy, home, and family.

I/We have the right to be free from imprisonment for the inability to pay debts.

I/We have the right to freedom of movement, choice of residence, and to leave a country.

I/We have the right to seek asylum from persecution.

I/We have the right to have a nationality.

I/We have the right to own property.

I/We have the right, as a man and a woman of marriageable age, to marry and have (found) a family.

I/We have the right, as a mother or as a child, to special protections.

I/We have the right, if an alien, to freedom from arbitrary expulsion from a country.

I/We have the right to freedom of thought, conscience and religion.

I/We have the right to freedom of expression, opinion, and the press.

I/We have the right to freedom from propaganda that advocates war, or that incites national, racial or religious hatred.

I/We have the right to free assembly and association.

I/We have the right to participate in the political life of the society.

I/We have the right, if I am/we are a member of an ethnic, religious, or linguistic minority, to enjoy my/our own culture, use my/our own language and practice my/our own religion.

I/We have the right to an adequate standard of living, including housing, clothing, and food.

I/We have the right to the highest attainable standard of physical and mental health.

I/We have the right to an education and the right to a human rights education.

I/We have the right to social security.

I/We have the right to work, under just and favorable conditions.

I/We have the right to form and participate in trade unions.

I/We have the right to participate in the cultural life of society.

I/We have the right to enjoy the benefits of scientific progress.

I/We have the right as "peoples" to self-determination (to determine our own political status; pursue economic and cultural development and use our own natural wealth and resources).

I/We have the right to a social and international order necessary to allow me/us to realize these rights.

I/We have the right to adequate rest and leisure.

In situations of armed conflict, I/we have legal protection under both human rights law and under applicable International Humanitarian Law.

Understanding Human Rights Legal Theory, History and Institutions

Introduction

"Recognition of the inherent dignity and of the equal and inalienable rights of all members of the human family is **the foundation** of freedom, justice and peace in the world."

—*U.N. Declaration of Human Rights (emphasis added)*

For millennia humankind has been striving to find freedom in relation to the powers, foreign or domestic, public or private, which try to influence, control, regulate, exploit, marginalize, or destroy persons. Human beings are somehow hardwired for freedom and the search to create their own reality in full human autonomy in an environment of peace and human security.

Countless lives have been lost, human beings harmed, cities destroyed, history erased, and churches, synagogues, temples and mosques destroyed by hate and sectarianism. Obscene amounts of money have been lost in crusades to destroy others with a goal of controlling or converting, or controlling to convert other peoples to the "true" way of life. Even in homogenous societies, issues arise pitting citizens against government, and people often assert "their rights" to get the government to treat them in a certain way. Even in places of relative peace where citizens have never seen war and violence, there are issues between human beings and their society's government, for every society has some kind of governance and norms, or standards of conduct to live by. People create or elect or accept a government which sets standards and requirements for the people to obey or conform to.

For the past two hundred forty years, the United States has been working within its own borders to legislate and apply, to interpret and judicially enforce a legal order which would fulfill the intent of the U.S. Constitution, an echoing call first uttered in the Declaration of Independence, with freedom and justice for all. It is a constant and evolving process, with new laws, new policies, new institutions, new issues, and new conflicts emerging all the time, in a world increasingly globalizing and interconnected by cyberspace. Part of that U.S. process involves participation in: creating, recognizing, and respecting international legal norms which have as their goal the respect for human dignity by one's own government; and preventing or resolving international conflicts in a peaceful manner, mindful of the two world wars and many genocides which have occurred at the hands of supposedly modern and civilized mankind.

For more than a hundred years, the international community, largely led by the U.S., has been in the process of participating in and helping the international community, in both global and regional organizations, to develop the concepts of human rights. The goal has always been to establish a minimum threshold standard of how governments should and may treat human beings, citizen or non-citizen, based solely on their inherent dignity as human beings. Most of this has happened since World War II, largely influenced by the horrors of the Holocaust and "man's inhumanity to man."

In the international community of nation states, there have been four phases of this U.S.-involved development of human rights, not necessarily one after another in sequence, but overlapping in time:

FOUR PHASES OF HUMAN RIGHTS DEVELOPMENT

1. Conceptualization, Articulation, and Development of the Concept of Human Rights. This involved questions of whether there is such a thing as a human right. If so, what is a human right? If so, where does it or do they come from? How many are there? What do they protect? How are they asserted and protected both by and from the government? How do they become part of national law?

2. Standards-setting: The Articulation in Writing of Human Rights Norms. This happened first in non-binding legal principles, such as in the Universal Declaration of Human Rights, followed by binding international agreements between states called treaties. These treaties are created by states to establish the standards of conduct which governments accept to follow internally and which demand other states to comply with. This phase continues in the international and regional community of nations. It also parallels the development of the International Humanitarian Law, part of the Law of Armed Conflict, a separate body of International Law.

3. Implementation Systems/Procedures/Mechanisms. History has well demonstrated that Human Rights written on paper and even in binding written treaties do not ensure that governments will respect and protect them. The international community recognized and realized: the need to set up international bodies to supervise the states in the transformation and implementation of human rights norms nationally; the need for a backup set of mechanisms to monitor internationally the states; and the need for mechanisms to hear written complaints about allegations and to require states to file reports with supervising bodies, so that they can be supervised, encouraged and given resources to improve. Note that the word used is "implementation," not "enforcement." The countries of the world did not want to use the word enforcement as it implies the use of coercive force against a state for how it treats its own people internally. "Implementation of human rights norms" encapsulates in legal terms the kind of force the international community wants to put forth. The international community has created treaties, and most treaties have supervising bodies created in the wording of the treaty. They have also set up bodies and mechanisms at the political and judicial levels to handle human rights issues, such as the U.N. Human Rights Council with its Special Mechanisms, such as special rapporteurs. This phase is about setting up systems to get states to comply with human rights norms. The U.S. has always been very much a part of this process.

4. The International Criminalization of Certain, Most Serious Human Rights Violations. This has evolved into the body of law, known as International Criminal Law (ICL). International Human Rights Law (IHRL) violations involve the fault of the state, i.e., the government for failing to comply with human rights norms among or by those who run a government. However, because acts are committed by individuals working for the state, IHRL did not initially lay any legal responsibility on individuals. Accountability was and is on the state.

However, along with the most serious violations of International Humanitarian Law (IHL), this phase sought to establish individual criminal responsibility for the worst human rights violations, such as torture, slavery, and genocide. Its aim was to deter individuals from committing these most serious violations by the threat of criminal prosecution and penal sanctions. The most serious human rights violations are considered to rise to the level of crimes against all of humankind. International crimes are crimes against all humankind. With the recent developments in International Criminal Law and the adoption of the International Criminal Court, the international community is attempting to undo the so-called "culture of impunity" and to replace it with a culture of human rights. Individual criminal responsibility, if properly implemented, is considered the best deterrent to the most serious human rights violations.

Having considered this continuous four-phase evolution, the following sections define human rights and the various principles and concepts involved in this academic area known as human rights, particularly International Human Rights Law.

THE CONCEPT AND DEFINITION OF HUMAN RIGHTS

Simply stated, human rights are legally enforceable claims or entitlements held by human beings as human beings for the protection of their inherent human dignity, i.e., their inherent worth. In fact and in law, there is no one universally and officially accepted definition of human rights. Several definitions are given below.

Human rights are claims or entitlements held by individual human beings as inherent attributes of the human personality. They are rights held by every human being in relation to government, state, and public power, based solely on being a human being. They are, in theory, legally enforceable claims that an individual can assert to get the government to do something or to refrain from doing something. In concept, they are limitations on the power of government in relation to the individual. They limit the exercise of power by government to only that which is granted to government by the people. In addition, human rights limit authorized power to be exercised only in a way that protects and advances, and does not harm human dignity and the development of the human personality. These rights are expressed in rules and principles that are found written into laws at the national and international levels.

The idea of human rights became necessary to keep governments from becoming tyrannical or despotic by limiting human freedoms. Living in the United States, it is easy to forget that until recent history, there has been little acceptance by governments of an individual's basic human rights derived from inherent human dignity. Rather, the history of the world has been characterized by sovereign kings or queens, emperors or empresses, or ruling elites, who would decide the fate of those over whom they ruled on the basis of their own whims. If a group of people were ruled by a kind and benevolent sovereign, they might be treated with respect. If not, they might experience oppression and hardship. People under the thumb of a cruel tyrant had no recourse but to suffer through his or her reign with hopes for some eventual relief. Aside from early experimentation with democracy in Greece, this scenario was typical.

Rights Exist Before Law Exists, and are not Given or Bestowed by the State

From the relatively modern concept of inalienable human rights based on inherent human dignity, there evolved the concept of government as formally and in law "recognizing" human rights rather than "creating" them. "Recognizing" reflects acceptance of the fact that human rights exist in every human being's situation without the need of any legislative action. Human beings were and are born with human rights. Laws do not create human rights; laws only recognize and protect human rights. All human beings are to have their rights protected from the "encroaching power of the state." This is expressly what the American colonists declared to England and to the world in the Declaration of Independence. That revered text which we celebrate every 4th of July states that government is created to protect human rights: "to secure these rights, governments are instituted among men, deriving their just powers from the consent of the governed; that whenever any form of government becomes destructive of these ends, it is the right of the people to alter or to abolish it, and to institute new government, laying its foundation on such principles, and organizing its powers in such form, as to them shall seem most likely to effect their safety and happiness."

Human rights in their modern philosophical sense were first articulated in such documents as the 1776 American Declaration of Independence, along with the 1789 French Declaration of the Rights of Man and of Citizen, commonly accepted as based on Natural Law. These documents present the philosophy that human beings are born with rights that they possess all their lives and that sovereigns, whatever or whoever they might be, may not violate those rights. In the Declaration of Independence, it was expressed as "all men are created equal and endowed...with certain unalienable rights, among them life, liberty, and the pursuit of happiness." These rights were not granted by the state or the king or the legislature. Human rights as a discipline took up this idea of rights as being what human beings possess as part of their nature and which pre-exist law.

This brings up the critical difference between human rights and so-called civil or constitutional rights or liberties. Human rights means something different from what in the U.S. are called "civil rights," "civil liberties," or "constitutional rights." Many civil rights, civil liberties, and constitutional rights do happen to be human rights. However, the concept of human rights includes much more. Americans tend to think of freedoms in domestic legal terms of civil rights or constitutional rights or civil liberties. They do not think of anything legal at the international level. These three types of rights are all rights granted by the sovereign, who gives them to individuals based on the belief that these rights are necessary for the proper ordering, harmonious functioning, and preservation of the society. However difficult, even the Constitution can be changed and individual rights could be repealed, i.e., thrown out.

By contrast, in modern theory, human rights are not granted by any sovereign, whether king or queen, president, prime minister, legislature, or parliament, dictator, or other legal authority. These rights exist inherently in each individual human being. The international human rights instruments in the "Primary Source Documents" section of each chapter make it clear that neither the nations of the world, nor the United Nations, nor any regional body, such as the Organization of American States, is creating or granting any rights by those instruments. Instead, they are merely providing for the articulation, respect, and protection of the rights that they thereby recognize in treaty as already existing in and held by the individual.

Constitutional liberties can be abrogated, or abolished, if the appropriate procedure in our U.S. Constitution is followed. The U.S. Bill of Rights could theoretically be thrown out, if the correct constitutional process is followed. Human rights, however, cannot be voted or legislated out, because they are inherent in Americans, too, because human rights belong to them by nature. If the government abolished the Constitution or the Bill of Rights, human rights would still exist in all Americans. The Declaration of Independence and other legal documents (treaties) in this work say so. That is the great truth celebrated in the U.S. every July 4.

Obvious in those treaties is that the "rock-bottom" basis for all human rights is human dignity, the inherent worth of the human being, merely for being human. Every country in the world now accepts the proposition that human rights exist and that human dignity is the basis of those rights. Countries may differ in many ways on where such dignity comes from and how human rights laws are to be interpreted and applied. But the existence of human rights, its basis in human dignity, and its related principle of equality are accepted as normative in all societies of the globe, even though the actual practice of states leaves much to be desired, and religious and ideological perspectives may warp implementation.

Conceptually, human rights as articulated in international instruments represent a balance of interests. They seek to articulate a fair balance between individual and government. On one hand is the need of human beings for freedom to do what they desire and become what they choose. On the other hand, reason dictates that a society must have some limitations on the conduct of individuals or there will be lawlessness, disorder, and the possible disintegration of society. Human rights seek to strike that balance between the needs of individuals to protect their freedom of human dignity and the legitimate needs of government to regulate the actions of some for the common good. This is particularly important in the war on terrorism. The standards themselves, set forth in the Primary Source Documents of this book, did not "fall from the sky" and are not the broadest and most liberal limitations on government conduct. They are, in fact, more of a minimum, common-denominator, and standard that all countries of the world would agree to, as limitations to be imposed upon their sovereignty. Human rights standards are limitations upon governments that are legally articulated and recognized by international organizations made up of governments, including the U.S. It might seem against the nature of any government institution to voluntarily limit itself and its power. But as the preamble to the U.N. Charter manifests, it was the voice of "We the peoples of the United Nations," not governments, who demanded this in light of the horrors of World War II, especially the Holocaust.

It has only been since the mid 1940s, with the end of World War II and the horrors of the Holocaust, that the global human rights movement and the Peoples of the world started to push governments for protection of human dignity of all human beings, by recognizing their inherent individual human rights. Protecting human dignity in the face of governmental powers means putting legal limits on the power of government. Human rights are limitations on the power of government.

Today, in light of the actions of the U.S. government exerting its power here and abroad in the war on terrorism, and with the initial indications of the new Trump administration, these limitations on the power of government are all the more necessary and need to be broadly known, understood, and promulgated in America. It was Lord Acton who said in 1887: "Power corrupts and absolute power corrupts absolutely." Given that the U.S. has come as close as any in history to being the most absolute power in the world, it behooves the U.S. and implicates all mankind to have an agreed system of values and norms for judging the rightness and justness of our government's action. The American people demand that governments respect and follow international law and not feel above it, in any exceptionalist sense. The international law of human rights and humanitarian law reflects those universal values and must be followed.

In the U.S., governments, Republican or Democrat, will always justify their actions, or to achieve "plausible deniability" when accused of wrongdoing. Each is capable and disposed to abusing power, usually in the name of good. A standard of conduct external to government is the necessary weapon of the free citizen to protect against the abuse of power by the state. The U.S. government's great system of checks and balances did not prevent human rights violations at Abu Gharib prison in Iraq, and is still only slowly and very lately resolving human rights issues at the Guantánamo Bay detainment facility in Cuba. The U.S. needs to set up a better bulwark against abuse of power by all branches of government; law consistent with international human rights legal obligations is suggested as the answer. Americans may, from time to time, need to protect themselves from their own government. The more one puts into place the concept of human rights to limit state power, the less people will have to resort to deadly and divisive rebellion, the seeds of which are often present in every society. This idea is reflected in the preamble of the Universal Declaration of Human Rights:

> "Whereas disregard and contempt for human rights have resulted in barbarous acts which have outraged the conscience of mankind, and the advent of a world in which human beings shall enjoy freedom of speech and belief and freedom from fear and want has been proclaimed as the highest aspiration of the common people,

> Whereas it is essential, if man is not to be compelled to have recourse, as a last resort, to rebellion against tyranny and oppression, that human rights should be protected by the rule of law..."

The theory of human rights is still in the process of being articulated in the U.S. and around the globe. One can, however, expound on some of the universally accepted doctrines and principles of human rights which constitute the theoretical basis of those rights, which are listed below.

It must be stated that rights exist outside of the concept of human rights law. There exist moral rights and some say divine rights as well. This work *only* addresses human law and the concept of human rights within that field of human law, particularly the law of nations, international law, as it relates to the United States of America.

Essential Characteristics of Human Rights

Human rights have several distinctive characteristics that distinguish them from any other type of legal rights. Human rights are legal rights and they are:

1. Inherent: Human rights are inherent attributes of the human personality. As stated, they inhere in, or are part of, the essential nature of human beings and are not created or bestowed by any earthly authority or constitution. In the Declaration of Independence this idea is expressed as human beings being "endowed" with such rights.

2. Universal: Human rights are universally held; they are held by all human beings, in that everyone has them. They are not an American right or a democratic right but are universally accepted philosophical and legal principles articulated by all the countries of the world. This is stated in our Declaration of Independence as "All men are created equal and endowed...with certain unalienable rights...."

3. Unalienable/Inalienable: Since these rights are not granted or legislated by any public or private authority, they cannot be taken away, that is, alienated, from the holder. The state has, in theory, no right to alienate them from a person. Indeed, the exercise of human rights can be limited by government for only certain reasons; the state may not extinguish one's human rights, nor may the state force a person to give them up. They inhere permanently in humans from birth (some say from conception) to death.

Prerequisite Principles of Human Rights

From these characteristics, there arise three necessary and related human rights principles that are prerequisites for the full respect for human rights by states:

1. Non-discrimination: Not only does everyone possess all human rights, but society must ensure that all people can exercise their rights without any discrimination based on their race, religion, color, sex, nationality, or other status. (See International Covenant on Civil and Political Rights (ICCPR), Primary Source Document 2)

2. Rule of law: Human rights can only be respected in a society characterized by "rule of law," meaning that law is the ultimate authority in society and no one is above the law. As Americans would say, it is "a society of laws and not of men." Human rights instruments, such as the ICCPR, Article 2.2, require states parties to legislate these rights into their national legal system to be legally enforceable against government, federal, state or local. No one in a society, even the President of the United States, can be above the law, even if Congress passed a law to that effect. All this is, of course, consistent with the United States Constitution. In America, nothing and no one may violate the Constitution, as it is now.

3. Effective domestic remedies: There must be effective domestic remedies for violations of rights. Without an effective and accessible legal remedy, there can be no legal human right. Human rights would be noble but illusory rights. In theory, human rights can only be protected if the holders of those rights or their representatives have accessible and effective legal remedies in the national "domestic" legal system to enforce their rights. Human rights instruments such as the ICCPR, Article 2.3, require states parties to establish legal procedures in national law to prevent or redress violations. These must be both accessible and effective. The remedies may be judicial, or administrative, so long as the latter has recourse to judicial scrutiny of administrative decision.

Collective or Group Rights

In its classic theory, human rights are individual. Each individual is said to be a "bearer" or "holder" of such rights individually, without regard to membership in any given society. It is up to each society (state) to set up its legal system so as to protect these individual rights for all.

In modern human rights theory, some hold that human rights can also be collective, or group rights. This theory is asserted especially, for example, to protect the rights of certain minority groups (racial, religious, linguistic, ethnic) and indigenous groups as a whole. In this theory, some argue that the group holds the human right for each of its members, collectively, whereas the other (and better) theory claims that each individual in the group/collective holds and exercises his or her individual human rights together with the other members of the group, and that human rights can theoretically only be individual. The theory of group or collective rights is not universally accepted, but is becoming more and more so, particularly in reference to indigenous peoples.

PRINCIPAL SOURCES OF HUMAN RIGHTS NORMS: TREATIES, CUSTOMARY INTERNATIONAL LAW, ETC.

Human rights have been articulated as legal rights primarily at the international level in and as part of the field of law known as public international law, also known as the law of nations. These norms are found in documents which are referred to as instruments. These instruments can set forth legally binding human rights norms, but some instruments set forth non-binding standards.

Human rights as a discipline is first and foremost articulated in legal principles and rules. Principles are broad general statements of desired goals of human rights. Rules are specific, legal, normative standards of conduct that, if followed, will result in conformity of state conduct with those principles.

There are two "material sources" where one finds human rights legal norms: human rights treaty instruments and customary international law norms. In addition to these binding legal norms, one also finds many rules, standards and principles in international documents which are not legally binding but are adopted to help states comply with their legal obligations, or to serve as the basis of a later binding treaty. These non-binding documents are identified by the following names: Resolutions, Declarations, Principles, Basic Principles, Code of Conduct, Standard Minimum Rules, and Guidelines.

International human rights treaties set forth what is referred to as "hard law," i.e., legally binding norms. Some of these non-legally binding documents are what is called "soft law." Again, these non-binding documents help states comply with their legal obligations, as a sort of road map to compliance with hard law obligations.

Treaties

The heart of human rights is found in treaties, which are contracts, agreements between or among countries to set standards of how government must act in relation to human beings for protection of human dignity. One's human rights are primarily set out in written international instruments called treaties. Treaty is a generic word for an international agreement which is governed by international law. Many other terms signify roughly the same thing as a treaty: an international legal instrument which creates binding legal obligations on states who choose to sign and ratify the treaty. The other names for a treaty instrument are as follows: covenant, convention, charter, statute agreement, pact, protocol. The last term, protocol, denotes a treaty which modifies an existing treaty. Later chapters discuss some of these different names for treaties, mostly using the terms "covenant" and "convention."

In the realm of international human rights law, it is necessary to keep in mind whether one is dealing with a document which is legally binding or non-legally binding. Accusing a country of violating human rights can only be done using a binding norm from a treaty to which the state is a "state party," or a customary international law norm, as explained below. Because the Universal Declaration of Human Rights (UDHR) is universally acknowledged as having ripened over the course of time into binding customary international law norms, even though it is a declaration and not a treaty, it has the status of "hard core" human rights norms. It is the only source of law that is an exception to citing a treaty as a normative document. Normally one would consider a "declaration" non-legally binding. The UDHR is normative, however.

It is necessary to understand treaties in order to understand human rights, humanitarian law, and international criminal law, all of which are covered in this text, even though the primary focus is on human rights texts. It is critical to keep in mind when looking at treaties that human rights treaties do not create any human rights; governments do not create any human rights.

Again, human rights are inherent; we are born with our rights as an attribute of our human personality and personhood. States do not create or give human rights. Human rights treaties are only the formal written recognition by states of the existence of these rights in the people, and along with the creation of treaties come the creation of certain mechanisms and procedures under the supervision of a designated body, all of it under international law. Moreover, these international treaty norms must be transformed or incorporated into the national legal system so that they become the domestic law of the state, and do not remain just international law. The international legal order is subsidiary to the national legal order and it is the state that is the primary protector of human rights. The international legal system is a backup, whenever the national law and legal system fails.

These questions relating to understanding a human rights treaty will be answered throughout this work:

1. What does a treaty look like?

2. How is a Treaty Instrument (Convention, Covenant, Charter, Pact, Agreement, Protocol) made?

3. How/when do treaties become international legal obligations "binding" on the U.S.?

4. How are treaties implemented (not enforced)?

5. How are treaties changed?

6. How can a state get out of treaty obligations (denunciation)?

7. What are the different parts of a treaty instrument and their function? (Anatomy of a treaty with treaty ICCPR excerpted as an example)

8. How are international human rights treaties interpreted and applied via:

   a. Vienna Convention of the Law of Treaties

   b. General Comments of Treaty Bodies

   c. U.S. Department of State Principles in Applying Human Rights

9. How are international human rights treaty norms transformed into U.S. national law?

10. Why do states, like the U.S., want to take on legal obligations under International Human Rights Law?

1. What does a treaty look like?

As an example, the following is a selection of parts of a treaty known as the International Covenant on Civil and Political Rights (ICCPR), which is covered more fully in the Primary Source Documents, all of which are good discussions of human rights law.

International Covenant on Civil and Political Rights
{excerpt}

Adopted and opened for signature, ratification and accession by General Assembly resolution 2200A (XXI) of 16 December 1966, entry into force 23 March 1976, in accordance with Article 49.

Preamble

The States Parties to the present Covenant,

Considering that, in accordance with the principles proclaimed in the Charter of the United Nations, recognition of the inherent dignity and of the equal and inalienable rights of all members of the human family is the foundation of freedom, justice and peace in the world,

Recognizing that these rights derive from the inherent dignity of the human person,

Recognizing that, in accordance with the Universal Declaration of Human Rights, the ideal of free human beings enjoying civil and political freedom and freedom from fear and want can only be achieved if conditions are created whereby everyone may enjoy his civil and political rights, as well as his economic, social and cultural rights,

Considering the obligation of States under the Charter of the United Nations to promote universal respect for, and observance of, human rights and freedoms,

...

Agree upon the following articles:

PART I

Article 1

1. All peoples have the right of self-determination. By virtue of that right they freely determine their political status and freely pursue their economic, social and cultural development.

...

Article 7

No one shall be subjected to torture or to cruel, inhuman or degrading treatment or punishment. In particular, no one shall be subjected without his free consent to medical or scientific experimentation.

...

Article 21

The right of peaceful assembly shall be recognized. No restrictions may be placed on the exercise of this right other than those imposed in conformity with the law and which are necessary in a democratic society in the interests of national security or public safety, public order (ordre public), the protection of public health or morals or the protection of the rights and freedoms of others.

Article 25

Every citizen shall have the right and the opportunity, without any of the distinctions mentioned in article 2 and without unreasonable restrictions:

(a) To take part in the conduct of public affairs, directly or through freely chosen representatives;

(b) To vote and to be elected at genuine periodic elections which shall be by universal and equal suffrage and shall be held by secret ballot, guaranteeing the free expression of the will of the electors;

(c) To have access, on general terms of equality, to public service in his country.

...

Article 28

1. There shall be established a Human Rights Committee (hereafter referred to in the present Covenant as the Committee). It shall consist of eighteen members and shall carry out the functions hereinafter provided.

2. The Committee shall be composed of nationals of the States Parties to the present Covenant who shall be persons of high moral character and recognized competence in the field of human rights, consideration being given to the usefulness of the participation of some persons having legal experience.

...

Article 40

1. The States Parties to the present Covenant undertake to submit reports on the measures they have adopted which give effect to the rights recognized herein and on the progress made in the enjoyment of those rights:

(a) Within one year of the entry into force of the present Covenant for the States Parties concerned;

(b) Thereafter whenever the Committee so requests.

2. All reports shall be submitted to the Secretary-General of the United Nations, who shall transmit them to the Committee for consideration. Reports shall indicate the factors and difficulties, if any, affecting the implementation of the present Covenant.

[End of treaty text excerpts]

ớ҄ớ҄ớ҄ớ҄ớ҄

2. How is a Treaty Instrument (Convention, Covenant, Charter, Pact, Agreement, Protocol) made?
Treaties are not just created by the administration of an international organization like the U.N. and forced upon the member states. Treaties are created by the collaborative sovereign voluntary consensual activity of individual nation states that gather together to fashion them. States draft and adopt treaties to which they may choose to become bound, or not, as their national self-interest or ruler dictates. In the following flow chart, the process of treaty-making is described. It is generally applicable to all human rights treaties, though some steps, such as an initial declaration of principle, do not apply to all treaties. Because almost all human rights treaties to which the U.S. is a party arise from the U.N. context, the following largely apply, except as noted.

Each treaty has its own historical, political, geopolitical, and legal context.

Steps in Treaty Creation and Implementation
Note: ↓ denotes a flow to the next step in the process.

Treaties are created by states in the context of an international intergovernmental organization such as the United Nations or the Organization of American States; the U.S. is a member state of both bodies.

> First Negotiation among states and adoption of a resolution approving a declaration of human rights principles by vote of the General Assembly (non-juridical, non-binding principles). Example: the U.N. Declaration on the Rights of the Child.
> (This pre-treaty declaration creation does not apply to all human rights treaties.)

> Someone in the international community makes a proposal in the IGO for interested states to come together to fashion a binding Treaty instrument covering a certain field of human rights; for example, children's rights. It is discussed by states internally, and if they agree, they join the other states in continuing the treaty-making, the so called "standard-setting" process, heading towards making new international law. Then arrangements are made for a diplomatic conference to gather the interested states.

The Diplomatic Conference, an assembly of all interested states, is held for negotiation and drafting of the articles of the text. Sometimes there is a model text presented as a starting point for negotiations. There is also the creation of the Preparatory Works (*Travaux Préparatoires*) which journals the legislative history of the drafting. Each part of the treaty is proposed, sometimes in different versions; when the assembly has finally chosen the text it feels is appropriate, it votes on that part, and moves on to the next part until the whole of the treaty text is arrived at that is acceptable to the states.

↓

Next the whole text is put to a vote. States vote to adopt the text; this sets and identifies the full official text. If it is rejected, the assembly continues its work, trying to find an acceptable text wording. If it is adopted by vote or consensus, the text is set and the assembly can proceed to the next step: signature by states.

↓

If the text is adopted, the treaty text is "open for signature" by states. This means it is open for states to sign the treaty by their official representative, who has "full powers" (Plenipotentiary) to act on behalf of the state, like signing a contract. Some states choose to have a signature and ratification process altogether and at the same time.

↓

States may sign the adopted "open for signature" instrument. Some sign and ratify at the same time. But unlike most contracts, which are binding upon signature, most signatures are made "*ad referendum*," meaning the treaty text must be submitted to the signer's government for the government to ratify the signing. This involves the internal laws of the signing state as to how the signature is ratified. It represents in theory all the people of a ratifying state approving and accepting to bind the state to complying with the treaty. Every state ratification process is different.

↓

After having signed, each of the 'signatory states' begins the process of ratification as per national legal requirements (constitution/law/administrative rule). States ratify, etc... the treaty under national or domestic law. Once a state finishes its ratification, it must submit its written instrument of ratification to a certain place called a depository.

↓

States deposit their Instrument of Ratification with the named depository, along with any instrument of reservations, declarations, and understandings ("RDU"/"RUD").

↓

Instrument submitted with Instrument of Ratification, may include an RDU:

- **A Reservation:** The reservation expresses the state's approving the treaty with a modification to a particular norm, usually meaning exclusion of that norm from the state's obligation.

- **A Declaration:** The declaration expresses the state's acceptance of the authority of the supervisory body to receive and decide complaints against it, or the scope of applicability or other qualification. (Caveat: This type of declaration is different from the declarations of principles like the UDHR; don't mistake them. This RDU declaration is a legal, juridical act and expression of the state that is submitted with the ratification/accession instrument.)

- **An Understanding or Interpretation:** An understanding or interpretation expresses the state's understanding or interpretation of the meaning of certain terms within the treaty.

- **Comment:** Sometimes states, when ratifying a treaty, will submit RDUs but one or more of them has been mislabeled; that is to say, a state may call a statement a reservation to the treaty when, in fact, it is not functionally a reservation but rather an understanding. The treaty body which is charged with supervision of the human rights treaty will apply the statement as it sees them functionally and legally as to what is expressed by the state, not necessarily as the state has named them.

As an example, the following is an actual U.S. Instrument of Ratification with RDUs, excerpts of the 1992 U.S. ratification of the ICCPR.

Instrument of Ratification

Formal Title: The International Covenant on Civil and Political Rights, signed on behalf of the United States on October 5, 1977.
Date Received from President: 02/23/1978 – 95th Congress (1977-1978)
Originating Organization: United Nations
Latest Senate Action: 04/02/1992 – 102nd Congress (1991-1992)
    Resolution of advice and consent to ratification agreed to in Senate by Division Vote.
Resolution of Ratification: Senate Consideration of Treaty Document 95-20

TEXT OF RESOLUTION OF ADVICE AND CONSENT TO RATIFICATION AS REPORTED BY THE COMMITTEE ON FOREIGN RELATIONS AND APPROVED BY THE SENATE:

Senate of the United States In Executive Session

2 April 1992

Resolved, (two-thirds of the Senators present concurring therein), That the Senate advise and consent to the ratification of the International Covenant on Civil and Political Rights, adopted by the United Nations General Assembly on 16 December 1966, and signed on behalf of the United States on 5 October 1977, (Executive E, 95-2), subject to the following Reservations, Understandings, Declarations and Proviso:

I. The Senate's advice and consent is subject to the following reservations:

(1) That Article 20 does not authorize or require legislation or other action by the United States that would restrict the right of free speech and association protected by the Constitution and laws of the United States.

...

(5) That the policy and practice of the United States are generally in compliance with and supportive of the Covenant's provisions regarding treatment of juveniles in the criminal justice system. Nevertheless, the United States reserves the right, in exceptional circumstances, to treat juveniles as adults, notwithstanding paragraphs 2 (b) and 3 of Article 10 and paragraph 4 of Article 14. The United States further reserves to these provisions with respect to individuals who volunteer for military service prior to age 18.

II. The Senate's advice and consent is subject to the following understandings, which shall apply to the obligations of the United States under this Covenant:

(1) That the Constitution and laws of the United States guarantee all persons equal protection of the law and provide extensive protections against discrimination. The United States understands distinctions based upon race, colour, sex, language, religion, political or other opinion, national or social origin, property, birth or any other status-as those terms are used in Article 2, paragraph 1 and Article 26-to be permitted when such distinctions are, at minimum, rationally related to a legitimate governmental objective. The United States further understands the prohibition in paragraph 1 of Article 4 upon discrimination, in time of public emergency, based "solely" on the status of race, colour, sex, language, religion or social origin not to bar distinctions that may have a disproportionate effect upon persons of a particular status.

...

(5) That the United States understand that this Covenant shall be implemented by the Federal Government to the extent that it exercises legislative and judicial jurisdiction over the matters covered therein, and otherwise by the state and local governments; to the extent that state and local governments exercise jurisdiction over such matters, the Federal Government shall take measures appropriate to the Federal system to the end that the competent authorities of the state or local governments may take appropriate measures for the fulfilment of the Covenant.

III. The Senate's advice and consent is subject to the following declarations:

(1) That the United States declares that the provisions of Articles 1 through 27 of the Covenant are not self-executing.

...

(3) That the United States declares that it accepts the competence of the Human Rights Committee to receive and consider communications under Article 41 in which a state party claims that another state party is not fulfilling its obligations under the Covenant....

Attest: Walter J. Stewart Secretary

[End of text excerpts]

ೋ∞ೋ∞ೋ∞ೋ∞ೋ∞

Looked at procedurally, the process looks like the following:
- Treaty is proposed
- Treaty conference to negotiate and draft text of treaty
- Text voted on for adoption
- Text adopted and opened for signature by states (adoption sets official text)
- Treaty signed by states and submitted for ratification at national level
- Treaty ratified by states (subject to RDUs)
- Treaty enters into force at pre-established time based on number of ratifications. Treaty is now binding on all states parties to it

3. How/when do treaties become international legal obligations which are "binding" on the U.S.?

↓

At the moment when the number of state ratifications set forth in the treaty has been reached and received by the depository, the treaty "enters into force." Every state that has ratified it at that time becomes a "state party" or "contracting party" to the treaty and is from that moment on obligated to comply with the treaty under international law.

↓

Other states who have not done so may sign and then accede or adhere to the instrument. They deposit their instrument of accession/adhesion with the designated depository. The date of entry into force for each such state is set forth in the treaty (e.g., 180 days after deposit of instrument of acceptance).

Looked at procedurally in another way:
- U.S. signs treaty; U.S. President or diplomat with full powers signs for U.S. indicating intent to ratify and become bound (Constitution Art. 2 sec. 2);
- U.S. Senate ratifies the treaty if it so chooses, and with or without reservations, declarations, and understandings;
- U.S. is now bound under international law if treaty has entered into force (EIF);
- If treaty is not "self-executing," these obligations do not enter into U.S. law until implementing legislation is passed by the U.S. Congress.

4. How are treaties implemented (note: not "enforced")?

↓

States parties to the instrument have set provision in the text for establishment of an implementation mechanism, called a supervisory organ; this is usually a Committee, Commission, Court (e.g., U.N. HRCee or American Commission on Human Rights). These organs are established and operate under the mandate and terms of reference in the instrument or as established by the parties or supervisory organ, such as rules of procedure or evidence. The states parties implement in good faith the treaty procedural obligation provisions at the international level: states report to the supervisory body individual/interstate complaints, general comments, country reports/on-site (in loco) investigation, thematic reports.

States begin the process of implementation into national or domestic law: transformation/incorporation of the treaty norms into national law so that international law then becomes national law.

In the discourse of international human rights law, one does not use the term "enforced," such as in "How is this treaty enforced?" One uses the term "implementation," which has the sense of fulfilling something. The international community does not want to use the term "enforce," because it suggests the use of coercive force against perceived violators. "How is this treaty implemented?" is the proper expression of the question.

5. How are treaties changed?

States can change a treaty by calling for an "amendment" or modification, which is done by creating a protocol by the same process as for creating a treaty. These can add a right or add a procedure or create a new supervisory body such as a court.

6. How can a state get out of treaty obligations (denunciation)?

States, because they are sovereign, can get out of a treaty by a process called "denunciation." The state can follow the terms of the Denunciation/Withdrawal clause in the treaty, and at the end of a certain time they are considered to no longer be bound by the treaty obligations.

A treaty can be terminated by the states parties if they should vote to do so, if the need for the treaty no longer exists, or when a newer or different treaty regime is created and becomes preferable.

7. What are the different parts of a treaty instrument and their functions?

An international human rights treaty is a carefully written, complex legal documents that looks very much like a complex contract. It is the expression of the will of all the states who participated in the negotiation and drafting of the treaty text. A treaty is made up of different parts, mostly a Preamble followed by many paragraph-like articles. After the Preamble, the substantive rights and procedural rights are set forth. Substantive rights are the human rights themselves, such as "Everyone has the right to life." Procedural rights are those which create the supervisory body and mechanisms for implementation, such as a written complaint procedure.

The main purpose of a treaty is to spell out, to express in written legal terms, what human rights are recognized by that instrument and what mechanism and procedures are being established to assure that the states parties fulfill their obligations to comply with it. Treaties involving International Humanitarian Law and International Criminal Law are also largely structured this way, though their purpose and juridical basis are a bit different.

THE ANATOMY OF A TREATY

(Treaty ICCPR excerpted as an example; see the full ICCPR text in Chapter 3)

The following are the different parts of a typical human rights treaty, particularly in the U.N. system. Each treaty starts with a title, which identifies what it is about. The title of the ICCPR is:

International Covenant on Civil and Political Rights

After the title comes the reference identifying the official text by adoption and open for signature date, and the U.N. resolution number wherein the General Assembly adopted that particular text. The text was adopted December 16, 1966. The date that the treaty came into effect and became legally binding was March 23, 1976, when the thirty-fifth state had ratified the treaty. That number was specified in the treaty text. See below. The treaty reference citation is:

Adopted and opened for signature, ratification and accession by General Assembly resolution 2200A (XXI) of 16 December 1966
Entry into force 23 March 1976, in accordance with Article 49

After the official reference information comes the Preamble (preamble means to "walk in front of" something). Examine the Preamble text of the ICCPR above. It starts with the words:

The States Parties to the present Covenant

Considering that, in accordance with the principles proclaimed in the Charter of the United Nations, recognition of the inherent dignity and of the equal and inalienable rights of all members of the human family is the foundation of freedom, justice and peace in the world.

The preamble is not part of the legally binding material in the treaty. It just sets up the background for the legal part. It is an explanation of how this treaty came to be and what it is about. Actually the five purposes of most preambles are: 1. Why the treaty is necessary; 2. The ideology behind the treaty; 3. The Goal of treaty; 4. The Basic Principles involved; and 5. A résumé of the substance of the treaty. The sentences in the preamble are called "*consideranda*" meaning "the things that must be considered" (considering, recognizing, realizing....). This language is helpful in interpreting the treaty by understanding its object and purpose. Next comes the words of obligation, the contractual agreement language that turns this document into a legally binding instrument:

Agree upon the following articles....

The words "agree upon the following articles" are the key words of obligation. States who ratify this treaty voluntarily accept to take on these obligations.

Article 1 of the ICCPR is the first substantive right, i.e., the right to self-determination,

Next comes the "non-discrimination clause," article 2.1,

> **Each State Party to the present Covenant undertakes to respect and to ensure to all individuals within its territory and subject to its jurisdiction the rights recognized in the present Covenant, without distinction of any kind, such as race, colour, sex, language, religion, political or other opinion, national or social origin, property, birth or other status.**

This says that the treaty applies to "all individuals within its territory and subject to its jurisdiction" and that no discrimination can be made in who gets to exercise these rights on the basis of their race, gender, etc. Next comes the "transformation clause." International human rights norms are to be transformed into national law so as to make them part of the fabric of the national legal system.

> **Where not already provided for by existing legislative or other measures, each State Party to the present Covenant undertakes to take the necessary steps, in accordance with its constitutional processes and with the provisions of the present Covenant, to adopt such other measures as may be necessary to give effect to the rights recognized in the present Covenant.**

Next comes the "effective domestic (national) remedies" clause, article 2.3,

> **Each State Party to the present Covenant undertakes:**
>
> **(a) To ensure that any person whose rights or freedoms as herein recognized are violated shall have an effective remedy, notwithstanding that the violation has been committed by persons acting in an official capacity;**

Rights are not rights unless they can be protected by law in a rule-of-law-based society with judicial and other implementation bodies and procedures. Important in article 2.3 is that the remedy must be real and effective in protecting against or remedying a violation. Any remedy which is not effective likely results in a human rights violation.

Article 3 is another substantive right. It states the human rights principle of equality which in this legal text becomes the human right to equality before the law between men and women. Everyone is equal. Men are not greater in rights than women.

> **The States Parties to the present Covenant undertake to ensure the equal right of men and women to the enjoyment of all civil and political rights set forth in the present Covenant.**

Article 4 is the "Derogation Clause." This clause is invoked if there occurs in a state party a public emergency which affects the very life of the nation and requires a temporary suspension of the exercise of certain rights in the treaty until the emergency is dealt with. This could be something such as, a military invasion by an enemy state, or a major earthquake paralyzing the capital city, or a massive flood. In such cases, the treaty allows the state to suspend certain rights; for example, freedom of movement, while the state deals with it. However, article 4 also sets forth the specific rights in the treaty which cannot be suspended under any circumstances, such as freedom from slavery or the denial of religious freedom. Article 4 reads in part:

> 1. In time of public emergency which threatens the life of the nation and the existence of which is officially proclaimed, the States Parties to the present Covenant may take measures derogating from their obligations under the present Covenant to the extent strictly required by the exigencies of the situation, provided that such measures are not inconsistent with their other obligations under international law and do not involve discrimination solely on the ground of race, colour, sex, language, religion or social origin.

> 2. No derogation from articles 6, 7, 8 (paragraphs 1 and 2), 11, 15, 16 and 18 may be made under this provision.

Article 5 sets forth the "abuse of rights clause" and "savings clause." Article 5.1 is the abuse of clause. It reads:

> Nothing in the present Covenant may be interpreted as implying for any State, group or person any right to engage in any activity or perform any act aimed at the destruction of any of the rights and freedoms recognized herein or at their limitation to a greater extent than is provided for in the present Covenant.

This article prevents a state from acting in such a way, feigning under the guise of protecting human rights, to actually limiting or preventing the exercise of rights. No state action is justified if it destroys or limits a right more than is allowed in the treaty under the limitations clauses.

The savings clause in article 5.2 reads:

> There shall be no restriction upon or derogation from any of the fundamental human rights recognized or existing in any State Party to the present Covenant pursuant to law, conventions, regulations or custom on the pretext that the present Covenant does not recognize such rights or that it recognizes them to a lesser extent.

This means roughly that the state parties cannot look to use another treaty or law in their legal system to justify restricting or suspending the rights in the treaty they have signed. This saves the effect of these treaty norms from limitation or suspension using some other national law as a pretext.

Articles 6 through 27 set forth the rest of the substantive human rights, such as torture, freedom of expression, the right to vote. Notice, however, that the substantive political human right is expressly reserved for citizens. (Every citizen shall have the right...)

Articles 27 through 44 are the implementation clause section of the treaty, establishing the supervisory body, the Human Rights Committee (HRC), and setting forth the various means and obligations of implementation, such as periodic state reports to the HRC and an inter-state complaint procedure.

Article 45 requires that the supervisory body report annually to the U.N. General Assembly on its activities so that the UNGA can be assured that it is fulfilling its mandate and operating within its terms of reference.

Article 48.1 is the "signature clause." 48.2 is the "ratification" and "deposit" clause. 48.3 and 48.4 constitute the "accession clause" and its deposit clause. 48.5 is the notification of all States Parties of when another state becomes a state party. It reads:

> 1. The present Covenant is open for signature by any State Member of the United Nations or member of any of its specialized agencies, by any State Party to the Statute of the International Court of Justice, and by any other State which has been invited by the General Assembly of the United Nations to become a Party to the present Covenant.

2. The present Covenant is subject to ratification. Instruments of ratification shall be deposited with the Secretary-General of the United Nations.

3. The present Covenant shall be open to accession by any State referred to in paragraph 1 of this article.

4. Accession shall be effected by the deposit of an instrument of accession with the Secretary-General of the United Nations.

5. The Secretary-General of the United Nations shall inform all States which have signed this Covenant or acceded to it of the deposit of each instrument of ratification or accession.

Article 49 is the "entry into force clause." It sets up the time at which a state party's legal obligations under the treaty commence. Only if the treaty has entered into force generally and has entered into force as to a particular state party, can one apply the treaty substantive and procedural norms to that state. This treaty required, as stated in this article, that thirty-five states ratify it in order for it to become legally binding, when it entered into force.

1. The present Covenant shall enter into force three months after the date of the deposit with the Secretary-General of the United Nations of the thirty-fifth instrument of ratification or instrument of accession.

2. For each State ratifying the present Covenant or acceding to it after the deposit of the thirty-fifth instrument of ratification or instrument of accession, the present Covenant shall enter into force three months after the date of the deposit of its own instrument of ratification or instrument of accession.

Article 50 is the "federal clause." It states what is the applicability of the treaty in states where there are federal systems with political sub-units like the U.S. with its fifty states, or Switzerland with its many Cantons. This says that when a state (country) ratifies a treaty and when it has entered into force as to that state, the norms are binding in and on all the political sub-units. Article 50 reads:

The provisions of the present Covenant shall extend to all parts of federal States without any limitations or exceptions.

Article 51 is the "amendment clause." This clause sets forth how the states can modify the treaty, such as by adding new substantive rights or new procedural rights. It requires one-third of the states to make a request for amendment before the amendment provision will be engaged. The process, similar to the negotiation and drafting of the treaty itself, is required. Amendments are done by adoption and by ratifying an instrument called a "protocol." The ICCPR has two protocols: the First Optional Protocol allows written complaints by victims of violations, if the state ratifies that protocol; the Second abolishes the death penalty.

Article 52 is a requirement of the U.N. Secretary-General to give certain notices to states parties about signatures, ratifications, accessions, and entry into force.

Article 53 is the "Official text clause." Article 53.1 states which language translations of the treaty are official texts. Only those official texts can be deposited as archives and cited in the official work of the U.N. and its treaty bodies.

The present Covenant, of which the Chinese, English, French, Russian, and Spanish texts are equally authentic, shall be deposited in the archives of the United Nations.

8. How is an international human rights treaty interpreted and applied using Vienna Convention of the Law of Treaties, General Comments of Treaty Bodies, and other tools?

The international instruments which set forth internationally recognized human rights and create an implementation mechanism/body are complex legal instruments drafted under International Law, which must be implemented according to that body of law and using the terminology of International Law. Every country must implement the treaties they sign and must interpret the treaty, because the language of the treaty text can be difficult to understand and the terms used may have special meanings, legal nuances, even meanings that occur only in the context of human rights law. Moreover, when dealing with international human rights law (IHRL), if one also includes consideration of a second body of law to an issue, such as International Humanitarian Law (IHL), the problem of terminology, interpretation, and application of legal norms, government standards of conduct gets even more complicated and sometimes confusing. This is the reason this text has included terminology, the meaning of legal terms in the field of International Human Rights Law, and International Humanitarian Law.

However, understanding the meaning of terms is a bit different from the science of "interpretation" of a treaty. One needs to know the meanings of terms, such as equality, but one also needs to know how to use other tools to help interpret and then apply the human rights texts to a real situation or planned situation.

As a continuing example, one can continue with the question as to whether the ICCPR norms concerning torture would apply to the alleged U.S. government water-boarding activities in Guantánamo or in Abu Ghraib Prison, Iraq under article 2.1 of the ICCPR. That treaty norm states:

Each State Party to the present Covenant undertakes to respect and to ensure to all individuals within its territory and subject to its jurisdiction the rights recognized in the present Covenant,

Article 7: No one shall be subjected to torture or to cruel, inhuman, or degrading treatment or punishment.

At first look, one would be likely to say no, that this treaty does not apply to the U.S., because neither Guantánamo nor Afghanistan are within the territory of the U.S. However, the answer is not so simple and has been highly contested. The U.S. government says no, that the ICCPR does not apply to the U.S. in this case. This is a very controversial issue at the time of this writing; it is a complex legal issue. It has two parts: whether the legal norms in the ICCPR apply to foreign lands under U.S. control (i.e., "Extra-territorial application"); and whether water-boarding constitutes torture, or whether it is ever a permissible limitation measure to protect public national security, which involves the meaning of torture in the ICCPR, and application of limitations clauses as it applies to the U.S.

Part of the answer to this question lies in many different legal sources which aid government, researchers, human rights treaty bodies, and activists to arrive at an answer. In the question raised above, other sources may be regarded as applicable, after first examining the text itself. The following are examples of the sources one would look at and are discussed more fully later in this work:
- The legislative history (known by the French expression, Travaux Préparatoires) of the treaty creation process, especially anything said by the U.S. or any other country about the territorial scope of application;
- The ratification instrument submitted by the U.S., especially the reservations declarations, and understandings;
- Any U.S. state reports submitted to the Human Rights Committee, along with List of Issues to be taken up, and U.S. responses to the List of Issues, and the Concluding Observations of the HRCee to the U.S. Report;
- The U.S. report and issues and Conclusions under other treaties such as the U.N. Convention against Torture;
- The jurisprudence of U.S. courts, such as the Supreme Court, in addressing the jurisdictional reach of the Constitution and U.S. laws;
- Decisions in cases handled by the treaty body such as the Human Rights Committee, and even of foreign and international forums, such as the International Court of Justice, European Court of Human Rights, and Inter-American Court of Human Rights, even if not legally binding;
- Writings of eminent scholars;
- Presidential Executive Orders concerning torture;
- Congressional Research Service memos;
- Department of State and Department of Defense records, particularly legal memoranda;
- Any other official statements or letters from the U.S. regarding the U.S. position;
- The practice of states in the international arena; how and what other nation-states do.

Two other sources one could consult which have a direct bearing on the interpretation and application of the ICCPR are briefly decribed below.

THE VIENNA CONVENTION ON THE LAW OF TREATIES (VCLT)

In International Law, the main text for explaining how a treaty is to be created, interpreted, and applied is the Vienna Convention on the Law of Treaties of 1980. This treaty is known as the 'treaty about treaties.' As a treaty, it was initially binding only on the states parties; but over the course of time, it has become accepted as binding on all states as a matter of Customary International Law. The U.S. accepts this, even though the U.S. has signed (1970), but never ratified the VCLT. The principles set forth in this treaty tell us how a treaty is interpreted. The following are excerpts from the VCLT with several articles bearing on how the ICCPR should be interpreted relative to any issue of interpreting and applying this treaty. Following is the excerpted text:

Vienna Convention on the Law of Treaties
{excerpt}

Done at Vienna on 23 May 1969.
Entered into force on 27 January 1980.

United Nations, Treaty Series, vol. 1155, p. 331

The States Parties to the present Convention,

Considering the fundamental role of treaties in the history of international relations,

Recognizing the ever-increasing importance of treaties as a source of international law and as a means of developing peaceful cooperation among nations, whatever their constitutional and social systems,

Noting that the principles of free consent and of good faith and the *pacta sunt servanda* rule are universally recognized,

Affirming that disputes concerning treaties, like other international disputes, should be settled by peaceful means and in conformity with the principles of justice and international law, Recalling the determination of the peoples of the United Nations to establish conditions under which justice and respect for the obligations arising from treaties can be maintained, Having in mind the principles of international law embodied in the Charter of the United Nations, such as the principles of the equal rights and self-determination of peoples, of the sovereign equality and independence of all States, of non-interference in the domestic affairs of States, of the prohibition of the threat or use of force and of universal respect for, and observance of human rights and fundamental freedoms for all, Believing that the codification and progressive development of the law of treaties achieved in the present Convention will promote the purposes of the United Nations set forth in the Charter, namely, the maintenance of international peace and security, the development of friendly relations and the achievement of cooperation among nations, Affirming that the rules of customary international law will continue to govern questions not regulated by the provisions of the present Convention,

Have agreed as follows:

PART I.
INTRODUCTION

Article 1 – Scope of the present Convention
The present Convention applies to treaties between States.

...

Article 18 – Obligation not to defeat the object and purpose of a treaty prior to its entry into force
A State is obliged to refrain from acts which would defeat the object and purpose of a treaty when:

(a) it has signed the treaty or has exchanged instruments constituting the treaty subject to ratification, acceptance or approval, until it shall have made its intention clear not to become a party to the treaty; or

(b) it has expressed its consent to be bound by the treaty, pending the entry into force of the treaty and provided that such entry into force is not unduly delayed....

PART III.
OBSERVANCE, APPLICATION AND INTERPRETATION OF TREATIES

SECTION 1. OBSERVANCE OF TREATIES

Article 26 – "Pacta sunt servanda"
Every treaty in force is binding upon the parties to it and must be performed by them in good faith.

Article 27 – Internal law and observance of treaties
A party may not invoke the provisions of its internal law as justification for its failure to perform a treaty. This rule is without prejudice to article 46....

SECTION 3. INTERPRETATION OF TREATIES

Article 31 – General rule of interpretation
A treaty shall be interpreted in good faith in accordance with the ordinary meaning to be given to the terms of the treaty in their context and in the light of its object and purpose.

The context for the purpose of the interpretation of a treaty shall comprise, in addition to the text, including its preamble and annexes:

(a) any agreement relating to the treaty which was made between all the parties in connection with the conclusion of the treaty;

(b) any instrument which was made by one or more parties in connection with the conclusion of the treaty and accepted by the other parties as an instrument related to the treaty.

3. There shall be taken into account, together with the context:

(a) any subsequent agreement between the parties regarding the interpretation of the treaty or the application of its provisions;

(b) any subsequent practice in the application of the treaty which establishes the agreement of the parties regarding its interpretation;

(c) any relevant rules of international law applicable in the relations between the parties.

4. A special meaning shall be given to a term if it is established that the parties so intended.

Article 32 – Supplementary means of interpretation
Recourse may be had to supplementary means of interpretation, including the preparatory work of the treaty and the circumstances of its conclusion, in order to confirm the meaning resulting from the application of article 31, or to determine the meaning when the interpretation according to article 31: (a) leaves the meaning ambiguous or obscure; or (b) leads to a result which is manifestly absurd or unreasonable....

[End text]

Source: http://www1.umn.edu/humanrts/instree/viennaconvention.html

The above text would be applied to the ICCPR in order to determine the interpretation and application of the treaty, particularly Article 7 on torture. Article 31.1 is the most important provision in this treaty. All treaties, both human rights and humanitarian law, must be interpreted "in good faith in accordance with the ordinary meaning to be given to the terms of the treaty in their context and in the light of its object and purpose." This must always be kept in mind when there is an issue about what the treaty language means. In applying this to the U.S., one must ask whether the government is interpreting the treaty text in good faith and if it is looking at the ordinary meaning of the terms in their context, in light of the object and purpose of the treaty.

Before moving on, one must also remember in the VCLT the Article 18 provision. This applies to states which have signed a treaty but have not yet ratified it. Again, a state signing a treaty signifies to the international community that with the signing, the state intends to then proceed with the process of ratification and to become legally bound to conform to its obligations. The question becomes: what, if any, obligation does a state have with regard to a treaty, if it has signed but not yet ratified the treaty? The answer is that the drafters did not want signing states to commit acts which would be contrary to the treaty object and purpose after having signed it. Therefore, they inserted a "soft obligation" in Article 18. This is important because the U.S. has a history of signing treaties and then not ratifying them. This goes to the question of what obligation the U.S. has in order to act in a way so as not to undermine a treaty it has signed, such as the Convention on Elimination of Discrimination against Women and the Convention on the Rights of the Child. The U.S., or any signatory, has an obligation to "refrain from acts which would defeat the object and purpose of a treaty."

GENERAL COMMENTS OF TREATY BODIES

Another authoritative source of material about interpretation and application of the ICCPR, used here just as an example, comes from the General Comments of the HRCee.

One of the functions of U.N. treaty bodies is to issue documents which explain the opinion of the members of the treaty bodies about the interpretation and application of human rights treaty norms. This is to give the states parties guidance on how states should interpret and apply the norms in a way that fulfills the state's legal obligations and avoids instances of claims of violation of the treaty by the state. The treaty bodies are made up of legal experts in human rights who work collaboratively. Much of the content of the general comments which they draft and issue, sometimes called "general recommendations" by some treaty bodies, comes from the jurisprudence of the committee from the cases it has decided from written claims of violations. Much comes from the periodic reports submitted to the body by the state parties. It basically tells states parties that if there is a claim of violation against the state party, this comment/recommendation shows how the committee will likely rule as to the interpretation and application of the article of the treaty allegedly violated. General comments are not treaties and are not legally binding.

Taking into consideration the periodic state reports as a start, the General Comments are authoritative interpretations of individual human rights or of the legal nature of human rights obligations in a treaty. They provide some orientation for the practical implementation of human rights norms and serve as a set of criteria for the treaty body to use for evaluating the progress of states in their implementation of the treaty rights. In questions of the interpretation of U.N. human rights treaties one should ascertain whether there are any general comments on the particular article at issue to lend guidance. Additionally, one should consider whether the issue involved brings into play more than one treaty. For example, in the issue set forth above regarding the prohibition of torture in the ICCPR, it is likely the comments of the Committee against Torture would be pertinent as well as those of the HRCee.

The following is an excerpt from General Comment 31 of the HRCee:

HUMAN RIGHTS COMMITTEE
Eightieth Session General Comment No. 31 [80]

The Nature of the General Legal Obligation Imposed on States Parties to the Covenant Adopted on 29 March 2004 (2187th meeting)

3. Article 2 defines the scope of the legal obligations undertaken by States Parties to the Covenant. A general obligation is imposed on States Parties to respect the Covenant rights and to ensure them to all individuals in their territory and subject to their jurisdiction (see paragraph 10 below). Pursuant to the principle articulated in article 26 of the Vienna Convention on the Law of Treaties, States Parties are required to give effect to the obligations under the Covenant in good faith.

The obligations of the Covenant in general and article 2 in particular are binding on every State Party as a whole. All branches of government (executive, legislative and judicial), and other public or governmental authorities, at whatever level-national, regional or local-are in a position to engage the responsibility of the State Party. The executive branch that usually represents the State Party internationally, including before the Committee, may not point to the fact that an action incompatible with the provisions of the Covenant was carried out by another branch of government as a means of seeking to relieve the State Party from responsibility for the action and consequent incompatibility. This understanding flows directly from the principle contained in article 27 of the Vienna Convention on the Law of Treaties, according to which a State Party 'may not invoke the provisions of its internal law as justification for its failure to perform a treaty'....

7. Article 2 requires that States Parties adopt legislative, judicial, administrative, educative and other appropriate measures in order to fulfill their legal obligations. The Committee believes that it is important to raise levels of awareness about the Covenant not only among public officials and State agents but also among the population at large.

...

10. States Parties are required by article 2, paragraph 1, to respect and to ensure the Covenant rights to all persons who may be within their territory and to all persons subject to their jurisdiction. This means that a State Party must respect and ensure the rights laid down in the Covenant to anyone within the power or effective control of that State Party, even if not situated within the territory of the State Party. As indicated in General Comment 15 adopted at the twenty-seventh session (1986), the enjoyment of Covenant rights is not limited to citizens of States Parties but must also be available to all individuals, regardless of nationality or statelessness, such as asylum seekers, refugees, migrant workers, and other persons, who may find themselves in the territory or subject to the jurisdiction of the State Party. This principle also applies to those within the power or effective control of the forces of a State Party acting outside its territory, regardless of the circumstances in which such power or effective control was obtained, such as forces constituting a national contingent of a State Party assigned to an international peace-keeping or peace-enforcement operation.

11. As implied in General Comment 29, the Covenant applies also in situations of armed conflict to which the rules of international humanitarian law are applicable. While, in respect of certain Covenant rights, more specific rules of international humanitarian law may be especially relevant for the purposes of the interpretation of Covenant rights, both spheres of law are complementary, not mutually exclusive.

The general comment cited can shed light on how the HRCee would interpret article 2 and 7 concerning waterboarding outside the U.S., as to the territorial scope of application of the ICCPR, including article 7.

The last tool to help in the interpretation and application of the ICCPR is a set of non-binding principles aimed at finely dissecting the ICCPR as it applies to the Limitation/Restriction clauses in that treaty. In the issue we are examining concerning waterboarding, the state will want to say that the measures of enhanced interrogation by infliction of pain are for the legitimate aim of protecting national security and public order. But since article 7 is an absolute human right such that no exceptions are allowed and such attempted justifications are not legitimate. One reads the General Comment to see if the HRC has spoken such as would shed light on the applicability of article 7 outside of the U.S.

OTHER SOURCES OF GUIDANCE ON INTERPRETATION AND UNDERSTANDING TREATIES (SO-CALLED SOFT LAW)

One can look at other sources of information which have been developed to help states and all interested others understand how to interpret and apply a treaty. There are numerous so-called "soft law" sets of principles and guidelines to help states interpret and harmonize their laws and comply with treaty norms. Soft law sources are not treaties and not legally binding but are expressly drafted to give guidance to states-parties. These documents can deal with one article or one function of the treaty, such as the limitations clauses or derogation periods. They come under many different names, often with the name of the place where they were formulated. One of those documents is examined in excerpted form below. This not well-known set of principles covers the interpretation and application of the limitations and derogations clauses of the ICCPR.

Though these principles are not legally binding, they are backed by very strong and credible legal scholarship, institutional acceptance and use, and are highly respected and generally accepted in the human rights legal community. They should be used in applying the limitations clauses or the derogation clauses of the ICCPR. They have been cited and applied outside of the context of the ICCPR. The reader is advised to read ICCPR Article 19.3 for sample human rights norms with a limitations clause in it. Article 4 of the ICCPR is the derogation clause of that treaty.

United Nations, Economic and Social Council, U.N. Sub-commission on Prevention of Discrimination and Protection of Minorities, Siracusa Principles on the Limitation and Derogation of Provisions in the international covenant on civil and Political rights, annex, U.N. Doc e/cn.4/1984/4 (1984).

...

Limitation Clauses

A. General Interpretative Principles Relating to the Justification of Limitations

1. No limitations or grounds for applying them to rights guaranteed by the Covenant are permitted other than those contained in the terms of the Covenant itself.

2. The scope of a limitation referred to in the Covenant shall not be interpreted so as to jeopardize the essence of the right concerned.

3. All limitation clauses shall be interpreted strictly and in favor of the rights at issue.

4. All limitations shall be interpreted in the light and context of the particular right concerned.

5. All limitations on a right recognized by the Covenant shall be provided for by law and be compatible with the objects and purposes of the Covenant.

6. No limitation referred to in the Covenant shall be applied for any purpose other than that for which it has been prescribed.

7. No limitation shall be applied in an arbitrary manner.

8. Every limitation imposed shall be subject to the possibility of challenge to and remedy against its abusive application.

9. No limitation on a right recognized by the Covenant shall discriminate contrary to Article 2, paragraph 1.

10. Whenever a limitation is required in the terms of the Covenant to be "necessary," this term implies that the limitation:

    (a) is based on one of the grounds justifying limitations recognized by the relevant article of the Covenant,

    (b) responds to a pressing public or social need,

    (c) pursues a legitimate aim, and

    (d) is proportionate to that aim. Any assessment as to the necessity of a limitation shall be made on objective considerations.

11. In applying a limitation, a state shall use no more restrictive means than are required for the achievement of the purpose of the limitation.

12. The burden of justifying a limitation upon a right guaranteed under the Covenant lies with the state.

13. The requirement expressed in Article 12 of the Covenant, that any restrictions be consistent with other rights recognized in the Covenant, is implicit in limitations to the other rights recognized in the Covenant.

14. The limitation clauses of the Covenant shall not be interpreted to restrict the exercise of any human rights protected to a greater extent by other international obligations binding upon the state.

*The term "limitations" in these principles includes the term "restrictions" as used in the Covenant.

B. Interpretative Principles relating to specific Limitation clauses

i. "prescribed by law"

15. No limitation on the exercise of human rights shall be made unless provided for by national law of general application which is consistent with the Covenant and is in force at the time the limitation is applied.

16. Laws imposing limitations on the exercise of human rights shall not be arbitrary or unreasonable.

17. Legal rules limiting the exercise of human rights shall be clear and accessible to everyone.

18. Adequate safeguards and effective remedies shall be provided by law against illegal or abusive imposition or application of limitations on human rights.

...

vi. "national security"

29. National security may be invoked to justify measures limiting certain rights only when they are taken to protect the existence of the nation or its territorial integrity or political independence against force or threat of force.

30. National security cannot be invoked as a reason for imposing limitations to prevent merely local or relatively isolated threats to law and order.

31. National security cannot be used as a pretext for imposing vague or arbitrary limitations and may only be invoked when there exists adequate safeguards and effective remedies against abuse.

32. The systematic violation of human rights undermines true national security and may jeopardize international peace and security. A state responsible for such violation shall not invoke national security as a justification for measures aimed at suppressing opposition to such violation or at perpetrating repressive practices against its population.

9. How are international human rights treaty norms transformed into U.S. national law?

A state which ratifies a human rights treaty must transform its international norms into national law. Each country has its own legal processes for transformation from international law to national law. There is a legal transformation process in U.S. law. On the following page is a chart of that process for the U.S.

10. Why do countries like the U.S. enter into treaties?

Why does a state like the U.S. take on legal obligations towards other states and subject itself to human rights complaints, which is really a limitation of the state's sovereignty and can be shaming or embarrassing? There are several reasons. One is that it makes a state look good in the eyes of the international community by being concerned with human rights both within the state and outside it. A more important reason is that states believe that by entering into a treaty system, they can increase their ability to address an issue, such as torture, or exploitation of children, together with other states. This is particularly so now, in light of globalization and so much transnational movement of people.

1. Treaty Norm:
Creation of an International Human Rights Treaty

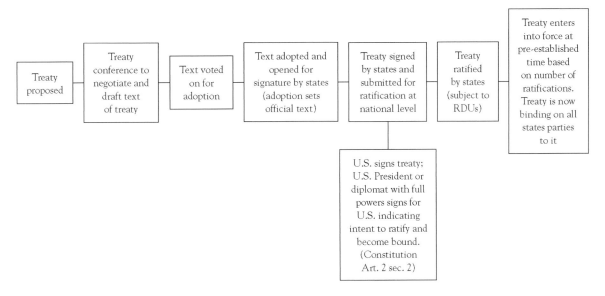

2. U.S. Treaty Ratification Process

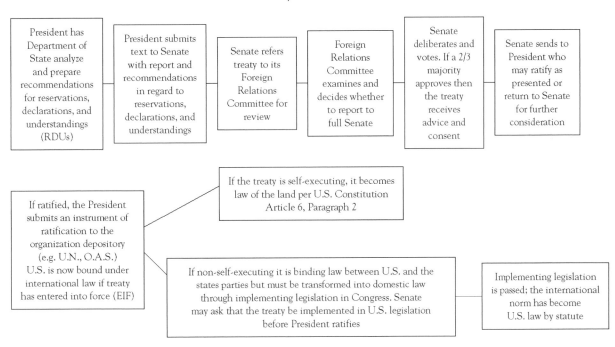

The U.S. enters into treaties, because it gives it a forum to work together with other states to address an issue of mutual concern and common national self-interest, such as human trafficking. When a state chooses to stay out of a treaty system, it has less ability to make an impact on the direction of the international law and policy in a given area; for example, the International Criminal Court (ICC). States sometimes stay out of a treaty system because of a strong domestic opposition to the treaty, such as has been the case of the U.S. and the Convention on the Rights of the Child, or because a state perceives that the treaty obligations will limit its power, activity, or strategy or economic interests in a certain sector, such as is the case with the U.S. regarding unwillingness to accept jurisdiction over it by the ICC or ratification of the ICESCR, simply because human rights places limitations on the power of states in relation to individuals. States do not, by their nature, like to limit their power and authority unless they perceive they will achieve something greater in their national or partisan political interest. Sometimes it is purely for internal political reasons that states choose to ratify or not to ratify a treaty, allowing the ruling government party to get elected or stay in power. State choices are not always principled and are too often principled on staying in power or getting elected. This dynamic exists in the U.S. as well.

More on Treaty Implementation:
The State Reporting System

Above, question 9 asked about how treaties are implemented internationally and nationally by the states parties under the supervisory setup in the treaty.

Human rights treaties are created by an inter-governmental organization, such as the U.N. As stated previously, the treaty sets up a supervising body to monitor and supervise the compliance of all the states parties to the norms of the treaty, both substantive and procedural. The treaty spells out the procedural obligations of the state as to how it implements the treaty. A state party implements a treaty in relation to the supervisory body by complying with its obligations to the treaty body at the international level and then transforming the norms into national law with effective domestic remedies to render those norms justiciable by local courts which ensure that the remedies are effective to protect against or redress violations.

I. Implementation Procedures (Procedural Human Rights)

Every human rights treaty delineates both substantive human rights and procedural human rights. Procedural Human Rights usually set up a supervisory body, such as the Committee against Torture, and spells out the procedural obligations for states, such as submitting periodic reports, and often includes an optional complaint procedure.

A. PERIODIC STATE REPORTS

This is principally done by requiring states party to a treaty to submit periodic state reports to a named supervising treaty body, a committee that bears the name or theme of the treaty, such as the Human Rights Committee that monitors States Parties on implementation of the ICCPR; Committee on Economic, Social and Cultural Rights monitors implementation of the ICESR; Committee on the Elimination of Racial Discrimination monitors CERD. In order to be complete, there exist supervising treaty bodies/committees for CEDAW (Women's human rights); CAT (torture); CRC (children); CMW (migrant workers); CRPD (persons with disabilities); CED (disappeared persons); and OPCAT has a Subcommittee on Prevention of Torture and other Cruel, Inhuman or Degrading Treatment or Punishment. The human rights treaty bodies are committees of independent human rights experts.

The U.S. reports only to those committees whose treaties it has signed and ratified; i.e., CAT, ICCPR, CERD, CRC (as ratifiers of two optional protocols to CRC; but not the original CRC). Most Americans are unaware that the U.S. still has not ratified: the original Convention on the Rights of the Child (CRC); the Convention on the Elimination of Discrimination against Women (CEDAW); the International Covenant on Economic, Social and Cultural Rights (ICESCR); the International Convention on the Protection of the Rights of All Migrant Workers and Members of Their Families (ICMW); the International Convention on the Rights of Persons with Disabilities (ICRPD); or the International Convention for the Protection of All Persons from Enforced Disappearance (ICED). Nonetheless, the U.S. is signatory to CRC (1995), CEDAW (1980), and ICESCR (1977), and may not act against the spirit of these treaties.

In a timely manner, there is follow-up on the country report by the committee in a process that leads to completion before the supervising body/committee. The state reports can be voluminous, as are some U.S. reports. (Some reports are sampled in the Chapter on the U.S. and U.N. and should be examined to get the feeling of how state reports are structured and what they cover.) From the state report, the supervising body/committee wants to know: how the state's implementation process is going; what problems the state is facing in implementation of the treaty; how the state is remedying those problems; what laws have been passed; what relevant case law there is; and anything else which would allow the supervising body/committee to be able to make observations and conclusions about how the state is doing, and to make recommendations as to how the state could address human rights issues. The supervising body/committee examines these state reports along with "shadow reports," usually submitted by NGOs, which add new facts, previously unmentioned problems, sometimes with augmented reporting that differs substantially from those facts submitted by governments in their state report. This is very much a consultative process in which NGOs are expected and allowed to contribute information to the treaty supervising body in its information-gathering process, and, in turn, the reporting state is often made more aware of what information human rights NGOs are turning over to the supervising body, and how the NGOs see the human rights problems.

After a state submits its periodic report, the supervising body reviews it, and can set a formal meeting with representatives of the state to discuss issues. The supervising body/committee often formulates lists of questions in advance to which states can submit answers. Then, after meetings in which the state and supervising body discuss the country's various human rights issues, the supervising body/committee often issues its conclusions and observations and recommendations, aimed at challenging the states to take actions or make laws, and recommends ways to improve the country's human rights circumstances. None of these recommendations are legally binding, but are offered as part of a process of improved domestic or national implementation of the treaty. Each human rights treaty has a similar reporting obligation. The purpose of the process is to assist countries in the domestic implementation of signed and ratified treaties. The various committees have only the good intention of states parties to enact treaties.

The most prominent reporting process is the Universal Periodic Review procedure before the U.N. Human Rights Council. The Council looks at a state's overall human rights record under all treaties, and even beyond human rights law. Every five years, every country in the world has its human rights record scrutinized by the Human Rights Council, but this is not a process based on the treaty body system.

B. COMPLAINT SYSTEM (Inter-state or Individual)

The second way a state party implements a treaty is by cooperating with any complaint systems written into the treaty body when there is a complaint lodged against the state. The term "complaint" is only one word for a written document alleging facts that claim that a state party has violated treaty norms. The terms "petitions," "communications," and "applications" are functionally the same thing as a complaint. They are documents submitted to the treaty body or to a court, asking that forum to apply the facts alleged to the treaty norms and the law and to find that a violation of the treaty has been committed by the state. Not all U.N. treaties have complaint systems, but they are moving in that direction. Most complaint systems operate functionally in a very similar manner. Some complaint procedures are state versus state complaints called inter-state complaints. One state party is alleging that another state party has committed a violation. There are individual complaints by the victims of the violation or those allowed by the rules to lodge a complaint, petition, communication, or application on the victims' behalf.

There is a kind of procedural similarity on the different complaint procedures in what is known as quasi-judicial procedure, which is what treaty bodies do. There are some human rights systems which do have judicial bodies, courts which can render binding judgments. However, the U.S. is not part of any such system, even though it has signed the American Convention on Human Rights of the Organization of American States, which does have a court.

Another point of cooperating with the supervisory body is in instances of *in loco* investigations, meaning "in place," wherein some investigators travel to a state where an incident occurred and search for evidence and testimony, or do research as to a particular issue. Sometimes in conjunction with deciding a case of alleged violation and sometimes for thematic reports a supervising body or persons are given a mandate by which it will go to a country where the violation occurred or investigate concerning a particular thematic issue, with the purpose of gathering information from primary sources and for examining local evidence.

Every treaty system is slightly different and yet largely the same as to its procedures and mechanisms. It must be remembered that these complaint procedures are subsidiary protections to national human rights systems. The complaint procedure is a back-up for when the national system has failed to protect. It is important to recognize that a human rights victim must first go through all accessible and effective domestic, legal, and other procedures to try to get relief at the national level, before filing at the level of international law.

The world of international human rights law largely uses the following procedural flow when someone submits a written complaint to the quasi-judicial or judicial body alleging a human rights violation:

In a human rights system which has a complaint mechanism, a party who has "standing" to file the complaint, petition, communication, or application submits ("lodges") a written submission alleging a violation with the secretariat of the forum or treaty body. It could be a commission, a court, or a committee.

The complaint is either Individual, by the victim or other person with standing, or a state filing against another state (Inter-state)

↓

The forum examines a complaint to see whether it meets the criteria for being admissible. This is called the admissibility stage, to determine whether the complaint meets the rules for cases, so that the body can take jurisdiction over the case and make a decision or not. All this is spelled out in the treaty and/or rules of procedure. The criteria for admissibility usually include the following:

↓

It will first determine whether the complaint is defective for certain reasons, such as, the complaint is submitted anonymously or is an abuse of the complaint process as merely a political attack or personal attack against someone, or full of vulgarity, or exists solely to embarrass the state.

↓

If defective, the forum will reject the complaint. If it is not defective, the forum will refer the complaint to the state for its position on the admissibility issue. With the state's response and admissions, denials, and arguments, the forum will determine if the case meets the admissibility criteria. Usual criteria for admissibility include:

Has the complainant exhausted all effective and accessible domestic remedies?

Has the complaint been filed within the permitted time limit since the last decision of the national courts?

Does the person or state filing the petition have "*Locus Standi*," legal standing to file it?

Is there already another case filed or pending in another human rights forum which is substantially the same case?

Is the matter of the complaint something that is within the legal scope of the treaty norm? (*ratione materiae*: Material Scope)

Did the event, i.e., the violation, occur at a time when the responding state was bound by the treaty? (*ratione temporis*: Temporal Scope)

Did the event, i.e., the violation, happen within the state party's territory or somewhere else where the state has jurisdiction? (*ratione loci*: Geographical Scope)

Has the complaint been filed against the proper party? (*ratione personae*: Personal Scope)

↓

If the forum decides that the case is admissible, it will "seize" the case and proceed to the next step. If inadmissible, it can be "stricken from the roll," i.e., dismissed.

Sometimes the complainant will request certain "provisional measures" at the start of the case to preserve the status quo or prevent an irremediable harm to the complainant while the case is being processed, such as in a death penalty case, or expulsion from the state to another state where the complainant will face torture. It may issue provisional measures and request the state to comply.

↓

If admissible: the forum explores the possibility of friendly settlement via a conciliation process. The forum arranges the conciliation process between petitioners, and the respondent state acts as an intermediator, seeking an "amicable settlement" consistent with human rights.

↓

If a friendly settlement is arrived at, which is consistent with respect for human rights, the forum stops the case and allows the state to implement the conciliation agreement, subject to its follow-up by the supervisory procedure power.

↓

If no friendly settlement is arrived at: Proceed to the "merits" of the case, the application of the facts to the law and a decision as to any violation.

↓

Evidence is submitted;

Hearings may be held;

The facts will be ascertained by the forum, and

The forum considers and deliberates on the merits;

↓

The forum arrives at a decision or reports on the merits as to application of law to the facts.

Sometimes it will also revisit admissibility.

It will decide if the merits show violation(s) or no violation;

↓

It will issue its decision which may call for monetary or other reparations for violations, or for a change of a law or whatever it feels will remedy the violation. In a Court, it will render its judgment, which will be binding upon the parties.

↓

State implements decision/judgment/views.

Most decisions and views are non-binding. Court Judgments are binding. If a violation was found, there can be follow-up supervision of the state by the political power in the IGO governing body.

Each international human rights petition system, global or regional, has its own specific rules of procedure, and one must examine the treaty, charter, statute, rules, and regulations, of a particular system to know exactly how it functions. The foregoing is a loose general schematic of how most complaint systems work.

The U.S. has accepted to be subject to only two complaint procedures at the time of this writing: the inter-state complaint in the ICCPR Article 41 which has never had one complaint filed between any states parties; and the charter based complaint procedure under the American Declaration of Human Rights in the Commission on Human Rights of the Organization of American States. See Chapter on the U.S. and U.N. and Chapter on the OAS.

To get a sense of a human rights complaint filed in an international human rights body, seeking a determination of whether the U.S. has violated human rights, there follows a short sample Petition which was filed against the U.S. in 2008 by U.S. lawyers working for NGOs. By using this actual Petition, the authors are not claiming that the U.S. was in fact legally responsible for any human rights violations alleged.

The following serves as a sample, highly excerpted international human rights Petition filed in the Inter-American Human Rights Commission against the U.S. concerning a Guantánamo Detainee, Djamel Ameziane:

A SAMPLE OF TREATY-BASED HUMAN RIGHTS COMPLAINT
{excerpt}

IN THE INTER-AMERICAN COMMISSION ON HUMAN RIGHTS

DJAMEL AMEZIANE,
Prisoner, U.S. Naval Station, Guantánamo Bay, Cuba

Petitioner,
v.
U.S.,
Defendant.

I. PRELIMINARY STATEMENT

Djamel Ameziane is a prisoner at the U.S. Naval Base at Guantánamo Bay, Cuba, where he has been held virtually incommunicado, without charge or judicial review of his detention, for six and a half years. While arbitrarily and indefinitely detained by the U.S. at Guantánamo, Mr. Ameziane has been physically and psychologically tortured, denied medical care for health conditions resulting from his confinement, prevented from practicing his religion without interference and insult, and deprived of developing his private and family life. The stigma of Guantánamo will continue to impact his life long after he is released from the prison. These harms, as well as the denial of any effective legal recourse to seek accountability and reparations for the violations he has suffered, constitute violations of fundamental rights under the American Declaration of the Rights and Duties of Man ("American Declaration"). The U.S. government, as a signatory to the Declaration, is obliged to respect these rights vis-à-vis Mr. Ameziane by virtue of holding him as its prisoner.

A citizen of Algeria. Mr. Ameziane left his home country in the 1990s to escape escalating violence and insecurity and in search of a better life. He went first to Austria, where he worked as a high-paid chef, and then to Canada, where he sought political asylum and lived for five years but was ultimately denied refuge. Fearful of being deported to Algeria and faced with few options, Mr. Ameziane went to Afghanistan. He fled that country as soon as the fighting began in October 2001, but was captured by the local police and turned over to U.S. forces, presumably for a bounty.

In February 2002, Mr. Ameziane was transferred from Kandahar to Guantánamo Bay, just weeks after the prison opened. As one of the first prisoners to arrive, Mr. Ameziane was held in Camp X-Ray — the infamous camp of the early regime at Guantánamo — in a small wire-mesh cage, exposed to the sun and the elements. In March 2007, he was transferred to Camp VI — the newest maximum security facility at Guantánamo — where, according to unclassified information to date, he sits in isolation all day, every day, in a small concrete and steel cell with no windows to the outside or natural light or air, and where he is slowly going blind.

During his imprisonment at Guantánamo, Mr. Ameziane has been interrogated hundreds of times. In connection with these interrogations, he has been beaten, subjected to simulated drowning, denied sleep for extended periods of time, held in solitary confinement, and subjected to blaring music designed to torture. His abuse and conditions of confinement have resulted in injuries and long-term health conditions for which he has never received proper treatment, despite repeated requests. Medical treatment has furthermore been withheld to coerce his cooperation in interrogations.

I. BACKGROUND AND CONTEXT
A. The U.S.' Response to September 11

10. Days after the attacks on the World Trade Center and the Pentagon on September 11, 2001, the Congress passed a joint resolution that broadly authorized the President to "use all necessary and appropriate force against those nations, organizations, or persons he determines planned, authorized, committed, or aided the terrorist attacks...in order to prevent any future acts of international terrorism by such nations, organizations, or persons." This resolution, the Authorization for the Use of Military Force ("AUMF"), provided the legal basis for the U.S.' military campaign against the Taliban regime in Afghanistan and the al Qaeda elements that supported it.

11. Two months later, on November 13, 2001, the President signed an executive order that defined a sweeping category of non-U.S. citizens whom the Department of Defense was authorized to detain in its "war against terrorism." The order provided that the President alone would determine which individuals fit within the purview of that definition and could be detained. It also explicitly denied all such detainees being held in U.S. custody anywhere the right to challenge any aspect of their detention in any U.S. or foreign court or international tribunal, and authorized trial by military commissions for individuals who would be charged.

...

II. STATEMENT OF FACTS

a. Background

Mr. Ameziane was born on April 14, 1967 in Algiers, the sixth in a close-knit family of eight brothers and sisters. Mr. Ameziane's brother remembers that as a child, Mr. Ameziane was quiet and loved to read, and was content to sit in his room for hours surrounded by stacks of books. Mr. Ameziane attended primary school, secondary school, and university in Algeria, and worked as a hydraulics technician after obtaining his university diploma.

...

III. ADMISSIBILITY

A. Mr. Ameziane's Petition is Admissible Under the Commission's Rules of Procedure.

74. Mr. Ameziane's petition is admissible in its entirety under the IACHR Rules. In particular, the Commission has jurisdiction ratione personae, ratione materiae, ratione temporis, and ratione loci to examine the petition, and Mr. Ameziane is exempt from the exhaustion of domestic remedies requirement under the terms of 31.2 of the IACHR Rules. The Commission should therefore reach a favorable admissibility finding and proceed in earnest to examine the merits of this grave case of human rights abuse.

...

IV. VIOLATIONS OF THE AMERICAN DECLARATION ON THE RIGHTS AND DUTIES OF MAN

A. The U.S. has Arbitrarily Deprived Mr. Ameziane of his Liberty and Denied his Right to Prompt Judicial Review in Violation of Article XXV of the American Declaration.

113. The ongoing detention of Mr. Ameziane as an "enemy combatant" — until recently without the prospect of court review — constitutes an arbitrary deprivation of his liberty and a denial of his right to prompt judicial review of the legality of his detention in violation of Article XXV of the American Declaration. While the U.S. Supreme Court recently

ruled in Boumediene that Guantánamo detainees have the right to habeas, as in 2004, the fact is that Mr. Ameziane remains imprisoned after more than six years, and a court has yet to examine the lawfulness of his detention, despite his best efforts to seek review. The violation of his right not to be arbitrarily detained and to have a court ascertain the legality of his detention without delay occurred years ago, and it will continue until the day that a U.S. federal court rules on his habeas petition.

Article XXV of the American Declaration provides:

> No person may be deprived of his liberty except...according to the procedures established by pre-existing law.

> ...Every individual who has been deprived of his liberty has the right to have the legality of his detention ascertained without delay by a court.

> These protections, like international human rights law in general, apply in all situations, including those of armed conflict. In the latter context, however, international humanitarian law may serve as the lex specialis in interpreting international human rights instruments, such as the American Declaration. Under international humanitarian law, certain deprivations of liberty, which would otherwise constitute violations of international human rights law, may be justified.

> ...

II. CONCLUSION AND PRAYER FOR RELIEF

232. For the aforementioned reasons, Petitioners respectfully request that the Honorable Commission:

1. With regard to Mr. Ameziane's request for precautionary measures:

a. Urgently issue the necessary and appropriate precautionary measures to prevent further irreparable harm to Mr. Ameziane's fundamental rights, in accordance with Sections VI.B.3 and VI.C.2:

2. With regard to Mr. Ameziane's individual petition against the U.S.:

a. Consider the admissibility and merits of this petition simultaneously, in accordance with Article 37(4) of the Commission's Rules of Procedure, given the serious and urgent nature of the case and the ongoing violations of Mr. Ameziane's fundamental rights;

b. Declare the petition admissible and find that the U.S. has violated Mr. Ameziane's rights enshrined in Articles I, III, V, VI, XI, XVIII, XXV, and XXVI of the American Declaration of the Rights and Duties of Man; and

c. Order the U.S. to provide prompt and adequate reparations for the violations suffered by Mr. Ameziane. The Petitioners thank the Commission for its careful attention to this pressing matter.

Dated: August 6, 2008 Respectfully submitted,

Pardiss Kebriaei

Shayana Kadidal

CENTER FOR CONSTITUTIONAL RIGHTS
666 Broadway, 7th Floor, New York, NY 10012
(Tel) 212-614-6452 (Fax) 212-614-6499

Viviana Krsticevic

Ariela Peralta

Francisco Quintana

Michael Camileri

CENTER FOR JUSTICE AND INTERNATIONAL LAW (CEJIL)
1630 Connecticut Ave, NW, Suite 401
Washington, D.C. 20009
(Tel) 202-319-3000   (Fax) 202-319-3019

[End Petition]

A sample of an actual Decision of an international human rights body in a case against the U.S. will be found in the Chapter on the OAS system.

One of the benefits of both the periodic reports and decision of cases by the supervisory body is what is referred to as General Comments or General Recommendations, referred to above as a help in interpreting treaties. The supervisory body distills the case law and its observation of the states reports and drafts and issues these General Comments to explain the body's understanding and application of the treaty. This informs states of the expert's views and what can be expected of the states in future reporting and responding to cases alleging violation.

II. Source of Human Rights Norms: Customary International Law

The second main source of material human rights norms is Customary International Law. This source of international law establishes binding legal norms. A legally binding customary law norm is said to exist if almost all countries of the world consistently act in a certain way in the international and domestic spheres (called "usage"), and that action is based on their belief (called *opinio juris*) that this practice is a matter of international law and not based on convenience or courtesy. When both of these elements of consistent practice and the *opinio juris* are established, we can say that a binding legal norm has "crystallized" or "ripened" in international law. An example is the human right against torture. The prohibition against torture is both a human right under the treaty known as the Convention against Torture, but is also as a recognized norm of customary international law binding on all states, even those who have not ratified the Torture Convention.

From these two sources of legal norms, treaty, and custom have come most of the human rights we now know as part of international human rights law. This doctrine of customary international law is based on the theory that states agreed to and consented to a rule of international law by the way they act and perceive that act as obligatory. They consent if they consistently and uniformly act a certain way and do so out of a sense of international legal obligation. This obligation is often expressed in their official pronouncements in international legal and political circles. Such objective action and subjective intention by states can be crystallized into a legal norm as long as there is no substantial persistent objection of the states to such a legal norm.

In theory, it is the intention of the international community that every country sign, ratify, and implement all these human rights norms by treaty and customary norms into national law at all levels, and create effective legal procedures and remedies in the national administrative and judicial system for violations of these norms. This goal is in process. It takes a long time. The United States, for example, signed the Genocide Convention in 1948 but did not ratify it until 1988. The process for each state (country) to make international human rights law part of national (domestic) law varies from country to country. The procedure in the United States is set forth in a flowchart above.

III. Source of Human Rights-Related Norms

A. General Principles of Law: There is another minor source of norms that does impact the field of international human rights law, but does not create substantive norms. It is a source of mostly procedural and ancillary norms: It is called General Principles of law. The principle of Exhaustion of Domestic Remedies is such a principle. Some principles are very important to the body of International Human Rights Law.

Basic/Functional International Human Rights Law Principles

The field of human rights is full of principles and rules. This comes with being part of international law. There are certain basic principles which apply to treaties. Most human rights norms are found in treaties, which are contractual agreements between two or more states (countries) governed by international law. Principles concerning the application and implementation of human rights treaties, whether they are global or regional or other international instruments (convention, charter, covenant, agreement, protocol) are listed below:

- *Pacta Sunt Servanda:* Latin expression meaning that agreements (*pacta*) must be kept (*sunt servanda*). Treaties are international legal agreements between two or more states. They are promises voluntarily made by one state to one or more other states. This principle says that states must keep their promises to each other and fulfill their obligations under the treaty. It is like saying treaties have to be obeyed by states conducting themselves according to the treaty.

- **Good Faith:** *Bona Fides:* This Latin expression has the meaning "in good faith." All parties to a treaty must accept and implement and interpret the treaty in good faith with the intent to achieve the object and purpose of the treaty. It is about the state's attitude towards its obligations.

- **Effectiveness:** Principle that states that you have to interpret and apply a treaty in a way that makes the treaty most effective in reaching the object and purpose of the treaty. An interpretation of the treaty that makes it ineffective in protecting human rights would violate the principle of effectiveness.

- **Proper interpretation:** Principle that states how to interpret the meaning of terms in a human rights treaty. When you try to interpret a treaty that is not clear, you must interpret it according to the plain meaning of words in their ordinary context consistent with the object and the purpose of the treaty. See the Vienna Convention on the Law of Treaties, which now states this as a legal rule.

- **Subsidiarity:** Principle that states the protection of individual human rights must be done primarily at the national level, in domestic courts under national law and that the international norms and mechanism are a backup system to be used only when the national level has not properly implemented them. The international system of protection of human rights is secondary or subsidiary to the national system. This usually means that a person who believes his or her human rights have been violated must first seek and exhaust all accessible and effective recourse in his or her national, administrative, and judicial system before taking the case to the international human rights mechanisms.

- *Pro Homine:* Most fundamental and important principle applicable to all human rights and all government action, and indeed all action of every member of society. This Latin expression means for or in favor of (hu)mankind. This is a principle of the application and interpretation of human rights law. Human rights, again, are protections of human beings from the abuse of power by government. They are meant to preserve human dignity. This principle means that human rights laws must be interpreted and applied in every situation and at all times in a way that is the most protective of human beings. In other words, all other things being equal, the protection of human beings takes precedence over the needs and desires of government. Because power corrupts and absolute power corrupts absolutely, and because governments have a tendency to usurp or abuse legal power, and oppress individuals and groups, this principle must always be kept in mind when examining the claims of a state versus the claims of human beings. States were created to protect the rights of humans, not vice versa. This principle applies to the whole process of human rights from their initial recognition to determining violation in a human rights committee, commission, or court. According to a Latin maxim: All law (including international law) is ultimately made for the sake of human beings, [therefore] all international human rights law and all national laws which implement them should be implemented, applied, and their violation adjudicated, with a view to best protecting human beings.

While this principle is classically expressed as *Pro Homine*, which means "for mankind," it is now sometimes seen as *Pro Persona*, to reflect non-sexist language.

• **Proportionality:** Where a state takes a measure that interferes with the exercise of human rights, the state's agents (such as police, legislators, judges, government bureaucrats) are only permitted to take measures; for example, enacting a criminal penalty for certain forms of expression, which constitute a reasonably and proportionally measured action in relation to the particular problem or social need. For example, a state enacting a measure imposing a life sentence for joy riding would be a human rights violation because the punishment is not proportional to the offense. Another example would be a general ordering an air attack to destroy a city of 200,000 because five enemy soldiers were somewhere in the city. This would be a disproportionate (as well as indiscriminate) attack because there is no proportionate relationship between the measure (killing 200,000 innocent civilians) and the objective (killing five enemy soldiers).

Proportionality limits the power of government to take any measures it wants and forces it to take only measures that cause minimal negative consequences against the dignity and freedom of human beings. In the United States, we do this when judging whether a government action violates the 8th amendment-constitutional prohibition against cruel or unusual punishment. See U.S. Supreme Court decision in *Graham v. Florida*, in case law Appendix.

Proportionality runs throughout all international law, and especially international human rights and humanitarian law. Whenever a state takes a measure; for example, surveillance of suspected terrorists, one has to ask whether the measure is proportional to the end sought to be achieved, even if the end aim is legitimate and constitutional. A disproportionate measure is an invalid measure. However laudable or important the government's aim, it may only interfere with freedom to the extent minimally necessary.

Freedom is the rule, limitation of freedom the exception, which must be justified by the government in a context of accountability and transparency.

• **Equality:** All individual human beings are equal, and all laws and procedures should treat them as equal human beings in all the human rights they hold. Women are equal to men. Other than for political human rights, like the right to vote, all persons in a society hold the same human rights, whether they are citizens, non-citizens, documented, or undocumented. Human rights, except for political rights, are border and nationality blind.

• **Non-discrimination:** By virtue of the inherent dignity and equality of each human person, no one should suffer discrimination on the basis of race, colour, ethnicity, gender, age, language, sexual orientation, religion, political or other opinion, national, social, or geographical origin, disability, property, birth, or other status as established by human rights standards. Everyone gets to exercise all human rights the same as everyone else with some exceptions (e.g., children). Discrimination is a difference in treatment of a person, such as a restriction, exclusion, exemption, or preference, based on some characteristic of that person where there is no reasonable and objective justification for the discrimination. All human rights treaties have non-discrimination.

• **Participation:** All people have the right to participate in and access information relating to the society and governmental decision-making processes that affect their lives and their well-being. A high degree of participation by communities is required of civil society, minorities, women, young people, indigenous peoples, and other identified groups to ensure a rights-based approach to governance. Everyone's voice is important, not just in voting, but in all matters affecting human rights, human security, and the quality of life and protection of human dignity.

• **Accountability:** The obligation or willingness to accept legal, political, or moral responsibility to society for one's actions. It means having one's actions subject to public examination and possibly suffering legal or political consequences for wrongdoing. For persons in government, it means having to be answerable to the people for how they fulfill their public duties, especially when they violate a society's norms. No one is above the law in a rule of law system, which the U.S. should hold itself to be.

- **Transparency:** The quality of a state government being open to monitoring, scrutiny, and examination in all its activities, subject usually to national security interest, resulting in the governed feeling that the government is open, public, accessible, accountable, fair, honest, and follows the rule of law. Government secrecy encourages the abuse of power and human rights violations. Unless the members of society can see what the government is doing, they cannot prevent or punish the government. Indeed, there are certain matters such as national security which require secrecy, but this must be the exception and always questioned by the people, the source of authority. Many governments including the U.S. are not sufficiently transparent and often hide behind security claims which are specious or exaggerated. Transparency gives people the information they need to judge the government consistent with its values, including human rights. Often governments deny or cover up human rights violations, as was proven in the U.S. Senate Select Committee on Intelligence in the declassified Torture Report.

OTHER PRINCIPLES

U.S. Department of State Key Principles in Applying Human Rights

The U.S. Department of State, through its Bureau of Democracy Human Rights and Labor (DRL), the focal point of human rights within the U.S. Government, has its own "principles" which it employs in dealing with international human rights. These are U.S. and not international legal principles. According to the Department of State website, these principles are as follows:

- First, *DRL strives to learn the truth and state the facts* in all of its human rights investigations, reports on country conditions, speeches, and votes in the U.N. and asylum profiles. Each year, DRL develops, edits, and submits to Congress a 5,000-page report on human rights conditions in over 190 countries that is respected globally for its objectivity and accuracy. DRL also provides relevant information on country conditions to the Immigration and Naturalization Service and immigration judges in asylum cases.

- Second, *DRL takes consistent positions* concerning past, present, and future abuses. With regard to past abuses, it actively promotes accountability. To stop ongoing abuses, the bureau uses an "inside-outside" approach that combines vigorous, external focus on human rights concerns (including the possibility of sanctions) with equally robust support for internal reform. To prevent future abuses, it promotes early warning and preventive diplomacy. Each year, DRL ensures that human rights considerations are incorporated into U.S. military training and security assistance programs; promotes the rights of women through international campaigns for political participation and full equality; conducts high-level human rights dialogues with other governments; coordinates U.S. policy on human rights with key allies; and raises key issues and cases through diplomatic and public channels.

- Third, *DRL forges and maintains partnerships* with organizations, governments, and multilateral institutions committed to human rights. The bureau takes advantage of multilateral fora to focus international attention on human rights problems and to seek correction. Each year, DRL provides significant technical, financial, or staff support for U.S. delegations to the annual meetings of several international human rights organizations; conducts regular consultations with Native American tribes and serves as the Secretary's principal advisor on international indigenous rights issues; maintains relations with the U.N. High Commissioner on Human Rights; and supports the creation of effective multilateral human rights mechanisms and institutions for accountability.

Source: http://www.state.gov/j/drl/hr/

IV. Other Helpful Sources

In determining what the international norm is, one can also look to the case law of international and even national courts as a subsidiary source of law. International case decisions, such as from the International Court of Justice and the

European Court of Human Rights and even national high courts as well, help in the interpretation of human rights law. One can also look into the writings of the most eminent legal scholars to help in interpreting norms.

CONCEPTS: RIGHTS AND OBLIGATIONS

POSITIVE AND NEGATIVE INDIVIDUAL RIGHTS AND THE STATE'S POSITIVE AND NEGATIVE OBLIGATIONS

Conceptually, most human rights have both a negative and a positive aspect to the exercise of the right, and positive and negative aspects of the state's obligation as to each right. All human rights norms have this duality. An example of a human right which can be both positive and negative is freedom of expression. The positive aspect of this right says, "I have a right to say x." That is a positive right to say something. The negative aspect of that right is the right not to have to express something: "I have a right not to reply to that question." So the right to freedom of expression is both a positive and a negative right. Positive rights give a person freedom to do something. For each positive right, there is a negative obligation of the state to refrain from interfering with that person's freedom. An example of violating that positive right would be not allowing that person to speak his opinions. Some rights are considered negative, either in allowing a person not to have to do something, or in prohibiting the state from doing something to someone, such as torturing someone. Everyone has the negative right not to be tortured and the negative right not to be forced to believe something in which one does not believe. Some negative rights require positive obligations by the state, such as to provide police to protect people's lives and property or schools to provide education.

Positive obligations, again, oblige the state to do something, and negative obligations oblige a state to refrain from doing something. Human rights obligations can be violated by states for doing nothing when there is a positive obligation to act. For example, the U.S. government has a negative obligation to avoid interfering with our human rights in the war on terrorism, and it has a positive obligation to protect our human right to life by taking positive measures to protect the U.S. from terrorist attacks. If the government did nothing to protect the U.S. it would violate its positive obligation to take steps to protect the U.S. from the harmful acts of others.

For all the individual rights we have and for all the obligations of state government, there are also duties, responsibilities on every member of society without which human rights cannot be realized. See "Duties" below. There are no human rights without human duties. Every human right has a correlative duty.

Four Legal Obligations Every State Must Fulfill Under International Human Rights Law
International law is based on the free consent of sovereign and equal states and expressed in the international community in legal agreements or custom. This consent gives rise to freely chosen legal obligations in relation to each other state party to the treaty or to all states under customary international law. There are four separate legal obligations which states, such as the United States, undertake to fulfill, and must fulfill to make human rights real and practical and not illusory and abstract only. These four obligations are:

1. Obligation to Respect Human Rights
State (national) government has the legal obligation to refrain, in any way, from interfering with individuals in the full enjoyment of their human rights. This obligation is the conscious recognition of the human rights of individuals and groups, and the conduct and treatment by the states consistent with such recognition.

2. Obligation to Protect Human Rights from the actions of others
State (national) government has the legal obligation to prevent or punish acts which result in violations committed by third parties, such as private individuals or groups or other non-state entities or actor or commercial interests.

3. Obligation to Ensure Human Rights by other states
States parties to a treaty and states bound by a customary international human rights norm have the legal obligation to act to ensure that all other states parties or other states bound by the customary norm respect and protect such human rights within their territory and all those outside their territory for whom the norms apply. Every state must actively and affirmatively cause other states and non-state actors to conduct themselves consistently with those norms, consistent with international law. The state's obligations are "*Erge Omnes,*" toward all other applicable states; see below.

4. Obligation to Fulfill by all things necessary and proper for full enjoyment

The state (national) government has the affirmative obligation to take administrative, budgetary, legislative, judicial, and other measures toward the full exercise and realization of all human rights. The state must take all necessary steps to ensure that all persons within its jurisdiction fully enjoy all substantive and procedural human rights all of the time.

States must fulfill all four of these obligations. Some of these obligations are negative, and some are positive. A state can violate its obligation by partially fulfilling an obligation that it has the capacity to fulfill completely.

Some scholarly sources only list three of the above four obligations, leaving out the obligation to ensure. The authors believe that states should fulfill all four.

V. OBLIGATIONS *REGE OMNES*

In international law, there are certain obligations deemed so important for the continued existence and development of the international community, and so necessary for the protection of human dignity, that they are known as obligations "*Rege Omens*." This Latin term means essentially "towards everyone." They are obligations of every state toward each other. The implication of this is that every state has the right to complain and call for action of other states when any other state is violating *Rege Omens* norms.

Refraining from torture, genocide, or slavery, for example, are considered obligations *Rege Omens*. They are also referred to as "Peremptory Norms" of conduct, which means that states cannot pass legislation inconsistent with such norms. Caveat: This is not the same, however, as "preemption" in the U.S. constitutional sense. Every state must comply with such obligations all the time, and they allow no abrogation, derogation, or exception for any reason.

Which obligations are *Rege Omens* is beyond the scope of this book. Generally speaking, the norms which give rise to *Rege Omens* obligations are called *Jus Cogens*. This term means a compelling or cogent right from which no limitation or derogation is possible.

Former Characterization of "Generations" of Human Rights

Most human rights have for many years been characterized as belonging to one of three so-called "generations" of human rights. This term was coined by a French jurist, Karel Vasak, for purposes of categorizing human rights as they had developed. This also had something to do with the Cold War and its influence on the development of the concept of human rights. It became common for people to speak of three "generations" of human rights. The "first generation" human rights consisted of the internationally accepted civil and political human rights.

The ICCPR contains internationally recognized civil and political rights. The "second generation" human rights consisted of the internationally accepted economic, social, and cultural rights (see Primary Source Document 3, the International Covenant on Economic, Social, and Cultural Rights). The West Bloc (non-communist) nations favored civil and political human rights, such as freedom of speech and religion, while the East Bloc states favored economic, social and cultural rights. The "third generation" human rights, also called "solidarity rights," were a mixture of new rights and ideas that were proclaimed as human rights but not universally accepted in the international community as such. These rights include the claimed right to peace, the right to a clean environment, the right to development, the right to humanitarian assistance, and the right to solidarity among nations. These rights find their way into very few legal treaties and are promoted primarily by developing countries.

The use of the term "generation" was never meant to imply any distinct historical difference or hierarchy of one generation over another. Over the years, however, the use of this term caused conceptual problems resulting in political controversy. In recent years, scholars and international organizations have discouraged the use of the term "generation" as a means of categorizing human rights. This shift is largely due to the development and articulation of the principles of interdependence, interrelatedness, and indivisibility of all human rights. One does, however, still see this term used in the older human rights literature and even in some new literature. For all intents and purposes, the body of international human rights law consists principally and primarily of first and second generation human rights.

The terms first, second, or third "generation" should not be used in human rights discourse. They are outmoded and inaccurate concepts which lead to confusion and misunderstanding.

Functional Principles

During the history of human rights, debates have arisen as to which rights were most important, whether there was a hierarchy of rights, whether a state could choose which rights it wished to recognize and implement, and how rights were related to each other. These theoretical principles arose because of certain political disagreements and problems in the way human rights were being used politically; in the way states were accusing their enemies of committing violations; and in the way states were claiming that they could only allow their citizens the enjoyment of certain types of human rights and not others. Certain principles have developed and been accepted in the field of human rights to ensure that human rights are recognized and implemented (one does not use the term "enforce") and discussed in a nonpolitical and functional way within the international community. The international community has developed human rights principles to help depoliticize them. These functional principles are interdependence, interrelatedness, and indivisibility:

Interdependence of human rights: Each human right is dependent on the enjoyment of each other right for its own enjoyment. Each right depends on each other right for any and all human rights to be enjoyed in reality. Thus, a state cannot deny a person any rights or that person's other rights will also fall. For example, freedom of movement is dependent on the right to adequate medical care. The right to fair trial is dependent on the right to equality before the law.

Interrelatedness of all human rights: All human rights are related to each other; for example, the right to adequate nourishment and freedom of speech, or freedom of religion and the right to vote. There is an intrinsic relationship between every human right and every other human right. They all have as their goal the protection of human dignity. One cannot try to separate them but must deal with all of them when addressing problems or alleged violations.

Indivisibility of human rights: All human rights form one indivisible body of norms that cannot be separated into different sets from which states may pick and choose what they will agree to follow. For example, one cannot say that his or her country's people are so poor that they can only have economic rights but not civil and political rights until all economic rights are fulfilled. Governments cannot divide rights in this way. Civil human rights are indivisible from political human rights, which are indivisible from economic rights, which are indivisible from social rights, which are indivisible from cultural rights, and so on. For most experts, the so-called "solidarity rights" (peace, development, solidarity, etc.) would not fit within the scope of this principle.

Other Human Rights Principles

Margin of Appreciation, sometimes referred to as Margin of Discretion, is largely a judicially created doctrine used in evaluating a specific factual situation in a court case to determine if a state has interfered with someone's human rights norm. This principle was judicially created within the European Convention on Human Rights system to allow the European Court to strike a fair balance between individual exercise of human rights in that Convention and the needs of states to deal with sometimes urgent and critical and complex problems on a basis where the state is given a benefit of the doubt, some leeway, some wiggle room, so to speak. It is not a term that has been used in relation to the U.S. In dealing with a human rights issue involving a European country, one would be wise to remember this doctrine. It has not been adopted in the Inter-American human rights system of which the U.S. is a member.

Human rights norms, again, constitute a balance between the needs of government to take care of matters of state and the freedom of human beings. International Human Rights Law gives the government a little leeway by applying a doctrine known as the Margin of Appreciation, sometimes referred to as a Margin of Discretion. This principle recognizes that the government is sometimes better placed than a human rights court, after the fact, to determine the most appropriate government response or measure to take. In adjudicating the correctness of the state action which interferes with someone's exercise of their rights, the adjudicator gives the state a certain judicial deference.

In essence, this means that where there is an alleged human rights violation, the government will be given the benefit of the doubt in the assessment of whether its actions were a legitimate restriction of human rights or whether they crossed the line and constituted human rights violations.

For example, police are told that a murderer is hiding somewhere in a large apartment building, and they evacuate every apartment and search the apartments without knocking. If a claim of violation of human rights is made, the forum that judges the legitimacy of the state action accords the government a margin of appreciation. If it finds that the search was not within the margin of appreciation, then it is a human rights violation. If it finds that the search was within the margin of appreciation, it is not a violation. There are some cases in the European Court of Human Rights system which relate to the U.S. and where one will encounter reference to this doctrine. Some argue for a general margin of appreciation doctrine in international law, but this has not been accepted. This would not be applied in the context of a U.S. human rights case in a U.S. forum nor should it be applied in discussion of U.S. compliance with an international norm.

VI. ABSOLUTE VS "PRIMA FACIE" HUMAN RIGHTS

Some human rights are absolute, meaning that they apply in all situations at all times, regardless of the circumstances. Some human rights are not absolute; they can be limited, restricted by the state, depending on the circumstances existing in a particular situation. These are called prima facie or conditional human rights. An example of an absolute human right is the freedom from torture. This type of right is seen in Article 7 of the ICCPR (Document 8) which reads: "No one shall be subjected to torture or to cruel, inhuman, or degrading treatment or punishment." When you read this article, there are no qualifiers, no limitations possible.

An example of a prima facie human right is the freedom of movement, as seen in Article 12 of the ICCPR, which reads:

12.1 Everyone lawfully within the territory of a State shall, within that territory, have the right to liberty of movement and freedom to choose his residence.

12.2 Everyone shall be free to leave any country, including his own.

12.3 The above-mentioned rights shall not be subject to any restrictions except those which are provided by law, are necessary to protect national security, public order (ordre public), public health or morals, or the rights and freedoms of others, and are consistent with the other rights recognized in the present Covenant.

Articles 12.1 and 12.2 state the norm as an absolute, but Article 12.3 renders it not absolute; that is, prima facie. Article 12.3 is a limitations clause. Any human rights norm which has a limitations clause (see below) in an international treaty is a conditional human right. The right is absolute, except for those express, specific situations spelled out in paragraph 3. States can limit the exercise of the freedom if the measure strictly complies with the limitations clause.

VII. LIMITATIONS/RESTRICTIONS (CLAUSE)

Some human rights norms are absolute and apply always and everywhere the same. Examples are the prohibition against torture and slavery. The only issues that arise with regard to absolute rights are the interpretation of the meaning of the terms. Examples would be whether water boarding is within the meaning of torture or not. At the U.S. domestic level, one applies the rules of interpretation, such as applying the Vienna Convention on Treaties, and one looks to the U.S. reservations, understandings, and declarations (RUDs) to see if there are any qualifications on how the member state, such as the U.S., interprets a norm or the meaning of a term such as "torture." Then one compares that to any Congressional implementing legislation, since the U.S. usually ratifies human rights treaties with RUDs, which among other things, declare that the treaty is non-self-executing, requiring implementing legislation. Finally, one compares that to the terms of the U.S. Constitution to determine constitutionality.

At the level of international law, when applying international human rights treaties, the situation of applying legal norms is different, only insofar as it is different for absolute and non-absolute, or "conditional" human rights norms. While absolute norms apply everywhere and always unconditionally, the same is not true of non-absolute or conditional human rights. Conditional human rights norms are those which have a limitation or restriction clause in them. (See ICCPR Article 19.3.) Article 19.3 is called a limitation clause or restriction cause. The limitation/restriction clause allows the state to take measures which restrict or limit the exercise of the substantive right, such as freedom of expression, so long as the measure fulfills certain criteria.

Real legal battles over human rights compliance are being fought principally within the context of the limitation/restriction clauses of those norms, such as ICCPR Art.19.3. Simply put, for example, with someone's exercise of their right to expression, where one can establish that the state has in fact interfered, the state will always try to show that there was a good legal reason, a legal justification, for why it has so interfered. An example would be the state trying to prevent anti-war protestors from demonstrating at the funeral of a dead American soldier. If the state tried to prevent such expression, would that be a justified limitation on freedom of expression under international human rights law? The international way of analyzing that issue is a bit different from the classical U.S. Constitutional analysis. Here one will see the international legal manner of analyzing such a limitation/restriction measure: these measures taken by a state, which interfere with an exercise of expression, and which are claimed to be legally justified, are called "limitations" or "restrictions." These measures limit or restrict the otherwise free exercise of one's expressions. They are the legal loopholes to human rights obligations of states. They allow in theory a fair balance between the freedom of the individual, on the one hand, versus the needs of state to regulate society in an orderly, harmonious, and productive way.

State measures, which interfere as a limitation/restriction with exercise of one's freedom of expression, are not necessarily violations of that human rights norm. These measures are usually claimed by the state to constitute legitimate government aims, such as protection of public safety, health, or national security, which can be permissible under the convention norms.

The legitimate aims which are applicable to a particular norm, such as ICCPR Article 19, are set forth in what are called limitation or restriction clauses. Again, Article 19.3 is known as the limitation or restriction clauses. Not all measures taken by states under the claim of legitimate restriction/limitation are valid under the human rights conventions. One must analyze the specific measure taken in order to determine if it is a permissible or legitimate restriction/limitation. If the limitation is not permissible as a matter of law, then a violation of the human rights norms of freedom of expression will normally be found.

There has developed an extensive international jurisprudence, particularly in the European Court of Human Rights, with its very advanced system of human rights jurisprudence, about how to analyze and thus determine whether a limitation measure is permissible under a convention article. Under international legal principles, the analysis of whether a state measure is a valid limitation/restriction measure expounds as follows:

First, one must determine whether the state's measure in fact interfered with the exercise of the substantive rights. Was there an "interference"? If one finds an interference, one will then ascertain whether the measure taken by the state meets the following criteria:

1. Prescribed by Law
Was the measure "prescribed by law"? This means that the measure is consistent with the Principle of Legality in that it meets all the following sub-criteria:

   a. It was issued by a proper legal authority who had the legal power and right to establish or take the measure under domestic (national) law;

   b. The measure is "accessible" to persons, in that they can find out what it is, and what is required; and

   c. It is sufficiently clear and precise enough that persons can know the foreseeable consequences of compliance or non-compliance, so as to be able to regulate their conduct accordingly.

2. Legitimate aim
By this is meant that the reason for which the state took the measure was to achieve a specific objective beneficial to society, whose object or "aim" is expressly listed in the limitation clause, such as, (viz. ICCPR Art. 19.3:) "for the protection of public order."

Human rights limitation/restriction clauses will be interpreted narrowly against the state. Only those aims listed in the limitation/restriction clause will serve to justify a measure of restriction/limitation. Note that not even national security constitutes a legitimate aim to restrict exercise of all human rights; for example, freedom of religion or belief in Article 18.

3. Necessity/necessary
Exercise of a right is the rule, and limitation of the exercise is an exception to the rule.

Assuming it is both prescribed by law and meets a legitimate aim or aims set forth in the limitation/restriction clause, in order for the measure to be permitted, it still must then pass the test of whether it is "necessary" to pass that measure to fulfill the state's obligations towards respect for and protection of human rights. This issue requires analysis of the measure in light of the following three criteria:

a. The measure meets a "pressing social need." Since freedom is the rule and limitation of freedom by the state is the exception, there must be a real and genuine need to take this measure to achieve the legitimate aim.

b. The measure must be "justified in principle." This means that the measure taken is really being taken for the reasons asserted by the state, and the measure is consistent with achieving respect for human rights. They cannot be used in a discriminatory way, nor for discriminatory purposes, nor be used to undermine any other human rights. The result of the limitation/restriction will end up being beneficial for both the society and the person affected.

c. The measure is "proportionate" to the goal sought to be achieved. In order to be accepted as a legitimate limit of the exercise of a right, the state is authorized to take on interference with individual freedom only to a degree that is necessary to meet the legitimate aim. There must be a relation of proportionality between the measure taken, such as a criminal punishment or disbanding of a group, and the legitimate aim; for example, control of violence or a threat to the rights and freedoms of others. One must always ask of all measures taken by states to restrict or control expression whether the measures are proportionate. Even if it is prescribed by law and there is a legitimate aim, there will be no pressing social need found if the measure taken is disproportionate to the aim. That will render the measure legally invalid and impermissible, and a violation will be found.

d. The measures must be relevant to the aim to be accomplished and sufficient to accomplish the aim. For a limitation/restriction measure to be legitimate and permissible to justify an interference on behalf of the state, the state must show it meets all of these above criteria.

From an International Law perspective, this is the method of analysis that applies to U.S. law, policy, and practice when judging whether the U.S. is in compliance with its international human rights law obligations, such as under the ICCPR.

Not all human rights treaties have limitation/restriction clauses. This analysis applies primarily to the ICCPR, which at this time is the most important general human rights treaty which is legally binding on the U.S., because the U.S. ratified it.

The U.S. has told the U.N. Human Rights Committee that its law, policy, and practice are in harmony with the norms of the ICCPR. The only way to determine this definitively from an international legal perspective is to apply the above criteria to U.S. law, policy, or practice.

Only when the U.S. law, policy, and practice fulfill the above criteria will they be in compliance with the international legal norms of the ICCPR.

The circumstances in which *prima facie* human rights can be limited are called permissible limitations or restrictions. Each *prima facie* right is defined within the article that sets forth the right and then the criteria for the limitation or restriction to be legally valid. In Article 12 of the ICCPR, the freedom of movement can be limited for such legitimate aims, such as public safety, public order, public health, or public morals. States can establish limitation measures on the exercise of such human rights so long as they are reasonably based on one of these specified aims, and no others, and the measure must have been established by proper legal authority and procedure, which are accessible, clear, and understandable to the public. Again, it must be stressed, this principle of limitations/restrictions represents the balance between individual freedoms and the just demands of society for the efficient and effective operation of government.

The battles over human rights violations take place primarily within the limitations clauses.

VIII. DEROGATION IN TIME OF PUBLIC EMERGENCY

Some human rights can be completely suspended in times of a serious and widespread public emergency affecting the very life and existence of a whole country, such as when the state is being invaded militarily by an enemy attack. Such suspension of human rights in times of public emergency is called derogation. Some human rights treaties contain derogations clauses. (See ICCPR Art. 4) International Human Rights Law recognizes the sometimes absolute need of the state government to suspend certain human rights for a certain period of time, so as to allow the state to deal with the public emergency. For example, if a country were being attacked militarily, a state could restrict freedom of movement or freedom of speech, for so long as it was necessary to protect the state. Only certain rights can be suspended like this. These are called "derogable rights." On the other hand, some human rights, such as freedom from slavery, cannot be suspended. These are called "non-derogable rights." The derogation clause of the treaty specifies which specific rights cannot be derogated, even in public emergency. (See ICCPR Art. 12.2.)

IX. CONCEPT OF THE DUTIES OF THE INDIVIDUAL

Many people mistakenly think that human rights are about what we can do with no one being able to stop the U.S. from doing it. These people see human rights as a license for everyone to do what they want, with no responsibility towards society. This is false. Society itself cannot continue to exist if everyone did what they wanted to do in the name of human rights. The truth is that in Human Rights Law, for every human right, there is a correlative duty. Everyone has human rights, and everyone has human duties towards others and society, without which society cannot function safely and develop. In theory, every human being has duties to society and the state, such as paying taxes and obeying the motor vehicle rules, without which the state could not ensure respect for human rights. [See Article 29.1 of the Universal Declaration of Human Rights]

The continued viability of a state that is supposed to protect human rights depends upon the fulfillment of citizens' duties to the state, unless unable or exempted. Human rights and human duties are interdependent. Rights and duties are two sides of the same coin. The coin is freedom. The connection of duties to human rights helps encourage the members of society to respect others' rights, as well as claim their own.

X. CONCEPTS OF CULTURAL RELATIVISM VS. UNIVERSALITY OF HUMAN RIGHTS

For many years, there was a great debate between different nations and groups regarding the issue of whether human rights were universal and had to be applied the same way to everyone everywhere (the doctrine of universality), or whether they were culturally varied in that each culture could interpret and apply them according to their cultural differences ("particularities" or "specificities"), known as the doctrine of cultural relativism. The interpretation and application of human rights internationally had been inconsistent and varied from culture to culture. This inconsistency has given rise to the claim by Western and developed states that human rights are universal and shall be applied in the same way to everyone in every society without regard to differences in religion, culture, language, customs, income level, or extent of poverty, or other differences. Those states, usually developing and Third World accused of violations, usually assert the defense of cultural relativism, which claims that human rights should be interpreted in different places in different ways depending on the particular culture, custom, religion, and so on, and not on a universal, one-size-fits-all basis. This debate is called "universality versus cultural relativism." In 1993 the international community announced at the United Nations Vienna Conference on Human Rights that the principle of universality of human rights was the internationally accepted one. This debate continues nonetheless. The United States accepts and supports the principle of universality. All human rights must be interpreted and applied to all people everywhere the same way, regardless of cultural particularities.

THE IMPORTANCE OF LEGAL PROTECTION
OF HUMAN RIGHTS

According to the preambles to the UDHR, ICCPR, and ICESCR, respect for human rights is "the foundation of freedom, justice, and peace in the world." This is a statement of vast significance. It says that respect for human rights is the legal foundation of freedom, justice, and peace in every country, including the United States. World War II taught the human race that it cannot let each state be the unaccountable god of all that happens within its territory, that the international community has an interest in and is affected by what happens in other states, and that there are international limits necessary for human civilization to continue. There are indeed various limitations, exceptions, and qualifications to the rather sweeping statement in the preambles of the UDHR, ICCPR, and ICESCR. However, the statement noted above is a fair statement of the general theory of the discipline known as human rights. Protection of human rights is necessary in order to preserve freedom, justice, and peace in the world. If one looks at almost every violent conflict scourging the earth today, the issue causing the conflict is always a perception of some that the human rights of others are being violated and no one is doing anything about it. Thus, there must be legal measures to prevent, stop, or remedy violations so that conflicts will not occur or will not be enflamed by a sense of irremediable injustice.

The International Bill of Rights

At the end of this chapter, one finds the documents which make up the International Bill of Rights. Three of them are treaties, the ICCPR, ICESCR, and First Protocol. The U.S. has ratified and is a state party to only one of these three treaties, the ICCPR. Even though the U.S. has signed but not ratified the ICESCR, the reader should be aware of it and push the U.S. to ratify it and work with it as the basis of U.S. discourse and debate over issues such as access to health care and education. The reader is invited to read all four of the instruments of the International Bill of Rights so as to have a command of the basic instruments articulating their rights. One can truthfully say that one has economic, social, and cultural human rights even though the U.S. has not ratified and accepted this as an international obligation, as most states of the world have.

In other chapters one finds other international human rights treaties with which one should become familiar, such as the Genocide Convention, Torture Convention, Convention on the Rights of the Child, Convention on Elimination of All Forms of Racism, and the Convention on Elimination of Discrimination against Women.

THE SPECTRUM OF ALL LAWS IN THE UNITED STATES AND WHERE INTERNATIONAL HUMAN RIGHTS LAWS FIT IN

As seen in the chart on page 54, international treaty law and customary law norms have a place in our legal system and have had such status since the founding of the country and its judiciary.

This chart shows the large spectrum of laws that regulate our society, from local municipal ordinances to international laws to international human rights norms applicable to the U.S. It shows how human rights norms, which constitute a body of law applicable in U.S., fit into and influence the U.S. legal system.

THE RELATIONSHIP AMONG INTERNATIONAL HUMAN RIGHTS LAW (IHRL), INTERNATIONAL HUMANITARIAN LAW (IHL), AND INTERNATIONAL CRIMINAL LAW (ICL)

As stated above, this text has as its principal focus the body of law known as International Human Rights Law (IHRL). However, of necessity, it also covers a bit of the body of law known as International Humanitarian Law (IHL) and International Criminal Law (ICL). The reason for this is that the reader or researcher of international issues, or even national issues, will often be looking at a situation which involves all three of these areas of International Law.

An example has been the siege of Aleppo, Syria in the years leading up to and including 2016. An armed conflict has been raging there, and the government of Syria has been dropping bombs on its own citizens while fighting the anti-government forces. Children were killed and hospitals were being destroyed, and earlier even chemical weapons had been used killing many civilians. Russia has been participating in the bombing.

In terms of International Law applicable to this tragic event, one cannot merely look at it in terms of the law of (1) International Humanitarian Law (IHL), simply because it happened during armed conflict. One must also make use of the field of (2) International Human Rights Law (IHRL) since it involves the acts of the Syrian Government towards its own citizens. Moreover, when judging the acts of military commanders and governmental authorities, the application of (3) International Criminal Law comes into play as to individuals' criminal responsibility; i.e., those who are responsible for the death and destruction. All three areas of law come into a convergence, and each and all three fields of law must be applied to such a situation.

Today one sees more and more of such situations of armed conflict under the title of IHL, which is itself part of the larger body of law known as The Law of Armed Conflict. The Law of Armed Conflict has two parts: the law as to when, under what circumstances a state may legally resort to force in International Law, called the *jus ad bellum* (example: self-defense); and the law applicable to the protection of victims and limitation of the methods and means of engaging in armed conflict, called the *jus in bello*, (example: mistreating a Prisoner of War). IHL is part of the *jus in bello*, which includes the Geneva Conventions of 1949 and their 1977 Protocols, and Hague Law customary international norms on methods and means of armed conflict. Some terms from this field are included in the dictionary, and some of the legal instruments from that field are included in the text where appropriate.

Under International Law both IHRL and IHL both apply to situations of armed conflict. Indeed, some human rights can be derogated, suspended in times of armed conflict, but not all human rights norms. Those norms that are "non-derogable" can never be suspended in war or in peace. Thus, in the second Iraq war in the early 2000s, when and where the U.S. had effective control of certain Iraqi territories, both IHL and IHRL applied. The U.S. government, however, held to a position that denied this applicability of both IHRL and IHL. The government claimed that only the IHL applied during armed conflict, and that the IHRL had no extra-territorial effect in Iraq. That is erroneous. This work takes a broader look at international situations that harm human beings and the law that mankind and his/her institutions have created to avoid such tragedy. Knowing these two areas of law and their interrelationship will help the reader to better comprehend the legal implications of a situation.

It doesn't take a brain surgeon to conclude that these bodies of law, even if applicable, have not been able to stop the apparent psychoses in this world. This is partly due to the ignorance of the American populace, and the legal community in general, about this body of law. Peoples cannot demand that their government play by certain rules when they have no idea what the rules are. Americans must understand that until we develop a greater awareness of these areas of law and demand that our government "play by the rules" in such devastating human activity as armed conflict, that history and tragedy will repeat and continue on tomorrow, and the slogan "never again" may never be realized in history.

Two additional reasons why this work includes Humanitarian Law with Human Rights Law are:

1. The U.S. has failed both, a. to teach Americans the basic principles of Humanitarian Law, as it is obligated to do under the Geneva Conventions, leaving Americans with no clue as to which rules of conflict apply to their government in extra-territorial armed conflict; and, b. for when Americans, soldier or civilian, may find themselves impacted by armed conflict. Article 144 of the Fourth Geneva Convention of 1949, to which the U.S. is a state party reads:

> ART. 144. – The High Contracting Parties undertake, in time of peace as in time of war, to disseminate the text of the present Convention as widely as possible in their respective countries, and, in particular, to include the study thereof in their programmes of military and, if possible, civil instruction, so that the principles thereof *may become known to the entire population*. Any civilian, military, police, or other authority, who in time of war assume responsibilities in respect of protected persons, must possess the text of the Convention and be specially instructed as to its provisions. [emphasis added]

2. The U.S. legal system, particularly the Supreme Court, has had to deal with these two areas of law (IHL and IHRL) in cases such as Rasul, Handi, Hamdan and Boumedienne in relation to the U.S. Constitution in the so-called war on terror.

I. THE RELATIONSHIP BETWEEN INTERNATIONAL HUMANITARIAN LAW (IHL) AND INTERNATIONAL HUMAN RIGHTS LAW (IHRL)

The relationship between these two bodies of law is important to keep in mind. They are not the same. Some people look at IHL as a subsidiary part of IHRL. This is not quite true. There is a substantial similarity in the goals of these two bodies of law regarding protecting humans from harm, but each has its own juridical structure. Human rights law recognizes inherent rights in all human beings in relation to a state's sovereign power. Individuals bear the rights. IHL does not create or recognize rights in individuals. It places obligations and limitations on states (and other parties with legal standing in armed conflict) to act a certain way regarding persons who are not citizens or residents of that state during armed conflict, such as a prisoner of war or civilian detainee. It is about obligations on states parties to limit the damage to non-military persons and objects under the principle of humanitarianism. It is to minimize human suffering during armed conflict.

This is so even though the seeds of human rights law are said to stem from the Declaration of Independence and the French Declaration of the Rights of Man and of Citizen, in an Enlightenment historical context. It started internationally after the 1868 Lieber Code, developed and enacted domestically within the U.S. context of its American Civil War, and was pulled into the bosom of the International Committee of the Red Cross (ICRC) in Europe under Henry

Dunant. When human rights law started with the UDHR in 1948, and two international covenants, the ICCPR and ICESCR, (the two bodies of law) evolved on separate courses under separate institutional cover, IHRL under the U.N. and regional bodies like the OAS, IHL under the supervision internationally of the ICRC, as they are today. The primary function of the ICRC is the monitoring of the parties to armed conflict to ensure their compliance with Humanitarian Law. Major tasks of the ICRC include visiting POW camps and other detention centers, and helping to locate missing persons.

It should be noted at this point that in international human rights and humanitarian law one rarely uses the term "war" any more. One uses the term "armed conflict." Technically, the term "war" refers to legal relationships between states, not armed violence. It signifies a breakup of diplomatic relations between two or more states, not bombs and bullets. IHL deals with any and all issues involving "armed conflict."

In explaining the relationship between IHL and IHRL, the ICRC describes it as follows:

> While IHL and human rights law have developed in their separate ways, some human rights treaties include provisions that come from IHL: for instance, the Convention on the Rights of the Child and its Optional Protocol on the involvement of children in armed conflict, and the Convention on Enforced Disappearance.

> IHL and International Human Rights Law are complementary bodies of international law that share some of the same aims. Both IHL and human rights law strive to protect the lives, the health, and the dignity of individuals, albeit from different angles, which is why, while very different in formulation, the essence of some of the rules is similar. For example, both IHL and human rights law prohibit torture or cruel treatment, prescribe basic rights for persons subject to criminal process, prohibit discrimination, contain provisions for the protection of women and children, and regulate aspects of the right to food and health. There are, however, important differences between them: their origins, the scope of their application, the bodies that implement them, and so on.

Temporal scope of application

While IHL applies exclusively in armed conflict...human rights law applies, in principle, at all times; i.e., in peacetime and during armed conflict.

IHL and human rights law share common substantive rules (such as the prohibition of torture), but they also contain very different provisions. IHL deals with many issues that are outside the purview of human rights law, such as the status of 'combatants' and 'prisoners of war,' the protection of the red cross and red crescent emblems, and the legality of specific kinds of weaponry. Similarly, human rights law deals with aspects of life that are not regulated by IHL, such as the freedom of the press, the right to assembly, to vote, to strike, and other matters. Furthermore, there are areas that are governed by both IHL and human rights law, but in different and sometimes contradictory ways. This is especially the case for the use of force and detention.

THE INTERPLAY OF IHL AND IHRL

The interplay of IHL and human rights law remains the subject of much legal attention, particularly because of its consequences for the conduct of military operations.

Although, generally speaking, these two branches of international law are complementary, the notion of complementarity cannot resolve the intricate legal issues of interplay that sometimes arise. In some instances, IHL and human rights rules might produce conflicting results when applied to the same facts, because they reflect the different circumstances for which they were primarily developed. *Source: https://www.icrc.org/en/document/what-difference-between-ihl-and-human-rights-law*

Though there are still problems and potential conflicts between the bodies of law, IHL and IHRL, a slow convergence is happening between them. When one is dealing with armed conflict situations, whether international or non-international, such as, civil wars or insurrections, one must keep in mind both IHRL and IHL. Armed conflict will always engage human rights law, because so many countries have ratified human rights instruments, and all armed conflicts see human rights violations, and few state violators and few individual perpetrators of international crimes are prosecuted. Hopefully, a greater awareness of this law will move the world, or at least the U.S. in a better direction. The relationship between IHL and IHRL is here to stay.

In closing this section and in order for the reader to get a taste of this body of law known as IHL, there follows the text of the basic principles of IHL. This is issued by the ICRC. It is a summary of all the Geneva Conventions and Protocols and all the other IHL customary law and treaties. All Americans are supposed to be taught these principles.

Basic rules of international humanitarian law in armed conflicts:
- Persons hors de combat (incapable of engaging in combat, such as a POW) and those who do not take a direct part in hostilities are entitled to respect for their lives and their moral and physical integrity. They shall in all circumstances be protected and treated humanely without any adverse distinction.
- It is forbidden to kill or injure an enemy who surrenders or who is hors de combat.
- The wounded and sick shall be collected and cared for by the party to the conflict which has them in its power. Protection also covers medical personnel, establishments, transports, and equipment. The emblem of the Red Cross or the red crescent is the sign of such protection and must be respected.
- Captured combatants and civilians under the authority of an adverse party are entitled to respect for their lives, dignity, personal rights, and convictions. They shall be protected against all acts of violence and reprisals. They shall have the right to correspond with their families and to receive relief.
- Everyone shall be entitled to benefit from fundamental judicial guarantees. No one shall be held responsible for an act he has not committed. No one shall be subjected to physical or mental torture, corporal punishment, or cruel or degrading treatment.
- Parties to a conflict and members of their armed forces do not have an unlimited choice of methods and means of warfare. It is prohibited to employ weapons or methods of warfare of a nature to cause unnecessary losses or excessive suffering.
- Parties to a conflict shall at all times distinguish between the civilian population and combatants in order to spare civilian population and property. Neither the civilian population as such nor civilian persons shall be the object of attack. Attacks shall be directed solely against military objectives.

Following is a chart showing the relationship of IHL and IHRL.

International Human Rights And Humanitarian Law Norm Chart

International Human Rights Law
Juridical basis: inherent human dignity. (during peacetime and during armed conflict, *except for rights derogated)

International Humanitarian Law
Juridical Basis: Humanitarianism. (only during armed conflict)

Universal Declaration of Human Rights

Global and regional human rights treaties , e.g. ICCPR, CAT, CERD, etc.*

And

Customary international human rights norms

Geneva Law
GC I, (Land); GC II, (Sea); GC III, (POW); GC IV, (Civilian); Prot. I; Prot. II. (protection of victims of armed conflict)

Other Treaties: Conventional Weapons, Cluster Munitions Cultural Property, ENMOD etc. (There are about 100 humanitarian law related legal instruments)

Hague Law 1899, 1907 (conduct of hostilities)

Laws and Customs of War (conduct of hostilities)

During armed conflict applicable international humanitarian law applies and so do all applicable human rights legal obligations, under customary law and all non derogable human rights treaty obligations, such as right to life, torture, cruel inhuman and degrading treatment or punishment, slavery, due process, freedom of religion. In addition, all derogable human rights which have not been officially derogated are also fully applicable during armed conflict, as if the case in the U.S. in 2010. The U.S. has not declared a period of derogation in the U.S. as a result of the war on terrorism as of December 2010.

STATES ARE EXPECTED TO RESPECT AND ENSURE RESPECT OF HUMANITARIAN LAW LEGAL OBLIGATIONS

Compliance is done by:

Domestic: military/legal system: Courts martial, military commissions, e.g. Army Field Manual, Doc. #106, and AFM 27-10. Suppress and Repress violations. Educate military and civilian populations (GC IV art. 144). Civil Litigation, e.g. ATCA, *see Kadic Case* in Appendix J.

International Committee of the Red Cross ("Promoter and Guardian of Humanitarian Law") monitors and reports on conflict compliance /visits detainees. HAS NO LEGAL ENFORCEMENT POWER.

Protecting Powers under GC s (e.g. GC IV art., Doc. #72)

UN General Assembly
UN Security Council
Human Rights Council
Intl Criminal Tribunals (Ad Hoc and ICC (U.S. Not a Party to ICC Stat.))
ICJ
Somewhat by: regional HR Systems
Civil Society

II. INTERNATIONAL CRIMINAL LAW (ICL): RELATIONSHIP/INTERPLAY WITH IHL AND IHRL, AN EVOLVING CONVERGENCE?

Terms and instruments of International Criminal Law are included in this text to familiarize the reader with this little known body of law. It includes *crimes against humanity, war crimes, crimes against peace,* and *torture.* As a body of law, it is basically the international criminalization of the worst violations of IHL and IHRL. It is the imposition of individual criminal responsibility on individuals, not governments, not the state. It says that certain acts are so terrible that they are an offense against all humankind, and the individuals who commit them should be held criminally accountable. They make the perpetrator an enemy of humankind, *hostis humani generis.* Piracy was the first international crime, slavery the second. Torture and genocide are modern international crimes one hears about still too often.

A few of the documents in this text are from the field of International Criminal Law. This book will only scratch the surface of IHL and ICL, but hopefully the reader will keep this broader international legal view in mind to apply to situations, not only in far off places, but in the U.S., too. That law applies here, too.

The U.S. has been a key proponent of International Criminal Law and was active in adjudicating the Nuremberg Trials which gave the U.S. much of the body of International Criminal Law, particularly war crimes, crimes against humanity, and crimes against peace. In addition, the U.S. helped articulate the Nuremberg principles, which state among other things that no one, military or civilian, is exempt from international criminal responsibility due to being a member of the government, or because one was simply following superior orders. International Criminal Law has continued to evolve and expand since then, with the major event being the adoption of the Rome Statute in 1998 and the creation of the International Criminal Court (ICC). But after being a key promoter of the ICC, the U.S. would not sign the Rome Statute until the last day of the Clinton Administration. When George W. Bush took office, he declared that the Rome Statute was dead on arrival, and that the U.S. would not sign and ratify it. He stated that the U.S. would "unsign" it, a process that does not exist within International Law. It remains signed but not ratified by the U.S. In fact, the reaction to the Rome Statute by the U.S. congressional establishment was so strong that Congress, pushed largely by the military, passed legislation entitled the American Service Member's Protection Act, whose aim was "to protect United States military personnel and other elected and appointed officials of the United States government against criminal prosecution by an international criminal court to which the United States is not party." It authorizes the U.S. President to use "all means necessary and appropriate to bring about the release of any U.S. or allied personnel being detained or imprisoned by, on behalf of, or at the request of the International Criminal Court." It has jokingly been called the "Hague Invasion Act."

Though not a party to the Rome Statute, the U.S. government participates in much activity of the Assembly of States parties, such as when they negotiated and drafted the definition of the Crime of Aggression. The U.S. also participated in many ways with the establishment and processes and prosecutions of the International Tribunal for the Former Yugoslavia (ICTY) and the International Tribunal for Rwanda (ICTR).

In the relationship of International Human Rights Law, Humanitarian Law, and International Criminal Law, there is evidence of a convergence of these fields of law, as new situations on the ground challenge and change the needs of law and justice. In more and more world events, particularly armed conflicts, a situation cannot be fully judged except in relation to all three of these fields of International Law. This creates controversy and legal argumentation, such as the U.S. military claiming that Humanitarian Law applies in certain military situations and human rights law does not. These issues are shown in the materials of this book and show the push and pull between the U.S. and the international community and between the U.S. civil society community and the U.S., especially as it acts abroad. A broad understanding of these three areas of law is important to the person seeking to judge government acts and use the most possible legal norms applicable. This convergence is likely to continue and will challenge the legal and political community in application and interpretation.

For this reason, this text has chosen to give the reader a little of all three of these fields of law, and others, assuming the reader wants as broad a legal understanding as possible. To quote Thomas Jefferson: "Educate and inform the whole mass of the people... They are the only sure reliance for the preservation of our liberty."

Primary Source Documents

I. UNIVERSAL DECLARATION OF HUMAN RIGHTS

The Universal Declaration of Human Rights is the key historical foundational instrument of international human rights law. It was adopted by the United National on December 10, 1948, a date which is celebrated in the U.S. and around the world as human rights day. The U.S. President issues a proclamation each December 10, in commemoration. It is the primary document used at the U.N. along with the Vienna Declaration and Programme of Action of 1993, in the work of the U.N. regarding human rights. The Universal Declaration of Human Rights is the first statement by the international community of nations of what were back then the commonly recognized human rights of every individual in every country. It is the most important and the fountainhead document of all human rights.

This instrument was originally drafted to be a non-legal instrument, but merely a declaration of principles, meaning that it would not create any binding legal obligations on states. But over the course of time and because of how states regard it and have acted under it, it has come to be considered as setting forth ("ripened into") binding legal norms under the doctrine of customary international law, at least as to what are known as the "hard core" human rights of the UDHR. Therefore, one can U.S. this instrument as a legal basis to accuse a state of violating its human rights.

All international and regional human rights instruments look to the UDHR as their touchstone, even though many legally binding treaties have been created to more fully flesh out human rights in different areas such as childrens' rights.

This instrument forms the foundational pillar of what is called the International Bill of Rights. The four documents of the Bill of Rights are those four which follow as primary documents, which are all treaties. This Declaration is the one human rights document every human being should read. Eleanor Roosevelt, an American, was a co-drafter of this Declaration. Following its adoption the General Assembly called upon all Member countries to publicize the text of the Declaration and to cause it to be disseminated, displayed, read and expounded principally in schools and other educational institutions, the U.S. has never done this.

[Text]

The Universal Declaration of Human Rights

Adopted and proclaimed by General Assembly resolution 217 A (III) of 10 December 1948

Preamble

Whereas recognition of the inherent dignity and of the equal and inalienable rights of all members of the human family is the foundation of freedom, justice and peace in the world,

Whereas disregard and contempt for human rights have resulted in barbarous acts which have outraged the conscience of mankind, and the advent of a world in which human beings shall enjoy freedom of speech and belief and freedom from fear and want has been proclaimed as the highest aspiration of the common people,

Whereas it is essential, if man is not to be compelled to have recourse, as a last resort, to rebellion against tyranny and oppression, that human rights should be protected by the rule of law,

Whereas it is essential to promote the development of friendly relations between nations,

Whereas the peoples of the United Nations have in the Charter reaffirmed their faith in fundamental human rights, in the dignity and worth of the human person and in the equal rights of men and women and have determined to promote social progress and better standards of life in larger freedom,

Whereas Member States have pledged themselves to achieve, in co-operation with the United Nations, the promotion of universal respect for and observance of human rights and fundamental freedoms,

Whereas a common understanding of these rights and freedoms is of the greatest importance for the full realization of this pledge,

Now, Therefore

THE GENERAL ASSEMBLY proclaims THIS UNIVERSAL DECLARATION OF HUMAN RIGHTS as a common standard of achievement for all peoples and all nations, to the end that every individual and every organ of society, keeping this Declaration constantly in mind, shall strive by teaching and education to promote respect for these rights and freedoms and by progressive measures, national and international, to secure their universal and effective recognition and observance, both among the peoples of Member States themselves and among the peoples of territories under their jurisdiction.

Article 1.
All human beings are born free and equal in dignity and rights. They are endowed with reason and conscience and should act towards one another in a spirit of brotherhood.

Article 2.
Everyone is entitled to all the rights and freedoms set forth in this Declaration, without distinction of any kind, such as race, colour, sex, language, religion, political or other opinion, national or social origin, property, birth or other status. Furthermore, no distinction shall be made on the basis of the political, jurisdictional or international status of the country or territory to which a person belongs, whether it be independent, trust, non-self-governing or under any other limitation of sovereignty.

Article 3.
Everyone has the right to life, liberty and security of person.

Article 4.
No one shall be held in slavery or servitude; slavery and the slave trade shall be prohibited in all their forms.

Article 5.
No one shall be subjected to torture or to cruel, inhuman or degrading treatment or punishment.

Article 6.
Everyone has the right to recognition everywhere as a person before the law.

Article 7.
All are equal before the law and are entitled without any discrimination to equal protection of the law. All are entitled to equal protection against any discrimination in violation of this Declaration and against any incitement to such discrimination.

Article 8.
Everyone has the right to an effective remedy by the competent national tribunals for acts violating the fundamental rights granted him by the constitution or by law.

Article 9.
No one shall be subjected to arbitrary arrest, detention or exile.

Article 10.
Everyone is entitled in full equality to a fair and public hearing by an independent and impartial tribunal, in the determination of his rights and obligations and of any criminal charge against him.

Article 11.
(1) Everyone charged with a penal offence has the right to be presumed innocent until proved guilty according to law in a public trial at which he has had all the guarantees necessary for his defence.

(2) No one shall be held guilty of any penal offence on account of any act or omission which did not constitute a penal offence, under national or international law, at the time when it was committed. Nor shall a heavier penalty be imposed than the one that was applicable at the time the penal offence was committed.

Article 12.
No one shall be subjected to arbitrary interference with his privacy, family, home or correspondence, nor to attacks upon his honour and reputation. Everyone has the right to the protection of the law against such interference or attacks.

Article 13.
(1) Everyone has the right to freedom of movement and residence within the borders of each state.

(2) Everyone has the right to leave any country, including his own, and to return to his country.

Article 14.
(1) Everyone has the right to seek and to enjoy in other countries asylum from persecution.

(2) This right may not be invoked in the case of prosecutions genuinely arising from non-political crimes or from acts contrary to the purposes and principles of the United Nations.

Article 15.
(1) Everyone has the right to a nationality.

(2) No one shall be arbitrarily deprived of his nationality nor denied the right to change his nationality.

Article 16.
(1) Men and women of full age, without any limitation due to race, nationality or religion, have the right to marry and to found a family. They are entitled to equal rights as to marriage, during marriage and at its dissolution.

(2) Marriage shall be entered into only with the free and full consent of the intending spouses.

(3) The family is the natural and fundamental group unit of society and is entitled to protection by society and the State.

Article 17.
(1) Everyone has the right to own property alone as well as in association with others.

(2) No one shall be arbitrarily deprived of his property.

Article 18.
Everyone has the right to freedom of thought, conscience and religion; this right includes freedom to change his religion or belief, and freedom, either alone or in community with others and in public or private, to manifest his religion or belief in teaching, practice, worship and observance.

Article 19.
Everyone has the right to freedom of opinion and expression; this right includes freedom to hold opinions without interference and to seek, receive and impart information and ideas through any media and regardless of frontiers.

Article 20.
(1) Everyone has the right to freedom of peaceful assembly and association.

(2) No one may be compelled to belong to an association.

Article 21.

(1) Everyone has the right to take part in the government of his country, directly or through freely chosen representatives.

(2) Everyone has the right of equal access to public service in his country.

(3) The will of the people shall be the basis of the authority of government; this will shall be expressed in periodic and genuine elections which shall be by universal and equal suffrage and shall be held by secret vote or by equivalent free voting procedures.

Article 22.

Everyone, as a member of society, has the right to social security and is entitled to realization, through national effort and international co-operation and in accordance with the organization and resources of each State, of the economic, social and cultural rights indispensable for his dignity and the free development of his personality.

Article 23.

(1) Everyone has the right to work, to free choice of employment, to just and favourable conditions of work and to protection against unemployment.

(2) Everyone, without any discrimination, has the right to equal pay for equal work.

(3) Everyone who works has the right to just and favourable remuneration ensuring for himself and his family an existence worthy of human dignity, and supplemented, if necessary, by other means of social protection.

(4) Everyone has the right to form and to join trade unions for the protection of his interests.

Article 24.

Everyone has the right to rest and leisure, including reasonable limitation of working hours and periodic holidays with pay.

Article 25.

(1) Everyone has the right to a standard of living adequate for the health and well-being of himself and of his family, including food, clothing, housing and medical care and necessary social services, and the right to security in the event of unemployment, sickness, disability, widowhood, old age or other lack of livelihood in circumstances beyond his control.

(2) Motherhood and childhood are entitled to special care and assistance. All children, whether born in or out of wedlock, shall enjoy the same social protection.

Article 26.

(1) Everyone has the right to education. Education shall be free, at least in the elementary and fundamental stages. Elementary education shall be compulsory. Technical and professional education shall be made generally available and higher education shall be equally accessible to all on the basis of merit.

(2) Education shall be directed to the full development of the human personality and to the strengthening of respect for human rights and fundamental freedoms. It shall promote understanding, tolerance and friendship among all nations, racial or religious groups, and shall further the activities of the United Nations for the maintenance of peace.

(3) Parents have a prior right to choose the kind of education that shall be given to their children.

Article 27.

(1) Everyone has the right freely to participate in the cultural life of the community, to enjoy the arts and to share in scientific advancement and its benefits.

(2) Everyone has the right to the protection of the moral and material interests resulting from any scientific, literary or artistic production of which he is the author.

Article 28.
Everyone is entitled to a social and international order in which the rights and freedoms set forth in this Declaration can be fully realized.

Article 29.
(1) Everyone has duties to the community in which alone the free and full development of his personality is possible.

(2) In the exercise of his rights and freedoms, everyone shall be subject only to such limitations as are determined by law solely for the purpose of securing due recognition and respect for the rights and freedoms of others and of meeting the just requirements of morality, public order and the general welfare in a democratic society.

(3) These rights and freedoms may in no case be exercised contrary to the purposes and principles of the United Nations.

Article 30.
Nothing in this Declaration may be interpreted as implying for any State, group or person any right to engage in any activity or to perform any act aimed at the destruction of any of the rights and freedoms set forth herein.

[End text]

Source: http://www.ohchr.org/EN/UDHR/Documents/UDHR_Translations/eng.pdf

2. INTERNATIONAL COVENANT ON CIVIL AND POLITICAL RIGHTS

It was always intended that the rights set forth in the UDHR would be transformed into binding legal instruments called treaties to make the obligations to protect human rights legally binding on all states who chose to become bound by them, as a "state-party. In 1966 the nations of the world gathered at the United Nations and drafted and adopted two treaties. The intent was to draft one treaty with all human rights in them. But largely because of the Cold War the international community could not agree on one instrument with all human rights, so they chose to create two instruments. One was the International Covenant on Civil and Political Rights. It is a general human rights treaty which treats only civil human rights and political human rights and it sets up a supervisory body, the Human Rights Committee, to monitor state compliance with its norms.

It was adopted at the U.N. in 1966 and entered into force in 1976. It is the most important treaty to which the U.S. is a state party and its obligations are legally binding on the U.S. since the U.S. ratified it in 1992. It has been the source of much controversy between the U.N. and the U.S. particularly in the context of the so-called war on terror. The U.S. has claimed that the ICCPR does not apply to any acts committed outside the U.S. The Human Rights Committee and most scholars claim it does apply anywhere the U.S. exercises "effective control" of an area, such as Guantánamo, or Gulf War Iraq.

This treaty should be applied to U/S. law, policy and practice even before applying the UDHR, which is also binding on the U.S. When the U.S. Senate ratified this treaty it also submitted reservations, declarations and understandings which substantially condition the extent of the U.S. obligations under it. It was declared to be "non-self-executing when ratified and no implementing legislation was ever enacted because the U.S. claimed its laws already fully protected the rights in the ICCPR.

[Text]

International Covenant on Civil and Political Rights

Adopted and opened for signature, ratification and accession by General Assembly resolution 2200A (XXI) of 16 December 1966, entry into force 23 March 1976, in accordance with Article 49

Preamble

The States Parties to the present Covenant,

Considering that, in accordance with the principles proclaimed in the Charter of the United Nations, recognition of the inherent dignity and of the equal and inalienable rights of all members of the human family is the foundation of freedom, justice and peace in the world,

Recognizing that these rights derive from the inherent dignity of the human person,

Recognizing that, in accordance with the Universal Declaration of Human Rights, the ideal of free human beings enjoying civil and political freedom and freedom from fear and want can only be achieved if conditions are created whereby everyone may enjoy his civil and political rights, as well as his economic, social and cultural rights,

Considering the obligation of States under the Charter of the United Nations to promote universal respect for, and observance of, human rights and freedoms,

Realizing that the individual, having duties to other individuals and to the community to which he belongs, is under a responsibility to strive for the promotion and observance of the rights recognized in the present Covenant,

Agree upon the following articles:

PART I

Article 1
1. All peoples have the right of self-determination. By virtue of that right they freely determine their political status and freely pursue their economic, social and cultural development.

2. All peoples may, for their own ends, freely dispose of their natural wealth and resources without prejudice to any obligations arising out of international economic co-operation, based upon the principle of mutual benefit, and international law. In no case may a people be deprived of its own means of subsistence.

3. The States Parties to the present Covenant, including those having responsibility for the administration of Non-Self-Governing and Trust Territories, shall promote the realization of the right of self-determination, and shall respect that right, in conformity with the provisions of the Charter of the United Nations.

PART II

Article 2
1. Each State Party to the present Covenant undertakes to respect and to ensure to all individuals within its territory and subject to its jurisdiction the rights recognized in the present Covenant, without distinction of any kind, such as race, colour, sex, language, religion, political or other opinion, national or social origin, property, birth or other status.

2. Where not already provided for by existing legislative or other measures, each State Party to the present Covenant undertakes to take the necessary steps, in accordance with its constitutional processes and with the provisions of the present Covenant, to adopt such laws or other measures as may be necessary to give effect to the rights recognized in the present Covenant.

3. Each State Party to the present Covenant undertakes:

(a) To ensure that any person whose rights or freedoms as herein recognized are violated shall have an effective remedy, notwithstanding that the violation has been committed by persons acting in an official capacity;

(b) To ensure that any person claiming such a remedy shall have his right thereto determined by competent judicial, administrative or legislative authorities, or by any other competent authority provided for by the legal system of the State, and to develop the possibilities of judicial remedy;

(c) To ensure that the competent authorities shall enforce such remedies when granted.

Article 3

The States Parties to the present Covenant undertake to ensure the equal right of men and women to the enjoyment of all civil and political rights set forth in the present Covenant.

Article 4

1 . In time of public emergency which threatens the life of the nation and the existence of which is officially proclaimed, the States Parties to the present Covenant may take measures derogating from their obligations under the present Covenant to the extent strictly required by the exigencies of the situation, provided that such measures are not inconsistent with their other obligations under international law and do not involve discrimination solely on the ground of race, colour, sex, language, religion or social origin.

2. No derogation from articles 6, 7, 8 (paragraphs I and 2), 11, 15, 16 and 18 may be made under this provision.

3. Any State Party to the present Covenant availing itself of the right of derogation shall immediately inform the other States Parties to the present Covenant, through the intermediary of the Secretary-General of the United Nations, of the provisions from which it has derogated and of the reasons by which it was actuated. A further communication shall be made, through the same intermediary, on the date on which it terminates such derogation.

Article 5

1. Nothing in the present Covenant may be interpreted as implying for any State, group or person any right to engage in any activity or perform any act aimed at the destruction of any of the rights and freedoms recognized herein or at their limitation to a greater extent than is provided for in the present Covenant.

2. There shall be no restriction upon or derogation from any of the fundamental human rights recognized or existing in any State Party to the present Covenant pursuant to law, conventions, regulations or custom on the pretext that the present Covenant does not recognize such rights or that it recognizes them to a lesser extent.

PART III

Article 6

1. Every human being has the inherent right to life. This right shall be protected by law. No one shall be arbitrarily deprived of his life.

2. In countries which have not abolished the death penalty, sentence of death may be imposed only for the most serious crimes in accordance with the law in force at the time of the commission of the crime and not contrary to the provisions of the present Covenant and to the Convention on the Prevention and Punishment of the Crime of Genocide. This penalty can only be carried out pursuant to a final judgement rendered by a competent court.

3. When deprivation of life constitutes the crime of genocide, it is understood that nothing in this article shall authorize any State Party to the present Covenant to derogate in any way from any obligation assumed under the provisions of the Convention on the Prevention and Punishment of the Crime of Genocide.

4. Anyone sentenced to death shall have the right to seek pardon or commutation of the sentence. Amnesty, pardon or commutation of the sentence of death may be granted in all cases.

5. Sentence of death shall not be imposed for crimes committed by persons below eighteen years of age and shall not be carried out on pregnant women.

6. Nothing in this article shall be invoked to delay or to prevent the abolition of capital punishment by any State Party to the present Covenant.

Article 7

No one shall be subjected to torture or to cruel, inhuman or degrading treatment or punishment. In particular, no one shall be subjected without his free consent to medical or scientific experimentation.

Article 8

1. No one shall be held in slavery; slavery and the slave-trade in all their forms shall be prohibited.

2. No one shall be held in servitude.

3.

   (a) No one shall be required to perform forced or compulsory labour;

   (b) Paragraph 3 (a) shall not be held to preclude, in countries where imprisonment with hard labour may be imposed as a punishment for a crime, the performance of hard labour in pursuance of a sentence to such punishment by a competent court;

   (c) For the purpose of this paragraph the term "forced or compulsory labour" shall not include:

      (i) Any work or service, not referred to in subparagraph (b), normally required of a person who is under detention in consequence of a lawful order of a court, or of a person during conditional release from such detention;

      (ii) Any service of a military character and, in countries where conscientious objection is recognized, any national service required by law of conscientious objectors;

      (iii) Any service exacted in cases of emergency or calamity threatening the life or well-being of the community;

      (iv) Any work or service which forms part of normal civil obligations.

Article 9

1. Everyone has the right to liberty and security of person. No one shall be subjected to arbitrary arrest or detention. No one shall be deprived of his liberty except on such grounds and in accordance with such procedure as are established by law.

2. Anyone who is arrested shall be informed, at the time of arrest, of the reasons for his arrest and shall be promptly informed of any charges against him.

3. Anyone arrested or detained on a criminal charge shall be brought promptly before a judge or other officer authorized by law to exercise judicial power and shall be entitled to trial within a reasonable time or to release. It shall not be the general rule that persons awaiting trial shall be detained in custody, but release may be subject to guarantees to appear for trial, at any other stage of the judicial proceedings, and, should occasion arise, for execution of the judgement.

4. Anyone who is deprived of his liberty by arrest or detention shall be entitled to take proceedings before a court, in order that that court may decide without delay on the lawfulness of his detention and order his release if the detention is not lawful.

5. Anyone who has been the victim of unlawful arrest or detention shall have an enforceable right to compensation.

Article 10

1. All persons deprived of their liberty shall be treated with humanity and with respect for the inherent dignity of the human person.

2.

   (a) Accused persons shall, save in exceptional circumstances, be segregated from convicted persons and shall be subject to separate treatment appropriate to their status as unconvicted persons;

   (b) Accused juvenile persons shall be separated from adults and brought as speedily as possible for adjudication.

3. The penitentiary system shall comprise treatment of prisoners the essential aim of which shall be their reformation and social rehabilitation. Juvenile offenders shall be segregated from adults and be accorded treatment appropriate to their age and legal status.

Article 11
No one shall be imprisoned merely on the ground of inability to fulfil a contractual obligation.

Article 12
1. Everyone lawfully within the territory of a State shall, within that territory, have the right to liberty of movement and freedom to choose his residence.

2. Everyone shall be free to leave any country, including his own.

3. The above-mentioned rights shall not be subject to any restrictions except those which are provided by law, are necessary to protect national security, public order (ordre public), public health or morals or the rights and freedoms of others, and are consistent with the other rights recognized in the present Covenant.

4. No one shall be arbitrarily deprived of the right to enter his own country.

Article 13
An alien lawfully in the territory of a State Party to the present Covenant may be expelled therefrom only in pursuance of a decision reached in accordance with law and shall, except where compelling reasons of national security otherwise require, be allowed to submit the reasons against his expulsion and to have his case reviewed by, and be represented for the purpose before, the competent authority or a person or persons especially designated by the competent authority.

Article 14
1. All persons shall be equal before the courts and tribunals. In the determination of any criminal charge against him, or of his rights and obligations in a suit at law, everyone shall be entitled to a fair and public hearing by a competent, independent and impartial tribunal established by law. The press and the public may be excluded from all or part of a trial for reasons of morals, public order (ordre public) or national security in a democratic society, or when the interest of the private lives of the parties so requires, or to the extent strictly necessary in the opinion of the court in special circumstances where publicity would prejudice the interests of justice; but any judgement rendered in a criminal case or in a suit at law shall be made public except where the interest of juvenile persons otherwise requires or the proceedings concern matrimonial disputes or the guardianship of children.

2. Everyone charged with a criminal offence shall have the right to be presumed innocent until proved guilty according to law.

3. In the determination of any criminal charge against him, everyone shall be entitled to the following minimum guarantees, in full equality:

(a) To be informed promptly and in detail in a language which he understands of the nature and cause of the charge against him;

(b) To have adequate time and facilities for the preparation of his defence and to communicate with counsel of his own choosing;

(c) To be tried without undue delay;

(d) To be tried in his presence, and to defend himself in person or through legal assistance of his own choosing; to be informed, if he does not have legal assistance, of this right; and to have legal assistance assigned to him, in any case where the interests of justice so require, and without payment by him in any such case if he does not have sufficient means to pay for it;

(e) To examine, or have examined, the witnesses against him and to obtain the attendance and examination of witnesses on his behalf under the same conditions as witnesses against him;

(f) To have the free assistance of an interpreter if he cannot understand or speak the language used in court;

(g) Not to be compelled to testify against himself or to confess guilt.

4. In the case of juvenile persons, the procedure shall be such as will take account of their age and the desirability of promoting their rehabilitation.

5. Everyone convicted of a crime shall have the right to his conviction and sentence being reviewed by a higher tribunal according to law.

6. When a person has by a final decision been convicted of a criminal offence and when subsequently his conviction has been reversed or he has been pardoned on the ground that a new or newly discovered fact shows conclusively that there has been a miscarriage of justice, the person who has suffered punishment as a result of such conviction shall be compensated according to law, unless it is proved that the non-disclosure of the unknown fact in time is wholly or partly attributable to him.

7. No one shall be liable to be tried or punished again for an offence for which he has already been finally convicted or acquitted in accordance with the law and penal procedure of each country.

Article 15
1 . No one shall be held guilty of any criminal offence on account of any act or omission which did not constitute a criminal offence, under national or international law, at the time when it was committed. Nor shall a heavier penalty be imposed than the one that was applicable at the time when the criminal offence was committed. If, subsequent to the commission of the offence, provision is made by law for the imposition of the lighter penalty, the offender shall benefit thereby.

2. Nothing in this article shall prejudice the trial and punishment of any person for any act or omission which, at the time when it was committed, was criminal according to the general principles of law recognized by the community of nations.

Article 16
Everyone shall have the right to recognition everywhere as a person before the law.

Article 17
1. No one shall be subjected to arbitrary or unlawful interference with his privacy, family, home or correspondence, nor to unlawful attacks on his honour and reputation.

2. Everyone has the right to the protection of the law against such interference or attacks.

Article 18
1. Everyone shall have the right to freedom of thought, conscience and religion. This right shall include freedom to have or to adopt a religion or belief of his choice, and freedom, either individually or in community with others and in public or private, to manifest his religion or belief in worship, observance, practice and teaching.

2. No one shall be subject to coercion which would impair his freedom to have or to adopt a religion or belief of his choice.

3. Freedom to manifest one's religion or beliefs may be subject only to such limitations as are prescribed by law and are necessary to protect public safety, order, health, or morals or the fundamental rights and freedoms of others.

4. The States Parties to the present Covenant undertake to have respect for the liberty of parents and, when applicable, legal guardians to ensure the religious and moral education of their children in conformity with their own convictions.

Article 19
1. Everyone shall have the right to hold opinions without interference.

2. Everyone shall have the right to freedom of expression; this right shall include freedom to seek, receive and impart information and ideas of all kinds, regardless of frontiers, either orally, in writing or in print, in the form of art, or through any other media of his choice.

3. The exercise of the rights provided for in paragraph 2 of this article carries with it special duties and responsibilities. It may therefore be subject to certain restrictions, but these shall only be such as are provided by law and are necessary:

(a) For respect of the rights or reputations of others;

(b) For the protection of national security or of public order (ordre public), or of public health or morals.

Article 20
1. Any propaganda for war shall be prohibited by law.

2. Any advocacy of national, racial or religious hatred that constitutes incitement to discrimination, hostility or violence shall be prohibited by law.

Article 21
The right of peaceful assembly shall be recognized. No restrictions may be placed on the exercise of this right other than those imposed in conformity with the law and which are necessary in a democratic society in the interests of national security or public safety, public order (ordre public), the protection of public health or morals or the protection of the rights and freedoms of others.

Article 22
1. Everyone shall have the right to freedom of association with others, including the right to form and join trade unions for the protection of his interests.

2. No restrictions may be placed on the exercise of this right other than those which are prescribed by law and which are necessary in a democratic society in the interests of national security or public safety, public order (ordre public), the protection of public health or morals or the protection of the rights and freedoms of others. This article shall not prevent the imposition of lawful restrictions on members of the armed forces and of the police in their exercise of this right.

3. Nothing in this article shall authorize States Parties to the International Labour Organisation Convention of 1948 concerning Freedom of Association and Protection of the Right to Organize to take legislative measures which would prejudice, or to apply the law in such a manner as to prejudice, the guarantees provided for in that Convention.

Article 23
1. The family is the natural and fundamental group unit of society and is entitled to protection by society and the State.

2. The right of men and women of marriageable age to marry and to found a family shall be recognized.

3. No marriage shall be entered into without the free and full consent of the intending spouses.

4. States Parties to the present Covenant shall take appropriate steps to ensure equality of rights and responsibilities of spouses as to marriage, during marriage and at its dissolution. In the case of dissolution, provision shall be made for the necessary protection of any children.

Article 24
1. Every child shall have, without any discrimination as to race, colour, sex, language, religion, national or social origin, property or birth, the right to such measures of protection as are required by his status as a minor, on the part of his family, society and the State.

2. Every child shall be registered immediately after birth and shall have a name.

3. Every child has the right to acquire a nationality.

Article 25

Every citizen shall have the right and the opportunity, without any of the distinctions mentioned in article 2 and without unreasonable restrictions:

(a) To take part in the conduct of public affairs, directly or through freely chosen representatives;

(b) To vote and to be elected at genuine periodic elections which shall be by universal and equal suffrage and shall be held by secret ballot, guaranteeing the free expression of the will of the electors;

(c) To have access, on general terms of equality, to public service in his country.

Article 26

All persons are equal before the law and are entitled without any discrimination to the equal protection of the law. In this respect, the law shall prohibit any discrimination and guarantee to all persons equal and effective protection against discrimination on any ground such as race, colour, sex, language, religion, political or other opinion, national or social origin, property, birth or other status.

Article 27

In those States in which ethnic, religious or linguistic minorities exist, persons belonging to such minorities shall not be denied the right, in community with the other members of their group, to enjoy their own culture, to profess and practise their own religion, or to use their own language.

PART IV

Article 28

1. There shall be established a Human Rights Committee (hereafter referred to in the present Covenant as the Committee). It shall consist of eighteen members and shall carry out the functions hereinafter provided.

2. The Committee shall be composed of nationals of the States Parties to the present Covenant who shall be persons of high moral character and recognized competence in the field of human rights, consideration being given to the usefulness of the participation of some persons having legal experience.

3. The members of the Committee shall be elected and shall serve in their personal capacity.

Article 29

1. The members of the Committee shall be elected by secret ballot from a list of persons possessing the qualifications prescribed in article 28 and nominated for the purpose by the States Parties to the present Covenant.

2. Each State Party to the present Covenant may nominate not more than two persons. These persons shall be nationals of the nominating State.

3. A person shall be eligible for renomination.

Article 30

1. The initial election shall be held no later than six months after the date of the entry into force of the present Covenant.

2. At least four months before the date of each election to the Committee, other than an election to fill a vacancy declared in accordance with article 34, the Secretary-General of the United Nations shall address a written invitation to the States Parties to the present Covenant to submit their nominations for membership of the Committee within three months.

3. The Secretary-General of the United Nations shall prepare a list in alphabetical order of all the persons thus nominated, with an indication of the States Parties which have nominated them, and shall submit it to the States Parties to the present Covenant no later than one month before the date of each election.

4. Elections of the members of the Committee shall be held at a meeting of the States Parties to the present Covenant convened by the Secretary General of the United Nations at the Headquarters of the United Nations. At that meeting, for which two thirds of the States Parties to the present Covenant shall constitute a quorum, the persons elected to the Committee shall be those nominees who obtain the largest number of votes and an absolute majority of the votes of the representatives of States Parties present and voting.

Article 31

1. The Committee may not include more than one national of the same State.

2. In the election of the Committee, consideration shall be given to equitable geographical distribution of membership and to the representation of the different forms of civilization and of the principal legal systems.

Article 32

1. The members of the Committee shall be elected for a term of four years. They shall be eligible for re-election if renominated. However, the terms of nine of the members elected at the first election shall expire at the end of two years; immediately after the first election, the names of these nine members shall be chosen by lot by the Chairman of the meeting referred to in article 30, paragraph 4.

2. Elections at the expiry of office shall be held in accordance with the preceding articles of this part of the present Covenant.

Article 33

1. If, in the unanimous opinion of the other members, a member of the Committee has ceased to carry out his functions for any cause other than absence of a temporary character, the Chairman of the Committee shall notify the Secretary-General of the United Nations, who shall then declare the seat of that member to be vacant.

2. In the event of the death or the resignation of a member of the Committee, the Chairman shall immediately notify the Secretary-General of the United Nations, who shall declare the seat vacant from the date of death or the date on which the resignation takes effect.

Article 34

1. When a vacancy is declared in accordance with article 33 and if the term of office of the member to be replaced does not expire within six months of the declaration of the vacancy, the Secretary-General of the United Nations shall notify each of the States Parties to the present Covenant, which may within two months submit nominations in accordance with article 29 for the purpose of filling the vacancy.

2. The Secretary-General of the United Nations shall prepare a list in alphabetical order of the persons thus nominated and shall submit it to the States Parties to the present Covenant. The election to fill the vacancy shall then take place in accordance with the relevant provisions of this part of the present Covenant.

3. A member of the Committee elected to fill a vacancy declared in accordance with article 33 shall hold office for the remainder of the term of the member who vacated the seat on the Committee under the provisions of that article.

Article 35

The members of the Committee shall, with the approval of the General Assembly of the United Nations, receive emoluments from United Nations resources on such terms and conditions as the General Assembly may decide, having regard to the importance of the Committee's responsibilities.

Article 36

The Secretary-General of the United Nations shall provide the necessary staff and facilities for the effective performance of the functions of the Committee under the present Covenant.

Article 37

1. The Secretary-General of the United Nations shall convene the initial meeting of the Committee at the Headquarters of the United Nations.

2. After its initial meeting, the Committee shall meet at such times as shall be provided in its rules of procedure.

3. The Committee shall normally meet at the Headquarters of the United Nations or at the United Nations Office at Geneva.

Article 38

Every member of the Committee shall, before taking up his duties, make a solemn declaration in open committee that he will perform his functions impartially and conscientiously.

Article 39

1. The Committee shall elect its officers for a term of two years. They may be re-elected.

2. The Committee shall establish its own rules of procedure, but these rules shall provide, inter alia, that:

(a) Twelve members shall constitute a quorum;

(b) Decisions of the Committee shall be made by a majority vote of the members present.

Article 40

1. The States Parties to the present Covenant undertake to submit reports on the measures they have adopted which give effect to the rights recognized herein and on the progress made in the enjoyment of those rights:

(a) Within one year of the entry into force of the present Covenant for the States Parties concerned;

(b) Thereafter whenever the Committee so requests.

2. All reports shall be submitted to the Secretary-General of the United Nations, who shall transmit them to the Committee for consideration. Reports shall indicate the factors and difficulties, if any, affecting the implementation of the present Covenant.

3. The Secretary-General of the United Nations may, after consultation with the Committee, transmit to the specialized agencies concerned copies of such parts of the reports as may fall within their field of competence.

4. The Committee shall study the reports submitted by the States Parties to the present Covenant. It shall transmit its reports, and such general comments as it may consider appropriate, to the States Parties. The Committee may also transmit to the Economic and Social Council these comments along with the copies of the reports it has received from States Parties to the present Covenant.

5. The States Parties to the present Covenant may submit to the Committee observations on any comments that may be made in accordance with paragraph 4 of this article.

Article 41

1. A State Party to the present Covenant may at any time declare under this article that it recognizes the competence of the Committee to receive and consider communications to the effect that a State Party claims that another State Party is not fulfilling its obligations under the present Covenant. Communications under this article may be received and considered only if submitted by a State Party which has made a declaration recognizing in regard to itself the competence of the Committee. No communication shall be received by the Committee if it concerns a State Party which has not made such a declaration. Communications received under this article shall be dealt with in accordance with the following procedure:

(a) If a State Party to the present Covenant considers that another State Party is not giving effect to the provisions of the present Covenant, it may, by written communication, bring the matter to the attention of that State Party. Within three months after the receipt of the communication the receiving State shall afford the State which sent the communication an explanation, or any other statement in writing clarifying the matter which should include, to the extent possible and pertinent, reference to domestic procedures and remedies taken, pending, or available in the matter;

(b) If the matter is not adjusted to the satisfaction of both States Parties concerned within six months after the receipt by the receiving State of the initial communication, either State shall have the right to refer the matter to the Committee, by notice given to the Committee and to the other State;

(c) The Committee shall deal with a matter referred to it only after it has ascertained that all available domestic remedies have been invoked and exhausted in the matter, in conformity with the generally recognized principles of international law. This shall not be the rule where the application of the remedies is unreasonably prolonged;

(d) The Committee shall hold closed meetings when examining communications under this article;

(e) Subject to the provisions of subparagraph (c), the Committee shall make available its good offices to the States Parties concerned with a view to a friendly solution of the matter on the basis of respect for human rights and fundamental freedoms as recognized in the present Covenant;

(f) In any matter referred to it, the Committee may call upon the States Parties concerned, referred to in subparagraph (b), to supply any relevant information;

(g) The States Parties concerned, referred to in subparagraph (b), shall have the right to be represented when the matter is being considered in the Committee and to make submissions orally and/or in writing;

(h) The Committee shall, within twelve months after the date of receipt of notice under subparagraph (b), submit a report:

> (i) If a solution within the terms of subparagraph (e) is reached, the Committee shall confine its report to a brief statement of the facts and of the solution reached;

> (ii) If a solution within the terms of subparagraph (e) is not reached, the Committee shall confine its report to a brief statement of the facts; the written submissions and record of the oral submissions made by the States Parties concerned shall be attached to the report. In every matter, the report shall be communicated to the States Parties concerned.

2. The provisions of this article shall come into force when ten States Parties to the present Covenant have made declarations under paragraph I of this article. Such declarations shall be deposited by the States Parties with the Secretary-General of the United Nations, who shall transmit copies thereof to the other States Parties. A declaration may be withdrawn at any time by notification to the Secretary-General. Such a withdrawal shall not prejudice the consideration of any matter which is the subject of a communication already transmitted under this article; no further communication by any State Party shall be received after the notification of withdrawal of the declaration has been received by the Secretary-General, unless the State Party concerned has made a new declaration.

Article 42
1.

> (a) If a matter referred to the Committee in accordance with article 41 is not resolved to the satisfaction of the States Parties concerned, the Committee may, with the prior consent of the States Parties concerned, appoint an ad hoc Conciliation Commission (hereinafter referred to as the Commission). The good offices of the Commission shall be made available to the States Parties concerned with a view to an amicable solution of the matter on the basis of respect for the present Covenant;

> (b) The Commission shall consist of five persons acceptable to the States Parties concerned. If the States Parties concerned fail to reach agreement within three months on all or part of the composition of the Commission, the members of the Commission concerning whom no agreement has been reached shall be elected by secret ballot by a two-thirds majority vote of the Committee from among its members.

2. The members of the Commission shall serve in their personal capacity. They shall not be nationals of the States Parties concerned, or of a State not Party to the present Covenant, or of a State Party which has not made a declaration under article 41.

3. The Commission shall elect its own Chairman and adopt its own rules of procedure.

4. The meetings of the Commission shall normally be held at the Headquarters of the United Nations or at the United Nations Office at Geneva. However, they may be held at such other convenient places as the Commission may determine in consultation with the Secretary-General of the United Nations and the States Parties concerned.

5. The secretariat provided in accordance with article 36 shall also service the commissions appointed under this article.

6. The information received and collated by the Committee shall be made available to the Commission and the Commission may call upon the States Parties concerned to supply any other relevant information.

7. When the Commission has fully considered the matter, but in any event not later than twelve months after having been seized of the matter, it shall submit to the Chairman of the Committee a report for communication to the States Parties concerned:

(a) If the Commission is unable to complete its consideration of the matter within twelve months, it shall confine its report to a brief statement of the status of its consideration of the matter;

(b) If an amicable solution to the matter on the basis of respect for human rights as recognized in the present Covenant is reached, the Commission shall confine its report to a brief statement of the facts and of the solution reached;

(c) If a solution within the terms of subparagraph (b) is not reached, the Commission's report shall embody its findings on all questions of fact relevant to the issues between the States Parties concerned, and its views on the possibilities of an amicable solution of the matter. This report shall also contain the written submissions and a record of the oral submissions made by the States Parties concerned;

(d) If the Commission's report is submitted under subparagraph (c), the States Parties concerned shall, within three months of the receipt of the report, notify the Chairman of the Committee whether or not they accept the contents of the report of the Commission.

8. The provisions of this article are without prejudice to the responsibilities of the Committee under article 41.

9. The States Parties concerned shall share equally all the expenses of the members of the Commission in accordance with estimates to be provided by the Secretary-General of the United Nations.

10. The Secretary-General of the United Nations shall be empowered to pay the expenses of the members of the Commission, if necessary, before reimbursement by the States Parties concerned, in accordance with paragraph 9 of this article.

Article 43
The members of the Committee, and of the ad hoc conciliation commissions which may be appointed under article 42, shall be entitled to the facilities, privileges and immunities of experts on mission for the United Nations as laid down in the relevant sections of the Convention on the Privileges and Immunities of the United Nations.

Article 44
The provisions for the implementation of the present Covenant shall apply without prejudice to the procedures prescribed in the field of human rights by or under the constituent instruments and the conventions of the United Nations and of the specialized agencies and shall not prevent the States Parties to the present Covenant from having recourse to other procedures for settling a dispute in accordance with general or special international agreements in force between them.

Article 45
The Committee shall submit to the General Assembly of the United Nations, through the Economic and Social Council, an annual report on its activities.

PART V

Article 46
Nothing in the present Covenant shall be interpreted as impairing the provisions of the Charter of the United Nations and of the constitutions of the specialized agencies which define the respective responsibilities of the various organs of the United Nations and of the specialized agencies in regard to the matters dealt with in the present Covenant.

Article 47
Nothing in the present Covenant shall be interpreted as impairing the inherent right of all peoples to enjoy and utilize fully and freely their natural wealth and resources.

PART VI

Article 48
1. The present Covenant is open for signature by any State Member of the United Nations or member of any of its specialized agencies, by any State Party to the Statute of the International Court of Justice, and by any other State which has been invited by the General Assembly of the United Nations to become a Party to the present Covenant.

2. The present Covenant is subject to ratification. Instruments of ratification shall be deposited with the Secretary-General of the United Nations.

3. The present Covenant shall be open to accession by any State referred to in paragraph 1 of this article.

4. Accession shall be effected by the deposit of an instrument of accession with the Secretary-General of the United Nations.

5. The Secretary-General of the United Nations shall inform all States which have signed this Covenant or acceded to it of the deposit of each instrument of ratification or accession.

Article 49
1. The present Covenant shall enter into force three months after the date of the deposit with the Secretary-General of the United Nations of the thirty-fifth instrument of ratification or instrument of accession.

2. For each State ratifying the present Covenant or acceding to it after the deposit of the thirty-fifth instrument of ratification or instrument of accession, the present Covenant shall enter into force three months after the date of the deposit of its own instrument of ratification or instrument of accession.

Article 50
The provisions of the present Covenant shall extend to all parts of federal States without any limitations or exceptions.

Article 51
1. Any State Party to the present Covenant may propose an amendment and file it with the Secretary-General of the United Nations. The Secretary-General of the United Nations shall thereupon communicate any proposed amendments to the States Parties to the present Covenant with a request that they notify him whether they favour a conference of States Parties for the purpose of considering and voting upon the proposals. In the event that at least one third of the States Parties favours such a conference, the Secretary-General shall convene the conference under the auspices of the United Nations. Any amendment adopted by a majority of the States Parties present and voting at the conference shall be submitted to the General Assembly of the United Nations for approval.

2. Amendments shall come into force when they have been approved by the General Assembly of the United Nations and accepted by a two-thirds majority of the States Parties to the present Covenant in accordance with their respective constitutional processes. 3. When amendments come into force, they shall be binding on those States Parties which have accepted them, other States Parties still being bound by the provisions of the present Covenant and any earlier amendment which they have accepted.

Article 52

1. Irrespective of the notifications made under article 48, paragraph 5, the Secretary-General of the United Nations shall inform all States referred to in paragraph I of the same article of the following particulars:

(a) Signatures, ratifications and accessions under article 48;

(b) The date of the entry into force of the present Covenant under article 49 and the date of the entry into force of any amendments under article 51.

Article 53

1. The present Covenant, of which the Chinese, English, French, Russian and Spanish texts are equally authentic, shall be deposited in the archives of the United Nations.

2. The Secretary-General of the United Nations shall transmit certified copies of the present Covenant to all States referred to in article 48.

[End text]

Source: http://www.ohchr.org/EN/ProfessionalInterest/Pages/CCPR.aspx

3. INTERNATIONAL COVENANT ON ECONOMIC, SOCIAL AND CULTURAL RIGHTS

This U.N. covenant is a general international human rights treaty which deals with economic, social and cultural rights. It was adopted in the U.N.at the same time as the ICCPR in 1966. It had been intended by the international community that one single general treaty be adopted covering civil, political, economic, social and cultural rights, but cold war politics and values prevented agreement between the East bloc and the West and it was decided to make them two separate covenants. The U.S. has signed but never ratified this treaty and for many years denied that there were such rights, and that they were, in any case "progressive" obligations aiming at a certain goal. It is not legally binding on the U.S. If the U.S. ratified this treaty it would apply to access to health care coverage.

[Text]

International Covenant on Economic, Social and Cultural Rights

Adopted and opened for signature, ratification and accession by General Assembly resolution 2200A (XXI) of 16 December 1966, entry into force 3 January 1976, in accordance with article 27

Preamble

The States Parties to the present Covenant,

Considering that, in accordance with the principles proclaimed in the Charter of the United Nations, recognition of the inherent dignity and of the equal and inalienable rights of all members of the human family is the foundation of freedom, justice and peace in the world,

Recognizing that these rights derive from the inherent dignity of the human person,

Recognizing that, in accordance with the Universal Declaration of Human Rights, the ideal of free human beings enjoying freedom from fear and want can only be achieved if conditions are created whereby everyone may enjoy his economic, social and cultural rights, as well as his civil and political rights,

Considering the obligation of States under the Charter of the United Nations to promote universal respect for, and observance of, human rights and freedoms,

Realizing that the individual, having duties to other individuals and to the community to which he belongs, is under a responsibility to strive for the promotion and observance of the rights recognized in the present Covenant,

Agree upon the following articles:

PART I

Article 1

1. All peoples have the right of self-determination. By virtue of that right they freely determine their political status and freely pursue their economic, social and cultural development.

2. All peoples may, for their own ends, freely dispose of their natural wealth and resources without prejudice to any obligations arising out of international economic co-operation, based upon the principle of mutual benefit, and international law. In no case may a people be deprived of its own means of subsistence.

3. The States Parties to the present Covenant, including those having responsibility for the administration of Non-Self-Governing and Trust Territories, shall promote the realization of the right of self-determination, and shall respect that right, in conformity with the provisions of the Charter of the United Nations.

PART II

Article 2

1. Each State Party to the present Covenant undertakes to take steps, individually and through international assistance and co-operation, especially economic and technical, to the maximum of its available resources, with a view to achieving progressively the full realization of the rights recognized in the present Covenant by all appropriate means, including particularly the adoption of legislative measures.

2. The States Parties to the present Covenant undertake to guarantee that the rights enunciated in the present Covenant will be exercised without discrimination of any kind as to race, colour, sex, language, religion, political or other opinion, national or social origin, property, birth or other status.

3. Developing countries, with due regard to human rights and their national economy, may determine to what extent they would guarantee the economic rights recognized in the present Covenant to non-nationals.

Article 3

The States Parties to the present Covenant undertake to ensure the equal right of men and women to the enjoyment of all economic, social and cultural rights set forth in the present Covenant.

Article 4

The States Parties to the present Covenant recognize that, in the enjoyment of those rights provided by the State in conformity with the present Covenant, the State may subject such rights only to such limitations as are determined by law only in so far as this may be compatible with the nature of these rights and solely for the purpose of promoting the general welfare in a democratic society.

Article 5

1. Nothing in the present Covenant may be interpreted as implying for any State, group or person any right to engage in any activity or to perform any act aimed at the destruction of any of the rights or freedoms recognized herein, or at their limitation to a greater extent than is provided for in the present Covenant.

2. No restriction upon or derogation from any of the fundamental human rights recognized or existing in any country in virtue of law, conventions, regulations or custom shall be admitted on the pretext that the present Covenant does not recognize such rights or that it recognizes them to a lesser extent.

PART III

Article 6

1. The States Parties to the present Covenant recognize the right to work, which includes the right of everyone to the opportunity to gain his living by work which he freely chooses or accepts, and will take appropriate steps to safeguard this right.

2. The steps to be taken by a State Party to the present Covenant to achieve the full realization of this right shall include technical and vocational guidance and training programmes, policies and techniques to achieve steady economic, social and cultural development and full and productive employment under conditions safeguarding fundamental political and economic freedoms to the individual.

Article 7

The States Parties to the present Covenant recognize the right of everyone to the enjoyment of just and favourable conditions of work which ensure, in particular:

(a) Remuneration which provides all workers, as a minimum, with:

(i) Fair wages and equal remuneration for work of equal value without distinction of any kind, in particular women being guaranteed conditions of work not inferior to those enjoyed by men, with equal pay for equal work;

(ii) A decent living for themselves and their families in accordance with the provisions of the present Covenant;

(b) Safe and healthy working conditions;

(c) Equal opportunity for everyone to be promoted in his employment to an appropriate higher level, subject to no considerations other than those of seniority and competence;

(d) Rest, leisure and reasonable limitation of working hours and periodic holidays with pay, as well as remuneration for public holidays

Article 8

1. The States Parties to the present Covenant undertake to ensure:

(a) The right of everyone to form trade unions and join the trade union of his choice, subject only to the rules of the organization concerned, for the promotion and protection of his economic and social interests. No restrictions may be placed on the exercise of this right other than those prescribed by law and which are necessary in a democratic society in the interests of national security or public order or for the protection of the rights and freedoms of others;

(b) The right of trade unions to establish national federations or confederations and the right of the latter to form or join international trade-union organizations;

(c) The right of trade unions to function freely subject to no limitations other than those prescribed by law and which are necessary in a democratic society in the interests of national security or public order or for the protection of the rights and freedoms of others;

(d) The right to strike, provided that it is exercised in conformity with the laws of the particular country.

2. This article shall not prevent the imposition of lawful restrictions on the exercise of these rights by members of the armed forces or of the police or of the administration of the State.

3. Nothing in this article shall authorize States Parties to the International Labour Organisation Convention of 1948 concerning Freedom of Association and Protection of the Right to Organize to take legislative measures which would prejudice, or apply the law in such a manner as would prejudice, the guarantees provided for in that Convention.

Article 9
The States Parties to the present Covenant recognize the right of everyone to social security, including social insurance.

Article 10
The States Parties to the present Covenant recognize that:

1. The widest possible protection and assistance should be accorded to the family, which is the natural and fundamental group unit of society, particularly for its establishment and while it is responsible for the care and education of dependent children. Marriage must be entered into with the free consent of the intending spouses.

2. Special protection should be accorded to mothers during a reasonable period before and after childbirth. During such period working mothers should be accorded paid leave or leave with adequate social security benefits.

3. Special measures of protection and assistance should be taken on behalf of all children and young persons without any discrimination for reasons of parentage or other conditions. Children and young persons should be protected from economic and social exploitation. Their employment in work harmful to their morals or health or dangerous to life or likely to hamper their normal development should be punishable by law. States should also set age limits below which the paid employment of child labour should be prohibited and punishable by law.

Article 11
1. The States Parties to the present Covenant recognize the right of everyone to an adequate standard of living for himself and his family, including adequate food, clothing and housing, and to the continuous improvement of living conditions. The States Parties will take appropriate steps to ensure the realization of this right, recognizing to this effect the essential importance of international co-operation based on free consent.

2. The States Parties to the present Covenant, recognizing the fundamental right of everyone to be free from hunger, shall take, individually and through international co-operation, the measures, including specific programmes, which are needed:

(a) To improve methods of production, conservation and distribution of food by making full use of technical and scientific knowledge, by disseminating knowledge of the principles of nutrition and by developing or reforming agrarian systems in such a way as to achieve the most efficient development and utilization of natural resources;

(b) Taking into account the problems of both food-importing and food-exporting countries, to ensure an equitable distribution of world food supplies in relation to need.

Article 12
1. The States Parties to the present Covenant recognize the right of everyone to the enjoyment of the highest attainable standard of physical and mental health.

2. The steps to be taken by the States Parties to the present Covenant to achieve the full realization of this right shall include those necessary for:

(a) The provision for the reduction of the stillbirth-rate and of infant mortality and for the healthy development of the child;

(b) The improvement of all aspects of environmental and industrial hygiene;

(c) The prevention, treatment and control of epidemic, endemic, occupational and other diseases;

(d) The creation of conditions which would assure to all medical service and medical attention in the event of sickness.

Article 13
1. The States Parties to the present Covenant recognize the right of everyone to education. They agree that education shall be directed to the full development of the human personality and the sense of its dignity, and shall strengthen the

respect for human rights and fundamental freedoms. They further agree that education shall enable all persons to participate effectively in a free society, promote understanding, tolerance and friendship among all nations and all racial, ethnic or religious groups, and further the activities of the United Nations for the maintenance of peace.

2. The States Parties to the present Covenant recognize that, with a view to achieving the full realization of this right:

(a) Primary education shall be compulsory and available free to all;

(b) Secondary education in its different forms, including technical and vocational secondary education, shall be made generally available and accessible to all by every appropriate means, and in particular by the progressive introduction of free education;

(c) Higher education shall be made equally accessible to all, on the basis of capacity, by every appropriate means, and in particular by the progressive introduction of free education;

(d) Fundamental education shall be encouraged or intensified as far as possible for those persons who have not received or completed the whole period of their primary education;

(e) The development of a system of schools at all levels shall be actively pursued, an adequate fellowship system shall be established, and the material conditions of teaching staff shall be continuously improved.

3. The States Parties to the present Covenant undertake to have respect for the liberty of parents and, when applicable, legal guardians to choose for their children schools, other than those established by the public authorities, which conform to such minimum educational standards as may be laid down or approved by the State and to ensure the religious and moral education of their children in conformity with their own convictions.

4. No part of this article shall be construed so as to interfere with the liberty of individuals and bodies to establish and direct educational institutions, subject always to the observance of the principles set forth in paragraph I of this article and to the requirement that the education given in such institutions shall conform to such minimum standards as may be laid down by the State.

Article 14
Each State Party to the present Covenant which, at the time of becoming a Party, has not been able to secure in its metropolitan territory or other territories under its jurisdiction compulsory primary education, free of charge, undertakes, within two years, to work out and adopt a detailed plan of action for the progressive implementation, within a reasonable number of years, to be fixed in the plan, of the principle of compulsory education free of charge for all.

Article 15
1. The States Parties to the present Covenant recognize the right of everyone:

(a) To take part in cultural life;

(b) To enjoy the benefits of scientific progress and its applications;

(c) To benefit from the protection of the moral and material interests resulting from any scientific, literary or artistic production of which he is the author.

2. The steps to be taken by the States Parties to the present Covenant to achieve the full realization of this right shall include those necessary for the conservation, the development and the diffusion of science and culture.

3. The States Parties to the present Covenant undertake to respect the freedom indispensable for scientific research and creative activity.

4. The States Parties to the present Covenant recognize the benefits to be derived from the encouragement and development of international contacts and co-operation in the scientific and cultural fields.

PART IV

Article 16

1. The States Parties to the present Covenant undertake to submit in conformity with this part of the Covenant reports on the measures which they have adopted and the progress made in achieving the observance of the rights recognized herein.

2.

(a) All reports shall be submitted to the Secretary-General of the United Nations, who shall transmit copies to the Economic and Social Council for consideration in accordance with the provisions of the present Covenant;

(b) The Secretary-General of the United Nations shall also transmit to the specialized agencies copies of the reports, or any relevant parts therefrom, from States Parties to the present Covenant which are also members of these specialized agencies in so far as these reports, or parts therefrom, relate to any matters which fall within the responsibilities of the said agencies in accordance with their constitutional instruments.

Article 17

1. The States Parties to the present Covenant shall furnish their reports in stages, in accordance with a programme to be established by the Economic and Social Council within one year of the entry into force of the present Covenant after consultation with the States Parties and the specialized agencies concerned.

2. Reports may indicate factors and difficulties affecting the degree of fulfilment of obligations under the present Covenant.

3. Where relevant information has previously been furnished to the United Nations or to any specialized agency by any State Party to the present Covenant, it will not be necessary to reproduce that information, but a precise reference to the information so furnished will suffice.

Article 18

Pursuant to its responsibilities under the Charter of the United Nations in the field of human rights and fundamental freedoms, the Economic and Social Council may make arrangements with the specialized agencies in respect of their reporting to it on the progress made in achieving the observance of the provisions of the present Covenant falling within the scope of their activities. These reports may include particulars of decisions and recommendations on such implementation adopted by their competent organs.

Article 19

The Economic and Social Council may transmit to the Commission on Human Rights for study and general recommendation or, as appropriate, for information the reports concerning human rights submitted by States in accordance with articles 16 and 17, and those concerning human rights submitted by the specialized agencies in accordance with article 18.

Article 20

The States Parties to the present Covenant and the specialized agencies concerned may submit comments to the Economic and Social Council on any general recommendation under article 19 or reference to such general recommendation in any report of the Commission on Human Rights or any documentation referred to therein.

Article 21

The Economic and Social Council may submit from time to time to the General Assembly reports with recommendations of a general nature and a summary of the information received from the States Parties to the present Covenant and the specialized agencies on the measures taken and the progress made in achieving general observance of the rights recognized in the present Covenant.

Article 22

The Economic and Social Council may bring to the attention of other organs of the United Nations, their subsidiary organs and specialized agencies concerned with furnishing technical assistance any matters arising out of the reports referred to in this part of the present Covenant which may assist such bodies in deciding, each within its field of competence, on the advisability of international measures likely to contribute to the effective progressive implementation of the present Covenant.

Article 23
The States Parties to the present Covenant agree that international action for the achievement of the rights recognized in the present Covenant includes such methods as the conclusion of conventions, the adoption of recommendations, the furnishing of technical assistance and the holding of regional meetings and technical meetings for the purpose of consultation and study organized in conjunction with the Governments concerned.

Article 24
Nothing in the present Covenant shall be interpreted as impairing the provisions of the Charter of the United Nations and of the constitutions of the specialized agencies which define the respective responsibilities of the various organs of the United Nations and of the specialized agencies in regard to the matters dealt with in the present Covenant.

Article 25
Nothing in the present Covenant shall be interpreted as impairing the inherent right of all peoples to enjoy and utilize fully and freely their natural wealth and resources.

PART V

Article 26
1. The present Covenant is open for signature by any State Member of the United Nations or member of any of its specialized agencies, by any State Party to the Statute of the International Court of Justice, and by any other State which has been invited by the General Assembly of the United Nations to become a party to the present Covenant.

2. The present Covenant is subject to ratification. Instruments of ratification shall be deposited with the Secretary-General of the United Nations.

3. The present Covenant shall be open to accession by any State referred to in paragraph 1 of this article.

4. Accession shall be effected by the deposit of an instrument of accession with the Secretary-General of the United Nations.

5. The Secretary-General of the United Nations shall inform all States which have signed the present Covenant or acceded to it of the deposit of each instrument of ratification or accession.

Article 27
1. The present Covenant shall enter into force three months after the date of the deposit with the Secretary-General of the United Nations of the thirty-fifth instrument of ratification or instrument of accession.

2. For each State ratifying the present Covenant or acceding to it after the deposit of the thirty-fifth instrument of ratification or instrument of accession, the present Covenant shall enter into force three months after the date of the deposit of its own instrument of ratification or instrument of accession.

Article 28
The provisions of the present Covenant shall extend to all parts of federal States without any limitations or exceptions.

Article 29
1. Any State Party to the present Covenant may propose an amendment and file it with the Secretary-General of the United Nations. The Secretary-General shall thereupon communicate any proposed amendments to the States Parties to the present Covenant with a request that they notify him whether they favour a conference of States Parties for the purpose of considering and voting upon the proposals. In the event that at least one third of the States Parties favours such a conference, the Secretary-General shall convene the conference under the auspices of the United Nations. Any amendment adopted by a majority of the States Parties present and voting at the conference shall be submitted to the General Assembly of the United Nations for approval.

2. Amendments shall come into force when they have been approved by the General Assembly of the United Nations and accepted by a two-thirds majority of the States Parties to the present Covenant in accordance with their respective constitutional processes.

3. When amendments come into force they shall be binding on those States Parties which have accepted them, other States Parties still being bound by the provisions of the present Covenant and any earlier amendment which they have accepted.

Article 30
Irrespective of the notifications made under article 26, paragraph 5, the Secretary-General of the United Nations shall inform all States referred to in paragraph I of the same article of the following particulars:

(a) Signatures, ratifications and accessions under article 26;

(b) The date of the entry into force of the present Covenant under article 27 and the date of the entry into force of any amendments under article 29.

Article 31
1. The present Covenant, of which the Chinese, English, French, Russian and Spanish texts are equally authentic, shall be deposited in the archives of the United Nations.

2. The Secretary-General of the United Nations shall transmit certified copies of the present Covenant to all States referred to in article 26.

[End Text]

Source: http://www.ohchr.org/EN/ProfessionalInterest/Pages/CESCR.aspx

☙❧☙❧☙❧☙❧

4. OPTIONAL PROTOCOL TO THE INTERNATIONAL COVENANT ON CIVIL AND POLITICAL RIGHTS

This instrument is a treaty which amends another treaty. It is a Protocol. It amends the ICCPR by adding a procedure the Human Right Committee which allows individual victims of violations of the rights in the ICCPR to file a complaint (called a "communication") against the accused state, but only if that state has ratified this Protocol. The U.S. has not ratified the Protocol because it does not want cases filed against it in the international arena. The U.S. has, though, accepted the competence of the Human Rights Committee to accept complaints filed by one state party against another state party. The U.S. was aware that no state has ever used this procedure against another state party before. This Protocol is part of the four instruments known as the International Bill of Rights. There is a Second Protocol to the ICCPR abolishing the death penalty.

[Text]

Optional Protocol to the International Covenant on Civil and Political Rights

Adopted and opened for signature, ratification and accession by General Assembly resolution 2200A (XXI) of 16 December 1966 entry into force 23 March 1976, in accordance with Article 9

The States Parties to the present Protocol,

Considering that in order further to achieve the purposes of the International Covenant on Civil and Political Rights (hereinafter referred to as the Covenant) and the implementation of its provisions it would be appropriate to enable the Human Rights Committee set up in part IV of the Covenant (hereinafter referred to as the Committee) to receive and consider, as provided in the present Protocol, communications from individuals claiming to be victims of violations of any of the rights set forth in the Covenant.

Have agreed as follows:

Article 1

A State Party to the Covenant that becomes a Party to the present Protocol recognizes the competence of the Committee to receive and consider communications from individuals subject to its jurisdiction who claim to be victims of a violation by that State Party of any of the rights set forth in the Covenant. No communication shall be received by the Committee if it concerns a State Party to the Covenant which is not a Party to the present Protocol.

Article 2

Subject to the provisions of article 1, individuals who claim that any of their rights enumerated in the Covenant have been violated and who have exhausted all available domestic remedies may submit a written communication to the Committee for consideration.

Article 3

The Committee shall consider inadmissible any communication under the present Protocol which is anonymous, or which it considers to be an abuse of the right of submission of such communications or to be incompatible with the provisions of the Covenant.

Article 4

1. Subject to the provisions of article 3, the Committee shall bring any communications submitted to it under the present Protocol to the attention of the State Party to the present Protocol alleged to be violating any provision of the Covenant.

2. Within six months, the receiving State shall submit to the Committee written explanations or statements clarifying the matter and the remedy, if any, that may have been taken by that State.

Article 5

1. The Committee shall consider communications received under the present Protocol in the light of all written information made available to it by the individual and by the State Party concerned.

2. The Committee shall not consider any communication from an individual unless it has ascertained that:

(a) The same matter is not being examined under another procedure of international investigation or settlement;

(b) The individual has exhausted all available domestic remedies. This shall not be the rule where the application of the remedies is unreasonably prolonged.

3. The Committee shall hold closed meetings when examining communications under the present Protocol.

4. The Committee shall forward its views to the State Party concerned and to the individual.

Article 6

The Committee shall include in its annual report under article 45 of the Covenant a summary of its activities under the present Protocol.

Article 7

Pending the achievement of the objectives of resolution 1514(XV) adopted by the General Assembly of the United Nations on 14 December 1960 concerning the Declaration on the Granting of Independence to Colonial Countries and Peoples, the provisions of the present Protocol shall in no way limit the right of petition granted to these peoples by the Charter of the United Nations and other international conventions and instruments under the United Nations and its specialized agencies.

Article 8

1. The present Protocol is open for signature by any State which has signed the Covenant.

2. The present Protocol is subject to ratification by any State which has ratified or acceded to the Covenant. Instruments of ratification shall be deposited with the Secretary-General of the United Nations.

3. The present Protocol shall be open to accession by any State which has ratified or acceded to the Covenant.

4. Accession shall be effected by the deposit of an instrument of accession with the Secretary-General of the United Nations.

5. The Secretary-General of the United Nations shall inform all States which have signed the present Protocol or acceded to it of the deposit of each instrument of ratification or accession.

Article 9
1. Subject to the entry into force of the Covenant, the present Protocol shall enter into force three months after the date of the deposit with the Secretary-General of the United Nations of the tenth instrument of ratification or instrument of accession.

2. For each State ratifying the present Protocol or acceding to it after the deposit of the tenth instrument of ratification or instrument of accession, the present Protocol shall enter into force three months after the date of the deposit of its own instrument of ratification or instrument of accession.

Article 10
The provisions of the present Protocol shall extend to all parts of federal States without any limitations or exceptions.

Article 11
1. Any State Party to the present Protocol may propose an amendment and file it with the Secretary-General of the United Nations. The Secretary-General shall thereupon communicate any proposed amendments to the States Parties to the present Protocol with a request that they notify him whether they favour a conference of States Parties for the purpose of considering and voting upon the proposal. In the event that at least one third of the States Parties favours such a conference, the Secretary-General shall convene the conference under the auspices of the United Nations. Any amendment adopted by a majority of the States Parties present and voting at the conference shall be submitted to the General Assembly of the United Nations for approval.

2. Amendments shall come into force when they have been approved by the General Assembly of the United Nations and accepted by a two-thirds majority of the States Parties to the present Protocol in accordance with their respective constitutional processes.

3. When amendments come into force, they shall be binding on those States Parties which have accepted them, other States Parties still being bound by the provisions of the present Protocol and any earlier amendment which they have accepted.

Article 12
1. Any State Party may denounce the present Protocol at any time by written notification addressed to the Secretary-General of the United Nations. Denunciation shall take effect three months after the date of receipt of the notification by the Secretary-General.

2. Denunciation shall be without prejudice to the continued application of the provisions of the present Protocol to any communication submitted under article 2 before the effective date of denunciation.

Article 13
Irrespective of the notifications made under article 8, paragraph 5, of the present Protocol, the Secretary-General of the United Nations shall inform all States referred to in article 48, paragraph I, of the Covenant of the following particulars:

(a) Signatures, ratifications and accessions under article 8;

(b) The date of the entry into force of the present Protocol under article 9 and the date of the entry into force of any amendments under article 11;

(c) Denunciations under article 12.

Article 14

1. The present Protocol, of which the Chinese, English, French, Russian and Spanish texts are equally authentic, shall be deposited in the archives of the United Nations.

2. The Secretary-General of the United Nations shall transmit certified copies of the present Protocol to all States referred to in article 48 of the Covenant.

Source: http://www.ohchr.org/EN/ProfessionalInterest/Pages/OPCCPR1.aspx

Chronology of U.S. Human Rights Moments & Events

Chapter 2

This **Chapter is About** a historical chronological overview of the United States in relation to human rights. Many of the events listed took place without any mention of or thought to the concept of human rights as we know it today, but nonetheless was about human rights; for example, the Emancipation Proclamation and the human right to equality. This chronological series of events and laws is followed by Primary Source Documents, including proclamations by U.S. Presidents, both Democratic and Republican, calling Americans to celebrate Human Rights/Bill of Rights Day and Week, December 10, the birthday of the UDHR.

This is Important Because Americans in 2017 should know what historical events shaped our country and who we are as a nation of diverse peoples. Ignoring history risks repeating its worst moments. It is important to understand that human rights are not values or laws which come from outside of the U.S. and are being forced upon U.S. by international institutions, such as the U.N. They are ideas based on American values which have been adopted in the U.S. and presented to the members of the international community, translated into principles, and transformed into concrete written human rights norms, with the direct and important contribution of the U.S. government, Democratic and Republican, and part of the fabric of America. The quotes of past Presidents about the connection to the Bill of Rights and the UDHR show the bi-partisan acceptance of the normative value of international human rights. The issues arise in their application to the realities faced by government. It is one thing to accept certain standards and values but another thing to regulate one's conduct to make it consistent with those values and norms, and comply with our international legal obligations. America's image is one of inconsistency between the words and action.

The following chronology shows how actively America has been involved both inside the U.S. and around the world in promoting and protecting human rights. It shows where human rights law is found in U.S. law, and focuses primarily on the national and federal level legal and political events involving human rights.

Quotes & Key Text Excerpts

When in the Course of human events it becomes necessary for one people to dissolve the political bands which have connected them with another and to assume among the powers of the earth, the separate and equal station to which the Laws of Nature and of Nature's God entitle them, a decent respect to the opinions of mankind requires that they should declare the causes which impel them to the separation.

We hold these truths to be self-evident, that all men are created equal, that they are endowed by their Creator with certain unalienable Rights, that among these are Life, Liberty and the pursuit of Happiness. — That to secure these rights, Governments are instituted among Men, deriving their just powers from the consent of the governed, — That whenever any Form of Government becomes destructive of these ends, it is the Right of the People to alter or to abolish it, and to institute new Government, laying its foundation on such principles and organizing its powers in such form, as to them shall seem most likely to effect their Safety and Happiness.

—*The Unanimous Declaration of the Thirteen United States of America, in Congress, July 4, 1776*

Four score and seven years ago our fathers brought forth on this continent, a new nation, conceived in Liberty, and dedicated to the proposition that all men are created equal. Now we are engaged in a great civil war, testing whether that nation, or any nation so conceived and so dedicated, can long endure. We are met on a great battle-field of that war. We have come to dedicate a portion of that field, as a final resting place for those who here gave their lives that that nation might live. It is altogether fitting and proper that we should do this. But, in a larger sense, we cannot dedicate — we cannot consecrate — we cannot hallow — this ground. The brave men, living and dead, who struggled here, have consecrated it, far above our poor power to add or detract. The world will little note, nor long remember what we say here, but it can never forget what they did here. It is for us the living, rather, to be dedicated here to the unfinished work which they who fought here have thus far so nobly advanced. It is rather for us to be here dedicated to the great task remaining before us — that from these honored dead we take increased devotion to that cause for which they gave the last full measure of devotion — that we here highly resolve that these dead shall not have died in vain — that this nation, under God, shall have a new birth of freedom — and that government of the people, by the people, for the people, shall not perish from the earth.

—*President Abraham Lincoln, Gettysburg Address, 1863*

What You Should Know

Human rights have figured in American history even before the Constitution. The Declaration of Independence, part of which begins this chapter as it began the country itself, was indeed one of the first political instruments in the world which espoused the natural law idea of the inherent, inalienable and universal fundamental human rights of all persons. It was in reaction to the human rights violations of Britain, called by the Founding Fathers "injuries and usurpations" that the famous founding document of what would become the United States of America was created. The Declaration of Independence even today is cited internationally as a source of the philosophy of human rights, along with the French Declaration of the Rights of Man and of citizen of 1779.

Every 4th of July the U.S. celebrates its highest national holiday: Independence Day. What do we celebrate? We celebrate a document, the Declaration of Independence, which declared the independence from Britain of thirteen colonies who perceived themselves thereafter as separate independent states. They would choose to come together in a federation under the Articles of Confederation and later culminating in the Constitution of the United States of America, the longest enduring constitution in the world. That would be followed by the Bill of Rights and statutes and regulations, sometimes engendered by, infused with, or in implementation of international law, particularly International Treaty Law, including International Human Rights Law, International Humanitarian Law, and International Criminal Law, among others. All of this was to constitute a political entity based on democracy, the will of the people, with a republican form of government, three separate bodies to act as checks and balances against each other to curtail the tendency to abuse of public power, under a rule of law system where no human being was above the law, law being the highest authority.

On December 10, 1948, the United States participated in the adoption of the U.N. resolution which set forth the first and foremost international instrument of human rights, the Universal Declaration of Human Rights (UDHR). This human rights instrument was the product of Americans working in the U.N. such as Eleanor Roosevelt, who served as the first member, first female member, first chairperson of the U.N. Human Rights Commission, and was one of three initial drafters of the UDHR. The Declaration of Independence, well known to Eleanor, was one philosophical source of the UDHR and reflected in its preamble.

Every year on December 10, the international community, including the U.S., celebrates the UDHR, the first international declaration about the fundamental human rights of all human beings, with a list of the then internationally recognized human rights. The President of the U.S. each year issues a proclamation around December 10, commemorating and reaffirming the UDHR and its place in America, and often referring to the Declaration of independence and Constitution and Bill of Rights, all as part of our Bill of Rights Day. The U.S. celebrates the UDHR on the same day in the same way it celebrates the Bill of Rights, rights which found their way into the UDHR.

Following the Chronology are Proclamations by U.S. Presidents, Republican and Democrat. These show how human rights, particularly in the UDHR, are linked to the Constitution and Bill of Rights, and have been part of American law and discourse accepted by both Democratic and Republican administrations, though often nuanced. Given that human rights are legal limitations on the power of state wielded by its government, it is not hard to understand why Republicans can get behind human rights. They are not the province of liberals. They stand squarely for a conservative notion: limiting the power of government for the protection of individual human dignity and maximizing human freedom. The presidential proclamations were given to the American people by former Presidents Obama, former Presidents George Bush junior and senior, and former President Ronald Regan, on the occasion of the December 10, Human Rights Day commemoration.

In accepting the UDHR as containing valid legal norms, the administrations proclaim that the norms in that instrument can be used to judge their government's performance, and can be used to judge other countries as well.

CHRONOLOGY OF HUMAN RIGHTS IN RELATION TO THE U.S.

By Tina M. Ramirez, © 2017

This Chronology of Human Rights in Relation to the U.S. highlights the major, historical human rights milestones for the U.S. including violations, actions, legislation and landmark court cases.

1215 Magna Carta signed by King John.

1619 First 20 African slaves sold as indentured servants to settlers in Virginia.

1628 British Petition of Rights signed by King Charles I.

1632 Lord Baltimore receives a charter for Maryland as a refuge for Catholics; founded in 1634.

1636 Roger Williams expelled from Massachusetts Bay Colony for religious dissension and establishes Providence Plantation in Rhode Island for religious freedom.

1638 Anne Hutchinson expelled from Massachusetts Bay Colony for religious dissension and establishes colony of Portsmouth.

1649 Maryland passes the Act Concerning Religion.

1654 Jews fleeing Spanish Inquisition arrive in New Amsterdam.

1660 Virginia enacts laws against Quakers.

1660 Mary Dyer hanged on Boston Commons for spreading Quaker principals.

1663 King Charles II grants royal charter recognizing the colony of Rhode Island and religious freedom.

1681 King Charles II grants William Penn charter to establish colony in Pennsylvania.

1682 Penn issues the Frame of Government recognizing religious liberty in Pennsylvania.

1689 John Locke publishes a "Letter of Toleration."

British Parliament adopts Bill of Rights.

1776 British Colonies issue Declaration of Independence.

1785 Virginia House of Burgesses adopts Statute of Religious Freedom drafted by Thomas Jefferson.

1787 Constitutional Convention adopts U.S. Constitution, enters into force in 1789.

1789 Judiciary Act of 1789 includes Alien Tort Claims Act, 28 USC sec. 1350.

1791 Congress passes Bill of Rights, the first ten amendments to the Constitution.

1807 Congress passes Slave Importation Act prohibiting further importation of slaves.

1830 Congress passes Indian Removal Act forcing Native Americans to relocate.

1831 Nat Turner leads a slave revolt in Virginia.

1848 Seneca Falls Convention drafts Declaration of Sentiments of women's rights.

1857 *Dred Scott v. Sandford* decided by Supreme Court.

1863 Civil War begins and President Lincoln signs Instructions for the Government of Armies of the U.S. in the Field or "Lieber Code" to regulate conduct of Union forces.

President Lincoln issues Emancipation Proclamation

President Lincoln gives Gettysburg Address

International Conference meets in Geneva and establishes the Red Cross.

1864 Diplomatic Conference passes First Geneva Convention protecting victims of conflict.

1865 Thirteenth Amendment passes and abolishes slavery; Freedmen's Bureau established.

Ku Klux Klan established in Pulaski, Tennessee.

1868 Fourteenth Amendment passes protecting equal protection and due process.

1870 Fifteenth Amendment passes protecting voting rights.

States pass "Jim Crow" laws beginning with Tennessee.

1882 Congress passes Chinese Exclusion Act.

1888 Congress passes the Scott Act restricting immigration by Chinese laborers into the U.S.

1889 First International Conference of American States held in Washington, D.C. established the International Union of American Republics (from October 1889 to April 1890).

1896 Supreme Court rules in *Plessy v. Ferguson*, upholding the constitutionality of state laws requiring racial segregation in private businesses, under the doctrine of "separate but equal." This would be the racial standard of the U.S. until *Brown v. Board of Education.*

1899 First Hague Peace Conference adopts revised Geneva Convention adding Regulations concerning the Laws and Customs of War on Land.

1907 Second Hague Peace Conference adopts revised Geneva Convention governing combatants.

1914 First World War begins.

1915-17 Armenian Genocide

1919 Treaty of Versailles concludes WWI and requires Kaiser Wilhelm II to be tried for a "supreme offense against international morality and the sanctity of treaties."

International Labor Organization (ILO) established.

1920 League of Nations established to maintain international peace.

Nineteenth Amendment passes and is ratified by required states giving women the right to vote.

1922 Supreme Court rules in *Ozawa v. U.S.* against Japanese right to naturalization.

Congress passes Cable Act restricting citizenship for women marrying foreigners.

1923 Treaty of Lausanne.

1924 Congress passes The Indian Citizenship or Snyder Act granting Native Americans born in the U.S. citizenship.

1926 Geneva Conference passes the Slavery Convention.

1929 Convention Relative to the Treatment of Prisoners of War adopted as Third Geneva Convention.

U.S. accedes to Slavery Convention.

1930 ILO adopts Convention Concerning Forced or Compulsory Labor (enters into force 1932).

1933 Congress passes President Franklin D. Roosevelt's "New Deal."

1934 Congress passes the Indian Reorganization Act.

1933 Adolph Hitler elected, National Socialist Party of Germany passes Nuremburg Laws against the Jewish population beginning the "Holocaust"; ends 1945.

1941 President Roosevelt gives "Four Freedoms" speech.

President Roosevelt and British Prime Minister Winston Churchill adopt Atlantic Charter.

Pearl Harbor attacked; U.S. enters World War II.

1942 At least 120,000 Japanese Americans forcibly moved to internment camps (until 1945).

1943 Congress repeals legislation excluding Chinese in and from the U.S.

1945 Charter of the United Nations adopted recognizing individual human rights and establishing the International Court of Justice.

Nuremburg war crimes tribunals begin under Nuremberg Charter, Rules and Principles.

1946 U.N. Economic and Social Council (ECOSOC) establishes U.N. Commission on Human Rights and U.N. Commission on the Status of Women.

1948 Charter of the Organization of American States (OAS) signed (enters into force in 1951) and OAS adopts Declaration of the Rights of Man.

U.N. General Assembly adopts Universal Declaration of Human Rights.

ILO adopts Convention on the Freedom of Association and Protection of the Right to Organize.

U.N. adopts Convention on the Prevention and Punishment of the Crime of Genocide (enters into force 1951).

U.S. signs Genocide Convention (ratified in 1988).

1949 Diplomatic Conference adopts four Geneva Conventions as international humanitarian law.

U.S. signs Four Geneva Conventions (ratifies all 1955).

Council of Europe founded.

1950 Council of Europe adopts European Convention on Human Rights (enters into force in 1953) establishing European Court of Human Rights.

1951 U.N. adopts Convention relating to the Status of Refugees (enters into force 1954).

1952 Congress passes the Immigration and Naturalization Act.

1953 U.N. adopts Convention on the Political Rights of Women (enters into force 1954).

U.S. signs Protocol to Slavery Convention (ratifies 1956).

1954 Supreme Court rules in *Brown v. Board of Education*.

The Johnson Amendment changes the U.S. tax code to prohibit certain tax-exempt organizations from endorsing or opposing political candidates.

1955 Rosa Parks refuses to give up her seat on the bus, beginning the Montgomery bus boycott.

1957 "Little Rock Nine" try to attend Little Rock Central High School but are blocked.

U.N. adopts Convention on Nationality of Married Women (enters into force 1958).

ILO adopts Convention Concerning Abolition of Forced Labor and Convention Concerning Indigenous and Tribal Populations.

Congress passes Civil Rights Act of 1957 related to voting rights.

1959 OAS creates Inter-American Commission on Human Rights headquartered in Washington, D.C.

1961 Council of Europe adopts European Social Charter.

1963 Martin Luther King Jr. participates in March on Washington and gives "I Have A Dream" speech.

24th Amendment passes and is ratified by required states ending poll taxes.

1964 Congress passes Civil Rights Act of 1964 protecting against racial or sexual discrimination.

1965 Congress passes Voting Rights Act of 1965.

U.N. adopts Convention on the Elimination of All Forms of Racial Discrimination (ICERD enters into force 1969).

1966 U.N. adopts International Covenant on Civil and Political Rights and its First Optional Protocol and the International Covenant on Economic, Social and Cultural Rights (ICCPR, First Optional Protocol and ICESCR enter into force 1976).

U.S. signs ICERD (ratifies 1994).

U.S. Supreme Court rules in *Miranda v. Arizona* that law enforcement must give suspects certain procedural rights.

1967 U.N. adopts a Protocol to the 1951 Refugee Convention (enters into force 1967).

U.S. accedes to Supplementary Convention on the Abolition of Slavery, the Slave Trade, and Institutions and Practices Similar to Slavery.

Detroit race riots begin, sparking riots throughout the U.S.

Congress passes Age Discrimination Act of 1967.

1968   U.N. General Assembly Convenes First International Conference on Human Rights in Tehran, Iran.

U.S. accedes to 1961 Protocol to Refugee Convention.

U.N. adopts Convention on the Non-Applicability of Statutory Limitations to War Crimes Against Humanity (enters into force 1970).

Supreme Court rules in *Green v. County School Board of New Kent County (Virginia)*.

1969   OAS adopts American Convention on Human Rights (enters into force in 1978) which calls for creation of an Inter-American Court of Human Rights.

1970   U.S. signs International Convention for the Suppression of Unlawful Seizure of Aircraft (ratified 1971).

1971   Supreme Court issues ruling in *Gillette v. United States* regarding the right of conscientious objection.

1972   Equal Rights Amendment to U.S. Constitution passes Congress but fails to be ratified by states.

U.S. Supreme Court decides *Furman v. Georgia* requiring national consistency in death penalty determination. Decision resulted in national moratorium on death penalty application.

1973   U.N. adopts Convention on Suppression and Punishment of the Crime of Apartheid (enters into force 1976).

U.S. signs International Convention on the Prevention and Punishment of Crimes Against International Protected Persons (1976).

Supreme Court rules in *Roe v. Wade* on privacy and abortion.

1975   Helsinki Conference on Security and Cooperation in Europe adopts Helsinki Final Act.

U.N. adopts Convention on Rights of Disabled Persons.

Congress passes Age Discrimination Act of 1975.

Congress establishes Commission on Security and Cooperation in Europe to monitor compliance with Helsinki Final Act and OSCE commitments.

1976   Congress over-rides a presidential veto and passes legislation amending the Foreign Assistance Act of 1961 to require an annual human rights report and Coordinator of Human Rights at the State Department (later to become the Assistant Secretary for the Bureau of Democracy, Human Rights and Labor).

Congress passes Foreign Sovereign Immunity Act (FSIA), 28 USC SEC 1330 etc., 1602-1611.

U.S. Supreme Court decides *Gregg v. Georgia*, finding state death penalty constitutional under 8th amendment, and setting two necessary criteria. Executions resume in U.S.

1977   U.S. signs American Convention on Human Rights, ICCPR (ratifies 1992) and ICESCR.

1978   U.S. Supreme Court rules in *California v. Bakke* limiting affirmative action.

Congress passes the Foreign Intelligence Surveillance Act to regulate how the government may obtain foreign intelligence.

1979   U.N. adopts Convention on the Elimination of All Forms of Discrimination Against Women (CEDAW enters into force 1981).

U.S. signs U.N. Convention Against the Taking of Hostages (ratifies 1984).

1980 U.S. signs Convention on Elimination of Discrimination of Women (CEDAW).

Filartiga v. Pena-Irala ruled U.S. District Courts could decide cases of human right violations ("torts in violation of international law") by aliens against other aliens found in U.S.

1981 Organization for African Unity (OAU) adopts African Charter on Human and People's Rights.

U.N. adopts Declaration on the Elimination of All Forms of Intolerance Based on Religion or Belief.

1984 U.N. adopts Convention Against Torture and Other Cruel, Inhuman or Degrading Treatment or Punishment (CAT) (enters into force 1987).

1986 Congress overrides presidential veto and places economic sanctions on South Africa.

U.N. adopts Declaration on the Right to Development.

1988 U.S. signs U.N. Torture Convention (ratifies 1994) and ratifies U.N. Genocide Convention.

Congress passes Civil rights Restoration Act over President Ronald Reagan's veto.

U.S. Supreme Court in *Thompson v. Oklahoma* finds that capital punishment on those 15 or under is unconstitutional.

1989 U.N. adopts Convention on the Rights of the Child (CRC enters into force 1990) and the Second Optional Protocol to the ICCPR regarding the death penalty (enters into force 1991).

U.S. Supreme Court rules in *Sanford v. Kentucky* allowing capital punishment of children 16 and over when crime committed.

1990 Congress passes Americans with Disabilities Act.

U.N. adopts International Convention on the Rights of All Migrant Workers and Members of Their Families (enters into force 2003).

Georgia Supreme Court upholds the state's Anti-Mask Act to safeguard the civil rights of the people.

1991 U.S. signs Refugee Convention and ratifies Abolition of Forced Labor Convention.

1992 U.N. General Assembly adopts Declaration on the Rights of Persons Belonging to National or Ethnic, Religious or Linguistic Minorities.

The acquittal of four white police officers caught on camera beating Rodney G. King, a black man, sparks "Los Angeles Riots," draws public attention to police brutality and racial injustice.

Congress passes the Torture Victims Protection Act.

1993 U.N. Security Council establishes the International Criminal Tribunal for the Former Yugoslavia.

Second World Conference on Human Rights adopts Vienna Declaration and Programme of Action.

U.N. General Assembly establishes the Office of the High Commissioner for Human Rights.

President Bill Clinton institutes "Don't Ask, Don't Tell" policy regarding homosexuals in military services.

Congress passes the Religious Freedom Restoration Act; signed into law by President Clinton.

1994 Rwandan genocide leaves one million, mostly Tutsis, dead; limited U.S. response.

U.N. Security Council establishes the International Criminal Tribunal for Rwanda.

1995 U.S. signs CRC.

Fourth World Conference on Women occurs in Beijing.

Dayton Peace Accords signed, bringing an end to armed conflict in former Yugoslavia under U.S. leadership; NATO led implementation force deployed to Bosnia-Herzegovina.

1996   Anti-terrorism and Effective Death Penalty Act, 28 USC Sec. 1605, creates exception to TVPA, allows civil suits by Americans against state sponsors of terrorism causing torture or extrajudicial killing.

Congress passes War Crimes Act to enforce criminal penalties for certain war crimes under the Geneva Convention.

1998   Diplomatic Conference on the Establishment of the International Criminal Court adopts Rome Statute Establishing an International Criminal Court (enters into force 2002).

U.S. signs International Convention for the Suppression of Terrorist Bombing (ratified 2002).

Congress passes the International Religious Freedom Act.

1999   U.S. ratifies Convention Concerning the Prohibition and Immediate Action for the Elimination of the Worst Forms of Child Labor (entered into force 2000).

2000   U.S. signs Rome Statute of the ICC ("unsigned" in 2001 by President Bush), International Convention for the Suppression of the Financing of Terrorism (ratified 2002), Optional Protocol to the CRC related to children in armed conflict (ratified 2002), U.N. Convention Against Transnational Crime and its Protocol to Prevent, Suppress and Punish Trafficking in Persons and Protocol Against the Smuggling of Migrants.

Congress passes the Religious Land Use and Institutionalized Persons Act (RLUIPA).

Congress passes the Trafficking Victims Protection Act.

Congress establishes Congressional Executive Commission on China to monitor human rights and the rule of law in China.

2001   World Conference Against Racism, Racial Discrimination, Xenophobia and Related Intolerance takes place in South Africa and produces The Durban Declaration and Programme of Action; the U.S. walks out.

Terrorist attack World Trade Center in New York, President George W. Bush declares "War on Terror."

Congress passes PATRIOT Act.

2002   U.S. ratifies First Optional Protocol to the CRC related to child soldiers and Second Optional Protocol to CRC related to Child Trafficking and Pornography.

Supreme Court rules in *Atkins v. Virginia*, that capital punishment of mentally ill is unconstitutional.

Congress passes American Serviceman's Protection Act.

U.S. opens Guantánamo Bay Detention Camp for suspected terrorist detainees.

2003   U.N. International Convention on the Protection of the Rights of All Migrant Workers and Members of Their Families enters into force. U.S. has not signed as of October 2010.

Iraq Abu Ghraib Prison scandal by U.S. soldiers and CIA breaks and is investigated.

2004   U.S. Supreme Court in *Rasul v. Bush* rules that U.S. District Courts have jurisdiction to determine legality of detention of non-citizen Guantánamo "enemy combatant" detainees.

U.S. Supreme Court in *Hamdi v. Rumsfeld* rules that U.S. citizen enemy combatant in Guantánamo has right to challenge detention before an impartial judge.

Congress passes Global Anti-Semitism Act and establishes a special envoy to combat and monitor concerns.

Secretary of State Colin Powell recognizes genocide in Darfur, Sudan.

2005 U.S. Supreme Court in *Roper v. Simmons*, overturning *Stanford v. Kentucky*, rules that all capital punishment of juveniles is unconstitutional.

U.N. Security Council adopts resolution referring Sudan to the International Criminal Court for human rights crimes in Darfur.

Congress passes Detainee Treatment Act to address concerns regarding interrogation techniques and prohibit inhumane treatment of detainees.

2006 U.N. Secretary General Kofi Annan leads an effort to reform Human Rights Commission.

U.N. adopts Convention on the Rights of Persons With Disabilities and International Convention for the Protection of All Persons from Enforced Disappearances.

U.S. Supreme Court rules in *Hamdan v. Rumsfeld* that military commission set up to try Guantánamo detainees lacked authority to do because of structure and procedure.

Congress passes the Military Commission Act in response to *Hamdi* decision to allow military commissions to try detainees and amend War Crimes Act of 1996 (was amended by President Obama in 2009).

2007 U.N. Human Rights Council established to replace former Commission; U.S. voted against its establishment.

U.N. adopts Declaration on the Rights of Indigenous Peoples.

2009 U.S. signs Convention on the Rights of Persons with Disabilities.

U.N. World Conference Against Racism or Durban II is held in Geneva.

President Obama issues executive orders to review and move individuals detained at the Guantánamo Bay Naval Base and begin the closure of the facility; calls for an end to interrogations at all detention facilities.

Congress passes the Hate Crimes Bill making gender identity and sexual orientation protected classes under hate crimes.

U.S. elected as member of the U.N. Human Rights Council (term expires 2012).

2010 Secretary Clinton announces Obama Administration's four point Human Rights Policy.

U.S. Supreme Court rules in *Samantar v. Yousuf* that FSIA does not provide immunity defense to individual torturers from a civil case in U.S. Federal court.

Supreme Court rules in *Graham v. Florida* prohibiting juvenile Life Without Possibility of Parole Sentences for non capital offenses.

Congress passes Patient Protection and Affordable Care Act.

U.S. undergoes first Universal Periodic Review in U.N. Human Rights Council.

U.S. Supreme Court hears *Skinner v. Switzer*, regarding death row inmate recourse to federal civil rights law to obtain DNA testing from state.

Assembly of States Parties to the International Criminal Court, with U.S. input, establishes the definition of the international crime of aggression for ICC jurisdictional purposes.

U.S. deals with issues of Ground Zero Mosque and threatened burning of Koran.

Supreme Court issues ruling in *Citizens United v. Federal Election Commission* that First Amendment allows corporations and unions to spend money on elections.

2011 U.S. completes Universal Periodic Review procedure by U.N. Human Rights Council by HRC vote adopting final Outcome Report.

Supreme Court issues ruling in *Miller v. Alabama* prohibiting life in prison without the possibility of parole sentence for juvenile homicide offenders.

President Obama declares 1996 DOMA Act unconstitutional and directs the Department of Justice to stop defending it in court.

A series of political protests and uprisings ignite throughout the Middle East in what becomes known as the Arab Spring.

President Obama and Secretary of State Hilary Clinton announce plans to make promotion of gay rights a priority in foreign policy.

U.N. Human Rights Council adopts Resolution 16/18 promoted by the U.S. on "Combatting Intolerance..." and Secretary Clinton works with OIC to launch "Istanbul Process" implementing the resolution.

Inter American Commission on Human Rights finds U.S. responsible for human rights violations under ADHR for domestic violence in *Jessica Lenahan (Gonzales) v. USA*.

Protests over social and economic inequality erupt in New York City, also known as Occupy Wall Street Movement.

Final U.S. military troops leave Iraq under U.S.-Iraq Status of Forces Agreement.

Supreme Court issues ruling in *CLS v. Martinez* regarding recognition of religious student group.

2012   U.S. Senate rejects ratification of the U.N. Convention on the Rights of Persons with Disabilities in a vote 61-38.

Terrorists attack diplomatic compounds in Benghazi, Libya, killing Ambassador Chris Stevens and three other Americans.

U.S. elected as member of the U.N. Human Rights Council (term expires 2015).

Black Lives Matter Movement emerges following death of black youth Trayvon Martin.

Supreme Court issues ruling in *Hosanna-Tabor Evangelical Lutheran Church and School v. EEOC* recognizing 1st amendment ministerial exception to employment law.

2013   With support from the OHCHR international experts issue the Rabat Plan of Action.

European Court of Human Rights issues judgment in *Al Masri v. the former Yugoslav Republic of Macedonia* against extraordinary rendition by U.S. to FYRM.

Supreme Court issues ruling in *Kiobel v. Royal Dutch Petroleum Co.* creating presumption that Alien Tort Claims Act does not apply to acts outside U.S.

Supreme Court issues ruling in *Shelby County v. Holder* finding formula for political subdivision mapping for voting to be unconstitutional.

Supreme Court issues ruling in *United States v. Windsor* finding DOMA unconstitutional and leaving marriage to the states.

2014   U.S. begins military operations against the Islamic State in the Levant (also referred to as ISIS or DAESH).

U.N. Commission of Inquiry issues report on human rights violations in the Democratic People's Republic of Korea (North Korea).

Supreme Court issues ruling in *Burwell v. Hobby Lobby* exempting for-profit corporations from the contraceptive mandate on religious grounds.

Senator Feinstein releases Executive Summary of the Senate Select Committee on Intelligence report on CIA detention and interrogation program.

2015   Supreme Court issues ruling in *Holt v. Hobbs* that a prison policy that prevents beard on a Muslim prisoner violates the Religious Land Use and Institutionalized Persons Act.

Congress passes USA Freedom Act, an overhaul of the National Security Council's intelligence gathering program.

Supreme Court issues ruling in *EEOC v. Abercrombie & Fitch Stores* regarding religious discrimination against Muslim woman job applicant for wearing veil.

Department of Justice issues report clearing police officer Darren Wilson of civil rights violations in the death of Michael Brown in Ferguson, MO.

Paris Agreement within the U.N. Framework Convention on Climate Change signed and entered into force in 2016; U.S. has ratified the treaty.

Supreme Court issues ruling in *Obergefell v. Hodges* regarding recognition of state licenses for same sex marriage.

Inter American Commission on Human Rights issues a Report on the Merits in *Kevin Cooper v. USA* regarding due process.

U.S. completes 2nd cycle of Universal Periodic Review in the U.N. Human Rights Council.

Congress passes McCain-Feinstein Amendment to National Defense Authorization Act to limit all national security interrogations to the techniques listed in Army Field Manual 2-22.3, prohibiting all enhanced interrogation techniques, including waterboarding.

2016   Inter American Commission on Human Rights issues a Report on the Merits in *Undocumented Workers v. USA* on the right to benefits for workplace injuries, under the ADHR.

Congress passes Iran Sanctions Act Extension; goes into law without President's signature.

Congress passes Frank R. Wolf International Religious Freedom Act.

The U.N. passes an historic resolution condemning settlements in Israel and East Jerusalem as illegal with the U.S. abstaining.

U.S. elected as member of the U.N. Human Rights Council (term expires 2019).

House and Senate pass resolutions declaring ISIL (DAESH) attacks on religious minorities in Iraq and Syria is genocide; Secretary Kerry also recognizes the genocide.

Congress passes North Korea Sanctions and Policy Enforcement Act; President Obama imposes sanctions for human rights violations.

Supreme Court issues ruling in *Utah v. Strieff* regarding use of evidence obtained by police in an unconstitutional search.

Supreme Court issues ruling in *Birchfield v. North Dakota* upholding breath test refusal penalties during arrests for drunk driving.

Supreme Court issues ruling in *Luis v. United States* invalidating partial freezing of defendant's assets under sixth amendment right to counsel of choice.

Supreme Court issues ruling in *Montgomery v. Louisiana* prohibiting state court mandatory sentences of life without parole for juvenile homicide offenders.

Supreme Court issues ruling in *Whole Woman's Health v. Hellerstedt* finding two abortion related provisions in a Texas law unconstitutional.

Congress overrides president's veto and pass Justice Against Sponsors of Terrorism Act, to allow a cause of action against a foreign government in U.S. courts for terrorism injury.

Supreme Court vacated the Court of Appeals in seven cases referred to as *Zubik v. Burwell* regarding religious exercise and health care coverage.

Supreme Court issues ruling in *Fisher v. University of Texas* finding race-conscious admissions program legal.

Supreme Court issues ruling in *United States v. Texas,* blocking the President's DACA and DAPA immigration programs created by Executive Order.

2017   President Trump issues two Executive Orders to address security concerns in immigration policy that temporarily halt processing immigrants from several Muslim majority countries; the 9th Circuit halted these orders for concerns that they target Muslim immigrants, and the President has appealed to the Supreme Court.

President Trump issues strict new immigration apprehension and removal enforcement policies, limiting use of prosecutorial discretion expanding number of those who can be apprehended and removed, resetting removal priorities, calling for hiring immigration agents, expanding the scope of expedited removals, and limiting humanitarian parole, and calling for local law enforcement collaboration agreements.

Secretary of State Tillerson does not personally present the annual Country Reports on Human Rights Practices, (which report on the human rights record of almost every state in the world and which serve as a basis of foreign policy and some U.S. laws), to Congress, as is usually done.

U.S. government threatens to pull out of U.N. Human Rights Council unless it eliminates perceived anti-Israel bias and treatment under agenda item 7, and over HRC failing to criticize certain violator states.

U.S. government pulls out of participating in cases against the U.S. before the Inter-American Commission of Human Rights.

President Trump pulls the U.S. out of the Paris Agreement on Climate Change, subject to future negotiations.

President Trump reacts militarily to Syrian use of chemical weapons against civilians, in an effort to limit Syria's further use of such unlawful tactics.

President Trump Executive Order countering the Johnson Amendment which prohibited political speech or support of candidates from tax exempt religious organizations.

Senate Foreign Relations Committee informs Secretary of State Tillerson that it will not confirm his State Department nominees unless they fully support human rights.

The Supreme Court opinion in *Trinity Lutheran Church v. Comer* ruled that the government may not exclude religious groups from grant programs simply because they are religious, allowing a religious school to benefit from a state-funded playground resurfacing program.

MORE HISTORY OF HUMAN RIGHTS IN THE U.S. EXPERIENCE

The concept of universal [human] rights developed by the 18th century political theorists nourished international law, as it also set the stage for American Constitutionalism. Indeed, international human rights law and the constitutional law of the United States are at bottom profoundly related: both seek to limit the authority of states to interfere with the inalienable rights of all individuals without discrimination.

—*Assistant Secretary of State John Shattuck, Initial Report of the United States of America to the U.N. Human Rights Committee under the International Covenant on Civil and Political Rights, July 1994.*

Given the long history of our country, it is indeed pretentious to give a short history of human rights in relation to the United States. It is particularly challenging in view of the incredible dynamic in the life of the United States since 9/11. So much has happened. So much has changed. But, as Jimmy Carter stated in his Farewell Address, the United States is a country which was created by human rights out of crisis and revolution. This nation was founded by people who fled oppression and persecution and came here for freedom. They believed they had rights and demanded that their rights be respected. When this did not happen, they separated themselves from their oppressor and formed their own society and government and went their own way to create America, the land of the free. This was expressed to the "Powers of the earth" in 1776, in the famous Declaration of Independence:

> When in the course of human events it becomes necessary for one people to dissolve the political bands that have connected them with another, and to assume among the Powers of the earth, the separate and equal station to which the Laws of Nature and of Nature's God entitle them, a decent respect to the opinions of mankind requires that they should declare the causes that impel them to separation.

> We hold these truths to be self-evident, that all men are created equal, that they are endowed by their Creator with certain unalienable rights, among these are Life, Liberty and the pursuit of Happiness. That to secure these rights, Governments are instituted among Men, deriving their just powers from the consent of the governed....

> The history of the present King of Great Britain is a history of repeated injuries and usurpations, all having in direct object the establishment of an absolute Tyranny over these States. To prove this, let Facts be submitted to a candid world.

> Here they set forth a specific list of "injuries and usurpations" by the King. An example of two of these is as follows:

> For depriving U.S. in many cases, of the benefits of Trial by Jury.

> He has plundered our seas, ravaged our Coasts, burnt our towns, and destroyed the lives of our people .... We, therefore, ... appealing to the Supreme Judge of the world for the rectitude of our intentions, do ... solemnly publish and declare, That these United Colonies are, and of Right ought to be Free and Independent States ....

> —*Declaration of Independence, in Congress July 4, 1776 (The unanimous Declaration of the thirteen United States of America)*

It has been said that the history of liberty is a history of limitations of governmental power, not the increase of it. Human rights, "unalienable rights," gave the U.S. the Declaration of Independence and the U.S. Constitution and Bill of Rights. History cannot argue against the fact that human rights abuses led to the drafting of the Declaration of Independence, which led to the founding of the United States. It gave proof that the United States of America was the first country to be created by human rights and for human rights. By this we mean that it was the awareness and consensus of the leaders of the thirteen colonies that all human beings had individual human rights just by being human, and that the human rights of all of the colonists were being violated by England. That led them to join together in united strength and to express the causes that would justify declaring their independence from England. In the Declaration of Independence, the

Founding Fathers together stated to England and the world that they would no longer tolerate the abuse of power resulting in human rights violations against colonists. They no doubt were mindful of the Magna Carta of 1212, which held budding ideas of the rights of the governed against the governor. The great experiment that was to be the United States of America was not only caused by (in reaction against) human rights violations. It also came into being for the protection of human rights in the colonies (and later the states) against any abuse of power by even their own respective governments. They held this view in common. The usurpation or abuse of power by government of any kind would no longer be tolerated in America. Government by the people and for the people was set on making government limited in ways that protected their unalienable right to life, liberty, and the pursuit of happiness. Our history has been a continuous battle and debate over how to balance the freedom of the individual and the needs of the state to protect those freedoms.

The Declaration of Independence did not create the United States. It only resulted in the thirteen colonies becoming separate and equal sovereign international states (e.g., the sovereign state of Massachusetts, the sovereign state of Virginia, etc.). They saw a need to join together with each other to form a union that could accomplish together what they could not do individually. That united entity would be granted authority to handle matters that would otherwise have been within their separate sovereignty, such as immigration, foreign affairs, and national defense from external threat. In their sovereignty as states, they chose to give up some of their sovereignty to a greater entity to become known as the "United States" of America. The Articles of Confederation of 1781 formed them into a confederation with limited central government.

The Constitution in 1789 gave them the legal political institution known as the United States of America, a separate and equal, sovereign, international federal state. This Constitution of the United States was legally a treaty, an international legal instrument, governed by international law, entered into freely by the thirteen colonies, which saw themselves as separate sovereign states. It had to be "ratified" by nine of the thirteen colonies before it entered into force, creating the greatest country in history. This country was known for its freedom and for being governed by law, not human power. This Constitution had its legal basis in international law, the source of the doctrine of sovereignty. This was consciously done by the Founding Fathers who knew international law, then called the law of nations or lex gentium. The Constitution is not only the organic instrument through which the U.S. was created; it is an international treaty which is governed by international law and must be interpreted and applied consistent with it, so long as not unconstitutionally. This fact is never discussed, but it is legally and historically true. One need only read the Federalist Papers to confirm this.

The U.S. is a federal state, meaning that it is composed of separate subunits called "states." Thus, the colonies first became individual international states and then became a federal republic of equal states, whereupon the individual states retained all the powers of international states, except those granted by the Constitution to the federal government. Most important of these was authority to engage in foreign affairs and national defense. In concept, this arrangement was a precursor of sorts to those individual sovereign states of the world who join together and limit their sovereignty for a common purpose, such as the protection of international human rights norms.

The Constitution contained only a few provisions to provide protection for the unalienable rights of the Declaration of Independence. It set forth a few civil liberties, such as establishing the right to habeas corpus (the right to challenge the lawfulness of one's arrest in a court of law); prohibiting bills of attainder (laws passed with the purpose of punishing one particular person); and prohibiting ex post facto legislation (making a law retroactive, therefore punishing people for breaking a law when it was not yet a law). In the Declaration of Independence, the signers clearly were cognizant of, and made reference to, international law as the basis of their right to secede. They believed that international law was based on the same natural law and Enlightenment philosophies that justified their claim to "unalienable rights." Although it was not yet called "human rights," the Founding Fathers clearly understood and meant this concept, even though the institution of slavery, the mistreatment of Indians, and the limited legal status of women were then still legal and social realities. The United States was nonetheless set upon a path toward achieving still greater rights of human beings, as the subsequent Civil War and civil rights and suffrage movements would attest. These movements helped catalyze national action for greater freedoms.

The Declaration of Independence is one of the two important historical documents that have provided the idea of human rights and its essential philosophy for the whole world. The other key document is the 1789 French Declaration of the Rights of Man and of Citizen. Even though it is not a legal document, the declaration has also established that all human beings are born equal and are created with their rights; that fundamental individual rights are not granted by state governments but are only recognized, respected, and protected by them; and that such protection is the first duty of government.

The United States was founded not only by human rights but also for the protection of the human rights of the colonists, as the subsequent Declaration of Rights (an early document that sought to insert the protection of certain individual freedoms into the Constitution), the Constitution and Bill of Rights would thereafter establish. In the 1791 amendments to the Constitution, Americans enjoyed a Bill of Rights to protect the citizenry from government. Along with the separation of powers, and checks and balances created by legal and institutional structure, Americans have enjoyed a system able to overcome major assaults on human rights, such as slavery and segregation, and to survive a civil war that would have ended most political enterprises.

The Constitution and the Bill of Rights would begin the U.S. legal experience of the protection of individuals from the power of the state. They reflected the belief in a government of limited powers, because human rights norms are limitations on how governments exercise power. Having learned about the abuse of power from its ties with England, the United States knew such legal restraints were necessary. The few individual rights provisions of the Constitution and the first ten amendments of the Bill of Rights, along with the Civil War amendments, would serve the United States as its protection of individual human freedom and as the precursors of modern human rights norms. Another important U.S. instrument in this equation was the Lieber Code, created at the time of the Civil War. This document, drafted by Professor Francis Lieber of Columbia University, established a code of conduct for the Union armed forces. This code set forth limitations on the military conduct of U.S. soldiers during the Civil War. It served as one of the founding documents of the field of international humanitarian law, which is the law of armed conflict. It established the principal of "military necessity," which set limits on the use of military power or force by a government so as to minimize the suffering, death, and destruction of war. This type of code is now embodied in the four Geneva Conventions and their various protocols. It is cited even in cases in other countries and legal systems.

The U.S. experience with human rights would take two tracks, one national and one international. On the national level, there are laws, such as the 1964 Civil Rights Act, and case decisions interpreting constitutionally based human rights, such as *Brown v. Board of Education*. On the international level, there is the U.S. participation in World War II; its participation in the Nuremberg trials of Nazi war crimes and the Tokyo trials of Japanese war crimes; and its involvement in the establishment of the United Nations and regional international human rights systems.

The United States has, perhaps more than any other state, given the world the foundations of human rights and many of the specific human rights norms, such as fair trial rights. It has given the field of human rights many of its greatest statespersons, scholars, and activists; created many nongovernmental organizations; and mobilized civil society in human rights issues both nationally and internationally. Although, none of this means that the United States has been free from committing its own human rights violations, the United States has, by and large, acted consistently with internationally recognized human rights norms, at least since the end of legal segregation until that ignominious day of 9/11 and the start of what has been called the war on terrorism. Since that date, human rights issues have come to the forefront, with claims and denials of human rights violations by the military, the CIA, the Immigration Service, the prison system, the President, and on and on. Much international criticism has been made against the U.S. for what others see as a double standard and attitude of being above the law, known as exceptionalism.

Since the shocking events of 9/11, a shift of political attitudes has changed U.S. participation in the world of human rights both domestically (i.e. abortion, capital punishment, and terrorism) and internationally (i.e. Israeli treatment of Palestinians or international terrorism, with arrest and detention of suspected terrorists outside the territory of the U.S. and certain interrogation techniques).

Although domestically, U.S. society is more often and more extensively oriented to the Constitution than to international human rights standards, it is slowly increasing its knowledge of these international norms. In addition, international bodies are increasing their activities regarding U.S. human rights practice and problems. Even in the U.S. Supreme Court one sees the increasing influence of international human rights norms. Institutionally, however, one has seen the gradual increase in the importance of the United Nations as it continued to develop international human rights standards and set up special mechanisms to monitor and resolve human rights issues, including those involving the U.S.

Primary Source Documents

Sample Human Rights Day Proclamations

The following proclamations show the recognition by the U.S. government, through the Head of State, of international human rights law in general and the Universal Declaration of Human Rights in particular, and of their context in the United Nations, and by both Republican and Democratic Presidents.

PRESIDENT RONALD REGAN
BY THE PRESIDENT OF THE UNITED STATES OF AMERICA
A PROCLAMATION, 1988

The second week in December commemorates two important dates. December 10 marks the 40th anniversary of the signing of the Universal Declaration of Human Rights, and December 15 marks the date almost 200 years ago when, in 1791, the first 10 amendments to the United States Constitution — our Bill of Rights — were ratified.

The human rights we regard today as inherent and unalienable were by no means universally accepted 2 centuries ago. Such rights as freedom of worship, speech, assembly, and the press were just beginning to be asserted by popular movements that would sweep Europe and elsewhere in the next century. The United States thus foreshadowed and fostered a powerful drive to improve the lot of mankind everywhere. During the drafting of our Constitution, Thomas Jefferson wrote that "a Bill of Rights is what people are entitled to against every government on earth."

Now, 200 years later, the Universal Declaration, enshrining many of the principles of our Founders, has become that worldwide Bill of Rights. Elaborating such a list of basic rights was one of the first tasks undertaken by the new United Nations Organization; the Chair of the drafting committee was Eleanor Roosevelt, who was later nominated for a Nobel Peace Prize for this work. Urging adoption of the Universal Declaration, then-Secretary of State George C. Marshall told the United Nations that "denials of basic human rights lie at the root of most of our troubles.... Governments which systematically disregard the rights of their own people," he said, "are not likely to respect the rights of other nations and other people." He called for adoption of the Universal Declaration as "a standard of conduct for U.S. all."

The Universal Declaration, like our own Bill of Rights, starts from the premises that civil liberties and political freedom are the birthright of all mankind and that all of U.S. are equal in the eyes of the law. Like our own Declaration of Independence, it also makes the inescapable connection between freedom, human rights, and government by the consent of the governed.

We are proud that the truths expressed by our Founding Fathers — America's source of strength, stability, and authority for more than 2 centuries — have also provided a standard for liberty and the rule of law emulated in dozens of other countries as well.

Despite this entrenched resistance of tyrants to practical guarantees of liberty, the Universal Declaration has done much to promote observance of human rights around the world. Over the past decade in particular we have seen great strides.

Now, Therefore, I, Ronald Reagan, President of the United States of America, by virtue of the authority vested in me by the Constitution and laws of the United States, do hereby proclaim December 10, 1988, as Human Rights Day, and December 15, 1988, as Bill of Rights Day, and I call upon all Americans to observe the week beginning December 10, 1988, as Human Rights Week.

PRESIDENT GEORGE H. W. BUSH
BY THE PRESIDENT OF THE UNITED STATES OF AMERICA
A PROCLAMATION, 1992

This week, as we commemorate the ratification of our Bill of Rights on December 15, 1791, we not only give thanks for our Nation's enduring legacy of liberty under law but also celebrate its role in promoting human rights around the world.

Our Bill of Rights guarantees, among other basic liberties, freedom of religion, speech, and the press. It affirms the right of the people to keep and bear arms; ensures that no person shall be deprived of life, liberty, or property without due process of law; and guarantees the right of citizens to be secure against unreasonable searches and seizure of their persons, houses, papers, and effects. The Bill of Rights also establishes fundamental rules of fairness in our Nation's judicial system, including the right to trial by jury, assistance of counsel, and freedom from cruel and unusual punishment. Finally, the Bill of Rights reserves to the States respectively, or to the people, those powers that are not delegated to the Federal Government by the Constitution.

Seventeen additional amendments have been added to our Constitution over the past 200 years, but the Bill of Rights has remained a shining symbol of our liberty — a standard against which we measure the legitimacy of American laws and institutions.

Over time, the Bill of Rights has proved to be a cornerstone as well: today we recognize that great document as the foundation of more recent charters of liberty, including the Universal Declaration of Human Rights, which was adopted by the General Assembly of the United Nations on December 10, 1948. Recognizing that respect for "the inherent dignity and...the equal and inalienable rights of all members of the human family is the foundation of freedom, justice, and peace in the world," signers of the Declaration affirmed that "everyone has the right to life, liberty, and the security of person." Signers likewise stated that "all are equal before the law and are entitled without any discrimination to equal protection of the law." They agreed to respect freedom of thought, conscience, and religion for all, without regard to race, nationality, gender, or belief, and declared that "everyone has the right to take part in the government of his country, directly or through freely chosen representatives." These principles were affirmed again in 1975, when the United States, Canada, and 33 European nations joined together in signing the Helsinki Final Act of the Conference on Security and Cooperation in Europe.

While we have made great progress toward the goals set forth at Helsinki and reaffirmed at subsequent CSCE meetings in Copenhagen, Geneva, and Moscow, we know that there is still much work to do in promoting the peaceful resolution of conflicts, the establishment of stable, democratic institutions of government, and universal compliance with international human rights agreements. When he proposed a Bill of Rights to our Constitution in 1789, James Madison sagely noted that such a document would strengthen democracy by preventing a tyranny of the majority, in which the will of a larger number of citizens might be levelled against the rights of the few. The resurgence of ethnic violence and bitter nationalist rivalries has underscored the urgency of protecting the rights of minorities. As it has done consistently in the past, the United States calls on all signatories to the Helsinki Final Act and the Universal Declaration of Human Rights to fulfill their solemn commitment to protect the rights of individuals, without regard to race, nationality, or creed.

Recognizing that egregious human rights violations continue not only in regions encompassed within the CSCE but also in other regions of the world, the United States also denounces any attempts to dilute or distort human rights agreements through the claim of particular socioeconomic circumstances or religious and cultural traditions. Having fought so long for recognition of an international human rights standard, one rooted in fundamental standards of morality and justice, we will not condone that consensus being undermined by those who claim that their particular economic, social, or political contexts relieve them of their obligation to protect the rights of individuals. The upcoming World Conference on Human Rights, which is to be held in June 1993, will provide the United States with another opportunity to reaffirm the universality of human rights and the common duty of all governments to uphold them.

Now, Therefore, I, George Bush, President of the United States of America, by virtue of the authority vested in me by the Constitution and laws of the United States, do hereby proclaim December 10, 1992, as Human Rights Day and December 15, 1992, as Bill of Rights Day, and call on all Americans to observe the week beginning December 10, 1992, as Human Rights Week. I urge all Americans to observe this week with appropriate ceremonies and activities.

ॐ৵৵ॐॐ৵৵ॐॐ

PRESIDENT GEORGE W. BUSH
BY THE PRESIDENT OF THE UNITED STATES OF AMERICA
A PROCLAMATION, 2001

The terrible tragedies of September 11 served as a grievous reminder that the enemies of freedom do not respect or value individual human rights. Their brutal attacks were an attack on these very rights. When our essential rights are attacked, they must and will be defended.

Americans stand united with those who love democracy, justice, and individual liberty. We are committed to upholding these principles, embodied in our Constitution's Bill of Rights, that have safeguarded U.S. throughout our history and that continue to provide the foundation of our strength and prosperity.

The heinous acts of terrorism committed on September 11 were an attack against civilization itself, and they have caused the world to join together in a coalition that is now waging war on terrorism and defending international human rights. Americans have looked beyond our borders and found encouragement as the world has rallied to join the American-led coalition. Civilized people everywhere have recognized that terrorists threaten every nation that loves liberty and cherishes the protection of individual rights.

Respect for human dignity and individual freedoms reaffirms a core tenet of civilized people everywhere. This important observance honoring our Bill of Rights and advocating human rights around the world allows all Americans to celebrate the universal principles of liberty and justice that define our dreams and shape our hopes as we face the challenges of a new era.

Now, Therefore, I, George W. Bush, President of the United States of America, by virtue of the authority vested in me by the Constitution and laws of the United States, do hereby proclaim December 10, 2001, as Human Rights Day; December 15, 2001, as Bill of Rights Day; and the week beginning December 9, 2001, as Human Rights Week. I call upon the people of the United States to honor the legacy of human rights passed down to U.S. from previous generations and to resolve that such liberties will prevail in our Nation and throughout the world as we move into the 21st century.

ॐ৵৵ॐॐ৵৵ॐॐ

PRESIDENT BARACK OBAMA
BY THE PRESIDENT OF THE UNITED STATES OF AMERICA
A PROCLAMATION, 2015

Sixty-seven years ago, the leaders of 48 countries from around the world declared with one voice that progress depends on defending human rights, and that a nation is strongest when the contributions of its whole citizenry are valued. Today, we celebrate the Universal Declaration of Human Rights — a milestone in our ongoing global march to uphold the inherent dignity and worth of every person. To honor the legacy of this historic document and to help ensure that its ideals endure for generations to come, we reaffirm our commitment to upholding the freedoms it safeguards, which are the birthright of all humanity.

When rights are suppressed, human potential is stifled. A nation draws upon new talents and ideas when opposition parties are fairly represented and those in power are accountable to their citizens at the ballot box. A free and independent press and a vibrant civil society can inform the public, expose corruption, and empower citizens to participate in self-governance. And when institutions are built to protect rights and freedoms, rather than serve the interests of those in power, those institutions can provide the stable foundation for stability needed for future generations to thrive.

In too many places around the world we see rights and freedoms denied. People are imprisoned for peaceful worship and girls are barred from attending school. LGBT individuals are subject to abuse because of who they are and who they love, and citizens are prevented from petitioning those in power for change. The United States of America stands in solidarity with those seeking to realize a brighter and freer future for themselves and their families, whether in their home country or as immigrants in a new land. We will continue to lift up the lives of all who yearn to exercise their inherent human rights and to shine a light on those still living in the darkest pockets of our world.

The strongmen of today will never extinguish the hope that persists around the world. Dissenters may be jailed, but ideas can never be imprisoned. Controlling access to information will not turn lies into truths, nor will it deter the longing for justice that stirs in every human soul. And refusing to recognize the basic dignity of every man, woman, and child - regardless of gender, background, race, ethnicity, sexual orientation, or belief — will only lend further momentum to the quest for equality that for generations has stirred hearts and spurred action. On this day, and every day, let U.S. remember our roots as one human family, forever dedicated to upholding the central tenets of the Universal Declaration of Human Rights.

Now, Therefore, I, Barack Obama, President of the United States of America, by virtue of the authority vested in me by the Constitution and the laws of the United States, do hereby proclaim December 10, 2015, as Human Rights Day and the week beginning December 10, 2015, as Human Rights Week. I call upon the people of the United States to mark these observances with appropriate ceremonies and activities.

U.S. State Department, Secretary of State & Human Rights

Chapter 3

This Chapter is About the part of the Executive branch of the U.S. government that deals with global issues, with the relation of the U.S. with other states, and with international organizations in foreign relations. This part of government mainly involves the Secretary of State, and the Department of State over which the Secretary presides. It constitutes America's face to the world and deals with how America appears and relates in the international community, and in one-on-one relationships with other countries.

This chapter is about the legal norms that apply to these relationships and to citizens, and what values underlie the policy of the U.S. in the global context. Public International Law and, particularly, International Human Rights Law, provides the dominant discourse for international relations. The State Department is a key voice of that discourse. Here you will learn about the activity of the Secretary of State and the Department of State in the area of human rights, focusing on the activity of the State Department's branch — the Bureau of Democracy, Human Rights and Labor. It discusses reports prepared by the Bureau for all sorts of human rights functions and bodies, including treaty bodies, the Universal Periodic Review, human trafficking, and the very important and comprehensive annual Country Reports.

This information reflects the situation of the transition to the new government in 2017. The information in this chapter could change, based on the administration's policies on human rights and its relationship to international human rights bodies (i.e., U.N. Human Rights Council). The sources listed throughout will provide updates as they happen.

This is Important Because the United States is not an island that exists by itself. It is a nation state, and member of an international community of states which seeks to solve common problems and preserve peace. Like every organization, body, or business, the international community needs rules and order that all members must follow in order to function. The International Human Rights Law, for example, is a set of norms that regulate how governments treat their people, both citizens and legal residents, and anyone under its jurisdiction. In relationship to the outside world, the U.S. Secretary of State is an extremely important position, because the U.S. is the most powerful state in the world. The Secretary of

State is the voice of America in the international arena. He or she defends the U.S. when it is criticized, and criticizes other states when they are violating human rights, in order to persuade those states to obey the human rights norms and change their conduct and policies. Much of the human rights work of the U.S. is done by the Secretary of State with heads of state and government officials around the world. The Department of State, which assists the U.S. through the Secretary in carrying out foreign policy, has many different parts that deal with human rights, but it is particularly the Bureau of Democracy, Human Rights, and Labor on which this chapter focuses. The Bureau's job is to publicize information that informs Americans and others of the U.S. role in human rights as it relates to the international realm, and what others are doing and saying about the U.S. with respect to its acts in the international arena. The executive branch of our government is tasked with carrying out the foreign policy of the U.S. according to the laws promulgated by Congress and the Constitution. How that branch acts, and what it says about the U.S., is important both to Americans and to those from other nations who look to America for leadership and guidance. It's important for all Americans to know what the government does to inform its citizens about what it does regarding human rights. The U.S., like every other nation, is not perfect and can improve its human rights record. However, before calling on the government to create change that will improve this great country, Americans have to learn about their own human rights, domestically and internationally. The State Department is the place where the U.S. most often and most extensively deals with human rights, and prepares what is said to the world about the U.S. and human rights.

Quotes & Key Text Excerpts

Promoting freedom and democracy and protecting human rights around the world are central to U.S. foreign policy. The values captured in the Universal Declaration of Human Rights and in other global and regional commitments are consistent with the values upon which the United States was founded centuries ago. The United States supports those persons who long to live in freedom and under democratic governments that protect universally accepted human rights. The United States uses a wide range of tools to advance a freedom agenda, including bilateral diplomacy, multilateral engagement, foreign assistance, reporting and public outreach, and economic sanctions. The United States is committed to working with democratic partners, international and regional organizations, non-governmental organizations, and engaged citizens to support those seeking freedom.

The Bureau of Democracy, Human Rights and Labor leads the U.S. efforts to promote democracy, protect human rights and international religious freedom, and advance labor rights globally.

Source: U.S. Department of State, Diplomacy in Action, https://www.state.gov/j/drl

❧❧❧❧❧❧❧❧

Washington, DC, January 11, 2017

...

I come before you at a pivotal time in both the history of our nation and our world. Nearly everywhere we look, people and nations are deeply unsettled. Old ideas and international norms which were well understood and governed behaviors in the past may no longer be effective in our time.

...

Our approach to human rights begins by acknowledging that American leadership requires moral clarity. We do not face an either/or choice on defending global human rights. Our values are our interests when it comes to human rights and humanitarian assistance. It is unreasonable to expect that every foreign policy endeavor will be driven by human rights considerations alone, especially when the security of the American people is at stake. But our leadership demands actions specifically focused on improving the conditions of people the world over, utilizing both aid and, where appropriate, economic sanctions as instruments of foreign policy.

And we must adhere to standards of accountability. Our recent engagements with the Government of Cuba was not accompanied by any significant concessions on human rights. We have not held them accountable for their conduct. Their leaders received much while their people received little. That serves neither the interest of Cubans nor Americans.

Abraham Lincoln declared that America is the "last best hope on Earth." Our moral light must not go out if we are to remain an agent of freedom for mankind. Supporting human rights in our foreign policy is a key component of clarifying to a watching world what America stands for.

In closing, let us also be proud about the ideals that define us and the liberties we have secured at great cost. The ingenuity, ideas, and culture of Americans who came before us made the United

States the greatest nation in history. So have their sacrifices. We should never forget that we stand on the shoulders of those who have sacrificed much and in some cases everything. They include our fallen heroes in uniform, our Foreign Service officers, and other Americans in the field who likewise gave all for their country.

—*Rex Tillerson, Testimony Before the Senate Foreign Relations Committee*

Source: U.S. Department of State, https://www.state.gov/secretary/remarks/2017/01/27394.htm

᪥᪥᪥᪥᪥᪥᪥᪥

The annual Country Reports on Human Rights Practices — the Human Rights Reports — cover internationally recognized individual, civil, political, and worker rights, as set forth in the Universal Declaration of Human Rights and other international agreements. The U.S. Department of State submits reports on all countries receiving assistance and all United Nations member states to the U.S. Congress in accordance with the Foreign Assistance Act of 1961 and the Trade Act of 1974.

Source: U.S. Department of State, Diplomacy in Action, https://www.state.gov/j/drl/rls/hrrpt

What You Should Know

Despite recent criticism about U.S. law, policy, and practice regarding human rights, the U.S. has been actively engaged in advancing the cause of human rights and freedom around the world. Unfortunately, those advancements are done behind the world stage and often not apparent to the American public. The Secretary of State, in conjunction with the State Department, shapes the President's foreign policy towards a more free, secure, and prosperous world, while protecting and supporting American interest abroad. The Department provides essential information to the President and the Secretary of State in order to implement human rights and foreign policy.

The Department of State focuses primarily outward in relation of the United States to the rest of the world. It deals with bilateral matters between the U.S. and foreign governments and between the U.S. and International Organizations, such as the U.N. It also looks inward sometimes, as it seeks to inform Americans about what the Government is doing in foreign relations, what is the government policy, what reports have been prepared by the State Department about human rights issues, and various human rights related topics, such as human trafficking or terrorism.

According to the U.S. government website, the State Department is responsible for handling the foreign affairs of the United States government. It was originally known as the Department of Foreign Affairs when it was created in 1789. It is the oldest of the cabinet-level agencies in the Executive Branch. It consists largely of diplomats and Foreign Service officers who carry out American foreign policy throughout the world. This task involves a multitude of issues ranging from trade and commerce to cultural interests and security measures, among other important things. The State Department interfaces with representatives of foreign governments, corporations, non-governmental organizations, and private individuals to advance U.S. interests all across the globe. It also produces information and materials to inform the public about matters of international concern like human rights. Human rights has become, and is, a pillar of U.S. foreign policy. That is not, however, to be presumed as unchangeable. Different administrations might have different policies or interpretations of the law. How well they act in harmony with the international legal standards, such as human rights and humanitarian law, is the issue.

The Department also issues U.S. passports and is a major influence concerning who can come into the United States and how long they can stay. It provides the personnel for embassies and consulates, and places people in the international organizations to represent the U.S. population.

The U.S. Department of State is a large organizational body with many integral and moving parts, addressing many subjects and many geographical areas. Primary Source Document 1, below, is an organizational chart of the State Department. Its head is the Secretary of State who assists the President (the Head of State of the U.S.) in the foreign affairs of this country.

The Secretary of State

The most visible voice of international human rights in the U.S. government is the Secretary of State. He or she regularly brings up human rights issues in meeting with heads of foreign states. Some of these issues are heard in the news, but much goes on behind closed diplomatic doors. Sometimes it is the Secretary who hears about human rights in the U.S. and fields criticisms of U.S. policy and practices, such as with immigration issues.

Human rights was a constant consideration of the U.S. administration under President Obama and was addressed both at home and abroad by Secretary of State John Kerry who was one of the most experienced in the U.S. government on the subject of Human Rights Law. Even when discussing domestic issues like police brutality, there was a focus on the social justice and constitutional law implications of crises, all of which are connected to international human rights norms without ever mentioning them.

The Secretary also introduces to the State Department the important Country Reports on Human Rights Practices. Every year upon presenting the Reports to Congress, the Secretary gives a summary of what salient human rights issues have arisen around the globe. For the 2016 summary, see Primary Source Document 3, below. In 2017 Secretary Tillerson broke tradition and did not present the Reports to Congress in person, but merely submitted his Preface. Some interpret this as exhibiting a lesser interest in the Country Reports and in human rights than shown by previous administrations.

Secretary of State Tillerson is a former oil company executive and engineer, with no diplomatic or governmental experience. He understands that human rights form part of American values and are important in the U.S. and the world, and are part of his job domain in the international political sphere. A quote from his Senate Foreign Relations Committee confirmation hearing is found in the Quote section at the beginning of this Chapter. In it he says, "Old ideas and international norms which were well understood and governed behaviors in the past may no longer be effective in our time." Some may interpret this as discrediting and delegitimizing the existing system of human rights norms, which may not sit well with the rest of the international community, which has fought so long to establish and achieve acceptance of those norms.

He continued: "We do not face an either/or choice on defending global human rights. Our values are our interests when it comes to human rights and humanitarian assistance. It is unreasonable to expect that every foreign policy endeavor will be driven by human rights considerations alone, especially when the security of the American people is at stake."

What this seems to say is that fundamental human rights, which are inherent and inalienable and are held by every human being on the face of the earth, may be treated as just one of the various values which must be considered and the subject of discussion, negotiation, and possible political compromise in a given situation. It is not to be expected that international issues will be looked at by human rights considerations alone. They seldom are. But neither should a government try to force a people to give up their human rights in exchange for another card in the deck, such as economic or military benefits.

Human rights cannot be bargained away, as they do not belong to the government. Once human rights become subject to any ethical, political, or geopolitical calculus, they are in danger. As discussed in Chapter 1, human rights are limitations on the power of government. Governments do not like limitations on their power and, if left to their own devices, will trade human rights for some monetary or hard power, or other benefit. Once human rights are given second place after any other value, including national security, the seeds of their destruction are sewn. When terrorists force a state to give up human rights in order to fight them, they have already won. Such rights are in danger. Moreover, since all human rights are indivisible, inter-related, and inter-dependent, if any are neutralized, all are. When the Secretary implies that new standards and new norms are needed in the world today, that implies that new norms will be less restrictive to governmental power. It is this attitude that manifests the precise reason for limitation of government power by human rights and other international norms.

Without understanding the human rights norms as recognized today, norms largely conceived, drafted, and promoted by Americans in the past, one cannot argue whether and how any of them should be changed or eliminated altogether. The reader is challenged to learn and debate the importance of fundamental human rights.

Bureau of Democracy, Human Rights, and Labor

The Department of State is a part of the executive branch of the U.S. government, under the President. It has within it many different branches. While these different branches all deal in areas related to human rights, there is one branch that deals primarily with what is happening within the context of the U.S, and globally as it relates specifically to human rights — the Bureau of Democracy, Human Rights and Labor (DRL). It is knowledgeable and informed about International Human Rights Law and institutions, and what occurs with respect to the U.S. and International Human Rights Law all around the world.

Its website offers much information for citizens, students and researchers who are interested in what the U.S. is doing and saying to the citizenry and the world regarding human rights, labor, and democracy with respect to specific issues and specific countries.

The Bureau website includes almost all the documents from the U.S. participation at the U.N. regarding then U.N. General Assembly and particularly the U.P.R. process of the U.S., as well as the documents from the U.N. treaty bodies such as the Committee against Racial Discrimination, Human Rights Committee, Committee on the Rights of the Child, Committee against Torture; and on the U.N. Human Rights Council Special Mechanisms.

The Bureau defines its role as follows:

The Bureau of Democracy, Human Rights and Labor Affairs (DRL) is a bureau within the United States Department of State. The bureau is under the purview of the Under Secretary of State for Civilian Security, Democracy, and Human Rights.

DRL's responsibilities include promoting democracy around the world, formulating U.S. human rights policies, and co-ordinating policy in human rights-related labor issues. The Office to Monitor and Combat Anti-Semitism is a separate agency included in the Bureau.

The Bureau is responsible for producing annual reports on the countries of the world with regard to religious freedom through its Office of International Religious Freedom and human rights. It also administers the U.S. Human Rights and Democracy Fund.

The head of the Bureau is the Assistant Secretary of State for Democracy, Human Rights, and Labor.

The bureau was formerly known as the Bureau of Human Rights and Humanitarian Affairs, but was reorganized and re-named in 1994, to reflect both a broader sweep and a more focused approach to the interlocking issues of human rights, worker rights, and democracy.

Source: U.S. Department of State, Diplomacy in Action

The Bureau is comprised of the following:
- Office of Country Reports and Asylum Affairs — Prepares the State Department's annual reports, including the Country Reports on Human Rights
- Office of International Religious Freedom — Supports the United States Ambassador-at-Large for International Religious Freedom
- Office of Policy Planning and Public Diplomacy
- Office for Africa — Monitors human rights in Africa
- Office for East Asia and the Pacific — Monitors human rights in East Asia
- Office for Near East Asia — Monitors human rights in the Middle East
- Office for Western Hemisphere — Monitors human rights in Latin America
- Office for South Central Asia — Monitors human rights in Central Asia
- Office of Global Programming
- Office of Multilateral and Global Affairs — Formulates and implements U.S. government policy on human rights in multilateral organizations, including the U.N. Human Rights Council, the U.N. General Assembly, the U.N. Security Council, the Office of the High Commissioner for Human Rights, the European Union, the Organization of American States, the African Union, and the Association of Southeast Asian Nations
- Office of International Labor Rights — Advises on policies and initiatives in tandem with the International Labour Organization
- Executive Office

The Bureau's mission is as follows: The protection of fundamental human rights was a foundation stone in the establish-ment of the United States over 200 years ago. Since then, a central goal of U.S. foreign policy has been the promotion of respect for human rights, as embodied in the Universal Declaration of Human Rights. The United States understands that the existence of human rights helps secure the peace, deter aggression, promote the rule of law, combat crime and corruption, strengthen democracies, and prevent humanitarian crises.

Because the promotion of human rights is an important national interest, the United States seeks to:
- Hold governments accountable to their obligations under universal human rights norms and international human rights instruments;
- Promote greater respect for human rights, including freedom from torture, freedom of expression, press freedom, women's rights, children's rights, and the protection of minorities;
- Promote the rule of law, seek accountability, and change cultures of impunity;
- Assist efforts to reform and strengthen the institutional capacity of the Office of the U.N. High Commissioner for Human Rights and the U.N. Human Rights [Council]; and
- Coordinate human rights activities with important allies, including the EU, and regional organizations.

This confirms the importance of the protection of human rights as being in the national interest, and thus having a central place in the Department of State and U.S. foreign policy.

The Bureau (DRL) applies *three key principles* to its work on human rights:

1. *DRL strives to learn the truth and state the facts* in all of its human rights investigations, reports on country conditions, speeches, and votes in the UN, and asylum profiles. Each year, DRL develops, edits, and submits to Congress a 5,000-page report on human rights conditions in over 190 countries that is respected globally for its objectivity and accuracy. DRL also provides relevant information on country conditions to the Immigration and Naturalization Service and immigration judges in asylum cases.

2. *DRL takes consistent positions* concerning past, present, and future abuses. With regard to past abuses, it actively promotes accountability. To stop ongoing abuses, the bureau uses an "inside-outside" approach that combines vigorous, external focus on human rights concerns (including the possibility of sanctions) with equally robust support for internal reform. To prevent future abuses, it promotes early warning and preventive diplomacy. Each year DRL ensures that human rights considerations are incorporated into U.S. military training and security assistance programs; promotes the rights of women through international campaigns for political participation and full equality; conducts high-level human rights dialogues with other governments; coordinates U.S. policy on human rights with key allies; and raises key issues and cases through diplomatic and public channels.

3. *DRL forges and maintains partnerships* with organizations, governments, and multilateral institutions committed to human rights. The bureau takes advantage of multilateral fora to focus international attention on human rights problems and to seek correction. Each year, DRL provides significant technical, financial, or staff support for U.S. delegations to the annual meetings of several international human rights organizations; conducts regular consultations with Native American tribes, and serves as the Secretary's principal advisor on international indigenous rights issues; maintains relations with the U.N. High Commissioner on Human Rights; and supports the creation of effective multilateral human rights mechanisms and institutions for accountability.

Source: https://www.state.gov/j/drl/hr/index.htm

One of the things the U.S. does through the administration to help democratize countries is to encourage the development of vibrant civil society organizations in countries low on democracy. The development of civil society organizations helps challenge governments to, among other things, respect human rights. CSOs can bring issues to the government's attention and propose changes to laws and policies to get them to align with international human rights standards. The Primary Source Documents below include a fact sheet prepared by DLR for the White House regarding the various ways the U.S. is helping CSOs through a variety of programs.

Among the many duties performed by DRL, the most important for human rights is the preparation of human rights related reports. The Bureau helps prepare reports that are essential to U.S. foreign policy and can incidentally help in the domestic awareness of human rights. The reports are for various purposes, addressed to various bodies, particularly inter-governmental organizations like the U.N., and are sometimes about other countries and also about the U.S. and its human rights laws, policies, and practices. It gathers the information for these reports from various agencies and branches of the U.S. government and sometimes from outside sources as well.

According to the DRL:

> Progress on human rights begins with a fundamental commitment to the dignity that is the birthright of every man, woman, and child. Progress in advancing human rights begins with the facts. The United States provides a record of the state of human rights in the world to raise awareness of the progress made, the ground lost, and the work that remains.
>
> These reports are an essential tool — for activists who courageously struggle to protect rights in communities around the world; for journalists and scholars who document rights violations and who report on the work of those who champion the vulnerable; and for governments, including our own, as they work to craft strategies to protect the human rights of more individuals in more places.

These reports include: Human Rights Reports; Trafficking-in-Person Reports; U.S. Treaty-body Reports; Universal Period Review; Advancing Freedom and Democracy Reports; and International Religious Freedom Reports.

DLR website on Reports: https://www.state.gov/j/ drl/rls/hrrpt/index.htm.

Reports about the human rights of other countries in the world, not the U.S., are: The Human Rights Country Reports; Trafficking-in-Person Reports; Advancing Freedom and Democracy Reports; and International Religious Freedom Reports.

Reports about the U.S. are: U.S. Treaty-body Reports and Universal Period Review Reports.

1. Country Reports on Human Rights Practices (Country Reports)

This report prepared by DLR is a major source of up-to-date information about the human rights records of almost every country in the world. According to the DLR, "The annual Country Reports on Human Rights Practices, also known as the Human Rights Reports, cover internationally recognized individual, civil, political, and worker rights, as set forth in the Universal Declaration of Human Rights and other international agreements."

Several of the Primary Source Documents, below, are from different parts of that Country Report Process, the Secretary's Preface, and the Overview; for example, Document 2 is a sample section of the 2016 Country Report. Document 6 is an excerpt from the 2016 Report on Russia.

2. Report to Congress on International Religious Freedom (CIRF Report)

This report, prepared by DLR is the annual Report to Congress on International Religious Freedom, also known as the International Religious Freedom Report, describes the status of religious freedom, government policies violating religious belief and practices of groups, religious denominations and individuals, and U.S. policies promoting religious freedom. It is used by the Administration in forming foreign policy. See an excerpt from this report in Chapter 8 on Freedom of Religion. This report is submitted in compliance with the International Religious Freedom Act of 1998, and is the official report of the U.S. Commission on International Religious Freedom, a bi-partisan body created by that Act.

Primary Source Documents in Chapter 14, Freedom of Thought, Conscience, Religion or Belief, include an excerpt of the USCIRF annual Report on Freedom of Religion.

3. Trafficking in Persons Report

The Trafficking in Persons (TIP) Report assesses governments on their efforts to combat trafficking in persons as defined in the U.N. Trafficking Protocol, including conduct involved in forced labor and trafficking of adults and children for commercial sexual exploitation. It is prepared by the U.S. Department of State, Office to Monitor and Combat Trafficking in Persons.

It is submitted in compliance with the Victims of Trafficking And Violence Prevention Act Of 2000.

Document 7, below, is an excerpt from the Department of State website report on Trafficking.

4. United States Universal Periodic Review National Report, and Related Documents

Since 2010, the DLR has been preparing documents for the U.S. for its human rights review in the U.N., known as the Universal Period Review. This report provides a partial snapshot of the human rights situation in the United States and shares some recent progress, while exploring opportunities to make further progress. The United States submitted its report to the U.N. High Commissioner for Human Rights in 2010 and again in 2015.

Primary Source Documents in Chapter 6, U.S., U.N. and Human Rights Law, include the U.S. National Reports prepared for the UPR Process and others prepared by the DLR.

The report reflects input collected during an extensive program of consultations with the American public in preparing these reports. Most likely, few Americans knew this process was going on. Many CSOs participated in these consultations, but submitted shadow reports about their concerns for their respective human rights records directly to the Office of High Commissioner to be considered in the U.S. UPR process.

The following Department of State calendar chart shows when and where the most recent consultations took place. These are in preparation for the year 2020, third cycle UPR process of the U.S. This process should have the attention of all U.S. CSOs who might wish to input this consultation process with their information and documentation of their concerns.

Calendar for UPR Working Group Civil Society Consultations — 2016
U.S. Department of State, Washington, D.C., 07-12-2016

Working Group	Topics	Lead Agencies	Tentative Date/Location
1	Civil Rights and Discrimination	U.S. Department of Justice – Civil Rights Division	August 4, 2016 10:30 AM - 1:00 PM U.S. Department of State 2201 C Street NW, Room 1105 Washington, DC RSVP to: UPR.civilrights@usdoj.gov
2	Criminal Justice	U.S. Department of Justice – Criminal Division	August 1, 2016 1:30-4:00 PM U.S. Department of State 2201 C Street NW, Room 1408 Washington, DC RSVP to: UPR.criminaljustice@usdoj.gov
3	Economic, Social, and Cultural Rights, Indigenous Peoples, and the Environment	U.S. Department of Housing and Urban Development U.S. Department of the Interior	August 17, 2016 10:00 AM - 4:00 PM U.S. Department of Housing and Urban Development 451 7th Street SW Washington, DC RSVP to: UPRWorkingGroup3@state.gov
4	National Security	U.S. Department of Defense Office of the Director of National Intelligence	June 9, 2016 2:00 PM - 5:00 PM U.S. Department of State 2201 C Street NW, Room 1408 Washington, DC
5	Immigration, Migrants, Trafficking, Labor, and Children	U.S. Department of Homeland Security U.S. Department of Labor	September 15, 2016 Washington, DC
6	Treaties, International Mechanisms, and Domestic Implementation	U.S. Department of State	April 27, 2016 10:00 AM - 12:00 PM U.S. Department of State 2201 C Street NW, Room 1482 Washington, DC

Note: updated 7/12/16

5. U.S. Treaty (Body) Reports

Chapter 6 of this work discusses the different treaty-based bodies to which the U.S., as a state party, must submit periodic states' reports. These are self-reporting by and about the U.S., based on the individual normative articles of the human rights treaties, such as the Convention against Torture. They are submitted to the treaty-body to allow it to evaluate how the U.S. is doing in complying with the subject treaty. These reports are long and detailed, and a valuable source of information about the U.S.

United Nations human rights treaties require states' parties to report periodically on the implementation of their treaty obligations. U.S. Government agencies collaborate to fulfill the United States' obligations.

6. Advancing Freedom and Democracy Report

The Advancing Freedom and Democracy Report describes U.S. efforts to support democracy and human rights in non-democratic countries and in those countries undergoing democratic transitions. This report is prepared by the DLR and is submitted in compliance with the ADVANCE Democracy Act of 2007.

According to the DLR: "The United States periodically produces additional reports on the specific human rights situations around the world. They include: the 2010 Anti-Semitism Compendium; the 2008 Contemporary Global Anti-Semitism Report; the 2006 Foreign Labor Trends Reports on Uzbekistan, the United Kingdom and India; the 2005 Report on Global Anti-Semitism; the 2001 Labor Diplomacy Report; and the 2001 Report on the Taliban's War Against Women."

Primary Source Documents

I. CHART (ORGANOGRAM) OF THE U.S. DEPARTMENT OF STATE

This chart shows the structure and different parts of the U.S. Department of State. It is particularly the last row on the right which deal with human rights. The Department of State should help the U.S. act in a way that results in the respect and protection of human rights outside the U.S. The Department itself should work as a model of human rights. Human rights norms bind governments to all those whom they serve and the government body should act consistent with International Human Rights Law.

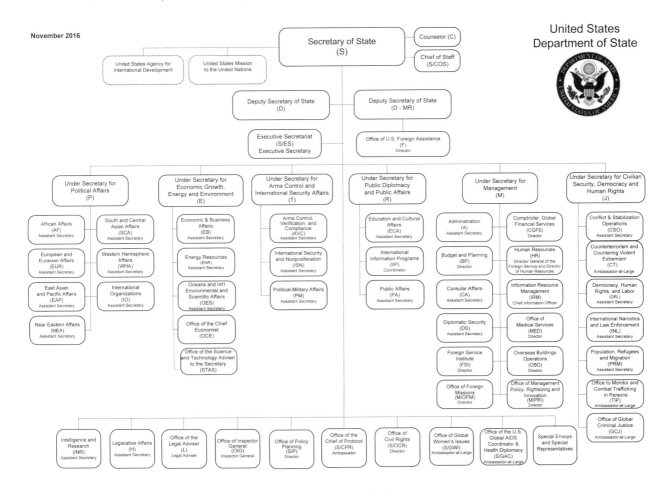

2. STATE DEPARTMENT REPORT OF A JOINT PRESS STATEMENT BY U.S. SECRETARY OF STATE REX TILLERSON, SECRETARY OF HOMELAND SECURITY JOHN KELLY, AND MEXICAN FOREIGN MINISTER LUIS VIDEGARAY CASO AND GOVERNMENT SECRETARY MIGUEL ANGEL OSORIO CHONG, FOREIGN MINISTRY, MEXICO, FEBRUARY 23, 2017

This is a report from the U.S. Department of State announcing a joint press statement from the meeting of Secretary of State Rex Tillerson, Secretary of Homeland Security John Kelly, and Mexican Foreign Minister Luis Videgaray Caso and Government Secretary Miguel Angel Osorio Chong, Foreign Ministry, Mexico in February 2017. This was a meeting between the U.S. government and the Mexican government over issues of mutual concern to both countries. From the U.S. side the issues were U.S. national security as to all the illegal immigrants coming in trough Mexico, about the new U.S. immigration deportation program, about the drug trade and about setting up methods of cooperation between the two countries to deal with the mutual problems. The main concern from the Mexican side is how the U.S. is treating the millions of Mexican nationals in the U.S. and the prospect of many of them being deported ("removed") back to Mexico, and many non-Mexicans also being removed to Mexico, and also the border wall which the U.S. President has promised to build at the Mexico-U.S. border. The purpose of this report is to show how human rights factor into this statement of what was discussed and of concern to both sides.

{Excerpt}

[Text]

Remarks
Rex W. Tillerson, Secretary of State
John Kelly, Secretary of Homeland Security
Mexican Foreign Secretary Luis Videgaray Caso, and
Mexican Government Secretary Miguel Angel Osorio Chong

Foreign Ministry
Mexico City, Mexico

February 23, 2017

Mexican Foreign Secretary Videgaray:

I would like to focus on the migratory topic. We have expressed to both Secretaries Tillerson and Kelly, first of all, our concern, concern to respect the rights of Mexicans living in the United States, and more specifically the human rights. And we have listened to a deep coincident on behalf of both secretaries that this is undoubtedly and a very positive situation that we will face this topic with the mechanics and with dialogues that will continue growing between both of us.

...

We have mentioned that all actions that our countries will decide in their regional security and safety issues or migrations have — they go beyond borders. Therefore, we have to get to a consensus as much as possible. But the Government of Mexico considered that the schemes of co-ordinations and the different mechanisms of co-operations that we have need a permanent dialogue that will set the needs of both countries. In this regard, we insist the need of maintaining the deportation schemes in an ordered fashion so as to guarantee the human rights of all Mexicans in your country.

...

SECRETARY KELLY:

The relationship between the United States and Mexico is among, I believe, the most critical in the world. Not only are we connected by 1,900 miles of border; we are also connected by trade, culture, history, and a commitment to democracy. We cooperate on a wide range of issues, including human rights, economics, energy, environment, climate, security, migration, trafficking, labor, promoting educational and cultural exchanges, and a wide variety of other endeavors.

...

Now, this is something I would really like you all to pay attention to because it is frequently misrepresented or misreported in the press. Let me be very, very clear: There will be no, repeat, no mass deportations. Everything we do in DHS will be done legally and according to human rights and the legal justice system of the United States. All deportations will be according to our legal justice system, which is extensive and includes multiple appeals. The focus of deportations will be on the criminal element that have made it into the United States.

...

[End Text]

Source: U.S. Department of State, Diplomacy in Action, https://www.state.gov/secretary/remarks/2017/02/268029.htm

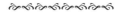

3. DEPARTMENT OF STATE COUNTRY REPORTS ON HUMAN RIGHTS PRACTICES, SECRETARY OF STATE'S PREFACE, 2016

This is the statement by the U.S. Secretary of State Rex W. Tillerson serving as a preface to the 2016 State Department Country Reports. It is the preface to his presentation of the report to the U.S. Congress in early 2017. The report concerns the human rights situation of almost every country in the world during the year 2016. It is primarily to inform the U.S. government, particularly the the Congress and White house and of the human rights record of every country reported so as to allow the President to know how foreign policy may be formulated and used to deal with other states to improve their human rights, and for Congress to pass legislation, both country specific and general to address human rights issues around the world. Globally it is an assessment of the state of the world and social and political trends. This Report is widely used in government and academia and even business. It is used in immigration court cases involving asylum and refugee issues to determine what is the human rights situation in a given country and whether that presents a danger to the alien before the court. An excerpt of an actual Country Report is found in a following Primary Source Document.

[Text]

2016 Department of State Country Reports on Human Rights Practices, Secretary of State's Preface

Secretary's Preface

Promoting human rights and democratic governance is a core element of U.S. foreign policy. These values form an essential foundation of stable, secure, and functioning societies. Standing up for human rights and democracy is not just a moral imperative but is in the best interests of the United States in making the world more stable and secure. The 2016 *Country Reports on Human Rights Practices* (The Human Rights Reports) demonstrate the United States' unwavering commitment to advancing liberty, human dignity, and global prosperity.

This year marks the 41st year the Department of State has produced annual Human Rights Reports. The United States Congress mandated these reports to provide policymakers with a holistic and accurate accounting of human rights conditions in nearly 200 countries and territories worldwide, including all member states of the United Nations and any country receiving U.S. foreign assistance. The reports cover internationally recognized individual civil, political, and worker rights, as set forth in the Universal Declaration of Human Rights and other international instruments.

The Human Rights Reports reflect the concerted efforts of our embassies and consulates to gather the most accurate information possible. They are prepared by human rights officers at U.S. missions around the world who review information available from a wide variety of civil society, government, and other sources. These reports represent thousands of work-hours as each country team collects and analyzes information. The Department of State strives to make the reports objective and uniform in scope and quality.

The Human Rights Reports are used by the U.S. Legislative, Executive, and Judicial Branches as a resource for shaping policy and guiding decisions, informing diplomatic engagements, and determining the allocation of foreign aid and security sector assistance. The Human Rights Reports are also used throughout the world to inform the work of human rights advocates, lawmakers, academics, businesses, multilateral institutions, and NGOs.

The Department of State hopes these reports will help other governments, civil society leaders, activists, and individuals reflect on the situation of human rights in their respective countries and work to promote accountability for violations and abuses.

Our values are our interests when it comes to human rights. The production of these reports underscores our commitment to freedom, democracy, and the human rights guaranteed to all individuals around the world.

I hereby transmit the Department of State's *Country Reports on Human Rights Practices for 2016* to the United States Congress.

Rex W. Tillerson
Secretary of State

[End Text]

Source: U.S. Department of State, Diplomacy in Action
https://www.state.gov/j/drl/rls/hrrpt/humanrightsreport/index.htm#wrapper

4. DEPARTMENT OF STATE COUNTRY REPORTS, WHY AND HOW THEY ARE PREPARED

This is an explanation by the State Department of why the annual Country Report on Human Rights Practices are prepared and how they are prepared. They show the amount of work that goes into the reports and why the report is prepared and submitted every year. The 2015 report is much more informative than the 2016 report. The 2016 webpage on "Why the Reports are Prepared" etc. can be found at https://www.state.gov/j/drl/rls/hrrpt/humanrightsreport/ index.htm#wrapper.

[Text]

HUMANRIGHTS.GOV

WHY THE REPORTS ARE PREPARED

This report is submitted to the Congress by the Department of State in compliance with Sections 116(d) and 502B(b) of the Foreign Assistance Act of 1961 (FAA), as amended. The law provides that the Secretary of State shall transmit to the Speaker of the House of Representatives and the Committee on Foreign Relations of the Senate by February 25 "a full and complete report regarding the status of internationally recognized human rights, within the meaning of subsection (a)...in countries that receive assistance under this part, and...in all other foreign countries which are members of the United Nations and which are not otherwise the subject of a human rights report under this Act." The report represents events for the calendar year 2015 only.

The Department has also included reports on several countries that do not fall into the categories established by these statutes and thus are not covered by the congressional requirement.

In the 1970s the United States formalized its role as an advocate for the promotion and protection of human rights. In 1976 Congress enacted legislation creating a Coordinator of Human Rights in the Department of State, a position later upgraded to Assistant Secretary. Legislation also requires that U.S. foreign and trade policy take into account countries' human rights and worker rights performance and that country reports be submitted to the Congress on an annual basis.

HOW THE REPORTS ARE PREPARED

The Department of State prepared this report using information from U.S. embassies and consulates abroad, foreign government officials, nongovernmental and international organizations, and published reports. U.S. diplomatic missions abroad prepared the initial drafts of the individual country reports, using information gathered throughout the year from a variety of sources, including government officials, jurists, the armed forces, journalists, human rights monitors, academics, and labor activists. This information gathering can be hazardous, and U.S. Foreign Service personnel regularly go to great lengths, under trying and sometimes dangerous conditions, to investigate reports of human rights abuses.

Once the initial drafts of the individual country reports were completed, the Bureau of Democracy, Human Rights, and Labor (DRL), in cooperation with other Department of State offices, worked to corroborate, analyze, and edit the reports, drawing on their own sources of information. These sources included reports provided by U.S. and other human rights groups, foreign government officials, representatives from the United Nations and other international and regional organizations and institutions, experts from academia, and the media. Bureau officers also consulted experts on worker rights, refugee issues, military and police topics, women's issues, and legal matters, among many others. The guiding principle was that all information be reported objectively, thoroughly, and fairly.

These reports are a resource for shaping policy; conducting diplomacy; and making assistance, training, and other government-related resource allocations. The reports serve also as a basis for U.S. government cooperation with private groups to promote the observance of internationally recognized human rights.

The Country Reports on Human Rights Practices cover internationally recognized civil and political rights, including those set forth in the Universal Declaration of Human Rights, as well as worker rights. As a whole, these include the rights not to be subjected to torture or other cruel, inhuman, or degrading treatment or punishment; to prolonged detention without charges; to disappearance or clandestine detention; and to other flagrant violations of the right to life, liberty, and the security of the person.

Universal human rights seek to incorporate respect for human dignity into the processes of government and law. All individuals have the right to nationality and the right to enjoy basic freedoms, such as freedoms of expression, association, peaceful assembly, movement, and religion or belief, without discrimination on the basis of race, religion, national origin, or gender. The right to join a free trade union is a necessary condition of a free society and economy. Thus the reports assess key internationally recognized worker rights, including the right of association, the right to organize and bargain collectively, the prohibition of forced or compulsory labor, the status of child labor practices, the minimum age for employment of children, discrimination with respect to employment, and acceptable work conditions.

DRL uses hyperlinks to other key human rights documents produced by the Department of State. Specifically, readers are asked to follow hyperlinks for complete information on religious freedom issues by consulting the *International Religious Freedom Report* and the *Trafficking in Persons Report*. Additionally linked are the Department of Labor's *Findings on the Worst Forms of Child Labor* report and several current publications produced by the Department's Consular Affairs Bureau on international child abductions, if applicable to the country in question.

[End Text]

Source: U.S. State Department, Diplomacy in Action
https://www.state.gov/j/drl/rls/hrrpt/humanrightsreport/index.htm#wrapper

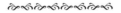

5. COUNTRY REPORTS ON HUMAN RIGHTS PRACTICES 2015, INTRODUCTION, DEPARTMENT OF STATE

This is the Introduction to the huge report known as the Country Report on Human Rights Practices. It is from the DRL and it introduces last year's annual report, the 2015 Country Reports. This is not the Introduction to the 2016 Report, which includes little information. The following is from the Obama Administration presentation by Secretary Kerry.

[Text]

This year marks the 40th anniversary of the annual *Country Reports on Human Rights Practices.*

One of the fundamental guarantees of the Universal Declaration of Human Rights is freedom of association — the freedom of people everywhere to form or join groups to protect their interests, advance their beliefs, and improve their communities.

Civil society encompasses almost all forms of organized social activity independent of government control: charitable groups that fight hunger and poverty; cultural organizations that promote the arts; professional organizations that set standards for their members; chambers of commerce that advocate for private business; labor unions that protect workers; environmental groups that champion clean water and air; neighborhood watch groups that prevent crime; and so on. Some civil society organizations provide services to people in a way that complements the work of governments, or fill a void where government is absent or negligent. Some provide advice to governments, suggesting programs and policies to make their countries more prosperous, just, and secure. Others help to hold governments accountable to their citizens by exposing problems like corruption and human rights abuses, and urging corrective action.

Over the last several decades, civil society has grown stronger in every part of the world. This has given ordinary citizens more power and responsibility. But it has also threatened governments that wish to monopolize power and evade responsibility. Such governments have been pushing back against citizen-led activism with increasing vigor and viciousness. In 2015, this global crackdown by authoritarian states on civil society deepened, silencing independent voices, impoverishing political discourse, and closing avenues for peaceful change.

Authoritarian governments stifle civil society because they fear public scrutiny, and feel threatened by people coming together in ways they cannot control. Since it would be embarrassing to admit this, they sometimes offer other, more reasonable sounding excuses for repressing or suppressing funding for non-governmental organizations. Here are some of the most common ones made in the last year, with a rejoinder to each:

"No one elected civil society — it is not representative or accountable." We expect governments to be elected and to answer to the people as a whole because governments have the power to coerce people to obey their decisions. Civil society organizations do not have that power — all they can do is to propose policies and ideas, something that people should have a right to come together to do, whether they represent a large or small segment of their societies. If governments — or the majority of people in a country — do not like what a civil society group is saying, they can ignore it. There is no need to prevent such a group from operating.

"Foreign funded NGOs threaten national sovereignty." It is true that some civil society organizations, especially in countries that do not yet have a tradition of private philanthropy, seek funding from outside their countries. But such organizations do not gain influence unless they also have strong roots in their communities. Where they are allowed to exist and raise funding for their work, such grass roots NGOs give their local constituencies a far bigger voice than they would otherwise have. Ironically, many of the governments that complain about foreign donations to their civil society accept large amounts of foreign assistance themselves, without conceding any loss of independence.

"The United States also regulates foreign funding of its civil society." This argument is generally made in reference to the U.S. Foreign Agent Registration Act, or FARA. But FARA only applies to people or organizations working under the direction or control of a foreign government or political party to represent that government's or party's interests in the United States. It does not apply to foreign funding of NGOs that provide services to the public or merely because such NGOs engage in advocacy inside the United States. The European Union, for example, funds civil society groups that, on their own initiative, lobby for various causes in the United States, such as the abolition of the death penalty and U.S. membership in the International Criminal Court. No U.S. law restricts such funding or imposes any special burdens on those receiving it.

"Regulating civil society is necessary to prevent financing of terrorism." It is true that fake charities have sometimes been used to channel funds to violent extremist groups. But most countries already have laws against terrorist financing. What is needed to enforce those laws is good intelligence and effective policing targeted against terrorists, not the imposition of stifling requirements on peaceful groups engaged in legitimate social service and activism.

In fact, a free and active civil society is often our strongest bulwark *against* the spread of violent extremism. Where there is injustice or suffering, civil society gives people peaceful means to organize against it, diminishing the appeal of the terrorists' argument that violence is the only viable way. Where violent extremist groups do seek to gain influence, local grass-roots civil society organizations can sometimes stand up against them more effectively than any government security agency. It is no surprise that one of the first things the terrorist organization Da'esh did when it took over the Syrian city of Raqqa was to kill or drive away civil society activists working to defend human rights and provide community services there. In fact, failed governance combined with repression of local civic activism helped Da'esh to take territory in Syria and Iraq and continued to provide an enabling environment for Da'esh and its affiliates, notably in the Sinai, Libya, and Yemen.

On the other hand, when governments take the criticism of civil society seriously, they can make progress against violent extremist groups. In Nigeria, Cameroon, Chad, and Niger, deadly attacks and abductions by Boko Haram continued to terrorize thousands of civilians. Nigerian security forces' heavy-handed tactics and abuses of civilians, including extrajudicial killings, contributed to the mutation of Boko Haram into an insurgency. Recognizing that it would not defeat Boko Haram as long as civilians felt threatened by security forces, the Nigerian government intensified its efforts to institute military reforms to better protect human rights and builds trust with civilian populations.

The strategies and tactics used to restrict civil society throughout the year varied.

Many governments continued to use direct and overt means to repress civil society within their countries.

Historically authoritarian regimes like the Democratic People's Republic of Korea (DPRK), Cuba, China, Iran, Sudan, and Uzbekistan continued to control political activity and ban or limit political opposition.

In Cuba, the constitution recognizes the Communist Party as the only legal party and "the superior leading force of society and of the state." State-orchestrated "acts of repudiation" prevented independent civil society groups and individuals from participating in meetings or events. State security continued its practice of arbitrary, short-term detentions to impede the exercise of freedoms of expression and peaceful assembly. The government also re-arrested several political prisoners it had released in January 2015 who had continued their activism during the year.

Members of Sudan's human rights community and civil society highlighted concerns including harassment, intimidation, detention, government restrictions on their ability to operate, and severe violations of religious freedom.

In China, repression and coercion markedly increased during the year against organizations and individuals involved in civil and political rights advocacy. The crackdown on the legal community was particularly severe. The All-China Federation of Trade Unions also undermined freedom of association by maintaining a variety of mechanisms to influence the selection of trade union representatives and undertaking activities to disrupt labor rights advocacy.

In Laos, the government continued to restrict individuals' rights to freedom of association. Political groups other than mass organizations approved by the Lao People's Revolutionary Party remained prohibited. The government occasionally tried to influence board membership of civil society organizations and forced some organizations to change their names to remove words it deemed sensitive, such as "rights."

Russia instituted a range of measures to suppress dissent. The government passed new repressive laws and selectively employed existing ones systematically to harass, discredit, prosecute, imprison, detain, fine, and suppress individuals and organizations engaged in activities critical of the government, including NGOs, independent media outlets, bloggers, the political opposition, and activists. Individuals and organizations that professed support for the government of Ukraine or opposed the Russian government's aggressive actions in Ukraine were especially targeted.

In Ukraine's region of Crimea, Russian occupation authorities deprived members of certain groups, in particular Ukrainians and Crimean Tatars, of the ability to speak out in support of their nationality and ethnicity and of opposition to the occupation, and subjected them to systematic harassment and discrimination. Occupation authorities subjected persons who refused Russian citizenship to discrimination in accessing education, health, and employment. Independent NGOs and media organizations have almost all been forced to flee the peninsula or go underground.

The political space in Rwanda and the overall human rights environment continued to shrink. There were reports of targeted killings, and an increasing number of reports of disappearances and harassment of civil society groups and opposition parties.

Public criticism of Democratic Republic of Congo government officials and government conduct or decisions regarding matters such as public affairs management, democracy, and corruption sometimes resulted in harsh responses, often from the National Intelligence Agency, and, less frequently, from provincial authorities and influential personalities.

In Venezuela, the law made insulting the president punishable by six to 30 months in prison, with those charged being held without bail pending trials, with lesser penalties for insulting lower-ranking officials. Venezuelan law provided that inaccurate reporting that disturbs the public peace was punishable by prison terms of two to five years. The requirement that the media disseminate only "true" information was undefined and open to politically motivated interpretation. Dozens of dissenting individuals have been detained and remain political prisoners, many awaiting due process.

Following weeks of protests throughout the Oromia Region in Ethiopia that began in late November, there have been reports of violent clashes between protesters and security forces resulting in deaths, injuries, the destruction of private property, and arbitrary detentions. There were reports of security forces arbitrarily detaining students on university campuses in connection with the protests.

The operating space for activists and NGOs in Azerbaijan remained severely constrained. Multiple sources reported a continuing crackdown on civil society, including intimidation, arrest, and conviction on charges widely considered politically motivated; criminal investigations into NGO activities; restrictive laws; and the freezing of bank accounts, which rendered many groups unable to function.

Another common strategy is to use overly broad counterterrorism or national security laws — or interpretation of those laws — to stifle civil society activity.

In Malaysia, the government selectively enforced laws, particularly the Sedition Act, which the Prime Minister had promised to repeal, reportedly in an effort to intimidate critics.? These efforts led to dozens of investigations, detentions, arrests, and charges against opposition politicians, civil society, journalists, and others.

The Government of Tajikistan took steps to eliminate political opposition in 2015. The Islamic Revival Party of Tajikistan (IRPT) lost its two parliamentary seats through elections that observers characterized as not administered in a fair manner. Following unrest in the capital in September, the Supreme Court officially banned the IRPT, forcing the closure of the IRPT's official newspaper, and prohibiting the distribution of any video, audio, or printed materials related to the party's activities.

In Turkey, the government has used anti-terror laws as well as a law against insulting the president to stifle legitimate political discourse and investigative journalism — prosecuting journalists and ordinary citizens and driving opposition media outlets out of business or bringing them under state control. Wide leeway granted to prosecutors and judges contributed to politically motivated investigations and court verdicts that were not consistent with the law or with rulings in similar cases.

Some governments deployed burdensome administrative and bureaucratic procedures as a means to restrict freedom of association and stifle civil society.

This year in central Asia, Tajikistan, Uzbekistan, and Kazakhstan passed or enacted new NGO legislation or related amendments that could restrict operating space for civil society organizations. Meanwhile, Turkmenistan already had and enforced a restrictive NGO law. In Hungary, international organizations and human rights NGOs continued to voice criticism of the systematic erosion of the rule of law, checks and balances, democratic institutions, transparency, and intimidation of independent civil society voices. There was also concern over the government's handling of large numbers of migrants and asylum seekers, sometimes marked by xenophobic rhetoric and a lack of humanitarian aid.

In Iran, the government restricted the operations of and did not cooperate with local or international human rights NGOs investigating alleged violations of human rights. By law NGOs must register with the Interior Ministry and apply for permission to receive foreign grants. Independent human rights groups and other NGOs faced continued harassment because of their activism as well as the threat of closure by government officials following prolonged and often arbitrary delays in obtaining official registration.

Authorities in Egypt used restrictive registration laws to investigate leading human rights organizations. The Ministry of Social Solidarity dissolved approximately 500 NGOs in 2015, largely linked to the Muslim Brotherhood. Remaining NGOs operate under tight scrutiny, with many reporting harassment by Egyptian authorities. The government also initiated investigations into the receipt of foreign funding by several human rights organizations. Human rights organizations claimed that these actions would force them to curtail their activities. In 2015, the Egyptian government sometimes imposed travel bans on human rights defenders and political activists.

A government board in Kenya canceled the licenses and froze the bank accounts of two NGOs for alleged links to terrorism. Critics accused the government of targeting the NGOs for their outspoken criticism of the government's human rights record. A later court decision ordered the government to unfreeze the NGOs' bank accounts.

In Cambodia, a Ministry of Interior directive prohibits publishers and editors from disseminating stories that insult or defame not just the king, but also government leaders and institutions. The government regularly cited national security concerns to justify restricting individuals' ability to criticize government policies and officials. In particular, the government routinely threatened to prosecute and arrest anyone who questioned the government's demarcation of the country's eastern border or suggested the government had ceded national territory to another country.

On November 26, the parliament of Uganda passed an NGO Act that aims "to provide a conducive and enabling environment" for NGOs and to "register, regulate, coordinate, and monitor" NGO activities. Parliament worked closely with civil society leaders on the bill and adopted most civil society recommendations in a parliamentary committee report. While most of this report was incorporated in the final bill, Parliament left intact a clause on "special obligations" that requires NGOs to receive approval from the local NGO monitoring committee and local governments before initiating activities and prohibits NGOs from engaging in acts "prejudicial to the interests of Uganda and the dignity of the people of Uganda."

In Nicaragua, domestic NGOs under government investigation reported problems accessing the justice system and delays in filing petitions, as well as pressure from state authorities. Many NGOs believed comptroller and tax authorities audited their accounts as a means of intimidation. While legally permitted, spot audits were a common form of harassment and often used selectively, according to NGOs.

In Bolivia, the president, vice president, and government ministers repeatedly criticized the work of NGOs and social organizations not allied with the government. Some NGOs alleged that government registration mechanisms were purposefully stringent in order to limit independent organizations in the country.

Vietnam's legal and regulatory framework established mechanisms for restricting the ability of NGOs to act and organize. The government used complex and politicized registration systems for NGOs and religious organizations to suppress unwelcome political and religious participation. Independent labor activists seeking to form unions separate from the Vietnam General Confederation of Labor or to inform workers of their labor rights also continued to face government harassment.

Pakistan's new policies governing the registration and activities of international NGOs included bans on their participation in "political activities" and "anti-state activities," but neither defined these terms nor indicated what body would be responsible for arbitrating claims against international NGOs. Many international NGOs expressed concern that authorities would use these prohibitions to curtail work on projects related to governance or human rights advocacy.

In Ecuador, the government continued to restrict independent media and civil society by using copyright laws to force takedown of web content.

The 2015 *Country Reports on Human Rights Practices* document these cases and hundreds more.

[End Text]

Source: U.S. Department of State, Diplomacy in Action website
https://www.state.gov/j/drl/rls/hrrpt/humanrightsreport/index.htm#wrapper

❦❦❦❦❦❦❦❦

6. COUNTRY REPORT ON HUMAN RIGHTS PRACTICES FOR 2016, DEPARTMENT OF STATE, RUSSIA

This is an excerpt from an actual 2016 Country Report about Russia. This type of report is done for every country covered by the Country Reports. The excerpt is part of the Executive Summary.

At the time of this writing, Russia and the U.S. were embroiled in a political controversy over possible interference with the 2016 presidential elections, and the issue of contact between members of the Trump administration and the Russian government. This Report informs Americans as to how the Department of State sees the human rights record of Russia for the year 2016.

{Excerpt}

[Text]

Country Reports on Human Rights Practices for 2016

Russia

Permalink: http://www.state.gov/j/drl/rls/hrrpt/humanrightsreport/index.htm?year=2016&dlid=265466

EXECUTIVE SUMMARY

The Russian Federation has a highly centralized, authoritarian political system dominated by President Vladimir Putin. The bicameral Federal Assembly consists of a directly elected lower house (State Duma) and an appointed upper house (Federation Council), both of which lacked independence from the executive. State Duma elections during 2016 and the presidential election in 2012 were marked by accusations of government interference and manipulation of the electoral process.

Security forces generally reported to civilian authorities, except in some areas of the North Caucasus.

The continuing occupation and purported "annexation" of Ukraine's Crimean Peninsula continued to affect the human rights situation significantly and negatively. The government continued to train, equip, and supply pro-Russian forces in eastern Ukraine, who were joined by numerous fighters from Russia. Credible observers attributed thousands of civilian deaths and injuries, as well as widespread abuses, to Russian-backed separatists in Ukraine's Donbas region, and to Russian occupation authorities in Crimea (see the *Country Reports on Human Rights* for Ukraine). Authorities also conducted politically motivated arrests, detentions, and trials of Ukrainian citizens in Russia, many of whom claimed to have been tortured. Human rights groups asserted that numerous Ukrainian citizens remained in Russia as political prisoners.

The most significant human rights problems were:

Restrictions on Political Participation and Freedom of Expression, Assembly, and Media: Authorities restricted citizens' ability to choose their government through free and fair elections and increasingly instituted a range of measures to suppress dissent. The government passed repressive laws and selectively employed existing ones to harass, discredit, prosecute, imprison, detain, fine, and suppress individuals and organizations critical of the government. Amendments to antiterrorism laws, known as the "Yarovaya package," granted authorities sweeping powers. Authorities especially targeted individuals and organizations that professed support for the government of Ukraine or opposed the Russian government's activities in Ukraine.

Suppression of Civil Society: Authorities further stymied the work of nongovernmental organizations (NGOs) through the "foreign agents" and "undesirable foreign organization" laws. Authorities also significantly expanded the definition of political activities to bring more NGOs under the "foreign agents" category. Authorities began fining NGOs for not disclosing "foreign agent" status, while courts closed NGOs for violations involving the foreign agents' list. Under the expanded definition of political activities, authorities added environmental and HIV-prevention organizations to the list.

Government Discrimination against Minorities: Authorities continued to discriminate against members of some religious and ethnic minorities; lesbian, gay, bisexual, transgender, and intersex (LGBTI) persons; and migrant workers. The Yarovaya package restricted "missionary activity," including preaching, proselytizing, disseminating religious materials, or engaging in interfaith discussion; authorities used it to harass religious minorities. Authorities utilized a law prohibiting "propaganda" of nontraditional sexual relations to minors to harass the LGBTI community.

Other problems included allegations of torture and excessive force by law enforcement officers that sometimes led to deaths; prison overcrowding, and substandard and life-threatening prison conditions; executive branch pressure on the judiciary; lack of due process in politically motivated cases; electoral irregularities; extensive official corruption; violence against women; limits on women's rights; trafficking in persons; discrimination against persons with disabilities; social stigma against persons with HIV/AIDS; and limitations on workers' rights.

The government failed to take adequate steps to prosecute or punish most officials who committed abuses, resulting in a climate of impunity.

Conflict in the North Caucasus between government forces, insurgents, Islamist militants, and criminals led to numerous abuses, including killings, torture, physical abuse, politically motivated abductions, and a general degradation in the rule of law. Ramzan Kadyrov's government in Chechnya generally did not investigate or prosecute abuses, and security forces committed abuses with impunity.

SECTION 1. RESPECT FOR THE INTEGRITY OF THE PERSON, INCLUDING FREEDOM FROM:

a. Arbitrary Deprivation of Life and other Unlawful or Politically Motivated Killings

There were several reports that the government or its agents committed arbitrary or unlawful killings. In the North Caucasus, both authorities and local militants reportedly carried out numerous extrajudicial killings (see section 1.g.).

Prison officials and police allegedly subjected inmates and suspects in custody to physical abuse that in some instances resulted in death (see section 1.c., Prison and Detention Center Conditions). On July 15, police in Ingushetia separately questioned Marem Daliyeva and her husband Magomed Daliyev for suspected involvement in a bank robbery. During the interrogation law enforcement officials insulted and threatened Daliyeva, then covered her head in a black bag, and took her to an undisclosed location for further questioning. They continued to hit her and administered electric shock to her hands and her abdomen. They returned her to the police station and held her for an additional two hours before she was released and learned that her husband had died during his questioning. As a result of complaints filed by Daliyeva, on July 19 the Investigative Committee opened a criminal case on exceeding authority and violating the rights of a citizen. As of August 12, the investigation had not yet determined responsibility for Daliyev's death or treatment during interrogation.

Physical abuse continued to be a problem in the armed forces. While there were no clear examples of physical abuse leading to death, there were cases of suspicious deaths. In one example, commanding officers deemed the death of conscript Andrey Shlychkov in March a suicide in their official account. The family claimed that senior officers beat the conscript to death, and then hanged him to suggest a suicide. The family claimed that accounts from fellow conscripts and bruising on Shlychkov's body supported this version. The Committee for the Social Protection of Servicemen in Bashkiriya was investigating the cause of death, and a criminal investigation into whether the case involved instigation to suicide was underway.

In February 2015 opposition politician Boris Nemtsov, deputy prime minister during the administration of Boris Yeltsin, was shot and killed on the streets of Moscow near the Kremlin. Authorities ultimately arrested five Chechens for the crime, with an additional suspect killed in an attempt to apprehend him in Chechnya. On October 3, the jury trial of the suspects began in a military court, with all five of the defendants pleading not guilty. One of the defendants, Zaur Dadayev, was formerly deputy commander of the North battalion of the Interior Troops of the Ministry of Internal Affairs in Chechnya. Reports indicated that Dadayev might have held a position within the ministry at the time of the killing. Dadayev confessed to the killing before recanting, claiming he had been tortured while in detention. He implied that he had received orders for Nemtsov's killing from Ruslan Geremeyev, another officer who served in the North battalion. The court summoned Geremeyev to testify as a witness on December 13, but Geremeyev did not appear in court.

Russian authorities were unable to identify Geremeyev's whereabouts. In December 2015 investigators charged Dadayev, Anzor Gubashev, Khamzat Bakhayev, Shadid Gubashev, and Temirlan Eskerkhanov with committing the murder as part of an organized group and illegally purchasing, carrying, transporting, and storing firearms.

The country played a significant military role in conflicts outside of its borders, in Syria and in eastern Ukraine, where human rights organizations attributed thousands of civilian deaths as well as other human rights abuses to Russian-backed separatists and Russian occupation authorities in Crimea (see *Country Reports on Human Rights* for Ukraine). Since September 2015 the country has conducted military operations including airstrikes in the continuing conflict in Syria. According to human rights organizations, the country's forces have taken actions such as bombing urban areas and humanitarian aid convoys during the conflict, including purposefully targeting civilians (see *Country Reports on Human Rights* for Syria).

In January a British public inquiry into the death in 2006 of Alexander Litvinenko, a former secret police (KGB) officer turned whistleblower and Putin critic, concluded that two Russian nationals, Andrey Lugovoy and Dmitriy Kuvtun, poisoned Litvinenko with a rare radioactive isotope, polonium 210, in London. The report also found it was probable that President Putin and the Federal Security Service (FSB) chief at the time, Nikolay Patrushev, had approved the killing, which was likely an FSB operation.

b. Disappearance

Enforced disappearances for both political and financial reasons continued in the North Caucasus (see section 1.g.). According to the 2016 report of the U.N. Working Group on Enforced or Involuntary Disappearances, there were 480 outstanding cases of enforced or involuntary disappearances in the country.

Security forces were allegedly responsible for the kidnapping and disappearance of asylum seekers from Central Asia, particularly Uzbekistan and Tajikistan (see section 2.d.).

c. Torture and Other Cruel, Inhuman, or Degrading Treatment or Punishment

Although the constitution prohibits such practices, numerous credible reports indicated that law enforcement personnel engaged in torture, abuse, and violence to coerce confessions from suspects, and authorities generally did not hold officials accountable for such actions. If law enforcement officers were prosecuted, they were typically charged with simple assault or exceeding their authority. According to human rights activists, judges often elected instead to use laws against abuse of power, because this definition, according to legal statutes, better captures the difference in authority between an officer of the law and the private individual who was abused.

There were reports of deaths as a result of torture (see section 1.a.).

Physical abuse of suspects by police officers was reportedly systemic and usually occurred within the first few days of arrest. Reports from human rights groups and former police officers indicated that police most often used electric shocks, suffocation, and stretching or applying pressure to joints and ligaments because those methods were considered less likely to leave visible marks. In the North Caucasus, local law enforcement organizations as well as federal security services reportedly committed torture (see section 1.g.).

In one example, on November 1, the independent news outlet *Meduza* published a letter written by jailed activist Ildar Dadin to his wife alleging that he and other inmates were being systematically tortured and threatened with death if they tried to complain. As of November 3, the head of the IK-7 prison in Segezha where Dadin was held, Sergey Kossiyev, had reportedly resigned, and the federal Investigative Committee announced that prosecutors had been sent to the prison to look into the allegations. Presidential spokesman Dmitriy Peskov said the allegations deserved "very close attention" and that President Putin would be informed about the matter. In 2015 Dadin was the first person to be convicted under a new legal provision that criminalizes repeated violations of the law on public events (see section 2.b).

Authorities reportedly tortured defendants and witnesses involved in high-profile trials. Ukrainians Mykola Karpyuk and Stanislav Klikh, convicted on May 26 for participating in military activities against Russian armed forces during the conflict in Chechnya in the 1990s, claimed that statements they made during the investigation were made under torture. According to Karpyuk authorities also threatened to kidnap and torture his son.

Arrests and court decisions related to police torture continued to come from the Republic of Tatarstan. On June 18, authorities arrested Nazilya Gainatullina, the head of the training department in the local federal penitentiary service in Tatarstan, for exceeding authority with the use of force. This arrest arose as a result of video footage released from a Kazan prison showing convicted criminals standing facing a wall while being hit by police officers.

Police and individuals operating with the tacit approval of authorities conducted attacks on political and human rights activists, critics of government policies, and persons linked to the opposition.

On March 9, a group of masked men beat two members of the Committee for the Prevention of Torture and six journalists traveling with them on a reporting tour between Ingushetia and Chechnya. The journalists included a Norwegian, a Swede, and six Russians, two of whom were human rights activists. According to Human Rights Watch (HRW), at least 15 men stopped the minibus carrying the eight persons and their driver. The attackers burned the group's minibus. All were injured, and five were hospitalized. No one has been prosecuted for the attack. While a government spokesperson called the attack "unacceptable," HRW reported that "authorities' utter failure to hold anyone to account" gave a green light to further attacks.

On March 16 in Chechnya, a mob of unidentified individuals attacked human rights defender Igor Kalyapin, head of the Committee for the Prevention of Torture. They hit him and threw eggs, antiseptic liquid, and flour on him. Local authorities investigated the attack but never filed charges.

Reports by refugees, NGOs, and the press suggested a pattern of police carrying out beatings, arrests, and extortions of persons whose ethnic makeup was assumed to be Romani, Central Asian, African, or of a Caucasus nationality.

There were multiple reports of authorities' detaining defendants for psychiatric evaluations for up to 30 days as a means of pressuring them or sending them for psychiatric treatment as a means of punishing them. On May 6, authorities forcibly removed Voronezh activist Dmitriy Vorobyovskiy from his home and took him to a psychiatric hospital where they tied him to a bed for three hours and injected him with unknown substances, according to his attorney. He remained in the hospital and has not yet been brought before a judge; no charges have been filed. Human rights groups called for his release, noting that his detention appeared linked to his frequent protests in Voronezh against the government and in support of political prisoners.

Nonlethal physical abuse and hazing continued to be a problem in the armed forces, although violations related to hazing in the military were fewer than in previous years. The NGO Union of Committees of Soldiers' Mothers confirmed that a decrease of incidents of "dedovshchina" (a pattern of hazing) in 2015 continued into 2016.

In March 2015 the St. Petersburg City Court found that military commissioners violated recruits' rights by not taking into account their medical files. There were continued problems with recruits medically unfit for duty being forced to enter into the army. NGOs reported complaints from conscripts drafted into service despite their claims of poor health. Soldiers returning from fighting in Ukraine also complained to NGOs of obstacles in receiving health care, because medical files had not been kept. Suicide among recruits continued to be a problem.

Prison and Detention Center Conditions

Conditions in prisons and detention centers varied but were sometimes harsh and life threatening. Overcrowding, abuse by guards and inmates, limited access to health care, food shortages, and inadequate sanitation were common in prisons, penal colonies, and other detention facilities.

Physical Conditions: Authorities held prisoners and detainees in the following types of facilities: temporary police detention centers, pretrial detention facilities, correctional labor colonies (ITKs), prisons (including prisons for those who violate ITK rules), medical correctional facilities, and educational labor colonies for juveniles. Correctional colonies varied according to security regime, from light to maximum security. Unofficial prisons, many of which were located in the North Caucasus, reportedly continued to operate. While the penal code establishes the separation of women and men, juveniles and adults, and pretrial detainees and convicts into separate quarters, there was anecdotal evidence that not all prison facilities followed these rules.

Prison overcrowding remained a serious problem. Although the federal minimum standard of space per person in detention is 26 square feet, Presidential Human Rights Council member Andrey Babushkin reported in October 2015 that inmates were being confined to spaces far below the mandatory minimum, particularly in prison facilities in larger cities. As of the end of 2015, according to the Prosecutor General's Office, 54 pretrial detention facilities in 24 regions of the country did not provide detainees the mandatory amount of space. The situation was particularly concerning in pretrial detention facilities in Moscow. As of December 2015, all facilities in Moscow were crowded beyond capacity and seven of them were overextended by 27 percent. The size of the country's prison population exacerbated the overcrowding. According to the most recent data available, prisons were operating at approximately 95 percent of capacity in 2014, up from 90 percent in 2013.

Penal Reform International reported conditions were generally better in women's colonies than in men's but remained substandard. Thirteen women's facilities also contained facilities for underage children of inmates who had no options for housing them with friends or relatives.

On April 27, Prosecutor General Yuriy Chayka announced that in 2015 approximately 4,000 individuals died in prison facilities and that the overwhelming majority of deaths were related to poor medical care. According to his report, 87 percent of deaths related to various diseases.

In the first six months of the year, 49 persons died in police stations, pretrial detention, or temporary detention, according to a tally maintained by the website *Russian Ebola*. Causes of death included medical conditions, suicide, and injuries sustained while in detention. In the second quarter of the year, 20 detainees died, nine of whom died in police stations, seven in temporary detention centers, and four in investigative detention. Of these deaths, authorities attributed nine to suicide and seven to "sudden deterioration of health." The remaining four died from a beating, a fire, an injury sustained while committing a crime, and torture, respectively.

The majority of deaths in prison and pretrial detention were reportedly related to a lack of quality care, according to a study conducted under the auspices of a presidential grant. A member of the monitoring commission conducting the study stated that the majority of prisoners' illnesses were associated with the detention environment, citing an example of a holding cell in a Krasnodar district court where the walls were covered in fungus and there was no ventilation.

In April a cancer-stricken female prison inmate in St. Petersburg died awaiting implementation of a European Court of Human Rights (ECHR) ruling ordering her transfer to a civil hospital. This was the second such death case in St. Petersburg. The ECHR found that the prison hospital did not provide adequate medical care, but a local district court refused to approve the transfer. At least three additional female cancer sufferers were in the prison hospital; two of them had similar ECHR transfer orders. On July 13, a 55-year-old prisoner, Nikolay Khozyashev, reportedly committed suicide in a penitentiary facility in Perm because prison officials were not providing medical assistance.

In the case of Sergey Magnitsky, a lawyer who died of medical neglect and abuse while in pretrial detention in 2009, authorities had not, as of year's end, brought those reportedly responsible for his death to justice. The investigation into the circumstances surrounding his death remained officially closed.

Prisoner-on-prisoner violence was also a problem. In some cases prison authorities encouraged prisoners to abuse certain inmates. On August 5, four inmates beat a 29-year-old prisoner in Primorskiy Kray, Anton Li. Prison officials brought Li to the hospital only the following day, and he fell into a coma after surgery. There were reports that the inmates carried out the attack under the instruction of prison employees. There were elaborate inmate-enforced caste systems in which certain groups, including informers, gay inmates, rapists, prison rape victims, and child molesters, were considered "untouchables." Prison authorities provided little or no protection to these groups.

Health, nutrition, ventilation, and sanitation standards varied among facilities but generally were poor. Potable water sometimes was rationed. Access to quality medical care remained a significant problem in the penal system.

Tuberculosis and HIV among the country's prison population remained significant problems. The Federal Penitentiary Services reported in 2015 that nearly 4 percent of the country's prison population was infected with tuberculosis, while the HIV rate among prisoners increased 6 percent compared with 2014. No new data were available for 2016. Prosecutor General Chayka stated that more than 62,000 detainees were infected with HIV. In January a local NGO filed a complaint with the prosecutor's office alleging that HIV-positive inmates in St. Petersburg, Murmansk, and Pskov Oblast had not received antiretroviral therapy since May 2015. Prison and health care officials acknowledged difficulties procuring the drugs but claimed that the problem was largely resolved. According to a prominent human rights advocate, suppliers were reluctant to sell the necessary drugs to prisons at the low procurement price set by the Ministry of Health. In May an HIV-infected prisoner demanded compensation for not being provided adequate medical treatment. The Ministry of Health did not order sufficient quantities of antiretroviral medicine for inmates in 2015, which, according to Prosecutor General Chayka, posed a serious threat to HIV-infected prisoners' lives. Although all correctional facilities had medical units or health centers, only 41 treatment facilities provided treatment for tuberculosis patients, down from 58 in 2014, and only nine prisons provided medical services for drug addiction.

In a 2012 pilot judgment in the case of *Ananyev v. Russia*, the ECHR noted that inadequate conditions of detention were a recurrent and systemic problem in the country and ordered the government to draft a binding implementation plan to remedy the situation. In 2012 the government submitted an action plan for implementing the court's ruling. Since release of the action plan, however, there have been no significant indications of progress. Prison conditions remained poor, as evidenced by the 44 ECHR judgments issued against the country in 2015 for inhuman and degrading prison conditions.

Administration: Both convicted inmates and inmates in pretrial detention facilities had visitation rights, but authorities could deny access to visitors depending on the circumstances. Authorities allowed prisoners serving a regular sentence four three-day visits with their spouses per year. By law those prisoners with harsher sentences are allowed fewer visitation rights. On occasion prison officials cancelled visits if the prison did not have enough space to accommodate them. The judge in a prisoner's case could deny the prisoner visitation rights. Authorities could also prohibit relatives deemed a security risk from visiting prisoners.

While prisoners could file complaints with public oversight commissions or with the Human Rights Ombudsman's Office, they were often afraid of reprisal. Prison reform activists reported that only prisoners who believed they had no other option risked the consequences of filing a complaint. Complaints that reached the oversight commissions often focused on minor personal requests.

There were no completely independent bodies to investigate credible allegations of inhuman conditions. In 2014 new members were added to public oversight commissions, but appointment and selection procedures prevented many human rights defenders from participating, decreasing the effectiveness of oversight commission observation in many regions. At the same time, authorities increased appointments of former military, police, and prison officials to oversight commissions, effectively placing them under the control of law enforcement agencies. According to activists and media reports, the independence of the oversight commissions varied by region. The newspaper *Vedomosti* reported that, after the selection of new members for the Moscow public oversight commission in 2013, the majority of commission members were former officers of the security services and former prison officials, rather than human rights activists who had historically made up the majority of commission members.

Independent Monitoring: There were no prison ombudsmen. The law regulating public oversight of detention centers allows public oversight commission representatives to visit facilities. According to the Russian Public Chamber, there were public oversight commissions in 81 regions with a total of 1,154 commission members. By law there should be five to 40 members on each commission. Authorities permitted only the oversight commissions to visit prisons regularly to monitor conditions. In October human rights activists expressed concern that several of the most active members of the commissions had been removed and replaced with individuals close to authorities, including many from law enforcement backgrounds. Notably, Dmitriy Komnov, who had overseen the prison where lawyer Sergei Magnitsky died in 2009, was elected to the Moscow public oversight commission. According to the NGO Committee for the Prevention of Torture, public oversight commissions were legally entitled to have access to all prison and detention facilities, including psychiatric facilities, but prison authorities often prevented them from accessing these facilities. The law does not establish procedures for federal authorities to respond to oversight commission findings or recommendations, which are not legally binding.

d. Arbitrary Arrest or Detention

While the law prohibits arbitrary arrest and detention, authorities engaged in arbitrary arrest and detention with impunity.

ROLE OF THE POLICE AND SECURITY APPARATUS

The Ministry of Internal Affairs, the FSB, the Investigative Committee, the Office of the Prosecutor General, and the National Guard are responsible for law enforcement at all levels of government. The FSB is responsible for security, counterintelligence, and counterterrorism as well as for fighting organized crime and corruption. The national police force under the Ministry of Internal Affairs is organized into federal, regional, and local levels. In April, President Putin established the Russian Federal National Guard Service. This new executive body, which is under the control of the president as the commander in chief, secures borders alongside the Border Guard, administers gun control, combats terrorism and organized crime, protects public order, and guards important state facilities. The National Guard also participates in armed defense of the county's territory together with the Ministry of Defense.

ARREST PROCEDURES AND TREATMENT OF DETAINEES

By law authorities may arrest and hold a suspect for up to 48 hours without court approval, provided there is evidence of the crime or a witness; otherwise, an arrest warrant is required. The law requires judicial approval of arrest warrants, searches, seizures, and detentions. Officials generally honored this requirement, although bribery or political pressure sometimes subverted the process of obtaining judicial warrants. After arrest, police typically take detainees to the nearest police station, where they inform them of their rights. Police must prepare a protocol stating the grounds for the arrest, and both detainee and police officer must sign it within three hours of detention. Police must interrogate detainees within the first 24 hours of detention. Prior to interrogation, a detainee has the right to meet with an attorney for two hours. No later than 12 hours after detention, police must notify the prosecutor. They must also give an opportunity to the detainee to notify his or her relatives by telephone unless a prosecutor issues a warrant to keep the detention secret. Police are required to release a detainee after 48 hours, subject to bail conditions, unless a court decides, at a hearing, to prolong custody in response to a motion filed by police not less than eight hours before the 48-hour detention period expires. The defendant and his or her attorney must be present at the court hearing.

By law police must complete their investigation and transfer a case to a prosecutor for arraignment within two months of a suspect's arrest, although an investigative authority may extend a criminal investigation for up to 12 months. Extensions beyond 12 months need the approval of the head federal investigative authority in the Ministry of Internal Affairs, the FSB, or the Investigative Committee. According to some defense lawyers, the two-month time limit often was exceeded, especially in cases with a high degree of public interest.

A number of problems related to detainees' ability to obtain adequate defense counsel. Federal law provides defendants the right to choose their own lawyers, but investigators generally did not respect this provision, instead designating lawyers friendly to the prosecution. These "pocket" defense attorneys agreed to the interrogation of their clients in their presence while making no effort to defend their clients' legal rights. In many cases, especially in more remote regions, defense counsel was not available for indigent defendants. Judges usually did not suppress confessions of suspects taken without a lawyer present. Judges at times freed suspects held in excess of detention limits, although they usually granted prosecutors' motions to extend detention periods.

Authorities generally respected the legal limitations on detention except in the North Caucasus. There were reports of occasional noncompliance with the 48-hour limit for holding a detainee. At times authorities failed to issue an official detention protocol within the required three hours after detention and held suspects longer than the legal detention limits. The practice was widespread in the North Caucasus (see section 1.g.) and unevenly applied.

Arbitrary Arrest: There were many reports of arbitrary arrest. On February 12 in Dagestan, police detained more than 30 men going to prayer at the local mosque. Witnesses told the independent online news site *Caucasian Knot* that the men were held until evening before being released. None of the men was charged with a crime.

Pretrial Detention: Observers noted that lengthy pretrial detention was a problem, but data on its extent was not available.

Detainee's Ability to Challenge Lawfulness of Detention before a Court: According to the law, a detainee may challenge the lawfulness of detention before an investigator, prosecutor, or court. The challenge can take the legal form of a referral or complaint. The defense typically submits a referral to ask for a certain procedural motion, be it with the prosecution or court, and a complaint is submitted with respect to action that was already taken. Using these instruments, a detainee or his or her lawyer can cause the prosecution or court to change the type of detention used (from arrest in a detention facility to house arrest, for example) or complain that a certain type of pretrial restraint is unlawful. The investigator and the court have absolute discretion to impose limits on the type of detention used if they have sufficient grounds to believe that the defendant will escape from prosecution, continue criminal activity, threaten witnesses or other individuals connected with the criminal case, destroy evidence, or otherwise hamper the investigation.

Statistics related to the number of successful challenges to the lawfulness of detention are not available. The judge typically agrees with the investigator's position and dismisses defense referrals or complaints on this problem.

Protracted Detention of Rejected Asylum Seekers or Stateless Persons: Authorities continued to detain asylum seekers while their cases were pending as well as all rejected asylum seekers prior to deportation or pending judicial review (see section 2.d.). Human rights NGOs reported authorities used protracted detention in such cases, including detention past the legal limit of 12 months.

Amnesty: In May, President Putin pardoned Lieutenant Nadiya Savchenko, a Ukrainian military pilot and Rada deputy, who was released in a prisoner swap in exchange for two Russian intelligence operatives. In March a politically motivated trial had found Savchenko guilty of killing two Russian journalists in Metalist, Ukraine. Putin also pardoned Ukrainian citizens Hennadiy Afanasyev and Yuriy Soloshenko, convicted for "plotting terrorist acts" and espionage, respectively, in a swap in June, this time for two journalists (see section 1.e., Political Prisoners and Detainees).

e. Denial of Fair Public Trial

The law provides for an independent judiciary, but judges remained subject to influence from the executive branch, the armed forces, and other security forces, particularly in high-profile or politically sensitive cases. The outcomes of some trials appeared predetermined.

The human rights ombudsman received 64,189 complaints in 2015, an 18 percent increase over 2014. The largest number of complaints (30 percent) alleged violations of criminal proceedings and violations during trials.

Judges were subject to pressures that could influence the outcome of cases. Former Supreme Court judge Tamara Morshchakova, in an interview on the Moscow Helsinki Group website on August 14, indicated that judges were concerned by how their rulings would be seen by higher courts and often consulted with contacts in the higher courts to make a decision that would not cause them to lose favor or be later overturned. Morshchakova also indicated that the number of individuals instructing judges on rulings was expanding to include local officials, not just superiors.

In many cases authorities reportedly did not provide witnesses and victims adequate protection from intimidation or threats from powerful criminal defendants.

TRIAL PROCEDURES

The defendant has a legal presumption of innocence. A judge typically hears trials (bench trials). Certain crimes, including terrorism, espionage, hostage taking, and inciting mass disorder, must be heard by panels of three judges. Judges acquitted less than 1 percent of defendants.

The law allows prosecutors to appeal acquittals, which they did in most cases. Prosecutors may also appeal what they regard as lenient sentences. Appellate courts reversed approximately 1 percent of sentences where the defendant had been found guilty and 37 percent where the defendant had been found not guilty and remanded them for a new trial, although these cases often ended in a second acquittal.

During trial the defense is not required to present evidence and is given an opportunity to cross-examine witnesses and call defense witnesses, although judges may deny the defense this opportunity. On March 24, the Jehovah's Witnesses organization in Tyumen appealed to the Russian Supreme Court regarding allegations of extremism against the church, in part because the lower courts refused to allow witnesses for the defense during the trial. Defendants in custody during a trial are confined to a caged area, which was replaced by glass enclosures in some courts. Defendants have the right to be present at the trial and the right to free interpretation as necessary from the moment charged through all appeals. Defendants have the right of appeal. Prior to trial, defendants receive a copy of their indictment, which describes the charges against them in detail. They also have the opportunity to review their criminal file following the completion of the criminal investigation. The law provides for the appointment of an attorney free of charge if a defendant cannot afford one, although the high cost of competent legal service meant that lower-income defendants often lacked competent representation. There were few qualified defense attorneys in remote areas of the country. Defense attorneys may visit their clients in detention, although defense lawyers claimed authorities electronically monitored their conversations and did not always provide them access to their clients. Defendants also have the right not to be compelled to testify or confess guilt.

POLITICAL PRISONERS AND DETAINEES

There were political prisoners in the country, and authorities detained and prosecuted individuals for political reasons. As of October 31, the Memorial Human Rights Center's updated list of political prisoners included 102 names, more than double the 50 individuals the organization listed in 2015. Those added to the list during the year included Maksim Panfilov, arrested on charges of participation in a mass disturbance and use of nonlethal force against government representatives in connection with the 2012 Bolotnaya Square case. The case concerned clashes between police and protesters at a demonstration on the eve of President Putin's inauguration in 2012. Blogger Aleksey Kungurov, who was accused of public justification of terrorism for his blog pieces criticizing Russian Aerospace Forces' activities in Syria, was also included. In June the *Chronicle of Current Events* published a list of 277 alleged political prisoners that included opposition politicians, human rights activists, environmental activists, religious believers, and bloggers. From this list, approximately one-third were members of the opposition, 40 percent had been prosecuted for religious beliefs, and 8 percent were bloggers or social activists.

On May 5, a blogger from Tver, Andrey Bubeyev, who was found guilty of extremism and calling for separatism, was sentenced to two years in a minimum-security penal colony for having reposted materials on social media against the country's involvement in Ukraine. On March 29, while Bubeyev was being held on remand, the Memorial Human Rights Center recognized him as a political prisoner.

On July 21, the Federal Penitentiary Service filed suit against opposition activist Alexey Navalny, requesting that his suspended sentence be changed to a real prison term in the Yves-Rocher case. On August 1, the Lyublinskiy District Court of Moscow declined to withdraw the suspended sentence. On November 16, the Supreme Court, referencing the European Court of Human Rights' ruling in February that Alexey Navalny's right to a fair trial had been violated, sent the case back to a lower court for review. Aleksey Navalny and his brother Oleg were found guilty of fraud in December 2014 in a case involving the Yves-Rocher company. Aleksey had received a suspended sentence of three and one-half years, while Oleg continued to serve a term of three and one-half years. Observers regarded both cases as politically motivated.

At least one reported political prisoner was held in a psychiatric facility. In July a district court in Chelyabinsk extended the period of mandatory treatment in a psychiatric hospital for Aleksey Moroshkin, a local activist, by six months. Authorities charged Moroshkin with public incitement to separatism via the internet for posting texts in April 2015 calling for the secession of the Ural region from the country. The Memorial Human Rights Center recognized Moroshkin as a political prisoner in July.

Once elected, many opposition politicians reported efforts by the ruling party to undermine their work or remove them from office, often through prosecution (see section 3).

After the country's attempted "annexation" of Crimea in 2014, judicial authorities began in 2015 to transfer court cases to Russia from occupied Crimea for trial. While there were no new notable cases during the year, the son of prominent exiled Crimean Tatar leader Mustafa Jemilev, Khaiser Jemilev, whom Russian authorities in 2014 transferred from the territory of occupied Crimea to Krasnodar Kray, charged with manslaughter, and sentenced in June 2015, was held in Russia until he completed his sentence in November.

On June 14, Putin pardoned Ukrainian citizens Hennadiy Afanasyev and Yuriy Soloshenko in a swap for two journalists held in Ukraine. Afanasyev was a codefendant in the case against Oleh Sentsov. In August 2015 the Northern Caucasus Military District Court sentenced Sentsov, a Ukrainian filmmaker, to 20 years in a prison camp after convicting him on terrorism charges widely seen as politically motivated. The other defendants in the case, Hennadiy Afanasyev, Oleksiy Chirniy, and Oleksandr Kolchenko, received sentences ranging from seven to 10 years. The men were detained in 2014 on suspicion that they were plotting terrorist acts in association with the Right Sector nationalist group. Soloshenko had been sentenced to six years in a penal colony for espionage.

There were reports that authorities filed politically motivated charges of treason and espionage against individuals, often in connection with the conflict in Ukraine. The government defines treason to include providing assistance to a foreign state or international organization directed against the country's national security. The Judicial Department under the Russian Supreme Court reported that in 2015, the most recent year for which the data is available, authorities convicted 28 persons on such charges, nearly twice as many as in the previous year. According to the NGO Moscow Public Supervisory Commission, several dozen scientists, entrepreneurs, police officers, and even mothers of small children were convicted of treason in the previous two years on charges classified as "secret" and heard in closed court proceedings.

CIVIL JUDICIAL PROCEDURES AND REMEDIES

Although the law provides mechanisms for individuals to file lawsuits against authorities for violations of civil rights, these mechanisms often did not work well. For example, the law provides that a defendant who has been acquitted after a trial has the right to compensation from the government. While this legal mechanism exists in principle, in practice it was very cumbersome to use. Persons who believed their civil rights had been violated typically sought redress in the ECHR after domestic courts had ruled against them. In 2015 the country passed a law enabling the Constitutional Court to review rulings from international human rights bodies and declare them "nonexecutable" if the court found that the ruling contradicts the constitution. In April the Constitutional Court for the first time declared a ruling by the ECHR, in which the ECHR ruled that the absolute ban on the voting rights of prisoners was in violation of the European Convention on Human Rights, to be nonexecutable under this law.

f. Arbitrary or Unlawful Interference with Privacy, Family, Home, or Correspondence

The law forbids officials from entering a private residence except in cases prescribed by federal law or when authorized by a judicial decision. The law also prohibits the collection, storage, utilization, and dissemination of information about a person's private life without his or her consent. While the law previously prohibited government monitoring of correspondence, telephone conversations, and other means of communication without a warrant, the "Yarovaya package" of amendments to antiterrorism laws came into effect on July 20. These amendments grant authorities sweeping new powers and require telecommunications providers to store all electronic and telecommunication data, including telephone calls, text messages, images, and videos, for six months. Metadata on all communications must be stored for three years and provided to law enforcement authorities upon request. The telecommunications provisions were scheduled to come into effect in July 2018. There were allegations that government officials and others engaged in electronic surveillance without appropriate authorization and entered residences and other premises without warrants.

g. Abuses in Internal Conflict

Violence continued in the North Caucasus republics, driven by separatism, interethnic conflict, jihadist movements, vendettas, criminality, excesses by security forces, and the activity of terrorists. Media reported that in 2015 the total number of deaths and injuries due to the conflicts in the North Caucasus decreased significantly compared with 2014 in all republics of the North Caucasus. According to human rights activists in the region, violence in Dagestan continued at a high level. Dagestan remained the most violent area in the North Caucasus, with approximately 60 percent of all casualties in the region in 2015. Local media described the level of violence in Dagestan as the result of Islamic militant insurgency tactics continuing from the Chechen conflict as well as of the high level of organized crime in the region.

Killings: *Caucasian Knot* reported that in 2015 at least 206 deaths and 49 injuries in the North Caucasus resulted from armed conflicts in the region. With 126 deaths from armed conflict in 2015, Dagestan was the most deadly region. Of the deaths in Dagestan, 97 were militants, 16 were civilians, and 13 were law enforcement officers. This represented a significant decrease from 2014, with the number of casualties in Dagestan down by just over half overall and by nearly 60 percent. The sharpest decrease in violent incidents took place in Chechnya, where the number of deaths decreased to 12 in 2015, compared with 52 in 2014, and the number of injuries fell from 65 to 16.

There continued to be reports that use of indiscriminate force by security forces resulted in numerous deaths or disappearances and that authorities did not prosecute the perpetrators. The Memorial Human Rights Center reported that, on January 1, the body of Khizir Yezhiyev, an economics professor at Grozny State Oil Technical University in Chechnya, was found in the woods near the village of Roshni-Chu in Urus-Martanovskiy district. The medical report stated he died from internal bleeding with six broken ribs, a pierced lung, and many visible injuries on his body. Official reports stated that he died from injuries after falling from a cliff. In December 2015 witnesses claimed to have seen security officials arrest Yezhiyev at a garage in Grozny and take him to an unknown location. According to a number of witnesses, the detainee was taken to one of Grozny's Zavodskiy district police headquarters.

Local militants continued to engage in violent acts against local security forces, often resulting in deaths.

Abductions: Government personnel, militants, and criminal elements continued to engage in abductions in the North Caucasus. According to the prosecutor general, as of 2011 there were more than 2,000 unsolved disappearances in the North Caucasus District. According to data from *Caucasian Knot*, the official list of missing persons in the North Caucasus contained 7,570 names. Local activists asserted that the number of missing persons in Chechnya was much higher than officially reported, potentially up to 20,000 individuals. Amnesty International (AI) reported that law enforcement agencies continued to rely on security operations as the primary method of combating armed groups and continued to be suspected of resorting to enforced disappearances, unlawful detention, as well as torture and other mistreatment of detainees.

There were also accounts of persons being detained by police or unknown individuals. The Memorial Human Rights Center reported that, on April 1, security forces removed from their homes two journalists and authors of "historical" and "linguistic" theories affirming the exceptional nature of the Chechen ethnicity and language, the antiquity of the Chechens, and their status as God's chosen people. On April 5, one of them posted on Facebook that he had not been abducted but was spending four days in the Oktyabrskoye District Department of Internal Affairs in Grozny, where he was detained to prevent his disappearance; the post was later removed. On April 6, the head of Chechnya, Ramzan Kadyrov, posted on Instagram that the authors had "apologized to the academic community and the clergy of Chechnya" for their writings.

In Chechnya the local Ministry of Public Health continued issuing genetic passports to relatives of individuals who were kidnapped or disappeared during the first and second Chechen conflicts. The genetic passport offers relatives the ability to identify remains that may belong to their family. Between January and July 2015, an estimated 32 Chechen residents received genetic passport, bringing the total to more than 300. Chechnya's Ministry of Internal Affairs claimed to have a database containing 3,016 missing persons, but human rights activists believed the actual number of missing persons to be higher.

Physical Abuse, Punishment, and Torture: Armed forces and police units reportedly abused and tortured both militants and civilians in holding facilities.

The Memorial Human Rights Center reported that in October 2015 police in the Dagestani village of Gotsali detained a 43-year-old man, seizing a hunting rifle with ammunition and planting a bag of marijuana on him. For two days his relatives were unable to locate him. At a hearing three days after his arrest, the man's relatives claimed he had to be carried into the courtroom because he could not walk on his own. Although he was supposed to be released after the hearing, the man was then charged on an administrative offense for speaking abusively and held for an additional three days. After 13 days in custody, the man reported that authorities had taken him with a bag over his head to an undisclosed location, subjected him to electric shocks, and urged him to confess to aiding insurgents.

Human rights groups noted authorities often did not act to address widespread reports of physical abuse of women.

The law requires relatives of terrorists to pay the cost of damages caused by an attack, which human rights advocates criticized as collective punishment. The Memorial Human Rights Center reported that Chechen Republic authorities have upheld the principle of collective responsibility in punishing the relatives of alleged members of illegal armed groups. In 2014 the head of the Chechen, Republic Kadyrov, posted on Instagram, "It shall no longer be said that parents are not responsible for the deeds of their sons and daughters. They will be responsible in Chechnya!" and, "If an insurgent murders a police officer or anyone else in Chechnya, his family will be immediately thrown out of Chechnya and banned from returning, and their home will be destroyed down to its very foundations."

The Memorial Human Rights Center and *Caucasian Knot* reported that, following an armed attack by two militants on a checkpoint in the village of Alkhan-Kala in Grozny's rural district in May, the homes of the attackers' families were set on fire. Local security officials arrested a journalist who photographed the burnt-out remains of one of the houses, allegedly on suspicion of collusion with Da'esh.

SECTION 2. RESPECT FOR CIVIL LIBERTIES, INCLUDING:

a. Freedom of Speech and Press

While the constitution provides for freedom of speech and press, the government increasingly restricted those rights. The government instituted several new laws that restrict both freedom of speech and press. Regional and local authorities used procedural violations and restrictive or vague legislation to detain, harass, or prosecute persons who criticized the government. The government exercised greater editorial control over state-controlled media than it had previously, creating a media landscape in which most citizens were exposed to predominantly government-approved narratives. Significant government pressure on independent media constrained coverage of numerous problems, especially the situation in Ukraine and Syria, LGBTI problems, the environment, elections, criticism of local or federal leadership, as well as issues of secessionism or federalism. Self-censorship in television and print media was increasingly widespread, particularly on points of view critical of the government or its policies. The government used direct ownership or ownership by large private companies with government links to control or influence major national media and regional media outlets, especially television.

Freedom of Speech and Expression: Government-controlled media frequently used terms such as "traitor," "foreign agent," and "fifth column" to describe individuals expressing views critical of or different from government policy, leading to a climate intolerant of dissent. Authorities also invoked a law prohibiting the "propaganda" of nontraditional sexual relations to minors to restrict the free speech of LGBTI persons and their supporters (see section 6).

Authorities continued to misuse the country's expansive definition of extremism as a tool to stifle dissent. As of November 9, the Ministry of Justice expanded its list of extremist materials to include 3,897 books, videos, websites, social media pages, musical compositions, and other items, an increase of nearly 800 items from 2015. According to the Investigative Committee, detectives referred more than 500 extremism cases to prosecutors in 2015, a number of which included charges of "extremism" levied against individuals for exercising free speech on social media and elsewhere.

In July 2015 journalist Alexander Sokolov of the independent news company RBK was arrested on a charge of participating in the activities of the People's Will Army, which was declared an extremist organization by the Moscow City Court. Sokolov maintained he was simply providing professional services to the group, such as registering its website. Sokolov had previously reported on state corruption and embezzlement connected with the construction of the Vostochnyy space center. In November 2015, the Memorial Human Rights Center recognized Sokolov as a political prisoner, demanding that the court drop its prosecution. In June, Human Rights Ombudswoman Tatyana Moskalkova appealed to the prosecutor general, requesting verification of the lawfulness and legality of the decisions taken in the case against Sokolov. On August 1, Reporters without Borders requested that authorities immediately release Sokolov. He remained in prison.

Press and Media Freedoms: The government increasingly restricted press freedom. As of 2015, the latest year for which data was available, the government and state-owned or state-controlled companies directly owned more than 60 percent of the country's 45,000 registered local newspapers and periodicals. The federal or local governments or progovernment individuals completely or partially owned approximately 66 percent of the 2,500 television stations, including all six national channels. Government-owned media outlets often received preferential benefits, such as rent-free occupancy of government-owned buildings. At many government-owned or controlled outlets, the state increasingly dictated editorial policy. A 2014 law, effective in January, restricts foreign ownership of media outlets to no more than 20 percent.

In May the owner of RBK, Mikhail Prokhorov, who was widely seen as under pressure from the government, fired the chief editors of RBK's newspaper, television channel, and web portal. Following several of RBK's high-profile investigations into corruption on the part of President Putin, his family, and alleged business associates, culminating in reporting on the "Panama Papers" scandal in April, the government allegedly demanded changes in the holding company's editorial policies. The editors in chief were replaced by new personnel from the state-owned TASS news agency. The new editors instructed staff that there would now be a "double line" editorial policy—a line that cannot be crossed—concerning certain types of topics, according to a transcript of an RBK staff meeting published by the newspaper *Meduza* and a source cited in Reuters.

In April the FSB raided the Prokhorov-owned ONEXIM Group's Moscow premises on suspicion of tax evasion. According to a number of analysts, the raids resulted from the government's displeasure with RBK's extended coverage of the Panama Papers leak of documents that detailed how private individuals and public officials used offshore accounts to conceal financial activity, at least some of questionable legality. The Ministry of Internal Affairs also opened a criminal case against RBK on suspicion of alleged fraud.

In July, Svetlana Bababeva, the chief editor of Gazeta.ru, one of the most widely read independent digital media sites in the country, was abruptly fired without explanation when her contract expired. Press reports subsequently indicated that the leadership of Rambler & Co, the media-holding firm that owns Gazeta.ru, faced government pressure to terminate Bababeva because of her opposition to the government and its policies.

Many newspapers ensured their financial viability by agreeing to various types of "support contracts" with government ministries, under which they agreed to provide positive coverage of government officials and policies in news stories. Absent direct government support, independent news publications reported difficulty attracting advertising and securing financial viability, since advertisers feared retaliation if their brands became linked to publications that criticized the government.

Violence and Harassment: Journalists continued to be subjected to arrest, imprisonment, physical attack, harassment, and intimidation as a result of their reporting. The Glasnost Defense Fund reported numerous actions against journalists in 2014, including five killings, 52 attacks, 107 detentions by law enforcement officers, 200 prosecutions, 29 threats against journalists, 15 politically motivated firings, and two attacks on media offices.

On July 12, the Federal Financial Monitoring Service, tasked with monitoring legal entities' and individuals' compliance with the country's terrorist and extremist financing laws, published a list of some 6,000 individuals on its website that included Crimean journalists Nikolay Semena and Anna Andriyevskaya from the Center for Journalistic Investigations. OSCE media freedom representative Dunja Mijatovic expressed concern over the government's placing of journalists on a list of alleged terrorists and extremists.

In September a criminal court in Chechnya's Shali District convicted *Caucasian Knot* journalist Zhalaudi Geriyev of drug possession for personal use and sentenced him to three years in prison. The defense maintained that the prosecutor's case was marred by inconsistencies and flawed evidence as well as by violations of the criminal procedure code. Although Geriyev had signed a confession while in custody, he completely recanted during the trial, claiming he signed the confession under duress. *Caucasian Knot* published a statement stating it believed the criminal case against Geriyev was fabricated and calling accusations of his drug use "completely far-fetched." The statement continued that the "absence of direct evidence" and the pressure placed on Geriyev suggested that the prosecution was "connected with his professional activities."

Journalists reporting in or on the North Caucasus remained particularly vulnerable to physical attacks for their reporting. Rumors also persisted of an alleged "hit list" that included prominent journalists such as Aleksey Venediktov, chief of the independent radio and news organization *Ekho Moskvy*.

There was no progress during the year in establishing accountability in a number of high-profile killings of journalists, including the 2004 killing of Paul Klebnikov, the 2006 killing of Anna Politkovskaya, or the 2009 killing of Natalia Estemirova.

Journalists and bloggers who uncovered various forms of government malfeasance also faced harassment, either in the form of direct threats to their physical safety or threats to their security or livelihood, often through legal prosecution. In March journalists on a reporting tour organized by the Committee for the Prevention of Torture were stopped and beaten by a group of masked assailants as they traveled from Ingushetia to Chechnya. No one was prosecuted for the attack (see section 1.c.).

Censorship or Content Restrictions: The government continued to use laws and decrees to censor or restrict media content.

According to the Glasnost Defense Fund and other NGOs, authorities used media's widespread dependence on the government for access to property, printing, and distribution services to discourage critical reporting. Approximately 90 percent of print media relied on state-controlled entities for paper, printing, and distribution services, and many television stations relied on the government for access to the airwaves and office space. Officials continued to manipulate the price of printing at state-controlled publishing houses to pressure private media rivals.

...

Section 3. Freedom to Participate in the Political Process

While the law provides citizens the ability to choose their government in free and fair periodic elections held by secret ballot and based on universal and equal suffrage, citizens could not fully do so because the government limited the ability of opposition parties to organize, register candidates for public office, access media, and conduct political campaigns.

The law allows regional authorities to abolish direct mayoral elections in major cities. Only nine of 83 regional capitals retained direct mayoral elections, although two previously elected mayors were still completing their terms. The law does not apply to Moscow and St. Petersburg, since the mayors of these cities have the status of governors.

After allegations of voter fraud in the 2011 State Duma elections sparked mass protests in Moscow and St. Petersburg, authorities sought to curtail the work of independent monitors and promote government-sponsored monitoring. The State Duma passed legislation in February allowing each party or candidate to have up to two election monitors present at each polling station, affirming the right of observers to use photography and video equipment, and banning the removal of observers without a court order. The legislation prohibited observers from being accredited to more than one polling station, sharply limiting the ability of civil society to monitor elections. Critics contended that the legislation makes it difficult for domestic election monitors to conduct surprise inspections due to provisions requiring observers to register with authorities, including the polling station they intend to monitor, three days before elections. The legislation also increased the registration requirements for journalists wishing to monitor elections. Such regulations hampered the work of independent or nonparty affiliated groups, whose monitors registered as journalists for their affiliated publications. The independent election-monitoring organization Golos reported that the number of independent observers decreased by half since 2011.

[End Text]

Source: U.S. Department of State website
https://www.state.gov/j/drl/rls/hrrpt/humanrightsreport/index.htm#wrapper

❧❧❧❧❧❧❧❧

7. SAMPLE DEPARTMENT OF STATE REPORT ON HUMAN TRAFFICKING, AFGHANISTAN

This is a sample report from the Department of State Report on Human Trafficking. It focuses on Afghanistan. In the past ten years the U.S. has become very involved in combatting the scourge of human trafficking. This happened because the U.S. came to realize, and could no longer deny, that human trafficking was happening in U.S. The U.S. has joined the global human rights movement to eradicate human trafficking. According to the DRL website:

> The Trafficking in Persons (TIP) Report is the U.S. Government's principal diplomatic tool to engage foreign governments on human trafficking. It is also the world's most comprehensive resource of governmental anti-human trafficking efforts and reflects the U.S. Government's commitment to global leadership on this key human rights and law enforcement issue. It represents an updated, global look at the nature and scope of trafficking in persons and the broad range of government actions to confront and eliminate it. The U.S. Government uses the TIP Report to engage foreign governments in dialogues to advance anti-trafficking reforms and to combat trafficking and to target resources on prevention, protection and prosecution programs. Worldwide, the report is used by international organizations, foreign governments, and nongovernmental organizations alike as a tool to examine where resources are most needed. Freeing victims, preventing trafficking, and bringing traffickers to justice are the ultimate goals of the report and of the U.S. Government's anti-human trafficking policy.

> In the TIP Report, the Department of State places each country onto one of three tiers based on the extent of their governments' efforts to comply with the "minimum standards for the elimination of trafficking" found in Section 108 of the TVPA. While Tier 1 is the highest ranking, it does not mean that a country has no human trafficking problem. On the contrary, a Tier 1 ranking indicates that a government has acknowledged the existence of human trafficking, made efforts to address the problem, and complies with the TVPA's minimum standards. Each year, governments need to demonstrate appreciable progress in combating trafficking to maintain a Tier 1 ranking.

{Excerpt}

[Text]

2016 Trafficking in Persons Report — Afghanistan

AFGHANISTAN: Tier 2 Watch List

Afghanistan is a source, transit, and destination country for men, women, and children subjected to forced labor and sex trafficking. Internal trafficking is more prevalent than transnational trafficking. Most Afghan trafficking victims are children who end up in carpet making and brick factories, domestic servitude, commercial sexual exploitation, begging, poppy cultivation, transnational drug smuggling, and assistant truck driving within Afghanistan, as well as in the Middle East, Europe, and South Asia. NGOs documented the practice of bonded labor, whereby customs allow families to force men, women, and children to work as a means to pay off debt or to settle grievances, sometimes for multiple generations with children forced to work to pay off their parents' debt. Some Afghan families knowingly sell their children into sex trafficking, including for *bacha baazi* — where men, including some government officials and security forces, use young boys for social and sexual entertainment. There are reports that some law enforcement officials, prosecutors, and judges accept bribes from or use their relationships with perpetrators of *bacha baazi* to allow them to escape punishment. Some families send their children to obtain employment through labor brokers and the children end up in forced labor. Opium-farming families sometimes sell their children to settle debts with opium traffickers. According to the government and the UN, insurgent groups forcibly recruit and use children as suicide bombers. Boys, especially those traveling unaccompanied, are particularly vulnerable to trafficking. Children in orphanages are also particularly vulnerable and were sometimes subjected to trafficking. Some entire Afghan families are trapped in debt bondage in the brick-making industry in eastern Afghanistan. Members of the Shia Hazara minority group were victims of forced recruitment and forced labor.

Men, women, and children in Afghanistan often pay intermediaries to assist them in finding employment, primarily in Iran, Pakistan, India, Europe, or North America; some of these intermediaries force Afghans into labor or prostitution. Afghan women and girls are subjected to sex trafficking and domestic servitude primarily in Pakistan, Iran, and India. The majority of Afghan victims in Pakistan are women and girls subjected to trafficking for the purpose of commercial sexual exploitation, including through forced marriages. Afghan boys and men are subjected to forced labor and debt bondage in agriculture and construction, primarily in Iran, Pakistan, Greece, Turkey, and the Gulf states. Some Afghan boys are subjected to sex trafficking in Greece after paying high fees to be smuggled into the country. In January 2016, an international organization reported the Iranian government and the Islamic Revolutionary Guards Corps (IRGC) coerced male Afghan migrants and registered refugees to fight in Syria in IRGC-organized and commanded militias by threatening them with arrest and deportation to Afghanistan. Some of those coerced into service were boys younger than the age of 18, some as young as 12, and have been used as combatants. Afghan boys are at high risk of sexual abuse by their employers in Iran and harassment or blackmailing by the Iranian security service and other government officials.

There were reports of women and girls from the Philippines, Pakistan, Iran, Tajikistan, Sri Lanka, and China subjected to sex trafficking in Afghanistan. Under the pretense of high-paying employment opportunities, some labor recruiting agencies lure foreign workers to Afghanistan, including from Sri Lanka, Nepal, India, Iran, Pakistan, and Tajikistan; the recruiters subject these migrants to forced labor after arrival.

In 2015, widespread and credible reporting from multiple sources indicated both the government and armed non-state groups in Afghanistan continued to recruit and use children in combat and non-combat roles. The U.N. verified and reported an increase in the number of children recruited and used in Afghanistan, mostly by the Taliban and other armed non-state actors. In January 2011, the Afghan government signed an action plan with the U.N. to end and prevent the recruitment and use of children by the Afghan National Defense and Security Forces (ANDSF), and in 2014, they endorsed a road map to accelerate the implementation of the action plan. Despite these efforts, there are still government cases of recruitment, most notably by the Afghan Local Police (ALP) and National Police (ANP). In a widely publicized case, a 10-year-old boy participated with Afghan local police forces in operations against the Taliban; local authorities publicly recognized the child, whom the Taliban later murdered. The media reported in some cases security force units used children as personal servants or support staff, and for sexual purposes. The abuse and sexual exploitation of children continues to be an issue of serious concern, as members of the Afghan security forces and other groups of non-state actors frequently sexually abuse and exploit young girls and boys.

[End Text]

Source: U.S. Department of State, Diplomacy in Action
https://www.state.gov/j/tip/rls/tiprpt/2016/index.htm

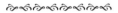

8. FACT SHEET: U.S. SUPPORT FOR CIVIL SOCIETY

This is a fact sheet to keep the public informed about the White House's efforts to encourage and assist Civil Society Organizations around the globe to promote democracy. These efforts are an attempt by the administration to create a climate in democracy deficient states that will foster human rights and encourage human rights defenders both organizational and individual.

[Text]

Fact Sheet: U.S. Support for Civil Society
The White House
U.S. Department of State, Washington, D.C.
09-22-2014

In September 2013, President Obama launched *Stand with Civil Society*, a global call to action to support, defend, and sustain civil society amid a rising tide of restrictions on its operations globally. Working in partnership with other governments, the philanthropic community, and multilateral initiatives, including the Community of Democracies and

Lifeline: Embattled CSO Assistance Fund, the United States Government has focused on three lines of effort over the past year: (1) promoting laws, policies, and practices that foster a supportive environment for civil society in accordance with international norms; (2) coordinating multilateral, diplomatic pressure to push back against undue restrictions on civil society; and (3) identifying innovative ways of providing technical, financial, and logistical support to promote a transparent and vibrant civil society. The United States is the largest supporter of civil society in the world, with more than $2.7 billion invested to strengthen civil society since 2010.

Today, President Obama deepened the United States' commitment to *Stand with Civil Society* by issuing a Presidential Memorandum to U.S. agencies engaged abroad. Specifically, the Presidential Memorandum directs U.S. agencies to defend and strengthen civil society abroad by: consulting regularly with civil society organizations to explain the views of the United States, seek their perspectives, utilize their expertise, and build strong partnerships to address joint challenges; resisting efforts by foreign governments to dictate the nature of U.S. assistance to civil society, the selection of individuals or entities to implement U.S. Government programs, or the selection of recipients or beneficiaries of those programs; opposing efforts by foreign governments to impose excessive restrictions on the freedoms of expression, peaceful assembly, and association; and creating greater opportunities for exchange and dialogue between governments and civil society. Through this directive, the President is mobilizing the U.S. Government to address the global crackdown on civil society.

The President also announced a new, groundbreaking initiative to support and connect civil society across the globe through the launch of Regional Civil Society Innovation Centers, in partnership with the Government of Sweden and the Aga Khan Development Network. Over the next two years, up to six networked Regional Civil Society Innovation Centers will be created worldwide. These Centers will connect civil society organizations at the regional and global level to each other, new partners, and resources; encourage peer-to-peer learning; provide civil society organizations and their networks with virtual and physical platforms to access tools and technologies that will bolster their work; and amplify civil society voices around the world. Civil society organizations, academia, and technology partners will provide additional financial and in-kind resources, as well as technical expertise, to enhance the value of the Centers to civil society.

The Administration is committing additional resources and taking new actions — in partnership with other governments, regional and multilateral institutions and bodies, the philanthropy community, and the private sector — to expand the space for civil society around the world and advance the *Stand with Civil Society Agenda*:

> Providing core funding for the Community of Democracies (CD). The United States will provide $3 million over three years in core funding to CD to strengthen the architecture for global diplomatic action when governments are considering new laws, regulations, or administrative measures that restrict civil society in a manner inconsistent with their international obligations and commitments, including those enshrined in the Universal Declaration of Human Rights, the International Covenant on Civil and Political Rights and the Financial Action Task Force. This funding will also help CD in its efforts to repeal or reform excessive restrictions on civil society through expert consultations and dialogue with civil society representatives from repressive environments.

> Operationalizing CD-UNITED (Using New Investments to Empower Democracy). The United States is supporting a groundbreaking effort that enables governments and organizations in CD to pool resources and co-finance projects that strengthen civil society and democracy worldwide. From training women activists in Central Asia to helping citizens and the media monitor elections in North Africa, CD-UNITED is making it easy for donors to team up and provide multilateral funding that supports civic engagement and citizen action. The new core funding for CD from the United States will allow CD-UNITED to build civil society partnerships and projects with courageous organizations in more countries around the world.

> Expanding the Legal Enabling Environment Program (LEEP). An increasing number of governments are inhibiting the free operation of civil society and cutting off civil society organizations' ability to receive funding from legitimate sources. In some cases, these restrictions arise out of the implementation of laws, regulations, and administrative measures that are being inappropriately applied; in other cases, the laws, regulations, and administrative measures are themselves problematic. The U.S. Gov-

ernment will expand the LEEP program, which is implemented by International Center for Not-for-Profit Law (ICNL), to further strengthen legal and regulatory environments for civil society by providing technical assistance, financial support to partner organizations, training, and expert research to mitigate restrictions on civil society.

Coordinating with the Open Government Partnership (OGP) to support civic participation and making government more responsive, effective, and accountable. OGP's 64 participating countries represent one-third of the world's population and have made more than 2,000 open government reform commitments since 2011. OGP National Action Plans (NAPs), developed through consultations between government and civil society, commit to advance transparency, accountability, citizen engagement, and technological innovation for good governance. The United States consulted with the general public, a broad range of civil society stakeholders, academia, and the private sector in developing its first two National Action Plans in 2011 and 2013. Globally, the United States works with participating countries to deepen engagement with civil society organizations to improve good governance in key thematic areas, such as the environment, health and education. The United States strongly supports the development of OGP's Rapid Response Policy to respond when participating countries do not fulfill their commitments to inclusive governance.

Consulting with civil society. Over the past year, the U.S. Government has held public and private consultations with civil society organizations to explore new approaches and partnerships around civil society sustainability and civic space. Consultations included a Partners' Forum in June on "The Challenge of Closing Space" and the Civil Society Forum of the African Leaders Summit in August. Most recently, in September, the Asia Civil Society Experience Summit in Indonesia (co-sponsored by the United Nations Development Programme and others) brought together over 150 participants from civil society, government, and the private sector from 21 countries across Asia. A joint statement by participating civil society organizations called on civil society to leverage information and communication technologies to strengthen regional coalitions; called on the international community to improve donor coordination and promote innovative partnerships with non-traditional actors; and called for civil society and international partners to engage local governments to collaborate with civil society to solve community problems.

Enhancing efforts with other governments and within intergovernmental bodies to protect civil society while combating terrorist activity. The United States is committed to working with relevant institutions and bodies, including the Financial Action Task Force (FATF), to implement laws on combating terrorist financing while working to protect the legitimate activities of civil society organizations from being disrupted. For example, the United States has worked closely with the FATF over the past year to increase engagement with civil society, including in the development of the FATF Non-Profit Organization Typology Report, and supports the inclusion of civil society during the important FATF anti-money laundering and counter-terrorism finance country assessment process. In the coming year, the Administration will continue to work with the FATF and seek continued consultation with the private sector to revise the FATF Best Practices on protecting non-profit organizations from abuse by terrorist organizations.

Expanding assistance to Lifeline: Embattled CSOs Assistance Fund. The Administration will contribute an additional $2 million to Lifeline, a multilateral initiative in which the United States participates. This builds on the $5 million that has been provided to date. The Czech Republic, Estonia, Latvia, Lithuania, the Netherlands, and Norway have also renewed their financial commitments to Lifeline. This funding will augment emergency assistance available to civil society organizations under threat and deliver more coordinated diplomatic engagement in priority countries. Since its founding in 2011, Lifeline has assisted 446 civil society organizations in 85 countries.

Developing the Next Generation of Civil Society through the establishment of an Asian Civil Society and Non-Profit Management Curriculum Program. The U.S. Government is partnering with Khon Kaen University in Thailand to establish Southeast Asia's first School for Civil Society and

Non-profit Management. This program will allow 140 university students per year, as well as 40 civil society leaders from throughout the Mekong Lower Basin, to complete a degree or certificate program that builds their non-profit management skills. Over the next three years, the University will develop Bachelor's and Master's degree programs as well as executive certification (non-degree) programs, and will serve as a regional hub for coordination, best practice exchange, and networking among civil society leaders.

Emerging Global Leaders Initiative: Atlas Corps Fellows. The United States Government and Atlas Corps will partner to bring 100 of the world's best social change leaders to the United States on a leadership development fellowship, each ranging from 6-18 months. As part of the program, Atlas Corps will convene fellows three times in Washington, D.C. for leadership training and place them at leading civil society organizations across the United States.

[End Text]

Source: whitehouse.gov
https://www.humanrights.gov/dyn/fact-sheet-u.s.-support-for-civil-society

U.N. Charter Based Bodies: Focus on Human Rights Council Universal Periodic Review

Chapter 4

This Chapter is About the close inter-relationship of the United Nations, human rights, and the U.S. It is the first of three chapters dealing with this subject. This chapter deals with human rights in the U.N. General Assembly and its Human Rights Council focusing on the Universal Periodic Review Process. Chapter 5 covers Human Rights Council Special Procedures and Complaint Procedure. And Chapter 6 discusses U.S., U.N., and Human Rights Law: Treaties and Treaty-based Bodies.

The chapter includes: what human rights treaties say; what U.N. bodies do; how, and to a certain extent why, the U.S. participates in the work of the U.N. and inter-relates with the people of the UN; what the U.S. says about itself as far as its law, policy, and practice; and how the international community, through these U.N. bodies, views U.S. law, policy, and practice, based on international legal norms which are binding on the U.S. in a very political world.

This is Important Because the United Nations is the main forum where the U.S. is most involved in Human Rights Law, Humanitarian Law, and International Criminal Law. The U.S. does this in different capacities:
- through complaints about another country's human rights practice;
- as a state party to a treaty submitting a report on its own human rights record;
- by being represented on administrative, political, or legal bodies which deal with human rights;
- by providing monetary and other resources to different bodies that the U.N. organization needs to function, such as an International Court.

This is important to the U.S. because:
- as a member of the U.N., the U.S. has its own human rights record examined by the international community at the U.N.;
- the U.S. plays an important role in examining the records of other countries;

- through participation in U.N. human rights processes, the U.S. can try to improve its own human rights record and promote better human rights practices by other states;
- the U.S. can recognize how its own human rights record needs improvement, as do all countries;
- the U.S. has served since World War II, more than any other country, as a model of human rights practices, and thus should set the best example possible;
- people should know and examine what the U.S. says about itself and the U.N. in the U.N. human rights processes, which exist to reduce conflict between nations due to human rights issues.

Human rights make up the dominant discourse at the United Nations, providing a measuring line for judging how nation states act regarding human rights. The U.S., more than any other state, has contributed to creating and engaging in the organs, instruments, policies, and procedures of the U.N. in the field of human rights.

Quotes & Key Text Excerpts

The United Nations General Assembly adopted the Universal Declaration of Human Rights sixty-eight years ago today to recognize and elevate the inherent dignity and inalienable rights of all individuals.

On this International Human Rights Day, we recommit ourselves to upholding universal respect for the fundamental freedoms of all humankind.

The Universal Declaration of Human Rights holds the promise of hope for the civilians who are caught in the crossfire of conflict, the citizens who fight against repressive governments, the families that are driven out of their homes and displaced by conflict, and the workers who are exploited for the profit of others. We stand in solidarity with those working to secure better and brighter futures, and commit to safeguarding their inalienable human rights in the pursuit of freedom, justice, and peace.

Today and every day, the United States will continue to urge all nations to observe the principles of liberty, democracy, free expression, and equal protection under the law without distinction based on race, creed, sexual orientation, political opinion, or faith. As we celebrate the progress we've made toward a more just world, we reaffirm our unwavering devotion to a universal value-preserving and protecting the equal and inalienable human rights of all people.

—*Secretary of State John Kerry*

Source: U.S. Department of State, Diplomacy in Action, Press Statement, Dec. 10, 2016. http://www.state.gov/secretary/remarks/2016/12/265040.htm

෯෯෯෯෯෯෯෯

The Charter of the United Nations is a guiding beacon along the way to the achievement of human rights and fundamental freedoms throughout the world. The immediate test is not only the extent to which human rights and freedoms have already been achieved, but the direction in which the world is moving. Is there a faithful compliance with the objectives of the Charter if some countries continue to curtail human rights and freedoms instead of to promote the universal respect for an observance of human rights and freedoms for all as called for by the Charter? The place to discuss the issue of human rights is in the forum of the United Nations. The United Nations has been set up as the common meeting ground for nations, where we can consider together our mutual problems and take advantage of our differences in experience. It is inherent in our firm attachment to democracy and freedom that we stand always ready to use the fundamental democratic procedures of honest discussion and negotiation. It is now as always our hope that despite the wide differences in approach we face in the world today, we can, with mutual good faith in the principles of the United Nations Charter, arrive at a common basis of understanding. We are here to join the meetings of this great international Assembly which meets in your beautiful capital of Paris. Freedom for the individual is an inseparable part of the cherished traditions of France. As one of the Delegates from the United States, I pray Almighty God that we may win another victory here for the rights and freedoms of all men.

—*Eleanor Roosevelt, The Struggle for Human Rights*

Source: http://www.americanrhetoric.com/speeches/eleanorroosevelt.htm

❦❦❦❦❦❦❦❦

The history of human rights as we know them today began in World War II. The world's reaction to the Holocaust and other horrors of the two major wars led all nations, including the United States, to come to grips with human rights. The main focus of the international human rights activity of the United States would be within the United Nations, which was established in San Francisco in 1945 upon the entry into force of the U.N. Charter. With its participation in the United Nations, a community of sovereign and equal states, the United States joined a larger political group because it saw from the lessons of World War II a need to impose some internationally accepted rules upon states so that holocausts would not happen again. It also saw the need for international cooperation to combat various violent evils that still threatened the world. It saw the increasing interconnectedness and interrelationship of nations.

—*Eleanor Roosevelt*

Source: American Rhetoric from Roosevelt to Reagan, Waveland Press: Prospect Heights, IL. 1987.

❦❦❦❦❦❦❦❦

And so I believe that at this moment we all face a choice. We can choose to press forward with a better model of cooperation and integration. Or we can retreat into a world sharply divided, and ultimately in conflict, along age-old lines of nation and tribe and race and religion.

I want to suggest to you today that we must go forward, and not backward. I believe that as imperfect as they are, the principles of open markets and accountable governance, of democracy and human rights and international law that we have forged remain the firmest foundation for human progress in this century. I make this argument not based on theory or ideology, but on facts — facts that all too often, we forget in the immediacy of current events.

...

Time and again, human beings have believed that they finally arrived at a period of enlightenment only to repeat, then, cycles of conflict and suffering. Perhaps that's our fate. We have to remember that the choices of individual human beings led to repeated world war. But we also have to remember that the choices of individual human beings created a United Nations, so that a war like that would never happen again. Each of us as leaders, each nation can choose to reject those who appeal to our worst impulses and embrace those who appeal to our best. For we have shown that we can choose a better history.

—*President Barack Obama, address to the U.N. General Assembly, 2016*

Source: http://time.com/4501910/president-obama-united-nations-speech-transcript

What You Should Know

THE UNITED NATIONS CHARTER AND HUMAN RIGHTS: HOW THE U.S. RELATES

The United Nations has increasingly become the global focus of human rights for all countries, including the United States. In recent decades, the U.S. seems almost to have perceived the U.N. as a political enemy or as a tool of those who hate the U.S. and its allies. In looking at the role of the U.S. in relation to the United Nations, one must look to the U.N. Charter, a document strongly influenced by the U.S. involvement in its formulation. The United Nations was founded in California, in the United States of America in 1945, and has its main headquarters in New York City, with another in Geneva, Switzerland. As an international inter-governmental organization (IGO), the U.N. is just that — an organization, like a club of governments, of states parties who choose to join it. It was created by the governments of certain countries like the U.S., but, as the Charter preamble states, it was created by the peoples of the world, not by governments. It functions globally as the world's institutional focus for compliance with human rights norms and laws. Its preamble reads: "We the peoples of the United Nations determined to save succeeding generations from the scourge of war, which twice in our lifetime has brought untold sorrow to mankind, and to reaffirm faith in fundamental human rights, in the dignity and worth of the human person, in the equal rights of men and women...."

From the beginnings of the U.N., at the very end of World War II, the United States acted as a prime mover for the creation of the United Nations Organisation in all fields, especially in human rights. Thus, the United States was instrumental in drafting and promoting the U.N. Charter, as well as the Universal Declaration of Human Rights. Eleanor Roosevelt served as one among several of the key drafters of that declaration, as well as a member of the U.N. Commission on Human Rights. The United Nations initiated the work of multilateral dealings with human rights problems among all nation states, whether a nation state was a U.N. member or not, and in a broad range of areas.

U.N. Charter and U.S. Legal Obligations

By ratifying the U.N. Charter more than seventy years ago, the United States became legally obligated to act to fulfill the purposes of the United Nations. Article 1.3 of the U.N. Charter states that one purpose is "to achieve international co-operation in solving international problems of an economic, social, cultural, or humanitarian character and in promoting and encouraging respect for human rights and for fundamental freedoms for all without distinction as to race, sex, language or religion." Under Article 55c, the United Nations is obligated to promote universal respect for, and observance of, human rights and fundamental freedoms for all without distinction as to race, sex, language, or religion. The international legal obligations of the United States as a member state in regard to human rights is set forth in the U.N. Charter, Article 56, which states that "all Members pledge themselves to take joint and separate action in cooperation with the [United Nations] Organization for the achievement of the purposes set forth in Article 55." The United States is thus legally obligated under the U.N. Charter to work toward these U.N. purposes both at home and globally. (See Primary Source Document 1)

The United States continues to act as a very committed and proactive member of various international organizations dealing with human rights. The United Nations Organization is the key institution, among others, to deal with human rights questions. It is an international intergovernmental institution, an organization, like a club of governments of the world. The United Nations Organisation is not an international government, nor is it a "one-world government." As a matter of law, it has no power over any member state other than that which the state gives it when it voluntarily ratifies the United Nations Charter. Most of the human rights norms that now exist are found in treaties, such as the ICCPR and CERD (the Convention on the Elimination of All Forms of Racial Discrimination), and were produced by the member states of the United Nations Organisation acting together as an international organization. The United States is and has been a prime mover and promoter of the human rights standard-setting, which leads to treaty-making activity of the international community.

U.S. in the U.N. General Assembly and on the U.N. Security Council and the International Court of Justice
U.S. representatives sit in the U.N. General Assembly and on the U.N. Security Council, where they deal with, among other issues of international importance, human rights in the geopolitical context. The U.S. is a permanent member of the Security Council. Americans have sat as judges on the International Court of Justice (ICJ), which, as the legal arm of the United Nations, has decided several cases relating to human rights. Up until recently, Professor Thomas Buergenthal, one of the most prominent and well-respected American human rights authorities in the world, sat as a judge on the ICJ. He has been succeeded by another well-respected American, Judge Joan E. Donaghue, who has an extensive human rights legal background, among other educational areas, including international law and diplomacy. The U.S. government has members sitting on, involved in, participating in issues before many United Nations human rights bodies, such as the Human Rights Council, which replaced the Commission on Human Rights in 2006.

The Universality of Human Rights: Vienna Conference on Human Rights
In 1993, the United States took on a very active and major state role in advancing the promotion and protection of human rights in the U.N. context at the Vienna Conference on Human Rights. At that U.N. conference, more than one hundred eighty countries of the world sought to update and rationalize international efforts and organizational systems to better protect human rights globally. It promoted the acceptance and primacy of the doctrine of "universality" of human rights, meaning that human rights apply to all peoples at all times in all countries, regardless of different customs, cultures, religions, and philosophies. This stood in direct opposition to any idea of "cultural relativism" which allowed for differing interpretations of human rights from culture to culture. This Conference resulted in the very important U.N. document known as the Vienna Declaration and Programme of Action which still sets the tone for human rights activity at the UN. (See Primary Source Document 2)

As previously mentioned, however, the United States had chosen to become legally bound by ratifying a few international human rights treaties. The U.S. has often not ratified human rights treaties, even when it was very active in the creation of those treaties. When the U.S. has ratified a human rights treaty, it has usually taken a very long time to do so. It took over forty years after it signed the treaty for the U.S. to ratify the Genocide Convention, and it took fifteen years after becoming a signatory to it for the U.S. to ratify the ICCPR. That glacially slow U.S. ratification process has continued into the new millennium.

Since September 11, 2001 and the so-called "war on terrorism," the U.S. seems to have alienated much of the world community, including some of its historically close friends. This alienation gets played out in the U.N. General Assembly and sometimes in the Security Council. The U.S. has been accused of not respecting international human rights and humanitarian law in its war on terrorism. The U.S. is perceived by many as judging itself above the law, and of considering itself an exceptionalist.

International Human Rights Standards as Legal Obligations: No State May Pick and Choose
On the other hand, in its addresses to the United Nations General Assembly (UNGA), the U.S. continues to defend its anti-terrorist actions against claims of violating international law, by claiming that its anti-terrorist actions serve to defend human rights as actions necessary to protect the U.S., its allies, and indeed the civilized world from damage and domination by religious and ideological extremists. The General Assembly has been pushing to get the U.S. and all countries to respect human rights in all measures taken to protect itself and others against terrorism. The General Assembly consistently reminds the U.S. that international human rights standards are legal obligations, and that no state may pick and choose which norms it wants to respect, and when. The outcry of support for and solidarity with the U.S. from much of the world after September 11, 2001 was a reminder from the international community that human rights treaties are "not a suicide pact," but rather a common source of strength. This international attitude communicates clearly that the U.S., like all countries, may not and must not disrespect human rights norms, simply because the U.S., particularly the executive branch of the U.S. government, perceives that it will lose its war against terrorism if it follows strictly the human rights standards against torture, or the right to a fair trial, or the right to protection from all forms of discrimination.

U.N. Global Counter Terrorism Strategy Four Pillars: Must Respect Human Rights
The U.N. has historically spent a great deal of time dealing with terrorism and security issues. In 2006, the U.N. General Assembly passed a unanimous resolution and Plan of Action to enhance national, regional, and international efforts to counter terrorism. The U.N. Global Counter Terrorism Strategy consists of four pillars:

1. addressing conditions conducive to the spread of terrorism;

2. preventing and combating terrorism;

3. building states' capacity to prevent and combat terrorism and strengthen the U.N. system's role in this regard;

4. ensuring respect for human rights and the rule of law as the fundamental basis of the fight against terrorism.

The U.N.'s collective voice for the nations of the world has declared that the war against terror must, in principle, be done in a way that respects human rights, even in the face of persons and groups who do not follow that principle. The General Assembly passes resolutions each year to review U.N. work against terrorism. Its 2016 resolution was entitled: "The United Nations Global Counter-Terrorism Strategy Review." With this resolution, the U.N. General Assembly recalled member states' attention to the following:

Recognizing that international cooperation and any measures taken by member states to prevent and combat terrorism, as well as to prevent violent extremism when conducive to terrorism, must fully comply with their obligations under international law, including the Charter, in particular the purposes and principles thereof, and relevant international conventions and protocols, in particular Human Rights Law, Refugee Law, and International Humanitarian Law.

Reaffirming that the acts, methods, and practices of terrorism in all its forms and manifestations are activities aimed at the destruction of human rights, fundamental freedoms, and democracy, at threatening territorial integrity and the security of states and at destabilizing legitimately constituted Governments, and that the international community should take the necessary steps to enhance cooperation to prevent and combat terrorism in a decisive, unified, coordinated, inclusive, and transparent manner.

Source: The U.N. Global Counter-Terrorism Strategy Review http://www.un.org/ga/search/view_doc.asp?symbol=A/70/L.55

RECENT SCANDALS AND U.S. MISUNDERTANDINGS/MISPERCEPTIONS OF U.N.

In light of the recent terrorist attacks in Turkey, Germany, France, and the U.S., this kind of dialogue and concerted U.N. action continues, but has unfortunately been misunderstood in the U.S., affecting public perceptions in the U.S. about the U.N. In addition, the U.N. Oil for Food scandal, sexual abuse by U.N. peace-keepers, and the apparent bureaucratic ineptitude and financial wastefulness of the U.N.'s international bureaucracy have already negatively influenced many Americans in the years leading up to and following 9/11. Many Americans also characterize the U.N. as anti-American and accuse it of acting as a platform for the "Castros" and the "Sadaam Husseins" of the world. In the Human Rights Council, the U.S. has been criticized for blindly supporting Israel, which has been a major target of human rights resolutions at the U.N. This has been very upsetting for many people in the U.S.

Many Americans state that they perceive the U.N. as an organization that not only does not advance the national self-interest of the U.S., but actually impedes U.S. interests. As U.S. administrations have seen themselves as a government trying to protect the nation, many Americans came to see the U.N. as standing in the nation's way, and believed the U.N. was unduly criticizing the U.S. for the measures the U.S. was taking to counter terrorism: e.g., the U.S. establishment of Guantánamo detention for terrorists without due process by deferring the accused to military courts; the CIA use of torture at black sites around the world; and the use of drones for assassinations and surveillance activity. All of these criticisms, however, were already subject of controversy in the U.S. as well.

With the 2008 election of President Obama, the mood, both in the U.S. and globally, changed to something more optimistic and positive, particularly with regards to hope for changes in U.S. human rights and humanitarian law policy. At the same time Barack Obama was being awarded the Nobel Peace prize, he had already decided, to the disappointment of many, to send more troops to war in Afghanistan, justifying a continuation of the U.S. war on terrorism. However, U.S. President Obama announced to the General Assembly that the U.S. was changing course regarding terrorist suspect detention. Obama worked to curtail U.S. military conflict in Afghanistan and Iraq, and for eight years, tried to get the U.S. to close the Guantánamo prison without success. Nonetheless, his regime was successful in making other serious policy changes for human rights.

With the election of Donald Trump in late 2016, a new era of anti-U.N. sentiment and action seemed to be dawning. The President's cabinet choices indicate a lessening interest in human rights issues in general, at least at the level of Secretary of State, within the U.S. Department of State, where U.S. interests mean taking on a more aggressive business attitude toward the world at large. President Trump's inaugural address declared "America First" as a sort of nationalist motto for his administration. Human rights issues seem to have been delegated away from the Department of State into the purview of the new U.S. Ambassador to the U.N., where the U.S. will continue to be engaged in the U.N.'s varying working bodies.

In 2017, U.S. President Trump spoke of considering use of "enhanced interrogation techniques," including waterboarding, even though key national security, military voices, and his own party's Congressional colleagues were warning against torture, such as waterboarding as directly illegal activity under domestic law. This bodes ill for U.S. relations with the international community, and for its still influential role and relationships within the U.N. The rule of law is essential in the world, and the notion that the U.S. threatens to keep its state safe by any means possible, without any reference to established principles of law, represents a danger to the whole world. It is exactly for this reason that the U.S. worked early on with other nations to create the U.N. to prevent just this kind of conflictual situation that abandons the rule of law.

Human Rights Council Special Mechanisms

The U.N. Human Rights Council (HRC)
In 2006, the U.N. General Assembly decided to scrap the politically compromised Commission on Human Rights, which was a charter-based organ organized under the United Nations Economic and Social Council (ECOSOC). The General Assembly in 2006 created by resolution 60/251, the Human Rights Council (HRC), as the inheritor of and replacement organ for the old Commission and Sub-Commission on Human Rights at the U.N. The HRC would soon become the primary global forum for discussion of and dealing with international human rights issues. The HRC is a subsidiary organ of the General Assembly, an inter-governmental body within the United Nations system responsible for strengthening the promotion and protection of human rights around the globe and for addressing situations of human rights violations and for making recommendations on them. The HRC is empowered to discuss all thematic human rights issues and country situations that require its attention throughout the year. It draws its 47 members from among the various United Nations Member States. Members of the HRC are elected by the U.N. General Assembly, and the HRC meets for its sessions at the U.N. Office in Geneva, Switzerland. Members are chosen with a deliberate attempt to represent all regions, cultures, and legal systems in the world. It also has a sub-body, known as the HRC Advisory Committee, made up of eighteen human rights experts, who serve as a sort of think-tank for the HRC.

The HRC and U.S. Administrations' Shifting Styles of Influence
A first example of how the U.S. participates and interacts in U.N. organs, the following is an anecdotal retelling of how the U.S., based on a specific U.S. President, interacts with issues at the HRC.

While the purpose of this Council is to create a more objective, impartial, and non-political forum to deal with human rights, it has turned out to be anything but. The U.S. began to participate in the dealings of the Council, even though it did not have an elected member on the Council. Early in the life of the Council, there was a bad relationship between the George W. Bush Administration and the Human Rights Council; the Bush Administration saw the Human Rights Council as a place for nation states to criticize the U.S. and its ally Israel.

Organization of Islamic Conferences (OIC) and the U.S. at the Human Rights Council: Example of U.S. Interactions
At the end of the Clinton Presidency and just before the George W. Bush Presidency, there developed at the HRC a representative bloc of 56 Muslim states, known as the Organization of Islamic Conferences (OIC), which sought to get the Council to condemn Israel and to support the Palestinians. The OIC moved the Council to spend what the U.S. and some other states considered an inordinate amount of time on Israeli-Palestinian issues, always ending up with condemnations of Israel. The U.S. criticized the Council for the poor human rights records of some of the countries the HRC's 47 members represented, inferring that, with such a composition of human rights violators, the Council could not be counted on to be objective, impartial, and effective. In 2007, the U.S. stopped attending and participating in the HRC sessions. It did, however, occasionally send one of its U.N. Mission staff to sit in on a session of particular interest to the U.S. In the U.S. view of the G.W. Bush era, the Human Rights Council was beyond repair.

With the election of Barack Obama, the mood within the Council became upbeat. The U.S. issued a Pledge to the U.N., to the world, and to Americans about its support of human rights and the international community, particularly with a view towards supporting the UN. It would rejoin participation with and attend the Human Rights Council sessions. In 2009, the General Assembly elected the U.S. to become a member of the HRC, which it accepted. The U.S. took its seat in 2010.

The U.S. co-drafted and proposed with Egypt a resolution on freedom of expression that was broadly received. This resolution was a directed response to one of the critical issues being dealt with by the Council, an issue seemingly unrelated to any issues involving Israel and the U.S. or even the U.S. war on terrorism: the so-called "defamation of religion" resolution. The "defamation of religion" resolution was an attempt by the Organization of Islamic Conferences and other states to pass a resolution condemning expressions deemed to be offensive to a religion, which was initially exclusively about Islam, but which later applied to all religions, even though everyone knew it was primarily about Islam. It was an attempt by the OIC to counter what it felt was the rising negative stereotyping of Islam as a religion of violence and terrorism, which had been leading to discrimination and violence against Muslims in various parts of the world. The U.S. and European Union took a position in opposition to the OIC on this issue, seeing it as a threat to freedom of expression and religion; that it was inconsistent with existing international human rights law. It voted against the OIC resolution each time it came up. Between 2007 and 2010, the resolution continued to be voted on and passed, as it also did in the General Assembly, but with diminishing support each time there was a vote. What had been presented as a resolution aimed at religious tolerance was not initially recognized as a two-edged sword which could undermine and curtail human rights, particularly in consideration of the areas of blasphemy and anti-proselytism laws.

The U.S. resolution 16/18, co-sponsored with Egypt, was an attempt to make the U.S. appear on the side of tolerance against negative stereotyping, while the new resolution asserted that one must adhere to international human rights standards, such as article 19 of the ICCPR, that guarantees: the right to hold opinions without interference; the right to freedom of expression, etc. The U.S. continued to oppose this OIC move regarding defamation of religion. Just as it seemed that support for the defamation resolution was waning in the HRC, in mid 2010, the Human Rights Council passed a different OIC-sponsored resolution aimed at creating a position of special investigator to work closely with and monitor mass media organizations "to ensure that they create and promote an atmosphere of respect and tolerance for religious and cultural diversity."

Then in 2011, the U.S. succeeded in passing the landmark Resolution 16/18 in the HRC, anchoring its legality in the ICCPR, which effectively sidetracked the "defamation of religion" movement and replaced it with the idea of "combating intolerance, negative stereotyping and stigmatization of, and discrimination, incitement to violence and violence against persons based on religion or belief." This gave rise to the two programs: The Istanbul Process and the Rabat Plan of Action, which continue to address this social phenomenon with dialogue based on that Resolution 16/18.

The following is **a second example** of how the U.S. participates and interacts in U.N. organs.

Although the Obama Administration was aware of the weaknesses and defects of the Human Rights Council, it believed it could make changes from within the HRC, if it could regain friends lost in the previous administration, and gain new ones. The U.S. presented itself as just one state like and equal to all other states which are obligated to follow the same legal standards and to be subject to the same scrutiny and same procedures as any other state. The U.S. tried to overcome the aura of exceptionalism which characterized the previous administrations in the eyes of many.

Since 2009, the U.S. attempted again to become a team player on the HRC, with the result of pleasing some Americans while displeasing others. The U.S. continued to walk a delicate line regarding Israel and the frequent HRC condemnations and investigations of Israel's conduct, such as, the Gaza Invasion in "Operation Cast Lead." In this matter, the Council called for an in-depth investigation as to whether Israel had committed international crimes. The HRC appointed Judge Richard Goldstone, who is Jewish, to lead the investigation which would bear his name. Israel denounced the investigation as biased, since it did not also cover Palestinian violence against Israel. The U.S. position held that the investigating panel was flawed with its results suspect. Whether the U.S. administration is Democratic or Republican, the U.S. rightfully maintains itself as a staunch ally of Israel. The U.S. tries to appear not to be so pro-Israel as to be un-objective or un-principled or unable to be a positive force in dealing with the Middle East crisis, particularly as related to questions on the Israel-Palestine situation. The issue of Israel and the impact of the settlements in the occupied territories and the so-called security wall continue to be within the HRC focus.

The Universal Periodic Review (UPR) Process

U.S. participation in the Human Rights Council would come to a peak in late 2010 and early 2011, when the U.S. was scheduled to have its general human rights record examined for the first time in history by an international inter-governmental human rights forum, i.e., the Universal Periodic Review (UPR) process. Every member country is legally required to go through this process at some point. The U.S. had appeared before "treaty-based bodies" such as the Human Rights Committee and Committee on the Elimination of Racial Discrimination (CERD), regarding its periodic human rights reports, but the UPR was to be a highly visible general examination of how the U.S. does or does not comply with international human rights norms, which include considerations of refugee law and international humanitarian law issues, such as Guantánamo detainees. The UPR process would bring the U.S. into the U.N.'s human rights dock, just like every other country.

When the Human Rights Council was established, the UPR process was one of its main features, i.e., every five years every country in the world would take a turn at having its human rights record examined by the current Human Rights Council, with the participation of non-Council states. In this way, no state could complain that the Council was picking on it or singling it out for political reasons. The U.S. UPR process can serve to illustrate how the UPR process works for all countries, especially since the U.S. recently successfully completed its second UPR process in 2015.

The UPR process always includes:

1. An assessment of the human rights situation in the country under review;

2. An expectation to implement the UPR recommendations and any voluntary pledges the country made in the 4.5 years between reviews;

3. An account of the implementation of the earlier recommendations and commitments made by the HRC for the *State under Review* or "SuR," and the start of a new assessment.

A random drawing took place that led to the establishment of a scheduled listing of all (the then) 192 states of the U.N., that set the time when each state must go through the UPR process. The U.S. UPR process was scheduled for November 5, 2010. The U.S. accepted this schedule and went along with the UPR procedure. (See Primary Source Documents 5 and 6.)

This process involves the State under Review (SuR) preparing a report of its own to submit to the Human Rights Council via the U.N. Office of the High Commissioner for Human Rights (OHCHR), which also prepares its own report on the State under Review to the HRC. The Universal Periodic Review of each country is based on three reports:

The national or state report: Without being obliged to do so, states are nevertheless expected to present a national report (of no more than 20 pages). When producing this report, they must follow the "General Guidelines for the Preparation of Information under the Universal Periodic Review." The states are also encouraged to gather information by engaging in a broad consultation process with all the relevant stakeholders at the national level. Stakeholders may include NGOs and other civil society actors, but also members of parliament or of the judicial system, and existing national human rights institutions. In order to prepare its national report, the U.S. State Department solicited participation from a broad spectrum of Americans in the UPR process. The U.S. held consultations across the United States and solicited input from NGOs, academic institutions, and others in civil society organizations. (See Primary Source Documents 7 and 9.)

A compilation report of United Nations information: The OHCHR compiles a summary, no more than 10 pages long, of information deriving from official U.N. documents (e.g., from treaty bodies, special procedures, or special agencies such as the UNDP and UNICEF, etc.) (See Primary Source Document 10.)

Summary of Stakeholder Submissions: Also prepared by the OHCHR, the Summary (report) is prepared for the 47 members of Human Rights Council which is shared with the Working Group, which is referred to as the Troika (three persons from countries randomly chosen) on the Universal Periodic Review. This summary, also prepared by the Office of the United Nations High Commissioner for Human Rights (OHCHR), includes a summary of 91 stakeholders' submissions (civil society groups) to the universal periodic review. This summary of stakeholder input is a ten-page summary of information provided by all other relevant stakeholders. The latter primarily include NGOs, NHRIs, defenders of human rights, academic institutions, regional organisations, and other representatives of civil society. (See Primary Source Document 11.)

The U.S. has passed twice (2010 and 2015) through the UPR process stages that culminate in a list of recommendations in an outcome report and a vote by the Human Rights Council on whether to accept the "outcome report" concerning the U.S. as a SuR.

In order to prepare its national report, the U.S. State Department solicited participation from a broad spectrum of Americans in the UPR process. The U.S. held consultations across the United States and solicited input from NGOs, academic institutions, and others in civil society organizations.

The U.N. OHCHR prepared a Compilation Report, which included information contained in the reports from other treaty bodies, HRC special procedures, including observations, and conclusions by the SuR, and other relevant U.N. documents. The HRC may also issue written questions to be answered, submitted by interested states in advance of the UPR hearing with the SuR. The UPR process is further explained below.

The Office of the High Commissioner for Human Rights also prepared a summary report of stakeholder contributions from these consultations and from sources beyond the U.S. national report. These reports, mainly submitted by civil society groups about their view of the U.S.' human rights record, are both general and specific on U.S. human rights topics. (See Primary Source Document 11.)

The United States appeared before the Council on November 5, 2010. The draft UPR outcome report/document by the Troika (Cameroon, Japan, and France) was adopted November 9, 2010. The final report/document appeared January 4, 2011. It contains the most recommendations of any country to have undergone the UPR process. On March 10, 2011, the U.S. submitted its formal responses to the recommendations of the Outcome Report. After vigorous debate, the Human Rights Council voted to adopt this Outcome Report on March 18, 2011. The U.S. accepted many recommendations and rejected many others. Over the next 4.5 years, the U.S. was expected to implement those accepted recommendations, as it would begin the UPR process again in 2015 (with the Troika of Saudi Arabia, The Netherlands, and Botswana), where its progress in implementation was evaluated, just as for every other state undergoing the UPR process every five years. In 2015, the U.S.' second cycle of the UPR process was held, with the same procedure of national consultations, national report, Compilation Report, Summary of Stakeholder submissions, advanced written questions, review proceedings, in Geneva with interactive dialogue, outcome document, follow-up, etc. The next UPR will be in 2020. More and more civil society organizations are participating in this process because of the importance of the U.S. in the field of human rights and based on opinions that the U.S. human rights record needs improvement.

Having gone through the UPR process twice, one can ask whether this process has caused any change in the U.S. law, policy, and practice. There is no U.N. enforcement power to make the U.S. do anything. It has only moral and political weight, and public perceptions to cause the U.S. to improve its human rights observance. It is believed that, since they want to look good and know they will be examined every five years, states have incentive to change. The Human Rights Council will want to know what states have done to implement the UPR recommendations when they appear at the next review; the hope is that they will be incentive enough to make changes.

Many Americans question whether the U.S. ought to be subject to the U.N. Human Rights Council, which is composed of so many states known to be gross human rights violators. However, there is always some evidence that suggests the U.S. itself has committed its share of human rights offenses, as well, since every state violates human rights to some extent— some more than others. The more appropriate question might relate to how far the U.S. will go in participating in this important Human Rights Council process.

Is the U.S. too important to the Council's survival and effectiveness? The HRC has not yet succeeded at fulfilling or achieving its purpose, at least, not as much as many would want and expect. Are politics and geopolitics too troublesome and complex for it to handle? Will the 2016 U.S. presidential election cause the U.S. to take a strong adversarial position regarding the HRC? It is possible that this Council could succumb to the geopolitical wrangling that characterizes international organizations. This, after all, is a body of governments judging other governments, some friendly, and some unfriendly to human rights, based on their human rights records. The U.S. is no innocent in human rights matters. Do the present Human Rights Council processes put the foxes in charge of guarding the chicken coop from other foxes? Time will tell. One could also rightly ask what alternatives the peoples of the United Nations have.

If the Council fails for too long to accomplish what it was created to do, i.e., promote human rights and fundamental freedoms, it will likely go the way of its predecessor. The Council is still in its infancy, and with the U.S. as a member again until 2019, it is anyone's guess as to how things will go for human rights at the United Nations. Promotion of respect for human rights is one of the stated purposes of the United Nations, set forth in its Charter. The U.S. will either help or hinder that goal. The world is waiting to see.

In 2010, the U.S. told the Human Rights Council:
The United States views participation in this UPR process as an opportunity to discuss with our citizenry and with fellow members of the Human Rights Council our accomplishments, challenges, and vision for the future on human rights. We welcome observations and recommendations that can help the U.S. on that road to a more perfect union. Delivering on human rights has never been easy, but it is work we will continue to undertake with determination, for human rights will always undergird our national identity and define our national aspirations.

This UPR process is an opportunity for American and international NGOs to input the international human rights processes to seek to influence the human rights direction of the U.S. Much depends on the attitude of the U.S. government as to how U.S. participation will go. If there is little domestic awareness of this process and the U.S. government position, or the response of the international community, one cannot expect much change in U.S. policy and practice.

We present our first Universal Periodic Review (UPR) report in the context of our commitment to help to build a world in which universal rights give strength and direction to the nations, partnerships, and institutions that can usher the U.S. toward a more perfect world, a world characterized by, as President Obama has said, "a just peace based on the inherent rights and dignity of every individual."

The ideas that informed and inform the American experiment can be found all over the world, and the people who have built it over centuries have come from every continent. The American experiment is a human experiment; the values, on which it is based, including a commitment to human rights, are clearly engrained in our own national conscience, but they are also universal.

Source: Introduction to the U.S. national UPR report submitted to the OHCHR, in 2010. (See Primary Source Document 7.)

Other U.N. Human Rights Organs

Besides the General Assembly, there are other organs of the U.N. which deal with human rights:
- the International Court of Justice with its opinions on human rights and humanitarian law issues such as the use of nuclear weapons, and Israel's security wall;
- the U.N. Security Council which increasingly deals with such issues as the Syrian civil war and the spread of DAESH/ISIS/ISIL, and the plight of North Korea. The Security Council's jurisdiction is limited to breaches of the peace, threats to the peace, and acts of aggression, but increasingly the Security Council (the least democratic part of the U.N., because any one of its five permanent members may veto and U.N. resolution) finds itself faced with human rights catastrophes which it proves unable to stop, even under its binding Chapter VII authority;
- many other U.N. and specialized agencies also deal with human rights:
  ○ the United Nations Educational, Scientific and Cultural Organisation (UNESCO), with which the U.S. has also had a rocky relationship;
  ○ the World Health Organization (WHO);
  ○ the Food and Agriculture Organisation (FAO);
  ○ the International Labour Organisation (ILO).

Primary Source Documents

I. THE CHARTER OF THE UNITED NATIONS ORGANISATION

The Charter of the United Nations Organisation, established in the United States of America when the U.N. Charter was adopted, entered into force in 1945. This Charter is the organic instrument of the UN, setting forth its purposes, powers, procedures, organs and financing. Its legal authority rests on the bits of sovereignty yielded by the countries of the world who believe that their national self-interest benefits from such an organization to provide a forum for discussion and resolution of problems common to the international community. The U.S. ratified the Charter and so it is a legal obligation of the U.S. to fulfill the obligations of the Charter. There are, however, many differences in how the U.S. and the U.N. see the Charter interpreted and applied. There is a complex dynamic between U.S. law, international law, and how human rights law under the U.N. is interpreted and applied. Most international legal obligations of the U.S. have their source in the U.N. Charter, as well as under international human rights treaties created together by states in the UN, entered into and ratified by the U.S. This Charter is neither the basis of a one-world government nor does it supercede the U.S. Constitution, which remains the supreme law of the U.S., though the U.S. Constitution has a place for international law within it.

{Excerpt}

U.N. Charter

WE THE PEOPLES OF THE UNITED NATIONS, DETERMINED
*   to save succeeding generations from the scourge of war, which twice in our lifetime has brought untold sorrow to mankind, and
*   to reaffirm faith in fundamental human rights, in the dignity and worth of the human person, in the equal rights of men and women and of nations large and small, and
*   to establish conditions under which justice and respect for the obligations arising from treaties and other sources of international law can be maintained, and
*   to promote social progress and better standards of life in larger freedom,

AND FOR THESE ENDS
*   to practice tolerance and live together in peace with one another as good neighbours, and
*   to unite our strength to maintain international peace and security, and
*   to ensure, by the acceptance of principles and the institution of methods, that armed force shall not be used, save in the common interest, and
*   to employ international machinery for the promotion of the economic and social advancement of all peoples,

HAVE RESOLVED TO COMBINE OUR EFFORTS TO ACCOMPLISH THESE AIMS

Accordingly, our respective Governments, through representatives assembled in the city of San Francisco, who have exhibited their full powers found to be in good and due form, have agreed to the present Charter of the United Nations and do hereby establish an international organization to be known as the United Nations.

CHAPTER I: PURPOSES AND PRINCIPLES

Article 1

The Purposes of the United Nations are:

1. To maintain international peace and security, and to that end: to take effective collective measures for the prevention and removal of threats to the peace, and for the suppression of acts of aggression or other breaches of the peace, and to bring about by peaceful means, and in conformity with the principles of justice and international law, adjustment or settlement of international disputes or situations which might lead to a breach of the peace;

2. To develop friendly relations among nations based on respect for the principle of equal rights and self-determination of peoples, and to take other appropriate measures to strengthen universal peace;

3. To achieve international co-operation in solving international problems of an economic, social, cultural, or humanitarian character, and in promoting and encouraging respect for human rights and for fundamental freedoms for all without distinction as to race, sex, language, or religion; and

4. To be a centre for harmonizing the actions of nations in the attainment of these common ends.

Article 2

The Organization and its Members, in pursuit of the Purposes stated in Article 1, shall act in accordance with the following Principles.

1. The Organization is based on the principle of the sovereign equality of all its Members.

2. All Members, in order to ensure to all of them the rights and benefits resulting from membership, shall fulfill in good faith the obligations assumed by them in accordance with the present Charter.

3. All Members shall settle their international disputes by peaceful means in such a manner that international peace and security, and justice, are not endangered.

4. All Members shall refrain in their international relations from the threat or use of force against the territorial integrity or political independence of any state, or in any other manner inconsistent with the Purposes of the United Nations.

5. All Members shall give the United Nations every assistance in any action it takes in accordance with the present Charter, and shall refrain from giving assistance to any state against which the United Nations is taking preventive or enforcement action.

6. The Organization shall ensure that states which are not Members of the United Nations act in accordance with these Principles so far as may be necessary for the maintenance of international peace and security.

7. Nothing contained in the present Charter shall authorize the United Nations to intervene in matters which are essentially within the domestic jurisdiction of any state or shall require the Members to submit such matters to settlement under the present Charter; but this principle shall not prejudice the application of enforcement measures under Chapter VII.

CHAPTER II: MEMBERSHIP

Article 3

The original Members of the United Nations shall be the states which, having participated in the United Nations Conference on International Organization at San Francisco, or having previously signed the Declaration by United Nations of 1 January 1942, sign the present Charter and ratify it in accordance with Article 110.

Article 4

1. Membership in the United Nations is open to all other peace-loving states which accept the obligations contained in the present Charter and, in the judgment of the Organization, are able and willing to carry out these obligations.

2. The admission of any such state to membership in the United Nations will be effected by a decision of the General Assembly upon the recommendation of the Security Council.

Article 5

A Member of the United Nations against which preventive or enforcement action has been taken by the Security Council may be suspended from the exercise of the rights and privileges of membership by the General Assembly upon the recommendation of the Security Council. The exercise of these rights and privileges may be restored by the Security Council.

Article 6

A Member of the United Nations which has persistently violated the Principles contained in the present Charter may be expelled from the Organization by the General Assembly upon the recommendation of the Security Council.

CHAPTER III: ORGANS

Article 7

1. There are established as principal organs of the United Nations: a General Assembly, a Security Council, an Economic and Social Council, a Trusteeship Council, an International Court of Justice and a Secretariat.

2. Such subsidiary organs as may be found necessary may be established in accordance with the present Charter.

Article 8

The United Nations shall place no restrictions on the eligibility of men and women to participate in any capacity and under conditions of equality in its principal and subsidiary organs.

CHAPTER IV: THE GENERAL ASSEMBLY

COMPOSITION

Article 9

1. The General Assembly shall consist of all the Members of the United Nations.

2. Each Member shall have not more than five representatives in the General Assembly.

FUNCTIONS and POWERS

Article 10

The General Assembly may discuss any questions or any matters within the scope of the present Charter or relating to the powers and functions of any organs provided for in the present Charter, and, except as provided in Article 12, may make recommendations to the Members of the United Nations or to the Security Council or to both on any such questions or matters.

Article 11

1. The General Assembly may consider the general principles of co-operation in the maintenance of international peace and security, including the principles governing disarmament and the regulation of armaments, and may make recommendations with regard to such principles to the Members or to the Security Council or to both.

2. The General Assembly may discuss any questions relating to the maintenance of international peace and security brought before it by any Member of the United Nations, or by the Security Council, or by a state which is not a Member of the United Nations in accordance with Article 35, paragraph 2, and, except as provided in Article 12, may make recommendations with regard to any such questions to the state or states concerned or to the Security Council or to both. Any such question on which action is necessary shall be referred to the Security Council by the General Assembly either before or after discussion.

3. The General Assembly may call the attention of the Security Council to situations which are likely to endanger international peace and security.

4. The powers of the General Assembly set forth in this Article shall not limit the general scope of Article 10.

Article 12

1. While the Security Council is exercising in respect of any dispute or situation the functions assigned to it in the present Charter, the General Assembly shall not make any recommendation with regard to that dispute or situation unless the Security Council so requests.

2. The Secretary-General, with the consent of the Security Council, shall notify the General Assembly at each session of any matters relative to the maintenance of international peace and security which are being dealt with by the Security Council and shall similarly notify the General Assembly, or the Members of the United Nations if the General Assembly is not in session, immediately the Security Council ceases to deal with such matters.

Article 13

1. The General Assembly shall initiate studies and make recommendations for the purpose of:

a. promoting international co-operation in the political field and encouraging the progressive development of international law and its codification;

b. promoting international co-operation in the economic, social, cultural, educational, and health fields, and assisting in the realization of human rights and fundamental freedoms for all without distinction as to race, sex, language, or religion.

c. The further responsibilities, functions and powers of the General Assembly with respect to matters mentioned in paragraph 1 (b) above are set forth in Chapters IX and X.

Article 14

Subject to the provisions of Article 12, the General Assembly may recommend measures for the peaceful adjustment of any situation, regardless of origin, which it deems likely to impair the general welfare or friendly relations among nations, including situations resulting from a violation of the provisions of the present Charter setting forth the Purposes and Principles of the United Nations.

VOTING

Article 18

1. Each member of the General Assembly shall have one vote.

2. Decisions of the General Assembly on important questions shall be made by a two-thirds majority of the members present and voting. These questions shall include: recommendations with respect to the maintenance of international peace and security, the election of the nonpermanent members of the Security Council, the election of the members of the Economic and Social Council, the election of members of the Trusteeship Council in accordance with paragraph 1 (c) of Article 86, the admission of new Members to the United Nations, the suspension of the rights and privileges of membership, the expulsion of Members, questions relating to the operation of the trusteeship system, and budgetary questions.

3. Decisions on other questions, including the determination of additional categories of questions to be decided by a two-thirds majority, shall be made by a majority of the members present and voting.

Article 19

A Member of the United Nations which is in arrears in the payment of its financial contributions to the Organization shall have no vote in the General Assembly if the amount of its arrears equals or exceeds the amount of the contributions due from it for the preceding two full years. The General Assembly may, nevertheless, permit such a Member to vote if it is satisfied that the failure to pay is due to conditions beyond the control of the Member.

...

Article 22

The General Assembly may establish such subsidiary organs as it deems necessary for the performance of its functions.

CHAPTER V: THE SECURITY COUNCIL

COMPOSITION

Article 23

1. The Security Council shall consist of fifteen Members of the United Nations. The Republic of China, France, the Union of Soviet Socialist Republics, the United Kingdom of Great Britain and Northern Ireland, and the United States of America shall be permanent members of the Security Council. The General Assembly shall elect ten other Members of the United Nations to be non-permanent members of the Security Council, due regard being specially paid, in the first instance to the contribution of Members of the United Nations to the maintenance of international peace and security and to the other purposes of the Organization, and also to equitable geographical distribution.

2. The non-permanent members of the Security Council shall be elected for a term of two years. In the first election of the non-permanent members after the increase of the membership of the Security Council from eleven to fifteen, two of the four additional members shall be chosen for a term of one year. A retiring member shall not be eligible for immediate re-election.

3. Each member of the Security Council shall have one representative.

FUNCTIONS and POWERS

Article 24

1. In order to ensure prompt and effective action by the United Nations, its Members confer on the Security Council primary responsibility for the maintenance of international peace and security, and agree that in carrying out its duties under this responsibility the Security Council acts on their behalf.

2. In discharging these duties the Security Council shall act in accordance with the Purposes and Principles of the United Nations. The specific powers granted to the Security Council for the discharge of these duties are laid down in Chapters VI, VII, VIII, and XII.

3. The Security Council shall submit annual and, when necessary, special reports to the General Assembly for its consideration.

Article 25

The Members of the United Nations agree to accept and carry out the decisions of the Security Council in accordance with the present Charter.

Article 26

In order to promote the establishment and maintenance of international peace and security with the least diversion for armaments of the world's human and economic resources, the Security Council shall be responsible for formulating, with the assistance of the Military Staff Committee referred to in Article 47, plans to be submitted to the Members of the United Nations for the establishment of a system for the regulation of armaments.

VOTING

Article 27

1. Each member of the Security Council shall have one vote.

2. Decisions of the Security Council on procedural matters shall be made by an affirmative vote of nine members.

3. Decisions of the Security Council on all other matters shall be made by an affirmative vote of nine members including the concurring votes of the permanent members; provided that, in decisions under Chapter VI, and under paragraph 3 of Article 52, a party to a dispute shall abstain from voting.

PROCEDURE

Article 28

1. The Security Council shall be so organized as to be able to function continuously. Each member of the Security Council shall for this purpose be represented at all times at the seat of the Organization.

2. The Security Council shall hold periodic meetings at which each of its members may, if it so desires, be represented by a member of the government or by some other specially designated representative.

3. The Security Council may hold meetings at such places other than the seat of the Organization as in its judgment will best facilitate its work.

CHAPTER VI: PACIFIC SETTLEMENT OF DISPUTES

Article 33

1. The parties to any dispute, the continuance of which is likely to endanger the maintenance of international peace and security, shall, first of all, seek a solution by negotiation, enquiry, mediation, conciliation, arbitration, judicial settlement, resort to regional agencies or arrangements, or other peaceful means of their own choice.

2. The Security Council shall, when it deems necessary, call upon the parties to settle their dispute by such means.

Article 34

The Security Council may investigate any dispute, or any situation which might lead to international friction or give rise to a dispute, in order to determine whether the continuance of the dispute or situation is likely to endanger the maintenance of international peace and security.

Article 35

1. Any Member of the United Nations may bring any dispute, or any situation of the nature referred to in Article 34, to the attention of the Security Council or of the General Assembly.

2. A state which is not a Member of the United Nations may bring to the attention of the Security Council or of the General Assembly any dispute to which it is a party if it accepts in advance, for the purposes of the dispute, the obligations of pacific settlement provided in the present Charter.

3. The proceedings of the General Assembly in respect of matters brought to its attention under this Article will be subject to the provisions of Articles 11 and 12.

Article 36

1. The Security Council may, at any stage of a dispute of the nature referred to in Article 33 or of a situation of like nature, recommend appropriate procedures or methods of adjustment.

2. The Security Council should take into consideration any procedures for the settlement of the dispute which have already been adopted by the parties.

3. In making recommendations under this Article the Security Council should also take into consideration that legal disputes should as a general rule be referred by the parties to the International Court of Justice in accordance with the provisions of the Statute of the Court.

Article 37

1. Should the parties to a dispute of the nature referred to in Article 33 fail to settle it by the means indicated in that Article, they shall refer it to the Security Council.

2. If the Security Council deems that the continuance of the dispute is in fact likely to endanger the maintenance of international peace and security, it shall decide whether to take action under Article 36 or to recommend such terms of settlement as it may consider appropriate.

Article 38

Without prejudice to the provisions of Articles 33 to 37, the Security Council may, if all the parties to any dispute so request, make recommendations to the parties with a view to a pacific settlement of the dispute.

CHAPTER VII: ACTION WITH RESPECT TO THREATS TO THE PEACE, BREACHES OF THE PEACE, AND ACTS OF AGGRESSION

Article 39

The Security Council shall determine the existence of any threat to the peace, breach of the peace, or act of aggression and shall make recommendations, or decide what measures shall be taken in accordance with Articles 41 and 42, to maintain or restore international peace and security.

Article 40

In order to prevent an aggravation of the situation, the Security Council may, before making the recommendations or deciding upon the measures provided for in Article 39, call upon the parties concerned to comply with such provisional measures as it deems necessary or desirable. Such provisional measures shall be without prejudice to the rights, claims, or position of the parties concerned. The Security Council shall duly take account of failure to comply with such provisional measures.

Article 41

The Security Council may decide what measures not involving the use of armed force are to be employed to give effect to its decisions, and it may call upon the Members of the United Nations to apply such measures. These may include complete or partial interruption of economic relations and of rail, sea, air, postal, telegraphic, radio, and other means of communication, and the severance of diplomatic relations.

Article 42

Should the Security Council consider that measures provided for in Article 41 would be inadequate or have proved to be inadequate, it may take such action by air, sea, or land forces as may be necessary to maintain or restore international peace and security. Such action may include demonstrations, blockade, and other operations by air, sea, or land forces of Members of the United Nations.

Article 43

1. All Members of the United Nations, in order to contribute to the maintenance of international peace and security, undertake to make available to the Security Council, on its call and in accordance with a special agreement or agree-

ments, armed forces, assistance, and facilities, including rights of passage, necessary for the purpose of maintaining international peace and security.

2. Such agreement or agreements shall govern the numbers and types of forces, their degree of readiness and general location, and the nature of the facilities and assistance to be provided. 3. The agreement or agreements shall be negotiated as soon as possible on the initiative of the Security Council. They shall be concluded between the Security Council and Members or between the Security Council and groups of Members and shall be subject to ratification by the signatory states in accordance with their respective constitutional processes.

Article 44

When the Security Council has decided to use force it shall, before calling upon a Member not represented on it to provide armed forces in fulfilment of the obligations assumed under Article 43, invite that Member, if the Member so desires, to participate in the decisions of the Security Council concerning the employment of contingents of that Member's armed forces.

Article 45

In order to enable the United Nations to take urgent military measures, Members shall hold immediately available national air-force contingents for combined international enforcement action. The strength and degree of readiness of these contingents and plans for their combined action shall be determined within the limits laid down in the special agreement or agreements referred to in Article 43, by the Security Council with the assistance of the Military Staff Committee.

Article 46

Plans for the application of armed force shall be made by the Security Council with the assistance of the Military Staff Committee.

Article 47

1. There shall be established a Military Staff Committee to advise and assist the Security Council on all questions relating to the Security Council's military requirements for the maintenance of international peace and security, the employment and command of forces placed at its disposal, the regulation of armaments, and possible disarmament.

2. The Military Staff Committee shall consist of the Chiefs of Staff of the permanent members of the Security Council or their representatives. Any Member of the United Nations not permanently represented on the Committee shall be invited by the Committee to be associated with it when the efficient discharge of the Committee's responsibilities requires the participation of that Member in its work.

3. The Military Staff Committee shall be responsible under the Security Council for the strategic direction of any armed forces placed at the disposal of the Security Council. Questions relating to the command of such forces shall be worked out subsequently.

4. The Military Staff Committee, with the authorization of the Security Council and after consultation with appropriate regional agencies, may establish regional sub-committees.

Article 48

1. The action required to carry out the decisions of the Security Council for the maintenance of international peace and security shall be taken by all the Members of the United Nations or by some of them, as the Security Council may determine.

2. Such decisions shall be carried out by the Members of the United Nations directly and through their action in the appropriate international agencies of which they are members.

Article 49

The Members of the United Nations shall join in affording mutual assistance in carrying out the measures decided upon by the Security Council.

Article 50

If preventive or enforcement measures against any state are taken by the Security Council, any other state, whether a Member of the United Nations or not, which finds itself confronted with special economic problems arising from the carrying out of those measures shall have the right to consult the Security Council with regard to a solution of those problems.

Article 51

Nothing in the present Charter shall impair the inherent right of individual or collective self-defence if an armed attack occurs against a Member of the United Nations, until the Security Council has taken measures necessary to maintain international peace and security. Measures taken by Members in the exercise of this right of self-defence shall be immediately reported to the Security Council and shall not in any way affect the authority and responsibility of the Security Council under the present Charter to take at any time such action as it deems necessary in order to maintain or restore international peace and security.

CHAPTER VIII: REGIONAL ARRANGEMENTS

Article 52

Nothing in the present Charter precludes the existence of regional arrangements or agencies for dealing with such matters relating to the maintenance of international peace and security as are appropriate for regional action provided that such arrangements or agencies and their activities are consistent with the Purposes and Principles of the United Nations.

CHAPTER IX: INTERNATIONAL ECONOMIC AND SOCIAL COOPERATION

Article 55

With a view to the creation of conditions of stability and well-being which are necessary for peaceful and friendly relations among nations based on respect for the principle of equal rights and self-determination of peoples, the United Nations shall promote:

a. higher standards of living, full employment, and conditions of economic and social progress and development;

b. solutions of international economic, social, health, and related problems; and international cultural and educational cooperation; and

c. universal respect for, and observance of, human rights and fundamental freedoms for all without distinction as to race, sex, language, or religion.

Article 56

All Members pledge themselves to take joint and separate action in co-operation with the Organization for the achievement of the purposes set forth in Article 55.

...

CHAPTER X: THE ECONOMIC AND SOCIAL COUNCIL

COMPOSITION

Article 61

1. The Economic and Social Council shall consist of fifty-four Members of the United Nations elected by the General Assembly.

2. Subject to the provisions of paragraph 3, eighteen members of the Economic and Social Council shall be elected each year for a term of three years. A retiring member shall be eligible for immediate re-election.

...

FUNCTIONS and POWERS

Article 62

1. The Economic and Social Council may make or initiate studies and reports with respect to international economic, social, cultural, educational, health, and related matters and may make recommendations with respect to any such matters to the General Assembly to the Members of the United Nations, and to the specialized agencies concerned.

2. It may make recommendations for the purpose of promoting respect for, and observance of, human rights and fundamental freedoms for all.

3. It may prepare draft conventions for submission to the General Assembly, with respect to matters falling within its competence.

4. It may call, in accordance with the rules prescribed by the United Nations, international conferences on matters falling within its competence.

...

PROCEDURE

Article 68

The Economic and Social Council shall set up commissions in economic and social fields and for the promotion of human rights, and such other commissions as may be required for the performance of its functions.

...

CHAPTER XIV: THE INTERNATIONAL COURT OF JUSTICE

Article 92

The International Court of Justice shall be the principal judicial organ of the United Nations. It shall function in accordance with the annexed Statute, which is based upon the Statute of the Permanent Court of International Justice and forms an integral part of the present Charter.

Article 93

1. All Members of the United Nations are ipso facto parties to the Statute of the International Court of Justice.

A state which is not a Member of the United Nations may become a party to the Statute of the International Court of Justice on conditions to be determined in each case by the General Assembly upon the recommendation of the Security Council.

Article 94

Each Member of the United Nations undertakes to comply with the decision of the International Court of Justice in any case to which it is a party.

1. If any party to a case fails to perform the obligations incumbent upon it under a judgment rendered by the Court, the other party may have recourse to the Security Council, which may, if it deems necessary, make recommendations or decide upon measures to be taken to give effect to the judgment.

....

CHAPTER XVI: MISCELLANEOUS PROVISIONS

Article 103

In the event of a conflict between the obligations of the Members of the United Nations under the present Charter and their obligations under any other international agreement, their obligations under the present Charter shall prevail.

Article 111

The present Charter, of which the Chinese, French, Russian, English, and Spanish texts are equally authentic, shall remain deposited in the archives of the Government of the United States of America. Duly certified copies thereof shall be transmitted by that Government to the Governments of the other signatory states.

IN FAITH WHEREOF the representatives of the Governments of the United Nations have signed the present Charter. DONE at the city of San Francisco the twenty-sixth day of June, one thousand nine hundred and forty-five.

Source: http://www.un.org/en/charter-united-nations

2. VIENNA DECLARATION AND PROGRAMME OF ACTION, 1993

The following is the entire text of the Vienna Declaration and Programme of Action, as adopted by the World Conference on Human Rights on 25 June 1993. The authors' bold sections highlight the important principles of the universality of human rights. The latter portions of the text represents how well the Vienna Declaration, in which the U.S. was a very significant partner, summarizes the human rights work the U.N. had completed up until 1993.

Vienna Declaration and Programme of Action

Adopted by the World Conference on Human Rights in Vienna on 25 June 1993

The World Conference on Human Rights,

Considering that the promotion and protection of human rights is a matter of priority for the international community, and that the Conference affords a unique opportunity to carry out a comprehensive analysis of the international human rights system and of the machinery for the protection of human rights, in order to enhance and thus promote a fuller observance of those rights, in a just and balanced manner,

Recognizing and affirming that all human rights derive from the dignity and worth inherent in the human person, and that the human person is the central subject of human rights and fundamental freedoms, and consequently should be the principal beneficiary and should participate actively in the realization of these rights and freedoms,

Reaffirming their commitment to the purposes and principles contained in the Charter of the United Nations and the Universal Declaration of Human Rights,

Reaffirming the commitment contained in Article 56 of the Charter of the United Nations to take joint and separate action, placing proper emphasis on developing effective international cooperation for the realization of the purposes set out in Article 55, including universal respect for, and observance of, human rights and fundamental freedoms for all,

Emphasizing the responsibilities of all States, in conformity with the Charter of the United Nations, to develop and encourage respect for human rights and fundamental freedoms for all, without distinction as to race, sex, language or religion,

Recalling the Preamble to the Charter of the United Nations, in particular the determination to reaffirm faith in fundamental human rights, in the dignity and worth of the human person, and in the equal rights of men and women and of nations large and small,

Recalling also the determination expressed in the Preamble of the Charter of the United Nations to save succeeding generations from the scourge of war, to establish conditions under which justice and respect for obligations arising from treaties and other sources of international law can be maintained, to promote social progress and better standards of life in larger freedom, to practice tolerance and good neighbourliness, and to employ international machinery for the promotion of the economic and social advancement of all peoples,

Emphasizing that the Universal Declaration of Human Rights, which constitutes a common standard of achievement for all peoples and all nations, is the source of inspiration and has been the basis for the United Nations in making advances in standard setting as contained in the existing international human rights instruments, in particular the International Covenant on Civil and Political Rights and the International Covenant on Economic, Social and Cultural Rights,

Considering the major changes taking place on the international scene and the aspirations of all the peoples for an international order based on the principles enshrined in the Charter of the United Nations, including promoting and encouraging respect for human rights and fundamental freedoms for all and respect for the principle of equal rights and self-determination of peoples, peace, democracy, justice, equality, rule of law, pluralism, development, better standards of living and solidarity,

Deeply concerned by various forms of discrimination and violence, to which women continue to be exposed all over the world,

Recognizing that the activities of the United Nations in the field of human rights should be rationalized and enhanced in order to strengthen the United Nations machinery in this field and to further the objectives of universal respect for observance of international human rights standards,

Having taken into account the Declarations adopted by the three regional meetings at Tunis, San José and Bangkok and the contributions made by Governments, and bearing in mind the suggestions made by intergovernmental and non-governmental organizations, as well as the studies prepared by independent experts during the preparatory process leading to the World Conference on Human Rights,

Welcoming the International Year of the World's Indigenous People 1993 as a reaffirmation of the commitment of the international community to ensure their enjoyment of all human rights and fundamental freedoms and to respect the value and diversity of their cultures and identities,

Recognizing also that the international community should devise ways and means to remove the current obstacles and meet challenges to the full realization of all human rights and to prevent the continuation of human rights violations resulting therefrom throughout the world,

Invoking the spirit of our age and the realities of our time which call upon the peoples of the world and all States Members of the United Nations to rededicate themselves to the global task of promoting and protecting all human rights and fundamental freedoms so as to secure full and universal enjoyment of these rights,

Determined to take new steps forward in the commitment of the international community with a view to achieving substantial progress in human rights endeavours by an increased and sustained effort of international cooperation and solidarity,

Solemnly adopts the Vienna Declaration and Programme of Action.

I

1. The World Conference on Human Rights reaffirms the solemn commitment of all States to fulfil their obligations to promote universal respect for, and observance and protection of, all human rights and fundamental freedoms for all in accordance with the Charter of the United Nations, other instruments relating to human rights, and international law. The universal nature of these rights and freedoms is beyond question.

In this framework, enhancement of international cooperation in the field of human rights is essential for the full achievement of the purposes of the United Nations.

Human rights and fundamental freedoms are the birthright of all human beings; their protection and promotion is the first responsibility of Governments.

2. All peoples have the right of self-determination. By virtue of that right they freely determine their political status, and freely pursue their economic, social and cultural development.

Taking into account the particular situation of peoples under colonial or other forms of alien domination or foreign occupation, the World Conference on Human Rights recognizes the right of peoples to take any legitimate action, in accordance with the Charter of the United Nations, to realize their inalienable right of self-determination. The World Conference on Human Rights considers the denial of the right of self-determination as a violation of human rights and underlines the importance of the effective realization of this right.

In accordance with the Declaration on Principles of International Law concerning Friendly Relations and Cooperation Among States in accordance with the Charter of the United Nations, this shall not be construed as authorizing or encouraging any action which would dismember or impair, totally or in part, the territorial integrity or political unity of sovereign and independent States conducting themselves in compliance with the principle of equal rights and self-determination of peoples and thus possessed of a Government representing the whole people belonging to the territory without distinction of any kind.

3. Effective international measures to guarantee and monitor the implementation of human rights standards should be taken in respect of people under foreign occupation, and effective legal protection against the violation of their human rights should be provided, in accordance with human rights norms and international law, particularly the Geneva Convention relative to the Protection of Civilian Persons in Time of War, of 14 August 1949, and other applicable norms of humanitarian law.

4. The promotion and protection of all human rights and fundamental freedoms must be considered as a priority objective of the United Nations in accordance with its purposes and principles, in particular the purpose of international cooperation. In the framework of these purposes and principles, the promotion and protection of all human rights is a legitimate concern of the international community. The organs and specialized agencies related to human rights should therefore further enhance the coordination of their activities based on the consistent and objective application of international human rights instruments.

5. All human rights are universal, indivisible and interdependent and interrelated. The international community must treat human rights globally in a fair and equal manner, on the same footing, and with the same emphasis. While the significance of national and regional particularities and various historical, cultural and religious backgrounds must be borne in mind, it is the duty of States, regardless of their political, economic and cultural systems, to promote and protect all human rights and fundamental freedoms.

6. The efforts of the United Nations system towards the universal respect for, and observance of, human rights and fundamental freedoms for all, contribute to the stability and well-being necessary for peaceful and friendly relations among nations, and to improved conditions for peace and security as well as social and economic development, in conformity with the Charter of the United Nations.

7. The processes of promoting and protecting human rights should be conducted in conformity with the purposes and principles of the Charter of the United Nations, and international law.

8. Democracy, development and respect for human rights and fundamental freedoms are interdependent and mutually reinforcing. Democracy is based on the freely expressed will of the people to determine their own political, economic, social and cultural systems and their full participation in all aspects of their lives. In the context of the above, the promotion and protection of human rights and fundamental freedoms at the national and international levels should be universal and conducted without conditions attached. The international community should support the strengthening and promoting of democracy, development and respect for human rights and fundamental freedoms in the entire world.

9. The World Conference on Human Rights reaffirms that least developed countries committed to the process of democratization and economic reforms, many of which are in Africa, should be supported by the international community in order to succeed in their transition to democracy and economic development.

10. The World Conference on Human Rights reaffirms the right to development, as established in the Declaration on the Right to Development, as a universal and inalienable right and an integral part of fundamental human rights.

As stated in the Declaration on the Right to Development, the human person is the central subject of development.

While development facilitates the enjoyment of all human rights, the lack of development may not be invoked to justify the abridgement of internationally recognized human rights.

States should cooperate with each other in ensuring development and eliminating obstacles to development. The international community should promote an effective international cooperation for the realization of the right to development and the elimination of obstacles to development.

Lasting progress towards the implementation of the right to development requires effective development policies at the national level, as well as equitable economic relations and a favourable economic environment at the international level.

11. The right to development should be fulfilled so as to meet equitably the developmental and environmental needs of present and future generations. The World Conference on Human Rights recognizes that illicit dumping of toxic and dangerous substances and waste potentially constitutes a serious threat to the human rights to life and health of everyone.

Consequently, the World Conference on Human Rights calls on all States to adopt and vigorously implement existing conventions relating to the dumping of toxic and dangerous products and waste and to cooperate in the prevention of illicit dumping.

Everyone has the right to enjoy the benefits of scientific progress and its applications. The World Conference on Human Rights notes that certain advances, notably in the biomedical and life sciences as well as in information technology, may have potentially adverse consequences for the integrity, dignity and human rights of the individual, and calls for international cooperation to ensure that human rights and dignity are fully respected in this area of universal concern.

12. The World Conference on Human Rights calls upon the international community to make all efforts to help alleviate the external debt burden of developing countries, in order to supplement the efforts of the Governments of such countries to attain the full realization of the economic, social and cultural rights of their people.

13. There is a need for States and international organizations, in cooperation with non-governmental organizations, to create favourable conditions at the national, regional and international levels to ensure the full and effective enjoyment of human rights. States should eliminate all violations of human rights and their causes, as well as obstacles to the enjoyment of these rights.

14. The existence of widespread extreme poverty inhibits the full and effective enjoyment of human rights; its immediate alleviation and eventual elimination must remain a high priority for the international community.

15. Respect for human rights and for fundamental freedoms without distinction of any kind is a fundamental rule of international human rights law. The speedy and comprehensive elimination of all forms of racism and racial discrimination, xenophobia and related intolerance is a priority task for the international community. Governments should take

effective measures to prevent and combat them. Groups, institutions, intergovernmental and non-governmental organizations and individuals are urged to intensify their efforts in cooperating and coordinating their activities against these evils.

16. The World Conference on Human Rights welcomes the progress made in dismantling apartheid and calls upon the international community and the United Nations system to assist in this process.

The World Conference on Human Rights also deplores the continuing acts of violence aimed at undermining the quest for a peaceful dismantling of apartheid.

17. The acts, methods and practices of terrorism in all its forms and manifestations as well as linkage in some countries to drug trafficking are activities aimed at the destruction of human rights, fundamental freedoms and democracy, threatening territorial integrity, security of States and destabilizing legitimately constituted Governments. The international community should take the necessary steps to enhance cooperation to prevent and combat terrorism.

18. The human rights of women and of the girl-child are an inalienable, integral and indivisible part of universal human rights. The full and equal participation of women in political, civil, economic, social and cultural life, at the national, regional and international levels, and the eradication of all forms of discrimination on grounds of sex are priority objectives of the international community.

Gender-based violence and all forms of sexual harassment and exploitation, including those resulting from cultural prejudice and international trafficking, are incompatible with the dignity and worth of the human person, and must be eliminated. This can be achieved by legal measures and through national action and international cooperation in such fields as economic and social development, education, safe maternity and health care, and social support.

The human rights of women should form an integral part of the United Nations human rights activities, including the promotion of all human rights instruments relating to women.

The World Conference on Human Rights urges Governments, institutions, intergovernmental and non-governmental organizations to intensify their efforts for the protection and promotion of human rights of women and the girl-child.

19. Considering the importance of the promotion and protection of the rights of persons belonging to minorities and the contribution of such promotion and protection to the political and social stability of the States in which such persons live,

The World Conference on Human Rights reaffirms the obligation of States to ensure that persons belonging to minorities may exercise fully and effectively all human rights and fundamental freedoms without any discrimination and in full equality before the law in accordance with the Declaration on the Rights of Persons Belonging to National or Ethnic, Religious and Linguistic Minorities.

The persons belonging to minorities have the right to enjoy their own culture, to profess and practise their own religion and to use their own language in private and in public, freely and without interference or any form of discrimination.

20. The World Conference on Human Rights recognizes the inherent dignity and the unique contribution of indigenous people to the development and plurality of society and strongly reaffirms the commitment of the international community to their economic, social and cultural well-being and their enjoyment of the fruits of sustainable development. States should ensure the full and free participation of indigenous people in all aspects of society, in particular in matters of concern to them. Considering the importance of the promotion and protection of the rights of indigenous people, and the contribution of such promotion and protection to the political and social stability of the States in which such people live, States should, in accordance with international law, take concerted positive steps to ensure respect for all human rights and fundamental freedoms of indigenous people, on the basis of equality and non-discrimination, and recognize the value and diversity of their distinct identities, cultures and social organization.

21. The World Conference on Human Rights, welcoming the early ratification of the Convention on the Rights of the Child by a large number of States and noting the recognition of the human rights of children in the World Declaration on the Survival, Protection and Development of Children and Plan of Action adopted by the World Summit for Chil-

dren, urges universal ratification of the Convention by 1995 and its effective implementation by States parties through the adoption of all the necessary legislative, administrative and other measures and the allocation to the maximum extent of the available resources. In all actions concerning children, non-discrimination and the best interest of the child should be primary considerations and the views of the child given due weight. National and international mechanisms and programmes should be strengthened for the defence and protection of children, in particular, the girl-child, abandoned children, street children, economically and sexually exploited children, including through child pornography, child prostitution or sale of organs, children victims of diseases including acquired immunodeficiency syndrome, refugee and displaced children, children in detention, children in armed conflict, as well as children victims of famine and drought and other emergencies. International cooperation and solidarity should be promoted to support the implementation of the Convention and the rights of the child should be a priority in the United Nations system-wide action on human rights.

The World Conference on Human Rights also stresses that the child for the full and harmonious development of his or her personality should grow up in a family environment which accordingly merits broader protection.

22. Special attention needs to be paid to ensuring non-discrimination, and the equal enjoyment of all human rights and fundamental freedoms by disabled persons, including their active participation in all aspects of society.

23. The World Conference on Human Rights reaffirms that everyone, without distinction of any kind, is entitled to the right to seek and to enjoy in other countries asylum from persecution, as well as the right to return to one's own country. In this respect it stresses the importance of the Universal Declaration of Human Rights, the 1951 Convention relating to the Status of Refugees, its 1967 Protocol and regional instruments. It expresses its appreciation to States that continue to admit and host large numbers of refugees in their territories, and to the Office of the United Nations High Commissioner for Refugees for its dedication to its task. It also expresses its appreciation to the United Nations Relief and Works Agency for Palestine Refugees in the Near East.

The World Conference on Human Rights recognizes that gross violations of human rights, including in armed conflicts, are among the multiple and complex factors leading to displacement of people.

The World Conference on Human Rights recognizes that, in view of the complexities of the global refugee crisis and in accordance with the Charter of the United Nations, relevant international instruments and international solidarity and in the spirit of burden-sharing, a comprehensive approach by the international community is needed in coordination and cooperation with the countries concerned and relevant organizations, bearing in mind the mandate of the United Nations High Commissioner for Refugees. This should include the development of strategies to address the root causes and effects of movements of refugees and other displaced persons, the strengthening of emergency preparedness and response mechanisms, the provision of effective protection and assistance, bearing in mind the special needs of women and children, as well as the achievement of durable solutions, primarily through the preferred solution of dignified and safe voluntary repatriation, including solutions such as those adopted by the international refugee conferences. The World Conference on Human Rights underlines the responsibilities of States, particularly as they relate to the countries of origin.

In the light of the comprehensive approach, the World Conference on Human Rights emphasizes the importance of giving special attention including through intergovernmental and humanitarian organizations and finding lasting solutions to questions related to internally displaced persons including their voluntary and safe return and rehabilitation.

In accordance with the Charter of the United Nations and the principles of humanitarian law, the World Conference on Human Rights further emphasizes the importance of and the need for humanitarian assistance to victims of all natural and man-made disasters.

24. Great importance must be given to the promotion and protection of the human rights of persons belonging to groups which have been rendered vulnerable, including migrant workers, the elimination of all forms of discrimination against them, and the strengthening and more effective implementation of existing human rights instruments. States have an obligation to create and maintain adequate measures at the national level, in particular in the fields of education, health and social support, for the promotion and protection of the rights of persons in vulnerable sectors of their populations and to ensure the participation of those among them who are interested in finding a solution to their own problems.

25. The World Conference on Human Rights affirms that extreme poverty and social exclusion constitute a violation of human dignity and that urgent steps are necessary to achieve better knowledge of extreme poverty and its causes, including those related to the problem of development, in order to promote the human rights of the poorest, and to put an end to extreme poverty and social exclusion and to promote the enjoyment of the fruits of social progress. It is essential for States to foster participation by the poorest people in the decision-making process by the community in which they live, the promotion of human rights and efforts to combat extreme poverty.

26. The World Conference on Human Rights welcomes the progress made in the codification of human rights instruments, which is a dynamic and evolving process, and urges the universal ratification of human rights treaties. All States are encouraged to accede to these international instruments; all States are encouraged to avoid, as far as possible, the resort to reservations.

27. Every State should provide an effective framework of remedies to redress human rights grievances or violations. The administration of justice, including law enforcement and prosecutorial agencies and, especially, an independent judiciary and legal profession in full conformity with applicable standards contained in international human rights instruments, are essential to the full and non-discriminatory realization of human rights and indispensable to the processes of democracy and sustainable development. In this context, institutions concerned with the administration of justice should be properly funded, and an increased level of both technical and financial assistance should be provided by the international community. It is incumbent upon the United Nations to make use of special programmes of advisory services on a priority basis for the achievement of a strong and independent administration of justice.

28. The World Conference on Human Rights expresses its dismay at massive violations of human rights especially in the form of genocide, "ethnic cleansing" and systematic rape of women in war situations, creating mass exodus of refugees and displaced persons. While strongly condemning such abhorrent practices it reiterates the call that perpetrators of such crimes be punished and such practices immediately stopped.

29. The World Conference on Human Rights expresses grave concern about continuing human rights violations in all parts of the world in disregard of standards as contained in international human rights instruments and international humanitarian law and about the lack of sufficient and effective remedies for the victims.

The World Conference on Human Rights is deeply concerned about violations of human rights during armed conflicts, affecting the civilian population, especially women, children, the elderly and the disabled. The Conference therefore calls upon States and all parties to armed conflicts strictly to observe international humanitarian law, as set forth in the Geneva Conventions of 1949 and other rules and principles of international law, as well as minimum standards for protection of human rights, as laid down in international conventions.

The World Conference on Human Rights reaffirms the right of the victims to be assisted by humanitarian organizations, as set forth in the Geneva Conventions of 1949 and other relevant instruments of international humanitarian law, and calls for the safe and timely access for such assistance.

30. The World Conference on Human Rights also expresses its dismay and condemnation that gross and systematic violations and situations that constitute serious obstacles to the full enjoyment of all human rights continue to occur in different parts of the world. Such violations and obstacles include, as well as torture and cruel, inhuman and degrading treatment or punishment, summary and arbitrary executions, disappearances, arbitrary detentions, all forms of racism, racial discrimination and apartheid, foreign occupation and alien domination, xenophobia, poverty, hunger and other denials of economic, social and cultural rights, religious intolerance, terrorism, discrimination against women and lack of the rule of law.

31. The World Conference on Human Rights calls upon States to refrain from any unilateral measure not in accordance with international law and the Charter of the United Nations that creates obstacles to trade relations among States and impedes the full realization of the human rights set forth in the Universal Declaration of Human Rights and international human rights instruments, in particular the rights of everyone to a standard of living adequate for their health and well-being, including food and medical care, housing and the necessary social services. The World Conference on Human Rights affirms that food should not be used as a tool for political pressure.

32. The World Conference on Human Rights reaffirms the importance of ensuring the universality, objectivity and non-selectivity of the consideration of human rights issues.

33. The World Conference on Human Rights reaffirms that States are duty-bound, as stipulated in the Universal Declaration of Human Rights and the International Covenant on Economic, Social and Cultural Rights and in other international human rights instruments, to ensure that education is aimed at strengthening the respect of human rights and fundamental freedoms. The World Conference on Human Rights emphasizes the importance of incorporating the subject of human rights education programmes and calls upon States to do so. Education should promote understanding, tolerance, peace and friendly relations between the nations and all racial or religious groups and encourage the development of United Nations activities in pursuance of these objectives. Therefore, education on human rights and the dissemination of proper information, both theoretical and practical, play an important role in the promotion and respect of human rights with regard to all individuals without distinction of any kind such as race, sex, language or religion, and this should be integrated in the education policies at the national as well as international levels. The World Conference on Human Rights notes that resource constraints and institutional inadequacies may impede the immediate realization of these objectives.

34. Increased efforts should be made to assist countries which so request to create the conditions whereby each individual can enjoy universal human rights and fundamental freedoms. Governments, the United Nations system as well as other multilateral organizations are urged to increase considerably the resources allocated to programmes aiming at the establishment and strengthening of national legislation, national institutions and related infrastructures which uphold the rule of law and democracy, electoral assistance, human rights awareness through training, teaching and education, popular participation and civil society.

The programmes of advisory services and technical cooperation under the Centre for Human Rights should be strengthened as well as made more efficient and transparent and thus become a major contribution to improving respect for human rights. States are called upon to increase their contributions to these programmes, both through promoting a larger allocation from the United Nations regular budget, and through voluntary contributions.

35. The full and effective implementation of United Nations activities to promote and protect human rights must reflect the high importance accorded to human rights by the Charter of the United Nations and the demands of the United Nations human rights activities, as mandated by Member States. To this end, United Nations human rights activities should be provided with increased resources.

36. The World Conference on Human Rights reaffirms the important and constructive role played by national institutions for the promotion and protection of human rights, in particular in their advisory capacity to the competent authorities, their role in remedying human rights violations, in the dissemination of human rights information, and education in human rights.

The World Conference on Human Rights encourages the establishment and strengthening of national institutions, having regard to the "Principles relating to the status of national institutions" and recognizing that it is the right of each State to choose the framework which is best suited to its particular needs at the national level.

37. Regional arrangements play a fundamental role in promoting and protecting human rights. They should reinforce universal human rights standards, as contained in international human rights instruments, and their protection. The World Conference on Human Rights endorses efforts under way to strengthen these arrangements and to increase their effectiveness, while at the same time stressing the importance of cooperation with the United Nations human rights activities.

The World Conference on Human Rights reiterates the need to consider the possibility of establishing regional and subregional arrangements for the promotion and protection of human rights where they do not already exist.

38. The World Conference on Human Rights recognizes the important role of non-governmental organizations in the promotion of all human rights and in humanitarian activities at national, regional and international levels. The World Conference on Human Rights appreciates their contribution to increasing public awareness of human rights issues, to the conduct of education, training and research in this field, and to the promotion and protection of all human rights

and fundamental freedoms. While recognizing that the primary responsibility for standard-setting lies with States, the conference also appreciates the contribution of non-governmental organizations to this process. In this respect, the World Conference on Human Rights emphasizes the importance of continued dialogue and cooperation between Governments and non-governmental organizations. Non-governmental organizations and their members genuinely involved in the field of human rights should enjoy the rights and freedoms recognized in the Universal Declaration of Human Rights, and the protection of the national law. These rights and freedoms may not be exercised contrary to the purposes and principles of the United Nations. Non-governmental organizations should be free to carry out their human rights activities, without interference, within the framework of national law and the Universal Declaration of Human Rights.

39. Underlining the importance of objective, responsible and impartial information about human rights and humanitarian issues, the World Conference on Human Rights encourages the increased involvement of the media, for whom freedom and protection should be guaranteed within the framework of national law.

II

A. Increased coordination on human rights within the United Nations system

1. The World Conference on Human Rights recommends increased coordination in support of human rights and fundamental freedoms within the United Nations system. To this end, the World Conference on Human Rights urges all United Nations organs, bodies and the specialized agencies whose activities deal with human rights to cooperate in order to strengthen, rationalize and streamline their activities, taking into account the need to avoid unnecessary duplication. The World Conference on Human Rights also recommends to the Secretary-General that high-level officials of relevant United Nations bodies and specialized agencies at their annual meeting, besides coordinating their activities, also assess the impact of their strategies and policies on the enjoyment of all human rights.

2. Furthermore, the World Conference on Human Rights calls on regional organizations and prominent international and regional finance and development institutions to assess also the impact of their policies and programmes on the enjoyment of human rights.

3. The World Conference on Human Rights recognizes that relevant specialized agencies and bodies and institutions of the United Nations system as well as other relevant intergovernmental organizations whose activities deal with human rights play a vital role in the formulation, promotion and implementation of human rights standards, within their respective mandates, and should take into account the outcome of the World Conference on Human Rights within their fields of competence.

4. The World Conference on Human Rights strongly recommends that a concerted effort be made to encourage and facilitate the ratification of and accession or succession to international human rights treaties and protocols adopted within the framework of the United Nations system with the aim of universal acceptance. The Secretary-General, in consultation with treaty bodies, should consider opening a dialogue with States not having acceded to these human rights treaties, in order to identify obstacles and to seek ways of overcoming them.

5. The World Conference on Human Rights encourages States to consider limiting the extent of any reservations they lodge to international human rights instruments, formulate any reservations as precisely and narrowly as possible, ensure that none is incompatible with the object and purpose of the relevant treaty and regularly review any reservations with a view to withdrawing them.

6. The World Conference on Human Rights, recognizing the need to maintain consistency with the high quality of existing international standards and to avoid proliferation of human rights instruments, reaffirms the guidelines relating to the elaboration of new international instruments contained in General Assembly resolution 41/120 of 4 December 1986 and calls on the United Nations human rights bodies, when considering the elaboration of new international standards, to keep those guidelines in mind, to consult with human rights treaty bodies on the necessity for drafting new standards and to request the Secretariat to carry out technical reviews of proposed new instruments.

7. The World Conference on Human Rights recommends that human rights officers be assigned if and when necessary to regional offices of the United Nations Organization with the purpose of disseminating information and offering training and other technical assistance in the field of human rights upon the request of concerned Member States. Human rights training for international civil servants who are assigned to work relating to human rights should be organized.

8. The World Conference on Human Rights welcomes the convening of emergency sessions of the Commission on Human Rights as a positive initiative and that other ways of responding to acute violations of human rights be considered by the relevant organs of the United Nations system.

Resources

9. The World Conference on Human Rights, concerned by the growing disparity between the activities of the Centre for Human Rights and the human, financial and other resources available to carry them out, and bearing in mind the resources needed for other important United Nations programmes, requests the Secretary-General and the General Assembly to take immediate steps to increase substantially the resources for the human rights programme from within the existing and future regular budgets of the United Nations, and to take urgent steps to seek increased extrabudgetary resources.

10. Within this framework, an increased proportion of the regular budget should be allocated directly to the Centre for Human Rights to cover its costs and all other costs borne by the Centre for Human Rights, including those related to the United Nations human rights bodies. Voluntary funding of the Centre's technical cooperation activities should reinforce this enhanced budget; the World Conference on Human Rights calls for generous contributions to the existing trust funds.

11. The World Conference on Human Rights requests the Secretary-General and the General Assembly to provide sufficient human, financial and other resources to the Centre for Human Rights to enable it effectively, efficiently and expeditiously to carry out its activities.

12. The World Conference on Human Rights, noting the need to ensure that human and financial resources are available to carry out the human rights activities, as mandated by intergovernmental bodies, urges the Secretary-General, in accordance with Article 101 of the Charter of the United Nations, and Member States to adopt a coherent approach aimed at securing that resources commensurate to the increased mandates are allocated to the Secretariat. The World Conference on Human Rights invites the Secretary-General to consider whether adjustments to procedures in the programme budget cycle would be necessary or helpful to ensure the timely and effective implementation of human rights activities as mandated by Member States.

Centre for Human Rights

13. The World Conference on Human Rights stresses the importance of strengthening the United Nations Centre for Human Rights.

14. The Centre for Human Rights should play an important role in coordinating system-wide attention for human rights. The focal role of the Centre can best be realized if it is enabled to cooperate fully with other United Nations bodies and organs. The coordinating role of the Centre for Human Rights also implies that the office of the Centre for Human Rights in New York is strengthened.

15. The Centre for Human Rights should be assured adequate means for the system of thematic and country rapporteurs, experts, working groups and treaty bodies. Follow-up on recommendations should become a priority matter for consideration by the Commission on Human Rights.

16. The Centre for Human Rights should assume a larger role in the promotion of human rights. This role could be given shape through cooperation with Member States and by an enhanced programme of advisory services and technical assistance. The existing voluntary funds will have to be expanded substantially for these purposes and should be managed in a more efficient and coordinated way. All activities should follow strict and transparent project management rules and regular programme and project evaluations should be held periodically. To this end, the results of such evaluation exer-

cises and other relevant information should be made available regularly. The Centre should, in particular, organize at least once a year information meetings open to all Member States and organizations directly involved in these projects and programmes.

Adaptation and strengthening of the United Nations machinery for human rights, including the question of the establishment of a United Nations High Commissioner for Human Rights

17. The World Conference on Human Rights recognizes the necessity for a continuing adaptation of the United Nations human rights machinery to the current and future needs in the promotion and protection of human rights, as reflected in the present Declaration and within the framework of a balanced and sustainable development for all people. In particular, the United Nations human rights organs should improve their coordination, efficiency and effectiveness.

18. The World Conference on Human Rights recommends to the General Assembly that when examining the report of the Conference at its forty-eighth session, it begin, as a matter of priority, consideration of the question of the establishment of a High Commissioner for Human Rights for the promotion and protection of all human rights.

B. Equality, dignity and tolerance

1. Racism, racial discrimination, xenophobia and other forms of intolerance

19. The World Conference on Human Rights considers the elimination of racism and racial discrimination, in particular in their institutionalized forms such as apartheid or resulting from doctrines of racial superiority or exclusivity or contemporary forms and manifestations of racism, as a primary objective for the international community and a worldwide promotion programme in the field of human rights. United Nations organs and agencies should strengthen their efforts to implement such a programme of action related to the third decade to combat racism and racial discrimination as well as subsequent mandates to the same end. The World Conference on Human Rights strongly appeals to the international community to contribute generously to the Trust Fund for the Programme for the Decade for Action to Combat Racism and Racial Discrimination.

20. The World Conference on Human Rights urges all Governments to take immediate measures and to develop strong policies to prevent and combat all forms and manifestations of racism, xenophobia or related intolerance, where necessary by enactment of appropriate legislation, including penal measures, and by the establishment of national institutions to combat such phenomena.

21. The World Conference on Human Rights welcomes the decision of the Commission on Human Rights to appoint a Special Rapporteur on contemporary forms of racism, racial discrimination, xenophobia and related intolerance. The World Conference on Human Rights also appeals to all States parties to the International Convention on the Elimination of All Forms of Racial Discrimination to consider making the declaration under article 14 of the Convention.

22. The World Conference on Human Rights calls upon all Governments to take all appropriate measures in compliance with their international obligations and with due regard to their respective legal systems to counter intolerance and related violence based on religion or belief, including practices of discrimination against women and including the desecration of religious sites, recognizing that every individual has the right to freedom of thought, conscience, expression and religion. The Conference also invites all States to put into practice the provisions of the Declaration on the Elimination of All Forms of Intolerance and of Discrimination Based on Religion or Belief.

23. The World Conference on Human Rights stresses that all persons who perpetrate or authorize criminal acts associated with ethnic cleansing are individually responsible and accountable for such human rights violations, and that the international community should exert every effort to bring those legally responsible for such violations to justice.

24. The World Conference on Human Rights calls on all States to take immediate measures, individually and collectively, to combat the practice of ethnic cleansing to bring it quickly to an end. Victims of the abhorrent practice of ethnic cleansing are entitled to appropriate and effective remedies.

2. Persons belonging to national or ethnic, religious and linguistic minorities

25. The World Conference on Human Rights calls on the Commission on Human Rights to examine ways and means to promote and protect effectively the rights of persons belonging to minorities as set out in the Declaration on the Rights of Persons belonging to National or Ethnic, Religious and Linguistic Minorities. In this context, the World Conference on Human Rights calls upon the Centre for Human Rights to provide, at the request of Governments concerned and as part of its programme of advisory services and technical assistance, qualified expertise on minority issues and human rights, as well as on the prevention and resolution of disputes, to assist in existing or potential situations involving minorities.

26. The World Conference on Human Rights urges States and the international community to promote and protect the rights of persons belonging to national or ethnic, religious and linguistic minorities in accordance with the Declaration on the Rights of Persons belonging to National or Ethnic, Religious and Linguistic Minorities.

27. Measures to be taken, where appropriate, should include facilitation of their full participation in all aspects of the political, economic, social, religious and cultural life of society and in the economic progress and development in their country.

Indigenous people

28. The World Conference on Human Rights calls on the Working Group on Indigenous Populations of the Sub-Commission on Prevention of Discrimination and Protection of Minorities to complete the drafting of a declaration on the rights of indigenous people at its eleventh session.

29. The World Conference on Human Rights recommends that the Commission on Human Rights consider the renewal and updating of the mandate of the Working Group on Indigenous Populations upon completion of the drafting of a declaration on the rights of indigenous people.

30. The World Conference on Human Rights also recommends that advisory services and technical assistance programmes within the United Nations system respond positively to requests by States for assistance which would be of direct benefit to indigenous people. The World Conference on Human Rights further recommends that adequate human and financial resources be made available to the Centre for Human Rights within the overall framework of strengthening the Centre's activities as envisaged by this document.

31. The World Conference on Human Rights urges States to ensure the full and free participation of indigenous people in all aspects of society, in particular in matters of concern to them.

32. The World Conference on Human Rights recommends that the General Assembly proclaim an international decade of the world's indigenous people, to begin from January 1994, including action-orientated programmes, to be decided upon in partnership with indigenous people. An appropriate voluntary trust fund should be set up for this purpose. In the framework of such a decade, the establishment of a permanent forum for indigenous people in the United Nations system should be considered.

Migrant workers

33. The World Conference on Human Rights urges all States to guarantee the protection of the human rights of all migrant workers and their families.

34. The World Conference on Human Rights considers that the creation of conditions to foster greater harmony and tolerance between migrant workers and the rest of the society of the State in which they reside is of particular importance.

35. The World Conference on Human Rights invites States to consider the possibility of signing and ratifying, at the earliest possible time, the International Convention on the Rights of All Migrant Workers and Members of Their Families.

3. The equal status and human rights of women

36. The World Conference on Human Rights urges the full and equal enjoyment by women of all human rights and that this be a priority for Governments and for the United Nations. The World Conference on Human Rights also underlines the importance of the integration and full participation of women as both agents and beneficiaries in the development process, and reiterates the objectives established on global action for women towards sustainable and equitable development set forth in the Rio Declaration on Environment and Development and chapter 24 of Agenda 21, adopted by the United Nations Conference on Environment and Development (Rio de Janeiro, Brazil, 3-14 June 1992).

37. The equal status of women and the human rights of women should be integrated into the mainstream of United Nations system-wide activity. These issues should be regularly and systematically addressed throughout relevant United Nations bodies and mechanisms. In particular, steps should be taken to increase cooperation and promote further integration of objectives and goals between the Commission on the Status of Women, the Commission on Human Rights, the Committee for the Elimination of Discrimination against Women, the United Nations Development Fund for Women, the United Nations Development Programme and other United Nations agencies. In this context, cooperation and coordination should be strengthened between the Centre for Human Rights and the Division for the Advancement of Women.

38. In particular, the World Conference on Human Rights stresses the importance of working towards the elimination of violence against women in public and private life, the elimination of all forms of sexual harassment, exploitation and trafficking in women, the elimination of gender bias in the administration of justice and the eradication of any conflicts which may arise between the rights of women and the harmful effects of certain traditional or customary practices, cultural prejudices and religious extremism. The World Conference on Human Rights calls upon the General Assembly to adopt the draft declaration on violence against women and urges States to combat violence against women in accordance with its provisions. Violations of the human rights of women in situations of armed conflict are violations of the fundamental principles of international human rights and humanitarian law. All violations of this kind, including in particular murder, systematic rape, sexual slavery, and forced pregnancy, require a particularly effective response.

39. The World Conference on Human Rights urges the eradication of all forms of discrimination against women, both hidden and overt. The United Nations should encourage the goal of universal ratification by all States of the Convention on the Elimination of All Forms of Discrimination against Women by the year 2000. Ways and means of addressing the particularly large number of reservations to the Convention should be encouraged. Inter alia, the Committee on the Elimination of Discrimination against Women should continue its review of reservations to the Convention. States are urged to withdraw reservations that are contrary to the object and purpose of the Convention or which are otherwise incompatible with international treaty law.

40. Treaty monitoring bodies should disseminate necessary information to enable women to make more effective use of existing implementation procedures in their pursuit of full and equal enjoyment of human rights and non-discrimination. New procedures should also be adopted to strengthen implementation of the commitment to women's equality and the human rights of women. The Commission on the Status of Women and the Committee on the Elimination of Discrimination against Women should quickly examine the possibility of introducing the right of petition through the preparation of an optional protocol to the Convention on the Elimination of All Forms of Discrimination against Women. The World Conference on Human Rights welcomes the decision of the Commission on Human Rights to consider the appointment of a special rapporteur on violence against women at its fiftieth session.

41. The World Conference on Human Rights recognizes the importance of the enjoyment by women of the highest standard of physical and mental health throughout their life span. In the context of the World Conference on Women and the Convention on the Elimination of All Forms of Discrimination against Women, as well as the Proclamation of Tehran of 1968, the World Conference on Human Rights reaffirms, on the basis of equality between women and men, a woman's right to accessible and adequate health care and the widest range of family planning services, as well as equal access to education at all levels.

42. Treaty monitoring bodies should include the status of women and the human rights of women in their deliberations and findings, making use of gender-specific data. States should be encouraged to supply information on the situation of women de jure and de facto in their reports to treaty monitoring bodies. The World Conference on Human Rights notes with satisfaction that the Commission on Human Rights adopted at its forty-ninth session resolution 1993/46 of 8 March 1993 stating that rapporteurs and working groups in the field of human rights should also be encouraged to do so.

Steps should also be taken by the Division for the Advancement of Women in cooperation with other United Nations bodies, specifically the Centre for Human Rights, to ensure that the human rights activities of the United Nations regularly address violations of women's human rights, including gender-specific abuses. Training for United Nations human rights and humanitarian relief personnel to assist them to recognize and deal with human rights abuses particular to women and to carry out their work without gender bias should be encouraged.

43. The World Conference on Human Rights urges Governments and regional and international organizations to facilitate the access of women to decision-making posts and their greater participation in the decision-making process. It encourages further steps within the United Nations Secretariat to appoint and promote women staff members in accordance with the Charter of the United Nations, and encourages other principal and subsidiary organs of the United Nations to guarantee the participation of women under conditions of equality.

44. The World Conference on Human Rights welcomes the World Conference on Women to be held in Beijing in 1995 and urges that human rights of women should play an important role in its deliberations, in accordance with the priority themes of the World Conference on Women of equality, development and peace.

4. The rights of the child

45. The World Conference on Human Rights reiterates the principle of "First Call for Children" and, in this respect, underlines the importance of major national and international efforts, especially those of the United Nations Children's Fund, for promoting respect for the rights of the child to survival, protection, development and participation.

46. Measures should be taken to achieve universal ratification of the Convention on the Rights of the Child by 1995 and the universal signing of the World Declaration on the Survival, Protection and Development of Children and Plan of Action adopted by the World Summit for Children, as well as their effective implementation. The World Conference on Human Rights urges States to withdraw reservations to the Convention on the Rights of the Child contrary to the object and purpose of the Convention or otherwise contrary to international treaty law.

47. The World Conference on Human Rights urges all nations to undertake measures to the maximum extent of their available resources, with the support of international cooperation, to achieve the goals in the World Summit Plan of Action. The Conference calls on States to integrate the Convention on the Rights of the Child into their national action plans. By means of these national action plans and through international efforts, particular priority should be placed on reducing infant and maternal mortality rates, reducing malnutrition and illiteracy rates and providing access to safe drinking water and to basic education. Whenever so called for, national plans of action should be devised to combat devastating emergencies resulting from natural disasters and armed conflicts and the equally grave problem of children in extreme poverty.

48. The World Conference on Human Rights urges all States, with the support of international cooperation, to address the acute problem of children under especially difficult circumstances. Exploitation and abuse of children should be actively combated, including by addressing their root causes. Effective measures are required against female infanticide, harmful child labour, sale of children and organs, child prostitution, child pornography, as well as other forms of sexual abuse.

49. The World Conference on Human Rights supports all measures by the United Nations and its specialized agencies to ensure the effective protection and promotion of human rights of the girl child. The World Conference on Human Rights urges States to repeal existing laws and regulations and remove customs and practices which discriminate against and cause harm to the girl child.

50. The World Conference on Human Rights strongly supports the proposal that the Secretary-General initiate a study into means of improving the protection of children in armed conflicts. Humanitarian norms should be implemented and measures taken in order to protect and facilitate assistance to children in war zones. Measures should include protection for children against indiscriminate use of all weapons of war, especially anti-personnel mines. The need for aftercare and rehabilitation of children traumatized by war must be addressed urgently. The Conference calls on the Committee on the Rights of the Child to study the question of raising the minimum age of recruitment into armed forces.

51. The World Conference on Human Rights recommends that matters relating to human rights and the situation of children be regularly reviewed and monitored by all relevant organs and mechanisms of the United Nations system and by the supervisory bodies of the specialized agencies in accordance with their mandates.

52. The World Conference on Human Rights recognizes the important role played by non-governmental organizations in the effective implementation of all human rights instruments and, in particular, the Convention on the Rights of the Child.

53. The World Conference on Human Rights recommends that the Committee on the Rights of the Child, with the assistance of the Centre for Human Rights, be enabled expeditiously and effectively to meet its mandate, especially in view of the unprecedented extent of ratification and subsequent submission of country reports.

5. Freedom from torture

54. The World Conference on Human Rights welcomes the ratification by many Member States of the Convention against Torture and Other Cruel, Inhuman or Degrading Treatment or Punishment and encourages its speedy ratification by all other Member States.

55. The World Conference on Human Rights emphasizes that one of the most atrocious violations against human dignity is the act of torture, the result of which destroys the dignity and impairs the capability of victims to continue their lives and their activities.

56. The World Conference on Human Rights reaffirms that under human rights law and international humanitarian law, freedom from torture is a right which must be protected under all circumstances, including in times of internal or international disturbance or armed conflicts.

57. The World Conference on Human Rights therefore urges all States to put an immediate end to the practice of torture and eradicate this evil forever through full implementation of the Universal Declaration of Human Rights as well as the relevant conventions and, where necessary, strengthening of existing mechanisms. The World Conference on Human Rights calls on all States to cooperate fully with the Special Rapporteur on the question of torture in the fulfilment of his mandate.

58. Special attention should be given to ensure universal respect for, and effective implementation of, the Principles of Medical Ethics relevant to the Role of Health Personnel, particularly Physicians, in the Protection of Prisoners and Detainees against Torture and other Cruel, Inhuman or Degrading Treatment or Punishment adopted by the General Assembly of the United Nations.

59. The World Conference on Human Rights stresses the importance of further concrete action within the framework of the United Nations with the view to providing assistance to victims of torture and ensuring more effective remedies for their physical, psychological and social rehabilitation. Providing the necessary resources for this purpose should be given high priority, inter alia, by additional contributions to the United Nations Voluntary Fund for Victims of Torture.

60. States should abrogate legislation leading to impunity for those responsible for grave violations of human rights such as torture and prosecute such violations, thereby providing a firm basis for the rule of law.

61. The World Conference on Human Rights reaffirms that efforts to eradicate torture should, first and foremost, be concentrated on prevention and, therefore, calls for the early adoption of an optional protocol to the Convention against Torture and Other Cruel, Inhuman and Degrading Treatment or Punishment, which is intended to establish a preventive system of regular visits to places of detention.

Enforced disappearances

62. The World Conference on Human Rights, welcoming the adoption by the General Assembly of the Declaration on the Protection of All Persons from Enforced Disappearance, calls upon all States to take effective legislative, administrative, judicial or other measures to prevent, terminate and punish acts of enforced disappearance. The World Conference on Human Rights reaffirms that it is the duty of all States, under any circumstances, to make investigations whenever

there is reason to believe that an enforced disappearance has taken place on a territory under their jurisdiction and, if allegations are confirmed, to prosecute its perpetrators.

6. The rights of the disabled person

63. The World Conference on Human Rights reaffirms that all human rights and fundamental freedoms are universal and thus unreservedly include persons with disabilities. Every person is born equal and has the same rights to life and welfare, education and work, living independently and active participation in all aspects of society. Any direct discrimination or other negative discriminatory treatment of a disabled person is therefore a violation of his or her rights. The World Conference on Human Rights calls on Governments, where necessary, to adopt or adjust legislation to assure access to these and other rights for disabled persons.

64. The place of disabled persons is everywhere. Persons with disabilities should be guaranteed equal opportunity through the elimination of all socially determined barriers, be they physical, financial, social or psychological, which exclude or restrict full participation in society.

65 Recalling the World Programme of Action concerning Disabled Persons, adopted by the General Assembly at its thirty-seventh session, the World Conference on Human Rights calls upon the General Assembly and the Economic and Social Council to adopt the draft standard rules on the equalization of opportunities for persons with disabilities, at their meetings in 1993.

C. Cooperation, development and strengthening of human rights

66. The World Conference on Human Rights recommends that priority be given to national and international action to promote democracy, development and human rights.

67. Special emphasis should be given to measures to assist in the strengthening and building of institutions relating to human rights, strengthening of a pluralistic civil society and the protection of groups which have been rendered vulnerable. In this context, assistance provided upon the request of Governments for the conduct of free and fair elections, including assistance in the human rights aspects of elections and public information about elections, is of particular importance. Equally important is the assistance to be given to the strengthening of the rule of law, the promotion of freedom of expression and the administration of justice, and to the real and effective participation of the people in the decision-making processes.

68. The World Conference on Human Rights stresses the need for the implementation of strengthened advisory services and technical assistance activities by the Centre for Human Rights. The Centre should make available to States upon request assistance on specific human rights issues, including the preparation of reports under human rights treaties as well as for the implementation of coherent and comprehensive plans of action for the promotion and protection of human rights. Strengthening the institutions of human rights and democracy, the legal protection of human rights, training of officials and others, broad-based education and public information aimed at promoting respect for human rights should all be available as components of these programmes.

69. The World Conference on Human Rights strongly recommends that a comprehensive programme be established within the United Nations in order to help States in the task of building and strengthening adequate national structures which have a direct impact on the overall observance of human rights and the maintenance of the rule of law. Such a programme, to be coordinated by the Centre for Human Rights, should be able to provide, upon the request of the interested Government, technical and financial assistance to national projects in reforming penal and correctional establishments, education and training of lawyers, judges and security forces in human rights, and any other sphere of activity relevant to the good functioning of the rule of law. That programme should make available to States assistance for the implementation of plans of action for the promotion and protection of human rights.

70. The World Conference on Human Rights requests the Secretary-General of the United Nations to submit proposals to the United Nations General Assembly, containing alternatives for the establishment, structure, operational modalities and funding of the proposed programme.

71. The World Conference on Human Rights recommends that each State consider the desirability of drawing up a national action plan identifying steps whereby that State would improve the promotion and protection of human rights.

72. The World Conference on Human Rights reaffirms that the universal and inalienable right to development, as established in the Declaration on the Right to Development, must be implemented and realized. In this context, the World Conference on Human Rights welcomes the appointment by the Commission on Human Rights of a thematic working group on the right to development and urges that the Working Group, in consultation and cooperation with other organs and agencies of the United Nations system, promptly formulate, for early consideration by the United Nations General Assembly, comprehensive and effective measures to eliminate obstacles to the implementation and realization of the Declaration on the Right to Development and recommending ways and means towards the realization of the right to development by all States.

73. The World Conference on Human Rights recommends that non-governmental and other grass-roots organizations active in development and/or human rights should be enabled to play a major role on the national and international levels in the debate, activities and implementation relating to the right to development and, in cooperation with Governments, in all relevant aspects of development cooperation.

74. The World Conference on Human Rights appeals to Governments, competent agencies and institutions to increase considerably the resources devoted to building well-functioning legal systems able to protect human rights, and to national institutions working in this area. Actors in the field of development cooperation should bear in mind the mutually reinforcing interrelationship between development, democracy and human rights. Cooperation should be based on dialogue and transparency. The World Conference on Human Rights also calls for the establishment of comprehensive programmes, including resource banks of information and personnel with expertise relating to the strengthening of the rule of law and of democratic institutions.

75. The World Conference on Human Rights encourages the Commission on Human Rights, in cooperation with the Committee on Economic, Social and Cultural Rights, to continue the examination of optional protocols to the International Covenant on Economic, Social and Cultural Rights.

76. The World Conference on Human Rights recommends that more resources be made available for the strengthening or the establishment of regional arrangements for the promotion and protection of human rights under the programmes of advisory services and technical assistance of the Centre for Human Rights. States are encouraged to request assistance for such purposes as regional and subregional workshops, seminars and information exchanges designed to strengthen regional arrangements for the promotion and protection of human rights in accord with universal human rights standards as contained in international human rights instruments.

77. The World Conference on Human Rights supports all measures by the United Nations and its relevant specialized agencies to ensure the effective promotion and protection of trade union rights, as stipulated in the International Covenant on Economic, Social and Cultural Rights and other relevant international instruments. It calls on all States to abide fully by their obligations in this regard contained in international instruments.

D. Human rights education

78. The World Conference on Human Rights considers human rights education, training and public information essential for the promotion and achievement of stable and harmonious relations among communities and for fostering mutual understanding, tolerance and peace.

79. States should strive to eradicate illiteracy and should direct education towards the full development of the human personality and to the strengthening of respect for human rights and fundamental freedoms. The World Conference on Human Rights calls on all States and institutions to include human rights, humanitarian law, democracy and rule of law as subjects in the curricula of all learning institutions in formal and non-formal settings.

80. Human rights education should include peace, democracy, development and social justice, as set forth in international and regional human rights instruments, in order to achieve common understanding and awareness with a view to strengthening universal commitment to human rights.

81. Taking into account the World Plan of Action on Education for Human Rights and Democracy, adopted in March 1993 by the International Congress on Education for Human Rights and Democracy of the United Nations Educational, Scientific and Cultural Organization, and other human rights instruments, the World Conference on Human Rights recommends that States develop specific programmes and strategies for ensuring the widest human rights education and the dissemination of public information, taking particular account of the human rights needs of women.

82. Governments, with the assistance of intergovernmental organizations, national institutions and non-governmental organizations, should promote an increased awareness of human rights and mutual tolerance. The World Conference on Human Rights underlines the importance of strengthening the World Public Information Campaign for Human Rights carried out by the United Nations. They should initiate and support education in human rights and undertake effective dissemination of public information in this field. The advisory services and technical assistance programmes of the United Nations system should be able to respond immediately to requests from States for educational and training activities in the field of human rights as well as for special education concerning standards as contained in international human rights instruments and in humanitarian law and their application to special groups such as military forces, law enforcement personnel, police and the health profession. The proclamation of a United Nations decade for human rights education in order to promote, encourage and focus these educational activities should be considered.

E. Implementation and monitoring methods

83. The World Conference on Human Rights urges Governments to incorporate standards as contained in international human rights instruments in domestic legislation and to strengthen national structures, institutions and organs of society which play a role in promoting and safeguarding human rights.

84. The World Conference on Human Rights recommends the strengthening of United Nations activities and programmes to meet requests for assistance by States which want to establish or strengthen their own national institutions for the promotion and protection of human rights.

85. The World Conference on Human Rights also encourages the strengthening of cooperation between national institutions for the promotion and protection of human rights, particularly through exchanges of information and experience, as well as cooperation with regional organizations and the United Nations.

86. The World Conference on Human Rights strongly recommends in this regard that representatives of national institutions for the promotion and protection of human rights convene periodic meetings under the auspices of the Centre for Human Rights to examine ways and means of improving their mechanisms and sharing experiences.

87. The World Conference on Human Rights recommends to the human rights treaty bodies, to the meetings of chairpersons of the treaty bodies and to the meetings of States parties that they continue to take steps aimed at coordinating the multiple reporting requirements and guidelines for preparing State reports under the respective human rights conventions and study the suggestion that the submission of one overall report on treaty obligations undertaken by each State would make these procedures more effective and increase their impact.

88. The World Conference on Human Rights recommends that the States parties to international human rights instruments, the General Assembly and the Economic and Social Council should consider studying the existing human rights treaty bodies and the various thematic mechanisms and procedures with a view to promoting greater efficiency and effectiveness through better coordination of the various bodies, mechanisms and procedures, taking into account the need to avoid unnecessary duplication and overlapping of their mandates and tasks.

89. The World Conference on Human Rights recommends continued work on the improvement of the functioning, including the monitoring tasks, of the treaty bodies, taking into account multiple proposals made in this respect, in particular those made by the treaty bodies themselves and by the meetings of the chairpersons of the treaty bodies. The comprehensive national approach taken by the Committee on the Rights of the Child should also be encouraged.

90. The World Conference on Human Rights recommends that States parties to human rights treaties consider accepting all the available optional communication procedures.

91. The World Conference on Human Rights views with concern the issue of impunity of perpetrators of human rights violations, and supports the efforts of the Commission on Human Rights and the Sub-Commission on Prevention of Discrimination and Protection of Minorities to examine all aspects of the issue.

92. The World Conference on Human Rights recommends that the Commission on Human Rights examine the possibility for better implementation of existing human rights instruments at the international and regional levels and encourages the International Law Commission to continue its work on an international criminal court.

93. The World Conference on Human Rights appeals to States which have not yet done so to accede to the Geneva Conventions of 12 August 1949 and the Protocols thereto, and to take all appropriate national measures, including legislative ones, for their full implementation.

94. The World Conference on Human Rights recommends the speedy completion and adoption of the draft declaration on the right and responsibility of individuals, groups and organs of society to promote and protect universally recognized human rights and fundamental freedoms.

95. The World Conference on Human Rights underlines the importance of preserving and strengthening the system of special procedures, rapporteurs, representatives, experts and working groups of the Commission on Human Rights and the Sub-Commission on the Prevention of Discrimination and Protection of Minorities, in order to enable them to carry out their mandates in all countries throughout the world, providing them with the necessary human and financial resources. The procedures and mechanisms should be enabled to harmonize and rationalize their work through periodic meetings. All States are asked to cooperate fully with these procedures and mechanisms.

96. The World Conference on Human Rights recommends that the United Nations assume a more active role in the promotion and protection of human rights in ensuring full respect for international humanitarian law in all situations of armed conflict, in accordance with the purposes and principles of the Charter of the United Nations.

97. The World Conference on Human Rights, recognizing the important role of human rights components in specific arrangements concerning some peace-keeping operations by the United Nations, recommends that the Secretary-General take into account the reporting, experience and capabilities of the Centre for Human Rights and human rights mechanisms, in conformity with the Charter of the United Nations.

98. To strengthen the enjoyment of economic, social and cultural rights, additional approaches should be examined, such as a system of indicators to measure progress in the realization of the rights set forth in the International Covenant on Economic, Social and Cultural Rights. There must be a concerted effort to ensure recognition of economic, social and cultural rights at the national, regional and international levels.

F. Follow-up to the World Conference on Human Rights

99. The World Conference on Human Rights on Human Rights recommends that the General Assembly, the Commission on Human Rights and other organs and agencies of the United Nations system related to human rights consider ways and means for the full implementation, without delay, of the recommendations contained in the present Declaration, including the possibility of proclaiming a United Nations decade for human rights. The World Conference on Human Rights further recommends that the Commission on Human Rights annually review the progress towards this end.

100. The World Conference on Human Rights requests the Secretary-General of the United Nations to invite on the occasion of the fiftieth anniversary of the Universal Declaration of Human Rights all States, all organs and agencies of the United Nations system related to human rights, to report to him on the progress made in the implementation of the present Declaration and to submit a report to the General Assembly at its fifty-third session, through the Commission on Human Rights and the Economic and Social Council. Likewise, regional and, as appropriate, national human rights institutions, as well as non-governmental organizations, may present their views to the Secretary-General on the progress made in the implementation of the present Declaration. Special attention should be paid to assessing the progress towards the goal of universal ratification of international human rights treaties and protocols adopted within the framework of the United Nations system.

Source: U.N. OHCHR, http://www.ohchr.org/EN/ProfessionalInterest/Pages/Vienna.aspx

๛๛๛๛๛๛๛๛

3. UNITED NATIONS: WHAT WE DO TO PROTECT HUMAN RIGHTS

How does the U.N. promote and protect human rights?

Protect Human Rights

The term "human rights" was mentioned seven times in the UN's founding Charter, making the promotion and protection of human rights a key purpose and guiding principle of the Organization. In 1948, the Universal Declaration of Human Rights brought human rights into the realm of international law. Since then, the Organization has diligently protected human rights through legal instruments and on-the-ground activities.

High Commissioner for Human Rights

The Office of the U.N. High Commissioner for Human Rights (OHCHR) has lead responsibility in the U.N. system for the promotion and protection of human rights. The office supports the human rights components of peacekeeping missions in several countries, and has many country and regional offices and centres. The High Commissioner for Human Rights regularly comments on human rights situations in the world and has the authority to investigate situations and issue reports on them.

Human Rights Council

The Human Rights Council, established in 2006, replaced the 60-year-old U.N. Commission on Human Rights as the key independent U.N. intergovernmental body responsible for human rights.

Human Rights Treaty Bodies

The human rights treaty bodies are committees of independent experts that monitor implementation of the core international human rights treaties

Special Procedures

The special procedures of the Human Rights Council are prominent, independent experts working on a voluntary basis, who examine, monitor, publicly report and advise on human rights from a thematic or country-specific perspective.

UNDG-HRM

The U.N. Development Group's Human Rights Mainstreaming Mechanism (UNDG-HRM) advances human rights mainstreaming efforts within the U.N. development system.

Special Advisers on the Prevention of Genocide and the Responsibility to Protect

The Special Adviser on the Prevention of Genocide acts as a catalyst to raise awareness of the causes and dynamics of genocide, to alert relevant actors where there is a risk of genocide, and to advocate and mobilize for appropriate action; the Special Adviser on the Responsibility to Protect leads the conceptual, political, institutional and operational development of the Responsibility to Protect.

What legal instruments help the U.N. protect human rights?

The International Bill of Human Rights

The Universal Declaration of Human Rights (1948) was the first legal document protecting universal human rights. Together with the International Covenant on Civil and Political Rights and the International Covenant on Economic, Social and Cultural Rights, the three instruments form the so-called International Bill of Human Rights. A series of international human rights treaties and other instruments adopted since 1945 have expanded the body of international human rights law.

Democracy

Democracy, based on the rule of law, is ultimately a means to achieve international peace and security, economic and social progress and development, and respect for human rights - the three pillars of the United Nations mission as set forth in the U.N. Charter. At the 2005 World Summit, all the world's governments reaffirmed "that democracy is a universal value based on the freely expressed will of people to determine their own political, economic, social and cultural systems and their full participation in all aspects of their lives" and stressed "that democracy, development and respect for all human rights and fundamental freedoms are interdependent and mutually reinforcing." Democratic principles are woven throughout the normative fabric of the United Nations. The 2009 Guidance Note on Democracy of the Secretary-General sets out the United Nations framework for democracy based on universal principles, norms and standards and commits the Organization to principled, coherent and consistent action in support of democracy.

What other U.N. offices and bodies are responsible for protecting human rights?

Security Council
The U.N. Security Council, at times, deals with grave human rights violations, often in conflict areas. The U.N. Charter gives the Security Council the authority to investigate and mediate, dispatch a mission, appoint special envoys, or request the Secretary-General to use his good offices. The Security Council may issue a ceasefire directive, dispatch military observers or a peacekeeping force. If this does not work, the Security Council can opt for enforcement measures, such as economic sanctions, arms embargos, financial penalties and restrictions, travel bans, the severance of diplomatic relations, a blockade, or even collective military action.

Third Committee of the General Assembly
The General Assembly's Third Committee (Social, Humanitarian and Cultural) examines a range of issues, including human rights questions. The Committee also discusses questions relating to the advancement of women, the protection of children, indigenous issues, the treatment of refugees, the promotion of fundamental freedoms through the elimination of racism and racial discrimination, and the right to self-determination. The Committee also addresses important social development questions.

Various Other U.N. Bodies
Different intergovernmental bodies and interdepartmental mechanisms based at the United Nations headquarters in New York, as well as the United Nations Secretary-General, address a range of human rights issues. The General Assembly, the Economic and Social Council (ECOSOC) and their subsidiary organs make policy decisions and recommendations to Member States, the United Nations system and other actors. The United Nations Permanent Forum on Indigenous Issues (UNPFII), an advisory body to the Economic and Social Council, has a mandate to discuss indigenous issues, including human rights. The Office of the High Commissioner for Human Rights interacts with and provides advice and support on human rights issues to these bodies and mechanisms. The Office also works to mainstream human rights in all areas of work of the Organization, including development, peace and security, peacekeeping and humanitarian affairs. Human rights issues are also addressed in the context of the post-conflict U.N. peacebuilding support activities

Secretary-General
The Secretary-General appoints special representatives, who advocate against major human rights violations:
- Special Representative of the Secretary-General for Children and Armed Conflict
- Special Representative of the Secretary-General on Sexual Violence in Conflict
- Special Representative of the Secretary-General on Violence Against Children

The 'Human Rights Up Front' Initiative (HRUF) is an initiative by the U.N. Secretary-General to ensure the U.N. system takes early and effective action, as mandated by the Charter and U.N. resolutions, to prevent or respond to serious and large-scale violations of human rights or international humanitarian law. The initiative underlines a shared responsibility among the various U.N. entities to work together to address such violations. HRUF seeks to achieve this by effecting change at three levels: cultural, operational and political. These changes are gradually transforming the way the U.N. understands its responsibilities and implements them. The initiative has been progressively rolled-out since late 2013. Through various presentations, letters and policy documents, the Secretary-General and Deputy Secretary-General have presented HRuF to the General Assembly and to staff and U.N. system leaders.

U.N. Peace Operations
Many United Nations peacekeeping operations and political and peacebuidling missions also include the human rights-related mandates aimed at contributing to the protection and promotion of human rights through both immediate and long-term action; empowering the population to assert and claim their human rights; and enabling State and

other national institutions to implement their human rights obligations and uphold the rule of law. Human rights teams on the ground work in close cooperation and coordination with other civilian and uniformed components of peace operations, in particular, in relation to the protection of civilians; addressing conflict-related sexual violence and violations against children; and strengthening respect for human rights and the rule of law through legal and judicial reform, security sector reform and prison system reform.

Commission on the Status of Women

The Commission on the Status of Women (CSW) is the principal global intergovernmental body dedicated to the promotion of gender equality and the advancement of women. U.N. Women, established in 2010, serves as its Secretariat.

Source: http://www.un.org/en/sections/what-we-do/protect-human-rights/index.html

4. U.N. GENERAL ASSEMBLY SAMPLE RESOLUTION ON HUMAN RIGHTS DEFENDERS

This document is a sample U.N. General Assembly (UNGA) resolution adopted by the Third Committee. Much of what the U.N. and its General Assembly accomplish happens by passing resolutions on particular subjects or countries. Resolutions express the collective attitude of those who vote. These resolutions are not legal instruments. They are political and administrative decisions of the different components of an international inter-governmental organization. The following is a sample resolution concerning the protection of human rights defenders.

Promotion and protection of human rights: human rights questions, including alternative approaches for improving the effective enjoyment of human rights and fundamental freedoms

Albania, Argentina, Armenia, Australia, Chile, Colombia, Dominican Republic, Georgia, Guatemala, Honduras, Hungary, Iceland, Ireland, Japan, Lebanon, Liechtenstein, Mexico, Mongolia, New Zealand, Norway, Palau, Panama, Paraguay, Switzerland, Ukraine, United States of America and Vanuatu: revised draft resolution

Recognizing the role of human rights defenders and the need for their protection

The General Assembly,

Guided by the purposes and principles of the Charter of the United Nations,

Guided also by the Universal Declaration of Human Rights, 1 the International Covenants on Human Rights2 and other relevant instruments,

Recalling its resolution 53/144 of 9 December 1998, by which it adopted by consensus the Declaration on the Right and Responsibility of Individuals, Groups and Organs of Society to Promote and Protect Universally Recognized Human Rights and Fundamental Freedoms,

Recalling also all other previous resolutions on this subject, including its resolutions 66/164 of 19 December

2011 and 68/181 of 18 December 2013 and Human Rights Council resolutions 22/6 of 21 March 2013 and 25/18 of 28 March 2014,

Reaffirming the importance of the Declaration and its implementation, and that promoting respect and support for the activities of human rights defenders is essential to the overall enjoyment of human rights,

Welcoming the steps taken by some States to promote and give full effect to the Declaration, as well as by the United Nations High Commissioner for Human Rights and some regional organizations in making the Declaration available and known to all stakeholders at the national and local levels in their respective languages, and underlining the need to promote and give full effect to the Declaration, including through its translation into the various languages and its further dissemination with a view to its implementation in all regions,

Emphasizing the important role that individuals and civil society institutions, including non-governmental organizations, groups and national human rights institutions, play at the local, national, regional and international levels in the promotion and protection of all human rights and fundamental freedoms for all,

Recognizing the substantial role that human rights defenders can play in supporting efforts to strengthen conflict prevention, peace and development through dialogue, openness, participation and justice, including by monitoring, reporting on and contributing to the promotion and protection of human rights,

Recognizing also the vital work of human rights defenders in promoting, protecting and advocating the realization of economic, social and cultural rights, and concerned that threats and attacks against human rights defenders, and hindrance of their work, have a negative impact on the realization of these rights, including as they relate to environmental and land issues as well as development,

Mindful that domestic law and administrative provisions and their application should not hinder, but enable the work of human rights defenders, including by avoiding any criminalization or stigmatization of the important activities and legitimate role of human rights defenders and the communities of which they are a part or on whose behalf they work, and by avoiding impediments, obstructions, restrictions or selective enforcement thereof contrary to relevant provisions of international human rights law,

Reaffirming that States have the primary responsibility and are under the obligation to protect all human rights and fundamental freedoms of all persons,

Reaffirming also that national legislation consistent with the Charter of the United Nations and other international obligations of the State in the field of human rights and fundamental freedoms is the juridical framework within which human rights defenders conduct their activities,

Gravely concerned that national security and counter-terrorism legislation as well as measures in other areas, such as laws regulating civil society organizations, are in some instances misused to target human rights defenders or hinder their work, endangering their safety in a manner contrary to international law,

Recognizing the urgent need to address, and to take concrete steps to prevent and stop, the use of legislation to hinder or limit unduly the ability of human rights defenders to exercise their work, including by reviewing and, where necessary, amending relevant legislation and its implementation in order to ensure compliance with the obligations and commitments of States under international human rights law,

Gravely concerned by the considerable and increasing number of communications received by special procedures of the Human Rights Council documenting the serious nature of the risks faced by human rights defenders, A/C.3/70/L.46/Rev.1 15-20296 3/7 including women human rights defenders, and the prevalence of impunity for violations and abuses against them in many countries, where they face threats, harassment and attacks and suffer insecurity, including through restrictions on the rights to freedom of opinion, expression, association or peaceful assembly, abuse of criminal or civil proceedings, or deplorable acts of intimidation and reprisal intended to prevent their cooperation with the United Nations and other international bodies in the field of human rights,

Gravely concerned also that human rights defenders are subject to attacks, threats and other abuses by non-State actors, and underlining the need for the human rights and fundamental freedoms of all persons, including human rights defenders, to be respected and protected,

Welcoming the steps taken by some States, including in follow-up to relevant resolutions, the universal periodic review under the Human Rights Council, special procedures, treaty bodies and regional human rights mechanisms, towards the improvement of dialogue between authorities and civil society and towards the adoption of national policies and legislation that serve to create a safe e and enabling environment and to recognize and protect human rights defenders, in particular from being prosecuted, in contravention of international human rights law, for peaceful activities, and against threats, harassment, intimidation, duress, arbitrary detention or arrest, enforced disappearance, violence and attacks by State and non-State actors,

Determined that dissenting views, including views on government and corporate policies related to or with an impact on human rights, may be expressed peacefully and communicated freely in society, online and offline, in accordance with international human rights law, and thereby emphasizing the importance of respecting all human rights of all, and stressing in this regard the importance of independent voices of civic activity, human rights education and independent, impartial and competent national judicial systems,

Stressing in particular that information and communication technologies are important tools for the promotion of human rights and reporting on human rights violations and abuses, and concerned that such technologies are increasingly being used to monitor and hamper the work of human rights defenders,

Strongly reaffirming that everyone has the right, individually and in association with others, to promote and strive for the protection and realization of human rights and fundamental freedoms at the national and international levels, as laid out in the Declaration, including in the context of promoting the implementation of the 2030 Agenda for Sustainable Development, 1. Stresses that the right of everyone to promote and strive for the protection and realization of human rights and fundamental freedoms without retaliation or fear thereof is an essential element in building and maintaining sustainable, open and democratic societies;

2. Calls upon all States to take all measures necessary to ensure the rights and safety of human rights defenders who exercise the rights to freedom of opinion, expression, peaceful assembly and association, which are essential for the promotion and protection of human rights;

3. Welcomes the work, and takes note with appreciation of the reports, of the Special Rapporteur of the Human Rights Council on the situation of human rights defenders;

4. Urges States to acknowledge through public statements, policies or laws the important and legitimate role of human rights defenders in the promotion of human rights, democracy and the rule of law as essential components of ensuring their recognition and protection, including by condemning unequivocally and publicly all cases of violence and discrimination against human rights defenders, including women human rights defenders;

5. Strongly condemns the violence against and the targeting, criminalization, intimidation, torture, disappearance, killing and thus silencing of human rights defenders for reporting and seeking information on human rights violations and abuses, and stresses the need to combat impunity by ensuring that those responsible for violations and abuses against human rights defenders, including against their legal representatives, associates and family members, are promptly brought to justice through impartial investigations;

6. Condemns all acts of intimidation and reprisal by State and non-State actors against individuals and groups, including against human rights defenders and their legal representatives, associates and family members, who seek to cooperate, are cooperating or have cooperated with subregional, regional and international bodies, including the United Nations, its representatives and mechanisms, in the field of human rights;

7. Urges non-State actors to respect the human rights and fundamental freedoms of all persons and to refrain from undermining the capacity of human rights defenders, including women human rights defenders, to operate free from hindrance and insecurity;

8. Strongly urges the release of persons detained or imprisoned, in violation of international human rights law, for exercising their human rights and fundamental freedoms, such as the rights to freedom of expression, peaceful assembly and association, including in relation to cooperation with the United Nations or other international mechanisms in the area of human rights, and demands that States take concrete and definitive steps to prevent and put an end to the practice of the arbitrary arrest and detention of human rights defenders;

9. Reaffirms the urgent need to respect, protect, facilitate and promote the work of those promoting and defending economic, social and cultural rights, as a vital factor contributing towards the realization of those rights, including as they relate to environmental and land issues as well as development;

10. Calls upon all States to create and maintain a safe and enabling environment for the defence of human rights and specifically to ensure that:

(a) The promotion and protection of human rights are not criminalized or met with limitations in contravention of international human rights law;

(b) Human rights defenders, their family members, associates and legal representatives are not prevented from enjoying universal human rights owing to their work, including by ensuring that all legal provisions, administrative measures and policies affecting them, including those aimed at preserving public safety, public order and public morals, are minimally restrictive, clearly defined, determinable, non-retroactive and compatible with relevant provisions of international human rights law;

(c) Measures to combat terrorism and preserve national security are in compliance with their obligations and commitments under international law, in particular under international human rights law, and do not hinder the work and safety of individuals, groups and organs of society engaged in promoting and defending human rights, while defining transparent and foreseeable criteria to identify clearly which offences qualify as terrorist acts;

(d) Where legislation and procedures governing the registration and funding of civil society organizations exist, they are transparent, non-discriminatory, expeditious, inexpensive, allow for the possibility to appeal and avoid requiring reregistration, and that such national provisions are in compliance with international human rights law;

(e) Procedural safeguards, including in criminal cases, are in place in accordance with international human rights law in order to avoid the use of unreliable evidence, unwarranted investigations and procedural delays, thereby effectively contributing to the expeditious closing of unsubstantiated cases, including against human rights defenders, and individuals are afforded the opportunity to lodge complaints directly with the appropriate authority, and respecting, inter alia, the right to be informed promptly and in detail of charges, the right to the presumption of innocence, the right to a fair and public hearing, the right to choose and communicate with counsel in confidence, the right to present witnesses and evidence and cross-examine prosecution witnesses and the right to appeal;

(f) Information, including on grave violations of human rights, held by public authorities, is not unnecessarily classified or otherwise withheld from the public, and urging States to adopt transparent, clear and action-oriented laws and policies that provide for the effective disclosure of information held by public authorities and a general right to request and receive such information, for which public access should be granted, except within narrow and clearly defined limitations;

(g) Provisions do not prevent public officials from being held accountable, and penalties for defamation are limited in order to ensure proportionality and reparation commensurate with the harm done;

(h) Information and communication technologies are not used in a manner that amounts to arbitrary or unlawful interference with the privacy of individuals or to threats against human rights defenders;

11. Encourages States to develop and put in place comprehensive and sustainable public policies and programmes that support and protect human rights defenders at all stages of their work, including their family members, associates and legal representatives;

12. Reaffirms the utility and benefit of consultations and dialogue with human rights defenders related to public policies and programmes, including for protection purposes, and encourages States to appoint focal points or to employ other relevant mechanisms for human rights defenders within the public administration;

13. Continues to express particular concern about systemic and structural discrimination and violence faced by women human rights defenders of all ages, and reiterates its strong call upon States to take appropriate, robust and practical steps to protect them and to integrate a gender perspective into their efforts to create a safe and enabling environment for the defence of human rights, as called for by the General Assembly in its resolution 68/181 of 18 December 2013;

14. Expresses concern about stigmatization and discrimination that target or affect individuals and associations defending the rights of persons belonging to minorities or espousing minority beliefs or views, or other groups vulnerable to dis-

crimination, and calls upon States to renounce firmly all discrimination and violence, underlining that such practices can never be justified on any grounds;

15. Reaffirms the right of everyone, individually and in association with others, to unhindered access to and communication with international bodies, in particular the United Nations, its representatives and mechanisms in the field of human rights, including the Human Rights Council, its special procedures, the universal periodic review mechanism and the treaty bodies, as well as regional human rights mechanisms;

16. Calls upon all States to take due note of the recommendations contained in the reports of the Secretary-General on cooperation with the United Nations, its representatives and mechanisms in the field of human rights;

17. Welcomes the efforts made by some States to investigate allegations of intimidation or reprisal and to bring perpetrators to justice, and encourages Governments to support such efforts;

18. Strongly calls upon all States to: (a) Refrain from, and ensure adequate protection from, any act of intimidation or reprisal against human rights defenders who cooperate, have cooperated or seek to cooperate with international institutions, including their family members and associates; (b) Fulfil the duty to end impunity for any such acts of intimidation or reprisals by bringing the perpetrators to justice and by providing an effective remedy for their victims; (c) Avoid legislation, measures and practices that have the effect of undermining the right reaffirmed in paragraph 15 of the present resolution;

19. Encourages all relevant regional organizations to consider the situation of human rights defenders and to develop and employ appropriate and effective guidelines and mechanisms for their protection, addressing violations and abuses by State and non-State actors;

20. Encourages leaders in all sectors of society and in their respective communities, including political, military, social and religious leaders and leaders in business and the media, to express public support for the important role of human rights defenders, including women human rights defenders, and the legitimacy of their work, and to condemn publicly any cases of violence and discrimination against human rights defenders, including women human rights defenders;

21. Underscores the responsibility of business enterprises to respect human rights, including the fundamental rights of human rights defenders to life, liberty and security of person, and their exercise of their rights to freedom of expression, peaceful assembly and association, and participation in public affairs, which are essential for the promotion and protection of human rights, including economic, social and cultural rights and the right to development, and urges enterprises to identify and address any adverse human rights impacts related to their activities through meaningful consultation with potentially affected groups and other relevant stakeholders in a manner consistent with the Guiding Principles on Business and Human Rights: Implementing the United Nations "Protect, Respect and Remedy" Framework;

22. Encourages national human rights institutions to pay due attention to the situation of human rights defenders, including through consultations with relevant stakeholders on issues such as legislation, policies and administrative measures that affect the defence of human rights, and to develop and support the documentation of violations and abuses against human rights defenders and their legal representatives, associates and family members;

23. Encourages the Office of the United Nations High Commissioner for Human Rights and the special procedures to continue the efforts related to the protection of human rights defenders, as laid out in relevant resolutions, including by offering assistance for the consideration of States in bringing their legislation and its application into line with international human rights law;

24. Encourages United Nations bodies, agencies and other entities, within their respective mandates and in cooperation with the Office of the United Nations High Commissioner for Human Rights and the Special Rapporteur, to address the situation of human rights defenders in their work in order to contribute to the effective implementation of the Declaration on the Right and Responsibility of Individuals, Groups and Organs of Society to Promote and Protect Universally Recognized Human Rights and Fundamental Freedoms;

25. Requests all concerned United Nations agencies and organizations, within their mandates, to provide all possible assistance and support to the Special Rapporteur for the effective fulfilment of his mandate, including in the context of country visits and through suggestions on ways and means of ensuring the protection of human rights defenders, including women human rights defenders;

26. Urges States to cooperate with and assist the Special Rapporteur in the performance of his mandate, including by responding without undue delay to the communications transmitted to them by the Special Rapporteur, and reiterates its call upon States with respect to responding favourably to the requests of the Special Rapporteur to visit their countries and to enter into a constructive dialogue with respect to the follow-up and implementation of recommendations, so as to enable the Special Rapporteur to fulfil his mandate even more effectively;

27. Requests the Special Rapporteur to continue to report annually on his activities to the General Assembly and the Human Rights Council, in accordance with his mandate;

28. Requests the Secretary-General to compile and regularly share information on the progress of implementation of the present resolution;

29. Decides to remain seized of the matter.

Source: United Nations; A/C.3/70/L.46/Rev.1; General Assembly Distr., Limited 18 November 2015 Original: English; Seventieth session Third Committee Agenda item 72 (b); http://www.un.org/ga/search/view_doc.asp?symbol=A/C.3/70/L.46/Rev.1

5. THE U.S. AND THE UNIVERSAL PERIODIC REVIEW PROCESS

The Universal Periodic Review (UPR) is a unique mechanism of the Human Rights Council (HRC) aimed at improving the human rights situation on the ground of each of the 193 United Nations (UN) Member States. Under this mechanism, the human rights situation of all U.N. Member States is reviewed every 5 years. 42 States are reviewed each year during three Working Group sessions dedicated to 14 States each. These three sessions are usually held in January/February, May/June and October/November. The result of each review is reflected in an "outcome report" listing the recommendations the State under review (SuR) will have to implement before the next review.

The UPR is a full-circle process comprised of 3 key stages:

1) Review of the human rights situation of the SuR;

2) Implementation between two reviews (5 years) by the SuR of the recommendations received and the voluntary pledges made;

3) Reporting at the next review on the implementation of those recommendations and pledges and on the human rights situation in the country since the previous review.

Q&A on the modalities of the UPR process:

What does the review consist of?

The review takes place in a Working Group in Geneva, Switzerland, and lasts 3.5 hours.

The Working Group is composed of all U.N. member-States and chaired by the President of the Human Rights Council. Other relevant stakeholders, such as NGOs, national institutions and U.N. agencies, can attend the Working Group but they cannot take the floor.

Each review starts with the presentation by the State under Review of its National Report and of its responses to the advance questions. Advance questions are questions submitted by States in writing ten days before the review.

Following this presentation, an interactive dialogue takes place during which States take the floor to ask questions and make recommendations on the human rights situation in the country under review. During this interactive dialogue, the State under Review takes the floor regularly to answer the questions and to comment on the recommendations.

At the end, the State under Review presents its concluding remarks.

The State under Review's overall speaking time throughout the review is 70 minutes. Other States have a total of 140 minutes.

What human rights obligations are addressed?

The Institutional-building text of the Human Rights Council, as set out in resolution A/HR C /R E S /5/1 of 18 June 2007, indicates that the review shall assess to what extent States respect their human rights obligations contained in:
- The Charter of the United Nations;
- The Universal Declaration of Human Rights;
- Human Rights instruments to which the State is party (human rights treaties ratified by the State concerned);
- Voluntary pledges and commitments made by the State (including those undertaken when presenting the candidature for election to the Human Rights Council); ? Applicable international humanitarian law

What is the review based on?

Three main documents are used to conduct the review of the State:
- A National Report of 20 pages prepared by the State concerned on the human rights situation in the country;
- A compilation of ten pages prepared by the Office of the High Commissioner on Human Rights (OHC HR) containing information from treaty bodies, special procedures and U.N. agencies such as UNDP and UNIC E F;
- A summary of ten pages prepared by the OHC HR containing information from the civil society.

These three documents are usually available on the OHC HR website six weeks before the start of the UPR working group.

How is the list of speakers established?

Every State willing to speak on a specific review is able to do so. The 140 minutes at hand for "reviewing States" are divided by the number of States interested in taking the floor. The lists of speakers for the 14 reviews of a given Working Group session open the week before the beginning of the session and States have four days to register. Then, each list is arranged in English alphabetical order and a letter is drawn by lot by the President of the Human Rights Council to decide where the list will begin.

States are able to swap places on the list. Those wishing to withdraw from a list have to inform the Secretariat at least 30 minutes before the beginning of the review to allow the latter to recalculate the speaking time provided to each delegation.

What is the troika and what does it do?

The troika consists of three countries' delegates assisting the review.

The troika members are selected by the drawing of lots among members of the Human Rights Council and from different regional groups. They can be delegation members or experts nominated by the selected State. E very State under review has a different troika.

The State under Review can request that one of the three members be from its Regional Group and/or that one of the troika members be substituted, although only on one occasion. Finally, a troika member may ask to be excluded from participation in a specific review.

According to a President's statement of 9 April 2008, the role of the troika is the following:

Before the review — The troika receives the written questions raised by States and relays them to the State under Review.

During the interactive dialogue — Troika members do not have a specific role during the interactive dialogue. However, they can take the floor as any delegation and make questions and recommendations.

The troika prepares the report of the Working Group, which contains a full account of the proceedings, with the involvement of the State under Review and with the assistance of the Secretariat. One of the troika members is then in charge of introducing the report before its adoption at the Working Group.

What is the "outcome" of the Working Group review and how is it adopted?

The 3.5 hour review results in a report prepared by the troika with the involvement of the State under Review (SuR) and the assistance of the Secretariat. The report contains the summary of the interactive dialogue, the responses by the SuR to the questions and recommendations and the full list of recommendations made by States.

The report is adopted a first time during the Working Group session a few days after the review. The adoption lasts for 30 minutes and is mainly procedural.

Once the report has been adopted during the Working Group session, it is then adopted by consensus a few months later at a plenary session of the Human Rights Council. One hour of the plenary is allocated to the adoption divided as such:
- 20 minutes to the SuR to reply to questions and issues that were not sufficiently addressed during the review and respond to recommendations that were raised by States during the interactive dialogue.
- 20 minutes to States to take the floor and express their opinion on the outcome of the review.
- 20 minutes to civil society, NGOs and National Human Rights Institutions (NHR Is), to make general comments.

What are the recommendations?

Recommendations are suggestions made to the State under Review to improve the human rights situation in the country. They can be of different nature and cover many issues. They are the key element of the review. During the first cycle, approximately 21'000 recommendations were made to 193 States.

According to HR C resolution A/HR C /R E S /5/1, States can accept or note recommendations but they cannot reject them. Responses to each recommendation must be clearly explained in writing in a specific document called "addendum." This addendum should be submitted to the Human Rights Council in advance of the adoption of the report at the Human Rights Council.

Who decides which State will be reviewed and when?

During the selection phase of the first UPR cycle, States were split per regional group. Subsequently, the list of each group was organised so that States selected first were those whose terms of membership were ending in June 2007, second those whose terms of membership were ending in June 2008 and third those who volunteered for the UPR. Then, the list of countries was re-organised in alphabetical order starting with the country drawn by lot by the President.

The order of review at the second cycle is exactly the same as during the first cycle. However, as there is now only 14 States reviewed per session, the composition of each Working Group session has changed.

What happens between two reviews?

The period between two reviews is called the "follow-up." It is the moment during which the State under Review implements the recommendations received.

The follow-up is the most critical and important phase of the whole UPR process as it is the one leading to the concrete realisation of the UPR goal, that is, the "improvement of the human rights situation on the ground." The success of this phase will also determine the efficiency and credibility of the mechanism and demonstrate States' engagement in the promotion and strengthening of human rights.

What is the focus of the second and subsequent cycles?

The reviews at the second and subsequent cycles look into the human rights situation in the country since the previous review and assess the level of implementation of the recommendations the State had previously received.

Can NGOs and NHRIs participate in the UPR process?

Yes. They can, inter alia, submit information which will be used to review the country and take the floor during the adoption of the report at the HR C session. However, they cannot take the floor during the review.

Where does the review take place?

The Universal Periodic Review process is held in Palais des Nations, Geneva, Switzerland.

6. LIST OF UNIVERSAL PERIODIC REVIEW TERMS AND TERMINOLOGY

This document comes from an NGO which focuses on the Universal Periodic Review (UPR). The terms used in the UPR process are challenging to understand. Becoming familiar with these terms will aid in understanding the many complex documents which are submitted to and come out of the Human Rights Council in the UPR process.

Addendum: The addendum is a document drafted by the State under Review containing their responses to the Working Group list of recommendations. An Addendum is limited to 2,675 words. The addendum is a secondary document to the Working Group Report.

Advance written questions: Advance questions are made by States and directed at the State under Review (SuR) about its human rights situation. These questions are submitted to a SuR through the troika, in writing, ten working days before the Working Group session. They are expected to be answered by the SuR during the presentation of its National Report during the review.

Basis of the review: The basis of the review is the elements taken into account to conduct the review of the human rights records of a given State. It consists of the Universal Declaration of Human, the United Nations Charter, the treaties to which the State is a party, the voluntary pledges and commitments the State has undertaken and international humanitarian law.

Civil Society (Organisations): Civil Society organisations are non-governmental and non-profit organisations working on a wide range of issues. They include NGOs but also a range of other entities, such as faith-based organisations, trade unions, academic groups, lawyers, human rights defenders, etc. Civil society has many opportunities to engage in the UPR process, notably through submitting information on the human rights situation, lobbying Permanent Missions in Geneva and their counterparts in-country, taking the floor during the adoption of the Working Group report at the Human Rights Council, and monitoring the implementation of recommendations on the ground.

Compilation of U.N. information: The Compilation of U.N. information is prepared by the Office of the High Commissioner for Human Rights (OHCHR). It summarises and compiles all information submitted to the OHC HR on a specific State under Review by U.N. agencies and other U.N. human rights mechanisms, such as Treaty Bodies and Special Procedures. The compilation also includes potential recommendations. It cannot exceed 5,350 words. (It is one of the three documents used to conduct the review of a State; see also the National Report and the Summary of other Stakeholders' information).

Consultations (National): Consultations are meetings that a State under Review should hold with representatives from civil society and the National Human Rights Institution in view of the drafting of their national report to the UPR. Consultations should also be held during the follow-up phase.

ECOSOC consultative status: ECOSOC status is granted by a NGO Committee in New York comprised of 19 Member States. It allows NGOs to access various human rights mechanisms, including the Universal Periodic Review. NGOs need E C OS OC status to enter U.N. premises, attend the review, make a statement (oral and written) during the adoption of the Working Group report, and organise parallel events at the UPR and the Human Rights Council. However, ECOSOC status is not needed for NGOs to submit a report on the human rights situation in the State under Review or to monitor and take part in the implementation of recommendations.

Extranet: The extranet is a website run by the Office of the High Commissioner for Human Rights and is only accessible by password. It contains organisational documents such as programmes of work, calendars of meetings and minutes of the Human Rights Council Bureau. Documents related to the Human Rights Council and the UPR, such as statements by States and NGOs, draft UPR Working Group reports and draft resolutions, can also be found on the extranet.

Follow-up: The Follow-up is a phase of the UPR process, between two reviews, during which the State under Review should take appropriate measures to implement the recommendations. Other stakeholders are encouraged to provide support as well as monitor the progress made.

General Debate: The General Debate is a discussion that takes place at the Human Rights Council under each agenda item. During the general debate on the UPR (item 6), States, national human rights institutions and civil society organisations take the floor to discuss UPR modalities. It is also the opportunity to provide feedback on the implementation of recommendations in a particular country. States usually present their Mid-term reports during the General Debate.

Human Rights Council: The Human Rights Council (HRC) is the United Nations body in charge of human rights. Located in Geneva, it meets three times per year to discuss a vast range of issues and country situations. It is composed of 47 members elected for three years by the General Assembly. It is also responsible for the organisation of the UPR .

Implementation: Implementation consists of the steps undertaken by a State to comply with the recommendations received during their review (see also Follow-up).

Institutional-building package: See Resolution 5/1.

Interactive dialogue: The interactive dialogue is the discussion taking place between the State under Review (SuR) and other States during the 3.5 hour review in the Working Group. States pose questions and make comments as well as put forward recommendations to the SuR. The SuR is expected to respond to those questions and comments during this dialogue.

International Humanitarian Law (IHL): International Humanitarian Law regulates the conduct of armed conflicts. It is supposed to protect persons who are not or are no longer participating in the hostilities (prisoners of war) and restricts the means and methods of warfare. The two main legal treaties in IHL are the Geneva Conventions and the Hague Convention. IHL is one of the five bases of the review of the UPR.

Item 6: Item of the Human Rights Council (HRC) agenda that is dedicated to the UPR . The HRC agenda has 10 items in total.

Mandate-Holders: See Special Rapporteur.

Mid-term Report: A mid-term report is a report submitted by a State, providing the Human Rights Council with information on the process of implementation of the recommendations. A voluntary update on the process of implementation is encouraged in paragraph 18 of Resolution 16/21. The report should be submitted two/three years after the review to the Office of the High Commissioner for Human Rights. States are encouraged to conduct broad consultations with all relevant stakeholders and reflect their perspectives in the report. Other stakeholders may also publish midterm reports about the human rights on the ground and the status of implementation of the recommendations by their government. Other stakeholders' reports cannot be submitted to OHCHR, but may be presented under Item 6 of the General Debate, posted on the organisations' own websites and/or on the website of UPR Info.

Modalities: Modalities are rules or guidelines governing the UPR . The main modalities of the UPR are contained in General Assembly Resolution 60/251 and Human Rights Council Resolutions 5/1 and 16/21.

Monitoring: Monitoring is the watching over by stakeholders, including civil society, the national institution for human rights and U.N. agencies, of the progress made by the Government to implement UPR recommendations.

National Human Rights Institution: The National Human Rights Institution (NHRI) is a State body with a constitutional and/or legislative mandate to protect and promote human rights. NHRIs should comply with the Paris Principles and are ranked according to their independence (from 'A' to 'C'). The NHRIs with an 'A' status enjoy greater access to the U.N. human rights bodies. NHRIs must apply for accreditation to the International Coordinating Committee. An ombudsman can be considered an NHRI.

National Report (or State Report): The national report is a report prepared by the Government of the State under Review about the human rights situation in the country. It should also include information regarding implementation of previous recommendations. The report cannot be longer than 10,700 words and should be submitted 12 weeks before the review. The national report is one of three documents used to conduct the review of a State. See also Compilation of U.N. information and Summary of Other Stakeholders' information.

Noted: According to Resolution 5/1, recommendations at the UPR can either be "supported" or "noted." Noted recommendations can, however, still be implemented and monitored, as part of the follow-up work of Governments and civil society.

Office of the High Commissioner for Human Rights (OHCHR): The OHC HR is the human rights branch of the United Nations. It is part of the United Nations Secretariat, with headquarters in Geneva. The OHC HR has offices in various countries and regions and works to ensure that international human rights standards are effectively implemented on the ground. It supports the work of the U.N. treaty bodies and the U.N. Human Rights Council. The High Commissioner for Human Rights is the head of the Office and leads the work of the United Nations on human rights.

Other Stakeholders: See Stakeholders.

Outcome: The outcome of the UPR consists of a set of documents published in the framework of the review of a country which includes the Working Group report, the addendum, and the statement delivered by the State under Review during the adoption of the Working Group report at the Human Rights Council.

Pre-sessions: UPR pre-sessions are meetings organised by UPR Info bringing together Permanent Missions, National Human Rights Institutions and Civil Society Organisations to discuss the human rights situation in the States coming up for review at the UPR. The pre-sessions take place one month prior to a State's review and provide a valuable platform for civil society to engage with U.N. member States and make their voice heard at the UPR.

Recommendation: Recommendations are suggestions made by States to a State under Review (SuR) on how to improve the human rights situations in their home countries. Recommendations can be very diverse in terms of actions contained and issues addressed. The SuR is expected to respond to all recommendations made to it by either accepting or noting them. SuR's responses to all recommendations should be submitted in writing prior to the adoption of the Working Group report at the Human Rights Council.

Recommending State: A Recommending State is a country which takes the floor during the review of a specific States to ask questions and make recommendations. For example: Country A recommends Country B "to ratify the International Covenant on Economic, Social and Cultural Rights." Country A would be the Recommending State in this example.

Report of the Working Group: The Working Group Report is the outcome of the review of a given State. It contains a full account of a State's review, including a summary of questions and comments made by States during the review as well as a complete list of all recommendations (including both accepted and noted recommendations). The troika and the State under Review assist the Human Rights Council (HRC) Secretariat in drafting this report. The list of recommendations is distributed online 48 hours after the review and adopted a few days after while the full draft report is available one week after the end of the Working Group session. The final version of the report is adopted by the HR C a few months later at a plenary session.

Resolution 16/21: This resolution by the Human Rights Council (HRC) was adopted in March 2011 following the Review of the HRC, which took place in 2010-2011. As a result of the Review, some modalities of the UPR were changed for the second cycle. Resolution 16/21 describes the changes and decisions made during the Review. It notably indicates that the second cycle of the UPR would begin in June 2012, that the cycle period changed from four (4) years to four and a half (4 1/2) years and that only 42 member states will be reviewed during the three (3) sessions of the Working Group. The resolution highlights that the second and subsequent cycles should focus on the implementation of the recommendations and the developments of the human rights situation in the State under Review.

Resolution 5/1: This resolution by the Human Rights Council (HRC) outlines the practices and guidelines to be followed during the UPR. It was adopted on 18 June 2007 following one year of negotiations within the HRC. It is also called the Institutional-building package.

Resolution 60/251: Resolution 60/251 is the U.N. General Assembly resolution establishing the Human Rights Council and the Universal Periodic Review. It was adopted on 15 March 2006 and was part of the U.N. reforms that replaced the Commission on Human Rights with the Human Rights Council.

Review: The Review is the examination by the UPR Working Group (WG) of whether U.N. member States are respecting the commitments they made and agreements they signed under international law. In particular, States are reviewed on their human rights obligations deriving from the United Nations Charter, the Universal Declaration of Human Rights, U.N. Human rights treaties ratified by the State concerned, international humanitarian law and any voluntary pledges and commitments made by the State. The WG will use the National Report, the Compilation of U.N. Information and the Summary of Other Stakeholders' Information to conduct the review. During the process, an interactive dialogue takes place between the State under Review and other States in which questions concerning the State under Review's human rights record is addressed and recommendations on how to improve the human rights situation in the country are submitted. During the review, the SuR has 70 minutes to speak, while the other States have 140 minutes.

Secretariat (HRC): The Human Rights Council Secretariat assists the Human Rights Council and the UPR in the organisation of the sessions. The HR C Secretariat is composed of staff from the Office of the High Commissioner for Human Rights.

Session (Working Group): See Working Group.

Side event: A side event is an unofficial meeting organised in the Palais des Nations in Geneva in parallel to a Human Rights Council or UPR session. A side event can be organised by a State, a national human rights institution, an NGO or the Office of the High Commissioner for Human Rights. The event usually discusses a specific human rights issue or the human rights situation in a specific country. It can also cover the launch of a publication.

Special Procedures: Special Procedures is a mechanism of the Human Rights Council (HR C) aiming to address either specific country situations or thematic issues in all parts of the world. The Office of the High Commissioner for Human Rights supports the mandate of the Special Procedures. Special Procedures can be an individual ("Special Rapporteur," "Independent Expert" or "mandate-holders") or a working group composed of five members. They are created by HRC resolutions and for a limited time. See also Special Rapporteur.

Special Rapporteur: Special Rapporteur (or Independent expert) is the title given to individuals bearing a specific mandate from the U.N. on a given country or thematic issue. Generally Special Rapporteurs examine, monitor, advise and publicly report on human rights issues falling under their mandate. They publish a yearly report to the Human Rights Council. The activities undertaken by Rapporteurs include, inter alia, responding to individual complaints, conducting studies, raising awareness and providing advice on technical cooperation at the country level. They can also conduct country missions but, first, they have to be invited by the Government concerned. Rapporteurs may not hold their positions for longer than six (6) years.

Stakeholders: Stakeholders are actors which take part in the UPR process. They include the State under Review, national institution for human rights, civil society, United Nations agencies, academics, parliamentarians, etc. Other Stakeholders: The term 'Other Stakeholders' is usually used at the UPR to designate actors, excluding States, that take part in the UPR process. It includes national institutions for human rights, civil society, United Nations agencies, academics, parliamentarians, etc.

State Report: See National Report.

State under Review (SuR): A SuR is a U.N. member State that is having its human rights record reviewed under the UPR.

Submission (NGO): Submissions are reports submitted by NGOs to the Office of the High Commissioner for Human Rights to be part of the Summary of Other Stakeholders' Information. Any civil society organisation, with or without E C OS OC status, can submit a report. NGOs can join together and submit joint reports. Individual reports are limited to 2,815 words while joint reports are limited to 5,630 words. Submissions are usually due 7 to 8 months before the review.

Summary of Other Stakeholders' Information: The Summary of Other Stakeholders' Information is a report compiled by the Office of the High Commissioner for Human Rights that summarises the information and recommendations contained in the NGO submissions. The compilation cannot exceed 5,350 words (It is one of the three documents used to conduct the review of a State; see also the National Report and the Compilation of U.N. information).

Technical assistance: Technical assistance is a request for help sought by a State from the United Nations (UN) or from other States. Technical assistance requests may include, but are not limited to, requests for staff, training programs in certain areas, help in drafting reports and requests to work together to develop programs. The U.N. has two voluntary funds to answer requests for technical assistance. See also Voluntary funds.

Treaty Bodies: Treaty bodies are committees of independent experts that monitor how core international human rights treaties and their optional protocols are being implemented by the State parties. States must have ratified a specific treaty in order to be reviewed by its relevant body. One example of a treaty body is the Human Rights Committee, which monitors the implementation of the International Covenant on Civil and Political Rights.

Troika: The troika assists the Working Group (WG) with the human rights review of a state. It is a group of three delegates from Human Rights Council members selected by drawing lots. A troika member may take the floor as any other delegation and ask questions and make recommendations during the interactive dialogue. The troika representatives have two main roles: (1) receive all written questions and/or issues raised by the WG and relays them to the State under Review (SuR) and (2) help preparing the report of the WG with the assistance of the U.N. Secretariat and the SuR. One Troika member is in charge of introducing the list of recommendations before its adoption at the WG.

Universal Periodic Review (UPR): The UPR is a United Nations human rights mechanism established by resolution 60/251 of the General Assembly to review the human rights records of all U.N. member States. E ach member state is reviewed every 4 1/2 years by the UPR Working Group. During the review process each State under Review is asked questions by their peers regarding their human rights record and also given recommendations on how to improve the human rights situation in their home country.

Voluntary pledges: Voluntary pledges are commitments made by a State under Review in the course of the UPR to do a specific action. Voluntary pledges can be made at different stages: during the drafting of the national report, during the review, and during the adoption of the Working Group report. For example, many States have made a voluntary pledge to submit a mid-term report on the implementation of recommendations received during their UPR review.

Voluntary Trust Fund for participation: The Fund for participation, or Fund 1, is a fund established by Human rights Council Resolution 6/17 to assist developing countries, particularly least developing countries, in their participation in the UPR process in Geneva. The Fund can cover the expenses of traveling costs to Geneva for delegation members and support trainings prior to the UPR.

Voluntary Trust Fund for Financial and Technical Assistance: The Voluntary Trust Fund for Financial and Technical Assistance, or Fund 2, is a fund established by Human Rights Council Resolution 6/17 to assist States in their implementation of UPR recommendations.

Webcast: The webcast is a live video streaming of a Human Rights Council or UPR session. The webcasts are then posted both on the OHC HR and UPR Info websites and are accessible by anyone.

Working Group: The UPR Working Group (WG) is the body that conducts the human rights review of States. In practice, all 193 U.N. member States, as well as the Holy See and the State of Palestine, are part of the group. The WG meets in Geneva, Switzerland three times per year with a total of fourteen (14) countries for each session to be reviewed. WG sessions usually take place in January, April, and October.

Working Group Report: See Report of the Working Group.

Source: https://www.upr-info.org/en/glossary#g

⌘⌘⌘⌘⌘⌘⌘⌘

7. REPORT OF THE UNITED STATES OF AMERICA TO HIGH COMMISSIONER FOR HUMAN RIGHTS ON THE UNIVERSAL PERIODIC REVIEW PROCESS

Known as the "national report," was the initial report filed by the U.S. in the 2010 Universal Periodic Review procedure. It is a statement that describes where the U.S., as a State under Review (SuR), sees itself regarding its attempt to ensure the full exercise by all persons under the jurisdiction of the U.S. of all internationally recognized human rights. Addressed to the Office of the High Commissioner for Human Rights in Geneva and transmitted to the Human Rights Council for consideration of the review, this document is considered, with the Compilation and Summary documents, as the principal basis for the Outcome Document (all three are below), which sets forth the Council's conclusions and recommendations. This national report is supposed to include opinions of Americans across the country, so as not to be a self-portrait by the government of itself.

Introduction

I.1 A more perfect union, a more perfect world

The story of the United States of America is one guided by universal values shared the world over-that all are created equal and endowed with inalienable rights. In the United States, these values have grounded our institutions and motivated the determination of our citizens to come ever closer to realizing these ideals. Our Founders, who proclaimed their ambition "to form a more perfect Union," bequeathed to U.S. not a static condition but a perpetual aspiration and mission.

We present our first Universal Periodic Review (UPR) report in the context of our commitment to help to build a world in which universal rights give strength and direction to the nations, partnerships, and institutions that can usher U.S. toward a more perfect world, a world characterized by, as President Obama has said, "a just peace based on the inherent rights and dignity of every individual."

The U.S. has long been a cornerstone of the global economy and the global order. However, the most enduring contribution of the United States has been as a political experiment. The principles that all are created equal and endowed with inalienable rights were translated into promises and, with time, encoded into law. These simple but powerful principles have been the foundation upon which we have built the institutions of a modern state that is accountable to its citizens and whose laws are both legitimated by and limited by an enduring commitment to respect the rights of individuals. It is our political system that enables our economy and undergirds our global influence. As President Obama wrote in the preface to the recently published National Security Strategy, "democracy does not merely represent our better angels, it stands in opposition to aggression and injustice, and our support for universal rights is both fundamental to American leadership and a source of our strength in the world." Part of that strength derives from our democracy's capacity to adopt improvements based upon the firm foundation of our principled commitments. Our democracy is what allows

U.S. to acknowledge the realities of the world we live in, to recognize the opportunities to progress toward the fulfillment of an ideal, and to look to the future with pride and hope.

The ideas that informed and inform the American experiment can be found all over the world, and the people who have built it over centuries have come from every continent. The American experiment is a human experiment; the values on which it is based, including a commitment to human rights, are clearly engrained in our own national conscience, but they are also universal.

Echoing Eleanor Roosevelt, whose leadership was crucial to the adoption of the Universal Declaration of Human Rights (UDHR), Secretary of State Hillary Clinton has reaffirmed that "[h]uman rights are universal, but their experience is local. This is why we are committed to holding everyone to the same standard, including ourselves." From the UDHR to the ensuing Covenants and beyond, the United States has played a central role in the internationalization of human rights law and institutions. We associate ourselves with the many countries on all continents that are sincerely committed to advancing human rights, and we hope this UPR process will help U.S. to strengthen our own system of human rights protections and encourage others to strengthen their commitments to human rights.

I.2 The United States and the Universal Periodic Review: approach and methodology

The ultimate objective of the UPR process, and of the U.N. Human Rights Council, is to enhance the protections for and enjoyment of human rights. Our participation signifies our commitment to that end, and we hope to contribute to it by sharing how we have made and will continue to make progress toward it. Some may say that by participating we acknowledge commonality with states that systematically abuse human rights. We do not. There is no comparison between American democracy and repressive regimes. Others will say that our participation, and our assessment of certain areas where we seek continued progress, reflects doubt in the ability of the American political system to deliver progress for its citizens. It does not. As Secretary Clinton said in a speech on human rights last year, "democracies demonstrate their greatness not by insisting they are perfect, but by using their institutions and their principles to make themselves . . . more perfect." Progress is our goal, and our expectation thereof is justified by the proven ability of our system of government to deliver the progress our people demand and deserve.

This document gives a partial snapshot of the current human rights situation in the United States, including some of the areas where problems persist in our society. In addressing those areas, we use this report to explore opportunities to make further progress and also to share some of our recent progress. For us, the primary value of this report is not as a diagnosis, but rather as a roadmap for our ongoing work within our democratic system to achieve lasting change. We submit this report with confidence that the legacy of our past efforts to embrace and actualize universal rights foreshadows our continued success.

8. This report is the product of collaboration between the U.S. Government and representatives of civil society from across the United States. Over the last year, senior representatives from more than a dozen federal departments and agencies traveled the country to attend a series of UPR consultations hosted by a wide range of civil society organizations. At these gatherings, individuals presented their concerns and recommendations and often shared stories or reports as they interacted with government representatives. Those conversations shaped the substance and structure of this report. Nearly a thousand people, representing a diversity of communities and viewpoints, and voicing a wide range of concerns, attended these gatherings in New Orleans, Louisiana; New York, New York; El Paso, Texas; Albuquerque, New Mexico; Window Rock, Arizona; the San Francisco Bay Area; Detroit, Michigan; Chicago, Illinois; Birmingham, Alabama; and Washington, D.C. Information about the process was also posted on the website of the U.S. Department of State (www.state.gov/g/drl/upr). Members of the public were encouraged to contribute questions, comments, and recommendations via that site, and many did so. The consultation process followed a familiar tradition of collaboration and discussion between government and civil society that is vital to the strength of our democracy. The U.S. Government is grateful to all those who hosted meetings and shared their views both in those consultations and online. We also welcome constructive comments and recommendations from other governments and non-governmental organizations through the UPR process.

II. The United States and human rights: normative and institutional background

II.1 Human Rights as the ends of government and the means of progress

9. The desire to live freely under a government that would respect and protect human rights was the fundamental motivation of our country's Founders-human rights have not only been part of the United States since the beginning, they were the reason our nation was created. From its adoption in 1789, the U.S. Constitution has been the central legal instrument of government and the supreme law of the land. The Constitution establishes the structure of government in the United States, starting with the fundamental principle that the will of the people is the basis of the legitimacy of government. The Constitution's first ten amendments, adopted in 1791 and known as the Bill of Rights, along with the Thirteenth, Fourteenth, and Fifteenth Amendments, adopted in the wake of the Civil War, protect many rights that, in the twentieth century, became recognized and protected under international human rights law. The principles enshrined in the Constitution and the system of government that it prescribes- including the checks and balances between the legislative, executive, and judicial branches, as well as the reservation of significant authority and autonomy for the fifty states joined together in a federal system- have been the basic building blocks of a government of the people, by the people, and for the people throughout U.S. history.

10. Since our founding, we have made tremendous progress in strengthening the protection of rights and in enhancing and expanding equal opportunities for their enjoyment. Just as the legitimacy of our government is grounded in the will of the people, the credit for progress accrues not only to our Constitution and the government it created, but also to the determination and commitment of our people. Throughout our history, our citizens have used the freedoms provided in the Constitution as a foundation upon which to advocate for changes that would create a more just society. The Constitution provided the means for its own amelioration and revision: its glaring original flaw of tolerating slavery, as well as denying the vote to women, have both been corrected through constitutional reform, judicial review and our democratic processes. Human rights- including the freedoms of speech, association, and religion-have empowered our people to be the engine of our progress.

II.2 Enduring commitments

11. As we look to the future, the United States stands committed to the enduring promises of protecting individual freedoms, fairness and equality before the law, and human dignity-promises that reflect the inalienable rights of each person. Our commitment to the rights protected in our Constitution is matched by a parallel commitment to foster a society characterized by shared prosperity. Finally, we are committed to the idea that the values behind the domestic promises articulated in our Constitution should also guide and inform our engagement with the world. Below, we address these commitments in turn.

III. A commitment to freedom, equality, and dignity

12. Article 1 of the Universal Declaration of Human Rights declares that "all human beings are born free and equal in dignity and rights" and that they are "endowed with reason and conscience." This basic truth suggests the kinds of obligations-both positive and negative-that governments have with regard to their citizens.

13. People should be free and should have a say in how they are governed. Governments have an obligation not to restrict fundamental freedoms unjustifiably, and governments need to create the laws and institutions that secure those freedoms.

14. People should enjoy fair treatment reflected in due process and equality before the law. Governments have an obligation not to discriminate or persecute and should establish mechanisms for protection and redress.

15. People should be treated with dignity. Governments have an obligation to protect the security of the person and to respect human dignity.

16. These obligations are what enable people to claim "life, liberty, and the pursuit of happiness" as their just entitlements. These same rights are encoded in international human rights law and in our own Constitution.

III.1 Freedom of expression, religion, association, and political participation

Freedom of expression

17. The United States maintains robust protections for freedom of expression. As a general matter, the government does not punish or penalize those who peacefully express their views in the public sphere, even when those views are critical of the government. Indeed, dissent is a valuable and valued part of our politics: democracy provides a marketplace for ideas, and in order to function as such, new ideas must be permitted, even if they are unpopular or potentially offensive. The United States has a free, thriving, and diverse independent press-a feature that existed before the advent of electronic and digital media and that continues today.

18. We also recognize that privacy is linked to free expression, in that individuals need to feel that they can control the boundaries of their self-disclosure and self-expression in order to be able to express themselves freely: surveillance, especially when practiced by a government, can lead to self-censorship. Although protecting the security of all citizens means that no individual can have an absolute right to privacy or expression, any limitations on these rights are determined in a public process, by representatives of the people in the legislature and by the courts.

Freedom of thought, conscience, and religion.

19. The desire for freedom from religious persecution has brought millions to our shores. Today, freedom of religion protects each individual's ability to participate in and share the traditions of his or her chosen faith, to change his or her religion, or to choose not to believe or participate in religious practice.

20. Citizens continue to avail themselves of freedom of religion protections in the Constitution and in state and federal law. For example, in a case this year, a Native American primary school student's right to wear his hair in a braid, in accordance with his family's religious beliefs, was upheld pursuant to a Texas religious freedom law.

21. The constitutional prohibition on the establishment of a religion by the government, along with robust protections for freedom of speech and association, have helped to create a multi-religious society in which the freedom to choose and practice one's faith, or to have no faith at all, is secure.

Freedom of association

22. In the United States, our vibrant civil society exists because people freely come together to meet and share interests and to advocate for political and other causes. In some cases, this takes the form of public gatherings, marches, or protests. In others, people establish or join organizations with a sustained purpose or agenda-today, there are more than 1.5 million non-profit organizations in the United States.

23. Freedom of association also protects workers and their right to organize. The labor movement in the United States has a rich history, and the right to organize and bargain collectively under the protection of the law is the bedrock upon which workers are able to form or join a labor union. Workers regularly use legal mechanisms to address complaints such as threats, discharges, interrogations, surveillance, and wages-and-benefits cuts for supporting a union. These legal regimes are continuously assessed and evolving in order to keep pace with a modern work environment. Our UPR consultations included workers from a variety of sectors, including domestic workers who spoke about the challenges they face in organizing effectively. Currently there are several bills in our Congress that seek to strengthen workers' rights-ensuring that workers can continue to associate freely, organize, and practice collective bargaining as the U.S. economy continues to change.

Freedom of political participation

24. Every person should have a say in how he or she is governed, and representative democracy has always been the essential foundation of our country's political system. When the United States was founded, only white men who owned property could vote. In the subsequent centuries, barriers fell for women, African Americans, Hispanics, Asian Americans, and Native Americans, and we continue to work to ensure universal enfranchisement in both law and fact.

25. After decades of work by women's rights groups and others, women obtained a constitutionally protected right to vote in 1920. Real protection of the right to vote for racial and ethnic minorities came many decades later with the enactment of the Voting Rights Act of 1965, a watershed moment in the fight for fairness in our election system. Nearly a century earlier, in the wake of the Civil War, the Fifteenth Amendment to the Constitution had granted the right to

vote to African-American men, although in practice that right continued to be obstructed and denied. Since the Voting Rights Act's passage, the United States has made substantial progress in breaking down racial barriers to voting, resulting in greater participation in elections and significant increases in the election of members of diverse racial and ethnic groups to public office.

26. The Voting Rights Act prohibits racial discrimination in voting, allowing the Department of Justice or a private citizen to challenge a voting practice as discriminatory in federal court. Under the Act, certain jurisdictions with histories of racial discrimination in voting require federal approval to implement any change affecting voting. The Act also ensures meaningful access to the franchise for non-English speaking citizens. In recent months, the Department of Justice has worked to strengthen enforcement of federal voting rights laws. The Department recently obtained consent decrees against some jurisdictions and concluded a settlement with another, and it is preparing to review thousands of redistricting plans that will be submitted after release of the 2010 Census results to ensure that voting districts are not drawn with the purpose or effect of marginalizing minority voters.

27. Other laws, such as the National Voter Registration Act of 1993 and the Help America Vote Act of 2002, help increase historically low registration rates of minorities and persons with disabilities that have resulted from discrimination, and protect the equal rights of all by facilitating complete and accurate voter rolls.

28. Several Members of Congress and other policymakers and advocates have promoted changes to our election administration system including proposals to establish a national mandate for universal voter registration; combat "deceptive practices" designed to deter legitimate voters from voting; require "permanent voter registration" systems; and require fail-safe procedures, so that eligible voters can correct inaccurate voter rolls and vote on the same day. Work continues toward having these proposals enacted into federal law.

III.2 Fairness and equality

29. The United States has always been a multi-racial, multi-ethnic, multi-religious society. Although we have made great strides, work remains to meet our goal of ensuring equality before the law for all. Thirty years ago, the idea of having an African-American president would not have seemed possible; today it is our reality. Our Attorney General, the nation's top law enforcement officer, is also African-American. Three of the last four Secretaries of State have been women, and two of the last three have been African-American. We have recently appointed our first Hispanic Supreme Court Justice, as well as several LGBT individuals to senior positions in the Executive Branch. And while individual stories do not prove the absence of enduring challenges, they demonstrate the presence of possibilities.

30. In 1947, W.E.B. DuBois testified before the U.N. General Assembly on the continued pervasive discrimination against African Americans in the United States. In the ensuing decades the U.S. civil rights movement emerged as a quintessential example of citizens using principles of non-violence, law, protest, and public debate to hold their government accountable and to demand that it deliver on their right to equal and fair treatment. The movement led to critical new laws prohibiting discrimination and seeking to ensure equal opportunity for all individuals. The progress in the decades since is a source of pride to our government and to our people. Indeed, our nation's struggle to banish the legacy of slavery and our long and continuing journey toward racial equality have become the central and emblematic narrative in our quest for a fair and just society that reflects the equality of all.

31. The United States aspires to foster a society in which, as Dr. Martin Luther King, Jr. put it, the success of our children is determined by the "content of their character." We are not satisfied with a situation where the unemployment rate for African Americans is 15.8%, for Hispanics 12.4%, and for whites 8.8%, as it was in February 2010. We are not satisfied that a person with disabilities is only one fourth as likely to be employed as a person without disabilities. We are not satisfied when fewer than half of African-American and Hispanic families own homes while three quarters of white families do. We are not satisfied that whites are twice as likely as Native Americans to have a college degree. The United States continues to address such disparities by working to ensure that equal opportunity is not only guaranteed in law but experienced in fact by all Americans.

32. In addition to our continuing quest to achieve fairness and equality for racial and ethnic minorities across our society, we wish to call attention to the following groups and issues.

Fairness, equality, and persons with disabilities

33. United States law and practice provide broad and effective protections against, and remedies for, disability-based discrimination. The most notable of these is the Americans with Disabilities Act of 1990 (ADA), the first national civil rights legislation in the world to unequivocally prohibit discrimination against persons with disabilities, which was amended in 2008 to ensure broader protections. The intent of these laws is to prohibit discrimination on the basis of disability and remove barriers to the full and equal inclusion of people with disabilities in U.S. society. These laws cover areas of life including education, health care, transportation, housing, employment, technology, information and communication, the judicial system, and political participation. To ensure implementation of these laws, a variety of technical assistance and remedies have been supported with federal funds. For example, training has been provided to the public and private sectors on implementation of the ADA; parent training information centers empower families to understand and claim their rights; and federally funded centers for independent living support the empowerment of individuals with disabilities to live where and with whom they choose in their communities. The Department of Justice and other federal departments and agencies have the authority to enforce these laws and, in this regard, receive complaints and utilize mediation and litigation as appropriate. On July 30, 2009, the United States signed the U.N. Convention on the Rights of Persons with Disabilities and is pursuing the necessary steps toward ratification, which the Administration strongly supports. Upon the 20th anniversary of the ADA, President Obama further demonstrated the nation's commitment to continued vigilance and improvement by announcing new regulations that increase accessibility in a variety of contexts and commit the federal government to hiring more persons with disabilities. Although we recognize that discrimination and access problems persist, which we are actively striving to address, the substantive equality of persons with disabilities in the United States has improved enormously in the past few decades.

Fairness, equality, and Lesbian, Gay, Bisexual and Transgender (LGBT) persons

34. In each era of our history there tends to be a group whose experience of discrimination illustrates the continuing debate among citizens about how we can build a more fair society. In this era, one such group is LGBT Americans. In 2003, reversing a prior decision, the Supreme Court struck down a state criminal law against sodomy, holding that criminalizing consensual private sexual practices between adults violates their rights under the Constitution.2 With the recent passage of the Matthew Shepard and James Byrd, Jr. Hate Crimes Prevention Act of 2009, the United States has bolstered its authority to prosecute hate crimes, including those motivated by animus based on sexual orientation, gender identity, or disability. Since 1998, employment discrimination based on sexual orientation has been prohibited in federal employment. Earlier this year, the Administration extended many benefits to the same-sex partners of federal employees, and supports the pending Domestic Partnership Benefits and Obligations Act, a law that would extend additional benefits currently accorded to married couples to same sex partners. Furthermore, President Obama is committed to the repeal of the "Don't Ask, Don't Tell" statute, which prevents gays and lesbians from serving openly in the military, and both the Chairman of the Joint Chiefs of Staff and the Secretary of Defense have testified at congressional hearings in support of its repeal. The President has also supported passage of the Employment Non-Discrimination Act, which would prohibit discrimination in employment based on sexual orientation or gender identity. Debate continues over equal rights to marriage for LGBT Americans at the federal and state levels, and several states have reformed their laws to provide for same-sex marriages, civil unions, or domestic partnerships. At the federal level, the President supports repeal of the Defense of Marriage Act.

Fairness, equality, and Muslim, Arab-American and South Asian American persons

35. We have worked to ensure fair treatment of members of Muslim, Arab-American, and South Asian communities. The U.S. Government is committed to protecting the rights of members of these groups, and to combating discrimination and intolerance against them. Examples of such measures include the Justice Department's formation of the 9/11 Backlash Taskforce and civil rights work on religious freedom (e.g., bringing a case on behalf of a Muslim school girl to protect her right to wear a hijab); the civil rights outreach efforts of the Department of Homeland Security; and the Equal Employment Opportunity Commission's enforcement efforts to combat backlash-related employment discrimination which resulted in over $5 million for victims from 2001-2006.

36. At our UPR consultations, including the meeting in Detroit, Michigan, Muslim, Arab-American, and South Asian citizens shared their experiences of intolerance and pressed for additional efforts to challenge misperceptions and discriminatory stereotypes, to prevent acts of vandalism, and to combat hate crimes. The federal government is committed

to ongoing efforts to combat discrimination: the Attorney General's review of the 2003 Guidance Regarding the Use of Race by Federal Law Enforcement Agencies (discussed below), as well as efforts to limit country-specific travel bans, are examples.

Fairness, equality, and women

37. As one of President Obama's first official acts, he signed into law the Lilly Ledbetter Fair Pay Act of 2009, which helps women who face wage discrimination recover their lost wages. Shortly thereafter, the President created the White House Council on Women and Girls to seek to ensure that American women and girls are treated fairly and equally in all matters of public policy. Thus, for instance, the Administration supports the Paycheck Fairness Act, which will help ensure that women receive equal pay for equal work. Our recent health care reform bill also lowers costs and offers greater choices for women, and ends insurance company discrimination against them. Moreover, the Administration established the first White House Advisor on Violence Against Women, appointed two women to the U.S. Supreme Court, and created an unprecedented position of Ambassador-at-Large for Global Women's Issues to mobilize support for women around the world. The Obama Administration strongly supports U.S. ratification of the Convention on the Elimination of all forms of Discrimination Against Women and is working with our Senate toward this end.

Fairness, equality, and Native Americans

38. The U.S. took the UPR process to "Indian Country." One of our UPR consultations was hosted on tribal land in Arizona, the New Mexico consultation addressed American Indian and Alaska Native issues, and other consultations included tribal representatives. The United States has a unique legal relationship with federally recognized tribes. By virtue of their status as sovereigns that pre-date the federal Union, as well as subsequent treaties, statutes, executive orders, and judicial decisions, Indian tribes are recognized as political entities with inherent powers of self-government. The U.S. government therefore has a government-to-government relationship with 564 federally recognized Indian tribes and promotes tribal self-governance over a broad range of internal and local affairs. The United States also recognizes past wrongs and broken promises in the federal government's relationship with American Indians and Alaska Natives, and recognizes the need for urgent change. Some reservations currently face unemployment rates of up to 80 percent; nearly a quarter of Native Americans live in poverty; American Indians and Alaska Natives face significant health care disparities; and some reservations have crime rates up to 10 times the national average. Today we are helping tribes address the many issues facing their communities.

39. In November of last year, President Obama hosted a historic summit with nearly 400 tribal leaders to develop a policy agenda for Native Americans where he emphasized his commitment to regular and meaningful consultation with tribal officials regarding federal policy decisions that have tribal implications. In March, the President signed into law important health provisions for American Indians and Alaska Natives. In addition, President Obama recognizes the importance of enhancing the role of tribes in Indian education and supports Native language immersion and Native language restoration programs.

40. Addressing crimes involving violence against women and children on tribal lands is a priority. After extensive consultations with tribal leaders, Attorney General Eric Holder announced significant reform to increase prosecution of crimes committed on tribal lands. He hired more Assistant U.S. Attorneys and more victim-witness specialists. He created a new position, the National Indian Country Training Coordinator, who will work with prosecutors and law enforcement officers in tribal communities. The Attorney General is establishing a Tribal Nations Leadership Council to provide ongoing advice on issues critical to tribal communities.

41. On July 29, 2010, President Obama signed the Tribal Law and Order Act, requiring the Justice Department to disclose data on cases in Indian Country that it declines to prosecute and granting tribes greater authority to prosecute and punish criminals. The Act also expands support for Bureau of Indian Affairs and Tribal officers. It includes new provisions to prevent counterfeiting of Indian-produced crafts and new guidelines and training for domestic violence and sex crimes, and it strengthens tribal courts and police departments and enhances programs to combat drug and alcohol abuse and help at-risk youth. These are significant measures that will empower tribal governments and make a difference in people's lives.

42. In April 2010, at the U.N. Permanent Forum on Indigenous Issues, U.S. Ambassador to the U.N. Susan Rice announced that the United States would undertake a review of its position on the U.N. Declaration on the Rights of Indigenous Peoples. That multi-agency review is currently underway in consultation with tribal leaders and with outreach to other stakeholders.

Fairness and equality at work

43. The United States is committed to continuing to root out discrimination in the workplace, and the federal government is committed to vigorously enforcing laws to that end. The Justice Department and the Equal Employment Opportunity Commission have reinvigorated efforts to enforce Title VII of the Civil Rights Act of 1964, which prohibits employment discrimination based on race, color, sex, national origin, and religion, and the Age Discrimination in Employment Act, which prohibits employment discrimination based on age. Both laws also prohibit retaliation against employees who bring charges of discrimination in the workplace.

44. In recognition of discrimination's long-term effects, for 45 years, working through the Department of Labor and other agencies, the federal government has required private companies with which it conducts significant business to take proactive steps to increase the participation of minorities and women in the workplace when they are underrepresented, and to ensure fairness in recruiting, hiring, promotion, and compensation. In May 2010, the Department of Labor chaired the first meeting since 2000 of the President's Committee on the International Labor Organization (ILO), which coordinates U.S. policy toward the ILO. The Committee agreed to work toward the successful ratification of ILO Convention No. 111 (to combat discrimination at work) and directed a subgroup to resume work on reviewing the feasibility of other conventions for ratification.

Fairness and equality in housing

45. The United States protects citizens from discrimination in housing through the Fair Housing Act of 1968, which prohibits discrimination in housing on the basis of race, color, religion, sex, national origin, familial status, or disability. Housing providers, both public and private, as well as other entities, such as municipalities, banks, and homeowners' insurance companies, are all covered by the Act. There is also a robust legal infrastructure in place for the investigation and prosecution of housing discrimination claims brought under the Act. Additionally, the 1974 Equal Credit Opportunity Act prohibits discrimination in the extension of credit, encompassing the actions of mortgage lenders and banks.

46. Following the recent economic crisis, the issue of predatory lending, and particularly discriminatory lending, is an area of enforcement focus. The recession in the United States was fueled largely by a housing crisis, which coincided with some discriminatory lending practices. The subsequent foreclosure crisis has disproportionately affected communities of color, and the federal government has focused resources and efforts to determine whether and where discrimination took place, as well as to ensure greater oversight going forward to prevent similar crises in the future. In this respect President Obama signed major financial reform legislation in 2010 that includes a new consumer protection bureau, among other provisions.

Fairness and equality in education

47. The United States is committed to providing equal educational opportunities to all children, regardless of their individual circumstances, race, national origin, ethnicity, gender, or disability. Consistent with this commitment, the federal government uses educational programs to ensure that federal dollars assist underserved students and develop strategies that will help such students succeed. The federal government has also taken steps to ensure that students with disabilities have access to technology, and to provide low-income students and students of color with increased access to early learning and college. In addition, the Department of Education administers and promotes programs that seek to provide financial aid to all students in need; promotes educational equity for women and students of color; assists school districts in offering educational opportunities to Native Hawaiians, American Indians, and Alaska Natives; and provides grants to strengthen historically Black colleges and universities and other institutions serving previously underserved populations.

48. Additionally, the Departments of Justice and Education enforce numerous laws, including the Civil Rights

Act of 1964, the Americans with Disabilities Act of 1990, the Patsy T. Mink Equal Opportunity in Education Act of 1972 (Title IX), and the Rehabilitation Act of 1973, that prohibit discrimination on the basis of race, color, national origin, sex, disability, and age with regard to education. In this capacity, the Justice Department is a party to more than 200 court cases addressing equal opportunities for students, and is involved in numerous out-of-court investigations, many of which have led to settlement agreements. The Department of Education investigates and resolves civil rights complaints filed by individuals, resolving 6,150 such complaints in the most recent fiscal year, and initiates compliance reviews where information suggests widespread discrimination. The Individuals with Disabilities Education Act (IDEA) requires public schools to make available to all eligible children with disabilities a free appropriate public education in the least restrictive environment appropriate to their individual needs.

49. The federal government is working closely with civil society groups-the representatives of which frequently raised the issue of education in our UPR consultations-and with state and local education authorities in our fifty states to address the factors that contribute to the education "achievement gap," and to ensure equality and excellence for all children in public schools, and particularly African-American and Hispanic children and children for whom English is a second language, who, like others, find linguistic discrimination a barrier to full participation.

Fairness and equality in law enforcement

50. The United States recognizes that racial or ethnic profiling is not effective law enforcement and is not consistent with our commitment to fairness in our justice system. For many years, concerns about racial profiling arose mainly in the context of motor vehicle or street stops related to enforcement of drug or immigration laws. Since the September 11, 2001 terrorist attacks, the debate has also included an examination of law enforcement conduct in the context of the country's effort to combat terrorism. Citizens and civil society have advocated forcefully that efforts by law enforcement to prevent future terrorist attacks must be consistent with the government's goal to end racial and ethnic profiling.

51. In addition to the U.S. Constitution, there are several federal statutes and regulations that impose limits on the use of race or ethnicity by law enforcement in their decision-making and enforcement activities. In particular, title VI of the Civil Rights Act of 1964, prohibits discrimination based on race, color or national origin in all federally assisted programs or activities, and 42 U.S.C. §14141 provides the Department of Justice with a cause of action to sue police departments for injunctive relief if they are engaging in a pattern or practice of unlawful conduct, including violations of non-discrimination mandates.

52. The U.S. Government's efforts to combat racial and ethnic profiling include increasing enforcement of federal anti-profiling statutes, as well as an examination of federal law enforcement policies and practices. In late 2009, the Attorney General initiated an internal review of the Justice Department's 2003 Guidance Regarding the Use of Race by Federal Law Enforcement Agencies to determine whether it is effective, and will recommend any changes that may be warranted.

53. On August 3, 2010, President Obama signed a law that reduces sentencing disparities between powder cocaine and crack cocaine offenses, capping a long effort-one discussed at our UPR consultations-that arose out of the fact that those convicted of crack cocaine offenses are more likely to be members of a racial minority.

54. The Administration is also committed to ensuring that the United States complies with its international obligations to provide consular notification and access for foreign nationals in U.S. custody, including the obligations arising from the Avena decision of the International Court of Justice.

III.3 Dignity

Safeguards for dignity in law enforcement and criminal justice

55. Law enforcement is one of the fundamental duties of any state. Our commitment to the inalienable rights of each person guides our efforts to ensure that our law enforcement system reflects and respects those rights.

56. The U.S. Constitution, as well as federal and state statutes, provides a number of substantive and procedural protections for individuals accused of committing crimes, those being held for trial, and those who are held in prisons or

jails. These include the right to be protected from unreasonable search and seizures, the right to due process under the law, the right to equal protection under the law, the right to an attorney, the right to remain silent during a criminal proceeding, the right to be protected from excessive bail in federal prosecutions, the right to be informed of the nature of the charges filed and of potential punishments, the right to a speedy and public trial, the right to cross-examine witnesses at trial, the right to an impartial jury of peers before someone can be sentenced to a year or more in prison, the right to be protected against being tried for the same crime twice, and the right to be free from cruel and unusual punishment in all prosecutions. (These constitutional rights are generally reflected, at times with different terminology, in international human rights law instruments to which the U.S. is party. In some respects, our constitutional rights go beyond those guaranteed in international law.)

57. These protections help to ensure that our process for determining criminal sanctions, including those that deprive individuals of their liberty, is fairly designed and implemented. Nonetheless many in civil society continue to raise concerns about our nation's criminal justice system at federal and state levels, including in the areas of capital punishment, juvenile justice, racial profiling, and racial disparities in sentencing. We are committed to continued vigilance in our effort to enforce the law in a manner consistent with the Constitution and with the rights and dignity of all citizens. Dignity and incarceration

58 The United States is committed to protecting the rights of incarcerated persons, and we regularly investigate, monitor compliance, and, where necessary, take legal action to secure the constitutional rights of incarcerated people, including the right to practice their religion.

59. We have also taken action to prevent assaults on the dignity of prisoners that may come from other prisoners. The independent National Prison Rape Elimination Commission, established by Congress under the Prison Rape Elimination Act, was charged with studying the impact of sexual assault in correction and detention facilities and developing national standards for the detection, prevention, reduction, and punishment of prison rape. In 2009, the Commission released its report which detailed progress made in improving the safety and security in these facilities as well as areas still in need of reform. The United States is working to address these issues. The Department of Justice is in the process of developing comprehensive regulations to effectively reduce rape in our nation's prisons.

60. In addition to working to ensure that prisons and jails meet constitutional standards, alternatives to incarceration are being utilized by states, including intensive probation supervision, boot camps, house arrest, and diversion to drug treatment. Dignity and criminal sanctions

61. The United States may impose the death penalty for the most serious crimes and subject to exacting procedural safeguards. Federal laws providing for the death penalty most often involve serious crimes in which death results. Several non-homicide crimes may also result in the imposition of a death sentence,

e.g., espionage, treason, and several carefully circumscribed capital offenses intended to target the threat of terrorist attacks resulting in widespread loss of life.

62. The federal government utilizes a system for carefully examining each potential federal death penalty case. This system operates to help ensure that the death penalty is not applied in an arbitrary, capricious, or discriminatory manner, and to promote indigent defendants receiving competent representation by qualified attorneys. Many of our states have adopted procedures of their own to provide experienced counsel for indigent defendants. In addition, existing federal law permits DNA testing in relevant federal and state cases.

63. In 2009, the death penalty was applied in 52 cases in the United States, about half the number of a decade earlier. The death penalty is authorized by 35 states, the federal government, and the U.S. military. There are currently 16 jurisdictions without the death penalty. While state governments retain primary responsibility for establishing procedures and policies that govern state capital prosecutions, the Supreme Court has excluded from application of the death penalty those offenders who, at the time of the offense, were under age 183 or had intellectual disabilities.4 Dignity and juvenile offenders

64. In 1974, Congress enacted the Juvenile Justice and Delinquency Prevention Act (JJDPA), to ensure that youth were not treated merely as "little adults," and that they received necessary and appropriate rehabilitative services in the least

restrictive environment consistent with public safety. The JJDPA created an office within the Justice Department dedicated to supporting federal, state, and local efforts to prevent juvenile crime, improving the juvenile justice system, and addressing the needs of juvenile crime victims. This office provides funding to states for system improvement, as well as funding for research to identify optimal prevention and intervention strategies for youth in the juvenile justice system or at risk of entering it. Our UPR consultations included direct testimony from juvenile offenders who underscored the importance of intervention strategies and programs to help juvenile offenders find education and employment so that they can become self-sufficient.

65. The Department of Justice also has a robust program to protect the rights of juveniles in juvenile justice facilities. For example, in July 2010, the Department entered an agreement with the State of New York regarding unconstitutional conditions in four upstate facilities. The agreement, in addition to limiting the kinds of restraints that can be used, mandates adequate mental health and substance abuse services.

66. In May 2010, the Supreme Court ruled that sentences of life imprisonment without the possibility of parole for juveniles who commit non-homicide offenses violate the Constitution's prohibition against cruel and unusual punishment.5

IV. A commitment to foster a society where citizens are empowered to exercise their rights

67. The paradigm elucidated in Franklin Roosevelt's 1941 "Four Freedoms" speech became a reference point for many in the international human rights movement. On subjects such as "freedom from want," the United States has focused on democratic solutions and civil society initiatives while the U.S. courts have defined our federal constitutional obligations narrowly and primarily by focusing on procedural rights to due process and equal protection of the law. But as a matter of public policy, our citizens have taken action through their elected representatives to help create a society in which prosperity is shared, including social benefits provided by law, so that all citizens can live what Roosevelt called "a healthy peacetime life." Often this has included safeguards for the most vulnerable in our society-including the young, the old, the poor, and the infirm. In the wake of the Civil War, legislation was passed to support the well-being of widows and veterans, and to provide land to former slaves. By the early 20th century, all of our states had recognized that children needed schooling in order to become free and engaged citizens and had instituted free education for all. During the Great Depression, new programs were introduced to ensure the security of those who could no longer work. In the 1960s, several administrations announced a "war on poverty," and programs were established to provide health care for seniors and the very poor. And this year saw the passage of major legislation that will greatly expand the number of Americans who have health insurance. In every case, the creation of these programs has reflected a popular sense that the society in which we want to live is one in which each person has the opportunity to live a full and fulfilling life. That begins, but does not end, with the exercise of their human rights.

IV.1 Education

68. Through the American Recovery and Reinvestment Act of 2009, the current Administration has made an unprecedented financial commitment of almost $100 billion to education. In November 2009, the

Administration announced the Race to the Top program, a $4.35 billion fund that is the largest competitive education grant program in U.S. history. It is designed to provide incentives to states to implement largescale, system-changing reforms that improve student achievement, narrow achievement gaps, and increase graduation and college enrollment rates. Additionally, Recovery Act funds are being used to promote high-quality early childhood education, provide an increase in available financial aid and loans for postsecondary school, and provide $12 billion for community colleges to give access to workers who need more education and training.

IV.2 Health

69. The United States has been the source of many significant innovations in modern medicine that have alleviated suffering and cured disease for millions in our own country and around the world. This year, we also made significant progress by enacting major legislation that expands access to health care for our citizens.

70. On March 23, 2010, President Obama signed the Affordable Care Act into law. The Act makes great strides toward the goal that all Americans have access to quality, affordable health care. The law is projected to expand health insur-

ance coverage to 32 million Americans who would otherwise lack health insurance, significantly reduces disparities in accessing high-quality care, and includes substantial new investments in prevention and wellness activities to improve public health. The law also includes important consumer protections, such as prohibiting insurance companies from denying coverage to people based on preexisting conditions or medical history, which disproportionately impacts older and sicker populations.

71. The law increases access to care for underserved populations by expanding community health centers that deliver preventive and primary care services. The law will also help our nation reduce disparities and discrimination in access to care that have contributed to poor health. For example, African Americans are 29 percent more likely to die from heart disease than non-Hispanic whites. Asian American men suffer from stomach cancer 114 percent more often than non-Hispanic white men. Hispanic women are 2.2 times more likely to be diagnosed with cervical cancer than non-Hispanic white women. American Indians and Alaska Natives are 2.2 times as likely to have diabetes as non-Hispanic whites. Additionally, these racial and ethnic groups accounted for almost 70 percent of the newly diagnosed cases of HIV and AIDS in 2003.6

72. The Act will reduce disparities like these through access to preventive services; investment in chronic disease control and prevention; enhanced data collection to support population-specific epidemiological research; and recruitment of health professionals from diverse backgrounds.

73. Implementation of the Affordable Care Act will help more Americans get the care they need to live healthy lives and ensure more Americans are free to learn, work, and contribute to their communities.

IV.3 Housing

74. The ability to access quality and affordable housing has a substantial impact on a person's health, education, and economic opportunities. Although we are fortunate to have a high-quality housing stock and a high percentage of homeownership, meeting our nation's housing needs will require continued effort, particularly in expanding the availability of affordable housing in all communities as our population grows. This was a topic frequently raised by citizens in our consultations, and our meetings in New York and New Orleans, included visits to public housing facilities and discussions with residents.

75. Federal housing assistance programs play an important role in covering the difference between the rents that low-income families are able to afford and the cost of rental housing. The main federal assistance programs to help households access affordable housing are the Housing Choice Voucher Program (Section 8), project-based Section 8 rental assistance, and public housing. These programs are intended to reduce housing costs to about 30 percent of household income.

76. We are creating new solutions to address the challenge of homelessness, which often coincides with other vulnerabilities such as mental illness. $190 million in new funding announced in July, 2010, will provide support to 550 local projects that will offer critically needed housing and support services to nearly 20,000 homeless individuals and families. This comes on top of the nearly $1.4 billion awarded last December to renew funding to more than 6,400 existing local programs. Moreover, the Homeless Prevention and Rapid Re-Housing Program, part of the Recovery Act, has helped prevent and end homelessness for nearly a half million people since it became law last year.

V. A commitment to values in our engagement across borders

77. The United States understands its role as a cornerstone in an international system of cooperation to preserve global security, support the growth of global prosperity, and progress toward world peace based on respect for the human rights and dignity of every person.

78. Our own efforts to build such a world include our role as the world's largest donor of development aid- including our commitment to disaster relief as seen recently in Haiti and Pakistan. And they include a commitment to using "smart power" in our foreign policy, including a focus on honest, determined diplomacy and on harnessing the full potential of international institutions to facilitate cooperation.

79. We also know that although we never welcome the use of force, wisdom and necessity will sometimes require it. As President Obama said in his Nobel Lecture, "To say that force may sometimes be necessary is not a call to cynicism-it is a recognition of history; the imperfections of man and the limits of reason."

80. The fundamental truth which grounds the principles of government enshrined in our Constitution- that each person is created with equal value from which flows inalienable rights-is not an exclusively American truth; it is a universal one. It is the truth that anchors the Universal Declaration of Human Rights, it is the truth that underpins the legitimate purposes and obligations not just of our government, but of all governments.

81. We are committed to that universal truth, and so we are committed to principled engagement across borders and with foreign governments and their citizens. This commitment includes, in the words of our Declaration of Independence, according "decent respect to the opinions of mankind," and seeking always to preserve and protect the dignity of all persons, because the values that we cherish apply everywhere and to everyone.

V.1 Values and National Security

82. The United States is currently at war with Al Qaeda and its associated forces. President Obama has made clear that the United States is fully committed to complying with the Constitution and with all applicable domestic and international law, including the laws of war, in all aspects of this or any armed conflict. We start from the premise that there are no law-free zones, and that everyone is entitled to protection under law. In his Nobel Lecture, the President made clear that "[w]here force is necessary, we have a moral and strategic interest in binding ourselves to certain rules of conduct...[E]ven as we confront a vicious adversary that abides by no rules...the United States of America must remain a standard bearer in the conduct of war."

Detention and treatment of detainees

83. On his second full day in office, President Obama acted to implement this vision by issuing three Executive Orders relating to U.S. detention, interrogation, and transfer policies and the Guantánamo Bay detention facility.

84. Executive Order 13491, Ensuring Lawful Interrogations, directed that individuals detained in any armed conflict shall in all circumstances be treated humanely and shall not be subjected to violence to life and person, nor to outrages upon personal dignity, whenever such individuals are in the custody or under the effective control of the United States Government or detained within a facility owned, operated, or controlled by the United States. Such individuals shall not be subjected to any interrogation technique or approach that is not authorized by and listed in Army Field Manural 2-22.3, which explicitly prohibits threats, coercion, physical abuse, and water boarding. The Order further directed the Central Intelligence Agency to close any detention facilities it operated, and not to operate any such detention facilities in the future. Individuals detained in armed conflict must be treated in conformity with all applicable laws, including Common Article 3 of the 1949 Geneva Conventions, which the President and the Supreme Court have recognized as providing "minimum" standards of protection in all non-international armed conflicts, including in the conflict with Al Qaeda.

85. The Executive Order also directed a review of all U.S. transfer policies to ensure that they do not result in the transfer of individuals to other nations to face torture or otherwise for the purpose, or with the effect, of undermining or circumventing the commitments or obligations of the United States to ensure the humane treatment of individuals in its custody or control. The resulting Task Force on transfer practices issued recommendations to the President regarding ways to strengthen existing safeguards in transfer policies, including that the State Department be involved in evaluating all diplomatic assurances; that mechanisms for monitoring treatment in the receiving country be further developed; and that the inspectors general of three key U.S. government Departments involved in transfers prepare annually a co-ordinated report on transfers conducted by each of their agencies in reliance on assurances. The United States is developing practices and procedures that will ensure the implementation of Task Force recommendations.

86. Thus, the United States prohibits torture and cruel, inhuman, or degrading treatment or punishment of persons in the custody or control of the U.S. Government, regardless of their nationality or physical location. It takes vigilant action to prevent such conduct and to hold those who commit acts of official cruelty accountable for their wrongful acts. The United States is a party to the Convention Against Torture, and U.S. law prohibits torture at both the federal and

state levels. On June 26, 2010, on the anniversary of adoption of the Convention Against Torture, President Obama issued a statement unequivocally reaffirming U.S. support for its principles, and committing the United States to continue to cooperate in international efforts to eradicate torture.

87. In issuing Executive Order 13492, Review and Disposition of Individuals Detained at the Guantánamo Bay Naval Base and Closure of Detention Facilities, the President announced the Administration's intention to close the Guantánamo Bay detention facilities. The President also created a task force to recommend the appropriate disposition of each detainee held at Guantánamo. The Task Force assembled large volumes of information from across the government to determine the proper disposition of each detainee. The Task Force examined this information critically, giving careful consideration to, among other things, the threat posed by the detainee, the reliability of the underlying information, any concerns about the post-transfer humane treatment of the detainee, and the interests of national security. Based on the Task Force's evaluations and recommendations, senior officials representing each agency responsible for the review reached unanimous determinations on the appropriate disposition for all detainees. Since January 2009, 38 detainees have resettled successfully in third countries, an additional 26 detainees have been repatriated, and one has been transferred to the United States for prosecution. The Administration remains committed to closure of the Guantánamo detention facility.

88. Executive Order 13493, Review of Detention Policy Options, established a task force to review and facilitate significant policy decisions regarding broader detention questions. This Special Task Force on Detention Policy has reviewed available options for the apprehension, detention, trial, transfer, release, or other disposition of individuals captured or apprehended in connection with armed conflicts and counterterrorism operations. As a matter of domestic law, the Obama Administration has not based its claim of authority to detain individuals at Guantánamo and in Afghanistan on the President's inherent constitutional powers, but rather on legislative authority expressly granted to the President by Congress in 2001. The Administration has expressly acknowledged that international law informs the scope of our detention authority. The President has also made clear that we have a national security interest in prosecuting terrorists, either before Article III courts or military commissions, and that we would exhaust all available avenues to prosecute Guantánamo detainees before deciding whether it would be appropriate to continue detention under the laws of war. Working with our Congress, we have revised our military commissions to enhance their procedural protections, including prohibiting introduction of any statements taken as a result of cruel, inhuman, or degrading treatment.

Privacy

89. Freedom from arbitrary and unlawful interference with privacy is protected under the Fourth Amendment to the Constitution and federal statutes. In addition, state and local laws and regulations provide robust protections of individuals' right to privacy and rigorous processes to ensure that investigative authorities are undertaken consistent with the Constitution.

90. Protecting our national interests may involve new arrangements to confronting threats like terrorism, but these structures and practices must always be in line with our Constitution and preserve the rights and freedoms of our people. Although the departments and agencies of the U.S. Government involved in surveillance and the collection of foreign intelligence information comply with a robust regime of laws, rules, regulations, and policies designed to protect national security and privacy, significant concerns in these areas have been raised by civil society, including concerns that relevant laws have been made outdated by technological changes, and that privacy protections need to be applied more broadly and methodically to surveillance.

91. The 2001 USA PATRIOT Act expanded intelligence collection authorities under the Foreign Intelligence Surveillance Act (FISA), which regulates electronic surveillance and physical searches conducted to acquire foreign intelligence information. The U.S. Executive Branch acknowledged in 2005 that the U.S. National Security Agency had been intercepting without a court order certain international communications where the government had a reasonable basis to conclude that one person was a member of, or affiliated with, Al Qaeda or a member of an organization affiliated with Al Qaeda and where one party was outside the United States. In response, considerable congressional and public attention focused on issues regarding the authorization, review, and oversight of electronic surveillance programs designed to acquire foreign intelligence information or to address international terrorism. Congress held hearings and enacted new legislation, including the 2007 Protect America Act and a series of amendments to FISA.

V.2 Values and Immigration

92. That immigrants have been consistently drawn to our shores throughout our history is both a testament to and a source of the strength and appeal of our vibrant democracy. As he left office, President Reagan remarked that the United States is "still a beacon, still a magnet for all who must have freedom, for all the pilgrims from all the lost places who are hurtling through the darkness, toward home." Over the last 50 years, the U.S. has accepted several million refugees fleeing persecution from all corners of the globe as well as many millions of immigrants seeking a better life or joining family. Today, the United States and other countries to which a significant number of people seek to emigrate face challenges in developing and enforcing immigration laws and policies that reflect economic, social, and national security realities. In addressing these issues we seek to build a system of immigration enforcement that is both effective and fair.

93. In 2009, the Department of Homeland Security (DHS) began a major overhaul of the U.S. immigration detention system in an effort to improve detention center management and prioritize health, safety, and uniformity among immigration detention facilities, while ensuring security and efficiency. As part of this effort, in conjunction with ongoing consultations with non-governmental organizations and outside experts, DHS issued revised parole guidelines, effective January 2010, for arriving aliens in expedited removal found to have a credible fear of persecution or torture. The new guidelines firmly establish that it is not in the public interest to detain those arriving aliens found to have a credible fear who establish their identities, and that they pose neither a flight risk nor a danger to the community.

94. Under section 287(g) of the Immigration and Nationality Act, DHS may delegate authority to state and local officers to enforce federal immigration law. DHS has made improvements to the 287(g) program, including implementing a new, standardized Memorandum of Agreement with state and local partners that strengthens program oversight and provides uniform guidelines for DHS supervision of state and local agency officer operations; information reporting and tracking; complaint procedures; and implementation measures. DHS continues to evaluate the program, incorporating additional safeguards as necessary to aid in the prevention of racial profiling and civil rights violations and improve accountability for protecting human rights.

95. A recent Arizona law, S.B. 1070, has generated significant attention and debate at home and around the world. The issue is being addressed in a court action that argues that the federal government has the authority to set and enforce immigration law. That action is ongoing; parts of the law are currently enjoined.

96. President Obama remains firmly committed to fixing our broken immigration system, because he recognizes that our ability to innovate, our ties to the world, and our economic prosperity depend on our capacity to welcome and assimilate immigrants. The Administration will continue its efforts to work with the U.S. Congress and affected communities toward this end.

V.3 Values and Trafficking

97. In June 2010, the United States issued its 10th annual Trafficking in Persons Report outlining the continuing challenges posed by human trafficking across the globe and, for the first time, included a ranking and full narrative of the United States. The narrative includes detailed information about U.S. anti-trafficking efforts undertaken by more than 10 federal agencies and its pursuit of policies, partnerships, and practices aimed at protecting victims, preventing trafficking, and prosecuting traffickers.

98. Hallmarks of the U.S. approach to combating human trafficking include a) vigorous prosecution of traffickers, and funding task forces throughout the nation comprised of local, state and federal law enforcement and a non-governmental victim service provider; b) a victim-centered approach that recognizes victims require specialized care and are an integral part of any investigation and/or prosecution; c) comprehensive victim services such as shelter, health care, mental health care, food, safety, legal services, interpretation, victim advocacy, immigration relief, education, job skills, employment placement, family reunification, and reintegration; d) temporary immigration relief and work authorization for victims assisting investigations and prosecutions and longer term immigration relief for certain victims and their family members which may then lead to permanent residence and citizenship; e) a coordinated identification and enforcement approach among labor, border, and criminal enforcement; and f) an expansive view of prevention activities that

includes strengthening labor protections and enforcement, addressing demand for commercial sex, and working with civil society to rid corporate supply chains of forced labor.

99. The U.S. stands out in terms of the sophistication and breadth of its anti-trafficking efforts. Furthermore, we provide substantial international assistance aimed at preventing trafficking in persons, protecting victims, and prosecuting traffickers.

VI. Conclusion

100. The United States views participation in this UPR process as an opportunity to discuss with our citizenry and with fellow members of the Human Rights Council our accomplishments, challenges, and vision for the future on human rights. We welcome observations and recommendations that can help U.S. on that road to a more perfect union. Delivering on human rights has never been easy, but it is work we will continue to undertake with determination, for human rights will always undergird our national identity and define our national aspirations.

Annex 1: Human Rights Treaty Ratification and Reporting The United States is at present Party to the following multilateral human rights related treaties:
- Slavery Convention and its amending Protocol;
- Supplementary Convention on the Abolition of Slavery, the Slave Trade and Institutions and Practices Similar to Slavery;
- Protocol Relating to the Status of Refugees;
- Inter-American Convention on the Granting of Political Rights to Women;
- Convention on the Political Rights of Women;
- Convention on the Prevention and Punishment of the Crime of Genocide;
- ILO Convention No. 105 concerning the Abolition of Forced Labor;
- International Covenant on Civil and Political Rights;
- Convention against Torture and Other Cruel, Inhuman or Degrading Treatment or Punishment;
- International Convention on the Elimination of All Forums of Racial Discrimination;
- ILO Convention 182 Concerning the Prohibition and Immediate Action for the Elimination of the Worst Forms of Child Labor;
- Optional Protocol to the Convention on the Rights of the Child on the Involvement of Children in Armed Conflict; and
- Optional Protocol to the Convention on the Rights of the Child on the Sale of Children, Child Prostitution, and Child Pornography.

The United States has signed but not ratified the following multilateral human rights treaties:
- International Covenant on Economic, Social and Cultural Rights;
- American Convention on Human Rights;
- Convention on the Elimination of All Forms of Discrimination Against Women;
- Convention on the Rights of the Child; and
- International Convention on the Rights of Persons with Disabilities.

In addition, the United States has entered into many bilateral treaties (including consular treaties and treaties of friendship, commerce and navigation) that contain provisions guaranteeing various rights and protections to nationals of foreign countries on a reciprocal basis. In some cases, these may be invoked directly in United States courts for that purpose.

Note that shorter forms of these complete treaty names are used in the UPR report, e.g., "Convention Against Torture."

In addition to accepting human rights obligations under the above-referenced treaties to which it is a party, the United States has made human rights commitments through numerous other instruments, including the 1948 Universal Declaration of Human Rights and the 1948 American Declaration of the Rights and Duties of Man.

The United States regularly submits lengthy and detailed reports on its implementation of several of the human rights treaties listed above, specifically the International Covenant on Civil and Political Rights, the Convention against Torture, the Convention on the Elimination of All Forums of Racial Discrimination, and the two Optional Protocols to the Convention on the Rights of the Child. A compilation of that reporting is posted on the State Department's website, at http://www.state.gov/g/drl/hr/treaties/index.htm Annex 2: Abbreviations

Source: Report of The United States of America to the High Commissioner for Human Rights on the Universal Periodic Review Process (2010 National Report) https://www.state.gov/documents/organization/146379.pdf

8. REPORT OF THE WORKING GROUP ON THE UNIVERSAL PERIODIC REVIEW, UNITED STATES OF AMERICA (UPR OUTCOME REPORT), 2011

This document is a written record of the U.S. UPR process and recommendations submitted to the Human Rights Council for its informal adoption, then submitted at an HRC session for formal adoption. This Working Group report is a good source for understanding what the U.S. hears from the International Community via the UN. Depending on the U.S. Administration's demeanor, it is the basis upon which the U.S. responds to suggestions and recommendations from the International Community. This is not a legal document as such, but a report by a UPR working group called a troika. The UPR process is about how the United States is complying with human rights and humanitarian law norms, and receiving recommendations by other states on how it could improve. Although the U.S. is not legally bound to follow it, including the recommendations, this document should be seriously considered by the State under Review and implemented as well as possible consistent with the domestic law, for the U.S. the Constitution. The UPR process is intended as a Feedback mechanism for a country's human rights self-improvement.

Supervising Body: United Nations, Human Rights Council

Comments: On November 5, 2010 the U.S. had its interactive dialogue session at the U.N. as part of the Universal Periodic Review Process. After that session, the randomly selected "Troika" of three countries (France, Cameroon and Japan) helped prepare a draft Outcome Document in November 2010, which summarized all the documentation and proceedings to that time and included all the recommendations of states to the U.S. for the U.S. to consider accepting and agreeing to put into effect. This was the most recommendations made of any of the states which had done the UPR process.

This Document was issued January 4, 2011, and is the Working Group's final Outcome report from the prepared draft. The U.S. needed to decide how to respond to this document and on March 10, 2011, the U.S. submitted its written response to the HRC. See Appendix K, #4. The U.S. decided which recommendations to accept and agree to put into practice.

The final Outcome document was presented and voted on by the Council and formally adopted on March 18, 2011. It should help guide the United States as to how to comply better with its human rights and humanitarian law obligations. The U.S. will be expected to exert its good faith efforts to put those accepted recommendations into practice. What it does will be considered at its next UPR in four years.

United Nations A/HRC/16/11 General Assembly 4 January 2011 Original: English
Human Rights Council
Sixteenth session
Agenda item 6
Universal Periodic Review

Report of the Working Group on the Universal Periodic Review United States of America
Previously issued as document A/HRC/WG.6/9/L.9. The annex to the present report is circulated as received.

Annex 3

Composition of the delegation

Introduction

1. The Working Group on the Universal Periodic Review (UPR), established in accordance with Human Rights Council resolution 5/1, held its ninth session from 1 to 12 November 2010. The review of the United States of America was held at the 9th meeting, on 5 November 2010. The delegation of the United States of America was headed jointly by the Honourable Esther Brimmer, Assistant Secretary, Bureau of International Organizations, Department of State; the Honourable Harold Hongju Koh, Legal Adviser, Office of the Legal Adviser, Department of State; and the Honourable Michael Posner, Assistant Secretary, Democracy, Human Rights and Labour, Department of State. At its 13th meeting, held on 9 November 2010, the Working Group adopted the report on the United States of America.

2. On 21 June 2010, the Human Rights Council selected the following group of rapporteurs (troika) to facilitate the review of the United States of America: Cameroon, France and Japan.

3. In accordance with paragraph 15 of the annex to resolution 5/1, the following documents were issued for the review of the United States of America:

    (a) A national report submitted/written presentation made in accordance with paragraph 15 (a) (A/HRC/WG.6/9/USA/1);

    (b) A compilation prepared by the Office of the United Nations High Commissioner for Human Rights (OHCHR) in accordance with paragraph 15 (b) (A/HRC/WG.6/9/USA/2);

    (c) A summary prepared by OHCHR in accordance with paragraph 15 (c) (A/HRC/WG.6/9/USA/3/Rev.1).

4. A list of questions prepared in advance by Plurinational State of Bolivia, the Czech Republic, Denmark, Germany, Japan, Latvia, Mexico, the Netherlands, Norway, the Russian Federation, Slovenia, Sweden, Switzerland and the United Kingdom of Great Britain and Northern Ireland was transmitted to the United States of America through the troika. Those questions are available on the extranet of the universal periodic review.

I. Summary of the proceedings of the review process

5. During the interactive dialogue, 56 delegations made statements. Additional statements, which could not be delivered during the interactive dialogue owing to time constraints, will be posted on the extranet of the universal periodic review when available.1 Recommendations made during the dialogue are found in section II of the present report.

A. Presentation by the State under review

6. The delegation expressed its pleasure at presenting its first UPR report and noted President Obama's and Secretary Clinton's deep commitment to multilateral engagement, human rights, and the rule of law. The story of the United States has been one of striving for a more perfect union. By admitting the possibility of imperfection, new opportunities to improve are revealed — the ability to do this has been and continues to be a source of national strength.

7. The United States explained that it encourages the involvement of its civil society, and works through law-abiding executives, democratic legislatures and independent courts to make progress. The United States expressed pride in its accomplishments, recognized that there remains room for further progress and reiterated its commitment to principled engagement with the international system to advance human rights at home and abroad.

B. Interactive dialogue and responses by the State under review

8. Cuba made recommendations.

9. The Bolivarian Republic of Bolivarian Republic of Venezuela expressed the hope that President Obama would make a commitment to human rights.

10. The Islamic Republic of Islamic Republic of Iran expressed concern over the situation of human rights and systematic violations committed by the United States at both the national and international levels.

11. The Russian Federation positively assessed the current Government's efforts to eliminate a number of human rights violations that had been committed in the course of the "fight against terrorism" and to join in the work of the Human Rights Council. On the other hand, in a number of areas, including, first of all, acceding to the international human rights treaties and ensuring human rights in the process of the fight against terrorism, additional efforts by the United States were required.

12. Nicaragua stated that the United States had made the use of force the cornerstone of its expansionist policy and that Latin America was one of its victims. It stated that the United States had violated human rights while pretending to be the world's guardian of human rights.

13. Indonesia noted positively the United States' commitment to freedom and equality, and welcomed the country's engagement with the Human Rights Council. It expressed its belief that the United States needed to make efforts to protect human rights in a balanced manner and to promote tolerance. Indonesia acknowledged the United States' contribution to the development of the United Nations norms.

14. The Plurinational State of Bolivia made recommendations.

15. Ecuador noted the Government's efforts to improve human rights, although the results had been limited.

16. The Democratic People's Republic of Korea remained concerned about the persistent reports of human rights violations committed by the United States at home and abroad.

17. Algeria stated that the election of a President of African descent had spoken louder than any statement about the United States' commitment to civil and political rights. Algeria noted that prison overcrowding was the norm and that prisons housed 60 per cent more inmates than they had been designed for.

18. Qatar welcomed the United States' efforts in combating racial and religious discrimination, providing social services and ensuring the enjoyment of economic, social and cultural rights.

19. Mexico recognized the robust institutional infrastructure for the protection of human rights.

20. Egypt expressed the hope of seeing concrete steps undertaken by the United States to ensure the protection of the human rights of the members of Muslim, Arab, AfricanAmerican and South Asian communities. It remained concerned about certain policies and practices in the human rights field.

21. China noted the Government's efforts in past years to promote and protect human rights and to make progress in health care and education. However, China expressed concern about the gaps in human rights legislation and the fact that the United States had not become a party to a number of core international human rights instruments. It was also concerned, inter alia, that the law enforcement agencies tended to use excessive force and that the incidence of poverty was higher among Afro-Americans, Latinos and Native Americans.

22. India commended the United States for its commitment to human rights and its acknowledgment of the remaining challenges. India was concerned about human rights abuses by business corporations and inquired about the United States' position on its Alien Tort Claims Act. It was concerned at the sexual harassment of women in the United States military and the disproportionately high conviction rates for African-Americans, as well as their low access to education, health and employment.

23. Bangladesh stated that, while progress had been made in the protection of civil and political rights, the protection of social and economic rights had not been fully recognized. It stated that the United States played a positive role internationally in supporting many countries' development efforts. Bangladesh was concerned at the recent enactment of an immigration law that might encourage discriminatory attitudes and ill treatment against migrants.

24. Malaysia appreciated the renewed commitment expressed by the Government to reengage on the full range of human rights, including through United States membership of the Human Rights Council. Malaysia stated that several issues, such as racial discrimination, racial profiling, religious intolerance and widening income equality, could be given more attention.

25. Brazil welcomed the measures announced by the United States to address violations of human rights that had been committed under its counter-terrorism policy. It noted with concern the rise in the number of persons living in poverty. Brazil encouraged the United States to investigate and address situations of forced labour against migrants.

26. Switzerland noted with satisfaction that several states had abolished the death penalty. Switzerland also noted, inter alia, that thousands of migrants had been detained in harsh conditions and without access to legal counselling for violations of immigration laws.

27. The Republic of Korea commended the Government's decision to close the Guantánamo Bay detention facility and to ban methods of interrogation that might not be in compliance with international law. It welcomed the adoption of legislation to expand access to health care for its citizens.

28. In addressing a number of observations and recommendations related to ratification of treaties, the delegation noted that its practice was to ensure that it could fully implement a treaty before it became a party to it and not to ratify unless it could do so. Under its Constitution, such ratification required approval of two thirds of the United States Senate. The United States was strongly committed to ratifying the CEDAW and the Convention on the Rights of Persons with Disabilities.

29. In response to questions regarding the creation of a national human rights institution, the U.S. delegation noted that this was an issue currently under consideration in the United States. The United States believed that multiple levels of complementary work at the federal and sub-federal levels and by different branches of government (executive, legislative and judicial) provided multiple and reinforcing protections for individual rights.

30. The United States then discussed other points raised by several countries: torture and the closing of the detention facility at Guantánamo Bay.

31. The delegation explained that the United States is unequivocally committed to the humane treatment of all individuals in detention, whether criminal detention or detainees in United States custody in armed conflict. Through Executive Orders, the President affirmed the United States commitment to abiding by the ban on torture and inhumane treatment, ordered CIA "black sites" closed, and instructed that any interrogations must be conducted consistent with United States treaty obligations and the revised Army Field Manual. President Obama also ordered a review to ensure that the detention facility at Guantánamo Bay fully complied with Common Article 3, and established a special interagency task force to review United States interrogation and transfer policies and to ensure that all United States. transfer practices comply with United States law, policy and international obligations and never result in the transfer of any individual to face torture.

32. The United States reaffirmed the President's commitment to closing the Guantánamo detention facility as quickly as possible, noting that the task has proven enormously complex and also involves United States allies, the courts, and the United States Congress. The United States expressed its gratitude to those countries that had accepted detainees for resettlement.

33. The delegation addressed questions related to its work to combat discrimination. The United States is committed to ensuring political participation by all qualified voters through enforcement of voting rights laws. The Justice Department will review redistricting plans after the 2010 Census to ensure that voting districts are not drawn with the purpose or effect of discriminating against minority voters. The United States explained its enforcement of laws to ensure equal access to housing, lending, credit, educational opportunities, and environmental justice. Although still grappling with the legacy of slavery and addressing problems of racial discrimination, the United States remains mindful of the need to address other inequalities as well.

34. The United States is committed to promoting equal rights for women. The delegation discussed the passage of the Lilly Ledbetter Fair Pay Act, the creation of an Ambassador-at-Large for Global Women's Issues, and other measures.

35. The delegation also noted important initiatives to ensure more robust protections for lesbian, gay, bisexual and transgender individuals. In addition to several non-legislative measures, the United States is seeking the legislative repeal of the Defence of Marriage Act and the "Don't Ask, Don't Tell law" and policy.

36. The United States continues to be a world leader in protecting disability rights. In addition to signing the Disabilities Convention, it vigorously enforces laws against architectural barriers and unnecessary institutionalization. In the past year, the United States filed or participated in more than a dozen lawsuits to promote full inclusion of persons with disabilities.

37. The delegation then addressed questions regarding the Arizona immigration law. The Justice Department had challenged this law on grounds that it unconstitutionally interferes with the federal Government's authority to set and enforce immigration policy, and litigation is ongoing in which a federal judge has enjoined the law. The United States expressed its commitment to advancing comprehensive immigration reform.

38. Thailand noted with appreciation that the United States had initiated the ratification process relating to a number of human rights instruments. It also welcomed the Government's efforts to address discrimination on various grounds and to promote equality before the law for all.

39. The Libyan Arab Jamahiriya was concerned at, inter alia, the racial discrimination and intolerance against persons with African, Arab Islamic and Latin American origins, the denial of the indigenous community of their rights, human rights violations resulting from its policies of occupation and invasion and the imposition of blockades. It was concerned over the large number of prisoners at Guantánamo, deprived of their right to a fair trial.

40. The United Kingdom of Great Britain and Northern Ireland noted that the United States had a strong record in human rights protection and welcomed U.S. recognition of the need to achieve greater equality for minorities, people with disabilities and LGBT individuals. It was concerned that the death penalty could sometimes be administered in a discriminatory manner and encouraged the United States to address those systemic issues. It asked about steps the United States had taken towards the ratification of Treaties and Optional Protocols to Conventions it had already signed. It encouraged the United States to redouble its efforts to ensure the closure of the Guantánamo detention facilities in a timely manner.

41. France welcomed the United States' pledge to ratify CEDAW and its intention to close the Guantánamo detention centre. It asked what measures had been taken in that regard and when the closure was expected.

42. Australia noted that the United States, in many ways, led by example in promoting human rights standards around the world. It expressed concern, however, at the country's continued use of the death penalty. It remained concerned about reports of violent crimes against persons of minority sexual orientation. Australia welcomed the United States' efforts to address the gap between the rights of Native and other Americans. Australia encouraged the United States to become a party to CRPD.

43. Belgium noted with regret that the death penalty was still applied by some 35 states. It expressed concern at the situation in the prison system, including violence against detainees; prison overpopulation and overrepresentation of some ethnic groups; and imprisonment, sometimes for life, without any possible reprieve for those who were minors when the acts were carried out.

44. The Sudan commended the United States' efforts to promote and protect human rights on its territory and globally. It commended the United States for its efforts to create the conditions necessary for the ratification of international conventions.

45. Austria stated that the United States had set positive examples in the protection of human rights at the national and international levels.

46. Bahrain noted the adoption of legislation on health care. Bahrain referred to the recommendations made by CAT on CAT's applicability in times of war and peace, and asked on the steps taken to implement that recommendation. It also referred to the recommendation made by CERD on the establishment of a national human rights institution.

47. Viet Nam noted the United States' commitment to strengthening its system of human rights protection. It expressed concern about the reported discrimination against migrants and foreigners, including Vietnamese migrants and students, and the lack of Government commitment to support many core international human rights instruments.

48. Ireland welcomed progressive developments in the United States including the Hate Crimes Prevention Act of 2009 and the work that is being conducted towards the ratification of the ILO Convention No. 111. Ireland noted that the United States remains one of the few countries in the world that continue to apply the death penalty. Ireland asked whether the United States intends to proceed to the introduction of a nation-wide moratorium on the death penalty. Ireland regretted that an increasing number of states within the United States have lifted moratoria on the death penalty and urged the United States to introduce a nation-wide moratorium. Ireland welcomed the United States' exclusion of the death penalty for crimes committed by minors and persons with an intellectual disability.

49. Morocco expressed appreciation for the United States' commitment to development assistance and referred to a number of programmes and innovative solutions concerning housing rights.

50. Cyprus noted with appreciation that the United States had signed the Rome Statute of ICC. It was concerned about the use of the death penalty and referred to the concerns expressed by a number of treaty bodies related to allegations of brutality and the use of excessive force by law enforcement officials against migrants.

51. Spain asked questions about the closing of the Guantánamo prison, the new regulations on military commissions and the right to a fair trial, and the guarantees for the remaining detainees; and about the United States' obligations related to consular access to foreign detainees, particularly in relation to the *Avena* ruling.

52. The delegation addressed issues raised by a number of states, including the relationship between human rights and national security, the death penalty, and indigenous issues. The United States was committed to establishing national security policies that respect the rule of law. It has redoubled its efforts over the past two years to ensure that all armed conflict operations comply fully with all applicable domestic and international law. Torture and cruel treatment are crimes in the United States and steps are taken to prosecute those who commit such acts. All individuals held in armed conflict are held lawfully. In response to a question from Spain, the United States said that all detainees in the U.S. and Guantánamo have robust access to habeas review by its federal courts.

53. United States targeting practices, including lethal operations conducted with the use of unmanned aerial vehicles, comply with all applicable law. To the extent that human rights law may apply in armed conflict or national actions taken in self-defence, in all cases, the United States works to ensure that its actions are lawful. The delegation noted first, that international human rights law and international humanitarian law are complementary, reinforcing, and animated by humanitarian principles designed to protect innocent life. Second, while the United States complied with human rights law wherever applicable, the applicable rules for the protection of individuals and the conduct of hostilities in armed conflict outside a nation's territory are typically found in international humanitarian law, which apply to government and non-government actors. Third, determining which international law rules apply to any particular government action during an armed conflict is highly fact-specific.

54. In answer to a number of questions regarding detainee treatment, the Defence Department has well-established procedures for reporting detainee abuse and investigates all credible allegations of abuse by United States forces. Between Iraq, Afghanistan, and Guantánamo, the United States has conducted hundreds of investigations regarding detainee abuse allegations, which have led to hundreds of disciplinary actions. All credible allegations of detainee abuse by United States forces have been thoroughly investigated and appropriate corrective action has been taken. The United States further noted its commitment to ensuring that it does not transfer individuals to torture in Iraq and elsewhere.

55. In response to comments from a number of countries regarding capital punishment, the delegation noted that while the matter is a subject of earnest debate in the United States, as a matter of law that punishment is permitted for the most serious crimes with appropriate safeguards. Recently, the United States Supreme Court has narrowed the class of individuals that can be executed, the types of crimes subject to the penalty, and the manner by which the punishment is administered so that it is not cruel and unusual. In response to questions from Mexico and the United Kingdom about consular notification and foreign nationals on death row, the United States noted its commitment, and pending federal legislation, to comply with the *Avena* ICJ judgment.

56. Turning to indigenous issues, the delegation noted the many challenges faced by Native Americans - poverty, unemployment, health care gaps, violent crime, and discrimination - and the laws and programmes it has in place to address these problems. The United States stated its belief that tribes and their members will flourish if they are empowered to

deal with the challenges they face. This conclusion is reflected in law and policy regarding tribal self-determination. President Obama hosted the White House Tribal Nations Conference at which he directed all agencies to submit plans for and progress reports on implementation of the Executive Order on Consultation and Coordination with Indian Tribal Governments. As a result, the level of tribal consultations is now at an historic high.

57. In response to questions from Australia, Cyprus, Finland, and Norway, the delegation noted the considerable attention that has been paid to the interagency consultations with tribal leaders as a part of the United States review of its position on the United Nations Declaration on the Rights of Indigenous Peoples. The decision to review its position was made in response to calls from tribes and other indigenous groups and individuals.

58. The United States has also taken numerous steps to address particular challenges faced by indigenous communities. These include health care reform, the settlement of certain claims, and improvements in criminal justice issues.

59. Denmark urged the Government to follow the recommendations of the international community that it ensure that state and federal authorities applied a moratorium on executions with a view to ultimately abolishing the death penalty nationwide. It would like to see the United States join the vast majority of States that adhered to ICESCR, CEDAW, CRC and OP-CAT.

60. Finland, while welcoming the progress made by the United States in enhancing the rights of indigenous peoples, including the ongoing review of its position on the United Nations Declaration on the Rights of Indigenous Peoples, asked how the Government was conducting the review and about the current situation with respect to the process. Finland also asked about measures undertaken to combat discrimination against women.

61. Ghana commended the United States for, inter alia, efforts that had transformed the country into a multi-racial, multi-ethnic and multi-religious society. It noted with appreciation that the Government continued to work to ensure that equal opportunity was not only guaranteed in law, but experienced by all Americans. Ghana, however, referred to the concerns expressed by several special procedures concerning ongoing structural discriminations.

62. Hungary recognized that the United States had a well-developed system of domestic human rights laws. However, the United States had limited obligations under the international human rights treaties. Hungary welcomed the change in the country's attitude towards ICC, and hoped for further steps to deepen relations with it.

63. Slovakia stated that the United States had been one of the prominent global defenders and promoters of human rights, dedicating significant resources to that commitment.

64. The Netherlands, while noting the Government's support for the ratification of CEDAW by the United States, noted with concern that no specific steps had been taken thus far to that end. The Netherlands also expressed concern at the use of death penalty in 35 states. The Netherlands commended the United States for having received many visits by Special Rapporteurs.

65. Turkey welcomed the decision of the United States to become a member of the Human Rights Council. Turkey expressed its belief that the increasing multilateral cooperation and engagement that the United States had embraced would contribute to global peace and stability and constitute an important factor for the protection of the human rights of those belonging to minority groups, in particular Muslims and immigrants.

66. Norway noted with appreciation the role that the United States played in the international human rights arena. It welcomed the answers provided by the United States to advance questions that it had posed. Norway stated that it looked forward to the transparent and inclusive follow-up in the universal periodic review implementation phase.

67. Sweden welcomed the repeal of the use of capital punishment in some states, but regretted the recurring sentencing to the death penalty and executions in many states. Sweden asked the United States to elaborate on the status of the death penalty and about the plans to impose an official moratorium on executions towards the complete abolition of the death penalty. It also asked about the measures taken by the United States to ensure the full enjoyment of the human rights of persons deprived of their liberty.

68. The Holy See noted that "Operation Streamline" against irregular migrants should be suspended and asked for information about the Government's decision to review its position on the United Nations Declaration on the Rights of Indigenous Peoples.

69. Italy noted with appreciation the Government's efforts to fight economic, social, gender and ethnic discrimination. It noted that the death penalty was still in force in 35 states, even though some states had applied a de facto moratorium.

70. With a view to strengthening the universal human rights system, Uruguay made recommendations.

71. The United States delegation noted that the United States criminal justice system is based on the protection of individual rights. The United States has acted to address a history of racially based law enforcement, through, among other things, enactment and enforcement of laws that prohibit discrimination based on race, colour or national origin by police departments that receive federal funds. The United States was working actively to study and address persistent racial and ethnic disparities in the U.S. criminal justice system and to implement appropriate corrective measures.

72. The United States assured delegations that it condemns racial and ethnic profiling in all of its forms, and is conducting a thorough review of policies and procedures to ensure that none of its law enforcement practices improperly target individuals based on race or ethnicity. With regard to Switzerland's concern for juveniles, the United States delegation noted that the United States Supreme Court recently decided that juvenile offenders convicted of crimes other than homicide may no longer be sentenced to life imprisonment without parole. The United States is committed to meeting its obligations under both international and domestic law for proper treatment of persons detained or incarcerated in the criminal justice system, including those in maximum security facilities. In response to inquiries from the Netherlands and Sweden about prison conditions, the United States confines inmates in prisons and community-based facilities that are safe, humane, and appropriately secure, and in response to questions from the Netherlands, Latvia and Denmark, noted that the United States has hosted visits from eight Special Procedures during the past three years.

73. The United States addressed additional questions regarding immigration. Over the last five years, it welcomed over 5.5 million new permanent residents and over 3.5 million new naturalized citizens, and resettled or granted asylum to nearly 425,000 refugees. It is committed to improving its immigration system. The Departments of Homeland Security (DHS) and Labour are working together to improve protections for migrants. In response to concerns from civil society regarding immigration detention and the removal process, DHS has undertaken major reforms to improve detention center management, health, safety, and uniformity among facilities. DHS's reforms are designed to ensure that detention was used only when appropriate, in light of legal requirements and the need to ensure public safety. In 2010 the United States lifted a 22-year ban on travel to the country by HIV-infected individuals. The United States delegation discussed recent programmes to combat international trafficking in persons.

74. In consultation with civil society and the United Nation High Commissioner for Refugees, the United States established that each arriving alien with a credible fear of persecution or torture would be considered for release; and that those who established their identity and did not pose a flight risk or a danger to the community would not be detained pending completion of their immigration proceedings. For detained aliens, the United States recognizes the need to improve conditions of confinement, medical care, and the ability to exercise their human rights. DHS is revising standards governing immigration detention conditions, implemented a new detainee locator system, and assigned new oversight personnel nationwide. In the context of immigration enforcement, the United States recognized concerns regarding racial and ethnic profiling by local law enforcement officials and reaffirmed its commitment and recent actions to combat profiling through significantly strengthened protections and training against such discrimination.

75. The Republic of Moldova underlined the important involvement of the United States in countering human trafficking. It noted with appreciation the fact that the number of applied death penalties had been decreasing and that the death penalty as a punishment was excluded for those offenders who were under the age of 18 at the time of the offence.

76. Trinidad and Tobago noted the Government's efforts to respect human rights, including those to eliminate all forms of racial discrimination, and the enactment of legislation in 2009 to combat gender-based wage discrimination.

77. New Zealand stated that the United States had demonstrated leadership in the promotion of human rights. It noted with appreciation that the United States had excluded the death penalty for those under 18 years of age at the time of

the offence, and those with intellectual disabilities. However, it noted that significant numbers of people continued to be executed. New Zealand welcomed the signing by the United States of CPRD.

78. Haiti deplored the difficulties encountered by persons of African descent who, for example, faced a high rate of unemployment and had lower income. Haiti asked about the Government's intention to set up a national human rights institution.

79. Israel expressed appreciation for the United States' significant contribution and commitment to the advancement and protection of human rights throughout the world. It also noted with appreciation the United States' engagement with stakeholders in a comprehensive consultation process.

80. Japan praised the United States for its efforts to tackle human rights issues in the unique context of its multi-racial, multi-national and multi-religious society. Japan was concerned about the alleged use of excessive force by law enforcement officials, especially against Latino and African-American persons.

81. Canada welcomed reinvigorated United States efforts to enforce its Civil Rights Act of 1964, which prohibited discrimination based on race, colour, sex, national origin and religion. It recognized the anti-human-trafficking efforts of the United States. Canada noted the major financial sector reform enacted by the United States that includes new consumer protections to address fairness in housing, and applauded the Affordable Health Care Act signed into law in March 2010. Canada noted with appreciation the active re-engagement in the Human Rights Council by the United States.

82. Germany asked how the United States was following up the recommendations of the treaty bodies on the ratification of CRC, Additional Protocols I and II to the Geneva Conventions and the Rome Statue of ICC. Germany noted that the United States did not have a national human rights institution.

83. Guatemala made recommendations.

84. Costa Rica acknowledged the United States' openness and commitment to the protection and promotion of the human rights of its people. Costa Rica noted with appreciation the constructive contribution of the United States in the formulation of international law and mechanisms. However, it noted the gap between the Government's ratification and contribution to international law.

85. The United States delegation responded to a number of questions and concerns regarding discrimination against Muslims, Arab Americans, and South Asians. The United States is committed to addressing negative stereotypes, discrimination and hate crimes through measures such as the creation of a 9/11 backlash taskforce, litigation to protect religious freedom including the right of school girls to wear the hijab, nationwide community outreach, and enforcement of employment discrimination laws. The United States is taking concrete measures to make border and aviation security measures more effective and targeted to eliminate profiling based on race, religion, or ethnicity.

86. Regarding online privacy, the United States recognized that new technologies like the Internet demand legitimate and effective law enforcement as well as protection of privacy, free expression, and the rule of law. Secretary Clinton was deeply committed to Internet Freedom at home and around the world, and to ensuring that the rights of free expression and association through the Internet were protected and defended.

87. Regarding questions related to economic, social and cultural rights, what Franklin Roosevelt described as "freedom from want," the United States has focused on democratic solutions and civil society initiatives while courts have defined constitutional obligations primarily by focusing on procedural rights to due process and equal protection of the law. As a matter of broader public policy, the United States is committed to help create a society in which prosperity is shared, including social benefits provided by law.

88. The United States is committed to working to pursue laws and policies that will build an economy and society that lifts up all Americans. The Government is taking on the structural inequalities that have too often held back some citizens. The United States is taking significant measures to ensure equal opportunities and access to areas including housing, education, and health care. The Government is actively responding to the foreclosure crisis by helping millions of

families restructure or refinance their mortgages to avoid foreclosure. The United States has taken important measures to help lift up every child in every school in the country, particularly those most disadvantaged. Recent legislation allowed schools to invest in technology, teacher development, and other measures. In 2010, President Obama signed into law the Affordable Care Act, which is projected to expand health insurance to 32 million Americans who would otherwise lack coverage.

89. The United States is also committed to enforcing employment and labor laws to protect workers' rights, has revitalized its engagement with ILO, and is renewing work on ratification of ILO conventions.

90. In closing, the United States delegation expressed its deep appreciation to civil society - not only for helping in the preparation of its report and presentation, but also in continuing to push the government to do better. United States civil society has been invaluable to the United States' Universal Periodic Review, and commended to other states active engagement with civil society throughout the process.

91. It is a testament to the steady erosion of barriers of race, gender, sexual orientation, religion, disability, and ethnicity that United States delegation members of such diversity were present to speak for the United States today. The United States is proud of its record of accomplishments, humbled by the recognition that more work remains, and remains committed to improvement and to continuing this dialogue going forward.

II. Conclusions and/or recommendations

92. In the course of the discussion, the following recommendations were made to the United States of America:

92.1. Ratify without reservations the following conventions and protocols: CEDAW; the ICESCR; the Convention on the Rights of the Child; the Convention on the Rights of Persons with Disabilities; the International Convention on the Protection of the Rights of All Migrant Workers and Members of Their Families; the International Convention for the Protection of All Persons from Enforced Disappearance; the Statute of the International Criminal Court; those of the ILO; the United Nations Declaration on Indigenous Peoples, and all those from the Inter-American Human Rights System (Bolivarian Republic of Venezuela);

92.2. Continue the process to ratify CEDAW and adhere to the other human rights fundamental instruments, such as the Statute of Rome of the International Criminal Court, the Convention on the Rights of the Child, the Optional Protocol to the Convention against Torture and the International Convention for the Protection of all Persons against Enforced Disappearance (France);

92.3. Ratify, until the next universal periodic review, ICESCR, the Convention on the Rights of the Child, Protocols I and II of the Geneva Conventions of 12 August 1949, ILO Conventions no. 87 (on freedom of association) and no. 98 (on the right to collective bargaining) as well as withdraw the reservation made to article 4 of the International Convention on the Elimination of Racial Discrimination (Russian Federation);

92.4. Ratify ICESCR and its Optional Protocol; the first Optional Protocol to the International Covenant on Civil and Political Rights, CEDAW, the Convention on the Rights of the Child, the Optional Protocol to the Convention against Torture, the Convention on the Rights of Persons with Disabilities, the Convention for the Protection of All Persons from Enforced Disappearance (Spain);

92.5. Continue its efforts to realise universal human rights by a) ratifying CEDAW; b) becoming a party to the United Nations Convention on the Rights of the Child; c) acceding to ICESCR; d) ratifying the United Nations Convention on the Rights of Persons with Disabilities (Canada);

92.6. Ratify the core human rights treaties, particularly the CRC, ICESCR, CEDAW and its Optional Protocol, the OP-CAT and the CMW and the CRPD with its Optional Protocol (Sudan);

92.7. Ratify the ICESCR, CEDAW and the Convention of the Rights of the Child at an early stage together with other important human rights conventions (Japan);

92.8. Ratify CEDAW, ICESCR, and CRC in token of its commitment to their implementation worldwide, as well as become party to other international human rights conventions as referred to in the OHCHR report (Indonesia);

92.9. Ratify all core international instruments on human rights, in particular ICESCR, CEDAW, the Convention on the Rights of the Child (Viet Nam);

92.10. Consider ratifying ICESCR, CEDAW and CRC at the earliest (India);

92.11. Consider undertaking necessary steps leading to ratification of the parent/umbrella United Nations Convention on the Rights of the Child and CEDAW respectively (Malaysia);

92.12. Ratify ICESCR (Democratic People's Republic of Korea, Ghana); Become a party to the ICESCR (Australia);

92.13. Proceed with ratifying the CRPD and CRC (Qatar);

92.14. Ratify, and ensure implementation into domestic law of CEDAW and CRC (Turkey);

92.15. Ratify the Convention on the Rights of the Child and the International Convention on the Protection of the Rights of All Migrant Workers and Members of Their Families (Haiti);

92.16. Endeavour to ratify international instruments that USA is not party, in particular among others the CRC, OP-CAT; CEDAW; and Rome Statute of the International Criminal Court (Costa Rica);

92.17. Ratify ICESCR, CEDAW, the Convention on the Rights of the Child; the Convention on the Rights of Persons with Disabilities and other core human rights treaties as soon as possible (China);

92.18. Ratify additional human rights treaties such as the ICESCR; the Convention of the Rights of the Child; the International Convention for the Protection of All Persons from Enforced Disappearances and the Convention on Rights of Persons with Disabilities in order to further strengthen their support to the United Nations Human Rights mechanisms (Netherlands);

92.19. Ratify the pending core international human rights instruments, in particular CRC, ICESCR, and its OP, CEDAW and its OP as well as CRPD, and others, and ensure their due translation into the domestic legislation and review existing ratifications with a view to withdraw all reservations and declarations (Slovakia);

92.20. Consider ratifying the treaties to which it is not a party, including the CEDAW, CRC, ICESCR, and CRPD (Republic of Korea);

92.21. Consider ratifying CEDAW, the Convention on the Rights of the Child, and the Convention on the Rights of Persons with Disabilities (Austria);

92.22. Consider prioritizing acquiescence to the Convention of the Rights of the Child, CEDAW, the ILO Convention No. 111 on Discrimination in Respect of Employment and Occupation so as to further strengthen its national framework for human rights, but also to assist in achieving their universality (Trinidad and Tobago);

92.23. Proceed with the ratification of Additional Protocols I and II of the Geneva Conventions of 1949, of the Convention on the Rights of the Child, of CEDAW as well as the Optional Protocol to the Convention against Torture (Cyprus);

92.24. Ratify at its earliest opportunity other core human rights instruments, particularly, those to which it is already a signatory, namely CEDAW, Convention on the Rights of the Child, ICESCR, and the Convention on the Rights of Persons with Disabilities (Thailand);

92.25. Ratify the ICESCR, CEDAW, CRC the CRPD, the Additional Protocol I and II (1977), to the Geneva Conventions, the ICC Statute, as well as the 1st and 2nd Protocol to the Hague Convention 1954 (Hungary);

92.26. Consider ratifying ILO Convention 100 on equal remuneration for men and women for work of equal value, and ILO Convention 111 on discrimination in employment and occupation (India);

92.27. Accede to ICESCR, the CRC and ILO convention No. 111 (Islamic Republic of Iran);

92.28. Consider ratifying the Rome Statute of the International Criminal Court and the Additional Protocols I and II of the Geneva Conventions (Austria);

92.29. Ratify the Convention on the Protection of the Rights of All Migrant Workers and Members of their Families and observe international standards in this regard (Egypt);

92.30. Consider signing the International Convention on the Protection of the Rights of All Migrant Workers and Members of Their Families (Turkey);

92.31. Accede to the International Convention on the Protection of the Rights of All Migrant Workers and Members of Their Families (Guatemala);

92.32. Complement its signature of ICESCR by ratifying it and recognizing the justiciability of these rights in its domestic legal systems (Egypt);

92.33. Swiftly ratify CEDAW (Finland); Ratify CEDAW (Democratic People's Republic of Korea, Ghana, Netherlands, New Zealand); Become a party to CEDAW (Australia);

92.34. Ratify the Convention on the Rights of the Child (Democratic People's Republic of Korea, New Zealand); Become a party to the Convention on the Rights of the Child (Australia);

92.35. Ratify the Convention on the Rights of Persons with Disabilities as a matter of priority (New Zealand); Become a party to the Convention on the Rights of Persons with Disabilities (Australia);

92.36. Proceed with the ratification process of the Rome Statute of the International Criminal Court at the earliest possible (Cyprus);

92.37. Ratify the 12 international human rights instruments to which it is not a party (Nicaragua);

92.38. Implement a program of ratification of all international human rights instruments, and then proceed to the incorporation of these in its internal legal system (Plurinational State of Bolivia);

92.39. Examine the possibility of ratifying the core human rights treaties to which the country is not yet a party and raising its reservations on those which it has ratified (Algeria);

92.40. Accede to international human rights instruments which is not yet acceded to (Libyan Arab Jamahiriya);

92.41. Continue the process to ratify and implement into domestic law the several international human rights instruments that still wait for this formal acceptance (Holy See);

92.42. Accede to the universal core treaties on human rights and those of inter-American system, in particular the recognition of the jurisdiction of the Inter-American Court on Human Rights (Brazil);

92.43. Consider the signing, ratification or accession, as corresponds, of the main international and Inter-American human rights instruments, especially the Convention on the Rights of the Child (Uruguay);

92.44. Withdraw all reservations and declarations on the international instruments to which it is a party that undermine its obligations or the purpose of the treaty (Spain);

92.45. Withdraw reservations, denunciations, and interpretations of the Covenant on Civil and Political Rights; the International Convention on the Elimination of All Forms of Racial Discrimination and the Convention against Torture, that undermine their compliance, and accept their individual procedures (Bolivarian Republic of Venezuela);

92.46. Withdraw reservations to the Convention against Torture (Brazil);

92.47. Consider lifting reservations to a number of ICCPR articles (Indonesia);

92.48. Take the necessary measures to consider lifting the United States reservation to article 5, paragraph 6 of the International Covenant on Civil and Political Rights that bans the imposition of the death penalty for crimes committed by persons under 18 (France);

92.49. Consider the withdrawal of all reservations and declarations that undermine the objective and spirit of the human rights instruments, in particular reservation to article 6 paragraph 5 of the International Covenant on Civil and Political Rights that bans the imposition of the death penalty to those who committed a crime when they were minors (Uruguay);

92.50. Withdraw the reservation to article 6, paragraph 5 of the International Covenant on Civil and Political Rights and consider further to abolish the death penalty in all cases (Austria);

92.51. Comply with its international obligations for the effective mitigation of greenhouse gas emissions, because of their impact in climate change (Bolivarian Republic of Venezuela);

92.52. Ensure the implementation of its obligations under international humanitarian law vis-à-vis Palestinian people. (Islamic Republic of Iran);

92.53. Respect the ruling of the International Court of Justice of the Hague, of 27 June 1986, which orders the United States Government to compensate Nicaragua for the terrorist acts that the people of Nicaragua suffered on those years from the part of the American President Ronald Reagan (Nicaragua);

92.54. Take appropriate action to resolve the obstacles that prevent the full implementation of the *Avena* Judgment of the International Court of Justice and, until this occurs, avoid the execution of the individuals covered in said judgment (Mexico);

92.55. Repeal the amendment which allows for slavery as a punishment (Bolivarian Republic of Venezuela);

92.56. Repeal the norms that limit freedom of expression and require journalists to reveal their sources, under penalty of imprisonment (Bolivarian Republic of Venezuela);

92.57. Abolish its extrajudicial and extraterritorial laws and refrain from the application of unilateral measures against other countries (Islamic Republic of Iran);

92.58. Make fully consistent all domestic anti-terrorism legislation and action with human rights standards (Islamic Republic of Iran);

92.59. Legislate appropriate regulations to prevent the violations of individual privacy, constant intrusion in and control of cyberspace as well as eavesdropping of communications, by its intelligence and security organizations (Islamic Republic of Iran);

92.60. Take effective legal steps to halt human rights violations by its military forces and private security firms in Afghanistan and other States (Islamic Republic of Iran);

92.61. Unconditionally abolish its extraterritorial legislation on human rights and other related matters against other countries including the 'North Korea Human Rights Act', as these legislations represent flagrant breach of their sovereignty and insulting violations of the dignity and the rights of the people (Democratic People's Republic of Korea);

92.62. Review, reform and adequate its federal and state laws, in consultation with civil society, to comply with the protection of the right to nondiscrimination established by the Convention on the Elimination of all Forms of Racial Discrimination, especially in the areas of employment, housing, health, education and justice (Plurinational State of Bolivia);

92.63. Modify the definition of the discrimination in the law to bring it in line with the ICERD and other international standards (China);

92.64. Review, with a view to their amendment and elimination, all laws and practices that discriminate against African, Arab and Muslim Americans, as well as migrants, in the administration of justice, including racial and religious profiling (Egypt);

92.65. Review its laws at the Federal and State levels with a view to bringing them in line with its international human rights obligations (Egypt);

92.66. Enact a federal crime of torture, consistent with the Convention, and also encompassing acts described as 'enhanced interrogation techniques' (Austria);

92.67. Take legislative and administrative measures to address a wide range of racial discrimination and inequalities in housing, employment and education

(Democratic People's Republic of Korea);

92.68. Take legislative and administrative measures to ban racial profiling in law enforcement (Democratic People's Republic of Korea);

92.69. Take legislative and administrative measures to end defamation of religion (Democratic People's Republic of Korea);

92.70. Take appropriate legislative and practical measures to improve living conditions through its prisons systems, in particular with regard to access to health care and education (Austria);

92.71. Consider raising to 18 years the minimum age for the voluntary recruitment to the armed forces, and explicitly define as a crime the violation of the provisions of the Optional Protocol to the Convention on the Rights of the Child on the involvement of children in armed conflict (Uruguay);

92.72. Establish a national human rights institution, in accordance with the Paris Principles (Egypt, Germany, Ghana, Sudan, Bolivarian Republic of Venezuela);

92.73. Implement recommendations of the United Nations human rights bodies concerning the establishment of an independent national human rights institute in line with the Paris Principles (Russian Federation); Taking necessary steps to establish an independent national human rights institution, in accordance with Paris Principles, in order to strengthen human rights at federal and state level in addition to the local level. (Qatar); Establish an independent national human rights institution in accordance with Paris Principles, to monitor compliance with international standards and to ensure coordination in implementing its human rights obligations between federal, state and local governments (Republic of Korea); Establishment of an independent national human rights institution compliant with Paris Principles at federal level with appropriate affiliated structures at state level (Ireland);

92.74. That a human rights institution at the federal level be considered in order to ensure implementation of human rights in all states (Norway);

92.75. End the blockade against Cuba2 (Cuba); Put an end to the infamous blockade against Cuba (Bolivarian Republic of Venezuela); Lift the economic, financial and commercial blockade against Cuba, which affects the enjoyment of the human rights of more than 11 million people (Plurinational State of Bolivia);

92.76. Lift the infamous economic, commercial and financial blockade as well as liberate immediately the five Cubans held in prison for 12 years (Nicaragua);

92.77. Put an end to the economic financial and commercial embargo against Cuba and Sudan (Sudan);

92.78. Unconditionally lift its measures of economic embargoes and sanctions unilaterally and coercively imposed upon other countries, as these measures are inflicting severe and negative impact on the human rights of the peoples (Democratic People's Republic of Korea);

92.79. Attempt to restrain any state initiative which approaches immigration issues in a repressive way towards the migrant community and that violates its rights by applying racial profiling, criminalizing undocumented immigration and violating the human and civil rights of persons (Guatemala);

92.80. Spare no efforts to constantly evaluate the enforcement of the immigration federal legislation, with a vision of promoting and protecting human rights (Guatemala);

92.81. Take the necessary measures in favor of the right to work and fair conditions of work so that workers belonging to minorities, in particular women and undocumented migrant workers, do not become victims of discriminatory treatment and abuse in the work place and enjoy the full protection of the labour legislation, regardless of their migratory status (Guatemala);

92.82. Adopt a fair immigration policy, and cease xenophobia, racism and intolerance to ethnic, religious and migrant minorities (Bolivarian Republic of Venezuela);

92.83. Implement concrete measures consistent with the Covenant on Civil and Political Rights, to ensure the participation of indigenous peoples in the decisions affecting their natural environment, measures of subsistence, culture and spiritual practices (Plurinational State of Bolivia);

92.84. Include and rank the human rights situation in the United States in the United States Annual Country Reports on Human Rights as was done for the annual report on trafficking of persons (Algeria);

92.85. Formulate goals and policy guidelines for the promotion of the rights of indigenous peoples and cooperation between government and indigenous peoples (Finland);

92.86. Undertake awareness-raising campaigns for combating stereotypes and violence against gays, lesbians, bisexuals and transsexuals, and ensure access to public services paying attention to the special vulnerability of sexual workers to violence and human rights abuses (Uruguay);

92.87. Incorporate human rights training and education strategies in their public policies (Costa Rica);

92.88. Invite United Nations Special Rapporteurs to visit and investigate Guantánamo Bay prison and United States secret prisons and to subsequently close them (Islamic Republic of Iran);

92.89. Consider the possibility of inviting relevant mandate holders as follow-up to the 2006 joint-study by the 5 special procedures, in view of the decision of the current Administration to close the Guantánamo Bay detention facility (Malaysia);

92.90. Respond and follow-up appropriately the recommendations formulated to the United States by the Special Rapporteur for the Protection of Human Rights and Fundamental Freedoms while Countering Terrorism (Mexico);

92.91. Accept individual applications procedures provided for in human rights instruments (Denmark);

92.92. In view of its positive cooperation with special procedures of the Human Rights Council, extend an open standing invitation to these procedures (Costa Rica); Issue a standing invitation to the Special Procedures of the Human Rights Council (Austria); Issue an open and standing invitation to the Special Procedures (Spain); Extend a standing invitation to all special procedures (Netherlands);

92.93. Consider extending a standing invitation to special procedures (Cyprus); (Denmark); (Republic of Korea);

92.94. End the discrimination against persons of African descent (Cuba);

92.95. Undertake studies to determine the factors of racial disparity in the application of the death penalty, to prepare effective strategies aimed at ending possible discriminatory practices (France);

92.96. Take appropriate legislative and practical measures to prevent racial bias in the criminal justice system (Austria);

92.97. Review the minimum mandatory sentences in order to assess their disproportionate impact on the racial and ethnic minorities (Haiti);

92.98. Devise specific programs aimed at countering growing Islamophobic and xenophobic trends in society (Egypt);

92.99. Eliminate discrimination against migrants and religious and ethnic minorities and ensure equal opportunity for enjoyment of their economic, social and cultural rights (Bangladesh);

92.100. End all forms of racial discrimination in terms of housing, education, health care, social security and labor (Libyan Arab Jamahiriya);

92.101. Ban, at the federal and state levels, the use of racial profiling by police and immigration officers (Plurinational State of Bolivia); Prohibit expressly the use of racial profiling in the enforcement of immigration legislation (Mexico);

92.102. Revoke the national system to register the entry and exit of citizens of 25 countries from the Middle-East, South Asia and North Africa, and eliminate racial and other forms of profiling and stereotyping of Arabs, Muslims and South Asians as recommended by CERD. (Sudan);

92.103. Ensure the prosecution and punishment, according to the law, of those responsible of racial hate and xenophobic criminal acts, as well as guarantee a fair compensation to the victims, such as the case of the Ecuadoreans Marcelo Lucero and Jose Sucuzhañay, murdered in the United States (Ecuador);

92.104. Make further efforts in order to eliminate all forms of discrimination and the abuse of authority by police officers against migrants and foreigners, especially the community of Vietnamese origin people in the United States (Viet Nam);

92.105. Avoid the criminalization of migrants and ensure the end of police brutality, through human rights training and awareness-raising campaigns, especially to eliminate stereotypes and guarantee that the incidents of excessive use of force be investigated and the perpetrators prosecuted (Uruguay);

92.106. Take administrative and legal measures against perpetrators of racially motivated acts, targeting migrants and minority communities (Bangladesh);

92.107. Adopt effective measures and an anti-discrimination Act to address racial problems (Ghana);

92.108. Prohibit and punish the use of racial profiling in all programs that enable local authorities with the enforcement of immigration legislation and provide effective and accessible recourse to remedy human rights violations occurred under these programs (Mexico);

92.109. Promote equal socio-economic as well as educational opportunities for all both in law and in fact, regardless of their ethnicity, race, religion, national origin, gender or disability (Thailand);

92.110. Repeal and do not enforce discriminatory and racial laws such as Law SB 1070 of the State of Arizona (Ecuador);

92.111. Adopt a comprehensive national work-plan to combat racial discrimination (Qatar);

92.112. Take measures to comprehensively address discrimination against individuals on the basis of their sexual orientation or gender identity (Australia);

92.113. That further measures be taken in the areas of economic and social rights for women and minorities, including providing equal access to decent work and reducing the number of homeless people (Norway);

92.114. Increase its efforts to effectively guarantee human rights of persons with disabilities, while welcoming the signing of the Convention and urging their prompt implementation (Costa Rica);

92.115. Consider taking further action to better ensure gender equality at work (Finland);

92.116. Continue its intense efforts to undertake all necessary measures to ensure fair and equal treatment of all persons, without regard to sex, race, religion, colour, creed, sexual orientation, gender identity or disability, and encourage further steps in this regard (Israel);

92.117. Respect the Cuban people's right to self-determination and cease its actions of interference and hostility against Cuba (Cuba);

92.118. A national moratorium on the death penalty is introduced with a view to completely abolish the penalty and, before such a moratorium is introduced, to take all necessary measures to ensure that any use of the death penalty complies with minimum standards under international law relating to the death penalty such as under article 6 and 14 of the International Covenant on Civil and Political Rights (Sweden);

92.119. Consider the possibility of announcing moratorium on the use of the death penalty (Russian Federation);

92.120. Establish a moratorium on the use of the death penalty at the federal and state level as a first step towards abolition (United Kingdom); Establish a moratorium on executions on the entire American territory, with a view to a definitive abolition of the death penalty (Belgium); Establish, at all levels, a moratorium on executions with a view to completely abolish the death penalty (Switzerland); Adopt a moratorium on the use of the death penalty with a view to abolishing capital punishment in federal and national legislations (Italy); Establish a moratorium to the death penalty with a view to its abolition (Uruguay); Impose a moratorium on executions with a view to abolishing the death penalty nationwide (New Zealand); Work towards a moratorium on executions with the view to abolishing the death penalty, in conformity with General Assembly resolution 62/149, adopted on 18 December 2007 (Netherlands);

92.121. Take all necessary measures in order to impose a moratorium on the use of the death penalty, with a view to abolishing it both at the federal and State levels (Cyprus);

92.122. Abolish the death penalty and in any event, establish a moratorium as an interim measure towards full abolition (Australia); Abolish capital punishment and, as a first step on that road, introduce as soon as practicable a moratorium on the execution of death sentences (Hungary); That steps be taken to set federal and state-level moratoria on executions with a view to abolish the death penalty nationwide (Norway);

92.123. Impose a nationwide moratorium on executions and commute existing death sentences to imprisonment term with a view to abolish the capital punishment entirely (Slovakia);

92.124. Consider abolishing death penalty (Turkey);

92.125. Abolish the death penalty (Germany);

92.126. Implement at the federal level a moratorium on executions (France);

92.127. Begin a process leading to the ending of the death penalty punishment (Ireland); Pursuing the process to abolishing the death penalty (Holy See);

92.128. Abolish as soon as possible the death penalty in the 35 Federal States where this brutal practice is authorized (Nicaragua);

92.129. Study the possibility for the Federal Government of campaigning in favour of applying the United Nations Moratorium on the death penalty (Algeria);

92.130. Establish a de jure moratorium of the death penalty at the federal level and in the military justice, in view of its abolition and as an example for the States that still retain it (Spain);

92.131. That, until a moratorium is applied, steps be taken to restrict the number of offences carrying the death penalty (Denmark);

92.132. A review of federal and state legislation with a view to restricting the number of offences carrying the death penalty (Norway);

92.133. Abolish the death penalty, which is also applied to persons with mental disabilities and commute those which have already been imposed (Bolivarian Republic of Venezuela);

92.134. End the prosecution and execution of mentally-ill persons and minors; (Cuba);

92.135. Extend the exclusion of death penalty to all crimes committed by persons with mental illness (Ireland);

92.136. Take legal and administrative measures to address civilian killings by the U.S. military troops during and after its invasion of Afghanistan and Iraq by investigating and bringing perpetrators to justice and remedying the victims and to close its detention facilities in foreign territories like Guantánamo, including CIA secret camps (Democratic People's Republic of Korea);

92.137. Prosecute the perpetrators of tortures, extrajudicial executions and other serious violations of human rights committed in Guantánamo, Abu Ghraib, Bagram, the NAMA and BALAD camps, and those carried out by the Joint Special Operations Command and the CIA (Cuba);

92.138. Heed the call of the High Commissioner to launch credible independent investigations into all reliable allegations made to date of violations of international human rights law committed by American forces in Iraq, including extrajudicial killings, summary executions, and other abuses (Egypt);

92.139. That measures be taken to eradicate all forms of torture and ill-treatment of detainees by military or civilian personnel, in any territory of jurisdiction, and that any such acts be thoroughly investigated (Norway);

92.140. Stop the war crimes committed by its troops abroad, including the killings of innocent civilians and prosecute those who are responsible (Cuba);

92.141. Halt immediately the unjustified arms race and bring to justice those responsible for all war crimes and massacres against unarmed civilians, women, children as well as acts of torture carried-out in prisons such as Abu Ghraib, Bagram and Guantánamo (Nicaragua);

92.142. Halt selective assassinations committed by contractors, and the privatization of conflicts with the use of private military companies (Bolivarian Republic of Venezuela);

92.143. End the use of military technology and weaponry that have proven to be indiscriminate and cause excessive and disproportionate damage to civilian life (Egypt);

92.144. Increases its efforts to eliminate alleged brutality and use of excessive force by law enforcement officials against, inter alia, Latino and African American persons and undocumented migrants, and to ensure that relevant allegations are investigated and that perpetrators are prosecuted (Cyprus);

92.145. Guarantee the complete prohibition of torture in all prisons under its control (Islamic Republic of Iran);

92.146. Define torture as a federal offense in line with the Convention against Torture and investigate, prosecute and punish those responsible of crimes of extraterritorial torture (Plurinational State of Bolivia);

92.147. Conduct thorough and objective investigation of facts concerning use of torture against imprisoned persons in the secret prisons of United States of America and detainees of the detention centres in Bagram and Guantánamo, bring those who are responsible for these violations to justice, and undertake all necessary measures to provide redress to those whose rights were violated, including payment of necessary compensation (Russian Federation);

92.148. Take measures to ensure reparation to victims of acts of torture committed under United States' control and allow access to the International Committee of the Red Cross to detention facilities under the control of the United States (Brazil);

92.149. Observe the Amnesty International 12 points program to prevent torture perpetrated by government agents (Ecuador);

92.150. Take measures with a view to prohibiting and punishing the brutality and the use of excessive or deadly force by the law enforcement officials and to banning torture and other ill-treatment in its detention facilities at home and abroad (Democratic People's Republic of Korea);

92.151. Strengthen oversight with a view to ending excessive use of force by law enforcement bodies, particularly when it is directed to the racial minorities and bring those responsible for violation of laws to justice (China);

92.152. Prevent and repress the illegitimate use of violence against detainees (Belgium);

92.153. Release the five Cuban political prisoners - arbitrarily detained, as acknowledged by the Working Group on Arbitrary Detentions in its Opinion No. 19/2005, serving unjust sentences that resulted from a politically manipulated trial in open disregard for the rules of due process (Cuba);

92.154. End the unjust incarceration of political prisoners, including Leonard Peltier and Mumia Abu-Jamal (Cuba);

92.155. Close Guantánamo and secret centers of detention in the world, punish agents that torture, disappear and execute persons who have been arbitrarily detained, and compensate victims (Bolivarian Republic of Venezuela);

92.156. Expedite efforts aimed at closing the detention facility at Guantánamo Bay and ensure that all remaining detainees are tried, without delay, in accordance with the relevant international standards (Egypt); Proceed with the closure of Guantánamo at the earliest possible date and bring to trial promptly in accordance with the applicable rules of international law the detainees held there or release them (Ireland);

92.157. Quickly close down Guantánamo prison and follow the provision of the United Nations Charter and the Security Council Resolution by expatriating the terrorist suspect to their country of origin (China);

92.158. The closure of Guantánamo prison as the detention conditions violate the UDHR and ICCPR and the European Convention on Human Rights (ECHR) and all other related human rights instruments (Sudan);

92.159. Close without any delay all detention facilities at the Guantánamo Bay as President Barack Obama has promised (Viet Nam);

92.160. Find for all persons still detained in the Guantánamo Bay detention center a solution in line with the United States obligations regarding the foundations of international and human rights law, in particular with the International Covenant on Civil and Political Rights (Switzerland);

92.161. Halt all transfer detainees to third countries unless there are adequate safeguards to ensure that they will be treated in accordance with international law requirements (Ireland);

92.162. Redouble its efforts to address sexual violence in correction and detention facilities as well as to address the problem of prison conditions, with a view to preserving the rights and dignity of all those deprived of their liberty (Thailand);

92.163. Reduce overcrowding in prisons by enlarging existing facilities or building new ones and/or making more use of alternative penalties (Belgium);

92.164. Ensure that detention centers for migrants and the treatment they receive meet the basic conditions and universal human rights law (Guatemala);

92.165. Further foster its measures in relation to migrant women and foreign adopted children that are exposed to domestic violence (Republic of Moldova);

92.166. Take effective measures to put an end to gross human rights abuses including violence against women, committed for decades by the United States military personnel stationed in foreign bases (Democratic People's Republic of Korea);

92.167. Take effective steps to put an end to child prostitution, and effectively combat violence against women and gun violence (Islamic Republic of Iran);

92.168. Define, prohibit and punish the trafficking of persons and child prostitution (Bolivarian Republic of Venezuela);

92.169. Insist more on measures aiming to combat the demand and provide information and services to victims of trafficking (Republic of Moldova);

92.170. Guarantee civilians to be tried by their natural judge and not by military commissions (Bolivarian Republic of Venezuela);

92.171. Prosecute or extradite for trial Luis Posada Carriles and dozens of other well-known terrorists living in impunity in the United States3 (Cuba);

92.172. Extradite the confessed terrorist Luis Posada Carriles (Bolivarian Republic of Venezuela);

92.173. Comply with the principles of international cooperation, as defined in Resolution 3074 of the General Assembly, for the extradition of persons accused of crimes against humanity and proceed to extradite former Bolivian authorities that are legally accused of such crimes, in order to be brought to trial in their country of origin (Plurinational State of Bolivia);

92.174. Make those responsible for gross violations of human rights in American prisons and prisons under the jurisdiction of America outside its territory accountable, compensate victims and provide them with remedies (Libyan Arab Jamahiriya);

92.175. Put on trial its gross violators of human rights and its war criminals and accede to ICC (Islamic Republic of Iran);

92.176. Respect the human rights of prisoners of war, guaranteed by the penal norms (Nicaragua);

92.177. Ensure the full enjoyment of human rights by persons deprived of their liberty, including by way of ensuring treatment in maximum security prisons in conformity with international law (Sweden);

92.178. Ensure the enjoyment of the right to vote both by persons deprived of their liberty and of persons who have completed their prison sentences (Sweden);

92.179. Review of alternative ways to handle petty crime and of measures to improve the situation of inmates in prisons (Algeria);

92.180. Incorporate in its legal system the possibility of granting parole to offenders under 18 sentenced to life imprisonment for murder (Switzerland);

Renounce to life in prison without parole sentences for minors at the moment of the actions for which they were charged and introduce for those who have already been sentenced in these circumstances the possibility of a remission (Belgium); Prohibit sentencing of juvenile offenders under the age of 18 without the possibility of parole at the federal and state level (Austria); Cease application of life imprisonment without parole for juvenile offenders and to review all existing sentences to provide for a possibility of parole (Slovakia);

92.181. Enact legislation to ensure that imprisonment is only used as a last resort when sentencing all juvenile offenders and provide systematic resocialisation support (Austria);

92.182. Incarcerate immigrants only exceptionally (Switzerland);

92.183. Investigate carefully each case of immigrants' incarceration (Switzerland);

92.184. Adapt the detention conditions of immigrants in line with international human rights law (Switzerland);

92.185. Ensure that migrants in detention, subject to a process of expulsion are entitled to counsel, a fair trial and fully understand their rights, even in their own language (Guatemala);

92.186. Ensure the right to habeas corpus in all cases of detention (Austria);

92.187. Guarantee the right to privacy and stop spying on its citizens without judicial authorization (Bolivarian Republic of Venezuela);

92.188. Adopt a set of legislative and administrative measures aimed at ensuring prohibition of the use by state and local authorities of modern technology for excessive and unjustified intervention in citizens' private life (Russian Federation);

92.189. Consider discontinuing measures that curtail human rights and fundamental freedoms (Bangladesh);

92.190. Take effective measures to counter insults against Islam and Holy Quran, as well as Islamophobia and violence against Moslems, and adopt necessary legislation (Islamic Republic of Iran);

92.191. Continue to create an enabling climate for religious and cultural tolerance and understanding at the grass roots level (Indonesia);

92.192. Recognize the right to association as established by ILO, for migrant, agricultural workers and domestic workers (Plurinational State of Bolivia);

92.193. Prevent slavery of agriculture workers, in particular children and women (Bolivarian Republic of Venezuela);

92.194. Decree maternity leave as mandatory (Bolivarian Republic of Venezuela);

92.195. Ensure the realization of the rights to food and health of all who live in its territory (Cuba);

92.196. Expand its social protection coverage (Brazil);

92.197. Continue its efforts in the domain of access to housing, vital for the realization of several other rights, in order to meet the needs for adequate housing at an affordable price for all segments of the American society (Morocco);

92.198. Reinforce the broad range of safeguards in favour of the most vulnerable groups such as persons with disabilities and the homeless to allow them the full enjoyment of their rights and dignity (Morocco); 92.199. End the violation of the rights of indigenous peoples (Cuba);

92.200. Guarantee the rights of indigenous Americans, and to fully implement the United Nations Declaration on the Rights of Indigenous Peoples (Islamic Republic of Iran);

92.201. Recognize the United Nations Declaration on the Rights of Indigenous Peoples without conditions or reservations, and implement it at the federal and state levels (Plurinational State of Bolivia);

92.202. Adopt and implement the United Nations Declaration on the Rights of Indigenous Peoples (Libyan Arab Jamahiriya);

92.203. Endorse the United Nations Declaration on the Rights of Indigenous Peoples when completing its national review process (Finland);

92.204. That the United Nations Declaration on the Rights of Indigenous People be used as a guide to interpret the State obligations under the Convention relating to indigenous peoples (Ghana);

92.205. Continue its forward movement on the Declaration of the Rights of Indigenous Peoples (New Zealand);

92.206. Guarantee the full enjoyment of the rights on natives of America in line with the United Nations Declaration on the Rights of Indigenous Peoples (Nicaragua);

92.207. End violence and discrimination against migrants (Cuba);

92.208. Prohibit, prevent and punish the use of lethal force in carrying out immigration control activities (Mexico);

92.209. Guarantee the prohibition of use of cruelty and excessive or fatal force by law enforcement officials against people of Latin American or African origin as well as illegal migrants and to investigate such cases of excessive use of force (Sudan);

92.210. Protect the human rights of migrants, regardless of their migratory status (Ecuador);

92.211. Reconsider restrictions on undocumented migrants' access to publicly supported health care (Brazil);

92.212. Reconsider alternatives to the detention of migrants (Brazil);

92.213. Ensure access of migrants to consular assistance (Brazil);

92.214. Make greater efforts to guarantee the access of migrants to basic services, regardless of their migratory status (Uruguay);

92.215. Put an end to its actions against the realization of the rights of peoples to a healthy environment, peace, development and self-determination (Cuba);

92.216. Raise the level of official development assistance to achieve the United Nations target of 0.7 percent of GDP and allow duty free-quota-free access to all products of all LDCs (Bangladesh);

92.217. Halt serious violations of human rights and humanitarian law including covert external operations by the CIA, carried out on the pretext of combating terrorism (Islamic Republic of Iran);

92.218. Do not prosecute those arrested for terrorist crimes or any other crime in exceptional tribunals or jurisdictions, but bring them to judicial instances legally established, with the protection of due process and under all the guarantees of the American Constitution (Ecuador);

92.219. Enact a national legislation that prohibits religious, racial and colour profiling particularly in context of the fight against terrorism (Qatar);

92.220. Smarten security checks so as to take into account the frequent homonymy specific to Moslem names so as to avoid involuntary discrimination against innocent people with such names because of namesakes listed as members of terrorist groups (Algeria);

92.221. Take positive steps in regard to climate change, by assuming the responsibilities arising from capitalism that have generated major natural disasters particularly in the most impoverished countries (Nicaragua);

92.222. Implement the necessary reforms to reduce their greenhouse gas emissions and cooperate with the international community to mitigate threats against human rights resulting from climate change (Plurinational State of Bolivia);

92.223. Inform Foreign Missions regularly of efforts to ensure compliance with consular notification and access for foreign nationals in United States custody at all levels of law enforcement (United Kingdom);

92.224. Abandon the State Department practice of qualifying other States according to its interpretation of human rights and contribute to the strengthening and effectiveness of the Universal Periodic Review as a fair and appropriate mechanism of the international community to evaluate the situation of human rights between States (Ecuador);

92.225. Continue consultations with non-governmental organisations and civil society in the follow up (Austria);

92.226. Persevere in the strengthening of its aid to development, considered as fundamental, in particular the assistance and relief in case of natural disasters (Morocco);

92.227. That the model legal framework expressed by the Leahy Laws be applied with respect to all countries receiving U.S.'s security assistance, and that the human rights records of all units receiving such assistance be documented, evaluated, made available and followed up upon in cases of abuse (Norway);

92.228. The removal of blanket abortion restrictions on humanitarian aid covering medical care given women and girls who are raped and impregnated in situations of armed conflict (Norway);

93. The response of the United States of America to these recommendations will be included in the outcome report adopted by the Council at its sixteenth session.

94. All conclusions and/or recommendations contained in the present report reflect the position of the submitting State(s) and/or the State under review. They should not be construed as endorsed by the Working Group as a whole.

...

[End Text]

Source: https://documents-dds-ny.un.org/doc/undoc/gen/g11/100/69/pdf/g1110069.pdf?OpenElement

ॐॐॐॐॐॐॐॐॐ

9. REPORT OF THE UNITED STATES OF AMERICA SUBMITTED TO THE U.N. HIGH COMMISSIONER FOR HUMAN RIGHTS IN CONJUNCTION WITH THE UNIVERSAL PERIODIC REVIEW, 2015

In 2015, the United States was up for its second cycle of UPR review. It had to go through the same formalities as it did in 2010 before the Human Rights Council. It needed to update its human rights record and speak to how it has sought to implement the Recommendations which it had accepted from the 2011 Outcome document. This is the latest pronouncement from the Obama administration of how the U.S. sees itself generally as to its human rights performance and what still lies ahead. Many American and international organizations submitted reports to the U.N. concerning the UPR process issues. Some are listed below. This is an amazingly complex and thorough process and requires consultation by the state with its civil society back home to get its input.

I. Introduction

1. As a nation founded on the human rights principles of equality under the law and respect for the dignity of the individual, the United States is firmly dedicated to the promotion of human rights.

2. Human rights are embedded in our Constitution, laws, and policies at every level, and governmental action is subject to review by an independent judiciary and debated by a free press and an engaged civil society. Not only do individuals within the United States have effective legal means to seek policy, administrative, and judicial remedies for human rights violations and abuses, the government itself pursues extensive and comprehensive enforcement actions to create systematic reform. Our federal system enables our nation to test new methods and strategies for promoting human rights at the state and local levels. While recognizing that there is more work to be done, we are constantly striving to create a fairer and more just society, as reflected in the programs and policies discussed in this report.

II. Methodology and Consultation Process

3. In our first UPR in 2010, the United States supported in whole or in part 173 of 228 recommendations. We have divided these recommendations into ten thematic areas and have structured Section III of this report accordingly. Working groups comprising experts from relevant federal agencies addressed each of the thematic areas, meeting periodically, assessing progress on the recommendations, and consulting with civil society to share updates and receive feedback.

4. This report responds to all recommendations that we supported in whole or in part, even where such recommendations fall outside the scope of the United States' human rights obligations and commitments.

III. Progress and Challenges

A. Domestic Mechanisms for Human Rights Implementation

Reviewing domestic laws and institutions Recommendations 65 and 74

5. The United States is committed to effective implementation of our human rights treaty obligations and has multiple mechanisms that provide for regular review of our federal and state laws and policies. We have, in recent years, improved engagement with state and local governments to foster better awareness of human rights obligations at the state, tribal, and local levels. State and local government officials have been members of recent U.S. delegations presenting reports on the Convention on the Elimination of All Forms of Racial Discrimination, the Optional Protocols to the Convention on the Rights of the Child, the International Covenant on Civil and Political Rights, and the Convention Against Torture. The United States intends to continue including state and local representatives, and we have invited them to several civil society consultations during this UPR cycle.

6. In addition, we have reminded federal, state, local, tribal, and territorial officials of our human rights treaty obligations and notified them of upcoming treaty reporting. For example, in 2014, the State Department wrote to state, local, territorial, and tribal officials to inform them of our upcoming presentations and this UPR. Federal officials have conducted targeted training sessions on human rights treaties for state and local officials, such as an August 2014 conference of state- and local-level employment nondiscrimination agencies. We have worked regularly with relevant associations, such as the 160-member International Association of Official Human Rights Agencies and the National Association of Attorneys General, to provide their members with information on U.S. human rights treaty obligations and commitments and to discuss the role they can play.

7. The United States has continued to receive and consider proposals for a national human rights institution. Although we do not have an NHRI, we have multiple protections and mechanisms to reinforce respect for human rights, including independent judiciaries at federal and state levels and numerous state, tribal, and local human rights institutions.

Human rights education, training, and engagement with civil society Recommendations 87 and 225

The United States continually works to improve human rights training for those in government. For instance, we held a 2014 roundtable on domestic violence, sexual assault, nondiscrimination, and human rights to educate U.S. government participants about U.S. human rights obligations and commitments relevant to these issues, helping them identify and understand relevant human rights resources.

Additionally, since 2012, we have convened interagency roundtable discussions on legal aid to explore ways in which civil legal aid can promote access to health services, housing, education, employment, family stability, and community well-being.

We also have a number of regular training programs related to the promotion and protection of human rights. For example, law enforcement and immigration screening personnel receive training on prohibitions of unlawful discrimination and racial or ethnic profiling, and on protections for those fleeing persecution, human trafficking, and certain other crimes.

Civil society plays a critical role in promoting human rights in the United States. Our laws and institutions create an enabling environment where civil society is encouraged to act freely without fear of reprisal. Consistent with our commitment to supporting free and robust civil society at home and around the world, we conduct frequent, in-depth consultations with civil society on issues related to our human rights record, including in preparation for this UPR (see Section II) and for treaty reports.

B. Civil Rights and Discrimination

Profiling and excessive use of force by law enforcement Recommendations 68, 101, 150-151, 208-209, and 219

8. The United States is dedicated to eliminating racial discrimination and the use of excessive force in policing. The vast majority of police officers in the United States are committed to respecting their fellow citizens' civil rights as they carry out difficult and dangerous work. But where there is individual or systemic officer misconduct, appropriate responses are required. In the past six years, the U.S. Department of Justice has opened more than 20 civil investigations into police departments that may be engaging in a pattern or practice of conduct that deprives persons of their rights. These investigations have focused on excessive force, discrimination, coercive sexual conduct, and unlawful stops, searches, and arrests. In the same time period, DOJ has reached 15 settlements with police departments.

9. On December 4, 2014, DOJ announced that its civil rights investigation into the Cleveland, Ohio, Division of Police had found a pattern or practice of unreasonable and unnecessary use of force. Consequently, DOJ and the city of Cleveland have committed to develop a court-enforceable agreement that will include an independent monitor to oversee necessary reforms. DOJ has taken similar action in the past five years, making public findings of discriminatory policing and/or excessive force and working toward long-term solutions in 13 states and jurisdictions.

10. In addition, in the last five years, DOJ has criminally prosecuted more than 335 individual police officers for misconduct, including use of excessive force, and obtained 254 convictions as of January 1, 2015.

11. We are also working to strengthen police-community relations. For example, in

Ferguson, Missouri, in addition to opening civil and criminal investigations after the August 2014 shooting of Michael Brown, DOJ sent mediators to create a dialogue between police, city officials, and residents to reduce tension in the community. In addition, DOJ is involved in a voluntary, independent, and objective assessment of the St. Louis County Police Department, looking at training, use of force, handling mass demonstrations, and other areas where reform may be needed.

12. As President Obama has said, "[t]he fact is, in too many parts of this country, a deep distrust exists between law enforcement and communities of color." At the President's request, the Attorney General convened roundtable discussions among law enforcement, elected officials, and community members in six cities in December 2014 and January 2015. The President also appointed a Task Force on 21st Century Policing, which is examining how to strengthen public trust and foster strong relationships between local law enforcement and the communities they protect.

13. In December 2014, DOJ announced an updated policy on profiling by federal law enforcement and state and local officers participating in federal law enforcement task forces. This policy instructs that law enforcement officers may not consider race, ethnicity, national origin, gender, gender identity, religion, or sexual orientation to any degree when making routine or spontaneous law enforcement decisions, unless the characteristics apply to a suspect's description. The policy applies a uniform standard to all federal law enforcement, national security, and intelligence activities conducted by law enforcement components.

Racial bias in the criminal justice system and mandatory minimum sentences Recommendations 96-97

14. The United States is taking steps to address the disproportionate percentage of minorities, particularly African-Americans, in the criminal justice system. For example, the Fair Sentencing Act of 2010 has reduced the disparity between more lenient sentences for powder cocaine charges and more severe sentences for crack cocaine charges (the latter of which are more frequently brought against racial minorities). Data from the U.S. Sentencing Commission through June 2014 indicate that 7,706 federal crack offenders' sentences have been reduced as a result of retroactive application of this change: of these offenders, an estimated 90 percent are African-American.

15. Lower penalty guidelines for all drug offenders went into effect in November 2014. The

USSC estimates that these changes will reduce penalties by an average of 11 months for 70 percent of newly-sentenced drug trafficking offenders, and that more than 40,000 currently imprisoned offenders may be eligible to have their sentences retroactively reduced by an average of 25 months.

16. With the Smart on Crime Initiative, launched in 2013, the Attorney General directed all federal prosecutors to, inter alia, reserve stringent mandatory minimum narcotics charges and repeat offender charges for only the most serious

offenders. This has contributed to less use of incarceration for less-serious drug offenses. DOJ is working with the U.S. Congress on legislation to reform mandatory minimum sentences and reduce their application to nonviolent offenders.

Discrimination based on religion and hate crimes Recommendations 64, 9899, 103, 106, 189, and 190-191

17. The United States is committed to preventing and effectively prosecuting hate crimes. In 2009, we enacted a powerful new tool, the Shepard-Byrd Hate Crimes Prevention Act, which enhanced federal prosecution for violent crimes motivated by religious, racial, or national origin bias and enabled federal prosecution of crimes based on sexual orientation, gender, gender identity, and disability. Over the last five years, DOJ has obtained convictions of more than 160 defendants on such charges, a nearly 50 percent increase over the previous five years. DOJ also continues to prosecute other hate crimes, and in 2014 assisted Kansas authorities in the investigation of a fatal shooting at a Kansas City Jewish community center. In January 2015, the FBI began collecting more detailed data on bias-motivated crimes, including those committed against Arab, Hindu, and Sikh individuals.

18. We continue to actively fight all forms of religious discrimination. For instance, in recent years, DOJ has received a large number of complaints involving members of Muslim communities alleging unfair obstacles to building or expanding places of worship. Ten of the 34 DOJ investigations in this area since 2010, and five of the six lawsuits, have involved mosques or Islamic schools. In one such case, DOJ filed an amicus brief in a state court and initiated a federal lawsuit to ensure that a mosque would be permitted to open and operate in Murfreesboro, Tennessee.

19. In 2013, DOJ successfully resolved two complaints alleging that Sikh individuals were denied access to county court systems because of their religious headwear. Those counties subsequently adopted policies that prohibit discrimination because of religious head coverings.

20. We continue our robust efforts to eliminate religious discrimination in employment: the U.S. Equal Employment Opportunity Commission is currently litigating a suit before the U.S. Supreme Court against an employer for refusing to hire a Muslim worker out of concern that she would request religious accommodation to wear a headscarf.

21. We also continue to seek input from affected communities on these issues. Federal prosecutors have been directly involved in outreach to members of Arab, Muslim, and Sikh communities, working to strengthen trust; to provide protection from hate crimes, bullying, and discrimination; and to make clear that the United States cannot conduct surveillance on any individual based solely on race, ethnicity, or religion. In addition, the U.S. Department of Homeland Security leads or participates in regular roundtable meetings among community leaders and federal, state, and local government officials to discuss the impact of its programs, policies, and procedures on members of diverse demographic groups, including religious minorities.

Racial discrimination in voting, employment, housing, education, and health Recommendations 62, 67, 94, 100, 107, 109, and 116

22. *Voting*—The right to vote is fundamental to democracy. Accordingly, ensuring equal access to the ballot box is critical, and the Voting Rights Act of 1965 remains our most powerful tool in this effort. Although the U.S. Supreme Court invalidated a key part of that law, which required prior federal review of changes to certain jurisdictions' voting practices, DOJ has recently filed three challenges to discriminatory practices in Texas and North Carolina asking that those states be required to clear future voting changes with DOJ or a federal court. In October 2014, a federal court found Texas' new voter identification law to be intentionally discriminatory against members of minority groups. DOJ has also vigorously enforced the voting rights of those belonging to language-minority groups, bringing or participating in cases to protect persons with limited English proficiency.

23. *Labor and Employment*—We are committed to protecting all individuals, including members of racial minorities, from workplace discrimination. From 2011-2013, EEOC received 293,086 individual complaints of discrimination, resolved 320,890 charges, and recovered a total of $1.1 billion for affected employees through the administrative process. Over this three-year period, EEOC filed 603 lawsuits on behalf of individuals subjected to workplace discrimination, resolved 817 such lawsuits, and recovered an additional $173.8 million for affected workers. In 2013, DOJ collected record civil penalties from employers in resolving employment discrimination claims based on citizenship status or national origin, and in 2014, it secured a record amount of back pay for these discrimination victims.

27. These robust enforcement efforts have produced tangible systemic results as well. For example, in 2014, in a case involving the hiring practices of the New York City Fire Department, DOJ obtained its largest-ever settlement in an employment discrimination case, resulting in jobs for some 290 eligible claimants and $98 million in monetary damages. In the last fiscal year, the Department of Labor recovered nearly 1,800 job offers and over $12 million in financial remedies for 23,000 workers for claims of racial and other forms of discrimination involving federal contractors.

28. *Housing*—We have aggressively pursued remedies for racial discrimination in housing and improved legal protections and policies to prevent such discrimination. Our Department of Housing and Urban Development is working to strengthen the housing market to bolster the economy and protect consumers, meet the need for quality affordable homes, utilize housing as a platform for improving quality of life, and build inclusive and sustainable communities free from discrimination. For example, in 2013, HUD published a proposed regulation to clarify program participants' obligation to take proactive steps to overcome historic patterns of segregation, promote fair housing choice, and foster inclusive communities. Under the proposed rule, HUD will collect data on patterns of integration and segregation to better identify potential fair housing issues.

29. The United States also aggressively enforces fair lending laws against lenders engaging in discriminatory practices. We have brought legal action to remedy such abuses and established a Financial Fraud Enforcement Task Force with state and local partners to proactively investigate these practices. Since 2010, DOJ has filed or resolved 26 lending matters. The resulting settlements have provided for over $900 million in monetary relief, including a $335 million settlement with Countrywide Financial and a $234.3 million settlement with Wells Fargo for racial and ethnic discrimination in mortgage loans; and a $98 million settlement with Ally Financial Inc. and Ally Bank for racial and ethnic discrimination in auto loans.

30. *Education*—We seek to ensure equal educational opportunities for all students by enforcing laws that prohibit discrimination in education, including on the basis of race, color, and national origin.

For example, in 2011, the U.S. government reached a resolution with the Los Angeles Unified School District in California, the second-largest public school district in the United States, to develop and implement a comprehensive plan to eliminate the disproportionate discipline of African-American students and others. Since then, the suspension rate in that school district has fallen significantly, including a more than 50 percent decrease for AfricanAmerican students.

31. Similarly, as a result of agreements, school districts in Kentucky and Delaware are working to eliminate the disproportionate discipline of African-American students and others, including by reviewing and revising discipline policies and improving collection of student discipline data. In 2014, we issued guidance to assist schools in administering discipline without discriminating on the basis of race, color, or national origin. In addition, DOJ monitors and seeks further relief as necessary in approximately 180 school districts that have a history of segregation and remain under court supervision.

32. We also have numerous laws allowing individuals to sue schools, school districts, or institutions of higher education to remedy individual cases of discrimination, beyond the systemic remedies pursued by the federal government. See Paragraphs 103-104 for more on education.

33. *Health*—We are committed to eliminating health disparities and promoting health, and we actively enforce federal civil rights laws to help ensure that all people have equal access to health care and social service programs. In 2011, the Department of Health and Human Services launched the United States' first plan to specifically address persistent racial and ethnic health disparities. By law, all persons in the United States, including persons without valid immigration status, are entitled to emergency health services.

34. For example, after securing a settlement in 2010, HHS monitored the University of Pittsburgh Medical Center for three years to ensure that closure of a hospital in a predominantly African-American community did not have a disparate impact on residents' access to health care. Additionally, HHS piloted a multi-state project to support hospitals in providing language access services to limited-English proficient populations in rural communities. During 2012-2013, HHS conducted compliance reviews of 45 such hospitals' language access programs. See Paragraphs 100-101 for more on health.

Discrimination against lesbian, gay, bisexual, and transgender individuals Recommendations 86 and 112

35. Equal protection of the rights of LGBT individuals is critically important to the United States, and we have made extraordinary strides to overcome obstacles and institutional biases that too often affect these individuals.

36. In a landmark 2013 ruling, *United States v. Windsor*, the U.S. Supreme Court struck down the federal government's ban on recognizing same-sex marriages. Since then, we have worked to implement that decision by treating married same-sex couples the same as married opposite-sex couples with respect to the relevant benefits and obligations, to the greatest extent possible under the law. As a result, married same-sex couples are now eligible for many federal benefits and recognition, including in the areas of taxation, immigration, student financial aid, and military and veterans' benefits. As of January 2015, same-sex couples can marry in 36 of our 50 states and the District of Columbia.

37. In the area of education, we have resolved a number of cases involving harassment of LGBT individuals in public schools. For example, in 2013, the U.S. government entered into a first-of-its kind settlement agreement with the Arcadia Unified School District in California to resolve allegations of discrimination against a transgender student. In 2014, the U.S. Department of Education released guidance describing the responsibilities of colleges, universities, and public schools to address sexual violence and other forms of sex discrimination, including discrimination based on gender identity.

38. In the area of policing, in 2014, DOJ's Community Relations Service launched transgender training for law enforcement officials that helps improve officer understanding and community relations.

39. In the area of employment, President Obama signed an order prohibiting federal contractors from discriminating against applicants and employees on the basis of sexual orientation or gender identity and adding gender identity as a prohibited basis for discrimination in federal employment. Furthermore, the U.S. government has taken the position that federal law prohibiting sex discrimination in employment extends to discrimination based on gender identity, including transgender status, and that LGBT workers stigmatized for failing to meet sex-based stereotypes may also pursue discrimination claims. In 2011, President Obama also announced the final repeal of the "Don't Ask, Don't Tell" law that barred gay men and lesbians from serving openly in the military.

Discrimination against persons with disabilities Recommendations 114 and 198

40. The United States has robust protections to prevent discrimination against persons with disabilities and has actively enforced these protections since our last report. In 2009, we launched an aggressive effort to eliminate unnecessary segregation of persons with disabilities, helping protect the rights of more than 46,000 individuals, including through groundbreaking agreements with six U.S. states. In 2013 alone, we participated in 18 such enforcement matters around the country.

41. The United States vigilantly protects the workplace rights of persons with disabilities. For example, in 2013, the EEOC obtained the largest jury verdict in its history ($240 million) on behalf of workers with intellectual disabilities who were subjected to verbal and physical abuse and poor living conditions by their employer. While the verdict was later reduced to comply with statutory limits, it restored the dignity of the workers and brought public attention to the treatment of persons with intellectual disabilities in U.S. workplaces. New regulations have also strengthened accountability for federal contractors' efforts to recruit persons with disabilities and protections for the equal employment rights of veterans, including disabled veterans.

42. The United States funds a network of independent agencies in all states and territories to protect the rights of people with disabilities and their families through legal representation, advocacy, referral, and education. These agencies are the largest providers of legally-based advocacy services to people with disabilities in the United States.

C. Criminal Justice

Prisons Recommendations 70, 145, 152, 162, 163, 174, 177-179, and 186

43. The United States continues to strive to improve living conditions throughout its confinement facilities. To that end, we ensure that all offenders housed in federal custody have access to medical care on-site, and in the community if needed.

44. In 2012, we issued regulations implementing the Prison Rape Elimination Act to prevent, detect, and respond to sexual abuse in federal, state, and local confinement facilities. These regulations include greater protections for juvenile offenders in adult facilities; new restrictions on crossgender observation and searches; minimum staffing ratios in juvenile facilities; expanded medical and mental health care, including reproductive health care, for victims of prison rape; greater protections for LGBT and gender non-conforming inmates; and independent audits of all covered facilities.

45. States must certify that all facilities under their operational control, including facilities run by private entities on behalf of the state, fully comply with these regulations; if they do not, they lose certain federal funding unless they pledge to devote that funding to compliance. Six states and one U.S. territory have been subjected to a five percent reduction in federal funding after declining to provide an assurance or certification of compliance.

46. In December 2014, we issued guidance to states and local agencies to strengthen the quality of education services provided to youth in confinement. It includes principles for improving education practices and addresses the educational and civil rights requirements applicable to confined youth, including those with disabilities.

47. We are committed to providing formerly incarcerated people with fair opportunities to rejoin their communities and become productive, law-abiding citizens. To this end, the Attorney General has called upon elected officials across the country to enact reforms to restore the voting rights of all who have served their terms in prison or jail, completed their parole or probation, and paid their fines.

48. The U.S. Constitution guarantees to individuals the right to petition a federal court for a writ of habeas corpus, and we provide state and federal prisoners, including those sentenced to capital punishment, a well-defined means to raise post-conviction claims in federal court if their constitutional rights were violated in lower courts. Habeas review in federal courts is an important vehicle for protecting the constitutional rights of both state and federal inmates.

Capital punishment Recommendations 95, 118, 134, and 135

49. U.S. constitutional restraints, in addition to federal and state laws and practices, limit the use of capital punishment to the most serious offenses, such as murder, in the most aggravated circumstances and with strict limitations. It is barred for any individual less than 18 years of age at the time of the crime and for individuals found by a court to have a significant intellectual disability. There are strict prohibitions against the use of any method of execution that would inflict cruel and unusual punishment and against imposition of the death penalty in a racially discriminatory manner. Federal and state laws require that sentencing decisions be individualized to the particular offender and offense. The President has directed DOJ to conduct a review of how the death penalty is being applied in the United States. Additionally, on January 23, the U.S. Supreme Court agreed to hear an argument, and is expected to rule in June 2015, on whether the lethal injection protocol used in executions by Oklahoma constitutes cruel and unusual punishment under the Eighth Amendment of our Constitution.

50. When an individual may be subject to capital punishment, the appellate process is substantial and thorough, with ample opportunity to challenge a conviction and penalty through direct appeal and habeas review. The Constitution requires that all criminal defendants, including capital defendants, receive effective assistance of counsel.

51. The number of states that have the death penalty, the number of persons executed each year, and the size of the population on death row have continued to decline since our last report. Currently, federal law and laws in 32 U.S. states provide for capital punishment. Since our last UPR, three states have repealed their capital punishment laws: Illinois (2011), Connecticut (2012), and Maryland (2013). Only seven states carried out a total of 35 executions in 2014- the lowest number of executions in the United States since 1994. The federal government has carried out no executions since our last UPR; in fact, it has not executed an inmate since 2003 and only three since 1963.

Criminal justice and international issues Recommendations 173 and 175

52. Through DOJ's Human Rights and Special Prosecutions Section and other U.S. agency components, we investigate and prosecute human rights violators and other international criminals. Recently, we obtained convictions of two U.S. citizens for unlawfully procuring citizenship after they concealed their participation in a 1982 massacre of civilians in a Guatemalan village, and another on the same charges after she concealed her participation in killings during the 1994 Rwandan genocide.

53. We also assess and carry out requests for international extradition in conformity with applicable extradition treaty provisions in force between the United States and the requesting state. We have extradited a number of persons accused of conduct constituting crimes such as genocide and war crimes, though such requests have been infrequent.

D. Indigenous Issues

Recommendations 83, 85, 199-203, 205, and 206

54. The United States has made substantial advances to better protect the rights of indigenous peoples domestically. In December 2010, President Obama announced our support for the U.N. Declaration on the Rights of Indigenous Peoples, following review and three informal consultations with tribal governments, indigenous groups, and NGOs.

55. We continue to engage in frequent and extensive domestic dialogues on matters of importance to indigenous peoples. In addition, we hold an annual White House Tribal Nations Conference with the leadership of tribal governments, where the President, the Vice President, many members of the Cabinet, dozens of senior U.S. officials, and hundreds of tribal leaders discuss issues such as tribal self-determination, including self-governance; health care; economic and infrastructure development; education; protection of land and natural resources; and other matters of priority to tribal governments. We also participated in the September 2014 World Conference on Indigenous Peoples, and were pleased that the four main priorities advocated by tribal government leaders were incorporated into the Outcome Document.

56. In 2013, President Obama issued an order creating the White House Council on Native American Affairs consisting of the heads of various federal agencies to improve high-level coordination on the pressing issues facing tribal communities.

57. In December 2014 we unveiled "Generation Indigenous," a major initiative to remove barriers to success for Native youth. It includes college and career readiness programs, leadership training, a listening tour by members of the President's cabinet to hear about the aspirations and concerns of Native youth, and a summit to discuss preservation of Native languages. The Department of the Interior, which educates 48,000 American Indian students across 23 states, issued a comprehensive reform plan in June 2014, and ED has proposed new education grants to better meet the needs of American Indian and Alaska Native students.

58. We have further taken action to address discrimination against members of tribal communities and Native individuals. DOL enforces non-discrimination in employment for these groups by federal contractors. Since our last UPR, DOJ has enforced civil rights laws on behalf of American Indians and Alaska Natives in several areas, including protection of religious practices, education, voting, fair lending, corrections, access to courts by non-English speaking Native individuals, hate crimes, sex trafficking, and excessive use of force by police.

59. Since 2010, we have enacted numerous laws to address the challenges facing American Indians and Alaska Natives. Most notable among these is the March 2013 reauthorization of the Violence Against Women Act, which strengthens provisions to address violence against American Indian and Alaska Native women. This reauthorization includes a critical new provision recognizing tribes' authority to prosecute in tribal courts those who commit acts of domestic violence on tribal lands irrespective of whether the perpetrator is Indian or non-Indian. Empowering indigenous peoples to address their challenges is a central principle of the UNDRIP, as well as sound policy. Additionally, a 2012 law gave greater control to tribes over tribal assets, including certain land leases, and a 2010 law enhances tribes' sentencing authority, strengthens defendants' rights, establishes new guidelines and training for officers handling domestic violence and sex crimes, improves services to victims, and seeks to help combat alcohol and substance abuse and help at-risk youth.

60. We have prioritized reaching settlement agreements with Indian tribes over trust mismanagement and other claims. These settlements to date total over $2.6 billion in compensation to more than 80 federally-recognized Indian tribes. In

addition, we settled an individual trust case for $3.4 billion and settled a landmark class-action lawsuit by Indian farmers and ranchers alleging that they were discriminated against in federal agricultural programs.

E. Immigration

Detention of migrants and immigration policies Recommendations 80, 82, 102, 144, 164, 183-185, and 212

61. On November 20, 2014, President Obama announced a series of executive actions on immigration and border security. These include: a plan to fundamentally alter our border security strategy; significant revisions to our immigration enforcement priorities; expansion of a policy to consider deferring removal, and providing work authorization, for certain individuals who arrived in the U.S. as children; and a new initiative to consider deferring removal, and providing work authorization, for certain parents of U.S. citizens and lawful permanent residents. Consistent with these actions, we are implementing a new enforcement and removal policy that continues to place top priority on threats to national security, public safety, and border security.

62. The United States continues to be a leader in extending protection to refugees and asylum seekers. In FY2014,4 we admitted 69,987 refugees and granted asylum to 25,199 individuals. We have also substantially increased grants of immigration protection for victims of torture, trafficking, domestic violence, child abuse, abandonment, or neglect, and other qualifying crimes.

63. From 2010 to 2014, among individuals who either arrived or were apprehended near the border shortly after entering the country without permission, the number of people who expressed a fear of returning to their country of origin increased by 469 percent. Other screenings for fear of return have also markedly increased. To address the substantial increase in individuals seeking protection, we have hired nearly 150 new asylum officers since October 2013 and plan to hire more officers.

64. We are also taking action to address specific concerns regarding racial profiling and use of force at the U.S.-Mexico border. In May 2014, U.S. Customs and Border Protection publicly released an updated Use of Force Policy, Guidelines, and Procedures Handbook, which requires training in the use of safe tactics, a requirement to carry less-lethal devices, and guidance on responding to thrown projectiles. CBP is launching a use-of-force incident-tracking system to better inform its responses to incidents.

65. The United States continues to provide due process guarantees throughout the immigration system, including in removal proceedings, where individuals are advised of their rights and other important information. While some individuals facing immigration proceedings are detained, that is only after an individualized determination that detention is appropriate or required by law. Many alternatives to detention are available and are used when appropriate. In FY2013, 37 percent of cases completed by the immigration courts involved an individual who was detained.

66. Since our first UPR, we have promulgated the 2011 Performance-Based National Detention Standards, which cover many facilities housing immigration detainees and establish minimum conditions of detention, including with respect to medical care, access to legal resources, visitation, recreation, correspondence, religious services, and grievance processes.

67. We have further prioritized the interview of and completion of asylum applications by unaccompanied children, consistent with the prioritization of the same population in immigration courts. Programs are being initiated to provide child advocates and representation to unaccompanied children in immigration proceedings in certain locations. We provide unaccompanied children with safe and appropriate residential environments until they are released to appropriate sponsors while their immigration cases proceed. While they are in our care, our facilities provide services such as food, clothes, basic education, recreation, and medical and legal assistance. Approximately 90 percent of all unaccompanied children were released to the care of a sponsor in FY2014. Once that occurs, they have a right under federal law - just like other children in their communities - to enroll in local public elementary and secondary schools, regardless of their or their sponsors' immigration status. We have also launched a program to provide refugee admission to certain children in El Salvador, Honduras, and Guatemala, providing a safe, orderly alternative to dangerous journeys from Central America.

Discrimination or violence against migrants and access to services Recommendations 79, 104-105, 108, 165, 167, 207, 210, 214, and 220

68. The United States has an unwavering commitment to respect the human rights of all migrants, regardless of their immigration status, and vigorously prosecutes crimes committed against migrants and enforces labor, workplace safety, and civil rights laws. All children have the right to equal access to public elementary and secondary education, regardless of their or their parents' immigration status, and such schools must provide meaningful access to their programs to persons with limited English proficiency, including migrants. In January 2015, we issued guidance to help schools ensure that English learner students can participate meaningfully and equally in education programs and services. Employers may not discriminate against employees or applicants based on their race, color, national origin, or, in certain cases, citizenship status.

69. Regardless of immigration status, victims of domestic violence have full access to a network of 1,600 domestic violence shelters and other supportive services, including community health centers and substance abuse, mental health, and maternal and child health programs.

70. VAWA specifically provides immigration protections for battered immigrants, allowing certain family members of U.S. citizens and lawful permanent residents who have been victims of domestic violence to independently petition for immigration status without the abuser's knowledge. This self-petitioning process removes one barrier to leaving that victims might face and shifts control over the immigration process to the victim, providing him or her with more options. In FY2014, 613 such self-petitions were granted.

71. The DHS Traveler Redress Inquiry Program provides a way for travelers who experience difficulties during their travel screening to seek redress, including those who believe they have been unfairly or incorrectly delayed, denied boarding, or identified for additional screening as a result of being placed on the terrorist watchlist or its subset, the No Fly List. DHS TRIP works with other government agencies as appropriate to make an accurate determination about any traveler who has sought redress. We are actively reviewing and revising the existing redress program to increase transparency for certain individuals, consistent with the protection of national and transportation security and classified and other sensitive information.

Consular access and notification Recommendations 54, 213, and 223

72. The United States has made significant efforts to meet the goal of across-the-board compliance with its consular notification and access obligations under the Vienna Convention on Consular Relations. The Federal Rules of Criminal Procedure were amended in December 2014 to facilitate compliance with our consular notification and access obligations, requiring judges to notify all defendants at their initial appearance in a federal case that non-U.S. citizens may request that a consular officer from the defendant's country of nationality be notified of the arrest, but that even without a defendant's request, a treaty or other international agreement may require consular notification. We have distributed more than 200,000 manuals on consular notification and access, which provide detailed instructions for police and prison officials engaged in detention or arrest of a foreign national, in order to comply with the VCCR and all relevant bilateral consular agreements. We distribute other free consular notification and access training materials and post them online, and have conducted nearly 900 outreach and training sessions on consular notification and access since 1998.

73. Legislation supported by the Administration that would bring U.S. into compliance with the ICJ's judgment in *Avena* has previously been introduced in the Senate, but has not been enacted into law.

F. Labor and Trafficking

Gender equality in the workplace Recommendation 115

74. U.S. law prohibits compensating men and women differently for the same or similar work, as well as any discrimination in compensation based on sex. However, the "gender gap" in pay persists. Full-time working women earn only about 78 percent of their male counterparts' earnings. We have established a high level task force to better respond to the issue, and continue to diligently enforce laws that address gender discrimination in pay in the workplace and seek justice for victims of sex-based wage discrimination.

75. For instance, from January 2010 to March 2013, the EEOC obtained more than $78 million in relief for such victims. From January 2010 to September 2014, DOL recovered more than $51 million in back wages and nearly 9,000 job opportunities on behalf of approximately 90,000 victims of discrimination, including gender discrimination. Additionally, in April 2014, President Obama signed an order prohibiting federal contractors from discriminating against employees who choose to discuss their compensation, and a Presidential Memorandum to advance equal pay through collection of compensation data collection. Private rights of action are also available to individuals who face gender discrimination in the workplace and wish to seek a remedy.

Human trafficking, including child prostitution Recommendations 168-169

76. We remain committed to combatting human trafficking, including commercial sexual exploitation of children, and have made great progress since our last report. For example, in FY2013, DHS initiated 987 criminal investigations with a nexus to human trafficking, and obtained 1,028 indictments and 828 convictions on charges arising from trafficking investigations. In FY2014, we granted special permission to remain in the country to 18,520 victims of various crimes, including human trafficking, and their family members. We also continue to prepare educational materials about trafficking; in January 2015, we published a guide for educators and school staff about the indicators of possible human trafficking and how to address and prevent child exploitation.

77. We have streamlined federal human trafficking investigations and prosecutions and have collaborated on a bilateral initiative with Mexican law enforcement to dismantle sex trafficking networks. We also aggressively investigate and prosecute those who commit forced labor and sex trafficking. In FY2013, DOJ charged 163 defendants with forced labor or sex trafficking. In the three prior years, DOJ brought 221 such cases, compared to 149 in the previous four-year period and 82 in the four-year period before that.

78. In addition to criminal prosecutions, we continue to enforce the rights of trafficking victims. For example, in a set of cases related to a single employment broker, we obtained significant relief (including $3.6 million and injunctive relief) on behalf of approximately 500 Thai agricultural workers who were trafficked to the United States. In the settlement, one employer offered some of the workers full-time employment, including profit-sharing and retirement benefits.

79. To assist trafficking victims in the United States, we have developed the first-ever Government-wide strategic action plan to strengthen services for trafficking victims, which is comprehensive, action-oriented, and designed to address the needs of all victims. Additionally, DHS has 26 full-time Victim Assistance Specialists in local investigative offices and more than 250 Victim Witness Coordinators. They work to ensure that possible human trafficking victims are rescued, transferred to safe locations, and provided with referrals for medical, mental health, and legal assistance.

Rights of agricultural and other workers Recommendations 81, 192, and 193

80. The United States vigorously enforces labor and employment laws without regard to a worker's immigration status. Furthermore, we combat employer efforts to discover the immigration status of workers during litigation, to prevent employers from threatening deportation, or otherwise intimidating workers or witnesses.

81. We vigorously enforce laws that prohibit employment discrimination against migrant workers on the basis of race, color, national origin, sex, religion, age, disability, or genetic information. We have initiated and favorably resolved numerous cases on behalf of female farmworkers who were subjected to sexual harassment. Wage laws generally set basic minimum wage and overtime pay standards. Safety laws require safeguards to prevent worker injury. Environmental laws prescribe how certain chemicals must be handled in the workplace. Our laws also generally prohibit discrimination against covered persons based upon citizenship or immigration status in hiring, firing, recruitment, or referral for a fee.

82. We have increased outreach to foreign workers, including agricultural workers, regarding their rights and how to pursue them, often by working cooperatively with NGOs and foreign governments-for example, through Consular Partnership agreements with a number of countries to provide information on U.S. labor and employment laws.

G. National Security

Counterterrorism efforts and intelligence-gathering Recommendations 58, 59, 90, 187, 188, and 217

The United States strives to protect privacy and civil liberties while also protecting national security. We have an extensive and effective framework of protections that applies to privacy and intelligence issues, including electronic surveillance. The Foreign Intelligence Surveillance Act governs, among other matters, electronic surveillance conducted within the United States for the purpose of gathering foreign intelligence or counterintelligence information. In establishing the Foreign Intelligence Surveillance Court, FISA sets forth a system of rigorous, independent judicial oversight of the activities it regulates to ensure that they are lawful and effectively address privacy and civil liberties concerns. Such activities are also subject to oversight by the U.S. Congress and entities in our Executive Branch.

83. Signals intelligence collection outside the FISA context is also regulated, and must have a valid foreign intelligence or counterintelligence purpose. In January 2014, the President issued Presidential Policy Directive-28, which enunciates standards for the collection and use of foreign signals intelligence. It emphasizes that we do not collect foreign intelligence for the purpose of suppressing criticism or dissent, or for disadvantaging any individual on the basis of ethnicity, race, gender, sexual orientation, or religion, and that agencies within our intelligence community are required to adopt and make public to the greatest extent feasible procedures for the protection of personal information of non-U.S. persons. It also requires that privacy and civil liberties protections be integral in the planning of those activities, and that personal information be protected at appropriate stages of collection, retention, and dissemination.

84. PPD-28 recognizes that all persons should be treated with dignity and respect, regardless of nationality or place of residence, and that all persons have legitimate privacy interests in the handling of their personal information collected through signals intelligence. It therefore requires U.S. signals intelligence activities to include appropriate safeguards for the personal information of all individuals.

85. Further, our intelligence community is required to report on such programs and activities to Congress, where these issues are vigorously debated. Agencies within our intelligence community have privacy and civil liberties officers. The National Security Agency, for example, has recently established a Civil Liberties and Privacy Officer who advises on issues including signals intelligence programs that entail the collection of personal information.

Military detention and transfer, operations, and accountability Recommendations 60, 66, 88, 89, 136-140, 142, 143, 146-149, 155-161, 166, 176, and 218

86. The United States is fully committed to ensuring that individuals it detains in any armed conflict are treated humanely. All U.S. military detention operations conducted in connection with armed conflict, including at Guantánamo Bay, are carried out in accordance with U.S. law, international humanitarian law including Common Article 3 of the Geneva Conventions of 1949, and other international laws, including the Convention Against Torture, as applicable.

87. The President has repeatedly reaffirmed his commitment to close the Guantánamo Bay detention facility. There were 242 detainees at Guantánamo at the beginning of this Administration. Since then, 116 have been transferred out of the facility, including 28 in 2014 and an additional five in January 2015. Currently, 122 detainees remain at Guantánamo, 54 of whom are designated for transfer. Out of the 68 others, ten are currently facing charges or serving criminal sentences; and the remaining 58 are eligible for review by the Periodic Review Board, which commenced in October 2013. The PRB has already conducted 12 hearings and two six-month file reviews, in which detainees participated with assistance from their personal representatives and private counsel. The PRB determined that continued detention of six of these detainees is no longer necessary, making them eligible for transfer, subject to appropriate security measures and consistent with our humane transfer policy. Two of these detainees have already been transferred to their countries of origin.

88. Under our standard military procedures, individuals detained by U.S. forces for more than 14 days are assigned an Internment Serial Number, starting a formal process of oversight and record keeping. Every ISN is reported to the International Committee of the Red Cross, and the ICRC is given access to these individuals as well as to all internment locations, including Guantánamo Bay, which the ICRC has visited more than 100 times since 2002.

89. All Guantánamo detainees can file a petition in U.S. federal court challenging the lawfulness of their detention. They have access to counsel and appropriate information to mount such a challenge.

90. Torture and cruel, inhuman or degrading treatment or punishment by U.S. personnel is prohibited at all times and in all places without exception. Immediately upon taking office in 2009, President Obama issued an Executive Order on ensuring lawful interrogations, which mandated that, consistent with the CAT and Common Article 3 of the 1949 Geneva Conventions, any individual detained in armed conflict by the United States or within a facility owned, operated, or controlled by the United States, in all circumstances, must be treated humanely. This Executive Order revoked legal opinions, including regarding the definition of torture, that previously had been relied upon in the context of the former CIA detention and interrogation program, which was ended by President Obama.

91. As a matter of fundamental policy and practice, we do not transfer any individual to a foreign country if it is more likely than not that the person would be tortured, after considering the totality of relevant factors. These include any allegations of prior or potential mistreatment of the individual by the receiving government, the receiving country's human rights record, whether posttransfer detention is contemplated, the specific factors suggesting that the individual in question is at risk of being tortured by officials in that country, whether similarly situated individuals have been tortured by the country under consideration, and, where applicable, any diplomatic assurances of humane treatment from the receiving country, including an assessment of their credibility. With respect to law of war detainee transfers, and in other contexts in which assurances are sought, it is U.S. practice to seek consistent, private access for post-transfer monitoring where post-transfer detention by the receiving state is anticipated, with minimal advance notice to the detaining government.

92. U.S. government personnel who are responsible for conducting interrogations receive training and are prohibited under U.S. law and policy from engaging in torture or cruel, inhuman, or degrading treatment, regardless of location. The Detainee Treatment Act of 2005, for example, prohibits subjecting persons detained under the law of war by the Department of Defense, or in a DoD facility, to any interrogation technique that is not authorized by and listed in U.S. Army Field Manual 2.22-3, and this prohibition is extended by executive order to all U.S. agencies detaining individuals in any armed conflict. Interrogations that comply with that Manual are consistent with U.S. and international legal obligations.

93. DoD has multiple accountability mechanisms in place to ensure that personnel adhere to law and policy in military operations and detention. DoD has conducted thousands of investigations and prosecuted or disciplined hundreds of service members for mistreatment of detainees and other related misconduct since 2001.

94. Regarding civilian prosecutions for potential abuses committed in armed conflict since September 11, 2001, DOJ conducted an extensive review led by Assistant U.S. Attorney John Durham of the treatment of 101 persons alleged to have been mistreated while in U.S. custody since the 9/11 attacks. That review generated two criminal investigations, but after examining a broad universe of allegations from multiple sources, the prosecutor concluded that the admissible evidence would not have been sufficient to obtain and sustain convictions beyond a reasonable doubt. DOJ has brought two cases and obtained convictions against two contractors for abuse of detainees in Afghanistan.

95. In December 2014, the U.S. Senate Select Committee on Intelligence released a declassified Executive Summary of its Report on the CIA's former detention and interrogation program. Harsh interrogation techniques highlighted in that Report are not representative of how the United States deals with the threat of terrorism today, and are not consistent with our values. The United States supports transparency and has taken steps to ensure that it never resorts to the use of those techniques again.

96. We are currently making efforts to accommodate Special Rapporteur on Torture Juan Mendez's request for a country visit. Last fall, we confirmed with Mr. Mendez our willingness to facilitate a visit to state and local facilities, per his request. With regard to his request to visit the Guantánamo Bay detention facility, we have extended an invitation for him to tour the facility and to observe operations there under the same conditions as other visitors, aside from the ICRC, which has regular access to Guantánamo detainees as described in Paragraph 89.

97. The United States continues to employ military commissions for the prosecution of certain offenses committed in the context of, and in association with, hostilities. All current military commission proceedings are required under U.S. law to apply fair trial safeguards, including the presumption of innocence; prohibitions on the use of evidence obtained by cruel, inhuman, or degrading treatment; restrictions on the admissibility of hearsay evidence and statements of the accused; the accused's right to discovery of evidence; and the standard of proving guilt beyond a reasonable doubt. A

conviction by a military commission is subject to multiple layers of review, including judicial review by civilian courts. In order to increase transparency and accountability, proceedings are now transmitted via video feed to locations at Guantánamo Bay and in the United States, so that the press and the public can view them with a 40-second delay to protect against the disclosure of classified information.

98. Finally, the United States takes scrupulous care to ensure that the use of military force, including through use of unmanned aerial vehicles, complies with the law of war, including the principles of distinction and proportionality. In addition, before we take any counterterrorism strike outside areas of active hostilities, it is U.S. policy that there must be near-certainty that no civilians will be killed or injured. Our counterterrorism policy requires that if at any time during the targeting process outside areas of active hostilities capture appears feasible, we must pursue capture instead; our preference is to detain, interrogate, and to prosecute when feasible.

H. Economic, Social, and Cultural Measures

Access to food and health care Recommendations 195-196

100. The United States has undertaken many initiatives domestically to promote food security and expand health care. The Affordable Care Act has increased health coverage options and quality through new consumer protections, the creation of the Health Insurance Marketplaces-a new means for uninsured people to enroll in health coverage-and additional support for state Medicaid and Children's Health Insurance Programs. It requires most health plans to cover ten categories of essential health benefits, including preventive services, maternity and prenatal care, hospitalizations, and mental health and substance use disorder services. It also reauthorized the Indian Healthcare Improvement Act, to address some of the health care access concerns in indigenous communities.

101. We are committed to expanding access to health care to all our citizens and as such, have made efforts to strengthen and protect our social and health care programs: Medicare for the elderly and disabled, and Medicaid for low-income individuals and families. Under the ACA, Medicare beneficiaries have saved billions of dollars on prescription drugs and have seen no increase in rates since 2013. Additionally, Medicare beneficiaries no longer have to pay costsharing for preventive services, and nearly nine million individuals have enrolled in coverage in state-run Medicaid programs since October 2013.

102. In FY2014, we invested more than $103 billion in domestic food assistance programs, serving one in four Americans during the year. Beneficiaries included about 46.5 million low-income individuals each month under the Supplemental Nutrition Assistance Program; about 8.3 million per month under the Special Supplemental Nutrition Program for Women, Infants and Children; over 30.3 million children each school day; and over 2.5 million elderly adults each year through the Older Americans Act nutrition programs. Emergency food providers received 785 million pounds of food through the Emergency Food Assistance Program. Substantial evidence demonstrates that these programs improve social, economic, and nutrition conditions for low-income Americans.

Access to education Recommendation 109

103. We are committed to equality of opportunity in education and to helping students succeed in school, careers, and life. To help increase educational excellence, support innovation and improvement, and address continuing challenges, ED has dedicated well over $1 billion to early childhood education, and also has launched a number of other programs and initiatives, including the Excellent Educators for All Initiative in July 2014, which directs states to submit plans in 2015 to help ensure that poor and minority children have equal access to experienced, qualified teachers. Also in 2014, we issued guidance to states, school districts, and schools to help ensure that students have equal access to educational resources, and launched the Performance Partnership Pilots program to test innovative, outcome-focused strategies for achieving significant improvements in educational, employment, and other key outcomes for disconnected youth.

104. In 2013, we issued guidance to institutions of higher education to help them promote diversity on their campuses. Guidance was also issued for elementary and secondary schools, school districts, and higher education institutions seeking to achieve a diverse student body. See Paragraphs 30-32 on racial discrimination in education.

Homelessness and access to housing, water, and sanitation Recommendations 113 and 197

105. *Housing and homelessness-*The United States is committed to ending homelessness, and has made great progress in this area. For example, in 2010, we launched Opening Doors, a strategic plan aimed at ending homelessness among veterans by the end of 2015; chronic homelessness by 2016; and homelessness for families, youth, and children by 2020; and setting a path to eradicate all types of homelessness in the United States. HUD's statistics show that since that launch, chronic homelessness has dropped 21 percent, homelessness among families has declined 15 percent, and homelessness among veterans has fallen by 33 percent. In 2016, the new National Housing Trust Fund is expected to begin distributing funds to increase and preserve affordable housing for very low-income and homeless individuals. Additionally, federal law guarantees immediate access to a free appropriate public education for children and youth experiencing homelessness.

106. *Water and sanitation-*In 2013, we competitively awarded $12.7 million to public water systems and wastewater systems. The funding helps provide water system staff with training and tools to enhance system operations and management practices, and it supports our continuing efforts to protect public health and promote sustainability in small communities. Through the U.S.-Mexico Border Water Infrastructure Grant Program, the United States and Mexico have been addressing critical water and sanitation infrastructure problems in the border region. During 2010-14, the program provided drinking water connections to 34,307 homes and wastewater connections to 403,634 homes. Between 2009 and 2013, we provided an additional 12,676 homes of indigenous persons with access to safe drinking water to decrease the risk of illness and improve quality of life.

Foreign and humanitarian assistance Recommendations 52, 226, and 227

107. Between October 2010 and September 2014, the United States provided more than $800 million in foreign assistance in response to natural disasters, nearly $400 million in disaster preparedness and risk reduction activities, and over $22 billion in humanitarian assistance out of a foreign assistance budget of over $207 billion during that period. Despite recent reductions in the foreign assistance budget, our response to natural disasters has remained steadfast, and we continue to be an international leader in both disaster response and preparedness.

108. As underscored by the "Leahy law," our partner nations' security forces' respect for human rights is critical. In 2014, the DoD "Leahy law" expanded the prohibition on DoD-funded activities to include not only training but also equipment and "other assistance" for members of a unit of a foreign security force for which there is credible information that the unit has committed a gross violation of human rights.

I. Environment Recommendations 51, 221, and 222

109. The United States is firmly committed to addressing the causes and impacts of climate change. The National Environmental Policy Act requires federal agencies to incorporate environmental considerations in their planning and decision-making processes. The President's Climate Action Plan has committed to cut carbon pollution and other greenhouse emissions; promote renewable energy development and use; cut waste in homes, businesses, and factories; conserve land and water resources; use sound science to manage climate impacts; launch a climate resilience toolkit and climate data initiative; and actively engage in international efforts to address global climate change.

110. Our new fuel economy standards for certain vehicles will reduce carbon pollution by over six billion tons, and we support renewable fuel standards and research and development investments to bring next-generation bio-fuels to the energy market. We are also working to reduce our greenhouse gas emissions from direct sources, such as facility energy use and fuel consumption by 28 percent by 2020, and to reduce our greenhouse gas emissions from indirect sources, such as employee commuting, by 13 percent by 2020.

111. As part of our domestic efforts to address climate change, we continue to focus attention on the environmental and health conditions of minority, low-income, and indigenous communities. This includes understanding the implications of climate change impacts on members of domestic minority, low-income, and indigenous communities; identifying populations and communities vulnerable to climate change; and seeking meaningful involvement and fair treatment of all our people, regardless of race, color, national origin, or income, in the design and evaluation of adaptation strategies.

112. Internationally, we are helping vulnerable countries adapt to climate change and enhance resilience of their communities and economies, including by providing $2.2 billion in adaptation assistance from 2010-2014. We are currently

working toward an ambitious, effective, and inclusive global climate change agreement in 2015 under which all countries would make emission reduction contributions.

J. Treaties and International Human Rights Mechanisms

Ratification of and reservations to human rights instruments Recommendations 1-11, 13-30, 33-35, 37-45, and 47-49

113. The United States is a party to numerous human rights treaties, and our reservations, understandings, and declarations to these treaties are limited, necessary, compatible with the objects and purposes of the respective instruments, and do not undermine compliance with our obligations.

114. Although we have not ratified any new human rights treaties since our last Report, we have taken steps to ratify the Convention on the Rights of Persons with Disabilities. The United States signed the CRPD in 2009 and transmitted it to the Senate for advice and consent to ratification in 2012. The Administration continues to support ratification of the CRPD with the reservations, understandings, and declarations included in the resolution of advice and consent passed by the Senate Foreign Relations Committee.

115. We support ratification of the Convention on the Elimination of All Forms of Discrimination Against Women, and have designated CEDAW as a priority among multilateral treaties for ratification. The United States signed CEDAW in 1979, and the President transmitted it to the Senate for advice and consent to ratification in 1980. The principles endorsed in CEDAW are consistent with our domestic and foreign policy objectives and are strongly supported in federal and state law.

116. The United States steadfastly supports the International Labour Organization Declaration on Fundamental Principles and Rights at Work. In the context of the Follow-up to the Declaration, we have demonstrated that U.S. workers enjoy those fundamental principles and rights. In May 2014, the President's Committee on the ILO pledged to redouble its efforts to ratify Convention 111 on Discrimination in Employment and Occupation, demonstrating our commitment to equal opportunity and treatment and the elimination of employment discrimination worldwide.

117. The United States is one of the strongest supporters of the Inter-American human rights system, and is the largest donor country to the Inter-American Commission on Human Rights. We actively participate in IACHR hearings and afford due consideration to the IACHR's recommendations.

Special procedures Recommendation 93

118. The United States accepts country visit requests by Special Procedures mandate holders as scheduling allows and has hosted nine such visits in the past five years. Also see Paragraph 97.

IV. Conclusion

119. The United States has a long history of promoting, protecting, and respecting human rights, beginning with our Declaration of Independence and our Constitution. We remain committed to improving implementation of our human rights obligations and commitments, through laws, policies, programs, training, and other mechanisms.

120. The United States is committed to an open, inclusive, and transparent review before the UPR working group, and continues to support strongly the UPR process and the U.N. human rights system. We look forward to hearing the recommendations of states, with a view to continuing our improvement and strengthening of human rights protections, in cooperation with civil society and the international community.

Annex I: Abbreviations

Abbreviation	Agency/Organization/Term
ACA	Affordable Care Act
CAT	Convention Against Torture and Other Cruel, Inhuman or Degrading Treatment or Punishment
CEDAW	Convention on the Elimination of All Forms of Discrimination Against Women

Abbreviation	Agency/Organization/Term
CIA	U.S. Central Intelligence Agency
CRPD	Convention on the Rights of Persons with Disabilities
DHS	U.S. Department of Homeland Security
DHS TRIP	U.S. Department of Homeland Security Traveler Redress Inquiry Program
DoD	U.S. Department of Defense
DOI	U.S. Department of the Interior
DOJ	U.S. Department of Justice
DOL	U.S. Department of Labor
ED	U.S. Department of Education
EEOC	U.S. Equal Employment Opportunity Commission
FISA	Foreign Intelligence Surveillance Act
HHS	U.S. Department of Health and Human Services
HUD	U.S. Department of Housing and Urban Development
IACHR	Inter-American Commission on Human Rights
ICRC	International Committee of the Red Cross
ILO	International Labour Organization
ISN	Internment Serial Number
LGBT	Lesbian, gay, bisexual and transgender
NGO	Non-governmental organization
NHRI	National Human Rights Institution
PPD-28	Presidential Policy Directive 28 - Signals Intelligence Activities
PRB	Periodic Review Board
UNDRIP	U.N. Declaration on the Rights of Indigenous Peoples
UPR	Universal Periodic Review
USSC	U.S. Sentencing Commission
VAWA	Violence Against Women Act
VCCR	Vienna Convention on Consular Relations

Annex II: Selected Civil Society Consultations

Topic	Date	Location
Convention on the Rights of the Child Protocols	Oct. 31, 2012	Washington, DC
Convention on the Rights of the Child Protocols	Jan. 15, 2013	Geneva, Switzerland
International Covenant on Civil and Political Rights (ICCPR)	Jan 10, 2012	Washington, DC
International Covenant on Civil and Political Rights (ICCPR)	May 30, 2013	Washington, DC
International Covenant on Civil and Political Rights (ICCPR)	March 12, 2014	Geneva, Switzerland
Access to Justice	April 1, 2014	Washington, DC
Indigenous Issues	April 24, 2014	Norman, Oklahoma
Civil Rights, Non-Discrimination, and Criminal Justice	July 9, 2012	Washington, DC
Civil Rights and Non-Discrimination	July 8, 2014	Washington, DC
Criminal Justice Issues	July 9, 2014	Washington, DC
Human Rights Treaties	Aug. 1, 2014	Washington, DC
Convention on the Elimination of Racial Discrimination (CERD)	Aug. 12, 2014	Geneva, Switzerland

Topic	Date	Location
Immigration, Trafficking, and Labor	Sept. 12, 2014	Washington, DC
Environmental Issues	Oct. 7, 2014	Berkeley, California
National Security	Oct. 14, 2014	Washington, DC
Convention Against Torture (CAT)	Oct. 14, 2014	Washington, DC
Convention Against Torture (CAT)	Nov. 11, 2014	Geneva, Switzerland
National Congress of American Indians	June 18-19, 2012	Lincoln, Nebraska
National Association of Counties	July 13-17, 2012	Pittsburgh, Pennsylvania

Annex III: Participating U.S. Federal Agencies

U.S. Department of Agriculture (USDA)
U.S. Department of Defense (DoD)
U.S. Department of Education (ED)
U.S. Department of Health and Human Services (HHS)
U.S. Department of Homeland Security (DHS)
U.S. Department of Housing and Urban Development (HUD)
U.S. Department of the Interior (DOI)
U.S. Department of Justice (DOJ)
U.S. Department of Labor (DOL)
U.S. Department of State (DOS)
U.S. Environmental Protection Agency (EPA)
U.S. Equal Employment Opportunity Commission (EEOC)
U.S. Interagency Council on Homelessness (USICH)
U.S. National Labor Relations Board (NLRB)
U.S. Office of the Director of National Intelligence (ODNI)

Annex IV: First Cycle UPR Recommendations Supported in Whole or in Part by the United States

Note: This document compiles in one place both the text of the recommendations supported by the United States during the first Universal Periodic Review (UPR) cycle, as they were listed in the UPR Working Group's January 2011 Report (A/HRC/16/11), and the comments and positions the United States articulated on those recommendations in its March 2011 response (A/HRC/16/11/Add.1). Because the second UPR cycle will focus on recommendations supported by the United States, this document omits those recommendations that the United States did *not* support in 2011. Although the titles of some headings and placement of some of the recommendations have been altered slightly, the recommendations, responses, and general substance remain unchanged.

GENERAL COMMENTS

Some recommendations ask the United States to achieve an ideal, e.g., end discrimination or police brutality, and others request action not entirely under the control of our Federal Executive Branch, e.g., adopt legislation, ratify particular treaties, or take action at the state level. Such recommendations enjoy our support, or our support in part, when we share the ideal that the recommendations express, are making serious efforts toward achieving their goals, and intend to continue to do so. Nonetheless, we recognize, realistically, that the United States may never completely accomplish what is described in the literal terms of the recommendation. We are also comfortable supporting a recommendation to do something that we already do, and intend to continue doing, without in any way implying that we agree with a recommendation that understates the success of our ongoing efforts.

Some countries added to their recommendations inaccurate assumptions, assertions, or factual predicates, some of which are contrary to the spirit of the UPR. In such cases, we have decided whether we support a recommendation by looking past the rhetoric to the specific action or objective being proposed. When we say we "support in part" such recommendations, we mean that we support the proposed action or objective but reject the often provocative assumption or assertion embedded in the recommendation.

The recommendations have been divided into ten subject matter categories:

(1) Civil Rights, Ethnic, and Racial Discrimination

(2) Criminal Justice Issues

(3) Indigenous Issues

(4) National Security

(5) Immigration

(6) Labor and Trafficking

(7) Economic, Social and Cultural Rights and Measures

(8) The Environment

(9) Domestic Implementation of Human Rights

(10) Treaties and International Human Rights Mechanisms

1. CIVIL RIGHTS, ETHNIC, AND RACIAL DISCRIMINATION

Recommendations the United States Supports:

Recommendations 68, 101, and 219: (68) Take legislative and administrative measures to ban racial profiling in law enforcement; (101) Ban, at the federal and state levels, the use of racial profiling by police and immigration officers; Prohibit expressly the use of racial profiling in the enforcement of immigration legislation; (219) Enact a national legislation that prohibits religious, racial and color profiling particularly in context of the fight against terrorism.

> U.S. position: Profiling — the invidious use of race, ethnicity, national origin, or religion — is prohibited under the U.S. Constitution and numerous pieces of national legislation.

Recommendation 95: Undertake studies to determine the factors of racial disparity in the application of the death penalty, to prepare effective strategies aimed at ending possible discriminatory practices.

Recommendation 96: Take appropriate legislative and practical measures to prevent racial bias in the criminal justice system.

Recommendation 97: Review the minimum mandatory sentences in order to assess their disproportionate impact on the racial and ethnic minorities.

Recommendation 106: Take administrative and legal measures against perpetrators of racially motivated acts, targeting migrants and minority communities.

> U.S. position: We support this recommendation insofar as it involves enforcing our laws, e.g., hate crimes legislation, and taking appropriate administrative actions.

Recommendations 107 and 111: (107) Adopt effective measures and an anti-discrimination act to address racial problems; (111) Adopt a comprehensive national work-plan to combat racial discrimination.

U.S. position: We have comprehensive Federal and State legislation and strategies to combat racial discrimination. We are working diligently toward better enforcement and implementation of these laws and programs.

Recommendations 86 and 112: (86) Undertake awareness-raising campaigns for combating stereotypes and violence against gays, lesbians, bisexuals and transsexuals, and ensure access to public services paying attention to the special vulnerability of sexual workers to violence and human rights abuses; (112) Take measures to comprehensively address discrimination against individuals on the basis of their sexual orientation or gender identity.

U.S. position: We agree that no one should face violence or discrimination in access to public services based on sexual orientation or their status as a person in prostitution, as these recommendations suggest. We have recently taken concrete steps to address discrimination on the basis of sexual orientation and gender identity, and are engaged in further efforts.

Recommendation 114: Increase its efforts to effectively guarantee human rights of persons with disabilities, while welcoming the signing of the Convention and urging their prompt implementation.

Recommendation 116: Continue its intense efforts to undertake all necessary measures to ensure fair and equal treatment of all persons, without regard to sex, race, religion, colour, creed, sexual orientation, gender identity or disability, and encourage further steps in this regard.

Recommendation 144: Increases its efforts to eliminate alleged brutality and use of excessive force by law enforcement officials against, inter alia, Latino and African American persons and undocumented migrants, and to ensure that relevant allegations are investigated and that perpetrators are prosecuted.

U.S. position: We support this recommendation insofar as it allows for the exercise of prosecutorial discretion.

Recommendation 151: Strengthen oversight with a view to ending excessive use of force by law enforcement bodies, particularly when it is directed to the racial minorities and bring those responsible for violation of laws to justice.

Recommendation 167: Take effective steps to put an end to child prostitution, and effectively combat violence against women and gun violence.

Recommendation 191: Continue to create an enabling climate for religious and cultural tolerance and understanding at the grass roots level.

Recommendation 198: Reinforce the broad range of safeguards in favor of the most vulnerable groups such as persons with disabilities and the homeless to allow them the full enjoyment of their rights and dignity.

Recommendation 209: Guarantee the prohibition of use of cruelty and excessive or fatal force by law enforcement officials against people of Latin American or African origin as well as illegal migrants and to investigate such cases of excessive use of force.

U.S. position: Law enforcement and immigration officers are lawfully permitted to use deadly force under certain exceptional circumstances; e.g., self-defense or defense of another person.

Recommendations the United States Supports in Part:

Recommendation 62: Review, reform and adequate its federal and state laws, in consultation with civil society, to comply with the protection of the right to nondiscrimination established by the Convention on the Elimination of all Forms of Racial Discrimination (CERD), especially in the areas of employment, housing, health, education and justice.

U.S. position: We disagree with some of the premises embedded in this recommendation, but we are committed to the objectives it states, in this case combating discrimination and promoting tolerance. While we recognize there is always room for improvement, we believe that our law is consistent with our CERD obligations. (See also the explanation of our positions regarding recommendations 65, 107, and 111.)

Recommendations 64, 67, 94, 98, 100, and 189: (64) Review, with a view to their amendment and elimination, all laws and practices that discriminate against African, Arab and Muslim Americans, as well as migrants, in the administration of justice, including racial and religious profiling; (67) Take legislative and administrative measures to address a wide range of racial discrimination and inequalities in housing, employment and education; (94) End the discrimination against persons of African descent; (98) Devise specific programs aimed at countering growing Islamophobic and xenophobic trends in society; (100) End all forms of racial discrimination in terms of housing, education, health care, social security and labor; (189) Consider discontinuing measures that curtail human rights and fundamental freedoms.

> U.S. position: See general comments, as well as the explanation of our positions regarding recommendations 107 and 111.

Recommendation 99: Eliminate discrimination against migrants and religious and ethnic minorities and ensure equal opportunity for enjoyment of their economic, social and cultural rights.

> U.S. position: A migrant's eligibility for full benefits under certain programs may depend on his/her lawful status.

Recommendation 103: Ensure the prosecution and punishment, according to the law, of those responsible of racial hate and xenophobic criminal acts, as well as guarantee a fair compensation to the victims, such as the case of the Ecuadoreans Marcelo Lucero and Jose Sucuzhañay, murdered in the United States.

> U.S. position: We support the recommendation as it regards investigating and, where appropriate, prosecuting persons who violate criminal laws. We cannot support the part of the recommendation asking that we "guarantee a fair compensation." Although mechanisms for remedies are available through our courts, we cannot make commitments regarding outcomes.

Recommendation 190: Take effective measures to counter insults against Islam and Holy Quran, as well as Islamophobia and violence against Moslems, and adopt necessary legislation.

> U.S. position: We take effective measures to counter intolerance, violence, and discrimination against all members of all minority groups, including Muslims. We cannot support this recommendation, however, to the extent that it asks U.S. to take legislative measures countering insults. Insults (unlike discrimination, threats, or violence) are speech protected by our Constitution.

2. CRIMINAL JUSTICE ISSUES

Recommendations the United States Supports:

Recommendation 70: Take appropriate legislative and practical measures to improve living conditions through its prisons systems, in particular with regard to access to health care and education.

Recommendation 145: Guarantee the complete prohibition of torture in all prisons under its control.

> U.S. position: U.S. law prohibits torture in all prisons and detention facilities under its control.

Recommendation 152: Prevent and repress the illegitimate use of violence against detainees.

> U.S. position: U.S. law prohibits mistreatment of detainees in U.S. custody, requires investigations of credible mistreatment allegations, and prescribes accountability measures for violations.

Recommendation 162: Redouble its efforts to address sexual violence in correction and detention facilities as well as to address the problem of prison conditions, with a view to preserving the rights and dignity of all those deprived of their liberty.

Recommendation 163: Reduce overcrowding in prisons by enlarging existing facilities or building new ones and/or making more use of alternative penalties.

Recommendation 177: Ensure the full enjoyment of human rights by persons deprived of their liberty, including by way of ensuring treatment in maximum security prisons in conformity with international law.

Recommendation 179: Review of alternative ways to handle petty crime and of measures to improve the situation of inmates in prisons.

Recommendations the United States Supports in Part:

Recommendation 118: A national moratorium on the death penalty is introduced with a view to completely abolish the penalty and, before such a moratorium is introduced, to take all necessary measures to ensure that any use of the death penalty complies with minimum standards under international law relating to the death penalty such as under article 6 and 14 of the International Covenant on Civil and Political Rights.

> U.S. position: We will continue to ensure that implementation of the death penalty complies with our international obligations; the portion asking that we end capital punishment does not enjoy our support.

Recommendations 134 and 135: (134) End the prosecution and execution of mentally-ill persons and minors; (135) Extend the exclusion of death penalty to all crimes committed by persons with mental illness.

> U.S. position: We cannot support Recommendation 134 with respect to prosecution. We support both recommendations with respect to executions regarding minors and persons with certain intellectual disabilities, but not regarding all persons with any mental illness.

Recommendation 150: Take measures with a view to prohibiting and punishing the brutality and the use of excessive or deadly force by the law enforcement officials and to banning torture and other ill-treatment in its detention facilities at home and abroad.

> U.S. position: See general comments, as well as explanations of the U.S. position for recommendations 145, 208, and 209.

Recommendation 173: Comply with the principles of international cooperation, as defined in Resolution 3074 of the General Assembly, for the extradition of persons accused of crimes against humanity and proceed to extradite former Bolivian authorities that are legally accused of such crimes, in order to be brought to trial in their country of origin.

> U.S. position: The first part of this recommendation enjoys our support; we cannot support the recommendation's second part ("proceed to extradite former Bolivian authorities..."). In addition, decisions on extradition cases are made on a case-by-case basis, consistent with our international legal obligations, and the United States cannot prejudge the outcome of any particular case.

Recommendations 174 and 175: (174) Make those responsible for gross violations of human rights in American prisons and prisons under the jurisdiction of America outside its territory accountable, compensate victims and provide them with remedies; (175) Put on trial its gross violators of human rights and its war criminals and accede to ICC.

> U.S. position: See general comments. In addition, we are committed to holding accountable persons responsible for human rights violations and war crimes. We cannot, however, support the portion of Recommendation 174 regarding compensation and remedies, because those are not always applicable. Nor can we support the part of Recommendation 175 that we accede to the Rome Statute, although we are engaging with State Parties to the Rome Statute on issues of concern.

Recommendation 178: Ensure the enjoyment of the right to vote both by persons deprived of their liberty and of persons who have completed their prison sentences.

U.S. position: We support this recommendation to the extent that some State laws conform to it. Most inmates do not have the right to vote, however, and former felons do not have the right to vote in some States.

Recommendation 186: Ensure the right to habeas corpus in all cases of detention.

U.S. position: We support this recommendation to the extent provided for under the U.S. Constitution and U.S. laws, and consistent with our international obligations.

3. INDIGENOUS ISSUES

Recommendations the United States Supports:

Recommendations 83, 200, 202, 203, 205, and 206: (83) Implement concrete measures consistent with the Covenant on Civil and Political Rights, to ensure the participation of indigenous peoples in the decisions affecting their natural environment, measures of subsistence, culture and spiritual practices; (200) Guarantee the rights of indigenous Americans, and to fully implement the United Nations Declaration on the Rights of Indigenous Peoples; (202) Adopt and implement the United Nations Declaration on the Rights of Indigenous Peoples; (203) Endorse the United Nations Declaration on the Rights of Indigenous Peoples when completing its national review process; (205) Continue its forward movement on the Declaration of the Rights of Indigenous Peoples; (206) Guarantee the full enjoyment of the rights on natives of America in line with the United Nations Declaration on the Rights of Indigenous Peoples.

U.S. position: We support these recommendations consistent with the "Announcement of U.S. Support for the United Nations Declaration on the Rights of Indigenous Peoples — Initiatives to Promote the Government-to-Government Relationship & Improve the Lives of Indigenous Peoples."

Recommendation 85: Formulate goals and policy guidelines for the promotion of the rights of indigenous peoples and cooperation between government and indigenous peoples.

Recommendations the United States Supports in Part:

Recommendation 199: End the violation of the rights of indigenous peoples.

U.S. position: See general comments.

Recommendation 201: Recognize the United Nations Declaration on the Rights of Indigenous Peoples without conditions or reservations, and implement it at the federal and state levels.

U.S. position: We cannot accept the first part of this recommendation ("Recognize ... without conditions"), but the second part ("implement ...") enjoys our support, consistent with the "Announcement of U.S. Support for the United Nations Declaration on the Rights of Indigenous Peoples — Initiatives to Promote the Government-to-Government Relationship & Improve the Lives of Indigenous Peoples."

4. NATIONAL SECURITY

Recommendations the United States Supports:

Recommendations 58 and 176: (58) Make fully consistent all domestic anti-terrorism legislation and action with human rights standards; (176) Respect the human rights of prisoners of war, guaranteed by the penal norms.

U.S. position: We support these recommendations insofar as they recommend compliance with our international law obligations.

Recommendations 66 and 146: (66): Enact a federal crime of torture, consistent with the Convention, and also encompassing acts described as 'enhanced interrogation techniques'; (146) Define torture as a federal offense in line with the Convention against Torture and investigate, prosecute and punish those responsible of crimes of extraterritorial torture.

> U.S. position: Existing Federal criminal laws comply with our obligations under the Convention against Torture.

Recommendation 89: Consider the possibility of inviting relevant mandate holders as follow up to the 2006 joint-study by the 5 special procedures, in view of the decision of the current Administration to close the Guantánamo Bay detention facility.

Recommendation 90: Respond and follow-up appropriately the recommendations formulated to the United States by the Special Rapporteur for the Protection of Human Rights and Fundamental Freedoms while Countering Terrorism.

Recommendation 139: That measures be taken to eradicate all forms of torture and ill treatment of detainees by military or civilian personnel, in any territory of jurisdiction, and that any such acts be thoroughly investigated.

Recommendation 149: Observe the Amnesty International 12 points program to prevent torture perpetrated by government agents.

> U.S. position: Some of the referenced points may not be fully applicable in every context.

Recommendations 159 and 160: (159) Close without any delay all detention facilities at the Guantánamo Bay as President Barack Obama has promised; (160) Find for all persons still detained in the Guantánamo Bay detention center a solution in line with the United States obligations regarding the foundations of international and human rights law, in particular with the International Covenant on Civil and Political Rights.

> U.S. position: We have made clear our desire to close the Guantánamo Bay detention facility and will continue to work with Congress, the courts, and other countries to do so in a responsible manner that is consistent with our international obligations. Until it is closed, this Administration will continue to ensure that operations there are consistent with our international legal obligations.

Recommendation 161: Halt all transfer detainees to third countries unless there are adequate safeguards to ensure that they will be treated in accordance with international law requirements.

Recommendation 188: Adopt a set of legislative and administrative measures aimed at ensuring prohibition of the use by state and local authorities of modern technology for excessive and unjustified intervention in citizens' private life.

> U.S. position: The U.S. Constitution's Fourth Amendment and existing U.S. law prohibit the use of modern technology for excessive and unjustified interference in individuals' private lives.

Recommendation 218: Do not prosecute those arrested for terrorist crimes or any other crime in exceptional tribunals or jurisdictions, but bring them to judicial instances legally established, with the protection of due process and under all the guarantees of the American Constitution.

> U.S. position: Persons who are charged with terrorist-related crimes are tried under legally established processes in either civilian courts or military commissions, depending on the nature of the crime and the individual. They are afforded all applicable protections under domestic and international law.

Recommendations the United States Supports in Part:

Recommendation 59: Legislate appropriate regulations to prevent the violations of individual privacy, constant intrusion in and control of cyberspace as well as eavesdropping of communications, by its intelligence and security organizations.

U.S. position: Our Constitution and laws contain appropriate rules to protect the privacy of communications, consistent with our international human rights obligations. See also the general comments.

Recommendations 60, 137, 138, 140, 155, 166, and 217: (60) Take effective legal steps to halt human rights violations by its military forces and private security firms in Afghanistan and other States; (137) Prosecute the perpetrators of tortures, extrajudicial executions and other serious violations of human rights committed in Guantánamo, Abu Ghraib, Bagram, the NAMA and BALAD camps, and those carried out by the Joint Special Operations Command and the CIA; (138) Heed the call of the High Commissioner to launch credible independent investigations into all reliable allegations made to date of violations of international human rights law committed by American forces in Iraq, including extrajudicial killings, summary executions, and other abuses; (140) Stop the war crimes committed by its troops abroad, including the killings of innocent civilians and prosecute those who are responsible; (155) Close Guantánamo and secret centers of detention in the world, punish agents that torture, disappear and execute persons who have been arbitrarily detained, and compensate victims; (166) Take effective measures to put an end to gross human rights abuses including violence against women, committed for decades by the United States military personnel stationed in foreign bases; (217) Halt serious violations of human rights and humanitarian law including covert external operations by the CIA, carried out on the pretext of combating terrorism.

U.S. position: The United States supports recommendations calling for prohibition and vigorous investigation and prosecution of any serious violations of international law, as consistent with existing U.S. law, policy, and practice. We reject those parts of these recommendations that amount to unsubstantiated accusations of ongoing serious violations by the United States. See also the general comments.

Recommendation 88: Invite United Nations Special Rapporteurs to visit and investigate Guantánamo Bay prison and United States secret prisons and to subsequently close them.

U.S. position: The United States has consistently invited United Nations Special Rapporteurs to tour the detention facility at Guantánamo, to observe detention conditions, and to observe military commission proceedings. That invitation remains. See also the general comments.

Recommendations 136, 147, 148, 156, and 157: (136) Take legal and administrative measures to address civilian killings by the U.S. military troops during and after its invasion of Afghanistan and Iraq by investigating and bringing perpetrators to justice and remedying the victims and to close its detention facilities in foreign territories like Guantánamo, including CIA secret camps; (147) Conduct thorough and objective investigation of facts concerning use of torture against imprisoned persons in the secret prisons of United States of America and detainees of the detention centres in Bagram and Guantánamo, bring those who are responsible for these violations to justice, and undertake all necessary measures to provide redress to those whose rights were violated, including payment of necessary compensation; (148) Take measures to ensure reparation to victims of acts of torture committed under United States' control and allow access to the International Committee of the Red Cross to detention facilities under the control of the United States; (156) Expedite efforts aimed at closing the detention facility at Guantánamo Bay and ensure that all remaining detainees are tried, without delay, in accordance with the relevant international standards; Proceed with the closure of Guantánamo at the earliest possible date and bring to trial promptly in accordance with the applicable rules of international law the detainees held there or release them; (157) Quickly close down Guantánamo prison and follow the provision of the United Nations Charter and the Security Council Resolution by expatriating the terrorist suspect to their country of origin.

U.S. position: We intend to close the Guantánamo Bay detention facility. The President has closed all CIA detention facilities and has prohibited CIA operation of such facilities. We allow the International Committee of the Red Cross access to individuals detained by the United States pursuant to armed conflict. We investigate allegations of torture, and prosecute where appropriate. We cannot accept portions of these recommendations concerning reparation, redress, remedies, or compensation.

Although mechanisms for remedies are available through U.S. courts, we cannot make commitments regarding their outcome. We cannot accept the part of Recommendation 136 that we close all detention centers; the United States maintains certain internment facilities abroad, consistent with applicable U.S. and international law. We cannot agree to the part of Recommendation 156 that we release all individuals detained pursuant to an armed conflict who are not promptly brought to trial. Regarding Recommendation 157, transfers of detainees to their home countries will only be conducted in accordance with our humane treatment policies.

Recommendation 142: Halt selective assassinations committed by contractors, and the privatization of conflicts with the use of private military companies.

> U.S. position: See general comments. Our contractors are not authorized to engage in direct hostilities or offensive operations or to commit assassinations. Like U.S. government personnel, contractors may only use force consistent with our international and domestic legal obligations. We have expressed support for the International Code of Conduct for Private Security Service Providers.

Recommendation 143: End the use of military technology and weaponry that have proven to be indiscriminate and cause excessive and disproportionate damage to civilian life.

> U.S. position: See general comments. In U.S. military operations, great care is taken to ensure that only legitimate objectives are targeted and that collateral damage is kept to a minimum.

Recommendation 187: Guarantee the right to privacy and stop spying on its citizens without judicial authorization.

> U.S. position: See general comments. We collect information about our citizens only in accordance with U.S. law and international obligations.

5. IMMIGRATION

Recommendations the United States Supports:

Recommendation 80: Spare no efforts to constantly evaluate the enforcement of the immigration federal legislation, with a vision of promoting and protecting human rights.

Recommendation 104: Make further efforts in order to eliminate all forms of discrimination and the abuse of authority by police officers against migrants and foreigners, especially the community of Vietnamese origin people in the United States.

Recommendation 108: Prohibit and punish the use of racial profiling in all programs that enable local authorities with the enforcement of immigration legislation and provide effective and accessible recourse to remedy human rights violations occurred under these programs.

Recommendation 144: Increases its efforts to eliminate alleged brutality and use of excessive force by law enforcement officials against, inter alia, Latino and African American persons and undocumented migrants, and to ensure that relevant allegations are investigated and that perpetrators are prosecuted.

> U.S. position: We support this recommendation insofar as it allows for the exercise of prosecutorial discretion.

Recommendation 164, 184, and 210: (164) Ensure that detention centers for migrants and the treatment they receive meet the basic conditions and universal human rights law; (184) Adapt the detention conditions of immigrants in line with international human rights law; (210) Protect the human rights of migrants, regardless of their migratory status.

> U.S. position: We support these recommendations insofar as they recommend compliance with our obligations under international human rights law.

Recommendation 165: Further foster its measures in relation to migrant women and foreign adopted children that are exposed to domestic violence.

Recommendation 183: Investigate carefully each case of immigrants' incarceration.

Recommendation 185: Ensure that migrants in detention, subject to a process of expulsion are entitled to counsel, a fair trial and fully understand their rights, even in their own language.

> U.S. position: We support these recommendations insofar as "entitled" to counsel means that a migrant in removal proceedings in immigration court enjoys the right to counsel at his/her own expense, and "fully understand their rights" means to have been provided information in a language they understand.

Recommendation 208: Prohibit, prevent and punish the use of lethal force in carrying out immigration control activities.

> U.S. position: Law enforcement and immigration officers are lawfully permitted to use deadly force under certain exceptional circumstances; e.g., self-defense or defense of another person.

Recommendation 212: Reconsider alternatives to the detention of migrants.

Recommendation 213: Ensure access of migrants to consular assistance.

> U.S. position: We support this recommendation understanding "consular assistance" to mean access consistent with Article 36 of the Vienna Convention on Consular Relations and similar provisions in bilateral consular agreements.

Recommendation 214: Make greater efforts to guarantee the access of migrants to basic services, regardless of their migratory status.

> U.S. position: We support this recommendation understanding that "basic services" refers to services such as primary education and emergency health services that are provided to migrants regardless of status.

Recommendation 220: Smarten security checks so as to take into account the frequent homonymy specific to Moslem names so as to avoid involuntary discrimination against innocent people with such names because of namesakes listed as members of terrorist groups.

Recommendation 223: Inform Foreign Missions regularly of efforts to ensure compliance with consular notification and access for foreign nationals in United States custody at all levels of law enforcement.

> U.S. position: We support this recommendation because it comports with the United States' general practice of widely disseminating information on its consular notification and access outreach and training efforts, including to foreign missions in the United States.

Recommendations the United States Supports in Part:

Recommendations 79 and 105: (79) Attempt to restrain any state initiative which approaches immigration issues in a repressive way towards the migrant community and that violates its rights by applying racial profiling, criminalizing undocumented immigration and violating the human and civil rights of persons; (105) Avoid the criminalization of migrants and ensure the end of police brutality, through human rights training and awareness-raising campaigns, especially to eliminate stereotypes and guarantee that the incidents of excessive use of force be investigated and the perpetrators prosecuted.

> U.S. position: See general comments. We will continue to both conduct human rights training and awareness campaigns and, where appropriate, bring civil or criminal actions regarding racial profiling, police brutality, and excessive use of force, and other actionable civil rights violations against immigrants. While unlawful presence in the U.S. is not a crime, and the federal government does not support state initiatives that aim to criminalize mere status, we cannot support the parts related to the

"criminalization" of migrants, as certain immigration offenses are subject to criminal sanction, e.g., illegal entry.

Recommendation 82: Adopt a fair immigration policy, and cease xenophobia, racism and intolerance to ethnic, religious and migrant minorities.

U.S. position: See general comments. It is consistent with our continuing efforts to improve our immigration policies and to eliminate xenophobia, racism, and intolerance in our society.

Recommendation 102: Revoke the national system to register the entry and exit of citizens of 25 countries from the Middle-East, South Asia and North Africa, and eliminate racial and other forms of profiling and stereotyping of Arabs, Muslims and South Asians as recommended by CERD.

U.S. position: See general comments. Our Constitution and numerous statutes prohibit the invidious use of race or ethnicity. The registration requirements of the National Security Entry-Exit Registration System are under review at this time.

Recommendation 207: End violence and discrimination against migrants.

U.S. position: See general comments.

6. LABOR AND TRAFFICKING

Recommendations the United States Supports:

Recommendation 115: Consider taking further action to better ensure gender equality at work.

U.S. position: We have comprehensive laws aimed at ensuring gender equality at work, and we are taking further action through the President's Equal Pay Taskforce.

Recommendation 168: Define, prohibit and punish the trafficking of persons and child prostitution.

Recommendation 169: Insist more on measures aiming to combat the demand and provide information and services to victims of trafficking.

Recommendation 192: Recognize the right to association as established by ILO, for migrant, agricultural workers and domestic workers.

U.S. position: We support the 1998 ILO Declaration on Fundamental Principles and Rights at Work, which reaffirms the commitment of all ILO Member States to respect, promote, and realize principles concerning fundamental rights in four categories including freedom of association and collective bargaining. Although not a party to ILO conventions 87 and 98 on those topics, we have robust laws addressing their fundamental principles.

Recommendation 193: Prevent slavery of agriculture workers, in particular children and women.

Recommendations the United States Supports in Part:

Recommendation 81: Take the necessary measures in favor of the right to work and fair conditions of work so that workers belonging to minorities, in particular women and undocumented migrant workers, do not become victims of discriminatory treatment and abuse in the work place and enjoy the full protection of the labor legislation, regardless of their migratory status.

U.S. position: Members of minority groups enjoy important anti-discrimination and labor protections. While labor laws apply to undocumented migrant workers, such individuals may not be entitled to certain types of remedies.

7. ECONOMIC, SOCIAL, AND CULTURAL RIGHTS AND MEASURES

Recommendations the United States Supports:

Recommendation 109: Promote equal socio-economic as well as educational opportunities for all both in law and in fact, regardless of their ethnicity, race, religion, national origin, gender or disability.

Recommendation 113: That further measures be taken in the areas of economic and social rights for women and minorities, including providing equal access to decent work and reducing the number of homeless people.

Recommendation 195: Ensure the realization of the rights to food and health of all who live in its territory.

> U.S. position: We are a non-party to the International Covenant on Economic, Social and Cultural Rights, and accordingly we understand the references to rights to food and health as references to rights in other human rights instruments that we have accepted. We also understand that these rights are to be realized progressively.

Recommendation 196: Expand its social protection coverage.

> U.S. position: The U.S. government seeks to improve the safety net that our country provides for the less fortunate.

Recommendation 197: Continue its efforts in the domain of access to housing, vital for the realization of several other rights, in order to meet the needs for adequate housing at an affordable price for all segments of the American society.

Recommendation 226: Persevere in the strengthening of its aid to development, considered as fundamental, in particular the assistance and relief in case of natural disasters.

8. THE ENVIRONMENT

Recommendations the United States Supports in Part:

Recommendations 51, 221, and 222: (51) Comply with its international obligations for the effective mitigation of greenhouse gas emissions, because of their impact in climate change; (221) Take positive steps in regard to climate change, by assuming the responsibilities arising from capitalism that have generated major natural disasters particularly in the most impoverished countries; (222) Implement the necessary reforms to reduce their greenhouse gas emissions and cooperate with the international community to mitigate threats against human rights resulting from climate change.

> U.S. position: See general comments. We disagree with premises embedded in these recommendations, but agree with their essential objectives (reduce greenhouse gas emissions and cooperate internationally).

9. DOMESTIC IMPLEMENTATION OF HUMAN RIGHTS

Recommendations the United States Supports:

Recommendation 65: Review its laws at the Federal and State levels with a view to bringing them in line with its international human rights obligations.

> U.S. position: We regularly engage in such reviews of our laws in light of our human rights obligations, including through the enforcement of our Federal civil rights laws and implementation of our domestic civil rights programs, litigation and judicial review, our reports to U.N. human rights treaty bodies, engagement with U.N. Special Procedures, and active discussions with civil society. Although the Federal government does not consistently or systematically review State laws, our civil rights mechanisms allow for review of State laws, as appropriate.

Recommendation 74: That a human rights institution at the federal level be considered in order to ensure implementation of human rights in all states.

> U.S. position: There are Federal and State institutions to monitor human rights; we are considering whether this network of protection is in need of improvement.

Recommendation 87: Incorporate human rights training and education strategies in their public policies.

> U.S. position: Programs at the Federal and State levels provide training on human rights, particularly on issues related to civil rights and non-discrimination; we are continuing to explore ways to strengthen such programs.

Recommendation 225: Continue consultations with non-governmental organizations and civil society in the follow up.

Recommendations the United States Supports in Part:

Recommendation 227: That the model legal framework expressed by the Leahy Laws be applied with respect to all countries receiving U.S.'s security assistance, and that the human rights records of all units receiving such assistance be documented, evaluated, made available and followed up upon in cases of abuse.

> U.S. position: This recommendation enjoys our support except for the last part regarding making our decision-making publicly available. We apply the Leahy laws (which impose human rights-related restrictions on assistance to foreign security forces) to all countries receiving U.S. security assistance, and we respond appropriately in cases of abuse. However, to do so, we consider information from all sources, including classified sources, and cannot make our decision-making public.

10. TREATIES AND INTERNATIONAL HUMAN RIGHTS MECHANISMS

Recommendations the United States Supports:

Recommendations 10, 11, 13, 14, 20, 21, 22, 26, 28, 30, 33, 34, 35, 39, 43, 47, 48, 49, and 93: (10) Consider ratifying ICESCR, CEDAW and CRC at the earliest; (11) Consider undertaking necessary steps leading to ratification of the parent/umbrella United Nations Convention on the Rights of the Child and CEDAW respectively; (13) Proceed with ratifying the CRPD and CRC; (14) Ratify, and ensure implementation into domestic law of CEDAW and CRC; (20) Consider ratifying the treaties to which it is not a party, including the CEDAW, CRC, ICESCR, and CRPD; (21) Consider ratifying CEDAW, the Convention on the Rights of the Child, and the Convention on the Rights of Persons with Disabilities; (22) Consider prioritizing acquiescence to the Convention of the Rights of the Child, CEDAW, the ILO Convention No. 111 on Discrimination in Respect of Employment and Occupation so as to further strengthen its national framework for human rights, but also to assist in achieving their universality; (26) Consider ratifying ILO Convention 100 on equal remuneration for men and women for work of equal value, and ILO Convention 111 on discrimination in employment and occupation; (28) Consider ratifying the Rome Statute of the International Criminal Court and the Additional Protocols I and II of the Geneva Conventions; (30) Consider signing the International Convention on the Protection of the Rights of All Migrant Workers and Members of Their Families; (33) Swiftly ratify CEDAW; Ratify CEDAW; Become a party to CEDAW; (34) Ratify the Convention on the Rights of the Child; Become a party to the Convention on the Rights of the Child; (35) Ratify the Convention on the Rights of Persons with Disabilities as a matter of priority; Become a party to the Convention on the Rights of Persons with Disabilities; (39) Examine the possibility of ratifying the core human rights treaties to which the country is not yet a party and raising its reservations on those which it has ratified; (43) Consider the signing, ratification or accession, as corresponds, of the main international and Inter-American human rights instruments, especially the Convention on the Rights of the Child; (47) Consider lifting reservations to a number of ICCPR articles; (48) Take the necessary measures to consider lifting the United States reservation to article 5, paragraph 6 of the International Covenant on Civil and Political Rights that bans the imposition of the death penalty for crimes committed by persons under 18; (49) Consider the withdrawal of all reservations and declarations that undermine the objective and spirit of the human rights instruments, in particular reservation to article 6 paragraph 5 of the International Covenant on Civil and Political Rights that bans the imposition of the death penalty to those who committed a crime when they were minors; (93) Consider extending a standing invitation to special procedures.

> U.S. position: We support the recommendations asking U.S. to ratify the Convention on the Elimination of All Forms of Discrimination against Women, the Convention on the Rights of Persons with Disabilities, and ILO Convention 111. We also support the recommendations that we ratify the Convention on the Rights of the Child, as we support its goals and intend to review how we could move toward its ratification. We also support recommendation urging deliberative treaty actions, such as that we "consider ratifying" them.

Recommendation 54: Take appropriate action to resolve the obstacles that prevent the full implementation of the *Avena* Judgment of the International Court of Justice and, until this occurs, avoid the execution of the individuals covered in said judgment.

> U.S. position: This recommendation is consistent with the longstanding U.S. policy of supporting the International Court of Justice and taking appropriate action to comply with judgments of the Court. The United States intends to continue to make best efforts to ensure compliance with the *Avena* judgment.

Recommendations the United States Supports in Part:

Recommendations 1-9, 15-19, 23, 24, 25, 27, 37, 38, 40, 41, and 42: (1) Ratify without reservations the following conventions and protocols: CEDAW; the ICESCR; the Convention on the Rights of the Child; the Convention on the Rights of Persons with Disabilities; the International Convention on the Protection of the Rights of All Migrant Workers and Members of Their Families; the International Convention for the Protection of All Persons from Enforced Disappearance; the Statute of the International Criminal Court; those of the ILO; the United Nations Declaration on Indigenous Peoples, and all those from the InterAmerican Human Rights System; (2) Continue the process to ratify CEDAW and adhere to the other human rights fundamental instruments, such as the Statute of Rome of the International Criminal Court, the Convention on the Rights of the Child, the Optional Protocol to the Convention against Torture and the International Convention for the Protection of all Persons against Enforced Disappearance; (3) Ratify, until the next universal periodic review, ICESCR, the Convention on the Rights of the Child, Protocols I and II of the Geneva Conventions of 12 August 1949, ILO Conventions no. 87 (on freedom of association) and no. 98 (on the right to collective bargaining) as well as withdraw the reservation made to article 4 of the International Convention on the Elimination of Racial Discrimination; (4) Ratify ICESCR and its Optional Protocol; the first Optional Protocol to the International Covenant on Civil and Political Rights, CEDAW, the Convention on the Rights of the Child, the Optional Protocol to the Convention against Torture, the Convention on the Rights of Persons with Disabilities, the Convention for the Protection of All Persons from Enforced Disappearance; (5) Continue its efforts to realise universal human rights by a) ratifying CEDAW; b) becoming a party to the United Nations Convention on the Rights of the Child; c) acceding to ICESCR; d) ratifying the United Nations Convention on the Rights of Persons with Disabilities; (6) Ratify the core human rights treaties, particularly the CRC, ICESCR, CEDAW and its Optional Protocol, the OP-CAT and the CMW and the CRPD with its Optional Protocol; (7) Ratify the ICESCR, CEDAW and the Convention of the Rights of the Child at an early stage together with other important human rights conventions; (8) Ratify CEDAW, ICESCR, and CRC in token of its commitment to their implementation worldwide, as well as become party to other international human rights conventions as referred to in the OHCHR report; (9) Ratify all core international instruments on human rights, in particular ICESCR, CEDAW, the Convention on the Rights of the Child; (15) Ratify the Convention on the Rights of the Child and the International Convention on the Protection of the Rights of All Migrant Workers and Members of Their Families; (16) Endeavour to ratify international instruments that USA is not party, in particular among others the CRC, OP-CAT; CEDAW; and Rome Statute of the International Criminal Court; (17) Ratify ICESCR, CEDAW, the Convention on the Rights of the Child; the Convention on the Rights of Persons with Disabilities and other core human rights treaties as soon as possible; (18) Ratify additional human rights treaties such as the ICESCR; the Convention of the Rights of the Child; the International Convention for the Protection of All Persons from Enforced Disappearances and the Convention on Rights of Persons with Disabilities in order to further strengthen their support to the United Nations Human Rights mechanisms; (19) Ratify the pending core international human rights instruments, in particular CRC, ICESCR, and its OP, CEDAW and its OP as well as CRPD, and others, and ensure their due translation into the domestic legislation and review existing ratifications with a view to withdraw all reservations and declarations; (23) Proceed with the ratification of Additional Protocols I and II of the Geneva Conventions of 1949, of the Convention on the Rights of the Child, of CEDAW as well as the Optional Protocol to the Convention against Torture; (24) Ratify at its earliest opportunity other core human rights instruments, particularly, those to which it is already a signatory, namely CEDAW, Convention on the Rights of the Child, ICESCR, and the Convention on the Rights of Persons with Disabilities; (25) Ratify the ICESCR, CEDAW, CRC the CRPD, the Additional Protocol I and II (1977), to the Geneva Conventions, the ICC Statute, as well as the 1st and 2nd Protocol to the Hague Convention 1954; (27) Accede to ICESCR, the CRC and ILO convention No. 111. (37) Ratify the 12 international human rights instruments to which it is not a party; (38) Implement a program of ratification of all international human rights instruments, and then proceed to the incorporation of these in its internal legal system; (40) Accede to international human rights instruments which is not yet acceded to; (41) Continue the process to ratify and implement into domestic law the several international human rights instruments that still wait for this formal acceptance; (42) Accede to the universal core treaties on human rights and those of interAmerican system, in particular the recognition of the jurisdiction of the Inter-American Court on Human Rights.

> U.S. position: We support the parts of these recommendations asking U.S. to ratify those treaties, identified above, of which the Administration is most committed to pursuing ratification. We cannot support the other portions. Nor can we support "without reservations" in Recommendation 1.

Recommendation 29: Ratify the Convention on the Protection of the Rights of All Migrant Workers and Members of their Families and observe international standards in this regard.

> U.S. position: We support the second part ("observe international standards ..."), understanding such standards to mean applicable international human rights law.

Recommendations 44 and 45: (44) Withdraw all reservations and declarations on the international instruments to which it is a party that undermine its obligations or the purpose of the treaty; (45) Withdraw reservations, denunciations, and interpretations of the Covenant on Civil and Political Rights; the International Convention on the Elimination of All Forms of Racial Discrimination and the Convention against Torture, that undermine their compliance, and accept their individual procedures.

> U.S. position: See general comments. We do not believe that any reservations, understandings, and declarations accompanying our ratification of international instruments undermine our obligations, or the treaty's object or purpose. We cannot support the part of Recommendation 45 regarding individual procedures.

Recommendation 52: Ensure the implementation of its obligations under international humanitarian law vis-à-vis Palestinian people.

> U.S. position: See general comments. The U.S. government complies with its international humanitarian law obligations, but we note that international humanitarian law governs conduct in the context of armed conflict, and cannot accept this recommendation's implication that we are in an armed conflict with the Palestinian people.

Annex V: U.S. Treaty Reports 2013-2014

Optional Protocols to the Convention on the Rights of the Child
Submitted January 25, 2010
Presented January 16, 2013

International Covenant on Civil and Political Rights (ICCPR)
Submitted December 30, 2011
Presented March 13-14, 2014

Convention on the Elimination of Racial Discrimination (CERD)
Submitted June 12, 2013
Presented August 13-14, 2014

Convention Against Torture and Other Cruel, Inhuman or Degrading Treatment or Punishment (CAT)
Submitted August 12, 2013
Presented November 12-13, 2014

[End Text]

Source: https://www.upr-info.org/en/review/United-States/Session-22-May-2015/National-report#top

10. COMPILATION PREPARED BY THE OFFICE OF THE UNITED NATIONS HIGH COMMISSIONER FOR HUMAN RIGHTS IN ACCORDANCE WITH THE ANNEX TO HUMAN RIGHTS COUNCIL RESOLUTION, 2015

This document is "a compilation of the information contained in reports of the [U.N.] treaty bodies and special procedures, including observations and comments by the State concerned, in reports of the United Nations High Commissioner for Human Rights, and in other relevant official United Nations documents." It is a record of all the U.S. has done in relation to the various human right bodies of the U.N, both charter-based and treaty-based. It lists all the treaties to which the U.S. is a state-party. It is a gauge of how much a state has invested and is involved in the human rights activity at the U.N. as a member of that organization. The Office of the High Commissioner for Human Rights prepares this document to inform the Human Rights Council of where the SuR stands for purposes of evaluating the SuR in the UPR process. The following Compilation is only about the U.S.

Compilation prepared by the Office of the United Nations High Commissioner for Human Rights in accordance with paragraph 15 (b) of the annex to Human Rights Council resolution 5/1 and paragraph 5 of the annex to Council resolution 16/21

United States of America

The present report is a compilation of the information contained in reports of the treaty bodies and special procedures, including observations and comments by the State concerned, in reports of the United Nations High Commissioner for Human Rights, and in other relevant official United Nations documents. It is presented in a summarized manner owing to word-limit constraints. For the full texts, please refer to the documents referenced. The report does not contain any opinions, views or suggestions on the part of the Office of the United Nations High Commissioner for Human Rights other than those contained in public reports and statements issued by the Office. It follows the general guidelines adopted by the Human Rights Council in its decision 17/119. Information included herein has been systematically referenced in endnotes. The report has been prepared taking into consideration the periodicity of the review, and developments during that period.

...

1. In 2011, the Special Rapporteur on the sale of children, child prostitution and child pornography recommended the ratification of the Convention on the Rights of the Child. The Special Rapporteur on the human right to safe drinking water and sanitation recommended that the United States of America ratify ICESCR and the Optional Protocol thereto, as well as the other core international human rights treaties it had not ratified to date. In 2013, the Committee on the Rights of the Child (CRC) recommended that the United States ratify OP-CRC-IC. In 2014, the Committee against Torture (CAT) and the Committee on the Elimination of Racial Discrimination (CERD) encouraged the United States to consider ratifying ICPPED. CERD also encouraged ratification of ICESCR, CEDAW, CRC, ICRMW and CRPD. In 2014, the Human Rights Committee (HR Committee) recommended that the United States reconsider its position regarding its reservations and declarations on the Covenant with a view to withdrawing them and encouraged it to consider acceding to ICCPR-OP2.

2. In 2014, the Working Group on the issue of human rights and transnational corporations and other business encouraged the Government to take steps to ratify the core ILO conventions. CERD called upon the United States to ratify the ILO Forced Labour Convention (No. 29) and ILO Minimum Age Convention (No. 138).

3. CRC reiterated its recommendation that the United States consider ratifying Additional Protocols I and II to the Geneva Conventions of 12 August 1949, and the Rome Statute of the International Criminal Court.

4. UNESCO encouraged the ratification of the 1960 Convention against Discrimination in Education.

5. UNHCR urged the United States to accede to the 1954 Convention relating to the Status of Stateless Persons, and the 1961 Convention on the Reduction of Statelessness.

B. Constitutional and legislative framework

6. UNESCO encouraged the United States to enshrine the right to education in its Constitution.

C. Institutional and human rights infrastructure and policy measures

7. The HR Committee recommended that the United States strengthen existing mechanisms mandated to monitor the implementation of human rights at federal, state, local and tribal levels, and consider establishing an independent national human rights institution, in accordance with the Paris Principles. CERD and CRC made a similar recommendation.

8. CERD recommended that the United States adopt a national action plan to combat structural racial discrimination.

9. CRC recommended the implementation of a national plan of action to combat the sale of children, child prostitution and child pornography and ensure that the National Strategy for Child Exploitation Prevention and Interdiction and related planning mechanisms cover all offences under OP-CRC-SC. CRC also encouraged those states that had not already done so to set up an office of the Child Advocate or Ombudsman to monitor the fulfilment of rights under OP-CRC-SC.

II. Cooperation with human rights mechanisms

A. Cooperation with treaty bodies

1. Reporting status

Treaty body	Concluding observations included in previous review	Latest report submitted since previous review	Latest concluding observations	Reporting status
CERD	March 2008	2013	August 2014	Combined tenth to twelfth reports due in 2017
HR Committee	July 2006	2013	March 2014	Fifth report due in 2019
CAT	May 2006	2013	November 2014	Sixth report due in 2018
CRC	June 2008 (OP-CRC-AC and OP-CRC-SC)	2010	February 2013	Combined third and fourth reports due in 2016 (OP-CRC-AC and OP-CRC-SC)

2. Responses to specific follow-up requests by treaty bodies

Concluding observations		Subject matter	Submitted in
Treaty body	Due in		
CERD	2015	Excessive use of force by law enforcement officials; — immigrants; and Guantánamo Bay	2015
HR Committee	2015	Accountability for past human rights violations; gun violence; — Guantánamo Bay; and surveillance of communications	2015
CAR	2015	Torture and ill-treatment; remedies and redress for victims	2015

B. Cooperation with special procedures

	Status during previous cycle	Current status
Standing invitation	No	No
Visits undertaken	Migrants (2007)	Sale of children (2010)
	Counter-terrorism (2007)	Violence against women (2011)
	Racism (2008)	Water and sanitation (2011)
	Extrajudicial, summary or arbitrary executions (2008)	Hazardous substances and wastes (2012)
	Mercenaries (2009)	Indigenous peoples (2012)
	Adequate housing (2009)	Transnational corporations and business (2013)
	African descent (2010)	
Visits agreed to in principle	Arbitrary detention	Arbitrary detention
	Sale of children	Torture
		Food
		Independence of judges and lawyers
		Discrimination against women
Visits requested	Water and sanitation	Foreign debt
	Violence against women	African descent
		Hazardous substances and wastes
Responses to letters of allegation and urgent appeals	In the period under review, 95 communications were sent. The Government replied to 56 communications.	
Follow-up reports and missions	Extrajudicial, summary or arbitrary executions; counter-terrorism	

10. The Special Rapporteur on torture and other cruel, inhuman or degrading treatment or punishment noted the invitation extended, but requested that the Government reconsider its terms, to enable him to visit every part of the detention facility at Guantánamo Bay and to conduct unmonitored interviews.

C. Cooperation with the Office of the United Nations High Commissioner for Human Rights

11. The United States made annual financial contributions to OHCHR activities, including the United Nations Voluntary Fund for Victims of Torture.

III. Implementation of international human rights obligations, taking into account applicable international humanitarian law

A. Equality and non-discrimination

In 2014, the United Nations High Commissioner for Human Rights urged the United States authorities to conduct in-depth examinations into how race-related issues were affecting law enforcement and the administration of justice, both at the federal and state levels. In 2013, special procedures mandate-holders called upon the Government to examine laws that could have a discriminatory impact on African Americans, and to ensure that such laws were in compliance with the country's international legal obligations.

12. CERD reiterated its concern that the definition of racial discrimination used in federal and state legislation and in court practice was not in line with the Convention. It called upon the United States to, inter alia, prohibit racial discrimination in all its forms and broaden the protection afforded by law.

13. CERD reiterated its concern at the lack of prohibition of racist hate speech and the underreporting of hate crimes.

14. The HR Committee and CERD remained concerned about the practice of racial profiling and surveillance by law enforcement officials targeting certain ethnic minorities. The HR Committee and CERD urged the State to combat racial profiling, inter alia by expanding protection against profiling on the basis of religion, religious appearance or national origin.

15. The Special Rapporteur on violence against women stated that multiple forms of discrimination against certain groups of women made them more vulnerable and exacerbated the negative consequences that violence had upon them. The implementation of policies and programmes must address the structural challenges which were often both the causes and consequences of violence against women.

B. Right to life, liberty and security of the person

17. While welcoming the increasing number of states that had abolished the death penalty, the HR Committee remained concerned about the continuing use of the death penalty and about racial disparities in its imposition. The Committee recommended that the United States consider establishing a moratorium at the federal level and engage with retentionist states with a view to achieving a nationwide moratorium. CAT made a similar recommendation. The HR Committee also recommended ensuring that retentionist states provide adequate compensation for persons who were wrongfully convicted. The United States voted against the draft General Assembly resolution on a moratorium on the use of the death penalty in 2014.

18. In 2012, the Special Rapporteur on extrajudicial, summary or arbitrary executions noted that the Government had supported the UPR recommendation to determine the factors in the racial disparity in the application of the death penalty and to prepare strategies aimed at ending discriminatory practices, indicating that further statistical analysis and studies on sentencing disparities were highly anticipated.

19. The Special Rapporteur called on the federal and state administrations to ensure that the death penalty was not imposed on the mentally ill. In 2014, two special procedures mandate holders stated that imposing capital punishment on individuals suffering from psychosocial disabilities was a violation of death penalty safeguards. The Secretary General stated that the use of untested means of execution had demonstrably increased the risk of executions amounting to cruel and unusual punishment.

20. In 2014, the United Nations High Commissioner for Human Rights expressed concern at the disproportionate number of young African Americans who had died in encounters with police officers, or who were in prisons and on death row. CERD reiterated its concern at the brutality and excessive use of force by law enforcement officials against members of racial and ethnic minorities, which had a disproportionate impact on African Americans and undocumented migrants crossing the United States-Mexico border. CAT expressed similar concerns.

21. CERD was concerned at the large number of gun-related deaths and injuries, which disproportionately affected members of racial and ethnic minorities, particularly African Americans. It urged the United States to reduce gun violence by, inter alia, adopting legislation expanding background checks for all private firearms transfers and reviewing the "stand your ground" laws. The HR Committee and the Special Rapporteur on violence against women, its causes and consequences made similar recommendations.

22. The HR Committee was concerned about the use of lethal force by Customs and Border Protection (CBP) officers and urged the State to ensure that the new CBP directive on the use of deadly force was enforced.

23. The Special Rapporteur on extrajudicial, summary or arbitrary executions reiterated his recommendation that the Government systematically track and publicly disclose information on civilian losses resulting from its international operations. CRC urged the State to prevent indiscriminate use of force, and ensure that children and families who were victims of attacks received compensation.

24. The Special Rapporteur reiterated his recommendations that the Government specify the basis for decisions to kill, rather than capture, "human targets" in the context of an armed conflict, and whether the State in which the killing took place had given consent. It should also specify procedural safeguards in place to ensure in advance that targeted killings complied with international law.

25. CAT regretted that a specific offence of torture had not yet been introduced and reiterated its recommendation that torture be criminalized at the federal level, and that penalties be commensurate with the gravity of that crime. The HR Committee was concerned about the lack of comprehensive legislation criminalizing all forms of torture. CAT reiterated its view that the United States should take effective measures to prevent acts of torture, not only in its sovereign territory but also in any territory under its jurisdiction.

26. In 2013, the Special Rapporteur on torture and other cruel, inhuman or degrading treatment or punishment urged the Government to ensure that solitary confinement was only imposed, if at all, in very exceptional circumstances, and indicated that keeping a person in solitary confinement for more than four decades clearly amounted to torture. CAT and the HR Committee were concerned about the practice of prolonged solitary confinement, and recommended, inter alia, that solitary confinement regimes be banned.

27. CAT urged the United States to ensure that no one was held in secret detention under its de facto effective control and reiterated that such detention constituted per se a violation of the Convention.

28. The Special Rapporteur on torture noted that, allegedly, around half of the detainees who remained indefinitely in detention at Guantánamo Bay had been cleared for transfer and resettlement; others had been designated for further indefinite detention. He also noted that recommendations made during the UPR called on the authorities to ensure that all remaining detainees be tried without delay or released. Several special procedures mandate holders stated that, even in extraordinary circumstances, when the indefinite detention of individuals, most of whom had not been charged, went beyond a minimally reasonable period of time, that constituted a flagrant violation of international human rights law and in itself constituted a form of cruel, inhuman and degrading treatment. The High Commissioner for Human Rights made similar remarks. In 2014, the Working Group on Arbitrary Detention considered that a two-year delay in allowing an individual to challenge his detention was a grave violation, further aggravated by his continued detention.

29. CAT recommended that the State party prevent and combat violence in prisons and places of detention. In 2011, the Special Rapporteur on violence against women took note of the general over-incarceration of women, commonly for non-violent crimes, and recommended considering alternatives to incarceration.

30. The HR Committee was concerned that domestic violence continued to be prevalent. CERD had similar concerns and called upon the United States to prevent and combat violence against women, particularly against American Indian and Alaska Native women, and provide them with access to justice and effective remedies. The Special Rapporteur on violence against women recommended, inter alia, that the State address the disproportionate impact that violence had on poor, minority and immigrant women; and re-evaluate mechanisms at federal, state, local and tribal levels for protecting victims and punishing offenders. CAT urged the State to eradicate sexual violence in the military. The Special Rapporteur on violence against women made similar recommendations.

31. The HR Committee urged the State to combat trafficking in persons by, inter alia, investigating allegations of trafficking and providing remedies to victims. CRC was concerned that the State was applying a very narrow definition of what constituted human trafficking and who was eligible for relief.

32. CRC was deeply concerned that protection services for sexually exploited children were severely lacking. It urged the United States to establish the specialist services required for children who had been trafficked, sold for sexual or economic exploitation or otherwise been victims of crimes under OP-CRC-SC. CRC recommended the prohibition of child prostitution and the sale of children at federal and state level, and the decriminalization of the involvement of children in prostitution. The Special Rapporteur on the sale of children made a similar recommendation.

33. The HR Committee was concerned about corporal punishment of children in schools, penal institutions, the home and all forms of child care at federal, state and local levels. The United States should, inter alia, put an end to corporal punishment in all settings and encourage non-violent forms of discipline as alternatives to corporal punishment.

34. CRC urged the State to prevent the sale of children for the purpose of child labour by, inter alia, combating the worst forms of child labour, especially in the agricultural sector.

35. CRC recommended that the United States raise the age of voluntary recruitment into the armed forces to 18 years, and enact a prohibition on arms exports to countries where children could be recruited into armed conflict.

C. Administration of justice, including impunity and the rule of law

36. The HR Committee urged the State to strengthen safeguards against wrongful sentencing to death and to ensure that retentionist states provided adequate compensation for persons who were wrongfully convicted; amend regulations and policies which had a racially disparate impact and ensure the retroactive application of the Fair Sentencing Act. CERD had similar concerns.

37. CAT recommended that the United States ensure that all instances of police brutality and excessive use of force by law enforcement officers were investigated promptly, effectively and impartially by an independent mechanism, with no institutional or hierarchical connection between the investigators and the alleged perpetrators; and provide effective remedies and rehabilitation to the victims.

38. The HR Committee recommended that the United States enact legislation to explicitly prohibit torture, ensure that the law provided for penalties commensurate with the gravity of such acts, and ensure the availability of compensation to victims of torture. CAT recommended that the United States ensure that appropriate rehabilitation programmes, including medical and psychological assistance, were provided to all victims of torture and ill-treatment; and that all relevant staff, including medical personnel, were trained to identify cases of torture in accordance with the Manual on the Effective Investigation and Documentation of Torture and Other Cruel, Inhuman or Degrading Treatment or Punishment (the Istanbul Protocol).

39. The Special Rapporteur on violence against women recommended the enactment of laws criminalizing sexual abuse and other misconduct towards prisoners, covering not only guards and correctional officers, but also all individuals who worked in prisons, including volunteers and government contractors, and strengthening institutional oversight to prevent rape and sexual abuse in prisons.

40. CERD reiterated its concern at the denial of access to justice, and adequate reparation or satisfaction for damages suffered, to indigenous women. It urged the United States to guarantee the right to access justice and effective remedies to all indigenous women who were victims of violence. CERD also reiterated its recommendation that the United States ensure that public legal aid systems were adequately funded and supervised.

41. In 2012 and 2013, the High Commissioner for Human Rights expressed disappointment at the failure to close the Guantánamo facility, and urged the Government to close it promptly. The HR Committee and several special procedures made similar remarks and calls. HR Committee also recommended that the system of administrative detention without charge or trial be ended and that any criminal cases against detainees held in Guantánamo and in Afghanistan be dealt with through the criminal justice system rather than military commissions. CAT and CERD had similar concerns.

42. HR Committee recommended that cases of unlawful killing, torture or other ill-treatment, unlawful detention or enforced disappearance during international operations be investigated, that perpetrators be prosecuted and that victims

be provided with remedies. The Special Rapporteur on extrajudicial, summary or arbitrary executions made similar remarks.

43. In 2014, the High Commissioner for Human Rights, the Special Rapporteur on the promotion and protection of human rights while countering terrorism and the Special Rapporteur on torture welcomed the release of the report of the United States Senate Select Committee on Intelligence on CIA interrogation practices. The Special Rapporteur on Torture noted that the release of the report contributed to fulfilling the obligations of the United States with respect to the truth. The Special Rapporteur on counter-terrorism stated that the individuals responsible for the criminal conspiracy revealed in the report must be brought to justice and face criminal penalties commensurate with the gravity of their crimes.

44. CRC urged the State party to investigate cases of torture and/or ill-treatment of detained children, and ensure that perpetrators were brought to justice and sanctioned with penalties commensurate with their crimes.

45. CERD was concerned at racial disparities in the juvenile justice system. It called upon the United States to address racial disparities in the application of disciplinary measures and ensure that juveniles were not transferred to adult courts and were separated from adults during pretrial detention and after sentencing. CERD reiterated its recommendation to abolish life imprisonment without parole for those under 18 at the time of the crime, and to commute the sentences of those currently serving such sentences. The HR Committee, CAT and CRC made similar recommendations.

46. CRC noted with concern that the United States continued to arrest and detain children in Department of Defense custody. The Committee urged the State to, inter alia, ensure that children under the age of 18 were handled by the juvenile justice system in all circumstances; grant UNICEF and other humanitarian agencies immediate and unimpeded access to detained children, and ensure that children in detention had access to free legal advisory assistance; ensure that no children were transferred to Afghan custody if there were substantial grounds for believing that there was a danger of their being subjected to torture and ill-treatment; and ensure that children detained in Department of Defense custody had access to adequate recovery and reintegration measures.

D. Right to privacy and family life

47. HR Committee was concerned about surveillance of communications in the interests of protecting national security and recommended, inter alia, that the State party ensure that any interference with the right to privacy complied with the principles of legality, proportionality and necessity, regardless of the nationality or location of the individuals whose communications were under direct surveillance. The Committee also recommended that the United States ensure that any interference with the right to privacy, family, home or correspondence be authorized by laws that, inter alia, specified in detail the precise circumstances in which any such interference might be permitted, the procedures for authorization, and the limit on the duration of surveillance; and provide for effective safeguards against abuse.

48. CERD remained concerned at the previous and continued removal of indigenous children from their families and communities through the United States child welfare system. It called upon the United States to enforce the Indian Child Welfare Act of 1978, to halt the removal of indigenous children from their families and communities.

E. Right to participate in public and political life

49. UNESCO stated that the United States should review its systems for protection of the confidentiality of journalists' sources.

50. CERD was concerned at the obstacles faced by individuals belonging to racial and ethnic minorities and indigenous peoples to effectively exercise their right to vote. It recommended that the State, inter alia; enforce federal voting rights law throughout the State; ensure that indigenous peoples could effectively exercise their right to vote; and ensure that all states reinstated voting rights for persons convicted of a felony who had completed their sentences.

F. Right to work and to just and favourable conditions of work

51. The Working Group on transnational corporations and other business called on the Government to ensure that all workers were able to exercise their rights in accordance with the ILO Declaration on Fundamental Principles and Rights at Work.

52. CERD called upon the United States to review its laws to protect migrant workers from exploitative working conditions and raise the minimum age for hazardous work in agriculture in line with international labour standards. The HR Committee and CRC made similar calls.

53. CRC was concerned at the dearth of legislation regarding child labour and child economic exploitation in the agricultural sector. It urged the United States to adopt a coordinated strategy for combating the worst forms of child labour, especially in the agricultural sector; and review laws at federal and state level to ensure that the minimum age of 16 years, with or without parental consent, also applied to small farms. The Working Group on transnational corporations and other business recommended that the rights of children be protected in the context of agricultural business activities.

G. Right to social security and to an adequate standard of living

54. While appreciating the steps taken to address homelessness, the HR Committee was concerned about the criminalization of people living on the street and of homeless people, and urged the State to, inter alia, abolish the related laws. CERD had similar concerns.

55. While acknowledging the positive steps taken by the State to address discrimination in access to housing, CERD remained concerned at the degree of racial segregation and poverty in neighbourhoods characterized by substandard conditions and services. It urged the State to investigate all cases of discriminatory practices and provide remedies.

56. In 2014, special procedures mandate-holders expressed concerns about household water disconnection in Detroit. In 2011, the Special Rapporteur on water and sanitation stated that the United States needed to develop a national water policy and make more efforts to reach the poorest segments of the population. The Special Rapporteur recommended the adoption of a comprehensive federal law on water and sanitation guaranteeing the rights to safe water and sanitation without discrimination.

H. Right to health

57. The HR Committee expressed concern about the exclusion of millions of undocumented immigrants and their children from coverage under the Affordable Care Act, and the limited coverage of undocumented immigrants and immigrants under Medicare and Children's Health Insurance. The HR Committee recommended facilitation of access to health care under the Affordable Care Act by undocumented immigrants, and immigrants and their families residing lawfully in the States for less than five years. CERD raised similar concerns.

58. The HR Committee said that the State should ensure that non-consensual use of psychiatric medication, electroshock and other restrictive and coercive practices was generally prohibited, and promote psychiatric care aimed at preserving the dignity of patients.

I. Right to education

59. While welcoming the formation of the Equity and Excellence Commission in 2011, CERD remained concerned that students from racial and ethnic minorities continued to attend segregated schools. CERD recommended, inter alia, the adoption of a plan to address racial segregation in schools and neighbourhoods and the promotion of racially integrated learning environments.

60. CRC was concerned that children detained in the United States detention facilities in Afghanistan had been almost totally deprived of access to education. It urged the State to provide all detained children under the age of 18 with access to education.

J. Minorities and indigenous peoples

61. In 2012, the Special Rapporteur on indigenous peoples noted that securing the rights of indigenous peoples to their lands was of central importance to their socioeconomic development, self-determination and cultural integrity. Despite positive aspects of existing legislation, new measures were needed to advance reconciliation with indigenous peoples and to provide redress for persistent deep-seated problems. Federal authorities should identify, develop and implement such measures in full consultation and coordination with indigenous peoples. The Special Rapporteur called for measures of reconciliation and redress, including initiatives to address outstanding claims regarding treaty violations or non-consensual takings of traditional lands and issues of self-governance, environmental degradation, language restoration and federal recognition.

62. The HR Committee welcomed the support for the United Nations Declaration on the Rights of Indigenous Peoples. It was however concerned about the insufficiency of consultation with indigenous peoples on matters of interest to their communities. The United States should protect the sacred areas of indigenous peoples against desecration, contamination and destruction and ensure that consultations were held with the indigenous communities that might be adversely affected by the State's development projects and exploitation of natural resources. CERD raised similar concerns through its early warning and urgent action procedure.

63. The Special Rapporteur on indigenous peoples noted the support of the United States for the United Nations Declaration on the Rights of Indigenous Peoples, and stated that the federal courts should interpret, or reinterpret, relevant doctrine, treaties and statutes in the light of the Declaration, in regard both to the nature of indigenous peoples' rights and the nature of federal power.

K. Migrants, refugees and asylum seekers

64. CAT was concerned at the use, under certain circumstances, of a mandatory detention system to hold asylum seekers and immigrants, on arrival, in prison-like detention facilities. The HR Committee recommended that policies of mandatory detention and deportation of certain categories of immigrants be reviewed. UNHCR urged the United States to, inter alia, utilize detention as a means of last resort for asylum-seekers.

65. The Special Rapporteur on violence against women recommended that the root causes of the increasing number of immigrant women in prisons and detention facilities be addressed.

66. CRC welcomed the Deferred Action for Childhood Arrivals program, under which unaccompanied children were provided with a temporary permit to remain in the United States. It recommended that the State party ensure, inter alia, that foreign immigrant children victims of offences covered by OP-CRC-SC were not returned or deported; that they were provided with all the necessary services for their recovery; and that every unaccompanied child was appointed an independent child advocate and was represented in all immigration court proceedings by a qualified attorney. CRC also recommended that the United States ensure that child labour legislation specifically focused on unaccompanied minor foreign nationals who had been brought to or who had arrived in the country for purposes amounting to economic exploitation. UNHCR urged the United States to, inter alia, refrain from using the detention of children for deterrence purposes and improve the repatriation procedures to ensure that returns were carried out in a safe and dignified manner.

67. CERD was concerned at the increased use of racial profiling to determine immigration status and to enforce immigration laws, and called upon the United States to, inter alia, guarantee access to legal representation in all immigration-related matters.

68. The Special Rapporteur on summary executions noted progress in tracking deaths of immigration detainees but indicated that the Government should also ensure accountability.

L. Environmental issues

69. CERD was concerned that individuals belonging to racial and ethnic minorities and indigenous peoples continued to be affected by the negative health impact of pollution caused by the extractive and manufacturing industries. It called upon the United States to ensure, inter alia, that federal legislation prohibiting environmental pollution was enforced, and any remaining radioactive and toxic waste cleaned up urgently. CERD also called upon the United States to prevent

activities of transnational corporations registered in the State which could have adverse effects on the enjoyment of human rights by local populations in other countries.

70. The Special Rapporteur on the implications for human rights of the environmentally sound management and disposal of hazardous substances and wastes recommended that the United States continue to assist the Marshall Islands to protect the environment and to secure hazardous sites, and guarantee the right to effective remedy through adequate compensation for past and future claims, and other forms of reparation.

M. Human rights and counter-terrorism

71. The HR Committee was concerned about the practice of targeted killings in extraterritorial counter-terrorism operations using unmanned aerial vehicles, and the lack of accountability for the resulting loss of life. It urged the United States to disclose the criteria for drone strikes, including the legal basis for specific attacks; to take all feasible measures to protect civilians in specific drone attacks and to track and assess civilian casualties, and all necessary precautionary measures in order to avoid such casualties; and provide victims or their families with an effective remedy where there had been a violation, including adequate compensation.

72. CRC recommended that a discretionary exemption from the "terrorist activity" bar be instituted to allow the favourable consideration of applications for asylum of former child soldiers, or refugee protection for them.

Unless indicated otherwise, the status of ratification of instruments listed in the table may be found on the official website of the United Nations Treaty Collection database, Office of Legal Affairs of the United Nations Secretariat, http://treaties.un.org/. Please also refer to the United Nations compilation on the United States of America from the previous cycle (A/HRC/WG.6/9/USA/2).

The following abbreviations are used in UPR documents:

ICERD	International Convention on the Elimination of All Forms of Racial Discrimination;
ICESCR	International Covenant on Economic, Social and Cultural Rights;
OP-ICESCR	Optional Protocol to ICESCR;
ICCPR	International Covenant on Civil and Political Rights;
ICCPR-OP 1	Optional Protocol to ICCPR;
ICCPR-OP 2	Second Optional Protocol to ICCPR, aiming at the abolition of the death penalty;
CEDAW	Convention on the Elimination of All Forms of Discrimination against Women;
OP-CEDAW	Optional Protocol to CEDAW;
CAT	Convention against Torture and Other Cruel, Inhuman or Degrading Treatment or Punishment;
OP-CAT	Optional Protocol to CAT;
CRC	Convention on the Rights of the Child;
OP-CRC-AC	Optional Protocol to CRC on the involvement of children in armed conflict;
OP-CRC-SC	Optional Protocol to CRC on the sale of children, child prostitution and child pornography;
OP-CRC-IC	Optional Protocol to CRC on a communications procedure;
ICRMW	International Convention on the Protection of the Rights of All Migrant Workers and Members of Their Families;
CRPD	Convention on the Rights of Persons with Disabilities;
OP-CRPD	Optional Protocol to CRPD;
ICPPED	International Convention for the Protection of All Persons from Enforced Disappearance.

[End Text]

Source: https://documents-dds-ny.un.org/doc/UNDOC/GEN/G15/039/92/PDF/G1503992.pdf; https://www.upr-info.org/sites/default/files/document/united_states/session_22_-_mai_2015/a_hrc_wg.6_22_usa_2_e.pdf

❧❦❧❦❧❦❧❦❧

II. REPORT OF THE WORKING GROUP ON THE UNIVERSAL PERIODIC REVIEW, 2015

This Document is the Outcome Report Document of the 2015 Universal Periodic Review of the U.S. It includes the recommendations submitted by the other countries. This is how the international community, in the context of the U.N. Human Rights Council, judges the U.S. record on compliance with international human rights norms which are applicable to the U.S. The Report was prepared by the Troika (three) of states assigned to this review: Botswana, the Netherlands and Saudi Arabia. The U.S. appeared for its Review and its oral presentation was given by State Department representatives; this was followed by interactive dialogue, and recommendations by the states who chose to do so. The Report is submitted to the Council for formal adoption. The next Review will be in 5 years, May 2020.

Report of the Working Group on the Universal Periodic Review

Introduction

1. The Working Group on the Universal Periodic Review, established in accordance with Human Rights Council resolution 5/1, held its twenty-second session from 4 to 15 May 2015. The review of the United States of America was held at the 11th meeting, on 11 May 2015. The delegation of the United States was headed by the United States Ambassador to the Human Rights Council, Keith Harper, and the Acting Legal Adviser, Department of State, Mary McLeod. At its 17th meeting, held on 15 May 2015, the Working Group adopted the report on the United States.

2. On 13 January 2015, the Human Rights Council selected the following group of rapporteurs (troika) to facilitate the review of the United States: Botswana, the Netherlands and Saudi Arabia.

3. In accordance with paragraph 15 of the annex to Human Rights Council resolution 5/1 and paragraph 5 of the annex to Council resolution 16/21, the following documents were issued for the review of the United States:

(a) A national report (A/HRC/WG.6/22/USA/1);

(b) A compilation prepared by the Office of the United Nations High Commissioner for Human Rights (OHCHR) (A/HRC/WG.6/22/USA/2);

(c) A summary prepared by OHCHR (A/HRC/WG.6/22/USA/3).

4. A list of questions prepared in advance by Azerbaijan, Belgium, China, Cuba, the Czech Republic, Denmark, Germany, Mexico, the Netherlands, Norway, Slovenia, Spain, Sweden, Switzerland and the United Kingdom of Great Britain and Northern Ireland was transmitted to the United States through the troika. These questions are available on the extranet of the Working Group.

I. Summary of the proceedings of the review process

A. Presentation by the State under review

5. The co-head of the United States delegation, Keith Harper, noted the importance of the universal periodic review mechanism and expressed pride in the record of the United States and its acknowledgement of its imperfections. He welcomed civil society's presence and engagement.

6. He highlighted the announcement of support of the United States for the United Nations Declaration on the Rights of Indigenous Peoples, as further explained in its statement of support and its enactment of laws to empower tribal governments to provide for public safety and to protect Native American women against domestic violence and sexual assault.

7. The other co-head of the United States delegation, Mary McLeod, noted that the United States had carefully considered the recommendations accepted from fellow States Members of the United Nations during its first universal periodic review and had taken many steps to implement them.

8. Ms. McLeod provided an outline of the democratic system in the United States, which allows for scrutiny, advocacy and debate to fuel progress and reform. She outlined federal efforts to end violence and discrimination against lesbian, gay, bisexual and transgender individuals, to prosecute crimes motivated by bias, to prohibit discrimination in federal employment and the military and to support efforts to ban the use of conversion therapy for minors. Progress had also been made at the state level.

9. She noted that, although there were many successes to report, there remained much work to be done, including in the light of the public release of the executive summary of the Senate Select Committee on Intelligence report on the former Central Intelligence Agency detention and interrogation programme.

10. She noted that, as President Obama had acknowledged, the United States had crossed a line and not lived up to its own values, and that it had taken responsibility for that. She added that the United States had since taken steps to clarify that the legal prohibition on torture applies everywhere and in all circumstances and to ensure that the United States never resorts to use of those harsh interrogation techniques again.

11. James Cadogan of the United States Department of Justice provided an overview of efforts to combat discrimination in the United States through laws like the Civil Rights Act of 1964 and the Voting Rights Act of 1965.

12. He noted that the recent tragic police-involved shootings or deaths of young African American men had renewed a longstanding and critical debate about the even-handed administration of justice.

13. The Department of Justice has prosecuted more than 400 law enforcement officials for excessive use of force in the past six years and has opened more than 20 investigations into discriminatory policing practices in various cities and states. A presidential task force has also been convened on the issue.

14. Work continues to combat discrimination in other areas, including in protecting an equal right to vote. The Department of Justice has recently brought challenges to racially discriminatory voting laws in North Carolina and Texas.

B. Interactive dialogue and responses by the State under review

15. During the interactive dialogue, 117 delegations made statements. The recommendations made during the dialogue can be found in section II of the present report. All written statements of the delegations, to be checked against delivery on the United Nations Webcast archives,5 are posted on the extranet of the Human Rights Council, when available.6

16. Kazakhstan made a statement.

17. Kenya was concerned with weak human rights monitoring mechanisms and digital data protection.

18. Latvia noted that the Convention on the Elimination of All forms of Discrimination against Women had been designated as a priority for ratification.

19. Lebanon commended the commitment of the United States to the principles of human rights established in constitutional law.

20. Libya commended the progress that had been achieved since the first universal periodic review report.

21. Liechtenstein took positive note of the efforts of the United States to protect national security and civil liberties.

22. Lithuania appreciated the consultation process of the Government of the United States with civil society.

23. Luxembourg made a statement.

24. Malaysia noted the findings of the Senate Intelligence Committee report on torture.

25. Mali welcomed the commitment of the United States to the implementation of international instruments obligations.

26. Mauritania encouraged the United States to strengthen its cooperation with the human rights mechanisms.

27. Mauritius commended the United States for its commitment in reviewing domestic laws and institutions.

28. Mexico acknowledged efforts for training of law enforcement officers on the prohibition of discrimination.

29. Montenegro noted the concerns of the Human Rights Committee about racial disparities in the imposition of the death penalty.

30. Morocco noted the efforts of the United States regarding the training of law enforcement officials to avoid racial profiling.

31. Namibia noted that three states had repealed capital punishment laws since the previous review cycle.

32. Nepal noted that the United States had pursued measures to combat racial and religious discrimination and hate crimes.

33. The Netherlands noted that no specific steps had been taken to ratify the Convention on the Elimination of All forms of Discrimination against Women.

34. New Zealand expressed concerns at the lack of full treaty-level protection for a number of vulnerable groups.

35. Nicaragua made a statement.

36. The Niger appreciated the support of the United States to OHCHR activities and its cooperation with human rights mechanisms.

37. Nigeria welcomed initiatives at fostering relations between law enforcement officers and communities.

38. Norway was concerned at the application of the death penalty.

39. Pakistan made a statement.

40. Panama appreciated the cooperation programme of the United States to eradicate all forms of child labour in Panama.

41. Paraguay acknowledged the invitation to the Special Rapporteur on torture and other cruel, inhuman or degrading treatment or punishment to visit Guantánamo, expecting that he could fulfil his mandate.

42. Peru highlighted the achievements on education, particularly the initiative entitled "Generation Indigenous."

43. The Philippines appreciated the increasing number of criminal convictions of human traffickers.

44. Poland welcomed efforts of the United States to comply with the recommendations made during the first review cycle.

45. Portugal was concerned at recent cases where executions by lethal injections had inflicted cruel punishment.

46. The Republic of Korea praised efforts to raise public awareness of human rights.

47. The Republic of Moldova welcomed measures aimed at greater protection for juvenile offenders.

48. The Czech Republic appreciated the consultations preceding the national report.

49. The Russian Federation regretted that the United States had paid insufficient attention to the recommendations made during the first review cycle.

50. Rwanda welcomed the increasing number of states that had abolished the death penalty.

51. Senegal noted the support of the United States to African countries affected by Ebola.

52. Serbia praised initiatives to expand access to health care.

53. Sierra Leone was concerned at protracted detentions and racial discrimination.

54. Singapore acknowledged efforts of the United States to comply with the recommendations made during the first review cycle.

55. Slovakia noted a moratorium on the death penalty on an ad hoc basis by the Federal Government.

56. Slovenia noted challenges, particularly non-discrimination, the prohibition of torture and mass surveillance.

57. The United States noted its view that torture and cruel, inhuman and degrading treatment and punishment are absolutely prohibited at all times and in all places under both international law and United States domestic law.

58. President Obama issued an executive order ending the Central Intelligence Agency's detention and interrogation programme and directing humane treatment of individuals detained in armed conflict. The United States has investigated allegations of torture or mistreatment since 11 September 2001.

59. In combating terrorism, the United States remains firmly committed to upholding its international obligations.

60. The United States is party to a number of human rights treaties and continues to explore whether and how to ratify additional treaties, including the Convention on the Rights of Persons with Disabilities and the Convention on the Elimination of All forms of Discrimination against Women.

61. While it is not at this time considering becoming a party to the Rome Statute of the International Criminal Court, the United States does engage with States parties on issues of concern, consistent with the requirements of United States law.

62. United States intelligence activities are authorized pursuant to a framework based on the rule of law, whereby statutes and other authorities established through democratic institutions govern its activities. United States intelligence collection programmes and activities are subject to stringent and multilayered oversight mechanisms.

63. Although the United States has federal laws and laws in the majority of states authorizing the death penalty for the most serious crimes that are within constitutional limits and consistent with its international obligations, defendants eligible for the death penalty receive heightened procedural safeguards over and above those enjoyed by all criminal defendants.

64. The recent trend in the United States is away from the use of capital punishment. No defendant found by a court to have significant intellectual and adaptive disabilities may be subject to capital punishment, either at the state or federal levels.

65. The United States seeks to prevent excessive uses of force and racial profiling in law enforcement by participating in the training of federal, state and local law enforcement officers across the country.

66. In December, the United States announced an updated policy applicable to all law enforcement activity under federal supervision, instructing that officers may not consider race or a number of other factors to any degree when making routine or spontaneous law enforcement decisions, unless those characteristics apply to a suspect's description.

67. The United States makes strong efforts to combat racial discrimination in education, strongly supporting diversity at all levels.

68. The United States seeks to address hate crimes, including through the ShepardByrd Hate Crimes Prevention Act, which greatly expanded the Federal Government's ability to prosecute bias-motivated violence.

69. There has been a trend away from corporal punishment in United States schools and parenting programmes, and home visitation providers stress positive discipline with parents, guiding them away from physical or violent punishment.

70. The United States has a strong commitment to preventing domestic violence, dating violence, sexual assault and stalking; assisting those who are survivors; and holding accountable those who commit such crimes. The Violence Against Women Act is designed to increase the availability of services for victims of violence and improve the criminal justice response.

71. South Africa encouraged the United States to implement the recommendations made during the first review cycle.

72. Spain welcomed efforts to close the Guantánamo military prison and welcomed the "Affordable Medical Care" Act.

73. The Sudan urged the Government to eliminate all forms of discrimination in all areas.

74. Sweden made a statement.

75. Switzerland noted the Senate report on methods of interrogation in the context of the fight against terrorism.

76. Thailand expressed concern at racial profiling by local law enforcement and immigration authorities.

77. The Former Yugoslav Republic of Macedonia welcomed initiatives to promote human rights at international forums.

78. Timor-Leste commended the Government for its support for the United Nations Declaration on the Rights of Indigenous Peoples.

79. Togo welcomed the law on access to health care and efforts to guarantee equal opportunities in education.

80. Trinidad and Tobago noted the need to rid the society of racial discrimination.

81. Tunisia noticed the efforts made in combating racism and hate crimes.

82. Turkey expressed concerns about poor protection services for sexually exploited children.

83. Ukraine noted the commitment to improving implementation of human rights obligations and adherence to the universal periodic review.

84. The United Kingdom of Great Britain and Northern Ireland urged closing the Guantánamo Bay detention facility.

85. Uruguay praised efforts to combat discrimination and a decline in the application of the death penalty in states.

86. Brazil referred to lesbian, gay, bisexual and transgender rights, immigration and border security and interferences to privacy.

87. Viet Nam highlighted the need to ratify the remaining core international human rights treaties.

88. Albania commended measures to counter intolerance, violence and discrimination.

89. Algeria commended efforts undertaken to eliminate racial discrimination.

90. Angola noted executive actions to improve the regulation of immigration.

91. Argentina expressed concern that the application of the death penalty was characterized by discrimination and arbitrariness.

92. Armenia appreciated the commitment of the United States to prevention of the crime of genocide.

93. Australia welcomed the efforts of the United States to better protect the rights of Native Americans.

94. Austria expressed concern that individuals continued to serve life sentences without parole for crimes committed when they were under 18 years of age.

95. Azerbaijan noted the concerns expressed by treaty bodies about torture and ill-treatment in detention.

96. Bangladesh noted concerns about racial profiling against religious minorities.

97. Belgium noted reports on health hazards for children working in farms.

98. Benin noted the progress made in wages equality.

99. Bosnia and Herzegovina noted steps concerning indigenous peoples and asked for the closure of the Guantánamo facility.

100. Botswana noted violence against women and encouraged addressing racial discrimination.

101. The Bolivian Republic of Venezuela made a statement.

102. Bulgaria noted efforts against racial discrimination.

103. Burkina Faso urged for improvement concerning the rights of women, children and migrants.

104. Cabo Verde noted the lack of progress regarding the ratification of treaties.

105. Canada commended prosecution against forced labour and human trafficking.

106. The United States said that it is committed to the effective implementation of its human rights obligations and welcomes input on ways to improve. Although it does not have a single national human rights institution, it has multiple complementary protections and mechanisms to reinforce respect for human rights, including through independent judiciaries at the federal and state levels and numerous state and local human rights institutions.

107. Recently, the Federal Government has increased engagement with state, local, tribal and territorial governments on United States human rights obligations. For example, the state of Illinois and the Federal Government have worked together to protect Illinois residents from discrimination by mortgage lenders and other forms of financial exploitation.

108. Additionally, states and cities of the United States often lead efforts to enforce antidiscrimination laws and implement important reforms. The city of Chicago's significant steps to respond to and prevent incidents of police misconduct include creating a reparations fund and formally apologizing to the victims of certain police violence. Chicago aims to improve relations among police and residents through training and a renewed commitment to community policing.

109. The United States has successfully challenged initiatives by states to criminalize mere undocumented presence in the country.

110. Non-citizens facing removal from the United States are afforded significant procedural protections and those detained can challenge immigration detention in court.

111. The United States is committed to accountability for Homeland Security personnel involved in any wrongdoing or misconduct, including excessive use of force.

112. For individuals detained pending removal proceedings and during the period reasonably necessary to remove them, the United States ensures that they are treated humanely and in a manner consistent with the United States Constitution, federal laws and policies and applicable international obligations.

113. It has established detailed immigration detention standards and remains committed to preventing abuses regarding detention conditions and bringing to justice those who commit them. More people than ever before are enrolled in alternatives to detention programmes.

114. The United States works aggressively to prevent and address human trafficking, through wide-ranging efforts, including those related to training and victims' services.

115. United States federal law prohibits all forms of housing-related discrimination on the basis of race, colour, religion, national origin, sex, disability or number of children.

116. The Government of the United States helps communities pursue alternatives to arrest and prosecution of individuals for various behaviours associated with homelessness by focusing on providing technical assistance and financial resources to help communities provide housing first.

117. In addressing homelessness, the United States has made it a priority first to meet the housing needs of families and individuals, and then provide other social support and assistance, setting an ambitious agenda to reduce all forms of homelessness within the decade and to reduce homelessness among military veterans by the end of 2015.

118. Chad noted concern related to recent events targeting the black community.

119. Chile valued measures implementing human rights standards.

120. China highlighted the deep-rooted human rights problems of the United States. 121. Congo made recommendations.

122. Costa Rica was concerned about racial discrimination and excessive use of force.

123. Côte d'Ivoire encouraged measures against discrimination and violence.

124. Croatia asked about measures against domestic violence and gender discrimination in the workplace.

125. Cuba made a statement.

126. Cyprus commended steps concerning indigenous peoples and human trafficking.

127. Romania noted the presentation of reports to treaty bodies.

128. The Democratic People's Republic of Korea was concerned about human rights violations by the United States.

129. The Democratic Republic of the Congo made a statement.

130. Denmark commended the Central Intelligence Agency report on interrogation practices in detention.

131. The Dominican Republic suggested preventing discrimination against indigenous and people of African descent.

132. Ecuador urged to prosecute torture.

133. Egypt made a statement.

134. El Salvador urged the United States to safeguard migrants' rights, namely, unaccompanied children.

135. Estonia noted the leadership of the United States on freedom of expression.

136. Fiji raised concern about life imprisonment for children convicted of murder.

137. Finland expected the State party to ratify the Convention on the Elimination of All forms of Discrimination against Women.

138. France made a statement.

139. Gabon encouraged the United States to continue fighting discrimination.

140. Germany made a statement.

141. Ghana commended the United States for its commitment to the universal periodic review.

142. Greece appreciated the commitment of the United States to improve implementation of its human rights obligations.

143. Guatemala noted the abolition of the death penalty in three states.

144. The Holy See acknowledged the efforts of the United States to protect human rights.

145. Honduras welcomed measures to protect unaccompanied migrant children.

146. Hungary noted that no human rights treaties had been ratified since 2010.

147. Iceland made a statement.

148. India noted deficiencies in law enforcement procedures.

149. Indonesia appreciated the engagement of the United States with the universal periodic review.

150. The Islamic Republic of Iran was concerned at the definition of racial discrimination.

151. Iraq welcomed efforts to combat religious discrimination.

152. Ireland was concerned by harsh death row conditions.

153. Israel noted the action plan to assist trafficking victims.

154. Italy appreciated the dedication of the United States to eliminate racial discrimination.

155. Japan noted that the United States had not ratified any human rights treaty since its first universal periodic review.

156. The Plurinational State of Bolivia made a statement.

157. Maldives made a statement.

158. Uzbekistan noted concerns about discrimination and the rights of migrants.

159. The United States said that the detainees held at the Guantánamo Bay facility continue to be detained lawfully, both as a matter of international law and under United States domestic law. At the same time, President Obama has stated that closing the Guantánamo detention facility is a national imperative.

160. The United States is fully committed to ensuring that the individuals it detains in any armed conflict are treated humanely in all circumstances, consistent with applicable United States treaty obligations, its domestic law and policy.

161. Eliminating sexual assault in the military through continuous assessment and improvement to prevention and response programmes remains one of the Department of Defense's top priorities.

162. United States forces go to extraordinary lengths to avoid civilian casualties, and the United States takes seriously and reviews all credible reports of civilian deaths and injuries.

163. The United States has worked steadily over the past several years to clarify, refine and strengthen its standards and procedures for counterterrorism operations outside the United States and areas of active hostilities.

164. As part of its ongoing immigration detention reform programmes, the United States has significantly improved health services for all persons in its custody, including women.

165. For unaccompanied children, the United States is fully committed to holding children only for the shortest amount of time necessary to complete immigration processing and to treating the children with dignity and respect during their time in United States custody.

166. By law, all persons in the United States, including undocumented migrants, are entitled to emergency health services, regardless of legal status.

167. The United States is taking steps to improve access to health care for members of racial and ethnic minorities, including through the enactment and implementation of the Affordable Care Act in 2010.

168. The United States is committed to promoting women's health and eliminating barriers to health-care services. The Government of the United States regularly reviews its policies to take all appropriate measures to improve the health and status of women and girls around the world, including survivors of sexual violence.

169. In all cases where the death penalty is or can be applied, the United States seeks to ensure the absence of racial discrimination and respect for legal and procedural safeguards.

170. Each United States federal agency has an official tribal consultation policy for matters directly affecting tribal nations. President Obama established the White House Council on Native American Affairs, composed of leaders of each of the cabinet-level agencies, who meet with tribes on a quarterly basis.

171. The United States introduced the initiative entitled "Generation Indigenous," a new effort to engage Native youth, and it will host a native youth conference in July 2015.

172. The United States remains committed to self-determination and selfgovernance, empowering tribes to make their own decisions about the future of their peoples.

173. The United States is committed to supporting tribes' efforts to recover their human remains, sacred and ceremonial objects and cultural property that has been stolen, looted or trafficked.

174. The United States is concerned about the pay gap between men and women, and President Obama has issued Executive Order 13665, intended to protect workers and job applicants from discrimination by federal contractors if they inquire about, disclose or discuss their compensation or that of another applicant or worker.

175. The United States welcomed and paid tribute to civil society groups for their vigorous engagement throughout the first and second cycles of the universal periodic review, noting that it fully supports and welcomes civil society's involvement.

II. Conclusions and recommendations

176. The following recommendations will be examined by the United States of America, which will provide responses in due time, but no later than the thirtieth session of the Human Rights Council, from 14 September to 2 October 2015:

176.1 Consider the ratification of those international human rights instruments to which the United States is still not a party (Peru);

176.2 Ratify the international human rights instruments to which it is not a party (Nicaragua);

176.3 Ratify all international human rights instruments to which it is not yet a State party (Plurinational State of Bolivia);

176.4 Take genuine steps towards the ratification of treaties and optional protocols to conventions that the United States has already signed, but not yet ratified (Germany);

176.5 Accelerate the ratification of outstanding international human rights legal instruments (Viet Nam);

176.6 Consider ratifying more human rights instruments (Israel);

176.7 Consider ratifying the core international human rights instruments and other relevant international conventions (Panama);

176.8 Work more to join the international treaties on human rights (Tunisia);

176.9 Withdraw all reservations to international human rights treaties and implement their provisions fully and in good faith (Russian Federation);

176.10 the Second Optional Protocol to the International Covenant on Civil and Political Rights, aiming at the abolition of the death penalty (TimorLeste);

176.11 Sign and ratify the Second Optional Protocol to the International Covenant on Civil and Political Rights, aiming at the abolition of the death penalty (Chile);

176.12 Consider the ratification of the Second Optional Protocol to the International Covenant on Civil and Political Rights, aiming at the abolition of the death penalty (Namibia);

176.13 Establish a formal moratorium on the death penalty with a view to ratifying the Second Optional Protocol to the International Covenant on Civil and Political Rights, aiming at the abolition of the death penalty (Australia);

176.14 Adhere to international legal instruments to which it is not yet a party, particularly the Second Optional Protocol to the International Covenant on Civil and Political Rights, aiming at the abolition of the death penalty (Gabon);

176.15 Ratify the International Covenant on Economic, Social and Cultural Rights (Uzbekistan) / Ratify as soon as possible the International Covenant on Economic, Social and Cultural Rights (China) / Become a State party to the International Covenant on Economic, Social and Cultural Rights (Trinidad and Tobago);

176.16 Step up efforts to ratify the International Covenant on Economic, Social and Cultural Rights, the Convention on the Elimination of All forms of Discrimination against Women and the Convention on the Rights of the Child (Philippines);

176.17 Consider ratifying the Convention on the Elimination of All forms of Discrimination against Women, the International Covenant on Economic, Social and Cultural Rights and also consider acceding to the Optional Protocol to the Convention against Torture and Other Cruel, Inhuman or Degrading Treatment or Punishment (Mauritius);

176.18 Proceed to the ratification of the Convention on the Rights of the Child, signed in 1995, the Convention on the Elimination of All forms of Discrimination against Women, signed in 1980, the International Covenant on Economic, Social and Cultural Rights, signed in 1977, and transpose them into national law (Luxembourg);

176.19 Promptly ratify the Convention on the Elimination of All forms of Discrimination against Women and the Convention on the Rights of Persons with Disabilities, as well as other core human rights conventions, such as the International Covenant on Economic, Social and Cultural Rights and the Convention on the Rights of the Child (Nepal);

176.20 Accede to the key international human rights instruments: the Convention on the Rights of the Child, the International Covenant on Economic, Social and Cultural Rights, the Convention on the Rights of Persons with Disabilities and the Convention on the Elimination of All forms of Discrimination against Women (Sierra Leone);

176.21 Consider ratification of the International Covenant on Economic, Social and Cultural Rights, the Convention on the Elimination of All forms of Discrimination against Women, the Convention on the Rights of the Child, the Convention on the Rights of Persons with Disabilities as well as the optional protocols to these conventions to which the United States is still not a party (Kazakhstan);

176.22 Reinforce its role as a global leader on human rights by becoming a party to the International Covenant on Economic, Social and Cultural Rights, the Convention on the Elimination of All forms of Discrimination against Women, the Convention on the Rights of the Child, and the Convention on the Rights of Persons with Disabilities (Australia);

176.23 Consider ratifying the International Covenant on Economic, Social and Cultural Rights, the Convention on the Rights of the Child and the Convention on the Elimination of All forms of Discrimination against Women (Bulgaria);

176.24 Consider early ratification of international conventions like the International Covenant on Economic, Social and Cultural Rights, the Convention on the Rights of the Child and the Convention on the Elimination of All forms of Discrimination against Women (India);

176.25 Expedite the ratification process of the Convention on the Rights of Persons with Disabilities and the Convention on the Elimination of All forms of Discrimination against Women and consider ratifying other international human rights conventions, particularly the International Covenant on Economic, Social and Cultural Rights, the Convention on the Rights of the Child and the International Convention on the Protection of the Rights of All Migrant Workers and Members of their Families (Indonesia);

176.26 Ratify the Convention on the Rights of the Child and the International Covenant on Economic, Social and Cultural Rights (Egypt);

176.27 Consider the ratification of the International Covenant on Economic, Social and Cultural Rights, the Convention on the Rights of the Child and the International Convention on the Elimination of All Forms of Discrimination against Women (Romania);

176.28 Ratify in due course instruments such as the International

Convention on the Protection of the Rights of All Migrant Workers and Members of their Families, the Convention on the Rights of the Child and the International Covenant on Economic, Social and Cultural Rights (Cabo Verde);

176.29 Ratify international human rights treaties particularly the Optional Protocol to the International Covenant on Economic, Social and Cultural Rights, the Convention on the Elimination of All forms of Discrimination against Women and the Convention on the Rights of the Child (Togo);

176.30 Ratify the core international human rights instruments, in particular the Convention on the Rights of the Child and the Convention on the Elimination of All forms of Discrimination against Women (Paraguay);

176.31 Ratify the Convention on the Elimination of All forms of Discrimination against Women and the Convention on the Rights of the Child and ensure their full implementation (Botswana);

176.32 Contribute to the universal application of the Convention on the Rights of the Child and the Convention on the Elimination of All forms of Discrimination against Women by ratifying these two important human rights conventions at an early stage (Iceland);

176.33 the Convention on the Rights of the Child, the International Convention on the Protection of the Rights of All Migrant Workers and Members of their Families, International Convention for the Protection of All Persons from Enforced Disappearance, the Convention on the Rights of Persons with Disabilities, the Convention on the Elimination of All forms of Discrimination against Women and the Rome Statute of the International Criminal Court (Ghana);

176.34 Consider the option of ratifying the relevant international conventions, mainly the Convention on the Elimination of All forms of Discrimination against Women, the Convention on the Rights of the Child and the International Convention for the Protection of All Persons from Enforced Disappearance (Democratic Republic of the Congo);

176.35 Urgently move to ratify the Convention on the Rights of Persons with Disabilities, the Convention on the Rights of the Child and the Convention on the Elimination of All forms of Discrimination against Women (New Zealand);

176.36 Ratify the Convention on the Rights of the Child, the Convention on the Elimination of All forms of Discrimination against Women, the Convention on the Rights of Persons with Disabilities and the Rome Statute of the International Criminal Court, as previously recommended (Hungary);

176.37 Continue to exert efforts to ratify major international human rights instruments, particularly including the Convention on the Elimination of All forms of Discrimination against Women and the Convention on the Rights of the Child (Republic of Korea);

176.38 Consider ratification of the Convention on the Rights of the Child, the Convention on the Elimination of All forms of Discrimination against Women, as well as the other core international human rights treaties that the United States is not a party to (the former Yugoslav Republic of Macedonia);

176.39 Ratify without delay the Convention on the Rights of Persons with Disabilities and the Convention on the Elimination of All forms of Discrimination against Women in accordance with its previously expressed commitment (Czech Republic);

176.40 Ratify the Convention on the Elimination of All forms of Discrimination against Women (Turkey) (Iraq) (Slovenia) (Bosnia and Herzegovina) (France) (Canada) / Ratify as soon as possible the Convention on the Elimination of All forms of Discrimination against Women (China) / Become a State Party to the Convention on the Elimination of All forms of Discrimination against Women (Trinidad and Tobago) / Ratify the Convention on the Elimination of All forms of Discrimination against Women as soon as possible (Japan);

176.41 Ratify the Convention on the Elimination of All forms of Discrimination against Women (Lebanon);

176.42 Speed up its national examination procedures with a view of prompt ratification of the Convention on the Elimination of All forms of Discrimination against Women (Latvia);

176.43 Ratify the Optional Protocol to the Convention against Torture and Other Cruel, Inhuman or Degrading Treatment or Punishment (Lebanon);

176.44 Ratify the Optional Protocol to the Convention against Torture and Other Cruel, Inhuman or Degrading Treatment or Punishment (Switzerland) (Denmark);

176.45 Ratify the Optional Protocol to the Convention against Torture and Other Cruel, Inhuman or Degrading Treatment or Punishment and take swift measures to ensure the human rights of convicts and persons in custody (Estonia);

176.46 Consider ratifying the Convention on the Rights of the Child and the Rome Statute of the International Criminal Court (Austria);

176.47 Ratify the Convention on the Rights of the Child (Mali);

176.48 Ratify the Convention on the Rights of the Child (Sweden) (TimorLeste) (Algeria) (Maldives) (France) (Portugal) (Slovenia) / Ratify as soon as possible the Convention on the Rights of the Child (China) (Japan) Become a party to the Convention on the Rights of the Child (Canada);

176.49 Ratify and implement into domestic law the Convention on the Elimination of All forms of Discrimination against Women, the Convention on the Rights of the Child and the Convention on the Rights of Persons with Disabilities (Estonia);

176.50 Expedite the ratification of the Convention on the Rights of the Child (Libya);

176.51 Pass legislation domestically to prohibit the passing of life imprisonment without the possibility of parole on offenders who were children at the time of offending, and ratify without any further delay the Convention on the Rights of the Child (Fiji);

176.52 Ratify the Convention on the Rights of the Child and the Optional Protocol to the Convention against Torture and Other Cruel, Inhuman or Degrading Treatment or Punishment (Czech Republic);

176.53 Ratify the major human rights instruments, in particular the Convention on the Rights of the Child and the International Convention on the Protection of the Rights of All Migrant Workers and Members of their Families (Honduras);

176.54 Ratify, among others, the Convention on the Rights of the Child, the Convention on the Rights of Persons with Disabilities, the International Convention on the Protection of the Rights of All Migrant Workers and Members of their Families / Accede to the American Convention on Human Rights and recognize the competence of the Inter-American Court of Human Rights (Chile);

176.55 Consider ratifying the Convention on the Rights of the Child and the International Convention on the Protection of the Rights of All Migrant Workers and Members of their Families (Burkina Faso);

176.56 Ratify the Convention on the Rights of the Child and the Convention on the Rights of Persons with Disabilities (Islamic Republic of Iran);

176.57 Improve the protection of children at national level by ratifying the Convention on the Rights of the Child and its Optional Protocols (Slovakia);

176.58 the Convention on the Rights of Persons with Disabilities (Guatemala) (Canada) (Bosnia and Herzegovina) / Ratify as soon as possible the Convention on the Rights of Persons with Disabilities (China);

176.59 Ratify the International Convention on the Protection of the Rights of All Migrant Workers and Members of their Families (Guatemala);

176.60 Consider ratifying the International Convention on the Protection of the Rights of All Migrant Workers and Members of their Families and the International Labour Organization Domestic Workers Convention, 2011 (No. 189) (Philippines);

176.61 Ratify the Convention on the Rights of Persons with Disabilities and the International Labour Organization Discrimination (Employment and Occupation) Convention, 1958 (No. 111) (Sudan);

176.62 Ratify the Arms Trade Treaty thus strengthening international regulation of the trade and transfer of conventional weapons, including small arms and light weapons (Trinidad and Tobago);

176.63 Ratify the Rome Statute of the International Criminal Court (New Zealand);

176.64 Ratify the Rome Statute of the International Criminal Court (TimorLeste) (Maldives) (France) (Guatemala) (Slovenia) / Become a State party to the Rome Statute of the International Criminal Court (Trinidad and Tobago);

176.65 Become a State party to the Rome Statute of the International Criminal Court (Chad);

176.66 Ratify and fully align its national legislation with all the obligations under the Rome Statute of the International Criminal Court (Latvia);

176.67 Ratify without delay the Rome Statute of the International Criminal Court (Fiji);

176.68 Take concrete steps towards ratifying the Rome Statute of the International Criminal Court as early as possible (Cyprus);

176.69 Boost the cooperation with the International Criminal Court with the objective to accede to the Rome Statute of the International Criminal Court (Luxembourg);

176.70 Ratify all international human rights conventions and protocols and those of the International Labour Organization and the Rome Statute of the International Criminal Court (Bolivarian Republic of Venezuela);

176.71 Ratify the fundamental International Labour Organization Forced Labour Convention, 1930 (No.29) and Minimum Age Convention, 1973 (No.138) (Uzbekistan);

176.72 Positively consider signing and ratifying the principal international and inter-American human rights instruments, as well as reviewing the reservations and declarations that may affect the object and purpose of such instruments (Uruguay);

176.73 Conduct human rights awareness-raising activities for law enforcement officers (Viet Nam);

176.74 Strengthen human rights education programmes and training for all civil servants, particularly for law enforcement and immigration officers, and combat impunity concerning abuses against defenceless persons (Costa Rica);

176.75 Create a national human rights institution (Senegal);

176.76 Set up a federal human rights institution (Congo) / Strengthen its institutional framework by establishing an independent human rights institution in accordance with the Principles relating to the status of national institutions for the promotion and protection of human rights (Paris Principles) (Tunisia) / Establish an independent national human rights institution in accordance with the Paris Principles (Paraguay);

176.77 Create a national human rights institution in conformity with the Paris Principles (Bolivarian Republic of Venezuela);

176.78 Establish an independent national human rights institution, in accordance with the Paris Principles (Poland);

176.79 Establish a centralized national human rights institution which is in line with the Paris Principles (Sierra Leone);

176.80 Consider the establishment of the independent national human rights institution (Republic of Korea);

176.81 Consider the establishment of a national human rights institution (Sudan);

176.82 Consider establishing a national human rights institution (India) / Consider establishing a national human rights institution in accordance with the Paris Principles (Nepal) / Consider the possibility of establishing an independent national human rights institution in line with the Paris Principles (Panama) / Consider establishing an independent national human rights institution in accordance with the Paris Principles to further improve coordination in the human rights sphere at the national level (Ukraine) / Consider establishing promptly a national human rights institution in accordance with the Paris Principles (Democratic Republic of the Congo) / Consider establishing a national human rights institution, in accordance to the Paris Principles (Indonesia);

176.83 Consider establishing national human rights institution (Kenya);

176.84 Consider establishing an independent national human rights institution, in accordance with the Paris Principles (Kazakhstan);

176.85 Accelerate the process of establishment of the national human rights institution (Gabon);

176.86 Establish a national human rights institution to provide national coherence to the efforts of promotion and protection of human rights (Morocco);

176.87 Create a human rights institution at the federal level in accordance with the Paris Principles as a national "focal point" for the promotion and protection of human rights (Hungary);

176.88 Continue strengthening the existing human rights monitoring mechanisms (Nepal);

176.89 Work towards the establishment of a national human rights institution in accordance with the Paris Principles (Philippines);

176.90 Establish a national human rights institution in accordance with the Paris Principles and adopt a national action plan to address structural racial discrimination (Chile);

176.91 Adopt an action plan consistent with the Durban Declaration and Programme of Action in an effort to eradicate racial discrimination effectively (Namibia);

176.92 Adopt and implement a national plan in accordance with the Durban Declaration and Programme of Action (Cuba);

176.93 Take all legal measures to adopt and implement a national racial justice plan consistent with the Durban Declaration and Programme of Action (Islamic Republic of Iran);

176.94 Undertake measures to combat racial discrimination, including adoption of a National Action Plan to Combat Racial Discrimination as recommended by the Committee on the Elimination of Racial Discrimination (South Africa);

176.95 Adopt and implement a national plan inspired by the Durban Declaration and Programme of Action, for the benefit especially of disadvantaged minorities, which are Afro-Americans and indigenous peoples (Cabo Verde);

176.96 Unconditionally abolish its extraterritorial legislation on human rights and related matters, including the "North Korea Human Rights Act" (Democratic People's Republic of Korea);

176.97 Interpret the Helms Amendment on the Allocation of Foreign Assistance in such a way that United States foreign assistance enables safe abortion for women and girls who have been raped and impregnated in conflict situations (Netherlands);

176.98 Clarify its interpretation of the Helms Amendment in order to be able to provide safe abortion for rape survivors (United Kingdom of Great Britain and Northern Ireland);

176.99 Allow foreign assistance to support safe abortion services, where legal in the host country. This should apply as a minimum in the cases of rape, incest and life endangerment, as is also permitted by existing United States federal law (Belgium);

176.100 Ensure that the United States international aid allows access to sexual and reproductive health services for women victims of sexual violence in conflict situations (France);

176.101 Put an end to all sanctions and unilateral coercive measures that violate sovereignty, the self-determination of the peoples and the full exercise of human rights, imposed to countries in all the regions of the world (Nicaragua);

176.102 Raise the level of official development assistance to achieve the United Nations target of 0.7 percent of gross domestic product (Bangladesh);

176.103 Repeal the Interventionist Decree against the Bolivarian Republic of Venezuela and unilateral coercive measures imposed on sovereign countries (Bolivarian Republic of Venezuela);

176.104 Respect the sovereignty and self-determination of the Bolivarian Republic of Venezuela (Bolivarian Republic of Venezuela);

176.105 Pursue the cooperation with international human rights mechanisms (Côte d'Ivoire);

176.106 Take further steps to implement the recommendations accepted during the first review cycle (Kazakhstan);

176.107 Consider the possibility of establishing a system to follow up on international recommendations, including universal periodic review accepted recommendations (Paraguay);

176.108 That a mechanism be established at the federal level to ensure comprehensive and coordinated compliance with international human rights instruments at the federal, local and state levels (Norway);

176.109 Issue a standing invitation to all special procedures of the Human Rights Council (Czech Republic) / Extend a standing invitation for special procedures mandate holders (Germany) / Extend a standing invitation to the special procedures (Guatemala);

176.110 Consider extending a standing invitation to all special procedures mandate holders of the Human Rights Council (Latvia);

176.111 Enhance further cooperation with human rights mechanisms, including issuing a standing invitation to special procedures and providing full access to the Special Rapporteur on torture and other cruel, inhuman or degrading treatment or punishment (Republic of Korea);

176.112 Consider issuing standing invitations to all special procedures and institute measures to ensure women are paid equally as men for the same work (Ghana);

176.113 End various forms of inequality (Egypt);

176.114 Improve domestic legislation towards a genuine gender equality in the working place (Congo);

176.115 Ensure that women receive equal pay for equal work so as to close the gender pay gap (Serbia);

176.116 Eliminate discrimination against women by introducing paid maternity leave and providing equal pay for women for the same work (Maldives);

176.117 Issue a decree on compulsory maternity leave and equal wages for men and women (Bolivarian Republic of Venezuela);

176.118 Put forward continued efforts in raising awareness and working towards addressing issues related to the racial discrimination (Republic of Korea);

176.119 Take administrative and legal measures against perpetrators of racially motivated acts (Bangladesh);

176.120 Strengthen the existing laws and legislation in order to combat different forms of discrimination, racism and hatred (Lebanon);

176.121 Take further measures to eliminate racial discrimination in all of its forms and manifestations, in particular, by prohibiting the practice of race profiling in law enforcement, as recommended by the United Nations treaty bodies (Kazakhstan);

176.122 Bring in line the definition of racial discrimination in federal and state legislation with the provisions of the International Convention on the Elimination of All Forms of Racial Discrimination (Ghana);

176.123 Combat better against racial discrimination (Senegal);

176.124 Invest further efforts in addressing the root causes of recent racial incidents and expand its capacity in reducing poverty in neighbourhoods experiencing sub/par public services, including access to adequate housing and public safety (Serbia);

176.125 End discrimination in law and practice against all minorities and migrants, particularly against women and children from poor families and take effective steps to prevent and combat violence against them (Islamic Republic of Iran);

176.126 Abolish any discriminatory measures that target Muslims and Arabs at airports (Egypt);

176.127 Continue to strengthen police-community relations with a view to reduce tension in the community (Montenegro);

176.128 Continue efforts in strengthening police-community relations (Rwanda);

176.129 Continue the efforts to examine how to strengthen public trust and foster strong relationships between local law enforcement and communities they serve (Albania);

176.130 Collaborate closely with marginalized communities to fix the problems in the justice system that continues to discriminate against them despite recent waves of protest over racial profiling and police killings of unarmed black men (Namibia);

176.131 Continue to take strong actions, including appropriate judicial measures, to counter all forms of discrimination and hate crimes, in particular those based on religion and ethnicity (Singapore);

176.132 Toughen its efforts to prevent religion and hate crimes as it is evident that the crimes are on the increase (Nigeria);

176.133 Continue its efforts in preventing and prosecuting hate crimes (Israel);

176.134 Continue to engage with the affected communities to provide protection to those most vulnerable to hate crimes and discrimination, and to better understand their circumstances (Singapore);

176.135 Strengthen the laws and mechanisms at the federal and state levels to further combat racial discrimination in all its forms as well as against hate speech and hate crimes, to ensure that people are protected therefrom; (Niger);

176.136 Prohibit racial discrimination and racist hate speech, as well as broaden the protection afforded by law (Azerbaijan);

176.137 Take concrete measures to combat racial discrimination in law enforcement and in the administration of justice (Maldives);

176.138 Take necessary measures to combat discriminatory practices against women and migrant workers in the labour market (Algeria);

176.139 Strengthen the existing mechanisms to prevent the excessive use of force and discriminatory practices in police work (Peru);

176.140 Take necessary measures to ensure that its commitment to eliminating racial discrimination is fully respected, particularly by law and order forces, as well as by the criminal justice system (Algeria);

176.141 Take necessary measures to fight against discriminatory practices of the police based on ethnic origin (France);

176.142 Address discrimination, racial profiling by the authorities, Islamophobia and religious intolerance by reviewing all laws and practices that violate the rights of minority groups, with a view to amending them (Malaysia);

176.143 Prohibit that federal authorities undertake racial profiles, and investigate the disproportionate use of lethal force against coloured people by state and local police (Plurinational State of Bolivia);

176.144 Double its efforts in combating violence and the excessive use of force by law enforcement officers based on racial profiling through training, sensitization and community outreach, as well as ensuring proper investigation and prosecution when cases occur (Malaysia);

176.145 That the process of round-table discussions among law enforcement, elected officials and community members, aimed to stem profiling and excessive use of force by the police should be stepped up to cover as many cities as possible (Nigeria);

176.146 Stop the practice of racial profiling in the judicial and law enforcement systems (Russian Federation);

176.147 Eliminate the practice of racial profiling and surveillance by law enforcement officials (Azerbaijan);

176.148 Effectively combat racial profiling and the use of excessive force by the police against coloured persons (Togo);

176.149 Combat racial profiling and Islamophobia on a non-discriminatory basis applicable to all religious groups (Pakistan);

176.150 Combat racial profiling, aSuRged by the Human Rights Committee and Committee on the Elimination of Racial Discrimination (Bangladesh);

176.151 Implement measures to assist states and local governments in combating excessive use of force by the police and eliminating racial profiling (Brazil);

176.152 Prohibit federal law enforcement authorities from engaging in racial profiling (Egypt);

176.153 Continue efforts at the federal and state levels aimed at overcoming racial discrimination, especially through the implementation of the Priority Enforcement Programme to guard against racial profiling of immigrants and other forms of racial discrimination (Holy See);

176.154 Adopt measures at the federal level to prevent and punish excessive use of force by law enforcement officials against members of ethnic and racial minorities, including unarmed persons, which disproportionately affect AfroAmerican and undocumented migrants (Mexico);

176.155 End police brutality against African Americans and rectify the judicial as well as socioeconomic systems that systematically discriminate against them (Pakistan);

176.156 Correctly address the root causes of racial discrimination and eliminate the frequently occurred excessive use of force by law enforcement against of African Americans and other ethnic minorities (China);

176.157 Continue implementing — at all levels — its policies and programmes aimed to eliminate discrimination on any ground, as well as the use of excessive or unreasonable force in policing (Croatia);

176.158 Take measures to put an end to police abuses, including the merciless killing of coloured people, and all racial discrimination (Democratic People's Republic of Korea);

176.159 Uphold its obligations to end all forms of racial discrimination in the country and protect the rights of African Americans against police brutality (Islamic Republic of Iran);

176.160 Take steps to eradicate discrimination and intolerance against any ethnic, racial or religious group and ensure equal opportunity for their economic, social and security rights (Turkey);

176.161 Take measures and comprehensive programmes aimed at developing sensitivities among cultures, creating the climate of mutual respect and expanding protection against all forms of discrimination, including profiling on the basis of race, religions or national origin (Indonesia);

176.162 Heighten efforts to promote non-discrimination of any kind, including discrimination on the basis of sexual orientation and gender identity (South Africa);

176.163 Keep promoting progress in lesbian, gay, bisexual, transgender and intersex issues, especially in preventing discrimination based on gender or sexual orientation (Israel);

176.164 Take affirmative steps to ensure that individuals' religious refusals are regulated to conform with international human rights standards that protect sexual and reproductive rights and the rights to equality and nondiscrimination on the basis of sex, gender, sexual orientation or gender identity (Sweden);

176.165 Abolish the death penalty in those states where it is still used (Nicaragua) / Abolish the death penalty in all states of the Union (Ecuador);

176.166 Abolish the death penalty (Costa Rica);

176.167 Abolish the death penalty (Plurinational State of Bolivia);

176.168 Continue efforts towards abolishing the death penalty (Austria);

176.169 Reduce gradually the number of persons sentenced to death, and ensure that efforts on this matter are pursued (Congo);

176.170 Introduce a moratorium at the federal level with view to achieving nationwide moratorium of capital punishment as a first step to abolishing such penalty (Lithuania);

176.171 Establish a federal moratorium on the death penalty with a view to the total abolition of the death penalty in the United States (Luxembourg); 176.172 Establish a moratorium on death penalty at the federal and states levels with a view to ultimately achieve nationwide legal abolition (Nepal);

176.173 Establish a moratorium on the death penalty aiming at its complete abolition in all states (Uruguay);

176.174 Establish a moratorium on the application of the death penalty aimed at its abolition and also condone the death penalty for an Argentinian citizen, Victor Saldano, who has been on death row since 1996 (Argentina);

176.175 Impose a moratorium on executions with a view to abolishing the death penalty at the federal and state levels (Namibia) / Institute a moratorium on the application of the death penalty with a view to abolition (Togo) / Establish, at the federal level, a moratorium on executions with a view to abolishing the death penalty (France) / Establish an official moratorium on the use of the death penalty (Montenegro) / Establish a moratorium on the application of the death penalty (Spain) / Impose a moratorium on executions and abolish the death penalty in all states of the United States (Turkey) / Ensure the establishment of a moratorium of the death penalty in those states that have not abolished it yet (Chile);

176.176 Work towards a moratorium on executions with a view of abolishing the death penalty (Rwanda);

176.177 That federal and state authorities impose a moratorium on executions with a view to abolishing the death penalty nationwide (Portugal);

176.178 Impose a moratorium on executions with a view to abolishing the death penalty nationwide (Iceland);

176.179 Impose a moratorium on executions with a view to abolishing the death penalty nationwide (Ireland);

176.180 Introduce a national moratorium on the death penalty aiming at complete abolition and take all necessary measures to ensure that the death penalty complies with minimum standards under international law. Exempt persons with mental illness from execution. Commit to ensuring that the origin of drugs being used is made public (Sweden);

176.181 Impose a moratorium on the use of the death penalty (Russian Federation);

176.182 Impose at least a moratorium on the death penalty (Azerbaijan);

176.183 Formally establish a moratorium on executions at the federal level while engaging with retentionist states to achieve a nationwide moratorium with the objective to ultimately abolish the death penalty nationwide (Germany);

176.184 Take all necessary steps to work towards an immediate moratorium on execution of the death penalty, with a view to a complete abolishment, in line with international human rights standards such as the right to live (Netherlands);

176.185 Take necessary steps to introduce a moratorium on the use of the death penalty at the federal and state levels (Slovakia);

176.186 Impose a moratorium on executions with a view to abolishing the death penalty for federal offences (New Zealand);

176.187 Impose a moratorium on executions with a view to abolishing the death penalty nationwide, and ensure that prosecutors in all jurisdictions cease pursuing death sentences (Estonia);

176.188 Continue efforts to establish a moratorium and eventually abolish capital punishment in all states (Sierra Leone);

176.189 Take into consideration the possibility of adopting a moratorium of capital executions at the state and federal levels, given that 26 states have abolished or adopted a moratorium on capital executions, (Italy);

176.190 Consider as a first step the application of a moratorium on executions, both at the state and federal levels, with a view to ultimately abolishing the death penalty (Cyprus) / Consider imposing an official moratorium on executions toward the complete abolition of the death penalty in the country (Greece);

176.191 Consider introducing at the federal level a moratorium on the use of the death penalty with a view to its permanent abolition (Holy See);

176.192 Consider adoption of a moratorium on the death penalty at the federal level (Uzbekistan);

176.193 A review of federal and state legislation to restrict the number of offences carrying the death penalty and steps towards federal- and state-level moratoriums on executions with a view to its permanent abolition (Norway);

176.194 Identify the root causes of ethnic disparities concerning especially those sentenced to capital punishment in order to find ways for eliminate ethnic discrimination in the criminal justice system (Angola);

176.195 Identify the factors of racial disparity in the use of the death penalty and develop strategies to end possible discriminatory practices (France);

176.196 When continuing to implement the death penalty, do not apply it to persons with intellectual disabilities (Spain);

176.197 Ensure that no person with a mental disability is executed (France);

176.198 Take specific measures in follow-up to the recommendations of the Human Rights Committee to the United States in 2014 with regards to capital punishment such as measures to avoid racial bias, to avoid wrongful sentencing to death and to provide adequate compensation if wrongful sentencing happens (Belgium);

176.199 Strengthen the justice sector in order to avoid imposing the death penalty on those persons wrongly convicted, and reconsider the use of methods which give raise to cruel suffering when this punishment is applied (Democratic Republic of the Congo);

176.200 Strengthen safeguards against wrongful sentencing to death and subsequent wrongful execution by ensuring, inter alia, effective legal representation for defendants in death penalty cases, including at the post conviction stage (Poland); 176.201 Continue the efforts on the progress towards the abolishment of the death penalty, based on the Department of Justice's review of how it is being applied in the country (Bulgaria);

176.202 Commit to full transparency on the combination of medicines used during executions by injection (France);

176.203 Put an end to unlawful practices which violate human rights, including extrajudicial executions and arbitrary detention, and close any arbitrary detention centres (Egypt);

176.204 Take legal and administrative measures to address civilian killings by the United States military troops during and after its invasion of Afghanistan and Iraq by bringing perpetrators to justice and remedying the victims (Democratic People's Republic of Korea);

176.205 Desist from extrajudicial killings such as drone strikes and ensure accountability for civilian loss of life resulting from extraterritorial counter terrorism operations (Malaysia);

176.206 Stop extrajudicial killings of citizens of the United States of America and foreigners, including those being committed with the use of remotely piloted aircraft (Russian Federation);

176.207 Use armed drones in line with existing international legal regimes and pay compensation to all innocent victims without discrimination (Pakistan);

176.208 Investigate and prosecute in courts the perpetrators of selective killings through the use of drones, which has cost the lives of innocent civilians outside the United States (Ecuador);

176.209 Punish those responsible for torture, drone killings, use of lethal force against African Americans and compensate the victims (Bolivarian Republic of Venezuela);

176.210 Strengthen safeguards against torture in all detention facilities in any territory under its jurisdiction, ensure proper and transparent investigation and prosecution of individuals responsible for all allegations of torture and ill-treatment, including those documented in the unclassified Senate summary on Central Intelligence Agency activities published in 2014 and provide redress to victims (Czech Republic);

176.211 Enact comprehensive legislation prohibiting all forms of torture and take measures to prevent all acts of torture in areas outside the national territory under its effective control (Austria);

176.212 Stops acts of torture by United States government officials, not only in its sovereign territory, but also on foreign soil (Maldives);

176.213 Prevent torture and ill-treatment in places of detention and (Azerbaijan);

176.214 Prevent the continued police brutality and excessive use of force by law enforcement officials, as well as analyse and eliminate its concrete reasons (Azerbaijan);

176.215 Take comprehensive measures to address the use of excessive force by the police and ensure the investigation and the prosecution of all such acts (Bulgaria);

176.216 Take further steps to end the use of excessive force in policing in all jurisdictions (Canada);

176.217 Respect the absolute prohibition on torture and take measures to guarantee punishment of all perpetrators (Costa Rica);

176.218 Ensure the independent and objective investigation of all cases of police arbitrariness, including murders, torture, arbitrary, detention, use of military equipment and seizure of property (Russian Federation);

176.219 Strengthen its measures to address police brutality in accordance with existing international standards governing the use of force (Thailand);

176.220 Take concrete measures to eliminate racial criteria in the approach of the law enforcement officials and combat the excessive use of force by the same officers (Angola);

176.221 Adopt legal and administrative measures necessary to make effective the investigation and sanction of cases of discriminatory police practices and the use of excessive force by security forces, along with the carrying out of awareness-raising campaigns (Argentina);

176.222 Continue consultations, investigations and reform programmes under way to eliminate racial discrimination and excessive use of force in policing (Australia);

176.223 Implement necessary measures to put an end to the disproportionate use of force against individuals and respect the right of peaceful protest (Turkey);

176.224 Ensure a sustained human rights training for law enforcement officers in order to curb killings, brutality and the excessive use of force targeting racial and ethnic minorities, particularly African Americans (Democratic Republic of the Congo);

176.225 Continue to vigorously investigate recent cases of alleged police-led human rights abuses against African Americans and seek to build improved relations and trust between United States law enforcement and all communities around the United States (Ireland);

176.226 Punish perpetrators of abuse and police brutality, which are increasingly alarming and constitute irrefutable acts of increasing racism and racial discrimination, particularly against African Americans, Latinos and women (Cuba);

176.227 Take appropriate measures to eliminate the excessive use of force by the law enforcement officers. We refer to the case of killing the Kazakh national, Kirill Denyakin, by a United States police officer in 2011 in Virginia (Kazakhstan);

176.228 Undertake additional measures to address the disproportionate impact of violence on poor, minorities and immigrant women (Botswana);

176.229 Investigate cases of deaths of migrants by customs and border patrols, particularly those where there have been indications of an excessive use of force, and ensure accountability and adequate reparation to the families of the victims (Mexico);

176.230 Adopt legislation expanding the verification of personal backgrounds for all acquisitions of firearms (Ecuador);

176.231 Eliminate gun violence (Azerbaijan);

176.232 Take necessary measures to reduce gun violence, concerned at the large number of gun-related deaths and injuries, which disproportionately affect members of racial and ethnic minorities (Iceland);

176.233 Consider the adoption of legislation to enhance the verification of the records for all fire arms transfers and the revision of the laws that stipulate selfdefence without limitations (Peru);

176.234 End the use of life imprisonment without parole for offenders under the age of 18 at the age of crime, regardless of the nature of that crime (Austria);

176.235 Abolish life imprisonment without the possibility of parole for nonviolent offenses (Benin);

176.236 Take further steps to improve the current conditions of its prisons (Japan);

176.237 Ensure consistent enforcement of consular notification at all levels of Government and support the passage of related legislation through Congress (United Kingdom of Great Britain and Northern Ireland);

176.238 Take further legislative steps towards meeting consular notification and access obligations under the Vienna Convention on Consular Relations, by intensifying already significant efforts made towards this goal, as referred in paragraphs 72 and 73 of the National Report (Greece);

176.239 Improve living conditions in prisons in particular in Guantánamo (Sudan);

176.240 Work and do all its best in order to close down the Guantánamo facility (Libya);

176.241 Immediately close the prison in Guantánamo and cease the illegal detention of terrorism suspects at its military bases abroad (Russian Federation);

176.242 Immediately close the Guantánamo facility (Maldives);

176.243 Close the Guantánamo prison and release all detainees still held in Guantánamo, unless they are to be charged and tried without further delay (Iceland);

176.244 Close Guantánamo and secret detention centres (Bolivarian Republic of Venezuela);

176.245 Close, as soon as possible, the detention centre at Guantánamo Bay and put an end to the indefinite detention of persons considered as enemy combatants (France);

176.246 Make further progress in fulfilling its commitment to close the Guantánamo detention facility and abide by the ban on torture and inhumane treatment of all individuals in detention (Malaysia);

176.247 Fully disclose the abuse of torture by its Intelligence Agency, ensure the accountability of the persons responsible, and agree to unrestricted visit by the Special Rapporteur on torture and other cruel, inhuman or degrading treatment or punishment to Guantánamo facilities (China);

176.248 Engage further in the common fight for the prohibition of torture, ensuring accountability and victims' compensation and enable the Special Rapporteur on torture and other cruel, inhuman or degrading treatment or punishment to visit every part of the detention facility at Guantánamo Bay and to conduct unmonitored interviews (Germany);

176.249 Take adequate measures to ensure the definite decommissioning of the Guantánamo Military Prison (Spain);

176.250 End illegal detentions in Guantánamo Bay or bring the detainees to trial immediately (Pakistan);

176.251 Put an end to the practice of secret detention (Azerbaijan);

176.252 Halt the detention of immigrant families and children, seek alternatives to detention and end use of detention for reason of deterrence (Sweden);

176.253 Consider alternatives to the detention of migrants, particularly children (Brazil);

176.254 Treat migrant children in detention with due respect to human rights and work with neighbouring countries to address migrant smuggling challenges in order to end human trafficking (Thailand);

176.255 Promote actions to eradicate sexual and domestic violence (Israel);

176.256 Guarantee the right to access to justice and effective remedies to all indigenous women who were victims of violence (the former Yugoslav Republic of Macedonia);

176.257 Continue to pay attention to violence against indigenous women by ensuring that all reports of violence, in particular sexual violence and rape against indigenous women, are thoroughly investigated, with a focus on ending impunity and bringing perpetrators before justice (Finland);

176.258 Redouble efforts to prevent sexual violence in the military and ensure effective prosecution of offenders and redress for victims (Slovenia);

176.259 Put an end to all United States military presence in foreign territories, which is the root cause of human rights abuses, including homicide and rape (Democratic People's Republic of Korea);

176.260 Conduct impartial and objective investigations of all cases of cruel treatment of adopted children in order to eliminate impunity for such crimes (Russian Federation);

176.261 Remove the agriculture exemption in the Fair Labour Standards Act which would raise the age for harvesting and hazardous work for hired children taking care to distinguish between farm owner and farm worker children (Belgium);

176.262 Repeal the Amendment of slavery against agricultural workers, especially women and children (Bolivarian Republic of Venezuela);

176.263 Ensure protection against exploitation and forced labour for all categories of workers, including farm and domestic workers, through such measures as a review of appropriate labour regulations (Canada);

176.264 Adapt its normative framework to ensure that all categories of workers enjoy protection from exploitation and forced labour (Algeria);

176.265 Prohibit corporal punishment of children in all settings, including the home and schools, and ensure that the United States encourages non-violent forms of discipline as alternatives to corporal punishment (Liechtenstein);

176.266 Prioritize the implementation of a plan of action to combat the sale of children and child prostitution (Trinidad and Tobago);

176.267 Increase the minimum age for voluntary recruitment into the armed forces to 18 years, and criminalize explicitly the violation of the provisions of the Optional Protocol to the Convention on the Rights of the Child on the involvement of children in armed conflict (Uruguay);

176.268 Continue to fight crimes of human trafficking (Lebanon);

176.269 Further increase the efforts to combat trafficking in persons (Armenia);

176.270 An increase in resources for nationwide anti-trafficking awareness programmes, including law enforcement training (Portugal);

176.271 Implement the strategic action plan on human trafficking as well as to strengthen services for trafficking victims (Sudan);

176.272 Establish, where appropriate, specialized services required for children and women who have been trafficked or sold for sexual exploitation (Canada);

176.273 Address trafficking in persons, and in particular sexual exploitation of children that results from this trafficking (Maldives);

176.274 Devise a national strategy for the reinsertion of former detainees and to prevent recidivism (Morocco);

176.275 Accelerate the process of passing a legislation to reform the mandatory minimum sentences begun with the Smart on Crime initiative (Nigeria);

176.276 Conduct in-depth examinations into how race-related issues are affecting law enforcement and the administration of justice (Ghana);

176.277 Conduct in-depth examinations into how race-related issues were affecting law enforcement and the administration of justice, both at the federal and state levels (Poland);

176.278 Establishing an independent commission chaired by a special Prosecutor to help identify and incarcerate the crimes perpetrated by individuals or groups based on racism (Libya);

176.279 Comply with the international cooperation principles laid down in General Assembly resolution 3074 (XXVIII) regarding the extradition of persons accused of crimes against humanity, and extradite former Bolivian authorities legally charged for their trial in the country of origin (Plurinational State of Bolivia);

176.280 Extradite Luis Posada Carriles and other terrorists sought by the Bolivarian Republic of Venezuela (Bolivarian Republic of Venezuela);

176.281 Investigate in a transparent manner all cases of human rights violations against protesters (Russian Federation);

176.282 Prosecute all Central Intelligence Agency operatives that have been held responsible for torture by the United States Senate Select Committee on Intelligence (Pakistan);

176.283 Allow an independent body to investigate allegations of torture and to end the impunity of perpetrators (Switzerland);

176.284 Prosecute and punish those responsible for torture (Cuba);

176.285 Investigate the Central Intelligence Agency torture crimes, which stirred up indignation and denunciation among people, to disclose all information and to allow investigation by international community in this regard (Democratic People's Republic of Korea);

176.286 Further ensure that all victims of torture and ill-treatment — whether still in United States custody or not — obtain redress and have an enforceable right to fair and adequate compensation and as full rehabilitation as possible, including medical and psychological assistance (Denmark);

176.287 Investigate the excessive use of force by the police and prosecute the responsible, with a view to putting an end to such practices (Egypt);

176.288 Investigate torture allegations, extrajudicial executions and other violations of human rights committed in Guantánamo, Abu Ghraib, Bagram, NAMA and BALAD camps and to subsequently close them (Islamic Republic of Iran);

176.289 Improve access to justice, including due process and redress, for victims of sexual violence in the military; this would include removing from the chain of command the decision about whether to prosecute cases of alleged assault (Denmark);

176.290 Adopt legal and administrative measures to make effective the investigation and sanction of violations of human rights during international operations, in which members of armed forces and other government agents participate (Argentina);

176.291 Ensure that youth in conflict with the law are handled by the juvenile justice system and have access to free legal advisory assistance (Republic of Moldova);

176.292 Ensure that children under 18 are handled by the juvenile justice system in all circumstances (Slovenia);

176.293 Fully respect and protect the right to privacy (Azerbaijan);

176.294 Take measures against arbitrary or illegal interferences in private life and correspondence (Costa Rica);

176.295 Take adequate and effective steps to guarantee against arbitrary and unlawful acquisition of this data (Kenya);

176.296 Review their national laws and policies in order to ensure that all surveillance of digital communications is consistent with its international human rights obligations and is conducted on the basis of a legal framework which is publicly accessible, clear, precise, comprehensive and nondiscriminatory (Liechtenstein);

176.297 Provide effective legal and procedural guarantees against collection and use by security services of personal information, including abroad (Russian Federation);

176.298 Take all necessary measures to ensure an independent and effective oversight by all government branches of the overseas surveillance operations of the National Security Agency, especially those carried out under the Executive Order 12333, and guarantee access to effective judicial and other remedies for people whose right to privacy would have been violated by the surveillance activities of the United States (Switzerland);

176.299 Ensure that all surveillance policies and measures comply with international human rights law, particularly the right to privacy, regardless of the nationality or location of those affected, including through the development of effective safeguards against abuses (Brazil);

176.300 Cease spying on communications and private data of people in the world (Bolivarian Republic of Venezuela);

176.301 Stop massive surveillance activities both inside and outside its territory to avoid violating the right to privacy of its citizens and those of other countries (China);

176.302 Suspend the interception, holding and use of communications, including the surveillance and extraterritorial interception and the scope of the surveillance operations against citizens, institutions and representatives of other countries, which violate the right to privacy, international laws and the principle of State sovereignty recognized in the Charter of the United Nations (Cuba);

176.303 Respect international human rights obligations regarding the right to privacy when intercepting digital communications of individuals, collecting personal data or requiring disclosure of personal data from third parties (Germany);

176.304 Strengthen the independent federal-level judicial and legislative oversight of surveillance activities of all digital communications with the aim of ensuring that the right of privacy is fully upheld, especially with regard to individuals outside the territorial borders of the United States (Hungary);

176.305 Respect the privacy of individuals outside the United States in the context of digital communications and data (Pakistan);

176.306 Amend visa application system by removing any requirements that violate the right to privacy (Egypt);

176.307 Improve the legal basis that would ensure respect for the privacy of individuals (Turkey);

176.308 Uphold a consistent and robust protection of religious freedom, including religious speech and conscientious objection, and provide for accommodation of religious views and actions regarding social issues (Holy See);

176.309 Guarantee the right by all residents in the country to adequate housing, food, health and education, with the aim of decreasing poverty, which affects 48 millions of people in the country (Cuba);

176.310 Amend laws that criminalize homelessness and which are not in conformity with international human rights instruments (Egypt);

176.311 Continue efforts to implement the human right to safe water and sanitation, ensuring this human right without discrimination for the poorest sectors of the population, including indigenous peoples and migrants (Spain);

176.312 Ensure compliance with the human right to water and sanitation according to General Assembly resolution 64/292 (Plurinational State of Bolivia);

176.313 While recognizing economic, social and cultural measures, strengthen efforts in ensuring equal access to health-care and social services (South Africa);

176.314 Continue efforts regarding access to the right to health (Spain);

176.315 Strengthen measures promoting access of vulnerable population to public and social and health services (Côte d'Ivoire);

176.316 Ensure equal access to equality maternal health and related services as an integral part of the realization of women's rights (Finland);

176.317 Further efforts in this positive direction with a view to strengthen national health-care programmes so that health care is easily accessible, available and affordable for all members of society (Serbia);

176.318 The removal of blanket restrictions on abortion for United States foreign assistance to permit its use for safe abortion in cases of rape, life or health endangerment and incest in countries where abortion is legal (Norway);

176.319 Continue to promote the right to education, including ensuring equal access to education for vulnerable groups (Armenia);

176.320 Take concrete steps to include the right to education in the Constitution (Maldives);

176.321 Guarantee the enjoyment of human rights of the minorities and vulnerable groups in the country, including the indigenous peoples and migrants (Nicaragua);

176.322 Fully implement the United Nations Declaration on the Rights of Indigenous Peoples, and remove discriminatory legal barriers (Egypt);

176.323 Implement the United Nations Declaration on the Rights of Indigenous Peoples (Plurinational State of Bolivia);

176.324 Regularly consult with indigenous peoples on matters of interest to their communities, to support their rights to traditionally owned lands and resources and to adopt measures to effectively protect sacred areas of indigenous peoples against environmental exploitation and degradation (Republic of Moldova);

176.325 Respond to the suggestion made by the special procedures in paragraph 69 (n) of document A/68/284 regarding cases of Alaska, Hawaii and Dakota (Pakistan);

176.326 Respect indigenous peoples and ethnic minorities' rights and interests; fully consult with them on their land, autonomy, environment, language and other issues; correct the historical injustice and offer compensation (China);

176.327 Continue its efforts for the implementation of its reform plan of June 2014 concerning the education of American Indian students and make use of education grant available to better meet the needs of American Indian and Alaskan native students (Albania);

176.328 Review regulations to ensure the protection against exploitation and forced labour of migrant workers (Plurinational State of Bolivia); 176.329 Review in depth its migration policy (Congo);

176.330 Further improve the rights of immigrants (Senegal);

176.331 Effectively respect for the rights of all migrant workers and their family members (Benin);

176.332 That special attention is given to protecting migrant workers from exploitative working conditions, specifically in the agricultural sector (Portugal);

176.333 Ensure the rights of migrant workers, especially in the sector of agriculture where the use of child labourers is a common practice (Holy See);

176.334 Avoid criminalization of migrants (Uruguay);

176.335 Facilitating access for undocumented immigrants and their children to health care under that Act (Portugal);

176.336 Consider the establishment of legislation providing for access to basic services for undocumented migrants, particularly health services, in conformity with the Affordable Care Act (Peru);

176.337 Consider reviewing the eligibility requirements to the public welfare system, so that the basic human rights of immigrants, including the undocumented, are guaranteed, in particular access to health for women and children (Honduras);

176.338 Guarantee the right to family reunification of migrants held in detention and continue with the efforts to protect the human rights of migrant persons, particularly their economic, social and cultural rights (Paraguay);

176.339 Ensure due process for all immigrants in immigration proceedings, using the principle of the best interest, especially in the case of families and unaccompanied children (Honduras);

176.340 Re-evaluate mechanisms at the federal, state and tribal levels, to address the disproportionate impact on immigrant women (Maldives);

176.341 Take up the commitment to address, in a framework of shared but differentiated responsibility and along with the international community, the world problem of climate change and its negative impact (Nicaragua);

176.342 Continue to actively participate in the climate change negotiations for a strong legally binding outcome of the United Nations Framework Convention on Climate Change process (Bangladesh);

176.343 Ensure federal legislation to prohibit environmental pollution and reduce greenhouse gas emissions to control climate change (Maldives).

177. All conclusions and recommendations contained in the present report reflect the position of the submitting State and the State under review. They should not be construed as endorsed by the Working Group as a whole.

[End Text]

Source: https://www.upr-info.org/sites/default/files/document/united_states/session_22_-_may_2015/a_hrc_wg.6_22_l.10.pdf

12. U.S. RESPONSE TO THE REPORT OF THE WORKING GROUP ON THE UNIVERSAL PERIODIC REVIEW: VIEWS ON CONCLUSIONS AND/OR RECOMMENDATIONS, VOLUNTARY COMMITMENTS AND REPLIES

This Document contains the responses of the U.S. to the views, conclusions and recommendations contained in the 2015 Outcome Document, above. It is the SuR's expression of what it accepts and does not accept. The decisions, views and recommendations made in the course of this process, while not legally binding upon states, should be taken seriously, except for those which are purely politically motivated by states antagonistic to the U.S. Indeed, even these should not be disregarded outright, but considered in light of helping the U.S. improve.

Addendum

1. The U. S. government has carefully reviewed the 343 recommendations received during its Universal Periodic Review. This response reflects our continuing efforts, in consultation with civil society, to promote, protect, and respect human rights for all.

2. Some recommendations ask U.S. to achieve an ideal, e.g., end discrimination or police brutality, and others request action not entirely within the power of our Federal Executive Branch, e.g., adopt legislation, ratify treaties, or act at the state level. We support or support in part these recommendations when we share their ideals, are making serious efforts to achieve their goals, and intend to continue doing so. Nonetheless, we recognize, realistically, that the United States may never completely accomplish what is described in these recommendations' literal terms.

3. We support recommendations to take actions we are already taking or have taken, and intend to continue taking, without in any way implying that our ongoing or prior efforts have been unsuccessful or that these actions are necessarily legally required. With respect to judicial remedies, we note that we cannot make commitments regarding, and do not control, the outcome of court proceedings.

4. Where recommendations include inaccurate assumptions, assertions, or factual predicates, we have decided whether we support them or support them in part by looking past their rhetoric to the proposed action or objective.

Civil Rights and non-discrimination

5. We support:
- 118,119,123,131,133,134,137,139,140,141,144,145,157,159,160,162,163,216,219, 222,225,228,276,277,281,287.
- 127,128,129. In December 2014, the President created the Task Force on 21stCentury Policing to make recommendations to strengthen police-community relations. Many state, local, and tribal law enforcement agencies are presently implementing many of those recommendations.

- 214,215,221,223. See general explanation in para. 6.
- 121,143,146,148,149,150,151,152,153,161,220. Profiling — the invidious use of irrelevant individual characteristics including race, ethnicity, national origin, or religion — is prohibited under our Constitution and federal government policy.
- 130. See explanation of #126, para. 6.

6. We support, in part:
- We note that we have federal, state, and tribal legislation and strategies in place to combat discrimination, including racial discrimination, and we take effective measures to counter intolerance, violence, and discrimination against members of all minority groups, including African-Americans, Muslims, Arabs, and indigenous persons:
- 113,125,154,155,227,321.
- 120,135,136. We cannot support these recommendations to the extent they ask U.S. to restrict constitutionally-protected belief or expression.
- 122,126,132,156,158,226. We disagree with some of these recommendations' premises, but we are committed to combating discrimination and hate crimes and promoting tolerance. Concerning #122, although we recognize there is always room for improvement, we believe that our law is consistent with our CERD obligations.
- 142,147. See explanation of #121, para. 5. The U.S. does not monitor communications to disadvantage individuals based on their ethnicity, race, gender, sexual orientation, or religion.
- 224. Although training largely occurs at the local level, the federal government promotes best practices through technical assistance, investigations, and agreements to reform police practices.
- 229. We cannot support parts of this recommendation concerning reparations.
- 308. We support this recommendation insofar as it recommends compliance with our domestic law and international human rights obligations, including regarding freedom of religion.

7. We do not support:
- 278.

Criminal justice

8. We support:
- 73,194,195,200,213,231,232,236,255,275.
- 74. We support human rights training for civil servants who need it, understanding that not all perform functions that require it (e.g., air-traffic controllers).
- 199. We support the second part of this recommendation to the extent provided for under our Eighth Amendment, which prohibits imposition of cruel and unusual punishment.

9. We support, in part:
- 198. We support consideration of these recommendations, noting that we may not agree with all of them.
- 230,233. We strongly support expanding the number of firearms transfers that are subject to background checks but with limited, common-sense exceptions (e.g., certain transfers between family members, temporary transfers for hunting/sporting).
- 51,234,235. Sentences of life without parole may not be imposed on juveniles for non-homicide crimes. The Administration supports federal legislation to eliminate life-without-parole sentences for juveniles in the federal criminal justice system. Concerning #235, we are not currently contemplating legislation to revise existing life-without-possibility-of-parole laws as applied to adult offenders.
- 180,196,197. We support these recommendations with respect to measures required to comply with U.S. obligations, and with respect to persons with certain intellectual disabilities, but not all persons with any mental illness.
- 218. We disagree with some of this recommendation's premises, but we are committed to combating discrimination and improper actions by law enforcement officials.

- 260. We disagree with some of this recommendation's premises, but we are committed to protecting the health and welfare of adopted children.
- 274. Recidivism is an important criminal justice concern, and we support and have undertaken efforts to address it, including through the Reentry Council.
- 279. See explanation of #280, para. 10.
- 291,292. The vast majority of matters involving youth are handled through the juvenile justice system. Factors weighed by courts deciding whether exceptional circumstances warrant trial as an adult include age/background, type/seriousness of the alleged offense, the juvenile's role, and prior record/past treatment. Concerning #291, juveniles have the right to free legal representation in all criminal and delinquency proceedings, and in many cases, it is also available for civil proceedings.

10. We do not support:
- 202.
- 13,165,166,167,168,169,170,171,172,173,174,175,176,177,178,179,181,182,183, 184,185,186,187,188,189,190,191,192,193,201, which concern abolition of the death penalty.
- 280. Decisions on extradition cases are made on a case-by-case basis, consistent with our international obligations, and we cannot prejudge the outcomes of particular cases.

Economic, social, and cultural rights and measures; indigenous issues; and the environment

11. We support:
- 124,257,313,315,316,317,319,327.
- 322,323,324,326. We support these recommendations consistent with our 2010 Announcement of Support for the UNDRIP.

12. We support, in part:
- 256. See general explanation in para. 3.
- 100. We support this recommendation's principle: addressing the needs of women who have been victims of sexual violence in conflict situations.
- 164. See explanation of #308, para. 6.
- 309,311,312,314. The U.S. is not a party to the ICESCR, and we understand the rights therein are to be realized progressively. We understand #311-312 as referencing a right to safe drinking water and sanitation, derived from the right to an adequate standard of living. We continue to improve our domestic laws and policies to promote access to housing, food, health, and safe drinking water and sanitation, with the aim of decreasing poverty and preventing discrimination. Concerning #312, we do not regard UNGA Resolution 64/292 as legally-binding.
- 310. We disagree with some of this recommendation's premises, but are committed to helping communities pursue alternatives to criminalizing homelessness. We believe our laws are consistent with our international obligations.
- 338. We support this recommendation insofar as it recommends compliance with our international human rights obligations.
- 341,342,343. We support these recommendations insofar as they encourage domestic action on climate change and international efforts to reach an agreement that is ambitious, inclusive, and applicable to all countries.

13. We do not support:
- 97,98,99,102,318,320,325.
- 335,336,337. Undocumented migrants in the U.S. have access to publicly-supported health care through Migrant Health Centers. Undocumented unaccompanied children are eligible for health care while in federal government-funded shelters.

National security

14. We support:
- 303.

- 239,240,242,244,246,249,251. We have clearly stated our desire to close the Guantánamo Bay detention facility and to continue working with Congress, the courts, and other countries to do so in a responsible manner that is consistent with our international obligations. Until it is closed, we will continue to ensure that operations there are consistent with our international obligations. Concerning #244 and 251, the U.S. does not operate secret detention centers. We allow the ICRC access to individuals we detain in armed conflict. We support #246 insofar as it recommends upholding our international obligations, and as consistent with domestic law and policy.
- 283,284. See explanation of #210, para. 15.
- 290. We support this recommendation insofar as it recommends upholding our international obligations, and as consistent with domestic law and policy. We take great care to ensure that our uses of force — including targeted strikes — conform to all applicable domestic and international law, including the law of war principles of proportionality and distinction.
- 293,294,295,296,307. We support these recommendations insofar as they recommend respect for ICCPR Article 17, which applies to individuals within a state's territory and subject to its jurisdiction. Our Constitution and laws contain appropriate protections for privacy of communications, consistent with our international human rights obligations, and we publicize our policies to the extent possible, consistent with national security needs. We frequently update and draft new laws, regulations, and policies to further protect individuals' privacy.

15. We support, in part:
- We support these recommendations insofar as they recommend upholding international obligations, and as consistent with domestic law and policy. We reject certain premises in these recommendations, which constitute unsubstantiated accusations of ongoing serious violations of international law:
- 203,211,212,217,258,286,288.
- 210,247,248. Consistent with international obligations and U.S. domestic law, we have conducted and will continue to conduct thorough independent investigations of credible allegations of torture, and to prosecute persons when there is sufficient legal basis. For example, DOJ conducted criminal investigations into alleged mistreatment of individuals in U.S. custody after the 2001 terrorist attacks, including appointment of a special prosecutor to investigate certain allegations, and brought several criminal prosecutions for abusing detainees and obtained the convictions of two contractors. In addition, DoD, CIA, and others have conducted numerous independent, rigorous investigations into detainee treatment, detention policy, and conditions of confinement. Concerning #247-248, we have extended an invitation to the Special Rapporteur on Torture to visit Guantánamo Bay consistent with the terms of other comparable visits to Guantánamo Bay.
- 204,205,206,207,209. See explanation of #290, para. 14. DoD investigates all credible allegations of misconduct by its personnel and pursues judicial or administrative action against alleged perpetrators as appropriate. For #205- 207 and 209, we conduct lethal, targeted action against al-Qaeda and its associated forces, including with remotely piloted aircraft, in order to prevent terrorist attacks on the U.S. and to save lives. Concerning #207 and 209, if we determine that non-combatants were killed or injured in a U.S. strike, we may, where appropriate, offer condolence or other *ex gratia* payments to those injured and the families of those killed. Concerning #209, we remain committed to investigating and prosecuting willful use of excessive force by law enforcement officers.
- 241,243,245,250. See explanation of #239, para. 14. We reject the premise in #241 and 250 that the U.S. engages in illegal detention of terrorism suspects. We support the parts of these recommendations asking that we close Guantánamo.
- 289. DoD has established victim-representation programs for sexual assault victims eligible for legal assistance, consistent with the findings of an independent study concluding that removing proceedings from the chain of command was not needed to improve the situation of victims.
- 297,298,299,304,305. We collect information only in accordance with U.S. law and international obligations. Presidential Policy Directive 28 states that all persons should be treated with dignity and respect, regardless of nationality or place of residence, and that all persons have legitimate privacy interests in the handling of their personal information. Our foreign intelligence oversight system is robust and transparent, and includes executive, legislative, and judicial bodies. We support #299 and 304-305 insofar as they recommend respect for the ICCPR, Article 17, which applies to individuals within a state's territory and subject to its jurisdiction.

16. We do not support:
- 208,259,267,282,285,300,301,302.

Immigration, migrants, trafficking, labor, and children

17. We support:
- 112,114,115,253,263,268,269,270,271,272,273,328,329,330,332,333,340.
- 138,264. U.S. federal labor and employment laws generally apply to all workers, regardless of immigration status.
- 254. Since perpetrators of human trafficking or migrant smuggling-related crimes can remain in neighboring countries, we rely on the support of foreign partners to combat both.
- 262. We support this recommendation insofar as it recommends prohibition of slavery for agricultural workers. All workers in the U.S., regardless of immigration status, are protected from forced labor by U.S. law, including our Thirteenth Amendment and the Trafficking Victims Protection Act.
- 266. We prioritize combating sex trafficking of minors and human trafficking generally, including through the National Strategy for Child Exploitation Prevention and Interdiction, scheduled for release in 2016, and the Attorney General's annual human trafficking report, which features recommendations for improvement in combating trafficking. The Justice for Victims of Trafficking Act, enacted in May 2015, authorizes the Attorney General to implement and maintain a National Strategy for Combating Human Trafficking.
- 331. We understand the reference to family members of migrant workers to mean those located within the U.S.

18. We support, in part:
- 306. See general explanation in para. 4.
- 116,117. U.S. law allows, but does not require, employers to offer paid maternity leave. The Family and Medical Leave Act entitles eligible employees to 12 weeks of unpaid, job-protected leave in a year for the birth and care of newborn or adopted/foster children.
- 252. We actively utilize alternatives to detention where appropriate, and are working to shorten detention families may face while their immigration proceedings are resolved. Conditions at Family Residential Centers are continually being evaluated and improved.
- 265. We support this recommendation insofar as it encourages non-violent forms of discipline. Excessive or arbitrary corporal punishment is prohibited under our Constitution, and we take effective measures to help ensure non-discrimination in school discipline policies and practices.
- 339. Noncitizens in the U.S. facing removal receive significant procedural protections. The best interest of a child is one factor in determinations by immigration judges. HHS provides care and placement for children who enter the U.S. without an adult guardian, considering the best interests of the child in all placement decisions.

19. We do not support:
- 261.
- 334. Although unlawful presence in the U.S. is not a crime, and the federal government does not support state initiatives intended to criminalize mere status, certain immigration offenses are subject to criminal sanction (e.g., illegal entry).

Treaties, international mechanisms, and domestic implementation

20. We support:
- 88,105,106,110.
- 1,7,12,17,21,23,24,25,27,31,32,34,35,38,39,40,41,42,46,47,48,49,50,55,56,58,60,61, 72,80,81,82,83,84. We support recommendation surging deliberative actions on treaties or domestic institutions, such as that we "consider" them. We support recommendations asking U.S. to ratify CEDAW, CRPD, and ILO Convention 111. We support recommendations asking U.S. to ratify the CRC, as we support its goals and intend to review how we could move toward its ratification. We understand recommendations here and in para. 21 urging that we accelerate ratification or review of certain treaties as not intended to prejudice appropriate review and consideration of them in accordance with constitutional procedures. We understand full implementation in #31 as consistent with any reservations, understandings, or declarations to which our ratification would be subject. Concerning #72, we do not believe that any of our reservations, understandings, and declarations on international instruments undermine our obligations or the treaties' object or purpose. Concerning #80-84,

although there are many efforts at all levels to improve and strengthen existing domestic institutions that monitor human rights, there are no current plans to establish a single national human rights institution.

- 62. We are preparing for Senate consideration of the ATT.
- 91,92,93,94,95. See general explanation in para. 6. We are working toward better enforcement and implementation of existing laws and programs, and will consider suggestions for further improvement on an ongoing basis, but at this time we do not have plans to develop a supplemental national action plan.
- 107. The federal government has established interagency working groups to coordinate follow-up to supported UPR recommendations and to consider recommendations by human rights treaty bodies.
- 237,238. We understand the recommendations to mean the Executive branch should support legislation to ensure compliance with obligations in VCCR Article 36 and the ICJ's judgment in *Avena*. 21. We support, in part:
- 2,3,4,5,6,8,14,16,18,19,20,22,26,28,29,30,33,36,37,45,52,53,54,57,70. We support the parts of these recommendations asking U.S. to ratify treaties, identified above, of which the Administration is most committed to pursuing ratification.
- 108. U.S. international human rights obligations are implemented through a comprehensive system of laws and policies at all levels of government. We are taking steps to strengthen federal-level coordination, and are considering ways to improve implementation.
- 111. We work with Special Rapporteurs to facilitate their visit requests on mutually agreed terms, and we expect two official trips in late 2015 and early 2016.

22. We do not support:

- 9,10,11,15,43,44,59,63,64,65,66,67,68,69,71,109.
- 75,76,77,78,79,85,86,87,89,90. See explanation of #80, para. 20.

Other recommendations

23. We received some recommendations that do not fit into specific categories. We do not support:

- 96,101,103,104.

[End Text]

Source: https://documents-dds-ny.un.org/doc/UNDOC/GEN/G15/207/66/PDF/G1520766.pdf?OpenElement

13. DECISION ADOPTED BY THE HUMAN RIGHTS COUNCIL: OUTCOME OF THE UNIVERSAL PERIODIC REVIEW OF THE UNITED STATES OF AMERICA

This Document is the Decision of the Human Rights Council adopting the Report of the Outcome of the UPR of the U.S. in 2015. The Council voted to adopt the Report of the Working Group, the Outcome Document. This finalizes the formal UPR process for the U.S. until the next one in 2020. In the meantime, the U.S. is expected to implement the recommendations it accepted in the previous document, which will form part of the next UPR process.

The Human Rights Council,

Acting in compliance with the mandate entrusted to it by the General Assembly in its resolution 60/251 of 15 March 2006, and with Human Rights Council resolutions 5/1 of 18 June 2007 and 16/21 of 21 March 2011, and President's statement PRST/8/1 of 9 April 2008, on the modalities and practices for the universal periodic review process,

Having conducted the review of the United States of America on 11 May 2015 in conformity with all relevant provisions contained in the annex to Council resolution 5/1,

Decides to adopt the outcome of the review of the United States of America, comprising the report thereon of the Working Group on the Universal Periodic Review (A/HRC/30/12), the views of the State concerning the recommendations and/or conclusions made, and its voluntary commitments and replies presented before the adoption of the outcome by the plenary to questions or issues not sufficiently addressed during the interactive dialogue held in the Working Group (A/HRC/30/12/Add.1 and A/HRC/30/2, chap. VI).

22nd meeting

24 September 2015 [Adopted without a vote.]

[End Text]

᠊ᠭᠥᠭᠥᠭᠥᠭᠥᠭᠥᠭᠥᠭᠥᠭᠥ

14. APPENDIX TO THE ADDENDUM TO THE REPORT ON THE SECOND UNIVERSAL PERIODIC REVIEW OF THE UNITED STATES OF AMERICA

This Document was submitted by the U.S. to the U.N. Office of the High Commissioner for Human Rights. It was in response to the OHCHR request for more detailed information on how the U.S. intended to implement the recommendations it had accepted from the 2015 UPR process, as found in the Outcome document, above. It is a detailed chart which must be read in conjunction with the Outcome document and the U.S. response to the views, observations and recommendations in that document. The OHCHR is asking for more detail of the unspecific responses the U.S. previously gave. This is part of the "follow-up" process to make sure states implement the recommendations and actually improve their human rights performance in reality.

Appendix to the Addendum
to the Report on the
Second Universal Periodic Review of the United States of America

This document is provided to the Office of the High Commissioner for Human Rights in response to its request for additional explanations, in more detail than we could provide under the strict word limit applicable to our Second Cycle UPR Addendum, of the U.S. positions on UPR recommendations that we supported in part. It is to be read in conjunction with our Second Cycle UPR Addendum.

****

Some recommendations ask us to achieve an ideal, e.g., end discrimination or police brutality, and others request action not entirely within the power of our Federal Executive Branch, e.g., adopt legislation, ratify treaties, or act at the state level. We support or support in part these recommendations when we share their ideals, are making serious efforts to achieve their goals, and intend to continue doing so. Nonetheless, we recognize, realistically, that the United States may never completely accomplish what is described in these recommendations' literal terms.

We support recommendations to take actions we are already taking or have taken, and intend to continue taking, without in any way implying that our ongoing or prior efforts have been unsuccessful or that these actions are necessarily legally required. With respect to judicial remedies, we note that we cannot make commitments regarding, and do not control, the outcome of court proceedings.

Where recommendations include inaccurate assumptions, assertions, or factual predicates, we have decided whether we support them or support them in part by looking past their rhetoric to the proposed action or objective.

#	Recommendation text	Position	Expanded Explanation
2	Ratify the international human rights instruments from which it is not a party.	Support in Part	We support the part of this recommendation asking us to ratify those treaties of which the Administration is most committed to pursuing ratification: the CEDAW, the CRPD, and ILO Convention 111. We also support the part of this recommendation asking us to ratify the CRC, as we support its goals and intend to review how we could move toward its ratification. We do not support the part of this recommendation related to other treaties. For more information, please refer to paragraphs 113-116 of our UPR Report.
3	Ratify all international human rights instruments to which it is not yet a State party.	Support in Part	Please refer to the explanation for recommendation #2.
4	Take genuine steps towards the ratification of Treaties and Optional Protocols to Conventions that the United States has already signed, but not yet ratified.	Support in Part	Please refer to the explanation for recommendation #2.
5	Accelerate the ratification of outstanding international human rights legal instruments.	Support in Part	Please refer to the explanation for recommendation #2. We understand the part of this recommendation asking us to accelerate ratification as not intended to prejudice appropriate

			review and consideration of these treaties in accordance with Constitutional procedures.
6	Consider ratifying more human rights instruments.	Support in Part	Please refer to the explanation for recommendation #2.
8	Work more to join the international treaties on human rights.	Support in Part	Please refer to the explanation for recommendation #2.
14	Adhere to international legal instruments to which it is not yet a party, particularly the Second Optional Protocol to the ICCPR.	Support in Part	Please refer to the explanation for recommendation #2.
16	Step up efforts to ratify ICESCR, CEDAW and CRC.	Support in Part	Please refer to the explanation for recommendation #2.
18	Proceed to the ratification of CRC, signed in 1995, CEDAW signed in 1980, ICESCR, signed in 1977, and transpose them into national law.	Support in Part	Please refer to the explanation for recommendation #2.
19	Promptly ratify CEDAW and CRPD, as well as other core human rights conventions such as the ICESCR and CRC.	Support in Part	Please refer to the explanation for recommendation #2.
20	Accede to the key international human rights instruments CRC, ICESCR, CRPD and CEDAW.	Support in Part	Please refer to the explanation for recommendation #2.
22	Reinforce its role as a global leader on human rights by becoming a party to the ICESCR, the CEDAW, the CRC, and the CRPD.	Support in Part	Please refer to the explanation for recommendation #2.
26	Ratify CRC and ICESCR.	Support in Part	Please refer to the explanation for recommendation #2.
28	Ratify in due course instruments, such as ICRMW, CRC and ICESCR.	Support in Part	Please refer to the explanation for recommendation #2.
29	Ratify international human rights treaties particularly the OP-ICESCR, CEDAW, and CRC.	Support in Part	Please refer to the explanation for recommendation #2.
30	Ratify the core international human rights instruments, in particular CRC and CEDAW.	Support in Part	Please refer to the explanation for recommendation #2.
33	Ratify CRC, ICRMW, ICPPED, CRPD, CEDAW and the Rome Statute.	Support in Part	Please refer to the explanation for recommendation #2.
36	Ratify CRC, CEDAW, CRPD and the ICC statute, as previously recommended.	Support in Part	Please refer to the explanation for recommendation #2.
37	Continue to exert efforts to ratify major international human rights instruments,	Support in Part	Please refer to the explanation for recommendation #2.

	particularly including CEDAW and CRC.		
45	Ratify OP-CAT and take swift measures to ensure the human rights of convicts and persons in custody.	Support in Part	We support the part of this recommendation asking us to promote, protect, and respect the human rights of those convicted of crimes and persons in custody. For more information, please refer to paragraphs 43-48 of our UPR Report. We do not support the part of this recommendation asking us to ratify the OP-CAT.
51	Pass legislation domestically to prohibit the passing of life imprisonment without the possibility of parole on offenders who were children at the time of offending, and ratify without any further delay the CRC.	Support in Part	We support the part of this recommendation asking us to ratify the CRC, as we support its goals and intend to review how we could move toward its ratification. Please refer to the explanation for recommendation #234.
52	Ratify the CRC and OP-CAT.	Support in Part	Please refer to the explanation for recommendation #2.
53	Ratify the major human rights instruments, in particular the CRC and ICRMW.	Support in Part	Please refer to the explanation for recommendation #2.
54	Ratify, among others, CRC, CRPD, ICRMW / Accede to the American Convention on Human Rights and recognize the competence of the Inter-American Court on Human Rights.	Support in Part	Please refer to the explanation for recommendation #2. We also do not support the part of this recommendation concerning the Inter-American Convention and Court. For more information, please refer to paragraph 117 of our UPR Report.
57	Improve the protection of children at national level by ratifying the Convention on the Rights of the Child and its Optional Protocols.	Support in Part	Please refer to the explanation for recommendation #2. We note that we have already ratified two of the Optional Protocols to the Convention on the Rights of the Child in 2002: the Optional Protocol on the Involvement of Children in Armed Conflict and the Optional Protocol on the Sale of Children, Child Prostitution, and Child Pornography.
70	Ratify all international human rights conventions and protocols, and those of the ILO and the Rome Statute.	Support in Part	Please refer to the explanation for recommendation #2.
91	Adopt an action plan consistent with the Durban Declaration and Programme of Action in an effort to eradicate racial discrimination effectively.	Support in Part	We support the part of this recommendation asking us to make efforts to eradicate racial discrimination. We have extensive Federal, state, and tribal legislation and strategies in place to combat all forms of discrimination, including racial discrimination. For more information, please refer to paragraphs 11-19 and 25-34 of our UPR Report. We are working diligently toward better enforcement and implementation of these laws and programs, and will consider suggestions for further improvement. We do not support the part of this recommendation referring to the Durban Declaration, and we do not at the current time have plans to develop a supplemental national action plan.
92	Adopt and implement a national plan in accordance with the Durban Declaration and Program of Action.	Support in Part	We support the aspect of this recommendation that is asking us to implement policies and strategies to combat racial discrimination. Please refer to the explanation for recommendation 91. We do not support the part of this recommendation referring to the Durban Declaration, and we do not at the current time have plans to develop a supplemental national action plan.
93	Take all legal measures to adopt and	Support	We support the aspect of this recommendation asking us to take legal measures to promote

	implement a national racial justice plan consistent with the Durban Declaration and Programme of Action.	in Part	justice without racial discrimination. Please refer to the explanation for recommendation #91. We do not support the part of this recommendation referring to the Durban Declaration, and we do not at the current time have plans to develop a supplemental national action plan.
94	Undertake measures to combat racial discrimination, including adoption of a National Action Plan to Combat Racial Discrimination as recommended by the Committee on the Elimination of Racial Discrimination.	Support in Part	We support the part of this recommendation asking us to undertake measures to combat racial discrimination. Please refer to the explanation for recommendation #91. We do not support the part of this recommendation asking us to adopt a national action plan, as we do not at the current time have plans to develop such a plan.
95	Adopt and implement a national plan inspired by the Durban Declaration and Program of Action, for the benefit especially of disadvantaged minorities, which are Afro-Americans and indigenous peoples.	Support in Part	We support the part of this recommendation asking us to implement policies and strategies for members of disadvantaged minorities, including African-Americans and indigenous individuals. Please refer to the explanation for recommendation #91. We do not support the part of this recommendation referring to the Durban Declaration, and we do not at the current time have plans to develop a supplemental national action plan.
100	Ensure that the US international aid allows access to sexual and reproductive health services for women victims of sexual violence in conflict situations.	Support in part	We support this recommendation in part in that U.S. foreign assistance funds are programmed in a manner consistent with applicable U.S. law and policy to support the needs of women who have been victims of sexual violence in conflict situations. This includes support through interventions such as family planning, post-exposure HIV prophylaxis, post-abortion care, fistula care, psychosocial support, community gender-based violence prevention, health provider training, and linkages with economic empowerment and livelihood programs.
108	That a mechanism be established at the federal level to ensure comprehensive and coordinated compliance with international human rights instruments at federal, local and state level.	Support in Part	We support the part of this recommendation asking us to establish a mechanism to coordinate efforts related to international human rights instruments at the federal level, as we have already taken steps to implement such mechanisms. For example, our interagency UPR Working Groups, under the leadership of the White House, are charged with reviewing UPR recommendations and related concluding observations and recommendations from treaty bodies and sharing best practices and information. We do not support the part of this recommendation asking us to create a single mechanism with respect to the state and local levels. U.S. international human rights obligations are implemented through a comprehensive system of laws and policies at all levels of government. Many state and local governments have their own human rights institutions and mechanisms. The U.S. Department of Justice also has statutory authority to investigate many allegations of human or civil rights violations or abuses by state or local government officials. We are considering ways to improve such implementation.
111	Enhance further co-operation with human rights mechanisms including issuing a standing invitation to special procedures and providing full access to the Special Rapporteur on Torture.	Support in Part	We support the part of this recommendation asking us to enhance further cooperation with human rights mechanisms. We have made reports to the treaty bodies for the Convention Against Torture, the Convention on the Elimination of All Forms of Racial Discrimination, the International Covenant on Civil and Political Rights, and two of the Optional Protocols to the Convention on the Rights of the Child since 2013. We also work regularly with Special Rapporteurs to facilitate their visits on mutually-agreed terms, and we are hosting one trip in

			the week of November 30-December 2 and another one in early 2016. We do not support the part of this recommendation referring to issuance of a standing invitation to special procedures. We are currently working with the Special Rapporteur on Torture to facilitate his visit request on mutually-agreed terms.
113	End various forms of inequality.	Support in Part	We support the part of this recommendation asking us to make efforts to achieve the ideal of equality. We are making serious efforts to reach this goal, and intend to continue doing so. For example, we note that we have federal, state, and tribal legislation and strategies in place to combat discrimination, including racial discrimination, and we take effective measures to counter intolerance, violence, and discrimination against members of all minority groups, including African-Americans, Muslims, Arabs, and indigenous persons. We support this recommendation "in part" because we recognize, realistically, that the United States may never completely accomplish what is described in this recommendation's literal terms.
116	Eliminate discrimination against women by introducing paid maternity leave and providing equal pay for women for the same work.	Support in Part	We support the part of this recommendation asking us to work toward eliminating discrimination against women and providing equal pay to women. We have comprehensive laws aimed at ensuring gender equality at work, and we aggressively enforce those laws, and we are taking further action to promote pay equity through the President's Equal Pay Taskforce. For more information, please refer to paragraphs 74-75 of our UPR Report. President Obama has called for the passage of federal legislation guaranteeing every working American paid family and medical leave to care for a new child, a seriously ill family member, or their own serious illness. U.S. law does not require employees to take any allotted leave; those who would prefer to return to the workplace sooner may do so. Under the Family and Medical Leave Act, eligible employees are entitled to take up to 12 workweeks of unpaid, job-protected leave in a 12-month period for the birth and care of a newborn child, or placement of a child for adoption or foster care and care of the newly placed child. Both mothers and fathers are entitled to take such leave. The leave can also be used for prenatal care or pregnancy-related incapacity. However, we support this recommendation "in part" because currently, U.S. law does not require provision of paid family leave for every individual employee. For more information, see: http://www.dol.gov/featured/paidleave/.
117	Issue a decree on compulsory maternity leave and equal wages for men and women.	Support in Part	We support the part of this recommendation asking us to work toward providing equal wages to women. President Obama signed two executive actions in 2014 aimed at ensuring fair pay for women. We do not support the part of this recommendation asking us to issue a decree on compulsory maternity leave. Please refer to the explanation for recommendation #116.
120	Strengthen the existing laws and legislation in order to combat different forms of discrimination, racism and hatred.	Support in Part	We support the part of this recommendation asking us to combat discrimination. We take effective measures at all levels of government to counter racial and religious discrimination and combat hate crimes, including through the Matthew Shepard/James Byrd, Jr., Hate Crimes Prevention Act of 2009. For more information, please refer to paragraphs 11-42 of our UPR Report. We do not support the parts of this recommendation that ask us to restrict Constitutionally-protected belief or expression.
122	Bring in line the definition of racial	Support	We support the aspect of this recommendation asking us to combat racial discrimination

	discrimination in federal and state legislation with the provisions of ICERD.	in Part	through our federal and state laws. For more information, please refer to paragraphs 11-19 and 25-34 of our UPR Report. We do not support the part of this recommendation implying that our federal and state laws are not in compliance with our international obligations: although we recognize there is always room for improvement, we believe that our law is consistent with our CERD obligations.
125	End discrimination in law and practice against all minorities and migrants, particularly against women and children from poor families and take effective steps to prevent and combat violence against them.	Support in Part	We support the part of this recommendation asking us to take effective steps to prevent and combat violence against women, children, and members of minorities. We also support the part of this recommendation asking us to make efforts to achieve the ideal of ending discrimination. We are making serious efforts to reach this goal, and intend to continue doing so. For more information, please refer to paragraphs 11-9, 25-34, 54-60, 68-71, 74-75, and 80-82 of our UPR Report. We support this recommendation "in part" because we recognize, realistically, that the United States may never completely accomplish what is described in this recommendation's literal terms.
126	Abolish any discriminatory measures that target Muslims and Arabs at airports.	Support in Part	We support the part of this recommendation asking us to prohibit measures that discriminate against Muslims and Arabs at airports. For more information, please refer to paragraph 71 of our UPR Report. We do not support the part of this recommendation implying that we currently have in place measures at U.S. airports that target or discriminate against Arabs or Muslims.
132	Toughen its efforts to prevent religion and hate crimes as it is evident that the crimes are on the increase.	Support in Part	We support the part of this recommendation asking us to toughen our ongoing efforts to prevent and punish hate crimes, including those motivated by religious hatred. For more information, please refer to paragraphs 20-24 of our UPR Report. We do not support the assertion in this recommendation that it is evident that hate crimes are on the rise in the United States.
135	Strengthen the laws and mechanisms at the federal and state level to further combat racial discrimination in all its forms as well as against hate speech and hate crimes, to ensure that people are protected therefrom.	Support in Part	Please refer to the explanation for recommendation #120.
136	Prohibit racial discrimination and racist hate speech, as well as broaden the protection afforded by law.	Support in Part	We support the part of this recommendation asking us to prohibit racial discrimination. Please refer to the explanation for recommendation #91. We do not support the parts of this recommendation that ask us to restrict Constitutionally-protected belief or expression.
142	Address discrimination, racial profiling by the authorities, Islamophobia and religious intolerance by reviewing all laws and practices that violate the rights of minority groups, with a view to amend them.	Support in Part	We support the part of this recommendation asking us to address discrimination and racial profiling by government authorities. We take effective measures to counter intolerance, violence, and discrimination against all members of all minority groups, including Muslims. Profiling – the invidious use of irrelevant individual characteristics including race, ethnicity, national origin, or religion – is prohibited under our Constitution and federal government policy. For more information, please refer to paragraphs 11-34 of our UPR Report. We do not support the part of this recommendation that asks us to restrict Constitutionally-protected belief or expression, and we do not support the implication of this recommendation that the

			laws of the United States currently violate the human rights of members of minority groups.
147	Eliminate the practice of racial profiling and surveillance by law enforcement officials.	Support in Part	We support the part of this recommendation asking us to work toward eliminating racial profiling. Please refer to the explanation for recommendation 142. For more information, please refer to paragraphs 9 and 11-16 of our UPR Report. We also support the part of this recommendation on surveillance to the extent it applies to unlawful surveillance in violation of U.S. law; however, we do not support this recommendation to the extent that it asks us to prohibit surveillance by law enforcement that is authorized by law or by a valid court order as part of a criminal investigation. The United States does not monitor communications to disadvantage individuals based on their ethnicity, race, gender, sexual orientation or religion.
154	Adopt measures at the federal level to prevent and punish excessive use of force by law enforcement officials against members of ethnic and racial minorities, including unarmed persons, which disproportionately affect Afro American and undocumented migrants.	Support in Part	We support the part of this recommendation asking us to prevent and punish excessive use of force by law enforcement. We have extensive Federal, state, and tribal legislation and strategies to combat all forms of discrimination, including racial discrimination. For more information, please refer to paragraphs 9, 11-16, and 64 of our UPR Report. We are working diligently toward better enforcement and implementation of these laws and programs, and will consider suggestions for further improvement. We do not support the implication of this recommendation that excessive use of force disproportionately affects undocumented migrants, as we are not aware of data on those impacts.
155	End police brutality against African Americans and rectify the judicial as well as socio-economic systems that systematically discriminate against them.	Support in Part	We support the part of this recommendation asking us to make efforts to end excessive use of force against African-Americans and to end discrimination in the criminal justice and other systems. We are making serious efforts to reach this goal, and intend to continue doing so. For more information, please refer to paragraphs 9, 11-19, 25-34, and 64 of our UPR Report. Please also refer to the explanation for recommendation #91. We support this recommendation "in part" because we recognize, realistically, that the United States may never completely accomplish what is described in this recommendation's literal terms.
156	Correctly address the root causes of racial discrimination and eliminate the frequently occurred excessive use of force by law enforcement against of African-Americans and other ethnic minorities.	Support in Part	We support the part of this recommendation asking us to make efforts to address the causes of racial discrimination. We also support the part of this recommendation asking us to work to eliminate use of excessive force against African-Americans and members of other minorities. We are making serious efforts to reach this goal, and intend to continue doing so. For more information, please refer to paragraphs 9, 11-16, and 64 of our UPR Report. Please also refer to the explanation for recommendation #91. We support this recommendation "in part" because we recognize, realistically, that the United States may never completely accomplish what is described in this recommendation's literal terms.
158	Take measures to put an end to police abuses, including the merciless killing of coloured people, and all racial discrimination.	Support in Part	We support the part of this recommendation asking us to take measures to end police abuses and racial discrimination. For more information, please refer to paragraphs 9, 11-19, 25-34, and 64 of our UPR Report. Please also refer to the explanation for recommendation #91. We do not support the part of this recommendation about the merciless killings of individuals by law enforcement.
164	Take affirmative steps to ensure that individuals' religious refusals are regulated to	Support in Part	We support this recommendation insofar as it recommends compliance with our domestic law and international human rights obligations, including regarding freedom of religion. We do

			conform with international human rights standards that protect sexual and reproductive rights and the rights to equality and non-discrimination on the basis of sex, gender, sexual orientation or gender identity.		not support the parts of this recommendation that ask us to restrict Constitutionally-protected belief or expression

180	Introduce a national moratorium on the death penalty aiming at complete abolition and take all necessary measures to ensure that the death penalty complies with minimum standards under international law. Exempt persons with mental illness from execution. Commit to ensuring that the origin of drugs being used is made public.	Support in Part	We support the part of this recommendation asking us to ensure that our implementation of capital punishment complies with international human rights obligations and commitments. We also support the part of this recommendation concerning exclusion from the death penalty with respect to prosecutions of persons with intellectual disabilities as defined by U.S. courts, but not regarding all persons with any mental illness. *See, e.g., Atkins v. Virginia*, 536 U.S. 304 (2002). For more information, please refer to paragraphs 48-54 of our UPR Report. We do not support the parts of this recommendation asking us to introduce a moratorium on the death penalty nor the part of this recommendation concerning the origin of drugs used for purposes of capital punishment.
196	When continuing to implement the death penalty, do not apply it to persons with intellectual disabilities.	Support in Part	We support this recommendation concerning exclusion from the death penalty with respect to prosecutions of persons with intellectual disabilities as defined by U.S. courts. *See, e.g., Atkins v. Virginia*, 536 U.S. 304 (2002). For more information, please refer to paragraph 49 of our UPR Report. We do not support this recommendation to the extent it is interpreted differently.
197	Ensure that no person with a mental disability is executed.	Support in Part	We also support the part of this recommendation concerning exclusion from the death penalty with respect to prosecutions of persons with intellectual disabilities as defined by U.S. courts, but not regarding all persons with any mental disability. *See, e.g., Atkins v. Virginia*, 536 U.S. 304 (2002). We do not support this recommendation to the extent it is interpreted differently.
198	Take specific measures in follow-up to the recommendations of the Human Rights Committee to the US in 2014 with regards to capital punishment such as measures to avoid racial bias, to avoid wrongful sentencing to death and to provide adequate compensation if wrongful sentencing happens.	Support in Part	We support this recommendation to the extent that it calls upon us to consider the non-binding 2014 recommendations from the Human Rights Committee. While we support measures to avoid racial bias and wrongful sentencing to death, and to provide adequate compensation in the event of wrongful sentencing, we do not support other parts of the recommendation, including the part asking that we take specific measures in follow-up to the recommendations on moratorium or abolishment of the death penalty.
203	Put an end to unlawful practices which violate human rights including extrajudicial executions and arbitrary detention, and close any arbitrary detention centres.	Support in Part	We support this recommendation to the extent that it calls upon the United States to uphold its obligations under international and domestic law. In particular, we support the part of this recommendation asking us to ensure that our practices do not violate human rights. We do not support the part of this recommendation that constitutes unsubstantiated allegations of ongoing serious violations of international law, or that implies that the United States engages in practices that violate human rights, including extrajudicial executions and arbitrary detention, or that we maintain arbitrary detention centers.
204	Take legal and administrative measures to address civilian killings by the US military	Support in Part	We support this recommendation to the extent that it calls upon the United States to uphold its obligations under international and domestic law. In particular, we support the part of this

	troops during and after its invasion of Afghanistan and Iraq by bringing perpetrators to justice and remedying the victims.		recommendation asking us to take appropriate measures to address any unlawful killings of civilians in armed conflict. We take great care to ensure that our uses of force – including targeted strikes – conform to all applicable domestic and international law, including the law of war principles of proportionality and distinction. The Department of Defense investigates all credible allegations of misconduct by its personnel and pursues judicial or administrative action against alleged perpetrators as appropriate. We do not support certain premises in this recommendation that constitute unsubstantiated accusations of ongoing serious violations of international law in Iraq and Afghanistan, or that suggest that there is a legal duty to remedy all victims in armed conflict. If we determine that non-combatants were killed or injured in a U.S. military operation, we may, where appropriate, offer condolence or other ex gratia payments to those injured and the families of those killed.
205	Desist from extrajudicial killings such as drone strikes and ensure accountability for civilian loss of life resulting from extraterritorial counter terrorism operations.	Support in Part	We support this recommendation to the extent that it calls upon the United States to uphold its obligations under international and domestic law, including in its counterterrorism operations. In particular, we support the part of this recommendation asking us to take appropriate measures to address any unlawful killings. The Department of Defense investigates all credible allegations of misconduct by its personnel and pursues judicial or administrative action against alleged perpetrators as appropriate. We do not support the part of this recommendation implicitly asking us to desist from lawful, targeted counterterrorism action or implying that such targeted action against al-Qaeda and its associated forces, including with remotely piloted aircraft, constitutes unlawful extrajudicial killing per se. We conduct lawful, targeted action against al-Qaeda and its associated forces, including with remotely piloted aircraft, as necessary to prevent terrorist attacks on the U.S. and to save lives. We take great care to ensure that our uses of force – including targeted strikes – conform to all applicable domestic and international law, including the law of war principles of proportionality and distinction.
206	Stop extrajudicial killings of citizens of the United States of America and foreigners, including those being committed with the use of remotely piloted aircraft.	Support in Part	Please refer to the explanation for recommendation #205.
207	Use armed drones in line with existing international legal regimes and pay compensation to all innocent victims without discrimination.	Support in Part	We support this recommendation to the extent that it calls upon the United States to uphold its obligations under international and domestic law. In particular, we support the part of this recommendation asking us to conduct military operations in line with existing international legal obligations. We take great care to ensure that our uses of force – including targeted strikes – conform to all applicable domestic and international law, including the law of war principles of proportionality and distinction. We do not support any premise underlying this recommendation that there is a legal duty to "pay compensation" to all victims in armed conflict. If we determine that non-combatants were killed or injured in a U.S. military operation, we may, where appropriate, offer condolence or other ex gratia payments to those injured and the families of those killed.

209	Punish those responsible for torture, drone killings, use of lethal force against African Americans and compensate the victims.	Support in Part	We support this recommendation to the extent that it calls upon the United States to uphold its obligations under international and domestic law. In particular, we support the part of this recommendation asking us to prosecute and punish individuals responsible for unlawful acts when appropriate. Please refer to the explanations of recommendations #204 and #205. We remain committed to investigating and prosecuting willful use of excessive force by law enforcement officers. We do not support certain premises in this recommendation, which constitute unsubstantiated accusations of ongoing serious violations of international law. We also do not support the part of this recommendation implying that targeted action against al-Qaeda and its associated forces, including with remotely piloted aircraft, is unlawful per se.
210	Strengthen safeguards against torture in all detention facilities in any territory under its jurisdiction, ensure proper and transparent investigation and prosecution of individuals responsible for all allegations of torture and ill-treatment, including those documented in the unclassified Senate summary on CIA activities published in 2014 and provide redress to victims.	Support in Part	We support this recommendation to the extent that it calls upon the United States to uphold its obligations under international and domestic law. In particular, we support the part of this recommendation asking us to investigate credible allegations of torture and to prosecute where appropriate.
211	Enact comprehensive legislation prohibiting all forms of torture and take measures to prevent all acts of torture in areas outside the national territory under its effective control.	Support in Part	We support this recommendation to the extent that it calls upon the United States to uphold its obligations under international and domestic law. Federal and state laws are already in place that criminalize acts that encompass torture throughout the United States. Additionally, 18 U.S.C. § 2340 et seq. provides federal criminal jurisdiction over an extraterritorial act or attempted extraterritorial act of torture committed under color of law if (1) the alleged offender is a national of the United States or (2) if the alleged offender is present in the United States, irrespective of the nationality of the victim or alleged offender.
212	Stops acts of torture by US Government officials, not only in its sovereign territory, but also in foreign soil.	Support in part	We support this recommendation insofar as it calls upon the United States to uphold its obligations under international and domestic law to prevent acts of torture. In particular, we support the part of this recommendation asking us to prohibit torture at all times and in all places. We do not support certain premises in this recommendation, which constitute unsubstantiated accusations of ongoing serious violations of international law.
217	Respect the absolute prohibition on torture and take measures to guarantee punishment of all perpetrators.	Support in Part	We support this recommendation insofar as it calls upon the United States to uphold its obligations under international and domestic law. In particular, we support the part of this recommendation asking us to respect the absolute prohibition on torture. We do not support the part of this recommendation that asks us to "guarantee" punishment. The Executive Branch of the U.S. government cannot make commitments regarding, and does not control, the outcome of court proceedings, which are based on the application of applicable law to the specific facts of each case.
218	Ensure the independent and objective investigation of all cases of police	Support in Part	We support the part of this recommendation asking us to ensure investigation of all credible allegations of police misconduct. We do not support the premise of this recommendation that
	arbitrariness, including murders, torture, arbitrary, detention, use of military equipment and seizure of property.		certain of these acts are always arbitrary, nor the part of this recommendation asking us to investigate activities by police that are permitted or authorized by law in certain circumstances (e.g., seizure of property pursuant to a lawfully-obtained court order).
224	Ensure a sustained human rights training for law enforcement officers in order to curb killings, brutality and the excessive use of force targeting racial and ethnic minorities, particularly African-Americans.	Support in Part	We support the part of this recommendation asking the federal government to conduct and promote human rights training. For more information, please refer to the explanation for recommendation #91. Although training largely occurs at the local level, the federal government promotes best practices through technical assistance, investigations, and agreements to reform police practices. We support this recommendation "in part" because we recognize, realistically, that the United States may never completely accomplish what is described in this recommendation's literal terms and because the federal government does not exercise control over the training of state and local law enforcement officers.
226	Punish perpetrators of abuse and police brutality, which are increasingly alarming and constitute irrefutable acts of increasing racism and racial discrimination, particularly against African-Americans, Latinos and women.	Support in Part	We support the part of this recommendation asking us to investigate credible allegations of abuses by law enforcement, and to prosecute officers responsible where appropriate. We note that we have federal, state, and tribal legislation and strategies in place to combat discrimination, including racial discrimination, and we take effective measures to counter intolerance, violence, and discrimination against members of all groups, including African-Americans, Latinos, and women. For more information, please refer to paragraphs 11-16 of our UPR Report. We do not support the part of this recommendation that implies that there is irrefutable evidence that incidents of abuse and racial discrimination are increasing, but we are committed to combating discrimination and promoting tolerance.
227	Take appropriate measures to eliminate the excessive use of force by the law enforcement officers. We refer to the case of killing the Kazakh national. Kirill Denyakin, by a US police officer in 2011 in Virginia.	Support in Part	We support the part of this recommendation asking us to take appropriate measures to combat excessive use of force by law enforcement. We note that we have federal, state, and tribal legislation and strategies in place to combat discrimination, including racial discrimination, and we take effective measures to counter intolerance, violence, and discrimination. For more information, please refer to paragraphs 11-16 of our UPR Report. We do not support the part of this recommendation regarding the particular case cited, as the Executive Branch of the U.S. government cannot make commitments regarding, and does not control, the outcome of court proceedings, which are based on the application of applicable law to the specific facts of each case.
229	Investigate cases of deaths of migrants by customs and border patrols, particularly those where there have been indications of an excessive use of force, and ensure accountability and adequate reparation to the families of the victims.	Support in Part	We support the part of this recommendation asking us to investigate cases of deaths of migrants in the custody of U.S. Customs and Border Protection, and to ensure accountability, where appropriate. We do not support the part of this recommendation concerning reparations. Although mechanisms for effective remedies are available through U.S. courts, the Executive Branch of the U.S. government cannot make commitments regarding, and does not control, the outcome of court proceedings, which are based on the application of applicable law to the specific facts of each case.
230	Adopt legislation expanding the verification of personal backgrounds for all acquisitions of firearms.	Support in part	We support the part of this recommendation concerning expanding the number of firearms transfers that are subject to background checks but with limited, common-sense exceptions (e.g., certain transfers between family members, temporary transfers for hunting/sporting).

233	Consider the adoption of legislation to enhance the verification of the records for all fire arms transfers and the revision of the laws that stipulate self-defence without limitations.	Support in Part	Please refer to the explanation for recommendation #230. We do not support the part of this recommendation asking us to revise laws that permit individuals to defend themselves when violently attacked.
234	End the use of life imprisonment without parole for offenders under the age of 18 at the age of crime, regardless of the nature of that crime.	Support in Part	We support the part of this recommendation concerning sentences of life imprisonment without parole imposed on juveniles for non-homicide crimes, which violate the Eighth Amendment's prohibition on cruel and unusual punishment. *See, e.g., Graham v. Florida*, 560 U.S. 48 (2011). Additionally, life without parole cannot be made mandatory for juvenile offenders, even those who have committed murder. *See, e.g., Miller v. Alabama*, 132 S. Ct. 2455 (2011). The United States has put forward legislative measures that would allow courts discretion to reduce a term of imprisonment imposed upon a juvenile defendant convicted of any offense after that defendant has served 20 years' incarceration. We do not support the part of this recommendation asking for complete elimination of life without parole sentences for juvenile offenders, as the United States is not currently contemplating legislative measures to completely eliminate the availability of life without parole sentences for juveniles.
235	Abolish life imprisonment without possibility of parole for non-violent offenses.	Support in Part	Please refer to the explanation for recommendation #234. We also do not support the part of this recommendation concerning life without parole sentences for non-violent adult offenders, as the United States is also not currently contemplating legislation to revise existing life without possibility of parole laws as they apply to adult offenders.
241	Immediately close the prison in Guantanamo and cease the illegal detention of terrorism suspects at its military bases abroad.	Support in Part	We support the part of this recommendation asking us to close the detention facility at Guantanamo Bay. The President has clearly stated our desire to close the detention facility and to continue working with Congress, the courts, and other countries to do so in a responsible manner that is consistent with our international obligations. Until it is closed, we will continue to ensure that operations there are consistent with our international obligations. For more information, please refer to paragraphs 87-99 of our UPR Report. We do not support the part of this recommendation implying that the U.S. engages in illegal detention of terrorism suspects.
243	Close the Guantanamo prison and release all detainees still held in Guantanamo, unless they are to be charged and tried without further delay.	Support in Part	Please refer to the explanation for recommendation #241. We do not support the part of this recommendation asking us to release all individuals detained at Guantanamo unless they are to be charged and tried without further delay. The detainees who remain at the Guantanamo Bay detention facility continue to be detained lawfully, both as a matter of international law and under U.S. domestic law. All U.S. military detention operations conducted in connection with armed conflict, including at Guantanamo Bay, are carried out in accordance with international humanitarian law, including Common Article 3 of the Geneva Conventions, and all other applicable international and domestic laws.
245	Close, as soon as possible, the detention centre at Guantanamo Bay and put an end to the indefinite detention of persons considered as enemy combatants.	Support in Part	Please refer to the explanation for recommendation #241. We do not support the part of the recommendation that calls for "an end to the indefinite detention of persons considered as enemy combatants." The detainees who remain at the Guantanamo Bay detention facility continue to be detained lawfully, both as a matter of international law and under U.S.

			domestic law. All U.S. military detention operations conducted in connection with armed conflict, including at Guantanamo Bay, are carried out in accordance with international humanitarian law, including Common Article 3 of the Geneva Conventions, and all other applicable international and domestic laws.
247	Fully disclose the abuse of torture by its Intelligence Agency, ensure the accountability of the persons responsible, and agree to unrestricted visit by the Special Rapporteur on Torture to Guantanamo facilities.	Support in Part	We support this recommendation to the extent that it calls upon the United States to uphold its obligations under international and domestic law. In particular, we support the part of this recommendation asking us to be as transparent as possible, consistent with the protection of national security, and to investigate credible allegations of torture. Please refer to the explanation for recommendation #210. For more information, please refer to paragraphs 87-99 of our UPR Report. We have extended an invitation to the Special Rapporteur on Torture to visit Guantanamo Bay consistent with the terms of other comparable visits. That invitation remains open. However, we do not support the part of this recommendation asking us to permit an unrestricted visit for the Special Rapporteur to Guantanamo due to security concerns.
248	Engage further in the common fight for the prohibition of torture, ensuring accountability and victims' compensation and enable the Special Rapporteur on torture to visit every part of the detention facility at Guantanamo Bay and to conduct unmonitored interviews.	Support in Part	We support the part of this recommendation asking us to engage further in the fight for the prohibition of torture. We do not support the part of this recommendation asking us to "ensure" compensation. Although mechanisms for remedies, including compensation, may be available through U.S.-based courts, the Executive Branch of the U.S. government cannot make commitments regarding, and does not control, the outcome of court proceedings, which are based on the application of applicable law to the specific facts of each case. Regarding the Special Rapporteur on torture, please refer to the explanation for recommendation #247.
250	End illegal detentions in Guantanamo Bay or bring the detainees to trial immediately.	Support in Part	Please refer to the explanation for recommendation #241. We do not support the part of this recommendation implying that the U.S. engages in illegal detention of terrorism suspects. As part of its conflict with al-Qaeda, the Taliban, and associated forces, the United States has captured and detained enemy combatants, and is permitted under the law of war to hold them until the end of hostilities. Thus, we also do not support the part of this recommendation asking us to bring all detainees to trial immediately.
252	Halt the detention of immigrant families and children, seek alternatives to detention and end use of detention for reason of deterrence.	Support in Part	We support the part of this recommendation asking us to seek alternatives to detention for immigrant families and children. We actively utilize alternatives to detention where appropriate, and are working to shorten the length of detention that families may face while their immigration proceedings are resolved. We have discontinued invoking general deterrence as a factor in custody determinations in cases involving families. Conditions at Family Residential Centers are continually being evaluated and improved to ensure a safe and productive environment. For more information, please refer to paragraphs 61-67 of our UPR Report. We do not support the part of this recommendation asking us to halt all detentions of immigrant families and children.
256	Guarantee the right to access to justice and effective remedies to all indigenous women who were victims of violence.	Support in Part	We support the part of this recommendation regarding access to justice. For more information, please refer to paragraphs 59 and 70 of our UPR Report. We do not support the part of the recommendation asking that we "guarantee" effective remedies. Although

			mechanisms for remedies may be available through U.S.-based courts, the Executive Branch of the U.S. government cannot make commitments regarding, and does not control, the outcome of court cases, which are based on the application of applicable law to the specific facts of each case.
258	Redouble efforts to prevent sexual violence in the military and ensure effective prosecution of offenders and redress for victims.	Support in Part	We support the part of this recommendation asking us to redouble efforts to prevent sexual violence in the military and ensure effective prosecution. Eliminating sexual assault from the military through continuous assessment and improvement to prevention and response programs remains one of the Department of Defense's top priorities. Within the past couple of years, the Department of Defense has implemented monumental reform efforts. Congress passed 33 sexual assault-related provisions in the National Defense Authorization Act for Fiscal Year 2014 that will improve the services provided to victims and the military's response capability. We do not support the part of this recommendation that asks us to "ensure" redress for all acts of sexual violence. Although mechanisms for remedies may be available through U.S.-based courts, the Executive Branch of the U.S. government cannot make commitments regarding, and does not control, the outcome of court cases, which are based on the application of applicable law to the specific facts of each case.
260	Conduct impartial and objective investigations of all cases of cruel treatment of adopted children in order to eliminate impunity for such crimes.	Support in Part	We support the part of this recommendation asking us to investigate all credible allegations of mistreatment of adopted children. We do not support the premise of the recommendation that there is impunity for such crimes in the United States.
265	Prohibit corporal punishment of children in all settings, including the home and schools, and that the United States encourage non-violent forms of discipline as alternatives to corporal punishment	Support in Part	We support the part of this recommendation asking us to encourage non-violent forms of discipline. We encourage creating positive school climates and equitable discipline practices, and we take effective measures to help ensure non-discrimination in school discipline policies and practices. Excessive or arbitrary corporal punishment in schools is prohibited under our Constitution, and 31 of the 50 States have outlawed corporal punishment in schools. We do not support the part of this recommendation related to the prohibition of corporal punishment in all settings.
274	Devise a national strategy for the re-insertion of former detainees and to prevent recidivism.	Support in Part	We support the part of this recommendation asking us to work to prevent recidivism. Recidivism is an important criminal justice concern, and we support and have undertaken efforts to address it, including through the Federal Interagency Reentry Council, led by the U.S. Department of Justice. We do not support the part of this recommendation asking us to devise a national strategy on this issue.
279	Comply with the international cooperation principles laid down in General Assembly Resolution 3074 regarding extradition of persons accused of crimes against humanity, and extradite former Bolivian authorities legally charged for their trail in the country of origin.	Support in Part	We support the part of this recommendation asking us to support the principle of cooperation when considering extradition of persons accused of crimes against humanity. We do not support the part of this recommendation asking us to extradite particular individuals, as we note that decisions on extradition cases are made on a case-by-case basis, consistent with our international obligations, and we cannot prejudge the outcomes of particular cases. For more information, please refer to paragraphs 52-53 of our UPR Report.

286	Further ensure that all victims of torture and ill-treatment – whether still in US custody or not - obtain redress and have an enforceable right to fair and adequate compensation and as full rehabilitation as possible, including medical and psychological assistance.	Support in Part	We support this recommendation to the extent that it calls upon the United States to uphold its obligations under international and domestic law. In particular, we support the part of this recommendation asking us to ensure that victims of torture have an enforceable right to fair and adequate compensation consistent with our obligations under the Convention Against Torture. For more information, please refer to paragraphs 87 and 91-96 of our UPR Report. We do not support certain premises in this recommendation, which constitute unsubstantiated accusations of ongoing serious violations of international law.
288	Investigate torture allegations, extrajudicial executions and other violations of human rights committed in Guantanamo, Abu Ghraib, Bagram, NAMA and BALAD camps and to subsequently close them.	Support in Part	We support this recommendation to the extent that it calls upon the United States to uphold its obligations under international and domestic law. In particular, we support the part of this recommendation asking us to investigate credible allegations of human rights violations. The Department of Defense investigates all credible allegations of misconduct by its personnel. For more information, please refer to paragraphs 87-96 of our UPR Report. We do not support certain premises in this recommendation, which constitute unsubstantiated accusations of serious violations of international law.
289	Improve access to justice, including due process and redress, for victims of sexual violence in the military; this would include removing from the chain of command the decision about whether to prosecute cases of alleged assault.	Support in Part	We support the part of this recommendation asking us to improve access to justice for victims of sexual assault in the military. Please refer to the explanation for recommendation #258. The Department of Defense has also established victim representation programs for sexual assault victims eligible for legal assistance. We do not support the part of this recommendation asking us to remove prosecutorial decisions from the chain of command in these cases, consistent with the findings of an independent study that doing so was not needed to improve victims' access to justice.
291	Ensure that youth in conflict with the law are handled by the juvenile justice system and have access to free legal advisory assistance.	Support in Part	We support the part of this recommendation asking that we provide free legal assistance to juveniles in criminal and delinquency proceedings. Juveniles have the right to free legal representation in all such proceedings, and in many cases, it is also available for civil proceedings. We do not support the part of this recommendation asking that all youthful offenders be handled through a juvenile justice system. Although the vast majority of criminal matters involving youth are handled through the juvenile justice system, factors weighed by courts deciding whether exceptional circumstances warrant trial as an adult include age/background, type/seriousness of the alleged offense, the juvenile's role, and prior record/past treatment.
292	Ensure that children under 18 are handled by the juvenile justice system in all circumstances.	Support in Part	We support this recommendation to the extent that the vast majority of criminal matters involving youth are handled through the juvenile justice system. Please refer to the explanation for recommendation #291.
297	Provide effective legal and procedural guarantees against collection and use by security services of personal information, including abroad.	Support in Part	We support this recommendation to the extent it applies to unlawful or arbitrary collection and use of personal information. The United States collects information only in accordance with U.S. law and international obligations. Additionally, President Obama has stated and set forth in Presidential Policy Directive 28 that all persons should be treated with dignity and respect, regardless of their nationality or place of residence, and that all persons have legitimate privacy interests in the handling of their personal information. The U.S. intelligence oversight

			system is robust and transparent, and includes executive, legislative, and judicial bodies. We do not support this recommendation to the extent it asks us to provide legal and procedural guarantees against collection and use of personal information that is authorized by law and necessary in furtherance of valid law enforcement or national security interests.
298	Take all necessary measures to ensure an independent and effective oversight by all Government branches of the overseas surveillance operations of the National Security Agency, especially those carried out under the Executive Order 12333, and guarantee access to effective judicial and other remedies for people whose right to privacy would have been violated by the surveillance activities of the United States.	Support in Part	We support this recommendation with respect to the importance of independent and effective oversight of U.S. intelligence operations. We collect information only in accordance with U.S. law and policy and our international obligations, including obligations contained in Article 17 of the ICCPR, within the scope of its application. The U.S. intelligence oversight system is robust and transparent. This system – which at various times and stages involves executive, legislative, and judicial bodies – provides for rigorous oversight of U.S. signals intelligence activities and procedures, including those pertaining to the use, retention and dissemination of personal information as set forth in Presidential Policy Directive-28. A new statute, the USA FREEDOM Act of 2015, was enacted in June 2015 and contains a number of provisions that modify U.S. surveillance authorities and other national security authorities through legislation, and increase transparency regarding the use of these authorities. The Act requires the declassification (or, where that is not possible, declassified summaries) of opinions by the Foreign Intelligence Surveillance Court or Court of Review that involve significant or novel interpretations of the law. It also increases the U.S. government's public reporting obligations regarding specific uses of FISA authorities, and permits recipients of FISA orders to make either annual or semiannual reports of the approximate aggregate number of FISA orders they have received. For more information, please refer to paragraphs 83-86 of our UPR Report.
299	Ensure that all surveillance policies and measures comply with international human rights law, particularly the right to privacy, regardless of the nationality or location of those affected, including through the development of effective safeguards against abuses.	Support in Part	We support this recommendation to the extent it recommends compliance with U.S. obligations contained in Article 17 of the ICCPR, which applies to individuals within a State's territory and subject to its jurisdiction. We note in this regard that U.S. efforts to safeguard the legitimate privacy interests of all persons in the conduct of signals intelligence activities extend, pursuant to Presidential Policy Directive 28, to all persons regardless of nationality or place of residence. Please refer to the explanation for recommendation #298 concerning additional safeguards.
304	Strengthen the independent federal-level judicial and legislative oversight of surveillance activities of all digital communications with the aim of ensuring that the right of privacy is fully upheld, especially with regard to individuals outside the territorial borders of the United States.	Support in Part	Please refer to the explanation for recommendation #298.
305	Respect the privacy of individuals outside the US in the context of digital communications and data.	Support in Part	Please refer to the explanation for recommendation #298.

306	Amend visa application system by removing any requirements that violate the right to privacy.	Support in Part	We support this recommendation insofar as it recommends respect for the ICCPR, Article 17, which applies to individuals within a State's territory and subject to its jurisdiction. We do not support the part of this recommendation that implies that the current U.S. visa application system violates any of our human rights obligations.
308	Uphold a consistent and robust protection of religious freedom, including religious speech and conscientious objection, and provide for accommodation of religious views and actions regarding social issues.	Support in Part	We support this recommendation insofar as it recommends compliance with our obligations under domestic law and international human rights law, including obligations regarding freedom of religion. We note that litigation on issues material to this recommendation is ongoing in U.S. courts. We support this recommendation "in part" because the Executive Branch of the U.S. government cannot make commitments regarding, and does not control, the outcome of court cases, which are based on the application of applicable law to the specific facts of each case.
309	Guarantee the right by all residents in the country to adequate housing, food, health and education, with the aim of decreasing poverty, which affects 48 millions of people in the country.	Support in Part	We support this recommendation to the extent that it asks us to improve access to adequate housing, food, health, and education with the aim of decreasing poverty in the United States. For more information, please refer to paragraphs 28-34 and 100-106 of our UPR Report. We do not support this recommendation to the extent it asks us to assume obligations under international instruments to which the United States is not a party. The United States is not a party to the International Covenant on Economic, Social, and Cultural Rights, and we understand that the rights therein are to be realized progressively.
310	Amend laws that criminalize homelessness and which are not in conformity with international human rights instruments.	Support in Part	We support this recommendation to the extent it asks us to help communities nationwide pursue alternatives to local legislation that allows for the arrest and prosecution of individuals for various behaviors associated with homelessness. For more information, please refer to paragraphs 28-29 and 205 of our UPR Report. We do not support the part of this recommendation that implies that current laws in the United States are not in conformity with our international human rights obligations. While we recognize there is always room for improvement, we believe that our laws are consistent with our international human rights obligations.
311	Continue efforts to implement the human right to safe water and sanitation, ensuring this human right without discrimination for the poorest sectors of the population, including indigenous peoples and migrants.	Support in Part	We support this recommendation to the extent that it asks us to improve access to safe drinking water and sanitation in the United States. For more information, please refer to paragraph 106 of our UPR Report. We do not support this recommendation to the extent it asks us to assume obligations under international instruments to which the United States is not a party. The United States is not a party to the International Covenant on Economic, Social and Cultural Rights, although we understand this recommendation as referencing the right to safe drinking water and sanitation, which is derived from the right to an adequate standard of living contained therein and is to be realized progressively.
312	Ensure compliance with the human right to water and sanitation according to General Assembly Resolution 64/292.	Support in Part	Please refer to the explanation for recommendation #311. Furthermore, General Assembly Resolution 64/292 is not a legally binding instrument.
314	Continue efforts regarding access to the right to health.	Support In Part	We support this recommendation to the extent that it asks us to improve access to health services in the United States. For more information, please refer to paragraphs 33-34, 44, 55,

			69, and 100-101 of our UPR Report. We do not support this recommendation to the extent it asks us to assume obligations under international instruments to which the United States is not a party. The United States is not a party to the International Covenant on Economic, Social, and Cultural Rights, and we understand the rights therein are to be realized progressively.
321	Guarantee the enjoyment of human rights of the minorities and vulnerable groups in the country, including the indigenous peoples and migrants.	Support in part	We support this recommendation to the extent it asks us to promote, protect, and respect the human rights of all individuals, including members of minorities and vulnerable groups, indigenous individuals, and migrants. We note that we have federal, state, and tribal legislation and strategies in place to combat discrimination, including racial discrimination, and we take effective measures to counter intolerance, violence, and discrimination against members of all minority groups, including African-Americans, Muslims, Arabs, and indigenous persons. For more information, please refer to paragraphs 25-42, 54-60, and 68-70 of our UPR Report. We do not support the possible implication of this recommendation that groups, rather than individuals, have human rights.
338	Guarantee the right to family reunification of migrants held in detention and continue with the efforts to protect the human rights of migrant persons, particularly their economic, social and cultural rights.	Support in Part	We support this recommendation insofar as it recommends compliance with our obligations under international human rights law. In particular, we support the part of this recommendation asking us to continue efforts to respect the human rights of migrants. For more information, please refer to paragraphs 61-70 of our UPR Report. We do not support the part of this recommendation that refers to a "right to family reunification," which is not a right recognized under our domestic laws or in any international binding instrument.
339	Ensure due process for all immigrants in immigration proceedings, using the principle of the best interest, especially in the case of families and unaccompanied children.	Support in Part	We support this recommendation to the extent it asks us to provide appropriate procedural safeguards in immigration proceedings, including those concerning unaccompanied children. Noncitizens in the U.S. facing removal receive significant procedural protections. The best interest of a child is an important consideration in many areas of U.S. law and in the exercise of prosecutorial discretion. We support this recommendation "in part," however, because it generally is one factor – not the only factor – in determinations made by an immigration judge or adjudicator in ensuring that interviews and hearings involving children are child-appropriate, and that the child is able to discuss freely the elements and details of his or her claim. The Department of Health and Human Services (HHS) provides care and placement for children who enter the United States without an adult guardian, considering the best interests of the child in all placement decisions. For more information, please refer to paragraphs 61-70 of our UPR Report.
341	Take up the commitment to address, in a framework of shared but differentiated responsibility and along with the international community, the world problem of climate change and its negative impact.	Support in Part	We support this recommendation insofar as it encourages domestic action on climate change and international efforts to reach an agreement that is ambitious, inclusive, and applicable to all countries. For more information, please refer to paragraphs 109-112 of our UPR Report. We do not support this recommendation to the extent it attempts to pre-judge the outcome of ongoing negotiations on the UN Framework Convention on Climate Change.
342	Continue to actively participate in the climate change negotiations for a strong legally binding outcome of the UNFCCC process.	Support in Part	Please refer to the explanation for recommendation #341.

343	Ensure federal legislation to prohibit environmental pollution and reduce greenhouse gas emissions to control climate change.	Support in Part	We support this recommendation insofar as it encourages domestic action on climate change and international efforts to reach an agreement that is ambitious, inclusive, and applicable to all countries. We also support the principle of this recommendation, which is to continue our efforts to reduce the impact of pollution and greenhouse gas emissions on the environment. For more information, please refer to paragraphs 109-112 of our UPR Report. We do not support the part of this recommendation asking us to introduce federal legislation to prohibit all environmental pollution.

Source: http://lib.ohchr.org/HRBodies/UPR/Documents/Session22/US/AdditionalInfo_US_22session.pdf

15. UNITED STATES U.N. HUMAN RIGHTS COUNCIL CANDIDATE 2017-2019, PLEDGE

This document is from the U.S. Department of State that was seeking a seat on the Human Rights Council for the years 2017-2019. It is a Pledge to the U.N. about how it will view and apply human rights if elected as a member of the Council. This states the U.S. position in different areas of human rights, such as persons with disabilities, racism, business and human rights. It also states: "The United States is committed to continued cooperation with the U.N.'s human rights mechanisms...by responding to inquiries, engaging in dialogues, and hosting visits. Since 2012, the United States has hosted seven official Special Rapporteur and Working Group visits." This pledge interestingly states that the U.S. "commits to continuing to engage in, and support, economic, social, and cultural rights..." even though the U.S. has not ratified the International Covenant on Economic, Social and Cultural Rights. The U.S. was elected to the Council for 2017-2019.

February 29, 2016

In the context of its decision to seek election to the U.N. Human Rights Council in November 2016, the United States issued the following pledge outlining its commitments to human rights around the world.

HUMAN RIGHTS COMMITMENTS AND PLEDGES OF THE UNITED STATES OF AMERICA

The deep commitment of the United States to championing the human rights enshrined in the Universal Declaration of Human Rights is driven by the founding values of our nation and the conviction that international peace, security, and prosperity are strengthened when human rights and fundamental freedoms are respected and protected. As the United States seeks to advance human rights and fundamental freedoms around the world, we do so cognizant of our own commitment to address challenges and to live up to our ideals at home and to meet our international human rights obligations.

The United States was pleased to participate in the second cycle of the Universal Periodic Review (UPR) at the Human Rights Council during our prior term on the Council. We are particularly pleased that we had the opportunity to work closely with civil society throughout that process, including at a town hall meeting in Geneva and several consultations in the United States. As we stated in our final report, the Government of the United States carefully reviewed the 343 recommendations received during its most recent UPR. Our response to these recommendations reflects our continuing endeavor to create, in the words of our Constitution, a more perfect union.

We, therefore, make the following pledges:

COMMITMENT TO ADVANCING AND SUPPORTING HUMAN RIGHTS IN THE U.N. SYSTEM

1. The United States commits to continuing its efforts in the U.N. system to be a strong advocate for all people around the world who suffer from discrimination, abuse, and oppression, and a stalwart defender of courageous individuals across the globe who work, often at great personal risk, on behalf of the rights of others.

2. The United States commits to continue working with determination for a balanced, credible, and effective U.N. Human Rights Council to advance the purpose and principles of the Universal Declaration of Human Rights. To that same end, in partnership with the international community, we will continue to promote universality, transparency, and objectivity in all of the Council's endeavors. The United States is proud of the work we have done building partnerships with numerous countries from every region to increase the Council's credibility, strengthen the Council as an institution, and create mechanisms to promote and protect human rights. During our first two terms on the Council, we were pleased to see broad support for such important cross-regional initiatives as the creation of two Special Rapporteurs, one on Freedom of Association and Assembly and another on the human rights situation in Iran, a resolution on women's right to a nationality, four resolutions on the human rights situation in Sri Lanka, the creation of a Working Group on Discrimination against Women in Law and Practice, as well as resolutions focusing on important issues such as early and forced marriage, and female genital mutilation. Similarly, we were pleased the Council took urgent action to address crisis situations in countries including Syria, Burundi, Libya, and the Central African Republic.

3. The United States is committed to advancing the promotion and protection of human rights and fundamental freedoms throughout the U.N. system, including in the U.N. General Assembly and its Third Committee. The United States will continue to strongly support the work of the U.N. human rights mechanisms — including Special Rapporteurs, Independent Experts Working Groups, and Commissions of Inquiry — and the dialogue that their reports engender. The United States will also continue to support the work of the human rights treaty bodies.

4. As we demonstrated during our extensive consultations with civil society during the UPR process, the United States recognizes and supports the vital role of civil society and human rights defenders in the promotion and protection of human rights. We also remain committed to promoting the effective involvement of non-governmental organizations in the work of the United Nations, including the Council, and other international organizations, as evidenced by our active engagement as a member of the U.N. NGO Committee.

5. As part of our commitment to the principle of the universality of human rights, the United States commits to working with our international partners in the spirit of openness, consultation, and respect and reaffirms that expressions of concern about the human rights situation in any country, our own included, are appropriate matters for international discussion.

6. The United States is committed to continuing its support for the Office of the U.N. High Commissioner for Human Rights (OHCHR) and remains one of the OHCHR's largest donors. In 2015, the United States provided $5.5 million to the OHCHR and its efforts to address violations of human rights worldwide, as well as almost $1.25 million to the U.N.

Voluntary Fund for Technical Cooperation in the Field of Human Rights, and $6.5 million to the Voluntary Fund for Victims of Torture. We anticipate making contributions to the UN's human rights activities in 2016 as well.

7. The United States is also committed to continuing its support of other U.N. bodies whose work contributes to the promotion of human rights. In 2015, in addition to our assessed contributions to U.N. organizations, the United States contributed voluntary funding to support a range of human rights efforts, such as through the U.N. Population Fund ($35 million), U.N. Democracy Fund ($4.2 million), and U.N. Women ($7.5 million).

8. The United States is committed to supporting implementation of the U.N. Global Counter Terrorism Strategy and the Secretary General's Plan of Action to Prevent ?Violent Extremism, both of which support respect for human rights and the rule of law. The United States also commits to promoting implementation of the HRC's resolution on "*Human Rights and Preventing and Countering Violent Extremism,*" adopted on October 1, 2015.

9. In conjunction with our domestic efforts, the United States remains committed to the promotion and protection of indigenous peoples in the work of the UN, including through continued attention to indigenous issues at the Human Rights Council and General Assembly.

COMMITMENT TO ADVANCING HUMAN RIGHTS, FUNDAMENTAL FREEDOMS, AND HUMAN DIGNITY AND PROSPERITY INTERNATIONALLY

1. The United States commits to continue supporting states in their implementation of human rights obligations, as appropriate, through human rights dialogue, exchange of experts, technical and inter-regional cooperation, and programmatic support of the work of non-governmental organizations.

2. The United States commits to continue its efforts to strengthen mechanisms in the international system to advance the rights, protection, and empowerment of women, including through support for U.N. Women; the implementation of Security Council Resolution 1325 and all subsequent resolutions related to Women, Peace and Security, and all relevant Human Rights Council and General Assembly resolutions related to elimination of all forms of violence against women and women's political participation; the work of the U.N. Commission on the Status of Women; and the work of the Inter-American Commission on Women.

3. The United States is committed to continuing to address stigma and discrimination in laws and policies and promote the human rights of persons regardless of their sexual orientation or gender identity and is pleased to support the efforts of the Special Rapporteur and unit of the Inter-American Commission on Human Rights to place greater regional focus on this area as well as the efforts undertaken to include sexual orientation and gender identity in the work of the U.N. Human Rights Council, General Assembly, and the Office of the High Commissioner for Human Rights.

4. The United States is committed to continuing to promote the human rights of persons with disabilities, including through measures advancing non-discrimination, inclusion, dignity, individual autonomy, equality of treatment, and accessibility.

5. The United States is dedicated to combating both overt and subtle forms of racism and racial and ethnic discrimination domestically and internationally. The United States is party to the International Convention on the Elimination of All Forms of Racial Discrimination, and is committed to seeing the goals of this convention fully realized and the obligations fully implemented by States Parties. Particular emphasis should be placed not only on eliminating any remaining legal barriers to equal rights and opportunities, but also on confronting the reality of continuing discrimination and inequality within institutions and societies. The United States also commits to actively supporting efforts related to the International Decade for People of African Descent.

6. The United States is committed to upholding our international obligations to prevent torture and cruel, inhuman or degrading treatment or punishment. The United States supports the work of the U.N. Special Rapporteur on Torture and the Committee Against Torture, and in 2015, the United States was proud to become a participant in the Group of Friends of the Convention Against Torture Initiative.

7. The United States commits to continuing to work to advance respect for workers' rights worldwide, including by: working with other governments and the International Labor Organization; promoting the adoption and implementation of policies, regulations and laws to achieve respect for internationally recognized worker rights; and providing funding for technical assistance projects to combat forced labor and other forms of human trafficking, advance the rights to freedom of association and collective bargaining, address workplace discrimination and exploitative working conditions, and build the capacity of worker organizations, employers, and governments to address labor issues.

8. The United States commits to promoting the ratification and implementation of the Protocol to Prevent, Suppress and Punish Trafficking in Persons, Especially Women and Children, supplementing the United Nations Convention against Transnational Organized Crime, including by promoting the effective involvement of non-governmental organizations in expert and treaty body meetings related to implementation of the Convention and Protocol, as well as continuing to advocate a victim-centered, trauma-informed, culturally-relevant, gender-responsive, and multi-disciplinary approach to combating all forms of trafficking in persons and to promoting the dignity, human rights and fundamental freedoms of trafficking victims.

9. The United States commits to continuing to promote freedom of religion for individuals of all religions or beliefs, particularly members of minority and vulnerable groups, through dedicated outreach, advocacy, training, and programmatic efforts, and to promote religious tolerance. The United States was pleased to support U.N. Human Rights Council resolution 16/18 ("Combating Intolerance, Negative Stereotyping and Stigmatization of, and Discrimination, Incitement to Violence, and Violence Against Persons Based on Religion or Belief") and its subsequent resolutions, and played an important role in subsequent Istanbul Process meetings and related work. The United States works to implement U.N. Human Rights Council resolution 16/18 through a series of programs intended to create a dialogue about the resolution and religious tolerance. The programs vary in scope bit focus on establishing a legal framework for religious tolerance, enforcing non-discrimination laws, and community engagement, including case studies and outreach exercises. We have conducted such workshops in Bosnia, Greece, Spain, and Indonesia for host country interlocutors, including lawyers, judges, government officials, NGO representatives, community leaders, and academics.

10. The United States commits to continuing to engage on, and support, economic, social, and cultural rights, including at the U.N. Human Rights Council, in the U.N. General Assembly and elsewhere, in terms consistent with human rights instruments we have accepted, including the Universal Declaration of Human Rights. In addition, the United States is committed to achieving the goals of the 2030 Agenda for Sustainable Development, including those related to ending extreme poverty, improving public health, increasing access to education and housing reducing violence and inequality, and expanding opportunity and protecting fundamental freedoms. We also continue to support both bilateral and multilateral international assistance programs that bolster food security, education, access to nondiscriminatory health care services and programs, safe drinking water, and other economic and social goods and services.

11. The United States is committed to continuing its leadership role in promoting business and human rights globally through multilateral fora, the forthcoming adoption of a National Action Plan on Responsible Business Conduct, and support of and engagement in multi-stakeholder initiatives. In 2011, the United States co-sponsored the resolution endorsing the U.N. Guiding Principles on Business and Human Rights. In September 2014, the United States began development of its own National Action Plan on Responsible Business Conduct, which seeks to promote responsible business conduct consistent with the U.N. Guiding Principles on Business and Human Rights and the OECD Guidelines for Multinational Enterprises. In January 2015, the United States published updates to the Federal Acquisition Regulation in alignment with the President's Executive Order "Strengthening Protections Against Trafficking in Persons in Federal Contracts" and related requirements in the Ending Trafficking in Government Contracting Act (set forth in the National Defense Authorization Act for 2013). The United States also takes a leading role in promoting accountability, transparency, and engagement on security and human rights through multi stakeholder initiatives. The United States is a founding member of the Open Government Partnership (OGP), the Voluntary Principles on Security and Human Rights, the International Code of Conduct Association for Private Security Companies (ICoCA), and the Montreux Document Forum (MDF). As part of its commitments in its OGP National Action Plan, the United States is working toward implementation of the Extractive Industry Transparency Initiative domestically.

12. The United States is also committed to the promotion and protection of human rights through regional organizations. Through our membership in the Organization for Security and Cooperation in Europe and the Organization of

American States, the United States commits to continuing efforts to uphold human rights and fundamental freedoms, and to strengthening and developing institutions and mechanisms for their protection. In particular recognition of its human rights commitments within the Inter-American system, the United States strongly supports the work of the Inter-American Commission on Human Rights, is its largest donor with $2.3 million contributed in 2015, and engages actively in proceedings on individual petitions filed against the United States, in thematic hearings, and with respect to the Commission's thematic and country reports.

13. The United States is the 2015-2017 President of the Community of Democracies (CD) and is leading efforts to support emerging democracies as they work to complete successful transitions. Themes for our presidency include democracy and security and democracy and development. CD working groups focus on issues such as the protection of civil society, freedom of expression, and development.

14. Recognizing the essential contributions of independent media to promoting the right to freedom of expression, exposing human rights violations and abuses, and promoting accountability and transparency in governance, the United States commits to continuing to champion freedom of expression and to promote media freedom and the protection of journalists worldwide. To this end, the United States leads and supports efforts at the Human Rights Council and U.N. General Assembly to protect and promote freedom of expression. In 2015, the United States co-sponsored a joint statement on freedom of artistic expression that over 50 countries supported. The United States supports initiatives on the safety of journalists, including the September 2014 HRC consensus resolution on that subject. In June 2012, the United States co-sponsored a consensus resolution at the Human Rights Council on Internet Freedom affirming that the same rights that people have offline must also be protected online, and co-sponsored a resolution in 2014 reaffirming these rights.

COMMITMENT TO ADVANCING HUMAN RIGHTS, FUNDAMENTAL FREEDOMS AND HUMAN DIGNITY AND PROSPERITY IN THE UNITED STATES

1. The United States executive branch is committed to working with the United States Senate to consider the ratification of the Convention on the Elimination of All Forms of Discrimination against Women, the Convention on the Rights of Persons with Disabilities, and ILO Convention 111, among other treaties.

2. The United States is committed to meeting its U.N. treaty obligations and participating in a meaningful dialogue with treaty bodies.

3. The United States is committed to continued cooperation with the UN's human rights mechanisms, as well as the Inter-American Commission on Human Rights and other regional human rights bodies, by responding to inquiries, engaging in dialogues, and hosting visits. Since 2012, the United States has hosted seven official Special Rapporteur and Working Group visits.

4. The United States is also strongly committed to continue our longstanding work to combat discrimination based on race, color, age, national origin, religion, gender, familial status, sexual orientation, gender identity, health status, and disability in various sectors in our society. Certain statutes also protect individuals who are members of language minority group or reside in institutions. Despite the achievements of the civil rights movement and many years of striving to achieve equal rights and equal opportunity for all, invidious discrimination still exists in our country and we continue to fight it through enforcement of myriad federal civil rights statutes, including the Civil Rights Act of 1964, the Voting Rights Act, the Fair Housing Act, Section 1557 of the Affordable Care Act, and numerous others.

5. The United States also continues its work to combat hate crimes, police misconduct, and human trafficking through federal and state prosecution of these crimes and strengthening of health and human service safety nets. Our federal hate crime statutes make it unlawful, among other things, to willfully cause bodily injury, or to attempt to do so, because of a person's race, color, religion, national origin, gender, sexual orientation, gender identity or disability. The United States Congress passed the Violence Against Women Reauthorization Act of 2013, Preventing Sex Trafficking and Strengthening Families Act of 2014, and the Justice for Victims of Trafficking Act of 2015 which further strengthened prevention, protection, and prosecution responses to human trafficking. The United States recognizes human trafficking as a violent crime and public health issue requiring a comprehensive response engaging the collaboration of criminal justice, health and social welfare, labor and education systems and institutions.

6. The United States' commitment to continuing to promote human prosperity and human rights and fundamental freedoms of all persons within the United States also includes protecting the rights of individuals with disabilities through enforcement of legislation such as the Americans with Disabilities Act, the Rehabilitation Act, and the Individuals with Disabilities Education Act.

7. The United States continues to work towards full racial equality. We are committed to ensuring that every American benefits from a local police force that protects and serves all members of the community, and we are working with state and local authorities to improve police training and build community trust. The United States enforces many laws that ensure that persons of every race have equal access to housing and credit through various statutes including the Fair Housing Act and Equal Credit Opportunity Act.

8. The United States is committed to strengthening government-to-government relationships with federally recognized tribes and furthering U.S. policy on indigenous issues. To that end, we support the United Nations Declaration on the Rights of Indigenous Peoples as explained in the "Announcement of U.S. Support for the United Nations Declaration on the Rights of Indigenous Peoples — Initiatives to Promote the Government-to-Government Relationship & Improve the Lives of Indigenous Peoples." While the Declaration is not legally binding, it carries considerable moral and political force and complements the government's ongoing efforts to address historical inequities faced by indigenous communities in the United States. Since 2009, the U.S. government has hosted an annual White House Tribal Nations Conference and in 2013 established the White House Council on Native American Affairs. In 2013, the Violence Against Women Reauthorization Act included an historic provision recognizing tribes' inherent power to exercise "special domestic violence criminal jurisdiction" over Indian or non-Indian perpetrators who commit acts of domestic violence or violate certain protection orders on tribal lands; the U.S. Department of Justice continues to coordinate with tribal governments to fully implement the new law. The United States played a leading role in shaping the outcome document of the September 2014 U.N. World Conference on Indigenous Peoples. In 2014, the United States provided over $290,000 of voluntary funding to U.N. Women, to support field-based projects protecting indigenous women and children from violence.

Source: U.S. Department of State, Diplomacy in Action, U.N. Human Rights Council Candidate 2017-2019.
https://www.state.gov/p/io/humanrights/

U.N. Human Rights Council Special Procedures & Complaint Procedure

Chapter 5

This Chapter is About a set of functions of the U.N. Human Rights Council (HRC), the main forum in which the U.S. is engaged in human rights. This includes its record both at home, and in relation to the records and issues of other countries. It is about what are called the Special Procedures, also called special mechanisms. These involve individuals or groups of persons who are given a mandate and authorization to help the HRC by providing it with certain information in dealing with states in regard to certain human rights situations. These special procedures mostly involve mandate holders known as special rapporteurs, independent experts, or working groups. This chapter discusses not only a communication procedure involving mandate holders to respond to certain urgent matters, but also a Human Rights Council complaint procedure for situations characterized by a systematic pattern of gross and reliably attested violations. Formerly called the 1503 procedure, the Complaint process is the new complaint procedure which improved upon the 1503 procedure.

This is Important Because the Human Rights Council is where the U.S. human rights record is brought not only before the international community in the UPR procedure, but also where the U.S. is involved in many special procedures of the Council. It is involved both as a country subject to a special procedure and as a country exercising the role of mandate-holder of a special procedure. Many times U.N. special procedures have taken place in the U.S. where an HRC special rapporteur or a working group has exercised its function in the U.S. during a special fact finding or assessment visit. This results in reports about the U.S. in certain areas such as racial discrimination, counterterrorism measures, or housing. In such cases, the international community is judging the U.S. constructively to help it advance its compliance with international human rights norms. This process involves procedures and reports which can yield information, observations, and recommendations which Americans need to know about to help the U.S. improve its human rights performance. The quote, below, by Nils Melzer concerning waterboarding shows the interaction of the international community with the U.S. as a voice calling the U.S. to comply with international human rights legal standards.

Quotes & Key Text Excerpts

The deep commitment of the United States to champion the human rights enshrined in the Universal Declaration of Human Rights is driven by the founding values of our nation and the conviction that international peace, security, and prosperity are strengthened when human rights and fundamental freedoms are respected and protected. As the United States seeks to advance human rights and fundamental freedoms around the world, we do so cognizant of our own commitment to live up to our ideals at home and to meet our international human rights obligations. In support of the United States candidacy for membership in the U.N. Human Rights Council, the United States made the following pledges:

* Commitment to Advancing Human Rights in the U.N. System;
* Commitment to Continue to Support Human Rights Activities in the U.N.;
* Commitment to Advancing Human Rights, Fundamental Freedoms, and Human Dignity and Prosperity Internationally;
* Commitment to Advancing Human Rights and Fundamental Freedoms in the United States.

Source U.S. Dept. of State, Diplomacy in Action, https://www.state.gov/j/drl/hr/unhrc/index.htm

The United States is committed to advancing the promotion and protection of human rights and fundamental freedoms throughout the U.N. system, including in the U.N. General Assembly and its Third Committee. The United States will continue to strongly support the work of the U.N. human rights mechanisms — including Special Rapporteurs, Independent Experts Working Groups, and Commissions of Inquiry — and the dialogue that their reports engender. The United States will also continue to support the work of the human rights treaty bodies....

The United States is committed to continued cooperation with the U.N.'s human rights mechanisms, as well as the Inter-American Commission on Human Rights and other regional human rights bodies, by responding to inquiries, engaging in dialogues, and hosting visits. Since 2012, the United States has hosted seven official Special Rapporteur and Working Group visits.

—U.N. Human Rights Council Candidate, Pledge, 2017-2019

Source: U.S. Department of State, Diplomacy in Action, https://www.state.gov/p/io/humanrights/index.htm

GENEVA (30 January 2017) — The United Nations Special Rapporteur on torture, Nils Melzer, has appealed to U.S. President Donald Trump not to reconsider the acceptability of waterboarding and other methods of torture used as interrogation techniques.

"Without any doubt, waterboarding amounts to torture," said the independent expert tasked by the Human Rights Council with monitoring and reporting on the use of torture and other cruel, inhuman, or degrading treatment or punishment around the world.

"Any tolerance, complacence, or acquiescence with such practice, however exceptional and well-argued, will inevitably lead down a slippery slope towards complete arbitrariness and brute force," Mr. Melzer cautioned.

"I urgently appeal to President Trump to carefully consider not only U.S. legal obligations, doctrine, and tradition, but also the consolidated legal and moral views of the entire international community before allowing the re-introduction of methods or interrogation that are more closely associated with barbarism than with civilization. I remain open to engage in a direct and constructive dialogue with the President."

The Special Rapporteur noted that the U.S. has always publicly affirmed its belief in the rule of law and respect for truth, and called on the Government to live up to the standards the nation has set both for itself and others.

"If the new Administration were to revive the use of torture, however, the consequences around the world would be catastrophic," he warned. "Should Mr. Trump follow through on all of his pledges, more countries are likely to follow his lead and get back into the torture business — an ultimate disgrace for all of humanity."

Three reasons why not to reinstate it

"First, waterboarding is a form of torture and, contrary to popular belief, torture simply does not work," Mr. Melzer emphasized.

"Torture is known to consistently produce false confessions and unreliable or misleading information," he said. "Faced with the imminent threat of excruciating pain or anguish, victims simply will say anything — regardless of whether it is true — to make the pain stop and try to stay alive."

The expert recalled the 2014 U.S. Senate Intelligence Committee Report, which concluded that the CIA's use of enhanced interrogation techniques, including waterboarding, was 'not an effective means of acquiring intelligence or gaining cooperation from detainees,' a conclusion echoed by countless law enforcement agencies and scientific studies worldwide.

"Second, even if torture did work, that does not make it legally or morally acceptable," he added. "Let us be clear: if you are looking for military advantage in war, you can argue that chemical weapons 'work,' or terrorism 'works' as well."

"However, all civilized peoples of this world have stood together to outlaw such abhorrent practices because, just as torture, they irreparably destroy the humanity and integrity not only of the victim, but also of the perpetrator and, ultimately of society as a whole," Mr. Melzer underscored.

Third, the expert stressed, "the use or incitement of torture and other cruel, inhuman, or degrading treatment or punishment has been absolutely prohibited in treaty law, such as the Convention against Torture, the International Covenant on Civil and Political Rights and the Geneva Conventions."

The Special Rapporteur noted that the prohibition is absolute, and breaches amount to internationally recognized crimes and, in armed conflict, even to war crimes.

"In my view," the human rights expert concluded, "the universal recognition of the absolute nature of this prohibition may well constitute the most fundamental achievement of mankind."

—Mr. Nils Melzer (Switzerland) was appointed by the U.N. Human Rights Council as the Special Rapporteur on torture and other cruel, inhuman, or degrading treatment or punishment in November 2016. Mr. Melzer has previously worked for the International Committee of the Red Cross and the Swiss Federal Department of Foreign Affairs and is currently the Human Rights Chair of the Geneva Academy of International Humanitarian Law and Human Rights.

Source: U.N. OHCHR, News and Events; http://www.ohchr.org/EN/NewsEvents/Pages/DisplayNews.aspx?NewsID=21129&LangID=E

What You Need To Know

A. Special Procedures/Mechanisms (U.N. HRC)

"Special Procedures" is the general name given to the mechanisms established by the Commission on Human Rights and assumed by its successor, the U.N. Human Rights Council (HRC), to address either specific country situations or thematic issues in all parts of the world. The term "Special Mechanisms" is also used.

The system of Special Procedures is a central element of the United Nations human rights machinery and covers all human rights: civil, cultural, economic, political, and social. A key feature of these mechanisms is that they can respond quickly to problems anywhere there are allegations of violations. Special Procedures allow for quicker action on the part of a human rights commission or council, as compared to the slow deliberative speed of the U.N. organs, such as the General Assembly. The Organization of American States (OAS) has its own "Special Mechanisms" processes that the Standing Rock Sioux Tribe, the Cheyenne River Sioux Tribe, and the Yankton Sioux Tribe, also known as the "Tribes," are currently working with.

The U.N. Office of the High Commissioner for Human Rights provides these mechanisms with personnel, policy, research, and logistical support for the discharge of their mandates. As of 30 September 2016, there are 43 thematic mandates and 14 country mandates. The U.N. Human Rights Council selects and offers to certain human rights experts a mandate to make a report or to investigate regarding a certain theme or country. Those who agree to act in such capacity are given a mandate by the Council empowering them to act, and are called "mandate-holders." The Special Procedures mandates usually call on mandate-holders to examine, monitor, advise, and publicly report on human rights situations in specific countries or territories, known as country mandates, or on major phenomena of human rights violations worldwide, known as thematic mandates. Various activities are undertaken by special procedures, including responding to individual complaints, conducting studies, providing advice for technical cooperation at the country level, engaging in general promotional activities, expert consultations, development of international human rights standards, advocacy, and raising public awareness.

Thematic mandates are renewed every three years, and country specific mandates are renewed every year, unless the HRC decides differently. Mandate-holders serve as experts in their personal capacity, for a maximum of six years and receive no salary. They tend to be academics, serving in the field of their specialty. They are independent, which helps them fulfill their mandate impartially in relationship to states. They network and share information both within and outside of the U.N. system. They can communicate their concerns through the media. In their country reports, they make recommendations to the government on how to improve in their subject area. They report on their work to the Human Rights Council annually and can even share with the General Assembly and the Security Council, if needed.

Special procedures involve either an individual called "Special Rapporteur," ("Independent Expert") or a working group, usually composed of five members (one from each global region). The mandates of the special procedures are established and defined by the resolution creating them. Mandate-holders of the special procedures serve in their personal capacity, and do not receive salaries or any other financial compensation for their work. The independent status of the mandate-holders is crucial in order to be able to fulfill their functions in all impartiality. Most Special Procedures mandate-holders also receive information on specific allegations of human rights violations and send communications based on so-called "urgent action" appeals or letters of allegation to governments asking for clarification and remedy. Their consideration of these urgent action communications about violations is directed more to address the broader structural nature of the problem.

Mandate-holders carry out country visits to investigate the human rights situation at the national level. In the past, there have been many U.S. visits of Special Rapporteurs and Working Groups to carry out investigations on certain U.S.

human rights practices. In its compilation of information on the US for the 2015 UPR process, the OHCHR reports that the following special procedures involved the U.S. and a visit to the U.S.: Special Rapporteur on the human rights of migrants (30 April-18 May 2007); Special Rapporteur on the promotion and protection of human rights and fundamental freedoms while countering terrorism (16-25 May 2007); Special Rapporteur on contemporary forms of racism, racial discrimination, xenophobia, and related intolerance (19 May-6 June 2008); Special Rapporteur on extrajudicial, summary, or arbitrary executions (16-30 June 2008); Working Group on the use of mercenaries as a means of violating human rights and impeding the exercise of the right of peoples to self-determination (20 July-3 August 2009); Special Rapporteur on adequate housing as a component of the right to an adequate standard of living (22 October-8 November 2009); Working Group of experts on people of African descent (25-29 January 2010); Special Rapporteur on Right to Safe Drinking Water and sanitation (2011); Special Rapporteur on the implications for human rights of the environmentally sound management and disposal of hazardous substances and wastes, U.S. Marshall Islands (27-30 March 2012) and the United States of America (24-27 April 2012); Special Rapporteur on the rights of indigenous peoples, (23 April to 4 May 2012); Special Rapporteur on Transnational corporations and business (2013).

All special procedure mandate-holders must comply with a written Code of Conduct, which controls how they act in fulfilling their mandate. This is to ensure their impartiality and objectivity and ensure state cooperation in facilitating, or at least not obstructing, their work. See Primary Source Document 1.

Since the UPR compilation report in 2015, there have been special rapporteur reports done on the issue of discrimination against women in law and in practice (2016), another by the Working Group of experts on people of African descent in 2016 (19 to 29 January 2016), and another by the Special Rapporteur in Trafficking in Persons, especially Women and Children (6-16 December 2016).

At the time of this writing, there were five Americans serving as mandate-holders in the HRC special procedures.

Source: Working with the United Nations Human Rights Programme A Handbook for Civil Society, http://www.ohchr.org/Documents/Publications/NgoHandbook/ngohandbook6.pdf

Thematic Special Procedures are mandated to investigate the situation of human rights in all parts of the world, irrespective of whether a particular government is a party to any of the relevant human rights treaties. This requires the mandate-holders to take the measures necessary to monitor and respond quickly to allegations of human rights violations against individuals or groups, either globally or in a specific country or territory, and to report on their activities to the HRC.

To summarize, the special procedures/mechanisms provide ways by which the HRC, and hence the U.N., is able intelligently, competently, impartially, and objectively: to analyze the issue involved or situation in a country; to give advice on the measures which should be taken by governments and others to protect human rights; to call attention of various U.N. organs and agencies and even the international community of the need to address a situation and the issues involved in that situation. Because they can act independently, mandate-holders can: provide an early warning call to action and call for preventative measures; advocate on behalf of victims; suggest appropriate reparations for violations; call into action governments, civil society, and other international organizations to address a problem.

Special procedures are Thematic and Country-specific; see following list.

43 Thematic Special Procedures

Working Groups:

    1. Working Group on people of African descent

    2. Working Group on arbitrary detention

    3. Working Group on enforced or involuntary disappearances

    4. Working Group on the use of mercenaries as a means of impeding the exercise of the right of peoples to self-determination

5. Working Group on the issue of human rights and transnational corporations and other business enterprises

6. Working Group on the issue of discrimination against women in law and in practice

Independent Experts:

7. Independent Expert on the enjoyment of human rights of persons with albinism

8. Independent Expert on the promotion of a democratic and equitable international order

9. Independent Expert on the effects of foreign debt and other related international financial obligations of states on the full enjoyment of human rights, particularly economic, social, and cultural rights

10. Independent Expert on human rights and international solidarity

11. Independent Expert on the enjoyment of all human rights by older persons

12. Independent Expert on protection against violence and discrimination based on sexual orientation and gender identity

Special Rapporteurs:

13. Special Rapporteur on adequate housing as a component of the right to an adequate standard of living, and on the right to non-discrimination in this context

14. Special Rapporteur on the sale of children, child prostitution, and child pornography

15. Special Rapporteur in the field of cultural rights

16. Special Rapporteur on the rights of persons with disabilities

17. Special Rapporteur on the right to education

18. Special Rapporteur on the issue of human rights obligations relating to the enjoyment of a safe, clean, healthy, and sustainable environment

19. Special Rapporteur on extrajudicial, summary, or arbitrary executions

20. Special Rapporteur on extreme poverty and human rights

21. Special Rapporteur on the right to food

22. Special Rapporteur on the rights to freedom of peaceful assembly and of association

23. Special Rapporteur on the promotion and protection of the right to freedom of opinion and expression

24. Special Rapporteur on freedom of religion or belief

25. Special Rapporteur on the implications for human rights of the environmentally sound management and disposal of hazardous substances and wastes

26. Special Rapporteur on the right of everyone to the enjoyment of the highest attainable standard of physical and mental health

27. Special Rapporteur on the situation of human rights defenders

28. Special Rapporteur on the independence of judges and lawyers

29. Special Rapporteur on the rights of indigenous peoples

30. Special Rapporteur on the human rights of internally displaced persons

31. Special Rapporteur on the human rights of migrants

32. Special Rapporteur on minority issues

33. Special Rapporteur on the right to privacy

34. Special Rapporteur on contemporary forms of racism, racial discrimination, xenophobia, and related intolerance

35. Special Rapporteur on contemporary forms of slavery, including its causes and its consequences

36. Special Rapporteur on the promotion and protection of human rights while countering terrorism

37. Special Rapporteur on torture and other cruel, inhuman, or degrading treatment or punishment

38. Special Rapporteur on trafficking in persons, especially women and children

39. Special Rapporteur on the promotion of truth, justice, reparation and guarantees of non-recurrence

40. Special Rapporteur on the negative impact of unilateral coercive measures on the enjoyment of human rights

41. Special Rapporteur on violence against women, its causes and consequences

42. Special Rapporteur on the human right to safe drinking water and sanitation

43. Special Rapporteur on the Right to Development

14 Country-specific Special Procedures

Independent Experts:

1. Independent Expert on the situation of human rights in Central African Republic

2. Independent Expert on the situation of human rights in Côte d'Ivoire

3. Independent Expert on the situation of human rights in Haiti

4. Independent Expert on the situation of human rights in Mali

5. Independent Expert on the situation of human rights in Somalia

6. Independent Expert on the situation of human rights in the Sudan

Special Rapporteurs:

7. Special Rapporteur on the situation of human rights in Belarus

8. Special Rapporteur on the situation of human rights in Cambodia

9. Special Rapporteur on the situation of human rights in Eritrea

10. Special Rapporteur on the situation of human rights in the Democratic People's Republic of Korea

11. Special Rapporteur on the situation of human rights in the Islamic Republic of Iran

12. Special Rapporteur on the situation of human rights in Myanmar

13. Special Rapporteur on the situation of human rights in the Palestinian territories occupied since 1967

14. Special Rapporteur on the situation of human rights in the Syrian Arab Republic

Urgent Action/Urgent Appeals and Mandate-Holder Communications

Noted above, special mechanisms can have complaint procedures allowing the mandate-holder to receive a communication of alleged violation(s), and thereupon the mandate-holder may communicate the urgency with a state where a violation is alleged to require urgent action. Most mandate-holders have an urgent action/appeal process to receive complaints directly. These appeals can come from individuals or groups and are addressed to the appropriate mandate-holder. This mini-complaint process allows the mandate-holder to interface quickly, to make contact with a state alleged to have violated or about to violate a right. When a mandate-holder receives an urgent action request, he/she can communicate with the state or even with a non-governmental organization or other non-state actors, to let them know that the alleged situation and country in which an alleged violation is taking place are being monitored/watched at an international level.

The U.N. Human Rights Council website explains this process as follows:

Communications
Special procedures mechanisms can intervene directly with Governments on allegations of violations of human rights that come within their mandates by means of letters which include urgent appeals and other communications. The intervention can relate to a human rights violation that has already occurred, is ongoing, or which has a high risk of occurring. The process involves sending a letter to the concerned state identifying the facts of the allegation, applicable international human rights norms and standards, the concerns and questions of the mandate-holder(s), and a request for follow-up action. Communications may deal with individual cases, general patterns and trends of human rights violations, cases affecting a particular group or community, or the content of draft or existing legislation, policy or practice considered not to be fully compatible with international human rights standards. In some cases, communications are also sent to inter-governmental organisations or non-state actors.

The decision to intervene is at the discretion of mandate-holders and will depend on the various criteria established under their respective mandates, as well as the criteria laid out in the Code of Conduct. The criteria will generally relate to: the reliability of the source and the credibility of information received; the details provided; and the scope of the mandate. Communications can be sent by mandate-holders irrespective of whether an alleged victim has exhausted domestic remedies and whether the concerned State has ratified an international or regional human rights instruments.

Submitting information to the special procedures
In order for a complaint to be assessed, the following information is needed:

1. Identification of the alleged victim(s)

2. Identification of the alleged perpetrators of the violation (if known), including substantiated information on all the actors involved, including non-state actors if relevant

3. Identification of the person(s) or organization(s) submitting the communication, if different from the victim (this information will be kept confidential)

4. Date, place, and detailed description of the circumstances of the incident(s) or violation. The information submitted can refer to violations that are said to have already occurred, that are on-going or about to occur

Other details pertaining to the specific alleged violation may be required depending on the mandate(s) to which the submission is addressed or relevant.

Communications that contain abusive language or that are obviously politically motivated are not considered. Communications should not be based solely on media reports.

To facilitate the consideration of alleged violations, the online form/questionnaire at the link "Online submission to special procedures" can be used, as can the questionnaires relating to several mandates be used by persons wishing to submit information. Communications are also considered even when they are not submitted in the form of a questionnaire. Such cases can be submitted by email to urgent-action@ohchr.org or by postal mail to:

OHCHR-UNOG
8-14 Avenue de la Paix
1211 Geneva 10
Switzerland

Source: U.N. OHCHR, Human Rights Council, http://www.ohchr.org/EN/HRBodies/SP/Pages/Communications.aspx

A sample urgent appeal procedure from the mandate-holder, the Special Rapporteur on Torture, reads as follows:

The Special Rapporteur will act upon receiving credible information suggesting that an individual or a group of individuals is at risk of torture at the hands, consent, or acquiescence of public officials.

Without drawing any conclusions as to the facts of the case, the Special Rapporteur will send a letter to the Minister of Foreign Affairs of the country concerned, urging the Government to ensure the physical and mental integrity of the person(s).

The Special Rapporteur also takes action when persons are feared to be at risk of:
- corporal punishment;
- means of restraint contrary to international standards;
- prolonged incommunicado detention;
- solitary confinement;
- "torturous" conditions of detention;
- the denial of medical treatment and adequate nutrition;
- imminent deportation to a country where there is a risk of torture, and
- the threatened use or excessive use of force by law enforcement officials.

Source: U.N. OHCHR, http://www.ohchr.org/EN/Issues/Torture/SRTorture/Pages/Appeals.aspx

See Primary Source Document 2.

The Special Rapporteur on Torture can also issue "allegation letters." Allegations of torture received by the Special Rapporteur which do not require immediate action are sent to Governments in the form of "allegation letters."

The Special Rapporteur requests that the Government clarify the substance of the allegations and to forward information on the status of any investigation (i.e., the findings of any medical examination, the identity of the persons responsible for the torture, the disciplinary and criminal sanctions imposed on them, and the nature and amount of compensation paid to the victims or their families).

Allegation letters may be sent in relation to systematic patterns of torture by identifying a specific group of victims or perpetrators; the use of particular methods of torture, and detention conditions amounting to ill-treatment.

Source: U.N. OHCHR, http://www.ohchr.org/EN/Issues/Torture/SRTorture/Pages/Allegation.aspx

Human Rights Council Complaint Procedure

In addition to the urgent appeal to a mandate-holder and the communication letter to the state, there is another useful process whenever and wherever there is a consistent pattern of gross and reliably attested human rights violations. It used to be called the 1503 procedure under the former Human Rights Commission. This complaint procedure is intended for the most egregious situations, and is not one of the Special Mechanisms. It is described in the Human Rights Council website as follows:

Pursuant to paragraph 94 of resolution 5/1, the Chairperson of the Working Group on Communications, together with the Secretariat, undertake an initial screening of communications based on the admissibility criteria set in paragraphs 85 to 88 of resolution 5/1. Manifestly ill-founded and anonymous communications are screened out. Communications not rejected in the initial screening are transmitted to the state concerned to obtain its views on the allegations of violations. Both the author of a communication and the state concerned are informed of the proceedings at each stage.

Two distinct working groups — the Working Group on Communications and the Working Group on Situations — are responsible, respectively, for examining written communications and bringing consistent patterns of gross and reliably attested violations of human rights and fundamental freedoms to the attention of the Council.

Criteria for a communication to be accepted for examination

A communication related to a violation of human rights and fundamental freedoms is admissible, provided that:

- It is not manifestly politically motivated and its object is consistent with the Charter of the United Nations, the Universal Declaration of Human Rights, and other applicable instruments in the field of Human Rights Law;
- It gives a factual description of the alleged violations, including the rights which are alleged to be violated;
- Its language is not abusive. However, such a communication may be considered if it meets the other criteria for admissibility after deletion of the abusive language;
- It is submitted by a person or a group of persons claiming to be the victims of violations of human rights and fundamental freedoms, or by any person or group of persons, including non-governmental organizations, acting in good faith in accordance with the principles of human rights, not resorting to politically motivated stands contrary to the provisions of the Charter of the United Nations and claiming to have direct and reliable knowledge of the violations concerned. Nonetheless, reliably attested communications shall not be inadmissible solely because the knowledge of the individual authors is second-hand, provided that they are accompanied by clear evidence:
  - that is not exclusively based on reports disseminated by mass media;
  - that does not refer to a case that appears to reveal a consistent pattern of gross and reliably attested violations of human rights already being dealt with by a special procedure, a treaty body, or other United Nations or similar regional complaints procedure in the field of human rights;
  - that domestic remedies have been exhausted, unless it appears that such remedies would be ineffective or unreasonably prolonged.

The process is confidential. It is not made public.

Source: U.N. OHCHR, Human Rights Council, http://www.ohchr.org/EN/HRBodies/HRC/ComplaintProcedure/Pages/HRC ComplaintProcedureIndex.aspx

Primary Source Documents

I. CODE OF CONDUCT FOR SPECIAL PROCEDURES MANDATE-HOLDERS OF THE HUMAN RIGHTS COUNCIL

This document is a Code of Conduct to be followed by all mandate holders in the Human Rights Council in the fulfillment of their work. It applies to all thematic rapporteurs, country specific rapporteurs, independent experts and working group members. This Code of Conduct was made in reaction to some states complaining against mandate holders for being biased and partial and not objective in carrying out their mandate. This Code is to assure that the Special Rapporteurs, Independent Experts and working group members act professionally, impartially and diplomatically. Since they are acting on behalf, and under the authority, of the Council they must do nothing to discredit the Council or adulterate the deliberations and actions of the Council.

[Text]

The Human Rights Council,

Guided by the aims and principles of the Charter of the United Nations and the Universal Declaration of Human Rights and recognizing the ensuing obligations inter alia of States to cooperate in promoting universal respect for human rights as enshrined therein,

Recalling the Vienna Declaration and Programme of Action adopted on 25 June 1993 by the World Conference on Human Rights,

Recalling also that in resolution 60/251 of 15 March 2006, entitled "Human Rights Council," the General Assembly:

(a) Reaffirmed that all human rights are universal, indivisible, interrelated, interdependent and mutually reinforcing and that all human rights must be treated in a fair and equal manner on the same footing and with the same emphasis;

(b) Acknowledged that peace and security, development and human rights are the pillars of the United Nations system and that they are interlinked and mutually reinforcing;

(c) Decided that members elected to the Council shall uphold the highest standards in the promotion and protection of human rights and shall fully cooperate with the Council;

(d) Stressed the importance of "ensuring universality, objectivity and non-selectivity in the consideration of human rights issues, and the elimination of double standards and politicization";

(e) Further recognized that the promotion and protection of human rights "should be based on the principles of cooperation and genuine dialogue and aimed at strengthening the capacity of Member States to comply with their human rights obligations for the benefit of all human beings,"

(f) Decided that "the work of the Council shall' be guided by the principles of universality, impartiality, objectivity, and non-selectivity, constructive international dialogue and cooperation, with a view to enhancing the promotion and protection of all human rights, civil, political, economic, social and cultural rights, including the right to development";

(g) Also decided that "the methods of work of the Council shall be transparent, fair and impartial and shall enable genuine dialogue, be results-oriented, allow for subsequent follow-up discussions to recommendations and their implementation and also allow for substantive interaction with special procedures and mechanisms";

Underlining the centrality of the notions of impartiality and objectivity, as well as the expertise of mandate-holders, within the context of special procedures, along with the need to give the required degree of attention to all human rights violations, wherever they may be taking place,

Bearing in mind that the efficiency of the system of special procedures should be reinforced through the consolidation of the status of mandate-holders and the adoption of principles and regulations taking the specificities of their mandate into consideration,

Considering that it is necessary to assist all stakeholders, including States, national human rights institutions, non-governmental organizations and individuals, to better understand and support the activities of mandate-holders,

Recalling articles 100, 104, 105 of the Charter of the United Nations, section 22 of article VI of the Convention on the Privileges and Immunities of the United Nations of 13 February 1946 and paragraph 6 of General Aésembly resolution 60/251,

Noting decision 1/102 of 30 June 2006, in which the Council decided to extend exceptionally for one year the mandates and mandate-holders of the special procedures of the Commission on Human Rights, of the Sub-Commission for the Promotion and Protection of Human Rights as well as the procedure established pursuant to Economic and Social Council resolution 1503 (XLVIII) of 27 May 1970,

Noting also decision 1/104 of 30 June 2006, in which the Council established the Open-ended Intergovernmental Working Group entrusted with the task of formulating recommendations on the issue of the review and possibly the enhancement and rationalization of all mandates, mechanisms, functions and responsibilities of the Commission on Human Rights, in order to maintain a regime of special procedures in accordance with paragraph 6 of General Assembly resolution 60/251,

Noting further resolution 2/1 of 27 November 2006, in which the Council requested the Open-ended Intergovernmental Working Group to "draft a code of conduct regulating the work of the special procedures,"

Considering that this code of conduct is an integral part of the review, improvement and rationalization called for in General Assembly resolution 60/251 that, inter alia, seeks to enhance the cooperation between Governments and mandate-holders which is essential for the effective functioning of the system,

Considering also that such a code of conduct will strengthen the capacity of mandate-holders to exercise their functions whilst enhancing their moral authority and credibility and will require supportive action by other stakeholders, and in particular by States,

Considering further that one should distinguish between, on the one hand, the independence of mandate-holders, which is absolute in nature, and, on the other hand, their prerogatives, as circumscribed by their mandate, the mandate of the Human Rights Council, and the provisions of the Charter of the United Nations,

Mindful of the fact that it is desirable to spell out, complete and increase the visibility of the rules and principles governing the behaviour of mandate-holders,

Noting the Regulations Governing the Status, Basic Rights and Duties of Officials other than Secretariat Officials, and Experts on Mission that was adopted by the General Assembly in resolution 56/280 of 27 March 2002,

Noting also the draft Manual of the United Nations Human Rights Special Procedures adopted in 1999 by the sixth annual meeting of mandate-holders, as revised,

Taking note of the deliberations and proposals of the Open-ended Intergovernmental Working Group on Review of Mandates,

1. Urges all States to cooperate with, and assist, the special procedures in the performance of their tasks and to provide all information in a timely manner, as well as respond to communications transmitted to them by the special procedures without undue delay;

2. Adopts the Code of Conduct for Special Procedures Mandate-Holders of the Human Rights Council, the text of which is annexed to the present resolution and whose provisions should be disseminated by the Office of the United Nations High Commissioner for Human Rights, to the mandate-holders, to the Member States of the United Nations and to other concerned parties.

Annex

DRAFT CODE OF CONDUCT FOR SPECIAL PROCEDURES MANDATE-HOLDERS OF THE HUMAN RIGHTS COUNCIL

Article 1 — Purpose of the Code of Conduct
The purpose of the present Code of Conduct is to enhance the effectiveness of the system of special procedures by defining the standards of ethical behaviour and professional conduct that special procedures mandate-holders of the Human Rights Council (hereinafter referred to as "mandate-holders") shall observe whilst discharging their mandates.

Article 2 Status of the Code of Conduct
1. The provisions of the present Code complement those of the Regulations Governing the Status, Basic Rights and Duties of Officials other than Secretariat Officials, and Experts on Mission (ST/SGB/2002/9) (hereinafter referred to as "the Regulations");

2. The provisions of the draft manual of United Nations Human Rights Special Procedures should be in consonance with those of the present Code;

3. Mandate-holders shall be provided by the United Nations High Commissioner for Human Rights, along with the documentation pertaining to their mission, with a copy of the present Code of which they must acknowledge receipt.

Article 3 — General principles of conduct
Mandate-holders are independent United Nations experts. While discharging their mandate, they shall:

(a) Act in an independent capacity, and exercise their functions in accordance with their mandate, through a professional, impartial assessment of facts based on internationally recognized human rights standards, and free from any kind of extraneous influence, incitement, pressure, threat or interference, either direct or indirect, on the part of any party, whether stakeholder or not, for any reason whatsoever, the notion of independence being linked to the status of mandate-holders, and to their freedom to assess the human rights questions that they are called upon to examine under their mandate;

(b) Keep in mind the mandate of the Council which is responsible for promoting universal respect for the protection of all human rights and fundamental freedoms for all, through dialogue and cooperation as specified in .General Assembly resolution 60/251 of 15 March 2006;

(c) Exercise their functions in accordance with their mandate and in compliance with the Regulations, as well as with the present Code;

(d) Focus exclusively on the implementation of their mandate, constantly keeping in mind the fundamental obligations of truthfulness, loyalty and independence pertaining to their mandate;

(e) Uphold the highest standards of efficiency, competence and integrity, meaning, in particular, though not exclusively, probity, impartiality, equity, honesty and good faith;

(f) Neither seek nor accept instructions from any Government, individual, governmental or non-governmental organization or pressure group whatsoever;

(g) Adopt a conduct that is consistent with their status at all times;

(h) Be aware of the importance of their duties and responsibilities, taking the particular nature of their mandate into consideration and behaving in such a way as to maintain and reinforce the trust they enjoy of all stakeholders;

(i) Refrain from using their office or knowledge gained from their functions for private gain, financial or otherwise, or for the gain and/or detriment of any family member, close associate, or third party;

(j) Not accept any honour, decoration, favour, gift or remuneration from any governmental or non-governmental source for activities carried out in pursuit of his/her mandate.

Article 4 — Status of mandate-holders
1. Mandate-holders exercise their functions on a personal basis, their responsibilities not being national but exclusively international.

2. When exercising their functions, the mandate-holders are entitled to privileges and immunities as provided for under relevant international instruments, including section 22 of article VI of the Convention on the Privileges and Immunities of the United Nations.

3. Without prejudice to these privileges and immunities, the mandate-holders shall carry out their mandate while fully respecting the national legislation and regulations of the country wherein they are exercising their mission. Where an issue arises in this regard, mandate-holders shall adhere strictly to the provisions of Regulation 1 (e) of the Regulations.

Article 5 — Solemn declaration
Prior to assuming their functions, mandate-holders shall make the following solemn declaration in writing:

"I solemnly declare that I shall perform my duties and exercise my functions from a completely impartial, loyal and conscientious standpoint, and truthfully, and that I shall discharge these functions and regulate my conduct in a manner totally in keeping with the terms of my mandate, the Charter of the United Nations, the interests of the United Nations, and with the objective of promoting and protecting human rights, without seeking or accepting any instruction from any other party whatsoever."

Article 6 — Prerogatives
Without prejudice to prerogatives for which provision is made as part of their mandate, the mandate-holders shall:

(a) Always seek to establish the facts, based on objective, reliable information emanating from relevant credible sources, that they have duly cross-checked to the best extent possible;

(b) Take into account in a comprehensive and timely manner, in particular information provided by the State concerned on situations relevant to their mandate;

(c) Evaluate all information in the light of internationally recognized human rights standards relevant to their mandate, and of international conventions to which the State concerned is a party;

(d) Be entitled to bring to the attention of the Council any suggestion likely to enhance the capacity of special procedures to fulfil their mandate.

Article 7 — Observance of the terms of the mandate
It is incumbent on the mandate-holders to exercise their functions in strict observance of their mandate and in particular to ensure that their recommendations do not exceed their mandate or the mandate of the Council itself.

Article 8 — Sources of information
In their information-gathering activities the mandate-holders shall:

(a) Be guided by the principles of discretion, transparency, impartiality, and even-handedness;

(b) Preserve the confidentiality of sources of testimonies if their divulgation could cause harm to individuals involved;

(c) Rely on objective and dependable facts based on evidentiary standards that are appropriate to the non-judicial character of the reports and conclusions they are called upon to draw up;

(d) Give representatives of the concerned State the opportunity of commenting on mandate-holders' assessment and of responding to the allegations made against this State, and annex the State's written summary responses to their reports.

Article 9 — Letters of allegation
With a view to achieving effectiveness and harmonization in the handling of letters of allegation by special procedures, mandate-holders shall assess their conformity with reference to the following criteria:

(a) The communication should not be manifestly unfounded or politically motivated;

(b) The communication should contain a factual description of the alleged violations of human rights;

(c) The language in the communication should not be abusive;

(d) The communication should be submitted by a person or a group of persons claiming to be victim of violations or by any person or group of persons, including non-governmental organizations, acting in good faith in accordance with principles of human rights, and free from politically motivated stands or contrary to, the provisions of the Charter of the United Nations, and claiming to have direct or reliable knowledge of those violations substantiated by clear information;

(e) The communication should not be exclusively based on reports disseminated by mass media.

Article 10 — Urgent appeals
Mandate-holders may resort to urgent appeals in cases where the alleged violations are time-sensitive in terms of involving loss of life, life-threatening situations or either imminent or ongoing damage of a very grave nature to victims that cannot be addressed in a timely manner by the procedure under article 9 of the present Code.

Article 11 — Field visits
Mandate-holders shall:

(a) Ensure that their visit is conducted in compliance with the terms of reference of their mandate;

(b) Ensure that their visit is conducted with the consent, or at the invitation, of the State concerned;

(c) Prepare their visit in close collaboration with the Permanent Mission of the concerned State accredited to the United Nations Office at Geneva except if another authority is designated for this purpose by the concerned State;

(d) Finalize the official programme of their visits directly with the host country officials with administrative and logistical back-up from the local United Nations Agency and/or Representative of the High Commissioner for Human Rights who may also assist in arranging private meetings;

(e) Seek to establish a dialogue with the relevant government authorities and with all other stakeholders, the promotion of dialogue and cooperation to ensure the full effectiveness of special procedures being a shared obligation of the mandate-holders, the concerned State and the said stakeholders;

(f) Have access upon their own request, in consultation with the Office of the High Commissioner for Human Rights and after a common understanding between the host Government and the mandate-holder, to official security protection during their visit, without prejudice to the privacy and confidentiality that mandate-holders require to fulfil their mandate.

Article 12 — Private opinions and the public nature of the mandate Mandate-holders shall:

(a) Bear in mind the need to ensure that their personal political opinions are without prejudice to the execution of their mission, and base their conclusions and recommendations on objective assessments of human rights situations;

(b) In implementing their mandate, therefore, show restraint, moderation and discretion so as not to undermine the recognition of the independent nature of their mandate or the environment necessary to properly discharge the said mandate.

Article 13 — Recommendations and conclusions
Mandate-holders shall:

(a) While expressing their considered views, particularly in their public statements concerning allegations of human rights violations, also indicate fairly what responses were given by the concerned State;

(b) While reporting on a concerned State, ensure that their declarations on the human rights situation in the county are at all times compatible with their mandate and the integrity, independence and impartiality which their status requires, and which is likely to promote a constructive dialogue among stakeholders, as well as cooperation for the promotion and protection of human rights;

(c) Ensure that the concerned government authorities are the first recipients of their conclusions and recommendations concerning this State and are given adequate time to respond, and that likewise the Council is the first recipient of conclusions and recommendations addressed to this body.

Article 14 — Communication with Governments
Mandate-holders shall address all their communications to concerned Governments through diplomatic channels unless agreed otherwise between individual Governments and the Office of the High Commissioner for Human Rights.

Article 15 — Accountability to the Council
In the fulfilment of their mandate, mandate-holders are accountable to the Council.

2. SPECIAL PROCEDURE'S QUESTIONNAIRE FOR ALLEGATIONS OF VIOLATIONS OF MIGRANTS' HUMAN RIGHTS

This document is a sample questionnaire prepared for the Special Procedure mandate holder on the rights of migrants. It is to help a person submit an urgent appeal to the mandate holder alleging that a state has violated or threatens to violate the human rights of migrants. It is aimed at getting the mandate holder to submit a communication to the government of the alleged violator state so as to let the state know the issue is before an international procedure, to get the government to obtain information concerning the problem, such as the whereabouts of a disappeared person, and to ask for a halt to violation or a remedy for violation. The person seeking urgent action fills in all the information, sends it in to the U.N. OHCHR and the mandate holder decides whether the issue is within the terms of reference for his mandate and whether he or she should send a communication with the state and engage in follow-up. Each mandate holder can have their own questionnaire, which is usually a link in the mandate holder's website at the U.N.

[Text]

Notes:

1. The objective of this questionnaire is to have access to precise information on alleged violations of the human rights of migrants. The Special Rapporteur may raise her concerns about the incidents reported and request Governments to make observations and comments on the matter.

2. Please indicate whether the information provided is confidential (in the relevant sections).

3. Should the information you wish to provide relate to conditions/policies/practices or laws (i.e. more general situations), which affect the human rights of migrants, please do not use this form. A special form will be provided at a later date to address the issue of good practice and/or negative developments with regards to the protection of the human rights of migrants. Meanwhile you may send that type of information without completing a form to the contact numbers indicated at the end of the questionnaire.

4. Do not hesitate to attach additional sheets, if the space provided is not sufficient.

QUESTIONNAIRE

1. GENERAL INFORMATION: (Please mark with an X when appropriate)
Does the incident involve an individual __ or a group__ ?

If it involves a group please state the number of people involved _____ and the characteristics of the group:
Number of Men _____ Number of Women _____ Number of Minors _____
Country in which the incident took place _____

Nationality of the victim(s) _____

2. IDENTITY OF THE PERSONS CONCERNED: Note: if more than one person is concerned, please attach relevant information on each person separately.

1. Family name: _____

2. First name: _____

3. Sex: __ male __ female

4. Birth date or age: _____

5. Nationality(ies): _____

6. Civil status (single, married, etc.):_____

7. Profession and/or activity (e.g. trade union, political, religious, humanitarian/solidarity/human rights, etc.)

8. Status in the country where the incident took place: Undocumented ___ Transit ___ Tourist ___ Student ___
Work Permit ___ Resident ___ Refugee ___ Asylum seeker ___ Temporary protection ___
Other (please specify) _____

3. INFORMATION REGARDING THE ALLEGED VIOLATION

1. Date: _____

2. Place: _____

3. Time: _____

4. The nature of the incident: Please describe the circumstances of the incident: _____
_____

5. Was any consular official contacted by the alleged victim or the authorities? (Please explain)
_____
_____
_____

6. Was the alleged victim aware of his/her right to contact a consular official of his/her country of origin? (Please explain)
_____
_____

7. Agents believed to be responsible for the alleged violation:
State Agents (specify) _____
Non-state Agents (specify)_____

If it is unclear whether they were state or non-state agents please explain why? If the perpetrators are believed to be State agents, please specify (military, police, agents of security services, unit to which they belong, rank and functions, etc.) and indicate why they are believed to be responsible; be as precise as possible: _____
_____
_____

If an identification as State agents is not possible, do you believe that Government authorities, or persons linked to them, are responsible for the incident, why? _____
_____
_____

4. STEPS TAKEN BY THE VICTIM, HIS/HER FAMILY OR ANY ONE ELSE ON HIS/HER BEHALF

(a) Indicate if complaints have been filed, when, by whom, and before which organ.

(b) Other steps taken:

(c) Steps taken by the authorities: Indicate whether or not, to your knowledge, there have been investigations by the State authorities; if so, what kind of investigations? Progress and status of these investigations; which other measures have been taken In case of complaints by the victim or its family, how have the organs dealt with them? What is the outcome of those proceedings? _____
_____
_____

5. IDENTITY OF THE PERSON OR INSTITUTION SUBMITTING THIS FORM
Institution ___ Individual ___ Name _____
Contact number or address (please indicate country and area code):
Fax: _____ Tel: _____ E-mail: _____
Date you are submitting this form: _____

The questionnaire should be sent to either of the following: Special Rapporteur on the Human Rights of Migrants Office of the High Commissioner for Human Rights, United Nations, 1211 Geneva 10 Switzerland, Fax: (+41 22) 917 90 06 E-mail: urgent-action@ohchr.org (please include in the subject box: Special Rapporteur HR Migrants)

[End Text]

ॐॐॐॐॐॐॐ

3. REPORT OF SPECIAL RAPPORTEUR ON ENVIRONMENTALLY SOUND MANAGEMENT AND DISPOSAL OF HAZARDOUS SUBSTANCES AND WASTES: MISSION TO THE MARSHALL ISLANDS AND THE UNITED STATES OF AMERICA*

This document shows the work of HRC special procedures focusing on human rights issues. Specifically, it is about the human rights of people living in the U.S. Marshall Islands and the effects of lingering nuclear radiation. This document is a report submitted by a Special Rapporteur to the Human Rights Council under his mandate on environmentally sound management and disposal of hazardous substances and wastes. It is a report about his visit to the U.S. Marshall Islands and U.S. mainland in 2012 aimed at assessing the "impact on human rights of the nuclear testing programme conducted in the Marshall Islands by the United States from 1946 to 1958." This report is focused on the harmful effects on human beings living in the Marshall Islands caused by nuclear testing conducted by the U.S. in 1946-58, and which is still causing serious harm to humans. The author of this report, a Human Rights Council Special Rapporteur, is a Romanian and an internationally recognized expert in sustainable development, with a PhD in soil science.

[Text]

Human Rights Council

Twenty-first session Agenda item 3

Promotion and protection of all human rights, civil, political, economic, social and cultural rights, including the right to development

Report of the Special Rapporteur on the implications for human rights of the environmentally sound management and disposal of hazardous substances and wastes, Calin Georgescu

Mission to the Marshall Islands (27-30 March 2012) and the United States of America (24-27 April 2012)

Summary

In the present report, submitted pursuant to Human Rights Council resolution 18/11, the Special Rapporteur on the implications for human rights of the environmentally sound management and disposal of hazardous substances and wastes gives his findings and makes recommendations on the basis of his visits to the Marshall Islands and the United States of America, during which he aimed to assess the impact on human rights of the nuclear testing programme conducted in the Marshall Islands by the United States from 1946 to 1958, focusing also on the efforts made by both Governments to mitigate its adverse effects.

The Special Rapporteur explores the adverse impact on human rights of the testing programme, in particular those resulting from hazardous substances and wastes. He discusses efforts to mitigate or eliminate these adverse effects, and concludes the report with his recommendations thereon.

* The summary of the present report is circulated in all official languages. The report itself, which is annexed to the summary, is circulated in the language of submission only.

Annex

Report of the Special Rapporteur on the implications for human rights of the environmentally sound management and disposal of hazardous substances and wastes on his mission to the Marshall Islands (27-30 March 2012) and the United States of America (24-27 April 2012)

I. Introduction

1. The Special Rapporteur on the implications for human rights of environmentally sound management and disposal of hazardous substances and wastes conducted a visit to the Marshall Islands from 27 to 30 March 2012, and to the United States of America from 24 to 27 April 2012. Both visits were carried out at the invitation of the respective Governments. The Special Rapporteur wishes to thank both Governments for their cooperation during the visits.

2. The Special Rapporteur conducted the two visits as part of his efforts to examine, in a spirit of cooperation and dialogue:

(a) the effects of the nuclear testing programme of the United States in the Marshall Islands between 1946 and 1958, when it was under United Nations trusteeship, on the enjoyment of human rights;

(b) the efforts made by both Governments to eliminate or mitigate the negative effects of the testing on the Marshallese population, and the sound management of hazardous substances and wastes associated with nuclear testing; and

(c) the lessons learned and additional measures necessary to ensure the full realization of the victims' right to an effective remedy. The findings of both visits are therefore presented in one comprehensive report.

3. During his four-day visit to the Marshall Islands, the Special Rapporteur met with the President, Christopher J. Loeak; members of the *Nitijela* (parliament); the Minister-in Assistance to the President; the Chief Secretary; the Assistant Attorney General; the Adviser on Nuclear Issues; representatives of the Environmental Protection Authority, the Ministry of Health, the Ministry of Resources and Development, and the Council of *Iroij* (elders); and the mayors and people

of Bikini, Enewetak, Rongelap and Utrok Atolls. The Special Rapporteur also had the opportunity to visit Ejit Island, to where the inhabitants of Bikini relocated, as well as certain places in Majuro where the former inhabitants of Enewetak and Utrok now reside. The Special Rapporteur also met with the Ambassador of the United States to the Marshall Islands, representatives of the United States Department of Energy, and members of academia and civil society.

4. The Special Rapporteur thanks the Ministry of Foreign Affairs for coordinating his visit to the Marshall Islands. He expresses his appreciation to the United Nations Joint Presence in Majuro and the Pacific Regional Office of the Office of the United Nations High Commissioner for Human Rights for their support during the visit. In addition, the Special Rapporteur expresses his sincere gratitude to civil society representatives who took the time to meet with him during his visit to the Marshall Islands. The Special Rapporteur was particularly honoured to receive the personal testimony of several of the survivors of the testing period, as well as accounts of descendants of those since deceased.

5. During his four-day visit to the United States of America, the Special Rapporteur met with representatives of the Department of State, the Department of Energy, the Department of Defense, the Senate Committee on Energy and Natural Resources and the National Cancer Institute, as well as with academics and members of civil society.

6. The Special Rapporteur thanks the Department of State for coordinating his visit and for its cooperation and flexibility in arranging the schedule. He also thanks the civil society representatives who took the time to meet with him during his visit.

7. The Special Rapporteur sent a questionnaire to the Government of the Marshall Islands and to that of the United States of America on 21 March 2012 to complement the information gathered during the course of his visits. He received their responses on 26 March and 24 April 2012, respectively.

8. While the Special Rapporteur acknowledges that many issues concerning nuclear testing in the Marshall Islands must be resolved, he emphasizes that the purpose of the present report is neither to apportion blame to either State nor to attempt to make a legal pronouncement on the nuclear testing programmes. Much has already been written in this vein and the Special Rapporteur wishes rather to stimulate constructive and forward-looking dialogue between the parties in the spirit of understanding, respect and reconciliation, for the benefit of the Marshallese people.

9. The Special Rapporteur is cognizant of the effects of the nuclear testing programme on the health of United States war veterans who were not necessarily aware of the consequences of their own exposure to hazardous substances and wastes. He also realizes that people in territories where other countries conducted similar nuclear testing programmes, for example in Algeria, French Polynesia and Kazakhstan, were affected.1 Such concerns, however, lay outside the scope of the present report, also owing to practical limitations. The report presents nonetheless an opportunity to provide good practices in the area of addressing the human rights impact of nuclear testing programmes generally and, in particular, to other States involved in such programmes and the populations whose rights may be affected.

II. Nuclear testing programme in the Marshall Islands

10. The Marshall Islands comprised 29 low-lying coral atolls and five islands, totaling 70 square miles of land scattered over 750,000 square miles of ocean. After centuries of successive colonial rule by Spain, Germany and Japan, the Marshall Islands was designated a Trust Territory pursuant to Security Council resolution 21 (1947), and the United States of America was designated as the Administering Authority. The Security Council designated the Trust Territory of the Pacific Islands, which comprised the present-day Marshall Islands, the Federated States of Micronesia, the Northern Mariana Islands and Palau as a strategic area, and placed it under the United Nations international trusteeship system. Under the terms of resolution 21 (1947), the United States was charged with fostering the development of political institutions, promoting economic, social and educational advancement, and moving the Trust Territory towards self-governance. Importantly, as the Security Council designated the Marshall Islands a "strategic area," it granted to the United States, as the Administering Authority, permission to militarize the territory. Notably, the Administering Authority was entrusted "to protect the land, resources, and health of Micronesia's inhabitants."

11. In article 16 of resolution 21 (1947), the Security Council, having approved the terms of trusteeship on 2 April 1947, provided that the Trusteeship Agreement would enter into force when approved by the Government of the United States of America after the completion of a due constitutional process. On 18 July 1947, the Congress of the United

States enacted a joint resolution accepting the Trusteeship Agreement, which was approved by the President the same day.

12. On 1 July 1946, before the Trusteeship Agreement came into force, the United States of America moved the 167 inhabitants of Bikini Atoll to the smaller Rongerik Atoll in order to commence nuclear tests, known as "Operation Crossroads." After enduring periods of near starvation and malnutrition due to limited food supplies on Rongerik Atoll, in 1948 they were relocated to Kwajalein Atoll, where they were housed in tents along the military airstrip. Soon after, they were moved again to Kili, a small island with no lagoon, no protective reef and no fishing grounds. Eventually, 139 Bikinians returned to Bikini Atoll in 1972, but were again moved to Kili Island and Ejit Island of Majuro Atoll owing to the radiation exceeding permissible levels on Bikini Atoll. The people of Bikini Atoll also decided not to return their homes. Indeed, in 1998, the International Atomic Energy Agency (IAEA) recommended that the Atoll not be permanently resettled under the present radiological conditions or until certain specified remediation action had been taken.2 The inhabitants of Rongelap Atoll also were evacuated in 1946, returned in 1957 and, ultimately, moved voluntarily from Rongelap in 1985.

13. Enewetak Atoll later became another testing site, and 145 people were moved to Ujelang Atoll. The detonation of the world's first hydrogen bomb vaporized one of the islands of Enewetak. The testing continued; on 1 March 1954, the Castle Bravo test resulted in a blast 1,000 times the explosive power of the bombing of Hiroshima on Bikini Atoll, making it the most powerful known detonation made by the United States. The nuclear weapon's high explosive yield created a fallout cloud that covered Rongelap Atoll (100 miles from the blast site) and Utrok Atoll (320 miles from the blast site).

14. Two months later, on 6 May 1954, the Marshallese people filed a petition with the United Nations Trusteeship Council regarding the nuclear testing, which received a hearing on 20 August 1954 (see chapter IV). In the petition, the Marshallese people were "not only fearful of the danger to their persons from these deadly weapons," but "also concerned for the increasing number of people removed from their land," and requested that "all experiments with lethal weapons in this area be immediately ceased." The United States of America continued its nuclear testing programme until 1958, conducting a total of 67 detonations throughout the territory of the Marshall Islands, mostly in Bikini (23) and Enewetak (43) Atolls, and accounting for 32 per cent of all atmospheric tests conducted by the United States. The Marshallese people were told that the tests were necessary for the eventual well-being of all people in the world.

15. The trusteeship of the United States of America was terminated pursuant to Security Council resolution 683 (1990), after the Council determined that the conclusion of a Compact of Free Association between the United States and the Marshall Islands fully satisfied the terms of the trusteeship agreement. Under the terms of the Compact, the Marshall Islands was established as a sovereign State in free association with the United States. The Compact granted the United States certain competencies, including full authority and responsibility for the security and defence of the Marshall Islands, including military operating rights and the use of certain areas. It also afforded the Marshall Islands certain privileges, for example on immigration and taxation, and provided for economic assistance, including eligibility for certain federal programmes.

16. According to information received from the United States of America, the Compact represents a continuation of the rights and obligations of the United States as elaborated in the Trusteeship Agreement, and provides a framework to achieve three main goals: (1) to secure self-government for the Marshall Islands; (2) to assist the Marshall Islands in its efforts towards attaining economic development and self-sufficiency; and (3) to ensure certain national security rights for all parties. The Compact was approved by the people of the Marshall Islands in a plebiscite held in 1983, and legislation on the Compact was passed by the United States Congress and signed into law by the President in 1986.

17. Under section 177 (a) of the Compact, the Government of the United States of America "accepts the responsibility for compensation owing to citizens of the Marshall Islands, for loss or damage to property and person of the citizens of the Marshall Islands, resulting from the nuclear testing program which the Government of the United States conducted in the Northern Marshall Islands between June 30, 1946, and August 18, 1958." Section 177 (b) requires, inter alia, the creation of a separate agreement for the just and adequate settlement of all claims and outlining provisions for medical surveillance, treatment programmes, radiological monitoring, and additional programmes and activities. Section 177 (c) of the Compact further provided for direct economic assistance to the Marshall Islands, including the establishment

of a $150 million fund for claims arising from the nuclear testing as well the provision of projects, programmes and technical assistance (see also chapter IV below).

III. Impact on the enjoyment of human rights

19. The nuclear testing resulted in both immediate and continuing effects on the human rights of the Marshallese. According to information received by the Special Rapporteur, radiation from the testing resulted in fatalities and in acute and long-term health complications. The effects of radiation have been exacerbated by near-irreversible environmental contamination, leading to the loss of livelihoods and lands. Moreover, many people continue to experience indefinite displacement.

A. Right to health

20. Radiation doses are not frequently encountered in everyday life, although people may be exposed to natural "background" radiation from the air, land, sea, foodstuffs and the human body itself, as well as from various beneficial practices, such as radiological medicine (for example, X-ray imaging or cancer radiotherapy). For the purposes of establishing international radiation protection standards, it is assumed that any increase in a dose of radiation, however minute, will result in a proportionate increase in the risk of cancer.

21. Human beings are exposed to radiation from the release of radioactive elements or radionuclides, generally through (a) rain washing hazardous radioactive materials out of the air in the form of acid rain; (b) direct external exposure to a nuclear explosion cloud; (c) direct external exposure to hazardous radioactive materials in the ground; (d) internal exposure from eating, drinking, or inhaling hazardous radioactive materials in food, water or air; or (e) internal and/or external exposure from contact with contaminated water. According to testimony from the survivors, in the immediate aftermath of the nuclear testing, white ash fell from the sky, and shortly thereafter people began to experience skin burns, hair loss, finger discolouration, nausea and other symptoms of acute radiation poisoning. They also provided testimony of observing and experiencing ailments that they had never experienced before, including cancers and growth retardation in children.

22. In response to the questionnaire (see paragraph 7 above), the United States Department of Energy stated that the development of thyroid disease, including thyroid cancer in the Marshall Islands, had been linked to the intake of radioactive iodine primarily as a consequence of ingesting hazardous fallout debris particles deposited on food surfaces, eating utensils, the hands and the face, and of drinking contaminated water.

23. In 2004, the National Cancer Institute of the United States conducted an expert assessment of the expected number of cancers among the Marshallese, and concluded in its report thereon that as much as 9 per cent of all cases of cancers expected to develop among those residents alive between 1948 and 1970 might be attributable to exposure to the radiation caused by nuclear tests. Specifically, according to the report, an estimated 530 "excess" cancers (namely those beyond the expected projections in a population) would be expected in the people living in the Marshall Islands during the testing period and, owing to the latency period of cancer, half of the malignancies had yet to be detected. A review report subsequently issued in 2010 significantly reduced the excess number of cancer cases to 170, lowering the percentage from 9 to 1.6 per cent. Owing to the current limitations of medical programmes, the assistance actually available to persons developing an excess cancer is unclear (see chapter IV below).

24. In the light of the lack of scientific consensus and the limited available data, the Special Rapporteur was unable to address fully the effects on the health of the first, second and subsequent descendants of the survivors of the nuclear tests. He observes that scientific contention focuses on whether low-level radiation can be linked to cancer; whether the effects of radiation are specific to the individual (given that certain people may have a predisposition to cancer without any radiation exposure from nuclear testing), or conversely whether certain people are particularly susceptible to radiation; and whether such radiation causes genetic and intergenerational harm (see Section IV below).

25. Both Governments provided the Special Rapporteur with an analysis by their respective experts, who reached differing conclusions on the safety of the islands for human habitation. In addition to the general consensus that Bikini and Enewetak Atolls are contaminated, assessments were conducted in other areas of the Marshall Islands; for example, between 1990 and 1994, the Marshall Islands Nationwide Radiological Study took in situ gamma spectrometry measurements and collected and analysed solid, plant and other food item samples from every inhabited island and many of the

larger uninhabited islands. Unfortunately, despite the comprehensive nature of the Study, issues were raised about its credibility and accuracy, leading the national parliament to adopt a resolution in which it did not accept the Study's findings.

26. Survivors of the tests provided compelling testimony about their psychological trauma from witnessing the explosions and their effect. Psychological stress and anxiety are recognized as a legitimate and serious health concern in populations where nuclear testing has been conducted. The Special Rapporteur understands that, although these health concerns are of a different nature to cancer, the fear of radiation itself is no less real. Consequently, the fear of some present-day inhabitants of the Marshall Islands of the radiation that they believe still contaminates their lands and affects their health should not be underestimated.

27. The Special Rapporteur also received information suggesting that the full effects of radiation on the right to health of Marshallese women may have been, and continues to be, underestimated. For example, the practice of women bathing in contaminated water may have been overlooked as a possible means of exposure, and cultural differences may also have resulted in an inadequate accounting of adverse reproductive outcomes. Studies show that pregnant women are particularly susceptible to thyroid cancer, with resultant negative effects on the health of the women and their infants.

28. The right to health is an inclusive right that extends to the underlying determinants of health, such as access to an adequate supply of safe food and to safe and potable water. The Marshallese diet consists primarily of seafood, supplemented by pandanus fruit, coconut and other fruits. The fallout from the nuclear testing contaminated local food supplies, leading to illnesses and, ultimately, the stigmatization of these foods. The United States of America informed people not to eat local foods and provided imported canned foods. Many people, however, continued to eat local foods for a variety of reasons (such as cultural customs and a lack of understanding of the adverse health effects), and succumbed to illnesses. Furthermore, given that the Marshallese derive much of their fresh water supply from coconuts, their access to safe drinking water was highly compromised during the testing period.

29. Some information indicates that, because of cultural differences and language barriers, Marshallese dietary customs were either unknown or ignored during the testing period. For example, the difference in dietary and other eating habits of men, women and children may have led to higher exposure of some members of the population, especially women. Women eat different parts of the fish to those eaten by men, especially bones and organ meat, in which certain radioactive isotopes tend to accumulate. The differences in the retention of radionuclides by coconut and land crabs were not recognized by the medical profession in the United States. Apparently, women were more exposed to radiation levels in coconut and other foods owing to their role in processing foods and weaving fiber to make sitting and sleeping mats, and handling materials used in housing construction, water collection, hygiene and food preparation, as well as in handicrafts.

30. The Special Rapporteur heard compelling testimony by women on their experience of returning from Rongelap Atoll, including on the alarmingly high rates of stillbirths, miscarriages, congenital birth defects and reproductive problems (such as changes in menstrual cycles and the subsequent inability to conceive, even in those who previously had no such difficulties). Some gave birth to babies that ultimately died from foetal disorders, and they still endured the shame and trauma they experienced as a result. The extent to which radionuclides were actually present in the breast milk of women exposed to the testing is unclear, making it also difficult to assess the risks to individuals who were breastfed by those women. The women also expressed their fears of reproduction and motherhood as a result of their exposure to radiation.

31. Several years after exposure, a high incidence of thyroid cancer was reported, as well as an unusually high prevalence of stunted growth among Marshallese children. The incidence of such cases was also supported by the number of claims before the Nuclear Claims Tribunal. Similar effects have been recorded in children in other irradiated environments, with a greater incidence of thyroid cancer due to the intake of iodine-131, particularly through drinking milk contaminated with iodine, an element that accumulates in the thyroid, thereby inhibiting growth and the child's cognitive abilities, which could lead to mental disability.

B. Displacement
32. The Special Rapporteur heard the accounts of women survivors of the shame that they had experienced during the relocation process, when they were subjected to examinations with Geiger counters while naked and hosed down with

liquid in the presence of their male relatives, as well as enduring on-site analysis of their pubic hair by American male personnel. In this context, many women, in particular those from Rongelap Atoll, were stigmatized, which affected their prospects for marriage and motherhood. In order to prevent such incidents from recurring, In the interests of non-recurrence the Special Rapporteur urges all States to adhere to the Guiding Principles on Internal Displacement, which identify the rights and guarantees relevant to the protection of persons from forced displacement and their protection and assistance during displacement, as well as during return or resettlement and reintegration. Guiding Principle 8, which declares that displacement should not be carried out in a manner that violates the rights to life, dignity, liberty and security of those affected, is particularly relevant.

33. Displacement due to the nuclear testing, especially of inhabitants from Bikini, Enewetak, Rongelap and Utrok Atolls, has created nomads who are disconnected from their lands and their cultural and indigenous way of life; for example, the Marshallese engaged in migratory practices to gather different types of cultural goods (ranging from fish, fruits and medicines to materials for housing) from the islands and atolls. Today, they are unable to perform these migratory practices and harvest their cultural goods because, in some cases, the islands and atolls have been contaminated by nuclear fallout. In addition, it should be considered that, in their matriarchal society, land is passed from mother to child; displacement from their lands has denied Marshallese women the right to exercise their cultural and other rights and their role as custodians of land in society.

34. The Marshallese have found it difficult to maintain their distinct cultural identity and the traditional bond to their lands. One of the challenges to assessing the loss of land use has been the differing concept of what constitutes land. The United States of America proposed to calculate land loss on the basis of commercial rent values. The Marshallese, as indigenous peoples, have a culturally distinctive relationship to land. In this context, the Special Rapporteur recalls the United Nations Declaration on the Rights of Indigenous Peoples, which the United States has endorsed. Specifically, article 26 of the Declaration underlines the right of indigenous peoples to the lands, territories and resources that they have traditionally owned, occupied or otherwise used or acquired. In this regard, States have an obligation to give legal recognition and protection to these lands, territories and resources, with due respect for the customs, traditions and land tenure systems of the indigenous peoples concerned. The Special Rapporteur encourages both States to use the Declaration as a basis for further discussions on unresolved land issues.

35. New thinking on the issue of redress includes concepts that encourage the consultation of groups, including indigenous groups, on what they deem fit or what they consider to be adequate redress, because the notion of monetary compensation is not appropriate in some contexts. In this connection, article 28 of the Declaration on the Rights of Indigenous Peoples affirms the right of indigenous peoples to redress, which may include restitution or, when this is not possible, just, fair and equitable compensation, for the lands, territories and resources that the indigenous peoples have traditionally owned or otherwise occupied or used, and that have been confiscated, taken, occupied, used or damaged without their free, prior and informed consent.

IV. Efforts to mitigate the impact of nuclear testing on the enjoyment of human rights

36. Various positive measures have been taken by the Government of the Marshall Islands and by that of the United States of America, to varying degrees of success, to address the issues of the right to an effective remedy; to health facilities, goods and services; and to environmental rehabilitation for the Marshallese people.

A. Right to an effective remedy
37. The Marshallese people filed a petition with the United Nations Trusteeship Council on 6 May 1954 (see paragraph 14 above). When the tests continued, the Marshallese filed another petition on 9 March 1956, in which they reiterated their previous concerns over the nuclear testing.

38. In response to the second petition, a representative of the United States of America answered that "nothing would please the United States more than to be able to comply with the wishes of the Marshallese people that the nuclear tests be discontinued in their islands, but this is not yet possible"; that "as long as there is a threat of...aggression, elementary prudence requires the United States to continue its tests"; and that "further tests are absolutely necessary for the eventual well-being of all the people of this world," reassuring that "all possible precautionary measures [would] be undertaken before such weapons are exploded." The Trusteeship Council voted to reaffirm its resolution 1082 (XIV) on the previous petition (T/PET/10/28) and to sanction the continuation of the tests, and recommended precautionary mea-

sures, settlement of all just claims of the former inhabitants of Bikini and Enewetak Atolls for loss of land, and that adequate provision be made for any losses arising as a result of the new series of tests.

39. After nearly 35 years without the possibility to return home, the people of Bikini Atoll filed a suit, *Juda v. United States of America*, under the Tucker Act, which vested jurisdiction to the United States Court of Federal Claims to hear the matter. The case was suspended temporarily in 1983 in the light of the negotiations on the Compact of Free Association (see paragraph 16 above) and, once it resumed, the court denied a motion to dismiss by the Government of the United States of America owing to lack of jurisdiction. Upon the entry into force of the Compact in 1986, however, an amended motion to dismiss the case was granted. Several suits filed thereafter were also dismissed on the grounds that the courts now lacked the jurisdiction owing to the existence of section 177 of the 1985 Compact, which governed the settlement of claims. As such, Marshallese citizens no longer had access to United States courts on any other potential and future claims.

40. Under section 177 of the Compact of Free Association, the United States of America agreed to provide $150 million for the Nuclear Claims Fund and established the Nuclear Claims Tribunal, with jurisdiction to render final judgements on all claims related to the nuclear testing programme past, present and future of the Government, citizens and nationals of the Marshall Islands. The Fund was projected to return at least $18 million per year, leaving the capital untouched; the Fund could thus continue to meet all claims in perpetuity. The United States and the Marshall Islands agreed to an amended version of the Compact, referred to as "Compact II" (or the Amended Compact) in 2003, which entered into force in 2004. Compact II primarily envisaged the gradual phasing out of economic assistance in order to reduce reliance on the United States and move towards self-sufficiency by increasing contributions to a trust fund. The major concern is that the fund set up under the original Compact was intended to cover not only personal injury claims but also property damages and remediation, which in some areas would require, at a minimum, the full amount initially injected into the fund. The Special Rapporteur received information that the United States continues to replenish the superfunds to provide compensation for irradiated property claims emanating from United States-dependent territories in the Pacific that suffered less damage than the Marshall Islands. He regrets that the Nuclear Claims Fund does not receive the same type of replenishment. Currently, the Nuclear Claims Fund contains less than $50,000, and award claims have been suspended.

41. The agreement for the implementation of section 177 of the Compact was enacted to, inter alia, "create and maintain, in perpetuity, means to address past, present, and future consequences of the Nuclear Testing Programme, including the resolution of resultant claims." The provision on changed circumstances under article IX of the agreement provides that additional funding may be requested from the United States Congress for loss or damage arising from the nuclear testing programme if such loss or damage is "discovered after the effective date" of the agreement and the "injury could not reasonably have been identified as of the effective date of the agreement" and failure to provide for the injuries would render the agreement "manifestly inadequate." Under article X, the Marshall Islands agreed to an espousal provision, which terminated any legal proceedings against the United States or its agents related to the nuclear weapons testing programme, and was intended to provide a full settlement of all claims, past, present and future. The tension between these provisions has hindered progress and created anxiety for the Marshallese on what the assistance envisaged by the Compact is supposed to entail, and for how long.

42. In 2000, the Marshall Islands brought the Changed Circumstances petition before the United States Congress, in which it stated, inter alia, that certain information, including subsequent declassified Department of Energy and Department of Defense documents, had not been available at the time of the negotiations on the Compact; the information apparently showed that the extent of radioactive fallout had been underestimated, and that advances in science and knowledge of radiogenic effects had provided more accurate assessments of the full impact of nuclear testing on people and the environment since the agreement came into force in 1986. The United States administration also presented its evaluation of the petition to Congress, asserting that the petition did not meet the set criteria for changed circumstances and hence there was no legal basis for considering additional funds. To date, Congress has not acted on the petition.

43. According to information received by the Special Rapporteur, some parties posit that the agreement on the implementation of section 177 offers full and final settlement of claims arising from the nuclear testing programme, while others contend that the overriding intent of Congress was to contemplate such action only if compensation has been just

and adequate; otherwise, there would have been no need for the changed circumstances provision. Even though resolving the legislative tension of the provisions contained in the Compact falls outside the scope of the present report, the Special Rapporteur emphasizes the right to an effective remedy as established in international human rights law, and calls on both States to fulfil this right. The Special Rapporteur is also of the view that interpretations of statutes should advance the course of justice.

44. Article 2.3 of the International Covenant on Civil and Political Rights requires that individuals have accessible and effective remedies to vindicate their rights. The Special Rapporteur recalls general comment No. 31 of the Human Rights Committee, in which the Committee pointed out that such remedies should be appropriately adapted so as to take into account the special vulnerability of certain categories of persons. The Committee also stressed the importance of establishing appropriate judicial and administrative mechanisms for addressing claims of rights violations. Article 2.3 moreover requires reparations to be provided to individuals whose rights have been violated.

45. The right to an effective remedy also requires that any person claiming a remedy have his or her right thereto determined by competent authorities (judicial, administrative, legislative or otherwise provided for by the legal system), and that the competent authority enforce such remedies when granted. The Special Rapporteur considers that, in order to give effect to the right to an effective remedy, competent authorities should not only be empowered to make binding decisions but should also have sufficient resources to effect the awards they make. Noting that the Nuclear Claims Tribunal was grossly underfunded, the President's Cancer Panel has called for increased funding, stating that "the U.S. Government should honor and make payments according to the judgment of the Marshall Islands Tribunal."

46. The Special Rapporteur welcomes the initiative taken by the Human Rights Council to address the issue of reparations by establishing, in its resolution 18/7, the mandate of Special Rapporteur on the promotion of truth, justice, reparations and guarantees of nonrecurrence, and concurs with its emphasis on the importance of a comprehensive approach incorporating the full range of judicial and non-judicial measures, including, among others, individual prosecutions, reparations, truth-seeking, institutional reform, or an appropriately conceived combination thereof, in order to, inter alia, ensure accountability, serve justice, provide remedies to victims, promote healing and reconciliation.

47. An opportunity exists to consider the issue within the international community. In his report on the effects of atomic radiation in the Marshall Islands, the Secretary-General indicates that the Organization stood ready to respond to any future instruction from Member States, adding that the General Assembly might wish to consider whether additional international efforts were appropriate for consolidating all the relevant available information on the effects of atomic radiation in the Marshall Islands into a final report of scientific findings on this regrettable episode in human history. If the Assembly wished to pursue that course, the United Nations Scientific Committee on the Effects of Atomic Radiation would be the appropriate international body to entrust with that responsibility.

B. Health services

48. Following the nuclear tests and subsequent exposure of individuals to fallout and radiation, in 1954, the Government of the United States of America implemented Project 4.1 to treat the people of the Marshall Islands. During the Project, many of the effects of radiation on human beings were documented, which contributed to global knowledge of this phenomenon. Serious concerns frequently raised by the Marshallese during the visit of the Special Rapporteur included that the Castle Bravo test (see paragraph 13 above) was a deliberate attempt to assess the effects of nuclear weapons on humans. With regard to human testing, the Special Rapporteur received information from survivors of the nuclear tests alleging that they were conducted without their prior and informed consent, in violation of article 7 of the International Covenant on Civil and Political Rights, and that the treatment received form the United States authorities had been degrading and culturally insensitive.

49. The Advisory Committee on Human Radiation Experiments was appointed in 1994 by President Clinton to investigate any unethical human experiments undertaken by personnel and/or agents of the United States of America and to make recommendations to ensure non-recurrence, if necessary. The Advisory Committee concluded that, with regard to the Marshall Islands, there was insufficient evidence to demonstrate intentional human testing on the Marshallese, except for two examples with minimal low-risk exposure. For the most part, however, consent for medical tests to monitor human health appears to have been neither sought nor obtained.

50. The Advisory Committee also highlighted the fact that there was evidence that demonstrated a lack of consideration for cultural appropriateness, and cautioned on the inherent conflicts posed by combining research with patient care, which could perhaps have been reduced by a clearer separation of the two activities and clearer disclosure to the subjects. The Advisory Committee recommended that, in such instances, the United States Government should deliver a personal, individualized apology and provide financial compensation to the subjects (or their next of kin) of human radiation experiments in which efforts were made by the U.S. Government to keep information secret from these individuals or their families, or from the public, for the purpose of avoiding embarrassment or potential legal liability, or both, and where this secrecy has had the effect of denying individuals the opportunity to pursue potential grievances.

It also noted that "one of the greatest harm from past experiments and intentional releases may be the legacy of distrust they created." Denial by the Government of the United States of access by Marshallese patients to medical files, and denial of access of Marshallese authorities to previously classified, then declassified, but unreadable scientific documentation, were cited as major concerns and a hindrance to open dialogue between the two parties. The Special Rapporteur raised the issue of access to information to United States authorities during his visit.

51. The Marshall Islands has a national care agency for its population (approximately 55,000 people) run by the Ministry of Health. Medical care is delivered mainly by an expatriate work force at primary and secondary care facilities on Ebeye Island (45 beds), Kwajalein Atoll (34 beds) and Majuro Atoll (90 beds), while smaller clinics on the remote outer islands provide limited primary care and pharmaceutical capabilities. The work force does not include any American doctors or nurses.

52. According to the World Health Statistics for 2011, the health infrastructure in the Marshall Islands comprises 27 beds per every 10,000 persons,16 a ratio comparable with that of global trends. In accordance with the best practices of integrated and coordinated approaches to reducing cancer morbidity and mortality through prevention, early detection, treatment, rehabilitation and palliation, the Marshall Islands developed a national comprehensive cancer control programme that focuses on primary and secondary prevention and medical care, and includes a cancer registry. Implementation of the programme has, however, been hampered by capacity constraints and insufficient resources, including lack of skilled personnel, transportation and pharmaceuticals. Diabetes is the single largest cause of death among Marshallese citizens, followed by cancer. A diet consisting primarily of canned and highly processed foods has been identified as a contributing factor to the high incidence of diabetes.

53. Efforts made by the Government of the United States of America deserve commendation, as some $600 million has been spent in various technical programmes. The amount also includes the contribution to the compensation proceeds under the Nuclear Claims Fund under the agreement on the implementation of section 177. Through the Department of Energy, the Government runs a medical programme that currently involves annual comprehensive medical screening and treating 138 patients (people who were living in Rongelap and Utrok Atolls at the time of the Castle Bravo test). Thirty one of the patients reside in the United States, the largest number in Hawaii. They may see a community doctor or be referred to regional or community hospitals for advanced diagnosis and care. Patients in the programme have a median age of 65; the youngest patient is 55 years of age; 60 per cent are women. The patients in the Marshall Islands live on 10 atolls; annual medical care and follow-up treatment are provided in close proximity to them. Patients with medical conditions that are potentially radiation-related findings and that cannot be diagnosed or handled in the Marshall Islands are referred to Hawaii. All related expenses for board and medical services are borne by the programme. The Department of Energy also operates the Whole-Body Counting Program, which carries out routine dose estimates on people who wish to assess their level of exposure to radionuclides.

54. The United States Department of the Interior also funds the 177 Health Care Program, which was established to meet the comprehensive health-care needs of people from Bikini, Enewetak, Rongelap and Utrok Atolls. People enrolled in the health programme of the Department of Energy are also entitled to coverage under the Program for conditions not covered by the former; the latter does not, however, treat cancer patients. According to information received by the Special Rapporteur, patients of the two programmes are generally satisfied with the quality of the services provided. There are concerns, however, regarding the scope of the programmes, which are limited to people who were residing in the islands at the time of the testing, thereby excluding their descendants.

55. The Marshallese are convinced that there is sufficient evidence — based on their own observations of changes to their reproductive functions — of intergenerational harm caused by radiation fallout. Their descendants are nonethe-

less still denied the benefits envisaged by Compact for the treatment of radiation effects. According to a recent report on the biological effects of ionizing radiation by the National Academy of Sciences, "although adverse health effects in children of exposed parents (attributable to radiation-induced mutations) have not been found, there are extensive data on radiation-induced transmissible mutations in mice and other organisms. Thus, there is no reason to believe that humans would be immune to this sort of harm." While the Special Rapporteur acknowledges these variations, he is nevertheless concerned that the right to health may be compromised. Regardless of the scientific debate on the link between exposure to low levels of radiation and cancer, he believes that a precautionary approach that emphasizes the likelihood of risk over conclusive proof may prove more prudent and protective of rights.

56. The position of the Government of the United States of America is that only the northern atolls were significantly affected; consequently, people from the southern atolls are not covered by any of the special programmes. They have therefore not been able to receive treatment, although they point out that other people similar to them, as "downwinders" from radiation fallout in the United States, receive compensation (on a presumptive basis) through the Radiation Exposure Compensation Act, even though they live even further downwind than those in the Marshall Islands. Cancer patients from the southern atolls are instead treated in a hospital run by the Government of the Marshall Islands that does not, however, offer dedicated oncology service.

57. The Special Rapporteur is concerned that scientific uncertainty may have the effect of shifting the burden of providing those affected by the nuclear fallout with health services from the United States of America to the Marshall Islands. In this regard, he is encouraged by the commitment made by the United States authorities to greater and meaningful discussions with the Marshallese on how the health dimensions may be addressed.

C. Environmental rehabilitation and monitoring

58. According to the United States Department of Energy, efforts to rehabilitate contaminated land in an environmentally sound and sustainable manner include a combined remedial strategy involving limited soil removal around housing and village areas, and treatment of agricultural areas with potassium, which has been recommended to atoll communities as a practical and effective solution to reduce levels of external and internal exposure. Moreover, treatment with potassium has been shown to be effective in reducing the uptake of cesium-137 in food crops for an extended period of time, and there is a proposed dose criterion for the treatment of contaminated sites in the Marshall Islands. The Department of Energy is implementing these methods to remediate contaminated land under the environmental monitoring programme for Bikini, Enewetak, Rongelap and Utrok Atolls.

59. Progress has been made in efforts to resettle the people of Rongelap Atoll under a memorandum of understanding signed by the people of Rongelap, the Marshall Islands and the United States of America. According to information received, however, there is still resistance in Rongelap among some people to the idea of resettlement. The Rongelapese raised the concern that restricting people's movements in an island is artificial (only about one third of the main island has been remediated and people claim to have received instructions from the United States authorities not to venture into the other parts of the island), and that the island should be remediated fully so people are not exposed to potential harm. People have also been warned not to consume food from the non-remediated areas of the island. The Department of Energy has conducted sampling of commonly consumed food; a report thereon is due early in 2013. Furthermore, a garden project has been launched to promote dietary change. Similarly, the Marshall Islands has an agricultural programme geared towards local food production. In 2008, the programme was partnered with civil society organizations in the Youth Food Initiative, the aim of which was to encourage the creation of backyard gardens in Majuro.

60. As mentioned above, IAEA recommended that Bikini Atoll not be resettled under the current radiological conditions, and stressed that remedial action would be necessary. It furthermore noted that there was a need to assess the radiological conditions of Enewetak. The Special Rapporteur is particularly concerned about the radioactive dump site on Runit Island. He received information indicating that the structural integrity of the nuclear waste container is substandard, and that the hazardous radioactive materials contained could seep and leach into the marine and terrestrial environment. He therefore calls on both the Governments to ensure that the impact of these hazardous substances and wastes on people's health and the environment is mitigated.

61. In addition to a lack of land, the Government of the Marshall Islands has identified the three-tier land tenure system as one of the challenges to resettlement programmes. The return, resettlement and reintegration of displaced people

should be intensified by a multisectoral comprehensive plan of action based on national consultations. Nevertheless, where return is not possible, other durable solutions should be explored.

62. As stated above, the Special Rapporteur was not able to address fully many of the issues concerning the Marshallese experience. Despite some divergence on significant matters by the parties, the Special Rapporteur is encouraged by the willingness he observed in both parties to improve the quality of life of the Marshallese people. He believes that the nuclear testing and the experiments have left a legacy of distrust in the hearts and minds of the Marshallese. The deep fissure in the relationship between the two Governments presents significant challenges; nonetheless the opportunity for reconciliation and progress, for the benefit of all Marshallese, is there to be taken.

V. Recommendations

63. The Special Rapporteur recommends that the Government and relevant State actors of the Marshall Islands:

(a) Carry out an independent, comprehensive radiological survey of the entire territory and, in this regard, request relevant United Nations agencies to undertake a study similar to the one conducted by IAEA on testing sites in other countries;

(b) Develop a comprehensive national health strategy and plan of action, on the basis of epidemiological evidence, addressing the health concerns of the whole population and, in particular, non-communicable diseases (such as cancer and diabetes), and build on the lessons learned from the National Comprehensive Cancer Control Plan for the period 2007-2012; the strategy and plan should pay special attention to women and children, and seek to overcome the barriers that women encounter in their access to health facilities, goods and services, including family planning and sexual and reproductive health services; support should also be sought for the renovation of the main hospital and provision of qualified medical personnel and oncology services;

(c) Consider taking the lead in regional consultations to address the burden of cancer and emerging non-communicable diseases in the Pacific;

(d) Ensure that impact assessments use reliable baseline studies for both environmental contaminants and human health conditions; impact assessments should be ongoing to monitor the evolving impact, and be carried out by competent, independent third parties;

(e) Engage in a broad consultative process, including with victims, families of victims, victims' associations and other relevant civil society actors, on outstanding issues and measures required to address any long-term human health and environmental effects of the testing, with particular emphasis on solutions aimed at reconciling the traditional land tenure system with durable solutions to displacement;

(f) Develop an economic diversification strategy to reduce overreliance on the Compact of Free Association, including by developing the tourism sector, and make a viability assessment of commercial exploitation of the medicinal and health properties of the pandanus fruit; ensure the implementation of mechanisms that strengthen the capacity of indigenous and tribal peoples to further their own development priorities are favoured; and establish programmes to support small-scale economic initiatives for women, including the necessary capacity-building;

(g) Promote good governance and transparency at the national and atoll administration levels, including through the disclosure of the use of Compact funds and other technical assistance; concurrently, strengthen public and private sector accountability; and develop a human rights policy and management framework, including annual reporting on their social, environmental and economic impact, with appropriate monitoring and evaluation;

(h) Consider creating partnerships with international academic institutions with a view to making the Marshall Islands a centre of excellence in environmental studies by means of the unique research, internship and secondment opportunities it provides, in such areas as climate change and marine biology;

(i) Seek international assistance to improve public infrastructure, including for water, sanitation and waste management facilities; and strengthen engagement with international agencies in these fields, including with the

United Nations Environmental Programme, to address the waste and chemicals management issues, nuclear or otherwise.

64. The Special Rapporteur recommends that the Government and relevant State actors of the United States of America:

(a) Continue to provide the Marshall Islands with assistance (financial, technical and otherwise) in order assist it to develop its health infrastructure and capacity further and to reduce the need for off-island referrals, including through the establishment of fellowship and technical training programmes; a nationwide medical survey; cancer and other health registries; and the infrastructure necessary to conduct early diagnosis and treatment for radiogenic diseases;

(b) Continue to assist the Marshall Islands in its efforts to protect the environment and to safeguard the rights of its people, by providing environmental information obtained by means of its monitoring operations; supporting Marshallese efforts to develop and sustain their own atmospheric, marine and terrestrial monitoring capabilities; strengthening the capacity of the Marshall Islands to address remaining threats and to protect its population from new dangers identified as a result of technological progress; assisting in the development of national public health and disaster response plans; and supporting the development of the educational and technical capacity to implement such plans fully;

(c) Support the Marshall Islands in conducting a comprehensive nationwide terrestrial and marine survey that identifies and maps the presence and concentration of radiogenic and other toxic substances remaining from the United States military activity in the Marshall Islands marine and terrestrial ecosystem, and continue to provide assistance and the means to secure, contain and remediate hazardous sites;

(d) Strengthen transparency and accountability mechanisms to ensure that individual atoll-administered funds are used to benefit the constituents intended, as well as the annual reporting mechanism used by the Marshall Islands to report to the United States Congress on the implementation and use of funds;

(e) Grant full access of the Marshall Islands to United States information and records regarding the environmental and human health ramifications of past and current United States military use of the islands, as well as full access to United States medical and other related records on the Marshallese, in accordance with the right to information and the principle of transparency;

(f) Guarantee the right to effective remedy for the Marshallese people, including by providing full funding for the Nuclear Claims Tribunal to award adequate compensation for past and future claims, and exploring other forms of reparation, where appropriate, such as restitution, rehabilitation and measures of satisfaction (for example, public apologies, public memorials and guarantees of nonrepetition); and consider the establishment of a truth and reconciliation mechanism or similar alternative justice mechanisms;

(g) Consider adopting a presumptive approach to groups currently excluded from the special programmes of the United States of America created to assist survivors of nuclear testing, whereby individuals exposed to nuclear fallout would be presumed to be eligible;

(h) Consider issuing a presidential acknowledgment and apology to victims, in accordance with the conclusion of the Advisory Committee on Human Radiation Experiments that the one of the greatest forms of harm from past experiments and intentional releases may be the legacy of distrust they created, and that, in such instances, the Government of the United States should deliver a personal and individualized apology.

65. The Special Rapporteur recommends that both the Governments of the Marshall Islands and of the United States of America maximize the benefits of the joint task force established to discuss progress in the implementation of the Compact of Free Association, emphasizing open and frank engagement to enhance accountability of both parties under the Compact.

66. The Special Rapporteur recommends that the international community, including relevant United Nations departments, funds and agencies:

Recall that the Marshall Islands were placed under the trusteeship of the United States of America by the international community, which therefore has an ongoing obligation to encourage a final and just resolution for the Marshallese people;

Acknowledge that the harm suffered by the Marshallese people has resulted in an increased global understanding of the movement of radionuclides through marine and terrestrial environments, and learn from the Marshallese experience with nuclear contamination, particularly the documentation prepared by the United States on the effects of nuclear exposure and medical research, which has contributed to the understanding of the relationship between radioiodine and thyroid cancer;

Support bilateral and multilateral action to assist the Marshall Islands in its efforts to regain use of traditional lands, including the knowledge and means to identify, assess, remediate and restore a sustainable way of life;

Promote regional and international assistance and cooperation in order to support the efforts of the Marshall Islands to guarantee the rights of affected communities, including through investment in the development of new technologies to remove environmental hazards and their subsequent impact on health;

(a) Support nationally-owned and nationally-led development plans and strategies, including through the provision of funding and technical assistance; to scale up small- and medium-enterprises; to mitigate the effects of climate change; and to monitor, secure and remove nuclear wastes on a scale and standard comparable to the clean-up of domestic testing sites in the United States, as part of an international response to nuclear legacy issues;

(b) Stand in international solidarity with the Marshallese people as they face the challenge of overcoming the legacy of nuclear testing.

[End text]

ॐ◌ॐ◌ॐ◌ॐ◌ॐ◌ॐ◌ॐ◌ॐ

4. END OF VISIT STATEMENT BY MARIA GRAZIA GIAMMARINARO, U.N. SPECIAL RAPPORTEUR IN TRAFFICKING IN PERSONS, ESPECIALLY WOMEN AND CHILDREN

This document is a written statement by the U.N. Special Rapporteur in Trafficking in Persons, especially Women and Children at the end of her visit to the U.S. in December 2016. Her goal was to assess what the U.S. has done to fight trafficking in persons. She will eventually write a report to present her assessment findings to the Human Rights Council. This statement is just her preliminary opinions about what she saw and the experience she had in the process of her official visit to the U.S. The Human Rights Council will receive her report and can consider it in its agenda. Again, a U.S. representative sits on the Council. This is a sample document of a Special Procedure at work in fighting against trafficking in human beings, with a focus on women and children.

[Text]

WASHINGTON, D.C., 19 December 2016—I am grateful to the Government of the United States of America for the invitation to carry out an official country visit from 6 to 16 December 2016. I would also like to thank the authorities I have met at the Federal, State and city levels, as well as the diplomatic community and businesses for their openness to engage in frank discussions with me. During my visit, I also had the opportunity to meet with representatives from civil society, who play an eminent role in assisting victims in this country, as well as with survivors, whom I would like to warmly thank for courageously sharing their painful experiences and aspirations with me.

Both U.S. citizens and foreign nationals mainly from Central America and South East Asia are trafficked within and into the U.S. While efforts to combat trafficking in persons have focused primarily on sexual exploitation thus far, trafficking for labor exploitation, domestic servitude as well as trafficking for the purpose of removal of organs and forced begging have also been brought to my attention. Women and girls, migrant workers and unaccompanied children, runaway youth, Native Americans, LGBTI individuals and domestic workers, including in diplomatic households, are particularly exposed to trafficking and exploitation. African American women and girls are disproportionately affected by involuntary domestic servitude.

To address the situation, the United States has developed an impressive number of laws and initiatives which focus on the protection of victims. Amongst these, I particularly welcome the Victims of Trafficking and Violence Protection Act (TVPA) of 2000 which provides for a long term form of immigration relief for trafficked persons — known as the T-visa, the TVPRA of 2008 which authorizes foreigners to apply for T-visa when they are, inter alia, unable to participate in a law enforcement interview because of physical or psychological trauma; and the TVPRA of 2013 which addresses child labor trafficking. The fact that the TVPA has been reauthorized with additional provisions for the protection of victims four times since 2000 is an indication of the Government's commitment to address emerging forms of trafficking in persons and adopt a victim centered approach. I further welcome the Preventing Sex trafficking and Strengthening Families Act of 2014 and the Justice for Victims of Trafficking Act of 2014 which enable survivors to provide formal input in Federal anti-trafficking policies and establish the Advisory Council on human trafficking that provides strategic advice to the Government. I now look forward to the implementation of the 2016 National Strategy for Child Exploitation, Prevention and Interdiction which assesses the nature and scope of the dangers facing children, including child sex trafficking.

However, I would urge the Federal authorities to close any protection gaps by ratifying without any delay the Convention on the Elimination of All Forms of Discrimination against Women, the Convention on the Rights of the Child, the International Covenant on Economic, Social and Cultural Rights, the International Convention on the Protection of the Rights of All Migrant Workers and Members of Their Families, and pertinent ILO conventions.

Since the ratification of the Palermo Protocol to prevent and punish trafficking in persons, the United States has championed the struggle against trafficking in persons worldwide. I particularly welcome the leadership of the United States in facilitating the first Security Council meeting dedicated to the issue of human trafficking in situations of conflict during its presidency of the United Nations Security Council in December 2015. At the international level, the unilateral compliance mechanism established by the Department of State's Office to Monitor and Combat Trafficking in Persons, which undertakes an annual assessment of the trafficking situation in States worldwide, is also a useful tool to promote and share good practices amongst States. In this context, I am encouraged by the Government's invitation extended to my mandate, the first of this kind since its inception, as it implies political will to strengthen a human rights based approach to the struggle against trafficking in persons.

Such an effort to adopt and revise legislation, train professionals, refine internal regulations demonstrate that anti-trafficking efforts are a long standing commitment in the U.S. Yet, the purpose of this country visit is also to shed light on persisting problems, issues to be dealt with, challenges faced, and to offer recommendations to address them in a spirit of cooperation.

Areas of concern:

Trafficking for Labour Exploitation

Unfortunately, official estimates of the total number of human trafficking victims in the United States are not available, which, in my view, prevents Federal authorities from having a comprehensive overview of the problem and allocating adequate resources in regions and sectors that require most attention. According to Polaris statistics, 75% of reported cases concerned sex trafficking, 13% labor trafficking, 3% sex and labor trafficking and 9% non-specified trafficking. The number of trafficked persons identified and supported is still low compared with the estimated dimension of trafficking, especially regarding trafficking for labor exploitation. During my visit, I was also repeatedly informed that labor exploitation of women and girls is generally accompanied by sexual abuse.

With these considerations in mind, I would like to offer the following preliminary recommendations:

There is a disproportionate focus on sex trafficking as opposed to trafficking for labor exploitation. While authorities justify this imbalance by highlighting the apparent ease to detect sex trafficking, there is a need for Federal and State authorities to engage in a more proactive and systematic effort to prioritize the detection of trafficking for forced labor and labour exploitation. Workers in the agriculture, hospitality and construction industries are particularly vulnerable to labor trafficking. They often work in precarious conditions on temporary or short-term contracts, on temporary visa if they are migrant workers, cumulating more than one job and encountering little opportunities to unionize to defend their rights, which expose them to labor exploitation. Mindful that many migrant victims of trafficking are undocumented, a coordinated approach based on the use of common indicators should be used by the different agencies to identify trafficking victims and to provide them with remedies including compensation.

The legal framework governing temporary visas for migrant workers, especially H-2A visa for temporary or seasonal agricultural work and H-2B visa for temporary or seasonal non-agricultural work visas, is of particular concern as it exposes applicants to the risk of exploitation, including human trafficking. Workers holding these temporary visas are tied to a specific employer who can exercise extensive control over them. Employers often confiscate passports, withhold wages, terminate contracts arbitrarily and threaten employees with job loss and deportation. Some live in deplorable housing conditions, commute long distance and enjoy low benefits. This is a serious problem in itself, but it is exacerbated by the fact that concerned workers may fear that if they report abuses, they will be deported or denied future visa applications. This situation creates vulnerabilities to labour exploitation, such as unsafe working conditions and isolation, especially in rural areas where there are fewer service providers. In order to prevent further harm, it will be essential to amend the regulation governing these temporary visas, as well as to those of Exchange visitor (J-1) and domestic workers (G-5) visas, and make visa "portable" to allow workers to change abusive employers.

Moreover, I am concerned that many recruitment agencies offer lower wages and benefits and charge future employees with recruitment fees. While some companies, notably in the electronic industry, have taken actions to address trafficking in their chains of supply, Federal authorities should better support business' efforts to establish and implement an unequivocal no fees policy. In many cases, workers can find themselves in an inextricable situation that makes reporting human rights violations, or voluntarily returning to their home countries impossible because of the debts they incur from recruitment agencies' fees, which often also includes migration and settlement expenses. A viable solution needs to be put in place to allow workers to report human trafficking without being afraid of losing their jobs or being deported. A confidential procedure protecting the workers' identity and privacy could be put in place to allow them to report abuses to law enforcement officers, while at the same time receiving services they are entitled to if they are recognized victims of human trafficking.

Diplomats and the staff of international organizations may bring domestic workers to the United States. As their work is performed in private households, where oversight is by nature limited, domestic workers are vulnerable to abuse and exploitation. I note with appreciation that migrant domestic workers employed by personnel working at foreign missions and international organizations are required to physically register (without their employer present) at the annual appointment at the Department of State which enables the review of their working conditions. I urge relevant authorities to take further steps to integrate the recommendations of the OSCE handbook on human trafficking for domestic servitude in diplomatic households, which provides useful guidance to address allegations or complaints regarding such exploitation.

A careful and extensive analysis of the root causes of human trafficking should allow Federal authorities to develop indicators and obtain greater results in identifying vulnerable people and preventing trafficking. Social and economic inequalities, humanitarian and economic situation in neighborhood countries, as much as the increasing stigmatization of migrants in the political discourse, make it essential for Federal authorities to engage in a more pro-active investigation approach on the basis of risk assessment. []. I also urge the Department of Interior to continue strengthening its prevention and outreach work by addressing root causes of trafficking of American Natives. The Department of Agriculture, which is one of the few Federal agencies that has a presence in every State, could also play a pertinent role in intensifying training of its staff and in closely monitoring companies that often employ seasonal and temporary workers and in conducting targeted labor inspections in the agriculture sector.

Trafficking for Sexual Exploitation

Adult and children are compelled to engage in commercial sex acts against their will by family members, individuals with whom they are romantically involved or gangs who have forced them into prostitution or lured them with a promise of a false job. Trafficked persons for sexual exploitation are U.S. citizens and foreign nationals alike. Sex trafficking of women and girls, runaway and homeless children, Native Americans, LGBTI individuals often occurs in fake massage parlours, via online ads or escort services, in residential brothels, on the street, or at hotels and motels.

Since 2007, the National Human Trafficking Hotline, operated by Polaris, has received reports of 14,588 sex trafficking cases inside the United States.

In the context of sexual exploitation, it is important to be aware that the way anti-trafficking action is currently implemented has an adverse impact on trafficked persons and potential victims of trafficking.

In this regard, I urge the government to stop the practice of arresting persons — especially women, girls and LGBTI — engaging in prostitution. The fear of prosecution, detention and expulsion is a major obstacle for trafficked persons who want to report their traffickers and exploiters. This is the main reason why I advocate for a human rights based approach to trafficking which includes the de-criminalization of those who engage in prostitution in States where it is illegal. Such an approach would be a powerful tool to ensure that victims are not arbitrarily arrested, or no longer afraid to report human rights violations. This terrible situation which can amount to slavery was repeatedly shared with me by trafficking survivors in the country throughout my visit. In this context, I encourage law enforcement officials to use their discretion to avoid arresting sex workers as they can be potential victims of sex trafficking.

I also wish to highlight that exemption from criminal liability is imperative for children. Federal law recognizes that minors under the age of 18 who engage in prostitution or other related offenses are victims of sex trafficking, without necessity to prove the illicit means used by traffickers. I urge States that have not yet done so, to pass safe harbour laws with the intended goal of ensuring that all minors involved in the sex industry are shielded from criminal prosecution. I also call for the systematic implementation of the non-punishment principle implying that trafficked persons — be they adults or children — must not be prosecuted for violations they are involved in as a direct consequence of their situation as trafficked persons.

With regards to post-conviction reliefs, some States have adopted vacatur laws which fall short of providing full remedies to trafficked persons, for instance by sealing criminal records rather than vacating convictions. Hence, there is a need for Federal authorities to adopt a law that would enable trafficking victims to vacate criminal convictions for acts they were compelled to commit.

Moreover, I look with interest at the recently established human trafficking initiative Court in New York, which makes it possible to dismiss a criminal case on grounds of prostitution and clear concerned individuals' criminal records. However, I regret that cases can only be brought to the Court as a consequence of an arrest for prostitution. I would recommend that victims and potential victims can directly access the Court on the basis of a complaint or a report.

In terms of immigration relief of trafficked persons, there is a need to speed up procedures for the granting of a T visa, U visa or a "Continued Presence." I urge Federal authorities to refrain from conditioning services and residence status to victims' cooperation with law enforcement authorities. I further urge the authorities to consider allowing persons waiting for such visas to access the labour market and support themselves during the lengthy waiting period. This will have a powerful impact on the process of regaining ownership of their lives, their sense of independence and freedom and their economic empowerment. Survival leadership is valid for any forms of trafficking, be it sexual or labour exploitation

Prevention

I am pleased to learn about the extensive awareness raising work undertaken by authorities at the Federal, State and local levels, as well as by CSOs and businesses to prevent human trafficking among population at risk, often developed in cooperation with trafficking survivors. These range from the Department of Homeland and Security's nationwide human trafficking awareness Blue Campaign for front-line responders at State, local, and tribal levels; the Department of Justice's guidance to immigration judges with respect, notably, to immigration court cases involving unaccompanied alien children, applied with professionalism and sensitivity by the judge I had the opportunity to meet in New York after observing a hearing at the New York Immigration Court; the Department of Health and Human Services' continued awareness raising campaigns and targeted training in the health care sector; the Department of Education's efforts to integrate trafficking information into school curricula; the Department of Agriculture and the Department of Health and Human Services' initiative to raise awareness for food and agricultural industry partners in rural communities; the Department of Defence's training for all its personnel, including troops prior to their deployment; the Department of Interior's task force to combat trafficking of Native American and Alaskan Native populations; and the Department of Transportation and the Department of Homeland and Security's human trafficking trainings for airline personnel and the car industry.

Furthermore, the "Know your rights" pamphlet delivered to temporary workers at U.S. embassies has been praised by numerous interlocutors, including trafficking survivors I met, which should encourage the authorities to continue to translate it into numerous languages and to share it widely with every individual entering the United States, regardless of the type of visa held.

Here, I would also like to mention what I consider pertinent additional measures to prevent human trafficking in the U.S., especially in relation to labour exploitation:

I welcome the U.S. Government's zero-tolerance policy on trafficking in persons for labour exploitation which notably consists of Executive Order 13627 which strengthens protections against trafficking in persons in Federal contracts and establishes specific requirements for Federal contractors and subcontractors to prevent trafficking in persons in government contracts. In this regard, I would suggest strengthening the responsibilities of labor attachés in U.S. embassies to help the Federal Government making sure the Federal Acquisitions Regulations and other pertinent laws are implemented in practice.

In addition, I welcome the California Transparency in Supply Chains Act, which requires companies to report on their actions to eradicate slavery and human trafficking in their supply chains, though it is urgent to strengthen its implementation. I am also hopeful that the National Action Plan on Responsible Business Conduct that aims "to promote and incentivize responsible business conduct, including with respect to transparency and anticorruption, in compliance with the U.N. Guiding Principles on Business and Human Rights and the OECD Guidelines on Multinational Enterprises," which is due to be released on 16 December 2016, will further strengthen the struggle against labor exploitation.

While welcoming the abovementioned initiatives, I note the considerable efforts that will now be required to implement and enforce them, including through raising awareness and building the capacity of contractors.

Finally, I would also like to pay tribute to civil society's commendable efforts to address labor trafficking, such as the Coalition of Immokalee Workers through its Fair Food Program which empowers farmworkers in Florida. It is now implemented in other States, and must be considered as an international benchmark.

Protection of Trafficked Persons

In order to protect the rights of victims and potential victims of trafficking, who are very often undocumented migrants, it is necessary to ensure consistency between anti-trafficking policy and immigration policy.

In general terms, walls, fences and laws criminalising irregular migration do not prevent human trafficking; on the contrary, they increase the vulnerabilities of people fleeing conflict, persecution, crisis situations and extreme poverty, who can fall easy prey to traffickers and exploiters. As President Obama made clear in his statement at the Summit on migrants and refugees in September 2016, "When desperate refugees pay cold-hearted traffickers for passage, it funds the same criminals who are smuggling arms, drugs and children and poses a challenge to [one country's] security." This is why I endorse calls for the establishment of safe and legal channels of migration as the main tool to prevent trafficking and exploitation.

Screening of trafficked persons and those at risk of trafficking in ports of entry should be undertaken by officials trained in identifying adequate channels for protection, including asylum, child protection and trafficking entitlements. These officials should be trained to provide affected people fleeing violence, humanitarian crisis and poverty with tailored solutions to enable them to rebuild their lives. I urge the authorities to adopt a protective approach, particularly when screening unaccompanied migrant children coming from neighboring and non-neighboring countries. In this respect, it is imperative that children exposed to violence and trafficking are not returned back to their countries. With regard to individuals awaiting deportation, I recommend that the Immigration and Customs Enforcement operates effective and consistent practices to identify situations of trafficking that had not been detected previously. Moreover, I am gravely concerned that unaccompanied migrant children placed in Office of Refugee Resettlement facilities have on occasions been released to sponsors who subsequently forced them to work or to engage in prostitution, as a result of inefficient background checks. U.S. Customs and Border Protection play a key role to stop transnational trafficking in persons and I thus urge the Federal authorities to provide adequate resources to ensure that CBS staff is duly trained to identify human trafficking victims.

In this regard, I am deeply troubled by the persisting practice of detaining children on immigration violations grounds. By no means can the detention of child victims be in the "best interest of the child," as prescribed by international human rights law. As a consequence, I urge relevant authorities to take appropriate measures to ensure adequate protection to minors, including by banning administrative detention of children, in particular for violations of immigration laws and regulations.

I further learnt that existing CSO-run shelters were only available for children and women. Similar services must be provided to protect male victims of trafficking who are currently sheltered in homeless centres throughout the country.

I also salute the dedication of civil society that provides psychological, legal and social assistance to victims and I encourage the Federal authorities to increase funding to non-profit organizations and to public agencies, especially those providing housing services, as the protection of victims should never be dependent on the goodwill of private funders who may change their priorities with no prior notice or explanations.

In relation to compensation, I am aware that under the TVPA, restitution is mandatory to trafficking victims. The Labor Department clarified that restitution can be provided to victims even if they are sent back to their home country. However, civil society organizations have reported a systemic failure to ensure compensation and I thus would urge the authorities to take additional positive measures in this regard.

Finally, I would like to highlight two general issues relating to the effectiveness of the whole anti-trafficking mechanisms: coordination and data collection. I have learnt of and met with a number of initiatives in the past two weeks, such as the Anti-Trafficking Coordination Teams (ACTeam) which brings together representatives from various Federal agencies in various cities across the country, as well as the San Francisco Mayor's Human Trafficking Task Force which adopts a broad human rights and victim-centered approach to address trafficking and protect sexually exploited peoples, including LGBTI individuals. While cooperation is key in addressing human trafficking, I note that coordination among Federal, State and local level agencies is often uneasy and I call for a more coordinated approach with universal anti-trafficking trainings to every entity. This would ensure effective anti-trafficking actions, including individualized victims' access to services and criminal investigations and prosecutions of human trafficking offenses. Additionally, I have found that data on trafficking is either lacking or collected in an uncoordinated manner, which in turn adversely impacts the understanding of the extent and prevalence of trafficking in persons in the U.S. I thus call on the authorities to develop a systematic and comprehensive data collection using common indicators and disaggregated data with a view to implementing a greater human rights oriented anti-trafficking response.

I thank you.

[End text]

Source: U.N. OHCHR Human Rights Council http://www.ohchr.org/EN/NewsEvents/Pages/DisplayNews.aspx?NewsID= 21049&LangID=E

༺༺༺༺༺༺༺

5. MESSAGE FROM HILAL ELVER, U.N. SPECIAL RAPPORTEUR ON RIGHT TO FOOD, AT THE RIGHT TO ADEQUATE FOOD EVENT, 2017

This document is a written statement of the video presentation of the U.N. Special Rapporteur on the Right To Food. It was given at an international conference on the Right to Food. The Special Rapporteur, a professor at the University of California, was exercising her broad mandate in creating awareness about the human right to food, largely in relation to the phenomenon of climate change. This presentation was not about the U.S. but about the right to food globally as affected by global warming. It is a sample document that shows how the U.N. Special Procedure mandate holders function in different contexts, but all in fulfillment of their mandates.

[Text]

The Right to Adequate Food Event

24 January 2017

Written text of the video message from Hilal Elver, Special Rapporteur on Right to Food

Dear distinguished participants and dear friends, I wish I would be with you there physically to discuss last 20 years of development in the area of right to food and accountability mechanism.

The human rights agenda was in forefront in two distinct periods during the 20th century. The first one was after WWII, when grim memories were fresh of catastrophic denial of human rights in Nazi Germany, Imperial Japan, and Fascist Italy. The 1948 Universal Declaration of Human Rights, followed by two legally binding Covenants (civil and political rights and economic, social and cultural rights) were major positive results of these years.

The second period was in 1990s when the Cold War ended and human rights again became prominent on the global policy agenda. Several high profile U.N. Global Conferences were held, the International Criminal Court was established, many other normative global initiatives took place. One of the notable highlights of this period was the Vienna World Conference on Human Rights in 1993 where the assembled governments endorsed the universality, indivisibility, interrelatedness and interdependence of all human rights. After that, at the 1996 World Food Summit these principles were endorsed, this time with respect to the right to adequate food.

More then 20 years ago it was widely acknowledged that the production oriented agricultural policies underpinned by the Green Revolution dramatically increased food production around the world, but this result was achieved at the expense of environmental degradation. Although over production period has credited with avoiding predicted famines in some parts of the world, it did not solve the problem of global hunger.

The reason that hunger and malnutrition persists is not because there is not enough food for everyone. Hunger persists because of poverty, social and economic inequality and inaccessibility to vital resources, as well as adverse impact of trade rules in developing countries and the predatory character of economic globalization. Many of the root causes of world hunger cannot and will not be overcome without the existence and implementation of normative principles of human rights.

Unfortunately, 20 years after the World Food Summit the recognition of the right to adequate food, is declining. It is becoming more difficult to embed the right to food concept in global regulatory frameworks than two decades ago. I will give two examples on that:

The first one was the failure to include the right food to 2015 Paris Climate Change Agreement, and the second one was the ignoring right to food language in 2030 Sustainable Development Goals.

In relation to Paris Climate Change Agreement we might refer to the "glass half empty, half dull" metaphor. Because, the human rights approach was first time affirmed in a climate change agreement but only in the Preamble, and then only after a long fight waged by the NGO community with the support of a few sympathetic States. This is a positive side.

On the down side, there was no mention of human rights in the operational provisions in the agreement. Moreover, regrettably, there was actually strong opposition to the inclusion of the right to food in the Paris text unlike some other rights that were explicitly mentioned in the Preamble.

This result was neither an accident nor an oversight. Rather it reflected the view that right to food approach was perceived as hostile to the interests of the big agro businesses. The agricultural lobby successfully excluded right to food from the text. Instead, the production approach to food security was explicitly repeated as it was in Article 2 of the UNFCCC. What I would consider, the international preoccupation with climate change has transferred the focus of concern to functional and quantitative solutions at the expense of normative and equity considerations. While climate justice played some role at Paris Agreement, unfortunately food justice was ignored.

However, recognition of the human right based approach is very important in climate change policies as many of the clean development mechanisms of the UNFCCC could have an adverse impact on the right to adequate food and the livelihood of many people, such as REDD+ about reforestation projects in order to reduce Green House Gas emission with the expense of local communities.

Similarly, biofuel is a poster child of benevolent climate change policies that is threatening peoples' right to food. It is important to insist on a human rights approach in response to climate change mitigation and adaptation policies and make a greater effort to protect access of all people to sufficient, healthy, and affordable food, while responding climate change.

However, there are further concerns relating to the application of new technologies to agriculture to eradicate hunger in time of climate change. For instance, efforts to increase food production by way on biotechnology and reliance on pesticides could have detrimental, sometimes unintended long-term consequences for the fulfillment of the right to adequate food and human health.

The second example of the strong resistance against human right language is the 2030 Sustainable Development Goals (SDGs). What would have been more appropriate to affirm the right to food in Goal No. 2 if the world really wants to "end hunger, achieve food security and improved nutrition and promote sustainable agriculture?" Unfortunately, it was an organized effort not to use clear human rights language and inventing some other concepts such as "no one left behind" and weakened the monitoring mechanism. These examples, among many, shows that we have entered a period in which supporting the right to food approach is becoming an uphill battle everywhere. The widespread rise of the chauvinistic nationalism, and the influence market driven thinking is making it unfashionable these days to support human rights.

The Committee of Food Security (CFS) is a unique international institutional framework within which civil society is strongly represented after revolutionary restructuring in 2009. But CFS is too young and in some senses too fragile to confront these problems directly. Meaningful participation in decision-making must be struggle against very powerful private sector mechanisms and big governments. The civil society mechanisms that exist need continuous support and vigilant attention. Repeating a commitment to a human rights approach needs to foregrounded in every document released by the CFS. Without an accountability mechanism, there is no way to protect peoples' right to adequate food, and access to food it will be treated as a charity demeaning to those who become dependent. Charity cannot realistically hope to prevail against big business. Only a vigorous program of human rights can have such a hope.

Finally there is also some good news to report. As we know, more than 25 countries now have implicit or explicit norms in their constitution dedicated to the protection of the right to adequate food, and many states have framework laws. Latin America is the leader of this trend, but we also see encouraging developments in Europe and other continents. Belgium presently has a right to food bill in its Parliament, I believe we should thank Olivier De Schutter for this achievement. In Italy, the Lombardy Region is championing the right to food. The cities of Milan and Torino are the leaders of this development making right to food a law. Additionally, Scotland is preparing a right to food bill soon to be put before lawmakers. Unfortunately, the European Convention of Human Rights, unlike some other regional human rights mechanisms (such as Americas, and Africa) does not have a provision affirming the right to food. This needs to be discussed publicly especially Europe while the Continent is struggling with ongoing refugee crises.

However, at sub-national levels in many cities throughout Europe, as well as in the United States and Canada there are signs that communities are beginning to appreciate the right to food, local food movement, as well as food sovereignty and democracy. There are growing efforts to mobilize people around these moral and normative ideas, which is enjoying some success despite strong resistance by many national governments and corporations. These political and economic actors do not like to impose legal accountability. They greatly prefer to rely on voluntary code of conduct to achieve corporate social responsibility. So far, with rare exceptions this reliance on voluntary compliance has been ineffective.

I would like to mention here the Peoples' Tribunal that took place last October in the Hague against Monsanto, one of the Big 6 pesticides and seed companies that is now really even bigger Big 3 due to recent mergers. At the tribunal, NGOs and human rights advocates listened to testimonies from experts and peoples from all over the world who described many human rights violations by big corporations. The distinguished European Court of Human Rights Judge Tulkens eloquently articulated the view that the progressive development of international human rights principles depend on their repetition and acknowledgment at various policymaking platforms. Therefore, as the Special Rapporteur part of our responsibility is to stress the necessity of the right to adequate food in all of our thematic reports and in every country visits, especially when we have opportunities to talk with government officials who are responsible for food policy.

Human rights principles became an important and powerful tool for victimized people after civil society organizations started to take them seriously in their efforts to oppose government actions. It was a difficult struggle at first. Many governments cynically considered that these principles of human rights would be just empty words that could be endorsed without any expectation that they would held accountable for their implementation. Unfortunately, influential Western based human rights NGOs such as Amnesty International and Human Rights Watch still do not fight hard or often enough, for economic, social and cultural rights.

But we are not discouraged, nor passive. We have very powerful right to food and food sovereignty civil society network around the world, wherever we go they are our partners, our ears, and our eyes. They teach us, remind us, and direct U.S. to wherever the human rights violations occur. We need to respect their voices in all of our deliberations and work. Taking this opportunity thank you all being there and keeping human rights agenda alive in this very difficult time.

[End Text]

Source: U.N. OHCHR, http://www.ohchr.org/Documents/Issues/Food/Event24Jan2017.pdf

֍֍֍֍֍֍֍֍

6. LETTER FROM PAMELA K. HAMAMOTO, U.S. AMBASSADOR TO THE U.N., TO U.N. SPECIAL RAPPORTEUR DAVID KAYE REGARDING THE U.S. POSITION ON ISSUES OF HUMAN RIGHTS AND CYBER GOVERNANCE

This letter is between the U.S. Ambassador to the U.N. and the U.N. Special Rapporteur on the promotion and protection of the right to freedom of opinion and expression, an American who holds a mandate from the HRC. Here, the international community in the office of the Special Rapporteur is interfacing with the U.S. government over how to govern the world of Information and Communications Technology (ICT) in a way that does not violate human rights. This puts the U.S. and the Rapporteur in a position to dialogue so that the Rapporteur will read and understand the U.S. position on this issue. The Special Rapporteur has presented the U.N.'s position on cyber governance to the U.S. The U.N. is seeking to steer the U.S. to help move the cyber and related technology world onto a path that protects human rights. It is about getting the U.S. to use its influence towards the private business sector of the ICT world regarding human rights issues such as privacy and expression and access to information, and to the internet itself. As is typical, the U.S. brings up the relation of this ICT sector to terrorism. This sets up the search for a balance between activity which protects human rights and activity which also allows legitimate business and access to information to function and prosper. Many issues come down to business versus human rights. The Special Rapporteur is arguing for the human rights side. There is also reference to the new business and human rights guidelines (Ruggie Principles) which need to be factored into the debate.

[Text]

THE PERMANENT MISSION OF THE UNITED STATES OF AMERICA TO THE UNITED NATIONS AND OTHER INTERNATIONAL ORGANIZATIONS IN GENEVA

February 4, 2016

Mr. David Kaye
Special Rapporteur on the promotion and protection of the right to freedom of opinion and expression,
Geneva, Switzerland

Dear Mr. Kaye:

The United States commends your initiative to focus the global community's attention on the pressing issues related to the responsibilities of the Information and Communication Technology (ICT) sector to respect the right to freedom of opinion and expression. We appreciate the opportunity to offer comments for consideration as you refine the project. The following submission, while not exhaustive, is intended to draw attention to areas that the United States views as critical to the success of this endeavor.

While the duty to protect human rights rests with States, the United States has championed efforts at the UN, the OECD, and in other multilateral and multi stakeholder fora to discuss the responsibilities of corporate actors to respect internationally-recognized human rights, as defined in the Guiding Principles on Business and Human Rights (UNGPs). In line with this position, President Obama announced in September 2014 that the United States would develop a National Action Plan (NAP) on Responsible Business Conduct, consistent with the UNGPs and the OECD Guidelines on Multinational Enterprises (OECD Guidelines). As part of the NAP process, the Administration issued an open call for submissions from external actors and launched a series of meetings to consult with stakeholders across the country. Officials made specific efforts to engage ICT companies in the process, fielding numerous submissions that addressed the human rights impacts of the ICT sector, and participating in one set of consultations in the California Bay Area, near the technology hub of Silicon Valley. The U.S. NAP is scheduled to be released this year and will be forwarded for consideration.

You may wish to examine the benefits and limitations of existing efforts to apply the UNGPs, the OECD Guidelines, and other related principles within the ICT sector, including, among others: government NAPs that address ICT issues; examples of human rights impact assessments or human rights due diligence conducted by ICT companies; indices that measure ICT companies' adherence to performance indicators based on these principles; and multi-stakeholder groups formed to foster transparency and accountability with respect to these principles. Your efforts to map this field are timely and useful as they will help avoid duplication of existing work, provide a clearinghouse of practical resources, evaluate the effectiveness of these efforts, and identify gaps and overlaps.

This initiative has particular relevance and urgency in light of the recent surge in attacks targeting civilians in Paris, Istanbul, San Bernardino, Jakarta, and elsewhere. These horrific events have intensified concerns regarding: (1) the use of the Internet and mobile tools to promote radical views, violence, and terrorist acts; (2) governmental capabilities to track such activities and respond with coordinated actions; and (3) the role of private companies that develop and deploy these technologies in combatting violent extremism. To address these concerns and others, such as cybercrime and cyberbullying, some ICT companies are working to develop policies and procedures to identify and address-in ways that respect and reinforce fundamental freedoms such as the freedom of expression-certain uses of their platforms that are illegal and/or in violation of their respective terms of service and community standards. Given the intensification of this discussion, you may wish to address this context directly in your work plan as companies struggle with these challenges. Recommendations from past reports issued by previous mandate holders may contain fresh meaning today when re-examined in this context.

There is a wide range of ICT companies, products, and services, each of which can create different opportunities and/or risks related to the freedom of opinion and expression. The United States views the effort to develop this taxonomy as useful and would suggest the following additions to the list of actors, products, and services set out in the call for submissions: cloud data services, big data analytics, and digital forensics. In addition, we would recommend further distinction within categories, such as "telecommunication" and "surveillance and cybersecurity," to identify relevant subcategories (e.g., mobile providers, Voice over Internet Protocol [VoIP] services, penetration testing, deep packet inspection, and DDoS-mitigation). More fine-tuned categories will help to better identify these related risks and opportunities.

In addition to the list of legal and policy matters identified in the call for submissions, we would also suggest that you consider the following topics: the impact of business and policy decisions by cloud providers that span diverse legal jurisdictions; the role of contract law in assigning responsibilities between relevant entities; the implications of advertising-based business models; and the reliance on users to flag content that violates terms of service. Furthermore, efforts within the private sector to address the legal and policy challenges of dual-use technologies also merit consideration, along with an analysis of the potential positive and negative effects these technologies have on the freedom of opinion and expression.

In addition to mapping the categories of actors in the ICT sector whose activities may implicate the right to freedom of opinion and expression, as well as the main legal issues raised, you may wish to include as part of this study an analysis of the ways that the right to freedom of opinion and expression online might be advanced through private sector engagement with civil society actors. For example, it may be prudent to better understand the importance of venues and mechanisms that foster dialogue and trust among ICT companies and other stakeholders, including governments, civil society, academics, and others, for helping the private sector understand the potential human rights impacts of their business operations. You may wish to consider examining the varied spaces available for such multi-stakeholder engagement, particularly between companies and civil society-such as the Internet Governance Forum at the global, regional, and national levels, the Freedom Online Coalition multi-stakeholder working groups, and the Global Network Initiative, to name just a few-and highlight examples of how stakeholders have leveraged these venues and mechanisms to identify ICT related human rights risks and work to mitigate their adverse impacts.

Sincerely,

Pamela K. Hamamoto, Ambassador

Source: U.N. OHCHR
http://www.ohchr.org/Documents/Issues/Expression/PrivateSector/USA.pdf

7. REPORT OF THE SPECIAL RAPPORTEUR ON THE SITUATION OF HUMAN RIGHTS IN THE DEMOCRATIC PEOPLE'S REPUBLIC OF KOREA

This document is a sample of a country-specific report, which is one of the special procedures of the U.N. Human Rights Council. It was prepared by the U.N. Special Rapporteur on the situation of human rights in the Democratic People's Republic of Korea, North Korea, to be presented to the HRC. The mandate holder, Marzuki Darusman of Indonesia, was reporting to the HRC on the possibility of criminal prosecution of the leaders of North Korea responsible for crimes against humanity on the North Korean people, which are international crimes. The focus is on how to prosecute using international criminal law and the possibility of using the International Criminal Court and other options. While this report does not directly involve the U.S., and human rights, it is a very important issue to U.S. foreign policy and diplomacy, and the U.S. would likely participate in some way in bringing about such prosecutions.

[Text]

Note by the Secretariat

The present report, submitted to the Human Rights Council pursuant to Council resolution 28/22, is the last to be submitted by the current mandate holder.

Two years have passed since the commission of inquiry on the situation of human rights in the Democratic People's Republic of Korea presented to the Human Rights Council its finding that crimes against humanities had been and were being committed in the country. Regrettably, the situation of human rights in the Democratic People's Republic of Korea has not improved, and the crimes against humanity documented by the commission of inquiry appear to continue. Nonetheless, the situation in the Korean peninsula appears to be improving, as seen in the increasing dialogue and interactions between the Democratic People's Republic of Korea and the Republic of Korea. Public discussions on the future of the Korean peninsula seem more visible, at least in the Republic of Korea. In this regard, the Special Rapporteur stresses that a framework on accountability measures for crimes against humanity and other human rights violations must be a component of discussions on the future of the Korean peninsula, including a unification scenario.

I. Introduction

1. Two years have passed since the commission of inquiry on the situation of human rights in the Democratic People's Republic of Korea presented to the Human Rights Council its finding that crimes against humanities had been and were being committed in the country (see A/HRC/25/63). Regrettably, the situation of human rights has not improved, and the crimes against humanity documented by the commission appear to continue. Nonetheless, the situation in the Korean peninsula appears to be improving, as seen in the increasing dialogue and number of interactions between the Democratic People's Republic of Korea and the Republic of Korea. Public discussions on the future of the Korean peninsula today are more visible, at least in the Republic of Korea.

2. In the present report, the Special Rapporteur describes how accountability for crimes against humanity should be ensured. Given the serious nature of these crimes, he urges the international community to take bold steps to address them while recalling its duty to prosecute such international crimes. In this way, the Special Rapporteur hopes that concrete steps aimed at preserving accountability for crimes against humanity committed in the Democratic People's Republic of Korea will be taken.

II. Latest developments

3. Since the previous report of the Special Rapporteur submitted to the Human Rights Council in March 2015 (A/HRC/28/71), there have been several important developments pertaining to the situation of human rights in the Democratic People's Republic of Korea.

A. Engagement with the international community

4. In the second of half of 2015, the Democratic People's Republic of Korea again showed willingness to engage with the international community on human rights, probably spurred by the upcoming debate in the General Assembly on the situation of human rights in the country.

5. In September 2015, the Government of the Democratic People's Republic of Korea invited the United Nations High Commissioner for Human Rights to visit the country and expressed its interest in continuing discussions on possible forms of technical assistance by the Office of the High Commissioner (OHCHR). In June 2015, a delegation of the European Union visited the country to hold a political dialogue with the authorities, including on improving the protection of human rights. In October, the Democratic People's Republic of Korea repatriated a national of the Republic of Korea and also permanent resident in the United States of America who had been detained since unlawfully entering the Democratic People's Republic of Korea in April 2015. During 2015, the Democratic People's Republic of Korea repatriated at least three more individuals to the Republic of Korea.

6. On 21 September 2015, the Special Rapporteur participated in a panel discussion on the situation of human rights in the Democratic People's Republic of Korea held during the thirtieth session of the Human Rights Council. The discussion, which was moderated by the former chairperson of the commission of inquiry, touched upon the issues of international abductions, enforced disappearances and related matters. The Democratic People's Republic of Korea, however, rejected the panel discussion, describing it as a politically motivated attempt to change the socialist system of the country.

7. On 17 December 2015, the General Assembly adopted resolution 70/172 on the situation of human rights in the Democratic People's Republic of Korea (119 Member States voted in favour, 19 against and 48 abstained). Like in its resolution 69/188, the Assembly called upon the Security Council to consider referring the situation of human rights in the country to the International Criminal Court.

8. On 10 December 2015, the High Commissioner addressed the Security Council, and briefed it on the situation of human rights in the Democratic People's Republic of Korea.

B. Developments in neighbouring countries

...

C. Efforts by the Office of the High Commissioner

1. Establishment of a field-based structure

17. On 23 June 2015, OHCHR opened its field-based structure in Seoul pursuant to Human Rights Council resolution 25/25. The Office is tasked with strengthening, monitoring and documenting the situation of human rights in the Democratic People's Republic of Korea, improving the engagement and capacity-building of stakeholders and maintaining the visibility of the situation. During the visits conducted by the Special Rapporteur to the Republic of Korea in September and November 2015, he had fruitful discussion with the staff members of the Office, which is now fully operational....

18. During his visits to the Republic of Korea and Japan, the Special Rapporteur was pleased to observe that officials and civil society actors in both countries were eager to support and cooperate with OHCHR. He reiterates his calls upon all stakeholders, including the Government of the Democratic People's Republic of Korea, to extend their full cooperation to OHCHR. In addition, he urges the Human Rights Council to ensure that the OHCHR field-based presence in Seoul can fulfil all aspects of its mandate effectively, including by ensuring that it is provided with adequate financial resources.

2. Dialogue on technical cooperation with the Government of the Democratic People's Republic of Korea

19. In September 2015, during the meeting between the High Commissioner and the Minister for Foreign Affairs of the Democratic People's Republic of Korea, the Minister invited the High Commissioner to pay a visit to the country. Subsequent discussions were held between the Government and OHCHR on a possible visit. The Special Rapporteur welcomes this positive development, and hopes that the visit be used as an opportunity to improve cooperation between the Government of the Democratic People's Republic of Korea and OHCHR. Such cooperation is critical to facilitate the implementation of the State's international human rights obligations, including the commitments it made during the universal periodic review, and is in accordance with the technical assistance mandate of OHCHR in Seoul.

3. Strategy on accountability

20. In 2014, the commission of inquiry found that crimes against humanity had been and were still being committed in the Democratic People's Republic of Korea. This confirmed the reports of various actors, including those who had left the Democratic People's Republic of Korea, members of civil society, and the current and previous mandate holders. In the two years since the report of the commission of inquiry, there has been no indication that the situation of human rights in the Democratic People's Republic of Korea has changed. Political prison camps remain in operation. Reports of torture and other violations against prisoners in political and ordinary prisons continue. Religious followers reportedly continue to face persecution, and persons attempting to flee the country appear to face harsher treatment than in earlier periods. Food insecurity remains a serious issue. ...

D. Accountability and future of the Korean peninsula

1. Discussions on unification

21. Since August 2015, relations between the two States on the Korean peninsula have improved, as witnessed by the increase in interaction and dialogue. At the same time, the Special Rapporteur noted that public discussions on a possible future unification seemed to be gaining momentum in the Republic of Korea. In addition, the Government of the Republic of Korea appears to be undertaking preparations, including a consideration of the implications of unification for the legal frameworks of the two States.

22. In this new context, the Special Rapporteur stresses that accountability for crimes against humanity must be part of any discussion about the future of the Korean peninsula, including the scenario of unification. International law requires that those who are responsible for crimes against humanity be held accountable. This will require a deep reflection on how to approach unification and accountability in a way that promotes long-term stability and strengthens the rule of law....

23. For the above reasons, crimes against humanity require prosecution at the national or international levels. As the term implies, crimes against humanity are a concern for all of humanity. Consequently, ensuring accountability for such crimes is an international as much as a Korean challenge and requires the international community to play a role....

24. A failure to address serious and systemic violations this has the potential to undermine the legitimacy and credibility of the system, and may therefore become a destabilizing factor. In addition, such a failure deprives victims of the justice and guarantees of non-repetition to which they are entitled. Persistent human rights issues, such as systematic discrimination and unequal distribution of wealth and services, must also be addressed. Furthermore, the justice and security sectors would require reform to meet international human rights standards, including through vetting. Without such reforms, prosecution would have little effect in the long term....

2. Responsibility to prosecute

25. With regard to accountability, the Special Rapporteur stresses that the finding by the commission of inquiry that crimes against humanity have been and are being committed in the Democratic People's Republic of Korea demands that the international community prosecute those responsible for such crimes, in particular those most responsible for their authorization, ordering and perpetration. In this regard, the Special Rapporteur highlights the preamble of the Rome Statute of the International Criminal Court, which states that "it is the duty of every State to exercise its criminal jurisdiction over those responsible for international crimes." Furthermore, in the Declaration of the high-level meeting of the General Assembly on the rule of law at the national and international levels, the Heads of State and Government and heads of delegation attending the meeting on 24 September 2012 committed to ensuring that impunity is not tolerated for crimes against humanity and gross violations of human rights law, and that such violations are properly investigated and appropriately sanctioned, including by bringing the perpetrators of any crimes to justice, through national mechanisms or, where appropriate, regional or international mechanisms, in accordance with international law.

26. By imposing an obligation to extradite or prosecute, various conventions obligate States to cooperate in combating impunity. An obligation to extradite or prosecute for, inter alia, crimes against humanity is also stipulated in article 9 of the Draft Code of Crimes against the Peace and Security of Mankind, according to which a State party in the territory of which an individual alleged to have committed a crime is found is to extradite or prosecute that individual.

27. The Special Rapporteur again stresses that the continuing situation in the Democratic People's Republic of Korea behoves the international community to take prosecutorial measures in relation to crimes against humanity committed in that country.

E. Structural and operational aspects of an effective process of accountability

1. Crimes against humanity

28. As the commission of inquiry noted, the prohibition of crimes against humanity forms part of the body of pre-emptory norms (*jus cogens*) that bind the entire international community as customary international law (see A/HRC/25/CRP.1, para. 1195). Consequently, individuals who commit crimes against humanity in the Democratic People's Republic of Korea may be held responsible on the basis of customary international law, even though the State is not a party to the Rome Statute of the International Criminal Court and has no provisions against crimes against humanity in its domestic criminal law. The Special Rapporteur also recalls that international law does not permit amnesties for crimes against humanity, particularly in relation to those most responsible for such crimes. Similarly, it is an established principle of international law that acting on the orders of a superior is not a defence for perpetrators of crimes against humanity (see ibid.).

2. Command and superior responsibility

29. The Special Rapporteur also recalls that, according to the principle of command and superior responsibility under international criminal law, military commander and civilian superiors are criminally responsible for failing to prevent or repress crimes against humanity committed by persons under their effective authority and control. Consequently, the criminal responsibility of the uppermost leadership of the Democratic People's Republic of Korea, including the Su-

preme Leader, for crimes against humanity must be considered, for ordering or instigating such crimes, even if lower-ranking officials carried out the crimes.

3. Principle of complementarity

30. With regard to the obligation to prosecute, it remains the rule that States have primary responsibility to exercise jurisdiction over serious crimes under international law. When national courts are unable to offer satisfactory guarantees of independence and impartiality or are materially unable or unwilling to conduct effective investigations or prosecution, international and internationalized criminal tribunals may exercise concurrent jurisdiction. International and internationalized tribunals are not, however, intended to stand in for domestic courts or to replace domestic obligations to investigate, prosecute and punish. This principle of complementarity rests on a combination of respect for State sovereignty and respect for the principle of universal jurisdiction. The principle allows States to exercise jurisdiction and to determine how to proceed with an alleged perpetrator on the basis of its own national law, while accepting that those who have committed international crimes may be prosecuted through international criminal bodies if national processes do not deliver justice.

4. Republic of Korea

31. The Special Rapporteur notes that the Republic of Korea appears to be well positioned to move forward with criminal proceedings, even if not all aspects of crimes against humanity found by the commission of inquiry could be addressed. The Republic of Korea has been a State party to the Rome Statute of the International Criminal Court since 13 November 2002. Furthermore, human rights constitute a major issue in the legal system of the Republic of Korea; Specifically, respect for human rights is a paramount consideration in the Constitution,. The universality of human rights is expressed in various international instruments that have been ratified by the Republic of Korea; consequently, the legal system of the Republic of Korea is protects human rights, and the principle of human rights guides how the legal system operates. Both the Government of the Republic of Korea and accused parties can refer to human rights norms in the legal system. To conform to international human rights standards, and to be credible to all parties, these processes must uphold strict safeguards of the rights of the defendant, including the presumption of innocence. Such a legal system also ensures the dignity of the rights of victims, while ensuring accountability for human rights violations.

32. The most important aspect of such legal prosecutions is that they be complemented by a broader transitional justice approach. Legal prosecution may ensure formal justice in some cases, but a legal system alone may not to be able to cope with the number of perpetrators. Furthermore, it might not be desirable to address all violations through prosecution. The disclosure of the whole truth and other mechanisms through which the dignity of victims can be restored may be equally important for a society to be able to face its past and move towards sustainable peace.

5. Principle of universal jurisdiction

33. The principle of "universal jurisdiction" may also allow for the prosecution of the leadership of the Democratic People's Republic of Korea in a third country. The principle establishes a territorial jurisdiction over persons for extraterritorial events where neither the victims nor alleged offenders are nationals of the forum State and no harm was allegedly caused to the forum State's own national interests. This principle is based on the notion that "certain crimes are so harmful to international interests that States are entitled — and even obliged — to bring proceedings against the perpetrator, regardless of the location of the crime and the nationality of the perpetrator or the victim."

34. In reality, the implementation of the above general principle remains limited, given that it depends on national law. States are entitled to grant their courts universal jurisdiction over certain crimes as a national decision. Consequently, the application of the principle of universal jurisdiction has not been uniform. Some States apply a narrow concept, allowing the prosecution only if the accused is available for trial, while others adopt a broader concept that allows for the initiation of proceedings even in the absence of the accused.

...

35. Despite challenges, prosecution based on the principle of universal jurisdiction might present the only opportunity to move forward on establishing criminal accountability, while the possibility of such prosecution may serve as a catalyst for other processes.

6. International Criminal Court

36. While pursuing prosecution in national courts, the Special Rapporteur remains convinced that the Security Council should refer the situation of human rights in the Democratic People's Republic of Korea to the International Criminal Court, as recommended by the commission of inquiry (A/HRC/25/63, para. 94(a)) and subsequently encouraged by the General Assembly in its resolutions 69/188and 70/172. The Security Council could refer the situation in the Democratic People's Republic of Korea to the International Criminal Court on the basis of article 13(b) of the Rome Statute and Chapter VII of the Charter of the United Nations.

37. In the event that the Security Council decided not to refer the situation to the International Criminal Court, the General Assembly could establish a tribunal (A/HRC/25/63, para. 87). In this regard, the General Assembly could rely on its residual powers recognized in, inter alia, its resolution 377 (V) ("Uniting for peace"), which provided that, if the Security Council, because of lack of unanimity of the permanent members, fails to exercise its primary responsibility for the maintenance of international peace and security in any case where there appears to be a threat to the peace, breach of the peace, or act of aggression, the Assembly should consider the matter immediately with a view to making appropriate recommendations to Members for collective measures....

F. Way forward

38. Given the gravity of the violations committed in the Democratic People's Republic of Korea, the international community is obliged to take steps to ensure accountability. As summarized above, there are various practical and legal issues to be further developed. In this regard, there are two main bodies central to moving the accountability agenda forward: the group of experts on accountability, and OHCHR in Seoul.

1. Group of experts on accountability

39. First, a group of independent experts should be formed. The group should have three main responsibilities:

(a) To establish the present state of international law and prevailing State practices on accountability;

(b) To determine an appropriate approach to ensure State accountability of crimes against humanity committed by the Government of the Democratic People's Republic of Korea;

(c) To recommend creative and practical mechanisms of accountability that are most effective in securing truth and justice for the victims of crimes against humanity in the Democratic People's Republic of Korea.

40. In recent years, there have been significant developments in international law with regard to accountability, such as the establishment of the International Criminal Court and other tribunals. Nonetheless, the Special Rapporteur notes with deep concern the prevalence of recourse to amnesties, sometimes in contravention of obligations under international human rights law. Against this background, the group should clearly lay down the international legal ground for accountability.

41. The fundamental steps leading to prosecution are to define crimes, to identify actors and to present evidence of criminal wrongdoing. The commission of inquiry laid the groundwork for these three steps. The urgent challenge now is to determine which methods can be most effectively utilized to hold perpetrators accountable, while allowing victims to know the truth of what happened in the past.

42. Since the commission of inquiry concluded its work, there has been no comprehensive analysis of which models could be most appropriate. Such an analysis should include a review of the types of courts available, advantages and disadvantages in the context of the Korean peninsula, and the possible scope of prosecution. The Special Rapporteur again stresses the importance of the International Criminal Court, while acknowledging that the Court is able to handle only the uppermost leadership....

43. In the course of its work, the group should consider experiences from other countries that have undergone transitional justice processes, in particular those where international criminal justice has been involved. At the same time, the group should provide advice that takes into account the unique situation of the Korean peninsula. As a guiding princi-

ple, the group should adopt a victim-centric approach to accountability and give due importance to the protection of the dignity of victims.

...

III. Conclusions and recommendations

46. Two years have passed since the commission of inquiry published its report, in which it found that crimes against humanity had been and were being committed in the Democratic People's Republic of Korea. Regrettably, it does not appear that the situation of human rights in the country has improved, and the crimes against humanity documented by the commission appear to continue. While the Democratic People's Republic of Korea has at times indicated its willingness to engage with the international community on some human rights issues, this has not yet led to any tangible improvement in the situation of human rights.

47. The period covered in the present report was characterized by greater interaction between the Democratic People's Republic of Korea and the Republic of Korea. Discussions on the possibility of unification among government actors and other parties in the Republic of Korea appear to be gaining traction.

48. The international community, while taking advantage of the opportunities for increased interaction between the Democratic People's Republic of Korea and the Republic of Korea, should also continue to take steps to facilitate holding to account those who have committed crimes against humanity.

49. The Special Rapporteur on the situation of human rights in the Democratic People's Republic of Korea calls upon the Human Rights Council:

(a) To extend the mandate of the Special Rapporteur, given that the situation of human rights in the Democratic People's Republic of Korea has hardly improved;

(b) To arrange to have an official communication, by the Human Rights Council, the Special Rapporteur or the United Nations High Commissioner for Human Rights, addressed to the Supreme Leader of the Democratic People's Republic of Korea to advise him and other senior leaders that they may be investigated and, if found to be responsible, held accountable for crimes against humanity committed under their leadership;

(c) To establish a group of independent experts with a mandate (i) to establish the present state of international law and prevailing State practices with regard to accountability; (ii) to determine an appropriate approach to ensure State accountability for crimes against humanity committed by the Government of the Democratic People's Republic of Korea; and (iii) to recommend creative and practical mechanisms of accountability to secure truth and justice for the victims of crimes against humanity in the Democratic People's Republic of Korea. Given the resource constraints faced by the Office of the High Commissioner and its field presence in Seoul, which has its own mandate, the group of experts should be established by the Human Rights Council;

(d) To ensure that the field presence of OHCHR in Seoul tasked with following up on the work of the commission of inquiry can function with independence, has sufficient financial resources and enjoys full cooperation with relevant Member States;

(e) To urge the Government of the Democratic People's Republic of Korea to invite the Special Rapporteur to undertake a visit to the country as soon as possible, without preconditions, in accordance with the terms of reference for country visits by special procedure mandate holders, and more generally to cooperate with the mandate;

(f) To task the Special Rapporteur or OHCHR with the formulation of a comprehensive policy on humanitarian assistance for the Democratic People's Republic of Korea.

50. The Special Rapporteur urges the Government of the Democratic People's Republic of Korea:

(a) To halt immediately the human rights violations identified by the commission of inquiry in its report;

(b) To resume dialogue with the Special Rapporteur, and to consider reissuing the invitations extended to all stakeholders concerned, including the Special Rapporteur;

(c) To establish substantive communications with OHCHR, including with a view to possible technical cooperation through the OHCHR field presence in Seoul;

(d) To engage genuinely in bilateral talks with the Republic of Korea and Japan, and to abide by the terms of bilateral agreements concluded, first and foremost in the interests of victims of human rights violations, including abductions, and their families;

(e) To cooperate with United Nations human rights mechanisms, including the Special Rapporteur, by granting them access to the country with a view to, inter alia, assisting in and assessing the implementation of the recommendations accepted by the State during the second cycle of the universal periodic review.

51. The Special Rapporteur calls upon Member States:

(a) To take concrete steps towards achieving accountability for those responsible for serious human rights violations in the Democratic People's Republic of Korea, including by means of referral by the Security Council of the situation in the country to the International Criminal Court;

(b) To make use of the principle of universal jurisdiction to realize and maximize the potential deterring effect of the findings and recommendations of the commission of inquiry, and thus to help to protect the population of the Democratic People's Republic of Korea from further crimes against humanity;

(c) To ensure that the Security Council holds regular briefings on the situation in the Democratic People's Republic of Korea, with the participation of the United Nations High Commissioner for Human Rights and other relevant experts, including the Special Rapporteur;

(d) To facilitate the work of the field-based structure and the Special Rapporteur, and to provide them with timely access to relevant information and potential witnesses, in particular those who have left the Democratic People's Republic of Korea, who may have information crucial to ensuring accountability;

(e) To involve fully civil society actors in the efforts of Member States to address the situation in the Democratic People's Republic of Korea;

(f) To protect persons from the Democratic People's Republic of Korea who have sought refuge in, or are transiting through, the territory of a Member State by abiding with the principle of non-refoulement.

52. The Special Rapporteur calls upon the United Nations system as a whole to address the grave human rights situation in the Democratic People's Republic of Korea in a coordinated and unified manner, in accordance with the Secretary-General's Human Rights Up Front initiative.

53. The Special Rapporteur calls upon civil society to continue its critical work in raising awareness of the situation of human rights in the Democratic People's Republic of Korea, including by reporting on human rights violations committed by the Government of the Democratic People's Republic of Korea.

54. The Special Rapporteur thanks all the partners and stakeholders who extended full cooperation and support during his mandate, and hopes that the common goal to improve the situation of human rights in the Democratic People's Republic of Korea will be achieved in the near future.

[End Text]

Source: U.N. OHCHR
http://www.ohchr.org/EN/Countries/AsiaRegion/Pages/KPIndex.aspx

8. ALLEGATION LETTER TO SPECIAL RAPPORTEURS JUAN MÉNDES AND DAINIUS PURAS REGARDING TWO JAPANESE TRANSGENDER PERSONS' IDENTITY

This document consists of an allegation letter sent by Human Rights Watch, a well known U.S. based NGO, addressed to two HRC special procedure mandate holders, both Special Rapporteurs: Juan Méndez, U.N. Special Rapporteur on torture and other cruel, inhuman or degrading treatment or punishment; and Dainius Puras, the U.N. Special Rapporteur on the Right of Everyone to the Enjoyment of the Highest Attainable Standard of Physical and Mental Health. It asks them to communicate with the government of Japan on behalf of transgender persons in Japan who wish to have their gender identity officially recognized and respected. It is up to the two Special Rapporteurs to decide whether and how to respond to this urgent appeal. NGOs such as HRW do much work in human rights advocacy, much of it is using the Special mechanisms of the HRC. These procedures are not often very effective but they can make a difference to advocates who will do everything possible to bring about respect for human rights all over the world using all available tools. Governments who know that an internal problem is being brought into an international forum like the HRC will sometimes grant such requests to avoid the so called "forum of shame," the public exposure and criticism of their alleged violations.

[Text]

April 1, 2016

Allegation Letter to U.N. Special Rapporteurs

Re: Legal Recognition of Transgender People in Japan

Complaint submitted to:
Juan Méndez, U.N. Special Rapporteur on torture and other cruel, inhuman or degrading treatment or punishment

Dainius Puras

U.N. Special Rapporteur on the right of everyone to the enjoyment of the highest attainable standard of physical and mental health

Human Rights Watch (the "complainant") submits that the provisions of the current Japanese legal gender recognition procedure and the manner in which it is implemented violate internationally protected human rights of transgender people in Japan, including the right to health and the prohibition on inhuman and degrading treatment or punishment. Human Rights Watch interviewed 38 transgender people in Japan between August and November 2015, as well as academic experts and psychiatrists who specialize in gender identity issues.

The Complainant
Human Rights Watch is an independent international human rights organization working to defend human rights of people worldwide. Our researchers investigate human rights abuses in some 90 countries around the world, including Japan, where we have an office.

The Alleged Victims
Transgender persons in Japan who wish to have their gender identity recognized on identification cards, school records, and other official documents and otherwise to be able to live their lives in a way that is consistent with their gender identity without being compelled to undergo psychiatric evaluation for the purposes of a diagnosis of a mental disorder.

State Agents Responsible
Japan Ministry of Health, Labor and Welfare
Japan Ministry of Education, Culture, Sports, Science and Technology

Summary
Legal gender recognition in Japan is regulated by Law No. 111 of 2003. The law came into effect one year after its promulgation, on July 16, 2004.

Law No. 111 requires a diagnosis of "Gender Identity Disorder" (GID) before any transgender person can apply to secure legal recognition of their appropriate gender. GID is defined in the law as "a person, despite his/her biological sex being clear, who continually maintains a psychological identity with an alternative gender, who holds the intention to physically and socially conform to an alternative gender." The process requires the person to be "medically diagnosed in such respects by two or more physicians generally recognized as holding competent knowledge and experience necessary for the task."

The legal gender recognition decision is made by the Family Court. An applicant to the court must, in addition to providing a certificate attesting to the fact that the individual has been diagnosed with GID, meet the following qualifications:
- Be 20 years old or older;
- Be presently unmarried;
- Not presently have any underage children;
- Not have gonads or permanently lack functioning gonads; and
- Have a physical form that is "endowed with genitalia that closely resemble the physical form of an alternative gender."

Cases of applicants who have been diagnosed with GID and are able to demonstrate that they meet all of the law's other criteria are adjudicated by the family court. While this legal recognition is a full legal transition from one gender to the other, court cases and research by Japanese nongovernmental organizations have revealed that in practice, even legally recognized transgender people face discrimination in, for example, adopting children and obtaining life insurance. That is to say, while Law No. 111 is on its own terms abusive, discriminatory and in need of reform, there is also a broader need to protect even those transgender people whose appropriate gender has been legally recognized from discrimination.

Law No. 111 is the first legal gender recognition procedure Japan has ever had, and its adoption represented a pivotal moment in Japan's public debate on sexual and gender minority issues. However, the procedure established under the law violates the rights of people in Japan who wish to be legally recognized as having a different gender from the one they were assigned at birth.

In a 2016 report, the Special Rapporteur on Torture noted that the refusal of transgender people's legal recognition in their appropriate gender, "leads to grave consequences for the enjoyment of their human rights, including obstacles to accessing education, employment, health care and other essential services." The report noted that: "In States that permit the modification of gender markers on identity documents abusive requirements can be imposed, such as forced or otherwise involuntary gender reassignment surgery, sterilization or other coercive medical procedures."

The legal requirements for transgender people in Japan to obtain a GID diagnosis, involve unnecessary, arbitrary, and burdensome tests. The mandatory psychiatric evaluation and the law's requirement that applicants be unmarried, sterile and lacking any children under 20 are inherently discriminatory. These conditions — and in particular the maltreatment many transgender people must accept in order to meet them — also amount to cruel and inhuman treatment and to a violation of transgender people's right to health. The law forces all transgender people who want to secure legal recognition of their appropriate gender to secure diagnosis of a psychological disorder, to refrain from having children at any point during the two decades prior to securing recognition and to be unmarried. It forces many would-be applicants-including those who would not otherwise choose to take these steps — to undergo physically transformative surgical interventions, undergo sterilization, and contemplate the breakup of existing marriages.

Law No. 111's requirements are particularly harmful for transgender children. It sets a mandatory minimum age of 20 for achieving legal gender recognition, and requires extra steps for people under 20 years of age to obtain a GID diagnosis (the first step in the process). Moreover, a GID diagnosis can only be given if the individual holds "the intention to physically and socially conform to an alternative gender," which sets children up to understand surgeries as inevitable and puts intense pressure on them to conform to gender stereotypes. These requirements cannot be squared with the principle that the best interests of children be a primary consideration in all administrative and legal decisions that impact them. Law No. 111 negatively impacts children' rights to physical integrity, privacy, and autonomy. These problems are also reflected in how Law No. 111 has been interpreted by the government with regard to gender non-conforming children in statements issued by the Ministry of Education, and the guidance issued to psychiatrists on GID patients.

Human Rights Watch has thoroughly documented the harmful impact of these interpretations of Law No. 111 by the Education Ministry in a forthcoming report about bullying and exclusion from education in Japan, which we will send to your offices this Spring. We are sending this letter now, in advance of our report, because the need for the special rapporteurs' intervention in Japan is urgent. This is because in 2016, a bi-partisan group of Japanese Members of Parliament will consider revisions to Law No. 111 that could relax the requirements for legal gender recognition in Japan.

The special rapporteurs' timely intervention in this matter could guide Japan to becoming a regional leader on human rights-based legal gender recognition for transgender people-and to eliminate ongoing patterns of cruel and inhuman treatment and violations of the right to health. Emerging international standards and best practices for legal gender recognition, including recommendations made by these special rapporteurs, call for a separation of legal recognition procedures from medical interventions while still providing health care support for those who wish to pursue medical interventions as part of their transition.

Recommendations

Human Rights Watch urges the special rapporteurs to encourage the government of Japan to implement three major recommendations related to improving access to legal gender recognition for transgender people, by:

Urging the Japanese government to revise or replace its legal gender recognition law in a way that is consistent with its international human rights obligations and in accordance with international best practices for legal gender recognition by separating the legal recognition process from medical interventions and GID diagnosis. The legal gender recognition process should be based on the self-declared gender identity of the applicant. Japan should also eliminate the legal requirements that transgender people be unmarried and without children under 20.

Urging the government to liaise with international health experts, including the Special Rapporteur on the Right to the Highest Attainable Standard of Health and the World Professional Association of Transgender Health in its efforts to revise or replace Law No. 111.

While these revisions are underway, instruct the Ministry of Education to issue an urgent clarifying interim directive with clear instructions for school officials to accommodate and respect gender identity of children without requiring a GID diagnosis or any consultation with medical experts. Parents may be consulted where appropriate but the child's gender identification should be the predominant factor in determining what accommodations are necessary.

International Law and Best Practices for Legal Gender recognition

International human rights standards are increasingly understood to require the separation of legal and medical processes of gender reassignment for transgender people. Several countries have adopted best practices that reflect this. Sweden, the Netherlands, Ireland, Colombia, Malta, and Denmark recently changed their legal recognition procedures to remove invasive medical requirements; Denmark and Malta, along with Argentina, do not require a medical diagnosis for legal gender recognition. Argentina and Malta are widely considered to set best standards in legal gender recognition procedures. Domestic lawmakers in some countries have adopted these standards in legislation, while in other cases domestic courts have required their application under existing legal frameworks.

In 2013, the U.N. Special Rapporteur on Torture stated that: "In many countries transgender persons are required to undergo often unwanted sterilization surgeries as a prerequisite to enjoy legal recognition of their preferred gender." The Special Rapporteur noted a trend of finding such compulsory sterilization a violation of human rights, including non-discrimination rights and physical integrity, and called upon governments to "to outlaw forced or coerced sterilization in all circumstances and provide special protection to individuals belonging to marginalized groups."

A 2012 Office of the High Commissioner for Human Rights (OHCHR) report, prepared in response to a 2011 Human Rights Council resolution calling for an end to violence and discrimination on the basis of sexual orientation and gender identity and expression, noted that "[r]egulations in countries that recognize changes in gender often require, implicitly or explicitly, that applicants undergo sterilization surgery as a condition of recognition. Some States also require that those seeking legal recognition of a change in gender be unmarried, implying mandatory divorce in cases where the individual is married."

In a 2014 joint statement, OHCHR, the World Health Organization, U.N. Program on HIV/AIDS (UNAIDS), the, U.N. Development Program, UNICEF, and UNFPA said: "States parties' obligation to respect the right to health requires that they abstain from imposing discriminatory practices. This includes an obligation to respect the rights of persons with disabilities and transgender and intersex persons, who also have the right to retain their fertility...." The agencies called on governments to "[p]rovide legal guarantees for full, free and informed decision-making and the elimination of forced, coercive and otherwise involuntary sterilization, and review, amend and develop laws, regulations and policies in this regard."

In a 2015 report, mandated by a 2014 Human Rights Council resolution on sexual orientation and gender identity, OHCHR recommended that states begin immediately "[i]ssuing legal identity documents, upon request, that reflect preferred gender, eliminating abusive preconditions, such as sterilization, forced treatment and divorce." The 2015 "Blueprint for the Provision of Comprehensive Care for Trans People in Asia and the Pacific," co-published by WHO, UNDP, USAID, PEPFAR, the Asia-Pacific Transgender Network, and the Health Policy Project recommended that governments "[t]ake all necessary legislative, administrative, and other measures to fully recognize each person's self-defined gender identity, with no medical requirements or discrimination on any grounds."

Similarly, principle 3 of the Yogyakarta Principles on the Application of International Human Rights Law in relation to Sexual Orientation and Gender Identity states that:

> Everyone has the right to recognition everywhere as a person before the law. Persons of diverse sexual orientations and gender identities shall enjoy legal capacity in all aspects of life. Each person's self-defined sexual orientation and gender identity is integral to their personality and is one of the most basic aspects of self-determination, dignity, and freedom. No one shall be forced to undergo medical procedures, including sex reassignment surgery, sterilization or hormonal therapy, as a requirement for legal recognition of their gender identity. No status, such as marriage or parenthood, may be invoked as such to prevent the legal recognition of a person's gender identity. No one shall be subjected to pressure to conceal, suppress, or deny their sexual orientation or gender identity.

In June 2013, the Parliamentary Assembly of the Council of Europe, a regional body comprised of 47 member states, passed Resolution 1945, calling for an end to coercive sterilization and castration. Transgender people are listed as one of the groups in the Council of Europe countries disproportionally affected by coercive sterilization.

International expert bodies have in recent years strengthened their positions against medical models for legal gender recognition. The World Professional Association for Transgender Health (WPATH), an international multidisciplinary professional association aimed at promoting evidence-based care, education, research, advocacy, public policy, and respect in transgender health and comprised of over 700 members worldwide, called for removal of any sterilization requirements as part of legal gender recognition in a 2010 statement. WPATH stated:

> No person should have to undergo surgery or accept sterilization as a condition of identity recognition. If a sex marker is required on an identity document, that marker could recognize the person's lived gender, regardless of reproductive capacity. The WPATH Board of Directors urges governments and other authoritative bodies to move to eliminate requirements for identity recognition that require surgical procedures.

In 2015 WPATH updated the statement, reiterating its condemnation of forced sterilization, and expanding its critique of arduous and medicalized procedures for legal gender recognition, saying: "No particular medical, surgical, or mental health treatment or diagnosis is an adequate marker for anyone's gender identity, so these should not be requirements for legal gender change" and "Marital status and parental status should not affect legal recognition of gender change, and appropriate legal gender recognition should be available to transgender youth."

As the special rapporteur on torture noted in his 2013 report, national courts in several countries have begun to reflect these standards in their decisions as well. The special rapporteur's report refers to the following domestic cases:

In 2009, the Austrian Administrative High Court ruled that mandatory gender reassignment, as a condition for legal recognition of gender identity, was unlawful.

In 2011, the Constitutional Court in Germany found that the requirement of gender reassignment surgery violated the rights to physical integrity and self-determination.

In 2012, the Swedish Administrative Court of Appeals ruled that forced sterilization could not be seen as voluntary.

In September 2014 the Norwegian Equality Body ruled that the Ministry of Health had provided no justification for the sterilization requirement in its gender recognition law, and thus the sterilization requirement was deemed to contravene the Anti-Discrimination Act.

Courts in some Asian countries have demonstrated a similar commitment to medical non-interference in legal gender recognition processes, including in the following cases:

In a 2007 judgment, the Nepal Supreme Court's definition of a third gender category situated it as a minority encompassing a broad range of identities for transgender and gender non-conforming people. A 2014 study found that respondents wrote in 16 different terms for their gender identities. The court made clear that the sole criterion for being legally recognized as third gender on documents and in government registers was an individual's "self-feeling." The judgment cited the right to recognition before the law, guaranteed by article 16 of the International Covenant on Civil and Political Rights, as well as the Yogyakarta Principles.

In 2013, India's Supreme Court stated that undertaking medical procedures should not be a requirement for legal recognition of gender identity. The court said: "Few persons undertake surgical and other procedures to alter their bodies and physical appearance to acquire gender characteristics of the sex which conform to their perception of gender, leading to legal and social complications since official record of their gender at birth is found to be at variance with the assumed gender identity." It continued: "Gender identity, therefore, refers to an individual's self-identification as a man, woman, transgender or other identified category." The court made it clear that mandatory sterilization was not acceptable: "no one shall be forced to undergo medical procedures, including SRS, sterilization or hormonal therapy, as a requirement for legal recognition of their gender identity."

In 2015, the Delhi High Court reinforced that, "Everyone has a fundamental right to be recognized in their gender" and that "gender identity and sexual orientation are fundamental to the right of self-determination, dignity and freedom."

Psychiatrists in Japan use both the International Classification of Diseases, which is published by the U.N. World Health Organization, and the Diagnostic and Statistical Manual (DSM), which is published by the American Psychiatric Association (APA). The DSM has eliminated the diagnosis of GID altogether, and the ICD's draft version for an upcoming revision proposes removing GID as well.

In 2012 the APA's board's changes to the latest DSM removed the term "Gender Identity Disorder." APA instead added the term "Gender Dysphoria" with the specific definition that it refers to emotional distress over "a marked incongruence between one's experienced/expressed gender and assigned gender." The APA specifically clarified: "It is important to note that gender nonconformity is not in itself a mental disorder. The critical element of gender dysphoria is the presence of clinically significant distress associated with the condition."

The World Health Organization is currently revising the ICD. When the new ICD is published in 2017, the global standards will no longer contain a diagnostic category for "Gender Identity Disorder," and all diagnostic codes related to experiences of transgender people will appear in a sexual health chapter, not the current mental disorders chapter.

The Facts and Alleged Violations in Japan's Pathologizing Approach to Gender Recognition

A. Mandatory Psychiatric Evaluation

Law No. 111 requires transgender people in Japan who seek legal recognition of their gender identity to obtain a diagnosis of "Gender Identity Disorder" (GID) as a prerequisite. Some people in Japan do understand their gender identity as a psychiatric condition and seek services accordingly. However, such a framework can stigmatize transgender people. Many of the people Human Rights Watch interviewed, including psychiatrists who work with transgender people, discussed this stigma. Our research also found that the process associated with obtaining a medical certificate for GID was itself burdensome and abusive.

Transgender people Human Rights Watch interviewed reported a variety of experiences in obtaining the GID diagnosis. For example, one was able to obtain the diagnosis certificate on their first visit to a psychiatrist, while in other instances clinic staff and psychiatrists forced applicants to undergo a lengthy and humiliating procedure. The 2012 edition of the Diagnosis and Treatment Guidelines for Gender Identity Disorder, which are non-binding, recommend three tests for a GID diagnosis: 1) a gender identity test, which is based on the testimony of the individual; 2) a biological gender test, which can contain an examination of chromosomes, an examination of hormonal action, an inspection of internal and external genitals, and "other examinations that doctors find necessary"; 3) and an exclusion of other diagnoses test to "confirm that the denial of gender identity/request for the surgery is not coming from schizophrenia nor other cultural, social, or occupational reasons." The only test that contains a reference to the time it can take is test 1, which "may last until enough information will be collected."

Kiyoshi M., a 24-year-old transgender man in Tokyo, told Human Rights Watch of his year-long effort to obtain the GID diagnosis four years ago, when he was 20 years old. On his first visit to a gender clinic in Tokyo, the psychiatrist told him to write his personal history, then return a few weeks later with a series of photos of himself from when he was a toddler through present day. "At every session I had to fill out a 100-question questionnaire," Kiyoshi M. said. According to him, the questions on the survey queried stereotypical understandings of gender-specific behaviors and appearances: "All of them were open ended questions about gender, such as 'when I was little, people told me I was____' or 'if my parent died, I would react by ____ .'"

Kiyoshi M. continued to visit that hospital for six months. "On my first time at the hospital, I told the doctor I wanted the diagnosis as soon as possible," he said. "But the doctor said to come every two weeks, then even after six months they needed more time and said they couldn't give [the diagnosis] to me so they told me to keep coming back." After six months, he gave up and started going to a second hospital in Tokyo, where the psychiatrist at the gender clinic tested him (through oral therapy sessions and interviews) for an additional six months before giving him the GID diagnosis. "Clinic staff constantly asked me at every step of the process — 'are you sure?'"

Yasuhiro D., a 30-year-old transgender man, traveled to a gender clinic 520 kilometers away from his home for six appointments over the course of two months, where he was subjected to psychiatric tests. "They showed me drawings and I had to talk to the therapist about them many times, it was extremely time consuming and repetitive" he said. "The drawings were of several people and they asked me which ones looked like my family members." Once he obtained the GID diagnosis certificate, he went to a clinic closer to Kyoto to request hormone therapy, but they told him he would have to redo all of the tests. "They said it was for a second opinion," Yasuhiro told Human Rights Watch. "Then after that second opinion was affirmative, they sent me to an external psychiatrist for a third opinion."

Hanae T., a 29-year-old transgender woman living in the Ishikawa Prefecture, told Human Rights Watch that it took her nearly a year to get the diagnosis. "I saw the psychiatrist almost the whole year. I kept seeing the psychiatrist until right before the beginning of 2011. It was in December 2010 that I got the diagnosis of GID," she said.

B. Coerced Sterilization and Compulsory Surgery

International human rights authorities have called for an identity-based model for legal recognition of gender. European regional human rights mechanisms have also developed a comparable body of work on this theme; while these have no authority over Japan's government, their work is a persuasive elucidation of the human rights arguments. Japan's legal recognition procedure is out of step with that recommended model on multiple levels, including because it effectively requires transgender people to undergo medical procedures in order to secure legal recognition of their gender identity. This has contradictory effects. To some extent the fact that gender-affirming medical procedures are available in Japan reflects advances in medical practices and the medical community's embrace of care for transgender people. But it also reinforces a pathological model that contributes to stigmatization of transgender people.

The policy of requiring individuals to be sterilized to gain legal recognition is a coercive practice that violates the rights to bodily integrity, health, and freedom from torture and other ill-treatment, among other human rights, as well as the fundamental human rights principles of autonomy and dignity.

Human Rights Watch interviewed transgender people in Japan who told U.S. that they would not have chosen sterilization if they had had the option to have their gender legally recognized without doing so. For example, Yasuhiro D., a 30-year-old transgender man in Osaka, told Human Rights Watch that the recent birth of his brother's second daughter made him reflect on how his reproductive rights were compromised in his quest to be legally recognized as a man. "Since I had my ovaries when my first niece was born, I even thought about stopping the hormones to make my body able to have children," Yasuhiro said. "I thought about this issue of having a child even as I sat waiting in the hospital for the SRS [sex reassignment surgery]. I didn't have any doubt that I wanted to live as a man, but I also wanted to preserve my ability to have a baby. I had to choose between being legally recognized for who I am and keeping my body the way I wanted it." He added, "I think a lot of transgender people want to have the surgery; however, having it as a prerequisite for LGR [legal gender recognition] means our reproductive rights are stripped away."

As Yasuhiro's account illustrates, compulsory surgery requires transgender individuals who seek legal gender recognition to make an unacceptable choice between exercising their right to recognition as a person before the law and their right to bodily autonomy.

Tamaki I., 27, a transgender woman in Osaka, said, "The hurdle is really high. I read that in America you don't need to have surgery to change your gender; you can just change your gender on the family register. If that comes true in Japan, I would want to change my gender right now. I can't understand why the government is asking for such high conditions. I do want to change my legal gender, but surgery has such a high risk, so I don't know yet."

Naoko R., 22, said, "I want to get my identification card changed. To change it on the family register, we have to get surgery. It's really a lot of pressure for me. It costs a lot, and I can't rely on my parents for help. My transgender friends are waiting for surgery, but I can't do that, so I feel like I'm becoming isolated, falling behind them. In Japan to be seen as GID we have to have a documented diagnosis. Everyone here [at the transgender support group Naoko attended] has some level of pressure about the surgery. Everyone thinks we'll have to undergo surgery in the future. That's very tough for us."

Kiyoshi M., who obtained the GID diagnosis after he spent a year visiting two clinics, and is currently taking hormones but has not had surgery explained: "Ideally I would want to just change my legal gender right now. All of these procedures are putting a lot of strain on my body that I don't want."

C. Age Restrictions on Legal Gender Recognition

Law No. 111 bars all transgender people who are younger than 20 from securing legal recognition of their gender identity. People under 20 can obtain a diagnosis (or in some cases, interviewees indicated that their psychiatrist issued them a "preliminary diagnosis) of GID, and interviewees told Human Rights Watch they used their GID diagnosis certificates to advocate for access to education according to their gender identity-including through restroom access and school uniforms according to their gender identity. In addition, the law adds an extra requirement that people under 20 need two signatures from physicians for a valid diagnosis. People who have reached Japan's age of majority (20) can independently pursue hormone treatment and surgical procedures-steps they are required by law to take in order to be legally recognized. After obtaining a GID diagnosis, a process which varies in length, the subsequent requisite medical procedures can take years and cost thousands of dollars, meaning legal gender recognition is sometimes not possible until the mid-20s even though people have expressed their gender identity and desire to legally transition more than a decade earlier.

The solution in Japan's case, however, is not simply to reduce the age at which applicants can pursue legal gender recognition under a procedure that continues to mandate GID diagnosis and medical interventions. Japan's process is coercive and invasive, and the combination of a lack of access to legal recognition for gender non-conforming children, the abuses they suffer as a result, and the rigid medical requirements for legal recognition as an adult creates significant anxiety for young people, which was evident in those Human Rights Watch interviewed.

Law No. 111's age limit is discriminatory, does not allow for the best interests of the child to be considered. This can have a harmful impact on children who are exploring and questioning their gender. A strict age limit can also violate the right to education for those transgender children who desire to attend school according to their gender identity.

In 2010 the Council of Europe Committee of Ministers called on member states to "ensure that the right to education can be effectively enjoyed without discrimination on grounds of sexual orientation or gender identity; this includes, in particular, safeguarding the right of children and youth to education in a safe environment, free from violence, bullying, social exclusion or other forms of discriminatory and degrading treatment related to sexual orientation or gender identity." In its 2015 statement on gender recognition, WPATH stated that "appropriate legal gender recognition should be available to transgender youth."

In the context of Japan's education system, the state's failure to accord legal recognition of transgender children's gender identity contributes to discrimination and degrading treatment of transgender children. Both the age restriction and the rigid medical criteria inflict significant harm on young people who instead need information, support, and safe spaces to explore and express gender-all elements of inclusive and supportive schools. What is more, the current requirement of mandatory medical procedures can cause gender non-conforming children to feel intense pressure to pursue otherwise unwanted medical procedures at a young age.

Japan's schools feature deeply -engrained gender separation and stereotypes. Nearly all junior high and high school students are required to wear gender-specific uniforms, and school activities are often gender-segregated. For children exploring their gender identity or those who identify as transgender, such an environment can be harsh. "The Japanese school system is really strict with the gender system," a transgender high school teacher told Human Rights Watch. "It imprints on students where they belong and don't belong — in later years when gender is firmly tracked, transgender kids really start suffering. They either have to conceal and lie or act like themselves and invite bullying and exclusion."

Additionally, Law No. 111's mandate of psychiatric and surgical intervention for transgender people who wish to secure legal recognition of their gender identity causes anxiety for some young people. Dozens of interviewees described to Human Rights Watch how their negative experiences in school when they were forced to dress and present as their birth-assigned sex instead of their gender identity informed their anxieties about the future, including university life and employment. Transgender children as young as 14 explained that while they do not necessarily want to undergo the medical procedures required by Law No. 111, they anxiously weigh that decision against continuing the abuse, discrimination, and exclusion they have already faced at school.

In 2015, the Ministry of Education sent a directive to all school boards titled "Regarding the Careful Response to Students with Gender Identity Disorder." The Education Ministry directive is non-binding, but sends a serious message from the ministry about schools' responsibility to care for transgender children. However, the directive's focus on diagnoses, and medical institutions as the primary source of information about gender and sexuality, reflects the government's continued reliance on the harmful pathological model of understanding transgender people's gender identity as enshrined in Law No. 111. For example, the 2015 Education Ministry directive states: "The diagnosis and advice from medical institutions is a very crucial opportunity for the school to get a professional knowledge."

In addition to the fact that the 2015 Education Ministry directive is predicated on a medical model and views children who are exploring and expressing their gender identity as "disordered," the directive's examples of support for schools to follow are not binding policy, but nonbinding recommendations. Human Rights Watch interviews with transgender children in Japan revealed that school officials issue varied responses to transgender students' requests to use facilities according to their gender identity, and in cases that occurred since its issuance, a piecemeal implementation of the new directive. Enshrining a right to legal recognition of gender based on their self-declared identity alone would substantially improve the situation for transgender children.

The right to recognition as a person before the law is articulated in the Universal Declaration of Human Rights and guaranteed in the International Covenant on Civil and Political Rights (ICCPR) and the Convention on the Rights of the Child. The right to preserve one's identity is guaranteed by article 8 of the Convention on the Rights of the Child, which specifies three aspects of identity-nationality, name, and family relations-but that list is not exhaustive. Together with the right to protection from arbitrary interference in privacy, such as ICCPR article 17, the right to preserve one's identity extends to the way one's identity is reflected on state-issued documents-including for children.

As the Convention on the Rights of the Child makes clear, "In all actions concerning children, whether undertaken by public or private social welfare institutions, courts of law, administrative authorities or legislative bodies, the best interests of the child shall be a primary consideration. This includes decisions about legal recognition of the gender identity of transgender children.

Article 12 of the Convention on the Rights of the Child provides that in determining the child's best interest, the child itself should be heard and taken into account:

1. States Parties shall assure to the child who is capable of forming his or her own views the right to express those views freely in all matters affecting the child, the views of the child being given due weight in accordance with the age and maturity of the child.

2. For this purpose, the child shall in particular be provided the opportunity to be heard in any judicial and administrative proceedings affecting the child, either directly, or through a representative or an appropriate body, in a manner consistent with the procedural rules of national law.

The Committee on the Rights of the Child has clarified the relation between articles 3 and 12 of the convention:

The purpose of article 3 is to ensure that in all actions undertaken concerning children, by a public or private welfare institution, courts, administrative authorities or legislative bodies, the best interests of the child are a primary consideration. It means that every action taken on behalf of the child has to respect the best interests of the child.... The Convention obliges States parties to assure that those responsible for these actions hear the child as stipulated in article 12. This step is mandatory.

Japan should make allowance for the fact that it may be in the best interest of many transgender children to change their legal gender before they reach 20 years old. The law should set no absolute minimum age for legal recognition of a transgender person's gender identity. Instead, in the case of children the individual circumstances of each child should be assessed to determine whether it is in that child's best interest to change their legal gender. The government should also amend its school-based policies and directives for transgender children to make it clear that no child should be required to provide a diagnosis of Gender Identity Disorder in order to wear uniforms, or access school facilities or activities according to his or her gender identity.

D. Discrimination on the Basis of Relationship Status and Parental Status

Japan's requirement that all applicants for legal gender recognition are single implies mandatory divorce for transgender people who wish to be recognized. Such a requirement is discriminatory, and has been condemned by major human rights bodies, including the 2011 and 2014 Human Rights Council resolution reports-both of which Japan voted for. The requirement that a transgender person not have biological children under the age of 20 if they wish to secure legal recognition of their gender identity violates transgender people's right to private and family life and the right to found a family, and discriminates on those grounds.

The revision of Law No. 111 in 2008 to clarify that transgender people seeking legal gender recognition must not have any children under 20 (previously the law mandated no children whatsoever), demonstrated that the government is willing to consider changes to the law, but it was an insufficient step.

Conclusion

Japan's current legal gender recognition procedure violates the rights of transgender people. It treats the fact of being transgender as a disorder-one that transgender people are required to certify that they suffer from as a prerequisite to securing legal recognition of their gender identity. It forecloses legal recognition to transgender people who are married, who have children or who have the capacity to reproduce. Not only is this discriminatory, but it forces many transgender people who want to secure legal recognition of their gender identity to contemplate invasive surgical procedures they may not want and, in some cases, requires the breakup of their families.

Human Rights Watch urges the Special Procedures mandate holders to urgently engage with the government of Japan to encourage it to separate the legal process for gender recognition from all gender-affirming healthcare-related procedures, to ensure the right of transgender children to secure recognition of their gender identity and to eliminate all discriminatory provisions from the law. Japan, a supporter of the human rights of lesbian, gay, bisexual, and transgender people globally, should become a regional leader in Asia on this issue by making transgender people's self-declared gender identity the sole criteria for legal recognition.

[End Text]

Source: Human Rights Watch Website, https://www.hrw.org/news/2016/04/01/hrw-allegation-letter-un-special-rapporteur

U.S., U.N. & Human Rights Law: Treaties & Treaty Bodies

Chapter 6

This **Chapter is About** the Human Rights treaties drafted and adopted by the states of the world at the U.N. to establish human rights norms for governments to follow. It is also about the institutional bodies created by the states parties to supervise the implementation of each of the treaties. These human rights treaty bodies are called committees. There are ten main human rights treaties in the U.N. human rights system, each with a supervising treaty body, made up of experts. This chapter is about what those treaty bodies do to ensure that the states who have ratified a treaty fulfill their obligations set forth in it, and the role the U.S. plays in fulfilling the U.S. obligations. Because of the large amount of material involved in all of the treaty bodies and their procedures, this chapter will focus only on the International Covenant on Civil and Political Rights (ICCPR), and its supervising body known as the Human Rights Committee, abbreviated HRCtee (also abbreviated "CCPR"). Information is provided to access materials for all the other U.N. treaty bodies. The Primary Source Documents in this chapter provide only small samples of the work of the bodies discussed; readers are encouraged to review the materials on treaties in Chapter 1 to deepen their understanding of treaties and their components.

This is Important Because human rights treaties are international contracts between states by which the U.S. accepts legal obligations as a member of the international community, as to how it acts in relation to human beings within its jurisdiction and control. Treaties are a source of U.S. law according to the Constitution and can be considered "the supreme law of the land" to the extent they are consistent with the Constitution. Most human rights treaties which the U.S. has ratified are within the context of the U.N. U.N. human rights treaties and treaty bodies show where the U.S. most specifically examines its own law and policy and practice of human rights. In the treaty bodies of the U.N., the U.S. is examined in the light of the treaties it told the world it will fulfill. This is where the policy, law and actions of the U.S. government are most finely scrutinized. It is in the results of these treaty bodies where Americans can find information to judge their country's human rights record in different areas such as torture, racial discrimination, or the rights of children. Americans who read the works of these treaty bodies will know what the U.S. is saying about itself and what the international community, through its human rights experts, is saying about the U.S. and human rights. These bodies have become increasingly important and confrontational in the context of the so-called "war on terrorism," as they challenge the U.S. to respect its human rights obligations while taking measures to counter terrorism.

Quotes & Key Text Excerpts

It is with great pleasure that the Government of the United States of America presents its Fourth Periodic Report to the United Nations Human Rights Committee concerning the implementation of its obligations under the International Covenant on Civil and Political Rights ("the Covenant" or "ICCPR"), in accordance with Covenant Article 40. The United States is committed to promoting and protecting human rights.

By no means is America perfect. But it is our commitment to certain universal values which allows U.S. to correct our imperfections, to improve constantly, and to grow stronger over time. Freedom of speech and assembly has allowed women, and minorities, and workers to protest for full and equal rights at a time when they were denied. The rule of law and equal administration of justice has busted monopolies, shut down political machines that were corrupt, ended abuses of power. Independent media have exposed corruption at all levels of business and government. Competitive elections allow U.S. to change course and hold our leaders accountable. If our democracy did not advance those rights, then I, as a person of African ancestry, wouldn't be able to address you as an American citizen, much less a President. Because at the time of our founding, I had no rights — people who looked like me. But it is because of that process that I can now stand before you as President of the United States.

—Remarks by President Obama at the New Economic School, Moscow, July 7, 2009.

ॐ∽⊙∽⊙∽⊙∽⊙

Treaty reporting is a way in which the Government of the United States can inform its citizens and the international community of its efforts to ensure the implementation of those obligations it has assumed, while at the same time holding itself to the public scrutiny of the international community and civil society.

As Secretary of State Hillary Clinton has stated, "Human rights are universal, but their experience is local. This is why we are committed to holding everyone to the same standard, including ourselves."

In implementing its treaty obligation under ICCPR Article 40, the United States has taken this opportunity to engage in a process of stock-taking and self-examination. The United States hopes to use this process to improve its human rights performance. Thus, this report is not an end in itself, but an important tool in the continuing development of practical and effective human rights strategies by the U.S. Government.

As President Obama has stated, "Despite the real gains that we've made, there are still laws to change and there are still hearts to open."

—Fourth Periodic Report of the United States of America to the United Nations Committee on Human Rights Concerning the International Covenant on Civil and Political Rights 2011

What You Need To Know

A. United Nations Human Rights Treaties

In the United Nations there have been many human rights treaties drafted, adopted, and ratified by states that choose to do so. The main human rights treaties are listed below. The right column includes the abbreviation for the body which supervises implementation of the treaty.

List of U.N. Human Rights Treaties

Abbreviation	Full name	Date of Adoption	Supervising body (Abbr.)
ICERD	International Convention on the Elimination of All Forms of Racial Discrimination	21 Dec 1965	CERD
ICCPR	International Covenant on Civil and Political Rights	16 Dec 1966	CCPR
ICESCR	International Covenant on Economic, Social and Cultural Rights	16 Dec 1966	CESCR
CEDAW	Convention on the Elimination of All Forms of Discrimination against Women	18 Dec 1979	CEDAW
CAT	Convention against Torture and Other Cruel, Inhuman or Degrading Treatment or Punishment	10 Dec 1984	CAT
CRC	Convention on the Rights of the Child	20 Nov 1989	CRC
ICMW	International Convention on the Protection of the Rights of All Migrant Workers and Members of Their Families	18 Dec 1990	CMW
CPED	International Convention for the Protection of All Persons from Enforced Disappearance	20 Dec 2006	CED
CRPD	Convention on the Rights of Persons with Disabilities	13 Dec 2006	CRPD
ICESCR-OP	Optional Protocol to the Covenant on Economic, Social and Cultural Rights	10 Dec 2008	CESCR
ICCPR-OP1	Optional Protocol to the International Covenant on Civil and Political Rights	16 Dec 1966	CCPR
ICCPR-OP2	Second Optional Protocol to the International Covenant on Civil and Political Rights, aiming at the abolition of the death penalty	15 Dec 1989	CCPR
OP-CEDAW	Optional Protocol to the Convention on the Elimination of Discrimination against Women	10 Dec 1999	CEDAW
OP-CRC-AC	Optional protocol to the Convention on the Rights of the Child on the involvement of children in armed conflict	25 May 2000	CRC
OP-CRC-SC	Optional protocol to the Convention on the Rights of the Child on the sale of children, child prostitution and child pornography	25 May 2000	CRC
OP-CRC-IC	Optional Protocol to the Convention on the Rights of the Child on a communications procedure	14 Apr 2014	CRC
OP-CAT	Optional Protocol to the Convention against Torture and Other Cruel, Inhuman or Degrading Treatment or Punishment	18 Dec 2002	SPT
OP-CRPD	Optional Protocol to the Convention on the Rights of Persons with Disabilities	12 Dec 2006	CRPD

These represent U.N. human rights treaties which the U.S. could chose to ratify. The U.S. has chosen to ratify only five of these treaties. Again, to ratify is to officially decide to become legally obligated to comply with it. The United States is a party to five core human rights treaties: the International Covenant on Civil and Political Rights (ICCPR); the International Convention on the Elimination of All Forms of Racial Discrimination (CERD); the Convention Against Torture and Other Cruel, Inhuman or Degrading Treatment or Punishment (CAT); and two optional protocols to the Convention on the Rights of the Child (CRC). As far as the CRC, the U.S. has ratified (acceded) not to the CRC treaty itself but only to the two Optional Protocols to the CRC, a most unusual status. The U.S. signed the treaty in 1995, but has never ratified it, making it the only state in the world which has not ratified it.

Treaties are either classified as general human rights treaties, such as the ICCPR and the ICESCR or sectoral treaties, meaning that they apply to particular groups of persons, such as children, women, migrants, racial groups, the disabled, and the disappeared. The main U.N. treaties are the ICCPR and the ICESCR. The ICCPR treats civil and political human rights such as freedom of expression, equality, the right to vote; the ICESCR treats, for example, the right to an adequate standard of living, including housing, work, education, health care, and social security.

The U.S. has ratified the ICCPR, and it is now part of U.S. law. The U.S. has had a long and unfriendly relationship with economic and social rights, calling them "not really rights," and just progressive aspirations; which has resulted in the U.S. not ratifying the ICESCR. The U.S. signed the ICESCR in 1976 and is one of five states who have signed but not ratified it. There are 165 states which have ratified it. Although the U.S. is constantly called to ratify it, political and economic reasons keep this from happening.

The text of the ICCPR and the ICESCR are included in the Primary Source Documents in Chapter 1. The reader is advised to read all of the U.N. human rights treaties to become aware of all the international human rights legal obligations which the U.S. should be following, and those not yet binding on the U.S. There should be a push to get the U.S. to ratify all of the human rights treaties so that it can truly be the champion of human rights. The U.S. compliance with its treaty obligations is still a work in progress, as it is for all countries.

In addition to being a state party to the ICCPR, the U.S. has not ratified the First Optional Protocol to the ICCPR because it does not want individual victims of U.S. violations to be able to file cases alleging violation by the U.S., though such cases can only be filed against the U.S. after the victim exhausts all domestic legal recourse in the U.S. first.

The text of the treaties listed are located in various chapters. See Appendix D: Alphabetical List of Primary Source Documents for specific locations.

For detailed information on these treaties and their treaty bodies, see the following websites:
- http://www.ohchr.org/EN/ProfessionalInterest/Pages/CoreInstruments.aspx
- http://www.ohchr.org/EN/HRBodies/Pages/HumanRightsBodies.aspx

When resorting to international human rights treaties as a basis to evaluate violations by the U.S. or any other state party, one must consider and factor in any treaty reservations, declarations, and understandings which accompanied the state's ratification or accession document. These could affect whether or not the state can be considered legally bound to act or not act in a certain way.

The Universal Declaration is not a treaty, so is not included here. It is a Declaration, not originally meant to create legal obligations, but it is now considered to contain binding legal norms under the doctrine of customary international law. The UDHR, however, served as the historical and philosophical basis for all these U.N. human rights treaties.

B. United Nations Human Rights Treaty Bodies

A treaty body is defined as a judicial organ (court or tribunal) or quasi-judicial organ (commission or committee) established by and within a treaty, under an international intergovernmental organization, to supervise and monitor compliance of states parties to the treaty norms.

Each state party to a treaty has an obligation to take steps to ensure that everyone in the state can enjoy the rights set out in the treaty. This is all about implementation. Treaty bodies are the U.N.'s way of seeing that this implementation becomes a reality and that states actually do create the conditions for implementing every right, so that it can be exercised by everyone. At the same time, it must be remembered that the international human rights legal system is subject to the principle of subsidiarity. This means that the international legal system and bodies are subsidiary to the national systems. It is at the national level, not international, that human rights are to be first and best protected. As we know, this does not always happen. The international legal system, including this U.N. treaty system, is a back up, a secondary system for when the state laws and mechanisms fail, as they sometimes do. Recourse to these international norms happens after the national system has tried and failed.

States are obligated by the terms of these treaties to transform the international norms into national norms and set up effective and accessible domestic legal procedures and remedies for protecting these rights. Even when states do transform the international norms into national law, there can still be failure to respect the norms. The international system attempts to get states to gradually improve their laws, policies, and practices by following the experts of the committees that function to see that a state complies with the terms of the treaty.

At the U.N., the different bodies which deal with human rights are known as either charter-based bodies or treaty-based bodies. Chapter 4 and 5 cover the U.N. Charter-based bodies and their procedures. This chapter covers the treaty-based bodies and procedures. All of these treaty bodies are structured similarly and set up in the text of the treaty as a body to supervise state implementation.

The ten U.N. human rights treaty bodies that monitor implementation of the core international human rights treaties are:
- Human Rights Committee (CCPR)
- Committee on Economic, Social and Cultural Rights (CESCR)
- Committee on the Elimination of Racial Discrimination (CERD)
- Committee on the Elimination of Discrimination against Women (CEDAW)
- Committee against Torture (CAT)
- Subcommittee on Prevention of Torture (SPT)
- Committee on the Rights of the Child (CRC)
- Committee on Migrant Workers (CMW)
- Committee on the Rights of Persons with Disabilities (CRPD)
- Committee on Enforced Disappearances (CED)

This chapter uses the ICCPR and the HRCtee as samples to represent all these different treaty bodies, though they are not all exactly the same. Each body sets its own rules and methods of work.

An example of a treaty article which sets up a treaty body is article 40 of the ICCPR. It states:

1. There shall be established a Human Rights Committee (hereafter referred to in the present Covenant as the Committee). It shall consist of eighteen members and shall carry out the functions hereinafter provided.

2. The Committee shall be composed of nationals of the states parties to the present Covenant who shall be persons of high moral character and recognized competence in the field of human rights, consideration being given to the usefulness of the participation of some persons having legal experience.

3. The members of the Committee shall be elected and shall serve in their personal capacity.

Each treaty body is set up by the states parties to the treaty once the treaty has entered into force. These bodies evolve over the course of time in light of the nature and amount of work they have before them. The independent experts who sit on them as members are not full-time employees of the U.N.; they are independent from the state government from their state of citizenship and independent of the U.N.

All of the treaties have the same type of article setting up the supervising body. Other articles of the treaty specify the powers and functions of the elected members.

These three main functions of the treaty bodies are explained in detail below.

1. Periodic State Reports

2. Complaints and Inquiries

3. General Comments

Periodic State Reports

In all of these treaties, one of the main procedural obligations on states parties is to submit a periodic state report to the committee. Article 40 of the ICCPR reads:

Article 40

1. The states parties to the present Covenant undertake to submit reports on the measures they have adopted which give effect to the rights recognized herein and on the progress made in the enjoyment of those rights: (a) Within one year of the entry into force of the present Covenant for the states parties concerned; (b) Thereafter whenever the Committee so requests.

2. All reports shall be submitted to the Secretary-General of the United Nations, who shall transmit them to the Committee for consideration. Reports shall indicate the factors and difficulties, if any, affecting the implementation of the present Covenant.

These periodic reports are human rights self-assessments taken by states in which they are supposed to be honest about how well or badly they are implementing all the articles in the treaty. Under article 40, the U.S. is expected to submit reports to the HRCtee every so often, supposedly every 5 years. The reporting process is very regimented and regulated. The report is to inform the committee as to what is going on in the state party in relation to the norms of the treaty.

According to the U.N., a simple way of disseminating information on what the treaty bodies do, particularly as to state reports, is found in the U.N. publication entitled *The Human Rights Treaty Bodies Protecting Your Rights*.

The Universal Declaration of Human Rights was adopted by the United Nations General Assembly in 1948. The Declaration laid the groundwork for the human rights structure that emerged in the following decades and of which the human rights expert committees, formally known as Treaty Bodies, are a key part. These committees are often described as the backbone of the international human rights protection system. Since 1948, states have adopted nine international human rights treaties and nine Optional Protocols.

United Nations Human Rights Expert Committees

When a state ratifies an international human rights treaty, it assumes the legal obligation to implement the treaty's provisions and abide by them. It also agrees to report periodically to the relevant committee on what progress it has made. For each treaty, there is a committee that reviews these reports and monitors how successfully states are implementing the rights in the treaty. The members of the committees are unpaid independent experts, nominated and elected by states. It is important that a committee's membership is drawn from different parts of the world, and from different cultural and legal backgrounds, and that there is balanced gender representation. Membership ranges from 10 to 25 experts, depending on the committee.

The Review Process

A state has to submit a report to the relevant committee every four to five years. States know well in advance when they are due to be reviewed, and when the public review session will take place. These sessions take place at the headquarters of the United Nations human rights office in Geneva, Switzerland. The review process, which takes several months, is as follows:

1. The state submits its written report.

2. A delegation from the state is invited to engage in a dialogue with the committee. This question and answer session, held in public, usually lasts one day.

3. A few days after the review, the committee issues its findings, known as Concluding Observations, highlighting progress as well as areas of concern, and making concrete recommendations for improvement.

4. The committee then sets a date by which it wants the state to report back on what steps it has taken to improve the human rights situation in the country . The committees work on a "reporting cycle" since Opportunity for input from Civil Society, National HR institutions, and U.N. system evaluation of how the treaty is being implemented in the country under review.

The exception to this process is the Subcommittee on the Prevention of Torture which does not consider state reports. Instead, it has a mandate to visit places where people are detained, including prisons, police stations, and mental health institutions, and advise on ways to prevent torture or cruel, inhuman or degrading treatment. That publication sets out the reporting cycle in a different way as follows:

- The Reporting Cycle Under the International Human Rights Treaties;
- Report — state party prepares and submits its report;
- List of Issues — The committee presents list of issues to the state party;
- Opportunity for input from Civil Society, National HR institutions, and U.N. system;
- Written Replies — state party submits written replies to list of issues;
- Dialogue — Constructive dialogue between the committee and state party delegation during session of the committee;
- Opportunity for input from Civil Society, National HR institutions, and U.N. system;
- Concluding Observations — The committee issues its concluding observations on the report, including recommendations;
- Follow-up — Procedure to follow-up on implementation of the committee's recommendations;
- Opportunity for input from Civil Society, National HR institutions, and U.N. system.

Follow-up to Reports

According to the HCtee procedure, after the adoption of the concluding observations, a follow-up procedure shall be employed in order to establish, maintain, or restore a dialogue with the state party. For this purpose and in order to enable the Committee to take further action, the Committee shall appoint a special rapporteur, who will report to the Committee. The special rapporteur will report with regard to the information received from the state party (within a specified deadline) as to the steps taken, if any, to meet the recommendations of the Committee. This sessional follow-up progress report will prompt the Committee plenary to make a determination of the date/deadline for the submission of the next report.

The Primary Source Documents in this chapter contain U.S. related documents from the HRCtee state reporting process, including the 2006 Concluding Observations of the HRCtee, the 2011 Fourth report, List of Issues and written replies, and Concluding Observations.

An increasing number of treaty bodies are now using a simplified reporting procedure based on a questionnaire sent by a committee to the state party. The state party's response forms the report required under the specific treaty. This procedure is simplified as it merges steps 1 and 2 in the cycle chart above into only one step. All documents of the reporting cycle are available at www.ohchr.org. This simplified reporting process can be seen in Primary Source Document 4.

It is important that states submit timely and informative reports. Officials from the respective ministries of the state under review are likely to be involved in preparing the information to submit to the committee. The United Nations Human Rights Office provides guidance on this, and there are substantive guidelines on how to prepare the report.

All committees welcome submissions from civil society groups, national human rights institutions, and United Nations bodies (for example, UNICEF, ILO, UNHCR, and U.N. Women). They can provide the committees with information and analysis at different stages of the review cycle. This helps the committee members get a more detailed understanding of the human rights situation in the country, so they can base their findings on multiple sources, not just the state's own evaluation of how it is doing.

NGOs submit "shadow reports" to the treaty body to help give a fuller or more accurate and correct picture of what is happening in a reporting state. Shadow reporting is an important tool for NGOs supporting women's human rights. By submitting a shadow report to a U.N. treaty body committee, NGOs can highlight issues not raised by their governments or point out where the government may be misleading the committee from the real situation. Shadow reports may be presented to all of the human rights treaty monitoring bodies. They may address the specific treaty articles or specifically mirror the country's common core document (CCD).

Treaty Reporting Guidelines

There are guidelines on how and what a state must submit in these reports. A document called the "Compilation of Guidelines on the Form and Content of Reports to be Submitted by states parties to the International Human Rights Treaties" has the guidelines for each of the treaty bodies. The compilation document with the guideline for the HRCtee as a sample set of guidelines is found in the Primary Source Document 2.

The last few U.S. reports to the HRCtee since 9/11 have been extremely interesting and full of contention between the U.S. government and the Committee, which has given an opinion that many of the U.S. anti-terrorism measures (e.g., waterboarding), and limitations of the treaty applies geographically (Guantánamo) are inconsistent with the treaty obligations of the U.S., with the U.S. arguing that the post 9/11 circumstances justify such extremes. Along with the Committee against Torture, one gets a very broad view of how these anti-terrorism measures have been evaluated by these treaty bodies in light of the treaty norms, much to the dissatisfaction of the U.S. government.

Both from the recommendations of the U.N. treaty bodies applicable to the U.S. and from the recommendations of states from the UPR outcome document, the U.S. government is getting many voices telling America how they think the government should change and act. The treaty body process is very important for the U.S. if it were sincere in wanting to improve its human rights record and with it its international image. It is fair to say that the U.S. is commonly perceived as not practicing what they preach and applying a double standard.

There is little scientific evidence of how much this treaty body process actually causes any change in the U.S. Every state reporting to treaty bodies wants to tell the world that it is the best human rights place on earth. To best evaluate these claims, one should review the state reports and the give and take with the Committee.

Complaints of Violations and Inquiries

A complaint is a written claim submitted to an international forum asking it to determine whether a state party to a treaty has violated the terms of that treaty These human rights bodies sometime provide for creation of a written complaint procedure, or one can be added by an optional protocol. They can handle complaints either from individuals against a state, or from one state party against another state party.

Several of the human rights treaties contain provisions to allow for state parties to complain to the relevant treaty body (Committee) about alleged violations of the treaty by another state party. These procedures have never been used.

When the U.S. ratified the ICCPR, it made a declaration accepting the power of the HRCtee to hear inter-state cases against it, knowing that it had never and probably would never file a case against it in that body.

Most committees can consider complaints by individuals who believe their rights have been violated. The following general conditions need to be met: 1. the state must have ratified the treaty in question; 2. the state must have agreed to be bound by the complaints process (often established in an Optional Protocol, such as the First Optional Protocol of the ICCPR); 3. the individual (or group of individuals) must have exhausted all the legal steps in their own country — the complaints process is the final option. Other specific conditions, known as admissibility criteria, apply depending on the treaty in question.

Chapter 1 explains the usual procedural flow of complaints. It includes a sample complaint petition. As stated above, the U.S. has not accepted the power of any treaty body to hear individual complaints against the U.S. Therefore, there are no decisions of any treaty body for cases against the U.S. However, in Primary Source Document 12 below, there is an excerpt of a decision of the HRCtee in *Ng v. Canada*. This was a case where a person who had committed murder in the U.S. had fled to Canada, and the U.S. was seeking his extradition back to the U.S. to face a capital murder charge. Mr.

Ng brought his case before the HRCtee by filing a complaint against Canada, which had accepted to be subject to complaints by individuals as a result of ratifying the Optional Protocol. The issues were mainly whether just sending Mr. Ng back to the U.S. by extradition to face trial and the death row syndrome of waiting years to be executed, and the very imposition of capital punishment, violated Canada's obligations under the ICCPR against torture, cruel, inhuman, and degrading treatment or punishment. The case has much to say about the U.S. and its system of criminal justice. This case presents the HRCtee's "views" as to whether a violation by Canada has been found.

Each treaty body with a complaint system has developed its jurisprudence, its case law; and this case law is used by the respective committees and sometimes by different committees, as the jurisprudence of that treaty body, which should be respected by states parties. This is because the decisions are not legally binding and are not judgments of a court, and there is no stare decisis principle involved. Again, these decisions are one of the bases of the general comments or recommendations of treaty bodies, thus increasing their importance.

The U.N. publication on treaty bodies answers the question of how you can file a complaint with a treaty body as follows:

If all above conditions are met, you can lodge a complaint with a specific committee. You don't need a lawyer, but legal advice may be helpful in drafting and submitting your complaint. You can also submit a complaint on behalf of an alleged victim, with her/his written consent. Sometimes consent is not needed; for example, if the alleged victim is in prison without access to the outside world, or is a victim of enforced disappearance.

One major change in the U.S. policy on human rights would be to get the U.S. to ratify all the U.N. human rights treaties and to accept the jurisdiction of all the treaty bodies to handle individual complaints against the U.S. The U.S. government does not want this exposure, which risks embarrassing international human rights scrutiny, because it knows that U.S. advocates will use this procedure after exhausting U.S. legal recourse. It is precisely this fear of exposure to the forum of shame that gets some states to change their ways. Again, this international system is only a back-up, a subsidiary system to keep government in check, using legal norms that the states themselves have chosen to accept and which they tell the world they will follow. If the U.S. were subject to all these treaty body complaint systems, it would affect how the government acts and what laws are passed and policies rolled out.

One other treaty body procedure described in the U.N. website is called the Inquiry procedure.

Inquiries

Upon receipt of reliable information on serious, grave, or systematic violations by a state party of the conventions they monitor, the Committee against Torture (article 20 CAT), the Committee on the Elimination of Discrimination against Women (article 8 of the Optional Protocol to CEDAW), the Committee on the Rights of Persons with Disabilities (article 6, Optional Protocol to CRPD), the Committee on Enforced Disappearances (article 33 of CED), the Committee on Economic, Social and Cultural Rights (article 11 of the Optional Protocol to ICESCR) and the Committee on the Rights of the Child (article 13 of the Optional Protocol on a communications procedure to CRC) may, on their own initiative, initiate inquiries if they have received reliable information containing well-founded indications of serious or systematic violations of the conventions in a state party.

1. The procedure may be initiated if the Committee receives reliable information indicating that the rights contained in the Convention it monitors are being systematically violated by the state party.

2. The Committee invites the state party to co-operate in the examination of the information by submitting observations.

3. The Committee may, on the basis of the state party's observations and other relevant information available to it, decide to designate one or more of its members to conduct an inquiry and report urgently to the Committee. Where warranted and with the consent of the state party concerned, an inquiry may include a visit to its territory.

4. The findings of the member(s) are then examined by the Committee and transmitted to the state party together with any comments and recommendations.

5. The state party is requested to submit its own observations on the Committee's findings, comments, and recommendations within a specific timeframe (usually six months) and, where invited by the Committee, to inform it of the measures taken in response to the inquiry.

6. The inquiry procedure is confidential, and the cooperation of the state party shall be sought at all stages of the proceedings.

General Comments/Recommendations of Human Rights Treaty Bodies

Each of the treaty bodies publishes its interpretation of the provisions of its respective human rights treaty in the form of "general comments" or "general recommendations." The Committee members use the decisions of the cases presented before it (jurisprudence) and the issues which appear before it in the periodic state reports, along with their own individual expert knowledge of human rights, to make their general comments. The General Comments tell how the articles of the treaty should be interpreted and applied. The committees are the most authoritative source of interpretation of the international human rights treaties. These comments play a key role in assisting states in implementing treaty obligations and in the development of international human rights law. It is a roadmap for state compliance.

These cover a wide range of subjects, from the comprehensive interpretation of substantive provisions, such as the right to life or the right to adequate food, to general guidance on the information that should be submitted in state reports relating to specific articles of the treaties.

General comments have also dealt with wider, cross-cutting issues, such as the role of national human rights institutions, the rights of persons with disabilities, violence against women, and the rights of minorities.

Source: OHCHR, http://www.ohchr.org/EN/HRBodies/TBPetitions/Pages/HRTBPetitions.aspx

In summary, there are many different bodies and procedures involved with human rights at the U.N., and with which the U.S. often engages or is engaged, and which could affect how the U.S. acts. It is difficult to determine how much change has occurred in the U.S. as a result of this interaction with the U.N. human rights treaty bodies and the Human Right Council. The issue is not how the U.S. acts, but rather, how can Americans become more aware of the bodies and their processes and become better informed citizens who work to make the U.S. recognize its violations and correct and improve itself as a state. The goal of this chapter is to offer the incentive and tools to become aware of human rights performance. These U.N. bodies provide a rich source of information about the U.S. and human rights, and humanitarian law and international criminal law.

Hopefully, once Americans examine this human rights picture and factor human rights into the dominant discourse of American society, the public debate will change on issues such as torture, police misconduct, gender equality, health care, immigration, and government surveillance. Currently, it is mostly through the many great human rights NGOs, including Amnesty International, Human Rights Watch, and Human Rights First, that Americans are educated in Human Rights Law.

There has been some attempt by the U.S. government to inform the (U.S.) states and other local leaders about these bodies, reports, and UPR process. Primary Source Document 13 is a letter from the U.S. Department of State legal advisors to states and other governmental bodies at all levels to make them aware of the treaty body and the U.S. activities there. Hopefully, informing constituents will be the next step.

Primary Source Documents

I. STATUS OF RATIFICATION OF U.N. HUMAN RIGHTS TREATIES

Treaty	Year	Signature	Ratification/ Accession	Key
International Convention on the Elimination of All Forms of Racial Discrimination	1969	1966	1994	***
International Covenant on Civil and Political Rights	1976	1977	1992	***
Optional Protocol to the International Covenant on Civil and Political Rights	1976	NA	NA	*
Second Optional Protocol to the International Covenant on Civil and Political Rights, aiming at the abolition of the death penalty	1991	NA	NA	*
International Covenant on Economic, Social and Cultural Rights	1976	1977	NA	**
Optional Protocol to the International Covenant on Economic, Social and Cultural Rights	2013	NA	NA	*
Convention on the Elimination of All Forms of Discrimination against Women	1981	1980	NA	**
Optional Protocol to the Convention on the Elimination of All Forms of Discrimination against Women	2000	NA	NA	*
Convention against Torture and Other Cruel, Inhuman or Degrading Treatment or Punishment	1987	1988	1994	***
Optional Protocol to the Convention against Torture and Other Cruel, Inhuman or Degrading Treatment or Punishment	2006	NA	NA	*
Convention on the Rights of the Child	1990	1995	NA	**
Optional Protocol to the Convention on the Rights of the Child on the involvement of children in armed conflict	2002	2000	2002	***
Optional Protocol to the Convention on the Rights of the Child on the sale of children, child prostitution and child pornography	2002	2000	2002	***
Optional Protocol to the Convention on the Rights of the Child on a communications procedure	2014	NA	NA	*
International Convention on the Protection of the Rights of All Migrant Workers and Members of their Families	2003	NA	NA	*
International Convention for the Protection of all Persons from Enforced Disappearance	2010	NA	NA	*
Convention on the Rights of Persons with Disabilities	2008	2009	NA	**
Optional Protocol to the Convention on the Rights of Persons with Disabilities	2008	NA	NA	*
Convention on the Rights of the Child	1990	1995	NA	*
Optional Protocol to the Convention on the Rights of the Child on a communications procedure	2014	NA	NA	*
International Convention on the Protection of the Rights of All Migrant Workers and Members of their Families	2003	NA	NA	*

Treaty	Year	Signature	Ratification/ Accession	Key
International Convention for the Protection of all Persons from Enforced Disappearance	2010	NA	NA	*
Convention on the Rights of Persons with Disabilities	2008	2009	NA	*
Optional Protocol to the Convention on the Rights of Persons with Disabilities	2008	NA	NA	*

Note: *** Treaty instruments which the U.S. has ratified, making the U.S. a state party to the treaty; ** Treaty instruments which the U.S. has signed and is therefore a signatory and for which the U.S. Senate has not yet ratified by its "advice and consent"; * Treaties which the U.S. has not signed.

Source: U.N. OHCHR, *Status of Ratification Interactive Dashboard, http://indicators.ohchr.org*

2. COMPILATION OF GUIDELINES ON THE FORM AND CONTENT OF REPORTS TO BE SUBMITTED BY STATES PARTIES TO THE INTERNATIONAL HUMAN RIGHTS TREATIES, 2009

This document from the U.N. sets forth guidelines for states when preparing and submitting their periodic reports for all the U.N. treaty bodies. It contains only the guidelines regarding the International Covenant on Civil and Political Rights. Guidelines for other treaty bodies can be found at the Source following this text. Because there are a lot of states involved and a lot of reports filed, the U.N., particularly the Office of the High Commissioner for Human Rights, wants a certain uniformity in the reports and so sets out guidelines. Each treaty body wrote its own rules and guidelines. This document contains the guidelines for all the treaty bodies but only the Human Rights Committee reporting procedure is covered. The rest of the treaty body guidelines can found in the whole document; see Source at the end of the text. When the U.S. is preparing its reports it is expected to follow these guidelines.

{Excerpt}

[Text]

International Human Rights Instruments

Report of the Secretary-General

In its resolutions 52/118 and 53/138, the General Assembly requested the Secretary-General to compile in a single volume the guidelines regarding the form and content of reports to be submitted by States parties that have been issued by the Human Rights Committee, the Committee on Economic, Social and Cultural Rights, the Committee on the Elimination of Discrimination against Women, the Committee on the Elimination of Racial Discrimination, the Committee on the Rights of the Child and the Committee against Torture. This compilation was prepared pursuant to that request and is being updated on a regular basis. In addition to the guidelines issued by the above bodies, the updated compilation contains guidelines for reports to be submitted to the Committee on Migrant Workers, and harmonized guidelines on reporting under the international human rights treaties, including guidelines on a common core document.

Chapter I

Harmonized Guidelines on Reporting Under The International Human Rights Treaties, Including Guidelines on a Core Document and Treaty-Specific Documents

Purpose of guidelines

1. These guidelines are intended to guide States parties in fulfilling their reporting obligations under:

- Article 40 of the International Covenant on Civil and Political Rights, reporting to the Human Rights Committee (CCPR)
- Articles 16 and 17 of the International Covenant on Economic, Social and Cultural Rights, reporting to the Committee on Economic, Social and Cultural Rights (CESCR)
- Article 9 of the International Convention on the Elimination of All Forms of Racial Discrimination, reporting to the Committee on the Elimination of Racial Discrimination (CERD)
- Article 18 of the Convention on the Elimination of All Forms of Discrimination against Women, reporting to the Committee on the Elimination of Discrimination Against Women (CEDAW)
- Article 19 of the Convention Against Torture and Other Cruel, Inhuman or Degrading Treatment and Punishment, reporting to the Committee Against Torture (CAT)
- Article 44 of the Convention on the Rights of the Child, reporting to the Committee on the Rights of the Child (CRC)
- Article 73 of the International Convention on the Protection of the Rights of All Migrant Workers and Members of Their Families, reporting to the Committee on Migrant Workers (CMW)

These guidelines do not apply to initial reports prepared by States under article 8 of the Optional Protocol to the Convention on the Rights of the Child on the involvement of children in armed conflict nor article 12 of the Optional Protocol to the Convention on the Rights of the Child on the sale of children, child prostitution and child pornography, although States may wish to consider the information provided in those reports when preparing their reports for the treaty bodies.

2. States parties to each of these human rights treaties undertake, in accordance with the provisions (reproduced in Appendix 1), to submit to the relevant treaty body initial and periodic reports on the measures, including legislative, judicial, administrative or other measures, which they have adopted in order to achieve the enjoyment of the rights recognized in the treaty.

3. Reports presented in accordance with the present harmonized guidelines will enable each treaty body and State party to obtain a complete picture of the implementation of the relevant treaties, set within the wider context of the State's international human rights obligations, and provide a uniform framework within which each committee, in collaboration with the other treaty bodies, can work.

4. The harmonized guidelines aim at strengthening the capacity of States to fulfil their reporting obligations in a timely and effective manner, including the avoidance of unnecessary duplication of information. They also aim at improving the effectiveness of the treaty monitoring system by:

(a) Facilitating a consistent approach by all committees in considering the reports presented to them;

(b) Helping each committee to consider the situation regarding human rights in every State party on an equal basis; and

(c) Reducing the need for a committee to request supplementary information before considering a report.

5. Where considered appropriate, and in accordance with the provisions of their respective treaties, each treaty body may request additional information from States parties for the purpose of fulfilling its mandate to review the implementation of the treaty.

6. The harmonized guidelines are divided into three sections. Sections I and II apply to all reports being prepared for submission to any of the treaty bodies, and offer general guidance on the recommended approach to the reporting process and the recommended form of reports, respectively. Section III provides guidance to States parties on the contents of reports, i.e. the common core document to be submitted to all treaty bodies and the treaty-specific document to be submitted to each treaty body.

I. THE REPORTING PROCESS

Purpose of reporting

7. The reporting system as described in these guidelines is intended to provide a coherent framework within which States can meet their reporting obligations under all of the international human rights treaties to which they are a party through a coordinated and streamlined process.

Commitment to treaties

8. The reporting process constitutes an essential element in the continuing commitment of a State to respect, protect and fulfil the rights set out in the treaties to which it is party. This commitment should be viewed within the wider context of the obligation of all States to promote respect for the rights and freedoms, set out in the Universal Declaration of Human Rights and international human rights instruments, by measures, national and international, to secure their universal and effective recognition and observance.

Review of the implementation of human rights at the national level

9. States parties should see the process of preparing their reports for the treaty bodies not only as an aspect of the fulfilment of their international obligations, but also as an opportunity to take stock of the state of human rights protection within their jurisdiction for the purpose of policy planning and implementation. The report preparation process thus offers an occasion for each State party to:

(a) Conduct a comprehensive review of the measures it has taken to harmonize national law and policy with the provisions of the relevant international human rights treaties to which it is a party;

(b) Monitor progress made in promoting the enjoyment of the rights set forth in the treaties in the context of the promotion of human rights in general;

(c) Identify problems and shortcomings in its approach to the implementation of the treaties; and

(d) Plan and develop appropriate policies to achieve these goals.

10. The reporting process should encourage and facilitate, at the national level, public scrutiny of government policies and constructive engagement with relevant actors of civil society conducted in a spirit of cooperation and mutual respect, with the aim of advancing the enjoyment by all of the rights protected by the relevant convention.

Basis for constructive dialogue at the international level

11. At the international level, the reporting process creates a basis for constructive dialogue between States and the treaty bodies. The treaty bodies, in providing these guidelines, wish to emphasize their supportive role in fostering effective national implementation of the international human rights instruments.

Collection of data and drafting of reports

12. All States are parties to at least one of the main international human rights treaties the implementation of which is monitored by independent treaty bodies (see paragraph 1), and more than seventy-five per cent are party to four or more. As a consequence, all States have reporting obligations to fulfil and should benefit from adopting a coordinated approach to their reporting for each respective treaty body.

13. States should consider setting up an appropriate institutional framework for the preparation of their reports. These institutional structures-which could include an inter-ministerial drafting committee and/or focal points on reporting within each relevant government department-could support all of the State's reporting obligations under the international human rights instruments and, as appropriate, related international treaties (for example, Conventions of the International Labour Organization and the United Nations Educational, Scientific and Cultural Organization), and could provide an effective mechanism to coordinate follow-up to the concluding observations of the treaty bodies. Such structures should allow for the involvement of sub-national levels of governance where these exist and could be established on a permanent basis.

14. Institutional structures of this nature could also support States in meeting other reporting commitments, for example to follow up on international conferences and summits, monitor implementation of the Millennium Development

Goals, etc. Much of the information collected and collated for such reports may be useful in the preparation of States' reports to the treaty bodies.

15. These institutional structures should develop an efficient system for the collection (from the relevant ministries and government statistical offices) of all statistical and other data relevant to the implementation of human rights, in a comprehensive and continuous manner. States can benefit from technical assistance from the Office of the United Nations High Commissioner for Human Rights (OHCHR) in collaboration with the Division for the Advancement of Women (DAW), and from relevant United Nations agencies.

Periodicity

16. In accordance with the terms of the relevant treaty, each State party undertakes to submit an initial report on the measures in place or taken to give effect to that treaty's provisions within a specified period after the treaty's entry into force for the reporting State. Thereafter, States parties are required to submit further reports periodically, in accordance with the provisions of each treaty, on the progress made during the reporting period. The periodicity of reports varies from treaty to treaty.

17. Reports under the revised reporting system will consist of two parts: the common core document and the treaty-specific document. In accordance with the different periodicity requirements of treaties, submission of these reports under different treaties may not be due at the same time. However, States could coordinate the preparation of their reports in consultation with the relevant treaty bodies with a view to submitting their reports not only in a timely manner, but with as little time lag between the different reports as possible. This will ensure that States receive the full benefit of submitting information required by several treaty bodies in a common core document.

18. States should keep their common core documents current. States should endeavour to update the common core document whenever they submit a treaty-specific document. If no update is considered necessary, this should be stated in the treaty-specific document.

II. THE FORM OF REPORTS

19. Information which a State considers relevant to assisting the treaty bodies in understanding the situation in the country should be presented in a concise and structured way. Although it is understood that some States have complex constitutional arrangements which need to be reflected in their reports, reports should not be of excessive length. If possible, common core documents should not exceed 60-80 pages, initial treaty-specific documents should not exceed 60 pages, and subsequent periodic documents should be limited to 40 pages. Pages should be formatted for A4-size paper, with 1.5 line spacing, and text set in 12 point Times New Roman type. Reports should be submitted in electronic form (on diskette, CD-ROM or by electronic mail), accompanied by a printed paper copy.

20. States may wish to submit separately copies of the principal legislative, judicial, administrative and other texts referred to in the reports, where these are available in a working language of the relevant committee. These texts will not be reproduced for general distribution, but will be made available to the relevant committee for consultation.

21. Reports should contain a full explanation of all abbreviations used in the text, especially when referring to national institutions, organizations, laws, etc., that are not likely to be readily understood outside of the State party.

22. Reports must be submitted in one of the official languages of the United Nations (Arabic, Chinese, English, French, Russian or Spanish).

23. Reports should be comprehensible and accurate when submitted to the Secretary-General. In the interests of efficiency, reports submitted by States whose official language is one of the official languages of the United Nations will not necessarily be edited by the Secretariat. Reports submitted by States whose official language is not one of the official languages of the United Nations may be edited by the Secretariat. Reports which, upon receipt, are found to be manifestly incomplete or require significant editing may be returned to the State for modification before being officially accepted by the Secretary-General.

III. THE CONTENT OF REPORTS

General

24. Both the common core document and the treaty-specific document form an integral part of each State's reports. Reports should contain information sufficient to provide each respective treaty body with a comprehensive understanding of the implementation of the relevant treaty by the State.

25. Reports should elaborate both the *de jure* and the *de facto* situation with regard to the implementation of the provisions of the treaties to which States are a party. Reports should not be confined to lists or descriptions of legal instruments adopted in the country concerned in recent years, but should indicate how those legal instruments are reflected in the actual political, economic, social and cultural realities and general conditions existing in the country.

26. Reports should provide relevant statistical data, disaggregated by sex, age, and population groups, which may be presented together in tables annexed to the report. Such information should allow comparison over time and should indicate data sources. States should endeavour to analyze this information insofar as it is relevant to the implementation of treaty obligations.

27. The common core document should contain information of a general and factual nature relating to the implementation of the treaties to which the reporting State is party and which may be of relevance to all or several treaty bodies. A treaty body may request that the common core document be updated if it considers that the information it contains is out of date. Updates may be submitted in the form of an addendum to the existing common core document or a new revised version, depending on the extent of the changes which need to be incorporated.

28. States preparing a common core document for the first time and which have already submitted reports to any of the treaty bodies may wish to integrate into the common core document information contained in those reports, insofar as it remains current.

29. The treaty-specific document should contain information relating to the implementation of the treaty which the relevant committee monitors. In particular, recent developments in law and practice affecting the enjoyment of rights under that treaty should be included, as well as — except for initial treaty-specific documents — a response to issues raised by the committee in its concluding observations or its general comments.

30. Each document may be submitted separately — though States are referred to consider paragraph 17 — the procedure for reporting will be as follows:

(a) The State party submits the common core document to the Secretary-General which is then transmitted to each of the treaty bodies monitoring the implementation of the treaties to which the State is party;

(b) The State party submits treaty-specific documents to the Secretary-General which are then transmitted to the specific treaty bodies concerned;

(c) Each treaty body considers the State party's report on the treaty the implementation of which it monitors, consisting of the common core document and the treaty-specific document, according to its own procedures.

FIRST PART OF REPORTS: THE COMMON CORE DOCUMENT

31. For convenience, the common core document should be structured using the headings contained in sections 1-3 in accordance with the guidelines. The common core document should include the following information.

1. General information about the reporting State

32. This section should present general factual and statistical information relevant to assisting the committees in understanding the political, legal, social, economic and cultural context in which human rights are implemented in the State concerned.

A. Demographic, economic, social and cultural characteristics of the State

33. States may provide background information on the national characteristics of the country. States should refrain from providing detailed historical narratives; it is sufficient to provide a concise account of key historical facts where these are necessary to assist the treaty bodies in understanding the context of the State's implementation of the treaties.

34. States should provide accurate information about the main demographic and ethnic characteristics of the country and its population, taking into account the list of indicators contained in the section "Demographic indicators" in Appendix 3.

35. States should provide accurate information on the standard of living of the different segments of the population, taking into account the list of indicators contained in the section "Social, Economic and Cultural Indicators" in Appendix 3.

B. Constitutional, political and legal structure of the State

36. States should provide a description of the constitutional structure and the political and legal framework of the State, including the type of government, the electoral system, and the organization of the executive, legislative and judicial organs. States are also encouraged to provide information about any systems of customary or religious law that may exist in the State.

37. States should provide information on the principal system through which non-governmental organizations are recognized as such, including through registration where registration laws and procedures are in place, granting of non-profit status for tax purposes, or other comparable means.

38. States should provide information on the administration of justice. They should include accurate information on crime figures, including inter alia, information indicating the profile of perpetrators and victims of crime and sentences passed and carried out.

39. Information submitted in respect of paragraphs 36 to 38 should take into account the list of indicators contained in the section "Indicators on the Political System" and "Indicators on Crime and the Administration of Justice" in Appendix 3.

2. General framework for the protection and promotion of human rights

C. Acceptance of international human rights norms

40. States should provide information on the status of all of the main international human rights treaties. Information may be organized in the form of a chart or table. It should include information on:

(a) *Ratification of main international human rights instruments.* Information on the status of ratification of the main international human rights treaties and optional protocols listed in Appendix 2, Section A, indicating if and when the State envisages acceding to those instruments to which it is not yet a party or which it has signed but has not yet ratified.

(i) Information on the acceptance of treaty amendments;

(ii) Information on the acceptance of optional procedures.

(b) *Reservations and declarations.* Where a State has entered reservations to any of the treaties to which it is a party, the common core document should provide information on:

(i) The nature and scope of such reservations;

(ii) The reason why such reservations were considered to be necessary and have been maintained;

(iii) The precise effect of each reservation in terms of national law and policy;

(iv) In the spirit of the World Conference on Human Rights and other similar conferences which encouraged States to consider reviewing any reservation with a view to withdrawing it,1 any plans to limit the effect of reservations and ultimately withdraw them within a specific time frame.

(c) *Derogations, restrictions, or limitations.* Where States have restricted, limited or derogated from the provisions of any of the treaties to which they are a party, the common core document should include information explaining the scope of such derogations, restrictions or limitations; the circumstances justifying them; and the timeframe envisaged for their withdrawal.

41. States may wish to include information relating to their acceptance of other international norms related to human rights, especially where this information is directly relevant to each State's implementation of the provisions of the main international human rights treaties. In particular, the attention of States is drawn to the following relevant sources of information:

(a) *Ratification of other United Nations human rights and related treaties.* States may indicate whether they are party to any of the other United Nations conventions related to human rights listed in Appendix 2, Section B;

(b) *Ratification of other relevant international conventions.* States are encouraged to indicate whether they are party to the international conventions relevant to human rights protection and humanitarian law listed in Appendix 2, Sections C to F;

(c) *Ratification of regional human rights conventions.* States may indicate whether they are party to any regional human rights conventions.

D. Legal framework for the protection of human rights at the national level

42. States should set out the specific legal context for the protection of human rights in the country. In particular, information should be provided on:

(a) Whether, and if so, which of the rights referred to in the various human rights instruments are protected either in the constitution, a bill of rights, a basic law, or other national legislation and, if so, what provisions are made for derogations, restrictions or limitations and in what circumstances;

(b) Whether human rights treaties have been incorporated into the national legal system;

(c) Which judicial, administrative or other authorities have competence affecting human rights matters and the extent of such competence;

(d) Whether the provisions of the various human rights instruments can be, and have been, invoked before, or directly enforced by, the courts, other tribunals or administrative authorities;

(e) What remedies are available to an individual who claims that any of his or her rights have been violated, and whether any systems of reparation, compensation and rehabilitation exist for victims;

(f) Whether any institutions or national machinery exist with responsibility for overseeing the implementation of human rights, including machinery for the advancement of women or intended to address the particular situations of children, the elderly, persons with disabilities, those belonging to minorities, indigenous peoples, refugees and internally-displaced persons, migrant workers, non-authorized aliens, non-citizens or others, the mandate of such institutions, the human and financial resources available to them, and whether policies and mechanisms for gender mainstreaming and corrective measures exist;

(g) Whether the State accepts the jurisdiction of any regional human rights court or other mechanism and, if so, the nature and progress of any recent or pending cases.

E. Framework within which human rights are promoted at the national level

43. States should set out the efforts made to promote respect for all human rights in the State. Such promotion may encompass actions by government officials, legislatures, local assemblies, national human rights institutions, etc, together with the role played by the relevant actors in civil society. States may offer information on measures such as dissemination of information, education and training, publicity, and allocation of budgetary resources. In describing these in the common core document, attention should be paid to the accessibility of promotional materials and human rights instruments, including their availability in all relevant national, local, minority or indigenous languages. In particular, States should provide information on:

(a) *National and regional parliaments and assemblies.* The role and activities of the national parliament and sub-national, regional, provincial or municipal assemblies or authorities in promoting and protecting human rights, including those contained in international human rights treaties;

(b) *National human rights institutions.* Any institutions created for the protection and promotion of human rights at the national level, including those with specific responsibilities with regard to gender equality for all, race relations and children's rights, their precise mandate, composition, financial resources and activities, and whether such institutions are independent;2

(c) *Dissemination of human rights instruments.* The extent to which each of the international human rights instruments to which the State is party have been translated, published and disseminated within the country;

(d) Raising human rights awareness among public officials and other professionals. Any measures taken to ensure adequate education and training in human rights for those with responsibilities for the implementation of the law, such as Government officials, police, immigration officers, prosecutors, judges, lawyers, prison officers, members of the armed forces, border guards, as well as teachers, medical doctors, health workers and social workers;

(e) Promotion of human rights awareness through educational programmes and Government-sponsored public information. Any measures taken to promote respect for human rights through education and training, including Government-sponsored public information campaigns. Details should be provided on the extent of human rights education within schools, (public or private, secular or religious) at various levels;

(f) Promotion of human rights awareness through the mass media. The role of the mass information media, such as the press, radio, television and internet, in publicizing and disseminating information about human rights, including the international human rights instruments;

(g) Role of civil society, including non-governmental organizations. The extent of the participation of civil society, in particular non-governmental organizations, in the promotion and protection of human rights within the country, and the steps taken by the Government to encourage and promote the development of a civil society with a view to ensuring the promotion and protection of human rights;

(h) *Budget allocations and trends.* Where available, budget allocations and budgetary trends, as percentages of national or regional budgets and gross domestic product (GDP) and disaggregated by sex and age for the implementation of the State's human rights obligations and the results of any relevant budget impact assessments;

(i) *Development cooperation and assistance.* The extent to which the State benefits from development cooperation or other assistance which supports human rights promotion, including budgetary allocations. Information on the extent to which the State provides development cooperation or assistance to other States which supports the promotion of human rights in those countries.

44. The reporting State may indicate any factors or difficulties of a general nature affecting or impeding the implementation of international human rights obligations at the national level.

F. Reporting process at the national level

45. States should provide information on the process by which both parts of their reports (common core document and treaty-specific documents) are prepared, including on:

(a) The existence of a national coordinating structure for reporting under the treaties;

(b) Participation of departments, institutions and officials at national, regional and local levels of governance and, where appropriate, at federal and provincial levels;

(c) Whether reports are made available to or examined by the national legislature prior to submission to the treaty monitoring bodies;

(d) The nature of the participation of entities outside of government or relevant independent bodies at the various stages of the report preparation process or follow-up to it, including monitoring, public debate on draft reports, translation, dissemination or publication, or other activities explaining the report or concluding observations of the treaty bodies. Such participants may include human rights institutions (national or otherwise), non-governmental organizations, or other relevant actors of civil society, including those persons and groups most affected by the relevant provisions of the treaties;

(e) Events, such as parliamentary debates and governmental conferences, workshops, seminars, radio or television broadcasts, and publications issued explaining the report, or any other similar events undertaken during the reporting period.

Follow-up to concluding observations of human rights treaty bodies

46. States should provide general information in the common core document on the measures and procedures adopted or foreseen, if any, to ensure effective follow-up to and wide dissemination of the concluding observations or recommendations issued by any of the treaty bodies after consideration of the State's reports, including any parliamentary hearing or media coverage.

G. Other related human rights information

47. States are invited to consider, where appropriate, the following additional sources of information for inclusion in their common core document.

Follow-up to international conferences

48. States may provide general information on follow-up to the declarations, recommendations, and commitments adopted at world conferences and subsequent reviews insofar as these have a bearing on the human rights situation in the country.

49. Where such conferences include reporting procedures (eg, the Millennium Summit), States may integrate the relevant information contained in those reports in the common core document.

3. Information on non-discrimination and equality and effective remedies

Non-discrimination and equality

50. States should provide in their common core document general information on the implementation of its obligations to guarantee equality before the law and equal protection of the law for everyone within their jurisdiction, in accordance with the relevant international human rights instruments, including information on the legal and institutional structures.

51. The common core document should include general factual information on measures taken to eliminate discrimination in all its forms and on all grounds, including multiple discrimination, in the enjoyment of civil, political, economic, social and cultural, rights, and on measures to promote formal and substantive equality for everyone within the jurisdiction of the State.

52. It should contain general information on whether the principle of non-discrimination is included as a general binding principle in a basic law, the constitution, a bill of rights or in any other domestic legislation and the definition of and

legal grounds for prohibiting discrimination (if not already provided in para. 42(a)) . Information should also be provided on whether the legal system allows for or mandates special measures to guarantee full and equal enjoyment of human rights.

53. Information should be provided on steps taken to ensure that discrimination in all its forms and on all grounds is prevented and combated in practice, including information on the manner and the extent to which the provisions of the existing penal laws, as applied by the courts, effectively implement the State parties' obligations under the principal human rights instruments.

54. States should provide general information regarding the human rights situation of persons belonging to specific vulnerable groups in the population.

55. States should provide information on specific measures adopted to reduce economic, social and geographical disparities, including between rural and urban areas, to prevent discrimination, as well as situations of multiple discrimination, against the persons belonging to the most disadvantaged groups.

56. States should provide general information on the measures, including educational programmes and public information campaigns, that have been taken to prevent and eliminate negative attitudes to, and prejudice against, individuals and groups which prevent them from fully enjoying their human rights.

57. States should provide general information on the implementation of their international obligations to guarantee equality before the law and equal protection of the law for everyone within their jurisdiction, in accordance with the international human rights instruments.

58. States should provide general information on the adoption of temporary special measures in specific circumstances to help accelerate progress towards equality. Where such measures have been adopted, States should indicate the expected timeframe for the attainment of the goal of equality of opportunity and treatment and the withdrawal of such measures.

Effective remedies

59. States should include general information in the common core document on the nature and scope of remedies provided in their domestic legislation against violations of human rights and whether victims have effective access to these remedies (if not already provided in para. 42(e)) .

SECOND PART OF REPORTS: THE TREATY-SPECIFIC DOCUMENT

60. The treaty-specific document should contain all information relating to States' implementation of each specific treaty which is relevant principally to the committee charged with monitoring the implementation of that treaty. This part of the report allows States to focus their attention on the specific issues relating to the implementation of the respective Convention. The treaty-specific document should include the information requested by the relevant committee in its most current treaty-specific guidelines. The treaty-specific document should include, where applicable, information on the steps taken to address issues raised by the committee in its concluding observations on the State party's previous report.

Appendix 1

Mandate of treaty bodies to request reports from States parties

...

International Covenant on Civil and Political Rights

Article 40

1. The States Parties to the present Covenant undertake to submit reports on the measures they have adopted which give effect to the rights recognized herein and on the progress made in the enjoyment of those rights:

    (a) Within one year of the entry into force of the present Covenant for the States Parties concerned;

    (b) Thereafter whenever the Committee so requests.

2. All reports shall be submitted to the Secretary-General of the United Nations, who shall transmit them to the Committee for consideration. Reports shall indicate the factors and difficulties, if any, affecting the implementation of the present Covenant.

3. The Secretary-General of the United Nations may, after consultation with the Committee, transmit to the specialized agencies concerned copies of such parts of the reports as may fall within their field of competence.

4. The Committee shall study the reports submitted by the States Parties to the present Covenant. It shall transmit its reports, and such general comments as it may consider appropriate, to the States Parties. The Committee may also transmit to the Economic and Social Council these comments along with the copies of the reports it has received from States Parties to the present Covenant.

5. The States Parties to the present Covenant may submit to the Committee observations on any comments that may be made in accordance with paragraph 4 of this article.

    (a) Within two years of the entry into force of the Convention for the State Party concerned;

    (b) Thereafter every five years.

2. Reports made under the present article shall indicate factors and difficulties, if any, affecting the degree of fulfilment of the obligations under the present Convention. Reports shall also contain sufficient information to provide the Committee with a comprehensive understanding of the implementation of the Convention in the country concerned.

3. A State Party which has submitted a comprehensive initial report to the Committee need not, in its subsequent reports submitted in accordance with paragraph 1 (b) of the present article, repeat basic information previously provided.

4. The Committee may request from States Parties further information relevant to the implementation of the Convention.

5. The Committee shall submit to the General Assembly, through the Economic and Social Council, every two years, reports on its activities.

6. States Parties shall make their reports widely available to the public in their own countries.

Appendix 2

Partial list of major international conventions relating to issues of human rights

A. Main international human rights conventions and protocols
- International Covenant on Economic, Social and Cultural Rights (ICESCR), 1966
- International Covenant on Civil and Political Rights (ICCPR), 1966
- International Convention on the Elimination of All Forms of Racial Discrimination, (ICERD), 1965
- Convention on the Elimination of All Forms of Discrimination against Women (CEDAW), 1979
- Convention against Torture and Other Cruel, Inhuman or Degrading Treatment or Punishment (CAT), 1984
- Convention on the Rights of the Child (CRC), 1989
- International Convention on the Protection of the Rights of All Migrant Workers and Members of Their Families, (ICMW), 1990
- Optional Protocol to the CRC on the involvement of children in armed conflict, 2000

- Optional Protocol to the CRC on the sale of children, child prostitution, and child pornography, 2000
- Optional Protocol to ICCPR, concerning individual petition, 1966
- Second Optional Protocol to ICCPR, concerning abolition of the death penalty, 1989
- Optional Protocol to CEDAW, concerning individual complaints and inquiry procedures, 1999
- Optional Protocol to CAT, concerning regular visits by national and international institutions to places of detention, 2002

...

Appendix 3

Indicators for assessing the implementation of human rights

Demographic indicators

Reporting States should provide accurate information, where available, about the main demographic characteristics and trends of its population, including the following. The information should cover at least the last five years and be disaggregated by sex, age, and main population groups.

- Population size
- Population growth rate
- Population density
- Population distribution by mother tongue, religion and ethnicity, in rural and urban areas
- Age-composition
- Dependency ratio (percentage of population under 15 and over 65 years of age)
- Statistics on births and deaths
- Life expectancy
- Fertility rate
- Average household size
- Proportion of single-parent households and households headed by women
- Proportion of population in rural and urban areas

Social, economic and cultural indicators

Reporting States should provide information reflecting the standard of living, including the following, covering at least the last five years and disaggregated by sex, age, and main population groups:

- Share of (household) consumption expenditures on food, housing, health and education
- Proportion of population below the national poverty line
- Proportion of population below the minimum level of dietary consumption
- Gini coefficient (relating to distribution of income or household consumption expenditure)
- Prevalence of underweight children under five years of age
- Infant and maternal mortality rates
- Percentage of women of child-bearing age using contraception or whose partner is using contraception
- Medical terminations of pregnancy as a proportion of live births
- Rates of infection of HIV/AIDS and major communicable diseases
- Prevalence of major communicable and non-communicable diseases
- Ten major causes of death
- Net enrolment ratio in primary and secondary education
- Attendance and drop-out rates in primary and secondary education
- Teacher-student ratio in public funded schools
- Literacy rates
- Unemployment rate
- Employment by major sectors of economic activity, including break-down between the formal and informal sectors
- Work participation rates

- Proportion of work force registered with trade unions
- Per capita income
- Gross domestic product (GDP)
- Annual growth rate
- Gross National Income (GNI)
- Consumer Price Index (CPI)
- Social expenditures (e.g., food, housing, health, education, social protection, etc.) as proportion of total public expenditure and GDP
- External and domestic public debt
- Proportion of international assistance provided in relation to the State budget by sector and in relation to GNI

Indicators on the political system

Reporting States should provide information on the following, covering at least the last five years and disaggregated by sex, age, and main population groups:

- Number of recognized political parties at the national level
- Proportion of population eligible to vote
- Proportion of non-citizen adult population registered to vote
- Number of complaints on the conduct of elections registered, by type of alleged irregularity
- Population coverage and breakdown of ownership of major media channels (electronic, print, audio, etc.)
- Number of recognized non-governmental organizations
- Distribution of legislative seats by party
- Percentage of women in parliament
- Proportions of national and sub-national elections held within the schedule laid out by law
- Average voter turnouts in the national and sub-national elections by administrative unit (eg, states or provinces, districts, municipalities and villages)

Indicators on crime and the administration of justice

Reporting States should provide information on the following, covering at least the last five years and disaggregated by sex, age, and main population groups:

- Incidence of violent death and life threatening crimes reported per 100,000 persons
- Number of persons and rate (per 100,000 persons) who were arrested/brought before a court\convicted\ sentenced\incarcerated for violent or other serious crimes (such as homicide, robbery, assault and trafficking)
- Number of reported cases of sexually motivated violence (such as rape, female genital mutilation, honour crimes and acid attacks)
- Maximum and average time of pre-trial detention
- Prison population with breakdown by offence and length of sentence
- Incidence of death in custody
- Number of persons executed under the death penalty per year
- Average backlog of cases per judge at different levels of the judicial system
- Number of police\security personnel per 100,000 persons
- Number of prosecutors and judges per 100,000 persons
- Share of public expenditure on police\security and judiciary
- Of the accused and detained persons who apply for free legal aid, the proportion of those who receive it
- Proportion of victims compensated after adjudication, by type of crime.

...

Chapter III

HUMAN RIGHTS COMMITTEE

A. Introduction

l. These guidelines replace all earlier versions issued by the Human Rights Committee, which may now be disregarded (CCPR/C/19/Rev. 1 of 26 August 1982, CCPR/C/5/Rev. 2 of 28 April 1995 and Annex VIII to the Committee's 1998 report to the General Assembly (A/53/40)) ; the Committee's general comment 2 (13) of 1981 is also superseded. The present guidelines do not affect the Committee's procedure in relation to any special reports which may be requested.

2. These guidelines will be effective for all reports to be presented after 31 December 1999.

3. The guidelines should be followed by States parties in the preparation of initial and all subsequent periodic reports.

4. Compliance with these guidelines will reduce the need for the Committee to request further information when it proceeds to consider a report; it will also help the Committee to consider the situation regarding human rights in every State party on an equal basis.

B. Framework of the Covenant concerning reports

1. Every State party, upon ratifying the Covenant, undertakes, under article 40, to submit, within a year of the Covenant's entry into force for that State, an initial report on the measures it has adopted which give effect to the rights recognized in the Covenant ("Covenant rights") and progress made in their enjoyment; and thereafter periodic reports whenever the Committee so requests.

2. For subsequent periodic reports the Committee has adopted a practice of stating, at the end of its concluding observations, a date by which the following periodic report should be submitted.

C. General guidance for contents of all reports

1. *The articles and the Committee's general comments.* The terms of the articles in Parts I, II and III of the Covenant must, together with general comments issued by the Committee on any such article, be taken into account in preparing the report.

2. *Reservations and declarations.* Any reservation to or declaration as to any article of the Covenant by the State party should be explained and its continued maintenance justified.

3. *Derogations.* The date, extent and effect of, and procedures for imposing and for lifting any derogation under article 4 should be fully explained in relation to every article of the Covenant affected by the derogation.

4. *Factors and difficulties.* Article 40 of the Covenant requires that factors and difficulties, if any, affecting the implementation of the Covenant should be indicated. A report should explain the nature and extent of, and reasons for every such factor and difficulty, if any such exist; and should give details of the steps being taken to overcome these.

5. *Restrictions or limitations.* Certain articles of the Covenant permit some defined restrictions or limitations on rights. Where these exist, their nature and extent should be set out.

6. *Data and statistics.* A report should include sufficient data and statistics to enable the Committee to assess progress in the enjoyment of Covenant rights, relevant to any appropriate article.

7. *Article 3.* The situation regarding the equal enjoyment of Covenant rights by men and women should be specifically addressed.

8. *Core document.* Where the State party has already prepared a core document, this will be available to the Committee: it should be updated as necessary in the report, particularly as regards "General legal framework" and "Information and publicity" (HRI/CORE/1, see chapter 1 of the present document) .

D. The initial report

1. General.

This report is the State party's first opportunity to present to the Committee the extent to which its laws and practices comply with the Covenant which it has ratified. The report should:

- Establish the constitutional and legal framework for the implementation of Covenant rights
- Explain the legal and practical measures adopted to give effect to Covenant rights
- Demonstrate the progress made in ensuring enjoyment of Covenant rights by the people within the State party and subject to its jurisdiction

2. Contents of the report.

1. A State party should deal specifically with every article in Parts I, II and III of the Covenant; legal norms should be described, but that is not sufficient: the factual situation and the practical availability, effect and implementation of remedies for violation of Covenant rights should be explained and exemplified.

2. The report should explain:

How article 2 of the Covenant is applied, setting out the principal legal measures which the State party has taken to give effect to Covenant rights; and the range of remedies available to persons whose rights may have been violated;

Whether the Covenant is incorporated into domestic law in such a manner as to be directly applicable;

If not, whether its provisions can be invoked before and given effect to by courts, tribunals and administrative authorities;

Whether the Covenant rights are guaranteed in a Constitution or other laws and to what extent; or

Whether Covenant rights must be enacted or reflected in domestic law by legislation so as to be enforceable.

3. Information should be given about the judicial, administrative and other competent authorities having jurisdiction to secure Covenant rights.

4. The report should include information about any national or official institution or machinery which exercises responsibility in implementing Covenant rights or in responding to complaints of violations of such rights, and give examples of their activities in this respect.

3. Annexes to the report.

1. The report should be accompanied by copies of the relevant principal constitutional, legislative and other texts which guarantee and provide remedies in relation to Covenant rights. Such texts will not be copied or translated, but will be available to members of the Committee; it is important that the report itself contains sufficient quotations from or summaries of these texts so as to ensure that the report is clear and comprehensible without reference to the annexes.

E. Subsequent periodic reports

1. There should be two starting points for such reports:

The concluding observations (particularly "Concerns" and "Recommendations") on the previous report and summary records of the Committee's consideration (insofar as these exist) ;

An examination by the State party of the progress made towards and the current situation concerning the enjoyment of Covenant rights by persons within its territory or jurisdiction.

2. Periodic reports should be structured so as to follow the articles of the Covenant. If there is nothing new to report under any article it should be so stated. 3

3. The State party should refer again to the guidance on initial reports and on annexes, insofar as these may also apply to a periodic report.

4. There may be circumstances where the following matters should be addressed, so as to elaborate a periodic report:

> There may have occurred a fundamental change in the State party's political and legal approach affecting Covenant rights: in such a case a full article-by-article report may be required;

> New legal or administrative measures may have been introduced which deserve the annexure of texts and judicial or other decisions.

F. Optional protocols

1. If the State party has ratified the Optional Protocol and the Committee has issued Views entailing provision of a remedy or expressing any other concern, relating to a communication received under that Protocol, a report should (unless the matter has been dealt with in a previous report) include information about the steps taken to provide a remedy, or meet such a concern, and to ensure that any circumstance thus criticized does not recur.

2. If the State party has abolished the death penalty the situation relating to the Second Optional Protocol should be explained.

G. The Committee's consideration of reports

1. General

> The Committee intends its consideration of a report to take the form of a constructive discussion with the delegation, the aim of which is to improve the situation pertaining to Covenant rights in the State.

2. List of issues

> On the basis of all information at its disposal, the Committee will supply in advance a list of issues which will form the basic agenda for consideration of the report. The delegation should come prepared to address the list of issues and to respond to further questions from members, with such updated information as may be necessary; and to do so within the time allocated for consideration of the report.

3. The State party's delegation

> The Committee wishes to ensure that it is able effectively to perform its functions under article 40 and that the reporting State party should obtain the maximum benefit from the reporting requirement. The State party's delegation should, therefore, include persons who, through their knowledge of and competence to explain the human rights situation in that State, are able to respond to the Committee's written and oral questions and comments concerning the whole range of Covenant rights.

4. Concluding observations

> Shortly after the consideration of the report, the Committee will publish its concluding observations on the report and the ensuing discussion with the delegation. These concluding observations will be included in the Committee's annual report to the General Assembly; the Committee expects the State party to disseminate these conclusions, in all appropriate languages, with a view to public information and discussion.

5. Extra information.

1. Following the submission of any report, subsequent revisions or updating may only be submitted:

(a) No later than 10 weeks prior to the date set for the Committee's consideration of the report (the minimum time required by the United Nations translation services) ; or

(b) After that date, provided that the text has been translated by the State party into the working languages of the Committee (currently English, Spanish and French) .

If one or other of these courses is not complied with, the Committee will not be able to take an addendum into account. This, however, does not apply to updated annexes or statistics.

2. In the course of the consideration of a report, the Committee may request or the delegation may offer further information; the secretariat will keep a note of such matters which should be dealt with in the next report.

1. The Committee may, in a case where there has been a long-term failure by a State party, despite reminders, to submit an initial or a periodic report, announce its intention to examine the extent of compliance with Covenant rights in that State party at a specified future session. Prior to that session it will transmit to the State party appropriate material in its possession. The State party may send a delegation to the specified session, which may contribute to the Committee's discussion, but in any event the Committee may issue provisional concluding observations and set a date for the submission by the State party of a report of a nature to be specified.

2. In a case where a State party, having submitted a report which has been scheduled at a session for examination, informs the Committee, at a time when it is impossible to schedule the examination of another State party report, that its delegation will not attend the session, the Committee may examine the report on the basis of the list of issues either at that session or at another to be specified. In the absence of a delegation, it may decide either to reach provisional concluding observations, or to consider the report and other material and follow the course in paragraph G. 4 above. 4

H. Format of the report

The distribution of a report, and thus its availability for consideration by the Committee, will be greatly facilitated if:

(a) The paragraphs are sequentially numbered;

(b) The document is written on A4-sized paper;

(c) Is single-spaced; and

(d) Allows reproduction by photo-offset (is on one side only of each sheet of paper) .

[End Text]

Source: http://www.un.org/ga/search/view_doc.asp?symbol=HRI/GEN/2/Rev. 6

3. GENERAL COMMENT NO. 30 OF THE U.N. HRC ON REPORTING OBLIGATIONS OF STATES PARTIES UNDER ARTICLE 40 OF THE COVENANT

This is a General Comment issued by the U.N. HRCtee reminding states parties to the ICCPR of their obligation to file their periodic states reports on time. This was issued because of the many overdue filings and failures to file periodic states report. It is a general comment on the meaning of article 40 of the ICCPR on the nature of the state party obligation to timely submit these reports so as to allow the HRCtee to supervise each state in the implementation of the ICCPR norms.

[Text]

General Comment No. 30 [75]
Reporting Obligations of States parties under article 40 of the Covenant
Adopted on 16 July 2002 (2025th meeting)

This General Comment would replace former General Comment 1

1. States parties have undertaken to submit reports in accordance with article 40 of the Covenant within one year of its entry into force for the States parties concerned and, thereafter, whenever the Committee so requests.

2. The Committee notes, as appears from its annual reports, that only a small number of States have submitted their reports on time. Most of them have been submitted with delays ranging from a few months to several years and some States parties are still in default, despite repeated reminders by the Committee.

3. Other States have announced that they would appear before the Committee but have not done so on the scheduled date.

4. To remedy such situations, the Committee has adopted new rules:

(a) If a State party has submitted a report but does not send a delegation to the Committee, the Committee may notify the State party of the date on which it intends to consider the report or may proceed to consider the report at the meeting that had been initially scheduled;

(b) When the State party has not presented a report, the Committee may, at its discretion, notify the State party of the date on which the Committee proposes to examine the measures taken by the State party to implement the rights guaranteed under the Covenant:

(v) If the State party is represented by a delegation, the Committee will, in presence of the delegation, proceed with the examination on the date assigned;

(vi) If the State party is not represented, the Committee may, at its discretion, either decide to proceed to consider the measures taken by the State party

(vii) to implement the guarantees of the Covenant at the initial date or notify a new date to the State party.

For the purposes of the application of these procedures, the Committee shall hold its meetings in public session if a delegation is present, and in private if a delegation is not present, and shall follow the modalities set forth in the reporting guidelines and in the rules of procedure of the Committee.

5. After the Committee has adopted concluding observations, a follow-up procedure shall be employed in order to establish, maintain or restore a dialogue with the State party. For this purpose and in order to enable the Committee to take further action, the Committee shall appoint a Special Rapporteur, who will report to the Committee.

6. In the light of the report of the Special Rapporteur, the Committee shall assess the position adopted by the State party and, if necessary, set a new date for the State party to submit its next report.

[End Text]

Source: http://tbinternet.ohchr.org/_layouts/treatybodyexternal/TBSearch.aspx?lang=en&treatyid=8&doctypeid=11

4. FOCUSED REPORTS BASED ON REPLIES TO LISTS OF ISSUES PRIOR TO REPORTING (LOIPR): IMPLEMENTATION OF THE NEW OPTIONAL REPORTING PROCEDURE (LOIPR PROCEDURE)

This document, from the Human Rights Committee, attempts to make the state reporting process more manageable and less cumbersome for states and more efficient for the members of the Committee. It is a new optional reporting procedure by which the

Committee attempts to solicit answers and information from states based on issue questions presented to the states before their presentation before the Committee. By answering all the questions and submitting their answers beforehand the state could fulfill its reporting obligation and not have to submit a bulkier and longer report covering issues which may not be of interest to the Committee. Usually the Committee has an idea of the most pressing issues involved with a state and wants to make sure the state responds with its position to that issue.

{Excerpt}

[Text]

Human Rights Committee
Ninety-ninth session
Geneva, 12-30 July 2010

I. Introductory remarks

1. At its ninety-seventh session, held in October 2009, the Committee started discussing its draft revised reporting guidelines. In this context, it decided to adopt a new reporting procedure whereby it would send States parties a list of issues (a so-called "list of issues prior to reporting" (LOIPR)) and consider their written replies in lieu of a periodic report (a so-called "focused report based on replies to a list of issues") . Under the new procedure, the State party's answer would constitute the report for the purposes of article 40 of the Covenant.

A. Potential added value of the LOIPR procedure

For States parties

2. The LOIPR procedure will facilitate the reporting process for States. The reporting burden will be alleviated in two ways:
   • Lists of issues will provide detailed guidance on the expected content of the report, thereby facilitating the drafting process
   • States will no longer be requested to submit both a report and written replies to a list of issues

3. Furthermore, the reporting process will be speedier for those States to which the LOIPR procedure will apply, as focused periodic reports drafted on the basis of an LOIPR will be given priority for consideration over other periodic reports, so as to ensure that they are considered within a maximum time frame of one year after submission.

For the Committee

4. The effectiveness of the Committee will be strengthened as follows:
   • This procedure will allow the Committee to receive more focused information and therefore assist it in improving its assessment of States parties' compliance with their Covenant obligations
   • The Committee will be able to reinitiate a dialogue with States that, owing to lack of financial and human resources, are long overdue in submitting their periodic report

B. Challenges to be taken into account

5. The preparation of LOIPRs will imply a significant increase in the workload of the Committee and the Secretariat. It will be necessary, therefore, at an initial stage, to take this difficulty into account and to assess the capacity of the Committee and the Secretariat in order to decide on the number of LOIPRs to be adopted at each session. In the long term, however, standard lists of issues will need to be prepared and adopted only for initial reports and for a limited number of periodic reports (those for States that have not accepted the new optional reporting procedure or from which the Committee continues to request a full report), and the workload will progressively diminish.

6. As long as both LOIPRs and a large number of standard lists of issues continue to be adopted by the Committee, additional meeting time will need to be provided for the Committee's country report task forces, which will adopt both the

standard lists of issues and LOIPRs. Furthermore, additional human resources will also be required from the Secretariat for the drafting of LOIPRs.

II. Principles and methodology underlying the implementation of the new optional reporting procedure

A. Pilot period

7. After a pilot period of five years (from November 2010), the Committee will appoint a working group to assess and review the new procedure in terms of its practicability, effectiveness and capacity to improve the examination of the human rights situation in the State parties.

B. States parties to which the new procedure will apply

8. The new procedure is not to be applied to initial reports of States parties or to periodic reports already submitted and awaiting consideration by the Committee.

9. The new procedure is optional, and States parties may decide to continue to submit their reports under the standard procedure.

10. All periodic reports, irrespective or being long overdue or not, potentially fall under the new LOIPR procedure, which should apply to as many State parties as possible. The Committee may decide, however, not to apply the LOIPR procedure to a State party when it deems that particular circumstances warrant a full report, including when a fundamental change in the State party's political and legal approach affecting Covenant rights has occurred; in such a case a full article-by-article report may be required.

C. Substance and format of the LOIPR

11. The LOIPR should include two sections:

(a) A first section, with standard paragraphs, on "General information on the national human rights situation, including new measures and developments relating to the implementation of the Covenant." This section will also provide the State party with an opportunity to highlight relevant positive developments. If not already provided in the common core document or when the information in the common core document is not up-to-date and if not raised under specific questions in the second section of the LOIPR, States parties may provide detailed information in this section on:

- Relevant new developments on the legal and institutional framework within which human rights are promoted and protected at the national level that have occurred since the previous periodic report, including any relevant case-law decisions
- New political, administrative and other measures taken to promote and protect human rights at the national level that have occurred since the previous report, including on any national human rights plans or programmes, and the resources allocated thereto, their means, objectives and results
- New measures and developments undertaken to implement the Covenant and the Committee's recommendations since the consideration of the previous report, including the necessary statistical data, as well as any events that occurred in the State party and are relevant under the Convention;

(b) A second section where questions are organized according to clusters of provisions as in the standard list of issues, highlighting specific issues depending on the situation of the concerned State party and the information available to the Committee, in particular, the recommendations included in the last concluding observations addressed to the State party as well any follow-up information provided by the State.

D. Information to be relied upon for the drafting of LOIPRs

12. It is proposed that, as is currently the case for the drafting and adoption of lists of issues by the Committee, a country file be compiled and provided by the Secretariat to members of the country report task force, which will then adopt LOIPRs. This country file should include, inter alia, the following:

- Previous report of the State party to the Committee
- Core document, including common core document if available
- Constitution of the State party
- Previous concluding observations of the Committee
- Summary records of consideration of last report
- Follow-up information, if available, and assessment by the Committee of this information
- Views under the Optional Protocol, if any, and information on follow-up given by the State party
- Concluding observations of other treaty bodies
- Reports of special procedures
- Universal periodic review documents
- Documents from regional organizations
- United Nations/Office of the United Nations High Commissioner for Human Rights information
- Reports from national human rights institutions (NHRIs) and from non-governmental organizations (NGOs)
- Any other document as deemed relevant by the Committee

E. Principles and methodology underlying the scheduling for adoption of LOIPRs and consideration of LOIPR-based focused reports

1. States parties should be given sufficient time to inform the Committee as to whether they agree to follow the new optional reporting procedure.

13. Notes verbales are to be sent by the Secretariat at the request of the Committee in which States will be given three months to inform the Committee as to whether they agree to follow the LOIPR procedure.

2. All stakeholders, in particular NHRIs and NGOs, should be given sufficient time to provide the Committee with relevant input prior to the drafting and adoption of LOIPRs.

14. The list of countries that will be examined according to the new procedure will be made public on the Office of the High Commissioner for Human Rights website, to the extent possible, at least nine months prior to the session during which the LOIPR is to be adopted by the Committee. 5

3. States parties should be given sufficient time to prepare their LOIPR-based focused reports.

15. States concerned will be given at least one year to reply to the LOIPR, i. e. to prepare their focused report under the LOIPR procedure.

4. LOIPR-based focused reports should be examined no later than one year after their submission.

16. While scheduling reports to be considered for its upcoming sessions, the Committee will prioritize only initial reports over reports based on LOIPR, in order to ensure that the time between the submission of the LOIPR-based report and its consideration is as short as possible, so as to avoid the loss of relevance of the LOIPR-based report, which would lead to the need for another list of issues and set of replies.

5. Consideration should be given to the capacity of the Committee and the Secretariat in order to determine the number of LOIPRs to be adopted at each session during the pilot period. In addition, both States that report regularly and States that are overdue in the submission of their reports may also be invited to follow the new optional reporting procedure.

17. Bearing in mind the need to continue adopting at each session standard lists of issues as well as LOIPRs, the Committee will only have the capacity to adopt five LOIPRs per session during the pilot period (therefore, country report task forces will adopt at each session 10 lists of issues: five standard lists of issues and five LOIPRs, i. e., 30 lists of issues, standard lists and LOIPRs combined, per year) .

18. The five States to which LOIPRs will be sent at each session will be selected according to the following cumulative criteria:

(a) The States concerned will primarily be selected from among the list of States whose report is due in 2013 and beyond and that have informed the Committee of their agreement to follow the new reporting procedure;

(b) LOIPRs may be drafted and sent to those States whose periodic report is at least 10 years overdue and that have agreed to the new reporting procedure;

(c) States will be selected in chronological order with regard to the date upon which their next periodic report is due and, when several reports are due on the same date, according to the date upon which they have informed the Committee of their wish to follow the optional reporting procedure.

F. Timetable for initial implementation of the new optional reporting procedure

19. 1 November 2010: The Committee will inform the following States parties of the initiation of the new optional reporting procedure and will request their agreement to follow this new procedure:

(a) All State parties whose reports are due in 2013 and beyond;

(b) All States parties whose reports are at least 10 years overdue.

20. Deadline for States to respond: 1 February 2011.

21. In case of failure to respond, States parties will be contacted and called for a consultation meeting with the Chairman of the Committee at a time deemed appropriate.

22. March 2011 (101st session): The Committee will make public its decision to adopt an LOIPR for States that have accepted the new optional procedure by the initial deadline of 1 February 2011. Depending on the number of States concerned and taking into account its capacity to adopt a specific number of LOIPRs at each session, the Committee will set a timetable for the drafting and adoption of lists of issues for future sessions.

23. So as to allow time for NHRIs and NGOs to provide relevant information to the Committee, the first five LOIPRs will be adopted at the October 2011 session. 6

24. The first five States parties regarding which LOIPRs will be adopted in October 2011 will be requested to submit their LOIPR-based report by 31 March 2013.

25. If received by the deadline (31 March 2013), the first focused reports will be scheduled for consideration in 2014.

[End Text]

Source: http://tbinternet.ohchr.org/_layouts/treatybodyexternal/Download.aspx?symbolno=CCPR/C/99/4&Lang=en **or**
http://www.ohchr.org/EN/HRBodies/CCPR/Pages/SimplifiedReportingProcedure.aspx

5. CONSIDERATION OF REPORTS SUBMITTED BY STATES PARTIES UNDER ARTICLE 40 OF THE COVENANT, CONCLUDING OBSERVATIONS OF THE HUMAN RIGHTS COMMITTEE, 2006

This is the final document of the U.N. HRCtee periodic reporting process with the U.S. It looks at the U.S. second and third periodic reports which were submitted and processed in 2006. The purpose of this document is for the HRCtee to express its concluding observations on everything that was submitted in the process of those two reports in 2006. It is here to set up a clearer and fuller review of the next set of documents regarding the fourth U.S. Periodic Report to the HRCtee. The recommendations are not legally binding on the U.S. but it is expected to make efforts to implement them because of the expertise of the Committee members acting as a body within their rules and authority.

{Excerpt}

[Text]

HUMAN RIGHTS COMMITTEE

Eighty-seventh session
10-28 July 2006

Consideration of reports submitted by states parties under Article 40 of the covenant

Concluding observations of the Human Rights Committee

UNITED STATES OF AMERICA

1. The Committee considered the second and third periodic reports of the United States of America (CCPR/C/USA/3) at its 2379th, 2380th and 2381st meetings (CCPR/C/SR. 2379-2381), held on 17 and 18 July 2006, and adopted the following concluding observations at its 2395th meeting (CCPR/C/SR. 2395), held on 27 July 2006.

A. Introduction

2. The Committee notes the submission of the State party's second and third periodic combined report, which was seven years overdue, as well as the written answers provided in advance. It appreciates the attendance of a delegation composed of experts belonging to various agencies responsible for the implementation of the Covenant, and welcomes their efforts to answer to the Committee's written and oral questions.

3. The Committee regrets that the State party has not integrated into its report information on the implementation of the Covenant with respect to individuals under its jurisdiction and outside its territory. The Committee notes however that the State party has provided additional material "out of courtesy." The Committee further regrets that the State party, invoking grounds of non-applicability of the Covenant or intelligence operations, refused to address certain serious allegations of violations of the rights protected under the Covenant.

4. The Committee regrets that only limited information was provided on the implementation of the Covenant at the State level.

GE. 06-45961

B. Positive aspects

5. The Committee welcomes the Supreme Court's decision in *Hamdan v. Rumsfeld* (2006) establishing the applicability of common article 3 of the Geneva Conventions of 12 August 1949, which reflects fundamental rights guaranteed by the Covenant in any armed conflict.

6. The Committee welcomes the Supreme Court's decision in *Roper v. Simmons* (2005), which held that the Eighth and Fourteenth Amendments forbid imposition of the death penalty on offenders who were under the age of 18 when their crimes were committed. In this regard, the Committee reiterates the recommendation made in its previous concluding observations, encouraging the State party to withdraw its reservation to article 6 (5) of the Covenant.

7. The Committee welcomes the Supreme Court's decision in *Atkins v. Virginia* (2002), which held that executions of mentally retarded criminals are cruel and unusual punishments, and encourages the State party to ensure that persons suffering from severe forms of mental illness not amounting to mental retardation are equally protected.

8. The Committee welcomes the promulgation of the National Detention Standards in 2000, establishing minimum standards for detention facilities holding Department of Homeland Security detainees, and encourages the State party to adopt all measures necessary for their effective enforcement.

9. The Committee welcomes the Supreme Court's decision in *Lawrence et al. v. Texas* (2003), which declared unconstitutional legislation criminalizing homosexual relations between consenting adults.

C. Principal subjects of concern and recommendations

10. The Committee notes with concern the restrictive interpretation made by the State party of its obligations under the Covenant, as a result in particular of (a) its position that the Covenant does not apply with respect to individuals under its jurisdiction but outside its territory, nor in time of war, despite the contrary opinions and established jurisprudence of the Committee and the International Court of Justice; (b) its failure to take fully into consideration its obligation under the Covenant not only to respect, but also to ensure the rights prescribed by the Covenant; and (c) its restrictive approach to some substantive provisions of the Covenant, which is not in conformity with the interpretation made by the Committee before and after the State party's ratification of the Covenant. (articles 2 and 40)

The State party should review its approach and interpret the Covenant in good faith, in accordance with the ordinary meaning to be given to its terms in their context, including subsequent practice, and in the light of its object and purpose. The State party should in particular (a) acknowledge the applicability of the Covenant with respect to individuals under its jurisdiction but outside its territory, as well as its applicability in time of war; (b) take positive steps, when necessary, to ensure the full implementation of all rights prescribed by the Covenant; and (c) consider in good faith the interpretation of the Covenant provided by the Committee pursuant to its mandate.

11. The Committee expresses its concern about the potentially overbroad reach of the definitions of terrorism under domestic law, in particular under 8 U.S.C. § 1182 (a) (3) (B) and Executive Order 13224 which seem to extend to conduct, e. g. in the context of political dissent, which, although unlawful, should not be understood as constituting terrorism (articles 17, 19 and 21) .

The State party should ensure that its counter-terrorism measures are in full conformity with the Covenant and in particular that the legislation adopted in this context is limited to crimes that would justify being assimilated to terrorism, and the grave consequences associated with it.

12. The Committee is concerned by credible and uncontested information that the State party has seen fit to engage in the practice of detaining people secretly and in secret places for months and years on end, without keeping the International Committee of the Red Cross informed. In such cases, the rights of the families of the detainees are also being violated. The Committee is also concerned that, even when such persons may have their detention acknowledged, they have been held incommunicado for months or years, a practice that violates the rights protected by articles 7 and 9. In general, the Committee is concerned by the fact that people are detained in places where they cannot benefit from the protection of domestic or international law or where that protection is substantially curtailed, a practice that cannot be justified by the stated need to remove them from the battlefield. (articles 7 and 9)

The State party should immediately cease its practice of secret detention and close all secret detention facilities. It should also grant the International Committee of the Red Cross prompt access to any person detained in connection with an armed conflict. The State party should also ensure that detainees, regardless of their place of detention, always benefit from the full protection of the law.

13. The Committee is concerned with the fact that the State party has authorized for some time the use of enhanced interrogation techniques, such as prolonged stress positions and isolation, sensory deprivation, hooding, exposure to cold or heat, sleep and dietary adjustments, 20-hour interrogations, removal of clothing and deprivation of all comfort and religious items, forced grooming, and exploitation of detainees' individual phobias. Although the Committee welcomes the assurance that, according to the Detainee Treatment Act of 2005, such interrogation techniques are prohibited by the present Army Field Manual on Intelligence Interrogation, the Committee remains concerned that (a) the State party refuses to acknowledge that such techniques, several of which were allegedly applied, either individually or in combination, over a protracted period of time, violate the prohibition contained by article 7 of the Covenant; (b) no sentence has been pronounced against an officer, employee, member of the Armed Forces, or other agent of the United States Government for using harsh interrogation techniques that had been approved; (c) these interrogation techniques may still be authorized or used by other agencies, including intelligence agencies and "private contractors"; and (d) the State party has provided no information to the fact that oversight systems of such agencies have been established to ensure compliance with article 7.

The State party should ensure that any revision of the Army Field Manual only provides for interrogation techniques in conformity with the international understanding of the scope of the prohibition contained in article 7 of the Covenant; the State party should also ensure that the current interrogation techniques or any revised techniques are binding on all agencies of the United States Government and any others acting on its behalf; the State party should ensure that there are effective means to follow suit against abuses committed by agencies operating outside the military structure and that appropriate sanctions be imposed on its personnel who used or approved the use of the now prohibited techniques; the State party should ensure that the right to reparation of the victims of such practices is respected; and it should inform the Committee of any revisions of the interrogation techniques approved by the Army Field Manual.

14. The Committee notes with concern shortcomings concerning the independence, impartiality and effectiveness of investigations into allegations of torture and cruel, inhuman or degrading treatment or punishment inflicted by United States military and non-military personnel or contract employees, in detention facilities in Guantánamo Bay, Afghanistan, Iraq, and other overseas locations, and to alleged cases of suspicious death in custody in any of these locations. The Committee regrets that the State party did not provide sufficient information regarding the prosecutions launched, sentences passed (which appear excessively light for offences of such gravity) and reparation granted to the victims. (articles 6 and 7)

The State party should conduct prompt and independent investigations into all allegations concerning suspicious deaths, torture or cruel, inhuman or degrading treatment or punishment inflicted by its personnel (including commanders) as well as contract employees, in detention facilities in Guantánamo Bay, Afghanistan, Iraq and other overseas locations. The State party should ensure that those responsible are prosecuted and punished in accordance with the gravity of the crime. The State party should adopt all necessary measures to prevent the recurrence of such behaviors, in particular by providing adequate training and clear guidance to its personnel (including commanders) and contract employees, about their respective obligations and responsibilities, in line with articles 7 and 10 of the Covenant. During the course of any legal proceedings, the State party should also refrain from relying on evidence obtained by treatment incompatible with article 7. The Committee wishes to be informed about the measures taken by the State party to ensure the respect of the right to reparation for the victims.

15. The Committee notes with concern that section 1005 (e) of the Detainee Treatment Act bars detainees in Guantánamo Bay from seeking review in case of allegations of ill-treatment or poor conditions of detention. (articles 7 and 10)

The State party should amend section 1005 of the Detainee Treatment Act so as to allow detainees in Guantánamo Bay to seek review of their treatment or conditions of detention before a court.

16. The Committee notes with concern the State party's restrictive interpretation of article 7 of the Covenant according to which it understands (a) that the obligation not to subject anyone to treatment prohibited by article 7 of the Covenant does not include an obligation not to expose them to such treatment by means of transfer, rendition, extradition, expulsion or refoulement; (b) that in any case, it is not under any other obligation not to deport an individual who may undergo cruel, inhumane or degrading treatment or punishment other than torture, as the State party understands the term; and (c) that it is not under any international obligation to respect a nonrefoulement rule in relation to persons it detains outside its territory. It also notes with concern the "more likely than not" standard it uses in non-refoulement procedures. The Committee is concerned that in practice the State party appears to have adopted a policy to send, or to assist in the sending of, suspected terrorists to third countries, either from the United States of America or other States' territories, for purposes of detention and interrogation, without the appropriate safeguards to prevent treatment prohibited by the Covenant. The Committee is moreover concerned by numerous well-publicized and documented allegations that persons sent to third countries in this way were indeed detained and interrogated while receiving treatment grossly violating the prohibition contained in article 7, allegations that the State party did not contest. Its concern is deepened by the so far successful invocation of State secrecy in cases where the victims of these practices have sought a remedy before the State party's courts (e.g. the cases of *Maher Arar v. Ashcroft* (2006) and *Khaled Al-Masri v. Tenet* (2006)). (article 7)

Source: http://www.refworld.org/docid/45c30bec9.html

కౌకౌకౌకౌకౌకౌ

6. FOURTH PERIODIC REPORT OF THE UNITED STATES OF AMERICA TO THE UNITED NATIONS COMMITTEE ON HUMAN RIGHTS CONCERNING THE INTERNATIONAL COVENANT ON CIVIL AND POLITICAL RIGHTS

This document is a state periodic report by the U.S. as a state party of the ICCPR treaty submitted to the U.N. HRCtee, a treaty body. It is required by article 40 of the ICCPR, and the fourth U.S. report submitted for the Committee's consideration. It is used by the Committee in supervising the U.S. compliance with the legal norm obligations in the ICCPR. It is about how the U.S. sees itself in relation to its law, policy and practice to the treaty norms, as well as fulfilling the treaty norms, the measures it has adopted, the progress it has made and what obstacles and problems exist. Every U.N. human rights treaty has a state reporting requirement with a certain procedure for processing the report, ultimately with recommendations to the state to help it implement the recommendations. The next few documents follow the process of the HRCtee in response to this Fourth Report. They are all connected.

{Excerpt}

[Text]

Fourth Periodic Report of the United States of America to the United Nations Committee on Human Rights Concerning the International Covenant on Civil and Political Rights

December 30, 2011

I. INTRODUCTION

...

2. Treaty reporting is a way in which the Government of the United States can inform its citizens and the international community of its efforts to ensure the implementation of those obligations it has assumed, while at the same time holding itself to the public scrutiny of the international community and civil society. As Secretary of State Hillary Clinton has stated, "Human rights are universal, but their experience is local. This is why we are committed to holding everyone to the same standard, including ourselves." In implementing its treaty obligation under ICCPR Article 40, the United States has taken this opportunity to engage in a process of stock-taking and self-examination. The United States hopes to use this process to improve its human rights performance. Thus, this report is not an end in itself, but an important tool in the continuing development of practical and effective human rights strategies by the U.S. Government. As President Obama has stated, "Despite the real gains that we've made, there are still laws to change and there are still hearts to open."

3. The organization of this periodic report follows the General Guidelines of the Human Rights Committee regarding the form and content of periodic reports to be submitted by States Parties as contained in document CCPR/C/2009/1. The information supplements that provided in the United States Initial Report of July 1994 (CCPR/C/81/Add. 4, published 24 August 1994, and HRI/CORE/1/Add. 49, published 17 August 1994, with related supplemental information and hearings), as well as the information provided by the United States in its combined Second and Third Periodic Report (CCPR/C/USA/3), and information provided by the U.S. delegation during Committee meetings considering that report (CCPR/C/SR/2379-2381) . It also takes into account the Concluding Observations of the Human Rights Committee published 18 December 2006 (CCPR/C/USA/CO/3/Rev. 1) . The United States has provided the text and explanations for reservations, understandings and declarations it undertook at the time it became a State Party to the Covenant in its prior reports. For purposes of brevity those descriptions and explanations will not be repeated in this report.

4. In this report, the United States has considered carefully the views expressed by the Committee in its prior written communications and public sessions with the United States. In the spirit of cooperation, the United States has provided as much information as possible on a number of issues raised by the committee and/or civil society, whether or not they bear directly on formal obligations arising under the Covenant. During preparation of this report, the U.S. Government has consulted with representatives of civil society and has sought information and input from their organizations. Civil

society representatives have raised a variety of concerns on many of the topics addressed in this report, a number of which are noted in the text of the report. The United States Government has also reached out to state, local, tribal, and territorial governments to seek information from their human rights entities on their programs and activities, which play an important part in implementing the Covenant and other human rights treaties. Information received from this outreach is referenced in some portions of the report and described in greater detail in Annex A to the Common Core Document.

...

Article 2 — Equal protection of rights in the Covenant

General Equal Protection

32. The enjoyment by all individuals within the United States of the rights enumerated in the Covenant without regard to race, color, sex, language, religion, political or other opinion, national or social origin, property, birth or other status, was discussed in paragraphs 77-100 of the United States Initial Report and paragraphs 26-59 of the combined Second and Third Periodic Report. While Articles 2 and 26 are not identical, there is overlap in their coverage. Therefore the material in this section relates to both Articles 2 and 26, as well as general related information.

33. The United States became a party to the International Convention on the Elimination of All Forms of Racial Discrimination on 20 November 1994, and the United States submitted its combined Initial, Second and Third Periodic Report to the United Nations Committee on the Elimination of Racial Discrimination (CERD Committee) in September 2000. The United States' combined Fourth, Fifth and Sixth Periodic Report was submitted to the Committee on 24 April 2007, and a United States delegation appeared before the CERD Committee concerning that Report at its 72nd Session, 18 February — 7 March 2008. The Committee's Concluding Observations and Recommendations, issued on 8 May 2008, can be found at CERD/C/USA/CO/6. The U.S. reports and Committee's Concluding Observations and Recommendations are available at http://www.state.gov/j/drl/hr/treaties/.

34. Classifications. Under the U.S. constitutional doctrine of equal protection, neither the federal government nor any state may deny any person equal protection under the law. The general rule is that legislative classifications are presumed valid if they bear some rational relation to a legitimate governmental purpose. See *FCC v. Beach Communication, Inc.*, 508 U.S. 307 (1993); *McGowan v. Maryland*, 366 U.S. 420, 425-36 (1961). The most obvious example is economic regulation. Both state and federal governments are able to apply different rules to different types of economic activities, and the courts will review such regulation under this standard. See, e. g., *Williamson v. Lee Optical Co.*, 348 U.S. 483 (1955). Similarly, the way in which a state government chooses to allocate its financial resources among categories of needy people will be reviewed under this highly deferential standard. See *Dandridge v. Williams*, 397 U.S. 471 (1970).

38. Corrective or affirmative action. In some circumstances, classification by race is permissible for certain purposes, such as redressing past racial discrimination and promoting diversity in educational settings. Because race has been recognized as a "suspect classification," individual classifications that distribute a benefit or a burden based on race will be subject to "strict scrutiny" by the courts. Where a government employer or other government entity has engaged in racial discrimination in the past, it will generally be permitted (and may sometimes be required) to consider race in a narrowly tailored fashion to correct the effects of its past conduct. See *Wygant v. Jackson Board of Education*, 476 U.S. 267 (1986). Government entities may also take race into account when necessary to address discriminatory acts of others when the effects of such discrimination are extended by government policies. See *City of Richmond v. J. A. Croson Co.*, 488 U.S. 469 (1989).

39. The United States Supreme Court has addressed affirmative action plans in the education context. In Grutter v. Bollinger, the Court recognized a compelling interest in achieving a genuinely diverse student body and held that race could be considered as a part of an effort to achieve that diversity, including by ensuring enrollment of a critical mass of minority students at universities and graduate schools. Specifically, the Court held that the University of Michigan Law School's interest in "assembling a class that is... broadly diverse" is compelling because "attaining a diverse student body is at the heart of [a law school's] proper institutional mission." Grutter, 539 U.S. 306 at 329 (2003). The Court found the Law School's program to be narrowly tailored to achieve this mission because it applied a flexible goal rather than a quota, because it involved a holistic individual review of each applicant's file, because it did not "unduly burden" indi-

viduals who were not members of the favored racial and ethnic groups, and because under the program, the Law School periodically reviewed its use of race to determine if it was still necessary. Id. at 342-43. At the same time, however, in Gratz v. Bollinger, 539 U.S. 244 (2003), the Court struck down the admissions policies of the University of Michigan's undergraduate affirmative action program, holding that they failed to give each applicant sufficient individualized consideration, and were therefore not "narrowly tailored" to meet the university's objective of achieving diversity. See 539 U. S. at 270.

...

Statutory Framework

42. General framework. A number of federal statutes prohibit discrimination by state or local governments; private entities in the areas of employment, housing, transportation, and public accommodation; and private entities that receive federal financial assistance. The federal government is actively engaged in the enforcement of such statutes against discrimination in the areas of employment, housing and housing finance, access to public accommodations, and education. In addition, most states and some localities also have laws prohibiting similar types of activity, and in many cases state and federal authorities have entered into work sharing arrangements to ensure effective handling of cases where state and federal jurisdiction overlaps. These are described in more detail in Annex A to the Common Core Document.

43. The most comprehensive federal statute, the Civil Rights Act of 1964, prohibits discrimination in a number of specific areas including: Title VI (prohibiting discrimination on the basis of race, color or national origin in programs and activities receiving federal financial assistance); and Title VII (prohibiting discrimination in employment on the basis of race, color, religion, sex or national origin). In addition, Title VIII of the Civil Rights Act of 1968 (the "Fair Housing Act") prohibits discrimination in the sale, rental and financing of dwellings and in other housing-related transactions on the basis of race, color, religion, sex, national origin, familial status, or disability. These provisions and other civil rights laws are enforced by a number of federal agencies, including the Department of Justice (DOJ), the Department of Education (ED), the Department of Labor, the Equal Employment Opportunity Commission (EEOC), the Department of Health and Human Services, and others. For example, among other things, DOJ's Civil Rights Division coordinates the U.S. government's enforcement of Title VI of the Civil Rights Act of 1964, 42 U. S. C. 2000d, which prohibits discrimination on the basis of race, color, or national origin in programs and activities receiving federal financial assistance. If a recipient of federal financial assistance is found to have discriminated and voluntary compliance cannot be achieved, the federal agency providing the assistance could either initiate fund termination proceedings or refer the matter to DOJ for appropriate legal action. Aggrieved individuals may file administrative complaints with the federal agency that provides funds to a recipient, or where the alleged discrimination is intentional, the individuals may file suit for appropriate relief in federal court. Title VI itself prohibits intentional discrimination. However, most funding agencies have regulations implementing Title VI that also prohibit recipient practices that have an unjustified discriminatory effect based on race, color, or national origin. More than 28 federal agencies have adopted regulations implementing Title VI.

...

III. COMMITTEE CONCLUDING OBSERVATIONS

502. The Committee recommended in paragraph 10 of its Concluding Observations that the United States review its approach to interpretation of the Covenant and, in particular (a) acknowledge the applicability of the Covenant with respect to individuals under its jurisdiction, but outside its territory, as well as its applicability in time of war; (b) take positive steps, when necessary, to ensure the full implementation of all rights prescribed by the Covenant; and (c) consider in good faith the interpretation of the Covenant provided by the Committee.

503. This set of observations and recommendations involves the interpretation of Article 2(1) of the Covenant, the question of the relationship between the Covenant and the international law of armed conflict, and the United States government's consideration of the views of the Committee with respect to the interpretation and application of the Covenant.

(a) Territorial Scope

504. Article 2(1) of the Covenant states that "[e]ach State Party to the present Covenant undertakes to respect and to ensure to all individuals within its territory and subject to its jurisdiction the rights recognized in the present Covenant, without distinction of any kind."

505. The United States in its prior appearances before the Committee has articulated the position that article 2(1) would apply only to individuals who were both within the territory of a State Party and within that State Party's jurisdiction. [9] The United States is mindful that in General Comment 31 (2004) the Committee presented the view that "States Parties are required by article 2, paragraph 1, to respect and to ensure the Covenant rights to all persons who may be within their territory and to all persons subject to their jurisdiction. This means that a State party must respect and ensure the rights laid down in the Covenant to anyone within the power or effective control of that State Party, even if not situated within the territory of the State Party." The United States is also aware of the jurisprudence of the International Court of Justice ("ICJ"), which has found the ICCPR "applicable in respect of acts done by a State in the exercise of its jurisdiction outside its own territory," as well as positions taken by other States Parties.

(b) Applicable Law

506. With respect to the application of the Covenant and the international law of armed conflict (also referred to as international humanitarian law or "IHL"), the United States has not taken the position that the Covenant does not apply "in time of war." Indeed, a time of war does not suspend the operation of the Covenant to matters within its scope of application. To cite but two obvious examples from among many, a State Party's participation in a war would in no way excuse it from respecting and ensuring rights to have or adopt a religion or belief of one's choice or the right and opportunity of every citizen to vote and to be elected at genuine periodic elections.

507. More complex issues arise with respect to the relevant body of law that determines whether a State's actions in the actual conduct of an armed conflict comport with international law. Under the doctrine of *lexspecialis*, the applicable rules for the protection of individuals and conduct of hostilities in armed conflict are typically found in international humanitarian law, including the Geneva Conventions of 1949, the Hague Regulations of 1907, and other international humanitarian law instruments, as well as in the customary international law of armed conflict. In this context, it is important to bear in mind that international human rights law and the law of armed conflict are in many respects complementary and mutually reinforcing. These two bodies of law contain many similar protections. For example prohibitions on torture and cruel treatment exist in both, and the drafters in each area have drawn from the other in developing aspects of new instruments; the Commentaries to Additional Protocol II to the Geneva Conventions make clear that a number of provisions in the Protocol were modeled on comparable provisions in the ICCPR. Determining the international law rule that applies to a particular action taken by a government in the context of an armed conflict is a fact-specific determination, which cannot be easily generalized, and raises especially complex issues in the context of non-international armed conflicts occurring within a State's own territory.

508. The United States understands, as it emphasized in its consultations with civil society organizations, that there have been concerns about a lack of adequate international legal protections for those the United States engages with overseas, particularly in armed conflict situations. In part to address these concerns, President Obama has taken a number of actions, which are discussed in more detail in response to the Committee's other Concluding Observations. Along with other actions, on January 22, 2009, President Obama issued three Executive Orders relating to U.S. detention and interrogation policies broadly and the Guantánamo Bay detention facility specifically. For example, Executive Order 13491 on Ensuring Lawful Interrogations, 74 Fed. Reg. 4894 (2009), which was adopted, *inter alia*, "to ensure compliance with the treaty obligations of the United States, including the Geneva Conventions," provides that

Consistent with the requirements of... the Convention Against Torture, Common Article 3, and other laws regulating the treatment and interrogation of individuals detained in any armed conflict, such persons shall in all circumstances be treated humanely and shall not be subjected to violence to life and person... whenever such individuals are in the custody or under the effective control of an officer, employee, or other agent of the United States Government or detained within a facility owned, operated, or controlled by a department or agency of the United States.

Id., Preamble and Sec. 3(a).

509. In addition, the United States Supreme Court has recognized the applicability of Common Article 3 of the Geneva Conventions to the conflict with Al Qaeda, Hamdan v. Rumsfeld, 548 U.S. 557, 630-631 (2006), and the United States has recently announced that it supports the principles set forth in Article 75 of Additional Protocol I to the Geneva Conventions of 1949 as a set of norms that it follows out of a sense of legal obligation in international armed conflict. It has also urged the U.S. Senate to provide advice and consent to ratification of Additional Protocol II to the Geneva Conventions, which contains detailed humane treatment standards and fair trial guarantees that apply to any criminal proceeding associated with the conduct of non-international armed conflict. The United States has recently conducted an extensive review and concluded that current U.S. military practices are consistent with Protocol II, as well as with Article 75 of Protocol I, including the rules within these instruments that parallel the ICCPR. The United States has continued to work to address concerns of the international community and civil society in regards to its actions abroad.

(c) Coordination with the Committee

510. The United States appreciates its ongoing dialogue with the Committee with respect to the interpretation and application of the Covenant, considers the Committee's views in good faith, and looks forward to further discussions of these issues when it presents this report to the Committee.

511. The Committee recommended in paragraph 11 of its Concluding Observations that the United States should ensure that its counter-terrorism measures are in full conformity with the Covenant, and in particular that the definitions of terrorism adopted under 8 U.S.C. 1182 (a) (3) (B) and Executive Order 13224 are limited to crimes that would justify being assimilated to terrorism, and the grave consequences associated with it.

512. The terms of the Immigration and Nationality Act (INA) relating to "terrorist activities" do not directly apply to criminal proceedings. The definition used in 8 U.S.C. 1182(a) (3) (B) is primarily used in the immigration context and is different from the definition found under U.S. criminal law (see, e. g., 18 U.S.C. 2331). Much of the conduct described in 8 U.S.C. 1182 is conduct covered under international conventions and protocols related to terrorism (e. g., hijacking, kidnapping, violent attacks on international protected persons, bombings). Furthermore, the INA authorizes the Executive to grant discretionary relief, in appropriate cases, to overcome some of the terrorism-related bars.

513. Executive Order 13224 provides legal authority for the United States to block the property of and freeze transactions with persons who commit, threaten to commit, or support terrorism. Section 3(d) of Executive Order 13224 defines the term "terrorism" as used in the Executive Order to mean an activity that:

(i) involves a violent act or an act dangerous to human life, property, or infrastructure; and

(ii) appears to be intended -

(A) to intimidate or coerce a civilian population;

(B) to influence the policy of a government by intimidation or coercion; or

(C) to affect the conduct of a government by mass destruction, assassination, kidnapping, or hostage-taking.

While the United States notes that there is no single definition of terrorism that has been accepted by the international community, the definition found in Executive Order 13224 is consistent with definitions found in the laws of other nations, the offenses covered in international counter-terrorism instruments (see, e. g., Article 2 of the International Convention for the Suppression of the Financing of Terrorism), and pertinent U.N. resolutions on combating terrorism (see, e. g., U.N. Security Council Resolution 1566, OP 3).

514. The Committee recommended in paragraph 12 of its Concluding Observations that the United States should immediately cease its practice of secret detention and close all secret detention facilities, grant the International Committee of the Red Cross prompt access to any person detained in connection with an armed conflict, and ensure that detainees, regardless of their place of detention, always benefit from the full protection of the law.

515. On January 22, 2009, President Obama issued three Executive Orders relating to U.S. detention and interrogation policies broadly and the Guantánamo Bay detention facility specifically. One of those orders, Executive Order 13491,

Ensuring Lawful Interrogations, *inter alia*, directed the Central Intelligence Agency (CIA) to close as expeditiously as possible any detention facilities it operated, and not to operate any such detention facilities in the future (section 4 (a) of E. O. 13491). Consistent with the Executive Order, CIA does not operate detention facilities. The Department of Defense (DoD) operates transit and screening facilities that are distinct from theater detention facilities. Consistent with the laws of war, the armed forces use these facilities to remove individuals from the immediate dangers of the battlefield so that appropriate military officials can determine who the detained persons are and whether they should be detained further. The majority of individuals are released from these facilities after the screening process determines that further detention is unnecessary. The small number of individuals not released shortly after capture are subsequently transferred to a theater internment facility structured for longer-term detention. Transit and screening sites are operated consistent with international legal obligations and U.S. law and policy, including Common Article 3 of the Geneva Conventions, the Detainee Treatment Act, and DoD Directive 2310. 01.

516. Executive Order 13491 further provides, *inter alia*, that individuals detained in any armed conflict shall in all circumstances be treated humanely (section 3(a)); and that such individuals in U.S. custody or effective control "shall not be subjected to any interrogation technique or approach, or any treatment related to interrogation, that is not authorized by and listed in Army Field Manual 2-22. 3" (section 3(b)).

517. The Executive Order additionally requires that:

All departments and agencies of the Federal Government shall provide the International Committee of the Red Cross (ICRC) with notification of, and timely access to, any individual detained in any armed conflict in the custody or under the effective control of an officer, employee, or other agent of the United States Government or detained within a facility owned, operated, or controlled by a department or agency of the United States Government, consistent with Department of Defense regulations and policies. (section 4(b)).

Department of Defense (DoD) Directive 2310. 01E ("The Department of Defense Detainee Program") states that the ICRC "shall be allowed to offer its services during an armed conflict, however characterized, to which the United States is a party."[10] Consistent with E. O. 13491 and DoD policy, the United States assigns internment serial numbers to all detainees held in U.S. custody in connection with armed conflict as soon as practicable and in all cases within 14 days of capture, and grants the ICRC access to such detainees. The ICRC is made aware of and has access to all U.S. law of war detention facilities.

518. The Supreme Court in Hamdan v. Rumsfeld, 548 U.S. 557, 630-631 (2006), determined that Common Article 3 to the 1949 Geneva Conventions protects "individuals associated with neither a signatory nor even a nonsignatory 'Power' who are involved in a conflict 'in the territory of' a signatory," and thus establishes a minimum standard applicable to the conflict with al Qaeda. Consistent with this ruling, and regardless of where an individual is detained, DoD Directive 2310. 01E states that it is Department of Defense policy that "[a]ll detainees shall be treated humanely and in accordance with U.S. law, the law of war, and applicable U.S. policy."[11] "All persons subject to this Directive [DoD Directive 2310. 01E] shall observe the requirements of the law of war, and shall apply, without regard to the detainee's legal status, at a minimum the standards articulated in Common Article 3 of the Geneva Conventions of 1949..."[12] Furthermore, Congress and the President have unambiguously declared that the United States shall not engage in torture or inhuman treatment. See e. g., Detainee Treatment Act, 42 U.S. C. 2000dd ("No individual in the custody or under the physical control of the United States Government, regardless of nationality or physical location, shall be subject to cruel, inhuman, or degrading treatment or punishment.").

519. Guantánamo. Another of the three Executive Orders, Executive Order 13492, requires that "[n]o individual currently detained at Guantánamo shall be held in the custody or under the effective control of any officer, employee, or other agent of the United States Government, or at a facility owned, operated, or controlled by a department or agency of the United States, except in conformity with all applicable laws governing the conditions of such confinement, including Common Article 3 of the Geneva Conventions."13] This Executive Order directed the Secretary of Defense to undertake a comprehensive review of the conditions of confinement at Guantánamo to assess compliance with Common Article 3 of the Geneva Conventions. Admiral Patrick Walsh, then Vice Chief of Naval Operations, assembled a team of experts from throughout the Department of Defense to conduct an assessment that considered all aspects of detention operations and facilities at Guantánamo. The review concluded that the conditions of detention at

Guantánamo were in conformity with Common Article 3 of the Geneva Conventions. [14] The United States has continued to ensure that the Guantánamo facility comports with Common Article 3 and all other applicable laws.

520. Afghanistan. The United States has strengthened the procedural protections for law of war detainees in Afghanistan, under a detention authority which includes those persons who "planned authorized, committed, or aided the terrorist attacks that occurred on September 11, 2001, and persons who harbored those responsible for those attacks" as well as "persons who were part of, or substantially supported, Taliban, al-Qaeda forces or associated forces that are engaged in hostilities against the United States or its coalition partners, including any person who has committed a belligerent act, or has directly supported hostilities, in aid of such enemy forces." In July 2009, the Department of Defense improved its review procedures for individuals held at the Detention Facility in Parwan (DFIP) at Bagram airfield, Afghanistan. The basis for the detainee's detention is reviewed 60 days after transfer to the DFIP, six months later, and periodically thereafter. These robust procedures improve the ability of the United States to assess whether the facts support the detention of each individual, and enhance a detainee's ability to challenge the basis of detention as well as the determination that continued internment is necessary to mitigate the threat posed by the detainee. For example, each detainee is appointed a personal representative, who is required to act in the best interests of the detainee and has access to all reasonably available information (including classified information) relevant to review board proceedings. Detainees can present evidence and witnesses if reasonably available, and the United States helps facilitate witness appearances in person, telephonically, or by video conferencing. The unclassified portions of review board proceedings are generally open, including to family, nongovernmental observers, and other interested parties. Determinations that a detainee meets the criteria for continued detention are reviewed for legal sufficiency by a Judge Advocate.

521. In paragraph 13 of its Concluding Observations, the Committee recommended that the United States ensure that any revision of the Army Field Manual provide only for interrogation techniques in conformity with the international understanding of the scope of the prohibition contained in article 7 of the Covenant; that the current interrogation techniques or any revised techniques are binding on all agencies of the United States Government and any others acting on its behalf; that there are effective means to file suit against abuses committed by agencies operating outside the military structure and that appropriate sanctions be imposed on its personnel who used or approved the use of now prohibited techniques; that the right to reparation of the victims of such practices is respected; and that the United States inform the Committee of any revisions of the interrogation techniques approved by the Army Field Manual.

522. The Army Field Manual is consistent with Article 7 of the Covenant. As noted above, in Executive Order 13491, the President ordered that, "[c]onsistent with the requirements of... the Convention Against Torture, Common Article 3, and other laws regulating the treatment and interrogation of individuals detained in any armed conflict," individuals detained in any armed conflict shall in all circumstances be treated humanely and shall not be subjected to violence to life and person (including murder of all kinds, mutilation, cruel treatment, and torture), nor to outrages upon personal dignity (including humiliating and degrading treatment), whenever such individuals are in the custody or under the effective control of an officer, employee, or other agent of the U.S. Government or detained within a facility owned, operated, or controlled by a department or agency of the United States. " (section 3(a)).

The President further ordered that an individual in the custody or under the effective control of an officer, employee, or other agent of the United States Government, or detained within a facility owned, operated, or controlled by a department or agency of the United States, in any armed conflict, shall not be subjected to any interrogation technique or approach, or any treatment related to interrogation, that is not authorized by and listed in Army Field Manual 2-22. 3. (section 3(b)).

The Order provided that in relying on the Army Field Manual, "officers, employees, and other agents of the United States Government..." "may not, in conducting interrogations, rely upon any interpretation of the law governing interrogation — including interpretations of Federal criminal laws, the Convention Against Torture, Common Article 3, Army Field Manual 2-22. 3, and its predecessor document, Army Field Manual 34-52 — issued by the Department of Justice between September 11, 2001, and January 20, 2009." (Section 3(c)).

523. Executive Order 13491 also revoked Executive Order 13440 (2007), which had interpreted Common Article 3 of the Geneva Conventions as applied to CIA detention and interrogation practices. The Order further provided that all executive directives, orders, and regulations inconsistent with Executive Order 13491, including but not limited to

those issued to or by the CIA from September 11, 2001 to January 20, 2009 concerning detention or the interrogation of detained individuals, were revoked to the extent of their inconsistency with that order.

524. Interrogations undertaken in compliance with Army Field Manual 2-22. 3 are consistent with U.S. domestic and international law obligations. For example, the Army Field Manual states that "[a]ll captured or detained personnel, regardless of status, shall be treated humanely, and in accordance with the Detainee Treatment Act of 2005 and DoD Directive 2310.1E... and no person in the custody or under the control of DoD, regardless of nationality or physical location, shall be subject to torture or cruel, inhuman, or degrading treatment or punishment, in accordance with and as defined in U.S. law." The Field Manual provides specific guidance, including a non-exclusive list of actions that are prohibited when used in conjunction with interrogations. Techniques that are not addressed in the Field Manual are considered prohibited. The Field Manual also provides guidance to be used while formulating interrogation plans for approval. It states: "[i]n attempting to determine if a contemplated approach or technique should be considered prohibited...consider these two tests before submitting the plan for approval:

- If the proposed approach technique were used by the enemy against one of your fellow soldiers, would you believe the soldier had been abused?
- Could your conduct in carrying out the proposed technique violate a law or regulation? Keep in mind that even if you personally would not consider your actions to constitute abuse, the law may be more restrictive.

If you answer yes to either of these tests, the contemplated action should not be conducted.

525. The Army Field Manual authorizes appropriate interrogation techniques for use by all U.S. agencies for detention in armed conflict. Executive Order 13491 established a Special Interagency Task Force on Interrogation and Transfer Policies to evaluate whether the Army Field Manual's interrogation techniques provided non-military U.S. agencies with an appropriate means of acquiring necessary intelligence and, if warranted, to recommend different guidance for those agencies. On August 24, 2009, the Attorney General announced that the Task Force had concluded that the Army Field Manual provides appropriate guidance on interrogation for military interrogators, and that no additional or different guidance was necessary for other agencies. The Task Force reaffirmed that, in the context of any armed conflict, interrogations by all U.S. agencies must comply with the techniques, treatments, and approaches listed in the Army Field Manual (without prejudice to authorized non-coercive techniques of law enforcement agencies). These conclusions rested on the Task Force's unanimous assessment, including that of the Intelligence Community, that the practices and techniques identified by the Army Field Manual or currently used by law enforcement provide adequate and effective means of conducting interrogations.

526. The Task Force concluded, moreover that the United States could improve its ability to interrogate the most dangerous terrorists by forming a specialized interrogation group, or High Value Detainee Interrogation Group (HIG), that would bring together the most effective and experienced interrogators and support personnel from law enforcement, the U.S. Intelligence Community, and the Department of Defense to conduct interrogations in a manner that will continue to strengthen national security consistent with the rule of law. The Task Force recommended that this specialized interrogation group develop a set of best practices and disseminate these for training purposes among agencies that conduct interrogations. In addition, the Task Force recommended that a scientific research program for interrogation be established to study the comparative effectiveness of interrogation approaches and techniques, with the goal of identifying the existing techniques that are most effective and developing new lawful techniques to improve intelligence interrogations.

527. U.S. obligations under the law of war do not mandate payment of reparations to individuals; however, the U.S. Government may, in certain circumstances, provide monetary payments or other forms of assistance to persons who suffer loss or injury due to combat or other operations. Such discretionary payments, often called "condolence" or "solatia" payments, do not constitute an admission of legal liability or settlement of any claim. In some circumstances, a claim based on one of several statutory authorities, including the Foreign Claims Act, 10 U.S. C. 2734, and the Military Claims Act, 10 U.S. C. 2733, may provide compensation to detainees for damage, loss, or destruction of personal property while detained.

528. Private suits for civil damages have been brought against private contractors by alleged victims of detainee abuse. See, e. g., *Saleh v. Titan*, 580 F. 3d 1 (D. C. Cir. 2009), cert. denied 131 S. Ct. 3055 (2011) (dismissing claims against pri-

vate contractor companies whose employees had worked as interrogators and translators at Abu Ghraib prison); *Al Shimari v. CACI international, Inc.*, 658 F. 3d 413 (4th Cir. 2011) (reversing and instructing district court to dismiss claims against private contractor); *Al-Quraishi v. L-3 Services, Inc*, 657 F. 3d 201 (4th Cir. 2011) (same); *Abbass v. CACI Premier Tech.*, Inc., No. 09-229 (D. D. C.) (case voluntarily dismissed). Former detainees and/or their families have also brought civil actions seeking damages from current or former government officials. Such claims, when asserted by aliens held outside the United States, have been repeatedly rejected by the courts. See, e.g., *Ali v. Rumsfeld*, 649 F.3d 762 (D.C. Cir. 2011); *Rasul v. Myers*, 563 F.3d 527 (D.C. Cir.), cert. denied, 130 S. Ct. 1013 (2009). Some courts, however, have suggested, over the government's opposition, that such claims when brought by citizens may proceed. See *Vance v. Rumsfeld, et al.*, Nos. 10-1687, 10-2442 (7th Cir. Aug. 8, 2011); *Padilla v. Yoo*, 633 F. Supp 2d 1005 (N.D. Cal. 2009), appeal pending. As noted above, detainees can attempt to seek monetary redress through an administrative claims process, under the Military Claims Act and the Foreign Claims Act. Investigations and prosecutions conducted by the U.S. government relating to claims of detainee abuse are addressed below.

529. The Committee recommended in paragraph 14 of the Concluding Observations that the United States should conduct prompt and independent investigations into all allegations concerning suspicious deaths, torture or cruel, inhuman or degrading treatment or punishment inflicted by its personnel (including commanders) as well as contract employees, in detention facilities in Guantánamo Bay, Afghanistan, Iraq and other overseas locations; that the United States should ensure that those responsible are prosecuted and punished in accordance with the gravity of the crime; that the United States should adopt all necessary measures to prevent the recurrence of such behaviors, in particular by providing adequate training and clear guidance to personnel (including commanders) and contract employees, about their respective obligations and responsibilities in line with article 7 and 10 of the Covenant; and that during the course of any legal proceedings, the United States should also refrain from relying on evidence obtained by treatment incompatible with article 7. The Committee has asked to be informed about the measures taken by the United States to ensure the respect of the right to reparation for the victims.

530. The United States does not permit its personnel to engage in acts of torture or cruel, inhuman or degrading treatment of people in its custody, either within or outside U.S. territory. This principle is embodied in multiple U.S. laws and has been forcefully reaffirmed by President Obama with respect to all situations of armed conflict, as discussed above.

531. The Obama Administration has released, in whole or in part, more than 40 OLC opinions and memoranda concerning national security matters as a result of litigation under the Freedom of Information Act. These include four previously classified memoranda released on April 16, 2009, which addressed the legality of various techniques used to interrogate terrorism suspects detained by the CIA and which President Obama revoked to the extent that they were inconsistent with Executive Order 13491.

532. The government of the United States, in various fora, has undertaken numerous actions relating to the alleged mistreatment of detainees. The bulk of the investigation and prosecution of allegations of mistreatment of detainees held in connection with counterterrorism operations, including administrative and criminal inquiries and proceedings, have been carried out by the Department of Defense and other U.S. government components that have jurisdiction to carry out such actions.

533. Department of Justice. The Department of Justice has successfully prosecuted two instances of detainee abuse in federal civilian court. In 2003, the U.S. Department of Justice brought criminal charges against David Passaro, a CIA contractor accused of brutally assaulting a detainee in Afghanistan in 2003. The CIA described his conduct as "unlawful, reprehensible, and neither authorized nor condoned by the Agency." The then Attorney General stated that "the United States will not tolerate criminal acts of brutality and violence against detainees." And the U.S. Attorney noted that the extraterritorial jurisdiction exercised by the United States is "[n]ot only vital to investigating and prosecuting terrorists, but also it is instrumental in protecting the civil liberties of those on U.S. military installations and diplomatic missions overseas, regardless of their nationality." See press release at http://www.justice.gov/opa/pr/2004/June/04_crm_414. htm. Following a jury trial, Passaro was convicted of felony assault. On August 10, 2009, the United States Court of Appeals for the Fourth Circuit upheld the conviction, holding that a U.S. federal court has jurisdiction over the trial of an American citizen for committing assaults on the premises of U.S. military missions abroad. In February 2010, the U.S. Supreme Court refused to hear an appeal by Passaro. Passaro was sentenced to 8 years and 4 months in prison.

534. In a second case, on February 3, 2009, Don Ayala, a U.S. contractor in Afghanistan, was convicted in U.S. federal court of voluntary manslaughter in the death of an individual whom he and U.S. soldiers had detained. See U.S. Attorney's Office Press Release at http://www.justice.gov/usao/vae/Pressreleases/02-FebruaryPDFArchive/09/20090203 ayalanr.html.

535. The United States Attorney's Office for the Eastern District of Virginia continues to investigate various allegations of abuse of detainees. In addition, the Attorney General announced on August 24, 2009, that he had ordered "a preliminary review into whether federal laws were violated in connection with interrogation of specific detainees at overseas locations." See http://www.justice.gov/ag/speeches/2009/ag-speech-0908241. html. Assistant U. S. Attorney John Durham assembled an investigative team of experienced professionals to recommend to the Attorney General whether a full investigation was warranted "into whether the law was violated in connection with the interrogation of certain detainees." Following a two-year investigation, on June 30, 2011, the Justice Department announced that it was opening a full criminal investigation into the deaths of two individuals in CIA custody overseas, and that it had concluded that further investigation into the other cases examined in the preliminary investigation was not warranted.

536. U.S. law provides several avenues for the domestic prosecution of U.S. Government officials and contractors who commit torture and other serious crimes overseas. For example, 18 U.S. C. 2340A makes it a crime to commit torture outside the United States. The War Crimes Act, 18 U.S. C. 2441, makes it a crime for any member of the U.S. armed forces or U.S. national to commit a "war crime," defined as, *inter alia*, "a grave breach in any of the international conventions signed at Geneva 12 August 1949" or certain enumerated breaches of common Article 3, whether inside or outside the United States. Similarly, under the provisions of the Military Extraterritorial Jurisdiction Act (MEJA), 18 U.S. C. 3261-3267, persons employed by or accompanying the Armed Forces outside the United States may be prosecuted domestically if they commit a serious criminal offense overseas. The MEJA specifically covers all civilian employees and contractors directly employed by the Department of Defense and, as amended in October 2004, those employed by other U.S. Government agencies, to the extent that such employment relates to supporting the mission of the Department of Defense overseas. See, e. g., 18 U.S. C. 3261(a) (criminal jurisdiction over felonies committed" while employed by or accompanying the Armed Forces outside the United States"); see also 10 U.S. C. 802(10) (military jurisdiction over "persons serving with or accompanying an armed force in the field" "[i]n time of declared war or a contingency operation"); National Defense Authorization Act for Fiscal Year 2005, Pub. L. No. 108-375 (2005 Act), Section 1206 Report at 10-13 (describing criminal and contractual remedies in detail)

...

549. In paragraph 15 of the Concluding Observations, the Committee recommended that the United States should amend section 1005 of the Detainee Treatment Act so as to allow detainees in Guantánamo Bay to seek review of their treatment or conditions of detention before a court.

550. The United States complies with the standards of Common Article 3 to the Geneva Conventions and the Convention Against Torture, at a minimum, in its detention operations, including those at Guantánamo. As noted, the President's Executive Order 13491, Ensuring Lawful Interrogations, provides that individuals detained in any armed conflict shall in all circumstances be treated humanely. As noted above, the United States has recently conducted an extensive review and concluded that current U.S. military practices are consistent with the requirements of Additional Protocol II and Article 75 of Additional Protocol I to the 1949 Geneva Conventions.

Source: U.S. Department of State, https://www.state.gov/j/drl/rls/179781.htm

7. COMMON CORE DOCUMENT FORMING PART OF THE REPORTS OF STATES PARTIES: UNITED STATES OF AMERICA, 2012

This document serves as a basic document used by the U.S. in all its treaty body reports. It is an informational foundation for the Committee to consider in conjunction with the full Fourth Report. It is submitted to all the treaties bodies to which the U.S. is a state party. The latest Common Core report was issued in 2012 and served as part of the fourth periodic state report process before the HRCtee in 2011-15. Primary Source Document 8 is the updated version.

{Excerpt}

[Text]

I. General information about the reporting State

A. Demographic, economic, social and cultural characteristics

1. Demographic indicators

The United States is a multi-racial, multi-ethnic, and multi-cultural society in which racial and ethnic diversity is ever increasing. Virtually every national, racial, ethnic, cultural, and religious group in the world is represented in the U.S. population. The United States decennial census in 2010 showed that from 2000 to 2010, the U.S. population grew by 27. 3 million (9.7%) to 308. 9 million. This represented a lower growth rate than was seen from 1990 to 2000 (13.2%), but was similar to the growth rate from 1980 to 1990 (9.8%). Regional growth was faster for the South and West than for the Midwest and Northeast. The West for the first time surpassed the population of the Midwest. Overall, the South and West accounted for 84. 4% of the U.S. population increase from 2000 to 2010. Over four fifths (83.7%) of the U.S. population in 2010 lived in the nation's 366 metropolitan areas — areas with core urban populations of 50,000 or more. http://www.census.gov/prod/cen2010/briefs/c2010br-01.pdf.

2. More than half the 27. 3 million population growth from 2000 to 2010 was due to a 15. 2 million population increase in the Hispanic or Latino population. 7 During this period, the Hispanic or Latino population grew by 43% from 35.3 million in 2000 to 50. 5 million in 2010 — from 13% to 16% of the total population. The non-Hispanic/Latino population grew at a relatively slower rate — about 5%. Within the non-Hispanic/Latino population, those who reported their race as White alone grew the most slowly (1%). While the non-Hispanic/Latino White alone population increased numerically from 194.6 million to 196.8 million over the 10-year period, its proportion of the total population declined from 69 percent to 64 percent.

3. In 2010, approximately 97% of all respondents reported only one race. From 2000 to 2010, all major race groups experienced increases in numbers, but the groups grew at different rates.

4. The Asian alone population was the fastest growing race group — growing by 43.3% from 10. 2 million to 14. 7 million — from 3.6% to 4.8% of the population. The Native Hawaiian and Pacific Islander (NHPI) alone population grew by more than a third, from 398,835 to 540,013, increasing its proportion of the population from 0. 1% to 0. 2%. The American Indian and Alaska Native (AIAN) alone population grew by 18% from 2. 5 to 2. 9 million, remaining at 0. 9% of the overall population. The Black or African American alone population grew by 12. 3% from 34. 7 million to 38. 9 million — increasing its proportion from 12. 3% to 12. 6%. The White only population (including White Hispanics/Latinos) grew by the smallest percentage — only 5. 7% — and was the only group to experience an actual decrease in its proportion of the population — from 75% to 72%. Of the 27. 3 million people added to the total population, the White alone population made up just under half of the growth — increasing by 12. 1 million. Within this White alone population, however, the vast majority of the growth was propelled by persons of Hispanic/Latino ethnicity.

...

II. General Framework for the protection and promotion of human rights

A. Acceptance of international human rights norms

104. The United States is committed to the cause of human rights. As a nation built on the moral truths of the Universal Declaration of Human Rights, the United States supported the adoption of that instrument. In addition, the United States is party to the International Covenant on Civil and Political Rights; the International Convention on the Elimination of All Forms of Racial Discrimination; the Convention against Torture and Other Cruel, Inhuman or Degrading Treatment or Punishment; the Optional Protocol to the Convention on the Rights of the Child on the involvement of

children in armed conflict; and the Optional Protocol to the Convention on the Rights of the Child on the sale of children, child prostitution and child pornography. The United States has also announced its support for the United Nations Declaration on the Rights of Indigenous Peoples.

105. Under our Constitution, treaty ratification requires not only executive approval, but also the consent of the U.S. Senate by a supermajority vote of two-thirds of those present and voting. For this reason, the United States has often pursued a practice of ?compliance before ratification, in contrast to the practice of ?ratification before compliance that some other nations may pursue. The Obama Administration supports ratification of the Convention on the Elimination of All Forms of Discrimination against Women (CEDAW) and the Convention on the Rights of Persons with Disabilities.

106. In addition to the international human rights instruments noted above, the United States is party to the Convention on the Prevention and Punishment of the Crime of Genocide; the Slavery Convention of 1926, as amended; the 1967 Protocol to the Convention relating to the Status of Refugees; the United Nations Convention against Transnational Organized Crime, including the Protocol against the Smuggling of Migrants by Land, Sea and Air; and the Protocol to Prevent, Suppress and Punish Trafficking in Persons, Especially Women and Children. The United States is also party to the Convention on the Civil Aspects of International Child Abduction and the Convention concerning the Prohibition and Immediate Action for the Elimination of the Worst Forms of Child Labour; and is a signatory to the Convention on Jurisdiction, Applicable Law, Recognition, Enforcement and Co-operation in respect of Parental Responsibility and Measures for the Protection of Children. The United States is party to the four 1949 Geneva Conventions for the Amelioration of the Condition of the Wounded and Sick in Armed Forces in the Field; the Amelioration of the Condition of Wounded, Sick and Shipwrecked Members of the Armed Forces at Sea; the Treatment of Prisoners of War; and the Protection of Civilian Persons in Time of War.

107. The United States is also a member of the Organization of American States and participates and cooperates actively in the proceedings of the Inter-American Commission on Human Rights. One of the seven Commissioners is from the United States.

B. Legal framework for the protection of human rights at the national level

108. The essential guarantees of human rights and fundamental freedoms within the United States are set forth in the Constitution and statutes of the United States, as well as the constitutions and statutes of the states and other constituent units. In practice, the enforcement of these guarantees ultimately depends on the existence of an independent judiciary with the power to invalidate acts by the other branches of government that conflict with those guarantees. Maintenance of a republican form of government with vigorous democratic traditions, popularly elected executives and legislatures, and the deep-rooted legal protection of freedoms of opinion, expression and the press all contribute to the protection of fundamental rights against governmental limitation and encroachment.

1. U.S. Constitution

109. The Constitution includes 27 amendments that have been added since 1791. Amending the Constitution requires approval by two-thirds of each house of the Congress, or by a national convention, followed by ratification by three-quarters of the states. The first 10 amendments provide for the basic protection of many of those individual rights that are fundamental to the democratic system of government. They remain at the heart of the United States legal system today, just as they were two centuries ago, although the specific rights they guarantee have been extensively elaborated by the judiciary over the course of time. Individuals may assert these rights against the government in judicial proceedings.

110. First Amendment guarantees freedom of religious exercise, speech and press, the right of peaceful assembly, and the right to petition the government to correct wrongs; and it prohibits laws respecting the establishment of religion. The Second Amendment protects a right to own firearms in certain circumstances. The Third Amendment provides that troops may not be quartered in a private home without the owner's consent. The Fourth Amendment guards against unreasonable searches, arrests, and seizures of persons and property.

111. The next four amendments deal with the system of justice. The Fifth Amendment forbids trial for a major crime except after indictment by a grand jury; it prohibits repeated trials for the same offence, forbids punishment without due process of law, and provides that an accused person may not be compelled to testify against him or herself. The Sixth Amendment guarantees the right to legal counsel for the accused in most criminal proceedings, and provides that witnesses shall be compelled to attend the trial and testify in the presence of the accused. The Seventh Amendment preserves trial by jury in many civil cases involving anything valued at more than 20 U.S. dollars. The Eighth Amendment forbids excessive bail or fines and cruel and unusual punishment.

112. The Ninth Amendment declares that the enumeration in the Constitution of certain rights shall not be construed to deny or disparage others retained by the people. The Tenth Amendment sets forth the federal and democratic nature of the United States system of government, providing that powers not delegated by the Constitution to the federal government, nor prohibited by it to the states, are reserved to the states or the people. The Tenth Amendment recognizes that the federal government is a government of limited jurisdiction, empowered to do only what the Constitution authorizes it to do, and that all other powers remain vested in the people, and in their duly constituted state governments.

113. Amendments to the Constitution subsequent to the original Bill of Rights cover a wide range of subjects. One of the most far-reaching is the Fourteenth Amendment, by which a clear and simple definition of citizenship was established and broadened guarantees of due process, equal treatment, and equal protection of the law were confirmed. This amendment, adopted in 1868, has been interpreted to apply most of the protections of the Bill of Rights to the states. By other amendments, the judicial power of the national government was limited; the method of electing the president was changed; slavery was forbidden; the right to vote was protected against denial because of race, color, sex, or previous condition of servitude; the congressional power to levy taxes was extended to incomes; and the election of United States Senators by popular vote was instituted.

114. The Constitution provides explicitly that the Constitution, laws, and treaties of the United States are the ?supreme Law of the Land. This clause means that when state constitutions or laws passed by state legislatures conflict with the federal Constitution, laws, or treaties, they have no force or effect. Decisions handed down by the Supreme Court of the United States and subordinate federal courts over the course of two centuries have confirmed and strengthened this doctrine of federal law supremacy.

2. State constitutions

115. As indicated above, the protections provided by the federal Constitution and statutes are applicable nationwide, generally providing a minimum standard of guaranteed rights for all persons in the United States. While the laws of individual states cannot detract from the protections afforded to their citizens by federal law, states are, except where prohibited by federal law or where it infringes on a protected federal right, free to offer their citizens greater protections of civil and political rights.

Historically, states individually or collectively have often led the federal government in the advancement and protection of civil and political rights. For example, starting with Vermont in 1777 and through 1862, most Northern states curtailed or abolished slavery before the federal Constitution did in 1865. Likewise, women first gained the right to vote in Wyoming Territory in 1869, while federal law did not extend that right until 1920.

More recently, in the latter half of the twentieth century, federal law and the federal courts played a more active role in civil rights protections. State courts, however, continue to play an important role in this arena. In many cases, in keeping with the federal system of government, individual state laws afford their citizens greater protections than the federal Constitution requires. See, e. g., *Prune Yard Shopping Center v. Robins*, 447 U.S. 74 (1980) (holding that broader state protections for free speech, protecting expression in a public shopping center, did not violate the federal Constitution). Broader state protections have been afforded in a number of areas, including free speech, religious liberty, property rights, victims' rights, and the provision of government services. State constitutions vary widely in length, detail, and similarity to the U.S. Constitution. As a result, a state court decision, while it may expand on a right protected by the U.S. Constitution, may rest on grounds very different from those on which a similar federal case would be decided.

116. Some state constitutions also provide greater protections against the establishment of religion than are provided by the First Amendment to the federal Constitution. For instance, based on the state constitution's broad prohibition of

governmental assistance to an institution not owned by the state, the Supreme Court of Nebraska found unconstitutional a statute under which public school books were lent to parochial schools, see *Gaffney v. State Department of Education*, 220 N. W. 2d 550 (Neb. 1974). On similar grounds, the Supreme Court of Idaho struck down a statute authorizing publicly provided transportation of students to non-public schools, see *Epeldi v. Engelking*, 488 P. 2d 860 (Id. 1971). In addition, while the U.S. Supreme Court has upheld the display of a nativity scene on public property as consistent with the First Amendment, the California Supreme Court has nonetheless held that the state constitution's ban on preference for religious sects prohibited the display of a lighted cross on public grounds in celebration of Christmas and Easter, compare *Lynch v. Donnelly*, 465 U.S. 668 (1984) with *Fox v. City of Los Angeles*, 587 P. 2d 663 (Cal. 1978).

Despite these examples, state courts are not uniform in their willingness to find greater protections within state constitutions than those guaranteed by the federal government. As is appropriate in a federal system, each state's protections are ultimately tailored by that state's democratic process. States are prohibited simply from subverting established federal protections.

3. Statutory law

There is no single statute or mechanism by which human rights and fundamental freedoms are guaranteed or enforced in the United States legal system. Rather, domestic law provides extensive protections through enforcement of the constitutional provisions cited above and a variety of statutes, which typically provide for judicial and/or administrative remedies. The basic federal statutes, some of which apply to private entities, include the following. Other statutes are referenced in the United States reports on individual treaties.

The 1866 and 1871 Civil Rights Acts (protecting property rights, freedom to contract, and providing federal remedies for private individuals subjected to unlawful discrimination by persons acting ?under color of law); The Civil Rights Act of 1964 (the most comprehensive federal statute, which prohibits discrimination in a number of areas, for example discrimination based on race, color, national origin, or religion in places of public accommodation; discrimination on the basis of race, color, or national origin in federally funded programs; and discrimination on the basis of race, color, national origin, sex, or religion in employment);

- The 1965 Voting Rights Act (invalidating discriminatory voter qualifications);
- The 1968 Fair Housing Act (providing the right to be free from discrimination in housing and the obligation for federal, state, and local governments to affirmatively further fair housing through the promotion of balanced living patterns and equal access to opportunity neighborhoods).
- Protection against violent acts undertaken because of actual or perceived race, color, religion, or national origin, or because of actual or perceived gender, disability, sexual orientation or gender identity is afforded by: The 2009 Matthew Shepard and James Byrd, Jr. Hate Crime Prevention Act.
- Similarly, in the area of sex discrimination, individuals benefit from the protections of the Equal Protection Clause, as well as statutes such as:
- The 1963 Equal Pay Act (equal pay for equal work);
- Title VII of the Civil Rights Act of 1964 (non-discrimination in employment based on sex);
- The Education Amendments of 1972 (non-discrimination in all federally-funded education programs and activities, including student recruitment, admissions, housing, counseling, financial and employment assistance, health and insurance benefits and services, and employment practices and benefits);
- The Equal Credit Opportunity Act (equal access and non-discrimination in housing, real estate and brokerage);
- The Pregnancy Discrimination Act of 1978 (non-discrimination in employment);
- The Public Health Service Act (prohibiting discrimination in federally assisted health training programs, projects for assistance in transition from homelessness, preventative health and health services block grants, community mental health services block grants, and substance abuse prevention and treatment block grants);
- The Social Security Act (prohibiting discrimination in maternal child and health services block grants);
- The Family Violence Prevention and Services Act;
- The Low-Income Energy Assistance Act of 1981;
- The Community Services Block Grant Act; and
- The 2010 Patient Protection and Affordable Care Act (nondiscrimination in obtaining health insurance — this act also covers discrimination on the basis of race, color, national origin, age, and disability).

121. Protection against age discrimination is provided by statutes such as the:
- Age Discrimination in Employment Act of 1967 (prohibiting discrimination in employment against workers or applicants 40 years of age or older); and
- Age Discrimination Act of 1975 (prohibiting discrimination based on age in federally funded programs).

123. Protection for persons with disabilities is provided by statutes such as the:
- Rehabilitation Act of 1973 (prohibiting disability discrimination in federal government employment and under any program or activity receiving federal financial assistance or conducted by a federal agency or the United States Postal Service);
- Civil Rights of Institutionalized Persons Act of 1980;
- The Americans with Disabilities Act of 1990 (although persons with disabilities have long been protected against disability-based discrimination by federal agencies or by programs and activities that receive federal financial assistance, this Act broadens these protections to include most public and private entities whether or not they receive federal financial assistance); this Act was recently amended by the Americans with Disabilities Amendments Act of 2008 to ensure a broad interpretation of ?disability and a broad interpretation of who is covered by the Act covers as an ?individual with a disability; and
- The Individual with Disabilities Education Act (requiring public schools to make available to all eligible children with disabilities a free appropriate public education in the least restrictive environment appropriate to their individual needs).

124. Protection from discrimination based on genetic information is provided by laws such as the:
- The Genetic Information Nondiscrimination Act of 2008 (preventing discrimination in employment or health insurance based on genetic information, including genetic testing and family medical history.) 125. Indian tribes are subject to the:
- Indian Civil Rights Act of 1968, which imposes on tribes such basic requirements as free speech protection, free exercise of religion, due process and equal protection.
- Recent permanent residents, temporary residents, asylees and refugees are protected by: The anti-discrimination provisions of the Immigration and Nationality Act, at 8 U.S. C. 1324b(a) (1) (B) from employment discrimination based on citizenship status;
- 8 U.S. C. 1324b(a) (1) (A) from discrimination based on place of birth, country of origin, ancestry, native language, accent or because they are perceived as foreign;
- Title VII of the Civil Rights Act of 1964 (nondiscrimination in employment based on national origin).

126. Most states and large cities as well as other jurisdictions, such as tribes, have adopted their own statutory and administrative schemes for protecting and promoting basic rights and freedoms. For the most part, state statutory protections mirror those provided by the U.S. Constitution and federal law. Typically, state constitutions and statutes protect individuals from discrimination in housing, employment, accommodations, credit and education. For example, a Minnesota statute prohibits discrimination in sales, rentals, or leases of housing. Minn. Stat. sec. 363. 03 (1992). Massachusetts makes it unlawful to refuse to hire or to discharge someone from employment on discriminatory grounds, or to discriminate in education. Mass. Ann. Laws ch. 151B, sec. 4; ch. 151C, sec 1 (1993). California requires that all persons be free and equal in accommodations, advantages, facilities, privileges and services of business establishments. Cal. Civ. Code sec. 51 (1993). Texas prohibits discrimination in credit or loans. Texas Revised Civil Statutes Annotated art. 5069-207 (1993) . State, local, tribal and territorial human rights laws and enforcement entities are described in greater detail in Annex A to this Common Core Document.

127. Prevention of the sale of children, child prostitution and child pornography and protection of the rights of victims is carried out through U.S. federal and state laws, both criminal and civil. Among the federal laws that provide for such prevention and protection are the following:
- The National Organ Transplant Act (prohibiting transfer of human organs for valuable consideration for use in human transplants if the transfer affects interstate commerce);
- The Trafficking Victims Protection Act of 2000, as amended (creating new crimes and enhanced penalties for existing crimes prohibiting trafficking in persons, including trafficking of children for sex and labor exploitation and providing protection of and assistance for victims);

- The Intercountry Adoption Act of 2000 (implementing the Hague Convention on Protection of Children and Cooperation in respect of Intercountry Adoption, including measures to prevent illegal adoptions);
- The Prosecutorial Remedies and Other Tools to end the Exploitation of Children Today Act of 2003 (strengthening law enforcement measures to address sexual crimes against children, including child pornography, child sex tourism and child abduction, and establishing a nationwide program to alert officials of a child abduction);
- The Adam Walsh Child Protection and Safety Act of 2006 (strengthening law enforcement measures to address sex offenders and to combat sex trafficking of children and sexual offenses against children and creating a national child abuse registry);
- The Providing Resources, Officers, and Technology to Eradicate Cyber Threats to Our Children Act of 2008 (addressing in particular online child obscenity and pornography);
- The Fair Labor Standards Act of 1938, as amended (establishing a minimum age for jobs in general and separately for jobs that have been determined to be particularly hazardous, and limiting hours that children are permitted to work).

128. Prevention of the recruitment and use of children in armed conflict in violation of the Optional Protocol on the involvement of children in armed conflict and protection and recovery of victims is carried out through U.S. federal and state laws, both criminal and civil. Among the federal laws that provide for such prevention and protection are the following:
- The U.S. Selective Service Act (precluding all mandatory recruitment into the U.S. military);
- 10 U.S. C. 505 (establishing seventeen as the minimum age for voluntary recruitment into U.S. armed forces);
- Child Soldiers Accountability Act of 2008 (creating criminal and immigration sanctions for persons recruiting or using child soldiers under the age of 15);
- Child Soldiers Prevention Act of 2008 (prohibiting specific types of military assistance and sales of military equipment to governments identified as recruiting and using child soldiers).

129. Protection against torture and cruel, inhuman or degrading punishment or treatment is provided by the Fifth, Eighth and Fourteenth Amendments to the U.S. Constitution and through U.S. federal and state laws, both criminal and civil. Applicable federal criminal statutes include the following:
- 18 U.S. C. § 2340 et seq. (providing extraterritorial jurisdiction over persons who commit or attempt to commit torture outside the United States if the alleged offender is a U.S. national or is present in the United States);
- 18 U.S. C. § 2441 (defining "war crimes" to include "grave breaches" of Common Article 3 of the Geneva Conventions, including specifically "torture" and "cruel and inhuman treatment");
- 18 U.S. C. § 242 (criminalizing deprivations of Constitutional rights, such as the rights to be free from unreasonable seizure, to be free from summary punishment or cruel and unusual punishment, and the right not to be deprived of liberty without due process of law).

130. Additional protection is provided by statues including the following:
- The Detainee Treatment Act of 2005 and the Military Commissions Acts of 2006 and 2009
- 10 U.S. C. § 948r, prohibiting admission of any statement obtained by the use of torture or by cruel, inhuman, or degrading treatment, as defined by the Detainee Treatment Act of 2005, in a military commission proceeding, except against a person accused of torture or cruel, inhuman, or degrading treatment as evidence that the statement was made;
- 42 U.S. C. § 2000dd, prohibiting cruel, inhuman and degrading treatment or punishment of those who are in the custody or under the physical control of the United States Government regardless of nationality or physical location;
- The Foreign Affairs Reform and Restructuring Act of 1998 (declaring the policy of the United States not to return any person to a country in which there are substantial grounds for believing the person would be in danger of being subjected to torture, regardless of whether the person is physically present in the United States).

4. Treaties and the national legal system

132. Duly ratified treaties are binding on the United States as a matter of international law and constitute the ?supreme Law of the Land under Article VI, cl. 2 of the U.S. Constitution. As a matter of U.S. domestic law, the way in which treaty provisions are implemented varies. In some instances, the United States may enact implementing legislation. Thus, for example, to implement the Genocide Convention, the United States Congress adopted the Genocide Convention Implementation Act of 1987, codified at 18 U.S. C. sec. 1091-93. When such legislation is necessary in order to implement U.S. obligations under a treaty, the United States practice with respect to certain treaties has been to enact the necessary legislation before depositing its instrument of ratification. It is for this reason, for example, that the United States did not deposit its instrument of ratification for the Convention against Torture until 1994, even though the Senate gave its advice and consent to ratification of that treaty in 1990, as Congress did not approve the necessary implementing legislation until May 1994. In other instances, the United States does not take any new legislative action to accompany its ratification because the substantive obligations set forth in a particular treaty are already reflected in existing domestic law. For example, because the human rights and fundamental freedoms guaranteed by the International Covenant on Civil and Political Rights (other than those to which the United States has taken a reservation) have long been protected as a matter of federal constitutional and statutory law, it was not considered necessary to adopt special implementing legislation to give effect to the Covenant's provisions in domestic law. Thus, that important human rights treaty was ratified in 1992 shortly after the Senate gave its advice and consent.

133. Given the subject matter of most treaties, they generally do not contain a provision that creates individually enforceable rights in the courts of the United States. Whether treaty provisions give rise to individually enforceable rights in U.S. courts depends on a number of factors, including the terms, structure, history and subject of the treaty.

134. Remedies are discussed below under Non-discrimination and Equality.

5. Institutions

(a) National institutions

135. Numerous national, state, local, tribal and territorial institutions exist with responsibility for overseeing implementation of human rights, including the advancement of the rights of women, children, the elderly, persons with disabilities, members of minority groups, indigenous peoples, refugees, and others. Such organizations are too numerous to name, but a few examples are set forth here. At the Presidential level, among other initiatives, President Obama has established the White House Council on Women and Girls to promote the fair and equal treatment of American women and girls in all matters of public policy; established the first White House Adviser on Violence Against Women; appointed a Senior Policy Advisor for Native American Affairs; and appointed a Special Assistant to the President for Disability Policy. Many federal government agencies include civil rights mandates as part of their missions, and the Equal Employment Opportunity Commission (EEOC), was specifically established to address issues of discrimination throughout the national workforce. In addition, most federal government departments and many state and local governmental departments and agencies have civil rights offices designed to ensure that civil rights are respected in the carrying out of those departments' missions. Nearly all the states, and some local jurisdictions, tribes, and territories have human rights or civil rights offices and/or commissions, which work to ensure that human rights and civil rights are respected within their jurisdictions. State, local, tribal and territorial organizations are described in greater detail in Annex A to this Common Core Document. In addition, as noted above, thousands of non-governmental organizations also work to ensure implementation of human rights.

(b) Regional human rights mechanisms

136. The Inter-American Commission on Human Rights was established under the Charter of the Organization of American States (OAS) ?to promote the observance and protection of human rights and to serve as a consultative organ of the Organization on these matters. (Article 106) The Commission is an autonomous organ of the OAS and a leading human rights body in the Western hemisphere. The Commission has authority to receive and evaluate individual complaints, make general recommendations, request information, prepare reports, and engage in similar investigatory and disseminating activities regarding the human rights compliance of all OAS states, including the United States.

137. The United States is a member of the OAS and participates and cooperates actively in the proceedings of the Inter-American Commission. One of the seven Commissioners is from the United States. The United States is one of

the Commission's most vocal supporters and defenders among all OAS Member States and is also one of its largest financial contributors, as a result of strong bipartisan Congressional support. The United States recognizes the Commission as an important mechanism for the promotion and protection of human rights in the Americas, in other States as well as our own.

C. Framework within which human rights are promoted at the national level

138. The United States promotes human rights in myriad ways through a variety of institutions and mechanisms at all levels of government and society. The U.S. Congress hears testimony on issues and enacts new legislation. The Executive Branch and the courts actively enforce the laws. The government also actively funds and pursues outreach and programmatic efforts to promote tolerance, mitigate and resolve problems, and assist those whose human rights have been violated. Examples of such activities are set forth in specific treaty reports.

139. Thousands of non-governmental organizations also act to promote human rights with funding from both governmental and private sources. While much has been accomplished, the United States fully recognizes that there is still work to be done to realize the full promise of the U.S. Constitution to ensure equality, equal opportunity and fundamental fairness for all people. The United States therefore continues to be dedicated to moving forward on all fronts toward these goals.

140. The United States continues to look at ways of improving human rights treaty implementation at all levels of government — federal, state and local. Numerous state and local governments within the United States have state and/or local civil rights and/or human rights organizations or commissions, many of which participate in the International Association of Official Human Rights Agencies. Many of these organizations also coordinate their employment and housing discrimination work with the federal government. Some Indian tribes and territorial governments also have such human rights organizations or commissions. Examples of activities at state, local, tribal and territorial levels are set forth in specific treaty reports and in the Annex to this Common Core Document. While these multiple levels of complementary protections and mechanisms serve to reinforce the ability of the United States to guarantee respect for human rights, we are nevertheless aware of the argument in favor of establishing a more comprehensive national human rights institution, and creating such a mechanism is currently being debated in the United States.

141. Information about human rights is readily available in the United States at the federal level as well as other levels. As a general matter, persons are well informed about their civil and political rights, including the rights of equal protection, due process, and non-discrimination. The scope and meaning of — and issues concerning enforcement of — individual rights are openly and vigorously discussed in the media, freely debated within the various political parties and representative institutions, and litigated before the courts at all levels. Federal agencies, as well as human rights agencies and entities at the state, local, tribal, and territorial levels engage in robust outreach and public education in the areas of civil rights and human rights.

142. All treaties, including human rights treaties, to which the United States is a Party, are published by the federal government, first in the Treaties and International Agreements Series (TIAS) and thereafter in the multi-volume United States Treaties (UST) series. Annually, the Department of State publishes a comprehensive listing of all treaties to which the United States is a Party, known as Treaties in Force (TIF). The constitutional requirement that the Senate give advice and consent to ratification of treaties ensures that there is a public record of treaty consideration, typically including a formal transmission of the treaty from the President to the Senate, a record of the Senate Foreign Relations Committee's public hearing and the Committee's report to the full Senate, together with the action of the Senate itself. By statute, 1 U.S.C. 112b(a), the Secretary of State is also required to transmit to the Congress the text of any international agreement (including the text of any oral international agreement, which agreement shall be reduced to writing), other than a treaty, to which the United States is a party within 60 days of the agreement's entry into force.

143. The texts of all human rights treaties (whether or not the United States has ratified) are published in numerous non-governmental compilations and computerized databases, and can be readily obtained from the government or virtually any public or private library. The United Nations Compilation of International Instruments on Human Rights (ST/HR/1) is also widely available. In addition, federal and state agencies have websites on which information about the agency structure and programs — including those of its office of civil rights — can be found. Many of the websites include relevant information in languages other than English, increasing dissemination to persons with limited English

proficiency within the United States, as well as to persons outside the United States who may be interested in the civil rights protections that the United States affords its citizens and residents.

144. The United States engages in active outreach to inform the public about the work of the United Nations and its various committees on human rights. Texts of human rights treaties to which the United States is party, committee documents and United States reports to U.N. human rights committees are made available on the State Department website, http://www.state.gov/g/drl/hr/treaties/index. htm. Copies of relevant documents are also widely distributed within the executive Branch of the U.S. Government, to federal judicial authorities, to relevant members of Congress and their staffs, and to state, territorial and tribal officials, and non-governmental human rights organizations. The State Department Legal Adviser has personally transmitted such information to the state governors, the governors of American Samoa, Guam, Northern Mariana Islands, Puerto Rico and the U.S. Virgin Islands, and the Mayor of the District of Columbia, as well as federally recognized Indian tribes. In addition to conveying information about the treaties and U.S. obligations thereunder, the Legal Adviser has reached out to states, territories, and tribes for information on their human rights and civil rights laws and programs, for purposes of treaty reporting. This outreach forms the basis for the Annex on State, Local, Tribal and Territorial Human Rights Organizations and Programs, attached to this Common Core Document. Also, as another example of the results of this outreach, the Legislature of the State of California passed a resolution requesting the Attorney General to publicize the text of the treaties and protocols among all city, county and state agencies; to prepare templates for use by cities, counties and state agencies for reporting purposes; and to transmit the resolution to appropriate U.S. and United Nations officials.

145. Government officials meet with civil society regularly to receive comments and input on programmatic efforts, as well as for the treaty reports. In recent years, as part of the universal periodic review (UPR) reporting process, as well as for individual treaty reports, the United States has engaged in unprecedented outreach to the public and human rights groups. The 2010 UPR consultations, hosted by a wide range of civil society organizations, involved nearly a thousand people, representing a diversity of communities throughout the United States, and voicing a wide range of viewpoints and concerns — input that informed not only the UPR Report but other treaty reports as well. Civil society organizations in the United States, which operate freely and openly, play a critical role in raising public awareness of human rights issues and pressing for continued progress on such issues.

146. Although there is no national educational curriculum in the United States, instruction in fundamental constitutional, civil, and political rights occurs throughout the educational system, from elementary and secondary school levels through postsecondary education. In a few areas, the U.S. Department of Education issues grants and may enter into contracts with third parties to develop training and instructional materials that may be used in schools or other educational institutions, or by parents to further education in the principles of human and civil rights. For example, the Department of Education supports grants to improve the quality of civics and government education, foster civic competence and responsibility, and improve the quality of civic and economic education. The program consists of two parts: We the People: The Citizen and the Constitution, and the Cooperative Civic Education and Economic Education Exchange Program. These programs are offered to elementary and secondary classrooms both nationally and internationally. Most institutions of higher education, public and private, include courses on constitutional law in their departments of political science or government. Constitutional law is a required subject in law school, and most law schools now offer advanced or specialized instruction in the areas of civil and political rights, nondiscrimination law, and related fields. Nearly every law school curriculum includes instruction in international law, including human rights law. Many textbooks have been published in the field, including documentary supplements containing the texts of the more significant human rights instruments. As noted above, the numerous non-governmental human rights advocacy groups in the United States also contribute to public understanding of domestic and international rights and norms at all levels of the educational spectrum. Financial information on federal spending on human rights and civil rights matters is contained in the individual treaty reports.

D. Reporting process at the national level

147. Preparation and submission of reports is coordinated by the federal government through the National Security Council and the Department of State. Those entities coordinate with all federal agencies with responsibilities relevant to the report on the contents and drafting of the document. They also meet as appropriate with Congressional committees to keep the committees apprised of the reporting process. The National Security Council and Department of State

also reach out to non-governmental entities, normally meeting with interested NGOs during the preparation for and drafting of the reports and seeking their input. Finally, the State Department reaches out to states, territories, tribes, and local jurisdictions to inform them of the treaty reporting process and to obtain their input. Outreach to the latter entities has normally been done through Governors, Attorneys General and other leaders of these jurisdictions, and also directly to human rights commissions and organizations through the International Association of Official Human Rights Agencies (IAOHRA). In 2009 and 2011, State Department officers attended the Board meeting of IAOHRA, and in 2010 a State Department officer spoke about the treaty reporting process at the IAOHRA Conference. A representative of the Los Angeles County Commission on Human Relations, who is also an IAOHRA Board member, was an adviser on the United States Delegation to the UPR Review in November 2010.

148. In connection with United States Government submission of reports to the appropriate United Nations Committees, many non-governmental organizations prepare and submit "shadow" reports on issues of particular concern to them. Those reports play an important role in the Committee's deliberations. Those reports and other publications are also covered in the media and circulated publicly in the United States and abroad.

149. Follow up to concluding observations involves similar coordination among federal departments and agencies, meetings with Congressional committees, and outreach to nongovernmental organizations and entities at state, local, tribal, and territorial levels.

E. Other related human rights information

150. The United States is committed to multilateral engagement on human rights through the United Nations and participates actively in numerous fora, including the Human Rights Council and the United Nations General Assembly as well as numerous international conferences in human rights and related areas. The commitments the United States has undertaken in such fora are numerous. They are implemented under U.S. laws, policies, and programs, including the legal and policy framework described in this report.

III. Information on non-discrimination and equality and effective remedies

151. The United States is a vibrant, multi-racial, multi-ethnic, and multi-cultural democracy, in which individuals have the right to be protected against discrimination based, *inter alia*, on race, color, and national origin in virtually every aspect of social and economic life. As noted above, the United States Constitution and federal laws prohibit discrimination based on race, color, or national origin in a broad array of areas, including education, employment, public accommodation, transportation, voting, housing and mortgage credit access, as well as in the military, and in programs receiving federal financial assistance; and protections also exist against discrimination based on sex, disability, and in some cases on sexual orientation and gender identity. Nondiscrimination obligations are imposed on federal contractors and subcontractors by Executive Order.

...

Source: U.S. Dept. of State, Diplomacy in Action, https://www.state.gov/documents/organization/251864.pdf

8. UPDATE TO THE COMMON CORE DOCUMENT, AS PART OF THE PERIODIC STATE REPORT PROCESS FOR COMING REPORTS TO THE DIFFERENT TREATY BODIES.

This updates the Committees and provides the latest information about the U.S. to consider with the state report. This report happened to be submitted to the Committee on the Rights of the Child during the U.S. state report process regarding the two Optional Protocols to the Convention on the Rights of the Child. It will be used with all the treaty bodies including the HRCtee. It should be read with the other primary source documents surrounding the U.S. Fourth Report of the HRCtee.

{Excerpt}

[Text]

Submitted with the Combined Third and Forth Periodic Report of the United States of America on the Optional Protocol to the Convention on the Rights of the Child on the Involvement of Children in Armed Conflict and the Optional

Protocol to the Convention on the Rights of the Child on the Sale of Children, Child Prostitution, and Child Pornography January 22, 2016 (re-submitted with revised Report, February 8, 2016)

Updates to the Common Core Document of the United States of America

January 23, 2016

The Common Core Document of the United States, which accompanies the periodic reports under all human rights treaties to which the United States is a party, was most recently submitted on December 30, 2011 with the Fourth Periodic Report of the United States of America to the United Nations Committee on Human Rights concerning the International Covenant on Civil and Political Rights, CCPR/C/USA/4. This document includes updates to specified paragraphs of the 2011 Common Core Document and Annex A to the Common Core Document: State, Local, Tribal, and Territorial Human Rights Organizations and Programs to provide more recent statistical and organizational information. 8 In addition, this document includes Table 1, which contains a list of the main international human rights conventions and protocols to which the United States is party, along with information on the reservations and understandings relating to those treaties. Because the next U.S. census will not take place until 2020, most population statistics included in this update are based on official intercensal population estimates and American Community Survey. 9 The United States is planning to produce a new Common Core Document to replace the 2011 Common Core Document once applicable data from the 2020 United States Census are published.

(77. 4%) White; 42. 16 million (13. 2%) African American/Black; 3. 96 million (1.2%) American Indian/Alaska Native (AIAN); 17. 34 million (5.4%) Asian; 741. 6 thousand (0.2%) Native Hawaiian/Other Pacific Islander (NHPI); and 8.0 million (2.5%) Two or More Races. Approximately 55. 4 million persons (17.4%) were of Hispanic origin, of which the large majority (88.1%) were White, 4.7% were African American/Black, and 2.9% were AIAN.

The total population increase from April 1, 2010 to July 1, 2014 was approximately 10.1 million.

The largest components of this growth by race were White at 46.7%, and Asian at 21.6%. Approximately 48.6% (4.9 million) of the change in population involved persons of Hispanic ethnicity.

Approximately 11. 4 million unauthorized immigrants were estimated to be living in the United States in January 2012, compared to 11. 5 million in January 2011. Of these, 42% had entered the United States in 2000 or later, and 59% were from Mexico. After Mexico, the leading source countries were El Salvador, Guatemala, Honduras, and the Philippines.

The estimate of the median age of the population in 2014 was 37.7, compared to 37.2 in the 2010 Census. The median age for all race and Hispanic origin groups rose during that period.

2. Social, economic, and cultural indicators

Update to paragraphs 11-13. Educational attainment. In 2014, it was estimated that 32.1% of persons 25 years and older in the United States were college graduates or higher — slightly higher than in 2010. For Asian Americans, the figure was 51.6%, for African Americans/Blacks 19.7%, and for non-Hispanic White Americans 33.6%. For Hispanic Americans, the figure was 14.4%. These percentages were higher than they were in 2010, when the total population with college degrees or higher was 28.1% and much higher than in 1970, when the population with college degrees was 10.7%.

In 2014, the estimates for those with high school diplomas or higher were 87% for all Americans, 86.3% for Asian Americans, 92% for non-Hispanic White Americans, 84.4% for African Americans/Blacks, and 65.3% for persons of Hispanic origin. Likewise, these percentage figures were higher than in 1970, when the total was only 52.3%.

Except for the Asian population, women generally were more likely than men to be high school graduates. For the Hispanic population this represents a change from 1970, when Hispanic women were less likely than Hispanic men to have high school diplomas. With regard to college, women overall were more likely to have a bachelor's or higher degree. Black or African American and Hispanic/Latino women were somewhat more likely than Black or African American and Hispanic men to have college degrees, while non-Hispanic White, and Asian women were slightly less likely than White and Asian men to have such degrees.

55.6% for African Americans/Blacks, 55.1% for White Americans, and 54.3% for Hispanic Americans. For men overall, it was 69.2%, and for women overall 57%.

Generally higher levels of education are associated with a greater likelihood of employment and a lower likelihood of unemployment. Individuals with higher levels of education are also generally more likely to be employed in higher paying jobs, such as management, professional, and related occupations, than are individuals with less education. Nonetheless, at nearly every level of education, African Americans and Hispanics were more likely to be unemployed than were Whites and Asian Americans.

3. Standard of living of different segments of the population

Update to paragraph 21. Real median household income for 2014 was $53,657, down from $57,357 in 2007, but not statistically different from the 2013 median of $54,462. The real median income for non-Hispanic White households declined by 1. 7% between 2013 and 2014, but for African American/Black, Asian American, and Hispanic households, changes from 2013 were not statistically significant. Median household income estimates for 2014 were: $60,256 for non-Hispanic White households, $35,398 for African American/Black households, $74,297 for Asian households, and $42,491 for Hispanic households.

The poverty rate in 2014 was 14.8%, not statistically different from 2013. In 2014, there were 46.7 million people in poverty — for the fourth year in a row, the number of people in poverty was not statistically different from the previous year's estimate. The 2014 poverty rate was 2.3 percentage points higher than in 2007, the year prior to the most recent recession.

Between 2013 and 2014, changes in the number of people in poverty and the poverty rate were not statistically significant for any race or Hispanic origin group. The 2014 poverty rate for non-Hispanic Whites was 10.1%, for African Americans/Blacks 26.2%, for Asians 12%, and for people of Hispanic origin, 23. 6%. In 2014, there were 46.7 million people in poverty — for the fourth year in a row, the figure was not statistically significant from the previous year's estimate. The 2014 poverty rate was 2.3% points higher than in 2007, the year prior to the most recent recession.

B. Constitutional, Political and Legal Structure of the State

1. Description of the constitutional structure and the political and legal framework Type of government

Update to paragraphs 35-36. Felony disenfranchisement. The Obama Administration is committed to providing formerly incarcerated people with fair opportunities to rejoin their communities and become productive, law-abiding citizens, including through restoring basic rights and encouraging inclusion in all aspects of society. To this end, in 2014, then Attorney General Holder called on elected officials across the country to enact reforms to restore the voting rights of all who have served their terms in prison or jail, completed their parole or probation, and paid their fines. Various changes have occurred in state practice since 2011. For example, in 2012, Iowa simplified its application process for felons seeking to restore their ability to vote, and South Carolina revoked voting rights for persons on felony probation. In 2013, Delaware repealed its five-year waiting period to vote for most offenses, and Virginia eliminated its waiting period and application for non-violent offenses. In 2015, Wyoming enacted a law requiring the Department of Corrections to issue a certificate of restoration of voting rights to certain non-violent felons being released from state prisons; the Governor of Kentucky signed an executive order that automatically restored the right to vote and hold public office to certain offenders once all terms of their sentences have been satisfied, excluding those convicted of violent crimes, sex crimes, bribery, or treason; and in settlement of litigation, California restored voting rights to felony offenders under community supervision.

Update to paragraph 38. In 2012, voter turnout was estimated to be 58%, below the voter turnout level of nearly 62% in 2008. In 2014 — a non-Presidential election year — turnout was estimated to have been nearly 36%.

Executive branch

Update to paragraph 50. The number for active duty military in 2012 was 1. 39 million, of which 202,876 were women. The figure for 2013 was 1. 37 million, of which 203,985 were women. The figure for 2014 was 1. 33 million, of which 200,692 were women.

Legislative branch

Update to paragraph 57. As of December 2015, the House of Representatives had 19 Standing Committees, and the Senate had 16.

Update to paragraph 64. The 114th Congress, which took office in January 2015, is one of the most diverse in American history. The Senate is 20% women, and 2% African American/Black, 4% Hispanic, and 1% Asian/Pacific Islander. The House is 20% Women, 10. 5% African American/Black, 7. 8% Hispanic, 2. 9% Asian/Pacific Islander, and 0. 4% American Indian.

Other governmental levels

Update to paragraph 81. According to the U.S. Census Bureau, the population of the District of Columbia in 2014 was 658,893.

2. Principal systems through which non-governmental organizations are recognized

Update to paragraph 90. The National Center for Charitable Statistics (NCCS) estimates that, as of November 2015, there were more than 1.5 million non-profit organizations in the United States, including 1,076,309 public charities, 103,430 private foundations, and 369,557 other types of non-profit organizations.

3. Information on administration of justice

Update to paragraphs 91-93. Crime rates. Crime rates in the United States continue to decrease.

Federal Bureau of Investigation (FBI) statistics for 2014 indicate that there were an estimated 1,165,383 violent crimes, an estimated rate of 365.5 per 100,000 population. The violent crime category includes murder, rape, robbery, and aggravated assault. For property crimes, the number was 8,277,829, a rate of 2,596. 1 per 100,000. Property crimes include burglary, larceny, theft, and motor vehicle theft. Arson is also a property crime, but data for arson are not included in property crime totals due to fluctuations in reporting. The figures for 2014 represent a continued reduction from prior years — specifically, for violent crimes a reduction of 9.6% in rate from 2010, and for property crimes a reduction of 11. 9% in rate from 2010. The homicide rate for 2014 was 4.5 per 100,000 inhabitants, down from 5.6 in 2001 and 4.8 in 2010.

Updates to paragraphs 94 and 95. Hate crimes. Based on the Matthew Shepherd and James Byrd, Jr. Hate Crime Prevention Act, in 2013, the FBI began collecting hate crimes statistics to include the bias categories of gender (male and female) and gender identity (transgender and gender nonconforming) in addition to the other bias categories of race, religion, disability, sexual orientation, and ethnicity. In 2014, 15,494 law enforcement agencies participated in the Hate Crime Statistics Program. Of these agencies, 1,666 reported 5,479 criminal incidents involving 6,418 offenses as being motivated by a bias toward a particular race, gender, gender identity, religion, disability, sexual orientation, or ethnicity. There were 5,462 single-bias incidents involving 6,681 victims. A percent distribution of victims by bias type showed that 48.3% of victims were targeted because of the offenders' racial bias, 18.7% were victimized because of the offenders' sexual-orientation bias, 17. 1% were targeted because of the offenders' religious bias, and 12. 3% were victimized due to ethnicity bias. Victims targeted due to their gender identity accounted for 1. 6% of single-bias incidents. The percentage of victims targeted due to their disability remained unchanged at 1.4%, while 0. 6% of victims were targeted because of their gender. There were 17 multiple-bias hate crime incidents involving 46 victims.

Of the 4,048 hate crime offenses classified as crimes against persons in 2014, intimidation accounted for 43. 1%, simple assault for 37. 4%, and aggravated assault for 19%. Four murders and nine rapes were also reported as hate crimes.

There were 2,317 hate crime offenses classified as crimes against property. The majority of these (73. 1%) were acts of destruction/damage/vandalism. Robbery, burglary, larceny-theft, motor vehicle theft, arson, and other offenses accounted for the remaining 26. 9% of crimes against property.

Beginning in 2013, law enforcement officers could report whether suspects were juveniles or adults, as well as the suspect's ethnicity when possible. Of the 1,875 offenders for whom ages were known, 81% were 18 years of age or older. Of the 5,192 known offenders, 52% were White, and 23. 2% were African American/Black. Race was unknown for 16%. Other races accounted for the remaining known offenders: 1. 1% AIAN; 0. 8% Asian; less than 0. 1% NHPI; and 6. 9% a group of multiple races. Of the 975 offenders for whom ethnicity was known, 47. 6% were not Hispanic or Latino, 6. 5% were Hispanic or Latino, and 1. 7% were in a group of multiple ethnicities. Ethnicity was unknown for 44. 2% of offenders.

Beginning in January 2015, the FBI began collecting more detailed data on bias-motivated crimes, including those committed against Arab, Hindu, and Sikh individuals. The expanded data will be featured in the Hate Crimes Statistics report for 2015.

To enhance the accuracy of hate crime reporting, representatives from the FBI's Uniform Crime Reporting (UCR) Program participated in five hate crime training sessions provided jointly by the Department of Justice (DOJ) and the FBI. Since April 2015, DOJ and the FBI have provided the training sessions to law enforcement agencies and community groups in several different areas of the county. UCR personnel also worked with states to ensure proper data submission and met with police agencies to provide training and discuss crime reporting issues.

In addition to releasing yearly hate crime statistics through its Uniform Crime Reporting (UCR) Program, the FBI also investigates incidents of bias-motivated crimes in violation of federal laws as part of its Civil Rights Program. These investigations are often worked in conjunction with local, state, tribal, and federal law enforcement partners and are referred for prosecution to local United States Attorney's Offices and/or DOJ's Civil Rights Division in Washington, D. C. The FBI investigates hate crimes that fall under federal jurisdiction, assists state and local authorities during their own investigations, and in some cases — with DOJ's Civil Rights Division — monitors developing situations to determine if federal action is appropriate.

DOJ continues to seek input on discrimination issues from affected communities, including Arab, Muslim, and Sikh communities, in an effort to strengthen trust and improve protection from hate crimes, bullying, and discrimination. The Department of Homeland Security (DHS) also leads or participates in regular roundtable meetings among community leaders and federal, state and local officials to help address concerns of members of diverse demographic groups.

Updates to paragraphs 96-100. In 2014, the prisoner population in the United States declined, from 1,577,000 at yearend 2013 to 1,561,500 at yearend 2014, reversing an increase that occurred between 2012 and 2013. The federal system held 13% of all prison inmates at yearend 2014, and the federal prison population accounted for almost a third of the total decline in the number of prisoners at yearend 2014, with 5,300 fewer prisoners in federal facilities on December 31, 2014, than on the same day in 2013. This was the second consecutive year of decline in the federal prison population. States held 10,100 fewer inmates at yearend 2014 than at yearend 2013.

On December 31, 2014, the number of persons sentenced to serve more than one year in state or federal prison facilities (1,508,600) decreased by 11,800 prisoners from yearend 2013 and by 44,900 from yearend 2009, when the U.S. prison population was at its peak. Admissions to state and federal prisons declined by 102,000 offenders (down almost 18%) between 2009 and 2014.

During 2014, federal prisons admitted 2,800 fewer sentenced prisoners than in 2013 (down 5. 2%) and released 300 fewer persons (down 0. 5%). State prisons released 12,600 more prisoners in 2014 than in 2013 (up 2. 2%) and admitted 519 fewer persons (down 0. 1%).

The imprisonment rate for all prisoners sentenced to more than a year in state or federal facilities decreased from 477 prisoners per 100,000 U.S. residents in 2013 to 471 per 100,000 in 2014. The number of males sentenced to more than one year decreased in 22 states and the federal prison system, and the sentenced female population decreased in 17 states and the federal prison system. The number of females sentenced to more than one year in state or federal prison increased by almost two percent between 2013 and 2014. This was the largest number of female prison inmates (106,200) since 2008 (106,400). An estimated 516,900 black males were in state or federal prison on December 31, 2014, on sentences of more than one year, which was 37% of the sentenced male prison population. White males made up an additional 32% of the male population (453,500 prison inmates), followed by Hispanic males (308,700 inmates or 22%). White females in state or federal prison at yearend 2014 (53,100 prisoners) outnumbered black (22,600) and Hispanic females (17,800) combined. Whites (50%) made up a greater share of the female prison population than blacks (21%); however, the imprisonment rate for black females (109 per 100,000 U.S. female residents) was twice the rate of white females (53 per 100,000).

Updates to paragraphs 101-103. Capital punishment. The number of states that have the death penalty, the number of persons executed each year, and the size of the population on death row have continued to decline since 2011. As of December 2015, federal law and the laws in 31 states provide for capital punishment. Connecticut abolished capital punishment in 2012; Maryland abolished it in 2013; and Nebraska took legislative action in 2015 to abolish it with regard to future cases.

The number of executions continues to decline. There were 43 executions in 2011 and 2012, 39 in 2013, and 35 in 2014 — down from 46 in 2010. In 2014, only seven states carried out executions. The decline continued into 2015. In 2015, 28 executions occurred in six states, the fewest executions since 1991. The federal government has not executed an inmate since 2003, and has executed only three inmates since 1964.

The death penalty continues to be an issue of active concern and debate, due to the disproportionate effects on minority populations and, in recent years, the use of particular lethal injection protocols. The U.S. Supreme Court, which upheld the constitutionality of Kansas' use of a particular three-drug lethal injection protocol in 2008, Baze v. Rees, 553 U.S. 35 (2008), also upheld the use of midazolam in Oklahoma's lethal injection procedure, finding that petitioners had failed to establish that the risk of harm was substantial when compared to any other known and available method of execution, Glossip v. Gross, 576 U.S. ___ (2015).

No defendant found by a court to have significant intellectual and adaptive disabilities, under criteria established by the U.S. Supreme Court, is subject to capital punishment, either at the state or federal level. The Supreme Court's 2002 ruling in Atkins v. Virginia has been further solidified in Hall v. Florida, 572 U.S. ___ (2014) and in Brumfield v. Cain, 576 U.S. ___ (2015), confirming that it would constitute cruel and unusual punishment in violation of the Eighth and Fourteenth Amendments to execute a defendant with significant intellectual and adaptive disabilities that became manifest before age 18.

Of prisoners under sentence of death at year end 2013, 56% were White and 42% were Black. The 389 Hispanic inmates under sentence of death accounted for 14% of inmates with a known ethnicity. Ninety-eight percent of inmates under sentence of death were male, and 2% were female. The race and sex of inmates under sentence of death remained relatively unchanged since 2000.

II. General Framework for the Protection and Promotion of Human Rights

A. Acceptance of international human rights norms

Update to paragraph 104. Human rights treaties. A list of the "Main international human rights conventions and protocols," to which the United States is party per Appendix 2(A) of the "Harmonized Reporting Guidelines," along with information on the reservations and understandings relating to those treaties, is contained in Table 1 to this document.

B Legal Framework for the protection of human rights at the national level

There are no updates.

Framework within which human rights are promoted at the national level Update to paragraphs 120-131. Statutory law. Recent laws and regulations that add protections against discrimination include:

In the area of sex and sexual-orientation discrimination:

- The Lilly Ledbetter Fair Pay Act of 2009;
- The Violence against Women Reauthorization Act of 2013;
- The 2015 Final Rule revised the regulatory definition of spouse under the Family and Medical Leave Act of 1993 (FMLA) so that eligible employees in legal same-sex marriages entered into in any U.S. state, or if entered into abroad, could have been entered into in any U.S. state, are able to take FMLA leave to care for their spouses or family members.

With regard to Indian tribes:
- The Tribal Law and Order Act of 2010;
- Title IX of the Violence Against Women Reauthorization Act of 2013: Safety for Indian Women;
- The Helping Expedite and Advance Responsible Tribal Home Ownership (HEARTH) Act of 2012.

In the area of prevention of the sale of children, child prostitution, and child pornography, and protection of the rights of victims:
- The Intercountry Adoption Universal Accreditation Act of 2012 (UAA);
- The Trafficking Victims Protection Reauthorization Act of 2013 (Title XII of the Violence against Women Reauthorization Act of 2013);
- The Preventing Sex Trafficking and Strengthening Families Act of 2014;
- The Justice for Victims of Trafficking Act of 2015.

Update to paragraph 144. The United States has continued to strengthen its active outreach to the public about the work of the United Nations and its committees on human rights. Texts of human rights treaties to which the United States is party, United States reports to U.N. Committees, and Committee Observations and Recommendations are made available on the State Department website, http://www.state.gov/j/drl/reports/treaties/, and are also widely distributed within the executive branch of the U.S. government, to federal judicial authorities, to relevant members of Congress and their staffs, and to state, territorial, and tribal officials, and non-governmental human rights organizations. The State Department Legal Adviser has personally transmitted such information annually to state governors, the governors of U.S. territories, the Mayor of the District of Columbia, and federally recognized Indian tribes, along with requests for information from those entities for purposes of treaty reporting. In addition, as noted below in the update to paragraph 136, the State Department is working actively with organizations such as the International Association of Official Human Rights Agencies and the National Association of Attorneys General (NAAG) to promote public knowledge of and input into U.N. human rights processes. Federal officials in other departments, such as the Departments of Justice, Homeland Security, Housing and Urban Development, and Labor, consistently work with their counterparts at state, local, tribal, and territorial levels, as well as with civil society, to coordinate public outreach, training, and programmatic activities. Many civil society organizations also publicize the U.S. reports and the Committee's Concluding Observations within the United States and work with state and local authorities and the public to promote awareness of human rights.

Update to paragraph 145. Civil society. Civil society continues to play a critical role in promoting human rights in the United States. Our laws and institutions create an enabling environment in which civil society is encouraged to act freely without fear of reprisal. Consistent with our commitment to supporting free and robust civil society at home and around the world, we conduct frequent, in-depth consultations with civil society on issues related to our human rights record. For example, in connection with recent human rights treaty reporting and the Universal Periodic Review (UPR), the United States has conducted at least 23 consultations with civil society since 2012 on issues such as non-discrimination; access to justice; criminal justice; indigenous issues; housing; the environment; and immigration, trafficking and labor. These consultations have been held in cities throughout the United States, as well as in Geneva, Switzerland in connection with presentations to U.N. Committees and the UPR mechanism, and with participation from a wide variety of federal agencies as well as state government representatives.

Update to paragraph 146. The Department of Education continues to support state and local efforts to improve civic learning and competence. In 2015, under the Supporting Effective Educator Development program, the Department of Education awarded grants to national nonprofit organizations to create learning and growth opportunities for educators serving students in high-need schools across a range of subject areas, including civics.

D. Reporting process at the national level

Update to paragraph 147. In recent years, the United States government has improved engagement with state and local governments to foster better awareness of human rights obligations at the state, tribal, and local levels. State and local government officials have been members of recent U.S. delegations presenting reports on the Convention on the Elimination of All Forms of Racial Discrimination, the Optional Protocols to the Convention on the Rights of the Child, the International Covenant on Civil and Political Rights, and the Convention Against Torture. The United States has also invited state, tribal, and local officials to consultations in connection with the UPR.

In addition, the federal government has reminded federal, state, local, tribal, and territorial officials of U.S. human rights treaty obligations and notified them of upcoming treaty reporting. For example, in 2014 and 2015, the State Department wrote to state, local, territorial, and tribal officials to inform them of upcoming U.S. human rights treaty presentations and the UPR. These and other letters to state, local, and tribal officials are available at http://www.state.gov/g/drl/hr/treaties/index. htm. Federal officials have conducted targeted training sessions on human rights treaties for state and local officials, such as at an August 2014 conference of state- and local-level employment non-discrimination agencies. The federal government has also worked regularly with relevant associations, such as the 160-member International Association of Official Human Rights Agencies and the National Association of Attorneys General (NAAG), to provide their members with information on U.S. human rights treaty obligations and commitments and to discuss the role they can play. A speech by Acting State Department Legal Adviser Mary McLeod before the NAAG Annual Conference in February 2015 is available at: http://www.state.gov/s/l/releases/remarks/239960. htm.

III. Information on Non-Discrimination and Equality and Effective Remedies

A. International legal obligations There are no updates.

B. Basic legal framework

1. U.S. Constitution and federal laws on discrimination and equality

Update to paragraph 159. The *Brown v. Board of Education* decision was issued in 1954, 62 years ago as of 2016.

Update to paragraph 162. In 2015, the U.S. Supreme Court ruled in Obergefell v. Hodges, 576 U.S. ___ (2015), that the Constitution guarantees same-sex couples the right to participate in the institution of marriage. Following this ruling, Attorney General Lynch announced that all federal benefits would be available equally to married same-sex couples in all 50 states, the District of Columbia, and the U.S. Territories. DOJ continues to work across the administration to fulfill its commitment to equal treatment for all Americans, including equal access to the benefits of marriage.

Update to paragraph 164. The Voting Rights Act of 1965 (VRA) remains the most powerful tool in protecting against discrimination in voting. Although the U.S. Supreme Court in 2013 invalidated the portion of the VRA that required prior federal review of changes to certain jurisdictions' voting practices, *Shelby County v. Holder*, 133 S. Ct. 2612 (2013), DOJ continues to protect against discrimination in voting through action under other federal laws and other provisions of the VRA. These include Section 2 of the VRA, which allows DOJ to challenge practices that limit voting rights on the basis of race, either intentionally or in result. DOJ has also made clear that it will work with Congress and other elected and community leaders to help formulate potential legislative proposals to improve voting rights protections. DOJ also vigorously enforces the voting rights of those belonging to language-minority groups, bringing or participating in cases to protect persons with limited English proficiency.

C. Legal remedies There are no updates.

D. Enforcement and prevention

1. Federal enforcement

Update to paragraph 174. DOJ's Civil Rights Division's Federal Coordination and Compliance Section (CRT/FCS) has responsibility for ensuring a coordinated and consistent approach to the enforcement of Title VI anti-discrimination provisions (which prohibit discrimination based on race, color, or national origin by entities receiving federal financial assistance). Although funding agencies are primarily responsible for investigating and making determinations on alleged violations by recipients of their funding, CRT/FCS guides federal policy, advises individual agencies, and in many cases staffs investigative efforts. As part of its reinvigorated civil rights enforcement, DOJ issued new guidance to federal funding agencies concerning their Title VI obligations, which include ensuring that recipients of federal financial assistance do not employ policies or methods of administration that have a disparate impact. http://www.justice.gov/sites/default/files/crt/legacy/2013/07/24/4yr_report.pdf. DOJ also committed to providing additional technical assistance to federal agencies in order to strengthen their Title VI enforcement efforts.

Update to paragraph 182. As of September 2015, the Equal Employment Opportunity Commission (EEOC) operated 53 offices across the country and was working closely with more than 90 Fair Employment Practice Agencies across the nation to process approximately 40,000 charges of employment discrimination under state and federal laws received annually from those agencies, in addition to the approximately 89,000 charges that it receives directly.

Update to paragraph 185. In 2015, Housing and Urban Development (HUD) published a regulation to clarify for cities and communities receiving federal funds their obligation to take proactive steps to overcome historic patterns of segregation, promote fair housing choice, and foster inclusive communities. Under the final affirmatively furthering fair housing rule, HUD will also collect data on patterns of integration and segregation in cities and communities to better identify potential patterns of segregation in order to help promote greater urban integration and equality.

Update to paragraph 186. As of September 2015, HUD was working with 88 Fair Housing Assistance Program (FHAP) agencies on the investigation and enforcement of complaints of housing discrimination.

2. Training and programs to prevent and eliminate negative attitudes and prejudice

Update to paragraph 191. As of September 2015, the Department of Education's Office of Elementary and Secondary Education funded 10 Equity Assistance Centers across the country to provide technical assistance and training to schools, districts, and other governmental agencies on issues related to equity in education.

Update to paragraph 196. The EEOC conducts approximately 3,700 educational, training, and outreach events per year, reaching approximately 350,000 people.

E. Human rights situation of persons belonging to specific vulnerable groups

Update to paragraph 198. Although some progress has been made, disparities in employment, home ownership and education continue exist. For example, although overall unemployment rates for American households have dropped since 2010, for the third quarter of 2015, the unemployment rate for Whites 16 years and over was 4. 5%, for African Americans/Blacks 9. 5%, and for Hispanics/Latinos 6. 5%. http://www.bls.gov/web/empsit/cpsee_e16. htm. In 2014, persons with disabilities continued to have a far lower participation rate in the labor force (17. 1%) than persons without disabilities (64. 6%). http://www.bls.gov/news. release/pdf/disabl.pdf. The disparities in home ownership also continue. In the third quarter of 2015, less than half of African Americans/Blacks and Hispanics/Latinos own homes, while slightly less than three-quarters of White Americans own homes.

American Indians and Alaska Natives

Update to paragraph 205. Poverty rates among Native Americans are the highest of any race group. The U.S. Census Bureau reported that 28. 3% of American Indian and Alaska Natives were living in poverty in 2014, not statistically different from the 2013 poverty rate. For the nation as a whole, the poverty rate in 2014 was 15. 5%.

Update to paragraph 207. President Obama has held Tribal Nations summits with tribal leaders every year during his Administration. In these summits, the President, the Vice President, many members of the Cabinet, dozens of senior U.S. officials, and hundreds of tribal leaders have discussed issues such as tribal self-determination, including self-governance; health care; economic and infrastructure development; education; protection of land and natural resources; and other matters of priority to tribal governments. Also in 2012, the President signed into law the HEARTH (Helping Expedite and Advance Responsible Tribal Home Ownership) Act that allows tribes to lease restricted lands for residential, business, public, religious, educational, and recreational purposes, thereby promoting tribal self-determination, self-governance, and economic development and home ownership. In addition, in 2013, President Obama issued an order creating the White House Council on Native American Affairs, consisting of the heads of various federal agencies, to improve high-level coordination on the pressing issues facing tribal communities. Finally, the 2013 reauthorization of the Violence Against Women Act strengthened provisions to address violence against American Indian and Alaska Native women, including a provision recognizing tribes' authority to prosecute in tribal courts those who commit acts of domestic violence in Indian country irrespective of whether the perpetrator is Indian or non-Indian. The Administration has also prioritized defending tribal water rights and reaching settlement agreements with Indian tribes over claims of trust mismanagement.

F. Special measures

Update to paragraph 216. In 2013, the Supreme Court followed prior precedent recognizing that colleges and universities have a compelling interest in achieving the educational benefits that flow from a racially and ethnically diverse student body and can lawfully pursue that interest in their admissions programs as long as the program is narrowly tailored to achieve that compelling interest, Fisher v. Texas, 133 S. Ct. 2411 (2013). On remand, the U.S. Court of Appeals for the Fifth Circuit upheld the University of Texas at Austin's limited consideration of race in undergraduate admissions to achieve the educational benefits of diversity. That decision has been appealed to the Supreme Court. Oral argument took place on December 9, 2015, and a decision is expected by the end of the 2015 Term. The United States filed a brief in support of the respondent university, setting forth, in great detail, the United States' critical interest in ensuring that educational institutions are able to provide the educational benefits of diversity. In September of 2013, the Departments of Education and Justice released joint guidance providing clarification to institutions of higher education in understanding and implementing lawful programs to promote diversity on their campuses, consistent with Fisher and prior Supreme Court decisions. They issued additional clarifying guidance in May of 2014.

[End Text]

Source: U.S. Department of State: Diplomacy in action, http://www.state.gov/documents/organization/252656.pdf

9. UNITED STATES WRITTEN RESPONSES TO QUESTIONS FROM THE UNITED NATIONS HUMAN RIGHTS COMMITTEE CONCERNING THE FOURTH PERIODIC REPORT

This document contains the written responses of the U.S. to specific issue questions posed by the HRCtee in response to the U.S. Fourth Report. It is to solicit answers to the questions which most concern the HRCtee in preparation for the U.S. appearing before the Committee for review. These questions all relate to specific articles of the ICCPR and issues that have been raised by the report and by shadow reports from non-governmental organizations.

{Excerpt}

[Text]

1. It is with great pleasure that the Government of the United States of America presents this information in response to the questions from the Human Rights Committee. The United States is pleased to participate in this process and has, in the spirit of cooperation, provided as much information as possible in response to the questions posed by the Committee, taking into consideration the page limit, even where the questions or information provided in response to them do not bear directly on obligations arising under the ICCPR. The United States further welcomes the opportunity to appear in person before the Committee in October 2013.

Constitutional and legal framework within which the Covenant is implemented (art. 2)

Issue 1. Please clarify the following issues:

a) the State party's understanding of the scope of applicability of the Covenant with respect to individuals under its jurisdiction but outside its territory; in times of peace, as well as in times of armed conflict;

b) which measures have been taken to ensure that the Covenant is fully implemented by State and local authorities;

c) whether the State party intends to reinvigorate Executive Order 13107/1998 titled "Implementation of Human Rights Treaties"

2. **Issue 1(a)**. With respect to the scope of applicability of the ICCPR, the United States refers the Committee to ¶¶ 504 — 510 of its Fourth Periodic Report (hereinafter "2011 Report").

3. **Issue 1(b)**. With respect to measures being taken to ensure that the ICCPR is fully implemented by state and local authorities, we refer the Committee to ¶¶ 31, 32, 215 and 216 of the U.S. Periodic Report filed with the Committee on Elimination of Racial Discrimination on June 13, 2013 (hereinafter "2013 CERD Report") and ¶¶ 120, 129 and Annex A of the Common Core Document (CCD).

4. **Issue 1(c)**. The United States is committed to domestic implementation of U.S. human rights obligations, including mainstreaming human rights into domestic policy and engaging in robust dialogue with U.S. civil society partners on U.S. human rights implementation. On December 18, 1998, President Clinton issued Executive Order 13107 regarding the implementation of human rights treaties. Consistent with this order, the White House leads a policy process that assists in the coordination of action by U.S. government agencies on the domestic implementation of U.S. human rights obligations and commitments, including with regard to U.S. periodic reporting to U.N. treaty bodies and the Universal Periodic Review process. Numerous other procedures exist to support coordination of human rights matters among relevant U.S. agencies. The United States continues to evaluate possible measures to enhance coordination within the U.S. government on U.S. implementation of human rights obligations.

Issue 2. Please clarify whether the State party will establish a national human rights institution with a broad human rights mandate, in line with the principles relating to the status of national institutions for the promotion and protection of human rights (the Paris Principles).

5. **Issue 2**. With regard to the issue of a national human rights institution, we refer the Committee to ¶ 129 of the CCD and ¶ 31 of the 2013 CERD Report.

Issue 3. Please clarify whether the State party will review its reservations to the Covenant with a view to withdrawing them.

6. **Issue 3**. At the time it became a Party to the ICCPR, the United States carefully evaluated the treaty to ensure that it could fully implement all of the obligations it would assume. The reservations taken by the United States to a few provisions of the ICCPR were crafted in close collaboration with the U.S. Senate to ensure that the United States could fulfil its international obligations under the ICCPR. We have no current plans to review or withdraw these reservations.

Non-discrimination and equal rights of men and women (arts. 2, paragraph 1, 3, and 26)

Issue 4. Please provide information on steps taken to address racial disparities in the criminal justice system, including the overrepresentation of individuals belonging to racial and ethnic minorities in prisons and jails. Please provide the Committee with the latest U.S. Department of Justice three-year report "on the nature and characteristics of contacts between U.S. residents and the police," and clarify whether the State party has conducted a study on the disparities between population groups, and if so, on the findings of such a study.

7. **Issue 4**. There is continuing concern regarding unwarranted racial disparities in some aspects of the justice system; the United States is committed to addressing these disparities. Several recent steps have been taken with regard to the criminal justice system. The Fair Sentencing Act of 2010 reduced the disparity between more lenient sentences for powder cocaine charges and more severe sentences for crack cocaine charges, which are more frequently brought against members of minority groups. We refer the Committee to ¶ 66 of the 2013 CERD Report for a discussion of the effects of this Act and its retroactive application. The Department of Justice (DOJ) intends to conduct further statistical analysis

and issue annual reports on sentencing disparities in the criminal justice system, and is working on other ways to increase system-wide monitoring. DOJ has pledged to work with the United States Sentencing Commission (USSC) on reform of mandatory minimum sentencing statutes and to implement the recommendations set forth in the USSC's 2011 report to Congress.

8. A recent USSC study indicates that sentence length is associated with some demographic factors such as race, but that additional analyses of all contributing factors are needed to determine whether demographic factors actually affect the length of sentences, http://www.ussc.gov/Legislative_and_Public_Affairs/Congressional_Testimony_and_Reports/Booker_Reports/2012_Booker/Part_E.pdf#page=1.

9. The Violent Crime Control and Law Enforcement Act of 1994, 42 U.S. C. 14141; the Omnibus Crime Control and Safe Streets Act of 1968, 42 U.S. C. 3789d; and Title VI of the Civil Rights Act, 42 U.S. C. 2000d, authorize the Attorney General (AG) to bring civil actions to eliminate patterns or practices of law enforcement misconduct, including racial discrimination. DOJ's Civil Rights Division (DOJ/CRT) investigates police departments, prisons, jails, juvenile correctional facilities, mental health facilities, and related institutions to ensure compliance with the law and brings lawsuits to enforce the laws, where necessary. DOJ/CRT's recent investigation of the New Orleans Police Department (NOPD), for instance, found a pattern or practice of unconstitutional conduct or violations of federal law in numerous areas; in 2012, DOJ/CRT reached one of the most comprehensive reform agreements in its history with the NOPD, http://www. justice.gov/crt/about/spl/nopd. php. Between 2009 and 2012, DOJ/CRT opened 15 investigations of police departments and currently is pursuing more than two dozen investigations. DOJ/CRT strongly prefers to work in a cooperative fashion with local governments and police departments to address unconstitutional policing, but does not hesitate to use litigation when cooperation proves elusive, see, e. g., http://www. justice.gov/crt/publications/accomplishments/at pp. 61-65. DOJ/CRT's work under 42 U.S. C. 14141 and Title VI also seeks to ensure equal access to the judicial system for Limited English Proficient (LEP) persons, *inter alia* through its Courts Language Access Initiative. Please see ¶¶ 66–68 of the 2013 CERD Report.

10. The latest DOJ three-year report on the nature and characteristics of contacts between U.S. residents and the police is Contacts between Police and the Public, 2008 (October 5, 2011), http://www.bjs.gov/content/pub/pdf/cpp08.pdf. DOJ's Bureau of Justice Statistics (BJS) has not conducted a specific study on the disparities between population groups.

Issue 5. Please clarify which steps have been taken to eliminate and combat all forms of racial profiling against Arabs, Muslims and South Asians, and whether the Guidance Regarding the Use of Race by Federal Law Enforcement Agencies covers profiling based on religion, religious appearance or national origin. Please provide information on the practices and justification of practices involving the surveillance of Muslims in the State party, given that it has not resulted in any prosecution. Please clarify whether plans are foreseen to review all relevant immigration enforcement programs, including the Immigration and Customs Enforcement Agreements of Cooperation in Communities to Enhance Safety and Security — Criminal Alien Program, the Secure Communities program, and 287(g) agreements, to determine whether they result in racial profiling. Please provide information on the number of complaints regarding racial profiling received annually by the Office of Civil Rights and Civil Liberties against Department of Homeland Security personnel, as well as the results of the investigations and disciplinary action undertaken. Please also provide information on steps taken to address discriminatory and unlawful use of "stop and frisk" practices by officers of the New York Police Department.

11. **Issue 5**. Profiling in law enforcement operations is premised on the erroneous assumption that any particular individual possessing one or more irrelevant personal characteristics is more likely to engage in misconduct than another individual who does not possess those characteristics. Profiling is generally an ineffective law enforcement technique and has a negative impact on the communities affected. Although the June 2003 Guidance Regarding the Use of Race by Federal Law Enforcement Agencies, by its terms, addresses only the use of race or ethnicity, the Department of Justice has created a working group to undertake a comprehensive review of that Guidance, which is ongoing. In addition, we note that new agents with the Federal Bureau of Investigation (FBI) are trained in how to properly conduct investigations and interviews in accordance with the laws, regulations, and Constitution of the U.S. —which prohibit invidious racial, ethnic, and religious profiling. Numerous U.S. government departments and agencies work to combat racial profiling against Arabs, Muslims, and South Asians. The Department of Homeland Security (DHS) Office for Civil Rights and Civil Liberties (CRCL) has trained over 4,000 state and local law enforcement and other personnel on cultural

awareness and best practices in community engagement through more than 75 training events. CRCL training covers religious and cultural practices of Sikh, Arab, and Muslim cultures, and effective policing without the use of ethnic or racial profiling. CRCL has also produced a training video, http://www.dhs.gov/civil-rights-and-civil-liberties-institute.

12. Further, through its Incident Community Coordination Team (ICCT), CRCL facilitates rapid communication between federal, state, and local authorities and communities that may have distinct civil rights and liberties concerns in the aftermath of any homeland security incident. Arab, Muslim, South Asian, Sikh, and Somali American community leaders have been frequent participants.

13. Within DHS, law enforcement agencies such as U.S. Customs and Border Protection (CBP) and U.S. Immigration and Customs Enforcement (ICE) are subject to strict rules and to investigations, where warranted, regarding incidents of assaults, harassment, threats, or profiling involving employees. CBP and Border Patrol Agents receive regular training in this area. DHS has also created trainings designed primarily for use by front-line state and local law enforcement agency personnel that directly address the risk of biased policing and how law enforcement officers and agencies can avoid illegal targeting of individuals based on race or ethnicity, http://www.ice.gov/secure_communities/crcl. htm.

14. With regard to the number of complaints, between October 2011 and May 2013, CRCL opened 42 complaints involving allegations of discrimination based on race, ethnicity, and/or national origin. Two complaints have been investigated and closed with recommendations for the DHS component agency or office involved and the other 40 complaints either remain pending or have been closed without recommendations. Please see ¶¶ 82–85 of the 2013 CERD Report for further discussion of racial profiling.

15. Through its Initiative to Combat Post 9-11 Discriminatory Backlash, DOJ/CRT has investigated over 800 incidents involving targeting of persons perceived to be Muslims or of Arab or South East Asian descent. Efforts to combat racial/ethnic profiling include increased enforcement of federal anti-profiling statutes and review of federal law enforcement policies and practices.

16. DOJ has been reviewing complaints from New York City community members regarding NYPD's stop-and-frisk program and has been closely monitoring Floyd v. City of New York, a case brought by private plaintiffs in the U.S. District Court for the Southern District of New York that challenges NYPD's stop-and-frisk practices on the grounds that they violate the Constitution and other laws. On June 12, 2013, DOJ filed a Statement of Interest in Floyd on the subject of fashioning an appropriate remedy so that, if the court does determine that NYPD's conduct is unlawful, that conduct can be effectively and sustainably corrected. As the Statement of Interest makes clear, DOJ takes no position as to whether NYPD's stop-and-frisk practices violate the law. Drawing on DOJ's extensive experience in facilitating wide-scale police reform, the Statement of Interest, among other things, sets forth the important function that an independent monitor can serve in cases involving systemic police misconduct.

Issue 6. Please provide information on the imposition of criminal penalties on people living on the streets. Please also provide information on the implementation of the 2009 Helping Families Save Their Home Act and the creation of durable alternatives to criminalization measures to address homelessness.

17. **Issue 6.** The 2009 Helping Families Save Their Homes Act (the 2009 Act) amended various federal laws and programs to help homeowners avoid foreclosure and otherwise assist borrowers retain their homes. The Act also reauthorized the Homeless Emergency Assistance and Rapid Transition to Housing (HEARTH) Act, which called for the U.S. Interagency Council on Homelessness (USICH) to "develop alternatives to laws and policies that prohibit sleeping, eating, sitting, resting, or lying in public spaces when there are no suitable alternatives, result in the destruction of property belonging to people experiencing homelessness without due process, or are selectively enforced against people experiencing homelessness." While criminalization of homelessness is driven by local measures and decisions, USICH and federal agencies provide leadership, technical assistance, and incentives urging communities to adopt alternatives.

18. "Opening Doors," the first federal strategic plan to prevent and end homelessness, urges cities to adopt constructive approaches to reduce criminalization of homelessness. In December 2010, USICH and DOJ's Access to Justice Initiative (DOJ/ATJ), with support from the Department of Housing and Urban Development (HUD), held a summit with local officials, law enforcement, business representatives, and advocates from around the country that resulted in rec-

ommendations for alternatives to criminalization that are detailed in a report released in April 2012, ??http://www.usich.gov/resources/uploads/_library/RPT_SoS_March2012.pdf. The report suggests that a combination of solutions involving coordination among communities and institutions and a variety of social, health, law enforcement, and justice providers, can help to achieve reductions in street homelessness, https://www.onecpd.info/resource/1966/2011-ahar- to-congress-and-supplemental-reports/.

19. DOJ/ATJ has also produced a guide to generate greater awareness of DOJ resources available to homeless people and those at risk of homelessness who are involved in the criminal justice system, http://www.justice.gov/atj/doj-resource-guide.pdf.

Issue 7. Please provide information on obstacles to access of undocumented migrants to health services and higher education institutions, and to federal and state programs addressing such obstacles.

20. **Issue 7.** The U.S. Department of Health and Human Services (HHS) provides technical assistance and investigates complaints to ensure that health care and human service providers that receive financial assistance from HHS comply with Title VI of the Civil Rights Act of 1964, which prohibits discrimination based on race, color or national origin. In 2000, HHS and the U.S. Department of Agriculture (USDA) issued policy guidance to reduce and eliminate barriers that discourage enrollment in Medicaid, the Children's Health Insurance Program, and other assistance programs. The guidance makes clear that Medicaid coverage of emergency services is available to undocumented immigrants, http://www.hhs.gov/ocr//resources/specialtopics/origin/policyguidanceregardinginquiriesintocitizenshipimmigrationstatus. html. In 2013 HHS released its Language Access Plan, promoting meaningful access by limited English proficiency individuals to HHS programs, including Medicare and programs established under Title I of the Affordable Care Act (ACA).

21. Under the Emergency Medical Treatment and Labor Act (EMTALA), any person who seeks emergency medical care at a participating hospital is generally guaranteed an appropriate medical screening exam and stabilizing treatment or an appropriate transfer to a medical facility that can provide such treatment, regardless of his or her ability to pay or immigration status.

22. With regard to education, federal law does not prohibit undocumented students from attending institutions of higher education in the U.S. In most states, undocumented students are allowed to enroll in public institutions and are charged out-of-state tuition, although a few states do not permit enrollment by undocumented students at publicly funded institutions. More than a dozen states have laws that allow undocumented students to pay in-state tuition provided, for example, that the student attended high school in that state, among other requirements. A few states also offer state financial aid to undocumented students.

23. The Administration's "Deferred Action for Childhood Arrivals" (DACA) policy, announced in June 2012, has also already provided temporary administrative relief from deportation, as well as work authorization, to over 365,000 immigrants.

....

Issue 11. Please provide information on:

a) whether the State party has instigated independent investigations into cases of torture or cruel, inhuman or degrading treatment or punishment of detainees in U.S. custody outside its territory. Please clarify whether those responsible have been prosecuted and sanctioned, and whether the State party has prosecuted former senior government and military officials who have authorized such torture and abuse;

b) whether the State party deems so-called "enhanced interrogation techniques," now prohibited by the State party, including "water boarding," to be in violation of article 7 of the Covenant. Please provide information on whether the State party has taken steps to prosecute officers, employees, members of the Armed Forces, or other agents of the U.S. Government, including private contractors, for having employed these techniques and what is being done to prevent the use of such techniques in the future. Please also clarify whether remedies have been offered to victims of such techniques;

c) the reasons why there is no legislation explicitly prohibiting torture within the territory of the State Party.

44. **Issue 11(a).** Under U.S. law, every U.S. official is prohibited from engaging in torture or in cruel, inhuman or degrading treatment or punishment, at all times, and in all places. The U.S. Armed Forces conduct prompt and independent investigations into all credible allegations concerning mistreatment of detainees. Detention facilities are inspected on a regular basis to ensure compliance with DoD regulations and to determine if improvements in operations are necessary. In addition, the U.S. Armed Forces have several independent criminal investigative agencies, whose function is to investigate allegations of criminal behavior.

45. Regarding allegations of mistreatment of detainees in U.S. military custody outside its territory, that violates the law of war, it is DoD policy that all reportable incidents allegedly committed by any DoD personnel or DoD contractor personnel will be promptly reported in accordance with specific guidelines; promptly and thoroughly investigated by proper authorities; and remedied by disciplinary or administrative action, when appropriate. On-scene commanders and supervisors are instructed to ensure that measures are taken to preserve evidence pertaining to any reportable incident. See DoD Directive 2311. 01E (DoD Law of War Program).

46. As noted in response to Issue 10, above, the U.S. government has undertaken numerous enforcement actions relating to alleged mistreatment of detainees. DOJ has investigated, charged, and prosecuted in federal civilian courts a number of cases involving alleged detainee abuse. For example, in 2004, DOJ brought criminal charges against David A. Passaro, a Central Intelligence Agency (CIA) contractor accused of brutally assaulting a detainee in Afghanistan in 2003. Please see ¶¶ 533-534 of the 2011 Report (concerning Passaro and the Ayala prosecution referenced in Issue 10 above).

47. In August 2009, the AG announced that he had ordered "a preliminary review into whether federal laws were violated in connection with interrogation of specific detainees at overseas locations," www.justice.gov/ag/speeches/2009/ag-speech-0908241. html. On June 30, 2011, following a two-year investigation, DOJ announced that it was opening a full criminal investigation into the deaths of two individuals in CIA custody overseas, and that it had concluded that further investigation into the other cases examined in the preliminary investigation was not warranted, www.justice.gov/opa/pr/2011/June/11-ag-861. html. These investigations, which were in addition to the DOJ prosecution efforts referenced below, were closed in 2012 after DOJ determined that the admissible evidence would not be sufficient to obtain and sustain a conviction beyond a reasonable doubt, http://www.justice.gov/opa//2012/August/12-ag-1067. html.

48. The CIA has also undertaken internal reviews relating to detainee treatment, the results of which are generally nonpublic. Where those reviews indicated potential violations of U.S. criminal laws, the CIA has referred those matters to DOJ. The U.S. Congress also has conducted extensive investigations into the treatment of detainees, http://www.levin. senate.gov/imo/media/doc/ supporting/2008/Detainees. 121108.pdf.

[End Text]

Source: U.S. Department of State, Diplomacy in Action, https://www.state.gov/j/drl/rls/212393. htm

10. CONCLUDING OBSERVATIONS ON THE FOURTH PERIODIC REPORT OF THE UNITED STATES OF AMERICA, HUMAN RIGHTS COMMITTEE, 2014

This document is the outcome of the process of the Fourth State report of the U.S. before the HRCTee. This constitutes the opinion of the Committee as to how the U.S. is doing in implementing the norms of the ICCPR, along with recommendations to the U.S. to help it improve compliance. This is the most important part of the supervising process of the treaty body and the most important document. The recommendations are not legally binding on the U.S. but the U. S, should implement them to show its good faith as a party to the treaty. This process is the U.S. speaking to the international community about its human rights record and the international community, through the U.N. HRCtee, telling the U.S. how it sees the U.S. doing. The reaction of the U.S. to the recommendations, how it implements them or not, tells a lot about how seriously the U.S. takes this process and its obligations under the different human rights treaties.

{Excerpts}

[Text]

Human Rights Committee

Concluding observations on the fourth periodic report of the United States of America*

1. The Committee considered the fourth periodic report of the United States of America (CCPR/C/USA/4 and Corr. 1) at its 3044th, 3045th and 3046th meetings (CCPR/C/SR. 3044, 3045 and 3046), held on 13 and 14 March 2014. At its 3061st meeting (CCPR/C/SR. 3061), held on 26 March 2014, it adopted the following concluding observations.

A. Introduction

2. The Committee welcomes the submission of the fourth periodic report of the United States of America and the information presented therein. It expresses appreciation for the opportunity to renew its constructive dialogue with the State party's high-level delegation, which included representatives of state and local governments, on the measures taken by the State party during the reporting period to implement the provisions of the Covenant. The Committee is grateful to the State party for its written replies (CCPR/C/USA/Q/4/Add. 1) to the list of issues (CCPR/C/USA/Q/4), which were supplemented by the oral responses provided by the delegation during the dialogue, and for the additional information that was provided in writing.

B. Positive aspects

3. The Committee notes with appreciation the many efforts undertaken by the State party and the progress made in protecting civil and political rights. The Committee welcomes in particular the following legislative and institutional steps taken by the State party:

(a) Full implementation of article 6, paragraph 5, of the Covenant in the aftermath of the Supreme Court's judgment in Roper v. Simmons, 543 U.S. 551 (2005), despite the State party's reservation to the contrary;

(b) Recognition by the Supreme Court in Boumediene v. Bush, 553 U.S. 723 (2008) of the extraterritorial application of constitutional habeas corpus rights to aliens detained at Guantánamo Bay;

(c) Presidential Executive Orders 13491 — Ensuring Lawful Interrogations, 13492 — Review and Disposition of Individuals Detained at the Guantánamo Bay Naval Base and Closure of Detention Facilities and 13493 — Review of Detention Policy Options, issued on 22 January 2009;

(d) Support for the United Nations Declaration on the Rights of Indigenous Peoples, announced by President Obama on 16 December 2010;

(e) Presidential Executive Order 13567 establishing a periodic review of detainees at the Guantánamo Bay detention facility who have not been charged, convicted or designated for transfer, issued on 7 March 2011.

C. Principal matters of concern and recommendations

Applicability of the Covenant at national level

4. The Committee regrets that the State party continues to maintain the position that the Covenant does not apply with respect to individuals under its jurisdiction, but outside its territory, despite the interpretation to the contrary of article 2, paragraph 1, supported by the Committee's established jurisprudence, the jurisprudence of the International Court of Justice and State practice. The Committee further notes that the State party has only limited avenues to ensure that state and local governments respect and implement the Covenant, and that its provisions have been declared to be non-self-executing at the time of ratification. Taken together, these elements considerably limit the legal reach and practical relevance of the Covenant (art. 2).

The State party should:

(a) Interpret the Covenant in good faith, in accordance with the ordinary meaning to be given to its terms in their context, including subsequent practice, and in the light of the object and purpose of the Covenant, and review its legal position so as to acknowledge the extraterritorial application of the Covenant under certain circumstances, as outlined, inter alia, in the Committee's general comment No. 31 (2004) on the nature of the general legal obligation imposed on States parties to the Covenant;

(b) Engage with stakeholders at all levels to identify ways to give greater effect to the Covenant at federal, state and local levels, taking into account that the obligations under the Covenant are binding on the State party as a whole, and that all branches of government and other public or governmental authorities at every level are in a position to engage the responsibility of the State party (general comment. No. 31, para. 4);

(c) Taking into account its declaration that provisions of the Covenant are non-self-executing, ensure that effective remedies are available for violations of the Covenant, including those that do not, at the same time, constitute violations of the domestic law of the United States of America, and undertake a review of such areas with a view to proposing to Congress implementing legislation to fill any legislative gaps. The State party should also consider acceding to the Optional Protocol to the Covenant, providing for an individual communication procedure.

(d) Strengthen and expand existing mechanisms mandated to monitor the implementation of human rights at federal, state, local and tribal levels, provide them with adequate human and financial resources or consider establishing an independent national human rights institution, in accordance with the principles relating to the status of national institutions for the promotion and protection of human rights (the Paris Principles) (General Assembly resolution 48/134, annex).

(e) Reconsider its position regarding its reservations and declarations to the Covenant with a view to withdrawing them.

Accountability for past human rights violations

5. The Committee is concerned at the limited number of investigations, prosecutions and convictions of members of the Armed Forces and other agents of the United States Government, including private contractors, for unlawful killings during its international operations, and the use of torture or other cruel, inhuman or degrading treatment or punishment of detainees in United States custody, including outside its territory, as part of the so-called "enhanced interrogation techniques." While welcoming Presidential Executive Order 13491 of 22 January 2009 terminating the programme of secret detention and interrogation operated by the Central Intelligence Agency (CIA), the Committee notes with concern that all reported investigations into enforced disappearances, torture and other cruel, inhuman or degrading treatment committed in the context of the CIA secret rendition, interrogation and detention programmes were closed in 2012, resulting in only a meagre number of criminal charges being brought against low-level operatives. The Committee is concerned that many details of the CIA programmes remain secret, thereby creating barriers to accountability and redress for victims (arts. 2, 6, 7, 9, 10 and 14).

The State party should ensure that all cases of unlawful killing, torture or other ill-treatment, unlawful detention or enforced disappearance are effectively, independently and impartially investigated, that perpetrators, including, in particular, persons in positions of command, are prosecuted and sanctioned, and that victims are provided with effective remedies. The responsibility of those who provided legal pretexts for manifestly illegal behavior should also be established. The State party should also consider the full incorporation of the doctrine of "command responsibility" in its criminal law and declassify and make public the report of the Senate Special Committee on Intelligence into the CIA secret detention programme.

Racial disparities in the criminal justice system

6. While appreciating the steps taken by the State party to address racial disparities in the criminal justice system, including the enactment in August 2010 of the Fair Sentencing Act and plans to work on reforming mandatory minimum

sentencing statutes, the Committee continues to be concerned about racial disparities at different stages in the criminal justice system, as well as sentencing disparities and the overrepresentation of individuals belonging to racial and ethnic minorities in prisons and jails (arts. 2, 9, 14 and 26).

The State party should continue and step up its efforts to robustly address racial disparities in the criminal justice system, including by amending regulations and policies leading to racially disparate impact at the federal, state and local levels. The State party should ensure the retroactive application of the Fair Sentencing Act and reform mandatory minimum sentencing statutes.

Racial profiling

7. While welcoming plans to reform the "stop and frisk" programme in New York City, the Committee remains concerned about the practice of racial profiling and surveillance by law enforcement officials targeting certain ethnic minorities and the surveillance of Muslims, undertaken by the Federal Bureau of Investigation (FBI) and the New York Police Department (NYPD), in the absence of any suspicion of wrongdoing (arts. 2, 9, 12, 17 and 26).

The State party should continue and step up measures to effectively combat and eliminate racial profiling by federal, state and local law enforcement officials, inter alia, by:

(a) Pursuing the review of its 2003 Guidance Regarding the Use of Race by Federal Law Enforcement Agencies and expanding protection against profiling on the basis of religion, religious appearance or national origin;

(b) Continuing to train state and local law enforcement personnel on cultural awareness and the inadmissibility of racial profiling; and

(c) Abolishing all "stop and frisk" practices.

Death penalty

8. While welcoming the overall decline in the number of executions and the increasing number of states that have abolished the death penalty, the Committee remains concerned about the continuing use of the death penalty and, in particular, racial disparities in its imposition that disproportionately affects African Americans, exacerbated by the rule that discrimination has to be proven on a case-by-case basis. The Committee is further concerned by the high number of persons wrongly sentenced to death, despite existing safeguards, and by the fact that 16 retentionist states do not provide for compensation for persons who are wrongfully convicted, while other states provide for insufficient compensation. Finally, the Committee notes with concern reports about the administration, by some states, of untested lethal drugs to execute prisoners and the withholding of information about such drugs (arts. 2, 6, 7, 9, 14 and 26) .

The State party should:

(a) Take measures to effectively ensure that the death penalty is not imposed as a result of racial bias;

(b) Strengthen safeguards against wrongful sentencing to death and subsequent wrongful execution by ensuring, inter alia, effective legal representation for defendants in death penalty cases, including at the post-conviction stage;

(c) Ensure that retentionist states provide adequate compensation for persons who are wrongfully convicted;

(d) Ensure that lethal drugs used for executions originate from legal, regulated sources, and are approved by the United States Food and Drug Administration and that information on the origin and composition of such drugs is made available to individuals scheduled for execution; and

(e) Consider establishing a moratorium on the death penalty at the federal level and engage with retentionist states with a view to achieving a nationwide moratorium.

The Committee also encourages the State party to consider acceding to the Second Optional Protocol to the International Covenant on Civil and Political Rights, aiming at the abolition of the death penalty, on the occasion of the 25th anniversary of the Protocol.

Targeted killings using unmanned aerial vehicles (drones)

9. The Committee is concerned about the State party's practice of targeted killings in extraterritorial counter-terrorism operations using unmanned aerial vehicles (UAV), also known as "drones," the lack of transparency regarding the criteria for drone strikes, including the legal justification for specific attacks, and the lack of accountability for the loss of life resulting from such attacks. The Committee notes the State party's position that drone strikes are conducted in the course of its armed conflict with Al-Qaida, the Taliban and associated forces in accordance with its inherent right of national self-defense, and that they are governed by international humanitarian law as well as by the Presidential Policy Guidance that sets out standards for the use of lethal force outside areas of active hostilities. Nevertheless, the Committee remains concerned about the State party's very broad approach to the definition and geographical scope of "armed conflict," including the end of hostilities, the unclear interpretation of what constitutes an "imminent threat," who is a combatant or a civilian taking direct part in hostilities, the unclear position on the nexus that should exist between any particular use of lethal force and any specific theatre of hostilities, as well as the precautionary measures taken to avoid civilian casualties in practice (arts. 2, 6 and 14).

The State party should revisit its position regarding legal justifications for the use of deadly force through drone attacks. It should:

(a) Ensure that any use of armed drones complies fully with its obligations under article 6 of the Covenant, including, in particular, with respect to the principles of precaution, distinction and proportionality in the context of an armed conflict;

(b) Subject to operational security, disclose the criteria for drone strikes, including the legal basis for specific attacks, the process of target identification and the circumstances in which drones are used;

(c) Provide for independent supervision and oversight of the specific implementation of regulations governing the use of drone strikes;

(d) In armed conflict situations, take all feasible measures to ensure the protection of civilians in specific drone attacks and to track and assess civilian casualties, as well as all necessary precautionary measures in order to avoid such casualties;

(e) Conduct independent, impartial, prompt and effective investigations of allegations of violations of the right to life and bring to justice those responsible;

(f) Provide victims or their families with an effective remedy where there has been a violation, including adequate compensation, and establish accountability mechanisms for victims of allegedly unlawful drone attacks who are not compensated by their home governments.

Gun violence

10. While acknowledging the measures taken to reduce gun violence, the Committee remains concerned about the continuing high numbers of gun-related deaths and injuries and the disparate impact of gun violence on minorities, women and children. While commending the investigation by the United States Commission on Civil Rights of the discriminatory effect of the "Stand Your Ground" laws, the Committee is concerned about the proliferation of such laws which are used to circumvent the limits of legitimate self-defense in violation of the State party's duty to protect life (arts. 2, 6 and 26).

The State Party should take all necessary measures to abide by its obligation to effectively protect the right to life. In particular, it should:

(a) Continue its efforts to effectively curb gun violence, including through the continued pursuit of legislation requiring background checks for all private firearm transfers, in order to prevent possession of arms by persons recognized as prohibited individuals under federal law, and ensure strict enforcement of the Domestic Violence Offender Gun Ban of 1996 (the Lautenberg Amendment); and

(b) Review the Stand Your Ground laws to remove far-reaching immunity and ensure strict adherence to the principles of necessity and proportionality when using deadly force in self-defense.

Excessive use of force by law enforcement officials

11. The Committee is concerned about the still high number of fatal shootings by certain police forces, including, for instance, in Chicago, and reports of excessive use of force by certain law enforcement officers, including the deadly use of tasers, which has a disparate impact on African Americans, and use of lethal force by Customs and Border Protection (CBP) officers at the United States-Mexico border (arts. 2, 6, 7 and 26).

The State Party should:

(a) Step up its efforts to prevent the excessive use of force by law enforcement officers by ensuring compliance with the 1990 Basic Principles on the Use of Force and Firearms by Law Enforcement Officials;

(b) Ensure that the new CBP directive on the use of deadly force is applied and enforced in practice; and

(c) Improve reporting of violations involving the excessive use of force and ensure that reported cases of excessive use of force are effectively investigated; that alleged perpetrators are prosecuted and, if convicted, punished with appropriate sanctions; that investigations are re-opened when new evidence becomes available; and that victims or their families are provided with adequate compensation.

Legislation prohibiting torture

12. While noting that acts of torture may be prosecuted in a variety of ways at both the federal and state levels, the Committee is concerned about the lack of comprehensive legislation criminalizing all forms of torture, including mental torture, committed within the territory of the State party. The Committee is also concerned about the inability of torture victims to claim compensation from the State party and its officials due to the application of broad doctrines of legal privilege and immunity (arts. 2 and 7).

The State party should enact legislation to explicitly prohibit torture, including mental torture, wherever committed, and ensure that the law provides for penalties commensurate with the gravity of such acts, whether committed by public officials or other persons acting on behalf of the State, or by private persons. The State party should ensure the availability of compensation to victims of torture.

Non-refoulement

13. While noting the measures taken to ensure compliance with the principle of non-refoulement in cases of extradition, expulsion, return and transfer of individuals to other countries, the Committee is concerned about the State party's reliance on diplomatic assurances that do not provide sufficient safeguards. It is also concerned at the State party's position that the principle of non-refoulement is not covered by the Covenant, despite the Committee's established jurisprudence and subsequent State practice (arts. 6 and 7).

The State party should strictly apply the absolute prohibition against refoulement under articles 6 and 7 of the Covenant; continue exercising the utmost care in evaluating diplomatic assurances, and refrain from relying on such assurances where it is not in a position to effectively monitor the treatment of such persons after their extradition, expulsion, transfer or return to other countries; and take appropriate remedial action when assurances are not fulfilled.

Trafficking and forced labour

14. While acknowledging the measures taken by the State party to address the issue of trafficking in persons and forced labour, the Committee remains concerned about cases of trafficking of persons, including children, for purposes of labour and sexual exploitation, and criminalization of victims on prostitution-related charges. It is concerned about the insufficient identification and investigation of cases of trafficking for labour purposes and notes with concern that certain categories of workers, such as farm workers and domestic workers, are explicitly excluded from protection under labour laws, thus rendering those categories of workers more vulnerable to trafficking. The Committee is also concerned that workers entering the United States of America under the H-2B work visa programme are also at a high risk of becoming victims of trafficking and/or forced labour (arts. 2, 8, 9, 14, 24 and 26).

The State party should continue its efforts to combat trafficking in persons, inter alia, by strengthening its preventive measures, increasing victim identification and systematically and vigorously investigating allegations of trafficking in persons, prosecuting and punishing those responsible and providing effective remedies to victims, including protection, rehabilitation and compensation. The State party should take all appropriate measures to prevent the criminalization of victims of sex trafficking, including child victims, insofar as they have been compelled to engage in unlawful activities. The State party should review its laws and regulations to ensure full protection against forced labour for all categories of workers and ensure effective oversight of labour conditions in any temporary visa programme. It should also reinforce its training activities and provide training to law enforcement and border and immigration officials, as well as to other relevant agencies such as labour law enforcement agencies and child welfare agencies.

Immigrants

15. The Committee is concerned that under certain circumstances mandatory detention of immigrants for prolonged periods of time without regard to the individual case may raise issues under article 9 of the Covenant. It is also concerned about the mandatory nature of the deportation of foreigners, without regard to elements such as the seriousness of crimes and misdemeanors committed, the length of lawful stay in the United States, health status, family ties and the fate of spouses and children staying behind, or the humanitarian situation in the country of destination. Finally, the Committee expresses concern about the exclusion of millions of undocumented immigrants and their children from coverage under the Affordable Care Act and the limited coverage of undocumented immigrants and immigrants residing lawfully in the United States for less than five years by Medicare and Children Health Insurance, all resulting in difficulties for immigrants in accessing adequate health care (arts. 7, 9, 13, 17, 24 and 26).

The Committee recommends that the State party review its policies of mandatory detention and deportation of certain categories of immigrants in order to allow for individualized decisions; take measures to ensure that affected persons have access to legal representation; and identify ways to facilitate access to adequate health care, including reproductive health-care services, by undocumented immigrants and immigrants and their families who have been residing lawfully in the United States for less than five years.

Domestic violence

16. The Committee is concerned that domestic violence continues to be prevalent in the State party, and that ethnic minorities, immigrants, American Indian and Alaska Native women are at particular risk. The Committee is also concerned that victims face obstacles to obtain remedies, and that law enforcement authorities are not legally required to act with due diligence to protect victims of domestic violence and often inadequately respond to such cases (arts. 3, 7, 9 and 26).

The State party should, through the full and effective implementation of the Violence against Women Act and the Family Violence Prevention and Services Act, strengthen measures to prevent and combat domestic violence and ensure that law enforcement personnel appropriately respond to acts of domestic violence. The State party should ensure that cases of domestic violence are effectively investigated and that perpetrators are prosecuted and sanctioned. The State party should ensure remedies for all victims of domestic violence and take steps to improve the provision of emergency shelter, housing, child care, rehabilitative services and legal representation for women victims of domestic violence. The State party should also take measures to assist tribal authorities in their efforts to address domestic violence against Native American women.

Corporal punishment

17. The Committee is concerned about corporal punishment of children in schools, penal institutions, the home and all forms of childcare at federal, state and local levels. It is also concerned about the increasing criminalization of students to deal with disciplinary issues in schools (arts. 7, 10 and 24).

The State party should take practical steps, including through legislative measures, where appropriate, to put an end to corporal punishment in all settings. It should encourage non-violent forms of discipline as alternatives to corporal punishment and should conduct public information campaigns to raise awareness about its harmful effects. The State party should also promote the use of alternatives to the application of criminal law to address disciplinary issues in schools.

Non-consensual psychiatric treatment

18. The Committee is concerned about the widespread use of non-consensual psychiatric medication, electroshock and other restrictive and coercive practices in mental health services (arts. 7 and 17).

The State party should ensure that non-consensual use of psychiatric medication, electroshock and other restrictive and coercive practices in mental health services is generally prohibited. Non-consensual psychiatric treatment may only be applied, if at all, in exceptional cases as a measure of last resort where absolutely necessary for the benefit of the person concerned, provided that he or she is unable to give consent, and for the shortest possible time without any long-term impact and under independent review. The State party should promote psychiatric care aimed at preserving the dignity of patients, both adults and minors.

Criminalization of homelessness

19. While appreciating the steps taken by federal and some state and local authorities to address homelessness, the Committee is concerned about reports of criminalization of people living on the street for everyday activities such as eating, sleeping, sitting in particular areas, etc. The Committee notes that such criminalization raises concerns of discrimination and cruel, inhuman or degrading treatment (arts. 2, 7, 9, 17 and 26).

The State party should engage with state and local authorities to:

(a) Abolish the laws and policies criminalizing homelessness at state and local levels;

(b) Ensure close cooperation among all relevant stakeholders, including social, health, law enforcement and justice professionals at all levels, to intensify efforts to find solutions for the homeless, in accordance with human rights standards; and

(c) Offer incentives for decriminalization and the implementation of such solutions, including by providing continued financial support to local authorities that implement alternatives to criminalization, and withdrawing funding from local authorities that criminalize the homeless.

Conditions of detention and use of solitary confinement

20. The Committee is concerned about the continued practice of holding persons deprived of their liberty, including, under certain circumstances, juveniles and persons with mental disabilities, in prolonged solitary confinement and about detainees being held in solitary confinement in pretrial detention. The Committee is furthermore concerned about poor detention conditions in death-row facilities (arts. 7, 9, 10, 17 and 24).

The State party should monitor the conditions of detention in prisons, including private detention facilities, with a view to ensuring that persons deprived of their liberty are treated in accordance with the requirements of articles 7 and 10 of the Covenant and the Standard Minimum Rules for the Treatment of Prisoners. It should impose strict limits on the use of solitary confinement, both pretrial and following conviction, in the federal system as well as nationwide, and abolish the practice in respect of anyone under the age of 18 and prisoners with serious mental illness. It should also bring the detention conditions of prisoners on death row into line with international standards.

Detainees at Guantánamo Bay

21. While noting the President's commitment to closing the Guantánamo Bay facility and the appointment of Special Envoys at the United States Departments of State and of Defense to continue to pursue the transfer of designated detainees, the Committee regrets that no timeline for closure of the facility has been provided. The Committee is also concerned that detainees held in Guantánamo Bay and in military facilities in Afghanistan are not dealt with through the ordinary criminal justice system after a protracted period of over a decade, in some cases (arts. 7, 9, 10 and 14).

The State party should expedite the transfer of detainees designated for transfer, including to Yemen, as well as the process of periodic review for Guantánamo detainees and ensure either their trial or their immediate release and the closure of the Guantánamo Bay facility. It should end the system of administrative detention without charge or trial and ensure that any criminal cases against detainees held in Guantánamo and in military facilities in Afghanistan are dealt with through the criminal justice system rather than military commissions, and that those detainees are afforded the fair trial guarantees enshrined in article 14 of the Covenant.

National Security Agency surveillance

22. The Committee is concerned about the surveillance of communications in the interest of protecting national security, conducted by the National Security Agency (NSA) both within and outside the United States, through the bulk phone metadata surveillance programme (Section 215 of the USA PATRIOT Act) and, in particular, surveillance under Section 702 of the Foreign Intelligence Surveillance Act (FISA) Amendment Act, conducted through PRISM (collection of communications content from United States-based Internet companies) and UPSTREAM (collection of communications metadata and content by tapping fiber-optic cables carrying Internet traffic) and the adverse impact on individuals' right to privacy. The Committee is concerned that, until recently, judicial interpretations of FISA and rulings of the Foreign Intelligence Surveillance Court (FISC) had largely been kept secret, thus not allowing affected persons to know the law with sufficient precision. The Committee is concerned that the current oversight system of the activities of the NSA fails to effectively protect the rights of the persons affected. While welcoming the recent Presidential Policy Directive/PPD-28, which now extends some safeguards to non-United States citizens "to the maximum extent feasible consistent with the national security," the Committee remains concerned that such persons enjoy only limited protection against excessive surveillance. Finally, the Committee is concerned that the persons affected have no access to effective remedies in case of abuse (arts. 2, 5 (1) and 17).

The State party should:

(a) Take all necessary measures to ensure that its surveillance activities, both within and outside the United States, conform to its obligations under the Covenant, including article 17; in particular, measures should be taken to ensure that any interference with the right to privacy complies with the principles of legality, proportionality and necessity, regardless of the nationality or location of the individuals whose communications are under direct surveillance;

(b) Ensure that any interference with the right to privacy, family, home or correspondence is authorized by laws that: (i) are publicly accessible; (ii) contain provisions that ensure that collection of, access to and use of communications data are tailored to specific legitimate aims; (iii) are sufficiently precise and specify in detail the precise circumstances in which any such interference may be permitted, the procedures for authorization, the categories of persons who may be placed under surveillance, the limit on the duration of surveillance; procedures for the use and storage of data collected; and (iv) provide for effective safeguards against abuse;

(c) Reform the current oversight system of surveillance activities to ensure its effectiveness, including by providing for judicial involvement in the authorization or monitoring of surveillance measures, and considering the establishment of strong and independent oversight mandates with a view to preventing abuses;

(d) Refrain from imposing mandatory retention of data by third parties;

(e) Ensure that affected persons have access to effective remedies in cases of abuse.

Juvenile justice and life imprisonment without parole

23. While noting with satisfaction the Supreme Court decisions prohibiting sentences of life imprisonment without parole for children convicted of non-homicide offences (*Graham v. Florida*), and barring sentences of mandatory life imprisonment without parole for children convicted of homicide offences (*Miller v. Alabama*) and the State party's commitment to their retroactive application, the Committee is concerned that a court may still, at its discretion, sentence a defendant to life imprisonment without parole for a homicide committed as a juvenile, and that a mandatory or non-homicide-related sentence of life imprisonment without parole may still be applied to adults. The Committee is also concerned that many states exclude 16 and 17 year olds from juvenile court jurisdictions so that juveniles continue to be tried in adult courts and incarcerated in adult institutions (arts. 7, 9, 10, 14, 15 and 24).

The State party should prohibit and abolish the sentence of life imprisonment without parole for juveniles, irrespective of the crime committed, as well as the mandatory and non-homicide-related sentence of life imprisonment without parole. It should also ensure that juveniles are separated from adults during pretrial detention and after sentencing, and that juveniles are not transferred to adult courts. It should encourage states that automatically exclude 16 and 17 year olds from juvenile court jurisdictions to change their laws.

Voting rights

24. While noting with satisfaction the statement by the Attorney General on 11 February 2014, calling for a reform of state laws on felony disenfranchisement, the Committee reiterates its concern about the persistence of state-level felon disenfranchisement laws, its disproportionate impact on minorities and the lengthy and cumbersome voting restoration procedures in states. The Committee is further concerned that voter identification and other recently introduced eligibility requirements may impose excessive burdens on voters and result in de facto disenfranchisement of large numbers of voters, including members of minority groups. Finally, the Committee reiterates its concern that residents of the District of Columbia (D. C.) are denied the right to vote for and elect voting representatives to the United States Senate and House of Representatives (arts. 2, 10, 25 and 26).

The State party should ensure that all states reinstate voting rights to felons who have fully served their sentences; provide inmates with information about their voting restoration options; remove or streamline lengthy and cumbersome voting restoration procedures; as well as review automatic denial of the vote to any imprisoned felon, regardless of the nature of the offence. The State party should also take all necessary measures to ensure that voter identification requirements and the new eligibility requirements do not impose excessive burdens on voters and result in de facto disenfranchisement. The State party should also provide for the full voting rights of residents of Washington, D. C.

Rights of indigenous peoples

25. The Committee is concerned about the insufficient measures taken to protect the sacred areas of indigenous peoples against desecration, contamination and destruction as a result of urbanization, extractive industries, industrial development, tourism and toxic contamination. It is also concerned about the restriction of access of indigenous peoples to sacred areas that are essential for the preservation of their religious, cultural and spiritual practices, and the insufficiency of consultation with indigenous peoples on matters of interest to their communities (art. 27).

The State party should adopt measures to effectively protect sacred areas of indigenous peoples against desecration, contamination and destruction and ensure that consultations are held with the indigenous communities that might be adversely affected by the State party's development projects and exploitation of natural resources with a view to obtaining their free, prior and informed consent for proposed project activities.

26. The State party should widely disseminate the Covenant, the text of its fourth periodic report, the written replies to the list of issues drawn up by the Committee and the present concluding observations among the judicial, legislative and administrative authorities, civil society and non-governmental organizations operating in the country, as well as the general public.

27. In accordance with rule 71, paragraph 5, of the Committee's rules of procedure, the State party should provide, within one year, relevant information on its implementation of the Committee's recommendations made in paragraphs 5, 10, 21 and 22 above.

28. The Committee requests the State party to provide in its next periodic report due to be submitted on 28 March 2019 specific, up-to-date information on the implementation of all its recommendations and on the Covenant as a whole. The Committee also requests the State party, when preparing its next periodic report, to continue its practice of broadly consulting with civil society and non-governmental organizations.

[End Text]

Source: U.S. State Dept. Diplomacy in Action, https://www.state.gov/documents/organization/235641.pdf

かゝゝかゝゝかゝ

II. ONE-YEAR FOLLOW-UP RESPONSE OF THE UNITED STATES OF AMERICA TO PRIORITY RECOMMENDATIONS OF THE HUMAN RIGHTS COMMITTEE ON ITS FOURTH PERIODIC REPORT ON IMPLEMENTATION OF THE INTERNATIONAL COVENANT ON CIVIL AND POLITICAL RIGHTS, 2015

This document is from the U.S. State Department to the U.N. HRCtee concerning the Fourth Periodic Report of the U.S. to the Committee, document. It is a follow up to the priority recommendations made to the U.S. in the HRCtee Concluding Observations (Primary Source Document 9).

{Excerpt}

[Text]

The Permanent Mission of the United States of America to the Office of the United Nations and other international organizations in Geneva presents its compliments to the Human Rights Committee and has the honor of conveying to the Committee the U.S. government's one year follow-up response to priority recommendations of the Human Rights Committee on the United States' fourth periodic report on implementation of the International Covenant on Civil and Political Rights,

The Permanent Mission of the United States avails itself of the opportunity to express once again the commitment of the United States to the protection and promotion of human rights and to the work of the Committee, and to renew to the Human Rights Committee the assurances of its highest consideration.

Enclosure:

As stated.

The Permanent Mission of the United States of America, Geneva, March 31, 2015

OHCTIR REGISTRY
1 APR 2015
DIPLOMATIC NOTE

One-year Follow-up Response of the United States of America to Priority Recommendations of the Human Rights Committee on its Fourth Periodic Report on Implementation of the International Covenant on Civil and Political Rights

Pursuant to the Committee's request, the United States provides the following informationObservations adopted March 26, 2014), focused primarily on measures taken subsequent to the Committee's recommendations and taking into consideration the Committee's follow-up guidelines.

Response to Committee Recommendation 5 — Accountability for past human rights violations:

1. The United States prohibits its personnel from engaging in acts of torture or cruel, inhuman, or degrading treatment of any person in its custody wherever they are held. It likewise does notpermit personnel to engage in unlawful killing, arbitrary detention, or forced disappearance. The United States takes vigilant action to prevent any such unlawful conduct by its personnel and to hold accountable any persons responsible for such acts. Successful prosecution, whether of civilian, military, or contract personnel, is dependent on the availability of evidence that will support conviction beyond a reasonable doubt. In addition, due process requires that the investigation and prosecution of these offenses must be conducted in accordance with the same legal standards applied to investigation and prosecution of other offenses. This is true for any prosecution in the United States, whether at the federal, state, or local level.

2. Federal Prosecutions: The following Federal prosecutions since the 1 10th session of the Committee supplement those enumerated in 181 of the Fourth Periodic Report and demonstrate the scope of criminal punishments available under U.S. law for misconduct of this nature by government personnel and contractors:

On December 20, 2014, the U.S. District Court for the Eastern District of California sentenced Bryan Robert Benson, a former police officer in Anderson, California, to five years in prison and three years of supervised release for violating the civil rights of a woman he arrested. According to court documents, while Benson was transporting the victim to jail, he stopped in a parking lot and sexually assaulted her. Benson was fired from his position with the Anderson Police Department as a result of his conduct. See http://www.justice.gov/opa/pr/former-anderson-california-police-officer-sentenced-five years- prison-sexually-assaulting.

...

3. The Department of Justice (DOJ) Human Rights and Special Prosecutions Section and the United States Attorneys' Offices pursue prosecutions of civilian personnel and contractors employed by the United States and allegedly involved in human rights violations. In addition to the convictions for unlawful killings and abuses committed by civilian personnel and contractors

On October 22, 2014, four civilian contractors — Dustin L. Heard, Evan S. Liberty, Nicholas A. Slatten, and Paul A. Slough — were convicted in U.S. District Court in

Washington, D. C., of charges that included murder, manslaughter, and weapons violations, in connection with the deaths of 14 civilians and the injuring of 20 others in Nisur Square in Baghdad, Iraq, in 2007 while the defendants were employed there by the former Blackwater USA. Slatten faces a mandatory sentence of life in prison. The other three face a mandatory minimum of 30 years in prison. This prosecution was reported as ongoing in 544 of the Fourth Periodic Report.

4. As reported during the 1 10th session and in LOIR 47, the Attorney General announced on August 30, 2012 the closure of investigations into the death of two individuals in U.S. custody at overseas locations following review of the treatment of 101 persons alleged to have been mistreated in U.S. government custody after the 9/11 attacks. The Department of Justice ultimately declined these cases for prosecution consistent with the Principles of Federal Prosecution, which require that each case be evaluated for a clear violation of a federal criminal statute with provable facts that reflect evidence of guilt beyond a reasonable doubt and a reasonable probability of conviction. See http://www.justice.gov/opa/pr/statement-attomeygeneral-eric-holder-closure-investigation-interrogation-certain-detainees.

5. State-Level Prosecutions: Accountability exists at all government levels in the United States.

The following examples of state and local prosecutions since the 1 10th session further demonstrate the scope of available criminal punishments:

Nicholas Dimauro, a former Atlanta, Georgia, police officer was convicted of using excessive force for beating a man while attempting to make an arrest. The man suffered a collapsed lung and several broken ribs. In December 2014, a Fulton County judge sentenced him to ten years in prison, plus five years' probation.

...

6. Prosecution of Military Personnel: As previously reported, the U.S. military investigates all credible allegations of misconduct by U.S. forces to determine the facts, including identifying those responsible for any violation of law, policy, or procedures; and multiple accountability mechanisms are in place to ensure that personnel adhere to those laws, policies, and procedures.

7. The Department of Defense (DOD) has conducted thousands of investigations since 2001 and it has prosecuted or disciplined hundreds of service members for misconduct, including mistreatment of detainees. For example, more than 70 investigations concerning allegations of detainee abuse by military personnel in Afghanistan conducted by DOD resulted in trial by courts-martial, close to 200 investigations of detainee abuse resulted in either non-judicial punishment or adverse administrative action, and many more were investigated and resulted in action at a lower level. The remainder were determined to be unsubstantiated, lacking in sufficient inculpatory evidence, or were included as multiple counts against one individual.

8. Effective Remedies: DOJ's Civil Rights Division (DOJ/CRT) continues to institute civil suits for equitable and declaratory relief pursuant to the Pattern or Practice of Police Misconduct provision of the Crime Bill of 1994, 42 U.S. C. 14141. Cases pursued since the 1 10th session that supplement those reported in 183 of the Fourth Periodic Report include:

On March 4, 2015, DOJ announced that its civil rights investigation into the Ferguson, Missouri, Police Department had found a pattern or practice of excessive force and discriminatory policing, among other violations. DOJ also announced that it did not find sufficient evidence to bring federal criminal civil rights charges against Officer Darren Wilson in the death of Michael Brown in Ferguson.

...

9. DOJ has taken similar action in the past five years, making public findings of discriminatory policing and/or excessive force and working toward long-term solutions in 14 states and jurisdictions. DOJ is also working to strengthen police-community relations. For example, in Ferguson, Missouri, in addition to opening civil and criminal investigations after the August 2014 shooting of Michael Brown, DOJ sent mediators to create a dialogue between police, city officials, and residents to reduce tension in the community. In addition, DOJ is involved in a voluntary, independent, and objective assessment of the St. Louis County (Missouri) Police Department, looking at training, use of force, handling mass demonstrations, and other areas where reform may be needed.

1 1. The following are examples of compensation or other effective remedy for victims of abuse pursued at the state level since the Committee's 1 10th session:

California:

In July 2014, the Board of Trustees of California State University, San Bernardino agreed to pay $2. 5 million to the parents of Bartholomew Williams to settle a wrongful death/excessive force suit. Williams, a graduate student at the university, was shot five times during a confrontation with police.

...

12. Command and Participant Responsibility: The Uniform Code of Military Justice, 10 U.S. C. 877, Article 77, provides that "Any person punishable under this chapter who (I) commits an offense punishable by this chapter, or aids, abets, counsels, commands, or procures its commission; or (2) causes an act to be done which if directly performed by him would be punishable by this chapter; is a principal." Although U.S. federal criminal law does not generally encompass the doctrine of command responsibility per se, DOJ can rely on conspiracy and aiding and abetting statutes to reach senior officials. Comparable state-level criminal law provisions also address conspiracy and participation offenses.

13. With respect to accountability for legal advice, the conduct of two senior DOJ officials in giving legal advice that justified the use of certain "enhanced interrogation techniques" following the 9/11 attacks was reviewed by an Associate Deputy Attorney General, a longtime career DOJ official. In a 69-page January 5, 2010 memorandum subsequently released publicly with limited redactions, he found that they had narrowly construed the torture statute, often failed to ex-

pose countervailing arguments, and overstated the certainty of their conclusions. He concluded that although they had exercised poor judgment, the evidence did not establish that they had engaged in professional misconduct.

14. Senate Select Committee on Intelligence Report: On December 9, 2014, the Senate Select Committee on Intelligence released its Findings and Conclusions and an Executive Summary of its Study of the CIA's former Detention and Interrogation Program. Upon the request of the Committee and in the interest of transparency, these documents, totaling over 500 pages, were declassified with minimal redactions to protect national security, leaving 93 percent of the released portion of the Study declassified. Harsh interrogation techniques highlighted in that Report are not representative of how the United States deals with the threat of terrorism today, and are not consistent with our values. The United States supports transparency and has taken steps to ensure that it never resorts to the use of those techniques again. See http://www.whitehouse.gov/the-press-office/2014/12/09/statement-president-re. port-senateselect-committee-intelligence.

Response to Committee Recommendation 10 — Gun violence:

15. The United States acknowledges that gun violence continues to be a serious concern in some communities across the nation. The Administration continues to support common-sense legislation to reduce the incidence of gun crime, including legislation that would close loopholes in the background check system and increase the number of firearms transactions subject to criminal background checks, create a specific firearms trafficking offense under federal law, restore and strengthen a federal assault weapons ban, and crack down on gun trafficking.

16. Federal Gun Control: In the absence of such legislation, as the United States reported during the Committee's I I (P session, the Administration has taken a number of executive actions designed to improve background checks and keep the most dangerous firearms out of the wrong hands, while continuing to push for other measures that require congressional action. On January 16, 2013, the President unveiled his plan to reduce gun violence, which included 23 executive actions. See President's plan entitled "Now is the Time" at http://www.whitehouse.gov/sites/default/files/docs/wh now is the time full.pdf.

17. In November 2013 the Administration announced that it had completed or made significant progress on all 23 executive actions. See Progress Report on the President's Executive Actions to Reduce Gun Violence, November 2013 at http://www.whitehouse.gov/sites/default/files/docs/novemberexecactions_progress reportfinal.pdf.

18. The Administration has also announced additional actions. See White House Fact Sheet:

Strengthening the Federal Background Check System to Keep Guns out of Potentially Dangerous Hands, January 3, 2014 at http://www.whitehouse.gov/ihe-press-office/2014/01/03/fact-sheetstrengthening-federal-background-check-system-keep-guns-out-p.

19. Guns and Domestic Violence: With respect to the Domestic Violence Offender Gun Ban, as amended and codified under 18 USC 922(g) (9) — known as the "Lautenberg amendment" — the United States reported to the Committee in March 2014 that DOJ had reviewed the guidelines for prosecutors with a view to ensuring the strict enforcement of the law banning persons convicted of misdemeanor crimes of domestic violence from owning firearms, in addition to enforcement of weapons legislation in general. DOJ's Bureau of Alcohol, Tobacco, Firearms and Explosives has primary investigative responsibility for such cases. United States Attorneys' Offices also work with state and local law enforcement to establish guidelines for handling these cases, which often arise in emergency situations, such as when a local officer responds to a domestic complaint and learns that a firearm is present and that one of the parties is prohibited to have the firearm under this statute. See http://www.justice.gov/usao/eousa/foia reading room/usamJtitle9/crm01117.htm.

20. The U.S. Supreme Court recently interpreted the federal firearms prohibition in United States v. Castleman, 134 S. Ct. 1405 (2014), upholding the federal law that makes it a crime for people convicted of misdemeanor domestic violence offenses, however minor, to possess guns. This decision addressed an important legal hurdle that had impeded recent prosecutions under 922(g) (9). See https://www.whitehouse.gov/blog/2014/03/28/supreme-eourt-decision-us-vcastleman-will-save-womens-lives.

21. Stand Your Ground: Attorney General Holder said in 2013 that "[I]it's time to question laws that senselessly expand the concept Of self-defense and sow dangerous conflict in our neighborhoods. These laws try to fix something that was never broken. There has always been a legal defense for using deadly force if- and the 'if is important — no safe retreat is available." See http://www.justice.gov/iso/opa/ag/ speeches/2013/ag-speech-130716. html.

22. As the United States clarified during the Committee's 110th session, the vast majority of criminal laws in the United States are enacted by state legislatures and enforced at the state and local levels. Although some states have adopted such laws, these laws are not uniform in their text or application and there has been limited information available on disparities in their application. Although some law enforcement groups have expressed concern that Stand Your Ground laws may have unintended consequences and inhibit the ability of law enforcement and prosecutors to hold violent criminals fully accountable for their acts, DOJ remains steadfast in its commitment to prosecute violations of federal criminal civil rights laws.

23. The United States Commission on Civil Rights has undertaken an investigation of the civil rights implications of Stand Your Ground laws with the focus of determining whether racial disparities exist in their application or enforcement. That investigation is ongoing. On October 17, 2014, the Commission conducted a public hearing involving a national panel of experts, which focused on "whether there is possible racial bias in the assertion, investigation and/or enforcement of justifiable homicide laws in states with Stand Your Ground provisions." The Commission is expected to issue a final report to the President and Congress concerning its findings, although no date has been set for the release of that report.

Response to Committee Recommendation MI 21 — Detainees at Guantánamo Bay

24. We preface this response by recalling the longstanding position of the United States that obligations under the Covenant apply only with respect to individuals who are both within the territory of a State Party and within its jurisdiction. The United States continues to have legal authority under the law of war to detain Guantánamo detainees until the end of hostilities, consistent with U.S. law and applicable international law, but it has elected, as a policy matter, to ensure that it holds them no longer than necessary to mitigate the threat they pose.

25. Closure of Guantánamo Bay Detention Facility: President Obama has repeatedly reaffirmed his commitment to close the Guantánamo Bay detention facility, most recently during his State of the Union address to the Congress on January 20, 2015 (available at http : //www.whitehouse.gov/the-press-office/2015/01 /20/remarks-president-state-union-address january-20-2015). He has emphasized that the continued operation of the facility weakens U.S. national security by draining resources, damaging relationships with key allies and partners, and emboldening violent extremists. See httn://www.white house.gov/the_pressoffice/Remarks-bythe-President-On-NationaI-Security-5-21-()9/. The United States is taking all feasible steps to reduce the detainee population at Guantánamo and to close the detention facility in a responsible manner that protects our national security.

26. Transfers: More than 80 percent of those at one time held at the Guantánamo Bay detention facility have been repatriated or resettled, including all detainees subject to court orders directing their release. Of the 242 detainees at Guantánamo at the beginning of this Administration, 116 have been transferred out of the facility, including 27 after adoption of the Committee's recommendations on March 26, 2014. This includes 12 Yemenis resettled in third countries since November 2014. More detainees were transferred out of the facility in 2014 than in any year since 2009, and the detainee population now stands at its lowest since 2002. Of the 122 who remain at Guantánamo, 56 are designated for transfer. Of the 66 others, ten are currently facing charges, awaiting sentencing, or serving criminal sentences, and the remaining 56 are eligible for review by the Periodic Review Board.

27. Periodic Review: The Periodic Review Board (PRB) process commenced in October 2013. The PRB is a discretionary, administrative interagency process to review whether continued detention of certain individuals detained at Guantánamo remains necessary to protect against a continuing significant threat to the security of the United States. As of March 24, 2015, the PRB had conducted 14 full hearings and three six-month file reviews, in which detainees participated with assistance from their personal representatives and, in some cases, private counsel. The PRB has determined that continued detention of eight of the detainees reviewed is no longer necessary to protect against a continuing significant threat to the United States. Two of these detainees were subsequently transferred to their countries of origin and

the remaining six are eligible for transfer subject to appropriate security assurances and consistent with our humane transfer policy.

28. Afghanistan: As of December 10, 2014, the Department Of Defense no longer operates detention facilities in Afghanistan.

29. Criminal Prosecutions: The United States remains of the view that in our efforts to protect our national security, both military commissions and federal courts can, depending on the circumstances of the specific case, provide tools that are both grounded in applicable law and effective. However, U.S. law currently precludes transfer of detainees from Guantánamo for prosecution in the United States.

30. As explained by the U.S. delegation during the Committee's 1 10th session, all current military commission proceedings at Guantánamo incorporate fundamental procedural guarantees that meet or exceed the fair trial safeguards required by Common Article 3 and other applicable law, and are further consistent with those in Additional Protocol Il of the 1949 Geneva Conventions. The 2009 Military Commissions Act also provides for the right to appeal final judgments rendered by a military commission to the U.S. Court of Military Commissions Review (CMCR). The detainee has a right to appeal that CMCR decision to the U.S. Court of Appeals for the District of Columbia Circuit and then the United States Supreme Court, both federal civilian courts consisting of life-tenured judges.

31. The United States is committed to ensuring the transparency of military commission proceedings. To that end, proceedings are now transmitted via video feed to locations at Guantánamo Bay and in the United States, so that the press and the public can view them, with a 40-second delay to protect against the disclosure of classified information. Court transcripts, filings, and other materials are also available to the public online via the Office of Military Commissions website.

32. There are no current plans to end prosecutions by military commissions. Since the Committee issued its recommendations in March 2014, the military commissions convened to try the defendants charged with the attacks on the USS COLE and on the United States on September 1 1, 2001 have continued with pretrial litigation. In each case more than 300 motions have been filed by the defendants challenging the structure of the commissions and the admissibility of evidence at trial, and presenting Constitutional questions, among other matters. On June 2, 2014, another case was referred to trial by military commission, against Iraqi citizen, Abd al Hadi al-Iraqi. The charges against al Hadi al-Iraqi include: denying quarter, attacking protected property, perfidy, attempted perfidy, and conspiracy. This case was referred to a commission that is not authorized to issue a capital sentence following a guilty verdict. A midlevel al Qaeda member convicted of a facilitating role in a terrorist bombing in Al Mukalla harbor of Yemen in 2002 will be sentenced between now and 2016 under a plea agreement.

Another mid-level al Qaeda member convicted of a facilitating role in a terrorist bombing in Jakarta, Indonesia in 2003 will be sentenced by early next year under a plea agreement that sets the remaining time of confinement at an additional 15 to 19 years. The explosion in Jakarta killed I I people and injured more than 80 others, with U.S. citizens among the injured.

Response to Committee Recommendation 22 — National Security Agency surveillance

33. Measures to Comply with Article 17 and Ensure That Any Interference is Authorized by Appropriate Laws and Complies with Legal Obligations: The United States takes extensive measures to ensure that its surveillance activities, irrespective of the context or purpose, comport with its domestic law and international legal obligations, including those with respect to Article 17 Of the Covenant. The right to protection of the law from arbitrary or unlawful interference with privacy, as enshrined in Article 17, is protected under the U.S. Constitution and U.S. laws. The United States understands this requirement to mean that, to be consistent with Article 17, an interference with privacy must be in accordance with transparent laws and must not be arbitrary. The Committee's recommendation implies that an interference under Article 1 7 has to be essential or necessary and be proportionate to achieve a legitimate objective. The United States notes that these legal concepts are derived from certain regional jurisprudence, are not broadly accepted internationally, go beyond that which is required by the text of Article 17, and are not supported by the travaux of the treaty. The United States again asserts its longstanding position that obligations under the Covenant apply only with respect to individuals who are both within the territory of the State Party and within its jurisdiction.

34. As explained by the U.S. delegation during the Committee's 1 10th session, our intelligence activities are authorized pursuant to a rule of law framework whereby statutes and other authorities established through democratic institutions govern our activities. U.S. intelligence collection programs and activities are subject to stringent and multilayered oversight mechanisms; all of the collection activities of U.S. intelligence agencies are carried out pursuant to valid foreign intelligence or counterintelligence purposes; we do not collect intelligence to suppress dissent, to provide a competitive advantage to U.S. companies or business sectors commercially, or to disadvantage any person on the basis of categories such as ethnicity, race, gender, sexual orientation, or religious belief. For detailed information on oversight and safeguards, please see our previous submissions to the Committee ("1 321-335 of the Fourth

Commissioner on Human Rights on privacy in the digital age (available at http://www.ohchr.org/Documents/Issues/Privacy/United%20States.pdf).

35. Recent Reforms: The United States has extensive and effective oversight to prevent abuse. Nevertheless, over the past 18 months, the United States has undertaken a comprehensive effort to examine and enhance the privacy and civil liberty protections embedded in our signals intelligence activities. As part of this process, we have sought — and benefitted from — a broad cross-section of views, ideas, and recommendations from oversight bodies, advocacy organizations, private companies, and the general public, as well as from discussions with foreign partners. This effort has resulted in strengthened privacy protections, new limits on the collection and use of signals intelligence, and increased transparency. To follow up on the reforms announced by President Obama, including those in the January 2014 Presidential Policy Directive (PPD-28) on signals intelligence activities, the Director of National Intelligence released a report in February 2015 that highlights the reforms the U.S. government has taken with respect to its signals intelligence practices and reflects an ongoing commitment to greater transparency. See http://icontherecord.tumblr.com/ppd-28/2015/overview.

36. As part of these reforms, we have: required that signals intelligence collection be as tailored as feasible and limited our Intelligence Community's ability to use signals intelligence collected in bulk to six specific purposes; begun an annual Cabinet-level review of signals intelligence priorities and requirements in light of potential risks to national security interests and relationships abroad; and required each Intelligence Community element to update or issue new policies and procedures that implement safeguards for all personal information collected through signals intelligence, regardless of nationality or place of residence, consistent with technical capabilities and operational needs.

37. In the last 18 months, we have increased transparency by declassifying and publicly releasing an unprecedented amount of information about current programs, much of which relates to the government's use of authorities granted under the Foreign Intelligence Surveillance Act (FISA). We have published the first Intelligence Community Annual Transparency Report, disclosing statistics on the government's use of National Security Letters and FISA authorities.

We have also declassified certain aggregate FISA data so that communications providers can disclose to the public additional information about how they respond to requests they receive from the government. We recently issued Principles of Intelligence Transparency, which are being implemented to further enhance transparency while protecting intelligence sources and methods. The United States government has also established a senior working group to continue to identify ways the Intelligence Community can increase transparency without harming national security.

38. Retention of Information: PPD-28 makes clear that all persons have legitimate privacy interests in the handling of their personal information in the context of signals intelligence activities. To that end, the President directed the U.S. government to apply protections to the personal information of non-U.S. persons, regardless of nationality or where they reside, that are comparable to those applied to U.S. persons, consistent with national security. The PPD specifically directs that the personal information of non-U.S. persons shall be retained only if the retention of comparable information concerning U.S. persons would be permitted. All agencies within the Intelligence Community must delete the personal information of non-U.S. persons collected through signals intelligence five years after collection unless the information has been determined to be relevant to, among other things, an authorized foreign intelligence or counterintelligence purpose, or if the Director of National Intelligence determines, after considering the views of the Office of the Director of National Intelligence's Civil Liberties Protection Officer and agency privacy and civil liberty officials, that continued retention is in the interest of national security. This new retention requirement is similar to the requirements applicable to personal information about U.S. citizens.

39. Dissemination of Information: Intelligence Community elements have always disseminated intelligence information because it is relevant to foreign intelligence requirements. All agency policies implementing PPD-28 now explicitly require that information about a person not be disseminated solely because he or she is a non-U.S. person and the Office of the Director of National Intelligence has issued a revised directive to all Intelligence Community elements to reflect this requirement. Intelligence Community personnel are now specifically required to -consider the privacy interests of non-U -S. persons when drafting and disseminating intelligence reports. In particular, signals intelligence information about the routine activities of a foreign person will not be disseminated by virtue of that fact alone unless it is otherwise responsive to an authorized foreign intelligence requirement. See http://www.dni.gov/files/documents/ ICD/ ICD%20203%20Analytic%20Standards.pdf.

40. Oversight and Compliance: Intelligence Community elements have always had strong training, oversight, and compliance programs to ensure the protection of privacy and civil liberties of U.S. persons. In response to PPD-28, Intelligence Community elements have added new training, oversight, and compliance requirements; developed mandatory training programs to ensure that intelligence officers know and understand their responsibility to protect the personal information of all people, regardless of nationality; added new oversight and compliance programs to ensure that these new rules are being followed properly, and now require the reporting of any significant compliance incident involving personal information, regardless of the person's nationality, to the Director of National Intelligence.

Source: U.S. Dept. of State, Diplomacy in Action, https://www.state.gov/documents/organization/242228.pdf

ะ~๕~ะ~๕~ะ~๕~ะ~๕

12. VIEWS ADOPTED BY THE COMMITTEE UNDER ARTICLE 5 (4) OF THE OPTIONAL PROTOCOL, CONCERNING COMMUNICATION NO. 469/1991: *Ng v. Canada*

This document is a sample case decision of a U.N. Treaty Body, the Human Rights Committee (HRCtee). The HRCtee is a quasi-judicial body made up of the 18 independent experts chosen by the states parties to the ICCPR. Its decisions are called "Views." The Committee presents its views as to whether the petition filed against Canada is admissible, meaning that it meets the criteria for the HRCtee to hear the case, and views as to the "merits" of the case (whether a violation of the treaty has, or has not, occurred). The Views of the HRCtee are not legally binding on the state party accused even if a violation is found and a remedy recommended.

Treaty bodies can set up complaint procedures to allow victims to bring a case against a state-party for alleged violations of the Treaty. The U. S has never had any cases filed against it in any U.N. treaty body complaint system because it has not accepted the power of any treaty body to accept any individual complaint cases against it. The U. S has accepted the jurisdiction ("competence") of the HRCtee to handle state versus state ("inter-state") cases against it but no state has ever filed a case against another state in the treaty bodies. This case was chosen as an example here because it involves the United States seeking the extradition of an American alleged murderer who fled to Canada and who is fighting against extradition to the U.S. to face a possible death penalty and experience the so called "Death Row Syndrome." He was sent back to the U.S. and prosecuted.

{Excerpt}

[Text]

Ng v. Canada
CCPR/C/49/D/469/1991
7 January 1994

Communication No. 469/1991: Canada

United Nations Human Rights Committee

Views of the Human Rights Committee under article 5, paragraph 4, of the Optional Protocol to the International Covenant on Civil and Political Rights

...

1. The author of the communication is Charles Chitat Ng, a British subject, born on 24 December 1960 in Hong Kong, and a resident of the United States of America, at the time of his submission detained in a penitentiary in Alberta, Canada, and on 26 September 1991 extradited to the U.S. He claims to be a victim of a violation of his human rights by Canada because of his extradition. He is represented by counsel.

2.1 The author was arrested, charged and convicted in 1985 in Calgary, Alberta, following an attempted store theft and shooting of a security guard. In February 1987, the U.S. formally requested the author's extradition to stand trial in California on 19 criminal counts, including kidnapping and 12 murders, committed in 1984 and 1985. If convicted, the author could face the death penalty.

2.2 In November 1988, a judge of the Alberta Court of Queen's Bench ordered the author's extradition. In February 1989, the author's habeas corpus application was denied, and on 31 August 1989 the Supreme Court of Canada refused the author leave to appeal.

2.3 Article 6 of the Extradition Treaty between Canada and the U.S. provides:

"When the offence for which extradition is requested is punishable by death under the laws of the requesting State and the laws of the requested State do not permit such punishment for that offence, extradition may be refused, unless the requesting State provides such assurances as the requested State considers sufficient that the death penalty shall not be imposed or, if imposed, shall not be executed."

Canada abolished the death penalty in 1976, except for certain military offences.

2.4 The power to seek assurances that the death penalty will not be imposed is discretionary and is conferred on the Minister of Justice pursuant to section 25 of the Extradition Act. In October 1989, the Minister of Justice decided not to seek these assurances.

2.5 The author subsequently filed an application for review of the Minister's decision with the Federal Court. On 8 June 1990, the issues in the case were referred to the Supreme Court of Canada, which rendered judgement on 26 September 1991. It found that the author's extradition without assurances as to the imposition of the death penalty did not contravene Canada's constitutional protection for human rights nor the standards of the international community. The author was extradited on the same day.

The complaint

3. The author claims that the decision to extradite him violates articles 6, 7, 9, 10, 14 and 26 of the [ICCPR] Covenant. He submits that the execution of the death sentence by gas asphyxiation, as provided for under California statutes, constitutes cruel and inhuman treatment or punishment per se, and that the conditions on death row are cruel, inhuman and degrading. He further alleges that the judicial procedures in California, inasmuch as they relate specifically to capital punishment, do not meet basic requirements of justice. In this context, the author alleges that in the U.S., racial bias influences the imposition of the death penalty.

The State party's initial observations and the author's comments thereon:

4.1 The State party submits that the communication is inadmissible ratione personae, loci and materiae.

4.2 It is argued that the author cannot be considered a victim within the meaning of the Optional Protocol, since his allegations are derived from assumptions about possible future events, which may not materialize and which are dependent on the law and actions of the authorities of the U.S. The State party refers in this connection to the Committee's views in communication No. 61/1979, where it was found that the Committee "has only been entrusted with the mandate of examining whether an individual has suffered an actual violation of his rights. It cannot review in the abstract whether national legislation contravenes the Covenant."

...

4.6 The State party finally submits that the author has failed to substantiate his allegations that the treatment he may face in the U.S. will violate his rights under the Covenant. In this connection, the State party points out that the imposition of the death penalty is not per se unlawful under the Covenant. As regards the delay between the imposition and the execution of the death sentence, the State party submits that it is difficult to see how a period of detention during which a convicted prisoner would pursue all avenues of appeal, can be held to constitute a violation of the Covenant.

5.1 In his comments on the State party's submission, counsel submits that the author is and was himself actually and personally affected by the decision of the State party to extradite him and that the communication is therefore admissible ratione personae. In this context, he refers to the Committee's views in communication No. 35/1978, and argues that an individual can claim to be a victim within the meaning of the Optional Protocol if the laws, practices, actions or decisions of a State party raise a real risk of violation of rights set forth in the Covenant.

5.2 Counsel further argues that, since the decision complained of is one made by Canadian authorities while the author was subject to Canadian jurisdiction, the communication is admissible ratione loci. In this connection, he refers to the Committee's views in communication No. 110/1981, where it was held that article 1 of the Covenant was "clearly intended to apply to individuals subject to the jurisdiction of the State party concerned at the time of the alleged violation of the Covenant."

5.3 Counsel finally stresses that the author does not claim a right not to be extradited; he only claims that he should not have been surrendered without assurances that the death penalty would not be imposed. He submits that the communication is therefore compatible with the provisions of the Covenant. He refers in this context to the Committee's views on communication No. 107/1981, where the Committee found that anguish and stress can give rise to a breach of the Covenant; he submits that this finding is also applicable in the instant case.

The Committee's consideration of and decision on admissibility:

6.1 During its forty-sixth session, in October 1992, the Committee considered the admissibility of the communication. It observed that extradition as such is outside the scope of application of the Covenant,h but that a State party's obligations in relation to a matter itself outside the scope of the Covenant may still be engaged by reference to other provisions of the Covenant. i The Committee noted that the author does not claim that extradition as such violates the Covenant, but rather that the particular circumstances related to the effects of his extradition would raise issues under specific provisions of the Covenant. Accordingly, the Committee found that the communication was thus not excluded ratione materiae.

6.2 The Committee considered the contention of the State party that the claim is inadmissible ratione loci. Article 2 of the Covenant requires States parties to guarantee the rights of persons within their jurisdiction. If a person is lawfully expelled or extradited, the State party concerned will not generally have responsibility under the Covenant for any violations of that person's rights that may later occur in the other jurisdiction. In that sense, a State party clearly is not required to guarantee the rights of persons within another jurisdiction. However, if a State party takes a decision relating to a person within its jurisdiction, and the necessary and foreseeable consequence is that this person's rights under the Covenant will be violated in another jurisdiction, the State party itself may be in violation of the Covenant. That follows from the fact that a State party's duty under article 2 of the Covenant would be negated by the handing over of a person to another State (whether a State party to the Covenant or not) where treatment contrary to the Covenant is certain or is the very purpose of the handing over. For example, a State party would itself be in violation of the Covenant if it handed over a person to another State in circumstances in which it was foreseeable that torture would take place. The foreseeability of the consequence would mean that there was a present violation by the State party, even though the consequence would not occur until later on.

...

7. On 28 October 1992, the Human Rights Committee therefore decided to join the question of whether the author was a victim within the meaning of article 1 of the Optional Protocol to the consideration of the merits. The Committee expressed its regret that the State party had not acceded to the Committee's request, under rule 86, to stay extradition of the author.

The State party's further submission on the admissibility and the merits of the communication.

8.1 In its submission dated 14 May 1993, the State party elaborates on the extradition process in general, on the Canada-U.S. extradition relationship and on the specifics of the present case. It also submits comments with respect to the admissibility of the communication, in particular with respect to article 1 of the Optional Protocol.

8.2 The State party recalls that:

"...extradition exists to contribute to the safety of the citizens and residents of States. Dangerous criminal offenders seeking a safe haven from prosecution or punishment are removed to face justice in the State in which their crimes were committed. Extradition furthers international cooperation in criminal justice matters and strengthens domestic law enforcement. It is meant to be a straightforward and expeditious process. Extradition seeks to balance the rights of fugitives with the need for the protection of the residents of the two States parties to any given extradition treaty. The extradition relationship between Canada and the U.S. dates back to 1794.... In 1842, the U.S. and Great Britain entered into the Ashburton-Webster Treaty, which contained articles governing the mutual surrender of criminals... This treaty remained in force until the present Canada-U.S. Extradition Treaty of 1976."

...

8.4 Extradition in Canada is governed by the Extradition Act and the terms of the applicable treaty. The Canadian Charter of Rights and Freedoms, which forms part of the constitution of Canada and embodies many of the rights protected by the Covenant, applies. Under Canadian law, extradition is a two-step process. The first involves a hearing at which a judge considers whether a factual and legal basis for extradition exists. The person sought for extradition may submit evidence at the judicial hearing. If the judge is satisfied with the evidence that a legal basis for extradition exists, the fugitive is ordered committed to await surrender to the requesting State. Judicial review of a warrant of committal to await surrender can be sought by means of an application for a writ of habeas corpus in a provincial court. A decision of the judge on the habeas corpus application can be appealed to the provincial court of appeal and then, with leave, to the Supreme Court of Canada. The second step in the extradition process begins following the exhaustion of the appeals in the judicial phase. The Minister of Justice is charged with the responsibility of deciding whether to surrender the person sought for extradition. The fugitive may make written submissions to the Minister, and counsel for the fugitive, with leave, may appear before the Minister to present oral argument. In coming to a decision on surrender, the Minister considers a complete record of the case from the judicial phase, together with any written and oral submissions from the fugitive, and while the Minister's decision is discretionary, the discretion is circumscribed by law. The decision is based upon a consideration of many factors, including Canada's obligations under the applicable treaty of extradition, facts particular to the person and the nature of the crime for which extradition is sought. In addition, the Minister must consider the terms of the Canadian Charter of Rights and Freedoms and the various instruments, including the Covenant, which outline Canada's international human rights obligations. Finally, a fugitive may seek judicial review of the Minister's decision by a provincial court and appeal a warrant of surrender, with leave, up to the Supreme Court of Canada. In interpreting Canada's human rights obligations under the Canadian Charter, the Supreme Court of Canada is guided by international instruments to which Canada is a party, including the Covenant.

8.5 With regard to surrender in capital cases, the Minister of Justice decides whether or not to request assurances to the effect that the death penalty should not be imposed or carried out on the basis of an examination of the particular facts of each case. The Extradition Treaty between Canada and the U.S. was not intended to make the seeking of assurances a routine occurrence; rather, assurances had to be sought only in circumstances where the particular facts of the case warrant a special exercise of discretion.

8.6 With regard to the abolition of the death penalty in Canada, the State party notes that:

"...certain States within the international community, including the U.S., continue to impose the death penalty. The Government of Canada does not use extradition as a vehicle for imposing its concepts of criminal law policy on other States. By seeking assurances on a routine basis, in the absence of exceptional circumstances, Canada would be dictating to the requesting State, in this case the U.S., how it should punish its criminal law offenders. The Government of Canada contends that this would be an unwarranted interference with the internal affairs of another State. The Government of Canada reserves the right... to refuse to extradite without assurances. This right is held in reserve for use only where exceptional circumstances exist. In the view of the Government of Canada, it may be that evidence showing that a fugitive would face certain or foreseeable violations of the Covenant would be one example of exceptional circumstances which would warrant the special measure of seeking assurances under article 6. However, the evidence presented by Ng during the extradition process in Canada (which evidence has been submitted by counsel for Ng in this communication) does not support the allegations that the use of the death penalty in the U.S. generally, or in the State of California in particular, violates the Covenant."

...

9.1 With regard to Mr. Ng's case, the State party recalls that he challenged the warrant of committal to await surrender in accordance with the extradition process outlined above, and that his counsel made written and oral submissions to the Minister to seek assurances that the death penalty would not be imposed. He argued that extradition to face the death penalty would offend his rights under section 7 (comparable to articles 6 and 9 of the Covenant) and section 12 (comparable to article 7 of the Covenant) of the Canadian Charter of Rights and Freedoms. The Supreme Court heard Mr. Ng's case at the same time as the appeal by Mr. Kindler, an American citizen who also faced extradition to the U.S. on a capital charge, and decided that their extradition without assurances would not violate Canada's human rights obligations.

9.2 With regard to the admissibility of the communication, the State party once more reaffirms that the communication should be declared inadmissible ratione materiae because extradition per se is beyond the scope of the Covenant. A review of the travaux preparatoires reveals that the drafters of the Covenant specifically considered and rejected a proposal to deal with extradition in the Covenant. In the light of the negotiating history of the Covenant, the State party submits that:

"...a decision to extend the Covenant to extradition treaties or to individual decisions pursuant thereto would stretch the principles governing the interpretation of human rights instruments in unreasonable and unacceptable ways. It would be unreasonable because the principles of interpretation which recognize that human rights instruments are living documents and that human rights evolve over time cannot be employed in the face of express limits to the application of a given document. The absence of extradition from the articles of the Covenant when read with the intention of the drafters must be taken as an express limitation."

...

10.1 On the merits, the State party stresses that Mr. Ng enjoyed a full hearing on all matters concerning his extradition to face the death penalty.

...

10.3 Finally, the State party observes that it is "in a difficult position attempting to defend the criminal justice system of the U.S. before the Committee. It contends that the Optional Protocol process was never intended to place a State in the position of having to defend the laws or practices of another State before the Committee."

10.4 With respect to the issue of whether the death penalty violates article 7 of the Covenant, the State party submits that:

"...article 7 cannot be read or interpreted without reference to article 6. The Covenant must be read as a whole and its articles as being in harmony... It may be that certain forms of execution are contrary to article 7. Torturing a person to death would seem to fall into this category, as torture is a violation of article 7. Other forms of execution may be in violation of the Covenant because they are cruel, inhuman or degrading. However, as the death penalty is permitted within the narrow parameters set by article 6, it must be that some methods of execution exist which would not violate article 7."

10.5 As to the method of execution, the State party submits that there is no indication that execution by cyanide gas asphyxiation, the chosen method in California, is contrary to the Covenant or to international law. It further submits that no specific circumstances exist in Mr. Ng's case which would lead to a different conclusion concerning the application of this method of execution to him; nor would execution by gas asphyxiation be in violation of the Safeguards guaranteeing protection of the rights of those facing the death penalty, adopted by the Economic and Social Council in its resolution 1984/50 of 25 May 1984.

...

11.2 As regards article 6 of the Extradition Treaty, counsel recalls that when the Treaty was signed in December 1971, the Canadian Criminal Code still provided for capital punishment in cases of murder, so that article 6 could have been invoked by either contracting State. Counsel submits that article 6 does not require assurances to be sought only in particularly "special" death penalty cases. He argues that the provision of the possibility to ask for assurances under article 6 of the Treaty implicitly acknowledges that offences punishable by death are to be dealt with differently, that different values and traditions with regard to the death penalty may be taken into account when deciding upon an extradition request and that an actual demand for assurances will not be perceived by the other party as unwarranted interference with the internal affairs of the requesting State. In particular, article 6 of the Treaty is said to "...allow the requested State...to maintain a consistent position: if the death penalty is rejected within its own borders...it could negate any responsibility for exposing a fugitive through surrender, to the risk of imposition of that penalty or associated practices and procedures in the other State." It is further submitted that "it is very significant that the existence of the discretion embodied in article 6, in relation to the death penalty, enables the contracting parties to honour both their own domestic constitutions and their international obligations without violating their obligations under the bilateral Extradition Treaty."

...

11. 4 As regards the extradition proceedings against Mr. Ng, counsel notes that his Federal Court action against the Minister's decision to extradite the author without seeking assurances never was decided upon by the Federal Court, but was referred to the Supreme Court to be decided together with Mr. Kindler's appeal. In this context, counsel notes that the Supreme Court, when deciding that the author's extradition would not violate the Canadian constitution, failed to discuss criminal procedure in California or evidence adduced in relation to the death row phenomenon in California.

...

11.7 The author refers to the Committee's decision of 28 October 1992 and submits that in the circumstances of his case, the very purpose of his extradition without seeking assurances was to foreseeably expose him to the imposition of the death penalty and consequently to the death row phenomenon. In this connection, counsel submits that the author's extradition was sought upon charges which carry the death penalty, and that the prosecution in California never left any doubt that it would indeed seek the death penalty. He quotes the Assistant District Attorney in San Francisco as saying that: "there is sufficient evidence to convict and send Ng to the gas chamber if he is extradited...."

11.8 In this context, counsel quotes from the judgment of the European Court of Human Rights in the Soering case:

"In the independent exercise of his discretion, the Commonwealth's attorney has himself decided to seek and persist in seeking the death penalty because the evidence, in his determination, supports such action. If the national authority with responsibility for prosecuting the offence takes such a firm stance, it is hardly open to the court to hold that there are no substantial grounds for believing that the applicant faces a real risk of being sentenced to death and hence experiencing the 'death row phenomenon.'"

Counsel submits that, at the time of extradition, it was foreseeable that the author would be sentenced to death in California and therefore be exposed to violations of the Covenant.

...

11.10 As to the method of execution in California, cyanide gas asphyxiation, counsel argues that it constitutes inhuman and degrading punishment within the meaning of article 7 of the Covenant. He notes that asphyxiation may take up to 12 minutes, during which condemned persons remain conscious, experience obvious pain and agony, drool and convulse and often soil themselves (reference is made to the execution of Robert F. Harris at San Quentin Prison in April

1992). Counsel further argues that, given the cruel character of this method of execution, a decision of Canada not to extradite without assurances would not constitute a breach of its Treaty obligations with the U.S. or undue interference with the latter's internal law and practices. Furthermore, counsel notes that cyanide gas execution is the sole method of execution in only three States in the U.S. (Arizona, Maryland and California), and that there is no evidence to suggest that it is an approved means of carrying out judicially mandated executions elsewhere in the international community.

...

Review of admissibility and consideration of merits:

13.1 In his initial submission, author's counsel alleged that Mr. Ng was a victim of violations of articles 6, 7, 9, 10, 14 and 26 of the Covenant.

13.2 When the Committee considered the admissibility of the communication during its forty-sixth session and adopted a decision relating thereto (decision of 28 October 1992), it noted that the communication raised complex issues with regard to the compatibility with the Covenant, ratione materiae, of extradition to face capital punishment, in particular with regard to the scope of articles 6 and 7 of the Covenant to such situations and their application in the author's case. It noted, however, that questions about the issue of whether the author could be deemed a "victim" within the meaning of article 1 of the Optional Protocol remained, but held that only consideration of the merits of all the circumstances under which the extradition procedure and all its effects occurred, would enable the Committee to determine whether Mr. Ng was indeed a victim within the meaning of article 1. The State party has made extensive new submissions on both admissibility and merits and reaffirmed that the communication is inadmissible because "the evidence shows that Ng is not the victim of any violation in Canada of rights set out in the Covenant." Counsel, in turn, has filed detailed objections to the State party's affirmations.

13.3 In reviewing the question of admissibility, the Committee takes note of the contentions of the State party and of counsel's arguments. It notes that counsel, in submissions made after the decision of 28 October 1992, has introduced entirely new issues which were not raised in the original communication, and which relate to Mr. Ng's conditions of detention in Canadian penitentiaries, the stress to which he was exposed as the extradition process proceeded, and alleged deceptive manoeuvres by Canadian prison authorities.

13.4 These fresh allegations, if corroborated, would raise issues under articles 7 and 10 of the Covenant, and would bring the author within the gambit of article 1 of the Optional Protocol. While the wording of the decision of 28 October 1992 would not have precluded counsel from introducing them at this stage of the procedure, the Committee, in the circumstances of the case, finds that it need not address the new claims, as domestic remedies before the Canadian courts were not exhausted in respect of them. It transpires from the material before the Committee that complaints about the conditions of the author's detention in Canada or about alleged irregularities committed by Canadian prison authorities were not raised either during the committal or the surrender phase of the extradition proceedings. Had it been argued that an effective remedy for the determination of these claims is no longer available, the Committee finds that it was incumbent upon counsel to raise them before the competent courts, provincial or federal, at the material time. This part of the author's allegations is therefore declared inadmissible under article 5, paragraph 2 (b), of the Optional Protocol.

13.5 It remains for the Committee to examine the author's claim that he is a "victim" within the meaning of the Optional Protocol because he was extradited to California on capital charges pending trial, without the assurances provided for in article 6 of the Extradition Treaty between Canada and the U.S. In this connection, it is to be recalled that:

(a) California had sought the author's extradition on charges which, if proven, carry the death penalty;

(b) the U.S. requested Mr. Ng's extradition on those capital charges;

(c) the extradition warrant documents the existence of a prima facie case against the author;

(d) U.S. prosecutors involved in the case have stated that they would ask for the death penalty to be imposed; and

(e) the State of California, when intervening before the Supreme Court of Canada, did not disavow the prosecutors' position. The Committee considers that these facts raise questions with regard to the scope of articles 6 and 7, in relation to which, on issues of admissibility alone, the Committee's jurisprudence is not dispositive. As indicated in the case of *Kindler v. Canada*, only an examination on the merits of the claims will enable the Committee to pronounce itself on the scope of these articles and to clarify the applicability of the Covenant and Optional Protocol to cases concerning extradition to face the death penalty.

14.1 Before addressing the merits of the communication, the Committee observes that what is at issue is not whether Mr. Ng's rights have been or are likely to be violated by the U.S., which is not a State party to the Optional Protocol, but whether by extraditing Mr. Ng to the U.S., Canada exposed him to a real risk of a violation of his rights under the Covenant. States parties to the Covenant will also frequently be parties to bilateral treaty obligations, including those under extradition treaties. A State party to the Covenant must ensure that it carries out all its other legal commitments in a manner consistent with the Covenant. The starting-point for consideration of this issue must be the State party's obligation, under article 2, paragraph 1, of the Covenant, namely, to ensure to all individuals within its territory and subject to its jurisdiction the rights recognized in the Covenant. The right to life is the most essential of these rights.

14.2 If a State party extradites a person within its jurisdiction in such circumstances, and if, as a result, there is a real risk that his or her rights under the Covenant will be violated in another jurisdiction, the State party itself may be in violation of the Covenant.

15.1 With regard to a possible violation by Canada of article 6 of the Covenant by its decision to extradite Mr. Ng, two related questions arise:

(a) Did the requirement under article 6, paragraph 1, to protect the right to life prohibit Canada from exposing a person within its jurisdiction to the real risk (i. e., a necessary and foreseeable consequence) of being sentenced to death and losing his life in circumstances incompatible with article 6 of the Covenant as a consequence of extradition to the U.S. ?

(b) Did the fact that Canada had abolished capital punishment except for certain military offences require Canada to refuse extradition or request assurances from the U.S., as it was entitled to do under article 6 of the Extradition Treaty, that the death penalty would not be imposed against Mr. Ng?

15.2 Counsel claims that capital punishment must be viewed as a violation of article 6 of the Covenant "in all but the most horrendous cases of heinous crime; it can no longer be accepted as the standard penalty for murder." Counsel, however, does not substantiate this statement or link it to the specific circumstances of the present case. In reviewing the facts submitted by author's counsel and by the State party, the Committee notes that Mr. Ng was convicted of committing murder under aggravating circumstances; this would appear to bring the case within the scope of article 6, paragraph 2, of the Covenant. In this connection the Committee recalls that it is not a "fourth instance" and that it is not within its competence under the Optional Protocol to review sentences of the courts of States. This limitation of competence applies a fortiori where the proceedings take place in a State that is not party to the Optional Protocol.

15.3 The Committee notes that article 6, paragraph 1, must be read together with article 6, paragraph 2, which does not prohibit the imposition of the death penalty for the most serious crimes. Canada did not itself charge Mr. Ng with capital offences, but extradited him to the U.S., where he faces capital charges and the possible (and foreseeable) imposition of the death penalty. If Mr. Ng had been exposed, through extradition from Canada, to a real risk of a violation of article 6, paragraph 2, in the U.S., this would have entailed a violation by Canada of its obligations under article 6, paragraph 1. Among the requirements of article 6, paragraph 2, is that capital punishment be imposed only for the most serious crimes, under circumstances not contrary to the Covenant and other instruments, and that it be carried out pursuant to a final judgement rendered by a competent court. The Committee notes that Mr. Ng was extradited to stand trial on 19 criminal charges, including 12 counts of murder. If sentenced to death, that sentence, based on the information which the Committee has before it, would be based on a conviction of guilt in respect of very serious crimes. He was over 18 years old when the crimes of which he stands accused were committed. Finally, while the author has claimed before the Supreme Court of Canada and before the Committee that his right to a fair trial would not be guaranteed in the judicial process in California, because of racial bias in the jury selection process and in the imposition of the death penalty, these claims have been advanced in respect of purely hypothetical events. Nothing in the file supports the contention that the author's trial in the Calaveras County Court would not meet the requirements of article 14 of the Covenant.

15.4 Moreover, the Committee observes that Mr. Ng was extradited to the U.S. after extensive proceedings in the Canadian courts, which reviewed all the charges and the evidence available against the author. In the circumstances, the Committee concludes that Canada's obligations under article 6, paragraph 1, did not require it to refuse Mr. Ng's extradition.

...

15.6 While States must be mindful of their obligation to protect the right to life when exercising their discretion in the application of extradition treaties, the Committee does not find that the terms of article 6 of the Covenant necessarily require Canada to refuse to extradite or to seek assurances. The Committee notes that the extradition of Mr. Ng would have violated Canada's obligations under article 6 of the Covenant if the decision to extradite without assurances had been taken summarily or arbitrarily. The evidence before the Committee reveals, however, that the Minister of Justice reached his decision after hearing extensive arguments in favour of seeking assurances. The Committee further takes note of the reasons advanced by the Minister of Justice in his letter dated 26 October 1989 addressed to Mr. Ng's counsel, in particular, the absence of exceptional circumstances, the availability of due process and of appeal against conviction and the importance of not providing a safe haven for those accused of murder.

15.7 In the light of the above, the Committee concludes that Mr. Ng is not a victim of a violation by Canada of article 6 of the Covenant.

16.1 In determining whether, in a particular case, the imposition of capital punishment constitutes a violation of article 7, the Committee will have regard to the relevant personal factors regarding the author, the specific conditions of detention on death row and whether the proposed method of execution is particularly abhorrent. In the instant case, it is contended that execution by gas asphyxiation is contrary to internationally accepted standards of humane treatment, and that it amounts to treatment in violation of article 7 of the Covenant. The Committee begins by noting that whereas article 6, paragraph 2, allows for the imposition of the death penalty under certain limited circumstances, any method of execution provided for by law must be designed in such a way as to avoid conflict with article 7.

16.2 The Committee is aware that, by definition, every execution of a sentence of death may be considered to constitute cruel and inhuman treatment within the meaning of article 7 of the Covenant; on the other hand, article 6, paragraph 2, permits the imposition of capital punishment for the most serious crimes. None the less, the Committee reaffirms, as it did in its general comment (44) on article 7 of the Covenant that, when imposing capital punishment, the execution of the sentence "must be carried out in such a way as to cause the least possible physical and mental suffering."

16.3 In the present case, the author has provided detailed information that execution by gas asphyxiation may cause prolonged suffering and agony and does not result in death as swiftly as possible, as asphyxiation by cyanide gas may take over 10 minutes. The State party had the opportunity to refute these allegations on the facts; it has failed to do so. Rather, the State party has confined itself to arguing that in the absence of a norm of international law which expressly prohibits asphyxiation by cyanide gas, "it would be interfering to an unwarranted degree with the internal laws and practices of the U.S. to refuse to extradite a fugitive to face the possible imposition of the death penalty by cyanide gas asphyxiation."

16.4 In the instant case and on the basis of the information before it, the Committee concludes that execution by gas asphyxiation, should the death penalty be imposed on the author, would not meet the test of "least possible physical and mental suffering," and constitutes cruel and inhuman treatment, in violation of article 7 of the Covenant. Accordingly, Canada, which could reasonably foresee that Mr. Ng, if sentenced to death, would be executed in a way that amounts to a violation of article 7, failed to comply with its obligations under the Covenant, by extraditing Mr. Ng without having sought and received assurances that he would not be executed.

16.5 The Committee need not pronounce itself on the compatibility with article 7 of methods of execution other than that which is at issue in this case.

17. The Human Rights Committee, acting under article 5, paragraph 4, of the International Covenant on Civil and Political Rights, is of the view that the facts as found by the Committee reveal a violation by Canada of article 7 of the Covenant.

18. The Human Rights Committee requests the State party to make such representations as might still be possible to avoid the imposition of the death penalty and appeals to the State party to ensure that a similar situation does not arise in the future.

[End Text]

Source: U.N. OHCHR, Selected Decisions of the Human Rights Committee, p. 94., http://www.ohchr.org/_layouts/15/Wopi Frame.aspx?sourcedoc=/Documents/Publications/SDecisionsVol5en.pdf&action=default&DefaultItemOpen=1

☙❧☙❧☙❧☙❧

13. LETTER FROM U.S. DEPARTMENT OF STATE, ACTING LEGAL ADVISOR TO GOVERNORS OF THE 50 STATES, CONCERNING U.S. GOVERNMENT TREATY BODY REPORTS, 2015

The purpose of this letter from the State Department is to make the governors of the 50 states aware of the U.N. treaty body reports submitted by the U.S., and the treaty bodies' concluding observations and recommendations. Some human rights issues arising in the U.S. periodic report to the treaty bodies occur in states, and violations are sometimes committed by agents of the state government and not the federal government. Under the federal clause of the human rights treaties, such as article 50 of the ICCPR, the treaty norms "shall extend to all parts of federal states without any limitations or exceptions." The State Department expects the states to become aware of the treaty norms and work internally and with the federal government to bring state law and practice into conformity with the particular treaties, something that does not always happen.

{Excerpt}

[Text]

United States Department of State
Washington, D. C. 20520
April 25, 2015

Dear Governor

I am writing to you as part of the U.S. Department of State's ongoing efforts to keep officials at all levels of government informed about U.S. human rights obligations and commitments. As you know, the United States has a long and proud tradition of advancing the protection of human rights around the globe. Our country also upholds these values by protecting human rights here at home, which we achieve not only through actions taken at the federal level, but also through the dedicated efforts of state, local, insular, and tribal governments in areas such as protecting civil and political rights, combating racial discrimination, and protecting children from harms like trafficking and prostitution. We thus believe it is important to distribute broadly information regarding the U.S. government's human rights obligations and commitments and our efforts to present and defend our country's human rights record to the international community.

Treaty Presentations
The United States is a party to five core human rights treaties: the International Covenant on Civil and Political Rights (ICCPR); the International Convention on the Elimination of All Forms of Racial Discrimination (CERD); the Convention Against Torture and Other Cruel, Inhuman or Degrading Treatment or Punishment (CAT); and two optional protocols to the Convention on the Rights of the Child (CRC). As part of our obligations under these treaties, the U.S. government must submit reports periodically to a committee of independent experts created by the terms of each of these treaties and then appear before that committee to present the report and answer questions. Over the last 12 months, the U.S. government made three such presentations in Geneva, Switzerland with respect to the following treaties: the ICCPR on March 13 and 14, 2014; the CERD on August 13 and 14, 2014; and the CAT on November 12 and 13, 2014.

These presentations were valuable opportunities to demonstrate to the world our country's commitment to protecting human rights domestically through our comprehensive system of laws, policies, and programs at all levels of government — federal, state, local, insular, and tribal. Reflecting our federal system of government, each of the U.S. delegations to these presentations featured not only senior officials from a range of federal agencies, but also elected or other high-level officials from state and local governments.

Shortly after each presentation, the respective committee issued a set of Concluding Observations & Recommendations (CORs), which presented the committee's views and recommendations on how the United States can further our implementation of the relevant treaty. Although these CORs are not legally binding, the United States carefully considers the views expressed by each committee, regardless of whether we agree with the factual or legal assertions on which they are based or whether they bear directly on obligations arising under the relevant treaty. These CORs provide constructive input from respected human rights actors in the international community and, as such, they merit consideration by officials at every level of government within the United States when taking actions or formulating and implementing policies that impact human rights.

In addition, CORs can serve as helpful reference points for consultations with civil society organizations and advocates on issues related to human rights in the United States. The federal government conducts civil society consultations in connection with the human rights treaty reporting process, which are important opportunities to receive input and feedback on ways that we can improve our implementation of human rights obligations and commitments. Similar human rights consultations could be useful at other levels of government.

The three sets of CORs from our 2014 presentations are available on the State Department website at:
- ICCPR: www.state.gov/documents/organization/235641.pdf
- CERD: www.state.gov/documents/organization/235644.pdf
- CAT: www.state.gov/documents/organization/234772.pdf

These documents can also be found, along with a wealth of other materials regarding U.S. human rights treaties and U.S. reports and presentations related to our human rights treaty obligations, at: www.state.gov/j/drl/reports/treaties/index. htm.

Upcoming Universal Periodic Review Presentation
The U.S. government will make its next human rights related presentation as part of the U.N. Human Rights Council's Universal Periodic Review (UPR) mechanism, on May I l, 2015, after filing our second UPR report on February 2, 2015. Unlike the treaty reporting process, the UPR is a process applicable to every U.N. Member State and UPR reports are filed approximately every five years. At the May presentation, other U.N. member states will have the opportunity to pose questions and make recommendations to the U.S. delegation related to implementation of our human rights obligations and commitments across a broad range of issues. The UPR provides the United States with the opportunity to reflect on the progress we have made in the promotion of human rights domestically, and to continue to consider ways to improve protection of human rights in our country. The content of our presentation, and the recommendations that we receive and ultimately support, will be available online at www.humanrights. gov.

2. Upcoming Reports on Children and Human Rights

We will also soon begin drafting our next human rights treaty reports, which will provide information on U.S. implementation of the two Optional Protocols to the Convention on the Rights of the Child (CRC) that were ratified by the United States in 2003: (l) the Optional Protocol to the CRC on the Involvement of Children in Armed Conflict and (2) the Optional Protocol to the CRC on the Sale of Children, Child Prostitution and Child Pornography. If you would like more information about these treaties, or if you have information relevant to your own jurisdiction's efforts to combat child trafficking, child prostitution and/or child pornography, we invite you to contact U.S. at the email address below. We would prefer to receive any such input — which could include descriptions of programs, significant prosecutions, or relevant data — by June l, 2015.

Many of the topics covered in this letter were addressed in my recent speech to the National Association of Attorneys General, which I invite you to read: www.state.gov/s/l/releases/remarks/239960. htm.

As with previous letters, we encourage you to share this letter broadly with other appropriate officials within your jurisdiction, such as the office of the attorney general, law enforcement agencies, human rights agencies or commissions, and county and local governments.

If you have any questions or comments, please feel free to contact U.S. through the State Department's Office of Intergovernmental Affairs at IGA humanrights@state. gov.

Best regards,

Mary E. McLeod
Acting Legal Adviser
U.S. Department of State

Attachment: U.S. Human Rights Presentations in 2014-15

cc: National Governors Association
National Association of Attorneys General
National Conference of State Legislatures
National Association of Counties
U.S. Conference of Mayors
International Association of Official Human Rights Agencies

Adopted by the Committee at its 110th session (10-28 March 2014).

Organization of American States: The U.S. & the Inter-American Human Rights System

Chapter 7

This **Chapter is About** an international inter-governmental organization, the Organization of American States (OAS), of which the U.S. is a founding member and still a funder. It is about a "regional" political system, one of whose components is a regional human rights system commonly known as the Inter-American Human Rights System, consisting of a human rights commission and a court.

This is Important Because the OAS membership comprises almost all states in North, Central, and South America, the entire western hemisphere; and the OAS has set up its own human rights system. As a member state of the OAS the U.S. participates in this human rights system by getting human rights complaints filed and decided against it, and having reports written by the Inter-American Commission about what the U.S. is doing to protect the human rights norms in that system, based on a human rights declaration, the American Declaration on Human Rights. The U.S. can influence the human rights performance of all member states through this international intergovernmental forum, particularly its human rights component. This can stabilize the region and protect democracy against harmful ideologies. In theory, it is the protector of the commonly shared values of this geographical area of the world. In practice, the U.S. has shown a stark inconsistency between what it says and how it acts in regards to the ADHR norms and the Inter-American Commission on Human Rights.

Quotes & Key Text Excerpts

Whereas,

The American peoples have acknowledged the dignity of the individual, and their national constitutions recognize that juridical and political institutions, which regulate life in human society, have as their principal aim the protection of the essential rights of man and the creation of circumstances that will permit him to achieve spiritual and material progress and attain happiness;

The American States have on repeated occasions recognized that the essential rights of man are not derived from the fact that he is a national of a certain state, but are based upon attributes of his human personality;

The international protection of the rights of man should be the principal guide of an evolving American law;

The affirmation of essential human rights by the American States together with the guarantees given by the internal regimes of the states establish the initial system of protection considered by the American States as being suited to the present social and juridical conditions, not without a recognition on their part that they should increasingly strengthen that system in the international field as conditions become more favorable, The Ninth International Conference of American States,

AGREES to adopt the following:

American Declaration of the Rights and Duties of Man

—*Organisation of American States, adopting resolution of the American Declaration on the Rights and Duties of Man, Bogata, Columbia 1948*

Source: http://www.oas.org/en/iachr/mandate/basics/declaration.asp

ॐॐॐॐॐ

The term "human rights" is broad and encompasses numerous, more specific issues under its general umbrella, such as the rights to free speech, to political participation, to a free and transparent system of justice, and others. Respect for human rights goes to the very heart of democracy. Over the course of five decades, the Inter-American Commission on Human Rights (IACHR) has advocated for justice and defended freedom throughout the Americas. The IACHR works with States to help strengthen the laws and institutions that provide human rights protections. The member countries of the OAS have affirmed their unequivocal commitment to democracy and human rights, and the Commission strives to ensure that this commitment produces tangible results.

Source: O.A.S. Human Rights website, http://www.oas.org/en/topics/human_rights.asp

ॐॐॐॐॐ

The United States is also committed to the promotion and protection of human rights through regional organizations. Through our membership in the Organization for Security and Cooperation in Europe and the Organization of American States, the United States commits to continuing efforts to uphold human rights and fundamental freedoms, and to strengthening and developing institutions and mechanisms for their protection. In particular recognition of its human rights commitments within the Inter-American system, the United States strongly supports the work of the Inter-American Commission on Human Rights, its largest donor with $2.3 million contributed in 2015, and engages actively in proceedings on individual petitions filed against the United States, in thematic hearings, and with respect to the Commission's thematic and country reports.

—*U.S. "pledges" to the U.N. Human Rights Council*

Source: http://www.state.gov/p/io/humanrights

❧❧❧❧❧❧❧❧

The United States and the Republic of Argentina renew their support for the Organization of American States (OAS) and the Inter-American Human Rights System. They note that their active engagement at the OAS is essential to advancing the shared values and goals of all member states.

Both countries affirm that OAS Charter principles — democracy, human rights, security, rule of law and development for all the peoples of the Americas — remain as enduring as its values remain sound.

The United States and Argentina are committed to working together towards strengthening the OAS, welcoming calls to focus the Organization on its core mandate of promoting and protecting human rights and democracy in all 35 OAS member states.

They underscore that the OAS has the responsibility to uphold the principles of the OAS Charter, the Inter-American Democratic Charter, and the American Declaration of the Rights and Duties of Man, and that all member states have a responsibility to fulfill their commitments and obligations under these instruments.

They also express an enduring commitment to supporting the independence, integrity, and effectiveness of the Inter-American Human Rights System, including the Commission and the Court, so as to promote and defend the human rights and dignity of all persons in the Americas.

The United States and Argentina have decided to work together towards achieving consensus among member states to make the OAS more relevant, efficient, effective, financially sound, and focused on delivering results that help to ensure a region that is more democratic, safe, and prosperous for all its people.

—*Joint Statement by Secretary of State John F. Kerry of the United States and Foreign Minister Susana Malcorra of the Republic of Argentina in Support of the Organization of American States and the Inter-American Human Rights System, March 23, 2016*

Source: http://www.state.gov/r/pa/prs/ps/2016/03/255059.htm

❧❧❧❧❧❧❧❧

Today, I'm personally pleased to return to the OAS, and on behalf of President Obama, underscore to all of you how deeply the United States values the partnerships that we have forged throughout this hemisphere. It's in large measure because of the relationships that we share in recent years that the Americas have stood in sharp contrast to more troubled and conflict-ridden regions of the world. Largely, the Americas have become more peaceful, more prosperous, and I am particularly encouraged by the theme of this year's conference — sustainable development — and the fact that this General Assembly will approve the Inter-American Program for Sustainable Development, which will jumpstart our region's implementation of the U.N. 2030 Agenda.

...

Protecting and advancing human rights remains a top priority as well. Many of our own nations, including my own, are redoubling our commitment to the Inter-American Commission on Human Rights. In 2013, this assembly agreed to seek full financing for the commission's operations and rapporteurs, and we all have a responsibility to both make good on that commitment and do all that we can to facilitate its critical work. For our part, the United States welcomed the productive site visits by the commission to Florida, Louisiana, and Missouri as part of its review on race and the criminal justice system.

Our hemisphere is also seeing encouraging trends with respect to transparency and accountability. More and more citizens are saying spontaneously, *"No mas"* to corruption within their governments, and are working to increase openness, expose abuses, and hold leaders to a higher standard. And we have seen the impact in many different places in the world in the last few years of corruption that steals the future from people in their own country.

—Secretary of State John Kerry, 46th Organization of American States General Assembly in Panama

Source: http://www.state.gov/secretary/remarks/2016/06/258461.htm

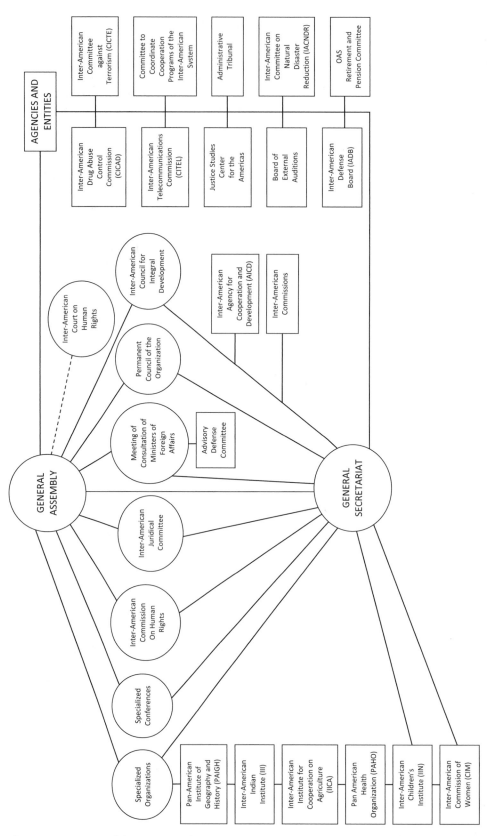

An organizational map (organogram) of the international inter-governmental organization known as the Organisation of American States (OAS), of which the U.S. is a member. Note the placement of the Inter-American Commission on Human Rights and the Inter-American Court of Human Rights.

What You Should Know

ORGANIZATION OF AMERICAN STATES
The Inter-American Human Rights System

Because the United Nations was very much limited in its human rights activity in the Cold War, there arose what are known as "regional" human rights systems. Regional systems are open only to member states within a particular geographical area. In theory, these regional systems can create and operate a human rights system more finely attuned to the differing issues and problems (particularities) of the states in a particular region. The Council of Europe was formed in 1950 of western European states, which adopted the European Convention for the Protection of Human Rights and Fundamental Freedoms and set up a human rights system that is the most advanced in the world today. The Organization of African Unity set up a regional system in the early 1980s.

The United States became a founding member of the Organization of American States (OAS), whose 1948 Charter set up an international intergovernmental organization for all countries in the Americas: North, South, and Central. The membership's initial states are: Argentina; Bolivia; Brazil; Chile; Colombia; Costa Rica; Cuba; Dominican Republic; Ecuador; El Salvador; Guatemala; Haiti; Honduras; Mexico; Nicaragua; Panama; Paraguay; Peru; United States of America; Uruguay; and Venezuela (Bolivarian Republic of). It subsequently grew to include the following 14 member states: Barbados, Trinidad and Tobago (1967); Jamaica (1969); Grenada (1975); Suriname (1977); Dominica (Commonwealth of), Saint Lucia (1979); Antigua and Barbuda, Saint Vincent and the Grenadines (1981); The Bahamas (Commonwealth of) (1982); St. Kitts and Nevis (1984); Canada (1990); Belize and Guyana (1991).

On May 2nd 1948, the OAS proclaimed the American Declaration of the Rights and Duties of Man (ADHR), the first regional human rights instrument applicable to the United States. The OAS established the Inter-American Commission on Human Rights in 1959. This body has its headquarters in Washington D.C. The OAS, among other goals, seeks to promote respect for human rights in the Americas and uses the ADHR as its basis of what those rights are. In 1965 the Commission was empowered to receive individual complaints ("petitions") against member states for violations. In 1970 the OAS Charter was amended so as to bootstrap the ADHR into being the legal basis in the Commissions for adjudicating petitions claiming violations. The Inter-American Commission was to become a formal charter organ of the OAS thereafter. The Commission still uses the ADHR as the legal basis for deciding cases against those states which are not party to the American Convention on Human Rights, as explained below.

In 1969, the OAS had adopted the American Convention on Human Rights, which entered into force in 1978. The United States signed the treaty in 1977, but it has never been ratified by the U.S. Senate. There have been two protocols to the ACHR, the first on adding economic and social rights, and the second on abolishing the death penalty. The ACHR sets forth a set of regional human rights substantive norms binding upon states that ratify it (twenty-three as of 2017).

Under the ACHR, individuals and certain groups can file petitions alleging violations against a state party that is bound by the treaty automatically upon the state's ratification of the ACHR. The ACHR also provides for petitions by one state party against another state ("inter-state petitions") if a state so expressly declared, upon ratification. Petitions by and against a state party are handled first by the Inter-American commission, which is a quasi-judicial body. A state party and the state Commission can refer the case to the Inter-American Court of Human Rights. The court has both contentious jurisdiction and advisory jurisdiction. Contentious jurisdiction involves cases of an individual versus a state or a state versus a state, alleging actual violation of one or more rights in the Convention. With advisory jurisdiction, the court interprets the ACHR or other treaty concerning the protection of human rights in the American states or, in response to a member states request, advises that state about the compatibility of its domestic laws with such treaties.

Cases filed either before the Inter-American Commission or the Inter-American Court of Human Rights must first be deemed admissible, that is, they must satisfy all the statutory ('legal') criteria for the Court or Commission to exercise its jurisdiction. These criteria include that the petitioner has exhausted all reasonably accessible and effective domestic remedies prior to filing. In contentious cases, the Commission or Court can request the state to take "provisional" or "interim" measures, such as stopping an execution or a deportation until the case is resolved. This happened in the recent 2015 *Cooper v. USA* case in order to spare the petitioner until the case could be decided by the Commission.

If the Court finds a violation of the Convention, it can enter judgment for the complainants that they be assured of the enjoyment of their human rights by the subject state, and it may award fair compensation to the injured party as reparations These can include so called "project of life" or "life project" damages for the loss of a victim's hopes and aspirations and life plans and potential.

The Obama Administration seemed to have taken a more serious and respectful posture towards the Inter-American system. However, in August 2010, the Inter-American Commission issued a press statement wherein it stated: "The Inter-American Commission on Human Rights (IACHR) deplores the forced transfer of Abdul Aziz Naji to Algeria from the United States Naval Base in Guantánamo, in breach of Precautionary Measures [259/02, granted on March 12, 2002]. The IACHR criticised the Obama Administration for sending this Guantánamo detainee back to where it determined he would likely suffer torture or other mistreatment. Naji had a case pending before the Commission against the U.S.

In cases filed by Guantánamo detainees against the U.S., the government has basically told the Inter-American Commission that it has no business looking into such issues or processing petitions.

The U.S. has never had any cases filed against it in the Inter-American Court because the U.S. has only signed but not ratified the Convention. A few cases have been filed against the U.S. in the Commission, under the ADHR. These have involved issues such as abortion, capital punishment, damage from the Granada and Panama invasions, interdictions (stop, arrest, return) of Haitian refugees on the high seas, and Guantánamo prisoners, and even the rights of Native Americans. These cases have been largely unsuccessful. Even in successful cases where the U.S. is found to have violated the ADHR, there is little evidence that its decisions were respected and implemented by the U.S. (see Primary Source Document 12.)

Most Americans know little about this human rights forum. As the existence of this human rights forum becomes better known, it may be increasingly resorted to by unsuccessful litigants in U.S. courts, who believe their grievances violate the ADHR's human rights norms. In U.S. case law, both the ACHR and the ADHR have been referred to, though not as a rule of decision. They are usually referred to as evidence of customary international law.

Regarding the U.S. and the "American Convention," since the U.S. has signed this Convention, it has an obligation under article 18 of the Vienna Conventions on the Law of Treaties to "refrain from acts which would defeat the object and purpose of the treaty." Thus, it cannot be said that the Inter-American Convention on Human Rights has no legal bearing on the U.S. government.

The U.S. continues to make positive statements about the importance, and even effectiveness, of the Inter-American system. The U.S. has the attitude, however, that action toward it is not legally binding and, therefore, it does not need to respond, or change its policy, as in, for example, treatment of prisoners in Guantánamo, immigration detention, or the death penalty.

The fact that the U.S. has not ratified the IACHR implies that it fears having to live by and conform to its norms, which are the most carefully and comprehensively drafted human rights norms of any regional human rights system. The U.S. failure to fully participate in this system, especially by not ratifying the binding legal instrument, makes the system less effective and leads to the contention of U.S. exceptionalism.

Should the U.S. ratify the American Convention, with appropriate reservations, declarations, and understandings, and get fully involved in the legal implementation of the IACHR, it will then be the role model the other state parties expect the U.S. to be. This institution and its human rights activity are all but invisible to the American public, leading to a lack of transparency and accountability, an attitude of exceptionalism, and minimal change in the U.S. human rights condition.

Primary Source Documents

I. CHARTER OF THE ORGANIZATION OF AMERICAN STATES

This is the international legal instrument which established the Organization of American States (OAS), a regional intergovernmental organization covering all states of North, Central and South America. The U.S. was a founding member and is still an active member. Adopted in 1948, it makes reference to fundamental rights and freedom applicable to the western hemisphere regional human rights system. It established the Inter-American Commission on Human Rights as an organ of the OAS. It was adopted the same year that the American Declaration on the Rights and Duties of Man were adopted.

{Excerpt}

Signed in Bogotá in 1948 and amended by the Protocol of Buenos Aires in 1967, by the Protocol of Cartagena de Indias in 1985, by the Protocol of Washington in 1992, and by the Protocol of Managua in 1993.

IN THE NAME OF THEIR PEOPLES, THE STATES REPRESENTED AT THE NINTH INTERNATIONAL CONFERENCE OF AMERICAN STATES,

Convinced that the historic mission of America is to offer to man a land of liberty and a favorable environment for the development of his personality and the realization of his just aspirations;

Conscious that that mission has already inspired numerous agreements, whose essential value lies in the desire of the American peoples to live together in peace and, through their mutual understanding and respect for the sovereignty of each one, to provide for the betterment of all, in independence, in equality and under law;

Convinced that representative democracy is an indispensable condition for the stability, peace and development of the region;

Confident that the true significance of American solidarity and good neighborliness can only mean the consolidation on this continent, within the framework of democratic institutions, of a system of individual liberty and social justice based on respect for the essential rights of man;

Persuaded that their welfare and their contribution to the progress and the civilization of the world will increasingly require intensive continental cooperation;

Resolved to persevere in the noble undertaking that humanity has conferred upon the United Nations, whose principles and purposes they solemnly reaffirm;

Convinced that juridical organization is a necessary condition for security and peace founded on moral order and on justice; and

In accordance with Resolution IX of the Inter-American Conference on Problems of War and Peace, held in Mexico City,

HAVE AGREED

upon the following CHARTER OF THE ORGANIZATION OF AMERICAN STATES

Part One
Chapter I
NATURE AND PURPOSES

Article 1

The American States establish by this Charter the international organization that they have developed to achieve an order of peace and justice, to promote their solidarity, to strengthen their collaboration, and to defend their sovereignty, their territorial integrity, and their independence. Within the United Nations, the Organization of American States is a regional agency.

The Organization of American States has no powers other than those expressly conferred upon it by this Charter, none of whose provisions authorizes it to intervene in matters that are within the internal jurisdiction of the Member States.

Article 2

The Organization of American States, in order to put into practice the principles on which it is founded and to fulfill its regional obligations under the Charter of the United Nations, proclaims the following essential purposes:

a) To strengthen the peace and security of the continent;

b) To promote and consolidate representative democracy, with due respect for the principle of nonintervention;

c) To prevent possible causes of difficulties and to ensure the pacific settlement of disputes that may arise among the Member States;

...

Chapter II
PRINCIPLES

Article 3

The American States reaffirm the following principles:

a) International law is the standard of conduct of States in their reciprocal relations;

b) International order consists essentially of respect for the personality, sovereignty, and independence of States, and the faithful fulfillment of obligations derived from treaties and other sources of international law;

c) Good faith shall govern the relations between States;

d) The solidarity of the American States and the high aims which are sought through it require the political organization of those States on the basis of the effective exercise of representative democracy;

e) Every State has the right to choose, without external interference, its political, economic, and social system and to organize itself in the way best suited to it, and has the duty to abstain from intervening in the affairs of another State. Subject to the foregoing, the American States shall cooperate fully among themselves, independently of the nature of their political, economic, and social systems;

f) The elimination of extreme poverty is an essential part of the promotion and consolidation of representative democracy and is the common and shared responsibility of the American States;

g) The American States condemn war of aggression: victory does not give rights;

h) An act of aggression against one American State is an act of aggression against all the other American States;

i) Controversies of an international character arising between two or more American States shall be settled by peaceful procedures;

j) Social justice and social security are bases of lasting peace;

k) Economic cooperation is essential to the common welfare and prosperity of the peoples of the continent;

l) The American States proclaim the fundamental rights of the individual without distinction as to race, nationality, creed, or sex;

m) The spiritual unity of the continent is based on respect for the cultural values of the American countries and requires their close cooperation for the high purposes of civilization;

n) The education of peoples should be directed toward justice, freedom, and peace.

Chapter III

...

Article 8

Membership in the Organization shall be confined to independent States of the Hemisphere that were Members of the United Nations as of December 10, 1985, and the non-autonomous territories mentioned in document OEA/Ser. P, AG/doc.1939/85, of November 5, 1985, when they become independent.

Article 9

A Member of the Organization whose democratically constituted government has been overthrown by force may be suspended from the exercise of the right to participate in the sessions of the General Assembly, the Meeting of Consultation, the Councils of the Organization and the Specialized Conferences as well as in the commissions, working groups and any other bodies established.

...

Chapter IV
FUNDAMENTAL RIGHTS AND DUTIES OF STATES

Article 17

Each State has the right to develop its cultural, political, and economic life freely and naturally. In this free development, the State shall respect the rights of the individual and the principles of universal morality.

Article 18

Respect for and the faithful observance of treaties constitute standards for the development of peaceful relations among States. International treaties and agreements should be public.

...

Article 45

The Member States, convinced that man can only achieve the full realization of his aspirations within a just social order, along with economic development and true peace, agree to dedicate every effort to the application of the following principles and mechanisms:

a) All human beings, without distinction as to race, sex, nationality, creed, or social condition, have a right to material well-being and to their spiritual development, under circumstances of liberty, dignity, equality of opportunity, and economic security;

b) Work is a right and a social duty, it gives dignity to the one who performs it, and it should be performed under conditions, including a system of fair wages, that ensure life, health, and a decent standard of living for the worker and his family, both during his working years and in his old age, or when any circumstance deprives him of the possibility of working;

c) Employers and workers, both rural and urban, have the right to associate themselves freely for the defense and promotion of their interests, including the right to collective bargaining and the workers' right to strike, and recognition of the juridical personality of associations and the protection of their freedom and independence, all in accordance with applicable laws;

d) Fair and efficient systems and procedures for consultation and collaboration among the sectors of production, with due regard for safeguarding the interests of the entire society;

e) The operation of systems of public administration, banking and credit, enterprise, and distribution and sales, in such a way, in harmony with the private sector, as to meet the requirements and interests of the community;

f) The incorporation and increasing participation of the marginal sectors of the population, in both rural and urban areas, in the economic, social, civic, cultural, and political life of the nation, in order to achieve the full integration of the national community, acceleration of the process of social mobility, and the consolidation of the democratic system. The encouragement of all efforts of popular promotion and cooperation that have as their purpose the development and progress of the community;

g) Recognition of the importance of the contribution of organizations such as labor unions, cooperatives, and cultural, professional, business, neighborhood, and community associations to the life of the society and to the development process;

h) Development of an efficient social security policy; and

i) Adequate provision for all persons to have due legal aid in order to secure their rights. Article 46

The Member States recognize that, in order to facilitate the process of Latin American regional integration, it is necessary to harmonize the social legislation of the developing countries, especially in the labor and social security fields, so that the rights of the workers shall be equally protected, and they agree to make the greatest efforts possible to achieve this goal.

...

Part Two
Chapter VIII
THE ORGANS

Article 53

The Organization of American States accomplishes its purposes by means of:

a) The General Assembly;

b) The Meeting of Consultation of Ministers of Foreign Affairs;

c) The Councils;

d) The Inter-American Juridical Committee;

e) The Inter-American Commission on Human Rights;

f) The General Secretariat;

...

Chapter XV
THE INTER-AMERICAN COMMISSION ON HUMAN RIGHTS

Article 106

There shall be an Inter-American Commission on Human Rights, whose principal function shall be to promote the observance and protection of human rights and to serve as a consultative organ of the Organization in these matters. An inter-American convention on human rights shall determine the structure, competence, and procedure of this Commission, as well as those of other organs responsible for these matters.

Article 145

Until the Inter-American Convention on Human Rights, referred to in Chapter XV, enters into force, the present Inter-American Commission on Human Rights shall keep vigilance over the observance of human rights.

Source: OAS, Charter of the Organization of American States, http://www.oas.org/en/sla/dil/inter_american_treaties_A-41_charter_OAS.asp

2. AMERICAN DECLARATION OF THE RIGHTS AND DUTIES OF MAN

This international instrument of the OAS first articulated human rights principles applicable to the states of the OAS. It is not a treaty and originally was not intended to create legal obligations. By a protocol to the Charter, the American Declaration was elevated to be the basis for human rights issues of the Inter-American Commission and is considered by the Commission as legally binding on all OAS member states, particularly those states which have not ratified the American Convention on Human Rights. It serves as the legal basis for cases filed against the U.S. in the Commission. The U.S. disputes this binding status. This is the oldest general human rights instrument in history, preceding the UDHR by some months in 1948.

[Text]

Preamble

All men are born free and equal, in dignity and in rights, and, being endowed by nature with reason and conscience, they should conduct themselves as brothers one to another.

The fulfillment of duty by each individual is a prerequisite to the rights of all. Rights and duties are interrelated in every social and political activity of man. While rights exalt individual liberty, duties express the dignity of that liberty.

Duties of a juridical nature presuppose others of a moral nature which support them in principle and constitute their basis.

Inasmuch as spiritual development is the supreme end of human existence and the highest expression thereof, it is the duty of man to serve that end with all his strength and resources.

Since culture is the highest social and historical expression of that spiritual development, it is the duty of man to preserve, practice and foster culture by every means within his power.

And, since moral conduct constitutes the noblest flowering of culture, it is the duty of every man always to hold it in high respect.

Chapter One—Rights

Article 1. Right to life, liberty and personal security
Every human being has the right to life, liberty and the security of his person.

Article 2. Right to equality before law
All persons are equal before the law and have the rights and duties established in this declaration, without distinction as to race, sex, language, creed or any other factor.

Article 3. Right to religious freedom and worship
Every person has the right freely to profess a religious faith, and to manifest and practice it both in public and in private.

Article 4. Right to freedom of investigation, opinion, expression and dissemination
Every person has the right to freedom of investigation, of opinion, and of the expression and dissemination of ideas, by any medium whatsoever.

Article 5. Right to protection of honor, personal reputation, and private and family life
Every person has the right to the protection of the law against abusive attacks upon his honor, his reputation, and his private and family life.

Article 6. Right to a family and to protection thereof
Every person has the right to establish a family, the basic element of society, and to receive protection therefore.

Article 7. Right to protection for mothers and children
All women, during pregnancy and the nursing period, and all children have the right to special protection, care and aid.

Article 8. Right to residence and movement
Every person has the right to fix his residence within the territory of the state of which he is a national, to move about freely within such territory, and not to leave it except by his own will.

Article 9. Right to inviolability of the home
Every person has the right to the inviolability of his home.

Article 10. Right to the inviolability and transmission of correspondence
Every person has the right to the inviolability and transmission of his correspondence.

Article 11. Right to the preservation of health and to well-being
Every person has the right to the preservation of his health through sanitary and social measures relating to food, clothing, housing and medical care, to the extent permitted by public and community resources.

Article 12. Right to education
Every person has the right to an education, which should be based on the principles of liberty, morality and human solidarity.

Likewise every person has the right to an education that will prepare him to attain a decent life, to raise his standard of living, and to be a useful member of society. The right to an education includes the right to equality of opportunity in every case, in accordance with natural talents, merit and the desire to utilize the resources that the state or the community is in a position to provide.

Every person has the right to receive, free, at least a primary education.

Article 13. Right to the benefits of culture

Every person has the right to take part in the cultural life of the community, to enjoy the arts and to participate in the benefits that result from intellectual progress, especially scientific discoveries.

He likewise has the right to the protection of his moral and material interests as regards his inventions or any literary, scientific or artistic works of which he is the author.

Article 14. Right to work and to fair remuneration

Every person has the right to work, under proper conditions, and to follow his vocation freely, in so far as existing conditions of employment permit.

Every person who works has the right to receive such remuneration as will, in proportion to his capacity and skill, assure him a standard of living suitable for himself and for his family.

Article 15. Right to leisure time and to the use thereof

Every person has the right to leisure time, to wholesome recreation, and to the opportunity for advantageous use of his free time to his spiritual, cultural and physical benefit.

Article 16. Right to social security

Every person has the right to social security which will protect him from the consequences of unemployment, old age, and any disabilities arising from causes beyond his control that make it physically or mentally impossible for him to earn a living.

Article 17. Right to recognition of juridical personality and civil rights

Every person has the right to be recognized everywhere as a person having rights and obligations, and to enjoy the basic civil rights.

Article 18. Right to a fair trial

Every person may resort to the courts to ensure respect for his legal rights. There should likewise be available to him a simple, brief procedure whereby the courts will protect him from acts of authority that, to his prejudice, violate any fundamental constitutional rights.

Article 19. Right to nationality

Every person has the right to the nationality to which he is entitled by law and to change it, if he so wishes, for the nationality of any other country that is willing to grant it to him.

Article 20. Right to vote and to participate in government

Every person having legal capacity is entitled to participate in the government of his country, directly or through his representatives, and to take part in popular elections, which shall be by secret ballot, and shall be honest, periodic and free.

Article 21. Right of assembly

Every person has the right to assemble peaceably with others in a formal public meeting or an informal gathering, in connection with matters of common interest of any nature.

Article 22. Right of association

Every person has the right to associate with others to promote, exercise and protect his legitimate interests of a political, economic, religious, social, cultural, professional, labor union or other nature.

Article 23. Right to property

Every person has a right to own such private property as meets the essential needs of decent living and helps to maintain the dignity of the individual and of the home.

Article 24. Right of petition

Every person has the right to submit respectful petitions to any competent authority, for reasons of either general or private interest, and the right to obtain a prompt decision thereon.

Article 25. Right of protection from arbitrary arrest

No person may be deprived of his liberty except in the cases and according to the procedures established by pre-existing law.

No person may be deprived of liberty for nonfulfillment of obligations of a purely civil character.

Every individual who has been deprived of his liberty has the right to have the legality of his detention ascertained without delay by a court, and the right to be tried without undue delay or, otherwise, to be released. He also has the right to humane treatment during the time he is in custody.

Article 26. Right to due process of law

Every accused person is presumed to be innocent until proved guilty.

Every person accused of an offense has the right to be given an impartial and public hearing, and to be tried by courts previously established in accordance with pre-existing laws, and not to receive cruel, infamous or unusual punishment.

Article 27. Right of asylum

Every person has the right, in case of pursuit not resulting from ordinary crimes, to seek and receive asylum in foreign territory, in accordance with the laws of each country and with international agreements.

Article 28. Scope of the rights of man

The rights of man are limited by the rights of others, by the security of all, and by the just demands of the general welfare and the advancement of democracy.

Chapter Two—Duties

Article 29. Duties to society

It is the duty of the individual so to conduct himself in relation to others that each and every one may fully form and develop his personality.

Article 30. Duties toward children and parents

It is the duty of every person to aid, support, educate and protect his minor children, and it is the duty of children to honor their parents always and to aid, support and protect them when they need it.

Article 31. Duty to receive instruction

It is the duty of every person to acquire at least an elementary education.

Article 32. Duty to vote

It is the duty of every person to vote in the popular elections of the country of which he is a national, when he is legally capable of doing so.

Article 33. Duty to obey the law

It is the duty of every person to obey the law and other legitimate commands of the authorities of his country and those of the country in which he may be.

Article 34. Duty to serve the community and the nation

It is the duty of every able-bodied person to render whatever civil and military service his country may require for its defense and preservation, and, in case of public disaster, to render such services as may be in his power.

It is likewise his duty to hold any public office to which he may be elected by popular vote in the state of which he is a national.

Article 35. Duties with respect to social security and welfare

It is the duty of every person to cooperate with the State and the community with respect to social security and welfare, in accordance with his ability and with existing circumstances.

Article 36. Duty to pay taxes

It is the duty of every person to pay the taxes established by law for the support of public services.

Article 37. Duty to work

It is the duty of every person to work, as far as his capacity and possibilities permit, in order to obtain the means of livelihood or to benefit his community. Article 38. Duty to refrain from political activities in a foreign country It is the duty of every person to refrain from taking part in political activities that, according to law, are reserved exclusively to the citizens of the state in which he is an alien.

Source: OAS, Inter-American Commission on Human Rights (IACHR), http://www.oas.org/en/iachr/mandate/Basics/declaration.asp

3. AMERICAN CONVENTION ON HUMAN RIGHTS (ACHR)

This regional general international human rights treaty, abbreviated ACHR, was adopted by the OAS in 1969. It is also called the Pact of San Jose. It binds only OAS states which have ratified it. The Convention established the Inter-American Court of Human Rights, a judicial body sitting in Costa Rica, which monitors implementation by both contentious cases and rendering advisory opinions. It is a very broad and specific human rights treaty. The U.S. has signed this treaty, and therefore is obligated to not to do anything to undermine its implementation. The U.S. has not ratified this treaty, however, so it not formally bound by it. There are two protocols that amend this Convention discussed below.

{Excerpt}

[Text]

Signed at the Inter-American Specialized Conference on Human Rights, San José, Costa Rica, Adopted November 22, 1969, entered into force July 18, 1978; O.A.S. Treaty Series No 36, at 1, O.A.S. Off. Rec. OEA/Ser. L./V/II. 23 doc.rev.2 Preamble

The American states signatory to the present Convention,

Reaffirming their intention to consolidate in this hemisphere, within the framework of democratic institutions, a system of personal liberty and social justice based on respect for the essential rights of man;

Recognizing that the essential rights of man are not derived from one's being a national of a certain state, but are based upon attributes of the human personality, and that they therefore justify international protection in the form of a convention reinforcing or complementing the protection provided by the domestic law of the American states;

Considering that these principles have been set forth in the Charter of the Organization of American States, in the American Declaration of the Rights and Duties of Man, and in the Universal Declaration of Human Rights, and that they have been reaffirmed and refined in other international instruments, worldwide as well as regional in scope;

Reiterating that, in accordance with the Universal Declaration of Human Rights, the ideal of free men enjoying freedom from fear and want can be achieved only if conditions are created whereby everyone may enjoy his economic, social, and cultural rights, as well as his civil and political rights; and

Considering that the Third Special Inter-American Conference (Buenos Aires, 1967) approved the incorporation into the Charter of the Organization itself of broader standards with respect to economic, social, and educational rights and resolved that an inter-American convention on human rights should determine the structure, competence, and procedure of the organs responsible for these matters,

Have agreed upon the following:

Part I
State Obligations and Rights Protected

Chapter I—General Obligations

Article 1. Obligation to Respect Rights
1. The States Parties to this Convention undertake to respect the rights and freedoms recognized herein and to ensure to all persons subject to their jurisdiction the free and full exercise of those rights and freedoms, without any discrimination for reasons of race, color, sex, language, religion, political or other opinion, national or social origin, economic status, birth, or any other social condition.

2. For the purposes of this Convention, "person" means every human being.

Article 2. Domestic Legal Effects
Where the exercise of any of the rights or freedoms referred to in Article 1 is not already ensured by legislative or other provisions, the States Parties undertake to adopt, in accordance with their constitutional processes and the provisions of this Convention, such legislative or other measures as may be necessary to give effect to those rights or freedoms.

Chapter II—Civil and Political Rights

Article 3. Right to Juridical Personality
Every person has the right to recognition as a person before the law.

Article 4. Right to Life
1. Every person has the right to have his life respected. This right shall be protected by law and, in general, from the moment of conception. No one shall be arbitrarily deprived of his life.

2. In countries that have not abolished the death penalty, it may be imposed only for the most serious crimes and pursuant to a final judgment rendered by a competent court and in accordance with a law establishing such punishment, enacted prior to the commission of the crime. The application of such punishment shall not be extended to crimes to which it does not presently apply.

3. The death penalty shall not be reestablished in states that have abolished it.

4. In no case shall capital punishment be inflicted for political offenses or related common crimes.

5. Capital punishment shall not be imposed upon persons who, at the time the crime was committed, were under 18 years of age or over 70 years of age; nor shall it be applied to pregnant women.

6. Every person condemned to death shall have the right to apply for amnesty, pardon, or commutation of sentence, which may be granted in all cases. Capital punishment shall not be imposed while such a petition is pending decision by the competent authority.

Article 5. Right to Humane Treatment
1. Every person has the right to have his physical, mental, and moral integrity respected.

2. No one shall be subjected to torture or to cruel, inhuman, or degrading punishment or treatment. All persons deprived of their liberty shall be treated with respect for the inherent dignity of the human person.

3. Punishment shall not be extended to any person other than the criminal.

4. Accused persons shall, save in exceptional circumstances, be segregated from convicted persons, and shall be subject to separate treatment appropriate to their status as unconvicted persons.

5. Minors while subject to criminal proceedings shall be separated from adults and brought before specialized tribunals, as speedily as possible, so that they may be treated in accordance with their status as minors.

6. Punishments consisting of deprivation of liberty shall have as an essential aim the reform and social readaptation of the prisoners.

Article 6. Freedom from Slavery

1. No one shall be subject to slavery or to involuntary servitude, which are prohibited in all their forms, as are the slave trade and traffic in women.

2. No one shall be required to perform forced or compulsory labor. This provision shall not be interpreted to mean that, in those countries in which the penalty established for certain crimes is deprivation of liberty at forced labor, the carrying out of such a sentence imposed by a competent court is prohibited. Forced labor shall not adversely affect the dignity or the physical or intellectual capacity of the prisoner.

3. For the purposes of this article, the following do not constitute forced or compulsory labor:

a. work or service normally required of a person imprisoned in execution of a sentence or formal decision passed by the competent judicial authority. Such work or service shall be carried out under the supervision and control of public authorities, and any persons performing such work or service shall not be placed at the disposal of any private party, company, or juridical person;

b. military service and, in countries in which conscientious objectors are recognized, national service that the law may provide for in lieu of military service;

c. service exacted in time of danger or calamity that threatens the existence or the well-being of the community; or

d. work or service that forms part of normal civic obligations.

Article 7. Right to Personal Liberty

1. Every person has the right to personal liberty and security.

2. No one shall be deprived of his physical liberty except for the reasons and under the conditions established beforehand by the constitution of the State Party concerned or by a law established pursuant thereto.

3. No one shall be subject to arbitrary arrest or imprisonment.

4. Anyone who is detained shall be informed of the reasons for his detention and shall be promptly notified of the charge or charges against him.

5. Any person detained shall be brought promptly before a judge or other officer authorized by law to exercise judicial power and shall be entitled to trial within a reasonable time or to be released without prejudice to the continuation of the proceedings. His release may be subject to guarantees to assure his appearance for trial.

6. Anyone who is deprived of his liberty shall be entitled to recourse to a competent court, in order that the court may decide without delay on the lawfulness of his arrest or detention and order his release if the arrest or detention is unlawful. In States Parties whose laws provide that anyone who believes himself to be threatened with deprivation of his liberty is entitled to recourse to a competent court in order that it may decide on the lawfulness of such threat, this remedy may not be restricted or abolished. The interested party or another person in his behalf is entitled to seek these remedies.

7. No one shall be detained for debt. This principle shall not limit the orders of a competent judicial authority issued for nonfulfillment of duties of support.

Article 8. Right to a Fair Trial

1. Every person has the right to a hearing, with due guarantees and within a reasonable time, by a competent, independent, and impartial tribunal, previously established by law, in the substantiation of any accusation of a criminal nature made against him or for the determination of his rights and obligations of a civil, labor, fiscal, or any other nature.

2. Every person accused of a criminal offense has the right to be presumed innocent so long as his guilt has not been proven according to law. During the proceedings, every person is entitled, with full equality, to the following minimum guarantees:

> a. the right of the accused to be assisted without charge by a translator or interpreter, if he does not understand or does not speak the language of the tribunal or court;

> b. prior notification in detail to the accused of the charges against him;

> c. adequate time and means for the preparation of his defense;

> d. the right of the accused to defend himself personally or to be assisted by legal counsel of his own choosing, and to communicate freely and privately with his counsel;

> e. the inalienable right to be assisted by counsel provided by the state, paid or not as the domestic law provides, if the accused does not defend himself personally or engage his own counsel within the time period established by law;

> f. the right of the defense to examine witnesses present in the court and to obtain the appearance, as witnesses, of experts or other persons who may throw light on the facts;

> g. the right not to be compelled to be a witness against himself or to plead guilty; and

> h. the right to appeal the judgment to a higher court.

3. A confession of guilt by the accused shall be valid only if it is made without coercion of any kind.

4. An accused person acquitted by a non-appealable judgment shall not be subjected to a new trial for the same cause.

5. Criminal proceedings shall be public, except insofar as may be necessary to protect the interests of justice.

Article 9. Freedom from Ex Post Facto Laws

No one shall be convicted of any act or omission that did not constitute a criminal offense, under the applicable law, at the time it was committed. A heavier penalty shall not be imposed than the one that was applicable at the time the criminal offense was committed. If subsequent to the commission of the offense the law provides for the imposition of a lighter punishment, the guilty person shall benefit therefrom.

Article 10. Right to Compensation

Every person has the right to be compensated in accordance with the law in the event he has been sentenced by a final judgment through a miscarriage of justice.

Article 11. Right to Privacy

1. Everyone has the right to have his honor respected and his dignity recognized.

2. No one may be the object of arbitrary or abusive interference with his private life, his family, his home, or his correspondence, or of unlawful attacks on his honor or reputation.

3. Everyone has the right to the protection of the law against such interference or attacks.

Article 12. Freedom of Conscience and Religion

1. Everyone has the right to freedom of conscience and of religion. This right includes freedom to maintain or to change one's religion or beliefs, and freedom to profess or disseminate one's religion or beliefs, either individually or together with others, in public or in private.

a. No one shall be subject to restrictions that might impair his freedom to maintain or to change his religion or beliefs.

3. Freedom to manifest one's religion and beliefs may be subject only to the limitations prescribed by law that are necessary to protect public safety, order, health, or morals, or the rights or freedoms of others.

4. Parents or guardians, as the case may be, have the right to provide for the religious and moral education of their children or wards that is in accord with their own convictions.

Article 13. Freedom of Thought and Expression

1. Everyone has the right to freedom of thought and expression. This right includes freedom to seek, receive, and impart information and ideas of all kinds, regardless of frontiers, either orally, in writing, in print, in the form of art, or through any other medium of one's choice.

2. The exercise of the right provided for in the foregoing paragraph shall not be subject to prior censorship but shall be subject to subsequent imposition of liability, which shall be expressly established by law to the extent necessary to ensure:

a. respect for the rights or reputations of others; or

b. the protection of national security, public order, or public health or morals.

3. The right of expression may not be restricted by indirect methods or means, such as the abuse of government or private controls over newsprint, radio broadcasting frequencies, or equipment used in the dissemination of information, or by any other means tending to impede the communication and circulation of ideas and opinions.

4. Notwithstanding the provisions of paragraph 2 above, public entertainments may be subject by law to prior censorship for the sole purpose of regulating access to them for the moral protection of childhood and adolescence.

5. Any propaganda for war and any advocacy of national, racial, or religious hatred that constitute incitements to lawless violence or to any other similar illegal action against any person or group of persons on any grounds including those of race, color, religion, language, or national origin shall be considered as offenses punishable by law.

Article 14. Right of Reply

1. Anyone injured by inaccurate or offensive statements or ideas disseminated to the public in general by a legally regulated medium of communication has the right to reply or to make a correction using the same communications outlet, under such conditions as the law may establish.

2. The correction or reply shall not in any case remit other legal liabilities that may have been incurred.

3. For the effective protection of honor and reputation, every publisher, and every newspaper, motion picture, radio, and television company, shall have a person responsible who is not protected by immunities or special privileges.

Article 15. Right of Assembly

The right of peaceful assembly, without arms, is recognized. No restrictions may be placed on the exercise of this right other than those imposed in conformity with the law and necessary in a democratic society in the interest of national security, public safety or public order, or to protect public health or morals or the rights or freedom of others.

Article 16. Freedom of Association

1. Everyone has the right to associate freely for ideological, religious, political, economic, labor, social, cultural, sports, or other purposes.

2. The exercise of this right shall be subject only to such restrictions established by law as may be necessary in a democratic society, in the interest of national security, public safety or public order, or to protect public health or morals or the rights and freedoms of others.

3. The provisions of this article do not bar the imposition of legal restrictions, including even deprivation of the exercise of the right of association, on members of the armed forces and the police.

Article 17. Rights of the Family

1. The family is the natural and fundamental group unit of society and is entitled to protection by society and the state.

2. The right of men and women of marriageable age to marry and to raise a family shall be recognized, if they meet the conditions required by domestic laws, insofar as such conditions do not affect the principle of nondiscrimination established in this Convention.

3. No marriage shall be entered into without the free and full consent of the intending spouses.

4. The States Parties shall take appropriate steps to ensure the equality of rights and the adequate balancing of responsibilities of the spouses as to marriage, during marriage, and in the event of its dissolution. In case of dissolution, provision shall be made for the necessary protection of any children solely on the basis of their own best interests.

5. The law shall recognize equal rights for children born out of wedlock and those born in wedlock.

Article 18. Right to a Name

Every person has the right to a given name and to the surnames of his parents or that of one of them. The law shall regulate the manner in which this right shall be ensured for all, by the use of assumed names if necessary.

Article 19. Rights of the Child

Every minor child has the right to the measures of protection required by his condition as a minor on the part of his family, society, and the state.

Article 20. Right to Nationality

1. Every person has the right to a nationality.

2. Every person has the right to the nationality of the state in whose territory he was born if he does not have the right to any other nationality.

3. No one shall be arbitrarily deprived of his nationality or of the right to change it.

Article 21. Right to Property

1. Everyone has the right to the use and enjoyment of his property. The law may subordinate such use and enjoyment to the interest of society.

2. No one shall be deprived of his property except upon payment of just compensation, for reasons of public utility or social interest, and in the cases and according to the forms established by law.

3. Usury and any other form of exploitation of man by man shall be prohibited by law.

Article 22. Freedom of Movement and Residence

1. Every person lawfully in the territory of a State Party has the right to move about in it, and to reside in it subject to the provisions of the law.

2. Every person has the right to leave any country freely, including his own.

3. The exercise of the foregoing rights may be restricted only pursuant to a law to the extent necessary in a democratic society to prevent crime or to protect national security, public safety, public order, public morals, public health, or the rights or freedoms of others.

4. The exercise of the rights recognized in paragraph 1 may also be restricted by law in designated zones for reasons of public interest.

5. No one can be expelled from the territory of the state of which he is a national or be deprived of the right to enter it.

6. An alien lawfully in the territory of a State Party to this Convention may be expelled from it only pursuant to a decision reached in accordance with law.

7. Every person has the right to seek and be granted asylum in a foreign territory, in accordance with the legislation of the state and international conventions, in the event he is being pursued for political offenses or related common crimes.

8. In no case may an alien be deported or returned to a country, regardless of whether or not it is his country of origin, if in that country his right to life or personal freedom is in danger of being violated because of his race, nationality, religion, social status, or political opinions.

9. The collective expulsion of aliens is prohibited.

Article 23. Right to Participate in Government

1. Every citizen shall enjoy the following rights and opportunities:

   a. to take part in the conduct of public affairs, directly or through freely chosen representatives;

   b. to vote and to be elected in genuine periodic elections, which shall be by universal and equal suffrage and by secret ballot that guarantees the free expression of the will of the voters; and

   c. to have access, under general conditions of equality, to the public service of his country.

2. The law may regulate the exercise of the rights and opportunities referred to in the preceding paragraph only on the basis of age, nationality, residence, language, education, civil and mental capacity, or sentencing by a competent court in criminal proceedings.

Article 24. Right to Equal Protection

All persons are equal before the law. Consequently, they are entitled, without discrimination, to equal protection of the law.

Article 25. Right to Judicial Protection

1. Everyone has the right to simple and prompt recourse, or any other effective recourse, to a competent court or tribunal for protection against acts that violate his fundamental rights recognized by the constitution or laws of the state concerned or by this Convention, even though such violation may have been committed by persons acting in the course of their official duties.

2. The States Parties undertake:

   a. to ensure that any person claiming such remedy shall have his rights determined by the competent authority provided for by the legal system of the state;

   b. to develop the possibilities of judicial remedy; and

   c. to ensure that the competent authorities shall enforce such remedies when granted.

Chapter III—Economic, Social, and Cultural Rights

Article 26. Progressive Development

The States Parties undertake to adopt measures, both internally and through international cooperation, especially those of an economic and technical nature, with a view to achieving progressively, by legislation or other appropriate means, the full realization of the rights implicit in the economic, social, educational, scientific, and cultural standards set forth in the Charter of the Organization of American States as amended by the Protocol of Buenos Aires.

Chapter IV—Suspension of Guarantees, Interpretation, and Application

Article 27. Suspension of Guarantees

1. In time of war, public danger, or other emergency that threatens the independence or security of a State Party, it may take measures derogating from its obligations under the present Convention to the extent and for the period of time strictly required by the exigencies of the situation, provided that such measures are not inconsistent with its other obligations under international law and do not involve discrimination on the ground of race, color, sex, language, religion, or social origin.

2. The foregoing provision does not authorize any suspension of the following articles: Article 3 (Right to Juridical Personality), Article 4 (Right to Life), Article 5 (Right to Humane Treatment), Article 6 (Freedom from Slavery), Article 9 (Freedom from Ex Post Facto Laws), Article 12 (Freedom of Conscience and Religion), Article 17 (Rights of the Family), Article 18 (Right to a Name), Article 19 (Rights of the Child), Article 20 (Right to Nationality), and Article 23 (Right to Participate in Government), or of the judicial guarantees essential for the protection of such rights.

3. Any State Party availing itself of the right of suspension shall immediately inform the other States Parties, through the Secretary General of the Organization of American States, of the provisions the application of which it has suspended, the reasons that gave rise to the suspension, and the date set for the termination of such suspension.

Article 28. Federal Clause

1. Where a State Party is constituted as a federal state, the national government of such State Party shall implement all the provisions of the Convention over whose subject matter it exercises legislative and judicial jurisdiction.

2. With respect to the provisions over whose subject matter the constituent units of the federal state have jurisdiction, the national government shall immediately take suitable measures, in accordance with its constitution and its laws, to the end that the competent authorities of the constituent units may adopt appropriate provisions for the fulfillment of this Convention.

3. Whenever two or more States Parties agree to form a federation or other type of association, they shall take care that the resulting federal or other compact contains the provisions necessary for continuing and rendering effective the standards of this Convention in the new state that is organized. Article 29. Restrictions Regarding Interpretation

4. No provision of this Convention shall be interpreted as:

> a. permitting any State Party, group, or person to suppress the enjoyment or exercise of the rights and freedoms recognized in this Convention or to restrict them to a greater extent than is provided for herein;

> b. restricting the enjoyment or exercise of any right or freedom recognized by virtue of the laws of any State Party or by virtue of another convention to which one of the said states is a party;

> c. precluding other rights or guarantees that are inherent in the human personality or derived from representative democracy as a form of government; or

> d. excluding or limiting the effect that the American Declaration of the Rights and Duties of Man and other international acts of the same nature may have.

Article 30. Scope of Restrictions

The restrictions that, pursuant to this Convention, may be placed on the enjoyment or exercise of the rights or freedoms recognized herein may not be applied except in accordance with laws enacted for reasons of general interest and in accordance with the purpose for which such restrictions have been established. Article 31. Recognition of Other Rights

Other rights and freedoms recognized in accordance with the procedures established in Articles 76 and 77 may be included in the system of protection of this Convention.

Chapter V—Personal Responsibilities

Article 32. Relationship between Duties and Rights

1. Every person has responsibilities to his family, his community, and mankind.

2. The rights of each person are limited by the rights of others, by the security of all, and by the just demands of the general welfare, in a democratic society.

Part II
Means of Protection

Chapter VI—Competent Organs

Article 33

The following organs shall have competence with respect to matters relating to the fulfillment of the commitments made by the States Parties to this Convention:

    a. the Inter-American Commission on Human Rights, referred to as "The Commission;" and

    b. the Inter-American Court of Human Rights, referred to as "The Court."

Chapter VII—Inter-American Commission on Human Rights

Section 1. Organization

Article 34

The Inter-American Commission on Human Rights shall be composed of seven members, who shall be persons of high moral character and recognized competence in the field of human rights.

Article 35

The Commission shall represent all the member countries of the Organization of American States.

Article 36

1. The members of the Commission shall be elected in a personal capacity by the General Assembly of the Organization from a list of candidates proposed by the governments of the member states.

...

Section 2. Functions

Article 41

The main function of the Commission shall be to promote respect for and defense of human rights. In the exercise of its mandate, it shall have the following functions and powers:

    a. to develop an awareness of human rights among the peoples of America;

    b. to make recommendations to the governments of the member states, when it considers such action advisable, for the adoption of progressive measures in favor of human rights within the framework of their domestic law and constitutional provisions as well as appropriate measures to further the observance of those rights;

    c. to prepare such studies or reports as it considers advisable in the performance of its duties;

    d. to request the governments of the member states to supply it with information on the measures adopted by them in matters of human rights;

e. to respond, through the General Secretariat of the Organization of American States, to inquiries made by the member states on matters related to human rights and, within the limits of its possibilities, to provide those states with the advisory services they request;

f. to take action on petitions and other communications pursuant to its authority under the provisions of Articles 44 through 51 of this Convention; and

g. to submit an annual report to the General Assembly of the Organization of American States.

Article 42

The States Parties shall transmit to the Commission a copy of each of the reports and studies that they submit annually to the Executive Committees of the Inter-American Economic and Social Council and the Inter-American Council for Education, Science, and Culture, in their respective fields, so that the Commission may watch over the promotion of the rights implicit in the economic, social, educational, scientific, and cultural standards set forth in the Charter of the Organization of American States as amended by the Protocol of Buenos Aires.

Article 43

The States Parties undertake to provide the Commission with such information as it may request of them as to the manner in which their domestic law ensures the effective application of any provisions of this Convention.

Section 3. Competence

Article 44

Any person or group of persons, or any non-governmental entity legally recognized in one or more member states of the Organization, may lodge petitions with the Commission containing denunciations or complaints of violation of this Convention by a State Party.

Article 45

Any State Party may, when it deposits its instrument of ratification of or adherence to this Convention, or at any later time, declare that it recognizes the competence of the Commission to receive and examine communications in which a State Party alleges that another State Party has committed a violation of a human right set forth in this Convention.

Communications presented by virtue of this article may be admitted and examined only if they are presented by a State Party that has made a declaration recognizing the aforementioned competence of the Commission. The Commission shall not admit any communication against a State Party that has not made such a declaration.

A declaration concerning recognition of competence may be made to be valid for an indefinite time, for a specified period, or for a specific case.

4. Declarations shall be deposited with the General Secretariat of the Organization of American States, which shall transmit copies thereof to the member states of that Organization.

Article 46

1. Admission by the Commission of a petition or communication lodged in accordance with Articles 44 or 45 shall be subject to the following requirements:

a. that the remedies under domestic law have been pursued and exhausted in accordance with generally recognized principles of international law;

b. that the petition or communication is lodged within a period of six months from the date on which the party alleging violation of his rights was notified of the final judgment;

c. that the subject of the petition or communication is not pending in another international proceeding for settlement; and

d. that, in the case of Article 44, the petition contains the name, nationality, profession, domicile, and signature of the person or persons or of the legal representative of the entity lodging the petition.

2. The provisions of paragraphs 1.a and 1.b of this article shall not be applicable when:

a. the domestic legislation of the state concerned does not afford due process of law for the protection of the right or rights that have allegedly been violated;

b. the party alleging violation of his rights has been denied access to the remedies under domestic law or has been prevented from exhausting them; or

c. there has been unwarranted delay in rendering a final judgment under the aforementioned remedies.

Article 47

The Commission shall consider inadmissible any petition or communication submitted under Articles 44 or 45 if:

a. any of the requirements indicated in Article 46 has not been met;

b. the petition or communication does not state facts that tend to establish a violation of the rights guaranteed by this Convention;

c. the statements of the petitioner or of the state indicate that the petition or communication is manifestly groundless or obviously out of order; or

d. the petition or communication is substantially the same as one previously studied by the Commission or by another international organization.

Section 4. Procedure

Article 48

1. When the Commission receives a petition or communication alleging violation of any of the rights protected by this Convention, it shall proceed as follows:

a. If it considers the petition or communication admissible, it shall request information from the government of the state indicated as being responsible for the alleged violations and shall furnish that government a transcript of the pertinent portions of the petition or communication. This information shall be submitted within a reasonable period to be determined by the Commission in accordance with the circumstances of each case.

b. After the information has been received, or after the period established has elapsed and the information has not been received, the Commission shall ascertain whether the grounds for the petition or communication still exist. If they do not, the Commission shall order the record to be closed.

c. The Commission may also declare the petition or communication inadmissible or out of order on the basis of information or evidence subsequently received.

d. If the record has not been closed, the Commission shall, with the knowledge of the parties, examine the matter set forth in the petition or communication in order to verify the facts. If necessary and advisable, the Commission shall carry out an investigation, for the effective conduct of which it shall request, and the states concerned shall furnish to it, all necessary facilities.

e. The Commission may request the states concerned to furnish any pertinent information and, if so requested, shall hear oral statements or receive written statements from the parties concerned.

f. The Commission shall place itself at the disposal of the parties concerned with a view to reaching a friendly settlement of the matter on the basis of respect for the human rights recognized in this Convention.

2. However, in serious and urgent cases, only the presentation of a petition or communication that fulfills all the formal requirements of admissibility shall be necessary in order for the Commission to conduct an investigation with the prior consent of the state in whose territory a violation has allegedly been committed.

Article 49

If a friendly settlement has been reached in accordance with paragraph 1.f of Article 48, the Commission shall draw up a report, which shall be transmitted to the petitioner and to the States Parties to this Convention, and shall then be communicated to the Secretary General of the Organization of American States for publication. This report shall contain a brief statement of the facts and of the solution reached. If any party in the case so requests, the fullest possible information shall be provided to it.

Article 50

1. If a settlement is not reached, the Commission shall, within the time limit established by its Statute, draw up a report setting forth the facts and stating its conclusions. If the report, in whole or in part, does not represent the unanimous agreement of the members of the Commission, any member may attach to it a separate opinion. The written and oral statements made by the parties in accordance with paragraph 1.e of Article 48 shall also be attached to the report.

2. The report shall be transmitted to the states concerned, which shall not be at liberty to publish it.

3. In transmitting the report, the Commission may make such proposals and recommendations as it sees fit.

Article 51

1. If, within a period of three months from the date of the transmittal of the report of the Commission to the states concerned, the matter has not either been settled or submitted by the Commission or by the state concerned to the Court and its jurisdiction accepted, the Commission may, by the vote of an absolute majority of its members, set forth its opinion and conclusions concerning the question submitted for its consideration.

2. Where appropriate, the Commission shall make pertinent recommendations and shall prescribe a period within which the state is to take the measures that are incumbent upon it to remedy the situation examined.

3. When the prescribed period has expired, the Commission shall decide by the vote of an absolute majority of its members whether the state has taken adequate measures and whether to publish its report.

Chapter VIII
Inter-American Court of Human Rights

Section 1. Organization

Article 52

1. The Court shall consist of seven judges, nationals of the member states of the Organization, elected in an individual capacity from among jurists of the highest moral authority and of recognized competence in the field of human rights, who possess the qualifications required for the exercise of the highest judicial functions in conformity with the law of the state of which they are nationals or of the state that proposes them as candidates.

2. No two judges may be nationals of the same state.

...

Section 2. Jurisdiction and Functions

Article 61

1. Only the States Parties and the Commission shall have the right to submit a case to the Court.

2. In order for the Court to hear a case, it is necessary that the procedures set forth in Articles 48 and 50 shall have been completed.

Article 62

1. A State Party may, upon depositing its instrument of ratification or adherence to this Convention, or at any subsequent time, declare that it recognizes as binding, ipso facto, and not requiring special agreement, the jurisdiction of the Court on all matters relating to the interpretation or application of this Convention.

2. Such declaration may be made unconditionally, on the condition of reciprocity, for a specified period, or for specific cases. It shall be presented to the Secretary General of the Organization, who shall transmit copies thereof to the other member states of the Organization and to the Secretary of the Court.

3. The jurisdiction of the Court shall comprise all cases concerning the interpretation and application of the provisions of this Convention that are submitted to it, provided that the States Parties to the case recognize or have recognized such jurisdiction, whether by special declaration pursuant to the preceding paragraphs, or by a special agreement.

Article 63

1. If the Court finds that there has been a violation of a right or freedom protected by this Convention, the Court shall rule that the injured party be ensured the enjoyment of his right or freedom that was violated. It shall also rule, if appropriate, that the consequences of the measure or situation that constituted the breach of such right or freedom be remedied and that fair compensation be paid to the injured party.

2. In cases of extreme gravity and urgency, and when necessary to avoid irreparable damage to persons, the Court shall adopt such provisional measures as it deems pertinent in matters it has under consideration. With respect to a case not yet submitted to the Court, it may act at the request of the Commission.

Article 64

1. The member states of the Organization may consult the Court regarding the interpretation of this Convention or of other treaties concerning the protection of human rights in the American states. Within their spheres of competence, the organs listed in Chapter X of the Charter of the Organization of American States, as amended by the Protocol of Buenos Aires, may in like manner consult the Court.

2. The Court, at the request of a member state of the Organization, may provide that state with opinions regarding the compatibility of any of its domestic laws with the aforesaid international instruments.

...

Section 3. Procedure

Article 66

1. Reasons shall be given for the judgment of the Court.

2. If the judgment does not represent in whole or in part the unanimous opinion of the judges, any judge shall be entitled to have his dissenting or separate opinion attached to the judgment.

Article 67

The judgment of the Court shall be final and not subject to appeal. In case of disagreement as to the meaning or scope of the judgment, the Court shall interpret it at the request of any of the parties, provided the request is made within ninety days from the date of notification of the judgment.

Article 68

1. The States Parties to the Convention undertake to comply with the judgment of the Court in any case to which they are parties.

2. That part of a judgment that stipulates compensatory damages may be executed in the country concerned in accordance with domestic procedure governing the execution of judgments against the state.

...

Source: OAS, Inter-American Commission on Human Rights (IACHR), http://www.oas.org/dil/treaties_B-32_American_Convention_on_Human_Rights.htm

☙☙☙☙☙☙☙☙

4. ADDITIONAL PROTOCOL TO THE AMERICAN CONVENTION ON HUMAN RIGHTS IN THE AREA OF ECONOMIC, SOCIAL AND CULTURAL RIGHTS

This Additional Protocol to the ACHR, adopted in 1988, known as the "Protocol of San Salvador," amends the ACHR in regard to economic, social and cultural rights implied within its Article 26. It is only open to OAS member states who are parties to the ACHR. The U.S. has not acceded to this legal instrument and so is not legally bound by it. The U.S. does not firmly accept that economic, social and cultural rights are human rights.

Preamble

The States Parties to the American Convention on Human Rights "Pact San José, Costa Rica,"

Reaffirming their intention to consolidate in this hemisphere, within the framework of democratic institutions, a system of personal liberty and social justice based on respect for the essential rights of man;

Recognizing that the essential rights of man are not derived from one's being a national of a certain State, but are based upon attributes of the human person, for which reason they merit international protection in the form of a convention reinforcing or complementing the protection provided by the domestic law of the American States;

Considering the close relationship that exists between economic, social and cultural rights, and civil and political rights, in that the different categories of rights constitute an indivisible whole based on the recognition of the dignity of the human person, for which reason both require permanent protection and promotion if they are to be fully realized, and the violation of some rights in favor of the realization of others can never be justified;

Recognizing the benefits that stem from the promotion and development of cooperation among States and international relations;

Recalling that, in accordance with the Universal Declaration of Human Rights and the American Convention on Human Rights, the ideal of free human beings enjoying freedom from fear and want can only be achieved if conditions are created whereby everyone may enjoy his economic, social and cultural rights as well as his civil and political rights;

Bearing in mind that, although fundamental economic, social and cultural rights have been recognized in earlier international instruments of both world and regional scope, it is essential that those rights be reaffirmed, developed, perfected and protected in order to consolidate in America, on the basis of full respect for the rights of the individual, the democratic representative form of government as well as the right of its peoples to development, self-determination, and the free disposal of their wealth and natural resources; and

Considering that the American Convention on Human Rights provides that draft additional protocols to that Convention may be submitted for consideration to the States Parties, meeting together on the occasion of the General Assembly of the Organization of American States, for the purpose of gradually incorporating other rights and freedoms into the protective system thereof,

Have agreed upon the following Additional Protocol to the American Convention on Human Rights "Protocol of San Salvador:" Article 1. Obligation to Adopt Measures

The States Parties to this Additional Protocol to the American Convention on Human Rights undertake to adopt the necessary measures, both domestically and through international cooperation, especially economic and technical, to the extent allowed by their available resources, and taking into account their degree of development, for the purpose of achieving progressively and pursuant to their internal legislations, the full observance of the rights recognized in this Protocol.

Article 2. Obligation to Enact Domestic Legislation
If the exercise of the rights set forth in this Protocol is not already guaranteed by legislative or other provisions, the States Parties undertake to adopt, in accordance with their constitutional processes and the provisions of this Protocol, such legislative or other measures as may be necessary for making those rights a reality.

Article 3. Obligation of nondiscrimination
The State Parties to this Protocol undertake to guarantee the exercise of the rights set forth herein without discrimination of any kind for reasons related to race, color, sex, language, religion, political or other opinions, national or social origin, economic status, birth or any other social condition.

Article 4. Inadmissibility of Restrictions
A right which is recognized or in effect in a State by virtue of its internal legislation or international conventions may not be restricted or curtailed on the pretext that this Protocol does not recognize the right or recognizes it to a lesser degree.

Article 5. Scope of Restrictions and Limitations
The State Parties may establish restrictions and limitations on the enjoyment and exercise of the rights established herein by means of laws promulgated for the purpose of preserving the general welfare in a democratic society only to the extent that they are not incompatible with the purpose and reason underlying those rights.

Article 6. Right to Work
1. Everyone has the right to work, which includes the opportunity to secure the means for living a dignified and decent existence by performing a freely elected or accepted lawful activity.

2. The State Parties undertake to adopt measures that will make the right to work fully effective, especially with regard to the achievement of full employment, vocational guidance, and the development of technical and vocational training projects, in particular those directed to the disabled. The States Parties also undertake to implement and strengthen programs that help to ensure suitable family care, so that women may enjoy a real opportunity to exercise the right to work.

Article 7. Just, Equitable, and Satisfactory Conditions of Work
The States Parties to this Protocol recognize that the right to work to which the foregoing article refers presupposes that everyone shall enjoy that right under just, equitable, and satisfactory conditions, which the States Parties undertake to guarantee in their internal legislation, particularly with respect to:

a. Remuneration which guarantees, as a minimum, to all workers dignified and decent living conditions for them and their families and fair and equal wages for equal work, without distinction;

b. The right of every worker to follow his vocation and to devote himself to the activity that best fulfills his expectations and to change employment in accordance with the pertinent national regulations;

c. The right of every worker to promotion or upward mobility in his employment, for which purpose account shall be taken of his qualifications, competence, integrity and seniority;

d. Stability of employment, subject to the nature of each industry and occupation and the causes for just separation. In cases of unjustified dismissal, the worker shall have the right to indemnity or to reinstatement on the job or any other benefits provided by domestic legislation;

e. Safety and hygiene at work;

f. The prohibition of night work or unhealthy or dangerous working conditions and, in general, of all work which jeopardizes health, safety, or morals, for persons under 18 years of age. As regards minors under the age of 16, the work day shall be subordinated to the provisions regarding compulsory education and in no case shall work constitute an impediment to school attendance or a limitation on benefiting from education received;

g. A reasonable limitation of working hours, both daily and weekly. The days shall be shorter in the case of dangerous or unhealthy work or of night work;

h. Rest, leisure and paid vacations as well as remuneration for national holidays.

Article 8. Trade Union Rights
1. The States Parties shall ensure:

a. The right of workers to organize trade unions and to join the union of their choice for the purpose of protecting and promoting their interests. As an extension of that right, the States Parties shall permit trade unions to establish national federations or confederations, or to affiliate with those that already exist, as well as to form international trade union organizations and to affiliate with that of their choice. The States Parties shall also permit trade unions, federations and confederations to function freely;

b. The right to strike.

2. The exercise of the rights set forth above may be subject only to restrictions established by law, provided that such restrictions are characteristic of a democratic society and necessary for safeguarding public order or for protecting public health or morals or the rights and freedoms of others. Members of the armed forces and the police and of other essential public services shall be subject to limitations and restrictions established by law.

3. No one may be compelled to belong to a trade union.

Article 9. Right to Social Security
1. Everyone shall have the right to social security protecting him from the consequences of old age and of disability which prevents him, physically or mentally, from securing the means for a dignified and decent existence. In the event of the death of a beneficiary, social security benefits shall be applied to his dependents.

2. In the case of persons who are employed, the right to social security shall cover at least medical care and an allowance or retirement benefit in the case of work accidents or occupational disease and, in the case of women, paid maternity leave before and after childbirth.

Article 10. Right to Health
Everyone shall have the right to health, understood to mean the enjoyment of the highest level of physical, mental and social well-being.

In order to ensure the exercise of the right to health, the States Parties agree to recognize health as a public good and, particularly, to adopt the following measures to ensure that right:

a. Primary health care, that is, essential health care made available to all individuals and families in the community;

b. Extension of the benefits of health services to all individuals subject to the State's jurisdiction;

c. Universal immunization against the principal infectious diseases;

d. Prevention and treatment of endemic, occupational and other diseases;

e. Education of the population on the prevention and treatment of health problems, and

f. Satisfaction of the health needs of the highest risk groups and of those whose poverty makes them the most vulnerable

Article 11. Right to a Healthy Environment
Everyone shall have the right to live in a healthy environment and to have access to basic public services.

The States Parties shall promote the protection, preservation, and improvement of the environment.

Article 12. Right to Food

1. Everyone has the right to adequate nutrition which guarantees the possibility of enjoying the highest level of physical, emotional and intellectual development.

2. In order to promote the exercise of this right and eradicate malnutrition, the States Parties undertake to improve methods of production, supply and distribution of food, and to this end, agree to promote greater international cooperation in support of the relevant national policies.

Article 13. Right to Education

1. Everyone has the right to education.

The States Parties to this Protocol agree that education should be directed towards the full development of the human personality and human dignity and should strengthen respect for human rights, ideological pluralism, fundamental freedoms, justice and peace. They further agree that education ought to enable everyone to participate effectively in a democratic and pluralistic society and achieve a decent existence and should foster understanding, tolerance and friendship among all nations and all racial, ethnic or religious groups and promote activities for the maintenance of peace.

The States Parties to this Protocol recognize that in order to achieve the full exercise of the right to education:

    a. Primary education should be compulsory and accessible to all without cost;

    b. Secondary education in its different forms, including technical and vocational secondary education, should be made generally available and accessible to all by every appropriate means, and in particular, by the progressive introduction of free education;

    c. Higher education should be made equally accessible to all, on the basis of individual capacity, by every appropriate means, and in particular, by the progressive introduction of free education;

    d. Basic education should be encouraged or intensified as far as possible for those persons who have not received or completed the whole cycle of primary instruction;

    e. Programs of special education should be established for the handicapped, so as to provide special instruction and training to persons with physical disabilities or mental deficiencies.

4. In conformity with the domestic legislation of the States Parties, parents should have the right to select the type of education to be given to their children, provided that it conforms to the principles set forth above.

5. Nothing in this Protocol shall be interpreted as a restriction of the freedom of individuals and entities to establish and direct educational institutions in accordance with the domestic legislation of the States Parties.

Article 14. Right to the Benefits of Culture

1. The States Parties to this Protocol recognize the right of everyone:

    a. To take part in the cultural and artistic life of the community;

    b. To enjoy the benefits of scientific and technological progress;

    c. To benefit from the protection of moral and material interests deriving from any scientific, literary or artistic production of which he is the author.

2. The steps to be taken by the States Parties to this Protocol to ensure the full exercise of this right shall include those necessary for the conservation, development and dissemination of science, culture and arts.

3. The States Parties to this Protocol undertake to respect the freedom indispensable for scientific research and creative activity.

4. The States Parties to this Protocol recognize the benefits to be derived from the encouragement and development of international cooperation and relations in the fields of science, arts and culture, and accordingly agree to foster greater international cooperation in these fields.

Article 15. Right to the Formation and the Protection of Families

The family is the natural and fundamental element of society and ought to be protected by the State, which should see to the improvement of its spiritual and material conditions.

Everyone has the right to form a family, which shall be exercised in accordance with the provisions of the pertinent domestic legislation.

3. The States Parties hereby undertake to accord adequate protection to the family unit and in particular:

a. To provide special care and assistance to mothers during a reasonable period before and after childbirth;

b. To guarantee adequate nutrition for children at the nursing stage and during school attendance years; c. To adopt special measures for the protection of adolescents in order to ensure the full development of their physical, intellectual and moral capacities;

d. To undertake special programs of family training so as to help create a stable and positive environment in which children will receive and develop the values of understanding, solidarity, respect and responsibility.

Article 16. Rights of Children

Every child, whatever his parentage, has the right to the protection that his status as a minor requires from his family, society and the State. Every child has the right to grow under the protection and responsibility of his parents; save in exceptional, judicially-recognized circumstances, a child of young age ought not to be separated from his mother. Every child has the right to free and compulsory education, at least in the elementary phase, and to continue his training at higher levels of the educational system.

Article 17. Protection of the Elderly

Everyone has the right to special protection in old age. With this in view the States Parties agree to take progressively the necessary steps to make this right a reality and, particularly, to:

a. Provide suitable facilities, as well as food and specialized medical care, for elderly individuals who lack them and are unable to provide them for themselves;

b. Undertake work programs specifically designed to give the elderly the opportunity to engage in a productive activity suited to their abilities and consistent with their vocations or desires;

c. Foster the establishment of social organizations aimed at improving the quality of life for the elderly.

Article 18. Protection of the Handicapped

Everyone affected by a diminution of his physical or mental capacities is entitled to receive special attention designed to help him achieve the greatest possible development of his personality. The States Parties agree to adopt such measures as may be necessary for this purpose and, especially, to:

a. Undertake programs specifically aimed at providing the handicapped with the resources and environment needed for attaining this goal, including work programs consistent with their possibilities and freely accepted by them or their legal representatives, as the case may be;

b. Provide special training to the families of the handicapped in order to help them solve the problems of coexistence and convert them into active agents in the physical, mental and emotional development of the latter;

c. Include the consideration of solutions to specific requirements arising from needs of this group as a priority component of their urban development plans;

d. Encourage the establishment of social groups in which the handicapped can be helped to enjoy a fuller life.

Article 19. Means of Protection

1. Pursuant to the provisions of this article and the corresponding rules to be formulated for this purpose by the General Assembly of the Organization of American States, the States Parties to this Protocol undertake to submit periodic reports on the progressive measures they have taken to ensure due respect for the rights set forth in this Protocol.

...

Source: OAS, Inter-American Commission on Human Rights (IACHR), http://www.oas.org/juridico/english/treaties/a-52.html

కా-కా-కా-కా-కా-కా

5. PROTOCOL TO THE AMERICAN CONVENTION ON HUMAN RIGHTS TO ABOLISH THE DEATH PENALTY

This is the 1990 OAS Protocol to the ACHR to Abolish the Death Penalty. Most of the states of the OAS have abolished capital punishment; only fifty-eight countries still have the death penalty. The U.S., which is not party to this OAS protocol, retains capital punishment/death penalty as an option at the federal level. Nineteen U.S. states and the District of Columbia have abolished the death penalty, and four more states have moratoria in place, leaving thirty U.S. states that retain the death penalty.

Preamble

The States parties to this protocol,

Considering:

That Article 4 of the American Convention on Human Rights recognizes the right to life and restricts the application of the death penalty;

That everyone has the inalienable right to respect for his life, a right that cannot be suspended for any reason;

That the tendency among the American States is to be in favor of abolition of the death penalty;

That application of the death penalty has irrevocable consequences, forecloses the correction of judicial error, and precludes any possibility of changing or rehabilitating those convicted;

That the abolition of the death penalty helps to ensure more effective protection of the right to life;

That an international agreement must be arrived at that will entail a progressive development of the American Convention on Human Rights, and

That States Parties to the American Convention on Human Rights have expressed their intention to adopt an international agreement with a view to consolidating the practice of not applying the death penalty in the Americas,

Have agreed to sign the following protocol to the American Convention on Human Rights to Abolish the Death Penalty:

Article 1

The States Parties to this Protocol shall not apply the death penalty in their territory to any person subject to their jurisdiction.

Article 2

No reservations may be made to this Protocol. However, at the time of ratification or accession, the States Parties to this instrument may declare that they reserve the right to apply the death penalty in wartime in accordance with international law, for extremely serious crimes of a military nature.

...

Source: OAS, Inter-American Commission on Human Rights (IACHR), http://www.oas.org/juridico/english/treaties/a-53.html

☙☙☙☙☙☙☙☙

6. ORGANIZATION OF AMERICAN STATES: REPORT ON THE 153RD SESSION OF THE INTER-AMERICAN COMMISSION ON HUMAN RIGHTS, DECEMBER 29, 2014

Following is the report by the Inter-American Commission on Human Rights on one of its sessions of activities which involved the U.S. in particular. It gives a description of the types of activities of the Commission, particularly the cases handled by that quasi-judicial body. The Jessica Lenahan (Gonzalez) v. U.S. case decision mentioned is Primary Source Document 12.

Washington, D.C.—The Inter-American Commission on Human Rights (IACHR) held its 153rd regular session from October 23 to November 7, 2014. The IACHR is made up of Tracy Robinson, Chair; Rose-Marie Belle Antoine, First Vice-Chair; Felipe González, Second Vice-Chair; José de Jesús Orozco Henríquez; Rosa María Ortiz; Paulo Vannuchi; and James Cavallaro. The Executive Secretary is Emilio Álvarez Icaza Longoria.

During the session, the IACHR worked on analyzing petitions, cases, and precautionary measures; studied various plans to address its procedural backlog; held 53 public hearings and 31 working meetings on cases and precautionary measures; and held meetings with representatives of States, petitioners, and civil society organizations from around the region, among other activities.

...

Human Rights Situation of Migrant and Refugee Children and Families in the United States

The Commission recently conducted a visit to the U.S. southern border as part of its ongoing efforts to monitor and report on the human rights situation of migrant and refugee children and families in the United States. In a hearing on the subject during this session, the petitioning organizations provided information on the practice of detaining children with their mothers; the lack of qualified, properly trained staff to attend to these families; violations of the right of migrant children and families to request and receive asylum; and expedited deportation proceedings, many of which are held without individuals having legal representation. The State alluded to efforts it has made to ensure the safety of migrant children and to the support given to countries of origin to apply policies that dissuade irregular migration, and referred to policies it had implemented in their home countries to deter irregular migration. The Commission lamented that Texas state authorities were not present at the hearing, and observed the need for direct cooperation on the causes of migration rather than deterrence measures, and for the adoption of measures to facilitate regular migration, especially in cases of family reunification. The IACHR reiterated that under international standards, measures other than detention must be adopted in the best interests of migrant children, with full respect for all their human rights, including the right to seek asylum or refuge.

Case 12.626 — Jessica Lenahan (Gonzales), United States — (Follow-Up on Recommendations)

The parties presented information regarding compliance with the recommendations contained in the Commission's merits decision of July 21, 2011. The petitioners, including Jessica Lenahan, shared information concerning pending challenges—including the ongoing failure, in the 15 years since the events that led to this case, to investigate the deaths of Leslie, Katherine, and Rebecca Gonzales and to grant reparations, implement policy reforms that address the root causes of violence against women, and engage meaningfully with the petitioners. The U.N. Special Rapporteur on violence against women, Rashida Manjoo, also participated in the hearing as part of the delegation of petitioners. In her statement, she stressed that violence against women is a pervasive human rights violation rooted in multiple, intersecting forms of discrimination, and must be addressed holistically. The State highlighted efforts to address violence against women at the federal level, including the adoption of the Violence against Women Act. It also reiterated the limitations in the U.S. federal system in relation to providing reparations and investigating the deaths of Jessica Lenahan's daughters. The State also suggested that a hearing be organized concerning the case of Jessica Lenahan during the March 2015 session. The Commission expressed its concern over the pending recommendations that have not been implemented by the State, particularly its failure to investigate the deaths of Leslie, Katherine, and Rebecca Gonzales. The IACHR reminded the State of Ms. Lenahan's right to a clarification of what happened to her three daughters and who is responsible for their deaths.

Reports of Racism in the United States Justice System

The Commission convened this hearing on its own initiative, as a result of its growing concern over the treatment of African-Americans by the United States criminal justice system and, particularly, by law enforcement officers. The IACHR received troubling information regarding the problem of racial profiling by law enforcement officials at the local, state, and federal levels. Petitioners mentioned specific programs based on racial profiling, such as the "stop-and-frisk" program in New York City, and state immigration laws passed in Arizona, Alabama, and elsewhere. They also noted the need to update the 2003 Department of Justice Guidance Regarding the Use of Race by Federal Law Enforcement Agencies. The IACHR also received information on the lack of criminal accountability in cases of excessive use of force by law enforcement officers. Carter Stewart, U.S. Attorney for the Southern District of Ohio, recognized that the United States disproportionately imprisons people of color and affirmed that the U.S. Attorney General is committed to addressing these disparities in the criminal justice system. In this regard, he mentioned the creation of a Racial Disparities Working Group and the "Smart on Crime Program" in which the Department of Justice, among other initiatives, modified charging policies in the case of defendants accused of certain nonviolent, low-level drug offenses and established community service measures as alternatives to incarceration. The Commission expressed its particular concerns as to the fact that in several states it is still possible to judge, sentence and imprison adolescents as adults, and as regards the effects of racial discrimination on adolescents, the abuse committed by the police. It also highlighted the need to prioritize prevention policies, data collection and analysis to study the causes of crime committed by youth, and to automatically expunge their registries or records.

Source: OAS, Inter-American Commission on Human Rights (IACHR), http://www.oas.org/en/iachr/media_center/PReleases /2014/131A.asp

7. INTER-AMERICAN COMMISSION ON HUMAN RIGHTS, THE RIGHT TO TRUTH IN THE AMERICAS

One of the functions of the experts on the OAS Inter-American Commission on Human Rights is to write reports on particular subjects deemed important to the Commission to help states comply with their human rights obligations. The following report is about the Right to Truth, that is the right of individuals to know the truth about what happened as a result of a human rights violation, such as the disappearance of loved ones.

{Excerpt}

Executive Summary

I. Introduction

1. Both the Inter-American Commission on Human Rights (hereinafter the "Inter-American Commission," the "Commission" or the "IACHR") and the Inter-American Court of Human Rights (hereinafter the "Inter-American Court" or the "Court") have emphasized the intrinsic relationship between democracy, and the observance of and respect for human rights. Some thirty years ago, the Inter-American Commission wrote that an analysis of the human rights situation in the countries of the region "enables [it] to affirm that only by means of the effective exercise of [...] democracy can the observance of human rights be fully guaranteed."

2. However, the history of the countries in this hemisphere is strewn with multiple and repeated breaks with the democratic and institutional order, non-international armed conflicts, civil wars and situations involving widespread violence that lingered for long periods of time and that in some cases continue to this day. Given the circumstances, mass and systematic violations of human rights have been frequent, as have serious violations of international humanitarian law (hereinafter "IHL"), committed by agents of the State, private parties operating with a State's support, tolerance or acquiescence, and members of illegal armed groups.

3. The absence of complete, objective, and truthful information about what transpired during those periods has been a constant, a policy of the State and even a "tactic of war," as in the case of the practice of forced disappearances. The Commission has noted: "[a] difficult problem that recent democracies have had to face has been the investigation of human rights violations under previous governments and the possibility of sanctions against those responsible for such violations."

4. The right to the truth has emerged in response to States' failure to clarify, investigate, prosecute and punish gross human rights and IHL violations. Through its efforts to combat impunity, the organs of the system have developed regional standards, which flesh out the right to the truth, and States and civil society have developed approaches and initiatives to implement them using a wide range of methods. Furthermore, the right to the truth is one of the pillars of the mechanisms of transitional justice.

5. In the present context, the IACHR has prepared this report in order to support the inter-American system's efforts to disseminate the principles on the right to the truth by systematizing the applicable framework of laws and examining a number of experiences undertaken in the region. Likewise, this report will serve as a springboard for discussion with a view to consolidating and improving the States' laws, policies and practices for addressing this issue. In addition, through this report the Commission is responding to the mandate that the OAS General Assembly entrusted to it in operative paragraph six of resolution AG/RES. 2175 (XXXVI-O/06) "Right to the truth."

6. This report has four chapters. The introductory chapter puts into context the relationship between democracy, human rights and truth, the importance of the right to the truth and describes the method used to prepare the report. In the second chapter, the Commission will explain the applicable legal framework, i.e., the inter-American system's norms and principles concerning the right to the truth. In the third chapter, the Commission will examine some initiatives undertaken by the States of the region as well as civil society, from the perspective of the principles and norms described in the second chapter. Finally, in chapter four, the Commission will offer pertinent conclusions and recommendations.

II. Legal framework: The conceptualization of the right to the truth in the Inter-American Human Rights System

7. The right to the truth is not expressly recognized in the inter-American human rights instruments. Nevertheless, since their inception both the IACHR and the Inter-American Court have established the substance of the right to the truth and the obligations it creates for States, based on a comprehensive analysis of a group of rights recognized in the American Declaration on the Rights and Duties of Man (hereinafter the "American Declaration") and the American Convention on Human Rights (hereinafter the "American Convention" or the "ACHR").

A. Development of the right to the truth as a response to the phenomenon of forced disappearance

8. Within the inter-American system, the right to the truth was initially linked to the widespread phenomenon of forced disappearance. Both the Inter-American Commission and Court have established that forced disappearance is a permanent or continuous violation of multiple rights, such as the right to personal liberty, to humane treatment, to life, and to recognition as a person before the law. Thus, a victim's disappearance and execution begin with his/her deprivation of liberty and the subsequent failure to provide information as to his/her whereabouts; it continues so long as the disappeared person's whereabouts have not been established or his/her remains identified. In short, both bodies have maintained that the practice of forced disappearance involves a gross abandonment of the essential principles upon which the inter-American human rights system is based and its prohibition is now accepted as jus cogens.

9. Given its implications, the phenomenon of forced disappearance, which remains a serious problem in the Americas,1 has been a matter of particular interest and concern for the Commission since its inception, given its mandate to monitor the human rights situation. Responding to this situation, both the IACHR and the Inter-American Court have established the obligations incumbent upon States in cases of forced disappearance, based on the inter-American human rights instruments. Central to these obligations is the duty to take all measures necessary to investigate and, where appropriate, punish those responsible, and to make fair and adequate reparations to the victim's next of kin. States also have an obligation to establish the facts of what happened, locate the victims' whereabouts or their remains, and inform the next of kin to that effect.

10. States are also obligated to conduct, ex officio, an effective search to establish the whereabouts of forcibly disappeared victims, in order to establish the truth of what happened. The IACHR has underscored the right of the family of victims of forced disappearance to know the truth of what happened to their loved ones, and the State's obligation to provide a simple, rapid, and efficient recourse that enables it to comply with that obligation.

11. Thus, the right to the truth first manifested itself as a right pertaining to relatives of victims of forced disappearance. The State's obligation is to take all measures necessary to establish what happened and to locate and identify the victims. The Commission has taken into account that determining the final whereabouts of the disappeared victim eases the anguish and suffering of his/her family members caused by the uncertainty as to the fate of their disappeared relative. Furthermore, receiving the bodies of their deceased loved ones is extremely important to their next of kin, given that it allows them to bury the victim according to their beliefs, as well as bring some degree of closure to the mourning process they have been living through all these years. The Court has held, therefore, that denying access to the truth concerning the fate of a disappeared loved one is a form of cruel and inhuman treatment to immediate family members, which explains the connection between a violation of the right to humane treatment and a violation of the right to know the truth.

B. Consolidation and content of the right to the truth in the inter-American system

12. The legal precedents of the IACHR and the Court, as explained in Chapter 2, supported by various reports and instruments developed by the United Nations (hereinafter the "UN"),

13. In this regard, the Commission and the Court have held that the right to the truth is directly connected to the rights to judicial guarantees and judicial protection, set forth in Articles XVIII and XXIV of the American Declaration, and Articles 8 and 25 of the American Convention. Likewise, in some cases the right to the truth is connected to the right of access to information, protected under Article IV of the American Declaration and Article 13 of American Convention.

14. Under those articles, the right to the truth has two dimensions. The first dimension is the right of the victims and their family members to know the truth about the events that led to serious violations of human rights, and the right to know the identity of those who played a role in the violations. This means that the right to the truth creates an obligation upon States to clarify and investigate the facts, prosecute and punish those responsible for cases of serious human rights violations, and, depending on the circumstances of each case, to guarantee access to the information available in State facilities and files concerning serious human rights violations.

15. Secondly, a principle has been established to the effect that the holders of this right are not just the victims and their family members, but also society as a whole. The Commission has maintained that greater society has the inalienable right to know the truth about past events, as well as the motives and circumstances in which aberrant crimes came to be committed, in order to prevent recurrence of such acts in the future.

16. In the instant report, the Commission examines the general principles pertaining to the right to the truth as interpreted by the organs of the inter-American system in keeping with the provisions of the aforementioned inter-American human rights instruments.

1. Right to a fair trial and judicial protection

17. The case law of the Inter-American Court sets forth that the right to the truth is regarded as a fundamental element of the right to a fair trial and judicial protection. The Commission, for its part, has written that the "right to the truth" is a basic and essential obligation of States Parties to the American Convention under Article 1(1) thereof, since a State's disregard of acts involving human rights violations means that, in practice, no protection system is in place to ensure that those responsible will be identified and, when appropriate, punished.

18. Thus, the right to the truth has been interpreted as a just expectation that a State must satisfy with respect to victims of human rights violations and their next of kin. Therefore, the purpose of fully ensuring the rights to judicial guarantees and judicial protection is to combat impunity, understood as "the overall lack of investigation, tracking down, capture, prosecution and conviction of those responsible for violating the rights protected by the American Convention." Other-

wise, the State's lack of due diligence "fosters chronic recidivism of human rights violations, and total defenselessness of victims and their relatives."4 Hence, victims of human rights violations or their relatives have the right to expect that everything necessary will be done to ascertain the truth of what happened through an effective investigation of the facts, prosecution of those responsible for the crimes, imposition of the appropriate punishments, and reparation of any damages and injuries that the relatives may have sustained.

19. The bodies of the system have also emphasized that the right to know the truth about what happened is not confined to the victims and their next of kin but also society as a whole. In the same vein, the Court has held that, in a democratic society, this right is a just expectation that the State must satisfy through performance of its obligation to investigate, on its own initiative, gross human rights violations and through public dissemination of the results of criminal prosecutions and investigations.

20. The Court has also pointed out that satisfaction of the collective dimension of the right to the truth requires a procedural examination of the most complete historical record possible, and a judicial determination as to the patterns of joint action and the identity of all those who, in one way or another, participated in the violations and their respective responsibility. Fulfillment of these obligations is necessary to guarantee a full reconstruction of the truth and a thorough investigation of the structures in which the human rights violations took place.

21. In view of the foregoing, the Commission stresses that no State measure adopted in the area of justice can mean that a human rights violation will go uninvestigated. The Court, too, has made the point that where grave human rights violations have been committed, the obligation to investigate cannot be ignored or made conditional on domestic legal acts or provisions of any kind. Accordingly, the instant report outlines the inter-American standards on the subject of amnesty laws and jurisdiction of military courts.

22. The Commission has held that the right to the truth cannot be curtailed by, inter alia, legislative measures such as amnesty laws. The IACHR has consistently maintained that the enforcement of amnesty laws that restrict access to justice in cases of serious human rights violations has two adverse effects. First, it renders ineffective the States' obligation to respect and observe the rights and freedoms recognized in the American Declaration and the American Convention and their obligation to ensure the free and full exercise of those rights and freedoms to all persons subject to their jurisdiction, without any form of discrimination, as required under Article 1(1) of the ACHR. Second, it hampers access to information concerning the facts and circumstances surrounding the violation of a fundamental right, eliminates the most effective means of ensuring the exercise of human rights — i.e., the prosecution and punishment of those responsible — and prevents the exercise of the legal remedies available under domestic law.

b. Incompatibility and illegitimacy of the military criminal justice system in cases of human rights violations

23. The military criminal justice system has been another means used to limit access to justice in the case of victims of human rights violations and their next of kin and to restrict their right to know the truth. Here, the organs of the inter-American human rights system have repeatedly and consistently held that military courts may not exercise jurisdiction to investigate and punish cases of human rights violations.

24. In transitional contexts, the rights to freedom of expression and access to information are of heightened importance. The Commission has held that States have an obligation to guarantee that victims and their family members have access to information concerning the circumstances surrounding serious human rights violations. The Commission has held that States have an obligation to guarantee that victims and their family members have access to information concerning the circumstances surrounding serious human rights violations. Both the Commission and the Court have emphasized that the right to be informed of events and have access to information is a right enjoyed by society in general as it is essential to the development of democratic systems.

25. The obligation of access to information in cases of serious human rights violations generates a set of affirmative obligations. First, as to the relevant legal framework, the organs of the inter-American system have held that, in imposing a limitation, the State has an obligation to set out, in a formal and material law, written in clear and precise language, the reasons for restricting access to certain information.

26. Second, the State should provide for a simple, prompt and effective judicial remedy, which in the event that a public authority denies information, determines whether an infringement of the right to information of the applicant took place and, if so, orders the appropriate institution to provide the information. Third, the Court has established that State officials have an obligation to help compile the evidence so that the objectives of an investigation can be achieved; they also must refrain from engaging in acts that obstruct the investigative process.

27. Fourth, the Commission has also pointed out that State efforts to ensure access to information must include the opening of archives so that the institutions investigating an event can conduct direct inspections; searches of official installations and inventories; advancing search operations that include searches of the places where the information could be; and holding hearings and questioning those who could know where the information is or those who could reconstruct what occurred, and other measures.

28. Finally, the right of access to information imposes on States the duty to preserve and facilitate access to State archives when they exist, and to create and preserve them when they have not been compiled or organized as such. In the event of gross violations of human rights, the information these archives can bring together has an undeniable value and is indispensable not only for pushing investigations forward but also for preventing these aberrant actions from being repeated.

C. Right to the truth as a measure of reparation

29. Because it is an obligation of States that emanates from the guarantees of justice, the right to the truth is another form of reparation in cases of human rights violations. In fact, acknowledgement of the facts is important, because it constitutes a form of recognizing the significance and value of persons as individuals, as victims and as holders of rights. Furthermore, knowledge of the circumstances of manner, time and place, motives and the identification of the perpetrators are fundamental to making full reparations to victims of human rights violations.

D. Importance of the Truth Commissions for the inter-American system

30. Truth Commissions (hereinafter "TC") are "official, temporary, non-judicial fact-finding bodies that investigate a pattern of abuses of human rights or humanitarian law, usually committed over a number of years." Both the Commission and the Court have placed emphasis on the importance of TC as non-judicial mechanisms of transitional justice whose purpose is to shed light on situations involving systematic human rights violations on a mass scale. On numerous occasions, both bodies have used information contained in the TC final reports as a source of information and as evidence in cases under consideration in the case and petition system.

31. The IACHR has repeatedly stressed its support for initiatives to investigate and shed light on situations involving systematic violations of human rights. The Commission has, therefore, applauded the creation of TC in the region and stressed their importance as a means to guarantee the right to the truth in both the individual and collective sense.

32. Along this same line of thinking, the Inter-American Court has written that the creation of a TC is one of a number of important mechanisms that enable a State to fulfill its obligation to guarantee the right to know the truth of what happened. In effect, the Court has maintained that, depending on the object, procedure, structure, and purpose of their mandate, those Commissions may contribute to the construction and preservation of the historical memory, the elucidation of the facts, and the determination of institutional, social, and political responsibilities during specific historical periods of a society.

III. National experiences. States' initiatives to meet obligations emanating from the right to the truth

A. Judicial mechanisms

33. As is explained in this report, the organs of the Inter-American human rights system have established that the guarantee of the right to the truth as a corollary of the right to a fair trial, judicial protection and, depending on the particular circumstances of each case, the right to freedom of expression, requires the judiciary to investigate and shed light on human rights violations and overcome legal or de facto obstacles standing in the way of prosecuting those responsible. In that context, some countries of the region have taken significant steps in prosecuting cases of serious human rights and

IHL violations and, in many instances, the instituting or re-instituting of judicial proceedings has been a direct consequence of decisions and positions of the organs of the Inter-American human rights system through friendly settlements, country reports or IACHR case decisions and Inter-American Court judgments.

B. Truth Commissions

34. In conjunction with judicial proceedings, TC contribute to moving forward in the joint effort to flesh out the truth about human rights violations in light of the historic, social and political context. At the same time, the work of TC is one way to recognize and dignify victims' experiences; and a fundamental source of information for instituting and continuing with judicial proceedings, as well as for public policy-making and mechanism-building aimed at providing adequate reparation to victims. In this regard, it has been noted that successful truth commissions have made contributions such as recognizing the victims as equal rights holders, giving them a voice and empowering them; fostering general social integration; and providing important information for the other measures of transitional justice. Moreover, the Court has held that even though these commissions do not replace the State's obligation to establish the truth through judicial proceedings, they involve determinations of the truth that complement each other, because each has its own meaning and scope, as well as particular potentials and constraints that depend on the context in which they arise and the specific cases and circumstances they analyze.

C. Importance of other complementary initiatives

35. In view of the high degree of complexity of the phenomena of mass and systematic human rights violations, other initiatives have greatly aided States' efforts in guaranteeing the right to the truth in the broadest sense. These initiatives have contributed to shedding light on human rights violations and officially recognizing them as a measure of reparation for the victims and their next of kin, of commemoration and remembrance for society in general. Even though this report mainly focuses on examining States' efforts, the Commission also discusses the crucial role that has been played by the victims, their representatives and civil society organizations in seeking, contributing to, designing and implementing and engaging in a wide range of initiatives aimed at upholding and demanding respect for the right to the truth.

36. The tireless efforts of the victims, their family members, human rights defenders, and civil society organizations, who have demanded and continue to demand truth, justice and reparation in cases of human rights violations, must be highlighted. In addition to efforts to conduct and support investigations into these acts, the victims and their representatives, human rights defenders and civil society organizations have played a crucial role in pushing forward and supporting the necessary reform of laws, policies and practices to overcome obstacles to the right to the truth. While this examination is not held up as exhaustive, the report does spotlight examples of creative initiative and engaging a variety of segments of the population, which reflect the enforcement of human rights standards in the quest for the truth and justice.

37. Additionally, there have been initiatives in the region aimed at public reflection and keeping the memory alive of the mass and systematic human rights violations of the past, as well as dignification of the victims. These efforts include senior government officials publically recognizing guilt and apologizing for gross human rights violations, erecting museums, memorials, archives and monuments with a view to remembering and commemorating these violations.

IV. Conclusions and Recommendations

38. The States of the Americas have been pioneers in the adoption of different mechanisms to tackle situations involving grave, mass and systematic human rights violations. However, determined measures are still needed to resolve those situations, and create the mechanisms required to fully redress victims and strengthen the rule of law. In order to accomplish those objectives, the kinds of legal and de facto obstacles mentioned throughout this report must be removed. Accordingly, the IACHR reaffirms its commitment to cooperating with the States in seeking solutions to the problems identified herein.

39. Based on the content of this report, the IACHR is recommending that the States:

1. Redouble efforts to guarantee the right to the truth in cases of grave violations of human rights and IHL. Accordingly, the Commission is urging the States to review their domestic laws and other norms, strike down those provisions that di-

rectly or indirectly hamper their compliance with their international obligations and adopt laws that guarantee the right to the truth.

2. In particular, redouble efforts to prevent the phenomenon of forced disappearance of persons and set in motion the mechanisms necessary to ensure that it is codified as a criminal offense; clarify what happened to the victims; determine their whereabouts; identify the exhumed bodies; and return the remains to the next of kin in accordance with their wishes, as well as through adequate mechanisms to ensure their participation in the process. The Commission recommends that the States ratify the Inter-American Convention on Forced Disappearance of Persons and the International Convention for the Protection of All Persons from Enforced Disappearance.

3. Eliminate all the legal and de facto obstacles that obstruct the institution and/or pursuit of judicial proceedings concerning serious human rights violations, including any amnesty laws which have been adopted and remain on the books.

4. Eliminate the use of the military criminal justice system for cases involving human rights violations.

5. Take the measures necessary to ensure the collaboration of all State institutions in declassifying and providing information in the judicial or non-judicial investigative proceedings in progress or those instituted in the future. In the case of serious violations of human rights or IHL in transnational or regional contexts, States must make all possible efforts to cooperate in providing official information to other States seeking to investigate, prosecute and punish those violations.

6. Provide the necessary political, budgetary, and institutional support to the official non-judicial initiatives to ascertain the truth, such as Truth Commissions. Specifically, States must ensure appropriate conditions for a Truth Commission to be established and function properly, and must take appropriate measures to implement Truth Commissions' recommendations effectively and within a reasonable period of time.

7. Continue events to memorialize the victims, make apologies, and acknowledge responsibility for the commission of human rights violations.

8. Systematize the efforts undertaken to guarantee the truth and implement broad campaigns to publicize them and make the results achieved public.

9. Adopt the measures necessary to classify, systematize, preserve and make available historical archives concerning serious violations of human rights and IHL.

[end of Executive Summary]

CHAPTER I
INTRODUCTION

A. Relationship between democracy, human rights and truth

40. The organs of the inter-American human rights system have emphasized the intrinsic relationship that exists between democracy, and the observance of and respect for human rights. Some thirty years ago, the Inter-American Commission on Human Rights (hereinafter the "Inter-American Commission," the "Commission" or the "IACHR") wrote that an analysis of the human rights situation in the countries of the region "enables [it] to affirm that only by means of the effective exercise of [...] democracy can the observance of human rights be fully guaranteed."

41. Representative democracy is the form of political organization that the member States of the Organization of American States (hereinafter the "OAS") have explicitly adopted. In its principles, the OAS Charter provides that "[t]he solidarity of the American States and the high aims which are sought through it require the political organization of those States on the basis of the effective exercise of representative democracy." Furthermore, "representative democracy is an indispensable condition for the stability, peace and development of the region." The countries of the American hemisphere later recommitted themselves to democratic government by adopting the Inter-American Democratic Charter, which provides that "the peoples of the Americas have a right to democracy and their governments have an obligation to promote and defend it." That legal instrument reflects the efforts to promote and strengthen democracy and the

mechanisms implemented to prevent and respond to situations that affect the evolution of the democratic political institutional process.

42. The Inter-American Democratic Charter reaffirms that "the promotion and protection of human rights is a basic prerequisite for the existence of a democratic society" and stipulates the following: [e]ssential elements of representative democracy include, inter alia, respect for human rights and fundamental freedoms, access to and the exercise of power in accordance with the rule of law, the holding of periodic, free, and fair elections based on secret balloting and universal suffrage as an expression of the sovereignty of the people, the pluralistic system of political parties and organizations, and the separation of powers and independence of the branches of government

43. However, the history of countries in this hemisphere is strewn with multiple and repeated breaks with the democratic and institutional order, non-international armed conflicts, civil wars and situations involving widespread violence that lingered for long periods of time and that in some cases continue to this day. Given the circumstances, massive and systematic violations of human rights have been frequent, as have serious violations of international humanitarian law (hereinafter "IHL"), committed by agents of the State, private parties operating with a State's support, tolerance or acquiescence, and members of illegal armed groups.

44. The absence of complete, objective and truthful information about what transpired during those periods has been a constant, a policy of the State and even a "tactic of war," as in the case of the practice of forced disappearances. The Commission has observed that "[a] difficult problem that recent democracies have had to face has been the investigation of human rights violations under previous governments and the possibility of sanctions against those responsible for such violations."

45. Given the situation, the OAS member States have recognized the importance of respecting and guaranteeing the right to the truth, i.e.: the right of victims of gross violations of human rights and serious violations of international humanitarian law, and their families and society as a whole, to know the truth regarding such violations to the fullest extent practicable, in particular the identity of the perpetrators, the causes and facts of such violations, and the circumstances under which they occurred.

46. The OAS General Assembly, too, has underscored the need for the States to provide effective mechanisms for all society and, in particular, for the victims' family members to know the truth regarding manifest violations of human rights and international humanitarian law, by adopting suitable measures to identify victims, especially in cases of serious or systematic human rights violations.

B. The importance of the right to the truth

47. The right to the truth has emerged in response to the States' failure to clarify, investigate, prosecute and punish serious violations of human rights and of IHL. This failure has been examined both by the IACHR and by the Inter-American Court of Human Rights (hereinafter the "Inter-American Court" or the "Court"), and by various organs of other international systems for the protection of human rights.

48. Furthermore, the right to the truth is one of the pillars of the mechanisms of transitional justice, defined as "the full range of processes and mechanisms associated with a society's attempts to come to terms with a legacy of large-scale past abuses, in order to ensure accountability, serve justice and achieve reconciliation." In transitional contexts in particular, reaching at a complete, 49. It has been written that truth, justice, reparations and guarantees of non-recurrence serve the pursuit of two intermediate or medium-term goals (recognizing victims and fostering trust) and two final goals (contributing to reconciliation and strengthening the rule of law). Although these pillars are mutually complementary, each has its own content and scope. Hence, truth is no substitute for justice, reparations or guarantees of non-recurrence.

C. Objective, method and structure of the present report

50. In the present context, the purpose of this report is to support the inter-American system's efforts to disseminate the principles on the right to the truth by systematizing the applicable framework of laws and examining a number of experiences undertaken in the region. Likewise, this report will serve as a springboard for discussion with a view to consolidating and improving the States' laws, policies and practices for addressing this issue. In addition, through this report the

Commission is responding to the mandate that the OAS General Assembly entrusted to it in operative paragraph six of resolution AG/RES. 2175 (XXXVI-O/06) "Right to the truth."

51. This report is the product of the information that the Commission has analyzed concerning the evolution of the right to the truth in the Americas. To do this, the IACHR has drawn on information provided by the States and civil society in the public hearings held by the Commission and other international mechanisms that monitor human rights, the cases and petitions filed with the inter-American human rights system, and the country and thematic reports prepared by the Commission. Likewise, to identify principles in this area the Commission has also used international decisions and recommendations by specialized international organizations.

52. This report has four chapters. This introductory chapter examines the relationship between democracy, human rights and truth, and the importance of the right to the truth. It also describes the method used to prepare the report. In the second chapter, the Commission will explain the applicable legal framework, i.e., the inter-American system's norms and principles concerning the right to the truth. In the third chapter, the Commission will examine some initiatives undertaken by the States of the region, from the perspective of the principles and norms described in the second chapter. Finally, in chapter four, the Commission will offer pertinent conclusions and recommendations.

...

210. In the United States, in 2004, activists and community members decided to create the Greensboro Truth and Reconciliation Commission for the purpose of examining the context, the causes and the consequences of what had taken place, as well as making recommendations for the community to recover from the tragedy in Greensboro, North Carolina, on November 3, 1979.[395] According to the International Center for Transitional Justice, the report approved by the Commission in 2006 is taught at local universities and "offers a community [which was] divided by suspicion and denial, the opportunity to begin to solve difficult problems related to race, social class and politics."

...

CHAPTER IV
CONCLUSIONS AND RECOMMENDATIONS

236. In this report, the Commission has outlined the evolution and principles of the inter-American human rights system with respect to the right to the truth. It has also examined some of the initiatives taken by the region's States in this area. According to these principles, the right to the truth follows from a set of rights recognized in international human rights instruments and its protection essentially depends on whether judicial mechanisms are set in motion when grave violations of human rights and of IHL are committed. The guarantee of the right to the truth also necessitates a body of political and legal measures aimed at shedding light on the human rights violations, making reparation to the victims and strengthening democratic institutions. In all these endeavors, the participation of and coordination with the victims, their family members, human rights defenders, civil society organizations and the general public are essential.

237. Precisely because of their history, the States of the Americas have been pioneers in the adoption of different mechanisms to tackle situations involving grave, massive and systematic human rights violations. However, as explained over the course of this report, determined measures are still needed to resolve those situations, and create the mechanisms required to fully redress victims and strengthen the rule of law. In order to accomplish those objectives, the kinds of legal and de facto obstacles mentioned in this report must be removed.

238. The IACHR reaffirms its commitment to cooperating with the States in seeking solutions to the problems identified. Various measures taken by States to guarantee the right to truth in the region and the recognition of the difficulties involved in prosecuting serious human rights violations and violations of IHL reflect an understanding and recognition of the existing problems and a commitment to effectively tackle the obstacles that the victims of these violations are up against.

239. These recommendations are made with a view to cooperating with the States in the region in adopting the measures that will guarantee the right to the truth in the Americas. Based on the content of this report, the IACHR is recommending that the States:

1. Redouble efforts to guarantee the right to the truth in cases of grave violations of human rights and IHL. Accordingly, the Commission is urging the States to review their domestic laws and other norms, strike down those provisions that directly or indirectly hamper their compliance with their international obligations and adopt laws that guarantee the right to the truth.

2. In particular, redouble efforts to prevent the phenomenon of forced disappearance of persons and set in motion the mechanisms necessary to ensure that it is codified as a criminal offense; clarify what happened to the victims; determine their whereabouts; identify the exhumed bodies; and return the remains to the next of kin in accordance with their wishes, as well as through adequate mechanisms to ensure their participation in the process. The Commission recommends that the States ratify the Inter-American Convention on Forced Disappearance of Persons and the International Convention for the Protection of All Persons from Enforced Disappearance.

3. Eliminate all the legal and de facto obstacles that obstruct the institution and/or pursuit of judicial proceedings concerning serious human rights violations, including any amnesty laws adopted that remain on the books.

4. Eliminate the use of the military criminal justice system for cases involving human rights violations.

5. Take the measures necessary to ensure the collaboration of all State institutions in declassifying and providing information in the judicial or non-judicial investigative proceedings in progress or those instituted in the future. In the case of serious violations of human rights or IHL in transnational or regional contexts, States must make all possible efforts to cooperate in providing official information to States seeking to investigate, prosecute and punish those violations.

6. Provide the necessary political, budgetary, and institutional support to the official non-judicial initiatives to ascertain the truth, such as Truth Commissions. Specifically, States must ensure appropriate conditions for a Truth Commission to be established and function properly, and must take appropriate measures to implement Truth Commissions' recommendations effectively and within a reasonable period of time.

7. Continue events to memorialize the victims, make apologies, and acknowledge responsibility for the commission of human rights violations.

8. Systematize the efforts undertaken to guarantee the truth and implement broad campaigns to publicize them and make the results achieved public.

9. Adopt the measures necessary to classify, systematize, preserve and make available historical archives concerning serious violations of human rights and International Humanitarian Law.

Source: Inter-American Commission on Human Rights OEA/Ser.L/V/II.152 Doc. 2 13 August 2014
http://www.oas.org/en/iachr/reports/pdfs/right-to-truth-en.pdf

8. U.S. CONGRESSIONAL RESEARCH SERVICE INFORMING THE LEGISLATIVE DEBATE SINCE 1914, ORGANIZATION OF AMERICAN STATES: BACKGROUND AND ISSUES FOR CONGRESS

The following document was prepared by the U.S. Congressional research service by a specialist on the O.A.S. to give members of Congress and certain others parts of the government information on which to base U.S. policy and budgeting.

{Executive Summary and Excerpts}

Peter J. Meyer
Analyst in Latin American Affairs August 22, 2016

Summary

The Organization of American States (OAS) is the oldest multilateral regional organization in the world. It was founded in 1948 by the United States and 20 Latin American nations to serve as a forum for addressing issues of mutual concern. Over time, the organization expanded to include all 35 independent countries of the Western Hemisphere (though Cuba currently does not participate). The organization's areas of focus have also shifted over time, evolving in accordance with the priorities of its member states. Today, the OAS concentrates on four broad objectives: democracy promotion, human rights protection, economic and social development, and regional security cooperation. It carries out a wide variety of activities to advance these goals, often providing policy guidance and technical assistance to member states.

U.S. Policy

Since the organization's foundation, the United States has sought to use the OAS to advance critical economic, political, and security objectives in the Western Hemisphere. Although OAS actions frequently reflected U.S. policy during the 20th century, this has changed to a certain extent over the past 15 years as Latin American and Caribbean governments have adopted more independent foreign policies. While the organization's goals and day-to-day activities are still generally consistent with U.S. policy toward the region, the United States' ability to advance its policy initiatives within the OAS has declined. Nevertheless, the United States has remained the organization's largest donor, contributing at least $58.5 million in FY2015—equivalent to nearly 42% of the total 2015 OAS budget.

As OAS decisions have begun to reflect the increasing independence of its member states, U.S. policymakers occasionally have expressed concerns about the direction of the organization. In recent years, some Members of Congress have criticized the OAS for failing to address the erosion of democratic institutions in some member states and have argued that the United States should withhold funding until the organization changes. Others maintain that the OAS remains an important forum for advancing U.S. relations with the other nations of the hemisphere and that U.S. policy should seek to strengthen the organization and make it more effective. Congressional Action Congress plays an important role in shaping U.S. policy toward the OAS. The FY2016 Consolidated Appropriations Act (P.L. 114-113) provided funding for the U.S. assessed contribution (membership dues) to the organization as well as $6.4 million in voluntary contributions to support democracy and development programs. Congress is now considering FY2017 appropriations measures.

...

Over the past several years, there has been considerable congressional debate over the role of the Organization of American States (OAS) in the Western Hemisphere and its utility for advancing U.S. objectives in the region. The United States helped found the OAS in 1948 in order to establish a multilateral forum in which the nations of the hemisphere could engage one another and address issues of mutual concern. In subsequent decades, OAS decisions often reflected U.S. policy as other member states sought to maintain close relations with the dominant economic and political power in the hemisphere. This was especially true during the early Cold War period, when the United States was able to secure OAS support for initiatives that were controversial in the region, such as a 1962 resolution to exclude Cuba from active participation as a result of its adherence to Marxism-Leninism and association with the communist bloc. OAS actions again aligned closely with U.S. policy in the 1990s following the end of the Cold War as a result of strong consensus among member states in support of initiatives designed to liberalize markets and strengthen democratic governance.

U.S. policymakers have responded to the United States' declining ability to advance its policy preferences within the OAS in a number of ways. Some Members of Congress contend that the OAS is failing in its mission to support democracy and human rights in Latin America. They have called on the U.S. government to use its influence in the organization to compel stronger action on these issues and occasionally have sought to withhold funding from the organization. Others argue that OAS actions continue to closely align with U.S. priorities in many cases and that defunding the OAS would amount to the United States turning its back on the Western Hemisphere. They have called for reforms to the OAS to make the organization more effective in carrying out its mission.

...

Current Priorities In 2014, the [OAS] General Assembly adopted a "Strategic Vision of the OAS," which reiterates that the four core pillars of the organization's mission are:

- strengthening democracy;
- promoting and protecting human rights;
- advancing integral development; and
- fostering multidimensional security.

Those priorities are relatively consistent with the Obama Administration's approach to the Western Hemisphere, which seeks to strengthen democracy and human rights, improve security and the rule of law, and promote prosperity and inclusive growth for all citizens of the region.

...

Human Rights Protection

Many analysts consider the inter-American human rights system to be the most effective part of the OAS. Unlike most of the organization's bodies, the Inter-American Commission on Human Rights (IACHR) and the Inter-American Court of Human Rights are autonomous, allowing them to execute their mandates to promote and protect human rights without needing to establish consensus among member states on every action. Consequently, advocates maintain, the two bodies are able to take on the "pivotal role of condemnation and early warning in response to situations that undermine the consolidation of democracy and rule of law" in the hemisphere.

In the first decades after its 1959 inception, the IACHR's documentation of human rights violations brought international attention to the abuses of repressive regimes. Although the human rights situation in the hemisphere has improved significantly as countries have transitioned away from dictatorships to democratic governments, the IACHR continues to play a significant role. Among other actions, the IACHR receives, analyzes, and investigates individual petitions alleging human rights violations. It received nearly 2,200 such petitions in 2015. It also issues requests to governments to adopt "precautionary measures" in certain cases where individuals or groups are at risk of suffering serious and irreparable harm to their human rights. The IACHR receives several hundred petitions for precautionary measures annually, and in 2015, it issued requests to governments in 38 cases. Additionally, the IACHR observes the general human rights situations in member states, conducting on-site visits to carry out in-depth analyses; publishing special reports when warranted; and noting in its annual report which countries' human rights situations deserve special attention, follow-up, and monitoring. In its most recent annual report (issued in March 2016 and covering 2015), the IACHR made special note of the human rights situations in Cuba, Guatemala, and Venezuela.

Since 1990, the IACHR has created rapporteurships to draw attention to emerging human rights issues and certain groups that are particularly at risk of human rights violations due to vulnerability and discrimination. There are currently 10 rapporteurships, which focus on freedom of expression; human rights defenders; economic, social, and cultural rights; and the rights of women, children, indigenous peoples, afro-descendants, prisoners, migrants, and lesbian, gay, bisexual, trans, and intersex (LGBTI) persons. These rapporteurships, particularly the Special Rapporteur for Freedom of Expression, have proven effective in drawing attention to potential abuses. The Inter-American Court of Human Rights, created in 1979, is an autonomous judicial institution charged with interpreting and applying the American Convention on Human Rights. Currently, 20 OAS member states accept the court's jurisdiction; the United States does not. According to a number of analysts, the Inter-American Court has played an important role in the development of international human rights case law, securing justice for individual victims while facilitating structural changes to prevent future violations. In 2014, for example, the Inter-American Court ruled that the Dominican Republic discriminated against Dominicans of Haitian descent and violated their rights to a nationality by expelling them from the country. The ruling ordered the Dominican government to provide legal documentation and financial compensation to the victims that brought the case, and to annul any law that deprives individuals born in the Dominican Republic from receiving Dominican citizenship.

Issues for Congress

Congress plays an important role in determining U.S. policy toward the OAS. As noted previously, the United States provided nearly 42% of the organization's funding in FY2015.

...

Policy issues that have drawn particular interest from some Members of Congress in recent years include the application of the Inter-American Democratic Charter, challenges to the inter-American human rights system, the management and budget of the OAS, the potential reintegration of Cuba into the inter-American system, and the rise of alternative regional organizations.

...

Challenges to the Inter-American Human Rights System

Background Despite the inter-American human rights system's reputation as one of the most effective parts of the OAS, it has faced a number of challenges in recent years. In June 2011, the Permanent Council established the "Special Working Group to Reflect on the Workings of the Inter-American Commission on Human Rights with a View to Strengthening the Inter-American System for the Protection of Human Rights." Although the special working group was ostensibly established to strengthen the inter-American human rights system, some civil society groups feared it would do the opposite. The impetus for the working group's creation — Brazil's negative reaction to an IACHR precautionary measure request — suggested that the review might be more focused on constraining the actions of the commission than supporting it. Some member states' presentations to the special working group reinforced this perception. They included calls to adopt more stringent criteria for granting precautionary measures, shift the focus of the IACHR's work away from individual cases toward general human rights promotion, remove the independent budget and staff of the Special Rapporteur for Freedom of Expression, and end the practice of identifying countries that have human rights situations that deserve special attention in the IACHR's annual report.

The special working group issued a report in December 2011 that provoked a mixed reaction in the hemisphere. While civil society groups welcomed some aspects of the report, they asserted that other portions "could trigger a process of weakening the inter-American human rights system." The report recognized that autonomy and independence are essential for the IACHR to carry out its mission, recommended that member states adopt the inter-American human rights treaties to assure the universality of the system, and called on the OAS to gradually increase the resources allocated to the human rights bodies. At the same time, the report included some member state suggestions that human rights defenders viewed as problematic. Despite these concerns, the 2012 General Assembly approved a resolution that welcomed the special working group's report, and instructed the Permanent Council to draw up proposals for its application to be presented to a special session of the General Assembly. The United States attached a footnote to the resolution that indicated it would not block consensus, but asserted that no efforts should be undertaken to force the implementation of the nonbinding recommendations.

The IACHR effectively vetoed the reform recommendations that human rights groups had viewed as most problematic by adopting a series of relatively minor changes to its rules of procedure, policies, and practices. Although countries such as Bolivia, Ecuador, and Venezuela tried to override the IACHR's decisions and push through more radical changes at a special session of the General Assembly in March 2013, the vast majority of OAS member states rejected the attempt. Subsequent efforts to push through extensive changes to the IACHR have also been rejected.

More recently, the IACHR has struggled to secure the resources necessary to carry out its mission. After warning member states for several months that it was facing a severe financial shortfall, the IACHR issued a press release in May 2016 noting that the commission would be suspending a number of its activities and would lose 40% of its personnel on July 31, 2016, unless it received an influx of additional funding. The IACHR receives roughly half of its annual funding from voluntary contributions, which fell from $6.2 million in 2013 to $2.9 million as of May 2016.

...

Policy Considerations

Members of Congress frequently have expressed support for the inter-American human rights system. In S. Rept. 114-79, for example, the Senate Appropriations Committee noted "the important role of the IACHR and the Inter-American Court of Human Rights in providing access to justice for victims of human rights violations." Congress also appropriated a $2 million voluntary contribution to the IACHR in FY2016 through the Consolidated Appropriations Act, 2016 (P.L. 114-113). The report (S.Rept. 114-290) accompanying the Senate Appropriations Committee's FY2017 foreign operations appropriations bill (S. 3117) recognizes the current budgetary challenges facing the IACHR and recommends a $7 million voluntary contribution for the commission. Despite these demonstrations of support for the IACHR, some analysts argue that the United States lacks credibility in defending the human rights body given its unwillingness to ratify the hemisphere's human rights treaties. The United States has signed only one such treaty—the American Convention on Human Rights. Although the Carter Administration submitted the treaty to the Senate for its advice and consent in 1978 (Treaty Doc. 95-21), the Senate has never approved ratification. Moreover, while the United States is currently subject to the jurisdiction of the IACHR under the American Declaration of the Rights and Duties of Man (adopted in 1948 alongside the OAS Charter), the U.S. government argues that the declaration does not create legally binding obligations. The reluctance of the United States and several other nations to ratify the American Convention has created a multi-tiered human rights system in the hemisphere that the IACHR and many OAS member states view as problematic.

Given these criticisms, some analysts argue that the United States could better assert leadership on human rights issues in the hemisphere by ratifying the various inter-American human rights treaties. A resolution introduced in May 2015 (H.Res. 285, Lewis) would express the sense of the House of Representatives that "the United States should fully support the Inter-American human rights system" and ratify hemispheric conventions. While subjecting the United States to the same legally binding obligations that the majority of the nations of the hemisphere already accept would likely increase U.S. credibility on the issue, some policymakers have raised concerns about potential conflicts with U.S. law and international interference in U.S. domestic affairs.

Alternatively, some observers contend that the U.S. government could demonstrate greater support for the inter-American human rights system by doing more to act on the IACHR's criticisms of various U.S. policies and its recommendations for improving human rights in the United States. The IACHR has issued recommendations to the United States in 22 cases over the past 11 years; as of 2015, the United States was in full compliance in 1 case, partial compliance in 10 cases, and noncompliance in 11 cases. If the U.S. government opts not to improve its compliance with IACHR recommendations, it will likely continue to face criticism from some in the hemisphere that it uses the IACHR to promote its interests without assuming any obligations.

Source: Congressional Research Service, 7-5700 www.crs.gov, R42639

9. ORGANIZATION OF AMERICAN STATES INTER-AMERICAN COMMISSION ON HUMAN RIGHTS TOWARDS THE CLOSURE OF GUANTÁNAMO

One of the crucial and contentious issues before the Inter-American Commission has been the U.S. waging of the so-called "War on Terror" and compliance with the O.A.S. human rights norms, particularly regarding the issue of detentions in Guantánamo, Cuba. Briefly stated, the position of the Inter-American Commission is that most if not all of the detentions are in violation of the norms of the ADHR as to prolonged and arbitrary arrest and detention and access to justice, and that the facility should be closed. The Commission has always held that what goes on in Guantánamo is within the human rights scope of the ADHR, as well as international humanitarian law. Following this report is the U.S. government's response to it.

Executive Summary

1. This report addresses the human rights situation of detainees held at the U.S. Naval Base in Guantánamo Bay, Cuba, a facility that has become a symbol of abuse around the world. The Inter-American Commission on Human Rights ("IACHR") was the first international instance to call upon the United States to take urgent steps to respect the basic

rights of the detainees. Just two months after the arrival of the first prisoners in January of 2002, the IACHR called upon the State to ensure that their legal status would be determined by a competent authority, so as to clarify the applicable legal regime and corresponding rights.

2. Since then, the IACHR has closely followed the situation through different mechanisms and has repeatedly called for the immediate closure of the detention facility. As a further and hopefully final step in the monitoring of the situation, the IACHR issues this report in which it provides an assessment of the current situation from a human rights perspective as the basis to issue recommendations designed to assist the State in taking the steps necessary to close the facility.

3. The report, following a rights-based approach, focuses on three main areas of concern. First, it addresses the major issues surrounding the detainees' right to personal integrity, from the authorized use of torture in the early years of the Guantánamo detentions to more current issues such as prison conditions at Camp 7 and the U.S. Government's response to the hunger strikes. The IACHR reiterates its finding that the continuing and indefinite detention of individuals in Guantánamo, without the right to due process, is arbitrary and constitutes a clear violation of international law; reasons of public security cannot serve as a pretext for the indefinite detention of individuals without charge or trial.

4. The report then examines the detainees' access to justice and whether the judicial remedies available are adequate and effective. It analyses important questions that were left unresolved by the landmark decision of the U.S. Supreme Court in Boumediene v. Bush, such as the scope of the executive's authority to detain individuals under the Authorization for the Use of Military Force (AUMF) as well as various substantive and procedural questions. The Commission outlines concerns with respect to the operation of presumptions and burdens of proof and their impact on access to effective remedies.

5. This chapter also assesses how military commissions operate in practice and the important challenges faced by detainees when exercising their right to legal representation. It further addresses the exclusive application of a separate regime to foreign Muslim men, an issue that presents an apparent targeting of individuals in relation to nationality, ethnicity and religion. In addition, this chapter analyses the functioning of the Periodic Review Board process established in 2011 as well as Inter-American Commission on Human Rights Towards the Closure of Guantánamo the lack of judicial review of claims relating to conditions of detention at Guantánamo.

6. Finally, the report looks at the various legal and political aspects involved in taking steps toward the closure of the detention facility and acknowledges some recent steps taken by the Executive. This chapter assesses the current situation of the three categories of detainees currently held at Guantánamo: detainees cleared for transfer; detainees facing criminal charges before military commissions; and detainees designated for continued detention. The IACHR analyzes the situation of the detainees from Yemen separately, an issue which is of key importance in the closure of the facility. It further elaborates on how transfers should be carried out in order to comply with international legal obligations and the principle of nonrefoulement. This chapter then analyzes the current state of proceedings before military commissions, a system that has proven to be slow, inefficient and out of line with due process guarantees.

7. The report concludes with some data that speaks for itself. According to official information, only 8% of Guantánamo detainees were characterized as "fighters" for Al-Qaeda or the Taliban; 93% were not captured by U.S. forces; and most were turned over to U.S. custody at a time in which the United States offered bounties for the capture of suspected terrorists. Only 1% of all prisoners ever held at Guantánamo have so far been convicted by a military commission; in two of those eight cases the material support conviction was overturned on appeal by federal courts. As of January 2015, the handful of ongoing prosecutions before military commissions remained stagnant at the pre-trial stage, having been in that stage for several years.

8. Based on its close analysis of the human rights situation of detainees held at Guantánamo Bay, in this report the IACHR issues a series of recommendations in order to encourage the United States to properly fulfill its international human rights commitments in taking the steps necessary to close Guantánamo. The Inter-American Commission also reiterates its call upon OAS Member States to consider receiving Guantánamo detainees in an effort to achieve the goal of closing the prison and to reaffirm the longstanding tradition of asylum and protection of refugees in the region. The recommendations are grouped following the same rights-based approach used in the analysis of the report.

9. With regard to the conditions of detention, the Inter-American Commission recommends that the United States ensure that detainees are held in accordance with international human rights standards; that conditions of detention are subject to accessible and effective judicial review; that detainees are provided with adequate medical, psychiatric and psychological care; and that their right to freedom of conscience and religion is respected. The Commission further recommends that the U.S. declassify all evidence of torture and ill-treatment; comply with the recommendations issued by the Committee Against Torture regarding the investigation of detainee abuse, redress for victims, and the end of the force-feeding of detainees; and establish an independent monitoring body to investigate the conditions of detention at Guantánamo Bay.

10. Concerning access to justice, the IACHR requests the United States to try detainees facing prosecution before military commissions in federal courts; ensure detainees' access to a proper judicial review of the legality of their detention; provide detainees and their counsel with all evidence used to justify the detention; and guarantee that attorney-client privilege is respected. The Commission also asks that Courts hearing such cases undertake a rigorous examination of the Government's evidence to ensure that any detention in this context is based on clear and convincing evidence.

11. Finally, the Inter-American Commission reiterates its call for the closure of Guantánamo. In order to fulfill this goal, the Commission recommends repealing the National Defense Authorization Act (NDAA) provisions that prohibit the transfer of Guantánamo detainees to the United States for prosecution, incarceration, and medical treatment; expediting the Periodic Review Board process; and accelerating detainees' transfers to their countries of origin or third countries in accordance with the principle of non-refoulement. The Commission further calls upon the United States Government to review the situation of the Yemeni detainees on an individual case-by-case basis; transfer detainees facing prosecution to the United States to be tried in federal courts; and transfer convicted detainees to federal prisons to serve the remainder of their sentences.

Source: Inter-American Commission on Human Rights OEA OAS/Ser.L/V/II. Doc. 20/15 3 June 2015
http://www.oas.org/en/iachr/reports/pdfs/Towards-Closure-Guantánamo.pdf

10. SUBMISSION OF THE GOVERNMENT OF THE UNITED STATES TO THE INTER-AMERICAN COMMISSION ON HUMAN RIGHTS WITH RESPECT TO THE DRAFT REPORT ON THE CLOSURE OF GUANTÁNAMO

Following is a letter from the U.S. State Department representative of the U.S. government in 2015, concerning the above Commission report being prepared about the U.S. and the Commission's position regarding detentions of persons at, and closure of, Guantánamo. It examines the continuing detentions in light of the norms of the ADHR.

Introduction

The Government of the United States appreciates the opportunity to comment on the draft report "Towards the Closure of Guantánamo." We appreciate the Commission's extensive efforts in preparing this draft report. The United States respects and supports the Commission and the strong sense of integrity and independence that historically has characterized its work. This response aims at assisting the Commission by providing general views of the United States on several of the matters addressed in the Commission's draft report. The lack of any specific objection to particular legal or factual propositions in the draft report should not be read as agreement with such propositions. In order to frame our substantive response to the Commission's draft report, we believe it important to offer some reflections on the legal framework the Commission has used in its discussion and analysis of U.S. law of war detention operations at Guantánamo. Subsequently, we will provide comments regarding the discussion of particular issues in the report.

Relevant International Legal Framework

All U.S. military detention operations conducted at Guantánamo Bay are carried out in accordance with the law of armed conflict, also known as the "law of war" or international humanitarian law (IHL), including Common Article 3 of the Geneva Conventions of 1949, and all other applicable international and domestic laws.

The detainees who remain at the Guantánamo Bay detention facility continue to be detained lawfully, both as a matter of international law and under U.S. domestic law. As a matter of international law, the United States is engaged not in a "war on terrorism," as characterized in the draft report, but in an ongoing armed conflict with al-Qaida, the Taliban, and associated forces. As part of this conflict, the United States has captured and detained enemy belligerents, and is permitted under the law of war to hold them until the end of hostilities. Further, as a matter of domestic law, this detention is authorized by the 2001 Authorization for Use of Military Force (AUMF) (U.S. Public Law 107-40), as informed by the laws of war. We object to the finding that U.S. detention operations at Guantánamo constitute arbitrary detention in violation of applicable international law. In both international and non-international armed conflicts, a State may detain enemy belligerents consistent with the law of armed conflict until the end of hostilities, and such detention is not arbitrary.

During situations of armed conflict, the law of war is the *lex specialis* and, as such, is the controlling body of law with regard to the conduct of hostilities and the protection of war victims. The law of war and international human rights law contain many provisions that complement one another and are in many respects mutually reinforcing. Further, despite the general presumption that specific law of war rules govern the entire process of planning and executing military operations in armed conflict, certain provisions of human rights treaties may apply in armed conflicts. For example, the obligations to prevent torture and cruel, inhuman, or degrading treatment or punishment in the Convention Against Torture (CAT) remain applicable in times of armed conflict and are reinforced by complementary prohibitions in the law of war. As our response in Section IV further demonstrates, the United States is fully committed to ensuring that individuals it detains in any armed conflict are treated humanely in all circumstances, consistent with applicable U.S. treaty obligations, U.S. domestic law, and U.S. policy.

The United States notes that many of the sources referred to by the Inter-American Commission do not give rise to binding legal obligations on the United States or are not within the Commission's mandate to apply with respect to the United States. The United States has undertaken a political commitment to uphold the American Declaration of the Rights and Duties of Man ("American Declaration"), a non-binding instrument that does not itself create legal rights or impose legal obligations on signatory states.

Article 20 of the Statute of the Inter-American Commission on Human Rights ("IACHR Statute") sets forth the powers of the Commission that relate specifically to OAS member States that, like the United States, are not parties to the legally binding American Convention on Human Rights ("American Convention"), including to pay particular attention to observance of certain enumerated human rights set forth in the American Declaration, to examine communications and make recommendations to the State, and to verify whether in such cases domestic legal procedures and remedies have been applied and exhausted. Further, the United States reiterates its understanding that the Commission lacks the authority to issue precautionary measures to a non-State Party to the American Convention.

Accordingly, we continue to have concerns about the jurisdictional competence of the Commission with respect to the United States and the law of war. Moreover, the Commission has cited jurisprudence of the Inter-American Court of Human Rights ("Inter-American Court") interpreting the American Convention. The United States has not accepted the jurisdiction of the Inter-American Court, nor, as previously noted, is it party to the American Convention. Accordingly, the jurisprudence of the Inter-American Court interpreting the Convention does not govern U.S. commitments under the American Declaration. Likewise, advisory opinions of the Inter-American Court interpreting other international agreements, such as the International Covenant on Civil and Political Rights (ICCPR), are not relevant.

Overview of United States' Efforts and Accomplishments
Regarding Guantánamo Closure

The United States continues to work toward the goal of closing the detention facility at Guantánamo Bay, a process that started under the Bush Administration, and is working assiduously to reduce the detainee population at Guantánamo and to close the facility in a responsible manner that protects national security. President Obama has repeatedly reaffirmed this commitment, including in his State of the Union Address in January 2015; he has stated that closing the detention facility at Guantánamo is a national security imperative and that its continued operation weakens our national security by draining resources, damaging our relationships with key allies and partners, and emboldening violent extremists. On January 22, 2009, President Obama signed Executive Order (E.O.) 13492, which ordered the closure of the detention facility at Guantánamo Bay. Pursuant to that order, the Department of Justice coordinated a special Guantánamo Review Task Force, which was established to review comprehensively information in the possession of the U.S. Government about the detainees in order to determine the appropriate disposition— transfer, prosecution, or other lawful disposition—for each of the 240 detainees subject to the review. It is important to note that a decision to designate a detainee for transfer does not reflect a decision that the detainee poses no threat, nor does it equate to a judgment that the U.S. Government lacks legal authority to hold the detainee. Rather, the decision reflects the best predictive judgment of senior government officials, based on the available information, that any threat posed by the detainee can be sufficiently mitigated through feasible and appropriate security measures in the receiving country. The United States continues to have legal authority to hold Guantánamo detainees in law of war detention until the end of hostilities, consistent with U.S. law and applicable international law, but has elected, as a policy matter, to ensure that it holds them no longer than necessary to mitigate the threat posed.

Subsequently, after working through numerous, complex issues associated with building a comprehensive process, the Periodic Review Board (PRB) process commenced in October 2013. The PRB consists of senior national security officials from the Departments of Defense, Homeland Security, Justice, and State, as well as from the Office of the Chairman of the Joint Chiefs of Staff and the Office of the Director of National Intelligence. The PRB process is a discretionary, administrative, interagency process that is reviewing the status of detainees at Guantánamo Bay to determine whether continued detention remains necessary to protect against a continuing significant threat to the security of the United States. In this way, the United States will ensure that any continued detention is carefully evaluated and justified. The PRB process thus makes an important contribution toward the Administration's goal of closing the Guantánamo Bay detention facility by ensuring a principled and sustainable process for reviewing the current circumstances and intelligence, and identifying whether additional detainees may be designated for transfer.

The PRB has conducted fourteen full hearings and three six-month file reviews. Eight of the full hearings have resulted in a final determination that law of war detention is no longer necessary, and one hearing is still pending a final determination.

Since 2002, more than 640 detainees have departed Guantánamo Bay to more than 40 countries, including OAS Member States. The United States is grateful to these governments for their support for U.S. efforts to close the Guantánamo Bay detention facility. All told, more than 80 percent of those at one time held at the Guantánamo Bay facility have been repatriated or resettled, including all detainees subject to final court orders directing their release. Of the 242 detainees at Guantánamo at the beginning of the Obama Administration, 116 have been transferred out of the facility. In 2014, 28 detainees were transferred from the facility, more than in any year since 2009. As of March 27, 2015, 122 detainees remain at the Guantánamo Bay detention facility, the lowest number since the initial weeks after the facility was opened. Of these, 56 are eligible for transfer, 10 are being prosecuted or have been convicted, with 2 currently awaiting sentencing, and the remaining 56 will be reviewed by the PRB.

Responses to Particular Issues Raised

A. Conditions of Detention

1. Prohibition on Torture and Cruel, Inhuman, or Degrading Treatment or Punishment
It is the clear position of the United States that torture and cruel treatment are categorically prohibited under domestic and international law, including human rights law and the law of armed conflict. The United States has taken important steps to ensure adherence to its legal obligations, establishing laws and procedures to strengthen the safeguards against torture and cruel treatment. For example, E.O. 13491, issued by President Obama during his first days in office, directs that, consistent with the Convention Against Torture and Common Article 3 of the 1949 Geneva Conventions, as well as U.S. law, any individual detained in armed conflict by the United States or within a facility owned, operated, or controlled by the United States, in all circumstances, must be treated humanely and must not be tortured or subjected to cruel, inhuman, or degrading treatment or punishment. The Executive Order also directs that no individual in U.S. custody in any armed conflict "shall . . . be subjected to any interrogation technique or approach, or any treatment related to interrogation, that is not authorized by and listed in Army Field Manual 2-22.3." The manual explicitly prohibits threats, coercion, and physical abuse. Interrogations undertaken in compliance with the Army Field Manual are consistent with U.S. domestic and international legal obligations. E.O. 13491 also revoked all previous executive directives

that were inconsistent with the Order, provided that no officer, employee, or agent of the U.S. Government could rely on any interpretation of the law governing interrogation issued by the Department of Justice between September 11, 2001, and January 20, 2009, and created a Special Task Force on Interrogations and Transfer Policies, which helped strengthen U.S. policies so that individuals transferred to other countries would not be subjected to torture.

The United States does not permit its personnel to engage in acts of torture or cruel, inhuman, or degrading treatment or punishment of any person in its custody either within or outside U.S. territory. As the United States recently reaffirmed in its presentation before the U.N. Committee Against Torture in November 2014, torture and cruel, inhuman, or degrading treatment or punishment are prohibited at all times in all places.

The Commission's draft report references the release of the declassified Executive Summary, Findings, and Conclusions of the Senate Select Committee on Intelligence Study of the Central Intelligence Agency's Detention and Interrogation Program ("SSCI Report"). The SSCI Report contains a review of a program that included interrogation methods used on terrorism suspects in secret facilities at locations outside of both the United States and Guantánamo Bay. Harsh interrogation techniques highlighted in that Report are not representative of how the United States deals with the threat of terrorism today, and are not consistent with our values. In E.O. 13491, President Obama prohibited the use of those techniques and ended the detention and interrogation program described in the SSCI Report. President Obama also determined that the Executive Summary, Findings, and Conclusions of the SSCI Report should be declassified, with appropriate redactions necessary to protect national security, because public scrutiny, debate, and transparency will help to inform the public's understanding of the program to ensure that the United States never resorts to these kinds of interrogation techniques again.

2. Accountability
The Department of Defense, the Central Intelligence Agency (CIA), the Department of Justice, and others have conducted numerous independent, rigorous investigations into detainee treatment, detention policy, and conditions of confinement since the September 11 attacks.

Reports have been issued by, among others, the Inspectors General of the Army, Navy, and CIA; Major General Ryder, the General Officer appointed by the Commander, U.S. Southern Command, for the purpose of investigating conditions of detention; an independent panel led by former Secretary of Defense James Schlesinger; the Senate Armed Services Committee; and the Senate Select Committee on Intelligence. For the sake of transparency and accountability, many of these reports were released to the public, to the extent consistent with national security and other applicable U.S. law and policy. These investigations led to hundreds of recommendations on ways to improve detention and interrogation operations, and the Department of Defense and the CIA have instituted processes to address these recommendations.

The U.S. military is, and has always been, required to investigate every credible allegation of abuse by U.S. forces in order to determine the facts, including identifying those responsible for any violation of law, policy, or procedures. The Department of Defense has multiple accountability mechanisms in place to ensure that personnel adhere to law and policy associated with military operations and detention.

The Department of Justice conducted preliminary reviews and criminal investigations into the treatment of individuals alleged to have been mistreated while in U.S. Government custody subsequent to the September 2001 terrorist attacks, brought criminal prosecutions in several cases, and obtained the conviction of a CIA contractor and a Department of Defense contractor for abusing detainees in their custody. Further, in August 2009, the Department of Justice commenced a preliminary review of the treatment of 101 persons alleged to have been mistreated while in U.S. Government custody subsequent to the September 11 attacks. That review, led by Assistant United States Attorney John Durham, who is a career federal prosecutor, generated two criminal investigations.

The Department of Justice ultimately declined those cases for prosecution consistent with the Principles of Federal Prosecution, which require that each case be evaluated for a clear violation of a federal criminal statute with provable facts that reflect evidence of guilt beyond a reasonable doubt and a reasonable probability of conviction.

With respect to accountability for legal advice, the conduct of two senior Department of Justice officials in giving legal advice that justified the use of certain "enhanced interrogation techniques" following the September 11 attacks was reviewed by an Associate Deputy Attorney General, a longtime career Department of Justice official. In a 69-page January 5, 2010 memorandum subsequently released publicly with limited redactions, he found that they had narrowly construed the torture statute, often failed to expose countervailing arguments, and overstated the certainty of their conclusions. He concluded that although they had exercised poor judgment, the evidence did not establish that they had engaged in professional misconduct.

3. Camp 7 Conditions

All U.S. military detention operations conducted in connection with armed conflict, including at Guantánamo Bay, are carried out in accordance with international humanitarian law, including Common Article 3 of the Geneva Conventions, and all other 7 applicable international and domestic laws. Camp 7 is a climate-controlled, single-cell facility currently used to house a small group of special detainees at Guantánamo captured during operations in the war against al-Qaida, the Taliban, and associated forces. The transfer of these detainees to Guantánamo Bay was announced in 2006. Individuals in this group are accused of plotting the September 11 attacks on the United States, the attack on the USS COLE, and various other attacks that have taken the lives of innocent civilians around the world. Facilities at Camp 7 or at any of the other camps are routinely maintained for habitability, which would include repairing or replacing equipment, plumbing, or structures in the interest of humane treatment consistent with applicable treatment standards.

The Department of Defense has been working closely with the International Committee of the Red Cross to facilitate increased opportunities for high-value Guantánamo detainees to communicate with their families. The addition of near-realtime communication is another step in the Department of Defense's efforts to assess continually and, where practicable and consistent with security requirements, improve conditions of confinement for detainees in its custody. The Department of Defense has concluded that increasing family contact for the high-value detainees can be done in a manner that is consistent with both humanitarian and security interests.

4. Role of Health Professionals

The Joint Medical Group at Guantánamo is committed to providing appropriate and comprehensive medical care to all detainees. The healthcare provided to the detainees being held at the Guantánamo Bay detention facility is comparable to that which our own service personnel receive while serving at Joint Task Force-Guantánamo. Detainees receive timely, compassionate, quality health care and have regular access to primary care and specialty physicians.

U.S. practice is consistent with principle No. 2 of the non-binding Principles of Medical Ethics relevant to the Role of Health Personnel in the Protection of Prisoners and Detainees against Torture and Other Cruel, Inhuman or Degrading Treatment or Punishment. Department of Defense physicians and health care personnel charged with providing care to detainees take their responsibility for the health of detainees very seriously. DoD Instruction 2310.08E, "Medical Program Support for Detainee Operations," June 6, 2006, states: "Health care personnel charged with the medical care of detainees have a duty to protect detainees' physical and mental health and provide appropriate treatment for disease. To the extent practicable, treatment of detainees should be guided by professional judgments and standards similar to those applied to personnel of the U.S. Armed Forces."

Military physicians, psychologists, and other health care personnel are held to the highest standards of ethical care and at no time have been released from their ethical obligations.

Department of Defense policy authorizes health care personnel qualified in behavioral sciences to provide consultative services to support authorized law enforcement or intelligence activities, including observation and advice on the interrogation of detainees when the interrogations are fully in accordance with applicable law and interrogation policy. These behavioral science consultants are not involved in the medical treatment of detainees and do not access medical records.

It is the policy of the United States to support the preservation of life by appropriate clinical means, in a humane manner, and in accordance with all applicable laws. To that end, the Department of Defense has established clinically appropriate procedures to address the medical care and treatment of individual detainees experiencing the adverse health effects of clinically significant weight loss, including those individuals who are engaged in hunger strikes. Involuntary feeding is used only as a last resort, if necessary to address significant health issues caused by malnutrition and/or dehydration. These procedures are administered in accordance with all applicable domestic and international laws pertaining to humane treatment.

...

5. Religious and Cultural Accommodations

Detainees at Guantánamo have the opportunity to pray five times each day. Prayer times are posted for the detainees, and arrows are painted in the living areas — in each cell and in communal areas — so that the detainees know the direction of Mecca. Once prayer call sounds, detainees receive 20 minutes of uninterrupted time to practice their faith. The guard force strives to ensure detainees are not interrupted during the 20 minutes following the prayer call, even if detainees are not involved in religious activity. The majority of detainees are in communal living accommodations, where they are able to pray communally. Even detainees who are in single cell living accommodations conduct prayer together.

Joint Task Force Guantánamo schedules detainee medical appointments, interviews, classes, legal visits, and other activities mindful of the prayer call schedule. Every detainee at Guantánamo is issued a personal copy of the Quran in the language of his choice. Strict measures are in place throughout the facility to ensure that the Quran is handled appropriately by U.S. personnel. The Joint Task Force recognizes Islamic holy periods like Ramadan by modifying meal schedules in observance of religious requirements. Special accommodations are made to adhere to Islamic dietary needs. Department of Defense personnel deployed to Guantánamo receive cultural training to ensure they understand Islamic practices.

6. Requests by the Commission to Visit the Guantánamo Bay Detention Facility

The United States is committed to being as open and transparent to the international community as possible. We have invited the Commission to visit the Guantánamo Bay detention facility and view the detention operations there. However, because of relevant security procedures in effect at the detention facility, we are unable to accommodate the Commission's request to meet with detainees held there. The United States continues to recognize the special role of the International Committee of the Red Cross (ICRC) under the Geneva Conventions of 1949 and grants it access to all detainees held at Guantánamo Bay. We value our relationship with the ICRC and address any concerns it may raise at all levels of the chain of command.

B. Access to Justice

1. Habeas Corpus

All Guantánamo Bay detainees have the ability to challenge the lawfulness of their detention in U.S. federal court through a petition for a writ of habeas corpus. Detainees have access to counsel and to appropriate evidence to mount such a challenge. Except in rare instances required by compelling security interests, all of the evidence relied upon by the government in habeas proceedings to justify detention is disclosed to the detainees' counsel, who have been granted security clearances to view the classified evidence, and the detainees may submit written statements and provide live testimony at their hearings via video link. The United States has the burden in these cases to establish its legal authority to hold the detainees. Detainees whose cases have been denied or dismissed continue to have access to counsel pursuant to the same terms applicable during pendency of proceedings.

With regard to the effectiveness of the habeas remedy afforded to Guantánamo detainees, the United States notes that the evidentiary issues and other procedural concerns raised in the draft report are matters within the expertise and purview of our independent federal judiciary, as the U.S. Supreme Court ruled in *Boumediene v. Bush*, 553 U.S. 723, 796 (2008). Many of the detainees at Guantánamo today have challenged their detention in U.S. federal courts. All of the detainees at Guantánamo who have prevailed in habeas proceedings under orders that are no longer subject to appeal have been either repatriated or resettled. To date, 32 detainees have been ordered released, and they were transferred from Guantánamo pursuant to U.S. federal court orders.

2. Military Commissions

The U.S. Government remains of the view that in our efforts to protect our national security, military commissions and federal courts can — depending on the circumstances of the specific prosecution — each provide tools that are both effective and legitimate. A statutory ban currently prohibits the use of funds to transfer Guantánamo detainees to the United States, however, even for prosecution in federal court.

All current military commission proceedings at Guantánamo incorporate fundamental procedural guarantees that meet or exceed the fair trial safeguards required by Common Article 3 and other applicable law, and are consistent with those in Additional Protocol II to the 1949 Geneva Conventions, as well.

These include: (1) innocence is presumed and the prosecution must prove guilt beyond a reasonable doubt; (2) there is a prohibition on the admission of any statement obtained by the use of torture or by cruel, inhuman, or degrading treatment in military commission proceedings, except against a person accused of torture or such treatment as evidence that the statement was made; (3) the accused has latitude in selecting defense counsel; (4) in capital cases, the accused is provided counsel "learned in applicable law relating to capital cases"; and (5) the accused has the right to pre-trial discovery.

The 2009 Military Commissions Act also provides for the right to appeal final judgments rendered by a military commission to the U.S. Court of Military Commissions Review, and subsequently to the U.S. Court of Appeals for the District of Columbia Circuit and then to the U.S. Supreme Court, both of which are federal civilian courts comprised of life-tenured judges.

Further, the United States is committed to ensuring the transparency of military commission proceedings. To that end, proceedings are now transmitted via video feed to locations at Guantánamo Bay and in the United States, so that the press and the public can view them, with a 40-second delay to protect against the disclosure of classified information. Court transcripts, filings, and other materials are also available to the public online via the Office of Military Commissions website, www.mc.mil.

C. Transfer Issues

1. Yemeni Detainees

Seventy-five of the remaining 122 detainees at Guantánamo are Yemeni nationals, 18 of whom are designated for transfer subject to appropriate security measures. An additional 30 Yemeni nationals are designated for "conditional detention," which means they are not approved for repatriation to Yemen at this time, but may be transferred to third countries if an appropriate resettlement option becomes available, or repatriated to Yemen in the future if security conditions improve. The current situation in Yemen precludes U.S. from repatriating Yemeni detainees at this time. Accordingly, we are vigorously engaging with partners and allies around the world for assistance in resettling these detainees. The U.S. Government, through intensive diplomatic efforts across the world, has found and continues to identify countries willing to resettle Yemeni detainees, including recent transfers of four individuals to Oman, three to Kazakhstan, three to Georgia, and one each to Slovakia and Estonia.

2. Non-refoulement

As a matter of fundamental policy and practice, the United States does not transfer any individual to a foreign country if it is more likely than not that the person would be tortured.

The United States' firm and long-standing commitment to this policy is demonstrated in many ways, such as in section 1242 of the Foreign Affairs Reform and Restructuring Act where it is explicitly stated, and in E.O. 13491, which required the formation of a special U.S. Government task force to study and evaluate the practices of transferring individuals to other nations in order to ensure consistency with all applicable laws and U.S. policies pertaining to treatment.

The United States considers the totality of relevant factors relating to the individual to be transferred and the proposed recipient government in question. Such factors include, but are not limited to:
- the individual's allegations of prior or potential mistreatment by the receiving government;
- the receiving country's human rights record;
- whether post-transfer detention is contemplated;
- the specific factors suggesting that the individual in question is at risk of being tortured by officials in that country;
- whether similarly situated individuals have been tortured by the country under consideration;
- and, where applicable, any diplomatic assurances of humane treatment from the receiving country (including an assessment of their credibility).

Humane treatment assurances are necessarily tailored to the specific context of a particular transfer. With respect to law of war detainee transfers, it is U.S. practice to obtain access for post-transfer monitoring where post-transfer detention by the receiving state is anticipated. Specifically, the United States seeks consistent, private access to the individual who has been transferred and thereafter detained, with minimal advance notice to the detaining government.

If the United States determines, after taking into account all relevant information, including any assurances received and the reliability of such assurances, that it is more likely than not that a person would be tortured if transferred to a foreign country, the United States would not approve the transfer of the person to that country.

Conclusion

We wish to again thank the Commission for the opportunity to comment on this draft report. We respectfully request that the Commission carefully consider the U.S. Government's response to the Commission's draft report as conveyed herein, and assimilate that response into the final report.

Source: U.S. Department of State, https://www.state.gov/documents/organization/258201.pdf

꿈꿈꿈꿈꿈꿈꿈

II. ORGANIZATION OF AMERICAN STATES, INTER-AMERICAN COMMISSION ON HUMAN RIGHTS, KEVIN COOPER V. UNITED STATES, OCTOBER 28, 2015

Primary Source Documents 11 and 12 are sample Inter-American Commission case decisions that show how contentious human rights cases are handled and what they say about the U.S. compliance with the norms of this regional human rights system of which the U.S. is a member. The first is an excerpt of a Report of the Merits rendered by the Inter-American Commission on Human Rights by a Kevin Cooper, a person on death row in the U.S., against the U.S., claiming that his due process and fair trial and racial equality rights under the ADHR were violated by the U.S. courts.

{Excerpt}

I. SUMMARY

1. On April 29, 2011, the Inter-American Commission on Human Rights ("the Inter-American Commission" or "the IACHR") received a petition and request for precautionary measures filed by Norman C. Hile and Katie C. De Witt of *Orrick, Herrington & Sutcliffe LLP* ("the petitioners") against the United States of America ("the State" or "the United States"). The petition was lodged on behalf of Kevin Cooper ("the alleged victim" or "Mr. Cooper") who is deprived of his liberty on death row in the state of California since 1985.

2. The petitioners contend that Mr. Cooper's rights to a fair trial and to due process of law recognized in Articles XVIII and XXVI of the American Declaration were violated. They assert, for example, that the processing of the crime scene was mishandled, that the District Attorney presented false evidence at trial, that the San Bernardino Sheriff's Department (SBSD) failed to disclose exculpatory information to the defense and planted and manipulated evidence, and that the District Court failed to conduct meaningful post-conviction proceedings. Petitioners further allege that court-appointed trial counsel committed numerous mistakes that materially prejudiced Mr. Cooper and that the alleged victim faced racism from the SBSD, the District Attorney and the community, in violation of the fundamental right to equality before the law recognized in Article II of the American Declaration. Petitioners assert that Mr. Cooper's execution by the United States would also constitute a violation of Article I of the American Declaration.

3. The State argues that all of Mr. Cooper's claims have been extensively considered by the courts of the state of California and the United States and that his conviction and sentence have been repeatedly upheld. The State also affirms that the alleged victim was not deprived of effective assistance of counsel at trial, but rather had "an extraordinarily vigorous and able defense" that protected his right to due process of law. Finally, according to the United States, the state of Cali-

fornia took precautions to protect Mr. Cooper from racial discrimination by granting the request to move the case out of San Bernardino County and the petitioners failed to allege any facts that support that Mr. Cooper's race played any role in his conviction and sentencing.

V. LEGAL ANALYSIS

A. Preliminary matters

104. Before embarking on its analysis of the merits in the case of Kevin Cooper, the Inter-American Commission considers it relevant to reiterate its previous rulings regarding the heightened scrutiny to be used in cases involving the death penalty. The right to life has received broad recognition as the supreme human right and as a *sine qua non* for the enjoyment of all other rights.

105. That gives rise to the particular importance of the IACHR's obligation to ensure that any deprivation of life that may arise from the enforcement of the death penalty strictly abides by the requirements set forth in the applicable instruments of the inter-American human rights system, including the American Declaration.1 That heightened scrutiny is consistent with the restrictive approach adopted by other international human rights bodies in cases involving the imposition of the death penalty,2 and it has been set out and applied by the Inter-American Commission in previous capital cases brought before it.

106. As the Inter-American Commission has explained, this standard of review is the necessary consequence of the specific penalty at issue and the right to a fair trial and all attendant due process guarantees:

> "due in part to its irrevocable and irreversible nature, the death penalty is a form of punishment that differs in substance as well as in degree in comparison with other means of punishment, and therefore warrants a particularly stringent need for reliability in determining whether a person is responsible for a crime that carries a penalty of death."

107. The Inter-American Commission will therefore review the petitioner's allegations in the present case with a heightened level of scrutiny, to ensure in particular that the rights to life, due process, and to a fair trial as prescribed under the American Declaration have been respected by the State. With regard to the legal status of the American Declaration, the IACHR reiterates that:

> "[t]he American Declaration is, for the Member States not parties to the American Convention, the source of international obligations related to the OAS Charter. The Charter of the Organization gave the IACHR the principal function of promoting the observance and protection of human rights in the Member States. Article 106 of the OAS Charter does not, however, list or define those rights. The General Assembly of the OAS at its Ninth Regular Period of Sessions, held in La Paz, Bolivia, in October, 1979, agreed that those rights are those enunciated and defined in the American Declaration. Therefore, the American Declaration crystallizes the fundamental principles recognized by the American States. The OAS General Assembly has also repeatedly recognized that the American Declaration is a source of international obligations for the member states of the OAS."
>
> ...
>
> B. Right to a fair trial and right to due process of law (Articles XVIII and XXVI of the American Declaration)

108. The American Declaration guarantees the right of all persons to a fair trial and to due process of law, respectively, in the following terms:

Article XXVI — Right to due process of law

Every accused person is presumed to be innocent until proved guilty.

Every person accused of an offense has the right to be given an impartial and public hearing, and to be tried by courts previously established in accordance with pre-existing laws, and not to receive cruel, infamous or unusual punishment.

Fair trial and due process violations

109. The petitioners allege that the mishandling and misprocessing of the crime scene by the San Bernardino Sheriff's Department deprived Mr. Cooper's defense team of the opportunity to conduct an independent analysis and reconstruction of the scene. They further state that the SBSD planted, manipulated and replaced evidence, and also failed to disclose exculpatory information to the defense. Petitioners further assert that the U.S. District Court for the Southern District failed to conduct meaningful post-conviction proceedings. Finally, petitioners allege that the rights to due process and fair trial were also violated given the draconian procedural restrictions imposed by the Antiterrorism and Effective Death Penalty Act (AEDPA) of 1996 that prohibits the filing and determination of otherwise meritorious constitutional claims unless the applicant can show, among other things, that "no reasonable factfinder would have found the applicant guilty of the underlying offense."

110. The United States argues that all of Mr. Cooper's claims have been extensively considered by the courts of the state of California and the United States and that his conviction and sentence have been repeatedly upheld. The State claims that in his various post-conviction petitions, Mr. Cooper pursued his rights in state and federal courts to raise the same issues that he raises before the IACHR. According to the State, at the alleged victim's request, post-conviction DNA tests were conducted, and they only served to further inculpate Mr. Cooper in the murders. Therefore, the State asserts that petitioners fail to establish that the courts of California and the United States were incapable of thoroughly considering Mr. Cooper's various petitions or deciding them in a fair and just fashion. Regarding the alleged procedural bars, according to the Government, few convicted prisoners have had the number of opportunities to challenge their conviction that Mr. Cooper has had. The State concludes that Mr. Cooper's inability to obtain the overturning of his conviction has not been the result of a failure of state and federal courts to conduct meaningful review over the past three decades, but rather because the evidence of Mr. Cooper's guilt is overwhelming.

...

C. Right to equality before the law (Article II of the American Declaration)

The American Declaration guarantees the right to equality before the law, in the following terms:

Article II — Right to equality before the law

All persons are equal before the law and have the rights and duties established in this Declaration, without distinction as to race, sex, language, creed or any other factor.

136. The petitioners contend that Mr. Cooper faced racism from the San Bernardino Sheriff's Department who ignored evidence implicating three white males, from the District Attorney who refused to allow the case to be transferred to a racially diverse forum, and from the community from which the jury that convicted and sentenced him was selected. They state that media coverage regarding Mr. Cooper's past history was particularly prejudicial and racially charged and that the change of venue to San Diego County was hardly an improvement given the extensive media coverage, proximity to the crime scene, and homogeneity of the population. Based on statistics, the petitioners note that a black person convicted of a capital crime is significantly more likely to receive the death penalty than a white person convicted of the same kind of offense.

137. The United States argue that the state of California took precautions to protect Mr. Cooper from racial discrimination by granting the request to move the case out of San Bernardino County, where the coverage of the murders and the pre-trial proceedings was significant. According to the State, the judge found that moving the trial into the north of the state would unreasonably exacerbate significant logistical considerations. It further states that the defense actively participated in the selection of an impartial jury to protect Mr. Cooper against discrimination, and a jury acceptable to the

defense and prosecution was chosen with ease. The State also asserts that the petitioners failed to allege any facts that support that Mr. Cooper's race played any role in his conviction and sentencing. Finally, according to the United States, statistical evidence is not sufficient by itself to cast doubt on Mr. Cooper's conviction and sentencing.

...

VII. FINAL CONCLUSIONS AND RECOMMENDATIONS

145. In accordance with the legal and factual considerations set out in this report, the Inter-American Commission concludes that the United States is responsible for the violation of the right to equality before the law (Article II), the right to a fair trial (Article XVIII), and the right to due process of law (Article XXVI) guaranteed in the American Declaration, with respect to Kevin Cooper. Consequently, should the State carry out the execution of Mr. Cooper, it would be committing a serious and irreparable violation of the basic right to life recognized in Article I of the American Declaration.

...

Accordingly,

THE INTER-AMERICAN COMMISSION ON HUMAN RIGHTS REITERATES THAT THE UNITED STATES:

1. Grant Kevin Cooper effective relief, including the review of his trial and sentence in accordance with the guarantees of due process and a fair trial enshrined in Articles I, II, XVIII and XXVI of the American Declaration;

2. Review its laws, procedures, and practices to ensure that people accused of capital crimes are tried and, if convicted, sentenced in accordance with the rights established in the American Declaration, including Articles I, II, XVIII, and XXVI thereof;

3. Ensure that the legal counsel provided by the State in death penalty cases is effective, trained to serve in death penalty cases, and able to thoroughly and diligently investigate all mitigating evidence; and

4. Given the violations of the American Declaration that the IACHR has established in the present case and in others involving application of the death penalty, the Inter-American Commission also recommends to the United States that it adopt a moratorium on executions of persons sentenced to death.

Source for full text: https://www.google.com/webhp?sourceid=chrome-instant&ion=1&espv=2&ie=UTF-8#q=Inter-American+commission+on+Human+Rights%2C+Cooper+v.+US

12. ORGANIZATION OF AMERICAN STATES, INTER-AMERICAN COMMISSION ON HUMAN RIGHTS, JESSICA LENAHAN (GONZALES) ET AL. V. UNITED STATES, JULY 21, 2011

The following report of the Inter-American Commission on Human Rights was issued on the merits of a formal written petition filed in the Commission by several human rights/civil liberties groups, such as the ACLU and Columbia Law School Human Rights Clinic and other human rights NGOs as petitioners on behalf of an American woman, Jessica Lenahan (Gonzales), against the U.S. concerning the failure of U.S. courts and law enforcement to prevent domestic violence leading to the death of her family members in the U.S. Many human rights NGOs and women's organisations and law school human rights clinics participated in and followed this case, and many filed friend of the court briefs in support of the petition. The U.N. Special Rapporteur on violence against women, Rashida Manjoo, also participated in the hearing as part of the delegation of petitioners. There have been many follow up ripple effects in the U.S. from this decision regarding domestic violence fostered by civil society and some local governments.

Following is the decision of the Commission as to whether it finds the U.S. in violation of the ADHR, and includes what happened after the decision was rendered as to the U.S. It is largely about the "positive obligations" of a state to act when a persons' rights have been impacted by private action, such as a homicide. This is an example of an international human rights body judging the U.S. for an event that took place within the U.S., but it is judged based on the international human rights norms of the regional human rights body, the O.A.S.. Note how the decision brings into consideration decisions from other international human rights systems such as the Council of Europe and even the U.N. system case law.

I. SUMMARY

1. This report concerns a petition presented to the Inter-American Commission on Human Rights (hereinafter the "Commission" or "IACHR") against the Government of the United States (hereinafter the "State" or the "United States") on December 27, 2005, by Caroline Bettinger-Lopez, Emily J. Martin, Lenora Lapidus, Stephen Mcpherson Watt, and Ann Beeson, attorneys-at-law with the American Civil Liberties Union. The petition was presented on behalf of Ms. Jessica Lenahan, formerly Jessica Gonzales, and her deceased daughters Leslie (7), Katheryn (8) and Rebecca (10) Gonzales.

2. The claimants assert in their petition that the United States violated Articles I, II, V, VI, VII, IX, XVIII and XXIV of the American Declaration by failing to exercise due diligence to protect Jessica Lenahan and her daughters from acts of domestic violence perpetrated by the ex-husband of the former and the father of the latter, even though Ms. Lenahan held a restraining order against him. They specifically allege that the police failed to adequately respond to Jessica Lenahan's repeated and urgent calls over several hours reporting that her estranged husband had taken their three minor daughters (ages 7, 8 and 10) in violation of the restraining order, and asking for help. The three girls were found shot to death in the back of their father's truck after the exchange of gunfire that resulted in the death of their father. The petitioners further contend that the State never duly investigated and clarified the circumstances of the death of Jessica Lenahan's daughters, and never provided her with an adequate remedy for the failures of the police. According to the petition, eleven years have passed and Jessica Lenahan still does not know the cause, time and place of her daughters' death.

3. The United States recognizes that the murders of Jessica Lenahan's daughters are "unmistakable tragedies." The State, however, asserts that any petition must be assessed on its merits, based on the evidentiary record and a cognizable basis in the American Declaration. The State claims that its authorities responded as required by law, and that the facts alleged by the petitioners are not supported by the evidentiary record and the information available to the Castle Rock Police Department at the time the events occurred. The State moreover claims that the petitioners cite no provision of the American Declaration that imposes on the United States an affirmative duty, such as the exercise of due diligence, to prevent the commission of individual crimes by private actors, such as the tragic and criminal murders of Jessica Lenahan's daughters.

4. In Report No. 52/07, adopted on July 24, 2007 during its 128th regular period of sessions, the Commission decided to admit the claims advanced by the petitioners under Articles I, II, V, VI, VII, XVIII and XXIV of the American Declaration, and to proceed with consideration of the merits of the petition. At the merits stage, the petitioners added to their allegations that the failures of the United States to conduct a thorough investigation into the circumstances surrounding Leslie, Katheryn and Rebecca's deaths also breached Jessica Lenahan's and her family's right to truth in violation of Article IV of the American Declaration.

5. In the present report, having examined the evidence and arguments presented by the parties during the proceedings, the Commission concludes that the State failed to act with due diligence to protect Jessica Lenahan and Leslie, Katheryn and Rebecca Gonzales from domestic violence, which violated the State's obligation not to discriminate and to provide for equal protection before the law under Article II of the American Declaration. The State also failed to undertake reasonable measures to protect the life of Leslie, Katheryn and Rebecca Gonzales in violation of their right to life under Article I of the American Declaration, in conjunction with their right to special protection as girl-children under Article VII of the American Declaration. Finally, the Commission finds that the State violated the right to judicial protection of Jessica Lenahan and her next-of kin, under Article XVIII of the American Declaration. The Commission does

not consider that it has sufficient information to find violations of articles V and VI of the American Declaration. As to Articles XXIV and IV of the American Declaration, it considers the claims related to these articles to have been addressed under Article XVIII of the American Declaration.

II. PROCEEDINGS SUBSEQUENT TO ADMISSIBILITY REPORT No. 52/07

6. In Report No. 52/07, adopted on July 24, 2007, the Commission declared Ms. Lenahan's petition admissible in respect to Articles I, II, V, VI, VII, XVIII and XXIV of the American Declaration and decided to proceed with the analysis of the merits of the case.

7. Report No. 52/07 was forwarded to the State and to the Petitioners by notes dated October 4, 2007. In the note to the petitioners, the Commission requested that they provide any additional observations they had within a period of two months, in accordance with Article 38(1) of the Commission's Rules of Procedure. In both notes, the Commission placed itself at the disposal of the parties with a view to reaching a friendly settlement of the matter in accordance with Article 38(4) of its Rules, and requested that the parties inform the Commission as soon as possible whether they were interested in this offer. In a communication dated October 12, 2007, the petitioners informed the Commission that they were amenable to engaging in friendly settlement discussions with the United States, which the Commission forwarded to the State on January 30, 2008. By letter dated October 15, 2007, Ms. Araceli Martínez-Olguin from the American Civil Liberties Union requested that all communications from the Commission pertaining to this matter be sent to her as well as to Mr. Watt and Ms. Bettinger-Lopez at their respective addresses.

8. In a communication dated March 24, 2008, the petitioners submitted to the Commission their final observations on the merits of the matter. The Commission forwarded to the State these observations by letter dated March 26, 2008, with a request pursuant to Article 38 (1) of its Rules to present any additional observations regarding the merits within two months. In a communication dated March 24, 2008, the petitioners also requested a merits hearing before the Commission during its 132º period of sessions. By letter dated August 4, 2008, the petitioners reiterated their request for a merits hearing during the 133º period of sessions, which was granted by the Commission on September 22, 2008. In a communication dated October 16, 2008, the State forwarded to the Commission its merits observations on this matter, which were transmitted to the petitioners on October 21, 2008.

9. The petitioners submitted additional observations and documentation to the Commission on October 21 and 22, 2008; March 12 and July 16, 2009; and January 11, February 20, and June 5, 2010; communications which were all duly forwarded to the State.

10. On August 3, 2009, the Commission requested the State to submit the complete investigation files and all related documentation in reference to the death of Simon Gonzales and of Leslie, Katheryn and Rebecca Gonzales, within a period of one month.

11. The State submitted additional observations to the Commission on April 9, 2010, which were duly forwarded to the petitioners.

12. The Commission convened a merits hearing pertaining to this case during its 133º ordinary period of sessions on October 22, 2008 with the presence of both parties.

13. During the processing of this case, the IACHR has received several *amicus curiae* briefs, which were all duly forwarded to the parties. In a communication dated July 6, 2007, Katherine Caldwell and Andrew Rhys Davies, attorneys for the firm Allen & Overy LLP, submitted an *amici curiae* brief, on behalf of several organizations, entities and international and national networks dedicated to the protection of the rights of women and children.4 In a communication dated January 4, 2008, Jennifer Brown and Maya Raghu from Legal Momentum; David S. Ettinger and Mary-Christine Sungalia from Horvitz & Levy LLP; and various local, national and international women's rights and human rights organizations,5 presented an *amicus curiae* brief. On October 15, 2008, the Commission received a supplemental *amicus cu-*

riae brief by Maya Raghu from Legal Momentum; David S. Ettinger and Mary-Christine Sungalia from Horvitz & Levy LLP; and various local, national and international women's rights and human rights organizations.

14. On April 11, 2011, the Commission also received a communication accrediting the University of Miami School of Law Human Rights Clinic as a co-petitioner, and Caroline Bettinger-Lopez as a representative of the Human Rights Clinic and lead counsel in the case. By communication dated April 18, 2011, Sandra Park from the Women's Rights Project of the American Civil Liberties Union was also accredited as co-counsel in the case. On July 6, 2011, the Commission received an additional communication accrediting Peter Rosenblum as co-counsel in the case and as Director of the Human Rights Clinic of Columbia Law School.

III. POSITIONS OF THE PARTIES

A. Position of the Petitioners

18. The petitioners allege that Jessica Lenahan, of Native-American and Latin-American descent, lived in Castle Rock, Colorado and married Simon Gonzales in 1990. In 1996, Simon Gonzales allegedly began adopting abusive behavior towards Jessica Lenahan and their three daughters Leslie, Katheryn and Rebecca (ages 7, 8 and 10). In 1999, after he attempted to commit suicide, Jessica Lenahan filed for divorce and started living separately from him.

19. They allege that after Jessica Lenahan separated from Simon Gonzales, he continued displaying erratic and unpredictable behavior that harmed her and their daughters. Between January and May, 1999, Simon Gonzales had several run-ins with the Castle Rock Police Department (hereinafter "CRPD"), among these, for road rage while driving with his daughters, for two break-ins to Jessica Lenahan's house, and for trespassing on private property and obstructing public officials at the CRPD station. The petitioners allege that by June 22, 1999, Simon Gonzales was a name that "the CRPD — a small police department in a small town — knew or should have known to be associated with domestic violence and erratic and reckless behavior."

20. Jessica Lenahan requested and obtained a restraining order from the Colorado Courts on May 21, 1999. The petitioners indicate that the temporary restraining order directed Simon Gonzales not to "molest or disturb the peace" of Jessica Lenahan or their children; excluded Simon Gonzales from the family home; and ordered him to "remain at least 100 yards away from this location at all times." The petitioners affirm that the front page of the temporary restraining order noted in capital letters that the reserve side contained "important notices for restrained parties and law enforcement officials." The reverse side of the temporary restraining order allegedly directed law enforcement officials as follows: "You shall use every reasonable means to enforce this restraining order....," according to the requirements of Colorado's mandatory arrest law. When the order was issued, the petitioners report that it was entered into the Colorado Bureau of Investigation's central registry of restraining orders, which is a computerized central database registry that is accessible to any state or local enforcement agency connected to the Bureau, including the Castle Rock Police Department.

21. Jessica Lenahan alleges that, despite the issuance of the temporary order, her former husband continued to terrorize her and the children. She called the CRPD to report this and other violations of the restraining order, but the police ignored most of her calls and in her words: "they would be dismissive of me, and they scolded me for calling them and asking for help."

22. On June 4, 1999, the state court made permanent the temporary restraining order, including slight changes such as granting Jessica Lenahan sole physical custody of the three girls and allowing Simon Gonzales occasional visitation or "parenting time."7 The petitioners claim that, upon Jessica Lenahan's request, the judge restricted Simon Gonzales' weekly contact with the girls to one "mid-week dinner visit," that Simon and Jessica Lenahan would previously arrange.

23. The petitioners allege that, in Colorado, as in other states, a restraining order represents a judicial determination that any violation of its terms threatens the safety of the domestic violence victim. As with Colorado's mandatory arrest law mentioned previously, restraining orders "are specifically meant to cabin police discretion in determining whether a threat exists in the face of evidence of such a violation."9

24. Despite the existence of the restraining order, the petitioners claim that on Tuesday, June 22, 1999, Simon Gonzales abducted his three daughters and their friend from the street in front of Jessica Lenahan's home. Simon Gonzales allegedly abducted his daughters in violation of the restraining order,since time for visitation had not been previously arranged with Jessica Lenahan. In response, over the next ten hours, Jessica Lenahan repeatedly contacted the CRPD to report the children missing, and to request the enforcement of her restraining order. According to the petition, the police continuously ignored her cries for help. During her conversations with various police officers from the CRPD, Jessica Lenahan clearly communicated that Simon Gonzales had abducted the children, in violation of a valid restraining order, that there was no pre-arranged dinner visit, and that she was concerned for the safety of her missing children.

25. The petition relates that Jessica Lenahan first called the police department on June 22nd, 1999, approximately at 5:50 p.m. seeking advice. During this conversation she communicated to the dispatcher that she did not know where her children were, that she thought perhaps her daughters had been taken by her ex-husband, and that this visit had not been pre-arranged as required by the restraining order. She also informed them that their friend Rebecca Robinson had also been taken. Around 7:40 p.m., Jessica Lenahan called the police department a second time noting that she held a restraining order against Simon Gonzales and that she was concerned over her children's safety.

26. The petitioners claim that at approximately 7:50 p.m., two hours after Jessica Lenahan first called the Castle Rock Police Department, Officer Brink and Sergeant Ruisi arrived at her house. Jessica Lenahan allegedly showed both officers a copy of the restraining order, which expressly directed them to arrest Simon Gonzales upon violation of the order. Jessica Lenahan explained to the officers that the judge had specifically noted in the order that the dinner visit was to be "pre-arranged" by the parties, that Simon Gonzales's normal visitation night was on Wednesday evenings, and that she had communicated to her former husband that he could not switch nights that week, since the girls had plans for their friend to sleep over.

27. Officer Brink allegedly held the restraining order in his hands and glanced at it briefly, and then communicated to Jessica Lenahan that there was nothing he could do because the children were with their father. The Officers promised Jessica Lenahan that they would drive by Simon Gonzales' apartment to see if he and the girls were there. The petitioners claim that shortly after 8:30 p.m., Jessica Lenahan was able to reach Simon Gonzales by phone and learned that he was with the girls at an amusement park in Denver, approximately 40 minutes from Castle Rock. She also received an alarming call from Simon Gonzales' girlfriend, Rosemary Young, asking questions about his mental health history, his capacity for harming himself or the children, and his access to firearms. Ms. Young also communicated that Simon Gonzales had threatened to drive off a cliff earlier that day.

28. After these calls, Jessica Lenahan became more alarmed and called the CRPD for a third time to communicate her concerns. The dispatcher allegedly communicated to Jessica Lenahan that an officer would be sent to her house, but the officer never arrived. Officer Brink did telephone Jessica Lenahan shortly thereafter, and she explained to him again that she had a restraining order, that it was "highly unusual," "really weird," and "wrong" for Simon Gonzales to have taken the girls to Denver on a weeknight, and that she was "so worried," particularly because it was almost bedtime and the girls were still not home.

29. Jessica Lenahan allegedly called the CRPD a fourth and a fifth time before 10:00 p.m., and requested several actions from Officer Brink including a) that an officer be dispatched to locate Simon Gonzales and the children in Denver, and to call the Denver police; b) to put on a statewide All Points Bulletin10 for Simon Gonzales and the missing children; and c) to contact Rosemary Young. Officer Brink allegedly refused to perform any of these three actions and asked Jessica Lenahan to wait until 10:00 p.m. to see whether Simon Gonzales returned with the children. In light of police inaction in the face of her concerns, Jessica Lenahan alleges that:

I was shocked when they responded that there was nothing they could do because Denver was of jurisdiction. I called back and begged them to put out a missing children alert or contact the Denver police, but they refused. The officer told me I needed to take this matter to divorce court and told me to call back if the children were not back home in a few hours. The officer said to me: "at least you know where the children are, they are with their father." I felt totally confused and humiliated. I called the police again and again that night.

30. Jessica Lenahan allegedly called the police department a sixth time around 10:00 p.m. to report that her children were still not home and again informed them about the restraining order. During the call, the dispatcher asked Jessica Lenahan to call back on a non-emergency line and scolded her stating that it was "a little ridiculous making U.S. freak out and thinking the kids are gone."11 Jessica Lenahan called again a seventh time at midnight to inform the CRPD that she was at her husband's apartment, that no one was home and she feared that her husband had "run off with my girls."12 The dispatcher told her that she would send an officer, but the officer never arrived.

31. Shortly thereafter, Jessica Lenahan drove to the CRPD where she met with Detective Ahlfinger, to whom she communicated again that she had a restraining order against Simon Gonzales, that she was afraid he had "lost it," and that he might be suicidal. According to the petitioners, inaction and indifference persisted in the response of the police even after Jessica Lenahan went to the Castle Rock Police Department and filed an incident report. The police simply replied that the father of the children had the right to spend time with them, even though she repeatedly mentioned the restraining order against him and that no visitation time had been agreed upon. She was only advised to wait until 10:00 p.m., and when she called at that time, her pleas were dismissed, and she was again told to wait, until 12:00 a.m.

32. The petitioners allege that approximately ten hours after Jessica Lenahan's first call to the police, Simon Gonzales drove up to and parked outside the police station at 3:15 a.m. on June 23, 1999, waited approximately 10-15 minutes, and then began shooting at the station. The police returned fire and shot and killed Simon Gonzales, and then discovered the bodies of Leslie, Katheryn and Rebecca in the back of Simon Gonzales' truck, apparently having been shot to death. The petitioners indicate that Jessica Lenahan trusted that the police would take action, and had she known the police would not do anything to locate her daughters, she would have undertaken steps to find them herself and avoid the tragedy.

33. After hearing about the shooting from Rosemary Young, Jessica Lenahan drove to the police station. 13 The petitioners allege that the officers refused to offer Jessica Lenahan any information on whether the girls were alive or not, and ignored her pleas to see the girls and identify them for about twelve hours. According to the petition, despite repeated pleas from the family, the deaths of Leslie, Katheryn and Rebecca Gonzales were never duly investigated by the State. Jessica Lenahan allegedly never learned any details of how, when and where her daughters died, their death certificates do not state this information, and therefore, she is still unable to include this information on their grave stones.

34. The petitioners claim that, to this day, Jessica Lenahan does not know whether the numerous bullets found inside of their bodies came from Simon Gonzales' gun or the guns of the police officers who fired upon the truck. She also alleges that she has never received any information as to why Simon Gonzales was approved to purchase a gun that night by the Federal Bureau of Investigations, since gun dealers cannot sell guns to individuals who are subject to a restraining order in the United States.

35. The petitioners claim that the investigations conducted by the authorities solely related to the shooting death of Simon Gonzales. According to them, these investigations summarily conclude that Simon Gonzales had murdered his children before the shootout at the CRPD station, yet provide little evidence to substantiate this conclusion. They claim that the evidence in these documents is insufficient to determine which bullets killed the Jessica Lenahan's daughters; those of the CRPD, or those of Simon Gonzales.

36. The petitioners allege that Jessica Lenahan and her family remain deeply traumatized by the deaths of Leslie, Katheryn and Rebecca Gonzales. The petitioners indicate that their sense of loss has been aggravated by the failure of Colorado and federal authorities to adequately investigate these deaths and respond with the information the family seeks. As set forth in the declaration of Jessica Gonzales' mother, Tina Rivera, the entire family has experienced great trauma and feels that closure to their tragedy will only come once questions surrounding the girls' deaths are answered.

37. The petitioners indicate that Jessica Lenahan filed suit in the United States District Court for the District of Colorado, a court of federal jurisdiction, alleging that the City of Castle Rock and several police officers had violated her rights under the Due Process Clause of the Fourteenth Amendment, claiming both substantive and procedural due process challenges. Firstly, in the realm of substantive due process, Jessica Lenahan argued that she and her daughters had a

right to police protection against harm from her husband. In the realm of procedural due process, she argued that she possessed a protected property interest in the enforcement of the terms of her restraining order and that the Castle Rock police officers' arbitrary denial of that entitlement without due process violated her rights. Jessica Lenahan also claimed that the City had failed to properly train its police officers in relation to the enforcement of restraining orders, and had a policy of "recklessly" disregarding the right to police protection created by such orders.

38. The District Court dismissed Jessica Lenahan's case, and on appeal a panel of judges of the Third Circuit Court of Appeals affirmed in part and reserved in part. This finding was then affirmed in a rehearing before all of the judges of the appellate court ("*en banc*" review).

39. Jessica Lenahan's case reached the Supreme Court, the highest court in the United States. On June 27, 2005, the Supreme Court rejected all of the claims presented by Jessica Lenahan, holding that her due process rights had not been violated. The Supreme Court held that despite Colorado's mandatory arrest law and the express and mandatory terms of her restraining order, Jessica Lenahan had no personal entitlement to police enforcement of the order under the due process clause.

40. The petitioners claim that, under the American Declaration, the judiciary had the obligation to provide a remedy for the police officers' failure to enforce the restraining order issued in favor of Jessica Lenahan in violation of state law and principles of international human rights law, which it failed to do. Moreover, the petitioners claim that the United States Supreme Court's decision in *Town of Castle Rock v. Gonzales* leaves Jessica Lenahan and countless other domestic violence victims in the United States without a judicial remedy by which to hold the police accountable for their failures to protect domestic violence victims and their children.

41. Regarding federal avenues, the petitioners mention two previous decisions from the United States Supreme Court, which read together with *Town of Castle Rock v. Gonzales*, allegedly severely limit access to such avenues for victims of domestic violence perpetrated by private actors.16 In regards to potential state remedies and due process for domestic violence victims, the petitioners argue that a civil tort suit under Colorado law against either the Town of Castle Rock or the individual officers involved, although technically available to Jessica Lehanan, would have had no possibility of success due to the doctrine of sovereign immunity. In regards to administrative channels, the petitioners claim that they have thoroughly reviewed a variety of Castle Rock sources, but have not located any information pointing to mechanisms available to file administrative complaints against the CRPD or the Town of Castle Rock.

42. The petitioners finally highlight that domestic violence is a widespread and tolerated phenomenon in the United States that has a disproportionate impact on women and negative repercussions on their children. They maintain that the failings of the Castle Rock Police Department in this case are representative of a larger failure by the United States to exercise due diligence in response to the country's domestic violence epidemic.17 The petitioners contend that Jessica Lenanan's claims are paradigmatic of those of numerous domestic violence victims in the United States, the majority of which are women and children, who pertain disproportionately to racial and ethnic minorities and to low-income groups. Even though the prevalence, persistence and gravity of the issue are recognized at the state and federal levels, and certain legislative measures have been adopted to confront the problem, the historical response of police officers has been to treat it as a family and private matter of low priority, as compared to other crimes. According to the petitioners, the present case demonstrates that police departments and governments still regularly breach their duties to protect domestic violence victims by failing to enforce restraining orders.

43. The petitioners also recently presented information to the Commission pertaining to two legal developments that they consider pertinent to the Commission's decision in this case. They highlight the 2009 sentence of the Inter-American Court of Human Rights in the case of *Claudia Ivette Gonzales and Others v. Mexico*, as a source of key principles of state responsibility in the context of violence against women. They particularly underscore the emphasis of this judgment on the obligation of States to act with due diligence towards acts of violence against women perpetrated by private actors. They also highlight that in April of 2009, the United States Department of Homeland Security articulated a new position recognizing the eligibility of foreign domestic violence victims for asylum in certain circumstances, thereby recognizing state responsibility to protect those victims.

44. The petitioners have presented their legal allegations under Articles I, II, IV, V, VI, VII, XVIII and XXIV of the American Declaration focusing on three main issues. First, they claim this case is about the United States' affirmative obligations under the American Declaration to exercise due diligence to protect domestic violence victims who are beneficiaries of court issued restraining orders when the government has knowledge that those victims, and their children, are in danger. Second, they affirm that this case is about the government's obligation to provide a remedy when it does not comply with its duty to protect. Third, they argue that this case is about a mother's right to truth, information and answers from the State as to when, where and how her daughters died after they were abducted in violation of a domestic violence restraining order, and the police ignored her calls for help.

B. Position of the State

45. The United States recognizes that the murders of Leslie, Katheryn and Rebecca Gonzales are "unmistakable tragedies."18 The State, however, underscores that any petition must be assessed on its merits, based on the evidentiary record and a cognizable basis in the American Declaration. The State claims that the facts alleged by the petitioners are not supported by the evidentiary record and that the petition has not demonstrated a breach of duty by the United States under the American Declaration. The State claims that the evidentiary record demonstrates that throughout the evening of June 22, 1999 and the early hours of June 23, 1999, the Castle Rock Police Department responded professionally and reasonably to the information Jessica Lenahan provided and that the information available at the time revealed no indication that Simon Gonzales was likely to commit a crime against his own children.

46. In response to the petitioners' overall description of the facts, the State argues that the petitioners' filings in this case present a "misleading, and in some instances, manifestly inaccurate portrayal of the facts."19 The State identifies three fundamental differences between the petitioners' claims and the actual record in this case.

IV. ANALYSIS

47. In this section, the Commission sets forth its findings of fact and law pertaining to the allegations advanced by the petitioners and the State. In its analysis and in accordance with article 43(1) of its Rules of Procedure, the Commission bases its findings on the arguments and evidence submitted by the parties, the information obtained during the two hearings before the IACHR related to this case, and information that is a matter of public knowledge.

48. First, the Commission proceeds to set forth the facts that it considers proven. Second, the Commission moves on to analyze whether the United States incurred international responsibility under Articles I, II, IV, V, VI, VII, XVIII and XXIV of the American Declaration, based on these facts.

A. Findings of Fact

49. After a comprehensive review of the arguments and evidence presented by the parties, the Commission concludes that the following facts have been proven:

1. The Existence of a Restraining Order against Simon Gonzales

50. The evidence presented to the Commission shows that at the time of the events subject to this petition, Jessica Lenahan possessed a valid restraining order against Simon Gonzales, initially granted on a temporary basis on May 21, 1999 and then rendered permanent on June 4, 1999. The initial order directed Simon Gonzales "not to molest or disturb the peace of the other party or any child;" excluded him from the family home; and ordered Simon Gonzales to remain at least 100 yards away from this location at all times. The Court further found that "physical or emotional harm" would result if Simon Gonzales were not excluded from the "home of the other party." The reserve side of the temporary restraining order reiterated the requirements of Colorado's mandatory arrest law, and contained important instructions for the restrained party and law enforcement officials which are discussed in detail *infra* in paras. 139-140.

51. When rendered permanent on June 4, 1999, the order granted Jessica Lenahan temporary sole physical custody of her three daughters. The order restricted Simon Gonzales' time with his daughters during the week to a "mid-week din-

ner visit" that Simon Gonzales and Jessica Lenahan had to previously arrange "upon reasonable notice." Simon Gonzales was also authorized parenting time with his daughters on alternating weekends starting after work on Friday evening and continuing through 7:00 p.m. on Sunday evening, and was entitled to two weeks of extended parenting time during the summer. After the order was rendered permanent, Jessica Lenahan and Simon Gonzales would normally arrange for him to have the children on Wednesday nights.

52. Any violation of its terms threatens the safety of the domestic violence victim. When the Colorado General Assembly passed mandatory arrest legislation in 1994, it held that "the issuance and enforcement of protection orders are of paramount importance in the state of Colorado because protection orders promote of protection orders are of paramount importance in the state of Colorado because protection orders promote safety, reduce violence, and prevent serious harm and death."

53. The State contends that Ms. Lenahan had access to remedies and that the case she filed was decided on the merits. Other valid legal claims, at the state and administrative level, may have been available to Jessica Lenahan, but she chose not to pursue them, and therefore, there is no way of knowing whether other legal theories she could have asserted would have resulted in an eventual

54. The State also describes a series of additional remedies and protections for victims of domestic violence at the national and state levels, entailing billions of dollars devoted to implementing programs related to domestic violence, as well as diverse laws that have been designed to improve the investigation of domestic violence cases. The State alleges that, at the national level, Congress has adopted three major pieces of legislation that recognize the seriousness of domestic violence and the importance of a nationwide response: the Violence against Women Act of 1994 (hereinafter "VAWA 1994"), the Violence against Women Act of 2000 (hereinafter "VAWA 2000"), and the Violence against Women and Department of Justice Reauthorization Act of 2005 (hereinafter "VAWA 2005").

55. The State alleges that the petitioners cite no provision of the American Declaration that imposes on the United States an affirmative duty, such as the exercise of due diligence, to prevent the commission of individual crimes by private parties. The petitioners cite case law of the Inter-American Court of Human Rights and of the Inter-American Commission on Human Rights, but these precedents cannot be interpreted to impose such a broad affirmative obligation upon the United States to prevent private crimes, such as the tragic and criminal murders of Leslie, Katheryn and Rebecca Gonzalez. The State moreover claims that the petitioners attempt unsuccessfully to argue that the entire corpus of international human right law and non-binding views of international bodies are embodied in obligations contained in the American Declaration, which in turn, are binding upon the United States. As a legal matter, the United States maintains that it is not bound by obligations contained in human rights treaties it has not joined and the substantive obligations enshrined in these instruments cannot be imported into the American Declaration.

56. In this regard, the State considers that the sentence of the Inter-American Court of Human Rights in the case of *Campo Algodonero* is based in very different legal and factual circumstances from those present in the case of Jessica Lenahan and her daughters. The State alleges that the facts driving this Court sentence centered on the systematic and consistent failure of the Mexican authorities to address the murders and disappearances of hundreds of women in Ciudad Juarez due to an official culture of discrimination and stereotyping; claims that are different from what has been presented in this case. Unlike the police in the case of *Campo Algodonero*, the CRPD officers had no reason to believe that any prevention measures where necessary in this case since Jessica Lenahan did not demonstrate concern for the physical safety of her children throughout her calls. The State also clarifies that the U.S. Department of Homeland Security's position is that under some circumstances, victims of domestic violence may satisfy all of the generally applicable requirements of asylum law; a position which does not translate into a general State recognition of responsibility related to human rights obligations pertaining to this issue.

57. The State emphasizes that "all States owe a moral and political responsibility to their populations to prevent and protect them from acts of abuse by private individuals."20 States around the world routinely prohibit and sanction such acts under their criminal laws, and the United States' commitment to preventing domestic violence and protecting victims is shown by the steps taken at the state and federal level to respond to domestic violence. For purposes of interpreting the

United States' legal obligations, however, the State notes that "it is essential to bear in mind that the judging of governmental action such as in this case has been and will remain a matter of domestic law in the fulfillment of a state's general responsibilities incident to ordered government, rather than a matter of international human rights law to be second-guessed by international bodies."

58. The State moreover alleges that the content of the due diligence standard that the petitioners would like the Commission to apply is substantively unclear. The content of the due diligence standard does not provide guidance to the State with respect to its "putative" duties to prevent private

violence other than the need to be "effective," which is the objective of all crime prevention measures. In the same vein, the State claims that even if the Commission applies the "due diligence" or a similar duty, the United States has met this standard.

V. ANALYSIS

59. In this section, the Commission sets forth its findings of fact and law pertaining to the allegations advanced by the petitioners and the State. In its analysis and in accordance with article 43(1) of its Rules of Procedure, the Commission bases its findings on the arguments and evidence submitted by the parties, the information obtained during the two hearings before the IACHR related to this case,21 and information that is a matter of public knowledge.22

60. First, the Commission proceeds to set forth the facts that it considers proven. Second, the Commission moves on to analyze whether the United States incurred international responsibility under Articles I, II, IV, V, VI, VII, XVIII and XXIV of the American Declaration, based on these facts.

A. Findings of Fact

61. After a comprehensive review of the arguments and evidence presented by the parties, the Commission concludes that the following facts have been proven:

62. The evidence presented to the Commission shows that at the time of the events subject to this petition, Jessica Lenahan possessed a valid restraining order against Simon Gonzales, initially granted on a temporary basis on May 21, 199923 and then rendered permanent on June 4, 1999.24 The initial order directed Simon Gonzales "not to molest or disturb the peace of the other party or any child;" excluded him from the family home; and ordered Simon Gonzales to remain at least 100 yards away from this location at all times.25 The Court further found that "physical or emotional harm" would result if Simon Gonzales were not excluded from the "home of the other party."26 The reserve side of the temporary restraining order reiterated the requirements of Colorado's mandatory arrest law,27 and contained important instructions for the restrained party and law enforcement officials which are discussed in detail *infra* in paras. 139-140.

4. Legal Process for Jessica Lenahan's Claims in the United States

63. When rendered permanent on June 4, 1999, the order granted Jessica Lenahan temporary sole physical custody of her three daughters.28 The order restricted Simon Gonzales' time with his daughters during the week to a "mid-week dinner visit" that Simon Gonzales and Jessica Lenahan had to previously arrange "upon reasonable notice." Simon Gonzales was also authorized parenting time with his daughters on alternating weekends starting after work on Friday evening and continuing through 7:00 p.m. on Sunday evening, and was entitled to two weeks of extended parenting time during the summer.29 After the order was rendered permanent, Jessica Lenahan and Simon Gonzales would normally arrange for him to have the children on Wednesday nights.

64. When the order was issued, it was entered into the Colorado Bureau of Investigation's central registry of restraining orders, which is a computerized central database registry that is accessible to any state or local enforcement agency connected to the Bureau, including the Castle Rock Police Department. In Colorado, like in other states, a restraining order represents a judicial determination that any violation of its terms threatens the safety of the domestic violence victim. When the Colorado General Assembly passed mandatory arrest legislation in 1994, it held that "the issuance and en-

forcement of protection orders are of paramount importance in the state of Colorado because protection orders promote safety, reduce violence, and prevent serious harm and death."

Simon Gonzales' Family and Criminal History prior to June 22, 1999

65. Throughout Jessica Lenahan's relationship with Simon Gonzales he demonstrated "erratic and emotionally" abusive behavior towards her and her daughters. Jessica Lenahan has described how "he would break our children's toys and other belongings, impose harsh discipline on the children and threaten to kidnap them, drive recklessly, exhibit suicidal behavior, and act verbally, physically, and sexually abusive to me." Simon Gonzales' frightening and destructive behavior continued despite Jessica Lenahan's efforts to separate from him, including forcing Jessica Lenahan to perform sexual favors for clothing and other necessities. He would also stalk her outside of her house, her job and on the phone "at all hours of the day and night," often while high on drugs, and break into her house.

66. Jessica Lenahan initially requested a restraining order from the District Court of Douglas County in Colorado, on May 21, 1999, due to Simon Gonzales' increasingly erratic and unpredictable behavior over the years. As justification, she indicated that Simon Gonzales had committed several incidents of violence against herself and her daughters, including trying to hang himself in the garage in the presence of his daughters and purposely breaking the children's belongings. She expressly indicated that she and her daughters were in imminent danger of "harm to my/our emotional health or welfare if the defendant is not excluded from the family home or the home of another." She requested to the Court that Simon Gonzales be allowed only limited contact with her to discuss "alteration of visits or matters concerning the children."

67. Simon Gonzales' criminal history shows that he had several run-ins with the police in the three months preceding June 22, 1999. Jessica Lenahan called the Castle Rock Police Department on at least four occasions during those months to report domestic violence incidents. She reported that Simon Gonzales was stalking her, that he had broken into her house and stolen her wedding rings, that he had entered into her house unlawfully to change the locks on the doors, and that he had loosened the water valves on the sprinklers outside her house so that water flooded her yard and the surrounding neighborhood. Simon Gonzales also received a citation for road rage on April 18, 1999, while his daughters were in his car without seatbelts, and his drivers' license had been suspended by June 23, 1999.

68. When Jessica Lenahan called the CRPD police on May 30, 1999 to report a break-in of her house perpetrated by Simon Gonzales, a CRPD officer was dispatched to her house. At this time, she showed the officer the restraining order and the CRPD later requested that Simon Gonzales come to the police station to discuss the violation of the restraining order. During the CRPD contact with Simon Gonzales, they described him in a police report as "uncooperative" and "initially refused to respond to the Police Department for questioning." When Simon Gonzales did go to the CRPD that day, he entered a restricted area, and was charged with trespass and with the obstruction of public officials. When he was asked by the officer to sign the summons, he "refused," and began to walk out of the lobby in an attempt to keep the officer from serving him the summons.

69. Prior to 1999, the Denver Police had taken Simon Gonzales to a hospital psychiatric facility in 1996 after he attempted suicide in front of Jessica Gonzales and their daughters. A non-extraditable warrant for Mr. Gonzales' arrest had also been issued in Larimer County by June 23, 1999.

70. On Tuesday June 22, 1999 in the evening, Simon Gonzales purchased a Taurus 9mm handgun with 9 mm ammunition, from William George Palsulich, who held a Federal Firearms License since 1992. Simon Gonzales went to Palsulich's house at 7:10 p.m on June 22, 1999 with Leslie, Katheryn and Rebecca Gonzales.30 Simon Gonzales successfully passed a background check processed through the Federal Bureau of Investigations the evening of June 22nd, 1999, which was required to purchase the gun.

3. Jessica Lenahan's Contacts with the Castle Rock Police Department during the Evening of June 22, 1999 and the Morning of June 23, 1999

71. At the time of the events, Jessica Lenahan worked as a janitor at a private cleaning business that serviced the CRPD and knew most of the officers, dispatchers and employees there. Not knowing the whereabouts of her daughters, the record before the Commission shows that Jessica Lenahan had eight contacts with the CRPD during the evening of June 22, 1999 and the morning of June 23, 1999. The eight contacts included four telephone calls she placed to the CRPD emergency line; one telephone call she placed to the CRPD non-emergency line at the request of a dispatcher; one phone call from a CRPD officer; a visit by two CRPD officers to her house after the first call; and a visit by her to the CRPD station. During each of these contacts, she reported to the police dispatchers that she held a restraining order against Simon Gonzales, that she did not know where her daughters were, that they were children, and that perhaps they could be with their father.

72. Jessica Lenahan first called the Castle Rock Police Station at 7:42 p.m. on the evening of June 22, 1999, to seek advice. During this call, Jessica Lenahan reported to the dispatcher the following:

I filed a Restraining Order against my husband and we had agreed that whatever night was best, I would let him have the dinner hour...and I don't know whether he picked them up today or not.... We're leaving but tonight there was no sign of him around or anything and the girls are gone and I don't know if I should go search through town for them.

73. During this call, Jessica Lenahan also communicated to the dispatcher that "the scary part" is that she did not know where her children were, that she was very upset and "I just don't know what to do." She indicated that she had last seen them at 5:30 p.m. and that the girls had a friend with them. As a response to this phone call, two officers were dispatched to Jessica Lenahan and Simon Gonzales' houses and drove around Castle Rock looking for his pick-up truck. During the visit of the officers, Jessica Lenahan explained that Simon Gonzales usually communicated with her when he picked up their daughters, but that he had not contacted her that night.

74. When Jessica Lenahan called the police station for a second time at 8:43 p.m., she informed them that she had learned that her husband had taken their daughters to Denver, outside of the Castle Rock police department jurisdiction, without her knowledge. CRPD Officer Brink returned Jessica Lenahan's telephone call, where she communicated that the girls were at Elitches Park in Denver with their father, that she did not consider this "cool" because two of the girls had school the next day, and that she considered this "highly unusual," "wrong," and "weird." Officer Brink in response advised her to inform the Court that her husband had violated their divorce decree, because based on the information she was offering he did not consider the restraining order violated. He closed the conversation by communicating to her that "at least you know where the kids are right now." At 8:49 p.m. an entry was made in the CRPD dispatch log of telephone calls reflecting Jessica Lenahan's children had been found as reported by her.

75. Jessica Lenahan called the CRPD a third time at 9:57 p.m. that evening. During this call, she informed the dispatcher that her kids were still not home, that she was upset, and that she "did not know what to do." She related to the dispatcher a conversation she had with Simon Gonzales that evening:

> I, I just told him [Simon Gonzales], I said, you know I would really like to call the cops cause they're looking for you cause we didn't know......And he said, we're at Elitches, we're fine. And I'm like, well why didn't you tell me. And he said, well cause I thought I had 'em over night and I said, no, you know you didn't.

76. During the call, the dispatcher asked Jessica Lenahan to call her back on a "non-emergency line." In response to Jessica Lenahan's concerns, the dispatcher communicated to her the following:

> I don't know what else to say, I mean......I wish you guys uh, I wish you would have asked or had made some sort of arrangements. I mean that's a little ridiculous making U.S. freak out and thinking the kids are gone...

77. To these comments from the dispatcher, Jessica Lenahan answered "well, I mean, I really thought the kids were gone too," that she was a "mess" and that she was "freaking out." The Dispatcher on duty encouraged Jessica Lenahan to try to call the suspect and then also to return a call to the police department. The same Dispatcher later reported that she "could tell [Jessica] Gonzales was nervous." The Dispatcher reported to investigators subsequently her belief that Simon Gonzales had a wish for a vengeance against the police department because of the contact he had with them recently, where he was charged with trespassing.

78. Another dispatcher reported to the state investigators after the shooting death of Simon Gonzales, that Jessica Lenahan also called around midnight to report that her daughters, ages 7, 8, and 10 were still not home. Dispatcher O'Neill indicates in the report that she detected from her conversations with Jessica Lenahan that "she was very worried about her children" and that "she wanted an officer to meet her" at her husband's apartment. Jessica Lenahan informed the dispatcher that Simon Gonzales had run off with the girls. Dispatcher O'Neill advised Jessica Lenahan that an officer would be dispatched and the officer was dispatched by Cpl. Patricia Lisk, but three other calls were pending and the officer was unable to respond.

79. Jessica Lenahan arrived at the police department at about 12:30 a.m, with her 13-year old son and "was crying." Jessica Lenahan spoke to the dispatchers telling them that "she didn't know what to do" about her children and that she was "scared for them." In response, Officer Aaron Ahlfinger was dispatched to the CRPD to speak to Jessica Lenahan and filed a missing person's report on the children and the truck. She reported to the Officer again that she had a restraining order against Simon Gonzales, that he had picked up their three daughters from her residence around 5:30 p.m that day, that she was afraid he had "lost it," and that he might be suicidal. She was worried that Simon Gonzales had abducted the children, but said "no" when the Officer asked her whether she believed Simon Gonzales would harm them. She informed the Officer that he might have taken the children to the Pueblo Area and that she had tried to reach him via his home and cell phone since 8:00 p.m., but that he was not answering, and that she was getting a message that the lines were disconnected. After Officer Ahlfinger left the station, he drove through Simon Gonzales' neighborhood, but did not see his vehicle in front of the residence and also called him on his home and cell phone.

80. An hour after Jessica Lenahan visited the CRPD station, at 1:40 a.m, Officer Ahlfinger requested that Dispatcher Lisk send an "Attempt to Locate BOLO" for Mr. Gonzales and his vehicle. After Officer Ahlfinger left, Dispatcher Lisk began investigating how to send the bulletin on the "attempt to locate" based on the information she had, but was unable to do so by the time Simon Gonzales arrived at license plate number for the truck he was driving through the Colorado Department of Motor Vehicles. Cpl. Lisk reported to one of the investigators after Simon Gonzales' shooting death that "she had other problems entering information into the screens for the attempt to locate, i.e., no physical descriptions on the children. Dispatcher Lisk reports that she spent a considerable time looking at CBI manuals and trying to determine how to enter the information while dispatching and answering other calls."

81. At approximately 3:25 a.m. Simon Gonzales drove his pick-up truck to the CRPD and fired shots through the window. There was an exchange of gunfire with officers from the station. In the course of this shooting, he was fatally wounded and killed, and when the officers approached the truck they discovered the bodies of three young girls subsequently identified as Leslie, Katheryn, and Rebecca Gonzales.

The Investigation of Leslie, Katheryn and Rebecca Gonzales' Deaths by the Authorities

82. The Colorado Bureau of Investigations (hereinafter "CBI") undertook a detailed investigation of the crime scene.31 The investigation report contains: 1) descriptions of the crime scene and how the integrity of the scene was protected by personnel on site, 2) the evidence collected at the crime scene, including evidence relating to the weapons used, and 3) descriptions of the bodies and physical locations of the victims inside the truck. The investigation was undertaken with the involvement of eight CBI crime scene agents, and other personnel on the scene within hours of the shooting.32 The report of this investigation does not contain any conclusions as to which bullets struck Leslie, Katheryn and Rebecca Gonzales or the time and place of their deaths.

83. A second investigation was undertaken at about 4:30 a.m. on June 23rd by the Critical Incident Team (hereinafter "CIT") of the 18th Judicial District, involving 18 members of the CIT, as well as a number of additional investigators.

This report includes descriptions of the interviews with the five officers involved in the shooting death of Simon Gonzales; interviews of 12 witnesses; an interview with Jessica Lenahan; an interview with Simon Gonzales' ex-girlfriend, Rosemary Young; and interviews with other relatives and acquaintances of Simon and Jessica Lenahan. The final report also includes a statement of Simon Gonzales' history; information regarding the autopsies of Simon Gonzales and his daughters; information regarding additional evidence secured from the homes of Simon Gonzales, Jessica Lenahan and Rosemary Young; a description of the physical evidence recovered from the crime scene; and a discussion of Simon Gonzales' possible motives for the shooting at the CRPD.

84. In its "summary of investigation" section, the CIT report states that as a result of the exchange of gunfire between the police officers and Simon Gonzales, "the 18th Judicial District Critical Incident Team was called out to investigate the circumstances surrounding the shooting."33 Regarding the death of Leslie, Katheryn and Rebecca Gonzales, the CIT report solely concludes that the "autopsies revealed that the three girls were shot at extremely close range and were not struck by any rounds fired by the officers. The exact location of the homicides of the children has not been determined. There were no injuries to any police officers, bystanders or witnesses. There is no information to indicate that there were any other suspects involved besides Simon James Gonzales."

85. The autopsy reports of Leslie, Katheryn and Rebecca before the Commission only confirm about Rebecca Gonzales that her cause of death was determined to be "brain injuries due to a through and through large caliber gunshot to the right side of the head;"34 and for both Katheryn and Leslie "brain injuries due to a through and through large caliber gunshot to the left side of the head."35 The autopsy reports do not identify which bullets, those of the CRPD or Simon Gonzales, struck Leslie, Katheryn and Rebecca Gonzales.

5. Legal Process for Jessica Lenahan's Claims in the United States

86. Jessica Lenahan filed suit on January 23, 2001, in the United States District Court for the District of Colorado, a court of federal jurisdiction, alleging that the City of Castle Rock and several police officers had violated her rights under the Due Process Clause of the Fourteenth Amendment, presenting both substantive and procedural challenges as described *supra* para. 37.

87. Accepting her allegations as true, the District Court dismissed her case regarding both claims. The Court held that "[w]hile the State may have been aware of the dangers that [the children] faced in the free world, it played no part in their creation, nor did it do anything to render [them] any more vulnerable to them," since Jessica Lenahan's daughters were not in the State's custody, but their father's.36 Therefore, the Court found that the plaintiffs had failed to state a claim since solely proving "inaction" from the police officers does not rise to the level of "conscience-shocking affirmative conduct or indifference," which is needed to support a violation of substantive due process.37 In the realm of procedural due process, the District Court held that the regulatory language of the mandatory arrest statute was not truly "mandatory," since it offered police officers discretion to determine whether probable cause exists, therefore, it considered that Jessica Lenahan did not have a protectable property interest in the enforcement of the order.

88. Thereafter, a panel of judges of the Tenth Circuit Court of Appeals affirmed in part and reversed in part the District Court decision. In regards to Jessica Lenahan's substantive due process challenge, the Court considered that Jessica Lenahan had failed to show that any affirmative actions by the defendants created or increased the danger to the victims; a requirement that the Court considered necessary to succeed on a substantive due process claim. The Tenth Circuit Court however reached a different conclusion in regards to Jessica Lenahan's procedural process claim, interpreting the Colorado Mandatory Arrest Statute as containing a mandatory duty to arrest, based on the use of the word "shall," when an officer has information amounting to probable clause that the order has been violated. The Court considered that the complaint in this case, viewed most favorably to Jessica Lenahan, indicated that defendant police officers used no reasonable means to enforce the restraining order, even though she communicated to the authorities that she held one, and that Simon Gonzales had taken his daughters in violation of this order. Therefore, under these circumstances, the Court concluded that Jessica Lenahan had effectively alleged a procedural due process claim with respect "to her entitlement to enforcement of the restraining order by every reasonable means."

89. This finding was then affirmed in a rehearing before all the judges of the court ("*en banc*" review). The Court underscored that Jessica Lenahan's entitlement to police enforcement of the restraining order arose when the order was issued by the state court, since it was granted based on the court's finding that "irreparable injury would result to the moving party if no order was issued." The Court considered that not only the order itself mandated that it be enforced, but the Colorado legislature had also passed a series of statutes to ensure its enforcement. It found that there was no question in this case that the restraining order mandated the arrest of Simon Gonzales under specified circumstances, or at a minimum required the use of reasonable means to enforce the order, which limited the police officers' discretion in its implementation. Among other findings, the Court ruled that "the statute promised a process by which [Jessica Lenahan's] restraining order would be given vitality through careful and prompt consideration of an enforcement request, and the constitution requires no less. Denial of that process drained all of the value from her property interest in the restraining order."

90. Jessica Lenahan's claims at the national level reached the United States Supreme Court, the highest judicial and appellate court in the United States. On June 27, 2005, the Supreme Court rejected all of Jessica Lenahan's claims by holding that under the Due Process Clause of the 14th Amendment of the U.S. Constitution, Colorado's law on the police enforcement of restraining orders did not give Jessica Lenahan a property interest in the enforcement of the restraining order against her former husband. In its analysis, the Supreme Court considered the Colorado Statute in question and the pre-printed notice to law enforcement officers on the restraining order, holding that a "well-established tradition of police discretion has long coexisted with apparently mandatory arrest statutes," and that the "deep-rooted nature of law-enforcement discretion, even in the presence of seemingly mandatory legislative commands," had been previously recognized by the United States Supreme Court.

91. The Supreme Court specifically noted that:

It is hard to imagine that a Colorado police officer would not have some discretion to determine that — despite probable cause to believe a restraining order has been violated — the circumstances of the violation or the competing duties of that officer or his agency counsel decisively against enforcement in a particular instance. The practical necessity for discretion is particularly apparent in a case such as this one, where the suspected violator is not actually present and his whereabouts are unknown.

6. Problem of Domestic Violence in the United States and Colorado

92. Throughout the processing of this case before the Commission, both parties have presented information related to the situation of domestic violence in the United States and the quality of the state response, as context to their claims.

93. Both parties recognize the gravity and prevalence of the problem of domestic violence in the United States, at the time of the events and the present. The petitioners highlight that in the United States between one and five million women suffer non-fatal violence at the hands of an intimate partner each year. The United States Government characterizes the problem as "acute" and "significant," and acknowledges that there were at least 3.5 million incidents of domestic violence in a four-year period, contemporary with the facts pertaining to this case. Available estimates only display part of the reality, since reports indicate that only about half of the domestic violence that occurs in the United States is actually reported to the police.

94. Studies and investigations presented by the parties reveal that women constitute the majority of domestic violence victims in the United States. Some sectors of the United States female population are at a particular risk to domestic violence acts, such as Native American women and those pertaining to low-income groups. Children are also frequently exposed to domestic violence in the United States, although definitive numbers are scarce.

95. Empirical research presented to the Commission also confirms that in order to regain control over departing spouses and children, batterers will escalate violence after the battered spouse attempts to separate from her abuser. In many cases and as part of the escalation of violence, the abduction of the children is a means to coerce the resumption of the marital relationship and/or reestablish the batterer's control.38 Therefore, when a battered parent seeks to leave an abu-

sive relationship, this is the time where the children are more at risk and more in need of legal protections and interventions from law enforcement agencies.

96. The Commission has also received information in the context of this case indicating that the problem of domestic violence in the United States was considered a "private matter," and therefore, undeserving of protection measures by law enforcement agencies and the justice system.39 Once domestic violence was finally recognized as a crime, women were still very unlikely to gain protection in the United States because of law enforcement's widespread under-enforcement of domestic violence laws. Very often, the police responded to domestic violence calls either by not taking any action, by purposefully delaying their response in the hope of avoiding confrontation, or, by merely attempting to mediate the situation and separate the parties so they could "cool off."

97. Therefore, the creation of the restraining order40 is widely considered an achievement in the field of domestic violence in the United States, since it was an attempt at the state level to ensure domestic violence would be treated seriously. A 2002 national survey found that female victims of intimate partner violence are significantly more likely than their male counterparts to obtain a protective or restraining order against their assailants. However, one of the most serious historical limitations of civil restraining orders has been their widespread lack of enforcement by the police. Police officers still tend to support "traditional patriarchal gender roles, making it difficult for them to identify with and help female victims."

98. To effectively address the problem of domestic violence, at the federal level, Congress has adopted three major pieces of legislation that recognize the seriousness of domestic violence and the importance of a nationwide response: the Violence against Women Act of 1994 (hereinafter "VAWA 1994"), the Violence against Women Act of 2000 (hereinafter "VAWA 2000") and the Violence against Women and Department of Justice Reauthorization Act of 2005 (hereinafter "VAWA 2005"). VAWA is a comprehensive legislative package including the requirement for states and territories to enforce protection orders issued by other states, tribes and territories. However, most laws that protect persons in the United States from domestic violence and provide civil remedies against perpetrators and other responsible parties are state and local laws and ordinances. Over the past two decades, states have adopted a host of new laws to improve the ways that the criminal and civil justice systems respond to domestic violence.

99. Finally, the petitioners have presented a series of available statistics pointing to the alarming rates of domestic violence in the State of Colorado, uncontested by the State. Approximately half of the murders in Colorado are committed by an intimate or former partner and the victims are disproportionately female. On average over a period of three years, 45 percent of female homicide victims statewide were killed by an intimate partner. The Denver Metro Domestic Violence Fatality Committee ("the Denver Committee") identified 54 domestic violence-related fatalities in Colorado for 1996; 52 for 1997; 55 for 1998; and 69 for 1999. Between 2000 and 2005, 17 children were killed during incidents related to domestic violence. In 2005, approximately 7,478 civil protection orders to protect from domestic violence were filed in the Colorado civil court system, and approximately 14,726 domestic violence cases were filed in Colorado county courts, constituting more than 20% of all the criminal cases filed.

100. The petitioners also presented evidence of newspaper coverage indicating that domestic violence-related fatalities continue to rise in Colorado with alarming frequency since the murder of Leslie, Katheryn and Rebecca Gonzales. Between December 2005 and September 2006, five domestic violence-related murders were reported in the state of Colorado, two of which occurred in Castle Rock. In December 2005, a woman was stabbed to death in Denver, Colorado by her ex-boyfriend. More specifically, on April 2006, another woman was found shot dead by her boyfriend in Pueblo, Colorado, who had been previously arrested twice for domestic violence and aggravated assault, and had four restraining orders against him. In September 2006, a woman and her daughter were killed by the husband of the former and the stepfather of the latter in Castle Rock, Colorado; and another woman was killed when her boyfriend dragged her behind a vehicle for more than a mile. The petitioners also presented evidence of newspaper coverage indicating that domestic violence-related fatalities continue to rise in Colorado with alarming frequency since the murder of Leslie, Katheryn and Rebecca Gonzales. Between December 2005 and September 2006, five domestic violence-related murders were reported in the state of Colorado, two of which occurred in Castle Rock. In December 2005, a woman was stabbed to death in Denver, Colorado by her ex-boyfriend. More specifically, on April 2006, another woman was found shot dead

by her boyfriend in Pueblo, Colorado, who had been previously arrested twice for domestic violence and aggravated assault, and had four restraining orders against him. In September 2006, a woman and her daughter were killed by the husband of the former and the stepfather of the latter in Castle Rock, Colorado; and another woman was killed when her boyfriend dragged her behind a vehicle for more than a mile.

B. Considerations of Law

101. The Commission now presents its conclusions as to the human rights violations claimed in this case under Articles I, II, IV, V, VI, VII, XVIII and XXIV of the American Declaration, based on the proven facts and the additional considerations advanced in this section.

1. The Right to Equality before the Law and the Obligation not to Discriminate (Article II), the Right to Life (Article I), and the Right to Special Protection (Article VII), established in the American Declaration

102. Article II of the American Declaration provides that:

All persons are equal before the law and have the rights and duties established in this Declaration, without distinction as to race, sex, language, creed or any other factor.

103. Article I of the American Declaration provides that:

Every human being has the right to life, liberty and the security of his person.

104. Article VII of the American Declaration, in turn, establishes that:

All women, during pregnancy and the nursing period, and all children, have the right to special protection, care and aid.

105. The petitioners argue that discrimination in violation of Article II of the American Declaration was the common thread in all of the State presumed failures to guarantee the rights of Jessica Lenahan and her daughters enumerated in said instrument. They contend that the State's failure to adequately respond to Jessica Lenahan's calls regarding the restraining order, to conduct an investigation into the death of Leslie, Katheryn and Rebecca Gonzales, and to offer her an appropriate remedy for the police failure to enforce this order, all constituted acts of discrimination and breaches to their right to equality before the law and non-discrimination under Article II of the American Declaration. They also contend that the State's duty to protect these victims from domestic violence was of broad reach, also implicating their right to life and their right to special protection under Articles I and VII of the American Declaration, given the factual circumstances of this case. The petitioners allege that the American Declaration imposes a duty on State parties to adopt measures to respect and ensure the full and free exercise of the human rights enumerated therein; a duty which under certain circumstances requires State action to prevent and respond to the conduct of private persons. They furthermore invoke the due diligence principle to interpret the scope of State obligations under the American Declaration in cases of violence against women; obligations they consider the State failed to discharge in this case.

106. The State, for its part rejects the petitioners' arguments by claiming that the tragic murders of Leslie, Katheryn and Rebecca Gonzales were not foreseen by anyone, and therefore, the State did act diligently to protect their lives, based on the information that the CRPD had available at the time of the events. The State also alleges that the state authorities adequately investigated the death of Leslie, Katheryn and Rebecca Gonzales, and therefore, did not incur in any discrimination. The State rejects the arguments presented by the parties related to the American Declaration and the applicability of the due diligence principle to the facts of this case by claiming that: a) the American Declaration is a non-binding instrument and its provisions are aspirational; b) that the American Declaration is devoid of any provision that imposes an affirmative duty on States to take action to prevent the commission of crimes by private actors; and that b) even though the due diligence principle has found expression in several international instruments related to the problem of violence against women, its content is still unclear.

107. The Commission has repeatedly established that the right to equality and non discrimination contained in Article II of the American Declaration is a fundamental principle of the inter-American system of human rights.41 The principle of non-discrimination is the backbone of the universal and regional systems for the protection of human rights.

108. As with all fundamental rights and freedoms, the Commission has observed that States are not only obligated to provide for equal protection of the law. They must also adopt the legislative, policy and other measures necessary to guarantee the effective enjoyment of the rights protected under Article II of the American Declaration.

109. The Commission has clarified that the right to equality before the law does not mean that the substantive provisions of the law have to be the same for everyone, but that the application of the law should be equal for all without discrimination. In practice this means that States have the obligation to adopt the measures necessary to recognize and guarantee the effective equality of all persons before the law; to abstain from introducing in their legal framework regulations that are discriminatory towards certain groups either in their face or in practice; and to combat discriminatory practices. The Commission has underscored that laws and policies should be examined to ensure that they comply with the principles of equality and non-discrimination; an analysis that should assess their potential discriminatory impact, even when their formulation or wording appears neutral, or they apply without textual distinctions.

110. Gender-based violence is one of the most extreme and pervasive forms of discrimination, severely impairing and nullifying the enforcement of women's rights. The inter-American system as well has consistently highlighted the strong connection between the problems of discrimination and violence against women.

111. In the same vein, the international and regional systems have pronounced on the strong link between discrimination, violence and due diligence, emphasizing that a State's failure to act with due diligence to protect women from violence constitutes a form of discrimination, and denies women their right to equality before the law. These principles have also been applied to hold States responsible for failures to protect women from domestic violence acts perpetrated by private actors. Domestic violence, for its part, has been recognized at the international level as a human rights violation and one of the most pervasive forms of discrimination, affecting women of all ages, ethnicities, races and social classes.

112. Various international human rights bodies have moreover considered State failures in the realm of domestic violence not only discriminatory, but also violations to the right to life of women. The Commission has described the right to life "as the supreme right of the human being, respect for which the enjoyment of all other rights depends." The importance of the right to life is reflected in its incorporation into every key international human rights instrument. The right to life is one of the core rights protected by the American Declaration which has undoubtedly attained the status of customary international law.

113. The Commission has also recognized that certain groups of women face discrimination on the basis of more than one factor during their lifetime, based on their young age, race and ethnic origin, among others, which increases their exposure to acts of violence. Protection measures are considered particularly critical in the case of girl-children, for example, since they may be at a greater risk of human rights violations based on two factors, their sex and age. This principle of special protection is contained in Article VII of the American Declaration.

114. In light of the parties' arguments and submissions, there are three questions before the Commission under Articles I, II and VII of the American Declaration that it will review in the following section. The first is whether the obligation not to discriminate contained in Article II of the American Declaration requires member States to act to protect women from domestic violence; understanding domestic violence as an extreme form of discrimination. The second question pertains to the content and scope of this legal obligation under the American Declaration in light of the internationally recognized due diligence principle, and when analyzed in conjunction with the obligations to protect the right to life and to provide special protection contained in Articles I and VII of the American Declaration. The third is whether this obligation was met by the authorities in this case.

a. Legal obligation to protect women from domestic violence under Article II of the American Declaration

115. The Commission begins analyzing this first question by underscoring its holding at the admissibility stage, that according to the well-established and long-standing jurisprudence and practice of the inter-American human rights system, the American Declaration is recognized as constituting a source of legal obligation for OAS member states, including those States that are not parties to the American Convention on Human Rights. These obligations are considered to flow from the human rights obligations of Member States under the OAS Charter. Member States have agreed that the content of the general principles of the OAS Charter is contained in and defined by the American Declaration, as well as the customary legal status of the rights protected under many of the Declaration's core provisions.

116. The inter-American system has moreover held that the Declaration is a source of international obligation for all OAS member states, including those that have ratified the American Convention. The American Declaration is part of the human rights framework established by the OAS member states, one that refers to the obligations and responsibilities of States and mandates them to refrain from supporting, tolerating or acquiescing in acts or omissions that contravene their human rights commitments.

117. As a source of legal obligation, States must implement the rights established in the American Declaration in practice within their jurisdiction. The Commission has indicated that the obligation to respect and ensure human rights is specifically set forth in certain provisions of the American Declaration. International instruments in general require State parties not only to respect the rights *enumerated therein, but also to ensure that individuals within their jurisdictions also exercise those rights.* The continuum of human rights obligations is not only negative in nature; it also requires positive action from States.

118. Consonant with this principle, the Commission in its decisions has repeatedly interpreted the American Declaration as requiring States to adopt measures to give legal effect to the rights contained in the American Declaration, including cases alleging violations under Article II. The Commission has not only required States to refrain from committing human rights violations contrary to the provisions of the American Declaration, but also to adopt affirmative measures to guarantee that the individuals subject to their jurisdiction can exercise and enjoy the rights contained in the American Declaration. The Commission has traditionally interpreted the scope of the obligations established under the American Declaration in the context of the international and inter-American human rights systems more broadly, in light of developments in the field of international human rights law since the instrument was first adopted, and with due regard to other rules of international law applicable to member states.

119. In its analysis of the legal obligations contained in the American Declaration, the Commission has also noted that a State can be held responsible for the conduct of non-State actors in certain circumstances. It has moreover held that the rights contained in the American Declaration may be implicated when a State fails to prevent, prosecute and sanction acts of domestic violence perpetrated by private individuals. Furthermore, the Commission notes that both the universal system of human rights and the inter-American system of human rights — referring to the International Covenant on Civil and Political Rights, the American Convention, and other international instruments - have underscored that the duty of the State to implement human rights obligations in practice can extend to the prevention and response to the acts of private actors.

120. In light of these considerations, the Commission observes that States are obligated under the American Declaration to give legal effect to the obligations contained in Article II of the American Declaration. The obligations established in Article II extend to the prevention and eradication of violence against women, as a crucial component of the State's duty to eliminate both direct and indirect forms of discrimination. In accordance with this duty, State responsibility may be incurred for failures to protect women from domestic violence perpetrated by private actors in certain circumstances.

121. The Commission also underscores that a State's breach of its obligation to protect women from domestic violence under Article II may also give rise to violations of the right to life established in Article I of the American Declaration,

and the duty to provide special protection under Article VII of the American Declaration in given cases. These principles will be reviewed in the following section.

b. The American Declaration, the Due Diligence Principle and Domestic Violence

122. The Commission notes that the principle of due diligence has a long history in the international legal system and its standards on state responsibility. It has been applied in a range of circumstances to mandate States to prevent, punish, and provide remedies for acts of violence, when these are committed by either State or non-State actors.

123. The Commission moreover observes that there is a broad international consensus over the use of the due diligence principle to interpret the content of State legal obligations towards the problem of violence against women; a consensus that extends to the problem of domestic violence. This consensus is a reflection of the international community's growing recognition of violence against women as a human rights problem requiring State action.

124. This consensus has found expression in a diversity of international instruments, including General Assembly resolutions adopted by consensus, broadly-approved declarations and platforms, treaties, views from treaty bodies, custom, jurisprudenc from the universal and regional systems, and other sources of international law. For example, the United Nations Human Rights Council, has underscored this year that States must exercise due diligence to prevent, investigate, prosecute and punish the perpetrators of violence against women and girl-children, and that the failure to do so "violates and impairs or nullifies the enjoyment of their human rights and fundamental freedoms."

125. The international community has consistently referenced the due diligence standard as a way of understanding what State's human rights obligations mean in practice when it comes to violence perpetrated against women of varying ages and in different contexts, including domestic violence. This principle has also been crucial in defining the circumstances under which a State may be obligated to prevent and respond to the acts or omissions of private actors. This duty encompasses the organization of the entire state structure — including the State's legislative framework, public policies, law enforcement machinery and judicial system - to adequately and effectively prevent and respond to these problems. Both the Inter-American Commission and the Court have invoked the due diligence principle as a benchmark to rule on cases and situations of violence against women perpetrated by private actors, including those pertaining to girl-children.

126. The evolving law and practice related to the application of the due diligence standard in cases of violence against women highlights in particular four principles. First, international bodies have consistently established that a State may incur international responsibility for failing to act with due diligence to prevent, investigate, sanction and offer reparations for acts of violence against women; a duty which may apply to actions committed by private actors in certain circumstances. Second, they underscore the link between discrimination, violence against women and due diligence, highlighting that the States' duty to address violence against women also involves measures to prevent and respond to the discrimination that perpetuates this problem. States must adopt the required measures to modify the social and cultural patterns of conduct of men and women and to eliminate prejudices, customary practices and other practices based on the idea of the inferiority or superiority of either of the sexes, and on stereotyped roles for men and women.

127. Third, they emphasize the link between the duty to act with due diligence and the obligation of States to guarantee access to adequate and effective judicial remedies for victims and their family members when they suffer acts of violence. Fourth, the international and regional systems have identified certain groups of women as being at particular risk for acts of violence due to having been subjected to discrimination based on more than one factor, among these girl-children, and women pertaining to ethnic, racial, and minority groups; a factor which must be considered by States in the adoption of measures to prevent all forms of violence.

128. The protection of the right to life is a critical component of a State's due diligence obligation to protect women from acts of violence. This legal obligation pertains to the entire state institution, including the actions of those entrusted with safeguarding the security of the State, such as the police forces. It also extends to the obligations a State may have to prevent and respond to the actions of non-state actors and private persons.

129. The duty of protection related to the right to life is considered especially rigorous in the case of girl-children. This stems, on the one hand, from the broadly-recognized international obligation to provide special protection to children, due to their physical and emotional development. On the other, it is linked to the international recognition that the due diligence duty of States to protect and prevent violence has special connotations in the case of women, due to the historical discrimination they have faced as a group.

130. In light of these considerations, the Commission observes that the evolving standards related to the due diligence principle are relevant to interpret the scope and reach of States' legal obligations under Articles I, II, and VII of the American Declaration in cases of violence against women and girl-children taking place in the domestic context. Cases of violence against women perpetrated by private actors require an integrated analysis of the State's legal obligations under the American Declaration to act with due diligence to prevent, investigate, sanction and offer remedies.

131. International and regional human rights bodies have also applied the due diligence principle to individual cases of domestic violence. The Inter-American Commission, for its part, established in the case of *Maria Da Penha Maia Fernandes v. Brazil* that the obligation of States to act with the due diligence necessary to investigate and sanction human rights violations applies to cases of domestic violence. The Commission interpreted the duty to act with due diligence towards domestic violence broadly, encompassing not only the prompt investigation, prosecution, and sanction of these acts, but also the obligation "to prevent these degrading practices." Furthermore, it found the existence of a general pattern of State tolerance and judicial inefficiency towards cases of domestic violence, which promoted their repetition, and reaffirmed the inextricable link between the problem of violence against women and discrimination in the domestic setting.

132. In the realm of prevention, the European Court of Human Rights and the CEDAW Committee have also issued a number of rulings finding States responsible for failures to protect victims from imminent acts of domestic violence when they have considered that the authorities knew of a situation of real and immediate risk to the wife, her children, and/or other family members, created by the estranged husband, and the authorities failed to undertake reasonable measures to protect them from harm. In determining the question of knowledge, one common feature of these rulings is that the State authorities had already recognized a risk of harm to the victim and/or her family members, but had failed to act diligently to protect them. The recognition of risk was reflected in the issuance of protection orders, the detention of the aggressor, assistance to the victim and/or her family members in the filing of complaints, and the institution of criminal proceedings, in response to the victim's and/or her family members repeated contacts with the authorities. This line of reasoning has also been followed by the European Court in cases where social services had already recognized a risk of harm to children who were abused in the home setting, and failed to adopt positive measures to prevent further abuse from taking place.

133. In several of these cases, the States have been held responsible for violations to the right to life when their authorities failed to undertake reasonable measures to protect children from domestic violence resulting in their death even though they knew or should have known of a situation of risk. Among these are cases where children were murdered by a parent in a domestic violence situation, and the authorities had already recognized the risk involved after one of their parents had filed complaints related to domestic violence.

134. In the analysis of the cases referred to, the European Court of Human Rights has advanced important principles related to the scope and content of the State's obligation to prevent acts of domestic violence. The European Court has considered the obligation to protect as one of reasonable means, and not results, holding the State responsible when it failed to take reasonable measures that had a real prospect of altering the outcome or mitigating the harm. The Court has established that authorities should consider the prevalence of domestic violence, its hidden nature and the casualties of this phenomenon in the adoption of protection measures; an obligation which may be applicable even in cases where victims have withdrawn their complaints. Given the nature of domestic violence, under certain circumstances authorities may have reason to know that the withdrawal of a complaint may signify a situation of threats on the part of the aggressor, or the State may at a minimum be required to investigate that possibility. Lastly, the Court has ruled that a State's failure to protect women from domestic violence breaches their right to equal protection of the law and that this failure does not need to be intentional.

135. As the Commission has previously held in cases involving the American Declaration, while the organs of the Inter-American System are not bound to follow the judgments of international supervisory bodies, their jurisprudence can provide constructive insights into the interpretation and application of rights that are common to regional and international human rights systems.

136. In the following section, the Commission will apply these considerations to the specific case of Jessica Lenahan and Leslie, Katheryn and Rebecca Gonzales.

c. Analysis of the response of the authorities in this case

137. Considering the specific circumstances of this case, the Commission proceeds to review: i) whether the state authorities at issue should have known that the victims were in a situation of imminent risk of domestic violence; and ii) whether the authorities undertook reasonable measures to protect them from these acts. The Commission's examination in this case will not be limited to the actions of just the Castle Rock Police Department, since the State's due diligence obligation requires the organization and coordination of the work of the entire State structure to protect domestic violence victims from imminent harm.

i. The authorities' knowledge that victims were in a situation of risk

138. The undisputed facts of this case show that Jessica Lenahan possessed a valid restraining order at the time of the events, initially granted by the justice system on a temporary basis on May 21, 1999, and then rendered permanent on June 4, 1999. The terms of the temporary order included both Jessica Lenahan and her daughters as beneficiaries and indicated expressly that "physical or emotional harm" would result if Simon Gonzales was not excluded from their home. When the order was rendered permanent, Jessica Lenahan was granted temporary sole physical custody of her three daughters. Simon Gonzales was also granted parenting time under the terms of the protection order, under certain conditions. Simon Gonzales' time with his daughters during the week was restricted to a "mid-week dinner visit" that Simon Gonzales and Jessica Lenahan had to previously arrange "upon reasonable notice."

139. The reverse side of the temporary order contained important notices for the restrained party and for law enforcement officials. The order indicated to the restrained party the following:

> ....IF YOU VIOLATE THIS ORDER THINKING THAT THE OTHER PARTY OR A CHILD NAMED IN THIS ORDER HAS GIVEN YOU PERMISSION YOU ARE WRONG, AND CAN BE ARRESTED AND PROSECUTED...

> THE TERMS OF THE ORDER CANNOT BE CHANGED BY AGREEMENT OF THE OTHER PARTY OR THE CHILD(REN). ONLY THE COURT CAN CHANGE THIS ORDER...

140. For law enforcement officials, the order stated the following, mirroring the terms of the Colorado Mandatory Arrest Statute in force at the time of the events:

> YOU SHALL USE EVERY REASONABLE MEANS TO ENFORCE THE RESTRAINING ORDER.

> YOU SHALL ARREST OR, IF AN ARREST WOULD BE IMPRACTICAL UNDER THE CIRCUMSTANCES, SEEK A WARRANT FOR THE ARREST OF THE RESTRAINED PERSON WHEN YOU HAVE INFORMATION AMOUNTING TO PROBABLE CAUSE THAT THE RESTRAINED PERSON HAS VIOLATED OR ATTEMPTED TO VIOLATE ANY PROVISION OF THIS ORDER.

> YOU SHALL ENFORCE THIS ORDER EVEN IF THERE IS NO RECORD OF IT IN THE CENTRAL REGISTRY.

> YOU ARE AUTHORIZED TO USE EVERY REASONABLE EFFORT TO PROTECT THE ALLEGED VICTIM AND THE ALLEGED VICTIM'S CHILDREN TO PREVENT FURTHER VIOLENCE.

141. The Commission considers that the issuance of this restraining order and its terms reflect that the judicial authorities knew that Jessica Lenahan and her daughters were at risk of harm by Simon Gonzales. The petitioners have construed this order before the Commission as a judicial determination of that risk upon breach of its terms; an allegation uncontested by the State. The order precludes even the parties from changing the terms by agreement, since only the relevant Court can change this order.

142. The Commission considers that the issuance of a restraining order signals a State's recognition of risk that the beneficiaries would suffer harm from domestic violence on the part of the restrained party, and need State protection. This recognition is typically the product of a determination from a judicial authority that a beneficiary — a woman, her children and/or other family members — will suffer harm without police protection. The United States itself acknowledges in its pleadings that it has adopted a series of measures at the federal and state levels to ensure that protection orders are effectively implemented by the police, since they represent an assessment of risk and a form of State protection.

143. Therefore, the Commission considers that the State's recognition of risk in this domestic violence situation through the issuance of a restraining order — and the terms of said order — is a relevant element in assessing the human rights implications of the State's action or inaction in responding to the facts presented in this case. It is a key component in determining whether the State authorities should have known that the victims were in a situation of imminent risk of domestic violence upon breach of the terms of the order. It is also an indicator of which actions could have been reasonably expected from the authorities.

144. With respect to the question of which actions could have reasonably been expected, the justice system included language in this order indicating that its enforcement terms were strict; and that law enforcement authorities were responsible for implementing this order when needed. The order expressly mandates law enforcement officials — by employing the word "shall" — to act diligently to either arrest or to seek a warrant for the arrest of the aggressor in the presence of information amounting to probable cause of a violation. The order authorizes and requires law enforcement officials to use every reasonable effort to protect the alleged victim and her children from violence.

145. In light of this judicial recognition of risk, and the corresponding need for protection, the State was obligated to ensure that its apparatus responded effectively and in a coordinated fashion to enforce the terms of this order to protect the victims from harm. This required that the authorities entrusted with the enforcement of the restraining order were aware of its existence and its terms; that they understood that a protection order represents a judicial determination of risk and what their responsibilities were in light of this determination; that they understood the characteristics of the problem of domestic violence; and were trained to respond to reports of potential violations. A proper response would have required the existence of protocols or directives and training on how to implement restraining orders, and how to respond to calls such as those placed by Jessica Lenahan.

ii. Measures undertaken to protect the victims

146. In this case, it is undisputed that Jessica Lenahan had eight contacts with the Castle Rock Police Department throughout the evening of June 22nd and the morning of June 23rd of 1999, and that during each of these contacts she informed the Castle Rock Police Department that she held this restraining order. She also informed them that she did not know the whereabouts of her daughters, that they were very young girls, and that she was afraid they had been picked up by their father without notice, along with their friend.

147. Therefore, in this case the CRPD was made aware that a restraining order existed. Knowing that this restraining order existed, they would have reasonably been expected to thoroughly review the terms of the order to understand the risk involved, and their obligations towards this risk. According to the requirements of the order itself, the CRPD should have promptly investigated whether its terms had been violated. If in the presence of probable cause of a violation, they should have arrested or sought a warrant for the arrest of Simon Gonzales as the order itself directed. This would have been part of a coordinated protection approach by the State, involving the actions of its justice and law enforcement authorities.

148. National law enforcement guidelines provided by the parties concerning the enforcement of restraining orders are instructive on the minimum measures that police authorities should have adopted to determine whether the order at issue had been violated. Guidelines from the International Association of Chiefs of Police,42 presented by the petitioners, provide that an officer must read an order in its entirety in determining its potential violation; that when a victim does not have a copy of her order, police officers should attempt to verify its existence; and that when missing, officers should attempt to locate and arrest the abuser and seize firearms subject to state, territorial, local or tribal prohibitions. There are some factors that police officers can weigh to determine the potential risk due to a restraining order violation, including threats of suicide from the aggressor; a history of domestic violence and violent criminal conduct; the separation of the parties; depression or other mental illness; obsessive attachment to the victim; and possession or access to weapons, among others. When an abuser has fled the scene, the guidelines instruct police officers to: determine whether the abuser's actions warrant arrest; and to follow departmental procedure for dealing with a criminal suspect who has fled the scene.

149. The Law Enforcement Training Manual published by the Colorado Coalition against Domestic Violence, mentioned by the State, offers similar guidelines to law enforcement officials when responding to potential restraining order violations in compliance with the Colorado Mandatory Arrest Statute. The Manual underscores as critical that the police should be trained on the complex dynamics of the problem of domestic violence in order to appropriately respond to victims' calls. For example, an aggressor's control tactics over the victim may include abusing the children, since they are often what is most important to the victim. The manual identifies red flags that indicate that life-threatening violence against the victim or her family members is more likely to occur: the separation or divorce of the parties; the obsessive possessiveness on the part of the aggressor; threats to commit suicide; the issuance of protection or restraining orders; depression on the part of the abuser; a prior history of criminal behavior on the part of the abuser; incidents related to stalking; and an aggressor's access to weapons. The manual indicates that police officers should not base their assessment of potential lethality on the victim's tone or demeanor, since it may not correspond to the seriousness of the situation, and may be the product of the unequal power relations inherent to domestic violence.

150. Based on a thorough review of the record, the Commission considers that the CRPD failed to undertake the mentioned investigation actions with the required diligence and without delay. Its response can be at best characterized as fragmented, uncoordinated and unprepared; consisting of actions that did not produce a thorough determination of whether the terms of the restraining order at issue had been violated.

151. The Commission presents below some observations concerning the CRPD response from the evidence presented by the parties.

152. First, the Commission does not have any information indicating that the police officers who responded to Jessica Lenahan's calls and those who visited her house ever thoroughly reviewed the permanent restraining order to ascertain its terms and their enforcement obligations. Available information indicates that they took note of the existence of the order based on the information that Jessica Lenahan provided throughout the evening, and their conclusions and biases regarding this information, and not on the actual terms of the order. For example, as soon as they heard from Jessica Lenahan that the protection order provided Simon Gonzales with parenting time, there was no follow-up to determine whether the terms of the order limited this parenting time. Jessica Lenahan told dispatchers and officers consistently, and repeatedly, throughout the evening of June 22nd and the morning of June 23rd that she was concerned over the whereabouts of her daughters. While Jessica Lenahan did indicate at a point in the evening that she did not think Simon Gonzalez would harm his daughters,43 the dispatchers and officers apparently applied only their personal perceptions in determining that the girls were safe because they were with their father. From the record, it is also evident that information pertaining to the existence of the restraining order was not adequately communicated between the dispatchers and police officers throughout the evening, and that Jessica Lenahan was consistently asked the same questions during each of her calls.

153. Second, by 8:49 p.m in the evening of June 22nd, Jessica Lenahan had informed the police that Simon Gonzales had taken the girls to another jurisdiction in Colorado without notice. However, the police officers' actions to locate Katheryn, Leslie and Rebecca were limited to Castle Rock until their bodies were found early the next morning. The po-

lice officers should have called the Denver police department to alert them of the situation, but they failed to do so. They knew by midnight that Simon Gonzales might have taken them to the Pueblo Area, but they failed to perform any actions to search for them there.

154. Third, the file before the Commission also shows that the police officers never did a thorough check of Simon Gonzales' previous criminal background and contacts with the police. This history displayed a pattern of emotional issues, and unpredictable behavior that would have been important in understanding the risk of a violation of the protection order.

155. Fourth, the information before the Commission indicates there were apparently no protocols or directives in place guiding police officers on how to respond to reports of potential restraining order violations involving missing children, which contributed to delays in their response. For example, the undisputed facts show that it took a dispatcher an hour — between 2:15 — 3:25 a.m. — to find the guidelines to enter an "Attempt to Locate BOLO" for Simon Gonzales and his vehicle. She also reported having problems entering information into the screens for the "Attempt to Locate" because she was missing crucial information such as the physical descriptions of the children. This information was never requested from Jessica Lenahan despite her eight contacts with the police during that evening.

156. Fifth, the lack of training of the Castle Rock police officers throughout the evening of June 22nd and the morning of June 23rd was evident. The response of the Castle Rock police officers, when assessed as a whole throughout this time period, displays misunderstandings and misinformation regarding the problem of domestic violence. Even the State concedes in its pleadings that, from the point of view of the CRPD, this situation appeared to be a "misunderstanding" between Mr. and Ms. Gonzales, and the officers had a sense of relief that the children were at least in a known location with their father, even though he was subject to a restraining order.

157. Some statements display that police officers did not understand the urgency or seriousness of the situation. When Jessica Lenahan called the CPRD for a third time at 9:57 p.m. to report that her children were still not home, the dispatcher asked her to call back on a "non-emergency line," and told her she wished that she and Simon Gonzales had made some arrangements since "that's a little ridiculous making U.S. freak out and thinking the kids are gone."

158. Sixth, the Commission notes that the police officers throughout the evening evidence that they did not understand that they were the ones responsible for ascertaining whether the restraining order had been violated. They kept on asking Jessica Lenahan to call them back throughout the evening, and to contact Simon Gonzalez herself, even though they were aware that this was a domestic violence situation. The State itself in its pleadings has presented as a defense that Jessica Lenahan never reported to the police officers that the restraining order had been violated. The Commission has manifested its concern on how States mistakenly take the position that victims are themselves responsible for monitoring the preventive measures, which leaves them defenseless and in danger of becoming the victims of the assailant's reprisals.

159. Seventh, the established facts also show systemic failures not only from the CRPD, but from the Federal Bureau of Investigations. On June 22, 1999, Simon Gonzales purchased a Taurus 9mm handgun with 9 mm ammunition, from William George Palsulich, who held a Federal Firearms License since 1992. Simon Gonzales contacted Palsulich at 6:00 p.m on June 22, 1999, in response to an advertisement Palsulich had placed in the newspaper concerning the sale of the gun, asking whether he could purchase the gun and ammunition. Simon Gonzales went to Palsulich's house at 7:10 p.m on June 22, 1999 with Leslie, Katheryn and Rebecca Gonzales to purchase this gun. The record before the Commission indicates that the seller processed a background check through the Federal Bureau of Investigations in order to make the sale to Simon Gonzalez. Palsulich initially had to decline the sale since the FBI refused the background check, but the FBI later called and informed Palsulich that the transaction had been approved. The State has not contested this point, nor it has indicated how the background check of a person, such as Simon Gonzales, subject to a restraining order and having a criminal history, could have been approved. The State has not explained either why the restraining order apparently did not show up in the review of data performed as part of the background check.

iii. Conclusions

160. Based on these considerations, the Commission concludes that even though the State recognized the necessity to protect Jessica Lenahan and Leslie, Katheryn and Rebecca Gonzales from domestic violence, it failed to meet this duty with due diligence. The state apparatus was not duly organized, coordinated, and ready to protect these victims from domestic violence by adequately and effectively implementing the restraining order at issue; failures to protect which constituted a form of discrimination in violation of Article II of the American Declaration.

161. These systemic failures are particularly serious since they took place in a context where there has been a historical problem with the enforcement of protection orders; a problem that has disproportionately affected women - especially those pertaining to ethnic and racial minorities and to low- income groups - since they constitute the majority of the restraining order holders. Within this context, there is also a high correlation between the problem of wife battering and child abuse, exacerbated when the parties in a marriage separate. Even though the Commission recognizes the legislation and programmatic efforts of the United States to address the problem of domestic violence, these measures had not been sufficiently put into practice in the present case.

162. The Commission underscores that all States have a legal obligation to protect women from domestic violence: a problem widely recognized by the international community as a serious human rights violation and an extreme form of discrimination. This is part of their legal obligation to respect and ensure the right not to discriminate and to equal protection of the law. This due diligence obligation in principle applies to all OAS Member States.

163. The States' duties to protect and guarantee the rights of domestic violence victims must also be implemented in practice. As the Commission has established in the past, in the discharge of their duties, States must take into account that domestic violence is a problem that disproportionately affects women, since they constitute the majority of the victims. Children are also often common witnesses, victims, and casualties of this phenomenon. Restraining orders are critical in the guarantee of the due diligence obligation in cases of domestic violence. They are often the only remedy available to women victims and their children to protect them from imminent harm. They are only effective, however, if they are diligently enforced.

164. In the case of Leslie, Katheryn and Rebecca Gonzales, the Commission also establishes that the failure of the United States to adequately organize its state structure to protect them from domestic violence not only was discriminatory, but also constituted a violation of their right to life under Article I and their right to special protection as girl-children under Article VII of the American Declaration. As with other obligations under the American Declaration, States are not only required to guarantee that no person is arbitrarily deprived or his or her life. They are also under a positive obligation to protect and prevent violations to this right, through the creation of the conditions that may be required for its protection. In the case of Leslie, Katheryn and Rebecca Gonzales, the State had a reinforced duty of due diligence to protect them from harm and from deprivations of their life due to their age and sex, with special measures of care, prevention and guarantee. The State's recognition of the risk of harm and the need for protection — through the issuance of a protection order which included them as beneficiaries — made the adequate implementation of this protection measure even more critical.

165. The State's duty to apply due diligence to act expeditiously to protect girl-children from right to life violations requires that the authorities in charge of receiving reports of missing persons have the capacity to understand the seriousness of the phenomenon of violence perpetrated against them, and to act immediately. In this case, the police appear to have assumed that Jessica Lenahan's daughters and their friend would be safe with Simon Gonzales because he was Leslie, Katheryn and Rebecca's father. There is broad international recognition of the connection between domestic violence and fatal violence against children perpetrated by parents, and the CRPD officers should have been trained regarding this link. The police officers should also have been aware that the children were at an increased risk of violence due to the separation of their parents, Simon Gonzales' efforts to maintain contact with Jessica Lenahan, and his criminal background. Moreover, the Commission knows of no protocols and/or directives that were in place to guide the police officers at hand on how to respond to reports of missing children in the context of domestic violence and protection

orders. The police officers' response throughout the evening was uncoordinated, and not conducive to ascertaining whether the terms of the order had been violated by Simon Gonzales.

166. As part of its conclusions, the Commission notes that when a State issues a protection order, this has safety implications for the women who requested the protection order, her children and her family members. Restraining orders may aggravate the problem of separation violence, resulting in reprisals from the aggressor directed towards the woman and her children, a problem which increases the need of victims to receive legal protection from the State after an order of this kind has been issued. Jessica Lenahan has declared before the Commission how she desisted from taking more actions to find her daughters that evening thinking that the State would do more to protect them, since she held a restraining order.

167. The Commission notes with particular concern the insensitive nature of some of the CRPD comments to Jessica Lenahan's calls, considering that in her contacts she demonstrated that she was concerned for the well-being of her daughters. For example, and as noted earlier, when Jessica Lenahan called the CPRD for a third time at 9:57 p.m. to report that her children were still not home, the dispatcher told her she wished that she and Simon Gonzales had made some arrangements since "that's a little ridiculous making U.S. freak out and thinking the kids are gone." Her pleas for police action became more disturbing as the evening progressed.44 The Commission accentuates that this form of mistreatment results in a mistrust that the State structure can really protect women and girl-children from harm, which reproduces the social tolerance toward these acts. The Commission also underscores the internationally-recognized principle that law enforcement officials "shall respect and protect human dignity and maintain and uphold the human rights of all persons in the performance of their duties.

168. The Commission reiterates that State inaction towards cases of violence against women fosters an environment of impunity and promotes the repetition of violence "since society sees no evidence of willingness by the State, as the representative of the society, to take effective action to sanction such acts."

169. The Commission also observes that the State's obligations to protect Jessica Lenahan and her daughters from domestic violence did not conclude that evening. They extended to offering Jessica Lenahan a remedy for these failures and to investigating the circumstances of Leslie, Katheryn and Rebecca Gonzales' death, as will be discussed in the following section.

170. Based on these considerations, the Commission holds that the systemic failure of the United States to offer a coordinated and effective response to protect Jessica Lenahan and her daughters from domestic violence, constituted an act of discrimination, a breach of their obligation not to discriminate, and a violation of their right to equality before the law under Article II of the American Declaration. The Commission also finds that the State failure to undertake reasonable measures to protect the life of Leslie, Katheryn and Rebecca Gonzales, and that this failure constituted a violation of their right to life established in Article I of the American Declaration, in relation to their right to special protection contained in Article VII of the American Declaration.

2. The right to judicial protection under Article XVIII

171. Article XVIII of the American Declaration provides:

Every person may resort to the courts to ensure respect for his legal rights. There should likewise be available to him a simple, brief procedure whereby the courts will protect him from acts of authority that, to his prejudice, violate any fundamental constitutional rights.

172. Article XVIII of the American Declaration establishes that all persons are entitled to access judicial remedies when they have suffered human rights violations. This right is similar in scope to the right to judicial protection and guarantees contained in Article 25 of the American Convention on Human Rights, which is understood to encompass: the right of every individual to go to a tribunal when any of his or her rights have been violated; to obtain a judicial investigation conducted by a competent, impartial and independent tribunal that establishes whether or not a violation has taken place; and the corresponding right to obtain reparations for the harm suffered.

173. The inter-American system has affirmed for many years that it is not the formal existence of such remedies that demonstrates due diligence, but rather that they are available and effective. Therefore, when the State apparatus leaves human rights violations unpunished and the victim's full enjoyment of human rights is not promptly restored, the State fails to comply with its positive duties under international human rights law. The same principle applies when a State allows private persons to act freely and with impunity to the detriment of the rights recognized in the governing instruments of the inter-American system.

i. Claims related to remedies for the non-enforcement of a protection order

174. The petitioners raise several claims related to the scope of the right to judicial protection under Article XVIII of the American Declaration. They claim that Jessica Lenahan's rights were violated because she has not obtained: a remedy for the non-enforcement of her protection order; adequate access to the United States Courts; and a diligent investigation into her daughters' deaths. As part of their claims related to the investigation, the petitioners also allege that Jessica Lenahan's and her next-of-kin's right to truth has been violated due to the State's failure to provide them information surrounding the deaths of Leslie, Katheryn and Rebecca Gonzales. The petitioners also raise these claims under the right to petition established in Article XXIV of the American Declaration, and the right to freedom of investigation, opinion, expression and dissemination under Article IV of the American Declaration.

175. The State for its part claims that Article XVIII of the American Declaration does not comprehend a right to a remedy related to the non-enforcement of restraining orders; that the United States' judicial system was available to Jessica Lenahan since her case was seen by the United States Supreme Court; that Jessica Lenahan had other valid legal avenues available to adjudicate facts related to the death of her daughters which she failed to pursue; and that the State undertook two extensive investigations following the tragic deaths of Leslie, Katheryn and Rebecca Gonzales which conformed to existing human rights standards. Concerning the right to truth, the State claims that the Commission should not rule on this claim under Article IV of the American Declaration since it was not raised at the admissibility stage.

176. The Commission will discuss how the obligations under Article XVIII apply to the given case in the following order: i) claims related to remedies for the non-enforcement of the protection order; and ii) claims related to the investigation of Leslie, Katheryn and Rebecca Gonzales' deaths, including allegations pertaining to access to information and the right to truth.

177. The Commission has identified the duty of State parties to adopt legal measures to prevent imminent acts of violence, as one side of their obligation to ensure that victims can adequately and effectively access judicial protection mechanisms. The Commission has identified restraining orders, and their adequate and effective enforcement, among these legal measures. According to this principle, the failures of the State in this case to adequately and effectively organize its apparatus to ensure the implementation of the restraining order also violated the right to judicial protection of Jessica Lenahan and Leslie, Katheryn and Rebecca Gonzales.

178. The Commission also considers that when there are State failures, negligence and/or omissions to protect women from imminent acts of violence, the State also has the obligation to investigate systemic failures to prevent their repetition in the future. This involves an impartial, serious and exhaustive investigation of the State structures that were involved in the enforcement of a protection order, including a thorough inquiry into the individual actions of the public officials involved. States must hold public officials accountable — administratively, disciplinarily or criminally - when they do not act in accordance with the rule of law.

179. The State should undertake this systemic inquiry on its own motion and promptly. A delay in this inquiry constitutes a form of impunity in the face of acts of violence against women and promotes their repetition.

180. The Commission does not have information indicating that the State authorities have undertaken any inquiry into the response actions of the Castle Rock police officers in their contacts with Jessica Lenahan throughout the evening of June 22nd and the morning of June 23rd. The Commission does not have information indicating either that any inquiry has been undertaken at the level of the Federal Bureau of Investigations for the approval of the gun-purchase. The two

investigations before the Commission appear to have focused exclusively on clarifying the circumstances of the shooting death of Simon Gonzales, and not on determining individual responsibilities on the part of public officials for failures to act in accordance with the relevant state and federal laws. Therefore, the Commission notes that the State responsibilities in this case were not met by the United States Supreme Court decision regarding Jessica Lenahan's constitutional claims and extended to investigating the systemic failures which occurred during the evening of June 22nd and the morning of June 23rd in enforcing the restraining order at issue.

ii. The investigation of Leslie, Katheryn and Rebecca's deaths, access to information, and the right to truth

181. The Commission has emphasized the principle that the ability of victims of violence against women to access judicial protection and remedies includes ensuring clarification of the truth of what has happened. Investigations must be serious, prompt, thorough, and impartial, and must be conducted in accordance with international standards in this area. In addition, the IACHR has established that the State must show that the investigation "was not the product of a mechanical implementation of certain procedural formalities without the State genuinely seeking the truth." The State is ultimately the one responsible for ascertaining the truth on its own initiative, and this does not depend on the efforts of the victim or her next-of-kin. In accordance with its special protection obligation and the due diligence principle, this obligation is particularly critical in cases implicating the right to life of girl-children.

182. The inter-American system has referred to the "Principles on the Effective Prevention and Investigation of Extra-legal, Arbitrary and Summary Executions," adopted by the Economic and Social Council of the United Nations by U.N. Resolution 1989/65, as guidelines that must be observed in the investigation of a violent death. These principles require that in cases such as that of Leslie, Katheryn and Rebecca Gonzales, the investigation of every suspicious death must have the following objectives: to identify the victim; to recover and analyze all the material and documentary evidence; to identify possible witnesses and collect their testimony; to determine the cause, manner and time of death, as well as the procedure, practice, or instruments which may have caused the death; to distinguish between natural death, accidental death, suicide, and homicide; and to identify and apprehend the person or persons who may have participated in the execution.

183. The regional system has also referred to the guidelines established in the United Nations Manual on the Effective Prevention and Investigation of Extra-Legal, Arbitrary and Summary Executions, noting that one of the most important aspects of a "full and impartial" investigation of an extralegal, arbitrary, or summary execution is gathering and analyzing the evidence for each suspicious death. To this end, the manual establishes that in relation to the crime scene, that investigators must, at a minimum, photograph that scene, any other physical evidence, and the body as found and after being moved; all samples of blood, hair, fibers, threads, or other clues should be collected and conserved; examine the area in search of footprints of shoes or anything else in the nature of evidence; and make a report detailing any observation of the scene, the actions of the investigators, and the disposition of all evidence collected. In addition, it is necessary to investigate the crime scene exhaustively, autopsies should be performed, and human remains must be analyzed rigorously by competent professionals.

184. In light of these international standards, the United States had the duty to undertake, on its own initiative, a prompt, thorough and separate investigation aimed at clarifying the cause, time and place of the deaths of Leslie, Katheryn and Rebecca Gonzales.

185. The petitioners claim that the investigations conducted by the authorities solely related to the shooting death of Simon Gonzales. According to them, these documents raise many unanswered questions and demonstrate the inadequate nature of the investigation into the death of the three girls. They claim that the evidence in these documents is insufficient to determine which bullets killed Jessica Lenahan's daughters, those of the CRPD or those of Simon Gonzales. The State, for its part, claims that in the wake of the tragedy two investigations were undertaken by the Colorado Bureau of Investigations and by the Critical Incident Team of the 18th Judicial District which were prompt, extensive and thorough. The State is surprised that the petitioners now argue that because there was no adequate investigation, the actual cause of the death of the Leslie, Katheryn and Rebecca Gonzales is unknown. The State considers that the petitioners' suggestion that the gunfire originating from the CRPD officers may have killed the children is contradictory to the evi-

dence amassed in the investigative reports mentioned by the State, which suggests that Simon Gonzales murdered the girl-children.

186. The established facts before the Commission reveal that two investigations were undertaken by the State related to the case at hand, one by the Colorado Bureau of Investigations and one by the Critical Incident Team of the 18th Judicial District, but these mainly focused on clarifying the facts surrounding the shooting death of Simon Gonzales, and not the murder of Leslie, Katheryn and Rebecca Gonzales. No investigation reports before the Commission indicate as their main objective the clarification of the circumstances related to the girl-children deaths. Documents related to the investigations conclude in summary fashion that Simon Gonzales murdered his daughters before the shooting at the CRPD station, and that they were not struck by any of the rounds fired by the police officers, but fail to provide any foundation for this premise.

187. Available information regarding the circumstances of the shooting leave doubt as to the conclusion that Simon Gonzales's bullets were the ones that killed his daughters. Each girl was found to be shot in the head and chest from multiple angles. The CIT investigation report reveals that several witness accounts mentioned hearing screams, two from female voices, at the time of the shooting in front of the Castle Rock Police Department. However, there is no indication in the record that these aspects were investigated. The investigations before the Commission also reveal important omissions such as the quick disposal of Simon Gonzales' truck, even though it contained blood, clothing and other evidence related to the girl-children, making the truck an important piece of evidence in the clarification of the circumstances of the girl-children's deaths.

188. An expert report prepared by Peter Diaczuk, a forensic scientist, presented by the petitioners on July 16, 2009 and uncontested by the State, reviews in detail documentation related to these two investigations and identifies significant irregularities pertaining to the inquiry into Leslie, Katheryn and Rebecca's deaths. He notes that the "incomplete handling, documentation, and analysis of the evidence in this case resulted in unnecessary uncertainty surrounding the time, place, and circumstances of the three girls' deaths;" and that "while many answers appeared within reach, law enforcement officials simply did not take the steps necessary to fully uncover them."

189. Professor Diaczuk in his report notes key differences between the quality of the investigation of elements found outside of Simon Gonzales' pick-up truck, and the evidence found inside the truck, where the three bodies of the girl-children were found. For example, he observes that even though law enforcement used care in photographing and documenting the outside crime scene and evidence found at the street level, near Simon Gonzales' body, the bodies of the girls and the interior of the truck were photographed hastily, without use of the proper lighting equipment or measurements. Even though important items of physical evidence at the crime scene were recognized, photographed, documented and collected, most of the items collected from inside of the truck were not routed to the laboratory for analysis, as opposed to the items collected outside the truck, which were properly analyzed. Professor Diaczuk highlights as a particularly troubling aspect the Colorado authorities' analysis and accounting of the firearm evidence found inside of Simon Gonzales' truck, noting that pursuant to investigatory procedures, a laboratory examination of all cases, projectiles and fragments — including those found inside and outside of the truck — was critical; but was not performed in this case. He furthermore notes that the truck in which the bodies of the girl-children were found was disposed of quickly, before time, location and circumstances surrounding the deaths of Jessica Lenahan's children were even recorded on their death certificates, even though inquiries into the girl-children's deaths were still pending.

190. Professor Diaczuk concludes overall that even if circumstantial evidence may have suggested to the authorities that Simon Gonzales was responsible for the deaths of the girl-children, the forensic analyses he reviewed do not sustain this conclusion, instead showing that the investigation of their deaths was prematurely concluded. He indicated that the death of each victim should have been treated as a separate occurrence, and investigated in its own right.

191. The Commission notes that the State has not challenged the expert report presented by Professor Peter Diaczuk. The State has responded overall to the petitioners' claims by stating that if the petitioners considered the investigation of the girl-children's deaths inappropriate and incomplete, they should have availed themselves of the Citizen Complaint Procedure of the Castle Rock Police Department. Regarding this State claim, the Commission established at the

admissibility stage that the State had not indicated how the alternative administrative remedy it mentions could have provided Jessica Lenahan with a different judicial redress for her pretentions, or how this could have been adequate and effective in remedying the violations alleged.

192. Regarding this issue, the Commission finally underscores that the State had the obligation to investigate the death of Leslie, Katheryn and Rebecca Gonzales as separate occurrences, on its own motion and initiative, and in a prompt, exhaustive and impartial manner.

193. The Commission has also identified the right to access information in respect to existing investigations as a crucial component of a victim's adequate access to judicial remedies. A critical component of the right to access information is the right of the victim, her family members and society as a whole to be informed of all happenings related to a serious human rights violation. The inter-American system has established that this right - the right to truth - is not only a private right for relatives of the victims, affording them a form of reparation, but also a collective right that ensures that society has access to information essential for the workings of democratic systems.

194. Eleven years have passed since the murders of Leslie, Katheryn and Rebecca Gonzales, and the State has not fully clarified the cause, time and place of their deaths. The State has not duly communicated this information to their family. The petitioners have presented information highlighting the challenges that Jessica Lenahan and her family members have faced to obtain basic information surrounding the circumstances of Leslie, Katheryn and Rebecca Gonzales' deaths. They also indicate that Leslie, Katheryn and Rebecca Gonzales' gravestones still do not contain information about the time and place of their death. In regards to concrete efforts, Jessica Lenahan's mother, Tina Rivera, has declared the following before the Commission:

> Despite our repeated requests for information and documentation about the circumstances of the deaths of Rebecca, Katheryn and Leslie in the days following their shooting, the CRPD gave U.S. nothing.... For several weeks, Jessica, Rosalie Ochoa, and I attempted to obtain information from the Castle Rock and Colorado officials. Jessica and Rosalie went to the Douglas County Court House several times to try to obtain the tapes of Jessica's 911 calls. They also made repeated in-person trips to the CRPD, requesting access to the police records from the night that my granddaughters were killed. They traveled to Denver General Hospital's mental health center and Simon Gonzales' employer to find more information about Simon Gonzales.... However, officials at the Douglas County Court House and CRPD were not cooperative and tried to dissuade U.S. from our efforts. We were denied access to the files and documents we sought. While denying our requests, the Police and Court House officials treated U.S. in a dismissive and harassing manner. We felt treated as criminals, not victims.

195. The Commission underscores that under the American Declaration, the State is obligated to investigate the circumstances surrounding Leslie, Katheryn and Rebecca Gonzales' deaths and to communicate the results of such an investigation to their family. Compliance with this State obligation is critical to sending a social message in the United States that violence against girl-children will not be tolerated, and will not remain in impunity, even when perpetrated by private actors.

196. In light of the considerations presented, the Commission finds that the United States violated the right to judicial protection of Jessica Lenahan and her next-of-kin under Article XVIII, for omissions at two levels. First, the State failed to undertake a proper inquiry into systemic failures and the individual responsibilities for the non-enforcement of the protection order. Second, the State did not perform a prompt, thorough, exhaustive and impartial investigation into the deaths of Leslie, Katheryn and Rebecca Gonzales, and failed to convey information to the family members related to the circumstances of their deaths.

197. The Commission considers that it does not have sufficient information to find the State internationally responsible for failures to grant Jessica Lenahan an adequate access to courts under Article XVIII. The Commission notes that Jessica Lenahan chose to raise her claims at the national level before federal courts. The undisputed facts show that her allegations reached the U.S. Supreme Court, the highest judicial instance and appellate court in the United States. The Supreme Court ruled on her claims on June 27, 2005. Even though this ruling was unfavorable to the victim, the record

before the Commission does not display that this legal process was affected by any irregularities, omissions, delays, or any other due process violations that would contravene Article XVIII of the American Declaration.

198. Regarding Articles XXIV and IV of the American Declaration, the Commission considers that the claims related to these articles were addressed under Article XVIII of the American Declaration.

V. CONCLUSIONS

199. Based on the foregoing considerations of fact and law, and having examined the evidence and arguments presented by the parties during the proceedings, the Commission concludes that the State failed to act with due diligence to protect Jessica Lenahan and Leslie, Katheryn and Rebecca Gonzales from domestic violence, which violated the State's obligation not to discriminate and to provide for equal protection before the law under Article II of the American Declaration. The State also failed to undertake reasonable measures to prevent the death of Leslie, Katheryn and Rebecca Gonzales in violation of their right to life under Article I of the American Declaration, in conjunction with their right to special protection as girl-children under Article VII of the American Declaration. Finally, the Commission concludes that the State violated the right to judicial protection of Jessica Lenahan and her next-of kin, under Article XVIII of the American Declaration.

200. The Commission does not find that it has sufficient information to find violations of articles V and VI. As to Articles XXIV and IV of the American Declaration, it considers the claims related to these articles to have been addressed under Article XVIII of the American Declaration.

VI. RECOMMENDATIONS

201. Based on the analysis and conclusions pertaining to the instant case, the Inter-American Commission on Human Rights recommends to the United States:

1. To undertake a serious, impartial and exhaustive investigation with the objective of ascertaining the cause, time and place of the deaths of Leslie, Katheryn and Rebecca Gonzales, and to duly inform their next-of-kin of the course of the investigation.

2. To conduct a serious, impartial and exhaustive investigation into systemic failures that took place related to the enforcement of Jessica Lenahan's protection order as a guarantee of their non-repetition, including performing an inquiry to determine the responsibilities of public officials for violating state and/or federal laws, and holding those responsible accountable.

3. To offer full reparations to Jessica Lenahan and her next-of-kin considering their perspective and specific needs.

4. To adopt multifaceted legislation at the federal and state levels, or to reform existing legislation, making mandatory the enforcement of protection orders and other precautionary measures to protect women from imminent acts of violence, and to create effective implementation mechanisms. These measures should be accompanied by adequate resources destined to foster their implementation; regulations to ensure their enforcement; training programs for the law enforcement and justice system officials who will participate in their execution; and the design of model protocols and directives that can be followed by police departments throughout the country.

5. To adopt multifaceted legislation at the federal and state levels, or reform existing legislation, including protection measures for children in the context of domestic violence. Such measures should be accompanied by adequate resources destined to foster their implementation; regulations to ensure their enforcement; training programs for the law enforcement and justice system officials who will participate in their execution; and the design of model protocols and directives that can be followed by police departments throughout the country.

6. To continue adopting public policies and institutional programs aimed at restructuring the stereotypes of domestic violence victims, and to promote the eradication of discriminatory socio-cultural patterns that impede women and children's full protection from domestic violence acts, including programs to train public officials in all branches of the administration of justice and police, and comprehensive prevention programs.

To design protocols at the federal and state levels specifying the proper components of the investigation by law enforcement officials of a report of missing children in the context of a report of a restraining order violation.

The following section VII of this case document is the Inter-American Commission's report of what happened after the Lenahan Report was rendered and sent to the U.S., finding the U.S. in violation of certain of Petitioner's rights and recommending corrective and reparative action. Special consideration should be given to response of the U.S, viewed in light of the selected quotations above, expressing that it is the U.S. policy to strengthen the Inter-American human rights system. Besides not ratifying the ACHR the U.S. does not implement decisions finding it in violation. The civil society follow-up to this case continues. See http://www.lawschool.cornell.edu/womenandjustice/DV-Resolutions.cfm.

According to the Columbia Law School Human Rights Clinic website: Since 2011, a number of local jurisdictions have invoked the Commission's decision in the Lenahan case as a basis for declaring freedom from domestic violence as a human right. While they vary in scope and content, these resolutions highlight both the local and international aspects of domestic violence. Efforts are underway to leverage these resolutions into changes in law and policy in several jurisdictions.

The Human Rights Clinic and Human Rights Institute are tracking these resolutions.

VII. ACTIONS SUBSEQUENT TO REPORT No. 114/10

202. On October 21, 2010, the IACHR adopted Report No. 114/10 on the merits of this case. This report was sent to the State on November 15, 2010, with a time period of two months to inform the Inter-American Commission on the measures adopted to comply with its recommendations. On the same date, the petitioners were notified of the adoption of the report.

203. On January 14, 2011, the State requested an extension to present its response to the merits report. The Commission granted an extension to the State until March 15, 2011 to present its observations, in accordance with Article 37(2) of the IACHR's Rules of Procedure.

204. The petitioners presented their observations regarding the report on January 28, 2011, which were forwarded to the State on February 15, 2011, with a one-month period to send its observations. The petitioners also forwarded additional information to the Commission on February 18, 2011, which was transmitted to the State for its information on March 11, 2011.

205. In the present case, the State requested an extension in which to present information, but did not do so within the time period provided. The petitioners, for their part, provided a series of observations with respect to the analysis and determinations made by the Commission in its merits report, concerning such issues as: ongoing violence against women in Castle Rock; the scope of the right to an adequate and effective remedy in United States courts; the reiteration of arguments concerning the applicability of Articles I, V, VI and VII of the American Declaration in the case; and the need for the United States to ensure compliance with its obligations under the American Declaration in a way that resolves the challenges of federalism. The petitioners also requested that the Commission adopt a number of more detailed recommendations and proposed measures of follow-up on compliance.

206. In accordance with the objectives of the individual case system and the applicable terms of the Commission's Rules of Procedure, in cases in which the IACHR has established a violation of the duties set forth in the American Declaration, it transmits the report to the State in question in order for the latter to report on compliance with the recommendations issued. The Commission notifies the petitioners as well, with the same objective of receiving information with respect to compliance with its recommendations. This phase of the proceedings does not serve as an opportunity to reopen questions that have been analyzed and decided by the Commission.

207. Given the lack of information from the State, the Commission must conclude that the recommendations issued have not been implemented, and that their compliance thus remains pending. The Commission is accordingly required to reiterate those recommendations and continue monitoring compliance.

208. With respect to the submissions of the petitioners, the information presented goes not toward issues of compliance but toward questions of law that, for the most part, were analyzed by the Commission.

209. The petitioners make one observation, however, that suggests a need for clarification as to the scope of the Commission's findings with respect to judicial protection. In their submission, the petitioners take issue with what they consider to have been an overly narrow reading of the right to an adequate and effective remedy in the United States court system. They claim that: "In the Commission's view, Ms. Lenahan's right to a remedy was not violated because she was able to present her allegations to the country's highest court and the legal process she followed was unaffected 'by any irregularities, omissions, delays or any other due process violations....'" [Citation omitted.] The petitioners also claim that this narrow view of the right to a remedy fails to take into consideration the long-standing jurisprudence of the inter-American human rights system, as well as guidance from other international authorities, recognizing that the right to a remedy must be effective, "not merely illusory or theoretical," and that it must be suitable to grant appropriate relief for the legal right that is alleged to have been infringed. They reiterate that taken together, three United States Supreme Court holdings — in the cases of *Castle Rock v. Gonzales, DeShaney v. Winnebago County Department of Social Services,* and *United States v. Morrison* — act as a categorical bar to victims and survivors of domestic violence initiating legal proceedings against government officials under the United States Constitution to vindicate their rights to be protected from such violence.

210. With respect to this point, the Commission considers it pertinent to reiterate certain aspects of its findings. On the one hand, the Commission was asked to pronounce upon the response that Jessica Lenahan encountered when she filed a federal suit under the due process clause of the Fourteenth Amendment. On this specific question, the Commission concluded that Ms. Lenahan was able to present her claims and be heard. This aspect of the Commission's analysis related to the claim that was in fact brought in the present case.

211. The petitioners have underlined concerns about limitations in the availability and scope of federal claims of action for victims of violence. These questions are important, and the Commission has taken due note of the restrictive approach employed by the Supreme Court in this regard. As the Special Rapporteur on Violence against Women of the United Nations indicated at the close of a recent visit to the United States:

Although VAWA's [Violence against Women's Act] intentions are laudable, there is little in terms of actual legally binding federal provisions which provide substantive protection or prevention for acts of domestic violence against women. This challenge has been further exacerbated by jurisprudence emanating from the Supreme Court. The effect of cases such as *DeShaney, Morrison* and *Castle Rock* is that even where local and state police are grossly negligent in their duties to protect women's right to physical security, and even where they fail to respond to an urgent call of assistance from victims of domestic violence, there is no constitutional or statutory remedy at the federal level.

212. The Commission also underscores, as established in the present report, that the inter-American system has affirmed for many years that it is not the formal existence of judicial remedies that demonstrates due diligence, but rather that they are available and effective. Therefore, when the State apparatus leaves human rights violations unpunished and the victim's full enjoyment of human rights is not promptly restored, the State fails to comply with its positive duties under international human rights law. The same principle applies when a State allows private persons to act freely and with impunity to the detriment of the rights recognized in the governing instruments of the inter-American system.

213. The key aspect of the Commission's analysis in this case did not deal with the scope of federal claims of action under national law, but rather with the deficiencies in the judicial response of the State at all levels to the concrete events of the present case. This analysis was centered on the obligation of the state to provide judicial remedies to Ms. Lenahan with respect to the non-enforcement of the protection order and the subsequent deaths of her daughters. This obligation covers a range of required responses on the part of the State that were not provided, beginning first with the duty to

respond to Ms. Lenahan's calls and complaints that her daughters were at risk due to the violation of the terms of the restraining order. That restraining order was the only means available to her at the state level to protect herself and her children in a context of domestic violence, and the police did not effectively enforce it. Given the failure to effectively enforce that restraining order, the state is required to investigate the circumstances in order to identify the reasons, remedy them where required, and hold those responsible to account. Further, as established in the Commission's report, the state is obliged to investigate and clarify the circumstances of the deaths of Leslie, Katheryn and Rebecca Gonzales, and to provide Jessica Lenahan access to that information. That investigation must be prompt, thorough and effective, and undertaken by the state at its own initiative. The state's failure to comply with the foregoing obligations gives rise to the requirement to adopt concrete measures to remedy the violations.

214. On April 4, 2011, the Commission transmitted Report No. 62/11 to the parties and requested the State to present information on compliance with the recommendations within one month from the date of transmittal. No further submission on this matter was received from either party. Accordingly, based on the information available, the Commission decided to ratify its conclusions and to reiterate its recommendations in this case, as set forth below.

VIII. FINAL CONCLUSIONS AND RECOMMENDATIONS

215. On the basis of the facts and information provided, the IACHR finds that the State has not taken measures toward compliance with the recommendations in the merits report in this case. Accordingly,

THE INTER-AMERICAN COMMISSION ON HUMAN RIGHTS REITERATES ITS RECOMMENDATIONS THAT THE UNITED STATES:

1. Undertake a serious, impartial and exhaustive investigation with the objective of ascertaining the cause, time and place of the deaths of Leslie, Katheryn and Rebecca Gonzales, and to duly inform their next-of-kin of the course of the investigation.

2. Conduct a serious, impartial and exhaustive investigation into systemic failures that took place related to the enforcement of Jessica Lenahan's protection order as a guarantee of their non-repetition, including performing an inquiry to determine the responsibilities of public officials for violating state and/or federal laws, and holding those responsible accountable.

3. Offer full reparations to Jessica Lenahan and her next-of-kin considering their perspective and specific needs.

4. Adopt multifaceted legislation at the federal and state levels, or to reform existing legislation, making mandatory the enforcement of protection orders and other precautionary measures to protect women from imminent acts of violence, and to create effective implementation mechanisms. These measures should be accompanied by adequate resources destined to foster their implementation; regulations to ensure their enforcement; training programs for the law enforcement and justice system officials who will participate in their execution; and the design of model protocols and directives that can be followed by police departments throughout the country.

5. Adopt multifaceted legislation at the federal and state levels, or reform existing legislation, including protection measures for children in the context of domestic violence. Such measures should be accompanied by adequate resources destined to foster their implementation; regulations to ensure their enforcement; training programs for the law enforcement and justice system officials who will participate in their execution; and the design of model protocols and directives that can be followed by police departments throughout the country.

6. Continue adopting public policies and institutional programs aimed at restructuring the stereotypes of domestic violence victims, and to promote the eradication of discriminatory socio-cultural patterns that impede women and children's full protection from domestic violence acts, including programs to train public officials in all branches of the administration of justice and police, and comprehensive prevention programs.

7. Design protocols at the federal and state levels specifying the proper components of the investigation by law enforcement officials of a report of missing children in the context of a report of a restraining order violation.

IX. PUBLICATION

216. In light of the above and in accordance with Article 47 of its Rules of Procedure, the IACHR decides to make this report public, and to include it in its Annual Report to the General Assembly of the Organization of American States. The Inter-American Commission, according to the norms contained in the instruments which govern its mandate, will continue evaluating the measures adopted by the United States with respect to the above recommendations until it determines there has been full compliance.

Done and signed in the city of Washington, D.C., on the 21th day of July 2011.

(Signed): José de Jesús Orozco Henríquez, First Vice President; Paulo Sérgio Pinheiro, Felipe González, Luz Patricia Mejía Guerrero, and María Silvia Guillén, Commission Members.

Source: http://www.oas.org/en/iachr/media_center/PReleases /2011/092.asp

13. SAVING THE ORGANIZATION OF AMERICAN STATES, SENATE, MARCH 12, 2015

This Congressional Record recording of Senator Leahy during the Congressional debate about the U.S. and the future of the OAS argues for a continued constructive engagement and cooperation with, and funding by, the U.S. in the work of the OAS. The Senator recognizes the positive human rights work of both the Inter-American Commission and the Court of Human Rights and the value of this organization to the U.S., particularly in relation to the OAS human rights work in protecting democracy in the Americas.
Mr. LEAHY. Mr. President, I want to speak briefly about an issue that all Senators should be concerned about, and that is the future of the Organization of American States.

The origin of the OAS dates to the First International Conference of American States held in Washington from October 1889 to April 1890. The OAS was formally established in 1948 with the signing of the OAS Charter, which entered into force in 1951.

As the OAS Charter states, its mission is to achieve among its members "an order of peace and justice, and to promote their solidarity, to strengthen their collaboration, and to defend their sovereignty, their territorial integrity, and their independence."

That is an important and inspiring responsibility, and no less so today than when the OAS was founded, although many of the challenges of one-half century ago have been replaced by new challenges today.

Today the OAS consists of 35 independent States and is, at least in composition and tradition, the primary political, judicial, and social governmental forum in this hemisphere. Another 69 States and the European Union have permanent observer status.

The OAS supports programs and activities in four principle areas to carry out its mission—democracy, human rights, security, and development—and it does so in a myriad of ways, some far more successfully than others.

Few here may be aware that the United States is by far the largest contributor to the OAS, paying 60 percent of its annual budget. Two other countries pay 22 percent and the remaining 32 countries together pay only 12 percent.

Of course, the United States has by far the largest economy and should pay its fair share, but no country should be assessed to pay more than 50 percent. Other members should also pay their fair share, and we should all expect the OAS to be competently managed and to deliver tangible results that justify its expenditures.

The OAS can be proud of the indispensable work of the Inter-American Human Rights Commission and the Inter-American Court, its internationally respected election observer missions, and other activities to support democracy and promote transparent and accountable governance. These priorities should be strengthened, as I will mention shortly.

But the reputation of the OAS as a hemispheric leader has taken a beating. This is partly due to ideological polarization driven primarily by the viscerally anti-United States rhetoric and policies of the leaders of four of its member States, and partly due to the fact that the OAS has failed to exercise effective leadership in response to key issues and events, while recent sub-hemispheric groupings have taken up much of the slack and become the region's principal fora.

The OAS has allowed itself to be spread too thin, accepting too many mandates from its member States without rigorous assessment of the costs and benefits. Scarce resources have been spent on employees—without regard to transparent hiring and promotion practices—some of whom contribute little to the organization. At the same time, the OAS is facing severe budget constraints and there is no monetary reserve to respond to contingencies. It is astounding that because some countries, including Brazil, stopped paying their quotas or are in arrears, and the OAS had nothing in reserve, it had to obtain a loan in order to pay employee salaries. This is not the kind of management the OAS needs; it is mismanagement.

The Inter-American Commission and the Inter-American Court play essential roles as institutions of last resort for victims of human rights violations in countries where impunity is the norm. When corrupt, dysfunctional judicial systems fail to provide access to justice for victims of crimes against humanity or other violations of human rights, the OAS helps fill that void. Likewise, the Special Rapporteur for Freedom of Expression plays a critical role at a time when some governments, such as Venezuela and Ecuador, are engaged in a systematic effort to intimidate and silence their critics in the independent press, while others, including Mexico and Honduras, fail to protect journalists from threats and attacks by gangs or violence related to drug trafficking.

Yet a shortage of funding and the failure of some member States to comply with the decisions of the Commission and the rulings of the Court undermine their effectiveness. Some governments have actively sought to weaken these key institutions by withholding financial support and proposing to limit the legal authority of the Commission and the Court. They and the Special Rapporteur for Freedom and Expression need sufficient resources to do their jobs, and it is time to establish a mechanism for sanctioning noncompliance.

The United States is not blameless, having signed but not yet ratified the American Convention on Human Rights. This provides a convenient excuse for other governments to accuse U.S. of hypocrisy as we urge their adherence to human rights norms. It is time for the Congress to act on this piece of unfinished business.

I would add, however, that the United States is part of the Inter-American Commission, as are all OAS member States, regardless of whether or not they have ratified the Convention. In fact, the United States has more cases at the Commission than any other country, and we strive to implement its decisions.

The OAS needs to strengthen its election monitoring capability—including insisting on timely and equal participation by opposition political parties, freedom of the press and association—to ensure a level playing field when some Latin governments refuse to allow early access by the OAS. Many Latin Americans are becoming cynical about the ability of democratic governments to deliver basic services in a manner that is transparent and accountable. Elected governments which are corrupt and neglect, or are unable to protect their people, erode support for democracy.

Similarly, the OAS and the Secretary General in particular need to respond swiftly to political crises, and exercise stronger leadership in defense of democratic institutions and human rights when they are under assault, consistent with the OAS Charter and the Inter-American Democratic Charter.

There is also the issue of hemispheric security. During the Cold War there was a single-minded, concerted effort to prevent the Soviet Union from gaining another foothold in Latin America. Countless innocent people were threatened, disappeared, tortured, or killed in the name of fighting communism by Central and South American security forces, many of them encouraged, trained and equipped by the United States, and only a token number of the individuals responsible have been punished.

Today the hemisphere faces new threats, such as drug cartels, gang violence, transnational crime, money laundering, and natural disasters. But the plans to address them like the Merida Initiative and the Alliance for Prosperity, while identifying such priorities as police and judicial reform, poverty, fiscal transparency, and corruption, tend to be long on goals and short on specifics of how to achieve them.

Cooperation on multi-dimensional security threats is not a matter of ideology. Cuba and the United States are already cooperating against drug-traffickers, as we are with other countries. But there is a lot more that can and should be done to identify the causes and develop and implement more effective regional strategies to address these problems.

Several Latin countries have made notable strides in the past decade and are providing greater opportunities for their people. The OAS can play a role in convening a debate, identifying solutions, and facilitating an alliance of key development organizations, including the Inter-American Development Bank and the Pan American Health Organization, to address areas of shared interest such as achieving sustained, equitable economic growth, strengthening public education and health, and protecting natural resources.

The OAS has an important, under-utilized role to play in interfacing with the wide range of civil society organizations which are essential to any democracy and are often under-appreciated, under-funded, and persecuted. With OAS offices throughout the hemisphere, its under-utilized employees could engage far more actively with academia, civil society, and the media. This should include any such entities that reject violence, not just those that are "registered" by local governments which sometimes use the registration process to silence legitimate voices whose views the government disagrees with.

Finally, the OAS needs to decide how to interact with other hemispheric multilateral organizations in a manner that strengthens the OAS and encourages cooperation. Cuba's suspension, and then refusal to return, provided an impetus for the creation of new entities like CELAC, the Community of Latin American and Caribbean States, that are anti-OAS and anti-United States and have sowed division within the hemisphere.

The next Secretary General of the OAS, who will be selected on March 18, has his work cut out for him. I say "him" because there is only one candidate, which says volumes about how the job is perceived. The Secretary General plays a crucial role as the strategic leader, but not the day-to-day manager, of the organization. The next Secretary General needs an Assistant Secretary General with the managerial expertise and mandate to right this sinking ship.

It will mean tough budgetary decisions, including the ability to say no to new programs and mandates and to focus instead on doing better at what it does best.

As soon as possible after they assume their positions I urge them to review Public Law 113-41, the "Organization of American States Revitalization and Reform Act of 2013." That Act, which received bipartisan support, identifies key issues that need to be addressed—many of which I have touched on here—and provides recommendations for how to address them.

I wish them both well because the people of every country in the hemisphere, including those whose governments have sought to harm the OAS, need the OAS. But absent significant and rapid reforms beginning with the quota issue, the OAS's decline may be irreversible.

Source: Congressional Record, https://www.congress.gov/congressional-record/2015/3/12/senate-section/article/s1489-1

Organization for Security & Cooperation in Europe (OSCE)

Chapter 8

This Chapter is About an international political organization called the Organization for Security and Cooperation in Europe. It is a political institution with a human rights component. The OSCE is a political system in which the U.S. is a member state even though the organizational focus is on post World War II Europe.

This is Important Because originally this organization allowed the U.S. to interface with countries of communist Central and Eastern Europe after WWII and during the Cold War, both to prevent a new war from breaking out and to try to encourage the communist countries to protect human rights and allow contact between family members in all countries, especially those behind the "iron curtain." This organization, which represents one billion people, is composed of the following participating States from Europe, Central Asia, and North America:

Albania, Andorra, Armenia, Austria, Azerbaijan, Belarus, Belgium, Bosnia and Herzegovina, Bulgaria, Canada, Croatia, Cyprus, Czech Republic, Denmark, Estonia, Finland, France, Georgia, Germany, Greece, Holy See, Hungary, Iceland, Ireland, Italy, Kazakhstan, Kyrgyzstan, Latvia, Liechtenstein, Lithuania, Luxembourg, Malta, Moldova, Monaco, Mongolia, Montenegro, Netherlands, Norway, Poland, Portugal, Romania, Russian Federation, San Marino, Serbia, Slovakia, Slovenia, Spain, Sweden, Switzerland. Tajikistan, the former Yugoslav Republic of Macedonia, Turkey, Turkmenistan, Ukraine, United Kingdom, United States, Uzbekistan

Quotes & Key Text Excerpts

Friends and colleagues, we meet in Hamburg today to reaffirm the same idea that tied us together in Helsinki 41 years ago: that our collective security is directly linked to the growth of our economies and the protection of basic human rights.

In our era as in the past, we advance the security and prosperity of our citizens when we advance the timeless principles that are at the heart of the OSCE — democratic governance and the rule of law; anti-corruption; respect for the sovereignty and territorial integrity of every state, no matter its size and power, and the dignity of every individual; and an unflinching stand against anti-Semitism, anti-Muslim, anti-Christian sentiment, and bigotry and intolerance of any kind.

These values literally can never be taken for granted. They have to be defended constantly, and they have to be so in word and deed. And that is exactly what we've done through the OSCE for four decades, and it is what we have to remain committed to achieving now and in the years to come.

Our task begins in actions where places of violence and assaults on human dignity persist, even where a clear path to peace is staring us in the face.

—Secretary of State John Kerry, Organization for Security and Cooperation in Europe (OSCE), December 8, 2016

Source: http://www.state.gov/secretary/remarks/2016/12/264970

꙰꙰꙰꙰꙰꙰꙰꙰

To start at that broad level, one of the things that my first couple of months have underscored to me is that as we look at the 57 countries that participate in the OSCE, there are a number of regional sub-groupings around trade, around other issues, around security, et cetera, but the OSCE remains this unique platform that cuts across all aspects of what within the OSCE is called comprehensive security, but meaning what we traditionally call hard security or political-military security, economic and environmental security, and human security, including human rights. It remains a unique platform in covering the broad range of issues, and it remains a unique platform in that it includes members of the EU, all the members of NATO, all the members of the Eurasian Customs Union. It includes a number of subgroups. And so it becomes this place where important conversations can happen between a large group of countries that collectively represent two-thirds of the world's economy — a billion people. It's a significant community that comes together.

—Ambassador Daniel Baer, U.S. Representative to the OSCE, Washington Foreign Press Center, 2013

Source: https://fpc.state.gov/217901.htm

What You Should Know

THE ORGANIZATION FOR SECURITY AND COOPERATION IN EUROPE (OSCE)

Formerly known as the Conference on Security and Cooperation in Europe (CSCE), this is the forum in which the U.S. has been particularly engaged in for many years regarding human rights. The U.S. helped create and sustain this prime forum for interaction between the U.S. and Russia today on human rights issues.

> The Organization for Security and Cooperation in Europe (OSCE) is a 56-member, pan-European, security organization. It is a key instrument for preventing conflict, promoting democracy, human rights and the rule of law, and encouraging open and transparent economies.
> *Source: http://www.state.gov/p/eur/rt/osce/*

At the end of World War II in Europe, many of the nations of eastern and Western Europe (thirty-five) and the United States and Canada established a political organization that was known as the Conference on Security and Cooperation in Europe (CSCE). It sought to establish the boundaries of post-war Europe, to draft political instruments regarding human rights obligations, and to create mechanisms for dealing with threats to security on both sides to minimize the risk of military action. The human rights component of this organization was based on the 1975 Helsinki Final Act. This document contains four chapters called "baskets." Each basket contains a number of principles. See Primary Source Document 1.

References to the member obligations on human rights are found primarily in the guiding principles contained in Baskets I and III. Principles VII and VIII refer to the member states' obligation to fulfill their obligations to respect human rights under existing international law. Because this is a political and not legal forum, they refer not to human rights obligations but to a state's "commitments." This Final Act of a conference was not a legal instrument, and the CSCE succeeded largely because everything was a matter of political and not legal obligation. However, the signing of the act was important historically and legally in the postwar struggle for human rights. It was the first international acknowledgement and acceptance by the USSR and its communist allies that they had an obligation, or a "commitment" to conform their conduct to international human rights standards. Initially this forum served as the meeting place of the two sides of the Iron Curtain and the principal place for discussions on human rights between the two sides, especially the United States and the Soviet Union during the Cold War era.

Since the CSCE's founding, numerous follow-up meetings and many documents concerning human rights have been issued from these meetings. These meetings consisted of the exchange of views concerning compliance of members with their human rights obligations and the expansion of the catalogue of human rights. These follow-up meetings gave rise to what is called the Helsinki Process. The 1989 Vienna follow-up document gave rise to the "Human Dimension Mechanism" of the CSCE, which consists of a multistage negotiation, fact-finding, and mediation process between states, as well as bilateral and multilateral negotiations and the use of missions of experts and rapporteurs to deal with specific issues and crises. This process is done in conjunction with the CSCE Office of the High Commissioner on National Minorities. This office was to provide early warning and take early action to prevent or end minority-based crises before they degenerate into serious conflicts.

In 1994, the name was changed to Organization for Security and Cooperation in Europe, OSCE. It is a very important human rights forum for the United States, which has always been a very active political player in this organization. The OSCE has served as the main political vehicle to become involved in, and engaged with, former communist countries in central and Eastern Europe. For example, it was the intense political pressure of the United States and its western European allies upon the former Soviet Union through the CSCE that caused the Soviets to permit the mass emigration of

Soviet Jews to Israel, the United States, and elsewhere in the late 1980s and early 1990s. There are now about fifty-three countries in the OSCE.

The OSCE has an Office for Democratic Institutions and Human Rights in Warsaw, Poland and the U.S. State Department engages in human rights activity in the OSCE context via that Office.

The OSCE approaches security through three dimensions: the politico-military, the economic and environmental, and the human.

The OSCE Institution is describes itself as follows:

The OSCE — the Organization for Security and Co-operation in Europe — is a forum for political dialogue on a wide range of security issues and a platform for joint action to improve the lives of individuals and communities. Through its comprehensive approach to security that encompasses the politico-military, economic and environmental, and human dimensions and its inclusive membership, the OSCE helps bridge differences and build trust between states by co-operating on conflict prevention, crisis management and post-conflict rehabilitation. With its institutions, expert units and network of field operations, the OSCE addresses issues that have an impact on our common security, including arms control, terrorism, good governance, energy security, human trafficking, democratization, media freedom and national minorities.

Institutions and Structures:
- Parliamentary Assembly
- High Commissioner on National Minorities
- Office for Democratic Institutions and Human Rights
- Representative on Freedom of the Media
- Court of Conciliation and Mediation
- Minsk Group
- Secretariat

Source: http://www.osce.org/whatistheosce/factsheet

The Parliamentary Assembly of the OSCE is the parliamentary dimension of the Organization for Security and Co-operation in Europe, whose 57 participating States span the geographical area from Vancouver to Vladivostok.

The primary task of the 323-member Assembly is to facilitate inter-parliamentary dialogue, an important aspect of the overall effort to meet the challenges of democracy throughout the OSCE area. Recognized as a regional arrangement under Chapter VIII of the United Nations Charter, the OSCE is a primary instrument for early warning, conflict prevention, crisis management, and post-conflict rehabilitation in its area. The Parliamentary Assembly, originally established by the 1990 Paris Summit to promote greater involvement in the OSCE by national parliaments in the participating States, also pursues other important objectives which are stated in the preamble of the Assembly's Rules of Procedure. They include:
- to assess the implementation of OSCE objectives by participating States;
- to discuss subjects addressed during meetings of the Ministerial Council and summit meetings of OSCE Heads of State or Government;
- to develop and promote mechanisms for the prevention and resolution of conflicts;
- to support the strengthening and consolidation of democratic institutions in OSCE participating States;
- to contribute to the development of OSCE institutional structures and of relations and co-operation between existing OSCE institutions.

Source: https://www.oscepa.org/about-osce-pa

There are four levels of OSCE decision-making platforms:
- Meetings of Heads of State or Government (Summits) take decisions, set priorities, and provide guidance at the highest political level.

- The Ministerial Council (MC), which gathers ministers of foreign affairs of the OSCE participating states, is the main decision-making and governing body of the OSCE between Summits.
- The Permanent Council (PC), meets regularly in Vienna to conduct political consultations and to govern the operational work of the Organization. This body also implements, within its area of competence, tasks defined and decisions taken at Summits and Ministerial Council meetings.
- The Forum for Security Co-operation (FSC) is an autonomous, decision-making body with a mandate set by Summit and Ministerial decisions. It covers fundamental politico-military agreements and helps to implement confidence- and security-building measures to regulate the exchange of military information and mutual verification between states.

According to the OSCE, its participating states have recognized that human rights are the birthright of all human beings, are inalienable, and are guaranteed by law. In promoting respect for human rights, ODIHR monitors governments' compliance with their human dimension commitments. The Office provides states with advice and assistance, and supports individuals and civil society with targeted training and education. ODIHR covers a broad spectrum of issues, ranging from the fundamental freedoms of religion or belief, movement, assembly, and association, to reporting on the use of the death penalty, monitoring trials, and preventing torture and other forms of ill-treatment.

The OSCE Office for Democratic Institutions and Human Rights (ODIHR) provides support, assistance, and expertise to participating states and civil society to promote democracy, rule of law, human rights, and tolerance and non-discrimination. ODIHR observes elections, reviews legislation, and advises governments on how to develop and sustain democratic institutions. The Office conducts training programmes for government and law-enforcement officials and non-governmental organizations on how to uphold, promote, and monitor human rights. The OSCE Office for Democratic Institutions and Human Rights (ODIHR) provides support, assistance, and expertise to participating states and civil society to promote democracy, rule of law, human rights, and tolerance and non-discrimination. ODIHR observes elections, reviews legislation, and advises governments on how to develop and sustain democratic institutions. The Office conducts training programmes for government and law-enforcement officials and non-governmental organizations on how to uphold, promote, and monitor human rights.

The OSCE openly monitored and observed the 2016 U.S. presidential elections. The OSCE International Election Observation Mission, STATEMENT OF PRELIMINARY FINDINGS AND CONCLUSIONS, is Primary Source Document 6 and represents OSCE efforts to protect democracy by free and fair elections in member states.

The OSCE has established a number of tools to monitor the implementation of commitments that participating states have undertaken in the field of human rights and democracy (the human dimension).

One of these tools, the so-called Human Dimension Mechanism, can be invoked on an ad hoc basis by any individual participating state or group of states. It is composed of two instruments: the Vienna Mechanism (established in the Vienna Concluding Document of 1989) and the Moscow Mechanism (established at the last meeting of the Conference on the Human Dimension in Moscow in 1991), the latter partly constituting a further elaboration of the Vienna Mechanism.

The Vienna Mechanism allows participating states, through an established set of procedures, to raise questions relating to the human dimension situation in other OSCE states.

The Moscow Mechanism provides for the additional possibility for participating states to establish ad hoc missions of independent experts to assist in the resolution of a specific human dimension problem, either on their own territory or in other OSCE participating states.

ODIHR is designated to provide support for the implementation of the Moscow Mechanism, and it maintains a list of experts appointed by some of the participating states who are available to carry out such investigations.

An example of the U.S. participating in this process took place in the 12 states of the European Community and the United States on the issue of reports of atrocities and attacks on unarmed civilians in Croatia and Bosnia-Herzegovina (1992).

In the U.S. government, there is a bi-partisan commission called the U.S. Helsinki Commission. It monitors what goes on in the OSCE, and its mission statement states:

We are a U.S. government agency that promotes human rights, military security, and economic cooperation in 57 countries in Europe, Eurasia, and North America. Nine Commissioners are members of the Senate, nine are members of the House of Representatives, and three are executive branch officials.

Source: https://www.csce.gov

Primary Source Documents

I. FINAL ACT HELSINKI, 1975

This political instrument was the final act of a Conference held in 1975 in Helsinki, Finland. It was entitled: the Conference on Security and Cooperation in Europe. It is not a legal document creating human rights legal norms, but a political document which recognized the commitment of all member states to fulfill their "obligations" under the international legal instruments involving human rights to which each was a state party. It was the basis of the interface between the "East" and the "West" during the Cold War for dealing with issues including human rights. It continued to be the main documentary basis for this institution when it changed its name to the Organization for Security and Cooperation in Europe.

{Excerpt}

Document 1. FINAL ACT OF HELSINKI 1975

The Conference on Security and Co-operation in Europe, which opened at Helsinki on 3 July 1973 and continued at Geneva from 18 September 1973 to 21 July 1975, was concluded at Helsinki on 1 August 1975 by the High Representatives of Austria, Belgium, Bulgaria, Canada, Cyprus, Czechoslovakia, Denmark, Finland, France, the German Democratic Republic, the Federal Republic of Germany, Greece, the Holy See, Hungary, Iceland, Ireland, Italy, Liechtenstein, Luxembourg, Malta, Monaco, the Netherlands, Norway, Poland, Portugal, Romania, San Marino, Spain, Sweden, Switzerland, Turkey, the Union of Soviet Socialist Republics, the United Kingdom, the United States of America and Yugoslavia.

During the opening and closing stages of the Conference the participants were addressed by the Secretary-General of the United Nations as their guest of honour. The Director-General of UNESCO and the Executive Secretary of the United Nations Economic Commission for Europe addressed the Conference during its second stage.

During the meetings of the second stage of the Conference, contributions were received, and statements heard, from the following non-participating Mediterranean States on various agenda items: the Democratic and Popular Republic of Algeria, the Arab Republic of Egypt, Israel, the Kingdom of Morocco, the Syrian Arab Republic, Tunisia.

Motivated by the political will, in the interest of peoples, to improve and intensify their relations and to contribute in Europe to peace, security, justice and cooperation as well as to rapprochement among themselves and with the other States of the world,

Determined, in consequence, to give full effect to the results of the Conference and to assure, among their States and throughout Europe, the benefits deriving from those results and thus to broaden, deepen and make continuing and lasting the process of détente,

The High Representatives of the participating States have solemnly adopted the following:

Questions relating to Security in Europe

The States participating in the Conference on Security and Co-operation in Europe,

Reaffirming their objective of promoting better relations among themselves and ensuring conditions in which their people can live in true and lasting peace free from any threat to or attempt against their security;

Convinced of the need to exert efforts to make détente both a continuing and an increasingly viable and comprehensive process, universal in scope, and that the implementation of the results of the Conference on Security and Cooperation in Europe will be a major contribution to this process;

Considering that solidarity among peoples, as well as the common purpose of the participating States in achieving the aims as set forth by the Conference on Security and Cooperation in Europe, should lead to the development of better and closer relations among them in all fields and thus to overcoming the confrontation stemming from the character of their past relations, and to better mutual understanding;

Mindful of their common history and recognizing that the existence of elements common to their traditions and values can assist them in developing their relations, and desiring to search, fully taking into account the individuality and diversity of their positions and views, for possibilities of joining their efforts with a view to overcoming distrust and increasing confidence, solving the problems that separate them and cooperating in the interest of mankind;

Recognizing the indivisibility of security in Europe as well as their common interest in the development of cooperation throughout Europe and among selves and expressing their intention to pursue efforts accordingly;

Recognizing the close link between peace and security in Europe and in the world as a whole and conscious of the need for each of them to make its contribution to the strengthening of world peace and security and to the promotion of fundamental rights, economic and social progress and well-being for all peoples;

Have adopted the following:

1. (a) Declaration on Principles Guiding Relations between Participating States The participating States, Reaffirming their commitment to peace, security and justice and the continuing development of friendly relations and co-operation;

Recognizing that this commitment, which reflects the interest and aspirations of peoples, constitutes for each participating State a present and future responsibility, heightened by experience of the past;

Reaffirming, in conformity with their membership in the United Nations and in accordance with the purposes and principles of the United Nations, their full and active support for the United Nations and for the enhancement of its role and effectiveness in strengthening international peace, security and justice, and in promoting the solution of international problems, as well as the development of friendly relations and cooperation among States;

Expressing their common adherence to the principles which are set forth below and are in conformity with the Charter of the United Nations, as well as their common will to act, in the application of these principles, in conformity with the purposes and principles of the Charter of the United Nations;

Declare their determination to respect and put into practice, each of them in its relations with all other participating States, irrespective of their political, economic or social systems as well as of their size, geographical location or level of economic development, the following principles, which all are of primary significance, guiding their mutual relations:

I. Sovereign equality, respect for the rights inherent in sovereignty

The participating States will respect each other's sovereign equality and individuality as well as all the rights inherent in and encompassed by its sovereignty, including in particular the right of every State to juridical equality, to territorial integrity and to freedom and political independence. They will also respect each other's right freely to choose and develop its political, social, economic and cultural systems as well as its right to determine its laws and regulations.

Within the framework of international law, all the participating States have equal rights and duties. They will respect each other's right to define and conduct as it wishes its relations with other States in accordance with international law and in the spirit of the present Declaration. They consider that their frontiers can be changed, in accordance with international law, by peaceful means and by agreement. They also have the right to belong or not to belong to international organizations, to be or not to be a party to bilateral or multilateral treaties including the right to be or not to be a party to treaties of alliance; they also have the right to neutrality.

...

VII. Respect for human rights and fundamental freedoms, including the freedom of thought, conscience, religion or belief

The participating States will respect human rights and fundamental freedoms, including the freedom of thought, conscience, religion or belief, for all without distinction as to race, sex, language or religion.

They will promote and encourage the effective exercise of civil, political, economic, social, cultural and other rights and freedoms all of which derive from the inherent dignity of the human person and are essential for his free and full development.

Within this framework the participating States will recognize and respect the freedom of the individual to profess and practice, alone or in community with others, religion or belief acting in accordance with the dictates of his own conscience.

The participating States on whose territory national minorities exist will respect the right of persons belonging to such minorities to equality before the law, will afford them the full opportunity for the actual enjoyment of human rights and fundamental freedoms and will, in this manner, protect their legitimate interests in this sphere.

The participating States recognize the universal significance of human rights and fundamental freedoms, respect for which is an essential factor for the peace, justice and well-being necessary to ensure the development of friendly relations and co-operation among themselves as among all States.

They will constantly respect these rights and freedoms in their mutual relations and will endeavour jointly and separately, including in co-operation with the United Nations, to promote universal and effective respect for them.

They confirm the right of the individual to know and act upon his rights and duties in this field.

In the field of human rights and fundamental freedoms, the participating States will act in conformity with the purposes and principles of the Charter of the United Nations and with the Universal Declaration of Human Rights. They will also fulfil their obligations as set forth in the international declarations and agreements in this field, including inter alia the International Covenants on Human Rights, by which they may be bound.

VIII. Equal rights and self-determination of peoples

The participating States will respect the equal rights of peoples and their right to self-determination, acting at all times in conformity with the purposes and principles of the Charter of the United Nations and with the relevant norms of international law, including those relating to territorial integrity of States.

By virtue of the principle of equal rights and self-determination of peoples, all peoples always have the right, in full freedom, to determine, when and as they wish, their internal and external political status, without external interference, and to pursue as they wish their political, economic, social and cultural development.

The participating States reaffirm the universal significance of respect for and effective exercise of equal rights and self-determination of peoples for the development of friendly relations among themselves as among all States; they also recall the importance of the elimination of any form of violation of this principle.

IX. Co-operation among States

The participating States will develop their co-operation with one another and with all States in all fields in accordance with the purposes and principles of the Charter of the United Nations. In developing their co-operation the participating States will place special emphasis on the fields as set forth within the framework of the Conference on Security and Co-operation in Europe, with each of them making its contribution in conditions of full equality.

They will endeavour, in developing their co-operation as equals, to promote mutual understanding and confidence, friendly and good-neighbourly relations among themselves, international peace, security and justice. They will equally endeavour, in developing their co-operation, to improve the well-being of peoples and contribute to the fulfilment of their aspirations through, inter alia, the benefits resulting from increased mutual knowledge and from progress and achievement in the economic, scientific, technological, social, cultural and humanitarian fields. They will take steps to promote conditions favourable to making these benefits available to all; they will take into account the interest of all in the narrowing of differences in the levels of economic development, and in particular the interest of developing countries throughout the world.

They confirm that governments, institutions, organizations and persons have a relevant and positive role to play in contributing toward the achievement of these aims of their cooperation.

They will strive, in increasing their cooperation as set forth above, to develop closer relations among themselves on an improved and more enduring basis for the benefit of peoples.

X. Fulfilment in good faith of obligations under international law

The participating States will fulfil in good faith their obligations under international law, both those obligations arising from the generally recognized principles and rules of international law and those obligations arising from treaties or other agreements, in conformity with international law, to which they are parties.

In exercising their sovereign rights, including the right to determine their laws and regulations, they will conform with their legal obligations under international law; they will furthermore pay due regard to and implement the provisions in the Final Act of the Conference on Security and Co-operation in Europe.

The participating States confirm that in the event of a conflict between the obligations of the members of the United Nations under the Charter of the United Nations and their obligations under any treaty or other international agreement, their obligations under the Charter will prevail, in accordance with Article 103 of the Charter of the United Nations.

All the principles set forth above are of primary significance and, accordingly, they will be equally and unreservedly applied, each of them being interpreted taking into account the others.

The participating States express their determination fully to respect and apply these principles, as set forth in the present Declaration, in all aspects, to their mutual relations and cooperation in order to ensure to each participating State the benefits resulting from the respect and application of these principles by all.

The participating States, paying due regard to the principles above and, in particular, to the first sentence of the tenth principle, "Fulfilment in good faith of obligations under international law," note that the present Declaration does not affect their rights and obligations, nor the corresponding treaties and other agreements and arrangements.

The participating States express the conviction that respect for these principles will encourage the development of normal and friendly relations and the progress of co-operation among them in all fields. They also express the conviction that respect for these principles will encourage the development of political contacts among them which in time would contribute to better mutual understanding of their positions and views.

The participating States declare their intention to conduct their relations with all other States in the spirit of the principles contained in the present Declaration.

(b) Matters related to giving effect to certain of the above Principles

(i) The participating States,

Reaffirming that they will respect and give effect to refraining from the threat or use of force and convinced of the necessity to make it an effective norm of international life, Declare that they are resolved to respect and carry out, in their relations with one another, inter alia, the following provisions which are in conformity with the Declaration on Principles Guiding Relations between Participating States:
- To give effect and expression, by all the ways and forms which they consider appropriate, to the duty to refrain from the threat or use of force in their relations with one another.
- To refrain from any use of armed forces inconsistent with the purposes and principles of the Charter of the United Nations and the provisions of the Declaration on Principles Guiding Relations between Participating States, against another participating State, in particular from invasion of or attack on its territory.

- To refrain from any manifestation of force for the purpose of inducing another participating State to renounce the full exercise of its sovereign rights.
- To refrain from any act of economic coercion designed to subordinate to their own interest the exercise by another participating State of the rights inherent in its sovereignty and thus to secure advantages of any kind.
- To take effective measures which by their scope and by their nature constitute steps towards the ultimate achievement of general and complete disarmament under strict and effective international control.
- To promote, by all means which each of them considers appropriate, a climate of confidence and respect among peoples consonant with their duty to refrain from propaganda for wars of aggression or for any threat or use of force inconsistent with the purposes of the United Nations and with the Declaration on Principles Guiding Relations between Participating States, against another participating State.
- To make every effort to settle exclusively by peaceful means any dispute between them, the continuance of which is likely to endanger the maintenance of international peace and security in Europe, and to seek, first of all, a solution through the peaceful means set forth in Article 33 of the United Nations Charter.

To refrain from any action which could hinder the peaceful settlement of disputes between the participating States.

(ii) The participating States, Reaffirming their determination to settle their disputes as set forth in the Principle of Peaceful Settlement of Disputes;

Have adopted the following:

Co-operation in Humanitarian and Other Fields

The participating States,

Desiring to contribute to the strengthening of peace and understanding among peoples and to the spiritual enrichment of the human personality without distinction as to race, sex, language or religion,

Conscious that increased cultural and educational exchanges, broader dissemination of information, contacts between people, and the solution of humanitarian problems will contribute to the attainment of these aims,

Determined therefore to cooperate among themselves, irrespective of their political, economic and social systems, in order to create better conditions in the above fields, to develop and strengthen existing forms of co-operation and to work out new ways and means appropriate to these aims,

Convinced that this co-operation should take place in full respect for the principles guiding relations among participating States as set forth in the relevant document, Have adopted the following:

1. Human Contacts The participating States, Considering the development of contacts to be an important element in the strengthening of friendly relations and trust among peoples,

Affirming, in relation to their present effort to improve conditions in this area, the importance they attach to humanitarian considerations,

Desiring in this spirit to develop, with the continuance of détente, further efforts to achieve continuing progress in this field

And conscious that the questions relevant hereto must be settled by the States concerned under mutually acceptable conditions,

Make it their aim to facilitate freer movement and contacts, individually and collectively, whether privately or officially, among persons, institutions and organizations of the participating States, and to contribute to the solution of the humanitarian problems that arise in that connexion,

Declare their readiness to these ends to take measures which they consider appropriate and to conclude agreements or arrangements among themselves, as may be needed, and Express their intention now to proceed to the implementation of the following:

(a) Contacts and Regular Meetings on the Basis of Family Ties

In order to promote further development of contacts on the basis of family ties the participating States will favourably consider applications for travel with the purpose of allowing persons to enter or leave their territory temporarily, and on a regular basis if desired, in order to visit members of their families.

Applications for temporary visits to meet members of their families will be dealt with without distinction as to the country of origin or destination: existing requirements for travel documents and visas will be applied in this spirit. The preparation and issue of such documents and visas will be effected within reasonable time limits, cases of urgent necessity-such as serious illness or death-will be given priority treatment. They will take such steps as may be necessary to ensure that the fees for official travel documents and visas are acceptable.

They confirm that the presentation of an application concerning contacts on the basis of family ties will not modify the rights and obligations of the applicant or of members of his family.

(b) Reunification of Families

The participating States will deal in a positive and humanitarian spirit with the applications of persons who wish to be reunited with members of their family, with special attention being given to requests of an urgent character-such as requests submitted by persons who are ill or old.

The receiving participating State will take appropriate care with regard to employment for persons from other participating States who take up permanent residence in that State in connexion with family reunification with its citizens and see that they are afforded opportunities equal to those enjoyed by its own citizens for education, medical assistance and social security.

...

(h) Expansion of Contacts

By way of further developing contacts among governmental institutions and non-governmental organizations and associations, including women's organizations, the participating States will facilitate the convening of meetings as well as travel by delegations, groups and individuals.

Follow-up to the Conference

The participating States,

Having considered and evaluated the progress made at the Conference on Security and Co-operation in Europe,

Considering further that, within the broader context of the world, the Conference is an important part of the process of improving security and developing co-operation in Europe and that its results will contribute significantly to this process,

Intending to implement the provisions of the Final Act of the Conference in order to give full effect to its results and thus to further the process of improving security and developing co-operation in Europe,

Convinced that, in order to achieve the aims sought by the Conference, they should make further unilateral, bilateral and multilateral efforts and continue, in the appropriate forms set forth below, the multilateral process initiated by the Conference,

1. Declare their resolve, in the period following the Conference, to pay due regard to and implement the provisions of the Final Act of the Conference:

(a) unilaterally, in all cases which lend themselves to such action;

(b) bilaterally, by negotiations with other participating States;

(c) multilaterally, by meetings of experts of the participating States, and also within the framework of existing international organizations, such as the United Nations Economic Commission for Europe and UNESCO, with regard to educational, scientific and cultural co-operation;

2. Declare furthermore their resolve to continue the multilateral process initiated by the Conference:

(a) by proceeding to a thorough exchange of views both on the implementation of the provisions of the Final Act and of the tasks defined by the Conference, as well as, in the context of the questions dealt with by the latter, on the deepening of their mutual relations, the improvement of security and the development of co-operation in Europe, and the development of the process of détente in the future;

(b) by organizing to these ends meetings among their representatives, beginning with a meeting at the level of representatives appointed by the Ministers of Foreign Affairs. This meeting will define the appropriate modalities for the holding of other meetings which could include further similar meetings and the possibility of a new Conference;

...

4. ...The original of this Final Act, drawn up in English, French, German, Italian, Russian and Spanish, will be transmitted to the Government of the Republic of Finland, which will retain it in its archives. Each of the participating States will receive from the Government of the Republic of Finland a true copy of this Final Act.

The text of this Final Act will be published in each participating State, which will disseminate it and make it known as widely as possible.

...

Wherefore, the undersigned High Representatives of the participating States, mindful of the high political significance which they attach to the results of the Conference, and declaring their determination to act in accordance with the provisions contained in the above texts, have subscribed their signatures below:

Done at Helsinki, on 1st August 1975

2. THE CHARTER OF PARIS FOR A NEW EUROPE, 1990

This Conference on Security and Co-operation in Europe (CSCE) document marks the end of the Cold War and the disintegration of the Soviet Union as a result of Perestroika and Glasnost. The Iron Curtain fell and a new Europe was rising, with many eastern and central European states wanting to come into the house of west Europe to create one house of Europe. The CSCE was the vehicle. This Charter declares a new era in Europe characterized by democracy and respect for human rights, and it marked a new era for the CSCE, which would soon thereafter become the OSCE.

Meeting of the Heads of State or Government of the participating States of the Conference on Security and Co-operation in Europe (CSCE): Austria, Belgium, Bulgaria, Canada, Cyprus, Czech and Slovak Federal Republic, Denmark, Finland, France, Germany, Greece, Holy See, Hungary, Iceland, Ireland, Italy, Liechtenstein, Luxembourg, Malta, Monaco, Netherlands, Norway, Poland, Portugal, Romania, San Marino, Spain, Sweden, Switzerland, Turkey, Union of Soviet Socialist Republics, United Kingdom, United States of America and Yugoslavia, Paris, 19-21 November 1990

A New Era of Democracy, Peace and Unity

We, the Heads of State or Government of the States participating in the Conference on Security and Co-operation in Europe, have assembled in Paris at a time of profound change and historic expectations. The era of confrontation and division of Europe has ended. We declare that henceforth our, relations will be founded on respect and co-operation.

Europe is liberating itself from the legacy of the past. The courage of men and women, the strength of the will of the peoples and the power of the ideas of the Helsinki Final Act have opened a new era of democracy, peace and unity in Europe.

Ours is a time for fulfilling the hopes and expectations our peoples have cherished for decades : steadfast commitment to democracy based on human rights and fundamental freedoms; prosperity through economic liberty and social justice; and equal security for all our countries.

The Ten Principles of the Final Act will guide U.S. towards this ambitious future, just as they have lighted our way towards better relations for the past fifteen years. Full implementation of all CSCE commitments must form the basis for the initiatives we are now taking to enable our nations to live in accordance with their aspirations.

Human Rights, Democracy and Rule of Law
We undertake to build, consolidate and strengthen democracy as the only system of government of our nations. In this endeavour, we will abide by the following:

Human rights and fundamental freedoms are the birthright of all human beings, are inalienable and are guaranteed by law. Their protection and promotion is the first responsibility of government. Respect for them is an essential safeguard against an overmighty State. Their observance and full exercise are the foundation of freedom, justice and peace.

Democratic government is based on the will of the people, expressed regularly through free and fair elections. Democracy has as its foundation respect for the human person and the rule of law. Democracy is the best safeguard of freedom of expression, tolerance of all groups of society, and equality of opportunity for each person.

Democracy, with its representative and pluralist character, entails accountability to the electorate, the obligation of public authorities to comply with the law and justice administered impartially. No one will be above the law.

We affirm that, without discrimination, every individual has the right to freedom of thought, conscience and religion or belief, freedom of expression, freedom of association and peaceful assembly, freedom of movement;

no one will be:
- subject to arbitrary arrest or detention,
- subject to torture or other cruel, inhuman or degrading treatment or punishment;

everyone also has the right:
- to know and act upon his rights,
- to participate in free and fair elections,
- to fair and public trial if charged with an offence,
- to own property alone or in association and to exercise individual enterprise,
- to enjoy his economic, social and cultural rights.

We affirm that the ethnic, cultural, linguistic and religious identity of national minorities will be protected and that persons belonging to national minorities have the right freely to express, preserve and develop that identity without any discrimination and in full equality before the law.

We will ensure that everyone will enjoy recourse to effective remedies, national or international, against any violation of his rights.

Full respect for these precepts is the bedrock on which we will seek to construct the new Europe.

Our States will co-operate and support each other with the aim of making democratic gains irreversible.

Economic Liberty and Responsibility
Economic liberty, social justice and environmental responsibility are indispensable for prosperity.

The free will of the individual, exercised in democracy and protected by the rule of law, forms the necessary basis for successful economic and social development. We will promote economic activity which respects and upholds human dignity.

Freedom and political pluralism are necessary elements in our common objective of developing market economies towards sustainable economic growth, prosperity, social justice, expanding employment and efficient use of economic resources. The success of the transition to market economy by countries making efforts to this effect is important and in the interest of U.S. all. It will enable U.S. to share a higher level of prosperity which is our common objective. We will co-operate to this end.

Preservation of the environment is a shared responsibility of all our nations. While supporting national and regional efforts in this field, we must also look to the pressing need for joint action on a wider scale.

Friendly Relations among Participating States
Now that a new era is dawning in Europe, we are determined to expand and strengthen friendly relations and co-operation among the States of Europe, the United States of America and Canada, and to promote friendship among our peoples.

To uphold and promote democracy, peace and unity in Europe, we solemnly pledge our full commitment to the Ten Principles of the Helsinki Final Act. We affirm the continuing validity of the Ten Principles and our determination to put them into practice. All the Principles apply equally and unreservedly, each of them being interpreted taking into account the others. They form the basis for our relations.

In accordance with our obligations under the Charter of the United Nations and commitments under the Helsinki Final Act, we renew our pledge to refrain from the threat or use of force against the territorial integrity or political independence of any State, or from acting in any other manner inconsistent with the principles or purposes of those documents. We recall that non-compliance with obligations under the Charter of the United Nations constitutes a violation of international law.

We reaffirm our commitment to settle disputes by peaceful means. We decide to develop mechanisms for the prevention and resolution of conflicts among the participating States.

With the ending of the division of Europe, we will strive for a new quality in our security relations while fully respecting each other's freedom of choice in that respect. Security is indivisible and the security of every participating State is inseparably linked to that of all the others. We therefore pledge to co-operate in strengthening confidence and security among U.S. and in promoting arms control and disarmament.

We welcome the Joint Declaration of Twenty-Two States on the improvement of their relations.

Our relations will rest on our common adherence to democratic values and to human rights and fundamental freedoms. We are convinced that in order to strengthen peace and security among our States, the advancement of democracy, and respect for and effective exercise of human rights, are indispensable. We reaffirm the equal rights of peoples and their right to self-determination in conformity with the Charter of the United Nations and with the relevant norms of international law, including those relating to territorial integrity of States.

We are determined to enhance political consultation and to widen co-operation to solve economic, social, environmental, cultural and humanitarian problems. This common resolve and our growing interdependence will help to overcome the mistrust of decades, to increase stability and to build a united Europe.

We want Europe to be a source of peace, open to dialogue and to co-operation with other countries, welcoming exchanges and involved in the search for common responses to the challenges of the future.

Security

Friendly relations among U.S. will benefit from the consolidation of democracy and improved security.

We welcome the signature of the Treaty on Conventional Armed Forces in Europe by twenty-two participating States, which will lead to lower levels of armed forces. We endorse the adoption of a substantial new set of Confidence- and Security-building Measures which will lead to increased transparency and confidence among all participating States. These are important steps towards enhanced stability and security in Europe.

The unprecedented reduction in armed forces resulting from the Treaty on Conventional Armed Forces in Europe, together with new approaches to security and cooperation within the CSCE process, will lead to a new perception of security in Europe and a new dimension in our relations. In this context we fully recognize the freedom of States to choose their own security arrangements.

Unity

Europe whole and free is calling for a new beginning. We invite our peoples to join in this great endeavour.

We note with great satisfaction the Treaty on the Final Settlement with respect to Germany signed in Moscow on 12 September 1990 and sincerely welcome the fact that the German people have united to become one State in accordance with the principles of the Final Act of the Conference on Security and Co-operation in Europe and in full accord with their neighbours. The establishment of the national unity of Germany is an important contribution to a just and lasting order of peace for a united, democratic Europe aware of its responsibility for stability, peace and co-operation.

The participation of both North American and European States is a fundamental characteristic of the CSCE; it underlies its past achievements and is essential to the future of the CSCE process. An abiding adherence to shared values and our common heritage are the ties which bind U.S. together. With all the rich diversity of our nations, we are united in our commitment to expand our co-operation in all fields. The challenges confronting U.S. can only be met by common action, co-operation and solidarity.

The CSCE and the World

The destiny of our nations is linked to that of all other nations. We support fully the United Nations and the enhancement of its role in promoting international peace, security and justice. We reaffirm our commitment to the principles and purposes of the United Nations as enshrined in the Charter and condemn all violations of these principles. We recognize with satisfaction the growing role of the United Nations in world affairs and its increasing effectiveness, fostered by the improvement in relations among our States.

Aware of the dire needs of a great part of the world, we commit ourselves to solidarity with all other countries. Therefore, we issue a call from Paris today to all the nations of the 7 world. We stand ready to join with any and all States in common efforts to protect and advance the community of fundamental human values.

Guidelines for the Future

Proceeding from our firm commitment to the full implementation of all CSCE principles and provisions, we now resolve to give a new impetus to a balanced and comprehensive development of our co-operation in order to address the needs and aspirations of out peoples.

Human Dimension

We declare our respect for human rights and fundamental freedoms to be irrevocable. We will fully implement and build upon the provisions relating to the human dimension of the CSCE.

Proceeding from the Document of the Copenhagen Meeting of the Conference on the Human Dimension, we will cooperate to strengthen democratic institutions and to promote the application of the rule of law. To that end, we decide to convene a seminar of experts in Oslo from 4 to 15 November 1991.

Determined to foster the rich contribution of national minorities to the life of our societies, we undertake further to improve their situation. We reaffirm our deep conviction that friendly relations among our peoples, as well as peace, justice, stability and democracy, require that the ethnic, cultural, linguistic and religious identity of national minorities be protected and conditions for the promotion of that identity be created. We declare that questions related to national minorities can only be satisfactorily resolved in a democratic political framework. We further acknowledge that the rights of persons belonging to national minorities must be fully respected as part of universal human rights. Being aware of the urgent need for increased cooperation on, as well as better protection of, national minorities, we decide to convene a meeting of experts on national minorities to be held in Geneva from 1 to 19 July 1991.

We express our determination to combat all forms of racial and ethnic hatred, antisemitism, xenophobia and discrimination against anyone as well as persecution on religious and ideological grounds.

In accordance with our CSCE commitments, we stress that free movement and contacts among our citizens as well as the free flow of information and ideas are crucial for the maintenance and development of free societies and flourishing cultures. We welcome increased tourism and visits among our countries.

The human dimension mechanism has proved its usefulness, and we are consequently determined to expand it to include new procedures involving, inter alia, the services of experts or a roster of eminent persons experienced in human rights issues which could be raised under the mechanism. We shall provide, in the context of the mechanism, for individuals to be involved in the protection of their rights. Therefore, we undertake to develop further our commitments in this respect, in particular at the Moscow Meeting of the Conference on the Human Dimension, without prejudice to obligations under existing international instruments to which our States may be parties.

We recognize the important contribution of the Council of Europe to the promotion of human rights and the principles of democracy and the rule of law as well as to the development of cultural co-operation. We welcome moves by several participating States to join the Council of Europe and adhere to its European Convention on Human Rights. We welcome as well the readiness of the Council of Europe to make its experience available to the CSCE.

Security

The changing political and military environment in Europe opens new possibilities for common efforts in the field of military security. We will build on the important achievements attained in the Treaty on Conventional Armed Forces in Europe and in the Negotiations on Confidence- and Security-building Measures. We undertake to continue the CSBM negotiations under the same mandate, and to seek to conclude them no later than the Follow-up Meeting of the CSCE to be held in Helsinki in 1992. We also welcome the decision of the participating States concerned to continue the CFE negotiation under the same mandate and to seek to conclude it no later than the Helsinki Follow-up Meeting. Following a period for national preparations, we look forward to a more structured cooperation among all participating States on security matters, and to discussions and consultations among the thirty-four participating States aimed at establishing by 1992, from the conclusion of the Helsinki Follow-up Meeting, new negotiations on disarmament and confidence and security building open to all participating States.

We call for the earliest possible conclusion of the Convention on an effectively verifiable, global and comprehensive ban on chemical weapons, and we intend to be original signatories to it.

We reaffirm the importance of the Open Skies initiative and call for the successful conclusion of the negotiations as soon as possible.

Although the threat of conflict in Europe has diminished, other dangers threaten the stability of our societies. We are determined to co-operate in defending democratic institutions against activities which violate the independence, sovereign equality or territorial integrity of the participating States. These include illegal activities involving outside pressure, coercion and subversion.

We unreservedly condemn, as criminal, all acts, methods and practices of terrorism and express our determination to work for its eradication both bilaterally and through multilateral co-operation. We will also join together in combating illicit trafficking in drugs.

Being aware that an essential complement to the duty of States to refrain from the threat or use of force is the peaceful settlement of disputes, both being essential factors for the maintenance and consolidation of international peace and security, we will not only seek effective ways of preventing, through political means, conflicts which may yet emerge, but also define, in conformity with international law, appropriate mechanisms for the peaceful resolution of any disputes which may arise. Accordingly, we undertake to seek new forms of co-operation in this area, in particular a range of methods for the peaceful settlement of disputes, including mandatory third-party involvement. We stress that full use should be made in this context of the opportunity of the Meeting on the Peaceful Settlement of Disputes which will be convened in Valletta at the beginning of 1991. The Council of Ministers for Foreign Affairs will take into account the Report of the Valletta Meeting.

Economic Co-operation

We stress that economic co-operation based on market economy constitutes an essential element of our relations and will be instrumental in the construction of a prosperous and united Europe. Democratic institutions and economic liberty foster economic and social progress, as recognized in the Document of the Bonn Conference on Economic Co-operation, the results of which we strongly support.

We underline that co-operation in the economic field, science and technology is now an important pillar of the CSCE. The participating States should periodically review progress and give new impulses in these fields.

We are convinced that our overall economic co-operation should be expanded, free enterprise encouraged and trade increased and diversified according to GATT rules. We will promote social justice and progress and further the welfare of our peoples. We recognize in this context the importance of effective policies to address the problem of unemployment.

We reaffirm the need to continue to support democratic countries in transition towards the establishment of market economy and the creation of the basis for self-sustained economic and social growth, as already undertaken by the Group of twenty-four countries. We further underline the necessity of their increased integration, involving the acceptance of disciplines as well as benefits, into the international economic and financial system.

We consider that increased emphasis on economic co-operation within the CSCE process should take into account the interests of developing participating States.

We recall the link between respect for and promotion of human rights and fundamental freedoms and scientific progress. Co-operation in the field of science and technology will play an essential role in economic and social development. Therefore, it must evolve towards a greater sharing of appropriate scientific and technological information and knowledge with a view to overcoming the technological gap which exists among the participating States. We further encourage the participating States to work together in order to develop human potential and the spirit of free enterprise.

We are determined to give the necessary impetus to co-operation among our States in the fields of energy, transport and tourism for economic and social development. We welcome, in particular, practical steps to create optimal conditions for the economic and rational development of energy resources, with due regard for environmental considerations.

We recognize the important role of the European Community in the political and economic development of Europe. International economic organizations such as the United Nations Economic Commission for Europe (ECE), the Bretton Woods Institutions, the Organisation for Economic Co-operation and Development (ECD), the European Free Trade Association (EFTA) and the International Chamber of Commerce (ICC) also have a significant task in promoting economic co-operation, which will be further enhanced by the establishment of the European Bank for Reconstruction and Development (EBRD). In order to pursue our objectives, we stress the necessity for effective co-ordination of the activities of these organizations and emphasize the need to find methods for all our States to take part in these activities.

Environment

We recognize the urgent need to tackle the problems of the environment and the importance of individual and co-operative efforts in this area. We pledge to intensify our endeavours to protect and improve our environment in order to restore and maintain a sound ecological balance in air, water and soil. Therefore, we are determined to make full use of the CSCE as a framework for the formulation of common environmental commitments and objectives, and thus to pursue the work reflected in the Report of the Sofia Meeting on the Protection of the Environment.

We emphasize the significant role of a well-informed society in enabling the public and individuals to take initiatives to improve the environment. To this end, we commit ourselves to promoting public awareness and education on the environment as well as the public reporting of the environmental impact of policies, projects and programmes.

We attach priority to the introduction of clean and low-waste technology, being aware of the need to support countries which do not yet have their own means for appropriate measures.

We underline that environmental policies should be supported by appropriate legislative measures and administrative structures to ensure their effective implementation.

We stress the need for new measures providing for the systematic evaluation of compliance with the existing commitments and, moreover, for the development of more ambitious commitments with regard to notification and exchange of information about the state of the environment and potential environmental hazards. We also welcome the creation of the European Environment Agency (EEA).

We welcome the operational activities, problem-oriented studies and policy reviews in various existing international organizations engaged in the protection of the environment, such as the United Nations Environment Programme (UNEP), the United Nations Economic Commission for Europe (ECE) and the Organisation for Economic Co-operation and Development (OECD). We emphasize the need for strengthening their co-operation and for their efficient co-ordination.

Culture
We recognize the essential contribution of our common European culture and our shared values in overcoming the division of the continent. Therefore, we underline our attachment to creative freedom and to the protection and promotion of our cultural and spiritual heritage, in all its richness and diversity.

In view of the recent changes in Europe, we stress the increased importance of the Cracow Symposium and we look forward to its consideration of guidelines for intensified cooperation in the field of culture. We invite the Council of Europe to contribute to this Symposium.

In order to promote greater familiarity amongst our peoples, we favour the establishment of cultural centres in cities of other participating States as well as increased cooperation in the audio-visual field and wider exchange in music, theatre, literature and the arts.

We resolve to make special efforts in our national policies to promote better understanding, in particular among young people, through cultural exchanges, co-operation in all fields of education and, more specifically, through teaching and training in the languages of other participating States. We intend to consider first results of this action at the Helsinki Follow-up Meeting in 1992.

Migrant Workers
We recognize that the issues of migrant workers and their families legally residing in host countries have economic, cultural and social aspects as well as their human dimension. We reaffirm that the protection and promotion of their rights, as well as the implementation of relevant international obligations, is our common concern.

Mediterranean
We consider that the fundamental political changes that have occurred in Europe have a positive relevance to the Mediterranean region. Thus, we will continue efforts to strengthen security and co-operation in the Mediterranean as an important factor for stability in Europe. We welcome the Report of the Palma de Mallorca Meeting on the Mediterranean, the results of which we all support.

We are concerned with the continuing tensions in the region, and renew our determination to intensify efforts towards finding just, viable and lasting solutions, through peaceful means, to outstanding crucial problems, based on respect for the principles of the Final Act.

We wish to promote favourable conditions for a harmonious development and diversification of relations with the non-participating Mediterranean States. Enhanced cooperation with these States will be pursued with the aim of promoting economic and social development and thereby enhancing stability in the region. To this end, we will strive together with these countries towards a substantial narrowing of the prosperity gap between Europe and its Mediterranean neighbours.

Non-governmental Organizations
We recall the major role that non-governmental organizations, religious and other groups and individuals have played in the achievement of the objectives of the CSCE and will further facilitate their activities for the implementation of the CSCE commitments by the participating States. These organizations, groups and individuals must be involved in an appropriate way in the activities and new structures of the CSCE in order to fulfil their important tasks.

New Structures and Institutions of the CSCE Process
Our common efforts to consolidate respect for human rights, democracy and the rule of law, to strengthen peace and to promote unity in Europe require a new quality of political dialogue and co-operation and thus development of the structures of the CSCE.

The intensification of our consultations at all levels is of prime importance in shaping our future relations. To this end, we decide on the following

We, the Heads of State or Government, shall meet next time in Helsinki on the occasion of the CSCE Follow-up Meeting 1992. Thereafter, we will meet on the occasion of subsequent follow-up meetings.

Our Ministers for Foreign Affairs will meet, as a Council, regularly and at least once a year. These meetings will provide the central forum for political consultations within the CSCE process. The Council will consider issues relevant to the Conference on Security and Co-operation in Europe and take appropriate decisions.

The first meeting of the Council will take place in Berlin.

A Committee of Senior Officials will prepare the meetings of the Council and carry out its decisions. The Committee will review current issues and may take appropriate decisions, including in the form of recommendations to the Council.

Additional meetings of the representatives of the participating States may be agreed upon to discuss questions of urgent concern.

The Council will examine the development of provisions for convening meetings of the Committee of Senior Officials in emergency situations.

Meetings of other Ministers may also be agreed by the participating States.

In order to provide administrative support for these consultations we establish a Secretariat in Prague.

Follow-up meetings of the participating States will be held, as a rule, every two years to allow the participating States to take stock of developments, review the implementation of their commitments and consider further steps in the CSCE process.

We decide to create a Conflict Prevention Centre in Vienna to assist the Council in reducing the risk of conflict.

We decide to establish an Office for Free Elections in Warsaw to facilitate contacts and the exchange of information on elections within participating States.

Recognizing the important role parliamentarians can play in the CSCE process, we call for greater parliamentary involvement in the CSCE, in particular through the creation of a CSCE parliamentary assembly, involving members of parliaments from all participating States. To this end, we urge that contacts be pursued at parliamentary level to discuss the field of activities, working methods and rules of procedure of such a CSCE parliamentary structure, drawing on existing experience and work already undertaken in this field.

We ask our Ministers for Foreign Affairs to review this matter on the occasion of their first meeting as a Council.

...

Procedural and organizational modalities relating to certain provisions contained in the Charter of Paris for a New Europe are set out in the Supplementary Document which is adopted together with the Charter of Paris.

We entrust to the Council the further steps which may be required to ensure the implementation of decisions contained in the present document, as well as in the Supplementary Document, and to consider further efforts for the strengthening of security and co-operation in Europe. The Council may adopt any amendment to the supplementary document which it may deem appropriate.

...

Wherefore, we, the undersigned High Representatives of the participating States, mindful of the high political significance we attach to the results of the Summit Meeting, and declaring our determination to act in accordance with the provisions we have adopted, have subscribed our signatures below:

Done at Paris, on 21 November 1990

⚜⚜⚜⚜⚜⚜⚜⚜

3. THE MOSCOW (HUMAN DIMENSION) MECHANISM, 1991

This document sets forth the terms of reference for a human rights related mechanism, one of the human dimension mechanisms. It set up a process for resolving human rights and other issues between members states. The goal was to avoid incidents giving rise to armed conflict between states and between the West and the East.

MOSCOW 1991 (Par. 1 to 16) as amended by ROME 1993 (Chapter IV, par. 5)

In order to strengthen and expand the human dimension mechanism described in the section on the human dimension of the CSCE in the Concluding Document of the Vienna Meeting and to build upon and deepen the commitments set forth in the Document of the Copenhagen Meeting of the Conference on the Human Dimension of the CSCE, the participating States adopt the following:

(1) The participating States emphasize that the human dimension mechanism described in paragraphs 1 to 4 of the section on the human dimension of the CSCE in the Vienna Concluding Document constitutes an essential achievement of the CSCE process, having demonstrated its value as a method of furthering respect for human rights, fundamental freedoms, democracy and the rule of law through dialogue and co-operation and assisting in the resolution of specific relevant questions.

In order to improve further the implementation of the CSCE commitments in the human dimension, they decide to enhance the effectiveness of this mechanism and to strengthen and expand it as outlined in the following paragraphs.

(2) The participating States amend paragraphs 42.1 and 42.2 of the Document of the Copenhagen Meeting to the effect that they will provide in the shortest possible time, but no later than ten days, a written response to requests for information and to representations made to them in writing by other participating States under paragraph 1 of the human dimension mechanism. Bilateral meetings, as referred to in paragraph 2 of the human dimension mechanism, will take place as soon as possible, and as a rule within one week of the date of the request.

(3) A resource list comprising up to six experts appointed by each participating State will be established without delay at the CSCE Institution. The experts will be eminent persons, including where possible experts with experience related to national minority issues, preferably experienced in the field of the human dimension, from whom an impartial performance of their functions may be expected. The experts will be appointed for a period of three to six years at the discretion of the appointing State, no expert serving more than two consecutive terms. Within four weeks after notification by the CSCE Institution of the appointment, any participating State may make reservations regarding no more than two

experts to be appointed by another participating State. In such case, the appointing State may, within four weeks of being notified of such reservations, reconsider its decision and appoint another expert or experts; if it confirms the appointment originally intended, the expert concerned cannot take part in any procedure with respect to the State having made the reservation without the latter's express consent. The resource list will become operational as soon as 45 experts have been appointed.

(4) A participating State may invite the assistance of a CSCE mission, consisting of up to three experts, to address or contribute to the resolution of questions in its territory relating to the human dimension of the CSCE. In such case, the State will select the person or persons concerned from the resource list. The mission of experts will not include the participating State's own nationals or residents or any of the persons it appointed to the resource list or more than one national or resident of any particular State. The inviting State will inform without delay the CSCE Institution when a mission of experts is established, which in turn will notify all participating States. The CSCE institutions will also, whenever necessary, provide appropriate support to such a mission.

(5) The purpose of a mission of experts is to facilitate resolution of a particular question or problem relating to the human dimension of the CSCE. Such mission may gather the information necessary for carrying out its tasks and, as appropriate, use its good offices and mediation services to promote dialogue and co-operation among interested parties. The State concerned will agree with the mission on the precise terms of reference and may thus assign any further functions to the mission of experts, inter alia, fact-finding and advisory services, in order to suggest ways and means of facilitating the observance of CSCE commitments.

(6) The inviting State will co-operate fully with the mission of experts and facilitate its work. It will grant the mission all the facilities necessary for the independent exercise of its functions. It will, inter alia, allow the mission, for the purpose of carrying out its tasks, to enter its territory without delay, to hold discussions and to travel freely therein, to meet freely with officials, nongovernmental organizations and any group or person from whom it wishes to receive information.

The mission may also receive information in confidence from any individual, group or organization on questions it is addressing.

The members of such missions will respect the confidential nature of their task. The participating States will refrain from any action against persons, organizations or institutions on account of their contact with the mission of experts or of any publicly available information transmitted to it. The inviting State will comply with any request from a mission of experts to be accompanied by officials of that State if the mission considers this to be necessary to facilitate its work or guarantee its safety.

(7) The mission of experts will submit its observations to the inviting State as soon as possible, preferably within three weeks after the mission has been established. The inviting State will transmit the observations of the mission, together with a description of any action it has taken or intends to take upon it, to the other participating States via the CSCE Institution no later than two weeks after the submission of the observations.

These observations and any comments by the inviting State may be discussed by the Committee of Senior Officials, which may consider any possible follow-up action. The observations and comments will remain confidential until brought to the attention of the Senior Officials. Before the circulation of the observations and any comments, no other mission of experts may be appointed for the same issue.

(8) Furthermore, one or more participating States, having put into effect paragraphs 1 or 2 of the human dimension mechanism, may request that the CSCE Institution inquire of another participating State whether it would agree to invite a mission of experts to address a particular, clearly defined question on its territory relating to the human dimension of the CSCE. If the other participating State agrees to invite a mission of experts for the purpose indicated, the procedure set forth in paragraphs 4 to 7 will apply.

(9) If a participating State (a) has directed an enquiry under paragraph 8 to another participating State and that State has not established a mission of experts within a period of ten days after the enquiry has been made, or (b) judges that the issue in question has not been resolved as a result of a mission of experts, it may, with the support of at least five other participating States, initiate the establishment of a mission of up to three CSCE rapporteurs. Such a decision will be ad-

dressed to the CSCE Institution, which will notify without delay the State concerned as well as all the other participating States.

(10) The requesting State or States may appoint one person from the resource list to serve as a CSCE rapporteur. The requested State may, if it so chooses, appoint a further rapporteur from the resource list within six days after notification by the CSCE Institution of the appointment of the rapporteur. In such case the two designated rapporteurs, who will not be nationals or residents of, or persons appointed to the resource list by any of the States concerned, will by common agreement and without delay appoint a third rapporteur from the resource list. In case they fail to reach agreement within eight days, a third rapporteur who will not be a national or resident of, or a person appointed to the resource list by any of the States concerned, will be appointed from the resource list by the ranking official of the CSCE body designated by the Council. The provisions of the second part of paragraph 4 and the whole of paragraph 6 also apply to a mission of rapporteurs.

(11) The CSCE rapporteur(s) will establish the facts, report on them and may give advice on possible solutions to the question raised. The report of the rapporteur(s), containing observations of facts, proposals or advice, will be submitted to the participating State or States concerned and, unless all the States concerned agree otherwise, to the CSCE Institution no later than two weeks after the last rapporteur has been appointed. The requested State will submit any observations on the report to the CSCE Institution, unless all the States concerned agree otherwise, no later than two weeks after the submission of the report.

The CSCE Institution will transmit the report, as well as any observations by the requested State or any other participating State, to all participating States without delay. The report will be placed on the agenda of the next regular meeting of the Committee of Senior Officials or of the Permanent Committee of the CSCE, which may decide on any possible follow-up action. The report will remain confidential until after that meeting of the Committee. Before the circulation of the report no other rapporteur may be appointed for the same issue.

(12) If a participating State considers that a particularly serious threat to the fulfilment of the provisions of the CSCE human dimension has arisen in another participating State, it may, with the support of at least nine other participating States, engage the procedure set forth in paragraph 10. The provisions of paragraph 11 will apply. (13) Upon the request of any participating State the Committee of Senior Officials or the Permanent Committee of the CSCE may decide to establish a mission of experts or of CSCE rapporteurs. In such case the Committee will also determine whether to apply the appropriate provisions of the preceding paragraphs. (14) The participating State or States that have requested the establishment of a mission of experts or rapporteurs will cover the expenses of that mission. In case of the appointment of experts or rapporteurs pursuant to a decision of the Committee of Senior Officials or of the Permanent Committee of the CSCE, the expenses will be covered by the participating States in accordance with the usual scale of distribution of expenses. These procedures will be reviewed by the Helsinki Follow-up Meeting of the CSCE.

(15) Nothing in the foregoing will in any way affect the right of participating States to raise within the CSCE process any issue relating to the implementation of any CSCE commitment, including any commitment relating to the human dimension of the CSCE.

(16) In considering whether to invoke the procedures in paragraphs 9 and 10 or 12 regarding the case of an individual, participating States should pay due regard to whether that individual's case is already sub judice in an international judicial procedure. Any reference to the Committee of Senior Officials in this document is subject to the decision of that Committee and the Council.

HELSINKI 1992 (Decisions, chapter VI, par. 7)

(7) In order to align the Human Dimension Mechanism with present CSCE structures and institutions the participating States decide that:

Any participating State which deems it necessary may provide information on situations and cases which have been the subject of requests under paragraphs 1 or 2 of the chapter entitled the "Human Dimension of the CSCE" of the Vienna Concluding Document or on the results of those procedures, to the participating States through the ODIHR — which can equally serve as a venue for bilateral meetings under paragraph 2 — or diplomatic channels. Such information may be discussed at Meetings of the CSO, at implementation meetings on Human Dimension issues and review conferences.

Source: http://www.osce.org/odihr/20066

4. THE VIENNA (HUMAN DIMENSION) MECHANISM, 1989

This is another human dimension mechanism (see Primary Source Document 3) used for resolving issues between member states. It permits states to request certain information from another member state where the requesting state has a concern about the requested state complying with its CSCE commitments, for example, regarding discriminatory treatment of a minority group. It also allows for a face to face state meeting to discuss the issues upon which information was requested. A Copenhagen amendment added time limits for states to act in.

("Human Dimension of the CSCE," par. 1 to 4)

The participating States,

Recalling the undertakings entered into in the Final Act and in other CSCE documents concerning respect for all human rights and fundamental freedoms, human contacts and other issues of a related humanitarian character,

Recognizing the need to improve the implementation of their CSCE commitments and their cooperation in these areas which are hereafter referred to as the human dimension of the CSCE,

Have, on the basis of the principles and provisions of the Final Act and of other relevant CSCE documents, decided:

to exchange information and respond to requests for information and to representations made to them by other participating States on questions relating to the human dimension of the CSCE. Such communications may be forwarded through diplomatic channels or be addressed to any agency designated for these purposes;

to hold bilateral meetings with other participating States that so request, in order to examine questions relating to the human dimension of the CSCE, including situations and specific cases, with a view to resolving them. The date and place of such meetings will be arranged by mutual agreement through diplomatic channels;

— that any participating State which deems it necessary may bring situations and cases in the human dimension of the CSCE, including those which have been raised it the bilateral meetings described in paragraph 2, to the attention of other participating States through diplomatic channels;

— that any participating State which deems it necessary may provide information on the exchanges of information and the responses to its requests for information and to representations (paragraph 1) and on the results of the bilateral meetings (paragraph 2), including information concerning situations and specific cases, at the meetings of the Conference on the Human Dimension as well as at the main CSCE Follow-up Meeting.

Copenhagen 1990 (Par. 42)

(42) The participating States recognize the need to enhance further the effectiveness of the procedures described in paragraphs 1 to 4 of the section on the human dimension of the CSCE of the Vienna Concluding Document and with this aim decide

(42.1) — to provide in as short a time as possible, but no later than four weeks, a written response to requests for information and to representations made to them in writing by other participating States under paragraph 1;

(42.2) — that the bilateral meetings, as contained in paragraph 2, will take place as soon as possible, as a rule within three weeks of the date of the request;

(42.3) — to refrain, in the course of a bilateral meeting held under paragraph 2, from raising situations and cases not connected with the subject of the meeting, unless both sides have agreed to do so.

5. U.S. POLICY AND THE ORGANIZATION FOR SECURITY AND COOPERATION IN EUROPE: REPORT TO THE CONGRESS, 2015

This document is from the U.S. Government, Department of State with information to help the U.S. government manage U.S. foreign policy towards the OSCE, of which it is a major funder. It discusses U.S. policy objectives advanced in 2014 through the OSCE and presents U.S. priorities for 2015 in that organization. This says how the U.S. views the OSCE in tarnation of the national interest and in light of the resources appropriated to keeping that organization functioning.

Report
Bureau Of European And Eurasian Affairs
March 2015

This report, submitted pursuant to Section 5 of the Act to Establish a Commission on Security and Cooperation in Europe, 22 U.S.C. 3005 (1976), as amended, discusses U.S. policy objectives advanced in 2014 through the Organization for Security and Cooperation in Europe (OSCE) and presents U.S. priorities for 2015.

U.S. Policy Objectives

The OSCE is the primary multilateral organization through which the United States advances comprehensive political-military, economic and environmental, and human dimension security and stability throughout Europe and Central Asia. U.S. leadership and robust engagement in the OSCE helps advance democratic reform and sustainable economic development, address regional and transnational threats, prevent and resolve conflicts, support civil society, promote tolerance and non-discrimination, and defend human rights and fundamental freedoms, including the freedom of expression exercised online and offline.

Preventing and Resolving Conflicts

In 2014, the OSCE played a pivotal role supporting the people of Ukraine's desire to live in a free, stable, and democratic society and in addressing Russia's blatant violation of Ukraine's sovereignty and territorial integrity. The OSCE deployed a Special Monitoring Mission comprised of 500 international monitors following Russia's intervention in Ukraine and occupation of Crimea. Participating States sent inspection teams into Ukraine under provisions of the Vienna Document. The Special Representative of the OSCE Chairmanship-in-Office in Ukraine and in the Trilateral Contact Group facilitated political dialogue and ceasefire efforts at the highest levels. The High Commissioner on National Minorities and Representative on Freedom of the Media supported civil society, documented abuses, and defended vulnerable populations in Crimea and other parts of Ukraine. The Office for Democratic Institutions and Human Rights (ODIHR) deployed its largest-ever Election Observation Mission to observe Ukraine's May presidential election and monitored October's parliamentary elections. ODIHR also conducted a Human Rights Assessment at the start of the crisis in and around Ukraine.

The United States supported key platforms of the OSCE: the 5+2 talks to address the Transnistrian conflict; the Minsk Group to resolve the Nagorno-Karabakh conflict; and the Geneva International Discussions on the conflict in Georgia. At the 2014 OSCE Ministerial Council, participating States agreed to a regional statement on the Transnistrian conflict calling for progress toward peaceful settlement. The Heads of Delegation of the Minsk Group co-chair countries also issued a statement calling on the sides to refrain from violence and work actively towards a lasting settlement.

The Ministerial Council adopted a decision that provides impetus to OSCE work to secure or reduce inventories of small arms and light weapons and stockpiles of conventional ammunition. The United States continued to seek updates to the Vienna Document in light of lessons learned during the ongoing crisis in and around Ukraine. We supported a widely-endorsed proposal to lower thresholds for notification of military activities, as well as proposals to increase inspections and evaluations. We also continued to support OSCE Vienna Document Chapter III (Risk Prevention) engagement in evolving crises, as demonstrated by extensive use of this measure with regard to the crisis in and around Ukraine.

Economic Development and Environmental Issues

Economic and environmental security in the OSCE region is a key objective for the United States. Toward this end, the United States advocated successfully at the 2014 Ministerial Council for the adoption of decisions aimed at preventing and countering corruption and reducing disaster risk. The United States supported the efforts of the Office of the Coordinator of Economic and Environmental Activities (OCEEA) to build the capacity of participating States to combat corruption, money-laundering, and the financing of terrorism.

Human Rights and Democracy

The United States worked closely with OSCE institutions to promote respect for human rights and fundamental freedoms. We engaged vigorously in the OSCE Permanent Council, at the annual Human Dimension Implementation Meeting (HDIM), and through other OSCE meetings to address the protection of human rights and fundamental freedoms and to defend the independence of ODIHR to pursue its mandate. The United States led efforts to push participating States to recognize the applicability of OSCE commitments on human rights and fundamental freedoms in the digital age, including media freedom and the protection of journalists. We continued to advocate for civil society and for its more robust involvement in human dimension activities. We supported ODIHR's full range of assistance to participating States and election monitoring missions by providing extra-budgetary support to ODIHR projects and recommending experts.

Fighting Intolerance and Discrimination

To underscore the importance of combatting anti-Semitism, the United States sent a Presidential Delegation to the OSCE's commemoration of the 10th anniversary of the Berlin conference on anti-Semitism. The participating States condemned all manifestations of anti-Semitism and committed themselves to enhanced efforts to combat anti-Semitism in a Ministerial Declaration in Basel in 2014. The Ministerial Council adopted decisions to prevent and combat violence against women and to develop the Action Plan for the Promotion of Gender Equality.

The OSCE's three Personal Tolerance Representatives visited Washington, DC in July 2014 and met with representatives from the Departments of State, Justice, and Education, as well as civil society and the Helsinki Commission. We worked closely with ODIHR and the OSCE's Tolerance Representatives to condemn and combat anti-Semitism and other hate-motivated crimes and discrimination against members of vulnerable populations, including persons belonging to racial, ethnic, and religious minorities; LGBT persons; women; people with disabilities; and migrants. We worked with ODIHR's Contact Point for Roma and Sinti issues to combat discrimination against members of the Romani minority.

Combating Trafficking in Persons

In 2014, the OSCE organized the 14th High-level Alliance against Trafficking in Persons conference to continue to advance the implementation of OSCE commitments and relevant international obligations to combat and prevent trafficking in human beings in all its forms. We contributed expertise and financial resources for the development of a handbook on methods to counter trafficking of domestic workers in diplomatic households and a report on how to leverage existing anti-money laundering tools to fight trafficking.

Countering Transnational Threats

The United States played a key role in negotiating two Ministerial declarations on countering foreign terrorist fighters and kidnapping and hostage-taking committed by terrorist groups. The United States assisted participating States in implementing their UNSCR 1540 non-proliferation commitments, supported OSCE's participation in the Global Counterterrorism Forum (GCTF), and supported OSCE border security initiatives throughout the OSCE region.

Field Activities

South-Eastern Europe

OSCE missions in South-Eastern Europe continued to help bring stability and development to their respective host countries and the region. In 2014, the missions facilitated elections, helped local authorities build strong independent institutions, promoted media freedom, and fostered youth and women's engagement in political processes.

Eastern Europe

The OSCE Mission to Moldova continued to coordinate the 5+2 negotiations on settlement of the Transnistrian conflict, help implement confidence-building measures, promote a free and pluralistic media environment, and fight trafficking in persons. The United States also advocated successfully to increase engagement in Ukraine by the OSCE and its institutions, including the Project Coordinator in Kyiv, in advancing reforms and in resolving the current crisis.

South Caucasus

In Armenia and Azerbaijan, the OSCE focused on justice- and security-sector reform, democratic institution building, and anti-corruption efforts. The strong mandate of the Office in Yerevan allowed it to implement meaningful programs in community policing, regulatory reform, and the new human rights action plan. The Project Coordinator in Baku carried out initiatives to prevent domestic violence, counter terrorism financing, protect the environment, train journalists, and protect trafficking victims. The United States continued to press the Project Coordinator in Baku to conduct programs in important areas of democratic development and governmental transparency and to engage with civil society. We continued to press to re-establish a meaningful OSCE presence in Georgia.

Central Asia

OSCE activities in Central Asia strengthened border security, bolstered civil society, promoted democracy and the rule of law, and improved regional trade and transport. The OSCE Border Management and Staff College in Dushanbe trained border guards from throughout the region, including Afghanistan. The OSCE Center in Almaty was downgraded to a Program Office in 2014, at the Government of Kazakhstan's insistence. The United States made clear that the OSCE Office should continue activities across all dimensions, and we are tracking the impact of the revised mandate with that concern in mind.

OSCE Budget and Scales of Contribution

On December 30, the OSCE participating States reached consensus on the 2015 unified budget of □141.2 million (a decrease of 0.8 percent from the 2014 level). The unified budget reflected an increase of 1.2 percent to ODIHR — a top U.S. priority....

The United States planned to maintain its levels of contribution at 11.5 percent for the Standard Scale and 14.0 percent for the Field Operations Scale for 2016-2018.

Advancing U.S. Priorities in 2015 and Beyond

The United States will continue to press OSCE participating States to uphold their commitments in all dimensions and promote cooperative, comprehensive security throughout the OSCE region. Our specific goals include:

- Continuing to leverage the OSCE and its institutions to resolve the crisis in Ukraine and promote Ukraine's long-term security, stability, democracy, and economic development;
- Strengthening respect for the exercise of human rights and fundamental freedoms and protecting the safety of journalists;
- Defending and promoting the role of civil society in advancing OSCE goals;
- Increasing the focus on combatting anti-Semitism and other forms of intolerance throughout the OSCE region;
- Increasing the focus on transparency, good governance, and anti-corruption in advancing economic and environmental security;
- Deploying OSCE resources where they are most needed;
- Achieving concrete steps toward resolving the protracted conflicts regarding Transnistria, Nagorno-Karabakh, and Georgia;

- Updating the Vienna Document to take into account lessons learned during the crisis in and around Ukraine and to reflect the current security environment in Europe;
- Supporting the OSCE's work to counter transnational threats and challenges such as terrorism, violent extremism, organized crime, threats to cyber security, and trafficking in persons;
- Drawing on the 40th anniversary of the Helsinki Final Act to emphasize the need for full implementation of existing OSCE commitments by participating States.

Source: U.S. Department of State, Diplomacy in Action
http://www.state.gov/p/eur/rls/rpt/249095.htm

6. OSCE - ODIHR REPORT ON THE 2016 U.S. ELECTIONS, JULY 17, 2017 (FINAL)

The right to vote is a fundamental human right held by every eligible American. There continue to exist national and international issues about who should be allowed to vote where US law and policy seem to deviate from the international standard. This document is an excerpt of the OSCE-Office of Democratic Institutions and Human Rights final election observer report on the U.S. Presidential election of 2016. It was prepared by the OSCE election observers who were present in the U.S. monitoring the democratic processes of the U.S. in action. One of the functions of the OSCE is to monitor elections in member states to assure that democracy is respected. They observe the election to determine if it is a "free and fair election" and meets democratic standards. The ODIHR also makes recommendations to the state on how to improve the election system process in member states of the O.S.C.E. This excerpt sets forth only the Executive Summary, Introduction and Acknowledgments and the Recommendations. These recommendations are not legally binding. The report briefly brings up the issue of Russian hacking in relation to the election.

[Text]

OSCE — ODIHR REPORT ON THE 2016 U.S. ELECTIONS
July 17, 2017

Office for Democratic Institutions and Human Rights

UNITED STATES OF AMERICA GENERAL ELECTIONS
8 November 2016

OSCE/ODIHR Election Observation Mission Final Report

I. EXECUTIVE SUMMARY

Following an invitation from the US government, the OSCE Office for Democratic Institutions and Human Rights (OSCE/ODIHR) deployed an Election Observation Mission (EOM) to observe the 8 November general elections.

The OSCE/ODIHR assessed the compliance of the election process with OSCE commitments, other international obligations and standards for democratic elections, as well as with domestic legislation. For election day, the OSCE/ODIHR EOM was joined by a delegation from the OSCE Parliamentary Assembly to form an International Election Observation Mission (IEOM).

The Statement of Preliminary Findings and Conclusions issued on 9 November 2016 concluded that "The 8 November general elections were highly competitive and demonstrated commitment to fundamental freedoms of expression, assembly and association. The presidential campaign was characterized by harsh personal attacks, as well as intolerant rhetoric by one candidate. Diverse media coverage allowed voters to make an informed choice. Recent legal changes and decisions on technical aspects of the electoral process were often motivated by partisan interests, adding undue obstacles for voters. Suffrage rights are not guaranteed for all citizens, leaving sections of the population without the right to vote. These elections were administered by competent and professional staff, including on election day, which was assessed positively by IEOM observers, despite some instances of long queues and malfunctioning voting equipment".

The election of the president and vice-president is indirect, conducted through an Electoral College that allows for a candidate to be elected without winning the popular vote nationwide. Both before and after the elections, several interlocutors expressed concern with this system. Concerning direct elections of Senators and Representatives, a number of interlocutors stated that the drawing of electoral district boundaries was largely driven by partisan interests. Almost all OSCE/ODIHR EOM interlocutors agreed that these elections took place in an increasingly polarized environment, with partisan animosity deepening, and against the backdrop of gridlock in Congress.

New Voting Technologies are used extensively across the country. Contrary to good practice, 15 states use Direct Recording Equipment machines that do not provide a voter-verified paper audit trail. This does not allow voters to ensure their votes have been recorded properly or authorities to conduct possible recounts. While some jurisdictions recently upgraded their voting systems, many election officials noted that NVT have not been replaced due to a lack of resources at the federal, state and local level, raising issues with the security, reliability and operability of the equipment. A number of concerns were raised by various stakeholders regarding gaps in security which could be used by malicious attackers with sufficient resources to gain unauthorized access. This, in combination with outdated equipment or voting and counting software, could lead to lost or inaccurately counted votes.

US citizens 18 years of age and older are eligible to vote. Some 4 million residents of US overseas territories and 600,000 residents of the District of Columbia do not have voting representation in Congress. In addition, residents of US overseas territories do not have the right to vote in presidential elections. More than 6 million convicts, including those who served their sentences as well as many facing trial, are disenfranchised, disproportionately impacting African Americans. These restrictions contravene the principle of universal and equal suffrage, as provided in OSCE commitments.

The legal framework is highly decentralized and complex, with significant variation between states. A number of previous OSCE/ODIHR recommendations remain unaddressed in the law and certain deficiencies in the legal framework persist, such as the disenfranchisement of citizens living in various territories, restrictions on the voting rights of convicted criminals, and infringements on secrecy of the ballot. In 2013, provisions of the Voting Rights Act were struck down, removing a timely and effective safeguard for the protection of rights for racial and linguistic minorities. A wide range of electoral litigation remained unresolved before election day, particularly with respect to voter registration and voter identification.

Individual states are responsible for administering elections with duties often delegated to some 10,500 jurisdictions across the country. The elections were administered by competent and committed staff and enjoyed broad public confidence. The work of the Election Assistance Commission (EAC) had a positive impact for state and county officials, enabling the exchange of best practices and providing standards for New Voting Technologies. A number of technical recommendations made by previous OSCE/ODIHR missions, as well as the 2014 Presidential Commission on Election Administration, were addressed.

Voter registration is active and implemented at the state level. Various initiatives have been undertaken to improve voter list accuracy and inclusiveness, often with bipartisan support. These included online registration, as well as inter-state projects to identify potential duplicate records and inaccuracies. Notwithstanding these measures, more than an estimated 35 million eligible voters were not registered for these elections, underscoring the need for continued efforts to enhance voter registration, particularly among marginalized communities. Voter identification rules are politically divisive and vary across the states, with 32 states requiring identification, of which 16 require photo identification. Provisional ballots are generally available if a voter does not have sufficient identification; however, eligibility is established only after the close of the polls, at times requiring additional information from the voter. A high volume of litigation regarding voter identification continued up to election day, generating confusion among voters and election officials regarding the application of the rules. Efforts to ensure the integrity of the vote are important, but should not lead to the disenfranchisement of eligible voters.

Candidate registration requirements vary considerably between states. A large number of candidates, including independents and representatives of small parties, were registered for congressional elections in an inclusive manner, providing voters with a variety of choice. Four presidential candidates were registered in a sufficient number of states to be elected. Variations in rules make it cumbersome for third party or independent candidates to register across all states for presidential elections.

Women are underrepresented in elected office. Women comprised 17 per cent of congressional candidates and hold 20 per cent of seats in the new Congress. This was the first time a major party nominated a woman as candidate for president but elements of the campaign were marked by misogynistic language. Women were well represented amongst electoral staff, including in decision making positions.

There are strong legal guarantees to ensure the right and opportunity to vote for persons with physical disabilities. While all polling stations are required to include specialized equipment to assist such voters, electoral staff were not always well trained in how to use the technology. Voting rights for persons with mental and intellectual disabilities vary considerably and some restrictions are at odds with international standards.

The campaign was dynamic and vivid, demonstrating a commitment to fundamental freedoms of expression, association and assembly. The campaign was dominated by the presidential race that largely focused on undecided voters in a small number of "battleground" states. The two major candidates offered distinct policy alternatives, but often used highly charged rhetoric and employed personal attacks. Intolerant speech by one candidate was frequent, including about women, minorities and people with disabilities. Both candidates faced scandals during the campaign that provoked widespread public debate about their qualifications for office. Third-party candidates received minimal attention.

The Federal Election Commission (FEC) oversees a campaign finance regime that imposes few actual limits on donations and does not limit expenditure. All financial reports are published expeditiously, but transparency is diminished by the absence of disclosure for some types of nonprofit organizations that play an important role in the campaign. Partisan decision making has limited the FEC's ability to reach decisions on key campaign finance issues or provide sanctions where violations occurred.

The media is pluralistic and vibrant, although increasingly polarized. A robust system of protection for media independence is in place, but hostility towards the media's role as a critical watchdog was voiced by one presidential candidate. The media extensively covered the campaign and a series of presidential debates attained record viewing. OSCE/ODIHR EOM media monitoring revealed partisan campaign coverage, in particular on cable television and in online spaces. Overall, the media provided voters with a wide range of information and enabled them to make an informed choice.

Legal measures are available to address electoral disputes and access to the courts is unrestricted. There is no fixed timeframe for resolving election-related disputes, which puts into question the effectiveness of a remedy, as provided for by OSCE commitments. Provisions on recounts vary widely and are often insufficiently defined, which can result in complaints not being addressed in a consistent and timely manner. Three state-wide recounts were requested by the presidential candidate Jill Stein on the grounds of alleged hacking from abroad, although no evidence was submitted at the time. One recount showed minimal discrepancies and the remaining two were suspended by the courts.

Most state law is silent on observation, leaving discretion to election officials. Restrictions on observation of early voting and election day are in place in 17 states. Citizen observers and party representatives were active and widespread throughout the country, providing an added layer of transparency and confidence in the election process.

More than one-third of voters are estimated to have cast their vote before election day, either in person or by post, including citizens abroad. Early voting enjoys broad public trust and a number of measures were implemented to ensure security. However, secrecy of the vote was not always guaranteed for postal voting and out-of-country voting by electronic means, contrary to OSCE commitments.

Election day procedures were generally followed and assessed positively by the IEOM observers. In a number of locations throughout the country long queues to access polling stations were observed. In numerous instances, multiple citizens intending to vote at a polling station were not found on the voter list, underlining systemic concerns with voter registration. Secrecy of the vote was not always guaranteed, generally where voters were not provided with ballot sleeves when using ballot scanners. Despite widespread concerns that voters would be intimidated at the polls, no serious incidents were observed by the IEOM or were reported to it. Polling officials were mainly co-operative, even in those areas that do not clearly provide for international observation. IEOM observers could not, however, fully observe procedures in 73 polling stations across 19 states.

In the days after the elections, a number of demonstrtions broke out in major cities and student campuses across the country. The demonstrators protested against the election of Mr. Trump and his use of divisive and offensive rhetoric. At the same time, civil rights groups reported an increase in hate crimes, primarily against racial and religious minorities.

Discussion of the alleged interference of the Russian government in the US elections became a key theme in the post-electoral period. Following reports from US intelligence agencies that alleged that the Russian government acted to influence the elections through malicious cyber activity, among other reasons, the US imposed sanctions on the Russian Federation and expelled Russian diplomats.

II. INTRODUCTION AND ACKNOWLEDGEMENTS

Following a timely invitation from the US government and based on the recommendation of a Needs Assessment Mission conducted from 16 to 20 May, the OSCE Office for Democratic Institutions and Human Rights (OSCE/ODIHR) established an Election Observation Mission (EOM) on 4 October to observe the 8 November general elections. 1 The EOM was headed by Ambassador Audrey Glover and consisted of 14 experts based in Washington, DC and 26 long-term observers (LTOs) deployed throughout the country.

On election day, the OSCE/ODIHR EOM joined efforts with an observer delegation from the OSCE Parliamentary Assembly (OSCE PA) to form an International Election Observation Mission (IEOM). Christine Muttonen was appointed by the OSCE Chairperson-in-Office as Special Co-ordinator and leader of the OSCE short-term observer mission. Makis Voridis headed the OSCE PA delegation. In total, 295 observers from 44 countries were deployed on election day, including 192 long-term and short-term observers by the OSCE/ODIHR, and a 103-member delegation from the OSCE PA. Opening was observed in 93 polling stations and voting was observed in 1,059 polling stations across the country. Counting was observed in 83 polling stations. This final report follows the Statement of Preliminary Findings and Conclusions, which was released at a press conference in Washington, DC on 9 November 2016. The OSCE/ODIHR EOM remained in the United States until 16 November and followed post-election day developments.

The OSCE/ODIHR EOM assessed compliance of the electoral process with OSCE commitments and other international standards and obligations for democratic elections and with national legislation. State and local elections were held concurrently with the general elections and were observed by the OSCE/ODIHR EOM only to the extent they impacted the general elections.

The OSCE/ODIHR EOM wishes to thank the government of the United States of America for the timely invitation to observe the elections, as well as the Department of State and the National Association of Secretaries of State and representatives of other federal and state institutions and election authorities for their assistance and support. The OSCE/ODIHR EOM also wishes to express its appreciation to international organizations and embassies accredited in the US, as well as political parties, media representatives and civil society organizations for their co-operation and support.

IV. ELECTORAL SYSTEM

The president and vice president are elected jointly for a four-year term. The election is indirect, conducted through an Electoral College comprised of 538 electors. All 50 states have a number of electors equivalent to their total representation in Congress, while the District of Columbia has three. The electors are nominated by parties and elected through a popular vote, largely through 'winner takes all' contests. The system allows for a candidate to win the popular vote nationwide while falling short of the majority of Electoral College votes. There is no federal law requiring electors to vote in line with their nominating party, but some state laws provide sanctions for so-called "faithless electors" or invalidate them. In these elections, a total of ten electors voted against the assigned vote from their electorate.

Both before and after the election, many OSCE/ODIHR EOM interlocutors expressed concern over the continued use of a system that separates the popular vote from winning the office of President. While any formal change to the Electoral College would require a constitutional amendment, several states have passed a National Popular Vote (NPV) act whereby states would pool their electoral votes in favour of the candidate that wins the national popular vote. For the NPV to take effect, states with a combined total of at least 270 electoral votes must join the initiative.

Senators and Representatives are directly elected, principally in "first-past-the-post" contests. Each state constitutes a single electoral district for the Senate, and elects two Senators who serve staggered six-year terms. At most, one Senator from each state may be elected at any election. Seats in the House are proportionally allocated to states according to their population, with a minimum of one per state. Representatives serve two-year terms.

Elections to the House are conducted in districts, which are revised every ten years, following a nationwide census. Districts must be drawn up on the basis of approximately equal population figures, ensuring an "equally effective voice" for voters. Redistricting based on the 2010 census has been the subject of sustained legal challenges, including several cases that remain ongoing. Some courts found that district boundaries were drawn on partisan or racial grounds, which undermined competitive elections and the principle of equal suffrage. In these elections, 8 candidates for the House ran unopposed. Positively, a number of states have established independent redistricting commissions and, in 2015, the Supreme Court held that an Independent Redistricting Commission established in Arizona was consistent with the Constitution. Such bodies can build public confidence in the process and remove partiality from final districting decisions.

V. LEGAL FRAMEWORK

In accordance with the federal system established in the Constitution, federal legislation provides minimum standards for elections, with implementation primarily regulated at state level. Federal and state court decisions also form an integral part of the legal framework. Electoral law, as a result, is decentralized and complex, with significant variations between states. The US is party to major international and regional instruments related to the holding of democratic elections.

Federal legislation includes the 1965 Voting Rights Act (VRA), which outlaws discriminatory law and practice on the grounds of ethnicity and language; the 1986 Uniformed and Overseas Citizens Absentee Voting Act and 2009 Military and Overseas Voting Empowerment Act (MOVE), which facilitate out-of-country voting; the 1984 Voting Accessibility for the Elderly and Handicapped Act and 1990 Americans with Disabilities Act, which promote access to the polls for people with disabilities; the 1993 National Voter Registration Act (NVRA), which facilitates voter registration; the 1971 Federal Election Campaign Act and 2002 Bipartisan Campaign Reform Act, which regulate campaign finance; and the 2002 Help America Vote Act (HAVA), which establishes minimum standards for administering elections, including for new voting technologies (NVT).

The Department of Justice (DoJ) monitors state implementation of federal election law and can bring enforcement suits in cases of non-compliance. In particular, Section 5 of the VRA requires jurisdictions with a history of discrimination to obtain federal pre-clearance of changes to electoral law from the DoJ or the federal district court in the District of Columbia. Unlike other sections of the VRA, Section 5 has an expiration date which, in 2006, was extended by Congress for 25 more years. In 2013, the Supreme Court, in Shelby County v. Holder, ruled that the formula to determine which jurisdictions are subject to pre-clearance (Section 4b) is unconstitutional as it is based on outdated information that does not necessarily reflect current circumstances. As a result, no jurisdiction was required to pre-clear election-related changes prior to these elections, with three exceptions that were covered by separate court orders.

The Shelby County decision removed a longstanding, timely and effective safeguard that protected racial and linguistic minorities from legal changes that have a discriminatory intent or impact. Since the ruling, a number of new registration, identification and voting arrangements were introduced that were challenged on the grounds of intent to suppress minority voters. The courts found adverse impacts on African American and Latino voters in several cases.

XI. ELECTION CAMPAIGN

Campaigning took place in an open atmosphere with respect for fundamental freedoms of expression and assembly. The campaign was dominated by the presidential race that largely focused on undecided voters in a small number of so-called "battleground" states, although the number of competitive states increased in the run-up to election day. While the main presidential candidates campaigned on immigration, trade, health care, job creation and foreign policy, congressional races primarily focused on local issues. The OSCE/ODIHR EOM noted a certain level of voter apathy in states with uncontested races.

Presidential and congressional candidates used campaign rallies, canvassing, advertising, social media, yard signs, door-knocking and phone calls to extensively reach out to voters and provide campaign information. While Ms. Clinton used a range of campaign methods, Mr. Trump departed from traditional methods, largely neglecting direct mail or canvassing and relying on his ability to leverage airtime and print space in the media. The Republican Party, however, did contribute to Mr. Trump's campaign through extensive voter-contact efforts. Third-party candidates received minimal attention.

The campaign was characterized by a high degree of partisan hostility between the two major presidential candidates. Both candidates used a tone that was confrontational, often employing personal attacks during campaign events and characterising each other as unfit for the office of president. Mr. Trump frequently used offensive and intolerant language, including against women, ethnic and racial communities, and people with disabilities. Mr. Trump also stated that, if elected, he would seek to put Ms. Clinton in jail. Ms. Clinton referred to a number of supporters of Mr. Trump as "deplorables". The negative rhetoric was often reflected in tightly contested congressional races. A few cases of disruptions at rallies were reported.

Mr. Trump alleged media bias against his campaign and repeatedly claimed that the electoral process was rigged. On several occasions, he appealed to his supporters to watch the polls and prevent fraud, raising fears of intimidation on election day. Mr. Trump's allegations of electoral fraud and his refusal to say that he would accept the election results were widely denounced as undermining the electoral process, including from within the Republican Party.

Mr. Trump's candidacy was deeply divisive among Republicans. The release of an audio tape on 7 October where Mr. Trump is heard boasting about having non-consensual sexual contact with women led many senior Republicans and congressional candidates to distance themselves from Mr. Trump. In response, Mr. Trump accused the Republican party leadership, including the Speaker of the House, of being disloyal. In the final days of the campaign, however, several senior Republicans re-joined Mr. Trump's campaign. The discord within the Republican Party contrasted with the sustained support lent by high profile Democrats to Ms. Clinton, including from President Obama and the First Lady.

The release by WikiLeaks on 7 October of thousands of emails from Ms. Clinton's campaign chairperson prompted renewed public discussion of her ties to financial institutions and wealthy donors, as well as her judgment on handling of matters of national security. US intelligence agencies accused the Russian government of being behind the hacking of the emails. (see Post-election Day Developments). On 28 October, the Federal Bureau of Investigation (FBI) announced that it received evidence from an unrelated case, that appeared to be "pertinent to the investigation" into Ms. Clinton's use of a private email server while Secretary of State. This featured prominently in the last days of the campaign. On 6 November, the FBI concluded that there was no case to bring against Ms. Clinton. Many electoral stakeholders opined that this contravened DoJ guidelines to remain neutral and maintain confidentiality in ongoing investigations in an election year.

XIII. MEDIA

A. MEDIA ENVIRONMENT

The media landscape is pluralistic and diverse, albeit increasingly polarized. The broadcast media include 1,780 commercial and public television stations and 15,489 radio stations. The environment is traditionally dominated by major television networks including CBS, NBC and ABC, with cable channels such as Fox News, CNN and MSNBC, growing in popularity. There are some 1,300 print publications, but media consumption, including on politics, in particular among young and middle aged groups, is shifting towards online media and social networks, primarily Facebook and Twitter.

Public service broadcasters are popular among more senior audiences. At the same time, National Public Radio (NPR) enjoys a significant and growing audience beyond traditional listeners. Most public TV stations are affiliates of the Public Broadcasting Service (PBS) and air programmes that commercial broadcasters tend not to offer, such as educational, cultural, and public affairs shows. Mostly financed through federal government subsidies, a continuous lack of resources jeopardizes the development of public service broadcasters.

In 1996 the Telecommunication Act was adopted and was the first major reform of telecommunications policy since 1934, which reduced Federal Communication Commission (FCC) regulations concerning cross ownership and effectively allowed for consolidation of the media market among big companies. At the same time, growing fragmentation of available media sources, in particular in the online sphere, has led to economic difficulties within the business model of traditional media and, according to several OSCE/ODIHR EOM interlocutors, a lower professional quality.

Journalists generally enjoy a high degree of freedom to undertake their activities. However, national security and counterterrorism measures implemented in recent years by the government, including attempts to compel reporters to reveal their sources on such issues have been reported by international organizations dealing with matters of freedom of expression. Positively, the OSCE Representative on Freedom of the Media (RFoM) welcomed legal reform that improved transparency and access to information, addressing other issues previously criticized by media organizations.

B. LEGAL FRAMEWORK

The First Amendment to the Constitution guarantees freedom of the press and expression, providing for a robust system of protection for media independence. It is further strengthened by various self-regulation mechanisms and decisions of the Supreme Court which affirm that no limitations should constrain freedom of speech. The 1996 Telecommunications Act, elements of the Code of Federal Regulations and FCC regulations outline several key principles for broadcasters to adhere to during elections.

Broadcasters (licensed stations, cable systems and direct broadcast satellite providers) are required to keep a publicly accessible "political file" reporting all requests to purchase airtime. In line with a prior OSCE/ODIHR recommendation, the range of media required to post their political files on the FCC website was expanded from only TV stations to include radio stations, cable systems and satellite operators. In the 60 days prior to general elections, commercial broadcasters are to provide "reasonable access" to all federal candidates who want to purchase airtime. All advertisements must include sponsorship identification and stations are not allowed to censor the content of a candidate's advertisement.

In addition, an "equal opportunity" rule stipulates that if a candidate for public office purchases airtime or is granted other channel's facilities, other candidates in that contest must be afforded equal conditions. There are several exemptions to this rule, such as newscast appearances, debates and scheduled or on-the-spot interviews that were introduced to protect editorial freedom. The FCC has interpreted that the equal opportunity rule applies only to candidates and not their supporters. As a consequence, commercial media exercised wide discretion with editorial policy.

Public broadcasters are subject to a general prohibition from endorsing or opposing candidates for public office and cannot air paid advertisements. In contrast, numerous publications, including major nationwide newspapers in an unprecedented manner, declared their political stance by officially endorsing or opposing presidential candidates.

The Commission on Presidential Debates (CPD), established in 1987 as an independent entity, is mandated to organize debates between presidential candidates. In these elections the CPD organized four debates between the two leading presidential and vice presidential candidates. Based on FEC regulations that require candidate selection to be made on the basis of "pre-established, objective" criteria, the CPD adopted guiding rules in October 2015. The criteria were legally challenged by Mr. Johnson and Ms. Stein. They argued that the criteria did not allow for a level playing field and resulted in only candidates from the two main parties participating. The debates were aired by all the major networks and attracted a large audience.

C. MEDIA MONITORING FINDINGS

The media election coverage was vibrant, extensive, and often visibly partisan, in particular on cable networks and in online spaces. A hostile atmosphere towards the media marked the electoral campaign, where their role as a critical watchdog was challenged by Mr. Trump, his campaign and some media outlets that supported his candidacy, such as Fox News and Breitbart. OSCE/ODIHR EOM quantitative and qualitative assessment revealed that the monitored media clearly prioritized presidential candidates from the two main parties, while the other two candidates each received less than two per cent of coverage on major broadcast media. Nevertheless, overall media reporting allowed voters to access a wide range of information on candidates and their positions, thus enabling them to make an informed choice.

The public broadcasters covered the candidates in a similar manner, airing documentaries produced by PBS and informative and analytical podcasts by NPR. In their newscasts, PBS and NPR provided significant coverage, with Mr. Trump receiving 42 and 38 per cent respectively, of mostly neutral and negative coverage, and Ms. Clinton receiving 31 and 27 per cent respectively, of mostly neutral coverage.

The three main national television networks provided the candidates with similar news coverage to the public broadcasters. Overall, Mr. Trump and his campaign, received between 42 to 48 per cent of prime-time news coverage, mostly neutral or negative in tone. Ms. Clinton received between 36 and 41 per cent of mainly neutral coverage. In contrast, cable networks often took a highly-partisan approach, in particular Fox News, that presented highly biased coverage against Ms Clinton (50 per cent of her coverage), especially in some talk shows.

While the newspapers often took a partisan approach in their coverage, such as the New York Times and USA Today that showed a high volume of negative coverage of Mr. Trump, some also offered a variety of well-researched and analytical reports. The rapidly developing online media sector, including social networks such as Facebook and Twitter, as well as a large number of non-traditional news websites featured prominently in the campaign. A high volume of dubious news, misinterpretations and distorted facts, were disseminated online, with higher intensity closer to election day. The sources of such news were often unclear.

XIX. POST- ELECTION DAY DEVELOPMENTS

A. POLITICAL DEVELOPMENTS

 As media reported a likely victory for Mr. Trump, a number of marches and demonstrations broke out in a range of major cities and student campuses, continuing after Ms. Clinton publicly conceded the election on 9 November and lasting several days. The demonstrators protested against the election of Mr. Trump and his use of divisive and offensive rhetoric. At the same time, civil rights groups reported an increase in hate crimes and cases of harassment and intimidation against members from racial and religious minority groups. The incidents also included attacks against Mr. Trump's supporters. On 21 November, in a development welcomed by the OSCE/ODIHR, the US Attorney General called for victims of such incidents to report them to law enforcement agencies and the Justice Department. While less widespread, protests continued until the time of the publication of this report.

Discussion of the alleged interference of the Russian government in the US elections was a key theme in the post-electoral period. On 29 December the FBI and DHS, expanding on the 7 October DHS statement, released a report detailing how they allege the Russian government acted to influence the US elections through malicious cyber activity. 112 On the same day, the US imposed sanctions on the Russian Federation, including the expulsion of 35 Russian diplomats. On 6 January 2017, the DHS published a declassified report, based on intelligence from the Central Intelligence Agency (CIA), FBI, and the National Security Agency (NSA), which accused the highest-levels of the Russian government of conducting "an influence campaign" to "undermine public faith in the US democratic process, denigrate Secretary Clinton, and harm her electability and potential presidency".113 The report further alleged that the Russian intervention developed a preference for Mr. Trump. Of note, it assessed that interference did not extend to the tallying of votes. In the aftermath of these reports, further statements and documents were released by media outlets alleging links between Mr. Trump and the Russian government that were strongly denied by Mr. Trump.

XX. RECOMMENDATIONS

These recommendations, as contained throughout the text, are offered with a view to enhance the conduct of elections in the United States and to support efforts to bring them fully in line with OSCE commitments and other international obligations and standards for democratic elections. These recommendations should be read in conjunction with past OSCE/ODIHR recommendations, in particular from the 2010 and 2012 Final Reports, which remain to be addressed. The OSCE/ODIHR stands ready to assist the authorities to further improve the electoral process and to address the recommendations contained in this and previous reports

A. PRIORITY RECOMMENDATIONS

1. To meet requirements regarding the equality of the vote, states should consider the establishment of independent redistricting commissions to draw district boundaries free from political interference. Such commissions should undertake broad public consultation and make recommendations on new boundaries well in advance of an election, allowing adequate time for any recourse to judicial review.

2. In order to ensure the right and opportunity to vote for all citizens, particularly national minorities, Congress should give urgent consideration to establish the formula to identify jurisdictions to be subject to Section Five of the Voting Rights Act, in line with the ruling in Shelby County v. Holder.

3. Restrictions on voting rights for persons with criminal convictions should be reviewed to ensure that all limitations are proportionate. Rights should be restored when sentences have been completed, with the law clarified and communicated to those affected. Pre-trial detainees should be provided with the means to vote.

4. Citizens resident in the District of Columbia and the US overseas territories should be provided with full representation rights in Congress. In addition, the right to vote in presidential elections should be extended to citizens resident in the US overseas territories.

5. Authorities should review existing measures to further reduce the number of unregistered voters, including addressing undue obstacles and burdensome procedures faced by marginalized sections of the population. Clear and accessible civic education programmes aimed at inclusive voter registration should be in place.

6. Legislation should be in place to guarantee the secrecy of the vote for in-person voting, including provisional and absentee voting.

7. States should refrain from introducing voter identification requirements that have or could have a discriminatory impact on voters. Consideration should be given to establishing federal standards for voter identification for both in-person and postal voting, to avoid possible discrimination and comply with the Voting Rights Act.

8. To improve transparency of campaign finance, disclosure of the sources of funding of nonprofit organizations that engage in campaign activities should be required. In addition, FEC rules regarding co-ordination should be reviewed and clarified to ensure that spending by outside groups is genuinely independent.

9. To help address security, functioning and reliability concerns of aging equipment, the authorities could allocate additional resources to upgrade or replace the existing electronic voting and counting systems.

10. Legislation should guarantee access in all states to international observers invited by the US authorities, to ensure full compliance with Paragraphs 8 of the 1990 OSCE Copenhagen Document and paragraph 25 of the 1999 OSCE Istanbul Document.

B. OTHER RECOMMENDATIONS

Election Administration

11. Election officials at the state and county level should be released from their duties if they are candidates in elections.

12. A thorough review of the obstacles faced in identifying, hiring and training poll workers should be conducted. States should ensure that resources for conducting elections, including hiring staff and establishing polling stations, are evenly allocated in all jurisdictions.

13. To further enhance the participation of voters with disabilities, comprehensive training and procedures should be developed. Specialized equipment already available at each polling station should be prepared and available throughout election day.

Voter Rights

14. States should review their legislation regarding voting rights for persons with disabilities. Blanket restrictions on the suffrage rights of persons with mental disabilities should be removed or be decided by courts on a case-by-case basis, depending on specific circumstances.

Voter Registration

15. Authorities should consider adopting formal procedures to ensure effective and continuous cyber-security measures to protect online voter registration systems.

16. Authorities should ensure that voter registers are maintained in full compliance with federal legislation. To ensure transparency of voter registration, the states could introduce oversight or audit procedures.

17. States not already participating in inter-state projects should consider doing so, to improve the accuracy of state voter registers across the country.

Candidate Registration

18. In line with good practice, the number of supporting signatures for candidate nomination should not exceed one per cent of registered voters. Additionally, federal legislation could clarify rules on nomination, such as appropriate advance deadlines, thereby promoting certainty for candidates.

Campaign Finance

19. Consideration could be given to reviewing the formula for the composition of the FEC in order to promote effective oversight and enforcement of campaign finance law.

20. The public financing system for presidential elections could be reformed, revising expenditure limits to make it more relevant to prevailing practice.

Media

21. Financial resources for public service broadcasters could be increased to provide space for impartial election reporting.

22. To provide viewers with an opportunity to see each of the candidates with a potential to win the presidency, consideration could be given to adjusting criteria for participation in the first presidential debate.

23. Freedom of the media to operate without any intimidation or pressure should be upheld.

Complaints and Appeals

24. States should introduce deadlines and effective measures in order for recounts to provide a timely remedy.

25. To avoid uncertainty during an election year, fundamental elements of electoral law should not be open to amendment less than one year before an election.

Early Voting

26. Jurisdictions should ensure the secrecy of postal ballots are always safeguarded when received by election officials by providing secrecy envelopes.

27. Where in-person early voting is used, states should ensure that the location and opening hours of polling stations provide, as far as possible, equal accessibility for all voters.

28. Federal authorities should develop secure voting methods, including for out-of-country voters, with a view to ensuring the secrecy of the vote while allowing for the expedient return of ballots.

New Voting Technologies

29. To prevent unauthorized access to voting equipment due to security gaps, election officials should consider a detailed and formalized examination of their storage, maintenance, testing and set-up procedures. Standardized post-election audits of electronic voting machines should be undertaken by manually examining randomly selected paper ballots and comparing the results to machine results. Reports of such processes should be made public.

30. To promote transparency and verifiability of electronic voting and counting systems, authorities should consider adopting legislation for the mandatory use of a voter-verifiable paper audit trail in elections.

31. Consideration should be given to enhance nationwide or inter-state mechanisms to provide comprehensive security of electronic voting and counting systems.

Election Day

32. Consideration should be given to the adoption of laws and regulations that set clear criteria for the determination of voter intent when ballots are counted or re-counted.

33. To enhance transparency, jurisdictions should consider promptly publishing results by polling station. When reporting preliminary results, the election officials should also include available information on how many provisional and absentee ballots are yet to be processed. The publication of preliminary and final election results should rest with state authorities.

[End text]

Source: OSCE-ODIHR, http://www.osce.org/odihr/elections/usa/294196?download=true

⋘⋙⋘⋙⋘⋙⋘⋙

7. MINISTERIAL COUNCIL, HAMBURG 2016, DECISION NO. 5/16 OSCE EFFORTS RELATED TO REDUCING THE RISKS OF CONFLICT STEMMING FROM THE USE OF INFORMATION AND COMMUNICATION TECHNOLOGIES

This document is an example of the work of the OSCE to prevent armed conflict. This Decision on behalf of the Organization is about measures to reduce the risk of conflict caused by the way a state uses information and communications technology. In light of the controversy surrounding the alleged Russian hacking during the 2016 U.S. Presidential election this Decision is very timely and emphasizes the threat potential created by cyber hacking, surveillance, misuse of cyberspace, false information, leaking harmful information, and infrastructure attacks. This document says that any efforts by OSCE participating States to reduce the risks of conflict stemming from the use of information and communication technologies must ensure that the measures will be consistent with: international law, including, inter alia, the U.N. Charter and the International Covenant on Civil and Political Rights; the Helsinki Final Act; and their responsibilities to respect human rights and fundamental freedoms.

Second day of the Twenty-Third Meeting MC(23) Journal No. 2, Agenda item 7

The Ministerial Council of the Organization for Security and Co-operation in Europe,

Reaffirming that efforts by OSCE participating States to reduce the risks of conflict stemming from the use of information and communication technologies will be consistent with: international law, including, inter alia, the U.N. Charter and the International Covenant on Civil and Political Rights; the Helsinki Final Act; and their responsibilities to respect human rights and fundamental freedoms,

Welcoming U.N. General Assembly resolution A/RES/70/237, and stressing the relevance to OSCE efforts to reduce the risks of conflict stemming from the use of information and communication technologies of the 2010, 2013 and 2015 reports of the United Nations Group of Governmental Experts on Developments in the Field of Information and Telecommunications in the Context of International Security,

Emphasizing the importance of OSCE confidence-building measures to reduce the risks of conflict stemming from the use of information and communication technologies to complement existing global, regional and subregional efforts in this field;

Emphasizing the importance of communication at all levels of authority to reduce the risks of conflict stemming from the use of information and communication technologies,

Recalling Permanent Council Decision No. 1039 of 26 April 2012, which established the OSCE framework for the development of CBMs designed to enhance inter-State co-operation, transparency, predictability, and stability, and to reduce the risks of misperception, escalation, and conflict that might stem from the use of information and communication technologies, and welcoming the work of the informal working group established pursuant to Permanent Council Decision No. 1039,

Building upon Permanent Council Decision No. 1106 of 3 December 2013 on an initial set of OSCE confidence-building measures to reduce the risks of conflict stemming from the use of information and communication technologies,

1. Endorses the adoption of Permanent Council Decision No. 1202 of 10 March 2016 on OSCE confidence-building measures to reduce the risks of conflict stemming from the use of information and communication technologies;

2. Stresses the importance of implementing existing OSCE confidence-building measures to reduce the risks of conflict stemming from the use of information and communication technologies and developing additional confidence-building measures in line with the Considerations set out in Permanent Council Decision No. 1202;

3. Welcomes the participating States' activities in the implementation of the existing OSCE confidence-building measures to reduce the risks of conflict stemming from the use of information and communication technologies, and notes in this respect the importance of continuously updating national contact points to facilitate pertinent communication and dialogue;

4. Encourages all participating States to contribute to the implementation of the OSCE confidence-building measures to reduce the risks of conflict stemming from the use of information and communication technologies;

5. Recognizes the importance of effective information exchange among participating States related to the OSCE confidence-building measures to reduce the risks of conflict stemming from the use of information and communication technologies and, inter alia, of ensuring rapid communication at technical and policy levels of authority, and of elaborating procedures for holding consultations in order to reduce the risks of misperception and of possible emergence of political or military tensions or conflict that may stem from the use of information and communication technologies;

6. Intends to explore, within the cross-dimensional, informal working group established pursuant to Permanent Council Decision No. 1039 under the auspices of the Security Committee, ways of strengthening the work of the OSCE as a practical platform for constructive and efficient implementation, and the possible development of further confidence-building measures to reduce the risks of conflict stemming from the use of information and communication technologies;

7. Invites participating States to make concrete proposals to this end by 30 June 2017;

8. Encourages relevant OSCE executive structures to assist participating States, upon their request, in the implementation of the OSCE confidence-building measures to reduce the risks of conflict stemming from the use of information and communication technologies, and to enhance pertinent national capabilities and processes, within available resources;

9. Welcomes the work undertaken by the 2016 OSCE German Chairmanship aimed at identifying how OSCE efforts to reduce the risks of conflict stemming from the use of information and communication technologies can be made more effective and can be intensified to promote an open, secure, stable, accessible and peaceful information and communication technologies environment in line with relevant OSCE commitments;

10. Underscores that further OSCE activities to reduce the risks of conflict stemming from the use of information and communication technologies, including those of relevant OSCE executive structures, should build on existing OSCE efforts, be in line with respective mandates and OSCE commitments, complement efforts by the United Nations, international and other regional fora, and be organized within available resources;

11. Invites the OSCE Partners for Co-operation to enhance dialogue on efforts to reduce the risks of conflict stemming from the use of information and communication technologies.

Source: http://www.osce.org/cio/288086

ॐ∽ॐ∽ॐ∽ॐ∽ॐ

8. OSCE MINISTERIAL COUNCIL, HAMBURG 2016: JOINT STATEMENT ON HUMAN RIGHTS AND FUNDAMENTAL FREEDOMS

This is a Joint Statement issued by all member states at the OSCE December 2016 Ministerial Council Meeting regarding the importance of human rights and fundamental freedoms, and lamenting the deterioration of the human rights situation in certain areas of the OSCE zone. It is a joint call to action to do something about that situation, particularly the stifling and persecuting of civil society members and organizations who work for human rights. It is a recognition of the connection between human rights and peace and security.

Ministerial Council Hamburg 2016
9 December 2016

23rd Ministerial Council   MC.DEL/41/16/Rev.1
Hamburg 8-9 December   12 December 2016

Closing Session

We make this statement in recognition that tomorrow, immediately following this Ministerial Council, we will observe Human Rights Day, marking the anniversary of the Universal Declaration of Human Rights. Instead of celebrating our achievements, we regret the further deterioration in parts of the OSCE region of respect for the exercise and enjoyment of those human rights, including the fundamental freedoms of expression and opinion, of association and peaceful assembly, and of thought, conscience, religion or belief. This is in sharp contrast to the commitments made by all participating States in the Helsinki Final Act and onwards, to respect human rights and fundamental freedoms, and promote universal and effective respect for them.

As pointed out in the Declaration adopted by the Parallel Civil Society Conference, the space for civil society is shrinking in our region, with numerous negative implications for the realization of the OSCE comprehensive security concept.

We commend all people and organisations that work tirelessly to ensure that the participating States implement our OSCE commitments on human rights and who hold governments to account. We speak here of civil society organisations, large and small, local, national and international, and also of courageous individuals who step forward to defend human rights.

There is no single model for human rights defenders. Examples include media workers, parliamentarians, lawyers, activists, bloggers and academics, alongside civil society organisations, but this list is not, and can never be, exhaustive. This group of brave individuals deserves our recognition and our deepest respect.

However, in certain parts of the OSCE region we continue to see severe restrictions placed on civil society organisations and attacks on human rights defenders. Legislation that restricts the work of civil society, and which results in criminal charges against and detention of people who have devoted their professional lives to the support of others. Lawyers who act in line with their professional obligations to defend individuals, only to subsequently face criminal charges themselves. Journalists who are silenced, through intimidation, legislation and restrictions on their work, and more worryingly through violent acts and murder.

So it is not enough just to give them our thanks. It is time for U.S. to stand up for their rights.

Where we see that another person's rights are at risk or under attack we must speak out and remind those governments of the commitments that they have freely made.

Whether it is a human rights defender facing reprisals for their actions, or whether it is someone who is being harassed, bullied or ridiculed because of who they are or what they stand for. We must challenge harmful stereotypes, combat myths with facts, and speak up for tolerance and non-discrimination. We must recall our commitments and hold ourselves and each other to account. There may be times when we are powerless to prevent injustice, but there must never be a time when we fail to protest.

We commend the work of the OSCE autonomous institutions, ODIHR, the HCNM and the RFOM, for their efforts to stand up for human rights, thereby contributing to our common security. Their institutional independence is essential to the promotion and protection of fundamental freedoms and human rights. To that end, they need to be equipped with adequate and sufficient means.

We will continue to take forward the principles that underpin both the UDHR, the international covenants and the Helsinki Final Act and stand up for human rights, across the OSCE region, and worldwide.

We also would like to express our sincere appreciation and thanks to the German Chairmanship for its tireless efforts to strengthen the Human Dimension.

On behalf of Albania, United States of America, Austria, Belgium, Bosnia and Herzegovina, Bulgaria, Canada, Cyprus, Croatia, Denmark, Spain, Republic of Estonia, Finland, France, Federal Republic of Germany, Georgia, United Kingdom, Greece, Hungary, Ireland, Iceland, Italy, Latvia, the former Yugoslav Republic of Macedonia, Lithuania, Luxembourg, Malta, Moldova, Montenegro, Norway, Netherlands, Poland, Portugal, Romania, San Marino, Serbia, Slovakia, Slovenia, Sweden, Switzerland, Czech Republic, and Ukraine.

Source: http://www.osce.org/cio/287976

Equality, Non-discrimination & Racism

Chapter 9

This Chapter is About the examination of the human rights to equality and non-discrimination in the context of state obligations to eliminate all forms of racism, as articulated in international human rights treaties, especially the International Convention on the Elimination of All Forms of Racial Discrimination. Overwhelmingly, international law sources support equality and non-discrimination as a means to address human rights deprivations in general. This chapter also discusses how states are obligated to work for the elimination of racism everywhere in all its forms.

This is Important Because, aware of catastrophic wars, genocides, etc., the international community addresses compellingly that discriminatory policies against equality of persons/peoples constitutes inequality in the exercise and enjoyment of the same human rights. Racially discriminatory policies constitute the root cause of violence in societies, leading to: the destabilization and erosion of security for all people to social disintegration; violent conflict, in some cases armed conflict; mass displacements; refugee flows; and nearly unfathomable human miseries. The international community recognizes the need for rights for all in order to draw attention to the many intolerances of racism, misogyny, ageism, nationalisms, exceptionalisms, soft and hard bigotries of all types, etc. with hopes for their elimination.

Only two human rights treaties use the term "elimination" in their titles: Convention on the Elimination of All Forms of Discrimination against Women (CEDAW); and International Convention on the Elimination of All Forms of Racial Discrimination (ICERD). Based on the international community's determination to eliminate human rights debasement by promoting human dignity and integrity, there is reason to consider that the full implementation of these two human rights treaties, by all nation states and without reservations, would do much to alleviate the suffering in the world.

Quotes & Key Text Excerpts

Article 1.

All human beings are born free and equal in dignity and rights.

Article 2.

Everyone is entitled to all the rights and freedoms set forth in this Declaration, without distinction of any kind, such as race, colour, sex, language, religion, political or other opinion, national or social origin, property, birth or other status.

Article 7.

All are equal before the law and are entitled without any discrimination to equal protection of the law. All are entitled to equal protection against any discrimination in violation of this Declaration and against any incitement to such discrimination.

—*Universal Declaration of Human Rights, 1948*

కించించించించి

Durban, South Africa, August-September 2001

Declaration

We declare that all human beings are born free, equal in dignity and rights and have the potential to contribute constructively to the development and well-being of their societies. Any doctrine of racial superiority is scientifically false, morally condemnable, socially unjust and dangerous, and must be rejected along with theories which attempt to determine the existence of separate human races;

We recognize that colonialism has led to racism, racial discrimination, xenophobia and related intolerance, and that Africans and people of African descent, and people of Asian descent and indigenous peoples were victims of colonialism and continue to be victims of its consequences. We acknowledge the suffering caused by colonialism and affirm that, wherever and whenever it occurred, it must be condemned and its reoccurrence prevented. We further regret that the effects and persistence of these structures and practices have been among the factors contributing to lasting social and economic inequalities in many parts of the world today;

We recognize that xenophobia against non-nationals, particularly migrants, refugees and asylum-seekers, constitutes one of the main sources of contemporary racism and that human rights violations against members of such groups occur widely in the context of discriminatory, xenophobic and racist practices;

Source: World Conference against Racism, Racial Discrimination, Xenophobia and Related Intolerance, 2001, http://www.un.org/WCAR/durban.pdf

కించించించించి

...

Racist hate speech can take many forms and is not confined to explicitly racial remarks....

The identification and combating of hate speech practices is integral to the achievement of the objectives of the Convention — which is dedicated to the elimination of racial discrimination in all its forms...

...On the qualification of dissemination and incitement as offences punishable by law, the Committee considers that the following contextual factors should be taken into account:

The content and form of speech: whether the speech is provocative and direct, in what form it is constructed and disseminated, and the style in which it is delivered.

The economic, social and political climate prevalent at the time the speech was made and disseminated, including the existence of patterns of discrimination against ethnic and other groups, including indigenous peoples. Discourses which in one context are innocuous or neutral may take on a dangerous significance in another: in its indicators on genocide the Committee emphasized the relevance of locality in appraising the meaning and potential effects of racist hate speech.

The position or status of the speaker in society and the audience to which the speech is directed. The Committee consistently draws attention to the role of politicians and other public opinion-formers in contributing to the creation of a negative climate towards groups protected by the Convention, and has encouraged such persons and bodies to adopt positive approaches directed to the promotion of intercultural understanding and harmony. The Committee is aware of the special importance of freedom of speech in political matters and also that its exercise carries with it special duties and responsibilities.

The reach of the speech, including the nature of the audience and the means of transmission: whether the speech was disseminated through mainstream media or the Internet, and the frequency and extent of the communication, in particular when repetition suggests the existence of a deliberate strategy to engender hostility towards ethnic and racial groups.

The objectives of the speech: speech protecting or defending the human rights of individuals and groups should not be subject to criminal or other sanctions.

...the Convention enshrines the obligation of States parties to prohibit and eliminate racial discrimination and to guarantee the right of everyone, without distinction as to race, colour, or national or ethnic origin, to equality before the law, notably in the enjoyment of civil, political, economic, social and cultural rights, including the rights to freedom of thought, conscience and religion, freedom of opinion and expression, and freedom of peaceful assembly and association.

...the expression of ideas and opinions made in the context of academic debates, political engagement or similar activity, and without incitement to hatred, contempt, violence or discrimination, should be regarded as legitimate exercises of the right to freedom of expression, even when such ideas are controversial.

School curricula, textbooks and teaching materials should be informed by and address human rights themes and seek to promote mutual respect and tolerance among nations and racial and ethnic groups.

...

The relationship between proscription of racist hate speech and the flourishing of freedom of expression should be seen as complementary and not the expression of a zero sum game where the priority given to one necessitates the diminution of the other. The rights to equality and freedom from discrimination, and the right to freedom of expression, should be fully reflected in law, policy and practice as mutually supportive human rights.

Source: UN, CERD/C/GC/37, International Convention on the Elimination of All Forms of Racial Discrimination, 26 September 2013, Committee on the Elimination of Racial Discrimination, General recommendation No. 35, Combating racist hate speech*, http://tbinternet.ohchr.org/_layouts/treatybodyexternal/TBSearch.aspx?Lang=en&TreatyID=6&DocTypeID=11

ॐ๛ॐ๛ॐ๛ॐ๛

"Four score and seven years ago our fathers brought forth on this continent, a new nation, conceived in liberty, and dedicated to the proposition that all men are created equal."

—President Abraham Lincoln, Gettysburg Address, November 19, 1863

ॐ๛ॐ๛ॐ๛ॐ๛

The United States has always been a multi-racial and multi-ethnic society, and its pluralism is increasing. We have made great strides over the years in overcoming the legacies of slavery, racism, ethnic intolerance, and destructive laws, policies, and practices relating to members of racial and ethnic minorities. Indeed, fifty years ago, the idea of having a Black/African American President of the United States would not have seemed possible; today, it is a reality. We recognize, however, that the path toward racial equality has been uneven, racial and ethnic discrimination still persists, and much work remains to meet our goal of ensuring equality for all. Our nation's Founders, who enshrined in our Constitution their ambition "to form a more perfect Union," bequeathed to U.S. not a static condition, but a perpetual aspiration and mission. This report shares our progress in implementing our undertakings under the CERD and on related measures to address racial discrimination.

Source: International Convention on the Elimination of All Forms of Racial Discrimination, 3 October 2013, Original: English, Committee on the Elimination of Racial Discrimination; Reports submitted by States parties under article 9 of the Convention; Seventh to ninth periodic reports of States parties due in 2011, United States of America [13 June 2013]

ॐ๛ॐ๛ॐ๛ॐ๛

Nothing in this Convention requires or authorizes legislation, or other action, by the United States of America prohibited by the Constitution of the United States as interpreted by the United States.

Source: U.S. reservations, declarations, and understandings, International Convention on the Elimination of All Forms of Racial Discrimination, 140 Cong. Rec. S7634-02 (daily ed., June 24, 1994). http://hrlibrary.umn.edu/usdocs/racialres.html

ॐ๛ॐ๛ॐ๛ॐ๛

The Working Group was informed that the federal structure of the United States has the virtue of allowing some states to explore more progressive policies to protect and promote the rights of people of African descent, which other states could benefit and learn from. Nevertheless, the Working Group also received information that the autonomy of the states and of local government also allows for the establishment of more regressive policies. While federal law provides a baseline of protection for civil and human rights, state laws can vary, and thus people of African descent enjoy different levels of protection of their rights depending on the state that they are living in.

The Working Group was also informed that some state and local governments have limited avenues and resources to ensure the realization of the rights of people of African descent. While state attorneys general and state civil rights commissions have a key role in combating Afrophobia and racial discrimination at the state level, the Working Group perceived disparities in the commitment levels and capacities of those institutions to implement state civil rights legislation.

Source: Report of the Working Group of Experts on People of African Descent on its mission to the United States of America
https://documents-dds-ny.un.org/doc/UNDOC/GEN/G16/183/30/PDF/G1618330.pdf?OpenElement

What You Should Know

As idealistic as it might sound, the international legal efforts to improve living enjoyment of all human rights came about and still comes about because persons/peoples struggle against the basic injustice of inequality derived from systemic and institutionalized discriminatory practices against persons/peoples, sometimes referred to as vulnerable groups. Discrimination against persons/peoples/vulnerable groups exists in public and in private, in state structures and in civil society. It is manifest in the political, civil, social, economic, and cultural order of human things public and private. Discrimination against persons or groups makes people uncomfortable. People duck and cover from injustices — until they cannot avoid those who suffer them anymore.

What or who is this discrimination against? It is the expression of indifference or fear or antipathy towards persons/peoples who have been stereotyped into groupings in a human pecking order based on questionable notions of tribe, race, gender orientation, cultural-national-social-ethnic origins, religion, etc. Even age, illnesses, and economic status can be demonized or scape-goated into ways to be discriminated against.

The international community through the U.N. and regional international organizations and civil society addresses human rights legally within an international framework that addresses domestic implementation of human rights treaties. Protection of the equality of human rights for all persons is the international community's primary task. By helping nation states address discrimination against persons/peoples within their domestic (human rights) legal systems, the U.N. has taken on the world-wide challenge of human rights. The international community in the U.N. and in regional systems and civil society groups endeavors to sensitize legalists in all nation states to existing inequality and discriminatory treatment of persons/peoples, by offering a legal framework to assist them in addressing their domestic human rights problems.

Understanding Equality

As a human right, equality has to do with equal treatment or equality before the law. The right to equality guarantees non-discrimination protections. The equality right and the non-discrimination right are intertwined principles that offer basic protection for all human rights. Article 2 of UDHR and ICCPR suggest that distinctions between persons and groups do not always mean there is discrimination, as long as distinctions are justified, reasonable, and with legitimate purpose. However, distinctions used for exclusion, restriction, suppression, preference, etc. whose purpose is nullifying, impairing recognition, enjoyment, or exercise of rights and freedoms by persons on an equal footing, constitute violations. Equality does not mean identical treatment in every instance. For example, someone of minor age, or who is incapacitated based on health or pregnancy have distinctively differing legal treatment needs. There sometimes exist needs for an affirmative action or preferential treatment for a time, to eliminate historic conditions of perpetuated discrimination and inequality. When applied to historically oppressed groups, it is not discrimination that is legalized, but a rather legitimate differentiation serving to recognize the group's distinctiveness within a limited context, as a means of examining reasonable and objectified criteria for their human rights cause.

Equality, as a human right, relates to essential human dignity; it is anti-superiority and anti-inferiority in classifications of human beings. Equality relates to unity or oneness in dignity of all members of the humanity, and is certainly the crux of thinking for the elimination of all forms of racial discrimination. No privileged group may bear human rights based on any notion of superiority vs. inferiority. Equality of treatment before the law must be consistent for all members of humanity, with only minor adjustments for the obvious lack of legal capacity of persons, such as the very young or someone with a physically-caused mental incapacity.

Equality is a principle of elementary justice that says all human beings are equal in value; that they all have the same intrinsic worth and the same human rights, and thus should be treated equally because of shared inherent human dignity. The expression, "equality before the law," means the right of an individual or groups of individuals to equal treatment in the administration of public policy or application of the law by law enforcement authorities or by ordinary courts of law. The principle of, and the right to, equality before the law is essential to the rule of law within democratic systems. Where there is this equality, no one can be above the law within a society of laws, without discriminatory exceptions for the powerful or highly influential, who have exactly the same rights, for example, to a fair trial, as everyone else before courts or tribunals.

Understanding Non-discrimination

Non-discrimination is obviously the opposite of discrimination, which refers to a hostile resistance, offensiveness, or indifference to a person's or group's enjoyment of all the same rights, freedoms, and protections, no matter who they are or where they come from, and anything that leads to "othering" them, i.e., denying their equality of status as persons. Discrimination has to be determined legally by facts exposing inequality.

Non-discrimination is a principle of human rights attached to equality. Non-discrimination communicates that no one may be denied the exercise and enjoyment of human rights based on the possession of characteristics, such as race, nationality, ethnicity, religion, language, sex, place of birth, social status, political, or other opinion, etc. States may not condition or limit human rights based on these kinds of characteristics. A state may not treat individuals or groups of persons differently regarding the enjoyment of human rights, unless there is a reasonable and objective justification for such a distinction to be made for which no other alternative can be found. The government would have to prove factually reasonable and objective justification for discriminating against someone's enjoyment and exercise of any human right.

The expression of a "non-discrimination clause" in human rights documents, such as treaties, conventions, covenants, instruments, declarations, etc. is use of the above-mentioned characteristics to reinforce listed specific substantive rights within a human rights document. A state must respect non-discrimination for any and all persons within its territorial jurisdiction, including for non-citizens.

Equality and Non-discrimination in International Law

1. U.N. Charter, 1945, universal respect for human rights/fundamental freedoms for all without distinction: preamble, paragraph 2; Article 1.2, 1.3; Article 2.1 (sovereign equality among all nations); Article 13.1b; Article 55c; Article 76c.

2. International Covenant on Civil and Political Rights, ICCPR, 1966, right to equality (before the law) and freedom from discrimination: Article 2.1; Article 3; Article 14.1 and 14.3; Article 20.2; Article 25; Article 26; Article 27.

3. International Covenant on Economic, Social and Cultural Rights, ICESCR, 1966, without discrimination of any kind as to race, colour, sex, language, religion, political or other opinion, national or social origin, property, birth or other status: Article 2.2; Article 3; Article 7a, I and 7c.

4. International Convention on the Elimination of All Forms of Racial Discrimination, CERD, 1965, any distinction, exclusion, restriction or preference based on race, colour, descent, or national or ethnic origin which has the purpose or effect of nullifying or impairing the recognition, enjoyment or exercise, on an equal footing, of human rights and fundamental freedoms in the political, economic, social, cultural or any other field of public life: Article 1.1; Article 5; treaty obligation to eliminate racial discrimination.

5. Convention on the Elimination of All Forms of Discrimination against Women, CEDAW, 1979, public and private non-discrimination: Article 1.

6. Convention on the Rights of the Child, CRC, 1989, non-discrimination: Article 2.1; disabled, Article 2.2; education, Article 29d; minority rights, Article 30.

7. Statute of the International Tribunal for the Former Yugoslavia, 1993, genocide prohibition: Article 4.2.

8. Statute of the International Tribunal for Rwanda, 1994, genocide prohibition: Article 2.2.

9. Rome Statute of the International Criminal Court, 1998, genocide prohibition: Article 6.

10. Four Geneva Conventions of 12 August 1949.

11. 1997 Protocols Additional to Geneva Conventions of 12 August 1949.

12. UDHR, 1948, prohibition of discrimination based on race, sex, language or religion; all born free and equal in dignity and rights: Article 1; Article 2; Article 7 (equality before the law without discrimination).

13. Convention on the Prevention and Punishment of the Crime of Genocide, 1948, prohibition of genocide as the ultimate negation of any right to equality: Article 2.

14. Declaration on the Elimination of All Forms of Intolerance and of Discrimination based on Religion or Belief, 1981, non-discrimination: Article 1.1, 1.2, 1.3; Article 2.1, 2.2; Article 4.2.

15. Declaration on the Rights of Persons Belonging to National or Ethnic, Religious and Linguistic Minorities, 1992, protection of minorities without discrimination: Preamble paragraph 6; Article 1.1, 1.2; Article 2.1.

16. U.N. Declaration on the Rights of Indigenous Peoples, UNDRIP, 2007.

17. African Charter on Human and Peoples' Rights, 1981, equality and non-discrimination: Article 2; Article 3; Article 18.3; Article 19.

18. African Charter on the Rights and Welfare of the Child, 1990, non-discrimination: Article 3; elimination of harmful social and cultural practices affecting welfare, dignity, normal growth and development, Article 21.1.

19. American Convention on Human Rights, 1969, non-discrimination: Article 1; equality: Article 8.2 and 24.

20. Inter-American Convention on the Prevention, Punishment, and Eradication of Violence against Women, 1994, women free from violence and non-discrimination: Articles 6a, 6b, Articles 7 & 8.

21. Inter-American Convention on the Elimination of All Forms of Discrimination against Persons with Disabilities, 1999, non-discrimination: Article II.

22. European Convention on Human Rights, 1950, enjoyment of rights and freedoms as non-discrimination: Article 14; non-discrimination: Protocol No. 12, 1 and 2.

23. European Social Charter, 1961, and European Social Charter (Revised), 1996, protection against poverty and exclusion: Article 30, non-discrimination "should": 3rd paragraph of preamble; non-discrimination in 1996 Revised: Article E, Part V.

24. Framework Convention for the Protection of National Minorities, 1995, respect, right to equality: Section II, Article 4.

Racism

Racism is the mistaken and gratuitous belief that the social construct of race is the primary factor in determining human characteristics and abilities, and that racial differences produce, again mistakenly and gratuitously, an inherent superiority of a particular race. Such a belief system leads to intolerance, discrimination, and persecution of those, because of skin tone, color, descent, or national or ethnic origin, deemed gratuitously to be inferior. A racist holds this attitude and some or all of these beliefs. In addition, racism is based on inaccurate assumptions, opinions, and actions resulting from the erroneous belief that "colors" the world in such a way as to arrive at the conclusion that one group is inherently superior or inferior to another. Such a belief system leads people to structure society or to maintain or retain structures within societies so that individuals and groups are excluded, restricted, or discriminated against on account of race or ethnic identification, while other favored groups hold on to privileges and perks at costs of the disfavored.

If equality is a foundational principle of human rights, and human dignity is both the origin, birthright, and realization of human rights; then every human being is equal with every other human being. Racism is completely inconsistent with the core of human rights and antithetical to the realization of all human rights. Racism represents danger to all human life. It creates intolerance, social divisions, strife, and violence, and can be a social symptom of genocidal tendencies.

International Convention on the Elimination of All Forms of Racial Discrimination (ICERD)

ICERD is the 1965 international human rights treaty dedicated to the complete dismantling of all racist and racially bigoted structures. Racism and racial discrimination are clearly understood as an historical issue of abuse, not an imagined history, in the same way as women and gender discrimination is based on lived history and not a product of imagination. Racial discrimination is and has been a cruel reality for centuries directed by dominant, sometimes a minority group itself, at a targeted group or groups of individuals, usually a minority, but sometimes a majority, as in the case of the majority of South African citizens living under apartheid.

ICERD Article 1 defines racial discrimination as "any distinction, exclusion, restriction or preference based on race, colour, descent or national or ethnic origin which has the purpose or effect of nullifying or impairing the recognition, enjoyment or exercise, on an equal footing, of human rights and fundamental freedoms in the political, economic, social, cultural, or any other field of public life."

The goal of the ICERD treaty is to push for the complete elimination of the phenomenon of discrimination against people based on racialized stereotypes in all its forms, both public and private, a phenomenon that transcends national, cultural, and religious boundaries. In racialized/racist societies, so-called "persons of color" have experiences of deprivations of human rights, higher rates of poverty, partial or total social exclusion, lower employment, deprivation or restrictions of the right to work, and other grievances, and sometimes deprivation of (full) citizenship rights, all of which have harmed and continue to harm stigmatized groups to the extent that implementation of an international human rights treaty had become necessary.

States party to ICERD are obligated to act to eliminate all forms of public and private racial discrimination. This certainly means the state must vet out all racist influences in public policy and law, but it does not mean the state will round up those who profess racist ideology in privacy. However, the state is required to address those who privately hold racial hatreds, to try to challenge racism, and to eliminate all forms of racial discrimination.

It is important to understand that racial discrimination within the ICERD frame of reference does not only relate to questions of racial discrimination due to skin color, but also relates directly to "distinctions, exclusions, restrictions, or preferences based on...descent or national or ethnic origin." ICERD is not about discrimination based only on skin pigmentation, skin flesh tone, or melanin, and all manner of pseudo-scientific misconceptions related to skin as an organ of the human body, but equally about discrimination based on descent, ethnicity, and nationality. ICERD is directed at the defense of political and civil rights, and economic, social, and cultural rights of migrants, immigrants, religious, and other minorities identified by nationality or ethnicity.

In addition to ICERD, ICCPR's Article 7 prohibition states: "No one shall be subjected to torture or to cruel, inhuman or degrading treatment or punishment." Threatening undocumented immigrants from specific nationalities with the violence of family separation exposes a state's hypocrisy; tearing families apart is cruel. So, in the consideration of equality and non-discrimination, one must also consider the Torture Convention (See Chapter 17), which parses the meanings of each category: torture; cruel treatment/punishment; inhuman treatment/punishment; degrading treatment/punishment. The international human rights frame of reference conveys how important it is to remind whole populations about the many hypocrisies countries embody whenever they become even momentarily silent in the defense of human rights, in an era when neo-nationalists move to discriminate against vulnerable persons and groups.

Despite the fact that racial discrimination still persists, it is important to recall that equality and racialized discrimination victims' rights are, and always have been, the same as everyone else's human rights. Because, however, racism is still unresolved, there is sometimes an attempt to emphasize, support, encourage, and advocate for reparations and affirmative action to restore personal ownership of human rights. An education in human rights is also essential for the elimination of all forms of illegal discrimination.

How the international community discusses the issue of racial discrimination

1. The Committee on the Elimination of Racial Discrimination (CERD): Treaty Body Reports; Handling Complaints; and Issuing General Comments

2. The ICCPR Human Rights Committee's (HR Committee)

3. Universal Periodic Review (UPR)

4. Report of the Special Rapporteur on contemporary forms of racism, racial discrimination, xenophobia and related intolerance, Doudou Diène, Mission to the United States of America, 2009

5. Human Rights Council Special Rapporteur on torture and other cruel, inhuman or degrading treatment or punishment 2016 — *Human Rights Council Special Rapporteur on extreme poverty and human rights anticipates an agreed upon visit to the United States of America, from December 4-15, 2017*

6. Working Group of Experts on People of African Descent

The Committee on the Elimination of Racial Discrimination (CERD) is the body of independent experts that meets twice annually, usually for three weeks at a time, as it monitors implementation of the Convention on the Elimination of All Forms of Racial Discrimination by its state parties.

All states parties submit regular reports to the Committee on how the rights are being implemented. States report every two years. The Committee examines each report and addresses its concerns and recommendations to the state party in the form of "concluding observations."

The ICERD treaty establishes three other mechanisms through which the Committee performs its monitoring functions: the early-warning procedure, the examination of inter-state complaints, and the examination of individual complaints.

The Committee also publishes its interpretation of the content of human rights provisions, known as general recommendations (or general comments), on thematic issues, and organizes thematic discussions.

U.N. discussions of non-discrimination with the U.S.
- The United States of America submitted its Seventh to Ninth Periodic Reports, as required under article 9 of the Convention, due in 2011, in June 2013. (See Primary Source Document 3.)
- The Committee on the Elimination of Racial Discrimination's (CERD) offered its Concluding observations on the U.S.A.'s combined seventh to ninth periodic reports in September 2014. (See Primary Source Document 4.) After affirming recent positive developments in the U.S. regarding legislative and policy developments to combat racial discrimination, CERD recommended elimination of the National Security Entry-Exit Registration System. The System had a War on Terrorism piece that required travelers from primarily Muslim-populated countries to be finger-printed, photographed, interviewed, and registered at their port of entry with information regarding their domestic information and plans in the U.S. The system was canceled because it led to no terrorist convictions of even one person. The CERD Committee also acknowledged: two Obama Executive orders to remove barriers for equal employment opportunities and improving Asian and Pacific Islander participation in federal programs and employment; the Fair Sentencing Act, a Hate Crimes Prevention Act, and the Lilly Ledbetter Fair Pay Act.

CERD Concerns and Recommendations
- Applicability of the Convention at the national level: recommends regarding lack of progress of sharing CERD information and withdrawing U.S. Article 2 reservations of the treaty;

- National human rights institution: Obama's Executive Order 13107 created Equality Working Group Initiative on Race and Gender to look at CERD. Yet there is the need for an NHRI to address all human rights issues in the U.S.;
- Special measures: regarding affirmative action as an example of type of recommended special measures needed;
- Racial profiling and illegal surveillance: as an ineffective law enforcement practice and a remaining concern;
- Racist hate speech and hate crimes: hate speech is protected speech in the U.S., except in incitement to imminent violence, unlike other countries; hate crimes go underreported; recommends: withdraw CERD Article 4 reservation; improve data collection system for statistical info-sharing; in-service for new recruits for hate crimes;
- Disparate impact of environmental pollution: racial and ethnic minorities and indigenous peoples disproportionately affected; recommends: federal legislation for anti-pollution enforcement; investigate polluters; clean-up radioactive/toxic waste; protect indigenous from transnational actions affecting their rights;
- Right to vote: restrictive voter ID laws, district gerrymandering, felon disenfranchisement laws; *Shelby v. Holder* decision by Supreme Court re: eliminating Voting Rights Act safeguards; no federal Senator in DC; recommend federal legislation to eliminate discriminatory impact of voting regulations; ensure voting rights, and other concerns of indigenous peoples; reinstate voting rights to felons in many conditions; full voting rights in DC;
- Criminalization of homelessness: disproportionate African Americans, Latino, Native American homeless harassed for loitering, camping, begging, etc.; recommends: abolish homelessness laws; intensify stakeholder involvement in solutions for problem; financial support for alternatives;
- Discrimination and segregation in housing: patterns of segregation and discrimination in housing against African Americans, minorities, ethnicity, etc.; poor housing stock; limited employment, health access; foreclosures; recommends: implement HUD Affirmatively Furthering Fair Housing with new housing programs; implement Fair Housing Act and Title VIII of Civil Rights Act; resources for HUD;
- Education: recommends: comprehensive plan for addressing racial segregation in schools/neighborhoods concretely with goals, timelines, etc.; federal funding of integrated learning environments; Equity and Excellence Commission recommendations to implement; reauthorize ESEA to solve segregation; work with education authorities and civil society groups;
- Right to health and access to health care: recommends: Affordable Care Act finance health-care services for racial, ethnic minorities outside system; sexual and reproductive health services to eliminate racial disparities re: maternal/infant mortality; improve monitoring and accountability mechanisms;
- Gun violence: recommends: legislative/policy measures to protect right to life and reduce violence; legislation for background checks; prohibit concealed guns in public, illegal gun sales; repeal Tiahrt Amendments; review Stand Your Ground laws; ensure necessity/proportionality in self-defence;
- Excessive use of force by law enforcement officials: recommends: prompt, effective investigation of alleged excess; prosecute perpetrators; reopen investigations when new evidence; compensation to victim's family; compliance with: Basic Principle on the Use of Force and Firearms by Law Enforcement Officials; new CBP directive;
- Immigrants: recommends: state to ensure fully guaranteed rights of non-citizens; abolish Operation Streamline; individualize assessments for decisions re: detention/deportation; guarantee access to lawyers; review laws /regulations to protect against worker exploitation/hazards, including farm work; enforce international labor standards and conditions oversight; ratify ILO Labour Office Convention No. 29 (1930);
- Violence against women: recommends: intensify protection of indigenous women; investigate all cases of violence; find appropriate remedies; previous recommendation of resources for violence prevention and services for victims; training in criminal justice system; awareness-raising campaigns;
- Criminal justice system: recommends effective elimination of racial disparities throughout criminal justice system; name and end laws/policies leading to racial disparities; national plans of action to eliminate structural discrimination; moratorium on death penalty; prevent incarceration of children with alternatives to incarceration;
- Juvenile justice: recommends addressing school discipline policies re: school-to-prison pipeline; get juveniles out of adult courts and separate from adults in jailing; abolish life imprisonment for juveniles;
- Guantánamo Bay: recommends ensured closure; fair trial for non-citizens; compliance re: human rights standards tor release from non-charged inmates;

- Access to legal aid: recommends: indigent defendants from racial/ethnic minorities need qualified lawyers funded/supervised; need stability/support for evictions/foreclosures/domestic violence, etc.;
- Rights of indigenous people: recommends: indigenous right to participate in public life/in decisions that affect them; recognize tribes; protect sacred sites/resource exploitation; implement Indian Child Welfare Act to halt removal of children from families/communities; implement Decision 1(68) Western Shoshone peoples;
- National action plan to combat racial discrimination: federal national action plan needed to eliminate structural racial discrimination; school curricula/textbooks, etc. to address human rights in promotion of understanding among racial/ethnic minority groups;
- General recommendations and comments include: more information on psychotropic drugs used with African American children in foster care; non-consensual psychiatric treatment, restrictive/coercive practices on minorities in mental health services; CERD implementation in U.S. non-autonomous territories; status of incarcerated Civil Rights era political activists; state party's declared recognition of CERD as competent experts; domestic ratification of CERD; ratification of other human rights treaties, especially CEDAW, ICESCR, CRC, ICRMW, CRPD, and ICPPED.

CERD General Recommendations

1. The issuance of the preceding General Recommendations by CERD experts takes place at the end of the process of reviewing Treaty Body Reports and Handling Complaints. Based on that entire process, experts, since 1972, have gone back to discuss again the treaty articles that came up as a result of review of various country reports. The give-and-take that goes on between the committee and countries always raises new questions for their clarification of the treaty's various articles and themes. Some questions arise or get expressed during each country's feedback process in the CERD Concerns and Recommendations. Having learned from many countries' difficulties implementing ICERD, the CERD committee since 1972 has chosen to make General Recommendations that serve as treaty article and thematic clarifications for all countries.

Here are some of the General recommendations, which are valuable to know in 2017:
- In 2011, General recommendation No. 34 on Racial discrimination against people of African descent, the experts clarified: Description; Rights; Measures of a general nature; The place and role of special measures; Gender-related dimensions of racial discrimination; Racial discrimination against children; Protection against hate speech and racial violence; Administration of justice; Civil and political rights; Access to citizenship; economic, social, and cultural rights; Measures in the field of education. As an example, under Administration of justice, the experts clarified:

> "Take all the necessary steps to secure equal access to the justice system for all people of African descent including by providing legal aid, facilitating individual or group claims, and encouraging non-governmental organizations to defend their rights.

> Introduce into criminal law the provision that committing an offence with racist motivation or aim constitutes an aggravating circumstance allowing for a more severe punishment.

> Ensure the prosecution of all persons who commit racially motivated crimes against people of African descent and guarantee the provision of adequate compensation for victims of such crimes.

> Also ensure that measures taken in the fight against crimes, including terrorism, do not discriminate in purpose or effect on the grounds of race and colour.

> Take measures to prevent the use of illegal force, torture, inhuman or degrading treatment or discrimination by the police or other law enforcement agencies and officials against people of African descent, especially in connection with arrest and detention, and ensure that people of African descent are not victims of practices of racial or ethnic profiling.

> Encourage the recruitment of people of African descent into the police and as other law enforcement officials.

Organize training programmes for public officials and law enforcement agencies with a view to preventing injustices based on prejudice against people of African descent."

- In 2005, General recommendation No. 30 on discrimination on non-citizens, the experts clarified: Responsibilities of States parties to the convention; Measures of a general nature; Protection against hate speech and racial violence; Access to citizenship; Administration of justice; Expulsion and deportation of non-citizens; Economic, social, and cultural rights. As an example, under Expulsion and deportation of non-citizens the experts clarified:

> "Ensure that laws concerning deportation or other forms of removal of non-citizens from the jurisdiction of the State party do not discriminate in purpose or effect among non-citizens on the basis of race, color, or ethnic or national origin, and that non-citizens have equal access to effective remedies, including the right to challenge expulsion orders, and are allowed effectively to pursue such remedies;

> Ensure that non-citizens are not subject to collective expulsion, in particular in situations where there are insufficient guarantees that the personal circumstances of each of the persons concerned have been taken into account;

> Ensure that non-citizens are not returned or removed to a country or territory where they are at risk of being subject to serious human rights abuses, including torture and cruel, inhuman or degrading treatment or punishment;

> Avoid expulsions of non-citizens, especially of long-term residents, that would result in disproportionate interference with the right to family life;"

Source: U.N. Office of the High Commissioner for Human Rights, Treaty bodies Search, http://tbinternet.ohchr.org/_layouts/ treatybodyexternal/TBSearch.aspx?Lang=en&TreatyID=6&DocTypeID=11

2. The ICCPR treaty's special mechanism has the Human Rights Committee (HRC) look at the full range of civil and political rights. In its Concluding observations on the fourth periodic report of the United States of America in 2014 on civil and political rights, including issues of racial discrimination, the HRC cited positive aspects of reform, and the following Principal matters of concern:
- Racial disparities in the criminal justice system: both acknowledging recent work, such as the Fair Sentencing Act of 2010, still concerned about racial disparities, such as overrepresentation of racial/ethnic minorities in prisons/jails; recommend on-going efforts in amending regulations/policies and retroactive application of Fair Sentencing Act.
- Racial profiling: recommends ending "stop and frisk" policy, still concerned about profiling and surveillance of certain minorities in absence of suspicion of wrongdoing; recommends review of 2003 Guidance Regarding the Use of Race by Federal Law Enforcement Agencies, and protect against profiling based on religion, religious appearance, national origin; train state, and local law enforcement re: cultural awareness and inadmissibility of racial profiling.
- and the Death penalty: concerned with racial disparities and disproportionate effect on African Americans, wrongful sentencing of death penalty, lack of compensation in some states for wrongful convictions, and untested lethal injections; recommend addressing all this at federal level; consider death penalty moratorium.

3. Universal Periodic Review recommendations 2015 were very close to the ICCPR treaty's special mechanism, except that the Human Rights Council (HRC) oversees review of the full spectrum of state obligations as adherents under many human rights treaties.

4. Report of the Special Rapporteur on contemporary forms of racism, racial discrimination, xenophobia, and related intolerance, Doudou Diène, Mission to the United States of America, 2009. The Rapporteur addressed public policies and measures to fight racism, etc. and also from the viewpoint of civil society groups and affected communities: Law enforcement and Racial profiling; Hate crimes; Education; Housing; Employment; Measures to prevent discrimination in the aftermath of the events of 11 September 2001; Measures taken in the aftermath of Hurricane Katrina; Immigration. This was followed by the Rapporteur's analysis and assessment and finally his recommendations for: Congress to estab-

lish a bipartisan commission to fight racism, etc.; government reassessment of related legislation; for U.S. DOJ Civil Rights Division, the EEOC, and HUD housing department to intensify enforcement civil rights laws; that consultation mechanisms be established at all levels of government to address racism, etc. at federal, state, and local levels; and much more. (See Primary Source Document 9)

5. Human Rights Council Special Rapporteur on torture and other cruel, inhuman, or degrading treatment or punishment 2016, Report of the Special Rapporteur, Addendum, Observations on communications transmitted to Governments and replies received. (See Chapter 17 for more information on torture.)

This refers to a Special Rapporteur on torture communication in 2016 that dealt with a few cases the U.S. is involved with. They are the cases that allege torture of African Americans and other minorities:

- Police Headquarters in the City of Chicago from 1972 through 1991, where petitioners were released, got formal apologies, financial, and other reparations for torture or physical abuse from Chicago City Council, after the Illinois Torture Inquiry and Relief Commission;
- concerning racial discrimination against Mr. Mumia Abu-Jamal, a person of African descent, and lack of access to appropriate medical treatment while in detention; He was eventually granted access to hepatitis C treatments in January 2017.
- concerning the deportation of Haitians, and in particular persons suffering from serious mental and physical illnesses and requiring appropriated specialized psychological and medical attention, to post-earthquake Haiti. The U.S. reply did not address risks of deportee women, persons with nonconforming gender identities, and persons suffering from chronic mental or physical illnesses who would be vulnerable to physical abuse and/or imprisonment or institutionalization in unsafe conditions upon return to Haiti; and that persons with serious health conditions were unable to access adequate medical treatment and facilities, specialized care, medications, nutrition, and stable and safe living conditions. The deportees were never asked any specific questions about any risks to torture or cruel or degrading treatment. The Special Rapporteur warned the U.S. that it was at risk of violating its non-refoulement obligation under Article 3 of the Convention Against Torture (CAT), and strongly urged the Government to refrain from carrying out further deportations in the absence of independent determinations under the CAT.

—Human Rights Council Special Rapporteur on extreme poverty and human rights anticipates an agreed upon visit to the United States of America from December 4-15, 2017

6. The Working Group of Experts on People of African Descent resulted from the World Conference against Racism, Racial Discrimination, Xenophobia, and Related Intolerance in 2001 and its adoption of the Durban Declaration and Programme of Action's inclusion of a request of the U.N. Human Rights Commission for a working group, which was established and began its work in 2002. It is considered part of Special Procedures under the U.N. Human Rights Council, i.e., the Working Group is an independent fact-finding and monitoring mechanism, and is also a Special Procedures mandate-holder, insofar as human rights experts, the Working Group may address specific country systems or thematic issues in response to allegations received. It may contact and intervene directly with governments by means of a letter on allegations of violations regarding individual cases, patterns and trends of human rights violations, cases affecting particular groups or communities, or regarding legislative drafts or actual legislation or practices incompatible with international human rights standards.

http://ap.ohchr.org/documents/E/HRC/resolutions/A_HRC_RES_9_14.pdf
http://www.ohchr.org/EN/Issues/Racism/WG AfricanDescent/Pages/Communications.aspx

The Working group had visited the U.S. in 2010. In 2016, The Working Group of Experts on People of African Descent completed a mission to the United States of America. (See Primary Source Document 7.) The delegation, made up of Mireille Fanon-Mendès-France, Sabelo Gumedze, and Ricardo Sunga III, visited Washington, DC; Baltimore, Maryland; Jackson, Mississippi; Chicago, Illinois; and New York City in mid to late January 2016. In DC, they met with representatives from the Department of State, the Department of Homeland Security, the Department of Housing and Urban Development, the Department of Health and Human Services, the Department of Labor, the Department of Justice, the Environmental Protection Agency, officials of the Equal Employment Opportunity Commission, the White House group working on African American issues, and staff of the congressional black caucus. In Maryland, they met with federal judges; in Mississippi, with Jackson mayor's office officials and the State Attorney General representatives; in Illinois, mayor's office officials and the police department officials; and in NYC with the State Attorney General. The Working Group also met with hundreds of African Americans from the cities and suburbia, and with lawyers, NGO representatives, and academics.

The Working Group's conclusions and recommendations were very forthright with their acknowledgements of significant positive steps and developments to improve circumstances for African Americans in the U.S., from the Patient Protection and Affordable Care Act to some relief on home foreclosure. Nonetheless, it also offered a very long list of conclusions for the U.S. to consider regarding African Americans' lives regarding: death penalty and its abolition; the epidemic of racial violence by the police, and the disparities in law enforcement policies; criminal records affecting employability for ex-criminals; reparations and a truth and reconciliation process re: racial bias and discrimination; over-incarceration; lack of tracking systems re: killings and excessive use of force by law enforcement; criminalization of homelessness and poverty; use of solitary confinement; excessively long prison sentences; imprisonment for minor offences; mandatory prison sentencing and zero tolerance policies; debts caused by fines and fees whose real purpose was to raise money for public security and law enforcement funding; juvenile justice and prosecution of children as adults; gap in human development indicators reflecting structural and institutional discrimination due to lack of employment opportunities; housing crisis due to excessively high rents or mortgages and gentrification; ineffective implementation of civil rights laws and over-complexity of legal recourse in federal, state, and county jurisdictions; lack of direct applicability of international human rights law and policies, which may not be invoked in national courts, as these laws and policies have been judicially and legislatively declared as non-self-executing treaties.

Recommendations for U.S. improvements by the Working Group of Experts on People of African Descent in 2016 include:

- establish an NHRI based on the Paris Principles with a division monitoring African Americans' human rights;
- fully ratify human rights treaties, with review and removal of any reservations, especially fully implement ICERD with realization of an action plan;
- align federal and state laws to the ICCPR and other human rights treaties with an agency established to specifically accomplish this goal;
- give effect to observations and recommendations, etc. of the various on-going U.N. human rights bodies;
- acknowledge history of racial discrimination, slavery's place in injustice and crimes against African Americans, Afrophobia, racism, xenophobia, and related intolerance;
- provide school curriculum in each state that reflects appropriately the history of the transatlantic trade of Africans, enslavement, and segregation;
- address the need for reparatory justice by educating for reconciliation and constructively open dialogue through the U.N. declared 2015-2024 International Decade for People of African Descent;
- pass U.S. HR 40 — the Commission to Study Reparation Proposals for African-Americans Act, perhaps by emulating the Caribbean Community's Ten-Point Action Plan on Reparations, with its formal apology, health initiatives, educational opportunities, effecting of an African knowledge programme, psychological rehabilitation, technology transfer and financial support, and debt cancellation;
- pass all pending criminal justice reform bills, including the End Racial Profiling Act and the Second Chance Reauthorization Act;
- follow through on the Sentencing Reform and Corrections Act of 2015;
- implement the recommendations in the final report of the President's Task Force on 21st Century Policing;
- ensure accountability for police violence against African Americans by improving and ensuring:
    - reporting of violations involving the excessive use of force and extrajudicial killings by the police;
    - independent investigation of reported or alleged cases of excessive use of force;
    - perpetrators are prosecuted and, if convicted, punished with appropriate sanctions;
    - investigations are re-opened when new evidence becomes available;
    - victims or their families are provided with remedies;
    - compliance with Basic Principles on the Use of Force and Firearms by Law Enforcement Officials of 1990
- realign and re-engage students who have been dismissed from educational institutions as part of a zero tolerance policy;

- revisit and review school security policies so that:
  - policing in schools can be abolished;
  - misdemeanor laws like school disturbance get repealed;
  - there are no more seclusion or restraint policies;
  - students get counseling and assistance for all kinds of issues related to health, mental health, disabilities, autism, attention deficit, hyperactivity, etc.
  - international human rights standards are learned and become normalized in schools;
- Juvenile Justice situations are addressed:
  - males and females are separated if in detention;
  - alternatives to youth imprisonment or detention are found and developed so that effective intervention and diversion becomes normative;
  - take family circumstances into account if imposing a sentence, with close attention to the best interests of the child;
  - excessive bail is prevented;
- develop community control of police via civilian boards that: works with community policing strategies and elects to showcase police whose skills are exemplary;
- investigate cases as to whether non-payment of court fines/fees are too much, causing arrests due to ripening civil contempt charges due to non-payment; if unpayable, fines/fees should be canceled;
- uphold the right to adequate standards of living, including adequate food, housing, and safe drinking water and sanitation;
- halt the demolition of public housing if replacement units have not been guaranteed with prior and informed consent and with the participation of the people affected;
- ban all solitary confinement as a human rights violation found in CAT;
- allow a visit by the Special Rapporteur on torture and other cruel, inhuman, or degrading treatment or punishment to independently monitor places of detention in the United States;
- repeal all laws that restrict voting rights, even of felons once their sentences are completed;
- raise awareness of and reduce crimes against the lesbian, gay, bisexual, transgender, queer; and intersex community, in particular against transgender women;
- respect asylum seekers by not imprisoning them while in their asylum process with guaranteed right to counsel and to an interpreter;
- strengthen the implementation of Executive Order 12898 achieving environmental protection for minority and low-income populations and for all communities.
- implement the Universal Periodic Review recommendations made to and accepted by the United States in 2015.

Rights to equality, non-discrimination, and the elimination of racism in U.S. domestic law

This section examines briefly the basis of public legal protections in the U.S. for equality and non-discrimination, and how racial discrimination is publicly not sanctioned, but privately goes almost unchallenged, based on U.S. Constitutional rights to freedom of thought and expression.

Equality

- The U.S. Declaration of Independence of 1776 is a legally binding document in the U.S. in exactly the same way that the U.N. Universal Declaration of Human Rights is legally binding for all human beings. They both embody such power that they are recognized as both customary national and international law for the U.S. In its preamble, the U.S. Declaration of Independence enshrined the phrase "We hold these truths to be self-evident, that all men are created equal, that they are endowed by their Creator with certain unalienable Rights, that among these are Life, Liberty and the pursuit of Happiness." It is in an eighteenth century English Enlightenment modality. In its Article 1, the UDHR, modeled very much on Jefferson's phrasing, reads as: "All human beings are born free and equal in dignity and rights. They are endowed with reason and conscience and should act towards one another in a spirit of brotherhood." It reads in a twentieth century vernacular that sounds agnostic.
- The U.S. Constitution differs from any treaty or document the United Nations has ever been involved in creating. The U.S. Constitution, as the foundational document for the initial creation of U.S. governance, has a

Bill of Rights in its first ten Amendments that have been expanded over time to twenty-seven Amendments; its Fourteenth Amendment, among other things, establishes "equal protection of the laws."

The United Nations, on the other hand, is an organization; its U.N. Charter establishes the United Nations Organization. Since the U.N. exists as an organizing vehicle for the creation of international treaties, especially in the legal field of human rights, it depends on its U.N. Charter member states to make real domestically or in national law any international human rights treaties States sign and/or ratify. Influential as it may be, the U.N. does not govern the U.S. nor any other country; also see Chapter 6.

Non-discrimination is directly constrained in the public sector, but not in the private sector. However, sometimes indirectly, the non-discrimination clause of the U.S. Constitution is applied to the private sector, if the state finds it has a compelling interest, compelling reason, as least restrictively as possible, in determining whether private parties behaved criminally towards an individual person's or persons' fundamental rights.

- The Fifth Amendment of the U.S. Constitution limits the power of the federal or state government to discriminate based on its "No person shall...be deprived of life, liberty, or property, without due process of law..."
- The Fourteenth Amendment explicitly forbids states violating rights to due process "...nor shall any State deprive any person of life, liberty or property, without due process of law..." as well as equal protection.
- The U.S. Equal Employment Opportunity Commission through Title VII of the Civil Rights Act of 1964 makes it illegal to discriminate against anyone on the basis of race, color, religion, national origin, or sex in employment; or to retaliate against someone because she/he complained about discrimination, or helped in investigating a discrimination complaint. Many laws and statutes protect persons in the U.S.; see https://www.eeoc.gov/laws/statutes;
- The U.S. Department of Justice Civil Rights Division works for Federal Protections against discrimination based on national origin, race, color, religion, disability, sex, and familial status. The DOJ suspects that illegal discrimination goes under-reported because victims do not know their legal rights in education, employment, housing, lending, public accommodations, law enforcement/police misconduct, for disabilities and voting; see https://www.justice.gov/crt/federal-protections-against-national-origin-discrimination-1.

Although the U.S. has signed and ratified International Convention on the Elimination of all Forms of Racial Discrimination (ICERD), its reservations to the treaty are a perfect expression of the problems of equality, non-discrimination and racial discrimination in the U.S.; see Primary Source Document 2. Although the U.S. has had a very significant role in the creation of human rights treaties around the world, it only ratifies those treaties insofar as it can easily circumvent them for enforcement in the U.S.

The U.S. has ratified international human rights treaties, and simultaneously has put all human rights treaties through a process of "reservations" to declare these treaties as non-self-executing. Why would the U.S. do this, if those treaties would improve and enhance the rights of its citizens? Does the U.S. believe the U.S. Constitution and our justice system already contain all the extensive and sufficient protections one needs for equality and non-discrimination before the law to be in compliance with ICERD? Why has the U.S. done very little to educate its people about the facts of human rights treaty ratification and then their subsequent non-implementation? Are the human rights to equality before the law and non-discrimination (and all other human rights) fully protected by the Constitution and laws of the United States? Yes...No...Perhaps. The apparent ambivalence is maddening.

During the One-Year Follow-up Response of the U.S. to Priority Recommendations of the Committee on the Elimination of Racial Discrimination in its Concluding Observations on the Combined Seventh to Ninth Periodic Reports of the United States of America, the U.S., under the Obama regime, responded with just a bit less obfuscation than usual to human rights issues related to:

- police use of force/excessive use of force;
- rights of non-citizens; detention and deportation; access to legal representation;
- migrant worker rights;
- closure of the Guantánamo Bay facility.

Given President Trump's first speech to Congress on February 28, 2017, the lack of reference to human rights is shockingly apparent. Fears regarding human rights violations are merited, and the following questions valid:

- What are the remaining controversies/critical issues or objections to the rights to equality, non-discrimination, and to the elimination of racism within the U.S. and international context?
- Why would the U.S. still hold on to any of its reservations to ICERD?
- Why doesn't the U.S. drop its many reservations to international human rights treaties, such as ICERD?

It is important to study U.S. issues related to racism, among other human rights, in an effort to acknowledge, address, and resolve. Those impacted by racism are not just victims of racism, but actively resist it, as evidenced by the protests against the deaths of young people at the hands of police authorities, and by activism by indigenous peoples as energy corporations and the U.S. government circumvent their rights to consultation and autonomy over their lands' many resources, including cultural resources. Black Lives Matter struggles as an organized movement, as do the current international indigenous peoples' movements, as exemplified by Standing Rock Sioux Tribe's, Cheyenne River Sioux Tribe's, and Yankton Sioux Tribe's request for Precautionary Measures for their protection on their own land in their struggle with the Dakota Access Pipeline (DAPL) forced through by the Trump administration in its first weeks in office.

The U.S. is now realizing that its people are paying keen attention to human rights issues related to inequality and discrimination. Americans demand more complete respect of all human rights as the legitimate basis of law everywhere, including the U.S., which one hopes is only momentarily adrift on important human rights questions.

Primary Source Documents:

I. INTERNATIONAL CONVENTION ON THE ELIMINATION OF ALL FORMS OF RACIAL DISCRIMINATION

In this Convention, the broad definition of the term "racial discrimination" is being "based on race, colour, descent, or national or ethnic origin." Note that Article 1, para. 4 is a reference to race-related affirmative action type measures. This article defines certain kinds of such measures as not constituting racial discrimination at all, subject to certain limitations. Also, the status and applicability of this instrument as to the United States may have changed since date of publication. For updates see: Web address: http://www1.umn.edu/humanrts/instree/d1cerd.htm or http://www.ohchr.org/Documents/ProfessionalInterest/cerd.pdf

International Convention on the Elimination of All Forms of Racial Discrimination, Adopted and opened for signature and ratification by General Assembly resolution 2106 (XX) of 21 December 1965, entry into force 4 January 1969, in accordance with Article 19

The States Parties to this Convention,

Considering that the Charter of the United Nations is based on the principles of the dignity and equality inherent in all human beings, and that all member states have pledged themselves to take joint and separate action, in co-operation with the Organization, for the achievement of one of the purposes of the United Nations which is to promote and encourage universal respect for and observance of human rights and fundamental freedoms for all, without distinction as to race, sex, language or religion, Considering that the Universal Declaration of Human Rights proclaims that all human beings are born free and equal in dignity and rights and that everyone is entitled to all the rights and freedoms set out therein, without distinction of any kind, in particular as to race, colour or national origin,

Considering that all human beings are equal before the law and are entitled to equal protection of the law against any discrimination and against any incitement to discrimination,

Considering that the United Nations has condemned colonialism and all practices of segregation and discrimination associated therewith, in whatever form and wherever they exist, and that the Declaration on the Granting of Independence to Colonial Countries and Peoples of 14 December 1960 (General Assembly resolution 1514 (XV)) has affirmed and solemnly proclaimed the necessity of bringing them to a speedy and unconditional end,

Considering that the United Nations Declaration on the Elimination of All Forms of Racial Discrimination of 20 November 1963 (General Assembly resolution 1904 (XVIII)) solemnly affirms the necessity of speedily eliminating racial discrimination throughout the world in all its forms and manifestations and of securing understanding of and respect for the dignity of the human person,

Convinced that any doctrine of superiority based on racial differentiation is scientifically false, morally condemnable, socially unjust and dangerous, and that there is no justification for racial discrimination, in theory or in practice, anywhere,

Reaffirming that discrimination between human beings on the grounds of race, colour or ethnic origin is an obstacle to friendly and peaceful relations among nations and is capable of disturbing peace and security among peoples and the harmony of persons living side by side even within one and the same State,

Convinced that the existence of racial barriers is repugnant to the ideals of any human society,

Alarmed by manifestations of racial discrimination still in evidence in some areas of the world and by governmental policies based on racial superiority or hatred, such as policies of apartheid, segregation or separation,

Resolved to adopt all necessary measures for speedily eliminating racial discrimination in all its forms and manifestations, and to prevent and combat racist doctrines and practices in order to promote understanding between races and to build an international community free from all forms of racial segregation and racial discrimination,

Bearing in mind the Convention concerning Discrimination in respect of Employment and Occupation adopted by the International Labour Organisation in 1958, and the Convention against Discrimination in Education adopted by the United Nations Educational, Scientific and Cultural Organization in 1960,

Desiring to implement the principles embodied in the United Nations Declaration on the Elimination of All Forms of Racial Discrimination and to secure the earliest adoption of practical measures to that end,

Have agreed as follows:

PART I

Article 1

1. In this Convention, the term "racial discrimination" shall mean any distinction, exclusion, restriction or preference based on race, colour, descent, or national or ethnic origin which has the purpose or effect of nullifying or impairing the recognition, enjoyment or exercise, on an equal footing, of human rights and fundamental freedoms in the political, economic, social, cultural or any other field of public life.

2. This Convention shall not apply to distinctions, exclusions, restrictions or preferences made by a State Party to this Convention between citizens and non-citizens.

3. Nothing in this Convention may be interpreted as affecting in any way the legal provisions of States Parties concerning nationality, citizenship or naturalization, provided that such provisions do not discriminate against any particular nationality.

4. Special measures taken for the sole purpose of securing adequate advancement of certain racial or ethnic groups or individuals requiring such protection as may be necessary in order to ensure such groups or individuals equal enjoyment or exercise of human rights and fundamental freedoms shall not be deemed racial discrimination, provided, however, that such measures do not, as a consequence, lead to the maintenance of separate rights for different racial groups and that they shall not be continued after the objectives for which they were taken have been achieved.

Article 2

1. States Parties condemn racial discrimination and undertake to pursue by all appropriate means and without delay a policy of eliminating racial discrimination in all its forms and promoting understanding among all races, and, to this end:

(a) Each State Party undertakes to engage in no act or practice of racial discrimination against persons, groups of persons or institutions and to ensure that all public authorities and public institutions, national and local, shall act in conformity with this obligation;

(b) Each State Party undertakes not to sponsor, defend or support racial discrimination by any persons or organizations;

(c) Each State Party shall take effective measures to review governmental, national and local policies, and to amend, rescind or nullify any laws and regulations which have the effect of creating or perpetuating racial discrimination wherever it exists;

(d) Each State Party shall prohibit and bring to an end, by all appropriate means, including legislation as required by circumstances, racial discrimination by any persons, group or organization;

(e) Each State Party undertakes to encourage, where appropriate, integrationist multiracial organizations and movements and other means of eliminating barriers between races, and to discourage anything which tends to strengthen racial division.

2. States Parties shall, when the circumstances so warrant, take, in the social, economic, cultural and other fields, special and concrete measures to ensure the adequate development and protection of certain racial groups or individuals belonging to them, for the purpose of guaranteeing them the full and equal enjoyment of human rights and fundamental freedoms. These measures shall in no case entail as a consequence the maintenance of unequal or separate rights for different racial groups after the objectives for which they were taken have been achieved.

Article 3

States Parties particularly condemn racial segregation and apartheid and undertake to prevent, prohibit and eradicate all practices of this nature in territories under their jurisdiction.

Article 4

States Parties condemn all propaganda and all organizations which are based on ideas or theories of superiority of one race or group of persons of one colour or ethnic origin, or which attempt to justify or promote racial hatred and discrimination in any form, and undertake to adopt immediate and positive measures designed to eradicate all incitement to, or acts of, such discrimination and, to this end, with due regard to the principles embodied in the Universal Declaration of Human Rights and the rights expressly set forth in article 5 of this Convention, inter alia:

(a) Shall declare an offence punishable by law all dissemination of ideas based on racial superiority or hatred, incitement to racial discrimination, as well as all acts of violence or incitement to such acts against any race or group of persons of another colour or ethnic origin, and also the provision of any assistance to racist activities, including the financing thereof;

(b) Shall declare illegal and prohibit organizations, and also organized and all other propaganda activities, which promote and incite racial discrimination, and shall recognize participation in such organizations or activities as an offence punishable by law;

(c) Shall not permit public authorities or public institutions, national or local, to promote or incite racial discrimination.

Article 5

In compliance with the fundamental obligations laid down in article 2 of this Convention, States Parties undertake to prohibit and to eliminate racial discrimination in all its forms and to guarantee the right of everyone, without distinction as to race, colour, or national or ethnic origin, to equality before the law, notably in the enjoyment of the following rights:

(a) The right to equal treatment before the tribunals and all other organs administering justice;

(b) The right to security of person and protection by the State against violence or bodily harm, whether inflicted by government officials or by any individual group or institution;

(c) Political rights, in particular the right to participate in elections to vote and to stand for election on the basis of universal and equal suffrage, to take part in the Government as well as in the conduct of public affairs at any level and to have equal access to public service;

(d) Other civil rights, in particular:

(i) The right to freedom of movement and residence within the border of the State;

(ii) The right to leave any country, including one's own, and to return to one's country;

(iii) The right to nationality;

(iv) The right to marriage and choice of spouse;

(v) The right to own property alone as well as in association with others;

(vi) The right to inherit;

(vii) The right to freedom of thought, conscience and religion;

(viii) The right to freedom of opinion and expression;

(ix) The right to freedom of peaceful assembly and association;

(e) Economic, social and cultural rights, in particular:

(i) The rights to work, to free choice of employment, to just and favourable conditions of work, to protection against unemployment, to equal pay for equal work, to just and favourable remuneration;

(ii) The right to form and join trade unions;

(iii) The right to housing;

(iv) The right to public health, medical care, social security and social services;

(v) The right to education and training;

(vi) The right to equal participation in cultural activities;

(f) The right of access to any place or service intended for use by the general public, such as transport hotels, restaurants, cafes, theatres and parks.

Article 6

States Parties shall assure to everyone within their jurisdiction effective protection and remedies, through the competent national tribunals and other State institutions, against any acts of racial discrimination which violate his human rights and fundamental freedoms contrary to this Convention, as well as the right to seek from such tribunals just and adequate reparation or satisfaction for any damage suffered as a result of such discrimination.

Article 7

States Parties undertake to adopt immediate and effective measures, particularly in the fields of teaching, education, culture and information, with a view to combating prejudices which lead to racial discrimination and to promoting understanding, tolerance and friendship among nations and racial or ethnical groups, as well as to propagating the purposes and principles of the Charter of the United Nations, the Universal Declaration of Human Rights, the United Nations Declaration on the Elimination of All Forms of Racial Discrimination, and this Convention.

PART II

Article 8

1. There shall be established a Committee on the Elimination of Racial Discrimination (hereinafter referred to as the Committee) consisting of eighteen experts of high moral standing and acknowledged impartiality elected by States Parties from among their nationals, who shall serve in their personal capacity, consideration being given to equitable geographical distribution and to the representation of the different forms of civilization as well as of the principal legal systems.

2. The members of the Committee shall be elected by secret ballot from a list of persons nominated by the States Parties. Each State Party may nominate one person from among its own nationals.

3. The initial election shall be held six months after the date of the entry into force of this Convention. At least three months before the date of each election the Secretary-General of the United Nations shall address a letter to the States Parties inviting them to submit their nominations within two months. The Secretary-General shall prepare a list in alphabetical order of all persons thus nominated, indicating the States Parties which have nominated them, and shall submit it to the States Parties.

4. Elections of the members of the Committee shall be held at a meeting of States Parties convened by the Secretary-General at United Nations Headquarters. At that meeting, for which two thirds of the States Parties shall constitute a quorum, the persons elected to the Committee shall be nominees who obtain the largest number of votes and an absolute majority of the votes of the representatives of States Parties present and voting.

5.

(a) The members of the Committee shall be elected for a term of four years. However, the terms of nine of the members elected at the first election shall expire at the end of two years; immediately after the first election the names of these nine members shall be chosen by lot by the Chairman of the Committee;

(b) For the filling of casual vacancies, the State Party whose expert has ceased to function as a member of the Committee shall appoint another expert from among its nationals, subject to the approval of the Committee.

6. States Parties shall be responsible for the expenses of the members of the Committee while they are in performance of Committee duties.

Article 9

1. States Parties undertake to submit to the Secretary-General of the United Nations, for consideration by the Committee, a report on the legislative, judicial, administrative or other measures which they have adopted and which give effect to the provisions of this Convention:

(a) within one year after the entry into force of the Convention for the State concerned; and

(b) thereafter every two years and whenever the Committee so requests. The Committee may request further information from the States Parties.

2. The Committee shall report annually, through the Secretary General, to the General Assembly of the United Nations on its activities and may make suggestions and general recommendations based on the examination of the reports and information received from the States Parties. Such suggestions and general recommendations shall be reported to the General Assembly together with comments, if any, from States Parties.

Article 10

1. The Committee shall adopt its own rules of procedure.

2. The Committee shall elect its officers for a term of two years.

3. The secretariat of the Committee shall be provided by the Secretary General of the United Nations.

4. The meetings of the Committee shall normally be held at United Nations Headquarters.

Article 11

1. If a State Party considers that another State Party is not giving effect to the provisions of this Convention, it may bring the matter to the attention of the Committee. The Committee shall then transmit the communication to the State Party

concerned. Within three months, the receiving State shall submit to the Committee written explanations or statements clarifying the matter and the remedy, if any, that may have been taken by that State.

2. If the matter is not adjusted to the satisfaction of both parties, either by bilateral negotiations or by any other procedure open to them, within six months after the receipt by the receiving State of the initial communication, either State shall have the right to refer the matter again to the Committee by notifying the Committee and also the other State.

3. The Committee shall deal with a matter referred to it in accordance with paragraph 2 of this article after it has ascertained that all available domestic remedies have been invoked and exhausted in the case, in conformity with the generally recognized principles of international law. This shall not be the rule where the application of the remedies is unreasonably prolonged.

4. In any matter referred to it, the Committee may call upon the States Parties concerned to supply any other relevant information.

5. When any matter arising out of this article is being considered by the Committee, the States Parties concerned shall be entitled to send a representative to take part in the proceedings of the Committee, without voting rights, while the matter is under consideration.

Article 12

1.

(a) After the Committee has obtained and collated all the information it deems necessary, the Chairman shall appoint an ad hoc Conciliation Commission (hereinafter referred to as the Commission) comprising five persons who may or may not be members of the Committee. The members of the Commission shall be appointed with the unanimous consent of the parties to the dispute, and its good offices shall be made available to the States concerned with a view to an amicable solution of the matter on the basis of respect for this Convention;

(b) If the States parties to the dispute fail to reach agreement within three months on all or part of the composition of the Commission, the members of the Commission not agreed upon by the States parties to the dispute shall be elected by secret ballot by a two-thirds majority vote of the Committee from among its own members.

2. The members of the Commission shall serve in their personal capacity. They shall not be nationals of the States parties to the dispute or of a State not Party to this Convention.

3. The Commission shall elect its own Chairman and adopt its own rules of procedure.

4. The meetings of the Commission shall normally be held at United Nations Headquarters or at any other convenient place as determined by the Commission.

5. The secretariat provided in accordance with article 10, paragraph 3, of this Convention shall also service the Commission whenever a dispute among States Parties brings the Commission into being.

6. The States parties to the dispute shall share equally all the expenses of the members of the Commission in accordance with estimates to be provided by the Secretary-General of the United Nations.

7. The Secretary-General shall be empowered to pay the expenses of the members of the Commission, if necessary, before reimbursement by the States parties to the dispute in accordance with paragraph 6 of this article.

8. The information obtained and collated by the Committee shall be made available to the Commission, and the Commission may call upon the States concerned to supply any other relevant information.

Article 13

1. When the Commission has fully considered the matter, it shall prepare and submit to the Chairman of the Committee a report embodying its findings on all questions of fact relevant to the issue between the parties and containing such recommendations as it may think proper for the amicable solution of the dispute.

2. The Chairman of the Committee shall communicate the report of the Commission to each of the States parties to the dispute. These States shall, within three months, inform the Chairman of the Committee whether or not they accept the recommendations contained in the report of the Commission.

3. After the period provided for in paragraph 2 of this article, the Chairman of the Committee shall communicate the report of the Commission and the declarations of the States Parties concerned to the other States Parties to this Convention.

Article 14

1. A State Party may at any time declare that it recognizes the competence of the Committee to receive and consider communications from individuals or groups of individuals within its jurisdiction claiming to be victims of a violation by that State Party of any of the rights set forth in this Convention. No communication shall be received by the Committee if it concerns a State Party which has not made such a declaration.

2. Any State Party which makes a declaration as provided for in paragraph 1 of this article may establish or indicate a body within its national legal order which shall be competent to receive and consider petitions from individuals and groups of individuals within its jurisdiction who claim to be victims of a violation of any of the rights set forth in this Convention and who have exhausted other available local remedies.

3. A declaration made in accordance with paragraph 1 of this article and the name of anybody established or indicated in accordance with paragraph 2 of this article shall be deposited by the State Party concerned with the Secretary-General of the United Nations, who shall transmit copies thereof to the other States Parties. A declaration may be withdrawn at any time by notification to the Secretary-General, but such a withdrawal shall not affect communications pending before the Committee.

4. A register of petitions shall be kept by the body established or indicated in accordance with paragraph 2 of this article, and certified copies of the register shall be filed annually through appropriate channels with the Secretary-General on the understanding that the contents shall not be publicly disclosed.

5. In the event of failure to obtain satisfaction from the body established or indicated in accordance with paragraph 2 of this article, the petitioner shall have the right to communicate the matter to the Committee within six months.

6.

(a) The Committee shall confidentially bring any communication referred to it to the attention of the State Party alleged to be violating any provision of this Convention, but the identity of the individual or groups of individuals concerned shall not be revealed without his or their express consent. The Committee shall not receive anonymous communications;

(b) Within three months, the receiving State shall submit to the Committee written explanations or statements clarifying the matter and the remedy, if any, that may have been taken by that State.

7.

(a) The Committee shall consider communications in the light of all information made available to it by the State Party concerned and by the petitioner. The Committee shall not consider any communication from a petitioner unless it has ascertained that the petitioner has exhausted all available domestic remedies. However, this shall not be the rule where the application of the remedies is unreasonably prolonged;

(b) The Committee shall forward its suggestions and recommendations, if any, to the State Party concerned and to the petitioner.

8. The Committee shall include in its annual report a summary of such communications and, where appropriate, a summary of the explanations and statements of the States Parties concerned and of its own suggestions and recommendations.

9. The Committee shall be competent to exercise the functions provided for in this article only when at least ten States Parties to this Convention are bound by declarations in accordance with paragraph I of this article.

Article 15

1. Pending the achievement of the objectives of the Declaration on the Granting of Independence to Colonial Countries and Peoples, contained in General Assembly resolution 1514 (XV) of 14 December 1960, the provisions of this Convention shall in no way limit the right of petition granted to these peoples by other international instruments or by the United Nations and its specialized agencies.

2.

(a) The Committee established under article 8, paragraph 1, of this Convention shall receive copies of the petitions from, and submit expressions of opinion and recommendations on these petitions to, the bodies of the United Nations which deal with matters directly related to the principles and objectives of this Convention in their consideration of petitions from the inhabitants of Trust and Non-Self-Governing Territories and all other territories to which General Assembly resolution 1514 (XV) applies, relating to matters covered by this Convention which are before these bodies;

(b) The Committee shall receive from the competent bodies of the United Nations copies of the reports concerning the legislative, judicial, administrative or other measures directly related to the principles and objectives of this Convention applied by the administering Powers within the Territories mentioned in subparagraph (a) of this paragraph, and shall express opinions and make recommendations to these bodies.

3. The Committee shall include in its report to the General Assembly a summary of the petitions and reports it has received from United Nations bodies, and the expressions of opinion and recommendations of the Committee relating to the said petitions and reports.

4. The Committee shall request from the Secretary-General of the United Nations all information relevant to the objectives of this Convention and available to him regarding the Territories mentioned in paragraph 2 (a) of this article.

Article 16

The provisions of this Convention concerning the settlement of disputes or complaints shall be applied without prejudice to other procedures for settling disputes or complaints in the field of discrimination laid down in the constituent instruments of, or conventions adopted by, the United Nations and its specialized agencies, and shall not prevent the States Parties from having recourse to other procedures for settling a dispute in accordance with general or special international agreements in force between them.

PART III

Article 17

1. This Convention is open for signature by any State Member of the United Nations or member of any of its specialized agencies, by any State Party to the Statute of the International Court of Justice, and by any other State which has been invited by the General Assembly of the United Nations to become a Party to this Convention.

2. This Convention is subject to ratification. Instruments of ratification shall be deposited with the Secretary-General of the United Nations.

Article 18

1. This Convention shall be open to accession by any State referred to in article 17, paragraph 1, of the Convention.

2. Accession shall be effected by the deposit of an instrument of accession with the Secretary-General of the United Nations.

Article 19

1. This Convention shall enter into force on the thirtieth day after the date of the deposit with the Secretary-General of the United Nations of the twenty-seventh instrument of ratification or instrument of accession.

2. For each State ratifying this Convention or acceding to it after the deposit of the twenty-seventh instrument of ratification or instrument of accession, the Convention shall enter into force on the thirtieth day after the date of the deposit of its own instrument of ratification or instrument of accession.

Article 20

1. The Secretary-General of the United Nations shall receive and circulate to all States which are or may become Parties to this Convention reservations made by States at the time of ratification or accession. Any State which objects to the reservation shall, within a period of ninety days from the date of the said communication, notify the Secretary-General that it does not accept it.

2. A reservation incompatible with the object and purpose of this Convention shall not be permitted, nor shall a reservation the effect of which would inhibit the operation of any of the bodies established by this Convention be allowed. A reservation shall be considered incompatible or inhibitive if at least two thirds of the States Parties to this Convention object to it.

3. Reservations may be withdrawn at any time by notification to this effect addressed to the Secretary-General. Such notification shall take effect on the date on which it is received.

Article 21

A State Party may denounce this Convention by written notification to the Secretary-General of the United Nations. Denunciation shall take effect one year after the date of receipt of the notification by the Secretary General.

Article 22

Any dispute between two or more States Parties with respect to the interpretation or application of this Convention, which is not settled by negotiation or by the procedures expressly provided for in this Convention, shall, at the request of any of the parties to the dispute, be referred to the International Court of Justice for decision, unless the disputants agree to another mode of settlement.

Article 23

1. A request for the revision of this Convention may be made at any time by any State Party by means of a notification in writing addressed to the Secretary-General of the United Nations.

2. The General Assembly of the United Nations shall decide upon the steps, if any, to be taken in respect of such a request.

Article 24

The Secretary-General of the United Nations shall inform all States referred to in article 17, paragraph 1, of this Convention of the following particulars:

(a) Signatures, ratifications and accessions under articles 17 and 18;

(b) The date of entry into force of this Convention under article 19;

(c) Communications and declarations received under articles 14, 20 and 23;

(d) Denunciations under article 21.

Article 25

1. This Convention, of which the Chinese, English, French, Russian and Spanish texts are equally authentic, shall be deposited in the archives of the United Nations.

2. The Secretary-General of the United Nations shall transmit certified copies of this Convention to all States belonging to any of the categories mentioned in article 17, paragraph 1, of the Convention.

Source: http://www.ohchr.org/EN/ProfessionalInterest/Pages/CERD.aspx

సొసొసొసొసొసొ

2. U.S. RESERVATIONS, DECLARATIONS, AND UNDERSTANDINGS, CONVENTION ON THE ELIMINATION OF ALL FORMS OF RACIAL DISCRIMINATION

The U.S. obligations under the Racial Discrimination Convention must be read in light of these RDUs. Note that the status and applicability of this instrument as to the United States may have changed since date of publication. For updates see: http://www1. umn.edu/humanrts/usdocs/racialres.html

I. The Senate's advice and consent is subject to the following reservations:

(1) That the Constitution and laws of the United States contain extensive protections of individual freedom of speech, expression and association. Accordingly, the United States does not accept any obligation under this Convention, in particular under Articles 4 and 7, to restrict those rights, through the adoption of legislation or any other measures, to the extent that they are protected by the Constitution and laws of the United States.

(2) That the Constitution and the laws of the United States establish extensive protections against discrimination, reaching significant areas of non-governmental activity. Individual privacy and freedom from governmental interference in private conduct, however, are also recognized as among the fundamental values which shape our free and democratic society. The United States understands that the identification of the rights protected under the Convention by reference in Article 1 to the fields of public life reflects a similar distinction between spheres of public conduct that are customarily the subject of governmental regulation, and spheres of private conduct that are not. To the extent, however, that the Convention calls for a broader regulation of private conduct, the United States does not accept any obligation under this Convention to enact legislation or take other measures under paragraph (1) of Article 2, subparagraphs (1)(c) and (d) of Article 2, Article 3 and Article 5 with respect to private conduct except as mandated by the Constitution and laws of the United States.

(3) That with reference to Article 22 of the Convention, before any dispute to which the United States is a party may be submitted to the jurisdiction of the International Court of Justice under this article, the specific consent of the United States is required in each case.

II. The Senate's advice and consent is subject to the following understanding, which shall apply to the obligations of the United States under this Convention: That the United States understands that this Convention shall be implemented by the Federal Government to the extent that it exercises jurisdiction over the matters covered therein, and otherwise by the state and local governments. To the extent that state and local governments exercise jurisdiction over such matters, the Federal Government shall, as necessary, take appropriate measures to ensure the fulfillment of this Convention.

III. The Senate's advice and consent is subject to the following declaration: That the United States declares that the provisions of the Convention are not self-executing.

Source: http://hrlibrary.umn.edu/usdocs/racialres.html

❧❧❧❧❧❧❧❧

3. INTERNATIONAL CONVENTION ON THE ELIMINATION OF ALL FORMS OF RACIAL DISCRIMINATION, 3 OCTOBER 2013

This is the U.S. government's 2013 report submitted to the Committee on the Elimination of Racial Discrimination (CERD), as part of a process all ICERD treaty parties go through. Instead of annual report submissions, the U.S. offers this three-year (7th through 9th) progress report that serves as an update to the CERD committee's concerns since its last periodic review before CERD.

{Excerpt}

Committee on the Elimination of Racial Discrimination

Reports submitted by States parties under article 9 of the Convention

Seventh to ninth periodic reports of States parties due in 2011, United States of America [13 June 2013]

I. Introduction

1. The Government of the United States of America welcomes the opportunity to report to the Committee on the Elimination of Racial Discrimination ("Committee") on measures giving effect to the undertakings of the United States under the International Convention on the Elimination of All Forms of Racial Discrimination (CERD), pursuant to article 9 thereof, and on related measures to address racial discrimination in the United States. This document, accompanied by the common core document and annex submitted on 30 December 2011, responds to the Committee's request for the seventh, eighth, and ninth periodic reports of the United States.

2. The United States has always been a multi-racial and multi-ethnic society, and its pluralism is increasing. We have made great strides over the years in overcoming the legacies of slavery, racism, ethnic intolerance, and destructive laws, policies, and practices relating to members of racial and ethnic minorities. Indeed, fifty years ago, the idea of having a Black/African American President of the United States would not have seemed possible; today, it is a reality. We recognize, however, that the path toward racial equality has been uneven, racial and ethnic discrimination still persists, and much work remains to meet our goal of ensuring equality for all. Our nation's Founders, who enshrined in our Constitution their ambition "to form a more perfect Union," bequeathed to U.S. not a static condition, but a perpetual aspiration and mission. This report shares our progress in implementing our undertakings under the CERD and on related measures to address racial discrimination.

3. This report and the accompanying common core document and Annex that the United States submitted in 2011 were prepared by the U.S. Department of State (DOS) with extensive input and assistance from numerous departments and agencies of the federal government. In preparing the report, we also solicited input from state, local, tribal and territorial jurisdictions and representatives of non-governmental organizations and public interest groups. Additionally, where possible throughout this report we have endeavoured to highlight and address examples of concerns raised by civil society regarding CERD implementation and initiatives that respond to those concerns. Our external consultation has taken many forms, including consultations related to United States participation in the universal periodic review and other outreach efforts. Both as a result of external consultation as well as our own internal reviews, we recognize that more can and should be done in many areas to implement our CERD obligations and related commitments more effectively.

4. Collaboration among federal government departments and agencies on the drafting of U.S. treaty reports has also resulted in the recognition that more can be done to support better coordination throughout the United States on strengthening understanding and respect for human rights. To this end, numerous federal government departments and agencies are participating in a newly established mechanism known as the Equality Working Group. The Group was launched in March 2012 by the Civil Rights Division of the Department of Justice (DOJ/CRT) in partnership with the Department of State's Bureau of Democracy, Human Rights, and Labour (DOS/DRL) to enhance the government's domestic implementation of our international human rights obligations and commitments relating to non-discrimination

and equal opportunity, with an initial focus on those commitments that relate to combating racial discrimination, including under the CERD.

5. The United States submitted its initial, second and third periodic reports as a single document to the Committee in September 2000, hereinafter "Initial U.S. Report" or "Initial Report," and made its presentation to the Committee on August 3 and 6, 2001. The fourth, fifth, and sixth periodic reports of the United States were also submitted as one document in April 2007 (hereinafter the "2007 Report"); the United States made its presentation to the Committee in February 2008, the Committee issued its concluding observations in May of 2008, and the United States submitted a one-year follow-up report on January 13, 2009. This report provides an update on progress since the submission of the prior reports. All these documents, and the Committee's observations with regard to these reports, may be viewed at http://www.state.gov/j/drl/reports/treaties/index.htm.

6. In an effort to be responsive to the Committee's reporting guidelines, CERD/C/2007/1, many subheadings in this report track those guidelines. However, given recent reports containing related information, including the common core document and annex as well as the comprehensive report on the International Covenant on Civil and Political Rights (ICCPR) submitted to the Human Rights Committee on December 30, 2011 (hereinafter "2011 U.S. ICCPR Report"), and given our desire to seek to respect the recommended 40-page limit, we have included cross references to other reports. Due to page constraints, some issues may not be addressed in the order or level of detail suggested in the Committee's guidelines. In addition, there are cases where we may not agree with the legal or factual premises underlying a given request for information or where concluding observations do not bear directly on obligations under the Convention; nevertheless, in the interest of promoting dialogue and cooperation, we have provided requested information to the degree possible. The Committee's concluding observations are addressed throughout the report.

II. Additional information relating to articles of the Convention

Article 1

A. Definitions of racial discrimination in domestic law and the Convention

7. Definition of racial discrimination in domestic law. Existing U.S. constitutional and statutory law and practice provide strong and effective protections against discrimination on the bases covered by article 1 of the Convention in all fields of public endeavour, and provide remedies for those who, despite these protections, become victims of discrimination. For discussion of U.S. constitutional provisions and laws providing protections against racial and ethnic discrimination, please see sections II and III of the common core document.

8. Prohibition of discriminatory effects or disparate impact. With regard to paragraph 10 of the Committee's concluding observations, although establishing a race discrimination violation of the U.S. Constitution requires proof of discriminatory intent, many U.S. civil rights statutes and regulations go further, prohibiting policies or practices that have discriminatory effects or disparate impact on members of racial or ethnic minorities or other protected classes. In cases involving disparate impact analysis, the inquiry is whether evidence establishes that a facially neutral policy, practice, or procedure causes a significantly disproportionate negative impact on the protected group and lacks a substantial legitimate justification. When facts support the use of disparate impact analysis, the United States is committed to using these valuable tools to address indirect discrimination. Laws that address disparate impact discrimination include:

- Title VII of the Civil Rights Act of 1964 (Title VII), prohibiting disparate impact in employment, as seen in the recent holding that New York City's use of examinations for fire-fighters had an unlawful disparate impact on Blacks/African Americans and Hispanics/Latinos. U.S. v. City of New York, NY, 683 F. Supp. 2d 77 (E.D.N.Y. 2009).
- The Voting Rights Act, which prohibits certain voting practices and procedures, including redistricting plans that have disparate impact on the basis of race, colour, or membership in a language minority group. For example, a recent enforcement action led to an agreement with Shannon County, South Dakota to ensure the voting rights of Lakota-speaking Native American voters with limited English proficiency.
- Title VI of the 1964 Civil Rights Act, 42 U.S.C. 2000d, and its implementing regulations, which prohibit practices that have the effect of discriminating by state or local governments or private entities receiving federal financial assistance, including schools, hospitals and health care facilities, law enforcement agencies, courts, and

creditors such as banks and credit card companies. For example, in 2010, the Department of Health and Human Services Office for Civil Rights (HHS/OCR) secured a settlement requiring the University of Pittsburgh Medical Center to ensure that closure of a hospital in a predominately Black/African American community did not have a disparate impact on the residents of that area. Other examples are noted below in the discussion under articles 2 and 5.

- The Fair Housing Act (Title VIII of the Civil Rights Act of 1968), which prohibits discrimination in the sale, rental, and financing of dwellings based, inter alia, on race, colour, or national origin; and the Equal Credit Opportunity Act, which prohibits creditors from discriminating against credit applicants on the basis of, inter alia, race, colour, or national origin. For example, in 2011, DOJ obtained its largest fair lending settlement, requiring Countrywide Financial Corporation to provide $335 million to some 230,000 Black/African American and Hispanic/Latino borrowers who were steered into sub-prime loans or forced to pay more for their mortgages than similarly-qualified White borrowers.

9. As part of its recently reinvigorated civil rights enforcement, in 2010 DOJ/CRT issued a letter to chief justices and administrators of state courts, clarifying the obligation under Title VI of courts that receive federal financial assistance to provide language assistance services to people with limited English language ability in all proceedings and court operations. DOJ also provides technical assistance to federal agencies to strengthen their Title VI enforcement efforts.

10. Examples of recent policy developments concerning disparate impact include the following. In 2013 the Department of Housing and Urban Development (HUD) published a final rule on the implementation of a discriminatory effects standard with regard to housing, designed to promote enforcement against housing practices that have an unjustified discriminatory effect, http://portal.hud.gov/hudportal/documents/huddoc?id=discriminatory effectrule.pdf. In April 2012, the Equal Employment Opportunity Commission (EEOC) issued guidance, inter alia, on the application of disparate impact analysis in cases involving employer use of arrest and conviction records in employment decisions — decisions that often have a disproportionate impact on racial minorities, Error! Hyperlink reference not valid.. Further examples of enforcement of laws against activities with unjustified discriminatory effect or disproportionate impact are found in the common core document and in the 2011 U.S. ICCPR Report (discussion under article 2).

11. Understanding of the phrase "public life." The United States understands that identification of the rights protected under the Convention by reference in article 1 to the fields of "public life" reflects a distinction between spheres of public conduct that are customarily subject to government regulation, and spheres of private conduct that may not be. With regard to this issue, and also in response to paragraph 11 of the Committee's concluding observations, at the time it became party to the CERD, the United States carefully evaluated the treaty to ensure that it could fully implement all of the obligations it would assume. In this case, the definition of "racial discrimination" under article 1 (1) of the Convention, the obligation imposed in article 2 (1) (d) to bring to an end all racial discrimination "by any persons, groups or organizations," and the specific requirements of paragraphs 2 (1) (c) and (d) and articles 3 and 5 could be read as imposing a requirement on States parties to take action to prohibit and punish purely private conduct of a nature generally held to lie beyond the proper scope of governmental regulation under U.S. law. For this reason, in close collaboration with the U.S. Senate, the United States crafted a formal reservation that U.S. undertakings in this regard are limited by the reach of constitutional and statutory protections under U.S. law as they may exist at any given time. We believe this reservation continues to be necessary, although we note that anti-discrimination laws in this area have broad reach. As described in greater detail in paragraph 154 of the common core document and also discussed below in the context of article 2, the protections against discrimination in the U.S. Constitution and federal laws reach significant areas of non-government activity, ranging from reliance on U.S. civil rights laws to prohibit private actors from engaging in racial or ethnic (national origin) discrimination in activities such as the sale or rental of private property, employment at private businesses, admission to private schools, and access to public facilities; or the use of the Immigration and Nationality Act's (INA) anti-discrimination provisions to protect authorized immigrants from discriminatory practices by private employers based on the workers' immigration status, how they look or speak, or where they are from. Similarly, many state anti-discrimination laws cover discriminatory practices by private employers, landlords, creditors, and educational institutions.

12. Differential treatment based on citizenship or immigration status. The United States strongly shares the Committee's view that citizens and noncitizens alike should enjoy protection of their human rights and fundamental freedoms. Although the Convention by its terms does not apply to "distinctions, exclusions, restrictions or preferences made by a

State Party between citizens and non-citizens," as a general matter the United States believes that every State must be vigilant in protecting the rights that noncitizens enjoy in the State, regardless of immigration status, as a matter of applicable domestic and international law.

13. As the common core document makes clear, the United States has one of the most open immigration systems in the world. Aliens within the United States, regardless of their immigration status, enjoy substantial protections under the U.S. Constitution. Many of these protections are shared on an equal basis with citizens, including protections against racial and national origin discrimination. The guarantee of equal protection of the laws under the Fifth and Fourteenth Amendments to the Constitution applies in some respects to aliens who have made an entry into the United States, even if such entry was unlawful. In addition to constitutional protections, which, for example, make it unlawful to deny elementary and secondary school children in the United States a free public education on the basis of their immigration status, see, e.g., Plyler v. Doe, 457 U.S. 202 (1982), many federal statutes prohibit discrimination against noncitizens. These include (1) section 274B(a)(1) of the INA, 8 U.S.C. 1324b (a)(1) (prohibiting employment discrimination against certain work authorized individuals, including some noncitizens, on the basis of national origin or citizenship status with respect to hiring, firing, or recruitment for a fee); (2) the protections of federal labour law; and (3) anti-discrimination employment laws, see EEOC Compliance Manual, Sec. 2, Threshold Issues, http://www.eeoc.gov/policy/docs/threshold.html#2-III-A-4 ("Individuals who are employed in the United States are protected by the EEO statutes regardless of their citizenship or immigration status."). In addition, the federal prohibition against discrimination based on race, colour, or national origin under Title VI of the Civil Rights Act applies to citizens and noncitizens alike. See DOJ/CRT Title VI Legal Manual, p. 6, http://www.justice.gov/crt/ about/cor/coord/vimanual.pdf.

14. The United States prioritizes elimination of racial discrimination against all individuals, both citizens and noncitizens alike. For example, in 2011 DOJ and the Department of Education (ED) issued guidance reminding public schools of their obligation under Plyler to enrol all students regardless of their or their parents' immigration status. DOJ and ED have since provided technical assistance to schools to help them fulfil these obligations. They have also investigated schools that are reportedly not following the rules leading, inter alia, to a recent settlement agreement with a Georgia school district that improperly notified parents that their children would be withdrawn from school for failure to provide social security numbers and failed to make enrolment procedures accessible to parents with limited English proficiency. Also in 2011, Alabama passed an immigration law (H.B. 56) that required the disclosure to schools of the immigration status of enrolling children and their parents. DOJ immediately travelled to Alabama to meet with parents, students, teachers, and other community leaders. DOJ challenged the law in Federal court, and private parties in a separate case also challenged the law. Ultimately, the court held that the disclosure provision (Section 28) of H.B. 56 violated the Equal Protection Clause of the U.S. Constitution and enjoined the operation of that section. United States v. Alabama, 691 F.3d 1269 (11th Cir. 2012); Hispanic Interest Coalition of Alabama v. Governor of Alabama, 691 F.3d 1236 (11th Cir. 2012).

15. DOJ investigates employment discrimination against noncitizens under the INA; the Office of Special Counsel for Immigration-Related Unfair Employment Practices (OSC) of DOJ/CRT works with local communities to prevent violations of, and to seek out and prosecute those who violate, anti-discrimination laws with regard to noncitizens. The United States also devotes substantial resources to assisting and providing services to noncitizens, for example, through the Department of Labour (DOL) Migrant Worker Partnership Program, designed to facilitate protection of the rights of noncitizens working in the United States. In addition, the EEOC enforces prohibitions against employment discrimination based on race and national origin without regard to immigration status; in recognition of the need to serve this vulnerable population more effectively, it created an Immigrant Worker Team in 2011 to develop policies for enforcement and outreach to immigrant groups. EEOC continues to prioritize serving vulnerable immigrant workers in its 2012 Strategic Plan and Strategic Enforcement Plan identifying agency priorities through FY 2016. For further discussion, see paragraphs 101-108 (Law with regard to Aliens) of the 2011 U.S. ICCPR Report and the discussion of noncitizens under article 5, below.

B. Information on special measures

16. The United States legal system provides for special measures when circumstances so warrant. See the discussion under article 2 below and the discussion in paragraphs 197 to 206 of the common core document. Recently, DOJ actively defended the undergraduate admission program of the University of Texas, which was challenged by two unsuccessful

White candidates for undergraduate admission. The Texas program adopts a holistic approach — examining race as one component among many — when selecting among applicants who are not otherwise eligible for automatic admission by virtue of being in the top ten percent of their high school classes. The U.S. Court of Appeals for the Fifth Circuit upheld the University's limited use of race as justified by a compelling interest in diversity and as narrowly tailored to achieve a critical mass of minority students. The Supreme Court heard arguments in the case, Fisher v. Texas, in October 2012, and is expected to decide the case by June 2013. In its amicus curiae brief, the Solicitor General argued, on a brief signed by several federal agencies, that, like the University, the United States has a compelling interest in the educational benefits of diversity, and that the University's use of race in freshman class admissions to achieve the educational benefits of diversity is constitutional.

Article 2

A. Brief description of legal framework and general policies

17. Racial discrimination by the government is prohibited at all levels. Prohibitions cover all public authorities and institutions as well as private organizations, institutions, and employers under many circumstances. For a description of the general legal framework and policies addressing racial discrimination, see paragraphs 142-175 of the common core document.

18. Recent laws relating to discrimination, including discrimination based on race, colour, and national origin, or minority groups, include:
- The Lilly Ledbetter Fair Pay Act, signed by President Obama in 2009, provides that the statute of limitations for bringing a wage discrimination claim, including claims alleging wage discrimination based on race or national origin, runs from the time an individual is "affected by application of a discriminatory compensation decision including each time wages, benefits, or other compensation is paid." The law overrides a Supreme Court decision in Ledbetter v. Goodyear Tire & Rubber Co., 500 U.S. 618 (2007).
- The Genetic Information Non-discrimination Act of 2008 governs the use of genetic information in health insurance and employment decisions. Protected genetic information includes genetic services (tests, counselling and education), genetic tests of family members, and family medical history. As it relates to racial and ethnic discrimination, this law prohibits an insurer or employer from refusing to insure or employ someone with a genetic marker for disease associated with certain racial or ethnic groups, such as sickle cell trait.
- The Matthew Shepard and James Byrd, Jr. Hate Crimes Prevention Act of 2009 (Shepard-Byrd Act) creates a new federal prohibition on hate crimes, 18 U.S.C. 249; simplifies the jurisdictional predicate for prosecuting violent acts undertaken because of, inter alia, the actual or perceived race, colour, religion, or national origin of any person; and, for the first time, allows federal prosecution of violence undertaken because of the actual or perceived gender, disability, sexual orientation or gender identity of any person.
- The American Recovery and Reinvestment Act of 2009 provided funding for programs that will help reduce discrimination and improve the lives of members of minority populations through education, training, and programs to end homelessness.
- The Patient Protection and Affordable Care Act (ACA) of 2010 provides many Americans access to health insurance. Section 1557 extends the application of federal civil rights laws to any health program or activity receiving federal financial assistance, any program or activity administered by an executive agency, or any entity established under Title 1 of the ACA.
- The Tribal Law and Order Act of 2010 gives tribes greater authority to prosecute and punish criminals; expands recruitment, retention, and training for Bureau of Indian Affairs (BIA) and tribal officers; includes new guidelines and training for domestic violence and sex crimes; strengthens tribal courts and police departments; and enhances programs to combat drug and alcohol abuse and help at-risk youth.
- The Claims Resolution Act of 2010 provides funding and statutory authorities for settlement agreements reached in the In re Black Farmers Discrimination Litigation (brought by Black/African American farmers who filed late claims in an earlier case concerning discrimination by the U.S. Department of Agriculture (USDA) in the award and servicing of farm loans), and also for several settlement agreements reached with regard to indigenous issues — the Cobell lawsuit (alleging U.S. government mismanagement of individual Indian money accounts), and four major Native American water rights cases.

- The Fair Sentencing Act of 2010 reduces sentencing disparities between powder cocaine and crack cocaine offenses, capping a long effort to address the fact that those convicted of crack cocaine offenses are more likely to be members of racial minorities.
- The financial reform legislation of 2010 includes a new consumer protection bureau that will help address the unjustified disproportionate effect of the foreclosure crisis on communities of colour.
- The Violence Against Women Reauthorization Act of 2013, signed by President Obama in March of this year, reauthorizes critical grant programs created by the original Violence Against Women Act (VAWA) and subsequent legislation, establishes new programs, and strengthens federal laws. Section 3 prohibits discrimination on the basis of, inter alia, actual or perceived race or national origin in any VAWA-funded program or activity.

B. Specific information on the legislative, judicial, administrative or other measures taken

19. To give effect to the undertaking to engage in no act or practice of racial discrimination against persons, groups of persons or institutions and to ensure that public authorities and public institutions act in conformity with this obligation. Federal agencies actively enforce federal non-discrimination laws against public authorities and institutions at all levels of government. The Violent Crime Control and Law Enforcement Act of 1994, 42 U.S.C. 14141; the Omnibus Crime Control and Safe Streets Act of 1968, 42 U.S.C. 3789d; and Title VI of the Civil Rights Act, 42 U.S.C. 2000d, authorize the Attorney General to bring civil actions to eliminate patterns or practices of law enforcement misconduct, including racial discrimination. DOJ/CRT investigates police departments, prisons, jails, juvenile correction facilities, mental health facilities, and related institutions to ensure compliance with the law and brings lawsuits to enforce the laws, where necessary. For example, a recent investigation of the New Orleans Police Department (NOPD) found a pattern or practice of unconstitutional conduct or violations of federal law in numerous areas, including: racial and ethnic profiling; failures to provide effective policing services to persons with limited English proficiency; unconstitutional stops, searches and arrests; gender-biased policing; and use of excessive force. In 2012, DOJ/CRT reached one of the most comprehensive reform agreements in its history to address these findings. See http://www.justice.gov/crt/about/spl/nopd.php. DOJ/CRT's work under 42 U.S.C.14141 and Title VI also seeks to ensure due process and equal protection in the administration of juvenile justice. For example, in 2012, DOJ entered into a settlement with the Juvenile Court of Memphis and Shelby County in Tennessee to address the disproportionate representation of Black/African-American children in almost every phase of the juvenile justice system and the system's need to respect all children's due process rights.

20. In the area of education, DOJ/CRT monitors and enforces approximately 200 federal school desegregation cases and actively combats discrimination against English Language Learner (ELL) students and their parents through enforcement of the Equal Educational Opportunities Act of 1973 (EEOA) and Title VI. During the last four years, CRT has pursued relief in 43 desegregation cases that integrate faculties, expand access to advanced courses, eliminate race-based extra-curricular activities, disrupt the "school-to-prison pipeline," halt segregative student transfers, open magnet schools, and close de facto single-race schools. During that time, CRT also reached 16 settlement agreements to ensure that states and school districts provide equal opportunities for students of all national origins regardless of their English language abilities.

21. DOJ/CRT also has sought to address one part of the "school-to-prison pipeline" problem by preventing students of colour from being excluded from school as a result of discriminatory suspensions and expulsions. In September 2010, CRT brought national attention to this critical issue by co-hosting with ED a first-of-its kind conference convening researchers, advocates and policy-makers to address best practices for keeping students in school.

22. DOJ/CRT also investigates and prosecutes cases of pattern or practice of employment discrimination by state or local government employers under Title VII. CRT filed 32 lawsuits under Title VII between 2009 and 2012, obtaining substantial relief for victims. It also launched a new pattern or practice initiative designed to use publicly available information in a systematic way to identify employers that should be investigated for potential pattern or practice of discrimination, without a referral from the EEOC. Primarily as a result of this initiative, by the end of October 2012, CRT was pursuing 28 active pattern or practice investigations, all of which had been initiated since January 2009.

23. In the area of voting, in addition to its usual work under Section 5 of the Voting Rights Act, since early 2011 DOJ/CRT has received approximately 2,200 redistricting plans for review under Section 5 to make sure they do not discriminate on the basis of, inter alia, race or ethnicity. In the past two years alone, CRT has blocked 14 voting changes because the jurisdiction had failed to show that the change complied with the Section 5 standards. These included 12 redistricting plans and two new photo identification requirements for voting.

24. DOJ/CRT has placed a priority on investigating allegations of discrimination against Arab Americans, South Asian Americans, and others perceived to be members of these groups. Many such complaints have been resolved informally. Others have resulted in lawsuits or settlements.

25. Other agencies, such as ED, HUD, DOL, EEOC, HHS and the Department of Homeland Security (DHS) also enforce non-discrimination laws related to race, colour, and national origin against public entities. Descriptions of these laws and their enforcement are found in other sections of this report and in paragraphs 159-175 of the common core document.

26. To give effect to the undertaking to prohibit and bring to an end racial discrimination by any persons, groups, or organizations: Civil rights laws, including 42 U.S.C. 1981 and 1982 and Titles II and VII of the Civil Rights Act of 1964, prohibit private actors from engaging in racial discrimination in making contracts or property transactions, such as the sale or rental of private property, the formation or terms of employment contracts, admission to private schools, and access to public facilities. In addition, enforcement against private parties who engage in discrimination is pursued under the Fair Housing Act and the Equal Credit Opportunity Act; Title VI of the 1964 Civil Rights Act (entities that receive federal funds); Executive Order 11246 (federal contractors and subcontractors); and the INA (discrimination on the basis of national origin or, for certain classes of "protected individuals," citizenship status). See paragraphs 159-175 of the common core document and other sections of this report for examples of such cases.

27. To give effect to the undertaking not to sponsor, defend or support racial discrimination by any persons or organizations. The U.S. government does not sponsor, defend, or support racial discrimination, and the Constitution, laws, and policies provide protections in this regard at all levels in the United States.

28. To review and if necessary amend or rescind governmental, national and local policies. Laws, regulations and policies in the United States are under continuous legislative and administrative review and revision, as well as judicial review, at all levels of government. For example:

- Universal periodic review (UPR) implementation — Federal government agencies are reviewing implementation of recommendations accepted by the United States during its first Universal Periodic Review before the U.N. Human Rights Council in November 2010, including through the creation of several thematic working groups focusing on a range of issues, including, inter alia, civil rights, criminal justice, indigenous issues, and immigration.
- The President created the National Equal Pay Enforcement Task Force to improve compliance with, public education regarding, and enforcement of equal pay laws. Task Force recommendations were announced in July 2010.
- Equality Working Group — As described above, this initiative is designed to enhance the government's domestic implementation of our international human rights treaty obligations and commitments that relate to non-discrimination and equal opportunity, including those in the CERD.
- DOJ — DOJ has indicated that it is reviewing the 2003 DOJ Guidance Regarding the Use of Race by Federal Law Enforcement Agencies.
- Following up on the report of the National Prison Rape Elimination Commission, in May 2012, DOJ issued a rule that sets national standards to prevent, detect, and respond to sexual abuse in confinement facilities. The rule, which is the first-ever federal effort to set standards to protect inmates in all correctional facilities at the federal, state, and local levels, is binding on the Federal Bureau of Prisons, and states that do not comply with the standards are subject to a 5 per cent reduction in funds otherwise received for prison operations.
- In 2011, the President sent a comprehensive legislative proposal to Congress that included restoration of the private right of action under Title VI (discussed in footnote 2 above). The language was included in S. 3322, introduced in the U.S. Senate in June 2012.
- For the purpose of reviewing thousands of redistricting plans under Section 5 of the Voting Rights Act to make sure they do not discriminate based on, inter alia, race or ethnicity, in 2011 DOJ made significant substantive

updates to its Section 5 procedures for the first time since 1987 and also updated its guidance to states and local jurisdictions, http://www.justice.gov/crt/about/vot/Policy_Guidance.php.

- The Attorney General has established and convened a Cabinet-Level Re-entry Council, a government-wide Council involving HUD, EEOC and other agencies to address both short- and long-term issues related to re-entry of those returning from prison and jail.

- DHS — U.S. Immigration and Customs Enforcement (ICE) is engaged in an on-going review and reform of immigration detention management policies and practices to ensure conditions of confinement consistent with the unique civil, rather than penal, authorities and purpose of immigration detention. The ICE Office of Detention Policy and Planning (ODPP) was established to spearhead ICE's detention reform initiative through both short- and long-term improvements (see the discussion of immigration detention under article 5, below).

- ICE is engaged in on-going data collection and research, data analysis, monitoring, oversight, and policy development to ensure that its immigration enforcement efforts, such as the Criminal Alien Program, Secure Communities, and the 287(g) program, do not become conduits for discriminatory policing. Steps taken by ICE include provision of awareness video briefings for state and local law enforcement to explain civil rights dimensions of immigration enforcement (including racial profiling, domestic violence and trafficking, limited English proficiency, etc.).

- As a result of a review, including consultation with affected communities, in April 2010 the Administration rescinded the DHS Transportation Security Administration (TSA) policy subjecting airline passengers from certain countries to secondary screening. Under the revised policy, passengers are selected for screening based on real-time, threat-based intelligence information covering all passengers traveling to the United States.

- As part of the Quadrennial Homeland Security Review, in July 2010 DHS realigned department program activities and organizational structure with mission goals. This review, which included dialogues with more than 20,000 stakeholders from all 50 states and the District of Columbia, incorporates civil rights and civil liberties protections.

- EEOC — EEOC has put in place a new strategic plan and accompanying enforcement plan to emphasize systemic and high impact litigation and to focus on national priority issues. Enforcement priorities for 2013-2016 include targeting "class-based recruitment and hiring practices that discriminate against racial and ethnic groups," and protecting immigrant, migrant, and other vulnerable workers, particularly with respect to "disparate pay, job segregation, harassment, trafficking, and discriminatory policies affecting vulnerable workers." This plan also requires increased coordination between EEOC and state and local government Fair Employment Practice Agencies (FEPAs) to enforce federal laws.

- The EEOC reviewed the quality and complaint processing times of agency decisions with regard to discrimination claims made against federal agencies.

- ED — ED will work with Congress on reauthorization of the Elementary and Secondary Education Act (ESEA) to promote the use of academic standards that prepare students to succeed in college and the workplace and accountability systems that recognize student growth and school progress, while continuing to close the achievement gap between students of different races and ethnicities. In March 2010, ED issued its recommendations for ESEA reauthorization, entitled A Blueprint for Reform.

- ED and DOJ issued guidance in December 2011 on the voluntary use of race in K-12 schools and higher education. The guidance helps ensure that integration does not end when a desegregation case is dismissed and that the benefits of educational diversity remain achievable for all students. ED's Office for Civil Rights (ED/OCR) also issued guidance concerning institutions' obligations under Title VI of the Civil Rights Act of 1964, as amended, and other laws to protect students from student-on-student harassment on the basis of race, colour, national origin, and other factors — guidance that clarifies the relationship between bullying and discriminatory harassment.

- HHS — As a result of an extensive review, in April 2011 HHS released its Action Plan to Reduce Racial and Ethnic Health Disparities. At the same time, the National Partnership for Action to End Health Disparities released its Stakeholder Strategy for Achieving Health Equity — a roadmap for eliminating health disparities through cooperative action.

- HUD — In 2011-12, HUD conducted an in-depth process involving stakeholders to update its regulations regarding its Affirmatively Furthering Fair Housing (AFFH) program, designed to combat racial and ethnic discrimination in housing. In 2013, HUD is drafting a proposed rule that will provide greater clarity on how jurisdictions and public housing authorities can improve access and advance the ability for all residents to make true housing choices. HUD is also working closely with communities and regions receiving regional planning grants to support decisions and actions that promote AFFH.

- DOL — Each year, DOL's Office of Federal Contract Compliance (OFCCP) audits the employment policies and practices of approximately 4,000 companies doing business with the federal government to ensure that these companies do not discriminate on the basis of, inter alia, race, colour, or national origin and to ensure that they take affirmative steps to recruit, hire, and promote minorities and women. In 2010, OFCCP enhanced its enforcement capability by hiring 200 additional investigators. It has also greatly increased its outreach to community organizations and the public and proposed changes to enhance the effectiveness of its audit process.

- EPA — EPA has led the government's efforts to re-energize the Federal Working Group on Environmental Justice (EJ IWG) under Executive Order 12898. In August 2011, 17 cabinet secretaries, agency administrators, and White House office heads signed a Memorandum of Understanding formally recommitting all agencies to environmental justice and establishing priorities, structures, and procedures for the IWG. The IWG conducted 20 community listening sessions across the country and, in 2012, 15 federal agencies issued final agency environmental justice strategies, implementation plans, and/or progress reports.

29. Legislative and judicial actions: The basic U.S. legal framework to address discrimination is described in paragraphs 142-148 and 153-155 of the common core document. Recent enactment of laws expanding human rights protections is noted above under article 2, section A. Judicial actions are described throughout this report.

30. To encourage, where appropriate, non-governmental organizations and institutions that combat racial discrimination and foster mutual understanding: Due to the open nature of U.S. society and its ever-increasing racial and ethnic diversity, a plethora of national, state, and local nongovernmental organizations and movements exist to promote racial and ethnic tolerance and coexistence in the United States. Government entities at all levels reach out to and work with such organizations in pursuing equal protection goals. For example, the newly established Equality Working Group creates a forum for dialogue between civil society and the federal government on issues of equality and human rights. DOJ's Community Relations Service (DOJ/CRS) engages with non-governmental organizations as it pursues its mission of mediation, technical assistance, and training to assist communities in avoiding racial and ethnic conflict, and to help resolve disputes when they occur. Other agencies throughout the federal government also work with non-governmental organizations, seeking their input and offering training and education to members of the public. States, local jurisdictions and tribal and territorial governments also engage with such organizations. Examples are noted in this report and in the Common core document and its annex.

C. Coordination among bodies mandated with combating racial discrimination

31. The issue of a national human rights institution, noted in paragraph 12 of the Committee's concluding observations, is discussed in the common core document in the section on Framework within which Human Rights are Promoted at the National Level. Although the United States does not have a single independent national human rights institution in accordance with the Paris Principles, multiple complementary protections and mechanisms serve to reinforce the ability of the United States to guarantee respect for human rights, including through our independent judiciary at both federal and state levels. Within the federal government, numerous departments and agencies are responsible for implementing U.S. human rights treaty obligations through the enforcement of domestic law, with DOJ/CRT playing a lead coordinating role. Numerous state and local governments within the United States have state and/or local civil rights and/or human rights organizations or commissions, many of which participate in the International Association of Official Human Rights Agencies. Some Indian tribes and territorial governments also have human rights organizations or commissions. The United States continues to examine ways to improve human rights treaty implementation at all levels of government.

32. With regard to the recommendation in paragraph 13 of the Committee's concluding observations that the United States establish appropriate mechanisms to ensure a coordinated approach towards the implementation of the Convention at the federal, state, and local levels, the United States fully agrees that mechanisms designed to strengthen coordination are critical, and numerous such mechanisms do exist. The framework within which human rights are promoted and coordinated in the United States is described in paragraphs 124-130 of the common core document. All federal agencies with mandates related to non-discrimination, including DOJ, EEOC, ED, HUD, DHS, DOL and others, coor-

dinate within the federal government, as well as with state and local authorities, human rights commissions, and non-governmental entities. For example, a hallmark of DOJ's civil rights work in this Administration is partnership and collaboration — strengthening relationships with other agencies, state Attorney General offices throughout the nation, and community and civil society partners to leverage resources and coordinate efforts to maximize impact. DOJ/CRT coordinates enforcement of Title VI of the Civil Rights Act of 1964 and assists other agencies with Title VI and other enforcement responsibilities, ensuring that recipients of federal financial assistance (including state and local governments) do not discriminate in their programs, including on the basis of race, colour and national origin. Over the last four years, DOJ has provided training, technical assistance, and counsel to civil rights offices in federal government agencies, and has reviewed other agencies' Title VI implementing regulations and guidance. DOJ has also created a Title VI Interagency Working Group, which facilitates interagency information sharing to strengthen Title VI enforcement efforts at the federal level. Additionally, several of the UPR Working Groups and the Equality Working Group were created with a view to further strengthening coordination and U.S. domestic implementation of human rights treaty obligations and commitments related to non-discrimination and equal opportunity.

D. Special measures

33. With regard to article 2, paragraph 2 and paragraph 15 of the Committee's concluding observations, the United States is committed to using all the tools at its disposal to address disparities in outcomes, across a host of indicators, that disproportionately impact members of racial and ethnic minorities, and the United States has in place measures that are race-based as well as measures that may be based on other factors, such as economic factors. Under the U.S. Constitution, classification by race is permissible in some circumstances for certain purposes, such as redressing past racial discrimination and promoting diversity in educational settings. A substantial number of federal ameliorative measures, including many described throughout this report, can be considered special measures for purposes of article 2, paragraph 2. Use of special measures is described further in paragraphs 197-206 of the common core document.

Article 3

Information on the legislative, judicial, administrative or other measures that give effect to the provisions of article 3, in particular

34. Measures to prevent, prohibit, and eradicate all practices of racial segregation. The United States condemns racial segregation and apartheid and undertakes to prevent, prohibit, and eradicate all practices of this nature. No such policies or practices are permitted, and it remains the U.S. position that such practices should be condemned and eradicated wherever found.

35. Measures to ensure proper monitoring of all trends that can give rise to racial segregation. As noted above, U.S. law reaches not only intentional discrimination but also certain facially neutral practices that may result in an unjustified disparate impact on members of a protected class. U.S. agencies, such as DOJ/CRT, the ED Office for Civil Rights (ED/OCR), the EEOC, and others, as well as state, territorial, tribal, and local agencies, monitor issues of segregation and discrimination to ensure that appropriate actions are taken under applicable law. The United States also collects census data in a manner that allows analysis by racial, ethnic, and other characteristics. Since the 2000 census, information has also been collected on Americans of Arab ancestry. Recognizing that racial segregation is a problem that in some cases has contributed to neighbourhoods of concentrated poverty, the Obama Administration has initiated programs, such as the Neighbourhood Revitalization Initiative, designed to support local communities in developing the tools needed to revitalize neighbourhoods of concentrated poverty into neighbourhoods of opportunity.

36. Measures to prevent and avoid as much as possible the discrimination prohibited under the Convention, in particular in the areas of education and housing. It is of concern that, in some cases, minorities are concentrated in areas or communities that may have sub-standard living conditions and/or services, and one of the missions of civil rights laws and authorities in the United States is to ensure that such situations are not the result of discriminatory policies or practices (direct or disparate impact) related to housing, education or other areas receiving federal financial assistance.

37. With regard to paragraphs 16 and 17 of the Committee's concluding observations, the causes and effects of de facto segregation and racial and ethnic disparities in housing and education, as well as in other aspects of American life, are issues of active study and concern. The United States continues its efforts to overcome not only current discrimination but

also the lingering effects of racism, intolerance, and destructive policies relating to members of minorities. Although it has been more than 40 years since the passage of the Fair Housing Act, housing discrimination and segregation continue to taint communities across the country. Far too many home seekers are shut out by housing providers' prejudice and stereotypes instead of being welcomed into communities that are diverse and thriving. Continuing discrimination affects Blacks/African Americans, Latinos/Hispanics, Arab Americans, Asian Americans, and other minority groups. DOJ/CRT has reinvigorated fair housing enforcement in recent years, working to ensure that local governments and private housing providers offer safe and affordable housing on a non-discriminatory basis, http://www.justice.gov/crt/publications/.

38. Housing: The Housing and Community Development Act of 1974 prohibits discrimination in allocation of community development funds on the basis, inter alia, of race, colour or national origin. Under the Fair Housing Act (FHA), HUD requires jurisdictions and other recipients not only to address discrimination, but also to take affirmative steps to overcome barriers to fair housing choice and equal access to opportunity. Thus, communities receiving federal funding must take specific actions to promote diverse, inclusive communities. HUD is working to clarify the FHA obligations and to provide more assistance and guidance for meeting them. HUD and DOJ are also emphasizing high impact litigation, and in 2011, DOJ and HUD achieved the largest residential fair lending settlement in U.S. history, requiring Countrywide Financial Corporation to pay $335 million in compensation for Black/African American and Hispanic/Latino victims of discriminatory mortgage lending practices from 2004 through 2008. In 2012, HUD investigated 81 cases involving steering and 11 cases involving redlining along with other efforts to combat housing discrimination by private actors.

39. Federal housing assistance programs play an important role in covering the difference between the rents that low-income families are able to afford and the cost of rental housing. In 2012, the U.S. provided $2.95 billion in Community Development Block Grants to support housing, $1 billion for the HOME program, $685 million in Native American Fair Housing Grants, and $5.8 billion to public housing programs, http://portal.hud.gov/hudportal/HUD?src=/fy2012 budget. Furthermore, 2,142,134 families received housing choice vouchers in 2012. In addition, HUD continues to help recipients of rental assistance in moving into higher-opportunity neighbourhoods. For example, the Baltimore Housing Mobility Program (BHMP) provides vouchers and counselling services to move individuals into neighbourhoods where less than 30 per cent of residents are members of a minority group, less than 10 per cent of residents live in poverty, and less than 5 per cent of all housing is public or HUD-assisted. In a recent study of BHMP, more than 95 per cent of new movers surveyed said that their new neighbourhoods were better or much better than their old neighbourhoods, and 63 per cent rated their new neighbourhoods as an excellent or very good place to raise children.

40. HUD is also creating new solutions to address the challenge of homelessness. In 2011, nearly 60 per cent of all sheltered homeless persons were minorities. Data from HUD's most recent count of homeless persons in January 2012 indicated a marginal decline in the estimated homeless population from 636,017 in 2009 to 633,782. In 2011, HUD estimated that there was a 7 per cent drop in homelessness among veterans, 40 per cent of whom are Black/African American or Hispanic/Latino. To help further combat homelessness, in 2009 Congress provided a one-time appropriation of $1.5 billion for the Homelessness Prevention and Rapid Re-Housing Program, which served nearly 1,378,000 people with services to prevent homelessness or rapidly re-house those who experienced homelessness. HUD currently manages several programs directly addressing homelessness, including the Continuum of Care program, the Emergency Shelter Grant program, and two programs targeting homeless veterans in collaboration with the Department of Veterans Affairs and the Department of Defense. Furthermore, in 2010, the U.S. Interagency Council on Homelessness published Opening Doors: Federal Strategic Plan to Prevent and End Homelessness — a comprehensive approach by 19 federal agencies to prevent and end veteran, chronic, and family and youth homelessness. This Plan presents 52 strategies based on best practices from around the country that build on the lesson that housing, health, education, and human service programs must be fully engaged and coordinated to prevent and end homelessness, http://www.usich.gov/.

41. Education: The United States also actively addresses de facto segregation in education — an issue not unrelated to residential segregation. Despite the promise of the Brown v Board of Education decision, far too many students still attend segregated schools with segregated faculties or unequal facilities. Even those enrolled in racially diverse schools too often are assigned to single-race classes, denied equal access to advanced courses, disciplined unfairly due to their race, or separated by race in prom and homecoming events. To ensure equal educational opportunities for all children, DOJ and ED enforce laws, such as Titles IV and VI of the Civil Rights Act of 1964, the Americans with Disabilities Act of 1990, the Patsy T. Mink Equal Opportunity in Education Act of 1972 (Title IX), and the Rehabilitation Act of 1973,

that prohibit discrimination in education, including on the basis of race, colour and national origin. DOJ/CRT monitors and seeks further relief, as necessary, in approximately 200 school districts that had a history of segregation and remain under court supervision. For example, since May 2011, CRT has been actively litigating to ensure that the Cleveland, Mississippi school district meets its long overdue obligation under U.S. law to desegregate its schools. CRT has argued that schools on the west side of the railroad tracks, which had been de jure segregated White schools until 1969 when the federal court ordered them to desegregate, still retain their character and reputation as White schools more than forty years later, while the formerly legally segregated schools on the east side of the tracks remain all Black/African American. Only one mile separates the all Black/African American schools from the high school and middle school with substantial White enrolments. CRT successfully asked the court to order the district to devise a new plan to desegregate its middle school and high school student bodies, as well as the faculties in all its schools. At a recent hearing, DOJ/CRT objected to the district's proposed plan and urged the court to order the immediate and effective desegregation of the middle and high schools.

42. CRT also investigates new allegations of discrimination and harassment, including those based on race, colour, and national origin, at all educational levels and, when appropriate, brings cases or intervenes in private suits. One example concerns complaints of severe harassment of Asian American students at South Philadelphia High School, including violent physical attacks against the students on school grounds. CRT engaged the school district, the Asian American Legal Defense and Education Fund, local advocacy organizations, the Pennsylvania Human Relations Commission, students, and the community in an extensive investigation of the school district's policies and practices regarding student-on-student harassment, leading to a December 2010 settlement agreement with the district to address and prevent such harassment. Advocates and students report that the school climate at South Philadelphia High School has improved since the agreement's implementation.

43. ED receives and resolves civil rights complaints filed by members of the public, receiving more than 15,674 complaints in Fiscal Years (FYs) 2011 and 2012, including more than 4,056 complaints alleging discrimination based on race, colour, or national origin. ED also initiates compliance reviews where information suggests widespread discrimination. Between FY 2009 and 2012, ED initiated more than 60 reviews specifically targeting Title VI discrimination issues.

44. The United States also assists school districts in voluntarily ending de facto segregation and avoiding racial isolation and in promoting diversity by (1) providing technical assistance in achieving these compelling government interests in ways that comply with non-discrimination laws, and (2) providing financial incentives to school districts for programs like magnet schools — schools with specialized courses or curricula that attract students from different areas with differing educational, economic, racial and ethnic backgrounds. ED/OCR conducts hundreds of technical assistance and outreach activities each year and offers assistance on its website in 20 languages. ED also administers higher education programs that provide financial aid to students in need; promotes educational equality for students who are members of minority groups; assists school districts in offering educational opportunities to Native Hawaiians, American Indians, and Alaska Natives; and provides grants to strengthen higher education institutions that serve populations historically underserved (e.g., minority serving institutions and historically Black colleges and universities). In May 2011, ED/OCR and DOJ/CRT jointly released guidance to remind school districts of the federal obligation to provide equal educational opportunities to all children residing within district boundaries, regardless of the actual or perceived citizenship or immigration status of the children and their parents or guardians. In December 2011, DOJ and ED also released two guidance documents on the voluntary use of race to achieve diversity and avoid racial isolation, one for school districts and one for colleges and universities.

45. In 2011, ED formed the Equity and Excellence Commission to recommend ways school finance can be improved to increase equity and achievement. The Commission issued a report containing its findings and recommendations in February 2013. The federal government is also working closely with civil society groups and state and local education authorities to address the factors that contribute to the achievement gap and to ensure equality for all children in public schools — particularly Black/African American and Hispanic/Latino children, and ELL students. In 2011, ED held a series of National Conversations on ELL education that brought together key stakeholders in six cities. President Obama and Dr. Jill Biden also convened the first White House Summit on Community Colleges in 2010 to discuss the role of community colleges in making higher education available to all. ED continued this dialogue by holding four regional community college summits and a Community College Virtual Symposium, which resulted in the production of four papers to assist community college leaders and practitioners in promoting college and career readiness for low-skill adults,

aligning secondary and postsecondary education, reforming remedial education programs to meet student needs more effectively, and increasing employer engagement at community colleges. In April 2012, ED released Investing in America's Future: A Blueprint for Transforming Career and Technical Education, which emphasizes improved data systems and incentives to identify and close participation and achievement gaps where they exist in career and technical education programs.

46. Through the American Recovery and Reinvestment Act of 2009, the Administration made an unprecedented financial commitment of almost $100 billion to education, including the Race to the Top (RTT) program. RTT provides incentives to states to implement large-scale, system-changing reforms to improve student achievement, narrow achievement gaps, and increase graduation and college enrolment rates. Recovery Act funds are also being used to increase available financial aid and loans for postsecondary school education, and to provide $12 billion for community colleges to enrol workers who need further education and training.

Article 4

A. Information on the legislative, judicial, administrative or other measures that give effect to the provisions of article 4, including enactment and enforcement of laws

47. With regard to article 4 and paragraph 18 of the Committee's concluding observations, the United States is deeply committed to combating racial discrimination. The United States has struggled to eliminate racial discrimination throughout our history, from abolition of slavery to our civil rights movement. We are not at the end of the road toward equal justice, but our nation is a far better and fairer place than it was in the past. The progress we have made has been accomplished without banning speech or restricting freedom of expression, assembly or association. We believe that banning and punishing offensive and hateful speech is neither an effective approach to combating intolerance, nor an appropriate role for government in seeking to promote respect for diversity. As President Obama stated in a speech delivered in Cairo, Egypt in June 2009, suppressing ideas never succeeds in making them go away. In fact, to do so can be counterproductive and even raise the profile of such ideas. We believe the best antidote to offensive and hateful speech is constructive dialogue that counters and responds to such speech by refuting it through principled arguments. In addition, we believe that governments should speak out against such offensive speech and employ tools to address intolerance that include a combination of robust legal protections against discrimination and hate crimes, proactive government outreach, education, and the vigorous defense of human rights and fundamental freedoms, including freedom of expression. It is incumbent upon both governments and members of society to model respect, welcome diversity of belief, and build respectful societies based on open dialogue and debate.

48. In light of this framework, the United States has long made clear its concerns over resorting to restrictions on freedom of expression, assembly, and association in order to promote tolerance and respect. This concern includes the restrictions contained in article 4 of the CERD to the extent that they might be interpreted as allowing or requiring restrictions on forms of expression that do not constitute incitement to imminent violence or "true threats" of violence. Indeed, these concerns were so fundamental that the United States took a reservation to article 4 and the corresponding provisions of article 7 when it became a party to the CERD, noting that it would not accept any obligation that could limit the extensive protections for such fundamental freedoms guaranteed in the U.S. Constitution.

49. Freedom of speech was critical to the achievement of equality in the United States. Many people complained that the words of Dr. Martin Luther King and other civil rights leaders were dangerous, and sought to ban them as disturbing the peace in communities where majorities of whites wanted to perpetuate racial segregation. When this issue was brought to the Supreme Court in the case of *New York Times v. Sullivan*, 376 U.S. 254 (1964), the Court ruled that an official in Alabama could not sue civil rights advocates over an advertisement that made negative statements about the police. Earlier in our history, the abolition of slavery was accelerated by the exhortations of preachers from pulpits and the writings of abolitionist pamphleteers. Today, in the United States, public expressions of hateful beliefs almost invariably draw larger and more powerful expressions of racial and religious equality and harmony. For example, a march by neo-Nazis that draws a dozen or so participants may be met with a peaceful interfaith vigil of hundreds of counter-demonstrators.

50. In short, we protect freedom of expression not only because it is enshrined in our Constitution as the law of the land, but also because our democracy depends on the free exchange of ideas and the ability to dissent. And we protect freedom of expression because the cost of stripping away individual rights is far greater than the cost of tolerating hateful

words. We also have grave concerns about how empowering government to ban offensive speech could easily be misused to undermine democratic principles.

51. Consistent with the First Amendment, we do not permit speech that incites imminent violence. This is a limited exception to freedom of expression, and such speech is only unlawful when it "is directed to inciting or producing imminent lawless action and is likely to incite or produce such action." *Brandenburg v. Ohio*, 395 U.S. 444, 447 (1969). Speech may also be restricted based on its content if it falls within the narrow class of "true threats" of violence. Moreover, numerous federal and state laws in the United States prohibit hate crimes. Federal statutes punish acts of violence or hostile acts motivated by bias based on race, ethnicity, or colour and intended to interfere with the participation of individuals in certain activities such as employment, housing, public accommodation, and use of public facilities. See, e.g., 19 U.S.C. 245 (federally protected activities), 18 U.S.C. 3631 (housing). In addition, 47 states have hate crimes laws, as do U.S. territories. The Matthew Shepard and James Byrd, Jr. Hate Crimes Prevention Act is a significant expansion of federal hate crimes laws. The Act creates a new criminal code provision, 18 U.S.C. 249, that criminalizes the wilful causing of bodily injury (or attempting to do so with fire, firearm, or other dangerous weapon) when the crime was committed because of the actual or perceived race, colour, religion, national origin of any person and that, unlike Section 245, does not require proof of intention to interfere with a federally protected activity. The law also provides funding and technical assistance to state, local and tribal jurisdictions to help them prevent, investigate, and prosecute hate crimes. Subsequent to enactment of the Shepard-Byrd Act, DOJ/CRT worked with U.S. Attorneys' Offices, the Federal Bureau of Investigation (FBI), and DOJ/CRS across the country to ensure that federal prosecutors, federal law enforcement agents, state and local law enforcement officers, non-governmental organizations, and interested members of the public were trained on the Act's requirements. Of particular importance, DOJ/CRT has trained law enforcement officers who are the first responders to assaults or other acts of violence so that they know what questions to ask and what evidence to gather at the scene to allow prosecutors to make an informed assessment of whether a case should be prosecuted as a hate crime.

52. In a memorandum to all United States Attorneys concerning the importance of the new Shepard-Byrd Hate Crimes Prevention Act, the Assistant Attorney General for the Civil Rights Division recognized that, unfortunately, hate crimes and the intolerance that breeds them remain all too prevalent in the United States. According to FBI statistics, in 2011 6,222 criminal incidents involving 7,254 offenses were reported as a result of bias toward a particular race, religion, sexual orientation, ethnicity/national origin, or physical or mental disability. See http://www.fbi.gov/about-us/cjis/ucr/hate-crime/2011/narratives/incidents-and-offenses. Of these, there were 6,216 single-bias incidents, of which 46.9 per cent were motivated by a racial bias, and 11.6 per cent were motivated by an ethnicity/national origin bias. Of the 4,623 hate crime offenses classified as crimes against persons, intimidation accounted for 45.6 per cent, simple assaults for 34.5 per cent, and aggravated assaults for 19.4 per cent. Four murders and seven forcible rapes were reported as hate crimes. Law enforcement agencies reported that 3,465 single-bias hate crime offenses were racially motivated. Of these offenses, 72 per cent were motivated by anti-Black bias, 16.7 per cent were motivated by anti-White bias, 4.8 per cent resulted from anti-Asian/Pacific Islander bias, 4.7 per cent were a result of bias against groups of individuals consisting of more than one race, and 1.9 per cent were motivated by anti-American Indian/Alaska Native (AI/AN) bias (Id. Table 1).

53. DOJ/CRT aggressively prosecutes hate crimes, including cross burnings, arsons, vandalisms, shootings, and assaults committed because of the victim's race. CRT convicted 140 defendants of federal hate crimes between 2009 and 2012, a 73 per cent increase over the previous 4 years. It has brought 15 cases charging 39 defendants under the Shepard-Byrd Act and has prosecuted cases in Arkansas, Kentucky, Michigan, Minnesota, Mississippi, New Mexico, New York, Ohio, South Carolina, Texas, and Washington. Cases under the Shepard-Byrd Act include: conviction in 2011 of two Arkansas men after they chased a group of Hispanic/Latino men and intentionally rammed their truck repeatedly into the victim's car; securing guilty pleas in 2010 against three men for assaulting a 22-year-old developmentally disabled Native American man in New Mexico, including branding a swastika into his arm and defacing his body with White supremacist symbols; securing guilty pleas in 2012 from three men involved in the fatal assault of an African American man in West Jackson, Mississippi; conviction of defendants in Shenandoah, Pennsylvania for assault of a Latino man after making racially charged comments; and securing the guilty plea in 2010 of a defendant who sent a series of threatening email communications to employees of five civil rights organizations that work to challenge discrimination against Latinos.

54. Through its post-9-11 discriminatory backlash initiative, DOJ/CRT has investigated over 800 incidents in which defendants targeted those they perceived to be Muslims or those they perceived to be of Arab or South East Asian descent.

CRT has also devoted enormous resources to the investigation and prosecutorial assessment of unsolved murders committed during the Civil Rights Era to determine whether perpetrators could be brought to justice in federal or state courts, and to bring closure to victims' family members even where no prosecution is possible.

55. DOJ engages in extensive outreach to educate people about their rights and available government services. One example includes the DOJ Community Relations Service newly revised Sikh Cultural Competency Training, designed to inform and educate communities experiencing tensions arising from incomplete knowledge of Sikh community neighbours and serve as a resource to help prevent violent hate crimes. In some areas, federal, state, and local authorities and community organizations have formed coalitions to track, prevent, and combat hate crimes. In 2010, the FBI devoted additional resources to combating hate crimes in cities most at risk for bias-motivated violence, working in collaboration with state and local law enforcement agencies and non-governmental partners.

56. The prosecution of hate crimes is only one element in broader efforts related to community engagement and empowerment. The U. S. Government works with state and local entities to educate young people through anti-bullying curricula and other educational programs aimed at eliminating hate among our nation's youth. Through these kinds of actions, the United States encourages communities and schools to address racism before it becomes fuel for violence. Active outreach programs also exist in communities, where federal, state, and local law enforcement officers work to build trust among different ethnic and racial groups, to understand sensitivities and break down stereotypes, and to increase dialogue. Finally, political leaders from the President to state and local officials speak out about intolerance and condemn such acts when they do occur. Discrimination and racist hatred have no place in our nation, and we are committed not only to combating these problems, but also to working with communities to prevent them from occurring in the first place.

B. Racial motives as aggravating circumstances under domestic penal legislation

57. The commission of a crime based on the victim's race, national origin, or ethnicity is an aggravating factor under many U.S. criminal statutes at both the federal and state levels. In 1994, the U.S. Congress passed the Hate Crimes Sentencing Enhancement Act, 28 U.S.C. 994, which required the U.S. Sentencing Commission to increase penalties for crimes committed because of animus toward a person's "actual or perceived race, colour, religion, national origin, ethnicity, gender, disability, or sexual orientation of any person." As described above, the federal criminal code treats certain bias motivated crimes as specific offenses. Most states either have specific hate crimes laws (see, e.g., Washington, New York and Massachusetts) or allow bias motivation in criminal offenses to be taken into account as aggravating circumstances in sentencing (see, e.g., Alabama, Arizona, California, and Florida). Penalty enhancement provisions generally apply to a wide range of violent acts, but in some states are limited to specific crimes, such as assault and battery.

Article 5

I. Information grouped under particular rights

58. Article 5 obligates States parties to prohibit and eliminate racial discrimination in all its forms and to guarantee the right of everyone to equality before the law, without distinction as to race, colour, or national or ethnic origin. The protections of the U.S. Constitution meet this fundamental requirement, as do laws, policies, and objectives of government at all levels. Article 5 specifically requires States parties to guarantee equality and non-discrimination in the enjoyment of certain enumerated rights. As noted in our prior CERD reports, article 5 does not affirmatively require States parties to provide or to ensure observance of each of the listed rights themselves, but rather to prohibit discrimination in the enjoyment of those rights to the extent they are provided in domestic law. In this respect, U.S. law fully complies with the requirements of the Convention. The U.S. continues to work to achieve the desired goals with regard to non-discrimination in each of the enumerated areas.

A. Equal treatment before tribunals and other organs administering justice

59. Independent and Effective Scrutiny of Claims: The Equal Protection Clause of the Fourteenth Amendment to the U.S. Constitution guarantees the right to equal treatment before organs administering justice in the United States. At all levels, claims of discrimination based on race, colour or national or ethnic origin, including claims made against offi-

cials, are investigated by independent authorities and are subject to independent and effective scrutiny by courts and/or administrative tribunals established to hear such claims.

60. The Sixth Amendment to the U.S. Constitution provides for the right to counsel in federal criminal prosecutions. In 2013, we commemorate the 50th anniversary of the landmark U.S. Supreme Court decision, Gideon v. Wainwright, which extended the right to counsel at government expense to individuals who cannot afford it for criminal prosecutions in state court. Over the years in a series of decisions since Gideon, the Supreme Court has recognized that the Sixth Amendment right to counsel applies in misdemeanour cases and in juvenile delinquency proceedings. By law, counsel for indigent defendants is provided without discrimination based on race, colour, ethnicity, and other factors. Federal, state, and local courts use a variety of methods to deliver indigent criminal defense services, including public defender programs, assigned counsel programs, and contract attorneys.

61. Although there is no right to counsel at government expense for civil matters, limited free civil legal assistance exists across the country, primarily through non-profit legal aid programs, such as those funded by the Legal Services Corporation (LSC), and pro bono initiatives led by the private bar. Established by Congress in 1974 as an independent non-profit corporation, LSC is the single largest funder of civil legal aid for low-income Americans. Its 134 grantees provide free legal assistance through more than 900 offices across the country and in U.S. territories. To leverage scarce resources, LSC encourages partnering with other funders of civil legal aid, including state and local governments, Interest on Lawyer's Trust Accounts (IOLTAs), state access to justice commissions (established in approximately half of the states), the private bar, philanthropic foundations, and businesses.

62. Regarding paragraph 22 of the Committee's concluding observations, the United States faces challenges in both its provision of legal representation to indigent criminal defendants and its provision of free and affordable civil legal services to the poor and middle class. We recognize that these challenges are felt acutely by members of racial and ethnic minorities.

63. To address these issues, DOJ established the Access to Justice Initiative (ATJ) in March 2010. ATJ's mission is to help the justice system efficiently deliver outcomes that are fair and accessible to all, irrespective of wealth and status. ATJ has worked to expand research and funding to improve the delivery of indigent defense services. In 2012, DOJ's Office of Justice Programs awarded nearly $3 million in grants for this purpose and has committed to approximately $2 million additional in 2013. ATJ has also worked to strengthen defender services in tribal courts and, in partnership with the BIA, has launched the Tribal Court Trial Advocacy Training Program, which provides free trainings to public defenders, prosecutors, and judges who work in tribal courts.

64. To strengthen civil legal services, ATJ is working with other federal agencies to determine whether existing federal safety-net grant programs could perform more successfully by incorporating legal services. Specifically, ATJ staff has established partnerships with agencies working to promote access to health and housing, education and employment, and family stability and community well-being, to remove unintended barriers that prevent legal aid providers from participating as grantees or sub-grantees. ATJ also supports expanded civil legal research through collaboration with legal scholars and the American Bar Foundation. ATJ is providing technical assistance to more than a dozen states considering creation of new access to justice commissions, which generally support civil legal services at the state level. Responding to a challenge from ATJ, the Conference of Chief Justices unanimously adopted a resolution in 2010 urging the approximately two dozen states without active commissions to establish them. ATJ staff has also worked with the American Bar Association (ABA) Resource Center for Access to Justice Initiatives, and the Public Welfare Foundation to develop a national strategy for establishing and strengthening commissions, and ATJ staff now serves on a new national ABA Access to Justice Commission Expansion Project Advisory Committee.

65. With regard to prevention of racial discrimination in the criminal justice system, the United States acts to assess and address the indicators of racial discrimination; eliminate laws that discriminate; develop training and other programs to foster dialogue and promote tolerance; and ensure equal access to law and justice at all stages of the complaint and hearing process. While laws and systems are in place to ensure equality of access to and treatment in the criminal justice system, the United States recognizes that racial and ethnic disparities continue to exist. Statistics relating to the crime rates of persons belonging to some minority groups, treatment of minorities in some cases by law enforcement personnel, and the proportion of minority persons in the justice and prison systems indicate the need for further understanding of the issues and for continued vigilance to make further progress in pursuing the goal of equality.

66. With regard to paragraph 20 of the Committee's concluding observations, a number of steps have been taken in recent years to address racial disparities in the administration and functioning of the criminal justice system. The Fair Sentencing Act, enacted in August 2010, reduced the disparity between more lenient sentences for powder cocaine charges and more severe sentences for crack cocaine charges, which are more frequently brought against minorities. Based on a request by the Attorney General, the Sentencing Commission voted to apply retroactively the guideline amendment implementing the Fair Sentencing Act. As of December 2012, 6,626 federal crack offenders' sentences had been reduced as a result of retroactive application of the Fair Sentencing Act. Of these, 93.5 per cent were Black/African American or Hispanic/Latino. DOJ also intends to conduct further statistical analysis and issue annual reports on sentencing disparities in the criminal justice system, and is working on other ways to implement increased system-wide monitoring steps. DOJ has also pledged to work with the Sentencing Commission on reform of mandatory minimum sentencing statutes and to implement the recommendations set forth in the Commission's 2011 report to Congress, Mandatory Minimum Penalties in the Federal Criminal Justice System. Finally, at the state and local level, many law enforcement authorities are implementing innovative solutions. For example, the Vera Institute for Justice has launched a program in several municipalities to help prosecutors' offices identify potential bias and to respond when bias is found.

67. Language access services are also critical in ensuring equal access to the judicial system for Limited English Proficient (LEP) persons. DOJ/CRT's Courts Language Access Initiative combines enforcement tools with policy, technical assistance, and collaboration in an effort to ensure that LEP parties receive interpretation and language services in court proceedings and operations. Noting the Supreme Court holding that failure to take reasonable steps to ensure meaningful access for LEP persons is a form of national origin discrimination, Lau v. Nichols, 414 U.S. 563 (1974), and based on the government's long commitment to that legal principle, in August 2010, the Assistant Attorney General for the Civil Rights Division sent a letter to all state chief justices and state court administrators concerning the need to bring state court language access policies and practices into compliance with Title VI of the Civil Rights Act of 1964 and the Omnibus Crime Control and Safe Streets Act of 1968. Among other things, the letter notes that language services must not be restricted to courtrooms; rather, meaningful access also extends to functions conducted in other court-managed offices, operations, and programs, such as intake or filing offices; cashiers; probation and parole offices; alternative dispute resolution programs; and detention facilities. Grant funds provided to the states by the Office of Justice Programs may be used to support language services for these purposes.

68. A recent study by the Sentencing Project, based on data from the DOJ Bureau of Justice Statistics (BJS), shows a shift in the racial makeup of U.S. prisons, suggesting that, while still stark, disparities in the prison population may be starting to diminish. Decline in incarceration rates was most striking for Black/African American women, dropping from six times the rate of White women in 2000 to 2.8 times in 2009 — a 30.7 per cent drop. For Black/African American men, the rate decreased by 9.8 per cent, from 7.7 times the rate of White men in 2000 to 6.4 in 2009. Incarceration rates for White men and women increased over the same period, rising 47.1 per cent for White women and 8.5 per cent for White men. By the end of the decade, Hispanic men were slightly less likely to be in prison, a drop of 2.2 per cent, but Hispanic women were imprisoned more frequently, an increase of 23.3 per cent.

69. With regard to paragraph 23 of the Committee's concluding observations, the situation regarding capital punishment in the United States, including the applicable limitations, the heightened procedural protections, and the decline in use of the death penalty is described in Part I B, section 3 of the common core document. Since submission of the common core document in 2011, enactment of legislation abolishing the death penalty by the states of Connecticut and Maryland has reduced to 32 the number of states that authorize capital punishment, in addition to the federal government and the U.S. Military. Eighteen states and the District of Columbia do not authorize the death penalty.

70. With respect to the Committee's comment concerning a potential moratorium on the death penalty, there is vigorous public debate in the United States on the death penalty. However, the use of the death penalty is a decision left to democratically elected governments at the federal and state levels. The U.S. Constitution grants states broad powers to regulate their own general welfare, including enactment and enforcement of criminal laws, public safety, and correction, and a number of states currently prohibit imposition of the death penalty either by law or by executive decision of the Governor. Any further decisions concerning a moratorium would have to be made separately at the federal level and by each of the 32 states that retain the death penalty.

71. With regard to paragraph 21 of the Committee's concluding observations, the U.S. Supreme Court has limited applicability of juvenile sentences of life without the possibility of parole (JLWOP) in two recent cases. In Graham v. Florida, 130 S. Ct. 2011 (2010), the Court ruled that application of JLWOP to juveniles who commit non-homicide offenses violates the Constitution's prohibition against cruel and unusual punishment. In *Miller v. Alabama*, 132 S.Ct. 2455 (2012), the Court held that sentencing schemes that mandate LWOP for those under 18 at the time of their crimes also violated the prohibition against cruel and unusual punishment, because mandating life without parole for juveniles prevents those meting out punishment from considering a juvenile's lessened culpability and greater capacity for change, and also runs afoul of the requirement for individualized sentencing for defendants facing the most serious penalties. States have responded to Miller in different ways, with courts in Louisiana and Illinois deciding that the ruling applies retroactively and courts in Michigan and Florida deciding that it does not. Iowa's governor has commuted life sentences for 38 individuals serving JLWOP sentences, and North Carolina and Pennsylvania have enacted legislative fixes. DOJ has provided to federal Public Defenders a list of all potentially affected persons in the federal system and is also considering possible federal legislation.

72. Like all criminal defendants in the United States, juveniles charged with homicide offenses are afforded extensive due process and other protections throughout the trial and sentencing process and are provided the ability to appeal their convictions and sentences to the fullest extent afforded by law. While the considerations vary from state to state, JLWOP sentences are generally imposed only after a judge determines, based upon numerous factors such as the juvenile's age, personal circumstances and background, the type and seriousness of the offense, the juvenile's role in the crime, and the juvenile's prior record/past treatment records, that the juvenile can be tried as an adult. A small group of states and the District of Columbia have prohibited JLWOP sentences for all juvenile offenders, and state courts in some jurisdictions have also reduced sentences.

73. Through its enforcement of the Civil Rights of Institutionalized Persons Act and the Violent Crime Control and Law Enforcement Act of 1994, DOJ vigorously protects the rights of juveniles who are incarcerated in facilities run by or for states, including those serving life sentences without parole. The 1974 Juvenile Justice and Delinquency Prevention Act is designed to ensure that youth are not treated merely as "little adults," and that they receive necessary and appropriate rehabilitative services in the least restrictive environment consistent with public safety. The Act created an office within DOJ dedicated to supporting federal, state, and local efforts to prevent juvenile crime, imprisonment in the juvenile justice system, and addressing the needs of juvenile crime victims. This office, the Office of Juvenile Justice and Delinquency Prevention, provides funding to states for system improvement and research to identify optimal prevention and intervention strategies for youth in the juvenile justice system or at risk of entering it. In addition to its traditional work in this area, DOJ/CRT is using authority under a section of the Violent Crime Control and Law Enforcement Act of 1994 to address civil rights violations that occur early in the juvenile justice process. Under this law, DOJ can determine whether youths' civil rights are being violated not only in detention facilities, but in juvenile arrests, juvenile courts, and juvenile probation systems as well. During the last four years, DOJ has used this authority to investigate the conduct of police in arresting children for school-based offenses, and to examine whether juvenile courts and probation systems comply with due process rights, the constitutional guarantee of equal protection, and federal laws prohibiting racial discrimination.

74. For example, under this authority, and based on an extensive investigation, including analysis of over 50,000 youth case files, DOJ/CRT found in 2012 that the juvenile court in Shelby County, Tennessee systemically violated the due process rights of all children who appear for delinquency proceedings, as well as the equal protection rights of African American children. CRT is working with the juvenile court to ensure wholesale reform. Using its authority to protect youths confined in juvenile detention facilities run by state or local governments, CRT also launched an investigation in Meridian, Mississippi that found a "school-to-prison pipeline" in which the rights of children were repeatedly and routinely violated. Children were systematically incarcerated for allegedly committing minor offenses, including school disciplinary infractions, and punished disproportionately without due process of law; the students most affected were Black/African American children and children with disabilities. When the local and state governments administering juvenile justice failed to enter into meaningful settlement negotiations, CRT filed a lawsuit to vindicate the children's rights. While the juvenile justice lawsuit is still pending, CRT reached a comprehensive settlement in a related federal lawsuit against the Meridian Public Schools to prevent and address racial discrimination in the school district's discipline practices. Under the settlement, the district will limit the use of discipline measures that remove students from the classroom, such as suspension; provide training to school personnel on non-discrimination and classroom management;

request law enforcement assistance only when necessary to protect safety; and collect and analyze data on discipline referrals and consequences to identify and address racial disparities.

75. Non-Discrimination in Terrorism Measures and Racial Profiling. In its fight against terrorism, the United States does not unlawfully discriminate against individuals based on race, colour or national or ethnic origin. U.S. anti-terrorism laws, which proscribe knowing or intentional participation in, or provision of material support to, violent unlawful conduct or formally designated Foreign Terrorist Organizations, do not discriminate on grounds of race, colour, or national or ethnic origin. In the aftermath of 9/11, the United States has stepped up its training of law enforcement officers with a view to combating prejudice that may lead to violence, making one of the focus areas for such training the increased bias against Arab Americans and others. The United States seeks to ensure that its laws and practices protect innocent people from violence, while at the same time living up to our commitment of fair treatment.

76. With regard to paragraph 24 of the Committee's concluding observations concerning measures to combat terrorism, the United States is committed to ensuring fairness before tribunals and other organs administering justice, including that all persons appearing before such organs are not discriminated against on grounds of race, colour, or national or ethnic origin.

77. With respect to enemy alien belligerents, the United States provided updated information relating to the Committee's concerns in the 2011 U.S. ICCPR Report, in particular in the discussion regarding habeas corpus, the operation of military commissions, and other proceedings contained in paragraphs 569-582. In brief, the United States has worked to ensure proper treatment of detainees at Guantánamo Bay, Cuba. On January 22, 2009, President Obama issued an Executive Order, entitled "Review and Disposition of Individuals Detained at the Guantánamo Bay Naval Base and Closure of Detention Facilities." That order requires that detention at Guantánamo conform to all applicable laws governing conditions of confinement, including common article 3 of the Geneva Conventions, see E.O. 13492, sec. 6. The Order also directed the Secretary of Defense to review the conditions of detention at Guantánamo. The resulting review by Admiral Walsh found that those conditions comply with, and often exceed, the requirements of common article 3. Moreover, each detainee held by the United States in military detention at Guantánamo Bay is entitled to petition the federal district courts for habeas corpus review of the lawfulness of his detention. Most Guantánamo detainees have availed themselves of this right, and the district and appellate courts have completed review of approximately 50 cases to date. With respect to military commissions, the Military Commissions Act of 2009 made many significant changes, including: prohibiting the admission at trial of statements obtained by use of torture or cruel, inhuman, or degrading treatment, except against a person accused of torture or such treatment as evidence that the statement was made; strengthening the restrictions on admission of hearsay evidence; stipulating that an accused in a capital case be provided with counsel learned in applicable law relating to capital cases; providing the accused with greater latitude in selecting his or her own military defense counsel; enhancing the accused's right to discovery; and establishing new procedures for handling classified information. Finally, regarding the Committee's concerns about non-refoulement to torture, as the United States explained in the 2011 U.S. ICCPR Report, beginning at paragraph 553, consistent with firm U.S. policy, the United States will not transfer any person to a country where it determines that it is more likely than not that the person will be tortured.

78. With respect to the Committee's concerns about the rights of noncitizens and equal treatment in the judicial system, as a matter of U.S. law, aliens within the United States, regardless of their immigration status, enjoy substantial protections under the U.S. Constitution and other domestic laws. Both DHS and DOJ have offices responsible for civil rights and civil liberties that help shape and implement policy, reach out to communities, and investigate and resolve complaints. For Fiscal Year 2012, the DHS Office for Civil Rights and Civil Liberties (CRCL) opened 256 new complaints (compared to 298 in FY 2011) and closed 281 complaints (compared to 219 in FY 2011) involving various DHS components such as ICE, U.S. Customs and Border Protection (CBP), the Transportation Security Administration (TSA), U.S. Citizenship and Immigration Services (USCIS), and others. A number of the closed complaints resulted in policy recommendations related to the protection of individuals' civil rights. Of the 256 new complaints, 26 involved abuse of authority, discrimination, or profiling.

79. DHS/CRCL also runs the CRCL Institute, which provides classroom and on-line training for DHS and other agencies in civil rights protections. In addition, DHS/CRCL, through its Community Engagement Section, engages in extensive outreach to the public and non-governmental organizations, including convening and participating in regular

roundtables with leaders from American Arab, Muslim, Sikh, Somali, Latino, South and Pacific Asian communities, among others, to discuss issues such as disaster preparedness, naturalization wait times, TSA airport screening, outreach to new immigrant communities, searches of electronic devices, and allegations of improper conduct toward Arab, Muslim, Sikh, South Asian and Somali American travellers at U.S. ports of entry. CRCL has established an Incident Community Coordination Team for communication with Arab, Muslim, Sikh, South Asian, and Somali American community leaders in the immediate aftermath of an incident.

80. With regard to paragraph 14 of the Committee's concluding observations concerning racial profiling, the United States recognizes that racial or ethnic profiling is not effective law enforcement practice and is not consistent with our commitment to fairness in our justice system. For many years, concerns about racial profiling arose mainly in the context of motor vehicle or street stops related to the enforcement of drug or immigration laws. More recently, and especially since 9/11, the debate has also included examination of law enforcement conduct in the effort to combat terrorism.

81. In addition to the U.S. Constitution, several federal statutes and regulations impose limits on the use of race or ethnicity by law enforcement, and the Obama Administration has vigorously relied on these tools to respond to such unlawful practices. These include Title VI of the Civil Rights Act of 1964 (prohibiting discrimination in all federally assisted programs or activities), and 42 U.S.C. 14141 (allowing suits against police departments for injunctive relief if they are engaging in a pattern or practice of unlawful conduct). Between 2009 and 2012, DOJ/CRT opened 15 investigations of police departments and currently is pursuing more than two dozen open investigations — the largest number at any one time in history, and involving larger police departments than ever before. In 2012 alone, CRT entered into far reaching, enforceable agreements with six jurisdictions to address serious policing challenges, the most agreements reached in a single year. If a violation is determined to exist, DOJ works with the law enforcement agency to revise policies and procedures and to provide training to ensure the constitutionality of police practices. Recent cases have included: the investigation of the New Orleans Police Department described above under article 5; an investigation of the Seattle Police Department that found an unlawful pattern or practice of excessive force and also raised concerns about discriminatory policing, leading to a court-approved settlement in September of 2012; and an investigation of the East Haven, Connecticut Police Department that found a pattern or practice of discriminatory policing against Hispanics/Latinos, targeting them for discriminatory traffic enforcement, leading to a settlement agreement providing for comprehensive reforms. The East Haven Police Department announced that the Department had hired its first Latino officer — a highly qualified bilingual woman, who will assist with building ties to the immigrant community.

82. DOJ/CRT strongly prefers to work in a cooperative fashion with local governments and police departments to address unconstitutional policing, and in almost every case, it is able to work in that manner to spur reform. DOJ also works with organizations that develop national standards for law enforcement, such as the International Association of Chiefs of Police. However, CRT does not hesitate to use litigation to combat racial profiling or other unlawful policing when cooperation proves elusive. For example, after lack of cooperation by the Maricopa County Sheriff's Office in an investigation of potential anti-Latino bias in policing and jail practices, DOJ filed a wide-ranging lawsuit. In December 2012, a federal court denied the County's motion to dismiss the case, and the litigation is continuing in 2013. In addition, in a case brought by DOJ, the Supreme Court struck down on pre-emption grounds three provisions of Arizona's immigration law, S.B. 1070 — section 3, which made it a crime to fail to carry valid immigration papers; section 5(c), which criminalized applying for or holding a job without proper immigration papers; and section 6, which was found to create an obstacle to federal law by authorizing state and local officers to make warrantless arrests of certain aliens, United States v. Arizona, 132 S. Ct. 2492 (2012). The Court also emphasized that there are serious constitutional questions regarding Section 2 of the Arizona law, which requires law enforcement officials to verify the immigration status of any person lawfully stopped or detained when they have reason to suspect that the person is here unlawfully. The Attorney General issued a statement assuring communities that DOJ will continue vigorously to enforce federal prohibitions against racial and ethnic discrimination, and DOJ is closely monitoring the impact of S.B. 1070 to ensure compliance with federal immigration law and applicable civil rights laws, including ensuring that law enforcement agencies and others do not implement the law in a manner that has the purpose or effect of discriminating against the Latino or any other community. See http://www.justice.gov/opa/pr/2012/June/12-ag-801.html.

83. DHS acts to ensure that its programs and activities are free of invidious racial or ethnic profiling. Certain immigration enforcement programs, including some of those in which DHS cooperates with state and local police to enforce federal immigration law, also contain clear prohibitions against racial and ethnic profiling. Under the 287(g) program, for

example, certain specially trained state and local law enforcement officers are authorized to enforce federal immigration law in jails and prisons. These officers receive specific training to ensure that they do not engage in racial profiling. Individuals alleging racial or ethnic profiling may file complaints with DHS/CRCL and ICE's Office of Professional Responsibility. DHS/CRCL is currently reviewing complaints alleging racial or ethnic profiling with regard to agency language access requirements and other issues in the ICE 287(g) program.

84. DHS continues to enhance its screening methodology; DHS security measures are tailored to specific intelligence about potential threats. These measures, which are part of a dynamic, threat-based process covering all passengers traveling to the United States, do not rely solely on a traveller's country of citizenship to determine the level of screening. Specific screening rules are reviewed quarterly by DHS/CRCL, the DHS Privacy Office, and the DHS Office of the General Counsel.

85. In addition, DHS/CRCL has created a special training program designed to increase the cultural competency of federal, state, local, and tribal law enforcement authorities. The training aims to increase communication, build trust, and encourage interactive dialogue among law enforcement officers and the diverse American communities, in which they work, including Arab, Muslim, South Asian, and Somali American communities, and is particularly designed to equip law enforcement personnel with enhanced competency in communicating with such communities. DOJ, the FBI, and the Coast Guard have also engaged in training for this purpose.

86. Recognizing public concerns related to the National Security Entry-Exit Registration System (NSEERS), DHS conducted several reviews of the program involving substantial consultations with the public and civil society. The reviews resulted initially in narrowing of the program's application and elimination of the domestic call-in portion of the program. As a result of further review and the development of new, enhanced security measures, in April 2011, DHS announced the official ending of the NSEERS registration process, http://www.dhs.gov/dhs-removes-designated-countries-nseers-registration-may-2011. In April 2012, DHS issued internal guidance on the treatment of individuals who were previously subject to, but failed to comply with, NSEERS requirements. It clarified that noncompliance with those requirements, in and of itself, is not a sufficient basis for negative immigration consequences. Rather, negative immigration consequences may apply only where DHS personnel have determined, based on the totality of the evidence, that the individual's NSEERS violation was wilful.

B. Security of person and protection by the State against violence or bodily harm

87. The U.S. Constitution and laws provide protection against violence or bodily harm through statutes such as the Violent Crime Control and Law Enforcement Act of 1994, the Civil Rights Acts, and federal "hate crimes" laws. Hate crimes are discussed under article 4, above.

88. Measures to prevent racially motivated acts of violence and ensure prompt response from the justice system. As described in paragraphs 166 and 177 of the common core document and above under article 4, DOJ/CRS assists state and local governments, private and public organizations, and community groups in preventing and resolving racial and ethnic tensions, incidents, and civil disorders, and restoring racial stability and harmony, through mediation, technical assistance and training. Other federal, state, and local agencies also engage in training and community outreach to prevent racially motivated acts of violence. Please see the discussion of outreach under article 7, below, for some of the measures taken.

89. Measures to prevent use of illegal force by police against protected groups. With regard to article 5 and paragraph 25 of the Committee's concluding observations, the Constitution and federal statutes prohibit racially discriminatory actions by law enforcement agencies, see, e.g., the Pattern or Practice of Police Misconduct provision of the Violent Crime Control and Law Enforcement Act of 1994, 42 U.S.C. 14141, and the Omnibus Crime Control and Safe Streets Act of 1968, 42 U.S.C. 3789d. Since 2009, the Administration has intensified its enforcement of these laws. Federal law prohibits the use of excessive force by any law enforcement officer against any individual in the United States, including members of racial and ethnic minorities, and undocumented migrants crossing U.S. borders. Victims of police brutality may seek legal remedies, such as criminal punishment of the perpetrator or civil damages. DOJ has successfully prosecuted law enforcement officers and public officials were sufficient evidence indicates that they wilfully violated a person's constitutional rights.

90. Depending on the location of the conduct, the actor, and other circumstances, any number of remedies, including the following, may be available:

- Criminal charges, which can lead to investigation and possible prosecution, 18 U.S.C. 242.
- Civil actions in federal or state court under the federal civil rights statute, 42 U.S.C. 1983, directly against state or local officials for money damages or injunctive relief.
- Suits for damages for negligence of federal officials and for negligence and intentional torts of federal law enforcement officers under the Federal Tort Claims Act, 28 U.S.C. 2671 et seq., or of state and municipal officials under comparable state statutes.
- Suits against federal officials directly for damages under provisions of the U.S. Constitution for "constitutional torts," see *Bivens v. Six Unknown Named Agents*, 403 U.S. 388 (1971); *Davis v. Passman*, 442 U.S. 228 (1979).
- Challenges to official action or inaction through judicial procedures in state courts and under state law, based on statutory or constitutional provisions.
- Suits for civil damages from participants in conspiracies to deny civil rights under 42 U.S.C. 1985.
- Claims for administrative remedies for alleged police misconduct.
- Federal civil proceedings under the pattern or practice provision of the Violent Crime Control and Law Enforcement Act of 1994, 42 U.S.C. 14141, or federal administrative and civil proceedings against law enforcement agencies receiving federal funds.
- Individual administrative actions or civil suits against law enforcement agencies receiving federal financial assistance under federal civil rights laws, see 42 U.S.C. 2000d (Title VI); 42 U.S.C. 3789d (Safe Streets Act).
- In the case of persons in detention or other institutionalized settings, federal civil proceedings under the Civil Rights of Institutionalized Persons Act of 1980 (CRIPA), 42 U.S.C. 1997.

91. The Administration aggressively enforces laws against police brutality and discriminatory policing. As noted above, DOJ investigates police departments, prisons and other institutions to ensure compliance with the law and brings legal action where necessary against both institutions and individuals. DOJ has convicted 254 such defendants for violating the civil rights laws between FY 2009 and FY 2012, a 13.4 per cent increase from the number convicted in the previous four years.

92. Within DHS, component agencies such as CBP and ICE are subject to strict restrictions and to investigations, when warranted, regarding incidents of assaults, harassment, threats, or shootings involving employees. State and local law enforcement agency personnel who exercise limited authority to help enforce U.S. immigration laws in prisons and jails under programs such as the ICE 287 (g) program are bound by similar restrictions, and ICE closely monitors their compliance, including through investigations by the ICE Office of Professional Responsibility. All law enforcement officers authorized to perform 287 (g) program functions in prisons and jails must pass a four-week training course at the ICE Academy, which includes coursework on the ICE Use of Force Policy, among other topics.

93. Finally, in addition to government-initiated actions, private litigants may sue law enforcement agencies for discriminatory police activities. See, e.g., *Elliot-Park v. Manglona*, 592 F. 3d 1003 (9th Cir. 2010) (failure to investigate an auto accident due to race of persons involved violated equal protection).

94. Encourage arrangements for communication and dialogue. DOJ/CRS provides conciliation services intended to prevent violence and reduce community tensions stemming from issues of race, colour, and national origin. CRS works directly with local law enforcement and minority communities to address actual or perceived instances of racial profiling, biased policing practices and policies, and the excessive use of force. This is done through a combination of mediation, training, and bringing law enforcement officials and minority community leaders together for facilitated problem-solving dialogues. DOJ/CRS has established a Law Enforcement Mediation Skills Program, designed to equip law enforcement officers with basic mediation and conflict resolution skills. In addition, the DOJ Office of Community Oriented Policing Services (COPS) is charged with advancing the practice of community policing at all levels. To that end, COPS has published more than 35 documents regarding anti-discrimination to help state and local law enforcement.

95. In addition, beginning in 2003, the DOJ Office for Victims of Crime (DOJ/OVC) funded a multiyear effort of the International Association of Chiefs of Police (IACP) to develop and implement a national strategy to create systemic change among law enforcement agencies in their response to victims, both in philosophy and practice. Under the En-

hancing Law Enforcement Response to Victims, the IACP developed and field-tested a comprehensive package of resources for local agencies to facilitate implementation of this shift. The strategy focuses on core elements of leadership, community partnering, training, and performance monitoring — with communication critical to each of those elements. Potential benefits of enhancing law enforcement's response to victims include: better citizen perception of community safety and increased confidence and trust in law enforcement, and greater willingness on the part of victims to cooperate with investigations. The resources are available at www.responsetovictims.org. DOJ, the DHS Federal Law Enforcement Training Center, and state and local agencies and training academies are also heavily involved in training law enforcement officers, including diversity training and training in defusing racially and ethnically tense situations. Law enforcement officers receive periodic training on these issues throughout their careers. The DHS CRCL Institute offers multiple training courses and materials, including materials on working effectively with Arab and Muslim Americans and others. DHS/CRCL also conducts robust and sustained engagement on a regular basis with communities throughout the United States whose civil rights and liberties may be affected by government policies, programs, or personnel. This community engagement takes a whole-of-government approach that ensures the participation of federal, state, and local authorities to address diverse community concerns and provide avenues of redress.

96. Many law enforcement agencies partner with NGOs to provide training to their officers. For example, the non-governmental American-Arab Anti-Discrimination Committee offers a Law Enforcement Outreach Program that has trained representatives of many federal law enforcement agencies, including the FBI, DHS, and the U.S. Park Police, in addition to training more than 20,000 individuals in academic institutions and industries such as the airlines. Local and state law enforcement agencies also reach out to community members.

97. Recruitment of minorities in law enforcement: According to the DOJ Bureau of Justice Statistics (BJS), Federal Law Enforcement Officers, 2008, members of minorities made up 34.3 per cent of all federal law enforcement officers in 2008. This representation included Hispanic/Latino officers (19.8 per cent), non-Hispanic Black/African American officers (10.4 per cent), Asians and Pacific Islander officers (3.0 per cent), and Native American officers (1.0 per cent). There were gains since 1996, when members of minorities made up only 28 per cent of officers, and 2004 when minorities made up 33.2 per cent. The largest gain occurred for Hispanic/Latino officers, who increased from 13.1 per cent in 1996 to 19.8 per cent in 2008, http://bjs.gov/content/pub/pdf/fleo08.pdf. While the composition of the law enforcement community overall now more closely represents that of the U.S. population as a whole, recognizing the importance of broad representation at all levels, police departments and law enforcement agencies continue to reach out to candidates from minority groups.

98. Return or removal to another country: Discussion of immigration relief and protection from removal available to asylum-seekers and other noncitizens in the United States is provided under article 13 of the 2011 U.S. ICCPR Report.

C. Political rights

99. The Fifteenth and Nineteenth Amendments to the U.S. Constitution and other U.S. laws guarantee the equal right to participate in elections, to vote and stand for election, to take part in the conduct of public affairs, and to have equal access to public service without regard to race or ethnicity. Consistent with the Convention, some distinctions are made on the basis of citizenship status. This section discusses recent initiatives to improve equal access to the political system, as well as some particular areas of concern.

100. Enforcement of voting rights: DOJ enforces statutes that protect the right to vote, including the Voting Rights Act of 1965 (VRA), the National Voter Registration Act of 1993 (NVRA), the Help America Vote Act of 2002 (HAVA), and the Uniformed and Overseas Citizens Absentee Voting Act of 1986 (UOCAVA), as amended by the Military and Overseas Voter Empowerment Act of 2009 (the MOVE Act). Among other protections, the VRA prohibits discrimination in voting on the basis of race, colour, or membership in a language minority group; requires certain covered jurisdictions to provide bilingual written materials and other assistance; and requires that voters who require assistance to vote by reason of blindness, disability, or inability to read or write be given assistance by a person of the voter's choice. Section 5 of the VRA requires that any changes in the election practices or procedures of the state and local jurisdictions it covers cannot take effect until those changes have been determined by either DOJ or a three-judge panel of the D.C. District Court to have neither discriminatory purpose nor effect. The NVRA contains a number of requirements for federal elections intended to increase the number of eligible citizens who register to vote and to ensure accurate and current registration lists. HAVA includes a number of minimum standards for election technology and election administration

in federal elections. UOCAVA and the MOVE Act protect the right to register and vote absentee in federal elections for members of the armed services, their families, and overseas citizens.

101. In 2011 and 2012, DOJ/CRT handled record numbers of new voting-related litigation matters, including vigilant enforcement of absentee voting protections for service members and overseas citizens, as well as challenges to state-wide redistricting plans and state photo identification requirements for voting where those changes would have a discriminatory effect. In addition, each year DOJ sends federal observers from the Office of Personnel Management, along with DOJ personnel, into the field to monitor elections around the country and throughout the election calendar, for federal, state, and local elections. The job of personnel deployed as observers is to monitor for violations of federal voting rights laws. In 2012, DOJ assigned more than 1,200 OPM observers and DOJ staff to monitor 101 elections, in 69 different jurisdictions, in 24 states.

102. With regard to paragraph 27 of the Committee's concluding observations, the situation regarding felony disenfranchisement in the United States is described in Part I B of the common core document. The U.S. Constitution generally assigns to the individual states, and not to the U. S. Congress, the responsibility for determining eligibility to vote. At the same time, Congress does have the power to regulate elections for federal offices and also the constitutional authority to eradicate discrimination in voting. Federal legislation addressing voting by former felons in federal elections has been proposed, but not enacted. As described in the common core document, a number of states have limited felony disenfranchisement or have otherwise facilitated the recovery of voting rights for those who can regain them.

103. Issues related to voting representation in Congress for residents of the District of Columbia and insular areas are addressed in paragraph 37 of the common core document.

104. Representation in federal workforce: Members of minorities are well represented in the federal workforce, although not always at levels that reflect their proportion of the overall population. The federal leadership under President Obama evidences broad racial and ethnic diversity. According to the EEOC's Annual Report on the Federal Workforce for FY 2010, the approximately 2.85 million members of the federal workforce include 65.5 per cent White, 7.9 per cent Hispanic/Latinos, 17.9 per cent Black/African Americans (higher than their percentage in the population overall), 5.9 per cent Asians, 0.4 per cent Native Hawaiian and Other Pacific Islanders, 1.6 per cent American Indian/Alaska Natives, and 0.8 per cent persons of two or more races. Over a period of 10 years, the number of Hispanics/Latinos in the total federal workforce has increased by 32.6 per cent, Asians by 37.2 per cent, and Blacks/African Americans by 11.6 per cent. In the same period, their participation in senior level positions also increased — Asians by 130.2 per cent, Hispanics/Latinos by 51.8 per cent, and Blacks/African Americans by 41.4 per cent. However, minority groups remain under-represented at senior levels, with Hispanics/Latinos holding 3.7 per cent, Blacks/African Americans 7.5 per cent, Asian Americans 4.5 per cent, American Indian/Alaska Natives 0.8 per cent, and Native Hawaiian/Pacific Islanders 0.07 per cent of the senior jobs. Recognizing that the federal workforce does not at all levels represent the people it serves, in August 2011 President Obama issued Executive Order 13583, requiring agencies to develop strategies to identify and remove existing barriers to equal employment opportunity in government recruitment, hiring, promotion, retention, professional development, and training. These requirements broadened the President's earlier action in 2009, through Executive Order 13515, to improve participation of Asian Americans and Pacific Islanders in federal programs and employment. In 2012, the EEOC issued practical guidance for federal employers on Asian American and Pacific Islander employment pursuant to E.O. 13515, http://www.eeoc.gov/federal/reports/aapi_practical_guide.cfm. In addition, in 2013 it issued a report compiling reported barriers to the advancement of Black/African American federal workers.

105. Representation in public office: Members of minorities are also represented in federal elected offices, but not at rates that reflect their proportions of the population. As all are aware, the highest office in the United States — the President — is held by a Black/African American, who was elected to a second four-year term in 2012. The proportions of minorities in Congress, as reported in the common core document, generally show modest growth from the levels described in the 2007 Report. In 2011, 10 of the state and territorial governors were members of racial or ethnic minorities — three Blacks/African Americans (Massachusetts, New York, and the U.S. Virgin Islands); three Hispanics/Latinos, one of whom was the first female Hispanic/Latina Governor in the United States (New Mexico, Nevada, and Puerto Rico); and four Asian and Pacific Islanders including one female (Louisiana, South Carolina, American Samoa and Guam). These numbers represent increases from those reported in 2007.

106. According to the 4th edition of the American Bar Association Directory of Minority Judges in the United States, published in 2008, of the approximately 60,000 judges and judicial officers in state, federal, and tribal courts (including in Puerto Rico, Guam, the U.S. Virgin Islands and the Commonwealth of the Northern Mariana Islands) in 2007, 4,169 were members of racial or ethnic minority groups (approximately 6.9 per cent). Of these, 1,751 were Black/African American, 1,452 were Hispanic/Latino American, 384 were Asian or Pacific Islander American, 35 were Native American (in state or federal courts), and 547 were Native American judges serving in tribal courts. This represents a modest increase from the 4,051 minority judges and judicial officers in 2000 and approximately 3,610 in 1997.

107. Involvement in development and implementation of policies and programs: As a matter of law and policy, governments at all levels in the United States endeavour to involve potentially affected persons in decisions concerning laws and policies that may affect them. Persons have access to their elected representatives to make their views known on legislation. Regulatory activity is accomplished through well-established, legally mandated processes that involve publication of proposed regulations and opportunity for public comment. This report contains numerous examples of programmatic outreach to the public to make members of the public aware of their rights and seek public input. With regard to indigenous peoples, U.S. law and policy mandate consultation with tribes in many areas, as described in the response to paragraphs 38 and 29 of the Committee's concluding observations, below.

108. Measures to promote awareness and eliminate obstacles to participation in public life. Robust opportunities for freedom of speech and the right to vote and participate in public life exist in the United States. Officials at all levels engage in active outreach to make the public aware of their rights and opportunities. Non-governmental organizations are also heavily involved in promoting awareness and encouraging involvement.

D. Other civil rights

109. Article 5(d) obligates States parties to ensure equality of enjoyment of a number of human rights and fundamental freedoms, including freedom of movement and residence; the right to leave and return to one's country; the right to nationality; the right to marriage and choice of spouse; the right to own property alone as well as in association with others; the right to inherit; the right to freedom of thought, conscience, and religion; the right to freedom of opinion and expression; and the right to freedom of peaceful assembly and association. These are guaranteed to persons in the United States without regard to race, ethnicity, or national origin, and interference with them may be criminally prosecutable under a number of statutes.

E. Economic, social and cultural rights — see web site source for complete text

II. Information by relevant groups of victims or potential victims of racial discrimination

A. Discussion of types of persons — see source for complete text

In furtherance of its reform of detention management policies and protections, and in addition to other detention reform initiatives noted under the discussion of policy reviews and revisions under article 2 above, ICE has accomplished the following:

- Created an Office of Detention Policy and Planning (ODPP) to coordinate reform efforts (2009).
- Established two advisory boards of local and national stakeholders, and secured on-going non-governmental organization collaboration on key reform initiatives (2009).
- Created the Detention Monitoring Council, which engages ICE senior leadership in the review of detention facility inspection reports, assessment of corrective action plans, and follow-up to ensure that remedial plans are implemented and to determine whether ICE should continue to use a particular facility (2010).
- Created the Enforcement and Removal Operations Public Advocate position to assist in timely resolution of immigration enforcement and detention problems or concerns.
- Initiated nationwide deployment of a new automated Risk Classification Assessment (RCA) instrument containing objective criteria to guide decision-making at detention facilities concerning whether an alien should be detained or released and, if detained, the alien's appropriate custody classification level (2012).
- Established an On-Site Detention Compliance Oversight Program, with a corps of more than 40 new federal Detention Service Managers, located at detention facilities housing more than 80 percent of the detainee

population, who monitor facilities to ensure compliance with ICE detention standards, report and respond to problems, and work with ICE field offices to address concerns (2010).

- Issued a new Transfer Directive that will minimize the long-distance transfer of detainees within ICE's detention system (2012).

- Improved alignment of detention capacity with DHS apprehension activity, resulting in a reduction in pre-final order long-distance transfers from the areas where detainees were apprehended (on-going).

- Issued a revised set of national detention standards, the 2011 Performance-Based National Detention Standards (PBNDS 2011), developed in collaboration with non-governmental stakeholders, to address more effectively the needs of ICE's detainee population for services such as medical and mental health care, legal resources, and protection against sexual abuse while maintaining a safe and secure detention environment (2012).

- Streamlined the process for clinical directors to authorize detainee health care treatment and installed regional managed care coordinators to provide expeditious and on-going case management for complex medical cases (2010).

- Established a toll-free hotline to address concerns from the public, including prosecutorial discretion requests, questions about immigration court cases and detention concerns (2012).

- Launched a Web-based detainee locator system enabling attorneys, family, and friends to find a detainee in ICE custody and to access information about visitation (2010).

- Issued a new Access Policy Directive establishing procedures for stakeholders to tour and visit detention facilities (2011).

- Distributed to all detention facilities a "Know Your Rights" video, developed by the American Bar Association, and self-help legal materials developed by various Legal Orientation Programs (2012).

- Opened Delaney Hall, a 450-bed civil detention facility in Essex, New Jersey, to provide low-risk detainees with improved conditions of confinement, including robust indoor and outdoor recreation, freedom of movement, and contact visitation (2011).

- Opened the Karnes County Civil Detention Center in Karnes City, Texas, which is the first facility designed and built from the ground up with ICE's civil detention reform standards in mind, to offer the least restrictive environment permissible to manage persons in administrative custody (2012) and

- Issued a Notice of Proposed Rulemaking, later required by section 1101 of the Violence Against Women Act of 2013, which amends the Prison Rape Elimination Act, 42 U.S.C. 15601-15609, to make it applicable to DHS and HHS detention and care facilities. The proposed rule sets standards to prevent, detect, and respond to sexual abuse in DHS confinement facilities. See 77 Fed. Reg. 75,300 (Dec 19, 2012); see also 78 Fed. Reg. 8987 (Feb. 7, 2013) (extending comment period) (2012-2013).

...

Indigenous peoples: General discussion of indigenous peoples is found in paragraphs 189-196 of the common core document. The Committee's concluding observations in paragraphs 38 and 29 raise concerns regarding activities to promote the culture and traditions of Native American, Native Hawaiian and Pacific Islander communities, and consultation with indigenous peoples.

Based on the government-to-government relationship between the United States and federally recognized tribes, the United States supports tribal authority over a broad range of internal and territorial affairs, including membership, culture, language, religion, education, information, social welfare, community and public safety, family relations, economic activities, lands and resource management, environment, and entry by non-members, as well as ways and means for financing these autonomous governmental functions. Many states also have comparable statutes. Federal laws and Executive Orders relevant to protection of tribal culture and traditions include:

- The American Indian Religious Freedom Act declares that "it shall be the policy of the United States to protect and preserve for American Indians their inherent right of freedom to believe, express, and exercise the traditional religions of the American Indian, Eskimo, Aleut, and Native Hawaiians," 42 U.S.C. 1996.

- The Native American Graves Protection and Repatriation Act (NAGPRA), 25 U.S.C. 3001 et seq., provides protection for certain cultural resources, including human remains, and funerary or sacred objects excavated or discovered on tribal or federal land.

- Federal law prohibits public schools, colleges, and universities from denying students equal educational opportunities because of their religion. See Title IV of the Civil Rights Act of 1964, 42 U.S.C. 2000c-6.

- Executive Order 13007 directs federal agencies to "accommodate access to and ceremonial use of Indian sacred sites by Indian religious practitioners."

- The Religious Freedom Restoration Act of 1993 (RFRA), 42 U.S.C. 2000bb, invalidates government action that substantially burdens religious exercise unless the action is justified by a compelling governmental interest.

- The Religious Land Use and Institutionalized Persons Act of 2000 (RLUIPA), 42 U.S.C. 2000cc et seq., protects individuals, houses of worship, and other religious institutions from discrimination in zoning and land marking laws, and requires that state and local institutions not place arbitrary or unnecessary restrictions on religious practice of prisoners or those who are institutionalized.

- The National Historic Preservation Act, 16 U.S.C. 470 et seq., provides for the recognition of historic properties of religious and cultural significance to Indian tribes and Native Hawaiian organizations. It also requires federal agencies to consider the effects of projects they carry out, financially assist, or license on historic properties and to consult Indian tribes and Native Hawaiian organizations that attach religious and cultural importance to such properties in that process. The Act also provides for federal funding for Tribal Historic Preservation Officers.

- The Tribal Law and Order Act of 2010 contains provisions to prevent counterfeiting of Indian-produced crafts.

- Executive Order 13592 directs federal agencies "to support activities that will strengthen the Nation by expanding educational opportunities and improving educational outcomes for all AI/AN students in order to fulfill our commitment to furthering tribal self-determination and to help ensure that AI/AN students have an opportunity to learn their Native languages and histories and receive complete and competitive educations that prepare them for college, careers, and productive and satisfying lives."

The U.S. government also recognizes the elected governments of the insular areas and strongly supports the preservation and maintenance of the insular areas' indigenous cultures, including languages and customs. In February 2012, pursuant to Presidential Executive Order 13537, the Office of Insular Affairs in DOI hosted the second annual meeting of the Interagency Group on Insular Areas. This group solicits information and advice from the elected leaders of Guam, American Samoa, the United States Virgin Islands, and the Commonwealth of the Northern Mariana Islands, and makes recommendations to the President annually, or as appropriate, on the establishment or implementation of federal programs concerning these Insular Areas. The results of the meeting are at http://www.doi.gov/oia/igia/2012/index.cfm.

Because it is crucial that U.S. agencies have input from tribal leaders before taking actions that significantly impact tribes, in 2009 President Obama signed the Presidential Memorandum on the implementation of Executive Order 13175, Consultation and Coordination with Indian Tribal Governments, directing all federal agencies to develop detailed plans of action to implement that Order. Numerous federal laws also require consultation with tribes and in some cases with the Native Hawaiian community, on matters that affect them, e.g., the Archaeological Resources Protection Act of 1979; NAGPRA, the National Historic Preservation Act, and the American Indian Religious Freedom Act. Many states also have comparable statutes. Although federal agencies' current consultation policies relative to federally recognized tribes are not generally applicable to the Native Hawaiian community and Indigenous Insular Communities, DOI is taking steps to improve outreach to and participation of those communities as well. This includes educating federal agencies concerning the importance of outreach to the Native Hawaiian community and the benefits of incorporating Native Hawaiian knowledge and experience in federal plans, and developing a DOI Native Hawaiian community consultation policy.

The U.S. government actively pursues outreach to tribes, including tribal consultations. President Obama himself has held four high-level conferences with more than 350 tribal leaders in 2009, 2010, 2011, and 2012 to discuss tribal government priorities. Federal agencies are implementing the consultation plans required by the Presidential Memorandum mentioned above. As a result, the number of tribal consultations is at a very high level, and DOI Bureaus and offices worked through thousands of issues with tribes in 2012. Several agencies have created new offices (VA, USDA) or tribal steering or advisory committees (Department of Energy, HHS) to ensure proper consultation. Some have also experimented with webinars and other online technologies to facilitate participation by tribal leaders. These innovations show the seriousness with which federal agencies are taking these consultations.

Recent and on-going agency consultations and other outreach to tribes include:

- At the direction of the Secretary of Agriculture, between July 2010 and April 2011, the USDA Office of Tribal Relations and the Forest Service engaged in listening sessions in more than 50 locations. Hundreds of tribal elected officials and tribal culture keepers provided recommendations to improve the Forest Service's protection of sacred sites. In December 2012, the Secretary of Agriculture released the resulting report on Indian Sacred Sites and joined the Departments of Defense, Energy and Interior in signing an MOU for access to and protection of sacred sites under a plan of action.

- In May 2011, EPA published its Policy on Consultation and Coordination with Indian Tribes.

- As part of the reissuance of the Cook Inlet National Pollutant Discharge Elimination System Wastewater General Permit for Oil and Gas facilities, EPA, through a contractor, collected traditional ecological knowledge from local tribes, leading to development of two new study requirements for the permit — additional ambient monitoring requirements and no discharge zones. The same template has been used to collect traditional knowledge from North Slope and Northwest Arctic communities regarding permits for discharge of wastewater associated with oil and gas exploration in the Chukchi and Beaufort Seas.

- In July 2010, the World Heritage Committee inscribed the Papahanaumokuakea Marine National Monument as the first mixed (natural and cultural) World Heritage Site in the United States. This was the result of active consultation with the Native Hawaiian community for whom this development has significant importance.

- The DOI Fish and Wildlife Service and DOJ are working with tribes to facilitate eagle feather possession for cultural and traditional uses and to promote coordination in wildlife investigations and enforcement efforts to protect golden and bald eagles. In October 2012, DOJ announced a new policy on this issue. In FY 2012, DOI awarded $8.95 million to support historic preservation for Indian tribes, Alaska Natives, and Native Hawaiian organizations. The National Park Service is also conducting tribal consultations in its consideration of a regulatory change that would allow gathering of plants and minerals on Park lands by members of federally recognized tribes for traditional uses.

- The federal government consults formally and informally with the Northwest Treaty Tribes when considering designation of critical habitat for endangered species, including salmon, to ensure that agencies are informed of relevant tribal science and any potential impacts on the tribes, including tribal treaty fishing rights.

- Since April 2010, ED has held 25 informal and formal regional consultations with tribal officials regarding reauthorization of the ESEA and implementation of Executive Order 13592, covering in particular the importance of preserving Native languages and the strengthening of tribes to participate meaningfully in the education of AI/AN public school children. Drawing from input received at these consultations, the Administration has proposed changes to the ESEA that support, inter alia, flexibility in the use of federal education funds to allow funding for Native language immersion and restoration, and expanded authority for tribal education agencies.

- The DHS Tribal Consultation and Coordination Plan of March 2010 expands the Department's commitment to close coordination with tribal partners across the nation on security initiatives, and continues to ensure direct involvement of tribes in developing regulatory policies, recommending grant procedures, and advising on key issues. Every component and office in the Department has identified a dedicated tribal liaison or point of contact. Further, DHS has formalized agreements with the Tohono O'odham Nation of Arizona, the Seneca Nation of Indians, the Kootenai Tribe of Idaho, and the Pascua Yaqui of Arizona to develop Western Hemisphere Travel Initiative compliant Enhanced Tribal Cards, which verify identity, tribal membership, and citizenship for the purpose of entering the United States by land or sea. This enhances safety and security at U.S. borders while facilitating legitimate travel and trade. CBP is continues to work with other tribes across the country on this initiative.

- Based on tribal consultations and public comment and the passage of the Helping Expedite and Advance Responsible Tribal Homeownership Act (HEARTH Act) in 2012, DOI issued regulations that will streamline the leasing process on Indian lands, spurring increased home ownership and expediting business and commercial development, including renewable energy projects. Two tribal governments have already taken advantage of the new law and regulations and many others are anticipated to follow their example.

...

110. The federal government has also cooperated with tribes to protect tribal lands and resources, including cooperative resource protection activities with the Sac and Fox Tribe on the Iowa River, restoration of the Klamath River through

possible dam removal in partnership with the Klamath River Basin tribes, and assistance to the Great Lakes Indian Fish and Wildlife Commission to assess the impact of land use and climate change on wetlands; a grant of $37.3 million in Recovery Act funds to tribes for wild land fire management and improvement of habitat and watersheds, plus grants of $213 million in Recovery Act funds by the Forest Service to benefit tribes and tribal lands; grants of more than $50 million in the past eight years for 400 conservation projects administered by 162 federally recognized tribes to benefit fish and wildlife resources and habitat; and many other grants and joint projects. In addition, 188 notices of decisions to repatriate human remains and cultural items were published in FY 2012. The Forest Service is also exercising its authority to assist tribes in reburial of over 3,000 sets of human remains and associated cultural items earlier removed from National Forests.

111. Many federal agencies continue to raise awareness of Indian law and policy. One example, "Working Effectively with Tribal Governments," is available to the public and state and local governments online at http://tribal. golearnportal.org/.

112. Regarding the recommendation in paragraph 29 of the Committee's concluding observations, the United States, in announcing its support for the United Nations Declaration on the Rights of Indigenous Peoples, went to great lengths to describe its position on various issues raised by the Declaration. Concerning the Committee's recommendation that the Declaration be used as a guide to interpret CERD treaty obligations, the United States does not consider that the Declaration — a non-legally binding, aspirational instrument that was not negotiated for the purpose of interpreting or applying the CERD — should be used to reinterpret parties' obligations under the treaty. Nevertheless, as stated in the United States announcement on the Declaration, the United States underlines its support for the Declaration's recognition in the preamble that indigenous individuals are entitled without discrimination to all human rights recognized in international law, and that indigenous peoples possess certain additional, collective rights.

113. In response to paragraph 30 of the Committee's concluding observations, the United States strongly supports accountability for corporate wrongdoing regardless of who is affected, and implements that commitment through its domestic legal and regulatory regime, as well as its deep and on-going engagement with governments, businesses, and NGOs in initiatives to address these concerns globally. The United States is a strong supporter of the business and human rights agenda, particularly regarding extractive industries whose operations can so dramatically affect the living conditions of indigenous peoples. In the context of extractive industries, one way we work to promote better business practices is through participation in the Voluntary Principles on Security and Human Rights Initiative (VPI), a multi-stakeholder initiative that promotes implementation of a set of principles that guides extractive companies on providing security for their operations in a manner that respects human rights. The Voluntary Principles discuss, inter alia, consultations with local communities, respect for human rights, and appropriate handling of allegations of human rights abuses in the context of maintaining the safety and security of business operations. The U.S. government has devoted significant resources to ensuring that the VPI has stable foundations to focus more effectively on implementation and outreach efforts. Working with other participants, the United States has helped develop an institutional framework to increase the efficiency and efficacy of VPI. Additionally, in the annual Country Reports on Human Rights Practices, the State Department has in recent years increased efforts to highlight the impacts and the lack of accountability surrounding the extraction of natural resources, including with regard to indigenous peoples.

114. Paragraph 19 of the Committee's concluding observations concerns Decision 1(68) related to the Western Shoshone. The United States respectfully refers the Committee to its 2007 Report and accompanying Annex II for a description of the history of this matter. In 2004, Congress passed a law (the Western Shoshone Land Claims Distribution Act) that authorized distribution of $145 million to qualifying Western Shoshone individuals. Distribution of the funds was completed on September 30, 2012. A total of 5,362 persons were determined eligible to participate in the Judgment, 902 appeals were filed, and final decisions were made by the Assistant Secretary for Indian Affairs. The Western Shoshone Judgment Act also established a Western Shoshone Scholarship, for which rules for eligibility are being drawn up. A total of 45 reports detailing the steps leading to completion of the fund distribution can be found at the IA website.

115. On March 1, 2011, the U.S. District Court for the District of Columbia granted a motion to dismiss in a case challenging the Western Shoshone Claims Distribution Act, Timbisha Shoshone Tribe v. Salazar, 766 F. Supp. 2d 175 (D.D.C. 2011). In this case, a number of individual members of the Timbisha Shoshone Tribe sued in the tribe's name claiming that the Distribution Act unlawfully takes tribal property by distributing the fund to individuals instead of to

the Western Shoshone Tribes, and violates the Equal Protection Clause of the U.S. Constitution because it impermissibly discriminates on the basis of race by distributing the fund to a group of descendants rather than to tribal members. The Court upheld the Distribution Act under a rational basis standard, finding that the classification was not a racial classification. The plaintiff appealed and, on May 15, 2012, the U.S. Court of Appeals for the D.C. Circuit concluded that the individuals who brought the suit (the Kennedy faction) had no standing to bring the case after the federal government recognized the Gholson faction, based on tribal election results, 678 F.3d 935 (D.C. Cir. 2012). The case was remanded with instructions to dismiss the complaint for lack of jurisdiction. The United States believes that it should not interfere in the internal dispute among the Western Shoshone, and that they have been properly compensated for the land at issue.

116. San Francisco Peaks: With regard to concerns that have been raised by the Committee concerning the decision of the United States Forest Service to grant the request of the operator of the Arizona Snow bowl ski area to make artificial snow from reclaimed waste water purchased from the City of Flagstaff, Arizona, the United States offers the following. This issue relates to a modification of a permit for operation of the Snow bowl ski area that has existed since 1937. In considering the modification, the Forest Service engaged in extensive consultations with interested and affected tribes, including the Acoma, Apache, Havasupai, Hopi, Hualapai, Navajo, Southern Paiute, Yavapai, and Zuni. In all, the Forest Service held approximately 41 meetings with tribal representatives, made more than 200 calls to tribal officials, and exchanged 245 letters with tribes as part of the consultation process. These consultations resulted in modifications to the permit to meet specific tribal concerns. In addition, in its decision the Forest Service committed itself to ensuring that the tribes continue to have access to the area for ceremonies and to harvest traditionally used forest products. The Forest Service also noted that, with the support of the tribes, it had previously worked to obtain wilderness status for the Kachina Peaks Wilderness, an 18,960-acre area of the mountain around Snow bowl, and also to remove 74,380 acres encompassing the San Francisco Peaks from mineral entry — all to preserve and protect those areas from future development. The Forest Service continues to seek frequent input of tribes pursuant to a Memorandum of Agreement in which the Forest Service committed, inter alia, to continue to allow the tribes access to the Peaks and to work with them periodically to inspect the condition of the religious and cultural sites on the Peaks and ensure that the tribes' religious activities on the Peaks are uninterrupted.

117. Several tribes objected to the Forest Service's decision and sued in federal courts under the Religious Freedom Restoration Act. Both the U.S. District Court for the District of Arizona and the U.S. Court of Appeals for the Ninth Circuit, however, found that the tribes' rights under the law did not preclude the federal government from authorizing this otherwise permissible activity on federal lands. The Court of Appeals noted that no plants, springs, natural resources, shrines with religious significance, or religious ceremonies would be physically affected by the artificial snow, and that the tribes would continue to have virtually unlimited access to the mountain, including the ski area, for religious and cultural purposes. A second suit, filed in 2009, was also dismissed at the district court level, a decision upheld by the Ninth Circuit Court of Appeals in February 2012. For further discussion of this matter, as well as an overall review of U.S. law and policy concerning consultations with tribes and U.S. legal protection of religious freedom, we respectfully refer the Committee to the discussions in this report, as well as to the U.S. Response, dated November 17, 2011, to the Office of the High Commissioner for Human Rights and the Special Rapporteur on the Rights of Indigenous Peoples.

118. Border Fence: In response to the Committee's March 2013 letter concerning the effects of the border fence on indigenous communities, in particular the Kickapoo Tribe of Texas, the Ysleta Del Sur Pueblo (Tigua) and the Lipan Apache (Nde), the U.S. government recognizes the potential impact that physical security barriers may have on local communities and landowners. More than 200 meetings and consultations have been held, including extensive consultations with American Indian tribes. For example, the government has consulted with the Ysleta Del Sur regarding access to cultural sites that may be affected by the fence. During the deployment of the fence, the DHS/CBP El Paso Sector Program Management Office met with representatives of the Ysleta Del Sur Pueblo and the construction company to ensure that native vegetation, especially the vegetation required for tribal ceremonies, was reseeded once the construction was completed. The Ysleta Del Sur Pueblo and the El Paso Sector also agreed to allow tribal access to the river and flood plain area for religious ceremonies. The Pueblo and the Sector have had a Memorandum of Agreement in place since March 14, 2005 to make allowances for the tribe's cultural and religious practices. In addition, DHS/CBP's Del Rio Sector staff meets with the Kickapoo tribe a few times each year to discuss issues related to tribal lands and border security, and to plan community events. CBP has not conducted outreach specifically related to the border fence with the

Kickapoo; their land is close to thirty miles away from the fence. CBP has not conducted outreach activities with the Lipan Apache tribe.

119. CBP trains its agents and officers in the cultural sensitivities involved in screening, inspection, and patrolling on tribal lands or with travellers transiting areas of operation near tribal artefacts. CBP is aware of the cultural and historic importance of the environments in which it works. CBP outreach encompasses training to respect and preserve the land and its history. An example is the discovery and preservation of two significant Tohono O'odham tribal archaeological areas in 2012. The cultural awareness of CBP to not disturb, but rather document the locations and notify the proper authorities, demonstrates a balance between conducting necessary law enforcement activities and preserving cultural heritage.

120. With regard to litigation, we are not aware of any instance in which lands held by any federally recognized tribe were acquired through eminent domain proceedings for the purposes of constructing the border fence and related infrastructure. The Ysleta del Sur Pueblo joined a number of non-tribal entities in challenging the portions of a U. S. law providing for the waiver of other U. S. laws (and related state and tribal laws) to facilitate construction of the border fence. Although the court rejected the legal position that such a waiver violated the U. S. Constitution, the court did fully consider the arguments. See *County of El Paso, Texas v. Chertoff*, No. 08-CA-196, 2008 WL 4372693 (W.D. Tex. Aug. 29, 2008), cert. denied, 129 S. Ct. 2789 (2009).

121. Minorities and descent-based communities: As noted in the common core document and throughout this report, despite the existence, implementation, and enforcement of myriad laws, policies, and programs designed to ensure equality for all, some members of racial and ethnic minorities, in particular Blacks/African Americans, Hispanics/Latinos, and Native Americans, continue to experience disproportionate levels of poverty, lower educational attainment, and other problems. Significant progress has been made in these areas, including as a result of the laws, policies and programs described throughout this report, but we recognize that we still have a great distance to go before we reach our goal.

122. Women: Committee guidelines request a description of factors affecting and difficulties experienced in ensuring the equal enjoyment by women, free from racial discrimination, of rights under the Convention. Discrimination based on sex, gender and race or ethnicity can take different forms, including race/ethnic-and gender-based violence, higher poverty rates for women of disadvantaged racial and ethnic groups, differences in educational attainment, and discrimination in the labour market, health care, and other areas. Minority women have made strides in a number of areas; for example, as noted in paragraph 13 of the common core document, in 2009 Hispanic/Latino women were more likely than Hispanic/Latino men to have college degrees or higher — a change from prior years back to 1970. From 1970 to 2009, the percentage of Black/African American women with college degrees also grew faster than that for Black/African American men. Despite gains, however, problems remain for women in general, including minority women — in particular with respect to discrimination in salary and promotions and harassment in employment; discrimination in sale and rental of housing; and violence against women. This section discusses gender related dimensions of race/ethnic discrimination with regard to two particular areas of concern expressed by the Committee — sexual violence and women's health issues.

123. In response to paragraph 26 of the Committee's concluding observations concerning sexual violence, individuals of every race, gender, and background face sexual violence; however, some communities are disproportionately affected. The United States believes that the best response to violence against women — the response most likely to empower survivors and hold offenders accountable — is a response driven and defined by the community served. Recognizing this, the United States provides grants to community organizations serving minority women who are survivors of sexual assault.

124. As noted by the Committee, an area of particular concern is violence against American Indian and Alaska Native women. Addressing such violence is an Administration priority. The problem stems at least in part from the fact that under U.S. law, tribal authorities have been prevented from exercising criminal jurisdiction over non-Indians on Indian lands, and are also limited in their criminal sentencing authority. Provisions proposed by DOJ and included in the 2013 reauthorization of VAWA address this situation with regard to certain common domestic abuse cases, as noted below.

125. Title XI of the 2005 reauthorization of VAWA, "The Safety for Indian Women Act," was designed to strengthen the capacity of Indian tribes and Alaska Natives communities to respond to violent crimes against women. Recognizing that more must be done, in July 2010 President Obama signed the Tribal Law and Order Act, which expands support for BIA and tribal officers; includes new guidelines and training for domestic violence and sex crimes; strengthens tribal courts and police departments; strengthens cooperation among tribal, state, and federal agencies; and enhances programs to combat drug and alcohol abuse and help at-risk youth. In April 2011, the Attorney General approved establishment of a National Coordination Committee to solicit advice about the complex issues surrounding the response to sexual violence in AI/AN communities and to advise DOJ's Office for Victims of Crime and other DOJ components about the unique cultural issues faced by AI/AN adult and child victims of sexual violence. The Committee, composed of representatives from tribal organizations and federal agencies, is developing recommendations to enhance the ability of federal agencies and tribal communities to address sexual violence against AI/AN adults and children. The 2013 reauthorization of VAWA, signed by President Obama in March of 2013, also significantly improves the safety of Native women and allows federal and tribal law enforcement agencies to hold more perpetrators of domestic violence accountable for their crimes.

126. Numerous federal agencies have programs aimed at preventing violence against Native American women. In FY 2012, the DOJ Office on Violence Against Women (OVW) awarded $36 million to more than 67 tribal governments and their designees to enhance the ability of tribes to respond to violent crimes, including sexual assault, domestic violence, dating violence and stalking, against AI/AN women; enhance victim safety; and develop education and prevention strategies. DOJ has also provided funding to establish a national clearinghouse on sexual assault for Native women — a one-stop shop where tribes can request on-site training and technical assistance in developing tribal sexual assault codes, establishing Sexual Assault Response Teams, and accessing tools to gain sexual assault forensic evidence collection certifications. In 2012, DOJ provided funding to four tribes to cross-designate tribal prosecutors to pursue violence against women cases in both tribal and federal courts. The Tribal Special Assistant U.S. Attorney initiative is another step in DOJ's on-going efforts to increase engagement, coordination, and action on public safety in tribal communities; it involves OVW, the Executive Office of U.S. Attorneys, and the U.S. Attorneys' Offices in Montana, Nebraska, New Mexico, North Dakota, and South Dakota. Many examples of actions taken to address violence against AI/AN women are listed in the Public Safety section of the December 2012 White House publication, "Continuing the Progress in Tribal Communities."

127. In FY 2010, HHS awarded $87 million through the Family Violence Prevention and Services Program in support of more than 1,600 tribal and community-based domestic violence prevention and service programs. Annually, these programs respond to more than 2.7 million calls to crisis hotlines, and provide emergency shelter and other services to more than 119,300 victims of domestic violence and 120,900 children. This funding also supports state, territorial, and tribal programs to prevent family violence and to provide immediate shelter and related assistance for victims of family violence and their dependents. Institutions such as the Asian and Pacific Islander Institute on Domestic Violence, the Institute on Domestic Violence in the African American Community, Casa de Esperanza: the National Latina Network of Healthy Families and Communities, and the National Indigenous Women's Resource Center, Inc. also raise awareness and improve services for minority communities.

128. With regard to educational institutions, in April 2011, Vice President Biden and Secretary of Education Duncan announced ED's issuance of guidance to make clear that under Title IX of the Education Amendments of 1972 discrimination can include sexual violence, and thus any school, college or university receiving federal funds is obligated to respond promptly and effectively to sexual violence. The guidance also provides practical enforcement strategies. In addition, ED's Office of Safe and Healthy Students uses the Internet, listservs, and trainings to elevate the awareness of educators, parents, and students about trafficking of children and to increase identification of trafficked children in schools. A toolkit on trafficking in persons, which will help school personnel better identify and serve students who are vulnerable to trafficking recruitment and students who have been victimized by trafficking, is expected to be available in late 2013. With regard to housing, DOJ and HUD actively enforce the Fair Housing Act's provisions against sexual harassment in housing, including pursuing many cases that involve minority women survivors of such harassment. HUD also issued guidance in 2011 to clarify that residents who are denied or evicted from housing as a result of domestic violence may have the basis to file discrimination complaints under the federal Fair Housing Act.

129. Through its Federal Law Enforcement Training Center (FLETC) and the ICE Victim Assistance Program (VAP), and with the assistance of non-government organizations, DHS actively trains its law enforcement personnel concerning issues related to violence against women in its immigration and law enforcement activities. All VAP providers must adhere to the DOJ Attorney General Guidelines for Victim and Witness Assistance 2011 Edition (rev. May 2012). VAP responds to victims' issues in crimes, including human trafficking, child pornography, child sex tourism, white collar crime, and human rights abuses; and DHS/CRCL's Compliance Branch investigates allegations of sexual assault, harassment, or abuse occurring in DHS detention facilities. DHS is also actively pursuing its "Blue Campaign" to combat human trafficking through enhanced public awareness and law enforcement training.

130. The BJS publication, "Criminal Victimization, 2011," indicates that the overall rate of violent crime declined from 32.1 to 22.5 victimizations per 1,000 persons age 12 and older from 2002 to 2011. This continues a long-term decline from 79.8 victimizations per 1,000 in 1993. Likewise, the rape/sexual assault rate fell from 1.5 per 1,000 persons in 2002 to 1.0 per 1,000 persons in 2010 and 0.9 per 1,000 persons in 2011. The study showed that violence against males and persons 24 and younger occurred at higher or somewhat higher rates than rates of violence against females and persons 25 and older. In 2011, no differences were detected in the rate of violence committed against Blacks/African Americans, Whites, or Hispanics/Latinos. However, the rate of serious violence (rape, sexual assault, robbery, and aggravated assault) for Blacks/African Americans was higher than the rate for Whites and Hispanics/Latinos. About half (49 per cent) of all violent crimes were reported to the police, with violent crimes against females more likely to be reported (58 per cent) than those against males (42 per cent). In January 2012, the Attorney General announced revisions to the Uniform Crime Report's definition of rape, which will lead to a more comprehensive statistical reporting of rape.

131. That violence against women is decreasing overall does not negate the serious problems experienced by women who are survivors of violence or the particular intensity of the problem for AI/AN women. The BJS National Crime Victimization Survey for 2011 indicates that the overall rate of violence for Native Americans is 45 per 1,000, with Native American males having a rate of 44 per 1,000 and Native American females with rates of 47 per 1,000.

132. With regard to paragraph 33 of the Committee's concluding observations, the United States recognizes that more can be done to increase women's access to health care, reduce unintended pregnancies, and support maternal and child health. As President Obama noted in his May 2009 speech at the University of Notre Dame, we must begin "reducing unintended pregnancies, and making adoptions more available, and providing care and support for women who do carry their child to term." In part to address these issues, the White House established the White House Council on Women and Girls in 2009. The United States is also increasing women's access to health care through the ACA which, inter alia, ensures that more women have access to health care services for healthy pregnancies, including screening for harmful conditions and smoking cessation and alcohol counselling programs.

133. The HHS Office of Population Affairs oversees the Title X Family Planning Program, which is the only federal grant program dedicated solely to providing individuals with comprehensive family planning and related preventive health services. This program is designed to provide access to contraceptive services, supplies, and information to all who want and need them. By law, priority is given to persons from low-income families. Title X-supported clinics also provide related preventive health services such as patient education and counselling; breast and cervical cancer screening; sexually transmitted disease (STD) and HIV prevention education, counselling, testing, and referral. In fiscal year 2012, Congress appropriated more than $297 million for family planning activities under Title X, and in calendar year 2012, 98 Title X grantees provided family planning services to approximately 5 million women and men through a network of more than 4,500 community-based clinics, including state and local health departments, tribal organizations, hospitals, university health centers, independent clinics, community health centers, faith-based organizations, and others. Approximately 75 per cent of U.S. counties have at least one clinic that provides Title X services.

134. Through its Personal Responsibility Education Program, HHS awards grants to state agencies to educate young people on both abstinence and contraception to prevent pregnancy and sexually transmitted infections, including HIV/AIDS. The program targets youth ages 10-19 who are homeless, in foster care, live in rural areas or in geographic areas with high teen birth rates, or are members of racial or ethnic minority groups. The program also supports pregnant youth and mothers under the age of 21.

135. In September 2010, HHS awarded $27 million to support pregnant and parenting teens and women in states and tribes across the country. Of these funds, $24 million was awarded to 17 states and tribes through the Pregnancy Assis-

tance Fund, created by the ACA. Also in September 2010, the HHS Office of Adolescent Health awarded $100 million in teen pregnancy prevention grants to support programs that have been found effective through rigorous research and to test new models and innovative strategies to prevent teen pregnancy. As of September 2012, a total of $12 million was awarded to 25 tribes, tribal organizations, and urban Indian organizations through the Tribal Maternal, Infant, and Early Childhood Home Visiting (MIECHV) Grant Program. This program also serves high risk American Indian and Alaska Natives, Native Hawaiians, Pacific Islanders, African American, Puerto Rican and other Hispanic ethnicities in high-need maternal and child health disparate communities. In FY 2011, MIECHV grants (totalling $250 million) were provided to every state.

136. To address the complex challenges to safe motherhood, the Maternal and Child Health Services Title V Block Grant Program provided $556 million in federal funds for comprehensive maternal health services, including access to prenatal and postnatal care for low-income and at-risk pregnant women. In 2009, more than 39 million individuals were served, including 2.5 million pregnant women, 4.1 million infants, 27.6 million children, and 1.9 million children with special health care needs. The HHS Health Resources Services Administration (HRSA) has also developed the Bright Futures for Women's Health and Wellness Initiative to encourage patient — provider relationships and better health among women across their lifespans. One of its target populations is underserved and minority women.

137. In July 2010, the United States issued a National HIV/AIDS Strategy and Federal Implementation Plan to: (1) reduce HIV incidence; (2) increase access to care and optimize health outcomes; and (3) reduce HIV related health disparities. Also, in March 2012 a working group was established by Presidential Memorandum to look at health-related disparities and the intersection of HIV/AIDS, violence against women and girls, and gender-related health disparities. To address disparities in HIV prevention and care involving racial and ethnic minorities and other marginalized populations, the United States is committed to reducing HIV-related mortality in communities at high risk for HIV infection; adopting community-level approaches to reduce HIV infection in high-risk communities; and reducing stigma and discrimination against people living with HIV.

138. The Black/African American infant mortality rate is twice as high as the national average. In May 2007, the HHS Office of Minority Health (OMH) launched A Healthy Baby Begins with You, a national campaign to raise awareness about infant mortality with an emphasis on the Black/African American community. Since 2008, OMH has held more than 60 awareness events (health fairs, community meetings, etc.), conducted media outreach, and launched a successful preconception education effort with colleges and universities, including training for more than 1,000 Preconception Peer Educators in more than 100 schools. In addition, in December 2012, OMH launched "Native Generations," a campaign to improve birth outcomes and lower infant mortality rates among AI/AN.

B. Racial discrimination mixed with other causes of discrimination

139. As noted in this report and in Section III B 1 of the common core document, most U.S. laws prohibit discrimination based on a number of different factors, including factors not covered by the Convention. Cases may be brought and won based on multiple types of discrimination.

Article 6

140. U.S. law offers numerous avenues for individuals to seek remedies for acts of racial discrimination. While litigation can be costly, lower-cost administrative remedies are also available in many cases at all levels. Available remedies are described in paragraphs 156-158 of the common core document and in the response to paragraph 25 of the Committee's concluding observations above.

141. As noted throughout this report, government agencies at all levels and civil society organizations engage in active outreach to provide information concerning rights and remedies. U.S. law and policy also seek to ensure that victims do not fear or endure reprisals for seeking relief from discrimination; retaliation is a basis for suit with regard to employment discrimination. Agencies train their enforcement officials to ensure that they are sufficiently alert to and aware of offenses with racial motives, and that victims can trust that police and judicial authorities will address complaints with fairness and effectiveness. We recognize that responses by authorities do not always meet the standards sought, and we commit to continue to improve outreach and services to victims of discrimination at all levels.

142. With regard to issues related to burden of proof in civil proceedings and paragraph 35 of the Committee's concluding observations, as noted above in response to paragraph 10 of the Committee's concluding observations, U.S. law does not invariably require proof of discriminatory intent. While a violation of the U.S. Constitution requires such proof, many of our most fundamental civil rights statutes and regulations go further, prohibiting policies or practices that have an unjustified disproportionate or disparate impact on racial or ethnic minorities and other protected classes. When the facts support the use of disparate impact theory, the United States is committed to using these valuable tools.

143. For example, under Title VII of the Civil Rights Act of 1964, as amended, the principal federal legislation prohibiting race-based employment discrimination, an employer may be liable for employment practices that are intentionally discriminatory (disparate treatment) or that are facially neutral but disproportionately screen out racial or other minorities, absent a demonstration that the challenged practice is job related for the position in question and consistent with business necessity. The burdens of proof in these two types of cases differ.

144. To prevail in a Title VII disparate treatment case, a plaintiff must establish that race or another protected characteristic was a motivating factor for an employment practice. Title VII follows the conventional rule of civil litigation in the United States, which requires the plaintiff to prove his or her case by a preponderance of the evidence. Typically, the plaintiff does this by establishing a prima facie case of discrimination and then by showing that the employer's asserted reason for the employment practice was a pretext for discrimination. A prima facie case of disparate treatment is relatively easy to establish, and therefore may create only a weak inference of discrimination. Its main function is to eliminate some of the more common non-discriminatory reasons for an employment decision, such as that the plaintiff was not qualified for the job. By eliminating these reasons, the prima facie case creates an inference of discrimination in the absence of evidence of a legitimate, non-discriminatory reason for the decision. By presenting evidence that the decision was taken for a non-discriminatory reason, the employer, in turn, can eliminate that inference. To prevail, the plaintiff bears the ultimate burden of proof in showing that the employer's action was motivated by discrimination. Often, this is accomplished by showing that the employer's stated reason for its action was really a pretext for discrimination.

145. A disparate impact claim, on the other hand, requires a plaintiff to isolate a specific employment practice and to show that it has a significant disparate impact on racial or ethnic minorities. In a disparate impact case, once there has been a sufficient showing of impact, the employer's only defense is to show that the action is job related for the position in question and justified by business necessity. An employer is in a much better position than the plaintiff to establish whether its policy is required for safe or efficient business operations, and therefore, the employer bears the burden of proof in showing business necessity. The employee ultimately has an opportunity to rebut the employer's business necessity case by showing that alternative policies or practices could satisfy the employer's needs with less impact on the affected group.

Article 7

146. The United States engages broadly and at all levels in measures to combat prejudice and promote understanding and tolerance.

147. Education and teaching: Development of educational curricula in the United States is decentralized, with primary responsibility for education at the state and local levels. Many schools feature human rights education, and some colleges, universities and law schools have special centers devoted to the study of human rights. Educational programs are often developed in partnership with NGOs, such as Amnesty International USA and the Education Caucus, a branch of the U.S. Human Rights Network. Although the federal government does not have authority to direct or control curricula or programs of instruction in schools, ED engages in initiatives to further the principles of human rights, civil responsibility, and character development, including knowledge about diverse cultures and religious traditions, tolerance, civility, and mutual respect. Recently ED began a civic learning and engagement initiative to encourage and strengthen high-quality civic education, including civic principles and civic, global, and intercultural literacy, http://www.ed.gov/civic-learning. ED's 2012 report on enhancing civic learning explains that, "[d]one well, civic education teaches students to communicate effectively, to work collaboratively, to ask tough questions, and to appreciate diversity."

148. Culture. Activities to promote cultural understanding, tolerance and friendship among groups are discussed throughout this report, including in the responses to Committee observations 29 and 38 concerning indigenous peoples, above.

149. Information. Although the United States does not have "State media," the federal agencies that address discrimination actively develop and disseminate publications and fact sheets designed to ensure that the issue of racial and ethnic equality is kept in the consciousness of the American public. Publications are available in multiple languages, including Chinese, Arabic, Haitian Creole, Korean, Russian, Spanish, Vietnamese, Farsi, Hindi, Laotian, Urdu, Tagalog, Hmong and Punjabi.

150. Racial and ethnic prejudice is also the focus of attention by both print media and other forms of public communication. Newspapers throughout the United States routinely publish articles on issues related to race and ethnicity, and the non-print media increasingly addresses these difficult issues as well. Training and continuing education is available for journalists through a number of organizations and associations.

151. With regard to paragraph 36 of the Committee's concluding observations, in recent years, the U.S. government has increased its outreach to state, tribal, and local human rights organizations concerning the roles they play in implementing U.S. human rights treaty obligations. For example, in 2009, DOS Legal Adviser Koh sent a memorandum to state governors providing information on our human rights treaty obligations and asking that they share the information with their Attorneys General and other relevant officials. Legal Adviser Koh also sent letters requesting input for U.S. human rights reports to state governors in 2010 and to tribal officials in 2011. We also have sought to improve coordination at all levels, working with the International Association of Official Human Rights Agencies. The DOS website contains considerable information relating to U.S. human rights treaty obligations, including the U.S. reports and the conclusions and observations adopted by the human rights treaty bodies.

152. Other outreach: Other U.S. agencies are also actively engaged in outreach to the public concerning the domestic protections that relate to, and in many cases implement, our CERD and other human rights treaty obligations and related commitments, including the following:
- DOJ — DOJ/CRS trains community leaders and law enforcement officers, and conducts community dialogues and mediations to prevent discrimination and to promote peace. CRS has also reached out to identify ways the NGO and law enforcement communities can work together to facilitate reporting, investigation, and prevention of hate crimes.
- HHS — HHS/OCR provides training and technical assistance to ensure that the more than 500,000 health care and human service programs that receive HHS funds comply with civil rights laws. In FY 2011 OCR provided training and technical assistance to more than 100,000 individuals, partnering with health agencies and professional associations.
- DHS — In addition to the many training programs it offers for law enforcement and other officials at all levels of government, DHS/CRCL conducts regular roundtables and meetings to bring together federal, state, and local government officials with community leaders to raise awareness of issues related to racial profiling and discrimination. In 2011, CRCL expanded engagement with new communities and in new geographic areas, increased engagement with youth, raised CRCL's online profile through social networking, continued to work with ethnic media outlets, and broadened DHS participation in major ethnic and religious community conventions and conferences.
- ED — ED/OCR conducts hundreds of technical assistance and outreach activities each year with institutions and individuals. Extensive materials are posted on ED's website in English and 19 other languages.
- EEOC — In addition to technical assistance programs provided to educate employers on anti-discrimination laws, the EEOC conducts extensive public outreach and awareness programs, including special efforts to reach historically underserved populations. In FY 2012, the EEOC conducted 3,992 no-cost events for the public, and nearly 1,000 other educational events for employers.

III. Additional issues raised by the Committee

153. Regarding the Committee's observations in paragraph 39 concerning the Durban Declaration and Program of Action, the concerns of the United States about the 2001 Durban Declaration and Programme of Action (DDPA) and its follow-up are well known. In 2009, after working to try to achieve a positive, constructive outcome in the Durban Review Conference that would get past the deep flaws of the Durban process to date to focus on the critical issues of racism, the United States withdrew from participating because the review conference's outcome document reaffirmed, in its entirety, the DDPA which unfairly singled out Israel and endorsed overbroad restrictions on freedom of expression that

run counter to the U.S. commitment to robust free speech. Regarding the Committee's observations in paragraph 40 concerning the optional declaration provided for in article 14, the United States remains aware of the possibility of making the optional declaration under article 14, but has not made a decision to do so. As noted in the 2007 Report, if such a declaration were contemplated, it would be submitted to the Senate for consent to ratification. With regard to the Committee's observations in paragraph 41 concerning ratification of the amendment to article 8, the United States has no plans to do so. The Committee's observations in paragraph 42 concerning making reports and observations readily available to the public are addressed in paragraph 5 of this report and in other discussions of outreach to the public. Its observations in paragraph 43 concerning consultation with civil society are addressed in paragraph 3 of this report.

Source: United Nations, International Convention on the Elimination of All Forms of Racial Discrimination, 3 October 2013, Original: English, Committee on the Elimination of Racial Discrimination, Reports submitted by States parties under article 9 of the Convention

4. INTERNATIONAL CONVENTION ON THE ELIMINATION OF ALL FORMS OF RACIAL DISCRIMINATION, 25 SEPTEMBER 2014

This is the CERD committee's response, with new and on-going concerns and recommendations along with thorough concluding observations, to the U.S. submission of its 7th through 9th periodic report.

{Excerpt}

Committee on the Elimination of Racial Discrimination Concluding observations on the combined seventh to ninth periodic reports of the United States of America

1. The Committee considered the seventh to ninth periodic reports of the United States of America, submitted in one document (CERD/C/USA/7-9), at its 2299th and 2300th meetings (CERD/C/SR.2299 and SR.2300), held on 13 and 14 August 2014. At its 2317th meeting, held on 26 August 2014, it adopted the following concluding observations.

A. Introduction

2. The Committee welcomes the combined seventh to ninth periodic reports submitted by the State party, which provides detailed information on the implementation of the recommendations contained in the previous concluding observations of the Committee (CERD/C/USA/CO/6).

3. The Committee also welcomes the supplementary information provided orally by the State party's large and diverse delegation to the issues raised by the Committee during the frank and constructive dialogue.

B. Positive aspects

4. The Committee notes with appreciation the legislative and policy developments in the State party to combat racial discrimination, since its last report, including:

(a) The termination of the National Security Entry-Exit Registration System in April 2011, as recommended by the Committee in its previous concluding observations (para. 14);

(b) The issuance of Executive Order 13583, requiring agencies to develop strategies to identify and remove existing barriers to equal employment opportunity in Government recruitment, hiring, promotion, retention, professional development and training, as well as Executive Order 13515 of October 2009 aimed at improving the participation of Asian Americans and Pacific Islanders in federal programmes and employment;

(c) The increased use of the "systemic initiative" by the Equal Employment Opportunity Commission to target "class-based recruitment and hiring practices that discriminate against racial and ethnic groups," which has resulted in an increased number of systemic lawsuits and financial settlements;

(d) The adoption of the Fair Sentencing Act, in August 2010, which has reduced, although not eliminated, the disparity between more lenient sentences for powder-cocaine charges and more severe sentences for crack-cocaine charges, which are more frequently brought against members of racial and ethnic minorities;

(e) The adoption of the Matthew Shepard and James Byrd, Jr. Hate Crimes Prevention Act, in October 2009, which, inter alia, creates a new federal prohibition on hate crimes and simplifies the jurisdictional predicate for prosecuting violent acts undertaken because of actual or perceived race, colour or national origin;

(f) The enactment of the Lilly Ledbetter Fair Pay Act, in January 2009, which overrides the Supreme Court decision in *Ledbetter v. Goodyear Tire & Rubber Co.* and enables the 180-day statute of limitations for bringing a wage discrimination claim to be reset with each payment of wages, benefits or other compensation.

C. Concerns and recommendations

Applicability of the Convention at the national level

5. While noting the applicability of the disparate impact doctrine in certain fields of life, the Committee remains concerned at its limited scope and applicability. It thus reiterates its previous concern that the definition of racial discrimination used in federal and state legislation, as well as in court practice, is not in line with article 1, paragraph 1, of the Convention on the Elimination of All Forms of Racial Discrimination, which requires States parties to prohibit and eliminate racial discrimination in all its forms, including practices and legislation that may not be discriminatory in purpose, but are discriminatory in effect (para. 10). The Committee expresses further concern at the lack of progress in withdrawing or narrowing the scope of the reservation to article 2 of the Convention and in prohibiting all forms of discriminatory acts perpetrated by private individuals, groups or organizations (para. 11) (arts. 1 (1), 2 and 6).

The Committee underlines the responsibility of the federal Government for the implementation of the Convention, and calls upon the State party to take concrete steps to:

(a) Prohibit racial discrimination in all its forms in federal and state legislation, including indirect discrimination, covering all fields of law and public life, in accordance with article 1, paragraph 1, of the Convention;

(b) Consider withdrawing or narrowing its reservation to article 2 of the Convention and broaden the protection afforded by law against all discriminatory acts perpetrated by private individuals, groups or organizations;

(c) Improve the system of monitoring and response by federal bodies to prevent and challenge situations of racial discrimination.

National human rights institution

6. While taking note of the creation of the Equality Working Group, the Committee reiterates its concern at the lack of an institutionalized coordinating mechanism with capacities to ensure the effective implementation of the Convention at the federal, state and local levels (para. 13). Noting the role that an independent national human rights institution can play in that regard, the Committee expresses regret at the lack of progress in establishing a national human rights institution, as recommended in its previous concluding observations (para. 12) (art. 2).

The Committee recommends that the State party create a permanent and effective coordinating mechanism, such as a national human rights institution established in accordance with the principles relating to the status of national institutions (the Paris Principles) (General Assembly resolution 48/134, annex) to ensure the full implementation of the Convention throughout the State party and the territories under its effective control, monitor compliance of domestic laws and policies with the provisions of the Convention and systematically carry out anti-discrimination training and awareness-raising activities at the federal, state and local levels.

Special measures

7. Taking note of the Supreme Court decision of April 2014 in *Schuette v. Coalition to Defend Affirmative Action* and the measures adopted by several states against the use of affirmative action in school admissions, the Committee expresses

concern at the increasing restrictions, based on race or ethnic origin, on the use of special measures as a tool to eliminate persistent disparities in the enjoyment of human rights and fundamental freedoms (art. 2 (2)).

The Committee reiterates its previous recommendation (para. 15) to adopt and strengthen the use of special measures, which is an obligation arising from article 2, paragraph 2, of the Convention, when circumstances warrant their use as a tool to eliminate the persistent disparities in the enjoyment of human rights and fundamental freedoms, based on race or ethnic origin. In that regard, it recommends that the State party take into account the Committee's general recommendation No. 32 (2009) on the meaning and scope of special measures in the International Convention on the Elimination of All Forms Racial Discrimination.

Racial profiling and illegal surveillance

8. While welcoming the acknowledgement by the State party that racial or ethnic profiling is not effective law enforcement practice and is inconsistent with its commitment to fairness in the justice system, the Committee remains concerned at the practice of racial profiling of racial or ethnic minorities by law enforcement officials, including the Federal Bureau of Investigation (FBI), the Transportation Security Administration, border enforcement officials and local police (arts. 2, 4 (c) and 5 (b)).

Recalling its general recommendation No. 31 (2001) on the prevention of racial discrimination in the administration and functioning of the criminal justice system, the Committee urges the State party to intensify efforts to effectively combat and end the practice of racial profiling by federal, state and local law enforcement officials, including by:

(a) Adopting and implementing legislation which specifically prohibits law enforcement officials from engaging in racial profiling, such as the End Racial Profiling Act;

(b) Swiftly revising policies insofar as they permit racial profiling, illegal surveillance, monitoring and intelligence gathering, including the 2003 Guidance Regarding the Use of Race by Federal Law Enforcement Agencies;

(c) Ending immigration enforcement programmes and policies which indirectly promote racial profiling, such as the Secure Communities programme and the Immigration and Nationality Act section 287(g) programme;

(d) Undertaking prompt, thorough and impartial investigations into all allegations of racial profiling, surveillance, monitoring and illegal intelligence-gathering; holding those responsible accountable; and providing effective remedies, including guarantees of non-repetition.

Racist hate speech and hate crimes

9. The Committee reiterates its concern at the lack of prohibition of racist hate speech, except for instances amounting to incitement to imminent violence or "true threats" of violence, as well as the wide scope of the reservations to article 4 of the Convention (para. 18). The Committee is also concerned at the underreporting of instances of hate crimes by the victims to the police, as well as by law enforcement officials to the FBI, given the voluntary nature to comply with the request of the FBI for hate crime statistics (arts. 2 and 4).

The Committee recommends that the State party:

(a) Consider withdrawing or narrowing its reservation to article 4 of the Convention, taking into account the Committee's general recommendation No. 35 (2013) on combating racist hate speech, which outlines diverse measures to effectively combat racist hate speech while protecting the legitimate right to freedom of expression;

(b) Improve its data collection system for statistics on complaints of hate crimes, including by officially requiring all law enforcement agencies to record and transmit all such instances to the FBI, disaggregated by factors such as race, ethnicity, age and religion, and regularly publicize such information;

(c) Ensure that all law enforcement officials and all new recruits are provided with initial and ongoing in-service training on the investigation and reporting of complaints of hate crimes;

(d) Provide statistical information concerning trends in instances of racist hate speech in its next periodic report so as to assess the impact of measures adopted by the State party in combating racist hate speech.

Disparate impact of environmental pollution

10. While welcoming the acknowledgment by the State party that low-income and minority communities are exposed to an unacceptable amount of pollution, as well as the initiatives taken to address the issue, the Committee is concerned that individuals belonging to racial and ethnic minorities, as well as indigenous peoples, continue to be disproportionately affected by the negative health impact of pollution caused by the extractive and manufacturing industries. It also reiterates its previous concern regarding the adverse effects of economic activities related to the exploitation of natural resources in countries outside the United States by transnational corporations registered in the State party on the rights to land, health, environment and the way of life of indigenous peoples and minority groups living in those regions (para. 30) (arts. 2 and 5 (e)).

The Committee calls upon the State party to:

(a) Ensure that federal legislation prohibiting environmental pollution is effectively enforced at state and local levels;

(b) Undertake an independent and effective investigation into all cases of environmentally polluting activities and their impact on the rights of affected communities; bring those responsible to account; and ensure that victims have access to appropriate remedies;

(c) Clean up any remaining radioactive and toxic waste throughout the State party as a matter of urgency, paying particular attention to areas inhabited by racial and ethnic minorities and indigenous peoples that have been neglected to date;

(d) Take appropriate measures to prevent the activities of transnational corporations registered in the State party which could have adverse effects on the enjoyment of human rights by local populations, especially indigenous peoples and minorities, in other countries.

Right to vote

11. The Committee is concerned at the obstacles faced by individuals belonging to racial and ethnic minorities and indigenous peoples to effectively exercise their right to vote, due, inter alia, to restrictive voter identification laws, district gerrymandering and state-level felon disenfranchisement laws. It is also concerned at the Supreme Court decision in *Shelby County v. Holder*, which struck down section 4 (b) of the Voting Rights Act and rendered section 5 inoperable, thus invalidating the procedural safeguards to prevent the implementation of voting regulations that may have discriminatory effect. It expresses further concern at the continued denial of the right of residents of the District of Colombia (D.C.), half of whom are African Americans, to vote for and elect representatives to the United States Senate and voting members to the House of Representatives (arts. 2 and 5 (c)).

The Committee recommends that the State party take effective measures to:

(a) Enforce federal voting rights legislation throughout the State party in ways that encourage voter participation, and adopt federal legislation to prevent the implementation of voting regulations which have discriminatory impact, in the light of the Supreme Court decision in *Shelby County v. Holder*;

(b) Ensure that indigenous peoples can effectively exercise their right to vote and address their specific concerns;

(c) Ensure that all states reinstate voting rights to persons convicted of felony who have completed their sentences; provide inmates with information about their voting restoration options; and review automatic denial of the right to vote to imprisoned felons, regardless of the nature of the offence;

(d) Provide for full voting rights of residents of Washington, D.C.

Criminalization of homelessness

12. While appreciating the measures taken by the federal and some state and local authorities to address homelessness, the Committee is concerned at the high number of homeless persons, who are disproportionately from racial and ethnic minorities, particularly African Americans, Hispanic/Latino Americans and Native Americans, and at the criminalization of homelessness through laws that prohibit activities such as loitering, camping, begging and lying down in public spaces (arts. 2 and 5 (e)).

The Committee calls upon the State party to:

(a) Abolish laws and policies making homelessness a crime;

(b) Ensure close cooperation among all relevant stakeholders, including social, health, law enforcement and justice professionals at all levels, to intensify efforts to find solutions for the homeless, in accordance with human rights standards;

(c) Offer incentives to decriminalize homelessness, including by providing financial support to local authorities that implement alternatives to criminalization, and withdrawing funding from local authorities that criminalize homelessness.

Discrimination and segregation in housing

13. While acknowledging the positive steps taken by the State party to address discrimination in access to housing and to reverse historical patterns of segregation, the Committee remains concerned at:

(a) the persistence of discrimination in access to housing on the basis of race, colour, ethnicity or national origin;

(b) the high degree of racial segregation and concentrated poverty in neighbourhoods characterized by sub-standard conditions and services, including poor housing conditions, limited employment opportunities, inadequate access to health-care facilities, underresourced schools and high exposure to crime and violence; and

(c) discriminatory mortgage-lending practices and the foreclosure crisis which disproportionately affected, and continues to affect, racial and ethnic minorities (arts. 3 and 5 (e)).

The Committee urges the State party to intensify its efforts to eliminate discrimination in access to housing and residential segregation based on race, colour ethnicity or national origin, by, inter alia:

(a) Ensuring the availability of affordable and adequate housing for all, including by effectively implementing the Affirmatively Furthering Fair Housing requirement by the Department of Housing and Urban Development, across all agencies administering housing programmes;

(b) Strengthening the implementation of legislation to combat discrimination in housing, such as the Fair Housing Act and Title VIII of the Civil Rights Act of 1968, including through the provision of adequate resources and increasing the capacity of the Department of Housing and Urban Development;

(c) Undertaking prompt, independent and thorough investigation into all cases of discriminatory practices by private actors, including in relation to discriminatory mortgage lending practices, steering and red-lining; holding those responsible to account; and providing effective remedies, including appropriate compensation, guarantees of non-repetition and changes in relevant laws and practices.

Education

14. While welcoming measures taken by the State party to address de facto racial segregation in education, such as the formation of the Equity and Excellence Commission in 2011, the Committee remains concerned that students from racial and ethnic minorities disproportionately continue to attend segregated schools with segregated or unequal facilities and that even those who are enrolled in racially diverse schools are frequently assigned to "single-race" classes, denied

equal access to advanced courses and disciplined unfairly and disproportionately due to their race, including referral to the criminal justice system. It also expresses concern at racial disparities in academic achievement, which contribute to unequal access to employment opportunities (arts. 3 and 5 (e)).

The Committee recommends that the State party intensify its efforts to ensure equal access to education by, inter alia:

(a) Developing and adopting a comprehensive plan to address racial segregation in schools and neighbourhoods, with concrete goals, timelines and impact assessment mechanisms;

(b) Increasing federal funding for programmes and policies that promote racially integrated learning environments for students;

(c) Effectively implementing the recommendations contained in the report of the Equity and Excellence Commission published in February 2013;

(d) Re-authorizing the Elementary and Secondary Education Act with provisions that support and encourage solutions to address school segregation;

(e) Continuing to work closely with state and local education authorities as well as civil society groups to strengthen measures to address the factors that contribute to the educational achievement gap.

Right to health and access to health care

15. While commending the adoption of the Patient Protection and Affordable Care Act in March 2010, the Committee is concerned that many states with substantial numbers of racial and ethnic minorities have opted out of the Medicaid expansion programme, following the Supreme Court decision of June 2012 in the *National Federation of Independent Business v. Sebelius* case, thus failing to fully address racial disparities in access to affordable and quality health care. It is also concerned at the exclusion of undocumented immigrants and their children from coverage under the Affordable Care Act, as well as the limited coverage of undocumented immigrants and immigrants residing lawfully in the United States for less than five years by Medicaid and Children's Health Insurance Programme, resulting in difficulties for immigrants in accessing adequate health care. It also reiterates its previous concern at the persistence of racial disparities in the field of sexual and reproductive health, particularly with regard to the high maternal and infant mortality rates among African American communities (para. 33) (art. 5 (e)).

The Committee recommends that the State party:

(a) Take concrete measures to ensure that all individuals, in particular those belonging to racial and ethnic minorities who reside in states that have opted out of the Affordable Care Act, undocumented immigrants and immigrants and their families who have been residing lawfully in the United States for less than five years, have effective access to affordable and adequate health-care services;

(b) Eliminate racial disparities in the field of sexual and reproductive health and standardize the data collection system on maternal and infant deaths in all states to effectively identify and address the causes of disparities in maternal and infant mortality rates; and

(c) Improve monitoring and accountability mechanisms for preventable maternal mortality, including by ensuring that state-level maternal mortality review boards have sufficient resources and capacity.

Gun violence

16. The Committee is concerned at the high number of gun-related deaths and injuries which disproportionately affect members of racial and ethnic minorities, particularly African Americans. It is also concerned at the proliferation of "Stand Your Ground" laws, which are used to circumvent the limits of legitimate self-defence, in violation of the State party's duty to protect life, and have a disproportionate and discriminatory impact on members of racial and ethnic minorities (arts. 2, 5 (b) and 6).

The Committee urges the State party to take effective legislative and policy measures to fulfil its obligation to protect the right to life and to reduce gun violence, including by adopting legislation expanding background checks for all private firearm transfers and prohibiting the practice of carrying concealed handguns in public venues; increasing transparency concerning gun use in crime and illegal gun sales, including by repealing the Tiahrt Amendments; and reviewing the Stand Your Ground laws to remove far-reaching immunity and ensure strict adherence to the principles of necessity and proportionality when deadly force is used for self-defence.

Excessive use of force by law enforcement officials

17. While recognizing the efforts made by the State party to intensify the enforcement of relevant laws, the Committee reiterates its previous concern at the brutality and excessive use of force by law enforcement officials against members of racial and ethnic minorities, including against unarmed individuals, which has a disparate impact on African Americans and undocumented migrants crossing the United States-Mexico border (para. 25). It also remains concerned that, despite the measures taken by the State party to prosecute law enforcement officials for criminal misconduct, impunity for abuses, in particular those committed by the Customs and Border Protection (CBP) against Hispanic/Latino Americans and undocumented migrants, remains a widespread problem (arts. 5 (b) and 6).

The Committee urges the State party to:

(a) Ensure that each allegation of excessive use of force by law enforcement officials is promptly and effectively investigated; that the alleged perpetrators are prosecuted and, if convicted, punished with appropriate sanctions; that investigations are re-opened when new evidence becomes available; and that victims or their families are provided with adequate compensation;

(b) Intensify its efforts to prevent the excessive use of force by law enforcement officials by ensuring compliance with the 1990 Basic Principles on the Use of Force and Firearms by Law Enforcement Officials, and ensure that the new CBP directive on the use of force is applied and enforced in practice;

(c) Improve the reporting of cases involving the excessive use of force and strengthen oversight of, and accountability for, inappropriate use of force;

(d) Provide, in its next periodic report, detailed information concerning investigations undertaken into allegations of excessive use of force by law enforcement officials, including the CBP, as well as their outcomes, including disciplinary or prosecutorial action taken against the perpetrator and remedies provided to victims or their families.

Immigrants

18. The Committee is concerned at the increasingly militarized approach to immigration law enforcement, leading to the excessive and lethal use of force by CBP personnel; increased use of racial profiling by local law enforcement agencies to determine immigration status and to enforce immigration laws; increased criminal prosecution for breaches of immigration law; mandatory detention of immigrants for prolonged periods of time; and deportation of undocumented immigrants without adequate access to justice. It is also concerned that workers entering the State party under the H-2B work visa programme are at high risk of becoming victims of trafficking and/or forced labour, and that some children from racial and ethnic minorities, particularly Hispanic/Latino children, are employed in the agriculture industry and may face harsh and dangerous conditions (arts. 2, 5 and 6).

The Committee calls upon the State party to ensure that the rights of non-citizens are fully guaranteed in law and in practice, by, inter alia:

(a) Abolishing "Operation Streamline" and dealing with any breaches of immigration law through the civil, rather than criminal immigration system;

(b) Undertaking thorough and individualized assessment for decisions concerning detention and deportation and guaranteeing access to legal representation in all immigration-related matters;

(c) Reviewing its laws and regulations in order to protect all migrant workers from exploitative and abusive working conditions, including by raising the minimum age for harvesting and hazardous work in agriculture under the Fair Labor Standards Act in line with international labour standards and ensuring effective oversight of labour conditions;

(d) Ratifying International Labour Office Convention No. 29 (1930) concerning Forced or Compulsory Labour and Convention No. 138 (1973) concerning Minimum Age for Admission to Employment.

Violence against women

19. While acknowledging the measures taken by the State party to reduce the prevalence of violence against women, the Committee remains concerned at the disproportionate number of women from racial and ethnic minorities, particularly African American women, immigrant women and American Indian and Alaska Native women, who continue to be subjected to violence, including rape and sexual violence. Additionally, it notes that while the Tribal Law and Order Act of 2010 has increased the length of sentences that tribal courts can hand down in criminal cases and the Violence Against Women Reauthorization Act of 2013 has expanded the jurisdiction of tribes over domestic violence and violence of protective orders committed on their lands, the jurisdiction is limited to those who live or work on reservations or who are married to or are in partnership with a tribal member. The Committee thus reiterates its previous concern that indigenous women are denied the right to access justice and to obtain adequate reparation or satisfaction for damages suffered (para. 26) (arts. 5 and 6).

The Committee calls upon the State party to intensify its efforts to prevent and combat violence against women, particularly American Indian and Alaska Native women, and ensure that all cases of violence against women are effectively investigated, perpetrators are prosecuted and sanctioned, and victims are provided with appropriate remedies. It also urges the State party to take measures to guarantee, in law and in practice, the right to access justice and effective remedies for all indigenous women who are victims of violence. It also reiterates its previous recommendation that the State party provide sufficient resources for violence prevention and service programmes; provide specific training for those working within the criminal justice system, including police officers, lawyers, prosecutors, judges and medical personnel; and undertake awareness-raising campaigns on the mechanisms and procedures available to seek remedies for violence against women.

Criminal justice system

20. While welcoming the measures taken by the State party to address racial disparities in the criminal justice system, such as the launch of the "Smart on Crime" initiative in August 2013, the Committee remains concerned that members of racial and ethnic minorities, particularly African Americans, continue to be disproportionately arrested, incarcerated and subjected to harsher sentences, including life imprisonment without parole and the death penalty. It expresses concern that the overrepresentation of racial and ethnic minorities in the criminal justice system is exacerbated by the use of prosecutorial discretion, the application of mandatory minimum drug-offence sentencing policies, and the implementation of repeat offender laws. The Committee is also concerned at the negative impact of parental incarceration on children from racial and ethnic minorities (arts. 2, 5 and 6).

The Committee calls upon the State party to take concrete and effective steps to eliminate racial disparities at all stages of the criminal justice system, taking into account the Committee's general recommendation No. 31 (2005) on the prevention of racial discrimination in the administration and functioning of the criminal justice system, by, inter alia:

(a) Amending laws and policies leading to racially disparate impacts in the criminal justice system at the federal, state and local levels and implementing effective national strategies or plans of action aimed at eliminating structural discrimination;

(b) Imposing a moratorium on the death penalty, at the federal level, with a view to abolishing the death penalty;

(c) Ensuring that the impact of incarceration on children and/or other dependents is taken into account when sentencing an individual convicted of a non-violent offence and promoting the use of alternatives to imprisonment.

Juvenile justice

21. The Committee is concerned at racial disparities at all levels of the juvenile justice system, including the disproportionate rate at which youth from racial and ethnic minorities are arrested in schools and referred to the criminal justice system, prosecuted as adults, incarcerated in adult prisons and sentenced to life imprisonment without parole. It also remains concerned that, despite the recent Supreme Court decisions which held that mandatory sentencing of juvenile offenders to life imprisonment without parole is unconstitutional, 15 states have yet to change their laws, and that discretionary sentences of life imprisonment without parole are still permitted for juveniles convicted of homicide (arts. 2, 5 and 6).

The Committee calls upon the State party to intensify its efforts to address racial disparities in the application of disciplinary measures, as well as the resulting "school-to-prison pipeline," throughout the State party and ensure that juveniles are not transferred to adult courts and are separated from adults during pretrial detention and after sentencing. It also reiterates its previous recommendation to prohibit and abolish life imprisonment without parole for persons who were under 18 years at the time of the crime, irrespective of the nature and circumstances of the crime committed, and to commute the sentences for those currently serving such sentences.

Guantánamo Bay

22. While welcoming the commitment made in January 2009 by the President of the United States to close the detention facilities at Guantánamo Bay, the Committee remains concerned that non-citizens continue to be arbitrarily detained without effective and equal access to the ordinary criminal justice system and at the risk of being subjected to torture or cruel, inhuman or degrading treatment or punishment (arts. 2, 5 and 6).

The Committee urges the State party to end the system of administrative detention without charge or trial and ensure the closure of the Guantánamo Bay facility without further delay. Recalling its general recommendation No. 30 (2004) on discrimination against non-citizens and general recommendation No. 31 (2005) on the prevention of racial discrimination in the administration and functioning of the criminal justice system, it also calls upon the State party to guarantee the right of detainees to a fair trial, in compliance with international human rights standards, and to ensure that any detainee who is not charged and tried is released immediately.

Access to legal aid

23. While welcoming the steps taken by the State party to improve access to justice by indigent persons, such as the Access to Justice Initiative launched in March 2010, the Committee remains concerned at the ongoing challenges faced by indigent persons belonging to racial and ethnic minorities to access legal counsel in criminal proceedings in practice. It also reiterates its concern at the lack of a generally recognized right to counsel in civil proceedings (para. 22), which disproportionately affects indigent persons belonging to racial and ethnic minorities, and hinders their seeking an effective remedy in matters such as evictions, foreclosures, domestic violence, discrimination in employment, termination of subsistence income or medical assistance, loss of child custody, and deportation (art. 6).

The Committee reiterates its previous recommendation that the State party adopt all necessary measures to eliminate the disproportionate impact of systemic inadequacies in criminal defence programmes on indigent defendants belonging to racial and ethnic minorities, including by improving the quality of legal representation provided to indigent defendants and ensuring that public legal aid systems are adequately funded and supervised. It also recommends that the State party allocate sufficient resources to ensure effective access to legal representation for indigent persons belonging to racial and ethnic minorities in civil proceedings, particularly with regard to proceedings that have serious consequences for their security and stability, such as evictions, foreclosures, domestic violence, discrimination in employment, termination of subsistence income or medical assistance, loss of child custody and deportation proceedings.

Rights of indigenous peoples

24. While acknowledging the steps taken by the State party to recognize the culture and traditions of indigenous peoples, including the support for the United Nations Declaration on the Rights of Indigenous Peoples announced by Presi-

dent Obama on 16 December 2010, the issuance of Executive Orders 13007 and 13175 and the high-level conferences organized by President Obama with tribal leaders, the Committee remains concerned at:

(a) Lack of concrete progress to guarantee, in law and in practice, the free, prior and informed consent of indigenous peoples in policy-making and decisions that affect them;

(b) The ongoing obstacles to the recognition of tribes, including high costs and lengthy and burdensome procedural requirements;

(c) Insufficient measures taken to protect the sacred sites of indigenous peoples that are essential for the preservation of their religious, cultural and spiritual practices against polluting and disruptive activities, resulting from, inter alia, resource extraction, industrial development, construction of border fences and walls, tourism and urbanization;

(d) The ongoing removal of indigenous children from their families and communities through the United States child welfare system;

(e) The lack of sufficient and adequate information from the State party on the measures taken to implement the recommendations of the Committee in its Decision 1(68) regarding the Western Shoshone peoples (CERD/C/USA/DEC/1), adopted under the Early Warning and Urgent Action Procedure in 2006, as well as the ongoing infringement of the rights of the Western Shoshone peoples (arts. 5 and 6).

Recalling its general recommendation No. 23 (1997) on indigenous peoples, the Committee calls upon the State party to:

(a) Guarantee, in law and in practice, the right of indigenous peoples to effective participation in public life and in decisions that affect them, based on their free, prior and informed consent;

(b) Take effective measures to eliminate undue obstacles to the recognition of tribes;

(c) Adopt concrete measures to effectively protect the sacred sites of indigenous peoples in the context of the State party's development or national security projects and exploitation of natural resources, and ensure that those responsible for any damages caused are held accountable;

(d) Effectively implement and enforce the Indian Child Welfare Act of 1978 to halt the removal of indigenous children from their families and communities;

(e) Take immediate action to implement the recommendations contained in Decision 1(68) on the Western Shoshone peoples and provide comprehensive information to the Committee on concrete measures taken in that regard.

National action plan to combat racial discrimination

25. While noting various measures taken by the State party to combat prejudice and promote understanding and tolerance, the Committee expresses concern at the absence of a national action plan to combat racial discrimination and to implement its recommendations. It is also concerned about the lack of inclusion of human rights in the school curricula (art. 7).

The Committee recommends that the State party adopt a national action plan to combat structural racial discrimination, and to ensure that school curricula, textbooks and teaching materials are informed by and address human rights themes and seek to promote understanding among racial and ethnic minority groups.

...

Source: United Nations CERD/C/USA/CO/7-9, International Convention on the Elimination of All Forms of Racial Discrimination, Committee on the Elimination of Racial Discrimination Concluding observations on the combined seventh to ninth periodic reports of the United States of America, https://www.state.gov/documents/organization/235644.pdf

⁂⁂⁂⁂⁂⁂⁂

5. ONE-YEAR FOLLOW-UP RESPONSE OF THE U.S. TO PRIORITY RECOMMENDATIONS OF THE COMMITTEE ON THE ELIMINATION OF RACIAL DISCRIMINATION IN ITS CONCLUDING OBSERVATIONS ON THE COMBINED SEVENTH TO NINTH PERIODIC REPORTS OF THE U.S.

The 2015 U.S. response to CERD Committee priority recommendations, based on its 7th through 9th report to CERD, is related to, among other issues, the urgency of heightened racial tensions as well as to reports of deaths and harassment of racial minorities due to apparent excessive police force in Ferguson, Missouri, Baltimore, Maryland, and Cleveland, Ohio. Members of the Committee are aware of the events going online in such large and important states such as the U.S.

1. Pursuant to the Committee's request, the United States provides the following information pertaining to the Committee's recommendations in paragraphs 17 (a) and (b), 18, and 22 of its Concluding Observations adopted on August 26, 2014, focusing to the extent possible on measures taken subsequent to the Committee's recommendations.

Recommendation 17(a) & (b) (Police use of force): The Committee urges the State party to:

(a) Ensure that each allegation of excessive use of force by law enforcement officials is promptly and effectively investigated; that the alleged perpetrators are prosecuted and, if convicted, punished with appropriate sanctions; that investigations are re-opened when new evidence becomes available; and that victims or their families are provided with adequate compensation.

2. U.S. federal, state, and local authorities take vigilant action to prevent use of excessive force by law enforcement officials and to hold accountable persons responsible for such use of force. It must be recognized that law enforcement officers have challenging and often dangerous jobs and that the vast majority of their interactions with civilians involve appropriate conduct. However, when there is improper conduct, the U.S. Department of Justice (DOJ) has criminal jurisdiction to investigate and prosecute use of excessive force by federal, state, and local officials that violates the U.S. Constitution or federal law. Successful prosecution of any case, including consideration of re-opening a case for prosecution, is dependent on the availability of evidence to support conviction beyond a reasonable doubt. DOJ also has civil jurisdiction to address state and local law enforcement patterns and practices that violate the Constitution or federal law, including the use of excessive force.

3. Federal Prosecutions: In the last six years, DOJ has brought criminal charges against more than 350 law enforcement officials. The following are recent examples of federal prosecutions involving the alleged use of excessive force by police against members of racial or ethnic minorities:

- On March 27, 2015, a federal grand jury indicted a Madison, Alabama, police officer for using unreasonable force against a man he was attempting to question. The indictment charged that the officer injured the victim, a man of South Asian descent, by slamming him into the ground.
- On June 18, 2015, DOJ charged a Miami Dade Police Detective with making traffic stops of three motorists, some of whom were Hispanic, to steal their money and property, in violation of the Fourth Amendment to the U.S. Constitution. The FBI is investigating the case with assistance from the Homestead, Florida Police Department.

4. State-Level Prosecutions: The following are recent examples of prosecutions at the state or local level involving the alleged use of excessive force by police against members of racial or ethnic minorities:

- Johnnie Riley, a former police officer with the Prince George's County Police Department in Maryland, was convicted of shooting Calvin Kyle, an African-American man, in the back in September 2012, after Kyle fled from a police car while handcuffed. In November 2014, the Prince George's County Circuit Court sentenced Riley to five years in prison.
- Michael Slager, a police officer in North Charleston, South Carolina, was indicted on June 8, 2015, by a Charleston County grand jury on a murder charge in the shooting death of Walter Scott, an African-American man.

- Ray Tensing, a former police officer for the University of Cincinnati in Cincinnati, Ohio, was indicted on July 29, 2015, by a Hamilton County grand jury on a murder charge in the shooting death of an African-American man, Samuel DuBose.

5. Effective Remedies: In addition to bringing criminal prosecutions, the DOJ Civil Rights Division continues to institute civil suits for equitable and declaratory relief pursuant to the pattern or practice of police misconduct provision of 42 U.S.C. § 14141. DOJ has opened more than 20 investigations of discriminatory policing and/or excessive force in the last six years and has reached 19 agreements with state or local law enforcement agencies, working toward long- term solutions in those jurisdictions.

Recent cases include:
- On March 4, 2015, DOJ issued a 100-page report finding that the Ferguson, Missouri, Police Department had engaged in a pattern or practice of excessive force and discriminatory policing, among other violations. DOJ's Civil Rights Division is negotiating an agreement for reform with the City, with the goal of focusing the Ferguson Police Department on public safety and constitutional policing.
- On May 8, 2015, following the death of Freddie Gray, DOJ announced the opening of a civil pattern or practice investigation into the Baltimore, Maryland, Police Department, focusing on the use of force; stops, searches and arrests; and whether there is a pattern of discriminatory policing. DOJ's Office of Community Oriented Policing Services (COPS) and Community Relations Service (CRS) will provide technical assistance to Baltimore to promote changes and improvements even as the investigation proceeds.
- Based on a two-year civil rights investigation that found a pattern and practice of unreasonable and unnecessary use of force by the Cleveland (Ohio) Division of Police, on May 26, 2015, DOJ announced an agreement with the City of Cleveland that requires sweeping changes to ensure community-oriented, bias-free, and transparent policing, including establishment of a Community Police Commission representative of the City's diverse communities, training for police officers, federal monitoring, and other requirements.

6. DOJ is also working proactively to prevent such incidents through training of police officers and helping to strengthen police-community relations. For example, in addition to opening civil and criminal investigations after the August 2014 shooting of Michael Brown in Ferguson, Missouri, DOJ sent mediators from CRS to create a dialogue between police, city officials, and residents to reduce tension in the community. DOJ has created a Collaborative Reform Initiative for Technical Assistance, which responds to requests from law enforcement for proactive, non- adversarial, and cost-effective technical assistance for agencies with significant law enforcement-related issues. Such assistance is currently being provided to police departments in Saint Louis County, Missouri; Fayetteville, North Carolina; and Salinas, California.

7. Effective remedies are also provided at the state level. The following are recent examples of compensation or other remedies for incidents involving members of racial or ethnic minorities:
- In October 2014, a jury in Colorado awarded $4.65 million to the family of Marvin Booker, who died after being shocked by an electronic control weapon and placed in a sleeper hold by Denver jail officers.
- In November 2014, the City of Cleveland, Ohio, agreed to pay $1.5 million each to the families of Timothy Russell and Malissa Williams, who died after a car chase during which police fired more than 100 shots at Russell's vehicle.
- In December 2014, a jury in California awarded $8 million to the family of Darren Burley, who died 12 days after a struggle with Los Angeles County Sheriff's deputies. The deputies acknowledged that they had punched Burley, used a stun gun on him, and used their body weight in order to handcuff him during an arrest.
- In May 2015, the City of Chicago, Illinois created a $5.5 million "reparations fund" for victims, most of whom were African-American or Hispanic, of police torture or physical abuse by former Chicago Police Commander Jon Burge or his subordinates between 1972 and 1991.
- In July 2015, New York City agreed to a $5.9 million settlement with the family of Eric Garner, who died after being placed in a chokehold during an arrest by Staten Island police officers in July 2014.

(b) Intensify its efforts to prevent the excessive use of force by law enforcement officials by ensuring compliance with the 1990 Basic Principles on the Use of Force and Firearms by Law Enforcement Officials, and ensure that the new Customs and Border Protection directive on the use of force is applied and enforced in practice.

8. Use of excessive force by law enforcement officials has increasingly become an issue of widespread public focus and concern in the United States in the face of a number of highly publicized recent incidents. Authorities at all levels have intensified their efforts to prevent such conduct through numerous mechanisms, including revised use of force policies; increased capacity for crisis intervention with specially-trained personnel; enhanced early warning systems to identify gaps in policy, training and supervision; increased community oversight; use of new types of equipment; and expedited investigations of misconduct complaints. In March 2015, President Obama's Task Force on 21st Century Policing released a report with approximately 60 recommendations, and in May 2015, a $20 million Body-Worn Camera Pilot Partnership Program was announced. The efforts being undertaken include a number of methods addressed in the 1990 Basic Principles on the Use of Force and Firearms by Law Enforcement Officials, and U.S. government policies on use of force by law enforcement officials are fully consistent with the Basic Principles and with the U.N. Code of Conduct for Law Enforcement Officials.

9. In addition, in December 2014, DOJ announced an updated policy on profiling applicable to all law enforcement activity under federal supervision. This policy instructs that law enforcement officers may not consider race, ethnicity, national origin, gender, gender identity, religion, or sexual orientation to any degree when making routine or spontaneous law enforcement decisions, unless the characteristics apply to a suspect's description.

10. There have also been recent legislative and policy efforts at the state and local levels to address and curb use of excessive force and discriminatory policing. The following are examples of such efforts:
- On April 19, 2015, the California Attorney General announced the development of an independently certified implicit-bias training program for law enforcement officers. The initiative aims to expose and alter subconscious prejudices that contribute to race discrimination in community law enforcement. Since 2014, numerous city-level law enforcement agencies around the country, including police departments in Dallas, Philadelphia, St. Louis, Chicago, and Los Angeles, have introduced implicit-bias education as part of officer training.
- On July 10, 2015, Rhode Island adopted the Comprehensive Community-Police Relationship Act. The new law combats discriminatory police practices through the imposition of monitoring and reporting requirements and search restrictions. Among its provisions are requirements that police departments record data on race at traffic stops and each compile an annual report for the Rhode Island Department of Transportation detailing that police department's responses to evidence of disparate enforcement.

11. With regard to the Department of Homeland Security (DHS) U.S. Customs and Border Protection (CBP) policy on use of force, DHS and CBP enforce strict standards of conduct applicable to all employees, whether they are on- or off-duty, investigate deaths resulting from use of force, and follow up on civil rights and civil liberties-related complaints. CBP has conducted comprehensive reviews of its use of force policies and practices, and continues actively to monitor and enforce those policies. On May 30, 2014, CBP released its current use of force handbook, along with an earlier Police Executive Research Forum report on use of force. Earlier, in 2010, CBP created a Use of Force Reporting System, which electronically tracks all lethal and non-lethal uses of force by agents and officers. On December 9, 2014, DHS also established a CBP Integrity Advisory Panel as a subcommittee of the Homeland Security Advisory Council, tasked with benchmarking CBP's progress in response to CBP use of force reviews and a report by the DHS Office of Inspector General, as well as identifying best practices from federal, state, local, and tribal law enforcement on incident prevention and transparency pertaining to incident response and discipline.

Recommendation 18 (Immigration policy):

The Committee calls upon the State party to ensure that the rights of non-citizens are fully guaranteed in law and in practice, including inter alia by:

(a) Abolishing "Operation Streamline" and dealing with any breaches of immigration law through civil, rather than criminal immigration system.

12. Operation Streamline is a law enforcement initiative aimed at deterring the increase in illegal crossings on the U.S. Southwest border by prosecuting certain non-citizens under 8 U.S.C. § 1325 ("improper entry by alien"). Most of those prosecuted had attempted to re-enter the United States without inspection after previously being ordered excluded or removed. The goal of Operation Streamline is to reduce rates of alien re-entry recidivism. The United States is commit-

ted to making sure that this type of enforcement activity is conducted in a manner consistent with U.S. human rights obligations.

13. Individuals subject to Operation Streamline are entitled to and afforded due process in all criminal proceedings under the U.S. Constitution and laws, including rights provided to all criminal defendants, and consistent with applicable international obligations. Each Streamline prosecution is conducted openly in federal court, with the benefit of legal representation; a thorough, transcribed plea dialogue and rights discussion; a right to demand a trial to make the government prove each element of each allegation beyond a reasonable doubt; a right to be heard at sentencing; and access to courts for higher-level review.

14. As of December 2014, only the Tucson, Del Rio, and Laredo sectors participate in Operation Streamline; the Yuma, El Paso, and Rio Grande Valley sectors discontinued using Operation Streamline between 2013 and 2014. However, U.S. Attorney's Offices in these sectors continue to prosecute misdemeanor cases under 8 U.S.C. § 1325.

(b) Undertaking thorough and individualized assessments for decisions concerning detention and deportation and guaranteeing access to legal representation in all immigration-related matters.

15. Decisions concerning detention and deportation are made on the basis of individualized assessments in light of the totality of the circumstances, and the United States provides avenues for relief and favorable discretion, consistent with U.S. international obligations. For example, in determining whether a removable non-citizen who is not subject to mandatory detention should be released, DHS and the DOJ Executive Office for Immigration Review undertake individualized assessments, considering factors that bear on whether the person is a flight risk or danger to the community, such as family, community ties, health, and criminal record.

16. On November 20, 2014, President Obama announced executive actions within his authority in order to improve the U.S. immigration system. In part, these actions are designed to prioritize removals of individuals who threaten U.S. national security, public safety, and border security, while allowing for the provision of temporary relief from removal on a discretionary and individualized basis to certain persons who have been in the United States for an extended period and meet certain guidelines for consideration, including national security and criminal background checks. Specifically, the reforms sought to: (1) expand the population eligible for consideration under Deferred Action for Childhood Arrivals (DACA) to people of any current age who had entered the United States before the age of 16 and had lived in the United States continuously since January 1, 2010; (2) extend the period of deferred action and work authorization under DACA from two years to three years; (3) allow parents of U.S. citizens and lawful permanent residents to request deferred action and employment authorization for three years under a new initiative, Deferred Action for Parents of Americans and Lawful Permanent Residents (DAPA), provided they have lived in the United States continuously since January 1, 2010, are not enforcement priorities, and pass required background checks; (4) focus enforcement priorities on the removal of national security, border security, and public safety threats; (5) implement a new Priority Enforcement Program in order to focus enforcement resources on those threats; (6) shift resources to the border; (7) modernize, improve, and streamline the legal immigration system; and (8) promote citizenship education and public awareness for lawful permanent residents.

17. DAPA and the modifications to DACA were challenged in federal court, leading to issuance of a preliminary injunction in February 2015 that temporarily blocked implementation of these two policies (but did not affect the original 2012 DACA policy). Despite the legal setback to two of these initiatives, the Obama Administration has taken tangible steps forward on its other immigration initiatives. For example, DHS has already implemented a regulation to provide work authorization for spouses of certain skilled workers on a pathway to citizenship and a policy memo clarifying standards for intracompany transfers for foreign workers. As co-chair of the interagency Task Force on New Americans, DHS' U.S. Citizenship and Immigration Services (USCIS) is working with federal, state and local stakeholders to strengthen the federal government's immigrant integration efforts by making them more strategic and deliberate. In April 2015, the Task Force issued a report, *Strengthening Communities by Welcoming All Residents: A Federal Strategic Action Plan on Immigrant & Refugee Integration*, which included a series of recommendations that USCIS and interagency partners are working to implement. USCIS launched one of these initiatives, the Citizenship Public Awareness Initiative, on July 6, 2015. In July 2015, the Administration also released a report entitled *Modernizing and Streamlining Our Legal Immigration System for the 21Century*, which includes new actions that federal agencies will undertake to improve the visa experience for families, workers, and people in need of humanitarian relief.

18. In November 2014, President Obama also announced his intention to focus immigration enforcement resources on criminals and persons who represent threats to our security and safety. DHS Secretary Jeh Johnson issued new department-wide enforcement and removal priorities directing the agency to focus its resources appropriately and effectively on individuals who pose the greatest risk to public safety, border security, and national security. Under this policy, the top priorities are on national security threats, convicted felons, gang members, and recent border crossers. Secondary priorities include those convicted of significant or multiple misdemeanors and those who are not apprehended at the border, but who entered or reentered the United States unlawfully after January 1, 2014. The third priority encompasses those who are non-criminals but who have failed to abide by a final order of removal issued on or after January 1, 2014. Individuals who do not fall into any of the priorities announced by Secretary Johnson will generally not be priorities for detention or removal.

19. Many procedural protections for individuals are provided in proceedings before an immigration judge, including the requirement that immigration judges advise individuals of their right to be represented at no expense to the government, and notify them of and provide them with a list of free legal services providers. Immigration judges must also advise individuals that they have a right to examine, and object to, the evidence against them; present evidence on their own behalf; cross-examine government witnesses; and appeal an adverse decision. Additionally, immigration judges cannot accept an admission of removability from individuals who are younger than 18 or who are incompetent to represent themselves, unless these individuals are accompanied by a qualified representative.

20. To promote access to legal representation, DOJ offers the Legal Orientation Program to detained individuals, and the Legal Orientation Program for Custodians of Unaccompanied Alien Children (including a national call center). These programs work with nonprofit organizations to explain immigration court procedures and basic legal information to detained individuals, and to inform custodians about their role and responsibilities to unaccompanied children in their care who are in removal proceedings. These providers also facilitate *pro bono* representation in removal proceedings and administrative appeals before the Board of Immigration Appeals. DOJ has also taken additional steps to encourage *pro bono* legal representation of respondents, including unaccompanied children, in removal proceedings, by implementing programs such as issuing guidance to immigration judges regarding facilitating *pro bono* representation; creating a Model Hearing Program for *pro bono* representatives; establishing Self-Help Legal Centers at Immigration Courts; establishing juvenile dockets in all 58 Immigration Courts across the country to expedite immigration proceedings involving juveniles; issuing guidance to immigration judges on how to handle cases involving unaccompanied children; and, in the fall of 2014, establishing, with the Corporation for National and Community Service, the "justice AmeriCorps" grants initiative to improve court efficiencies in facilitating representation of unaccompanied children and identifying potential trafficking victims. Additionally, DOJ continues to implement its nationwide policy to provide enhanced procedural safeguards to detained individuals in immigration proceedings who may be mentally incompetent to represent themselves. These safeguards include: competency hearings; independent psychiatric or psychological examinations; and, for individuals deemed mentally incompetent to represent themselves, provision of qualified representatives. DOJ is also moving forward with regulatory initiatives that it initially proposed on September 17, 2014, related to *Separate Appearances for Custody and Bond Proceedings* and a *List of Pro Bono Legal Service Providers for Aliens in Immigration Proceedings*, and considering draft regulations for public comment that would streamline the process for legitimate entities to get approval to offer low-cost or pro-bono legal services and represent people in immigration court proceedings. Both initiatives, once promulgated as final rules, are expected to encourage legal representation of individuals in immigration proceedings.

21. On June 24, 2015, DHS Secretary Johnson announced a substantial change in the Department's detention practices with respect to families with children apprehended at the border. The new approach recognizes that, once a family has established initial eligibility for asylum or other relief under U.S. law, long-term detention of the family is an inefficient use of DHS resources and should be discontinued. Building on additional reforms announced on May 13, 2015, regarding the operation of family detention facilities, Secretary Johnson announced that families who are successful in stating a case of credible or reasonable fear of persecution in their home countries will generally be released on an appropriate monetary bond or other appropriate condition of release and that these credible or reasonable fear interviews will take place within a reasonable time frame. Additionally, bond criteria will be to set at a level that is reasonable and realistic, taking into account the family's ability to pay, risk of flight, and public safety. DHS is effectively transitioning the facilities into processing centers at which DHS can release those found eligible to apply for relief or protection within an average of approximately 20 days under reasonable conditions designed to achieve their appearance in immigration

proceedings. DHS is also setting up a federal advisory committee of outside experts, in the fields of detention management, public health, children and family services, and mental health, to advise DHS concerning family detention facilities, and is working with non-governmental organizations to ensure that families are provided with adequate access to legal services and other appropriate social services while in DHS custody.

(c) Reviewing its laws and regulations in order to protect all migrant workers from exploitative and abusive working conditions, including by raising the minimum age for harvesting and hazardous work in agriculture under the Fair Labor Standards Act in line with international labour standards, and ensuring effective oversight of labour conditions.

22. The protection of migrant workers is vital to the United States, and we are committed to ensuring that all such workers in the United States receive the protections to which they are entitled under our Constitution and laws, consistent with applicable international obligations.

23. As previously reported to the Committee, U.S. laws that apply to migrant workers prohibit discrimination in employment on the bases of race, color, national origin (ethnicity), sex (including pregnancy, sex stereotyping, and gender identity), religion, age, disability, or genetic information (including family medical history). In addition, the Equal Employment Opportunity Commission (EEOC) recently held that federal law protects workers from discrimination on the basis of sexual orientation. Under U.S. law, most migrant workers also have the right to advocate as a group for better pay or working conditions, with or without the assistance of a labor organization, and to bargain collectively through representatives of their own choosing. Migrant workers, including most agricultural workers, are entitled to a minimum wage for hours worked. Safety laws require safeguards to prevent worker injury. Environmental laws prescribe how certain chemicals must be handled in the workplace.

24. U.S. federal labor and employment laws generally apply to all workers located in the United States, regardless of immigration status. When investigating violations, U.S. labor enforcement agencies do not ask about the immigration status of the workers in question. The EEOC, the National Labor Relations Board (NLRB), and the Department of Labor (DOL) also combat employer efforts to discover the immigration status of workers during litigation in order to prevent employers from threatening deportation or otherwise intimidating the charging parties or witnesses.

25. Temporary foreign workers brought into the United States in accordance with the Immigration and Nationality Act also acquire protection under the visa programs under which they are admitted. For instance, foreign workers performing agricultural labor or services of a temporary or seasonal nature (H-2A visa) must: (1) be paid the higher of the federal or state minimum wage, the adverse effect wage rate, the local prevailing wage, or the agreed-upon collective bargaining rate; (2) receive a copy of the work contract; and (3) receive a guaranteed offer to work or be paid for a total number of hours equal to at least 75 percent of the work period specified in the contract. Federal agencies conduct outreach to migrant communities about their rights under U.S. laws, often in concert with civil and human rights groups that provide assistance to these communities. Agencies make materials available in offices and on-line in a variety of languages, and provide language assistance to those who need it to protect their rights.

26. As reported in our 2013 periodic report, DOL has established formal partnerships with foreign embassies and consulates of countries that are major countries of origin for migrant workers. Since 2013, DOL has renewed its partnerships with Costa Rica, the Dominican Republic, El Salvador, Mexico, and Nicaragua, and concluded a new partnership agreement with Belize. The EEOC has entered into similar partnerships, including with Mexico and the Philippines, and the NLRB has such partnerships with Mexico, Ecuador, Colombia, and the Philippines.

27. All workers, regardless of immigration status, are protected from forced labor by the U.S. criminal code, the Thirteenth Amendment to the U.S. Constitution, and the Trafficking Victims Protection Act (TVPA). Certain victims of trafficking and related crimes, such as forced labor, who assist law enforcement in the investigation or prosecution, and who meet other requirements, may be eligible to receive humanitarian immigration benefits allowing them to remain temporarily in the United States, with the possibility of obtaining permanent residence. Protecting children, in particular, from labor that is unsafe, unhealthy, or detrimental to their education and general wellbeing is a priority and a shared responsibility among the federal government and state and local governments. There are minimum age requirements under federal and state laws. All states have rules regarding the employment of young workers. In addition, some states

have separate minimum wage requirements. When federal and state rules differ, the rules that provide the most protection will apply.

28. As reported to the Committee during the August 2014 presentation, in 2011, DOL sought comments on whether to amend and expand the list of agricultural occupations considered too hazardous for the employment of children under age 16. DOL received more than 10,000 comments on the proposed rule. Many were from parents who own or operate farms, who believed that the proposal would limit the ability of their own children to work legally and gain hands-on experience on their farms. Other commenters, including nearly 200 members of Congress and a number of agricultural education instructors, were concerned that the rule would undermine American farming traditions and the preparation of the next generation of farmers and ranchers. Although DOL also received comments supporting the proposed rule, in light of the thousands of comments expressing profound concerns, in April 2012, DOL announced that it would withdraw the proposed rule. This decision to withdraw the rule was based on the Obama Administration's commitment to listening and responding to the comments of Americans in the public comment process.

29. In connection with this decision, DOL affirmed its intention to work to promote the safety and health of children employed as farm workers, including by collaborating with farming organizations to develop educational programs that address hazardous agricultural work practices and conditions. The U.S. government has also intensified efforts to combat unlawful forms of child labor and to protect the greatest number of young agricultural workers. For example, in 2014, the Environmental Protection Agency (EPA) proposed modifications to its Worker Protection Standard to better protect the nation's two million farm workers and their families from pesticide exposure. The revised standard proposed to afford farm workers, including children, health protections similar to those already enjoyed by workers in other industries, and would generally prohibit children under 16 from handling pesticides. EPA has indicated that it will publish a final rule revising its Worker Protection Standard by fall 2015.

30. Concurrent with President Obama's November 2014 executive actions, an Interagency Working Group for the Consistent Enforcement of Federal Labor, Employment, and Immigration Laws was established. Through this working group, DOL, DHS, DOJ, EEOC, and NLRB put forth a six-month action plan that seeks to enhance coordination in cases where federal responsibilities to enforce labor, employment, and immigration laws may overlap, ensure that workers who cooperate with labor and employment enforcement may continue to do so without fear of retaliation, ensure that unscrupulous parties do not attempt to misuse immigration enforcement or labor laws to thwart worker protections, and ensure the effective enforcement of these laws.

(d) Ratifying ILO Convention No.29 concerning Forced or Compulsory Labour and ILO Convention No.138 concerning Minimum Age for Admission to Employment.

31. The 1998 ILO Declaration on Fundamental Principles and Rights at Work confirms that all ILO Members have an obligation, arising from the very fact of membership in the Organization, to respect, promote, and realize in good faith the principles concerning the fundamental rights that are the subject of the ILO's eight core conventions, including the elimination of all forms of forced or compulsory labor and the effective abolition of child labor. Although the United States has not ratified the majority of those conventions, the United States has demonstrated, in its follow-up reports under the Declaration, that U.S. workers do enjoy the fundamental principles and rights at work.

32. Under U.S. practice, prior to the President's transmitting any ILO convention to the U.S. Senate for advice and consent to ratification, a careful review of the convention is undertaken by the Tripartite Advisory Panel on International Labor Standards (TAPILS), a sub-group of the President's Committee on the ILO comprising representatives from the U.S. government and from employer and worker organizations. This review considers whether U.S. law and practice, at both the state and federal levels, are in full conformity with the convention's provisions. Because of the issues considered in the review, the review process for each convention is complex, thorough, and often lengthy. The United States ratified ILO Convention 105 on the abolition of forced labor in 1991, and ILO Convention 182 on the worst forms of child labor in 1999.

33. TAPILS began a review of ILO Convention 29 on forced or compulsory labor when it began its review of Convention 105, but decided to concentrate on Convention 105. TAPILS has not completed reviews of either Convention 29 or Convention 138, and neither Convention has been transmitted by the President to the Senate for advice and consent to ratification.

Recommendation 22 (Guantánamo):

The Committee urges the State party to end the system of administrative detention without charge or trial and ensure the closure of the Guantánamo Bay facility without further delay. Recalling its general recommendation No.30 (2004) on non-citizens and general recommendation No.31 (2005) on the prevention of racial discrimination in the administration and functioning of the criminal justice system, it also calls upon the State party to guarantee the right of detainees to a fair trial in compliance with international human rights standards, and to ensure that any detainee who is not charged and tried is released immediately.

34. We preface this response by noting that the United States is committed, in the interest of promoting dialogue and cooperation, to providing information in response to the Committee's requests to the degree practicable, even where we may not agree that a given request bears directly on obligations under the Convention. The United States continues to have legal authority to detain Guantánamo detainees until the end of hostilities, consistent with U.S. law and applicable international law, but it has elected, as a policy matter, to ensure that it holds individuals no longer than necessary to mitigate the threat they pose.

35. President Obama has repeatedly reaffirmed his commitment to close the Guantánamo Bay detention facility, including during his State of the Union address to Congress on January 20, 2015. He has emphasized that the continued operation of the facility weakens U.S. national security by draining resources, damaging relationships with key allies and partners, and emboldening violent extremists. The United States is taking all feasible steps to reduce the detainee population at Guantánamo and to close the detention facility in a responsible manner that protects our national security.

36. More than 80 percent of those at one time held at the Guantánamo Bay detention facility have been repatriated or resettled, including all detainees subject to court orders directing their release. Of the 242 detainees at Guantánamo at the beginning of the Obama Administration, 122 have been transferred out of the facility. More detainees were transferred out of the facility in 2014 than in any year since 2009, and the detainee population now stands at its lowest since 2002. Of the 116 who remain at Guantánamo, 53 are designated for transfer, subject to appropriate security and humane treatment conditions. Of the 63 others, ten are currently facing charges, awaiting sentencing, or awaiting possible further appellate review of the sentences, and the remaining 53 are eligible for review by the Periodic Review Board (PRB). The PRB process, which has been underway since October 9, 2013, is a discretionary, administrative interagency process to review whether continued law of war detention of certain detainees at Guantánamo Bay remains necessary to protect against a continuing significant threat to the security of the United States. The PRB has conducted 20 hearings and six six-month file reviews, in which detainees are able to participate with their Personal Representatives and, in some cases with their Private Counsel.

37. The majority of Guantánamo detainees designated for transfer are Yemeni nationals, and in light of the current security situation in Yemen, the United States recognizes the need to identify appropriate resettlement solutions for that population as part of broader transfer efforts.

38. The United States remains of the view that in our efforts to protect our national security, both military commissions and federal courts can, depending on the circumstances of the specific case, provide appropriate processes for criminal prosecution that are both grounded in applicable law and effective. U.S. law currently precludes the transfer of detainees from Guantánamo for prosecution in the United States. All current military commission proceedings at Guantánamo incorporate fundamental procedural guarantees that meet or exceed the fair trial safeguards required by Common Article 3 of the 1949 Geneva Conventions and other applicable law, and that are further consistent with those in Additional Protocol II to the 1949 Geneva Conventions. A conviction by a military commission is subject to multiple layers of review, including judicial review by federal civilian courts consisting of life-tenured judges.

39. All Guantánamo detainees have the ability to challenge the lawfulness of their detention in U.S. Federal court through a petition for a writ of *habeas corpus*. Detainees have access to independent legal counsel and to appropriate evidence to mount such a challenge. The United States is fully committed to ensuring that individuals we detain in any armed conflict are treated humanely in all circumstances, consistent with applicable U.S. treaty obligations, U.S. domestic law, and U.S. policy.

Source: One-Year Follow-up Response of the United States of America to Priority Recommendations of the Committee on the Elimination of Racial Discrimination in its Concluding Observations on the Combined Seventh to Ninth Periodic Reports of the United States of America 2015https://www.state.gov/documents/organization/247415.pdf

6. FOURTH, FIFTH AND SIXTH-PERIODIC REPORTS OF THE UNITED STATES OF AMERICA TO THE COMMITTEE ON THE ELIMINATION OF RACIAL DISCRIMINATION

The Fourth, Fifth and Sixth US Periodic Reports to the CERD Committee made in 2007 during the George W. Bush administration are mentioned here for comparative reference only. The reports are not reprinted here, but the reader is encouraged to access them at http://www.state.gov/g/drl/rls/cerd_report/83404.htm, and compare and contrast them with the Seventh, Eighth and Ninth Reports of 2013-2015 submitted during the Obama regime.See Primary Source Documents 3 and 5.

7. CONCLUDING OBSERVATIONS OF THE COMMITTEE ON THE ELIMINATION OF RACIAL DISCRIMINATION — UNITED STATES OF AMERICA, MAY 8, 2008

The 2008 CERD Concluding Observations on the U.S. Report on ICERD, like Document 6, is mentioned here for comparative reference only, and can be accessed at http://www.state.gov/documents/organization/107361.pdf . The reader is encouraged to compare and contrast these 2008 observations with the 2014 observations in Primary Source Document 4. Note that even though the CERD Committee uses the same format for both the 2008 and 2014 observation/ recommendation reports, which are about equal in length, the 2008 report is more generalized than the 2014 report, which has many more observations and recommendations, reflecting how much serious effort had been made on non-discrimination issues by the US government in the intervening years.

8. REPORT OF THE WORKING GROUP OF EXPERTS ON PEOPLE OF AFRICAN DESCENT ON ITS MISSION TO THE UNITED STATES OF AMERICA

The report transmitted herewith contains the findings of the Working Group of Experts on People of African Descent on its visit to the United States of America from 19 to 29 January 2016. In it, the Working Group presents the current legal, institutional and policy framework, and measures taken to prevent racism, racial discrimination, xenophobia, Afrophobia and related intolerance faced by people of African descent in the United States, underscoring positive developments as well as gaps in implementation. The Working Group describes the situation, highlights good practices and the main challenges identified, and makes concrete recommendations.

{Excerpt}

Note by the Secretariat

I. Introduction

1. At the invitation of the Government of the United States of America, the Working Group of Experts on People of African Descent undertook a visit to the United States from 19 to 29 January 2016. The members of the delegation were Mireille Fanon-Mendès-France, Sabelo Gumedze and Ricardo Sunga III.

2. The Working Group visited Washington, D.C.; Baltimore, Maryland; Jackson, Mississippi; Chicago, Illinois; and New York City. The Working Group met with representatives of several government departments and offices, including the Department of State, the Department of Homeland Security, the Department of Housing and Urban Development, the Department of Health and Human Services, the Department of Labor, the Department of Justice and the Environ-

mental Protection Agency. The Working Group also met with officials of the Equal Employment Opportunity Commission, in Washington, D.C.

3. In Baltimore, the Working Group met with the Maryland federal judges. In Jackson, the Working Group met with officials of the Office of the Mayor and the Office of the Attorney General of the State of Mississippi. In Chicago, the Working Group met with the Attorney General of the State of Illinois, and with representatives of the Office of the Mayor of the City of Chicago and the Chicago Police Department. In New York City, the Working Group met with the Office of the Attorney General of the State of New York. The Working Group also met with officials of the White House working on African American issues and with staff of the congressional black caucus and interacted with a member of the United States Senate. In all the cities that the Working Group visited, it also met with hundreds of African Americans from communities with a large population of people of African descent living in the suburbs, as well as with lawyers, academics and representatives of non-governmental organizations.

4. The Working Group thanks the Government for its invitation and for its cooperation during the visit. In particular, the Working Group thanks the Office of Human Rights and Humanitarian Affairs at the Department of State for its support. The Working Group would also like to warmly thank the U.S. Human Rights Network for coordinating meetings with civil society in different parts of the country, and all the people who shared their views on the human rights situation of African Americans in the country.

5. The Working Group regrets that it was not given access, contrary to the terms of reference for special procedure mandate holders, to Mississippi State Penitentiary (Parchman Farm) as had been requested. Visits to such facilities provide opportunities to obtain views and to make recommendations regarding measures needed to address violations and to improve compliance with international law. Failure to permit and facilitate such visits undermines the responsibility of the United States to cooperate with the United Nations human rights mechanisms. The Working Group also regrets that it was not possible to meet with all of the high-level state and local-level authorities, as had been requested.

II. Background

A. Historical overview

6. The history of people of African descent in the United States is well documented. The first enslaved Africans were brought to the American colonies in the early part of the seventeenth century. Slavery became an entrenched institution, with Africans making up one fifth of the population of the American colonies by 1775. The issuance in 1863 of the Emancipation Proclamation, which declared that all enslaved persons within the rebellious states were free, was followed by the Thirteenth Amendment to the Constitution of the United States of America, which outlawed the practice of enslavement, the Fourteenth Amendment to the Constitution, in 1868, granting full United States citizenship to all persons born or naturalized in the United States, including African Americans, and the Fifteenth Amendment to the Constitution, in 1870, prohibiting denial of the right to vote on the basis of race. 7. Despite these legal and constitutional developments, the prevalence of "Jim Crow" laws — laws at the state and local levels that enforced racial segregation and persecution, primarily in the southern states — perpetuated political disenfranchisement, social and economic exploitation, violence and the overall subjugation of people of African descent until the 1960s. Lynching was a form of racial terrorism that has contributed to a legacy of racial inequality that the United States must address. Thousands of people of African descent were killed in violent public acts of racial control and domination and the perpetrators were never held accountable.

8. The civil rights movement from 1954 to 1968 was another important era in the struggle for rights by people of African descent in the country. The Montgomery bus boycott, the Selma to Montgomery marches, and many non-violent protests and acts of civil disobedience throughout the country led to further legislative developments, including but not limited to the Civil Rights Act of 1964, which prohibited, among other things, discrimination based on race or colour; the Voting Rights Act of 1965, which sought to overcome the legal barriers to the exercise of voting rights by African Americans; and the Fair Housing Act of 1968, which prohibited discrimination in the purchase or renting of property.

9. The 2010 United States census indicated that there were 43.21 million African Americans, constituting 14 per cent of the United States population. The July 2015 estimates indicated that there were 46.28 million African Americans, constituting 14.4 per cent of the United States population. Despite substantial changes since the end of the enforcement

of Jim Crow and the fight for civil rights, a systemic ideology of racism ensuring the domination of one group over another continues to impact negatively on the civil, political, economic, social and cultural rights of African Americans today.

II. Legal framework and steps taken for the protection of the human rights of people of African descent

A. Legal framework

10. The United States has ratified two of the international instruments related to the fight against racial discrimination: the International Covenant on Civil and Political Rights and the International Convention on the Elimination of All Forms of Racial Discrimination. Despite having also signed other relevant instruments, such as the International Covenant on Economic, Social and Cultural Rights, the Convention on the Elimination of All Forms of Discrimination Against Women, the Convention on the Rights of the Child and the Convention on the Rights of Persons with Disabilities, which could enhance the protection and recognition of the rights of people of African descent, the internal processes for ratification of these instruments have been stalled for a long time. The United States has not signed and ratified any of the human rights treaties that would allow United States citizens to present individual complaints to the United Nations human rights treaty bodies or to the Inter-American Court of Human Rights. The United States is subject to the individual complaints procedure in the Inter-American Commission on Human Rights. The Working Group was informed that due to the standing declarations by the United States considering the International Covenant on Civil and Political Rights, the International Convention on the Elimination of All Forms of Racial Discrimination and the Convention against Torture and Other Cruel, Inhuman or Degrading Treatment or Punishment as non-self-executing, courts in general in the United States are reluctant to consider international human rights treaties and jurisprudence when these are invoked as independent legal arguments. Owing to these factors, human rights treaties are generally not recognized as giving rise to individually enforceable rights in United States courts.

11. In its first report to the United States, in 2010, the Working Group provided an overview of the strong legal framework in place to combat racial discrimination. The Working Group recognizes that the country's Constitution, particularly its Thirteenth, Fourteenth and Fifteenth Amendments, in combination with civil rights legislation and the Supreme Court's jurisprudence, have provided people of African descent with legal tools to combat interpersonal and institutional discrimination. However, having listened to African Americans in different parts of the country, the Working Group considers that civil rights laws are not being fully implemented, and even if fully implemented, they are insufficient to overcome and transform the institutional and structural racial discrimination and racism against people of African descent. Mass incarceration, police violence, housing segregation, disparity in the quality of education, labour market segmentation, political disenfranchisement and environmental degradation continue to have detrimental impacts on people of African descent, despite the application of civil rights laws. 12. The Working Group was informed that the federal structure of the United States has the virtue of allowing some states to explore more progressive policies to protect and promote the rights of people of African descent, which other states could benefit and learn from. Nevertheless, the Working Group also received information that the autonomy of the states and of local government also allows for the establishment of more regressive policies. While federal law provides a baseline of protection for civil and human rights, state laws can vary, and thus people of African descent enjoy different levels of protection of their rights depending on the state that they are living in. 13. The Working Group was also informed that some state and local governments have limited avenues and resources to ensure the realization of the rights of people of African descent. While state attorneys general and state civil rights commissions have a key role in combating Afrophobia and racial discrimination at the state level, the Working Group perceived disparities in the commitment levels and capacities of those institutions to implement state civil rights legislation.

B. Institutional and policy measures

14. While there is no exclusive federal authority charged specifically with monitoring and advancing the situation of people of African descent, the Working Group was informed about measures that several federal agencies were undertaking to enforce civil rights laws. In general, authorities at the federal and state levels acknowledged that racial discrimination was a great challenge in the United States and acknowledged the need to adopt focused policies to address existing gaps in order to tackle institutional and structural racism. One example is My Brother's Keeper, a White House initiative launched in February 2014 to address opportunity gaps that African American boys and young men face in re-

gard to their access to basic health care, good nutrition, high-quality education, and labour opportunities, and in reduction of violence.

15. Another measure was the creation of a task force to identify best practices and to make recommendations to the President on how policing practices can promote effective crime reduction while building public trust. The task force released its report on 18 May 2015 with a set of recommendations divided into six pillars: building trust and legitimacy, policy and oversight, technology and social media, community policing and crime reduction, training and education, and officer wellness and safety. The report adopted positive recommendations on key issues such as racial profiling, the use of force, the independence of investigations into killings by police officers, data collection, civilian oversight of law enforcement agencies and police workforce diversity, among others. The recommendations are not binding on state and local agencies.

16. The Civil Rights Division of the Department of Justice has been focusing on tackling racial bias in law enforcement through civil rights investigations into local police departments. Since 2009, the Department of Justice has opened 22 investigations and has reached 16 agreements to reform unconstitutional policing practices. In 2010, the United States Attorney General created the Office for Access to Justice to address the crisis in the provision of indigent legal defence that continues to have a specific impact on African Americans and other minorities. In 2016, the Attorney General launched a set of reforms to the criminal justice system known as the Roadmap to Re-entry, which is aimed at reducing the existing high level of recidivism and at improving public health, child welfare, employment, education, housing and other key reintegration outcomes for those who have served their time in the federal prison system.

17. One of the most important policy developments since the 2010 report of the Working Group has been the adoption of the Patient Protection and Affordable Care Act, which has allowed 2.3 million African American adults to gain medical health insurance.

18. In 2015, the Department of Housing and Urban Development released a new rule — Affirmatively Furthering Fair Housing — which provides planning tools to communities that are taking actions to overcome historic patterns of segregation. The Equal Employment Opportunity Commission issued new guidance on the application of disparate impact analysis in cases involving the use by employers of arrest and conviction records in employment decisions, which often have a disproportionate impact on racial minorities. Under this guidance, for example, the Equal Employment Opportunity Commission filed a lawsuit against BMW Manufacturing Co., alleging that the company excluded African American workers from employment at a disproportionate rate when the company's new logistics contractor applied BMW's criminal conviction records guidelines to incumbent logistics employees. In 2015, a United States district court ordered the company to pay $1.6 million and provide job opportunities to alleged victims of racial discrimination.

19. The landmark decision of the Supreme Court in June 2016 in Fisher v. University of Texas at Austin et al., which upheld an affirmative action policy at the University of Texas, permitting the inclusion of race as one of the components to be considered during the applications process, is a positive development with longer-term policy implications. IV. Manifestations of racial discrimination A. The criminal justice system and barriers to civil and political participation

20. The Working Group is deeply concerned at the alarming levels of police brutality and excessive use of lethal force by law enforcement officials, committed with impunity against people of African descent in the United States. In addition to the most recent and well-known cases of killings of unarmed African Americans — such as the cases of Eric Garner, Michael Brown, Tamir Rice, Walter Scott, Freddie Gray and Laquan McDonald — the Working Group received information about many other similar cases. The Working Group met with a considerable number of relatives of African Americans allegedly killed by police officers that are still seeking justice for their loved ones, including Tyrone West, Tyron Lewis, Jonathan Sanders, Oscar Grant, Tony Robinson, Marlon Brown, India Kager, Ronald Johnson, Mohamed Bah, Rekia Boyd, Sandra Bland and Alonso Smith.

21. Despite efforts made by the Department of Justice, there is still a lack of an official national system to track killings committed by law enforcement officials. Federal authorities commented that the main reason for this problem is that the 18,000 police departments and law enforcement agencies in the United States are not obliged to report these types of incidents. The Department of Justice was aware of this information gap and informed the Working Group that, notwithstanding the need for legislation, it was also building a system to track information nationwide. To date, the system had not been launched.

22. In the absence of a public national system to track cases of killings by police officers, the Guardian newspaper's "The Counted" database identified a total of 1,136 people killed by the police in 2015, of whom 302 were African Americans. African Americans were killed at twice the rate of white, Hispanic and Native Americans. In addition, about 25 per cent of the African Americans killed were unarmed, compared to 17 per cent of the white people. The Washington Post database of police shootings registered 990 people shot dead in 2015, of whom 38 were unarmed African Americans. Excessive and disproportionate use of force against African Americans also includes the use of tasers and heavy-handed assaults by law enforcement officers, which also have debilitating consequences for victims; there is no national system to track such incidents, either.

23. The Working Group is deeply concerned about the low number of cases where police officers have been held accountable for these crimes, despite the evidence. The Guardian reported that only 18 law enforcement officers were charged with crimes in relation to the 1,136 killings registered in 2015. One in every four killings by police officers that occurred in the first quarter of 2015 remain unresolved more than a year later, and 69 per cent of the 289 cases of killings by the police in the first three months of 2015 have now been ruled justified or accidental. The final report of the President's Task Force on 21st Century Policing acknowledged some of the obstacles in tackling impunity related to killings by police officers and recommended mandatory external and independent criminal investigations and the use of external and independent prosecutors in cases of police use of force resulting in injury or death.

24. Killings of unarmed African Americans by the police is only the tip of the iceberg in what is a pervasive racial bias in the justice system. The Working Group heard testimonies that African Americans face a pattern of police practices which violate their human rights: they are disproportionately targeted for police surveillance, and experience and witness public harassment, excessive force and racial discrimination. Due to racial bias, there is fear of approaching the police for help and there is also a failure on the part of the State to provide protection. The Working Group heard testimonies from African Americans based on their experience that from an early age they are treated by the State as a dangerous criminal group and face a presumption of guilt rather than of innocence. The rapid negative escalation of situations and the excessive use of force disproportionately used on African Americans demonstrates this concern. The Working Group heard reports that racial profiling is a rampant practice among law enforcement officials. During the country visit, the Working Group was informed about and observed the excessive control and supervision targeting all levels of the lives of African Americans. This control has been reinforced since September 2001 by the introduction of the Patriot Act, and affects not only United States citizens but also has a disparate impact on the detention, treatment and deportation of undocumented migrants, including people of African descent, who enter the United States.

25. The report by the Department of Justice on the Ferguson Police Department, released on 4 March 2015, confirmed that these practices are used. On the basis of police data on stops, searches and arrests, the report documented that although African Americans constitute 67 per cent of the population in Ferguson, 85 per cent of traffic stops, 90 per cent of tickets and 93 per cent of arrests made by the Ferguson police in 2012-2014 were against African Americans. One of the main conclusions of the report was that " Ferguson's law enforcement practices are shaped by the City's focus on revenue rather than by public safety needs. This emphasis on revenue has compromised the institutional character of Ferguson's police department, contributing to a pattern of unconstitutional policing... Further, Ferguson's police and municipal court practices both reflect and exacerbate existing racial bias, including racial stereotypes. Ferguson's own data establish clear racial disparities that adversely impact African Americans. The evidence shows that discriminatory intent is part of the reason for these disparities."

26. Similarly, a report issued in April 2016 by the Police Accountability Task Force in Chicago concluded that racism was one of the main factors that could explain the pattern of arrests without justification, detentions without legal counsel, and physical and verbal abuse, including deaths and injuries, against African Americans committed by members of the Chicago Police Department. The report shows that despite African Americans constituting only one third of the city's population, 74 per cent of the 404 people shot by the Chicago police between 2008 and 2015 were black, three out of every four people on whom Chicago police officers used tasers between 2012 and 2015 were African Americans, and 72 per cent of the investigative street stops that did not lead to arrests in the summer of 2014 were carried out on African Americans. The report emphasizes that the Chicago Police Department's own data give "validity to the widely held belief that the police have no regard for the sanctity of life when it comes to people of colour."

27. The Working Group recognizes steps taken at the federal and state level to end racial profiling. In 2014, the City of New York withdrew an appeal in connection with the landmark Floyd v. City of New York case and agreed to join a remedial process ordered by a federal judge, who had found the City liable for a decade-long pattern of discriminatory and unconstitutional stop-and-frisk practices that disproportionately affected the black and Latino communities. In a recent report by the independent monitor of the remedial process, it was underscored that despite the recent reductions in the absolute number of stops recorded by the New York Police Department and the adoption of a set of preventive measures, there were still major challenges ahead in ensuring that written changes in policies were carried out in practice.

28. The Department of Justice, as recommended by the Committee on the Elimination of Racial Discrimination reviewed the 2003 guidance regarding the use of race by federal law enforcement agencies and adopted in 2014 new guidance that also prohibits law enforcement biases based on ethnicity, gender, national origin, religion, sexual orientation or gender identity. The new guidance eliminates the exception made in the former guidance regarding the use of racial profiling in cases of national security threats and in enforcing laws protecting the integrity of the nation's borders.

29. Although crime rates in the United States have been decreasing for the last 20 years, the federal and state prison and local jail population has soared to over 2.2 million people, with another 7 million on parole or probation. African Americans are overrepresented in the penitentiary system, accounting for 36 per cent of sentenced federal and state prisoners. African American women constitute 21 per cent of the imprisoned female population. The incarceration rate for African American males is 5.9 times higher than the rate for white males, while the rate for African American females is 2.1 times higher than the rate for white females. The Sentencing Project has underscored that if current trends continue, one of every three black American males born today can expect to go to prison in his lifetime.

30. Thousands of young African Americans, particularly those living under the poverty line and with low levels of educational attainment, have been placed in detention centres, without addressing the root causes of crime, guaranteeing better security to the communities where they lived or offering them effective rehabilitation.

31. The Working Group was informed that the "War on Drugs" had had a devastating impact on African Americans and that mass incarceration was considered a system of racial control that operated in a similar way to how Jim Crow laws once operated.

32. The Working Group observed that the federal authorities, and some state authorities, have recognized that mass incarceration has been ineffective and have started taking measures to curb some of its negative impacts. At the federal level, the Administration has worked to enhance common-sense sentencing reforms by reducing disparities in the mandatory minimums for crack and powder cocaine possession (Fair Sentencing Act of 2010) and by modernizing the federal sentencing guidelines for drug crimes. The majority of states have also lowered sentences for drug and property crimes and have increased opportunities for early release.

33. The Working Group was also informed about the serious disadvantages that individuals with criminal records or a history of incarceration face when they go back to their communities, in accessing employment, housing, health, safety net programmes and welfare assistance. For example, African Americans with criminal records are 50 per cent less likely to receive an interview request or job offer than individuals without criminal records. Furthermore, white men with a criminal record had more positive responses in job applications than African American men with no criminal record even when their work experience was the same. Individuals with records of low-level non-violent offences may be denied public housing assistance, and individuals with a felony drug record are fully or partially excluded from food stamps (the Supplemental Nutrition Assistance Program, also known as SNAP) in 30 states.

34. Acknowledging this problem, the Federal Government has put in place some re-entry programmes. The Working Group was informed that the Office of Personnel Management had modified its rules to delay inquiries into criminal history until later in the federal hiring process. Grantees of the Department of Labor's Re-entry Employment Opportunities programme are able to use grant funds to pay non-profit legal services centres to assist programme participants with mitigating the impact of criminal records, and the Department of Housing and Urban Development intends providing funds for organizations to assist with expunging, sealing and/or correcting juvenile or adult records. Nevertheless, the Working Group was informed that federal and state re-entry programmes are underfunded in terms of meeting the needs of the 600,000 prisoners released each year.

35. The Working Group is concerned about inadequate conditions of detention and about particularly serious barriers in accessing health treatment, including mental health treatment. A large number of prisoners in Pennsylvania, who have been diagnosed with hepatitis C and are primarily of African descent, have reportedly not received appropriate medication due to the high costs of treatment. The Working Group heard testimonies of labour impositions on inmates, who earned around 15 to 20 cents per hour of work. African American communities emphasized that the privatization of detention centres might tend to privilege the earning of profits, by sacrificing adequate detention conditions. The Working Group also heard how the mass incarceration of African American men and women had had a devastating impact on their children.

36. The Working Group commends the landmark Supreme Court decisions that banned the application of the death penalty for children under 18 years of age (*Roper v. Simmons*), that prohibited life sentences without parole imposed on juveniles convicted of non-homicide offences (*Graham v. Florida*) and that considered unconstitutional mandatory life sentences without parole for children under 17 years of age convicted for homicide (*Miller v. Alabama*). Nevertheless, the Working Group is concerned that life imprisonment sentences can still be imposed on children convicted of homicide, that in 15 states children can still be tried as adults, and that around 10,000 children are housed in adult prisons and jails on any given day in the United States. According to the Equal Justice Initiative, 70 per cent of the children sentenced to life in prison are African Americans.

37. Solitary confinement or restrictive housing is an extensive practice in the United States. The Liman Program at Yale University estimated that approximately 80,000 to 100,000 inmates were being held in restrictive housing in federal and state penitentiaries in the fall of 2014. Based on the results of the National Inmate Survey 2011-2012, the Bureau of Justice Statistics of the Department of Justice estimated that 18 per cent of the inmates in federal and state prisons affirmed having been placed in solitary confinement during the course of 12 months. A study made by the New York City Department of Health and Mental Hygiene on the records of first-time inmates in the New York City jail system between 2011 and 2013 found that African Americans were 2.52 times more likely than whites to be put in solitary confinement.

38. The Working Group acknowledges that on 25 January 2016, the President of the United States, Barack Obama, announced the adoption of a set of recommendations made by the Department of Justice on the use of solitary confinement in the federal prison system. The Department of Justice recommended important measures, such as the ending of solitary confinement for juveniles and for inmates who have committed low-level infractions, the placement of inmates with serious mental illness in alternative forms of housing, limitations on the use of punitive segregation, the introduction of the principle of less restrictive conditions for inmates who face legitimate threats inside the prison, and the establishment of a data system to report on the use of solitary confinement. The Working Group was also informed about some reforms made at the state level (namely in Colorado, New Mexico, Virginia and Washington) aimed at restricting the use of solitary confinement. Notwithstanding these positive steps, the Working Group is concerned that the recommendations made by the Department of Justice are not binding and are only applicable to the federal prison system.

39. The Working Group was also informed that race was a significant factor in death penalty cases in the United States. African Americans represent 41.7 per cent of the death row population and 34.6 per cent of defendants executed since 1976 in the United States. Studies also reveal that there is a strong correlation between race and the decision to impose the death penalty. Despite the fact that a vast majority (90 per cent) of homicides in the United States are intraracial, out of the 1,359 inmates executed in the United States (in the period from the 1976 reinstatement of capital punishment to 2013), only 17 were white defendants convicted for killing African Americans, while 230 were African American defendants convicted for killing white persons.

40. The racial composition of the jury is one of the main identified causes of racial bias in the application of the death penalty. While the Constitution of the United States of America entitles defendants to trial by an impartial jury, a common pattern in many states is that minorities are underrepresented on capital punishment juries. The Working Group acknowledges the recent ruling (*Foster v. Chatman*) considered that prosecutors had violated *Batson v. Kentucky* (1986) regarding race-based in which the Supreme Court discrimination in jury selection.

41. The dangerous ideology of white supremacy inhibits social cohesion among the United States population. Hate crime groups, including white supremacist terror groups, are still active in the United States, targeting African Americans, as was seen in the attack at a church in Charleston in 2015. The Confederate flag is considered as a symbol of hate for many African Americans and they have led campaigns to have it removed, however it still is used by some local au-

thorities. 42. The Working Group was also concerned that voter ID laws with increased identification requirements and limits on early voting and registration in several states served to discriminate against minorities such as African Americans, contrary to the spirit of the Voting Rights Act of 1965. In 2013, the Supreme Court, in its decision in *Shelby v. Holder*, struck down parts of the Voting Rights Act, thereby making it easier to put in place voting restrictions at the state and local levels.

B. Disparities in access to education, health, housing and employment

43. The cumulative impact of racially motivated discrimination faced by African Americans in the enjoyment of their rights to education, health, housing and employment, among other economic, social, cultural and environmental rights, has had serious consequences for their overall well-being. Racial discrimination continues to be systemic and rooted in an economic model that denies development to the poorest African American communities. More than 10 million (26 per cent) of African Americans remain mired in poverty, and of that figure, almost half (12 per cent) live in what is known as "deep poverty."

44. The Working Group is concerned about reports that across the country there are police officers in schools, without appropriate training, arresting children for minor offences and dealing with behaviour that previously would be handled as part of a school disciplinary process, resulting in the criminalization of children's behaviour and severe punishment. The police have the authority to detain, frisk and arrest children in school. For example, a black female student was violently arrested by a school resource officer at Spring Valley High School in South Carolina in 2015. Zero tolerance policies and heavy-handed efforts to increase security in schools have led to the excessive penalization and harassment of African American children through racial profiling. African American children are more likely to face harsh disciplinary measures than white children and are being pushed out of school into the criminal justice system — a phenomenon that has been described sadly as the "school to prison pipeline."

45. The Working Group is concerned by the underfunding and closure of schools, particularly those in poor neighbourhoods with significant African American populations. The Working Group was particularly concerned to learn of threats to close Chicago State University, a historically black university.

46. In school curricula, the historical facts concerning the period of colonization, the transatlantic trade in Africans, and enslavement, which have been crucial to the organization of contemporary American society, are not sufficiently covered in all schools. The curricula in some states fail to address adequately the root causes of racial inequality and injustice. This contributes to the structural invisibility of African Americans.

47. The Working Group also received information about de facto segregation of schools. This segregation appears to be nurtured by a culture rooted in the legacy of racial inequality and by failure to address the history of racial injustice, enslavement and the Jim Crow laws.

48. The Working Group noted that a number of factors contributed to the disparities faced by African Americans in realizing the right to the enjoyment of the highest attainable standard of health, which included lack of access to health insurance coverage, lack of access to preventive services and care, and shortcomings related to a lack of diversity and of cultural competency among those giving the care. While the implementation of the Patient Protection and Affordable Care Act has led to 20 million people getting health insurance coverage, states with some of the widest health disparities in the country have rejected expansion of Medicaid, one of the main tools to cover the uninsured. Nine out of ten people who fall into the coverage gap live in the South, and black adults are more likely than any other racial group to be affected. The impact of social determinants such as lack of access to good-quality and healthy housing conditions, lack of education and employment, and transportation barriers also continued to serve as impediments to full enjoyment of the right to health.

49. The Working Group learned that African Americans had limited access to food variety, including to healthy food, as they were concentrated in poor neighbourhoods with food outlets selling unhealthy and even expired food. African Americans have the highest rates of obesity, which is linked to "food deserts."

50. The Working Group is concerned about the persistence of a de facto residential segregation in many of the metropolitan areas in the United States. In the Working Group's meeting with the Department of Housing and Urban Develop-

ment, a series of maps were shown which not only starkly depicted high concentrations of African American families in low-income neighbourhoods and districts, but also reflected the correlation between racial segregation and socioeconomic disparities in access to health, education, and even access to adequate food, between the African American population and the white population. The Working Group was informed that people of African descent were more likely than other people with similar borrower characteristics to be victims of predatory lending, to receive higher-cost loans and to lose their homes to foreclosure. The Department of Housing and Urban Development recognizes that although the most blatant forms of housing discrimination have declined since the 1970s because of the implementation of the Fair Housing Act, the forms of discrimination that persist raise the costs of housing searches for members of minorities and restrict their housing options.

51. The Working Group was also informed about "racial steering," a practice employed by real estate brokers to guide prospective property buyers either towards or away from neighbourhoods on the basis of their race. In many of the places it visited, the Working Group heard from civil society that gentrification had had a detrimental and disparate impact on African Americans.

52. African American people are also concerned that they are disproportionately exposed to environmental hazards that impact on their health and standard of living. They are often forced to live in disadvantaged areas with hazardous environments (e.g. in proximity to industrial toxicity, power stations, flood zones and so on) and without access to social and commercial facilities. The most polluting industrial facilities, across a range of sectors from farming and mining to manufacturing, are more likely to be situated in poor and minority neighborhoods, including those of people of African descent. For instance, the Working Group is concerned about the possible health risks to African Americans on account of the incinerator project in Curtis Bay, Baltimore, and the lead-contaminated water in Flint, Michigan. The Working Group was also informed about the destruction of public housing in some cities; at the same time, public funding for new houses appears to be insufficient to meet the demands for new housing.

53. According to the Department of Housing and Urban Development, in 2015, of the more than half a million homeless people in the United States, African Americans constituted 40.4 per cent. They also constituted 27.8 per cent of the homeless people who were unsheltered.

54. Despite the recovery of the United States economy, the impact of the 2008 and 2009 recession on African Americans is still very much present. The unemployment rate among African Americans is almost twice the national unemployment rate. The Working Group is particularly concerned about the level of unemployment among young African Americans without a high school degree. In 2014, the annual income for African Americans was just under half the income of white Americans who are not Hispanic.

55. People of African descent continue to be underrepresented in management positions. In 2013, they accounted for only 7 per cent of workers in management occupations. Instead, African Americans disproportionately work in temporary jobs with less security and lower salaries. Nearly half a million African Americans earn the minimum wage. The Equal Employment Opportunity Commission continues to receive more than 30,000 complaints a year concerning racial discrimination.

C. Multiple forms of discrimination

56. The Working Group studied intersectionality of the different forms of discrimination faced by people of African descent and heard experiences of racial discrimination based on ethnicity, religion, socioeconomic status, sex and gender identity. The Working Group is particularly concerned by the increasing number of murders of transgender women of African descent and the increasing level of violence affecting them. Racial discrimination also disparately impedes the ability of African American women to maintain overall good health, control their sexuality and reproduction, survive pregnancy and childbirth, and parent their children. African American women in the United States die from pregnancy-related complications at a rate three to four times higher than that of white women. The Working Group is particularly concerned about the fact that 37 per cent of the households headed by African American women live below the poverty line.

57. The Working Group of Experts on People of African Descent shares the findings of the Working Group on the issue of discrimination against women in law and in practice in respect of African American women. In particular, the Work-

ing Group of Experts on People of African Descent is concerned at the disproportionate number of African American women subjected to heightened levels of violence, including rape and sexual violence. It also deplores reports of police brutality and the increased number of killings of African American women by the police. Furthermore, it is disturbed at the persistent fatal consequences for women of the lack of gun control, particularly in cases of domestic violence.

V. Conclusions and recommendations

A. Conclusions

58. The Working Group welcomes the work of the bureaus and offices in all government departments and agencies, which implement the civil rights laws through the investigation of complaints, litigation, and the issuance of guidance, and by securing remedies, including compensation.

59. The Working Group acknowledges the Office for Access to Justice, of the Department of Justice, for its work to improve justice for all Americans, and the Civil Rights Division, also of the Department of Justice, for its work on investigations into excessive use of force by the police and on patterns of discrimination. The Working Group welcomes the steps taken to reform the criminal justice system and combat racial discrimination and disparities through initiatives including the Fair Sentencing Act; the Department's Smart on Crime and re-entry initiatives; the report and recommendations of the President's Task Force on 21st Century Policing, to strengthen community-police relationships across the country; the new Guidance for Federal Law Enforcement Agencies Regarding the Use of Race, Ethnicity, Gender, National Origin, Religion, Sexual Orientation or Gender Identity; and the enforcement guidance on the consideration of arrest and conviction records in employment decisions under title VII of the Civil Rights Act of 1964.

60. The Working Group also noted that during its visit, the Government adopted a series of executive actions to reduce the use of solitary confinement at the federal level by prohibiting the solitary confinement of juveniles, diverting inmates with serious mental illness to alternative forms of housing, and establishing that inmates should be housed in the least restrictive settings, among other issues. These changes are part of a larger effort to implement criminal justice reforms, including those now pending in Congress. 61. The Working Group noted White House initiatives such as My Brother's Keeper and the White House Initiative on Educational Excellence for African Americans, aimed at addressing opportunity gaps and improving educational outcomes for African Americans.

62. The Working Group noted the new report by the Charles Colson Task Force on Federal Corrections, which concluded that punitive mandatory sentences for drug crimes represent the primary driver for prison overcrowding.

63. The Working Group welcomes the abolition of the death penalty in three additional states since the Working Group's visit to the United States in 2010, as this form of torture and inhumane punishment is disproportionately used against African Americans.

64. The Working Group noted the important development in the area of health with the adoption of the Patient Protection and Affordable Care Act, which has allowed 2.3 million African American adults to gain medical health insurance.

65. The Working Group noted some positive developments at the state and local levels. The Working Group welcomes the measures taken in New York City that prohibit employers from asking about criminal history until an employee is hired. These measures also allow the issuance of municipal identification cards for undocumented migrants, and create a policy of issuing desk appearance tickets for certain offenders as an alternative to imprisonment for a misdemeanour offence. The Working Group also noted the decision to end the stop and frisk policy.

66. Similarly, the Working Group welcomes the steps taken in Illinois to combat the home foreclosure crisis that had especially affected African Americans. The Working Group also welcomes the measures taken by the mayor of Chicago to foster accountability in the police department following the Laquan McDonald case.

67. The Working Group welcomes the growing human rights movement in the United States, which has successfully advocated for social change. Following the epidemic of racial violence by the police, civil society networks such as Black Lives Matter, together with other activists, are strongly advocating for racial justice, legal and policy reforms, and citizen control over policing and other areas which directly target African Americans.

68. Despite the positive measures, the Working Group remains extremely concerned about the human rights situation of African Americans. In particular, the legacy of colonial history, enslavement, racial subordination and segregation, racial terrorism and racial inequality in the United States remains a serious challenge, as there has been no real commitment to reparations and to truth and reconciliation for people of African descent. Contemporary police killings and the trauma that they create are reminiscent of the past racial terror of lynching. Impunity for State violence has resulted in the current human rights crisis and must be addressed as a matter of urgency.

69. Racial bias and disparities in the criminal justice system, mass incarceration and the tough-on-crime policies disproportionately impact African Americans. Mandatory minimum sentencing and the disproportionate punishment of African Americans including with the death penalty are of grave concern.

70. The Working Group identified some of the main barriers to tackling impunity for killings by the police as: (a) the lack of independence of the initial investigations, which in the majority of cases are conducted by the same police department that the alleged perpetrator is a member of; (b) the wide discretion of prosecutors to determine when and how to present charges; and (c) the fact that some federal, state and county practices are not in line with international standards as regards the use of force.

71. The surge in incarceration has been driven since the 1980s by changes in criminal justice policies as part of the so-called "War on Drugs." Policies enacted at the federal and state levels emphasizing harsher sentencing rules (such as the more frequent use of mandatory minimums and of "three strikes" rules), longer prison sentences and higher conviction rates have been applied with a racial bias, with deep collateral damage on African Americans.

72. Disparities in the enforcement of policies can be found in the different approaches adopted by states to address issues such as racial profiling, the presence of police in schools, the criminalization of homelessness, limitations on the use of lethal force by law enforcement officials, the use of solitary confinement and the prosecution of juvenile offenders as adults, among others. The United States is also not acting with due diligence to protect the rights of African Americans, as evidenced by the lack of gun control and the stand-your-ground laws, among other things.

73. The Working Group is concerned about the lack of an official and reliable national system to track killings and excessive use of force committed by law enforcement officials while on duty. The Working Group is also deeply concerned about the low number of cases in which police officers have been held accountable. It identified that the federal, state and county regulations that are not in line with international standards on the use of force and firearms are some of the main barriers to police accountability.

74. Mass incarceration has had a disproportionately high impact on people of African descent. The devastating impact of the "War on Drugs" has led to mass incarceration and is compared by African Americans to enslavement, due to the exploitation and dehumanization of African Americans. The costs of mass incarceration practices must be measured in human lives — particularly the generations of young black men and women who serve long prison sentences and are lost to their families and to society at large.

75. The Working Group is also concerned about the criminalization of poverty, which disproportionately affects African Americans. There has been an increase in the imprisonment of people for minor offences and of those who are unable to pay debts due to increases in fines and fees. They are detained in debtor prisons and made to work off their debt. As illustrated by the Department of Justice investigation of the Ferguson Police Department, in some jurisdictions the imposition of fines is a way to secure revenues rather than to maintain public security. This creates numerous problems for individuals and families. There is also an excessive punishment of poor children for minor offences.

76. State laws establishing mandatory minimum sentences and zero tolerance policies have been applied with racial bias. Thousands of young African Americans have been placed in detention centres, without addressing the root causes of crime, or guaranteeing better security to their communities; nor have they been offered effective rehabilitation. People who have served their time in prison continue to be stigmatized when they are released. Their criminal records impede them from finding a job, getting adequate housing or accessing social programmes, and from voting. Some re-entry programmes are not well funded, and re-entry programmes are not present countrywide.

77. Racial profiling is a rampant practice and seriously damages the trust between African Americans and law enforcement officials. Also, some parts of the media routinely portray African Americans as criminals and this negatively impacts the perception that society in general has of African Americans. These practices not only erode trust but also lead to fatal consequences. For example, Philando Castile was stopped by law enforcement dozens of times before he was eventually shot and killed.

78. The Working Group expresses deep concern about the continued existence of the death penalty in 31 states and at the federal level.

79. While noting the recent executive actions on solitary confinement, the Working Group remains concerned about its use in prisons, juvenile detention centres and foster care, at both the federal and state levels. The Working Group is particularly concerned about its negative impact on children.

80. The Working Group is concerned about the underage prosecution of children as adults in the United States. Children are detained in adult prisons and jails, putting them at risk of sexual assault and abuse. Juveniles should be treated as juveniles, no matter what crime they are alleged to have committed, and must be held in a juvenile facility. The Working Group is also concerned at the use of police in schools and at school discipline being criminalized, subjecting African American children in particular to severe punishments. These practices are a violation of children's human rights and should be eliminated.

81. The persistent gap in almost all the human development indicators, such as life expectancy, income and wealth, level of education, and even food security, between African Americans and the rest of the United States population, reflects the level of structural and institutional discrimination that creates de facto barriers for people of African descent to fully exercise their human rights.

82. Geographic location and zip code can determine to some extent the future of young African Americans. People from poor black neighbourhoods are more likely to face lower educational attainment, more exposure to violence and crime, a tense interaction with the police, fewer employment opportunities, environmental degradation and also low life expectancy rates.

83. African Americans in many cities are facing a housing crisis, in which people are not able to pay their rents or mortgages, and even less to purchase a new house, and are subsequently subject to de facto gentrification.

84. The Working Group acknowledges that federal civil rights legislation, put in place in the 1960s and 1970s, has had a positive impact by redressing individual and even institutional cases of racial discrimination. However, hearing the testimonies of African Americans in different parts of the country, the Working Group is concerned about the implementation of civil rights laws not being sufficiently effective to overcome and transform the structural racial discrimination against African Americans.

85. The complex organizational structure of the legal system, with the independence of federal, state and county jurisdictions, and the lack of direct and the lack or direct applicability of international human rights law and policies, creates gaps that impact deeply on the human rights of African Americans.

86. The Working Group is concerned that international human rights treaties cannot be invoked in national courts, as in most cases there is no enabling legislation and they have been declared non-self-executing.

87. The following recommendations are intended to assist the United States in its efforts to combat all forms of racism, racial discrimination, Afrophobia, xenophobia and related intolerance.

B. Recommendations

88. The Working Group reiterates the recommendation that it made after its visit to the United States of America in 2010 to establish a national human rights commission in accordance with the principles relating to the status of national institutions for the promotion and protection of human rights (Paris Principles). The Government should establish within this body a specific division to monitor the human rights of African Americans.

89. In addition to the above, the Working Group urges the Government of the United States of America to consider the ratification of the core international human rights treaties to which the United States is still not a party, with a view to removing any gaps in the protection and full enjoyment of rights therein. It also encourages the United States to ratify regional human rights treaties and to review the reservations related to the treaties that it has signed or ratified.

90. Federal and state laws should be adopted that incorporate the International Covenant on Civil and Political Rights and other international human rights treaties, as well as regional treaties. To this end, an inter-agency body should be created, composed of high-level officials from the executive, the legislature and the judiciary at both the federal and the state levels, who will take steps to give effect to the decisions, resolutions, views, observations and recommendations of United Nations human rights bodies such as the Human Rights Council, the treaty bodies and special procedures, and of regional human rights bodies.

91. There is a profound need to acknowledge that the transatlantic trade in Africans, enslavement, colonization and colonialism were a crime against humanity and are among the major sources and manifestations of racism, racial discrimination, Afrophobia, xenophobia and related intolerance. Past injustices and crimes against African Americans need to be addressed with reparatory justice.

92. Monuments, memorials and markers should be erected to facilitate public dialogue. Education must be accompanied by acts of reconciliation, to overcome acts of racial bigotry and legacies of racial injustice. Federal and state legislation should be passed recognizing the negative impact of enslavement and racial injustice.

93. During the International Decade for People of African Descent, public forums or hearings should be held with African Americans in order to create a constructive and open dialogue in which organizations and social movements can share experiences and engage with policymakers and institutions of the local, state and federal government on ways to address the crisis being experienced by American society.

94. The Working Group encourages Congress to pass H.R. 40 — the Commission to Study Reparation Proposals for African-Americans Act — which would establish a commission to examine enslavement and racial discrimination in the colonies and the United States from 1619 to the present and to recommend appropriate remedies. The Working Group urges the United States to consider seriously applying analogous elements contained in the Caribbean Community's Ten-Point Action Plan on Reparations, which includes a formal apology, health initiatives, educational opportunities, an African knowledge programme, psychological rehabilitation, technology transfer and financial support, and debt cancellation.

95. The Working Group encourages the Government of the United States of America to elaborate a national action plan to fully implement the International Convention on the Elimination of All Forms of Racial Discrimination and comprehensively address racism affecting African Americans.

96. The Government should increase engagement with human rights organizations and civil society and should fund them with the aim of implementing the universal periodic review recommendations made to and accepted by the United States.

97. The Working Group urges the Government to ensure that recent policies undertaken to address racial disparities will be further implemented at the federal and state levels.

98. The Working Group urges Congress to expedite the passing of all pending criminal justice reform bills, including the End Racial Profiling Act and the Second Chance Reauthorization Act. It also welcomes the bipartisan support for bill S.2123 — the Sentencing Reform and Corrections Act of 2015 — which among other things proposes drastically reducing the use of mandatory minimum sentencing and in the Working Group's opinion is crucial to achieving comprehensive criminal justice reform.

99. The Working Group recommends urgent action to ensure accountability for police violence against African Americans: by improving the reporting of violations involving the excessive use of force and extrajudicial killings by the police, and ensuring that reported cases of excessive use of force are independently investigated; by ensuring that alleged perpetrators are prosecuted and, if convicted, are punished with appropriate sanctions; by ensuring that investigations are

re-opened when new evidence becomes available; and by ensuring that victims or their families are provided with remedies. The Working Group also calls for implementation of the recommendations in the final report of the President's Task Force on 21st Century Policing.

100. The Working Group recommends that the Government step up its efforts to prevent excessive use of force by law enforcement officials by ensuring compliance with the Basic Principles on the Use of Force and Firearms by Law Enforcement Officials, of 1990.

101. Security policies in schools should be revisited. Policing in schools should be abolished.

102. Misdemeanour laws affecting schoolchildren should be repealed, such as the misdemeanour law in South Carolina under which school disturbance constitutes a misdemeanour.

103. The use of restraint and seclusion in schools should be prohibited. Early counselling should be given to students with mental health issues. Special attention and protection must be given to students with autism, attention deficit hyperactivity disorder and other similar disabilities.

104. The Working Group recommends that the Government develop guidelines on how to ensure that school discipline policies and practices are in compliance with international human rights standards. Positive Behavioural Interventions and Supports and restorative practices in school discipline should be used in order to reduce disciplinary incidents and improve learning in schools.

105. Males should be separated from females in detention. Younger prisoners should be separated from adults. Alternatives to imprisonment for youth, such as intervention and diversion, should be explored.

106. In imposing sentences, the welfare of the family of the accused should be taken into account, with particular attention given to the best interests of the child.

107. Appropriate measures should be adopted to prevent excessive bail. Alternatives to detention should also be explored.

108. Community policing strategies should be developed to give the community control of the police that are there to protect and serve them. The Working Group recommends that communities establish boards that would elect police officers they want playing this important role.

109. Before non-payment of a court fine or fee is treated as a civil contempt of court charge, it should first be determined whether the individual has the ability to pay. Imprisonment should not be offered as a way of paying off the debt. If the debt cannot be paid, the fee should not be levied.

110. The Working Group also recommends that the prison reform processes and policies include specific policies to address the increasing rate of incarceration of African American women.

111. Solitary confinement should be banned absolutely for being in violation of international human rights law standards, particularly those found in the Convention against Torture and Other Cruel, Inhuman or Degrading Treatment or Punishment and in the Standard Minimum Rules for the Treatment of Prisoners.

112. The Working Group recommends that the Government allow independent monitoring of places of detention in the United States, and in this connection that it consider inviting the Special Rapporteur on torture and other cruel, inhuman or degrading treatment or punishment. As part of a call for greater expression of commitment to the rights of detainees, the Working Group takes the opportunity to urge the Government to ratify the Optional Protocol to the Convention against Torture and Other Cruel, Inhuman or Degrading Treatment or Punishment, which creates a mechanism for unrestricted and unannounced visits to places of detention.

113. International human rights standards should be observed in the criminal justice system. The Working Group recommends the abolition of the death penalty throughout the United States.

114. The Working Group calls upon the Government to ensure that all states repeal laws that restrict voting rights. In particular, it urges reinstatement of the voting rights of persons convicted of a felony who have completed their sentences.

115. Targeted measures should be developed to raise awareness of and reduce crimes against the lesbian, gay, bisexual, transgender, queer and intersex community, in particular against transgender women.

116. Asylum seekers should not be imprisoned pending a determination of their application for refugee status. The right to counsel and the right to an interpreter should be respected at all times.

117. The Working Group recommends extending access to affordable health care to a greater part of the population. Health policies and programmes should place particular priority on access to quality and affordable health care with targeted goals for reducing the maternal mortality of African American women.

118. Consistently, the school curriculum in each state should reflect appropriately the history of the transatlantic trade in Africans, enslavement and segregation.

119. The Department of Education should study zero tolerance policies and their disparate impact on African American students. A task force should be created to specifically focus on realigning and re-engaging students who have been dismissed from educational institutions as part of a zero tolerance policy.

120. The Working Group recommends upholding the right to adequate standards of living, including adequate food, housing, and safe drinking water and sanitation. The Government should immediately halt the demolition of public housing if replacement units have not been guaranteed. All such activities must be undertaken only through prior and informed consent and with the participation of the people affected.

121. The Working Group urges the Government to strengthen the implementation of Executive Order 12898, including through the allocation of adequate resources.

122. The Government of the United States of America should undertake a review of policies to improve protection of the environment and ensure that environmental justice is provided.

123. The Working Group encourages the Government to undertake impact-oriented activities in the framework of the International Decade for People of African Descent (2015-2024).

Source: Report of the Working Group of Experts on People of African Descent on its mission to the United States of America
http://www.ushrnetwork.org/sites/ushrnetwork.org/files/unwgepad_us_visit_final_report_9_15_16.pdf

9. U.N. GENERAL ASSEMBLY, HUMAN RIGHTS COUNCIL, 28 APRIL 2009, RACISM, RACIAL DISCRIMINATION, XENOPHOBIA AND RELATED FORMS OF INTOLERANCE, FOLLOW-UP TO AND IMPLEMENTATION OF THE DURBAN DECLARATION AND PROGRAMME OF ACTION

This is the 2009 Report of the Special Rapporteur, Doudou Diène, as a result of his Mission to the United States of America, on contemporary forms of racism, racial discrimination, xenophobia and related intolerance in the U.S. It demonstrates how continuously aware the international community is in its analysis, assessment and recommendations regarding equality and non-discrimination issues related to racism, as well as the international community's willingness to assist the U.S. with these issues. The Obama administration was receptive to Special Rapporteur Diène's Mission and eventual Report.

Report of the Special Rapporteur on contemporary forms of racism, racial discrimination, xenophobia and related intolerance, Doudou Diène, Mission to the United States of America, 2009

Summary

At the invitation of the Government, the Special Rapporteur visited the United States of America from 19 May to 6 June 2008. During the mission, the Special Rapporteur visited Washington, D.C., New York, Chicago, Omaha, Los Angeles, New Orleans and the Louisiana and Mississippi Gulf Coast, Miami and San Juan (Puerto Rico).

The Special Rapporteur had extensive meetings with state institutions, including the Supreme Court, civil society organizations active in the field of racism, minority communities and victims of racism.

The Special Rapporteur formulates several recommendations, including that:

(a) Congress establish a bipartisan commission to evaluate the progress and failures in the fight against racism and the ongoing process of resegregation, particularly in housing and education, and to find responses to check these trends;

(b) The Government reassess existing legislation on racism, racial discrimination, xenophobia and related intolerance in view of two main guidelines: addressing the overlapping nature of poverty and race or ethnicity; and linking the fight against racism to the construction of a democratic, egalitarian and interactive multiculturalism, in order to strengthen inter-community relations;

(c) The Government should intensify its efforts to enforce federal civil rights laws;

(d) The Government clarify to law enforcement officials the obligation of equal treatment and, in particular, the prohibition of racial profiling.

Annex

Report submitted by the special rapporteur on contemporary forms of racism, racial discrimination, xenophobia and related intolerance, doudou diÈne, on his mission to the united states of America (19 May-6 June 2008)

Introduction

1. At the invitation of the Government, the Special Rapporteur visited the United States of America from 19 May to 6 June 2008 ((Washington, D.C., New York, Chicago, Omaha, Los Angeles, New Orleans and the Louisiana and Mississippi Gulf Coast, Miami and San Juan, Puerto Rico). He held extensive meetings with federal authorities at the executive, legislative and judicial branches as well as with local authorities (see appendix).

2. Apart from the agenda with state institutions, including the Supreme Court, the Special Rapporteur also had extensive meetings with civil society organizations active in the area of racism and xenophobia, minority communities as well as victims of racism and racial discrimination.

3. The Special Rapporteur wishes to express his gratitude to the Government of the United States for its full cooperation and openness throughout the visit as well as a particular appreciation to Justice Stephen Breyer at the Supreme Court. He also wishes to express his sincere thanks to all civil society organizations that actively participated and contributed to the success of his mission. In particular, he wishes to thank Global Rights for its support throughout the mission.

I. GENERAL BACKGROUND

A. Historical and political context

4. The first inhabitants of North America are believed to have arrived crossing from the Bering Strait towards the end of the last Ice Age. Before the advent of European explorers in the late 15th century, a population of one to two million people is believed to have populated North America. Epidemic diseases brought by the Europeans and violence obliterated many Native American peoples.

5. The United States of America became an independent State after the American Revolutionary War (1775-1783). The three documents that emerged from independence — the Declaration of Independence (1776), the United States

Constitution (1787) and the Bill of Rights (1791) — are among the first formal legally-binding documents recognizing inalienable individual rights such as freedom of religion, freedom of expression and freedom of assembly.

6. The contradictions between the agrarian and slave-based South and the manufacturing, liberalizing and generally anti-slavery North exploded when the Republican candidate, Abraham Lincoln, won the 1860 presidential election. By that time, 4 million slaves and 488,000 free blacks lived in the United States alongside 27 million whites. While the American Civil War (1861-1865) brought about the legal end of slavery and the adoption of the fourteenth amendment to the Constitution, including the equal protection clause, differential treatment to blacks living in the South would continue well into the twentieth century. Jim Crow laws were enacted in many States, legitimated by the "separate but equal" doctrine legitimated by the Supreme Court in *Plessy v. Fergunson*.

7. The "separate but equal" doctrine remained until the emergence of the civil rights movement in the mid-twentieth century. Though the starting point of the movement is difficult to trace, the landmark decision by the Supreme Court on *Brown v. Board of Education* in 1954, striking down racial segregation in schools, certainly had a fundamental impact in unleashing the changes that took place in subsequent years. The movement culminated in the adoption of the Civil Rights Act of 1964, a milestone document that set the institutional framework for the protection of human rights in contemporary United States of America.

B. Demographic, ethnic and religious composition

8. According to the U.S. Census Bureau, in 2006 the United States had a population of around 299 million, composed as follows: 73.9 percent white, 12.4 percent black or African American, 4.4 percent Asian, 0.8 percent American Indian and Alaska Native, 0.1 percent Native Hawaiian and other Pacific Islander, 6.3 percent of other races and 2 percent of people with two or more races. The U.S. Census Bureau correctly does not define Hispanic or Latinos as a race, as individuals of South and Central American origin may be of any race. In 2006 Hispanics or Latinos composed 14.8 percent of the population.

9. In 2007, the foreign-born population in the United States (those not U.S. citizens or U.S. nationals at birth) amounted to approximately 38 million people, or 12.6 percent of the total population. 42.5 percent of those foreign born residents were naturalized citizens. Out of the foreign born population, 47.5 percent are Hispanics, 23.4 percent are Asians, 20.3 percent are non-Hispanic whites and 7.8 percent are blacks.

C. International human rights instruments

10. The United States is party to the International Covenant on Civil and Political Rights (ICCPR), the International Convention on the Elimination of All Forms of Racial Discrimination (ICERD) and other international human rights instruments. With respect to both the ICCPR and the ICERD, the United States has adopted a number of formal reservations, understandings and declarations. In the case of ICERD, with respect to Articles 4 and 7, and in the case of ICCPR, with respect to Article 20, the United States has taken treaty reservations to these provisions, explaining that their scope is at odds with the extensive protections contained in the U.S. Constitution and U.S. laws in the areas of individual freedom of speech, expression and association.

D. Methodology

11. The Special Rapporteur carried out extensive meetings with authorities at the executive, legislative and judiciary branches to collect their views and opinions as well as information concerning government programmes, legislation and judicial decisions. Additionally, an agenda with civil society organizations, communities and associations representing minority groups, victims of discrimination, journalists and student leaders was organized.

12. The Special Rapporteur structured his meetings around three questions: (i) Is there still racism, racial discrimination, xenophobia and related intolerance in the United States? (ii) If so, who are their main victims and what are their main manifestations and expressions? (iii) What are or should be the governmental policies and programmes to fight these phenomena at the political, legal and cultural levels?

II. LEGAL FRAMEWORK

13. The fourteenth amendment of the Constitution, adopted on the aftermath of the Civil War, contains an Equal Protection Clause that formally recognizes the principle of equality before the law. It provides that "[No State shall] *deny to any person within its jurisdiction the equal protection of the laws.*" The fifteenth amendment, ratified on 3 February 1870, further extends the right to vote to all races.

14. The civil rights movement in the 1960s led to the signature by President Lyndon B. Johnson of the Civil Rights Act in 1964. The Act constitutes a historic landmark in the elimination of *de jure* racial discrimination in the country and to set up the institutional and legal structure to combat discrimination. The Act also set up the Commission on Civil Rights, which was mandated to inter alia investigate denials of the right to vote, study and collect information concerning legal developments constituting a denial of equal protection of the laws under the Constitution and appraise the laws and policies of the Federal Government in this regard. The Act was further complemented by the Civil Rights Act of 1968, which prohibited discrimination in the sale, rental, and financing of housing.

15. The enforcement of non-discrimination provisions of the Constitution and federal legislation is primarily carried out by the Civil Rights Division at the Department of Justice, which is composed of over 700 staff. The Civil Rights Division carries out enforcement actions in areas that include criminal cases, disability rights, education, employment, housing and voting. Other Federal agencies are also involved in the enforcement of equal protection legislation, such as the Equal Employment Opportunity Commission and the Office of Fair Housing and Equal Opportunity at the Department of Housing and Urban Development.

III. Public policies AND MEASURES to fight racism, racial discrimination, xenophobia and related intolerance

A. Law enforcement

16. Law enforcement in the United States involves agencies at the federal, state and local levels. While the Special Rapporteur met with several officials at the local level, his analysis is based primarily on agencies, and policies developed, at the Federal level.

17. Racial discrimination by law enforcement agencies is prohibited by the Constitution and federal statutes. These include the Violent Crime Control and Law Enforcement Act of 1994 and the Omnibus Crime Control and Safe Streets Act of 1968. Officials at the Civil Rights Division of the Department of Justice underscored the fundamental importance that it attaches to combating police misconduct, including racial discrimination by police officers, which amounts to approximately half of its Criminal Section's caseload.

18. Officials at the Civil Rights Division as well as at the Department of Homeland Security highlighted the importance of training of law enforcement officials. A Federal Law Enforcement Training Center exists since 1970 and currently provides law enforcement training to over 80 Federal agencies. Particular trainings focusing on cultural awareness and relations with minority communities have also been developed.

19. In what concerns overrepresentation of minorities in the criminal justice system, it was recognized that disparities in incarceration rates exist between minorities, particularly African Americans, and whites. However, as the United States affirmed in its latest periodic report to the Committee on the Elimination of Racial Discrimination (CERD), the reasons for such disparities are complex and do not necessarily indicate differential treatment of persons in the criminal justice system.

Racial profiling

20. The Supreme Court has produced solid jurisprudence prohibiting racial profiling. For example, in *Wren v. United States* (1996), the Court stated that "the Constitution prohibits selective enforcement of the law based on considerations such as race," making explicit reference to the Equal Protection Clause. In *United States v. Armstrong* (1996), repeating *Oyler v. Boles* (1962), the Court further affirmed that "the decision whether to prosecute may not be based on 'an unjustifiable standard such as race, religion, or other arbitrary classification." The ruling in *United States v. Montero-Camargo* (1996) further cautioned against the use of factors that are facially race-neutral but in effect can be discriminatorily used against minorities (e.g. searches against individuals living in "high-crime" areas that are also predominantly inhabited by minorities).

21. In June 2003, responding to a call made by President Bush in his State of the Union address in 2001, the Department of Justice issued a *Guidance Regarding the Use of Race by Federal Law Enforcement Agencies* prohibiting the use of race or ethnicity in law enforcement practices, the first time such guidelines have been issued. The guidance was formally adopted by the Department of Homeland Security in June 2004. Officials at the Civil Rights Division highlighted that the guidelines were also incorporated in the training modules that all law enforcement officials have to undergo. While officials recognized that the guidelines do not create rights that can be affirmed in court, they highlighted that racial profiling violates the equal protection clause of the Constitution, which therefore offers overarching protection against this practice.

B. Hate crimes

22. According to the U.S. Criminal Code, crimes motivated by race, color, religion or national origin can be investigated and prosecuted by federal authorities only when the crime occurs because of the victim's participation in a federally protected activity (e.g. public education, employment, etc). In cases that do not meet the latter requirement, the jurisdiction lies at the state level. Apart from federal regulations, 47 states have laws on hate crimes.

23. The number of hate crimes reported in the United States has decreased from 8,063 reported incidents in 2000 to 7,624 reported incidents in 2007, a fact that was highlighted by officials at the Civil Rights Division. The trend in the past two years is however the opposite, with a 6 percent increase from 2005 to 2007. In 2001, a peak of 9,730 such incidents was reached (a 20 percent increase in comparison to 2000), which the FBI Hate Crimes Statistics relates to the aftermath of 9/11. The number of yearly reported incidents fell back to its normal trend from 2002.

24. In 2007, 3,642 incidents (48.8 percent of total) were motivated by race (68 percent of which were anti-Black); 1,426 incidents (19.1 percent of total) were motivated by religion (65.2 percent of which were anti-Jewish and 10.8 percent anti-Islamic); and 1,102 incidents (14.7 percent of total) were related to ethnicity or national origin (43.5 percent of which were anti-Hispanic).

25. Officials highlighted the prompt and decisive action of the Civil Rights Division in the aftermath of 9/11 by quickly bringing a number of cases against perpetrators of hate crimes. In particular, 32 "9/11 backlash" cases were brought, involving 42 offenders, 35 of whom were convicted. This response, which involved cooperation with state and local officials, is considered as a key factor in explaining the rapid drop in the number of hate crimes after the peak reached in the aftermath of 9/11.

C. Education

26. Educational policy at the federal level is carried out by the Department of Education. An Office for Civil Rights within the Department is mandated "to ensure equal access to education and to promote educational excellence throughout the nation through vigorous enforcement of civil rights." This Office enforces several federal laws that prohibit discrimination, including Titles VI of the Civil Rights Act of 1964 (discrimination on the basis of race, color and national origin). The Office for Civil Rights enforces this law in all institutions, including elementary and secondary schools, colleges and universities that receive funds from the Department of Education.

27. An important piece of federal legislation in the domain of education is the No Child Left Behind Act, which was enacted by Congress in 2002. One of its key objectives is to promote more accountability in public schools and to improve the performance of students. In this regard, it also explicitly addresses the need to close the achievement gap between white and minority students. Recent data indicates that although the achievement gap is still large, it has narrowed in recent years.

D. Housing

28. Extensive legislation to prevent discrimination on housing and lending has been set up over the past decades. This includes the Fair Housing Act (Title VIII of the Civil Rights Act of 1968), which prohibits discrimination in the sale, rental or financing of housing on the basis of race, color, religion, sex, familial status or national origin. The Act expanded the protections offered by the Civil Rights Act of 1964 (Title VI), which prohibited discrimination in programs

and activities receiving federal financial assistance but refrained from regulating private conduct in the domain of housing.

29. Federal laws on fair housing are administered and enforced by the Office of Fair Housing and Equal Opportunity (FHEO) at the Department of Housing and Urban Development (HUD). The number of complaints filed with HUD and the Fair Housing Assistance Program (which provides grants to State and local fair housing enforcement agencies) has increased substantially in the last ten years, from 5,818 complaints in 1998 to 10,154 in 2007. However, it is not evident whether this reflects an increase in housing discrimination or better knowledge of fair housing laws and willingness to report cases of discrimination. In 2007, 43 percent of complaints were based on disability, 37 percent on race, 14 percent on family status and 14 percent on national origin.

30. The Special Rapporteur was informed of a number of programs carried out by HUD to promote equal housing opportunity, including financial assistance to public and private institutions carrying out monitoring and enforcement activities of fair housing laws. HUD also has a constant output of relevant research and advocacy materials, which are used not only to raise awareness regarding existing legislation, but also to monitor and inform relevant stakeholders regarding emerging trends and challenges.

31. The Civil Rights Division at the Department of Justice also carries out enforcement of fair housing laws. As an example of the role played by the Division, the Special Rapporteur was informed of two initiatives. The Fair Housing Testing Program uses paired testing techniques to detect cases of discrimination in the housing market. In addition, by launching operation *Home Sweet Home* in 2006, the Department of Justice committed to conduct a record number of tests to expose and combat discriminatory practices in housing.

E. Employment

32. Discrimination related to employment on the basis of race, color, religion, sex, or national origin is prohibited under the Civil Rights Act of 1964 (Title VII). The enforcement of these provisions, along with other legislation prohibiting employment discrimination is conducted by the Equal Employment Opportunity Commission (EEOC). The EEOC has a total staff of some 2200 employees in 52 offices throughout the country and a budget of around US$ 330 million, which allows it to file around 80,000 charges per year. In 2007, charges related to employment discrimination based on race were 37 percent of the total whereas national origin represented 11.4 percent of all charges.

33. In his meeting with the Vice-Chair of EEOC, the Special Rapporteur was informed about the E-RACE Initiative (Eradicating Racism and Colorism from Employment). The Initiative has some clearly defined goals, including to improve data collection in order to better identify, investigate and prosecute allegations of discrimination, improve the quality of EEOC's litigation, develop strategies to tackle emerging issues of race and color discrimination, promote voluntary compliance to eradicate race and color discrimination.

34. The EEOC also shared with the Special Rapporteur some of the issues of concern for the Commission. Particular emphasis was placed on the emergence of subtle forms of discrimination, which are harder to identify and to act upon. Reference was also made to the persistence of discrimination and the consistency in the number of racial discrimination charges filed every year since 1964.

35. The Special Rapporteur also met, at the Department of Labor, with the Assistant Secretary for Employment Standards and the Civil Rights Enforcement Division. The Department enforces compliance of federal contractors to laws that prohibit discrimination. The Special Rapporteur was informed that the Department plays an active role in investigating federal contractors rather than simply responding to complaints. It also develops partnerships with the EEOC and other bodies to improve enforcement actions.

F. Measures to prevent discrimination in the aftermath of the events of 11 September 2001

36. Many officials have noted symbolic and concrete actions taken to prevent discrimination against people of Arab and Muslim descent in the aftermath of 9/11, starting with the remarks made by President Bush during a visit to the Islamic Center on 17 September 2001. These community outreach efforts were described as a best practice in the fight against

terrorism by the Special Rapporteur on the promotion and protection of human rights and fundamental freedoms while countering terrorism in his report on the United States.

37. The Special Rapporteur was briefed on the *Initiative to Combat Post 9/11 Discriminatory Backlash*, designed by the Department of Justice to combat violations of civil rights against Arab, Muslim, Sikh and South-Asian Americans. Key strategies within this programme include measures to ensure that cases of discrimination are reported and handled promptly, identifying policies that might involve bias crimes and discrimination and reaching out to affected communities to inform them of existing mechanisms. Two special positions were created at the Civil Rights Division: a Special Counsel for Post 9/11 National Origin Discrimination and a Special Counsel for Religious Discrimination.

38. Experts from the Department of Homeland Security also highlighted some initiatives developed after 9/11 to prevent discrimination against people of Arab and Muslim descent. Reference was made to the *Guidance Regarding the Use of Race by Federal Law Enforcement Agencies*, in particular its provision that "in investigating or preventing threats to national security or other catastrophic events [...] Federal law enforcement officers may not consider race or ethnicity except to the extent permitted by the Constitution and laws of the United States." The Special Rapporteur was also informed of the Traveller Redress Inquiry Program, which allows the public to clarify problems of misidentifications with individuals placed on watch lists.

G. Measures taken in the aftermath of Hurricane Katrina

39. Since the Special Rapporteur received allegations concerning possible racial bias in reconstruction efforts in the aftermath of Hurricane Katrina, he raised the issue with several Government authorities in order to collect additional information from some of the federal agencies and visited affected areas.

40. The Civil Rights Division of the Department of Justice highlighted its proactive role in the aftermath of Katrina, reflected in the launching of Operation Home Sweet Home in February 2006. While the initiative had a nationwide focus, it initially concentrated on the areas where Katrina victims were relocated, increasing the reach of its testing programme to identify cases of housing discrimination. Emphasis was also place in areas where a surge of hate crimes had occurred, as these crimes are often correlated with housing discrimination.

41. The Department of Housing and Urban Development noted actions developed to provide adequate housing to those displaced by Katrina. These include additional disaster-relief funding for the affected areas; limited extensions of a foreclosure moratorium; grants for home-owners whose houses were damaged or destroyed; and funding to local public housing projects. The Office of Fair Housing and Equal Opportunity at HUD also developed proactive actions to raise awareness in the Gulf coast region about fair housing obligations, in cooperation with the Federal Emergency Management Agency (FEMA), which leads relief efforts.

42. The Special Rapporteur also makes reference to the United States latest periodic report to CERD, which analyzed concerns about the disparate effects of Katrina on racial or ethnic minorities. In the report, the United States stated that "recognizing the overlap between race and poverty in the United States, many commentators conclude nonetheless that the post-Katrina issues were the result of poverty (i.e., the inability of many of the poor to evacuate) rather than racial discrimination *per se*."

H. Immigration

43. The Special Rapporteur met with the Office of Citizenship at the U.S. Citizenship and Immigration Service (CIS), and was briefed concerning CIS's policy to reinvigorate assimilation efforts, particularly in what concerns English proficiency of migrants. Officials pointed out that they viewed assimilation of migrants into the United States as a key element for integration into the labor market, the educational system and social life more broadly, but this did not imply the abandonment of cultural or religious diversity, upon which the United States was founded. The Special Rapporteur was informed that CIS had intensified its efforts to diminish the backlog in citizenship applications and thus respond more rapidly to applicants.

44. CIS officials referred to the naturalization exam, which has been recently reformed in order to become more uniform nationwide. The naturalization test contains an English reading and writing section as well as questions on U.S. history

and government. CIS produces and distributes study materials to help immigrants prepare for the test. Information guides are also available to new immigrants with information on rights and responsibilities as well as practical help on issues such as employment education and taxes.

45. Immigrants are entitled to some constitutionally-protected rights regardless of their immigration status. In *Plyler v. Doe*, the Supreme Court established that denying free public education to children on the basis of immigration status is unlawful. Furthermore, although the Immigration and Nationality Act protects only documented migrants from employment discrimination, unfair documentary practices and retaliation, EEOC noted several judicial decisions that prevent courts from disclosing the immigration status of plaintiffs in employment discrimination cases.

IV. VIEWS OF CIVIL SOCIETY AND COMMUNITIES CONCERNED

A. Law enforcement

46. One of the key issues mentioned by civil society was the weak record of civil rights enforcement by the Federal Government. In particular, reference was made to the limited number of cases filed by the Civil Rights Division of the Department of Justice, especially when compared to previous administrations. This has led to a growing perception of discredit by civil society organizations in the Division's commitment to enforce civil rights laws.

Racial disparities in the criminal justice system

47. The most critical issue of concern raised by civil society organizations, minority communities and victims themselves was related to racial disparities in the criminal justice system. Interlocutors pointed to an overrepresentation of individuals belonging to racial and ethnic minorities in the criminal justice system. While in mid-2007 black males constituted around 12.5 percent of the population, they comprised 38.9 percent of the number of people in U.S. prisons and jails. Black males are therefore 6.5 more likely to be incarcerated than white, non-Hispanic males. While many civil society organizations agreed that part of the explanation to these disparities is related to social factors, particularly the overlap of poverty and race, it was pointed out that racial discrimination also plays a key role in explaining this phenomenon.

48. Studies have identified racial disparities at several stages of law enforcement activities. A key example is traffic stops. A report by the Department of Justice recently found that whereas white, black and Hispanic drivers were stopped by the police at similar rates, black and Hispanic drivers were approximately 2.5 times more likely to be searched; the rate of arrests was two times higher for blacks and 50 percent higher for Hispanics; blacks were 3.5 times more likely and Hispanics were almost 2 times more likely to experience use of police force. Another example concerns sentencing outcomes. A majority of studies show evidence of racially discriminatory sentencing; in particular, that individuals belonging to minorities tend to be disadvantaged in terms of the decision to incarcerate or not and in receiving harsher sentences than white individuals with comparable social and economic status.

49. Mandatory minimum penalties have been pointed out as an important factor that promotes racial bias. A striking example refers to mandatory minimum sentences for possession of crack and powder cocaine. These sentences establish more severe penalties for persons arrested for possessing or selling crack cocaine, 81 percent of whom are African American, than for those in possession of or selling powder cocaine, 71.8 percent of whom are white or Hispanic.

50. Civil society also pointed to evidences of racial bias in the application of the death penalty. In 2005, African Americans comprised nearly 42 percent of the number of death row inmates but only around 12 percent of the general population. The key factor that shows evidence of racial bias in the death penalty, according to many organizations, is the race of the victim. Nationwide, even though the absolute number of murders of blacks and whites is similar, some 80 percent of people on death row have been convicted of crimes against white victims. Interlocutors pointed to the critical situation in some states. In Alabama, for example, whereas 65 percent of all murders involve black victims, 80 percent of people currently awaiting execution in the state were convicted of crimes in which the victims were white.

51. Juvenile justice was an issue of concern for civil society organizations, particularly when it represents an entry point into criminal justice (see subsection III.C). The rate of detention of youth in 2003 was five times higher for African Americans and two times higher for Hispanics than for whites. The Special Rapporteur was also presented with data concerning the disproportional representation of African American youth in several stages of the juvenile justice pro-

cess, including arrests, detentions, petitions and prison. Reference was made to the issue of sentencing of youth to life without parole, which is applied in 39 states, as well as on reported racial bias in these practices, particularly in certain states. In the 25 states for which data is available the rate of African Americans serving life without parole sentences is on average 10 times higher than whites, relative to the state population. In California, the rate is 18 times that of white youth. Even after controlling for differences in murder arrest rates, racial disparities remain.

Racial profiling

52. Civil society generally refers to two main forms of racial profiling. First, a particular form of the practice targets predominantly African-American or Hispanic minorities, generally but not exclusively in stops and searches by local and state police. Second, in the context of counter-terrorism policies, racial profiling practices have reportedly targeted primarily people of Arab, Muslim, South Asian or Middle-Eastern descent, particularly in air travel and border control.

53. Some civil society accounts point to widespread existence of racial profiling. It has been suggested that approximately 32 million people in the United States report having been victims of this practice. While exact numbers may be difficult to assert, it was a common recognition among virtually all interlocutors that the practice of racial profiling continues to exist. Numerous anecdotal accounts of victims of racial profiling in stop and search operations by the police were heard, including a testimony by an African American Member of Congress victim of such an incident.

54. Several organizations expressed concern at the National Special Entry-Exit Registration Program (NSEERS), put in place in 2002. The special registration program required male non-citizens over the age of 16 and from 25 countries to register with local immigration authorities. Twenty-four of these countries have a majority Muslim population. While the initial requirements of re-registration after 30-days and one year of continuous presence in the United States have been suspended, the program continues to be considered by civil society as discriminatory on the basis of national origin and religious background.

55. Civil society organizations expressed criticisms regarding recent attempts to address the issue. The *Guidance Regarding the Use of Race by Federal Law Enforcement Agencies* issued by the Department of Justice was criticized, particular because it "does not cover profiling based on religion, religious appearance or national origin; does not apply to local law enforcement agencies; does not include any enforcement mechanism; does not require data collection; does not specify any punishment for federal officers who disregard it; contains a blanket exception for cases of 'threat to national security and other catastrophic events' and 'in enforcing laws and protecting the integrity of the Nations' borders'."

B. Hate crimes

56. Interlocutors highlighted that the main weakness of federal hate crimes legislation is the dual requirement that needs to be met for the Federal Government to be able to investigate and prosecute a case: bias-motivated violence and relation to a federally protected activity. In cases that do not meet these requirements, the jurisdiction lies at the state level. However, many states lack the capacity and resources to thoroughly investigate and prosecute such crimes. In this regard, a Local Law Enforcement Hate Crimes Prevention Act designed to strengthen the role of the Federal Government in the investigation and prosecution of such crimes and to expand the grounds for protection was approved in the House of Representatives and the Senate in 2007. However, it was withdrawn after an expression by the White House that the President would veto the bill, which was seen as "unnecessary and constitutionally questionable."

57. While many interlocutors expressed concern regarding the number of hate crimes in the United States, some NGOs highlighted that the government response has in general been more vigorous than in other countries.

C. Education

De facto school segregation

58. One of the most important decisions by the U.S. Supreme Court in the fight for racial equality was *Brown v. Board of Education* prohibiting school segregation. However, interlocutors pointed out that despite the end of *de jure* segregation and positive changes, particularly in the 1960-1980 period, the trend has since been reversed. The percentage of black students in predominantly minority schools, which was 77 percent in 1968 and decreased to 63 percent in 1988, had

surged to 73 percent in 2005. Civil society organizations expressed concern at recent U.S. Supreme Court decisions — *Parents Involved in Community Schools v. Seattle School District* and *Meredith v. Jefferson County Board of Directors* — that ruled that race-conscious integration measures are unconstitutional. In the view of many NGOs, these race-conscious measures are a necessary measure to ensure racial integration and made an essential contribution to de-segregation of schools, particularly in the South. Some organizations also pointed out that the rise of segregation also has an impact on the quality of education received by students belonging to minorities. Furthermore, a concern was expressed that the Court may have abandoned the notion that racial diversity can be considered a compelling interest that justifies the use of race-based criteria. This view is present in the dissenting opinion of Justice Breyer in the *Community Schools* case.

Achievement gaps

59. Civil society representatives highlighted that while the achievement gap between students belonging to minorities and white students has narrowed in the past years, it is still in a similar level to 1990. The introduction of the No Child Left Behind Act placed high emphasis on educational performance; however, interlocutors highlighted the negative incentives created by the Act and its disproportionate effects on minority children. In particular, it was argued that the focus on standardized performance tests that penalize schools that underperform creates an incentive for schools to push out low-performing, at-risk students — a group that is composed disproportionately of minorities — in order to improve the overall school performance.

Schools as an entry point to the criminal justice system

60. Many NGOs used the metaphor of the "school to prison pipeline" to refer to the failure of the school system to educate pupils adequately, serving rather as a conduit to juvenile and criminal justice. Among the chief causes of this phenomenon, interlocutors referred to the widespread application of Zero Tolerance Policies, which call for severe punishment for minor infractions. These measures are considered to have gone beyond reasonable policies to prevent violence in school, leading to what is considered to be an overreliance on disciplinary methods (e.g. suspensions and expulsions) and the criminalization of school misbehaviour (i.e. by referring students with non-violent behaviour to juvenile courts). In Texas, for example, "disruptive behaviour" corresponds to 17 percent of school arrests and "disorderly conduct" comprised 26 percent of such arrests. In meetings with parents of students that were disciplined, the Special Rapporteur was informed of several practices that exist in some school districts, such as the issuing of fines by the police to students with inappropriate behaviour, regular searches and reported cases of excessive use of force by police officers inside schools. Civil society pointed to racial disparities in the application of these disciplinary measures. For example, whereas African-American children represent only 17 percent of public school enrolment, they constitute 32 percent of out-of-school suspensions. Some studies have also indicated that African-American students are more likely than white students to be suspended, expelled or arrested for the same kind of school conduct.

D. Housing

61. Concerns about fair housing expressed by civil society generally focus on two major issues: direct discriminatory practices and structural factors that have an impact, even if unintended, on the housing situation of minorities.

62. According to interlocutors, direct discriminatory practices in housing continue to exist. Data produced in paired testing, which allows for a comparison of treatment between whites and persons of color when they have similar qualifications, identified subtle forms of direct discrimination. This includes the practice of "steering" members of racial or ethnic groups towards neighbourhoods primarily occupied by those same groups, prohibited under the Fair Housing Act. Steering practices have generally contributed to a persistence of residential segregation. Direct discrimination has also been detected in rental and sale of houses as well as in mortgage lending, with people of colour being more likely to receive higher cost or subprime loans than white borrowers with similar income and other characteristics.

63. Concerns were expressed that the FHEO, which is the key agency responsible for acting on complaints of housing discrimination, only finds reasonable cause for discrimination in a small number of complaints and that the period of investigation is often surpasses the 100-day mark set by Congress. It should be noted, however, that a number of cases are resolved through the conciliation and settlement processes which are encouraged under the Fair Housing Act. At the same time, enforcement actions by the Civil Rights Division at the Department of Justice were also criticized due to the limited number of cases it has initiated. Another problem raised by civil society is the large number of unreported cases

of fair housing violations due to lack of knowledge of Fair Housing laws. While the Special Rapporteur was informed by HUD of many awareness-raising initiatives, civil society deemed them insufficient to educate the public.

64. A particular dimension of the housing problem highlighted by civil society lies in homelessness. The Special Rapporteur visited the Skid Row area in Los Angeles, interacting with a number of homeless persons and civil society support groups. Interlocutors highlighted the disproportionate impact of homelessness among minorities, particular African Americans, as also highlighted by the Human Rights Committee in its 2006 of the United States periodic report. This problem is often reinforced by the reduction of funds for the construction of public housing. In addition, relations between law enforcement and homeless persons were also highlighted as an important problem, particularly with regard to the enforcement of minor law enforcement violations which often take a disproportionately high number of African American homeless persons to the criminal justice system.

65. The issue of residential segregation was directly observed by the Special Rapporteur, who examined the issue in-depth in his visits outside the capital. Despite some progresses in the 1980-2000 period, they contributed little to change the overall static patterns of residential segregation in the country. Furthermore, civil society noted that residential segregation has a direct impact on school segregation and that the two problems should be tackled together.

E. Employment

66. Interlocutors stated that ethnic disparities in employment and, more generally, poverty levels have fundamental consequences for the overall situation of racial and ethnic minorities in the United States. Whereas the unemployment rate for non-Hispanic whites in 2007 was 5.2 percent, it was 12.6 percent for American Indians or Alaskan Natives, 12 percent for African-Americans and 7.3 percent for Hispanics.

67. While many interlocutors pointed these disparities in unemployment level as an indication of the interplay of race and socio-economic status, concerns over forms of direct and indirect discrimination in employment were also raised. One of the issues that was raised concerns the legal remedies available to undocumented migrants (see subsection III.h). Another issue of concern regards the lack of protection for certain occupations, particularly domestic and agricultural workers, which disproportionately affect Africa-Americans and Hispanics. In some cases, these occupations may be excluded from the legal protections offered by a number of statutes, such as minimum wages, overtime pay and job safety.

68. Civil society organizations pointed to inadequate enforcement of Title VII of the Civil Rights Act of 1964, which prohibits employment discrimination based on race, color, religion, sex and national origin, highlighting a the limited number of Title VII cases filed by the Civil Rights Division of the Department of Justice. In particular, reference was made to the low percentage of cases referred to the Civil Rights Division by the EEOC that are actually taken up.

F. Discrimination in the aftermath of the events of 11 September 2001

69. The Special Rapporteur met with several representatives of the Arab, Sikh, Middle Eastern and South Asian communities in the United States to hear their views concerning the situation after 9/11. Their common view was that their situation had deteriorated quickly in the aftermath of 9/11, particularly due to the extension of national security measures that in their view discriminate against these communities. One of the major concerns regards instances of racial profiling, particularly in airports, as well as programs such as NSEERS (see section III.A above).

70. An increase in cases of discrimination and harassment in the workplace was also reported, not only towards people of Arab or Muslim descent, but also against Sikhs. Serious concern was expressed regarding the long delay in the processing of citizenship applications, which had been disproportionately high for individuals of Arab, Middle Eastern or South Asian descent.

71. More broadly, these organizations referred to overall negative perceptions of the American public towards Muslims. Reference was made to a recent USA Today/Gallup poll that showed that 39 percent of Americans felt at least some prejudice against Muslims and that 22 percent would not want Muslims as neighbors. While a number of organizations welcomed outreach initiatives developed by the Government in the aftermath of 9/11, they expressed the need for comprehensive actions to address issues of stereotyping and concrete policy changes in areas that have a discriminatory impact on individuals of Arab, Sikh, Middle Eastern and South Asian descent.

G. Measures taken in the aftermath of Hurricane Katrina

72. The Special Rapporteur travelled to New Orleans, as well as the Louisiana and Mississippi Gulf coast, in order to hear local civil society, community leaders and residents about their concerns in the aftermath of Katrina. In addition, he visited different neighborhoods that were severely affected by the storm, including the 9th Ward of New Orleans. He also met with the Mayor of New Orleans, with whom he discussed the reconstruction efforts and implications for minorities.

73. Data from the U.S. Census Bureau show the massive impact of Hurricane Katrina in the entire Gulf coast. In the State of Louisiana, 1.3 million people were displaced, with a dramatic depopulation of New Orleans as a whole. However, data indicate the disproportionately high impact of Katrina for African-Americans. For example, whereas the population of whites in New Orleans decreased approximately 39 percent after Katrina, the population of Africa-Americans declined around 69 percent. The ethnic makeup of the city also changed: African-Americans formed around 67.3 percent of the population before Katrina and comprised only 58.8 percent after the hurricane.

74. Interlocutors in the Gulf coast, including displaced families, argued that the Federal Government is not fulfilling its obligation to create adequate conditions for the return of the displaced, particularly in terms of housing. Serious concerns were voiced regarding the demolition of public housing and substitution by private development projects. The demolition of public housing in New Orleans was deemed to have a particularly grave impact for the African-American population, which constitutes the vast majority of public housing residents.

75. Another issue of concern in the reconstruction phase is employment. According to interlocutors, the combination of the surge in unemployment rates after Katrina and the arrival of a large population of migrant workers, particularly of Hispanic origin, both documented and undocumented, have created a vulnerable environment where workers have been exposed to exploitation and substandard conditions of employment. Ethnic tensions emerged in this context between some African-American and Hispanic individuals, particularly in the context of low wages and stiffened competition for jobs. Attempts to instrumentalize and overstate these tensions were also made, particularly by certain local politicians.

76. Interlocutors also mentioned cases of excessive use of force by law enforcement officials and military personnel in the early days after Katrina; arbitrary detention of persons who attempted to evacuate the city; inadequate treatment of inmates, particularly in the Orleans Parish Prison; and allegations of racially discriminatory results of decisions by the Army Corp of Engineers to increase the height of the levies in predominantly white neighbourhoods.

H. Immigration

77. The Special Rapporteur held a number of meetings with migrant workers across the country as well as civil society organizations working with migrant workers. In all of the meetings, migrant workers, particularly those who are undocumented, expressed serious concerns about their vulnerability and dire conditions.

78. The major issue raised was the disappointment with Congress' failure to approve the comprehensive immigration reform package put forward by the President. Migrant workers expressed the view that the regularization of their status would have represented improved protection and enforcement of their rights. This relates to their serious concern at the lack of legal protection they face, partly a result of the U.S. Supreme Court decision in *Hoffman Plastic Compounds, Inc. v. NLRB*, in which the Court ruled that the National Labour Relations Board did not have the authority to order that employers award back pay for work not performed to undocumented workers victims of unfair labour practices. This decision is allegedly being used by lower courts in cases that restrict the rights of undocumented workers in other domains, including access to justice.

79. Serious concern was expressed by several civil society organizations regarding worksite immigration enforcement by Immigration and Customs Enforcement (ICE) officials, particularly regarding allegations of the use of an individual's appearance to determine which individuals in a worksite or community should be screened for immigration status. Concerns were also expressed regarding cooperation agreements between ICE and local law enforcement agencies that allow the latter to enforce immigration laws, which could have serious implications in generating distrust among communities and local police.

V. ANALYSIS AND ASSESSMENT

80. Racism and racial discrimination have profoundly and lastingly marked and structured American society. The United States has made decisive progress in the political and legal combat against racism, through the resistance of communities of victims, the exemplary and powerful struggle of civil rights movements and the growing political confrontation of racism. However, the historical, cultural and human depth of racism still permeates all dimensions of life of American society.

81. The Special Rapporteur noted a strong awareness at all levels of government and society regarding the challenges in the fight against racism. He interprets this finding as a direct legacy of the continuous and determined struggle of the civil rights movement. In particular, he noted the recognition by authorities of the persistence of different manifestations of racism in the country and willingness to tackle this phenomenon. The Special Rapporteur considers awareness and open recognition of manifestations of racism as a precondition of any efforts to adequately tackle the problem. In particular, he commends the United States for the quantity and quality of information on issues related to his mandate, produced both by State institutions and civil society, and including racially- and ethnically-disaggregated data on demographic, social and cultural indicators. This information is essential for identifying trends and designing effective public policies.

82. The legacy of the civil rights movement is also reflected in the solid and comprehensive legal framework put in place in the country, particularly after the adoption of the Civil Rights Act of 1964 and extended in a variety of federal and local statutes and institutions. The Special Rapporteur would also like to note the central role played historically by the U.S. Supreme Court in the fight against racial discrimination, starting in *Brown v. Board of Education* and expanded thereafter. The legal and institutional frameworks are in any State the first lines of defence against racism, not only enforcing the obligation to equal treatment, but also giving victims access to remedies and, ultimately, to justice.

83. The vitality of civil society is a third decisive element that contributes to the fight against racism. The Special Rapporteur was impressed with the quality of the work conducted by NGOs across the country, playing a key role in holding governments accountable to its obligation to enforce civil rights laws.

84. The Special Rapporteur identified a number of challenges in the fight against racism that should be addressed, both at the Federal and local levels.

85. Throughout his mission and in the analysis of documents, the Special Rapporteur was exposed to three broad types of issues: instances of direct racial discrimination; laws and policies that are *prima facie* non-discriminatory, but that have disparate effects for certain racial or ethnic groups; and problems that arise from the overlap of class, specifically poverty, and race or ethnicity.

86. Instances of direct discrimination and concrete racial bias still exist and are most pronounced with regards to law enforcement agencies. Despite the clear illegality of racial profiling under the fourteenth amendment, recent evidence shows practices that still prevail in law enforcement, such the disparity in the rate of arrests of minority and white drivers stopped by the police (see para. 52). In the educational system, evidence also shows racial bias in the type of disciplinary action given to white or minority students (see para. 64). In the justice system, evidence of racial bias in conviction rates and length of sentences of both juvenile and criminal courts exist (see paras. 50-55). In addition, programs such as NSEERS have clear ethnic or religious connotations (see para. 58). Direct discrimination was also found in many studies that used paired testing techniques, particularly in the areas of housing and employment. While these cases do not directly involve discrimination by state agents, strong enforcement of human rights is required. The Special Rapporteur notes that the right institutions are already in place to enforce existing laws, however, more robust efforts are required to increase the number of cases taken up every year, creating an important deterrent against future discrimination.

87. The Special Rapporteur also noted some laws and policies that are *prima facie* non-discriminatory but they have disparate effects for certain racial or ethnic groups. The key example of such practices is mandatory minimum sentences (see para. 53 above). While the Special Rapporteur welcomes the decision of the U.S. Sentencing Commission to revise the sentencing guidelines for crack cocaine offences, additional work needs to be done to review mandatory minimum sentences for crack cocaine, which disproportionately affect African-Americans.

88. Socio-economic indicators show that poverty and race or ethnicity continue to overlap in the United States. In 2007, whereas 9 percent of non-Hispanic whites were below the poverty level, 24.7 percent of African-Americans, 25.3 percent of American Indian and Alaskan Native and 20.7 percent of Hispanics were in that situation. This reality is a direct legacy of the past, in particular slavery, segregation, the forcible resettlement of Native Americans, which was confronted by the United States during the civil rights movement. However, whereas the country managed to establish equal treatment and non-discrimination in its laws, it has yet to redress the socio-economic consequences of the historical legacy of racism. While noting some progress in this area, particularly in what concerns the representation and participation of racial and ethnic minorities in the high echelons of the political, economic and cultural arenas and the emergence of a middle class within minority groups, the Special Rapporteur underlines that much still needs to be done in this area.

89. The overlap between poverty and race in the United States creates structural problems that go far beyond patterns of income. Rather, it interacts with a number of mutually reinforcing factors, such as poor educational attainment, low-paying wages and inadequate housing, which create a vicious cycle of marginalization and exclusion of minorities. The overrepresentation of minorities in inferior schools, more vulnerable neighbourhoods, the juvenile justice system and the criminal justice system are to a large extent linked to their overall socio-economic situation. At the same time, these trends also contribute to reinforce prejudices and stereotypes, such as an association of minorities to criminality or to poor educational performance.

90. The consequences of the overlap of poverty and race were clearly seen in the aftermath of Hurricane Katrina. Minorities, as the poorest segments of the population, lived in more vulnerable neighbourhoods and were more exposed to the effects of the storm. It is thus not unexpected that these groups suffered from disproportional displacement or loss of their homes. Katrina therefore illustrates the pernicious effects of socio-economic marginalization and shows the need for a robust and targeted governmental response to ensure that racial disparities are addressed.

91. The Special Rapporteur also noted that the socio-economic marginalization of racial or ethnic minorities has become more acute due to what he perceived as a slow process of *de facto* re-segregation in many areas of the American society. In particular, in his visits to metropolitan areas, he noted the striking pattern of ethnic and racial cleavages that persist and which are being reinforced by processes such as gentrification in neighbourhoods historically inhabited by minorities. A related aspect is the process of re-segregation in public schools. Several studies have shown that the present level of segregation is similar to that of the late 1960s. These processes not only contribute to keep racial groups physically separated, but also affect the marginalization of public services in areas that are predominantly attended by minorities. Ultimately, this creates an obstacle in the most important means of promoting equality of opportunity, which is to offer quality education for all students. In this regard, the Special Rapporteur is particularly concerned about the retraction of affirmative action policies, which make a tangible contribution to enhancing diversity and integration in schools.

92. The Special Rapporteur would like to make specific reference to the situation of Native Americans, which have been the first people to be historically discriminated in the continent. He was particularly sensitive to the statements made by the Principal Chief of the Cherokee Nation, Mr. Chad Smith, whom the Special Rapporteur met in Miami, as well as other indigenous leaders met in Omaha and Los Angeles, who highlighted the dire socio-economic conditions faced by many Native Americans and the difficulties in preserving their cultural heritage. He recalls the need for constant vigilance for the situation of Native Americans, which should be the subject of particular attention in view of the historical legacy of discrimination against them.

93. The situation in Puerto Rico also merits particular attention by the Government in view of its specificity. A number of particular elements should be borne in mind with regards to Puerto Rico: the ethnic dimension, including the racial make-up of the population and the situation of the black minority in the island; the cultural dimension, including the Hispanic origin of the population; and the political dimension, in particular the specific political status enjoyed by Puerto Rico in the United States. It is therefore essential that specific actions, in line with Puerto Rico's specificities, be undertaken to fight racism in the island.

94. The Special Rapporteur recalls the idea that he has put forward in many of his reports concerning the need to go beyond a legal strategy that guarantees non-discrimination. While essential, the legal strategy is only the first stage in the fight against racism. A long-term strategy needs to address the root causes of the phenomenon, particularly in terms of

intellectual constructs, prejudices and perceptions. To fight these manifestations, the only effective solution is to link the fight against racism to the deliberate politically conscious construction of a democratic, egalitarian and interactive multiculturalism. In his views, this is the most important problem the United States needs to face. A key notion in this regard is the need to promote interaction among different communities as an important means to create tolerance and mutual understanding, strengthening the social networks that hold a society together. Racial or ethnic communities in the United States still experience very little interaction with each other: racially-delimited neighbourhoods, schools and churches prevail. The promotion of more interaction among racial minorities is an essential step that needs to be taken to address the root causes of racism in the United States.

95. This notion of interactions among communities is also central to understand that the problem of racism in the United States is not solely that between a white majority and minorities, but also occurs among minorities themselves. In particular, many minority groups have been isolated, competing for jobs and social services. Apart from enforcing civil rights laws robustly, promoting more interaction among minorities themselves is an essential step in the fight against racism in the United States.

96. During the drafting of this report the United States elected President Barack Obama as its next Head of State. The Special Rapporteur would like to underscore the importance of this event in giving new visibility to minorities in the country. It further corroborates the view expressed in this report that the United States has made fundamental progress in the past decades in giving visibility to members of minorities in the political, economic and cultural arena. More significantly, this election is the outer reflection of the slow but profound transformation process in the deeper layers of consciousness of every citizen of the United States from all racial and ethnic communities, in the individual confrontation to racism in all dimensions and instances of everyday life.

VI. RECOMMENDATIONS

97. Congress should establish a bipartisan Commission to evaluate the progress and failures in the fight against racism and the ongoing process of re-segregation, particularly in housing and education, and to find responses to check these trends. In this process, broad participation from civil society should be ensured.

98. The Government should reassess existing legislation on racism, racial discrimination, xenophobia and related intolerance in view of two main guidelines: addressing the overlapping nature of poverty and race or ethnicity; and linking the fight against racism to the construction of a democratic, egalitarian and interactive multiculturalism, in order to strengthen inter-community relations.

99. The Federal Government, in particular the Civil Rights Division of the Department of Justice, the Equal Employment Opportunities Commission and the Office of Fair Housing and Equal Opportunity of the Department of Housing and Urban Development should intensify their efforts to enforce federal civil rights laws in their respective domains.

100. Since the fight against racism needs to take place at the federal, state and local levels of government, the Special Rapporteur recommends that adequate consultation mechanisms be put in place for a coordinated approach at all levels of Government.

101. As a matter of urgency, the Government should clarify to law enforcement officials the obligation of equal treatment and, in particular, the prohibition of racial profiling. This process would benefit from the adoption by Congress of the End Racial Profiling Act. State Governments should also adopt comprehensive legislation prohibiting racial profiling.

102. To monitor trends regarding racial profiling and treatment of minorities by law enforcement, federal, state and local governments should collect and publicize data about police stops and searches as well as instances of police abuse. Independent oversight bodies should be established within police agencies, with real authority to investigate complaints of human rights violations in general and racism in particular. Adequate resources should also be provided to train police and other law enforcement officials.

103. Mandatory minimum sentences should be reviewed to assess disproportionate impact on racial or ethnic minorities. In particular, the different minimum sentences for crack and powder cocaine should be reassessed.

104. In order to diminish the impact of socio-economic marginalization of minorities in what concerns their access to justice, the Government should improve, including with adequate funding, the state of public defenders.

105. The Special Rapporteur recommends that complementary legislation be considered to further clarify the responsibility of law enforcement and criminal justice officials not only to protect human rights, but as key agents in the fight against racism.

106. In view of the recent recommendations by the Human Rights Committee, the Committee Against Torture and the Committee on the Elimination of Racial Discrimination, and considering that the use of life imprisonment without parole against young offenders, including children, has had a disproportionate impact for racial minorities, federal and state governments should discontinue this practice against persons under the age of eighteen at the time the offence was committed.

107. The Government should intensify funding for testing programs and "pattern and practice" investigations to assess discrimination, particularly in the areas of housing and employment. Robust enforcement actions should be taken whenever civil rights violations are found.

108. The Department of Education, in partnership with state and local agencies, should conduct an impact assessment of disciplinary measures in public schools, including the criminalization of school misbehaviour, and revisit those measures that are disproportionately affecting racial or ethnic minorities.

109. Special measures to promote the integration of students in public schools as well as to reduce the achievement gap between white and minority students should be developed, in accordance with article 2, paragraph 2, of ICERD.

110. The Federal Government and the States of Louisiana, Alabama and Mississippi should increase its assistance to the persons displaced by Hurricane Katrina, particularly in the realm of housing. The principle that "competent authorities have the primary duty and responsibility to establish conditions, as well as provide the means, which allow internally displaced persons to return voluntarily, in safety and with dignity, to their homes or places of habitual residence" should be respected.

Source: Report of the Special Rapporteur on contemporary forms of racism, racial discrimination, xenophobia and related intolerance, Doudou Diène, Mission to the United States of America, 2009
http://www2.ohchr.org/english/bodies/hrcouncil/docs/11session/A.HRC.11.36.Add.3.pdf

Rights of Indigenous Peoples

Chapter 10

This Chapter is About the indigenous peoples' on-going struggles to enjoy all their human rights, with full cognizance of their human dignity and their distinctiveness as indigenous peoples and individuals. Indigenous peoples' human rights issues are distinct from minority rights groups' issues because, although indigenous peoples often constitute a minority group within a nation state, they are sometimes the majority within the countries where their ancestors have always lived. The factors that distinguish indigenous peoples' human rights from minority rights are: indigenous peoples are the descendants of identifiable (ab)original peoples on the lands on the four continents in which they live; their identity and human rights are still recognized as under constant threat since the onset of the civil, political, economic, social, and cultural primarily-European-settler/colonial expansion, which began in the late middle ages of European history.

This is Important Because as disparate peoples, indigenous peoples have struggled for centuries for recognition of their on-going status as indigenous peoples. In the 20th-21st centuries, their legal struggles have emerged within the U.N. and regional international human rights systems, with their uniqueness serving to reintroduce the international community, nation states and their governments to many new insights into human rights and states' responsibilities, including: recognizing the validity of indigenous peoples' own legal systems within their home territories by national governments; supporting their adjudication of their own law within their own territories; helping to develop their natural resources, including their rights to cultural capital; supporting their right to status as consultative partners and participants in all decision-making processes that affect them and their territories, etc.

This is important in the United States because the indigenous peoples' current human rights international and domestic struggle for their own survival is historically and dramatically reinvigorating human rights as a primary source of law, both internationally and domestically. U.S. domestic laws affecting indigenous peoples' human rights must evolve and be updated so as to address a multitude of human rights, if any concept of our common humanity is to survive. In the U.S., indigenous peoples' rights are at a critical moment, and the human rights violations of indigenous peoples continue to be uncovered, especially within the influential U.S.

Primary Source Documents

Quotes & Key Text Excerpts

Recognizing and reaffirming that indigenous individuals are entitled without discrimination to all human rights recognized in international law, and that indigenous peoples possess collective rights which are indispensable for their existence, well-being and integral development as peoples,

Article 1

Indigenous peoples have the right to the full enjoyment, as a collective or as individuals, of all human rights and fundamental freedoms as recognized in the Charter of the United Nations, the Universal Declaration of Human Rights and international human rights law.

—*UN Declaration on the Rights of Indigenous Peoples, Preamble excerpt and Art 1.*

Source: United Nations, Human Rights Council, Working Group on the Universal Periodic Review, Ninth Session, Geneva, 1-12 November 2010 National report submitted in accordance with paragraph 15 (a) of the annex to Human Rights Council resolution 5/1; United States of America

᠀᠁᠀᠁᠀᠁᠀᠁

The U.S. took the UPR process to "Indian Country." One of our UPR consultations was hosted on tribal land in Arizona; the New Mexico consultation addressed American Indian and Alaska Native issues; and other consultations included tribal representatives. The United States has a unique legal relationship with federally recognized tribes. By virtue of their status as sovereigns that pre-date the federal Union, as well as subsequent treaties, statutes, executive orders, and judicial decisions, Indian tribes are recognized as political entities with inherent powers of self-government. The U.S. government therefore has a government-to-government relationship with 564 federally recognized Indian tribes and promotes tribal self-governance over a broad range of internal and local affairs. The United States also recognizes past wrongs and broken promises in the federal government's relationship with American Indians and Alaska Natives, and recognizes the need for urgent change. Some reservations currently face unemployment rates of up to 80 percent; nearly a quarter of Native Americans live in poverty; American Indians and Alaska Natives face significant health care disparities; and some reservations have crime rates up to 10 times the national average. Today we are helping tribes address the many issues facing their communities.

In November of last year, President Obama hosted a historic summit with nearly 400 tribal leaders to develop a policy agenda for Native Americans where he emphasized his commitment to regular and meaningful consultation with tribal officials regarding federal policy decisions that have tribal implications. In March, the President signed into law important health provisions for American Indians and Alaska Natives. In addition, President Obama recognizes the importance of enhancing the role of tribes in Indian education and supports Native language immersion and Native language restoration programs.

Addressing crimes involving violence against women and children on tribal lands is a priority. After extensive consultations with tribal leaders, Attorney General Eric Holder announced significant reform to increase prosecution of crimes committed on tribal lands. He hired more Assistant U.S. Attorneys and more victim-witness specialists. He created a new position, the National Indian Country Training Coordinator, who will work with prosecutors and law enforcement officers in tribal communities. The Attorney General is establishing a Tribal Nations Leadership Council to provide ongoing advice on issues critical to tribal communities.

On July 29, 2010, President Obama signed the Tribal Law and Order Act, requiring the Justice Department to disclose data on cases in Indian Country that it declines to prosecute and granting tribes greater authority to prosecute and punish criminals. The Act also expands support for Bureau of Indian Affairs and Tribal officers. It includes new provisions to prevent counterfeiting of Indian-produced crafts and new guidelines and training for domestic violence and sex crimes, and it strengthens tribal courts and police departments and enhances programs to combat drug and alcohol abuse and help at-risk youth. These are significant measures that will empower tribal governments and make a difference in people's lives.

In April 2010, at the U.N. Permanent Forum on Indigenous Issues, U.S. Ambassador to the U.N. Susan Rice announced that the United States would undertake a review of its position on the U.N. Declaration on the Rights of Indigenous Peoples. That multi-agency review is currently underway in consultation with tribal leaders and with outreach to other stakeholders.

Source: United Nations, Human Rights Council, Working Group on the Universal Periodic Review, Ninth Session, Geneva, 1-12 November 2010 National report submitted in accordance with paragraph 15 (a) of the annex to Human Rights Council resolution 5/1; United States of America

ᠵᡜᠵᡜᠵᡜᠵᡜ

In 2012, the Special Rapporteur on indigenous peoples noted that securing the rights of indigenous peoples in their lands was of central importance to their socioeconomic development, self-determination, and cultural integrity. Despite positive aspects of existing legislation, new measures were needed to advance reconciliation with indigenous peoples and to provide redress for persistent deep-seated problems. Federal authorities should identify, develop, and implement such measures in full consultation and coordination with indigenous peoples. The Special Rapporteur called for measures of reconciliation and redress, including initiatives to address outstanding claims regarding treaty violations or non-consensual takings of traditional lands and issues of self-governance, environmental degradation, language restoration, and federal recognition.

The HR Committee welcomed the support for the United Nations Declaration on the Rights of Indigenous Peoples. It was, however, concerned about the insufficiency of consultation with indigenous peoples on matters of interest to their communities. The United States should protect the sacred areas of indigenous peoples against desecration, contamination, and destruction, and ensure that consultations were held with the indigenous communities that might be adversely affected by the State's development projects and exploitation of natural resources. CERD raised similar concerns through its early warning and urgent action procedure.

The Special Rapporteur on indigenous peoples noted the support of the United States for the United Nations Declaration on the Rights of Indigenous Peoples, and stated that the federal courts should interpret, or reinterpret, relevant doctrine, treaties, and statutes in the light of the Declaration, in regard both to the nature of indigenous peoples' rights and the nature of federal power.

Source: United Nations, Human Rights Council, Working Group on the Universal Periodic Review, Twenty-second session, 4-15 May 2015, Compilation prepared by the Office of the United Nations High Commissioner for Human Rights in accordance with paragraph 15 (b) of the annex to Human Rights Council resolution 5/1 and paragraph 5 of the annex to Council resolution 16/21, United States of America

ᠵᡜᠵᡜᠵᡜᠵᡜ

With the passage of the Tribal Law and Order Act, we are witnessing tangible progress toward a healthier, brighter future for Native Americans. I want to reaffirm the Justice Department's commitment and my own commitment to building and sustaining healthy and safe tribal communities; to renewing our nation's enduring promise to American Indians and Alaska Natives; to respecting the sovereignty and self-determination of tribal governments; and to ensuring that the progress we have achieved in recent years is not derailed.

—Attorney General Eric Holder, 2010

The rights of the Sioux peoples are recognized and affirmed in their treaties, agreements, and other constructive arrangements with the United States, in various court decisions, in the U.S. Constitution, and in international human rights instruments. Despite such recognition, their rights are being violated by decisions made with respect to the pipeline project traversing un-ceded Sioux territory.

The total lack of presence and action by the United States government, at the federal level, is a concern that must be addressed. We remind the United States of their ratification of the International Covenant on Civil and Political Rights as well as the 2010 public pronouncement of support for the U.N. Declaration on the Rights of Indigenous Peoples and their 22 September 2014 reiteration of commitment to the U.N. Declaration at the World Conference on Indigenous Peoples. We call on the United States to take urgent action on the alarming situation in North Dakota, including the criminalization of indigenous peoples in their peaceful attempts to safeguard their human rights and fundamental rights.

Source: Columbia University Institute for the Study of Human Rights, U.N. Permanent Forum on Indigenous Issues Statement on the Dakota Access Pipeline, http://www.humanrightscolumbia.org/news/un-permanent-forum-indigenous-issues-issues-statement-dakota-access-pipeline-0

What You Need To Know

The Very Long Struggle for Indigenous Peoples' Rights

A brief historical timeline of indigenous peoples' subjugation to colonizing powers and emergence on the international human rights stage is presented below. The human rights perspective includes recognition that indigenous groups or native peoples have been discriminated against for centuries, at least since the onslaught of primarily, but not solely, European settler-colonialism, with major efforts to forcibly assimilate indigenous peoples into what in many situations became dominant colonial societies. Those colonizing nations included: Portugal, Spain, United Kingdom, Russia, France, Belgium, Germany, Italy, the Netherlands, Denmark, Norway, Sweden, Austria-Hungary, Turkey/Ottoman Empire, Japan, and the U.S.A.

1920s

Nearly a century ago, in 1923 and 1924 in Geneva, Switzerland at the League of Nations, indigenous leaders from the Six Nations of the Iroquois Cayuga Chief Deskaheh and Maori leader W.T. Ratana of New Zealand both tried individually and unsuccessfully to bring international attention to their peoples' oppression and extreme difficulties. These two leaders, from different regions of the earth, were denied access to speak in any officially recognized capacity at the League of Nations, whose authorities were willing and excited to have their photo taken alongside them, but who offered no substantial support to their two causes. These two indigenous leaders laid claim to representing peoples being harmed by Canada, the U.S. and New Zealand. The League of Nations, whose successor would become the post-World War II United Nations Organisation in 1945, was the premier international organization of its time, but was flummoxed by the requests of these two men who came to them to communicate their peoples' need for international assistance at distant ends of the earth. Nonetheless undeterred, their attempts to raise their issues, although blocked from the League of Nations, were registered very favorably within the news media of that time.

1940s-1950s

Even after the birth of the United Nations and post-1948 UDHR, as the U.N. relegated indigenous populations and concerns to U.N. efforts for the elimination of racial discrimination and for the end of slavery, the Bolivian delegation in 1948, in the third session of the U.N. General Assembly, submitted a measure relating to aboriginal populations, which evolved into a proposal to study indigenous populations, but led to nothing practical in the end. It was not until the 1950s that indigenous peoples were finally acknowledged within international fora, when the International Labour Organization whose interest in indigenous peoples culminated in the 1957 ILO Convention No. 107, entitled "Convention Concerning the Protection and Integration of Indigenous and Other Tribal and Semi-Tribal Populations in Independent Countries." The ILO, still from within an assimilationist frame of reference that viewed indigenous peoples among many other minorities, had become aware of forced labor among native peoples early in the 1950s. It was not until 1989 that the ILO's assimilationist mindset dissipated, allowing them to include clear recognition of gender equality and non-discrimination within the adoption of ILO Convention No. 169, known as the Convention concerning Indigenous and Tribal Peoples in Independent Countries.

1960s and 1970s

With official decolonization of European empires and the emergence of new nation states into the 1960s and 1970s, indigenous organizations, through their very public political actions, brought public media attention to extreme human rights abuse toward indigenous peoples by governments that had broken treaties, and were still seizing and violating sacred lands. They exposed to the international community indigenous peoples' long suffering from discrimination, marginalization, gross violations of human rights, their enforced duress to extreme under-development with regard to economic control over their own resources, education, and illiteracy, to over-incarceration, economic exploitation, forced assimilation to the point of genocide or near-genocide, etc., even massacres against indigenous peoples. By the late 1960s, non-governmental organizations and the U.N. were finally ready to listen to indigenous peoples.

In 1971, still within its framework of viewing indigenous peoples based on racial discrimination and minority status, the Sub-Commission on Prevention of Discrimination and Protection of Minorities included a chapter entitled "Measures taken in connection with the protection of indigenous peoples," which recommended a broader study, which in turn led the Economic and Social Council to authorize the Sub-Commission on Human Rights to study comprehensively the problem of discrimination against indigenous populations, i.e., to create the Working Group on Indigenous Populations. By 1972, a study of indigenous populations' human rights issues was underway. The resulting report was named the Martinez Cobo Study, named for its Special Rapporteur, whose investigation consulted with indigenous peoples throughout nearly a decade, i.e., indigenous groups from Asia, Australia, and the Pacific to the Arctic and the Americas and the Caribbean.

1980s-2017

The Martinez Cobo report was submitted in portions to the U.N. Sub-Commission between 1981 and 1983. In the full 1984 report, "It has been pointed out...that basic United Nations texts contain no explicit or specific mention of indigenous populations." In its conclusions, there was a call for clarification: for a special legal status for indigenous populations; to end indigenous peoples' ad hoc classification, especially since indigenous rights already come to be examined annually at the U.N. There was a call for action in holistic thinking in areas of concern for indigenous populations on health, housing, education, language, culture with reference to indigenous cultural, social, and legal institutions, employment, land, political rights, religious rights and practices, equality, and discrimination, and the need for consultation with, and very importantly, by participation of indigenous peoples on these issues. In 1985, the Voluntary Fund for Indigenous Populations was established. The year 1989 saw the adoption of ILO Convention No. 169 concerning Indigenous and Tribal Peoples in Independent States, which, in its first article, enshrined the importance of indigenous self-identification as criterion for determining indigenous groups, wherein tribal peoples' conditions distinguish them by their own customs, traditions, and special laws.

The 1990s and 2000s saw developments to acquire more profound respect and important steps forward for indigenous peoples internationally: the U.N. proclamation of 1993 as the International Year of World's Indigenous People; with the Working Group on Indigenous Populations' release of the Draft Declaration on the Rights of Indigenous Peoples approved by the Sub-Commission and then the Commission on Human Rights in 1995 establishing a Working Group to fine-tune and finalize the declaration; with the U.N. Proclamation of an International Decade of the World's Indigenous People from 1995 to 2004 thematically emphasizing partnership-in-action with the goals: of raising awareness of indigenous issues; of integrating and solidifying indigenous concerns into intergovernmental agendas, by creating a permanent niche within and across the U.N. system; of creating a strong push for national governments to integrate indigenous peoples' rights into domestic agendas.

Throughout the 1990s, indigenous peoples consolidated documentation of human rights violations against them, all the while educating the public with this information via international forums. The U.N. proclaimed August 9 as the International Day of the World's Indigenous People. It also established a fellowship programme for indigenous people through the Office of the High Commissioner on Human Rights (OHCHR). In 2000, the Economic and Social Council established a U.N. high level body called U.N. Permanent Forum on Indigenous Issues (UNPFII) first discussed in the Vienna Conference of 1993. The UNPFII mandate includes facilitating open discussions of indigenous concerns among country representatives and indigenous peoples, usually focused on human rights: indigenous cultures; economic and social development; the environment; education; health, etc. In 2001, the U.N. Commission on Human Rights appointed a Special Rapporteur on the rights of indigenous peoples, Rodolfo Stavenhagen, a Mexican anthropologist whose successor in 2008 was S. James Anaya, a law professor and Native American, whose thorough report on his mission to the U.S. in April-May 2012 led to his final report to the U.N. in August 2012. The current United Nations Special Rapporteur on the rights of indigenous peoples since 2014 is Victoria Tauli Corpuz, a Kankanaey Igorot indigenous people's leader from the Cordillera Region in the Philippines, a former Chair of the U.N. Permanent Forum on Indigenous Issues, and one of the drafters of the U.N. Declaration on the Rights of Indigenous Peoples. She focuses in 2017 on all issues affecting indigenous peoples, with an emphasis on state governments representatives' overcoming the lack of effective implementation of the always necessary consultation and free, prior, and informed consent of indigenous peoples in all state activities affecting them, especially in legislative measures and measures for natural resource development and investment projects. In addition, in her 2016 report, Special Rapporteur Tauli Corpuz began a thematic analysis of the impact of international investment agreements on the rights of indigenous peoples, coming to the conclusion that without consultation with indigenous groups, agreements like the Trans-Pacific Partnership, end up "limiting democratic space by effectively transferring public decision-making powers over economic, social, and cultural governance to corporate actors."

The Special Rapporteur reports annually on the human rights and fundamental freedoms of indigenous peoples. Unfinished business of the 1990s included: a finalized Declaration itself; on-going resistance to indigenous concerns from nation states, such as Canada, Australia, New Zealand, and the U.S. that were all officially overcome by 2010, by which time all four countries signed and accepted the U.N. Declaration on the Rights of Indigenous Peoples. The 2000s also saw the U.N. proclamation for the second Decade of the World's Indigenous People from 2005 to 2014 with a small fund for small-scale projects. The replacement of the Working Group by the Expert Mechanism on the Rights of Indigenous Peoples, made up of five experts, took place. The Expert Mechanism works as a subsidiary of the U.N. Human Rights Council which had supplanted the previous Human Rights Commission and Sub-Commission. In 2002 and 2003, the U.N. established a Voluntary Fund for Indigenous and Local Communities, and a Voluntary Fund to support the UNPFII, where more than 1,500 indigenous persons from all over the world participate annually.

Consultation with and participation by indigenous peoples in all issues has been the consistent political frame of reference and cornerstone from which indigenous peoples work to realize full human rights. Such collaboration or cooperation among westernized or powerful nations with their varied indigenous peoples constitutes both a unique factor and a factor of some difficulty to powerful nations in the international process that led to the emergence from the U.N. of the U.N. Declaration on the Rights of Indigenous Peoples in 2007. Insistence on consultation for, by, and with indigenous peoples as collectives of people(s) proves to be enlightening for people who are not indigenous-identified, a concept that many struggle to understand.

The United Nations Declaration on the Rights of Indigenous Peoples (UNDRIP)

Existentially, many indigenous groups around the world continue to experience marginalization, deprivation of their land, and resources and means of living, with confiscation of land with burial grounds, holy places, and rituals, almost always for the purpose of industrialized extraction of minerals, for taking of water rights and other natural resources, for (re)settlement, or for transit/transport purposes. Indigenous groups' rights to preserve identity, language, culture, religion, and way of life and even to just continue to exist as distinct peoples with collective identities, i.e., their dignity as individuals and as cultural groups, is endangered and under constant threat in many countries. In order to protect indigenous peoples, the U.N.'s now defunct Commission on Human Rights, moved by many human rights NGOs and indigenous groups themselves, mandated its Sub-Commission to prepare studies and to propose specific human rights standards aimed at protecting the human rights of indigenous peoples by 1988. A Draft Declaration resulted, which established a universal framework of standards for the survival, dignity, well-being, and rights of indigenous peoples everywhere.

In 2006, the U.N. Human Rights Council, in its first session as the replacement body for the former Commission and Sub-Commission on Human Rights, adopted the Declaration on the rights of indigenous people with 30 members in favor, 2 against, with 12 abstentions. The Organisation of African Unity (OAU) adopted a decision to negotiate to resolve concerns regarding: the definition of indigenous peoples; their self-determination; land and resources ownership; the establishment of distinctly indigenous political and economic institutions; and national and territorial integrity of indigenous groups.

Unique to the declaration is its inclusion of both individual and collective rights, with emphases on cultural rights to identity, rights to education, health, employment, language, among others, perhaps most importantly the right to full and effective participation in all matters that concern them in their economic, social, and cultural development. The declaration guarantees the right to remain distinct from the dominant cultures around them. The draft caused a lot of controversy initially, as it was seen by some state representatives as too favorable to indigenous groups' power to self-manage their affairs without adequate consideration of state/national governmental interests.

The U.N. Declaration on the Rights of Indigenous Peoples was negotiated slowly and carefully over two decades and was not open for adoption until 2007, and has been adopted by 143 states, with 4 Anglophone states, i.e., Australia, Canada, New Zealand, and the United States, voting against it at that time. Only 11 nation states abstained from the vote, the largest of which is the Russian Federation. The four English-speaking countries originally voting against the declaration have long histories dating back to their colonial periods whose histories survive as indigenous groups recollect them through traditional means.

The declaration has nine key sections: foundational rights; life and security; language, culture, and spirituality; education, information, and employment; participation; development, economics, and social rights; rights to country, resources; rights to our knowledge; and self-governance. Self-governance relates to the human rights to life and security and self-determination: guaranteed participation in decision-making affecting indigenous peoples protects human rights to land and country; to resources, such as water, land use, forests, extractable minerals, metals, and energy sources; to resources of cultural capital, such as ancestral or traditional knowledge bases, such as traditional foods and medicines; to development and social rights.

Australia and Canada have made progress in coming to recognize domestically through their federal courts that its aboriginal peoples have title to lands as traditional indigenous peoples. The centuries-old colonial claim to *terra nullius*, i.e., whereby under-crowded land was claimed to belong to no one, or was territory with apparently no state sovereignty over it, or which was deemed unsettled and unclaimed by any prior sovereign, is being thoroughly delegitimized as a fiction created by the settler-colonial European powers. Australia finally rejected *terra nullius* claims made by British colonizers.

Doing away with stereotypes of indigenous peoples

First of all, it is important to set aside stereotypes regarding indigenous peoples. Indigenous peoples are contemporary people, who do, in fact, understand completely human rights from the western frame of reference, which traces human rights as descendent from natural rights, from conceptions of social contract theory, from the common good, equality, etc., and as related to individuals. After all, indigenous peoples had been living under European colonial and post-colonial nations in some cases for five hundred years, and these legal concepts are nothing new to them. Indigenous peoples know that individual human rights exist. Yet their distinct frame of reference has really only begun to be appreciated as valid and legally informative in the last generation.

Collective Human Rights

Unique to indigenous thinking on human rights is, in some sense, the permeation of all the natural world into one's, and presumably into everyone's, identity. Nature informs indigenous peoples' identity, perspectives, frames of reference, and world views. There is an insistence on an understanding of identity as both communitarian and individual with a strong sense of group cultural rights and individual rights. The collective rights are easily and almost indistinguishably as important as individual rights. Euro-centric emphases on individual rights can seem a bit foreign and narrow-minded within indigenous societies, as this communal attribute serves as a critique and counter-point to western tendencies toward individualism. The universality of human rights attachment to groups or even to all persons together makes more sense for indigenous persons than an individualized framework of human rights attachments. For indigenous peoples, groups bear human rights just as individuals bear them.

Communicating the existence of indigenous peoples' human rights has been considered by many as too politically sensitive and divisive an issue in many countries that have indigenous people, such as the United States, which has Native Americans, Eskimos, and Native Hawaiians as separately identified indigenous groups. Yet, as one delves more deeply into indigenous peoples' thinking-through on human rights issues, discussion usually creates an integrative effect and even a distinctive affect regarding human identity as derivative from within nature, not at all Eurocentric, which historically tends to characterize human identity as a dominant force over nature for exploitative purposes. Both unique and true as systems of normative belief, the thinking-through of indigenous groups' rights is neither simplistic, idealized, nor offered as a panacea. The authors' characterization of indigenous peoples' attitudes toward human rights as a "thinking-through" process is perhaps a bit simplistic. However, as soon as attachments to nature are disrupted from within the mindset, the world goes severely awry and out of balance. Destruction of nature, instead of nature's maintenance, has severe consequences within indigenous thinking-through. For example, it is unimaginable to make a conscious decision to destroy meadows to build a skyscraper someone will have to be responsible for and maintain for hundreds of years. Such a decision would suggest no thinking-through. (There is an irony that indigenous Americans are sometimes hired in skyscraper construction.) Yet indigenous attachments to the natural world, to long-range thinking about land "ownership" and resource use and development, can initially, for Euro-centric thinkers, seem idiosyncratic or out of the mainstream.

Indigenous reflections on human rights reveal a conceptual expansion of human rights thinking regarding identity formation based on the group's/community's responsible integration of customs and traditions regarding family and extended kinship loyalties, deference, and mutual respect for others, especially in honoring and relying on group elders. The need to share life and to honor others; to work together collaboratively; to offer and expect compassion and corrections to and from others in attempting harmonious relationships with one another and in the surrounding natural world... all of this is simply integrated habitually, peaceably, seriously, and more responsibly than in what seems to indigenous peoples as an unduly ambitious (= not humble) and hyperactive westernized world. In the Euro-centric thinking on human rights, one wants to realize and enjoy one's own rights; in contrast, among indigenous peoples, human rights attach themselves inter-generationally to people, and relate to nature, to sources of knowledge, to language knowledge, to seriousness and humor, to customs and traditions, etc. There is something integrated and holistic in indigenous leaders' human rights thinking-through, aimed at the harmonious, to a consensus-building in decision-making that acts as counterpoint or contrast to the intrusive, divisive, polarizing, or erratic themes of much of westernized life. This Weltanschauung or world view constitutes how indigenous peoples interpret human rights as normative within their communal lives.

The definition of indigenous peoples is a working definition

It was agreed that it is important to reject the idea of any formal definition of indigenous peoples. This is the common position of indigenous peoples, as a result of years of discussion and debate within the Working Group on Indigenous Populations. Definitions were considered neither desirable, nor necessary, nor helpful at the international level. For indigenous peoples, it might not even have been possible, and certainly seems foolish to define "indigenous peoples" who live in ninety of the world's countries with more than 370 million indigenous peoples residing in them. In the end, once all indigenous rights are finally respected, enjoyed, and protected, the word "indigenous" could be replaced by specific names of indigenous groups.

An individual's membership in a tribal group constitutes a part of a community's sovereign right and power to make all kinds of decisions without reference to the external states' involvement. Being indigenous refers to: a group's presence/occupation of at least a part of ancestral lands or a region; to a group's common ancestry with the land's original occupants; to a group's historic attachment to a common culture in general that manifests religion, tribal systematization, common traditions of dress, livelihood, life style, etc.; to a mother-tongue or language, which is not necessarily the only language, but which is included as a preferred, habitual, general, normative part of daily language; and other relevant factors associated with indigenous peoples.

In lieu of a definition of what 'indigenous' means, Article 33 of the United Nations Declaration on the Rights of Indigenous Peoples offers that self-identification by indigenous peoples among themselves defines their identity. ILO Convention No. 169 aligned self-identification and self-determination of tribal peoples within independent countries whose social, cultural, and economic conditions distinguish them from other sections of national populations. Indigenous refers to those whose own customs, traditions, special laws/regulations, social, cultural, economic, and political institutions can trace back to original peoples on the land/region, no matter the state's current borders or boundaries, whether established by colonialism, conquest, or some other process external to the tribe. Indigenous communities, peoples, and nations are sometimes too simplistically understood as native societies within territories conquered by European colonizers. These groups consider themselves distinct from the dominant population and are determined to preserve ancestral traditions and rights in the Americas, Polynesia, Oceania, Asia, Australia, New Zealand, and the Arctic territories, that include Canada, the Scandinavian countries of Norway, Sweden, and Finland, and Denmark's territory of Greenland. Indigenous peoples need not be characterized as ethnic minorities, since in places such as Bolivia and Guatemala indigenous populations constitute majority populations within their countries.

The working definition: Indigenous communities, peoples, and nations are those which, having a historical continuity with pre-invasion and pre-colonial societies that developed on their territories, consider themselves distinct from other sectors of the societies now prevailing on those territories, or parts of them. They form at present non-dominant sectors of society and are determined to preserve, develop, and transmit to future generations their ancestral territories, and their ethnic identity, as the basis of their continued existence as peoples, in accordance with their own cultural patterns, social institutions, and legal system.

"Indigenous Peoples" in the end is just the international technical concept used for people who would otherwise have been known as Native Peoples, Autochthonous Peoples, Aborigines, Aboriginal Peoples, First Nations, and in the Americas, where they can nonetheless still sometimes inaccurately be called Indians.

The goal in coming decades is that with the successful enjoyment of all human rights, people will recognize without prejudice proper indigenous peoples' names, such as:
- Makoa, Kunama, Zulu, Baka, Namaqua, Amazigh, Mulonga, Bubi, Afar, Twa, Ogoni, Hutu, Chokwe, Tutsi, Ogiek, Bagwere, Bujeba, Lomwe, Benadiri, Maasai, Ayoup, Tuareg, Duala, or any other of Africa's approximately two hundred indigenous peoples;

or from the more than two hundred Caribbean's peoples' and North, Central, and South Americas' native peoples' names, such as:
- Garífuna, Chichimeca Jonaz, Inuit, Innu, Chippewa, Kuna, Mapuche, Choctaw, Taíno, Guanahatabey, Tepehuán, Onondaga, Ch'orti', Kickapoo, Wichí, Tojolabal, Warao, Lakota, Lenca, Ixcatec, Shawanwa, etc.

or from Oceania's and Asia's hundreds of indigenous peoples, such as:
- Tao, Altayans, Maní, Igorot, Semang, Thao, Atí, Adamanese, Ainu, Sakha, Wanniyala-Aetto, Papuans, Tibetans, Maori, Rarotongan, Fiji, Chamorros, etc.

or from Europe's, such as:
- Tatars, Vascos, Saami, Veps, Krymchaks, Karaites.

For more information on the international community's many indigenous peoples, visit: https://www.cs.mcgill.ca/~rwest/link-suggestion/wpcd_2008-09_augmented/wp/l/List_of_indigenous_peoples.htm

International law concerning indigenous rights
- The UDHR, the International Covenant on Civil and Political Rights (ICCPR) and the International Covenant on Economic, Social and Cultural Rights (ICESCR) and the International Convention on the Elimination of All Forms of Racial Discrimination (ICERD) all affirm the right to self-determination. Thus, indigenous people are entitled to determine their own social, cultural, and economic development, as well as to respect for all the other rights listed in those treaties.
- The United Nations Declaration on the Rights of Indigenous Peoples (UNDRIP), although not a legally binding treaty, articulates and interprets clearly rights applicable to indigenous peoples and serves to inform nation states in treaty implementation related to indigenous peoples.
- Latin American and African national courts and regional international courts have used the above-listed treaties, UNDRIP, and the ILO Indigenous and Tribal Peoples Convention, 1989 (No. 169) in the area of collective indigenous peoples' rights for their physical and cultural survival, with reference to ancestral lands, territories, and resources.
- Within the OAS system, the Inter-American Human Rights Commission in 1990 established the Office of the Rapporteur on the Rights of Indigenous Peoples, whose current Rapporteur is Francisco José Eguiguren Praeli, due to the exposed vulnerability from the preceding decades and generations to gross violations of their human rights as indigenous peoples, such as was the case of Guatemala.

Special Mechanisms/Procedures related to Indigenous Peoples

Perhaps more than any other bearers of human rights, indigenous peoples have worked hard to embed themselves into the processes of the U.N. and the OAS in order to exercise their collective and individual rights. The following are the various Special Mechanisms or Procedures in play within the U.N. and the OAS at the time of publication.

U.N. Permanent Forum on Indigenous Issues (UNPFII)

UNPFII is an advisory body of experts to the Economic and Social Council at the U.N. Established in 2000, by ECOSOC Resolution 2000/22, the UNPFII was a response to the 1993 Vienna World Conference on Human Rights. UNPFII has a mandate to monitor and deal with indigenous peoples' issues related to: economic and social development; indigenous culture; the environment; health; education; and human rights. They give advice and make recommendations to ECOSOC, and to other U.N. organs on indigenous issues. They promote and prepare information dissemination and coordinate indigenous peoples' issues within the U.N. system, and have held annual two-week sessions, usually in Geneva, since 2002. In 2017, at its 15th session, the UNPFII recommended to member states: recognition of language rights via language policy development to promote/protect indigenous languages with full immersion methods, language nests, and nomadic schooling with an aim to collecting and disseminating baseline information on the status of indigenous languages in close cooperation with indigenous peoples concerned. Very broadly to states, U.N. and supportive groups; UNPFII recommended support and funding to revitalize indigenous language fluency along with information and communications technology in indigenous languages and other language projects. UNPFII commended Canada's unqualified endorsement of the U.N. Declaration on the Rights of Indigenous Peoples; the initiation of national dialogue in Guatemala for constitutional reforms for recognition of indigenous justice systems, among many other items.

Expert Mechanism on the Rights of Indigenous Peoples (EMRIP)

In 2007, the Human Rights Council (HRC) established a subsidiary body to itself, called the Expert Mechanism on the Rights of Indigenous Peoples (EMRIP) via Resolution 6/36. EMRIP, as five HRC-appointed independent experts on the rights of indigenous peoples, completes thematic studies and research for the HRC and has given advice and recommendations to the HRC since 2009 on issues concerning indigenous peoples' right to education that promotes and protects their languages and culture, and thereby the rights and identity of indigenous peoples, and how to realize that right to education. In 2011, EMRIP submitted a progress report to the HRC on the very specific right to participate in decision-making with focus on extractive industries. In 2012, EMRIP submitted the previous two reports, plus a report on its questionnaire for states on best practices to reach the goals of the U.N. Declaration on the Rights of Indigenous Peoples. EMRIP has done a study on access to justice in the promotion/protection of indigenous peoples' rights. EMRIP's experts are of indigenous origin, of gender balance, and from varied areas of the world. Financed by the Voluntary Fund for Indigenous Populations, EMRIP meets annually in July with representatives from indigenous groups and organizations, academics, civil society groups, and inter-governmental organizations and states representatives. A member from UNPFII and the Special Rapporteur are also usually present.

Special Rapporteur on the Rights of Indigenous Peoples

In 2001, the former Commission on Human Rights appointed, as part of the special procedures system, Special Rapporteur on the rights of indigenous people, whose mandate is: to promote between states and indigenous peoples any good practice, such as laws, programs, agreements that cause respect for and implementation of indigenous peoples' human rights; to develop country reports on overall conditions of human rights of indigenous peoples; to address specific cases in countries where alleged human rights violations are occurring via formal contact with governments involved and others; to conduct/contribute thematic studies that promote/protect indigenous peoples' rights. Subsequent Special Rapporteurs follow up on recommendations from predecessors' reporting or earlier work, and report all activities to the HRC.

From 2001 to 2008, the first Special Rapporteur on the rights of indigenous peoples was Rodolfo Stavenhagen, a highly respected Mexican anthropologist. From 2008 to 2014, S. James Anaya, a law professor and Native American, whose thorough reporting on his mission to the U.S. in April-May 2012 led to his final report to the U.N. in August 2012. Special Rapporteur Anaya also created an impressively large archive of data and reports related to indigenous peoples. (See Document 3: Index of Reports...on the Rights of Indigenous Peoples.) The current United Nations Special Rapporteur on the rights of indigenous peoples since 2014 is Victoria Tauli Corpuz, a Kankanaey Igorot indigenous people's leader from the Cordillera Region in the Philippines, a former Chair of the U.N. Permanent Forum on Indigenous Issues, and one of the drafters of the U.N. Declaration on the Rights of Indigenous Peoples. (See Primary Source Documents 2 and 5 for Special Rapporteur Reports)

International Investment Agreements as too adversarial and possible exploitation of indigenous peoples' resources: extraction of mineral, energy, forestry, water, agricultural, cultural resources, etc.

The 2016 Special Rapporteur's (Victoria Tauli Corpuz) Report on the rights of indigenous peoples (See Primary Source Document 5) "provides an analysis of the impacts of international investment agreements, including bilateral investment treaties and investment chapters of free trade agreements, on the rights of indigenous peoples." After the mention of visits completed to Lapland, Honduras, and Brazil in 2015 and 2016, she expounds in a third progression of reports on the theme of international investment agreements' structure as negatively impacting the lives and the human rights of indigenous peoples. She uses questionnaires sent to U.N. states members, indigenous peoples, civil society groups, and various formal indigenous groups and experts in Asia, Africa, North and South America, Europe, etc. working on this issue alongside sustainable development in her research that leads to reports. The goal of the reports has been to gain insight into how to enhance promotion of coherent international investment law and human rights law, with states realizing their duties to protect indigenous peoples' rights by not allowing obstruction of rights by thousands of multi-stakeholder investors which operate within home states or host states. The problem with these agreements relates to their structuring into such agreements overly favorable terms for investors with apparently full no-risk protections and security for return on investments as a legitimate expectation. An investor-state gets access to external arbitration in cases of alleged violations of contract or alleged failures of investment without any requirement to exhaust domestic legal remedies, and in procedures which have only minimal transparency. Contractual language allows investors to gain billions of dollars in awards that can never be litigated domestically, and which have investors able to seize what for them are overseas investments, especially in the extractive and energy industries, thereby exploiting indigenous peoples' mineral, energy, forest, and water resources. Megaregional free trade agreements, like the TPP, represent the danger. On the contrary, states are obliged to make use of UNDRIP to form, oversee, and protect culturally appropriate mechanisms to effect indigenous peoples' participation in all decision-making affecting their rights, specifically because of their very long history as marginalized and oppressed groups. Indigenous peoples are generally very pro-development economically. One might say they have become in the contemporary era very savvy on this issue in relation to sustainable development, a global theme of ever-increasing importance.

Guiding Principles on Business and Human Rights: Protect, Respect, and Remedy Framework

The U.N. has reaffirmed since 2011 that there is independent corporate responsibility to respect indigenous peoples' rights with the incorporation of Guiding Principles on Business and Human Rights, as can be attested by these already incorporated standards into Guidelines on Multinational Corporations of the Organization for Economic Cooperation and Development (OECD). Since the 2007 UNDRIP, multi-stakeholder investors are required to seek free, prior, and informed consent from affected indigenous peoples before getting any approval or before undertaking investment, through good-faith consultations. Despite these normative standards, interests in mining, hydroelectric, agribusiness, oil, gas, and even solar sectors continue to violate and ignore indigenous peoples' land, cultural, and self-governance rights, despite recommendations and case decisions within regional and international human rights bodies. Multinational corporations are fully aware of these normative standards, but work to obfuscate them, ignore them, as do states with inadequate implementation of many international human rights standards. Governments weakly challenge international investment agreements. With those agreements, wealthy interests choose to ignore property rights of indigenous peoples that are protected under international human rights law.

Examples of Investor-State Settlements: The Growing List of Cases that Ignore and/or Deny International Human Rights Law

The Special Rapporteur's 2016 Report cites the following examples of investor-state settlements impacting indigenous peoples' human rights:

- *Burlington Resources Inc. v. Ecuador* (2010): oil/gas company sued Ecuador, breach related to protection/security due to indigenous people protests; Ecuador avoided indigenous rights arguments. In parallel case, in Inter-American Commission on Human Rights, and in Inter-American Court of Human Rights, decisions ruled that there was a failure to consult indigenous peoples to obtain their free, prior, and informed consent; threat to indigenous peoples survival.
- *Chevron v. Ecuador* (2014): Ecuadoran Courts decided that Chevron pay $8.6 billion for indigenous peoples' suffering, but Chevron took legal actions to avoid payment. Inter-American Commission on Human Rights took precautionary measures to require Ecuador to protect indigenous groups from threatened human rights.

- *Von Pezold and Border Timbers v. Zimbabwe* (2015): Zimbabwe confiscated German and Swiss companies' land for four indigenous communities. Although acknowledging that state and company had human rights obligations, the International Centre for Settlement of Investment Disputes tribunal rejected Zimbabwe's defense, because it dominated indigenous communities' leaders' claimants' independence as prejudiced, due to affiliations with the government; due to tribunal's inability to determine whether people were indigenous and tribunal's lack of competence re: indigenous peoples' rights. The tribunal was unpersuaded by international human rights law obligations.

- *Glamis Gold v. United States* (2009); An arbitration panel ruled against company access to sacred area of Quechuan tribal nation in southern California/Arizona border area; test of the limits of treaty breach when U.S. deals with investors' expectations; tribunal did not engage in international human rights arguments for indigenous peoples.

- *Grand River Enterprise Six Nations, Ltd v. United States* (2011): Canadian Haudenosaunee Nations' individuals owned tobacco companies and wanted U.S. authorities to consult them as collectivities on U.S. policies affecting them. Tribunal rejected this opinion, because consultations should have taken place with native tribes on U.S. side of the border whose sovereign interests were affected by tobacco commerce.

- *South American Silver Mining v. Plurinational State of Bolivia* (in Permanent Court of Arbitration): Bolivia confiscated 10 mining concessions from a UK company with a bilateral investment treaty with Bolivia, and wanted $386 million in compensation due to state's failure to provide protection/security in investment treaty. The company claimed efforts to consult with indigenous communities for their consent, but accused Bolivia of fomenting a small group's opposition. Bolivia claimed public interest action to revert ownership to state, based on legal principles of proportionality and necessity out of concern for company's security and to restore public order for indigenous groups; tempered company's expectations with domestic laws re: indigenous rights and bilateral investment treaty missing systematic interpretation of Vienna Convention on the law of treaties; company project violated UNDRIP rights; company had fabricated indigenous consent; customary international law puts human rights primacy over investor protections; cited Inter-American Court of Human Rights decision in *Sawhoyamaxa v. Paraguay*, which ruled that state's human rights obligations and land restitution to indigenous groups is a public purpose or interest; and also U.N. Charter Article 103 applies. Company invoked multiple cases that avoided international human rights law arguments, and that ILO Indigenous and Tribal Peoples Convention No. 169, and UNDRIP are not customary international law; preference for UNDRIP leads to degrade investor protections.

- *Bear Creek Mining Corp. v. Peru* is similar to preceding case, but is argued under free trade agreement between Canada and Peru; company felt forced to withdraw with Aymara indigenous protests, but seeks $500 million; claims Peru acted out of expediency and capitulation to violence; company claimed intention to consult and environmental permitting; Peruvian domestic law serves to implement ILO Convention No. 169; case denied in the end;

Special Rapporteur 2016 Report recommendations regarding international investment agreements include:
- States must not lose regulatory powers in them; maintain entitlement to make counterclaims for relief from investor interference with state's human rights obligations; States should ratify: U.N. Convention on Transparency in Treaty-based Investor-State Arbitration;
- Mechanisms are necessary to regulate and mandate respect for human rights;
- Their policy objectives should include respect for human rights; include human rights assessments;
- Indigenous peoples' human rights needs to be included:
  - Appropriate consultation procedures/mechanisms for indigenous peoples in drafting, negotiating, and approving investment agreements;
  - Use Guiding Principles on Business and Human Rights on right to food;
  - Use and respect ICESCR and "clean hands" doctrine in dealings with indigenous peoples;
- Jurisdiction should prohibit:
  - Anything that does not comply with human rights law,
  - Shell/mailbox companies;
  - Investment protections before consultations with indigenous peoples.

OAS Special Mechanism

In the Americas, the Organization of American States (OAS), the regional international organization of the Americas, has its own Special Mechanisms that have recently allowed the Standing Rock Sioux Tribe, the Cheyenne River Sioux Tribe, and the Yankton Sioux Tribe, known as the "Tribes," to make use of. The Tribes have petitioned and requested that the Inter-American Commission on Human Rights (IACHR) call on the United States to adopt *precautionary measures* to prevent irreparable harm to the Tribes, their members, and others resulting from the ongoing and imminent construction of the Dakota Access Pipeline ("DAPL"), and from the harassment and violence being perpetrated against people gathered in prayer and protest in opposition to DAPL. (See Primary Source Document 6)

The IACHR, a seven-member commission elected by the OAS General Assembly to no more than two four-year terms, is an autonomous organ of the OAS. It exists, according to its statute, to promote the observance/defense of human rights and as an OAS advisory body to address states parties to the American Convention on Human Rights, and to non-members states as well. By mandate, the IACHR: requests information from governments; responds to government inquiries in an advisory capacity; makes recommendations to governments; authorizes studies and reports; conducts on-site observations in countries; submits its prepared reports annually to the OAS General Assembly; among other expansive functions. It is a monitoring and compliance body of the OAS that may make quasi-judicial decisions on individual cases of petition, but seems to have greater influence over countries with human rights issues through its thematic reporting process. The IACHR, as a part-time body whose commissioners are employed full-time elsewhere, usually in other countries, only meets in short sessions three times annually. There are country Rapporteurs assigned to the seven commissioners; and thematic Rapporteurs on LGBTI, women, children, Afro-descendants, migrant workers, persons in detention, human rights defenders, and indigenous peoples.

2015 UPR — U.S. Reporting

The U.S., in its country report submitted to the U.N. as part of its 2015 Universal Periodic Review, in response to the section on Indigenous issues (based on Recommendations 83, 85, 199-203, 205, and 206 from its 2010 UPR), addressed:

- its substantial advances to better protect the rights of indigenous peoples domestically, e.g., President Obama's announcement of support for the U.N. Declaration on the Rights of Indigenous Peoples and three informal consultations with tribal governments, indigenous groups, and NGOs;
- frequent and extensive domestic dialogues on matters of importance to indigenous peoples, e.g., annual White House Tribal Nations Conference with tribal governments' leadership of, where discussions addressed issues: tribal self-determination; self-governance; health care; economic and infrastructure development; education; protection of land and natural resources; and other matters, all of which indigenous leaders shared at September 2014 World Conference on Indigenous Peoples, and were pleased that the four main priorities advocated by tribal government leaders were incorporated into the Outcome Document;
- The 2013 order, issued by President Obama, creating the White House Council on Native American Affairs with heads of various federal agencies to improve high-level coordination on the pressing issues facing tribal communities;
- "Generation Indigenous," an initiative to remove barriers to success for Native youth, launched in December 2014: college and career readiness programs; leadership training; a listening tour for members of the President's cabinet to hear aspirations and concerns of Native youth; preservation of Native languages; Department of the Interior's 48,000 American Indian students across 23 states to get a comprehensive reform plan in June 2014; new education grants to better meet the needs of American Indian and Alaska Native students;
- further action taken to address discrimination against tribal communities and Native individuals: Department of Labor enforcement of non-discrimination in employment by federal contractors and Department of Justice enforcement of civil rights laws on behalf of American Indians and Alaska Natives, i.e., protection of religious practices, education, voting, fair lending, corrections, access to courts for non-English-speakers, re: hate crimes, sex trafficking, and excessive use of force by police;
- March 2013 reauthorization of the Violence Against Women Act, part of which addresses violence against American Indian and Alaska Native women: with a new tribal authority recognition to prosecute in tribal courts any acts of domestic violence on tribal lands irrespective to perpetrator as Indian or non-Indian; empowerment to all challenges addressed in UNDRIP; 2012 law giving greater control to tribes over tribal assets, e.g., land leases; 2010 law enhancement of tribal sentencing authority, strengthening of defendants' rights, new guidelines, and

training for officers re: domestic violence and sex crimes, improvement of services to victims, and help to combat alcohol and substance abuse, and help at-risk youth;

- prioritization to reach settlement agreements with tribes over trust-mismanagement, etc., already $2.6 billion in compensation to more than 80 federally-recognized Indian tribes; an individual trust case for $3.4 billion; settled a landmark class-action lawsuit by Indian farmers and ranchers alleging that they were discriminated against in federal agricultural programs.

Source: United Nations, General Assembly, Human Rights Council, Working Group on the Universal Periodic Review, Twenty-second session, 15 May 2015, A/HRC/WG.6/22/USA/1, 13 February 2015, National report submitted in accordance with paragraph 5 of the annex to Human Rights Council resolution 16/21, United States of America

Current international conflicts: International Investment Agreements, TPP, and Indigenous Peoples' right to full and effective participation in all matters that concern them in their economic, social, cultural development

- The Trans-Pacific Partnership (TPP): Although blocked in its present form, the TPP could be resurrected as a trade treaty in some other form. Since eleven of its twelve state signers have indigenous peoples within them, indigenous peoples' groups have been expressing concerns regarding the lack of protections for their rights in relation to foreign investors, and that their consultative status is ignored in the TPP. The TPP contains no reference to human rights at all, much less any human rights impact assessments. The only indigenous people referred to in the TPP are the Maori of New Zealand in New Zealand's exception chapter.

U.S. Constitution, Congress, Executive Branch, U.S. Supreme Court Decisions and Indigenous Peoples' Rights in the U.S.

- The U.S., after its successful secession from Great Britain in the late 18th century, inherited treaties and treaty-making powers with Indian tribes that got land and resources from them in exchange for tribal retention of rights and sovereignty over land and resources they had not given up.
- Since Article I, section 8 of the U.S. Constitution states that Congress has the federal power to regulate commerce with the Indian tribes, a priority over state level legislatures: in the late 18th century and early 19th century, the Supreme Court recognized Indian tribes as inherently sovereign nations with ancestral lands and with powers of self-government, although subordinated to U.S. governmental plenary powers, which eventually led to unilateral actions to restrict still existent sovereignty, while dispossessing them of ancestral lands. Eventually diminished to trusteeships and "domestic dependent nations," the commerce clause was used as a means of indigenous dispossession of land and resources.
- Many of the Supreme Court's decisions during this period enshrine justices' attitudes toward Indians as backward, inferior savages and conquered peoples, reducing them to peoples in need of protective status, while sometimes affirming original notions of Indian sovereignty and rights to self-government.
- After 1871, the U.S. stopped dealing in treaties with Indian tribes, as it established trans-continental control over all its territories. Instead of retaining indigenous sovereignty and self-rule, U.S. law and policy aimed to assimilate and acculturate indigenous peoples into the dominant society and to manage them on reservations, settlements, rancherias, and pueblos.
- In 1887, the Dawes General Allotment Act broke up tribal lands into individual plots, which eventually led to greater land loss and land sales that turned some reservations into patchworks of territory, causing impoverishment and social problems.
- Congress finally granted U.S. citizenship to all Indians in 1924.
- In 1934, the Congress passed the Indian Reorganization Act (IRA), as an act of major reform to secure land and to establish reservation-based governance under the federal Secretary of the Interior, but still based on a model of total assimilation into the dominant society.
- In the 1950s the U.S. government moved to end the special status of Indian tribes in a policy known as "termination," which tried to privatize lands and terminate tribal federal recognition status and self-governing powers. By the time the "termination" policy ended, more land was lost, and indigenous peoples were more impoverished.
- In the 1960s-1970s, native peoples exercised their desire to hold on to and to recover their cultural institutions, including self-governance with some success, as policy started to accommodate these aspirations. In 1970, President Nixon spoke to Congress in support of a future determined by Indian acts and decisions. In 1975, the

Indian Self-Determination and Education Assistance Act was followed in 1978 by the Indian Child Welfare Act, which guaranteed indigenous custody of their own children. Also in 1978, the American Indian Religious Freedom Act required federal officials to consult with tribes on any actions affecting indigenous practice of religion.

- In 1990, the Native American Graves Protection and Repatriation Act required the return of indigenous remains and sacred objects to appropriate groups. Also, 1990 saw passage of the Native American Languages Act to develop programs for use and recovery of indigenous languages. Other laws protective of culture, religion, economic and natural resource development, and education and civil rights were passed in the 1990s. In addition, indigenous-related programs and agencies exist within the U.S. government with efforts to appoint indigenous persons to high positions in government, such as the Assistant Secretary for Indian Affairs at the head of the Bureau of Indian Affairs. President Obama created a position of Senior Policy Advisor for Native American Affairs.

In 2017, most people within the U.S. experience images of Native Americans that don't match stereotypes of them as relics from a distant past, due to tremendous strife and resistance in North Dakota. In 2014, Lakota-Sioux tribes began protesting a culture and life-threatening decision-making process that never consulted them or included their input, as required by international and U.S. domestic law regarding running an oil pipeline through sacred territories, under rivers and lakes in North Dakota. In the summer and fall of 2016, the world's media attention was finally drawn to North Dakota and Standing Rock. After years of protests against DAPL, the Dakota Access Pipeline, under construction through their indigenous lands, looked to be stopped, at least temporarily, with the new decision by the Army Corps of Engineers to reroute it away from the Sioux-Lakota indigenous lands. At least temporarily, the indigenous peoples of North America felt a victory. In late January 2017, President Trump stated he wanted to fast-track DAPL. The water protectors are prepared for a protracted struggle for their indigenous rights. Like all indigenous peoples, the Lakota-Sioux peoples are used to struggling for their rights. They have been actively involved in the international indigenous human rights struggle for decades, and are ready to exhaust domestic legal remedies, even as they keep informed and turn to international human rights systems, such as the U.N. and the OAS.

In addition, the Tohono O'odham Nation, a U.S. recognized Native American tribe, has a reservation that runs along seventy-five miles of the U.S.-Mexico border in southwest Arizona. The tribe of about 28,000 members are against the building of the security wall that President Trump's 2017 executive order calls for. They are resisting because they have not been consulted in any way, and because a permanent wall could cut through tribal lands and divide families who would no longer be able to cross freely back and forth across the borderline between countries.

Current indigenous issues in the U.S. include the Dakota Access Pipeline and the Standing Rock Sioux Tribe, Cheyenne River Sioux Tribe, and Yankton Sioux Tribe's *precautionary measures* (See OAS Special Mechanism above) and issues outlined in The United Nations Special Rapporteur on the rights of indigenous peoples, James Anaya, Primary Source Document 2.

Like those human rights covenants on women, children, immigrants, and those discriminated against based on racist notions about color, social class, and culture, indigenous peoples' struggles for respect for their human dignity is the basis of law embodied in international human rights law. As more is demanded from the U.S. Constitution, which stands behind human rights norms, the United States should act positively and constructively to promote and protect the rights of indigenous peoples in the U.S.

Primary Source Documents

I. DECLARATION ON THE RIGHTS OF THE INDIGENOUS PEOPLES

The U.S. was one of four countries to vote against the United Nations Declaration on the Rights of Indigenous Peoples (UNDRIP) in 2008. In 2010, the U.S. was the last of those four countries to support it. Although, as a declaration, UNDRIP is not a legally binding treaty, this declaration articulates legal groundwork and interprets indigenous peoples' rights. It informs U.S. citizens about the historical and current neglect of U.S. native peoples in the U.S., and the direction the U.S. intends to take in support of human rights of indigenous peoples.

Human Rights Council Resolution 2006/2.

Working group of the Commission on Human Rights to elaborate a draft declaration in accordance with paragraph 5 of the General Assembly resolution 49/214 of 23 December 1994

The Human Rights Council,

Recalling Commission on Human Rights resolution 1995/32 of 3 March 1995, in which it established an open-ended intersessional working group with the sole purpose of elaborating a draft United Nations declaration on the rights of indigenous peoples, considering the draft contained in the annex to resolution 1994/45 of the Sub-Commission on the Promotion and Protection of Human Rights, for consideration and adoption by the General Assembly within the first International Decade of the World's Indigenous People,

Aware that the working group of the Commission on Human Rights to elaborate a draft declaration in accordance with paragraph 5 of the General Assembly resolution 49/214 of 23 December 1994 has held 11 sessions between 1995 and 2006,

Considering that the General Assembly, in its resolution 59/174 of 20 December 2004, urges all parties involved in the process of negotiation to do their utmost to carry out successfully the mandate of the working group and to present to the General Assembly for adoption as soon as possible a final draft United Nations declaration on the rights of indigenous peoples,

Stressing that paragraph 127 of the outcome document of the 2005 World Summit, adopted by the General Assembly in its resolution 60/1 of 16 September 2005, reaffirms the commitment of the international community to adopt a final draft United Nations declaration on the rights of indigenous peoples as soon as possible,

Taking note of the report of the working group on its eleventh session, which took place in Geneva from 5 to 16 December 2005 and from 30 January to 3 February 2006 (E/CN.4/2006/79),

Welcoming the conclusion of the Chairperson-Rapporteur in paragraph 30 of the report of the working group and his proposal as contained in annex I to the report,

1. *Adopts* the United Nations Declaration on the Rights of Indigenous Peoples as proposed by the Chairperson-Rapporteur of the working group of the Commission on Human Rights to elaborate a draft declaration in accordance with paragraph 5 of the General Assembly resolution 49/214 of 23 December 1994 in annex I to the report of the working group on its eleventh session (E/CN.4/2006/79);

2. *Recommends* to the General Assembly that it adopt the following draft resolution:

The General Assembly,

Taking note of Human Rights Council resolution 2006/2 of 29 June 2006, in which the Council adopted the text of the United Nations Declaration on the Rights of Indigenous Peoples,

1. *Expresses its appreciation* to the Council for the adoption of the United Nations Declaration on the Rights of Indigenous Peoples;

2. *Adopts* the Declaration as contained in the annex to Council resolution 2006/2 of 29 June 2006.

[Adopted by a recorded vote of 30 votes to 2, with 12 abstentions. The voting was as follows:

In favour: Azerbaijan, Brazil, Cameroon, China, Cuba, Czech Republic, Ecuador, Finland, France, Germany, Guatemala, India, Indonesia, Japan, Malaysia, Mauritius, Mexico, Netherlands, Pakistan, Peru, Poland, Republic of Korea, Romania, Saudi Arabia, South Africa, Sri Lanka, Switzerland, United Kingdom of Great Britain and Northern Ireland, Uruguay, Zambia

Against: Canada, Russian Federation

Abstaining: Algeria, Argentina, Bahrain, Bangladesh, Ghana, Jordan, Morocco, Nigeria, the Philippines, Senegal, Tunisia, Ukraine.]

Annex

UNITED NATIONS DECLARATION ON THE RIGHTS OF INDIGENOUS PEOPLES

Affirming that indigenous peoples are equal to all other peoples, while recognizing the right of all peoples to be different, to consider themselves different, and to be respected as such,

Affirming also that all peoples contribute to the diversity and richness of civilizations and cultures, which constitute the common heritage of humankind,

Affirming further that all doctrines, policies and practices based on or advocating superiority of peoples or individuals on the basis of national origin, racial, religious, ethnic or cultural differences are racist, scientifically false, legally invalid, morally condemnable and socially unjust,

Reaffirming also that indigenous peoples, in the exercise of their rights, should be free from discrimination of any kind,

Concerned that indigenous peoples have suffered from historic injustices as a result of, inter alia, their colonization and dispossession of their lands, territories and resources, thus preventing them from exercising, in particular, their right to development in accordance with their own needs and interests,

Recognizing the urgent need to respect and promote the inherent rights of indigenous peoples which derive from their political, economic and social structures and from their cultures, spiritual traditions, histories and philosophies, especially their rights to their lands, territories and resources,

Further recognizing the urgent need to respect and promote the rights of indigenous peoples affirmed in treaties, agreements and other constructive arrangements with States,

Welcoming the fact that indigenous peoples are organizing themselves for political, economic, social and cultural enhancement and in order to bring an end to all forms of discrimination and oppression wherever they occur,

Convinced that control by indigenous peoples over developments affecting them and their lands, territories and resources will enable them to maintain and strengthen their institutions, cultures and traditions, and to promote their development in accordance with their aspirations and needs,

Recognizing also that respect for indigenous knowledge, cultures and traditional practices contributes to sustainable and equitable development and proper management of the environment,

Emphasizing the contribution of the demilitarization of the lands and territories of indigenous peoples to peace, economic and social progress and development, understanding and friendly relations among nations and peoples of the world,

Recognizing in particular the right of indigenous families and communities to retain shared responsibility for the upbringing, training, education and well-being of their children, consistent with the rights of the child,

Recognizing also that indigenous peoples have the right freely to determine their relationships with States in a spirit of co-existence, mutual benefit and full respect,

Considering that the rights affirmed in treaties, agreements and constructive arrangements between States and indigenous peoples are, in some situations, matters of international concern, interest, responsibility and character,

Also considering that treaties, agreements and other constructive arrangements, and the relationship they represent, are the basis for a strengthened partnership between indigenous peoples and States,

Acknowledging that the Charter of the United Nations, the International Covenant on Economic, Social and Cultural Rights and the International Covenant on Civil and Political Rights affirm the fundamental importance of the right of self-determination of all peoples, by virtue of which they freely determine their political status and freely pursue their economic, social and cultural development,

Bearing in mind that nothing in this Declaration may be used to deny any peoples their right of self-determination, exercised in conformity with international law,

Convinced that the recognition of the rights of indigenous peoples in this Declaration will enhance harmonious and cooperative relations between the State and indigenous peoples, based on principles of justice, democracy, respect for human rights, non-discrimination and good faith,

Encouraging States to comply with and effectively implement all their obligations as they apply to indigenous peoples under international instruments, in particular those related to human rights, in consultation and cooperation with the peoples concerned,

Emphasizing that the United Nations has an important and continuing role to play in promoting and protecting the rights of indigenous peoples,

Believing that this Declaration is a further important step forward for the recognition, promotion and protection of the rights and freedoms of indigenous peoples and in the development of relevant activities of the United Nations system in this field,

Recognizing and reaffirming that indigenous individuals are entitled without discrimination to all human rights recognized in international law, and that indigenous peoples possess collective rights which are indispensable for their existence, well-being and integral development as peoples,

Solemnly proclaims the following United Nations Declaration on the Rights of Indigenous Peoples as a standard of achievement to be pursued in a spirit of partnership and mutual respect,

Article 1
Indigenous peoples have the right to the full enjoyment, as a collective or as individuals, of all human rights and fundamental freedoms as recognized in the Charter of the United Nations, the Universal Declaration of Human Rights and international human rights law.

Article 2

Indigenous peoples and individuals are free and equal to all other peoples and individuals and have the right to be free from any kind of discrimination, in the exercise of their rights, in particular that based on their indigenous origin or identity.

Article 3

Indigenous peoples have the right of self-determination. By virtue of that right they freely determine their political status and freely pursue their economic, social and cultural development.

Article 4

Indigenous peoples, in exercising their right to self-determination, have the right to autonomy or self-government in matters relating to their internal and local affairs, as well as ways and means for financing their autonomous functions.

Article 5

Indigenous peoples have the right to maintain and strengthen their distinct political, legal, economic, social and cultural institutions, while retaining their rights to participate fully, if they so choose, in the political, economic, social and cultural life of the State.

Article 6

Every indigenous individual has the right to a nationality.

Article 7

1. Indigenous individuals have the rights to life, physical and mental integrity, liberty and security of person.

2. Indigenous peoples have the collective right to live in freedom, peace and security as distinct peoples and shall not be subjected to any act of genocide or any other act of violence, including forcibly removing children of the group to another group.

Article 8

1. Indigenous peoples and individuals have the right not to be subjected to forced assimilation or destruction of their culture.

2. States shall provide effective mechanisms for prevention of, and redress for:

(a) Any action which has the aim or effect of depriving them of their integrity as distinct peoples, or of their cultural values or ethnic identities;

(b) Any action which has the aim or effect of dispossessing them of their lands, territories or resources;

(c) Any form of forced population transfer which has the aim or effect of violating or undermining any of their rights;

(d) Any form of forced assimilation or integration by other cultures or ways of life imposed on them by legislative, administrative or other measures;

(e) Any form of propaganda designed to promote or incite racial or ethnic discrimination directed against them.

Article 9

Indigenous peoples and individuals have the right to belong to an indigenous community or nation, in accordance with the traditions and customs of the community or nation concerned. No discrimination of any kind may arise from the exercise of such a right.

Article 10

Indigenous peoples shall not be forcibly removed from their lands or territories. No relocation shall take place without the free, prior and informed consent of the indigenous peoples concerned and after agreement on just and fair compensation and, where possible, with the option of return.

Article 11

1. Indigenous peoples have the right to practice and revitalize their cultural traditions and customs. This includes the right to maintain, protect and develop the past, present and future manifestations of their cultures, such as archaeological and historical sites, artefacts, designs, ceremonies, technologies and visual and performing arts and literature.

2. States shall provide redress through effective mechanisms, which may include restitution, developed in conjunction with indigenous peoples, with respect to their cultural, intellectual, religious and spiritual property taken without their free, prior and informed consent or in violation of their laws, traditions and customs.

Article 12

1. Indigenous peoples have the right to manifest, practice, develop and teach their spiritual and religious traditions, customs and ceremonies; the right to maintain, protect, and have access in privacy to their religious and cultural sites; the right to the use and control of their ceremonial objects; and the right to the repatriation of their human remains.

2. States shall seek to enable the access and/or repatriation of ceremonial objects and human remains in their possession through fair, transparent and effective mechanisms developed in conjunction with indigenous peoples concerned.

Article 13

1. Indigenous peoples have the right to revitalize, use, develop and transmit to future generations their histories, languages, oral traditions, philosophies, writing systems and literatures, and to designate and retain their own names for communities, places and persons.

2. States shall take effective measures to ensure this right is protected and also to ensure that indigenous peoples can understand and be understood in political, legal and administrative proceedings, where necessary through the provision of interpretation or by other appropriate means.

Article 14

1. Indigenous peoples have the right to establish and control their educational systems and institutions providing education in their own languages, in a manner appropriate to their cultural methods of teaching and learning.

2. Indigenous individuals, particularly children, have the right to all levels and forms of education of the State without discrimination.

3. States shall, in conjunction with indigenous peoples, take effective measures, in order for indigenous individuals, particularly children, including those living outside their communities, to have access, when possible, to an education in their own culture and provided in their own language.

Article 15

1. Indigenous peoples have the right to the dignity and diversity of their cultures, traditions, histories and aspirations which shall be appropriately reflected in education and public information.

2. States shall take effective measures, in consultation and cooperation with the indigenous peoples concerned, to combat prejudice and eliminate discrimination and to promote tolerance, understanding and good relations among indigenous peoples and all other segments of society.

Article 16

1. Indigenous peoples have the right to establish their own media in their own languages and to have access to all forms of non-indigenous media without discrimination.

2. States shall take effective measures to ensure that State-owned media duly reflect indigenous cultural diversity. States, without prejudice to ensuring full freedom of expression, should encourage privately-owned media to adequately reflect indigenous cultural diversity.

Article 17
1. Indigenous individuals and peoples have the right to enjoy fully all rights established under applicable international and domestic labour law.

2. States shall in consultation and cooperation with indigenous peoples take specific measures to protect indigenous children from economic exploitation and from performing any work that is likely to be hazardous or to interfere with the child's education, or to be harmful to the child's health or physical, mental, spiritual, moral or social development, taking into account their special vulnerability and the importance of education for their empowerment.

3. Indigenous individuals have the right not to be subjected to any discriminatory conditions of labour and, inter alia, employment or salary.

Article 18
Indigenous peoples have the right to participate in decision-making in matters which would affect their rights, through representatives chosen by themselves in accordance with their own procedures, as well as to maintain and develop their own indigenous decision-making institutions.

Article 19
States shall consult and cooperate in good faith with the indigenous peoples concerned through their own representative institutions in order to obtain their free, prior and informed consent before adopting and implementing legislative or administrative measures that may affect them.

Article 20
1. Indigenous peoples have the right to maintain and develop their political, economic and social systems or institutions, to be secure in the enjoyment of their own means of subsistence and development, and to engage freely in all their traditional and other economic activities.

2. Indigenous peoples deprived of their means of subsistence and development are entitled to just and fair redress.

Article 21
1. Indigenous peoples have the right, without discrimination, to the improvement of their economic and social conditions, including, inter alia, in the areas of education, employment, vocational training and retraining, housing, sanitation, health and social security.

2. States shall take effective measures and, where appropriate, special measures to ensure continuing improvement of their economic and social conditions. Particular attention shall be paid to the rights and special needs of indigenous elders, women, youth, children and persons with disabilities.

Article 22
1. Particular attention shall be paid to the rights and special needs of indigenous elders, women, youth, children and persons with disabilities in the implementation of this Declaration.

2. States shall take measures, in conjunction with indigenous peoples, to ensure that indigenous women and children enjoy the full protection and guarantees against all forms of violence and discrimination.

Article 23
Indigenous peoples have the right to determine and develop priorities and strategies for exercising their right to development. In particular, indigenous peoples have the right to be actively involved in developing and determining health, housing and other economic and social programmes affecting them and, as far as possible, to administer such programmes through their own institutions.

Article 24

1. Indigenous peoples have the right to their traditional medicines and to maintain their health practices, including the conservation of their vital medicinal plants, animals and minerals. Indigenous individuals also have the right to access, without any discrimination, to all social and health services.

2. Indigenous individuals have an equal right to the enjoyment of the highest attainable standard of physical and mental health. States shall take the necessary steps with a view to achieving progressively the full realization of this right.

Article 25

Indigenous peoples have the right to maintain and strengthen their distinctive spiritual relationship with their traditionally owned or otherwise occupied and used lands, territories, waters and coastal seas and other resources and to uphold their responsibilities to future generations in this regard.

Article 26

1. Indigenous peoples have the right to the lands, territories and resources which they have traditionally owned, occupied or otherwise used or acquired.

2. Indigenous peoples have the right to own, use, develop and control the lands, territories and resources that they possess by reason of traditional ownership or other traditional occupation or use, as well as those which they have otherwise acquired.

3. States shall give legal recognition and protection to these lands, territories and resources. Such recognition shall be conducted with due respect to the customs, traditions and land tenure systems of the indigenous peoples concerned.

Article 27

States shall establish and implement, in conjunction with indigenous peoples concerned, a fair, independent, impartial, open and transparent process, giving due recognition to indigenous peoples' laws, traditions, customs and land tenure systems, to recognize and adjudicate the rights of indigenous peoples pertaining to their lands, territories and resources, including those which were traditionally owned or otherwise occupied or used. Indigenous peoples shall have the right to participate in this process.

Article 28

1. Indigenous peoples have the right to redress, by means that can include restitution or, when this is not possible, of a just, fair and equitable compensation, for the lands, territories and resources which they have traditionally owned or otherwise occupied or used, and which have been confiscated, taken, occupied, used or damaged without their free, prior and informed consent.

2. Unless otherwise freely agreed upon by the peoples concerned, compensation shall take the form of lands, territories and resources equal in quality, size and legal status or of monetary compensation or other appropriate redress.

Article 29

1. Indigenous peoples have the right to the conservation and protection of the environment and the productive capacity of their lands or territories and resources. States shall establish and implement assistance programmes for indigenous peoples for such conservation and protection, without discrimination.

2. States shall take effective measures to ensure that no storage or disposal of hazardous materials shall take place in the lands or territories of indigenous peoples without their free, prior and informed consent.

3. States shall also take effective measures to ensure, as needed, that programmes for monitoring, maintaining and restoring the health of indigenous peoples, as developed and implemented by the peoples affected by such materials, are duly implemented.

Article 30

1. Military activities shall not take place in the lands or territories of indigenous peoples, unless justified by a significant threat to relevant public interest or otherwise freely agreed with or requested by the indigenous peoples concerned.

2. States shall undertake effective consultations with the indigenous peoples concerned, through appropriate procedures and in particular through their representative institutions, prior to using their lands or territories for military activities.

Article 31

1. Indigenous peoples have the right to maintain, control, protect and develop their cultural heritage, traditional knowledge and traditional cultural expressions, as well as the manifestations of their sciences, technologies and cultures, including human and genetic resources, seeds, medicines, knowledge of the properties of fauna and flora, oral traditions, literatures, designs, sports and traditional games and visual and performing arts. They also have the right to maintain, control, protect and develop their intellectual property over such cultural heritage, traditional knowledge, and traditional cultural expressions.

2. In conjunction with indigenous peoples, States shall take effective measures to recognize and protect the exercise of these rights.

Article 32

1. Indigenous peoples have the right to determine and develop priorities and strategies for the development or use of their lands or territories and other resources.

2. States shall consult and cooperate in good faith with the indigenous peoples concerned through their own representative institutions in order to obtain their free and informed consent prior to the approval of any project affecting their lands or territories and other resources, particularly in connection with the development, utilization or exploitation of their mineral, water or other resources.

3. States shall provide effective mechanisms for just and fair redress for any such activities, and appropriate measures shall be taken to mitigate adverse environmental, economic, social, cultural or spiritual impact.

Article 33

1. Indigenous peoples have the right to determine their own identity or membership in accordance with their customs and traditions. This does not impair the right of indigenous individuals to obtain citizenship of the States in which they live.

2. Indigenous peoples have the right to determine the structures and to select the membership of their institutions in accordance with their own procedures.

Article 34

Indigenous peoples have the right to promote, develop and maintain their institutional structures and their distinctive customs, spirituality, traditions, procedures, practices and, in the cases where they exist, juridical systems or customs, in accordance with international human rights standards.

Article 35

Indigenous peoples have the right to determine the responsibilities of individuals to their communities.

Article 36

1. Indigenous peoples, in particular those divided by international borders, have the right to maintain and develop contacts, relations and cooperation, including activities for spiritual, cultural, political, economic and social purposes, with their own members as well as other peoples across borders.

2. States, in consultation and cooperation with indigenous peoples, shall take effective measures to facilitate the exercise and ensure the implementation of this right.

Article 37

1. Indigenous peoples have the right to the recognition, observance and enforcement of Treaties, Agreements and Other Constructive Arrangements concluded with States or their successors and to have States honour and respect such Treaties, Agreements and other Constructive Arrangements.

2. Nothing in this Declaration may be interpreted as to diminish or eliminate the rights of Indigenous Peoples contained in Treaties, Agreements and Constructive Arrangements.

Article 38

States in consultation and cooperation with indigenous peoples, shall take the appropriate measures, including legislative measures, to achieve the ends of this Declaration.

Article 39

Indigenous peoples have the right to have access to financial and technical assistance from States and through international cooperation, for the enjoyment of the rights contained in this Declaration.

Article 40

Indigenous peoples have the right to have access to and prompt decision through just and fair procedures for the resolution of conflicts and disputes with States or other parties, as well as to effective remedies for all infringements of their individual and collective rights. Such a decision shall give due consideration to the customs, traditions, rules and legal systems of the indigenous peoples concerned and international human rights.

Article 41

The organs and specialized agencies of the United Nations system and other intergovernmental organizations shall contribute to the full realization of the provisions of this Declaration through the mobilization, inter alia, of financial cooperation and technical assistance. Ways and means of ensuring participation of indigenous peoples on issues affecting them shall be established.

Article 42

The United Nations, its bodies, including the Permanent Forum on Indigenous Issues, and specialized agencies, including at the country level, and States, shall promote respect for and full application of the provisions of this Declaration and follow up the effectiveness of this Declaration.

Article 43

The rights recognized herein constitute the minimum standards for the survival, dignity and well-being of the indigenous peoples of the world.

Article 44

All the rights and freedoms recognized herein are equally guaranteed to male and female indigenous individuals.

Article 45

Nothing in this Declaration may be construed as diminishing or extinguishing the rights indigenous peoples have now or may acquire in the future.

Article 46

1. Nothing in this Declaration may be interpreted as implying for any State, people, group or person any right to engage in any activity or to perform any act contrary to the Charter of the United Nations.

2. In the exercise of the rights enunciated in the present Declaration, human rights and fundamental freedoms of all shall be respected. The exercise of the rights set forth in this Declaration shall be subject only to such limitations as are determined by law, in accordance with international human rights obligations. Any such limitations shall be non-discriminatory and strictly necessary solely for the purpose of securing due recognition and respect for the rights and freedoms of others and for meeting the just and most compelling requirements of a democratic society.

3. The provisions set forth in this Declaration shall be interpreted in accordance with the principles of justice, democracy, respect for human rights, equality, non-discrimination, good governance and good faith.

Sources: http://www.unhchr.ch/html/menu2/10/c/ind/ind_sub.htm#chrw; United Nations Declaration on the Rights of Indigenous Peoples, http://www.un.org/esa/socdev/unpfii/documents/DRIPS_en.pdf

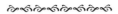

2. REPORT OF THE SPECIAL RAPPORTEUR, JAMES ANAYA, ON THE RIGHTS OF INDIGENOUS PEOPLES

This is the impressively thorough Special Rapporteur on the Rights of Indigenous Peoples James Anaya's final report to the UN after his official US visit in 2012. It covers history, contemporary federal legislation and policy, specific on-going disadvantaged conditions, and a renewal of U.S. interest in UNDRIP as a direction all three branches of government might embrace.

{Excerpt}

United Nations, General Assembly, Human Rights Council, Twenty-first session, Agenda item 3

Promotion and protection of all human rights, civil, political, economic, social and cultural rights, including the right to development, A/HRC/21/47/Add.1, Distr.: General 30 August 2012, Original: English

Addendum

The situation of indigenous peoples in the United States of America

Summary

In this report the Special Rapporteur examines the human rights situation of indigenous peoples in the United States, on the basis of research and information gathered, including during a visit to the country from 23 April to 4 May 2012. During his mission, the Special Rapporteur held consultations with United States officials as well as with indigenous peoples, tribes, and nations in Washington, D.C., Arizona, Alaska, Oregon, Washington state; South Dakota and Oklahoma, both in Indian country and in urban areas. Appendices I and II to this report include, respectively, summaries of information provided by the Government and of information submitted by indigenous peoples, organizations and individuals in connection with the mission.

The Special Rapporteur concludes that indigenous peoples in the United States — including American Indian, Alaska Native and Native Hawaiian peoples — constitute vibrant communities that have contributed greatly to the life of the country; yet they face significant challenges that are related to widespread historical wrongs, including broken treaties and acts of oppression, and misguided government policies, that today manifest themselves in various indicators of disadvantage and impediments to the exercise of their individual and collective rights.

Significant federal legislation and programmes that have been developed over the last few decades, in contrast to early exercises of federal power based on misguided policies, constitute good practices that in significant measure respond to indigenous peoples' concerns. Especially to be commended are the many new initiatives taken by the executive to advance the rights of indigenous peoples in the last few years.

The Special Rapporteur finds, however, that existing federal programmes need to be improved upon and their execution made more effective. Moreover, new measures are needed to advance toward reconciliation with indigenous peoples and address persistent deep-seated problems related to historical wrongs, failed policies of the past and continuing systemic barriers to the full realization of indigenous peoples' rights.

The United Nations Declaration on the Rights of Indigenous Peoples is an important impetus and guide for improving upon existing measures to address the concerns of indigenous peoples in the United States, and for developing new measures to advance toward reconciliation. The Declaration, which is grounded in widespread consensus and fundamental human rights values, should be a benchmark for all relevant decision-making by the federal executive, Congress, and the judiciary, as well as by the states of the United States. The Special Rapporteur makes a series of recommendations in this regard.

The Special Rapporteur would like to thank the United States Government, especially the Department of State, for the cooperation it provided for the mission. He would also like to express his deep gratitude to representatives of indigenous peoples, nongovernmental organizations and academic institutions — named in appendix II- whose assistance in planning and carrying out of this visit was indispensible. The Special Rapporteur is grateful to the indigenous peoples that welcomed him into their communities and for the hospitality he received. Finally, the Special Rapporteur is grateful to the Office of the High Commissioner for Human Rights and the Support Project for the Special Rapporteur on Indigenous Peoples at the University of Arizona for their assistance in carrying out the mission and preparing this report.

Annex

Report of the Special Rapporteur on the rights of indigenous peoples, James Anaya, on the situation of indigenous peoples in the United States of America

I. The indigenous peoples of the United States

1. The indigenous peoples of the United States include a vast array of distinct groups that fall under the generally accepted designation of Native Americans, which include American Indians and Alaska Natives; also included are the people indigenous to Hawaii, or Native Hawaiians. These indigenous peoples form tribes or nations — terms used interchangeably in this report — and other communities with distinctive cultural and political attributes.

A. The diverse indigenous nations, tribes and communities

2. Broadly speaking, Native Americans living in the contiguous United States constitute tribes or nations with diverse cultural and ethnic characteristics that can be grouped geographically. Linguistic families and other cultural markers, however, cross rough geographic categories, and within these categories differences abound. For historical and other reasons, Alaska Natives and Native Hawaiians are considered distinct from Native Americans in the contiguous United States.

3. The United States presently recognizes and maintains what it refers to as government-to-government relations with approximately 566 American Indian and Alaska Native tribes and villages, around 230 of these being Alaskan Native groups. For the most part each of these tribes and villages determines its own membership. While having some form of federal recognition, Native Hawaiians do not have a similar status under United States law as that of American Indians and Alaska Native groups. Many other groups in the United States that identify as indigenous peoples have not been federally recognized, although some of these have achieved recognition at the state level.

4. It is estimated that prior to colonization, the indigenous population within the territory that now constitutes the United States numbered several million, and represented diverse cultures and societies speaking hundreds of languages and dialects. After the arrival of Europeans, the indigenous population suffered significant decline due to the effects of disease, war, enslavement and forced relocations.

5. Today, according to United States census data people who identify as Native American represent approximately 1.7 per cent of the overall population of the United States, with 5.2 million persons identifying as American Indian that this number significantly exceeds the number of those who are enrolled or registered members of federally recognized indigenous groups. In addition, there are roughly a half a million persons that identify entirely or partly as Native Hawaiians.

6. Characteristically, the federally recognized tribes have reservations or other lands that have been left to or set aside for them, and over which they exercise powers of self- government. While the land holdings vary significantly among the tribes, in all cases they pale in comparison to the land areas once under their possession or control. Still, the diminished landholdings provide some physical space and material bases for the tribes to maintain their cultures and political institutions, and to develop economically.

7. While many indigenous persons live on reservations or other Native-controlled land areas, many others live in urban areas beyond the boundaries of indigenous lands. It is quite common, however, for indigenous persons living in urban ar-

eas to maintain close ties to the land-based communities of the tribes with which they are affiliated, and to develop bonds of community with other indigenous persons in their urban settings.

8. Several indigenous peoples live in border areas and face unique challenges, especially tribes living along the United States-Mexico border, where heightened border security measures implemented by the federal Government in recent years have increasingly made cross-border contact between members of the same tribes very difficult.

B. The contributions of indigenous peoples to the broader society, despite negative stereotypes

9. Within the United States stereotypes persist that tend to render Native Americans relics of the past, perpetuated by the use of Indian names by professional and other high- profile sports teams, caricatures in the popular media and even mainstream education on history and social studies. Throughout his mission, the Special Rapporteur heard complaints from indigenous representatives about such stereotypes, and about how they obscure understanding of the reality of Native Americans today and instead help to keep alive racially discriminatory attitudes.

10. Beyond the stereotypes, one readily sees vibrant indigenous communities, both in reservation and other areas, including urban areas, which have contributed to the building of the country and continue to contribute to the broader society. Of course their greatest contribution is in the vast expanses of land that they gave up, through treaty cessions and otherwise, without which the United States and its economic base would not exist. Native Americans have also added to the defence and security of the United States and are represented among the ranks of the United States military services at a rate higher than that of any other ethnic group.

11. Today, indigenous peoples in the United States face multiple disadvantages, which are related to the long history of wrongs and misguided policies that have been inflicted upon them. Nonetheless, American Indians, Alaska Natives and Native Hawaiians have survived as peoples, striving to develop with their distinct identities intact, and to maintain and transmit to future generations their material and cultural heritage. While doing so, they add a cultural depth and grounding that, even while often going unnoticed by the majority society, is an important part of the country's collective heritage. Further, the knowledge that they retain about the country's landscapes and the natural resources on them, along with their ethic of stewardship of the land, are invaluable assets to the country, even if not fully appreciated.

II. United States law and policy regarding indigenous peoples

12. Laws and policies related to indigenous peoples have developed over centuries since the colonial era, and today they comprise a complex array of decisions by the United States Congress, the executive branch of the federal Government and the federal courts, in particular the United States Supreme Court.

A. The basic framework

13. The Constitution of the United States (1787) makes little reference to indigenous peoples, the principal mention being in its article I, section 8, which provides Congress the power to "regulate commerce with ...with the Indian Tribes." This provision signals that, within the federal structure of government of the United States, competency over matters relating to indigenous peoples rests at the federal, as opposed to state, level.

14. Looking beyond the constitutional text to historical practice, the colonial era law of nations and reason, the United States Supreme Court established, in a series of early 19th century cases, foundational principles about the rights and status of Indian tribes that largely endure today. Supreme Court doctrine recognizes that Indian tribes are inherently sovereign with powers of self-government; indeed they are "nations" with original rights over their ancestral lands. Within this same body of doctrine, however, the sovereignty and original land rights of tribes are deemed necessarily diminished and subordinated to the power of United States, as a result of discovery or conquest by the European colonial powers or the successor United States.

15. The federal power to regulate commerce with the Indian tribes is thereby enlarged to one that is deemed plenary in nature and that can be used to unilaterally modify or extinguish tribal sovereignty or land rights. This power is also related to and justified by a duty of protection the federal Government is deemed to have over Indian tribes, in a so- called trusteeship. In all, tribes are sovereign nations with certain inherent powers of self- government and original rights, but

they are rendered, in words penned by the famous Supreme Court Justice John Marshall, "domestic dependent nations," subject to the overriding power of the federal Government.

16. While acknowledging positive characteristics of the rights-affirming strain of this judicial doctrine, the Special Rapporteur notes that the rights-limiting strain of this doctrine is out of step with contemporary human rights values. As demonstrated by a significant body of scholarly work, the use of notions of discovery and conquest to find Indians rights diminished and subordinated to plenary congressional power is linked to colonial era attitudes toward indigenous peoples that can only be described as racist. Early Supreme Court decisions themselves reveal perceptions of Indians as backward, conquered peoples, with descriptions of them as savages and an inferior race.

17. At times, however, the Supreme Court and lower courts have been protective of indigenous peoples' rights by affirming original Indian rights to the extent consistent with operative doctrine, or more often by enforcing treaty terms, legislation, or executive decisions that are themselves protective of indigenous rights.

B. The evolution of federal policy and legislation

18. Federal legislative and executive action, in the exercise of the broad authority over indigenous affairs affirmed by the Supreme Court, has evolved over time along with shifting policy objectives shaped by historical circumstances and prevailing attitudes of the time.

19. After achieving its independence, the United States continued the practice that had been established by Great Britain and other colonial powers of treaty-making with Indian tribes. These treaties were means both by which the United States or its colonial precursors acquired land from Indian tribes, as well as means by which the tribes retained rights over lands and resources not ceded. The treaties, moreover, dealt with diverse issues and provided a foundation for the United States' relations with tribes on the basis of their recognition as nations with inherent sovereignty.

20. Although the United States ceased dealing with Indian tribes through treaties in 1871, after having consolidated its control over the territory it had acquired across the continent, many of the historical treaties with tribes continue in force as part of federal law and to define United States-tribal relations. At the same time, numerous flagrant violations of historical treaties constitute some of the principal wrongdoings committed by the United States towards indigenous peoples, which was a recurring subject of concern raised to the Special Rapporteur during his visit.

21. Subsequent to the end of the treaty-making era, United States law and policy was characterized by a series of steps aimed at acculturating indigenous peoples in the ways of the dominant society and diluting or eliminating their sovereignty and collective rights over lands and resources. In the late nineteenth century, a vast government bureaucracy emerged under a United States Commissioner of Indian Affairs to consolidate and manage the system of reservations, pueblos, rancherias and settlements that were home to the surviving indigenous peoples in the country.

22. Under the Dawes General Allotment Act of 1887, tribal landholdings were broken up into individual plots that could become alienable, which eventually resulted in a substantial further loss of Indian land and a complex system of interspersed Indian and non- Indian titled land that now characterizes tenure within many reservations. The Dawes Act resulted in even greater impoverishment and social upheaval among the tribes, and thus, after conferring United States citizenship on all Indians in 1924, Congress passed the Indian Reorganization Act of 1934 as a major reform measure.

23. The Indian Reorganization Act included provisions to secure the Indian land base from further erosion and provided for establishing reservation-based governments akin to local municipalities under the authority of the Secretary of Interior of the federal Government, on the basis of model constitutions that were developed by the Secretary. While providing a degree of self-government, the Act was considered a transitional measure to prepare the Indians for, in the words of its chief architect, United States Indian Commissioner John Collier, "real Indian tribes today continue under the IRA regime.

24. In the 1950s the United States Government attempted to complete its programme of assimilation with tribes and convert their lands to private ownership. The termination policy was eventually abandoned, but not before several tribes lost federal recognition and their self-governing status, and saw their landholdings dissipate, with invariably devastating social and economic consequences that are still apparent today.

The contemporary federal legislative and policy regime

25. In the face of past federal programmes of assimilation and acculturation, Native Americans continued to make clear their determination, as they still do, to hold on to and recover their own distinctive cultures and institutions of self-government as a basis for their development and place in the world. With this resolve eventually came a change in federal policy, as it moved to reflect, if not entirely accommodate, indigenous peoples' own aspirations. In 1970, the President of the United States advanced this change in a message to Congress, in which he affirmed, "The time has come to break decisively with the past and to create the conditions for a new era in which the Indian future is determined by Indian Acts and Indian

26. The contemporary thrust of federal policy is marked by several pieces of major legislation, including the Indian Self-Determination and Education Assistance Act of 1975, by which tribes are able to assume the planning and administration of federal programmes that are devised for their benefit; the Indian Child Welfare Act of 1978, which favours indigenous custody of indigenous children; the American Indian Religious Freedom Act of 1978, which directs federal officials to consult with tribes about actions that may affect religious practices; the Native American Graves Protection and Repatriation Act of 1990, which directs federal agencies and museums to return indigenous remains and sacred objects to appropriate indigenous groups; and the Native American Languages Act of 1990, which provides support for the use and recovery of indigenous languages through educational programmes. A number of other laws provide protections for indigenous religion and culture, and still others address Indian economic and natural resource development, education and civil rights.

27. In alignment with the existing federal legislation, there are dozens of executive directives and programmes that apply specifically to indigenous peoples, many of which are listed in appendix I, and that reflect a significant level of dedication on the part of the Government to indigenous concerns within the self-determination policy framework.

28. Several agencies throughout the Government are dedicated specifically to indigenous affairs, the principal one being the Department of Interior, which includes the Bureau of Indian Affairs. Under federal law, pursuant to its historical protectorate, or trusteeship, the United States holds in trust the underlying title to the Indian lands within reservations and other lands set aside by statute or treaty for the tribes. The Department is responsible for overseeing some 55 million surface acres and the subsurface mineral resources in some 57 million acres.

29. There are numerous other indigenous-specific agencies and programmes in various parts of the Government. Notably, and especially in recent years, the Government has made an important, increased effort to appoint indigenous individuals to high-level government positions dealing with indigenous affairs, including the position of Assistant Secretary for Indian Affairs, which heads the Bureau of Indian Affairs. Also significantly, in 2009, the position of Senior Policy Advisor for Native American Affairs was created to advise the President on issues related to indigenous peoples.

III. The disadvantaged conditions of indigenous peoples: The present day legacies of historical wrongs

30. United States laws and policies in the last few decades undoubtedly have contributed to halting the erosion of indigenous identities, and have weighed in favour of placing indigenous peoples on a path toward greater self-determination, as well as economic and social health. Nonetheless, the conditions of disadvantage persist with the continuing effects of a long history of wrongs and past, misguided policies.

A. Economic and social conditions

31. At the close of the Special Rapporteur's mission to the United States, he received a manila envelope stuffed with letters written by students from a class at White River High School in South Dakota, a school where a majority of the students are from the nearby reservation of the Rosebud Sioux Tribe. In a cover letter the class's teacher explained that the students "would like to feel they have a voice as it is so desolate here that it is sometimes hard to remember there is an outside world. Despite all the hardships here, these kids are so incredibly resilient and talented."

32. The teacher's words were a poignant introduction to the first letter in the stack, which was from a 15-year-old girl who lamented: Life here is very hand to mouth. Out here, we don't have the finer things. You get what you get and you don't throw a fit. And I'm going to be honest with you, sometimes I don't eat. I've never told anyone this before, not even

my mom, but I don't eat sometimes because I feel bad about making my mom buy food that I know is expensive. And you know what? Life is hard enough for my mom, so I will probably never tell her. My parents have enough to worry about. I do not know what you can do, but try your very best to help us. Please help us. We can do this. Yes we can!

33. The evident hardship combined with resilience was reflected in the other letters, giving a highly personalized gloss on the conditions of disadvantage faced by indigenous peoples in the United States. These conditions vary widely among the diverse indigenous tribes, nations and communities. United States census data and other available statistics, however, show Native Americans to fare much worse along social and economic indicators than any other ethnic group in the country.

34. For example, Native Americans, especially on reservations, have disproportionately education, 77 per cent of Native Americans aged 25 or older hold a high school diploma or alternative credential as compared with 86 per cent of the general population, while 13 per cent of Native Americans hold a basic university degree as compared to

35. The image now often popularized of Native Americans flush with cash from casinos is far from the norm. A number of tribes do have casino operations as part of economic development efforts, taking advantage of special exemptions from ordinary state regulation and taxation that are available to them under federal law. Most tribes, however, do not have casinos and, of those that do, only a handful have reaped substantial riches sufficient to significantly reduce poverty levels.

B. Violence against women

36. The continuing vulnerabilities of indigenous communities are highlighted by alarmingly high rates of violence Department of Justice estimates that indigenous women are more than twice as likely as all other women to be victims of violence and that one in three of them will be raped during her lifetime.

Estimates are that nearly 80 per cent of the rapes of indigenous women are by non- indigenous men, many of who have made their way into indigenous communities but who are not presently subject to indigenous prosecutorial authority because of their non- indigenous status. Congress has yet to pass key reforms in the Violence Against Women Act that would bolster tribes' ability to prosecute these cases. In order to get away from violent situations, many victims are forced to leave their homes and communities, which is particularly troubling in the context of indigenous peoples. As one Tinglit woman expressed, "when I left, I didn't just leave my family. I left my culture behind... I ran away from my traditions, from my songs, my dances, and my heritage."

C. Lands, resources and broken treaties

37. The conditions of disadvantage of indigenous peoples undoubtedly are not mere happenstance. Rather, they stem from the well-documented history of the taking of vast expanses of indigenous lands with abundant resources, along with active suppression of indigenous peoples' culture and political institutions, entrenched patterns of discrimination against them and outright brutality, all of which figured in the history of the settlement of the country and the building of its economy.

38. Many Indian nations conveyed land to the United States or its colonial predecessors by treaty, but almost invariably under coercion following warfare or threat thereof, and in exchange usually for little more than promises of government assistance and protection that usually proved illusory or worse. In other cases, lands were simply taken by force or fraud. In many instances treaty provisions that guaranteed reserved rights to tribes over lands or resources were broken by the United States, under pressure to acquire land for non- indigenous interests. It is a testament to the goodwill of Indian nations that they have uniformly insisted on observance of the treaties, even regarding them as sacred compacts, rather than challenge their terms as inequitable.

39. In nearly all cases the loss of land meant the substantial or complete undermining of indigenous peoples' own economic foundations and means of subsistence, as well as cultural loss, given the centrality of land to cultural and related social patterns. Especially devastating instances of such loss involve the forced removal of indigenous peoples from their ancestral territories, as happened for example, with the Choctaw, Cherokee and other indigenous people who were re-

moved from their homes in the south-eastern United States to the Oklahoma territory in a trek through what has been called a "trail of tears," in which many of them perished.

40. Another emblematic case involves the Black Hills in South Dakota, part of the ancestral territory of the Lakota people that, under the Treaty of Fort Laramie of 1868, was reserved to the Lakota and other tribes known collectively as the Sioux Nation. Following the discovery of gold in the area, in 1877 Congress passed an act reversing its promise under the treaty and vesting ownership of the Black Hills to the Government. The Lakota and other Sioux tribes have refused to accept payment required in accordance with a 1980 Supreme Court decision and continue to request the return of the Black Hills; this is despite the fact that the people of these tribes are now scattered on several reservations and are some of the poorest among any group in the country. Today, the Black Hills are national forest and park lands, although they still hold a central place in the history, culture, and worldviews of surrounding tribes and at the same time serve as a constant visible reminder of their loss.

41. In addition to millions of acres of lands lost, often in violation of treaties, a history of inadequately controlled extractive and other activities within or near remaining indigenous lands, including nuclear weapons testing and uranium mining in the western United States, has resulted in widespread environmental harm, and has caused serious and continued health problems among Native Americans. During his visit, the Special Rapporteur also heard concerns about several currently proposed projects that could potentially cause environmental harm to indigenous habitats, including the Keystone XL pipeline and the Pebble Mine project in Alaska's Bristol Bay watershed. By all accounts the Pebble Mine would seriously threaten the sockeye salmon fisheries in the area if developed according to current plans.

42. In many places, including in Alaska and the Pacific Northwest in particular, indigenous peoples continue to depend upon hunting and fishing, and the maintenance of these subsistence activities is essential for both their physical and their cultural survival, especially in isolated areas. However, indigenous peoples face ever-greater threats to their subsistence activities due to a growing surge of competing activities, restrictive state and federal regulatory regimes, and environmental harm.

D. Sacred places

43. With their loss of land, indigenous peoples have lost control over places of cultural and religious significance. Particular sites and geographic spaces that are sacred to indigenous peoples can be found throughout the vast expanse of lands that have passed into government hands. The ability of indigenous peoples to use and access their sacred places is often curtailed by mining, logging, hydroelectric and other development projects, which are carried out under permits issued by federal or state authorities. In many cases, the very presence of these activities represents a desecration.

44. A case that has been reviewed in detail by the Special Rapporteur involves the San Francisco Peaks in Northern Arizona, an area sacred to the Navajo, Hopi and other indigenous peoples, where under a federal permit the brought to the attention of the Special Rapporteur can be found in appendix II. The desecration and lack of access to sacred places inflicts permanent harm on indigenous peoples for whom these places are essential parts of identity.

E. The removal of children from indigenous environments

45. Historically, added to the taking of indigenous lands was the direct assault on indigenous cultural expression that was carried out or facilitated by the federal and state governments. Likely the programme of this type with the most devastating consequences, which are still felt today, was the systematic removal of indigenous children from their families to place them in government or church-run boarding schools, with the objective of expunging them of their indigenous identities. Captain Richard Pratt, founder of the Carlisle Indian school, coined the phrase, "kill the Indian in him, save the man," in instituting the boarding school policy in the 1880s which continued well into the mid 1900s.

46. Emotional, physical, and sexual abuse within the boarding schools has been well- documented. Typically, upon entering a boarding school, indigenous children had their hair cut, were forced to wear uniforms and were punished for speaking their languages or practising their traditions. The compounded effect of generations of indigenous people, including generations still living, having passed through these schools cuts deep in indigenous communities throughout the United States, where social problems such as alcoholism and sexual abuse are now pervasive and loss of language is widespread.

47. Additionally, a pattern of placing indigenous children in non-indigenous care under state custody proceedings, with similar effects on indigenous individuals and communities, continued until well into the 1970s, only to be blunted by passage of the Indian Child Welfare Act in 1978, federal legislation that advances a strong presumption of indigenous custody for indigenous children but that continues to face barriers to its implementation.

F. Open wounds of historical events

48. The open wounds left by historical events are plentiful, alive in intergenerational memory if not experience. The Special Rapporteur heard emotional testimony from a direct descendant of victims of one of the most well-known atrocities committed against Native Americans, the massacre at Sand Creek in 1864. Scores of Cheyenne and Arapaho were attacked by surprise and massacred by some 700 armed United States troops. Previously, the tribes had signed a treaty with the United States, under which they willingly gave up their arms and flew a flag of truce at the Sand Creek camp. No action was ever taken against those responsible for the massacre and, despite the promises made in a later treaty of reparations for the descendants of the victims at Sand Creek, none has yet been made.

49. A more recent incident that continues to spark feelings of injustice among indigenous peoples around the United States is the well-known case of Leonard Peltier, an activist and leader in the American Indian Movement, who was convicted in 1977 following the deaths of two Federal Bureau of Investigation agents during a clash on the Pine Ridge Reservation in South Dakota. After a trial that has been criticized by many as involving numerous due process problems, Mr. Peltier was sentenced to two life sentences for murder, and has been denied parole on various occasions. Pleas for presidential consideration of clemency by notable individuals and institutions have not borne fruit. This further depletes the already diminished faith in the criminal justice system felt by many indigenous peoples throughout the country.

G. Self-government

50. Many indigenous representatives in all the locations visited by the Special Rapporteur stressed the importance to the health and well-being of their peoples of securing and recovering the various expressions and practices of their cultures, including indigenous languages, and of being able to transmit their cultures and identities to future generations, along with securing ties to land and natural resources and enhancing self-government capacity.

51. As noted in paragraphs 25-29 and in appendix I, several government programmes are in place to address the concerns of indigenous peoples and to provide them substantial assistance. Indigenous leaders stressed to the Special Rapporteur, however, that the solution lies fundamentally in further strengthening indigenous peoples' ability to develop and implement their own programmes for economic development and job creation, education, preservation and development of cultural expressions and knowledge, and public order, including the protection of indigenous women and children.

52. Yet, the government policy of indigenous self-determination in place for several decades has not abated problematic restrictions that have been imposed on indigenous peoples' self-government. As a general matter, the sovereignty of federally-recognized Indian tribes, as far as it goes, displaces the authority of the states over so-called Indian country, that is, reservation and other lands under Indian control. But United States courts have continued to see the inherent sovereignty of tribes, and hence their self-governance authority, as an implicitly diminished sovereignty, and this view has served to limit the powers of tribal regulatory and judicial authorities especially in relation to non-indigenous persons. Additionally, tribal sovereignty may succumb to substantial state sovereignty

53. Judicially-established limitations on tribal sovereignty are in addition to those imposed by Congress, especially under acts devised under the earlier eras of assimilation. These include the Major Crimes Act of 1885, which established paramount federal jurisdiction over certain crimes committed in Indian country, whether by an indigenous or non-indigenous person; and Public Law 280 of 1953, which extended state criminal and civil jurisdiction to Indian country in specified states.

54. Especially in light of inadequate state and federal law enforcement on reservations, these jurisdictional limits imposed on indigenous tribes result in situations in which, as one tribal judge lamented, "we can't police and punish people who come into the community and cause harm to that community and its people." The Special Rapporteur also heard numerous frustrations based on concerns that jurisdictional limitations send the constant message to tribes that their in-

stitutions are incompetent and inferior, no matter how capable they have demonstrated themselves to be. Further impeding self-governance capacity are financial constraints.

55. It is important to note, however, that despite these impediments, many tribal governments and justice systems are gaining strength, and the Special Rapporteur was impressed by the determination of tribes to continue build their governance institutions. During the Special Rapporteur's consultation in Oklahoma, the Principal Chief of the Cherokee Nation put it this way: "As the Principal Chief of the largest Indian Tribe in the United States, my vision for our people is one of becoming great."

H. Recognition

56. In order for its powers of sovereignty, or self-government, to be recognized and officially functional within the United States legal system, or to be eligible for assistance designated for Indian tribes, an indigenous group must have specific recognition by the federal Government. A number of indigenous peoples, for reasons related to the same cluster of historical events that have broadly affected indigenous peoples in the country, lack such federal recognition and hence are especially disadvantaged. Several of these are tribes that were stripped of their federal status as a result of the termination policies of the 1950s.

57. Unrecognized indigenous groups have been striving to achieve federal recognition for decades, principally through an administrative process provided for this purpose by the Department of the Interior. Concerns regarding the cost and the length of the federal recognition process, and the challenges faced by lack of recognition, were repeatedly brought to the attention of the Special Rapporteur. Indigenous groups have invested millions of dollars and filed thousands of documents in support of their claims. Figures about the pace of the recognition process yield differing perspectives. Nonetheless, as described by one Senator "it is not a system that is working under any stretch of the imagination."

I. Alaska

58. Indigenous peoples in Alaska have federal recognition within a unique legal regime that developed under a specific set of circumstances. In 1971 Congress enacted the Alaska Native Claims Settlement Act (ANCSA), which extinguished "all claims of aboriginal title," as well as "any aboriginal hunting and fishing rights that may exist," throughout Alaska. The act set up a system of native-run corporations with assets provided under the settlement, and Alaska Natives born as of the date of the act were given shares in the corporations.

59. With its design of replacing rights in land and resources with individual shares in corporations, ANCSA can be seen as being driven by the policy of assimilation that had long been in place and that presumably was coming to an end around the time of the act's adoption (see paras. 21-24 above). Yet ANCSA continues to define realities for indigenous peoples in Alaska, leaving in its aftermath precarious conditions for indigenous peoples in their ability to maintain the subsistence and cultural patterns that have long sustained them amid abundant fish and wildlife resources, or to craft their own vehicles of self- determination.

60. Subsequent federal legislation has done little to restore Alaska Native hunting and fishing rights, but instead has left indigenous hunting and fishing subject to the same regulatory regime that applies to non-indigenous activities. And this regulatory regime is a highly complex, difficult one to navigate, in which both the federal Government and the state play a part, with the state in effect having a dominant role. The matter of subsistence hunting and fishing remains crucial both for cultural purposes and for food security. However, subsistence activities are subject to a state regulatory regime that allows for, and appears to often favour, competing land and resource uses such as mining and other activities, including hunting and fishing for sport, that may threaten natural environments and food sources.

61. Representatives of Alaska Native tribal governments, villages, corporations and organizations with whom the Special Rapporteur met coincided in the view that ANCSA was faulty in its inception. There were divergent views, however, about the extent to which the corporations can and are being responsive to the needs and aspirations of Alaska Natives, within the limitations of the corporate model. The Special Rapporteur did find indications that in many respects the native-run corporations are functioning to provide important economic and other benefits to Alaska Natives.

62. At the same time, the Special Rapporteur was struck by indications about how the economic and cultural transformations accelerated by ANCSA have bred or exacerbated social ills among indigenous communities, manifesting themselves, for example, in high rates of suicide, alcoholism, and violence.

63. Several Alaska Native representatives expressed to the Special Rapporteur the view that the problem runs deeper than ANCSA, to the incorporation of Alaska into the United States as a federal state through procedures that allegedly were not in compliance with the right of the indigenous people of Alaska to self-determination.

J. Hawaii

64. Also uniquely vulnerable are the indigenous people of Hawaii, having experienced a particular history of colonial onslaught and resulting economic, social and cultural upheaval. They benefit from some federal programmes available to Native Americans, but they have no recognized powers of self-government under federal law. And they have little by way of effective landholdings, their lands largely having passed to non-indigenous ownership and control with the aggressive patterns of colonization initiated with the arrival of the British explorer James Cook in 1778. Indigenous Hawaiians have diffuse interests in lands "ceded' to the United States and then passed to the state of Hawaii, under a trust that is specified in the 1959 Statehood Admission Act and now managed by the Office of Hawaiian Affairs.

65. Remarkably, the United States Congress in 1993 issued an apology "to Native Hawaiians on behalf of the people of the United States for the overthrow of the Kingdom of Hawaii on January 17, 1893 with the participation of agents and citizens of the United the "inherent sovereignty of the Native Hawaiian people" and called for "reconciliation" efforts.

66. The call for reconciliation, however, remains unfilled, while a growing movement of indigenous Hawaiians challenges the legitimacy and legality of the annexation of Hawaii following the overthrow, as well as the process by which Hawaii moved from its designation as a non-self-governing territory under United Nations supervision, to being incorporated into the United States as one of its federal states in 1959. In the meantime, indigenous Hawaiians see their sacred places under the domination of others, and they continue to fare worse than any other demographic group in Hawaii in terms of education, health, crime, and employment.

IV. More needs to be done

A. Welcomed, but still not sufficient, government initiatives

67. The Special Rapporteur acknowledges the high level of attention to indigenous peoples' concerns that is represented by numerous acts of Congress and federal executive programmes (see paras. 25-29 above and appendix I). Such attention represents some acknowledgment of the historical debt acquired toward the country's first peoples, and partially fulfils historical treaty commitments.

68. It is evident that the federal executive has taken steps in recent years to strengthen these programmes, in addition to its new initiatives to develop consultation policies and open spaces of dialogue with tribes; to strengthen support for the recovery of indigenous languages; to settle outstanding claims for mismanagement indigenous assets held in trust by the Government; to increase funding for federal programmes; to address the problem of violence against indigenous women; to clean up environmental pollution caused by natural resource extraction; to assist tribes with acquiring land to restore their land bases; and to enhance tribal capacity and cooperative arrangements in the area of law and order, among others.

69. The Special Rapporteur notes however, concerns that were raised with him about the adequacy of effective implementation of the highly developed body of law and government programmes concerning indigenous peoples. While welcoming improved consultation procedures, for example, a number of indigenous leaders complained that they have yet to see significant change in the decision-making of government agents about matters of crucial concern to their peoples, in particular decisions about lands that are outside of indigenous-controlled areas but that nonetheless affect their access to natural or cultural resources or environmental well-being.

70. The Special Rapporteur also repeatedly heard concerns about a lack of sufficient funding for housing, health, education, environmental remediation, women's health and safety, language and other programmes, concerns that were

raised by both federal officials and representatives of indigenous peoples. Also pointed out were complicated or confusing bureaucratic procedures, and an inadequate understanding and awareness among government officials about tribal realities or even about the content of relevant laws and policies themselves.

71. The Special Rapporteur observes, nonetheless, that the overall thrust of the policy underlying the federal legislation and programmes adopted in the last few decades — a policy of advancing indigenous self-determination and development with respect for cultural identity — is generally in line with the aspirations expressed by indigenous peoples. The problems signalled are that the laws and programmes do not go far enough to meet those aspirations and that they are underfunded or inadequately administered. The Special Rapporteur takes special note, moreover, that they fail to go so far as to ultimately resolve persistent, deep-seated problems.

B. The need for determined action within a programme of reconciliation

72. It is evident that numerous matters relating to the history of misdealing and harm inflicted on indigenous peoples are still unresolved. In all his consultations with indigenous peoples during his visit to the United States, it was impressed upon the Special Rapporteur that historical wrongs continue to live in intergenerational memory and trauma, and that, together with current systemic problems, they still inflict harm. Across the United States, he heard of specific unresolved problems of historical origins and systemic dimensions, and indigenous representatives made abundantly clear that these problems continue to breed disharmony, dislocation and hardship.

73. The Special Rapporteur is of the firm view that, unless genuine movement is made toward resolving these pending matters, the place of indigenous peoples within the United States will continue to be an unstable, disadvantaged and inequitable one, and the country's moral standing will suffer. Determined action should take place within a cross-cultural, encompassing programme of reconciliation, aimed at closing the latent wounds and building just and equitable conditions, and at providing needed redress consistent with the United States' human rights obligations.

74. The Special Rapporteur notes that the Government took a step that could be one on a path toward reconciliation, when in 2010 Congress adopted a resolution of apology to the indigenous peoples of the country, following in the spirit of the apology previously issued to Native Hawaiians (para. 65 above). Acknowledging widespread wrongdoing, the Apology states: "The United States, acting through Congress … apologizes on behalf of the people of the United States for the many instances of violence, maltreatment and neglect inflicted on Native Peoples by citizens of the United States [and] expresses its regret." The apology also "urges the President to acknowledge the wrongs of the United States against Indian tribes in the history of the United States in order to bring healing to this appropriations act, and apparently few indigenous people, much less the public in general, were made aware of it.

75. Such an apology should not go unnoticed. Rather, it should be a point of public awakening and mark a path toward reconciliation, a path for concrete steps to address issues whose resolution is essential to defeating disharmony, and a path toward more enlightened framing of relations between indigenous peoples and the United States.

76. Among the pending issues that should be addressed with firm determination, within a programme of reconciliation, are the severed or frayed connections with culturally significant landscapes and sacred sites, such as those resulting from the taking of the Black Hills or from environmental pollution in countless places; imposed limitations on indigenous self-governance capacity, such as that preventing indigenous authorities from acting with full force to combat violence against women; the pathologies left by the removal of indigenous children from their communities; and other persistent symbols of subordination, such as the refusal of the United States thus far to make good on its long- standing promise to provide reparations for the Sand Creek massacre. Also to be addressed are the pervasive problems left in the aftermath of Alaska Statehood and the Alaska Native Claims Settlement Act, and the still not remedied, yet acknowledged, suppression of indigenous Hawaiian sovereignty.

77. The Special Rapporteur notes the previous significant effort made by the United States to comprehensively resolve the grievances of Indian tribes by its creation in 1946 of the Indian Claims Commission and by extending the Commission's authority widely to include claims based on "fair and honourable dealings," inter alia. Over its life the Commission determined hundreds of land claims based on treaties or ancestral occupation, but the only remedies provided under the relevant statute were for monetary compensation upon a finding of extinguishment or taking of rights, a product of the assimilationist frame of thinking of the period in which the Commission was created, which left many fundamental is-

sues unresolved or further complicated. Still the establishment of the Commission represents the capacity of the United States to take sweeping action to address evident wrongs on the basis of prevailing policy preferences.

78. What is now needed is a resolve to take action to address the pending, deep-seated concerns of indigenous peoples, but within current notions of justice and the human rights of indigenous peoples. Exemplifying the kind of restorative action to be taken consistent with contemporary human rights values is the return of the sacred Blue Lake to Taos Pueblo and the restoration of land to the Timbisha Shoshone Tribe. Both land areas were restored from land under federal administration, with no consequence for any individual property interests. Another exemplary action is the more recent initiative to transfer management of national park lands to the Oglala Sioux Tribe in South Dakota. Such measures reveal a needed understanding of the centrality of land and geographic spaces to the physical and cultural well-being of indigenous peoples, in accordance with standards now prevailing internationally and accepted by the United States.

V. The significance of the Declaration on the Rights of Indigenous Peoples

79. The United Nations Declaration on the Rights of Indigenous Peoples stands as an important impetus and guide for measures to address the concerns of indigenous peoples in the United States and to move toward reconciliation. An authoritative instrument with broad support, the Declaration marks a path toward remedying the injustices and inequitable conditions faced by indigenous peoples, calling on determined action to secure their rights, within a model of respect for their self-determination and distinctive cultural identities.

80. The Declaration represents a global consensus among Governments and indigenous peoples worldwide that is joined in by the United States as well as by indigenous peoples in the country. It was adopted by the General Assembly with the affirmative votes of an overwhelming majority of United Nations Member States amid expressions of celebration by indigenous peoples from around the world. At the urging of indigenous leaders from throughout the country, the United States declared its support for the Declaration on 16 December 2010, reversing its earlier position.

81. By its very nature, the Declaration on the Rights of Indigenous Peoples is not legally binding, but it is nonetheless an extension of the commitment assumed by United Nations Member States — including the United States — to promote and respect human rights under the United Nations Charter, customary international law, and multilateral human rights treaties to which the United States is a Party, including the International Covenant on Civil and Political Rights, and the International Convention on the Elimination of All Forms of Racial Discrimination.

82. Whatever its precise legal significance, the Declaration embodies a convergence of common understanding about the rights of indigenous peoples, upon a foundation of fundamental human rights, including rights of equality, self-determination, property and cultural integrity. It is a product of more than two decades of deliberations in which the experiences and aspirations of indigenous peoples worldwide, along with failures and successes of the relevant laws and policies of States, were closely examined, with a view toward promoting human rights.

83. With these characteristics, the Declaration is now part of United States domestic and foreign policy, as made clear in the United States' announcement that its endorsement of the instrument:
- reflects the U.S. commitment to work with [indigenous] tribes, individuals, and communities to address the many challenges they face. The United States aspires to improve relations with indigenous peoples by looking to the principles embodied in the Declaration in its dealings with federally recognized tribe, while also working, as appropriate, with all indigenous individuals and communities in the United States.
- Moreover, the United States is committed to serving as a model in the international community in promoting and protecting the collective rights of indigenous peoples as well as the human rights of all individuals.

84. As part of United States domestic and foreign policy, an extension of international human right commitments, and reflecting a commitment to indigenous peoples in the United States, the Declaration should now serve as a beacon for executive, legislative and judicial decision-makers in relation to issues concerning the indigenous peoples of the country. All such decision-making should incorporate awareness and close consideration of the Declaration's terms. Moreover, the Declaration is an instrument that should motivate and guide steps toward still-needed reconciliation with the country's indigenous peoples, on just terms.

VI. Conclusions and recommendations

85. Indigenous peoples in the United States — including American Indian, Alaska Native and Native Hawaiian peoples — constitute vibrant communities that have contributed greatly to the life of the country. Yet they face significant challenges that are related to widespread historical wrongs and misguided government policies that today manifest themselves in various indicators of disadvantage and impediments to the exercise of their individual and collective rights.

Existing federal legislation and executive programmes

86. Many acts of Congress and federal programmes that have been developed over the last few decades — in contrast to earlier exercises of federal power based on misguided policies — constitute good practices that in significant measure respond to indigenous peoples' concerns. Especially to be commended are the many new initiatives taken by the executive to advance the rights of indigenous peoples in the last few years.

The need to build on good practices and advance toward reconciliation

87. Relevant authorities should take steps to address the concerns of indigenous leaders that, in certain respects, federal legislation protective of their rights is not adequately implemented and that federal programmes are not adequately funded or administered.

88. Further, the federal executive and Congress should respond to initiatives promoted by indigenous peoples for new or amended legislation and programmes, in accordance with the international human rights commitments of the United States.

89. Despite positive aspects of existing legislation and programmes, new measures are needed to advance reconciliation with indigenous peoples and to provide redress for persistent deep-seated problems. Federal authorities should identify, develop and implement such measures in full consultation and coordination with indigenous peoples.

90. Measures of reconciliation and redress should include, inter alia, initiatives to address outstanding claims of treaty violations or non-consensual takings of traditional lands to which indigenous peoples retain cultural or economic attachment, and to restore or secure indigenous peoples' capacities to maintain connections with places and sites of cultural or religious significance, in accordance with the United States international human rights commitments. In this regard, the return of Blue Lake to Taos Pueblo, the restoration of land to the Timbisha Shoshone, the establishment of the Oglala Sioux Tribal Park, and current initiatives of the National Park Service and the United States Forest Service to protect sacred sites, constitute important precedents or moves in this direction.

91. Other measures of reconciliation should include efforts to identify and heal particular sources of open wounds. And hence, for example, promised reparations should be provided to the descendants of the Sands Creek massacre, and new or renewed consideration should be given to clemency for Leonard Peltier.

92. Issues of self-governance, environmental degradation, language restoration, and federal recognition, as well as the particular concerns of indigenous peoples in urban settings and border areas, among other matters, should also be addressed.

The United Nations Declaration on the Rights of Indigenous Peoples

93. The United Nations Declaration on the Rights of Indigenous Peoples is an important impetus and guide for improving upon existing measures to address the concerns of indigenous peoples in the United States, and for developing new measures to advance toward reconciliation. The Declaration represents an international standard accepted by the United States, at the urging of indigenous peoples from across the country, and is an extension of the United States historical leadership and commitment to promote human rights under various sources of international law. With these characteristics, the Declaration is a benchmark for all relevant decision- making by the federal executive, Congress, and the judiciary, as well as by the states of the United States.

The federal executive

94. The federal executive should work closely with indigenous leaders, at all levels of decision-making, to identify and remove any barriers to effective implementation of existing government programmes and directives, and to improve upon them. In this regard, efforts should be made to ensure coordinated and clear delineation of tasks among the various government agencies working on indigenous issues, effective means of interaction and consultation with indigenous peoples, and coherent, coordinated federal executive action on indigenous issues.

95. In keeping with the expressed commitment of the United States to the principles of the Declaration on the Rights of Indigenous Peoples and its related international human rights obligations, the President should consider issuing a directive to all executive agencies to adhere to the Declaration in all their decision- making concerning indigenous peoples.

96. Independently of such a presidential directive, given that the Declaration has already been adopted as part of United States policy, all executive agencies that touch upon indigenous affairs should become fully aware of the meaning of the Declaration with respect to their respective spheres of responsibility, and they should ensure that their decisions and consultation procedures are consistent with the Declaration. To this end there should be a crosscutting executive level campaign to ensure awareness about the content and meaning of the Declaration.

97. In following up to the apology resolution adopted by Congress in 2010, which directs the President to pursue reconciliation with the country's indigenous peoples, the President should develop, in consultation with them, a set of relevant initiatives in accordance with paragraphs 87-92 above. As an initial measure, the President should make the apology resolution widely known among indigenous peoples and the public at large, in a way that is appropriate to the sensitivities and aspirations of indigenous peoples, and within a broader programme that contributes to public education about indigenous peoples and the issues they face.

Congress

98. Congress should act promptly on legislative proposals advocated by indigenous leaders for the protection of their peoples' rights, and ensure that any legislation concerning indigenous peoples is adopted in consultation with them. Particular, immediate priority should be placed on legislation advocated by indigenous peoples and proposed by the executive to extend protection for indigenous women against violence by, inter alia, enlarging the law enforcement capacities of tribal authorities.

99. Following up to the hearing on the Declaration held by the Senate Committee on Indian Affairs on 9 June 2011, Congress should hold hearings to educate its members about the Declaration on the Rights of Indigenous Peoples and to consider specific legislative measures that are needed to fully implement the rights affirmed therein. Attention should be paid to aspects of already existing legislation that should be reformed, and to new legislation that could advance needed measures of reconciliation. Consideration should also be given to providing judicial remedies for infringements of rights incorporated in the Declaration.

100. Congress should, in consultation with indigenous peoples, enact legislative reforms or altogether new legislation as required to achieve the reconciliation called for in its apology resolution of 2010.

101. Any legislation adopted by Congress should be in alignment with the human rights standards represented by the Declaration. To this end Congress should consider adopting a resolution affirming the Declaration as the policy of United States and declaring its resolve to exercise its power to advance the principles and goals of the Declaration.

102. At a minimum, Congress should continuously refrain from exercising any purported power to unilaterally extinguish indigenous peoples' rights, with the understanding that to do so would be morally wrong and against United States domestic and foreign policy, and that it would incur responsibility for the United States under its international human rights obligations.

The federal judiciary

103. The federal judiciary, in particular the United States Supreme Court, has played a significant role in defining the rights and status of indigenous peoples. While affirming indigenous peoples' rights and inherent sovereignty, it has also

articulated grounds for limiting those rights on the basis of colonial era doctrine that is out of step with contemporary human rights values.

104. Consistent with well-established methods of judicial reasoning, the federal courts should discard such colonial era doctrine in favour of an alternative jurisprudence infused with the contemporary human rights values that have been embraced by the United States, including those values reflected in the United Nations Declaration on the Rights of Indigenous Peoples. Furthermore, just as the Supreme Court looked to the law of nations of the colonial era to define bedrock principles concerning the rights and status of indigenous peoples, it should now look to contemporary international law, to which the Declaration is connected, for the same purposes.

105. Accordingly, the federal courts should interpret, or reinterpret, relevant doctrine, treaties and statutes in light of the Declaration, both in regard to the nature of indigenous peoples' rights and the nature of federal power.

The states of the United States

106. Although competency over indigenous affairs rests at the federal level, states of the United States exercise authority that in various ways affects the rights of indigenous peoples. Relevant state authorities should become aware of the rights of indigenous peoples affirmed in the Declaration on the Rights of Indigenous Peoples, and develop state policies to promote the goals of the Declaration and to ensure that the decisions of state authorities are consistent with it.

Indigenous peoples' authorities

107. Indigenous authorities should endeavour to educate the members of their tribes, nations or communities about the Declaration and its contents. They should apply the Declaration in their own self-governance, as well as use it as a common point of understanding in dealings with federal and state legislative, executive and judicial authorities.

Alaska and Hawaii

108. The situations in Alaska and Hawaii are each unique and merit particular attention and action on the part of the United States to secure the rights of indigenous peoples there. The Special Rapporteur intends to address these situations further in future communications with the United States.

Appendix I

Summary of information on federal programmes, policies, legislation and other initiatives related to indigenous peoples submitted to the Special Rapporteur by Government representatives, agencies and departments

Executive Orders

1. Executive Order No. 13007 — Indian Sacred Sites of 1996: Calls on federal agencies responsible for management of federal lands, to accommodate, to the extent practicable, access to and ceremonial use of Indian sacred sites by Indian religious practitioners and avoid adversely affecting the physical integrity of such sites, and where appropriate, maintain the confidentiality of sacred sites.

2. Executive Order 13175 Consultation and Coordination with Indian Tribal Governments of 2000: Aims to establish regular and meaningful consultation and collaboration with tribal officials in the development of certain federal policies related to tribes, to strengthen the United States government-to-government relationships with Indian tribes, and to reduce the imposition of unfunded mandates upon Indian tribes.

3. Presidential Memorandum of November 5, 2009: Directs each agency to submit to the Director of the Office of Management and Budget (OMB), within 90 days, a detailed plan of actions the agency will take to implement the policies and directives of Executive Order 13175.

4. The plan should be developed after consultation by the agency with Indian tribes and tribal officials as described in Executive Order 13175. Further, each agency head must submit to the Director of the OMB, within 270 days after No-

vember 5, 2009, and annually thereafter, a progress report on the status of each action included in its plan together with any proposed updates to its plan.

5. Executive Order 13592 Improving American Indian and Alaska Native Educational Opportunities and Strengthening Tribal Colleges and Universities of 2011: Establishes the White House Initiative on American Indian and Alaska Native Education chaired by the Secretaries of Interior and Education. Its purpose is to help expand educational opportunities and improve educational outcomes for American Indian and Alaska Native students including instruction in indigenous languages, cultures and histories and preparation for college and career building.

Legislation

6. Omnibus Appropriations Act H.R. 2764-526, Sec. 699B of 2008: Establishes an Advisor for Activities Relating to Indigenous Peoples Internationally who is required to advise the Director of United States Foreign Assistance and the Administrator of USAID on matters relating to indigenous peoples, and who should represent the United States Government on such matters in meetings with foreign governments and multilateral institutions.

7. Tribal Law and Order Act of 2010: Improves the capacity of tribal governments to deal with domestic violence and sex crimes, alcohol and substance abuse, strengthens services to victims, and provides enhanced tribal sentencing authority. The Act also expands recruitment and retention of Bureau of Indian Affairs and tribal officers and provides new guidelines and training for officers handling domestic violence and sex crimes. Establishes the Office of Tribal Justice within the Justice Department.

8. Claims Resolution Act of 2010: Authorizes and funds the Cobell v. Salazar settlement agreement (regarding alleged mismanagement of Indian trust accounts). Additionally, it included four water settlements for seven tribes in Arizona, Montana and New Mexico and provisions for over $1 billion for new water infrastructure projects to meet drinking water supply needs and rehabilitation of existing, aging infrastructure. To date, there are 26 congressionally enacted Indian water rights settlements.

9. Patient Protection and Affordable Care Act (PPACA) of (2010): Authorizes new and expanded programmes and services to American Indian and Alaska Natives through the Indian Health Service to make health care accessible and affordable. Created permanent authorization for the Indian Health Care Improvement Act (IHCIA), which is the legal authority for the provision of health care to American Indians and Alaska Natives.

10. American Recovery and Reinvestment Act of 2009: Provides more than $3 billion to help tribal communities renovate schools on reservations, promote job creation, improve housing and support health and policing services.

11. Indian Arts and Crafts Amendments Act of 2010: Amends the Indian Arts and Crafts Act, which makes illegal to sell, offer, or display for sale any art or craft product falsely suggesting it was Indian made. The Act empowers federal law enforcement officers to enforce this prohibition and it differentiates among penalties bases on the price of goods involved in the offense.

Legislative proposals

12. Proposed American Jobs Act: Intended to provide employment opportunities and tax cuts to small businesses and employees. Within Indian Country, the Act will serve to provide tax cuts to Native American-owned businesses, the extension of payroll tax cuts to Native American workers, the extension of unemployment insurance, subsidized employment opportunities for Native American youth and adults, community rebuilding and revitalization, and expansion of high-speed internet.

13. S. 1925 — Proposed Violence Against Women Reauthorization Act: Title IX addresses violence perpetrated against American Indian and Alaska Native women by restoring concurrent tribal criminal jurisdiction over all persons who commit misdemeanor domestic and dating violence in Indian Country and clarifies tribal court authorities to issue and enforce civil protection orders.

14. H.R. 4970 — Proposed Violence Against Women Reauthorization Act: Among other measures, would authorize Native American victims of domestic violence or Indian Tribes on behalf of Indian victims to seek protection orders from United States district courts against suspects of abuse.

Other Executive/White House Initiatives

15. Presidential Proclamation of National Native American Heritage Month November of 2011: Proclamation to celebrate the rich and diverse ancestry of American Indians and Alaska Natives and their contributions to the United States.

16. Presidential Website: Winning the Future — President Obama and the Native American Community: Serves to assist Native Americans and Alaska Natives navigate federal government programmes and policies. The site contains a resource center designed to bring together over 25 different agencies and departments into one, navigable location. See http://www.whitehouse.gov/nativeamericans

17. White House Tribal Nations Conferences 2009-2011: Over the past three years, the President has hosted three White House Tribal Conferences that brought together Cabinet Secretaries and senior Administration officials with leaders invited from all the federally recognized tribes in order to strengthen the relationship between the United States Government and tribal governments. Issues discussed by representatives from federal agencies and tribal leaders include job creation and tribal economies; promotion of safe and strong tribal communities; protection of natural resources and respect of cultural rights; and social issues including health care, education, housing, and infrastructure.

18. Office of National Drug Control Policy (ONDCP)/High Intensity Drug Trafficking Area Program: Provides funding for enforcement and drug prevention efforts nationwide including Native American projects in Oregon, Arizona, New York and Oklahoma. The ONDCP engaged in a consultation process for the National Northern Border Counternarcotics Strategy in five northern states which included federal, state and tribal officials.

19. America's Great Outdoors and the Call to Action: Presidential initiative that includes the support of tribal historic preservation efforts and tribal cultural traditions. Grants support tribes in fulfilling responsibilities under the National Historic Preservation Act including conducting surveys of historic places, maintaining historic site inventories, nominating properties to the National Register of Historic Places, and reviewing Federal agency undertakings under Section 106 of the National Historic Preservation Act.

20. White House Rural Council: Works across federal agencies to address challenges faced by tribal communities in the area of sustainable economic development and to promote economic prosperity in Indian Country.

21. Let's Move! in Indian Country is a comprehensive initiative dedicated to solving the problem of obesity within a generation, so that children born today will grow up healthier and able to pursue their dreams.

Department of Agriculture

22. USDA Office of Tribal Relations (OTR): Established in 2009 to serve as point of contact between the Department and all federally recognized tribal governments, tribal communities, individual tribal members, as well as state-recognized tribal governments. OTR is responsible for working with all departmental agencies to build a collaborative and integrated approach to issues, programmes and services addressing the needs of American Indians and Alaskan Natives, including Tribal consultation.

23. USDA Action Plan for Tribal Consultation and Collaboration: Outlines actions the Department intends to take to develop consultation processes across all departmental agencies at a regional level regarding their different programmes and services, which would include a reporting, accountability and performance assessment structure for these consultation processes.

24. Sacred Sites Policy Review: Review by the USDA's Office of Tribal Relations (OTR) and the Forest Service of the effectiveness of existing policies and procedures for the protection of Native American sacred sites on National Forest System Lands, which involved national and regional level listening sessions with tribal governments and traditional cul-

tural practitioners to gather recommendations. A final report with recommendations for needed action at the level of USDA will be developed in consultation with tribal governments and cultural practitioners.

25. USDA Rural Development: Provided for investment in business in Indian Country through multiple programmes that included $7.6 million for their Business & Industry Loan Guarantee programme and $4.2 million in grants to support economic development. The

USDA also provided over $50 million through Natural Resources Conservation Service programmes to improve and benefit trust lands across the country.

26. Internet Access: Both the Department of Agriculture and the Department of Commerce have dedicated programmes to bring high-speed, affordable broadband into tribal communities and have awarded loans and grants worth over $1.5 billion for projects to benefit tribal areas.

27. Keepseagle v. Vilsack settlement of 2010: The Government reached a $760 million settlement with Native American farmers and ranchers who sued the Department of Agriculture for discrimination in loan programmes. In addition to monetary damages and debt relief awarded to Native American farmers, the settlement contained programmatic reforms including the establishment of a Council on Native American Farming and Ranching that responds directly to the Secretary of Agriculture, technical assistance to help access farm loan programmes, a moratorium on further collection of delinquent loans during the pendency of the settlement process and an additional round of loan servicing after completion of the claims process.

Department of Interior

28. Department of the Interior Action Plan and Tribal Consultation Policy: Developed by a joint federal-tribal team. Provides for a Department-wide tribal governance officer, early tribal involvement in the design of actions implicating tribal interests.

29. Department of the Interior Indian Loan Guaranty Insurance and Interest Subsidy Program: Established by the Indian Finance Act of 1974 to stimulate American Indian and Alaska Native economic enterprises and employment. In fiscal year 2011, the programme made over 46 loan guarantees, totalling more than $78 million.

30. Department of the Interior Indian Water Rights Office leads, coordinates, and manages the Department's Indian water rights settlement program.

31. National Commission on Indian Trust Administration and Reform: The Secretary of the Interior appointed five prominent American Indians to service on the Commission. The Commission will undertake an evaluation of Interior's trust management of Native American trust funds.

32. Department of the Interior Pilot program to reduce crime on Indian reservations: Engages reservation communities experiencing high crime rates to reduce violent crime, juvenile delinquency, and criminal behaviour.

33. Proposed Lease Reforms: Aims to simplify the leasing process on tribal lands and enhance tribally driven renewable solar and wind energy projects.

34. Management of Indian trust lands: Over 11 million acres belong to individual Indians and nearly 44 million acres are held in trust for Indian tribes. On these lands, the Department manages over 109,000 leases.

Office of the Special Trustee for American Indians

35. The Office of the Special Trustee for American Indians manages approximately $3.7 billion in trust funds from leases, use permits, land sales and income from financial assets. The Office has a Trust Beneficiary Call Center to implement the Cobell v. Salazar decision, which provides the Department with the ability to resolve trust claims. The call centre uses a toll-free phone number to provide comprehensive account information to beneficiaries. The Office also has a Trust Asset and Accounting Management System, an integrated database containing land title documents, including supporting revenue distribution, invoicing, acquisitions and all legal details relating to land transactions.

Bureau of Indian Affairs

36. Water Rights Negotiation/Litigation Program: A programme of the Bureau of Indian Affairs (BIA) to provide funds to the United States and tribes for activities associated with securing or defending federally reserved Indian water rights through negotiations and/or litigation. It primarily provides funds for necessary documentation, expert witnesses and technical reports to further water rights claims.

37. Water Management, Planning, and Pre-Development Program: A BIA programme for assisting tribes in managing, conserving and utilizing trust water resources, primarily by providing funds for necessary technical research, studies and other information for Indian tribes.

38. High Priority Performance Goal crime reduction initiative of 2009: Programme implemented by the Bureau of Indian Affairs in collaboration with tribal law enforcement officials intended to reduce violent crime in four targeted reservations by five percent over a 24-month period. The initiative was expanded to two additional reservations.

Bureau of Indian Education

39. The Bureau of Indian Education funds 183 elementary and secondary schools on 64 reservations throughout the United States, serving approximately 42,000 Indian students. Of these, 58 are tribally-operated under contracts or grants. The Bureau also funds or operates off-reservation boarding schools and provides higher education scholarships to Indian students.

United States Geological Survey

40. Technical Training in Support of Native American Relations (TESNAR): A programme that provides grants for the development and implementation of technical training, by USGS scientists, for the employees of Tribes and tribal organizations in order to strengthen the technical capacity of Tribes in managing tribal natural and cultural resources.

Bureau of Reclamation

41. Native American Affairs Program: A programme of the Bureau of Reclamation (BOR) that provides support for Indian water rights negotiations and the realization of various irrigation, water development, drought relief and other services and programmes implemented by the BOR.

42. Water Rights Settlement Projects: Provides support for Indian water rights settlements, including serving as the construction entity for water supply projects approved as part of enacted settlements.

43. Bureau of Reclamation/ Rural Water Projects: Works with Indian tribes to assess their water supply needs, including for domestic uses, and to address these needs by designing and constructing water supply projects. Construction of water projects to provide safe and reliable domestic water supplies to Indian tribes, and other local entities, are ongoing in several states.

U.S. Fish & Wildlife Service

44. Tribal Wildlife Grants Program: Provided approximately 360 grants to nearly 200 tribal governments to conserve, protect and enhance fish, wildlife, plants and habitats.

National Park Service

45. Agreements on gathering of traditional plants and minerals: The National Park Service is preparing to issue a rule to authorize agreements between Park Service and federally-recognized tribes to permit limited gathering of plants and minerals for traditional purposes.

46. Proposed Tribal National Park: The National Park Service is working with the Oglala Sioux Tribe to develop legislation to establish the first tribal national park in the South Unit of the Badlands National Park, which is located entirely in the Pine Ridge Indian Reservation.

47. National Park Service Management Policies: Management policies and other official guidelines such as Director's Order # 53 — Special Park Uses, direct officials to respect the government-to-government relationship, to provide access to and use of Indian sacred sites, and to ensure that consultation to ascertain and address the concerns of Indian tribes and tribal traditional religious practitioners is carried out when actions that may have an effect on Indian tribes and their cultural traditions are proposed.

48. National Park Service Shared Beringian Heritage Program: United States and Russian joint cooperation for the protection of the area's natural, cultural resources and the rights of indigenous peoples in both countries. The National Park Service is to consult with Alaska indigenous peoples regarding initiatives under the program.

Bureau of Land Management

49. BLM Tribal Consultation Policy: Developed in response to Executive Order 13175 with the purpose to identify the cultural values, the religious beliefs, the traditional practices, and the legal rights of Native American people which could be affected by BLM actions on Federal lands.

50. BLM — 8100 Manual and Handbook: Instructs BLM managers on identification and management of cultural resources on public lands. Provides for tribal consultation to identify and manage sacred sites, including providing access to such sites.

51. BLM/Co-management Agreements: Provides for co-management agreements to manage areas of significant value to Tribes. These have included co-management agreement with the Pueblo de Cochiti in New Mexico to manage the Kasha-Katuwe Tent Rocks National Monument; and a co-management agreement with Taos Pueblo, New Mexico to jointly manage the "Wild Rivers Section" of the Rio Grande.

52. BLM Cultural Resources Management program: Provides for repatriation to Native American peoples of human remains and cultural items held in BLM's collections and enhancing management of culturally significant sites on public lands.

Department of Justice

53. Violence Against Women Federal/Tribal Prosecution Task Force: Composed of federal and tribal prosecutors that facilitate and coordinate action between the Justice Department and tribal governments regarding the prosecution of violent crimes against women in Indian Country including the development of recommendations and resource materials on prosecutions of these offenses.

54. Coordinated Tribal Assistance Solicitation: Provides a single streamlined application process for tribal government-specific grant programmes administered by the Office of Justice Programs, Community Oriented Policing Services, and the Office on Violence Against Women.

55. Consideration of Policy Regarding Eagle Feathers: Departments of Justice and the Interior have worked to facilitate tribal members' access to eagle feathers for religious and cultural purposes and to address concerns over the effects of federal laws protecting eagles on tribal and cultural practices.

Department of Homeland Security

56. Tribal Relations Program: Seeks to include tribal governments in many facets of homeland security and emergency management, through joint law enforcement operations with Customs and Border Protection and improved response to disasters affecting tribal members and tribal lands.

Department of Labor

57. Indian and Native American Program/ Employment and Training Administration: Provides funding for tribes and Native American non-profit organizations to provide employment and training services to unemployed and low-income Native Americans, Alaska Natives, and Native Hawaiians.

Department of Commerce

58. The Minority Business Development Agency of the Department of Commerce: Funded six Native American Business Enterprise Centers in Arizona, California, New Mexico, North Dakota, Washington and Oklahoma.

Department of the Treasury

59. Community Development Financial Institutions Fund (CDFI) — Native Initiatives Program: Designed to increase capital, credit, and financial services for Native populations across the nation and build the capacity of Native community development financial institutions to provide financial products and services to Native Communities.

Department of Housing and Urban Development

60. Section 184 Loan Guarantee Program: Based on the Housing and Community Development Act of 1992, the programme provides home ownership opportunities to American Indians and Alaska Native living on trust or restricted lands.

61. Native Hawaiian Housing Block Grant Program Section 184A Loan Guarantee Program for Native Hawaiians: Provides access to private financing on Hawaiian home lands and promotes homeownership, property rehabilitation and new home constructions for eligible Native Hawaiian individuals.

62. Native American Housing Needs Assessment: Study undertaken by Housing and Urban Development that included regional and national outreach meetings with tribal housing stakeholders to seek input on methodology for survey of housing needs.

63. Indian Housing Block Grant (IHBG) Program: Provides annual funding to Native American tribes or tribally designated housing authority to make housing assistance available to low-income Indian families. IHBG was established through the Native American Housing Assistance and Self-Determination Act of 1996.

64. Indian Community Development Block Grant (ICDBG) Program: Provides grants to improve housing and economic opportunities in Native American and Alaskan Native communities.

65. Rural Housing and Economic Development (RHED) Program: Provides for rural housing and economic development activities at the state and local levels including reservation and tribal communities in rural areas.

66. Tribal Colleges and Universities Program (TCUP): Assists Tribal Colleges and Universities to build, expand, renovate and equip their facilities and support their role as service providers for health programmes, job training and economic development.

67. Resident Opportunity and Self-Sufficiency (ROSS) Program: Provides funding for job training and support services to assist public housing residents to transition from welfare to work.

68. Department of Housing and Urban Development Tribal Government-to-Government Consultation Policy of 2001: Enhances communication and coordination between the Department and federally recognized Indian tribes or Alaska Native tribes.

Department of Veterans Affairs

69. Home Loans to Native American Veterans: The Department of Veterans Affairs Loan Guaranty Service works with federally-recognized tribes to provide loans to Native American Veterans for the purchase, construction, or improvement of homes located on federally-recognized trust land.

Department of Energy

70. Office of Indian Energy/ Indian Country Energy and Infrastructure Working Group: An informal group of tribal leaders who provide advice and input to the Office of Indian Energy and Department of Energy on energy development issues in Indian Country.

71. Office of Indian Energy: Engaged in the development of programmes for tribal energy education, strategic and targeted technical assistance for tribes on renewable energy project deployment, transmission and electrification, innovative project development, and best practices forums.

72. Strategic Technical Assistance Response Team (START): An initiative of the Office of Indian Energy Policy and Programs (DOE-IE) that advances modern clean energy project development in Indian Country.

73. Department of Energy Technical Assistance and Grants: Technical assistance and grants to help Native American communities develop renewable energy resources and energy efficiency.

74. Tribal Energy Program: Provides funds to tribes to undertake assessments of energy efficiency of tribal buildings and provide training for assessing clean energy options.

75. American Indian Research and Education Initiative: Department of Energy facilitated partnership between the American Indian Higher Education Consortium and the American Indian Science and Engineering Society to bring science, technology, engineering, and mathematics research and education funding to Native American students in tribal colleges and universities.

Department of Health and Human Services

76. Tribal Advisory Committee: Established by the Secretary to improve services, outreach, and consultation efforts with tribes.

77. Indian Health Service and Health Resources and Services Administration/ National Health Service Corp program: Seeks to improve the recruitment and retention of health care providers in the Indian health care system.

78. Special Diabetes Program for Indians: Provides funding to Indian Health Service, tribal, and urban Indian health programmes for community-driven strategies to address diabetes treatment.

79. National Action Alliance for Suicide Prevention: Developed new task forces to address and improve suicide prevention programmes in American Indians and Alaska Native communities.

80. Indian Health Service Sexual Assault Policy and Protocol: Establishes a standard of care for sexual assault victims who seek clinical services within an Indian Health Service operated hospital; seeks to ensure that care is culturally sensitive, patient-centered, and needs are addressed with a coordinated response from the community. The policies also assist in evidence collection for possible use in the criminal justice system.

81. Administration for Native Americans/U.S. Department of Health & Human Services: Promotes self-sufficiency for Native Americans by providing discretionary grant funding for community-based projects, and training and technical assistance to eligible tribes and Native organizations. Conducted a Language Symposium in September 2011 to build and share best practices, discuss challenges and barriers and identify necessary resources to support language and culture in Native communities.

Department of Education

82. National Advisory Council on Indian Education: Advises the Secretary of Education on the funding and administration of Department programmes relevant to American Indians and Alaska Natives and reports to Congress on any recommendations that the Council considers appropriate for the improvement of federal education programmes that include or may benefit Native Americans.

Environmental Protection Agency

83. Office of Air and Radiation: Supported initiatives for tribal involvement in the designation and application of Clean Air Act standards within Indian Country.

84. Indian Environmental General Assistance Program: Provides technical and financial assistance to tribes to develop and administer federal environmental programmes.

85. EPA Targeted Grants: Provided $12 million in grants to 83 tribes to establish Tribal Environmental Response Programs to address contamination on tribal lands.

86. Border 2012 Program: Provides for the improvement and expansion of clean water and wastewater management capacity to tribal communities in border areas.

87. Tribal Solid Waste Interagency Workgroup: Environmental Protection Agency, in collaboration with the Bureau of Indian Affairs, Indian Health Service, Department of Defense and United States Department of Agriculture, provides financial assistance to tribes to manage new solid waste initiatives.

88. EPA-Tribal Science Council: Partnership with tribal representatives to integrate Environmental Protection Agency and tribal interests, including the integration of traditional ecological knowledge in environmental science, policy and decision-making.

89. EPA-Policy on Consultation and Coordination: Provides for consultation with federally recognized tribal governments when Environmental Protection Agency actions and decisions may affect tribal interests. The EPA has developed a guide to consulting with Indian Tribal Governments for Federal Government personnel.

90. Toxics Release Inventory (TRI) Reporting for Facilities Located in Indian Country and Clarification of Additional Opportunities Available to Tribal Governments under the TRI Program: Requires each facility located in Indian country to submit TRI reports to the Agency and the appropriate Tribe, rather than to the State in which the facility is located. The rule also provides Tribes with the opportunity to request that facilities located in their lands be added to the TRI and that a particular chemical be added or deleted from the TRI chemical list.

91. Health and Environment Impacts of Uranium Contamination in the Navajo Nation (June 2008): Five-year plan developed by the Bureau of Indian Affairs, Department of Energy, Nuclear Regulatory Commission, Environmental Protection Agency and Indian Health Service at the request of the House Committee on Oversight and Government Reform to address the public health and environmental impacts from historical uranium mining on the Navajo Reservation.

92. National Environmental Justice Advisory Council: Currently developing a national tribal and indigenous peoples' environmental justice policy to improve the Agency's effectiveness when addressing the environmental justice concerns of federally-recognized tribes, tribal members, state-recognized tribes, indigenous organizations, and other indigenous stakeholders.

93. National Tribal Operations Committee (NTOC): Works to ensure more affective representation of tribal interests within the NTOC and stronger connections between the NTOC and regional and subject matter tribal partnership groups including air, water and science councils.

94. American Indian Environmental Office (AIEO): Supports implementation of federal environmental laws consistent with the federal trust responsibility, the government-to- government relationship, and Agency's 1984 Indian Policy. It participates in the Arctic Council Indigenous Peoples Contaminant Action Program (IPCAP), which intends to build awareness and capacity among Arctic indigenous communities to better understand their contaminant exposures and to more effectively engage in governmental efforts to address exposure issues.

95. Border 2020 Program: American Indian Environmental Office collaborates with the Office of International and Tribal Affairs (OITA) in conducting effective coordination and formal government-to-government consultation with United States border tribes and in outreach to Mexican border indigenous communities.

96. North American Tribal/First Nations/Indigenous Climate Change Adaptation Project: American Indian Environmental Office is a lead partner with other federal agencies, the Canadian government, and a Canadian indigenous not-for-profit organization in an effort to design a workshop scheduled for September 2012 to focus on climate change adaptation needs of North American indigenous communities in the area of food security and traditional plant use.

Department of Transportation

97. Indian Reservations Roads Program: Provides funds for planning, designing, construction, and maintenance activities on Indian Reservation Roads. The programme is jointly administered by the Bureau of Indian Affairs (BIA) and the Federal Highway Administration's Federals Lands Highway Office.

98. Public Transportation on Indian Reservations Program/Tribal Transit Program: Provides a total of $45 million in direct funding to federally recognized tribes to support tribal public transportation in rural areas.

The Special Rapporteur met with representatives of the following federal departments, offices, bureaus, agencies, and other institutions during his visit to the United States from 23 April to 4 May 2012

Federal Level

Department of State
- United States Agency for International Development
- Bureau of International Organizations, Office of Human Rights and Humanitarian Affairs
- Bureau of Democracy, Human Rights, and Labor
- Office of the Legal Adviser
- Office of the Special Representative for Global Intergovernmental Affairs
- Office of Global Women's Issues
- Office to Monitor and Combat Trafficking in Persons
- Bureau of Western Hemisphere Affairs

Department of the Interior
- Bureau of Indian Affairs
- The Bureau of Indian Education
- Bureau of Land Management
- National Park Service
- Bureau of Reclamation
- Office of the Special Trustee for American Indians
- The United States Geological Survey
- International Affairs Coordinator for the Office of the Assistant Secretary — Indian Affairs

Department of Justice
- Office of Tribal Justice

The White House
- Senior Policy Advisor for Native American Affairs
- Advisor on Violence Against Women
- Office of Intergovernmental Affairs and Public Engagement and Others

Department of Health and Human Services
- Director, Indian Health Service
- Chief Medical Officer, Indian Health Service Office of the General Counsel
- Office of Multilateral Affairs

Environmental Protection Agency

- American Indian Environmental Office, including its Tribal/Indigenous Peoples Environmental Justice Work Group
- Assessment and Remediation Division, Office of Superfund Remediation and Technology Innovation
- Office of Solid Waste and Emergency Response
- Cross-Cutting Issues Law Office of General Counsel

Department of Housing and Urban Development
- Office of Native American Programs
- Office of Public and Indian Housing
- Office of Fair Housing and Equal Opportunity
- Secretary for Public Affairs
- Office of International and Philanthropic Innovation • Office of Policy Development and Research

United States Department of Agriculture
- Office of Tribal Relations
- Natural Resources and Environment • Forest Service
Department of Education

State Level
- Office of the Governor of South Dakota
- Office of the Governor of Alaska

Appendix II

Summary of information and allegations presented by indigenous peoples, groups, and organizations to the Special Rapporteur on the rights of indigenous peoples

1. During his mission, the Special Rapporteur held consultations with United States officials as well as with indigenous peoples, tribes, and nations in Washington, D.C.; Arizona; Alaska; Oregon; Washington state; South Dakota; and Oklahoma, both in Indian country and in urban areas. The Special Rapporteur is very grateful for the assistance he received from the National Congress of American Indians; the Navajo Nation; the Indian Law Resource Center; the International Indian Treaty Council; the University of Arizona Indigenous Peoples Law and Policy Program; the Alaska Native Heritage Center; Port Graham Village; Chickaloon Village; the Curyung Tribal Council; the National Indian Child Welfare Association; the Cowlitz Indian Tribe; the University of Tulsa; and Sinte Gleska University for their assistance in planning key consultations in the various locations visited. He would also like to thank the numerous individuals who provided essential assistance in this regard, in particular, Dalee Sambo Dorough (Alaska), Armstrong Wiggins (Washington, D.C.), William Means (South Dakota), Andrea Carmen (Alaska), Melissa Clyde (Oregon), Gabe Galanda (Oregon), Bill Rice (Oklahoma), and Seanna Howard and Robert Williams, Jr. (Arizona).

2. The Special Rapporteur received the following information either in person during his consultations or via electronic or other means. The submissions are divided roughly by the region of their origin for organizational purposes.

Northeast and Washington, D.C.

3. Seneca Nation of Indians: United States has frequently breached treaty promises to the Seneca Nation; Government infringement on Seneca rights, including the construction of the Kinzua Dam and the violation of treaty-protected lands rights, waters rights, and resources rights, and the right to economic development.

4. Algonquin Confederacy of the Quinnipiac Tribal Council, Inc.: Discriminatory practices and removal of Quinnipiac artifacts and landmarks from traditional territories.

5. Haudenosaunee Ska-Roh-Reh: Contaminated drinking water; barriers to practising traditional religion; treaty breach by the United States Government.

6. Association of American Indian Affairs: Stronger protection needed for sacred sites; reform is needed for the federal recognition process; promotion of international repatriation with recommended modalities; call to create a Special U.S./Tribal Nations Joint Commission on Implementation of the United Nations Declaration on the Rights of Indigenous Peoples.

7. Ramapough Lunaape Nation: Industrial pollution threatens the health and well-being of community; state recognition by resolution has been achieved but federal recognition is still lacking.

8. Maine Indian Tribal — State Commission (MITSC): Maine Indian Claims Settlement Act and Maine Implementing Act create structural inequalities that limit the self- determination of Maine tribes; structural inequalities contribute to Maine tribal members experiencing extreme poverty, high unemployment, short life expectancy, poor health, limited educational opportunities and diminished economic development.

9. Members of the Beaver Clan, Onondaga Nation: Report on sexual violence and criminal acts against indigenous children.

10. Indian Law Resource Center: Highlights areas of Government policy that present significant concerns for indigenous peoples located in the United States and elsewhere including the effect of United States' foreign policy on indigenous peoples in other countries; recommendations are made for policy change that would bring the United States into compliance with the United Nations Declaration on the Rights of Indigenous Peoples.

Southeast region

11. Lummi Nation: Need for protection of sacred sites and repatriation of ancestral remains.

12. Council of the Original Miccosukee Simanolee Nation Aboriginal People: Affirm rights to land, culture and way within the context of historical violations by the Government.

13. Choctaw Nation of Florida: Historical taking of lands and treaty breach issues.

14. Yamasi People: Need for sustainable development and peaceful and productive communication between indigenous peoples and the Government regarding environmental issues.

Midwest and Great Lakes region

15. Keweenaw Bay Indian Community (KBIC): Mining activities, including prospective mining development, is negatively affecting indigenous lands and waters within the Anishinaabeg territory and established reservation homelands, which includes the destruction of the sacred place, Migi zii wa sin (Eagle Rock).

16. Anishinaabe representative: Increased mining in the Great Lakes region is a growing threat to native communities on both sides of the United States/Canada border.

17. Native American Alliance of Ohio (NAAO): Report that "documentary genocide," the practice of eliminating recognition of native peoples, is taking place in Ohio.

South Dakota and broader Great Plains region (including submissions at Sinte Gleska University consultation)

18. Sioux Nation Treaty Council: Contamination from extractive industries including gold mining, uranium mining and strip mining for coal in treaty territory; breach of the 1868 Fort Laramie Treaty; high rates of cancer among indigenous people of the Northern Great Plains; misrepresentation of Sioux peoples by non-indigenous person; proposed war games in Buffalo Gap National Grasslands.

19. Cheyenne River Sioux Tribe: Uncertainty remains regarding compensation stemming from the Tribal Equitable Compensation Act (TECA) and P.L. 106-511, an act to provide for equitable compensation for the Cheyenne River Sioux Tribe, and for other purposes.

20. Lakota People's Law Project: Native children are taken from their families in violation of the Indian Child Welfare Act and this is reflected by the disproportionately high rate of Native American children in foster care.

21. Chief Iron Eagle, Nakota Sioux Fire (Yankton Sioux Reservation): Lack of adequate legal recourse to address treaty breach and sovereignty issues faced by indigenous peoples in the United States.

22. Black Hills Sioux Nation Treaty Council and Owe Aku International Justice Project: Treaty violation of the 1868 Fort Laramie Treaty; laws and policies in the United States do not extend equal rights to Native peoples and nations; inadequate implementation of the United Nations Declaration on the Rights of Indigenous Peoples by the United States Government.

23. Oceti Sakowin Omniciye and Treaty of 1805 Task Force: United States Government in violation of the 1805 Treaty, the first treaty between the Dakota, Lakota, & Nakota and the Government.

24. Mandan, Hidatsa, and Arikara Nation (Fort Berthold Reservation): Need to streamline process for federal review and approval of individual Indian tribes mineral leases while maintaining trust responsibility; Bakken Formation can provide numerous benefits to the Mandan, Hidatsa, and Arikara Nation and its members but must be developed in a way that does not harm community.

25. Nueta, Hidatsa, & Sahnish Allottee Economic Development Corporation: Environmental degradation resulting from oil development in the area; lack of corporate responsibility regarding oil development in Fort Berthold; lack of consultation regarding development of the Garrison Dam / Lake Sakakawea Project.

26. Ihanktonwan Dakota: Self-government and self-determination in light of the United Nations Declaration on the Rights of Indigenous Peoples; Doctrine of Discovery in addition to a patchwork of federal statutes, regulations and policies create foremost barriers to self- determination.

27. American Indian Movement Interpretative Center: Concerns regarding development activities in the Penokee Range and Bad River Watershed of Wisconsin; opposition to the Keystone XL Pipeline Project; concerns regarding effects of uranium mining in the Navajo Nation; call for the immediate release of Leonard Peltier.

28. Community for the Advancement of Native Studies: Underrepresentation of Native American students in higher education and as teachers and administrators in the South Dakota education system; discriminatory practices within the state education system.

29. Sisseton and Wahpeton representative: Treaty information 1668-1817; information regarding the Waldron-Black Tomahawk Controversy and the Status of "Mixed Bloods" among the Teton Sioux.

30. Emerson Elk, Fred Sitting Up, Bill Means, Shawn Bordeaux, and Sam Mato: Indigenous identity theft is taking place through academic colonialism, legislation, agency rule making, and other activities.

31. Oahe Landowners Board of Directors: Inadequate compensation for the dispossession of indigenous lands as part of the Oahe Dam and Reservoir Project.

32. Cante Wanjila: Inability of Native Americans incarcerated in federal, state and private prisons to freely practise their traditional religions without discrimination, harassment, indifference and racial profiling.

33. Ihanktonwan Treaty Steering Committee: Continued interest in the seven treaties the tribe has with the federal government; lack of consultation by the United States Government regarding the Keystone XL Pipeline Project, poor groundwater quality due to uranium mining; mismanagement of tribal lands by the Government; land dispossession.

34. National Boarding School Healing Project: Information regarding the experiences of American Indians attending boarding schools during the years of 1920 to 1960 in the northern plains region; accounts of emotional, physical and sexual abuse and neglect of children and separation from families and communities.

35. Native American Women's Health Education Resource Center: Native American and Alaska Native women are often denied due process within courts and health care services following a sexual assault; denial of health services based on race; need for improved standard of care for sexual assault victims, including the collection of forensic evidence to assist with the prosecution process.

36. Bryce in the Woods: Historical overview of Lakota economic system and secretarial orders regarding Cheyenne River Sioux Tribe lands.

37. Chief Arvol Looking Horse and Indigenous Elders and Medicine Peoples: Call for United States Government to acknowledge indigenous peoples' right to self-determination, respect their religious and cultural practices, and include indigenous peoples in consultation and decision-making processes.

38. International Indian Treaty Council: Failure of the United States Government to fully accept the rights to self-determination and free, prior and informed consent of indigenous peoples; importance of implementation of Committee for the Elimination of Racial Discrimination concluding observations regarding the Western Shoshone indigenous peoples and nuclear testing, toxic and dangerous waste storage and other activities carried out in areas of spiritual or cultural significance to indigenous peoples; the United Nations Declaration as a framework for a "new jurisdiction" for redress of treaty violations; proposed language to strengthen and recognize treaty rights within the proposed American Declaration on the Rights of Indigenous Peoples.

39. President of the Rosebud Sioux Tribe: Non-consultation by state and federal authorities regarding the development of the Keystone XL Pipeline Project; treaty breach of the 1851 and 1868 Fort Laramie Treaty; loss of lands due to the General Allotment Act 1887; call for improved implementation of the United Nations Declaration on the Rights of Indigenous Peoples.

40. Rosebud Sioux Tribe member: Concerns regarding Indian health-care services, home energy costs, the Supplemental Nutrition Assistance Program (SNAP), and the Keystone XL Pipeline Project.

41. Owe Aku (Bring Back the Way): Environmental degradation caused by uranium, oil and gas development; lack of free, prior and informed consent; treaty violations by the United States Government; genocide by the Government in Lakota homelands.

42. Oglala Sioux Tribe: Infringement on treaty lands by construction and operation of Keystone XL Pipeline Project; negative environmental consequences if the pipeline is constructed and operated; provided several resolutions from native nations and organizations opposing the Keystone XL Pipeline Project.

43. Chief Iron Eagle, Nakota Sioux Fire: Working to address issues related to treaty rights for the Nakota people.

44. Standing Rock Sioux Tribe:
   • Resolution opposing the original route of the development of the Keystone XL Pipeline Project through the Standing Rock Sioux Tribe aboriginal homelands and the new proposed route through the Lakota Homelands.
   • Obstruction of the right to education; need to improve intellectual development of Lakota children.

45. Sicangu Lakota Nation: Complex federal and state laws and regulations negatively affect tribal sovereignty and hinder economic development of indigenous peoples.

46. Chief Oliver Red Cloud: Taking of lands after the ratification of the 1868 Fort Laramie Treaty; Indian Reorganization Act promoted colonialism and assimilation of Native Americans.

47. Lakota Rose LaPlante: South Dakota Department of Social Service is in non- compliance with the Indian Child Welfare Act.

48. International Native Indian Programs Incorporated (INIPI): Alleged misuse of funds on the Pine Ridge Reservation.

49. Cante Tenza Okolakiciye — Strong Heart Warrior Society, Free & Independent Lakota Nation and Elders: Call for the United States Government to investigate alleged graft and corruption within the Oglala Sioux Tribal Government as well as elder abuse by Oglala Sioux tribal members.

50. Unites Sioux Tribes Development Corporation: Difficulties with gaming compacts and tribal-state relations.

51. Mniwakhanwozu Oyate: Presentation is in his native language, with attachment of an article of Sinte Gleksa University hosting the Special Rapporteur on the rights of indigenous peoples.

52. Sheryl Lightfoot (Ojibwe): United States Government qualified support for the United Nations Declaration on the Rights of Indigenous Peoples appears to be an active process of self-exemption and a pre-emptive strike against implementation that preserves the status quo while also offering some relief from transnational and domestic political pressure.

53. Lawrence Swallow: Indian Reorganization Act constitutions do not reflect culture or identity of indigenous peoples; inadequate management of land claims; physical abuse of children.

Oklahoma and South-Central region (including submissions at Tulsa consultation)

54. Lipan Apache Band of Texas: Community members of El Calaboz Rancheri´a are harassed by United States Government agents working along the United States-Mexico border; lack of free, prior and informed consent regarding seizure and destruction traditional ranchería lands.

55. Osage Indians: Wrongful transfer of headrights in the Osage Mineral Trust to non-Indians and corporations.

56. United Keetoowah Band of Cherokee: Overview of the Western/Arkansas Cherokee people; current status of the United Keetoowah Band of Cherokees, the band's history, and how it has staved off termination attempts.

57. Kickapoo Tribe of Oklahoma: Difficulties of tribal members in obtaining a 1-872 card and using the card for entry into the United States; need to protect and respect Native American religious practices, customs, and observances; encroachment of urban areas on wildlife habitat that inhibits hunting and gathering; delays in placing newly acquired tribally owned lands into trust status.

58. Sac and Fox Nation: Refusal by the Department of the Interior to acknowledge the rights granted to the Nation through their Federal Corporate Charter undermines self- determination; proposed pump station for the Keystone XL Pipeline Project threatens water sources and gravesites; violation of Native American Graves Protection and Repatriation Act by the state of Pennsylvania.

59. Tusekia Harjo Band of the Seminole Nation of Oklahoma: Outlines the negative effects of discrimination on the social conditions of American Indians; many Indians have lost faith in law enforcement and justice systems in Indian Country; mistreatment of Indians in state and federal courts; need to implement United Nations Declaration on the Rights of Indigenous Peoples as a means to end discrimination.

60. Muscogee (Creek) Nation representative: Unequal treatment in economic for opportunities inhibits economic development, which is connected to social, political and legal issues for Muscogee (Creek) Nation.

61. Cherokee Nation representative: Tribal courts are not afforded the same respect as federal and state courts; tribal court judges and justices are viewed and treated with less esteem than their federal and state counterparts.

62. Executive Director Choctaw/Cherokee: Federal recognition is a flawed and arbitrary process with the primary objective being forced assimilation.

63. Chickasaw Nation Department of Justice: Compacting with the United States as one of the original "demonstration" tribes with Indian Health Services proved to be a positive and empowering experience in self-governance; recent challenges to tribal self governance by federal and state agencies; protection of natural resources; and litigation connected to water rights agreements.

64. Euchee (Yuchi) Tribe: Tribe is not federally recognized but is trying to gain federal recognition, which it sees as critical to its self-determination.

65. Principal Chief Cherokee Nation: Department of the Interior adoption of a tribal consultation policy; resolution of longstanding breach of Indian Trust lawsuits; national criminal justice training program; preservation and revitalization of native languages; ongoing problems, including violence against indigenous women.

66. Prairie Band Potawatomi: State taxation of Native American veterans domiciled in Indian Country violates the Soldiers and Sailors Civil Relief Act of 1940.

67. Descendants of the Sand Creek Massacre: Call for the United States Government to make reparations in connection to the 1864 Sand Creek Massacre near Fort Lyon, Colorado.

68. Gregory Bigler (Tribal Court Judge): Lack of jurisdiction over non-Indians; jurisdiction questions over activities within the Tribes'/Nations' territory; inability to craft solutions for some criminal and certain juvenile cases due to limited resources.

69. Walter R. Echo-Hawk (Chief Justice for the Supreme Court of the Kickapoo Tribe of Oklahoma; Justice of the Supreme Court of the Pawnee Nation): Discusses multiple aspects of federal Indian law and policy that require strengthening or could benefit from reform in light of the U.N. Declaration on the Rights of Indigenous Peoples.

70. Haskell Indian Nations University Student Senate: Chronic underfunding undermines Native American education and institutions; call for improved federal support for Native American education.

71. Wetlands Preservation Organization: Development threatens the Wakarusa Wetlands; forced relocation of plants and animals creates an environmental and social threat.

72. Ponca Tribe Business Committee: Pollutants from the Continental Carbon Company facility in Ponca City, Oklahoma continued to interfere, with the Ponca peoples' health and the use of their property.

73. National Indian Youth Council (Dr. Kay McGowan): Governments, including the United States, that have systematically used boarding school programmes to diminish their indigenous populations and the need to systematically redress the damage of such programmes.

74. Indigenous Environment Network: Overview of difficulties involved in living in the modern world and yet staying rooted to tradition, particularly in light of continuing racism toward Indians and development of the Keystone XL Pipeline Project, which threatens archaeological and historical sites.

75. Tribal Towns of the Muscogee (Creek) Nation (Hickory Grounds): Making efforts to protect, preserve and maintain sacred historical sites in the aboriginal homelands of the Muscogee people.

76. Ponca Tribe of Oklahoma member: Provided information regarding treaties with the United States beginning in 1858 and 1865, which ceded thousands of acres of land.

Pacific Northwest region (including submission at Portland consultation)

77. Columbia River Intertribal Fish Commission: Importance of the Columbia River and its fish population to Northwest Coastal Indians is reinforced by a map showing the various native peoples associated with the river.

78. Snoqualmie Tribal Elder: Violations of Snoqualmie tribal member's civil and human rights due to banishment from the tribe and lack of due process.

79. Métis Consulting, LLC: Métis descendants excluded from consultation and planning process regarding Fort Vancouver Barracks Transfer; continued occupation by the United States Army and U.S. National Park Service of Métis traditional lands that were confiscated in 1846.

80. National Indian Child Welfare Association: Current national trends in American Indian and Alaska Native child welfare policy and practice; disproportionate rate of American Indian and Alaska Native children in United States state foster care systems.

81. Seattle Human Rights Commission: Poor social and economic conditions of Seattle urban Indian populations include high rates of accidental deaths, diabetes, liver disease, alcohol-related deaths, infant mortality, poverty, homelessness and lower education achievement.

82. City of Seattle Native American Employees Association (CANOES): Violence against native women is a serious concern in the Pacific Northwest as women have very few resources aimed at preventing such violence or assisting victims of violence.

83. Honor the Earth /1000 Nations: Lack of compliance with essential elements of the United Nations Declaration on the Rights of Indigenous peoples undermines sacred sites protection and religious freedoms; militarization of Indian Country.

84. Cowlitz Tribe: Efforts to consolidate their land base and engage in economic development opportunities following their "restoration" to federal recognition, having previously been terminated during the 1950s.

85. Makah Tribe Chairman: Barriers to indigenous management of natural resources, especially marine resources; need to integrate tribal governments into higher levels of natural resource management at federal level, especially energy, land and ocean management.

Southwest region (including submissions at Tucson consultation)

86. San Carlos Apache Tribe representative: Opposition to a land exchange process that would facilitate mining in the Oak Flat area in Arizona's Tonto National Forest, a region that has cultural, social, religious and political significance to for the Apache and other indigenous peoples.

87. Chairman of the Tohono O'odham Nation: Increased border security and other restrictive measures have made travel difficult across the United States-Mexico border for tribal members and restricted freedom of movement; and the proposed Rosemont Copper mine threatens cultural and archaeological sites containing numerous funerary and sacred objects.

88. Gente de l'ioti, A.C.: Tohono O'odham Nation exercise of the right to self- determination is severely restricted by the presence of United States federal agents on the Nation's main reservation; the United States Customs and Border Patrol regularly violate the rights of indigenous peoples that reside in near the United States-Mexico border.

89. Tohono O'odham (Mexico): The Tohono O'odham peoples in Mexico and the United States were separated by metal barriers installed by the United States Government without consultation; the Department of Homeland Security fails to recognize the right of indigenous people to freely enter and exit the Tohono O'odham reservation.

90. Individual from Tohono O'odham: Deaths of immigrants crossing on Tohono O'odham Nation; access to water as a human right.

91. O'odham Voice Against the Wall: Failure to adequately recognize and protect the human rights of indigenous peoples whose communities span the United States-Mexico border.

92. Leonard Peltier Defense Offense Committee: Concerns regarding the health, safety and reintegration of Leonard Peltier.

93. Keepers of the Secret (from Havasupai Tribe): Current ban on uranium mining does not protect Havasupai territory and drinking water sources.

94. Navajo Nation Office of the Vice President: The goal of the Navajo Nation is to develop an educational system that endorses Navajo culture by sustaining the language while promoting academic success; the Navajo nation is moving for-

ward to create and operate a school system specifically designed to meet the needs of Navajo students despite disparities among the funding levels for state and private education systems and the Navajo Nation education system.

95. Navajo Nation Human Rights Commission: The United States frequently allows for the desecration and economic exploitation of indigenous peoples' sacred sites, including the San Francisco Peaks located in Flagstaff, Arizona for the benefit on non-indigenous peoples, business owners and the non-indigenous public to the detriment of indigenous peoples.

96. Navajo Nation Corrections Project and International Indian Treaty Council: High rate of Native Americans incarcerated in state and federal prisons; Native peoples are often denied access to traditional religious and spiritual ceremonies and services while incarcerated; wrongful conviction and prosecutorial misconduct of Leonard Peltier.

97. Dine' bi Siihasin: Mismanagement of housing programmes in the Navajo Nation result in discrimination and oppression.

98. Chihene Nde Nation: Due to lack of federal recognition, the tribe is having great difficulty protecting sacred and ancient sites from being excavated and looted.

99. Pueblo of Laguna: Indigenous transmission of knowledge to future generations is difficult without access to traditional lands, language and cultural practices; uranium mining has contaminated water sources and threatens many sacred sites.

100. Nahuacalli and Tonatierra Project: Rights of indigenous peoples are threatened by Arizona Senate Bill 1070, the North American Free Trade Agreement, and the Doctrine of Discovery.

101. Native American Church of North America, Inc.: Concerns regarding health and sustainability of naturally occurring peyote in peyote gardens; reoccurring issues for peyote users and harvesters include wrongful arrest, confiscation, prejudicial treatment in family custody cases, and discrimination in employment.

102. Native American Directions: The Tucson Unified School District's Mexican American Studies program is a good example how a school district should reflect the community that it serves.

103. Indigenous Elders and Medicine Peoples Council: A recent report regarding the USDA Forest Service Policies and Procedures fails to provide meaningful and effective direction for the development of policies for the protection of indigenous sacred sites.

104. Indigenous Youth Experience Council: United States Government has statutory and treaty obligations as well as standing agreements to protect the sacred places of indigenous peoples.

105. National Congress of American Indians: Importance of "Carcieri Fix" to restore the benefits provided by the Indian Reorganization Act and to remove the uncertainty surrounding development and strategic planning in Indian Country; support for reform of federal surface leasing regulations for American Indian lands; important that tribes have equal access to states of all programmes.

106. Indian Law Resource Center, National Congress of American Indians Task Force on Violence Against Women, National Indigenous Women's Resource Center, Inc., and Clan Star, Inc.: Violence against American Indian and Alaska Native women and girls in the United States has reached epidemic levels in Indian Country and Alaska Native villages.

107. Morning Star Institute: Hundreds of Native American sacred places, heritage languages and cultures are endangered; Native Americans encounter serious barriers when attempting to exercise their cultural rights.

108. Inter Tribal Council of Arizona: Mining in the Oak Flat area will result in the destruction of sacred sites, notably mining in any part of the ecosystem will negatively affect the religious and cultural integrity of the area as a whole.

109. Black Mesa United-Dzilijiin Bee Ahota, Inc. (BMU-DzBA): Strip mining and related activities threaten Black Mesa, a sacred mountain, and area drinking water sources.

110. International Council of Thirteen Indigenous Grandmothers: Mining threatens the survival of indigenous cultures, contaminates soil and drinking water; government, financial institutions and decision-making bodies should have better implementation of free, prior and informed consent with regard to indigenous peoples.

111. Representative of boarding school survivors, Leo Killsback: Boarding schools and forced assimilation created historical trauma that is now imbedded in the contemporary lives of Native Americans.

112. Tewa Women United: Extractive industry threaten natural resources including water, air and land in New Mexico; Historical Document Retrieval and Assessment Project document.

113. Honor Our Pueblo Existence: Indigenous peoples in the Southwest region of the United States live in the shadow of a violent culture created by Government and military projects to research, develop, and manufacture weapons of mass destruction.

114. Black Mesa Water Coalition: Department of the Interior has a trust responsibility to indigenous communities to protect drinking water sources.

115. Individual from Navajo reservation: Need to protect indigenous peoples' right to water.

116. Wooden Shoe People representative: Working to bring attention to the non-binding apology to Native Americans on behalf of the citizens of the United States that was included in the 2010 Department of Defense Appropriations Bill.

117. Pueblo of Jemez, New Mexico: The Jemez Pueblo has never ceded or abandoned the Indian title to the Valles Caldera, which is critically important to the group for both spiritual and resource reasons. Jemez Pueblo has never been compensated for the taking of these lands by the United States.

118. National Indian Youth Council:
- The contemporary legal framework for prosecuting domestic violence in Indian Country is in adequate; tribes need criminal and full civil jurisdiction over non- Indian offenders in order to protect Native women against violence;
- Urban Indians are frequently landholders of allotments, and given current emphasis on extractive industries, mineral extraction, and energy policy, off and near reservation Indian are affected by on-reservation policymaking; and
- United States Government consistently ignores urban Indians generally, and in the following areas, specifically: the right to participation, violence against women, cultural and spiritual issues, education and related services, and person sovereignty.

119. Forgotten People organization:
- Failures of the United States Government to remediate conditions in the Hopi Partition Land and the area affected by the Bennett Freeze, which was lifted in 2009 with inadequate funding for rehabilitation or the protection of water rights;
- Mental, physical and psychological trauma resulting from the Bennett Freeze including youth suicide and mental illness;
- Expropriation of land and for energy resource exploitation;
- Health and remediation issues related to uranium mining on the Navajo Nation;
- Land and animal confiscation;
- Extractive industries and the contamination of water sources and high rates of cancer and contamination resulting from abandoned uranium mines;
- Destruction of spiritual and sacred sites on Black Mesa as the result of mining;
- Forced relocation of the people from Black Mesa has resulted in the inability to practise traditional religion, which is based on a spiritual relationship with ancestral lands;

- Threats to indigenous peoples while they are attempting to protect burial and sacred sites; destruction of sacred sites; and
- Opposition to Senate Bill 2109/House Resolution 4067, Little Colorado River Water Rights Settlement and its potential benefits for the Navajo Generating Station (NGS) owners and Peabody Coal Company; settlement grants a waiver without redress for past, present and future contamination of our water sources.

Alaska (including submissions at Anchorage consultation)

120. Native Village of Point Hope: Importance of accessibility to subsistence resources including whales, seals, polar bears and fish; negative repercussions of military activities and radiation on village population and wildlife; high poverty rates and substance abuse in area.

121. Alaska-Hawaii Alliance for Self Determination: Self-determination for Native Alaska and Hawaiian peoples; government and corporate practices are abusive toward indigenous natural resources and cultural practices.

122. Chugachmiut Tribal Consortium: High rate of suicide among Alaska Natives; intergenerational stress and related long-term consequences on children and communities.

123. Indian Law Resource Center: Legal barriers regarding violence against Native American and Alaska Native women include the lack of jurisdiction over non-Indians, lack of adequate response to violence against Alaska Native women due to jurisdictional limitations created by United States law, and ramifications of Public Law 280.

124. Native Village of Eklutna: Need to balance subsistence needs of indigenous peoples with development of urban areas in Alaska.

125. Akiak Native Community and Akiak IRA Council: Restrictions on king salmon fishing inhibit families and elders from gathering a sufficient fish supply for the winter; confusing fishing regulations hinder some indigenous peoples from harvesting fish.

126. Yupiit Nation, Akiak Native Community: The Alaska Native Claims Settlement Act restricts traditional fishing activities; request for Congressional hearings to examine high rates of suicide, domestic violence, sexual assault, accidental death, and health issues in Alaska Native communities.

127. Iñupiat Community of the Arctic Slope: Maps of Arctic Slope area; proposed oil and gas exploration development; information about possible oil spill in Arctic Ocean.

128. Kenaitze Indian Tribe Community members:
- Status of Alaska Native peoples is distinct from indigenous peoples in the contiguous United States; Alaska Natives must be afforded rights of self- determination and self-government.
- The United States provided false and misleading information regarding the United Nations list of Non-Self-Governing Territories.

129. NANA Regional Corporation: Importance of the Declaration on the Rights of Indigenous Peoples and the promotion of indigenous rights domestically; need to protect and promote subsistence activities at the federal and state levels; Kuskokwim river king salmon closure places severe stress on the food security of Yupiit households in the region; economic barriers to rural economic development; diminishing population of indigenous language speakers.

130. Alaska Native and Indigenous Faculty Council: Significant disparities exist between Alaska Natives and other Alaskans.

131. Ahtna, Inc.: Ongoing adverse land title and subsistence disputes are exacerbated by differential enforcement of property laws and a lack of enforcement of trespass laws.

132. Sealaska Corporation: The equitable settlement of Native land claims is fundamentally an issue of Native rights, but also of job fairness and self-determination; the importance to pursue subsistence activities, both to preserve aspects

of culture and to ensure food security; the legal framework governing subsistence in Alaska significantly hampers the ability of Alaska Natives to access their traditional foods.

133. Native Village of Paimiut, Yupiaq: Alaska Natives Commission: Final Report, Volume I, Anchorage, Alaska (May 1994).

134. Occupy Bearing Sea: Commercial fishing is having damaging effects on native fishing practices; North Pacific Fisheries Management Council needs to enact policies to protect native fishing.

135. Yup'ik Eskimo Dillingham community member: Pebble Mine Project will have devastating consequences on the Bristol Bay cultural landscape and salmon stocks used for subsistence harvest.

136. Atmautluak Traditional Council: Call to the Special Rapporteur on the rights of indigenous peoples to review the denial of the right to self-determination regarding the situation of Alaska and Hawaii.

137. Native Village of Unalakleet community member: Off-shore oil and gas development threatens indigenous communities that rely on marine mammals and fish as primary sources of food; flooding and erosion related to climate change; lack of education; high suicide rates; and lack of self-government.

138. Alaska Federation of Natives: Need for food security is a basic human right and a vital part of Alaska indigenous cultures; provided information regarding way to empower indigenous people to have an active and meaningful role in issues that affect them.

139. Chickaloon Village Traditional Council; Chickaloon Native Village: Proposed Usibelli coal mine threatens indigenous lands and culture.

140. Chickaloon Village community members:
- Negative effects of Alaska Native Claims Settlement Act on indigenous families and culture.
- Education at the Ya Ne Dah Ah school includes traditional Athabascan culture, history, language in addition to math, reading, and writing while creating relationships between elders and young people of the village.
- Importance of language in Athabascan culture, tradition and spirituality.
- Indigenous lands and watersheds that support salmon habitat should be protected from the negative effects of coal mining and related activities.
- Concern regarding environmental degradation and mental health issues related to the proposed coal mine.
- Mental health of village residents is not being adequately considered under the Rapid Health Impact Assessment of the Wishbone Hill Coal Mining Project.
- Importance of several rivers and creeks in area to indigenous peoples including Moose Creek, Buffalo Creek, Eska Creek, Chickaloon and King rivers.
- Federal Indian law and the Alaska Native Claims Settlement Act have undermined efforts of Alaskan tribes to realize self-determination, to promote native education, and to assert tribal sovereignty.

141. Second International Indigenous Women's Symposium on Environmental and Reproductive Health:
- Gwich'in Arctic Village; Venetie Tribal Government, Alaska; Resistance of Environmental Destruction on Indigenous Lands (REDOIL): Tribal challenges to oil and mining industries; right to a healthy environment; need to protect environment and traditional food resources, particularly caribou.
- Gwich'in Steering Committee: Importance of Arctic National Wildlife Refuge and the Porcupine Caribou Herd for the Gwich'in Nation who are a remote and traditional people; threats to communities from oil and gas development.
- Resistance of Environmental Destruction on Indigenous Lands (REDOIL): Dramatic increase in respiratory ailments in native communities has occurred due to industrial activities, particularly mining.
- International Indian Treaty Council; North-South Indigenous Network Against Pesticides; Indigenous Women's Environmental and Reproductive Health Initiative; and the Native Village of Savoonga: Negative effects of environmental toxins on the health, well-being, and cultures of indigenous peoples particularly

indigenous women, children and future generations; framework for assessing United States laws, policies and practices regarding the production, use export, and disposal and dumping of environmental toxins.

- Elim Students Against Urainium: Uranium exploratory activities damaging effects on the Tubutulik River and Norton Bay watersheds.
- Importance of traditional medicine and how it can be used to achieve better physical and mental health for Alaskan Natives.
- Alaska Inter-Tribal Council: Expression of political will by Atmautluak Traditional Council and Native Village of St. Michael to be reinstated to the list of non-self-governing territories.

142. Curyung Tribal Council and community members:
- Background and history of Curyung tribe; value of subsistence;
- Information regarding the proposed Pebble Mine Project; risks of Pebble Mine Project; potential negative effects of oil spills;
- Efforts by the tribe regarding environmental and economic issues, particularly preservation of populations of marine resources;
- Tribal resolutions that provide for protection of the Bristol Bay watershed; tribal resolution to re-instate Alaska to the list of Non-Self-Governing Territories; and
- Pebble Partnership Report; Bristol Bay Regional Vision Statement; and the Environmental Protection Agency Bristol Bay Watershed Assessment

143. Nunamta Aulukestai: Potential harm regarding with offshore drilling in the Bristol Bay region; risks to regional indigenous peoples, wildlife and natural resources from the Pebble Mine Project; environmental reports regarding the Pebble Mine Project; and information regarding opposition to the Pebble Mine Project.

144. Bristol Bay Native Corporation: Information on Pebble Mine Project; Bristol Bay Native Corporation opposition to Pebble Mine Project; concerns regarding unacceptable environmental effects of the project; and information regarding the importance of responsible resource development.

145. Bristol Bay Vision: Report that documents a yearlong effort by the residents of Bristol Bay to create a vision for their schools and community.

146. Atmautluak Traditional Council: Resolution declaring the tribe's sovereignty.

147. Knugank Tribe: The tribe was omitted from the list of federally recognized tribes in 1993, which inhibits efforts to promote sovereignty and the exercise the right to self- govern; and the inability of the tribe to gain title to a traditional cemetery.

148. Qutekcak Tribe: As a result of historical circumstances and administrative errors, Qutekcak Native Community has not been allowed federal recognition.

149. Knikatnu, Inc.: Concerns regarding the proposed Susitna-Watana Hydroelectric Project, No. 14241; concerns regarding wildlife management and declining wildlife populations in Alaska and effects on indigenous peoples.

150. Alaska Native Tribal Health Consortium: The Southeast Alaska Regional Suicide Prevention Task Force is developing coping strategies to reduce the high rate of suicide among Alaska Natives.

California

151. La Cuna de Aztlan Sacred Sites Protection Circle: Development of solar power projects threatens sacred sites in Eastern Riverside and San Bernardino counties.

152. Kawaiisu Tribe of Tejon, Kawaiisu National Council: Lack of recognition and treaty breach contribute to the tribe's inability to exercise its right to full and effective participation in matters related to culture, land and territories; tribe opposes corporate ownership of grave goods, artifacts and cultural sites.

153. American Indian Rights and Resources Organization (Temecula Indians): Damaging effects of disenrollment, banishment, and denial of tribal membership, including exclusion from participation in regularly schedule elections for the Tribal Council.

154. Tosobol Clan (Temecula Indians): Allottee disenrollment and membership results in denial of access to housing, education, and health assistance; banishment and exclusion are barriers to accessing on-reservation allotments.

155. Sherwood Valley Rancheria: Opposes certain aspects of the Marine Life Protection Act (MLPA), which places restrictions and regulations on the gathering of native foods including seaweed, abalone, smelt and salmon along the coastline.

156. Nuumu Yadoha Language Program (Hupa Mattole Indian): Lack of recognition has negative consequences on health and education programmes for small California Indian groups.

157. Tübatulabal Tribal Chairwomen: Certain tribes in California that have allotment lands and are seeking federal recognition; state government has created a definition for "California Native American Tribes" that includes both federally and non-federally recognized tribes.

158. Winnemem Wintu Tribe: Tribe is unable to conduct a spiritual ceremony for young girls due to refusal by the U.S. Forest Service to effectuate a mandatory closure of a small section of the McCloud River.

159. InterTribal Sinkyone Wilderness Council: The Marine Life Protection Act (MLPA) is an example of a successful collaboration between the state of California and North Coast Indian Tribes developing regulations that will protect the continuation of traditional tribal gathering, harvesting and fishing in designated marine protected areas outside of reservation lands.

160. California Traditional Basket Weavers: Information about the traditional methods of basket weaving by Native Californians; traditional basket weavers and their children suffer from health conditions caused by high levels of mercury in the water and soil of California's Central Valley

161. Juaneño Band of California Mission Indians: Ineligibility of members of terminated tribes to direct health care from Indian Health Services, educational scholarships and other benefits directed by the United States for the welfare and advancement of Indian people.

162. Viejas Band of Kumeyaay Indians: Lack of consultation regarding the proposed development of wind farm; proposed construction of industrial-seized wind turbines on lands traditionally used and occupied by area tribes that are home to sacred sites and burial grounds.

163. Basket Weavers In Action and Indigenous Youth Foundation; California Traditional Basket Weavers: Indigenous people in California suffer from serious health problems caused by exposure toxins, pollutants and pesticides in areas where Tule reeds are gathered for basket making.

164. AIM-WEST: Indigenous peoples in the United States face challenges to protecting sacred sites, as well as the ability to exercise the freedom of religion; hate crimes and violence against Native women, the insensitive use of American Indians as mascots in sports images, and team names by non-native schools, and imprisonment of Leonard Peltier.

Hawaii

165. Indigenous Peoples and Nations: Importance of self-determination for Alaska and Hawaiian Natives.

166. Commission on the Restitution of the Hawaiian Government in Exile: Resolution calling for fact finding commission on the political status of Hawaii to compel the United States to fulfill its treaty obligations to the Hawaiian people and to the United Nations.

167. Indigenous Hawaiian individuals: Native Hawaiians experience loss of traditional lands, territories and culture; The plight of native Hawaiian people as presented in a short documentary film: occupation of the Hawaiian Islands; justification for Hawaiian self- governance and self-determination.

168. Koani Foundation — Ke Aupuni O Hawaii: Joint resolution of political will of the people of the Hawaiian islands asserting the international legal and political status of the Hawaiian Islands; Hawaiian Sovereignty Elections Council Report.

Source: United Nations, General Assembly, A/HRC/21/47/Add.1, 30 August 2012; Human Rights Council, Twenty-first session, Agenda item 3, Promotion and protection of all human rights, civil, political, economic, social, and cultural rights, including the right to development; Report of the Special Rapporteur on the rights of indigenous peoples, James Anaya; Addendum, The situation of indigenous people in the United States of America.
http://www.ohchr.org/Documents/HRBodies/HRCouncil/RegularSession/Session21/A-HRC-21-47-Add1_en.pdf

3. OUTCOME DOCUMENT OF THE HIGH-LEVEL PLENARY MEETING OF THE GENERAL ASSEMBLY KNOWN AS THE WORLD CONFERENCE ON INDIGENOUS PEOPLES

This Outcome Document from the first World Conference on Indigenous Peoples (UNWCIP), 22-23 September 2014 in New York, shares perspectives and best practices on the realization of the rights of indigenous peoples, and is a way to pursue objectives of the United Nations Declaration on the Rights of Indigenous Peoples (UNDRIP). Through this process, member states commit to seek ways to implement pieces of the Outcome Document they find feasible at the national or local level, such as developing measures to address violence against indigenous women, or "respecting the contributions of indigenous peoples to ecosystem management and sustainable development, including knowledge acquired through experience in hunting, gathering, fishing, pastoralism and agriculture, as well as their sciences, technologies and cultures…" among many other issues.

United Nations, A/RES/69/2, General Assembly Sixty-ninth session, Agenda item 65, Distr.: General 25 September 2014, Resolution adopted by the General Assembly on 22 September 2014

1. We, the Heads of State and Government, ministers and representatives of Member States, reaffirming our solemn commitment to the purposes and principles of the Charter of the United Nations, in a spirit of cooperation with the indigenous peoples of the world, are assembled at United Nations Headquarters in New York on 22 and 23 September 2014, on the occasion of the high-level plenary meeting of the General Assembly known as the World Conference on Indigenous Peoples, to reiterate the important and continuing role of the United Nations in promoting and protecting the rights of indigenous peoples.

2. We welcome the indigenous peoples' preparatory processes for the World Conference, including the Global Indigenous Preparatory Conference held in Alta, Norway, in June 2013. We take note of the outcome document of the Alta Conference1 and other contributions made by indigenous peoples. We also welcome the inclusive preparatory process for the high-level plenary meeting, including the comprehensive engagement of the representatives of indigenous peoples.

3. We reaffirm our support for the United Nations Declaration on the Rights of Indigenous Peoples, adopted by the General Assembly on 13 September 2007,2 and our commitments made in this respect to consult and cooperate in good faith with the indigenous peoples concerned through their own representative institutions in order to obtain their free, prior and informed consent before adopting and implementing legislative or administrative measures that may affect them, in accordance with the applicable principles of the Declaration.

4. We reaffirm our solemn commitment to respect, promote and advance and in no way diminish the rights of indigenous peoples and to uphold the principles of the Declaration.

5. In addition to the Declaration, we recall the other major achievements of the past two decades in building an international framework for the advancement of the rights and aspirations of the world's indigenous peoples, including the es-

tablishment of the Permanent Forum on Indigenous Issues, the creation of the Expert Mechanism on the Rights of Indigenous Peoples and the establishment of the mandate of the Special Rapporteur on the rights of indigenous peoples. We commit ourselves to giving due consideration to recommendations and advice issued by those bodies in cooperation with indigenous peoples.

6. We encourage those States that have not yet ratified or acceded to the International Labour Organization Indigenous and Tribal Peoples Convention, 1989 (No. 169),3 to consider doing so. We recall the obligation of ratifying States under the Convention to develop coordinated and systematic action to protect the rights of indigenous peoples.

7. We commit ourselves to taking, in consultation and cooperation with indigenous peoples, appropriate measures at the national level, including legislative, policy and administrative measures, to achieve the ends of the Declaration and to promote awareness of it among all sectors of society, including members of legislatures, the judiciary and the civil service.

8. We commit ourselves to cooperating with indigenous peoples, through their own representative institutions, to develop and implement national action plans, strategies or other measures, where relevant, to achieve the ends of the Declaration.

9. We commit ourselves to promoting and protecting the rights of indigenous persons with disabilities and to continuing to improve their social and economic conditions, including by developing targeted measures for the aforementioned action plans, strategies or measures, in collaboration with indigenous persons with disabilities. We also commit ourselves to ensuring that national legislative, policy and institutional structures relating to indigenous peoples are inclusive of indigenous persons with disabilities and contribute to the advancement of their rights.

10. We commit ourselves to working with indigenous peoples to disaggregate data, as appropriate, or conduct surveys and to utilizing holistic indicators of indigenous peoples' well-being to address the situation and needs of indigenous peoples and individuals, in particular older persons, women, youth, children and persons with disabilities.

11. We commit ourselves to ensuring equal access to high-quality education that recognizes the diversity of the cultures of indigenous peoples and to health, housing, water, sanitation and other economic and social programmes to improve well-being, including through initiatives, policies and the provision of resources. We intend to empower indigenous peoples to deliver such programmes as far as possible.

12. We recognize the importance of indigenous peoples' health practices and their traditional medicine and knowledge.

13. We commit ourselves to ensuring that indigenous individuals have equal access to the highest attainable standard of physical and mental health. We also commit ourselves to intensifying efforts to reduce rates of HIV and AIDS, malaria, tuberculosis and non-communicable diseases by focusing on prevention, including through appropriate programmes, policies and resources for indigenous individuals, and to ensure their access to sexual and reproductive health and reproductive rights in accordance with the Programme of Action of the International Conference on Population and Development, the Beijing Platform for Action and the outcome documents of their review conferences.

14. We commit ourselves to promoting the right of every indigenous child, in community with members of his or her group, to enjoy his or her own culture, to profess and practise his or her own religion or to use his or her own language.

15. We support the empowerment and capacity-building of indigenous youth, including their full and effective participation in decision-making processes in matters that affect them. We commit ourselves to developing, in consultation with indigenous peoples, policies, programmes and resources, where relevant, that target the well-being of indigenous youth, in particular in the areas of health, education, employment and the transmission of traditional knowledge, languages and practices, and to taking measures to promote awareness and understanding of their rights.

16. We acknowledge that indigenous peoples' justice institutions can play a positive role in providing access to justice and dispute resolution and contribute to harmonious relationships within indigenous peoples' communities and within society. We commit ourselves to coordinating and conducting dialogue with those institutions, where they exist.

17. We commit ourselves to supporting the empowerment of indigenous women and to formulating and implementing, in collaboration with indigenous peoples, in particular indigenous women and their organizations, policies and programmes designed to promote capacity-building and strengthen their leadership. We support measures that will ensure the full and effective participation of indigenous women in decision-making processes at all levels and in all areas and eliminate barriers to their participation in political, economic, social and cultural life.

18. We commit ourselves to intensifying our efforts, in cooperation with indigenous peoples, to prevent and eliminate all forms of violence and discrimination against indigenous peoples and individuals, in particular women, children, youth, older persons and persons with disabilities, by strengthening legal, policy and institutional frameworks.

19. We invite the Human Rights Council to consider examining the causes and consequences of violence against indigenous women and girls, in consultation with the Special Rapporteur on violence against women, its causes and consequences, the Special Rapporteur on the rights of indigenous peoples and other special procedures mandate holders within their respective mandates. We also invite the Commission on the Status of Women to consider the issue of the empowerment of indigenous women at a future session.

20. We recognize commitments made by States, with regard to the United Nations Declaration on the Rights of Indigenous Peoples, to consult and cooperate in good faith with the indigenous peoples concerned through their own representative institutions in order to obtain their free and informed consent prior to the approval of any project affecting their lands or territories and other resources.

21. We also recognize commitments made by States, with regard to the Declaration, to establish at the national level, in conjunction with the indigenous peoples concerned, fair, independent, impartial, open and transparent processes to acknowledge, advance and adjudicate the rights of indigenous peoples pertaining to lands, territories and resources.

22. We recognize that the traditional knowledge, innovations and practices of indigenous peoples and local communities make an important contribution to the conservation and sustainable use of biodiversity. We acknowledge the importance of the participation of indigenous peoples, wherever possible, in the benefits of their knowledge, innovations and practices.

23. We intend to work with indigenous peoples to address the impact or potential impact on them of major development projects, including those involving the activities of extractive industries, including with the aim of managing risks appropriately.

24. We recall the responsibility of transnational corporations and other business enterprises to respect all applicable laws and international principles, including the Guiding Principles on Business and Human Rights: Implementing the United Nations "Protect, Respect and Remedy" Framework and to operate transparently and in a socially and environmentally responsible manner. In this regard, we commit ourselves to taking further steps, as appropriate, to prevent abuses of the rights of indigenous peoples.

25. We commit ourselves to developing, in conjunction with the indigenous peoples concerned, and where appropriate, policies, programmes and resources to support indigenous peoples' occupations, traditional subsistence activities, economies, livelihoods, food security and nutrition.

26. We recognize the importance of the role that indigenous peoples can play in economic, social and environmental development through traditional sustainable agricultural practices, including traditional seed supply systems, and access to credit and other financial services, markets, secure land tenure, health care, social services, education, training, knowledge and appropriate and affordable technologies, including for irrigation and water harvesting and storage.

27. We affirm and recognize the importance of indigenous peoples' religious and cultural sites and of providing access to and repatriation of their ceremonial objects and human remains in accordance with the ends of the Declaration. We commit ourselves to developing, in conjunction with the indigenous peoples concerned, fair, transparent and effective mechanisms for access to and repatriation of ceremonial objects and human remains at the national and international levels.

28. We invite the Human Rights Council, taking into account the views of indigenous peoples, to review the mandates of its existing mechanisms, in particular the Expert Mechanism on the Rights of Indigenous Peoples, during the sixty-ninth session of the General Assembly, with a view to modifying and improving the Expert Mechanism so that it can more effectively promote respect for the Declaration, including by better assisting Member States to monitor, evaluate and improve the achievement of the ends of the Declaration.

29. We invite the human rights treaty bodies to consider the Declaration in accordance with their respective mandates. We encourage Member States to include, as appropriate, information on the situation of the rights of indigenous peoples, including measures taken to pursue the objectives of the Declaration, in reports to those bodies and during the universal periodic review process.

30. We welcome the increasingly important role of national and regional human rights institutions in contributing to the achievement of the ends of the Declaration. We encourage the private sector, civil society and academic institutions to take an active role in promoting and protecting the rights of indigenous peoples.

31. We request the Secretary-General, in consultation and cooperation with indigenous peoples, the Inter-Agency Support Group on Indigenous Peoples' Issues and Member States, to begin the development, within existing resources, of a system-wide action plan to ensure a coherent approach to achieving the ends of the Declaration and to report to the General Assembly at its seventieth session, through the Economic and Social Council, on progress made. We invite the Secretary-General to accord, by the end of the seventieth session of the Assembly, an existing senior official of the United Nations system, with access to the highest levels of decision-making within the system, responsibility for coordinating the action plan, raising awareness of the rights of indigenous peoples at the highest possible level and increasing the coherence of the activities of the system in this regard.

32. We invite United Nations agencies, funds and programmes, in addition to resident coordinators, where appropriate, to support the implementation, upon request, of national action plans, strategies or other measures to achieve the ends of the Declaration, in accordance with national priorities and United Nations Development Assistance Frameworks, where they exist, through better coordination and cooperation.

33. We commit ourselves to considering, at the seventieth session of the General Assembly, ways to enable the participation of indigenous peoples' representatives and institutions in meetings of relevant United Nations bodies on issues affecting them, including any specific proposals made by the Secretary-General in response to the request made in paragraph 40 below.

34. We encourage Governments to recognize the significant contribution of indigenous peoples to the promotion of sustainable development, in order to achieve a just balance among the economic, social and environmental needs of present and future generations, and the need to promote harmony with nature to protect our planet and its ecosystems, known as Mother Earth in a number of countries and regions.

35. We commit ourselves to respecting the contributions of indigenous peoples to ecosystem management and sustainable development, including knowledge acquired through experience in hunting, gathering, fishing, pastoralism and agriculture, as well as their sciences, technologies and cultures.

36. We confirm that indigenous peoples' knowledge and strategies to sustain their environment should be respected and taken into account when we develop national and international approaches to climate change mitigation and adaptation.

37. We note that indigenous peoples have the right to determine and develop priorities and strategies for exercising their right to development. In this regard, we commit ourselves to giving due consideration to all the rights of indigenous peoples in the elaboration of the post-2015 development agenda.

38. We invite Member States and actively encourage the private sector and other institutions to contribute to the United Nations Voluntary Fund for Indigenous Peoples, the Trust Fund on Indigenous Issues, the Indigenous Peoples Assistance Facility and the United Nations Indigenous Peoples' Partnership as a means of respecting and promoting the rights of indigenous peoples worldwide.

39. We request the Secretary-General to include relevant information on indigenous peoples in his final report on the achievement of the Millennium Development Goals.

40. We request the Secretary-General, in consultation with the Inter-Agency Support Group on Indigenous Peoples' Issues and Member States, taking into account the views expressed by indigenous peoples, to report to the General Assembly at its seventieth session on the implementation of the present outcome document, and to submit at the same session, through the Economic and Social Council, recommendations regarding how to use, modify and improve existing United Nations mechanisms to achieve the ends of the United Nations Declaration on the Rights of Indigenous Peoples, ways to enhance a coherent, system-wide approach to achieving the ends of the Declaration and specific proposals to enable the participation of indigenous peoples' representatives and institutions, building on the report of the Secretary-General on ways and means of promoting participation at the United Nations of indigenous peoples' representatives on the issues affecting them.

—4th plenary meeting 22 September 2014

Source: http://www.un.org/en/ga/69/meetings/indigenous/#&panel1-1
For U.S. commentary, see: http://www.un.org/en/ga/69/meetings/indigenous/pdf/WCIP-Outcome-Document-Rev3.pdf

ৡ৾৶৾ৡ৾৶৾ৡ৾৶৾ৡ৾৶৾

4. REPORT OF THE SPECIAL RAPPORTEUR ON THE RIGHTS OF INDIGENOUS PEOPLES 2016

In this 2016 Report of the Special Rapporteur on the Rights of Indigenous Peoples, Ms. Victoria Tauli Corpuz summarizes her 1. activities since her last report including details on three countries visited, and 2. on-going analysis and reporting on the detrimental impact on indigenous peoples due to international investment agreements, with appropriate conclusions and recommendations.

{Excerpt}

Report of the Special Rapporteur on the Rights of Indigenous Peoples

I. Introduction

1. The present report is submitted to the Human Rights Council by the Special Rapporteur on the rights of indigenous peoples pursuant to Council resolutions 15/14 and 24/9. In the report, she provides a brief summary of her activities since her previous report (A/HRC/30/41) and offers a thematic analysis of the impact of international investment agreements on the rights of indigenous peoples.

II. Activities of the Special Rapporteur

A. Country visits

2. Since the thirtieth session of the Council, the Special Rapporteur carried out three official country visits — to Lapland in August 2015, Honduras in November 2015 and Brazil in March 2016 — the reports of which will be issued as addenda to the present report.

B. Report on environmental conservation measures

3. The Special Rapporteur will present a thematic report on environmental conservation measures and their impact on indigenous peoples' rights to the General Assembly at its seventy-first session.

III. International investment agreements

A. Background

4. In her 2015 report to the General Assembly (A/70/301), the Special Rapporteur concluded that the protections that international investment agreements provide to foreign investors can have significant impacts on indigenous peoples'

rights. In order to gain further insights into the issue she sent questionnaires to States Members of the United Nations, indigenous peoples and civil society organizations and, in cooperation with the International Work Group for Indigenous Affairs, the Asia Indigenous Peoples Pact, the Columbia Center on Sustainable Investment and the Indigenous Peoples' International Centre for Policy Research and Education (Tebtebba), organized a series of regional and global consultations with indigenous peoples and experts in the area of international investment law and human rights.

5. This research indicates that there are significant impacts on indigenous peoples' rights as a result of the international investment regime, in addition to the impacts of the investments themselves. These impacts are manifested in the subordination of those rights to investor protections, generally as a result of a phenomenon referred to as regulatory chill and serious deficiencies in the dispute resolution process instituted by the investment regime.

6. The present report is the second of three that the Rapporteur dedicates to this issue. She has previously introduced the topic and touched on some of the impacts of international investment agreements on indigenous peoples' rights and the more systemic issues associated with the international investment law regime. In the present report, she seeks to further contextualize and examine those impacts by focusing on cases involving such agreements and rights. In her final report, she will reflect on the standards of protections that those agreements afford and contextualize them in the light of developments in international human rights law and the sustainable development agenda as they pertain to indigenous peoples.

7. In doing so, the Special Rapporteur seeks to promote coherence in international investment law and international human rights law and ensure that State fulfilment of duties pertaining to indigenous peoples' rights is not obstructed by protections afforded to investors.

B. Overview of international investment agreements

8. The international investment regime consists of 3,268 international investment agreements, comprising almost 3,000 bilateral investment treaties and more than 300 investment chapters of bilateral or regional free trade agreements. These agreements, between States, provide legal protections to investors of "home States" for their investments in "host States."

9. International investment agreements tend to follow a standard format, with provisions on: prohibiting expropriation or "regulatory taking" without compensation; national treatment or non-discrimination, meaning that foreign investors are treated no less favourably than domestic investors; "most favoured nation treatment," requiring the same standard of treatment available to other foreign investors; "fair and equitable treatment," or "minimum international standards of treatment," which can be very broad in scope, generally including protection of investors' "legitimate expectations"; and full protection and security for investments.

10. International investment agreements also typically provide investors with access to an investor-State dispute settlement process, whereby investors can bring arbitration cases against a host State for alleged failures to protect their investments in accordance with the provisions in the agreements. There is generally no obligation to exhaust domestic remedies or appeals system, and minimal transparency or opportunities for third-party intervention. Awards are enforceable through the acquisition of a State's overseas assets, are not subject to any financial limitations and can run into billions of dollars.

11. According to the United Nations Conference on Trade and Development (UNCTAD), cancellations or alleged violations of contracts and revocation or denial of licences are among the most commonly challenged State actions, with approximately 30 per cent of all settlements relating to the extractive and energy industries, which account for most new investments. The majority of such cases are taken against States with significant populations of indigenous peoples in whose territories the exploited mineral, energy or forest resources are located.

12. Recent years have seen a growing number of megaregional free trade agreements, with scopes that extend far beyond trade to include investment and regulatory dimensions, essentially forming global economic structural agreements. The most recent is the Trans-Pacific Partnership. Its investment chapter, containing many of the standard provisions in the model bilateral investment treaty of the United States of America, is one of its most controversial features. It has been

widely criticized, including by Special Rapporteurs, for limiting democratic space by effectively transferring public decision-making powers over economic, social and cultural governance to corporate actors.

IV. Indigenous peoples' rights

A. Overview

13. Under international human rights law, indigenous peoples are recognized as peoples vested with the right to self-determination, as affirmed in the International Covenant on Civil and Political Rights, the International Covenant on Economic, Social and Cultural Rights and the International Convention on the Elimination of All Forms of Racial Discrimination, by virtue of which they are entitled to determine their own social, cultural and economic development. The rights affirmed under those treaties, which have been widely adopted, take on particular characteristics when interpreted in the light of indigenous peoples' distinct realities, needs, world views and historical contexts and the *jus cogens* prohibition of racial discrimination. The United Nations Declaration on the Rights of Indigenous Peoples offers the clearest articulation and interpretation of those rights as they pertain to indigenous peoples.

14. This is reflected in the jurisprudence of the United Nations human rights treaty bodies, which instruct States to use the United Nations Declaration on the Rights of Indigenous Peoples when implementing their treaty obligations. The treaties have also been interpreted by national and regional courts and commissions in Latin America and Africa in the light of the provisions of the Declaration and the International Labour Organization (ILO) Indigenous and Tribal Peoples Convention, 1989 (No. 169), indicating the universal applicability of those instruments and signalling the emergence of customary international law in the area of indigenous peoples' rights.

15. The concept of "indigenous peoples" is not defined under international law. However, its generally accepted characteristics include: self-identification as an indigenous people; the existence of and desire to maintain a special relationship with ancestral territories; distinct social, economic or political systems from mainstream society, which may be reflected in language, culture, beliefs and customary law; and a historically non-dominant position within society. This applies irrespective of State nomenclature.

16. Indigenous peoples' territorial and property rights are *sui generis* in nature, encompassing the territories and resources that they have traditionally owned, occupied or otherwise used or acquired, including the right to own, use, develop and control resources. Those collective rights exist irrespective of State titles and are premised on: their status as self-determining peoples entitled to the lands and resources necessary for their physical and cultural survival; their customary land tenure regimes; and long-term possession of ancestral territories.

17. Consequently, States are obliged to establish culturally appropriate mechanisms to enable the effective participation of indigenous peoples in all decision-making processes that directly affect their rights. To ensure this, international human rights law standards require good-faith consultations to obtain their free, prior and informed consent. This requirement applies prior to the enactment of legislative or administrative measures, the development of investment plans or the issuance of concessions, licences or permits for projects in or near their territories.

18. Human rights bodies have consequently clarified that economic growth or national development cannot be used as a basis for non-consensual infringements on the territorial and cultural rights of indigenous peoples. This is reinforced by the *erga omnes* nature of the right of all peoples to self-determination, the prohibition of racial discrimination and the fact that their protection is a matter of public interest.

B. Recognition and enforcement

19. Indigenous peoples are among the most marginalized and discriminated against groups in the world. The international framework protecting their rights emerged largely in response to that reality. Significant advances have been made in some jurisdictions in relation to the recognition of their rights, in particular in Latin America, and varying degrees of recognition are afforded in the domestic regulatory frameworks of other countries. However, throughout much of Asia and Africa, the rights recognized as pertaining to groups that meet the characteristics of indigenous peoples under international law tend to fall short of those recognized under international human rights law standards and, in many cases, the international law category "indigenous peoples" is not officially recognized.

20. Even in countries where international human rights law standards have been incorporated into domestic law, further steps are necessary to adjust the law to fully meet these international standards and ensure their enforcement. The associated "implementation gap" between law and practice is often symptomatic of power imbalances between vulnerable indigenous peoples and powerful political elites who seek to benefit from exploitation of resources found in their territories.

21. This power imbalance is generally mirrored in the relationship between institutions established to protect indigenous peoples' rights and those responsible for promoting and facilitating natural resource exploitation. Therefore, even in jurisdictions with advanced legal frameworks, deep-rooted structural discrimination and vested interests can render ineffective the legal protections afforded to indigenous peoples.

C. Business and indigenous peoples' rights

22. The Guiding Principles on Business and Human Rights affirm the independent corporate responsibility to respect indigenous peoples' rights as recognized in international human rights law. This responsibility is bolstered by the incorporation of the Principles into standards, such as the Organization for Economic Cooperation and Development (OECD) Guidelines on Multinational Corporations. A growing body of standards exists in relation to investment that affects indigenous peoples' lands, including performance standards of most international financial institutions, such as the International Finance Corporation, and apply to private banks that adhere to the Equator Principles, which require clients to respect indigenous peoples' rights, including free, prior and informed consent. The World Bank has included the requirement for such consent in its draft revised policy. However, other banks, such as the African Development Bank and the Brazilian Development Bank, have yet to develop safeguard policies for indigenous peoples.

23. The standards of a growing number of multi-stakeholder initiatives include respect for indigenous peoples' rights, as affirmed under the United Nations Declaration on the Rights of Indigenous Peoples, and consequently require free, prior and informed consent prior to approving or undertaking an investment. Some extractive industry bodies and companies sourcing palm oil, sugar, soy and other resources have also made policy progress towards the recognition of rights recognized in the Declaration, including the requirement for such consent, as has the United Nations Global Compact. Those developments reflect the general acknowledgement by transnational corporations of their responsibility to respect indigenous peoples' rights.

24. However, implementation of those commitments remains poor, and issues remain surrounding the interpretation of indigenous peoples' rights, in particular the right to give or withhold free, prior and informed consent.

25. Tackling the underlying issue of corporate participation in violations of indigenous peoples' rights would contribute significantly to addressing the current imbalance and incoherence in international law. Mechanisms have been proposed to address business and human rights, such as arbitration tribunals dedicated to providing a remedy for affected peoples and individuals. Discussions at the intergovernmental level on a treaty on business and human rights have also raised many of the issues witnessed in the context of promoting investor obligations under international investment agreements.

V. Impacts on indigenous peoples' rights of investments, international investment agreements and investor-State dispute settlements

A. Impact of investments on indigenous peoples

26. The Special Rapporteur's research reveals an alarming number of cases in the mining, oil and gas, hydroelectric and agribusiness sectors whereby foreign investment projects have resulted in serious violations of indigenous peoples' land, self-governance and cultural rights. Those violations, which can extend to crimes against humanity, have been addressed extensively in the recommendations and jurisprudence of international and regional human rights bodies.

27. Typically, the host States involved employ economic development policies aimed at the exploitation of energy, mineral, land or other resources that are predominantly located in the territories of indigenous peoples. The government agencies responsible for implementing those policies regard such lands and resources as available for unhindered exploitation and actively promote them as such abroad to generate capital inflows. Recognition of indigenous peoples' rights in

the domestic legal framework is either non-existent, inadequate or not enforced. Where they exist, institutions mandated to uphold indigenous peoples' rights are politically weak, unaccountable or underfunded. Indigenous peoples lack access to remedies in home and host States and are forced to mobilize, leading to criminalization, violence and deaths. They experience profound human rights violations as a result of impacts on their lands, livelihoods, cultures, development options and governance structures, which, in some cases, threaten their very cultural and physical survival. Projects are stalled and there is a trend towards investor-State dispute settlements related to fair and equitable treatment, full protection and security and expropriation.

28. Despite significant developments in the recognition of indigenous peoples' rights and safeguards under international human rights law, investment in those sectors is generating "increasing and ever more widespread effects on indigenous peoples' lives" as the legal vacuum arising from the lack of recognition or enforcement of their land rights facilitates arbitrary land expropriation, enabling national and local officials to make those lands available for investment projects. At the same time, the vast majority of those lands are protected under international investment agreements, and related investor-State dispute settlement disputes in agribusiness and extractive sectors are expected in Africa and Asia, while in Latin America there is a growing number of claims concerning settlements in relation to such activities in or near indigenous territories.

29. Special Rapporteurs, United Nations treaty bodies and the Inter-American Commission on Human Rights have made numerous recommendations urging home States to adopt regulatory measures for companies domiciled in their jurisdictions aimed at preventing, sanctioning and remedying violations of indigenous peoples' rights abroad for which those companies are responsible or in which they are complicit.

30. The Inter-American Commission on Human Rights has noted that addressing related jurisdictional issues may require negotiations between States during bilateral or other agreements and before foreign companies are accepted for business.

B. Impacts of international investment agreements and investor-State dispute settlements

31. International investment agreements can have serious impacts on indigenous peoples' rights as a result of three main interrelated issues: (a) the failure to adequately address human rights in the preambles and substantive provisions of such agreements; (b) the actual or perceived threat of enforcement of investor protections under investor-State dispute settlement arbitration, leading to regulatory chill; and (c) the exclusion of indigenous peoples from the drafting, negotiation and approval processes of agreements and from the settlement of disputes.

32. These potential impacts of international investment agreements must be considered in the light of the current inadequate recognition and lack of enforcement of indigenous peoples' rights in domestic legal frameworks. Such agreements, and investor-State dispute settlements, tend to block necessary advances and developments in domestic legal frameworks as they relate to investment activity. They limit the State's will and freedom to impose and enforce human rights obligations on transnational corporations and to progressively realize human rights. By entrenching investor protections, they also entrench rights-denying aspects of extant legislative frameworks and contribute to preventing the needed reform from a human rights perspective.

33. International Human Rights Law and international investment agreements play significant roles in governing the behaviour of host States in relation to resource extraction in or near indigenous peoples' territories. Agreements serve to protect and regulate property rights of investors related to the exploitation or use of land and resources. Those rights can come into direct conflict with the pre-existing — but not necessarily formally recognized and titled — inherent customary law and possession-based property rights of indigenous peoples protected under international human rights law.

34. International Human Rights Law recognizes that in certain contexts restrictions can be placed on indigenous peoples' property rights. However, to be legitimate, such restrictions must be: (a) established by law; (b) necessary; (c) proportional to their purpose; and (d) non-restrictive to the peoples' survival. It affirms that, in the context of indigenous peoples' property rights, these conditions imply that good-faith consultations must be held to obtain free, prior and informed consent before any measures affecting those property rights can be considered legitimate.

35. Inadequate respect and protections for indigenous peoples' land and free, prior and informed consent rights when granting rights to investors over their territories are the root causes for subsequent and broader violations of indigenous peoples' rights. In such contexts, international investment agreements that fail to recognize international human rights law obligations contribute to the subordination of indigenous peoples' rights to investor protections, as those protections become an obstacle to future recognition of indigenous peoples' pre-existing rights.

36. In order to address the perverse situation that arises when indigenous peoples are prevented from realizing their land and resource rights owing to protections afforded to investors, a former Special Rapporteur has stressed:

That resolving [indigenous peoples'] land rights issues should at all times take priority over commercial development. There needs to be recognition not only in law but also in practice of the prior right of traditional communities. The idea of prior right being granted to a mining or other business company rather than to a community that has held and cared for the land over generations must be stopped, as it brings the whole system of protection of human rights of indigenous peoples into disrepute.

37. International investment agreements that have facilitated and protected investments in indigenous territories are often accompanied by the deployment of military and private security services. The effects of this are a major concern in many jurisdictions, in particular those with histories of low-intensity conflict. As a result, under international human rights law, and as reflected in article 30 of the United Nations Declaration on the Rights of Indigenous Peoples, military activities should not take place in the lands or territories of indigenous peoples, unless justified by a relevant public interest or otherwise freely agreed to or requested by the indigenous peoples concerned. However, such security presences are effectively mandated under certain existing interpretations of the provisions of such agreements on full protection and security, leading to a direct conflict between international investment law and international human rights law.

38. In some cases, international investment agreements, and measures deemed necessary to facilitate their implementation, have triggered large-scale conflict and significant loss of life. On 1 January 1994, when the North American Free Trade Agreement came into effect and triggered privatization of indigenous peoples' communal lands, the Zapatista National Liberation Army, composed of indigenous peoples from Chiapas, initiated an armed rebellion, calling the Agreement a "death sentence" for indigenous peoples.

39. Some 14 years later, the free trade agreement between the United States and Peru was used as a pretext for a series of neo-liberal legislative decrees, 10 of which had seriously negative implications for Amazonian indigenous peoples' territorial rights. The refusal of the Government of Peru to accept proposals made by indigenous peoples triggered mobilization, resulting in the tragic deaths of 30 people when the military was deployed in response.

40. Consideration of investor-State dispute settlement claims where indigenous peoples' rights are involved affords the opportunity to assess the practices of tribunals, the arguments made by States and investors and the space available for indigenous peoples' participation and the ways in which international investment agreements can come into conflict with international human rights law.

C. Examples of investor-State dispute settlements involving indigenous peoples' rights

41. In the International Centre for Settlement of Investment Disputes case *Burlington Resources Inc. v. Ecuador* (2010) the oil and gas company claimed that Ecuador had failed to meet its obligations to give its operations full protection and security against indigenous peoples' opposition and at times violent protests. The State argued that the indigenous peoples' actions had been a case of force majeure and did not address the issue of indigenous peoples' rights in its defence. The security aspect of the claim was rejected on procedural grounds without addressing the indigenous rights issues. The case was also subject to parallel consideration by the Inter-American Commission on Human Rights and the Inter-American Court of Human Rights. In 2012, the Court ruled that the failure to consult the indigenous peoples and obtain their free, prior and informed consent, and the use of force by the State, had put the indigenous peoples' survival at risk.

42. In *Chevron v. Ecuador* (2014), the company took a series of arbitration cases to avoid paying damages awarded by Ecuadorian courts in 2011. The $8.6 billion award followed a class action suit addressing harms suffered by indigenous peoples as a result of environmental contamination. The case demonstrates the extremely broad and potentially indigenous

rights-denying interpretation of "investment" as including a lawsuit in domestic courts and payments to affected people arising from the lack of remediation. Precautionary measures were subsequently sought from the Inter-American Commission on Human Rights seeking to prevent any action arising from the investor-State dispute settlement award that would contravene, undermine, or threaten the human rights of the concerned indigenous communities.

43. In *Von Pezold and Border Timbers v. Zimbabwe* (2015), the company claimed expropriation under the bilateral investment treaties between Germany and Zimbabwe and between Switzerland and Zimbabwe in the context of the State's taking of land. Four indigenous communities, whose traditional lands were the subject of proceedings, submitted an amicus submission claiming that the State and the company had human rights obligations towards them. In its preliminary order of June 2012, the International Centre for Settlement of Investment Disputes tribunal acknowledged their claims to the lands and that its determinations may well have an impact on the interests of the indigenous communities. However, the tribunal rejected their amicus submission on the grounds that: (a) the communities and their chiefs lacked "independence," as they were associated with people affiliated to the Government, and therefore the claimants may be unfairly prejudiced by their participation; (b) it was not in a position to decide if they were indigenous or not and lacked the competence to interpret indigenous peoples' rights; (c) it was not persuaded that consideration of international human rights law obligations, including, article 26 of the United Nations Declaration on the Rights of Indigenous Peoples was part of its mandate, and rules of general international law did not necessarily extend to international human rights law; and (d) neither the State nor the company had raised indigenous rights issues. It concluded that the putative rights of the indigenous communities as "indigenous peoples" under international human rights law was a matter outside of the scope of the dispute.

44. In *Glamis Gold v. United States* (2009), an arbitration panel found against the company, which had been refused access to a sacred area of the Quechan tribal nation. The decision hinged on the tribunal's position that its role was to assess if the customary international law standard of fair and equitable treatment had been breached and not to assess if the State had fairly balanced the competing rights of the Quechan nation and the company. It held that the State had been justified in relying upon the opinion of the professionals it had engaged and that, as the investor's expectations had not been induced by the State in a quasi-contractual manner, they did not trigger a treaty breach. The decision also pointed to the significance of the highly regulated environment in California with respect to environmental measures in general and mineral exploration in particular, which should have tempered the investor's expectations. The tribunal accepted the Quechan amicus submission but did not engage with its argument that international human rights law as it pertained to indigenous peoples was applicable in the case.

45. In *Grand River Enterprise Six Nations, Ltd. v. the United States* (2011), a tobacco company owned by members of the Canadian Haudenosaunee nations challenged measure taken by the United States. One of the issues raised by the company was the absence of prior consultation in relation to some of the measures. While finding that no expropriation had occurred, the tribunal stated that it may well be that there does exist a principle of customary international law requiring governmental authorities to consult indigenous peoples as collectivities on governmental policies or actions significantly affecting them. As the enterprise was owned by individuals, the tribunal held that it did not have to address the issue of prior consultation. It did, however, add that a good case could be made that consultations should have occurred with governments of the native American tribes or nations in the United States, whose members and sovereign interests could, and apparently are, being affected by the measures to regulate commerce in tobacco.

46. In the Permanent Court of Arbitration case *South American Silver Mining v. the Plurinational State of Bolivia*, the company is seeking $387 million for the alleged expropriation of 10 mining concessions and violations of fair and equitable treatment, pursuant to the bilateral investment treaty between the United Kingdom of Great Britain and Northern Ireland and the Plurinational State of Bolivia. The company holds that it made legitimate efforts with the communities to achieve an overall consent and that opposition to the project is from a small group of illegal miners and certain indigenous organizations, with the Government fomenting conflict. It argues that the communities have repeatedly requested it to move forward with the project, and alleges that the Plurinational State of Bolivia failed to provide full protection and security, noting its "patently unreasonable" decision not to prosecute indigenous leaders, given the implications for its investment.

47. The Plurinational State of Bolivia responded that: (a) it had acted in the public interest and had been justified in reverting ownership to the State in accordance with the principles of proportionality and necessity, to avoid security con-

cerns arising out of indigenous peoples' opposition to the project and to restore public order; (b) it was enforcing domestic legislation that should have tempered the company's legitimate expectations, as the State made no commitment to stability; (c) the project violates rights recognized in the United Nations Declaration on the Rights of Indigenous Peoples; (d) the company had attempted to fabricate consent in total disregard for the right to self-government of the concerned indigenous peoples; (e) the bilateral investment treaty had no applicable law clause, so there should be "systemic interpretation" in accordance with article 31 (3) (c) of the Vienna Convention on the law of treaties, including human rights obligations towards indigenous peoples under national and international law, as this would be consistent with the evolving nature of standards around fair and equitable treatment, full protection and security, arbitrariness and expropriation; and (f) customary international law recognizes the primacy of human rights over investor protections, citing the ruling of the Inter-American Court of Human Rights in *Sawhoyamaxa v. Paraguay* and Article 103 of the Charter of the United Nations.

48. In response, the company contends that: (a) the State failed to show how the systemic interpretation would result in having to degrade the protections granted to the company under the treaty to uphold the putative rights of indigenous communities under international law; (b) the United Nations Declaration on the Rights of Indigenous Peoples, OECD Guidelines and the Guiding Principles on Business and Human Rights are non-binding instruments, while the ILO Indigenous and Tribal Peoples Convention, 1989 (No. 169), the Inter-American Commission on Human Rights and the jurisprudence of the Inter-American Court of Human Rights are not binding on the United Kingdom, and consequently they are not rules of international law applicable to relations between the parties; (d) the State failed to demonstrate that protection of indigenous peoples' rights had advanced to the level of "*erga omnes* obligations" or why human rights trump investor protections.

49. The company invoked the view of Canada in *Grand River Enterprise Six Nations, Ltd. v. the United States* (see para. 48) that the ILO Indigenous and Tribal Peoples Convention, 1989 (No. 169) and the United Nations Declaration on the Rights of Indigenous Peoples do not form part of customary international law, and the decisions of previous tribunals in *Glamis Gold v. United States* (see para. 47) not to rule on the applicability of indigenous rights and in *Von Pezold and Border Timbers v. Zimbabwe* (see para. 46) that indigenous rights do not fall under the scope of bilateral investment treaties. The company holds that an exception maintaining preference for indigenous peoples' rights over investor protections would be necessary to "degrade" investor protections and points to the standard Maori exception employed in the bilateral investment treaties of New Zealand as evidence of this.

50. In the International Centre for Settlement of Investment Disputes case *Bear Creek Mining Corp. v. Peru*, the company is claiming over $500 million for alleged indirect expropriation, lack of fair and equitable treatment, discrimination and lack of full protection and security for its presumptive mining rights at the Santa Ana concession, under the free trade agreement between Peru and Canada. The claim was made following indigenous peoples' protests, which gave rise to the withdrawal of its mining concession.

51. According to the company, the protests, some of which turned violent, were politically motivated involving an anti-foreign and anti-mining movement that gained support from the Aymara indigenous people. It claims that, rather than assess the social and environmental conditions, the Government of Peru acted out of political expediency and capitulated to extreme violence. The company states that it intended to comply with environmental permitting and corporate social responsibility and had consulted the indigenous communities that supported the project and that would benefit significantly as a result of employment and revenues.

52. The State's response addressed the nature of the investment, the necessity of its actions and the absence of adequate consultation and free, prior and informed consent. It argued that the project had not constituted an investment as permissions to proceed were still pending, including the approval of the environmental social impact assessment. Consequently, the company had never held rights to mine. The indigenous peoples' protests had paralyzed major cities in Puno, Peru, for more than a month and the violent social unrest had been due to deep-rooted indigenous community opposition to mining activities and not, as the company alleged, "puppet shows staged by politicians" or "political theatre." It states that the revocation of the concession had therefore been a non-discriminatory and necessary exercise of its police powers aimed at guaranteeing public safety.

53. Addressing the consultation and consent requirements, the State argues that the company had been responsible for engaging with and learning the concerns of the indigenous peoples affected by the project but had failed to consult with

and obtain the consent of all the affected indigenous peoples and communities, as it had been required to do under relevant international human rights law standards, Peruvian law, practices recommended by the Government of Canada and the International Council on Mining and Metals guidelines. In that regard, it argues that Peruvian law serves to implement the ILO Indigenous and Tribal Peoples Convention, 1989 (No. 169), which requires prior consultation and in practice is a "consent" requirement. It states that it was incumbent on the company not only to go through the motions of consulting with affected indigenous communities, and that it must in fact obtain prior approval as, without that approval or consent, the project cannot succeed. It also states that the company would not have obtained consent had the months of violent protests in opposition to it been predicted. Instead, the company's support had come from a handful of communities in the area of influence of the project and not from the neighbouring communities that would also be affected by the project and who opposed it. This selective and divisive approach to consultation served to fuel discontent and conflict with cross border implications.

54. The Colombia Centre on Sustainable Investment submitted an application to file a written submission in the case, but was denied by the tribunal. The amicus submission had pointed to the inconsistency between the investor's understanding of what is meant by "an investment" and the definition in the free trade agreement. Furthermore, it had raised the consequent non-applicability of the fair and equitable treatment standard and the failure to demonstrate legitimate expectations, even if that standard had been applied. Similarly, it had pointed to the central role that the requirement to seek and obtain free, prior and informed consent should play in the assessment of the facts and the determination of the award, and the urgency of ensuring compliance with this requirement, in the light of the extensive mining-related social conflict throughout Peru. According to the submission, providing compensation to the company would be equivalent to granting it a right to exploitation and would disregard indigenous peoples' rights.

D. Observations on investor-State dispute settlements

55. A number of observations can be made with regard to the above cases. Firstly, in all of the cases where an award was issued, international human rights law as it pertains to indigenous peoples' rights was not considered a source of applicable law. With the exception of *Glamis Gold v. United States*, indigenous peoples' rights and interests were effectively ignored by tribunals and considered immaterial to proceedings, despite the fact that violations of their rights and efforts to assert them had been core issues underpinning the disputes in question, and the decisions could have had potentially profound impacts on their rights and well-being.

56. The decision in that case is regarded as forward-looking in terms of ensuring respect for the protection of indigenous peoples' sacred spaces and demonstrating that awards can be sensitive to and inclusive of indigenous peoples' issues. The tribunal's decision that a 50 per cent reduction in the projected earnings, arising from a measure aimed at protecting indigenous peoples' sacred places, did not constitute indirect expropriation and that the measures did not constitute a "manifestly arbitrary" denial of justice, supports this view.

57. However, the tribunal essentially ignored the position articulated in the Quechan nation amicus submission that international human rights law as it pertained to the rights arising in the case should be considered applicable law. A related critique is that the tribunal relied heavily on the robust legislative history in California relating to the environment in the determination of what constituted an investor's legitimate expectation, thereby setting a dangerous precedent in jurisdictions that do not have such a history.

58. How a tribunal would respond to such an argument is unknown. An alternative argument could be that, in States where the rule of law is weak, legislative reform to respect human rights is inevitable once the political environment matures sufficiently. As State obligations in relation to indigenous peoples exist under international human rights law, a reasonable investor should expect that they will eventually be implemented, as any expectation that they will not is blatantly unjust and lacks legitimacy. A clearer position on behalf of the tribunal, that a State maintains the right to regulate in order to protect its indigenous peoples' rights, as recognized under international human rights law, would have avoided this ambiguity.

59. One reason provided for the failure of tribunals to address indigenous rights was the State's failure to raise human rights issues in its arguments, a view also expressed by tribunals in other cases. This contrasts with the pending cases of *Bear Creek Mining Corp. v. Peru* and *South American Silver Mining v. the Plurinational State of Bolivia*, in which the States place significant emphasis on indigenous peoples' rights, in particular consultation and free, prior and informed consent

rights, as meriting consideration by the tribunals. This development points to a potential synergy between affording protection to indigenous peoples' rights in domestic regulation and international investment agreements and reducing the risk of potentially costly lawsuits in the context of measures affecting investor protections.

60. These cases also raise important issues regarding corporate and State responsibilities in relation to consultations seeking to establish the free, prior and informed consent of indigenous peoples, and the relationship that such consent has in establishing an investment over which an investor can claim protection. In doing so, the cases give tribunals an opportunity to address an issue of fundamental importance to indigenous peoples' rights and to ensuring greater coherence between the international investment law and international human rights law. An overarching issue that arises relates to the role of corporate human rights due diligence in determining legitimate expectations in contexts where social conflict and rights violations appear inevitable in the absence of free, prior and informed consent.

61. The cases also illustrate the frequent tensions that arise between the international human rights law and international investment law regimes. In *Burlington Resources Inc. v. Ecuador*, the contrast is striking between the findings of the Inter-American Court of Human Rights that the State used unnecessary and excessive force against the indigenous peoples, thereby threatening their existence, and the claim by the company involved in the investor-State dispute settlement that the State had not used sufficient force to protect its investment from those indigenous peoples, with neither the company nor the State seeing fit to address indigenous peoples' rights in their arguments.

62. The number of investor-State dispute settlement cases involving indigenous peoples' rights is growing, a fact that could be related to the speculative nature of such settlements, which encourages investors, in particular risk-taking extractive companies, to seek ever broader interpretations of the protections surrounding international investment agreements. Similarly, the expectation among risk-adverse States that the trend will continue reduces the probability that States will take urgently needed measures to recognize, protect, respect and fulfil indigenous peoples' rights, including by addressing historical injustices in relation to land claims.

63. The Inter-American Court of Human Rights decision in *Sawhoyamaxa indigenous community v. Paraguay* is illustrative of this. The State argued that it could not implement land restitution programmes aimed at guaranteeing indigenous peoples' rights because of protections afforded to investors under its bilateral investment treaty with Germany. The Court ruled that the treaty had to be interpreted in the light of the State's human rights obligations and that the taking of land for restitution to indigenous people could be justified as a "public purpose or interest." While it is one of the few cases that has attempted to reconcile obligations under international investment law and international human rights law, it offers no guidance on the extent to which the investor should be compensated or what considerations should determine when compensation is or is not required. This points to the need for further guidance from human rights bodies on these matters.

64. The limited and inconsistent role that tribunals attribute in their deliberations to amicus submissions of indigenous peoples also emerges from the cases. The basis in *Von Pezold and Border Timbers v. Zimbabwe* for rejecting the amicus submission raises a number of profound concerns should it guide future tribunals, as South American Silver suggests it should.

65. The notion that indigenous peoples must demonstrate "independence" from the State in relation to matters pertaining to their rights is inconsistent with the State's role as the duty-bearer in relation to those rights. Equally alarming, and contrary to international human rights law, is the tribunal's dismissal of the fundamental role of self-identification in the determination of what constitutes an indigenous people.

66. The tribunal essentially distanced itself from any damage that its decision could have on indigenous rights, acknowledging that its ruling could affect those rights but holding that they were outside the scope of the dispute and not part of the applicable law. This amounts to the subordination of indigenous peoples' rights to investor protections, with no option provided for participation or appeal. Such arguments go to the core of the legitimacy crisis that the international investment law system is facing. Justifications based on a lack of competence in relation to indigenous rights are further evidence of the system's deficiencies.

67. All of the above reflects the fact that, at its core, the investor-State dispute settlement system is adversarial and based on private law, in which affected third-party actors, such as indigenous peoples, have no standing and extremely

limited opportunities to participate. Amicus submissions and participations at the request of States are grossly inadequate in a context where States and investors are involved in causing and benefiting from harm to indigenous peoples' rights.

68. In their responses to questionnaires, a number of States pointed to the approach adopted by the European Union, which is to a degree reflected in chapter 8 of the Comprehensive Economic and Trade Agreement between Canada and the European Union, as a step towards reforming dispute resolution systems. Among its improved features is a revised model for appointing State party-nominated arbitrations, eliminating conflicts of interest arising from arbitrators who also act as council and expert, and gaining access to a full appellate review after awards have been rendered. The approach of Brazil in its recent bilateral investment treaties, which do not provide access to investor-State dispute settlements and instead rely on a combination of mediation and diplomatic approaches and State to State arbitration, is also noteworthy.

69. In addition to acknowledging the need to reform dispute resolution systems, States emphasized the need to guarantee the regulatory space necessary for the realization of indigenous peoples' rights, including the requirement for prior consultation with the objective of free, prior and informed consent. The responses suggest that the intent and expectation of home and host States when entering into international investment agreements was not to place limitations on their ability to fulfil indigenous peoples' rights, the presumption being that the State maintains the right to regulate without facing compensation demands and that, where necessary, protections afforded to investors must be balanced in a proportionate manner against the duty to protect indigenous peoples' rights. The Special Rapporteur encourages more States to respond to her questionnaires, which are available in English, French and Spanish and will inform her final report on the issue.

VI. Trans-Pacific Partnership

70. In 2015, the Trans-Pacific Partnership agreement was signed by 12 countries from three continents that, together, account for a large part of global trade. Of those countries, 11 have significant populations of indigenous peoples, a growing number of which are negatively affected by large-scale foreign investment projects in their territories. Those peoples have expressed their concerns in relation to the lack of protections for their rights vis-à-vis those of foreign investors, and the imbalance in remedies. They have also criticized the absence of consultation in the negotiation of the Partnership and the lack of any human rights impact assessments. As pointed out by the Waitangi Tribunal, the failure to adequately consult on the Partnership "harms the relationship [with indigenous peoples] and increases the probability of a low-trust and adversarial relationship going forward." In that regard, indigenous peoples are demanding good-faith consultations prior to ratification as they fear that, unless adequate protections are included, the Partnership will facilitate projects and activities that lead to further conflict and serious violation of rights to lands, territories and natural resources, including their rights to traditional knowledge.

71. The Trans-Pacific Partnership includes no reference to human rights. While it does refer to the right to regulate in relation to "environmental, health or other regulatory objectives," it qualifies this by holding that measures have to be "consistent with" its investment chapter, effectively reducing the scope of this right to that determined by expansive interpretations of broad investment protections.

72. The Maori of New Zealand are the only indigenous people addressed in the exception chapter. The provision permits "favourable treatment to Maori" and excludes interpretation of the Treaty of Waitangi from investor-State dispute settlements. However, the Maori regard the exception to be inadequate. Having expressed its concerns in relation to the potential impacts of investor-State dispute settlements, the Waitangi Tribunal recommended that the Maori participate in the appointment of arbitrators where their rights are affected.

73. Implicit in the Maori Trans-Pacific Partnership exception is the recognition that their rights, and by extension those of other indigenous peoples, can be negatively affected by investor protections under the Partnership and its investor-State dispute settlement mechanism. So too is the fact that those protections afforded to the Maori under the exception are essentially denied to all other affected indigenous peoples owing to the absence of exceptions for them.

74. One of the issues that indigenous peoples have highlighted in relation to the Partnership is its impact on their control over their traditional knowledge, as the rights of corporations that hold intellectual property rights are strengthened

in the relevant chapter of the Partnership, while traditional knowledge rights that fall outside of the intellectual property regime are afforded no protection. Experience to date demonstrates that, in the absence of adequate safeguards, traditional knowledge can be commercialized. Similar concerns exist in relation to genetic resources and biodiversity.

75. An exception, allowing parties to take measures in relation to traditional knowledge in accordance with their international obligations, is included in the exception chapter, but in practice it can be ignored or interpreted to have little relevance by arbitrators. Requirements under international human rights law and international environmental law in relation to equitable benefit sharing and a general requirement for free, prior and informed consent of indigenous peoples were not included in the Trans-Pacific Partnership, with consent only referenced where national law already requires it.

76. The effects of the Trans-Pacific Partnership, whereby investor rights are entrenched and indigenous rights are constrained, could have a particularly profound impact on indigenous peoples in the many resource-rich Partnership countries, given the huge number of extractive industry, forestry, palm oil and energy companies based in Australia, Canada, Malaysia, New Zealand and the United States. These resources are often in areas of ongoing dispute and conflict between indigenous peoples and foreign investors.

VII. Conclusions and recommendations

A. Conclusions

77. Foreign investment can contribute to economic growth and development. However, there is a long-standing debate as to the conditions necessary for developing countries to benefit from such investment, and the extent to which international investment agreements facilitate those conditions.

78. Modern international public order requires development to be sustainable and consistent with human rights and democratic principles. While some initial steps have been taken to attempt to incorporate those policy objectives into international investment agreements, through reference to the unencumbered right of the State to regulate in the public interest in the preambles and substantive provisions of model bilateral investment treaties, references to human rights in those agreements are rare and the broader response of the international investment law regime to date has been inadequate. Its legitimacy continues to be questioned as a result.

79. The research that the Special Rapporteur conducted in preparing the present report, including workshops and questionnaires, indicates that foreign and domestic investment has a serious impact on indigenous peoples' rights, even in the absence of international investment agreements. Guaranteeing indigenous peoples' rights will therefore require not only reforms within the international investment law regime, but also far more proactive engagement on the part of States in terms of realizing their human rights obligations. However, her research also indicates that such agreements can, and in a growing number of contexts do, compound, contribute to and exacerbate those serious impacts.

80. As concluded by the Waitangi Tribunal in the context of the Trans-Pacific Partnership, even when an exception is included with the intention of protecting indigenous peoples' rights:

> We are not in a position to reach firm conclusions on the extent to which investor-State dispute settlements under the Trans-Pacific Partnership may prejudice Maori Treaty rights and interests, but we do consider it a serious question worthy of further scrutiny and debate and dialogue between the Treaty partners. We do not accept the Crown's argument that claimant fears in this regard are overstated.

81. Harmonizing international investment law with international human rights law is a fundamental precondition to addressing this legitimacy crisis, to respecting indigenous peoples' rights and to ensuring a coherent body of international law. By ensuring that international investment agreements do not restrict regulatory space, and by taking measures to protect indigenous peoples' rights in the context of investor activities, States can prevent costly investor-State dispute settlement cases and eliminate uncertainty around the limits that international investment law places on both State and indigenous peoples' sovereignty. In addition, by invoking international human rights law arguments in settlement disputes, States will increase the pressure on investors to conduct adequate human rights due diligence prior to initiating settlement disputes.

82. A synergy therefore exists between protecting the State's right to regulate in the public interest and ensuring the protection of indigenous peoples' rights, as recognizing indigenous peoples' rights provides a means through which States can limit the abrogation of control over decisions pertaining to natural resources to foreign investors and to tribunals charged with protecting their interests.

83. The Special Rapporteur believes that it is possible to develop a system of international investment law that reduces risk to indigenous peoples' rights and serves to benefit them and the State, while providing greater investment security to foreign investors. Both short- and longer-term reforms, at the level of international investment law and in domestic regulatory frameworks of home and host States, and in the policies, practices and obligations of investors, will be necessary in order to realize this.

84. Strong arguments exist for radically reforming the system of investor-State dispute settlements and to reform the investment dispute system. Mechanisms aimed at resolving disputes between investors and States that extend to affected communities and individuals through the use of fact-finding and mediation, and possibly through judicial powers, modelled on a body such as the Inter-American Court of Human Rights, have been proposed.

85. The outdated belief of States that they are in a position to guarantee security for investors while ignoring the human rights of indigenous peoples must be debunked. Investors must take responsibility for assessing the social and political risk associated with their investments. Otherwise, their expectations cannot be legitimate. Dispute resolution systems can no longer exclude those who are most affected by the disputes they purportedly resolve, otherwise their awards lack legitimacy. Full and effective participation of indigenous peoples in accordance with their right to give or withhold consent, together with ensuring equity of remedies, are key principles in moving beyond the current unbalanced and incoherent system. The Special Rapporteur encourages cooperation and creative thinking in that regard and looks forward to developing her final report, in which she will examine the interplay of investor protections and indigenous peoples' rights and consider how human rights and sustainable development approaches can help inform the future of international investment law.

B. Recommendations

Contents of international investment agreements

86. International investment agreements must include properly constructed clauses in relation to the right to regulate. These clauses should:

   (a) Avoid the use of qualifying language with respect to the right to regulate in the public interest;

   (b) Preserve that right in a manner explicitly consistent with the State duties to protect, respect and fulfil indigenous peoples' rights in accordance with international law obligations, including international human rights law;

   (c) Apply to all investor protection standards, such as fair and equitable treatment, full protection and security and indirect expropriation;

   (d) Be explicit that bona fide measures in the pursuit of human rights do not constitute a breach of international investment agreements and are non-compensable.

87. Mechanisms should be developed to amend existing international investment agreements to include the right to regulate and to mandate respect for human rights.

88. International investment agreements should include respect for human rights as a policy objective in their preambles.

89. Where the right to regulate is not sufficiently protected in international investment agreements, general exceptions for measures aimed at the promotion of equality and addressing long-term historic discrimination, or specific exceptions and investor-State dispute settlement carve-outs in relation to measures addressing indigenous peoples' rights, should be included. Specific exceptions should be developed in cooperation with indigenous peoples.

90. Jurisdiction clauses should prohibit claims taken:

(a) In relation to investments that do not comply with the law, including international human rights law;

(b) By shell or mailbox companies established in jurisdictions purely or primarily to take advantage of such protections in international investment agreements.

91. Investment protection, such as fair and equitable treatment, full protection and security and expropriation prohibitions, should only apply to established investments. They should not apply before consultations have been conducted to obtain indigenous peoples' free, prior and informed consent or before contractual agreements are entered into with the concerned indigenous peoples.

92. International investment agreements and interpretative text should entitle States to file counterclaims for affirmative relief arising from investor interference with their obligations under international human rights law.

Negotiation process

93. In accordance with the recommendations of the Special Rapporteur in her 2015 report to the General Assembly (A/70/301):

(a) Appropriate consultation procedures and mechanisms should be developed in cooperation with indigenous peoples in relation to the drafting, negotiation and approval of international investment agreements, and their right to consultation should be guaranteed prior to the ratification of the Trans-Pacific Partnership;

(b) Human rights impact assessments should be conducted of all trade and investment agreements, following the impact assessments carried out as part of the Guiding Principles on Business and Human Rights developed by the Special Rapporteur on the right to food.

94. States should negotiate international investment agreements in accordance with their international cooperation obligations under the International Covenant on Economic, Social and Cultural Rights and in keeping with the "clean hands" doctrine in relation to indigenous peoples' rights.

95. States should negotiate international investment agreements in accordance with their international cooperative on obligations under international human rights law, and in keeping with the "clean hands" doctrine, through the conduct of human rights impact assessments, appropriate due diligence and knowledge generation in relation to all potential impacts on indigenous peoples' rights, both at home and abroad.

Investment dispute settlement

96. Investment dispute settlement bodies addressing cases having an impact on indigenous peoples' rights should promote the convergence of human rights and international investment agreements by:

(a) Adopting approaches based on international human rights law when weighing up all rights related to a given dispute, addressing issues of necessity based on human rights imperatives such as the elimination of racial discrimination, applying the principle of proportionality and acknowledging the profound impacts of large-scale projects on indigenous peoples' self-determination rights and well-being;

(b) According due consideration to international human rights law when interpreting investment protections and the definition of an investment and ensuring that their decisions respect the State's duty to regulate under that law, irrespective of whether the right to regulate is explicitly affirmed in the relevant international investment agreements;

(c) Taking into account the human rights responsibilities of investors as outlined in the Guiding Principles on Business and Human Rights;

(d) Ensuring that applicable law includes all international human rights law treaties ratified by either State party, and the United Nations Declaration on the Rights of Indigenous Peoples as an interpretative guide for their application to indigenous peoples;

(e) Attaching weight to the legitimate expectations of States in relation to their ability to protect indigenous peoples' rights;

(f) Recognizing the right of intervention of the indigenous peoples concerned through amicus submissions and by according full consideration to their arguments;

(g) Interpreting investor State contract clauses, including stabilization clauses, covered by such agreements through umbrella clauses, in a manner that does not place limitations on the State's ability to protect indigenous peoples' rights;

(h) Being cognizant of foreign corporations' contribution to violations of indigenous peoples' rights and the jurisdictional, financial, cultural, technical, logistical and political obstacles facing indigenous peoples when attempting to hold them to account;

(i) Avoiding awards that contribute to regulatory chill in relation to indigenous peoples' rights or effectively endorse corporate involvement in indigenous rights' harms;

(j) Refusing to accept commercial confidentiality in all but the most extreme situations as a barrier to transparency in the context of regulatory actions related to fundamental human rights.

97. States should:

(a) Promote the above practices through interpretative text;

(b) Ratify the United Nations Convention on Transparency in Treaty-based Investor-State Arbitration;

(c) Appoint arbitrators with knowledge of indigenous peoples' rights and cooperate jointly to interpret relevant international investment agreements in relation to indigenous peoples' rights;

(d) Avoid including umbrella clauses in bilateral investment treaties;

(e) Strengthen their human rights arguments when responding to investor-State dispute settlement claims, emphasizing their duty to regulate in order to protect indigenous peoples' rights and the corporate responsibility to respect those rights.

Corporate obligations

98. International investment agreements should:

(a) Address the corporate responsibility to respect human rights, including the requirement to conduct human rights due diligence, and to prevent, mitigate and remedy human rights' harms in which they may be involved, in particular in relation to vulnerable groups such as indigenous peoples;

(b) Protect only bona fide investments. If evidence exists of inadequate human rights due diligence or corporate contribution to indigenous rights harms, there should be express provisions for the denial of the benefits of investor protection in terms of access to investor-State dispute settlements through a duty on tribunals to decline jurisdiction, with mechanisms to vitiate corporate rights in such contexts;

(c) Require public reporting by corporations in relation to the potential impact of their operations on indigenous peoples' rights and measures taken to prevent and mitigate such impacts.

99. States should consider:

(a) Incorporating the provisions of international investment agreements in relation to corporate responsibility into domestic law to enable their enforcement;

(b) Developing a mechanism for reviewing corporate compliance with their responsibility to respect human rights, drawing from existing processes, including United Nations treaty and charter bodies, OECD national contact points and international financial institutions' inspection panels, with a view to ensuring due weight is given to findings in any related investment dispute claims.

100. Investors should:

(a) Operate under the assumption that regulatory frameworks continuously evolve to progressively realize the human rights of indigenous peoples, as explicitly required by international human rights law;

(b) Support the transition toward a model of investment that promotes the realization of human rights.

Complementary measures necessary to mitigate the impacts of international investment agreements

101. International and regional human rights bodies should continue to issue recommendations addressing the responsibilities of home and host States to regulate corporate behaviour and consider developing general recommendations or advisory opinions on the responsibility of home States in relation to indigenous peoples' rights and the intersection of investment protection and human rights.

102. Home States should adopt and enforce extraterritorial regulation in relation to the impacts of their corporations on indigenous peoples overseas and ensure they are held to account for any rights violations, including the denial of protections under international investment agreements.

103. Host States must comply with their duty to regulate in relation to indigenous peoples' rights to:

(a) Lands, territories and resources, necessitating demarcation based on customary land tenure, possession and use;

(b) Restitution of land, territories and resources taken without free, prior and informed consent;

(c) Self-determination, by virtue of which they can determine their own social, cultural and economic development and maintain and develop their institutions, customs and decision-making processes;

(d) Good-faith prior consultation to give or withhold free, prior and informed consent in relation to measures affecting their rights;

(e) Their beliefs and traditional knowledge;

(f) A permanent and enduring way of life of their own choosing.

104. Governmental bodies responsible for protecting indigenous peoples' rights should ensure that information is made available to foreign investors addressing the need to respect indigenous peoples' rights and the State's obligation to progressively realize those rights.

105. Indigenous peoples could consider publicly declaring their expectations with regard to any potential investment projects in their territories, for example, through consultation and free, prior and informed consent protocols, thereby influencing potential investor's legitimate expectations.

106. International financial institutions, including the World Bank, must implement their performance standards in a manner consistent with developments in international human rights law standards, including in relation to the requirement for free, prior and informed consent.

107. In order to suspend or terminate an international investment agreement that affects indigenous peoples' rights, States could invoke article 62 (2) of the Vienna Convention on the law of treaties in relation to a fundamental change in

circumstances, such as the recognition of indigenous peoples within their borders. To do so, they would need to show that:

(a) such recognition was not foreseen when the agreement was entered into, which could be explained by the evolving understanding of States in Asia and Africa as to what constitutes an indigenous people in those regions;

(b) the change radically transforms the extent of obligations still to be performed under the treaty, as could be the case given the requirement to obtain indigenous peoples' free, prior and informed consent to investment plans; and

(c) the change is not the result of a breach by the party invoking it either of an obligation under the treaty or of any other international obligation owed to any other party to the treaty, a threshold that is not met by the recognition of indigenous peoples' rights within the host State.

Long-term reform

108. Longer-term reform of international investment law necessitates a shift in thinking about the purpose and nature of international investment agreements and dispute resolution mechanisms. Rather than viewing their role as purely, or even perhaps primarily, to protect investor rights, they need to be understood within a broader public policy and the international law framework, commensurate with our stage of economic globalization and interdependence, such that legitimate investor protections work in harmony with indigenous and human rights rather than acting as a constraint upon long-term public policy objectives and serving to further fragment the international order. This will involve redesigning aspects of the international investment law system that are not fit for purpose. The objective should be to protect the legitimate rights of investors and the need for reasonable predictability, while also guaranteeing the State's right to regulate and protect fundamental human rights, and ensuring that the rights of the most vulnerable are not subordinated to the economic interests of the most powerful.

Source: A/HRC/33/42 Report of the Special Rapporteur on the rights of indigenous peoples
http://www.ohchr.org/EN/HRBodies/HRC/RegularSessions/Session33/Pages/ListReports.aspx

ﬤﬥﬤﬥﬤﬥﬤﬥ

5. REQUEST FOR PRECAUTIONARY MEASURES PURSUANT TO ARTICLE 25 OF THE IACHR RULES OF PROCEDURE CONCERNING SERIOUS AND URGENT RISKS OF IRREPARABLE HARM ARISING OUT OF CONSTRUCTION OF THE DAKOTA ACCESS PIPELINE

This request for precautionary measures mechanism from the OAS' Inter-American Commission on Human Rights was invoked when the Standing Rock Sioux Tribe, Cheyenne River Sioux Tribe, and Yankton Sioux Tribe and their supporters were experiencing harm in North Dakota at Dakota Access Pipeline DAPL protests. TigerSwan, a private contractor working with police, was labeling Native American protesters as insurgents. A precautionary measure is a request for rapid response by the IACHR, in serious and urgent situations, to take actions to avoid irreparable harm to persons or groups of persons in the 35 OAS member states. The lawfulness of the request stems from Article 106 of the OAS Charter, under which the Commission's principal function is "to promote the observance and protection of human rights." It is also reflected in Article 41.b of the American Convention on Human Rights, as well as in Article 18.b of the IACHR Statute and in the Inter-American Convention on Forced Disappearance of Persons.

December 2, 2016
Mr. Emilio Álvarez Icaza Longoria
Executive Secretary
Inter-American Commission on Human Rights

Honorable Mr. Álvarez:

By this request, the Standing Rock Sioux Tribe, the Cheyenne River Sioux Tribe, and the Yankton Sioux Tribe (the "Tribes") respectfully request that this Commission call on the United States to adopt precautionary measures to prevent irreparable harm to the Tribes, their members, and others resulting from the ongoing and imminent construction of the Dakota Access Pipeline ("DAPL"), and from the harassment and violence being perpetrated against people gathered in prayer and protest in opposition to DAPL.

The construction and operation of DAPL would cause serious and irreparable harm to lands and waters that are sacred to the Tribes, central to the survival of their culture, and essential to their physical integrity and health. As such, granting the easement allowing the final stage of construction would cause imminent, serious and irreparable violations of the Tribes' rights to culture, life, liberty and personal security, health, water, property, and equality before the law. Because the United States has failed to meaningfully consult with the Tribes in granting permits for the pipeline, or to perform an adequate assessment of the environmental and social effects of granting the permits, granting the final easement would also seriously and irreparably violate the Tribes' rights to information and participation in government. Finally, ongoing and escalating violence and harassment of peaceful protesters by state and local police forces, and private security guards, and the continued failure of the United States to ensure the safety of the protesters, pose an immediate threat of grave and irremediable violation of the Tribes' and others' rights to life, liberty and personal security, health, peaceable assembly, association, and protection from arbitrary arrest.

Beneficiaries

The beneficiaries of this request are the members of the Standing Rock Sioux Tribe, the Cheyenne River Sioux Tribe, the Yankton Sioux Tribe, as well as some members of other tribes, and other individuals, peacefully praying and protesting in opposition to DAPL.

...

Standing Rock Sioux Tribe, Cheyenne River Sioux Tribe, Yankton Sioux Tribe

Request for Precautionary Measures

December 2, 2016

Source: Standing Rock Sioux Tribe, Cheyenne River Sioux Tribe, Yankton Sioux Tribe Request for Precautionary Measures, December 2, 2016, https://turtletalk.files.wordpress.com/2016/12/standing-rock-cheyenne-river-yankton-sioux-tribes-request-for-precautionary-measures-final-dec-02-2016.pdf

Rights of the Child

Chapter 11

This Chapter is About understanding what constitutes the Rights of the Child in international human rights law with reference to both the legal theoretical basis of children's rights, and the special rights of children in International Humanitarian Law, i.e., their rights in areas of armed conflict. Additionally, this chapter will examine the status of children's rights within U.S. domestic law.

This is Important Because without a fully integrated international and domestic legal understanding of what the rights of the child are and how to use them, there is grave risk that childhood, and children and their rights could devolve into mere control mechanisms over children as extensions of adult property rights, which has historically led to their abuse, neglect, and exploitation. Without sufficient attention paid to their agency as persons, or to the full range of their political, civil, economic, social, and cultural rights and needs, children might become stymied in their development. Even as their survival and protection are of great and immediate importance, so is the continuous development of her or his human integrity and dignity equally urgent, not as a mere aspirational abstract concept, but as a fact of life within the child's experience. The vision of, and law related to, the rights of the child is to protect children, and also to ensure their development to full realization of all their rights.

It is important that the globalization of children's rights be supported and implemented by the U.S. within all institutions affecting children, for it is most often within civil, social, cultural, and institutional settings, such as schools, health care facilities, sports, social clubs, foster care, legal procedures in police custody and the courts, within the family, etc., that a child experiences her or his continuous, undisturbed development toward the full ripening of their eventual adult human rights as opposed to the neglect or violation of those same rights unique to children. Children everywhere gain social awareness of their own agency to realize rights and to act to protect the rights of those around them. Children's rights must not remain merely academic and aspirational; children need to experience their human rights appropriate to their age and stage of development. Nor should children's rights be left entirely in the hands of legalists, politicians, non-governmental, or civil society organizations, or even parents whose rights regarding their children's welfare are assured within human rights law and appropriately guaranteed and properly understood.

A knowledgeable understanding of children's rights law can be, for children, a stepping stone into understanding other fields of study, especially of international human rights as law, an absolute necessity for assurance that governments respect human rights and human dignity. No child can stand up for rights if he or she does not know they exist. For parents, other responsible adults, and their governments, understanding children's rights could inspire them to understand and stand up for all human rights. The rights of the child and her or his guardians and human rights education (HRE) connect inextricably in childhood; the only remedy for ignorance of, for, and about human rights is HRE, which has to begin in childhood.

Quotes & Key Text Excerpts

Recognizing that the United Nations has, in the Universal Declaration of Human Rights and in the International Covenants on Human Rights, proclaimed and agreed that everyone is entitled to all the rights and freedoms set forth therein, without distinction of any kind, such as race, colour, sex, language, religion, political or other opinion, national or social origin, property, birth or other status,

Recalling that, in the Universal Declaration of Human Rights, the United Nations has proclaimed that childhood is entitled to special care and assistance,

Convinced that the family, as the fundamental group of society and the natural environment for the growth and well-being of all its members and particularly children, should be afforded the necessary protection and assistance so that it can fully assume its responsibilities within the community,

Recognizing that the child, for the full and harmonious development of his or her personality, should grow up in a family environment, in an atmosphere of happiness, love, and understanding,

Considering that the child should be fully prepared to live an individual life in society, and brought up in the spirit of the ideals proclaimed in the Charter of the United Nations, and in particular in the spirit of peace, dignity, tolerance, freedom, equality, and solidarity,

Bearing in mind that, as indicated in the Declaration of the Rights of the Child, "the child, by reason of his physical and mental immaturity, needs special safeguards and care, including appropriate legal protection, before as well as after birth, —

...

Have agreed as follows:

...

Article 2

1. States Parties shall respect and ensure the rights set forth in the present Convention to each child within their jurisdiction without discrimination of any kind, irrespective of the child's or his or her parent's or legal guardian's race, colour, sex, language, religion, political or other opinion, national, ethnic or social origin, property, disability, birth or other status.

2. States Parties shall take all appropriate measures to ensure that the child is protected against all forms of discrimination or punishment on the basis of the status, activities, expressed opinions, or beliefs of the child's parents, legal guardians, or family members.

Article 3

1. In all actions concerning children, whether undertaken by public or private social welfare institutions, courts of law, administrative authorities or legislative bodies, the best interests of the child shall be a primary consideration.

2. States Parties undertake to ensure the child such protection and care as is necessary for his or her well-being, taking into account the rights and duties of his or her parents, legal guardians, or other individuals legally responsible for him or her, and, to this end, shall take all appropriate legislative and administrative measures.

The U.S. has signed, but not yet ratified this treaty.

—*U.N. Convention on the Rights of the Child, preamble and articles 2 and 3*

෯෨෯෨෯෨෯෨෯

Encouraged by the overwhelming support for the Convention on the Rights of the Child, — for the promotion and protection of the rights of the child,

Reaffirming that the rights of children require special protection, and calling for continuous improvement of the situation of children without distinction, as well as for their development and education in conditions of peace and security,

Disturbed by the harmful and widespread impact of armed conflict on children and the long-term consequences it has for durable peace, security and development,

Condemning the targeting of children in situations of armed conflict and direct attacks on objects protected under international law, including places that generally have a significant presence of children, such as schools and hospitals,

Noting the adoption of the Rome Statute of the International Criminal Court, in particular, the inclusion therein as a war crime, of conscripting or enlisting children under the age of 15 years or using them to participate actively in hostilities in both international and non-international armed conflict,

Considering therefore that to strengthen further the implementation of rights recognized in the Convention on the Rights of the Child there is a need to increase the protection of children from involvement in armed conflict,...

Noting that article 1 of the Convention on the Rights of the Child specifies that, for the purposes of that Convention, a child means every human being below the age of 18 years unless, under the law applicable to the child, majority is attained earlier,

Convinced that an optional protocol to the Convention that raises the age of possible recruitment of persons into armed forces and their participation in hostilities will contribute effectively to the implementation of the principle that the best interests of the child are to be a primary consideration in all actions concerning children,

Noting that the twenty-sixth International Conference of the Red Cross and Red Crescent in December 1995 recommended, inter alia, that parties to conflict take every feasible step to ensure that children below the age of 18 years do not take part in hostilities,

Welcoming the unanimous adoption, in June 1999, of International Labour Organization Convention No. 182 on the Prohibition and Immediate Action for the Elimination of the Worst Forms of Child Labour, which prohibits, inter alia, forced or compulsory recruitment of children for use in armed conflict,....

Optional Protocol to the Convention on the Rights of the Child on the Involvement of Children in Armed Conflict, 2002

Considering that, in order to further achieve the purposes of the Convention on the Rights of the Child and the implementation of its provisions, especially articles 1, 11, 21, 32, 33, 34, 35, and 36, it would be appropriate to extend the measures that States Parties should undertake in order to guarantee the protection of the child from the sale of children, child prostitution, and child pornography,

Considering also that the Convention on the Rights of the Child recognizes the right of the child to be protected from economic exploitation and from performing any work that is likely to be hazardous or to interfere with the child's education, or to be harmful to the child's health or physical, mental, spiritual, moral or social development,

Gravely concerned at the significant and increasing international traffic in children for the purpose of the sale of children, child prostitution, and child pornography,

Deeply concerned at the widespread and continuing practice of sex tourism, to which children are especially vulnerable, as it directly promotes the sale of children, child prostitution, and child pornography,

Recognizing that a number of particularly vulnerable groups, including girl children, are at greater risk of sexual exploitation, and that girl children are disproportionately represented among the sexually exploited,

Concerned about the growing availability of child pornography on the Internet and other evolving technologies, and recalling the International Conference on Combating Child Pornography on the Internet, held in Vienna in 1999, in particular its conclusion calling for the worldwide criminalization of the production, distribution, exportation, transmission, importation, intentional possession, and advertising of child pornography, and stressing the importance of closer cooperation and partnership between Governments and the Internet industry,

Believing that the elimination of the sale of children, child prostitution, and child pornography will be facilitated by adopting a holistic approach, addressing the contributing factors, including underdevelopment, poverty, economic disparities, inequitable socio-economic structure, dysfunctioning families, lack of education, urban-rural migration, gender discrimination, irresponsible adult sexual behaviour, harmful traditional practices, armed conflicts, and trafficking in children,

Believing also that efforts to raise public awareness are needed to reduce consumer demand for the sale of children, child prostitution, and child pornography; and believing further in the importance of strengthening global partnership among all actors and of improving law enforcement at the national level,

Noting the provisions of international legal instruments relevant to the protection of children, including the Hague Convention on Protection of Children and Cooperation in Respect of Intercountry Adoption, the Hague Convention on the Civil Aspects of International Child Abduction, the Hague Convention on Jurisdiction, Applicable Law, Recognition, Enforcement and Cooperation in Respect of Parental Responsibility and Measures for the Protection of Children, and International Labour Organization Convention No. 182 on the Prohibition and Immediate Action for the Elimination of the Worst Forms of Child Labour,

Encouraged by the overwhelming support for the Convention on the Rights of the Child, demonstrating the widespread commitment that exists for the promotion and protection of the rights of the child,

Recognizing the importance of the implementation of the provisions of the Programme of Action for the Prevention of the Sale of Children, Child Prostitution and Child Pornography; and the Declaration and Agenda for Action adopted at the World Congress against Commercial Sexual Exploitation of Children, held in Stockholm from 27 to 31 August 1996, and the other relevant decisions and rec-ommendations of pertinent international bodies,

Taking due account of the importance of the traditions and cultural values of each people for the pro-tection and harmonious development of the child,

Have agreed as follows....

Optional Protocol to the Convention on the Rights of the Child on the Sale of Children, Child Prosti-tution, and Child Pornography

—*Convention on the Rights of the Child: Protocol on Involvement of Children in Armed Conflict; Protocol on the Sale of Children, Child Prostitution and Child Pornography*

ॐॐॐॐॐॐॐॐ

The United States is committed to effective implementation of our human rights treaty obligations and has multiple mechanisms that provide for regular review of our federal and state laws and poli-cies. We have, in recent years, improved engagement with state and local governments to foster better awareness of human rights obligations at the state, tribal, and local levels. State and local gov-ernment officials have been members of recent U.S. delegations presenting reports on the Conven-tion on the Elimination of All Forms of Racial Discrimination, the Optional Protocols to the Convention on the Rights of the Child, the International Covenant on Civil and Political Rights, and the Convention Against Torture. The United States intends to continue including state and local rep-resentatives, and we have invited them to several civil society consultations during this UPR cycle.

...

We remain committed to combatting human trafficking, including commercial sexual exploitation of children, and have made great progress since our last report.

—*United States of America National report submitted in accordance with paragraph 5 of the annex to Human Rights Council resolution 16/21*

ॐॐॐॐॐॐॐॐ

Children and families should never be in immigration detention —

GENEVA (14 December 2016) — Governments should stop placing children and families in immi-gration detention, a group of U.N. human rights experts has said in a call to mark International Mi-grants' Day on 18 December. The detention of children has been increasing amid rhetoric and policies that seek to criminalise undocumented migrants, including children. However, there is never a justification for such detention.

Every day, thousands of children — sometimes with families — are locked up in immigration deten-tion in over one hundred countries around the world, including both developed and developing countries. Such an experience can be devastating for a child and is not a legitimate response under in-ternational human rights law.

The Committee on the Rights of the Child has held that under the U.N. Convention on the Rights of the Child, which has been ratified by 196 states, states cannot justify detaining migrant children because they are unaccompanied or separated from their families. States also cannot justify detaining children on the basis that their parents need to be detained and that it is the only way to keep the family together.

We are concerned that some States appear to be working on the erroneous assumption that detention is sometimes in the best interests of the child or that the Convention on the Rights of the Child, which allows for detention as an exceptional measure in the juvenile justice context, somehow permits it. We are similarly concerned about attempts to justify immigration detention as an important measure to reduce the occurrence of children running away once in a transit or destination country. This notion is neither child rights-compliant nor evidence-based.

Let us be clear: immigration detention is *never* in the best interests of the child. This view has been repeatedly expressed by the Committee on the Rights of the Child, the Committee on Migrant Workers, the Working Group on Arbitrary Detention, and the Special Rapporteur on the Human Rights of Migrants, who have called on States to immediately cease any kind of migration-related detention of children and families. This is also the position of all 22 U.N., intergovernmental and civil society members of the Inter-Agency Working Group to End Child Immigration Detention.

The reasons why immigration detention is not in the best interests of the child are many. Most importantly, children in immigration detention will often be traumatised, and will struggle to understand why they are, as they see it, being 'punished' when they have done nothing wrong. Even short periods of detention have an adverse and long-lasting effect on a child's development, on their physical and mental well-being, and might aggravate previous trauma experienced in the countries of origin or transit.

Immigration detention is a clear child rights violation, and States must prohibit it by law and cease the practice quickly and completely. States must adopt alternatives to detention for children and their families that are non-custodial and community-based. These alternatives are better suited for the next steps of a child's life, whether they stay in the host country, are re-settled in a third country, or are returned to their country of origin if that is in their best interests. The prohibition of child migration-related detention and the duty to implement alternatives should be guaranteed by law and effectively fulfilled in practice.

Unaccompanied migrant children should be the main responsibility of child protection agencies and not of migration authorities, and they should be placed in the national alternative care system, preferably in family-type care rather than in institutional care. Such a system should benefit from substantial investments to be in a position to respond to this new task. Unaccompanied migrant children should quickly be appointed a competent and appropriately trained, legal guardian tasked with protecting their best interests in *loco parentis*, including through the appointment of a lawyer to represent them in the various proceedings that they may face.

When applying alternatives to detention, States need to make sure that they respect the children's rights, including their rights to education, to the enjoyment of the highest attainable standard of health, to an adequate standard of living, and to rest, leisure, and play.

We note the commitment by States in the *New York Declaration on Refugees and Migrants* to work towards ending the practice of immigration detention of children. As the Global Compacts on refugees and migration are being developed, we are calling for a clear, unified, and child-rights approach on this issue, and look forward to supporting States in implementing this commitment as a priority. We encourage States to exchange information on the good practices on alternatives to immigration detention of children which already exist.

States need to have their priorities clear: the protection of children and youth, and the principle of family unity are more important than the protection of borders.

—*Special Rapporteur on the human rights of migrants, Mr. François Crépeau; Chair of the Committee on the Protection of the Rights of All Migrant Workers and Members of Their Families, Mr. Jose S. Brillantes; Chair of the Committee on the Rights of the Child, Mr. Benyam Dawit Mezmur; Chair of the Working Group on Arbitrary Detention, Mr Sètondji Roland Adjovi through the Office of the High Commissioner for Human Rights, 18 December 2016*

❧❧❧❧❧❧❧❧❧

Understanding the legal extent of the freedom of children as persons, parental authority over their own children, and state responsibilities for protecting children and promoting their rights constitutes how U.S. domestic law addresses the issue of children's rights in the U.S.

—*John J. Garman, Law Professor, Faulkner University Jones School of Law*

Source: http://scholar.valpo.edu/cgi/viewcontent.cgi?article=1173&context=vulr

❧❧❧❧❧❧❧❧❧

In every U.S. jurisdiction, children are prosecuted in adult courts and sentenced to adult prison terms. Fourteen states have no minimum age for adult prosecution, while others set the age at 10, 12, or 13. Some states automatically prosecute youth age 14 and above as adults. Fifteen states give discretion to the prosecuting attorney, not a judge, to decide whether a youth is to be denied the services of the juvenile system. Tens of thousands of youth under the age of 18 are being held in adult prisons and jails across the country. The U.S. remains the only country to sentence people under the age of 18 to life without the possibility of parole.

In 2015, there was some movement toward reducing the number of children tried as adults. In Illinois, a new law ended the automatic transfer of children under 15 to adult court. New Jersey increased the minimum age to be tried as an adult from 14 to 15. California, for the first time in 40 years, improved the statutory criteria judges use in transfer hearings, which could reduce the number of youth tried as adults.

—*Human Rights Watch, "Youth in the Criminal Justice System," 2015*

Source: https://www.hrw.org/world-report/2016/country-chapters/united-states#9edf78

❧❧❧❧❧❧❧❧❧

In the United States, there is no constitutional provision or national law prohibiting states from subjecting children under age 18 to the adult criminal justice system, imposing adult criminal sentences, or incarcerating children in adult prison facilities. As a result, each year approximately 200,000 children are tried as adults, and on any given day thousands are incarcerated in adult jails and prisons. In addition to the human rights violations inherent in trying and imposing criminal punishments on children, once in the adult system, children in adult jails and prisons face disproportionately high rates of physical and sexual abuse and solitary confinement. By far, the vast majority of the youth who are criminalized and incarcerated in adult facilities are racial and ethnic minorities. Youth in adult prisons are at high risk of physical and sexual assault.

—*Melody Hanes, U.S. State Department Office of Juvenile Justice and Delinqency Prevention, reporting to the Inter-American Commission on Human Rights, Human Rights Situation of Children Deprived of Liberty with Adults in the United States; OAS videos; CUNY School of Law, Youth Justice.*

Source: http://www.law.cuny.edu/academics/clinics/hrgj/projects/youth-justice-project.html

❧❧❧❧❧❧❧❧❧

Children of African descent in the U.S. continue to be a vulnerable population marginalized by persistent race, gender, and economic discrimination in violation of their human rights in the ICERD, CRC, CEDAW, ICESCR, and ICCPR. The ICERD Committee issued its 2014 Concluding Observations requesting that the U.S. government provide, in its next periodic review, detailed information regarding the rate at which African-American (hereinafter referred to as AAi) children in foster care are prescribed psychotropic medications. Foster care children are often a silent voice, particularly AA girls, who are the subject of this report. This submission will focus on the over-medication of psychotropic drugs on girls in foster care of African descent and its impact on her healthy development and dignity.

—*The Franklin Law Group, P.C., Baltimore, Maryland*

Source: http://tbinternet.ohchr.org/Treaties/CAT/Shared%20Documents/USA /INT_CAT_NHS_USA_18527_E.pdf

෩ඏ෩ඏ෩ඏ෩ඏ

An estimated 300,000 - 500,000 predominately Hispanic children harvest produce in the heat, exposed to pesticides, using repetitive motions for 10-14 hours a day. The high school dropout rate for these children is 4x the national rate. Due to exemptions to the Fair Labor Standards Act in 1938, the U.S. federal child laws are minimal for agriculture. The federal standard is 12 and younger in some cases. In many situations, we have young girls working in fields with adult men where there are little regulations and reported abuse. These issues are well documented with written and video reports by numerous organizations. Despite these reports, the CARE bill which seeks to equalize the child labor laws has failed to leave the Congressional House Committee on Education and the Workforce since 2001.

Source: http://juliaperezauthor.com/uploads/SenateCommitte_StateofHumanRights_Dec2014.pdf

What You Should Know

The Rights of the Child in International Human Rights Law and in International Humanitarian Law

The United Nations Convention on the Rights of the Child, in 1989, known as the CRC, was the culmination of decades-long, broad international efforts to protect children through implementable, internationally recognized, normative legal standards. Poland acted as the first nation to bring up the subject to the U.N. for recognition of the rights of children. Children's rights law recognizes certain rights unique to children that require respect and reassurance in fulfillment of all human rights of all persons in all societies who are under eighteen years of age. As sectoral/sectorial rights, i.e., as a specific social sector or group sorted out from among other sectors/groups, children's rights do not apply to everyone of every age, but only to persons' rights whose youth and maturity need both protection and empowerment to counter and combat historical abuse, neglect, or exploitation as children. The rights of children are addressed in the nearly unanimous ratification of the CRC, and within domestic law and societal practice around the world.

Every country on the planet has ratified the Convention on the Rights of the Child, except, the U.S. Although the U.S. was inextricably involved in CRC's development and formulation, and even though the U.S. signed the CRC in 1994, the U.S. has yet to present it for U.S. Senate ratification. In what to some nation states seems a contradictory stance, the U.S. has signed and ratified the two optional protocols to the CRC: the (1st) Optional Protocol to the Convention on the Rights of the Child on the Involvement of Children in Armed Conflict with its concerns for children in armed conflict, an attempt to prohibit child soldiers; and the (2nd) Optional Protocol to the Convention on the Rights of the Child on the Sale of Children, Child Prostitution, and Child Pornography. The U.S. was eager to ratify the two Optional Protocols as means to act against the "child-soldier" phenomenon internationally and against the sale of children, child prostitution, and child pornography, both internationally and nationally. The U.N. Committee on the Rights of the Child responds to periodic state reports from the U.S. under these two protocols, with encouragement and recommendations to fully ratify the CRC, especially since the two optional protocols are understood as derivative from the CRC.

The CRC's sectorial referencing of children's rights integrates both ICCPR and ICESCR legal ideas and norms within it. The CRC's focus on the whole child reveals that there is more to the rights of children than traditional notions of care and protection of children.

The object and purpose of the CRC is to recognize human rights of children in four areas of concern:

- survival rights, i. e., the right to life, survival, health, and the right to access to health care facilities;
- rights to development, i.e., the right to free, equal education, vocational education; the right to respect from those in authority over them for the child's human dignity; the right to access to information, mass media aimed at social, spiritual, moral, physical, mental health or well-being; the right to children's materials created to enhance understanding; the right to cultural, artistic, recreational and free time activities; and the right to freedom of thought, conscience, and religion, the only area that requires parental involvement, although nothing prevents parents from being involved in all aspects of child development;
- special protection rights, e.g., the right to protection from economic exploitation; from sexual exploitation or abuse; from cruelty; from any form of physical or mental violence, injury, abuse, negligent treatment, maltreatment; from hazards in any workplace environment; from anything that interferes with the child's education; from torture or other cruel, inhuman or degrading treatment or punishment; from capital punishment, and from life imprisonment; and
- participation rights, i.e., the right to respect for the child's opinions; the right to develop his or her own views and to express those views in matters that affect him or her; to freedom of expression, and freedom of thought, conscience, and religion; to freedom of association and to peaceful assembly.

Orphans, children with mental or physical disabilities or handicaps, and children from minority groups are entitled to protection or special care or special rights, and the right to enjoy her or his own culture, religion, and language. Refugee children, whether accompanied or unaccompanied by family, have special rights for legal protection and humanitarian assistance under the CRC, and under other protective international refugee human rights and humanitarian law instruments.

The U.S. was key in proposing, drafting, and promoting rights to personal freedoms expressed in the CRC, those that are especially reminiscent of the U.S. Bill of Rights, such as freedom of expression, religion, association, assembly, and even privacy. Ironically, the U.S., because it has not yet ratified the CRC, may not, for the time being, contribute to shaping the CRC's further development. The U.S. may not serve as a member of the U.N. Committee on the Rights of the Child until it ratifies the treaty.

Below is the UNICEF listing of children's rights in first person format, as derived from the articles of the CRC, as a means for students to engage in their meaning more directly:

Children's rights as derived from articles of the Convention on the Rights of the Child:

Article 1 – As someone under eighteen years of age, I (we) have these rights.

Article 2 – I (we) have these rights, no matter who I am (we are), wherever I (we) live, whatever my (our) parents do, whatever language I (we) speak, whatever my (our) religion is, whether I am (we are) a boy or girl, whatever my (our) culture is, whether I (we) have a disability, whether I am (we are) rich or poor. I (we) should be treated fairly on any basis.

Article 3 – All adults should do what is best for me (us). When adults make decisions, they should think about how their decisions will affect me (us).

Article 4 – The government has a responsibility to make sure my (our) rights are protected. They must help my (our) families to protect my (our) rights and create an environment where I (we) can grow and reach my (our) potential.

Article 5 – My (our) family has the responsibility to help me (us) learn to exercise my (our) rights, and to ensure that my (our) rights are protected.

Article 6 – I (we) have the right to be alive.

Article 7 – I (we) have the right to a name, and this should be officially recognized by the government. I (we) have the right to a nationality (to belong to a country).

Article 8 – I (we) have the right to an identity — an official record of who I am (we are). No one should take this away from me (us).

Article 9 – I (we) have the right to live with my (our) parent(s), unless it is bad for me (us). I (we) have the right to live with a family who cares for me (us).

Article 10 – If I (we) live in a different country than my (our) parents do, I (we) have the right to be together in the same place.

Article 11 – I (we) have the right to be protected from kidnapping.

Article 12 – I (we) have the right to give my (our) opinion, and for adults to listen and take it seriously.

Article 13 – I (we) have the right to find out things and share what I (we) think with others, by talking, drawing, writing or in any other way, unless it harms or offends other people.

Article 14 – I (we) have the right to choose my (our) own religion and beliefs. My (our) parents should help me (us) decide what is right and wrong, and what is best for me (us).

Article 15 – I (we) have the right to choose my (our) own friends and join or set up groups, as long as it isn't harmful to others.

Article 16 – I (we) have the right to privacy.

Article 17 – I (we) have the right to get information that is important to my (our) well-being, from radio, newspaper, books, computers, and other sources. Adults should make sure that the information I am (we are) getting is not harmful, and help me (us) find and understand the information I (we) need.

Article 18 – I (we) have the right to be raised by my (our) parent(s) if possible.

Article 19 – I (we) have the right to be protected from being hurt and mistreated, in body or mind.

Article 20 – I (we) have the right to special care and help if I (we) cannot live with my (our) parents.

Article 21 – I (we) have the right to care and protection if I (we) are adopted or in foster care.

Article 22 – I (we) have the right to special protection and help if I am/we are a refugee (if I (we) have been forced to leave my (our) home and live in another country), as well as all the rights in this Convention.

Article 23 – I (we) have the right to special education and care if I (we) have a disability, as well as all the rights in this Convention, so that I (we) can live a full life.

Article 24 – I (we) have the right to the best health care possible, safe water to drink, nutritious food, a clean and safe environment, and information to help me (us) stay well.

Article 25 – If I (we) live in care or in other situations away from home, I (we) have the right to have these living arrangements looked at regularly to see if they are the most appropriate.

Article 26 – I (we) have the right to help from the government if I am/we are poor or in need.

Article 27 – I (we) have the right to food, clothing, a safe place to live, and to have my (our) basic needs met. I (we) should not be disadvantaged so that I (we) can't do many of the things other kids can do.

Article 28 – I (we) have the right to a good quality education. I (we) should be encouraged to go to school to the highest level I (we) can.

Article 29 – My (our) education should help me (us) use and develop my (our) talents and abilities. It should also help me (us) learn to live peacefully, protect the environment, and respect other people.

Article 30 – I (we) have the right to practice my (our) own culture, language, and religion, or any I (we) choose. Minority and indigenous groups need special protection of this right.

Article 31 – I (we) have the right to play and rest.

Article 32 – I (we) have the right to protection from work that harms me (us), and is bad for my (our) health and education. If I (we) work, I (we) have the right to be safe and paid fairly.

Article 33 – I (we) have the right to protection from harmful drugs and from the drug trade.

Article 34 – I (we) have the right to be free from sexual abuse.

Article 35 – No one is allowed to kidnap or sell me (us).

Article 36 – I (we) have the right to protection from any kind of exploitation (being taken advantage of).

Article 37 – No one is allowed to punish me (us) in a cruel or harmful way.

Article 38 – I (we) have the right to protection and the right to freedom from war. Children under 15 may not be forced to go into the army or take part in war.

Article 39 – I (we) have the right to help if I (we)'ve been hurt, neglected or badly treated.

Article 40 – I (we) have the right to legal help and fair treatment in the justice system that respects my (our) rights.

Article 41 – If the laws of my (our) country provide better protection of my (our) rights than the articles in this Convention, those laws should apply.

Article 42 – I (we) have the right to know my (our) rights. Adults should know about these rights and help me (us) learn about them, too.

Articles 43 to 54 – These articles explain how governments and international organizations like UNICEF will work to ensure children are protected with their rights.

Hard Human Rights Law

International legal documents that address children's rights and function as hard human rights law for ratifying nations are contained in:
- Convention on the Rights of the Child (CRC)
- Optional Protocol to the Convention on the Rights of the Child on the Involvement of Children in Armed Conflict (OP1 CRC) or (OP-CRC-AC)
- Optional Protocol to the Convention on the Rights of the Child on the Sale of Children, Child Prostitution, and Child Pornography (OP2 CRC)

In addition to the two substantive protocols; in 2011, there was a Complaint ('communication') procedure introduced by the Third Optional Protocol to the CRC. The U.S. has not ratified that third Protocol, whose purpose creates the individual complaints procedure to bring it in line with other treaty-based human rights regimes as the mechanism for direct contact with the Committee on the CRC and for implementing and monitoring state obligations for the CRC and its Protocols. Direct complaints to the Committee on the CRC are only receivable from parties to this third CRC Protocol.

- Optional Protocol to the CRC on a Communications Procedure (OP3 CRC) or (OP-CRC-IC)
- The ICCPR's articles No. 18.4, 23.4, 24, 26
- Article 24

    1. Every child shall have, without any discrimination as to race, colour, sex, language, religion, national or social origin, property or birth, the right to such measures of protection as are required by his status as a minor, on the part of his family, society, and the State.

    2. Every child shall be registered immediately after birth and shall have a name.

    3. Every child has the right to acquire a nationality.

- International Labour Organization (ILO) Convention N. 182 concerning the Prohibition and Immediate Action for the Elimination of the Worst Forms of Child Labour 2000.
- ICESCR: The International Covenant on Economic, Social and Cultural Rights contains provisions relating to children and maternity. ICESCR, 1976, although itself a treaty, was directly influential in understanding the later CRC. ICESCR's Articles 10 (child labour and exploitation); 13, 14 (child's education) are contained within it. The U.S. has signed the ICESCR, but has not ratified it, so those norms are not legally binding on the U.S. It should be argued as customary international law or as help in undertanding the economic, social, and cultural rights norms of the UDHR. This convention addresses many of the same rights that are within the CRC.

Hard Humanitarian Law applicable to the rights of children:
- Certain provisions of the Fourth Geneva Convention of 1949 and 1977 Protocols and customary humanitarian law;
- Refugee Law applicable to the rights of children — 1951 Convention Relating to the Status of Refugees and 1967 Protocol Relating to the Status of Refugees;
- Report by the Special Rapporteur on the sale of children, child prostitution, and child pornography on her mission to the United States of America (12-27 October 2010);
- U.S. federal law that does not explicitly proscribe the sale of children per se, but rather only forbids sale of children for specific purposes, such as for child pornography, child prostitution, and adoption;
- Child prostitution has been mainly addressed by fifty states' legislation, wherein federal law applies only insofar as interstate or foreign commerce is affected, and that there are extensive government-funded studies underway designed to get a better understanding of the problem;
- There is still criminalization of children who are victims of commercial sexual exploitation, i.e., children are charged with crimes in which they have been victims. Some states' legislation is aimed at extending protection to child victims of commercial sexual exploitation;
- There is no uniformity in the definition of a child for the purpose of child pornography. In some states, a child is a person under 16 years old or 17 years old, depending on the nature of acts involved;
- Combined Third and Fourth Periodic Report of the U.S. on the Optional Protocols to the Convention on the Rights of the Child on the Involvement of Children in Armed Conflict and the Sale of Children, Child Prostitution, and Child Pornography;
- The U.N. Committee Against Torture strongly criticized the U.S. for state laws and policies that incarcerate juveniles in adult jails and prisons under conditions that endanger their safety and well-being. The Committee also recommended ending taser use and solitary confinement for youth; separating incarcerated youth from adults; ending the sentencing of life without parole to youth; and ending the detrimental effects of U.S. criminal detention by adopting international standards emphasizing alternatives to imprisonment;
- The U.S. is a Member State of the Organization of American States and adopted the American Declaration of the Rights and Duties of Man. It is also a signatory to the American Convention on Human Rights. The Inter-American Commission on Human Rights develops reports and handles cases regarding children. See Chapter 7 on the OAS Human Rights System.
- U.S. Reports to the Committee on the Rights of the Child:
  - Initial Report Concerning the Optional Protocol on the Involvement of Children in Armed Conflict (OPAC);
  - Initial Report Concerning the Optional Protocol on the Sale of Children, Child Prostitution, and Child Pornography.

Soft Human Rights Law

The following international legal documents function as so-called soft human rights law, since they are the articulation of underlying legal principles consistent with international human rights law in the field of children's rights:
- The Declaration on the Rights of the Child in 1959;
- Minimum Rules for the Administration of Juvenile Justice aka "Beijing Rules";
- Guidelines for the Prevention of Juvenile Delinquency in 1990, also known as the "Riyadh Guidelines";
- U.N. Human Rights Council, Thirty-second session, Agenda item 3, Promotion and protection of all human rights, civil, political, economic, social, and cultural rights, including the right to development, 2016 A/HRC/32/L.30/Rev.1 32/... Realizing the equal enjoyment of the right to education by every girl.

The Committee also issues General Comments on the articles of the CRC and certain topics regarding children. See Primary Source Document 8.

Rights of the Child within U.S. Domestic Law
Even though there exists no extant list of legal rights of children cited in the U.S. Constitution, it is a given that children learn their rights usually in school, solely related to the amendments to the U.S. Constitution, known as the Bill of Rights. There is a long history in America of a so-called "child welfare movement" that predates the formation of the

U.S. There is in the larger U.S. culture only a historically pejorative sense of the rights of the child (except for those who have studied the rights of the child), and a state of profound confusion among most children and their guardians as to their human rights as children.

U.S. domestic legal documents:
- The U.S. Constitution

Federal Supreme Court judgments that affect the rights of children:
- *In re Gault* 387 U.S. 1 (1967) held for the first time that children/juveniles in legal proceedings have due process rights, such as the right to legal counsel, against self-incrimination, to challenge witnesses, etc.... Justice Abraham Fortas was a strong advocate of children's rights.
- *Tinker v. Des Moines Independent Community School District*, (1969) U.S. Supreme Court ruled 7-2 that students' free speech rights are to be protected: "Students don't shed their constitutional rights at the school house gates."
- *Thompson v. Oklahoma*, 487 U.S. 815 (1988) The U.S. Supreme Court placed a first moratorium on the execution of juveniles, based on constitutional prohibition of cruel and unusual punishment and evolving standards of decency that mark the progress of a maturing society.
- *Roper v. Simmons*, 543 U.S. 551, 575 (2005) The U.S. Supreme Court abolished juvenile death penalty in the U.S. This could allow the U.S. to drop its reservation to the ICCPR Article 6 that eliminates capital punishment for juveniles/children. Justice Anthony Kennedy cited instances of international law and laws of other civilized nations, and related British-influenced legal thinking as supportive and confirmative of the Supreme Court's finding that juvenile death penalty constituted cruel and unusual punishment.
- *Graham v. Florida*, 130 S.Ct. 2011 (2010) The U.S. Supreme Court held that sentencing juveniles to life in prison without the possibility of parole for crimes other than homicide is categorically forbidden as a violation of the Eighth Amendment. The Court considered international human rights law and normative sources, something which is found not to be binding precedent, but reaffirmed the wisdom of the Court's holding as to a modern view of the rights of the child in the U.S.

Legislative efforts
- Juvenile Justice and Delinquency Prevention Act 1974 (reauthorized in 2002) tried to improve outcomes for youth and community safety; Congress tried to address and enhance youth and community safety outcomes in multi-state juvenile justice systems and changed how states approach juvenile justice with the creation of federal standards for custody and care.
- Child Welfare and Adoption Assistance Act (1980) sought to enhance family preservation with an eye toward helping keep families together or family reunification and to keep children out of foster care or other placement options, unless adoption proved necessary, with a federal subsidy in the case of adoption. Judicial review, special needs children, plans for the future of children in foster care, and possible matching federal funds were addressed.
- Adoption and Safe Families Act (ASFA) of 1997 was a reform of the Child Welfare and Adoption Assistance Act, and an attempt to enhance adoption possibilities for special needs children and a general shift of reference towards focus on the child's health over the needs and rights of biological parents.

Full understanding of children's rights domestically is impeded by the fact that the U.S. has not broadened its understanding of the rights of children, nor has it promulgated, nor has it yet ratified into domestic law some key international instruments it helped formulate as normative internationally, such as the Convention on the Rights of the Child (CRC), the International Covenant on Economic, Social and Cultural Rights (ICESCR), and the Convention on the Elimination of All Forms of Discrimination against Women (CEDAW). Nonetheless, because the U.S. has ratified the CRC Optional Protocols, and is signatory to the others, the U.S. is obligated to not violate any of the principles or purposes of these documents.

Concerns, Objections and Controversies Surrounding the CRC: Difficulties Unique to the U.S.
In 2017, the United States is still unprepared to ratify and adhere to the Convention on the Rights of the Child with or without reservations.

The lack of children's rights resources, especially with regard to HRE, as sectorial rights within the U.S., is the primary cause for confusion for children and adults in the U.S.

In addition, there is great confusion among people in the U.S. regarding the role of international law in general. For example, in *Sosa v. Alvarez-Machain*, a case not directly related to children's rights, Justice David Souter stated that the ICCPR, although constructed as a binding ratified, bona fide covenant/treaty of the U.S. as a matter of international law, the U.S.'s reservation to the treaty enacts that the ICCPR is a non-self-executing human rights treaty and therefore, non-binding on the U.S. This is confusing, because, if it is a ratified U.S. treaty law aligned with the U.S. Constitution, then why is it ignored? Why did the ratifying Senate specifically disallow its interpretation into federal courts? Since the ICCPR refers to children's rights in several articles, is not the ICCPR's disavowal to enact international law into U.S. law a great source of confusion to persons in the U.S.? Is this phenomenon due to distrust of the treaty itself, or due to an unjustified fear of the international community, where countries embrace it into their domestic law? Or is the ratification-then-nullification of a treaty related to its usefulness by the U.S. Executive Branch as an additional tool to pressure other governments to comply with human rights law, while the U.S. chooses not to enforce it within its own borders? Or does the institutionalization of human rights, including children's rights throughout the world, provide a vehicle to the U.S. economic gain of some kind? It is a confusion that needs clarification by government.

In the case of the Convention on the Rights of the Child, does the U.S. not fully ratify the CRC because of the incurring costs related to its implementation? As with other human rights treaties, is non-implementatation really less risky than implementation? Is deliberate non-implementation of a fully ratified international human rights treaty legal or illegal? Does opening the U.S. to CRC implementation really create risk? Has the security and risk-averse era of the last decades made the U.S. insecure about opening its systems to examination of the U.S.'s real human rights issues, all of which affect children? Does the U.S. have justifiable fear of an intrusion by the U.N. into its systems that serve to protect children's rights? The Committee on the Rights of the Child already serves without controversy in monitoring U.S. progress on our adherence to the two Optional Protocols to the CRC, regarding child soldiers and child trafficking, etc. The U.S. regularly submits reports to this CRC committee, among other U.N. monitoring committees, and benefits from the U.N.'s several feedback processes and mechanisms. With the U.N. having no enforcement power other than that of the ratifying state itself, what would the U.S. realistically fear from the U.N. with ratification of the CRC? Is it legal for the U.S. to ignore the CRC main treaty and still ratify protocols to that treaty?

Human rights treaties, such as the CRC, tend not to spell out hard-and-fast rules. Instead, they remain generalized in terminology, so that countries, states, and cultures can interpret the treaties in order to realize them within their domestic spheres, which usually includes generating new domestic law upon ratification. As an old constitutional democracy, the U.S. is reticent to respond to generalizing treaties, such as the CRC. Even though the U.S. and U.S.-based non-governmental organizations (NGOs) played major roles in the development, expression, promotion, and standard-setting process in the field of children's human rights; as of 2017, the U.S. is the only country not to ratify the CRC, but expresses an intent to eventually ratify. The U.S. fully understands that, under the Vienna Convention on the Law of Treaties, it bears an obligation to refrain from acts that would defeat the object and purpose of the CRC treaty. Since the U.N. only requires implementation of ratified human rights treaties, it never speaks of treaty enforcement procedures and offers no sanctions for failures to enforce human rights norms. Those norms depend for their implementation/enforcement on ratifying states/governments, something only nation states can do.

Opposition to the CRC in the U.S. is largely concerned with perceived interference with U.S. sovereignty as it relates to how American law, primarily state law, deals with children. Additionally, the CRC is unfortunately misinterpreted as interference with the rights of parents to decide in absolute terms all questions related to raising their children. Some U.S. adults have not yet understood that implementation of children's rights depends on state and parental support. Some also imagine that there exist ways for the international community to enforce human rights law, which is not the case, as the U.N. has no enforcement mechanisms, no threat of force in its purview. The U.N. depends on states that ratify to implement treaties domestically. Some U.S. politicians are skilled at creating crippling wedge issues related to the U.N., its treaty-making role in human rights, which includes the CRC.

Because the CRC unequivocally supports an inherent right to life for a sectorial group of persons under age eighteen without mention of the unborn fetus, some see in this an inference that the CRC supports abortion rights. However, this question is deliberately left aside so that states party may make their own decisions on this matter. Because the right to an education, to a human rights education, and the prohibition of abusive physical and mental violence, abuse, and negligence are clearly acknowledged in the CRC, some see an intrusion into their community's or family's religious lives and discipline. The CRC offers a visionary challenge to strengthen families and to emphasize the responsible role of parents in very generalized ways. It does not attack parents but defers to parental roles on questions of conscience and religious matters.

The goals of the CRC are: to challenge those in power through the establishment of a variety of domestic norms to enhance the best interests of children; to eliminate all forms of neglect or maltreatment of children; to support parents in protecting children's survival and special protection rights; and to assist in pro-active capacities of children to develop and participate in decisions affecting them as children heading toward adulthood.

Despite the controversies surrounding the CRC, there are calls to begin teaching international human rights law (HRE) in the U.S. within K-12 social studies curricula. Among the many human rights taught and examined, the CRC vision and normative status is most immediately relevant to young people. Ratification and domestic implementation of the CRC as the world's first universally ratified human rights treaty with or without reservations is an important step.

Primary Source Documents

I. CONVENTION ON THE RIGHTS OF THE CHILD (CRC)

The Convention on the Rights of the Child is considered by many as customary international law, just like the Geneva Conventions, the UDHR, etc. The U.S. has signed the CRC, but to date, is the only country who has not ratified it. As the first legally binding universal code on the rights of children, these proclaimed rights correspond to all children below the age of eighteen globally or universally. And, under principles of international law contained in the Vienna Convention on the Law of Treaties, the U.S. should act consistently with legal instruments it has signed, as an indication of good faith.

Preamble

The States Parties to the present Convention,

Considering that, in accordance with the principles proclaimed in the Charter of the United Nations, recognition of the inherent dignity and of the equal and inalienable rights of all members of the human family is the foundation of freedom, justice and peace in the world,

Bearing in mind that the peoples of the United Nations have, in the Charter, reaffirmed their faith in fundamental human rights and in the dignity and worth of the human person, and have determined to promote social progress and better standards of life in larger freedom,

Recognizing that the United Nations has, in the Universal Declaration of Human Rights and in the International Covenants on Human Rights, proclaimed and agreed that everyone is entitled to all the rights and freedoms set forth therein, without distinction of any kind, such as race, colour, sex, language, religion, political or other opinion, national or social origin, property, birth or other status,

Recalling that, in the Universal Declaration of Human Rights, the United Nations has proclaimed that childhood is entitled to special care and assistance,

Convinced that the family, as the fundamental group of society and the natural environment for the growth and well-being of all its members and particularly children, should be afforded the necessary protection and assistance so that it can fully assume its responsibilities within the community,

Recognizing that the child, for the full and harmonious development of his or her personality, should grow up in a family environment, in an atmosphere of happiness, love and understanding,

Considering that the child should be fully prepared to live an individual life in society, and brought up in the spirit of the ideals proclaimed in the Charter of the United Nations, and in particular in the spirit of peace, dignity, tolerance, freedom, equality and solidarity,

Bearing in mind that the need to extend particular care to the child has been stated in the Geneva Declaration of the Rights of the Child of 1924 and in the Declaration of the Rights of the Child adopted by the General Assembly on 20 November 1959 and recognized in the Universal Declaration of Human Rights, in the International Covenant on Civil and Political Rights (in particular in articles 23 and 24), in the International Covenant on Economic, Social and Cultural Rights (in particular in Article 10) and in the statutes and relevant instruments of specialized agencies and international organizations concerned with the welfare of children,

Bearing in mind that, as indicated in the Declaration of the Rights of the Child, "the child, by reason of his physical and mental immaturity, needs special safeguards and care, including appropriate legal protection, before as well as after birth,"

Recalling the provisions of the Declaration on Social and Legal Principles relating to the Protection and Welfare of Children, with Special Reference to Foster Placement and Adoption Nationally and Internationally; the United Nations Standard Minimum Rules for the Administration of Juvenile Justice (The Beijing Rules); and the Declaration on the Protection of Women and Children in Emergency and Armed Conflict,

Recognizing that, in all countries in the world, there are children living in exceptionally difficult conditions, and that such children need special consideration,

Taking due account of the importance of the traditions and cultural values of each people for the protection and harmonious development of the child,

Recognizing the importance of international co-operation for improving the living conditions of children in every country, in particular in the developing countries,

Have agreed as follows:

PART I

Article 1
For the purposes of the present Convention, a child means every human being below the age of eighteen years unless under the law applicable to the child, majority is attained earlier.

Article 2
1. States Parties shall respect and ensure the rights set forth in the present Convention to each child within their jurisdiction without discrimination of any kind, irrespective of the child's or his or her parent's or legal guardian's race, colour, sex, language, religion, political or other opinion, national, ethnic or social origin, property, disability, birth or other status.

2. States Parties shall take all appropriate measures to ensure that the child is protected against all forms of discrimination or punishment on the basis of the status, activities, expressed opinions, or beliefs of the child's parents, legal guardians, or family members.

Article 3
1. In all actions concerning children, whether undertaken by public or private social welfare institutions, courts of law, administrative authorities or legislative bodies, the best interests of the child shall be a primary consideration.

2. States Parties undertake to ensure the child such protection and care as is necessary for his or her wellbeing, taking into account the rights and duties of his or her parents, legal guardians, or other individuals legally responsible for him or her, and, to this end, shall take all appropriate legislative and administrative measures.

3. States Parties shall ensure that the institutions, services and facilities responsible for the care or protection of children shall conform with the standards established by competent authorities, particularly in the areas of safety, health, in the number and suitability of their staff, as well as competent supervision.

Article 4
States Parties shall undertake all appropriate legislative, administrative, and other measures for the implementation of the rights recognized in the present Convention. With regard to economic, social and cultural rights, States Parties shall undertake such measures to the maximum extent of their available resources and, where needed, within the framework of international co-operation.

Article 5

States Parties shall respect the responsibilities, rights and duties of parents or, where applicable, the members of the extended family or community as provided for by local custom, legal guardians or other persons legally responsible for the child, to provide, in a manner consistent with the evolving capacities of the child, appropriate direction and guidance in the exercise by the child of the rights recognized in the present Convention.

Article 6

States Parties recognize that every child has the inherent right to life. States Parties shall ensure to the maximum extent possible the survival and development of the child.

Article 7

The child shall be registered immediately after birth and shall have the right from birth to a name, the right to acquire a nationality and as far as possible, the right to know and be cared for by his or her parents. States Parties shall ensure the implementation of these rights in accordance with their national law and their obligations under the relevant international instruments in this field, in particular where the child would otherwise be stateless.

Article 8

States Parties undertake to respect the right of the child to preserve his or her identity, including nationality, name and family relations as recognized by law without unlawful interference. Where a child is illegally deprived of some or all of the elements of his or her identity, States Parties shall provide appropriate assistance and protection, with a view to speedily re-establishing his or her identity.

Article 9

States Parties shall ensure that a child shall not be separated from his or her parents against their will, except when competent authorities subject to judicial review determine, in accordance with applicable law and procedures, that such separation is necessary for the best interests of the child. Such determination may be necessary in a particular case such as one involving abuse or neglect of the child by the parents, or one where the parents are living separately and a decision must be made as to the child's place of residence. In any proceedings pursuant to paragraph 1 of the present article, all interested parties shall be given an opportunity to participate in the proceedings and make their views known.

States Parties shall respect the right of the child who is separated from one or both parents to maintain personal relations and direct contact with both parents on a regular basis, except if it is contrary to the child's best interests.

Where such separation results from any action initiated by a State Party, such as the detention, imprisonment, exile, deportation or death (including death arising from any cause while the person is in the custody of the State) of one or both parents or of the child, that State Party shall, upon request, provide the parents, the child or, if appropriate, another member of the family with the essential information concerning the whereabouts of the absent member(s) of the family unless the provision of the information would be detrimental to the well-being of the child. States Parties shall further ensure that the submission of such a request shall of itself entail no adverse consequences for the person(s) concerned.

Article 10

1. In accordance with the obligation of States Parties under Article 9, paragraph 1, applications by a child or his or her parents to enter or leave a State Party for the purpose of family reunification shall be dealt with by States Parties in a positive, humane and expeditious manner. States Parties shall further ensure that the submission of such a request shall entail no adverse consequences for the applicants and for the members of their family.

2. A child whose parents reside in different States shall have the right to maintain on a regular basis, save in exceptional circumstances, personal relations and direct contacts with both parents. Towards that end and in accordance with the obligation of States Parties under Article 9, paragraph 2, States Parties shall respect the right of the child and his or her parents to leave any country, including their own, and to enter their own country. The right to leave any country shall be subject only to such restrictions as are prescribed by law and which are necessary to protect the national security, public order (ordre public), public health or morals or the rights and freedoms of others and are consistent with the other rights recognized in the present Convention.

Article 11

1. States Parties shall take measures to combat the illicit transfer and non-return of children abroad.

2. To this end, States Parties shall promote the conclusion of bilateral or multilateral agreements or accession to existing agreements.

Article 12

1. States Parties shall assure to the child who is capable of forming his or her own views the right to express those views freely in all matters affecting the child, the views of the child being given due weight in accordance with the age and maturity of the child.

2. For this purpose, the child shall in particular be provided the opportunity to be heard in any judicial and administrative proceedings affecting the child, either directly, or through a representative or an appropriate body, in a manner consistent with the procedural rules of national law.

Article 13

1. The child shall have the right to freedom of expression; this right shall include freedom to seek, receive and impart information and ideas of all kinds, regardless of frontiers, either orally, in writing or in print, in the form of art, or through any other media of the child's choice.

2. The exercise of this right may be subject to certain restrictions, but these shall only be such as are provided by law and are necessary:

(a) For respect of the rights or reputations of others; or

(b) For the protection of national security or of public order (ordre public), or of public health or morals.

Article 14

1. States Parties shall respect the right of the child to freedom of thought, conscience and religion.

2. States Parties shall respect the rights and duties of the parents and, when applicable, legal guardians, to provide direction to the child in the exercise of his or her right in a manner consistent with the evolving capacities of the child.

3. Freedom to manifest one's religion or beliefs may be subject only to such limitations as are prescribed by law and are necessary to protect public safety, order, health or morals, or the fundamental rights and freedoms of others.

Article 15

1. States Parties recognize the rights of the child to freedom of association and to freedom of peaceful assembly.

2. No restrictions may be placed on the exercise of these rights other than those imposed in conformity with the law and which are necessary in a democratic society in the interests of national security or public safety, public order (ordre public), the protection of public health or morals or the protection of the rights and freedoms of others.

Article 16

1. No child shall be subjected to arbitrary or unlawful interference with his or her privacy, family, home or correspondence, nor to unlawful attacks on his or her honour and reputation.

2. The child has the right to the protection of the law against such interference or attacks.

Article 17

States Parties recognize the important function performed by the mass media and shall ensure that the child has access to information and material from a diversity of national and international sources, especially those aimed at the promotion of his or her social, spiritual and moral well-being and physical and mental health. To this end, States Parties shall:

(a) Encourage the mass media to disseminate information and material of social and cultural benefit to the child and in accordance with the spirit of Article 29;

(b) Encourage international co-operation in the production, exchange and dissemination of such information and material from a diversity of cultural, national and international sources;

(c) Encourage the production and dissemination of children's books;

(d) Encourage the mass media to have particular regard to the linguistic needs of the child who belongs to a minority group or who is indigenous;

(e) Encourage the development of appropriate guidelines for the protection of the child from information and material injurious to his or her well-being, bearing in mind the provisions of articles 13 and 18.

Article 18
1. States Parties shall use their best efforts to ensure recognition of the principle that both parents have common responsibilities for the upbringing and development of the child. Parents or, as the case may be, legal guardians, have the primary responsibility for the upbringing and development of the child. The best interests of the child will be their basic concern.

2. For the purpose of guaranteeing and promoting the rights set forth in the present Convention, States Parties shall render appropriate assistance to parents and legal guardians in the performance of their child-rearing responsibilities and shall ensure the development of institutions, facilities and services for the care of children.

3. States Parties shall take all appropriate measures to ensure that children of working parents have the right to benefit from child-care services and facilities for which they are eligible.

Article 19
1. States Parties shall take all appropriate legislative, administrative, social and educational measures to protect the child from all forms of physical or mental violence, injury or abuse, neglect or negligent treatment, maltreatment or exploitation, including sexual abuse, while in the care of parent(s), legal guardian(s) or any other person who has the care of the child.

2. Such protective measures should, as appropriate, include effective procedures for the establishment of social programmes to provide necessary support for the child and for those who have the care of the child, as well as for other forms of prevention and for identification, reporting, referral, investigation, treatment and follow-up of instances of child maltreatment described heretofore, and, as appropriate, for judicial involvement.

Article 20
1. A child temporarily or permanently deprived of his or her family environment, or in whose own best interests cannot be allowed to remain in that environment, shall be entitled to special protection and assistance provided by the State.

2. States Parties shall in accordance with their national laws ensure alternative care for such a child.

3. Such care could include, inter alia, foster placement, kafalah of Islamic law, adoption or if necessary placement in suitable institutions for the care of children. When considering solutions, due regard shall be paid to the desirability of continuity in a child's upbringing and to the child's ethnic, religious, cultural and linguistic background.

Article 21
States Parties that recognize and/or permit the system of adoption shall ensure that the best interests of the child shall be the paramount consideration and they shall:

(a) Ensure that the adoption of a child is authorized only by competent authorities who determine, in accordance with applicable law and procedures and on the basis of all pertinent and reliable information, that the adoption is permissible in view of the child's status concerning parents, relatives and legal guardians and that, if required, the persons concerned have given their informed consent to the adoption on the basis of such counselling as may be necessary;

(b) Recognize that inter-country adoption may be considered as an alternative means of child's care, if the child cannot be placed in a foster or an adoptive family or cannot in any suitable manner be cared for in the child's country of origin; (c) Ensure that the child concerned by inter-country adoption enjoys safeguards and standards equivalent to those existing in the case of national adoption;

(d) Take all appropriate measures to ensure that, in inter-country adoption, the placement does not result in improper financial gain for those involved in it;

(e) Promote, where appropriate, the objectives of the present article by concluding bilateral or multilateral arrangements or agreements, and endeavour, within this framework, to ensure that the placement of the child in another country is carried out by competent authorities or organs.

Article 22

1. States Parties shall take appropriate measures to ensure that a child who is seeking refugee status or who is considered a refugee in accordance with applicable international or domestic law and procedures shall, whether unaccompanied or accompanied by his or her parents or by any other person, receive appropriate protection and humanitarian assistance in the enjoyment of applicable rights set forth in the present Convention and in other international human rights or humanitarian instruments to which the said States are Parties.

2. For this purpose, States Parties shall provide, as they consider appropriate, co-operation in any efforts by the United Nations and other competent intergovernmental organizations or non-governmental organizations co-operating with the United Nations to protect and assist such a child and to trace the parents or other members of the family of any refugee child in order to obtain information necessary for reunification with his or her family. In cases where no parents or other members of the family can be found, the child shall be accorded the same protection as any other child permanently or temporarily deprived of his or her family environment for any reason, as set forth in the present Convention.

Article 23

1. States Parties recognize that a mentally or physically disabled child should enjoy a full and decent life, in conditions which ensure dignity, promote self-reliance and facilitate the child's active participation in the community.

2. States Parties recognize the right of the disabled child to special care and shall encourage and ensure the extension, subject to available resources, to the eligible child and those responsible for his or her care, of assistance for which application is made and which is appropriate to the child's condition and to the circumstances of the parents or others caring for the child.

3. Recognizing the special needs of a disabled child, assistance extended in accordance with paragraph 2 of the present article shall be provided free of charge, whenever possible, taking into account the financial resources of the parents or others caring for the child, and shall be designed to ensure that the disabled child has effective access to and receives education, training, health care services, rehabilitation services, preparation for employment and recreation opportunities in a manner conducive to the child's achieving the fullest possible social integration and individual development, including his or her cultural and spiritual development.

4. States Parties shall promote, in the spirit of international cooperation, the exchange of appropriate information in the field of preventive health care and of medical, psychological and functional treatment of disabled children, including dissemination of and access to information concerning methods of rehabilitation, education and vocational services, with the aim of enabling States Parties to improve their capabilities and skills and to widen their experience in these areas. In this regard, particular account shall be taken of the needs of developing countries.

Article 24

1. States Parties recognize the right of the child to the enjoyment of the highest attainable standard of health and to facilities for the treatment of illness and rehabilitation of health. States Parties shall strive to ensure that no child is deprived of his or her right of access to such health care services.

2. States Parties shall pursue full implementation of this right and, in particular, shall take appropriate measures:

(a) To diminish infant and child mortality;

(b) To ensure the provision of necessary medical assistance and health care to all children with emphasis on the development of primary health care;

(c) To combat disease and malnutrition, including within the framework of primary health care, through, inter alia, the application of readily available technology and through the provision of adequate nutritious foods and clean drinking water, taking into consideration the dangers and risks of environmental pollution;

(d) To ensure appropriate pre-natal and post-natal health care for mothers;

(e) To ensure that all segments of society, in particular parents and children, are informed, have access to education and are supported in the use of basic knowledge of child health and nutrition, the advantages of breast feeding, hygiene and environmental sanitation and the prevention of accidents;

(f) To develop preventive health care, guidance for parents and family planning education and services.

3. States Parties shall take all effective and appropriate measures with a view to abolishing traditional practices prejudicial to the health of children.

4. States Parties undertake to promote and encourage international co-operation with a view to achieving progressively the full realization of the right recognized in the present article. In this regard, particular account shall be taken of the needs of developing countries.

Article 25
States Parties recognize the right of a child who has been placed by the competent authorities for the purposes of care, protection or treatment of his or her physical or mental health, to a periodic review of the treatment provided to the child and all other circumstances relevant to his or her placement.

Article 26
1. States Parties shall recognize for every child the right to benefit from social security, including social insurance, and shall take the necessary measures to achieve the full realization of this right in accordance with their national law.

2. The benefits should, where appropriate, be granted, taking into account the resources and the circumstances of the child and persons having responsibility for the maintenance of the child, as well as any other consideration relevant to an application for benefits made by or on behalf of the child.

Article 27
1. States Parties recognize the right of every child to a standard of living adequate for the child's physical, mental, spiritual, moral and social development.

2. The parent(s) or others responsible for the child have the primary responsibility to secure, within their abilities and financial capacities, the conditions of living necessary for the child's development.

3. States Parties, in accordance with national conditions and within their means, shall take appropriate measures to assist parents and others responsible for the child to implement this right and shall in case of need provide material assistance and support programmes, particularly with regard to nutrition, clothing and housing.

4. States Parties shall take all appropriate measures to secure the recovery of maintenance for the child from the parents or other persons having financial responsibility for the child, both within the State Party and from abroad. In particular, where the person having financial responsibility for the child lives in a State different from that of the child, States Parties shall promote the accession to international agreements or the conclusion of such agreements, as well as the making of other appropriate arrangements.

Article 28

1. States Parties recognize the right of the child to education, and with a view to achieving this right progressively and on the basis of equal opportunity, they shall, in particular:

(a) Make primary education compulsory and available free to all;

(b) Encourage the development of different forms of secondary education, including general and vocational education, make them available and accessible to every child, and take appropriate measures such as the introduction of free education and offering financial assistance in case of need;

(c) Make higher education accessible to all on the basis of capacity by every appropriate means;

(d) Make educational and vocational information and guidance available and accessible to all children;

(e) Take measures to encourage regular attendance at schools and the reduction of drop-out rates.

2. States Parties shall take all appropriate measures to ensure that school discipline is administered in a manner consistent with the child's human dignity and in conformity with the present Convention.

3. States Parties shall promote and encourage international cooperation in matters relating to education, in particular with a view to contributing to the elimination of ignorance and illiteracy throughout the world and facilitating access to scientific and technical knowledge and modern teaching methods. In this regard, particular account shall be taken of the needs of developing countries.

Article 29

1. States Parties agree that the education of the child shall be directed to:

(a) The development of the child's personality, talents and mental and physical abilities to their fullest potential;

(b) The development of respect for human rights and fundamental freedoms, and for the principles enshrined in the Charter of the United Nations;

(c) The development of respect for the child's parents, his or her own cultural identity, language and values, for the national values of the country in which the child is living, the country from which he or she may originate, and for civilizations different from his or her own;

(d) The preparation of the child for responsible life in a free society, in the spirit of understanding, peace, tolerance, equality of sexes, and friendship among all peoples, ethnic, national and religious groups and persons of indigenous origin;

(e) The development of respect for the natural environment.

2. No part of the present article or Article 28 shall be construed so as to interfere with the liberty of individuals and bodies to establish and direct educational institutions, subject always to the observance of the principles set forth in paragraph 1 of the present article and to the requirements that the education given in such institutions shall conform to such minimum standards as may be laid down by the State.

Article 30

In those States in which ethnic, religious or linguistic minorities or persons of indigenous origin exist, a child belonging to such a minority or who is indigenous shall not be denied the right, in community with other members of his or her group, to enjoy his or her own culture, to profess and practise his or her own religion, or to use his or her own language.

Article 31

1. States Parties recognize the right of the child to rest and leisure, to engage in play and recreational activities appropriate to the age of the child and to participate freely in cultural life and the arts.

2. States Parties shall respect and promote the right of the child to participate fully in cultural and artistic life and shall encourage the provision of appropriate and equal opportunities for cultural, artistic, recreational and leisure activity.

Article 32

1. States Parties recognize the right of the child to be protected from economic exploitation and from performing any work that is likely to be hazardous or to interfere with the child's education, or to be harmful to the child's health or physical, mental, spiritual, moral or social development.

2. States Parties shall take legislative, administrative, social and educational measures to ensure the implementation of the present article. To this end, and having regard to the relevant provisions of other international instruments, States Parties shall in particular:

(a) Provide for a minimum age or minimum ages for admission to employment;

(b) Provide for appropriate regulation of the hours and conditions of employment;

(c) Provide for appropriate penalties or other sanctions to ensure the effective enforcemnt of the present article.

Article 33

States Parties shall take all appropriate measures, including legislative, administrative, social and educational measures, to protect children from the illicit use of narcotic drugs and psychotropic substances as defined in the relevant international treaties, and to prevent the use of children in the illicit production and trafficking of such substances.

Article 34

States Parties undertake to protect the child from all forms of sexual exploitation and sexual abuse. For these purposes, States Parties shall in particular take all appropriate national, bilateral and multilateral measures to prevent:

(a) The inducement or coercion of a child to engage in any unlawful sexual activity;

(b) The exploitative use of children in prostitution or other unlawful sexual practices;

(c) The exploitative use of children in pornographic performances and materials.

Article 35

States Parties shall take all appropriate national, bilateral and multilateral measures to prevent the abduction of, the sale of or traffic in children for any purpose or in any form.

Article 36

States Parties shall protect the child against all other forms of exploitation prejudicial to any aspects of the child's welfare.

Article 37

States Parties shall ensure that:

(a) No child shall be subjected to torture or other cruel, inhuman or degrading treatment or punishment. Neither capital punishment nor life imprisonment without possibility of release shall be imposed for offences committed by persons below eighteen years of age;

(b) No child shall be deprived of his or her liberty unlawfully or arbitrarily. The arrest, detention or imprisonment of a child shall be in conformity with the law and shall be used only as a measure of last resort and for the shortest appropriate period of time;

(c) Every child deprived of liberty shall be treated with humanity and respect for the inherent dignity of the human person, and in a manner which takes into account the needs of persons of his or her age. In particular, every child deprived of liberty shall be separated from adults unless it is considered in the child's best interest not to do so and shall have the right to maintain contact with his or her family through correspondence and visits, save in exceptional circumstances;

(d) Every child deprived of his or her liberty shall have the right to prompt access to legal and other appropriate assistance, as well as the right to challenge the legality of the deprivation of his or her liberty before a court or other competent, independent and impartial authority, and to a prompt decision on any such action.

Article 38

1. States Parties undertake to respect and to ensure respect for rules of international humanitarian law applicable to them in armed conflicts which are relevant to the child.

2. States Parties shall take all feasible measures to ensure that persons who have not attained the age of fifteen years do not take a direct part in hostilities.

3. States Parties shall refrain from recruiting any person who has not attained the age of fifteen years into their armed forces. In recruiting among those persons who have attained the age of fifteen years but who have not attained the age of eighteen years, States Parties shall endeavour to give priority to those who are oldest.

4. In accordance with their obligations under international humanitarian law to protect the civilian population in armed conflicts, States Parties shall take all feasible measures to ensure protection and care of children who are affected by an armed conflict.

Article 39

States Parties shall take all appropriate measures to promote physical and psychological recovery and social re-integration of a child victim of: any form of neglect, exploitation, or abuse; torture or any other form of cruel, inhuman or degrading treatment or punishment; or armed conflicts. Such recovery and re-integration shall take place in an environment which fosters the health, self-respect and dignity of the child.

Article 40

1. States Parties recognize the right of every child alleged as, accused of, or recognized as having infringed the penal law to be treated in a manner consistent with the promotion of the child's sense of dignity and worth, which reinforces the child's respect for the human rights and fundamental freedoms of others and which takes into account the child's age and the desirability of promoting the child's re-integration and the child's assuming a constructive role in society.

2. To this end, and having regard to the relevant provisions of international instruments, States Parties shall, in particular, ensure that:

(a) No child shall be alleged as, be accused of, or recognized as having infringed the penal law by reason of acts or omissions that were not prohibited by national or international law at the time they were committed;

(b) Every child alleged as or accused of having infringed the penal law has at least the following guarantees:

(i) To be presumed innocent until proven guilty according to law;

(ii) To be informed promptly and directly of the charges against him or her, and, if appropriate, through his or her parents or legal guardians, and to have legal or other appropriate assistance in the preparation and presentation of his or her defence;

(iii) To have the matter determined without delay by a competent, independent and impartial authority or judicial body in a fair hearing according to law, in the presence of legal or other appropriate assistance and, unless it is considered not to be in the best interest of the child, in particular, taking into account his or her age or situation, his or her parents or legal guardians;

(iv) Not to be compelled to give testimony or to confess guilt; to examine or have examined adverse witnesses and to obtain the participation and examination of witnesses on his or her behalf under conditions of equality;

(v) If considered to have infringed the penal law, to have this decision and any measures imposed in consequence thereof reviewed by a higher competent, independent and impartial authority or judicial body according to law;

(vi) To have the free assistance of an interpreter if the child cannot understand or speak the language used;

(vii) To have his or her privacy fully respected at all stages of the proceedings.

3. States Parties shall seek to promote the establishment of laws, procedures, authorities and institutions specifically applicable to children alleged as, accused of, or recognized as having infringed the penal law, and, in particular:

(a) The establishment of a minimum age below which children shall be presumed not to have the capacity to infringe the penal law;

(b) Whenever appropriate and desirable, measures for dealing with such children without resorting to judicial proceedings, providing that human rights and legal safeguards are fully respected.

4. A variety of dispositions, such as care, guidance and supervision orders; counselling; probation; foster care; education and vocational training programmes and other alternatives to institutional care shall be available to ensure that children are dealt with in a manner appropriate to their well-being and proportionate both to their circumstances and the offence.

Article 41
Nothing in the present Convention shall affect any provisions which are more conducive to the realization of the rights of the child and which may be contained in:

(a) The law of a State party; or

(b) International law in force for that State.

PART II

Article 42
States Parties undertake to make the principles and provisions of the Convention widely known, by appropriate and active means, to adults and children alike.

Article 43
1. For the purpose of examining the progress made by States Parties in achieving the realization of the obligations undertaken in the present Convention, there shall be established a Committee on the Rights of the Child, which shall carry out the functions hereinafter provided.

2. The Committee shall consist of ten experts of high moral standing and recognized competence in the field covered by this Convention. The members of the Committee shall be elected by States Parties from among their nationals and shall serve in their personal capacity, consideration being given to equitable geographical distribution, as well as to the principal legal systems.

3. The members of the Committee shall be elected by secret ballot from a list of persons nominated by States Parties. Each State Party may nominate one person from among its own nationals.

...

Article 44

1. States Parties undertake to submit to the Committee, through the Secretary-General of the United Nations, reports on the measures they have adopted which give effect to the rights recognized herein and on the progress made on the enjoyment of those rights:

(a) Within two years of the entry into force of the Convention for the State Party concerned;

(b) Thereafter every five years.

Reports made under the present article shall indicate factors and difficulties, if any, affecting the degree of fulfilment of the obligations under the present Convention. Reports shall also contain sufficient information to provide the Committee with a comprehensive understanding of the implementation of the Convention in the country concerned.

A State Party which has submitted a comprehensive initial report to the Committee need not, in its subsequent reports submitted in accordance with paragraph 1 (b) of the present article, repeat basic information previously provided.

The Committee may request from States Parties further information relevant to the implementation of the Convention.

The Committee shall submit to the General Assembly, through the Economic and Social Council, every two years, reports on its activities.

6. States Parties shall make their reports widely available to the public in their own countries.

Article 45
In order to foster the effective implementation of the Convention and to encourage international cooperation in the field covered by the Convention:

(a) The specialized agencies, the United Nations Children's Fund, and other United Nations organs shall be entitled to be represented at the consideration of the implementation of such provisions of the present Convention as fall within the scope of their mandate. The Committee may invite the specialized agencies, the United Nations Children's Fund and other competent bodies as it may consider appropriate to provide expert advice on the implementation of the Convention in areas falling within the scope of their respective mandates. The Committee may invite the specialized agencies, the United Nations Children's Fund, and other United Nations organs to submit reports on the implementation of the Convention in areas falling within the scope of their activities;

...

༺๛༺๛༺๛༺๛

2. OPTIONAL PROTOCOL TO THE CONVENTION ON THE RIGHTS OF THE CHILD ON THE INVOLVEMENT OF CHILDREN IN ARMED CONFLICT (OP-CRC-AC)

The U.S. has ratified the Optional Protocol to the CRC on the involvement of Children in Armed Conflict (OP-CRC-AC) but not the CRC main treaty.

Adopted and opened for signature, ratification and accession by General Assembly resolution A/RES/54/263 of 25 May 2000, entry into force 12 February 2002

The States Parties to the present Protocol,

Encouraged by the overwhelming support for the Convention on the Rights of the Child, demonstrating the widespread commitment that exists to strive for the promotion and protection of the rights of the child,

Reaffirming that the rights of children require special protection, and calling for continuous improvement of the situation of children without distinction, as well as for their development and education in conditions of peace and security,

Disturbed by the harmful and widespread impact of armed conflict on children and the long-term consequences it has for durable peace, security and development,

Condemning the targeting of children in situations of armed conflict and direct attacks on objects protected under international law, including places that generally have a significant presence of children, such as schools and hospitals,

Noting the adoption of the Rome Statute of the International Criminal Court, in particular, the inclusion therein as a war crime, of conscripting or enlisting children under the age of 15 years or using them to participate actively in hostilities in both international and non-international armed conflict,

Considering therefore that to strengthen further the implementation of rights recognized in the Convention on the Rights of the Child there is a need to increase the protection of children from involvement in armed conflict,

Noting that Article 1 of the Convention on the Rights of the Child specifies that, for the purposes of that Convention, a child means every human being below the age of 18 years unless, under the law applicable to the child, majority is attained earlier,

Convinced that an optional protocol to the Convention that raises the age of possible recruitment of persons into armed forces and their participation in hostilities will contribute effectively to the implementation of the principle that the best interests of the child are to be a primary consideration in all actions concerning children,

Noting that the twenty-sixth International Conference of the Red Cross and Red Crescent in December 1995 recommended, inter alia, that parties to conflict take every feasible step to ensure that children below the age of 18 years do not take part in hostilities,

Welcoming the unanimous adoption, in June 1999, of International Labour Organization Convention No. 182 on the Prohibition and Immediate Action for the Elimination of the Worst Forms of Child Labour, which prohibits, inter alia, forced or compulsory recruitment of children for use in armed conflict,

Condemning with the gravest concern the recruitment, training and use within and across national borders of children in hostilities by armed groups distinct from the armed forces of a State, and recognizing the responsibility of those who recruit, train and use children in this regard,

Recalling the obligation of each party to an armed conflict to abide by the provisions of international humanitarian law,

Stressing that the present Protocol is without prejudice to the purposes and principles contained in the Charter of the United Nations, including Article 51, and relevant norms of humanitarian law,

Bearing in mind that conditions of peace and security based on full respect of the purposes and principles contained in the Charter and observance of applicable human rights instruments are indispensable for the full protection of children, in particular during armed conflict and foreign occupation,

Recognizing the special needs of those children who are particularly vulnerable to recruitment or use in hostilities contrary to the present Protocol owing to their economic or social status or gender,

Mindful of the necessity of taking into consideration the economic, social and political root causes of the involvement of children in armed conflict,

Convinced of the need to strengthen international cooperation in the implementation of the present Protocol, as well as the physical and psychosocial rehabilitation and social reintegration of children who are victims of armed conflict,

Encouraging the participation of the community and, in particular, children and child victims in the dissemination of informational and educational programmes concerning the implementation of the Protocol,

Have agreed as follows:

Article 1
States Parties shall take all feasible measures to ensure that members of their armed forces who have not attained the age of 18 years do not take a direct part in hostilities.

Article 2
States Parties shall ensure that persons who have not attained the age of 18 years are not compulsorily recruited into their armed forces.

Article 3
1. States Parties shall raise the minimum age for the voluntary recruitment of persons into their national armed forces from that set out in Article 38, paragraph 3, of the Convention on the Rights of the Child, taking account of the principles contained in that article and recognizing that under the Convention persons under the age of 18 years are entitled to special protection.

2. Each State Party shall deposit a binding declaration upon ratification of or accession to the present Protocol that sets forth the minimum age at which it will permit voluntary recruitment into its national armed forces and a description of the safeguards it has adopted to ensure that such recruitment is not forced or coerced.

3. States Parties that permit voluntary recruitment into their national armed forces under the age of 18 years shall maintain safeguards to ensure, as a minimum, that:

(a) Such recruitment is genuinely voluntary;

(b) Such recruitment is carried out with the informed consent of the person's parents or legal guardians;

(c) Such persons are fully informed of the duties involved in such military service;

(d) Such persons provide reliable proof of age prior to acceptance into national military service.

4. Each State Party may strengthen its declaration at any time by notification to that effect addressed to the Secretary-General of the United Nations, who shall inform all States Parties. Such notification shall take effect on the date on which it is received by the Secretary-General.

5. The requirement to raise the age in paragraph 1 of the present article does not apply to schools operated by or under the control of the armed forces of the States Parties, in keeping with articles 28 and 29 of the Convention on the Rights of the Child.

Article 4
1. Armed groups that are distinct from the armed forces of a State should not, under any circumstances, recruit or use in hostilities persons under the age of 18 years.

2. States Parties shall take all feasible measures to prevent such recruitment and use, including the adoption of legal measures necessary to prohibit and criminalize such practices.

3. The application of the present article shall not affect the legal status of any party to an armed conflict.

Article 5
Nothing in the present Protocol shall be construed as precluding provisions in the law of a State Party or in international instruments and international humanitarian law that are more conducive to the realization of the rights of the child.

Article 6
1. Each State Party shall take all necessary legal, administrative and other measures to ensure the effective implementation and enforcement of the provisions of the present Protocol within its jurisdiction.

2. States Parties undertake to make the principles and provisions of the present Protocol widely known and promoted by appropriate means, to adults and children alike.

3. States Parties shall take all feasible measures to ensure that persons within their jurisdiction recruited or used in hostilities contrary to the present Protocol are demobilized or otherwise released from service. States Parties shall, when

necessary, accord to such persons all appropriate assistance for their physical and psychological recovery and their social reintegration.

Article 7

1. States Parties shall cooperate in the implementation of the present Protocol, including in the prevention of any activity contrary thereto and in the rehabilitation and social reintegration of persons who are victims of acts contrary thereto, including through technical cooperation and financial assistance. Such assistance and cooperation will be undertaken in consultation with the States Parties concerned and the relevant international organizations.

2. States Parties in a position to do so shall provide such assistance through existing multilateral, bilateral or other programmes or, inter alia, through a voluntary fund established in accordance with the rules of the General Assembly.

Article 8

1. Each State Party shall, within two years following the entry into force of the present Protocol for that State Party, submit a report to the Committee on the Rights of the Child providing comprehensive information on the measures it has taken to implement the provisions of the Protocol, including the measures taken to implement the provisions on participation and recruitment.

2. Following the submission of the comprehensive report, each State Party shall include in the reports it submits to the Committee on the Rights of the Child, in accordance with Article 44 of the Convention, any further information with respect to the implementation of the Protocol. Other States Parties to the Protocol shall submit a report every five years.

3. The Committee on the Rights of the Child may request from States Parties furthe information relevant to the implementation of the present Protocol.

Article 9

1. The present Protocol is open for signature by any State that is a party to the Convention or has signed it.

2. The present Protocol is subject to ratification and is open to accession by any State. Instruments of ratification or accession shall be deposited with the Secretary-General of the United Nations.

3. The Secretary-General, in his capacity as depositary of the Convention and the Protocol, shall inform all States Parties to the Convention and all States that have signed the Convention of each instrument of declaration pursuant to Article 3.

Article 10

1. The present Protocol shall enter into force three months after the deposit of the tenth instrument of ratification or accession.

2. For each State ratifying the present Protocol or acceding to it after its entry into force, the Protocol shall enter into force one month after the date of the deposit of its own instrument of ratification or accession.

...

Source: Optional Protocol to the Convention on the Rights of the Child on the involvement of children in armed conflict, http://www.ohchr.org/EN/ProfessionalInterest/Pages/OPACCRC.aspx

⌘⌘⌘⌘⌘⌘⌘⌘

3. INSTRUMENT OF RATIFICATION OF THE UNITED STATES OF AMERICA WITH RESERVATIONS, DECLARATIONS, AND UNDERSTANDINGS, FIRST OPTIONAL PROTOCOL TO THE CONVENTION ON THE RIGHTS OF THE CHILD ON THE INVOLVEMENT OF CHILDREN IN ARMED CONFLICT

This legal instrument in U.S. and international law expresses a declaration (the terms) under which the U.S. ratifies and thus accepts legal obligations of the Optional Protocol to the Convention on the Rights of the Child on the Involvement of Children in

Armed Conflict. The U.S. made reservations, declarations, and understandings (RDU) to the OP-CRC-AC (aka First Optional Protocol to the CRC) that are legally binding on the U.S., and U.S. obligations under the First Optional Protocol to the CRC must be read in light of these RDUs. The U.S. has expressly stated that the CRC itself creates no obligations on the U.S. although two of the three optional protocols to the CRC are legally normative.

U.S. Ratification of CRC OP on Children in Armed Conflict With RUDs

Declaration:

GEORGE W. BUSH
President of the United States of America

TO ALL TO WHOM THESE PRESENTS SHALL COME, GREETING:

CONSIDERING THAT: The Optional Protocol to the Convention on the Rights of the Child on the Involvement of Children in Armed Conflict, was adopted by the United Nations General Assembly on May 25, 2000 and signed on behalf of the United States on July 5, 2000; and

The Senate of the United States of America by its resolution of June 18, 2002, two-thirds of the Senators present concurring therein, gave its advice and consent to ratification of the Optional Protocol, subject to the following understandings:

The Government of the United States of America declares, pursuant to Article 3 (2) of the Optional Protocol to the Convention on the Rights of the Child on the Involvement of Children in Armed Conflict that —

(A) the minimum age at which the United States permits voluntary recruitment into the Armed Forces of the United States is 17 years of age;

(B) The United States has established safeguards to ensure that such recruitment is not forced or coerced, including a requirement in section 505 (a) of title 10, United States Code, that no person under 18 years of age may be originally enlisted in the Armed Forces of the United States without the written consent of the person's parent or guardian, if the parent or guardian is entitled to the person's custody and control;

(C) each person recruited into the Armed Forces of the United States receives a comprehensive briefing and must sign an enlistment contract that, taken together, specify the duties involved in military service; and

(D) all persons recruited into the Armed Forces of the United States must provide reliable proof of age before their entry into military service.

Understandings:

(1) NO ASSUMPTION OF OBLIGATIONS UNDER THE CONVENTION ON THE RIGHTS OF THE CHILD — The United States understands that the United States assumes no obligations under the Convention on the Rights of the Child by becoming a party to the Protocol.

(2) IMPLEMENTATION OF OBLIGATION NOT TO PERMIT CHILDREN TO TAKE DIRECT PART IN HOSTILITIES — The United States understands that, with respect to Article 1 of the Protocol —

(A) the term "feasible measures" means those measures that are practical or practically possible, taking into account all the circumstances ruling at the time, including humanitarian and military considerations;

(B) the phrase "direct part in hostilities"

(i) means immediate and actual action on the battlefield likely to cause harm to the enemy because there is a direct causal relationship between the activity engaged in and the harm done to the enemy; and

(ii) does not mean indirect participation in hostilities, such as gathering and transmitting military information, transporting weapons, munitions, or other supplies, or forward deployment; and

(C) any decision by any military commander, military personnel, or other person responsible for planning, authorizing, or executing military action, including the assignment of military personnel, shall only be judged on the basis of all the relevant circumstances and on the basis of that person's assessment of the information reasonably available to the person at the time the person planned, authorized, or executed the action under review, and shall not be judged on the basis of information that comes to light after the action under review was taken.

(3) MINIMUM AGE FOR VOLUNTARY RECRUITMENT — The United States understands that Article 3 of the Protocol obligates States Parties to the Protocol to raise the minimum age for voluntary recruitment into their national armed forces from the current international standard of 15 years of age.

(4) ARMED GROUPS — The United States understands that the term "armed groups" in Article 4 of the Protocol means nongovernmental armed groups such as rebel groups, dissident armed forces, and other insurgent groups.

(5) NO BASIS FOR JURISDICTION BY ANY INTERNATIONAL TRIBUNAL — The United States understands that nothing in the Protocol establishes a basis for jurisdiction by any international tribunal, including the International Criminal Court.

Source: Optional Protocol to the Convention on the Rights of the Child on the Involvement of Children in Armed Conflict, New York, 25 May 2000 United States Of America: Ratification, https://treaties.un.org/doc/Treaties/2000/11/20001114%2003-38%20AM/Related%20Documents/CN.1361.2002-Eng.pdf or http://indicators.ohchr.org

4. OPTIONAL PROTOCOL TO THE CONVENTION ON THE RIGHTS OF THE CHILD ON THE SALE OF CHILDREN, CHILD PROSTITUTION, AND CHILD PORNOGRAPHY [SECOND] (OP-CRC-SC)

The U.S. has ratified the Optional Protocol to the CRC on the Sale of Children, Child Prostitution, and Child Pornography [Second] (OP-CRC-SC), but not the CRC main treaty.

[Text]

The States Parties to the present Protocol,

Considering that, in order further to achieve the purposes of the Convention on the Rights of the Child and the implementation of its provisions, especially articles 1, 11, 21, 32, 33, 34, 35 and 36, it would be appropriate to extend the measures that States Parties should undertake in order to guarantee the protection of the child from the sale of children, child prostitution and child pornography,

Considering also that the Convention on the Rights of the Child recognizes the right of the child to be protected from economic exploitation and from performing any work that is likely to be hazardous or to interfere with the child's education, or to be harmful to the child's health or physical, mental, spiritual, moral or social development,

Gravely concerned at the significant and increasing international traffic in children for the purpose of the sale of children, child prostitution and child pornography,

Deeply concerned at the widespread and continuing practice of sex tourism, to which children are especially vulnerable, as it directly promotes the sale of children, child prostitution and child pornography,

Recognizing that a number of particularly vulnerable groups, including girl children, are at greater risk of sexual exploitation and that girl children are disproportionately represented among the sexually exploited,

Concerned about the growing availability of child pornography on the Internet and other evolving technologies, and recalling the International Conference on Combating Child Pornography on the Internet, held in Vienna in 1999, in particular its conclusion calling for the worldwide criminalization of the production, distribution, exportation, transmission, importation, intentional possession and advertising of child pornography, and *stressing* the importance of closer cooperation and partnership between Governments and the Internet industry,

Believing that the elimination of the sale of children, child prostitution and child pornography will be facilitated by adopting a holistic approach, addressing the contributing factors, including underdevelopment, poverty, economic disparities, inequitable socio-economic structure, dysfunctioning families, lack of education, urban-rural migration, gender discrimination, irresponsible adult sexual behaviour, harmful traditional practices, armed conflicts and trafficking in children,

Believing also that efforts to raise public awareness are needed to reduce consumer demand for the sale of children, child prostitution and child pornography, and believing further in the importance of strengthening global partnership among all actors and of improving law enforcement at the national level,

Noting the provisions of international legal instruments relevant to the protection of children, including the Hague Convention on Protection of Children and Cooperation in Respect of Intercountry Adoption, the Hague Convention on the Civil Aspects of International Child Abduction, the Hague Convention on Jurisdiction, Applicable Law, Recognition, Enforcement and Cooperation in Respect of Parental Responsibility and Measures for the Protection of Children, and International Labour Organization Convention No. 182 on the Prohibition and Immediate Action for the Elimination of the Worst Forms of Child Labour,

Encouraged by the overwhelming support for the Convention on the Rights of the Child, demonstrating the widespread commitment that exists for the promotion and protection of the rights of the child,

Recognizing the importance of the implementation of the provisions of the Programme of Action for the Prevention of the Sale of Children, Child Prostitution and Child Pornography and the Declaration and Agenda for Action adopted at the World Congress against Commercial Sexual Exploitation of Children, held in Stockholm from 27 to 31 August 1996, and the other relevant decisions and recommendations of pertinent international bodies,

Taking due account of the importance of the traditions and cultural values of each people for the protection and harmonious development of the child, Have agreed as follows:

Article 1
States Parties shall prohibit the sale of children, child prostitution and child pornography as provided for by the present Protocol.

Article 2
For the purposes of the present Protocol:

(a) Sale of children means any act or transaction whereby a child is transferred by any person or group of persons to another for remuneration or any other consideration;

(b) Child prostitution means the use of a child in sexual activities for remuneration or any other form of consideration;

(c) Child pornography means any representation, by whatever means, of a child engaged in real or simulated explicit sexual activities or any representation of the sexual parts of a child for primarily sexual purposes.

Article 3
1. Each State Party shall ensure that, as a minimum, the following acts and activities are fully covered under its criminal or penal law, whether such offences are committed domestically or transnationally or on an individual or organized basis:

(a) In the context of sale of children as defined in Article 2:

(i) Offering, delivering or accepting, by whatever means, a child for the purpose of:

    a. Sexual exploitation of the child;

    b. Transfer of organs of the child for profit;

    c. Engagement of the child in forced labour;

(ii) Improperly inducing consent, as an intermediary, for the adoption of a child in violation of applicable international legal instruments on adoption;

    (b) Offering, obtaining, procuring or providing a child for child prostitution, as defined in Article 2;

    (c) Producing, distributing, disseminating, importing, exporting, offering, selling or possessing for the above purposes child pornography as defined in Article 2.

4. Subject to the provisions of the national law of a State Party, the same shall apply to an attempt to commit any of the said acts and to complicity or participation in any of the said acts.

3. Each State Party shall make such offences punishable by appropriate penalties that take into account their grave nature.

4. Subject to the provisions of its national law, each State Party shall take measures, where appropriate, to establish the liability of legal persons for offences established in paragraph 1 of the present article. Subject to the legal principles of the State Party, such liability of legal persons may be criminal, civil or administrative.

5. States Parties shall take all appropriate legal and administrative measures to ensure that all persons involved in the adoption of a child act in conformity with applicable international legal instruments.

Article 4

1. Each State Party shall take such measures as may be necessary to establish its jurisdiction over the offences referred to in Article 3, paragraph 1, when the offences are committed in its territory or on board a ship or aircraft registered in that State.

2. Each State Party may take such measures as may be necessary to establish its jurisdiction over the offences referred to in Article 3, paragraph 1, in the following cases:

    (a) When the alleged offender is a national of that State or a person who has his habitual residence in its territory;

    (b) When the victim is a national of that State.

3. Each State Party shall also take such measures as may be necessary to establish its jurisdiction over the aforementioned offences when the alleged offender is present in its territory and it does not extradite him or her to another State Party on the ground that the offence has been committed by one of its nationals.

4. The present Protocol does not exclude any criminal jurisdiction exercised in accordance with internal law.

Article 5

1. The offences referred to in Article 3, paragraph 1, shall be deemed to be included as extraditable offences in any extradition treaty existing between States Parties and shall be included as extraditable offences in every extradition treaty subsequently concluded between them, in accordance with the conditions set forth in such treaties.

2. If a State Party that makes extradition conditional on the existence of a treaty receives a request for extradition from another State Party with which it has no extradition treaty, it may consider the present Protocol to be a legal basis for extradition in respect of such offences. Extradition shall be subject to the conditions provided by the law of the requested State.

3. States Parties that do not make extradition conditional on the existence of a treaty shall recognize such offences as extraditable offences between themselves subject to the conditions provided by the law of the requested State.

4. Such offences shall be treated, for the purpose of extradition between States Parties, as if they had been committed not only in the place in which they occurred but also in the territories of the States required to establish their jurisdiction in accordance with Article 4.

5. If an extradition request is made with respect to an offence described in Article 3, paragraph 1, and the requested State Party does not or will not extradite on the basis of the nationality of the offender, that State shall take suitable measures to submit the case to its competent authorities for the purpose of prosecution.

Article 6
1. States Parties shall afford one another the greatest measure of assistance in connection with investigations or criminal or extradition proceedings brought in respect of the offences set forth in Article 3, paragraph 1, including assistance in obtaining evidence at their disposal necessary for the proceedings.

2. States Parties shall carry out their obligations under paragraph 1 of the present article in conformity with any treaties or other arrangements on mutual legal assistance that may exist between them. In the absence of such treaties or arrangements, States Parties shall afford one another assistance in accordance with their domestic law.

Article 7
States Parties shall, subject to the provisions of their national law:

(a) Take measures to provide for the seizure and confiscation, as appropriate, of:

(i) Goods, such as materials, assets and other instrumentalities used to commit or facilitate offences under the present protocol;

(ii) Proceeds derived from such offences;

(b) Execute requests from another State Party for seizure or confiscation of goods or proceeds referred to in subparagraph (a);

(c) Take measures aimed at closing, on a temporary or definitive basis, premises used to commit such offences.

Article 8
1. States Parties shall adopt appropriate measures to protect the rights and interests of child victims of the practices prohibited under the present Protocol at all stages of the criminal justice process, in particular by:

(a) Recognizing the vulnerability of child victims and adapting procedures to recognize their special needs, including their special needs as witnesses;

(b) Informing child victims of their rights, their role and the scope, timing and progress of the proceedings and of the disposition of their cases;

(c) Allowing the views, needs and concerns of child victims to be presented and considered in proceedings where their personal interests are affected, in a manner consistent with the procedural rules of national law;

(d) Providing appropriate support services to child victims throughout the legal process;

(e) Protecting, as appropriate, the privacy and identity of child victims and taking measures in accordance with national law to avoid the inappropriate dissemination of information that could lead to the identification of child victims;

(f) Providing, in appropriate cases, for the safety of child victims, as well as that of their families and witnesses on their behalf, from intimidation and retaliation;

(g) Avoiding unnecessary delay in the disposition of cases and the execution of orders or decrees granting compensation to child victims.

2. States Parties shall ensure that uncertainty as to the actual age of the victim shall not prevent the initiation of criminal investigations, including investigations aimed at establishing the age of the victim.

3. States Parties shall ensure that, in the treatment by the criminal justice system of children who are victims of the offences described in the present Protocol, the best interest of the child shall be a primary consideration.

4. States Parties shall take measures to ensure appropriate training, in particular legal and psychological training, for the persons who work with victims of the offences prohibited under the present Protocol.

5. States Parties shall, in appropriate cases, adopt measures in order to protect the safety and integrity of those persons and/or organizations involved in the prevention and/or protection and rehabilitation of victims of such offences.

6. Nothing in the present article shall be construed to be prejudicial to or inconsistent with the rights of the accused to a fair and impartial trial.

Article 9
1. States Parties shall adopt or strengthen, implement and disseminate laws, administrative measures, social policies and programmes to prevent the offences referred to in the present Protocol. Particular attention shall be given to protect children who are especially vulnerable to such practices.

2. States Parties shall promote awareness in the public at large, including children, through information by all appropriate means, education and training, about the preventive measures and harmful effects of the offences referred to in the present Protocol. In fulfilling their obligations under this article, States Parties shall encourage the participation of the community and, in particular, children and child victims, in such information and education and training programmes, including at the international level.

3. States Parties shall take all feasible measures with the aim of ensuring all appropriate assistance to victims of such offences, including their full social reintegration and their full physical and psychological recovery.

4. States Parties shall ensure that all child victims of the offences described in the present Protocol have access to adequate procedures to seek, without discrimination, compensation for damages from those legally responsible.

5. States Parties shall take appropriate measures aimed at effectively prohibiting the production and dissemination of material advertising the offences described in the present Protocol.

Article 10
1. States Parties shall take all necessary steps to strengthen international cooperation by multilateral, regional and bilateral arrangements for the prevention, detection, investigation, prosecution and punishment of those responsible for acts involving the sale of children, child prostitution, child pornography and child sex tourism. States Parties shall also promote international cooperation and coordination between their authorities, national and international non-governmental organizations and international organizations.

2. States Parties shall promote international cooperation to assist child victims in their physical and psychological recovery, social reintegration and repatriation.

3. States Parties shall promote the strengthening of international cooperation in order to address the root causes, such as poverty and underdevelopment, contributing to the vulnerability of children to the sale of children, child prostitution, child pornography and child sex tourism.

4. States Parties in a position to do so shall provide financial, technical or other assistance through existing multilateral, regional, bilateral or other programmes.

Article 11

Nothing in the present Protocol shall affect any provisions that are more conducive to the realization of the rights of the child and that may be contained in:

(a) The law of a State Party;

(b) International law in force for that State.

Article 12

1. Each State Party shall, within two years following the entry into force of the present Protocol for that State Party, submit a report to the Committee on the Rights of the Child providing comprehensive information on the measures it has taken to implement the provisions of the Protocol.

2. Following the submission of the comprehensive report, each State Party shall include in the reports they submit to the Committee on the Rights of the Child, in accordance with Article 44 of the Convention, any further information with respect to the implementation of the present Protocol. Other States Parties to the Protocol shall submit a report every five years.

3. The Committee on the Rights of the Child may request from States Parties further information relevant to the implementation of the present Protocol.

Article 13

1. The present Protocol is open for signature by any State that is a party to the Convention or has signed it.

2. The present Protocol is subject to ratification and is open to accession by any State that is a party to the Convention or has signed it. Instruments of ratification or accession shall be deposited with the Secretary-General of the United Nations.

...

Source: Optional Protocol to the Convention on the Rights of the Child on the Sale of Children, Child Prostitution, and Child Pornography [Second] (OP-CRC-SC), http://www.ohchr.org/EN/ProfessionalInterest/Pages/OPSCCRC.aspx

❦❦❦❦❦❦❦❦

5. INSTRUMENT OF RATIFICATION OF THE UNITED STATES OF AMERICA WITH RESERVATIONS, DECLARATIONS, AND UNDERSTANDINGS, SECOND OPTIONAL PROTOCOL TO THE CONVENTION ON THE RIGHTS OF THE CHILD ON THE SALE OF CHILDREN, CHILD PROSTITUTION, AND CHILD PORNOGRAPHY

This is the legal instrument under US and international law that expresses a reservation (terms) under which the United States ratifies and thus accepts legal obligations under the Optional Protocol to the Convention on the Rights of the Child on the Sale of Children, Child Prostitution and Child Pornography. The U.S. Senate made reservations, declarations, and understandings (RDU) to the OP-CRC-SC (aka Second Optional Protocol to the CRC) that are legally binding on the U.S. insofar as they are consistent with the object and purpose of the Second Optional Protocol to the CRC, and U.S. obligations under the Second Optional Protocol to the CRC must be read in light of these RDUs. The U.S. has expressly stated in this instrument that the CRC itself creates no obligations on the U.S. although two of the three optional protocols to the CRC are legally normative.

[Text]

Reservation:

"To the extent that the domestic law of the United States does not provide for jurisdiction over an offense described in Article 3 (1) of the Protocol if the offense is committed on board a ship or aircraft registered in the United States, the obligation with respect to jurisdiction over that offense shall not apply to the United States until such time as the United States may notify the Secretary-General of the United Nations that United States domestic law is in full conformity with the requirements of Article 4 (1) of the Protocol.

The Senate's advice and consent is subject to the following understandings:

(1) NO ASSUMPTION OF OBLIGATIONS UNDER THE CONVENTION ON THE RIGHTS OF THE CHILD – The United States understands that the United States assumes no obligations under the Convention on the Rights of the Child by becoming a party to the Protocol.

(2) THE TERM "CHILD PORNOGRAPHY" – The United States understands that the term "sale of children" as defined in Article 2(a) of the Protocol, is intended to cover any transaction in which remuneration or other consideration is given and received under circumstances in which a person who does not have a lawful right to custody of the child thereby obtains de facto control over the child.

(3) THE TERM "CHILD PORNOGRAPHY" – The United States understands the term "child pornography," as defined in Article 2(c) of the Protocol, to mean the visual representation of a child engaged in real or simulated sexual activities or of the genitalia of a child where the dominant characteristic is depiction for a sexual purpose.

(4) THE TERM "TRANSFER OF ORGANS FOR PROFIT" – The United States understands that –

(A) the term "transfer of organs for profit," as used in Article 3(1)(a)(i) of the Protocol, does not cover any situation in which a child donates an organ pursuant to lawful consent; and

(B) the term "profit," as used in Article 3(1)(a)(i) of the Protocol, does not include the lawful paymeasonable amount associated with the transfer of organs, including any payment for the expense of travel, housing, lost wages, or medical costs.

(5) THE TERMS "APPLICABLE INTERNATIONAL LEGAL INSTRUMENTS" AND "IMPROPERLY INDUCING CONSENT" –

(A) UNDERSTANDING OF "APPLICABLE INTERNATIONAL LEGAL INSTRUMENTS" – The United States understands that the term "applicable international legal instruments" in Articles 3 (1) (a) (ii) and 3 (5) of the Protocol refers to the Convention on Protection of Children and Co-operation in Respect of Intercountry Adoption done at The Hague on May 29, 1993 (in this paragraph referred to as "The Hague Convention").

(B) NO OBLIGATION TO TAKE CERTAIN ACTION – The United States is not a party to The Hague Convention, but expects to become a party. Accordingly, until such time as the United States becomes a party to The Hague Convention, it understands that it is not obligated to criminalize conduct proscribed by Article 3(1)(a)(ii) of the Protocol or to take all appropriate legal and administrative measures required by Article 3(5) of the Protocol.

(C) UNDERSTANDING Of "IMPROPERLY INDUCING CONSENT" – The United States understands that the term "Improperly inducing consent" in Article 3(1)(a)(ii) of the Protocol means knowingly and willfully inducing consent by offering or giving compensation for the relinquishment of parental rights.

(6) IMPLEMENTATION OF THE PROTOCOL IN THE FEDERAL SYSTEM OF THE UNITED STATES – The United States understands that the Protocol shall be implemented by the Federal Government to the extent that it exercises jurisdiction over the matters covered therein, and otherwise by the State and local governments. To the extent that State and local governments exercise jurisdiction over such matters, the Federal Government shall as necessary, take appropriate measures to ensure the fulfillment of the Protocol.

Source: United Nations Human Rights Office of the High Commissioner, Status of Ratification Interactive Dashboard
http://indicators.ohchr.org

6. U.S. INITIAL REPORTS CONCERNING THE OPTIONAL PROTOCOL TO THE CONVENTION ON THE RIGHTS OF THE CHILD ON THE INVOLVEMENT OF CHILDREN IN ARMED CONFLICT

This is the U.S. Department of State's prepared report to the U.N. Committee on the Rights of the Child pursuant to Article 8 of the Optional Protocol on the Involvement of Children in Armed Conflict.

U.S. Initial Reports Concerning the Optional Protocol to the Convention on the Rights of the Child on the involvement of children in armed conflict

Initial Report Concerning the Optional Protocol on the Involvement of Children in Armed Conflict

I. Introduction

1. The Government of the United States of America welcomes this opportunity to report to the Committee on the Rights of the Child on measures giving effect to its undertakings under the Optional Protocol to the Convention on the Rights of the Child on the Involvement of Children in Armed Conflict ("the Protocol"), in accordance with Article 8 thereof. The organization of this initial report follows the General Guidelines of the Committee on the Rights of the Child regarding the form and content of initial reports to be submitted by States Parties (CRC/OP/AC/1, 12 October 2001).

2. The Protocol deals reasonably with the issues of minimum ages for compulsory recruitment, voluntary recruitment, and direct participation in hostilities, while fully protecting the military recruitment and readiness requirements of States Parties that rely on national voluntary armed forces.

3. The Protocol raises the minimum age for military conscription to 18 years. The Protocol also calls for governments to set a minimum age for voluntary recruitment above the current international standard of 15 years and to report on measures to ensure that recruitment is truly voluntary. States Parties must take "all feasible measures" to ensure that members of their armed forces who are not yet 18 do not take a "direct" part in hostilities. States that become party to the Protocol also agree to "take all feasible measures to prevent" in their territory the recruitment and use of persons younger than 18 in hostilities by non-governmental armed groups, including by adopting legal measures to prohibit and criminalize such practices.

4. Another important provision of the Protocol is its promotion of international cooperation and assistance in the rehabilitation and social reintegration of children who have been victimized by armed conflict.

5. No implementing legislation is required with respect to U.S. ratification of the Protocol since current U.S. law meets the standards in the Protocol.

6. The Protocol is subject to ratification or open for accession by any State, i.e., it is not limited to States Parties to the Convention on the Rights of the Child. By ratifying the Protocol, the United States does not become party to the Convention on the Rights of the Child, or assume any rights or obligations under that Convention.

II. Information on Measures and Developments Relating to the Implementation of the Protocol

Article 1 – Direct Participation in Hostilities

7. The Protocol requires States Parties to "take all feasible measures" to ensure that members of their armed forces under age 18 do not take "a direct part in hostilities." At the time the United States deposited its instrument of ratification, it expressed the following understanding of the meaning of the terms "feasible" and "direct part in hostilities:"

With respect to Article 1, the United States understands that the term "feasible measures" means those measures that are practical or practically possible, taking into account all the circumstances ruling at the time, including humanitarian and military considerations. The United States understands the phrase "direct part in hostilities" to mean immediate and actual action on the battlefield likely to cause harm to the enemy because there is a direct causal relationship between the activity engaged in and the harm done to the enemy. The phrase "direct participation in hostilities" does not mean indirect participation in hostilities, such as gathering and transmitting military information, transporting weapons, munitions and other supplies, or forward deployment. The United States further understands that any decision by any military commander, military personnel, or any other person responsible for planning, authorizing, or executing military action, including the assignment of military personnel, shall only be judged on the basis of that person's assessment of the information reasonably available to the person at the time the person planned, authorized, or executed the action under review, and shall not be judged on the basis of information that comes to light after the action under review was taken.

8. This understanding is based upon the negotiating history of Article 1 of the Protocol. The language in Article 1 is drawn from Article 38(2) of the Convention on the Rights of the Child, and Article 77(2) of the Protocol Additional to the Geneva Conventions of 12 August 1949, relating to the Protection of Victims of International Armed Conflicts (Protocol 1), which both require that States Parties take all "feasible measures" to ensure that children under the age of 15 do not take a "direct part in hostilities."

9. The terminology used in Article 1 of the Protocol recognizes that in exceptional cases it will not be "feasible" for a commander to withhold or prevent a soldier under the age of 18 from taking a part in hostilities. The term "feasible" is understood in the law of armed conflict to mean that which is "practicable or practically possible taking into account all circumstances ruling at the time, including humanitarian and military considerations." This is the definition used in Article 3(10) of the Protocol to the 1980 Conventional Weapons Convention Concerning the Use of Mines, Booby-Traps and Other Devices (Protocol II), adopted at Geneva October 10, 1980. It is also the generally accepted meaning of the term in Protocol I to the Geneva Conventions. Indeed, a number of States (e.g., Canada, Germany, Ireland, Italy, Netherlands, and Spain) included such a definition of "feasible" in understandings that accompanied their instruments of ratification to Protocol I to the Geneva Conventions.

10. The standard set out in Article 1 also recognizes that there is no prohibition concerning indirect participation in hostilities or forward deployment. The term "direct" has been understood in the context of treaties relating to the law of armed conflict (including International Committee of the Red Cross (ICRC) commentaries on the meaning of the provisions of Protocol I to the Geneva Conventions) to mean a direct causal relationship between the activity engaged in and the harm done to the enemy at the time and place where the activity takes place.

11. Throughout negotiations of Article 77(2) of Protocol I to the Geneva Conventions, Article 38(2) of the Convention on the Rights of the Child, and Article 1 of this Protocol, some delegations, as well as the ICRC, repeatedly attempted to replace "all feasible measures" with "necessary" or a variant thereof and to remove the reference to "direct." However, other delegations, including the United States, insisted that there should be no deviation from existing treaties using the same terminology.

12. For example, during negotiation of the Convention on the Rights of the Child, the ICRC explained its position in the Working Group as follows:

The Working Group could have taken advantage of the adoption of Article 20 [subsequently renumbered as Article 38] to improve protection by prescribing that the States Party to the present Convention take all "necessary" measures instead of "all feasible" measures. In other words, the text which was finally approved means that voluntary participation by children is not totally prohibited. During the Diplomatic Conference (1974-1977) [concerning Protocol I to the Geneva Conventions], the ICRC had proposed the words 'necessary measures' but this was, unfortunately, not accepted. Protocol I, Article 77 speaks of 'feasible measures'.

Likewise, the Working Group could have strengthened protection by removing the word 'direct'. The ICRC suggested this too during the Diplomatic Conference but the proposal was not approved. This being the case, it can reasonably be inferred from the present Article 20 of the Draft Convention that indirect participation, for example gathering and transmitting military information, transporting weapons, munitions and other supplies is not affected by the provision.

Written Statement of the ICRC, 22 January 1987 (UN Doc. E.CN.4/1987/WG.1/WP.4).

13. Prior to U.S. ratification of the Protocol, U.S. law and practice had been to assign all recruits after basic training, including those aged 17, to a unit, but not based on whether that unit might be deployed into hostilities. Accordingly, the United States generally supported an age 17 standard for participation in hostilities. Prior to the January 2000 negotiat-

ing session of the Protocol, however, the Department of Defense reviewed its practice and decided that it could support adoption of a rule that would require that the United States take all "feasible measures" to ensure that persons under the age of 18 would not take "a direct part in hostilities." The Department of Defense determined that it could execute its national security responsibilities under the obligation of Article 1 of the Protocol, as the terms of Article 1 (with respect to the meaning of "all feasible measures" and "take a direct part in hostilities") are currently understood under the law of armed conflict.

14. At the final session of negotiations, just before adoption of the Protocol, the U.S. delegation made a statement regarding its understanding of Article 1 that the U.N. Working Group summarized as follows:

As for participation in hostilities, the terms in Article 1, with their roots in international humanitarian law and the law of armed conflict, were clear, well understood and contextually relevant. The United States of America would take all steps it feasibly could to ensure that under-18-year-old service personnel did not take a direct part in hostilities. While the standard recognizes that, in exceptional cases, it might not be feasible for a commander to withhold or remove such a person from taking a direct part in hostilities, the United States believed that it was an effective, sensible and practical standard that would promote the object that all sought: protecting children and ensuring that the protocol had the widest possible adherence and support.

Working Group on Involvement of Children in Armed Conflict, Report on Its Sixth Session, U.N. Doc. E/CN.4/2000/74, para. 131.

15. In contrast, other delegations expressed disappointment that the Protocol did not bar "indirect" participation in hostilities and that the discretionary power granted to States through use of the term "feasible measures" weakened the Protocol. Id. At paras. 106, 116, 121-22, 135, 143, 148 (statements by the ICRC, Italy, Belgium, Ethiopia, the Russian Federation, and Portugal). The Russian delegation acknowledged that since States were not required to prohibit participation, but only called on to take "all feasible measures" to prevent such participation, the Protocol left States open to the possibility in any emergency of involving persons under 18 years of age in hostilities. Id. At para. 131.

16. For the United States, the restriction to "take all feasible measures" to ensure that members of the U.S. Armed Forces who have not attained 18 years of age do not take "a direct part in hostilities" affects, on a year-to-year basis, approximately 1,500 17-year-old service members. Virtually all 17-year-olds who enter the U.S. Armed Forces are high school seniors and are placed in the Delayed Entry Program until after they earn a high school diploma. When they enter basic training, only about 7,500 of those entering the U.S. Armed Forces are still 17 years old. On average, initial training lasts from 4 to 6 months depending on the Service, and nearly 80% of the 17-year-olds turn 18 during this period. Thus, after this training is completed, on average about 1,500 17-year-old service members will be fully trained and ready for operational assignment.

17. To implement the terms of Article 1 of the Protocol, U.S. Military Services have adopted an implementation plan. The implementation plans have been tailored to meet the unique mission requirements of each Service. The implementation plans went into effect in January 2003. The plans relate to the date (not year) of birth of the individual. Summaries of each Service implementation plan, and the U.S. Coast Guard practice, follow:

Army. The Army will not assign soldiers outside the United States, either on permanent or temporary duty orders, until they reach their eighteenth birthdate. For those soldiers under eighteen who were already overseas at the time the implementation plan went into effect, commanders were to take all feasible measures to ensure these soldiers not take a direct part in hostilities until they reached 18 years of age.

Navy. Sailors who have not reached their eighteenth birthdate will not be assigned to ships and squadrons that are scheduled to deploy at a date earlier than their eighteenth birthday.

Air Force. The Air Force will not assign airmen who have not reached their eighteenth birthdate to hostile fire/imminent danger areas.

Marine Corps. The Marine Corps has directed commanders who have operational and administrative control of Marines who have not reached their eighteenth birthdate to track and manage the assignment of those Marines such that all feasible measures are taken to ensure they do not take a direct part in hostilities. This responsibility may not be delegated below the battalion or squadron commander level.

Coast Guard. The Coast Guard has five core missions: maritime security, maritime safety, protection of natural resources, maritime mobility, and national defense. Under Title 14 of the U.S. Code, the Coast Guard is a "military service and a branch of the armed forces of the United States at all times." The Coast Guard exercises its duties as a military service primarily in two of its core missions: maritime security and national defense. Since its inception, the Coast Guard has participated in every major U.S. armed conflict. Coast Guard units have and continue to participate in Operations Iraqi Freedom and Enduring Freedom.

In accordance with 10 U.S.C 505 and Coast Guard policy, a seventeen year-old may apply for entry to the Coast Guard only if that person obtains written consent from his or her custodial parent or guardian, is a legally emancipated minor, or is married. Written consent must be executed before a notary public, recruiter-in-charge, or recruiter. If not legally separated or divorced, consent must be given by both parents (or the surviving parent, if one parent is deceased). If the parents are legally separated or divorced or if one parent is missing, consent must be given by the custodial parent. If both parents are deceased or if custody was awarded to an individual other than the parents, consent must be given by the legally appointed guardian. Otherwise, all applicants must be at least eighteen years old. Waivers for minimum age are not authorized (therefore, no one under seventeen years of age may apply for entry to the Coast Guard). It should also be noted that under Coast Guard policy, recruiters must verify an applicant's documents to ensure they meet the minimum age requirements by carefully examining birth certificates.

The Coast Guard does not have a written policy establishing a rule for "all feasible measures" to ensure enlistees do not take part in armed conflict. However, it is Coast Guard practice not to assign recent, non-rate basic training graduates directly to conflict areas or to any of the Coast Guard cutters serving in those regions.

Article 2 – Forced or Compulsory Recruitment

18. Article 2 prohibits States Parties from forcibly or compulsorily recruiting into military service anyone under 18. The United States does not permit compulsory recruitment of any person under 18 for any type of military service. While inactive, the U.S. selective service system remains established in law and provides for involuntary induction at and after age 18. See The Military Selective Service Act, 50 U.S.C. App. 451 et seq. By law, the Selective Service System is an independent agency, separate from the Department of Defense.

19. The general scope of Article 2 of the Protocol is substantially identical to Article 3 of the Convention (No. 182) for Elimination of the Worst Forms of Child Labor, adopted by the International Labor Conference on June 17, 1999, which, inter alia, requires that States Parties take immediate and effective measures to secure the elimination of forced or compulsory recruitment of children under the age of 18 for use in armed conflict. ILO Convention No. 182 entered into force with respect to the United States on December 2, 2000.

Article 3 – Voluntary Recruitment

20. Article 3(1) obliges States Parties to raise the minimum age for voluntary recruitment into their national armed forces from 15 years, which is the minimum age provided in Article 38(3) of the Convention on the Rights of the Child and in Article 77(2) of Protocol I to the Geneva Conventions. The United States expressed the following understanding in order to clarify the nature of the obligation it assumed under Article 3(1):

The United States understands that Article 3 obliges States Parties to raise the minimum age for voluntary recruitment into their national armed forces from the current international standard of age 15.

21. Article 3(1) states that in raising the age for voluntary recruitment States Parties shall "take account" of the "principles" contained in Article 38(3) of the Convention on the Rights of the Child and recognize that persons under the age of 18 are entitled to special protection. In this regard, Article 38(3) states that "[i]n recruiting among those persons who have attained the age of fifteen years but who have not attained the age of eighteen years, States Parties shall endeavour to give priority to those who are oldest." This provision is compatible with the long-standing U.S. practice of permitting 17-year-olds, but not those who are younger, to volunteer for service in the Armed Forces. The Department of Defense goal is that at least 90% of new recruits should have high school diplomas, but many enlistment contracts are signed with high school seniors who may be as young as 17. While waiting for graduation, these individuals are placed in the Delayed

Entry Program. Most of these individuals turn 18 before graduating from high school and shipping to basic training. Of the nearly 175,000 new enlistees each year, only about 7,500 (just over 4%) are 17 when they ship to basic training, and nearly all of those (80%) will turn 18 while in training. At no time since 1982 has the percentage of 17-year-old recruits into the Armed Forces exceeded 8%. Qualified 17-year-olds will remain an integral part of the U.S. military's recruiting efforts into the foreseeable future, but it is not expected that their numbers will fluctuate significantly, or dominate the Armed Forces' recruiting pool. No one under age 17 is eligible for recruitment, including for participation in the Delayed Entry Program.

22. Article 3(2) provides that each State Party effects the increase in minimum age by depositing a binding declaration to that effect upon ratification, and by providing a description of the safeguards it maintains to ensure that such recruitment is not forced or coerced. The United States submitted the following declaration in conjunction with the deposit of its instrument of ratification of the Protocol:

Pursuant to Article 3(2) of the Protocol, the United States declares that the minimum age at which the United States permits voluntary recruitment into the Armed Forces of the United States is 17 years of age. The United States has established safeguards to ensure that such recruitment is not forced or coerced, including a requirement in section 505(a) of title 10, United States Code, that no person under 18 years of age may be originally enlisted in the Armed Forces of the United States without the written consent of the person's parent or guardian, if the parent or guardian is entitled to the person's custody and control. . . . Moreover, each person recruited into the Armed Forces of the United States receives a comprehensive briefing and must sign an enlistment contract that, taken together, specify the duties involved in military service. All persons recruited into the Armed Forces of the United States must provide reliable proof of age before their entry into the military service.

23. The "comprehensive briefing" referred to in the U.S. declaration cited above is conducted through the Military Entrance Processing Command (MEPCOM), which gives each applicant a briefing that outlines applicable regulations based on Title 10 of the U.S. Code, and the enlistment form (DD Form 4). This briefing is outlined in the MEPCOM Regulation 601-23, which also includes a list of questions that each applicant must be asked (e.g., do you understand that you are joining the Army for 6 years?). The briefing also defines fraudulent enlistments and associated penalties.

24. The MEPCOM also has programs that check to ensure that the date of birth entered by a recruiter falls into the age window outlined by Title 10, MEPCOM regulations, and other joint military service regulations. Additionally, each recruiter is required to obtain an original (or certified) government document that states the individual's age. Typically, this is an original birth certificate. If the individual is 17 years old, the recruiter is required to witness both parents' signatures. If a parent is divorced, then only one signature, i.e., of a custodial parent, is required provided the custodial parent can produce the original (raised seal) divorce decree.

25. Article 3(3) further describes safeguards that States are required to maintain, including ensuring that such recruitment is genuinely voluntary; requiring the informed consent of the person's parents or legal guardians; fully informing such recruits of the duties involved in military service; and requiring reliable proof of age prior to acceptance into national military service. U.S. law and policy, described above, meets these requirements.

26. Article 3(5) provides that military schools are exempt from the requirements of this article. By its terms, this exemption extends to military schools, regardless of whether or not individuals attending these facilities are members of the armed forces. In this regard, U.S. law specifies a minimum age of 17 for admission to military academies. See, e.g., 10 U.S.C. 4346.

Article 4 – Non-governmental Actors
27. Article 4(1) provides that armed groups, distinct from the armed forces of a State, "should" not recruit or use in hostilities persons under the age of 18. Article 4(2) requires that States Parties take "all feasible measures" to prevent in their territory the recruitment and use in hostilities of persons under the age of 18 by "armed groups, distinct from the armed forces of a State," including by the enactment of legislation to ensure that such recruitment and use is punishable as a criminal offense under their national laws. Additionally, Article 4(3) provides that "the application of the present article under this Protocol shall not affect the legal status of any party to an armed conflict."

28. In order to clarify the nature of the obligation assumed under Article 4, the United States submitted the following understanding with its instrument of ratification of the Protocol:

The United States understands that the term "armed groups" in Article 4 of the Protocol means nongovernmental armed groups such as rebel groups, dissident armed forces, and other insurgent groups.

29. Consistent with Article 4, U.S. law already prohibits insurgent activities by nongovernmental actors against the United States, irrespective of age. See 18 U.S.C. 2381, et seq. U.S. law also prohibits the formation within the United States of insurgent groups, again irrespective of age, which have the intent of engaging in armed conflict with foreign powers. See 18 U.S.C. 960.

Article 5 – Savings Clause
30. Article 5 is a savings clause. The article states that nothing in the Protocol is to be construed as precluding provisions in the law of a State Party, international instruments or international humanitarian law that might provide more favorable treatment with respect to the rights of children.

Article 6 – National Implementation
31. Article 6 obliges States Parties to ensure effective implementation and enforcement of obligations accepted under the Protocol within their respective jurisdictions; to ensure wide dissemination of the Protocol; to take all feasible measures to demobilize children employed in contravention of the terms of the Protocol; and "when necessary" accord to such children "appropriate assistance" for their physical and psychological recovery, and their social reintegration.

32. As a matter of good administration, the Department of Defense issued an internal directive providing guidance to its components on the Protocol's requirements. It will not be necessary for the United States to demobilize or provide appropriate assistance to U.S. children, since the United States does not utilize children in contravention of the terms of the Protocol.

Article 7 – International Cooperation and Assistance
33. Article 7(1) obliges States Parties to undertake to cooperate in the implementation of the Protocol, including in the prevention of any act contrary to the Protocol and in the demobilization, rehabilitation, and social reintegration of persons who are victims of acts contrary to the Protocol through, inter alia, technical cooperation and financial assistance. Article 7(2) specifies that States Parties "in a position to do so" shall provide financial, technical or other assistance through existing multilateral, bilateral or other programs.

34. The United States has contributed substantial resources to international programs aimed at preventing the recruitment of children and reintegrating child ex-combatants into society and is committed to continue to develop rehabilitation approaches that are effective in addressing this serious and difficult problem. The United States applies a definition of child ex-combatants in keeping with the Cape Town Principles of 1997, which cover any child associated with fighting forces in any capacity, whether or not he or she ever bore arms. In this regard, United States programming adopts a broad approach by seeking to include all children affected by armed conflict rather than singling out for separate services former child combatants. It also espouses the principle that family reunification and community reintegration are both goals and processes of recovery for former child combatants. United States programming aimed at assisting children affected by war addresses the disarmament, demobilization, rehabilitation and integration into civilian society of former child combatants; the prevention of recruitment of children; and the recovery and rehabilitation of children affected by armed conflict, including activities to identify separated children, protect them from harm, provide appropriate interim care, carry out tracing for family reunification, arrange alternate care for children who cannot be reunited, reform their legal protections and facilitate community reintegration. The Protocol serves as a means for encouraging such programs and constitutes an important tool for increasing assistance to children who are affected by armed conflict.

35. Through the United States Agency for International Development (USAID), the United States has contributed over $10 million over the past several years toward the demobilization of child combatants and reintegration into their communities. A few noteworthy accomplishments sponsored by USAID in conjunction with implementing partners include the following:
  • In Angola, enhanced child protection and psycho-social services, increased access to basic services and livelihood opportunities, and integrated lessons learned into national policies and legislation for children.

Supported the development and implementation of an innovative methodology and program for training parents, teachers and other child caretakers to identify and address emotional and psychological problems caused by conflict-related stress and trauma.

- In Afghanistan, conducted a program to provide emotional support for war-affected children, including child ex-combatants, through non-formal education activities, opportunities to play, training in vocational skills, and psychosocial recovery and well-being. Such programs seek to instill a sense of security, encourage positive social interactions, enable children to participate in the recovery and development of their community, provide opportunities for emotional expression, teach non-violent approaches to conflict resolution, sensitize communities to the needs and legal rights of children, and facilitate the social integration and protection of all children, including those who have participated in or been affected by armed conflict.

- In Colombia, promoted successful reintegration of child ex-combatants into society through (1) the establishment of safe houses/centers around the country where groups of 20 to 25 ex-combatants live, study, and receive needed counseling, and (2) the creation of a network of registered NGOs to provide confidential support upon "graduation" from the centers. Simultaneously supported consolidation of the legal framework for the protection of child ex-combatants and provided relevant training to judges, public defenders, human rights ombudsman representatives, and local, regional, and national authorities. Helped develop protocols, guidelines, manuals, and an information management system to monitor and evaluate the program. Supported development and implementation of a national strategy to prevent child recruitment focused on high-risk indigenous and Afro-Colombian youth based on community strengthening, including community income-generation and social infrastructure projects.

...

36. Since 2001, the U.S. Department of Labor (USDOL) has provided approximately $24 million towards preventing the recruitment of child combatants and promoting the economic reintegration of former child soldiers and war-affected youth. A few noteworthy achievements supported by USDOL in conjunction with implementing partners include the following:

- In Angola, launched a three-year, $4 million program in 2005 to provide literacy, life skills, and primary school equivalency education to 24,025 youth, including war-affected children.
- In Afghanistan, enrolled nearly 3,400 underage former soldiers in community-based reintegration programs combining informal education, skills training, and psycho-social support.

...

Article 8 — State Parties

37. Article 8 provides that States Parties shall submit, within two years following the entry into force of the Protocol for that State Party, a report to the Committee on the Rights of the Child providing comprehensive information on the measures it has taken to implement the provisions of the Protocol.

38. Initial U.S. reporting under Article 8 is limited to reporting on the measures the United States has taken to implement the provisions of the Protocol. The United States has no obligation to comply with any additional reporting requirements contained in Article 44 of the Convention on the Rights of the Child, nor is the Committee on the Rights of the Child competent to request information from the United States on any matter other than implementation of the Protocol.

39. Article 8(2) also creates separate supplemental reporting requirements for States Parties to the Convention on the Rights of the Child (i.e., to include reports on implementation of the Protocol within supplemental reports submitted under the Convention on the Rights of the Child) and for States that are not parties to the Convention on the Rights of the Child (i.e., to submit supplemental reports on any further information with respect to implementation of the Protocol every five years). Additionally, Article 8(3) draws from Article 44(4) of the Convention on the Rights of the Child when it permits the Committee on the Rights of the Child to request further information relevant to the implementation of the Protocol.

40. The Protocol grants the Committee on the Rights of the Child no authority other than receiving reports and requesting additional information as set forth above. During the negotiations, States rejected proposals that would have permit-

ted the Committee, inter alia, to hold hearings, initiate confidential inquiries, conduct country visits, and transmit findings to the State Party concerned.

41. This report is submitted in accordance with U.S. obligations under Article 8 of the Protocol.

Article 9 – Signature and Ratification

42. Article 9 provides that the Protocol is subject to ratification or open for accession by any State, i.e., it is not limited to parties to the Convention on the Rights of the Child. During the negotiations of the Protocol, the United Nations Legal Counsel provided a legal opinion which confirmed that under the rules of the law of treaties there was no legal impediment to an instrument which is entitled "optional protocol" being open to participation by States that had not also established, or which did not also establish, their consent to be bound by the convention to which that instrument was said to be an optional protocol. The U.N. opined that there is no necessary legal impediment to an instrument which is entitled "optional protocol" being open to participation by States which have not also established, or which do not also establish, their consent to be bound by the convention, to which that instrument is said to be an "optional protocol."

U.N. Office of Legal Affairs, 18 January 2000. Cf., also, "Rights of the Child," Report of the Working Group on a draft optional protocol to the Convention on the Rights of the Child on involvement of children in armed conflict on its sixth session, E/CN.4/2000/74 (27 March 2000), para 82.

43. Consistent with the fact that the Protocol is an independent international agreement, the following understanding was attached to the U.S. instrument of ratification:

The United States understands that the Protocol constitutes an independent multilateral treaty, and that the United States does not assume any obligations under the Convention on the Rights of the Child by becoming a party to the Protocol.

Article 10 – Instrument of Ratification

44. The United States deposited its instrument of ratification of the Protocol on December 23, 2002. The Protocol entered into force with respect to the United States on January 23, 2003.

Article 11 – Denunciation

45. The United States has taken no steps to denounce the Protocol.

Source: U.S. Department of State, Diplomacy in Action, Initial report Concerning the Optional Protocol on the Involvement of Children in Armed Conflict, https://www.state.gov/j/drl/rls/83929.htm or https://www.state.gov/j/drl/rls/c22156.htm or https://www.state.gov/documents/organization/84649.pdf

7. U.S. INITIAL REPORTS CONCERNING THE OPTIONAL PROTOCOL TO THE CONVENTION ON THE RIGHTS OF THE CHILD ON THE SALE OF CHILDREN, CHILD PROSTITUTION AND CHILD PORNOGRAPHY

This is the U.S. Department of State's prepared report to the U.N. Committee on the Rights of the Child pursuant to Article 12 of the Optional Protocol on the Sale of Children, Child Prostitution and Child Pornography.

[Text; footnotes omitted]

I. INTRODUCTION

1. The Government of the United States of America welcomes this opportunity to report to the Committee on the Rights of the Child on measures giving effect to its undertakings under the Optional Protocol to the Convention on the Rights of the Child on the sale of children, child prostitution and child pornography (the "Protocol"), in accordance with Article 12 thereof. The organization of this initial report follows the General Guidelines of the Committee on the

Rights of the Child regarding the form and content of initial reports to be submitted by States Parties (CRC/OP/SA/1, 4 April 2002).

2. It is especially important for the United States that the Protocol contains effective and practical strategies to prosecute and penalize those who commit crimes involving child prostitution, child pornography and trafficking in children. The Protocol is subject to ratification by any State Party or signatory to the Convention on the Rights of the Child. Thus, the United States was able to become a party to the Protocol because it had signed the Convention on the Rights of the Child in February 1995, although the United States assumed no obligation under the Convention on the Rights of the Child by becoming a party to the Protocol. The U.S. instrument of ratification is attached at Annex I.

3. Prior to U.S. ratification of the Protocol, U.S. federal and state law satisfied the substantive requirements of the Protocol. Accordingly, no new, implementing legislation was required to bring the United States into compliance with the substantive obligations that it assumed under the Protocol, although a technical legal lacuna caused the United States to enter a reservation with respect to offenses committed on board a ship or aircraft registered in the United States. The provisions of the Protocol are not self-executing under U.S. domestic law, with one exception. That exception is Article 5, discussed below, which permits States Parties to consider the offenses covered by Article 3(1) as extraditable offenses in any existing extradition treaty between States Parties.

II. INFORMATION ON MEASURES AND DEVELOPMENTS RELATING TO THE IMPLEMENTATION OF THE PROTOCOL

Article 1 – Prohibition of Sale of Children, Child Pornography and Child Prostitution
4. Article 1 provides that "States Parties shall prohibit the sale of children, child prostitution and child pornography as provided for by the present Protocol." By its terms, Article 1 is introductory in nature and creates no obligations aside from those set forth in the remaining articles.

Article 2 – Definitions
5. Article 2 defines "sale of children," "child prostitution" and "child pornography."

6. Article 2(a) defines sale of children as "any act or transaction whereby a child is transferred by any person or group of persons to another for remuneration or other consideration."

7. To clarify the definition of sale of children in Article 2(a) the following understanding accompanied the U.S. instrument of ratification:

The United States understands that the term "sale of children," as defined in Article 2(a) of the Protocol, is intended to cover any transactions in which remuneration or other consideration is given and received under circumstances in which a person who does not have a lawful right to custody of the child thereby obtains de facto authority over the child.

8. With this understanding, as more fully discussed in the analysis of Article 3, U.S. law is consistent with the obligations of the Protocol with respect to the sale of children.

9. Article 2(b) defines child prostitution as "the use of a child in sexual activities for remuneration or any other form of consideration." As more fully described in the analysis of Article 3, the definition set forth in the Protocol is consistent with U.S. federal and state law and practice.

10. Article 2(c) defines child pornography as "any representation, by whatever means, of a child engaged in real or simulated explicit sexual activities or any representation of the sexual parts of a child, the dominant characteristic of which is depiction for a sexual purpose." A number of delegations, including those of the European Union, Japan, and the United States, stated their understanding that the term "any representation" meant "visual representation." Delegations, including the U.S. delegation, also stated their understanding that the term "sexual parts" meant "genitalia." These understandings were included in the negotiating record of the final session.

11. To confirm this meaning of Article 2(c), the following understanding accompanied the U.S. instrument of ratification:

The United States understands the term, "child pornography," as defined in Article 2(c) of the Protocol, to mean the visual representation of a child engaged in real or simulated sexual activities or of the genitalia of a child where the dominant characteristic is depiction for a sexual purpose.

12. With this understanding, as more fully discussed in the analysis of Article 3, U.S. law is consistent with the obligations of the Protocol with respect to child pornography.

Article 3 – Criminalization

13. Article 3(1) provides that States Parties shall ensure that the following acts are covered under their criminal or penal law and punishable by appropriate penalties, taking into account the grave nature of such offenses:

- in the context of sale of children, the offering, delivering, or accepting by whatever means a child for the purpose of sexual exploitation of the child, transfer of organs for profit, or engagement of the child in forced labor (Article 3(1)(a)(i));
- in the context of sale of children, "improperly inducing consent, as an intermediary, for the adoption of a child in violation of applicable international instruments on adoption" (Article 3(1)(a)(ii));
- offering, obtaining, procuring or providing a child for child prostitution (Article 3(l)(b)); and
- producing, distributing, disseminating, importing, exporting, offering, selling, or possessing for these purposes child pornography (Article 3(1)(c)).

14. As discussed below, these acts violate criminal statutes under U.S. federal and state laws.

Article 3(1)(a)(i)a – Sexual Exploitation

15. The requirement to criminalize the sale of a child for purposes of sexual exploitation largely overlaps with the requirement to criminalize acts concerning child prostitution and child pornography. The term "sexual exploitation" is not defined, but it was generally understood during the negotiations that the term means prostitution, pornography, or other sexual abuse in the context of the sale of children.

16. In the United States, the Federal and State Governments have enacted criminal laws to protect children from sexual exploitation by adults. For example, federal and state laws prohibiting child sexual abuse and statutory rape laws are used to prosecute adults who sexually exploit children for the above-described purposes. Moreover, as set forth in detail in the analysis of Article 3(1)(b) and 3(1)(c), federal and state law prohibit exploitation of children for purposes of prostitution and pornography. Additionally, federal law prohibits trafficking in children for sexual purposes. 18 U.S.C. 1591, which was passed as part of the Trafficking Victims Protection Act of 2000, criminalizes all sex trafficking of children, regardless of whether fraud, force or coercion was used in the offense. There is no requirement that the sex trafficking cross state lines, provided it can be shown that the conduct is in or affecting interstate or foreign commerce. In addition, under 18 U.S.C. 2423(a), it is prohibited to transport in interstate commerce any individual under age 18 with the intent that the "individual engage in prostitution or in any sexual activity for which any person can be charged with a criminal offense." Attempts to do so are prohibited by 18 U.S.C. 2423(e). As an example of a state law, see, e.g., NMSA [New Mexico] 1978, 30-6A 1-4, Sexual Exploitation of Children. During its Legislative Session 2007, New Mexico is also proposing a bill similar to 18 U.S.C. 1591 to criminalize the trafficking of persons. In Utah, child prostitution is a second-degree felony punishable by 1 to 15 years in prison. Section 76-10-1306, Utah Code Annotated. Also, enticement of a child to engage in sexual activity over the Internet is a second-degree felony punishable by 1 to 15 years in prison. Section 76-5-401, Utah Code Annotated. Idaho punishes the following offenses: Sexual abuse of a child under the age of 16 years, I.C. 18-1506, Ritualized abuse of a child, I.C. 18-1506A, Sexual exploitation of a child, I.C. 18-1507, Lewd conduct with minor child under sixteen, I.C. 18-1508, Sexual battery of a minor child under eighteen years of age, I.C. 18-1508A.

Article 3(1)(a)(i)b – Transfer of Organs of the Child for Profit

17. During the negotiations, States limited the scope of the Protocol with respect to organ trafficking to situations where (1) the sale of a child occurred and (2) the organs of that child were subsequently extracted and sold for a profit.

18. U.S. federal law contains comprehensive protections against trafficking in the organs of a child. U.S. federal law criminalizes acquiring, receiving, or otherwise transferring any human organ for valuable consideration for use in human transplantation if the transfer affects interstate commerce. 42 U.S.C. 274e (National Organ Transplant Act of 1984, as

amended). The federal proscription is limited to transfers affecting interstate commerce because "laws governing medical treatment, consent, definition of death, autopsy, burial, and the disposition of dead bodies are exclusively State law." S.Rep. 98-382, 98th Cong., 2nd Sess. 1984. Nonetheless, the phrase "affecting interstate commerce" is generally interpreted broadly by U.S. courts.

19. While U.S. state law may not always criminalize the sale of organs per se, the situation addressed in the Protocol would inevitably fall within the scope of one or more criminal state statutes. Since the transfer of organs of a child must be within the context of the sale of a child, situations involving the lawful consent of a child to donate an organ in which the transfer does not involve valuable consideration are not prohibited. Accordingly, depending on the nature of the crime and state law, the conduct prohibited by the Protocol would constitute assault, and might also be battery, maiming, child abuse or criminal homicide.

20. Consequently, to clarify the scope of the obligation to criminalize the transfer of organs in Article 3 the United States expressed the following understanding in its instrument of ratification:

The United States understands that the term "transfer of organs for profit" as used in Article 3(l)(a)(i) of the Protocol, does not cover any situation in which a child donates an organ pursuant to lawful consent. Moreover, the United States understands that the term "profit," as used in Article 3(1)(a)(i) of the Protocol, does not include the lawful payment of a reasonable amount associated with the transfer of organs, including any payment for the expense of travel, housing, lost wages, or medical costs.

Article 3(1)(a)(i)c – Engagement of the Child in Forced Labor

21. The Protocol requires States Parties to criminalize the conduct of both the seller and buyer of a child in the context of a sale, i.e., (1) acts of arranging for a buyer of a child (seller's conduct), (2) delivering the child pursuant to a sale (the seller's conduct or the conduct of his/her agent), and (3) accepting the child pursuant to the sale (the buyer's conduct). Since "offering, delivering or accepting" a child for the purpose of forced labor must take place in the context of a sale, criminal penalties are required under Article (3)(1)(a)(i)c where the transaction has been completed.

22. U.S. federal law, consistent with the requirements of Article 3(1)(a)(i)c, criminalizes the sale of a child for the purpose of engagement in forced labor. Forced labor is specifically prohibited by 18 U.S.C. 1589, which was passed as part of the Trafficking Victims Protection Act of 2000. Section 1589 criminalizes providing or obtaining the labor or services of a person by (1) threats of serious harm to, or physical restraint against, that person or another person; (2) by means of any scheme, plan, or pattern intended to cause the person to believe that, if the person did not perform such labor or services, that person or another person would suffer serious harm or physical restraint, or (3) by means of the abuse or threatened abuse of the law or the legal process. Congress passed 1589 in response to the Supreme Court's narrow interpretation of the involuntary servitude statute, 18 U.S.C. 1584, in United States v. Kozminski, 487 U.S. 931 (1988) (holding that the statutory prohibition against involuntary servitude is limited to cases involving compulsion of services by use or threatened use of physical or legal coercion). In addition to the forced labor statute, other provisions of the U.S. Code provide criminal penalties for peonage, enticement into slavery, involuntary servitude, and trafficking with respect to peonage, slavery, involuntary servitude, or forced labor, sex trafficking, as discussed above, and unlawful conduct with respect to documents in furtherance of trafficking, peonage, slavery, involuntary servitude, or forced labor. See 18 U.S.C. 1581, 1583, 1584, 1590, 1591, and 1592. Attempts to commit such crimes are penalized under 18 U.S.C. 1594. These laws reach any such conduct that takes place anywhere in the United States. Federal law further criminalizes interstate kidnapping (18 U.S.C. 1201). The kidnapping statutes punish individuals who kidnap others, including minors, across state lines. Also, New Mexico is proposing a bill during its Legislative Session 2007 to criminalize the trafficking of persons, including provisions to prohibit forced labor of children, and will include provisions to penalize the seller and the buyer. Idaho law prohibits human trafficking for sexual purposes or for labor. I.C. 18-18-8501 through 18-8505.

23. The provisions of 18 U.S.C. 241, the federal civil rights conspiracy statute, prohibits conspiracies to violate the Thirteenth Amendment. The Thirteenth Amendment prohibits slavery and involuntary servitude and has been interpreted very broadly. "The undoubted aim of the Thirteenth Amendment . . . was not merely to end slavery but to maintain a system of completely free and voluntary labor throughout the United States." Pollock v. Williams, 322 U.S. 4, 17 (1944). It has been construed to grant Congress the "power to pass all laws necessary and proper for abolishing all badges and incidents of slavery." Civil Rights Cases, 109 U.S. 3, 20 (1883). In Jones v. Alfred H. Mayer Co., 392 U.S. 409, 440

(1968), the Supreme Court declared that Congress has the power "rationally to determine what are the badges and the incidents of slavery." Furthermore, under the Thirteenth Amendment, Congress may reach conduct by private individuals as well as governments.

24. Finally, a person who "aids, abets, counsels, commands, induces or procures" the commission of one of these federal offenses is punishable as a principal under 18 U.S.C. 2. Accordingly, those who take part in a portion of the transaction resulting in the sale of a child for the purpose of forced labor will also be subject to punishment under U.S. anti-trafficking laws in combination with 2. Such conduct when involving two or more persons could also incur conspiracy liability under 18 U.S.C. 371.

Article 3(1)(a)(ii) – Improperly Inducing Consent as an Intermediary for Adoption in Violation of Applicable International Legal Instruments on Adoption

25. The obligation contained in Article 3(l)(a)(ii) to criminalize "improperly inducing consent, as an intermediary, for the adoption of a child in violation of applicable international legal instruments on adoption" is drawn from the Convention on Protection of Children and Co-operation in respect of Intercountry Adoption (the "Hague Convention"), adopted May 29, 1993. The Hague Convention (Article 4(c)(3)) requires that an adoption within the scope of the Convention shall take place only if the competent authorities of the State of origin determine, inter alia, that consent has not been induced by payment or compensation of any kind.

26. During the final session of negotiations of the Protocol, both Japan and the United States stated their understanding that "applicable international instruments on adoption" meant the Hague Convention. Further, both countries stated their understanding that, since they were not parties to that instrument, they would not be bound to penalize the conduct barred by the Hague Convention, i.e., improperly inducing consent. The United States further stated that it understood the term "improperly inducing consent" to mean knowingly and willfully inducing consent by offering or giving compensation for the relinquishment of parental rights. These understandings are reflected in the negotiating record of the last session. No delegation stated a contrary understanding.

27. On September 20, 2002, the United States Senate gave its advice and consent to ratification of the Hague Convention. The Executive Branch is expected to deposit the instrument of ratification for the Convention as soon as it is able to carry out all of the obligations of the Convention. If the United States were to ratify the Hague Convention, it would have an obligation under the Protocol to criminalize the conduct specified in Article 3(1)(a)(ii). The implementing legislation with respect to the Hague Convention would criminalize an intermediary's knowing and willful inducement of consent by offering or giving compensation for the relinquishment of parental rights. See Intercountry Adoption Act of 2000, 404, P.L. 106-279.

28. The U.S. Government has issued final regulations necessary to meet Convention obligations, notably 22 C.F.R. 96. Application of the regulations is underway; accrediting entities have been identified and engaged and they are in the process of accrediting adoption service providers. New immigration rules also need to be promulgated and/or put into effect by the Department of Homeland Security, which exercises authority over immigration matters. Once these processes are complete, the United States will be in a position to carry out obligations under the Convention. Currently, it is estimated that this will occur, and that the United States will be able to deposit its instrument of ratification sometime in 2007. Up-to-date status information is available on the web at http://www.travel.state.gov/family/adoption/convention/convention_462.html.

29. In order to clarify the nature of U.S. obligations under Article 3(1)(a)(ii), the following understanding accompanied the U.S. instrument of ratification:

The United States understands that the term "applicable international legal instruments" in Articles 3(1)(a)(ii) and 3(5) of the Protocol refers to the Convention on Protection of Children and Co-operation in Respect of Intercountry Adoption done at the Hague on May 29, 1993 (in this paragraph referred to as "The Hague Convention"). The United States is not a party to The Hague Convention, but expects to become a party. Accordingly, until such time as the United States becomes a party to The Hague Convention, it understands that it is not obligated to criminalize conduct proscribed by Article 3(1)(a)(ii) of the Protocol or to take all appropriate legal and administrative measures required by Article 3(5) of the Protocol. The United States further understands that the term "improperly inducing consent" in Article 3(1)(a)(ii) of the Protocol means knowingly and willfully inducing consent by offering or giving compensation for the relinquishment of parental rights.

Article 3(1)(b) – Child Prostitution

30. Child prostitution is not legal anywhere in the United States. Under U.S. federal law, the Mann Act, 18 U.S.C. 2421, prohibits transporting a person across foreign or state borders for the purpose of prostitution. In addition to this general prohibition, federal law specifically prohibits transportation across foreign or state borders of any individual under age 18 with the intent that the "individual engage in prostitution or in any sexual activity for which any person can be charged with a criminal offense." 18 U.S.C. 2423. Federal laws further prohibit enticing, persuading, inducing, etc., any person to travel across a state boundary for prostitution or for any sexual activity for which any person may be charged with a crime, 18 U.S.C. 2422, and travel with intent to engage in any sexual act with one under age 18, 18 U.S.C. 2423(b). The newest federal legal tool in the fight against child prostitution is 18 U.S.C. 1591, which prohibits sex trafficking of children. Sex trafficking is defined as causing a person to engage in a commercial sex act through force, fraud, or coercion, or where the victim is under 18. The term "commercial sex act" means any sex act, on account of which anything of value is given to or received by anyone. For offenses involving persons under the age of 18, there is no requirement of force, fraud, or coercion. There are additional penalties if the victim is younger than 14. Furthermore, unlike the Mann Act, there is no requirement that any person be transported across foreign or state borders.

31. In addition, all 50 states prohibit prostitution activities involving minors under the age of 18. State child prostitution statutes specifically address patronizing a child prostitute, inducing or employing a child to work as a prostitute, or actively aiding the promotion of child prostitution. See, e.g., NMSA [New Mexico] 1978, 30-6A (4), Sexual Exploitation of Children by prostitution; in Utah, child prostitution is a second-degree felony punishable by 1 to 15 years in prison. Section 76-10-1306, Utah Code Annotated.

Article 3(1)(c) – Child Pornography

32. U.S. federal and state criminal laws also prohibit the child pornography activities proscribed by Article 3(1)(c).

33. Federal law prohibits the production, distribution, receipt, and possession of child pornography, if the pornographic depiction was produced using any materials that had ever been transported in interstate or foreign commerce, including by computer, or if the image was transported interstate or across a U.S. border. 18 U.S.C. 2251-2252A. Conspiracy and attempts to violate the federal child pornography laws are also chargeable federal offenses. Thus, federal law essentially reaches all the conduct proscribed by this Article.

34. More specifically, 18 U.S.C. 2251 establishes as criminal offenses the use, enticement, employment, coercion, or inducement of any minor to engage in "any sexually explicit conduct for the purpose of producing any visual depiction" of that conduct. That provision further prohibits the transportation of any minor in interstate or foreign commerce with the intent that the minor engage in sexually explicit conduct for the purpose of producing any visual depiction of such conduct. Parents, legal guardians and custodians are punishable under this provision if they permit a minor to engage in sexually explicit conduct for the purpose of producing a visual depiction of that conduct that the parent or guardian knows or has reason to know will be transported or has been transported in interstate or foreign commerce. The provision also subjects to criminal penalty those who produce and reproduce the offending material, as well as those who advertise seeking/offering to receive such materials or seeking/offering participation in visual depictions of minors engaged in sexually explicit conduct.

35. Federal law also prohibits (1) the transfer, sale, purchase, and receipt of minors for use in production of visual depictions of minors engaged in sexually explicit conduct, 18 U.S.C. 2251A; (2) knowingly transporting, shipping, receiving, distributing, or possessing any visual depiction involving a minor in sexually explicit conduct, 18 U.S.C. 2252 and 2252A; (3) the use of a minor to produce child pornography for importation into the United States, and the receipt, distribution, sale, or possession of child pornography intending that the visual depiction will be imported into the United States, 18 U.S.C. 2260. For purposes of these statutes, a minor is defined as anyone under age 18. 18 U.S.C. 2256(1).

36. Sexually explicit conduct is defined in these federal statutes as "actual or simulated (A) sexual intercourse, including genital-genital, oral-genital, anal-genital, or oral-anal, whether between persons of the same or opposite sex; (B) bestiality; (C) masturbation; (D) sadistic or masochistic abuse; or (E) lascivious exhibition of the genitals or pubic area of any person." 18 U.S.C. 2256(2). Further, each state has enacted laws addressing child pornography. The precise scopes of

these statutes vary from state to state; however, they all prohibit the visual depiction by any means of a child engaging in sexually explicit conduct. While the exact wording of the statutes may differ, all state statutes address the following three areas: (1) production: employment or use of a minor to engage in or assist in any sexually explicit conduct for the purpose of producing a depiction of that conduct; (2) trafficking: distributing, transmitting or selling child pornography; and (3) procurement: inducing or persuading a minor to be the subject of child pornography. Under NMSA 1978, 30-6A (3), Sexual Exploitation of Children, New Mexico state law prohibits the production, distribution, receipt, and possession of child pornography, and under NMSA 1978, 30-37-3.2, Child Solicitation by a Computer, it prohibits the soliciting of a minor, by computer, to engage in sexual intercourse, sexual contact, or in a sexual obscene performance. For the purposes of determining jurisdiction, child solicitation by computer is committed in New Mexico if a computer transmission either originates or is received in New Mexico. In Utah, possession, production or distribution of child pornography is a second-degree felony punishable by 1 to 15 years in prison. Section 76-5a-4, Utah Code Annotated. Enticement of a child to engage in sexual activity over the Internet is also a second-degree felony punishable by 1 to 15 years in prison. Section 76-5-401, Utah Code Annotated.

Article 3(2) – Ancillary Criminal Liability

37. The Protocol does not obligate States to criminalize attempts to commit acts covered by Article 3(1) or complicity or participation in such acts. Article 3(2) provides that "subject to the provisions of a State Party's national law, the same shall apply to an attempt to commit any of these acts and to complicity or participation in any of these acts." The phrase "subject to the provisions of a State Party's national law" was specifically incorporated into Article 3(2) to reflect the fact that practice with respect to the coverage of attempts differs in national laws.

38. Under 18 U.S.C. 2, aiding and abetting the commission of an offense against the United States is a criminal offense. Federal and state laws do not, however, criminalize all attempts to commit the offenses covered by the Protocol. (E.g., many U.S. states do not criminalize attempts to commit prostitution.)

39. In sum, although U.S. law does not always punish the attempt to commit, or all forms of participation in, Article 3(1) offenses, U.S. law is consistent with the requirements of Article 3(2).

Article 3(3) – Effective Sanction

40. U.S. federal and state laws punish the conduct proscribed by the Protocol with sufficient severity as required by Article 3(3). For example, federal offenses cited above, by which the United States would implement the Protocol's requirement to criminalize the conduct described in Article 3(1), are felonies. For 18 U.S.C. 1584 (involuntary servitude) and 1589 (forced labor), the term of imprisonment is up to 20 years, but if death results or if the violation includes kidnapping or an attempt to kidnap, aggravated sexual abuse or an attempt to commit aggravated sexual abuse, or an attempt to kill, the defendant may be sentenced to any term of years or life. Penalties for sex trafficking of children are even more severe. 18 U.S.C. 1591 provides for a mandatory minimum of 15 years imprisonment and a maximum penalty of life imprisonment for child sex trafficking if the victim is under 14 years of age, and a mandatory minimum of 10 years imprisonment and a maximum of 40 years imprisonment if the victim is between the ages of 14 and 18.

41. The statute relating to sexual exploitation of minors (which prohibits producing and advertising child pornography), 18 U.S.C. 2251, provides for a range of penalties, including fines and sentences ranging from 15 years to life imprisonment; the statute prohibiting selling or buying of children for the purpose of producing child pornography, 18 U.S.C. 2251A, has a mandatory minimum penalty of 30 years imprisonment and a maximum penalty of life imprisonment; the statutes covering activities related to material involving the sexual exploitation of children and child pornography (the statutes are slightly different, but both generally cover child pornography offenses other than production, which is covered by 2251), 18 U.S.C. 2252 and 2252A, provide for penalties ranging from a maximum of 40 years imprisonment (for knowing distribution, transportation, receipt, etc., of child pornography, with a prior qualifying conviction), a mandatory minimum of 5 years imprisonment for knowing distribution, transportation, receipt, etc., of child pornography, and a maximum imprisonment of not more than 10 years for possession of child pornography without a prior qualifying conviction (possession of child pornography with a prior qualifying conviction is punishable by a mandatory minimum term of 10 years imprisonment and a maximum term of 20 years imprisonment). The prohibition of the production or use of sexually explicit depictions of a minor for importation into the United States, 18 U.S.C. 2260, contains penalties ranging from a mandatory minimum of 5 years and a maximum of 15 years for a first offense not involving production and a man-

datory minimum of 15 years imprisonment and a maximum penalty of 30 years for a first offense involving production to a mandatory minimum of 35 years and a maximum of life for a third offense involving production.

42. The statutes relating to transportation for purposes of prostitution or criminal sexual activity, 18 U.S.C. 2421-2423, provide for fines and terms of imprisonment ranging from not more than 10 years imprisonment (18 U.S.C. 2421-transportation of any individual for prostitution or criminal sexual activity) to life imprisonment (18 U.S.C. 2422(b)-enticement of a minor to engage in criminal sexual activity; 18 U.S.C. 2423(a)-transportation of a minor to engage in criminal sexual activity). Both 18 U.S.C. 2422(b) and 2423(a) have a 10 year mandatory minimum term of imprisonment. Additionally, as noted above, 18 U.S.C. 1591 provides for a mandatory minimum of 15 years imprisonment and a maximum penalty of life imprisonment for child sex trafficking.

43. With regard to the transfer of organs, 42 U.S.C. 274e(b) provides for a substantial fine and/or a term of imprisonment of not more than five years.

Article 3(4) – Liability of Legal Persons

44. Article 3(4) requires States Parties, where appropriate and subject to provisions of their national law, to establish liability (whether criminal, civil, or administrative) of legal persons for the offenses established in Article 3(1).

45. Generally, under U.S. law, a corporation is criminally liable for the acts of its employees or agents if the employee's or agent's acts (1) lie within the scope of employment and (2) are motivated at least in part by an intent to benefit the corporation. See United States v. Sun Diamond, 138 F.3d 961, 970 (D.C. Cir. 1998). Liability can be imputed to the corporation even though the employee's conduct was not within the employee's actual authority (provided it was within his "apparent authority") and even though it may have been contrary to the corporation's stated policies. See United States v. Hilton Hotels, Inc., 467 F.2d 1000, 1004 (9th Cir. 1972). Accordingly, U.S. law is consistent with Article 3(4) since a State Party is required to establish corporate liability "where appropriate" and "subject to provisions of its national law."

Article 4 – Jurisdiction

46. Article 4 provides that each State Party shall take measures as may be necessary to establish jurisdiction over criminal conduct identified in Article 3(1) concerning the sale of children, child prostitution, and child pornography when the offense is committed in its territory or on board a ship or aircraft registered in that State (Article 4(1)). Each State Party is also required to establish jurisdiction when the alleged offender is present in its territory and it does not extradite him to another State Party on the ground that the offense has been committed by one of its nationals (Article 4(3)). Article 4 further provides that each State Party may, but is not obligated to, establish jurisdiction in the following cases: (1) when the alleged offender is a national of that State or has his habitual residence in that country (Article 4(2)(a)) and (2) when the victim is a national of that State (Article 4((2)(b)).

47. The general nature of the U.S. obligations under the Protocol was clarified by the following U.S. understanding:

The United States understands that the Protocol shall be implemented by the Federal Government to the extent that it exercises jurisdiction over the matters covered therein, and otherwise by the State and local governments. To the extent that State and local governments exercise jurisdiction over such matters, the Federal Government shall, as necessary, take appropriate measures to ensure the fulfillment of the Protocol.

Article 4(1) – Territorial, Ship, and Aircraft Jurisdiction

48. Article 4(1) obligates States to take "such measures as may be necessary" to establish jurisdiction over the offenses referred to in Article 3(1), when the offenses are committed in its territory or on board a ship or aircraft registered in that State.

49. Federal laws criminalizing the offenses described in the Protocol confer jurisdiction over such offenses committed on U.S. territory. Additionally, U.S. laws extend special maritime and territorial criminal jurisdiction (18 U.S.C 7) over crimes involving (among others) sexual abuse, (18 U.S.C. 2241-2245), child pornography (18 U.S.C. 2252 and 2252A), assault (18 U.S.C. 113), maiming (18 U.S.C. 114), murder (18 U.S.C. 1111), and manslaughter (18 U.S.C. 1112). Special maritime and territorial jurisdiction extends to any vessel or aircraft belonging in whole or in part to the United States, or any citizen or corporation thereof, while such vessel or aircraft is on or over the high seas or any other waters within the admiralty or maritime jurisdiction of the United States and out of the jurisdiction of any particular State. Spe-

cial maritime jurisdiction also extends to any place outside of the jurisdiction of any nation with respect to an offense by or against a national of the United States. Additionally, federal law extends special aircraft jurisdiction over the following crimes (among others) if committed on aircraft registered in the United States (49 U.S.C. 46501, 46506): assault (18 U.S.C. 113), maiming (18 U.S.C. 114), murder (18 U.S.C. 1111), manslaughter (18 U.S.C. 1112), and attempts to commit murder or manslaughter (18 U.S.C. 1113). For cases not covered by special aircraft or special maritime and territorial jurisdiction, U.S. law extends jurisdiction in other ways. U.S. law extends jurisdiction over transportation in foreign commerce of any individual who has not attained the age of 18 years with the intent to cause the person to be used to produce child pornography and the transportation in foreign commerce of child pornography images (18 U.S.C. 2251, 2252, and 2252A). U.S. law also prohibits travel with intent to engage in illicit sexual conduct (defined as a commercial sex act with a person under 18 or a sexual act with a person under 18 that would be in violation of federal law had it happened in the special maritime and territorial jurisdiction of the United States) (18 U.S.C. 2423(b), or engaging in illicit sexual conduct in foreign places (18 U.S.C. 2423(c)). U.S. law also applies extraterritorially to child pornography offenses where there is an intent to import the images to the United States (18 U.S.C. 2260). U.S. law also broadly extends criminal jurisdiction over vessels used in peonage and slavery (18 U.S.C. 1582, 1585-1588), while the statute outlawing child sex trafficking applies in cases in or affecting foreign commerce as well (18 U.S.C. 1591).

50. Accordingly, while U.S. law provides a broad range of bases on which to exercise jurisdiction over offenses covered by the Protocol that are committed "on board a ship or aircraft registered in" the United States (emphasis added), U.S. jurisdiction in such cases is not uniformly stated for all crimes covered by the Protocol, nor is it always couched in terms of "registration" in the United States. Therefore, the reach of U.S. jurisdiction may not be co-extensive with the obligation contained in this Article. This is a minor technical discrepancy. As a practical matter, it is unlikely that any case would arise which could not be prosecuted due to the lack of maritime or aircraft jurisdiction. The United States did not, therefore, delay ratification of the Protocol for this reason, but instead entered a reservation at the time of ratification that suspended the obligation that the United States establish jurisdiction over any covered offenses that may fall within this technical gap until the United States has enacted the necessary legislation to establish such jurisdiction. Accordingly, the following reservation accompanied the U.S. instrument of ratification:

Subject to the reservation that, to the extent that the domestic law of the United States does not provide for jurisdiction over an offense described in Article 3(1) of the Protocol if the offense is committed on board a ship or aircraft registered in the United States, the obligation with respect to jurisdiction over that offense shall not apply to the United States until such time as the United States may notify the Secretary-General of the United Nations that United States domestic law is in full conformity with the requirements of Article 4(1) of the Protocol.

Article 4(2) – Nationality and Passive Personality Jurisdiction
51. With respect to Article 4(2), some federal laws provide for the assertion of jurisdiction over U.S. nationals for covered offenses committed outside the United States, e.g., 18 U.S.C. 1585 (seizure, detention, transportation, or sale of slaves); 18 U.S.C. 1587 (possession of slaves aboard vessel). However, U.S. extraterritorial jurisdiction based on nationality of the offender does not reach all offenses set forth in the Protocol. Also, federal law generally does not provide for the assertion of extraterritorial jurisdiction where the victim is a U.S. national. Nonetheless, since Article 4(2) is permissive rather than obligatory, U.S. law is consistent with the requirements of the provision.

Article 4(3) – Jurisdiction Where Extradition is Denied on Grounds of Nationality
52. The requirement of Article 4(3)-that States Parties that do not extradite their nationals must have a means of asserting jurisdiction over them-does not apply to the United States. The United States does not deny extradition on the grounds that the person sought is a U.S. national, and the Secretary of State may order the extradition of a U.S. citizen under an extradition treaty if the other requirements of the treaty are met. See 18 U.S.C. 3196. Accordingly, this paragraph does not require any change in current U.S. law or practice.

Article 5 – Extradition
53. Article 5 addresses the legal framework for extradition of alleged offenders and contains standard provisions that effectively amend existing U.S. bilateral extradition treaties to include the offenses defined in Article 3(1) as extraditable offenses for purposes of those treaties. The Article is generally modeled on similar provisions contained in other multilateral conventions to which the United States is a party, such as the 1988 United Nations Convention against Illicit Traffic in Narcotic Drugs and Psychotropic Substances.

54. Article 5(1) provides that the offenses described in Article 3(1) will be "deemed to be included as extraditable offenses" in preexisting extradition treaties between States Parties to the Protocol and will be included in future extradition treaties. The effect of Article 5(1) on the bilateral extradition treaties to which the U.S. is a party is to expand any lists of extraditable offenses to include the offenses described in Article 3(1) of the Protocol.

55. Articles 5(2) and (3) concern extradition requests when no bilateral extradition treaty exists between the requesting and requested State. If, under the law of the requested State, a treaty is required for extradition, that State may at its option consider the Protocol as the treaty that provides the legal basis for extradition. If, on the other hand, the law of the requested State permits extradition without a treaty, it must extradite subject to the conditions established by its law. Under U.S. law, with very limited statutory exceptions, a treaty is generally required for extradition from the United States. Article 5(2) does not provide an obligatory basis for extradition. Moreover, since the United States has a general regime for extradition by treaty, no obligation exists under Article 5(3) to extradite to States with which the United States does not have an extradition treaty.

56. Article 5(4) provides that for purposes of extradition between States Parties, offenses shall be treated as if they occurred within the States required to assert jurisdiction in accordance with Article 4. This provision is understood to require a Party to determine extraditability by assessing whether the conduct would be criminal if it had been committed in its territory. Under U.S. extradition law, precisely this type of analysis is undertaken in assessing whether the dual criminality standard has been satisfied. See, e.g., Collins v. Loisel, 259 U.S. 309 (1922); Bozilov v. Seifert, 983 F.2d 140 (9th Cir. 1993); United States v. Casamento, 887 F.2d 1141 (2d Cir. 1989); Emami v. United States District Court, 834 F.2d 1444 (9th Cir. 1987).

57. Article 5(5) provides that if a request for extradition of an alleged offender found within its jurisdiction is refused on the basis of the nationality of the offender, the State shall "take suitable measures" to submit the case to its competent authorities for prosecution. As stated above, since the United States does not deny extradition on the basis of nationality, the United States is in compliance with Article 5(5) of the Protocol.

Article 6 – Mutual Legal Assistance

58. This article provides for general mutual legal assistance between States Parties in connection with investigations or criminal or extradition proceedings brought in respect of the offenses established in Article 3(1). The article is modeled on other multilateral conventions, to which the United States is a party, including the International Convention for the Suppression of Terrorist Bombing and the Convention against Torture and Other Cruel, Inhuman or Degrading Treatment or Punishment. Article 6(1) provides that States Parties "shall afford one another the greatest measure of assistance in connection with investigations or criminal or extradition proceedings" concerning Article 3(1) offenses, including the supply of evidence at their disposal necessary for the proceedings. While not expressly stated, it was generally understood that the law of the requested state applies to determine the scope of the assistance that would be afforded.

59. Article 6(2) provides that the obligation contained in Article 6(1) shall be carried out "in conformity with" any treaties or arrangements on mutual legal assistance. In the event that no treaty or other arrangement on mutual legal assistance is in effect between the respective States, assistance would be provided in accordance with the domestic law of the requested State.

60. The United States has Mutual Legal Assistance Treaties (MLATs) with more than 50 countries and could offer assistance to those countries to the extent provided for under each MLAT. In the absence of a treaty, 28 U.S.C. 1782 permits a U.S. district judge to order the production of evidence for a proceeding in a foreign or international tribunal, including criminal investigations conducted before formal accusation. Accordingly, this Article can be implemented on the basis of U.S. law and treaties.

Article 7 – Seizure and Confiscation

61. Article 7 provides that States parties shall, "subject to the provisions of their national law" take, "as appropriate," measures: (1) to provide for the seizure and confiscation of goods used to commit offenses under the Protocol or proceeds derived from such offenses (Article 7(1)); (2) to execute requests from another State Party for seizure and confiscation of such goods or proceeds (Article 7(2)); and (3) aimed at closing on a temporary or definitive basis premises used to commit such offenses.

62. Given that the obligations of Article 7 are subject to the limits of a State Party's laws and that each State Party is obligated to take only such measures as are appropriate, U.S. ratification did not require implementing legislation. Existing U.S. law contains several provisions authorizing forfeiture for offenses covered by the Protocol. 18 U.S.C. 1594 authorizes criminal forfeiture and civil (in rem, non-conviction-based) forfeiture for violations of federal laws prohibiting forced labor and child sex trafficking. 18 U.S.C. 2253 and 2254 authorize, respectively, criminal and civil forfeiture for violations of federal child pornography laws. 18 U.S.C. 2428 authorizes criminal and civil forfeiture for violations of federal laws prohibiting transportation and enticement for criminal sexual activity and travel for illicit sexual conduct. These provisions all authorize forfeiture of all property, real and personal, used or intended to be used to commit or to facilitate the commission of the offense, and all property constituting or derived from proceeds of the offense. Sections 2253 and 2254 also authorize forfeiture of the pornographic depictions themselves. Most of the offenses that are predicates for these forfeiture statutes are also predicates for money laundering prosecutions pursuant to 18 U.S.C. 1956 and 1957. The money laundering statutes prohibit certain domestic and international financial transactions with the proceeds of specified predicate offenses, and international movement of money for the purpose of committing such offenses. Property involved in money laundering, and property traceable to such property, are forfeitable under 18 U.S.C. 981 (civil forfeiture) and 18 U.S.C. 982 (criminal forfeiture).

63. Certain other U.S. statutes authorize forfeiture of obscene materials, not limited to materials involving children. 18 U.S.C. 1467, as amended in July 2006 by the Adam Walsh Child Protection and Safety Act of 2006, authorizes civil and criminal forfeiture of obscene materials, real or personal property constituting or traceable to proceeds of obscenity offenses, and real or personal property used to commit or to promote the commission of such offenses. 19 U.S.C. 1305 authorizes civil forfeiture of obscene materials being imported into the United States.

64. Thus, consistent with Article 7, existing federal statutes authorize forfeiture of obscene and pornographic materials, proceeds derived from the subject offenses, and real and personal property used to commit the offenses. See, e.g., Alexander v. United States, 509 U.S. 544 (1993) (forfeiture of businesses and real estate connected with the sale of obscene materials); United States v. Parcels of Property Located at 14 Leon Drive, 2006 WL 1476060 (M.D. Ala. May 25, 2006) (civil forfeiture under 18 U.S.C. 2254 of residence used for child sexual exploitation); United States v. Ownby, 926 F. Supp. 558 (W.D. Va. 1996), aff'd 131 F.3d 138 (4th Cir. 1997) (forfeiture under 18 U.S.C. 2253(a)(3) of a house used to store pornography of juveniles engaged in sexually explicit conduct); United States v. Krasner, 841 F. Supp. 649 (M.D. Pa. 1993) (forfeiture pursuant to 18 U.S.C. 982 of a business involved in laundering the proceeds of obscenity offenses).

65. Neither federal nor state law generally provides for the forfeiture of all proceeds and instrumentalities of wholly foreign offenses covered by the Protocol in a U.S. criminal or civil (in rem non-conviction-based) forfeiture proceeding. However, U.S. law does provide for the execution of foreign confiscation orders and judgments for any foreign offense for which there would be forfeiture under U.S. federal law, if that offense had been committed within the United States. See 28 U.S.C. 2467. As set forth in paragraphs 62 through 64, supra, this means that the United States can enforce foreign confiscation orders and judgments against the proceeds and instrumentalities of offenses set forth in the Protocol as to which forfeiture is authorized under U.S. law. The only prerequisite for such assistance is that both the United States and the party requesting the assistance are parties to a treaty or agreement that provides for confiscation or forfeiture assistance, as this Protocol does.

Article 8 – Protection of Child Victims

66. Article 8(1) provides that State Parties shall adopt "appropriate" measures to protect the rights and interests of child victims of the practices prohibited under the Protocol at all stages of the criminal justice process, in particular by: (1) recognizing the vulnerability of child victims and adopting procedures to recognize their special needs (Article 8(1)(a)); (2) informing child victims of their rights and the progress and disposition of related proceedings (Article 8(1)(b)); (3) allowing the views, needs and concerns of child victims to be presented in proceedings where their personal interests are affected, "in a manner consistent with the procedural rules of national law" (Article 8(1)(c)); (4) providing "appropriate" support services to child victims throughout the legal process (Article 8(1)(d)); (5) protecting, "as appropriate," the privacy and identity of child victims and taking measures "in accordance with national law" to avoid the "inappropriate" dissemination of information that could lead to the identification of child victims (Article 8(1)(e)); (6) providing, in "appropriate cases," for the safety of child victims, family members, and witnesses (Article 8(1)(f)); and (7) avoiding "unnecessary" delay in the disposition of cases and the execution of orders or decrees granting compensation to child victims (Article 8(1)(g)).

67. During the negotiations, delegations generally recognized that the protections to be afforded children under Article 8(1) are necessarily a matter of discretion under national law. As described below, federal and state law provides extensive protection for child victims in the criminal justice process as contemplated by Article 8(1).

68. With regard to Article 8(1)(a), U.S. law at both the federal and state levels recognizes the special needs of child victims and witnesses. For example, in federal cases, 18 U.S.C. 3509(b) provides various alternatives for live, in-court testimony when it is determined that a child cannot or should not testify. Additionally, all states provide special accommodation for child victims and witnesses, including the use of videotaped or closed-circuit testimony, child interview specialists, and developmentally-appropriate questioning. See, e.g., Colorado Revised Statutes 18-3-413.5; North Dakota Century Code, 31-04-04.1. New Mexico law, NMSA 1978 30-9-17, provides for videotaped depositions of alleged victims who are under sixteen years of age in lieu of direct testimony. Utah uses Children's Justice Centers to interview child victims of sexual or serious physical abuse. These Centers provide a safe, home-like, child-friendly facility with interviewers trained in child interviewing protocols to minimize the trauma for the child. Section 67-5b -101, et seq., Utah Code Annotated. In addition, nationwide, there are over 600 Child Advocacy Centers (CACs) supported by various combinations of federal, state, and local funds that use a similar approach. In order to reduce the need for multiple child-interviews by the various disciplines involved in a case, which can be traumatic to the child, CACs utilize a multidisciplinary approach, with one key interviewer observed and provided questions by the rest of the team in one interview. The Federal Government also aids states in reducing the trauma to child sexual abuse victims through funding to states under the Children's Justice Act, established in the Victims of Crime Act (VOCA), and the Child Abuse Prevention and Treatment Act (CAPTA) (42 U.S.C. 5101 et seq; 42 U.S.C. 5116 et seq).

69. With respect to Article 8(1)(b), federal and state law also provides for informing child victims of their rights and the progress of their cases. For example, the general Federal Guidelines for Treatment of Crime Victims and Witnesses in the Criminal Justice System provide that law enforcement personnel should ensure that victims are informed about the role of the victim in the criminal justice system, as well as the scheduling of their cases and advance notification of proceedings in the prosecution of the accused. The Federal Government also helps provide for appropriate notification of victims through funding to states under the Victims of Crime Act (VOCA) and technical assistance programs. The promotion by the Federal Government of state compliance is also an "appropriate measure" to protect the rights referred to in Article 8(1)(b). Guidelines and statutes at the state level further provide extensive procedures for victim notification of the victim's rights and of the scheduling of proceedings. See, e.g., Iowa Victim Rights Act, 1997 Ia. HF 2527, 6-14; NM Const., Art. II 24, [New Mexico] Victims Rights, NMSA 1978 31-26-4, Victim Rights.

70. With respect to Article 8(1)(c), federal and state law allows the views and needs of child victims to be presented in a manner consistent with the procedural rules of national law. For example, at the federal level, 18 U.S.C. 3509 specifically provides for the preparation of a victim impact statement to be used to prepare the pre-sentence report in sentencing offenders in cases in which the victim was a child. Through guidelines and statutes, states provide for victims' presentation of their views at different stages of proceedings. See, e.g., Iowa Victim Rights Act, 1997 Ia. HF 2527, 17.

71. Both federal and state laws also provide appropriate support services throughout the legal process consistent with the provisions of Article 8(1)(d). For example, at the federal level, 18 U.S.C. 3509(g) provides for the use of multidisciplinary child abuse teams "when it is feasible to do so." Likewise, in order to "protect the best interests of the child,"18 U.S.C. 3509(h) provides for the appointment of a guardian ad litem for a child who has been a victim of or witness to a crime involving abuse or exploitation. ("Exploitation" is defined as child prostitution or pornography.) CAPTA requires that all States receiving the Basic State Grant under CAPTA provide a guardian ad litem to all child abuse victims involved in court proceedings related to their victimization (42 U.S.C. 5106(a)(b)(2)(xiii)). Additionally, all states provide special accommodations and support services, including the appointment of guardians ad litem or other support persons. See, e.g., California Penal Code 1348.5; HRS 587-2 (Hawaii).

72. Federal and state laws further provide for protecting, "as appropriate," the privacy of child victims in accordance with national law, as required by Article 8(1)(e). Both federal and state laws attempt to provide for the privacy of child victims. See, e.g., 18 U.S.C. 3509(d), "confidentiality of information," which provides detailed procedures for keeping the name of or any other information about a child confidential; 18 U.S.C. 3509(m), which provides for images of child pornography to remain in the care, custody, and control of the government or the court during criminal proceedings, thereby minimizing further dissemination of the images; and Iowa Code 915.36. While modalities of protection of pri-

vacy may vary from state to state, the Protocol requires only that a Party provide the level of protection deemed "appropriate." Given this flexibility, current U.S. law meets the requirements of this provision.

73. With respect to Article 8(l)(f), U.S. law and policy provide, "in appropriate cases," for the safety of child victims, as well as that of their families and witnesses on their behalf, from intimidation and retaliation. In the United States at both the federal and state levels there is a general policy of attempting to establish promptly the criminal responsibility of service providers, customers, and intermediaries in child prostitution, child pornography, and child abuse, in part in order to provide for the safety of victims and their families. Additionally, at both the federal and state levels, safe havens may be provided on a discretionary basis for children escaping from sexual exploitation, as well as protection for those who provide assistance to victims of commercial exploitation from intimidation and harassment. See, e.g., Federal Witness Protection Act, 18 U.S.C. 3521; HRS 587-2 (Hawaii).

74. The U.S. judicial procedure at both the federal and state levels provides protection against unnecessary delay in the disposition of cases and the execution of orders granting awards to child victims, consistent with the provisions of Article 8(l)(g). In all U.S. criminal cases, the Sixth Amendment to the Constitution requires a speedy trial. Additionally, many states as well as the Federal Government have enacted speedy trial laws, which set strict time deadlines for the charging and prosecution of criminal cases. See Speedy Trial Act, 18 U.S.C. 3161 et seq.

75. Also, the immigration laws of the United States bear important protections for child victims of trafficking. For example, the Immigration and Nationality Act, as amended by section 107 of the Trafficking Victims Protection Act of 2000, provides for a "T visa" that allows victims of severe forms of trafficking in persons to remain in the United States and to receive certain kinds of public assistance to the same extent as refugees. See 8 U.S.C. 1101(a)(15)(T); 8 CFR 214.11. After three years in T status, victims of human trafficking may apply for permanent residency. In addition, subject to some limitations, eligible child victims of trafficking may apply for lawful immigration status for their parents. The immigration laws also provide that a child victim of trafficking may not be removed from the United States based solely on information provided by the trafficker and sets forth robust confidentiality protections for child trafficking victims. See 8 U.S.C. 1367.

76. Furthermore, administered by the Office of Refugee Resettlement (ORR) in the U.S. Department of Health and Human Services, the Unaccompanied Refugee Minors (URM) program was developed in 1979 to address the needs of thousands of children from Southeast Asia who entered the United States as refugees without a parent or a guardian to care for them. Since 1980, over 12,000 minors have entered the URM program. Currently, ORR has over 600 minors in URM care. Two lead voluntary agencies, the Lutheran Immigration and Refugee Services (LIRS) and the United States Conference of Catholic Bishops (USCCB) work in conjunction with ORR on the URM program, and there are currently 19 URM affiliate sites. Those currently eligible for the URM program include minors who are unaccompanied refugees, Amerasians, Cuban and Haitian entrants, asylees, and victims of a severe form of trafficking. In addition, accompanied minors can become eligible for URM program services after arrival in the United States through a reclassification process, e.g., through family breakdown, age re-determination, a death in the family, or a grant of asylum.

77. Each child in the care of this program is eligible for the same range of child-welfare benefits as non-refugee children. Depending on their individual needs, minors are placed in home foster care, group care, independent living, or residential treatment. The URM program assists unaccompanied minors in developing appropriate skills to enter adulthood and to achieve economic and social self-sufficiency. Services provided through the program include English language training, career planning, health/mental needs, socialization skills/adjustment support, family reunification, residential care, education/training, and ethnic/religious preservation. Individuals must be under the age of 18 in order to qualify for the program, but can in most cases remain in the program until age 20 or 21, depending on state guidelines for emancipation.

Article 8(2) through 8(6)
78. Article 8 further provides that States Parties shall, with respect to the offenses prohibited under the Protocol: (1) ensure that uncertainty as to the actual age of the victim not prevent the initiation of a criminal investigation (Article 8(2)); (2) ensure that the best interest of the child be a primary consideration in the treatment of child victims by the criminal justice system (Article 8(3)); (3) "take measures" to ensure "appropriate" training, in particular legal and psychological, for the persons who work with child victims (Article 8(4)); and (4) "in appropriate cases," adopt measures in

order to protect the safety and integrity of the persons and/or organizations involved in the prevention and/or protection and rehabilitation of child victims (Article 8(5)).

79. U.S. federal and state law satisfies each of these requirements. With respect to Article 8(2), nothing in U.S. federal or state law prohibits an investigation of exploitation of a child from going forward when the age of the child is unknown, or when it is unclear if the victim is, in fact, an adult. In fact, it is common for investigations in the United States to try to determine the child's age while investigating all aspects of the case.

80. With respect to Article 8(3), it is a general policy underlying both federal and state law that the best interests of the child are a primary consideration in the treatment of child victims. In many cases, laws have been passed with the child victim's best interest specifically in mind. See, e.g., Rhode Island Children's Bill of Rights, R.I. Gen. Laws 42-72-15; Hawaii Child Protective Act, HRS 587.

81. Article 8(4) and 8(5) are flexible; in view of the broad scope of the provision, the obligations were qualified, i.e., "take measures to ensure appropriate" training and protect the safety of the child in "in appropriate cases." Consistent with these articles, it is a general policy of the Federal and State Governments at all levels to provide training for those who work with child victims, and to adopt measures where appropriate to protect those involved with prevention of such offenses and the protection and rehabilitation of children. The United States also satisfies its obligations by providing federal funding to states where such training is needed. These federal funds are administered by, inter alia, the Department of Health and Human Services (HHS) and the Department of Justice's Office of Juvenile Justice and Delinquency Prevention (OJJDP) and Office of Victims of Crime (OVC). Similar provisions exist at the state level. See, e.g., Ark. Stat. Ann. 20-82-206 (Arkansas); Idaho Code 16-1609A.

82. Article 8(6) is a savings clause. It states that nothing in it shall be construed as prejudicial to the rights of the accused to a fair and impartial trial. The provisions in United States law that provide for a fair and impartial trial are grounded in the United States Constitution. Nothing in this Protocol would or could undermine those fundamental human rights and civil rights protections of people brought before courts in the United States.

Article 9 – Prevention
83. Article 9 provides that States Parties shall, with respect to the offenses referred to in the Protocol, (1) adopt or strengthen, implement, and disseminate laws, policies, and programs to prevent the offenses (Article 9(1)); (2) promote awareness in the public at large, including children, about "the preventive measures and harmful effects of the offences" (Article 9(2)); (3) take all "feasible" measures with "the aim" of ensuring "all appropriate" assistance to victims of such offenses, including their full social reintegration, and their full physical and psychological recovery (Article 9(3)); (4) ensure that child victims have access to adequate procedures to seek compensation (Article 9(4)); and (5) take "appropriate" measures "aimed at" effectively prohibiting advertisement of the offenses covered by the Protocol (Article 9(5)).

84. The United States meets the requirements of Article 9. With respect to Articles 9(1) and 9(2), it is a priority commitment for the United States at both the federal and state levels to strengthen and implement laws to prevent the offenses prohibited by the Protocol. It is also a policy priority for the United States to create a climate through education, social mobilization, and development activities to ensure that parents and others legally responsible for children are able to protect children from sexual exploitation. In April 2006, the United States Government in partnership with three U.S. non-governmental organizations held a mid-term review to take stock of United States' efforts in combating child sexual exploitation since the 2001 Second World Congress on the Commercial Sexual Exploitation of Children in Yokohama. A report, including areas for improvement, was produced from mid-term review and will be submitted for the 2007 Third World Congress.

85. With respect to measures to ensure appropriate assistance to victims, including their full social integration and full physical and psychological recovery, a wide range of federal and state programs satisfy the standards set forth in Article 9(3). The Federal Government provides many types of aid to such agencies and comparable organizations that serve children. The Family and Youth Services Bureau of the Department of Health and Human Services (HHS) administers grant programs supporting a variety of locally based youth services. These services include youth shelters, which provide emergency shelter, food, clothing, outreach services, and crisis intervention for victimized youths; "transitional living programs" for homeless youth, which assist these youth in developing skills and resources to live independently in society; and education and prevention grants to reduce sexual abuse of runaway, homeless, and street youth. HHS's Chil-

dren's Bureau administers the Chafee Independent Living Program, providing concrete support such as housing and education for children who "age out" of the foster care system at age 18.

86. The Justice Department's Office of Juvenile Justice and Delinquency Prevention oversees the Model Court Project under which local courts have put in place a variety of reforms to strengthen their abilities to improve court decision-making in abuse and neglect cases, and to work more closely with the child welfare agencies to move children out of foster care and into safe, stable, permanent homes.

87. HHS's Children's Bureau supports research on the causes, prevention, and treatment of child abuse and neglect; demonstration programs to identify the best means of preventing maltreatment and treating troubled families; and the development and implementation of training programs. Grants are provided nationwide on a competitive basis to state and local agencies and organizations. Projects have focused on every aspect of the prevention, identification, investigation, and treatment of child abuse and neglect. HHS's Children's Bureau also administers the Community-Based Child Abuse Prevention program which provides funding to states for the maintenance of a statewide prevention network and the provision of prevention services at the local level, as well as the Court Improvement Program focusing on the work of the courts in child welfare cases.

88. State child protection agencies ensure the safety of children and youth who require protective custody, making placement recommendations and coordinating assessments and interviews of children and adults with appropriate law enforcement and licensing agencies. Victim assistance programs provide victimized youth with assistance in dealing with the court system, emotional support, and referrals to additional resources. Such services enable these youth both to address the immediate consequences of their victimization and to reenter society. The routine operation of state child welfare agencies also serves these aims.

89. With regard to the requirement under Article 9(4) that States Parties ensure access by child victims to adequate procedures for seeking compensation, there is mandatory restitution for victims in these cases under federal law. 18 U.S.C. 1593 provides for mandatory restitution for any trafficking offense, including the crimes of forced labor and sex trafficking. In addition, 18 U.S.C. 2259 provides for mandatory restitution for any offense involving the sexual exploitation of children, including selling and buying of children. There are also civil remedies available to victims of trafficking and sexual exploitation. See 18 U.S.C. 1595 and 2255. The Victims of Crime Act (VOCA) funds support more than 4,000 victim services programs across the country, and many of these provide services for child victims. In addition, VOCA supports state victim compensation programs for which child victims or their caretakers can apply.

90. Consistent with the provisions of Article 9(5), U.S. law contains certain restrictions on advertising that are appropriate under our legal system. For example, 18 U.S.C. 2251 proscribes advertising child pornography when the child pornography actually exists for sale or distribution. Advertising or promoting child prostitution could, in some circumstances, be punished under federal law if it aids and abets child prostitution or constitutes a conspiracy to violate child prostitution laws.

91. The Department of Justice has formed and funded 42 anti-trafficking task forces in 25 states and territories. The task forces are primarily intended to lead to the identification and rescue of more victims of human trafficking by providing for support staff, training programs, interpreter/translator services, and liaisons with U.S. Attorneys' Offices and other agencies concerned with the identification and rescue of trafficking victims.

92. One initiative to protect children from sexual exploitation is the Innocence Lost Initiative, which combats child prostitution in the United States. The Innocence Lost Initiative is a partnership between the Criminal Division of the Department of Justice, the Federal Bureau of Investigation, and the National Center for Missing & Exploited Children. Part of this initiative is an intensive week-long training program on the investigation and prosecution of child prostitution cases, held for members of multi-disciplinary teams from cities across the United States. The program brings state and federal law enforcement agencies, prosecutors, and social services providers all from one city to be trained together. This grouping and training is designed to cultivate cooperation, partnership, and an effective integration among the critical enforcement entities in each city. As of September 30, 2006, the Innocence Lost Initiative has resulted in 241 open investigations, 614 arrests, 129 criminal informations or grand jury indictments, and 106 convictions in both the federal and state systems.

Article 10 – International Cooperation and Assistance

93. Article 10 provides that States Parties shall undertake international cooperation for: (1) the prevention, detection, investigation, prosecution, and punishment of those responsible for acts involving the sale of children, child prostitution, child pornography, and sex tourism (Article 10(1)); (2) the rehabilitation and social reintegration of children who have been victims of such practices (Article 10(2)); and (3) addressing the root causes of the vulnerability of children to these crimes (Article 10(3)). Article 10 does not, however, require States Parties to provide a specific type or amount of assistance. Article 10(4) specifies that States Parties "in a position to do so" shall provide financial, technical, or other assistance through existing multilateral, regional, bilateral, or other programs.

94. With regard to Article 10(1), the United States regularly engages in bilateral and multilateral efforts to deter and prevent the increasing international traffic in children for labor and sexual exploitation. In an effort to attack this issue at its source, the United States has worked with foreign governments and non-governmental organizations (NGO's) to inform potential victims of the risks posed to them by the traffic in women and children, the tactics criminal groups use to coerce victims and conduct such traffic, and the ways in which victims can seek assistance in the United States. The United States has also funded deterrence and public information campaigns abroad in countries such as Cambodia, Costa Rica, Brazil, Belize, and Mexico targeted at U.S. child sex tourists.

95. Additionally, pursuant to bilateral and multilateral legal assistance treaties with foreign governments, the United States regularly cooperates with law enforcement agencies of other countries to counteract child prostitution, pornography, and sale of children, as well as sex tourism. The United States funds training for law enforcement and consular officials of foreign countries in the areas of trafficking in persons, child sex tourism, and sexual exploitation of women and children. The United States also supports deterrent programs that encourage innovative partnerships among governments, labor, industry groups, and NGOs to end the employment of children in hazardous or abusive conditions. Examples of these innovative partnerships include: cooperation with the government of South Korea to replicate a San Francisco-based model offenders prevention program targeted at persons who are arrested for soliciting sexual services from prostituted persons; cooperation with travel and tourism companies both in the U.S. and abroad to support an ethical code of conduct to protect children from commercial sexual exploitation, which was developed by a U.S. NGO in partnership with Nordic tour operators; and cooperation between an international faith-based organization, UNICEF and the Madagascar ministries of Population, Tourism and Education to conduct a survey of the types of child labor and sexual exploitation that will lead to a nationwide anti-trafficking campaign.

96. In 2003, President Bush launched a $50 million Initiative on Trafficking in Persons (POTUS Initiative) to support organizations that rescue, shelter, and provide services to women and children who are victims of trafficking. This initiative has funded projects in Brazil, Cambodia, India, Indonesia, Mexico, Moldova, Sierra Leone, and Tanzania. In 2007, New Mexico and the State of Chihuahua, Mexico will enter into a bilateral agreement to create an initiative similar to the POTUS Initiative. It will include the establishment of a joint task force and the sharing of resources and information regarding organized criminal trafficking networks.

97. The United States contributes to a wide array of programs that support the elimination of child labor worldwide, including programs to address the sexual exploitation of children. In particular, since 1995, the U.S. Government has provided approximately $500 million for technical assistance projects aimed at eliminating exploitative child labor around the world. Of this amount, over $191 million has been awarded to the International Labor Organization and other grantees to address the trafficking of children for commercial sexual exploitation and labor in Asia, Africa, Latin America and the Caribbean, the Middle East, and Europe. These projects promote educational and training opportunities for child laborers or children at risk of engaging in exploitative labor. The projects also aim to develop comprehensive regional and national strategies to combat trafficking, improve law enforcement capacity to arrest and prosecute traffickers, enhance support to victims of trafficking, and increase awareness of both at-risk populations and policymakers to trafficking.

98. With regard to Articles 10(2) and 10(3), the United States is committed to working with other governments to address the root causes of these crimes and to developing rehabilitation approaches that are effective. The United States funds and supports international initiatives to provide vocational training for children and income-generating opportunities for their families and assists various countries in developing, implementing, and enforcing national policies to combat child labor and sex crimes. In addition, the United States supports and funds a variety of international initiatives

to safeguard children from hazardous or abusive working conditions, including projects that assist exploited children and provide them and their families with a variety of social services. The United States has recently provided funds to expand existing shelters and rehabilitation programs, including in Morocco for former child maids, in India for children of prostituted women, as well as in the Philippines and Gabon for trafficked children.

99. Through various components of the Department of Justice, the U.S. has trained foreign law enforcement officials in numerous countries on investigating and prosecuting child sex trafficking and has worked with governments to develop model anti-trafficking legislation.

100. For example, the Civil Rights Division sent prosecutors to Ukraine and Mexico and its victim witness coordinator to the Republic of Georgia to share the experiences of the United States in combating human trafficking and assisting victims. Several countries, such as Poland, Thailand, Venezuela, Azerbaijan, the United Kingdom, Brazil, India, Russia, China, Bhutan, Bulgaria, the Netherlands, Kazakhstan, Turkmenistan, Nepal, and Bangladesh, sent representatives to the United States to learn more about this global issue through meetings with Civil Rights Division attorneys and victim staff.

101. The Child Exploitation and Obscenity Section (CEOS) of the U.S. Department of Justice Criminal Division, in partnership with the Office of Overseas Prosecutorial Development and Training and the State Department, regularly provides training for foreign delegates on child exploitation offenses as part of the State Department's International Visitor Program. These training sessions range from providing an overview of U.S. child exploitation laws, including child protection statutes, to how to investigate and prosecute human trafficking cases successfully.

102. In 2006, CEOS presented 24 training sessions to delegates from around the world. CEOS discussed these issues with delegates from countries such as Indonesia, Brazil, Ecuador, China, France, Germany, and Saudi Arabia, to name a few.

103. Moreover, CEOS trial attorneys regularly perform extensive overseas training programs. For example, in May 2006, a CEOS trial attorney was a member of a training team sent to Latvia to train law enforcement on human trafficking. Members of the team traveled to several cities throughout Latvia, including the capital city of Riga to train an audience of Latvian judges, police, and prosecutors on numerous topics related to human trafficking. These topics included an overview of U.S. laws, a discussion of appropriate investigative techniques, and a primer on the international response to human trafficking, including a discussion of relevant international treaties. This program was part of a continuing effort in Latvia to support the fight against trafficking in persons.

104. In 2006, CEOS attorneys conducted similar training programs in Nigeria, Armenia, and Indonesia, and from July to November 2006, a CEOS attorney served as the Intermittent Legal Advisor for Human Trafficking in the Republic of Indonesia.

105. The United States is also a Party to the U.N. Protocol to Prevent, Suppress and Punish Trafficking in Persons, Especially Women and Children. The United States signed the Protocol on December 13, 2000, and it entered into force for the United States on December 3, 2005. The Protocol calls for information exchange in certain circumstances (Art. 10). The general provisions of the Transnational Organized Crime Convention, to which the United States is also a Party, apply to the Protocol and contain provisions on extradition (Art. 16) and mutual legal assistance (Art. 18).

106. Additionally, since the Trafficking Victims Protection Act (TVPA) was passed in The 2000, the United States has submitted annual Trafficking in Persons Reports to the U.S. Congress on foreign governments' efforts to eliminate severe forms of trafficking in persons. The Report is a major tool for advancing international cooperation to combat human trafficking and raising global awareness on the issue. The 2006 Report assessed the efforts of 149 countries to combat trafficking in persons, including their efforts to prosecute traffickers, protect victims, and prevent the crime. A government that fails to make significant efforts to bring itself into compliance with the minimum standards for eliminating trafficking, as established in the TVPA, receives a "Tier 3" assessment in the Report. Such an assessment may trigger the withholding of U.S. non-humanitarian, non-trade-related foreign assistance to that country.

Source: U.S. Department of State, Diplomacy in Action, https://www.state.gov/j/drl/rls/84467.htm or https://www.state.gov/documents/organization/84647.pdf

՞ѕ-՞ѕ-՞ѕ-՞ѕ-՞ѕ

8. COMMITTEE ON THE RIGHTS OF THE CHILD, GENERAL COMMENT NO. 20 (2016) ON THE IMPLEMENTATION OF THE RIGHTS OF THE CHILD DURING ADOLESCENCE

The U.N. Committee on the Rights of the Child, which supervises the implementation of the Convention on the Rights of the Child and its three Protocols has as one of its tasks to write general comments on how the CRC is to be interpreted and applied. It issues general comments on different subjects within its mandate. In this general comment the subject is adolescents and human rights under the CRC. It is to help the states parties to the CRC best understand the treaty and how the Committee will view certain subjects before it, such as a complaint alleging a violation.

Committee on the Rights of the Child

General comment No. 20 (2016) on the implementation of the rights of the child during adolescence

I. Introduction

1. The Convention on the Rights of the Child defines a child as every human being below the age of 18 years unless under the law applicable to the child majority is attained earlier, and emphasizes that States should respect and ensure the rights embodied in the Convention to each child within their jurisdiction without discrimination of any kind. While the Convention recognizes the rights of all persons under 18 years, the implementation of rights should take account of children's development and their evolving capacities. Approaches adopted to ensure the realization of the rights of adolescents differ significantly from those adopted for younger children.

2. Adolescence is a life stage characterized by growing opportunities, capacities, aspirations, energy and creativity, but also significant vulnerability. Adolescents are agents of change and a key asset and resource with the potential to contribute positively to their families, communities and countries. Globally, adolescents engage positively in many spheres, including health and education campaigns, family support, peer education, community development initiatives, participatory budgeting and creative arts, and make contributions towards peace, human rights, environmental sustainability and climate justice. Many adolescents are at the cutting edge of the digital and social media environments, which form an increasingly central role in their education, culture and social networks, and hold potential in terms of political engagement and monitoring accountability.

3. The Committee observes that the potential of adolescents is widely compromised because States parties do not recognize or invest in the measures needed for them to enjoy their rights. Data disaggregated by age, sex and disability are not available in most countries to inform policy, identify gaps and support the allocation of appropriate resources for adolescents. Generic policies designed for children or young people often fail to address adolescents in all their diversity and are inadequate to guarantee the realization of their rights. The costs of inaction and failure are high: the foundations laid down during adolescence in terms of emotional security, health, sexuality, education, skills, resilience and understanding of rights will have profound implications, not only for their individual optimum development, but also for present and future social and economic development.

4. In the present general comment, the Committee provides guidance to States on the measures necessary to ensure the realization of the rights of children during adolescence, cognizant also of the 2030 Agenda for Sustainable Development. It highlights the importance of a human rights-based approach that includes recognition and respect for the dignity and agency of adolescents; their empowerment, citizenship and active participation in their own lives; the promotion of optimum health, well-being and development; and a commitment to the promotion, protection and fulfilment of their human rights, without discrimination.

5. The Committee recognizes that adolescence is not easily defined, and that individual children reach maturity at different ages. Puberty occurs at different ages for boys and girls, and different brain functions mature at different times. The process of transitioning from childhood to adulthood is influenced by context and environment, as reflected in the wide variation in cultural expectations of adolescents in national legislations, which afford different thresholds for entry into adult activities, and across international bodies, which employ a variety of age ranges to define adolescence. The

present general comment does not seek, therefore, to define adolescence, but instead focuses on the period of childhood from 10 years until the 18th birthday to facilitate consistency in data collection.1

6. The Committee notes that several of its general comments have a particular resonance for adolescents, notably those relating to adolescent health and development, HIV/AIDS, eradicating practices that are harmful to women and children, unaccompanied and separated children and juvenile justice. The Committee emphasizes the particular significance for adolescents of the recommendations arising from the day of general discussion on digital media and children's rights. The present general comment has been developed to provide an overview on how the Convention in its entirety needs to be understood and implemented in respect of all adolescents and should be read together with other general comments and with documents arising from the day of general discussion.

II. Objectives

7. The objectives of the present general comment are:

(a) To provide States with guidance on the legislation, policies and services needed to promote comprehensive adolescent development consistent with the realization of their rights;

(b) To raise awareness of the opportunities afforded by and challenges faced during adolescence;

(c) To enhance understanding of and respect for the evolving capacities of adolescents and the implications for the realization of their rights;

(d) To strengthen the case for greater visibility and awareness of adolescents and for investment to enable them to realize their rights throughout the course of their lives.

III. The case for a focus on adolescents

8. The Committee draws States parties' attention to the powerful case for a focus on adolescents to promote the realization of their rights, strengthen their potential contribution to positive and progressive social transformation and overcome the challenges they face in the transition from childhood to adulthood in an increasingly globalized and complex world.

9. Adolescents are on a rapid curve of development. The significance of the developmental changes during adolescence has not yet been as widely understood as that which occurs in early years. Adolescence is a unique defining stage of human development characterized by rapid brain development and physical growth, enhanced cognitive ability, the onset of puberty and sexual awareness and newly emerging abilities, strengths and skills. Adolescents experience greater expectations surrounding their role in society and more significant peer relationships as they transition from a situation of dependency to one of greater autonomy.

10. As they move through their second decade, children begin to explore and forge their own individual and community identities on the basis of a complex interaction with their own family and cultural history, and experience the creation of an emergent sense of self, often expressed through language, arts and culture, both as individuals and through association with their peers. For many, that process takes place around and is significantly informed and influenced by their engagement with the digital environment. The process of construction and expression of identity is particularly complex for adolescents as they create a pathway between minority and mainstream cultures.

Recognizing adolescence as part of the life course

11. In order to ensure the optimum development of every child throughout childhood, it is necessary to recognize the impact that each period of life has on subsequent stages. Adolescence is a valuable period of childhood in its own right but is also a critical period of transition and opportunity for improving life chances. Positive early childhood interventions and experiences facilitate optimal development as young children become adolescents. However, any investment in young people risks being wasted if their rights throughout adolescence do not also receive adequate attention. Furthermore, positive and supportive opportunities during adolescence can be used to offset some of the consequences

caused by harm suffered during early childhood, and build resilience to mitigate future damage. The Committee therefore underlines the importance of a life-course perspective.

Challenging environment

12. Reaching adolescence can mean exposure to a range of risks, reinforced or exacerbated by the digital environment, including substance use and addiction, violence and abuse, sexual or economic exploitation, trafficking, migration, radicalization or recruitment into gangs or militias. As they approach adulthood, adolescents need suitable education and support to tackle local and global challenges, including poverty and inequality, discrimination, climate change and environmental degradation, urbanization and migration, ageing societies, pressure to perform in school and escalating humanitarian and security crises. Growing up in more heterogeneous and multi-ethnic societies, as a consequence of increased global migration, also requires greater capacities for Period of health risks

13. Although adolescence is generally characterized by relatively low mortality compared to other age groups, the risk of death and disease during the adolescent years is real, including from preventable causes such as childbirth, unsafe abortions, road traffic accidents, sexually transmitted infections, including HIV, interpersonal injuries, mental ill health and suicide, all of which are associated with certain behaviours and require cross-sectoral collaboration.

IV. General principles of the Convention

14. The general principles of the Convention provide the lens through which the process of implementation should be viewed, and act as a guide for determining the measures needed to guarantee the realization of the rights of children during adolescence.

A. Right to development

15. The Committee emphasizes the importance of valuing adolescence and its associated characteristics as a positive developmental stage of childhood. It regrets the widespread negative characterization of adolescence leading to narrow problem-focused interventions and services, rather than a commitment to building optimum environments to guarantee the rights of adolescents and support the development of their physical, psychological, spiritual, social, emotional, cognitive, cultural and economic capacities.

16. States, together with non-State actors, through dialogue and engagement with adolescents themselves, should promote environments that acknowledge the intrinsic value of adolescence and introduce measures to help them to thrive, explore their emerging identities, beliefs, sexualities and opportunities, balance risk and safety, build capacity for making free, informed and positive decisions and life choices, and successfully navigate the transition into adulthood. An approach is required that builds on strengths and recognizes the contribution that adolescents can bring to their lives and those of others, while addressing the barriers that inhibit those opportunities.

17. Factors known to promote the resilience and healthy development of adolescents include: (a) strong relationships with and support from the key adults in their lives; (b) opportunities for participation and decision-making; (c) problem-solving and coping skills; (d) safe and healthy local environments; (e) respect for individuality; and (f) opportunities for building and sustaining friendships. The Committee emphasizes that opportunities for adolescents to build and benefit from such social assets will enhance their capacities to contribute to the realization of their rights, including by maintaining good physical and mental health, avoiding risky behaviour, recovering from adversity, succeeding in school, showing tolerance, creating friendships and exercising leadership.

Respect for evolving capacities

18. Article 5 of the Convention requires that parental direction and guidance be provided in a manner consistent with the evolving capacities of the child. The Committee defines evolving capacities as an enabling principle that addresses the process of maturation and learning through which children progressively acquire competencies, understanding and increasing levels of agency to take responsibility and exercise their rights. The Committee has argued that the more a child knows and understands, the more his or her parents will have to transform direction and guidance into reminders and gradually to an exchange on an equal footing.

19. The Committee emphasizes that the right to exercise increasing levels of responsibility does not obviate States' obligations to guarantee protection. Gradual emergence from the protection of the family or another care environment, together with relative inexperience and lack of power, can render adolescents vulnerable to violations of their rights. The Committee stresses that engaging adolescents in the identification of potential risks and the development and implementation of programmes to mitigate them will lead to more effective protection. By being guaranteed the right to be heard, to challenge rights violations and to seek redress, adolescents are enabled to exercise agency progressively in their own protection.

20. In seeking to provide an appropriate balance between respect for the evolving capacities of adolescents and appropriate levels of protection, consideration should be given to a range of factors affecting decision-making, including the level of risk involved, the potential for exploitation, understanding of adolescent development, recognition that competence and understanding do not necessarily develop equally across all fields at the same pace and recognition of individual experience and capacity.

B. Non-discrimination

21. The Committee has identified multiple forms of discrimination, many of which have particular implications in adolescence and necessitate an intersectional analysis and targeted holistic measures. Adolescence itself can be a source of discrimination. During this period, adolescents may be treated as dangerous or hostile, incarcerated, exploited or exposed to violence as a direct consequence of their status. Paradoxically, they are also often treated as incompetent and incapable of making decisions about their lives. The Committee urges States to ensure that all of the rights of every adolescent boy and girl are afforded equal respect and protection and that comprehensive and appropriate affirmative action measures are introduced in order to diminish or eliminate conditions that result in direct or indirect discrimination against any group of adolescents on any grounds. States are reminded that not every differentiation of treatment will constitute discrimination, if the criteria for such differentiation are reasonable and objective and if the aim is to achieve a purpose that is legitimate under the Convention.

C. Best interests

22. The right of the child to have his or her best interests taken into account as a primary consideration is a substantive right, an interpretative legal principle and a rule of procedure, and it applies to children both as individuals and as a group. All measures of implementation of the Convention, including legislation, policies, economic and social planning, decision-making and budgetary decisions, should follow procedures that ensure that the best interests of the child, including adolescents, are taken as a primary consideration in all actions concerning them. In the light of its general comment No. 14 (2013) on the right of the child to have his or her best interests taken as a primary consideration, the Committee stresses that, when determining best interests, the child's views should be taken into account, consistent with their evolving capacities and taking into consideration the child's characteristics. States parties need to ensure that appropriate weight is afforded to the views of adolescents as they acquire understanding and maturity.

D. Right to be heard and to participation

23. In accordance with article 12 of the Convention, States parties should introduce measures to guarantee adolescents the right to express views on all matters of concern to them, in accordance with their age and maturity, and ensure they are given due weight, for example, in decisions relating to their education, health, sexuality, family life and judicial and administrative proceedings. States should ensure that adolescents are involved in the development, implementation and monitoring of all relevant legislation, policies, services and programmes affecting their lives, at school and at the community, local, national and international levels. The online environment provides significant emerging opportunities for strengthening and expanding their engagement. The measures should be accompanied by the introduction of safe and accessible complaint and redress mechanisms with the authority to adjudicate claims made by adolescents, and by access to subsidized or free legal services and other appropriate assistance.

24. The Committee emphasizes the importance of participation as a means of political and civil engagement through which adolescents can negotiate and advocate for the realization of their rights, and hold States accountable. States should adopt policies to increase opportunities for political participation, which is instrumental in the development of active citizenship. Adolescents can connect with peers, engage in political processes and increase their sense of agency

to make informed decisions and choices, and therefore need to be supported in forming organizations through which they can participate in a variety of means, including digital media. If States decide to lower the voting age to under 18 years, they should invest in measures that support adolescents to understand, recognize and fulfil their role as active citizens, including through citizenship and human rights education and by identifying and addressing barriers to their engagement and participation.

25. The Committee notes that adults' understanding and awareness of adolescents' right to participation is important for adolescents' enjoyment of that right, and it encourages States to invest in training and awareness-raising, particularly for parents and caregivers, professionals working with and for adolescents, policymakers and decision makers. Support is needed to enable adults to become mentors and facilitators so that adolescents can take greater responsibility for their own lives and the lives of those around them.

V. Adolescents requiring particular attention

26.Certain groups of adolescents may be particularly subject to multiple vulnerabilities and violations of their rights, including discrimination and social exclusion. All measures taken in respect of legislation, policies and programmes focused on adolescents should take into consideration intersecting violations of rights and the compounded negative effects on the adolescents concerned.

Girls

27.During adolescence, gender inequalities become more significant. Manifestations of discrimination, inequality and stereotyping against girls often intensify, leading to more serious violations of their rights, including child and forced marriage, early pregnancy, female genital mutilation, gender-based physical, mental and sexual violence, abuse, exploitation and trafficking. Cultural norms ascribing lower status to girls can increase the likelihood of confinement to the home, lack of access to secondary and tertiary education, limited opportunities for leisure, sport, recreation and income generation, lack of access to cultural life and the arts, burdensome domestic chores and childcare responsibilities. In many countries, girls report lower levels of health and life satisfaction indicators than boys, a difference that gradually increases with age.

28. States need to invest in proactive measures to promote the empowerment of girls, challenge patriarchal and other harmful gender norms and stereotyping and legal reforms in order to address direct and indirect discrimination against girls, in cooperation with all stakeholders, including civil society, women and men, traditional and religious leaders and adolescents themselves. Explicit measures are needed in all laws, policies and programmes to guarantee the rights of girls on an equal basis with boys.

Boys

29. Traditional concepts of masculinity and gender norms linked to violence and dominance can compromise boys' rights. These include the imposition of harmful initiation rites, exposure to violence, gangs, coercion into militia, extremist groups and trafficking. The denial of their vulnerability to physical and sexual abuse and exploitation also poses pervasive and significant barriers to boys gaining access to sexual and reproductive health information, goods and services, and a consequent lack of protective services.

30. The Committee urges States to introduce measures to address such rights violations, and encourages them to challenge negative perceptions of boys, promote positive masculinities, overcome cultural values based on machismo and promote greater recognition of the gender dimension of the abuses they experience. States should also recognize the importance of engaging with boys and men, as well as girls and women, in all measures introduced to achieve gender equality.

Adolescents with disabilities

31. The Committee has previously highlighted the widespread prejudice, exclusion, social isolation and discrimination faced by many children with disabilities.3 Adolescents with disabilities are, in many States, commonly excluded from opportunities available to other adolescents. They can be barred from participating in social, cultural and religious rites of passage. Significant numbers are denied access to secondary or tertiary education or vocational training, and consequent acquisition of the social, educational and economic skills necessary for future employment and freedom from pov-

erty. They are widely denied access to sexual and reproductive health information and services and may be subjected to forced sterilization or contraception, which is in direct violation of their rights and can amount to torture or ill-treatment. Adolescents with disabilities are disproportionately vulnerable to physical and sexual violence, as well as child or forced marriage, and are routinely denied access to justice or redress.

32. States parties should introduce measures to overcome such barriers, guarantee equal respect for the rights of adolescents with disabilities, promote their full inclusion and facilitate effective transitions from adolescence to adulthood, consistent with article 23 of the Convention and the recommendations in general comment No. 9 (2006) on the rights of children with disabilities. Adolescents with disabilities should, in addition, be provided with opportunities for supported decision-making in order to facilitate their active participation in all matters concerning them.

Lesbian, gay, bisexual, transgender and intersex adolescents

33. Adolescents who are lesbian, gay, bisexual, transgender and intersex commonly face persecution, including abuse and violence, stigmatization, discrimination, bullying, exclusion from education and training, as well as a lack of family and social support, or access to sexual and reproductive health services and information.4 In extreme cases, they face sexual assault, rape and even death. These experiences have been linked to low self-esteem, higher rates of depression, suicide and homelessness.

34. The Committee emphasizes the rights of all adolescents to freedom of expression and respect for their physical and psychological integrity, gender identity and emerging autonomy. It condemns the imposition of so-called "treatments" to try to change sexual orientation and forced surgeries or treatments on intersex adolescents. It urges States to eliminate such practices, repeal all laws criminalizing or otherwise discriminating against individuals on the basis of their sexual orientation, gender identity or intersex status and adopt laws prohibiting discrimination on those grounds. States should also take effective action to protect all lesbian, gay, bisexual, transgender and intersex adolescents from all forms of violence, discrimination or bullying by raising public awareness and implementing safety and support measures.

Minority and indigenous adolescents

35. The inadequate attention paid to and the insufficient respect shown for the cultures, values and world vision of adolescents from minority and indigenous groups can lead to discrimination, social exclusion, marginalization and non-inclusion in public spaces. This increases the vulnerability of minority and indigenous adolescents to poverty, social injustice, mental health issues, including disproportionately high suicide rates, poor educational outcomes and high levels of detention within the criminal justice system.

36. The Committee urges States parties to introduce measures to support adolescents from minority and indigenous communities so that they can enjoy their cultural identities and build on the strengths of their cultures to become active contributors to family and community life, paying particular attention to the rights of adolescent girls. In so doing, States should address the comprehensive recommendations contained in the Committee's general comment No. 11 (2009) on indigenous children and their rights under the Convention.

VI. General measures of implementation

37. In accordance with general comments No. 5 (2003) on general measures of implementation of the Convention (arts. 4, 42 and 44, para. 6) and No. 19 (2016) on public budgeting for the realization of children's rights (art. 4), the Committee draws attention to States parties' obligations to implement the following measures to establish the framework for the realization of the rights of children during adolescence. The experience and perspectives of adolescents themselves should be fully recognized and taken seriously in the development of all such measures, including:

(a) Comprehensive and multisectoral national strategies rooted in the Convention, with a dedicated focus on adolescents, to address the structural social and economic roots underlying the rights violations adolescents face and ensure a coordinated approach across government ministries;

(b) Monitoring implementation to ensure that the rights of adolescents are respected in legislation, policy and services;

(c) Collecting data disaggregated at a minimum by age, sex, disability, ethnicity and socioeconomic condition, to render the lives of adolescents visible, the Committee recommends that States agree on common indicators against which to monitor progress in the implementation of adolescents' rights;

(d) Transparent budgetary commitments to ensure that adolescents are duly considered when balancing competing spending priorities and complying with the principles of sufficiency, effectiveness, efficiency and equality;

(e) Training for all professionals working with and for adolescents on the Convention and its associated obligations, with a focus on the competencies needed to work with adolescents in accordance with their evolving capacities;

(f) Dissemination of accessible information about children's rights and how to exercise them through, inter alia, the school curriculum, the media, including digital media, and public information materials, making particular efforts to reach out to adolescents in marginalized situations.

VII. Definition of the child

38. The Convention prohibits any gender-based discrimination, and age limits should be equal for girls and boys.

39. States should review or introduce legislation recognizing the right of adolescents to take increasing responsibility for decisions affecting their lives. The Committee recommends that States introduce minimum legal age limits, consistent with the right to protection, the best interests principle and respect for the evolving capacities of adolescents. For example, age limits should recognize the right to make decisions in respect of health services or treatment, consent to adoption, change of name or applications to family courts. In all cases, the right of any child below that minimum age and able to demonstrate sufficient understanding to be entitled to give or refuse consent should be recognized. The voluntary and informed consent of the adolescent should be obtained whether or not the consent of a parent or guardian is required for any medical treatment or procedure. Consideration should also be given to the introduction of a legal presumption that adolescents are competent to seek and have access to preventive or time-sensitive sexual and reproductive health commodities and services. The Committee emphasizes that all adolescents have the right to have access to confidential medical counselling and advice without the consent of a parent or guardian, irrespective of age, if they so wish. This is distinct from the right to give medical consent and should not be subject to any age limit.

40. The Committee reminds States parties of the obligation to recognize that persons up to the age of 18 years are entitled to continuing protection from all forms of exploitation and abuse. It reaffirms that the minimum age limit should be 18 years for marriage, recruitment into the armed forces, involvement in hazardous or exploitative work and the purchase and consumption of alcohol and tobacco, in view of the degree of associated risk and harm. States parties should take into account the need to balance protection and evolving capacities, and define an acceptable minimum age when determining the legal age for sexual consent. States should avoid criminalizing adolescents of similar ages for factually consensual and non-exploitative sexual activity.

VIII. Civil rights and freedoms

Birth registration
41. The lack of birth registration can result in significant additional complications during adolescence, such as the denial of basic services, the inability to prove nationality or receive an identification document, a heightened risk of being exploited or trafficked, a lack of necessary safeguards in the criminal justice and immigration systems and the underage conscription into the armed forces. Adolescents who have not been registered at birth or immediately after should be provided with free late birth certificates and civil registration.

Freedom of expression
42. Article 13 of the Convention affirms that children have the right to freedom of expression and that the exercise of that right may be subject only to the restrictions set out in article 13 (2). The obligation of parents and caregivers to provide appropriate guidance in accordance with the evolving capacities of adolescents should not interfere with adolescents' right to freedom of expression. Adolescents have the right to seek, receive and impart information and ideas and use the means of their dissemination, including spoken, written and sign language and such non-verbal expression as im-

ages and objects of art. Means of expression include, for example, books, newspapers, pamphlets, posters, banners, digital and audiovisual media, as well as dress and personal style.

Freedom of religion

43. The Committee urges States parties to withdraw any reservations to Article 14 of the Convention, which highlights the right of the child to freedom of religion and recognizes the rights and duties of parents and guardians to provide direction to the child in a manner consistent with his or her evolving capacities (see also Art. 5). In other words, it is the child who exercises the right to freedom of religion, not the parent, and the parental role necessarily diminishes as the child acquires an increasingly active role in exercising choice throughout adolescence. Freedom of religion should be respected in schools and other institutions, including with regard to choice over attendance in religious instruction classes, and discrimination on the grounds of religious beliefs should be prohibited.

Freedom of association

44. Adolescents want and need to spend an increasing amount of time with their peers. The associated benefits are not merely social but also contribute towards competencies that are foundational for successful relationships, employment and community participation, building, inter alia, emotional literacy, a sense of belonging, skills such as conflict resolution and strengthened trust and intimacy. Association with peers is a major building block in adolescent development, the value of which should be recognized within the school and learning environment, recreational and cultural activities and opportunities for social, civic, religious and political engagement.

45. States should guarantee that adolescents' right to freedom of association and peaceful assembly in all its forms is fully respected, consistent with the restrictions delineated in article 15 (2) of the Convention, including through the provision of safe spaces for both girls and boys. Legal recognition should be afforded to adolescents to establish their own associations, clubs, organizations, parliaments and forums, both in and out of school, form online networks, join political parties and join or form their own trade unions. Measures should also be introduced to protect adolescent human rights defenders, particularly girls, who often face gender-specific threats and violence.

Privacy and confidentiality

46. The right to privacy takes on increasing significance during adolescence. The Committee has repeatedly raised concerns about violations of privacy in respect of, for example, confidential medical advice; space for and belongings of adolescents in institutions; correspondence and other communications, either in the family or other forms of care; and exposure of those involved in criminal proceedings. The right to privacy also entitles adolescents to have access to their records held by educational, health-care, childcare and protection services and justice systems. Such information should only be accessible in compliance with due process guarantees and to individuals authorized by law to receive and use it. States should, through dialogue with adolescents, ascertain where breaches of privacy have taken place, including in relation to personal engagement in the digital environment and the use of data by commercial and other entities. States should also take all appropriate measures to strengthen and ensure respect for the confidentiality of data and the privacy of adolescents, consistent with their evolving capacities.

Right to information

47. Access to information encompasses all forms of media but particular attention needs to be given to the digital environment, as adolescents increasingly use mobile technology and as social and digital media become the primary means through which they communicate and receive, create and disseminate information. Adolescents use the online environment, inter alia, to explore their identity, learn, participate, express opinions, play, socialize, engage politically and discover employment opportunities. In addition, the Internet provides opportunities for gaining access to online health information, protective support and sources of advice and counselling and can be utilized by States as a means of communicating and engaging with adolescents. The ability to access relevant information can have a significant positive impact on equality. The recommendations from the days of general discussion on the media in 1996 and 2014 have particular resonance for adolescents.5 States should adopt measures to ensure that all adolescents have access, without discrimination, to different forms of media and support and promote equal access to digital citizenship, including through the promotion of accessible formats for adolescents with disabilities. Training and support should be provided as part of the basic education curriculum to ensure the development of adolescents' digital, information and media and social literacy skills.

48. The digital environment can also expose adolescents to risks, such as online fraud, violence and hate speech, sexist speech against girls and lesbian, gay, bisexual, transgender and intersex adolescents, cyberbullying, grooming for sexual exploitation, trafficking and child pornography, over-sexualization and targeting by armed or extremist groups. This should not however restrict adolescents' access to the digital environment. Instead, their safety should be promoted through holistic strategies, including digital literacy with regard to online risks and strategies for keeping them safe, strengthened legislation and law enforcement mechanisms to tackle abuse online and fight impunity, and training parents and professionals who work with children. States are urged to ensure the active engagement of adolescents in the design and implementation of initiatives aimed at fostering online safety, including through peer mentoring. Investment is needed in the development of technological solutions on prevention and protection and the availability of assistance and support. States are encouraged to require businesses to undertake child-rights due diligence with a view to identifying, preventing and mitigating the impact of risks on children's rights when using digital media and information and communications technology.

IX. Violence against children

Protection from all forms of violence

49. The Committee refers States parties to the recommendations in general comments No. 13 (2011) on the right of the child to freedom from all forms of violence and No. 18 (2014) on harmful practices for comprehensive legislative, administrative, social and educational measures to bring an end to all forms of violence, including a legal prohibition on corporal punishment in all settings, and to transform and bring an end to all harmful practices. States parties need to create more opportunities for scaling up institutional programmes on prevention and rehabilitation

X. Family environment and alternative care

Support for parents and caregivers

50. The role of parents and caregivers in providing security, emotional stability, encouragement and protection to children remains important throughout adolescence. The Committee emphasizes that States' obligations to render appropriate assistance to parents and caregivers, as outlined in articles 18 (2) and (3) of the Convention, and to assist parents in providing the support and living conditions necessary for optimum development consistent with article 27 (2), have equal application to parents of adolescents. Such support should respect the rights and evolving capacities of adolescents and the increasing contribution they make to their own lives. States should ensure that they do not, in the name of traditional values, tolerate or condone violence, reinforce unequal power relations within family settings and, therefore, deprive adolescents of the opportunity to exercise their basic rights.

51. The Committee draws States parties' attention to the significance of a growing divide between the environments in which adolescents live, characterized by the digital era and globalization, and those in which their parents or caregivers grew up. Adolescents are exposed to and inevitably influenced by a global commercial world, unmediated or regulated by parental or community values, that can inhibit intergenerational understanding. This changing context poses challenges to the capacity of parents and caregivers to communicate effectively with adolescents and provide guidance and protection in a manner that takes into account the current realities of their lives. The Committee recommends that States undertake research with adolescents and their parents and caregivers into the nature of guidance, assistance, training and support needed to help address the intergenerational divergence of experience.

Adolescents in alternative care

52. There is significant evidence of poor outcomes for adolescents in large long-term institutions, as well as in other forms of alternative care, such as fostering and small group care, albeit to a much lesser degree. These adolescents experience lower educational attainment, dependency on social welfare and higher risk of homelessness, imprisonment, unwanted pregnancy, early parenthood, substance misuse, self-harm and suicide. Adolescents in alternative care are commonly required to leave once they reach 16-18 years of age and are particularly vulnerable to sexual abuse and exploitation, trafficking and violence as they lack support systems or protection and have been afforded no opportunities to acquire the skills and capacities to protect themselves. Those with disabilities are often denied opportunities for community living and are transferred to adult institutions, where they are at increased risk of being subjected to continuing violations of their rights.

53. States should commit strongly to and invest more in supporting adolescents in alternative care. Preference for foster and small homes needs to be complemented with the measures necessary to tackle discrimination, ensure regular reviews of adolescents' individual situations, support their education, give them a real voice in the processes affecting them and avoid multiple moves. States are urged to ensure that institutionalization is used only as a measure of last resort and to ensure the appropriate protection of all children living in institutions, including through access to confidential complaints mechanisms and justice. States should also adopt measures to support the independence and improve the life chances of adolescents in alternative care and address the particular vulnerabilities and insecurities they face as they become old enough to leave such care.

54. Adolescents leaving alternative care require support in preparing for the transition, gaining access to employment, housing and psychological support, participating in rehabilitation with their families where that is in their best interest and gaining access to after-care services consistent with the Guidelines for the Alternative Care of Children.

Adolescent-headed families

55. A significant number of adolescents are the primary caregivers of their families, either because they themselves are parents or because their parents have died or disappeared or are absent. Articles 24 and 27 of the Convention require that adolescent parents and caregivers be provided with basic knowledge of child health, nutrition and breastfeeding, and appropriate support to assist them in fulfilling their responsibilities towards the children they are responsible for and, when needed, material assistance with regard to nutrition, clothing and housing. Adolescent caregivers need extra support in order to enjoy their rights to education, play and participation.

In particular, States should introduce social protection interventions at key stages of the life cycle and respond to the specific requirements of adolescent caregivers.

XI. Basic health and welfare

Health care

56. Health services are rarely designed to accommodate the specific health needs of adolescents, a problem that is compounded by the lack of demographic and epidemiological data and statistics disaggregated by age, sex and disability. When adolescents seek help, they often experience legal and financial barriers, discrimination, lack of confidentiality and respect, violence and abuse, stigma and judgmental attitudes from health-care personnel.

57. Adolescents' health outcomes are predominantly a consequence of social and economic determinants and structural inequalities, mediated by behaviour and activity, at the individual, peer, family, school, community and societal levels. Accordingly, States parties, in collaboration with adolescents, should undertake comprehensive multi-stakeholder reviews of the nature and extent of adolescent health problems and the barriers they face in gaining access to services, as a basis for future comprehensive health policies, programmes and public health strategies.

58. Mental health and psychosocial problems, such as suicide, self-harm, eating disorders and depression, are primary causes of ill health, morbidity and mortality among adolescents, particularly among those in vulnerable groups. Such problems arise from a complex interplay of genetic, biological, personality and environmental causes and are compounded by, for example, experiences of conflict, displacement, discrimination, bullying and social exclusion, as well as pressures concerning body image and a culture of "perfection." The factors known to promote resilience and healthy development and to protect against mental ill health include strong relationships with and support from key adults, positive role models, a suitable standard of living, access to quality secondary education, freedom from violence and discrimination, opportunities for influence and decision-making, mental health awareness, problem-solving and coping skills and safe and healthy local environments. The Committee emphasizes that States should adopt an approach based on public health and psychosocial support rather than overmedicalization and institutionalization. A comprehensive multi-sectoral response is needed, through integrated systems of adolescent mental health care that involve parents, peers, the wider family and schools and the provision of support and assistance through trained staff.

59. The Committee urges States to adopt comprehensive gender and sexuality-sensitive sexual and reproductive health policies for adolescents, emphasizing that unequal access by adolescents to such information, commodities and services amounts to discrimination. Lack of access to such services contributes to adolescent girls being the group most at risk of

dying or suffering serious or lifelong injuries in pregnancy and childbirth. All adolescents should have access to free, confidential, adolescent-responsive and non-discriminatory sexual and reproductive health services, information and education, available both online and in person, including on family planning, contraception, including emergency contraception, prevention, care and treatment of sexually transmitted infections, counselling, pre-conception care, maternal health services and menstrual hygiene.

60. There should be no barriers to commodities, information and counselling on sexual and reproductive health and rights, such as requirements for third-party consent or authorization. In addition, particular efforts need to be made to overcome barriers of stigma and fear experienced by, for example, adolescent girls, girls with disabilities and lesbian, gay, bisexual, transgender and intersex adolescents, in gaining access to such services. The Committee urges States to decriminalize abortion to ensure that girls have access to safe abortion and post-abortion services, review legislation with a view to guaranteeing the best interests of pregnant adolescents and ensure that their views are always heard and respected in abortion-related decisions.

61. Age-appropriate, comprehensive and inclusive sexual and reproductive health education, based on scientific evidence and human rights standards and developed with adolescents, should be part of the mandatory school curriculum and reach out-of-school adolescents. Attention should be given to gender equality, sexual diversity, sexual and reproductive health rights, responsible parenthood and sexual behaviour and violence prevention, as well as to preventing early pregnancy and sexually transmitted infections. Information should be available in alternative formats to ensure accessibility to all adolescents, especially adolescents with disabilities.

HIV/AIDS

62. Adolescents are the only age group in which death due to AIDS is increasing. Adolescents may face challenges in gaining access to antiretroviral treatment and remaining in treatment; the need to gain the consent of guardians in order to access HIV-related services, disclosure and stigma are some barriers. Adolescent girls are disproportionately affected, representing two thirds of new infections. Lesbian, gay, bisexual and transgender adolescents, adolescents who exchange sex for money, goods or favours and adolescents who inject drugs are also at a higher risk of HIV infection.

63. The Committee encourages States to recognize adolescents' diverse realities and ensure that they have access to confidential HIV testing and counselling services and to evidence-based HIV prevention and treatment programmes provided by trained personnel who fully respect the rights of adolescents to privacy and non-discrimination. Health services should include HIV-related information, testing and diagnostics; information on contraception and the use of condoms; care and treatment, including antiretroviral and other medicines and related technologies for the care and treatment of HIV/AIDS; advice on suitable nutrition; spiritual and psychosocial support; and family, community and home-based care. Consideration should be given to reviewing HIV-specific legislation that criminalizes the unintentional transmission of HIV and the non-disclosure of one's HIV status.

Drug use among adolescents

64. Adolescents are more likely to be initiated into drug use and can be at a higher risk of drug-related harm than adults, and drug use initiated in adolescence more often leads to dependence. Those identified at greatest risk of drug-related harm are adolescents in street situations, those excluded from school, those with histories of trauma, family breakdown or abuse, and those living in families coping with drug dependence. States parties have an obligation to protect adolescents from the illicit use of narcotic drugs and psychotropic substances. States parties should ensure adolescents' right to health in relation to the use of such substances, as well as tobacco, alcohol and solvents, and put in place prevention, harm-reduction and dependence treatment services, without discrimination and with sufficient budgetary allocation. Alternatives to punitive or repressive drug control policies in relation to adolescents are welcome. Adolescents should also be provided with accurate and objective information based on scientific evidence aimed at preventing and minimizing harm from substance use.

Injuries and a safe environment

65. Unintended injuries or injuries due to violence are a leading cause of death and disability among adolescents. Most of the unintentional injuries result from road traffic crashes, drowning, burns, falls and poisoning. To reduce risk, States parties should develop multisectoral strategies that include legislation requiring the use of protective equipment, policies on driving while intoxicated and on licensing, programmes on education, skills development and behaviour change, adaptations to the environment, and the provision of care and rehabilitation services for those who suffer injuries.

Adequate standard of living

66. The impact of poverty has profound implications during adolescence, sometimes leading to extreme stress and insecurity and to social and political exclusion. Strategies imposed on or adopted by adolescents to address economic hardship can include dropping out of school, being involved in child or forced marriage, becoming involved in sexual exploitation, trafficking, hazardous or exploitative work or work that interferes with education, becoming members of a gang, being recruited into militias and migrating.

67. States are reminded of the right of every child to a suitable standard of living for physical, mental, spiritual, moral and social development, and are urged to introduce social protection floors that provide adolescents and their families with basic income security, protection against economic shocks and prolonged economic crises and access to social services.

XII. Education, leisure and cultural activities

Education

68. Guaranteeing the right to universal, quality and inclusive education and training is the single most important policy investment that States can make to ensure the immediate and long-term development of adolescents, and a growing body of evidence testifies to the positive impact of secondary education in particular States are encouraged to introduce widely available secondary education for all as a matter of urgency and to make higher education accessible to all on the basis of capacity by every appropriate means.

69. The Committee is deeply concerned at the challenges faced by many States to achieve equality in the enrolment of girls and boys and keep girls in school beyond primary education. Investment in girls' secondary education, a commitment necessary to comply with articles 2, 6 and 28 of the Convention, also serves to protect girls from child and forced marriage, sexual exploitation and early pregnancy, and contributes significantly towards the future economic potential of girls and their children. Investment should also be made in strategies that promote positive gender relations and social norms; address sexual and gender-based violence, including within schools; and promote positive role models, family support and the economic empowerment of women, to overcome the legal, political, cultural, economic and social barriers that represent barriers for girls. Furthermore, States should recognize that a growing number of boys are not enrolling and are not remaining in school, identify the causes and adopt appropriate measures to support boys' continued participation in education.

70. The Committee notes with concern the numbers of adolescents in marginalized situations who are not given the opportunity to make the transition to secondary education, such as adolescents living in poverty; lesbian, gay, bisexual, transgender and intersex adolescents; adolescents belonging to minorities; adolescents with psychosocial, sensory or physical disabilities; adolescents who are migrating; adolescents in situations of armed conflict or natural disasters; and adolescents in street situations or working. Proactive measures are necessary to end discrimination of marginalized groups in gaining access to education, including by establishing cash transfer programmes, respecting minority and indigenous cultures and children from all religious communities, promoting inclusive education for children with disabilities, combating bullying and discriminatory attitudes within the education system and providing education in refugee camps.

71. Efforts need to be made to consult adolescents on the barriers impeding their continued participation in school, given the high levels of early school leaving while still illiterate or without obtaining qualifications. The Committee has observed the following contributory factors: fees and associated costs; family poverty and lack of adequate social protection schemes, including adequate health insurance; lack of adequate and safe sanitation facilities for girls; exclusion of pregnant schoolgirls and adolescent mothers; persistent use of cruel, inhuman and degrading punishments; lack of effective measures to eliminate sexual harassment in school; sexual exploitation of girls; environments not conducive to girls' inclusion and safety; inappropriate teaching pedagogies; irrelevant or outdated curricula; failure to engage students in their own learning; and bullying. In addition, schools often lack the flexibility needed for adolescents to be able to combine work and/or family care responsibilities with their education, without which they may be unable to continue to meet the associated costs of schooling. Consistent with article 28 (1) (e) of the Convention and Sustainable Development Goal 4, States should introduce comprehensive and proactive measures to address all these factors and improve enrolment and attendance, reduce early school leaving and provide opportunities to complete education for those who have left.

72. The Committee draws attention to its general comment No. 1 (2001) on the aims of education, in which it asserts the need for education to be child-centred, child-friendly and empowering and emphasizes the importance of a more collaborative and participatory pedagogy. Curricula for secondary education should be designed to equip adolescents for active participation, develop respect for human rights and fundamental freedoms, promote civic engagement and prepare adolescents to lead responsible lives in a free society. To develop adolescents' fullest potential and keep them in school, consideration should be given to how learning environments are designed, to ensure they capitalize on adolescents' capacity for learning, motivation to work with peers and empowerment, and focus on experiential learning, exploration and limit testing.

Transitions from education to training and/or decent work

73. Significant numbers of adolescents are not in education, training or employment, leading to disproportionate levels of unemployment, underemployment and exploitation as they move towards adulthood. The Committee urges States to support out-of-school adolescents in a manner appropriate to their age to facilitate the transition to decent work, including by ensuring consistency between education and labour laws, and to adopt policies to promote their future employment. In line with article 28 (1) (d) adolescents, States should make educational and vocational information and guidance available and accessible to adolescents.

74. Both formal and informal education and training need to be designed for the twenty-first century skills required in the modern labour market, including integrating soft and transferrable skills into the curricula; expanding opportunities for experiential or practical learning; developing vocational training based on labour market demand; establishing public-private sector partnerships for entrepreneurship, internships and apprenticeships; and providing guidance on academic and vocational opportunities. States should also disseminate information on employment rights, including rights in relation to membership in trade unions and professional associations.

Leisure, recreation and the arts

75. Adolescents' right to rest and leisure and to engage and participate freely in play, recreational and artistic activities, both online and offline, are fundamental to their exploration of identity, enabling adolescents to explore their culture, forge new artistic forms, create relationships and evolve as human beings. Leisure, recreation and the arts give adolescents a sense of uniqueness that is fundamental to the rights to human dignity, optimum development, freedom of expression, participation and privacy. The Committee notes with regret that those rights are widely neglected in adolescence, especially for girls. Fear of and hostility towards adolescents in public spaces, and a lack of adolescent-friendly urban planning, educational and leisure infrastructure, can inhibit the freedom to engage in recreational activity and sports. The Committee draws the attention of States to the rights embodied in article 31 of the Convention and its recommendations in general comment No. 17 (2013) on the right of the child to rest, leisure, play, recreational activities, cultural life and the arts.

XIII. Special protection measures

Migration

76. Growing numbers of adolescent girls and boys migrate, either within or outside their country of origin, in search of improved standards of living, education or family reunification. For many, migration offers significant social and economic opportunities. However, it also poses risks, including physical harm, psychological trauma, marginalization, discrimination, xenophobia and sexual and economic exploitation and, when crossing borders, immigration raids and detention. Many adolescent migrants are denied access to education, housing, health, recreation, participation, protection and social security. Even where rights to services are protected by laws and policies, adolescents may face administrative and other obstacles in gaining access to such services, including: demands for identity documents or social security numbers; harmful and inaccurate age-determination procedures; financial and linguistic barriers; and the risk that gaining access to services will result in detention or deportation. The Committee refers States parties to its comprehensive recommendations elaborated in respect of migrant children.

77. The Committee stresses that article 22 of the Convention recognizes that refugee and asylum-seeking children require special measures if they are to enjoy their rights and benefit from the additional safeguards given to them through the international refugee protection regime. Those adolescents should not be subjected to expedited removal procedures but rather be considered for entry into the territory and should not be returned or refused entry before a determi-

nation of their best interests has been made and a need for international protection has been established. In line with the obligation under article 2 to respect and ensure the rights of every child within their jurisdiction, irrespective of status, States should introduce age- and gender-sensitive legislation governing both unaccompanied and separated refugee and asylum-seeking adolescents, as well as migrants, underpinned by the best interests principle, prioritizing the assessment of protection needs over the determination of immigration status, prohibiting immigration-related detention and referring to the recommendations in general comment No. 6 (2005) on the treatment of unaccompanied and separated children outside their country of origin, addressing the particular vulnerability of those adolescents. States should also introduce measures to address the factors driving adolescents to migrate and the vulnerabilities and rights violations faced by adolescents left behind when parents migrate, including dropping out of school, child labour, vulnerability to violence and criminal activities and burdensome domestic responsibilities.

Trafficking

78. Many adolescents are at risk of being trafficked for economic reasons or for sexual exploitation. States are urged to establish a comprehensive and systematic mechanism for collecting data on the sale of, trafficking in and abduction of children, ensuring that the data is disaggregated and paying particular attention to children living in the most vulnerable situations. States should also invest in rehabilitation and reintegration services and psychosocial support for child victims. Attention should be paid to the gender-based dimensions of vulnerability and exploitation. Awareness-raising activities, including through social media, need to be conducted in order to make parents and children aware of the dangers of both domestic and international trafficking. States are urged to ratify the Optional Protocol to the Convention on the Rights of the Child on the sale of children, child prostitution and child pornography and to harmonize legislation accordingly.

Conflict and crisis

79. Situations of armed conflict and humanitarian disasters result in the breakdown of social norms and family and community support structures. They force many displaced and crisis-affected adolescents to assume adult responsibilities and expose them to risks of sexual and gender-based violence, child and forced marriage and trafficking. Furthermore, adolescents in such situations are likely to be denied education, skills training, safe employment opportunities and access to appropriate sexual and reproductive health services and information, and to face isolation, discrimination and stigma, mental health and risk-taking behaviour.

80. The Committee is concerned about the failure of humanitarian programmes to address the specific needs and rights of adolescents. It urges States parties to ensure that adolescents are provided with systematic opportunities to play an active role in the development and design of protection systems and reconciliation and peacebuilding processes. Explicit investment in post-conflict and transition reconstruction should be seen as an opportunity for adolescents to contribute to the economic and social development, resilience-building and peaceful transition of the country. In addition, emergency preparedness programmes should address adolescents, recognizing both their vulnerability and right to protection, and their potential role in supporting communities and helping to mitigate risk.

Recruitment into armed forces and groups

81. The Committee expresses deep concern about the fact that adolescent boys and girls are being recruited, including through the use of social media, by States' armed forces, armed groups and militias, and urges all States parties to ratify the Optional Protocol to the Convention on the Rights of the Child on the involvement of children in armed conflict. It is also concerned about adolescents' vulnerability to being enticed by terrorist propaganda, extremist views and involvement in terrorist activities. Research with adolescents should be undertaken to explore the factors driving their engagement in such activities and States should take appropriate action in response to the findings, paying particular attention to measures promoting social integration.

82. States should ensure the recovery and gender-sensitive reintegration of adolescents who are recruited into armed forces and groups, including those in migration situations, and prohibit the recruitment or use of adolescents in all hostilities as well as peace or ceasefire negotiations and agreements with armed groups.6 States should support opportunities for adolescent participation in peace movements and peer-to-peer approaches to non-violent conflict resolution rooted in local communities, to ensure the sustainability and cultural appropriateness of interventions. The Committee urges States parties to take firm measures to ensure that cases of conflict-related sexual violence, sexual exploitation and abuse and other human rights abuses against adolescents are promptly and duly addressed.

83. The Committee recognizes that, in many parts of the world, adolescents are recruited into gangs and pandillas, which often provide social support, a source of livelihood, protection and a sense of identity in the absence of opportunities to achieve such goals through legitimate activities. However, the climate of fear, insecurity, threat and violence posed by gang membership threatens the realization of the rights of adolescents and is a major factor contributing to adolescent migration. The Committee recommends that more emphasis be placed on the development of comprehensive public policies that address the root causes of juvenile violence and gangs, instead of aggressive law enforcement approaches. Investment is needed in prevention activities for at-risk adolescents, interventions to encourage adolescents to leave gangs, rehabilitation and reintegration of gang members, restorative justice and the creation of municipal alliances against crime and violence, with an emphasis on the school, the family and social inclusion measures. The Committee urges States to give due consideration to adolescents forced to leave their country for reasons related to gang violence and to afford them refugee status.

Child labour

84. The Committee emphasizes that all adolescents have the right to be protected from economic exploitation and the worst forms of child labour, and urges States to implement the provisions of article 32 (2) of the Convention, as well as the International Labour Organization Minimum Age Convention, 1973 (No. 138), and the Worst Forms of Child Labour Convention, 1999 (No. 182).

85. The introduction to age-appropriate forms of work plays an important developmental role in the lives of adolescents, equipping them with skills and enabling them to learn responsibilities and, where necessary, to contribute to their families' economic well-being and support their access to education. Action against child labour should comprise comprehensive measures, including school-to-work transitions, social and economic development, poverty eradication programmes and universal and free access to quality, inclusive primary and secondary education. It should be underlined that adolescents, once they reach the national legal minimum working age, which should be aligned with international standards and with compulsory education, have the right to perform light work under appropriate conditions, with due respect accorded to their rights to education and to rest, leisure, play, recreational activities, cultural life and the arts.

86. The Committee recommends that States adopt a transitional approach towards achieving a balance between the positive role of work in adolescents' lives while ensuring their right to compulsory education, without discrimination. Schooling and the introduction to decent work should be coordinated to facilitate both in the lives of adolescents, according to their age and the effective mechanisms introduced to regulate such work, and give redress when adolescents are the victims of exploitation. The protection from hazardous work of all children under 18 years of age should be stipulated, with a clear list of specific harmful work. Efforts directed at preventing harmful work and working conditions should be made as a matter of priority, paying special attention to girls involved in domestic labour and other often "invisible" workers.

Justice for adolescents

87. Adolescents may come into contact with justice systems through conflict with the law, as victims or witnesses of crime or for other reasons, such as care, custody or protection. Measures are needed to reduce adolescents' vulnerability both as victims and perpetrators of crimes.

88. States parties are urged to introduce comprehensive juvenile justice policies that emphasize restorative justice, diversion from judicial proceedings, alternative measures to detention and preventive interventions, to tackle social factors and root causes, consistent with articles 37 and 40 of the Convention, and the United Nations Guidelines for the Prevention of Juvenile Delinquency. The focus should be on rehabilitation and reintegration, including for those adolescents involved in activities categorized as terrorism, in line with the recommendations in general comment No. 10 (2007) on children's rights in juvenile justice. Detention should be used only as a measure of last resort and for the shortest appropriate period of time, and adolescents should be detained separately from adults. The Committee emphasizes the imperative to ban the death penalty and prohibit life imprisonment for anyone convicted of a crime committed when under the age of 18 years. The Committee is seriously concerned at the number of States seeking to lower the age of criminal responsibility and encourages States to raise progressively the age of criminal responsibility to 18 years.

XIV. International cooperation

89. The Committee stresses that implementation of the Convention is a cooperative exercise for the States parties, and highlights the need for international cooperation. The Committee encourages States parties to contribute and use, as appropriate, technical assistance from the United Nations and regional organizations in implementing the rights of adolescents.

XV. Dissemination

90. The Committee recommends that States disseminate widely the present general comment to all stakeholders, in particular parliament and all levels of government, including within ministries, departments and municipal/local authorities, and to all adolescents. The Committee also recommends that the present general comment be translated into all relevant languages, in adolescent-friendly versions and in formats accessible to adolescents with disabilities.

Source: http://tbinternet.ohchr.org/_layouts/treatybodyexternal/

9. OPTIONAL PROTOCOL TO THE CONVENTION ON THE RIGHTS OF THE CHILD ON A COMMUNICATIONS PROCEDURE (OP3 CRC) OR (OP-CRC-IC)

This Optional Protocol to the Convention on the Rights of the Child on a communications procedure has not been signed or ratified by the US. Nonetheless, it authorizes the CRC Committee to create procedures for individuals to make communications/contacts/submissions to the CRC Committee as complaints against States parties to the CRC and/or its protocols.

Adopted and opened for signature, ratification and accession by General Assembly resolution A/RES/66/138 of 19 December 2011. Entered into force on 14 April 2014

The States parties to the present Protocol,

Considering that, in accordance with the principles proclaimed in the Charter of the United Nations, the recognition of the inherent dignity and the equal and inalienable rights of all members of the human family is the foundation of freedom, justice and peace in the world,

Noting that the States parties to the Convention on the Rights of the Child (hereinafter referred to as "the Convention") recognize the rights set forth in it to each child within their jurisdiction without discrimination of any kind, irrespective of the child's or his or her parent's or legal guardian's race, colour, sex, language, religion, political or other opinion, national, ethnic or social origin, property, disability, birth or other status,

Reaffirming the universality, indivisibility, interdependence and interrelatedness of all human rights and fundamental freedoms,

Reaffirming also the status of the child as a subject of rights and as a human being with dignity and with evolving capacities,

Recognizing that children's special and dependent status may create real difficulties for them in pursuing remedies for violations of their rights,

Considering that the present Protocol will reinforce and complement national and regional mechanisms allowing children to submit complaints for violations of their rights,

Recognizing that the best interests of the child should be a primary consideration to be respected in pursuing remedies for violations of the rights of the child, and that such remedies should take into account the need for child-sensitive procedures at all levels,

Encouraging States parties to develop appropriate national mechanisms to enable a child whose rights have been violated to have access to effective remedies at the domestic level,

Recalling the important role that national human rights institutions and other relevant specialized institutions, mandated to promote and protect the rights of the child, can play in this regard,

Considering that, in order to reinforce and complement such national mechanisms and to further enhance the implementation of the Convention and, where applicable, the Optional Protocols thereto on the sale of children, child prostitution and child pornography and on the involvement of children in armed conflict, it would be appropriate to enable the Committee on the Rights of the Child (hereinafter referred to as "the Committee") to carry out the functions provided for in the present Protocol,

Have agreed as follows:

Part I

General provisions

Article 1
Competence of the Committee on the Rights of the Child

1. A State party to the present Protocol recognizes the competence of the Committee as provided for by the present Protocol.

2. The Committee shall not exercise its competence regarding a State party to the present Protocol on matters concerning violations of rights set forth in an instrument to which that State is not a party.

3. No communication shall be received by the Committee if it concerns a State that is not a party to the present Protocol.

Article 2
General principles guiding the functions of the Committee

In fulfilling the functions conferred on it by the present Protocol, the Committee shall be guided by the principle of the best interests of the child. It shall also have regard for the rights and views of the child, the views of the child being given due weight in accordance with the age and maturity of the child.

Article 3
Rules of procedure

1. The Committee shall adopt rules of procedure to be followed when exercising the functions conferred on it by the present Protocol. In doing so, it shall have regard, in particular, for article 2 of the present Protocol in order to guarantee child-sensitive procedures.

2. The Committee shall include in its rules of procedure safeguards to prevent the manipulation of the child by those acting on his or her behalf and may decline to examine any communication that it considers not to be in the child's best interests.

Article 4
Protection measures

1. A State party shall take all appropriate steps to ensure that individuals under its jurisdiction are not subjected to any human rights violation, ill-treatment or intimidation as a consequence of communications or cooperation with the Committee pursuant to the present Protocol.

2. The identity of any individual or group of individuals concerned shall not be revealed publicly without their express consent.

Part II

Communications procedure

Article 5
Individual communications

1. Communications may be submitted by or on behalf of an individual or group of individuals, within the jurisdiction of a State party, claiming to be victims of a violation by that State party of any of the rights set forth in any of the following instruments to which that State is a party:
- The Convention;
- The Optional Protocol to the Convention on the sale of children, child prostitution and child pornography;
- The Optional Protocol to the Convention on the involvement of children in armed conflict.

2. Where a communication is submitted on behalf of an individual or group of individuals, this shall be with their consent unless the author can justify acting on their behalf without such consent.

Article 6
Interim measures

1. At any time after the receipt of a communication and before a determination on the merits has been reached, the Committee may transmit to the State party concerned for its urgent consideration a request that the State party take such interim measures as may be necessary in exceptional circumstances to avoid possible irreparable damage to the victim or victims of the alleged violations.

2. Where the Committee exercises its discretion under paragraph 1 of the present article, this does not imply a determination on admissibility or on the merits of the communication.

Article 7 – Admissibility
The Committee shall consider a communication inadmissible when:

1. The communication is anonymous;

2. The communication is not in writing;

3. The communication constitutes an abuse of the right of submission of such communications or is incompatible with the provisions of the Convention and/or the Optional Protocols thereto;

4. The same matter has already been examined by the Committee or has been or is being examined under another procedure of international investigation or settlement;

5. All available domestic remedies have not been exhausted. This shall not be the rule where the application of the remedies is unreasonably prolonged or unlikely to bring effective relief;

6. The communication is manifestly ill-founded or not sufficiently substantiated;

7. The facts that are the subject of the communication occurred prior to the entry into force of the present Protocol for the State party concerned, unless those facts continued after that date;

8. The communication is not submitted within one year after the exhaustion of domestic remedies, except in cases where the author can demonstrate that it had not been possible to submit the communication within that time limit.

Article 8
Transmission of the communication

1. Unless the Committee considers a communication inadmissible without reference to the State party concerned, the Committee shall bring any communication submitted to it under the present Protocol confidentially to the attention of the State party concerned as soon as possible.

2. The State party shall submit to the Committee written explanations or statements clarifying the matter and the remedy, if any, that it may have provided. The State party shall submit its response as soon as possible and within six months.

Article 9
Friendly settlement

1. The Committee shall make available its good offices to the parties concerned with a view to reaching a friendly settlement of the matter on the basis of respect for the obligations set forth in the Convention and/or the Optional Protocols thereto.

2. An agreement on a friendly settlement reached under the auspices of the Committee closes consideration of the communication under the present Protocol.

Article 10
Consideration of communications

1. The Committee shall consider communications received under the present Protocol as quickly as possible, in the light of all documentation submitted to it, provided that this documentation is transmitted to the parties concerned.

2. The Committee shall hold closed meetings when examining communications received under the present Protocol.

3. Where the Committee has requested interim measures, it shall expedite the consideration of the communication.

4. When examining communications alleging violations of economic, social or cultural rights, the Committee shall consider the reasonableness of the steps taken by the State party in accordance with article 4 of the Convention. In doing so, the Committee shall bear in mind that the State party may adopt a range of possible policy measures for the implementation of the economic, social and cultural rights in the Convention.

5. After examining a communication, the Committee shall, without delay, transmit its views on the communication, together with its recommendations, if any, to the parties concerned.

Article 11 – Follow-up
1. The State party shall give due consideration to the views of the Committee, together with its recommendations, if any, and shall submit to the Committee a written response, including information on any action taken and envisaged in the light of the views and recommendations of the Committee. The State party shall submit its response as soon as possible and within six months.

2. The Committee may invite the State party to submit further information about any measures the State party has taken in response to its views or recommendations or implementation of a friendly settlement agreement, if any, including as deemed appropriate by the Committee, in the State party's subsequent reports under article 44 of the Convention, article 12 of the Optional Protocol to the Convention on the sale of children, child prostitution and child pornography or article 8 of the Optional Protocol to the Convention on the involvement of children in armed conflict, where applicable.

Article 12
Inter-State communications

1. A State party to the present Protocol may, at any time, declare that it recognizes the competence of the Committee to receive and consider communications in which a State party claims that another State party is not fulfilling its obligations under any of the following instruments to which the State is a party:

    1. The Convention;

2. The Optional Protocol to the Convention on the sale of children, child prostitution and child pornography;

3. The Optional Protocol to the Convention on the involvement of children in armed conflict.

4. The Committee shall not receive communications concerning a State party that has not made such a declaration or communications from a State party that has not made such a declaration.

5. The Committee shall make available its good offices to the States parties concerned with a view to a friendly solution of the matter on the basis of the respect for the obligations set forth in the Convention and the Optional Protocols thereto.

6. A declaration under paragraph 1 of the present article shall be deposited by the States parties with the Secretary-General of the United Nations, who shall transmit copies thereof to the other States parties. A declaration may be withdrawn at any time by notification to the Secretary-General. Such a withdrawal shall not prejudice the consideration of any matter that is the subject of a communication already transmitted under the present article; no further communications by any State party shall be received under the present article after the notification of withdrawal of the declaration has been received by the Secretary-General, unless the State party concerned has made a new declaration.

Part III

Inquiry procedure

Article 13
Inquiry procedure for grave or systematic violations

1. If the Committee receives reliable information indicating grave or systematic violations by a State party of rights set forth in the Convention or in the Optional Protocols thereto on the sale of children, child prostitution and child pornography or on the involvement of children in armed conflict, the Committee shall invite the State party to cooperate in the examination of the information and, to this end, to submit observations without delay with regard to the information concerned.

2. Taking into account any observations that may have been submitted by the State party concerned, as well as any other reliable information available to it, the Committee may designate one or more of its members to conduct an inquiry and to report urgently to the Committee. Where warranted and with the consent of the State party, the inquiry may include a visit to its territory.

3. Such an inquiry shall be conducted confidentially, and the cooperation of the State party shall be sought at all stages of the proceedings.

4. After examining the findings of such an inquiry, the Committee shall transmit without delay these findings to the State party concerned, together with any comments and recommendations.

5. The State party concerned shall, as soon as possible and within six months of receiving the findings, comments and recommendations transmitted by the Committee, submit its observations to the Committee.

6. After such proceedings have been completed with regard to an inquiry made in accordance with paragraph 2 of the present article, the Committee may, after consultation with the State party concerned, decide to include a summary account of the results of the proceedings in its report provided for in article 16 of the present Protocol.

7. Each State party may, at the time of signature or ratification of the present Protocol or accession thereto, declare that it does not recognize the competence of the Committee provided for in the present article in respect of the rights set forth in some or all of the instruments listed in paragraph 1.

8. Any State party having made a declaration in accordance with paragraph 7 of the present article may, at any time, withdraw this declaration by notification to the Secretary-General of the United Nations.

Article 14
Follow-up to the inquiry procedure

1. The Committee may, if necessary, after the end of the period of six months referred to in article 13, paragraph 5, invite the State party concerned to inform it of the measures taken and envisaged in response to an inquiry conducted under article 13 of the present Protocol.

2. The Committee may invite the State party to submit further information about any measures that the State party has taken in response to an inquiry conducted under article 13, including as deemed appropriate by the Committee, in the State party's subsequent reports under article 44 of the Convention, article 12 of the Optional Protocol to the Convention on the sale of children, child prostitution and child pornography or article 8 of the Optional Protocol to the Convention on the involvement of children in armed conflict, where applicable.

Part IV

Final provisions

Article 15
International assistance and cooperation

1. The Committee may transmit, with the consent of the State party concerned, to United Nations specialized agencies, funds and programmes and other competent bodies its views or recommendations concerning communications and inquiries that indicate a need for technical advice or assistance, together with the State party's observations and suggestions, if any, on these views or recommendations.

2. The Committee may also bring to the attention of such bodies, with the consent of the State party concerned, any matter arising out of communications considered under the present Protocol that may assist them in deciding, each within its field of competence, on the advisability of international measures likely to contribute to assisting States parties in achieving progress in the implementation of the rights recognized in the Convention and/or the Optional Protocols thereto.

Article 16
Report to the General Assembly

The Committee shall include in its report submitted every two years to the General Assembly in accordance with article 44, paragraph 5, of the Convention a summary of its activities under the present Protocol.

Article 17
Dissemination of and information on the Optional Protocol

Each State party undertakes to make widely known and to disseminate the present Protocol and to facilitate access to information about the views and recommendations of the Committee, in particular with regard to matters involving the State party, by appropriate and active means and in accessible formats to adults and children alike, including those with disabilities.

Article 18
Signature, ratification and accession

1. The present Protocol is open for signature to any State that has signed, ratified or acceded to the Convention or either of the first two Optional Protocols thereto.

2. The present Protocol is subject to ratification by any State that has ratified or acceded to the Convention or either of the first two Optional Protocols thereto. Instruments of ratification shall be deposited with the Secretary-General of the United Nations.

3. The present Protocol shall be open to accession by any State that has ratified or acceded to the Convention or either of the first two Optional Protocols thereto.

4. Accession shall be effected by the deposit of an instrument of accession with the Secretary-General.

Article 19 – Entry into force
1. The present Protocol shall enter into force three months after the deposit of the tenth instrument of ratification or accession.

2. For each State ratifying the present Protocol or acceding to it after the deposit of the tenth instrument of ratification or instrument of accession, the present Protocol shall enter into force three months after the date of the deposit of its own instrument of ratification or accession.

Article 20
Violations occurring after the entry into force

1. The Committee shall have competence solely in respect of violations by the State party of any of the rights set forth in the Convention and/or the first two Optional Protocols thereto occurring after the entry into force of the present Protocol.

2. If a State becomes a party to the present Protocol after its entry into force, the obligations of that State vis-à-vis the Committee shall relate only to violations of the rights set forth in the Convention and/or the first two Optional Protocols thereto occurring after the entry into force of the present Protocol for the State concerned.

Article 21 – Amendments
1. Any State party may propose an amendment to the present Protocol and submit it to the Secretary-General of the United Nations. The Secretary-General shall communicate any proposed amendments to States parties with a request to be notified whether they favour a meeting of States parties for the purpose of considering and deciding upon the proposals. In the event that, within four months of the date of such communication, at least one third of the States parties favour such a meeting, the Secretary-General shall convene the meeting under the auspices of the United Nations. Any amendment adopted by a majority of two thirds of the States parties present and voting shall be submitted by the Secretary-General to the General Assembly for approval and, thereafter, to all States parties for acceptance.

2. An amendment adopted and approved in accordance with paragraph 1 of the present article shall enter into force on the thirtieth day after the number of instruments of acceptance deposited reaches two thirds of the number of States parties at the date of adoption of the amendment. Thereafter, the amendment shall enter into force for any State party on the thirtieth day following the deposit of its own instrument of acceptance. An amendment shall be binding only on those States parties that have accepted it.

Article 22 – Denunciation
1. Any State party may denounce the present Protocol at any time by written notification to the Secretary-General of the United Nations. The denunciation shall take effect one year after the date of receipt of the notification by the Secretary-General.

2. Denunciation shall be without prejudice to the continued application of the provisions of the present Protocol to any communication submitted under articles 5 or 12 or any inquiry initiated under article 13 before the effective date of denunciation.

Article 23
Depositary and notification by the Secretary-General

1. The Secretary-General of the United Nations shall be the depositary of the presdent Protocol.

2. The Secretary-General shall inform all States of:
  • Signatures, ratifications and accessions under the present Protocol;

- The date of entry into force of the present Protocol and of any amendment thereto under article 21;
- Any denunciation under article 22 of the present Protocol.

Article 24 – Languages

1. The present Protocol, of which the Arabic, Chinese, English, French, Russian and Spanish texts are equally authentic, shall be deposited in the archives of the United Nations.

2. The Secretary-General of the United Nations shall transmit certified copies of the present Protocol to all States.

Source: United Nations Human Rights Office of the High Commissioner, http://www.ohchr.org/EN/ProfessionalInterest/Pages/ OPICCRC.aspx

Women's and Girls' Rights

Chapter 12

This Chapter is About the issue of discrimination against women's and girls' human rights in all spheres of life as a matter of concern within international human rights law and U.S. domestic law.

This is Important Because 1) although women and men share the same human rights, discrimination based on gender and race have long been understood and acknowledged universally as political, civil, social, economic, and cultural realities that must be addressed systemically, in such a way as to reform totally and dismantle entirely every institution that stymies and denies women their human rights, and 2) although the U.S. is a signatory of the Convention on the Elimination of All Forms of Discrimation against Women (CEDAW) since July 1980, it is one of only seven countries that has not ratified it.

Quotes & Key Text Excerpts

Whereas recognition of the inherent dignity and of the equal and inalienable rights of all members of the human family is the foundation of freedom, justice and peace in the world,...

Whereas the peoples of the United Nations have in the Charter reaffirmed their faith in fundamental human rights, in the dignity and worth of the human person and in the equal rights of men and women....

Article 2

Everyone is entitled to all the rights and freedoms set forth in this Declaration, without distinction of any kind, such as race, colour, sex, language, religion, political or other opinion, national or social origin, property, birth or other status....

Article 7

All are equal before the law and are entitled without any discrimination to equal protection of the law. All are entitled to equal protection against any discrimination in violation of this Declaration and against any incitement to such discrimination...etc....

Source: Universal Declaration of Human Rights 1948

ॐ✦ॐ✦ॐ✦ॐ✦

Article 2

1. Each State Party to the present Covenant undertakes to respect and to ensure to all individuals within its territory and subject to its jurisdiction the rights recognized in the present Covenant, without distinction of any kind, such as race, colour, sex, language, religion, political or other opinion, national or social origin, property, birth or other....

Article 3

The States Parties to the present Covenant undertake to ensure the equal right of men and women to the enjoyment of all civil and political rights set forth in the present Covenant....

Source: International Covenant on Civil and Political Rights 1966

ॐ✦ॐ✦ॐ✦ॐ✦

Article 2.2

The States Parties to the present Covenant undertake to guarantee that the rights enunciated in the present Covenant will be exercised without discrimination of any kind as to race, colour, sex, language, religion, political or other opinion, national or social origin, property, birth or other status....

Article 3

The States Parties to the present Covenant undertake to ensure the equal right of men and women to the enjoyment of all economic, social and cultural rights set forth in the present Covenant.

Article 7

The States Parties to the present Covenant recognize the right of everyone to the enjoyment of just and favourable conditions of work which ensure, in particular: (a) Remuneration which provides all workers, as a minimum, with: (i) Fair wages and equal remuneration for work of equal value without distinction of any kind, in particular women being guaranteed conditions of work not inferior to those enjoyed by men, with equal pay for equal work; ....

Article 10

The States Parties to the present Covenant recognize that:

1. The widest possible protection and assistance should be accorded to the family, which is the natural and fundamental group unit of society, particularly for its establishment and while it is responsible for the care and education of dependent children. Marriage must be entered into with the free consent of the intending spouses.

2. Special protection should be accorded to mothers during a reasonable period before and after childbirth. During such period working mothers should be accorded paid leave or leave with adequate social security benefits....

Source: International Covenant on Economic, Social and Cultural Rights 1966

∞∞∞∞∞∞∞∞

Article 1

...discrimination against women shall mean any distinction, exclusion, or restriction made on the basis of sex which has the effect or purpose of impairing or nullifying the recognition, enjoyment or exercise by women, irrespective of their marital status, on a basis of equality of men and women, of human rights and fundamental freedoms in the political, economic, social, cultural, civil or any other field.

Article 2

"States Parties condemn discrimination against women in all its forms, agree to pursue by all appropriate means and without delay a policy of eliminating discrimination against women and, to this end, undertake:

(a) To embody the principle of the equality of men and women in their national constitutions or other appropriate legislation if not yet incorporated therein and to ensure, through law and other appropriate means, the practical realization of this principle;

(b) To adopt appropriate legislative and other measures, including sanctions where appropriate, prohibiting all discrimination against women;

(c) To establish legal protection of the rights of women on an equal basis with men and to ensure through competent national tribunals and other public institutions the effective protection of women against any act of discrimination;

(d) To refrain from engaging in any act or practice of discrimination against women and to ensure that public authorities and institutions shall act in conformity with this obligation;

(e) To take all appropriate measures to eliminate discrimination against women by any person, organization or enterprise;

(f) To take all appropriate measures, including legislation, to modify or abolish existing laws, regulations, customs and practices which constitute discrimination against women;

(g) To repeal all national penal provisions which constitute discrimination against women.

Article 5

...to ensure that family education includes a proper understanding of maternity as a social function and the recognition of the common responsibility of men and women in the upbringing and development of their children, it being understood that the interest of the children is the primordial consideration in all cases.

Article 10

States Parties shall take all appropriate measures to eliminate discrimination against women in order to ensure to them equal rights with men in the field of education...the same conditions for career and vocational guidance, for access to studies...ensured in pre-school, general, technical, professional and higher technical education,...access to the same curricula,...examinations...the elimination of any stereotyped concept of the roles of men and women at all levels and in all forms of education by encouraging coeducation and other types of education which will help to achieve this aim...by the revision of textbooks and school programs...and...teaching methods.... The same opportunities to...scholarships and...grants...to participate actively in sports and physical education...access to educational information to help ensure the health and well-being of families, including information and advice on family planning.

Source: Convention on the Elimination of All Forms of Discrimination Against Women 1965, entry into force 1969, 1979 (full text of CEDAW at the end of this chapter)

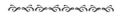

Wherever the Special Rapporteur went, officials asked her why she decided to visit the United States. She explained that based on information received from diverse sources, she was convinced that there were serious issues of custodial sexual misconduct in United States prisons that had to be investigated. Many felt nevertheless that special rapporteurs should concentrate on crisis situations around the world rather than focus on countries where human rights protection is more or less ensured. The Special Rapporteur maintains that the notion that human rights protections are only for societies that are in crisis should be contested. Human rights protections are not only applicable during emergencies, but are also required in societies perceived to be crisis-free. Although the United States has a comparatively high level of political freedom, some aspects of its criminal justice system pose fundamental human rights questions. Other special rapporteurs have also stressed this point.

Source: United Nations Special Rapporteur on violence against women, its causes and consequences Radhika Coomaraswamy

The U.S., which is a leading State in formulating international human rights standards, is allowing its women to lag behind, said the U.N. Working Group on discrimination against women in law and practice in a news release issued by the Office of the U.N. High Commissioner for Human Rights (OHCHR).

Source: U.N. News Centre, "Women in U.S. lagging behind in human rights, U.N. experts report after 'myth-shattering' visit," http://www.un.org/apps/news/story.asp?NewsID=52797#.WHaRynfMwdU

స్కాస్కాస్కాస్కాస్కా

[C]ommunities that give their daughters the same opportunities as their sons, they are more peaceful, they are more prosperous, they develop faster, they are more likely to succeed.

—*President Barack Obama, July 25, 2015*

స్కాస్కాస్కాస్కాస్కా

We are here to advance the cause of women and to advance the cause of democracy and to make it absolutely clear that the two are inseparable. There cannot be true democracy unless women's voices are heard. There cannot be true democracy unless women are given the opportunity to take responsibility for their own lives. There cannot be true democracy unless all citizens are able to participate fully in the lives of their country.

—*Hillary Clinton, Women in Democracy Conference, Vienna, July 1997*

What You Should Know

In the U.S. domestic scene, 1980s domestic politicians viewed the Convention on the Elimination of All Forms of Discrimination Against Women (CEDAW) as a very politically controversial treaty. The U.S. Senate was reluctant to ratify CEDAW due to concerns that included interpretation of certain articles; for example, those referring to affirmative action considerations for women and persons of color. Some opponents questioned whether this treaty was necessary at all, considering the strong gender equality laws already enacted in U.S. law. However, since the 1980s, effort to globalize economy coincides with growing women's awareness in international political, economic, social, cultural, and civil human rights.

Awareness continues to expand in understanding the realities of discrimination against women, not merely as victims, but as agents of their own human rights: to protection from and prevention of gender discrimination and how the threat of sexual violence feeds into gender discrimination; to advancing reproductive and sexual rights; and to women's political, civil, economic and social rights. Women continue to stand historically at the center of cultural politics. Women seek and succeed in participating in all areas of civil society in many countries, including the U.S., and seek unabashedly empowerment, equality, and non-discrimination, even though there still exist the stymying effects of sexism in women's efforts for complete equality and freedom from all forms of discrimination.

Although there is no way yet to clarify the role discrimination may have played against women in the 2016 U.S. presidential election, that election can serve as an example of the stymying of women's empowerment expectations in the U.S. In the middle of the U.S. presidential campaign from November 30 through December 2015, the U.N. Working Group on the issue of discrimination against women in law and in practice, led by experts Eleonora Zielinska, Frances Raday, and Alda Facio, witnessed and noted "the political rhetoric of some of the candidates...included unprecedented hostile stereotyping of women; ...violent attacks to prevent women from exercising their rights to reproductive health; ...significant and disparate worsening of the economic situation of women, in particular women of colour." Although a woman eventually won the popular vote for presidency of the U.S. in November 2016, she was still deprived the presidency due to an arcane political electoral system wherein, for the fifth time in its history, the U.S. popular vote went unearned by the elected president. Even though candidate H. R. Clinton had won nearly three million more votes than her rival, D. Trump, she was deprived the presidency through the archaic 18th century electoral college system, which is not based on a national popular vote, but on the popular vote within each state, whose electors are mandated to vote for the candidate who won the popular vote in each state. For the second time in recent U.S. presidential elections, U.S. voters encountered the perplexing dilemma of an electoral system wherein individual votes do not count as having equal weight per person in the U.S. Even though it has happened to male candidates four times before her, like the so-called Tom Bradley Effect in California that posed a question of racism's role in an election for governor in 1982, it is unclear what role sexism toward women played in the election results. The election's extenuated circumstances were complicated by an untimely hacker release of emails supposedly embarrassing only to Clinton, and accusations of Russian interference in the U.S. election were alleged. A deeply divided public was unsettled by many human rights issues related to economy, racial discrimination, equality, etc..., but did gender discrimination play a role in H. R. Clinton's loss as the first woman to run for the office of U.S. president? Did people vote against her in any part due to the fact that she is a woman? It is an unanswerable question at the time of this writing, but the issue exposes the ambivalent emotion that women, just like persons of 'color' are forced to face existentially in the U.S. Even though women as leaders have risen in many areas of civil society and in politics in the U.S. and the world as the primary voices in the quest and challenge for equal justice for women under international and U.S. law, has the U.S. adequately addressed its history of discrimination against women?

Women's and Girls' Rights in International Law and Their Importance

The question might seem confusing, since women and men share the same human rights. However, discrimination based on gender and race have long been understood and acknowledged universally as political, civil, social, economic, and cultural realities that must be addressed systemically, in such a way as to reform totally and dismantle entirely every institution that stymies and denies women their human rights.

Despite the importance of discrimination against women's and girls' human rights in all spheres of life as a matter of concern within international human rights law and U.S. domestic law, the U.S., although a signatory of CEDAW since July 1980, is one of only seven countries that has not ratified it.

There are three international treaties, two of which are international human rights treaties, whose purpose is to eliminate horrific realities: Convention on the Elimination of All Forms of Discrimination Against Women (CEDAW), which has to do with the elimination of discrimination against women and girls; and International Convention on the Elimination of All Forms of Racial Discrimination (ICERD), which addresses the elimination of the scourge of racism.

In the CEDAW, the Convention on the Elimination of All Forms of Discrimination Against Women human rights treaty, one reads: "States Parties shall take all appropriate measures to eliminate discrimination against women in...." Gender discrimination against women is clearly understood as a historical issue, not an imagined history, in the same way as racism's history is not a product of imagination. Instead, it is and has been a cruel reality for many centuries. The goal of the treaty is to push for the elimination of the phenomenon of discrimination against women in all its forms, a phenomenon that transcends national, cultural, and religious boundaries. Generally, women more than men have experienced deprivation of human rights, higher rates of poverty, partial or total social exclusion, lower employment, deprivation of the right to work, and even deprivation of (full) citizenship, all of which have harmed and continue to harm women, to the extent that implementation of an international human rights treaty had become necessary to eliminate all violence and bias directed against women and girls simply because they are female.

Because women's and girls' rights are the same as everyone else's human rights, there is not a separate list of human rights to be addressed only for women. However, because misogyny is a continuous fact of human history, there is sometimes an attempt to emphasize, support, and encourage women's and especially girls' personal ownership of human rights. In the following list of rights, the human rights are equally valid for men and especially boys, whose education in human rights is also essential.

I/We have the right to be myself/ourselves and to resist gender stereotypes.

I/We have the right to express myself/ourselves with originality and enthusiasm.

I/We have the right to take risks, to strive freely, and to take pride in success.

I/We have the right to accept and appreciate my/our body/bodies.

I/We have the right to have confidence in myself/ourselves and to be safe in the world.

I/We have the right to prepare for interesting work and economic independence.

International Human Rights Law instruments that address concerns of women:

International Bill of Human Rights
- UDHR (1948)
- ICCPR (1966)
- ICESCR (1966)

Treaties that specifically address discrimination against women:
- Declaration on the Elimination of Discrimination against Women (1967)
- Convention on the Elimination of All Forms of Discrimination against Women (1979) (CEDAW)

- Convention on the Rights of the Child (Art. 2) (1989)(CRC)
- Convention on the Protection of the Rights of All Migrant Workers and Members of Their Families (Art. 7) (1990) (CMW)
- Convention on the Rights of Persons with Disabilities (Art. 6) (2008) (CRPD)
- International Convention on the Elimination of All Forms of Racial Discrimination (1965) (CERD) regarding gender-related dimensions of racial discrimination, via the Committee on the Elimination of Racial Discrimination, does take into account gender factors or issues which may be interlinked with racial discrimination.

International Humanitarian Law concerns addressed via U.N. Security Council Resolutions: As a result of the 1990s war in Bosnia, Herzegovina, the Rwandan Genocide, and eventual armed conflict in Sierra Leone, and Democratic Republic of Congo, SCR 1325 (2000) and SCR 1820 on women and peace and security acknowledged the inordinate impact of war on women; that women had been excluded from participation in the peace process; that women should and do play pivotal roles in conflict management, resolution, and sustaining peace. SCR 1325 led to ensured collaboration/coordination throughout the U.N. system with agencies and a Special Adviser on Gender Issues and Advancement of Women. In SCR 1820, (2008) U.N. Security Council acknowledged rape/sexual violence as war crimes, crimes against humanity. SCR 1888 (2009) requires U.N. peacekeeping missions to protect women and children from sexual violence and appointed a special representative on sexual violence during armed conflict. SCR 1889 (2009), SCR 2106 (2013) removed impunity for sexual violence during armed conflict. SCR 2122 (2013) reinforced women's leadership in conflict resolution and peacebuilding. In summary, demands in the following areas are being implemented:

- Women's participation in decision-making at all levels;
- Rejection of violence as an impediment to women's advancement to equal rights;
- Equality of women and men under the rule of law;
- Security forces and systems protect and prevent against violence based on gender;
- Appropriate mechanisms provide protection from violence in refugee/displaced person camps;
- Recognition of systemic discrimination causes burdens on women/girls;
- Recognition of sexual violence as a tactic of war as a war crime, crime against humanity, and an act of genocide to be excluded from any amnesty provisions;
- Incorporation of women's full and equal participation in peace-building processes;
- Identification of parties suspected of patterns of sexual violence during armed conflict.

United Nations monitoring mechanisms for reporting on issues related to women:

- Convention against Torture and Other Cruel, Inhuman or Degrading Treatment or Punishment (1984) (CAT) via its Committee against Torture also regularly addresses issues of violence against women and girls.
- U.N. Human Rights Council, via its Working Group on the issue of discrimination against women in law and in practice 2010. The Report of the Working Group on the issue of discrimination against women in law and in practice on its mission to the United States of America, 2016 is an example of how the U.N. monitors the rights of women.
- U.N. Special Rapporteur on violence against women, its causes and consequences 1994, 2011. In 1999 the Rapporteur, Ms. Radhika Coomaraswamy, issued the Report of the Mission to the United States of America on the issue of violence against women in state and federal prisons/immigration detention facilities for women after a visit to Washington, DC and the states of New York, New Jersey, Connecticut, Georgia, California, Michigan, and Minnesota, and arrived at findings of critical concern regarding: lack of minimal standards equally applicable to all prisons; use of instruments of restraints, such as shackles or leg-irons; inconsistent training for correctional officers re: many issues, including sexual misconduct; inadequate health care; parenting issues; inconsistency in grievance procedures; private industry using prison labor; privatization of prisons. The Rapporteur made specific recommendations for the federal government and for each state visited.
- Report of the Special Rapporteur on violence against Women, its causes and consequences — Addendum — Mission to the U.S., A/HRC/17/26/Add.5 (June 2011)
- In their Universal Periodic Review 2010 and 2015, the U.S. committed to ratifying CEDAW.

- The U.N. Committee on the Elimination of Racial Discrimination, a body of independent experts, monitors implementation of the Convention on the Elimination of all Forms of Racial Discrimination. States parties submit reports to the committee every two years, which include women's rights concerns.
- The U.N. Human Rights Committee, a body of human rights experts, monitors implementation of the ICCPR treaty. It holds three sessions yearly in Geneva, Switzerland. All states parties submit regular reports, usually every four years, on their implementation of human rights, including those of women.
- The U.N. Commission on the Status of Women, (CSW), since 1946, is the established functional commission of the U.N. Economic and Social Council (ECOSOC) that holds annually a two-week session to discuss progress and gaps in women's issues among U.N. members, civil society groups, and other U.N. entities. The CSW is the intergovernmental body of the U.N. that continuously promotes empowerment for women and gender equality rights. Since 1996, CSW monitors and reviews implementation of the Bejing Declaration and Platform for Action, thereby mainstreaming gender perspectives within all U.N. activity. Since 2015, it contributes to ECOSOC's 2030 Agenda for Sustainable Development with its efforts to accelerate and realize gender equality and empowerment for women.
- United Nations General Assembly, Sixty-eighth session, Item 28 (a) of the provisional agenda, Advancement of Women A/68/340, Pathways to, Conditions and Consequences of Incarceration for Women 2013.

The following are *regional* international human rights law instruments concenrning women:

Organization of African Unity (OAU):
- African (Banjul) Charter on Human and Peoples' Rights (Articles 2, 18) (1981)
- Protocol on the Rights of Women in Africa (Maputo Protocol) (2003)

Organization of American States (OAS):
- Charter of OAS (Chapter II, Article 3 (1) (1967))
- American Convention on Human Rights (Article 1) (1969)
- Inter-American Convention on the Prevention, Punishment and Eradication of Violence Against Women (Belém do Pará Convention) (1994)

Council of Europe:
- European Convention on Human Rights and Fundamental Freedoms (Art. 14) (1950)
- Council of Europe Convention on Preventing and Combating Violence Against Women and Domestic Violence (Istanbul Convention) (2011)

Regional political organizations have protocols, resolutions, and declarations pertaining to women's human rights:
- Association of Southeast Asian Nations
- South Asian Association for Regional Cooperation
- Economic Community of West African States
- Southern African Development Community

The most recent report of the U.N. Human Rights Council, Working Group on the issue of discrimination against women in law and in practice can serve as an example of international legal thinking and how the rest of the world occasionally views U.S. culture. As applied to women's concerns, this kind of monitoring/reporting is an invaluable benefit to countries. The Working Group's mandate since 2010 had them report back to countries visited and to the U.N. Human Rights Council after consultations with states and other actors regarding laws and practices that discriminate against women as well as legal actions that create practices that succeed in eliminating discrimination. The Working Group laid out the following information in 2016 after a visit to the U.S. in 2015. They acknowledged good practices/progress in U.S. as follows:

Regarding domestic violence and asylum:
- U.S. President Obama's concession that in immigration court, domestic violence can constitute valid grounds for asylum when foreign governments fail to protect victims (Ironically, courts do not apply the same standard of a "duty to protect" by U.S. officials.)

- Matter of A-R-C-G- et al., Respondents, Decided August 26, 2014, U.S. Department of Justice Executive Office for Immigration Review Board of Immigration Appeals, Cite as 26 I&N Dec. 388 (BIA 2014) Interim Decision #3811 — The Board of Immigration Appeals held for the first time that survivors of domestic violence may qualify for asylum in the United States based on the harm they have suffered.

Regarding women's reproductive health:

- Many individual U.S. states extended more protections, such as universal paid maternity leave, and complete accessibility to reproductive health care, and passed laws intended to expand insurance coverage for contraceptive services, including (in some states) coverage for over-the-counter contraceptives, and coverage of sterilization services for men or women seeking it.

Regarding public and political representation:

- The Obama presidential years saw the largest increase in female participation in representative government...and three of the Supreme Court justices are women.

Regarding economic and social rights:

- Women are a driving economic force constituting nearly half of the U.S. labor force.
- Working mothers account for two-thirds of household earnings.
- Immigrant women workers are often at the forefront of protest for and attainment of wage increases for all workers.

Regarding employment protections:

- The federal Pregnancy Discrimination Act, under Title VII anti-discrimination laws, forbids discrimination based on pregnancy.
- Recent U.S. Supreme Court decisions re: women's abortion rights
- *Whole Woman's Health v. Hellerstedt* 2016 struck down Texas' attempts to close down all abortion facilities by requiring their conversion into surgical units and by mandating abortion doctors to have admitting privileges at local hospitals, because these two restrictions unnecessarily reduced access to women's health services throughout Texas.
- *Planned Parenthood of Southeastern Pennsylvania v. Casey* 1992 stated abortion restrictions could not impose an undue burden on a woman seeking to end a pregnancy.

Regarding access to health care:

- Affordable Care Act (ACA) passed in 2010

The Working Group recognized gaps/problems in U.S. as follows:

Regarding women's reproductive health:

- Some U.S. states persist in threatening legal protections for reproductive health rights of women: by passing laws intended to defund family planning services and access to women's contraceptives; by passing laws intended to restrict or ban abortion or to require pre-abortion counseling; and by targeting abortion providers with excessive regulation.

Regarding public and political representation:

- Although the Obama presidential years saw the largest increase in female participation in representative government, 2016 saw only four women out of fifteen cabinet members; only 19.4% of Congressional representatives are women; only 24.9% of state legislative representatives are women. The U.S. in 2016 was globally ranked 72 out of 194 countries for women's public and political representation, due in part to complex adversities women face in political fundraising;

Regarding economic and social rights, although women constitute nearly half of the U.S. labor force, and working mothers account for two-thirds of household earnings:

- Women were the most negatively impacted by the subprime mortgage collapse of 2008;
- Women in poverty increased 2.4% in the last decade;

- Subsequent decrease in funding for social services has deeply impacted minority women and single mothers;
- Standards for workplace accommodation for pregnant women, post-natal mothers, and persons with care responsibilities are not mandatory, as required by international human rights law;
- The gender wage gap is 21%, with education increasing women's earnings but not eliminating the gap, not even with the highest levels of educational attainment;
- Domestic workers in the U.S., frequently undocumented and immigrant, are overwhelmingly women workers vulnerable to verbal and physical abuse and wage theft.

Regarding access to health care:
- There is still no universal health coverage in the country;
- Maternal mortality rates in the United States increased 136% since 1990, with Afro-American women nearly four times more likely to die in childbirth.

Regarding women's general safety, the Special Rapporteur on violence against women in her report on her visit to the United States in 2011 found that women in detention:
- Are over-incarcerated;
- Experience sexual violence in prison;
- Pregnant women are sometimes shackled;
- Are too often in solitary confinement;
- Incarcerated women with dependent children lack options for custodial sentencing;
- Native-American women experience high rates of violence;
- Afro-American women experience an increased number of homicides by the police;
- Transgender women are mistreated in detention and often wrongfully placed with males.

The Working Group's conclusions for the U.S.: establish an independent national human rights institution (NHRI) in compliance with the Paris Principles; address proactively the rights of vulnerable women, such as Native American, Afro-American, Hispanic, ethnic minorities, migrant, LBTQ, in poverty, with disabilities, and/or elderly.

As nation states seek ways to bring home international human rights standards via regional human rights agreements that fight isolation and ignorance about women's rights, countries are making some progress in regional international human rights legal systems by joining together the same international human rights norms for men and women to articulate claims leading to legal judgments or sanctions by regional human rights bodies.

In the Inter-American Commission on Human Rights (IACHR), the following cases are important:
- *In re Campo Algondonero*, 2009 — The IACHR found that Mexico had violated human rights of the Algondonero, et. al. family by failing to investigate the killings of three young women in the city of Ciudad Juarez, Mexico, on the border with El Paso, Texas. The IACHR considered Mexico's failure to investigate violations of the 1978 American Convention of Human Rights and the 1994 Inter-American Convention on the Prevention, Punishment, and Eradication of Violence Against Women (Convention of Belém do Pará). For the first time, the Court: considered states' affirmative obligations to respond to violence against women by private actors; looked at the cases at issue in the context of mass violence against women and structural discrimination; and found that gender-based violence can constitute gender discrimination.
- *Jessica Lenahan (Gonzales) v. United States* — In 2011, the IACHR found the U.S. responsible for human rights violations in a case after Lenahan, a domestic violence survivor, who had exhausted U.S. domestic remedies in a lawsuit against her local police department when the 2005 U.S. Supreme Court found that Lenahan had no right to police enforcement of the 1999 restraining order issued against the father of her three children, whom he abducted and eventually murdered. Since the decision, in the U.S., invoking the IACHR's decision regarding a human right to freedom from domestic abuse is affecting legal discussion and domestic policy regarding non-enforcement of a protection order.

In the Inter-American Court on Human Rights, the following cases carry weight:
- *Karen Atala Riffo v. Chile* — In 2012, IACHR conclusions found there was discriminatory treatment and arbitrary interference in the private and family life of Ms. Karen Atala Riffo, a Chilean judge and a lesbian mother of three

daughters. In 2001, separated from her husband, she reached a settlement with her ex-husband that she would retain custody of the children. When she came out as a lesbian in 2005, the ex-husband sued for custody. Subsequently, the Supreme Court of Chile awarded the husband custody, citing her orientation as putting the development of her children at risk. The Inter-American Court found that the State violated the American Convention on Human Rights, a first case the Court took regarding LGBT rights.

- *Bevacqua and S. v. Bulgaria*, 2008, *Opuz v. Turkey*, 2009, and dozens more European cases establish a caseload of decisions moving to eliminate discrimination against women, moving toward some justice and protections for women within the European system, often in cases of domestic violence.

In Latin America:

- Mexico's Supreme Court and Colombia's Constitutional Court: decisions for reproductive rights, including access to abortion;
- Uruguay, Mexico, Colombia, Argentina, and Brazil have expanded same-sex couples' rights via legislation and judicial decisions;
- Nicaragua and the Dominican Republic (amended constitution) banned abortion under all circumstances; Chile's Constitutional Court banned morning-after pill in public health facilities; FGM among Embera-Chami aboriginal group spurred debate on limits of cultural sovereignty v. human rights norms;
- HR networks: Red Alas; Latin American Human Rights Clinicians' Network; Bring Human Rights Home Lawyers' Network; U.S. Human Rights Clinicians' Network.

Women's and Girls' Rights within U.S. Domestic Law and Their Importance

In colonial America women, started demanding a "vote and voyce" as early as 1648, when Margaret Brent, the first female lawyer in colonial Maryland and Virginia, after years of success in the legal profession and with the acquisition of land and property, was denied her vote and voice by Governor Thomas Green. It is still a struggle in the U.S. for women to get official acknowledgement of their equality under the law, as there is still no articulated guarantee within the U.S. Constitution for equal rights for women, although in civil society the movement is strong for gender equality. The U.S. Constitution's Nineteenth Amendment guarantees women's right to vote.

Nonetheless, many U.S. federal laws guarantee women's equal rights or needs for special protections. They include:

- Equal Pay Act of 1963;
- Title VII of the Civil Rights Act which creates non-discrimination;
- Title IX law that prohibits sex discrimination in education (1972);
- Pregnancy Discrimination Act of 1978 that amends Title VII of the Civil Rights Act of 1964;
- The Family Violence Prevention and Services Act (FVPSA) (1984);
- The Violence Against Women Act (VAWA) (1994), reauthorized in 2005 to allocate funds for victims and to prevent their homelessness; and in 2013 to include protections for Native American women on tribal lands, for lesbians and for immigrant women;
- Lily Ledbetter Fair Pay Restoration Act (2009) which allows victims, usually women, of pay discrimination to file a complaint with the government against their employer within 180 days of their last paycheck;
- Anti-stalking laws existing in U.S. individual states.

The U.S. Equal Employment Opportunity Commission (EEOC) exists to enforce federal laws related to discrimination against job applicants or an employees based on race, color, religion, sex (including pregnancy, gender identity, and sexual orientation), national origin, age (40 or older), disability or genetic information. It is also illegal to discriminate against a person who complained about, filed a charge of concerning, or participated in an employment discrimination investigation or lawsuit.

U.S. Department of Justice (DOJ), Office on Violence Against Women (OVW), a component of the DOJ, tries to lead in reducing violence against women; in administering justice for women; in strengthening services to women victims of domestic violence, dating violence, sexual assault, and stalking.

Many domestic and international civil society advocacy organizations exist to address women's equality concerns regarding their rights in employment, reproductive rights, poverty, public breastfeeding, pregnancy, etc. Below is a mere sampling of such groups:

- National Organization of Women (NOW)
- League of Women Voters
- American Association of University Women (AAUW)
- Association of Women's Rights in Development (AWID)
- Object
- American Civil Liberties Union (ACLU), Written statement submitted by the ACLU to the U.N. Commission on the Status of Women

The Main Objections to Women's and Girls' Rights within the U.S. Context

The vision of human rights starts and ends with the quality of relationships between persons/sectoral groups and those who govern them. The state's right to exist rests with the ability of the state to promote, protect, and defend the rights of all the people under its jurisdiction. Is this vision aspirational or normative? In human rights treaties, aspiration and normative thinking converge and coalesce.

People have a difficult time acknowledging patriarchal prejudice against women. This is dangerous in echelons of power, where women's concerns are often barely represented, sometimes completely omitted. The U.S., sometimes liberal and progressive in terms of innovation and creativity to resolve crises, sometimes honestly conservative, conventional, and tradition-bound in its conceptions of leadership for stability, often forget about women's rights. Even as the U.S. still holds in high regard an uncritically prevalent notion of its own exceptionalism that stems from 19th-20th century myth-making about itself, when it comes to the human rights of women and girls, (and so-called persons of color, children, the variant gender-oriented, the poor, the homeless, etc.,) the U.S. proves time and again that it is still tied to patriarchal institutionalized attitudes that derive from within family, religion, education, and government, that put unnecessarily into play human rights to equality and non-discrimination of women and girls. Ambivalence towards another myth, that of prosperity within an American dream, need not mute any of our rights which include equality and non-discrimination. There is sometimes an anti-democratic pecking order mentality that Americans embrace, incarnate, fail to acknowledge, and therefore fail to disassemble and eliminate in terms of bias towards women (and other groups). International human rights norms continually pose a question: Why would it ever be lawful for agents of the state to withhold full respect for, to neglect, to disregard, or to violate women's and girls' human rights to equality and non-discrimination, especially when women and girls make up the majority of persons on the planet? In this chapter, one might have finally gotten the insight that women and girls struggle daily and existentially from and with prejudice that favors males over females. All states at some point neglect, pacify, disfavor, or violate women's rights. In international human rights treaties, the rights to equality and non-discrimination are understood as requiring the "elimination of all forms of discrimination against women." In international human rights law (IHRL), the vision is as clear as the principal treaty named to address the problem. How will the U.S. ever get past its ambivalence towards human rights treaties it has signed and sometimes ratified, if it hatches occasional malevolent scapegoating of the United Nations? On the issue of women's and girls' equal rights, one may ask: Is the U.S. lagging behind other countries in its promotion, protection, and defense of women's human rights?

Main objections by the U.S. to full ratification of internationally binding human rights treaties, such as CEDAW:

- *Ratifiers do not necessarily respect the rights of women.* There is some truth to this statement. Even though 96% of countries have ratified CEDAW, only the U.S. and Palau have signed it without ratifying. The Vatican, Sudan, Iran, and Somalia have not acceded to CEDAW in any way. Only 22 of the 192 ratifying countries have enacted national plans. Women are still under-represented in government. However, the U.S. is a well-resourced democratic republic with many civil society institutions that can easily model democratic human rights behaviors more easily than in many countries. The expectation of inclusion of women within leadership is a cultural norm within the U.S. The U.S. could easily ratify CEDAW and other human rights treaties without reservation.
- *Human history is replete with stereotypes about women and men.* Even the 1948 U.N. Declaration of Human Rights employed "man" in reference to rights holders. However, objections were made leading to finalization of the UDHR which used terms such as "person," "human being," and "everyone." Its preamble referenced "equal rights

of men and women." Only during the 1970s did women take high office at the U.N., which declared 1976-1985 as the Decade for Women.

- *Religious or cultural belief systems are in conflict with equality and non-discrimination rights of women and girls.* Nonetheless, human rights speak directly to counter the logic and injustice of religious or cultural traditions that suppress women's rights. Human rights could have been considered counter-cultural a few generations ago. However, because of their internationalized transparency and international legal promotion and location within effective international treaty law, and because they exist to promote civil, political, economic, social, and cultural rights, and do not exist to oppress minority rights; human rights can no longer be considered counter-cultural. On the contrary, religious and cultural sub-groups whose belief systems suppress women/girls' rights are now considered counter-cultural. For example, groups like white supremacist organizations or even the American Alt-Right whose bigotries were once tolerated as part of cultural or religious belief are now generally far from the center of dominant U.S. culture. As a softer example of counter-culture, some families homeschool their children due to fears about public education or exposure to people outside their group. Homeschoolers are considered counter-cultural insofar as they avoid public schools, an undeniable part of traditional U.S. culture. Human rights are considered a part of international customary law, of which the elimination of all forms of discrimination against women is an essential part.

- *Religion-based doctrines teach that women are subordinate.* However, whenever religious leaders promote this notion, they are challenged more frequently as mere culture-based bad habits from within religions and among theologians, as well as from within the larger culture. Respect for the right to freedom of expression and conscience allows religious leaders time to learn to compare diverse cultural and religious norms, that are sometimes relativist in nature, and time to realize that equality and non-discrimination are non-threatening concepts as unifying and reasonable measures of universal human rights norms. Although States parties may put forth reservations to CEDAW related to freedom of religion, such reservations are allowed only for an interim that allows time for equality and non-discrimination principles to be legally applied domestically, leading to greater clarifications, but ultimately leading to the elimination and uprooting of all forms of discrimination against women. Treaty reservations are supposed to be dropped eventually in favor of women's equal rights.

- *Women's rights compete with others' rights.* This is a fallacy. Women are not at war with anyone to take anything away from anyone. Rather women and/or men stand, with all their human rights intact, at the center of the human family in the constant search for ways to exercise equity and non-discrimination for everyone in the family.

- *Women will be conscripted into the military, into armed combat.* The U.S. has already legitimated women's full participation in the military. Men only in the U.S. are still required to register for the draft. There is no active conscription in the U.S. at this time. Military service is entirely voluntary at this moment.

- *A husband will no longer have to support a wife economically, and Social Security benefits for wives and widows will disappear.* Rights to marriage and spousal support are realigning legally in dramatic ways within the U.S. and elsewhere, due to new legalities of equality and non-discrimination established in favor of same-sex marriage. The benefits of marital status are not so much in flux as much as marriage, divorce, and alimony are being measured by the economics within new forms of marriage.

Primary Source Documents

I. CONVENTION ON THE ELIMINATION OF ALL FORMS OF DISCRIMINATION AGAINST WOMEN (CEDAW)

Presently, 187 out of 194 UN member nations have ratified the Convention on the Elimination of All Forms of Discrimination Against Women (CEDAW); Sudan, Somalia, Iran, Palau, Tonga, and the U.S. are the seven non-ratifiers, although Palau and the U.S. are signatories. The U.S. signed CEDAW in 1980 under the Carter administration. Since 1980 CEDAW has stayed within the confines of the Senate Commission on Foreign Relations, where it has been looked at in hearings on five occasions. Nevertheless, under certain principles of international law in the Vienna Convention on the Law of Treaties, the U.S. should act consistently with legal instruments it has signed, as an indication of its good faith intent to act accordingly, until ratification.

The States Parties to the present Convention,

Noting that the Charter of the United Nations reaffirms faith in fundamental human rights, in the dignity and worth of the human person and in the equal rights of men and women,

Noting that the Universal Declaration of Human Rights affirms the principle of the inadmissibility of discrimination and proclaims that all human beings are born free and equal in dignity and rights and that everyone is entitled to all the rights and freedoms set forth therein, without distinction of any kind, including distinction based on sex,

Noting that the States Parties to the International Covenants on Human Rights have the obligation to ensure the equal rights of men and women to enjoy all economic, social, cultural, civil and political rights,

Considering the international conventions concluded under the auspices of the United Nations and the specialized agencies promoting equality of rights of men and women,

Noting also the resolutions, declarations and recommendations adopted by the United Nations and the specialized agencies promoting equality of rights of men and women,

Concerned, however, that despite these various instruments extensive discrimination against women continues to exist,

Recalling that discrimination against women violates the principles of equality of rights and respect for human dignity, is an obstacle to the participation of women, on equal terms with men, in the political, social, economic and cultural life of their countries, hampers the growth of the prosperity of society and the family and makes more difficult the full development of the potentialities of women in the service of their countries and of humanity,

Concerned that in situations of poverty women have the least access to food, health, education, training and opportunities for employment and other needs,

Convinced that the establishment of the new international economic order based on equity and justice will contribute significantly towards the promotion of equality between men and women,

Emphasizing that the eradication of apartheid, all forms of racism, racial discrimination, colonialism, neo-colonialism, aggression, foreign occupation and domination and interference in the internal affairs of States is essential to the full enjoyment of the rights of men and women,

Affirming that the strengthening of international peace and security, the relaxation of international tension, mutual co-operation among all States irrespective of their social and economic systems, general and complete disarmament, in particular nuclear disarmament under strict and effective international control, the affirmation of the principles of justice, equality and mutual benefit in relations among countries and the realization of the right of peoples under alien and colonial domination and foreign occupation to self-determination and independence, as well as respect for national sovereignty and territorial integrity, will promote social progress and development and as a consequence will contribute to the attainment of full equality between men and women,

Convinced that the full and complete development of a country, the welfare of the world and the cause of peace require the maximum participation of women on equal terms with men in all fields,

Bearing in mind the great contribution of women to the welfare of the family and to the development of society, so far not fully recognized, the social significance of maternity and the role of both parents in the family and in the upbringing of children, and aware that the role of women in procreation should not be a basis for discrimination but that the upbringing of children requires a sharing of responsibility between men and women and society as a whole,

Aware that a change in the traditional role of men as well as the role of women in society and in the family is needed to achieve full equality between men and women,

Determined to implement the principles set forth in the Declaration on the Elimination of Discrimination against Women and, for that purpose, to adopt the measures required for the elimination of such discrimination in all its forms and manifestations,

Have agreed on the following:

PART I

Article 1
For the purposes of the present Convention, the term "discrimination against women" shall mean any distinction, exclusion or restriction made on the basis of sex which has the effect or purpose of impairing or nullifying the recognition, enjoyment or exercise by women, irrespective of their marital status, on a basis of equality of men and women, of human rights and fundamental freedoms in the political, economic, social, cultural, civil or any other field.

Article 2
States Parties condemn discrimination against women in all its forms, agree to pursue by all appropriate means and without delay a policy of eliminating discrimination against women and, to this end, undertake:

(a) To embody the principle of the equality of men and women in their national constitutions or other appropriate legislation if not yet incorporated therein and to ensure, through law and other appropriate means, the practical realization of this principle;

(b) To adopt appropriate legislative and other measures, including sanctions where appropriate, prohibiting all discrimination against women;

(c) To establish legal protection of the rights of women on an equal basis with men and to ensure through competent national tribunals and other public institutions the effective protection of women against any act of discrimination;

(d) To refrain from engaging in any act or practice of discrimination against women and to ensure that public authorities and institutions shall act in conformity with this obligation;

(e) To take all appropriate measures to eliminate discrimination against women by any person, organization or enterprise;

(f) To take all appropriate measures, including legislation, to modify or abolish existing laws, regulations, customs and practices which constitute discrimination against women;

(g) To repeal all national penal provisions which constitute discrimination against women.

Article 3

States Parties shall take in all fields, in particular, in the political, social, economic and cultural fields, all appropriate measures, including legislation, to ensure the full development and advancement of women, for the purpose of guaranteeing them the exercise and enjoyment of human rights and fundamental freedoms on a basis of equality with men.

Article 4

1. Adoption by States Parties of temporary special measures aimed at accelerating de facto equality between men and women shall not be considered discrimination as defined in the present Convention, but shall in no way entail as a consequence the maintenance of unequal or separate standards; these measures shall be discontinued when the objectives of equality of opportunity and treatment have been achieved.

2. Adoption by States Parties of special measures, including those measures contained in the present Convention, aimed at protecting maternity shall not be considered discriminatory.

Article 5

States Parties shall take all appropriate measures:

(a) To modify the social and cultural patterns of conduct of men and women, with a view to achieving the elimination of prejudices and customary and all other practices which are based on the idea of the inferiority or the superiority of either of the sexes or on stereotyped roles for men and women;

(b) To ensure that family education includes a proper understanding of maternity as a social function and the recognition of the common responsibility of men and women in the upbringing and development of their children, it being understood that the interest of the children is the primordial consideration in all cases.

Article 6

States Parties shall take all appropriate measures, including legislation, to suppress all forms of traffic in women and exploitation of prostitution of women.

PART II

Article 7

States Parties shall take all appropriate measures to eliminate discrimination against women in the political and public life of the country and, in particular, shall ensure to women, on equal terms with men, the right:

(a) To vote in all elections and public referenda and to be eligible for election to all publicly elected bodies;

(b) To participate in the formulation of government policy and the implementation thereof and to hold public office and perform all public functions at all levels of government;

(c) To participate in non-governmental organizations and associations concerned with the public and political life of the country.

Article 8

States Parties shall take all appropriate measures to ensure to women, on equal terms with men and without any discrimination, the opportunity to represent their Governments at the international level and to participate in the work of international organizations.

Article 9

1. States Parties shall grant women equal rights with men to acquire, change or retain their nationality. They shall ensure in particular that neither marriage to an alien nor change of nationality by the husband during marriage shall automatically change the nationality of the wife, render her stateless or force upon her the nationality of the husband.

2. States Parties shall grant women equal rights with men with respect to the nationality of their children.

PART III

Article 10
States Parties shall take all appropriate measures to eliminate discrimination against women in order to ensure to them equal rights with men in the field of education and in particular to ensure, on a basis of equality of men and women:

(a) The same conditions for career and vocational guidance, for access to studies and for the achievement of diplomas in educational establishments of all categories in rural as well as in urban areas; this equality shall be ensured in pre-school, general, technical, professional and higher technical education, as well as in all types of vocational training;

(b) Access to the same curricula, the same examinations, teaching staff with qualifications of the same standard and school premises and equipment of the same quality;

(c) The elimination of any stereotyped concept of the roles of men and women at all levels and in all forms of education by encouraging coeducation and other types of education which will help to achieve this aim and, in particular, by the revision of textbooks and school programmes and the adaptation of teaching methods;

(d) The same opportunities to benefit from scholarships and other study grants;

(e) The same opportunities for access to programmes of continuing education, including adult and functional literacy programmes, particularly those aimed at reducing, at the earliest possible time, any gap in education existing between men and women;

(f) The reduction of female student drop-out rates and the organization of programmes for girls and women who have left school prematurely;

(g) The same Opportunities to participate actively in sports and physical education;

(h) Access to specific educational information to help to ensure the health and well-being of families, including information and advice on family planning.

Article 11
1. States Parties shall take all appropriate measures to eliminate discrimination against women in the field of employment in order to ensure, on a basis of equality of men and women, the same rights, in particular:

(a) The right to work as an inalienable right of all human beings;

(b) The right to the same employment opportunities, including the application of the same criteria for selection in matters of employment;

(c) The right to free choice of profession and employment, the right to promotion, job security and all benefits and conditions of service and the right to receive vocational training and retraining, including apprenticeships, advanced vocational training and recurrent training;

(d) The right to equal remuneration, including benefits, and to equal treatment in respect of work of equal value, as well as equality of treatment in the evaluation of the quality of work;

(e) The right to social security, particularly in cases of retirement, unemployment, sickness, invalidity and old age and other incapacity to work, as well as the right to paid leave;

(f) The right to protection of health and to safety in working conditions, including the safeguarding of the function of reproduction.

2. In order to prevent discrimination against women on the grounds of marriage or maternity and to ensure their effective right to work, States Parties shall take appropriate measures:

(a) To prohibit, subject to the imposition of sanctions, dismissal on the grounds of pregnancy or of maternity leave and discrimination in dismissals on the basis of marital status;

(b) To introduce maternity leave with pay or with comparable social benefits without loss of former employment, seniority or social allowances;

(c) To encourage the provision of the necessary supporting social services to enable parents to combine family obligations with work responsibilities and participation in public life, in particular through promoting the establishment and development of a network of child-care facilities;

(d) To provide special protection to women during pregnancy in types of work proved to be harmful to them.

3. Protective legislation relating to matters covered in this article shall be reviewed periodically in the light of scientific and technological knowledge and shall be revised, repealed or extended as necessary.

Article 12
1. States Parties shall take all appropriate measures to eliminate discrimination against women in the field of health care in order to ensure, on a basis of equality of men and women, access to health care services, including those related to family planning.

2. Notwithstanding the provisions of paragraph I of this article, States Parties shall ensure to women appropriate services in connection with pregnancy, confinement and the post-natal period, granting free services where necessary, as well as adequate nutrition during pregnancy and lactation.

Article 13
States Parties shall take all appropriate measures to eliminate discrimination against women in other areas of economic and social life in order to ensure, on a basis of equality of men and women, the same rights, in particular:

(a) The right to family benefits;

(b) The right to bank loans, mortgages and other forms of financial credit;

(c) The right to participate in recreational activities, sports and all aspects of cultural life.

Article 14
1. States Parties shall take into account the particular problems faced by rural women and the significant roles which rural women play in the economic survival of their families, including their work in the non-monetized sectors of the economy, and shall take all appropriate measures to ensure the application of the provisions of the present Convention to women in rural areas.

2. States Parties shall take all appropriate measures to eliminate discrimination against women in rural areas in order to ensure, on a basis of equality of men and women, that they participate in and benefit from rural development and, in particular, shall ensure to such women the right:

(a) To participate in the elaboration and implementation of development planning at all levels;

(b) To have access to adequate health care facilities, including information, counselling and services in family planning;

(c) To benefit directly from social security programmes;

(d) To obtain all types of training and education, formal and non-formal, including that relating to functional literacy, as well as, inter alia, the benefit of all community and extension services, in order to increase their technical proficiency;

(e) To organize self-help groups and co-operatives in order to obtain equal access to economic opportunities through employment or self employment;

(f) To participate in all community activities;

(g) To have access to agricultural credit and loans, marketing facilities, appropriate technology and equal treatment in land and agrarian reform as well as in land resettlement schemes;

(h) To enjoy adequate living conditions, particularly in relation to housing, sanitation, electricity and water supply, transport and communications.

PART IV

Article 15
1. States Parties shall accord to women equality with men before the law.

2. States Parties shall accord to women, in civil matters, a legal capacity identical to that of men and the same opportunities to exercise that capacity. In particular, they shall give women equal rights to conclude contracts and to administer property and shall treat them equally in all stages of procedure in courts and tribunals.

3. States Parties agree that all contracts and all other private instruments of any kind with a legal effect which is directed at restricting the legal capacity of women shall be deemed null and void.

4. States Parties shall accord to men and women the same rights with regard to the law relating to the movement of persons and the freedom to choose their residence and domicile.

Article 16
1. States Parties shall take all appropriate measures to eliminate discrimination against women in all matters relating to marriage and family relations and in particular shall ensure, on a basis of equality of men and women:

(a) The same right to enter into marriage;

(b) The same right freely to choose a spouse and to enter into marriage only with their free and full consent;

(c) The same rights and responsibilities during marriage and at its dissolution;

(d) The same rights and responsibilities as parents, irrespective of their marital status, in matters relating to their children; in all cases the interests of the children shall be paramount;

(e) The same rights to decide freely and responsibly on the number and spacing of their children and to have access to the information, education and means to enable them to exercise these rights;

(f) The same rights and responsibilities with regard to guardianship, wardship, trusteeship and adoption of children, or similar institutions where these concepts exist in national legislation; in all cases the interests of the children shall be paramount;

(g) The same personal rights as husband and wife, including the right to choose a family name, a profession and an occupation;

(h) The same rights for both spouses in respect of the ownership, acquisition, management, administration, enjoyment and disposition of property, whether free of charge or for a valuable consideration.

2. The betrothal and the marriage of a child shall have no legal effect, and all necessary action, including legislation, shall be taken to specify a minimum age for marriage and to make the registration of marriages in an official registry compulsory.

PART V

Article 17

1. For the purpose of considering the progress made in the implementation of the present Convention, there shall be established a Committee on the Elimination of Discrimination against Women (hereinafter referred to as the Committee) consisting, at the time of entry into force of the Convention, of eighteen and, after ratification of or accession to the Convention by the thirty-fifth State Party, of twenty-three experts of high moral standing and competence in the field covered by the Convention. The experts shall be elected by States Parties from among their nationals and shall serve in their personal capacity, consideration being given to equitable geographical distribution and to the representation of the different forms of civilization as well as the principal legal systems.

2. The members of the Committee shall be elected by secret ballot from a list of persons nominated by States Parties. Each State Party may nominate one person from among its own nationals.

3. The initial election shall be held six months after the date of the entry into force of the present Convention. At least three months before the date of each election the Secretary-General of the United Nations shall address a letter to the States Parties inviting them to submit their nominations within two months. The Secretary-General shall prepare a list in alphabetical order of all persons thus nominated, indicating the States Parties which have nominated them, and shall submit it to the States Parties.

4. Elections of the members of the Committee shall be held at a meeting of States Parties convened by the Secretary-General at United Nations Headquarters. At that meeting, for which two thirds of the States Parties shall constitute a quorum, the persons elected to the Committee shall be those nominees who obtain the largest number of votes and an absolute majority of the votes of the representatives of States Parties present and voting.

5. The members of the Committee shall be elected for a term of four years. However, the terms of nine of the members elected at the first election shall expire at the end of two years; immediately after the first election the names of these nine members shall be chosen by lot by the Chairman of the Committee.

6. The election of the five additional members of the Committee shall be held in accordance with the provisions of paragraphs 2, 3 and 4 of this article, following the thirty-fifth ratification or accession. The terms of two of the additional members elected on this occasion shall expire at the end of two years, the names of these two members having been chosen by lot by the Chairman of the Committee.

7. For the filling of casual vacancies, the State Party whose expert has ceased to function as a member of the Committee shall appoint another expert from among its nationals, subject to the approval of the Committee.

8. The members of the Committee shall, with the approval of the General Assembly, receive emoluments from United Nations resources on such terms and conditions as the Assembly may decide, having regard to the importance of the Committee's responsibilities.

9. The Secretary-General of the United Nations shall provide the necessary staff and facilities for the effective performance of the functions of the Committee under the present Convention.

Article 18

1. States Parties undertake to submit to the Secretary-General of the United Nations, for consideration by the Committee, a report on the legislative, judicial, administrative or other measures which they have adopted to give effect to the provisions of the present Convention and on the progress made in this respect:

    (a) Within one year after the entry into force for the State concerned;

    (b) Thereafter at least every four years and further whenever the Committee so requests.

2. Reports may indicate factors and difficulties affecting the degree of fulfilment of obligations under the present Convention.

Article 19

1. The Committee shall adopt its own rules of procedure.

2. The Committee shall elect its officers for a term of two years.

Article 20

1. The Committee shall normally meet for a period of not more than two weeks annually in order to consider the reports submitted in accordance with article 18 of the present Convention.

2. The meetings of the Committee shall normally be held at United Nations Headquarters or at any other convenient place as determined by the Committee.

Article 21

1. The Committee shall, through the Economic and Social Council, report annually to the General Assembly of the United Nations on its activities and may make suggestions and general recommendations based on the examination of reports and information received from the States Parties. Such suggestions and general recommendations shall be included in the report of the Committee together with comments, if any, from States Parties.

2. The Secretary-General of the United Nations shall transmit the reports of the Committee to the Commission on the Status of Women for its information.

Article 22

The specialized agencies shall be entitled to be represented at the consideration of the implementation of such provisions of the present Convention as fall within the scope of their activities. The Committee may invite the specialized agencies to submit reports on the implementation of the Convention in areas falling within the scope of their activities.

PART VI

Article 23

Nothing in the present Convention shall affect any provisions that are more conducive to the achievement of equality between men and women which may be contained:

(a) In the legislation of a State Party; or

(b) In any other international convention, treaty or agreement in force for that State.

Article 24

States Parties undertake to adopt all necessary measures at the national level aimed at achieving the full realization of the rights recognized in the present Convention.

Article 25

1. The present Convention shall be open for signature by all States.

2. The Secretary-General of the United Nations is designated as the depositary of the present Convention.

3. The present Convention is subject to ratification. Instruments of ratification shall be deposited with the Secretary-General of the United Nations.

4. The present Convention shall be open to accession by all States. Accession shall be effected by the deposit of an instrument of accession with the Secretary-General of the United Nations.

Article 26

1. A request for the revision of the present Convention may be made at any time by any State Party by means of a notification in writing addressed to the Secretary-General of the United Nations.

2. The General Assembly of the United Nations shall decide upon the steps, if any, to be taken in respect of such a request.

Article 27

1. The present Convention shall enter into force on the thirtieth day after the date of deposit with the Secretary-General of the United Nations of the twentieth instrument of ratification or accession.

2. For each State ratifying the present Convention or acceding to it after the deposit of the twentieth instrument of ratification or accession, the Convention shall enter into force on the thirtieth day after the date of the deposit of its own instrument of ratification or accession.

Article 28

1. The Secretary-General of the United Nations shall receive and circulate to all States the text of reservations made by States at the time of ratification or accession.

2. A reservation incompatible with the object and purpose of the present Convention shall not be permitted.

3. Reservations may be withdrawn at any time by notification to this effect addressed to the Secretary-General of the United Nations, who shall then inform all States thereof. Such notification shall take effect on the date on which it is received.

Article 29

1. Any dispute between two or more States Parties concerning the interpretation or application of the present Convention which is not settled by negotiation shall, at the request of one of them, be submitted to arbitration. If within six months from the date of the request for arbitration the parties are unable to agree on the organization of the arbitration, any one of those parties may refer the dispute to the International Court of Justice by request in conformity with the Statute of the Court.

2. Each State Party may at the time of signature or ratification of the present Convention or accession thereto declare that it does not consider itself bound by paragraph I of this article. The other States Parties shall not be bound by that paragraph with respect to any State Party which has made such a reservation.

3. Any State Party which has made a reservation in accordance with paragraph 2 of this article may at any time withdraw that reservation by notification to the Secretary-General of the United Nations.

Article 30

The present Convention, the Arabic, Chinese, English, French, Russian and Spanish texts of which are equally authentic, shall be deposited with the Secretary-General of the United Nations.

IN WITNESS WHEREOF the undersigned, duly authorized, have signed the present Convention.

Source: U.N. Office of the High Commissioner on Human Rights
http://www.ohchr.org/EN/ProfessionalInterest/Pages/CERD.aspx

2. CONVENTION ON THE POLITICAL RIGHTS OF WOMEN, JULY 7, 1954

The United States took twenty-three years to ratify the 1953 Convention on the Political Rights of Women, which it did so in 1976.

The Contracting Parties,

Desiring to implement the principle of equality of rights for men and women contained in the Charter of the United Nations,

Recognizing that everyone has the right to take part in the government of his country directly or indirectly through freely chosen representatives, and has the right to equal access to public service in his country, and desiring to equalize the status of men and women in the enjoyment and exercise of political rights, in accordance with the provisions of the Charter of the United Nations and of the Universal Declaration of Human Rights,

Having resolved to conclude a Convention for this purpose,

Hereby agree as hereinafter provided:

Article 1
Women shall be entitled to vote in all elections on equal terms with men, without any discrimination.

Article 2
Women shall be eligible for election to all publicly elected bodies, established by national law, on equal terms with men, without any discrimination.

Article 3
Women shall be entitled to hold public office and to exercise all public functions, established by national law, on equal terms with men, without any discrimination.

Article 4
1. This Convention shall be open for signature on behalf of any Member of the United Nations and also on behalf of any other State to which an invitation has been addressed by the General Assembly.

2. This Convention shall be ratified and the instruments of ratification shall be deposited with the Secretary-General of the United Nations.

Article 5
1. This Convention shall be open for accession to all States referred to in paragraph I of article IV.

2. Accession shall be effected by the deposit of an instrument of accession with the Secretary-General of the United Nations.

Article 6
1. This Convention shall come into force on the ninetieth day following the date of deposit of the sixth instrument of ratification or accession.

2. For each State ratifying or acceding to the Convention after the deposit of the sixth instrument of ratification or accession the Convention shall enter into force on the ninetieth day after deposit by such State of its instrument of ratification or accession.

Article 7
In the event that any State submits a reservation to any of the articles of this Convention at the time of signature, ratification or accession, the Secretary-General shall communicate the text of the reservation to all States which are or may become Parties to this Convention. Any State which objects to the reservation may, within a period of ninety days from the date of the said communication (or upon the date of its becoming a Party to the Convention), notify the Secretary-General that it does not accept it. In such case, the Convention shall not enter into force as between such State and the State making the reservation.

Article 8
1. Any State may denounce this Convention by written notification to the Secretary-General of the United Nations. Denunciation shall take effect one year after the date of receipt of the notification by the Secretary General.

2. This Convention shall cease to be in force as from the date when the denunciation which reduces the number of Parties to less than six becomes effective.

Article 9

Any dispute which may arise between any two or more Contracting States concerning the interpretation or application of this Convention, which is not settled by negotiation, shall at the request of any one of the parties to the dispute be referred to the International Court of Justice for decision, unless they agree to another mode of settlement.

Article 10

The Secretary-General of the United Nations shall notify all Members of the United Nations and the non-member States contemplated in paragraph I of article IV of this Convention of the following:

(a) Signatures and instruments of ratification received in accordance with article IV;

(b) Instruments of accession received in accordance with article V;

(c) The date upon which this Convention enters into force in accordance with article VI;

(d) Communications and notifications received in accordance with article VII;

(e) Notifications of denunciation received in accordance with paragraph I of article VIII;

(f) Abrogation in accordance with paragraph 2 of article VIII.

Article 11

1. This Convention, of which the Chinese, English, French, Russian and Spanish texts shall be equally authentic, shall be deposited in the archives of the United Nations.

2. The Secretary-General of the United Nations shall transmit a certified copy to all Members of the United Nations and to the non-member States contemplated in paragraph I of article IV.

Source: United Nations Treaty Collection: Convention on the Political Rights of Women, New York, 31 March 1953, https://treaties.un.org/pages/ViewDetails.aspx?src=TREATY&mtdsg_no=XVI-1&chapter=16&lang=en or http://hrlibrary .umn.edu/instree/e2cprw.htm

3. DECLARATION ON THE ELIMINATION OF VIOLENCE AGAINST WOMEN, 1993

The Declaration on the Elimination of Violence Against Women is the 1993 UN General Assembly resolution that generated the most widely understood and utilized definition of "violence against women" and expressed anew the right of women and girls to live a life free of the threat of violence.

The General Assembly,

Recognizing the urgent need for the universal application to women of the rights and principles with regard to equality, security, liberty, integrity and dignity of all human beings,

Noting that those rights and principles are enshrined in international instruments, including the Universal Declaration of Human Rights, the International Covenant on Civil and Political Rights, the International Covenant on Economic, Social and Cultural Rights, the Convention on the Elimination of All Forms of Discrimination against Women and the Convention against Torture and Other Cruel, Inhuman or Degrading Treatment or Punishment,

Recognizing that effective implementation of the Convention on the Elimination of All Forms of Discrimination against Women would contribute to the elimination of violence against women and that the Declaration on the Elimination of Violence against Women, set forth in the present resolution, will strengthen and complement that process,

Concerned that violence against women is an obstacle to the achievement of equality, development and peace, as recognized in the Nairobi Forward-looking Strategies for the Advancement of Women, in which a set of measures to combat violence against women was recommended, and to the full implementation of the Convention on the Elimination of All Forms of Discrimination against Women,

Affirming that violence against women constitutes a violation of the rights and fundamental freedoms of women and impairs or nullifies their enjoyment of those rights and freedoms, and concerned about the long-standing failure to protect and promote those rights and freedoms in the case of violence against women,

Recognizing that violence against women is a manifestation of historically unequal power relations between men and women, which have led to domination over and discrimination against women by men and to the prevention of the full advancement of women, and that violence against women is one of the crucial social mechanisms by which women are forced into a subordinate position compared with men,

Concerned that some groups of women, such as women belonging to minority groups, indigenous women, refugee women, migrant women, women living in rural or remote communities, destitute women, women in institutions or in detention, female children, women with disabilities, elderly women and women in situations of armed conflict, are especially vulnerable to violence,

Recalling the conclusion in paragraph 23 of the annex to Economic and Social Council resolution 1990/15 of 24 May 1990 that the recognition that violence against women in the family and society was pervasive and cut across lines of income, class and culture had to be matched by urgent and effective steps to eliminate its incidence,

Recalling also Economic and Social Council resolution 1991/18 of 30 May 1991, in which the Council recommended the development of a framework for an international instrument that would address explicitly the issue of violence against women,

Welcoming the role that women's movements are playing in drawing increasing attention to the nature, severity and magnitude of the problem of violence against women,

Alarmed that opportunities for women to achieve legal, social, political and economic equality in society are limited, inter alia, by continuing and endemic violence,

Convinced that in the light of the above there is a need for a clear and comprehensive definition of violence against women, a clear statement of the rights to be applied to ensure the elimination of violence against women in all its forms, a commitment by States in respect of their responsibilities, and a commitment by the international community at large to the elimination of violence against women,

Solemnly proclaims the following Declaration on the Elimination of Violence against Women and urges that every effort be made so that it becomes generally known and respected:

Article 1
For the purposes of this Declaration, the term "violence against women" means any act of gender-based violence that results in, or is likely to result in, physical, sexual or psychological harm or suffering to women, including threats of such acts, coercion or arbitrary deprivation of liberty, whether occurring in public or in private life.

Article 2
Violence against women shall be understood to encompass, but not be limited to, the following:

(a) Physical, sexual and psychological violence occurring in the family, including battering, sexual abuse of female children in the household, dowry-related violence, marital rape, female genital mutilation and other traditional practices harmful to women, non-spousal violence and violence related to exploitation;

(b) Physical, sexual and psychological violence occurring within the general community, including rape, sexual abuse, sexual harassment and intimidation at work, in educational institutions and elsewhere, trafficking in women and forced prostitution;

(c) Physical, sexual and psychological violence perpetrated or condoned by the State, wherever it occurs.

Article 3

Women are entitled to the equal enjoyment and protection of all human rights and fundamental freedoms in the political, economic, social, cultural, civil or any other field. These rights include, inter alia:

(a) The right to life;

(b) The right to equality;

(c) The right to liberty and security of person;

(d) The right to equal protection under the law;

(e) The right to be free from all forms of discrimination;

(f) The right to the highest standard attainable of physical and mental health;

(g) The right to just and favourable conditions of work;

(h) The right not to be subjected to torture, or other cruel, inhuman or degrading treatment or punishment.

Article 4

States should condemn violence against women and should not invoke any custom, tradition or religious consideration to avoid their obligations with respect to its elimination. States should pursue by all appropriate means and without delay a policy of eliminating violence against women and, to this end, should:

(a) Consider, where they have not yet done so, ratifying or acceding to the Convention on the Elimination of All Forms of Discrimination against Women or withdrawing reservations to that Convention;

(b) Refrain from engaging in violence against women;

(c) Exercise due diligence to prevent, investigate and, in accordance with national legislation, punish acts of violence against women, whether those acts are perpetrated by the State or by private persons;

(d) Develop penal, civil, labour and administrative sanctions in domestic legislation to punish and redress the wrongs caused to women who are subjected to violence; women who are subjected to violence should be provided with access to the mechanisms of justice and, as provided for by national legislation, to just and effective remedies for the harm that they have suffered; States should also inform women of their rights in seeking redress through such mechanisms;

(e) Consider the possibility of developing national plans of action to promote the protection of women against any form of violence, or to include provisions for that purpose in plans already existing, taking into account, as appropriate, such cooperation as can be provided by non-governmental organizations, particularly those concerned with the issue of violence against women;

(f) Develop, in a comprehensive way, preventive approaches and all those measures of a legal, political, administrative and cultural nature that promote the protection of women against any form of violence, and ensure that the re-victimization of women does not occur because of laws insensitive to gender considerations, enforcement practices or other interventions;

(g) Work to ensure, to the maximum extent feasible in the light of their available resources and, where needed, within the framework of international cooperation, that women subjected to violence and, where appropriate, their children have specialized assistance, such as rehabilitation, assistance in child care and maintenance, treatment, counselling, and health and social services, facilities and programmes, as well as support structures, and should take all other appropriate measures to promote their safety and physical and psychological rehabilitation;

(h) Include in government budgets adequate resources for their activities related to the elimination of violence against women;

(i) Take measures to ensure that law enforcement officers and public officials responsible for implementing policies to prevent, investigate and punish violence against women receive training to sensitize them to the needs of women;

(j) Adopt all appropriate measures, especially in the field of education, to modify the social and cultural patterns of conduct of men and women and to eliminate prejudices, customary practices and all other practices based on the idea of the inferiority or superiority of either of the sexes and on stereotyped roles for men and women;

(k) Promote research, collect data and compile statistics, especially concerning domestic violence, relating to the prevalence of different forms of violence against women and encourage research on the causes, nature, seriousness and consequences of violence against women and on the effectiveness of measures implemented to prevent and redress violence against women; those statistics and findings of the research will be made public;

(l) Adopt measures directed towards the elimination of violence against women who are especially vulnerable to violence;

(m) Include, in submitting reports as required under relevant human rights instruments of the United Nations, information pertaining to violence against women and measures taken to implement the present Declaration;

(n) Encourage the development of appropriate guidelines to assist in the implementation of the principles set forth in the present Declaration;

(o) Recognize the important role of the women's movement and non-governmental organizations world wide in raising awareness and alleviating the problem of violence against women;

(p) Facilitate and enhance the work of the women's movement and non-governmental organizations and cooperate with them at local, national and regional levels;

(q) Encourage intergovernmental regional organizations of which they are members to include the elimination of violence against women in their programmes, as appropriate.

Article 5
The organs and specialized agencies of the United Nations system should, within their respective fields of competence, contribute to the recognition and realization of the rights and the principles set forth in the present Declaration and, to this end, should, inter alia:

(a) Foster international and regional cooperation with a view to defining regional strategies for combating violence, exchanging experiences and financing programmes relating to the elimination of violence against women;

(b) Promote meetings and seminars with the aim of creating and raising awareness among all persons of the issue of the elimination of violence against women;

(c) Foster coordination and exchange within the United Nations system between human rights treaty bodies to address the issue of violence against women effectively;

(d) Include in analyses prepared by organizations and bodies of the United Nations system of social trends and problems, such as the periodic reports on the world social situation, examination of trends in violence against women;

(e) Encourage coordination between organizations and bodies of the United Nations system to incorporate the issue of violence against women into ongoing programmes, especially with reference to groups of women particularly vulnerable to violence;

(f) Promote the formulation of guidelines or manuals relating to violence against women, taking into account the measures referred to in the present Declaration;

(g) Consider the issue of the elimination of violence against women, as appropriate, in fulfilling their mandates with respect to the implementation of human rights instruments;

(h) Cooperate with non-governmental organizations in addressing the issue of violence against women.

Article 6

Nothing in the present Declaration shall affect any provision that is more conducive to the elimination of violence against women that may be contained in the legislation of a State or in any international convention, treaty or other instrument in force in a State.

Source: University of Minnesota Human Rights Library, http://hrlibrary.umn.edu/instree/e4devw.htm or United Nations, General Assembly, A/RES/48/104, 20 December 1993, http://www.un.org/documents/ga/res/48/a48r104.htm or http://www.un.org/ga/search/view_doc.asp?symbol=A/RES/48/104

4. CONVENTION ON THE NATIONALITY OF MARRIED WOMEN, AUGUST 11, 1958

This 1958 Convention on the Nationality of Married Women addresses the legal ambiguity, conflicts, questions of change of nationality related to marriage and divorce within the international legal system. Regarding married women's full citizenship rights, the treaty provides a legal framework for securing the nationality of married women. The treaty protects married women's citizenship rights, as previously expressed in the Universal Declaration of Human Rights article 15 regarding the right to a nationality. The treaty acknowledges that women have the complete right to retain, renounce, or change citizenship on equal terms with men, no longer allowing any threat of arbitrary deprivation of nationality due to marriage or divorce.

The Contracting States,

Recognizing that, conflicts in law in practice with reference to nationality arise as a result of provisions concerning the loss or acquisition of nationality by women as a result of marriage, of its dissolution or of the change of nationality by the husband during marriage,

Recognizing that, in article 15 of the Universal Declaration of Human Rights, the General Assembly of the United Nations has proclaimed that "everyone has the right to a nationality" and that "no one shall be arbitrarily deprived of his nationality nor denied the right to change his nationality,"

Desiring to co-operate with the United Nations in promoting universal respect for, and observance of, human rights and fundamental freedoms for all without distinction as to sex,

Hereby agree as hereinafter provided:

Article 1

Each Contracting State agrees that neither the celebration nor the dissolution of a marriage between one of its nationals and an alien, nor the change of nationality by the husband during marriage, shall automatically affect the nationality of the wife.

Article 2

Each Contracting State agrees that neither the voluntary acquisition of the nationality of another State nor the renunciation of its nationality by one of its nationals shall prevent the retention of its nationality by the wife of such national.

Article 3

1. Each Contracting State agrees that the alien wife of one of its nationals may, at her request, acquire the nationality of her husband through specially privileged naturalization procedures; the grant of such nationality may be subject to such limitations as may be imposed in the interests of national security or public policy.

2. Each Contracting State agrees that the present Convention shall not be construed as affecting any legislation or judicial practice by which the alien wife of one of its nationals may, at her request, acquire her husband's nationality as a matter of right.

Article 4

1. The present Convention shall be open for signature and ratification on behalf of any State Member of the United Nations and also on behalf of any other State which is or hereafter becomes a member of any specialized agency of the United Nations, or which is or hereafter becomes a Party to the Statute of the International Court of Justice, or any other State to which an invitation has been addressed by the General Assembly of the United Nations.

2. The present Convention shall be ratified and the instruments of ratification shall be deposited with the Secretary-General of the United Nations.

Article 5

1. The present Convention shall be open for accession to all States referred to in paragraph I of article 4.

2. Accession shall be effected by the deposit of an instrument of accession with the Secretary-General of the United Nations.

Article 6

1. The present Convention shall come into force on the ninetieth day following the date of deposit of the sixth instrument of ratification or accession.

2. For each State ratifying or acceding to the Convention after the deposit of the sixth instrument of ratification or accession, the Convention shall enter into force on the ninetieth day after deposit by such State of its instrument of ratification or accession.

Article 7

1. The present Convention shall apply to all non-self-governing, trust, colonial and other non-metropolitan territories for the international relations of which any Contracting State is responsible; the Contracting State concerned shall, subject to the provisions of paragraph 2 of the present article, at the time of signature, ratification or accession declare the non-metropolitan territory or territories to which the Convention shall apply ipso facto as a result of such signature, ratification or accession.

2. In any case in which, for the purpose of nationality, a non-metropolitan territory is not treated as one with the metropolitan territory, or in any case in which the previous consent of a non-metropolitan territory is required by the constitutional laws or practices of the Contracting State or of the non-metropolitan territory for the application of the Convention to that territory, that Contracting State shall endeavour to secure the needed consent of the non-metropolitan territory within the period of twelve months from the date of signature of the Convention by that Contracting State, and when such consent has been obtained the Contracting State shall notify the Secretary-General of the United Nations. The present Convention shall apply to the territory or territories named in such notification from the date of its receipt by the Secretary-General.

3. After the expiry of the twelve-month period mentioned in paragraph 2 of the present article, the Contracting States concerned shall inform the Secretary-General of the results of the consultations with those non-metropolitan territories for whose international relations they are responsible and whose consent to the application of the present Convention may have been withheld.

Article 8

1. At the time of signature, ratification or accession, any State may make reservations to any article of the present Convention other than articles 1 and 2.

2. If any State makes a reservation in accordance with paragraph 1 of the present article, the Convention, with the exception of those provisions to which the reservation relates, shall have effect as between the reserving State and the other Parties. The Secretary-General of the United Nations shall communicate the text of the reservation to all States which are or may become Parties to the Convention. Any State Party to the Convention or which thereafter becomes a Party may notify the Secretary-General that it does not agree to consider itself bound by the Convention with respect to the State making the reservation. This notification must be made, in the case of a State already a Party, within ninety days from the date of the communication by the Secretary-General; and, in the case of a State subsequently becoming a Party, within ninety days from the date when the instrument of ratification or accession is deposited. In the event that such a notification is made, the Convention shall not be deemed to be in effect as between the State making the notification and the State making the reservation.

3. Any State making a reservation in accordance with paragraph 1 of the present article may at any time withdraw the reservation, in whole or in part, after it has been accepted, by a notification to this effect addressed to the Secretary-General of the United Nations. Such notification shall take effect on the date on which it is received.

Article 9

1. Any Contracting State may denounce the present Convention by written notification to the Secretary-General of the United Nations. Denunciation shall take effect one year after the date of receipt of the notification by the Secretary-General.

2. The present Convention shall cease to be in force as from the date when the denunciation which reduces the number of Parties to less than six becomes effective.

Article 10

Any dispute which may arise between any two or more Contracting States concerning the interpretation or application of the present Convention which is not settled by negotiation, shall, at the request of any one of the parties to the dispute, be referred to the International Court of Justice for decision, unless the parties agree to another mode of settlement.

Article 11

The Secretary-General of the United Nations shall notify all States Members of the United Nations and the non-member States contemplated in paragraph 1 of article 4 of the present Convention of the following:

   (a) Signatures and instruments of ratification received in accordance with article 4;

   (b) Instruments of accession received in accordance with article 5;

   (c) The date upon which the present Convention enters into force in accordance with article 6;

   (d) Communications and notifications received in accordance with article 8;

   (e) Notifications of denunciation received in accordance with paragraph 1 of article 9;

   (f) Abrogation in accordance with paragraph 2 of article 9.

Article 12

1. The present Convention, of which the Chinese, English, French, Russian and Spanish texts shall be equally authentic, shall be deposited in the archives of the United Nations.

2. The Secretary-General of the United Nations shall transmit a certified copy of the Convention to all States Members of the United Nations and to the non-member States contemplated in paragraph 1 of article 4.

෨෨෨෨෨෨෨෨

5. REPORT OF THE WORKING GROUP ON THE ISSUE OF DISCRIMINATION AGAINST WOMEN IN LAW AND IN PRACTICE ON ITS MISSION TO THE UNITED STATES OF AMERICA

This formal 2016 Report of the Working Group on the Issue of Discrimination Against Women in Law and in Practice on its Mission to the United States of America addresses both the adequacy/inadequacy of women's equality and of women's enjoyment/frustration of human rights in the U.S. The Working Group draws conclusions and makes strategic recommendations for improving women's human rights in the U.S., specifically: absence of equality provision in the US Constitution; social and economic rights; marital status issues; gun violence; ratification of international/regional conventions; achievements in prohibiting discrimination in employment, education, marriage rights, and health/reproductive health issues; and gender-based violence, with special notice of issues affected by poverty and violence, the situation of minority, migrant, incarcerated, sex-working women.

United Nations, General Assembly, A/HRC/32/44/Add.2, Human Rights Council

Thirty-second session, Agenda item 3, Promotion and protection of all human rights, civil, political, economic, social and cultural rights, including the right to development,

I. Introduction

A. The visit

1. The Working Group on the issue of discrimination against women in law and in practice visited the United States of America from 30 November to 11 December 2015 at the invitation of the Government. The Working Group met with various concerned stakeholders in Washington, D.C., Austin and McAllen (Texas), Montgomery and Lowndes County (Alabama) and Salem and Portland (Oregon). The experts wish to thank the federal and state authorities as well as civil society organizations for their assistance in the organization of this visit.

2. In Washington, D.C., the Group met with representatives of the Departments of State, Labor, Health and Human Services, Education, Justice, Homeland Security and Housing and Urban Development; the White House Council on Women and Girls; the White House Advisor on Violence against Women; the Equal Employment Opportunity Commission; and the Office of Personnel Management. The Working Group also met with members of Congress, a judge of the Superior Court of the District of Columbia and a member of the National Association of Women Judges. In Austin, the Working Group met with representatives of the Commission for Women, the Office of the Speaker of the Texas House of Representatives and state trial judges. In McAllen, it met with the office of the Assistant City Manager. In Montgomery, it met with the Lieutenant Governor, a judge of the Middle District Court and a legislator. In Salem, it met with the Attorney General and the Office of Child Care. In Portland, it met with a District Court judge and the Oregon Commission for Women, including the Commissioner.

3. During its visit, the Working Group met with numerous non-governmental organizations, visited the Coffee Creek Penitentiary (Oregon), health centres, abortion clinics, childcare centres and relief nurseries. The Working Group would like to express its sincere gratitude for the exceptional level of cooperation and support extended by civil society during the visit.

B. Context

4. The visit of the Working Group took place at a moment when the political rhetoric of some of the candidates for the presidency in the upcoming elections included unprecedented hostile stereotyping of women; when there were increasingly restrictive legislative measures at the state level and violent attacks to prevent women from exercising their rights

to reproductive health;1 and when there was a significant and disparate worsening of the economic situation of women, in particular women of colour.

5. The Working Group acknowledges the commitment of the United States to liberty, so well represented by the Statue of Liberty, which symbolizes both womanhood and freedom. Nevertheless, in the global context, women in the United States do not take their due place as citizens of the world's leading economy, which has one of the highest per capita incomes. In the United States, women fall behind as regards their public and political representation, their economic and social rights and their health and safety protections.

6. Coming as it did at a time when the economy already had a high level of socioeconomic inequality, the global economic crisis further increased economic insecurity for the middle and lower deciles of the population and had a significantly adverse impact on women, in particular women of colour. Government recovery policies to boost the economy resulted in decreased expenditures on critical social protection programmes, many of which were essential for women.

7. The experts are fully aware of the diversity of the United States and of its political and legal framework, which combines federal and state legislation. Accordingly, the Working Group, rather than reviewing multitudinous provisions, and in view of the word limit on documents, comprehensively seeks to extract the key features of national policy, selected examples of state policy, the most recent trends in women's political, civil, social and economic situation and the achievements and obstacles encountered in promoting gender equality.

II. Legal, institutional and policy framework for women's equality and human rights

A. Legal framework

1. Ratification of conventions at the international and regional levels

8. The United States ratified the International Covenant on Civil and Political Rights (1992), the International Convention on the Elimination of All Forms of Racial Discrimination (1994), the Convention against Torture and Other Cruel, Inhuman or Degrading Treatment or Punishment (1994) and the Optional Protocols to the Convention on the Rights of the Child on the sale of children, child prostitution and child pornography and on the involvement of children in armed conflict (2002).

9. The Working Group deeply regrets that the United States has not ratified the Convention on the Elimination of All Forms of Discrimination against Women and its Optional Protocol. In 2010 and 2015, in the framework of the universal periodic review, the Government committed to ratifying the Convention but has not yet done so. The Working Group notes that resistance to ratification of the Convention reflects, inter alia, the opposition of a powerful sector of society to the Convention's formulation of women's international human right to equality. The United States is one of only seven countries in the world which have not ratified the Convention. Even in the absence of ratification, many of the Convention standards are entrenched, inter alia, in the Universal Declaration of Human Rights and in the International Covenant on Civil and Political Rights and are hence binding on the United States. Nevertheless, the Working Group is of the unreserved opinion that ratification of the Convention is crucial, on both the domestic and the global level, in order to confirm the commitment of the United States to substantive equality for women in all spheres of life. At the domestic level, ratification is essential in order to provide all women in the country with "missing" rights and protections guaranteed under the Convention, such as universal paid maternity leave, accessible reproductive health care and equal opportunity in standing for political election. The Working Group welcomes in this regard the initiatives undertaken by "Cities for CEDAW," which has started a process of incorporating Convention principles at the local level.

10. The Working Group also deeply regrets that the United States has not ratified other major international and regional human rights instruments that have a direct impact on the rights of women, such as the International Covenant on Economic, Social and Cultural Rights; the Convention on the Rights of the Child; the International Convention on the Protection of the Rights of All Migrant Workers and Members of Their Families; the Convention on the Rights of Persons with Disabilities; and the Inter-American Convention on the Prevention, Punishment and Eradication of Violence against Women "Convention of Belém do Pará." It further regrets that it is not party to the Equal Remuneration Convention, 1951 (No. 100), the Workers with Family Responsibilities Convention, 1981 (No. 156), the Indigenous

and Tribal Peoples Convention, 1989 (No. 169), the Maternity Protection Convention, 2000 (No. 183) and the Domestic Workers Convention, 2011 (No. 189) of the International Labour Organization (ILO).

2. Main achievements in prohibiting discrimination and violence against women

11. The experts recognize the very significant protection for women's rights under federal legislation and under the Constitution and greatly appreciate landmark decisions, in particular of the Supreme Court, which have created benchmarks in prohibiting sex discrimination. They note, in particular, the following.

Employment rights
12. The Equal Pay Act of 1963 requires that men and women in the same workplace be given equal pay for equal work.

13. Title VII of the Civil Rights Act of 1964 prohibits employment discrimination, including sexual harassment, based on race, colour, religion, sex or national origin by employers with 15 or more employees.

14. The Pregnancy Discrimination Act of 1978, amending Title VII, prohibits sex discrimination on the basis of pregnancy and clarifies that employment discrimination on the basis of pregnancy, childbirth or related medical conditions constitutes sex discrimination under Title VII.

15. The Family and Medical Leave Act (1993) provides employees with the right to take unpaid, job-protected leave of 12 workweeks in a 12-month period, including for the birth of a child and to care for the newborn, within one year of the birth.

16. The Lilly Ledbetter Fair Pay Restoration Act (2009) and Executive Order 13665 (2014) promote pay transparency and provide more effective procedures for challenging unequal pay.

Education
17. Title IX of the Education Amendments of 1972 prohibits sex discrimination in federally funded educational programmes.

Same-sex marriage
18. In its 2015 landmark decision in *Obergefell v. Hodges*, the Supreme Court recognized same-sex marriage as a constitutional right under the Fourteenth Amendment to the Constitution.

Right to health
19. The adoption of the Affordable Care Act in 2010 expanded access to health care for many uninsured citizens, with the biggest gains for the poor, minorities and low-wage workers. The legislation marked significant progress in women's enjoyment of the right to health. The Act also established crucial protections against discriminatory practices by health insurance plans in terms of charges and coverage relating to women's reproductive health needs as well as provisions for coverage of provider screening and counselling for domestic violence.

Violence against women
20. The Violence against Women Act of 1994 as last reauthorized in 2013, is a key resource to prevent gender-based violence, specifically domestic violence, sexual assault, date violence and stalking (see A/HRC/17/26/Add.5 and Corr.1, paras. 67-71). There are also statutory protections at state and local levels. The last reauthorization of the Act created earmarked funding to support sexual assault response teams and to train law enforcement officers and prosecutors in how to deal with sexual assault, and explicitly barred discrimination based on gender identity or sexual orientation

21. The Working Group also notes the adoption in 2012 of the National Standards to Prevent, Detect, and Respond to Prison Rape, pursuant to the Prison Rape Elimination Act (2003).

22. The experts welcome the significant legislative and judicial measures taken in the past decades aimed at eliminating discrimination and violence against women. Nonetheless, the Working Group notes that significant gaps remain in many of these legal frameworks and makes recommendations for further measures to guarantee gender equality in the workplace, in family status, in the right to health and as regards violence against women.

3. Challenges

Absence of an equality provision in the Constitution

23. The Working Group regrets that political resistance has consistently blocked efforts to pass an equal rights amendment, which would entrench women's right to equality in the Constitution. Constitutional guarantee is considered by leading human rights experts as crucial to secure women's right to equality and is included in almost all constitutions globally. According to a poll in 2012, 91 per cent of people in the United States think that the Constitution should include equal rights for men and women.

24. An equal rights amendment is also essential to demonstrate genuine political will to attain substantive equality between women and men, to pre-empt legislative reversal of gains made in the protection of women's right to equality and to further strengthen the review power of the Supreme Court to strike down discrimination against women.

Marital status

25. Family law is the prerogative of the states; there are therefore numerous laws relating to marriage across the country. Most states set the age of marriage at 18 without parental consent and 16 with parental consent and under certain conditions. Mississippi is the only state where women can marry without parental consent at the age of 15, and men at 17.

26. Although polygamy has been illegal in all states since 1862 (Morrill Anti-Bigamy Act), some cases of polygamy have been reported, especially in Utah and Colorado, However, in December 2013, a District Court in Utah ruled, in the case *Brown v. Buhman*, that Utah's anti-polygamy law was unconstitutional on the basis of the First Amendment to the Constitution which guarantees, among other rights, religious freedom.

Guns and gender-based violence

27. A series of federal and state laws have aimed at keeping guns out of the hands of the most dangerous domestic violence offenders. The strongest state laws prohibit domestic abusers and stalkers from buying or possessing guns, require background checks for all gun sales and create processes to ensure that abusers and stalkers surrender the guns already in their possession. However, federal prohibitions apply to abusers who are currently or formerly married to their victims and those who live with or formerly lived with their victims, but do not prohibit dating partners or misdemeanant stalkers from buying or possessing guns. The experts regret that existing regulations have done little to curb the problem of guns and their role in violence against women, in particular intimate partner homicides, but welcome the actions announced by the executive in January 2016 to reduce gun violence by increasing background checks for purchasers.

Rights to reproductive and sexual health

28. The experts regret that throughout the years, women in the United States have seen their rights to sexual and reproductive health significantly eroded. Since the 1973 decision by the Supreme Court in *Roe v. Wade* that a woman has a constitutional right to choose to terminate a pregnancy in the first trimester prior to viability, other Supreme Court decisions have opened the door to, inter alia, greater state regulation of abortion, barring abortion counselling and referral by family planning programmes funded under Title X of the federal Public Health Service Act; establishing the "undue burden test" providing that state regulations can survive constitutional review so long as they do not place a "substantial obstacle in the path of a woman seeking an abortion of a nonviable foetus"; and deciding that lawmakers can overrule a doctor's medical judgment and that the "State's interest in promoting respect for human life at all stages in the pregnancy" can outweigh a woman's interest in protecting her health. Women's rights to sexual and reproductive health are constantly being challenged.

29. At the time of writing, the Supreme Court was reviewing a case (*Whole Woman's Health v. Hellerstedt*) which had major implications for the future of access to essential reproductive health care in the United States. The expert group deeply hopes that this decision will reinstate the fundamental right of women to access reproductive and sexual health services in accordance with their constitutional rights. The Working Group is also concerned that the Supreme Court's recognition, in the *Hobby Lobby* case, of an exemption from the obligation of an employer to provide insurance that included contraception on the grounds of freedom of religion will deprive some women of the possibility of accessing contraceptives. A similar case, *Zubik v. Burwell*, concerning contraception and religious refusals, was also being heard by the Supreme Court.

30. Furthermore, the Working Group deplores the adoption in 1973 of the Helms Amendment to the Foreign Assistance Act, which was intended to prohibit foreign aid extended by the United States from being used to pay for the use of abortion "as a method of family planning," but is being used to justify a complete ban on using those funds for abortions, even when a pregnancy is a result of rape or incest or when a pregnancy is a threat to the life of a woman or girl. The Working Group also regrets the adoption in 1976 of the Hyde Amendment prohibiting the use of certain federal funds for abortions except in cases of rape, incest or preserving the life of the mother.

Social and economic rights

31. The Working Group regrets the important gaps in the legal framework which prevent women in the United States from fully enjoying their economic and social rights, including their equal right to work.

B. Access to justice

32. The courts play a central role in determining women's ability to enjoy and exercise the rights accorded to them by law. In the United States, there has been an increase in awareness of the need for gender diversity and gender-sensitive adjudication in judiciaries. Since the beginning of his mandate, the President has appointed more than 130 women judges. The Supreme Court has three women among its nine justices, for the first time in its history. Of the 170 active judges currently sitting on the 13 federal courts of appeal, 60 are women (35 per cent).

33. A severe problem for women litigants is access to justice: free legal counsel and aid are not systematically available for women living in poverty, and when legal aid is partially provided to the most destitute, it is allegedly of very poor quality. The experts hope that the White House Legal Aid Interagency Roundtable established in September 2015 will propose concrete solutions and have an adequate budget to address this gap.

34. The institution of the class action, which has allowed large numbers of women to access compensation for discrimination or injury caused by powerful corporations, is being eroded, with particular impact on women's legal resources for fighting gender discrimination, as demonstrated in the Supreme Court's rejection in 2013 of a class action suit against Wal-Mart Stores Inc. for discrimination, brought on behalf of about one million female workers. The justices held that the petitioners had failed to identify a common corporate policy that had led to gender discrimination against workers at thousands of Wal-Mart and Sam's Club stores across the country.

35. The Working Group also remains concerned at the particular difficulties faced by Native American women in accessing justice. The nature of the interaction between federal, state and tribal jurisdictions has meant that crimes committed by non-indigenous men on reservations often go unpunished. To address this situation, in July 2010, the Tribal Law and Order Act was passed with the aim of clarifying responsibilities and increasing coordination among the various law enforcement agencies.19 The reauthorization of the Violence against Women Act in 2013 was an attempt to remedy the criminal justice response to violence against Native American women. However, the Working Group received reports that these laws are not being fully and effectively implemented, resulting in a persistent failure of the justice system to respond adequately to acts of violence against Native American women (see CERD/C/USA/CO/7-9 and A/HRC/17/26/Add.5 and Corr.1).

36. The experts recommend that the issue of substantive equality for women in court proceedings be revisited and reinvigorated and that access to justice for all, with adequate legal representation, be regarded as a civil right which, where necessary, should be publicly funded.

C. Institutional framework and policies at the federal level

1. Institutional framework

37. The Government has considerably strengthened the institutional structure to promote women's rights and gender equality, including through the White House Council on Women and Girls and the White House Advisor on Violence against Women, which have reinforced the Civil Rights Division and the Office on Violence against Women within the Department of Justice; and the Office on Women's Health, the Family Violence Prevention and Services Division and the Office of Minority Health within the Department of Health and Human Services. Other departments and federal

entities also play a key role such as the Department of Labor, the Equal Employment Opportunity Commission, the Office of Personnel Management and the Commission on Civil Rights.

38. The Working Group observed during its visit that federal and state authorities had very limited knowledge of international human rights standards and mechanisms. It regrets that no national human rights institution has been established in accordance with the principles relating to the status of national institutions for the promotion and protection of human rights (the Paris Principles). The Working Group notes that six inter-agency working groups exist, under the leadership of the White House, to coordinate the review of the recommendations of the universal periodic review and concluding observations of treaty bodies, but regrets the absence of a mechanism which would coordinate and monitor the implementation of the recommendations of special procedures mandate holders.

2. Policies

39. The Working Group acknowledges that the promotion of gender equality and the empowerment of women and girls has been at the forefront of the current administration's policies. Indeed, the Government has been working to combat discrimination, eliminate violence against women and girls, expand access to women's health care, including sexual and reproductive health and rights, support women-owned businesses and women entrepreneurs and encourage women's economic and political leadership. Several of these policies are detailed in the Government's report on the implementation of the Beijing Declaration and Platform for Action.

III. Participation of women in political and public life and in economic and social life, and access to health

A. Participation in political and public life

40. Despite the current administration's commitment to advancing women's rights, adequate representation for women in political life is far from being achieved and, indeed, only 4 out of 15 Cabinet members are women.

41. Women hold 19.4 per cent of the seats in the House of Representatives and 20 per cent in the Senate. Between 2004 and 2015, the number of women in the Senate increased from 14 to 20 and the number of women in the House grew from 60 to 84. This represents the highest level of legislative representation ever achieved by women in the United States. However, it still puts the country at only 96 in the global ranking. Women of colour make up 7.4 per cent (32 of 435 representatives) of the House. There is only one woman of colour serving in the Senate, but not a single African-American woman.

42. Only six states have female governors: New Hampshire, New Mexico, Oklahoma, Oregon, Rhode Island and South Carolina. The share of state senate seats held by women is largest in Arizona (43.3 per cent) and smallest in South Carolina (2.2 per cent). The share of seats in the state house or assembly held by women is largest in Colorado (46.2 per cent) and smallest in Oklahoma (12.9 per cent).

43. According to several of the interlocutors whom the Working Group met during its visit, the low level of representation of women in elected political posts is due partly to the greater difficulties women face in fundraising for campaigns. The financing of political campaigns has increasingly played a major role in recent decades and has drastically altered the landscape of elections and political participation. The experts observed that women's difficulty in fundraising is considered to result from complex causes. In particular, it is a result of exclusion from the predominantly male political networks that promote funding.

Interlocutors also attribute women's low rate of election to negative stereotypes and biased presentation of women in the media, which adversely affect both women's fundraising ability and their political candidacy. The experts consider the objective difficulties women face in raising campaign funding to be a serious limitation on women's opportunities for political representation, and are deeply concerned that the removal of limits on campaign contributions by the Supreme Court in 2014 threatens to exacerbate this situation.

44. In this regard, the Working Group welcomes the initiatives undertaken by states and cities that have started programmes for public financing of campaigns. One method, which its supporters call "Clean Money, Clean Elections," gives each candidate who chooses to participate a fixed amount of money. Some interlocutors have pointed out that, in

order to effectively give women an equal chance, competing private funding would have to be restricted. The Working Group encourages the efforts deployed by voluntary organizations, such as Emily's List, which promote women candidates. The Working Group recalls that, in accordance with international human rights standards, temporary special measures have been adopted in many democratic countries to ensure more adequate representation of women in politics.

45. Furthermore, while more women currently vote than men, it is essential to ensure that women continue to have access to the voting booth. Today, a patchwork of state laws is making it more and more difficult to exercise the right to vote. For instance, officials in Ohio, Texas and North Carolina have manipulated rules to keep part of the population away from the polls. The Working Group welcomes the efforts deployed by the League of Women Voters which has, for instance, successfully challenged the Florida state legislature for redrawing congressional districts for a particular party's benefit. The Working Group is concerned that changes in voter identification laws, such as those in Alabama, which increase bureaucratic requirements for voter identification, are particularly problematic for women who have changed their name after marriage, and reductions in the number of voting centers can make registration and voting less accessible for the poor, a majority of whom are women. A counter example and good practice is the State of Oregon, which has facilitated voter registration and voting by mail.

B. Participation in economic and social life

46. Women's participation in the workforce has played a key role in the country's economic growth in the last decades. Women constitute nearly half of the labour force in the United States, and 57 per cent of women are labour force participants. Mothers are more likely to provide significant financial support to their families than ever before, with nearly two thirds of women being primary or co-breadwinners for their families. Among dual-earner couples, 29 per cent of women earned as much as or more than their husbands. Women today are more likely than men to graduate from college, and are as likely to obtain advanced degrees.

47. However, while women have made great achievements in education and have increased their workforce participation, the Working Group is concerned that their crucial labour force participation and educational achievements are not accompanied by equal economic returns, especially as reflected in the wage gap and the high numbers of women earning the minimum or beneath minimum wage. It notes that, in practice, discrimination against women in employment continues; women's work is valued less and provides less favourable terms and conditions of work, including salary and promotion. Furthermore, it considers that, despite the prohibition of discrimination in employment and the establishment of the Equal Employment Opportunity Commission, the legal system does not provide women with a level playing field, failing to secure the workplace accommodations necessary for women to fulfil both reproductive and productive roles.

48. The Working Group regrets the persistence of a corporate culture that perpetuates gender stereotypes. The Working Group was informed that women own over one third of the firms in the United States, most of them small and medium-size businesses, and that these businesses face greater barriers in obtaining low-cost capital from sources such as the Small Business Administration and clearly need support to achieve equal economic potential. The federal Government has a stated goal of awarding 5 per cent of federal contracts to women-owned businesses; it is reported that this goal was reached for the first time only in 2015.

49. The Working Group recognizes the gains for women's equal opportunity in employment made under the equal protection guarantees of the Fourteenth and Fifth Amendments and the prohibition against employment discrimination contained in Title VII of the Civil Rights Act of 1964. It also appreciates the decisions of the Supreme Court in sex discrimination cases in which the Court has rejected the use of gender stereotypes and recognized the legitimacy of affirmative action and the discriminatory effect of sexual harassment and gender hostility in the workplace. However, in another of its decisions, the Court has made it more difficult for women to prove discrimination. In equal protection cases under the Fourteenth Amendment, the Court has traditionally applied intermediate scrutiny rather than strict scrutiny. In Title VII cases, the Court has developed two principal models for proving claims of employment discrimination. The "disparate treatment" model focuses on an employer's intent to discriminate. Alternately, the "disparate impact" model, a facially neutral employment practice, may violate Title VII even if there is no evidence of an employer's intent to discriminate. Both models require the plaintiff to establish a prima facie case of discrimination, and the burden then shifts to the employer to articulate a defence. Ultimately, however, the plaintiff retains the burden of persuasion to

establish that the employer's assertion of a legitimate, non discriminatory reason for its actions was a mere pretext. The Supreme Court has also recently circumscribed the effectiveness of using class action suits in employment discrimination claims (see para. 33).

50. The gender wage gap is 21 per cent, and during the last decade little improvement has been made in closing it despite the Equal Pay Act of 1963. Research has shown that a woman working every year between the ages of 25 and 65 will have lost $420,000 over her working life because of the earnings gap. Education increases women's earnings but does not eliminate the gap, which is in fact larger for those with the highest levels of educational attainment. In her lifetime, a woman with an advanced degree in such fields as law or medicine can expect to earn $2 million less than her male peers. The wage gap affects women's income throughout their lives, affecting their financial security and independence and increasing pension poverty.

51. The wage gap may be attributed both to vertical discrimination in wage scales and to horizontal discrimination as a result of a gender-segregated labour market. In order to address the latter, international human rights standards require equal pay for work of equal value. However, in the United States, neither federal nor state equal pay laws have required equal pay for work of equal value. Exceptionally, California has now set a precedent with the California Fair Pay Act of 2015, which legislates the right to equal pay for work of equal value.

52. Women's earnings also differ considerably by ethnicity: African-American, Native American and Hispanic women have the lowest earnings. Across the largest racial and ethnic groups in the United States, Asian/Pacific Islander women have the highest median annual earnings, at $46,000, followed by white women ($40,000). Native American and Hispanic women have the lowest earnings, at $31,000 and $28,000, respectively. Data also indicate that women of colour are less likely to attain a bachelor's degree or higher than other women.

53. The expert group is concerned that, although the Pregnancy Discrimination Act of 1978 established that pregnancy discrimination is sex discrimination under Title VII, between 1997 and 2011, the number of pregnancy discrimination complaints filed with the Equal Employment Opportunity Commission increased by 46 per cent and pregnant women have largely continued to lose their requests for remedy. The experts hope that the 2014 guidelines issued by the Commission and the decision of the Supreme Court in 2015 in *Young v. United Parcel Service* will improve access to justice for pregnancy-related discrimination.

54. The Working Group is appalled by the lack of mandatory standards for paid maternity leave, which is required in international human rights law. The Family and Medical Leave Act, which gives employees of companies with more than 50 employees the right to take unpaid, job-protected leave of 12 workweeks in a 12-month period, cannot be regarded as in lieu of paid maternity leave and falls far short of international human rights standards, which require that maternity leave must be paid leave for a minimum of 14 weeks; best practice is the provision of paid leave for fathers too. Some form of paid parental leave is provided by legislation in three states, but only for six weeks and not at full pay. Attempts by the current administration to provide paid maternity leave for federal employees have not yet been successful. The United States is one of only two countries in the world without mandatory paid maternity leave for all women workers.

55. The Working Group is also concerned at the unequal division of family caregiving work, demonstrated by the fact that women are nine times more likely than men to work part-time for family care reasons. Part-time work means lower earnings (and lower social security contributions); part-time workers are also much less likely to have access to paid leave of any kind or to benefit from employer contributions to employer-provided health insurance or pension plans. Women are also three times more likely than men to report having left their job because of caregiving responsibilities (6 per cent compared with 2 per cent, according to a survey of people aged 45-74 undertaken in 2013 by the American Association of Retired People). A study by MetLife (2011) estimated that women with caregiving responsibilities who were over the age of 50 would lose $324,044 in income and benefits over their lifetime if they completely exit the workforce for caregiving reasons. The Working Group considers that the public budget should provide facilities for childcare and after-school care and facilities for the elderly and disabled that are affordable and accessible, to allow adults with care responsibilities — women and men — to work in full-time employment.

56. The percentage of women in poverty has increased over the past decade — from 12.1 per cent to 14.5 per cent — at a higher rate than for men; this has predominantly affected women of colour, single-parent families and older women.

As noted previously by other United Nations experts, the subprime mortgage market disparately targeted the poor and, in particular, poor women, thus contributing to the increase in women's poverty.

57. The Working Group suggests that both federal and state governments address this problem urgently, by promoting employment for women, raising the minimum wage and eliminating the wage gap. Residual poverty should be addressed through the social security system and, given the country's economic strength, there should be a policy of zero tolerance for relegating people to poverty.

58. Furthermore, many stakeholders complained that minimum wages have lost value as a living wage. The majority of minimum wage earners are women working full time and as the sole source of income for their families. The Working Group regards the raising of the minimum wage to the level of a living wage to be one of the most appropriate ways both to reduce the wage gap and to reduce poverty among working women. The Working Group welcomes recent efforts by the Government in this regard.

59. The Working Group is also concerned at the situation of the estimated 2.5 million domestic workers in the United States, According to the National Domestic Workers Alliance, the overwhelming number of them are women, frequently immigrant women, many of whom are undocumented. During their visit, the experts heard dreadful testimonies from workers in this group who were victims of verbal and physical abuse and wage theft.

The Working Group welcomes the initiatives taken by civil society organizations to improve conditions for domestic workers through a domestic workers' bill of rights. Wage theft also affects other low-income and migrant workers (such as those in manufacturing, construction and some service jobs). The Working Group welcomes the recent increase in the budget of the Wage and Hour Division within the Department of Labor to support investigations.

60. The Working Group recalls that international human rights standards require establishing social protection floors for core economic and social rights, providing paid maternity leave and taking all appropriate measures to produce de facto equality between all women and men in the labour market. It is not for the Working Group to suggest how these minimum standards should be achieved, but only to point out that the United States, the economic leader of the world, lags behind in providing a safety net and a decent life for those of its women who do not have access to independent wealth, high salaries or economic support from a partner or family.

C. Access to health care

61. The Working Group praises the cconsiderable progress achieved by the adoption of the Affordable Care Act. However, it regrets the absence of universal health insurance coverage. The experts also regret the decision of the Supreme Court to allow states to opt out from the expansion of their Medicaid thresholds, as foreseen by the Act. Too many women pay a high price, sometimes with their lives, for this considerable coverage gap, which has strong regional and ethnic disparities. According to official data from 2015, 28 per cent of the people living in poverty are still uninsured. This affects primarily women and, in particular, African-American and Hispanic women, who are thus prevented from accessing basic preventive care and treatments.

62. Furthermore, immigrants, including immigrant women, must wait five years before they can access Medicaid and undocumented migrants are completely excluded from health care, with the exception of emergency care, including labour and delivery and care available at community and migrant health centres and through HIV/AIDS and maternal and child health programmes. During their visit, the experts observed that Texas and Alabama do not allow immigrants lawfully residing in those states to enrol in Medicaid even after completing the federal waiting period of five years. The experts heard appalling testimonies of migrant women who had been diagnosed with breast cancer but could not afford the appropriate treatment. The Health Equity and Access under the Law (HEAL) for Immigrant Women and Families Act, currently before Congress, would expand access to health care for immigrants, particularly women and children. The Working Group also regretted to learn about the serious inadequacies of health-care facilities to treat women with disabilities, and calls for improvement in this regard.

63. The Working Group deplores the substantial disparities that persist in the prevalence of certain diseases, such as obesity, cancer and HIV/AIDs, according to ethnicity, sex and level of education. Black women, for instance, experience the highest rates of hypertension and obesity compared with other ethnic group. The experts also regret that the

vast majority of lesbian, bisexual, transgender and intersex persons report having experienced discrimination by health-care providers, including refusal of care, harsh language and physical roughness.

64. The experts are also concerned at the results of a study which showed that, after a period of consistent decline, the suicide rate among women increased between 1999 and 2014 from 4 per 100,000 population to 5.8. Suicide is a very worrying public health issue, and concerned authorities should address it urgently.

Sexual and reproductive health

65. Women's empowerment is intrinsically linked to their ability to control their reproductive lives (A/HRC/32/44). The Working Group would like to recall that according to international human rights standards, including the Convention on the Elimination of All Forms of Discrimination against Women, which the United States has signed but not ratified, States must take all appropriate measures to ensure women's equal right to decide freely and responsibly on the number and spacing of their children, which includes women's right to access contraceptives.

66. The Working Group welcomes the requirement in the Affordable Care Act that new private health plans must cover contraceptive counselling, without out-of-pocket costs. Despite the Government's efforts, and a significant drop in teenage pregnancy, the Working Group remains concerned that the rate of teenage pregnancy is substantially higher than in other Western industrialized nations and that ethnic and geographic disparities in teen birth rates persist.

67. The experts were informed that, being a prerogative of each state, there is no national policy on sex education and adequate and quality sex education in school. Oregon, for example, does provide sex education, but it is lacking in many curricula. According to interlocutors, in many schools only abstinence is taught in place of scientifically based sex education, which is a key element of health policy.

68. Although women have a right under federal law to terminate a pregnancy in various circumstances, including the constitutional guarantee under *Roe v. Wade*, ever-increasing barriers are being created to prevent their access to abortion procedures. Women's access to reproductive health services has been truncated in some states by the imposition of serious constraints. These take the form of unjustified medical procedures, such as compelling women to undergo ultrasounds or to endure medically unnecessary waiting periods; withholding early-pregnancy abortion medications; and imposing burdensome conditions for the licensing and operation of clinics resulting in the closing of clinics across the country, leaving women without access to sexual and reproductive health services. Furthermore, marketplace insurance coverage for the legal termination of pregnancy is far from universal. Thus, insurance will frequently not be available for women who wish to exercise their right to terminate their pregnancy in the first trimester. These restrictions have a disproportionate and discriminatory impact on poor women. As the experts observed during their visit to the Rio Grande Valley in Texas, one of the poorest regions in the country, immigrant women face severe barriers in accessing sexual and reproductive health services. The adoption of the Woman's Health Protection Act would prohibit states from enacting unconstitutional restrictions on reproductive health-care providers that block access to safe and legal abortion services by requiring all hospitals to provide these services and insurance schemes to provide coverage for abortions, to which women have a right under United States law.

69. The Working Group is also concerned that an increasing number of states are targeting women's health providers for exclusion from key federal health programmes, including the Title X Family Planning Program, the Centers for Disease Control and Prevention programmes on sexually transmitted infections under section 318 (of the Public Health Service Act and Medicaid. At least 17 states have taken such action since 2011; 10 of these states have taken official action to block certain women's health providers, such as Planned Parenthood, from participating in Medicaid.

70. In addition, many of the clinics work in conditions of constant threats, harassment and vandalism, too often without any kind of protection from law enforcement officials, as the experts observed during their visits to Texas and Alabama. Alabama has a history of serious violence against abortion providers, including the killing in 1993 of Dr. David Gunn, the first doctor to be murdered for performing abortions in the United States. The massacre in the Colorado family planning centre that occurred just before the start of the visit once again demonstrated the extreme hostility and danger faced by family planning providers and patients. The experts are concerned at the stigma attached to reproductive and sexual health care, which leads to acts of violence, harassment and intimidation against those seeking or providing such care. The Working Group reminds the Government of its due diligence obligation and encourages it to investigate and prosecute violence or threats of violence occurring in this context.

71. The experts reiterate that the enjoyment of the right to freedom of religion or belief cannot be used to justify gender discrimination and, therefore, should not be used as a justification for hindering the realization of women's right to the enjoyment of the highest attainable standard of physical and mental health (ibid.). Laws on religious or conscience-based refusals to provide reproductive health care in the United States should be reconciled with international human rights standards. Refusal to provide sexual and reproductive health services on the grounds of religious freedom should not be permitted where such refusal would effectively deny women immediate access to the highest attainable standard of reproductive health care and affect the implementation of rights to which they are entitled under both international human rights standards and domestic law.

72. The Working Group expresses serious concern at the increase in the maternal mortality rate in the United States. According to the United Nations, the rate increased by 136 per cent between 1990 and 2013. This global number hides distressing ethnic and socioeconomic disparities. African-American women are nearly four times more likely to die in childbirth. States with high poverty rates have a 77 per cent higher maternal mortality rate. Concerned authorities should continue to elaborate adequate policies to address this issue.

73 The Working Group is surprised at the extremely high levels of cesarean deliveries in the United States (32.2 per cent of deliveries). According to the World Health Organization, the ideal rate of caesarean sections should be between 10 per cent and 15 per cent. When medically necessary, a caesarean section can effectively prevent maternal and newborn mortality; however, when the rate goes above 10 per cent, there is no evidence that mortality rates improve. The experts would encourage the concerned authorities to address this issue carefully and take measures to prevent the performance of caesarian sections for non-medical reasons.

74. The Working Group welcomes the progressive policies introduced by several states to promote access to reproductive and sexual health care. A 2014 report provides a compendium of proactive policy solutions on reproductive health issues ranging from access to contraception and termination of pregnancy to promoting comprehensive sexuality education and improving maternal health. Its author recommends that these solutions be widely adopted. The Working Group also notes with satisfaction the law passed in 2015 in Oregon that allows pharmacists to prescribe contraceptives, thus facilitating access to family planning measures

IV. Gender-based violence and women victims of multiple forms of discrimination

75. Despite the considerable efforts deployed in the past two decades at the legal, institutional and policy levels and some positive achievements to prevent and respond to gender-based violence, stakeholders have unanimously denounced the alarmingly persistent high levels of such violence in the United States.

Poverty and violence
76. The Working Group observed that poverty may result in homelessness, which exposes women to higher levels of violence and vulnerability. During the visit, interlocutors pointed out that victims of domestic violence were often among the homeless, either because they had been evicted as a result of the violence or because they had fled from their violent partner. Solutions should include effective protection orders, increased availability of shelters, housing support, and prioritizing eligibility for aid for single-mother households and those facing heavy unpaid care burdens.

Gun violence
77. The Working Group is troubled at the persistent, fatal consequences for women of the lack of gun control, in particular in cases of domestic violence. Women in the United States are 11 times more likely to be murdered with a firearm than women in other high-income countries. Over the past 25 years, more intimate partner homicides have been committed with guns than with all other weapons combined. When a gun is present in a domestic violence situation, it increases the risk of homicide for women by 500 per cent. In 35 states, persons convicted of domestic violence misdemeanours or subject to restraining orders are not prohibited from acquiring guns. Federal law (and the law in most states) allows domestic abusers and stalkers to easily evade gun prohibitions by purchasing guns from unlicensed, private sellers. Forty-one states do not require all prohibited domestic abusers to relinquish guns they already own.

Minority women

78. The Working Group is deeply concerned at the disproportionate number of women from ethnic minorities, particularly African-American, Native American and immigrant women, who are subjected to heightened levels of violence, including rape and sexual violence (see CERD/C/USA/CO/7-9 and A/HRC/17/26/Add.5 and Corr.1). Relevant authorities stressed the difficulties in obtaining accurate data on various immigrant and refugee communities, who may fear reporting to law enforcement officials. Indigenous women are more than twice as likely as all other women to be victims of violence, and one in three of them will be raped during her lifetime. It is estimated that nearly 80 per cent of the rapes of indigenous women are by non-indigenous men (A/HRC/21/47/Add.1). The experts also deplore reports of police brutality and the increased number of homicides of African-American women by the police.

79. Lesbian, bisexual, transgender and intersex persons face heightened exposure to hate crimes and physical violence. Sexual orientation-based hate crimes made up about 21 per cent of hate crimes reported by law enforcement in 2013 to the Uniform Crime Reporting Program of the Bureau of Justice Statistics. This percentage is probably an underestimate given that a number of lesbian, bisexual, transgender and intersex survivors of hate violence may not report their abuse to the police.

Migrant women in detention centres

80. The Working Group is extremely concerned at the situation of migrant women in detention centres, in particular women with minor children who are in prolonged detention. According to the information received, some detention facilities are not complying with federal mandates and agency policies. Regarding women seeking asylum, the Commission on Civil Rights noted that the expedited removal process was fundamentally unfair as it did not afford detained immigrants the proper ability to obtain counsel and that the process should be improved to ensure that those who genuinely feared persecution could exercise their right to seek asylum in the United States. The Working Group also received allegations of sexual abuse and assault of women detainees, as well as mistreatment by Customs and Border Protection officials. Migrant women are often victims of trafficking and violence, including sexual violence, during their journey to the United States. The experts received complaints that appropriate health-care services were not systematically provided to these women in a timely manner, despite the horrifying physical and emotional ordeals they endured and in violation of detention standards. The experts also received complaints of migrant transgender women being mistreated in detention and often wrongfully placed with males.

Incarcerated women

81. The Working Group shares the concerns expressed by the Special Rapporteur on violence against women, its causes in consequences in the report on her visit to the United States (A/HRC/17/26/Add.5 and Corr.1) regarding women in detention (overincarceration, sexual violence, shackling of pregnant women, solitary confinement, lack of alternatives to custodial sentences for women with dependent children, inappropriate access to health care and inadequate re-entry programmes). The Working Group is also concerned at the negative effects of the Prison Litigation Reform Act on the ability of prisoners to seek protection of their rights; the Act requires prisoners to exhaust all internal complaint procedures before bringing an action in federal court. While welcoming the adoption of the National Standards to Prevent, Detect, and Respond to Prison Rape, pursuant to the Prison Rape Elimination Act (2003), the Working Group expresses serious concern at reports that their implementation at the state level continues to be a substantial challenge.

Women in prostitution/sex workers

82. The criminalization of women in prostitution/sex workers in most of the country exposes them further to violence, places them in a situation of injustice, vulnerability and stigma and is contrary to international human rights standards. As the Committee on the Elimination of Discrimination against Women has systematically reiterated, women should not be criminalized for being in a situation of prostitution. Furthermore, as stipulated in the Protocol to Prevent, Suppress and Punish Trafficking in Persons, Especially Women and Children, supplementing the United Nations Convention against Transnational Organized Crime (the Palermo Protocol), efforts should be deployed to discourage the demand that fosters all forms of exploitation of women.

V. Conclusions and recommendations

A. Conclusions

83. The Working Group greatly appreciates the invitation by the Government of the United States for the visit, which opened the door to an open and frank exchange regarding both good practices and gaps in women's enjoyment of their human rights in the United States.

84. The experts are of the opinion that, in a global context, women in the United States do not take their due place as citizens of the world's leading economy, which has one of the highest per capita incomes. In the United States, women are left behind in terms of international standards as regards their public and political representation, their economic and social rights and their health and safety protections.

85. The experts welcome the genuine support expressed by the current administration for the cause of women's equality and its undertaking to ratify the Convention on the Elimination of All Forms of Discrimination against Women. However, the experts regret the failure to implement these aims. As many stakeholders have underscored, the extreme polarization of politics has profoundly affected the ability of the Government to ratify the Convention and to introduce measures to guarantee women's human rights.

86. At the domestic level, ratification of the Convention is essential in order to provide all women in the United States with the rights and protections guaranteed therein. It is a myth that women already enjoy all those rights and protections under United States law. There are "missing" rights and protections to which women would be entitled under the Convention, such as universal paid maternity leave, accessible reproductive health care and equal opportunity in standing for political election.

87. The United States, which is a leading State in terms of formulating international human rights standards, is allowing its women to lag behind in the respect for these standards. While all women are victims of these "missing" rights, women who are poor; Native American, African-American, Hispanic and Asian women; women who are members of ethnic minorities; migrant women; lesbian, bisexual, transgender or intersex persons; women with disabilities; and older women are in a situation of heightened vulnerability.

88. The ability to address these challenges is limited by a range of factors. Such obstacles include lack of political will to pass essential legislation; women's limited representation in leadership positions in Congress and in business; a strong conservative religious lobby which opposes reproductive rights; gun lobbies which oppose gun control; and discriminatory gender norms perpetuating a culture that allows discrimination against women to flourish. Women's underrepresentation and negative representation in the media also present major challenges and reinforce existing gender biases.

B. Recommendations

89. In a spirit of cooperation and collaboration, the Working Group makes the following recommendations to the federal and state authorities, as relevant, with a view to strengthening measures designed to guarantee gender equality, the empowerment of women and the promotion and protection of women's human rights.

Legal framework
90. With regard to the legal framework, the Working Group recommends:

(a) Ratifying the Convention on the Elimination of All Forms of Discrimination against Women;

(b) Adopting an equal rights amendment which would entrench women's right to equality in the Constitution;

(c) Reinforcing existing legislation in order to eliminate all forms of sex discrimination in employment, to pre-empt restrictive interpretation of the laws which prejudice women's access to remedies and to allow class action suits for employment discrimination claims on the basis of overall data against large corporations;

(d) Amending the Equal Pay Act to include the right to equal pay for work of equal value, with the implementation provisions recommended in the report of the Working Group submitted to the Human Rights Council at its twenty-sixth session, in 2014 (A/HRC/28/28);

(e) Mandating 14 weeks of paid maternity leave for all women workers in public and private employment, taking into account that best practice is payment from a social security fund which does not impose a direct financial burden on employers;

(f) Ratifying the ILO Domestic Workers Convention, 2011 (No. 189) and applying its provisions to ensure that domestic work is decent work;

(g) Making sure that women can, in practice, exercise their existing constitutional right, reaffirmed in *Roe v. Wade*, to choose to terminate a pregnancy in the first trimester;

(h) Ensuring that the provisions of the Affordable Care Act regarding insured access to contraceptives are universally enforced;

(i) Repealing the Helms Amendment and, in the meantime, issuing an executive order clarifying the scope of the existing legislation and clarifying women's right to insured reproductive health care for termination of pregnancy in cases of risk to life or to health (physical and mental), a pregnancy resulting from rape or other unlawful intercourse, teenage pregnancy or severe fetal impairment;

(j) Repealing the Hyde Amendment;

(k) Adopting the Woman's Health Protection Act;

(l) Disallowing conscientious objection by health-care personnel, providers and insurers to performing procedures to which women are legally entitled and for which there is no easily accessible, affordable and immediate alternative health provider;

(m) Expanding access to health care for immigrants via, for instance, the adoption of the Health Equity and Access under the Law (HEAL) for Immigrant Women and Families Act;

(n) Ensuring that women in prostitution/sex workers are not criminalized;

(o) Amending gun control laws to effectively protect women against gun violence;

(p) Changing laws to ensure that the legal age of marriage is 18, in all cases, for both women and men.

Access to justice

91. With regard to access to justice, the Working Group recommends:

(a) Ensuring further gender diversity and gender-sensitive adjudication in judiciaries;

(b) Revisiting and reinvigorating substantive equality for women in court proceedings and ensuring access to justice for all without discrimination, with adequate legal representation regarded as a civil right which, where necessary, should be publicly funded;

(c) Ensuring systematic accountability in cases of police brutality, noting in particular the frequency of police brutality against African-American women;

(d) Empowering Native American tribes to ensure justice in their communities through the exercise of full criminal jurisdiction within their lands;

(e) Ensuring the implementation of the National Standards to Prevent, Detect, and Respond to Prison Rape.

Institutional framework

92. Regarding the institutional framework, the Working Group recommends:

(a) Establishing an independent human rights institution in compliance with the Paris Principles, which should include a woman's rights commission;

(b) Establishing a high-level inter-agency working group on human rights implementation with a mandate to oversee and coordinate the implementation of the human rights obligations and commitments of the United States domestically, including the implementation of the recommendations of special procedures mandate holders.

Policies

93. With regard to public and political life, the Working Group recommends:

(a) Applying temporary special measures to ensure gender equality in public and political representation, at both the executive and legislative branches, as well as in the judiciary;

(b) Introducing initiatives to encourage the participation of women in elected positions, including by provision of public funding for election campaigns.

94. With regard to economic and social life, the Working Group recommends:

(a) Developing policies to address occupational segregation, both vertical and horizontal;

(b) Providing facilities for childcare and after-school care and facilities for the elderly and disabled which are affordable and accessible to all women without discrimination, to allow adults with care responsibilities — women and men — to work in full-time employment;

(c) Raising the minimum wage to a living wage level;

(d) Facilitating access to capital and increasing the level of federal contract procurement for businesses owned by women, and taking measures to combat a corporate culture that perpetuates gender stereotypes;

(e) Ensuring that the Wage and Hour Division within the. Department of Labor undertakes proper investigations, and increasing supervision to hold employers who violate the rights of vulnerable women workers to account;

(f) Addressing the legacies of racism and persistent forms of racial discrimination and ethnic disparities in every sphere of life (inequalities in access to education, employment, housing and health care).

95. With regard to health, the Working Group recommends:

(a) Increasing funding of clinics under the Title X Family Planning Program in order to expand coverage for low-income women who lack insurance so they can access preventive care, including sexual and reproductive health services, and to reduce maternal mortality;

(b) Preventing politically motivated actions to exclude women's health providers from federally supported public health programmes;

(c) Taking additional measures to make contraception available and accessible at no cost, in particular for teenagers, with a view to combating teenage pregnancy;

(d) Considering reviewing the eligibility requirements for the public welfare system so that the basic human rights of immigrants, including the undocumented, are guaranteed, in particular access to health care for women and children;

(e) Addressing the root causes of increased maternal mortality, in particular among African-American women;

(f) Ensuring adequate, scientifically based sex education in school curricula;

(g) Ensuring mandatory human rights education in schools, including the promotion of gender equality, the elimination of violence against women and harmful gender stereotypes as well as the legacy of slavery and racism;

(h) Combating the stigma attached to reproductive and sexual health care, which leads to acts of violence, harassment and intimidation against those seeking or providing reproductive health care, and duly investigate and prosecute violence or threats of violence;

(i) Taking steps to reconcile United States laws on religious or conscience-based refusals to provide reproductive health care with international human rights standards and to prohibit refusal to provide sexual and reproductive health services on the grounds of religious freedom where such refusal would effectively deny women immediate access to the highest attainable standard of health care, and to implement the rights to which women are entitled under both international human rights standards and domestic law.

96. With regard to violence against women and safety, the Working Group recommends:

(a) Implementing fully the Violence against Women Act of 2013;

(b) Ensuring effective protection orders, increased availability of shelters, culturally and linguistically responsive programmes and housing support, prioritizing eligibility particularly for single-mother households and those facing heavy, unpaid care burdens;

(c) Ending detention of migrant women with children and establishing accountability mechanisms and adequate gender-sensitive training of Customs and Border Protection officials;

(d) Seeking alternatives to custodial sentences for mothers of dependent children.

97. With regard to women in the media, the Working Group recommends:

(a) Strengthening the enforcement of the Federal Communications Commission Equal Employment Opportunity rules;

(b) Promoting the training of journalists regarding gender equality and women's rights, to try to combat harmful gender stereotyping in the media.

Source: https://documents-dds-ny.un.org/doc/UNDOC/GEN/G16/172/75/PDF/G1617275.pdf

6. U.N. WORKING GROUP ON THE ISSUE OF DISCRIMINATION AGAINST WOMEN IN LAW AND IN PRACTICE FINALIZES COUNTRY MISSION TO THE UNITED STATES, 2015

This December 2015 U.N. High Commissioner on Human Rights press release, issued at the end of 10-day Working Group on the Issue of Discrimination Against Women in Law and in Practice on its Mission to the United States of America, offers early insight into women's human rights issues in the U.S.

WASHINGTON DC (11 December 2015)—At the end of a 10-day mission to the United States, in which the expert group's delegation, comprised of Eleonora Zielinska, Frances Raday and Alda Facio held meetings in Washington DC and visited the states of Alabama, Oregon and Texas, Frances Raday delivered the following statement:

We want to express our sincere appreciation to the Government of the United States for having invited U.S. to conduct this country visit. We are grateful to all our interlocutors, officials at the Federal and state levels and members of civil society, including women's organisations, practitioners and individual women who shared their experiences with us.

U.S. Women in Global Context

In its greatly appreciated invitation to our expert group, the United States opened the door to a frank interchange regarding both good practices and gaps in U.S. women's enjoyment of international human rights. We acknowledge the United States' commitment to liberty, so well represented by the Statue of Liberty which symbolizes both womanhood and freedom. Nevertheless, in global context, U.S. women do not take their rightful place as citizens of the world's leading economy, which has one of the highest rates of per capita income. In the U.S., women fall behind international standards as regards their public and political representation, their economic and social rights and their health and safety protections.

In 2010 and 2015, in the framework of its Universal Periodic Review, the U.S. government committed to ratify the Convention on the Elimination of All of Forms of Discrimination Against Women (CEDAW) but this commitment has not yet been implemented. Resistance to ratification of CEDAW reflects the opposition of a powerful sector of society to the Convention's formulation of women's international human right to equality. This political resistance has also consistently blocked efforts to pass an Equal Rights Amendment, which would entrench women's right to equality in the U.S. Constitution. We strongly urge ratification of CEDAW and adoption in the Constitution of women's right to equality and non-discrimination as defined in the Convention.

The U.S. is one of only seven countries which have not ratified CEDAW. Even in the absence of ratification of CEDAW, many of its standards are entrenched in the Universal Declaration of Human Rights, the International Covenant on Civil and Political Rights(1) and in customary international law, and are hence binding on the U.S. Nevertheless, we are of the unreserved opinion that ratification of CEDAW is crucial, on both the domestic and the global levels, in order to confirm the U.S. commitment to substantive equality for women in all spheres of life. At the domestic level, ratification is essential in order to provide all U.S. women with rights and protections guaranteed under CEDAW. There is a myth that women already enjoy all these rights and protections under U.S. law. However, there are missing rights and protections such as universal paid maternity leave, accessible reproductive health care and equal opportunity in standing for political election.

We welcome the Cities for CEDAW initiatives which have started a process of incorporating CEDAW principles at the local level. This not only has intrinsic value for the women and men in those cities but it also serves to demonstrate the sustainability of women's international human rights standards in the U.S. context and can act as a lever for their further expansion.

As regards resistance to CEDAW, our visit is particularly timely at a moment when the political rhetoric of some of the candidates for the Presidency in the upcoming elections has included unprecedented hostile stereotyping of women; when there are increasingly restrictive legislative measures in some states and violent attacks to prevent women's access to exercise of their reproductive rights; and when there is an increase in the rate of women living in poverty, a persistent wage gap and increasingly precarious employment.

Public and Political Life

Four out of 15 members of cabinet are women. Women hold 19.4% of Congressional seats and their representation in state legislatures varies widely between 12.9% and 46.2%, with an average of 24.9%. This represents the highest level of legislative representation ever achieved by women in the United States. However, it still places the country at only 72 in global ranking.

According to several interlocutors, the low level of representation for women in elected political posts is partly due to the greater difficulties women face in fundraising for campaigns. The role of money in political campaigns has grown significantly in the last decades and has drastically altered the landscape for elections and political participation. Women's difficulty in fundraising is considered to result from complex causes. In particular, it is a result of exclusion from the predominantly male political networks that promote funding. It also results from underlying factors, such as negative stereotypes and biased presentation of women in the media, which adversely affect both women's fundraising ability and their political candidacy. It is our view that the claim that women have lesser political ambition should not be regarded as unrelated to all the other factors since these must act as a rational deterrent to women's political involvement. Our group regards the objective difficulties women face in raising campaign funding as a serious limitation on women's opportunities for political representation and is deeply concerned that the removal of limits on campaign funding by the Supreme Court threatens to exacerbate this situation. A small number of states and cities have started to use programs for public financing of campaigns. One method, which its supporters call "Clean Money, Clean Elections," gives each candidate who chooses to participate a fixed amount of money. Some interlocutors have pointed out that, in order to effectively give women an equal chance, competing private funding would have to be restricted. The Group encourages the efforts deployed by some voluntary organisations, such as Emily's List, which promote women candidates. We would like to recall that, in accordance with international human rights law requirements, temporary special measures have been adopted in many democratic countries to ensure more adequate representation of women in politics.

It is essential to ensure women's continued access to the voting booth. At present women vote in higher percentages than men. Our group is concerned that changes in voter identification laws, such as those in Alabama, which increase bureaucratic requirements for voter identification, in particular problematic for women who change their name in marriage and reduce the number of voting centers, can make registration and voting less accessible for the poor, of whom a majority are women. A counter example and good practice is the state of Oregon which has facilitated voter registration and voting by mail.

The courts play a central role in determining women's ability to enjoy and exercise the rights accorded to them by law. There has been an increase in global awareness of the need for gender diversity and gender sensitive adjudication in judiciaries. In the U.S., the number of women justices has increased significantly, with women justices constituting three out of the nine Supreme Court justices(2) and women constituting over a third of the judges in federal and in state courts. While the presence of female judges does not guarantee judicial decision-making which is in substance gender-sensitive, the importance of diversity remains and the increase in the number of women judges is a positive trend. A severe problem for women litigants is in access to justice: free legal counsel and aid is not systematic for women living in poverty and when legal aid is partially provided to the most destitute, it is allegedly of very poor quality. Furthermore, the institution of the class action which has allowed large numbers of women to access compensation for discrimination or injury caused by powerful corporations, is being eroded. Our group recommends that the issue of substantive equality for women in court proceedings be revisited and reinvigorated and that access to justice for all, with adequate legal representation, be regarded as a civil right which, where necessary, should be publically funded.

Economic and Social Life

The global economic crisis created a serious challenge for the realization of economic and social rights in the United States and had a significantly adverse impact on women. As noted previously by other U.N. independent experts, the subprime mortgage market had disparately targeted the poor and, in particular, poor women. Subsequent government policies to boost the economy resulted in decreased expenditures on critical social protection programs, many of which are essential for women. These cuts had a disproportionately negative impact on minority women and single mothers.

Women constitute nearly half of the U.S. labour force, at a participation rate of 57.0%, and have been an important factor in driving the last decades of U.S. economic growth. Furthermore, working mothers account for two thirds of household earnings. Our expert group is concerned that this crucial labour force participation by women is not accompanied by equal economic opportunity and we are shocked by the lack of mandatory standards for workplace accommodation for pregnant women, post-natal mothers and persons with care responsibilities, which are required in international human rights law.

The gender wage gap is 21%, affecting women's income throughout their lives, increasing women's pension poverty. During the last decade little improvement has been made in closing it. Education increases women's earnings but does not eliminate the gap, which is in fact largest for those with the highest levels of educational attainment. Women's earnings differ considerably by ethnicity: Afro-American, Native American and Hispanic women have the lowest earnings. Despite the existence of the 1963 Equal Pay Act and Title VII, federal law does not require equal pay for work of equal value. However, California has now set a precedent with its 2015 California Fair Pay Act thus applying for the first time in U.S. legislation the right to equal pay for work of equal value, which is required by international human rights law. Minimum wages have lost value as a living wage and the majority of minimum wage earners are women. Many are working full time and are the sole breadwinners for their families. Interlocutors regard the raising of the minimum wage to the level of a living wage as one of the most appropriate ways both to reduce the wage gap and reduce poverty amongst working women.

The estimated 2.5 million domestic workers in the U.S. are overwhelmingly women, frequently immigrant women many of whom are undocumented. We learned that many of these workers are vulnerable to verbal and physical abuse and to wage theft. We welcome the initiatives taken by the CSOs to improve conditions for domestic workers through a domestic workers' bill of rights. The Group calls for the U.S. to ratify the ILO Domestic Workers Convention and apply its provisions to ensure that domestic work is decent work. This does not capture the situation of other informal economy spaces, such as tip employees and seasonal jobs, where minimum conditions of employment should also be regulated.

An additional severe problem is lack of enforcement. Wage theft, particularly in manufacturing, construction, and some service jobs impacts low-income and migrant workers, in particular undocumented women. Our group welcomes the recent increase in the budget of the Wage and Hour Division (U.S. Department of Labor) to support investigations and urges the government to increase supervision and to hold employers who violate the rights of these particularly vulnerable women workers to account.

The 1993 Family and Medical Leave Act provides employees with the right to take unpaid, job-protected leave of twelve workweeks in a 12-month period, including for the birth of a child and to care for the newborn child within one year of birth; A significant number of employees are not covered by the Act because it is restricted, amongst other things, to employers who have more than 50 employees. However, even for those employees whom it covers, this provision falls far beneath international human rights standards, which require that maternity leave must be paid leave, with best practice being the provision of additional paid leave for fathers too. The U.S. is one of only two countries in the world without a mandatory paid maternity leave for all women workers. As of 2014, paid maternity leave is provided by legislation in 3 states and in Federal government employment but it is only for six weeks, which is beneath the international minimum of 14 weeks. The Group regards it as vital that 14 weeks paid maternity leave for pregnancy birth and post natal related needs be guaranteed for all women workers in public and private employment and advises that best practice is payment from a social security fund which does not impose the direct burden on employers.

Caring responsibilities fall primarily on women and women are reported to be far more likely than men to work only part time for family care reasons. Our expert group considers that the public budget should provide childcare, after-school and also elder and disabled facilities, which are affordable and accessible, to allow adults with care responsibilities, women and men, to work in full time employment.

The percentage of women in poverty has increased over the past decade, from 12.1% to 14.5%, with a higher rate of poverty than men, affecting predominantly ethnic minorities, single parent families and older women. We suggest that both Federal and state governments address this problem urgently, by promoting employment for women, raising the minimum wage and eliminating the wage gap. Residual poverty should be addressed through the social security system and, given the country's economic strength, there should be a policy of zero tolerance for the relegation of people to poverty.

Poverty may result in homelessness which exposes women to higher levels of violence and vulnerability. Furthermore, interlocutors pointed out that victims of domestic violence are often numbered amongst the homeless, either because they have been evicted as a result of the violence or because they have fled from their violent partner. Solutions should include effective protection orders, increased availability of shelters, housing support, prioritizing eligibility particularly for single mother households and those facing heavy unpaid care burdens.

We were informed that women own over one third of U.S. firms, mainly in small and medium size businesses. These businesses face greater barriers in obtaining low cost capital from sources such as the Small Business Administration and clearly need support in order to achieve equal economic potential. However, the Small Businesses Administration has a stated goal of awarding only 5% of federal contracts to women-owned businesses. Furthermore, it is reported that this goal has never been reached in practice.

International Human Rights Law requires the establishment of social protection floors for core economic and social needs, provision for paid maternity leave, and the taking of all appropriate measures to produce de facto equality between all women and men in the labour market and in women-owned businesses. It is not for our group to suggest how these minimum standards should be achieved but only to point out how the United States, as economic leader of the world, lags behind in providing a safety net and a decent life for those of its women who do not have access to independent wealth, high salaries or economic support from a partner or family.

Access to Health Care

The group acknowledges the legislative and institutional(3) efforts deployed towards improving the enjoyment of women's right to health. In particular, we welcome the steps taken by the current administration to expand access to health care for many uninsured citizens through the Affordable Care Act (ACA) passed in 2010(4), aimed at reducing the cost of health insurance and augmenting access to health care through the expansion of Medicaid, thus reducing the number of uninsured. ACA also established crucial protections against discriminatory practices consisting, inter alia, of charging women more for health insurance than men due to perceived higher costs associated with women's reproductive health needs.

Despite this considerable progress, there is still no universal health coverage in the country, and too many women pay the price, sometimes with their lives, of this considerable coverage gap with strong regional and ethnic disparities. According to the information we received, a third of the people living in poverty are still uninsured, affecting primarily women, in particular Afro-American and Hispanic women, preventing them from accessing basic preventive care and treatments. Furthermore, there are restrictions for immigrants, including immigrant women to access Medicaid during a five year waiting period and there is perpetual exclusion of undocumented migrants from any health care with the limited exception of emergency care. According to various stakeholders we met, Texas and Alabama do not allow lawfully residing immigrants to enrol in Medicaid even after completion of the federal waiting period of five years. We heard appalling testimonies of migrant women who were diagnosed with breast cancer but could not afford the appropriate treatment. The Group hopes that the Health Equity and Access under the Law (HEAL) for Immigrant Women and Families Act, currently before Congress, would expand access to health care for immigrants, particularly for women and children. Our Group also regretted to learn about the serious inadequacies of health care facilities to treat women with disabilities and calls for improvement.

Reproductive Health and Rights

Our expert Group is concerned at the increase in maternal mortality rates in the United States. According to U.N. reports, the ratio increased by 136% between 1990 and 2013. These numbers also hide distressing ethnic and socio-economic disparities. Afro-American women are nearly four times more at risk to die in childbirth. States with high poverty rates have a 77% higher maternal mortality rate. We strongly encourage concerned authorities to continue their efforts to identify the root causes and elaborate adequate policies to address this issue.

Our group welcomes the ACA's requirement that new private health plans cover contraceptive counselling, without out-of-pocket costs. However, we are concerned that the Supreme Court's recognition, in Hobby Lobby, of an exemption on grounds of freedom of religion to opt out of contraceptive insurance for employees, will deprive some women of the possibility of accessing contraceptives. The Group would like to recall that, under international human rights law, states must take all appropriate measures to ensure women's equal right to decide freely and responsibly on the number and spacing of their children which includes women's right to access contraceptives.

Our Group was informed that, being a prerogative of each state, adequate and quality sex education in schools was lacking in many curricula. We learned that in many schools, only abstinence was taught instead of providing objective and scientifically based sex education which is a key element of health policy. However, we were pleased to learn that in Oregon for instance, sex education is included in the school curriculum.

Women's reproductive rights include the constitutional guarantee under Roe v. Wade for a woman to be able to choose to terminate a pregnancy in the first trimester prior to viability. Although women have a legal right to terminate a pregnancy under federal law, ever increasing barriers are being created to prevent their access to abortion procedures. In 1976 the Hyde Amendment prevented federal Medicaid and Medicare coverage for the termination of a pregnancy except in cases where the life of the woman is in danger, in cases of rape and incest. Women's access to reproductive health services has been truncated in some states by imposition of severe barriers. These take the form of unjustified medical procedures, such as compelling women to undergo ultrasounds or to endure groundless waiting periods, withholding of early pregnancy abortion medications, imposing burdensome conditions for the licensing of clinics, which have resulted in the closing of clinics across the country leaving women without geographical access to sexual and reproductive health services. These restrictions have a disproportionate and discriminatory impact on poor women. As we observed during our visit in the Rio Grande Valley, one of the poorest regions in the country, immigrant women face severe barriers in accessing sexual and reproductive health services. Furthermore, the marketplace insurance coverage for a safe and legal termination of pregnancy is far from universal. Thus, insurance will frequently not be available for women who wish to exercise their right to terminate their pregnancy in the first trimester.

In addition, many of the clinics work in conditions of constant threats, harassment and vandalising, too often without any kind of protection measures by law enforcement officials, as we observed during our visits to Texas and Alabama. Alabama has a history of severe violence against abortion providers including the killing of Dr. David Gunn, in 1993, the first doctor to be murdered for performing abortions in the United States. The recent massacre in the Colorado family planning centre, which occurred just before the start of our visit, once again demonstrated the extreme hostility and danger faced by family planning providers and patients.

We encourage the adoption of the Woman's Health Protection Act, which would prohibit states from enacting restrictions on reproductive health care providers that interfere with women's personal decision making and block access to safe and legal abortion services; and to require all hospitals to provide these services and insurance schemes to provide coverage for abortions to which women have a right under U.S. law. We also encourage increased funding of clinics under the Title X Family Planning Program(5) in order to expand coverage for low-income women who lack insurance in order for them to access preventive care, including sexual and reproductive health services, and in order to reduce maternal mortality.

We urge the authorities to combat the stigma attached to reproductive and sexual health care, which leads to violence, harassment and intimidation against those seeking or providing reproductive health care, and to investigate and prosecute violence or threats of violence. We wish to recall, as independent United Nations human rights experts have consistently stressed, that freedom of religion cannot be used to justify discrimination against women, and therefore should not be regarded as a justification for denying women's right to enjoyment of the highest attainable standard of health. We encourage steps to reconcile U.S. laws on religious or conscience-based refusals to provide reproductive health care with international human rights law and to prohibit refusal to provide sexual and reproductive health services on grounds of religious freedom, where such refusal will effectively deny women immediate access to the health care to which they are entitled under both international human rights law and U.S. law.

Women's Safety

Our group acknowledges the significant efforts deployed at the legislative(6) and institutional(7) levels to lower the prevalence of violence against women. We share the concerns expressed by the Special Rapporteur on violence against women in her report on her visit to the United States in 2011(8), regarding, inter alia, women in detention (over-incarceration, sexual violence, shackling of pregnant women, solitary confinement, lack of alternatives to custodial sentences for women with dependent children, inappropriate access to health care and inadequate re-entry programmes) as well as the alarming high rates of violence against Native-American women. We also share the concerns of the Special Rapporteur regarding the fatal consequences for women of lack of gun control, in particular in cases of domestic violence. Our group also deplores police brutality and the increased number of homicides of Afro-American women by the police. Our attention was also drawn to numerous cases of violence against LBTQ women, including homicides.

We are extremely concerned at the situation of migrant women in detention centers, in particular women with minor children who are in prolonged detention. According to the information received, detention facilities are not complying with federal mandates and agency policies. We received allegations of women being subjected to an "expedited removal process" which in spite of the credible fear of return exception, results in the denial of many legitimate asylum claims. We also received allegations of sexual abuse and assault of women detainees, as well as mistreatment from CBP officials. Migrant women are often victims of trafficking and violence, including sexual violence during their journey to the United States. We regretted to learn that appropriate health care services are not systematically provided to these women in a timely manner despite the horrifying physical and emotional ordeals endured. We also received complaints of transgender women being mistreated in detention often wrongfully placed with males. The group encourages the establishment of accountability mechanisms and adequate gender sensitive training as well as the release of women and children from detention.

The criminalization of women in prostitution in most of the country places them in a situation of injustice, vulnerability and stigma and is contrary to international human rights law. As the CEDAW Committee has systematically reiterated, women should not be criminalized for being in a situation of prostitution. Furthermore, as stipulated in the Palermo Protocol, efforts should be deployed to discourage the demand that fosters all forms of exploitation of women.

Conclusions

We want to reiterate our gratitude to the Government for inviting our expert group to conduct this visit and for engaging in frank and open dialogue. The current administration has demonstrated its will to cooperate with the international human rights mechanisms: the UPR, the Committee on the Elimination of Racial Discrimination, the Human Rights Committee and the Committee against Torture and has invited numerous special procedures. Nonetheless, we note that there is no proper institutional framework to follow-up on recommendations received. In this regard, we would like to insist on the importance of establishing an independent human rights institution in compliance with the Paris Principles (which should include a woman's rights commission).

While the current administration has consistently expressed its unconditional support for the cause of women's equality, we regret to observe a gap between rhetoric and reality. As many stakeholders have underscored, the extreme polarisation of politics is profoundly affecting the ability of the Government to ratify CEDAW and to guarantee women's human rights. We understand the complexity of federalism but this cannot be regarded as a justification for failure to secure these rights. Under the Vienna Declaration, these rights are universal, indivisible and inalienable.

The United States, which is a leading state in formulating international human rights standards, is allowing its women to lag behind international human rights standards. Although there is a wide diversity in state law and practice, which makes it impossible to give a comprehensive report, we could discern an overall picture of women's missing rights. While all women are the victims of these missing rights, women who are poor, belong to Native American, Afro-American and Hispanic ethnic minorities, migrant women, LBTQ women, women with disabilities and older women are disparately vulnerable.

These preliminary findings and conclusions will be developed and presented in a more comprehensive report to the Human Rights Council in June 2016.

The U.N. Working Group on the issue of discrimination against women in law and in practice was created by the Human Rights Council in 2011 to identify, promote and exchange views, in consultation with States and other actors, on good practices related to the elimination of laws that discriminate against women. The Group is also tasked with developing a dialogue with States and other actors on laws that have a discriminatory impact where women are concerned. The Working Group is composed of five independent experts: the Current Chair-Rapporteur Eleonora Zielinska (Poland), the Vice-Chair Alda Facio (Costa Rica) and the other members Emna Aouij (Tunisia), Kamala Chandrakirana (Indonesia), and Frances Raday (Israel/United Kingdom).

Source: U.N. High Commissioner on Human Rights Press Release, 11 December 2015 http://www.ohchr.org/EN/NewsEvents/Pages/DisplayNews.aspx?NewsID=16872&LangID=E

7. INTER-AMERICAN CONVENTION ON THE PREVENTION, PUNISHMENT AND ERADICATION OF VIOLENCE AGAINST WOMEN "CONVENTION OF BELÉM DO PARÁ"

This is excerpted from the Inter-American Convention on the Prevention, Punishment and Eradication of Violence Against Women "Convention of Belem Do Para," a regional treaty of the Organization of American States. The U.S. did not sign or ratify this treaty.

THE STATES PARTIES TO THIS CONVENTION,

RECOGNIZING that full respect for human rights has been enshrined in the American Declaration of the Rights and Duties of Man and the Universal Declaration of Human Rights, and reaffirmed in other international and regional instruments;

AFFIRMING that violence against women constitutes a violation of their human rights and fundamental freedoms, and impairs or nullifies the observance, enjoyment and exercise of such rights and freedoms;

CONCERNED that violence against women is an offense against human dignity and a manifestation of the historically unequal power relations between women and men;

RECALLING the Declaration on the Elimination of Violence against Women, adopted by the Twenty-fifth Assembly of Delegates of the Inter-American Commission of Women, and affirming that violence against women pervades every sector of society regardless of class, race or ethnic group, income, culture, level of education, age or religion and strikes at its very foundations:

CONVINCED that the elimination of violence against women is essential for their individual and social development and their full and equal participation in all walks of life; and

CONVINCED that the adoption of a convention on the prevention, punishment and eradication of all forms of violence against women within the framework of the Organization of American States is a positive contribution to protecting the rights of women and eliminating violence against them,

HAVE AGREED to the following:

CHAPTER I

Definition and Scope of Application

Article 1
For the purposes of this Convention, violence against women shall be understood as any act or conduct, based on gender, which causes death or physical, sexual or psychological harm or suffering to women, whether in the public or the private sphere.

Article 2
Violence against women shall be understood to include physical, sexual and psychological violence:

a. that occurs within the family or domestic unit or within any other interpersonal relationship, whether or not the perpetrator shares or has shared the same residence with the woman, including, among others, rape, battery and sexual abuse;

b. that occurs in the community and is perpetrated by any person, including, among others, rape, sexual abuse, torture, trafficking in persons, forced prostitution, kidnapping and sexual harassment in the workplace, as well as in educational institutions, health facilities or any other place; and

c. that is perpetrated or condoned by the state or its agents regardless of where it occurs.

CHAPTER II

Rights Protected

Article 3
Every woman has the right to be free from violence in both the public and private spheres.

Article 4

Every woman has the right to the recognition, enjoyment, exercise and protection of all human rights and freedoms embodied in regional and international human rights instruments. These rights include, among others:

a. The right to have her life respected;

b. The right to have her physical, mental and moral integrity respected;

c. The right to personal liberty and security;

d. The right not to be subjected to torture;

e. The rights to have the inherent dignity of her person respected and her family protected;

f. The right to equal protection before the law and of the law;

g. The right to simple and prompt recourse to a competent court for protection against acts that violate her rights;

h. The right to associate freely;

i. The right of freedom to profess her religion and beliefs within the law; and

j. The right to have equal access to the public service of her country and to take part in the conduct of public affairs, including decision-making.

Article 5

Every woman is entitled to the free and full exercise of her civil, political, economic, social and cultural rights, and may rely on the full protection of those rights as embodied in regional and international instruments on human rights. The States Parties recognize that violence against women prevents and nullifies the exercise of these rights.

Article 6

The right of every woman to be free from violence includes, among others:

a. The right of women to be free from all forms of discrimination; and

b. The right of women to be valued and educated free of stereotyped patterns of behavior and social and cultural practices based on concepts of inferiority or subordination.

CHAPTER III

Duties of the States

Article 7

The States Parties condemn all forms of violence against women and agree to pursue, by all appropriate means and without delay, policies to prevent, punish and eradicate such violence and undertake to:

a. refrain from engaging in any act or practice of violence against women and to ensure that their authorities, officials, personnel, agents, and institutions act in conformity with this obligation;

b. apply due diligence to prevent, investigate and impose penalties for violence against women;

c. include in their domestic legislation penal, civil, administrative and any other type of provisions that may be needed to prevent, punish and eradicate violence against women and to adopt appropriate administrative measures where necessary;

d. adopt legal measures to require the perpetrator to refrain from harassing, intimidating or threatening the woman or using any method that harms or endangers her life or integrity, or damages her property;

e. take all appropriate measures, including legislative measures, to amend or repeal existing laws and regulations or to modify legal or customary practices which sustain the persistence and tolerance of violence against women;

f. establish fair and effective legal procedures for women who have been subjected to violence which include, among others, protective measures, a timely hearing and effective access to such procedures;

g. establish the necessary legal and administrative mechanisms to ensure that women subjected to violence have effective access to restitution, reparations or other just and effective remedies; and

h. adopt such legislative or other measures as may be necessary to give effect to this Convention.

Article 8
The States Parties agree to undertake progressively specific measures, including programs:

a. to promote awareness and observance of the right of women to be free from violence, and the right of women to have their human rights respected and protected;

b. to modify social and cultural patterns of conduct of men and women, including the development of formal and informal educational programs appropriate to every level of the educational process, to counteract prejudices, customs and all other practices which are based on the idea of the inferiority or superiority of either of the sexes or on the stereotyped roles for men and women which legitimize or exacerbate violence against women;

c. to promote the education and training of all those involved in the administration of justice, police and other law enforcement officers as well as other personnel responsible for implementing policies for the prevention, punishment and eradication of violence against women;

d. to provide appropriate specialized services for women who have been subjected to violence, through public and private sector agencies, including shelters, counseling services for all family members where appropriate, and care and custody of the affected children;

e. to promote and support governmental and private sector education designed to raise the awareness of the public with respect to the problems of and remedies for violence against women;

f. to provide women who are subjected to violence access to effective readjustment and training programs to enable them to fully participate in public, private and social life;

g. to encourage the communications media to develop appropriate media guidelines in order to contribute to the eradication of violence against women in all its forms, and to enhance respect for the dignity of women;

h. to ensure research and the gathering of statistics and other relevant information relating to the causes, consequences and frequency of violence against women, in order to assess the effectiveness of measures to prevent, punish and eradicate violence against women and to formulate and implement the necessary changes; and

i. to foster international cooperation for the exchange of ideas and experiences and the execution of programs aimed at protecting women who are subjected to violence.

Article 9
With respect to the adoption of the measures in this Chapter, the States Parties shall take special account of the vulnerability of women to violence by reason of, among others, their race or ethnic background or their status as migrants, refugees or displaced persons. Similar consideration shall be given to women subjected to violence while pregnant or who are disabled, of minor age, elderly, socioeconomically disadvantaged, affected by armed conflict or deprived of their freedom.

CHAPTER IV

Inter-American Mechanisms of Protection

Article 10
In order to protect the rights of every woman to be free from violence, the States Parties shall include in their national reports to the Inter-American Commission of Women information on measures adopted to prevent and prohibit violence against women, and to assist women affected by violence, as well as on any difficulties they observe in applying those measures, and the factors that contribute to violence against women.

Article 11
The States Parties to this Convention and the Inter-American Commission of Women may request of the Inter-American Court of Human Rights advisory opinions on the interpretation of this Convention.

Article 12
Any person or group of persons, or any nongovernmental entity legally recognized in one or more member states of the Organization, may lodge petitions with the Inter-American Commission on Human Rights containing denunciations or complaints of violations of Article 7 of this Convention by a State Party, and the Commission shall consider such claims in accordance with the norms and procedures established by the American Convention on Human Rights and the Statutes and Regulations of the Inter-American Commission on Human Rights for lodging and considering petitions.

CHAPTER V

General Provisions

Article 13
No part of this Convention shall be understood to restrict or limit the domestic law of any State Party that affords equal or greater protection and guarantees of the rights of women and appropriate safeguards to prevent and eradicate violence against women.

Article 14
No part of this Convention shall be understood to restrict or limit the American Convention on Human Rights or any other international convention on the subject that provides for equal or greater protection in this area.

Article 15
This Convention is open to signature by all the member states of the Organization of American States.

Article 16
This Convention is subject to ratification. The instruments of ratification shall be deposited with the General Secretariat of the Organization of American States.

Article 17
This Convention is open to accession by any other state. Instruments of accession shall be deposited with the General Secretariat of the Organization of American States.

Article 18
Any State may, at the time of approval, signature, ratification, or accession, make reservations to this Convention provided that such reservations are:

a. not incompatible with the object and purpose of the Convention, and

b. not of a general nature and relate to one or more specific provisions.

Article 19

Any State Party may submit to the General Assembly, through the Inter-American Commission of Women, proposals for the amendment of this Convention.

Amendments shall enter into force for the states ratifying them on the date when two-thirds of the States Parties to this Convention have deposited their respective instruments of ratification. With respect to the other States Parties, the amendments shall enter into force on the dates on which they deposit their respective instruments of ratification.

Article 20

If a State Party has two or more territorial units in which the matters dealt with in this Convention are governed by different systems of law, it may, at the time of signature, ratification or accession, declare that this Convention shall extend to all its territorial units or to only one or more of them.

Such a declaration may be amended at any time by subsequent declarations, which shall expressly specify the territorial unit or units to which this Convention applies. Such subsequent declarations shall be transmitted to the General Secretariat of the Organization of American States, and shall enter into force thirty days after the date of their receipt.

Article 21

This Convention shall enter into force on the thirtieth day after the date of deposit of the second instrument of ratification. For each State that ratifies or accedes to the Convention after the second instrument of ratification is deposited, it shall enter into force thirty days after the date on which that State deposited its instrument of ratification or accession.

Article 22

The Secretary General shall inform all member states of the Organization of American States of the entry into force of this Convention.

Article 23

The Secretary General of the Organization of American States shall present an annual report to the member states of the Organization on the status of this Convention, including the signatures, deposits of instruments of ratification and accession, and declarations, and any reservations that may have been presented by the States Parties, accompanied by a report thereon if needed.

Article 24

This Convention shall remain in force indefinitely, but any of the States Parties may denounce it by depositing an instrument to that effect with the General Secretariat of the Organization of American States. One year after the date of deposit of the instrument of denunciation, this Convention shall cease to be in effect for the denouncing State but shall remain in force for the remaining States Parties.

Article 25

The original instrument of this Convention, the English, French, Portuguese and Spanish texts of which are equally authentic, shall be deposited with the General Secretariat of the Organization of American States, which shall send a certified copy to the Secretariat of the United Nations for registration and publication in accordance with the provisions of Article 102 of the United Nations Charter.

IN WITNESS WHEREOF the undersigned Plenipotentiaries, being duly authorized thereto by their respective governments, have signed this Convention, which shall be called the Inter-American Convention on the Prevention, Punishment and Eradication of Violence against Women "Convention of Belém do Pará."

DONE IN THE CITY OF BELEM DO PARA, BRAZIL, the ninth of June in the year one thousand nine hundred ninety-four.

Immigration, Migrant Workers, Refugees & Asylum

Chapter 13

This Chapter is About immigration, migrant workers, and refugees and asylum, controversial subjects not only in the U.S., but also globally, especially in Europe and the Middle East, particularly in the context of the war on terror and the real fear of terrorists coming into a country to do harm.

This is Important Because immigrants, migrant workers, and refugees are the bearers of human rights like every other human being, wherever they are. Sometimes national laws and policies affect these people in ways that engage and violate their human rights; for example, freedom of movement or the right to work. Immigrants, migrant workers, and refugees have been beaten, murdered, abused, and commercially and sexually exploited all over the world. Given their large number in the U.S., especially of undocumented immigrants, this issue was key in the 2016 presidential election, and Congress has been unable to legislate to remediate this problem.

The U.S. has long had extensive and evolving law and policy regarding these groups — how to lawfully immigrate, what to do about those who do so unlawfully, and how one goes about claiming and proving refugee status and seeking a grant of asylum in the U.S. This chapter is especially important because, at present, the system is not working.

Quotes & Key Text Excerpts

Give me your tired, your poor, Your huddled masses yearning to breathe free,

The wretched refuse of your teeming shore. Send these, the homeless, tempest-tossed to me, I lift my lamp beside the golden door!

—*Emma Lazarus, "New Colossus," poem about Statue of Liberty*

Source: https://www.howtallisthestatueofliberty.org/what-is-the-quote-on-the-statue-of-liberty/

Article 1

All human beings are born free and equal in dignity and rights. They are endowed with reason and conscience and should act towards one another in a spirit of brotherhood.

Article 2

Everyone is entitled to all the rights and freedoms set forth in this Declaration, without distinction of any kind, such as race, colour, sex, language, religion, political or other opinion, national or social origin, property, birth or other status. Furthermore, no distinction shall be made on the basis of the political, jurisdictional or international status of the country or territory to which a person belongs, whether it be independent, trust, non-self-governing or under any other limitation of sovereignty.

Article 3

Everyone has the right to life, liberty and security of person.

Article 14

1. Everyone has the right to seek and to enjoy in other countries asylum from persecution.

Article 29

1. Everyone has duties to the community in which alone the free and full development of his personality is possible

—*The Universal Declaration of Human Rights*

The States Parties to the present Covenant,

Considering that, in accordance with the principles proclaimed in the Charter of the United Nations, recognition of the inherent dignity and of the equal and inalienable rights of all members of the human family is the foundation of freedom, justice and peace in the world,

Recognizing that these rights derive from the inherent dignity of the human person,

Recognizing that, in accordance with the Universal Declaration of Human Rights, the ideal of free human beings enjoying civil and political freedom and freedom from fear and want can only be achieved if conditions are created whereby everyone may enjoy his civil and political rights, as well as his economic, social and cultural rights,

Article 2

Each State Party to the present Covenant undertakes to respect and to ensure to all individuals within its territory and subject to its jurisdiction the rights recognized in the present Covenant, without distinction of any kind, such as race, colour, sex, language, religion, political or other opinion, national or social origin, property, birth or other status.

Article 9

Everyone has the right to liberty and security of person. No one shall be subjected to arbitrary arrest or detention. No one shall be deprived of his liberty except on such grounds and in accordance with such procedure as are established by law.

...

Anyone who is deprived of his liberty by arrest or detention shall be entitled to take proceedings before a court, in order that that court may decide without delay on the lawfulness of his detention and order his release if the detention is not lawful.

Article 10

All persons deprived of their liberty shall be treated with humanity and with respect for the inherent dignity of the human person.

...

Article 13

An alien lawfully in the territory of a State Party to the present Covenant may be expelled therefrom only in pursuance of a decision reached in accordance with law and shall, except where compelling reasons of national security otherwise require, be allowed to submit the reasons against his expulsion and to have his case reviewed by, and be represented for the purpose before, the competent authority or a person or persons especially designated by the competent authority.

Article 14

All persons shall be equal before the courts and tribunals. In the determination of any criminal charge against him, or of his rights and obligations in a suit at law, everyone shall be entitled to a fair and public hearing by a competent, independent and impartial tribunal established by law.

Article 26

All persons are equal before the law and are entitled without any discrimination to the equal protection of the law. In this respect, the law shall prohibit any discrimination and guarantee to all persons equal and effective protection against discrimination on any ground such as race, colour, sex, language, religion, political or other opinion, national or social origin, property, birth or other status.

—*The International Covenant on Civil and Political Rights*

Source: http://www.ohchr.org/en/professionalinterest/pages/ccpr.aspx

I had always hoped that this land might become a safe and agreeable asylum to the virtuous and per-secuted part of mankind, to whatever nation they might belong.

—*President George Washington*

Remember, remember always, that all of us, and you and I especially, are descended from immigrants and revolutionists.

—*President Franklin D. Roosevelt*

You who are so-called illegal aliens must know that no human being is 'illegal.' That is a contradiction in terms. Human beings can be beautiful or more beautiful, they can be fat or skinny, they can be right or wrong, but illegal? How can a human being be illegal?

—*Elie Wiesel, Nobel Laureate, Holocaust Survivor*

What You Should Know

Values and Immigration

In its 2010 National Report to the U.N. Human Rights Council for its Universal Periodic Review Process, the U.S. government stated to the Council the following, concerning human rights and values involved in immigration in America:

> That immigrants have been consistently drawn to our shores throughout our history is both a testament to and a source of the strength and appeal of our vibrant democracy. As he left office, President Reagan remarked that the United States is "still a beacon, still a magnet for all who must have freedom, for all the pilgrims from all the lost places who are hurtling through the darkness, toward home." Over the last 50 years, the U.S. has accepted several million refugees fleeing persecution from all corners of the globe as well as many millions of immigrants seeking a better life or joining family. Today, the United States and other countries to which a significant number of people seek to emigrate face challenges in developing and enforcing immigration laws and policies that reflect economic, social, and national security realities. In addressing these issues, we seek to build a system of immigration enforcement that is both effective and fair.

Since that time, the subject of immigration, migrant workers, and refugees has been very controversial, and the U.S. Congress has tried to address it without success. It is an issue that has divided America and took center stage in the 2016 presidential election. It is a critical issue facing many countries in the world.

Under international law, every state has sovereignty. One aspect of the right to sovereignty is the right to determine and legislate who can enter and stay in the country and under what conditions. Every state can determine the criteria for admissibility as to who can enter the country as an immigrant or other status, such as tourist, and set rules for who can be excluded and how one can lose legal status and be subject to removal, once called deportation.

Let it be emphasized at the outset that nothing in international law forces a state to let certain persons enter or remain in the state. Sovereignty allows the state this sole prerogative. The U.S. has copious and complex legislation and regulations on immigration, migrant workers, and refugees. The Constitution itself gives "plenary" power over these areas to Congress for legislation to be carried out by the administration with the compliance of state governments. But more and more, it has become clear that the problems have outstripped the law, and the sheer size of these alien populations has become unmanageable and problematic. In light of historical injustices to these groups, international law has much to say about this topic and the protection that states and the international community must give to these populations.

Definitions

Migrant/Immigration

Immigration is about immigrants, and immigrants are a certain kind of people based on their action of migrating. The term migrant can be understood as "any person who lives temporarily or permanently in a country where he or she was not born, and has acquired some significant social ties to this country." For some, this definition may be too narrow when considering that, according to some states' policies, a person can be considered as a migrant even when she/he is born in the country. When migrants arrive at the border with the intent to enter another country, they are immigrants. An immigrant is a person who enters a country with the intent to reside indefinitely or permanently in that state in which he or she is not a citizen. Persons who come as tourists or for short visits or limited work assignments are not immigrants. They can, however, change their intent after entering and become immigrants whether legally or illegally. Immigrants are either "documented," also called "legal immigrants," or are without lawful and documented authorization and are thus not lawful immigrants, commonly called "undocumented" or "illegal immigrants." This latter term should not be used, because no person can be called illegal, which implies a criminal act or criminalization of a person. Being in the U.S. without legal status may or may not be the result of a criminal act. The exclusion or removal of aliens from the U.S. is a civil administrative matter and not a criminal matter.

Migrants are people who make choices about when to leave and where to go, even though these choices are sometimes extremely limited or even coerced.

The definition of migrant in international law is broad. This broad definition of migrants reflects the current difficulty in distinguishing between migrants who leave their countries because of political persecution, conflicts, economic problems, environmental degradation, or a combination of these reasons, and those who do so in search of conditions of survival or well-being that does not exist in their place of origin. The definition also attempts to define migrant population in a way that takes new situations into consideration.

Migrant Worker
The U.N. Convention on the Rights of Migrants defines a migrant worker as a "person who is to be engaged, is engaged, or has been engaged in a remunerated activity in a State of which he or she is not a national."

America has many migrant workers. The need for laws applicable to them is obvious.

Globally, the issue of migrant workers has become so serious that the international community has adopted a human rights treaty seeking to protect their rights.

Refugees
It is important not to confuse the terms immigrants, aliens, migrants, and refugees. They are not the same. In United States law, a refugee is defined as "any person who is outside any country of such person's nationality, or in the case of a person having no nationality, is outside any country in which such person last habitually resided, and who is unable or unwilling to return to, and is unable or unwilling to avail himself or herself of the protection of that country because of persecution or a well-founded fear of persecution on account of race, religion, nationality, membership in a particular social group, or political opinion...." This is similar to the international definition found in the 1951 Refugee Convention, below:

> [a person who] owing to well-founded fear of being persecuted for reasons of race, religion, nationality, membership of a particular social group or political opinion, is outside the country of his nationality and is unable, or owing to such fear, is unwilling to avail himself of the protection of that country; or who, not having a nationality and being outside the country of his former habitual residence as a result of such events, is unable or, owing to such fear, is unwilling to return to it.

A person who meets those criteria is known as a convention refugee, as opposed to a non-convention refugee, such as a person fleeing a civil war. Most persons one sees on television reports are not convention refugees, especially if they are fleeing generalized violence. They may still need legal protection but not under the refugee/asylum legal framework.

In a non-legal sense, a refugee is a person who flees from his country to another, seeking safety and protection from the things from which he fled (persecution, civil war, poverty). A person is seeking refuge from harm. For the conventional refugee, the harm is the violation of his or her human rights by his or her own government that is supposed to be protecting and respecting the human rights of its citizens.

Most often, refugee is used in the United States to describe someone who is seeking asylum in the United States. Asylum is legal protection offered by one country to someone who fled from another country because of persecution, and who meets all the criteria of the status of refugee. Refugee in this sense is a legal status. In order to receive asylum in the United States, a person first has to meet the criteria of being a refugee under U.S. law.

Source: https://www.uscis.gov/laws/immigration-and-nationality-act

Main issues: who gets permission to enter the U.S. as either immigrants or non-immigrants; how and when do persons lose their legal status to be in the U.S.; which aliens are removable persons; how and why are aliens apprehended; when and how are aliens detained; what legal recourse do aliens have to challenge removal, the right to work, the right to public benefits, the rights of their children, legal or illegal, separation of families; and when do aliens become citizens. All of these issues are covered by U.S. law.

U.S. Law

The U.S. Constitution granted all power over immigration to the federal government, specifically to Congress. Congress has been legislating in this area for a long time. The main source of U.S. legislation on aliens and nationality is found in title 8 of the United States Code, and is based on the Immigration and Nationalty Act of 1952. According to the U.S. Customs and Immigration Service (USCIS), which is the agency of the Department of Homeland Security charged with handling immigration:

> The Immigration and Nationality Act, or INA, was created in 1952. Before the INA, a variety of statutes governed immigration law but were not organized in one location. The McCarran-Walter bill of 1952, Public Law No. 82-414, collected and codified many existing provisions and reorganized the structure of immigration law. The Act has been amended many times over the years, but is still the basic body of immigration law.

Source: https://www.uscis.gov/laws/immigration-and-nationality-act

Much of the migrant worker law has been covered by non-immigrant visas, though much of the alien migrant workers are covered by the Immigration Reform and Control Act of 1986, which made it illegal to knowingly hire undocumented aliens or others lacking identity and government authorization.

Several other amendments have changed immigration law; but in the 21st century, with an estimated 11.1 million undocumented aliens in the U.S., Congress has been struggling to come up with a comprehensive immigration law, which both republicans and democrats accept. The U.S. Congress has been unable to pass a comprehensive immigration bill which would include some kind of legal status for the estimated undocumented aliens living in the U.S.

Because of the Congressional stalemate, President Obama tried to get around the logjam by issuing Executive Orders. He created a procedure granting Deferred Action on Childhood Arrivals, the DACA program. This program allowed many young, undocumented who were brought to the U.S. as children, to be able to obtain a quasi legal, though temporary status in the U.S. Many people received DACA status. The Obama administration then sought to create another program for parents of U.S. citizens and permanent residents with approved visa petitions, who were in the U.S. unlawfully. This would allow them to stay in the U.S. until they could become legalized. It was called the Deferred Action for Parents of Americans and Lawful Permanent Residents (DAPA) program. The objective of the two programs was to protect certain young aliens and family unity while awaiting Congress to pass legislation allowing these people to immigrate or at least legalize lawfully. These programs were brought to court by certain state governors, and the U.S. Supreme Court ruled against the Obama administration and continued the injunction against both programs, excepting those persons who had already been granted DACA status.

Refugee law is also found in the U.S. Code title 8, sec. 1158, and in title 8 of the Code of Federal Regulations, and it defines a refugee and the conditions under which the U.S., through the Attorney General, can grant asylum to a refugee under the statute. It also indicates bars and exclusions to refugee status and granting asylum.

International Law Sources

The following international laws are applicable to immigrants, migrants workers, and refugees:

International Human Rights Law:
- Universal Declaration of Human Rights (as customary international law, at least regarding 'hard core' rights)
- International Covenant on Civil and Political Rights
- International Covenant on Economic, Social and Cultural Rights (even though not legally binding, it should be cited because of its extensive acceptance by most nations of the world)

- International Convention on the Elimination of all Forms of Racial Discrimination (which defines race as including "race, colour, descent, or national or ethnic origin")
- International Convention against Torture, Cruel, Inhuman or Degrading Treatment or Punishment (most particularly regarding detention issues)
- Convention on the Rights of the Child
- Convention on the Protection of All Rights of Migrant Workers and Their Families
- Convention on the Prevention and Punishment of the Crime of Genocide

This list is not comprehensive; there are other treaties, such as on nationality and statelessness, and discrimination against women, which might apply in certain situations.

International Humanitarian Law:
- Geneva Convention IV of 1949 (protection of civilians in armed conflict)
- Protocols I and II of 1977 to the Geneva Conventions (protection of civilians in armed conflict)

International Refugee Law:
- Convention Relating to the Status of Refugees 1951
- Protocol to the Convention Relating to Refugees 1967
- Cartagena Declaration on Refugees 1984 (non-binding on U.S., applies to states in western hemisphere including the U.S. as a regional concept of treatment of refugees)
- The Principle of Non-Refoulement, which is a principle of customary international law prohibiting the expulsion, deportation, return, or extradition of an alien to his state of origin or another state where there is a risk that his life or freedom would be threatened for discriminatory reasons. It is applied in treaty law in Article 33 of the Refugee Convention and Article 3.1 of the Torture Convention.

International Criminal Law:

It is conceivable that certain acts, such as a widespread or systematic attack on migrants, could engage international criminal responsibility in certain situations. The U.S. interfaces with the international community in several places where international human rights law and refugee and humanitarian law come into play and is the dominant discourse of an issue.

1. The United Nations

The U.S. is involved in these areas of law regarding aliens at the U.N. through: treaty bodies and the Human Rights Council.

a. Treaty Bodies

The human rights treaty bodies ratified by the U.S. are: the Human Rights Committee under the ICCPR; the Committee on Elimination of Racial Discrimination under ICERD; the Committee against Torture under the Torture Convention; the Committee on the Rights of the Child under the Convention on the Rights of the Child.

U.S. law, policy, and practice is evaluated in light of international legal standards in regards to periodic states' reports by the U.S.

An example of a state report on immigration submitted to a treaty body can be seen in the following excerpt, taken from the U.S. Fourth Report to the Human Rights Committee:

Law with regard to aliens:

101. As noted in the Second and Third Periodic Report, under United States immigration law, an alien is "any person not a citizen or national of the United States," 8 U.S.C. 1101(a) (3). As a matter of U.S. law, aliens within the territory of the United States, regardless of their immigration status, enjoy robust protections under the U.S. Constitution and other domestic laws. Many of these protections are shared on an equal basis with citizens, including a broad range of

protections against racial and national origin discrimination. In particular, the Supreme Court has held that the equal protection and due process protections of the Fourteenth Amendment "are universal in their application, to all persons within the territorial jurisdiction, without regard to any differences of race, of color, or of nationality." *Yick Wo v. Hopkins*, 118 U.S. 356,369 (1886). Similarly, the Court has held that aliens are "person[s]" within the meaning of the due process protections of the Fifth Amendment. See Kwong Hai Chew, 344 U.S. at 596 &n.5; *Zadvydas v. Davis*, 533 U.S. 678, 693 (2001) ("[T]he Due Process Clause applies to all 'persons' within the United States, including aliens, whether their presence here is lawful, unlawful, temporary, or permanent.") Among other protections afforded to aliens within the United States, aliens, like citizens, are entitled to the constitutional guarantee against cruel and unusual punishment and slavery and involuntary servitude.

102. In addition to the constitutional protections afforded to aliens, many federal statutes provide aliens with further protections against discrimination. Many of these statutes were enacted because of the recognition that aliens may be especially vulnerable and may require additional protections against discrimination, particularly in the employment arena. These federal civil rights laws prohibit discrimination on the basis of race, color, and national origin, and apply to both citizens and aliens.

Law with regards to removal (expulsion) of aliens:

257. Removal. Aliens who are physically present in the United States may be placed in "removal" proceedings under the INA. Aliens who were admitted (inspected and authorized by an immigration officer upon arrival) are charged as "deportable" when placed into removal proceedings. See 8 U.S.C. 1227 et seq. Aliens who have not been admitted are charged as "inadmissible." See 8 U.S.C. 1182 et seq.

258. Removal hearing. In general, proceedings before an immigration judge commence when DHS issues a Notice to Appear (NTA), charging the alien as deportable or inadmissible and thus removable from the United States. 8 U.S.C. 1229; 8 C.F.R. 239.1(a). An alien who concedes removability may apply for relief from removal provided he or she meets the statutory requirements for such relief. An alien who has not applied for discretionary relief or voluntary departure may be ordered removed from the United States by the immigration judge.

259. In cases where an alien was legally admitted to the United States and deportability is at issue, the burden is on the government to establish by clear and convincing evidence that the alien is deportable. 8 U.S.C. 1229a(c)(3)(A). When an alien has been charged as inadmissible, the burden is on the alien to prove that he or she is clearly and beyond doubt entitled to be admitted to the United States, or that by clear and convincing evidence, he or she is lawfully present in the United States pursuant to a prior admission. 8 U.S.C. 1229a(c)(2)(A)(B).

260. Upon issuance of the NTA, DHS may either take an alien into custody upon issuance of a warrant, or may release the alien on bond or conditional release. 8 U.S.C. 1226(a); 8 C.F.R. 236.1. DHS may revoke its authorization of conditional release or release on bond at any time as a matter of discretion. 8 U.S.C. 1226(b); 8 C.F.R. 236.1(c)(9). For a discussion of custody/release authority, see the discussion under Article 9 above.

261. DHS is obligated by statute to take into custody any alien convicted of certain criminal offenses or who has engaged in terrorist activity, 8 U.S.C. 1226(c), 1226a, but may release the alien if such release is deemed necessary to provide protection to a witness or potential witness cooperating in a major criminal investigation, and DHS decides that the alien's release will not pose a danger to the safety of people or property and that the alien is likely to appear for scheduled proceedings. See 8 U.S.C. 1226 (c) (2).

262. Removal hearings are open to the public, except that the immigration judge may, due to lack of space, or for the purpose of protecting witnesses, parties, the public interest, or abused alien spouses, limit attendance or hold a closed hearing in any specific case. 8 C.F.R. 1003.27. Proceedings may also be closed to the public upon a showing by DHS that information to be disclosed in court may harm the national security or law enforcement interests of the United States, 8 C.F.R. 1003.27(d), 1240.11.

263. At the outset of a proceeding, the immigration judge must advise the alien of his or her right to representation, provide information on pro-bono counsel, and inform the alien that he or she will have the opportunity to examine and object to evidence and to cross-examine witnesses. 8 C.F.R. 1240.10(a)(1)-(4). The immigration judge must also place the

alien under oath, read the facts alleged in the NTA to the alien, and request that the alien admit or deny each factual allegation, 8 C.F.R. 1240(b)(5), (c).

264. During the removal proceedings, the immigration judge has the authority to determine whether an alien is inadmissible or deportable, to grant relief from removal (e.g., voluntary departure, asylum, cancellation of removal), and to determine the country to which an alien should be removed. 8 C.F.R. 1240.10-12. An alien in removal proceedings retains the right to representation by qualified counsel at the alien's choosing, at no expense to the government. 8 U.S.C. 1229a (b) (2)-(4). An alien must also be afforded a competent, impartial interpreter if the alien is not able to communicate effectively in English. 8 C.F.R. 1240.5.

271. Relief and protection from removal. A number of forms of relief are available to aliens who are subject to removal. Aliens in removal proceedings who are eligible to receive an immigrant visa have a visa immediately available to them, and those who are not inadmissible may be able to adjust status to that of an LPR in removal proceedings. 8 U.S.C. 1255(a), 1255(i). Waivers are available for some grounds of inadmissibility. For example, a discretionary waiver of inadmissibility is available under section 212(h) of the INA for certain criminal grounds of inadmissibility. To qualify, the alien applicant must demonstrate that he or she is the spouse, parent, son, or daughter of a U.S. citizen or lawful permanent resident of the United States and that the U.S. citizen or lawful permanent resident family member would suffer extreme hardship if the alien applicant were removed from the United States. 8 U.S.C. 1182 (h) (1)(b). Both lawful permanent residents (LPR) and non-permanent residents may be eligible for a form of relief called "cancellation of removal" under 8 U.S.C. 1229b. The Immigration Court may cancel the removal of an LPR if the alien has been an LPR for at least five years, has resided continuously in the United States for at least seven years after having been admitted in any status, and has not been convicted of an aggravated felony. 8 U.S.C. 1229b(a). Cancellation of removal is also available to a non-permanent resident who is inadmissible or deportable from the United States if the alien has been physically present in the United States for a continuous period of not less than ten years immediately preceding the date of such application, has been a person of good moral character during such period, has not been convicted of certain criminal offenses, and establishes that removal would result in "exceptional and extremely unusual hardship" to the alien's spouse, parent, or child, who is a U.S. citizen or LPR. 8 U.S.C. 1229b (b).

Primary Source Document 6 is a General Recommendation from another treaty body, the Committee on the Elimination of Racial Discrimination, applicable to the U.S. as a state party to the Race Convention.

b. U.N. Human Rights Council

This organ of the General Assembly is the focus of human rights generally at the U.N.

At the Human Rights Council, issues regarding immigrants are treated both in the special mechanisms, such as a special rapporteur on the human rights of Migrants (See report of Jorge Bustamonte, below) ; or in the Universal Periodic Review process. The above quote at the start of this narrative was from the 2010 U.S. national report in that process. It is the U.S. government speaking to the international community about how we see ourselves in relation to our international human rights obligations in light of our national laws and policies. Another except from the U.S. National UPR report, this one from 2015, can be found in Primary Source Document 7.

The U.S. also deals with the U.N. High Commissioner for Refugees on refugee issues, primarily regarding people in other countries wanting to come to the U.S. as refugees. And, issues regarding immigrants, etc. can also come up in the activity of the U.N. General Assembly.

In 2011, the U.S. government submitted its Fourth Report to the U.N. Human Rights Committee on its implementation of the ICCPR. This included the articles on equality, not discrimination and expulsion of aliens. The U.S. government stated:

> The U.S. also deals with international refugee issues through the office of the U.N. High Commissioner on Refugees. The U.S. processes refugee applications in many countries of the world where people are seeking to legally enter the U.S. as refugees or their relatives.

2. Organisation of American States

Another place where the U.S. faces international human rights norms applicable to immigrants, both legal and non-legal, is in the Organisation of American States, of which the U.S. is a founding member. Most Americans know little about the OAS or Inter-American Commission on Human Rights, the focus of human rights in North, Central, and South America. The I-A Commission is headquartered in Washington DC and has a U.S. citizen sitting as a Commissioner on that body.

The Commission has authority to receive, process, and decide written complaints called Petitions, alleging that a state like the U.S. has violated one or more of the human rights in the ADHR. A whole decision of one recent case filed on behalf of "Undocumented Immigrants against the U.S." is among the Primary Source Documents. This Report on the Merits of a Petition alleging the U.S. has violated the ADHR shows how the international (regional) human rights system scrutinized an actual situation to determine if the U.S. followed the ADHR or not. It also shows the responses and attitude of the U.S. government to that Petition system. This system receives little respect from the U.S. government who looks at the process as trying to apply norms which it does not consider to be legally binding on the U.S. and hence not deserving compliance.

In the OAS, there is a Convention on Human Rights, but the U.S. is not a state party to that treaty. It has signed the treaty but never ratified it.

It is particularly in regards to the activity of the Inter-American Commission on Human Rights that the U.S. faces application of norms under the American Declaration of the Rights and Duties of Man, called the American Declaration of Human Rights. The I-A Commission writes comments about immigration in general, applicable to all the American states, but it also has sent members to do on-site reporting specifically about immigration in U.S. law, policy, and practice in relation to the ADHR norms. See Primary Source Documents.

While every immigrant is not a citizen of the U.S., every alien is a human being and therefore is a holder of, and entitled to the exercise of, all human rights, with the exception of Political Human Rights. Human rights are not based on citizenship, though the ICCPR allows the exercise of the right to vote and run for office to citizens of a country in deference to the state's sovereignty, as it must. Americans should learn what human rights are, and work to assure that U.S. laws and policies are consistent with international standards.

Immigrants have all human rights every one else has, except for political rights. There is a tendency to think of immigrants as aliens and not part of "us." Some Americans think that human rights just belong to citizens. This is not how human rights law works. It deals with and recognizes rights held by individual human beings in a society, not by citizens alone. These are the terms that states have accepted in ratifying international human rights treaties.

Immigrants, migrant workers, and refugees all have the same human rights as all American citizens, except political rights. This includes the right to due process of law, freedom from arbitrary detention, and equality before the law; these rights should be exercised without discrimination based on race, religion, or national origin or other status. While none of these human rights give any person the right to enter or stay in the U.S., these rights must be recognized, respected, and protected for all those living in the U.S.

Primary Source Documents

I. U.N. DECLARATION ON THE HUMAN RIGHTS OF INDIVIDUALS WHO ARE NOT NATIONALS OF THE COUNTRY IN WHICH THEY LIVE

This first document is a 1985 Declaration of human rights principles applicable to all persons not citizens of the country in which they find themselves for any reason. Because it is a declaration it is not legally binding upon the U.S., but it does express the common understanding of the international community that everyone has human rights even in places where they are not citizens. It means that all aliens have human rights. This declaration should be read in the context of all modern human rights treaties, which all apply to and recognize rights in every alien under the non-discrimination clause in all human rights treaties.

[Text]

The General Assembly,

Considering that the Charter of the United Nations encourages universal respect for and observance of the human rights and fundamental freedoms of all human beings, without distinction as to race, sex, language or religion, Considering that the Universal Declaration of Human Rights proclaims that all human beings are born free and equal in dignity and rights and that everyone is entitled to all the rights and freedoms set forth in that Declaration, without distinction of any kind, such as race, colour, sex, language, religion, political or other opinion, national or social origin, property, birth or other status,

Considering that the Universal Declaration of Human Rights proclaims further that everyone has the right to recognition everywhere as a person before the law, that all are equal before the law and entitled without any discrimination to equal protection of the law, and that all are entitled to equal pro- tection against any discrimination in violation of that Declaration and against any incitement to such discrimination,

Being aware that the States Parties to the International Covenants on Human Rights undertake to guarantee that the rights enunciated in these Covenants will be exercised without discrimination of any kind as to race, colour, sex, language, religion, political or other opinion, national or social origin, property, birth or other status,

Conscious that, with improving communications and the development of peaceful and friendly relations among countries, individuals increasingly live in countries of which they are not nationals, Reaffirming the purposes and principles of the Charter of the United Nations,

Recognizing that the protection of human rights and fundamental freedoms provided for in international instruments should also be ensured for individuals who are not nationals of the country in which they live,

Proclaims this Declaration:

Article 1
For the purposes of this Declaration, the term "alien" shall apply, with due regard to qualifications made in subsequent articles, to any individual who is not a national of the State in which he or she is present.

Article 2
1. Nothing in this Declaration shall be interpreted as legitimizing the illegal entry into and presence in a State of any alien, nor shall any provision be interpreted as restricting the right of any State to promulgate laws and regulations concerning the entry of aliens and the terms and conditions of their stay or to establish differences between nationals and

aliens. However, such laws and regulations shall not be incompatible with the international legal obligations of that State, including those in the field of human rights.

2. This Declaration shall not prejudice the enjoyment of the rights accorded by domestic law and of the rights which under international law a State is obliged to accord to aliens, even where this Declaration does not recognize such rights or recognizes them to a lesser extent.

Article 3
Every State shall make public its national legislation or regulations affecting aliens.

Article 4
Aliens shall observe the laws of the State in which they reside or are present and regard with respect the customs and traditions of the people of that State.

Article 5
1. Aliens shall enjoy, in accordance with domestic law and subject to the relevant international obligation of the State in which they are present, in particular the following rights:

> (a) The right to life and security of person; no alien shall be subjected to arbitrary arrest or detention; no alien shall be deprived of his or her liberty except on such grounds and in accordance with such procedures as are established by law;

> (b) The right to protection against arbitrary or unlawful interference with privacy, family, home or correspondence;

> (c) The right to be equal before the courts, tribunals and all other organs and authorities administering justice and, when necessary, to free assistance of an interpreter in criminal proceedings and, when prescribed by law, other proceedings;

> (d) The right to choose a spouse, to marry, to found a family;

> (e) The right to freedom of thought, opinion, conscience and religion; the right to manifest their religion or beliefs, subject only to such limitations as are prescribed by law and are necessary to protect public safety, order, health or morals or the fundamental rights and freedoms of others;

> (f) The right to retain their own language, culture and tradition;

> (g) The right to transfer abroad earnings, savings or other personal monetary assets, subject to domestic currency regulations.

2. Subject to such restrictions as are prescribed by law and which are necessary in a democratic society to protect national security, public safety, public order, public health or morals or the rights and freedoms of others, and which are consistent with the other rights recognized in the relevant international instruments and those set forth in this Declaration, aliens shall enjoy the following rights:

> (a) The right to leave the country;

> (b) The right to freedom of expression;

> (c) The right to peaceful assembly;

> (d) The right to own property alone as well as in association with others, subject to domestic law.

3. Subject to the provisions referred to in paragraph 2, aliens lawfully in the territory of a State shall enjoy the right to liberty of movement and freedom to choose their residence within the borders of the State.

4. Subject to national legislation and due authorization, the spouse and minor or dependent children of an alien lawfully residing in the territory of a State shall be admitted to accompany, join and stay with the alien.

Article 6.

No alien shall be subjected to torture or to cruel, inhuman or degrading treatment or punishment and, in particular, no alien shall be subjected without his or her free consent to medical or scientific experimentation.

Article 7

An alien lawfully in the territory of a State may be expelled therefrom only in pursuance of a decision reached in accordance with law and shall, except where compelling reasons of national security otherwise require, be allowed to submit the reasons why he or she should not be expelled and to have the case reviewed by, and be represented for the purpose before, the competent authority or a person or persons specially designated by the competent authority. Individual or collective expulsion of such aliens on grounds of race, colour, religion, culture, descent or national or ethnic origin is prohibited.

Article 8

1. Aliens lawfully residing in the territory of a State shall also enjoy, in accordance with the national laws, the following rights, subject to their obligations under Article 4:

(a) The right to safe and healthy working conditions, to fair wages and equal remuneration for work of equal value without distinction of any kind, in particular, women being guaranteed conditions of work not inferior to those enjoyed by men, with equal pay for equal work;

(b) The right to join trade unions and other organizations or associations of their choice and to participate in their activities. No restrictions may be placed on the exercise of this right other than those prescribed by law and which are necessary, in a democratic society, in the interests of national security or public order or for the protection of the rights and freedoms of others;

(c) The right to health protection, medical care, social security, social services, education, rest and leisure, provided that they fulfil the requirements under the relevant regulations for participation and that undue strain is not placed on the resources of the State.

2. With a view to protecting the rights of aliens carrying on lawful paid activities in the country in which they are present, such rights may be specified by the Governments concerned in multilateral or bilateral conventions.

Article 9

No alien shall be arbitrarily deprived of his or her lawfully acquired assets.

Article 10

Any alien shall be free at any time to communicate with the consulate or diplomatic mission of the State of which he or she is a national or, in the absence thereof, with the consulate or diplomatic mission of any other State entrusted with the protection of the interests of the State of which he or she is a national in the State where he or she resides.

Source: United Nations, General Assembly, A/RES/40/144, 13 December 1985, http://www.un.org/documents/ga/res/40/ a40r144.htm

2. THE RIGHTS OF NON CITIZENS ON THE HUMAN RIGHTS OF INDIVIDUALS WHO ARE NOT NATIONALS OF THE COUNTRY IN WHICH THEY LIVE, OFFICE OF THE UNITED NATIONS HIGH COMMISSIONER FOR HUMAN RIGHTS, 2006

International Human Rights Law and sometimes Refugee Law applies to the field of immigration and determines the rights and status of those who are not citizens of the country in which they are living. This U.N. publication, written primarily by an American law professor, is about the human rights held by every human being in the world. This includes persons in the U.S. who are not U.S. citizens, whether they are documented or undocumented.

As it pertains to the U.S. this document is less about who can enter and stay in the U.S., and more about how the U.S. and all state governments must treat non-U.S. citizens as human beings who possess inherent human dignity. The U.S. determines who enters and who can stay in this country and has the right to deport, so long as keeping consistent with national and international law. How states such as the U.S. treat human beings in their territory is a matter of international human rights law as permitted by the U.S. Constitution.

Contents

...

INTRODUCTION

All persons should, by virtue of their essential humanity, enjoy all human rights. Exceptional distinctions, for example between citizens and non-citizens, can be made only if they serve a legitimate State objective and are proportional to the achievement of that objective.

Citizens are persons who have been recognized by a State as having an effective link with it. International law generally leaves to each State the authority to determine who qualifies as a citizen. Citizenship can ordinarily be acquired by being born in the country (known as *jus soli* or the law of the place), being born to a parent who is a citizen of the country (known as jus sanguinis or the law of blood), naturalization or a combination of these approaches.

A non-citizen is a person who has not been recognized as having these effective links to the country where he or she is located. There are different groups of non-citizens, including permanent residents, migrants, refugees, asylum-seekers, victims of trafficking, foreign students, temporary visitors, other kinds of non-immigrants and stateless people. While each of these groups may have rights based on separate legal regimes, the problems faced by most, if not all, non-citizens are very similar. These common concerns affect approximately 175 million individuals worldwide — or 3 per cent of the world's population.

Non-citizens should have freedom from arbitrary killing, inhuman treatment, slavery, arbitrary arrest, unfair trial, invasions of privacy, refoulement, forced labour, child labour and violations of humanitarian law. They also have the right to marry; protection as minors; peaceful association and assembly; equality; freedom of religion and belief; social, cultural and economic rights; labour rights (for example, as to collective bargaining, workers' compensation, healthy and safe working conditions); and consular protection. While all human beings are entitled to equality in dignity and rights,

States may narrowly draw distinctions between citizens and non-citizens with respect to political rights explicitly guaranteed to citizens and freedom of movement.

For non-citizens, there is, nevertheless, a large gap between the rights that international human rights law guarantees to them and the realities that they face. In many countries, there are institutional and pervasive problems confronting non-citizens. Nearly all categories of non-citizens face official and non-official discrimination. While in some countries there may be legal guarantees of equal treatment and recognition of the importance of non-citizens in achieving economic prosperity, non-citizens face hostile social and practical realities. They experience xenophobia, racism and sexism; language barriers and unfamiliar customs; lack of political representation; difficulty realizing their economic, social and cultural rights-particularly the right to work, the right to education and the right to health care; difficulty obtaining identity documents; and lack of means to challenge violations of their human rights effectively or to have them remedied. Some non-citizens are subjected to arbitrary and often indefinite detention. They may have been traumatized by experiences of persecution or abuse in their countries of origin, but are detained side by side with criminals in prisons, which are frequently overcrowded, unhygienic and dangerous. In addition, detained non-citizens may be denied contact with their families, access to legal assistance and the opportunity to challenge their detention. Official hostility-often expressed in national legislation-has been especially flagrant during periods of war, racial animosity and high unemployment. For example, the situation has worsened since 11 September 2001, as some Governments have detained non-citizens in response to fears of terrorism. The narrow exceptions to the principle of non-discrimination that are permitted by international human rights law do not justify such pervasive violations of non-citizens' rights. The principal objective of this publication is to highlight all the diverse sources of international law and emerging international standards protecting the rights of non-citizens, especially:

- The relevant provisions of the International Convention on the Elimination of All Forms of Racial Discrimination and other human rights treaties;
- The general comments, country conclusions and adjudications by the Committee on the Elimination of Racial Discrimination and other treaty bodies;
- The reports of the United Nations Commission on Human Rights thematic procedures on the human rights of migrants and racism;
- The relevant work of such other global institutions as the International Labour Organization and the Office of the United Nations High Commissioner for Refugees; and The reports of regional institutions, such as the European Commission against Racism and Intolerance.

Chapter I examines the general principle of equality for non-citizens. Chapter II explains in greater detail the sources and extent of specific non-citizen rights, including universal rights and freedoms; civil and political rights; and economic, social and cultural rights. Chapter III discusses the application of these rights to particular groups of non-citizens, such as stateless persons, refugees and asylum-seekers, non-citizen workers, and children.

I. THE GENERAL PRINCIPLE OF EQUALITY FOR NON-CITIZENS

International Human Rights Law is founded on the premise that all persons, by virtue of their essential humanity, should enjoy all human rights without discrimination unless exceptional distinctions-for example between citizens and non-citizens-serve a legitimate State objective and are proportional to the achievement of that objective. Any approach to combating discrimination against non-citizens should take into account:

(a) The interest of the State in specific rights (e.g., political rights, right to education, social security, other economic rights);

(b) The different non-citizens and their relationship to that State (e.g., permanent residents, migrant workers, asylum-seekers, temporary residents, tourists, undocumented workers); and

(c) Whether the State's interest or reason for distinguishing between citizens and non-citizens or among non-citizens (e.g., reciprocity, promoting development) is legitimate and proportionate.

"All persons are equal before the law and are entitled without any discrimination to the equal protection of the law." (International Covenant on Civil and Political Rights, Art. 26)

A. International Covenant on Civil and Political Rights

The International Covenant on Civil and Political Rights provides an example of the general principle of equality that underlies international human rights law as it relates to non-citizens, and the narrow nature of exceptions to that principle. According to its article 2 (1), each State party:

> "undertakes to respect and to ensure to all individuals within its territory and subject to its jurisdiction the rights recognized in the present Covenant, without distinction of any kind, such as race, colour, sex, language, religion, political or other opinion, national or social origin, property, birth or other status."

Moreover, article 26 states that:

> "All persons are equal before the law and are entitled without any discrimination to the equal protection of the law. In this respect, the law shall prohibit any discrimination and guarantee to all persons equal and effective protection against discrimination on any ground such as race, colour...national or social origin...or other status."

The Human Rights Committee has explained that:

> "the rights set forth in the Covenant apply to everyone, irrespective of reciprocity, and irrespective of his or her nationality or statelessness. Thus, the general rule is that each one of the rights of the Covenant must be guaranteed without discrimination between citizens and aliens."

Human Rights Committee: "the general rule is that each one of the rights of the Covenant must be guaranteed without discrimination between citizens and aliens."

The Human Rights Committee has also observed that the rights of non-citizens may be qualified only by such limitations as may be lawfully imposed under the International Covenant on Civil and Political Rights. Specifically, the Covenant permits States to draw distinctions between citizens and non-citizens with respect to two categories of rights: political rights explicitly guaranteed to citizens and freedom of movement. With regard to political rights, article 25 establishes that "every citizen" shall have the right to participate in public affairs, to vote and hold office, and to have access to public service.

Regarding freedom of movement, article 12 (1) grants "the right to liberty of movement and freedom to choose [one's] residence" only to persons who are "lawfully within the territory of a State"-that is, apparently permitting restrictions on undocumented migrants.

B. International Convention on the Elimination of All Forms of Racial Discrimination

The International Convention on the Elimination of All Forms of Racial Discrimination also illustrates the narrow nature of exceptions to the general principle of equality. It indicates that States may make distinctions between citizens and non-citizens, but-unlike the International Covenant on Civil and Political Rights-it requires all non-citizens to be treated similarly. It defines racial discrimination in article 1 (1):

> "the term 'racial discrimination' shall mean any distinction, exclusion, restriction or preference based on race, colour, descent, or national or ethnic origin which has the purpose or effect of nullifying or impairing the recognition, enjoyment or exercise, on an equal footing, of human rights and fundamental freedoms in the political, economic, social, cultural or any other field of public life."

Article 1 (2) and (3) of the Convention, however, seems at first to limit its application with regard to discrimination against non-citizens. Article 1 (2) states: "This Convention shall not apply to distinctions, exclusions, restrictions or preferences made by a State Party to this Convention between citizens and noncitizens." Article 1 (3) refines article 1 (2) by stating that: "Nothing in this Convention may be interpreted as affecting in any way the legal provisions of States Parties concerning nationality, citizenship or naturalization, provided that such provisions do not discriminate against any particular nationality." (emphasis added)

The Committee on the Elimination of Racial Discrimination indicated in its general recommendation XI, however, that these provisions need to be read in the light of the totality of human rights law:

"Article 1, paragraph 2, must not be interpreted to detract in any way from the rights and freedoms recognized and enunciated in other instruments, especially the Universal Declaration of Human Rights, the International Covenant on Economic, Social and Cultural Rights and the International Covenant on Civil and Political Rights."

In its concluding observations regarding States' reports as well as its opinions on individual communications, the Committee has further underscored the need for States parties to:

- Publicly condemn any acts of intolerance or hatred against persons belonging to particular racial, ethnic, national or religious groups, and promote a better understanding of the principle of non-discrimination and of the situation of non-citizens;

- Make sure that non-citizens enjoy equal protection and recognition before the law; Focus on the problems faced by non-citizens with regard to economic, social and cultural rights, notably in areas such as housing, education and employment; Guarantee the equal enjoyment of the right to adequate housing for both citizens and non-citizens, as well as guarantee that non-citizens have equal access to social services that ensure a minimum standard of living;

- Take measures to eliminate discrimination against non-citizens in relation to working conditions and language requirements, including rules and practices in employment that may be discriminatory in effect; and Apply international and regional standards pertaining to refugees equally, regardless of the nationality of the asylum-seeker, and use all available means, including international cooperation, to address the situation of refugees and displaced persons, especially regarding their access to education, housing and employment.

In August 2004, the Committee adopted general recommendation XXX on discrimination against non-citizens. Some of its main principles are summarized here and the recommendation is reproduced in full in the annex below. States are under an obligation to guarantee equality between citizens and non-citizens in the enjoyment of their civil, political, economic, social and cultural rights to the extent recognized under international law and enunciated especially in the Universal Declaration of Human Rights, the International Covenant on Economic, Social and Cultural Rights, and the International Covenant on Civil and Political Rights; Differential treatment based on citizenship or immigration status will constitute discrimination if the criteria for such differentiation are not applied pursuant to a legitimate aim and are not proportional to the achievement of this aim; States must abstain from applying different standards of treatment to different categories of non-citizens, such as female non-citizen spouses of citizens and male non-citizen spouses of citizens; Immigration policies and any measures taken in the struggle against terrorism must not discriminate, in purpose or effect, on grounds of race, colour, descent, or national or ethnic origin; States have a duty to protect non-citizens from xenophobic attitudes and behaviour; States are obliged to ensure that particular groups of non-citizens are not discriminated against with regard to access to citizenship or naturalization and that all non-citizens enjoy equal treatment in the administration of justice; Deportation or other removal proceedings must not discriminate among non-citizens on the basis of race or national origin and should not result in disproportionate interference with the right to family life; Non-citizens must not be returned or removed to a country or territory where they are at risk of being subject to serious human rights abuses; Obstacles to non-citizens' enjoyment of economic, social and cultural rights, notably in education, housing, employment and health, must be removed.

Committee on the Elimination of Racial Discrimination: "States parties are under an obligation to guarantee equality between citizens and non-citizens in the enjoyment of [their civil, political, economic, social and cultural] rights...."

General recommendation XXX builds upon all the previous protections for non-citizens and their interpretations not only by the Committee on the Elimination of Racial Discrimination, but also by the Human Rights Committee and other human rights institutions. Accordingly, general recommendation XXX provides a comprehensive elaboration of the human rights of non-citizens as a guide to all countries and particularly those that have ratified the Convention. The more detailed implications of each paragraph of this recommendation are discussed in chapter II below.

The Committee on the Elimination of Racial Discrimination has indicated that States may draw distinctions between citizens and non-citizens only if such distinctions do not have the effect of limiting the enjoyment by non-citizens of the rights enshrined in other instruments. For example, in A (FC) and Others v. Secretary of State for the Home Department, nine terrorism suspects successfully challenged their detention, alleging that the United Kingdom of Great Britain and Northern Ireland had violated article 5 (the right to liberty and security) of the European Convention on Human

Rights. Differential treatment based on citizenship or immigration status will constitute forbidden discrimination if the criteria for such differentiation are inconsistent with the objectives and purposes of the International Convention on the Elimination of All Forms of Racial Discrimination; are not proportional to the achievement of those objectives and purposes; or do not fall within the scope of article 1 (4) of the Convention, which relates to special measures. For example, a Tunisian permanent resident married to a Danish citizen was denied a loan by a Danish bank because he was not a Danish citizen. The Committee noted that the Tunisian was denied the loan "on the sole ground of his non-Danish nationality and was told that the nationality requirement was motivated by the need to ensure that the loan was repaid. In the opinion of the Committee, however, nationality is not the most appropriate requisite when investigating a person's will or capacity to reimburse a loan. The applicant's permanent residence or the place where his employment, property or family ties are to be found may be more relevant in this context. A citizen may move abroad or have all his property in another country and thus evade all attempts to enforce a claim of repayment." Accordingly, the Committee found that the Tunisian had suffered discrimination.

C. International Covenant on Economic, Social and Cultural Rights

Like article 2 (1) of the International Covenant on Civil and Political Rights, article 2 (2) of the International Covenant on Economic, Social and Cultural Rights declares that States parties guarantee the rights enunciated in the Covenant "without discrimination of any kind as to race, colour...national or social origin...or other status." Article 2 (3), however, creates an exception to this rule of equality for developing countries: "Developing countries, with due regard to human rights and their national economy, may determine to what extent they would guarantee the economic rights recognized in the present Covenant to non-nationals." As an exception to the rule of equality, article 2 (3) must be narrowly construed, may be relied upon only by developing countries and only with respect to economic rights. States may not draw distinctions between citizens and non-citizens as to social and cultural rights.

D. Regional bodies

Regional human rights law is largely consistent with the protections provided by global standards, but reveals several important elaborations on those standards as well as particular exceptions to the general principle of equality. Article 5 (1) of the Convention for the Protection of Human Rights and Fundamental Freedoms (European Convention on Human Rights), for example, reiterates the global principle of the right to liberty and security of person, but elaborates upon that standard by providing that "[n]o one shall be deprived of his liberty" except in certain specified cases and only "in accordance with a procedure prescribed by law." The list of exceptions to the right to liberty in article 5 (1) is exhaustive and only a narrow interpretation of those exceptions is consistent with the aim of article 5, namely to protect the individual from arbitrary detention.

The European Court of Human Rights has found a distinction between European "citizens" and individuals of non-European nationality with regard to deportation permissible. In *C. v. Belgium*, a Moroccan citizen who had lived in Belgium for 37 years was ordered to be deported owing to convictions for criminal damage, possession of drugs and conspiracy. He claimed discrimination on grounds of race and nationality in violation of article 14 of the European Convention because "his deportation amounted to less favourable treatment than was accorded to criminals who, as nationals of a member State of the European Union, were protected against such a measure in Belgium." The Court found no violation of article 14 of the European Convention because such preferential treatment was "based on an objective and reasonable justification, given that the member States of the European Union form a special legal order, which has...established its own citizenship."

E. National constitutions

Some national constitutions guarantee rights to "citizens," whereas international human rights law would-with the exception of the rights of public participation and of movement and economic rights in developing countries-provide rights to all persons.

II. SPECIFIC RIGHTS OF NON-CITIZENS

A. Fundamental Rights and Freedoms
1. Right to life, liberty and security of the person

Protection from arbitrary detention; freedom from torture and cruel, inhuman or degrading treatment or punishment; right of detained non-citizens to contact consular officials

Non-citizens have an inherent right to life, protected by law, and may not be arbitrarily deprived of life. They also have the right to liberty and security of the person. All individuals, including non-citizens, must be protected from arbitrary detention. If non-citizens are lawfully deprived of their liberty, they must be treated with humanity and with respect for the inherent dignity of their person. They must not be subjected to torture or to cruel, inhuman or degrading treatment or punishment, and may not be held in slavery or servitude. Detained non-citizens have the right to contact consular officials and the receiving State must notify them of this right.

States are obliged to respect the human rights of detainees, including legal protections, irrespective of whether they are in the territory of the State in question. Where persons find themselves within the authority and control of a State and where a circumstance of armed conflict may be involved, their fundamental rights may be determined in part by reference to international humanitarian law as well as international human rights law. States must allow a competent tribunal to determine the legal status of each detainee pursuant to international humanitarian law, in particular article 5 of the Geneva Convention relative to the Treatment of Prisoners of War. Where it may be considered that the protections of international humanitarian law do not apply, however, such persons remain the beneficiaries at least of the non-derogable protections under international human rights law. In short, no person under the authority and control of a State, regardless of his or her circumstances, is devoid of legal protection for his or her fundamental and non-derogable human rights. If the legal status of detainees is not clarified, the rights and protections to which they may be entitled under international or domestic law cannot be said to be the subject of effective legal protection by the State. So-called international zones administered by States to detain non-citizens, and where such non-citizens are denied legal or social assistance, are a legal fiction and a State cannot avoid its international human rights responsibilities by claiming that such areas have extraterritorial status. States and international organizations must also ensure that measures taken in the struggle against terrorism do not discriminate in purpose or effect on grounds of race or national or ethnic origin. States may nonetheless arrest or detain non-citizens against whom action is being taken with a view to deportation or extradition, regardless of whether such detention is reasonably considered necessary, for example, to prevent those non-citizens from committing offences or fleeing.

2. Protection from refoulement

Non-citizens enjoy the right to be protected from refoulement, or deportation to a country in which they may be subjected to persecution or abuse. This principle of non-refoulement exists in a number of international instruments with slightly varying coverage. Expulsions of non-citizens should not be carried out without taking into account possible risks to their lives and physical integrity in the countries of destination. With regard to non-refoulement, article 3 of the Convention against Torture and Other Cruel, Inhuman or Degrading Treatment or Punishment provides:

"1. No State Party shall expel, return ('refouler') or extradite a person to another State where there are substantial grounds for believing that he would be in danger of being subjected to torture.

"2. For the purpose of determining whether there are such grounds, the competent authorities shall take into account all relevant considerations including, where applicable, the existence in the State concerned of a consistent pattern of gross, flagrant or mass violations of human rights."

In assessing whether an expulsion order violates article 3, it must be determined whether the individual concerned would be exposed to a real and personal risk of being subjected to torture in the country to which he or she would be returned. All relevant considerations-including the existence of a consistent pattern of gross, flagrant or mass violations of human rights-must be taken into account pursuant to article 3 (2), but the lack of such a pattern does not mean that a person might not be subjected to torture in his or her specific circumstances. The risk of torture must be assessed on grounds that go beyond mere theory or suspicion. It does not, however, have to meet the test of being highly probable. A person subject to an expulsion order is required to establish that he or she would be in danger of being tortured and that the grounds for so believing are substantial in the way described above, and that such danger is personal and present. The following information, while not exhaustive, would also be pertinent to determining whether an expulsion order violates article 3 of the Convention:

(a) Is the State concerned one in which there is evidence of a consistent pattern of gross, flagrant or mass violations of human rights (see Art. 3, para. 2)?

(b) Has the person claiming a violation of article 3 been tortured or maltreated by or at the instigation of or with the consent or acquiescence of a public official or other person acting in an official capacity in the past? If so, was this in the recent past?

(c) Is there medical or other independent evidence to support a claim by the person that he or she has been tortured or maltreated in the past? Has the torture had after-effects?

(d) Has the situation referred to in (a) above changed? Has the internal situation in respect of human rights altered?

(e) Has the person engaged in political or other activity within or outside the State concerned which would appear to make him or her particularly vulnerable to the risk of being placed in danger of torture were he or she to be expelled, returned or extradited to the State in question?

(f) Is there any evidence as to the credibility of the person? This analysis was used by the European Court of Human Rights in *Chahal v. The United Kingdom* in determining whether a Sikh leader of Indian nationality would be at risk of ill-treatment if he were deported from the United Kingdom to India.

The wording of article 3 (1) of the Convention against Torture is similar to, but not entirely congruent with, that of article 33 (1) of the Convention relating to the Status of Refugees. Whereas the former provides protection from refoulement only to persons who are in danger of becoming victims of torture, the latter provides protection against refoulement for persons in danger of falling victim to various kinds of persecution.

Torture victims cannot be expected to recall entirely consistent facts relating to events of extreme trauma, but they must be prepared to advance such evidence as there is in support of such a claim.

3. Liberty of movement and the right to enter one's own country

Persons do not have the right to enter or to reside in countries of which they are not citizens. However, non-citizens who are lawfully within the territory of a State have the right to liberty of movement and free choice of residence. Restrictions and other quotas on where such non-citizens can settle in a State-especially those restrictions and quotas that might involve an element of compulsion-may violate their right to liberty of movement. States are encouraged to ensure that the geographical distribution of non-citizens within their territory is made according to the principle of equity and does not lead to the violation of their rights as recognized under the International Convention on the Elimination of All Forms of Racial Discrimination. Asylum-seekers should be guaranteed freedom of movement wherever possible. All non-citizens shall be free to leave a State.

Article 12 (4) of the International Covenant on Civil and Political Rights provides that "[n]o one shall be arbitrarily deprived of the right to enter his own country." The Human Rights Committee has broadly interpreted this provision to give rights to stateless persons who are resident in a particular State and others with a long-term relationship with the country, but who are not citizens. States are urged to ensure that the residence permits of non-citizens who are long-term residents are withdrawn only under exceptional and clearly defined circumstances, and that adequate recourse to appeal against such decisions is made available. Requiring lawfully permanent residents of a State to obtain return visas to re-enter that State may not comply with article 12 (4). Any State with such a provision should review its legislation to ensure compliance with article 12 (4).

4. Protection from arbitrary expulsion

A non-citizen may be expelled only to a country that agrees to accept him or her and shall be allowed to leave for that country.

Instruments such as the United Nations Declaration on the Rights of Individuals who are not Nationals of the Country in which They Live, which is non-binding, and Protocol No. 4 to the European Convention on Human Rights prohibit the collective expulsion of non-citizens. Any measure that compels non-citizens, as a group, to leave a country is prohibited except where such a measure is taken on the basis of a reasonable and objective examination of the particular case of each individual non-citizen in the group. In other words, the procedure for the expulsion of a group of non-citizens must afford sufficient guarantees demonstrating that the personal circumstances of each of those non-citizens concerned has been genuinely and individually taken into account. Hence, for example, if one member of a group of non-citizens is found not to qualify for refugee status because there is a safe country of origin and is ordered to be deported, the other members of the group cannot be ordered to be deported unless they too are individually deemed not to qualify for refugee status.

There is, nonetheless, significant scope for States to enforce their immigration policies and to require departure of un-lawfully present persons, such as those who remain in a State longer than the time allowed by limited-duration permits. Yet that discretion is not unlimited and may not be exercised arbitrarily. The case of *Winata and Lan Li v. Australia*, for example, concerned a stateless married couple from Indonesia who had lost their Indonesian citizenship and had been residing in Australia for many years. After overstaying their visas, the couple faced deportation, but petitioned both on their own behalf and on behalf of their 13-year-old son, who was an Australian citizen. The Human Rights Committee found that deportation of the couple would amount to a violation of their rights under article 17 of the International Covenant on Civil and Political Rights in conjunction with article 23, and a violation of the rights of their son under article 24 (1). It also found that, while the mere fact that non-citizen parents have a child who is a citizen does not by itself make the proposed deportation of the parents arbitrary, the fact that the child in this case had grown up in Australia since his birth 13 years before, "attending Australian schools as an ordinary child would and developing the social relationships inherent in that," the State had the burden of showing additional factors justifying the deportation of both parents that went "beyond a simple enforcement of its immigration law in order to avoid a characterization of arbitrariness."

Non-citizens-even non-citizens suspected of terrorism-should not be expelled without allowing them a legal opportunity to challenge their expulsion. The International Covenant on Civil and Political Rights, however, provides the right to certain procedural protections in expulsion proceedings (art. 13) only to noncitizens "lawfully in the territory of a State party."

5. Freedom of thought and conscience

Right to hold and express opinions; right of peaceful assembly; freedom of association

Non-citizens have the right to freedom of thought and conscience, as well as the right to hold and express opinions. They also have the right to peaceful assembly and freedom of association. Membership in political parties, for example, should be open to non-citizens.

6. Protection from arbitrary interference with privacy, family, home or correspondence

Non-citizens may not be subjected to arbitrary or unlawful interference with their privacy, family, home or correspondence. Article 8 of the European Convention on Human Rights, for example, states:

> "1. Everyone has the right to respect for his private and family life, his home and his correspondence."

> "2. There shall be no interference by a public authority with the exercise of this right except such as is in accordance with the law and is necessary in a democratic society in the interests of national security, public safety or the economic well-being of the country, for the prevention of disorder or crime, for the protection of health or morals, or for the protection of the rights and freedoms of others."

Where a non-citizen has real family ties in the territory of a State from which he or she is ordered to be deported and the deportation would jeopardize those ties, the deportation is justified with regard to article 8 only if it is proportionate to the legitimate aim pursued. In other words, the deportation is justified only if the interference with family life is not excessive compared to the public interest to be protected. The public interest often balanced against the right to respect for family life is the State's interest in maintaining public order. It arises in the context of non-citizens convicted of criminal offences. There is no right of a migrant non-citizen to enter or to remain in a particular country after having committed a serious criminal offence, but to remove a person from a country where close members of his or her family are living may amount to an infringement of the right to respect for family life as guaranteed in article 8 (1) of the Convention, especially where the individual concerned poses little danger to public order or security.

A number of States, however, continue to discriminate with regard to the capacity of women to pass on their nationality to their children and several have made reservations to article 9 of the Convention. Such States may allow women to pass on their nationality to their children only if they are unmarried or their husbands are stateless.

Parents should be able to transmit their nationality to their children regardless of their sex and of whether they are married to the other parent. At the same time, the principle of *jus soli* (citizenship based on the place of birth) has become the international norm governing the nationality of children born to non-citizen parents, especially if they would otherwise be stateless. Children of non-citizens whose legal status has not yet been determined should be protected from any difficulties in acquiring citizenship.

B. Civil and political rights
1. Right to recognition and equal protection before the law

Equality before courts and tribunals; entitlement to a fair and public hearing; freedom from subjection to retrospective penal legislation

Non-citizens are entitled to equal protection and recognition before the law. They shall be equal before the courts and tribunals, and shall be entitled to a fair and public hearing by a competent, independent and impartial tribunal established by law in the determination of any criminal charge against them or of their rights and obligations in a suit at law. Non-citizens shall not be subjected to retrospective penal legislation and may not be imprisoned for failure to fulfil a contractual obligation.

2. Right to acquire, maintain and transmit citizenship

States should take effective measures to ensure that all non-citizens enjoy the right to acquire citizenship without discrimination. Hence, States should not discriminate against particular groups of non-citizens on the basis of race or ethnic or national origin with regard to naturalization or the registration of births, and should eliminate from their legislation all discrimination between men and women with regard to the acquisition and transmission of nationality. Non-citizen spouses of citizens should be able to acquire citizenship in the same manner regardless of their sex. Article 9 of the Convention on the Elimination of All Forms of Discrimination against Women provides that:

> "1. States Parties shall grant women equal rights with men to acquire, change or retain their nationality. They shall ensure in particular that neither marriage to an alien nor change of nationality by the husband during marriage shall automatically change the nationality of the wife, render her stateless or force upon her the nationality of the husband.

> "2. States Parties shall grant women equal rights with men with respect to the nationality of their children."

Governments should pay greater attention to immigration policies that have a discriminatory effect on persons of a particular national or ethnic origin, and are encouraged to investigate possible barriers to naturalization, in terms of both the procedure and the lack of motivation to apply for citizenship.

3. Protection from discrimination on the basis of sex

States should eliminate from their legislation all discrimination between men and women with regard to the acquisition and transmission of nationality. The nationality and immigration laws of several countries discriminate between the capacity of male and female citizens to marry and live with their non-citizen spouses. For example, Mauritius adopted an immigration law which provided that, if a Mauritian woman married a man from another country, the husband must apply for residence in Mauritius and that permission may be refused. If, however, a Mauritian man married a foreign woman, the foreign woman was automatically entitled to residence in Mauritius. The Human Rights Committee held that Mauritius had violated the International Covenant on Civil and Political Rights by discriminating between men and women without adequate justification and by failing to respect the family's right to live together. Non-citizen spouses of citizens should be able to acquire citizenship in the same manner regardless of their sex, in keeping with article 5(d) (iii) of the International Convention on the Elimination of All Forms of Racial Discrimination.

C. Economic, social and cultural rights
1. Rights of non-citizens as members of minorities

Right to enjoy one's culture, profess and practise one's religion, and use one's language Since non-citizens are often of a different national or racial origin than citizens, States are encouraged to consider non-citizens as belonging to national minorities, and to ensure that they enjoy the rights that arise from such status.

Examples of the rights that non-citizens enjoy as members of minorities can be found in several legal instruments and in the jurisprudence of their monitoring bodies. For example, the Human Rights Committee has stated that "where aliens constitute a minority within the meaning of article 27 of the [International] Covenant on Civil and Political Rights, they shall not be denied the right, in community with other members of their group, to enjoy their own culture, to profess and practise their own religion and to use their own language." The rights of national and racial minorities to enjoy such rights, therefore, cannot be restricted to citizens.

In addition, the United Nations Declaration on the Rights of Persons Belonging to National or Ethnic, Religious and Linguistic Minorities, although not legally binding, elaborates upon the rights of national and ethnic minorities, which has been interpreted to include migrant communities.

Under the Rome Statute of the International Criminal Court, the Court apparently has jurisdiction to protect non-citizens from persecution and abuses committed with intent to cause annihilation of their national group. Article 5 of the Rome Statute lists the four crimes that fall within the Court's jurisdiction: the crime of genocide, crimes against humanity, war crimes and the crime of aggression. Article 6 defines genocide as certain acts "committed with intent to destroy, in whole or in part, a national, ethnical, racial or religious group, as such." These acts are, therefore, crimes within the jurisdiction of the Court. In addition, under article 7, "persecution against any identifiable group or collectivity on political, racial, national, ethnic, cultural, religious, gender...or other grounds that are universally recognized as impermissible under international law" are also considered crimes against humanity.

Non-citizens enjoy the right to freedom of religion. Furthermore, States are urged to take measures necessary to prevent practices that deny non-citizens their cultural and ethnic identity, such as requirements that noncitizens change their name in order to be naturalized. Article 15 of the International Covenant on Economic, Social and Cultural Rights obliges States to take steps to ensure that everyone, regardless of citizenship, enjoys the right to take part in cultural life. Non-citizens have the right to marry when at marriageable age.

2. Right to health, education, housing, a minimum standard of living and social security

States must avoid different standards of treatment with regard to citizens and non-citizens that might lead to the unequal enjoyment of economic, social and cultural rights. Governments shall take progressive measures to the extent of their available resources to protect the rights of everyone-regardless of citizenship-to: social security; an adequate standard of living including adequate food, clothing, housing, and the continuous improvement of living conditions; the enjoyment of the highest attainable standard of physical and mental health; and education.

States should take effective measures to ensure that housing agencies and private landlords refrain from engaging in discriminatory practices.

Educational institutions must be accessible to everyone, without discrimination, within the jurisdiction of a State party. This "principle of non-discrimination extends to all persons of school age residing in the territory of a State party, including non-nationals, and irrespective of their legal status."Furthermore, "the prohibition against discrimination enshrined in article 2 (2) of the [International] Covenant [on Economic, Social and Cultural Rights] is subject to neither progressive realization nor the availability of resources; it applies fully and immediately to all aspects of education and encompasses all internationally prohibited grounds of discrimination."

III. RIGHTS OF SELECTED NON-CITIZEN GROUPS

Different categories of undocumented non-citizens, such as stateless persons, refugees and asylum-seekers, undocumented economic migrants, women being trafficked into prostitution, and children, must each be dealt with in a manner appropriate to their particular situation.

A. Stateless persons

Some non-citizens are stateless. They either never acquired citizenship of the country of their birth or lost their citizenship, and have no claim to the citizenship of another State. Such persons include individuals native to the country of their residence who failed to register for citizenship during a specified period and have been denied it since then; and children born in States that recognize only the *jus sanguinis* principle of acquiring citizenship to non-citizen parents of States that recognize only the jus soli principle. The rights of stateless persons are enunciated in a number of international instruments, including the Convention relating to the Status of Stateless Persons and the Convention on the Reduction of Statelessness. The status of stateless persons-especially stateless persons who have been precluded from applying for residence permits or citizenship-should be regularized by, for example, simplifying procedures for applying for residence permits and through campaigns to make it clear that stateless persons would not risk expulsion when identifying themselves to the authorities. States should also seek to reduce the number of stateless persons, with priority for children, inter alia by encouraging parents to apply for citizenship on their behalf. Stateless persons should not be involuntarily repatriated to the countries of origin of their ancestors. Individuals who have taken the citizenship of a country other than their native country should be able to acquire citizenship of their native country.

Under article 12 (4) of the International Covenant on Civil and Political Rights, stateless persons should not be arbitrarily deprived of their right to enter their country of residence or a country with which they have a long-term relationship.

The rights of stateless persons are enunciated in a number of international instruments, including the Convention relating to the Status of Stateless Persons and the Convention on the Reduction of Statelessness

B. Refugees and asylum-seekers

Five United Nations instruments form the basis of the rights of refugees in international human rights law: the 1951 Convention relating to the Status of Refugees and its 1967 Protocol; the Statute of the Office of the High Commissioner for Refugees; the Declaration on Territorial Asylum; and the Handbook on Procedures and Criteria for Determining Refugee Status.

International standards pertaining to refugees and asylum-seekers should be applied equally, regardless of the nationality of the asylum-seeker or refugee. Conditions in refugee shelters and conditions of detention faced by undocumented migrants and asylum-seekers should meet international standards. States should ensure that individuals caught in an illegal situation, such as asylum-seekers who are in a country unlawfully and whose claims are not considered valid by the authorities, are not treated as criminals.

The 2003 report of the Special Rapporteur on the human rights of migrants focused particularly on the detention of migrants and the conditions of their detention. Concerns included detention of asylum-seekers; prolonged detention periods; the arbitrary nature of detention decisions; detention on the basis of unspecified allegations related to terrorism or national security; detention of trafficking victims; detention of migrant children; absence of legal assistance and judicial review procedures; detention with ordinary criminals; solitary confinement; methods of restraint threatening physical integrity; detention in inappropriate facilities;

overcrowding and poor hygienic conditions; lack of medical care; lack of education for young detainees; and other problems.

1. Refugees

The 1951 Convention relating to the Status of Refugees and its 1967 Protocol provide that refugees should be entitled to treatment at least as favourable as that accorded to citizens with respect to: religion (art. 4); protection of intellectual property (art. 14); access to courts and legal assistance (art. 16); rationing measures (art. 20); elementary education (art.

22 (1)); public relief and assistance (art. 23); labour legislation and social security (art. 24); as well as fiscal charges (art. 29). The Convention and its Protocol also require that States parties accord to refugees treatment no less favourable than that accorded to non-citizens generally with respect to exemption from legislative reciprocity (art. 7 (1)); acquisition of property (art. 13); non-political and non-profit-making associations and trade unions (art. 15); wage-earning employment (art. 17); self-employment (art. 18); liberal professions (art. 19); housing (art. 21); post-elementary education (art. 22 (2)); and freedom of movement (art. 26). Employment, housing and social assistance should not be denied to recognized refugees, especially on grounds of their ethnicity.

States must ensure a more rigorous supervision of the application of measures aimed at facilitating the integration of refugees, particularly at the local level. Some States have made positive efforts to create a comprehensive integration plan for new arrivals and offer them tools they will need for success in the society of the State.

2. Asylum-seekers

Certain rights apply particularly to asylum-seekers. Eligibility for asylum should not depend on the ethnic or national origin of applicants. Asylum-seekers should not be left in a destitute condition while awaiting examination of their asylum claims, since such poor conditions could reinforce prejudice, stereotypes and hostility towards asylum applicants. The procedure for determining eligibility for asylum should not be slow and States should ensure that applicants are given access to sufficient legal assistance. States should be encouraged to provide free legal advice to applicants. Time limits for registration to lodge asylum claims should not be so short as to deprive persons of the protection to which they are entitled under international law. International Human Rights Law is also relevant in the context of defining adequate reception standards for asylum-seekers. Asylum-seekers should be granted the right to work. The human rights of asylum-seekers are also protected by regional human rights instruments in Africa, Europe and the Americas that apply to all persons residing within the jurisdiction of their respective States parties, regardless of their legal status in the country of asylum.

The holding of asylum-seekers in detention should be avoided to the greatest extent possible, particularly in the cases of persons arriving with families. Where detention does occur, it should not be for an indefinite period, and careful attention should be paid to the accommodation and facilities provided for the families-particularly the children-of asylum-seekers held in detention.

Asylum-seekers and refugees should not be detained alongside convicted criminals, nor should they be detained for lack of identity papers or their uncertainty about travel routes into the receiving State. Wherever possible, asylum-seekers should be guaranteed freedom of movement.

C. Non-citizen workers and their families

Everyone-regardless of citizenship-has the right to work and Governments are obliged to take progressive measures to safeguard this right. Non-citizens who are lawfully present in a State are entitled to treatment equal to that enjoyed by citizens in the realm of employment and work. Everyone, including non-citizens, has the right to just and favourable conditions of work, and international standards that provide protection in treatment and conditions at work in areas such as safety, health, hours of work and remuneration apply to all workers regardless of citizenship or status. States must ensure the right of everyone to establish and join trade unions. Non-citizen workers should not be barred from holding trade union office and their right to strike should not be restricted.

1. International Labour Organization (ILO)

International Labour Organization (ILO) conventions and recommendations (for example, on collective bargaining, discrimination, workers' compensation, social security, working conditions and environment, abolition of forced labour and child labour) generally protect the rights of all workers irrespective of citizenship. The eight fundamental ILO conventions and the recommendations that accompany them apply to all workers regardless of citizenship. Several ILO instruments specifically protect migrant workers and their

families. The most significant are: Convention No. 97 concerning migration for employment; Convention No. 143 concerning working conditions and equal treatment of migrant workers; and Convention No. 118 concerning equality of treatment in social security. In many instances, the conventions guarantee certain rights-e.g., equal remuneration and minimum wage with respect to past employment and maintenance of social security benefits-to non-citizens regardless of the legality of the migrant's presence in the territory. Other rights are extended only to those persons lawfully within a territory, e.g., rights to equal opportunities and vocational training.

ILO Convention No. 143 provides specific guidance as to the treatment of irregular migrants and those migrants who are employed unlawfully. In laying out the minimum norms applicable to such persons, article 1, for example, establishes that States parties must "respect the basic human rights of all migrant workers" regardless of their migratory status or legal situation. The Committee of Experts on the Application of Conventions and Recommendations has interpreted these rights to be the fundamental human rights enshrined in the International Bill of Human Rights, the International Convention on the Protection of the Rights of All Migrant Workers and Members of Their Families, and the ILO Declaration on Fundamental Principles and Rights at Work.

2. International Convention on the Protection of the Rights of All Migrant Workers and Members of Their Families

The International Convention on the Protection of the Rights of All Migrant Workers and Members of Their Families, of which ILO Conventions Nos. 97 and 143 formed the basis, protects all migrant workers and their families, but does not generally include international organization employees, foreign development staff, refugees, stateless persons, students and trainees (arts. 1 and 3).

The Convention provides for: Non-discrimination (art. 7); Freedom for migrants to leave any country and to enter their country of origin (art. 8); The right to life (art. 9); Freedom from torture and ill-treatment (art. 10); Freedom from slavery or forced labour (art. 11); Freedom of thought, conscience and religion (art. 12); Freedom of opinion and expression (art. 13); Freedom from arbitrary or unlawful interference with privacy, family, home, correspondence or other communications (art. 14); Property rights (art. 15); Liberty and security of person (art. 16); The right of migrants deprived of their liberty to be treated with humanity (art. 17); A fair and public hearing by a competent, independent and impartial tribunal (art. 18); The prohibition of retroactive application of criminal laws (art. 19); The prohibition of imprisonment for failure to fulfill a contract (art. 20); The prohibition of the destruction of travel or identity documents (art. 21); The prohibition of expulsion on a collective basis or without fair procedures (art. 22); The right to consular or diplomatic assistance (art. 23); The right to recognition as a person before the law (art. 24); Equality of treatment between nationals and migrant workers as to work conditions and pay (art. 25); The right to participate in trade unions (art. 26); Equal access to social security (art. 27); The right to emergency medical care (art. 28); The right of a child to a name, birth registration and nationality (art. 29); and Equality of access to public education (art. 30).

In addition, States parties must ensure respect for migrants' cultural identity (art. 31); the right to repatriate earnings, savings and belongings (art. 32); and information about rights under the Convention (art. 33).

3. Inter-American Court of Human Rights

The Inter-American Court of Human Rights has confirmed the applicability of international labour standards to non-citizens, and particularly to non-citizens in irregular status. In an opinion issued in September 2003, the Court held that non-discrimination and the right to equality are jus cogens that are applicable to all residents regardless of immigration status. Hence, Governments cannot use immigration status as a justification for restricting the employment or labour rights of unauthorized workers, such as rights to social security. The Court found that Governments do have the right to deport individuals and refuse to offer jobs to people who do not possess employment documents, but held that, once an employment relationship has been initiated, unauthorized workers become entitled to all the employment and labour rights that are available to authorized workers.

The Court stated:

> "...the migratory status of a person cannot constitute a justification to deprive him of the enjoyment and exercise of human rights, including those of a labour-related nature. When assuming an employment relationship, the migrant acquires rights that must be recognized and ensured because he is an employee, irrespective of his regular or irregular status in the State where he is employed. These rights are a result of the employment relationship."

Inter-American Court of Human Rights: "Non-discrimination and the right to equality are jus cogens that are applicable to all residents regardless of immigration status."

4. Committee on the Elimination of Racial Discrimination

The Committee on the Elimination of Racial Discrimination has frequently expressed concern that non-citizens who serve as domestic workers are subjected to debt bondage, other illegal employment practices, passport deprivation, illegal confinement, rape and physical assault.8 States are urged to put an end to the practice of employers retaining the passports of their foreign employees, in particular domestic workers...

Victims of trafficking

Non-citizens are often the target of trafficking. Persons who emigrate through irregular channels, such as smuggling and trafficking networks, risk suffocating in containers or drowning when an overloaded ship sinks. Adequate assistance and support, including formal protection, aid and education, should be provided to victims of trafficking.

E. Non-citizen children

Article 2 of the Convention on the Rights of the Child provides that "States Parties shall respect and ensure the rights set forth in the present Convention to each child within their jurisdiction without discrimination of any kind . . . " The Committee on the Rights of the Child encourages States to continue and strengthen their efforts to integrate the right to non-discrimination that is enshrined in article fully in all relevant legislation, and to ensure that this right is effectively applied in all political, judicial and administrative decisions and in projects, programmes and services which have an impact on all children, including non-citizen children and children belonging to minority groups. The Committee recommends that States should develop comprehensive and coordinated policies to address the developing phenomenon of immigration, including public information campaigns to promote tolerance; monitor and collect data on racially motivated acts; and study the situation of non-citizen children, especially in the school system, and the effectiveness of measures taken to facilitate their integration. States should also take effective measures to address discriminatory attitudes or prejudices, in particular towards non-citizen children, fully and effectively implement legal measures to prevent discrimination that are already adopted, and ensure that their legislation is in full compliance with article 2 of the Convention on the Rights of the Child.

Citizenship based on the place of birth has emerged as the overriding international norm governing the nationality of children born to non-citizen parents, in particular if they would otherwise be stateless.

Children of non-citizens have the right to a name and the right to acquire a nationality. Under article 7 of the Convention on the Rights of the Child, a child "shall be registered immediately after birth and shall have the right from birth to a name, the right to acquire a nationality...States Parties shall ensure the implementation of these rights...in particular where the child would otherwise be stateless." In view of the nearly universal ratification of the Convention, the principle of jus soli (citizenship based on the place of birth) has emerged as the overriding international norm governing the nationality of children born to noncitizen parents, in particular if they would otherwise be stateless. The right of parents to transmit their citizenship to their children must be enforced without discrimination as to the sex of the parent. Article 7 of the Convention also requires transmittal of citizenship from a parent to his or her adopted child. Article 7 should be read in conjunction with article 8 (preservation of identity, including nationality, name and family relations), article 9 (avoiding separation from parents), article 10 (family reunification) and article 20 (continuity of upbringing of children deprived of their family environment). Within the holistic approach recommended by the Committee on the Rights of the Child for the interpretation of the Convention, those articles should be understood according to the general principles of the Convention as reflected in articles 2 (right to non-discrimination), 3 (principle of the best interests of the child), 6 (right to life and development) and 12 (right to respect for the child's views in all matters affecting the child and opportunity to be heard in any judicial or administrative proceedings affecting the child).

Children of non-citizens are entitled to those measures of protection required by their status as minors. Children of non-citizens without legal status should not be excluded from schools, and schools that allow children of non-citizens to be educated in programmes designed in their country of origin should be encouraged.

With specific regard to asylum-seekers who are children, the Convention on the Rights of the Child provides important guidance for designing and implementing reception policies under the "best interest" principle. States must guarantee: special protection and care to child asylum-seekers with respect to their special needs; avoidance of detention for asylum-seekers under 18 years of age; and access of children to legal and psychological assistance, including by enabling contact with non-governmental organizations offering such assistance. Asylum-seekers and refugees who are children should not be placed in institutions that are not equipped to provide the special care they require. Such children should not be the subject of discrimination in the enjoyment of economic, social and cultural rights such as access to education, health care and social services. States should ensure the full economic, social and cultural rights of all non-citizen children in detention without discrimination — especially the right to education — and ensure their right to integration into society. Conclusions and recommendations.

Almost all advocacy for non-citizens has focused on the rights of discrete groups, such as asylum-seekers, refugees, stateless persons, trafficked persons, etc. Unfortunately, however, little has been done to identify the common plights, needs and approaches for redress of the various non-citizen groups. Indeed, diverse groups of non-citizens — and their respective advocacy and interest groups — have traditionally seen themselves as separate and their problems as unique, despite similar goals and common circumstances. In addition, international law and mechanisms relating to non-citizens have, until recently, focused on non-citizen subgroups while neglecting broader protections for non-citizens as a whole. For example, various United Nations institutions have designated special rapporteurs on such themes as trafficking, migrants, indigenous people, refugees, and racial discrimination and xenophobia. Similarly, several treaties have been designed to protect trafficked persons, migrant workers, indigenous and tribal peoples, refugees, and stateless persons. While all of these measures are essential and do not overlap so much as to be rendered unnecessary, a unified effort for the protection of non-citizens is nonetheless needed.

A primary objective of any international effort to protect the rights of non-citizens begins by demonstrating, as indicated by this publication, that without clear, comprehensive standards governing the rights of non-citizens, their implementation by States and more effective monitoring of compliance, the discriminatory treatment of non-citizens in contravention of relevant international human rights instruments will continue.

Furthermore, since the seven principal human rights treaties deal with many of the problems encountered by non-citizens, States should pursue universal ratification and implementation of those treaties, particularly the International Convention on the Protection of the Rights of All Migrant Workers and Members of Their Families. States, as appropriate, should also ratify and implement such other relevant treaties as the Protocol relating to the Status of Refugees; ILO Conventions Nos. 97, 118, 143, etc.; the Conventions on the Reduction of Statelessness and relating to the Status of Stateless Persons; the Vienna Convention on Consular Relations and its Optional Protocols; Protocols Nos. 4 and 7 to the European Convention on Human Rights; and the European Framework Convention for the Protection of National Minorities. States should be encouraged to abide by the Declaration on the Human Rights of Individuals Who are not Nationals of the Country in which They Live.

Since problems relating to the treatment of non-citizens arise under each of the seven principal human rights treaties, it would be desirable for the treaty bodies to coordinate their work more effectively. One approach would be for the treaty bodies to prepare joint general comments/recommendations that would establish a consistent, structured approach to the protection of the rights of non-citizens. At a minimum, treaty bodies that have adopted specific standards should consider updating them and those bodies that have yet to issue interpretive guidance relating to non-citizens should do so. In addition, treaty bodies should intensify their dialogues with States parties with regard to the rights accorded to, and the actual situation faced by, non-citizens within their respective spheres of concern.

[Footnotes omitted]

Annex

Committee on the Elimination of Racial Discrimination, general recommendation XXX (2004) on discrimination against non-citizens

The Committee on the Elimination of Racial Discrimination,

Recalling the Charter of the United Nations and the Universal Declaration of Human Rights, according to which all human beings are born free and equal in dignity and rights and are entitled to the rights and freedoms enshrined therein without distinction of any kind, and the International Covenant on Economic, Social and Cultural Rights, the International Covenant on Civil and Political Rights and the International Convention on the Elimination of All Forms of Racial Discrimination,

Recalling the Durban Declaration in which the World Conference against Racism, Racial Discrimination, Xenophobia and Related Intolerance recognized that xenophobia against non-nationals, particularly migrants, refugees and asylum-seekers, constitutes one of the main sources of contemporary racism and that human rights violations against members of such groups occur widely in the context of discriminatory, xenophobic and racist practices,

Noting that, based on the International Convention on the Elimination of All Forms of Racial Discrimination and general recommendations XI and XX, it has become evident from the examination of the reports of States parties to the Convention that groups other than migrants, refugees and asylum-seekers are also of concern, including undocumented non-citizens and persons who cannot establish the nationality of the State on whose territory they live, even where such persons have lived all their lives on the same territory,

Having organized a thematic discussion on the issue of discrimination against non-citizens and received the contributions of members of the Committee and States parties, as well as contributions from experts of other United Nations organs and specialized agencies and from non-governmental organizations,

Recognizing the need to clarify the responsibilities of States parties to the International Convention on the Elimination of All Forms of Racial Discrimination with regard to non-citizens,

Basing its action on the provisions of the Convention, in particular article 5, which requires States parties to prohibit and eliminate discrimination based on race, colour, descent, and national or ethnic origin in the enjoyment by all persons of civil, political, economic, social and cultural rights and freedoms, Affirms that:

1. RESPONSIBILITIES OF STATES PARTIES TO THE CONVENTION

Article 1, paragraph 1, of the Convention defines racial discrimination. Article 1, paragraph 2, provides for the possibility of differentiating between citizens and non-citizens. Article 1, paragraph 3, declares that, concerning nationality, citizenship or naturalization, the legal provisions of States parties must not discriminate against any particular nationality;

Article 1, paragraph 2, must be construed so as to avoid undermining the basic prohibition of discrimination; hence, it should not be interpreted to detract in any way from the rights and freedoms recognized and enunciated in particular in the Universal Declaration of Human Rights, the International Covenant on Economic, Social and Cultural Rights and the International Covenant on Civil and Political Rights;

Article 5 of the Convention incorporates the obligation of States parties to prohibit and eliminate racial discrimination in the enjoyment of civil, political, economic, social and cultural rights. Although some of these rights, such as the right to participate in elections, to vote and to stand for election, may be confined to citizens, human rights are, in principle, to be enjoyed by all persons. States parties are under an obligation to guarantee equality between citizens and non-citizens in the enjoyment of these rights to the extent recognized under international law;

Under the Convention, differential treatment based on citizenship or immigration status will constitute discrimination if the criteria for such differentiation, judged in the light of the objectives and purposes of the Convention, are not applied pursuant to a legitimate aim, and are not proportional to the achievement of this aim. Differentiation within the scope of article 1, paragraph 4, of the Convention relating to special measures is not considered discriminatory;

States parties are under an obligation to report fully upon legislation on non-citizens and its implementation. Furthermore, States parties should include in their periodic reports, in an appropriate form, socio-economic data on the non-citizen population within their jurisdiction, including data disaggregated by gender and national or ethnic origin; Recommends,

Based on these general principles, that the States parties to the Convention, as appropriate to their specific circumstances, adopt the following measures:

2. MEASURES OF A GENERAL NATURE

Review and revise legislation, as appropriate, in order to guarantee that such legislation is in full compliance with the Convention, in particular regarding the effective enjoyment of the rights mentioned in article 5, without discrimination;

Ensure that legislative guarantees against racial discrimination apply to non-citizens regardless of their immigration status, and that the implementation of legislation does not have a discriminatory effect on non-citizens;

Pay greater attention to the issue of multiple discrimination faced by non-citizens, in particular concerning the children and spouses of non-citizen workers, to refrain from applying different standards of treatment to female non-citizen spouses of citizens and male non-citizen spouses of citizens, to report on any such practices and to take all necessary steps to address them;

Ensure that immigration policies do not have the effect of discriminating against persons on the basis of race, colour, descent, or national or ethnic origin;

Ensure that any measures taken in the fight against terrorism do not discriminate, in purpose or effect, on the grounds of race, colour, descent, or national or ethnic origin and that non-citizens are not subjected to racial or ethnic profiling or stereotyping;

3. PROTECTION AGAINST HATE SPEECH AND RACIAL VIOLENCE

Take steps to address xenophobic attitudes and behaviour towards non-citizens, in particular hate speech and racial violence, and to promote a better understanding of the principle of non-discrimination in respect of the situation of non-citizens;

Take resolute action to counter any tendency to target, stigmatize, stereotype or profile, on the basis of race, colour, descent, and national or ethnic origin, members of "non-citizen" population groups, especially by politicians, officials, educators and the media, on the Internet and other electronic communications networks and in society at large;

4. ACCESS TO CITIZENSHIP

Ensure that particular groups of non-citizens are not discriminated against with regard to access to citizenship or naturalization, and to pay due attention to possible barriers to naturalization that may exist for long-term or permanent residents;

Recognize that deprivation of citizenship on the basis of race, colour, descent, or national or ethnic origin is a breach of States parties' obligations to ensure non-discriminatory enjoyment of the right to nationality;

Take into consideration that in some cases denial of citizenship for long-term or permanent residents could result in creating disadvantage for them in access to employment and social benefits, in violation of the Convention's anti-discrimination principles;

Reduce statelessness, in particular statelessness among children, by, for example, encouraging their parents to apply for citizenship on their behalf and allowing both parents to transmit their citizenship to their children;

Regularize the status of former citizens of predecessor States who now reside within the jurisdiction of the State party;

5. ADMINISTRATION OF JUSTICE

18. Ensure that non-citizens enjoy equal protection and recognition before the law and in this context, to take action against racially motivated violence and to ensure the access of victims to effective legal remedies and the right to seek just and adequate reparation for any damage suffered as a result of such violence;

19. Ensure the security of non-citizens, in particular with regard to arbitrary detention, as well as ensure that conditions in centres for refugees and asylum-seekers meet international standards;

20. Ensure that non-citizens detained or arrested in the fight against terrorism are properly protected by domestic law that complies with international human rights, refugee and humanitarian law;

21. Combat ill-treatment of and discrimination against non-citizens by police and other law enforcement agencies and civil servants by strictly applying relevant legislation and regulations providing for sanctions and by ensuring that all officials dealing with non-citizens receive special training, including training in human rights;

22. Introduce in criminal law the provision that committing an offence with racist motivation or aim constitutes an aggravating circumstance allowing for a more severe punishment;

23. Ensure that claims of racial discrimination brought by non-citizens are investigated thoroughly and that claims made against officials, notably those concerning discriminatory or racist behaviour, are subject to independent and effective scrutiny;

24. Regulate the burden of proof in civil proceedings involving discrimination based on race, colour, descent, and national or ethnic origin so that once a non-citizen has established a prima facie case that he or she has been a victim of such discrimination, it shall be for the respondent to provide evidence of an objective and reasonable justification for the differential treatment;

The Rights of Non-citizens

6. EXPULSION AND DEPORTATION OF NON-CITIZENS

25. Ensure that laws concerning deportation or other forms of removal of non-citizens from the jurisdiction of the State party do not discriminate in purpose or effect among non-citizens on the basis of race, colour or ethnic or national origin, and that non-citizens have equal access to effective remedies, including the right to challenge expulsion orders, and are allowed effectively to pursue such remedies; 26. Ensure that non-citizens are not subject to collective expulsion in particular in situations where there are insufficient guarantees that the personal circumstances of each of the persons concerned have been taken into account;

27. Ensure that non-citizens are not returned or removed to a country or territory where they are at risk of being subject to serious human rights abuses, including torture and cruel, inhuman or degrading treatment or punishment;

28. Avoid expulsions of non-citizens, especially of long-term residents, that would result in disproportionate interference with the right to family life; ...

7. ECONOMIC, SOCIAL AND CULTURAL RIGHTS

29. Remove obstacles that prevent the enjoyment of economic, social and cultural rights by non-citizens, notably in the areas of education, housing, employment and health;

30. Ensure that public educational institutions are open to non-citizens and children of undocumented immigrants residing in the territory of a State party;

31. Avoid segregated schooling and different standards of treatment being applied to non-citizens on grounds of race, colour, descent, and national or ethnic origin in elementary and secondary school and with respect to access to higher education;

32. Guarantee the equal enjoyment of the right to adequate housing for citizens and non-citizens, especially by avoiding segregation in housing and ensuring that housing agencies refrain from engaging in discriminatory practices;

33. Take measures to eliminate discrimination against non-citizens in relation to working conditions and work requirements, including employment rules and practices with discriminatory purposes or effects; 34. Take effective measures to

prevent and redress the serious problems commonly faced by non-citizen workers, in particular by non-citizen domestic workers, including debt bondage, passport retention, illegal confinement, rape and physical assault;

35. Recognize that, while States parties may refuse to offer jobs to non-citizens without a work permit, all individuals are entitled to the enjoyment of labour and employment rights, including the freedom of assembly and association, once an employment relationship has been initiated until it is terminated;

36. Ensure that States parties respect the right of non-citizens to an adequate standard of physical and mental health by, inter alia, refraining from denying or limiting their access to preventive, curative and palliative health services;

37. Take the necessary measures to prevent practices that deny non-citizens their cultural identity, such as legal or de facto requirements that non-citizens change their name in order to obtain citizenship, and to take measures to enable non-citizens to preserve and develop their culture;

38. Ensure the right of non-citizens, without discrimination based on race, colour, descent, and national or ethnic origin, to have access to any place or service intended for use by the general public, such as transport, hotels, restaurants, cafés, theatres and parks;

39. The present general recommendation replaces general recommendation XI (1993). ISBN-13: 978-92-1-154175

Source: Office of the United Nations High Commissioner for Human Rights, The Rights of Non-Citizens, 2006
http://www.ohchr.org/Documents/Publications/noncitizensen.pdf

3. U.S. DEPT. OF STATE PRIORITY ENFORCEMENT PROGRAM WITH DHS MEMO ON ENFORCEMENT PRIORITIES

The following document is the Department of Homeland Security memo of instructions on priorities for thearrest (apprehension), detention, and removal of certain types of aliens from the U.S. Because there are so many undocumented aliens and so many legal aliens who lose their legal status by breaking certain laws, the DHS has to narrow its focus to arrest and remove these aliens who are the most harmful to our society, especially convicted criminals. This is also about the PEP program, which seeks to engage communities to work with the federal agencies to that end. This is executive administrative action.

The Department of Homeland Security's (DHS) Priority Enforcement Program (PEP) enables DHS to work with state and local law enforcement to take custody of individuals who pose a danger to public safety before those individuals are released into our communities. PEP was established at the direction of DHS Secretary Jeh Johnson in a November 20, 2014, memorandum, entitled Secure Communities. PEP focuses on convicted criminals and others who pose a danger to public safety.

How it works
PEP begins at the state and local level when an individual is arrested and booked by a law enforcement officer for a criminal violation and his or her fingerprints are submitted to the FBI for criminal history and warrant checks. This same biometric data is also sent to U.S. Immigration and Customs Enforcement (ICE) so that ICE can determine whether the individual is a priority for removal, consistent with the DHS enforcement priorities described in Secretary Johnson's November 20, 2014 Secure Communities memorandum. Under PEP, ICE will seek the transfer of a removable individual when that individual has been convicted of an offense listed under the DHS civil immigration enforcement priorities, has intentionally participated in an organized criminal gang to further the illegal activity of the gang, or poses a danger to national security.

What are DHS' priorities for removal?
PEP builds upon the enforcement priorities set forth in the [following] November 20, 2014, Memorandum from DHS Secretary Jeh Johnson entitled *Policies for the Apprehension, Detention and Removal of Undocumented Immigrants.*

Secretary, U.S. Department of Homeland Security, Washington, DC 20528

Homeland Security November 20, 2014

MEMORANDUM FOR:

Thomas S. Winkowski, Acting Director U.S. Immigration and Customs Enforcement
R. Gil Kerlikowske, Commissioner U.S. Customs and Border Protection
Leon Rodriguez, Director U.S. Citizenship and Immigration Services
Alan D. Bersin, Acting Assistant Secretary for Policy

FROM: Jeh Charles Johnson, Secretary of the Department of Homeland Security
SUBJECT: Policies for the Apprehension, Detention and Removal of Undocumented Immigrants

This memorandum reflects new policies for the apprehension, detention, and removal of aliens in this country. This memorandum should be considered Department-wide guidance, applicable to the activities of U.S. Immigration and Customs Enforcement (ICE), U.S. Customs and Border Protection (CBP), and U.S. Citizenship and Immigration Services (USCIS). This memorandum should inform enforcement and removal activity, detention decisions, budget requests and execution, and strategic planning.

In general, our enforcement and removal policies should continue to prioritize threats to national security, public safety, and border security. The intent of this new policy is to provide clearer and more effective guidance in the pursuit of those priorities. To promote public confidence in our enforcement activities, I am also directing herein greater transparency in the annual reporting of our removal statistics, to include data that tracks the priorities outlined below. www.dhs.gov

The Department of Homeland Security (DHS) and its immigration components — CBP, ICE, and USCIS — are responsible for enforcing the nation's immigration laws. Due to limited resources, DHS and its Components cannot respond to all immigration violations or remove all persons illegally in the United States. As is true of virtually every other law enforcement agency, DHS must exercise prosecutorial discretion in the enforcement of the law. And, in the exercise of that discretion, DHS can and should develop smart enforcement priorities, and ensure that use of its limited resources is devoted to the pursuit of those priorities. DHS's enforcement priorities are, have been, and will continue to be national security, border security, and public safety. DHS personnel are directed to prioritize the use of enforcement personnel , detention space, and removal assets accordingly.

In the immigration context, prosecutorial discretion should apply not only to the decision to issue, serve, file, or cancel a Notice to Appear, but also to a broad range of other discretionary enforcement decisions, including deciding: whom to stop, question, and arrest; whom to detain or release; whether to settle, dismiss, appeal, or join in a motion on a case; and whether to grant deferred action, parole, or a stay of removal instead of pursuing removal in a case. While DHS may exercise prosecutorial discretion at any stage of an enforcement proceeding, it is generally preferable to exercise such discretion as early in the case or proceeding as possible in order to preserve government resources that would otherwise be expended in pursuing enforcement and removal of higher priority cases. Thus, DHS personnel are expected to exercise discretion and pursue these priorities at all stages of the enforcement process-from the earliest investigative stage to enforcing final orders of removal-subject to their chains of command and to the particular responsibilities and authorities applicable to their specific position.

Except as noted below, the following memoranda are hereby rescinded and superseded: John Morton, Civil Immigration Enforcement: Priorities for the Apprehension, Detention, and Removal of Aliens, March 2, 2011; John Morton, Exercising Prosecutorial Discretion Consistent with the Civil Enforcement Priorities of the Agency for the Apprehension, Detention and Removal of Aliens, June 17, 20 11; Peter Vincent, Case-by-Case Review of Incoming and Certain Pending Cases, November 17, 2011; Civil Immigration Enforcement: Guidance on the Use of Detainers in the Federal, State, Local, and Tribal Criminal Justice Systems, December 21, 2012; National Fugitive Operations Program: Priorities, Goals, and Expectations, December 8, 2009.

A. Civil Immigration Enforcement Priorities

The following shall constitute the Department's civil immigration enforcement priorities:

Priority 1 (threats to national security, border security, and public safety)
Aliens described in this priority represent the highest priority to which enforcement resources should be directed:

(a) aliens engaged in or suspected of terrorism or espionage, or who otherwise pose a danger to national security;

(b) aliens apprehended at the border or ports of entry while attempting to unlawfully enter the United States;

(c) aliens convicted of an offense for which an element was active participation in a criminal street gang, as defined in 18 U.S.C. § 52 l(a), or aliens not younger than 16 years of age who intentionally participated in an organized criminal gang to further the illegal activity of the gang;

(d) aliens convicted of an offense classified as a felony in the convicting jurisdiction, other than a state or local offense for which an essential element was the alien's immigration status; and

(e) aliens convicted of an "aggravated felony," as that term is defined in section 101(a)(43) of the Immigration and Nationality Act at the time of the conviction.

The removal of these aliens must be prioritized unless they qualify for asylum or another form of relief under our laws, or unless, in the judgment of an ICE Field Office Director, CBP Sector Chief or CBP Director of Field Operations, there are compelling and exceptional factors that clearly indicate the alien is not a threat to national security, border security, or public safety and should not therefore be an enforcement priority.

Priority 2 (misdemeanants and new immigration violators)
Aliens described in this priority, who are also not described in Priority 1, represent the second-highest priority for apprehension and removal. Resources should be dedicated accordingly to the removal of the following:

(a) aliens convicted of three or more misdemeanor offenses, other than minor traffic offenses or state or local offenses for which an essential element was the alien's immigration status, provided the offenses arise out of three separate incidents;

(b) aliens convicted of a "significant misdemeanor," which for these purposes is an offense of domestic violence ; 1 sexual abuse or exploitation; burglary; U.N. lawful possession or use of a firearm; drug distribution or trafficking; or driving under the influence; or if not an offense listed above, one for which the individual was sentenced to time in custody of 90 days or more (the sentence must involve time to be served in custody, and does not include a suspended sentence);

(c) aliens apprehended anywhere in the United States after unlawfully entering or re-entering the United States and who cannot establish to the satisfaction of an immigration officer that they have been physically present in the United States continuously since January 1, 2014 ; and

(d) aliens who, in the judgment of an ICE Field Office Director, USCIS District Director, or USCIS Service Center Director, have significantly abused the visa or visa waiver programs.

These aliens should be removed unless they qualify for asylum or another form of relief under our laws or, unless, in the judgment of an ICE Field Office Director, CBP Sector Chief, CBP Director of Field Operations, USCIS District Director, or users Service Center Director, there are factors indicating the alien is not a threat to national security, border security, or public safety, and should not therefore be an enforcement priority.

Priority 3 (other immigration violations)
Priority 3 aliens are those who have been issued a final order of removal on or after January 1, 2014. Aliens described in this priority, who are not also described in Priority 1 or 2, represent the third and lowest priority for apprehension and removal. Resources should be dedicated accordingly to aliens in this priority. Priority 3 aliens should generally be removed unless they qualify for asylum or another form of relief under our laws or, unless, in the judgment of an immigration officer, the alien is not a threat to the integrity of the immigration system or there are factors suggesting the alien should not be an enforcement priority....

B. Apprehension, Detention, and Removal of Other Aliens Unlawfully in the United States

Nothing in this memorandum should be construed to prohibit or discourage the apprehension, detention, or removal of aliens unlawfully in the United States who are not identified as priorities herein. However, resources should be dedicated, to the greatest degree possible, to the removal of aliens described in the priorities set forth above, commensurate with the level of prioritization identified. Immigration officers and attorneys may pursue removal of an alien not identified as a priority herein, provided, in the judgment of an ICE Field Office Director, removing such an alien would serve an important federal interest.

C. Detention

As a general rule, DHS detention resources should be used to support the enforcement priorities noted above or for aliens subject to mandatory detention by law. Absent extraordinary circumstances or the requirement of mandatory detention, field office directors should not expend detention resources on aliens who are known to be suffering from serious physical or mental illness, who are disabled, elderly, pregnant, or nursing, who demonstrate that they are primary caretakers of children or an infirm person, or whose detention is otherwise not in the public interest. To detain aliens in those categories who are not subject to mandatory detention, DHS officers or special agents must obtain approval from the ICE Field Office Director. If an alien falls within the above categories and is subject to mandatory detention, field office directors are encouraged to contact their local Office of Chief Counsel for guidance.

D. Exercising Prosecutorial Discretion

Section A, above, requires DHS personnel to exercise discretion based on individual circumstances. As noted above, aliens in Priority l must be prioritized for removal unless they qualify for asylum or other form of relief under our laws, or unless, in the judgment of an ICE Field Office Director, CBP Sector Chief, or CBP Director of Field Operations, there are compelling and exceptional factors that clearly indicate the alien is not a threat to national security, border security, or public safety and should not therefore be an enforcement priority. Likewise, aliens in Priority 2 should be removed unless they qualify for asylum or other forms of relief under our laws, or unless, in the judgment of an ICE Field Office Director, CBP Sector Chief, CBP Director of Field Operations, USCIS District Director, or USCIS Service Center Director, there are factors indicating the alien is not a threat to national security, border security, or public safety and should not therefore be an enforcement priority. Similarly, aliens in Priority 3 should generally be removed unless they qualify for asylum or another form of relief under our laws or, unless, in the judgment of an immigration officer, the alien is not a threat to the 5 integrity of the immigration system or there are factors suggesting the alien should not be an enforcement priority.

In making such judgments, DHS personnel should consider factors such as: extenuating circumstances involving the offense of conviction; extended length of time since the offense of conviction; length of time in the United States; military service; family or community ties in the United States; status as a victim, witness or plaintiff in civil or criminal proceedings; or compelling humanitarian factors such as poor health, age, pregnancy, a young child, or a seriously ill relative. These factors are not intended to be dispositive nor is this list intended to be exhaustive. Decisions should be based on the totality of the circumstances.

E. Implementation

The revised guidance shall be effective on January 5, 2015. Implementing training and guidance will be provided to the workforce prior to the effective date. The revised guidance in this memorandum applies only to aliens encountered or apprehended on or after the effective date, and aliens detained, in removal proceedings, or subject to removal orders who have not been removed from the United States as of the effective date. Nothing in this guidance is intended to modify USCIS Notice to Appear policies, which remain in force and effect to the extent they are not inconsistent with this memorandum.

F. Data

By this memorandum I am directing the Office of Immigration Statistics to create the capability to collect, maintain, and report to the Secretary data reflecting the numbers of those apprehended, removed, returned, or otherwise repatriated by any component of DHS and to report that data in accordance with the priorities set forth above. I direct CBP, ICE, and USCIS to cooperate in this effort. I intend for this data to be part of the package of data released by DHS to the public annually.

G. No Private Right Statement

These guidelines and priorities are not intended to, do not, and may not be relied upon to create any right or benefit, substantive or procedural, enforceable at law by any party in any administrative, civil, or criminal matter.

Source: U.S. Immigration and Customs Enforcement, Priority Enforcement Program, https://www.ice.gov/pep and Secretary, U.S. Department of Homeland Security, Jeh Charles Johnson, November 20, 2014, https://www.dhs.gov/sites/default/files/publications/14_1120_memo_prosecutorial_discretion.pdf

༄༅༄༅༄༅༄༅

4. GENERAL COMMENT NO. 15 OF THE U.N. HRC ON THE POSITION OF ALIENS UNDER THE COVENANT (ON CIVIL AND POLITICAL RIGHTS)

The Human Rights Committee is the U.N. treaty body elected by states parties to the ICCPR to supervise the states in implementing the ICCPR. One of its tasks is to draft and issue General Comments on the interpretation and application of the articles of the ICCPR. These serve as roadmaps for states parties on how to comply with the treaty norms. This document explains how aliens should be regarded as holders of rights under the treaty, how they can exercise them, and how to seek an effective remedy for violations.

[Text]

GENERAL COMMENT 15

The position of aliens under the Covenant (Twenty-seventh session, 1986),

Compilation of General Comments and General Recommendations Adopted by Human Rights Treaty Bodies, U.N. Doc. HRI/GEN/1/Rev.1 at 18 (1994).

1. Reports from States parties have often failed to take into account that each State party must ensure the rights in the Covenant to "all individuals within its territory and subject to its jurisdiction" (art. 2, para. 1). In general, the rights set forth in the Covenant apply to everyone, irrespective of reciprocity, and irrespective of his or her nationality or statelessness.

2. Thus, the general rule is that each one of the rights of the Covenant must be guaranteed without discrimination between citizens and aliens. Aliens receive the benefit of the general requirement of nondiscrimination in respect of the rights guaranteed in the Covenant, as provided for in article 2 thereof. This guarantee applies to aliens and citizens alike. Exceptionally, some of the rights recognized in the Covenant are expressly applicable only to citizens (art. 25), while article 13 applies only to aliens. However, the Committee's experience in examining reports shows that in a number of countries other rights that aliens should enjoy under the Covenant are denied to them or are subject to limitations that cannot always be justified under the Covenant.

3. A few constitutions provide for equality of aliens with citizens. Some constitutions adopted more recently carefully distinguish fundamental rights that apply to all and those granted to citizens only, and deal with each in detail. In many States, however, the constitutions are drafted in terms of citizens only when granting relevant rights. Legislation and case law may also play an important part in providing for the rights of aliens. The Committee has been informed that in some States fundamental rights, though not guaranteed to aliens by the Constitution or other legislation, will also be extended to them as required by the Covenant. In certain cases, however, there has clearly been a failure to implement Covenant rights without discrimination in respect of aliens.

4. The Committee considers that in their reports States parties should give attention to the position of aliens, both under their law and in actual practice. The Covenant gives aliens all the protection regarding rights guaranteed therein, and its requirements should be observed by States parties in their legislation and in practice as appropriate. The position of aliens would thus be considerably improved. States parties should ensure that the provisions of the Covenant and the rights under it are made known to aliens within their jurisdiction.

5. The Covenant does not recognize the right of aliens to enter or reside in the territory of a State party. It is in principle a matter for the State to decide who it will admit to its territory. However, in certain circumstances an alien may enjoy the protection of the Covenant even in relation to entry or residence, for example, when considerations of non-discrimination, prohibition of inhuman treatment and respect for family life arise.

6. Consent for entry may be given subject to conditions relating, for example, to movement, residence and employment. A State may also impose general conditions upon an alien who is in transit. However, once aliens are allowed to enter the territory of a State party they are entitled to the rights set out in the Covenant.

7. Aliens thus have an inherent right to life, protected by law, and may not be arbitrarily deprived of life. They must not be subjected to torture or to cruel, inhuman or degrading treatment or punishment; nor may they be held in slavery or servitude. Aliens have the full right to liberty and security of the person. If lawfully deprived of their liberty, they shall be treated with humanity and with respect for the inherent dignity of their person. Aliens may not be imprisoned for failure to fulfill a contractual obligation. They have the right to liberty of movement and free choice of residence; they shall be free to leave the country. Aliens shall be equal before the courts and tribunals, and shall be entitled to a fair and public hearing by a competent, independent and impartial tribunal established by law in the determination of any criminal charge or of rights and obligations in a suit at law. Aliens shall not be subjected to retrospective penal legislation, and are entitled to recognition before the law. They may not be subjected to arbitrary or unlawful interference with their privacy, family, home or correspondence. They have the right to freedom of thought, conscience and religion, and the right to hold opinions and to express them. Aliens receive the benefit of the right of peaceful assembly and of freedom of association. They may marry when at marriageable age. Their children are entitled to those measures of protection required by their status as minors. In those cases where aliens constitute a minority within the meaning of article 27, they shall not be denied the right, in community with other members of their group, to enjoy their own culture, to profess and practice their own religion and to use their own language. Aliens are entitled to equal protection by the law. There shall be no discrimination between aliens and citizens in the application of these rights. These rights of aliens may be qualified only by such limitations as may be lawfully imposed under the Covenant.

8. Once an alien is lawfully within a territory, his freedom of movement within the territory and his right to leave that territory may only be restricted in accordance with article 12, paragraph 3. Differences in treatment in this regard between aliens and nationals, or between different categories of aliens, need to be justified under article 12, paragraph 3. Since such restrictions must, inter alia, be consistent with the other rights recognized in the Covenant, a State party cannot, by restraining an alien or deporting him to a third country, arbitrarily prevent his return to his own country (art. 12, para. 4).

9. Many reports have given insufficient information on matters relevant to article 13. That article is applicable to all procedures aimed at the obligatory departure of an alien, whether described in national law as expulsion or otherwise. If such procedures entail arrest, the safeguards of the Covenant relating to deprivation of liberty (arts. 9 and 10) may also be applicable. If the arrest is for the particular purpose of extradition, other provisions of national and international law may apply. Normally an alien who is expelled must be allowed to leave for any country that agrees to take him. The particular rights of article 13 only protect those aliens who are lawfully in the territory of a State party. This means that national law concerning the requirements for entry and stay must be taken into account in determining the scope of that protection, and that illegal entrants and aliens who have stayed longer than the law or their permits allow, in particular, are not covered by its provisions. However, if the legality of an alien's entry or stay is in dispute, any decision on this point leading to his expulsion or deportation ought to be taken in accordance with article 13. It is for the competent authorities of the State party, in good faith and in the exercise of their powers, to apply and interpret the domestic law, observing, however, such requirements under the Covenant as equality before the law (art. 26).

10. Article 13 directly regulates only the procedure and not the substantive grounds for expulsion. However, by allowing only those carried out "in pursuance of a decision reached in accordance with law," its purpose is clearly to prevent arbi-

trary expulsions. On the other hand, it entitles each alien to a decision in his own case and, hence, article 13 would not be satisfied with laws or decisions providing for collective or mass expulsions. This understanding, in the opinion of the Committee, is confirmed by further provisions concerning the right to submit reasons against expulsion and to have the decision reviewed by and to be represented before the competent authority or someone designated by it. An alien must be given full facilities for pursuing his remedy against expulsion so that this right will in all the circumstances of his case be an effective one. The principles of article 13 relating to appeal against expulsion and the entitlement to review by a competent authority may only be departed from when "compelling reasons of national security" so require. Discrimination may not be made between different categories of aliens in the application of article 13.

Source: Office of the High Commissioner for Human Rights, CCPR General Comment No. 15: The Position of Aliens Under the Covenant, 11 April 1986, http://www.refworld.org/docid/45139acfc.html

৵৽৵৽৵৽৵৽

5. GENERAL COMMENT NO. 35 OF THE U.N. HRC ON LIBERTY AND SECURITY OF PERSONS UNDER THE COVENANT (ON CIVIL AND POLITICAL RIGHTS)

Like Primary Source Document 4, this is a General Comment issued by the Human Rights Committee to all states parties. It is largely in reaction to the growing practice of governments forcibly detaining aliens. It emphasizes that freedom and liberty are the rule and detention is the exception and must be justified by the state in the context of the object and purpose of the ICCPR treaty.

Human Rights Committee
International Covenant on Civil and Political Rights CCPR/C/GC/35
General comment No. 35, Article 9 (Liberty and security of person)

I. General remarks

Article 9 recognizes and protects both liberty of person and security of person. In the Universal Declaration of Human Rights, article 3 proclaims that everyone has the right to life, liberty and security of person. That is the first substantive right protected by the Universal Declaration, which indicates the profound importance of article 9 of the Covenant both for individuals and for society as a whole. Liberty and security of person are precious for their own sake, and also because the deprivation of liberty and security of person have historically been principal means for impairing the enjoyment of other rights.

1. Liberty of person concerns freedom from confinement of the body, not a general freedom of action. Security of person concerns freedom from injury to the body and the mind, or bodily and mental integrity, as further discussed in paragraph 9 below. Article 9 guarantees those rights to everyone. "Everyone" includes, among others, girls and boys, soldiers, persons with disabilities, lesbian, gay, bisexual and transgender persons, aliens, refugees and asylum seekers, stateless persons, migrant workers, persons convicted of crime, and persons who have engaged in terrorist activity.

2. Paragraphs 2 to 5 of article 9 set out specific safeguards for the protection of liberty and security of person. Some of the provisions of article 9 (part of paragraph 2 and the whole of paragraph 3) apply only in connection with criminal charges. But the rest, in particular the important guarantee laid down in paragraph 4, i.e. the right to review by a court of the legality of detention, applies to all persons deprived of liberty.

3. Deprivation of liberty involves more severe restriction of motion within a narrower space than mere interference with liberty of movement under article 12. Examples of deprivation of liberty include police custody, *arraigo*, remand detention, imprisonment after conviction, house arrest, administrative detention, involuntary hospitalization, institutional custody of children and confinement to a restricted area of an airport, as well as being involuntarily transported. They also include certain further restrictions on a person who is already detained, for example, solitary confinement or the use of physical restraining devices. During a period of military service, restrictions that would amount to deprivation of liberty for a civilian may not amount to deprivation of liberty if they do not exceed the exigencies of normal military service or deviate from the normal conditions of life within the armed forces of the State party concerned.

4. Deprivation of personal liberty is without free consent. Individuals who go voluntarily to a police station to participate in an investigation, and who know that they are free to leave at any time, are not being deprived of their liberty.

5. States parties have the duty to take appropriate measures to protect the right to liberty of person against deprivation by third parties. States parties must protect individuals against abduction or detention by individual criminals or irregular groups, including armed or terrorist groups, operating within their territory. They must also protect individuals against wrongful deprivation of liberty by lawful organizations, such as employers, schools and hospitals. States parties should do their utmost to take appropriate measures to protect individuals against deprivation of liberty by the action of other States within their territory.

6. When private individuals or entities are empowered or authorized by a State party to exercise powers of arrest or detention, the State party remains responsible for adherence and ensuring adherence to article 9. It must rigorously limit those powers and must provide strict and effective control to ensure that those powers are not misused, and do not lead to arbitrary or unlawful arrest or detention. It must also provide effective remedies for victims if arbitrary or unlawful arrest or detention does occur.

7. The right to security of person protects individuals against intentional infliction of bodily or mental injury, regardless of whether the victim is detained or non-detained. For example, officials of States parties violate the right to personal security when they unjustifiably inflict bodily injury. The right to personal security also obliges States parties to take appropriate measures in response to death threats against persons in the public sphere, and more generally to protect individuals from foreseeable threats to life or bodily integrity proceeding from any governmental or private actors. States parties must take both measures to prevent future injury and retrospective measures, such as enforcement of criminal laws, in response to past injury. For example, States parties must respond appropriately to patterns of violence against categories of victims such as intimidation of human rights defenders and journalists, retaliation against witnesses, violence against women, including domestic violence, the hazing of conscripts in the armed forces, violence against children, violence against persons on the basis of their sexual orientation or gender identity, and violence against persons with disabilities. They should also prevent and redress unjustifiable use of force in law enforcement, and protect their populations against abuses by private security forces, and against the risks posed by excessive availability of firearms. The right to security of person does not address all risks to physical or mental health and is not implicated in the indirect health impact of being the target of civil or criminal proceedings.

II. Arbitrary detention and unlawful detention

10. The right to liberty of person is not absolute. Article 9 recognizes that sometimes deprivation of liberty is justified, for example, in the enforcement of criminal laws. Paragraph 1 requires that deprivation of liberty must not be arbitrary, and must be carried out with respect for the rule of law.

11. The second sentence of paragraph 1 prohibits arbitrary arrest and detention, while the third sentence prohibits unlawful deprivation of liberty, i.e., deprivation of liberty that is not imposed on such grounds and in accordance with such procedure as are established by law. The two prohibitions overlap, in that arrests or detentions may be in violation of the applicable law but not arbitrary, or legally permitted but arbitrary, or both arbitrary and unlawful. Arrest or detention that lacks any legal basis is also arbitrary. Unauthorized confinement of prisoners beyond the length of their sentences is arbitrary as well as unlawful; the same is true for unauthorized extension of other forms of detention. Continued confinement of detainees in defiance of a judicial order for their release is arbitrary as well as unlawful.

12. An arrest or detention may be authorized by domestic law and nonetheless be arbitrary. The notion of "arbitrariness" is not to be equated with "against the law," but must be interpreted more broadly to include elements of inappropriateness, injustice, lack of predictability and due process of law, as well as elements of reasonableness, necessity and proportionality. For example, remand in custody on criminal charges must be reasonable and necessary in all the circumstances. Aside from judicially imposed sentences for a fixed period of time, the decision to keep a person in any form of detention is arbitrary if it is not subject to periodic re-evaluation of the justification for continuing the detention.

13. The term "arrest" refers to any apprehension of a person that commences a deprivation of liberty, and the term "detention" refers to the deprivation of liberty that begins with the arrest and continues in time from apprehension until re-

lease. Arrest within the meaning of article 9 need not involve a formal arrest as defined under domestic law. When an additional deprivation of liberty is imposed on a person already in custody, such as detention on unrelated criminal charges, the commencement of that deprivation of liberty also amounts to an arrest.

14. The Covenant does not provide an enumeration of the permissible reasons for depriving a person of liberty. Article 9 expressly recognizes that individuals may be detained on criminal charges, and article 11 expressly prohibits imprisonment on ground of inability to fulfil a contractual obligation. Other regimes involving deprivation of liberty must also be established by law and must be accompanied by procedures that prevent arbitrary detention. The grounds and procedures prescribed by law must not be destructive of the right to liberty of person. The regime must not amount to an evasion of the limits on the criminal justice system by providing the equivalent of criminal punishment without the applicable protections. Although conditions of detention are addressed primarily by articles 7 and 10, detention may be arbitrary if the manner in which the detainees are treated does not relate to the purpose for which they are ostensibly being detained. The imposition of a draconian penalty of imprisonment for contempt of court without adequate explanation and without independent procedural safeguards is arbitrary.

15. To the extent that States parties impose security detention (sometimes known as administrative detention or internment) not in contemplation of prosecution on a criminal charge, the Committee considers that such detention presents severe risks of arbitrary deprivation of liberty. Such detention would normally amount to arbitrary detention as other effective measures addressing the threat, including the criminal justice system, would be available. If, under the most exceptional circumstances, a present, direct and imperative threat is invoked to justify the detention of persons considered to present such a threat, the burden of proof lies on States parties to show that the individual poses such a threat and that it cannot be addressed by alternative measures, and that burden increases with the length of the detention. States parties also need to show that detention does not last longer than absolutely necessary, that the overall length of possible detention is limited and that they fully respect the guarantees provided for by article 9 in all cases. Prompt and regular review by a court or other tribunal possessing the same attributes of independence and impartiality as the judiciary is a necessary guarantee for those conditions, as is access to independent legal advice, preferably selected by the detainee, and disclosure to the detainee of, at least, the essence of the evidence on which the decision is taken.

...

18. Detention in the course of proceedings for the control of immigration is not per se arbitrary, but the detention must be justified as reasonable, necessary and proportionate in the light of the circumstances and reassessed as it extends in time. Asylum seekers who unlawfully enter a State party's territory may be detained for a brief initial period in order to document their entry, record their claims and determine their identity if it is in doubt. To detain them further while their claims are being resolved would be arbitrary in the absence of particular reasons specific to the individual, such as an individualized likelihood of absconding, a danger of crimes against others or a risk of acts against national security. The decision must consider relevant factors case by case and not be based on a mandatory rule for a broad category; must take into account less invasive means of achieving the same ends, such as reporting obligations, sureties or other conditions to prevent absconding; and must be subject to periodic re-evaluation and judicial review. Decisions regarding the detention of migrants must also take into account the effect of the detention on their physical or mental health. Any necessary detention should take place in appropriate, sanitary, non-punitive facilities and should not take place in prisons. The inability of a State party to carry out the expulsion of an individual because of statelessness or other obstacles does not justify indefinite detention. Children should not be deprived of liberty, except as a measure of last resort and for the shortest appropriate period of time, taking into account their best interests as a primary consideration with regard to the duration and conditions of detention, and also taking into account the extreme vulnerability and need for care of unaccompanied minors.

Source: United Nations, International Covenant on Civil and Political Rights, CCPR/C/GC/35, Human Rights Committee, 16 December 2014, http://www.refworld.org/docid/553e0f984.html

6. GENERAL RECOMMENDATION XXX ON DISCRIMINATION AGAINST NON-CITIZENS ISSUED BY THE COMMITTEE ON ELIMINATION OF RACIAL DISCRIMINATION (CERD), 2005

The U.N. Committee on Elimination of Racial Discrimination, which supervises implementation of the International Convention on Elimination of All Forms of Racial Discrimination, issues "general recommendations," similar to the general comments of the HRCee (See Primary Source Documents 4 and 5). This document discusses racial discrimination against certain immigrants, "non citizens."

[Text]

Sixty-fifth session (2005)

General recommendation XXX on discrimination against non-citizens

The Committee on the Elimination of Racial Discrimination,

Recalling the Charter of the United Nations and the Universal Declaration of Human Rights, according to which all human beings are born free and equal in dignity and rights and are entitled to the rights and freedoms enshrined therein without distinction of any kind, and the International Covenant on Economic, Social and Cultural Rights, the International Covenant on Civil and Political Rights and the International Convention on the Elimination of All Forms of Racial Discrimination,

Recalling the Durban Declaration in which the World Conference against Racism, Racial Discrimination, Xenophobia and Related Intolerance, recognized that xenophobia against non-nationals, particularly migrants, refugees and asylum-seekers, constitutes one of the main sources of contemporary racism and that human rights violations against members of such groups occur widely in the context of discriminatory, xenophobic and racist practices,

Noting that, based on the International Convention on the Elimination of All Forms of Racial Discrimination and general recommendations XI and XX, it has become evident from the examination of the reports of States parties to the Convention that groups other than migrants, refugees and asylum-seekers are also of concern, including undocumented non-citizens and persons who cannot establish the nationality of the State on whose territory they live, even where such persons have lived all their lives on the same territory,

Having organized a thematic discussion on the issue of discrimination against non-citizens and received the contributions of members of the Committee and States parties, as well as contributions from experts of other United Nations organs and specialized agencies and from non-governmental organizations,

Recognizing the need to clarify the responsibilities of States parties to the International Convention on the Elimination of All Forms of Racial Discrimination with regard to non-citizens,

Basing its action on the provisions of the Convention, in particular article 5, which requires States parties to prohibit and eliminate discrimination based on race, colour, descent, and national or ethnic origin in the enjoyment by all persons of civil, political, economic, social and cultural rights and freedoms,

Affirms that:

I. Responsibilities of States parties to the Convention

1. Article 1, paragraph 1, of the Convention defines racial discrimination. Article 1, paragraph 2 provides for the possibility of differentiating between citizens and non-citizens. Article 1, paragraph 3 declares that, concerning nationality, citizenship or naturalization, the legal provisions of States parties must not discriminate against any particular nationality;

2. Article 1, paragraph 2, must be construed so as to avoid undermining the basic prohibition of discrimination; hence, it should not be interpreted to detract in any way from the rights and freedoms recognized and enunciated in particular in

the Universal Declaration of Human Rights, the International Covenant on Economic, Social and Cultural Rights and the International Covenant on Civil and Political Rights;

3. Article 5 of the Convention incorporates the obligation of States parties to prohibit and eliminate racial discrimination in the enjoyment of civil, political, economic, social and cultural rights. Although some of these rights, such as the right to participate in elections, to vote and to stand for election, may be confined to citizens, human rights are, in principle, to be enjoyed by all persons. States parties are under an obligation to guarantee equality between citizens and non-citizens in the enjoyment of these rights to the extent recognized under international law;

4. Under the Convention, differential treatment based on citizenship or immigration status will constitute discrimination if the criteria for such differentiation, judged in the light of the objectives and purposes of the Convention, are not applied pursuant to a legitimate aim, and are not proportional to the achievement of this aim. Differentiation within the scope of article 1, paragraph 4, of the Convention relating to special measures is not considered discriminatory;

5. States parties are under an obligation to report fully upon legislation on non-citizens and its implementation. Furthermore, States parties should include in their periodic reports, in an appropriate form, socio-economic data on the non-citizen population within their jurisdiction, including data disaggregated by gender and national or ethnic origin;

Recommends,

Based on these general principles, that the States parties to the Convention, as appropriate to their specific circumstances, adopt the following measures:

II. Measures of a general nature

6. Review and revise legislation, as appropriate, in order to guarantee that such legislation is in full compliance with the Convention, in particular regarding the effective enjoyment of the rights mentioned in article 5, without discrimination;

7. Ensure that legislative guarantees against racial discrimination apply to non-citizens regardless of their immigration status, and that the implementation of legislation does not have a discriminatory effect on non-citizens;

8. Pay greater attention to the issue of multiple discrimination faced by non-citizens, in particular concerning the children and spouses of non-citizen workers, to refrain from applying different standards of treatment to female non-citizen spouses of citizens and male non-citizen spouses of citizens, to report on any such practices and to take all necessary steps to address them;

9. Ensure that immigration policies do not have the effect of discriminating against persons on the basis of race, colour, descent, or national or ethnic origin;

10. Ensure that any measures taken in the fight against terrorism do not discriminate, in purpose or effect, on the grounds of race, colour, descent, or national or ethnic origin and that non-citizens are not subjected to racial or ethnic profiling or stereotyping;

III. Protection against hate speech and racial violence

11. Take steps to address xenophobic attitudes and behaviour towards non-citizens, in particular hate speech and racial violence, and to promote a better understanding of the principle of non-discrimination in respect of the situation of non-citizens;

12. Take resolute action to counter any tendency to target, stigmatize, stereotype or profile, on the basis of race, colour, descent, and national or ethnic origin, members of "non-citizen" population groups, especially by politicians, officials, educators and the media, on the Internet and other electronic communications networks and in society at large;

IV. Access to citizenship

13. Ensure that particular groups of non-citizens are not discriminated against with regard to access to citizenship or naturalization, and to pay due attention to possible barriers to naturalization that may exist for long-term or permanent residents;

14. Recognize that deprivation of citizenship on the basis of race, colour, descent, or national or ethnic origin is a breach of States parties' obligations to ensure non-discriminatory enjoyment of the right to nationality;

15. Take into consideration that in some cases denial of citizenship for long-term or permanent residents could result in creating disadvantage for them in access to employment and social benefits, in violation of the Convention's anti-discrimination principles;

16. Reduce statelessness, in particular statelessness among children, by, for example, encouraging their parents to apply for citizenship on their behalf and allowing both parents to transmit their citizenship to their children;

17. Regularize the status of former citizens of predecessor States who now reside within the jurisdiction of the State party;

V. Administration of justice

18. Ensure that non-citizens enjoy equal protection and recognition before the law and in this context, to take action against racially motivated violence and to ensure the access of victims to effective legal remedies and the right to seek just and adequate reparation for any damage suffered as a result of such violence;

19. Ensure the security of non-citizens, in particular with regard to arbitrary detention, as well as ensure that conditions in centres for refugees and asylum-seekers meet international standards;

20. Ensure that non-citizens detained or arrested in the fight against terrorism are properly protected by domestic law that complies with international human rights, refugee and humanitarian law;

21. Combat ill-treatment of and discrimination against non-citizens by police and other law enforcement agencies and civil servants by strictly applying relevant legislation and regulations providing for sanctions and by ensuring that all officials dealing with non-citizens receive special training, including training in human rights;

22. Introduce in criminal law the provision that committing an offence with racist motivation or aim constitutes an aggravating circumstance allowing for a more severe punishment;

23. Ensure that claims of racial discrimination brought by non-citizens are investigated thoroughly and that claims made against officials, notably those concerning discriminatory or racist behaviour, are subject to independent and effective scrutiny;

24. Regulate the burden of proof in civil proceedings involving discrimination based on race, colour, descent, and national or ethnic origin so that once a non-citizen has established a prima facie case that he or she has been a victim of such discrimination, it shall be for the respondent to provide evidence of an objective and reasonable justification for the differential treatment;

VI. Expulsion and deportation of non-citizens

25. Ensure that laws concerning deportation or other forms of removal of non-citizens from the jurisdiction of the State party do not discriminate in purpose or effect among non-citizens on the basis of race, colour or ethnic or national origin, and that non-citizens have equal access to effective remedies, including the right to challenge expulsion orders, and are allowed effectively to pursue such remedies;

26. Ensure that non-citizens are not subject to collective expulsion, in particular in situations where there are insufficient guarantees that the personal circumstances of each of the persons concerned have been taken into account;

27. Ensure that non-citizens are not returned or removed to a country or territory where they are at risk of being subject to serious human rights abuses, including torture and cruel, inhuman or degrading treatment or punishment;

28. Avoid expulsions of non-citizens, especially of long-term residents, that would result in disproportionate interference with the right to family life;

VII. Economic, social and cultural rights

29. Remove obstacles that prevent the enjoyment of economic, social and cultural rights by non-citizens, notably in the areas of education, housing, employment and health;

30. Ensure that public educational institutions are open to non-citizens and children of undocumented immigrants residing in the territory of a State party;

31. Avoid segregated schooling and different standards of treatment being applied to non-citizens on grounds of race, colour, descent, and national or ethnic origin in elementary and secondary school and with respect to access to higher education;

32. Guarantee the equal enjoyment of the right to adequate housing for citizens and non-citizens, especially by avoiding segregation in housing and ensuring that housing agencies refrain from engaging in discriminatory practices;

33. Take measures to eliminate discrimination against non-citizens in relation to working conditions and work requirements, including employment rules and practices with discriminatory purposes or effects;

34. Take effective measures to prevent and redress the serious problems commonly faced by non-citizen workers, in particular by non-citizen domestic workers, including debt bondage, passport retention, illegal confinement, rape and physical assault;

35. Recognize that, while States parties may refuse to offer jobs to non-citizens without a work permit, all individuals are entitled to the enjoyment of labour and employment rights, including the freedom of assembly and association, once an employment relationship has been initiated until it is terminated;

36. Ensure that States parties respect the right of non-citizens to an adequate standard of physical and mental health by, inter alia, refraining from denying or limiting their access to preventive, curative and palliative health services;

37. Take the necessary measures to prevent practices that deny non-citizens their cultural identity, such as legal or de facto requirements that non-citizens change their name in order to obtain citizenship, and to take measures to enable non-citizens to preserve and develop their culture;

38. Ensure the right of non-citizens, without discrimination based on race, colour, descent, and national or ethnic origin, to have access to any place or service intended for use by the general public, such as transport, hotels, restaurants, cafés, theatres and parks;

39. The present general recommendation replaces general recommendation XI (1993).

Source: United Nations Office of the High Commissioner for Human Rights, CERD General Recommendation XXX on Discrimination Against Non Citizens, 1 October 2002, http://www.refworld.org/publisher,CERD,GENERAL,,45139e084,0.html

꿍ᅰ꿍ᅰ꿍ᅰ꿍ᅰ

7. STATEMENT OF THE U.S. GOVERNMENT, REPORT OF THE UNITED STATES OF AMERICA SUBMITTED TO THE U.N. HIGH COMMISSIONER FOR HUMAN RIGHTS IN CONJUNCTION WITH THE UNIVERSAL PERIODIC REVIEW, 2015

In 2015 the U.S. government appeared before the U.N. Human Rights Council for its Universal Periodic Review, like every other country is obligated to do every five years. Before appearing it had to submit a report about how the U.S. was doing in respecting human rights. The report covered many topics including immigration detention. Here is what the U.S. says about its policy and practice, in response to several recommendations for improvement, made to the U.S. by other countries.

{Excerpt}

...

E. Immigration

Detention of migrants and immigration policies Recommendations 80, 82, 102, 144, 164, 183-185, and 212 61.

On November 20, 2014, President Obama announced a series of executive actions on immigration and border security. These include: a plan to fundamentally alter our border security strategy; significant revisions to our immigration enforcement priorities; expansion of a policy to consider deferring removal, and providing work authorization, for certain individuals who arrived in the U.S. as children; and a new initiative to consider deferring removal, and providing work authorization, for certain parents of U.S. citizens and lawful permanent residents. Consistent with these actions, we are implementing a new enforcement and removal policy that continues to place top priority on threats to national security, public safety, and border security.

62. The United States continues to be a leader in extending protection to refugees and asylum seekers. In FY2014, 1 we admitted 69,987 refugees and granted asylum to 25,199 individuals. We have also substantially increased grants of immigration protection for victims of torture, trafficking, domestic violence, child abuse, abandonment, or neglect, and other qualifying crimes.

63. From 2010 to 2014, among individuals who either arrived or were apprehended near the border shortly after entering the country without permission, the number of people who expressed a fear of returning to their country of origin increased by 469 percent. Other screenings for fear of return have also markedly increased. To address the substantial increase in individuals seeking protection, we have hired nearly 150 new asylum officers since October 2013 and plan to hire more officers.

64. We are also taking action to address specific concerns regarding racial profiling and use of force at the U.S.-Mexico border. In May 2014, U.S. Customs and Border Protection publicly released an updated Use of Force Policy, Guidelines, and Procedures Handbook, which requires training in the use of safe tactics, a requirement to carry less-lethal devices, and guidance on responding to thrown projectiles. CBP is launching a use-of-force incident-tracking system to better inform its responses to incidents. Fiscal years begin on October 1 of the prior calendar year and end on September 30.

65. The United States continues to provide due process guarantees throughout the immigration system, including in removal proceedings, where individuals are advised of their rights and other important information. While some individuals facing immigration proceedings are detained, that is only after an individualized determination that detention is appropriate or required by law. Many alternatives to detention are available and are used when appropriate. In FY2013, 37 percent of cases completed by the immigration courts involved an individual who was detained. 66. Since our first UPR, we have promulgated the 2011 Performance-Based National Detention Standards, which cover many facilities housing immigration detainees and establish minimum conditions of detention, including with respect to medical care, access to legal resources, visitation, recreation, correspondence, religious services, and grievance processes.

67. We have further prioritized the interview of and completion of asylum applications by unaccompanied children, consistent with the prioritization of the same population in immigration courts. Programs are being initiated to provide child advocates and representation to unaccompanied children in immigration proceedings in certain locations. We provide unaccompanied children with safe and appropriate residential environments until they are released to appropri-

ate sponsors while their immigration cases proceed. While they are in our care, our facilities provide services such as food, clothes, basic education, recreation, and medical and legal assistance. Approximately 90 percent of all unaccompanied children were released to the care of a sponsor in FY2014. Once that occurs, they have a right under federal law — just like other children in their communities — to enroll in local public elementary and secondary schools, regardless of their or their sponsors' immigration status. We have also launched a program to provide refugee admission to certain children in El Salvador, Honduras, and Guatemala, providing a safe, orderly alternative to dangerous journeys from Central America. Discrimination or violence against migrants and access to services

Recommendations 79, 104-105, 108, 165, 167, 207, 210, 214, and 220

68. The United States has an unwavering commitment to respect the human rights of all migrants, regardless of their immigration status, and vigorously prosecutes crimes committed against migrants and enforces labor, workplace safety, and civil rights laws. All children have the right to equal access to public elementary and secondary education, regardless of their or their parents' immigration status, and such schools must provide meaningful access to their programs to persons with limited English proficiency, including migrants. In January 2015, we issued guidance to help schools ensure that English learner students can participate meaningfully and equally in education programs and services. Employers may not discriminate against employees or applicants based on their race, color, national origin, or, in certain cases, citizenship status.

69. Regardless of immigration status, victims of domestic violence have full access to a network of 1,600 domestic violence shelters and other supportive services, including community health centers and substance abuse, mental health, and maternal and child health programs.

70. VAWA specifically provides immigration protections for battered immigrants, allowing certain family members of U.S. citizens and lawful permanent residents who have been victims of domestic violence to independently petition for immigration status without the abuser's knowledge. This self-petitioning process removes one barrier to leaving that victims might face and shifts control over the immigration process to the victim, providing him or her with more options. In FY2014, 613 such self-petitions were granted.

71. The DHS Traveler Redress Inquiry Program provides a way for travelers who experience difficulties during their travel screening to seek redress, including those who believe they have been unfairly or incorrectly delayed, denied boarding, or identified for additional screening as a result of being placed on the terrorist watchlist or its subset, the No Fly List. DHS TRIP works with other government agencies as appropriate to make an accurate determination about any traveler who has sought redress. We are actively reviewing and revising the existing redress program to increase transparency for certain individuals, consistent with the protection of national and transportation security and classified and other sensitive information. Consular access and notification Recommendations 54, 213, and 223

72. The United States has made significant efforts to meet the goal of across-the-board compliance with its consular notification and access obligations under the Vienna Convention on Consular Relations. The Federal Rules of Criminal Procedure were amended in December 2014 to facilitate compliance with our consular notification and access obligations, requiring judges to notify all defendants at their initial appearance in a federal case that non-U.S. citizens may request that a consular officer from the defendant's country of nationality be notified of the arrest, but that even without a defendant's request, a treaty or other international agreement may require consular notification. We have distributed more than 200,000 manuals on consular notification and access, which provide detailed instructions for police and prison officials engaged in detention or arrest of a foreign national, in order to comply with the VCCR and all relevant bilateral consular agreements. We distribute other free consular notification and access training materials and post them online, and have conducted nearly 900 outreach and training sessions on consular notification and access since 1998.

73. Legislation supported by the Administration that would bring U.S. into compliance with the ICJ's judgment in *Avena* has previously been introduced in the Senate, but has not been enacted into law.

Source: Report of the United States of America, submitted to the U.N. High Commissioner for Human Rights In Conjunction with the Universal Periodic Review, https://www.state.gov/documents/organization/237460.pdf

8. REPORT ON IMMIGRATION IN THE UNITED STATES: DETENTION AND DUE PROCESS, INTER-AMERICAN COMMISSION ON HUMAN RIGHTS

The U.S. is a member of the Organization of American States and subject to human rights scrutiny by the Inter-American Commission on Human Rights. That Commission, which included a U.S. law professor-commissioner, drafted and issued a report about its view of the U.S. immigration law and policy judged by the normative standards of the American Declaration on Human Rights. It is meant to help the U.S. see itself more objectively and hear ways suggested by the I-A Commission on how to improve its compliance with the ADHR.

Report on Immigration in the United States: Detention and Due Process

[Throughout this report, the Commission will use the terms "migrant" and "immigrant" interchangeably. The migrants or immigrants will be referred to as either "undocumented" or "unauthorized," again interchangeably. Finally, the Commission will use the terms "alien" and "noncitizen" also interchangeably.]

I. INTRODUCTION

1. In keeping with Article 58 of its Rules of Procedure, the Inter-American Commission on Human Rights (hereinafter "the Inter-American Commission," "the Commission," or "the IACHR") is presenting this report as a diagnostic analysis of the human rights situation with respect to immigrant detention and due process in the United States and to make recommendations so that immigration practices in that country conform to international human rights standards.

2. The United States hosts the largest number of international immigrants in the world. According to the International Organization for Migration (IOM), in 2005 the United States had a total of 38.4 million international migrants. Many of those migrants came to the United States through formal and legal channels. The Department of Homeland Security (DHS) estimates that as of January 2008 there were 12.6 million legal permanent residents (LPRs) in the United States; another 1,107,126 were added in 2008. Every year, many legal permanent residents are granted U.S. citizenship. In 2008, 1,046,539 persons became naturalized citizens. The United States is also one of the leading countries for granting asylum and resettling refugees. In 2008, the United States granted asylum to 22,930 persons and resettled 60,108 refugees.

3. According to government figures, as of January 2009, there were approximately 10.8 million undocumented immigrants living in the United States. Of those, some 4 million came after January 2000; the other 6.8 million arrived in the 1980s and 1990s. Nearly half of all undocumented immigrants entered the United States legally, but remained in the country after their visas expired. Approximately 5 million children in the United States have at least one undocumented parent, 3 million of whom are U.S.-born citizens.

4. Under U.S. immigration law, there are a number of ways an undocumented immigrant can regularize his or her status. For example, an immigrant may seek asylum; seek withholding of removal (non-refoulement); qualify for adjustment of status, qualify for cancellation of removal, qualify for a "T" visa as a victim of human trafficking, qualify for a "U" visa as a victim of domestic violence or other violent crime, seek a waiver of inadmissibility, or qualify for Special Immigrant Juvenile Status. Some who are believed to be undocumented may even actually have derivative or acquired U.S. citizenship. Moreover, deportable LPRs who are detained likewise often have potential forms of relief to remain in the United States.

5. In an effort to control the influx of new immigrants, since the mid-1990s the United States stepped up efforts to detect, detain and deport undocumented immigrants and criminally-convicted legal immigrants, including LPRs. In 1996, the U.S. Congress passed the Illegal Immigration Reform and Immigrant Responsibility Act (IIRIRA) and the Antiterrorism and Effective Death Penalty Act (AEDPA) which significantly expanded the use of mandatory detention without bond, added to the list of crimes that subject legal immigrants, including legal permanent residents (LPRs), to mandatory deportation, and generally created a more stringent approach to immigration policy. 6. In the aftermath of September 11, 2001 and with the passage of the Homeland Security Act of 2002, the new Department of Homeland Security (DHS) took responsibility for the duties of the former Immigration and Naturalization Services (INS). Under the

newly created DHS, the government established Immigration and Customs Enforcement (ICE) as the principal domestic immigration enforcement and detention agency. 7. The focus of this report is on ICE's civil immigration operations. Since 2002, with the creation of DHS and ICE, the federal government has taken a stricter enforcement approach to civil immigration violations. In a 2003 memorandum to its field office directors, the Office of Detention and Removal Operations (DRO), a subsection of ICE, announced "Operation Endgame," a ten year strategic plan to achieve a "100% removal rate." Through a series of programs, including partnerships with state and local law enforcement, the number of those deported rose from 189,026 in FY2001 to 358,886.

In FY2008 ICE detention of noncitizens practically doubled, from approximately 209,000 in FY2001 to 378,582 in FY2008. The IACHR was of the view that this increase in immigration-related detention warranted investigation to ascertain whether the immigration policies and practices were compatible with the United States' international obligations in the area of human rights. Pursuant to Article 18(g) of its Statute and Article 55 of its Rules of Procedure, the IACHR conducted a series of in loco observations to investigate the conditions under which immigrants are held in custody in the United States. The Inter- American Commission drew upon other sources of information as well. With respect to the visits to detention centers, and based on the provisions of its Rules of Procedure that govern the "on-site observations" (articles 53 to 55), the IACHR filed a request with the Government of the United States seeking authorization for a visit to observe the conditions under which immigrants are held in detention. The United States Government invited the Inter-American Commission to visit four detention facilities in the summer of 2008. However, the IACHR was unable to make the visits at that time because of the conditions that the United States Government set and to which the Inter-American Commission did not agree.

10. In December 2008, the United States Mission to the Organization of American States contacted the IACHR to resume discussion of a possible visit to the immigrant detention centers in the country. Steps were taken so that the Inter-American Commission was able to perform those visits according to its rules and practices. In the week of July 20 to 24, 2009, a delegation from the IACHR visited detention centers in Arizona and Texas. In all, the delegation visited two shelters for unaccompanied minors, one family detention facility, and three adult detention facilities. The centers visited were the following: ƒ Southwest Key Unaccompanied Minor Shelter (Phoenix, Arizona) ƒ Florence Service Processing Center (Florence, Arizona) ƒ Pinal County Jail (Florence, Arizona) ƒ T. Don Hutto Family Residential Center (Taylor, Texas) ƒ Willacy Detention Facility (Raymondville, Texas) ƒ International Education Services Unaccompanied Minor Shelter (Los Fresnos, Texas)

11. The IACHR would like to thank ICE and the Office of Refugee Resettlement (ORR) for the cooperation they provided to enable the Inter-American Commission to conduct the mission and for their willingness to answer the delegation's questions.

12. Nevertheless, the IACHR denounces the decision of the Sheriff of Maricopa County, in Phoenix, Arizona, who refused to grant access to the delegation. While the IACHR is aware that the Maricopa County jail houses persons arrested under an agreement that allows the state to enforce federal civil immigration laws, it is a universally accepted principle of international human rights law that States must comply with their international obligations in good faith and may not invoke internal rules as a pretext for noncompliance. This good faith principle implies that States must open their doors to agencies that monitor the observance of human rights, so that those agencies can check the situation and properly perform their mission.

13. As for other sources, the Inter-American Commission took into account the information received during the thematic hearing held in October 2007, during its 130th regular session. There, an advocacy group for immigrants in the United States informed the IACHR of alleged violations of human rights in the detention of migrant families, unaccompanied children, asylum seekers and other vulnerable immigrant groups.

14. The Inter-American Commission also consulted experts on immigration in the United States, international organizations, attorneys and defenders of the rights of migrant persons, to get their views on the topic of this report. The IACHR also spoke with former detainees and their families and sent out a questionnaire for the State, persons and civil society organizations in various parts of the country to answer.

15. Thereafter, the Inter-American Commission held two more thematic hearings on problems of enforcement of immigrations laws and due process for detained immigrants in the United States, as well as a working meeting on detainees

with mental disabilities or disorders. The IACHR did an exhaustive analysis of the research and reports of State agencies, nonprofit organizations and the media to get a broader perspective on the concerns regarding current policies and practices in immigrant detention and due process in the United States.

16. Following the IACHR's visits to the immigrant detention facilities, ICE organized two briefings for the Inter-American Commission in October 2009: one that concerned ICE's plans to reform the immigrant detention system, and another on changes to the local enforcement program under the 287(g) agreement, which will be examined later in this report.

17. Notwithstanding the more detailed findings included throughout the body of this report, one of the IACHR's main concerns is the increasing use of detention based on a presumption of its necessity, when in fact detention should be the exception. The United States Supreme Court itself has upheld the constitutionality of mandatory detention in immigration cases that have not been decided, even though the violations being alleged are civil in nature and despite the loss of liberty that detention presupposes.

18. As will be explained, the Inter-American Commission is convinced that in many if not the majority of cases, detention is a disproportionate measure and the alternatives to detention programs would be a more balanced means of serving the State's legitimate interest in ensuring compliance with immigration laws. The IACHR is disturbed by the rapid increase in the number of partnerships with local and state law enforcement for purposes of enforcing civil immigration laws. The Inter-American Commission finds that ICE has failed to develop an oversight and accountability system to ensure that these local partners do not enforce immigration law in a discriminatory manner by resorting to racial profiling and that their practices do not use the supposed investigation of crimes as a pretext to prosecute and detain undocumented migrants.

19. For those cases in which detention is strictly necessary, the IACHR is troubled by the lack of a genuinely civil detention system, where the general conditions are commensurate with human dignity and humane treatment, and featuring those special conditions called for in cases of non-punitive detention. The Inter-American Commission is also disturbed by the fact that the management and personal care of immigration detainees is frequently outsourced to private contractors, yet insufficient information is available concerning the mechanisms in place to supervise the private contractors.

20. The IACHR is also disturbed by the impact that detention has on due process, mainly with respect to the right to an attorney which, in turn, affects one's right to seek release. To better guarantee the right to legal representation and, ultimately, to due process, stronger programs offering alternatives to detention are needed and the Legal Orientation Program must be expanded nationwide. The Inter-American Commission is particularly troubled by the lack of legal representation provided or facilitated ex officio by the State for cases of unaccompanied children, immigrants with mental disabilities and other persons unable to represent themselves.

II. DRAFT REPORT AND RESPONSE OF THE UNITED STATES

21. The IACHR discussed and approved a draft version of this report on August 2, 2010. Pursuant to Article 60(a) of its Rules of Procedure, the report was sent to the United States on September 1, 2010 with a request that it submit its observations within a one month time period. After an extension was requested and granted by the Inter-American Commission, the State submitted its response on October 19, 2010.

22. In its response, the State expresses its appreciation for the opportunity to comment on the draft report, and its satisfaction for being able to facilitate the Commission's visits to detention facilities and the consultations that took place during 2008 and 2009. The United States indicates that since the research for this report was completed, the Department of Homeland Security of the Obama Administration launched its own comprehensive review of the immigration enforcement policy system, which in its opinion has resulted in important changes in the immigration enforcement policy arena. 23. The United States highlights its pride in being a nation of immigrants, and values the contributions made by migrants to its economy, culture and social fabric, and points out that one out of five of the 190 million migrants in the world live in this country. The State adds: Immigration is an issue of critical importance to the United States, and accordingly is extensively addressed by U.S. law and policy. International law recognizes that every state has the sovereign

right to control admission to its territory, and to regulate the admission and expulsion of foreign nationals consistent with any international obligations it has undertaken.

This principle has long been recognized as a fundamental attribute of state sovereignty. Immigration detention can be an important tool employed by States in exercising their sovereignty, as they ensure public safety and remove as expeditiously as possible individuals who may pose a threat to the security of the country or the safety of its citizens and lawful residents. Accordingly immigration detention, provided it is employed in a manner consistent with a State's international human rights obligations, is permitted under international law.

24. However, the State then goes on to express its opinion in the sense that "contrary to the Commission's assertions, neither the American Declaration of the Rights and Duties of Man nor international law generally establish a presumption of liberty for undocumented migrants who are present in a country in violation of that country's immigration laws." The United States stresses the importance of enforcing immigration laws and policies "in a lawful, professional, safe, and humane manner that respects the human rights of migrants regardless of their immigration status." The State agrees with the Commission that it has an obligation to ensure the human rights of all immigrants, documented and undocumented alike, but it also considers that many of the sources referred to by the Inter-American Commission do not give rise to binding legal obligations on the United States. According to the position of the State, the American Declaration is "a non-binding instrument that does not itself create legal rights or impose legal obligations on signatory states." It is also the opinion of the State that Article 20 of the Statute of the Inter-American Commission "sets forth the powers of the Commission that relate specifically to OAS member states which, like the United States, are not parties to the legally binding American Convention on Human Rights," which includes "pay[ing] particular attention to observance of certain enumerated human rights set forth in the American Declaration, to examine communications and make recommendations to the state, and to verify whether in such cases domestic legal procedures and remedies have been applied and exhausted."

25. The United States reiterates "its respect of and support for the Commission and the strong sense of integrity and independence which historically has characterized its work." It also requests "that in keeping with its mandate under Article 20 of the IACHR Statute, the Commission center its review of applicable international standards on the American Declaration and U.S. observance of the rights enumerated therein." The United States considers that the jurisprudence of the Inter-American Court of Human Rights interpreting the American Convention does not govern U.S. commitments under the American Declaration and that, likewise, "the advisory opinions of the Inter- American Court interpreting other international agreements, such as the International Covenant on Civil and Political Rights (ICCPR) are not relevant."

26. In its response, the State further mentions that in October 2009, the Department of Homeland Security issued a report which identifying some of the same concerns raised by the IACHR in its report. The United States indicates that this report was based on information gathered from 25 separate facility tours; discussions with detainees and employees; meetings with over 100 non-governmental organizations, and Federal, State, and local officials; and the review of data and reports from governmental agencies and human rights organizations. As explained by the State, the DHS report describes the "unique challenges associated with the rapid expansion of ICE's detention capacity from fewer than 7,500 beds in 1995 to over 30,000 today, as the result of congressional and other mandates" and it also "outlines core findings and key recommendations for building a new ICE detention system designed to hold, process, and prepare individuals for removal — as compared to the punitive purpose of criminal incarceration." The State further explains that in following up the DHS report, "sweeping reforms to transform the immigration detention system" would be undertaken, based on several key principles to be applied by ICE: — Prioritize efficiency throughout the removal process to reduce detention costs, minimize the length of stays, and ensure fair proceedings; — Detain aliens in settings commensurate with the risk of flight and danger they present; — Be fiscally prudent when carrying out detention reform; — Provide sound medical and mental health care to detainees; — Provide the necessary federal oversight of detention facilities; and — Ensure Alternatives to Detention (ATD) are cost-effective and promote a high rate of compliance with orders to appear and removal orders.

27. The United States refers also to the creation of the Office of Detention Policy and Planning (ODPP) within ICE "to coordinate the agency-wide detention reform effort and transform the vision for reform into concrete and measurable actions and goals." Some of the accomplishments referred to by the State in its response are the following: — Creation of

ODPP to coordinate the overall reform effort; — Design and test of a new risk assessment tool and intake process to inform and systematize nationwide decision making about who is detained and who is released; — Preparation of comprehensive policies and guidance and creation of important efficiencies in the ATD program allowing the enrollment of more potentially successful participants; — Drafting of a new set of detention standards, currently under review, that would make conditions of confinement in its facilities less penal in the short term for more than half of the detainees; — Elimination of delays associated with detainees health care by revising our Treatment Authorization Process; — Development of a new Medical Classification Scheme by working with members of the Director's Advisory Group on Health Care; — Launching of an Online Detainee Locator System (ODLS); and — Training of more than 40 new federal employees posted at each major detention facility.

28. Additionally, the State mentions that the Director of ICE "issued four nationwide policies that have significantly impacted how ICE uses and prioritizes its resources consistent with reform principles." These policies include the Civil Immigration Enforcement Memorandum; the Parole of Arriving Aliens with A Credible Fear of Persecution; the National Fugitive Operations Program; and the Guidance Regarding the Handling of Removal Proceedings of Aliens with Pending or Approved Applications or Petitions. The United States also underscores that "ICE is committed to providing transparency, consistency across facilities, and efficiency in the resolution of disputes," to which end it "has continually updated its website with policy reform announcements, newly issued policy memoranda, and statistics, and has posted draft policy guidance to solicit public feedback." The State response asserts that DHS and ICE authorities remain fully committed to comprehensive immigration reform, and that they have held "dozens of meetings with Members of Congress, participated in more than 40 roundtable discussions and listening sessions across the United States, and met with over 1,000 different immigration stakeholders."

29. The considerations by the State summarized above are more general in nature. The more specific observations to the IACHR Report will be reflected as appropriate and analyzed in the respective sections of this document. The full text of the observations of the United States —as requested in its October 19, 2010 letter— is available in the website of the Inter-American Commission.

30. The Inter-American Commission appreciates the response of the State, and the positive engagement with the inter-American system of human rights. However, with respect to the position of the United States interpreting the nature of the American Declaration, it must be reiterated that it is indeed an instrument that generates international obligations in the framework of the OAS Charter, taking into account the IACHR´s Statute. The IACHR has held before that for Member States that have yet to ratify the American Convention, the expression of their obligations in the sphere of human rights is set forth in the American Declaration; accordingly, such obligations have been interpreted in relation to the OAS Charter generally, and the American Declaration more specifically. The Inter-American Commission has also explained that it may interpret and apply the pertinent provisions of the American Declaration in light of current developments in the field of international human rights law, as evidenced by treaties, custom and other relevant sources of international law.

As it stated previously in a general report: The international law of human rights is a dynamic body of norms evolving to meet the challenge of ensuring that all persons may fully exercise their fundamental rights and freedoms. In this regard, as the International Covenants elaborate on the basic principles expressed in the Universal Declaration of Human Rights, so too does the American Convention represent, in many instances, an authoritative expression of the fundamental principles set forth in the American Declaration. While the Commission clearly does not apply the American Convention in relation to member States that have yet to ratify that treaty, its provisions may well be relevant in informing an interpretation of the principles of the Declaration.

31. As for the structure of the report, Section III will present the relevant international standards on the human rights of immigrants; Section IV will contain the IACHR's observations and concerns with regard to immigration detention, certain immigration enforcement procedures, detention conditions and the impact on due process; in section V the Inter-American Commission will make its final conclusions and recommendations as to how best to overcome the problems that the current system poses with respect to the international human rights obligations undertaken by the United States. Throughout the report and as pertinent, the IACHR will make reference to certain particularly vulnerable groups where immigration detention is concerned, such as unaccompanied children, migrant families, those seeking asylum, persons with mental disabilities or disorders, and others.

III. RELEVANT INTERNATIONAL STANDARDS ON THE HUMAN RIGHTS OF IMMIGRANTS

32. The United States has an obligation to ensure the human rights of all immigrants, documented and undocumented alike; this includes the rights to personal liberty, to humane treatment, to the minimum guarantees of due process, to equality and nondiscrimination and to protection of private and family life. In its Advisory Opinion on the Juridical Condition and Rights of the Undocumented Migrants, the Inter-American Court of Human Rights (I/A Court H.R.) described the basic principles of human rights that must inform the immigration policies of the OAS member states. Specifically, the Court wrote that States may establish mechanisms to control undocumented migrants' entry into and departure from their territory, which must always be applied with strict regard for the guarantees of due process and respect for human dignity. It also held that the States have the obligation to respect and to ensure respect for the human rights of all persons under their respective jurisdictions, in the light of the principle of equality and non-discrimination, irrespective of whether such persons are nationals or foreigners.

A. Right to personal liberty .

33. The American Declaration of the Rights and Duties of Man (the "American Declaration") provides that every human being has the right to liberty and the right to protection against arbitrary arrest. Article XXV of the American Declaration states that "no person may be deprived of liberty for non-fulfillment of obligations of a purely civil character. "The American Convention on Human Rights (the "American Convention") also provides for the right to personal liberty.

34. In general, the paramount principle where the right to personal liberty is concerned is that pre-trial detention is an exceptional measure. The IACHR will make reference to the relevant international standards developed with respect to criminal proceedings, and then introduce the specific standards that concern immigration-related detention, which is eminently civil in nature. For cases involving criminal proceedings, the Inter-American Commission has developed the criteria that must be met in order for preventive detention (or detention pending trial) to be compatible with the right to personal liberty. As the IACHR wrote:

The precautionary measures are established only when they are necessary for the proposed objectives. The pre-trial detention is not an exception to this rule. In compliance with the principle of exceptionality, the pre-trial detention will be appropriate when it is the only way to ensure the purposes of the process and when it has been demonstrated that less damaging measures would be unsuccessful to such purposes. Therefore, if possible, the pre-trial detention has to be replaced for a lower severity measure.

35. Similarly, the Inter-American Commission has held that the principle of necessity that must regulate preventive detention implies that the authority that ordered the measure must sufficiently prove the reasons why the existence of indications of criminal responsibility has any bearing on the efficient course of the investigations in the case in question. It also implies establishing the reasons why it is appropriate to impose preventive detention rather than a less severe measure. This determination must be made on a case-by-case basis.

36. In the universal human rights system, Article 9(1) of the International Covenant on Civil and Political Rights (ICCPR), ratified by the United States, reads as follows: "Everyone has the right to liberty and security of person. No one shall be subjected to arbitrary arrest or detention." The United Nations Human Rights Committee, which oversees the Covenant's implementation, observes that "the notion of 'arbitrariness' must not be equated with 'against the law' but be interpreted more broadly to include such elements as inappropriateness and injustice."

37. The Human Rights Committee has also held that "remand in custody could be considered arbitrary if it is not necessary in all the circumstances of the case, for example to prevent flight or interference with evidence: the element of proportionality becomes relevant in this context (...)." Thus, the determination as to whether detention is an appropriate measure must be done on the basis of a case-by-case analysis; a State has to consider all the less invasive or intrusive ways of accomplishing its objective before detention can be admissible. Article 9(1) also requires that the State periodically revisit the decision to keep a person in custody to determine whether it still has sufficient grounds to justify the detention. The Human Rights Committee suggests two possible grounds for continuing pre-trial detention: if the person refuses to cooperate with the investigation or there is a likelihood of flight.

38. In the case of immigration detention, the standard for the exceptionality of pre-trial detention must be even higher because immigration violations ought not to be construed as criminal offenses. The United Nations Special Rapporteur on the Human Rights of Migrant Workers wrote, "Irregular migrants are not criminals per se and should not be treated as such."

39. In effect, to be in compliance with the guarantees protected in Articles I and XXV of the American Declaration, member States must enact immigration laws and establish immigration policies that are premised on a presumption of liberty — the right of the immigrant to remain at liberty while his or her immigration proceedings are pending — and not on a presumption of detention. Detention is only permissible when a case- specific evaluation concludes that the measure is essential in order to serve a legitimate interest of the State and to ensure that the subject reports for the proceeding to determine his or her immigration status and possible removal. The argument that the person in question poses a threat to public safety is only acceptable in exceptional circumstances in which there are certain indicia of the risk that the person represents. The existence of a criminal record is not sufficient to justify the detention of an immigrant once he or she has served his or her criminal sentence. Whatever the case, the particular reasons why the immigrant is considered to pose a risk have to be explained. The arguments in support of the appropriateness of detention must be set out clearly in the corresponding decision.

40. The IACHR also underscores the fact that the detention review procedures must respect the guarantees of due process, including the defendant's right to an impartial hearing in decisions that affect his or her fate, his or her right to present evidence and refute the State's arguments, and the opportunity to be represented by counsel.

41. Furthermore, since the State's use of immigration detention must be premised on a presumption of the right to personal liberty, then alternatives to detention programs (such as GPS monitoring), bond or release should also be regarded as a reasonable measure that is proportional to the legitimate end that the State seeks to achieve.

42. Specifically, in the case of immigrants the Human Rights Committee observed that illegal entry by itself would not justify detention for a period. For its part, the United Nations Working Group on Arbitrary Detention has also summarized the basic requirements for detention of immigrants to be permissible: It was felt that States should be reminded that detention shall be the last resort and permissible only for the shortest period of time and that alternatives to detention should be sought whenever possible. Grounds for detention must be clearly and exhaustively defined and the legality of detention must be open for challenge before a court and regular review within fixed time limits. Established time limits for judicial review must even stand in "emergency situations" when an exceptionally large number of undocumented immigrants enter the territory of a State. Provisions should always be made to render detention unlawful if the obstacle for identifying immigrants in an irregular situation or carrying out removal from the territory does not lie within their sphere, for example, when the consular representation of the country of origin does not cooperate or legal considerations — such as the principle of non-refoulement barring removal if there is a risk of torture or arbitrary detention in the country of destination — or factual obstacles — such as the unavailability of means of transportation — render expulsion impossible.

43. Apart from the basic right to personal liberty that all immigrants enjoy, various international instruments have established specific restrictions regarding the detention of certain persons who are members of more vulnerable groups. The IACHR will now summarize the specific international standards on the right to personal liberty with respect to some of these groups.

Asylum seekers

44. The 1951 Convention relating to the Status of Refugees (hereinafter "the Convention on Refugees") allows very little margin for restrictions on freedom of movement.56 Article 31 of the Convention on Refugees reads as follows:

1. The Contracting States shall not impose penalties, on account of their illegal entry or presence, on refugees who, coming directly from a territory where their life or freedom was threatened in the sense of article 1, enter or are present in their territory without authorization, provided they present themselves without delay to the authorities and show good cause for their illegal entry or presence.

2. The Contracting States shall not apply to the movements of such refugees restrictions other than those which are necessary and such restrictions shall only be applied until their status in the country is regularized or they obtain admission into another country. The Contracting States shall allow such refugees a reasonable period and all the necessary facilities to obtain admission into another country.

45. When interpreting the Convention on Refugees, the Office of the United Nations High Commissioner for Refugees (hereinafter the "UNHCR") concluded that "[a]s a general principle asylum-seekers should not be detained" and that "[t]here should be a presumption against detention." The UNHCR underscores the fact that under Article 31, "detention should only be resorted to in cases of necessity." As the UNHCR wrote, detention of asylum seekers may be resorted to only on grounds prescribed by law, to verify identity; to determine the elements on which the claim to refugee status or asylum is based; to deal with cases where refugees or asylum-seekers have destroyed their travel and/or identity documents or have used fraudulent documents in order to mislead the authorities of the State in which they intend to claim asylum; or to protect national security or public order.

46. The UNHCR concludes that "[d]etention should therefore only take place after a full consideration of all possible alternatives (...)."

47. In those cases in which an asylum seeker's detention is deemed necessary, the UNHCR has established that such detention "should not constitute an obstacle to an asylum-seekers' possibilities to pursue their asylum application." It has also observed that the following minimal procedural guarantees must be observed: (i) to receive prompt and full communication of any order of detention, together with the reasons for the order, and their rights in connection with the order, in a language and in terms which they understand; (ii) to be informed of the right to legal counsel. Where possible, they should receive free legal assistance; (iii) to have the decision subjected to an automatic review before a judicial or administrative body independent of the detaining authorities. This should be followed by regular periodic reviews of the necessity for the continuation of detention, which the asylum-seeker or his representative would have the right to attend; (iv) either personally or through a representative, to challenge the necessity of the deprivation of liberty at the review hearing, and to rebut any findings made. Such a right should extend to all aspects of the case and not simply the executive discretion to detain; v) to contact and be contacted by the local UNHCR Office, available national refugee bodies or other agencies and an advocate. The right to communicate with these representatives in private, and the means to make such contact should be made available.

48. The Inter-American Commission has observed that in cases in which asylum seekers are detained, "the longer detention as a preventive measure continues, the greater the resulting burden on the rights of the person deprived of liberty."

2. Migrant families and unaccompanied children

49. Under Article V of the American Declaration, "[e]very person has the right to the protection of the law against abusive attacks upon his...private and family life." Under Article VII, "[a]ll women, during pregnancy and the nursing period, and all children have the right to special protection, care and aid." The need to guarantee these rights has a direct bearing on the appropriateness of detaining migrant families and children. Given the provisions of Articles V and VII, mandatory detention of a child's mother or father must be considered on a case-by-case basis, analyzing whether the measure is proportional to the end the State seeks to achieve and taking the best interests of the child into account.

50. Given the intrinsic protection of family life recognized in Articles V, VI and VII of the American Declaration, it is possible to conclude that families and pregnant women who seek asylum ought not to be detained; and if they are detained, they ought not to be subjected to prison-like conditions.

51. Under international standards, unaccompanied minors ought not to be detained either. In its Advisory Opinion on the Juridical Condition and Human Rights of the Child, the Inter-American Court adopted the principle of the "best interests of the child," established in the United Nations Convention on the Rights of the Child as the primary consideration when a member State is contemplating a measure that might affect minors under its jurisdiction.66 The principle of exceptionality governing deprivation of liberty in general and deprivation of liberty for immigration violations, carries even more weight when children are involved. Only in the most extreme cases could such a measure be justified.

52. Article 37(b) of that Convention, which the United States signed but is not party to, provides that "[t]he arrest, detention or imprisonment of a child shall be in conformity with the law and shall be used only as a measure of last resort and for the shortest appropriate period of time."

53. The United Nations Special Rapporteur on the Human Rights of Migrant Workers observes that in the unusual case where children must be detained, ...detention of children is permitted only as a measure of last resort and only when it is in the best interest of the child, for the shortest appropriate period of time and in conditions that ensure the realization of the rights enshrined in the Convention on the Rights of the Child...Children under administrative custodial measures should be separated from adults, unless they can be housed with relatives in separate settings...Should the age of the migrant be in dispute, the most favourable treatment should be accorded until it is determined whether he/she is a minor.

54. In the "Revised Guidelines on Applicable Criteria and Standards relating to the Detention of Asylum Seekers," the UNHCR concludes that "minors who are asylum-seekers should not be detained." If, for some extraordinary reason children are detained, they ought not to be held in prison-like conditions.

55. The UNHCR also concluded that unaccompanied children who are detained should benefit from the same minimum procedural guarantees of due process that asylum seekers enjoy and a legal guardian or adviser should be appointed for them.

B. Right to due process and access to justice

56. Under Article XXVI of the American Declaration, "[e]very person accused of an offense has the right to be given an impartial and public hearing...." The IACHR has maintained that Article XXVI also applies to immigration proceedings. As the Inter-American Commission wrote: "to deny an alleged victim the protection afforded by Article XXVI simply by virtue of the nature of immigration proceedings would contradict the very object of this provision and its purpose to scrutinize the proceedings under which the rights, freedoms and well-being of the persons under the State's jurisdiction are established."

57. Article 8 of the American Convention reaffirms the rights recognized in Article XXVI of the American Declaration. During any proceeding that can result in a penalty of any kind, all persons are equally entitled to the following minimum guarantees: the right to a hearing, with due guarantees and within a reasonable time by a competent, independent, and impartial tribunal; prior notification in detail to the accused of the charges against him; the right not to be compelled to be a witness against oneself or to plead guilty; the right of the accused to be assisted without charge by a translator or interpreter; the right of the accused to be assisted by legal counsel of his own choosing, and to communicate freely and privately with his counsel; the right of the defense to examine witnesses present in the court and to obtain their appearance as witnesses, experts or other persons who may throw light on the facts; and the right to appeal the judgment to a higher court. While many of these guarantees are articulated in a language that is more germane to criminal proceedings, they must be strictly enforced in immigration proceedings as well, given the circumstances of such proceedings and their consequences.

58. The IACHR has observed that the due process rights set forth in Article 8 of the American Convention "establish a baseline of due process to which all immigrants, whatever their situation, have a right." Immigrants are at a real disadvantage that can adversely affect due process unless special countervailing measures are taken to reduce or eliminate the procedural handicaps with which immigrants are encumbered.

59. In its Advisory Opinion on the "Juridical Condition and Rights of the Undocumented Migrants" the Inter-American Court highlighted the following: [...] for "the due process of law" a defendant must be able to exercise his rights and defend his interests effectively and in full procedural equality with other defendants.... To accomplish its objectives, the judicial process must recognize and correct any real disadvantages that those brought before the bar might have, thus observing the principle of equality before the law and the courts and the corollary principle prohibiting discrimination. The presence of real disadvantages necessitates countervailing measures that help to reduce or eliminate the obstacles and deficiencies that impair or diminish an effective defense of one's interests. Absent those countervailing measures, widely recognized in various stages of the proceeding, one could hardly say that those who have the disadvantages enjoy a true opportunity for justice and the benefit of the due process of law equal to those who do not have those disadvantages.

1. Right to judicial protection and to a habeas corpus petition

60. The United Nations Working Group on Arbitrary Detention concluded that "where people have been detained, expelled or returned without being provided with legal guarantees, their continued detention and subsequent expulsion are to be considered as arbitrary." The United Nations Special Rapporteur on the Human Rights of Migrant Workers has urged the States to avoid the use of detention facilities and of legal mechanisms and methods of interception and/or deportation that curtail judicial control of the lawfulness of the detention and other rights, such as the right to seek asylum.

61. Article XVIII of the American Declaration provides that "[e]very person may resort to the courts to ensure respect for his legal rights. There should likewise be available to him a simple, brief procedure whereby the courts will protect him from acts of authority that, to his prejudice, violate any fundamental constitutional rights." Similarly, Article XXV provides that "[e]very individual who has been deprived of his liberty has the right to have the legality of his detention ascertained without delay by a court ...."

62. The Inter-American Court has held that "writs of habeas corpus and of amparo are among those judicial remedies that are essential for the protection of various rights whose derogation is prohibited by [the American Convention] and that serve, moreover, to preserve legality in a democratic society."

In the case of Rafael Ferrer- Mazorra and in light of the rights protected under the American Declaration, the Inter-American Commission emphasizes the fact that access must be provided to a judicial review of the detention, "as it provides effective assurances that the detainee is not exclusively at the mercy of the detaining authority."

2. Right to seek asylum

63. Article XXVII of the American Declaration provides that "every person has the right, in case of pursuit not resulting from ordinary crimes, to seek and receive asylum in foreign territory, in accordance with the laws of each country and with international agreements."

In order to comply with Article XXVII, the domestic procedures by which a refugee seeks asylum must be adequate and effective. The adequacy of the internal procedures not only involves the formal rights of due process in immigration proceedings, but also the effects that detention can have on the asylum seeker's guarantees of due process.

C. The right to humane treatment during detention

64. Thus far, the IACHR has established that immigration detention must be the exception and must be applied in conformity with certain requirements. The Inter- American Commission has also underscored the relevant guarantees of due process and access to justice. In this section, the IACHR will focus on the detention conditions that must be present in those exceptional cases in which deprivation of liberty is necessary, taking into consideration general criteria regarding humane treatment as well as those special guarantees that must be afforded to ensure that immigration detentions, which are civil in nature, do not become punitive.

65. Under Article XXV of the American Declaration, every person who has been deprived of his liberty "has the right to humane treatment during the time he is in custody." In interpreting the rights protected in the Article XXV clause that concerns the right to humane treatment, and the right to the security of one's person protected under Article I of the American Declaration, the Inter-American Commission has made frequent reference to the United Nations Minimum Rules for the Treatment of Prisoners and to the Body of Principles for the Protection of All Persons under Any Form of Detention or Imprisonment. Recently, the IACHR approved its own set of "Principles and Best Practices on the Protection of Persons Deprived of Liberty in the Americas" (hereinafter the "Inter-American Principles on Detention"), which explain the protections afforded under Article XXV of the American Declaration.

66. Principle II of the Inter-American Principles on Detention states that "[u]nder no circumstances shall persons deprived of liberty be discriminated against for reasons of race, ethnic origin, nationality, color, sex, age, language, religion, political or other opinion, national or social origin, economic status, birth, physical, mental, or sensory disability, gender, sexual orientation, or any other social condition." That same principle provides that measures can and must be taken to

protect vulnerable groups, such as pregnant women, persons with physical, mental or sensory disabilities, and that these measures shall be "subject to review by a judge or other competent, independent, and impartial authority."

67. The Inter-American Principles on Detention offer specific guidelines on basic provisions — such as the rights to food, drinking water, sleeping quarters, hygiene, clothing and educational activities, recreation, religious freedom and visits — so as to ensure that all persons held in the custody of a state receive humane treatment. The Inter-American Principles on Detention prohibit overcrowding in prisons and detention facilities, which is regarded as a violation of Article 5 of the American Convention.

68. The ICCPR also establishes general prohibitions against incarceration in inhumane conditions. Article 7 reads as follows: "No one shall be subjected to torture or to cruel, inhuman or degrading treatment or punishment..." Article 10(1) of the Covenant similarly provides that "[a]ll persons deprived of their liberty shall be treated with humanity and with respect for the inherent dignity of the human person." As to the legal implications that ICCPR Article 10 has for undocumented migrants, the United Nations Special Rapporteur on the Human Rights of Migrant Workers underscored the fact that "detention of migrants on the grounds of their irregular status should under no circumstances be of a punitive nature."

69. When determining whether the obligation to provide humane treatment has been observed, consideration must be given to the question of whether the conditions of detention to which immigrants deprived of their liberty are subjected take into account their status and needs. For example, in *C v. Australia*, the Human Rights Committee concluded that Article 7 had been violated because a person seeking asylum had been detained for such a prolonged period as to cause him mental illness.

70. The next sections describe the specific rights that follow from the obligation to provide humane treatment. Where necessary, the special needs of immigrants are explained.

1. Right to medical care

71. In keeping with the legal obligations regarding humane treatment prescribed in Article XXV of the American Declaration, Principle IX(3) of the Inter-American Principles on Detention provides that: All persons deprived of liberty shall be entitled to an impartial and confidential medical or psychological examination, carried out by qualified medical personnel immediately following their admission to the place of imprisonment or commitment, in order to verify their state of physical or mental health and the existence of any mental or physical injury or damage; to ensure the diagnosis and treatment of any relevant health problem; or to investigate complaints of possible ill-treatment or torture. The medical or psychological information shall be entered into the respective official register, and when necessary taking into account the gravity of the findings, it shall be immediately transmitted to the competent authority.

72. Principle X sets out guidelines on the range of medical, psychiatric and dental services to which immigration detainees should have access, from basic care to prolonged, ongoing treatment in the case of the most serious afflictions. Under Principle X, special measures are to be provided to treat the health needs of vulnerable groups like the elderly, women, children and detainees with physical or mental disabilities. This Principle establishes that "the provision of health services shall, in all circumstances, respect the following principles: medical confidentiality; patient autonomy; and informed consent to medical treatment in the physician-patient relationship."

73. The Inter-American Principles also spell out specific requirements on involuntary seclusion and solitary confinement in the case of persons with mental disabilities:

In cases of involuntary seclusion of persons with mental disabilities it shall be ensured that the measure is authorized by a competent physician; carried out in accordance with officially approved procedures; recorded in the patient's individual medical record; and immediately notified to their family or legal representatives. Persons with mental disabilities who are secluded shall be under the care and supervision of qualified medical personnel.

74. The United Nations Committee on Economic, Social and Cultural Rights, the body that supervises the International Covenant on Economic, Social and Cultural Rights (ICESCR), which the United States has signed, has reiterated that detainees must have equal and nondiscriminatory access to medical care and attention:

States are under the obligation to respect the right to health by, inter alia, refraining from denying or limiting equal access for all persons, including prisoners or detainees, minorities, asylum seekers and illegal immigrants, to preventive, curative and palliative health services; abstaining from enforcing discriminatory practices as a State policy; and abstaining from imposing discriminatory practices relating to women's health status and needs.

75. When examining the specific medical needs of immigration detainees, the United Nations Special Rapporteur on the Human Rights of Migrant Workers recommended the following to the States:

Ensuring the presence in holding centres of a doctor with appropriate training in psychological treatments. Migrants should have the possibility of being assisted by interpreters in their contacts with doctors or when requesting medical attention. Detention of migrants with psychological problems, as well as those belonging to vulnerable categories and in need of special assistance, should be only allowed as a measure of last resort, and they should be provided with adequate medical and psychological assistance.

2. Right to be separated from criminal inmates

76. In keeping with the legal obligations on humane treatment set forth in Article XXV of the American Declaration, Principle XIX of the Inter-American Principles on Detention requires strict separation of the various categories of persons deprived of their liberty:

In particular, arrangements shall be made to separate men and women; children and adults; the elderly; accused and convicted; persons deprived of liberty for civil reasons and those deprived of liberty on criminal charges. In cases of deprivation of liberty of asylum or refugee status seekers, and in other similar cases, children shall not be separated from their parents. Asylum or refugee status seekers and persons deprived of liberty due to migration issues shall not be deprived of liberty in institutions designed to hold persons deprived of liberty on criminal charges.

77. The United Nations Special Rapporteur on the Human Rights of Migrant Workers recommends "ensuring that migrants under administrative detention are placed in a public establishment specifically intended for that purpose or, when this is not possible, in premises other than those intended for persons imprisoned under criminal law."

3. Right to be notified of transfer to other detention establishments

78. In keeping with the legal obligations on humane treatment set forth in Article XXV of the American Declaration, Principle IX(4) of the Inter-American Principles on Detention spells out safeguards to ensure that:

The transfers of persons deprived of liberty shall be authorized and supervised by the competent authorities, who shall, in all circumstances, respect the dignity and fundamental rights of persons deprived of liberty, and shall take into account the need of persons to be deprived of liberty in places near their family, community, their defense counsel or legal representative, and the tribunal or other State body that may be in charge of their case. The transfers shall not be carried out in order to punish, repress, or discriminate against persons deprived of liberty, their families or representatives; nor shall they be conducted under conditions that cause physical or mental suffering, are humiliating or facilitate public exhibition.

79. Under the U.N. Body of Principles, an immigrant in custody and transferred to another facility "shall be entitled to notify or to require the competent authority to notify members of his family or other appropriate persons of his choice of his (...) transfer and of the place where he is kept" and "shall also be promptly informed of his right to communicate by appropriate means with a consular post or diplomatic mission of the State of which he is a national (...)."

80. When transfer is ordered, special consideration is to be given to the impact that transfer will have on the right to protection of the family and the right to due process. When an immigrant has been in a country for some time, he or she should be held in custody in a place close to his or her habitual place of residence, in order to safeguard those rights. Article VI of the American Declaration provides that "every person has the right to establish a family, the basic element of society, and to receive protection therefore." The Inter-American Commission has written that "[i]t is a right so basic to the Convention that it is considered to be non-derogable even in extreme circumstances." The IACHR has repeatedly held that "visiting rights are a fundamental requirement for ensuring respect of the personal integrity and freedom of the

inmate and, as a corollary, the right to protection of the family for all the affected parties (...) [and that] because of the exceptional circumstances of imprisonment, the state must establish positive provisions to effectively guarantee the right to maintain and develop family relations."

81. Apart from the right to family, the location of the detention facility can frequently affect an immigrant's due process rights, including his or her right to be represented by an attorney. Only under exceptional circumstances should immigrants in custody who have secured legal representation be transferred outside the jurisdiction in which they were apprehended; it is the government's responsibility to demonstrate to an independent court the need to transfer the immigrant in custody. Moreover, the State must ensure that the transfers are based on objective grounds and answer objective needs. Specifically, it is impermissible for immigration detainees to be transferred to a jurisdiction that would be more likely to issue an order of removal.

4. Right to have duly trained and qualified personnel and independent supervision at the place of detention

82. Principle XX of the Inter-American Principles on Detention establish guidelines regarding the training required for personnel working in and supervising places of detention or imprisonment. Principle 29 of the United Nations Body of Principles for the Protection of All Persons under Any Form of Detention or Imprisonment provides that "places of detention shall be visited regularly by qualified and experienced persons appointed by, and responsible to, a competent authority distinct from the authority directly in charge of the administration of the place of detention or imprisonment."

83. In particular, immigrants that have to be detained must be accommodated in facilities in which the officials who have custody have been given the proper training in:

psychological aspects relating to detention, cultural sensitivity and human rights procedures, and ensuring that centres for the administrative detention of migrants are not run by private companies or staffed by private personnel unless they are adequately trained and the centres are subject to regular public supervision to ensure the application of international and national human rights law.

5. Right to an established disciplinary policy and to due process

84. Principle XXII of the Inter-American Principles on Detention provides that: "disciplinary sanctions, and the disciplinary procedures adopted in places of deprivation of liberty shall be subject to judicial review and be previously established by law and shall not contravene the norms of international human rights law." Principle 30 of the United Nations Body of Principles for the Protection of All Persons under Any Form of Detention or Imprisonment provides that:

1. The types of conduct of the detained or imprisoned person that constitute disciplinary offences during detention or imprisonment, the description and duration of disciplinary punishment that may be inflicted and the authorities competent to impose such punishment shall be specified by law or lawful regulations and duly published. 2. A detained or imprisoned person shall have the right to be heard before disciplinary action is taken. He shall have the right to bring such action to higher authorities for review.

85. The Inter-American Principles on Detention set out strict guidelines on the use of confinement or isolation measures:

Solitary confinement shall only be permitted as a disposition of last resort and for a strictly limited time, when it is evident that it is necessary to ensure legitimate interests relating to the institution's internal security, and to protect fundamental rights, such as the right to life and integrity of persons deprived of liberty or the personnel.

In all cases, the disposition of solitary confinement shall be authorized by the competent authority and shall be subject to judicial control, since its prolonged, inappropriate or unnecessary use would amount to acts of torture, or cruel, inhuman, or degrading treatment or punishment.

86. Finally, any bodily searches or inspections "shall comply with criteria of necessity, reasonableness and proportionality."

6. The right to an effective procedure for petition and response

87. Principle VII of the Inter-American Principles on Detention reads as follows:

Persons deprived of liberty shall have the right of individual and collective petition and the right to a response before judicial, administrative, or other authorities. This right may be exercised by third parties or organizations, in accordance with the law.

This right comprises, amongst others, the right to lodge petitions, claims, or complaints before the competent authorities, and to receive a prompt response within a reasonable time. It also comprises the right to opportunely request and receive information concerning their procedural status and the remaining time of deprivation of liberty, if applicable.

Persons deprived of liberty shall also have the right to lodge communications, petitions or complaints with the national human rights institutions; with the Inter-American Commission on Human Rights; and with the other competent international bodies, in conformity with the requirements established by domestic law and international law.

88. The United Nations Special Rapporteur on the Human Rights of Migrant Workers underscores the point that immigration detainees must be assured effective access to judicial recourse in the event that the petition mechanism fails to correct any violation of the right to humane treatment.

7. Obligation to investigate deaths that occur during detention

89. Principle XXIII(3) of the Inter-American Principles on Detention reads as follows: Member States of the Organization of American States shall carry out serious, exhaustive, impartial, and prompt investigations in relation to all acts of violence or situations of emergency that have occurred in places of deprivation of liberty, with a view to uncovering the causes, identifying those responsible, and imposing the corresponding punishments on them. States shall take appropriate measures and make every effort possible to prevent the recurrence of acts of violence or situations of emergency in places of deprivation of liberty.

90. Principle 34 of the United Nations Body of Principles for the Protection of All Persons under Any Form of Detention or Imprisonment states that: Whenever the death or disappearance of a detained or imprisoned person occurs during his detention or imprisonment, an inquiry into the cause of death or disappearance shall be held by a judicial or other authority, either on its own motion or at the instance of a member of the family of such a person or any person who has knowledge of the case. When circumstances so warrant, such an inquiry shall be held on the same procedural basis whenever the death or disappearance occurs shortly after the termination of the detention or imprisonment. The findings of such inquiry or a report thereon shall be made available upon request, unless doing so would jeopardize an ongoing criminal investigation. 8. Specific rights of asylum seekers in detention

91. The right to seek asylum is internationally recognized, as are the special risks and threats that might be entailed. Therefore, the UNHCR has established additional guidelines to govern the treatment of asylum seekers in the event they are taken into custody. The UNHCR notes that the general principles of humane treatment apply with equal force to asylum seekers, but emphasizes that they also need to be afforded certain protections specific to their condition:

(i) the initial screening of all asylum-seekers at the outset of detention to identify trauma or torture victims, for treatment in accordance with Guideline 7.

(ii) the segregation within facilities of men and women; children from adults(unless these are relatives); (iii) the use of separate detention facilities to accommodate asylum- seekers. The use of prisons should be avoided. If separate detention facilities are not used, asylum-seekers should be accommodated separately from convicted criminals or prisoners on remand. There should be no co-mingling of the two groups;

(iv) the opportunity to make regular contact and receive visits from friends, relatives, religious, social and legal counsel. Facilities should be made available to enable such visits. Where possible such visits should take place in private unless there are compelling reasons to warrant the contrary;

(v) the opportunity to receive appropriate medical treatment, and psychological counseling where appropriate;

(vi) the opportunity to conduct some form of physical exercise through daily indoor and outdoor recreational activities;

(vii) the opportunity to continue further education or vocational training;

(viii) the opportunity to exercise their religion and to receive a diet in keeping with their religion;

(ix) the opportunity to have access to basic necessities i.e. beds, shower facilities, basic toiletries etc.;

(x) access to a complaints mechanism, (grievance procedures) where complaints may be submitted either directly or confidentially to the detaining authority. Procedures for lodging complaints, including time limits and appeal procedures, should be displayed and made available to detainees in different languages.

9. Adherence to U.N. Principles for the detention of unaccompanied children

92. Article VII of the American Declaration recognizes every child's right to "special protection, care and aid." Inasmuch as the rights of the child and his or her particular vulnerability are internationally recognized, the United Nations Special Rapporteur on the Human Rights of Migrant Workers has advised States to adhere strictly to the United Nations Rules for the Protection of Juveniles Deprived of their Liberty and the United Nations Standard Minimum Rules for the Administration of Juvenile Justice.

93. Article 37(d) of the United Nations Convention on the Rights of the Child provides that "[e]very child deprived of his or her liberty shall have the right to prompt access to legal and other appropriate assistance, as well as the right to challenge the legality of the deprivation of his or her liberty before a court or other competent, independent and impartial authority, and to a prompt decision on any such action."

...

V. FINAL CONCLUSIONS AND RECOMMENDATIONS

415. On the basis of the investigation set forth in this report, and on the updated information and observations presented by the United States, the Inter-American Commission will proceed to its final conclusions and the corresponding recommendations. The observations presented by the United States to the draft version of this report have been very valuable in assessing those areas in which advances have already been made, and where immigration reform is producing concrete results toward compliance with international human rights obligations. The IACHR encourages the State to continue such reforms and to broaden them with a view to enhancing the protection of all persons under its jurisdiction.

416. Throughout this report, the Inter-American Commission has expressed its concern with the increasing use of detention of migrants based on a presumption of its necessity, when in fact detention should be the exception. The United States Supreme Court itself has upheld the constitutionality of mandatory detention in immigration cases that have not been decided, despite the fact that the violations alleged are civil in nature, and despite the loss of liberty that detention presupposes.

417. The IACHR is preoccupied by the rapid increase in the number of partnerships with local and state law enforcement for purposes of enforcing civil immigration laws. The Inter-American Commission finds that ICE has failed to develop an oversight and accountability system to ensure that these local partners do not enforce immigration law in a discriminatory manner by resorting to racial profiling and that their practices do not use the supposed investigation of crimes as a pretext to prosecute and detain undocumented migrants. In this regard, the October 2010 observations of the United States point to the implementation of performance-based standards. The Inter- American Commission will be very interested in analyzing the result of the application of those standards as part of the follow-up to the recommendations of this report.

418. It must be reiterated that detention is a disproportionate measure in many if not the majority of cases, and that the programs that provide for alternatives to detention constitutes a more balanced way for the State to ensure compliance with immigration laws. Another concern the IACHR sets forth in this report is the impact of detention on due process, mainly with respect to the right to legal counsel which directly affects the right to seek release. To better guarantee the right to legal representation and, ultimately, to due process, the IACHR considers that stronger programs offering alternatives to detention are needed and the Legal Orientation Program must be expanded nationwide. In this regard, the

October 2010 observations of the United States indicate initiatives to broaden its alternative to detention programs, an initiative which the IACHR welcomes.

419. In this report the IACHR also stresses that even in those cases in which detention is strictly necessary, there is no genuinely civil system where the general conditions comply with standards of respect for human dignity and humane treatment; there is also a lack of the special conditions required for in cases of non-punitive detention.

As developed above, the IACHR is further troubled by the frequent outsourcing of the management and personal care of immigration detainees to private contractors.

A. Interior Enforcement Recommendations

420. The Inter-American Commission acknowledges the significant challenges that the federal government faces in administering such a complex, expansive system of immigration enforcement and removal. Given the human rights concerns identified in this report, the IACHR offers the following recommendations for how the State can improve its current policies and practices with respect to immigration enforcement, detention, and due process, so as to enhance the protection of immigrants' basic human rights. The Inter- American Commission urges DHS to expend the financial and human resources required to achieve vigorous central oversight, accountability and control over the many aspects of ICE's civil immigration operations. This will require significant increases in ICE personnel to provide direct, in-person, daily supervision of the various facets of ICE's civil immigration operations.

1. Federal Enforcement Programs

421. Given ICE's new emphasis on investigation of employers, the IACHR urges the State to devote the necessary resources to lower the error rate in its E-Verify system, which is used to determine an employee's work authorization. Further, the Inter- American Commission urges the State to standardize the employment audits and make them more transparent, so as to give workers access to the audit process, to give them a reasonable period of time to prove that their work status is valid and to implement stricter supervision of employers to make certain that they are not engaging in prohibited practices, such as taking adverse employment action when social security numbers do not initially match or failing to inform workers of their rights under the program. The IACHR urges the State to prioritize worksite control in the case of those employers who commit abuses of employees. If an unauthorized immigrant is apprehended at his or her workplace, the State must guarantee strict enforcement of the humanitarian guidelines issued by ICE.

422. With respect to ICE's Fugitive Operations program (FOT), the Inter- American Commission recommends the elimination of home raids, unless the targeted immigrant fugitive has a serious criminal record or poses another identifiable, serious risk to the safety of the community. To the extent that FOTs continue to execute home raids, the IACHR urges that ICE require:

a. that the raid be carried out exclusively by FOT officers based on reliable evidence;

b. that the FOT officers identify themselves as "immigration officials" before seeking entry to the dwelling;

c. that the FOT officers present individualized administrative arrest warrants issued by an independent judge before seeking to enter the residence, and

d. that the FOT officers not be permitted to arrest collateral persons who are not named in the administrative arrest warrant.

423. Finally, the Inter-American Commission urges the State to eliminate the use of removal quotas to evaluate and promote ICE personnel, in order to prevent a deviation from ICE's priorities, which are that the focus should be on immigrants with serious criminal records.

2. State and Local Partnership Enforcement Programs

424. This section includes the recommendations of the IACHR with respect to ICE's programs to enforce civil immigration law through state and local partners (287(g), Jail Enforcement, Criminal Alien Program, and Secure Communities Program).

425. The IACHR recommends that ICE eliminate 287(g) authorization for Task Force Enforcement, as the federal authorities are unable to properly monitor to prevent and combat the use of racial profiling and the negative effects on security and crime prevention. The Inter-American Commission also recommends that the United States Department of Justice (DOJ) replace its April 3, 2002 memorandum — in which it found that local law enforcement agencies have an inherent authority to enforce federal civil immigration laws — and return its position to the DOJ policy announced in 1996.661

426. First, the Inter-American Commission recommends that the state and local partners only be permitted to participate in enforcement of civil immigration laws once an individual has been criminally convicted or the criminal proceeding has been fully adjudicated. Second, the IACHR urges ICE to require participating LEAs to collect essential data that may indicate racial-profiling of the persons whose immigration statuses are reviewed and to periodically report to ICE on this matter. This data should include: the total number of arrests and the total number of persons with respect to whom the charges were dropped. In both cases, it should be possible to break down the information by type of charge or accusation and the person's ethnic origin. Third, the Inter-American Commission urges ICE to establish transparent instructions to its state and local coordination teams and other appropriate bodies, so that these data can be diligently reviewed to identify possible patterns of racial-profiling. Also, appropriate follow-up investigations should be conducted and training provided to and corrective action taken against the participating LEAs. Fourth, the IACHR recommends that ICE conduct unannounced inspections of partner LEAs to review their implementation of the partnership agreements. Finally, the Inter-American Commission strongly urges ICE to publish the data it compiles from the participating LEAs, so the public can monitor and be satisfied that racial-profiling is not being used in a discriminatory manner within these programs.

427. Finally, the IACHR urges federal and local authorities to refrain from passing laws that use criminal offenses to criminalize immigration, and from developing administrative or other practices that violate the fundamental principle of nondiscrimination and the immigrants' rights to due process of law, personal liberty, and humane treatment. The Inter-American Commission also underscores the need to find appropriate ways to amend the law recently enacted in Arizona to adapt it to international human rights standards for the protection of immigrants.

B. Detention recommendations

1. Mandatory detention of arriving aliens and deportable immigrants with criminal convictions

428. The IACHR urges the State to eliminate the practice of mandatory detention for broad classes of immigrants, including "arriving aliens" and deportable, legal immigrants (including LPRs) with criminal convictions but who have served their sentence.

2. Custody determinations and alternatives to detention

429. The Inter-American Commission urges the State to develop a risk assessment tool premised upon a presumption for release and to establish clear criteria to determine whether detention is in order. Those criteria should be dictated exclusively by procedural factors in order to ensure that detention does not become punitive (for example, when there is a flight risk). Public safety can only be invoked when the persons in question have criminal records and under no circumstances can be invoked in the case of persons who have only committed immigration infractions. Whatever the case, the determination of whether a person should be incarcerated ought to be done on a case-by- case basis, taking into account the person's circumstances and sufficiently substantiating the reasons why the decision was not based on a presumption of liberty. This decision should be subject to judicial review.

430. The risk assessment tool should be designed to place each person in the least restrictive environment necessary to fulfill the State's goals at each stage of the proceedings and should feature an evaluation of any humanitarian needs a person might have. The humanitarian considerations regarding vulnerable groups, including families, children, the elderly, asylum seekers, victims of human trafficking, of persecution and of other serious crimes, and persons with physical

or mental health problems, should create a strong presumption in favor of the need to be released or placed in an appropriate environment other than civil detention or the current detention system. Persons in vulnerable groups should only be placed in civil detention or under the current detention system in extraordinary, carefully defined circumstances. Furthermore, the case-by-case risk assessment should consider the likelihood of a person's success on the merits of his or her claims to remain in the United States.

431. As part of an individualized risk assessment, the IACHR recommends that immigrants be permitted to be represented by counsel, to present evidence and to appeal any decision on his or her risk assessment to an immigration judge. The Inter-American Commission also recommends that risk assessment determinations be automatically reviewed on a defined, periodic basis and that these reviews take into account the State's increased burden of proof when detention continues over time; pertinent developments in the proceedings on the merits should also be factored in wherever relevant.

432. The risk assessment tool should present a broad spectrum of custody determinations, including: release, bond, telephone reporting, in-person reporting, case manager meetings, unannounced home visits, GPS monitoring, house detention, residential group living, civil detention, and detention in a secured facility. The IACHR recognizes that this will require the State to develop expansive, robust, community-based Alternatives to Detention programs. The Inter-American Commission urges the State to significantly increase its funding for such programs, while gradually abandoning its current approach of mass detention. In order for the Alternatives to Detention programs to be successful, the IACHR recommends that such programs include meaningful case management by properly trained personnel and assistance in accessing social service organizations.

433. The State must also guarantee that in the event persons are found to be in violation of immigration law or are not granted legal status, they are to be deported from the United States in a manner that is respectful of their human rights.

3. Civil detention system

434. The IACHR urges the State to significantly curtail prison-like detention conditions. Accordingly, the Inter-American Commission urges the State to carry through with its commitment to develop a genuinely civil detention system. The IACHR recommends that each facility house only small groups, in such a way that the State is able to provide for their basic needs and protect the human rights of all detained immigrants. Furthermore, the State should locate civil detention facilities near urban centers in order to ensure that detainees have meaningful access to legal representation.

435. The Inter-American Commission urges the State to design and implement proper oversight and monitoring mechanisms by federal immigration authorities, to ensure that those centers that are run by private firms comply with international standards on immigration detention.

C. Civil detention conditions

436. The IACHR urges the State to make the new civil detention standards into legally enforceable regulations that depart from the ACA criminal detention standards, so that they constitute the guarantee necessary to ensure that the human rights of immigrant detainees are respected. The Inter-American Commission offers some recommendations concerning the elements necessary for the detention system to be truly civil in nature:

a. The facility must provide detainees meaningful privacy, freedom of movement within the facility grounds, and access to outdoor recreation (open to the sky without obstruction). The facility must provide ample access to all three during normal daytime hours, except under extraordinary circumstances such as a demonstrable security risk. The detainees' sleeping quarters must not have the appearance of a prison cell.

b. Visitation space must be sufficient to accommodate a reasonable amount of visitors, based on the size of the detention population, and provide basic facilities. Detainees should be permitted to receive unplanned visitors and to have in-person, contact visits.

c. Facilities must provide adequate space for confidential meetings with attorneys and mental health practitioners, so that these meetings can happen in an efficient and timely manner. Detainees should be permitted to meet with their attorneys and mental health practitioners 7 days a week during normal waking hours. Attorney-client meetings should not have any set time limit.

d. Detainees must be permitted to have confidential phone conversations with their attorneys and consulates, with only well grounded restrictions on the time or frequency of such calls.

e. Facilities must provide appropriate space for legal orientation group meetings. Facilities should actively seek out and accommodate potential legal orientation providers. ICE should approve legal orientation presenters based on objective, transparent criteria.

f. Detainees represented by law students, BIA accredited representatives, and law graduates, must be provided with the same access to counsel as detainees represented by attorneys.

g. Law libraries must be up to date, with internet access and access to electronic immigration case information. Facilities must provide ample quiet work space and office materials for detainees to work on their cases. Detainees should be permitted to freely access the law library during normal work hours with no set time limits, demand and space providing.

h. Mail regarding legal matters must be kept confidential, delivered to detainees expeditiously, and if necessary opened by the detainee in front of facility staff. i. Detainees should be allowed to wear their own clothing.

j. Detention employees should not wear prison-type uniforms. k. Detention employees should not be called "guards" and detainees should not be referred to as "inmates."

l. Detainees should eat meals at normal meal-time hours and have sufficient time to complete their meals. Facilities should be open to detainee suggestions for nutritious meals that correspond to the detainees' cultural preferences.

m. Detainees should not be shackled or handcuffed, either in the facility or during transport, unless there is a specific, individualized reason. Detainees should not be shackled during immigration court proceedings.

n. The use of segregation, either for disciplinary or administrative purposes, must be strictly prohibited.

o. Detainees should have broad access to internet, e-mail, and phone communication free of charge. All forms of communication must be kept in good working order.

p. Detainees should be allowed to keep possessions that are not illegal or dangerous with them in their room. "Contraband" policies should be revised to enable detainees to accept basic, legal items such as postage stamps, envelopes, care-packages from family members and legal representatives. Detainees must have unfettered access to their legal documents.

q. Detainees should be given the option of participating in organized daily activities, indoor and outdoor. The facility should actively encourage outside organizations to provide regular activities to the detainee population.

r. Facilities should provide detainees with access to programmatic activities, including educational, English language, and skills-based programs.

s. Detainees should be provided a quiet space to practice their religion. Facilities must make accommodations with respect to dress, schedule, and dietary considerations. The facility should reach out to the greater religious community to make regular visits and perform religious services for the detainee population.

t. Detainees must be provided with a means to register their grievances and suggestions directly to facility authorities both verbally and in writing.

1. Medical and mental health care

437. The IACHR first recommends that when designing and implementing a new health care system, the DIHS and other providers of health care services for immigrant detainees do away with the current model of emergency care. The

Inter-American Commission recommends that the DIHS establish a new protocol which gives primacy to the medical care decisions of the attending, qualified medical, dental and mental health personnel. Moreover, the IACHR suggests that DIHS establish an independent review panel, which would permit detainees to appeal denials of care.

438. As the State is currently developing a civil detention system, the Inter- American Commission is recommending that the facilities be located near urban centers, where qualified medical personnel are available. The IACHR urges the State to earmark sufficient funds so that each facility has a clinic and medical staff to provide comprehensive health care services, including dental and mental health care. The Inter-American Commission recommends that detainees have direct access to the medical, dental and mental health care clinics in the facilities, so that they can make appointments and receive emergency treatment.

439. Finally, the IACHR urges the State to immediately end the practice of placing detainees with mental health issues in administrative segregation. The Inter- American Commission urges the State to place detainees with mental health issues in environments and with treatment commensurate with their needs.

D. Due process recommendations

440. The IACHR is offering the following recommendations with a view to contributing to the protection of detained immigrants' due process rights in immigration proceedings. The Inter-American Commission is recommending that the State greatly reduce the use of expedited removal when adjudicating immigrants' claims. In particular, the IACHR urges the State to eliminate the application of expedited removal in the case of all vulnerable groups and asylum seekers who demonstrate a credible fear at the time of their first interview at the border or entry point. The Inter-American Commission is also recommending the elimination of expedited removal in the case of immigrants apprehended within 100 miles of an international land border and within 14 days of entering the country. At a minimum, the State should have the burden of proof to demonstrate that the immigrant has been in the United States for less than 14 days.

441. The IACHR underscores the point that if detention is appreciably decreased, particularly detention in prison-like conditions, the problem of a dearth of legal representation would substantially improve. In any event, the Inter-American Commission is recommending that the State devote significant additional resources to improve access to legal representation. The IACHR first recommends that the State appoint government-funded counsel, or at a minimum specially trained guardians ad litem for all minors and persons with mental illnesses in immigration proceedings. Second, the Inter-American Commission recommends that the State expand its Legal Orientation Program nationwide for both detained and non-detained immigrants. Finally, the State should earmark financial resources to support non-profit legal service organizations with their pro bono representation programs and to provide them the means to represent persons with complex and meritorious cases.

442. With respect to stipulated orders of removal, the IACHR recommends that apprehended immigrants have the opportunity to consult with legal counsel before consenting to an order of removal. The Inter-American Commission further recommends that the State eliminate ICE's role in presenting this option to an apprehended immigrant. Rather, an immigration judge, with proper interpretation in a language understood by the apprehended person, should present this option to an individual at the first hearing in the proceeding. This option should draw a clear distinction between a "stipulated order of removal" and "voluntary departure." As part of this new procedure, the State should establish a protocol by which it is a judge who decides whether the immigrant understood the consequences of consenting to the stipulated removal and that the immigrant can only give his or her consent in the presence of a judge.

443. To ensure that every immigrant receives a fair hearing, conducted close to where family and support resources may be located, the IACHR recommends that the State require that a completed "Notice to Appear" (NTA) be promptly filed in the jurisdiction where an individual was apprehended, eliminating the possibility of ICE moving the immigrants to a jurisdiction in which the likelihood of securing an order of removal is much greater. This would also have the effect of reducing the number of transfers within the system and would ensure that detainees are notified of the charges against them.

444. The Inter-American Commission recommends that the State create a strong presumption against transferring migrant detainees outside the jurisdiction of apprehension. To the extent that transfers are necessary, the IACHR urges the State to require that a detainee be provided sufficient advance notice and that it establish a mechanism by which a

detainee can turn to an immigration judge to challenge a transfer based on family, legal representation or other humanitarian considerations.

445. With respect to the release on bond process, the Inter-American Commission recommends that the State eliminate the current regulation which establishes ICE's right to an automatic stay of the appeal if ICE establishes an initial bond of US$10,000 or higher. Further, the State should establish a reasonable ceiling bond amount which ICE district offices may not exceed, so that a better balance is struck between the State's interest in appearance at all hearings and the resources the detainee has to post bond. Both the Department of Justice (DOJ) and the DHS should develop mechanisms to review the bond process to ensure that these dual goals are met.

446. The IACHR urges the State to significantly limit the use of video- teleconferencing in immigration proceedings. Video-conferencing should not be used for proceedings in which decisions are made on the merits or in any other hearing that requires the determination of the immigrant's credibility or other subjective analysis.

447. With respect to immigrants held after an order of removal has been issued (post-order of removal detention), the Inter-American Commission urges the State to enact regulations which affirmatively establish the State's proactive compliance with the U.S. Supreme Court's decisions in *Zadvydas v. Davis* and *Clark v. Martinez*. The IACHR recommends that the State ensures that post-order of removal detainees receive prompt, meaningful 90-day custody reviews. If release is not ordered during this custody review, a specific, written explanation of the detainees' refusal to cooperate and/or specific, written reasons why ICE believes removal is likely in the reasonably foreseeable future should be required. The Inter-American Commission urges the State to create an automatic review at the six-month post-order deadline established by the Supreme Court for when a post-order of removal detainee must be released. The IACHR recommends that the six-month post-order review be conducted by an immigration judge or the appropriate federal court.

E. Recommendations on families and unaccompanied children

448. The Inter-American Commission is recommending that ICE codify its current practice of placing families apprehended at or near the border to normal immigration proceedings, pursuant to INA § 240. In the case of those few families that must be subjected to detention, the IACHR is recommending that the State transfer custody of the families to the ORR and implement a range of services comparable to those that currently exist for unaccompanied children. Finally, the Inter-American Commission is urging the State to transform the new guidelines for parole of asylum seekers into federal regulations.

449. In an effort to respect the rights of the family and adhere to the "best interests of the child" principle, the IACHR further recommends that the federal government coordinate with state and local governments to ensure that detained immigrants are able to maintain custody of their U.S. citizen children while in detention (in light of other factors and unless there is an independent reason the parent is a risk to the child) and are permitted time and autonomy to make custody decisions with respect to U.S. citizen children if the parent is scheduled for removal from the United States.

450. The Inter-American Commission recommends that the ORR ensure that the other contract shelters provide levels of care and a range of services similar to that observed at the Southwest Key Shelter in Phoenix, Arizona, and the International Educational Services, Inc. Shelter in Los Fresnos, Texas. The IACHR urges the State to provide sufficient funding and place more shelters in urban areas where the necessary qualified medical, mental health, social service, educational, and legal professionals can be identified and retained to provide consistent, quality care to the unaccompanied children. The Inter-American Commission recommends that the State codify the Flores standards into federal regulations, with a focus on the best interests of the child principle.

451. The IACHR urges the State to earmark the necessary resources to fully implement the reforms introduced in 2008 under the TVPRA. In particular, the Inter- American Commission underscores the importance of screening unaccompanied children from Mexico and Canada for asylum seekers, victims of trafficking, and victims of other forms of persecution and criminal activity. To effectively identify possible victims, the IACHR urges the State to ensure that such screenings are conducted in a conducive environment, by trained personnel, with an age-appropriate screening template. This screening should not be conducted by agents in ICE's Customs and Border Protection or any other uniformed police unit.

452. With respect to unaccompanied children's due process rights, the Inter- American Commission urges the State to appoint an attorney, at the State's expense, to represent unaccompanied children in immigration proceedings. The IACHR further urges the State to enact regulations that prohibit DHS or ICE officials from obtaining an unaccompanied child's health records or records of other social service consultations.

453. With respect to unaccompanied minors repatriated to their home country, the Inter-American Commission recommends that the repatriation process be transferred to the exclusive jurisdiction of the ORR. The IACHR urges the State to continue to improve its repatriation protocols with other States Parties to ensure that unaccompanied minors are repatriated safely and into a safe home environment.

...

Finally, in concluding this report, the Inter-American Commission thanks all the persons who assisted in its preparation and drafting, including the many organizations of civil society, immigration advocates, experts, and individuals who supplied valuable time and information. The IACHR also once again expresses its appreciation to the United States for its cooperative approach which facilitated the visits and made the investigation reflected in this report possible, and also for its constructive and informative observations that contributed to strengthen the above findings.

The Inter-American Commission reiterates that the State must comply fully with the international human rights obligations under the American Declaration, as interpreted and developed in the inter-American system. As indicated in the October 2010 observations by the United States, reflected in this report, some of the specific concerns of the Inter-American Commission are being addressed thorough immigration reform, which means that compliance with some of these recommendations is already underway. Within the framework of its functions and competencies, the IACHR will follow up on full compliance with these recommendations, and offers the United States its collaboration and advice to that effect.

Source: Organization of American States, Inter-American Commission on Human Rights, OEA/Ser.L/V/II., Doc. 78/10, 30 December 2010, Report on Immigration in the United States: Detention and Due Process, https://www.oas.org/en/iachr/migrants/docs/pdf/Migrants2011.pdf

ॐ∽ॐ∽ॐ∽ॐ∽ॐ

9. INTER-AMERICAN COMMISSION ON HUMAN RIGHTS, REPORT NO. 50/16 ON MERITS, UNDOCUMENTED WORKERS V. UNITED STATES

This report is an actual case decision of a petition filed in the Inter-American Commission on Human Rights against the United States by undocumented aliens who were working in the U.S. and were injured on the job. This is a report from the Commission on the merits of the petition. This case shows how the Inter-American Commission analyzes a case, determines the facts, how it addresses U.S. and state constitutions and laws, and how it applies the norms of the American Declaration of Human Rights to the facts of the case and determines the "merits" of the case, whether there was or was not a violation of one or more of the norms in the ADHR, and what remedies it recommends, and follow-up and the response of the U.S. The decisions of the Commission are arguably not legally binding but should be respected by the U.S.

{Excerpt}

INTER AMERICAN COMMISSION ON HUMAN RIGHTS
REPORT No. 50/16 CASE 12.834
MERITS (PUBLICATION)

UNDOCUMENTED WORKERS

v.

UNITED STATES
NOVEMBER 30, 2016

I. SUMMARY

1. On November 1, 2006, the Inter-American Commission on Human Rights (the "Inter-American Commission" or the "IACHR") received a petition from the University of Pennsylvania School of Law, the American Civil Liberties Union Foundation, and the National Employment Law Project (the "petitioners") against the United States of America (the "State" or "United States"), on behalf of, among others, Leopoldo Zumaya and Francisco Berumen Lizalde, foreign undocumented workers who had resided in the United States.

2. The petitioners claim that the presumed victims were excluded from employment rights and remedies available to their documented counterparts. The presumed victims have allegedly been directly affected by the United States' denial of equal rights based on immigration status in their efforts to seek enforcement of their employment and labor rights. The petitioners contend that a decision of the United States Supreme Court, *Hoffman Plastic Compounds, Inc. v. National Labor Relations Board*, 535 U.S. 137 (2002) ("*Hoffman*"), made the issue of immigration status relevant to workplace rights and encouraged employers to claim that undocumented immigrant workers lack legal rights in contexts beyond that discussed in Hoffman, which related to the freedom of association of undocumented workers. These other contexts, petitioners claim, include: access to compensation for workplace injuries, freedom from workplace discrimination, and entitlement to hold an employer responsible for a workplace injury. Within these contexts, they claim that the presumed victims were denied full protection for their labor rights and denied due process.

3. The State contends that the petitioners have not exhausted domestic remedies, noting that remedies are available in state courts, and therefore the case should be dismissed. In the alternative, the State argues that it has a sovereign right to deny permission to work to those "illegally present" in the country or to those who have not obtained authorization to work. Consequently, the State maintains that federal and state law recognizes the difficulty in providing backpay for work that was not done when it could not have lawfully been done. Further, the State claims that the petitioners have "overstated" the impact of Hoffman and that undocumented workers are still entitled to protection under the National Labor Relations Act ("NLRA"), including wage compensation and medical benefits. The State affirms its commitment to protecting all workers against employment and labor violations, regardless of whether they possess authorization to work.

4. In Report No. 134/11, adopted by the IACHR on March 20, 2011 during its Period of Sessions, the Commission declared petition 1190-06 admissible, without prejudging the merits of the matter, with respect to Articles II (Right to equality before law), XVI (Right to social security), XVII (Right to recognition of juridical personality and civil rights), and XVIII (Right to fair trial) of the American Declaration of the Rights and Duties of Man ("American Declaration") with regard to Leopoldo Zumaya and Francisco Berumen Lizalde. It published this report and included it in its Annual Report to the General Assembly of the Organization of American States. The petition was then registered as Case No. 12.834.

5. In the instant report, after analyzing the position of the petitioners and the State, and the available information, the Inter-American Commission concludes that the United States is responsible for violating Articles II and XVI of the American Declaration with respect to Leopoldo Zumaya and Francisco Berumen Lizalde and for additionally violating Mr. Lizalde's rights under Articles XVII and XVIII. As such, it recommends that the State: provide Messrs. Zumaya and Lizalde with adequate monetary compensation to remedy the violations sustained in the present report; ensure all federal and state laws and policies, on their face and in practice, prohibit any and all distinctions in employment and labor rights based on immigration status and work authorization, once a person commences work as an employee; prohibit employer inquiries into the immigration status of a worker asserting his or her employment and labor rights in litigation or in administrative complaints; ensure that undocumented workers are granted the same rights and remedies for violations of their rights in the workplace as documented workers; establish a procedure whereby undocumented workers involved in workers' compensation proceedings, or their representatives, may request the suspension of their deportations until the resolution of the proceedings and the workers have received the appropriate medical treatment ordered by the presiding courts; and improve and enhance the detection of employers who violate labor rights and exploit undocumented workers and impose adequate sanctions against them.

II. PROCEEDINGS BEFORE THE IACHR
SUBSEQUENT TO ADMISSIBILITY REPORT

6. By communications of December 21, 2011, the Inter-American Commission transmitted the admissibility report to the parties and in accordance with the Rules of Procedure in force at the time, the Commission set a deadline of three months for the petitioners to present additional observations on the merits and, at the same time, placed itself at the disposition of the parties with a view to reaching a friendly settlement of the matter.

7. On July 31, 2013, the petitioners submitted additional information on the merits, the pertinent parts of which were duly forwarded to the State by note dated September 6, 2013. The Inter-American Commission set a deadline of four months for the State to submit its observations. On April 24, 2014, the IACHR transmitted a note to the State, in which it reiterated the request for information on the merits.

8. On June 27, 2014, the IACHR received the United States' response on the merits, the pertinent parts of which were duly forwarded to the petitioners on September 5, 2014.

9. Meanwhile, the petitioners requested a hearing on the merits during the Period of Sessions, March 7-22, 2013, and again during the 153 Period of Sessions, October 23-November 7, 2014; these requests were not granted due to the large number of requests received. The Commission granted the petitioners' request for the 154 Period of Sessions and held a hearing on the merits of the case on March 16, 2015.

III. POSITIONS OF THE PARTIES

A. The petitioners

10, The petitioners indicate that the present complaint challenges government-sanctioned discrimination against undocumented immigrant workers5 in the United States. Petitioners represent two undocumented workers who sustained injuries while on the job in Pennsylvania and Kansas, respectively, and were allegedly excluded from employment rights and remedies available to their documented counterparts. They claim that this discrimination stems from the U.S. Supreme Court's decision in *Hoffman Plastic Compounds, Inc. v. National Labor Relations Board*. In that case, petitioners assert that undocumented workers' right to an effective remedy for violation of their freedom of association was limited: from Hoffman and onward, undocumented workers illegally fired in retaliation for exercising this right are no longer able to access the remedy of back-pay under the NLRA.

11. Petitioners contend that the impact of Hoffman has extended beyond the denial of freedom of association for undocumented workers and that employers have been encouraged to claim that undocumented immigrant workers lack legal rights in other contexts, including those in dispute in the present case. Although U.S. federal law protects a worker's right to be free from discrimination based on sex, color, race, religion, and national origin, the petitioners argue that, following Hoffman, a number of state courts have either eliminated or severely limited state-law based workplace protections for undocumented workers. Petitioners indicate that these rights and remedies are often exclusively provided by state law and include access to compensation for workplace injuriess, freedom from workplace discrimination, and entitlement to hold an employer responsible for a workplace injury. Further, petitioners claim that in some states where an individual may sue in tort for injury or wrongful death, these benefits have also been limited — including in Pennsylvania and Kansas.

12. The petitioners also allege that, in addition to limiting or eliminating the workplace rights of undocumented workers, a further consequence of Hoffman has been the intimidation of undocumented workers to discourage them from asserting their rights through the judicial system. More specifically, the petitioners contend that because Hoffman had the effect of making immigration status relevant to workplace rights, employer-defendants often seek discovery of immigrant worker-plaintiffs' immigration status, an action which chills immigrants' willingness to pursue their workplace rights. According to the petitioners, allowing this discovery results in the State's tacit condoning of this intimidation and exploitation of immigrant workers' rights.

1. Presumed Victims

a. Leopoldo Zumaya

13. Petitioners indicate that Leopoldo Zumaya, a Mexican national, worked on a farm in Pennsylvania picking apples for 14 months, from September 2003 to November 2004. In his Declaration, Mr. Zumaya stated that, "It was common knowledge that my employer knowingly accepted false documents and employed approximately fifteen undocumented workers when I worked there. My employer accepted my documents [at hiring] and knew that I was undocumented."

14. In November 2004, Mr. Zumaya fell from a tree and severely fractured his left leg. He had to undergo three separate surgeries so that doctors could insert a metal plate and six screws in his ankle and leg and to try to repair torn ligaments. Mr. Zumaya's employer initially paid his medical benefits, but when it became clear he would not return to work soon, his employer indicated that his benefits would be suspended. He was deemed physically able to return to sedentary work; however, due to his physical limitations, he was unable to find work.

15. Mr. Zumaya therefore retained an attorney to represent him in a workers' compensation claim against his former employer. He was advised to settle with his employer, and ultimately did so for the amount of $35,000. According to the petitioners, had Mr. Zumaya been a U.S. citizen, he would have been eligible to receive a settlement value of between U.S. $85,000- 100,000 in workers' compensation benefits.

16. Prior to the issuance of the admissibility report, Mr. Zumaya returned to Mexico. The petitioners report that he suffers from chronic regional pain disorder and sustained permanent nerve damage, which continues to affect him.

b. Francisco Berumen Lizalde

17. Petitioners affirm that Francisco Berumen Lizalde, also a national of Mexico, worked as a painter in Kansas for eight months, from March through November 2005. In November 2005, he fell from scaffolding and fractured his hand, which rendered him unable to work. Mr. Lizalde received medical care for his injury, consisting of surgery and the placement of a cast on his hand. He also received four checks from his employer's insurance company to cover medical expenses.

18. Shortly after Mr. Lizalde filed for workers' compensation benefits and before he was able to be seen by a doctor to determine the extent of his disability, he was arrested and charged with document fraud, on the basis that he used a false social security number to obtain employment He was subsequently jailed for one month, convicted of this crime (a felony under U.S. law), and deported to Mexico in February 2006. During the time he was in jail, Mr. Lizalde was unable to see a doctor and therefore unable to have the cast removed until he returned to Mexico.

19. After returning to Mexico, Mr. Lizalde reports that he still does not have full movement or strength of his hand. He has undergone physical therapy in Mexico for his hand and is paying the full costs of such treatment.

2. Legal Argument: Rights to equality before the law, recognition of juridical personality and civil rights, and right to a fair trial (Articles II, XVII, and XVIII of the American Declaration)

20. The petitioners submit that the United States' failure to ensure equal redress and access to justice for violations of its labor and employment laws and protection of undocumented workers from discrimination by non-state actors violates its obligations under Articles II, XVII, and XVIII of the American Declaration to the detriment of the two presumed victims, Mr. Zumaya and Mr. Lizalde. Petitioners acknowledge that compensation for workplace injury is governed by state, not federal, law; however, they assert that the American Declaration imposes an obligation on the federal government to guarantee fundamental human rights at both the national and local levels. Furthermore, they assert that the state laws implicated in the present case are being interpreted in a discriminatory manner because of the analysis and precedent established by the U.S. Supreme Court in Hoffman and that current practices inhibit access to justice for undocumented workers.

21. According to the petitioners, Mr. Zumaya had his entitlement to wage-loss benefits, provided under the workers' compensation scheme, prematurely limited because he had not been authorized to work at that time, despite the fact that he had been fully engaged in the employment relationship when he sustained the injury. The petitioners claim that Mr. Zumaya was forced to accept a settlement for a fraction of his claim, due to a decision of the Pennsylvania Supreme

Court finding that an unauthorized worker is not entitled to wage loss benefits once it was determined that the person could return to work, even though there was no work available to him with the physical restrictions imposed by his workplace injury. The petitioners assert that had Mr. Zumaya been authorized to work in the United States, his settlement would have been far greater, allowing him to continue physical therapy and support himself pending employment that did not require him to exceed his physical capabilities.

22. Petitioners argue that, with regard to Mr. Lizalde, he was unable to pursue his claim for disability or to secure payments for medical care after his workplace injury given that he was prosecuted and deported shortly after filing a workers' compensation claim. Additionally, petitioners call into question the circumstances and timing of Mr. Lizalde's arrest, advancing a "strong suspicion" that he was turned in to immigration authorities as a result of filing a workers' compensation claim.

23. In both cases, the petitioners claim that, as illustrated through the experiences and declarations of the alleged victims in this case as well as their lawyers, employers are often aware of the undocumented status of immigrant workers and are "more than willing" to use that information to defeat claims, deny work, and otherwise harm workers who file claims against them. Petitioners maintain that, even in states where undocumented workers are legally entitled to workers' compensation benefits with no limitations, local and federal law enforcement cooperate with employers and insurance companies to deny them those benefits. Additionally, petitioners submit that undocumented workers also rationally fear deportation as a result of disclosing their full identities and immigration status during legal proceedings against their employer.

24. The climate of fear surrounding undocumented workers n the United States regarding the consequences of taking action against employers who have violated workers' human rights is what petitioners label the "in terrorem" effect. Akin to a chilling effect, they affirm that it discourages undocumented workers from asserting workplace rights out of fear of adverse immigration enforcement actions.

25. To combat or overcome this fear, the petitioners report that the United States, through its relevant agencies, has developed two policies designed to keep immigration authorities from interfering with workers' exercise of their labor rights. The first policy is a field manual for U.S. Immigration and Customs Enforcement (ICE) agents on how to question persons during labor disputes to avoid the chilling effect described above; the second is a Memorandum of Understanding (MOU) with the U.S. Department of Labor (DOL), the purpose of which is to preclude the involvement of immigration enforcement in labor disputes. However, the petitioners claim that ICE "often fails to follow its own policy of non-involvement in labor disputes," conducting workplace raids in the middle of or immediately following a DOL investigation against the employer.

26. Petitioners additionally emphasize the irrelevance of immigration status and related matters to the issues in labor disputes and workplace rights, in addition to the chilling effect of such disclosures. Petitioners cite a number of cases in which they allege that courts "contemplating the in terrorem effect of discovery related to plaintiffs' immigration status" have come to the same conclusions, upon considering "the overwhelmingly detrimental impact of potential harassment, intimidation, and threats against plaintiffs such discovery causes." To support this argument, petitioners cite cases in which courts found that granting discovery requests for information related to immigration status would allow illegal and condemnable actions by employers to go unreported and unsanctioned.

27. Lastly, the petitioners claim that in the years following Hoffman, remedies available to undocumented workers under federal law are no longer guaranteed. This lack of remedies, they maintain, translates into a denial of undocumented workers' rights under these statutes. Even though the petitioners recognize that "most litigation ultimately results in undocumented workers being found eligible for remedies under federal statutes," they argue that Hoffman and cases following it have emboldened employers to disclose their workers' immigration status and argue against their eligibility for workers' compensation on the basis of their immigration status. Importantly, petitioners assert that "the uncertainty of the outcome has forced undocumented workers to litigate and re-litigate supposedly guaranteed remedies on a case-by-case basis and in various contexts, with varying rates of success." According to the petitioners, this litigation and mixed outcomes threaten undocumented workers' rights and simultaneously serve to discourage them from claiming their rights.

28. The petitioners conclude that, as a result of the above, the United States has failed in its affirmative obligation to ensure that Messrs. Zumaya and Lizalde were not discriminated against in the realization of their labor rights and that they had effective access to justice. Thus, according to the petitioners, the State has violated their rights to equality before law, recognition of juridical personality and civil rights, and to a fair trial, as set forth in Articles II, XVII, and XVIII of the American Declaration.

B. The State

29. The State does not dispute the factual circumstances of either Mr. Zumaya's or Mr. Lizalde's case. It does, however, dispute the petitioners' claims concerning the availability of remedies and maintains that the petition sets forth no human rights violations, as explained in more detail below.

30. The United States submits that it is fully committed to the protection of all workers, including undocumented persons. The State details the efforts it makes through its various agencies, outlined below, to pursue enforcement of labor and employment laws against employers who violate these laws, regardless of whether the victims of those violations are lawfully present and entitled to work in the United States.

1. Labor Protection Efforts

31. The State cites as examples of its enforcement efforts those undertaken by the Department of Labor (DOL), National Labor Relations Board (NLRB), and the Equal Employment Opportunity Commission (EEOC). According to the State, the DOL administers and enforces more than 180 federal laws for the protection and advancement of workers in the United States. Of these 180, two major statutes it enforces are the Fair Labor Standards Act (FLSA), administered by its Wage and Hour Division, and the Occupational Safety and Health Act (OSH Act), administered by the Occupational Safety and Health Administration (OSHA). The FLSA prescribes standards for wages and overtime pay, and the OSH Act prescribes a set of regulations and safety and health standards that public sector employers must meet. With regard to the health and safety conditions in private industries, the State asserts that OSHA or OSHA-approved state programs regulate those workplace conditions.

32. In addition to the work performed by the DOL internally, the State maintains that the Department engages bilaterally with nations of origin for undocumented workers. The State alleges that these consultations have resulted in DOL initiatives to inform migrant workers about applicable labor protections under United States laws. Further, the State cites a number of joint declarations it has with other States, including Mexico, Costa Rica, El Salvador, Guatemala, Nicaragua, and Belize, on mutual commitments to inform workers about their labor rights in the United States and to foster environ- ments in which these rights are respected.

33. The State also refers to the work of the NLRB in enforcing the National Labor Relations Act (NLRA). The State affirms that the NLRA guarantees covered employees the right to form, join, decertify, or assist a labor organization and to bargain collectively through representatives of their own choosing or to refrain from such activities. According to the State, employers must not interfere with rights under the NLRA, and employees, labor organizations, and employers themselves may file charges alleging unfair labor practices with the NLRB. The NLRB, in turn, investigates the claims and makes findings on the merits and recommendations, which include "make-whole remedies, such as reinstatement and backpay for discharged workers." As examples of the types of sanctions that the NLRB may impose, the State mentions that an employer may be ordered to recognize and bargain with a labor organization or to comply with informational remedies, such as the posting of a notice by the employer promising not to violate the law.

34. Regarding the EEOC, the State explains that it is the entity responsible for enforcing federal, anti-discrimination laws that make it illegal to discriminate against a job applicant or an employee on account of the person's race, color, religion, sex (including pregnancy), national origin, age (40 or older), disability, or genetic information. According to the State, it is also illegal to discriminate against a person for having: complained about discrimination, filed a charge of discrimination, or participated in an employment discrimination investigation or lawsuit. The State asserts that federal anti-discrimination laws apply to all types of work situations, including hiring, firing, promotions, harassment, training, wages, and benefits.

35. On the topic of ICE's enforcement actions and general agency guidelines, the State informs that on April 30, 2009, ICE announced a revised Worksite Enforcement Strategy, which promotes, among other things, "integrity in the immigration system and an equitable enforcement program," prioritizing the "most egregious violators, including employers who abuse and exploit their workers, traffic in persons, or create false identity documents." The State assures that "ICE is actively committed to effective labor law enforcement promoting proper wages and working conditions for all covered workers regardless of their immigration status." Further, the State claims that ICE refrains from engaging in civil worksite enforcement activities at worksites that are the subject of an existing DOL investigation of labor disputes "during the pendency of the investigation and any related proceeding."

2. Legal Argument: Rights to equality before the law, recognition of juridical personality and civil rights, and a fair trial (Articles II, XVII, and XVIII of the American Declaration)

36. The State maintains that there has been no violation of the presumed victims' rights under the American Declaration because Hoffman does not impact the rights of workers who suffer on-the-job injuries in Pennsylvania and Kansas. The State submits that it has a sovereign right to deny permission to work to those illegally present in the country or to those who have not obtained authorization to work. Thus, the State submits that, consistent with this principle, federal and state laws recognize the difficulty in providing backpay for work that was not done when it could not lawfully have been done.

37. According to the State, the Supreme Court's decision in Hoffman leaves its decision in *Sure-Tan, Inc. v. National Labor Relations Board* undisturbed, namely the finding that the NLRA applies to undocumented workers. The State asserts that this ruling had no impact on the NLRB's ability to order companies to cease unlawful activities under the NLRA.

38. To support this position, the State cites a July 2002 memorandum issued by the General Counsel of the NLRB to NLRB regional offices. In this memo, the State indicates that it was made clear that Hoffman did not affect other actions the NLRB could take against employers acting unlawfully. In the memo, the General Counsel advised that the NLRB could still seek to award backpay for work that was actually performed and to enforce cease and desist orders, subject to contempt proceedings for non-compliance. The State insists that the General Counsel both in this memorandum and in subsequent instructions emphasized the point that regional offices should presume that employees are lawfully authorized to work and should not set out on sua sponte investigations to determine the charging party's immigration status in the U.S. The State also maintains that Hoffman did not impact the laws enforced by DOL or the work of the EEOC.

39. Further, the State argues that federal and administrative court decisions subsequent to Hoffman have confirmed the principle that employers in the United States may not illegally discriminate against employees, even when those employees are undocumented workers.

40. Additionally, the State contends that Hoffman concerned the unavailability of only one particular remedy under one particular statute — backpay for the period between termination of employment for union activities and when the NLRB found that the employer acted unlawfully. However, the State asserts that Hoffman does not even implicate the claims of Petitioners, who seek compensation through state workers' compensation systems for injuries they suffered while working; thus, there is a basic factual distinction that separates the cases.

41. Notwithstanding this factual distinction, the State maintains that the two jurisdictions implicated in this case, Pennsylvania and Kansas, are not hostile or adverse towards undocumented workers and, based on precedent, would likely have upheld the presumed victims' rights. With regard to Pennsylvania, the State refutes Petitioners' claims regarding *Reinforced Earth Co. v. Workers' Compensation Appeal Board*, stating that the decision does not cite *Hoffman* and "implicitly rejects" extending Hoffman to the Pennsylvania workers' compensation scheme. Moreover, the State highlights that the decision expressed the principle that undocumented workers are eligible for workers' compensation, including medical expenses and wage-loss compensation, even where a worker obtained employment using fraudulent documentation.

42. With regard to Kansas, the State likewise refutes the Petitioners' arguments that Kansas has erected procedural barriers to undocumented workers' access to workers' compensation. The State maintains that the case cited as support by the Petitioners, *Doe v. Kansas Department of Human Resources*, involves a claim by an undocumented worker for workers' compensation that was upheld. Further, the State affirms that this case does not mention *Hoffman* in its decision.

43. Based on the above, the State requests that the Commission dismiss the case, as it submits that no violation of the American Declaration has occurred. The Commission notes that the State included arguments concerning the admissibility of the case in its response, but given that the admissibility decision was made by the Commission in 2011, these are untimely and it is not pertinent to consider them.

IV. ESTABLISHED FACTS

44. In application of Article 43(1) of its Rules of Procedure, the IACHR will examine the arguments and evidence provided by the petitioners and the State. In addition, it will take into consideration publicly available information.

A. Presumed Victims

45. In November 2004, Mr. Zumaya was injured on the job, at a farm in Pennsylvania, while picking apples. He fell from a tree and severely fractured his left leg. Mr. Zumaya had worked on this farm for 14 months and did not have authorization to work in the United States.

46. As a result of this injury, Mr. Zumaya had to have three operations. In the first operation, a metal plate and six screws were inserted in his leg; in the second, the screws were removed; and the third was to fix a torn ligament in the front of his leg. Mr. Zumaya suffers chronic pain in his leg and sustained permanent nerve damage from the fall.

47. Mr. Zumaya's employer initially paid for his medical expenses, but when it became apparent he could no longer go back to work, his employer ceased these payments.29 The employer's insurance company also refused payment of workers' compensation benefits due to his undocumented status. Mr. Zumaya retained counsel to bring a workers' compensation claim against his employer and was advised by his attorney to accept a settlement for $35,000.

48. In November 2005, Mr. Lizalde was injured on the job when he fell from scaffolding and fractured his hand. Mr. Lizalde had been working as a painter in Kansas for eight months. Mr. Lizalde received medical care for the injury he sustained, through the insurance of his employer. Such care consisted of surgery on his hand which was then placed in a cast. He also received four checks from his employer's insurance company in the amount of $470 each, for a total of $1,880, to cover medical expenses.

49. Shortly after filing a workers' compensation claim in December 2005 and prior to a doctor's appointment to determine the full extent of the disability, Mr. Lizalde was arrested and charged with document fraud. He was detained for more than a month in jail, convicted of the felony and deported to Mexico in February 2006. While in jail, Mr. Lizalde did not have access to medical care and was unable to get his cast removed until after he was in Mexico, at his own cost.

50. Prior to being deported, Mr. Lizalde retained counsel to preserve his right to workers' compensation benefits. Nonetheless, within days of filing Mr. Lizalde's claim, his lawyer was contacted and informed that Mr. Lizalde had been prosecuted and deported. His lawyer was further informed that, given that Mr. Lizalde's presence is required to pursue his claim, Mr. Lizalde had to choose between possible prosecution and conviction for illegal reentry or to forego his legal rights to workers' compensation, including disability compensation and medical treatment.

B. *Hoffman Plastic Compounds, Inc. v. NLRB*

51. Given that the parties center many of their arguments around the impact of the U.S. Supreme Court case *Hoffman Plastic Compounds, Inc. v. NLRB* ("*Hoffman*"), the Commission considers it pertinent to include a brief description of this case.

52. In *Hoffman*, the U.S. Supreme Court considered whether an undocumented worker, Mr. Jose Castro, who presented fraudulent documents to prove his authorization to work and was later fired along with other workers in retaliation for union-organizing activities, could be eligible to receive backpay and other relief to remedy the labor violation. In the first instance, the NLRB had found that the layoff of these employees by employer Hoffman Plastic Compounds violated the NLRA and ordered backpay and other relief. At a later compliance hearing, Mr. Castro testified that he had never been legally admitted nor authorized to work in the United States, and on this basis, the Administrative Law Judge (AU) presiding over the case determined that the Board was precluded from ordering backpay as a remedy for Mr. Castro.

53. In September 1998, the NLRB reversed the AL's decision with respect to backpay. The Board held that "the most effective way to accommodate and further the immigration policies embodied in the Immigration Reform and Control Act of 1986 is to provide the protections and remedies of the NLRA to undocumented workers in the same manner as to other employees." The NLRB determined that Mr. Castro was entitled to backpay in the amount of $66,951, plus interest, calculated from the date of Mr. Castro's termination of employment to the date that Hoffman first learned of Castro's undocumented status.

54. Hoffman next appealed to the U.S. Court of Appeals for the District of Columbia ("Court of Appeals"). A panel of the Court of Appeals denied the petition for review initially; after a re-hearing en banc, the court again denied the petition for review and upheld the NLRB's order.

55. Hoffman then appealed to the U.S. Supreme Court, which granted certiorari and ultimately held (in a 5-4 vote) that "Federal immigration policy, as expressed by Congress in IRCA, foreclosed the Board [NLRB] from awarding backpay to an undocumented alien who has never been legally authorized to work in the United States."

56. In so ruling, the Supreme Court relied heavily on its previous ruling in *Sure-Tan, Inc. v. NLRB* ("*Sure-Tan*"). In the *Sure-Tan* case, six of seven workers were undocumented and all six voted for a certain union as the collective bargaining representative with their employer, Sure-Tan, Inc. The employer filed objections to the election with the NLRB, which overruled them. After receiving notification of the overruling, the president of Sure-Tan, Inc. sent a letter to the Immigration and Naturalization Service (INS) and requested that it check into the immigration status of a number of its employees, claimants included. Based on the subsequent investigation realized by the INS, five of the workers involved voluntarily exited from the U.S. to avoid deportation.

57. The Supreme Court in *Sure-Tan* determined, inter alia, that:

a. "The NLRA's terms — defining 'employee' to include 'any employee,' and not listing undocumented aliens among the few groups of specifically exempted workers — fully support [the interpretation of the NLRB]. Similarly extending the NLRA's coverage to undocumented aliens is consistent with its purpose of encouraging and protecting the collective bargaining process;"

b. "The Board's interpretation of the NLRA as applying to unfair labor practices committed against undocumented aliens is reasonable, and thus will be upheld;"

c. "Enforcement of the NLRA with respect to undocumented alien employees is compatible with the INA's purpose in restricting immigration so as to preserve jobs for American workers, since, if there is no advantage as to wages and employment conditions in preferring illegal alien workers, any incentive for employers to hire illegal aliens is lessened. In turn, if the demand for undocumented aliens declines, there may then be fewer incentives for aliens themselves to enter in violation of the federal immigration laws;"

d. "[P]etitioners committed an unfair labor practice under § 8(a)(3) of the NLRA by constructively discharging their undocumented alien employees through reporting the employees to the INS in retaliation for participating in union activities;" and

e. With regard to the NLRB's remedial order, including the figure of backpay, "the [Seventh Circuit] Court of Appeals erred in its modification of [this] order…[b]y directing the Board to impose a minimum backpay award without regard to the employees' actual economic losses or legal availability for work, the court exceeded its limited authority of review under the NLRA. A backpay remedy must be tailored to expunge only actual, not speculative, consequences of an unfair labor practice."

58. With regard to (e), the Supreme Court in *Sure-Tan* found that the "main deficiency" in the Seventh Circuit Court of Appeals' decision for review was the amount of backpay ordered, not that backpay was ordered. Specifically, the Supreme Court's objection to the Court of Appeals' decision in *Sure-Tan* was that the latter failed to take into consideration "the period of time these particular employees might have continued working before apprehension by the INS and without affording the petitioners any opportunity to provide mitigating evidence" in calculating an estimate amount of backpay. As the Supreme Court explained:

[T]he Court of Appeals recognized…in computing backpay, the employees must be deemed "unavailable for work" (and the accrual of backpay therefore tolled) during any period when they were not lawfully entitled to be present and employed in the United States. The Court of Appeals assumed that, under these circumstances, the employees would receive no backpay, and so awarded a minimum amount of backpay that would effectuate the underlying purposes of the Act by providing some relief to the employees as well as a financial disincentive against the repetition of similar discriminatory acts in the future.

59. Notwithstanding this reasoning and its own determination of the "probable unavailability of the Act's more effective remedies" in that case, the Supreme Court in *Sure-Tan* found that the Seventh Circuit Court of Appeals "plainly exceeded its limited authority under the Act" by directing the Board to impose a minimum backpay award without regard to the employees' actual economic losses or legal availability for work."

60. The Supreme Court in *Hoffman* departed from the *Sure-Tan* ruling on the point of backpay, determining that "There is no reason to think that Congress intended to permit backpay where but for an employer's unfair labor practices, an alien-employee would have remained in the United States illegally, and continued to work illegally, all the while successfully evading apprehension by immigration authorities." The Court concluded in Hoffman that "allowing the [NLRB] to award backpay to illegal aliens would unduly trench upon explicit statutory prohibitions critical to federal immigration policy, as expressed in IRCA. It would encourage the successful evasion of apprehension by immigration authorities, condone prior violations of the immigration laws, and encourage future violations." As a result, Jose Castro, the undocumented worker illegally fired by Hoffman in retaliation for union-organizing, was denied backpay.

C. Situation of Undocumented Workers in the United States

61. Prior to continuing to its analysis on the merits of this case, the Commission deems it relevant to provide an updated snapshot on the situation of undocumented workers in the United States. Reports suggest that the population of "unauthorized immigrants" in the United States is approximately 11,022,000 as of 2013. The top country of origin is Mexico, with 6,194,000, or 56% of this population, accounting for 71% when combined with the countries of Central America. A Pew study reports that, as of 2012, unauthorized immigrants accounted for 3.5% of the U.S. population, 26% of all immigrants, and 5.1% of the U.S. labor force consisting of 8.1 million who were working or looking for work.

62. According to this same study, in terms of the top industries in which unauthorized immigrants work, as of 2012, 62% held service, construction, and production jobs, which is twice the share of U.S. born workers in those same industries. To break this figure down, nearly 33% held service jobs as a janitor, child care worker or cook, almost double the share of U.S. born workers in those types of occupations (17%); 15% held construction or extraction jobs, triple the share of U.S. workers (5%); and 14% were employed in production, installation, and repair, more than half of the share of U.S. born workers (9%). Unauthorized immigrants only constitute 2% of the workers in management, professional, and office support occupations.

63. According to the U.S. Bureau of Labor Statistics, there were 4,585 workers who died from work-related injuries in 2013. Of those, 879 or 19% involved foreign-born workers, of whom Mexican workers accounted for 41% (360 persons) and Central American workers for 14% (123 persons), for a joint total of 55% (483) or 10.5% of all work-related fatalities. Further, in 2013, of the non-fatal occupational injuries in private industry recorded by the race or ethnic origin of the worker (immigration situation is not recorded), approximately 21-22% were workers classified as "Hispanic" or "Hispanic and another race."

64. For its part, OSHA has acknowledged that immigrant and "hard to reach" workers are employed in some of the most inherently dangerous jobs: in its Fiscal Year 2014-2018 Strategic Plan, it explained, "OSHA has made outreach to Latino and other limited English proficiency workers — a population that typically experiences a higher rate of injuries, illnesses, and fatalities in the workplace — a priority by working with community- and faith- based groups, employers, unions, consulates, the medical community, health and safety professionals, and government representatives."

65. Undocumented workers also contributed an estimated $11.84 billion in state and local taxes in 2012. This includes sales and excise taxes from the purchase of goods, such as gasoline and clothing, and services, which account for more than $7 billion of the $11.84. Undocumented immigrants also pay property taxes, directly as property owners or indirectly as renters, accounting for approximately $3.6 billion (of the $11.84). Regarding contributions to the social secu-

rity fund, in 2010 the U.S. Social Security Administration' (SSA) estimated that there was a $12 billion surplus of tax revenue paid into the system, attributable to the earnings of unauthorized workers.

66. In the United States, the Commission observes that the Immigration Reform and Control Act of 1986 (IRCA) was enacted to "control and deter illegal immigration to the United States" and explicitly prohibited employers from knowingly hiring undocumented workers. Also, for the first time in U.S. history, IRCA established sanctions for U.S. employers who knowingly hire undocumented workers. Under IRCA, employers are required to verify the work authorization of prospective employees. This review process, effective November 6, 1986, and onward, consists of requiring all employers to complete a form (known as the "I-9") each time they seek to hire a person to perform work in the United States. In order to complete the I-9, prospective employees need to provide two forms of identification to the employer.

67. The standard of review that employers must apply when examining documentation presented by a prospective employee is whether the document "reasonably appears on its face to be genuine." As mentioned above, failure to comply with these requirements may lead to fines and other sanctions. It is the State's responsibility to ensure that employers in all U.S. states comply with the requirements established under IRCA and to sanction those employers who fail to comply. This system was in place at the time of hiring for both Mr. Zumaya and Mr. Lizalde.

V. LEGAL ANALYSIS

68. In addressing the allegations raised by the petitioners in this case, the Inter-American Commission emphasizes that it is necessary to consider the provisions of the American Declaration in the broader context of both the inter-American and international human rights systems. The Inter-American Commission considers this necessary in light of developments in the field of international human rights law since the Declaration was adopted and having regard to other relevant rules of international law applicable to (ICEAFRD), to which it is a Party. Pursuant to the principles of treaty interpretation, the Inter-American Court of Human Rights has likewise endorsed an interpretation of international human rights instruments that takes into account developments in the corpus juris of international human rights law over time and in present-day conditions.

69. Developments in the corpus of international human rights law relevant to interpreting and applying the American Declaration may in turn be drawn from the provisions of other prevailing international and regional human rights instruments. In particular, this includes the American Convention on Human Rights, which, in many instances, may be considered to represent an authoritative expression of the fundamental principles set forth in the American Declaration. While the Commission clearly does not apply the American Convention in relation to Member States that have yet to ratify that treaty, its provisions may well be relevant in informing an interpretation of the Declaration.

70. The petitioners claim that the State has violated the rights of Messrs. Zumaya and Lizalde under various Articles of the American Declaration. As concluded in the admissibility report in this matter, the IACHR is competent to examine and pronounce upon these allegations against the State of the United States. The Declaration is a source of legal obligation for application by the Inter-American Commission to the United States on the basis of its commitment to uphold respect for human rights as provided in the Charter of the Organization of American States (OAS). The United States deposited its instrument of ratification of the OAS Charter on June 19, 1951. Article 20 of the Inter-American Commission's Statute, as well as the Rules of Procedure of the Inter-American Commission, authorize the IACHR to examine the alleged violations of the Declaration raised by the petitioners against the State, which relate to acts or omissions that transpired after the State joined the OAS.

A. Right to equality before law (Article II of the American Declaration)

71. Article II of the American Declaration provides as follows:

Article II. All persons are equal before the law and have the rights and duties established in this Declaration, without distinction as to race, sex, language, creed or any other factor.

72. The Commission has repeatedly established that the right to equality and non-discrimination contained in Article IIs a fundamental principle of the inter-American human rights system ("IAHRS"). The principle of non-discrimination is the backbone of the universal and regional systems for the protection of human rights. As with all fundamental

rights and freedoms, the Commission has observed that States are not only obligated to provide for equal protection of the law78, but they must also adopt the legislative, policy, and other measures necessary to guarantee the effective enjoyment of the rights protected under Article II of the American Declaration.

73. The notion of equality set forth in the American Declaration relates to the application of substantive rights and to the protection to be given to them in the case of acts by the State or others. The Commission has clarified that the right to equality before the law does not necessarily mean that the substantive provisions of the law have to be the same for everyone, but that the application of the law should be equal for all without discrimination. In practice this means that States have the obligation to adopt the measures necessary to recognize and guarantee the effective equality of all persons before the law; to abstain from introducing in their legal framework regulations that are discriminatory towards certain groups either on their face or in practice; and to combat discriminatory practices.

74. The Commission has previously recognized that while Article II does not prohibit all distinctions in treatment in the enjoyment of protected rights and freedoms, it does require that any permissible distinctions be based upon objective and reasonable justification, that they further a legitimate objective, "regard being had to the principles which normally prevail in democratic societies, and that the means are reasonable and proportionate to the end sought." Regard should also be given to the fact that "one of the American Declaration's objectives...was to assure in principle 'the equal protection of the law to nationals and aliens alike in respect to the rights set forth.'" In this regard, the Commission takes note of similar conclusions reached by U.N. treaty bodies, which have interpreted the prohibition of discrimination to include non-nationals, regardless of their legal status and authorization to work.

75. The Commission also takes into account evolving standards in the area of discrimination, and considers that what has been expressed by the Human Rights Committee under the ICCPR is equally applicable in the inter-American system:

The Committee believes that the term "discrimination" as used in the Covenant should be understood to imply any distinction, exclusion, restriction, or preference which is based on any ground such as race, colour, sex, language, religion, political or other opinion, national or social origin, property, birth or other status, and which has the purpose or effect of nullifying or impairing the recognition, enjoyment or exercise by all persons, on an equal footing, of all rights and freedoms.

76. Regarding employment of undocumented workers, the Commission deems it pertinent to state at the outset that neither the State nor individuals in a State are obligated to offer employment to undocumented workers. In other words, the State and individuals, such as employers, can abstain from establishing an employment relationship with migrants in an irregular situation. However, upon assuming an employment relationship, the Commission considers that the protections accorded by law to workers, with the range of rights and obligations covered, must apply to all workers without discrimination, including on the basis of documented or undocumented status.

77. In the present case, the Commission finds that Mr. Zumaya and Mr. Lizalde, who assumed an employment relationship and were later injured on the job, experienced treatment different than that given to documented workers when they sought to obtain workers' compensation for their injuries and to access justice.

78. This difference in treatment is not attributable to a facial distinction in the laws but rather to a "distinction, exclusion, or preference" in their implementation, which has the practical effect of pairing the rights of undocumented workers. As the State has put forth and petitioners acknowledge, there are several laws that protect workers and mechanisms in place to enforce these laws, and on the face of these laws it does not matter whether the worker involved has work authorization. However, the Commission observes that, despite the terms of these laws and mechanisms, neither Mr. Zumaya nor Mr. Lizalde were able to obtain full benefits under workers' compensation programs, including medical benefits.

79. The "distinction, exclusion, or preference" is notable in the precedents established in both jurisdictions, Pennsylvania and Kansas, as well as in the actions and practices of both State and non-State actors. There are two seminal cases that were repeatedly cited by both the Petitioners and the State in their submissions. These cases demonstrate the reach of Hoffman, and thus are important to mention here.

80. In the first case, *Reinforced Earth Co. v. Workers' Compensation Appeals Board* ("*Reinforced Earth*"), an undocumented worker (the "claimant") employed as a maintenance helper sustained a head, neck, and back injuiy. As part of the job, the claimant routinely cut and welded iron, repaired motors, and lifted heavy steel beams. As a result of his injuries, the claimant was unable to return to work, and following termination from employment, his employer was ordered to pay claimant's total disability payments, medical expenses, to remain responsible for claimant's medical expenses, and pay claimant's litigation costs. The employer appealed this order several times, eventually reaching the Pennsylvania Supreme Court, seeking a suspension in the claimant's benefits and the extension of a blanket "public policy exception" that would exempt undocumented workers from coverage under the IRCA, which had been denied on appeals below.

81. The Pennsylvania Supreme Court, in ruling on the case, held that it would not consider announcing a public policy exception with respect to the receipt of workers' compensation benefits by undocumented workers, as the legislature has already spoken on the issue and to do so would be to exceed its powers, engaging in an "exercise of judicial legislation." However, the Court reversed in one key area; under Pennsylvania law, when an employer or insurer seeks to terminate or modify disability benefits, the employer or insurer must show medical evidence of a change in condition and evidence of a referral (or referrals) to an open job or jobs, "which fits in the occupational category for which the claimant has been given medical clearance," such as light work or sedentary work. In Reinforced Earth, the Court eliminated the second requirement for employers and insurers specifically when the claimant is an undocumented worker, finding that "when an employer seeks to suspend the workers' compensation benefits that have been granted to an employee who is an unauthorized alien, a showing of job availability by the employer is not required."

Clarifying its position, the Court affirmed that while the employer may seek suspension of the total disability compensation claimant was granted, the employer may not seek a suspension of medical benefits awarded, "as the provisions of [the section providing for payment of reasonable surgical and medical services] apply to injuries whether or not loss of earning power occurs."

82. In the second case, *Doe v. Kansas Department of Human Resources*, an undocumented worker from Mexico, Delia Butanda, sustained injuries on the job at a meatpacking plant. She filed a claim for workers' compensation using the false name (Victoria Acosta) and social security number she originally used to obtain employment at the plant. Ms. Butanda was awarded over $57,000 in compensation for her injuries. Later, as the result of a "referral from the Kansas Insurance Department," the Workers' Compensation Division's Fraud and Abuse Unit discovered Ms. Butanda's real identity. Subsequently, in an administrative decision later affirmed by the Kansas Supreme Court, Ms. Butanda was found to have committed a "fraudulent or abusive act" in obtaining workers' compensation benefits through the use of this assumed identity, an action which also amounted to concealment of a material fact. As a result of this discovery, her compensatory benefits were suspended.

83. Notably, in its decision, the Kansas Supreme Court acknowledged that Ms. Butanda's employer, NBP, "knew or should have known" that she was an undocumented worker and "yet was willing to look the other way when it hired her;" nonetheless, the Court reasoned that NBP's complicity was irrelevant in the determination of the culpability of Ms. Butanda for her fraudulent actions. agency may properly calculate the amount of benefits owed, or face prosecution for fraud if caught.

84. However, such disclosure automatically triggers violations of IRCA.101 Further, as a result of Doe, any awards made in Kansas prior to the discovery of the use of a false identity may be set aside or suspended, meaning that the final award may be modified not on the basis of the injury or employer wrongdoing or knowledge — actual or implied — of workers' immigration status, but rather an action made at the outset of the employment relationship.

85. Experts have warned that, as the result of Doe and similar cases, undocumented immigrants will be "deterred" from making workers' compensation claims because the process "risks intervention by federal immigration officials." They also caution that "despite any complicity and causation on their behalf, unscrupulous employers will benefit with lower labor costs," and "unauthorized workers [have] more reason to cling to their assumed identities [thereby] promot[ing] identity fraud."

86. The Commission takes note of two cases in other jurisdictions within the United States that restrict access to equal remedies for undocumented workers. In *Balbuena v. IDR Realty, LLC*, the highest state court in New York found that, based on *Hoffman*, an injured undocumented worker was precluded from claiming lost wages derived from income

earned in the United States but could seek wages based on income that could be earned in the worker's home country. In *Sanchez v. Eagle Alloy*, the Michigan Supreme Court denied review of an appellate court decision finding that, based on Hoffman, due to the workers' commission of a crime (use of false identities), the weekly wage-loss benefits of the two undocumented workers involved, who were fired after being injured on the job, should be suspended.

87. Finally, in a more recent decision of the NLRB and in light of the significant jurisprudence on these issues at both state and federal levels in the United States, the Commission deems important to mention the case of *Mezonos Maven Bakery, Inc. and Puerto Rican Legal Defense and Education Fund* ("*Mezonos*"). In Mezonos, the NLRB found that even where it is undisputed that the employer, not the employees, violated IRCA, the undocumented employees who are wrongfully fired are still foreclosed from being awarded backpay on the basis of this violation. The NLRB made clear that its hands were tied, "regardless of the merits of [claimants'] arguments," as the Supreme Court in *Hoffman* used "1RCA violator-neutral" language — i.e., regardless of which party, employer or employee, committed the violation — and noted that it would be unable to even order such a remedy, as the Court in Hoffman found that a backpay award "lies beyond the bounds of the Board's remedial discretion." Lastly, the NLRB in Mezonos summarized Hoffman's ruling as, where undocumented workers are involved and "[without regard to] which party violates the law, the result is an unlawful employment relationship [between an employer and an undocumented worker]." As such, the NLRB may not encroach upon federal law by "legitimizing" that illegal relationship through awards designed to remedy labor violations.

88. As mentioned above, the difference in treatment is not only attributable to legal precedent but also to the practice of local and federal officials. In this regard, in the cases of both Mr. Zumaya and Mr. Lizalde, local and federal officials collaborated with private individuals (employers and insurance agencies) to enforce the infraction of immigration laws; however, these actions took place only following the initiation of workers' compensation claims by both workers and to the detriment of the processing of these claims. The Commission considers that the actions of the State in this context had the effect of extinguishing the two workers' compensation claims, a scenario that would have not taken place but for their irregular migratory situation: Mr. Lizalde was deported prior to the conclusion of the claim and it was in this context that the insurance agency of Mr. Zumaya's employer refused to pay him workers' compensation benefits.

89. In the present case, the Commission observes that, despite the State's argument that benefits other than lost wages are still available to undocumented workers post-Hoffman, neither Mr. Zumaya nor Mr. Lizalde received full medical benefits for the injuries they sustained. Further, the foregoing analysis makes plain that the State subjected the two victims, Messrs. Zumaya and Lizalde, as non-nationals lacking authorization to work, to a legal regime in relation to their workers' compensation proceedings that is fundamentally distinct from that applicable to other national and/or authorized workers.

90. The Commission therefore considers that the State has failed to ensure that the protections in the law for workers, including remedies for labor rights violations, are recognized and applied without discrimination to every worker. The Commission acknowledges that the State has the prerogative to prosecute persons who commit social security fraud, but it emphasizes that such prosecution is irrelevant to and in no way should affect the right of an undocumented injured worker to receive and enjoy labor rights, such as to workers' compensation, once the person has assumed an employment relationship in the U.S.

91. In the Commission's view and based on the record in this case, the State has not shown that this difference in treatment is based upon an objective and reasonable justification, that it furthers a legitimate objective, or that the means are reasonable and proportionate to the end sought. The State has described in broad strokes a number of programs and mechanisms to protect workers and enforce violations of labor laws against employers. However, the State does not provide any concrete link between the general and the specific; it has failed to show any measures taken to ensure the effective equality of Messrs. Zumaya and Lizalde in obtaining workers' compensation benefits equal to those received by similarly-situated, documented peers or in combatting the identified discriminatory practices.

92. Based on the above, in denying the two victims access to remedies equal to that of other injured workers, the Commission considers that the State has denied them the protection of equality before the law, in violation of Article II of the American Declaration.

B. Rights to juridical personality and to enjoy basic civil rights and to a fair trial (Articles XVII and XVIII of the American Declaration)

93. Articles XVII and XVIII of the American Declaration provide as follows Article XVII. Every person has the right to be recognized everywhere as a person having rights and obligations, and to enjoy the basic civil rights.

Article XVIII. Every person may resort to the courts to ensure respect for his legal rights. There should likewise be available to him a simple, brief procedure whereby the courts will protect him from acts of authority that, to his prejudice, violate any fundamental constitutional rights.

94. With regard to the right to juridical personality and to enjoy basic civil rights, enshrined in Article XVII of the American Declaration, the Commission highlights that this right implies the recognition of every person as entitled to rights and obligations based on the sole condition of being human. As such, this right is an essential requirement or condition for the enjoyment of all rights, and it likewise imposes important limits to State action. The Commission observes that the failure to recognize juridical personality harms human dignity because it renders a person vulnerable to non-observance of his or her rights by the State or other individuals.

95. The Commission highlights that the American Declaration, unlike other international instruments, specifically includes within Article XVII the right to "enjoy the basic civil rights," one of which is the right to work. The Charter of the Organization of American States (hereinafter "OAS Charter" or the "Charter") first established this right in its Article 45 (b), providing that "[work is a right and a social duty." The Charter further establishes that this right must be observed under "proper conditions," defined as those that "ensure life, health and a decent standard of living for the worker and his family, both during his working years and in his old age, or when any circumstance deprives him of the possibility of working."

96. In the present, the Commission finds that workers' compensation programs and the benefits provided through them fall squarely within the concept of "proper conditions" as prescribed in the OAS Charter. Payments for medical care due to injuries suffered on the job and disability payments, among others, are precisely those types of conditions that ensure life, health, and a decent standard of living when a circumstance, such as an accident, deprives a worker of the possibility of working. In addition, the failure to remedy the wrong with the correct or proportionate redress in the situation of these undocumented workers constitutes an impermissible failure to recognize their juridical personality. In effect, this failure creates a legal limbo in which the violations committed against them are not recognized under the law.

97. Based on a review of this Commission's decisions and principles of international law, the IACHR considers that undocumented workers should not be denied protection of their human Rights by the State on the basis of infractions of immigration regulations. In other words, it does not follow that an infraction of (civil) domestic legislation in one area should be used to deprive that person of the protection of his or her rights in another. The IACHR emphasizes that an infraction of a State's immigration laws does not exempt the State from complying with its obligations imposed by both domestic and international law to remedy the violation of labor rights. To find otherwise would be to provide for an indirect, yet highly effective, way of discriminating against undocumented migrant workers by denying them juridical personality and creating legal inequality between persons.

98. As this Commission has recognized previously, both Articles XVII and XVIII are predicated upon the recognition and protection by a State of an individual's fundamental civil and constitutional rights. Article XVIII further prescribes a fundamental role for the courts of a State in ensuring and protecting these basic rights. For its part, Article XVIII of the American Declaration establishes that all persons are entitled to access judicial remedies when they have suffered human rights violations. This right is similar in scope to the right to judicial protection and guarantees contained in Article 25 of the American Convention on Human Rights, which is understood to encompass: the right of every individual to go to a tribunal when any of his or her rights have been violated; to obtain a judicial investigation conducted by a competent, impartial and independent tribunal that establishes whether or not a violation has taken place; and the corresponding right to obtain reparations for the harm suffered.

99. The Commission has affirmed for many years that it is not the formal existence of judicial remedies that demonstrates due diligence, but rather that they are adequate and effective. The "effectiveness" of a judicial remedy has two aspects: one is normative and the other is empirical. The normative aspect deals with the remedy's suitability, or its ability to determine whether a violation of human rights occurred, and its capacity to yield positive results or responses, principally measured in terms of whether it offers the possibility to provide adequate redress, for human rights violations.

100. The second aspect, the empirical nature of the remedy, refers to the political or institutional conditions that enable a legally recognized remedy to "fulfill its purpose" or "produce the result for which [it] was designed." In this regard and as the Commission has previously stated, a remedy is not effective when it is "illusory," excessively onerous for the victim, or when the State has not ensured its proper enforcement by the judicial authorities.

101. Thus, when the State apparatus leaves human rights violations unpunished and the victim's full enjoyment of human rights is not promptly restored, the State fails to comply with its positive duties under international human rights law. The same principle applies when a State allows private persons to act freely and with impunity to the detriment of the rights recognized in the governing instruments of the IAHRS.

102. The Commission further maintains that there is a direct connection between the suitability of available judicial remedies, as mentioned above, and the real possibility of observance of economic, social, and cultural rights. The IACHR has identified the principle of equality of arms as an integral part of the right to a fair trial, given that the types of relationships governed by social rights usually give rise to and presuppose conditions of inequality between the parties in a dispute — such as between workers and employers or the beneficiary of a social service and the State that provides the service. That inequality often translates into disadvantages in the framework of judicial proceedings.

103. The IACHR considers that real inequality between the parties in a proceeding engages the duty of the State to adopt all the necessary measures to lessen any deficiencies that thwart the effective protection of the rights at stake. The Inter-American Commission has also noted that the particular circumstances of a case may determine that guarantees additional to those explicitly prescribed in the pertinent human rights instruments are necessary to ensure a fair trial. For the IACHR this includes recognizing and correcting any real disadvantages that the parties in a proceeding might have, thereby observing the principle of equality before the law and the prohibition of discrimination.

104. In the context of the specific case, Messrs. Lizalde and Zumaya filed their workers' compensation claims pursuant to serious work-related injuries that affected their physical integrity with lasting consequences. The interests at stake therefore dealt not only with their social and economic rights generally, but also very concretely with their personal integrity and involved their need for ongoing medical treatment.

105. In the present case, the Commission observes that Mr. Lizalde did not have access to a full and fair hearing by the courts. He initially had access to a workers' compensation mechanism; however, his deportation prior to the conclusion of the workers' compensation proceeding he initiated was a principal factor in rendering the second element — the empirical nature — of the judicial remedy null. Upon being deported, the workers' compensation proceeding could not produce the result for which it was designed, as Kansas law requires the worker to be physically present in order to continue his/her case. For his part, Mr. Zumaya was advised by his lawyer to accept a settlement with his employer for less than what experts estimate he would have received were he a U.S. citizen.

106. Regarding the situation of Mr. Lizalde, the State argues that, while it may be more difficult, it is not impossible to continue a worker's compensation claim after being deported, and, regardless, Mr. Lizalde and his lawyers did not try to pursue the proceedings once he was deported by way of requesting humanitarian parole to allow his entry into the U.S.

107. On this point, the IACHR notes that it is possible for a deported person to apply for a non-immigrant visa or for humanitarian parole, which would allow for entry into the country thus satisfying the requirement of presence to continue a workers' compensation claim. However, the IACHR also notes that undocumented workers would likely be subject to certain bars on their readmission under a non-immigrant visa., In order to overcome these bars, they would, at the time of requesting a non-immigrant visa, also have to submit requests for waivers of their inadmissibility. By way of example, the steps required to apply for the latter, humanitarian parole, include the following: (1) an application for a travel document (Form 131), which includes a filing fee of $360 per parole applicant; (2) since parolees may not work, locating a sponsor in the U.S., and having him or her complete and file Form 1-134, Affidavit of Support; and (3) mailing these documents, fees, and a supporting explanation of why the person should be granted humanitarian parole to one of two locations in the state of Texas. While the U.S. government does not specify the time frame to analyze and decide upon requests for humanitarian parole, it does state that if no response is received within 120 days, then only on or after the 121st day may the applicant, by mail only, contact the Parole Branch, the unit that adjudicates these requests.

108. In short, both processes to return to the United States are complex, costly, and potentially time-consuming, making them — for many deported or voluntarily-departed workers, and certainly the two workers in this case — unduly burdensome. Furthermore, there are no guarantees that such applications will be granted.

109. The Commission also finds that these hurdles allow for undocumented workers to be exploited and discriminated against with little to no guarantees of judicial protection. In this regard, the Commission takes note of the views espoused by U.S. Supreme Court justice Breyer in his dissenting opinion in *Hoffman*, where he recognized the high possibility of exploitation of undocumented workers "if no real penalties existed for labor law violations [committed against undocumented workers] beyond a posting [of cease and desist orders] and the possibility of a contempt charge for repeat offenders."

110. Based on its review .of international law and precedents within the inter-American system, the IACHR finds that once a person, regardless of migratory situation or authorization to work, enters into an employment relationship, he or she has the same rights as all other workers, and States are obligated to respect, protect, and guarantee these rights.

111. The Commission's analysis of the merits of this case indicates that the judicial branch of the State has not fully recognized the victims' right to non-discrimination and Mr. Lizalde's right to juridical personality, nor has it afforded the victims adequate or effective protection of their rights as workers, as provided for under the American Declaration. While the victims were able to file claims for workers' compensation and to file suits against their employers for failure to comply with the terms of the workers' compensation, any relief available from the courts is conditioned, reduced, or denied based on the migratory situation of the workers, a condition which may not be legitimately used to deprive workers harmed on the job from the right to a remedy for a serious injury.

112. In reaching this conclusion, the Commission takes into consideration the situation of both workers. In the case of Mr. Lizalde, who was unable to obtain full medical benefits and unlike Mr. Zumaya did not reach a settlement with his employer, the State has demonstrated that the existence of a worker's compensation suit is not enough to suspend a deportation, thus heightening the risk that undocumented workers' rights will not be adequately processed via the judicial system. In the case of Mr. Zumaya, the Commission takes into account the allegations of the petitioners and the State, but it considers that it lacks sufficient elements to find a violation of Mr. Zumaya's rights under Articles XVII and XVIII of the American Declaration. Specifically, it lacks information on the terms of and reasons for the settlement he reached with his employer as well as the consequences of this settlement on the claims presented before the IACHR. Despite the lack of information with respect to Mr. Zumaya's settlement, sufficient evidence was presented by the parties regarding the uncertainty faced by undocumented workers over the outcome of their claims. In this regard, the Commission recognizes that undocumented workers have had varying rates of success on their claims, given that the workers' compensation system in the United States is a patchwork of fifty different systems, with varying interpretations of the effect of the *Hoffman* decision.

113. In this regard, the Commission points to the Concluding Observations of the U.N. Committee on the Elimination of Racial Discrimination (CERD) on the United States, which support its conclusion in the present case: in pertinent part, the CERD stresses that decisions such as that of *Hoffman* from the U.S. Supreme Court "have further eroded the ability of workers belonging to racial, ethnic and national minorities to obtain legal protection and redress in cases of discriminatory treatment at the workplace, unpaid or withheld wages, or work-related injury or illnesses."

114, Based on the foregoing, the Commission finds that the State is responsible for violations of Mr. Lizalde's rights under Articles XVII and XVIII of the American Declaration.

C. Right to Social Security (Article XVI of the American Declaration)

115. Article XVI of the American Declaration establishes that "Every person has the right to social security which will protect him from the consequences of unemployment, old age, and any disabilities arising from causes beyond his control that make it physically or mentally impossible for him to earn a living."

116. As explained in the preceding section, the OAS Charter provides in Article 45 (b) that "proper [working] conditions" are those that "ensure life, health and a decent standard of living for the worker and his family, both during his

working years and in his old age, or when any circumstance deprives him of the possibility of working." The Commission also deems pertinent to note here that Article 45 (h) of the Charter explicitly calls for the "development of an efficient social security policy," and Article 46, on the subject of regional integration, deems it necessary for Member States to "harmonize social legislation...especially in the labor and social security fields, so that workers shall be equally protected."

117. The Commission considers that the right of all workers to receive benefits arising from the employment relationship, such as those included within workers' compensation schemes, is one of a group of economic and social rights that must accompany civil and political liberties for the full protection of human rights, such as the rights to property or to juridical personality. Benefits such as access to medical treatments and services paid by the employer to cover the cost of healing injuries sustained on the job, as well as disability payments to provide a source of income for the injured worker to support himself or herself during the time in which the disability prevents him or her from working, are critical and necessary to meet the social security standards established in the OAS Charter and Article XVI of the American Declaration.

Access to medical treatment and services also relates to the right to personal integrity. These benefits are earned by workers and form part of workers' compensation. The Commission therefore considers that workers' compensation programs, generally, as they exist in the states of the United States, seek to provide protections to workers during vulnerable times, and as such clearly fall within the scope of "social security."

118. The Inter-American Court has endorsed a similar position. In its Advisory Opinion on the Juridical Condition and Rights of Undocumented Migrants, it cited social security as a right which all workers irrespective of migratory status possess and one that assumes a "fundamental importance...yet [is] frequently violated." The Commission finds illustrative the view put forth by Judge Sergio Garcia Ramirez in his concurring opinion, citing social security as a "particularly important" right, as one that contributes to determining the "general framework for the provision of services and for the protection and welfare of those that provide them."

119. Labor rights are also human rights. The Commission notes that the right to social security, along with others, is similar to the provisions of other international instruments in this regard. For example, the United States is a Member Country of the International Labour Organization (ILO), which is a specialized agency within the United Nations.

120. In its Note on the Dignity and Rights of Migrant Workers in an Irregular Situation, the ILO has clarified that "unless otherwise stated, all international labour standards cover all workers irrespective of their nationality or immigration status. Lack of labor protection for migrant workers in an irregular situation undermines protection generally for lawfully resident migrant workers as well as national workers."

Further, the United States, as a member of the ILO, is obliged "to respect, to promote and to realize" the principles contained in the ILO Declaration on Fundamental Principles and Rights at Work, which was adopted in 1998 ("1998 ILO Declaration"). One of these fundamental principles centers on eliminating discrimination in hiring, assignment of tasks, working conditions, pay, benefits, promotions, lay-offs and termination of employment.

121. Additionally, the Commission notes that the United States is a signatory to the North American Agreement on Labor Cooperation (NAALC), the supplemental labor accord to the North American Free Trade Agreement (NAFTA). The three signatories — Canada, Mexico, and the United States — agreed in the NAALC to commit themselves to promote 11 labor principles that apply to "workers" (including non-citizens). These principles include: prevention of occupational injuries and illnesses; compensation in cases of occupational injuries and illnesses, and protection of migrant workers. Thus, not only under inter-American standards but also through other international treaties and conventions does the U.S. have the obligation to ensure that all workers have effective access to social security programs that protect and provide remedies for workers injured on the job.

122. Lastly, the Commission observes that there are two programs run by the U.S. Social Security Administration (SSA) that benefit workers whose injuries have rendered them unable to work for at least 12 months, in addition to other individuals. However, the Commission observes that these programs were not available to the two victims and would not be available to the many undocumented workers who reside in the U.S. temporarily. The first program, Social Security Disability Insurance (SSDI), which pays benefits to injured workers and members of their families, only becomes available if

the person worked a required number of quarters (three-month periods) preceding the claim. The number of quarters required depends on the person's age at the time of the event causing the disability, and in the cases of both Mr. Zumaya and Mr. Lizalde, the required amount would have been 20 quarters or five years. The second program, Supplemental Security Income (SSI), makes monthly payments to persons who have low income and few resources and who are age 65 or older, blind, or disabled; as a non-citizen, a person must prove that he or she is a "qualified alien" and that he or she also meets a condition that allows qualified aliens to receive SSI benefits.

123. Therefore, in light of the fact that neither Mr. Zumaya nor Mr. Lizalde was able to recover their full benefits under the workers' compensation programs applicable in Pennsylvania and Kansas, respectively, and due to the contrary decisions reached by federal and state courts on the issue, the IACHR finds that the United States has failed to ensure the right to social security of these two workers. Thus, the Commission finds that the State has violated Article XVI of the American Declaration to the detriment of Messrs. Zumaya and Lizalde.

VI. ACTIONS SUBSEQUENT TO REPORT No. 83/15

124. On December 29, 2015, the Inter-American Commission electronically approved Report No. 83/15 on the merits of this matter, which comprises paragraphs 1 to 123 supra, with the following recommendations to the State:

1. Provide Messrs. Zumaya and Liza1de with adequate monetary compensation to remedy the violations sustained in the present report;

2. Once a person commences work as an employee, ensure all federal and state laws and policies, on their face and in practice, prohibit any and all distinctions in employment and labor rights based on immigration status and work authorization;

3. Prohibit employer inquiries into immigration status of a worker asserting his or her employment and labor rights in litigation or in administrative complaints;

4. Ensure that undocumented workers are granted the same rights and remedies for violations of their rights in the workplace as documented workers;

5. Establish a procedure whereby undocumented workers involved in workers' compensation proceedings, or their representatives, may request the suspension of their deportations until the resolution of the proceedings and the workers have received the appropriate medical treatment ordered by the presiding courts; and

6. Improve and enhance the detection of employers who violate labor rights and exploit undocumented workers and adequately sanction them.

125. On January 21, 2016 the report was transmitted to the State with a time period of two months to inform the Inter-American Commission on the measures taken to comply with its recommendations. On that same date, the petitioners were notified of the adoption of the report.

126. By letter dated March 18, 2016 the United States provided its response. Firstly, the State contended that several of the recommendations of the Commission "already reflect U.S. law, policy, and action in this area" as was stated in its submissions during the merits stage. In general, the State pointed out that

> ...these include aggressive enforcement of a robust system of laws that protect workers' rights and prohibit many forms of discrimination and retaliation against workers based on their undocumented status; ongoing efforts to combat employer efforts to discover the immigration status of workers during litigation, investigation of claims, and administrative proceedings; and conducting investigations at worksites and enforcing labor laws, without regard to the worker's immigration status. Our immigration law and policies include safeguards for the protection of various classes of victims and vulnerable individuals. Further, our immigration authorities work collaboratively with labor and employment agencies to ensure consistent enforcement of the law.

127. On the other hand, the State indicated that "other recommendations" of Report 83/15 "do not seem feasible for federal implementation, in that they implicate questions of U.S. state law or otherwise fall within the purview of state authorities for their implementation; or require a change in federal or state jurisprudence."

128. The State further affirmed that the recommendations of the Commission are "not requirements under international law." Lastly, the State reiterated its disagreement with the Commission's assertion that there has been a violation of its legal international obligations in this case. The State did not provide information with respect to measures taken in response to the specific recommendations.

129. On June 10, 2016 the Inter-American Commission approved Report No. 29/16 containing the final conclusions and recommendations indicated infra. As set forth in Article 47.1 of its Rules of Procedure, on July 5, 2016, the IACHR transmitted the report to the State with a time period of one month to present information on compliance with the final recommendations. On the same date the IACHR transmitted the report to the petitioners and also requested their observations on compliance with the final recommendations.

130. The State did not provide information with respect to compliance with the final recommendations. Also, no response was received within the stipulated period from the petitioners.

VII. FINAL CONCLUSIONS AND RECOMMENDATIONS

131. On the basis of the foregoing analysis, the Inter-American Commission finds that the State is responsible for violating the human rights of Messrs. Zumaya and Liza1de under Articles II and XVI of the American Declaration by not fully recognizing the victims' rights to non-discrimination and social security.

The Commission further finds that, as Mr. Lizalde was unable to pursue his workers' compensation claim in the judicial system, the State has also violated his right to juridical personality and a fair trial, enshrined in Articles XVII and XVIII of the American Declaration.

132. Based upon these conclusions,

THE INTER-AMERICAN COMMISSION ON HUMAN RIGHTS REITERATES THAT THE UNITED STATES:

1. Provide Messrs, Zumaya and Lizalde with adequate monetary compensation to remedy the violations sustained in the present report;

2. Once a person commences work as an employee, ensure all federal and state laws and policies, on their face and in practice, prohibit any and all distinctions in employment and labor rights based on immigration status and work authorization;

3. Prohibit employer inquiries into immigration status of a worker asserting his or her employment and labor rights in litigation or in administrative complaints;

4. Ensure that undocumented workers are granted the same rights and remedies for violations of their rights in the workplace as documented workers;

5. Establish a procedure whereby undocumented workers involved in workers' compensation proceedings, or their representatives, may request the suspension of their deportations until the resolution of the proceedings and the workers have received the appropriate medical treatment ordered by the presiding courts; and

6. Improve and enhance the detection of employers who violate labor rights and exploit undocumented workers and adequately sanction them.

VIII. PUBLICATION

133. In light of the above and in accordance with Article 47.3 of its Rules of Procedure, the IACHR decides to make this report public, and to include it in its Annual Report to the General Assembly of the Organization of American States. The Inter-American Commission, according to the instruments which govern its mandate, will continue evaluating the measures adopted by the United States with respect to the above recommendations until it determines there has been full compliance.

Done and signed in Panama City, Panama on the 30' day of the month of November, 2016.

[Signed]:

Francisco Jose Eguiguren, First Vice President; Margarette May Macaulay, Second Vice President; Jose de Jesus Orozco Henriquez, Paulo Vannuchi, Esmeralda E. Arosema Bernal de Troititio, and Enrique Gil Botero, Commissioners.

The undersigned, Paulo Abrao, Executive Secretary of the Inter-American Commission on Human Rights, in keeping with Article 49 of the Commission's Rules of Procecrur, certifies that/thrs)is an accurate copy of the original deposited in the archive of the IACHR Secretariat.

Paulo Abrao, Executive Secretary

Source: Inter-American Commission on Human Rights, IACHR, OEA/Ser.L/II.159, Doc. 59, 30 November 2016, REPORT No. 50/16, Case 12.834, Report on Merits (Publication), Undocumented Workers, United States of America, http://www.oas. org/en/iachr/decisions/2016/USPU12834EN.pdf

⬞⬞⬞⬞⬞⬞⬞⬞⬞

10. REPORT OF THE JORGE BUSTAMANTE, SPECIAL RAPPORTEUR TO THE U.N. HUMAN RIGHTS COUNCIL ON THE HUMAN RIGHTS OF MIGRANTS, ON HIS MISSION TO THE UNITED STATES OF AMERICA, 2007

This report is by a U.N. Special Rapporteur on the Human Rights of Migrants, based on his visit to the U.S. on behalf of the U.N. Commission on Human Rights, the predecessor of the U.N. Human Rights Council. A special rapporteur is a person with expertise in a particular topic who is selected and receives a mandate from a body such as the Commission and visits a country, writes up a report and presents it to the mandating body, here the Commission on Human Rights. This is part of the special mechanisms of the U.N. human rights system.

[Footnotes omitted]

Promotion and Protection of All Human Rights, Civil, Political, Economic, Social and Cultural Rights, Including the Right to Development

SUMMARY

The present report is submitted in accordance with resolution 2001/52 of the Commission on Human Rights following the official visit of the Special Rapporteur on the human rights of migrants to the United States of America (the U.S.) between 30 April and 18 May 2007. The purpose of the mission was to examine and report on the status of the human rights of migrants living in the U.S. For the purposes of this report, "migrants" refers to all non-citizens living in the U.S., including, among others, undocumented non-citizens and non-citizens with legal permission to remain in the country, such as legal permanent residents, work visa holders, and persons with refugee status. The Special Rapporteur thanks the Government of the U.S. for extending an invitation for him to conduct such a mission. The Special Rapporteur was disappointed, however, that his scheduled and approved visits to the Hutto Detention Center in Texas and the Monmouth detention centre in New Jersey were subsequently cancelled without satisfactory explanation.

While noting the Government's interest in addressing some of the problems related to the human rights of migrants, the Special Rapporteur has serious concerns about the situation of migrants in the country, especially in the context of specific aspects of deportation and detention policies, and with regard to specific groups such as migrant workers in New Orleans and the Gulf Coast in the aftermath of Hurricane Katrina, migrant farm workers, and migrants in detention facilities. The Special Rapporteur wishes to highlight the fact that cases of indefinite detention — even of migrants fleeing adverse conditions in their home countries — were not uncommon according to testimonies he received. The Special Rapporteur learned from human rights advocates about the lack of due process for non-citizens in U.S. deportation proceedings and their ability to challenge the legality or length of their detention; as well as about the conditions of detained asylum-seekers, long-term permanent residents and parents of minors who are U.S. citizens. In some cases immigrant detainees spend days in solitary confinement, with overhead lights kept on 24 hours a day, and often in extreme heat and cold. According to official sources, the U.S. Government detains over 230,000 people a year-more than three times the number of people it held in detention nine years ago.

The Special Rapporteur notes with dismay that xenophobia and racism towards migrants in the U.S. has worsened since 9/11. The current xenophobic climate adversely affects many sections of the migrant population, and has a particularly discriminatory and devastating impact on many of the most vulnerable groups in the migrant population, including children, unaccompanied minors, Haitian and other Afro-Caribbean migrants, and migrants who are, or are perceived to be, Muslim or of South Asian or Middle Eastern descent.

The Special Rapporteur notes that the U.S. lacks a clear, consistent, long-term strategy to improve respect for the human rights of migrants. Although there are national laws prohibiting discrimination, there is no national legislative and policy framework implementing protection for the human rights of migrants against which the federal and local programmes and strategies can be evaluated to assess to what extent the authorities are respecting the human rights of migrants.

In light of numerous issues described in this report, the Special Rapporteur has come to the conclusion that the U.S. has failed to adhere to its international obligations to make the human rights of the 37.5 million migrants living in the country (according to Government census data from 2006) a national priority, using a comprehensive and coordinated national policy based on clear international obligations. The primary task of such a national policy should be to recognize that, with the exception of certain rights relating to political participation, migrants enjoy nearly all the same human rights protections as citizens, including an emphasis on meeting the needs of the most vulnerable groups. The Special Rapporteur has provided a list of detailed recommendations and conclusions, stressing the need for an institution at the federal level with a mandate solely devoted to the human rights of migrants, a national body that truly represents the voices and concerns of the migrant population, and which could address underlying causes of migration and the human rights concerns of migrants within the U.S.

[End of summary]

[Text of Report; footnotes omitted]

Report of the Special Rapporteur on the Human Rights of Migrants, Jorge Bustamante, on His Mission to the United States of America

...

Pursuant to his mandate the Special Rapporteur on the human rights of migrants visited the United States of America (the U.S.) from 30 April to 18 May at the invitation of the Government.

Inhabiting a large geographic area, the migrant population of the U.S. is complex. Hence, the Special Rapporteur did not have time to conduct a comprehensive investigation of all the issues related to the various migrant populations residing in the U.S. The Special Rapporteur met with a great variety of organizations, State, national and local agencies, officials, and individuals. These included the following: the Indigenous Front of Binational Organizations and California Rural Legal Assistance; religious leaders and representatives; people whose homes were raided by the Department of Homeland Security's agency for Immigration and Customs Enforcement; the National Immigration Law Centre; members of the Youth Justice Coalition; Homies Unidos (which led tours of Pico Union, MacArthur Park and Koreatown in Los Angeles); the Florence detention centre in Arizona; officials at the U.S. Border Patrol; Nogales, Arizona; Dr. Bruce Parks, Pima County's Medical Examiner (who provided statistics and information about migrant deaths due to exposure); the Coalición de Derechos Humanos and other non-governmental organizations (NGOs) in the Phoenix area, including the Macehalli Day Labor Center and the Florence Immigrant and Refugee Rights Project; members of local Native American groups; advocates for migrant domestic workers in Maryland and elsewhere; the Farmworker Association of Florida in Immokalee; (while in Florida he also discussed detention and deportation procedures with the Haitian community); the U.S. Human Rights Network and several of its member organizations; community members and advocates. Furthermore, numerous migrants provided testimonials about conditions directly experienced by themselves or by their migrant family members.

During his visit, the Special Rapporteur toured the U.S. border with Mexico and watched U.S. immigration officials at work. He met there with officials from the U.S. Customs and Border Protection (CBP), a division of the Department of Homeland Security (DHS), spending half a day with Border Patrol officers at the San Diego sector. In Los Angeles the Special Rapporteur conducted site visits, listened to presentations and witnessed community testimony on the system of immigration enforcement (including on raids and detention, workers' rights, deportation procedures, and the criminalization of immigrants).

In Tucson, Arizona, the Special Rapporteur met with advocates and lawyers who informed him of the practice of subjecting immigrants to disproportionate criminal charges in addition to civil charges for violation of the immigration laws of the U.S. In particular, the Special Rapporteur learned that immigration authorities and federal prosecutors are now charging some non-citizens with civil violations for being in the country illegally, as well as for the overly-broad charge of "self-smuggling" themselves into the country. This latter criminal charge is defined as a felony and therefore the migrant can be sentenced to prison upon conviction.

In Atlanta, Georgia, the Special Rapporteur attended a regional NGO briefing, "Directly Impacted Community Members Briefing and Press Conference," organized by the National Network of Immigrant and Refugee Rights and its member organizations the Georgia Latino Alliance for Human Rights (GLAHR), the Latin American and Caribbean Community Center (LACCC) and the American Civil Liberties Union (ACLU) of both Georgia and New York. He also attended a reception in Atlanta where he was able to meet with Georgia State Representatives and Senators. During the NGO briefings in Atlanta, the Special Rapporteur heard from migrants and migrant human rights advocates from different organizations and who travelled from across the southern U.S., including the Mississippi Immigrant Rights Alliance (MIRA), the New Orleans Workers' Center for Racial Justice, the Southern Poverty Law Center (SPLC), Queer Progressive Agenda (QPA), Raksha (South Asian community organization), the Mexican American Legal Defense and Education Fund (MALDEF), the Georgia Department of Education Program, and the Roman Catholic Archdiocese of Atlanta. Migrants and NGO advocates from these and other organization informed the Special Rapporteur of the plight of migrants in the south of the U.S., where the migrant population is booming.

The Special Rapporteur also attended a public hearing in New York on the rights of migrants organized by the ACLU of New York, regional NGOs and grass-roots organizations. In New York, the Special Rapporteur heard several individuals testify about the post-9/11 backlash, including the experiences of the some 750 migrants arrested and subjected to arbitrary and lengthy detention subsequent to the September 11, 2001 attacks on the U.S.

The visit concluded with meetings with senior officials of the Department of Homeland Security and the State Department in Washington, D.C. On the last day of his visit, the Special Rapporteur was informed that the cancellation of his visits to the detention facilities in Texas and New Jersey was due to a pending lawsuit filed against both facilities, in which the U.S. Government was not allowed to interfere. A statement was subsequently published in the press suggesting that the cancellation was because the "Special Rapporteur declined the invitation"; the Special Rapporteur made clear that this latter allegation was false.

8. Migrant rights issues raised in these various meetings included, but were not limited to, the following: indefinite detention; arbitrary detention; mandatory detention; deportation without due process; family separation; anti-immigrant legislation; racial profiling; linguistic, racial, ethnic, gender and sexual-orientation discrimination; State violence; wage theft; forced labour; limited access to health and education; the growing anti-immigrant climate (including the

post-9/11 backlash); and significant limitations on due process and judicial oversight. Most of these issues are addressed in this report.

I. INTERNATIONAL LAW AND STANDARDS

9. Since the early stages of the nation State, control over immigration has been understood as an essential power of government. In recent history, governments have allowed limits to be placed on their power regarding immigration policy, recognizing that it may only be exercised in ways that do not violate fundamental human rights. Therefore, while international law recognizes every State's right to set immigration criteria and procedures, it does not allow unfettered discretion to set policies for detention or deportation of non-citizens without regard to human rights standards.

A. Right to fair deportation procedures

10. The governmental power to deport should be governed by laws tailored to protect legitimate national interests. U.S. deportation policies violate the right to fair deportation procedures, including in cases in which the lawful presence of the migrant in question is in dispute, as established under article 13 of the International Covenant on Civil and Political Rights (ICCPR). These deportation policies, particularly those applied to migrants lawfully in the U.S. who have been convicted of crimes, also violate (a) international legal standards on proportionality; (b) the right to a private life, provided for in article 17 of the ICCPR; and (c) article 33 of the Convention relating to the Status of Refugees, which prohibits the return of refugees to places where they fear persecution, with very narrow exceptions.

11. The ICCPR, which the U.S. ratified in 1992, states in article 13 (to which the U.S. has entered no reservations, understandings or declarations): "An alien lawfully in the territory of a State Party to the present covenant may be expelled therefrom only in pursuance of a decision reached in accordance with law and shall, except where compelling reasons of national security otherwise require, be allowed to submit the reasons against his expulsion and to have his case reviewed by, and be represented for the purpose before, the competent authority or a person or persons especially designated by the competent authority."

12. The Human Rights Committee, which monitors State compliance with the ICCPR, has interpreted the phrase "lawfully in the territory" to include non-citizens who wish to challenge the validity of the deportation order against them. In addition, the Committee has made this clarifying statement: "... if the legality of an alien's entry or stay is in dispute, any decision on this point leading to his expulsion or deportation ought to be taken in accordance with article 13." and further: "An alien must be given full facilities for pursuing his remedy against expulsion so that this right will in all the circumstances of his case be an effective one."

13. Similarly, article 8, paragraph 1 of the American Convention on Human Rights, which the U.S. signed in 1977, states that "Every person has the right to a hearing, with due guarantees and within a reasonable time, by a competent, independent, and impartial tribunal, previously established by law...for the determination of his rights and obligations of a civil, labor, fiscal, or any other nature."

14. Applying this standard, the Inter-American Commission on Human Rights has stated that detention and deportation proceedings require "as broad as possible" an interpretation of due process requirements and include the right to a meaningful defence and to be represented by an attorney.

15. Because U.S. immigration laws impose mandatory deportation without a discretionary hearing where family and community ties can be considered, these laws fail to protect the right to private life, in violation of the applicable human rights standards.

16. Article 16, paragraph 3, of the Universal Declaration of Human Rights and article 23, paragraph 1, of the ICCPR state that "The family is the natural and fundamental group unit of society and is entitled to protection by society and the State." Furthermore, article 23, paragraph 3 states that the right of men and women to marry and found a family shall be recognized. This right includes the right to live together. Article 17, paragraph 1 of the International Covenant on Civil and Political Rights states that "No one shall be subjected to arbitrary or unlawful interference with his privacy, family or correspondence...."

17. As the international body entrusted with the power to interpret the ICCPR and decide cases brought under its Optional Protocol, the Human Rights Committee has explicitly stated that family unity imposes limits on the power of States to deport.

18. The American Declaration of the Rights and Duties of Man features several provisions relevant to the question of deportation of non-citizens with strong family ties. Article V states that "Every person has the right to the protection of the law against abusive attacks upon . . . his private and family life." Under article VI, "Every person has the right to establish a family, the basic element of society, and to receive protection therefor." The American Convention on Human Rights, to which the U.S. is a signatory, contains analogous provisions. The case of *Wayne Smith and Hugo Armendáriz v. United States of America*, which came before the Inter-American Commission on Human Rights in 2006 relies on several of these provisions to challenge the U.S. policy of deporting non-citizens with criminal convictions without regard to family unity. In light of these international standards, the U.S. has fallen far behind the practice of providing protection for family unity in deportation proceedings.

19. Moreover, the rights of children to live together with their parents are violated by the lack of deportation procedures in which the State's interest in deportation is balanced against the rights of the children.

U.S. mandatory deportation laws harm the human rights of children of non-citizen parents.

20. U.S. restrictions on relief for refugees convicted of crimes violate the Convention and the Protocol relating to the Status of Refugees.3 The U.S. provides two forms of relief for refugees fleeing persecution-withholding of removal, which provides bare protection against refoulement, and more robust asylum relief, which provides a pathway to permanent residence. Although petitioners' cases do not involve claims for refugee protection, a discussion of the effect of U.S. immigration laws on non-citizens with criminal convictions would be incomplete without an exploration of the effect of the laws on noncitizen refugees.

Even the weaker form of relief-withholding of removal-is per se unavailable to non-citizens with aggravated felonies sentenced to an aggregate term of at least five years' imprisonment and to those whom the Attorney General determines have been convicted of a particularly serious crime. U.S. law denies these refugees even a hearing for their refugee claims, instead denying relief on a categorical basis. U.S. laws therefore contravene the due process and substantive protections of the Declaration of the Rights and Duties of Man and the Convention and the Protocol relating to the Status of Refugees, which allow for exceptions to non-refoulement in only a narrow set of cases and after individualized hearings.

B. Right to liberty of person

21. Pursuant to the Immigration and Nationality Act, U.S. Immigration and Customs Enforcement (ICE) may detain non-citizens under final orders of removal only for the period necessary to bring about actual deportation. Additionally, two U.S. Supreme Court decisions, *Zadvydas v. Davis*, and *Clark v. Martinez*, placed further limits on the allowable duration of detention. As a result of those decisions, ICE may not detain an individual for longer than six months after the issuance of a final removal order if there is no significant likelihood of actual deportation (for example, because the home country refuses repatriation) in the reasonably foreseeable future.

22. Although these two court decisions limit the ability of ICE to detain non-citizens indefinitely, in practice, U.S. policy is a long way out of step with international obligations. Immigration enforcement authorities have failed to develop an appropriate appeals procedure, and for all practical purposes have absolute discretion to determine whether a non-citizen may be released from detention. Furthermore, those released from detention as a result of a post-order custody review are released under conditions of supervision, which in turn are monitored by ICE deportation officers. Again, ICE officers have absolute authority to determine whether an individual must return to custody. Given that these discretionary decisions are not subject to judicial review, current U.S. practices violate international law.

23. The Special Rapporteur wishes to stress that international conventions require that the decision to detain someone should be made on a case-by-case basis after an assessment of the functional need to detain a particular individual. He notes that the individual assessment of cases does not appear to be sufficient and that detention policies in the U.S. con-

stitute serious violations of international due process standards. Based on individual testimonies, the Government's own admissions and reports he received, the Special Rapporteur notes that the violations include:

- Failing to promptly inform detainees of the charges against them
- Failing to promptly bring detainees before a judicial authority
- Denying broad categories of detainees release on bond without individualized assessments
- Subjecting detainees to investigative detention without judicial oversight
- Denying detainees access to legal counsel

24. In sum, in the current context the U.S. detention and deportation system for migrants lacks the kinds of safeguards that prevent certain deportation decisions and the detention of certain immigrants from being arbitrary within the meaning of the International Covenant on Civil and Political Rights (ICCPR), which the U.S. has signed and ratified.

C. Labour rights

25. The labour rights of migrants affected by conditions in certain portions of the labour market, including the tomato workers in Florida and migrants in regions of the country devastated by Hurricane Katrina, are also included in the Universal Declaration of Human Rights and ICCPR. The U.S. Government has committed itself to protecting these rights.

III. UNITED STATES OF AMERICA, IMMIGRATION POLICY AND PRACTICE

A. Legal and political background

26. With regard to deportation policy, under current U.S. immigration law, individuals arriving in the U.S. without the necessary visas or other legal permission to enter, including asylum-seekers and refugees, are subject to mandatory detention. In addition, persons subject to deportation procedures after being lawfully present in the U.S., including legal permanent residents who have been convicted of crimes, are subject to detention.

All of these persons are detained in immigration detention centres, county jails or private prisons under contract with immigration enforcement agencies for months, and sometimes years.

According to testimonies heard by the Special Rapporteur, U.S. citizens erroneously identified as noncitizens, long-time lawful permanent residents, non-citizen veterans, and vulnerable populations with a regular legal status have also been detained for months without sufficient due process protections, including fair individualized assessments of the reasons for their detention.

27. In 2006, the Department of Homeland Security arrested over 1.6 million migrants, including both undocumented migrants and legal permanent residents, of which over 230,000 were subsequently held in detention.

28. On average, there are over 25,000 migrants detained by immigration officials on any given day. The conditions and terms of their detention are often prison-like: freedom of movement is restricted and detainees wear prison uniforms and are kept in a punitive setting. Many detainees are held in jails instead of detention centres, since the U.S. uses a combination of facilities owned and operated by ICE, prison facilities owned and operated by private prison contractors and over 300 local and county jails from which ICE rents beds on a reimbursable basis. As a result, the majority of non-criminal immigrants are held in jails where they are mixed in with the prison's criminal population. This is the case despite the fact that under U.S. law an immigration violation is a civil offence, not a crime. The mixture of criminal and immigrant detainees in these jails can result in the immigrants being treated in a manner that is inappropriate to their status as administrative, as opposed to criminal, pretrial or post-conviction inmates.

29. In 1996, the Immigration and Naturalization Service had a daily detention capacity of 8,279 beds. By 2006, that had increased to 27,500 with plans for future expansion. At an average cost of US$ 95 per person per day, immigration detention costs the U.S. Government U.S. $ 1.2 billion per year.

30. ICE reported an average stay of 38 days for all migrant detainees in 2003. Asylum-seekers granted refugee status, spend an average of 10 months in detention, with the longest period in one case being three and a half years. There are instances of individuals with final orders of removal who languish in detention indefinitely, such as those from countries with whom the U.S. does not have diplomatic relations or that refuse to accept the return of their own nationals. Under U.S. law, migrant detainees about whom the U.S. has certain national security concerns are subject to the possibility of indefinite detention, in contravention of international standards.

31. Migrants in detention include asylum-seekers, torture survivors, victims of human trafficking, long-term permanent residents facing deportation for criminal convictions based on a long list of crimes (including minor ones), the sick, the elderly, pregnant women, transgender migrants detained according to their birth sex rather than their gender identity or expression, parents of children who are U.S. citizens, and families. Detention is emotionally and financially devastating, particularly when it divides families and leaves spouses and children to fend for themselves in the absence of the family's main financial provider.

32. Immigrants are also often transferred to remote detention facilities, which interferes substantially with access to counsel and to family members and often causes great financial and emotional hardship for family members who are not detained. Thousands of those held in immigration detention are individuals who, by law, could be released.

33. Detention has not always been the primary enforcement strategy relied upon by the U.S. immigration authorities, as it appears to be today. In 1954, the Immigration and Naturalization Service announced that it was abandoning the policy of detention except in rare cases when an individual was considered likely to be a security threat or flight risk. This reluctance to impose needless confinement was based on the concepts of individual liberty and due process, long recognized and protected in the American legal system, and also enshrined in international human rights standards.

34. Sweeping changes in immigration laws in 1996 drastically increased the number of people subject to mandatory, prolonged and indefinite detention. The increasing reliance of the U.S. authorities on detention as an enforcement strategy has meant that many individuals have been unnecessarily detained for prolonged periods without any finding that they are either a danger to society or a flight risk. These practices have continued despite attempts by the U.S. Supreme Court to limit the Government's discretion to indefinitely detain individuals.

35. Certain provisions of the Immigration and Nationality Act, as amended by two laws passed in 1996 (the Antiterrorism and Effective Death Penalty Act (AEDPA) and the Illegal Immigration Reform and Immigrant Responsibility Act (IIRAIRA)) require mandatory detention, pending removal proceedings, of virtually any non-citizen who is placed in proceedings on criminal grounds, as well as of persons who arrive at the country's borders in order to seek asylum from persecution without documentation providing for their legal entry into the country. These two laws have significantly increased the number of migrants subject to mandatory detention on a daily basis, since AEDPA requires the mandatory detention of non-citizens convicted of a wide range of offences, and IIRAIRA has further expanded the list of offences for which mandatory detention is required.

36. As a result of these legislative changes, minor drug offences-such as possession of paraphernalia- as well as minor theft or other property-related offences, can result in mandatory detention and in the past decade the use of detention as an immigration enforcement mechanism has become more the norm than the exception in U.S. immigration enforcement policy.

37. The policy of mandatory detention also strips immigration judges of the authority to determine during a full and fair hearing whether or not an individual presents a danger or a flight risk. Instead, certain previous convictions (and in some cases, merely the admission of having committed an offence) automatically trigger mandatory detention without affording non-citizens an opportunity to be heard as to whether or not they merit release from custody.

38. This policy also deprives immigration judges-and even the Department of Homeland Security-of the authority to order the release of an individual, even when it is clear that he or she poses no danger or flight risk that would warrant such detention.

39. In its landmark decision, *Zadvydas v. Davis*, the Supreme Court held that indefinite immigration detention of non-citizens who have been ordered deported but whose removal is not reasonably foreseeable would raise serious constitutional problems.

40. Prior to Zadvydas, the Government had a policy of detaining individuals even when there was virtually no chance they would actually be removed (this has been especially common with migrants from countries such as Cuba, Iraq, the Islamic Republic of Iran, the Lao People's Democratic Republic, the former Soviet Union and Viet Nam). The Government often referred to these individuals as "lifers," in recognition of the fact that their detention was indefinite and potentially permanent. In the aftermath of Zadvydas, new regulations were promulgated in order to comply with the Supreme Court's decision. Under these regulations, if the Department of Homeland Security cannot remove a migrant within the 90-day removal period, the Government is required to provide a post-order custody review to determine if the individual can be released. If the individual remains in detention six months after the removal order has become final, another custody review is to be conducted. Once it is determined that removal is not reasonably foreseeable, the regulations require the individual to be released under conditions of supervision.

41. Unfortunately, many problems plague the post-order custody review process. For example, some detainees never receive notice of their 90-day or 6-month custody reviews, and therefore do not have the opportunity to submit documentation in support of their release. Others never receive timely custody reviews at either the 90-day or 6-month mark. In addition, decisions to continue detention are often based on faulty reasoning and erroneous facts, ignore the law outlined by the Supreme Court in Zadvydas, or are essentially rubber-stamp decisions that fail to cite any specific evidence in support of their conclusion.

42. Frequently, these decisions ignore documentation (including letters from the detained individual's consulate) that proves that there is no significant likelihood of removal in the reasonably foreseeable future. In other cases, the Department of Homeland Security has failed to present evidence of the likelihood of removal and instead blames detainees for failing to facilitate their own removal.

43. The Special Rapporteur notes that according to the law, individuals can be released on parole regardless of their immigration status. In practice, however, because migrants are not entitled to a review of their custody by an immigration judge, or are subjected to rubber-stamp administrative custody review decisions, their detention is essentially mandatory.

44. The Special Rapporteur acknowledges that the mission for the Department of Homeland Security is to "lead the unified national effort to secure America" through its Immigration and Customs Enforcement agency (ICE). ICE is the largest investigative branch of the Department of Homeland Security; and seeks to protect the U.S. against terrorist attacks by targeting undocumented immigrants, whom the agency considers to be "the people, money and materials that support terrorism and other criminal activities."

45. In that context, the ICE has recently shifted its approach to enforcement by bringing criminal charges against employers of irregular migrant workers, seizing their assets and charging them with money laundering violations.

B. Deportation policy

46. With regard to deportation policy, following changes to U.S. immigration law in 1996, non-citizens in the U.S. have been subjected to a policy of mandatory deportation upon conviction of a crime, including very minor ones. These persons are not afforded a hearing in which their ties to the U.S., including family relationships, are weighed against the Government's interest in deportation. According to Government sources, hundreds of thousands of persons have been deported since these laws went into effect in 1996.

One case that has been brought to the attention of the Special Rapporteur is that of a male migrant, originally from Haiti, who enlisted in the U.S. military in 1970. A lawful permanent resident, or green card holder, this individual served his adopted country for four years. Now a 52-year-old veteran with four U.S. citizen sons, two of whom are in the military themselves, he faces mandatory deportation because he was convicted of the possession and sale of small amounts of crack cocaine in the mid-1990s, for which he spent 16 months in prison.

Some 672,593 immigrants in the U.S. — many of whom, like the Haitian migrant described above, were legal residents — have been deported from the country under the 1996 legislation that requires mandatory deportation of non-citizens convicted of a crime after they have served their sentence. It does not matter whether the non-citizen has lived in the U.S. legally for decades, built a home and family, run a business, or paid taxes. And these laws do not apply only to serious crimes, but also to minor offences.

C. Local enforcement operations

57. While migration is a federal matter, ICE is actively seeking the assistance of State and local law enforcement in enforcing immigration law. Under a recent federal law, ICE has been permitted to enter into agreements with state and local law enforcement agencies through voluntary programmes which allow designated officers to carry out immigration law enforcement functions. These state and local law enforcement agencies enter into a memorandum of understanding (MOU) or a memorandum of agreement (MOA) that outlines the scope and limitation of their authority. According to ICE, over 21,485 officers nationwide are participating in this programme, and more than 40 municipal, county, and state agencies have applied. In 2006, this programme resulted in 6,043 arrests and so far in 2007, another 3,327.

58. Local law enforcement agencies that have signed MOUs so far are:
- Florida Department of Law Enforcement (the first to enter into the agreement)
- Alabama Department of Public Safety
- Arizona Department of Corrections
- Los Angeles, County Sheriff's Department
- San Bernardino County Sheriff-Coroner Department

D. Detention and removal system

On 2 November 2005 the Department of Homeland Security announced to the public a multi-year plan called the Secure Border Initiative (SBI) to increase enforcement along the U.S. borders and to reduce illegal migration. The SBI is divided into two phases.

The first phase includes a restructuring of the detention and removal system through the expansion of expedited removal and the creation of the "catch and return" initiative, in addition to greatly strengthening border security through additional personnel and technology.

The second phase, the interior enforcement strategy, was unveiled to the public on 20 April 2006. It is through this initiative that U.S. Immigration and Customs Enforcement (ICE) has expanded operations that target undocumented workers and individuals who are in violation of immigration law. The operations also target all non-citizens, including refugees, legal permanent residents, and others with permission to reside in the U.S., who have any of a long list of criminal offences on their records, including minor offences, which result in the mandatory detention and deportation of these individuals in accordance with the immigration laws passed in 1996.

The primary goal of the IES is to "Identify and remove criminal aliens, immigration fugitives and other immigration violators." According to the Office of Detention and Removal Operations:

The Special Rapporteur heard accounts from victims that ICE officials entered their homes without a warrant, denied them access to lawyers or a phone to call family members and coerced them to sign "voluntary departure "agreements.

Many who are subject to these raids and subsequent mandatory detention are long-time permanent residents who know far more about the country from which they are facing removal-the U.S.-than the country to which they may be removed. Although lawful permanent status is not terminated with detention, but only when a final order of removal is entered against an individual, lawful residents can be detained until there is a final resolution in their case.

E. Mandatory detention

Detention impairs an individual's ability to obtain counsel and present cases in removal proceedings. In 2005, 65 per cent of immigrants appeared at their deportation hearings without benefit of legal counsel. Despite the adversarial and legally complex nature of removal proceedings and the severe consequences at stake, detainees are not afforded appointed counsel.

Moreover, detention impacts an individual's ability to earn income, thereby also impeding the ability to retain counsel. To make matters worse, the Department of Homeland Security often transfers detainees hundreds or thousands of miles away from their home cities without any notice to their attorneys or family members, which violates the agency's own administrative regulations on detention and transfer of detainees. Non-citizens are often detained in particularly remote locations. Many private attorneys are put off from taking cases where clients are detained in such locations. Onerous distances, inflexible visitation schedules and advance notice scheduling requirements by facilities are all obstacles that impede the ability of detainees to secure and retain legal assistance.

Detention severely impairs the right of a respondent in removal proceedings to present evidence in her or his own defence. Extensive documentation is often required, including family ties, employment history, property or business ties, rehabilitation or good moral character. Obtaining admissible supporting documents from family members, administrative agencies, schools and hospitals, can be burdensome for anyone, but often practically impossible for detainees. Access to mail and property is often limited and can also create significant obstacles for detainees.

Faced with the prospect of mandatory and prolonged detention, detainees often abandon claims to legal relief from removal, contrary to international standards that require non-citizens to be able to submit reasons against their deportation to the competent authorities. Mandatory detention operates as a coercive mechanism, pressuring those detained to abandon meritorious claims for relief in order to avoid continued or prolonged detention and the onerous conditions and consequences it imposes.

U.S. immigration law allows for detention of migrants that is often neither brief nor determinate, and adjudication of defences against removal can be complicated and lengthy. An appeal to the Board of Immigration Appeals by either party extends the period of mandatory detention for many additional months. A petition for review to the Court of Appeals also extends mandatory detention, often for a period of years. A non-citizen is subject to mandatory detention even after being granted relief by the immigration judge, simply upon the filing of a notice of intent to appeal by Government counsel. In fact, it is often the most meritorious cases that take the longest to adjudicate, and in which migrants spend the longest amount of time in detention. Often the cases subject to continuing appeals are cases where individuals may have the strongest ties to the U.S. and risk the severest consequences if removed.

Immigration laws are known for being particularly complex. It may take a non-citizen subject to mandatory detention months and sometimes years to ultimately prove that he or she was not deportable.

In one case a lawful permanent resident of the U.S. was detained for approximately three and a half years, subject to mandatory detention, for offences that the Court of Appeals for the Ninth Circuit ultimately found not to constitute deportable offences. Three and a half years after being placed in the custody of the Department of Homeland Security and charged as having been convicted of an aggravated felony, this person was released by the Department, as it was clear that nothing in his case made him removable and that removal proceedings would therefore be terminated.

The Security Through Regularized Immigration and a Vibrant Economy Act of 2007 (the STRIVE Act), introduced by Congress on 22 March 2007, is an example of recently proposed legislation that would further expand mandatory detention and indefinite immigration detention, and was an attempt to create comprehensive immigration reform through policy. It required that the Department of Homeland Security significantly increase the number of facilities for the detention of non-citizens, adding a minimum of 20 detention facilities with the capacity to detain an additional 20,000 non-citizens.

The STRIVE Act would have essentially overruled the limitations on indefinite detention outlined by the U.S. Supreme Court in *Zadvydas v. Davis* by specifically authorizing the Department of Homeland Security to indefinitely detain certain non-citizens who have been ordered removed, even when their removal is not reasonably foreseeable. The STRIVE Act would also have increased the number of people subject to mandatory detention by further expanding the kinds of crimes that constitute an aggravated felony and providing the basis for such detention. During the Special Rapporteur's mission to the U.S. the bill died in the Congressional Subcommittee on 5 May 2007 as it did not come to a vote.

Despite efforts by activists, community members, lawyers, and other advocates to repair the significant damage resulting from the legislation introduced in 1996, the legislation and its effects have not been reversed nor mitigated. Moreover, at both state and federal levels, the anti-immigrant climate has resulted in legislation that leads to increased mandatory detention of non-citizens even before they are in Department of Homeland Security custody.

For example, in November 2006, Arizona voters approved Proposition 100, which became effective on 7 December 2006 upon its codification in Arizona Revised Statutes §13-3961. That section now provides that a person who is in criminal custody shall be denied bail "if the proof is evident or presumption great" that the person is guilty of a serious felony offence and the person "has entered or remained in the U.S. illegally." In addition to the serious due process and equal protection issues this provision raises, by mandating different treatment for non-citizens and citizens in criminal proceedings and requiring state officials with little understanding of the complexity of immigration laws to enforce those laws, it also virtually ensures the eventual transfer of these individuals to Department of Homeland Security custody (even if they are never convicted), further increasing the number of people potentially subject to mandatory, prolonged, and indefinite detention.

87. Without the ability to comply uniformly with the current regulations there can be no reasonable expectation that ICE has the capacity to handle its large caseload resulting in part from the efforts of the Department of Homeland Security to secure the border.

III. THE PLIGHT OF MIGRANT WORKERS:
THE CASE OF HURRICANE KATRINA

A. Background

88. In the aftermath of Hurricane Katrina, which devastated New Orleans and other areas of the U.S. Gulf Coast in 2005, several hundred thousand workers, mostly African Americans, lost their jobs and their homes, and many became internally displaced persons (IDPs). Since the storm, these IDPs have faced tremendous structural barriers to returning home and to finding the employment necessary to rebuild their lives. Without housing, they cannot work; without work, they cannot afford housing. Since Hurricane Katrina, tens of thousands of migrant workers, most of them undocumented, have arrived in the Gulf Coast region to work in the reconstruction zones. They have made up much of the labour to rebuild the area, to keep businesses running and to boost tax revenue. To support their families, migrant workers often work longer hours for less pay than other labourers. For some migrant workers, wages continue to decrease.

Jobs are becoming scarcer because the most urgent work, gutting homes and removing debris, is mostly finished.

89. These migrant workers, like their original local counterparts, are finding barriers to safe employment, fair pay, and affordable housing, and in some cases, experience discrimination and exploitation amounting to inhuman and degrading treatment. In fact, many workers are homeless or living in crowded, unsafe and unsanitary conditions, harassed and intimidated by law enforcement, landlords and employers alike.

90. Migrant workers on the Gulf Coast are experiencing an unprecedented level of exploitation. They often live and work amid substandard conditions, homelessness, poverty, environmental toxicity, and the constant threat of police and immigration raids, without any guarantee of a fair day's pay. They also face structural barriers that make it impossible to hold public or private institutions accountable for their mistreatment; most have no political voice.

...

94. As noted above, the Universal Declaration of Human Rights, the International Covenant on Civil and Political Rights (ICCPR), the International Covenant on Economic, Social and Cultural Rights (ICESCR), and the International Convention on the Protection of the Rights of All Migrant Workers and Members of Their Families establish workers' rights to (a) a safe and healthful workplace, (b) compensation for workplace injuries and illnesses, (c) freedom of association and the right to form trade unions and bargain collectively, and (d) equality of conditions and rights for immigrant workers.

95. Immigrant workers, including those who migrated to work in the regions affected by Katrina, often experience violations of these rights. Lack of familiarity with U.S. law and language difficulties often prevent them from being aware of their rights as well as specific hazards in their work. Immigrant workers who are undocumented, as many are, risk deportation if they seek to organize to improve conditions. Fear of drawing attention to their immigration status also prevents them from seeking protection from Government authorities for their rights as workers. In 2002, the Supreme Court stripped undocumented workers of any remedies if they are illegally fired for union organizing activity. Under international law, however, undocumented workers are entitled to the same labour rights, including wages owed, protection from discrimination, protection for health and safety on the job and back pay, as are citizens and those working lawfully in a country.

96. Furthermore, pre- and post-Katrina policies and practices of local, state and federal government agencies have had a grossly disproportionate impact on migrants of colour, in violation of the U.S. Government's obligations under the Convention on the Elimination of All Forms of Racial Discrimination (CERD) and other human rights norms that the U.S. has ratified.

B. Institutional responsibility

97. Personal stories recounted to the Special Rapporteur illuminate the commonality of the struggles faced by migrant workers but also the institutional responsibility, and how both policies and practices perpetuate structural and institutional racism and xenophobia. Across the city of New Orleans, workers — both returning internally displaced persons and new migrant workers — list calamities that have become routine: homelessness, wage theft, toxic working conditions, joblessness, police brutality, and layers of bureaucracy. These shared experiences with structural racism unite low-wage workers across racial, ethnic, and industry lines.

Thousands of workers now live in the same conditions: they sleep in the homes they are gutting or in abandoned cars that survivors were forced to leave behind; they are packed in motels, sometimes 10 to a room; and they live on the streets. Most migrant workers were promised housing by their employers but quickly found upon arrival that no housing accommodation had been made available. Instead, they were left homeless.

98. By all accounts, state and local governments have turned a blind eye to this dismal housing situation. Although the city depends on migrant workers to act as a flexible, temporary workforce, it also made no arrangements to provide them with temporary housing. As a result, the workers who are rebuilding New Orleans often have nowhere to sleep.

99. The federal Government has sent mixed messages. On the one hand, it relaxed the immigration law requirements relating to hiring practices, thereby sending a message to contractors that hiring undocumented workers was permissible if not condoned. On the other hand, federal authorities failed to assure these workers and their family members that they would not be turned over to immigration authorities.

100. New migrant workers on the Gulf Coast have experienced a range of problems relating to wage theft which include:
   • Non-payment of wages for work performed, including overtime
   • Payment of wages with cheques that bounce due to insufficient funds
   • Inability to identify the employer or contractor in order to pursue claims for unpaid wages
   • Subcontractors — often migrants themselves — who want to but cannot pay wages because they have not been paid by the primary contractor (often a more financially stable white contractor)

101. These conditions are particularly salient for migrant workers, especially if they are undocumented as they are more easily exploitable. They may be hired for their hard manual labour and then robbed of their legally owed wages. The situation is exacerbated by the complexity of local employment structures. Because there are multiple tiers of subcontractors, often flowing from a handful of primary contractors with federal Government contracts, workers often do not know the identities of their employers. This is typical of the growing contingent of low-wage workers throughout the country. In New Orleans, workers explained that without knowing the identity of their employer, they cannot pursue wage claims against them.

...

IV. CONCLUSIONS

104. Contrary to popular belief, U.S. immigration policy did not become more severe after the terrorist attacks on September 11. Drastic changes made in 1996 have been at work for more than a decade, affecting communities across the nation and recent policy changes simply exacerbate what was put in motion then. Also, contrary to popular belief, these policies do not target only undocumented migrants — they apply to citizens born in the U.S. of undocumented parents and long-term lawful permanent residents (or green card holders) as well.

105. Not only have immigration laws become more punitive — increasing the types of crimes that can permanently sever a migrant's ties to the U.S. — but there are fewer ways for migrants to appeal for leniency. Hearings that used to happen in which a judge would consider a migrant's ties to the U.S., particularly their family relationships, were stopped in 1996. There are no exceptions available, no matter how long an individual has lived in the U.S. and no matter how much his spouse and children depend on him for their livelihood and emotional support.

106. Throughout the history of the U.S., many different kinds of non-citizens have been made subject to mandatory detention. People with lawful permanent resident status (or green card holders), including those who have lived lawfully in the U.S. for decades, are subject to deportation. So are other legal immigrants — refugees, students, business people, and those who have permission to remain because their country of nationality is in the midst of war or a humanitarian disaster. Undocumented non-citizens are also subject to mandatory detention and deportation regardless of whether they have committed a crime.

107. A primary principle of U.S. immigration law is that U.S. citizens can never be denied entry into the country; neither can they ever be forcibly deported from the U.S. By contrast, non-citizens, even those who have lived in the country legally for decades, are always vulnerable to mandatory detention and deportation.

108. In the wake of Hurricane Katrina, migrant workers from across the U.S. travelled to New Orleans. Ultimately, the voices of workers in post-Katrina New Orleans demonstrate that the actions and inactions of federal, state, and local governments and the actions of the private reconstruction industry have created deplorable working and living conditions for people striving to rebuild and return to the city. Because these workers are migrant, undocumented, and displaced they have little chance to hold officials and private industry accountable (e.g., many cannot vote, and displaced workers in New Orleans continue to experience barriers to voting) except through organized, collective action.

V. RECOMMENDATIONS

109. The Special Rapporteur would like to make the following recommendations to the [U.S.] Government.

On general detention matters

110. Mandatory detention should be eliminated; the Department of Homeland Security should be required to make individualized determinations of whether or not a non-citizen presents a danger to society or a flight risk sufficient to justify their detention.

111. The Department of Homeland Security must comply with the Supreme Court's decision in *Zadvydas v. Davis* and *Clark v. Martinez*. Individuals who cannot be returned to their home countries within the foreseeable future should be released as soon as that determination is made, and certainly no longer than six months after the issuance of a final order. Upon release, such individuals should be released with employment authorization, so that they can immediately obtain employment.

112. The overuse of immigration detention in the U.S. violates the spirit of international laws and conventions and, in many cases, also violates the actual letter of those instruments. The availability of effective alternatives renders the increasing reliance on detention as an immigration enforcement mechanism unnecessary. Through these alternative programmes, there are many less restrictive forms of detention and many alternatives to detention that would serve the country's protection and enforcement needs more economically, while still complying with international human rights law and ensuring just and humane treatment of migrants. Create detention standards and guidelines

113. At the eighty-seventh session of the Human Rights Committee in July 2006, the U.S. Government cited the issuance of the National Detention Standards in 2000 as evidence of compliance with international principles on the treatment of immigration detainees. While this is indeed a positive step, it is not sufficient. The U.S. Government should create legally binding human rights standards governing the treatment of immigration detainees in all facilities, regardless of whether they are operated by the federal Government, private companies, or county agencies.

114. Immigration detainees in the custody of the Department of Homeland Security and placed in removal proceedings, should have the right to appointed counsel. The right to counsel is a due process right that is fundamental to ensuring fairness and justice in proceedings. To ensure compliance with domestic and international law, court-appointed counsel should be available to detained immigrants.

115. Given that the difficulties in representing detained non-citizens are exacerbated when these individuals are held in remote and/or rural locations, U.S. Immigration and Customs Enforcement (ICE) should ensure that the facilities where non-citizens in removal proceedings are held, are located within easy reach of the detainees' counsel or near urban areas where the detainee will have access to legal service providers and pro bono counsel. Deportation issues impacting due process and important human rights

116. U.S. immigration laws should be amended to ensure that all non-citizens have access to a hearing before an impartial adjudicator, who will weigh the non-citizen's interest in remaining in the U.S. (including their rights to found a family and to a private life) against the Government's interest in deporting him or her. Detention/deportation issues impacting unaccompanied children

117. The Government should urge lawmakers to pass the Unaccompanied Alien Child Protection Act of 2007 reintroduced in March 2007.

118. Children should be removed from jail-like detention centres and placed in home-like facilities. Due care should be given to rights delineated for children in custody in the American Bar Association "Standards for the Custody, Placement, and Care; Legal Representation; and Adjudication of Unaccompanied Alien Children in the U.S."

119. Temporary Protected Status (TPS) should be amended for unaccompanied children whose parents have TPS, so they can derive status through their parents. Situation of migrant women detained in the U.S.

120. In collaboration with legal service providers and non-governmental organizations that work with detained migrant women, ICE should develop gender-specific detention standards that address the medical and mental health concerns of migrant women who have survived mental, physical, emotional or sexual violence.

121. Whenever possible, migrant women who are suffering the effects of persecution or abuse, or who are pregnant or nursing infants, should not be detained. If these vulnerable women cannot be released from ICE custody, the Department of Homeland Security should develop alternative programmes such as intense supervision or electronic monitoring, typically via ankle bracelets. These alternatives have proven effective during pilot programmes. They are not only more humane for migrants who are particularly vulnerable in the detention setting or who have family members who require their presence, but they also cost, on average, less than half the price of detention. Judicial review

122. The U.S. should ensure that the decision to detain a non-citizen is promptly assessed by an independent court.

123. The Department of Homeland Security and the Department of Justice should work together to ensure that immigration detainees are given the chance to have their custody reviewed in a hearing before an immigration judge. Both departments should revise regulations to make clear that asylum-seekers can request these custody determinations from immigration judges.

124. Congress should enact legislation to ensure that immigration judges are independent of the Department of Justice, and instead part of a truly independent court system.

125. Families with children should not be held in prison-like facilities. All efforts should be made to release families with children from detention and place them in alternative accommodation suitable for families with children.

On migrant workers

126. The Government should ensure that state and federal labour policies are monitored, and their impact on migrant workers analysed. Policymakers and the public should be continually educated on the human needs and human rights of workers, including migrant workers. In this context, the Special Rapporteur strongly recommends that the U.S. consider ratifying the International Convention on the Protection of the Rights of All Migrant Workers and Members of Their Families.

127. A human services infrastructure should be built in disaster-affected communities to comprehensively meet the needs of workers facing substandard housing and homelessness, wage theft, unsafe working conditions and health issues.

128. Effective oversight of the enforcement of applicable labour laws by state and federal agencies should be ensured.

129. Existing health and safety laws should be assiduously enforced in order to curb exploitative hiring and employment practices by contractors.

130. Improved health and safety conditions should be ensured in places that are known to employ migrant workers, compensation for workers and health care for injured migrant workers should be provided, and the significant incidences of wage theft combated.

131. Local law enforcement and federal immigration authorities must cease harassing and racially profiling migrant workers. Law enforcement should instead focus on helping to promote the rights of workers, including the rights of migrant workers.

Source: United Nations, General Assembly, A/HRC/7/12/Add.2, Human Rights Council, Seventh session, Agenda item 3, 5 March 2008, Promotion and Protection of All Human Rights, Civil, Political, Economic, Social and Cultural Rights, Including the Right to Development, Report of the Special Rapporteur on the human rights of migrants, Jorge Bustamante, Mission to the United States of America, http://www.refworld.org/docid/47d647462.html

⊱⊰⊱⊰⊱⊰⊱⊰

II. CONVENTION RELATING TO THE STATUS OF REFUGEES

This international treaty is part of International Refugee Law. It is the primary source instrument of refugee law and is usually applied along with the 1967 Protocol which follows in Primary Source Document 12. This is the treaty that defines what is a refugee and sets norms regarding asylum and what rights refugees have. Note the precise and narrow definition of refugee and the five grounds from which a refugee can flee persecution: race, religion, nationality, political opinion and membership in a particular social group. Only those who are persecuted on these five grounds are true convention refugees, and subject to a grant of asylum, at the discretion of the state. This treaty only applied to refugees after World War II in Europe. It did not apply elsewhere. Only with Primary Source Document 12 did it start to apply globally.

[Text]

Preamble

The High Contracting Parties,

Considering that the Charter of the United Nations and the Universal Declaration of Human Rights approved on 10 December 1948 by the General Assembly have affirmed the principle that human beings shall enjoy fundamental rights and freedoms without discrimination,

Considering that the United Nations has, on various occasions, manifested its profound concern for refugees and endeavoured to assure refugees the widest possible exercise of these fundamental rights and freedoms,

Considering that it is desirable to revise and consolidate previous international agreements relating to the status of refugees and to extend the scope of and the protection accorded by such instruments by means of a new agreement,

Considering that the grant of asylum may place unduly heavy burdens on certain countries, and that a satisfactory solution of a problem of which the United Nations has recognized the international- scope and nature cannot therefore be achieved without international co-operation,

Expressing the wish that all States, recognizing the social and humanitarian nature of the problem of refugees, will do everything within their power to prevent this problem from becoming a cause of tension between States, Noting that the United Nations High Commissioner for Refugees is charged with the task of supervising international conventions providing for the protection of refugees, and recognizing that the effective co-ordination of measures taken to deal with this problem will depend upon the co-operation of States with the High Commissioner,

Have agreed as follows:

Chapter I—General Provisions

Article 1. Definition of the term "refugee"

A. For the purposes of the present Convention, the term "refugee, shall apply to any person who:

(1) Has been considered a refugee under the Arrangements of 12 May 1926 and 30 June 1928 or under the Conventions of 28 October 1933 and 10 February 1938, the Protocol of 14 September 1939 or the Constitution of the International Refugee Organization;

Decisions of non-eligibility taken by the International Refugee Organization during the period of its activities shall not prevent the status of refugee being accorded to persons who fulfil the conditions of paragraph 2 of this section;

(2) As a result of events occurring before I January 1951 and owing to well-founded fear of being persecuted for reasons of race, religion, nationality, membership of a particular social group or political opinion, is outside the country of his nationality and is unable, or owing to such fear, is unwilling to avail himself of the protection of that country; or who, not having a nationality and being outside the country of his former habitual residence as a result of such events, is unable or, owing to such fear, is unwilling to return to it.

In the case of a person who has more than one nationality, the term "the country of his nationality" shall mean each of the countries of which he is a national, and a person shall not be deemed to be lacking the protection of the country of his nationality if, without any valid reason based on well-founded fear, he has not availed himself of the protection of one of the countries of which he is a national.

B. (1) For the purposes of this Convention, the words "events occurring before I January 1951" in Article 1, section A, shall be understood to mean either (a) "events occurring in Europe before I January 1951"; or (b) "events occurring in Europe or elsewhere before I January 1951"; and each Contracting State shall make a declaration at the time of signature, ratification or accession, specifying which of these meanings it applies for the purpose of its obligations under this Convention.

(2) Any Contracting State which has adopted alternative (a) may at any time extend its obligations by adopting alternative (b) by means of a notification addressed to the Secretary-General of the United Nations.

C. This Convention shall cease to apply to any person falling under the terms of section A if:

(1) He has voluntarily re-availed himself of the protection of the country of his nationality; or

(2) Having lost his nationality, he has voluntarily reacquired it; or

(3) He has acquired a new nationality, and enjoys the protection of the country of his new nationality; or (4) He has voluntarily re-established himself in the country which he left or outside which he remained owing to fear of persecution; or

(5) He can no longer, because the circumstances in connection with which he has been recognized as a refugee have ceased to exist, continue to refuse to avail himself of the protection of the country of his nationality;

Provided that this paragraph shall not apply to a refugee falling under section A (I) of this article who is able to invoke compelling reasons arising out of previous persecution for refusing to avail himself of the protection of the country of nationality;

(6) Being a person who has no nationality he is, because the circumstances in connection with which he has been recognized as a refugee have ceased to exist, able to return to the country of his former habitual residence;

Provided that this paragraph shall not apply to a refugee falling under section A (I) of this article who is able to invoke compelling reasons arising out of previous persecution for refusing to return to the country of his former habitual residence.

D. This Convention shall not apply to persons who are at present receiving from organs or agencies of the United Nations other than the United Nations High Commissioner for Refugees protection or assistance.

When such protection or assistance has ceased for any reason, without the position of such persons being definitively settled in accordance with the relevant resolutions adopted by the General Assembly of the United Nations, these persons shall ipso facto be entitled to the benefits of this Convention.

E. This Convention shall not apply to a person who is recognized by the competent authorities of the country in which he has taken residence as having the rights and obligations which are attached to the possession of the nationality of that country.

F. The provisions of this Convention shall not apply to any person with respect to whom there are serious reasons for considering that.

> (a) He has committed a crime against peace, a war crime, or a crime against humanity, as defined in the international instruments drawn up to make provision in respect of such crimes;

> (b) He has committed a serious non-political crime outside the country of refuge prior to his admission to that country as a refugee;

> (c) He has been guilty of acts contrary to the purposes and principles of the United Nations.

Article 2. General obligations
Every refugee has duties to the country in which he finds himself, which require in particular that he conform to its laws and regulations as well as to measures taken for the maintenance of public order.

Article 3. Non-discrimination
The Contracting States shall apply the provisions of this Convention to refugees without discrimination as to race, religion or country of origin.

Article 4. Religion
The Contracting States shall accord to refugees within their territories treatment at least as favourable as that accorded to their nationals with respect to freedom to practise their religion and freedom as regards the religious education of their children.

Article 5. Rights granted apart from this Convention
Nothing in this Convention shall be deemed to impair any rights and benefits granted by a Contracting State to refugees apart from this Convention.

Article 6. The term "in the same circumstances"
For the purposes of this Convention, the term "in the same circumstances" implies that any requirements (including requirements as to length and conditions of sojourn or residence) which the particular individual would have to fulfil for

the enjoyment of the right in question, if he were not a refugee, must be fulfilled by him, with the exception of requirements which by their nature a refugee is incapable of fulfilling.

Article 7. Exemption from reciprocity

Except where this Convention contains more favourable provisions, a Contracting State shall accord to refugees the same treatment as is accorded to aliens generally.

After a period of three years' residence, all refugees shall enjoy exemption from legislative reciprocity in the territory of the Contracting States.

Each Contracting State shall continue to accord to refugees the rights and benefits to which they were already entitled, in the absence of reciprocity, at the date of entry into force of this Convention for that State.

The Contracting States shall consider favourably the possibility of according to refugees, in the absence of reciprocity, rights and benefits beyond those to which they are entitled according to paragraphs 2 and 3, and to extending exemption from reciprocity to refugees who do not fulfil the conditions provided for in paragraphs 2 and 3.

5. The provisions of paragraphs 2 and 3 apply both to the rights and benefits referred to in articles 13, 18, 19, 21 and 22 of this Convention and to rights and benefits for which this Convention does not provide.

Article 8. Exemption from exceptional measures

With regard to exceptional measures which may be taken against the person, property or interests of nationals of a foreign State, the Contracting States shall not apply such measures to a refugee who is formally a national of the said State solely on account of such nationality. Contracting States which, under their legislation, are prevented from applying the general principle expressed in this article, shall, in appropriate cases, grant exemptions in favour of such refugees.

Article 9. Provisional measures

Nothing in this Convention shall prevent a Contracting State, in time of war or other grave and exceptional circumstances, from taking provisionally measures which it considers to be essential to the national security in the case of a particular person, pending a determination by the Contracting State that that person is in fact a refugee and that the continuance of such measures is necessary in his case in the interests of national security.

Article 10. Continuity of residence

1. Where a refugee has been forcibly displaced during World War II and removed to the territory of a Contracting State, and is resident there, the period of such enforced sojourn shall be considered to have been lawful residence within that territory.

2. Where a refugee has been forcibly displaced during World War II from the territory of a Contracting State and has, prior to the date of entry into force of this Convention, returned there for the purpose of taking up residence, the period of residence before and after such enforced displacement shall be regarded as one uninterrupted period for any purposes for which uninterrupted residence is required.

Article 11. Refugee seamen

In the case of refugees regularly serving as crew members on board a ship flying the flag of a Contracting State, that State shall give sympathetic consideration to their establishment on its territory and the issue of travel documents to them or their temporary admission to its territory particularly with a view to facilitating their establishment in another country.

Chapter II—Juridical Status

Article 12. Personal status

1. The personal status of a refugee shall be governed by the law of the country of his domicile or, if he has no domicile, by the law of the country of his residence.

2. Rights previously acquired by a refugee and dependent on personal status, more particularly rights attaching to marriage, shall be respected by a Contracting State, subject to compliance, if this be necessary, with the formalities required

by the law of that State, provided that the right in question is one which would have been recognized by the law of that State had he not become a refugee.

Article 13. Movable and immovable property
The Contracting States shall accord to a refugee treatment as favourable as possible and, in any event, not less favourable than that accorded to aliens generally in the same circumstances, as regards the acquisition of movable and immovable property and other rights pertaining thereto, and to leases and other contracts relating to movable and immovable property.

Article 14. Artistic rights and industrial property
In respect of the protection of industrial property, such as inventions, designs or models, trade marks, trade names, and of rights in literary, artistic and scientific works, a refugee shall be accorded in the country in which he has his habitual residence the same protection as is accorded to nationals of that country. In the territory of any other Contracting States, he shall be accorded the same protection as is accorded in that territory to nationals of the country in which he has his habitual residence.

Article 15. Right of association
As regards non-political and non-profit-making associations and trade unions the Contracting States shall accord to refugees lawfully staying in their territory the most favourable treatment accorded to nationals of a foreign country, in the same circumstances.

Article 16. Access to courts
1. A refugee shall have free access to the courts of law on the territory of all Contracting States.

2. A refugee shall enjoy in the Contracting State in which he has his habitual residence the same treatment as a national in matters pertaining to access to the courts, including legal assistance and exemption from cautio judicatum solvi.

3. A refugee shall be accorded in the matters referred to in paragraph 2 in countries other than that in which he has his habitual residence the treatment granted to a national of the country of his habitual residence.

Chapter III—Gainful Employment

Article 17. Wage-earning employment
The Contracting States shall accord to refugees lawfully staying in their territory the most favourable treatment accorded to nationals of a foreign country in the same circumstances, as regards the right to engage in wage-earning employment.

In any case, restrictive measures imposed on aliens or the employment of aliens for the protection of the national labour market shall not be applied to a refugee who was already exempt from them at the date of entry into force of this Convention for the Contracting State concerned, or who fulfils one of the following conditions:

> (a) He has completed three years' residence in the country;

> (b) He has a spouse possessing the nationality of the country of residence. A refugee may not invoke the benefit of this provision if he has abandoned his spouse;

> (c) He has one or more children possessing the nationality of the country of residence.

3. The Contracting States shall give sympathetic consideration to assimilating the rights of all refugees with regard to wage-earning employment to those of nationals, and in particular of those refugees who have entered their territory pursuant to programmes of labour recruitment or under immigration schemes.

Article 18. Self-employment
The Contracting States shall accord to a refugee lawfully in their territory treatment as favourable as possible and, in any event, not less favourable than that accorded to aliens generally in the same circumstances, as regards the right to en-

gage on his own account in agriculture, industry, handicrafts and commerce and to establish commercial and industrial companies.

Article 19. Liberal professions

1. Each Contracting State shall accord to refugees lawfully staying in their territory who hold diplomas recognized by the competent authorities of that State, and who are desirous of practising a liberal profession, treatment as favourable as possible and, in any event, not less favourable than that accorded to aliens generally in the same circumstances.

2. The Contracting States shall use their best endeavours consistently with their laws and constitutions to secure the settlement of such refugees in the territories, other than the metropolitan territory, for whose international relations they are responsible.

Chapter IV—Welfare

Article 20. Rationing

Where a rationing system exists, which applies to the population at large and regulates the general distribution of products in short supply, refugees shall be accorded the same treatment as nationals.

Article 21. Housing

As regards housing, the Contracting States, in so far as the matter is regulated by laws or regulations or is subject to the control of public authorities, shall accord to refugees lawfully staying in their territory treatment as favourable as possible and, in any event, not less favourable than that accorded to aliens generally in the same circumstances.

Article 22. Public education

1. The Contracting States shall accord to refugees the same treatment as is accorded to nationals with respect to elementary education.

2. The Contracting States shall accord to refugees treatment as favourable as possible, and, in any event, not less favourable than that accorded to aliens generally in the same circumstances, with respect to education other than elementary education and, in particular, as regards access to studies, the recognition of foreign school certificates, diplomas and degrees, the remission of fees and charges and the award of scholarships.

Article 23. Public relief

The Contracting States shall accord to refugees lawfully staying in their territory the same treatment with respect to public relief and assistance as is accorded to their nationals.

Article 24. Labour legislation and social security

1. The Contracting States shall accord to refugees lawfully staying in their territory the same treatment as is accorded to nationals in respect of the following matters;

   (a) In so far as such matters are governed by laws or regulations or are subject to the control of administrative authorities: remuneration, including family allowances where these form part of remuneration, hours of work, overtime arrangements, holidays with pay, restrictions on home work, minimum age of employment, apprenticeship and training, women's work and the work of young persons, and the enjoyment of the benefits of collective bargaining;

   (b) Social security (legal provisions in respect of employment injury, occupational diseases, maternity, sickness, disability, old age, death, unemployment, family responsibilities and any other contingency which, according to national laws or regulations, is covered by a social security scheme), subject to the following limitations:

      (i) There may be appropriate arrangements for the maintenance of acquired rights and rights in course of acquisition;

(ii) National laws or regulations of the country of residence may prescribe special arrangements concerning benefits or portions of benefits which are payable wholly out of public funds, and concerning allowances paid to persons who do not fulfil the contribution conditions prescribed for the award of a normal pension.

2. The right to compensation for the death of a refugee resulting from employment injury or from occupational disease shall not be affected by the fact that the residence of the beneficiary is outside the territory of the Contracting State.

3. The Contracting States shall extend to refugees the benefits of agreements concluded between them, or which may be concluded between them in the future, concerning the maintenance of acquired rights and rights in the process of acquisition in regard to social security, subject only to the conditions which apply to nationals of the States signatory to the agreements in question.

4. The Contracting States will give sympathetic consideration to extending to refugees so far as possible the benefits of similar agreements which may at any time be in force between such Contracting States and non-contracting States.

Chapter V—Administrative Measures

Article 25. Administrative assistance
1. When the exercise of a right by a refugee would normally require the assistance of authorities of a foreign country to whom he cannot have recourse, the Contracting States in whose territory he is residing shall arrange that such assistance be afforded to him by their own authorities or by an international authority.

2. The authority or authorities mentioned in paragraph I shall deliver or cause to be delivered under their supervision to refugees such documents or certifications as would normally be delivered to aliens by or through their national authorities.

3. Documents or certifications so delivered shall stand in the stead of the official instruments delivered to aliens by or through their national authorities, and shall be given credence in the absence of proof to the contrary.

4. Subject to such exceptional treatment as may be granted to indigent persons, fees may be charged for the services mentioned herein, but such fees shall be moderate and commensurate with those charged to nationals for similar services.

5. The provisions of this article shall be without prejudice to articles 27 and 28.

Article 26. Freedom of movement
Each Contracting State shall accord to refugees lawfully in its territory the right to choose their place of residence and to move freely within its territory subject to any regulations applicable to aliens generally in the same circumstances.

Article 27. Identity papers
The Contracting States shall issue identity papers to any refugee in their territory who does not possess a valid travel document.

Article 28. Travel documents
1. The Contracting States shall issue to refugees lawfully staying in their territory travel documents for the purpose of travel outside their territory, unless compelling reasons of national security or public order otherwise require, and the provisions of the Schedule to this Convention shall apply with respect to such documents. The Contracting States may issue such a travel document to any other refugee in their territory; they shall in particular give sympathetic consideration to the issue of such a travel document to refugees in their territory who are unable to obtain a travel document from the country of their lawful residence.

2. Travel documents issued to refugees under previous international agreements by Parties thereto shall be recognized and treated by the Contracting States in the same way as if they had been issued pursuant to this article.

Article 29. Fiscal charges

1. The Contracting States shall not impose upon refugees duties, charges or taxes, of any description whatsoever, other or higher than those which are or may be levied on their nationals in similar situations.

2. Nothing in the above paragraph shall prevent the application to refugees of the laws and regulations concerning charges in respect of the issue to aliens of administrative documents including identity papers.

Article 30. Transfer of assets

1. A Contracting State shall, in conformity with its laws and regulations, permit refugees to transfer assets which they have brought into its territory, to another country where they have been admitted for the purposes of resettlement.

2. A Contracting State shall give sympathetic consideration to the application of refugees for permission to transfer assets wherever they may be and which are necessary for their resettlement in another country to which they have been admitted.

Article 31. Refugees unlawfully in the country of refuge

1. The Contracting States shall not impose penalties, on account of their illegal entry or presence, on refugees who, coming directly from a territory where their life or freedom was threatened in the sense of Article 1, enter or are present in their territory without authorization, provided they present themselves without delay to the authorities and show good cause for their illegal entry or presence.

2. The Contracting States shall not apply to the movements of such refugees restrictions other than those which are necessary and such restrictions shall only be applied until their status in the country is regularized or they obtain admission into another country. The Contracting States shall allow such refugees a reasonable period and all the necessary facilities to obtain admission into another country.

Article 32. Expulsion

1. The Contracting States shall not expel a refugee lawfully in their territory save on grounds of national security or public order.

2. The expulsion of such a refugee shall be only in pursuance of a decision reached in accordance with due process of law. Except where compelling reasons of national security otherwise require, the refugee shall be allowed to submit evidence to clear himself, and to appeal to and be represented for the purpose before competent authority or a person or persons specially designated by the competent authority.

3. The Contracting States shall allow such a refugee a reasonable period within which to seek legal admission into another country. The Contracting States reserve the right to apply during that period such internal measures as they may deem necessary.

Article 33. Prohibition of expulsion or return ("refoulement")

1. No Contracting State shall expel or return ("refouler") a refugee in any manner whatsoever to the frontiers of territories where his life or freedom would be threatened on account of his race, religion, nationality, membership of a particular social group or political opinion.

2. The benefit of the present provision may not, however, be claimed by a refugee whom there are reasonable grounds for regarding as a danger to the security of the country in which he is, or who, having been convicted by a final judgement of a particularly serious crime, constitutes a danger to the community of that country.

Article 34. Naturalization

The Contracting States shall as far as possible facilitate the assimilation and naturalization of refugees. They shall in particular make every effort to expedite naturalization proceedings and to reduce as far as possible the charges and costs of such proceedings.

Chapter VI—Executory and Transitory Provisions

Article 35. Co-operation of the national authorities with the United Nations
1. The Contracting States undertake to co-operate with the Office of the United Nations High Commissioner for Refugees, or any other agency of the United Nations which may succeed it, in the exercise of its functions, and shall in particular facilitate its duty of supervising the application of the provisions of this Convention.

2. In order to enable the Office of the High Commissioner or any other agency of the United Nations which may succeed it, to make reports to the competent organs of the United Nations, the Contracting States undertake to provide them in the appropriate form with information and statistical data requested concerning:

    (a) The condition of refugees,

    (b) The implementation of this Convention, and

    (c) Laws, regulations and decrees which are, or may hereafter be, in force relating to refugees.

Article 36. Information on national legislation
The Contracting States shall communicate to the Secretary-General of the United Nations the laws and regulations which they may adopt to ensure the application of this Convention.

Article 37. Relation to previous conventions
Without prejudice to Article 28, paragraph 2, of this Convention, this Convention replaces, as between Parties to it, the Arrangements of 5 July 1922, 31 May 1924, 12 May 1926, 30 June 1928 and 30 July 1935, the Conventions of 28 October 1933 and 10 February 1938, the Protocol of 14 September 1939 and the Agreement of 15 October 1946.

Chapter VII—Final Clauses Article

38. Settlement of disputes
Any dispute between Parties to this Convention relating to its interpretation or application, which cannot be settled by other means, shall be referred to the International Court of Justice at the request of any one of the parties to the dispute.

...

Source: The UN Refugee Agency, UNHCR, Convention and Protocol Relating to the Status of Refugees, Text of the 1951 Convention; Text of the 1967 Protocol; Resolution 2198 (XXI) adopted by the UN General Assembly, http://www.unhcr.org/en-us/protection/basic/3b66c2aa10/convention-protocol-relating-status-refugees.html

12. PROTOCOL RELATING TO THE STATUS OF REFUGEES

This 1967 instrument is called a protocol, which is a treaty which modifies or amends a base treaty. This Protocol amends and modifies the 1951 Convention Relating to the Status of Refugees. It expands the geographical scope of the 1951 Refugee Convention to include anyone anywhere who fulfills the criteria for refugee status in a country which becomes a party to this treaty.

[Text]

The Protocol was taken note of with approval by the Economic and Social Council in resolution 1186 (XLI) of 18 November 1966 and was taken note of by the General Assembly in resolution 2198 (XXI) of 16 December 1966. In the same resolution the General Assembly requested the Secretary-General to transmit the text of the Protocol to the States mentioned in Article 5 thereof, with a view to enabling them to accede to the Protocol

ENTRY INTO FORCE: 4 October 1967, in accordance with Article 8

The States Parties to the present Protocol,

Considering that the Convention relating to the Status of Refugees done at Geneva on 28 July 1951 (hereinafter referred to as the Convention) covers only those persons who have become refugees as a result of events occurring before I January 1951,

Considering that new refugee situations have arisen since the Convention was adopted and that the refugees concerned may therefore not fall within the scope of the Convention,

Considering that it is desirable that equal status should be enjoyed by all refugees covered by the definition in the Convention irrespective of the dateline I January 1951,

Have agreed as follows:

Article 1. General provision
The States Parties to the present Protocol undertake to apply articles 2 to 34 inclusive of the Convention to refugees as hereinafter defined.

2. For the purpose of the present Protocol, the term "refugee" shall, except as regards the application of paragraph 3 of this article, mean any person within the definition of article I of the Convention as if the words "As a result of events occurring before 1 January 1951 and ..." and the words "... as a result of such events," in Article 1 A (2) were omitted.

3. The present Protocol shall be applied by the States Parties hereto without any geographic limitation, save that existing declarations made by States already Parties to the Convention in accordance with article I B (I) (a) of the Convention, shall, unless extended under article I B (2) thereof, apply also under the present Protocol.

Article 2. Co-operation of the national authorities with the United Nations
1. The States Parties to the present Protocol undertake to co-operate with the Office of the United Nations High Commissioner for Refugees, or any other agency of the United Nations which may succeed it, in the exercise of its functions, and shall in particular facilitate its duty of supervising the application of the provisions of the present Protocol.

2. In order to enable the Office of the High Commissioner or any other agency of the United Nations which may succeed it, to make reports to the competent organs of the United Nations, the States Parties to the present Protocol undertake to provide them with the information and statistical data requested, in the appropriate form, concerning:

  (a) The condition of refugees;

  (b) The implementation of the present Protocol;

  (c) Laws, regulations and decrees which are, or may hereafter be, in force relating to refugees.

Article 3. Information on national legislation
The States Parties to the present Protocol shall communicate to the Secretary-General of the United Nations the laws and regulations which they may adopt to ensure the application of the present Protocol.

Article 4. Settlement of disputes
Any dispute between States Parties to the present Protocol which relates to its interpretation or application and which cannot be settled by other means shall be referred to the International Court of Justice at the request of any one of the parties to the dispute.

Article 5. Accession
The present Protocol shall be open for accession on behalf of all States Parties to the Convention and of any other State Member of the United Nations or member of any of the specialized agencies or to which an invitation to accede may have been addressed by the General Assembly of the United Nations. Accession shall be effected by the deposit of an instrument of accession with the Secretary-General of the United Nations.

Article 6. Federal clause

In the case of a Federal or non-unitary State, the following provisions shall apply:

(a) With respect to those articles of the Convention to be applied in accordance with article I, paragraph 1, of the present Protocol that come within the legislative jurisdiction of the federal legislative authority, the obligations of the Federal Government shall to this extent be the same as those of States Parties which are not Federal States;

(b) With respect to those articles of the Convention to be applied in accordance with article I, paragraph 1, of the present Protocol that come within the legislative jurisdiction of constituent States, provinces or cantons which are not, under the constitutional system of the Federation, bound to take legislative action, the Federal Government shall bring such articles with a favourable recommendation to the notice of the appropriate authorities of States, provinces or cantons at the earliest possible moment;

(c) A Federal State Party to the present Protocol shall, at the request of any other State Party hereto transmitted through the Secretary-General of the United Nations, supply a statement of the law and practice of the Federation and its constituent units in regards to any particular provision of the Convention to be applied in accordance with article I, paragraph 1, of the present Protocol, showing the extent to which effect has been given to that provision by legislative or other action.

Article 7. Reservations and declarations

At the time of accession, any State may make reservations in respect of article IV of the present Protocol and in respect of the application in accordance with article I of the present Protocol of any provisions of the Convention other than those contained in articles 1, 3, 4, 16(1) and 33 thereof, provided that in the case of a State Party to the Convention reservations made under this article shall not extend to refugees in respect of whom the Convention applies.

Source: The U.N. Refugee Agency, UNHCR, Convention and Protocol Relating to the Status of Refugees, Text of the 1951 Convention; Text of the 1967 Protocol; Resolution 2198 (XXI) adopted by the UN General Assembly, http://www.unhcr.org/en-us/protection/basic/3b66c2aa10/convention-protocol-relating-status-refugees.html

13. INTERNATIONAL CONVENTION ON THE PROTECTION OF THE RIGHTS OF ALL MIGRANT WORKERS AND THEIR FAMILIES

This relatively new human rights instrument seeks to protect the migrant workers rights from exploitation and discrimination and mistreatment. The U.S. has not signed or ratified this treaty because of the sensitivity of the subject in America. Migrant workers and their families, even the children, are historically an exploited and vulnerable group of persons. This treaty seeks to recognize and set a supervision framework for their protection.

{Excerpt}

[Text]

Adopted by General Assembly resolution 45/158 of 18 December 1990

Preamble

The States Parties to the present Convention,

Taking into account the principles embodied in the basic instruments of the United Nations concerning human rights, in particular the Universal Declaration of Human Rights, the International Covenant on Economic, Social and Cultural Rights, the International Covenant on Civil and Political Rights, the International Convention on the Elimination of All Forms of Racial Discrimination, the Convention on the Elimination of All Forms of Discrimination against Women and the Convention on the Rights of the Child, *Taking into account* also the principles and standards set forth in the relevant instruments elaborated within the framework of the International Labour Organisation, especially the Convention concerning Migration for Employment (No. 97), the Convention concerning Migrations in Abusive Conditions and the Promotion of Equality of Opportunity and Treatment of Migrant Workers (No.143), the Recommendation concerning Migration for Employment (No. 86), the Recommendation concerning Migrant Workers (No.151), the Convention concerning Forced or Compulsory Labour (No. 29) and the Convention concerning Abolition of Forced Labour (No. 105),

Reaffirming the importance of the principles contained in the Convention against Discrimination in Education of the United Nations Educational, Scientific and Cultural Organization,

Recalling the Convention against Torture and Other Cruel, Inhuman or Degrading Treatment or Punishment, the Declaration of the Fourth United Nations Congress on the Prevention of Crime and the Treatment of Offenders, the Code of Conduct for Law Enforcement Officials, and the Slavery Conventions,

Recalling that one of the objectives of the International Labour Organisation, as stated in its Constitution, is the protection of the interests of workers when employed in countries other than their own, and bearing in mind the expertise and experience of that organization in matters related to migrant workers and members of their families,

Recognizing the importance of the work done in connection with migrant workers and members of their families in various organs of the United Nations, in particular in the Commission on Human Rights and the Commission for Social Development, and in the Food and Agriculture Organization of the United Nations, the United Nations Educational, Scientific and Cultural Organization and the World Health Organization, as well as in other international organizations,

Recognizing also the progress made by certain States on a regional or bilateral basis towards the protection of the rights of migrant workers and members of their families, as well as the importance and usefulness of bilateral and multilateral agreements in this field,

Realizing the importance and extent of the migration phenomenon, which involves millions of people and affects a large number of States in the international community,

Aware of the impact of the flows of migrant workers on States and people concerned, and desiring to establish norms which may contribute to the harmonization of the attitudes of States through the acceptance of basic principles concerning the treatment of migrant workers and members of their families,

Considering the situation of vulnerability in which migrant workers and members of their families frequently find themselves owing, among other things, to their absence from their State of origin and to the difficulties they may encounter arising from their presence in the State of employment,

Convinced that the rights of migrant workers and members of their families have not been sufficiently recognized everywhere and therefore require appropriate international protection,

Taking into account the fact that migration is often the cause of serious problems for the members of the families of migrant workers as well as for the workers themselves, in particular because of the scattering of the family,

Bearing in mind that the human problems involved in migration are even more serious in the case of irregular migration and convinced therefore that appropriate action should be encouraged in order to prevent and eliminate clandestine movements and trafficking in migrant workers, while at the same time assuring the protection of their fundamental human rights,

Considering that workers who are non-documented or in an irregular situation are frequently employed under less favourable conditions of work than other workers and that certain employers find this an inducement to seek such labour in order to reap the benefits of unfair competition,

Considering also that recourse to the employment of migrant workers who are in an irregular situation will be discouraged if the fundamental human rights of all migrant workers are more widely recognized and, moreover, that granting certain additional rights to migrant workers and members of their families in a regular situation will encourage all migrants and employers to respect and comply with the laws and procedures established by the States concerned,

Convinced, therefore, of the need to bring about the international protection of the rights of all migrant workers and members of their families, reaffirming and establishing basic norms in a comprehensive convention which could be applied universally,

Have agreed as follows:

Part I: Scope and Definitions

Article 1
1. The present Convention is applicable, except as otherwise provided hereafter, to all migrant workers and members of their families without distinction of any kind such as sex, race, colour, language, religion or conviction, political or other opinion, national, ethnic or social origin, nationality, age, economic position, property, marital status, birth or other status.

2. The present Convention shall apply during the entire migration process of migrant workers and members of their families, which comprises preparation for migration, departure, transit and the entire period of stay and remunerated activity in the State of employment as well as return to the State of origin or the State of habitual residence.

Article 2
For the purposes of the present Convention:

1. The term "migrant worker" refers to a person who is to be engaged, is engaged or has been engaged in a remunerated activity in a State of which he or she is not a national.

(a) The term "frontier worker" refers to a migrant worker who retains his or her habitual residence in a neighbouring State to which he or she normally returns every day or at least once a week;

(b) The term "seasonal worker" refers to a migrant worker whose work by its character is dependent on seasonal conditions and is performed only during part of the year;

(c) The term "seafarer," which includes a fisherman, refers to a migrant worker employed on board a vessel registered in a State of which he or she is not a national;

(d) The term "worker on an offshore installation" refers to a migrant worker employed on an offshore installation that is under the jurisdiction of a State of which he or she is not a national;

(e) The term "itinerant worker" refers to a migrant worker who, having his or her habitual residence in one State, has to travel to another State or States for short periods, owing to the nature of his or her occupation;

(f) The term "project-tied worker" refers to a migrant worker admitted to a State of employment for a defined period to work solely on a specific project being carried out in that State by his or her employer; (g) The term "specified-employment worker" refers to a migrant worker:

(i) Who has been sent by his or her employer for a restricted and defined period of time to a State of employment to undertake a specific assignment or duty; or

(ii) Who engages for a restricted and defined period of time in work that requires professional, commercial, technical or other highly specialized skill; or

(iii) Who, upon the request of his or her employer in the State of employment, engages for a restricted and defined period of time in work whose nature is transitory or brief; and who is required to depart from the State of employment either at the expiration of his or her authorized period of stay, or earlier if he or she no longer undertakes that specific assignment or duty or engages in that work;

(h) The term "self-employed worker" refers to a migrant worker who is engaged in a remunerated activity otherwise than under a contract of employment and who earns his or her living through this activity normally working alone or together with members of his or her family, and to any other migrant worker recognized as self-employed by applicable legislation of the State of employment or bilateral or multilateral agreements.

Article 3
The present Convention shall not apply to:

(a) Persons sent or employed by international organizations and agencies or persons sent or employed by a State outside its territory to perform official functions, whose admission and status are regulated by general international law or by specific international agreements or conventions;

(b) Persons sent or employed by a State or on its behalf outside its territory who participate in development programmes and other co-operation programmes, whose admission and status are regulated by agreement with the State of employment and who, in accordance with that agreement, are not considered migrant workers;

(c) Persons taking up residence in a State different from their State of origin as investors;

(d) Refugees and stateless persons, unless such application is provided for in the relevant national legislation of, or international instruments in force for, the State Party concerned;

(e) Students and trainees;

(f) Seafarers and workers on an offshore installation who have not been admitted to take up residence and engage in a remunerated activity in the State of employment.

Article 4
For the purposes of the present Convention the term "members of the family" refers to persons married to migrant workers or having with them a relationship that, according to applicable law, produces effects equivalent to marriage, as well as their dependent children and other dependent persons who are recognized as members of the family by applicable legislation or applicable bilateral or multilateral agreements between the States concerned.

Article 5
For the purposes of the present Convention, migrant workers and members of their families:

(a) Are considered as documented or in a regular situation if they are authorized to enter, to stay and to engage in a remunerated activity in the State of employment pursuant to the law of that State and to international agreements to which that State is a party;

(b) Are considered as non-documented or in an irregular situation if they do not comply with the conditions provided for in subparagraph (a) of the present article.

Article 6
For the purposes of the present Convention:

(a) The term "State of origin" means the State of which the person concerned is a national;

(b) The term "State of employment" means a State where the migrant worker is to be engaged, is engaged or has been engaged in a remunerated activity, as the case may be;

(c) The term "State of transit,' means any State through which the person concerned passes on any journey to the State of employment or from the State of employment to the State of origin or the State of habitual residence.

Part II: Non-discrimination with Respect to Rights

Article 7
States Parties undertake, in accordance with the international instruments concerning human rights, to respect and to ensure to all migrant workers and members of their families within their territory or subject to their jurisdiction the

rights provided for in the present Convention without distinction of any kind such as to sex, race, colour, language, religion or conviction, political or other opinion, national, ethnic or social origin, nationality, age, economic position, property, marital status, birth or other status.

Part III: Human Rights of All Migrant Workers and Members of their Families

Article 8

1. Migrant workers and members of their families shall be free to leave any State, including their State of origin. This right shall not be subject to any restrictions except those that are provided by law, are necessary to protect national security, public order (ordre public), public health or morals or the rights and freedoms of others and are consistent with the other rights recognized in the present part of the Convention.

2. Migrant workers and members of their families shall have the right at any time to enter and remain in their State of origin.

Article 9

The right to life of migrant workers and members of their families shall be protected by law.

Article 10

No migrant worker or member of his or her family shall be subjected to torture or to cruel, inhuman or degrading treatment or punishment.

Article 11

1. No migrant worker or member of his or her family shall be held in slavery or servitude.

2. No migrant worker or member of his or her family shall be required to perform forced or compulsory labour.

3. Paragraph 2 of the present article shall not be held to preclude, in States where imprisonment with hard labour may be imposed as a punishment for a crime, the performance of hard labour in pursuance of a sentence to such punishment by a competent court.

4. For the purpose of the present article the term "forced or compulsory labour" shall not include:

(a) Any work or service not referred to in paragraph 3 of the present article normally required of a person who is under detention in consequence of a lawful order of a court or of a person during conditional release from such detention;

(b) Any service exacted in cases of emergency or calamity threatening the life or well-being of the community;

(c) Any work or service that forms part of normal civil obligations so far as it is imposed also on citizens of the State concerned.

Article 12

1. Migrant workers and members of their families shall have the right to freedom of thought, conscience and religion. This right shall include freedom to have or to adopt a religion or belief of their choice and freedom either individually or in community with others and in public or private to manifest their religion or belief in worship, observance, practice and teaching.

2. Migrant workers and members of their families shall not be subject to coercion that would impair their freedom to have or to adopt a religion or belief of their choice.

3. Freedom to manifest one's religion or belief may be subject only to such limitations as are prescribed by law and are necessary to protect public safety, order, health or morals or the fundamental rights and freedoms of others.

4. States Parties to the present Convention undertake to have respect for the liberty of parents, at least one of whom is a migrant worker, and, when applicable, legal guardians to ensure the religious and moral education of their children in conformity with their own convictions.

Article 13

1. Migrant workers and members of their families shall have the right to hold opinions without interference.

2. Migrant workers and members of their families shall have the right to freedom of expression; this right shall include freedom to seek, receive and impart information and ideas of all kinds, regardless of frontiers, either orally, in writing or in print, in the form of art or through any other media of their choice.

3. The exercise of the right provided for in paragraph 2 of the present article carries with it special duties and responsibilities. It may therefore be subject to certain restrictions, but these shall only be such as are provided by law and are necessary:

(a) For respect of the rights or reputation of others;

(b) For the protection of the national security of the States concerned or of public order (ordre public) or of public health or morals;

(c) For the purpose of preventing any propaganda for war;

(d) For the purpose of preventing any advocacy of national, racial or religious hatred that constitutes incitement to discrimination, hostility or violence.

Article 14

No migrant worker or member of his or her family shall be subjected to arbitrary or unlawful interference with his or her privacy, family, correspondence or other communications, or to unlawful attacks on his or her honour and reputation. Each migrant worker and member of his or her family shall have the right to the protection of the law against such interference or attacks.

Article 15

No migrant worker or member of his or her family shall be arbitrarily deprived of property, whether owned individually or in association with others. Where, under the legislation in force in the State of employment, the assets of a migrant worker or a member of his or her family are expropriated in whole or in part, the person concerned shall have the right to fair and adequate compensation.

Article 16

1. Migrant workers and members of their families shall have the right to liberty and security of person.

2. Migrant workers and members of their families shall be entitled to effective protection by the State against violence, physical injury, threats and intimidation, whether by public officials or by private individuals, groups or institutions.

3. Any verification by law enforcement officials of the identity of migrant workers or members of their families shall be carried out in accordance with procedure established by law.

4. Migrant workers and members of their families shall not be subjected individually or collectively to arbitrary arrest or detention; they shall not be deprived of their liberty except on such grounds and in accordance with such procedures as are established by law.

5. Migrant workers and members of their families who are arrested shall be informed at the time of arrest as far as possible in a language they understand of the reasons for their arrest and they shall be promptly informed in a language they understand of any charges against them.

6. Migrant workers and members of their families who are arrested or detained on a criminal charge shall be brought promptly before a judge or other officer authorized by law to exercise judicial power and shall be entitled to trial within a reasonable time or to release. It shall not be the general rule that while awaiting trial they shall be detained in custody, but release may be subject to guarantees to appear for trial, at any other stage of the judicial proceedings and, should the occasion arise, for the execution of the judgement.

7. When a migrant worker or a member of his or her family is arrested or committed to prison or custody pending trial or is detained in any other manner:

(a) The consular or diplomatic authorities of his or her State of origin or of a State representing the interests of that State shall, if he or she so requests, be informed without delay of his or her arrest or detention and of the reasons therefor;

(b) The person concerned shall have the right to communicate with the said authorities. Any communication by the person concerned to the said authorities shall be forwarded without delay, and he or she shall also have the right to receive communications sent by the said authorities without delay;

(c) The person concerned shall be informed without delay of this right and of rights deriving from relevant treaties, if any, applicable between the States concerned, to correspond and to meet with representatives of the said authorities and to make arrangements with them for his or her legal representation.

8. Migrant workers and members of their families who are deprived of their liberty by arrest or detention shall be entitled to take proceedings before a court, in order that that court may decide without delay on the lawfulness of their detention and order their release if the detention is not lawful. When they attend such proceedings, they shall have the assistance, if necessary without cost to them, of an interpreter, if they cannot understand or speak the language used.

9. Migrant workers and members of their families who have been victims of unlawful arrest or detention shall have an enforceable right to compensation.

Article 17
1. Migrant workers and members of their families who are deprived of their liberty shall be treated with humanity and with respect for the inherent dignity of the human person and for their cultural identity. 2. Accused migrant workers and members of their families shall, save in exceptional circumstances, be separated from convicted persons and shall be subject to separate treatment appropriate to their status as unconvicted persons. Accused juvenile persons shall be separated from adults and brought as speedily as possible for adjudication.

3. Any migrant worker or member of his or her family who is detained in a State of transit or in a State of employment for violation of provisions relating to migration shall be held, in so far as practicable, separately from convicted persons or persons detained pending trial.

4. During any period of imprisonment in pursuance of a sentence imposed by a court of law, the essential aim of the treatment of a migrant worker or a member of his or her family shall be his or her reformation and social rehabilitation. Juvenile offenders shall be separated from adults and be accorded treatment appropriate to their age and legal status.

5. During detention or imprisonment, migrant workers and members of their families shall enjoy the same rights as nationals to visits by members of their families.

6. Whenever a migrant worker is deprived of his or her liberty, the competent authorities of the State concerned shall pay attention to the problems that may be posed for members of his or her family, in particular for spouses and minor children.

7. Migrant workers and members of their families who are subjected to any form of detention or imprisonment in accordance with the law in force in the State of employment or in the State of transit shall enjoy the same rights as nationals of those States who are in the same situation.

8. If a migrant worker or a member of his or her family is detained for the purpose of verifying any infraction of provisions related to migration, he or she shall not bear any costs arising therefrom.

Article 18
1. Migrant workers and members of their families shall have the right to equality with nationals of the State concerned before the courts and tribunals. In the determination of any criminal charge against them or of their rights and obliga-

tions in a suit of law, they shall be entitled to a fair and public hearing by a competent, independent and impartial tribunal established by law.

2. Migrant workers and members of their families who are charged with a criminal offence shall have the right to be presumed innocent until proven guilty according to law.

3. In the determination of any criminal charge against them, migrant workers and members of their families shall be entitled to the following minimum guarantees:

(a) To be informed promptly and in detail in a language they understand of the nature and cause of the charge against them;

(b) To have adequate time and facilities for the preparation of their defence and to communicate with counsel of their own choosing;

(c) To be tried without undue delay;

(d) To be tried in their presence and to defend themselves in person or through legal assistance of their own choosing; to be informed, if they do not have legal assistance, of this right; and to have legal assistance assigned to them, in any case where the interests of justice so require and without payment by them in any such case if they do not have sufficient means to pay;

(e) To examine or have examined the witnesses against them and to obtain the attendance and examination of witnesses on their behalf under the same conditions as witnesses against them;

(f) To have the free assistance of an interpreter if they cannot understand or speak the language used in court;

(g) Not to be compelled to testify against themselves or to confess guilt.

4. In the case of juvenile persons, the procedure shall be such as will take account of their age and the desirability of promoting their rehabilitation.

5. Migrant workers and members of their families convicted of a crime shall have the right to their conviction and sentence being reviewed by a higher tribunal according to law.

6. When a migrant worker or a member of his or her family has, by a final decision, been convicted of a criminal offence and when subsequently his or her conviction has been reversed or he or she has been pardoned on the ground that a new or newly discovered fact shows conclusively that there has been a miscarriage of justice, the person who has suffered punishment as a result of such conviction shall be compensated according to law, unless it is proved that the non-disclosure of the unknown fact in time is wholly or partly attributable to that person.

7. No migrant worker or member of his or her family shall be liable to be tried or punished again for an offence for which he or she has already been finally convicted or acquitted in accordance with the law and penal procedure of the State concerned.

Article 19

1. No migrant worker or member of his or her family shall be held guilty of any criminal offence on account of any act or omission that did not constitute a criminal offence under national or international law at the time when the criminal offence was committed, nor shall a heavier penalty be imposed than the one that was applicable at the time when it was committed. If, subsequent to the commission of the offence, provision is made by law for the imposition of a lighter penalty, he or she shall benefit thereby. 2. Humanitarian considerations related to the status of a migrant worker, in particular with respect to his or her right of residence or work, should be taken into account in imposing a sentence for a criminal offence committed by a migrant worker or a member of his or her family.

Article 20

1. No migrant worker or member of his or her family shall be imprisoned merely on the ground of failure to fulfill a contractual obligation.

2. No migrant worker or member of his or her family shall be deprived of his or her authorization of residence or work permit or expelled merely on the ground of failure to fulfill an obligation arising out of a work contract unless fulfillment of that obligation constitutes a condition for such authorization or permit.

Article 21

It shall be unlawful for anyone, other than a public official duly authorized by law, to confiscate, destroy or attempt to destroy identity documents, documents authorizing entry to or stay, residence or establishment in the national territory or work permits. No authorized confiscation of such documents shall take place without delivery of a detailed receipt. In no case shall it be permitted to destroy the passport or equivalent document of a migrant worker or a member of his or her family.

Article 22

1. Migrant workers and members of their families shall not be subject to measures of collective expulsion. Each case of expulsion shall be examined and decided individually.

2. Migrant workers and members of their families may be expelled from the territory of a State Party only in pursuance of a decision taken by the competent authority in accordance with law.

3. The decision shall be communicated to them in a language they understand. Upon their request where not otherwise mandatory, the decision shall be communicated to them in writing and, save in exceptional circumstances on account of national security, the reasons for the decision likewise stated. The persons concerned shall be informed of these rights before or at the latest at the time the decision is rendered.

4. Except where a final decision is pronounced by a judicial authority, the person concerned shall have the right to submit the reason he or she should not be expelled and to have his or her case reviewed by the competent authority, unless compelling reasons of national security require otherwise. Pending such review, the person concerned shall have the right to seek a stay of the decision of expulsion.

5. If a decision of expulsion that has already been executed is subsequently annulled, the person concerned shall have the right to seek compensation according to law and the earlier decision shall not be used to prevent him or her from re-entering the State concerned.

6. In case of expulsion, the person concerned shall have a reasonable opportunity before or after departure to settle any claims for wages and other entitlements due to him or her and any pending liabilities. 7. Without prejudice to the execution of a decision of expulsion, a migrant worker or a member of his or her family who is subject to such a decision may seek entry into a State other than his or her State of origin.

8. In case of expulsion of a migrant worker or a member of his or her family the costs of expulsion shall not be borne by him or her. The person concerned may be required to pay his or her own travel costs.

9. Expulsion from the State of employment shall not in itself prejudice any rights of a migrant worker or a member of his or her family acquired in accordance with the law of that State, including the right to receive wages and other entitlements due to him or her.

Article 23

Migrant workers and members of their families shall have the right to have recourse to the protection and assistance of the consular or diplomatic authorities of their State of origin or of a State representing the interests of that State whenever the rights recognized in the present Convention are impaired. In particular, in case of expulsion, the person concerned shall be informed of this right without delay and the authorities of the expelling State shall facilitate the exercise of such right.

Article 24

Every migrant worker and every member of his or her family shall have the right to recognition everywhere as a person before the law.

Article 25

1. Migrant workers shall enjoy treatment not less favourable than that which applies to nationals of the State of employment in respect of remuneration and:

(a) Other conditions of work, that is to say, overtime, hours of work, weekly rest, holidays with pay, safety, health, termination of the employment relationship and any other conditions of work which, according to national law and practice, are covered by these terms;

(b) Other terms of employment, that is to say, minimum age of employment, restriction on work and any other matters which, according to national law and practice, are considered a term of employment. 2. It shall not be lawful to derogate in private contracts of employment from the principle of equality of treatment referred to in paragraph 1 of the present article.

3. States Parties shall take all appropriate measures to ensure that migrant workers are not deprived of any rights derived from this principle by reason of any irregularity in their stay or employment. In particular, employers shall not be relieved of any legal or contractual obligations, nor shall their obligations be limited in any manner by reason of such irregularity.

Article 26

1. States Parties recognize the right of migrant workers and members of their families:

(a) To take part in meetings and activities of trade unions and of any other associations established in accordance with law, with a view to protecting their economic, social, cultural and other interests, subject only to the rules of the organization concerned;

(b) To join freely any trade union and any such association as aforesaid, subject only to the rules of the organization concerned;

(c) To seek the aid and assistance of any trade union and of any such association as aforesaid.

2. No restrictions may be placed on the exercise of these rights other than those that are prescribed by law and which are necessary in a democratic society in the interests of national security, public order (ordre public) or the protection of the rights and freedoms of others.

Article 27

1. With respect to social security, migrant workers and members of their families shall enjoy in the State of employment the same treatment granted to nationals in so far as they fulfill the requirements provided for by the applicable legislation of that State and the applicable bilateral and multilateral treaties. The competent authorities of the State of origin and the State of employment can at any time establish the necessary arrangements to determine the modalities of application of this norm.

2. Where the applicable legislation does not allow migrant workers and members of their families a benefit, the States concerned shall examine the possibility of reimbursing interested persons the amount of contributions made by them with respect to that benefit on the basis of the treatment granted to nationals who are in similar circumstances.

Article 28

Migrant workers and members of their families shall have the right to receive any medical care that is urgently required for the preservation of their life or the avoidance of irreparable harm to their health on the basis of equality of treatment with nationals of the State concerned. Such emergency medical care shall not be refused them by reason of any irregularity with regard to stay or employment.

Article 29

Each child of a migrant worker shall have the right to a name, to registration of birth and to a nationality.

Article 30

Each child of a migrant worker shall have the basic right of access to education on the basis of equality of treatment with nationals of the State concerned. Access to public pre-school educational institutions or schools shall not be refused or limited by reason of the irregular situation with respect to stay or employment of either parent or by reason of the irregularity of the child's stay in the State of employment.

Article 31

1. States Parties shall ensure respect for the cultural identity of migrant workers and members of their families and shall not prevent them from maintaining their cultural links with their State of origin.

2. States Parties may take appropriate measures to assist and encourage efforts in this respect.

Article 32

Upon the termination of their stay in the State of employment, migrant workers and members of their families shall have the right to transfer their earnings and savings and, in accordance with the applicable legislation of the States concerned, their personal effects and belongings.

Article 33

1. Migrant workers and members of their families shall have the right to be informed by the State of origin, the State of employment or the State of transit as the case may be concerning:

(a) Their rights arising out of the present Convention;

(b) The conditions of their admission, their rights and obligations under the law and practice of the State concerned and such other matters as will enable them to comply with administrative or other formalities in that State.

2. States Parties shall take all measures they deem appropriate to disseminate the said information or to ensure that it is provided by employers, trade unions or other appropriate bodies or institutions. As appropriate, they shall co-operate with other States concerned.

3. Such adequate information shall be provided upon request to migrant workers and members of their families, free of charge, and, as far as possible, in a language they are able to understand.

Article 34

Nothing in the present part of the Convention shall have the effect of relieving migrant workers and the members of their families from either the obligation to comply with the laws and regulations of any State of transit and the State of employment or the obligation to respect the cultural identity of the inhabitants of such States.

Article 35

Nothing in the present part of the Convention shall be interpreted as implying the regularization of the situation of migrant workers or members of their families who are non-documented or in an irregular situation or any right to such regularization of their situation, nor shall it prejudice the measures intended to ensure sound and equitable-conditions for international migration as provided in part VI of the present Convention.

Part IV: Other Rights of Migrant Workers and Members of their Families who are Documented or in a Regular Situation

Article 36

Migrant workers and members of their families who are documented or in a regular situation in the State of employment shall enjoy the rights set forth in the present part of the Convention in addition to those set forth in part III.

Article 37

Before their departure, or at the latest at the time of their admission to the State of employment, migrant workers and members of their families shall have the right to be fully informed by the State of origin or the State of employment, as appropriate, of all conditions applicable to their admission and particularly those concerning their stay and the remunerated activities in which they may engage as well as of the requirements they must satisfy in the State of employment and the authority to which they must address themselves for any modification of those conditions.

Article 38

1. States of employment shall make every effort to authorize migrant workers and members of the families to be temporarily absent without effect upon their authorization to stay or to work, as the case may be. In doing so, States of employment shall take into account the special needs and obligations of migrant workers and members of their families, in particular in their States of origin.

2. Migrant workers and members of their families shall have the right to be fully informed of the terms on which such temporary absences are authorized.

Article 39

1. Migrant workers and members of their families shall have the right to liberty of movement in the territory of the State of employment and freedom to choose their residence there.

2. The rights mentioned in paragraph 1 of the present article shall not be subject to any restrictions except those that are provided by law, are necessary to protect national security, public order (ordre public), public health or morals, or the rights and freedoms of others and are consistent with the other rights recognized in the present Convention.

Article 40

1. Migrant workers and members of their families shall have the right to form associations and trade unions in the State of employment for the promotion and protection of their economic, social, cultural and other interests.

2. No restrictions may be placed on the exercise of this right other than those that are prescribed by law and are necessary in a democratic society in the interests of national security, public order (ordre public) or the protection of the rights and freedoms of others.

Article 41

1. Migrant workers and members of their families shall have the right to participate in public affairs of their State of origin and to vote and to be elected at elections of that State, in accordance with its legislation.

2. The States concerned shall, as appropriate and in accordance with their legislation, facilitate the exercise of these rights.

Article 42

1. States Parties shall consider the establishment of procedures or institutions through which account may be taken, both in States of origin and in States of employment, of special needs, aspirations and obligations of migrant workers and members of their families and shall envisage, as appropriate, the possibility for migrant workers and members of their families to have their freely chosen representatives in those institutions.

2. States of employment shall facilitate, in accordance with their national legislation, the consultation or participation of migrant workers and members of their families in decisions concerning the life and administration of local communities.

3. Migrant workers may enjoy political rights in the State of employment if that State, in the exercise of its sovereignty, grants them such rights.

Article 43

1. Migrant workers shall enjoy equality of treatment with nationals of the State of employment in relation to:

(a) Access to educational institutions and services subject to the admission requirements and other regulations of the institutions and services concerned;

(b) Access to vocational guidance and placement services;

(c) Access to vocational training and retraining facilities and institutions;

(d) Access to housing, including social housing schemes, and protection against exploitation in respect of rents;

(e) Access to social and health services, provided that the requirements for participation in the respective schemes are met;

(f) Access to co-operatives and self-managed enterprises, which shall not imply a change of their migration status and shall be subject to the rules and regulations of the bodies concerned;

(g) Access to and participation in cultural life.

2. States Parties shall promote conditions to ensure effective equality of treatment to enable migrant workers to enjoy the rights mentioned in paragraph 1 of the present article whenever the terms of their stay, as authorized by the State of employment, meet the appropriate requirements.

3. States of employment shall not prevent an employer of migrant workers from establishing housing or social or cultural facilities for them. Subject to Article 70 of the present Convention, a State of employment may make the establishment of such facilities subject to the requirements generally applied in that State concerning their installation.

Article 44

1. States Parties, recognizing that the family is the natural and fundamental group unit of society and is entitled to protection by society and the State, shall take appropriate measures to ensure the protection of the unity of the families of migrant workers.

2. States Parties shall take measures that they deem appropriate and that fall within their competence to facilitate the reunification of migrant workers with their spouses or persons who have with the migrant worker a relationship that, according to applicable law, produces effects equivalent to marriage, as well as with their minor dependent unmarried children.

3. States of employment, on humanitarian grounds, shall favourably consider granting equal treatment, as set forth in paragraph 2 of the present article, to other family members of migrant workers.

Article 45

1. Members of the families of migrant workers shall, in the State of employment, enjoy equality of treatment with nationals of that State in relation to:

(a) Access to educational institutions and services, subject to the admission requirements and other regulations of the institutions and services concerned;

(b) Access to vocational guidance and training institutions and services, provided that requirements for participation are met;

(c) Access to social and health services, provided that requirements for participation in the respective schemes are met;

(d) Access to and participation in cultural life.

2. States of employment shall pursue a policy, where appropriate in collaboration with the States of origin, aimed at facilitating the integration of children of migrant workers in the local school system, particularly in respect of teaching them the local language.

3. States of employment shall endeavour to facilitate for the children of migrant workers the teaching of their mother tongue and culture and, in this regard, States of origin shall collaborate whenever appropriate.

4. States of employment may provide special schemes of education in the mother tongue of children of migrant workers, if necessary in collaboration with the States of origin.

Article 46

Migrant workers and members of their families shall, subject to the applicable legislation of the States concerned, as well as relevant international agreements and the obligations of the States concerned arising out of their participation in customs unions, enjoy exemption from import and export duties and taxes in respect of their personal and household effects as well as the equipment necessary to engage in the remunerated activity for which they were admitted to the State of employment:

(a) Upon departure from the State of origin or State of habitual residence;

(b) Upon initial admission to the State of employment;

(c) Upon final departure from the State of employment;

(d) Upon final return to the State of origin or State of habitual residence.

Article 47

1. Migrant workers shall have the right to transfer their earnings and savings, in particular those funds necessary for the support of their families, from the State of employment to their State of origin or any other State. Such transfers shall be made in conformity with procedures established by applicable legislation of the State concerned and in conformity with applicable international agreements.

2. States concerned shall take appropriate measures to facilitate such transfers.

Article 48

1. Without prejudice to applicable double taxation agreements, migrant workers and members of their families shall, in the matter of earnings in the State of employment:

(a) Not be liable to taxes, duties or charges of any description higher or more onerous than those imposed on nationals in similar circumstances;

(b) Be entitled to deductions or exemptions from taxes of any description and to any tax allowances applicable to nationals in similar circumstances, including tax allowances for dependent members of their families.

2. States Parties shall endeavour to adopt appropriate measures to avoid double taxation of the earnings and savings of migrant workers and members of their families.

Article 49

1. Where separate authorizations to reside and to engage in employment are required by national legislation, the States of employment shall issue to migrant workers authorization of residence for at least the same period of time as their authorization to engage in remunerated activity.

2. Migrant workers who in the State of employment are allowed freely to choose their remunerated activity shall neither be regarded as in an irregular situation nor shall they lose their authorization of residence by the mere fact of the termination of their remunerated activity prior to the expiration of their work permits or similar authorizations.

3. In order to allow migrant workers referred to in paragraph 2 of the present article sufficient time to find alternative remunerated activities, the authorization of residence shall not be withdrawn at least for a period corresponding to that during which they may be entitled to unemployment benefits.

Article 50

1. In the case of death of a migrant worker or dissolution of marriage, the State of employment shall favourably consider granting family members of that migrant worker residing in that State on the basis of family reunion an authorization to stay; the State of employment shall take into account the length of time they have already resided in that State.

2. Members of the family to whom such authorization is not granted shall be allowed before departure a reasonable period of time in order to enable them to settle their affairs in the State of employment.

3. The provisions of paragraphs I and 2 of the present article may not be interpreted as adversely affecting any right to stay and work otherwise granted to such family members by the legislation of the State of employment or by bilateral and multilateral treaties applicable to that State.

Article 51

Migrant workers who in the State of employment are not permitted freely to choose their remunerated activity shall neither be regarded as in an irregular situation nor shall they lose their authorization of residence by the mere fact of the termination of their remunerated activity prior to the expiration of their work permit, except where the authorization of residence is expressly dependent upon the specific remunerated activity for which they were admitted. Such migrant workers shall have the right to seek alternative employment, participation in public work schemes and retraining during the remaining period of their authorization to work, subject to such conditions and limitations as are specified in the authorization to work.

Article 52

1. Migrant workers in the State of employment shall have the right freely to choose their remunerated activity, subject to the following restrictions or conditions.

2. For any migrant worker a State of employment may:

(a) Restrict access to limited categories of employment, functions, services or activities where this is necessary in the interests of this State and provided for by national legislation;

(b) Restrict free choice of remunerated activity in accordance with its legislation concerning recognition of occupational qualifications acquired outside its territory. However, States Parties concerned shall endeavour to provide for recognition of such qualifications.

3. For migrant workers whose permission to work is limited in time, a State of employment may also:

(a) Make the right freely to choose their remunerated activities subject to the condition that the migrant worker has resided lawfully in its territory for the purpose of remunerated activity for a period of time prescribed in its national legislation that should not exceed two years;

(b) Limit access by a migrant worker to remunerated activities in pursuance of a policy of granting priority to its nationals or to persons who are assimilated to them for these purposes by virtue of legislation or bilateral or multilateral agreements. Any such limitation shall cease to apply to a migrant worker who has resided lawfully in its territory for the purpose of remunerated activity for a period of time prescribed in its national legislation that should not exceed five years.

4. States of employment shall prescribe the conditions under which a migrant worker who has been admitted to take up employment may be authorized to engage in work on his or her own account. Account shall be taken of the period during which the worker has already been lawfully in the State of employment.

Article 53

1. Members of a migrant worker's family who have themselves an authorization of residence or admission that is without limit of time or is automatically renewable shall be permitted freely to choose their remunerated activity under the same conditions as are applicable to the said migrant worker in accordance with Article 52 of the present Convention.

2. With respect to members of a migrant worker's family who are not permitted freely to choose their remunerated activity, States Parties shall consider favourably granting them priority in obtaining permission to engage in a remunerated activity over other workers who seek admission to the State of employment, subject to applicable bilateral and multilateral agreements.

Article 54

1. Without prejudice to the terms of their authorization of residence or their permission to work and the rights provided for in articles 25 and 27 of the present Convention, migrant workers shall enjoy equality of treatment with nationals of the State of employment in respect of:

(a) Protection against dismissal;

(b) Unemployment benefits;

(c) Access to public work schemes intended to combat unemployment;

(d) Access to alternative employment in the event of loss of work or termination of other remunerated activity, subject to Article 52 of the present Convention.

2. If a migrant worker claims that the terms of his or her work contract have been violated by his or her employer, he or she shall have the right to address his or her case to the competent authorities of the State of employment, on terms provided for in Article 18, paragraph 1, of the present Convention.

Article 55
Migrant workers who have been granted permission to engage in a remunerated activity, subject to the conditions attached to such permission, shall be entitled to equality of treatment with nationals of the State of employment in the exercise of that remunerated activity.

Article 56
1. Migrant workers and members of their families referred to in the present part of the Convention may not be expelled from a State of employment, except for reasons defined in the national legislation of that State, and subject to the safeguards established in part III.

2. Expulsion shall not be resorted to for the purpose of depriving a migrant worker or a member of his or her family of the rights arising out of the authorization of residence and the work permit.

3. In considering whether to expel a migrant worker or a member of his or her family, account should be taken of humanitarian considerations and of the length of time that the person concerned has already resided in the State of employment.

Part V: Provisions Applicable to Particular Categories of Migrant Workers and Members of their Families

Article 57
The particular categories of migrant workers and members of their families specified in the present part of the Convention who are documented or in a regular situation shall enjoy the rights set forth in part m and, except as modified below, the rights set forth in part IV.

Article 58
1. Frontier workers, as defined in Article 2, paragraph 2 (a), of the present Convention, shall be entitled to the rights provided for in part IV that can be applied to them by reason of their presence and work in the territory of the State of employment, taking into account that they do not have their habitual residence in that State.

2. States of employment shall consider favourably granting frontier workers the right freely to choose their remunerated activity after a specified period of time. The granting of that right shall not affect their status as frontier workers.

Article 59
1. Seasonal workers, as defined in Article 2, paragraph 2 (b), of the present Convention, shall be entitled to the rights provided for in part IV that can be applied to them by reason of their presence and work in the territory of the State of employment and that are compatible with their status in that State as seasonal workers, taking into account the fact that they are present in that State for only part of the year.

2. The State of employment shall, subject to paragraph 1 of the present article, consider granting seasonal workers who have been employed in its territory for a significant period of time the possibility of taking up other remunerated activi-

ties and giving them priority over other workers who seek admission to that State, subject to applicable bilateral and multilateral agreements.

Article 60

Itinerant workers, as defined in Article 2, paragraph 2 (A), of the present Convention, shall be entitled to the rights provided for in part IV that can be granted to them by reason of their presence and work in the territory of the State of employment and that are compatible with their status as itinerant workers in that State.

Article 61

1. Project-tied workers, as defined in Article 2, paragraph 2 (of the present Convention), and members of their families shall be entitled to the rights provided for in part IV except the provisions of Article 43, paragraphs I (b) and (c), Article 43, paragraph I (d), as it pertains to social housing schemes, Article 45, paragraph I (b), and articles 52 to 55.

2. If a project-tied worker claims that the terms of his or her work contract have been violated by his or her employer, he or she shall have the right to address his or her case to the competent authorities of the State which has jurisdiction over that employer, on terms provided for in Article 18, paragraph 1, of the present Convention.

3. Subject to bilateral or multilateral agreements in force for them, the States Parties concerned shall endeavour to enable project-tied workers to remain adequately protected by the social security systems of their States of origin or habitual residence during their engagement in the project. States Parties concerned shall take appropriate measures with the aim of avoiding any denial of rights or duplication of payments in this respect.

4. Without prejudice to the provisions of Article 47 of the present Convention and to relevant bilateral or multilateral agreements, States Parties concerned shall permit payment of the earnings of project-tied workers in their State of origin or habitual residence.

Article 62

1. Specified-employment workers as defined in Article 2, paragraph 2 (g), of the present Convention, shall be entitled to the rights provided for in part IV, except the provisions of Article 43, paragraphs I (b) and (c), Article 43, paragraph I (d), as it pertains to social housing schemes, Article 52, and Article 54, paragraph 1 (d).

2. Members of the families of specified-employment workers shall be entitled to the rights relating to family members of migrant workers provided for in part IV of the present Convention, except the provisions of Article 53.

Article 63

1. Self-employed workers, as defined in Article 2, paragraph 2 (h), of the present Convention, shall be entitled to the rights provided for in part IV with the exception of those rights which are exclusively applicable to workers having a contract of employment.

2. Without prejudice to articles 52 and 79 of the present Convention, the termination of the economic activity of the self-employed workers shall not in itself imply the withdrawal of the authorization for them or for the members of their families to stay or to engage in a remunerated activity in the State of employment except where the authorization of residence is expressly dependent upon the specific remunerated activity for which they were admitted.

Part VI: Promotion of Sound, Equitable, Humane and Lawful Conditions in Connection with International Migration of Workers and Members of Their Families

Article 64

1. Without prejudice to Article 79 of the present Convention, the States Parties concerned shall as appropriate consult and co-operate with a view to promoting sound, equitable and humane conditions in connection with international migration of workers and members of their families.

2. In this respect, due regard shall be paid not only to labour needs and resources, but also to the social, economic, cultural and other needs of migrant workers and members of their families involved, as well as to the consequences of such migration for the communities concerned.

Article 65

1. States Parties shall maintain appropriate services to deal with questions concerning international migration of workers and members of their families. Their functions shall include, inter alia:

(a) The formulation and implementation of policies regarding such migration;

(b) An exchange of information. consultation and co-operation with the competent authorities of other States Parties involved in such migration;

(c) The provision of appropriate information, particularly to employers, workers and their organizations on policies, laws and regulations relating to migration and employment, on agreements concluded with other States concerning migration and on other relevant matters;

(d) The provision of information and appropriate assistance to migrant workers and members of their families regarding requisite authorizations and formalities and arrangements for departure, travel, arrival, stay, remunerated activities, exit and return, as well as on conditions of work and life in the State of employment and on customs, currency, tax and other relevant laws and regulations.

2. States Parties shall facilitate as appropriate the provision of adequate consular and other services that are necessary to meet the social, cultural and other needs of migrant workers and members of their families.

Article 66

1. Subject to paragraph 2 of the present article, the right to undertake operations with a view to the recruitment of workers for employment in another State shall be restricted to:

(a) Public services or bodies of the State in which such operations take place;

(b) Public services or bodies of the State of employment on the basis of agreement between the States concerned;

(c) A body established by virtue of a bilateral or multilateral agreement.

2. Subject to any authorization, approval and supervision by the public authorities of the States Parties concerned as may be established pursuant to the legislation and practice of those States, agencies, prospective employers or persons acting on their behalf may also be permitted to undertake the said operations.

Article 67

1. States Parties concerned shall co-operate as appropriate in the adoption of measures regarding the orderly return of migrant workers and members of their families to the State of origin when they decide to return or their authorization of residence or employment expires or when they are in the State of employment in an irregular situation.

2. Concerning migrant workers and members of their families in a regular situation, States Parties concerned shall co-operate as appropriate, on terms agreed upon by those States, with a view to promoting adequate economic conditions for their resettlement and to facilitating their durable social and cultural reintegration in the State of origin.

Article 68

1. States Parties, including States of transit, shall collaborate with a view to preventing and eliminating illegal or clandestine movements and employment of migrant workers in an irregular situation. The measures to be taken to this end within the jurisdiction of each State concerned shall include:

(a) Appropriate measures against the dissemination of misleading information relating to emigration and immigration;

(b) Measures to detect and eradicate illegal or clandestine movements of migrant workers and members of their families and to impose effective sanctions on persons, groups or entities which organize, operate or assist in organizing or operating such movements;

(c) Measures to impose effective sanctions on persons, groups or entities which use violence, threats or intimidation against migrant workers or members of their families in an irregular situation.

2. States of employment shall take all adequate and effective measures to eliminate employment in their territory of migrant workers in an irregular situation, including, whenever appropriate, sanctions on employers of such workers. The rights of migrant workers vis-à-vis their employer arising from employment shall not be impaired by these measures.

Article 69

1. States Parties shall, when there are migrant workers and members of their families within their territory in an irregular situation, take appropriate measures to ensure that such a situation does not persist. 2. Whenever States Parties concerned consider the possibility of regularizing the situation of such persons in accordance with applicable national legislation and bilateral or multilateral agreements, appropriate account shall be taken of the circumstances of their entry, the duration of their stay in the States of employment and other relevant considerations, in particular those relating to their family situation.

Article 70

States Parties shall take measures not less favourable than those applied to nationals to ensure that working and living conditions of migrant workers and members of their families in a regular situation are in keeping with the standards of fitness, safety, health and principles of human dignity.

Article 71

1. States Parties shall facilitate, whenever necessary, the repatriation to the State of origin of the bodies of deceased migrant workers or members of their families.

2. As regards compensation matters relating to the death of a migrant worker or a member of his or her family, States Parties shall, as appropriate, provide assistance to the persons concerned with a view to the prompt settlement of such matters. Settlement of these matters shall be carried out on the basis of applicable national law in accordance with the provisions of the present Convention and any relevant bilateral or multilateral agreements.

Part VII: Application of the Convention

Article 72

1. (a) For the purpose of reviewing the application of the present Convention, there shall be established a Committee on the Protection of the Rights of All Migrant Workers and Members of Their Families (hereinafter referred to as "the Committee");

(b) The Committee shall consist, at the time of entry into force of the present Convention, of ten and, after the entry into force of the Convention for the forty-first State Party, of fourteen experts of high moral standing, impartiality and recognized competence in the field covered by the Convention.

2. (a) Members of the Committee shall be elected by secret ballot by the States Parties from a list of persons nominated by the States Parties, due consideration being given to equitable geographical distribution, including both States of origin and States of employment, and to the representation of the principal legal systems. Each State Party may nominate one person from among its own nationals;

(b) Members shall be elected and shall serve in their personal capacity.

...

Article 73

1. States Parties undertake to submit to the Secretary-General of the United Nations for consideration by the Committee a report on the legislative, judicial, administrative and other measures they have taken to give effect to the provisions of the present Convention:

(a) Within one year after the entry into force of the Convention for the State Party concerned;

(b) Thereafter every five years and whenever the Committee so requests.

2. Reports prepared under the present article shall also indicate factors and difficulties, if any, affecting the implementation of the Convention and shall include information on the characteristics of migration flows in which the State Party concerned is involved.

...

4. States Parties shall make their reports widely available to the public in their own countries.

Article 74

1. The Committee shall examine the reports submitted by each State Party and shall transmit such comments as it may consider appropriate to the State Party concerned. This State Party may submit to the Committee observations on any comment made by the Committee in accordance with the present article. The Committee may request supplementary information from States Parties when considering these reports.

...

Article 76

1. A State Party to the present Convention may at any time declare under this article that it recognizes the competence of the Committee to receive and consider communications to the effect that a State Party claims that another State Party is not fulfilling its obligations under the present Convention. Communications under this article may be received and considered only if submitted by a State Party that has made a declaration recognizing in regard to itself the competence of the Committee. No communication shall be received by the Committee if it concerns a State Party which has not made such a declaration....

Source: United Nations Human Rights, Office of the High Commissioner, General Assembly resolution 45/158, 18 December 1990: International Convention on the Protection of the Rights of All Migrant Workers and Members of Their Families, http://www.ohchr.org/EN/ProfessionalInterest/Pages/CMW.aspx

⊱⊰⊱⊰⊱⊰⊱⊰

14. A PLEDGE OF SUPPORT FOR REFUGEE PROTECTION BY NATIONAL SECURITY LEADERS, RETIRED MILITARY LEADERS, AND FORMER GOVERNMENT LEADERS, ON WORLD REFUGEE DAY

This document is a letter dated June 20, 2016, arguing for the U.S. government to support the global protection of refugees. It is signed by former U.S. governmental, military and national security leaders and discusses how the U.S. should view and support the protection of refugees as in our national interest and consistent with our core values.

Refugee Protection, Syrian Refugees

Washington, D.C. — In honor of World Refugee Day, 28 of the nation's most prominent national security leaders, retired military leaders, and former government officials today publicly called on the United States to reaffirm its commitment to protecting refugees. The call came through a signed statement of principles organized by Human Rights First, affirming the importance of refugee resettlement for advancing U.S. national security interests and upholding American values. Signers of today's open statement organized by Human Rights First include: Former Secretary of State Madeleine K. Albright; Former Secretary of Homeland Security Michael Chertoff; Former Secretary of Defense and U.S. Senator William S. Cohen; Former Secretary of Defense Chuck Hagel; Former Director of the CIA General Michael V. Hayden, U.S. Air Force (Ret.); Former Director of the National Counterterrorism Center Michael E. Leiter; Former U.S. Senator Carl M. Levin; Former Commander of U.S. Army Europe General David M. Maddox, U.S. Army (Ret.); Former Director of the National Counterterrorism Center Matthew G. Olsen; Former Secretary of Defense William J. Perry; Former NATO Supreme Allied Commander Admiral James G. Stavridis, U.S. Navy (Ret.); Former Homeland Security Advisor Frances F. Townsend; and many others.

The statement of principles reads:

The world today is gripped by the worst refugee crisis since World War II. Some sixty million people — half of them children — have fled persecution and violence, the highest number ever recorded. From Syria to Burma to Eritrea, desperate people are seeking freedom from brutal regimes, lawless militias, and genocidal terrorist groups. Thousands have died trying to find safety and millions are struggling to survive.

The United States has long been a refuge for those seeking safety and freedom, and for a simple reason: Americans believe their compassion and openness are sources not of weakness but strength. The demonstration of these qualities accords with the core ideals on which our nation was founded, and on which our greatness rests. For more than two centuries, the idea of America has pulled toward our shores those seeking liberty, and it has ensured that they arrive in the open arms of our citizens. That is why the Statue of Liberty welcomes the world's "huddled masses yearning to breathe free," and why President Reagan stressed the United States as "a magnet for all who must have freedom, for all the pilgrims from all the lost places who are hurtling through the darkness."

Today there are many hurtling through that darkness.

Yet despite America's role as the global leader in resettling refugees, many voices call for closed doors rather than open arms. To give in to such impulses would represent a mistake of historic proportions. Now is the time for the United States to reaffirm its commitment to protecting refugees.

Americans are rightly concerned not only for the security of refugees but their own as well. For this reason, refugees are vetted more thoroughly than any other category of traveler seeking to arrive in the United States. The security process includes screenings by national and international intelligence agencies, fingerprint and other biometric data checks against terrorist and criminal databases, and multiple rounds of interviews.

As we ensure the safety of our own citizens, we should recognize that refugees serve as a source of national renewal. Fleeing horrors today, they will tomorrow emerge as patriotic citizens who give back to the country that welcomed them in their time of desperation. And accepting refugees demonstrates, at a time when it is so sorely needed, that America leads the world in marching toward a better future.

We believe:
- The United States should provide refuge to those fleeing violence and persecution, consistent with our nation's founding ideals.
- Accepting refugees, and encouraging other countries to do so, advances U.S. interests by supporting the stability of our allies struggling to host large numbers on their own.
- Welcoming refugees, regardless of their religion or race, exposes the falseness of terrorist propaganda and counters the warped vision of extremists.
- The United States must not abandon those targeted by terrorists because they worked with American troops and diplomats in support of our missions in Iraq and Afghanistan.
- Religious bans and tests are un-American and have no place in our immigration and refugee policies.
- American leadership is essential in addressing the global refugee crisis.

Sincerely,

(Names in alphabetical order)

Madeleine K. Albright
Former Secretary of State

Stephen J. Hadley
Former National Security Advisor to President George W. Bush

Leon E. Panetta
Former Secretary of Defense and Director, Central Intelligence Agency

William J. Burns
Former Deputy Secretary of State

Chuck Hagel
Former Secretary of Defense and U.S. Senator

William J. Perry
Former Secretary of Defense

Michael Chertoff
Former Secretary of Homeland Security

General Michael V. Hayden, U.S. Air Force, (Ret.)
Former Director, Central Intelligence Agency

Thomas R. Pickering
Former Undersecretary of State for Political Affairs

Derek Chollet
Former Assistant Secretary of Defense for International Security Affairs

Fred C. Hof
Former U.S. Ambassador & Special Advisor for transition in Syria

Kori N. Schake
Former Deputy Director for Policy Planning, U.S. State Department

Henry Cisneros
Former Secretary of Housing and Urban Development

Robert Kagan
Co-Founder, Project for the New American Century

Randy Scheunemann
Former Director, Project for the New American Century

William S. Cohen
Former Secretary of Defense and U.S. Senator

David J. Kramer
Former Assistant Secretary of State for Democracy, Human Rights, and Labor

Eric Schwartz
Former Assistant Secretary of State for Population, Refugees, and Migration

Ryan C. Crocker
Former U.S. Ambassador to Afghanistan, Iraq, Pakistan, Syria, Kuwait, and Lebanon

Mark Lagon
President, Freedom House
Former Ambassador at Large, Office to Monitor and Combat Trafficking in Persons

John Shattuck
Former Assistance Secretary of State for Democracy, Human Rights, and Labor and U.S. Ambassador to Czech Republic

Tom Daschle
Former U.S. Senator

Michael E. Leiter
Former Director, National Counterterrorism Center

Admiral James G. Stavridis, U.S. Navy (Ret.)
Former NATO Supreme Allied Commander
Former Commander, U.S. Southern Command

Michele A. Flournoy
Former Under Secretary of Defense for Policy

Carl M. Levin
Former U.S. Senator

Frances F. Townsend
Former Homeland Security Advisor to President George W. Bush

Richard Fontaine
President, Center for a New American Security

General David M. Maddox, U.S. Army (Ret.)
Former Commander in Chief, U.S. Army Europe

Paul D. Wolfowitz
Former Deputy Secretary of Defense

Robert S. Ford
Former Ambassador to Syria and Algeria

Matthew G. Olsen
Former Director, National Counterterrorism Center

Source: Statement of Principle on America's Commitment to Refugees, http://www.humanrightsfirst.org/sites/default/files/statement-on-americas-commitment-to-refugees.pdf

Freedom of Thought, Conscience, Religion or Belief

By Tina M. Ramirez

Chapter 14

This Chapter is About the freedom of thought, conscience, religion or belief — a universally accepted human right protected under Article 18 of both the Universal Declaration of Human Rights and the International Covenant on Civil and Political Rights. In the United States, this freedom is often referred to as "religious freedom" and is considered the first freedom because it was the First Amendment to the Constitution in the Bill of Rights. Religious freedom has a long and storied history in America and served as an inspiration for the international standard later adopted by the United Nations in Article 18 of the UDHR and ICCPR. This chapter will discuss the First Amendment protection of religious freedom within the American legal and historic context of commitment to this right, and also describe the international framework for protecting this freedom and how the U.S. has engaged in that process through the nation's foreign policy.

This is Important Because we live in an interconnected world where individuals of different beliefs are in constant contact with one another, living their lives based on the beliefs that form the basis of their identity and place in the world. One's religion or belief cannot be easily separated from their identity, conscience, moral decisions, or orientation to the world. The very nature of opposing truth claims requires a space where every person has the equal freedom to explore and challenge truth claims to determine what they believe and how those beliefs will orient their lives. The freedom to believe or not believe, to express one's beliefs or not, and to hold a conscientious objection to actions that run counter to one's beliefs, are fundamental human rights and are necessary for peace, stability and security in the world today.

Religion is an important aspect of human culture. According to the Pew Research Center, around 80% of Americans follow some religion or belief. The freedom of religion or belief is distinct from other human rights because it is about what happens inside of a person. While other human rights regulate the outside — how someone is treated physically — freedom of religion or belief protects the conscience of humanity where determinations of right and wrong are made. It relates to the orientation of the individual to the ultimate truths of reality, the individual's place in the world, and the external expression of those truths or beliefs. Freedom of religion or belief protects both the internal and external aspects of an individual's religion or belief, including the expression of ideas about non-belief. As such, it ensures that there is always a public space for religious truth claims and the way in which those truth claims may influence public and private behavior.

Quotes & Key Text Excerpts

Congress shall make no law respecting an establishment of religion, or prohibiting the free exercise thereof; or abridging the freedom of speech, or of the press, or the right of the people peaceably to assemble, and to petition the Government for a redress of grievances.

—*First Amendment to the U.S. Constitution (Bill of Rights)*

Everyone has the right to freedom of thought, conscience and religion; this right includes freedom to change his religion or belief, and freedom, either alone or in community with others and in public or private, to manifest his religion or belief in teaching, practice, worship and observance.

—*Universal Declaration of Human Rights 1948 (UDHR), Art. 18*

Whereas, Almighty God hath created the mind free; That all attempts to influence it by temporal punishments or burthens, or by civil incapacitations tend only to beget habits of hypocrisy and meanness, and therefore are a departure from the plan of the holy author of our religion, who being Lord, both of body and mind yet chose not to propagate it by coercions on either, as was in his Almighty power to do...

—*Statute of Virginia for Religious Freedom 1786*

...The citizens of the United States of America have a right to applaud themselves for having given to mankind examples of an enlarged and liberal policy — a policy worthy of imitation. All possess alike liberty of conscience and immunities of citizenship. It is now no more that toleration is spoken of as if it were the indulgence of one class of people that another enjoyed the exercise of their inherent natural rights, for, happily, the Government of the United States, which gives to bigotry no sanction, to persecution no assistance, requires only that they who live under its protection should demean themselves as good citizens in giving it on all occasions their effectual support....May the children of the stock of Abraham who dwell in this land continue to merit and enjoy the good will of the other inhabitants — while every one shall sit in safety under his own vine and fig tree and there shall be none to make him afraid.

—*President George Washington's Letter to a Hebrew Congregation, 1790*

In the future days, which we seek to make secure, we look forward to a world founded upon four essential human freedoms. The first is freedom of speech and expression — everywhere in the world. The second is freedom of every person to worship God in his own way — everywhere in the world.

The third is freedom from want — which, translated into world terms, means economic understandings which will secure to every nation a healthy peacetime life for its inhabitants — everywhere in the world. The fourth is freedom from fear — which, translated into world terms, means a world-wide reduction of armaments to such a point and in such a thorough fashion that no nation will be in a position to commit an act of physical aggression against any neighbor — anywhere in the world. That is no vision of a distant millennium. It is a definite basis for a kind of world attainable in our own time and generation. That kind of world is the very antithesis of the so-called new order of tyranny which the dictators seek to create with the crash of a bomb.

—*President Franklin D. Roosevelt, excerpted from the State of the Union Address to the Congress, January 6, 1941, "Four Freedoms Speech"*

ഇം-ഇം-ഇം-ഇം-ഇം-ഇം-ഇം

The right to freedom of religion undergirds the very origin and existence of the United States. Many of our Nation's founders fled religious persecution abroad, cherishing in their hearts and minds the ideal of religious freedom. They established in law, as a fundamental right and as a pillar of our Nation, the right to freedom of religion. From its birth to this day, the United States has prized this legacy of religious freedom and honored this heritage by standing for religious freedom and offering refuge to those suffering religious persecution.

(2) Freedom of religious belief and practice is a universal human right and fundamental freedom articulated in numerous international instruments, including the Universal Declaration of Human Rights, the International Covenant on Civil and Political Rights, the Helsinki Accords, the Declaration on the Elimination of All Forms of Intolerance and Discrimination Based on Religion or Belief, the United Nations Charter, and the European Convention for the Protection of Human Rights and Fundamental Freedoms.

—*International Religious Freedom Act of 1998*

What You Need To Know

The freedom of thought, conscience, religion or belief is one of the first human rights recognized in the world, and has attained the status of a standard of normative International Law. As such, regardless of whether a country has signed the ICCPR, it can never deny an individual their freedom of thought, conscience, religion or belief. There are absolutely no limitations permitted on the freedom to have or hold a belief and this freedom cannot be taken away even when an individual is imprisoned. Only the manifestation of those beliefs can be limited, and only exceptionally.

World history is replete with religious conflict and intolerance. Perhaps because religion or belief is such an important part of our humanity, it has taken millennia to come to a place where it is finally recognized as a universal human right for all people. As such, freedom of religion or belief entails the freedom for all people to hold truth claims — and that includes competing claims, including those which may be deemed offensive.

Freedom of religion or belief is an important litmus test or canary in the coal mine for other human rights. Violations of this freedom involve limitations of other rights and when this freedom is protected, other rights benefit as well. Religious freedom is also important for what it does not protect — no one may justify violence in the name of religion on the basis of exercising their freedom of religion or belief. Freedom of religion or belief protects the internal conscience of having or holding a religion or belief unequivocally, but there are limitations on the expression of religion or belief and those limitations do not permit any actions that would nullify the right itself.

In a world where global conflict increasingly exhibits religious factors, understanding the scope of freedom of religion or belief and its influence on other human rights and freedoms is essential. Given the alarming rise of terrorist attacks on Americans which are justified in the name of religion as well as the rise of other human rights that compete with the traditional space for freedom of religion or belief, there is, at any rate, a real danger for the contours of this freedom to become increasingly blurred. Unless we pay attention, its basic principles may in the long run even be turned upside down.

America is unique in that religious freedom was enshrined as the first freedom articulated in the Bill of Rights and has had a prominent place throughout our nation's history. Though other nations at times recognized the importance of protecting this freedom for others, such as Cyrus the Great who issued the first known Edict of Toleration for religious minorities, no country has given more value to the human right as America has.

From its earliest days, America was a refuge for those fleeing religious persecution. From the French Huguenots to the Puritans of England, and many others, Protestant communities were fleeing the religious wars that characterized Europe at the time. Unfortunately, the early colonies did not always respect the freedom of others. Laws in some of the British colonies justified religious persecution to protect their own denominations. For instance, in the Massachusetts Bay Colony, Quaker Mary Dyer was sentenced to death and hanged for blasphemy in the mid 1600s. The colony provided no space for opposing religious views and banished Baptists Roger Williams and Anne Hutchison as well as many Catholics. Anti-Catholic sentiment was widespread because of the persecution many Protestants had experienced under Catholics in Europe.

In spite of these challenges, several colonies were founded on the basis of religious freedom and the concepts they established were influential in America's adoption of the First Amendment. After being banished from the Massachusetts Bay Colony, Roger Williams established Rhode Island where he guaranteed religious freedom for everyone. The Colony became a haven for many religious dissenters since the government was not permitted to engage in matters of religious belief. William Penn established Pennsylvania similarly, guaranteeing religious freedom in his Frame of Government, which also outlines several other ideas reflecting internationally accepted human rights. And Lord Baltimore established the colony of Maryland with protections for religious freedom, but only for Christians. Under the Maryland Toleration Act, anyone who denied Christianity or blasphemed the religion could be sentenced to death.

On January 16, 1786 the Virginia Statue for Religious Freedom, authored by Thomas Jefferson, was passed in the state's General Assembly. This Statute set the tone for the constitutional basis for religious freedom and provides insight into the intent and scope of its protection. Jefferson's Statute recognizes that no one should be coerced to believe or practice the tenants of a particular religion by threats of legal punishment. It goes on to say that no one should be forced to attend religious services or pay taxes to a church; individuals should be free to worship as they please without discrimination. The Statute states that everyone should be free to profess their beliefs and that any infringement of this law would constitute a violation of natural law.

Jefferson's Statute inspired protections for religious freedom enshrined in the Constitution and Bill of Rights. Following Independence, several states continued to have established churches and public support for religion was common long after the Constitution was adopted. The scope of the First Amendment protection for religious freedom has been defined by many cases throughout U.S. history. And though established in law, the fears and divisions over religion were not resolved with the Constitution. Anti-Catholic sentiment continued to grow and was a central component of the mid-1800s Know Nothing Political Party. Beginning in 1875, 37 states passed constitutional amendments that forbid government funds from being spent on sectarian schools. These have become known as Blaine Amendments for the anti-Catholic Senator who led an effort to pass the law as a constitutional amendment, which was narrowly defeated in the Senate. Supreme Court justices have recognized the anti-Catholic bigotry rooted in the Blaine Amendments and there are various challenges seeking to overturn them as unconstitutional. When, in 1922, Oregon passed a law that sought to eliminate Catholic schools, the Supreme Court deemed it unconstitutional.

Mormons have also faced banishment and discrimination. In 1833 Mormons were evicted from one county in Missouri, and then the governor ordered them to be exterminated. In 1838, a Mormon settlement in Missouri was attacked leaving several dead. The Mormons fled to Illinois and later Utah to escape persecution with their founding leader, Joseph Smith, being attacked and killed in Illinois.

The U.S. has a long and storied history of conscience protections, from individuals who hold deep religious beliefs about serving in the military, to the refusal of Jehovah's Witnesses to pledge allegiance to the American flag, and protections for conscience in the health care industry established in the wake of the Supreme Court's decision on abortion in *Roe v. Wade.*

In 1661, the Massachusetts Bay Colony exempted men from military service on religious grounds, and in 1701, the Quakers were given a group exemption from military service by William Penn. The Quakers and Mennonites have deep traditions of pacifism, which have led to various accommodations throughout U.S. history to protect their conscientious objection to military service. During the Revolutionary War (1775-83) Quakers refused to pay taxes because they might support the war effort and were consequently often arrested and imprisoned.

By the Civil War, both the North and the South had options for certain groups of religious conscientious objectors to pay a fine or find a substitute to be exempted from military service. Since the amount was too high for the majority of conscientious objectors, it was not a viable option for most. By World War One, the Selective Service Act of 1917 recognized the right of conscientious objectors to abstain from duties that forced them to bear arms and the legislation expanded the groups that qualified for a conscientious objection beyond the traditional religious groups such as Quakers and Mennonites. By World War Two, the Selective Training and Service Act of 1940 further expanded groups protected to include men with religious training and beliefs, and provided alternative forms of service through the Civilian Public Services, which were often run by pacifists.

The Supreme Court began to look at cases involving the right to conscientious objection in the 1940s and by 1971, they had reached two important decisions that had a significant impact on the rights of individuals to conscientious objection. In 1965, the Supreme Court ruled in *U.S. v. Seeger* that anyone with a "sincere and meaningful belief" should be exempted from military service. Justice Tom Clark, in writing the opinion of the Court, argued that "religion or belief" with reference to a "Supreme Being" as outlined in the law for those seeking exemption should be broadly construed. He wrote, "We believe that under this construction, the test of belief 'in a relation to a Supreme Being' is whether a given belief that is sincere and meaningful occupies a place in the life of its possessor parallel to that filled by the orthodox belief in God of one who clearly qualifies for the exemption."

In 1966, a man named Cassius Clay, who is better known by his religious name "Muhammed Ali," objected to the military draft on the basis of his beliefs as a Muslim in the Nation of Islam. Despite his claim of conscientious objection, the local draft board and then the Kentucky State Appeals Board rejected his claim. During that process, a Kentucky judge advised the Department of Justice that Ali should be exempted, but was ignored. Ali was eventually convicted of draft evasion, sentenced to five years in prison and a $10,000 fine. At first, he appealed the case to the Fifth Circuit Court, which he lost, and then he appealed to the Supreme Court. Finally, in 1971 the Supreme Court reviewed Ali's case and in a surprising decision, reversed the initial decision and determined that Ali should be granted religious exemption from military service in *Cassius Clay v. U.S.* In his appeal, Ali had claimed that he was willing to fight for Islam only in accordance with the beliefs of the Nation of Islam. As the Court reviewed the teachings of the Nation of Islam, they determined that Ali was not selectively determining who he would or would not fight for, but rather had a general or categorical belief against war. They determined that his belief in fighting for Islam was based on a hypothetical and abstract view of a future holy war that may be of a spiritual and not physical nature. The Court held that while selective objections to military service did not qualify for exemption, general objections did.

Currently, according to the Unified Military Training and Service Act as amended (50 U.S.C. App. § 456(j)), the law states the following with respect to conscientious objection to military service:

> (j) Nothing contained in this title shall be construed to require any person to be subject to combatant training and service in the armed forces of the United States who, by reason of religious training and belief, is conscientiously opposed to participation in war in any form. As used in this subsection, the term "religious training and belief" does not include essentially political, sociological, or philosophical views, or a merely personal moral code. Any person claiming exemption from combatant training and service because of such conscientious objections whose claim is sustained by the local board shall, if he is inducted into the armed forces under this title, be assigned to noncombatant service as defined by the President, or shall, if he is found to be conscientiously opposed to participation in such noncombatant service, in lieu of such induction, be ordered by his local board, subject to such regulations as the President may prescribe, to perform for a period equal to the period prescribed in section 4(b) such civilian work contributing to the maintenance of the national health, safety, or interest as the Director may deem appropriate and any such person who knowingly fails or neglects to obey any such order from his local board shall be deemed, for the purposes of section 12 of this title, to have knowingly failed or neglected to perform a duty required of him under this title. The Director shall be responsible for finding civilian work for persons exempted from training and service under this subsection and for the placement of such persons in appropriate civilian work contributing to the maintenance of the national health, safety, or interest.

Protections for individuals with a conscientious objection have been applied to many other areas as well, such as the rights of health care workers and businesses who hold objections to abortion. In 1973, Congress passed what has become known as the Church Amendment as part of the Public Health Service Act. The Church Amendment (42 U.S.C. §300a-7(b-e)) provided conscientious protections for health care workers in hospitals receiving funding from the federal government who "decline to participate in abortions or sterilizations on account of religious beliefs or moral convictions." Several additional legal protections have passed since the Church Amendment, including protections for religious educational institutions opposed to abortion (1988 Civil Rights Restoration Act, 20 U.S.C. §1687), and protection for federal employees who have a conscientious objection to participating in executions of capital crimes (18 U.S.C. §3597). In 2004, under the Hyde-Weldon Amendment (Sec. 507 (d) of the Consolidated Appropriations Act of 2016, Pub. L. No. 114-113), Congress protected the conscience rights of health care workers, hospitals, health insurance companies, and other health care institutions from supporting abortions when using federal or state funds. And in 2010, as Congress passed the Patient Protection and Affordable Care Act, amendments were included to once again protect insurers, providers, and others from being forced to include abortion as an essential benefit in their health care plans (42 U.S.C. §18023) or participate in physician assisted suicide (42 U.S.C. §18113).

In spite of these conscience protections, President Obama issued regulations implementing the legislation that required certain abortifacient drugs to be included in the essential services in the new health care plans. Many religious institutions and businesses argued that providing abortifacient drugs would be in contravention of their conscience rights and subsequently several cases were filed to challenge these new regulations. The list of Supreme Court cases below outlines the results of several of these cases, where the Supreme Court upheld the conscience rights of individuals, businesses, and religious institutions opposed to providing or aiding in abortion. Importantly, in none of these cases was anyone denied access to abortion or abortifacient drugs; however, they were not permitted to violate the conscience of their employers in seeking provision of these services.

Another area where the conscience rights of individuals have been affected is in the area of same sex marriage laws. As states across the U.S. have passed laws recognizing same-sex marriage, several challenges have arisen when businesses in those states refuse to provide services for same-sex marriage ceremonies because in doing so, they feel it would violate their deeply held religious belief in the sacrament of marriage as a heterosexual union. Importantly, the issue at stake in these laws is not whether businesses can refuse services for any other purpose, including the person's sexual orientation. The issue in these objections is whether businesses may choose not to participate in a religious ceremony that they have a religious objection to. So far, the various same-sex marriage laws passed across the country have not fully addressed the intersection of religious freedom and new categories of rights such as equal protection for individuals on the basis of their sexual orientation in states that have adopted same-sex marriage laws. As a result, it is likely that we will see more development on the exemptions applied to individuals with a conscientious objection through the courts in the coming years, particularly as more areas are being affected by these laws, including in the provision of social services. In states that have not provided religious exemptions for certain services, organizations such as Catholic Charities who have a religious objection to placing children in the homes of couples from same-sex marriages, have been forced to close their operations involved in foster care and adoption services in Massachusetts, Illinois and the District of Columbia. In the midst of these challenges, several states looked for ways to address the need for religious exemptions to protect individuals and businesses with conscientious objections to certain issues. On March 26, 2015, then-Governor Mike Pence of Indiana signed the Religious Freedom Restoration Act into law, which provided RFRA protection to the state and included businesses in those receiving protection from government burdens on religious exercise. An amendment was added to the bill shortly thereafter to protect individuals from discrimination on the basis of sexual orientation. A similar law was vetoed in Arizona prior to the Indiana law's passage.

Religion has held a unique role in the American experience and protection for the individual right to freedom of religion continues to evolve in laws and policies throughout the U.S., particularly as new categories of rights emerge and need to be addressed in light of the prevailing protections on religious freedom. Recent statements from the U.N. independent expert on sexual orientation and gender identity and Chai Feldblum, a member of the U.S. Equal Employment and Opportunity Commission have pitted gay rights against the rights of religious freedom, and claimed that religious freedom can be restricted. In the coming years, these issues will require greater attention from the courts and legislators. From the earliest colonies to the ideals enshrined in the Constitution and Bill of Rights, lawmakers have navigated through a variety of challenges to ensure a protected and neutral space for individuals to explore and practice their religion or beliefs. This unique experience has provided a substantial basis for the international standard for religious freedom later adopted by the United Nations and continues to serve as a model for many nations in the world today.

1. U.S. Domestic Framework for Freedom of Religion or Belief

a. Constitutional Right to Freedom of Religion

There are three areas in the Constitution that relate to religious freedom. These include the only reference in the Constitution itself, in Article VI, and the two amendments to the Constitution.

Article VI of the Constitution states that, "...no religious test shall ever be required as a qualification to any office or public trust under the United States."

Religious freedom is guaranteed in the First Amendment to the Constitution,

"Congress shall make no law respecting an establishment of religion, or prohibiting the free exercise thereof; or abridging the freedom of speech, or of the press; or the right of the people peaceably to assemble, and to petition the Government for a redress of grievances."

The first part of this guarantee is known as the "establishment clause" and guarantees that the *federal* government cannot establish an official religion or take any action that would make the federal government the arbiter of religious truth claims. The second part of this guarantee is known as the "free exercise clause" and guarantees that the federal government will not make any law that prohibits the exercise of religion.

The Fourteenth Amendment to the Constitution expands on the First Amendment by guaranteeing "equal protection" for all citizens,

"All persons born or naturalized in the United States, and subject to the jurisdiction thereof, are citizens of the United States and of the State where in they reside. No State shall make or enforce any law which shall abridge the privileges or immunities of citizens of the United States; nor shall any State deprive any person of life, liberty, or property, without due process of law; nor deny to any person within its jurisdiction the equal protection of the laws."

These laws have been further defined in various court cases. Importantly, the reference to a "wall of separation between church and state" was used in a letter by then-President Thomas Jefferson to the Danbury Baptist Church in Rhode Island. The president's response referred to his perspective that the issue they wrote him about was a matter for the state for which the president was unable to interfere since the first amendment related to what the federal government could or could not do, rather than what the states could do. Much later, Jefferson's statement was referred to in various Supreme Court cases that have since defined the legal landscape for the first amendment's establishment clause. The constitutional right to religious freedom is protected by courts at all levels throughout the U.S. In addition, the Department of Justice has a Civil Rights Division focused specifically on addressing cases involving violations of this right.

b. Domestic Legislation on Freedom of Religion
The following is a list of legislation that has shaped and refined the scope of religious freedom in U.S. law.

1954: *Johnson Amendment* — In 1954, then-Senator Lyndon B. Johnson put forward an amendment to a bill on the Internal Revenue Code which prohibits any non-profit organization registered as a 501(c)3 from "influencing legislation, and which does not participate in or intervene in (including the publishing or distributing of statements), any political campaign on behalf of any candidate for public office." It extends the prohibition against 501(c)3 groups from influencing legislation to also prohibiting them from intervening in a political campaign on behalf of a candidate. (President Trump has stated that he will invalidate the Johnson Amendment because of claims that it has a chilling effect on the speech of religious leaders regarding political issues in their congregations, thus violating their freedom of speech and religion.)

1993: *Religious Freedom Restoration Act* — In response to Smith, Congress passed RFRA, reinforcing the Sherbert-Yoder test on laws affecting the Free Exercise of Religion and stating that regardless of whether a law is generally applicable, it must not "substantially burden" religion. Furthermore, it must be justified as the "least restrictive means" for achieving a "compelling government interest." It currently only applies to federal laws.

2000: *Religious Land Use and Institutionalized Persons Act* — RLUIPA was unanimously passed by both houses of Congress and signed into law by President Bill Clinton. RLUIPA sought to address inadequacies in RFRA by limiting restrictions by state and local governments that posed a substantial burden on religious exercise without demonstrating that the restriction was the least restrictive means of furthering a compelling government interest. It provided specific free exercise protection to ensure the rights of prisoners were respected while incarcerated or confined. It also ensured that cities could not use burdensome zoning law restrictions to restrict the free exercise of churches and other institutions use of their property.

c. Domestic Case Law on Freedom of Religion
The following is a non-exhaustive list of various court cases that have shaped and refined the scope of religious freedom in U.S. law.

1879: *Reynolds v. United States* — the Supreme Court made its major first decision on the Free Exercise Clause, upholding a federal law banning polygamy in the territories despite Mormon religious practices of polygamy.

1940: *Cantwell v. State of Connecticut* — the Supreme Court incorporated the Free Exercise Clause through the 14th Amendment's Due Process Clause to protect against actions taken by the states; the decision protected religious actions such as proselytism.

1943: *West Virginia State Board of Education v. Barnette* — the Supreme Court ruled that forcing children to salute the American flag constituted a violation of their freedom of speech and religion under the first amendment.

1947: *Everson v. Board of Education of Ewing* — the Supreme Court incorporated the Establishment Clause through the 14th Amendment's Due Process Clause and expanded its protection to the states; establishes that neither a state nor the federal government may pass laws which aid one or all religions or preference one over another.

1961: *Torcaso v. Watkins* — the Supreme Court clarified that religious tests may not be used for any public office in the United States.

1963: *Murray v. Curlett* — the Supreme Court rules that school prayer was an unconstitutional violation of the Establishment Clause.

1963: *Sherbert v. Verner* — the Supreme Court overturned a state law that denied unemployment benefits to a Seventh-Day Adventist whose religious beliefs forbade him from working on the Sabbath.

1971: *Lemon v. Kurtzman* — the Supreme Court established what has come to be known as the "Lemon Test," which requires three factors to determine if a law is consistent with the Establishment Clause. Such laws would have a secular purpose, have as their primary effect to neither advance nor inhibit religion, and would not create an excessive government entanglement with religion.

1972: *Wisconsin v. Yoder* — the Supreme Court protected the parental rights of Amish parents to direct their child's education and not be forced to comply with a compulsory school attendance law.

1990: *Employment Division, Oregon Department of Human Resources v. Smith* — the Supreme Court ruled that there was no protection under the Free Exercise Clause from a "neutral law of general applicability" and did not permit Native Americans to use peyote in its religious services.

1992: *Lee v. Weisman* — the Supreme Court ruled that schools cannot sponsor a member of the clergy to conduct even non-denominational prayers at a graduation.

1993: *Church of Lukumi Babalu Aye v. City of Hialeah* — the Supreme Court upholds the right of Santeria members to practice animal sacrifice at worship services.

2000: *Santa Fe Independent School District v. Doe* — the Supreme Court reaffirmed its decision in Lee v. Weisman, ruling that student-led and initiated public prayer at a football game violated the Establishment Clause.

2001: *Good News Club v. Milford Central School* — the Supreme Court ruled that religious clubs should be permitted to meet on school campuses and that it would not violate the Establishment Clause.

2002: *Zelman v. Simmons-Harris* — the Supreme Court ruled that parents could use public funds (in the form of vouchers) to choose to send their children to religiously-affiliated schools.

2005: *Cutter v. Wilkinson* — the Supreme Court ruled that facilities that accept funds from the federal government cannot deny prisoners accommodations that are necessary for their religious exercise since doing so would impose a substantial burden on prisoners' rights under RLUIPA.

2005: *Van Orden v. Perry* — the Supreme Court ruled that a monument of the Ten Commandments displayed at the Texas State Capitol did not violate the Establishment Clause because the monument had a secular historic purpose. The Court had an opposite opinion in *McCreary County v. ACLU of Kentucky*, which was decided at the same time because the purpose of the monument in question was of a primarily religious character.

2010: *Christian Legal Society v. Martinez* — the Supreme Court ruled that student campus organizations could not limit their membership to their faith community if it would discriminate against individuals on the basis of their sexual orientation.

2012: *EEOC v. Hosanna-Tabor Evangelical Lutheran Church and School, Michigan* — The Supreme Court ruled unanimously against the EEOC and in favor of protecting the ministerial exception for religious institutions to discriminate in their hiring practices for the purposes of obtaining ministerial staff that adhere to their religious beliefs. The "ministerial exception" includes teachers as well as other religious leaders.

2014: *Town of Greece v. Galloway* — the Supreme Court ruled that government bodies can choose to have a time of prayer before public meetings as long as it permitted expressions from all faiths equally.

2014: *Burwell v. Hobby Lobby* — the Supreme Court rules that a private business owned by individuals with a religious objection to abortion will not be forced to violate their conscience by providing abortifacient drugs in employee health care plans; the health care regulations were applied in a manner that violated the Religious Freedom Restoration Act. (There are another 50 pending lawsuits that will be affected by this decision, including religious universities and other institutions.)

2015: *Holt v. Hobbs* — the Supreme Court ruled unanimously that an Arkansas prison policy was in violation of RLUIPA because it prevented a Muslim prisoner from growing a beard in accordance with his religious beliefs.

d. Freedom of Religion in Foreign Policy

Congress passed the International Religious Freedom Act of 1998 (IRFA) that made the promotion of religious freedom a priority in the nation's foreign policy. The law defined the scope of religious freedom on the basis of Article 18 of the UDHR and ICCPR. IRFA established various mechanisms to help prioritize religious freedom in foreign policy, including an Office of International Religious Freedom within the State Department's Bureau of Democracy, Human Rights and Labor, headed by an Ambassador at Large for International Religious Freedom. The Office was tasked with issuing a special report on the status of religious freedom in countries worldwide and designating countries that commit systematic, ongoing and egregious violations of religious freedom as "Countries of Particular Concern" or CPCs. CPC designations require the President to respond with specific sanctions, however the requirement may be waived for national security reasons. In addition, the legislation makes foreign diplomats who have been involved in particularly severe violations of religious freedom ineligible for visas or admission to the U.S. The law has only been used once, when in 2005, the State Department denied then-Chief Minister of Gujarat State in India, Narendra Modi, a visa to enter the U.S. due to his failure to stop large-scale and deadly anti-Muslim riots that occurred in his state in 2004. Modi, who has since become Prime Minister of India, was later permitted to travel to the U.S. in spite of the previous denial under IRFA.

Aiding the Office of International Religious Freedom in this effort, IRFA established the U.S. Commission on International Religious Freedom, headed by ten politically appointed commissioners, which included the Ambassador at Large as a non-voting member. The primary task of USCIRF was to determine recommendations for CPC designation. IRFA also gave the Commission authority to request a study on the treatment of asylum applicants with claims of religious persecution who have been denied their petitions and faced expedited removal from the U.S. The Commission subsequently published a study on its findings related to Expedited Removal, which was influential in changes to U.S. refugee and asylum policies to ensure that those with a legitimate claim of religious persecution were not illegally removed from the U.S. The legislation also established the position of a Special Advisor on International Religious Freedom within the White House National Security Council.

In 2016, Congress passed the Frank R. Wolf International Religious Freedom Act, which was signed into law by President Barack Obama on December 16, 2016. The Wolf bill was named for the congressman who had authored the original IRFA legislation in 1998. The amended law boosted the Ambassador's position within the State Department, who will now report directly to the Secretary of State. The Wolf bill also mandated that all diplomats are trained in international religious freedom, and the Office of International Religious Freedom was required to publish an annual list of individuals imprisoned because of their religion or belief around the world. The bill included language that recognized the rights of atheists and other non-religious persons as individuals protected under religious freedom, which includes the freedom not to participate in any religion.

Religious freedom is also addressed within several other forums — the Executive Congressional Commission on China, the Helsinki Commission, and through the various U.S. Missions to the United Nations. In the 2016 authorization bill for the State Department — the first to be passed since 2002, Congress called on the State Department to ensure that no U.N. member should be on the Human Rights Council if they have been designated as a CPC under IRFA.

There has also been a longstanding tradition of religious freedom throughout U.S. refugee policies to prioritize certain persecuted groups. And the U.S. has recognized various instances where genocide and other crimes against humanity were occurring in foreign countries, which implicates a moral responsibility to respond. In 2004, the U.S. recognized the situation in Darfur, Sudan, as genocide, and again in 2016, the U.S. recognized the situation in Iraq and Syria as genocide for the violence by Islamic State militants against Yazidi, Christian and other religious communities. In response to the 2004 designation, then-President George Bush appointed a Special Envoy to negotiate what became known as the Comprehensive Peace Agreement between North and South Sudan, ending a civil war that had lasted several decades. As of this writing, there has been no formal response to the 2016 genocide designation.

e. Reports to the U.N. on Freedom of Religion
The U.S. submitted its first report to the U.N. Human Rights Council under the Universal Periodic Review mechanism in 2010. The second report was submitted in 2015 addressed recommendations from the first UPR.

2. International Framework for Freedom of Religion or Belief

The right to freedom of religion or belief is protected in various documents internationally and in every regional human rights system. The most widely accepted international norms for this freedom are found in Article 18 of both the Universal Declaration of Human Rights and the International Covenant on Civil and Political Rights. Importantly, there are two key components of Article 18 of the UDHR and ICCPR: the freedom to have a religion or belief, and the freedom to manifest those beliefs in practice.

a. International Treaties on Freedom of Religion
The following Declaration and treaties protect the freedom of religion or belief to varying degrees:

Universal Declaration of Human Rights 1948 (UDHR),

Art. 2: Everyone is entitled to all the rights and freedoms set forth in this Declaration, without distinction of any kind, such as race, colour, sex, language, religion, political or other opinion, national or social origin, property, birth or other status. Furthermore, no distinction shall be made on the basis of the political, jurisdictional or international status of the country or territory to which a person belongs, whether it be independent, trust, non-self-governing or under any other limitation of sovereignty.

Art. 18: Everyone has the right to freedom of thought, conscience and religion; this right includes freedom to change his religion or belief, and freedom, either alone or in community with others and in public or private, to manifest his religion or belief in teaching, practice, worship and observance.

Article 18 of the UDHR is legally binding on all states as a matter of customary international law.

International Covenant on Civil and Political Rights 1966 (ICCPR),

Art. 2(1): Each State Party to the present Covenant undertakes to respect and to ensure to all individuals within its territory and subject to its jurisdiction the rights recognized in the present Covenant, without distinction of any kind, such as race, colour, sex, language, religion, political or other opinion, national or social origin, property, birth or other status.

Art. 18:

1. Everyone shall have the right to freedom of thought, conscience and religion. This right shall include freedom to have or to adopt a religion or belief of his choice, and freedom, either individually or in community with others and in public or private, to manifest his religion or belief in worship, observance, practice and teaching.

2. No one shall be subject to coercion, which would impair his freedom to have or to adopt a religion or belief of his choice.

3. Freedom to manifest one's religion or beliefs may be subject only to such limitations as are prescribed by law and are necessary to protect public safety, order, health, or morals or the fundamental rights and freedoms of others.

4. The States Parties to the present Covenant undertake to have respect for the liberty of parents and, when applicable, legal guardians to ensure the religious and moral education of their children in conformity with their own convictions.

Article 18 of the ICCPR is the most important international human rights norm concerning freedom of religion applicable to the U.S. It can be analyzed and applied along with any First Amendment issue because by caselaw, courts should always try to interpret and apply U.S. law in a manner consistent with international law, which the ICCPR constitutes.

Art. 27: In those States in which ethnic, religious or linguistic minorities exist, persons belonging to such minorities shall not be denied the right, in community with the other members of their group, to enjoy their own culture, to profess and practise their own religion, or to use their own language.

Helsinki Final Act 1975, Principle VII:

The participating States will respect human rights and fundamental freedoms, including the freedom of thought, conscience, religion or belief, for all without distinction as to race, sex, language or religion.

American Convention on Human Rights, 1969, Art 12:

1. Everyone has the right to freedom of conscience and of religion. This right includes freedom to maintain or to change one's religion or beliefs, and freedom to profess or disseminate one's religion or beliefs, either individually or together with others, in public or in private.

2. No one shall be subject to restrictions that might impair his freedom to maintain or to change his religion or beliefs.

3. Freedom to manifest one's religion and beliefs may be subject only to the limitations prescribed by law that are necessary to protect public safety, order, health, or morals, or the rights or freedoms of others.

4. Parents or guardians, as the case may be, have the right to provide for the religious and moral education of their children or wards that is in accord with their own convictions.

This article comes from the Inter-American human rights system under the Organization of American States, which covers almost all states in the western Hemisphere. The U.S. has signed but not ratified this regional human rights treaty.

Because the U.S. has not ratified the American Convention on Human Rights, Article 12 of that treaty is not legally binding on the U.S. However, having signed that treaty the U.S. has a "soft obligation" under the Vienna Convention on the Law of Treaties, not to act in a manner inconsistent with it. Arguably, however Article III of the American Declaration on the Rights and Duties of Man, also from the OAS, can be used as a norm to judge the U.S. freedom of religion action under the OAS Inter-American legal standards. Article III of the American Declaration, which is not a treaty, reads:

Article III. Every person has the right freely to profess a religious faith, and to manifest and practice it both in public and in private.

b. Human Rights Committee General Comments and Case Law
The Human Rights Committee is the treaty body that reviews compliance of member states with the International Covenant on Civil and Political Rights. The Committee receives reports from member states every three years with the status of the treaty in their country. In addition, the Committee issues General Comments about the scope of provisions in the treaty as needed. And the Committee receives complaints from member states that have accepted its jurisdiction in the First Optional Protocol to the ICCPR to accept the individual complaint mechanism for the treaty.

General Comment 22 is the most important document defining the scope of Article 18 of the ICCPR. In it, freedom of religion or belief is defined as a right for theists and atheists or other non-believers and new religious communities. The Comment explains the scope of limitations to this freedom, and ensures that states do not justify any limitations not permitted or such as may be justified on the basis of a particular religious moral code. This General Comment is found in the Primary Source Document 2.

c. Additional International Documents on Freedom of Religion

The United Nations adopted the Declaration on the Elimination of All Forms of Intolerance and of Discrimination Based on Religion or Belief in 1981. The Declaration was originally intended to be a treaty, but in the end it did not receive sufficient support. The International Convention on the Elimination of All Forms of Racism was separated off from the original treaty work and two documents emerged — the 1981 Declaration and the Racism Convention. The 1981 Declaration clarifies the scope of freedom of religion or belief further, and establishes the principal that religion is a protected class in discrimination. The 1992 Declaration on the Rights of Persons Belonging to National or Ethnic, Religious or Linguistic Minorities also provides protections for the freedom of religion or belief of minority communities.

U.N. Declaration on the Elimination of All Forms of Intolerance and of Discrimination Based on Religion or Belief 1981 (U.N. 1981 Dec.), Art. 1:

(1) Everyone shall have the right to freedom of thought, conscience and religion. This right shall include freedom to have a religion or whatever belief of his choice, and freedom, either individually or in community with others and in public or private, to manifest his religion or belief in worship, observance, practice and teaching.

(2) No one shall be subject to coercion which would impair his freedom to have a religion or belief of his choice.

(3) Freedom to manifest one's religion or belief may be subject only to such limitations as are prescribed by law and are necessary to protect public safety, order, health or morals or the fundamental rights and freedoms of others.

d. Related Human Rights Instruments

There are several additional human rights treaties that include provisions to protect freedom of religion or belief. These include protections for refugees, minorities, women, and children.

The Refugee Convention

Article 4. The Contracting States shall accord to refugees within their territories treatment at least as favorable as that accorded to their nationals with respect to freedom to practice their religion and freedom as regards the religious education of their children.

Article 33 (1) No Contracting State shall expel or return ("refouler") a refugee in any manner whatsoever to the frontiers of territories where his life or freedom would be threatened on account of his race, religion, nationality, membership of a particular social group or political opinion. (2) The benefit of the present provision may not, however, be claimed by a refugee whom there are reasonable grounds for regarding as a danger to the security of the country in which he is, or who, having been convicted by a final judgment of a particularly serious crime, constitutes a danger to the community of that country.

Convention on the Rights of the Child

Article 14.1. States Parties shall respect the right of the child to freedom of thought, conscience and religion. 2. States Parties shall respect the rights and duties of the parents and, when applicable, legal guardians, to provide direction to the child in the exercise of his or her right in a manner consistent with the evolving capacities of the child. 3. Freedom to manifest one's religion or beliefs may be subject only to such limitations as are prescribed by law and are necessary to protect public safety, order, health or morals, or the fundamental rights and freedoms of others.

Article 30. In those States in which ethnic, religious or linguistic minorities or persons of indigenous origin exist, a child belonging to such a minority or who is indigenous shall not be denied the right, in community with other members of his or her group, to enjoy his or her own culture, to profess and practise his or her own religion, or to use his or her own language.

Additionally, other treaties include general protections against discrimination on the basis of religion. This includes the 1992 Declaration on the Rights of Persons Belonging to National or Ethnic, Religious and Linguistic Minorities, General Assembly resolution 47/135 (1992 Minorities Declaration) http://www.un-documents.net/a47r135.htm, the CEDAW, and the ICESCR, Art. 2(2).

e. Mechanisms: Special Rapporteur for Freedom of Religion or Belief

The Human Rights Council is mandated to appoint an independent expert with the title Special Rapporteur for freedom of religion or belief to monitor this human right. The mandate was originally created under authorized under Resolution 1986/20 focused on religious intolerance, and in 2000, the mandate was changed to its current title, and endorsed by ECOSOC decision 2000/261 and General Assembly Resolution 55/97. The mandate has been renewed since. Under Human Rights Council Resolution 6/37, the Special Rapporteur has been mandated to promote the legal standard globally, identify obstacles and propose recommendations to improve respect for it, examine violations of the right, and apply a gender perspective. The Special Rapporteur may use country visits, communications with foreign governments and annual reports to carry out his/her mandate.

There have been five individuals to fill this post since its inception: Mr. Angelo d'Almeida Ribeiro (1986-1993), Mr. Abdelfattah Amor (1993-2004), Ms. Asma Jahangir (2004-2010), Mr. Heiner Bielefeldt (2010-2016), and Mr. Ahmed Shaheed (Nov 1, 2016 — present).

Country visits often provide in-depth reporting on the situation and can be an important tool to move countries toward greater respect of this freedom. The Special Rapporteurs have also offered important insight and analysis into the freedom of religion or belief on a number of topics. For instance, a report on the scope of Article 20 and the "incitement to religious hatred" in the context of Article 18 helped the U.N. move away from dangerous resolutions that provided legal cover for blasphemy laws. The Special Rapporteur's reports on conversion have helped describe how the right is an aspect of the forum internum and the forum externum, which is important because as a matter of the former, the right is inviolable and no restrictions are permitted. This is because conversion occurs inside a person, in their seat of conscience before it is expressed publicly. The other various reports offer important insights on a number of topics, from how women are affected by violations of this freedom to how to navigate counter-terrorism laws or regulate school education in a manner consistent with this freedom.

f. Human Rights Council and UPR

The Human Rights Council is a body within the General Assembly comprised of 47 member states that monitor and promote human rights worldwide. The United States has been a member of the Council and subject to the Council's Universal Periodic Review mechanism for member states twice — in 2011 and 2015 respectively. Excerpts from the review are below. Many of the recommendations and responses focus on issues relating to the rights of Muslims in a post-9/11 environment.

Beginning in 1999, Pakistan, on behalf of a voting bloc of 57 Muslim-majority countries, began proposing resolutions condemning a concept they referred to as the "defamation of religions" within the Human Rights Commission. Originally proposed as a "defamation of Islam" resolution, the title quickly changed; however, the intent was still the same. The OIC sought legal protection from verbal challenges to Islam that they deemed offensive; to many observers, they were seeking international justification for blasphemy and apostasy laws. The resolutions passed under the racism agenda item at the U.N. from 1999 to 2005. In 2006, the Council adopted a similar resolution, but called on certain special rapporteurs to provide an analysis of the concept "defamation of religions" with respect to Article 20 of the ICCPR and whether or to what extent, the concept addressed incitement against individuals on the basis of religion.

Article 20 of the ICCPR states:

1. Any propaganda for war shall be prohibited by law.

2. Any advocacy of national, racial or religious hatred that constitutes incitement to discrimination, hostility or violence shall be prohibited by law.

Article 20 places a burden on the state parties to the treaty to prohibit by law any instances that amount to incitement to violence against individuals on the basis of their national, racial or religious heritage. According to the original intent of Article 20, it was meant to prevent violence against religious or other communities such as occurred during the Holocaust against the Jewish community. It has been used in reference to the Rwandan genocide when public media incited violence against ethnic communities. Importantly, the article is not a blanket restriction on provocative speech, but rather on speech intended to incite violence of a very high threshold.

From 2007 to 2009, support for the resolution weakened as international advocates and officials, including from the U.S., argued that the concept of "defamation of religions" was flawed and inconsistent with international law. In particular, it was argued that the concept conflated race (an immutable characteristic) with religion (a choice), that the freedom of religion or belief protects the right of individuals and not religion or beliefs and therefore there can be no protection for religions from being defamed but only individuals, and that the concept of defamation provides cover for blasphemy and apostasy laws that are inconsistent with the freedom to choose and change one's religion or beliefs and has a chilling effect on speech and religious expression — especially for those who may dissent from the majority or from minority communities.

By 2011, the resolution had lost significant support. At the same time, two prominent members of the Pakistani government who were both opposed to the states' own blasphemy laws were brutally murdered. In the wake of their deaths the U.S. and others opposed to the resolutions moved to adopt a new resolution. The U.S.-led effort led to the adoption by consensus of Resolution 16/18 titled, "Combating intolerance, negative stereotyping and stigmatization of, and discrimination, incitement to violence, and violence against persons based on religion or belief" in March 2011. The new resolution was adopted under the agenda item for religious intolerance and focused on the proscription in Article 20 of the ICCPR for states to take measures to prevent incitement of religious hatred that amounts to discrimination, hostility or violence.

Following the U.S.-led effort to pass Resolution 16/18, Secretary of State Hillary Clinton attended an OIC event in Istanbul where she called on leaders there to join her in battling religious discrimination. The meeting launched what has come to be known as the Istanbul Process whereby the Secretary of State proposed a list of best practices for preventing religious discrimination and violence. The Istanbul Process focused on both freedom of religion or belief and the freedom of expression in Article 19 of the ICCPR. Resolution 16/18 and the Istanbul Process marked a positive shift away from the defamation of religions concept, which conflated race and religion and attempted to protect religions over individuals. In doing so, it also moved the international community away from any legal justification of blasphemy and apostasy laws. However, vague references to "incitement" and "negative stereotyping" coupled with references to print and other materials in the resolution could easily be misinterpreted without stronger and more robust declarations about the scope of freedom of religion or belief with respect to religious expression and permissible limitations.

Shortly after the adoption of Resolution 16/18, the Office of the U.N. High Commissioner for Human Rights sought recommendations from non-governmental organizations regarding how best to implement the resolution. The first discussion took place in Rabat, Morocco and by 2013 the Rabat Plan was adopted by the UN, which laid out a three-part test for determining whether a speech prohibition was valid. The conditions were based on Articles 19 and 20, with little consideration for the scope of Article 18 on freedom of religion or belief. The Rabat Plan's focus on limitations to expression — regardless of the religious nature and rights of religious speech — was therefore quite distinct from the Istanbul Process, which focused on Articles 18 and 20. The Plan also did not clarify the difference between incitement and provocation, which have often been conflated in discussions surrounding limitations on religious expression. This could lead states to restrict religious speech deemed offensive on the basis that it is provocative, even though statements that are provocative may not rise to the level of incitement intended to cause violence, which has often been the case with legal restrictions on religious expression in the form of blasphemy, apostasy and anti-conversion. The Rabat Plan did, however, highlight the problematic nature of blasphemy laws and recognized that freedom of religion or belief does not include a right to have a religion or belief that is free from criticism or ridicule.

In spite of the various discussions that have largely resolved the discussion of the defamation of religions concept, blasphemy and apostasy laws remain a challenge internationally, as do other laws limiting religious speech under the guise of "hate speech." One significant issue with the defamation of religions resolutions which relates to similar discussions in the U.S. involves the way this concept sought to justify government interference in religion and determination of theology in so far as they determined what religious ideas were offensive. In the U.S., the Establishment Clause protects individuals from the federal government making decisions on matters of theology or religious belief.

g. Counter-Terrorism Measures and Religion

In the wake of the terrorist attacks on the United States on September 11, 2001, President Bush incorporated respect for religious freedom as a priority in his National Security Strategy (NSS). Based on popular research, including from the Pew Research Center, countries that lack religious pluralism and respect for religious freedom were found to be less stable and more prone to religion-related conflict and extremism. Conversely, respect for religious freedom has been shown to be an important indicator of a country's resiliency to the ideologies that lead to extremism. With this in mind, under President Bush the NSS reflected how America's historic culture of pluralism and respect for religious freedom serves as an important model for countries navigating the role of religion in society and developing policies that prevent and counter extremism. The language regarding religious freedom was not found in President Obama's NSS. President Trump has made some statements reflecting a move towards its inclusion.

Religion can be a motivating factor in conflict and it can also be utilized by religious leaders to incite their followers to violence. When, as is often the case, extremist groups actively employ religious terminology in their recruitment efforts and frame their groups' purposes and existence around religious ideology, the religious dimension of violent extremism cannot be ignored. It is important to recall that the international human right to freedom of religion or belief does not protect religion or religious ideas; it protects the individual's right to have and manifest their beliefs. Moreover, it does not include any protection for religious practices that violate the rights and freedoms of others, such as a religious claim that one may kill someone who refuses to convert to their belief.

Recent attempts to train members of societies prone to religious extremism in human rights and religious freedom have shown a tendency to provide communities the tools they need to dampen or prevent extremist attitudes thus lessening chances of violence. In Sudan and Iraq — two countries highly prone to religious extremism that the U.S. has engaged on the issue of religiously motivated and targeted genocide — it was found that when members of civil society fully embrace the human right to freedom of religion or belief, they are able to apply this right to their various spheres of influence in ways that increase public support for the right, mitigate conflict, and increase opportunities for minority faith communities.

Importantly, when freedom of religion or belief is advanced among diverse groups working in collaboration with one another across religious and ideological lines, there is a significant decrease in the push and pull factors that lead people into violent extremism. This is because societies that work together across religious and socioeconomic lines to encourage tolerance, increase pluralistic literacy, and increase respect freedom of religion or belief are communities that are resilient against extremist ideologies and violence against vulnerable populations. The results of recent programs have offered substantial support for expanding efforts to advance freedom of religion or belief within other efforts aimed at preventing and countering violent extremism.

h. Refugee Policy

The International Religious Freedom Act of 1998 establishes processes to ensure that consular officers and others involved in adjudicating cases for refugee admissions which involve persons who faced religious persecution, are not biased in any way toward the refugee applicant and are aware that religious persecution is a legitimate claim for refugee admission. Moreover, IRFA calls on consular officers to utilize the annual IRF reports published on each country to provide information about the situation affecting individuals who claim religious persecution. Each year, when providing a report to Congress on the Proposed Refugee Admissions for the year, the State Department highlights the communities eligible for consideration of admission based on religious persecution and the general concerns regarding religious persecution in each region where the U.S. refugee admissions program is active, in accordance with IRFA as well as the North Korean Human Rights Act of 2004, which has the DPRK listed as a country of particular concern for violations of religious freedom. Religious persecution is one of the five primary claims for individuals seeking refuge under international refugee law, which enables them to be referred to the U.S.

In 1989, Congress passed what has come to be known as the Lautenberg Amendment, which recognized certain minority religious communities from the former Soviet Union for refugee admission on the basis of a well founded and established fear of religious persecution under the priority two classification for groups. Under Lautenberg, Jews, Evangelical Christians, Ukranian Catholics, and Orthodox communities from Eurasia and the Baltics can more easily access the U.S. refugee program if they have close family in the U.S. Since 2004, the Lautenberg Amendment has also included religious minorities from Iran as well. In addition, the State Department has recognized Cubans who are facing religious persecution as a priority two group for refugee consideration.

In 2007, Senators Ted Kennedy and Gordon Smith introduced the Refugee Crisis in Iraq Act that was included as an amendment to the 2008 Defense Authorization Bill. The Iraq Act provided that religious minorities from Iraq qualify as a priority two group due to religious persecution. It seems that the State Department did not prioritize Iraqi religious minorities in processing under President Obama. The original Senate bill focused primarily on Iraqis who had worked with the U.S. military in Iraq; however, it also gave preference to persecuted religious minorities:

"Priority 2 refugees of special humanitarian concern under the refugee resettlement priority system shall include…(4) Iraqis who are members of a religious or minority community and have close family members (as described in sections 201(b)(2)(A)(i) or 203(a) of the Immigration and Nationality Act (8 U.S.C. 1151(b)(2)(A)(i) and 1153(a))) in the United States….(b)Identification of other persecuted groups…"

In 2017, President Trump issued an executive order to prioritize persecuted religious communities who represented minority communities in their country of origin from seven countries after a brief period where the refugee admissions program in those countries would be paused. Individuals may also be given priority access to the U.S. refugee admissions program based on humanitarian concerns, including by request of the President, which relates to the 2017 Executive Order from President Trump. That Executive Order was the subject of Federal Court litigation at the time of this writing.

Primary Source Documents

I. AN ACT FOR ESTABLISHING RELIGIOUS FREEDOM

This historical document shows how freedom of religion and its protection was an important part of the American historical record. Written by Thomas Jefferson it was an act passed by the General Assembly of the State of Virginia, many of whose people had experienced religious persecution. This act served as the forerunner of the first amendment protections for religious freedom under the U.S. Constitution. This Act is rooted in Jefferson's philosophy. Today this act can be looked at, along with the First Amendment, in light of the international legal norms in texts such as the Universal Declaration of Human Rights and the International Covenant on Civil and Political Rights, which are arguably the progeny of this act. This is because the U.S. was very instrumental in influencing the drafting of the international human rights norms including freedom of religion.

[Text]

Virginia, January 16, 1786

Whereas, Almighty God hath created the mind free;

That all attempts to influence it by temporal punishments or burthens, or by civil incapacitations tend only to beget habits of hypocrisy and meanness, and therefore are a departure from the plan of the holy author of our religion, who being Lord, both of body and mind yet chose not to propagate it by coercions on either, as was in his Almighty power to do,

That the impious presumption of legislators and rulers, civil as well as ecclesiastical, who, being themselves but fallible and uninspired men have assumed dominion over the faith of others, setting up their own opinions and modes of thinking as the only true and infallible, and as such endeavouring to impose them on others, hath established and maintained false religions over the greatest part of the world and through all time;

That to compel a man to furnish contributions of money for the propagation of opinions, which he disbelieves is sinful and tyrannical;

That even the forcing him to support this or that teacher of his own religious persuasion is depriving him of the comfortable liberty of giving his contributions to the particular pastor, whose morals he would make his pattern, and whose powers he feels most persuasive to righteousness, and is withdrawing from the Ministry those temporary rewards, which, proceeding from an approbation of their personal conduct are an additional incitement to earnest and unremitting labours for the instruction of mankind;

That our civil rights have no dependence on our religious opinions any more than our opinions in physics or geometry,

That therefore the proscribing any citizen as unworthy the public confidence, by laying upon him an incapacity of being called to offices of trust and emolument, unless he profess or renounce this or that religious opinion, is depriving him injuriously of those privileges and advantages, to which, in common with his fellow citizens, he has a natural right,

That it tends only to corrupt the principles of that very Religion it is meant to encourage, by bribing with a monopoly of worldly honours and emoluments those who will externally profess and conform to it;

That though indeed, these are criminal who do not withstand such temptation, yet neither are those innocent who lay the bait in their way;

That to suffer the civil magistrate to intrude his powers into the field of opinion and to restrain the profession or propagation of principles on supposition of their ill tendency is a dangerous fallacy which at once destroys all religious liberty because he being of course judge of that tendency will make his opinions the rule of judgment and approve or condemn the sentiments of others only as they shall square with or differ from his own;

That it is time enough for the rightful purposes of civil government, for its officers to interfere when principles break out into overt acts against peace and good order;

And finally, that Truth is great, and will prevail if left to herself, that she is the proper and sufficient antagonist to error, and has nothing to fear from the conflict, unless by human interposition disarmed of her natural weapons free argument and debate, errors ceasing to be dangerous when it is permitted freely to contradict them:

Be it enacted by General Assembly that no man shall be compelled to frequent or support any religious worship, place, or ministry whatsoever, nor shall be enforced, restrained, molested, or burthened in his body or goods, nor shall otherwise suffer on account of his religious opinions or belief, but that all men shall be free to profess, and by argument to maintain, their opinions in matters of Religion, and that the same shall in no wise diminish, enlarge or affect their civil capacities. And though we well know that this Assembly elected by the people for the ordinary purposes of Legislation only, have no power to restrain the acts of succeeding Assemblies constituted with powers equal to our own, and that therefore to declare this act irrevocable would be of no effect in law; yet we are free to declare, and do declare that the rights hereby asserted, are of the natural rights of mankind, and that if any act shall be hereafter passed to repeal the present or to narrow its operation, such act will be an infringement of natural right.

[End Text]

Source: Library of Virginia, Education and Outreach Division, http://www.virginiamemory.com/docs/ReligiousFree.pdf

☙☙☙☙☙☙☙

2. GENERAL COMMENT NO. 22 OF THE U.N. HRC ON THE RIGHT TO FREEDOM OF THOUGHT, CONSCIENCE AND RELIGION

The Human Rights Committee (aka Committee on Civil and Political Rights or CCPR), as the body of independent experts that monitors implementation of the International Covenant on Civil and Political Rights (ICCPR) by states parties to it, publishes general comments in thematic issues as interpretations of the content of human rights provisions in the ICCPR. This is Human Rights Committee's General Comment No. 22, addressing the right to freedom of thought, conscience and religion.

[Text]

(Art. 18) : 30/07/93. CCPR/C/21/Rev.1/Add.4

1. The right to freedom of thought, conscience and religion (which includes the freedom to hold beliefs) in article 18.1 is far-reaching and profound; it encompasses freedom of thought on all matters, personal conviction and the commitment to religion or belief, whether manifested individually or in community with others. The Committee draws the attention of States parties to the fact that the freedom of thought and the freedom of conscience are protected equally with the freedom of religion and belief. The fundamental character of these freedoms is also reflected in the fact that this provision cannot be derogated from, even in time of public emergency, as stated in article 4.2 of the Covenant.

2. Article 18 protects theistic, non-theistic and atheistic beliefs, as well as the right not to profess any religion or belief. The terms "belief" and "religion" are to be broadly construed. Article 18 is not limited in its application to traditional religions or to religions and beliefs with institutional characteristics or practices analogous to those of traditional religions. The Committee therefore views with concern any tendency to discriminate against any religion or belief for any reason, including the fact that they are newly established, or represent religious minorities that may be the subject of hostility on the part of a predominant religious community.

3. Article 18 distinguishes the freedom of thought, conscience, religion or belief from the freedom to manifest religion or belief. It does not permit any limitations whatsoever on the freedom of thought and conscience or on the freedom to have or adopt a religion or belief of one's choice. These freedoms are protected unconditionally, as is the right of everyone to hold opinions without interference in article 19.1. In accordance with articles 18.2 and 17, no one can be compelled to reveal his thoughts or adherence to a religion or belief.

4. The freedom to manifest religion or belief may be exercised "either individually or in community with others and in public or private." The freedom to manifest religion or belief in worship, observance, practice and teaching encompasses a broad range of acts. The concept of worship extends to ritual and ceremonial acts giving direct expression to belief, as well as various practices integral to such acts, including the building of places of worship, the use of ritual formulae and objects, the display of symbols, and the observance of holidays and days of rest. The observance and practice of religion or belief may include not only ceremonial acts but also such customs as the observance of dietary regulations, the wearing of distinctive clothing or headcoverings, participation in rituals associated with certain stages of life, and the use of a particular language customarily spoken by a group. In addition, the practice and teaching of religion or belief includes acts integral to the conduct by religious groups of their basic affairs, such as the freedom to choose their religious leaders, priests and teachers, the freedom to establish seminaries or religious schools and the freedom to prepare and distribute religious texts or publications.

5. The Committee observes that the freedom to "have or to adopt" a religion or belief necessarily entails the freedom to choose a religion or belief, including the right to replace one's current religion or belief with another or to adopt atheistic views, as well as the right to retain one's religion or belief. Article 18.2 bars coercion that would impair the right to have or adopt a religion or belief, including the use of threat of physical force or penal sanctions to compel believers or non-believers to adhere to their religious beliefs and congregations, to recant their religion or belief or to convert. Policies or practices having the same intention or effect, such as, for example, those restricting access to education, medical care, employment or the rights guaranteed by article 25 and other provisions of the Covenant, are similarly inconsistent with article 18.2. The same protection is enjoyed by holders of all beliefs of a non-religious nature.

6. The Committee is of the view that article 18.4 permits public school instruction in subjects such as the general history of religions and ethics if it is given in a neutral and objective way. The liberty of parents or legal guardians to ensure that their children receive a religious and moral education in conformity with their own convictions, set forth in article 18.4, is related to the guarantees of the freedom to teach a religion or belief stated in article 18.1. The Committee notes that public education that includes instruction in a particular religion or belief is inconsistent with article 18.4 unless provision is made for non-discriminatory exemptions or alternatives that would accommodate the wishes of parents and guardians.

7. In accordance with article 20, no manifestation of religion or belief may amount to propaganda for war or advocacy of national, racial or religious hatred that constitutes incitement to discrimination, hostility or violence. As stated by the Committee in its General Comment 11 [19], States parties are under the obligation to enact laws to prohibit such acts.

8. Article 18.3 permits restrictions on the freedom to manifest religion or belief only if limitations are prescribed by law and are necessary to protect public safety, order, health or morals, or the fundamental rights and freedoms of others. The freedom from coercion to have or to adopt a religion or belief and the liberty of parents and guardians to ensure religious and moral education cannot be restricted. In interpreting the scope of permissible limitation clauses, States parties should proceed from the need to protect the rights guaranteed under the Covenant, including the right to equality and non-discrimination on all grounds specified in articles 2, 3 and 26. Limitations imposed must be established by law and must not be applied in a manner that would vitiate the rights guaranteed in article 18. The Committee observes that paragraph 3 of article 18 is to be strictly interpreted: restrictions are not allowed on grounds not specified there, even if they would be allowed as restrictions to other rights protected in the Covenant, such as national security. Limitations may be applied only for those purposes for which they were prescribed and must be directly related and proportionate to the specific need on which they are predicated. Restrictions may not be imposed for discriminatory purposes or applied in a discriminatory manner. The Committee observes that the concept of morals derives from many social, philosophical and religious traditions; consequently, limitations on the freedom to manifest a religion or belief for the purpose of protecting morals must be based on principles not deriving exclusively from a single tradition. Persons already subject to certain legitimate constraints, such as prisoners, continue to enjoy their rights to manifest their religion or belief to the

fullest extent compatible with the specific nature of the constraint. States parties' reports should provide information on the full scope and effects of limitations under article 18.3, both as a matter of law and of their application in specific circumstances.

9. The fact that a religion is recognized as a state religion or that it is established as official or traditional or that its followers comprise the majority of the population, shall not result in any impairment of the enjoyment of any of the rights under the Covenant, including articles 18 and 27, nor in any discrimination against adherents to other religions or non-believers. In particular, certain measures discriminating against the latter, such as measures restricting eligibility for government service to members of the predominant religion or giving economic privileges to them or imposing special restrictions on the practice of other faiths, are not in accordance with the prohibition of discrimination based on religion or belief and the guarantee of equal protection under article 26. The measures contemplated by article 20, paragraph 2 of the Covenant constitute important safeguards against infringement of the rights of religious minorities and of other religious groups to exercise the rights guaranteed by articles 18 and 27, and against acts of violence or persecution directed towards those groups. The Committee wishes to be informed of measures taken by States parties concerned to protect the practices of all religions or beliefs from infringement and to protect their followers from discrimination. Similarly, information as to respect for the rights of religious minorities under article 27 is necessary for the Committee to assess the extent to which the right to freedom of thought, conscience, religion and belief has been implemented by States parties. States parties concerned should also include in their reports information relating to practices considered by their laws and jurisprudence to be punishable as blasphemous.

10. If a set of beliefs is treated as official ideology in constitutions, statutes, proclamations of ruling parties, etc., or in actual practice, this shall not result in any impairment of the freedoms under article 18 or any other rights recognized under the Covenant nor in any discrimination against persons who do not accept the official ideology or who oppose it.

11. Many individuals have claimed the right to refuse to perform military service (conscientious objection) on the basis that such right derives from their freedoms under article 18. In response to such claims, a growing number of States have in their laws exempted from compulsory military service citizens who genuinely hold religious or other beliefs that forbid the performance of military service and replaced it with alternative national service. The Covenant does not explicitly refer to a right to conscientious objection, but the Committee believes that such a right can be derived from article 18, inasmuch as the obligation to use lethal force may seriously conflict with the freedom of conscience and the right to manifest one's religion or belief. When this right is recognized by law or practice, there shall be no differentiation among conscientious objectors on the basis of the nature of their particular beliefs; likewise, there shall be no discrimination against conscientious objectors because they have failed to perform military service. The Committee invites States parties to report on the conditions under which persons can be exempted from military service on the basis of their rights under article 18 and on the nature and length of alternative national service.

⊱⊷⊰⊱⊷⊰⊱⊷⊰

3. DECLARATION ON THE ELIMINATION OF ALL FORMS OF INTOLERANCE AND OF DISCRIMINATION BASED ON RELIGION OR BELIEF

This document is a non-binding declaration adopted in the U.N. General Assembly which declares some of the content of the human right to freedom of religion or belief in order to bring an end to all forms of intolerance and discrimination against anyone, based on their religion or belief. It is a declaration of the international community that religious intolerance and discrimination are human rights violations. It calls everyone, not just states, to be tolerant and not discriminate against people because of what religion or beliefs they hold. There was an attempt at the U.N. to create a legally binding treaty to protect freedom of religion or belief but it was so politically controversial that it had to be abandoned. However, the General Assembly chose to do something to express the international consensus on this human right and the problems of intolerance and discrimination by issuing the declaration of principles of what is included in the human right to freedom of religion or belief. It has gathered a lot of weight over the year since it was adopted by the UNGA and is usually cited along with articles 18 of the Universal Declaration of Human Rights and of the International Covenant on Civil and Political Rights. These articles can be found in Chapter 1, Primary Source Documents 1 and 2. This Declaration fleshes out those articles.

[Text]

Declaration on the Elimination of All Forms of Intolerance and of Discrimination Based on Religion or Belief, Proclaimed by General Assembly resolution 36/55 of 25 November 1981

The General Assembly,

Considering that one of the basic principles of the Charter of the United Nations is that of the dignity and equality inherent in all human beings, and that all Member States have pledged themselves to take joint and separate action in co-operation with the Organization to promote and encourage universal respect for and observance of human rights and fundamental freedoms for all, without distinction as to race, sex, language or religion,

Considering that the Universal Declaration of Human Rights and the International Covenants on Human Rights proclaim the principles of nondiscrimination and equality before the law and the right to freedom of thought, conscience, religion and belief,

Considering that the disregard and infringement of human rights and fundamental freedoms, in particular of the right to freedom of thought, conscience, religion or whatever belief, have brought, directly or indirectly, wars and great suffering to mankind, especially where they serve as a means of foreign interference in the internal affairs of other States and amount to kindling hatred between peoples and nations,

Considering that religion or belief, for anyone who professes either, is one of the fundamental elements in his conception of life and that freedom of religion or belief should be fully respected and guaranteed,

Considering that it is essential to promote understanding, tolerance and respect in matters relating to freedom of religion and belief and to ensure that the use of religion or belief for ends inconsistent with the Charter of the United Nations, other relevant instruments of the United Nations and the purposes and principles of the present Declaration is inadmissible,

Convinced that freedom of religion and belief should also contribute to the attainment of the goals of world peace, social justice and friendship among peoples and to the elimination of ideologies or practices of colonialism and racial discrimination,

Noting with satisfaction the adoption of several, and the coming into force of some, conventions, under the aegis of the United Nations and of the specialized agencies, for the elimination of various forms of discrimination,

Concerned by manifestations of intolerance and by the existence of discrimination in matters of religion or belief still in evidence in some areas of the world,

Resolved to adopt all necessary measures for the speedy elimination of such intolerance in all its forms and manifestations and to prevent and combat discrimination on the ground of religion or belief,

Proclaims this Declaration on the Elimination of All Forms of Intolerance and of Discrimination Based on Religion or Belief:

Article 1

1. Everyone shall have the right to freedom of thought, conscience and religion. This right shall include freedom to have a religion or whatever belief of his choice, and freedom, either individually or in community with others and in public or private, to manifest his religion or belief in worship, observance, practice and teaching.

2. No one shall be subject to coercion which would impair his freedom to have a religion or belief of his choice.

3. Freedom to manifest one's religion or belief may be subject only to such limitations as are prescribed by law and are necessary to protect public safety, order, health or morals or the fundamental rights and freedoms of others.

Article 2

1. No one shall be subject to discrimination by any State, institution, group of persons, or person on the grounds of religion or other belief.

2. For the purposes of the present Declaration, the expression "intolerance and discrimination based on religion or belief" means any distinction, exclusion, restriction or preference based on religion or belief and having as its purpose or as its effect nullification or impairment of the recognition, enjoyment or exercise of human rights and fundamental freedoms on an equal basis.

Article 3
Discrimination between human being on the grounds of religion or belief constitutes an affront to human dignity and a disavowal of the principles of the Charter of the United Nations, and shall be condemned as a violation of the human rights and fundamental freedoms proclaimed in the Universal Declaration of Human Rights and enunciated in detail in the International Covenants on Human Rights, and as an obstacle to friendly and peaceful relations between nations.

Article 4
1. All States shall take effective measures to prevent and eliminate discrimination on the grounds of religion or belief in the recognition, exercise and enjoyment of human rights and fundamental freedoms in all fields of civil, economic, political, social and cultural life.

2. All States shall make all efforts to enact or rescind legislation where necessary to prohibit any such discrimination, and to take all appropriate measures to combat intolerance on the grounds of religion or other beliefs in this matter.

Article 5
1. The parents or, as the case may be, the legal guardians of the child have the right to organize the life within the family in accordance with their religion or belief and bearing in mind the moral education in which they believe the child should be brought up.

2. Every child shall enjoy the right to have access to education in the matter of religion or belief in accordance with the wishes of his parents or, as the case may be, legal guardians, and shall not be compelled to receive teaching on religion or belief against the wishes of his parents or legal guardians, the best interests of the child being the guiding principle.

3. The child shall be protected from any form of discrimination on the ground of religion or belief. He shall be brought up in a spirit of understanding, tolerance, friendship among peoples, peace and universal brotherhood, respect for freedom of religion or belief of others, and in full consciousness that his energy and talents should be devoted to the service of his fellow men.

4. In the case of a child who is not under the care either of his parents or of legal guardians, due account shall be taken of their expressed wishes or of any other proof of their wishes in the matter of religion or belief, the best interests of the child being the guiding principle. 5. Practices of a religion or belief in which a child is brought up must not be injurious to his physical or mental health or to his full development, taking into account article 1, paragraph 3, of the present Declaration.

Article 6
In accordance with article I of the present Declaration, and subject to the provisions of article 1, paragraph 3, the right to freedom of thought, conscience, religion or belief shall include, inter alia, the following freedoms:

(a) To worship or assemble in connection with a religion or belief, and to establish and maintain places for these purposes;

(b) To establish and maintain appropriate charitable or humanitarian institutions;

(c) To make, acquire and use to an adequate extent the necessary articles and materials related to the rites or customs of a religion or belief;

(d) To write, issue and disseminate relevant publications in these areas;

(e) To teach a religion or belief in places suitable for these purposes;

(f) To solicit and receive voluntary financial and other contributions from individuals and institutions;

(g) To train, appoint, elect or designate by succession appropriate leaders called for by the requirements and standards of any religion or belief;

(h) To observe days of rest and to celebrate holidays and ceremonies in accordance with the precepts of one's religion or belief;

(i) To establish and maintain communications with individuals and communities in matters of religion and belief at the national and international levels.

Article 7
The rights and freedoms set forth in the present Declaration shall be accorded in national legislation in such a manner that everyone shall be able to avail himself of such rights and freedoms in practice.

Article 8
Nothing in the present Declaration shall be construed as restricting or derogating from any right defined in the Universal Declaration of Human Rights and the International Covenants on Human Rights.

[End Text]

Source: U.N. website, http://www.un.org/documents/ga/res/36/a36r055.htm

4. DECLARATION ON THE RIGHTS OF PERSONS BELONGING TO NATIONAL OR ETHNIC, RELIGIOUS AND LINGUISTIC MINORITIES, 1992

This document is a non-binding statement of human rights principles about the human rights of religious, ethnic, national or linguistic minority groups. In its concern for the rights of various types of minority groups who were subject to mistreatment in the larger society the UNGA in 1992 adopted this Declaration which included the rights of religious minorities. It allowed religious minorities to practice and preserve their faith or belief and not be forced to assimilate to the dominant religion or suppress their own practice. It can be read along with article 27 of the ICCPR. Though this instrument is not a treaty and therefore not legally binding it has come to be broadly accepted in the international community as having political and moral authority.

[Text]

Declaration on the Rights of Persons Belonging to National or Ethnic, Religious and Linguistic Minorities

Adopted by General Assembly resolution 47/135 of 18 December 1992

The General Assembly,

Reaffirming that one of the basic aims of the United Nations, as proclaimed in the Charter, is to promote and encourage respect for human rights and for fundamental freedoms for all, without distinction as to race, sex, language or religion,

Reaffirming faith in fundamental human rights, in the dignity and worth of the human person, in the equal rights of men and women and of nations large and small,

Desiring to promote the realization of the principles contained in the Charter, the Universal Declaration of Human Rights, the Convention on the Prevention and Punishment of the Crime of Genocide, the International Convention on the Elimination of All Forms of Racial Discrimination, the International Covenant on Civil and Political Rights, the International Covenant on Economic, Social and Cultural Rights, the Declaration on the Elimination of All Forms of Intolerance and of Discrimination Based on Religion or Belief, and the Convention on the Rights of the Child, as well as other relevant international instruments that have been adopted at the universal or regional level and those concluded between individual States Members of the United Nations,

Inspired by the provisions of article 27 of the International Covenant on Civil and Political Rights concerning the rights of persons belonging to ethnic, religious and linguistic minorities,

Considering that the promotion and protection of the rights of persons belonging to national or ethnic, religious and linguistic minorities contribute to the political and social stability of States in which they live,

Emphasizing that the constant promotion and realization of the rights of persons belonging to national or ethnic, religious and linguistic minorities, as an integral part of the development of society as a whole and within a democratic framework based on the rule of law, would contribute to the strengthening of friendship and cooperation among peoples and States,

Considering that the United Nations has an important role to play regarding the protection of minorities,

Bearing in mind the work done so far within the United Nations system, in particular by the Commission on Human Rights, the Sub-Commission on Prevention of Discrimination and Protection of Minorities and the bodies established pursuant to the International Covenants on Human Rights and other relevant international human rights instruments in promoting and protecting the rights of persons belonging to national or ethnic, religious and linguistic minorities,

Taking into account the important work which is done by intergovernmental and non-governmental organizations in protecting minorities and in promoting and protecting the rights of persons belonging to national or ethnic, religious and linguistic minorities,

Recognizing the need to ensure even more effective implementation of international human rights instruments with regard to the rights of persons belonging to national or ethnic, religious and linguistic minorities,

Proclaims this Declaration on the Rights of Persons Belonging to National or Ethnic, Religious and Linguistic Minorities:

Article 1
1. States shall protect the existence and the national or ethnic, cultural, religious and linguistic identity of minorities within their respective territories and shall encourage conditions for the promotion of that identity.

2. States shall adopt appropriate legislative and other measures to achieve those ends.

Article 2
1. Persons belonging to national or ethnic, religious and linguistic minorities (hereinafter referred to as persons belonging to minorities) have the right to enjoy their own culture, to profess and practise their own religion, and to use their own language, in private and in public, freely and without interference or any form of discrimination.

2. Persons belonging to minorities have the right to participate effectively in cultural, religious, social, economic and public life.

3. Persons belonging to minorities have the right to participate effectively in decisions on the national and, where appropriate, regional level concerning the minority to which they belong or the regions in which they live, in a manner not incompatible with national legislation.

4. Persons belonging to minorities have the right to establish and maintain their own associations.

5. Persons belonging to minorities have the right to establish and maintain, without any discrimination, free and peaceful contacts with other members of their group and with persons belonging to other minorities, as well as contacts across frontiers with citizens of other States to whom they are related by national or ethnic, religious or linguistic ties.

Article 3
1. Persons belonging to minorities may exercise their rights, including those set forth in the present Declaration, individually as well as in community with other members of their group, without any discrimination.

2. No disadvantage shall result for any person belonging to a minority as the consequence of the exercise or non-exercise of the rights set forth in the present Declaration.

Article 4

1. States shall take measures where required to ensure that persons belonging to minorities may exercise fully and effectively all their human rights and fundamental freedoms without any discrimination and in full equality before the law.

2. States shall take measures to create favourable conditions to enable persons belonging to minorities to express their characteristics and to develop their culture, language, religion, traditions and customs, except where specific practices are in violation of national law and contrary to international standards.

3. States should take appropriate measures so that, wherever possible, persons belonging to minorities may have adequate opportunities to learn their mother tongue or to have instruction in their mother tongue.

4. States should, where appropriate, take measures in the field of education, in order to encourage knowledge of the history, traditions, language and culture of the minorities existing within their territory. Persons belonging to minorities should have adequate opportunities to gain knowledge of the society as a whole.

5. States should consider appropriate measures so that persons belonging to minorities may participate fully in the economic progress and development in their country.

Article 5

1. National policies and programmes shall be planned and implemented with due regard for the legitimate interests of persons belonging to minorities.

2. Programmes of cooperation and assistance among States should be planned and implemented with due regard for the legitimate interests of persons belonging to minorities.

Article 6

States should cooperate on questions relating to persons belonging to minorities, inter alia, exchanging information and experiences, in order to promote mutual understanding and confidence.

Article 7

States should cooperate in order to promote respect for the rights set forth in the present Declaration.

Article 8

1. Nothing in the present Declaration shall prevent the fulfilment of international obligations of States in relation to persons belonging to minorities. In particular, States shall fulfil in good faith the obligations and commitments they have assumed under international treaties and agreements to which they are parties.

2. The exercise of the rights set forth in the present Declaration shall not prejudice the enjoyment by all persons of universally recognized human rights and fundamental freedoms.

3. Measures taken by States to ensure the effective enjoyment of the rights set forth in the present Declaration shall not prima facie be considered contrary to the principle of equality contained in the Universal Declaration of Human Rights.

4. Nothing in the present Declaration may be construed as permitting any activity contrary to the purposes and principles of the United Nations, including sovereign equality, territorial integrity and political independence of States.

Article 9

The specialized agencies and other organizations of the United Nations system shall contribute to the full realization of the rights and principles set forth in the present Declaration, within their respective fields of competence.

[End Text]

Source: U.N. OHCHR, http://www.ohchr.org/EN/ProfessionalInterest/Pages/Minorities.aspx

❧✦❧✦❧✦❧✦❧

5. THE REPORT OF THE SPECIAL RAPPORTEUR ON FREEDOM OF RELIGION OR BELIEF

This document is an excerpt from a report by the U.N. Special Rapporteur on Freedom of Religion or Belief. This is a special mechanism of the U.N. Human Rights Council. The special rapporteur is an expert on the law of human rights and freedom of religion or belief. Part of his mandate is to produce reports on different subjects or issues of freedom of religion or belief. This is just a sample of his report to show the work of a special rapporteur in educating the international community, here the Human Rights Council, in the concepts of freedom of religion, in order to advance the world's understanding of and respect for this human right, which has been called the "linchpin of all human rights."

[Text]

Selected Excerpts from the Report of the Special Rapporteur on freedom of religion or belief, Heiner Bielefeldt, December 24, 2012, A/HRC/22/51

15. Although people from all religious or belief backgrounds may be exposed to anti-minority victimization when living in a minority situation, certain religious communities have a particularly long-lasting history of discrimination, harassment and even persecution. Human rights violations perpetrated against members of religious or belief minorities are multifaceted in motives and settings while the perpetrators may be States or non-State actors or both.... These violations account for the need for concerted action.

...

18. For example, minority protection systems that were developed in the framework of bilateral or multilateral peace agreements typically resulted in political or legal safeguards on behalf of specifically listed minority groups and their members. Although these safeguards might have provided practical advantages for the identified minority groups, such protection systems were not always human rights-based. Instead of building on the principles of universality, freedom and equality, they typically protected only the members of certain predefined groups. Moreover, the political context of bilateral or multilateral agreements harboured the risk that the specific minorities were seen as receiving protection by certain foreign powers. As a result, some of these minority protection mechanisms were eventually turned against the very groups they were supposed to protect.

19. The human rights- based approach also differs from theologically defined concepts of minority protection in which different status positions may depend on the degree of closeness to, or distance from, the predominant religion of the State. This would again result in reserving protection for a predefined list of religious communities while not appropriately taking into account the right to freedom of religion or belief of those individuals or groups who do not, or do not seem to, fit into the setting of theologically accepted religions, such as members of other minorities, individual dissenters, minorities within minorities, atheists or agnostics, converts or people with unclear religious orientation.

23. In the context of human rights, the identity of a person or a group must always be defined in respect of the self-understanding of the human beings concerned, which can be very diverse and may also change over time. While generally applying to different (ethnic, linguistic, etc.) categories of identity, this principle of respecting every person's self-understanding is even more pronounced when it comes to defining religious or belief identities, since the development of such identities relates to the human right to freedom of thought, conscience, religion or belief.

24. Measures used to promote the identity of a specific religious minority always presuppose respect for the freedom of religion or belief of all of its members. Thus, the question of how they wish to exercise their human rights remains the personal decision of each individual. Strictly speaking, this means that the State cannot guarantee the long-term development or identity of a particular religious minority. Instead, what the State can and should do is create favourable conditions for persons belonging to religious minorities to ensure that they can take their faith-related affairs in their own hands in order to preserve and further develop their religious community life and identity.

29. Besides problems of direct and open discrimination, members of religious minorities may also suffer from hidden forms of discrimination, such as structural or indirect discrimination.

[End Text]

Source: U.N. OHCHR, http://www.ohchr.org/Documents/Issues/Religion/A.HRC.22.51_English.pdf

෯෨෯෨෯෨෯෨෯

6. RESOLUTION ADOPTED BY THE HUMAN RIGHTS COUNCIL, COMBATING INTOLERANCE, NEGATIVE STEREOTYPING AND STIGMATIZATION OF, AND DISCRIMINATION, INCITEMENT TO VIOLENCE AND VIOLENCE AGAINST, PERSONS BASED ON RELIGION OR BELIEF

This is a resolution of the U.N. Human Rights Council regarding the very contentious issue known as "defamation of religion." That term is not a legal term nor a human rights concept. For some years many Muslim states had been trying and succeeding in getting the Council to pass resolutions condemning defamation of religion, and calling for obligating states to ban any expressions which harmed the sensitivities of believers of a religion, particularly Islam. This was largely in the wake of 9/11 when there was violence and discrimination in the U.S. and elsewhere in the world against Muslims. The resolution which was sought by the bloc known as the organization of Islamic Conference (OIC) came to be seen as a move which would, if accepted, have undermined the validity and theoretical underpinnings of all human rights. The U.S. decided to try to change the dialogue away from defamation of religion by introducing this resolution in the Council in 2011. It was adopted and focused attention on the concept of combating intolerance, negative stereotyping and stigmatization of, and discrimination, incitement to violence and violence against, persons based on religion or belief. After that was adopted the so called Istanbul Process was instigated by Secretary of State Hillary Clinton to provide a forum for states to discuss how to implement resolution 16/18. This was a landmark resolution in the field of religious freedom and freedom of expression. The issue at stake involves the interaction between the right to freedom of expression and the right to freedom of religion.

[Text]

Resolution adopted by the Human Rights Council, adopted March 24, 2011

16/18

Combating intolerance, negative stereotyping and stigmatization of, and discrimination, incitement to violence and violence against, persons based on religion or belief

The Human Rights Council,

Reaffirming the commitment made by all States under the Charter of the United Nations to promote and encourage universal respect for and observance of all human rights and fundamental freedoms without distinction as to, inter alia, religion or belief,

Reaffirming also the obligation of States to prohibit discrimination on the basis of religion or belief and to implement measures to guarantee the equal and effective protection of the law,

Reaffirming further that the International Covenant on Civil and Political Rights provides, inter alia, that everyone shall have the right to freedom of thought, conscience and religion or belief, which shall include freedom to have or to adopt a religion or belief of his choice, and freedom, either individually or in community with others and in public or private, to manifest his religion or belief in worship, observance, practice and teaching,

Reaffirming the positive role that the exercise of the right to freedom of opinion and expression and the full respect for the freedom to seek, receive and impart information can play in strengthening democracy and combating religious intolerance,

Deeply concerned about incidents of intolerance, discrimination and violence against persons based on their religion or belief in all regions of the world,

Deploring any advocacy of discrimination or violence on the basis of religion or belief,

Strongly deploring all acts of violence against persons on the basis of their religion or belief, as well as any such acts directed against their homes, businesses, properties, schools, cultural centres or places of worship,

Concerned about actions that willfully exploit tensions or target individuals on the basis of their religion or belief,

Noting with deep concern the instances of intolerance, discrimination and acts of violence in many parts of the world, including cases motivated by discrimination against persons belonging to religious minorities, in addition to the negative projection of the followers of religions and the enforcement of measures that specifically discriminate against persons on the basis of religion or belief,

Recognizing the valuable contribution of people of all religions or beliefs to humanity and the contribution that dialogue among religious groups can make towards an improved awareness and understanding of the common values shared by all humankind,

Recognizing also that working together to enhance implementation of existing legal regimes that protect individuals against discrimination and hate crimes, increase interfaith and intercultural efforts, and to expand human rights education are important first steps in combating incidents of intolerance, discrimination and violence against individuals on the basis of religion or belief,

1. Expresses deep concern at the continued serious instances of derogatory stereotyping, negative profiling and stigmatization of persons based on their religion or belief, as well as programmes and agendas pursued by extremist organizations and groups aimed at creating and perpetuating negative stereotypes about religious groups, in particular when condoned by Governments;

2. Expresses its concern that incidents of religious intolerance, discrimination and related violence, as well as of negative stereotyping of individuals on the basis of religion or belief, continue to rise around the world, and condemns, in this context, any advocacy of religious hatred against individuals that constitutes incitement to discrimination, hostility or violence, and urges States to take effective measures, as set forth in the present resolution, consistent with their obligations under international human rights law, to address and combat such incidents;

3. Condemns any advocacy of religious hatred that constitutes incitement to discrimination, hostility or violence, whether it involves the use of print, audio-visual or electronic media or any other means;

4. Recognizes that the open public debate of ideas, as well as interfaith and intercultural dialogue, at the local, national and international levels can be among the best protections against religious intolerance and can play a positive role in strengthening democracy and combating religious hatred, and convinced that a continuing dialogue on these issues can help overcome existing misperceptions;

5. Notes the speech given by Secretary-General of the Organization of the Islamic Conference at the fifteenth session of the Human Rights Council, and draws on his call on States to take the following actions to foster a domestic environment of religious tolerance, peace and respect, by:

(a) Encouraging the creation of collaborative networks to build mutual understanding, promoting dialogue and inspiring constructive action towards shared policy goals and the pursuit of tangible outcomes, such as servicing projects in the fields of education, health, conflict prevention, employment, integration and media education;

(b) Creating an appropriate mechanism within Governments to, inter alia, identify and address potential areas of tension between members of different religious communities, and assisting with conflict prevention and mediation;

(c) Encouraging training of Government officials in effective outreach strategies; (d) Encouraging the efforts of leaders to discuss within their communities the causes of discrimination, and evolving strategies to counter these causes;

(e) Speaking out against intolerance, including advocacy of religious hatred that constitutes incitement to discrimination, hostility or violence;

(f) Adopting measures to criminalize incitement to imminent violence based on religion or belief;

(g) Understanding the need to combat denigration and negative religious stereotyping of persons, as well as incitement to religious hatred, by strategizing and harmonizing actions at the local, national, regional and international levels through, inter alia, education and awareness-building;

(h) Recognizing that the open, constructive and respectful debate of ideas, as well as interfaith and intercultural dialogue at the local, national and international levels, can play a positive role in combating religious hatred, incitement and violence;

6. Calls upon all States:

(a) To take effective measures to ensure that public functionaries in the conduct of their public duties do not discriminate against an individual on the basis of religion or belief;

(b) To foster religious freedom and pluralism by promoting the ability of members of all religious communities to manifest their religion, and to contribute openly and on an equal footing to society;

(c) To encourage the representation and meaningful participation of individuals, irrespective of their religion, in all sectors of society;

(d) To make a strong effort to counter religious profiling, which is understood to be the invidious use of religion as a criterion in conducting questionings, searches and other law enforcement investigative procedures;

7. Encourages States to consider providing updates on efforts made in this regard as part of ongoing reporting to the Office of the United Nations High Commissioner for Human Rights;

8. Calls upon States to adopt measures and policies to promote the full respect for and protection of places of worship and religious sites, cemeteries and shrines, and to take measures in cases where they are vulnerable to vandalism or destruction;

9. Calls for strengthened international efforts to foster a global dialogue for the promotion of a culture of tolerance and peace at all levels, based on respect for human rights and diversity of religions and beliefs, and decides to convene a panel discussion on this issue at its seventeenth session, within existing resources.

[End Text]

Source: http://www2.ohchr.org/english/bodies/hrcouncil/docs/16session/A.HRC.RES.16.18_en.pdf

7. INTERNATIONAL RELIGIOUS FREEDOM ACT OF 1998

This federal statute established religious freedom as a pillar of U.S. foreign policy. It provided for the establishment of the bipartisan Commission on International Religious Freedom, an Ambassador-at-Large for International Religious Freedom, and the issuance of an annual report on the freedom of religion throughout the world, with emphasis on the realities of religious persecution and discrimination and with recommendations, policy-implementation, and program development to promote religious freedom.

[Text]

International Religious Freedom Act (Excerpts)

SEC. 2. FINDINGS; POLICY. [22 USC 6401.]

(a) FINDINGS.—Congress makes the following findings:

(1) The right to freedom of religion undergirds the very origin and existence of the United States. Many of our Nation's founders fled religious persecution abroad, cherishing in their hearts and minds the ideal of religious freedom. They established in law, as a fundamental right and as a pillar of our Nation, the right to freedom of religion. From its birth to this day, the United States has prized this legacy of religious freedom and honored this heritage by standing for religious freedom and offering refuge to those suffering religious persecution.

(2) Freedom of religious belief and practice is a universal human right and fundamental freedom articulated in numerous international instruments, including the Universal Declaration of Human Rights, the International Covenant on Civil and Political Rights, the Helsinki Accords, the Declaration on the Elimination of All Forms of Intolerance and Discrimination Based on Religion or Belief, the United Nations Charter, and the European Convention for the Protection of Human Rights and Fundamental Freedoms.

(3) Article 18 of the Universal Declaration of Human Rights recognizes that "Everyone has the right to freedom of thought, conscience, and religion. This right includes freedom to change his religion or belief, and freedom, either alone or in community with others and in public or private, to manifest his religion or belief in teaching, practice, worship, and observance." Article 18(1) of the International Covenant on Civil and Political Rights recognizes that "Everyone shall have the right to freedom of thought, conscience, and religion. This right shall include freedom to have or to adopt a religion or belief of his choice, and freedom, either individually or in community with others and in public or private, to manifest his religion or belief in worship, observance, practice, and teaching." Governments have the responsibility to protect the fundamental rights of their citizens and to pursue justice for all. Religious freedom is a fundamental right of every individual, regardless of race, sex, country, creed, or nationality, and should never be arbitrarily abridged by any government.

(4) The right to freedom of religion is under renewed and, in some cases, increasing assault in many countries around the world. More than one-half of the world's population lives under regimes that severely restrict or prohibit the freedom of their citizens to study, believe, observe, and freely practice the religious faith of their choice. Religious believers and communities suffer both government-sponsored and government-tolerated violations of their rights to religious freedom. Among the many forms of such violations are state-sponsored slander campaigns, confiscations of property, surveillance by security police, including by special divisions of "religious police," severe prohibitions against construction and repair of places of worship, denial of the right to assemble and relegation of religious communities to illegal status through arbitrary registration laws, prohibitions against the pursuit of education or public office, and prohibitions against publishing, distributing, or possessing religious literature and materials.

(5) Even more abhorrent, religious believers in many countries face such severe and violent forms of religious persecution as detention, torture, beatings, forced marriage, rape, imprisonment, enslavement, mass resettlement, and death merely for the peaceful belief in, change of or practice of their faith. In many countries, religious believers are forced to meet secretly, and religious leaders are targeted by national security forces and hostile mobs.

(6) Though not confined to a particular region or regime, religious persecution is often particularly widespread, systematic, and heinous under totalitarian governments and in countries with militant, politicized religious majorities.

(7) Congress has recognized and denounced acts of religious persecution through the adoption of the following resolutions:

(A) House Resolution 515 of the One Hundred Fourth Congress, expressing the sense of the House of Representatives with respect to the persecution of Christians worldwide.

(B) Senate Concurrent Resolution 71 of the One Hundred Fourth Congress, expressing the sense of the Senate regarding persecution of Christians worldwide.

(C) House Concurrent Resolution 102 of the One Hundred Fourth Congress, expressing the sense of the House of Representatives concerning the emancipation of the Iranian Baha'i community.

(b) POLICY.—It shall be the policy of the United States, as follows:

(1) To condemn violations of religious freedom, and to promote, and to assist other governments in the promotion of, the fundamental right to freedom of religion.

(2) To seek to channel United States security and development assistance to governments other than those found to be engaged in gross violations of the right to freedom of religion, as set forth in the Foreign Assistance Act of 1961, in the International Financial Institutions Act of 1977, and in other formulations of United States human rights policy.

(3) To be vigorous and flexible, reflecting both the unwavering commitment of the United States to religious freedom and the desire of the United States for the most effective and principled response, in light of the range of violations of religious freedom by a variety of persecuting regimes, and the status of the relations of the United States with different nations.

(4) To work with foreign governments that affirm and protect religious freedom, in order to develop multilateral documents and initiatives to combat violations of religious freedom and promote the right to religious freedom abroad.

(5) Standing for liberty and standing with the persecuted, to use and implement appropriate tools in the United States foreign policy apparatus, including diplomatic, political, commercial, charitable, educational, and cultural channels, to promote respect for religious freedom by all governments and peoples.

[End Text]

Source: IRFA 2016, https://www.congress.gov/bill/114th-congress/house-bill/1150/text?format=txt

8. FRANK R. WOLF INTERNATIONAL RELIGIOUS FREEDOM ACT

This is a federal legislation named in honor of Senator Frank Wolf, a strong supporter in Congress of religious freedom. It is an amendment to the International Religious Freedom Act of 1998, the previous primary document above. It expressed the sense of Congress that the position of Ambassador at large for religious freedom should be elevated to the level of Secretary in the State Department and also the sense that Congress understood that freedom of religion or belief includes the right to protect theistic and non-theistic beliefs as well as the right not to profess or practice any religion. It also called for training of all U.S. foreign service officers in freedom of religion.

[Text]

(Sec. 2) This bill amends the International Religious Freedom Act of 1998 (IRFA) to state in the congressional findings that the freedom of thought and religion is understood to protect theistic and non-theistic beliefs as well as the right not to profess or practice any religion.

TITLE I—DEPARTMENT OF STATE ACTIVITIES

(Sec. 101) In order to promote religious freedom as a U.S. foreign policy interest, the Ambassador at Large for International Religious Freedom: (1) shall coordinate international religious freedom policies across all U.S. programs and activities, and (2) is urged to participate in any interagency processes in which the promotion of international religious freedom policy can advance U.S. national security interests.

The bill expresses the sense of Congress that the Department of State should consider elevating the office of International Religious Freedom and the position of the Ambassador at Large for International Religious Freedom to the Office of the Secretary.

(Sec. 102) The deadline for submitting the Annual Report on International Religious Freedom is changed from September 1 to May 1 (or the first day thereafter on which the appropriate House of Congress is in session).

Such report shall include information about:

- severe violations of religious freedom in a country where a government does not exist or does not control its territory;
- identification of prisoners in a country;
- action taken by a government to censor religious content, communications, or worship activities online;
- persecution of human rights advocates seeking to defend the rights of members of religious groups or highlight religious freedom violations, including prohibitions on ritual animal slaughter or male infant circumcision; and
- country-specific analysis of the impact of U.S. actions on religious freedom.

The executive summary of each such report shall include: (1) information about a country in which a non-state actor is designated as an entity of particular concern for religious freedom, and (2) a Special Watch List that shall identify each country that engages in or tolerates severe violations of religious freedom but which the President determines does not meet all the criteria for designation as a country of particular concern for religious freedom.

The bill expresses the sense of Congress that given that the annual Country Reports on Human Rights Practices no longer contain updated information on religious freedom conditions globally, it is important that the State Department and the Commission on International Religious Freedom work together to fulfill the original intent of the IRFA.

(Sec. 103) The Foreign Service Act of 1980 is amended to direct the State Department to develop a curriculum for, and the Director of the George P. Shultz National Foreign Affairs Training Center to begin, mandatory training on religious freedom for all Foreign Service officers. The State Department shall submit a plan within 180 days for undertaking such training.

(Sec. 104) The commission shall make publicly available lists of persons who are imprisoned, detained, disappeared, placed under house arrest, tortured, or subject to forced renunciations of religious faith by the government of a foreign country or by a non-state actor that the commission recommends for designation as a country or entity of particular concern for religious freedom.

TITLE II—NATIONAL SECURITY COUNCIL

(Sec. 201) The National Security Act of 1947 is amended to express the sense of Congress that there should be within the National Security Council staff a Special Adviser to the President on International Religious Freedom with primary responsibility to serve as a religious freedom resource for executive branch officials.

TITLE III—PRESIDENTIAL ACTIONS

(Sec. 301) The President: (1) concurrent with the annual review of the status of religious freedom in foreign countries required under the IFRA, shall identify any non-state actors operating in a reviewed country or surrounding region that have engaged in particularly severe violations of religious freedom, (2) shall designate each such non-state actor as an entity of particular concern for religious freedom, and (3) shall submit a report detailing the reasons for such designation.

The bill expresses the sense of Congress that the State Department should work with Congress to create new political, financial, and diplomatic tools to address severe violations of religious freedom by non-state actors.

The President shall, with respect to each non-state actor designated as an entity of particular concern for religious freedom, determine the specific officials or members who are responsible for such violations.

(Sec. 302) The deadline for such annual review is changed from September 1 to not later than 90 days after a review is submitted.

The President shall designate as a country of particular concern for religious freedom a country that appears on the special watch list in more than two consecutive annual reports.

(Sec. 303) The President's report on action taken in response to violations of religious freedom or on designation of a country as a country of particular concern for religious freedom shall include: (1) an evaluation of the impact on the advancement of U.S. interests in democracy, human rights, and security; and (2) a description of policy tools being applied in the country, including programs that target democratic stability, economic growth, and counter-terrorism.

(Sec. 304) The waiver of specified presidential actions subsequent to the designation of a country as a country of particular concern for religious freedom is limited to 180 days. The bill prescribes additional presidential waiver authority after such 180-period.

The bill expresses the sense of Congress that: (1) ongoing waivers do not fulfill the purposes of the IRFA; and (2) the President, the State Department, and other executive branch officials should find ways to address existing violations through presidential actions.

(Sec. 305) The bill directs the President to publish in the Federal Register: (1) any designation of a non-state actor as an entity of particular concern for religious freedom, and (2) the identities of individuals responsible for severe violations of religious freedom by non-state actors.

TITLE IV—PROMOTION OF RELIGIOUS FREEDOM

(Sec. 401) The bill expresses the sense of Congress that: (1) the State Department should make specified assistance available to promote international religious freedom, and (2) preference for such assistance should be given to projects targeting religious freedom violations in countries designated as countries of particular concern for religious freedom and in countries on the special watch list.

TITLE V—DESIGNATED PERSONS LIST FOR PARTICULARLY SEVERE VIOLATIONS OF RELIGIOUS FREEDOM

(Sec. 501) The State Department shall establish the Designated Persons List for Particularly Severe Violations of Religious Freedom of foreign individuals who are sanctioned (through visa denials, financial sanctions, or other measures) for ordering or otherwise directing particularly severe violations of freedom religion. The State Department shall submit the initial list within 180 days and provide updates every 180 days.

TITLE VI—MISCELLANEOUS PROVISIONS

(Sec. 601) The bill express the sense of Congress that U.S. institutions of higher education operating campuses outside the United States or establishing educational entities with foreign governments, particularly with or in countries that engage in or tolerate severe violations of religious freedom, should adopt a voluntary code of operating conduct that should:

- uphold the right of freedom of religion of their employees and students;
- ensure that the religious views and peaceful practice of religion in no way affect the status of a worker's or faculty member's employment or a student's enrollment; and
- make every effort in all negotiations, contracts, or memoranda of understanding engaged in with a foreign government to protect academic freedom and the rights enshrined in the U.N. Declaration of Human Rights.

The bill expresses the sense of Congress that the President's annual national security strategy report should (1) promote international religious freedom as a foreign policy and national security priority; and (2) be a guide for the strategies and activities of relevant federal agencies, including the Department of Defense quadrennial defense review.

[End Text]

Source: Congress.gov, https://www.congress.gov/bill/114th-congress/house-bill/1150

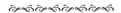

9. REPORT OF THE COMMISSION ON INTERNATIONAL RELIGIOUS FREEDOM, 2015, RUSSIA

This document is a small part of the CIRF annual report on the religious freedom record of Russia. All states in the world are the subject of the annual freedom of religion report of this Bi-Partisan U.S. Commission. It is done to help the administration formulate foreign policy. The information is gathered in the country as much as possible, especially through the U.S. embassies and consulates. This sample shows the work of the Commission in seeking to help the U.S. government work for freedom of religion world-wide. It also shows the work done by U.S. ambassadors interfacing with the Russian leaders and others to try to encourage better respect for religious freedom in the country. The legal basis of the reports is the international human rights law found in the UDHR and the ICCPR. The report judges the actions of Russia using international Human Rights Law, not the U.S. Constitution.

{Excerpt}

[Text]

RUSSIA 2015 INTERNATIONAL RELIGIOUS FREEDOM REPORT

Executive Summary

The constitution provides for freedom of religion, guaranteeing equal rights irrespective of religious belief and the right to worship and profess one's religion, but by law officials may prohibit the activity of a religious association for violating public order or engaging in "extremist activity." The law states Christianity, Islam, Judaism, and Buddhism are the country's four "traditional" religions and recognizes the special role of the Russian Orthodox Church (ROC). The government generally did not restrict the activities of Jewish or Christian groups with a longer presence in the country but imposed restrictions limiting the activities of Muslims and other religious groups such as Jehovah's Witnesses, Pentecostals, and Scientologists. Government actions included detaining, fining, and imprisoning members of minority religious groups. Police conducted raids on minority religious groups in private homes and places of worship, confiscating religious publications and property, and blocked their websites. Authorities applied anti-extremism laws to revoke the registration of minority religious groups and imposed restrictions that infringed on the practices of minority religious groups and their ability to purchase land, build places of worship, and obtain restitution of properties confiscated during the Soviet era. The government continued to declare some religious materials of minority religious groups extremist, adding two Muslim publications to the extremist list. A prosecutor also seized books from a Jewish school to examine them for extremist content. The government later amended the law to make it illegal to declare the key texts, or "holy books" of the four "traditional" religions as extremist. The Ministry of Justice (MOJ) declared a Jewish charity organization a "foreign agent," requiring the organization to add this designation to its website and all its publications. The government granted privileges to the ROC that were accorded to no other religious group.

There were incidents of violence related to religion, including attacks on religious adherents resulting in death or severe injury and vandalism of synagogues, cemeteries, and mosques. In Dagestan, an imam was shot and killed in front of a mosque, and in Moscow the director of the Museum of the History of Jews in Russia survived after being shot in the head outside of his office. Unlike in previous years, there were no reports of anti-Semitic acts or slogans during nationalist demonstrations.

The U.S. Ambassador and embassy officials met with a range of government officials, including the foreign ministry's special representative for human rights, to discuss the treatment of minority religious groups, the use of the law on extremism to restrict the activities of religious groups, and the revocation of registration of some religious organizations. The Ambassador met with senior representatives of the four "traditional" religious groups, including the patriarch and the head of external relations of the ROC, the chair of the Federation of Jewish Communities, the chair of the Russia Muftis Council, and the Papal Nuncio to discuss religious freedom issues. Embassy representatives regularly engaged with officials from "traditional" and minority religious groups, including rabbis, muftis, Protestant pastors, Catholic priests, U.S. missionaries, Mormons, Buddhists, Jehovah's Witnesses, Scientologists, Falun Gong adherents, Hare Krishnas, and nongovernmental organizations (NGOs) to promote interfaith cooperation and religious tolerance and discuss religious freedom developments, including specific cases.

Section I. Religious Demography

The U.S. government estimates the population at 142.4 million (July 2015 estimate). The most recent figures from a 2013 poll by the Levada Center, an NGO research organization, reports 68 percent of Russians consider themselves Orthodox, while 7 percent identify as Muslim. Religious groups constituting less than 5 percent of the population each include Buddhists, Protestants, Roman Catholics, Jews, The Church of Jesus Christ of Latter-day Saints (Mormons), Jehovah's Witnesses, Hindus, Bahais, the International Society of Krishna Consciousness (Hare Krishnas), pagans, Tengrists, Scientologists, and Falun Gong adherents. The 2010 census estimates the number of Jews at 150,000;

...

Government Practices

Government authorities continued to detain, imprison, and fine members of minority religious groups. Police conducted raids on the private homes and places of worship of minority religious groups, disrupting religious services and confiscating religious publications they deemed "extremist." Authorities revoked the status of some minority religious groups, forcing them to suspend their activities, and imposed a number of restrictions that infringed on the religious practices of other minority religious groups, in particular Muslims, Jehovah's Witnesses, Pentecostals, and Scientologists, including limiting their ability to obtain land and build places of worship. The MOJ declared a Jewish charity organization to be a "foreign agent." The government granted privileges to the ROC that were accorded to no other religious group.

In April Baptist pastor Pavel Pilipchuk was imprisoned for five days in Orel after refusing to pay a fine for organizing an open air meeting for worship without informing the city administration beforehand. He was initially fined 20,000 rubles ($271) in 2014, and the court doubled the fine for nonpayment.

In January a member of the Church of Evangelical Christians-Baptists was arrested in Tomsk and charged with holding an unauthorized public event after police found him handing out copies of the New Testament and Psalms to people on the street. A court fined the man 10,000 rubles ($136).

On November 23, the Moscow city court banned the activity of the Church of Scientology of Moscow and ordered that it be dissolved. The court accepted the MOJ's argument that the term Scientology was trademarked and thus could not be considered a religious organization covered by the constitution's freedom of religion clause. The MOJ also stated the Church of Scientology conducted its business in St. Petersburg, contrary to the charter identifying Moscow as the location of all activity.

Throughout the year, authorities attempted to dissolve a number of minority religious associations on grounds they were conducting extremist activity.

On August 5, the Supreme Court confirmed the Krasnodar Regional Court's decision to ban Jehovah's Witnesses in Krasnodar Territory.

In February the Supreme Court upheld a local government ban on hijabs in schools in the region of Mordovia, dismissing the appeal of the Muslim community of Mordovia. Mordovian Minister of Education Dmitry Livanov said he believed children wearing hijabs should study at religious schools. Representatives of the Mordovian Muslim community stated the ban violated their constitutional right to freedom of faith.

Across the country, police with the support of local authorities conducted raids on minority religious groups, in private homes and places of worship, confiscating and destroying religious literature and other property.

Religious minorities said local authorities utilized the country's anti-extremism laws to ban sacred and essential religious texts. The MOJ's list of extremist materials grew to 3,209 entries from 2,500 at the end of 2014, including 69 texts from the Jehovah's Witnesses, four from Falun Gong, and seven from Scientology. Items added to the list of extremist materials included neo-Nazi internet videos, the book Islamic Aqeedah by Jamila Muhammad Zina, and some materials by Archbishop of the Russian Orthodox Autonomous Church Andrey Maklakov.

In October security forces raided the offices of the Church of Scientology of Moscow, stating the organization used office recording devices and video cameras to conduct surveillance of members of the church. Authorities opened a criminal investigation, which was continuing at year's end.

In January the Ambassador met with Archbishop Ivan Yurkovich, the Papal Nuncio, to discuss the state of Roman Catholicism in the country and the relationship between the Catholic Church and the ROC.

Embassy officials met with U.S. missionaries and religious workers to inquire about their experiences with immigration, registration, and police authorities, as well as with local populations, as a gauge of religious freedom.

Representatives from the embassy and the consulates in St. Petersburg,

Yekaterinburg, and Vladivostok met regularly with rabbis and leaders of the Jewish community, muftis and other Islamic leaders, Protestant pastors, Catholic priests, Mormons, Jehovah's Witnesses, Scientologists, Falun Gong adherents, Hare Krishnas, and Buddhists. These discussions covered developments related to religion and religious freedom, including legislation, government practices, and specific religious freedom cases.

[End Text]

Source: U.S. Department of State, Diplomacy in Action, 2015 Freedom of Religion Report, https://www.state.gov/j/drl/rls/irf/2015/eur/256235.htm

᪻᪻᪻᪻᪻᪻᪻᪻

l0. REPORT OF THE UNITED STATES OF AMERICA, SUBMITTED TO THE U.N. HIGH COMMISSIONER FOR HUMAN RIGHTS IN CONJUNCTION WITH THE UNIVERSAL PERIODIC REVIEW, 2015

These following statements were made by the U.S. government during the Universal Periodic Review process at the U.N. Human Rights Council in 2015. These statements were made in the U.S. national report regarding the policy position of the U.S. towards certain enumerated recommendations made in 2010 by various states to the U.S, on how to improve its human rights performance. See Chapter 4 on the UPR process at the U.N. Human Rights Council regarding that Outcome Document and recommendations.

{Excerpt}

[Text]

Report of the United States of America Submitted to the U.N. High Commissioner for Human Rights In Conjunction with the Universal Periodic Review

2015

[2010 Outcome Report]
Recommendations 64, 98-99, 103, 106, 189, and 190-191

20. The United States is committed to preventing and effectively prosecuting hate crimes. In 2009, we enacted a powerful new tool, the Shepard-Byrd Hate Crimes Prevention Act, which enhanced federal prosecution for violent crimes motivated by religious, racial, or national origin bias and enabled federal prosecution of crimes based on sexual orientation, gender, gender identity, and disability. Over the last five years, DOJ has obtained convictions of more than 160 defendants on such charges, a nearly 50 percent increase over the previous five years. DOJ also continues to prosecute other hate crimes, and in 2014 assisted Kansas authorities in the investigation of a fatal shooting at a Kansas City Jewish community center. In January 2015, the FBI began collecting more detailed data on bias-motivated crimes, including those committed against Arab, Hindu, and Sikh individuals.

21. We continue to actively fight all forms of religious discrimination. For instance, in recent years, DOJ has received a large number of complaints involving members of Muslim communities alleging unfair obstacles to building or expanding places of worship. Ten of the 34 DOJ investigations in this area since 2010, and five of the six lawsuits, have involved mosques or Islamic schools. In one such case, DOJ filed an amicus brief in a state court and initiated a federal lawsuit to ensure that a mosque would be permitted to open and operate in Murfreesboro, Tennessee.

22. In 2013, DOJ successfully resolved two complaints alleging that Sikh individuals were denied access to county court systems because of their religious headwear. Those counties subsequently adopted policies that prohibit discrimination because of religious head coverings.

23. We continue our robust efforts to eliminate religious discrimination in employment: the U.S. Equal Employment Opportunity Commission is currently litigating a suit before the U.S. Supreme Court against an employer for refusing to hire a Muslim worker out of concern that she would request religious accommodation to wear a headscarf.

24. We also continue to seek input from affected communities on these issues. Federal prosecutors have been directly involved in outreach to members of Arab, Muslim, and Sikh communities, working to strengthen trust; to provide protection from hate crimes, bullying, and discrimination; and to make clear that the United States cannot conduct surveillance on any individual based solely on race, ethnicity, or religion. In addition, the U.S. Department of Homeland Security leads or participates in regular roundtable meetings among community leaders and federal, state, and local government officials to discuss the impact of its programs, policies, and procedures on members of diverse demographic groups, including religious minorities.

Recommendations 68, 101, and 219: (68) Take legislative and administrative measures to ban racial profiling in law enforcement; (101) Ban, at the federal and state levels, the use of racial profiling by police and immigration officers; Prohibit expressly the use of racial profiling in the enforcement of immigration legislation; (219) Enact a national legislation that prohibits religious, racial and color profiling particularly in context of the fight against terrorism.

> **U.S. position:** Profiling — the invidious use of race, ethnicity, national origin, or religion — is prohibited under the U.S. Constitution and numerous pieces of national legislation.

Recommendation 116: Continue its intense efforts to undertake all necessary measures to ensure fair and equal treatment of all persons, without regard to sex, race, religion, colour, creed, sexual orientation, gender identity or disability, and encourage further steps in this regard.

Recommendation 191: Continue to create an enabling climate for religious and cultural tolerance and understanding at the grass roots level.

Recommendations 64, 67, 94, 98, 100, and 189: (64) Review, with a view to their amendment and elimination, all laws and practices that discriminate against African, Arab and Muslim Americans, as well as migrants, in the administration of justice, including racial and religious profiling; (67) Take legislative and administrative measures to address a wide range of racial discrimination and inequalities in housing, employment and education; (94) End the discrimination against persons of African descent; (98) Devise specific programs aimed at countering growing Islamophobic and xenophobic trends in society; (100) End all forms of racial discrimination in terms of housing, education, health care, social security and labor; (189) Consider discontinuing measures that curtail human rights and fundamental freedoms.

> **U.S. position:** See general comments, as well as the explanation of our positions regarding recommendations 107 and 111.

Recommendation 99: Eliminate discrimination against migrants and religious and ethnic minorities and ensure equal opportunity for enjoyment of their economic, social and cultural rights.

> **U.S. position:** A migrant's eligibility for full benefits under certain programs may depend on his/her lawful status.

Recommendation 190: Take effective measures to counter insults against Islam and Holy Quran, as well as Islamophobia and violence against Moslems, and adopt necessary legislation.

> **U.S. position:** We take effective measures to counter intolerance, violence, and discrimination against all members of all minority groups, including Muslims. We cannot support this recommendation, however, to the extent that it asks U.S. to take legislative measures countering insults. Insults (unlike discrimination, threats, or violence) are speech protected by our Constitution.

Recommendation 82: Adopt a fair immigration policy, and cease xenophobia, racism and intolerance to ethnic, religious and migrant minorities.

> **U.S. position:** See general comments. It is consistent with our continuing efforts to improve our immigration policies and to eliminate xenophobia, racism, and intolerance in our society.

Recommendation 102: Revoke the national system to register the entry and exit of citizens of 25 countries from the Middle-East, South Asia and North Africa, and eliminate racial and other forms of profiling and stereotyping of Arabs, Muslims and South Asians as recommended by CERD.

> **U.S. position:** See general comments. Our Constitution and numerous statutes prohibit the invidious use of race or ethnicity. The registration requirements of the National Security Entry-Exit Registration System are under review at this time.

[End Text]

Source: U.S. Department of State, Diplomacy in Action, https://www.state.gov/j/drl/upr/2015/237250.htm

II. FOURTH PERIODIC REPORT OF THE U.S. TO THE U.N. HUMAN RIGHTS COMMITTEE ON HUMAN RIGHTS CONCERNING THE ICCPR

This document is an excerpt from the Fourth periodic state report submitted by the U.S. to the U.N. Human Rights Committee in fulfillment of its obligation under article 40 of the ICCPR. This excerpt is from the U.S. report regarding article 18 of the ICCPR. These reports are to be submitted about every four to five years. This is the latest report submitted to the HRCtee. This is the U.S. self-disclosing to the U.N. about how it is doing regarding its implementation of the ICCPR, particularly article 18 on freedom of religion or belief. It shines a light on what is happening within the U.S. in the area of freedom of religion judged by international human rights standards.

{Excerpt}

[Text]

Fourth Periodic Report of the U.S. to the U.N. Human Rights Committee on Human Rights Concerning the ICCPR dated 12/30/11, Article 18

Article 18 — Freedom of thought, conscience and religion

336. The First Amendment to the U.S. Constitution provides that Congress shall make no law respecting an establishment of religion, or prohibiting the free exercise thereof; or abridging the freedom of speech. This amendment is made applicable to state and local governments by the Fourteenth Amendment of the Constitution. Freedom of thought and conscience is protected by the guarantee of freedom of speech and opinion. See, e.g., *Wooley v. Maynard*, 430 U.S. 705, 714 (1977) (noting that "the right of freedom of thought [is] protected by the First Amendment"). The U.S. Supreme Court has "identified the individual's freedom of conscience as the central liberty that unifies the various Clauses in the First Amendment." *Wallace v. Jaffree*, 472 U.S. 38, 50 (1985). Forty years later, the Supreme Court declared that the "heart of the First Amendment is the notion that an individual should be free to believe as he will, and that in a free society one's beliefs should be shaped by his mind and his conscience rather than coerced by the State." *Abood v. Detroit Bd. of Educ.*, 431 U.S. 209, 234-35 (1977).

337. The right to freedom of thought and conscience, including the right to non-belief, is in many circumstances subsumed within freedom of religion. The government may not force a person to profess a belief or disbelief in a particular religion. *Torcaso v. Watkins*, 367 U.S. 488, 495 (1961) (Maryland requirement that to hold public office a person must state a belief in God violated the First and Fourteenth Amendments of the U.S. Constitution). Writing for the Supreme Court, Justice Stevens stated: "[T]he individual freedom of conscience protected by the First Amendment embraces the

right to select any religious faith or none at all. This conclusion derives support not only from the interest in respecting the individual's freedom of conscience, but also from the conviction that religious beliefs worthy of respect are the product of free and voluntary choice by the faithful," *Wallace v. Jaffree*, 472 U.S. 38, 53 (1985). For more general information regarding non-discrimination on the basis of religion, please see the discussion above under Article 2.

338. By Executive Order 13498 of February 5, 2009, President Obama created an Advisory Council on Faith-based and Neighborhood Partnerships, and renamed and refocused the White House Office of Faith-based and Neighborhood Partnerships (Office). The Council is a resource for non-profits and community organizations, both secular and faith-based. The mission of the Council, as laid out in the Executive Order, is to "bring together leaders and experts in fields related to the work of faith-based and neighborhood organizations in order to: identify best practices and successful modes of delivering social services; evaluate the need for improvements in the implementation and coordination of public policies relating to faith-based and other neighborhood organizations; and make recommendations to the President, through the Executive Director [of the Office], for changes in policies, programs, and practices that affect the delivery of services by such organizations and the needs of low-income and other underserved persons in communities at home and around the world." The Office forms partnerships between governments at all levels and non-profit voluntary organizations, both secular and faith-based, more effectively to serve Americans in need. The Office has coordinated President Obama's national fatherhood agenda; built partnerships between federal agencies and local nonprofits on, for example, supporting the inclusion of faith-based organizations so they are a part of the government's disaster response efforts; brought people together across religious lines (e.g., working with groups on more than 4,000 interfaith service projects in 2009); and helped to lead the Administration's efforts on interfaith cooperation abroad. The Office has also worked to help local organizations respond to the economic crisis, from implementing foreclosure prevention programs to strengthening nonprofit capacity building. The Office coordinates 12 federal centers for faith-based and neighborhood partnerships. Each center forms partnerships between its agency and faith-based and neighborhood voluntary organizations to advance specific goals. For example, the Department of Education's Center for Faith-based and Neighborhood Partnerships empowers faith-based and community organizations to apply for federal grants by supplying resources and training, but it does not make the decisions about which groups will be funded. Those decisions are generally made through a careful competitive process established by each grant program.

339. Charitable status for taxation and solicitation. The U.S. Constitution limits the government's ability to regulate the activities of religious organizations. There has been no change in the law with regard to the lack of a requirement for religious organizations to register with any federal government agency in order to operate. Likewise, the law has not changed with regard to the tax-exempt status of religious and other charitable organizations as described in paragraphs 320 — 322 of the Second and Third Periodic Report.

340. Religious Freedom Restoration Act. As noted in paragraph 314 of the Second and Third Periodic Report, the Religious Freedom Restoration Act of 1993 (RFRA), 42 U.S.C. 2000(b)(b), which invalidates government action that substantially burdens religious exercise unless the action is the least restrictive means of furthering a compelling government interest, applies to actions by the federal government, but not to the states. The Supreme Court held in City of Boerne v. Flores, 521 U.S. 507 (1997), that the attempt by Congress to make the RFRA applicable to the states exceeded congressional authority. In response to this decision many states have adopted their own versions of the RFRA to ensure that religious exercise is not burdened by state action, including Alabama, Arizona, Connecticut, Florida, Idaho, Illinois, New Mexico, Oklahoma, Rhode Island, South Carolina, and Texas.

341. In Gonzales v. O Centro Espirita Beneficiente Uniao Do Vegetal, 546 U.S. 418 (2006), the Supreme Court held that the RFRA required the federal government to permit the importation, distribution, possession and use of a hallucinogenic controlled substance for religious purposes by the Uniao Do Vegetal church, even where Congress had found the substance to have a high potential for abuse and to be unsafe for use even under medical supervision, and where its importation and distribution would violate an international treaty. The Court held that the RFRA requires courts to examine individual religious freedom claims and to grant exceptions to generally-applicable laws (in this case, the Controlled Substances Act) where no compelling government interest in regulating the activity can be shown.

342. Religious Land Use and Institutionalized Persons Act. In response to The City of Boerne case, Congress enacted the Religious Land Use and Institutionalized Persons Act of 2000 (RLUIPA), 114 Stat. 804, imposing a requirement on states that in most circumstances burdens on religion through land use regulation and burdens on the religious exercise

of prisoners must, as with RFRA, be justified by a compelling governmental interest and must be accomplished through the least restrictive means. Lower courts have continued to uphold RLUIPA against constitutional challenges. See, e.g., Westchester Day School v. Mamaroneck, 504 F.3d 338 (2d Cir. 2007) (upholding land use provisions of RLUIPA under the Establishment Clause, the Commerce Clause, and the Tenth Amendment); Van Wyhe v. Reisch, 581 F.3d 639 (8th Cir. 2009) (upholding prisoner provision of RLUIPA under the Spending Clause as valid condition imposed on states for receipt of federal funding).

343. As noted above, indigenous representatives have raised the issue of the practice of Native American religious activities in prisons. As a general matter, RLUIPA has removed barriers to the religious practices of Native Americans and others, where the prisoner demonstrates a substantial burden on religious exercise, and where the prohibition is not necessary and narrowly tailored to meet a compelling government interest. However, in 2008, the Ninth Circuit Court of Appeals heard a case involving a total prohibition on group worship for maximum security prisoners. Greene v. Solano County Jail, 513 F.3d 982 (2008). The court remanded the case for a determination whether such a total prohibition is the least restrictive means to maintain jail security, and a settlement was reached at that time.

344. Religion and public schools. State-sponsored religious speech in public schools is generally severely restricted by the Constitution, while at the same time genuinely private religious speech by students at schools is strongly protected. See, e.g., Prince v. Jacoby, 303 F.3d 1074 (9th Cir. 2002) (student-created Bible club had constitutional right to the same access to school facilities for its meetings that other student-initiated clubs were given). As discussed above under Article 2, Hearn and U.S. v. Muskogee Public School District (E.D. Okla. 2004) involved an action against a school district that had barred a Muslim girl from wearing a hijab to school. The resulting consent decree protects the rights of students to wear religious garb. DOJ also obtained a settlement in a case in which another girl was harassed by a teacher and students because she was a Muslim.

345. In September 2009, DOJ/CRD opened an investigation involving an altercation between a Black student and a Muslim student in a Michigan school district. Ultimately, several other students jumped into the fight and attacked the Muslim student. During the fight, the Muslim student's hijab was snatched from her head, and the students who attacked her allegedly shouted several religious and national origin epithets. CRD entered into an agreement with the district that required the district to mediate the conflict resolution process for all students involved in the altercation and engage the services of a nonprofit dispute resolution organization to assist with addressing tensions between the Black and Muslim communities. In 2008, CRD entered into two agreements with a district in Arizona resolving a complaint from a parent alleging religious and national origin discrimination. The complaint alleged that a male student was harassed by other students for being from the Middle East and a Muslim. The agreements addressed harassment directed at the student and required the school district to revise its non-discrimination policies and procedures. In May 2007, CRD reached an agreement with a Texas school district that allows Muslim high school students to say their midday prayers at the school. The agreement stemmed from CRD's investigation of a complaint alleging that the school had denied the students' requests to pray during lunch in an unused space and had prohibited them from saying their prayers in a corner of the cafeteria, even though the school permitted other groups of students to gather during the lunch hour.

346. With regard to governmental funding, where an educational benefit, such as a scholarship, is provided directly to a student, and the student is then free to use it toward education at the school of his or her choice, whether public or private, secular or religious, the Supreme Court has found that the non-Establishment principle of the Constitution is not violated. Second, where the government itself gives aid directly to a private or religious school, the aid will pass constitutional muster if the aid is secular in nature, is distributed in a neutral manner without regard to religion, and where the aid is not used by the recipient for religious purposes. The law in this area has not changed substantially since the submission of the Second and Third Periodic Report.

347. Federal funding of religious charities. As noted in paragraph 317 of the Second and Third Periodic Report, Congress has enacted numerous provisions permitting federal funding of religiously affiliated charities. For example, religious organizations are permitted to participate in certain welfare grant programs under Section 104 of the Personal Responsibility and Work Opportunity Reconciliation Act of 1996, 110 Stat. 2105 (1996). In addition, executive branch agencies that administer social services programs have adopted rules implementing Executive Order 13279 that prohibit discrimination against religious organizations in the selection of grant recipients. Religious organizations are permitted to participate in systems where beneficiaries receive vouchers to redeem at any of a number of service providers

regardless of whether their services are secular or religious; and are also permitted to participate in direct grant systems, as long as the religious providers do not discriminate against beneficiaries on the basis of their religious beliefs or require beneficiaries to participate in any religious activities, and as long as the programs sufficiently segregate religious and secular activities in a manner that ensures that the government funds do not subsidize religious activities. When the government itself makes decisions about which schools to send aid, it must ensure that such aid is not diverted to religious uses. See, e.g., Mitchell v. Helms, 530 U.S. 793 (2000). The law with regard to these areas has not changed significantly since the last report.

348. Government sponsored religious displays. As noted in paragraph 572 of the Initial Report and paragraph 318 of the Second and Third Periodic Report, the law regarding government-sponsored religious displays remains fact-specific. In Pleasant Grove City Utah v. Summum, 555 U.S. 460 (2009), the Supreme Court upheld Pleasant Grove's denial of a request by the Summum religious organization to erect a monument containing the seven Aphorisms of Summum in a public park in which a Ten Commandments monument already stood. The Court held that the placement of privately donated, permanent monuments in a public park is a form of government speech not subject to scrutiny under the Free Speech Clause of the Constitution. The Court did not resolve whether the city's display of the Ten Commandments violated the Establishment Clause. In Salazar v. Buono, 130 S.Ct. 1803 (2010), the Supreme Court ordered a federal appeals court to reconsider an order that would have forced removal of a large cross placed on land in the Mojave National Preserve 75 years earlier, following World War I. A plurality of the court found that the intent of the cross was not to set the state's imprimatur on a particular creed, but rather to honor fallen soldiers, a cause that had become entwined in the public consciousness.

349. Religion and employment. Title VII of the Civil Rights Act of 1964 requires employers to accommodate the sincerely held religious observances and practices of their employees so long as the accommodation does not impose an undue hardship. The law also contains exceptions for religious employers so that, for example, a church may prefer coreligionists in hiring. Although it is not an expressly stated exception in the statute, courts have often held that individuals employed by religious institutions in a clergy or "ministerial" capacity cannot bring EEO claims. However, the scope and application of this exemption is the subject of a case currently pending before the U.S. Supreme Court, which will be decided in the 2011-12 term. See EEOC v. Hosanna-Tabor Evangelical Lutheran Church and School, 597 F. 3d 769 (6th Cir. 2010), cert. granted, 131 S. Ct. 1783 (2010). The EEOC investigates allegations of religious discrimination in employment and occasionally files lawsuits to protect the rights of those who are harmed. Workers also may file their own lawsuits. Examples of recent lawsuits include: a complaint by a Muslim worker about harassment that included slurs and questions about whether he was a terrorist because of his faith, EEOC v. Sunbelt Rentals, Inc., No. PJM 04-cv-2978 (D. Md.) (settled Oct. 16, 2009 for $46,641 to the employee); and a lawsuit challenging an employer's refusal to grant leave to, and eventual termination of, a worker who sought time off to observe his Sabbath, EEOC v. Staybridge Suites, No. A:08-cv-02420 (W.D. Tenn.) (settled Sept. 14, 2009 for $70,000). Further description of EEOC enforcement against employment discrimination based on religion is contained in the discussion of Article 20, below.

350. Religious Freedom within the Armed Forces. Within the United States Armed Forces, service members are allowed free access to any and all religious denominations of their choosing, as are all persons under U.S. authority. The military goes to great lengths to accommodate these religious needs. Title 10 of the U.S. Code prescribes chaplains for each of the Military Departments for the function of providing religious services to meet the needs of the Military Members of that Department.

351. The 202 Department of Defense-approved Ecclesiastical Endorsing Agencies, supporting Chaplains from around 200 different religious denominations, indicate the strength of support to the broad diversity of religions in the U. S. military. Through the process of "Appointment of Chaplains for the Military Departments" (Department of Defense Instruction (DoDI) 1304.19), any given Ecclesiastical Endorsing Agency that meets IRS section 501(c)(3) exempt status, and a few additional basic uniform support standards, can establish a Chaplainship for a military officer in its faith. Minority faiths often have a high ratio of chaplain support. In September 2009, 180 Catholic Priests supported the nearly 284,000 Catholics in the U. S. military, for a ratio of 1 Chaplain to every 1,578 Catholics. There are three Chaplains for the U. S. military's 5,358 Buddhists (a ratio of 1 to 1,786), eight Chaplains serving the military's 3,540 Muslims (a ratio of 1 to 443), and 17 rabbis serving the 4,712 Jews (a ratio of 1 to 277). These numbers of believers are based on self-reporting by service members.

352. Military Chaplains are charged with leading those of their own faith. They also are mandated "to advise and assist commanders in the discharge of their responsibilities to provide for the free exercise of religion in the context of military service as guaranteed by the Constitution." Chaplains also must be willing to "support directly and indirectly the free exercise of religion by all members of the Military Services, their family members, and other persons authorized to be served by the military chaplaincies," without proselytizing to them. As well, they must "perform their professional duties as Chaplains in cooperation with Chaplains from other religious traditions." (DoDI 1304.28). For individuals within the military seeking to exercise their religious freedom, "[i]t is DoD policy that requests for accommodation of religious practices should be approved by commanders when accommodation will not have an adverse impact on mission accomplishment, military readiness, unit cohesion, standards, or discipline." (DoDI 1300.17, "Accommodation of Religious Practices Within the Military Services").

353. International Religious Freedom. The International Religious Freedom Act of 1998, as amended, provides that United States policy is to promote, and to assist other governments in the promotion of, religious freedom. That Act requires the President annually to designate countries of particular concern for religious freedom; it also amended the Immigration and Nationality Act to make foreign government officials who have committed severe violations of religious freedom ineligible to receive visas or be admitted into the United States. 8 U.S.C. 1182(a)(2)(G). In September 2011, the following countries were listed as countries of particular concern: Burma, China, Eritrea, Iran, North Korea, Saudi Arabia, Sudan and Uzbekistan. Following designation, the United States will seek to work with the designated countries to bring about change through various means, possibly including negotiation of bilateral agreements or application of sanctions. The United States Report on Religious Freedom for July — December 2010, released on September 13, 2011, can be accessed at: www.state.gov/j/drl/rls/irf/2010_5/index.htm.

[End Text]

Source: U.S. Department of State, Diplomacy in Action, https://www.state.gov/j/drl/rls/179781.htm

☙☙☙☙☙☙☙

12. PRESIDENT TRUMP'S REMARKS AT THE NATIONAL PRAYER BREAKFAST

With the 2016 election of Donald Trump as U.S. president a new discourse on religious freedom began. President Trump in the first few weeks of his administration attended the National Prayer Breakfast in Washington D.C. and chose that occasion to speak about freedom of religion or belief from his own perception. The follow is an excerpted version of that speech as related to freedom of religion or belief. It shows that religious freedom is important to this President.

{Excerpt}

President Trump's Remarks at the National Prayer Breakfast, Feb. 2, 2017

...I was blessed to be raised in a churched home. My mother and father taught me that to whom much is given much is expected. I was sworn in on the very bible from which my mother would teach U.S. as young children. And that faith lives on in my heart every single day.

The people in this room come from many, many backgrounds. You represent so many religions and so many views. But we are all united by our faith in our Creator and our firm knowledge that we are all equal in His eyes. We are not just flesh and bone and blood. We are human beings, with souls. Our Republic was formed on the basis that freedom is not a gift from government, but that freedom is a gift from God.

It was the great Thomas Jefferson who said, "The God who gave U.S. life, gave U.S. liberty." Jefferson asked, "Can the liberties of a nation be secure when we have removed a conviction that these liberties are the gift of God?"

Among those freedoms is the right to worship according to our own beliefs. That is why I will get rid of, and totally destroy, the Johnson Amendment and allow our representatives of faith to speak freely and without fear of retribution. I will do that — remember.

Freedom of religion is a sacred right, but it is also a right under threat all around us, and the world is under serious, serious threat in so many different ways. And I've never seen it so much and so openly as since I took the position of President. The world is in trouble, but we're going to straighten it out. Okay? That's what I do. I fix things. We're going to straighten it out....

We have seen unimaginable violence carried out in the name of religion. Acts of wanton slaughter against religious minorities. Horrors on a scale that defy description. Terrorism is a fundamental threat to religious freedom. It must be stopped, and it will be stopped. It may not be pretty for a little while. It will be stopped.

...We have seen peace-loving Muslims brutalized, victimized, murdered and oppressed by ISIS killers. We have seen threats of extermination against the Jewish people. We have seen a campaign of ISIS and genocide against Christians, where they cut off heads. Not since the Middle Ages have we seen that. We haven't seen that, the cutting off of heads. Now they cut off their heads, they drown people in steel cages. Haven't seen this — I haven't seen this. Nobody has seen this for many, many years.

All nations have a moral obligation to speak out against such violence. All nations have a duty to work together to confront it and to confront it viciously, if we have to. So I want to express clearly today to the American people that my administration will do everything in its power to defend and protect religious liberty in our land. America must forever remain a tolerant society where all faiths are respected, and where all of our citizens can feel safe and secure. We have to feel safe and secure.

In recent days, we have begun to take necessary action to achieve that goal. Our nation has the most generous immigration system in the world. But there are those that would exploit that generosity to undermine the values that we hold so dear. We need security. There are those who would seek to enter our country for the purpose of spreading violence or oppressing other people based upon their faith or their lifestyle. Not right. We will not allow a beachhead of intolerance to spread in our nation. You look all over the world and you see what's happening.

So in the coming days, we will develop a system to help ensure that those admitted into our country fully embrace our values of religious and personal liberty, and that they reject any form of oppression and discrimination. We want people to come into our nation, but we want people to love U.S. and to love our values — not to hate U.S. and to hate our values. We will be a safe country. We will be a free country. And we will be a country where all citizens can practice their beliefs without fear of hostility or fear of violence. America will flourish as long as our liberty and, in particular, our religious liberty is allowed to flourish.

America will succeed as long as our most vulnerable citizens — and we have some that are so vulnerable — have a path to success. And America will thrive as long as we continue to have faith in each other and faith in God.

That faith in God has inspired men and women to sacrifice for the needy, to deploy to wars overseas, and to lock arms at home, to ensure equal rights for every man, woman and child in our land. It's that faith that sent the pilgrims across the oceans, the pioneers across the plains, and the young people all across America to chase their dreams. They are chasing their dreams. We are going to bring those dreams back. As long as we have God, we are never, ever alone. Whether it's the soldier on the night watch or the single parent on the night shift, God will always give U.S. solace and strength and comfort.

We need to carry on and to keep carrying on. For U.S. here in Washington, we must never, ever stop asking God for the wisdom to serve the public according to his will. That's why President Eisenhower and Senator Carlson had the wisdom to gather together 64 years ago to begin this truly great tradition. But that's not all they did together. Let me tell you the rest of the story. Just one year later, Senator Carlson was among the members of Congress to send to the President's desk a joint resolution that added "under God" to our Pledge of Allegiance. That's a great thing. Because that's what we are and that is what we will always be, and that is what our people want: one beautiful nation, under God.

Thank you. God bless you. And God bless America. Thank you very much. Thank you. Thank you.

[End Text]

Source: https://www.whitehouse.gov/the-press-office/2017/02/02/remarks-president-trump-national-prayer-breakfast